The GATF
Encyclopedia of
Graphic Communications

The GATF Encyclopedia of Graphic Communications

Richard M. Romano
Editor-in-Chief

Frank J. Romano
Editor

Peter Oresick
Director, GATF Press

Thomas M. Destree, Erika L. Kendra
Associate Editors

Robert J. Romano
Technical Illustrator

GATF*Press*
Pittsburgh

Library of Congress Catalog Card Number: 97-74138
International Standard Book Number: 0-88362-190-8
International Standard Book Number: 0-88362-215-7 (Leather-Bound Edition)

Printed in the United States of America

Order No. 1306

GATF*Press*
Graphic Arts Technical Foundation
200 Deer Run Road
Sewickley, PA 15143-2600
Phone: 412/741-6860
Fax: 412/741-2311
http://www.gatf.org

Table of Contents

The Story of Print: The First 500 Years xiii

A 1

B 49

C 107

D 211

E 267

F 295

G 347

H 377

I 399

J 449

K 455

L 463

M 495

N 533

O 543

P 569

Q 657

R 661

S 687

T 761

U 795

V 803

W 815

X 843

Y 847

Z 849

Time Line of Communications History 851

Bibliography 939

About the Authors 941

About GATF 943

Other Books Available from GATFPress 945

Dedication

For Joanne Lois Romano
The woman in all of our lives

Richard, Robert, Frank Romano

Preface

World Color proudly supports the Graphic Arts Technical Foundation's contributions to our industry. GATF is an integral provider of relevant and comprehensive information and training, providing us with the tools and knowledge we use daily in the graphic arts.

In appreciation for the valuable role that GATF plays in our industry, World Color is pleased to contribute the printing for the first edition of *The GATF Encyclopedia of Graphic Communications*.

Robert G. Burton
Chairman, President, and Chief Executive Officer
World Color Press, Inc.

WORLD COLOR™
DIGITAL DIVISION

Preface

Boise Cascade, as a leading manufacturer of quality papers, is pleased to partner with the industry's leading resource for technical information—the Graphic Arts Technical Foundation.

This encyclopedia is another tangible benefit of GATF's excellent educational outreach. Boise Cascade is proud to donate the paper for the first edition of *The GATF Encyclopedia of Graphic Communications,* a landmark reference for the graphic communications industry both today and for many years to come.

N. David Spence
Senior Vice President & General Manager, Paper Division
Boise Cascade Corporation

Boise Cascade

Foreword

For almost 75 years, the Graphic Arts Technical Foundation has kept the graphic communications industries informed about reproduction and related technology. Through publications, seminars, and electronic media, GATF has educated several generations of graphic arts professionals.

With the *GATF Encyclopedia of Graphic Communications,* GATF broadens its base of education. The information in this comprehensive volume extends to the public as well. With over 10,000 terms, a history of the printing industry, and a detailed time line, it is the most extensive resource ever published on virtually every aspect of visual communication.

A project as complex as this could only be accomplished by combining the talents of GATF's technical and editorial resources with the talents of Frank and Richard Romano. As a team effort, the result speaks for itself.

We would also like to acknowledge the contribution of the industry. Printing was donated by World Color Press and paper was donated by Boise Cascade. Thus, the *GATF Encyclopedia of Graphic Communications* is truly a collaboration between suppliers, industry and associations, working together to inform, educate, and advance graphic communications.

George H. Ryan
President
Graphic Arts Technical Foundation

Acknowledgments

It takes a village to make an encyclopedia.

We thank the faculty at the Rochester Institute of Technology, especially Professors Frank Cost, Sam Hoff, Barry Lee, and Werner Rebsamen for their assistance.

We thank the following students for helping in many ways: Jacquie Bailey, Eric Cohen, Chris Hahn, Eric Kenly, Peter Muir, Tim Peretta, and Charles White.

We thank the RIT administration for providing the environment that supports research and publishing, especially Provost Stanley McKenzie.

We thank the Mary Flagler Cary Charitable Trust for their support of education, especially Ned Ames.

We thank Mike Bruno, the dean of the American graphic arts industry, for his contribution and inspiration.

We thank Pat Mills, who started typing the manuscript of what was thought to be a simple glossary in 1990 and helped convert it to a relational database.

We thank Jim Cavuoto of Micro Publishing Press for sharing his knowledge.

We thank the Graphic Arts Technical Foundation, with its talented and supportive staff of industry experts, and its farsighted management, especially George Ryan, president, and John Sweeney, vice president and director of marketing.

We thank the tireless and professional publications staff who brought this volume into being, especially Erika Kendra, technical editor, and Tom Destree, editor in chief, with editorial assistance from Frances Wieloch, editor of *GATFWorld;* Pamela Groff, senior technical writer; adjunct editor Kristin Kovacic; and adjunct proofreaders Martha Sheppard and Lawrence Oresick.

We thank World Color Press, especially Laura Gale, for their commitment to the education and future of their industry.

And, last but not least, we thank the person who MADE this project a quest, and kept its vision from beginning to end: Peter Oresick, GATF*Press* director.

Richard M. Romano
Frank J. Romano

The Story of Print: The First 500 Years

Oriental Roots

The invention of printing depended on the invention and refinement of paper, which occurred in China over several centuries. The Chinese had developed "rag" paper—a cheap scrap-cloth and plant-fiber substitute for bark, reed, and bamboo strips and expensive silk paper—by about 105 AD. Chinese prisoners are thought to have passed this technology on to their Arab captors in the 8th century, and the secrets of the craft were revealed to Europeans in the 12th and 13th centuries.

The printing process may date back as far as 100 AD. By inking covered marble surfaces and placing paper on them, the Chinese were able to "print" designs and symbols. By the year 500, wood blocks were used in some parts of the Orient to reproduce ideographic symbols. Blocks may have been used to print textiles in India as early as 400 BC. Books were block printed in China about the 9th century AD. The idea of using raised blocks of wood to create an impression on a substrate (initially clay) derived from seals (used in impressing signatures). The Chinese word for "print" is the same as that for "seal."

The earliest known printed book is the *Diamond Sutra,* printed by Wang Chieh in 868. Many other books, most in roll form but one in the cut-sheet form we are familiar with today, have been found that date from around the same time. The idea of printing was adopted by religious communities to promote their doctrines with prayers, hymns, and other ecclesiastical materials. The other primary use of printing, dating from around 969 or earlier, was the production of playing cards, supposedly invented by bored members of an Oriental harem. In the 10th century, the emperor financed the printing of the Chinese classics, which led to a widespread revival of learning and education during the time of the Sung dynasty (known as the Sung Renaissance). Also, in the 10th century, printing was applied to the production of paper currency, which had the effect of introducing the concept of inflation to China.

Block printing had a dramatic effect on Chinese culture and the democratization of knowledge. By 972, approximately 5,000 volumes of the Buddhist canon had been printed, and hundreds of volumes of dynastic histories appeared soon after that time, followed by encyclopedias, dictionaries, and compilations of literature. But because of a prohibition on the use of printing for commercial purposes, all printed texts were given away by the government. This stifled the further development of printing technology.

Between 1058 and 1061, Pi Sheng used clay, and later tin, to create movable type. The nature of the Chinese language (the lack of a true alphabet and the presence of more than 40,000 "characters") made the practical use of movable type a near impossibility. Pi Sheng's type did not catch on in the East until 200 years later.

Metal type was invented in 1403 in Korea, because of a lack of hardwood, and it was endorsed by the Korean emperor T'ai Tsung as an aid to government and the preservation of civilization. (He never read the "Congressional Record.")

Movable metal type could have taken off in China with the adoption of a simplified, 24-character alphabet devised by King Sajong of Korea, but interest in Chinese provincialism prevented this. Typesetting as we now know it only became popular in China after Gutenberg's invention in the mid-15th century. Then, the techniques of Eastern typography—first carried from Korea to Europe—were introduced by missionaries. What goes around comes around.

However, knowledge of typographic printing did not reach Europe directly from the East. In the early 14th century, Uighurs, who lived on the borders of Mongolia and Turkestan, created a set of Uighur typefaces, carved on wooden cubes. As a nomadic people usually considered to have been the educators of other Mongolian peoples, it is surprising that this skill had not spread to Europe. An obstacle in its progress toward Europe may have been the Islamic religion, which accepted paper to record the word of Allah but refused reproduction by artificial means.

Early Letterforms

Egyptian papyri dating from the Fifth Dynasty (2300 BC) contain the earliest known examples of calligraphy. The hieratic script, created to facilitate speed in writing, derived from a simplified pictorial or hieroglyphic lettering.

In ancient Greece, writers used both a formal script for literary works and a more utilitarian cursive hand to keep accounts. The Greek book hand combined capitals, based on the stiff geometric forms used in stone inscription, with rounded, more easily inscribed uncial letters. What we now recognize as capital letters were developed and perfected before the 1st century AD by Roman painters and stonecutters. The inscriptions on Roman columns and monuments are as legible and elegant today as any printed letterform.

By the first millennium AD, the legacy of letters had moved from stone to papyrus or vellum (calf or lamb skin), and the quill or pen had become its defining tool. A comparison of scribal styles over the centuries reveals a wide spectrum of forms, but one that gained considerable currency was the uncial script, an adaptation of Roman capitals with smooth, round letterforms and the first intimations of ascenders and descenders. The uncial form reached its height with the Irish Book of Kells of the 8th century.

By the 5th century, a form known to paleographers as *half-uncial* was popular in written books. It was more upright than original uncial scripts, with pronounced ascenders and descenders. Half-uncials employed contrasting letterforms at the beginnings of lines, a development which leads directly to upper- and lowercase letters.

The key event in this evolution of the letterform was the rise of Charlemagne's empire and the subsequent growth of scholarship in the 9th century. Charlemagne's court advisors led a wide-reaching reform of written styles. The most visible of these was the Caroline minuscule, a small, round, open script with well-defined characters, which is entirely recognizable as lowercase. Under the direction of the Anglo-Saxon scholar Alcuin of York, this distinctive script evolved at Charlemagne's court at Aachen. Square capitals or uncials were used for initial letters and titling. The increase in scholarship and literacy during this period allowed the Caroline minuscule to become the predominant scholarly letterform in the Holy Roman Empire. Charlemagne's renaissance gave us the first uniform written communication.

After Charlemagne, scripts evolved away from the elegant simplicity of the Caroline script with the rise of "national hands"—writing specific to a country or geographic area. By the Gothic period of the 12th to 15th centuries, which was centered in northern Europe, manuscript production and illumination had reached a high art. Gothic scripts (black letter, textura, or fraktur) emulated the forms of Gothic architecture with heavy-handed elaboration and ornamentation. These letterforms are dark and obscure, in opposition to the clarity and openness of the Caroline minuscule.

Advent of the Printing Press

Prior to the advent of the printing press in the 15th century, books were written on vellum because of its durability. Since books took more than a year to produce, paper at that time was too flimsy. The first printed books to show up for sale were Bibles and religious tracts. The next books to attract buyers were the "humanist" texts brought back from Byzantium by the Crusaders. Then came other texts of antiquity.

The distribution of books was poorly organized, and there was a low literacy rate in Europe. People who could not read had access to book culture only through traveling raconteurs who stood in the marketplace and read from books as a means of making a living.

From its European debut sometime in the 12th century, paper gradually proved to be a viable alternative to animal skin vellum and parchment. As literacy expanded, rag paper became increasingly cheap and plentiful. Population growth created a large amount of discarded linen for fiber, and the appetite for books increased with expansion in trade and in government.

Scribal monks sanctioned by the church had overseen the maintenance and hand-copying of sacred texts for centuries, but the secular world began to create its own version of the professional scribe. New scriptoria, or writing rooms, employed virtually every literate cleric who wanted work.

The church had from the beginning embraced the power of print. The church copied indulgences, theological texts, and how-to manuals for inquisitions, and this solidified the church's influence. But the church had more difficulty controlling the activities of printers than scribes. Printed copies of Martin Luther's theses (1517), for example, were widely and rapidly disseminated, prompting far-reaching discussions that became the foundation for opposition to the church's role as interpreter of spiritual truth. Bibles printed in vernacular languages rather than Latin fueled the Protestant Reformation; one's relationship with God could be direct and personal. Print became the tool of change.

The printing press was not a single invention. It was the aggregation of technologies known for years before Johannes Gutenberg, who gets credit for an invention that is thought to have been developed simultaneously in Holland and Prague. The developments brought together by Gutenberg in his pursuit of printing were:

1. The adaptation for printing of the wine, or olive oil, screw-type press that had been in use for many years throughout Europe and Asia.
2. The development of oil-based inks. These had been around since the 10th century, impressed on vellum with woodblocks. Handwritten religious manuscripts used an egg-based tempura that was unsuitable for printing with metal type.
3. The development of a punch and mold system that allowed the mass production of the movable type used to reproduce a page of text. These letters would be put together in a type tray which was then used to print a page or pages of text. If a letter broke down, it could be replaced. When the printing of the copies of one page was finished, the type could be reused for the next page or the next book.
4. The adaptation of wood block-print technology—xylography—known in Europe since the return of Marco Polo from Asia at the end of the 13th century.
5. The development of mass production paper-making techniques.

By mid-century, plague (the Black Death) had killed off many scribes, and those who were left demanded high fees. Thus, it was time for someone to bring these elements together to invent a mechanical method for the reproduction of writing.

Johannes Gutenberg. Johannes Gensfleisch zur Laden zum Gutenberg (1400–1468) was born into a patrician family of the city of Mainz, Germany. His early training was in goldsmithing, the craft of his father, Friele zum Gensfleisch. Gutenberg took his mother's last name for his own, following the custom that one son should carry on the mother's family name. As the son of a patrician and craftsman of Mainz, he was in a privileged position.

Beyond this, there are very few direct pieces of information about the person who invented the most important communication system of all time. Most of the information about his life comes from documents of financial or legal transactions. Exiled from Mainz in the course of a struggle between the guilds of that city and the patricians, Gutenberg moved to Strassburg (now Strasbourg, France) between 1428 and 1430, and records put his presence there from 1434 to 1444. He engaged in crafts such as gem cutting, stone polishing, and metalworking, and he taught them to a number of business associates.

In 1438, Gutenberg was working on a mass production technique for mirrors. He had borrowed a significant amount of money from business partners to invest in the manufacture and selling of mirrors at a pilgrim convention in Aachen. Unfortunately, the partners discovered that Gutenberg had gotten the year of the festival wrong; it was actually two years away. In compensation, his partners asked him to teach them something else that he had been secretly working on. A five-year contract was then drawn up between Gutenberg and Hans Riffe, Andreas Dritzehn, and Andreas Heilmann. A clause stated that in case of the death of one of the partners his heirs were not to enter the partnership, only compensated financially. When Dritzehn died in 1438, his heirs sued Gutenberg, demanding to be made partners. They lost the suit, but the trial revealed that Gutenberg was working on an invention that had something to do with metal casting, a press with a screw mechanism, and paper. Witnesses testified that a carpenter named Conrad Saspach had built a wooden press, and Hans Dünne, a goldsmith, declared that he had sold to Gutenberg, in 1436, 100 guilders' worth of casting materials. This very tantalizing fragment offers only a glimpse into history.

After March 1444, Gutenberg's activities are unknown for a number of years. In October 1448, Gutenberg was back in Mainz to borrow more money from a relative, and

A bas-relief on a monument to Gutenberg in Mainz, Germany.

in 1450, Gutenberg went into partnership with a wealthy Mainz money-broker, Johann Fust. Fust invested 800 guilders—a substantial capital investment—to become a partner.

Gutenberg hired Peter Schöffer, eventually Fust's son-in-law, as his assistant. They set type for a Turkenkalender (Turkish calendar), which was printed in 1454, and two indulgences. Two years later Fust invested an

Johann Fust

additional 800 guilders in installment payments for a partnership in the "work of the book," with the work itself as collateral. Fust and Gutenberg became estranged as Fust, apparently, wanted a quick return on his investment, while Gutenberg aimed at perfection. Fust foreclosed.

Fust won the suit against him, the record of which is preserved, in part, in what is called the Helmasperger Notariatsinstrument (the Helmasperger notarial instrument), dated November 6, 1455. Gutenberg was ordered to pay Fust the total sum of the two loans plus compound interest (probably totaling 2,020 guilders). It has been said that this settlement ruined Gutenberg, but recent scholarship suggests that it favored him, allowing him to operate a printing shop through the 1450s and '60s.

The work of the book mentioned in the trial refers to the 42-line Bible that is Gutenberg's masterpiece. It is called the 42-line Bible because most of its pages are 42 lines long. It was completed in 1455 at the latest. The sale of the 42-line Bible alone would have produced many times over the sum owed Fust by Gutenberg, and there exists no explanation as to why these assets were not counted among Gutenberg's property at the trial. Fust gained control of the Bible and of the type for Gutenberg's second masterpiece, the Psalter, and some of Gutenberg's printing equipment.

Fust continued to print, using Gutenberg's materials, with the assistance of Peter Schöffer, his son-in-law, who was Gutenberg's skilled assistant and a witness against him at the 1455 trial.

After the Fust foreclosure in 1455, Gutenberg literally disappears from record. We know that in 1462 the city of Mainz was attacked, and many of the workmen from the Gutenberg shop went to other cities, taking with them the skill and craft of

Peter Schöffer

printing, which is how this art spread throughout Europe.

Gutenberg's financial status in his last years has been debated, but he was probably not destitute. In 1465, Adolf, the archbishop of Mainz, pensioned Gutenberg, giving him an annual measure of grain, wine, and clothing and exempting him from certain taxes. Elector Adolph von

Nassau made him a member of his court just before Gutenberg died in Mainz in 1468, and his last possessions were recorded by a friend, Konrad Hummery: "sundry forms, letters, instruments, tools and other things related to the work of printing . . . which have belonged and still belong to me [Gutenberg]." Gutenberg was buried in the cemetery of the Franciscan church in Mainz.

The Bible. Gutenberg had designed a Latin Bible that remains an almost perfect specimen of the printing art, though no printed material was ever credited to Gutenberg during his lifetime. The Gutenberg Bible is also called the Mazarin Bible, because it was later discovered in the library of Cardinal Mazarin of France, is identified as the earliest printed book from movable type, and is so called after its printer.

A page from Gutenberg's bible.

Gutenberg's Bible had no title page, no page numbers, and no artifacts to distinguish it from the work of a manuscript copyist, as other contemporary works exhibited. In the manuscript era, books were costly. No single person could own more than a few of them. There was no need for title pages and none existed. Usually a manuscript began with the name of the author and his subject at the head of the opening paragraph. Sometimes it ended with the name of the scribe and of the place and the date of completion. The preliminary statement of author and subject (the incipit) was occasionally omitted; the scribe's record (the colophon) was rarely there. With the increase of book production, the need for these distinguishing characteristics became common. For the convenience of booksellers and readers, both items were printed on the first leaf of the book, the origin of the modern title page. Publishers endeavored to win favor with readers by continuous improvement. Books selected at random from successive decades will show an evolution from the barest of text to the addition of title page, introduction, table of contents, footnotes, maps, illustrations, tables, commentary, index, colophon, and errata.

It is agreed that Gutenberg's Bible, though economic in its use of space, displays a technical proficiency not substantially improved upon before the 19th century.

There were at least two type fonts created for the Bible. The first was probably a font that would set 36 lines to a page. One indulgence of 31 lines from 1454 is set in this type style; a calendar and an entire Bible are also set in this font. At first it was considered that this Bible predated the Gutenberg Bible. It now appears that the entire font was given to Albrecht Pfister, who took it to Bamberg, Germany, and printed a Bible in 1461. There are 14 copies of the 36-line Bible extant, one at the Plantin-Moretus Museum in Antwerp, Belgium.

The second type font was the 42-line font. An indulgence of 30 lines from 1455 uses this type style. It is now believed that the Gutenberg Bible started out as 40 lines to the page. After about 60 pages had been set, the quantity of Bibles was increased, and the number of lines was increased to 41, then 42 to conserve paper. The first volume contains 324 leaves, and the second volume has 319. Of the original 180 copies, 135 were printed on paper, 45 on vellum. There were three purchases of paper and four stocks, based on watermarks that were used.

An analysis shows that two-color printing was attempted but discontinued, and the addition of color was left to an illuminator. The Bible was printed in 1455 and illumination and hand-worked initials were completed by August 15, 1456. The first run of 180 two-volume Gutenberg Bibles sold for 30 florins each, or about three years' wages. Some Bibles were sold unbound so that purchasers could use their favorite binders. The original Bible that served as the master copy has never been identified, but the text of every Bible printed from 1455 to the end of the 15th century was based on the 42-line Bible. Forty original copies are still in existence.

The Psalter. The first printed book to bear the name of its printer is a magnificent Psalter completed in Mainz on August 14, 1457, which lists Johann Fust and Peter Schöffer—no mention of Gutenberg. The Psalter is decorated with hundreds of two-color initial letters and delicate scroll borders that were printed (not illuminated) in a most ingenious technique based on multiple inkings of metal blocks. Most experts agree that it would have been impossible for Fust and Schöffer alone to have invented and executed the intricate technical approach necessary to execute this process between November 6, 1455, when Gutenberg lost control of his printing establishment, and August 14, 1457, when the Psalter appeared.

Thus, it was probably Gutenberg's genius that was responsible for the Psalter. It is suggested that he may also have had a hand in the creation of copper engraving, in which he may have recognized a method for producing pictorial matrices from which to cast reliefs that could be set with the type, initial letters, and calligraphic scrolls.

The Catholicon. This was a popular religious dictionary and was printed in Mainz in 1460, in an edition of 748 pages in two columns of 66 lines each. The book has a colophon:

> *By the help of the most high, at whose bidding the tongues of children become eloquent, and who often reveals to the lowly what he conceals from the wise; this noble book, Catholicon, in the year of our Lord's incarnation 1460, in mother city of Mainz of the renowned German nation . . . without the help of reed stylus or quill, but by a wonderful concord, proportion and measure of punches and forms has been printed and finished . . .*

It is now believed that Gutenberg helped to set up a print shop in Elville, near Mainz, where the Catholicon was produced in three printings from 1460 to 1469. It is also believed that he wrote the colophon.

The invention. Gutenberg's lasting innovation was, of course, the efficient molding and casting of movable metal type. Each letter was carved into the end of a steel punch, which was then hammered into a copper blank. The engraved copper impression was inserted into a mold, and a molten alloy made of lead, antimony, and tin was poured in. The alloy cooled quickly, and the resulting reverse image of the letter attached to a lead base could be handled in minutes. The width of the character varied according to the letter's size. The base of an "i," for example, would be narrower than the base of an "m". This emphasized the visual impact of words and clusters of words, rather than evenly spaced letters.

Gutenberg foresaw the profit-making potential for a printing press that used movable metal type. Secular scribes simply could not keep up with the commercial demand for books. Gutenberg also saw strong market potential in selling indulgences, the passports to Heaven offering written dispensation from sin that the Church sold to fund crusades, buildings, and other projects. Gutenberg sought to make his work appear as close as possible to handwritten manuscripts. His style of calligraphed type, his use of abbreviations and special symbols, and his use of hand-drawn illustrations in bibles and prayer books, all followed the practices of the scribes. To reproduce this "look," Gutenberg fashioned a font of 292 characters, far larger than the fonts of today. Pressruns of 200,000 indulgences were common.

Gutenberg's method of using movable type endured almost unchanged for five centuries. In fact, hobbyists today continue to handset type, and a few printers still routinely set a line of metal type for imprinting.

Gutenberg's Bible, in 1455, marked the beginning of mass communication, and the effect it had upon the world is comparable, in modern times, to the effect of computers and telecommunications. Books proliferated and spurred changes in society. Literacy increased; standards were written and enforced; languages were recorded; and maps charted the world. The world shrank as people moved from a knowledge base centered on images and aural communication to one centered on the printed word and reading.

Laurens Janszoon Coster. Coster, also spelled Koster, (c. 1370–1440) is said to be a Dutch rival of Johannes Gutenberg as the inventor of printing. In the 19th century some Dutch scholars believed that Coster was the real inventor of book printing and that Gutenberg had stolen the idea from him. In Coster's home town, Haarlem, his statue still stands in the central square.

Coster is said to have printed with movable type as early as 1430, but proof is lacking. No surviving specimen attributed to him bears his name—documentation also

Laurens Janszoon Coster.

missing in the case of Gutenberg. Coster's printing achievement was not recorded until a century after his death, and his method of typecasting was said to be casting in sand from wooden molds.

His last name means "sacristan," a title for an official of the Great Church of Haarlem. He is mentioned several times in records between 1417 and 1434 as alderman, tax assessor, and treasurer and is presumed to have died in a plague that struck Haarlem in 1440. In Gutenberg's case there are references to him and proximity to specific printed products. Coster does not have even that body of evidence.

Printing and the Renaissance

At almost the same time as the emergence of movable type in Germany, northern Italy was experiencing the beginnings of the Renaissance. The humanist movement, initiated by Petrarch in the late 14th century, represented a surge in the study and dissemination of the classics—secular rather than religious texts. When the printing press arrived in Italy in the 1460s, printers did as they had done in Germany: they emulated the letterforms of the scribes. The Italian scribal hand was not the heavy medieval black letter script, but instead the light *littera antiqua* of the humanist scholars. In the years between 1465 and 1500, Italian printers adopted, developed, and perfected what we now know as the roman type style.

The first printers in Italy were Sweynheym and Pannartz, who set up their shop in 1464 near Rome. They came from Germany, where they had worked for Gutenberg, but then quickly adopted the Italian humanist script as their model. The type they produced had semi-gothic characteristics, but closely followed Italian calligraphic models.

The real center of Italian printing and culture was Venice. Printing began in Venice in 1469 with the granting of a five-year exclusive license to John de Spira (also de Speyer and van Speier). De Spira died before he could make much of his monopoly, but in the year that he was active he produced a printing typeface that is clearly roman.

Nicolas Jenson. Nicolas Jenson (c.1420–1480) was a publisher and printer best known as the person who developed the roman typeface. Apprenticed as a painter and then a cutter of dies for coinage, Jenson later became master of the French Royal Mint at Tours. In 1458 he went to Mainz and probably learned printing in Gutenberg's shop in Eltville. In 1470 he opened a printing office in Venice, and, in the first work he produced, the printed roman lowercase letter took on the proportions, shapes, and form that marked its transition from an imitation of handwriting to the typographic style that has remained in use throughout the centuries.

Jenson's type is remarkably similar to that of John de Spira; they each may have used a similar manuscript hand as a model. Jenson's rounder, slighter, roman letter results in a gray, not a black page. The roman style is a typical Renaissance product, just as the black letter is a Gothic style.

Aldus Manutius. Aldus Pius Manutius (1452–1516) was the foremost editor, printer, and publisher of the Renaissance. He was born at Bassiano, south of Rome. Between 1467 and 1473 he was a student in the Faculty of Arts in the University of Rome, where he developed a passion for the classics. In the late 1470s he attended the University of Ferrara, where he studied Greek under humanist educator Battista Guarino. From 1480 he was employed as tutor to the children of the Duke of Carpi, near Ferrara. He moved to Mirandola in 1482 to stay with his friend, the cabalist Giovanni Pico, whose nephew Alberto Pio, the prince of Carpi, granted Aldus the funds to set up a printing press for the promotion of Greek scholarship.

In 1489 Aldus abandoned teaching for publishing and moved to Venice, where he entered into a partnership with Andrea Torresano, who provided experience and resources, and Pierfrancesco Barbarigo, who provided financial and political support. In 1490 the Aldine Press was founded, with a staff of Greek scholars, compositors, and printers. Aldus did most of the work, but he probably owned only 10% of the firm. He improved his position by marrying Maria Torresano in 1505. Aldus was succeeded in the publishing business by his youngest son, Paolo, and his grandson Aldo II, who ran the firm until 1598.

Aldus had begun his career as a teacher and saw a need for the publication of Greek and Latin classics—works ranked high on the Renaissance humanist agenda. Many of the works of ancient Rome and Greece had been published by the end of the 15th century but a large number were not in print. Because of Aldus, works of numerous Greek and Latin authors were published for the first time, and works by others appeared in better editions than had previously been available. During the first twenty years of his press, he published the works of Aristotle, Thucydides, Herodotus, Sophocles, Euripides, Theocritus, Homer, and Hesiod; Latin authors published include Virgil, Horace, Juvenal, Persius, Martial, Cicero, Ovid, Catullus, and Pliny—the foundation of Greek and Latin classics.

The Aldine Press also introduced many printing innovations. Bolognese typecutter and goldsmith Francesco Griffo advanced typeface design beyond simple imitation of hand-drawn characters, applying his punch-cutting art in the type for *De Aetna,* by Pietro Bembo (1493), and the *Hypnerotomachia Poliphili* (1499), by Francisco Colonna. His most famous achievement was the development of italic type around 1500.

Aldus experimented with a number of Greek and Latin types, many of his own design. Aldus's punches were cut for him by Griffo. The first two fonts used by Aldus were modeled on the writing of the Greek scribe Immanuel Rhusotas, and the third one was from Aldus's editorial collaborator Cretan Marcus Musurus. The last was a simplified version that represented Griffo's interpretation of Aldus's own handwriting. Aldus did not revolutionize roman type as much as he refined it. Griffo's types are quite similar to those of de Spira and Jenson, and historians believe that they are variations on common ancestors.

Aldus was the first to adopt italic as a printing font. The italic type was based on the cursive but legible hand called Cancelleresca used in the government offices of Venice and other Italian city-states. In addition to its aesthetic qualities, italic had an economic advantage: it allowed the printer to squeeze a greater number of characters on a line. Aldus's fonts had great influence on the development of typography over the centuries.

Aldus's anchor and dolphin signature symbol became a well-known printer's mark; it appeared in the first edition of *Hypnerotomachia Poliphili* in 1499. The anchor and dolphin symbol is called an impresa, a form of pictorial puzzle popular in Renaissance Italy. Today it would be called an icon. The picture illustrates a motto, a saying of the emperor Augustus: *Festina lente*, "Make haste slowly." The anchor was symbolic of slowness and the dolphin of speed, an apt description of the printer's style of working.

Aldus's anchor and dolphin signature symbol.

Aldus's books were printed in three different sizes: folios, quartos, and octavos. The terms refer to the number of times a large sheet of paper was folded to produce a given number of printed pages; the greater the number of folds, the smaller the resulting pages. The most famous of Aldus's printings was the *editiones princepes* (first printed editions) of Aristotle. The five volumes, published in folio between 1495 and 1498, contained all of Aristotle's works except for the *Poetics* and the *Rhetoric*. Classical authors were typically published with marginal commentaries, or glosses, by other writers, which resulted in large and cumbersome folio volumes. After 1500 Aldus began producing smaller books without glosses. The octavo-sized volume, the precursor of the modern pocket book, was an innovation popularized by Aldus.

The popularity of the octavo format is evident from Aldus's production record: he printed 55 editions in the folio format, 48 in octavo, and 29 of his editions were quartos. He experimented with a sextodecimo and a trecesimo-secundo edition. A typical edition ran 1,000 to 2,000 copies.

The price of an Aldine Latin octavo was equivalent to one days' salary of a Venetian schoolmaster, about five times the price of a modern hardcover. Publishing was a lucrative business, and demand for Aldine texts was high. The pace of work in Aldus's shop was such that "with both hands occupied and surrounded by pressmen who are clamorous for work, there is scarcely even time to blow my nose."

Aldus was representative of the second wave of humanism, a movement dedicated to placing classical culture at the center of education, ethics, and public life. Earlier humanists, such as Francesco Petrarca (1304–74) and Lorenzo Valla (1407–57), had focused on works in Latin, which were more immediately accessible because Latin was already the language of academic discourse throughout Europe. In the 15th century, increasing contact with Byzantium inspired a revival of interest in Greek, a revival that gained momentum with the fall of Constantinople in 1453, when many Byzantine scholars fled to Italy bringing their manuscript libraries with them. The humanist curriculum of Greek and Latin classics dominated European education until the 20th century. It has been said that Aldus Manutius may have started the Renaissance.

After the death of Aldus, book production leadership shifted to France, although German firms remained powerful, and Venice boasted 150 presses. Printers in this era functioned as typecutters, publishers, and booksellers.

Johann Gutenberg first used movable type about 1450; by the end of the century, presses had been established in over 200 communities, and as many as 40,000 different items had been printed for a total of 12 million copies. Books usually appeared as quartos bound between wooden boards and decorated copiously with woodcuts. Print runs were small, averaging less than 500. Thomas a Kempis's *Imitation of Christ* (1471) was a best seller, and had almost 100 editions by 1500. The vernacular had advanced by that time, but most 15th-century productions were religious works in Latin. An *incunabulum,* or *incunable* (Latin for "cradle"), is any book, pamphlet, or broadside printed during the 15th century—the beginning of the European printing industry. Many incunabula were destroyed during the Reformation and Counter Reformation, so the value of surviving copies is high. The British Museum Library and the Bibliothèque Nationale have two of the largest collections outside of Germany.

English Printing: William Caxton. William Caxton (1422–91) was born in the Weald of Kent. In 1438, he became apprenticed to Robert Large, a textile merchant who became the mayor of London in 1439. After Large's death in 1441, Caxton moved to Bruges, Belgium, the center for trade between the English and Flemish, and built up a thriving textile business. He attained prominence as a merchant and by 1463 was acting governor of the Merchant Adventurers in the Low Countries. In 1464 he attempted unsuccessfully to renew a wool treaty with Phillip, Duke of Burgundy. Four years later, Caxton successfully completed the trade negotiations with Charles the Bold, Phillip's successor. Caxton was hired as an advisor to Charles's new duchess, the former Princess Margaret of York, sister of Edward IV.

About 1471, Caxton visited Cologne, where he learned the art of printing from one of Gutenberg's workmen. Later he founded a press in Bruges, before returning to England. In 1476, he set up England's first printing press. Caxton had been a prolific translator and found the printing press a marvelous way to advance his mission of promoting popular literature. In 1477, Caxton's press at Westminster produced *Dictes or Sayenges of the Phylosophers*, the first dated book printed in England. Caxton ultimately published more than ninety books, including the first edition of Chaucer's *Canterbury Tales*.

It was at the request of Duchess Margaret that he resumed translation of a popular French romance, *The Recuyell of the Historyes of Troye* by Raoul le Fèvre. *The Recuyell* is the first printed book in the English language (1474). His next publication, *The Game and Play of Chess Moralised* (1476), was a translation of the first major European work on chess, and was the first printed book in English to make extensive use of woodcuts.

Caxton was an enthusiastic editor and he determined the diction, spelling, and usage for all the books he printed. English suffered from so much regional variation that Caxton's contributions as an editor and printer have given him credit for standardizing the English language.

The typefaces used by Caxton were all variations of black letter or Gothic type. His earlier works were set in an early form of French *lettre bâtarde*. By 1490, he had acquired a more round and open typeface, a textura originated by Parisian printer Antoine Verard and later favored by Caxton's successor, Wynkyn de Worde.

16th–17th Centuries:
Innovations in Type and Illustration

Simon de Colines. Simon de Colines (1480–1546) was a partner of printer Henri Estienne. Colines married Estienne's widow and was in charge of the press until Estienne's son Robert entered the business in 1526, at which time Colines set up his own shop. In 1528 he began to use italic type and publish many Greek and Latin classics. He is credited with the design of italic and Greek fonts and of a roman face for St. Augustine's *Sylvius* (1531), from which the Garamond types were derived. In 1525 he published the notable *Grandes Heures de Simon de Colines*, with decorations by Geoffroy Tory.

Claude Garamond. The French type designer Claude Garamond (1490–1561) was apprenticed about 1510 to Antoine Augerau, and by 1520 he was working with the typefounder Geoffroy Tory. Garamond was one of the first punch cutters to work independently of printers, influencing European punch cutters for 150 years.

His first romans and *grecs du roi* were cut for the firm of Robert Estienne. He designed many typefaces in renais-

sance roman styles, as well as two italics. His Greek type set the pattern for Greek printing until the early 19th century.

Many of his punches survive today at the Plantin-Moretus Museum in Antwerp and at the Imprimerie Nationale in Paris. Though most of today's typefaces called Garamonds are actually based on the work of Jean Jannon, there are a few bearing Garamond's name that are based directly on his work, and countless others, including Jan Tschichold's Sabon, that owe large elements of their design to Garamond.

In 1545 Garamond began to publish books. Apparently he was not successful in business, for he died in poverty.

Henri Estienne. Henri Estienne II (1528–1598) was the grandson of Henri Estienne, founder of the family printing firm in Paris, and son of Robert Estienne, who had left Paris to establish a printing firm in Geneva. Educated in classical literature, Henri Estienne II traveled in Italy, England, and Flanders, studying ancient manuscripts and visiting scholars. He joined his father in Geneva and began publishing the results of his own research in printed editions of ancient Greek texts.

In 1566 Estienne published his most famous work—a Latin edition of the work of Greek historian Herodotus, accompanied by a French translation. Designed to show how the strange stories in Herodotus were paralleled by equally strange contemporary ones, these translations were satirical of Estienne's own age. Estienne was arrested in Geneva, tried, and forced to cancel offending pages. Even so, the book went through twelve editions in sixteen years. After 1583 he spent much time away from his home, wandering from city to city in search of a patron. The later publications of his press suffered from neglect. He died on a visit to France.

Jean Jannon. The French punch cutter and printer Jean Jannon, born in 1580, designed a series of Baroque romans and italics. Much of Jannon's original material survives at the Imprimerie Nationale in Paris, where his typefaces are known as Caractères de l'Université. They wound up there when Cardinal Richelieu attacked the Protestant stronghold of Sedan and confiscated Jannon's print shop. The types were used in 1890 for the centennial of the French Revolution, since they were thought to be Garamond's. Beatrice Warde discovered the error in the 1920s, but by then many Jannon types were issued as Garamond types.

Robert Granjon. From the middle of the 16th until well into the 18th century, the most notable type designers in Europe were known more for their refinements on Garamond's modifications of earlier faces than for innovations of their own. One of the few who attempted new approaches was Robert Granjon (1523–1588), who tried—with his type called *Civilité*—to create a major typeface different from roman, italic, and Gothic. He envisioned it as a national type for the use of French printers. Reminiscent of a cursive gothic, it found minor acceptance as a display face and was not utilized in book printing.

Christophe Plantin. Christophe Plantin (1520–1589) learned bookbinding and bookselling in Normandy and started a printing business in Antwerp in 1549. His many publications were distinguished by their excellent typography, and he was original in using copper, instead of wood, engravings for book illustrations.

Christopher Plantin designed his formats to suit his markets and recognized publishing and distribution as being separate from printing. His *Biblia Polyglotta,* which would fix the original text of Old and New Testaments, was supported by Philip II of Spain in spite of clerical opposition. It appeared in eight volumes during 1569–1572.

When Antwerp was plundered by the Spaniards in 1576 and Plantin had to pay a ransom, he established a branch office in Paris. Then, in 1583, he settled in Leiden as the typographer of the new university of the states of Holland, leaving his business in Antwerp to his sons-in-law, John Moretus and Francis van Raphelengius. In 1585, Plantin returned to Antwerp. After his death, the business was carried on by Moretus. The House of Plantin stood for 300 years. In 1876 the city of Antwerp acquired the buildings and their contents and created the Plantin-Moretus Museum.

Christoffel Van Dijck. Born in 1606, Christoffel Van Dijck was a Dutch punch cutter who designed several Baroque romans and italics. He set the standard for Dutch oldstyle typography, which greatly influenced William Caslon in his type designs. Most of Van Dijck's material has been destroyed, but the remaining punches and matrices are at Johann Enschende en Zonen, in Haarlem, Netherlands.

Philippe Grandjean. In 1692, King Louis directed that a typeface be designed for the exclusive use of the royal printer. The design was the work of a committee of the Academy of Sciences, whose members ignored calligraphic models in favor of analytical and mathematical principles. The type, *Romain du Roi* (King's roman), was then cut by Philippe Grandjean. There is at least a legend that King Louis refused a request from the King of Sweden for a set of the punches.

The 18th Century

William Caslon. William Caslon (1692–1766) was born in the village of Cradley, in Worcestershire, England. He was an apprentice engraver in London at the age of 13; by age 24 he had become a successful independent engraver.

In 1720, Caslon began his career in type design by accepting a commission to create a typeface for the New Testament in Arabic. His subsequent roman typeface set an example for beauty and readability for all later type. His first specimen sheet in 1734 displayed 38 of his type fonts and led to the virtual cessation of importing Dutch types, on which English printers had formerly relied. His typefaces, noted for their legibility, are among the best "utility" faces ever produced.

Caslon expanded his business into Britain's first major type foundry, moving, in 1737, into the Chiswell Street Foundry, where his family would continue in the trade for over 120 years. Caslon type fell into disuse at the start of the 19th century. But in 1844, Charles Whittingham initiated a Caslon revival by using the typeface for the Chiswick Press publication of *The Diary of Lady Willoughby.* This revival was taken up in America by L. J. Johnson, who copied the Caslon face in 1858 under the name Old Style. The Caslon typeface remains one of the most popular of all time.

John Baskerville. Baskerville (1706–1775) was born in Worcestershire, too. He began engraving tombstones and working as a calligrapher at the age of 17. He entered the japanning (lacquering) trade in Birmingham in 1740 and built up a considerable fortune in less than a decade.

Baskerville took up printing and typefounding as a hobby, seeking to improve upon the typefaces of William Caslon. His first edition, *Virgil,* was published in 1757, in royal quarto (12.5×10-in. format). Later books in quarto included the works of Horace, Lucretius, Terence, and Catullus. Baskerville's typeface designs were delicate, with contrast in stroke widths, requiring advances in printing technology which he also pioneered. In particular, he is credited with the technique of "sock"—pressing the wet printed sheets between copper plates, thereby smoothing the paper and drying the ink.

His other innovations include the use of wove paper, the invention of rich inks that were truly black, generous space between lines, and wide letterspacing within display lines made up of capitals. He also introduced glossy paper instead of the rough, antique laid paper of the time. Baskerville's work was known for its rather plain, unornamented style. His beautiful round roman typeface, modeled on his earlier penmanship, had an important influence on type design. His typefaces are considered a transition between the old style type such as Caslon and the modern type style exemplified by Bodoni.

He was printer to Cambridge University from 1758 to 1768. His folio Bible of 1763 ranks as the finest example of printing in the 18th century.

Giambattista Bodoni. Giambattista Bodoni (1740–1813) was born into a printing family in Saluzzo, Italy. At the age of 18, he was hired by the Vatican printing house in Rome. By 1768, he was given the position of director of the press of Ferdinand, Duke of Parma, which he retained for the rest of his life.

The Evolution of Typefaces

The first printed types were derived from medieval lettering, with ornate capitals, wedge-shaped serifs, and thick strokes. These typefaces are called "blackletter" and they evolved from the Carolingian miniscule by a gradual narrowing and flowing of lines with pens made from feathers. The blackletter used by Gutenberg in his first Bible is called textura. Other kinds of blackletter are fraktur, bastarda and rotunda. Fraktur was in use in Germany well into the 1900s.

Old style type had its origins in Renaissance humanism. The main characteristics include low contrast with diagonal stress, and "bracketed" serifs (serifs with a curved join to the vertical stem of the letter). The earliest (Venetian or Renaissance) old style typefaces have very minimal contrast, and a sloped crossbar on the lowercase "e." One such is Bruce Rogers' Centaur (1916), based on Jenson's roman. Monotype's Bembo (1929) is based on the work of Francesco Griffo for Aldus. Italics were independent designs. Arrighi's italic (1524) is seen today as the italic form of Centaur. The italic form of Bembo is based on the italic of Tagliente (1524). Baroque oldstyle type (17th century) has more contrast, with a variable axis, and more slope to the italic. Garamond and Caslon are good examples of oldstyle types.

"Transitional" type is has a place between old style and modern. Distinguishing features of transitional typefaces include vertical stress and slightly higher contrast than old style typefaces, combined with horizontal serifs. Philippe Grandjean's "Romain du Roi" for the French Crown around 1702, and Pierre Simon Fournier's work around 1750 and John Baskerville's work from 1757 onwards typify this category. Transitional types evolved towards "modern" designs where contrast is accentuated and serifs are more flattened. Richard Austin (Bell), William Martin (Bulmer) and Miller & Richard (Scotch Roman) are British designers with transitional transitionals, as such.

"Modern" typefaces are distinguishable by their stark vertical stress and strong contrast. Modern serifs and horizontals are very thin, almost hairline thickness. The first designer was Giambattista Bodoni, of Parma, Italy. The most common "modern" typefaces are the many re-interpretations of Bodoni's work. Didot and its re-interpretation by J.E. Walbaum (1800) is not commonly in use.

Sans serif type made its first appearance around 1815–1817. It is distingushed by simple letterforms with relatively uniform stroke weight, lacking significant contrast, often geometric in its basic design. Sans Serif (gothic or grotesque) letters have no serifs, as the name states. Low contrast and absence of serifs make most sans serif typefaces harder to read for general text. Gothic or grotesque are both generic names for sans serif (but Letter Gothic is a slab serif type).

Sans serif italics are usually a sloped or mechanically obliqued style of the plain letters. The most common sans is Helvetica (1951, Meidinger) with a wide range of weights and widths. Other ubiquitous sans serif types include Univers (Frutiger, 1952–1970), Arial (Monotype), Franklin Gothic (M.F. Benton, 1903) and Frutiger (Frutiger, 1975). The Art Deco movement in the 1920s and 1930s introduced geometrical shapes as the basis for sans serif designs. Some sans faces do not fall into neat sans serif categories. Eric Gill's 1928 Gill Sans has an architectural quality with greater contrast and humanistic design which makes it more appropriate than most sans typefaces for text applications.

Slab Serif (Egyptian) faces have square rectangular serifs, often the same thickness as the body strokes. Many of the most popular slab serif forms have been created by adding slab serifs to sans faces by the same designer (Adrian Frutiger's 1977 Glypha from his Univers, Herb Lubalin's 1974 Lubalin Graph from his and Tom Carnase's Avant Garde). Other slab serif faces include Berthold City (Trump, 1930), Memphis (Weiss, 1930), Serifa (Frutiger, 1968) and Silica (Stone, 1990).

The Clarendons or Ionics are an offspring of the slab serif typefaces in which the square serifs are bracketed. These are often used in newspaper work, because the serifs hold up well under printing conditions which has made them very popular for newspaper use. The most famous member of this sub-family is Century Schoolbook (Morris Fuller Benton, 1924–35).

Fat Face types are an offshoot from the moderns, intended for display purposes. The first such types appeared from 1810–1820 and further exaggerated the contrast of modern typefaces, with slab-like vertical lines and extra emphasis of any vertical serifs, which often acquired a wedge shape. Bodoni Ultra, Normande and Elephant are all examples of fat face types which are based on early to mid-19th Century originals

Wood type is carved from wood, cut perpendicular to the grain and distinguished by stark contrasts, an overall dark color, and a lack of fine lines. Faces may be unusually compressed or extended. Many wood types have an "Old West" or Victorian feel, because they are most strongly associated with America in the 1870–1900 period. Some of the wood types most popular today are those in an Adobe collection of 1990, which includes Cottonwood, Ironwood and Juniper, among others.

Script typefaces are based on handwriting with either a flexible steel nib pen, or a broad-edged pen, and is modelled after calligraphic handwriting. Common scripts based on steel nib styles include Shelley (Carter, 1972), Coronet (Middleton, 1937–38), and Snell Roundhand (Carter, 1965, based on Snell (1694). Script faces based more on the broad-edged tradition include Park Avenue (Smith, 1933). There are also monoline scripts, which lack significant contrast in the letter strokes, such as Freestyle Script.

Brush typefaces look as if they were drawn as sign-painted lettering, such as Balloon (Kaufmann, 1939),

---

The Evolution of Typefaces *(continued)*

Brush Script (Smith, 1942), and Dom Casual (Dom, 1952). Brushwork can also be the basis for script, as with Present Script (Sallaway, 1974) and Mistral (Excoffon, 1953)

The Victorian era, from 1880 to World War I, was characterized by an ornamental style of art, with organic, asymmetrical, intricate and flowing lines that in some cases was somewhat overwhelming. It evolved into an "Art Nouveau" movement that produced distinctive typography, including Arnold Boecklin (Weisert, 1904), Artistik, Desdemona, Galadriel and Victorian.

Art Deco found beauty in geometric simplicity. Appearing in the 1920s and 30s, Art Deco usually means sans serif type based on a Bauhaus model. Popular faces are Futura (Renner, 1927–39), Spartan (Mergenthaler), and Kabel (Koch, 1927–30). A recent Art Deco display face is ITC Anna (1991).

Many of the most interesting typefaces of the twentieth century do not fit easily into the above categories.

They reflect the integration of different styles. Times New Roman (Morison/Lardent, 1931) has old style, transitional and modern elements. Zapf's Palatino (1948) and Zapf Renaissance (1987) are modern typefaces with the spirit of Renaissance letterforms.

Revivals of old style show modern influences in the proportions or lettershapes and include the Granjon-inspired Galliard (Carter, 1978) and Minion (Slimbach, 1989). Aldo Novarese's Eurostile (1964) takes sans serif forms and distorts them towards square and rectangular shapes. Zapf's 1958 Optima is a delicious blend of sans serif frames with calligraphic covering. Shannon (Holmes & Prescott Fishman, 1981) is a sans serif based on Celtic manuscript letterforms.

Several designers have re-interpreted ancient Greek lettering for a modern sans serif alphabet, most popularly Carol Twombly's Lithos (1989), and Matthew Carter's Skia GX (1994).

Bodoni was the most successful early proponent of the "modern" typeface, distinguished by a strong contrast between the thin and thick strokes, and vertical, rather than oblique, shading. His books were produced for the wealthy and the aristocracy, and they were more advanced in elegance and refinement than anything else being printed in Europe. Intended more for show, his publications were often inaccurate and difficult to read. His Greek typefaces, as seen in his masterful edition of Homer, are more successful. His enormous collection of typefaces was published posthumously in the two-volume *Manuale Tipografico* (Parma, 1818).

Into the 19th Century: Technological Advances

The 500 years after Gutenberg consisted of improvements on and mechanization of the typesetting and printing processes. In the 19th century, type was still inserted character-by-character into a composing stick, which comprised a line of type. The characters from the composing stick were then transferred as a unit to a metal or wooden tray called a galley. After the galley of type was proofed with ink, it was broken down into pages, and running heads, folios, etc., were added. Each page of type was then locked up, to be sent for platemaking or to the pressroom if the material was going to be printed directly from type. Presses at that time were flatbed, or platen, presses in which the type was locked onto a flat platen and the substrate was pressed over it, either sheet by sheet, or, later, by a rotating cylinder.

In 1725, Scottish printer William Ged invented a process for making plates from locked-up metal type by creating an intermediate mold of the entire page or pages. It was refined and officially named stereotyping shortly afterward by Firmin Didot. In stereotyping, the metal type is covered with a wet paper or mat, and pressure is applied to stamp the impression of the type into the mat. The paper or mat is allowed to dry and placed in a casting machine, where molten metal is poured to cast an entire page of type as a single plate.

In 1800, Lord Stanhope had a cast-iron screw press made. Its strength was such that it could print two folio pages at a time. A few years later, Friedrich König built a wood prototype of an iron press, where a cylinder rolled across the type. Far less pressure was required because only one fraction of the type was in contact with the roller any time. When König hooked up his press to the steam engine, it printed 1,100 large sheets per hour. He enlisted the help of *The Times* of London, which then had a circulation of 10,000, and soon eight men worked his press at 4,000 copies an hour. In time, a press that fed paper from a roll printed 12,000 copies per hour. Platen presses continued to have their place in small jobbing work—business cards and stationery.

In 1846, the American printer Richard Hoe created a cylinder-type press (in contrast to the flatbed type previously employed), in which the type could be locked into place on a rotating cylinder. In 1869 English printers began using curved stereotype plates on cylinder-based presses, which replaced assembled type forms.

But as mass communication advanced, printing technology raced to keep pace.

Mass Communication. For several centuries after the invention of movable type, the most important product of the printing press was the book. Beginning in the 18th century, new kinds of publications were born. Early newspapers consisted of about four pages of hard-to-read type. Circulation was limited, confined to the small number of people who were both literate and able to afford them. This situation changed dramatically during the 19th century, when the newspaper became a mass-produced medium, a product of Industrial Revolution technology. One of the distinguishing characteristics of the Industrial Revolution was the use of new sources of energy, with steam power taking on a growing importance. König's steam-powered press printed in one-third the time that the hand press required.

The development of the mass-circulation newspaper was further stimulated by 19th-century inventions for the rapid gathering and dissemination of news. Railroads and steamships conveyed reporters to scenes of newsworthy events. The telegraph quickly relayed their stories back to the newsroom and made stories less verbose—senders were charged by the word. The news gathering power of the telegraph was enhanced by transatlantic cables. The telephone, by the end of the century, further assisted reporters and their newspapers.

Paper Evolves. Papermaking technology improved rapidly throughout the 19th century to fuel printing growth. The introduction of chlorine for bleaching meant that white paper could be manufactured from colored linen and cotton rags, increasing the range of available raw materials.

As the century progressed, the demand for paper increased dramatically, and other sources were sought. Esparto grass from Spain and North Africa became a valued commodity for papermaking. When it was realized that wood pulp could be used as a source, large-scale paper manufacture become possible. A machine was developed that could pulp logs using grindstones revolving in water, but because the pulp contained large amounts of impurities, the first wood pulp papers were of very poor quality. It was found that these impurities could be removed by boiling the wood pulp with various chemical reagents: soda and sulfite in the 1850s, sulfate in the 1880s. The use of wood pulp allowed papermakers to increase their production, and larger and faster papermaking machines were developed.

Vegetable fibers, which in Europe came principally from flax and hemp, were shredded and reduced to a pulp in water; a screen was dipped in the pulp and removed with a thin layer of pulp. As the water drained off, the pulped fibers meshed and matted into a sheet, which was then dried and pressed. The first mechanical papermaking process was invented in 1798 by Nicolas Louis Robert, a Frenchman who devised a machine with an endless wire-mesh web that was turned by hand and dipped into a vat of pulp, lifting out a pulp layer. The mesh vibrated to shake off excess water and to lock the fibers together. The pulp layer was then squeezed through rollers and dried. Robert traveled to England seeking backers for his idea. In 1805 a practical commercial machine was built by the Fourdrinier brothers,

Henry and Sealy, and Bryan Donkin. The screen end of a modern papermaking machine is still called a fourdrinier.

Lithography: Alois Senefelder. Alois Senefelder (1771–1834) of Germany was the inventor of lithography. His invention of a new printing process came about by chance while he was seeking a method of reproducing plays and musical scores. He was experimenting on Bavarian limestone in place of the more costly copper. Writing in reverse on a piece of limestone with greasy chalk and then dampening the stone, he found that an inked roller would deposit ink only on the chalk. His experiments led to the discovery that polished stone, when properly inked and treated with chemicals would transfer

Litho stones.

its image onto paper. Thus was born stone printing, or, as Senefelder called it, chemical printing, the forerunner of lithography. The practical aspects of lithography were immediately apparent, and in 1799 the prince-elector of Bavaria gave Senefelder an exclusive fifteen-year privilege to exploit his invention. Just one year after Senefelder submitted his model for an automated press in 1817, the first lithograph was published in the United States by Bass Otis.

Senefelder's work on copper plates was unsuccessful until an accident led to his discovery in 1796. Senefelder records that he jotted down a laundry list with grease pencil on a piece of Bavarian limestone. It occurred to him that if he etched away the rest of the surface, the markings would be left in relief. Two years of experimentation eventually led to the discovery of flat-surface printing (modern lithography). In 1818 he documented his discovery in *Vollständiges Lehrbuch der Steindruckerey (A Complete Course of Lithography):* "I had just ground a stone plate smooth in order to treat it with etching fluid and to pursue on it my practice in reverse writing, when my mother asked me to write a laundry list for her. The laundress was waiting, but

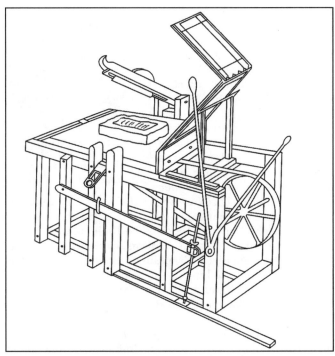

An early lithographic press invented by Alois Senefelder.

we could find no paper...I wrote the list hastily on the clean stone...As I was preparing afterwards to wash the writing from the stone...I became curious to see what would happen with writing made thus of prepared ink, if the stone were now etched with aqua fortis (nitric acid). I thought that possibly the letters would be left in relief and admit of being inked and printed like book types or wood-cuts."

Later in the development of lithography, plates of zinc, iron, brass and copper were ground with pumice and chalk and wrapped around a cylinder to substitute for stone. Photography later made it possible to fix an image onto a photosensitive plate by exposure through a negative. In off-set lithographic printing, the first image is printed onto a rubber blanket before being transferred to the stock.

Photography. French inventor Joseph Nicephore Niépce (1765–1833), the first person to make a permanent photographic image, was interested in lithography. Studying the work of Alois Senefelder, Niépce tried to improve the process by using tin plates to perfect a form of photolithography. Research advanced slowly and drained the funds of his trust. He did find a way to fix images using acid baths. A breakthrough came in 1822 when he made a permanent image using a camera obscura. After exposing coated pewter plates to a camera image, he used the vapors from heated iodine crystals to darken the silver and heighten contrast.

Louis Daguerre was a theater set painter known for the realism of his large canvases, which he showcased in spectacles called "dioramas." Forming a partnership with

Niépce in 1829, Daguerre set out to create a practical photographic process. Niépce, in failing health, died penniless in 1833, having solved the basic problem of reproducing nature by light, and having invented the first photomechanical reproduction process. Daguerre built on this knowledge, and, by 1837, after nine years of work, he devised the daguerreotype. Adhering a thin sheet of polished silver to a copper plate, he made it light-sensitive by exposing it to the vapors from heated iodine crystals. Exposures of 15–30 minutes were needed to make an impression. This latent (invisible) image was developed by treating it with mercury vapor. Fixed in a solution of salt and hot water, the positive image became permanent.

Daguerre unveiled his invention in 1839, after an Englishman named William Henry Fox Talbot announced the development of a process called photography. The daguerreotype could only be seen in certain lights and from particular angles, and unlike Talbot's negative-positive process, the daguerreotype could not be mass-produced. But there was no comparison between Daguerre's pictures and the crude, grainy photos produced by Talbot.

In partnership with his brother-in-law, Daguerre began manufacturing the Giroux camera which, packaged with Daguerre's 79-page instruction manual, was soon in high demand and shipped around the world. Users improved Daguerre's basic methods. The introduction of fast achromatic lenses, large apertures, and an improved development process utilizing mercury and bromide chlorine vapors brought exposure time down to two minutes. But by 1851 this art form would be forgotten.

William Talbot's contributions were the introduction of the negative-positive process and the use of paper as a production medium. Talbot sought a chemical means to produce a permanent image. By 1835 he had devised a method of making ordinary paper sensitive to light. He called it the calotype. After dipping a sheet in a diluted salt solution, he dried it and then immersed it in silver nitrate solution. The resulting chemical combination formed light-sensitive silver chloride. Placing the sheet in a camera, he exposed it for 30 minutes. The image was made permanent with a salt or potassium iodide bath which washed away much of the unexposed silver chloride. He switched to Sir John Herschel's more effective hypo sulfite of soda, or "hypo," as a fixer.

The problem in applying silver chloride solutions to glass is that it will not adhere. In 1848, Niépce de St. Victor, cousin of Nicephore Niépce, mixed egg whites with potassium iodide, potassium bromide, and a little salt. He spread the solution on a glass plate, let it dry, and dipped it in silver nitrate. The plate, still wet, was exposed in a camera and then developed. Known as albumen photography, this process was also used to make the first commercially manufactured printing papers. British sculptor Frederick Scott Archer replaced albumen with collodion in 1851. Dissolving gun cotton in a solution of ether and alcohol, he added silver iodide and iron iodide. The dried plate was immersed in silver nitrate and distilled water. The collodion process spread during the next 30 years. Using this process, photographers captured the Civil War as images for all time.

Print in the United States

Religious and political freedom were rallying cries for those Europeans who were drawn to the American colonies. In 1638, Reverend Joseph Glover and his wife Elizabeth sailed for America to set up a press at Cambridge, Massachusetts. Reverend Glover returned to England to recruit a pressman and order equipment and supplies. He died on the way back to America, and his assistant Stephen Daye (1594–1668), took over. Daye, a locksmith whose son Matthew was a printer's apprentice, brought the continent's first press to Cambridge. The Dayes printed a broadside and an almanac in their first year. In 1640 they produced 1,700 copies of the first book printed in the colonies, the *Bay Psalm Book*. The printing press quickly became central to political and religious expression in the New World. Print was at the heart of the dissemination and defense of visionary ideas that shaped the American Revolution.

"Revolutionary" Printing. During the Middle Ages publishing was a monopoly of the monasteries and universities. To stem the dissemination of unpopular ideas, governments granted publishing monopolies to corporations and guilds, some of which endured for centuries. French printers became subject to licensing regulations as early as 1474. Censorship policies were poorly enforced, and thousands of unlicensed tracts were published in both Europe and North America. The growth in the size of the reading public prompted the creation of circulating libraries in England by the 1720s, making booksellers a force in the growth of publishing. With the appearance of the novel, individual authors gained wide followings, and the heightened demand for books led to the separation of the publishing and selling functions.

As more presses were established in many colonies, it became difficult to monitor them, and laws became less rigid. Presses, once confined to the capitals of the colonies, began to multiply as the colonies became immersed in the fight for freedom. In America, Isaiah Thomas and others utilized the press to rally citizen support for the Revolutionary War. Thomas, a writer and owner of a press, was in demand to establish presses in other places. He issued his paper *Massachusetts Spy* with the challenge, "Americans!—Liberty or Death!—Join or Die!"

By 1783, after the war, the number of presses multiplied even faster. As a result of the important role the press played in the war, the government made "freedom of the press" an important agenda of the new nation. Unrestricted printing presses gave rise to the printing of pamphlets, newspapers, and books, and after the establishment of peace, the press flourished. Most people who owned a printing press published either their own books or their own newspapers—their own opinions, their own propaganda.

Benjamin Franklin. Benjamin Franklin was born in Boston on January 17, 1706, into a Puritan family. His father, Josiah, was a candlemaker and mechanic who raised 13 children—survivors of his 17 children by two wives. With less than two years of formal schooling, Franklin was pressed into his father's trade. He devoured books at home, and, after being apprenticed to his brother  James, printer of *The New England Courant*, he read virtually every book that came to the shop. He absorbed the values and philosophy of the English Enlightenment. Like his favorite author, Joseph Addison, whose essays in the *Spectator* he memorized, Franklin added good sense, tolerance, and urbanity to his Puritan ethic.

At age 16, Franklin secretly wrote articles for the *Courant* signed "Silence Dogood," in which he satirized the Boston authorities and society. In one essay he argued that "hypocritical Pretenders to Religion" more injured the commonwealth than those "openly Profane." At one point James Franklin was imprisoned for similar statements, and Benjamin Franklin carried on the paper himself. He refused to suffer his brother's domineering attitude and in 1723 ran away to Philadelphia. Though penniless and unknown, Franklin soon found a job as a printer. After a year he went to England, where he became a master printer, sowed the wild oats of youth, astonished Londoners with his swimming feats, and lived among the aspiring writers and thinkers of London. Returning to Philadelphia in 1726, he soon owned his own newspaper, the *Pennsylvania Gazette*, and began to print *Poor Richard's Almanack* (1732). His business expanded further when he contracted to do the public printing of the province, and he established partnerships with printers in other colonies. He also operated a book shop and became clerk of the Pennsylvania Assembly and postmaster of Philadelphia. In 1748, Franklin, at age 42, retired to live off the income from his businesses, managed mostly by others.

The sayings of "Poor Richard" are well known: "Early to bed and early to rise make a man healthy, wealthy, and wise." In his *Autobiography*, Franklin summarized his view of how the poor man may improve himself by hard work, thrift, and honesty. *Poor Richard's Almanack* sold widely in America, and a version known as *The Way to Wealth* was translated into many languages. In 1727, Franklin began his career as a civic leader by organizing a club of tradesmen called the Junto, which met for discussion on how to build their own businesses, insure the growth of Philadelphia, and improve the quality of life. Franklin led the Junto in founding a library (1731), a fire company (1736), a learned society (1743), a college (later the University of Pennsylvania, 1749), and an insurance company and a hospital (1751). The group also carried out plans for paving,

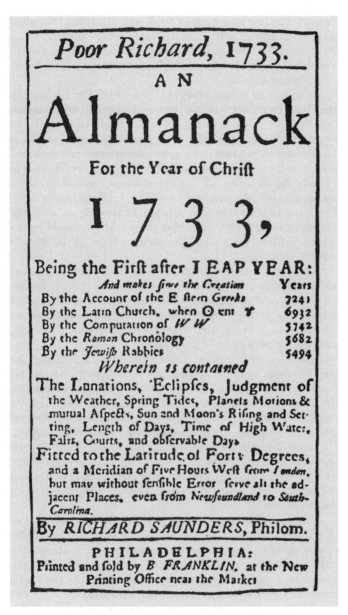

Poor Richard's Almanac.

cleaning, and lighting the streets and for making them safe with a nightwatch and a voluntary militia.

Franklin began another career in 1740 when he invented a fireplace called the Franklin stove, which soon heated buildings in Europe and North America. He read about electricity, and the experiments he proposed showed that lightning was in fact a form of electricity. His famous kite experiment, in which he flew a kite with the wire attached to a key during a thunderstorm, further established that laboratory-produced static electricity was akin to a previously mysterious and terrifying natural phenomenon. The Royal Society in London published these discoveries, and the lightning rods he invented appeared on buildings all over America and Europe. Franklin became

world famous. In Ben Franklin's simultaneous careers as printer, publisher, moralist, essayist, civic leader, scientist, inventor, politician, statesman, diplomat, businessman, and philosopher, he was a symbol of the American character. He was elected to the Royal Society in 1756 and to the French Academy of Sciences in 1772. His achievements included a theory of heat absorption, a stove, charting the Gulf Stream, tracking storm paths, and inventing bifocal lenses.

In 1751, Franklin was elected to the Pennsylvania Assembly and began over 40 years as a public official. He had intended to enlist political support for his various civic enterprises, but politics soon engulfed him. He opposed the Proprietary Party that sought to preserve the power of the Penn family in Pennsylvania affairs, and as the legislative strategist and recorder for the so-called Quaker Party, he defended the powers of elected representatives.

Franklin did not initially contemplate separation from Britain, which he regarded as having the freest, best government in the world. In the Plan of Union, which he presented in 1754 to the Albany Congress, he proposed partial self-government for the American colonies. A year later Franklin supported the ill-fated expedition of General Edward Braddock to recapture Fort Duquesne, and he persuaded the Quaker-dominated Pennsylvania Assembly to pass the colony's first militia law. He himself led a military expedition to the Lehigh Valley, where he established forts to protect frontiersmen from French and Indian raiders.

Franklin saw that colonial and ministerial ideas of governing were far apart. When he went to England in 1757 as agent of the Pennsylvania Assembly, he was alarmed to hear Lord Granville of the Privy Council declare that for the colonies, the king's instructions were "the Law of the Land: for the King is the Legislator of the Colonies." In England from 1757 to 1762, Franklin worked to persuade British officials to limit proprietary power in Pennsylvania. He enjoyed English social and intellectual life, attended meetings of the Royal Society, visited David Hume in Scotland, heard orchestras play the works of Handel, made tours of Europe, and received honorary degrees from the universities of St. Andrews (1759) and Oxford (1762). He created a pleasant family life at his Craven Street boarding house in London.

At home from 1762 to 1764, Franklin traveled throughout the colonies, reorganizing the American postal system. He built a new house on Market Street in Philadelphia—reconstructed and open to visitors today—and provided for his family, which included the former Deborah Read, his wife since 1730, their daughter Sally, who married Richard Bache and had a large family of her own, and his illegitimate son, William. As governor of New Jersey in 1762, William became a Loyalist during the American Revolution, estranged from his father.

In 1764 Franklin lost his seat in the assembly in a scurrilous campaign, but his party sent him to England in 1764 to petition that Pennsylvania be taken over as a royal colony. The crisis precipitated by the Stamp Act (1765) pushed that effort into the background and propelled Franklin into a new role as chief defender of American rights in Britain. At first he advised obedience to the act until it could be repealed, but news of violent protest against it in America stiffened his own opposition. After repeal of the Stamp Act, Franklin reaffirmed his desire to see the union of mother country and colonies "secured and established," but he also warned that "the seeds of liberty are universally found and nothing can eradicate them." He opposed the Townshend Acts (1767) because such "acts of oppression" would "sour American tempers" and perhaps even "hasten their final revolt." When the British Parliament passed the Tea Act (1773), which hurt colonial merchants, Franklin protested in a series of political essays, including "An Edict by the King of Prussia" and "Rules by Which a Great Empire May Be Reduced to a Small One." As these satires circulated in England, Franklin wrote his sister: "I have held up a Looking-Glass in which some of the Ministers may see their ugly faces, and the Nation its Injustice." In 1773, Franklin's friends in Massachusetts, against his wishes, published letters by Governor Thomas Hutchinson that Franklin had obtained in confidence. Exposed as a dishonest schemer, Franklin was denounced before the Privy Council in 1774 and stripped of his postmaster's office. Although he continued to work for conciliation, the Boston Tea Party and Britain's oppressive response to it soon doomed such efforts. In March 1775, Franklin sailed for home.

From April 1775 to October 1776, Franklin served on the Pennsylvania Committee of Safety and in the Continental Congress, submitted articles of confederation for the united colonies, proposed a new constitution for Pennsylvania, and helped draft the Declaration of Independence. He signed the Declaration, thus becoming a revolutionary at the age of 70. Franklin and his two grandsons sailed for France in 1776, where he gained critical French aid for the Revolutionary War. Parisian literary and scientific circles hailed him as a living embodiment of Enlightenment virtues. Wigless and dressed in plain brown clothes, he was called Le Bonhomme Richard.

France wanted to injure Britain but could not afford to help the American rebels unless eventual success seemed assured. Franklin worked behind the scenes to send war supplies across the Atlantic, thwart British diplomacy, and make friends with influential French officials. He overcame his own doubts about the possibly dishonest dealings of his fellow commissioner (Silas Deane) in channeling war materials to American armies, but the third commissioner, Arthur Lee, bitterly condemned both Deane and Franklin. Despite these quarrels, in 1778, following news of the American victory at Saratoga, the three commissioners were able to sign the vital alliance with France.

Franklin became the first American minister to France, and for seven years he acted as diplomat, purchasing agent, recruiting officer, loan negotiator, admiralty court, and intelligence chief. He was the main representative of the new United States in Europe and oversaw the dispatch of French armies and navies to North America, supplied American armies with French munitions, outfitted John Paul Jones—whose ship *Bonhomme Richard* was named in Franklin's honor—and secured loans from the nearly bankrupt French treasury.

The loss at Yorktown (1781) persuaded British leaders that they could not win the war, and Franklin made secret contact with peace negotiators sent from London. In these negotiations he proposed treaty articles close to those finally agreed to, such as complete American independence, access to the Newfoundland fishing grounds, evacuation of British forces from all occupied areas, and a western boundary on the Mississippi River. With John Jay, Franklin represented the United States in signing the Treaty of Paris (1783), by which the world's foremost power (Great Britain) recognized the independence of the world's newest nation.

Franklin came home in 1785. In his 80th year he was suffering from painful bladder stones but accepted election for three years as president of Pennsylvania and resumed active roles in the Pennsylvania Society for Promoting the Abolition of Slavery, the American Philosophical Society, and the University of Pennsylvania.

At the Constitutional Convention of 1787, although he was too weak to stand, Franklin's good humor and gift for compromise helped to prevent bitter disputes. Franklin's final public pronouncements urged ratification of the Constitution and approved the inauguration of the new federal government under his admired friend George Washington. He wrote friends in France that "we are making Experiments in Politicks," but that American "affairs mend daily and are getting into good order very fast." Still cheerful and optimistic, Benjamin Franklin died in Philadelphia on April 17, 1790.

In his will he left 800 pounds, to gain interest for 100 years, to the cities of Boston and Philadelphia to aid in the education of young people. At the turn of the century both cities erected Franklin Institutes and put some of the money back in the bank for another 100 years. In the 1990s the funds were used to enhance the institutes.

He was the quintessential American and defined the spirit of a nation. His epitaph, which he penned when he was in his forties, asked that he be remembered for one thing—that he was a printer.

Robert Hoe. Robert Hoe (1784–1833) emigrated to New York City from England in 1803 and became a partner with two brothers, Matthew and Peter Smith, in a newly founded enterprise, Smith, Hoe and Company, manufacturers of printers' equipment. Among Hoe's innovations was the introduction of the "Washington" press, with a cast-iron frame to replace the wooden frame in presses. In 1829 he began improving upon the Napier cylinder press imported from England, finally supplanting British-made presses in the United States. Hoe also acquired rights to a steam-powered press patented by Isaac Adams and manufactured it.

19th Century America: The Industrial Revolution of Type

Until the 19th century Gutenberg's print technology had not changed dramatically. In the early 1800s the development of continuous rolls of paper, a steam-powered press, and a way to use iron instead of wood for building presses all added to the efficiency of printing. Printing advances made it possible for newspaperman Benjamin Day to drop the price of his *New York Sun* to a penny in 1833. Some historians point to this "penny press" as the first true mass medium, designed to "lay before the public, at a price well within the means of everyone, all the news of the day." Typesetting, however, had not changed at all.

Before the 19th century, printers cast a foundry type which they reused after every printing. The compositor set the type in a "stick" (hand-held tray) which he held in his left hand. With his right, he placed the letters in reading sequence with the tops towards himself. He could feel with his fingers the nicks along the bottom of the type and know that they were facing the right way. He put blocks of type metal between words—brass for a 1-point space, copper for a ½-pt. space, and stainless steel for a ¼-pt. space.

James Clephane: Godfather of the Typewriter and the Linotype.

James Ogilvie Clephane played a major role in the bringing about of these two monumental inventions. Born in Washington in 1842 of Scottish descent, he was a highly competent shorthand writer. He was private secretary to Secretary of State Seward during the Civil War and then was admitted to the bar of the Supreme Court. But his legal activities were concentrated on court reporting—transcribing court testimony. Clephane sought a way to transcribe his notes quickly and in the multiple forms that cases in the highest tribunal demanded. The answer was not quick to come.

The typewriter was patented in 1867. It had been invented in Milwaukee by Christopher Sholes and two associates and built commercially in 1874. Clephane is reputed to have worn out the first two typewriters himself. The typewriter had solved only some of Clephane's problems. He could transcribe his shorthand rapidly, but it still took just as long for the printer to deliver copies. Clephane thought it would save time if somehow a machine could link with lithographic printing or make stereotypes to cast metal type. He sought the aid of Charles Moore to build such a machine. Moore went to a machine shop in Baltimore owned by August Hahl. Ottmar Mergenthaler, Hahl's cousin, felt he could improve the machine. Mergenthaler delivered the machine to Moore and Clephane, and it produced sharp characters, properly spaced on an endless narrow strip, ready for transfer to a lithographer's stone. Sometimes a line of type would slip in the printing process. After much experimentation, it was decided that the solution lie in making a stereotype plate for final production. In trying to solve Clephane's and Moore's problems, Mergenthaler had some ideas of his own.

Ottmar Mergenthaler and the Linotype.

Apprenticed to a watchmaker in his native Germany at the age of 14, Ottmar Mergenthaler (1854–1899) emigrated to the United States in 1872 and became a citizen in 1878. His "writing" machine developed for James Clephane used a keyboard to assemble lines of matrices prior to casting a one-piece slug in molten metal. After every job, the slugs were remelted for the next job. From this prototype, Mergenthaler received financial backing from groups of newspaper publishers. A group of publishers headed by Whitelaw Reid bought controlling interest in the National Typographic Company, which later was renamed the Mergenthaler Linotype Company. The first machine was installed in the *New York Tribune* in 1886.

Mergenthaler could not solve the problem of automatic justification, since the answer was a patent owned by J. W. Shuckers for the variable wedge, later called the spaceband. Eventually the Linotype company acquired the company that had the patent, and the Linotype machine enjoyed almost two decades without serious competition. A group of engineers from Linotype started the Intertype Company in 1911, when some of the original patents expired. For the next 70 years these two companies controlled typesetting machinery around the world, with minor competition from Monotype and Ludlow.

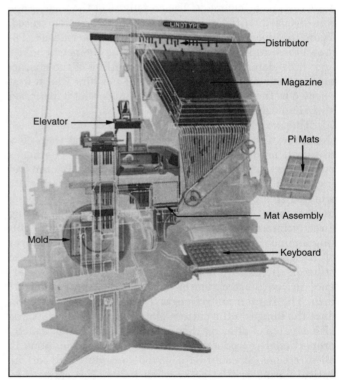

The recirculating matrix principle of the Linotype linecasting machine. This "x-ray" view shows the flow of matrices.

Linn Boyd Benton Mechanizes Typefounding.

Linn Boyd Benton (1844–1932) invented the enabling technology for mechanized typesetting. Benton completed his self-instruction in typefounding and had a mind that could deal with decimal fractions and measurements of ten-thousandths of an inch. His 1882 patent was a multiple mold for casting leads and slugs. He began to work on a typesetting machine with automatic justification. He devised a system, based on his "self-spacing type," that shortened the time required for justification by reducing the number of character widths in a font of type. Printing type after that was cast to predetermined widths. By 1884 his foundry (Benton Waldo, and Company of Milwaukee) was using the first version of a pantograph machine he invented for engraving steel punches. A patent for the third version came in 1885.

As his son Morris was entering Cornell in 1892, twenty-three American type foundries, including the Benton firm, merged to form the American Type Founders Company (ATF). Linn Benton moved to New York where the new company had its offices. Morris Fuller Benton helped his father to further develop the punch- and matrix-engraving machines. He became ATF's chief type designer in 1900. He was one of the most prolific typeface designers in history.

A key step in type production was to get the characters to an appropriate size for making patterns. Each drawing for a typeface was placed in a special delineating machine invented by Linn Benton. It was a refined pantograph with a microscope attachment. The crosshairs of the microscope were focused on the outline of the character being traced. Then the operator, looking through the microscope, followed the outline of the design by moving the pencil holder and, in so doing, traced an enlarged outline of the character. Benton's patent application for the machine was at first rejected by the Patent Office on the grounds that it described a mechanical impossibility.

The next step was to create a pattern plate for each character. These were made either in wax and then electrotyped, or directly in metal, depending on whether a punch or a matrix was required. In Milwaukee, Benton had invented a pantographic machine for his type foundry. He adapted this punch-cutting machine for matrix engraving in the early 1900s, when ATF decided that engraving directly into a matrix blank was more practical than cutting a punch. Matrices could be cut for different point sizes of a type simply by adjusting the reproduction ratio between the pattern and the cutting tool. Allowable tolerance in the construction of this head was within 0.0002 inch. The Benton matrix engraver could accurately reproduce the image on the pattern plate in any type size. It was also capable of altering that image, deviating from exactly proportional reproductions by infinitesimal gradations in all directions. It could be adjusted to compensate for the optical variables that occur when letter sizes change. As print historian, D. B. Updike wrote, "a design for a type alphabet that may be entirely successful for the size for which it is drawn, cannot be successfully applied to all other sizes of the same series. Each size is a law unto itself, and is often bettered by modifications in the original design."

Benton's machine could scale a drawing to the required size, compress or expand the characters, and vary the weight slightly to compensate for the larger or smaller size—this last being a crude form of the "optical scaling" once done by skilled typographers. In optical scaling, the thickest strokes retain the same relative thickness at any size, but the thinnest strokes are not simply scaled up or down with the rest of the type, but made thicker at small sizes and thinner at large display sizes, so as to provide the best compromise between art and readability. Only the 36-point size of a typeface was cut exactly proportional to the pattern plate. Going down in size, the face was actually extended in width but not in height, and above 36-point, the letters were condensed relative to the standard.

Each size of ATF's American Caslon, in sizes from 6 to 48 point, was photographically proportional to the pattern plate. The Stempel foundry used a Benton matrix engraver with three sets of patterns for each typeface. Adjustments on the machine itself were only used to widen characters in the very smallest point sizes. The unfinished matrix went to a fitter, who made final adjustments on Benton's matrix fitting machine. The matrix as delivered from the Benton engraving machine required very precise trimming in order to be absolutely straight and on the proper baseline. ATF's type was then cast from a mixture of tin, antimony, lead, and a small amount of copper.

When Linn Benton was eighty-six years old, he received a patent for an improvement in the larger printing types used for newspaper headings. His inventions revolutionized the typefounding art, and placed ATF in a position of leadership. Morris Benton remained at ATF for another five years after his father's death, but it was a difficult period for the company. Profits had begun to decline, and the 1930s brought a brush with bankruptcy. In 1937, Morris Benton retired from ATF.

Tolbert Lanston and the Monotype. The Monotype is a machine used for mechanical typesetting that consists of two separate mechanisms (a keyboard and a typecaster), casts type consisting of individual characters, and sets justified lines (lines that are spaced out to uniform length). It was invented and patented in 1887 by Tolbert Lanston (1844–1913), around the same time that the Linotype was put into operation. Monotype's keyboard consists of banks of keys that, when tapped, operate a complicated system of valves, pipes, levers, and punches to perforate a moving paper ribbon. The width of each character tapped is registered on a scale so that the operator can determine how many justifying keys must be depressed in order to justify the line. Once the paper ribbon has been perforated, it is placed on the caster; compressed air is passed through the punched holes to position a case containing matrices over a mold. Each combination of punched holes positions the matrix case to produce a particular character and at the same time adjust the mold width to suit the unit width of the character. Each character is cast as the ribbon unwinds until a complete line of characters and spaces is produced.

Paper Tower

Justifying Scale

Em Rack

The Monotype keyboard (left), caster (center), and mat case (right).

The line is then delivered onto a galley, or tray, at the side of the machine. It is said that Lanston got the idea for separating the input and the output mechanisms because of a device invented by a fellow worker at the Census Bureau—Herman Hollerith had developed the punch card and tabulating machine.

Harder metals are used for this single-type composition than are used in line-composing machines (e.g., Linotype). The versatility of the composition of individual characters and the ability to cast new type caused the Monotype system to be widely used throughout the world, particularly for book work and the setting of tabular material. Production of the Monotype began in Salfords, England in 1902.

By the early decades of the 20th century, companies like Monotype and Linotype held a virtual monopoly on commercial printing, and they kept it right up to the digital era. Where type had once been cut and cast by individual printers, it was later "issued" by the Monotype Corporation and others.

Beginning with the original typeface Imprint (1912) and Plantin (1913), many contemporary typefaces were adapted and developed for Monotype machine composition. This was followed by a large-scale program of typeface development that is still unique in the history of typography. Under the guidance of Stanley Morison, beginning in 1922, Monotype continued a program of type revivals, cutting typefaces such as Baskerville, Bell, Bembo, Ehrhardt and Fournier. Monotype also developed new typefaces, producing many well-known and important designs: Perpetua (1929), Gill Sans (1929–1931), and Joanna, by Eric Gill (1930–1931), Centaur by Bruce Rogers (1929), and, perhaps the most well-known and most widely used typeface in the world, Times New Roman (1932). Monotype's Times New Roman is the "father" to all versions of Times.

By this time, the "point" measurement system had finally reached standardization due to the work of Nelson Hawkes and the new power of a single type foundry (ATF). Previously, different sizes of type had simply been called by different names. Thus "Brevier" was the British name for 8-pt. type of any style. Unfortunately, these names were not standardized internationally; 8-pt. type was called "Petit Texte" by the French and "Testino" by the Italians. This naming system also created confusion, such as "English" referring both to black letter type and a 14-pt. size; "English English" was thus a 14-pt. black letter. Pierre Simon Fournier had first proposed a comprehensive point system in 1737, with later refinements, but what was adopted was the later version developed by Francois Ambroise Didot. This put approximately 72 points to the inch (and now exactly 72 points to the inch on PostScript systems).

The Typewriter. Typewriter patents date to 1713. The first typewriter said to have worked was built by Pellegrino Turri in 1808. The "writing ball" of Danish pastor Malling Hansen (1870) looked like a pincushion and probably predated the IBM Selectric. Friedrich Wilhelm Nietzsche's mother and sister gave him a Hansen as a gift, but he hated it like everything else.

The "Sholes & Glidden Type Writer" was produced by the gunmakers E. Remington & Sons in Ilion, New York, from 1874–1878. It was not a great success (about 5,000 were sold), but it founded a worldwide industry.

The idea began at a machine shop in Milwaukee, Wisconsin, in 1868. A local publisher-politician-philosopher-tinkerer named Christopher Latham Sholes spent hours at the machine shop with fellow tinkerers, eager to participate in the Age of Invention. Sholes was working on a machine to automatically number the pages in books, when one of his colleagues suggested the idea might be extended to a device to print the entire alphabet. An article from *Scientific American* was passed around, and the gentlemen nodded in agreement that "typewriting" (the phrase coined in the magazine) was the wave of the future.

Sholes thought of a simple device with a piece of printer's type mounted on a little rod, mounted to strike upward to a flat plate which would hold a piece of carbon paper sandwiched with a piece of stationery. The impact of the type should produce an impression on the paper.

With the key of an old telegraph instrument mounted on its base, Sholes would tap down on his model, and the type jumped up to hit the carbon and paper against the glass plate. There was no space bar, line advance, or any other normal typewriter feature. Those were all to come. In 1868, the mere idea of type striking against paper to produce an image was totally new. Sholes proceeded to construct a machine to do the whole alphabet. The prototype was eventually sent to Washington as the required patent model.

Sholes's basic mechanism was an "up-strike" design. The actual printing type is mounted on the end of a "typebar." Pressing the key swings the typebar up toward the cylindrical platen against a ribbon for inking. The typing was, therefore, hidden from view, and so the machine was called a "blind-writer." The carriage was hinged so the user could check his work.

Investor and con man James Densmore provided the marketing impetus that eventually brought the machine to Remington. Sholes lacked the patience required to perfect the machine and penetrate the marketplace, so he sold all of his rights to Densmore, whose belief in the machine kept the enterprise afloat. Remington agreed to produce the device beginning in 1873. The "Glidden" part of the typewriter's name came from Carlos Glidden, who had assisted

Sholes at the Milwaukee machine shop. The original typewriter was heavily decorated with colorful decals and gold paint. A foot treadle was provided for the carriage return. It looked like an old sewing machine. In fact, William Jenne, the Remington engineer who set up the typewriter factory had been transferred from Remington's sewing machine division.

A table model was also offered with a handle at the side instead of the foot pedal. The original Sholes & Glidden used the QWERTY keyboard, but it typed in capitals only. The keyboard was designed to separate frequently used pairs of letters so that the typebars would not clash and get stuck at the printing point.

In 1878, the No. 2 machine was introduced. It typed both upper- and lowercase, using a shift key. Gone were the decorated panels in favor of a black open frame (which turned out to be quieter), establishing the archetype open-black-box look typewriters would have for decades to come. It took another decade, but the Remington No. 2 became a success, and the typewriter Industry was born.

The Sholes & Glidden, like many early typewriters, is an understroke or "blind" writer: the typebars are arranged in a circular basket under the platen (the printing surface) and type on the bottom of the platen. This means that the typist (confusingly called a "typewriter" herself in the early days) has to lift up the platen to see her work. Another example of an understroke typebar machine is the Caligraph of 1880, the second typewriter to appear on the American market. The Smith Premier (1890) is another example of a full-keyboard understroke typewriter that was very popular in its day.

The QWERTY keyboard came to be called the "Universal" keyboard, as the alternative keyboards fought a losing battle against the QWERTY momentum. But not all early typewriters used the QWERTY system, and many did not even type with typebars, such as the ingenious Hammond, introduced in 1881. The Hammond had its own keyboard, the two-row, curved "Ideal" keyboard. (Universal Hammonds were also soon made available). The Hammond prints from a type shuttle—a single C-shaped piece of vulcanized rubber containing all letters and figures. The shuttle can easily be exchanged when you want to use a different typeface. There is no cylindrical platen as on typebar typewriters; the paper is hit against the shuttle by a hammer, and then the paper collects in a basket. The Hammond gained a solid base of loyal customers. These well-engineered machines lasted, through electrification and a name change to "Varityper," right up to the beginning of the word processor era.

Other machines typing from a single type element rather than typebars included the Crandall (1881) and the Blickensderfer. The effort to create a visible rather than "blind" machine led to many ingenious ways of getting the typebars to the platen. Examples of early visible writers include the Williams and the Oliver. The Daugherty-Visible of 1891 was the first frontstroke typewriter (a machine in which the typebars rest below the platen and hit the front of it). With the Underwood of 1895, this style of typewriter began to gain ascendancy. By the 1920s, virtually all typewriters were look-alikes: frontstroke, QWERTY, typebar machines printing through a ribbon, using one shift key and four banks of keys. The most popular Underwood was the No. 5.

Mark Twain and the Paige typesetter. Mark Twain first heard about James Paige and his automatic typesetting machine in 1880, at which time he invested $5,000 in it. By 1887 Twain had invested a total of $50,000, and as principal investor was paying about $3,000 a month. Believing that there were millions in mechanical typesetting, he bought the rights to the machine outright in 1889, and within a few more years, the machine, as chief among a series of bad speculations, bankrupted him. The Paige machine had over 18,000 separate parts, and it was designed to set (with the help of two operators) over 8,000 ems an hour. Before the Paige could be made to work consistently, the Linotype machine swept the market.

In his autobiography, Twain boasted, "I was the first person in the world that ever had a telephone in his house." He also wrote, "I was the first person in the world to apply the typemachine to literature." He started typing occasional letters on the machine in 1874, and he had a manuscript typed by a secretary later that year. When in 1905 an installment of his autobiography mentioning his experience with a typewriter appeared in *The North American Review,* Remington quickly seized the opportunity to use his remarks in an advertisement for its machine. Mark Twain was the first person to submit a novel in typed form to a publisher (*Life on the Mississippi,* 1883), but he did not type it himself—it was a typed copy of his handwritten manuscript. His autobiography says *Tom Sawyer* was his first book submitted in typescript. He remembered it wrong, and research by Twain historians has proven otherwise. The Paige typesetter now sits in the basement of the Mark Twain house in Hartford, Connecticut.

Halftones and the printing of pictures. Richard Leach, an English physician, was frustrated by the limitations of wet-plate photography. In 1871 he developed the gelatin-bromide dry plate. By 1878, faster dry plates were commercially produced that could be developed long after exposure. Heavy darkroom equipment disappeared. Exposure time dropped to fractions of seconds, allowing handheld cameras to be used. Dry plates were universally adopted.

In the late 1870s in Rochester, New York, a bank clerk and amateur photographer named George Eastman began making experimental gelatin emulsions in his mother's kitchen. By 1879 he patented a machine for coating dry plates with emulsion and started part-time commercial production in a loft. In 1881 Eastman quit the bank and became a full-time manufacturer. He developed emulsions of increasing sensitivity and stability. Eastman realized that photographic processes were not accessible to everyone. With William H. Walker, he invented rolled paper film

which became the model for contemporary roll films. A year later, in 1885, Eastman patented a machine that coated a continuous roll of paper with an emulsion. A double-coating process allowed the emulsion to be removed from the paper after development and transferred to a durable gelatin-collodion film. Prints were sharp and free from paper grain distortion. Eastman wanted a camera that anyone could use. In 1888 he introduced the Kodak portable box camera with the marketing slogan, penned by Eastman himself, "You press the button, we do the rest."

Outfitted with a simple lens and a paper roll of 100 pictures, photographers did not need to fuss with camera settings, focus, or development. After exposing the film, the entire camera was shipped back to Eastman's factory. The film was developed, camera reloaded, and mailed back to the customer with mounted prints. The Kodak was a success. In 1889 the company introduced flexible celluloid film and the popularity of photography soared. It was the Kodak Brownie camera, in 1900, that firmly lodged Kodak and photography in the world's collective consciousness. Selling for one dollar each, the Brownie made Kodak a household name and global institution.

Thomas Dallmeyer's variable focus lens in 1899 helped make photography a more exacting science. In 1907, Frenchmen Auguste and Louis Lumière developed a simpler color photography system. The brothers were pioneers in motion picture camera and projection systems, and they established the 35-mm standard.

The turn of the century also saw the development of the halftone process by Frederich Eugene Ives, which permitted newspapers and magazines to add photographic images to their pages. Printing presses lay down a film of ink that is uniform in thickness and in density of color. The printed reproduction of a continuous-tone image, one that, as in a photograph, has a range of light and dark values that blend seamlessly together, is created by patterns of minute dots too small for the human eye to resolve individually, but which together appear as tonal gradations of gray. The dots are larger and closer together in the shadow (or dark) areas, smaller and farther apart in lighter (or highlight) areas. Dot patterns are created using a special halftone screen of glass or later plastic, closely ruled with two sets of opaque lines at right angles to each other. The screen disperses the light reflected from an original image into discrete dots of varying size, which are reproduced on a film negative that is then used to expose a sensitized plate to form a positive printing image. Halftone plates are made in relief for letterpress printing.

In 1924, the Leitz 24×36-mm camera, the Leica, used 35-mm motion-picture stock, making the camera portable and easy to use. In 1861, James Clerk Maxwell, a Scottish doctor, had shown that all color hues derive from three primary colors. He projected three monochromatic slides of the Scottish flag from three different projectors. The combined images produced an exact color representation of the flag. The advent of Kodachrome, Agfacolor, and other commercial films in the 1930s eliminated making a color print from three negatives, which were converted into three layers of colored gelatin and combined.

In 1947, Edwin Land introduced instant film and founded the Polaroid Land Company. In 1950, Kodak's Kodachrome film was widely marketed for the amateur photographer. Instant color film, developed by Elkin Blout and Howard Rogers of Polaroid, was released in 1963.

In 1963, D. Gregg at Stanford University created a forerunner to digital photography. The videodisk camera could photograph and store images for several minutes. In 1979, Philips and Sony collaborated on the videodisk. Using computer technology, sound and images were digitally recorded and then imprinted as micro-pits on a plastic disk. A laser then optically scanned the information and converted it into pictures and sound on a home TV. Although a superior technology, the video disk languished commercially as videotape dominated the video market. With the release of the compact disc (CD) audio technology in the 1980s, the video disk reemerged as digital photography. In 1986, Kodak succeeded in creating a sensor that could record 1.4 million picture elements, or megapixels. In the 1990s the first digital cameras appeared for commercial use.

20th-Century Type Innovators

Eric Gill. Eric Gill (1882–1940), stone carver, wood engraver, essayist, and typographer, was born in Brighton, England. His father was a curate and his mother a singer. Early in life he displayed a talent for drawing and an eye for proportion, inspiring his family to enroll him in an art school in Chichester. In 1900 his father apprenticed him to the architect of the Ecclesiastical Commissioners. He began to study lettering in evening classes with Edward Johnston. After three years he abandoned architecture to start his own business in letter cutting and stone carving. In 1907 he joined an artists' community in Ditchling, Sussex, where he had his first experiences with printing and typography. In 1925 Stanley Morison approached Gill with the idea of creating a new typeface for the Monotype Corporation. Consequently Gill designed Perpetua and a sans serif, Gill Sans, which has become the leading British sans serif, sometimes described as the "national typeface of England." Although he never considered himself primarily a typographer, he designed eleven typefaces of beauty and subtlety and wrote an influential "Essay on Typography."

Frederic W. Goudy. Goudy (1865–1947) taught himself printing and typography while working as a bookkeeper. In 1895, in partnership with an English teacher, C. Lauren Hooper, he set up the Camelot Press in Chicago, which printed the chapbook for Stone & Kimball publishers, widely praised for its fine design. He sold the first typeface he designed, called Camelot, to a Boston printer for $10. In 1903, with his wife, Bertha, and Will Ransom, he started the Village Press in Park Ridge, Illinois. Goudy and the Village Press landed in Marlborough, NY in 1923. The workshop and type foundry burned in 1939.

From 1920 to 1940 he was art director of the Lanston Monotype Company. He produced such faces as Goudy Old Style, Kennerley, Garamond, and Forum for the American Type Founders and Lanston companies. He was the author of *The Alphabet* (1918), *Elements of Lettering* (1922), *Typologia* (1940), and the autobiographical *A Half-Century of Type Design and Typography*, 1895–1945 (1946).

Goudy is credited with personally designing over 120 typefaces. His type is reminiscent of Jenson's famous model from 1470. Goudy set the standard for contemporary type designers with new, distinctive types, while remaining faithful to the old models, particularly those of the Venetian Renaissance.

Stanley Morison. Stanley Morison (1889–1967), born in Wanstead, Essex, is best remembered for his design of Times New Roman, which first appeared in print in 1932 in London's *Times*. Later it was called the most successful new typeface of the first half of the 20th century. He was typographic adviser to Monotype Corporation and Cambridge University Press; editor of *The Fleuron*, a typographic journal; and author of *Four Centuries of Fine Printing* and *First Principles of Typography*.

Morison joined Monotype in 1922 for their revival of a Garamond type (actually a revival of a revival cut by Jean Jannon in the 1620s). Over the next nine years and under Morison's direction, Monotype released revivals of roughly a dozen historic roman faces, including Centaur, a revival of Jenson's type designed by the American Bruce Rogers; Bembo and Poliphilus, adapted from Francesco Griffo's roman types; and eventually in 1931 Morison's own Times New Roman, based on 17th century styles.

Morison was not so much a designer as a champion of designs. One of his greatest achievements was the rediscovery of Francesco Griffo's work, especially the type in Pietro Bembo's *De Aetna* of 1495. Before Morison, few typographic scholars had much to say about the Aldine types, generally preferring Jenson's specimens. Blaming the poor reputation of Griffo's type on the poor specimens that had come down to contemporary scholars, Morison encouraged the development of Monotype's Bembo, released in 1929, and demonstrated that it was this type that had been the model for the popular French old-faces of Claude Garamond in the mid-16th century. Bembo was one of the most popular revivals ever released by Monotype. In Morison's words, "In the pages of *De Aetna* the type, then new, looks almost as fresh as if it had come off a present-day typecaster."

Paul Renner. Paul Renner (1878–1956) was a painter, typographer, typeface designer, and teacher. Between 1908 and 1917 he designed thousands of books for German publishers. In the 1920s he began to support modern styles of typography. Renner is best known for designing the typeface Futura, which became a standard for what was known as New Typography.

Renner was not directly affiliated with the Bauhaus school; instead, between 1926 and 1933, he was principal of the Printing Trade School in Munich, and co-founder of the Master School for Germany's Print. He gathered a staff of leading typographers, including Jan Tschichold and Georg Trump. Renner's progressive views on art and design brought him into conflict with the Nazis. His polemical booklet of 1932, "Kulturbolschewismus?," in which he attacked Nazi cultural policy, led to his arrest as a "Cultural Bolshevist" and his eventual dismissal from his teaching post in Munich. In his forced retirement, Renner continued to design typefaces and write about typography.

Dawn of a New Age:
Offset Lithography and Phototypesetting

An American printer, Ira W. Rubel, of Nutley, New Jersey, accidentally discovered offset lithography in 1904 and soon built a press to exploit it. The process was developed separately in the U.S. by Ira Rubel, Alex Sherwood, and by Charles and Albert Harris. In lithography, the image is printed indirectly by "offsetting" it first onto a rubber-covered cylinder, called a blanket, from which the image is then printed. It is the most widely used commercial printing process and is sometimes called photolithography.

Don't Call It Cold Type. Non-hot-metal typesetting was called cold type because it described the preparation of type by machines resembling typewriters, but which were capable of producing justified lines of type. Justification was achieved in several ways. In the IBM MT/SC Selectric Composer, a first typing calculated the total measurement of the type characters up to the beginning of the justification zone and caused a code to appear. A final typing determines the automatic adjustment of the spaces between the words to obtain justification.

In the Friden (later Singer) Justowriter (1950s), there were two units. The keyboard on which the uncoded, unjustified proofing copy was typed simultaneously perforated a paper tape with the code for the letters, as well as, for each line, the code for the amount of space between the words as indicated by a calculator. The tape then controlled, on a second unit of the machine, the electric typing of the final justified copy.

The Addressograph-Multigraph Varityper (1930s) was also a typewriter with proportional fonts and required two typings for justification. The Headliner (1950s) was used to set display type photographically. Cold type was a step on the road to phototypesetting.

On the Road to Typesetting Automation. The first major technology that brought us to the age of computer automation was the TeleTypeSetter System (TTS) of 1934. Frank Gannett supported the development of a counting keyboard that kept track of character widths so an operator could justify a linecaster line offline; a transmission system that communicated the data to remote sites, printed the copy out, and also punched a paper tape (with TTS code); and a device that attached to the linecaster so that it could run from the paper tape automatically. This labor-saving technology was restricted from use by typographical unions and only came into general use after World War II, when newspapers faced competition from radio and television.

Typesetting by photography was proposed as early as 1866. Hungarian engineer Eugene Porzolt designed the first photocomposing machine in 1894. The decline of letterpress relief printing and the increase in offset lithography at the beginning of the 20th century spurred research into the development of photocomposition systems, dispensing with metal typecasting. One device was patented in Japan by Nobuo Morisawa in 1925, but phototypesetting machines did not become available commercially until the 1950s.

Louis Marius Moyroud (1914–) and René Alphonse Higonnet (1902–1983) developed the first practical phototypesetting machine. Born in Moirans, Isère, France, Moyroud attended engineering school from 1929 to 1936 and graduated as an engineer from École Nationale Supérieure des Arts et Métiers of Cluny, France. He served in the military as a second lieutenant from 1936 to 1938 and as a first lieutenant in 1939 and 1940. He joined the LMT Laboratories, a subsidiary in Paris of ITT, in 1941 and left in 1946 to spend all of his time on photocomposition.

Higonnet was born in Valence, Drôme, France. The son of a teacher, he was educated at the Lycée de Tournon and the electrical engineering school of Grenoble University. He was granted a scholarship by the International Institute of Education in New York in 1922, went to Carleton College in Minnesota for one year, and subsequently spent one term at Harvard. He was an engineer with the Matériel Téléphonique, a French subsidiary of ITT, from 1924 to 1948. He then became a transmission engineer and worked on long-distance cables: in Paris–Strasbourg, London–Brussels, and Vienna–Budapest. He was also associated with the patent and information department of ITT.

Moyroud and Higonnet demonstrated their first phototypesetting machine, the Lumitype—later known as the Photon—in September 1946 and introduced it to America in 1948. The Photon was refined under the direction of the Graphic Arts Research Foundation and released in 1954.

The first book to be composed by the Photon, *The Wonderful World of Insects,* was printed in 1953. Composed without the use of metal type, it might someday rank in historical importance with the first book printed from movable type, the Gutenberg Bible.

Harris Intertype's Fotosetter made its debut in 1949. The Fotosetter was an adaptation of a linecasting machine that embedded a small film negative in each brass matrice and photographed one at a time. Mergenthaler tried something similar with an abortive device that tried to photograph the reference side of a line of mats. Typeface masters for photocomposition were then on film; the characters projected onto photo-sensitive paper or film. Lenses were used to adjust the size of the type image, scaling the type to the desired size. The technology allowed new freedoms, such as overlapping characters for kerning and tracking.

The Fotosetter, a recirculating-matrix phototypesetter.

Second-generation phototypesetters made their debut in 1954 with the introduction of the Photon 200 machine. It used a spinning film matrix containing all of the characters in a font, a stroboscopic light source, and a system of lenses for focusing images of type in the desired sizes onto sensitized paper.

The Computer Age. By the 1960s such machines were being combined with early computers, which automatically prepared tapes with end-of-line (hyphenation and justification) and page design decisions, for high-speed operation.

The earliest computer-based systems each had their own command language for communicating with output devices. Although these machines had advantages, they also had problems. None of the command languages handled graphics at all, and they all had their own formats for fonts—film, glass, or plastic, and later digital.

In the 1960s the term "computer" described a room full of big machines, probably from IBM, RCA, Burroughs, Univac, or DEC, as typesetting began to be automated. RCA offered a cathode-ray tube (CRT) machine, called the Videocomp, made in Germany by Hell (later merged with Linotype). This inspired IBM to fund the development of the IBM 2680, a CRT-based machine, made for IBM by Alphanumeric Inc. Alphanumeric acquired Autologic to make the machine, which Photon sold for a while as the Photon 7000.

In the late 1960s Mergenthaler purchased special-purpose computers (Lineasec and Justape) to drive its lead-casting Linotype machines. The computers came from a Massachusetts company named Compugraphic, a spinoff from Photon. Photon was the leading phototypesetter man-

ufacturer and its president, Bill Garth, wanted to produce a small, inexpensive typesetting machine, but his board of directors preferred large, expensive machines. Garth left Photon and founded Compugraphic with Ellis Hanson. At Compugraphic, Garth arranged to buy back from Mergenthaler the rights to the justifying machine that Compugraphic had been making for them. Then he used the processor logic and hardware to directly drive small phototypesetters, first the 2961 and then the 4961—the names derived from the number of fonts on-line (2 or 4), the characters in the font (90), the TTS code level (6) and the number of lenses (1).

This growing market was of course noticed by Harris Intertype, Mergenthaler Linotype, and Monotype, who had been the only makers of lead-casting type machines for years. They set about making their own phototypesetters.

Harris Intertype's second-generation phototypesetter, the Fototronic, was about 8 ft. long, 4 ft. wide, and 6 ft. high. The fonts were on six dinner-plate-sized glass discs spinning at high speed at the ends of radial arms that rotated around when a type face change was called for. The back of the machines would generally be built into the wall of a darkroom. These monsters were used by newspapers well into the 1980s.

Mergenthaler's first phototypesetter, the Linofilm, came out in 1954. The Linofilm Quick was released in 1964, but it also did not sell well. By 1970 the company produced a phototypesetter called the VIP, which held six fonts (later eighteen) at a time and selected sizes from 5 to 36 points with a moving zoom lens. (Special "double-sized" font strips could be used to set type from 35 to 72 points.) Adjustment of the zoom mechanism was critical, and the VIP had a reputation for variation in type sizes from one machine to another. The type fonts for the VIP were on film strips a little larger than a business card. This became the best-seller that Mergenthaler had long coveted.

Direct-Input Phototypesetting. The Photon 200B had actually been a device that integrated the input and output. The operator typed on a keyboard and sent the lines to be output. Both the Mergenthaler Linofilm and the Harris Fototronic had special-purpose keyboards with proprietary tape coding. For productivity, larger users wanted standard six-level TTS paper tape, which was being used extensively by the early 1960s. This gave rise to a number of tape-operated phototypesetters.

In 1971 Compugraphic introduced the CompuWriter, a $6,950 keyboard and phototypesetter in one. It sold like hotcakes and spawned over twenty competitors. Mergenthaler had the Linocomp and later the CRTronic. AM Varityper had the Comp/Set and later the Comp/Edit. Alphatype had the Alphatronic; Itek had the Quadritek; and Berthold had the Diatype and later the Diatronic. From 1971 until 1985 the industry went through its direct-input phase, while tape-operated and then floppy disk systems also evolved as well. Later, video monitors and floppy disks were added to the direct input systems.

The CRT Typesetter. It had become obvious to Alphanumeric, in 1969, that the IBM mainframe computer needed to run its phototypesetter—the IBM 2680—was going to restrict its sales volume. Alphanumeric had become its own best customer, operating its machines on a service bureau basis in major cities. The company decided to spin off its typesetter development and replace the IBM mainframe with a minicomputer controller. Alphanumeric bought a small company called Autologic, and engineer Hank Bechard was named president. He sold a major share of the company to Volt Inc.

Autologic machines were fast, wide-output machines and had been first offered through Photon as the Photon 7000 (the numbers being the last digits of Photon's office phone number). Autologic machines continued after the demise of Photon and carved a major place in the market for newspaper production. 100-pica-wide machines (16+ inches) allowed them to set an entire newspaper page in one pass with no need for pasteup. By mid-1995 Autologic no longer produced any hardware, but the company continued to market its newspaper pagination software. In 1996 Autologic merged with Information International Incorporated to form Autologic International.

The first marketable CRT typesetter was actually the German-made Hell Digiset, which was introduced in the U.S. by RCA. RCA had a computer division and saw the CRT as a perfect match. They called it the Videocomp. When RCA got out of the computer business, the machine was marketed by Information International.

Harris had the Harris CRT, but it only sold a few units. Mergenthaler Linotype Company worked with CBS Labs to create the Linotron 1010, which was used by the Government Printing Office and Wright Patterson Air Force Base, but it was not a commercial success. In 1967 Mergenthaler Linotype acquired the K. S. Paul device invented by Peter Purdy and Ronald McIntosh and called it the Linotron 505. The company would later introduce the 303, 606, 404, and 101.

By 1972 over thirty models of machines to set type photographically were on the market from a number of companies, including Autologic, Compugraphic, AM Varityper, Autologic, Information International, Itek, Star Parts, Harris Intertype, Graphic Systems Inc., Monotype, Friden (then Singer), Mergenthaler Linotype, and Photon. Without a computer to drive them, phototypesetters were just like linecasting machines, requiring skilled people to input to them on "counting" keyboards that required the operator to make all decisions and produced paper tape. A computer allowed the typesetters' decisions to be programmed, and this reduced the involvement of the operator.

Front-End Systems. By the 1970s, there were front-end systems being developed by firms like Atex, DEC, Penta, Datalogics, Quadex, Bedford Computer, Information International, IBM, and others. These systems automatically hyphenated, justified, kerned, tracked, indented, spaced, and eventually formatted pages. A high-speed output device then could produce camera-ready pages with all text in position.

This led to the need for even faster phototypesetters. CRT typesetters were very expensive, but in 1973 Compugraphic introduced the Videosetter at about $30,000, and in 1977 Mergenthaler Linotype introduced the Linotron 202 at about $50,000. This led to another twenty or so midrange CRT setters, including the Autologic APS-5 and Micro 5, the Compugraphic 8600, the AM Varityper 6400, the Alphatype CRS and others.

The Imagesetter Is Born. In 1978 Monotype introduced the Lasercomp, the first device to use a laser in a pure raster output device. Photon had shown an early laser phototypesetter that only handled characters as did Compugraphic with the Videosetter in 1975. Mergenthaler had an abortive laser system called the Omnitech that used zinc oxide coated paper in 1979. But Monotype had the first imagesetter capable of text and images. However, there was no front end on earth capable of sending to output a page of text and images, and it did not sell well.

By the early 1980s major typesetting suppliers were experimenting with the integration of text and images on modified CRT or laser devices. The solution to their problem came in 1985 with Adobe's PostScript page description language. The raster image processor (RIP) was born and now pages started to be assembled with desktop computers. Within a few years there were imagesetters from Varityper, Ultra, Alphatype, Linotype, Autologic, Dainippon Screen, Scitex, Scangraphic, ECRM, and others.

The Advent of "Computer-to" Technologies. Once an established standard for page output was popularized, more and more pages were output to film with all elements in position. This increased the use of scanners and color workstations and led to color printers for proofing. Experiments with computer-to-plate started in the early 1980s, but products did not reach the market until 1992. In 1991 on-press computer-to-plate exposure was pioneered by Heidelberg and Presstek. In 1993, digital color presses from Indigo and Xeikon allowed short runs of plain-paper color printing. New technologies are predicted to go directly to press cylinder and bypass plates as such. All of this has been possible because of the laser and laser dot technology. Text and images are just agglomerations of dots. Thus the printing industry enters a new century with a totally digital orientation.

Typefaces: An Art Reborn. In the past typefaces were dedicated to particular typesetting machines. The advent of PostScript in 1985 and especially the opening of the Type 1 format in 1989 created a deluge in new type fonts that could be used on virtually any laser printer, imagesetter, or other PostScript output device. Traditional foundries yielded to new entrepreneurial foundries, and thousands of new typefaces, many variations on existing letterforms, have flourished.

The Monotype and Linotype machines spawned a revival in typeface, and the more recent developments in phototypesetting and digital typography have contributed to its spread. Adobe Systems' PostScript technology, now the industry standard for digital type, has served to put "old-face" types on millions of desktop computers and laser printers. PostScript's strength is in its ability to render letterforms suitable for whatever the latest output technology happens to be at the time.

Conclusion

Both the Internet and interactive multimedia are providing ways of employing the printed word that add new possibilities to print's role in culture. The printed word is now used for real-time social interaction (email) and for individualized navigation through interactive documents (portable document formats). It is difficult to gauge the social and cultural impact of new media without historical distance, but these innovations will likely trigger another major transformation in the use, influence, and character of human communication.

Depending on the date you select—most use 1455 when the Gutenberg Bible finished printing—the printing and publishing industry is well over 500 years old. The evolution of the letterform, type design, printing technology, photography, mass communication, and humanity's quest for knowledge and understanding are all intertwined.

A

A, a
The first letter of the Latin and English alphabets, derived from the Greek *alpha*. The form of the uppercase *A* derives from the North Semitic letter *aleph*, later adopted by the Greeks and ultimately by the Romans. The lowercase *a* derives from the Latin cursive letter *a* and comes down in its current form thanks to Carolingian and Florentine influences.

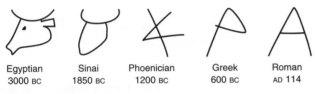

| Egyptian 3000 BC | Sinai 1850 BC | Phoenician 1200 BC | Greek 600 BC | Roman AD 114 |

The evolution of the letter A.

AA
See *Author's Alteration*.

AAP
Abbreviation for *Association of American Publishers*, a trade organization that developed a *SGML* application called the Electronic Manuscript Standard, for the electronic publication of books and articles. See *Standard Generalized Markup Language (SGML)*.

A-B Box
A device used in computer networks to allow a printer or other such peripheral to be used by more than one computer.

Abend
Shorthand term for an *abortive end* or *abnormal end*, an abrupt end to a computer operation or routine due to an error or operator intervention. See also *Abort*.

Aberration
The blurring of a photographic image caused by improperly focusing the camera lens. A specific form of aberration is called *chromatic aberration*, a dispersion of colors that varies slightly from lens to lens. Chromatic aberration typically manifests itself as concentric rings of colors on the edge of an image. Keeping the lens curvature within tolerances can eliminate this problem. See *Newton's Rings* and *Achromat*.

Ablation
In computing, a means of writing data to an *optical disc* by using a laser to etch small pits into a thin layer of aluminum.

Ablation Plate
A type of printing *plate* used in *offset lithography* in which the images are burned onto the plate by laser *diode*s directed

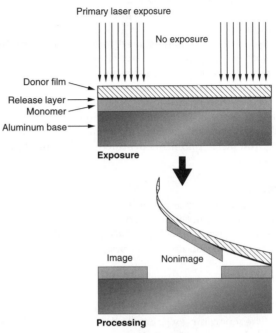

Ablation plate.

by computer data. The plate comprises either a metal or a polyester base, with a thin coating that can be selectively burned by the laser. Its primary advantage is the elimination of a post-exposure chemical treatment. This means that ablation plates can be imaged directly on the press, and that all plates for a job can be produced at the same time and in alignment with each other. (See *Plate: Offset Lithography*.)

Abort
To prematurely terminate a computer routine or operation. An operation may be aborted by the user or by the computer system because of an error or other condition that makes further processing impossible.

Aborts Last Command
In many computer applications, the feature (commonly known as an *undo* command) in which the computer or application stores a copy of the file in its *buffer* before executing a command. If the user is not happy with the result(s) of that command, s/he can call up the copy of the file from the buffer. Most programs only allow one level of undo.

Abrasion
The frictional rubbing of one substance or material against another, frequently causing wear or other damage.

Abrasion Resistance
A property of paper referring to the degree to which a paper can maintain its surface and structural integrity under

prolonged rubbing, scratching, and scuffing. Abrasion resistance is important not only for packaging papers and paperboard, which must be able to withstand sliding and other abrasive forces encountered in shipping and handling, but also for writing and typing papers, which may need to stand up to an eraser.

Abrasion resistance is measured in a laboratory by rotating a paper sample under abrasive wheels for a set length of time, and then measuring the sample's change in weight. Wet or dry abrasion resistance tests can be performed.

The term *abrasion resistance* also refers to a printing ink's ability to resist scuffing and scratching with increased handling, an important consideration in the printing of packaging and other materials destined to be subjected to abrasive forces.

Abrasiveness

A property of a substance or material describing the extent to which it will scratch another surface. To guard against abrasive substances, many papers, *substrate*s, and ink films need to possess a certain degree of *abrasion resistance*.

A/B Roll

In video editing, a device comprising two video sources (such as videotapes or videodiscs) and a single video recorder. The operator switches between the two input video signals by means of a *digital video effects generator* to add special *transition*s such as *wipe*s and *dissolve*s between different scenes. Digital video editing software such as Adobe Premiere also allows a type of A/B roll editing or transitioning between different video signals.

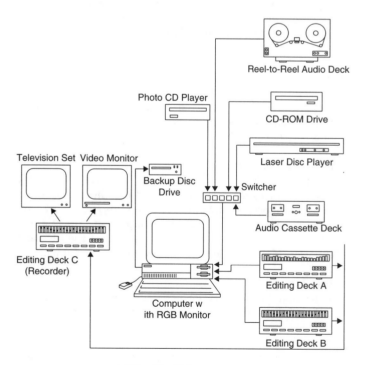

A/B roll editing system.

ABS

Abbreviation of *acrylonitrile-butadiene-styrene*, a variety of plastic produced by the copolymerization of styrene.

Absolute Address

In computing, an indication of a file's location in *machine code*, which the computer can read directly. Also known as *machine address* and *effective address*.

Absolute Coordinates

In graphic design, the location of a point in terms of its *x, y,* and *z* distance from a predetermined point of origin.

Absolute Humidity

A measure of the total weight of water vapor present in the atmosphere, which affects a paper's structural properties. See *Humidity* and *Relative Humidity*.

Absolute Point

In computing, the smallest individually addressable point on a display screen, usually a *pixel*.

Absolute Register

The greatest extent to which all printed image elements or colors conform to their position on the original. See *Register*.

Absolute Vector

In computer graphics, a line or line segment with end points defined in terms of *absolute coordinates*.

Absorbance

Alternate term for *absorptance*. See *Absorptance*.

Absorbency

A property of any porous material, such as paper, to absorb a fluid, be it ink, water, oil, or other substance. A paper's degree of *ink absorbency* varies according to the type of ink to be printed on it. Its moisture absorbency varies according to its *filler* content, the degree of *sizing*, and its *finish*. See *Ink Absorbency* and *Moisture Content*.

Absorptance

In *color*, a term descriptive of the relation between the light that is absorbed by a surface and the total light striking the surface. The perception of color is possible because different atoms absorb only certain wavelengths of light, and reflect light back in the opposite wavelengths. So, a substance that is perceived as *red* absorbs light in the *green* and *blue* wavelengths and reflects red back to the viewer. Also called *absorbance*. (See *COLOR PLATES 13–15*.)

Absorption

The penetration of a fluid into the surface of a solid, as in a paper's ability to absorb ink, water, etc., which may be more or less desirable depending on the printing process and the intended end-use properties of the printed piece. See *Absorbency*.

Abstract

In publishing, a short summary of a book or article. In academic journal publishing, abstracts are printed in separate volumes to enable researchers to easily determine the usefulness of a particular article of study.

ABUI

Abbreviation for *Association of Banyan Users International*. See *Association of Banyan Users International (ABUI)*.

Accelerated Aging

A process used to estimate the *permanence* of paper or other *substrate*. Depending on a paper's chemical composition, it can have varying levels of longevity. Since normal aging is not practical, procedures have been developed to simulate the aging process in a much shorter period of time. Accelerated aging uses either the "dry method," in which a paper sample is aged in a 105°C oven for a set period of time, and examined for reduced strength, brittleness, reduced *tearing resistance*, *folding endurance*, etc., or the "moist method," which ages the paper at 90°C at 25% *relative humidity*. The fibers of *cellulose* that make up a paper deteriorate more rapidly in the presence of moisture, so it is believed that the moist method more closely approximates the natural aging of a paper. (See also *Permanence*.)

Accelerating Tray

In *binding and finishing*, a part of the machine used in *gathering* to increase the speed with which the *signature*s are fed into the chain. See *Gathering*.

Accelerator

A substance or process that expedites the rate at which another process is carried out. For example, a chemical ink *drier* or a high-temperature oven are two means of accelerating the drying of a printing ink.

In computing, especially in the *Windows* environment, the term *accelerator* refers to a keyboard shortcut, or a keystroke that initiates a function without needing to search out the menu containing the function.

Accelerator Board

See *Graphics Accelerator*.

Accent

A mark placed over, under, or through a character as a guide to pronunciation. In languages other than English, an accent refers to a mark that indicates a specific sound, stress, or pitch to distinguish the pronunciation of words otherwise identically spelled.

Originally, the term *accent* meant accented characters—the combination of a character and its appropriate accent—such as the ñ, pronounced as "ny" in Spanish or the ç, pronounced as an "s" in French. These accents, the tilde and the cedilla respectively, combine with the letter to form a specialized character, primarily for pronunciation.

In typesetting, most accented characters do not exist as a single unit but are formed by combining letters and accents. Following are some common accents:

Acute	´
Angstrom	°
Macron	¯
Cedilla	¸
Circumflex	ˆ
Dieresis (or Umlaut)	¨
Grave	`
Breve	˘
Tilde	~
Caron (or Hacek or Clicka)	ˇ
Overdot	·

The accent is stored as a separate character in most cases, with zero width (no *escapement* value). Thus, it "floats" above or below a character position. Accents used in this manner are designed for the *weight*, style, and height (*cap* and *lowercase*) of a *typeface*. There are two methods for keying accented characters: either with an individual key that indicates the complete character or with two separate keys, one for the accent and one for the character. In the latter case, the output device selects the accent, positions it with no escapement, and then positions the character, which escapes normally. For example:

$$´ + e = é$$

An accent set in this way is called a *centered accent*, *floating accent*, or *piece accent*. When the accent is set with a character, the software computes an escapement value for the accent so that it is centered over the character. A *pre-positioned accent* or *fixed accent* is given a fixed escapement value so that it appears centered over a particular character (or characters of similar width). Thus, two separate accents of similar design would be used with characters of dissimilar escapement value.

In *color*, the term *accent* refers to a small application of an additional color to complement and add interest and vibrancy to a larger, less intense color. The greater the intensity of the added color, the smaller the amount needed to attract the desired degree of attention. Likewise, the less intense the color, the greater the amount needed.

Acceptance Sampling

The evaluation and comparison of a quantity or set of materials or products to quality standards as a means of gauging their acceptability. Also known as *inspection*.

Acceptance Testing

In computer hardware and software development, a means of ensuring that a piece of equipment or a software application meets the requirements of the user(s).

Access

In computing, to find and retrieve a specific computer file. *Access* also refers to the communication between a *CPU* and an attached peripheral device.

Access Area

In a computer disk drive, a mechanical device containing one or more *read/write head*s.

Access Code

Alternate term for a *password*. See *Password*.

Access Control

In networking, hardware and software that monitor system activity and operation, grant or refuse users access, and take care of all automated administrative tasks for the network.

Access Method (AM)

In networking, the means by which connected nodes are granted access to the network transmission medium. The software/hardware configuration comprising the access method typically regulates which messages get sent at which time, usually as a means of avoiding collisions between messages. Some common access methods include *CSMA*, *token passing*, etc.

Access Protocol

In networking, the set of rules used by the network to avoid collisions between transmitted messages. The access protocol defines the means by which *node*s can access the transmission medium at a particular time. Also known as the *media-access control protocol*.

Access Rights

In networking, system resources and/or operations that a connected *node* is allowed to use, as determined by the network administrator. Examples of rights granted to a user include file creation, deletion, editing, etc. Different users may have different rights, depending upon their standing in a particular organization.

Access Server

See *Server*.

Access Time

In computing, a measure of the time required to retrieve data from a storage medium. (The term also refers to the time required to write data to a storage medium.) A *hard disk*, for example, has an access time of less than 20 *millisecond*s. Other types of devices, such as *floppy disk*s, removable cartridges, and especially *CD-ROM*s have longer access times. A storage medium with the shortest access time is *flash memory*, with an access time as low as 250 *nanosecond*s. Access time is also known as *seek access time*. Access time can also vary on a single device; therefore, tests to gauge access time measure *average access time*, or the amount of time it takes to retrieve randomly positioned data.

Accordion Fold

In *binding and finishing*, a term for a type of fold consisting of two or more *parallel fold*s, with adjacent folds in opposite directions such that the folds open and close much like the bellows of an accordion. Also called a *fanfold* and, in England, a *concertina fold* or *over-and-back fold*. See *Folding*.

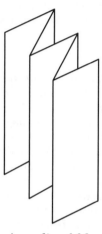

Accordion fold.

Account

In networking, usually on *local area network*s, a record of *access rights*, time spent connected to the network, etc., kept for each user who is granted access to the network. An account may be strictly for administrative or security purposes, or for purposes of billing.

Account Executive

In advertising, the individual in charge of a particular advertising campaign with a client. Account executives are responsible for all aspects of an ad campaign, from design, layout, media buying, etc.

Accounting

In networking, the management and tracking of which users or nodes make use of which network resources, often for security and/or billing purposes. Accounting can take into account such things as connect time, space used for file storage, service requests, etc.

Accounting Software

In computing, any application program designed to facilitate a company or individual's accounting procedures. Such programs usually allow data entry, as well as various means of generating period reports, such as end-of-year reports on outgo and income, balance sheets, income statements, and records of accounts payable and receivable.

Account Policy

In networking, the rules defining which users are allowed access to which network resources, and whether or not they must pay for extended (or even any) privileges.

Accumeter Gluer/Moistener

In **binding and finishing**, a mechanical device that is used to apply an **adhesive** and/or water to a printed **web** to prevent the formation of **gusset**s and to facilitate **folding**. Adhesive applied to the **spine** of a **book block** helps hold the **signature**s together during subsequent binding operations.

Accumulator

Alternate term for a computer's **register**. See **Register** (last definition).

Accuracy

A measure of the degree to which something is free from error. In scientific measurements, accuracy refers to the degree to which a specific measurement agrees with a predetermined measurement of the same or similar elements. In this sense, accuracy should not be confused with **precision**.

Accurate Screens

A system developed by Adobe Systems, Inc., for calculating high-quality **PostScript** halftone **screen angles**, comprising **supercell** screen-calculation algorithms. See **Screen Angles**.

Acetate

A family of **solvent**s used in printing inks; also known as **ester**s.

The term *acetate* is also used to refer to **cellulose acetate**, a type of plastic film used as a printing **substrate**, an overlay on **mechanical**s, **overlay color proof**s, and other artwork, or overhead transparencies.

Acetate Butyrate

A **thermoplastic** material used as a **substrate** in **screen printing**.

Acetate Proof

Alternate term for an **overlay color proof**. See **Overlay Color Proof**.

Acetic Acid

An organic acid (chemical formula $C_2H_4O_2$) that is characterized by a pungent scent and produced by a variety of means. It is the primary constituent of vinegar, and it is used to synthesize **acetate**, a transparent plastic film. Acetic acid is also used to test the acid resistance of materials.

Acetone

A **solvent** in the **ketone** family (chemical formula CH_3COCH_3) used in the manufacture of printing inks for **gravure** and **flexography** packaging. Acetone is also used in **screen printing** both as an ink thinner and as a solvent used to remove **lacquer** and lacquer-adhered stencils from screen fabrics. Acetone is the fastest-drying solvent in the ketone family.

ACF

Alternate term for **advanced communications function**. See **Advanced Communications Function**.

ACF/NCP

Abbreviation for **advanced communication function** for the **network control program**. See **Network Control Program**.

Achromat

In photography, a camera lens that has been modified to reduce or eliminate **chromatic aberration** by focusing two different **color**s (such as blue-violet and yellow) simultaneously. Chromatic aberration, which manifests itself as a blurring of colors, is caused by the refraction of light of different wavelengths (colors) as it passes through a curved lens and strikes a flat photographic plate or photographic emulsion. By grinding a lens so that two prominent colors are in common focus, the blurring effect can be minimized. Achromat lenses are found in nearly all cameras these days. Achromat lenses are also referred to as **apochromatic**.

Achromatic

Possessing no **color** or **hue** or, in other words, absorbing or reflecting all wavelengths of light in equal amounts. The term also describes a printed material that contains only black, white, and/or gray, the *achromatic colors*. In **subtractive color theory**, a white pigment reflects all the light that hits it, absorbing no colors, while black pigments absorb all the light that strikes it, reflecting no light back to the observer. Between these extremes are the grays, which can be produced either by mixing white and black, or by mixing complementary colors. (Light itself, by the way, cannot actually be gray.) Achromatic colors are also known as **neutral colors**.

Achromatic Color Removal (ACR)

An obsolete term for **gray component replacement**. See **Gray Component Replacement (GCR)**.

Acid

A substance that yields hydrogen (H^+) ions when added to a solution. Acids typically have a corrosive effect on many substances. The **acidity** of a solution is described in terms of **pH**, a scale running from 1–14, where 7 is defined as neutral, with acidity increasing as pH decreases. Acids turn litmus paper red, and neutralize **alkali**s, those substances occupying the opposite end of the pH scale. A substance capable of functioning both as an acid and an alkali is referred to as **amphoteric**. See **pH**.

Acid Dye

A variety of **colorant** comprising salts of organic acids, used in the **screen printing** of textiles.

Acid-Free Paper

See **Alkaline Paper**.

Acidity

The extent to which a solution is an *acid*. See *Acid* and *pH*.

Acid Number

A unit used to measure the amount of potassium hydroxide (chemical formula KOH) needed to neutralize the free *acid*s found in oils, waxes, or *resin*s. A high degree of acidity is undesirable in many printing applications, and the addition of a high-*pH* substance (called a base) is needed to counteract the acidity of a substance. Acid number is measured in milligrams of KOH needed to neutralize one gram of oil, wax, or resin.

Acid Paper

A type of paper that is slightly acidic. Most paper is acid paper, since it is produced using bleaching agents, *sizing* materials (in particular, acid-rosin sizing, which is the chemical that, although useful for imparting water resistance to paper, is also responsible for rapid aging, yellowing, and deteriorating), and *coating*s that impart to the paper a degree of acidity. The disadvantages of acid paper include low *permanence*; acid paper tends to deteriorate very rapidly, perhaps in as short a time as 50 years or less. There has been much interest in recent years (especially from librarians and archivists) in *alkaline paper* (also called *acid-free paper*), the advantage of which is its much longer permanence (as long as 200 years). The lack of acids in papers is also believed to be more environmentally sound. The disadvantages of alkaline paper include its incompatibility with acid-based offset press *dampening system*s (when acids and bases intermingle, they react, sometimes quite strongly), especially when *calcium carbonate* is used as a *filler* or a coating. Alkaline sizing materials (such as alkyl ketene dimer and alkyl succinic anhydride) are beginning to be used in place of acid-rosin sizing.

New developments are removing the stumbling blocks to alkaline paper, and some experts have predicted that in the near future acid paper will no longer be available. (See also *Alkaline Paper*.)

Acidity and alkalinity occupy opposite ends of the *pH* scale. A solution with a pH of 7 is defined as neutral, one with a pH of less than 7 is defined as an acid, and a solution with a pH of greater than 7 is defined as a base (or an alkaline solution). See *pH*.

Acid Resist

See *Resist*.

ACK

In telecommunications, an abbreviation for *acknowledge*. See *Acknowledge (ACK)*.

Acknowledge (ACK)

In telecommunications and networking, a character used by some network *protocol*s to indicate that a message has been received intact. If no ACK is received by the sending device—or if the sender receives a *negative acknowledgment (NAK)*—the original message is resent. If an ACK is received, the next message can be sent.

Acknowledgment

In computer applications, any audible or visible signal generated by a program indicating that a particular screen element or function has been activated or selected.

Acoustic Coupler

An early form of a *modem* comprising a device into which a conventional telephone handset can be plugged. The audio tones from the handset can then be encoded for transmission. Alternately, encoded tones can be decoded upon reception.

Acoustic Tablet

A type of computer input device in which sonic signals produced by a sound-emitting *stylus* are converted to electrical signals which, in turn, are converted to *digital* information and processed by the computer.

Acquire

In publishing, to purchase the reprint rights to a book, article, photograph, artwork, etc.

In imaging, to *acquire* means to obtain a digital image from an analog source, such as from a *scanner* or *video capture board*. Acquire may be used synonymously with *import*, save that the latter typically refers to an image already in digital form.

ACR

Abbreviation of *achromatic color removal*, an obsolete term for *gray component replacement*. See *Gray Component Replacement (GCR)*.

Acrobat

A program developed by Adobe Systems, Inc., for creating, editing, distributing, and viewing *Portable Document Format* files. See *Portable Document Format (PDF)*.

Acronym

In typography, a set of of letters that form a pronounceable word, each letter also standing for another word, such as *NASA*, which stands for *National Aeronautic and Space Administration*, or *TIFF*, which stands for *Tagged Image File Format*. Stylistically, an acronym is typeset in all capital letters, usually without periods between the letters.

Often, an acronym will enter the lexicon of a language as a word in its own right, and after a while it may not even be obvious that it is an acronym. For example, the word *laser* began life as an acronym for *light amplification by stimulated emission of radiation*.

Across-the-Cover

In *foil stamping*, the movement of the foil in a direction parallel to the front-to-back direction of the book cover. See also *Head-to-Foot*.

Across-the-Grain
See *Against-the-Grain*.

Acrylate
A *monomer* (chemical structure $CH_2{=}CH{-}C{-}O{-}$) used in *ultraviolet curing ink*.

Acrylic
Generic term for a family of thermoplastic *resin*s, derived from the *ester*s of amides of acrylic or methacrylic acid, used in printing inks and adhesives for packaging applications and as modifiers in *polyvinyl chloride* materials. Acrylic resins are widely used for their strength, rigidity, and their compatibility with other plastics, and are also the basis of Lucite and Plexiglas. Acrylic films are also used as *substrate*s in *screen printing*. See *Acrylic Ink* and *Acrylic Adhesive*. See also *Resin*.

Acrylic Adhesive
A type of *adhesive* material produced from *acrylic* polymers. Acrylic materials (such as solutions of copolymers of alkyl acrylates as well as small amounts of acrylic acid, acrylonitrile, or acrylamide) adhere readily to a variety of surfaces and are used in many types of *pressure-sensitive adhesive*s. Environmental regulations have resulted in the development of emulsion polymers, waterborne acrylic resins that are used as adhesive materials in packaging because of their high tack and good age-resistance characteristics. Acrylic resins are also used in *hot-melt adhesive*s.

Acrylic Emulsion
A type of water-based latex coating material produced from *acrylic* polymers.

Acrylic Ink
An ink produced from *acrylic* polymers and used in various printing processes. Acrylic solution resins are used in *paste ink*s for *offset lithography* and *screen printing*. They also produce excellent *halftone dot*s because of their color fidelity and fast setting times. Acrylic paste inks are widely used in the printing of cartons used for packaging.

Acrylic substances are widely used in solvent-based *liquid ink*s for *flexography*, and their resistance to discoloration, heat, and abrasion, as well as their strength, yields excellent results when printed on paper, paperboard, and various plastic substrates. Often, adding *nitrocellulose* to acrylic-based liquid solvent inks improves heat resistance and compatibility with other laminating materials.

Acrylic polymers are also used in water-based liquid inks, which are largely replacing solvent-based inks in flexography and *gravure*, primarily for environmental reasons. Acrylic inks are widely used for outdoor applications because of the weather resistance and durability of acrylic polymers.

ACS
Abbreviation for *Advanced Communications Service*. See *Advanced Communications Service (ACS)*.

Actinic Rays
Short-wavelength rays of light—such as ultraviolet light—responsible for the chemical reactions that take place in and *cure* photosensitive materials, such as photographic printing plate coatings, photographic emulsions, plastic films, and radiation-cured inks. Actinic rays are commonly produced by arc lamps, photographic flood bulbs, mercury vapor lamps, etc. Actinic rays are also known as *Actinic Light*. (See *Photopolymer*, *Photopolymer Plate*, and *Ultraviolet Curing Ink*.)

Activate
In computing, especially by means of a *graphical user interface (GUI)*, to make a *window* active, usually by clicking within it or on its title bar. See *Active*.

Active
In computer applications or operating systems, descriptive of any screen element, function, or *window* that the user has selected (or *activate*d) and which can be acted on in some fashion.

Active Hub
In networking, a point of distribution of a network (or *hub*) that boosts signals transmitted from point to point on the network. See *Hub*. See also *Passive Hub*.

Active-Matrix
A type of *liquid crystal display (LCD)* in which each *pixel* is controlled by its own transistor and consequently has faster screen updates and allows the display to be clearly viewed at wider angles. See also *Passive-Matrix*. See *Liquid Crystal Display (LCD)*.

Active Page
In computing, the portion of a computer's *video memory* displayed on a monitor at any given time. A computer stores all the data it needs for a particular file in *video memory*, which is divided into a number of sections called pages. The active page is the one currently on the screen.

Active Play
A *videodisc* that has been recorded using the *constant angular velocity* technique. See *Constant Angular Velocity (CAV)*.

Activity Ratio
In database management, a measure of file usage expressed as the ratio of records used to the total number of records in the file.

Actual Basis Weight
The *basis weight* of a quantity of paper as measured under prevailing environmental conditions. Actual basis weight can differ from the specified basis weight due to variations in the papermaking process and the influence of variable *moisture content* on paper weight. (See *Basis Weight*.)

ACU

Abbreviation for *Automatic Calling unit*. See *Automatic Calling Unit (ACU)*.

Acutance

A measure of the sharpness of the edge of a printed image against a background or the *substrate* on which it is printed.

Acute Accent

In typography, a right-pointing *accent* (´) placed over a character such as "é." The accent pointing in the opposite direction is called a *grave accent*. See *Accent*.

Adaptable Fraction

Alternate term for a *shilling fraction*, or *fake fraction*. See *Shilling Fraction* and *Fractions*.

Adapter

Any device used to connect two cords, connectors, or devices that otherwise will not connect to each other.

An *adapter* is also any component, such as an *add-on card*, which increases the ability for a computer to perform certain tasks, such as process graphics faster (see *Graphics Adapter*, for example).

An *adapter* is also any component or device that controls a specific piece of hardware attached to the computer, such as a *joystick* or *digitizing tablet*.

Adaptive Differential Pulse Code Modulation (ADPCM)

In multimedia and telecommunications, a file-encoding format used for storing or transmitting digitized audio or speech.

Essentially, the ADPCM method determines the difference between two *PCM*-coded voice signals. This difference is encoded using a filter and is transmitted at a rate lower than the standard 64 *kilobits per second*.

During encoding, the audio signal is sampled 8000 times per second, and three or four *bit*s (in contrast to the 8 bits required for PCM encoding) are used to encode the difference between two consecutive samples.

Adaptive Routing

In networking, a means of transmission in which the system can dynamically determine the most expedient path or route to take from one node to another.

ADB

Abbreviation for *Apple Desktop Bus*. See *Apple Desktop Bus (ADB)*.

ADC

See *Analog-to-Digital Converter*.

Ad Card

Alternate term for a *fact title*. See *Fact Title*.

ADCCP

Abbreviation for *advanced data communications control procedures*. See *Advanced Data Communications Control Procedures (ADCCP)*.

Ad Complaint

A grievance filed by an advertiser or publisher with the printer about inferior quality of a printed advertisement. Ad complaints often result in a *makegood*, or a reprinting and rerunning of the ad, free of charge.

A/D Converter

See *Analog-to-Digital Converter*.

Addition

Alternate term for an *extension*. See *Extension*.

Addition Agent

A substance—commonly an organic compound—added to an *electroplating* solution to alter the characteristics of the layer of deposited metal. They are commonly used in the electrolytic baths for *gravure cylinder* copperplating to inhibit the growth of copper crystals, which contribute to undesirable degrees of surface *roughness*.

Additive Color Primaries

In *color*, wavelengths of light corresponding to the colors *red, green, and blue*, which can be combined to produce other colors, such as yellow, orange, violet, etc. Colors produced using these primaries differ from *subtractive color primaries*. See *Additive Color Theory*. See COLOR PLATE 2. (See also *Subtractive Color Primaries*.)

Additive Color Theory

In *color*, intermediate colors created by mixing the *additive color primaries*, or light having wavelengths that correspond to *red, green, and blue*. Each of these colors occupies about one-third of the visible spectrum of light; when mixed together in equal proportions, they form *white light*. (*Subtractive color theory* involves the use of colorants rather than light which, although producing roughly the same effect, works on a very different principle; see *Subtractive Color Theory*.) See COLOR PLATES 1 and 2.

Color television sets and computer monitors are two examples of displays that produce all the colors discernible to the human eye by means of additive colors. Varying the intensities of the three primaries produces all the shades in between. For example, red light plus green light (with no blue) produces yellow; red light plus blue light (with no green) produces magenta; blue light plus green light (with no red) produces cyan.

Different proportions also increase the range of colors that can be produced. For example, 2 parts red to 1 part green produces orange; 2 parts green to 1 part red produces chartreuse; 1 part blue to 1 part green to 4 parts red produces brown. These effects occur because light is essentially a wave, and different colors have different wavelengths.

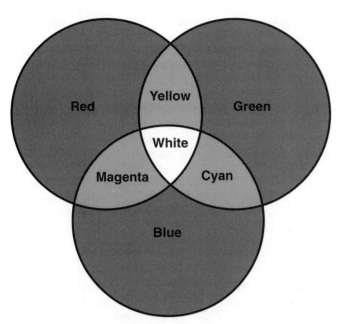

Additive color theory.

When lights possessing different wavelengths are combined with each other, the waves interfere with each other, crests and troughs (of the waves of light) enhancing and/or cancelling each other. The resultant combined wave will have a new wavelength, which will correspond to the new color. Colors can also be "cancelled out" by combining a color and its opposite hue in equal proportions. The opposite of red is cyan, the opposite of blue is yellow, and the opposite of green is magenta.

Color printing uses the subtractive colors. It is the difference between the additives and the subtractives that makes color reproduction from computer-generated originals difficult.

Additive Plate

A type of printing *plate* that is used in *offset lithography*, in contrast to a *subtractive plate*, in which light shined through a photographic negative hardens and renders insoluble the image areas on the plate, the nonimage areas remaining soluble. The coating in the nonimage areas then needs to be removed—or subtracted—from the surface of the plate following exposure. Additive plates require the addition of a special image-strengthening material to the image areas to keep them durable. See *Plate: Offset Lithography*.

Add-Noise Filter

In graphics and digital image manipulation, a function of many image-editing programs that allows the user to distort an image so as to make it look like a *coarse grain*ed photograph.

Add-On Device

Alternate term for a *peripheral*. See *Peripheral*.

Address

In computing, a character, set of characters, or other code identifying the location of a particular data set on a computer storage medium or in the computer memory. An address refers to the location of a particular file, as well as to the specific position of the *cursor*, the main memory location, a peripheral device, or any other physical aspect of a computer system.

Addressability

A term referring to the smallest discrete unit (such as a *pixel*) that a computer display can address.

Addressable Location

In computing, any portion of a computer's memory where data can be stored and retrieved.

Addressable Photo Elements

In *digital photography*, the *pixel*s of an image, equivalent to the number of active light-sensing elements in a *CCD array* multiplied by the total number of horizontal scan lines in an image.

Addressable Point

On a computer display, the smallest point (such as the *pixel*) that can be described in terms of device coordinates.

Addressable Resolution

A measure of the number of *pixel*s, or *spot*s, that a *film recorder*'s light source can place on a line of film. The higher the addressable resolution, the clearer and sharper the image. (See *Resolution*.)

Address Bus

In computing, a channel from a computer's *CPU* to its memory through which flow the *address*es of data (but not the data itself). The number of wires available in the address bus determines the amount of memory that can be directly addressed, each line bearing one *bit* of address data.

Addressing

In computing, the act of assigning a particular data set a unique location in the main memory, each data set thus having an *address* used to store and retrieve it. See *Address*.

Address Register

In computing, a portion of the computer's memory in which the *address*—or location—of an instruction is stored. The address register is also a portion of a computer's memory (or an attached device) used to store the locations of memory, peripheral devices, or other physical components of a system.

Address Resolution Protocol (ARP)

In networking and telecommunications, a *protocol* within a network (especially one using *TCP/IP* and *AppleTalk*) that allows a **host** to locate the physical **address** of a particular node when only the logical address is known. Essentially, ARP makes use of a **network interface card**, a table that maps logical addresses to physical addresses. When a node needs to send a message, it checks to see if physical address data is already present; if not, it sends an ARP request.

Add-Subtract Time

In computing, the amount of time it takes a **CPU** to perform an addition or subtraction operation, exclusive of the time it takes to acquire the data from storage and put the result back into storage.

Add Thin Space

A code or specification used in computerized typesetting to indicate where a **thin space** should be inserted, for use in **justification**. See **Thin Space**.

ADF

Abbreviation for **automatic document feeder**. See **Automatic Document Feeder**.

Adherend

Any surface, material, or substance that is affixed to another surface, material, or substance.

Adhering

In **screen printing**, the process of attaching an indirect film to the screen fabric. See **Screen Printing**.

Adhering Liquid

A lacquer-based **solvent** used in **screen printing** to attach the **stencil** to the screen fabric. See **Screen Printing**.

Adhesion

A property of a substance that describes its ability to stick to another material, either mechanically or chemically, as in the ability of a printing ink to adhere to the surface of a paper. (See also **Cohesion**.) The term **ultimate adhesion** is used to refer to the strength of the bond produced by an **adhesive** substance. See also **Mechanical Adhesion**, **Peel Adhesion**, **Shear Adhesion**, **Specific Adhesion**, **Ultimate Adhesion**, and **Adhesive**.

Adhesion Buildup

An increase in the **peel adhesion** (the force required to remove a **pressure-sensitive label**) of an adhesive material over time.

Adhesion Test

Any of a wide range of tests performed to gauge the efficacy of a printed ink film or adhesive coating. The **cross-hatch test** is one commonly used ink adhesion test.

Adhesive

Of a substance, possessing properties of **adhesion**. See **Adhesion**.

In papermaking, *adhesive* is an alternate term for a **binder** used in **coated paper**. See **Binder** and **Coating**.

An *adhesive* is a specific substance capable of adhering to a surface, or of facilitating the attachment of two surfaces or substances in varying degrees of permanence or application.

TYPES OF ADHESIVES

Adhesive materials are widely used in **binding and finishing** for adhering pages together and in adhering pages to covers, and in packaging for the forming, sealing, and labeling of boxes, cartons, bags, and other packaging materials. There is a wide variety of adhesives available, the specific variety for a particular end-use being dictated primarily by cost, the nature of the **substrate**, and the specific end-use requirements. There are three general classes of adhesive: water-based adhesives, hot-melt adhesives, and solvent-based adhesives.

Water-Based Adhesives. The most prevalent adhesives are those that are water borne, their popularity due to their lack of toxicity, their low cost, and their strength. Natural water-based adhesives include those based on starches, in particular corn starch. Such adhesives are derived from raw flour or starch, or, more commonly, the acid hydrolysis of the starch molecule, in which it is broken down into smaller units. At this point, it can be combined with other materials, such as tackifiers (primarily borate salts, sodium hydroxide, sodium silicate, and plasticizers and other fillers). Starch-based adhesives are often used for the forming and sealing of **corrugated board** used in shipping cartons, the winding of cardboard tubes, the forming and sealing of bags, and the adhesion of labels on cans. A variety of starch-based adhesive called jelly gum is used to affix labels on bottles. Jelly gums are particularly compatible with high-speed labeling equipment.

Casein, derived from precipitated cow's milk, is also used in some types of adhesive, in particular beer-bottle labeling, as it is especially resistant to cold-water immersion during beer production, and the adhesive is easily removed during glass-bottle reclamation. Casein adhesives are also used (with special synthetic **elastomer**s) in the adhesion of aluminum foil to paper.

Other infrequently used natural adhesives include animal proteins and animal glues, the latter derived from collagen extracted from animal tissues. Once quite popular, these animal-based adhesives are used only in certain specialty applications, as the advancement of synthetic adhesives far surpasses their performance characteristics.

Natural rubbers and latexes are also used, especially in self-seal applications for candy wrappers and envelopes, among other uses.

Synthetic water-based adhesives are the most widely used in packaging. Synthetic adhesives are derived from resin-based **emulsion**s such as a suspension of polyvinyl acetate in water. Additives such as protective colloids and plasticizers, fillers, solvents, preservatives, and other materials are often added to impart a desired set of properties, such as water resistance or adhesion to metals and plastics as well as to paper and paperboard. The cost-effectiveness of such adhesives has also ensured their proliferation in the packaging industry. Recent developments in the use of **acrylic** polymers with vinyl acetate copolymers have also improved the adhesion properties of these adhesives.

Hot-Melt Adhesives. *Hot-melt adhesives* are based on thermoplastic polymers (such as the copolymers of ethylene and vinyl acetate) that melt when heated, are applied in the molten state, and form a strong bond when cooled. Waxes are often added to these adhesives to lower the **viscosity** of the melt, facilitating the application of the adhesive, and to regulate the speed at which the material sets. Hot-melts based on **polyethylene** are not useful in as broad a range of applications as ethylene-vinyl acetate-based adhesives but are widely used in the sealing of bags and cases. Amorphous **polypropylene** is also used in some applications—specifically in the bonding of paper to paper to produce water-resistant wrappings or shipping tape—but the weakness of these adhesives makes them unsuitable for many other uses.

Newer hot-melt adhesives based on copolymers of styrene and butadiene have emerged in recent years, and have found application in **pressure-sensitive adhesive**s for tape and labels, as well as in plastic soft-drink bottles.

The advantages of hot-melt adhesives—adhesion by simple cooling, coupled with their ability to flow into gaps and join ill-fitting surfaces—easily outweigh their disadvantages, which include reduced strength at elevated temperatures. In addition, the wide variety of materials used for hot-melts imparts the ability to adhere to nearly any surface. Hot-melt adhesives are the most widely used adhesives in binding, especially **perfect binding**.

Solvent-Based Adhesives. Due to a variety of cost and environmental factors, solvent-borne adhesives are only used in specialized applications where water-borne or hot-melt adhesives are inappropriate or ineffectual. Solutions of rubber-resin materials are often used for pressure-sensitive labels and tapes, but other less expensive and environmentally safer types of adhesives are gradually edging out such formulations. Similarly, solvent-borne polyurethane adhesives (now used in the sealing of plastic films such as plastic bags, snack wrappers, and boil-in-bag dinners) are also being edged out by other adhesive systems. Acrylic polymers, for example, are now *de rigueur* in potato chip bags. A type of "warm-melt" polyurethane (containing no solvent vehicle) is now being used in some food-packaging applications.

See also **Cold Temperature Adhesive**, **Hot Temperature Adhesive**, **Layflat Adhesive**, **Permanent Adhesive**, **Pressure-Sensitive Adhesive**, **Removable Adhesive**, and **Temporary Adhesive**.

ADHESIVE APPLICATION

As there are many different types of adhesives and surfaces to which adhesive is applied, so too is there a large number of devices and configurations for applying the adhesive.

There are generally several categories of adhesive applicating systems.

Circulating vs. Noncirculating. The most common system is the noncirculating system, which is used to apply both cold water-borne and hot-melt adhesives. A noncirculating system essentially comprises a parallel series of guns, each one attached to the main tank by individual hoses. The adhesive is pumped to each gun though the hose, and the adhesive is applied by the nozzle of the gun. In a circulating system, one single hose connects all the guns in series, the hose running in a loop out of the main tank, though the guns, then back into the tank. (A kind of hybrid system is known as an internally circulating system, in which a single hose circulates the adhesive within the device, but each gun is at the terminal of offshoot hoses that form dead ends.)

Cold-Glue vs. Hot-Melt Systems. In a cold-glue system, hoses pump the fluid adhesive to applicator heads that apply the adhesive to the substrate in bead, spray, or droplet form (depending upon the requirement) by means of attachments or special configurations on the applicator heads.

In a hot-melt system, an additional requirement is needed: melting the adhesive. The most common configuration for melting devices is a tank melter, or essentially a large pot or tank in which cold adhesive can be added and melted into liquid form. Small tank melters hold about eight pounds of adhesive, while larger units can hold up to several hundred pounds. The sides of the tank are lined with a thermally conductive substance, and the adhesive melts first along the sides of the tank. Internal circulation from the pumping mechanism works to distribute the heat throughout the interior of the tank. A variation on the tank melter is a grid melter, in which dimensional patterns are used to increase the surface area of the heated surface. Grid melters provide a much greater melt rate than straight tank melters. Various other configurations can also be utilized to keep the adhesive cool or warm, depending upon the chemistry of the adhesive. Some adhesives need to be "premelted" and kept in a liquid form before application, while some degrade quickly when melted and need to be kept cool until just prior to application. The delivery of the molten adhesive to the dispenser can be effected either using piston-driven or gear-driven pumping devices. The dispensing mechanism itself can be some variety of extrusion gun. A conventional extrusion gun essentially pumps the molten adhesive through a nozzle onto the substrate. Automatic extrusion guns use timers and other controllers to dispense adhesive at set rates. Manual systems require human intervention. Web-extrusion guns use the same basic principle of the extrusion gun coupled with patterned blades to apply a film of adhesive to a moving substrate. The thickness of the film and the pattern in which it is applied can be adjusted. Labels, tapes, envelopes, and other such continuous substrates commonly utilize web-extrusion guns. A third type of dispensing device utilizes rotating wheels and rollers to apply adhesive to a substrate.

Delivery Rate. In the application of an adhesive, it is necessary to determine the **MIDR**, or the *maximum instantaneous delivery rate* (also called the **IPDR**, or *instantaneous pump delivery rate*) or the amount of adhesive that a pump needs to feed to the dispensing guns, assuming the guns were continuously extruding adhesive. The commonly used units for MIDR are pounds per hour (lb/h) or grams per minute (g/min). The MIDR is calculated using the size of the bead that a gun is required to lay down, and the speed with which this can be accomplished.

Adhesive Binding
Alternate term for *perfect binding*. See *Perfect Binding*.

Adhesive Bleed
A seeping or oozing of the *adhesive* material from pressure-sensitive label stock caused by *cold-flow* or pressure produced by clamps or other means. Also called *ooze*, *adhesive ooze*, and *adhesive strike-through*.

Adhesive-Coated Paper
A type of *coated one side* paper in which the coating is an adhesive or glue, which can either be permanently sticky, or only become sticky with the application of moisture, heat, or other condition.

Adhesive Ooze
Alternate term for *adhesive bleed*. See *Adhesive Bleed*.

Adhesive Residue
A sticky deposit remaining on a surface to which a *pressure-sensitive adhesive* substance has been applied and removed, due to a low degree of *cohesion* in the adhesive material. *Adhesive residue* also refers to the adhesive remaining on a water-applied *decal* after attachment to a surface.

Adhesive Strike-Through
Alternate term for *adhesive bleed*. See *Adhesive Bleed*.

Adjacency
In *optical character recognition (OCR)*, a condition in which two characters are spaced too close together for the scanner to read them as individual characters.

Adjacency Effect
The property of the eye that causes the same color to look different when surrounded by or adjacent to other colors. A color appears darker when surrounded by a lighter color, or lighter when surrounded by a darker color. (See COLOR PLATE 18.)

Adjacent Colors
Alternate term for *analogous colors*. See *Analogous Colors*.

Adjustable Fabric Holder
In *screen printing*, the part of the *chase* (or screen printing frame) to which the screen fabric can be attached and moved forward or backward, for accurate control of screen tension or register. See *Chase*. Also called an *adjustable frame*.

Adjustable Frame
See *Adjustable Fabric Holder*.

Adjustable Stroke
In *screen printing*, the mechanical control of the distance travelled by the *squeegee*.

ADO
Abbreviation for *Ampex Digital Optics*. See *Ampex Digital Optics (ADO)*.

Adobe Acrobat
See *Acrobat* and *Portable Document Format (PDF)*.

Adobe Font Metrics (AFM)
The specification developed by Adobe Systems, Inc., for *PostScript* fonts which stores (as a text file) typographic information such as character widths, *kern pair*s, and character *bounding box*es.

Adobe Illustrator
See *Illustrator*.

Adobe PageMaker
See *PageMaker*.

Adobe Photoshop
See *Photoshop*.

Adobe Type Manager™
Abbreviated *ATM*, a software program or system extension manufactured by Adobe Systems that is used to enhance the display of *screen font*s on computer monitors. Essentially, ATM uses the *outline font*s (or *printer font*s) rather than *bitmap font*s, which not only allows for the creation of screen fonts in any type size, but also reduces the memory and processing power needed for bitmaps. ATM also handles the downloading of fonts to a computer printer.

ADP
Abbreviation for *automatic data processing*. See *Automatic Data Processing (ADP)*.

ADPCM
See *Adaptive Differential Pulse Code Modulation (ADPCM)*.

Adsorption
A concentrated layer of molecules or particles of a solid, liquid, gas, or dissolved substance, in particular that of particles of a *pigment* in an ink *vehicle* that can hamper the effective dispersion of other additives, such as *drier*s.

Adsorption also refers to the condition in which any liquid or gaseous molecules congregate on the surface of another substance.

ADTV
Abbreviation for **advanced-definition television**. See **Advanced-Definition Television (ADTV)**.

Advanced Communication Function
A line of sophisticated networking applications developed by IBM for IBM systems. Abbreviated **ACF**.

Advanced Communications Service (ACS)
In networking, a large-scale data communications network developed by AT&T.

Advanced Data Communications Control Procedures (ADCCP)
In networking and telecommunications, a bit-oriented standard **ANSI** communications protocol.

Advanced Peer-to-Peer Networking (APPN)
A network **protocol** used in IBM's **Systems Network Architecture (SNA)** that allows connected nodes to communicate without the need for a centralized **host**. APPN also features **dynamic routing**, and is used on a variety of networks, such as **Ethernet**, **Token Ring**, **FDDI**, **ISDN**, etc. APPN is based on the older **Advanced Program-to-Program Communications (APPC)**.

Advanced Program-to-Program Communications (APPC)
In networking, a session **protocol** used by IBM's **Systems Network Architecture (SNA)** that allows programs utilized by the network to communicate with each other without the need for **terminal emulation**, or on a **peer-to-peer** basis. The standards for APPC are described in **LU6.2**.

Advanced Run-Length Limited Encoding
In computing, a means of storing data on a **hard disk** that increases the capacity of **run-length limited encoding** by more than 25%. See **Run-Length Limited Encoding**. Abbreviated **ARLL**.

Advanced Technology-Compatible
See **AT-Compatible**.

Advance Feed
In the days of paper tape-based typesetting systems, a term descriptive of a paper tape whose feed hole was positioned slightly toward the front of the frame of code holes.

Advance on Royalties
In publishing, a fee paid to an author upon signing a contract for publication and/or upon delivery of a final manuscript (often, half of an agreed-upon advance is paid upon signing, and half is paid upon delivery and acceptance of the manuscript). The amount of the advance is subtracted from the author's share of **royalties** accrued from the sale of copies of the publication. When royalties received have exceeded the amount of the advance, the publication is said to have "earned out." If an advance is not completely paid off by royalties, it is not often asked to be returned, the publisher merely absorbing the loss. In some rare cases, an advance paid upon signing a contract is revoked due to delivery of an unacceptable and unpublishable manuscript. Also known simply as an **advance** and an **advance payment against royalties**.

Advertisement
In publishing and broadcasting, any document or production designed specifically to encourage readers or viewers to purchase a product or service.

Advertising Agency
A company that designs and produces **advertisement**s.

AES
Abbreviation for **Audio Engineering Society**. See **Audio Engineering Society (AES)**.

AES/EBU
Abbreviation for **Audio Engineering Society/European Broadcast Union**, a standard for the connection of stereo, digital and audio signals through shielded three-wire cables using an XLR microphone **jack**.

Affinity
Any tendency for one substance or material to be attracted to or by another substance or material.

The term *affinity* is also used to describe the bond between an **adhesive** and an **adherend**.

AFM
See **Adobe Font Metrics (AFM)**.

A4
A standard metric paper size used in Europe that corresponds most closely to the United States standard letter size of 8½×11 in. A4-size paper is equal to 210×297 mm, or 8.27×11.69 in. See **A Series**.

A4-Display
A computer monitor that displays a page equivalent to **A4**-size paper (or 210×297 mm). A diagonal screen dimension of at least 16 inches is required. A4-size paper is the European equivalent of United States letter-size (8½×11 in.) paper.

AFP
Abbreviation for *Advanced Function Printing*.

In networking, *AFP* is also an abbreviation for **AppleTalk Filing Protocol**. See **AppleTalk Filing Protocol (AFP)**.

AFP also refers to a module added to Novell's NetWare networking software that provides support for ***AppleTalk Filing Protocol***, allowing connected Mac users to easily access network files and applications.

Aftermarket

In computing, the market created for a variety of peripheral hardware devices and software programs after the advent and sale of a specific type of computer.

After-Tack

A property of a printing ink that describes its ability to develop ***tack***, or stickiness, after it appears to have dried.

Afterword

A portion of the ***back matter*** of a book providing a quick summary of the main text, or additional material uncovered by the author after the preparation of the main text. An afterword is often found in successive editions of a book, serving as a means of updating the material without having to revise and reset the main text itself. See ***Book Typography***.

Against-the-Grain

The direction perpendicular to the orientation of the paper fibers (or ***grain***), also called ***across-the-grain***, as opposed to ***with-the-grain***. See ***Grain***.

Agate

The original name for 5½-point type. Originally, ***type size*** was expressed using names, not numbers. Although this tradition is no longer in use, the term *agate* is still used to refer to 5½-point type, especially when describing the type used in newspaper classified advertising.

Newspapers also used agate type to measure display advertising as a means of determining ad rates. There are 14 agate lines per inch. Ad rates are typically "per line, per column," thus a 2-column, 2-inch ad would be 56 agate lines ($2 \times 14 \times 2 = 56$). The width of the column commonly depends on the newspaper.

Although the smallest type typically used is 6 point, agate is used by newspapers to squeeze more text on a page but, due to its decreased size and reduced legibility, is not commonly recommended.

FOR SALE 1988 Toyota 4Runner. 115,000 miles. Great condition. Make offer or trade for computer. Call 555-8888 after 7pm.
FOR LEASE 2BR apartment in Back Bay. A/C, deck and other features. $2,000 per month. Call 555-3333 after 6pm.
WANTED 1989 Stretch Yugo. Call 555-8888 after 7pm.
LOST Fuzzy teddy bear about 12 in. high. Brown with red belt. Answers to "Sweeney." Call 555-3388 after 6pm.
FOR SALE 1990 Cadillac Seville. 34,000 miles. Mint condition. Mint color. Best offer. Call 555-8888 after 5pm.

Agate type.

Agent

Any chemical, physical or mechanical substance or material used to enhance or facilitate a desired effect, such as an ***emulsifying agent***, or a ***wetting agent***.

In multimedia, an *agent* is any animated figure that explains how to operate a particular software application.

In computing, an *agent* is also any program designed to perform a repetitive task, much like a ***macro***. Also known, in this sense, as a ***softbot***, a contraction of ***software robot***.

An *agent* is also a person responsible for procuring work for clients, or for procuring ***talent*** to work on specific (usually freelance) projects. Examples are literary agents, employment agents, etc.

Age Resistance

The ability of a substance—such as an ink film, a ***substrate***, or printed piece—to resist deteriorating upon exposure to oxygen, heat, light, or internal chemical action. Also known as ***permanence***.

Age Stability

A property of a printing ink that determines its ability to retain its optical and structural properties at a particular temperature for a specified period of time.

Agfa FotoFlow

A ***color management system***—a set of computer programs or utilities that ensure consistent color throughout the prepress processes by calibrating the color relationships among the scanners, monitors, printers, imagesetters, and other devices in the chain from input to output—developed by Agfa. FotoFlow comprises a set of utilities and applications, the most important of which is FotoTune, a program that uses "ColorTags," a series of CIE-based device profiles, to match colors between different devices. In particular, the ColorLinks feature allows the merging of ColorTags to convert from ***color space*** to color space quickly and accurately. (See ***Color Management System [CMS]***.)

Agglomerate

Any mass of things gathered together, commonly used to refer to a cluster of undispersed particles of printing ink ***pigment*** or other additives. Such undispersed particles can have deleterious effects not only on the dispersion of other substances in the ink (such as ***drier***s), but also on the performance of the ink in a printing process. This condition is sometimes found in inks used in ***screen printing***. A string of such clusters is referred to as an ***aggregate***.

Aggregate

Any sum or mass of particular objects, used to refer to a string or chain of clusters of undispersed particles of printing ink ***pigment***. Such clusters can have deleterious effects on the dispersion of other additives in the ink and on the performance of the ink in a printing operation. An individual cluster of pigment particles is referred to as an ***agglomerate***.

Aggressiveness

The measure of how quickly and with what degree of tackiness an ***adhesive*** material forms a bond with another surface or substance.

Aging

The changes in color, structure, gloss, or other properties in a (printed) substance over time. See **Permanence**.

In **screen printing**, *aging* refers to the **curing** of printed decorations onto textiles by means of moist heat as a way of ensuring the **colorfastness** of the colorant and removing the stiffness of the textile fibers, which is characteristic of air-dried decorations.

AI

Abbreviation for **artificial intelligence**. See **Artificial Intelligence (AI)**.

AIF

Common **file extension** for files saved in the **audio interchange file format**. See **Audio Interchange File Format (AIFF)**.

AIFF

Abbreviation for **audio interchange file format**. See **Audio Interchange File Format (AIFF)**.

AIP Cube

A model of a **virtual reality** system created by MIT that plots three variables—autonomy, interaction, and presence—on a three-axis coordinate system. Autonomy describes the system's ability to receive and react to external stimuli, such as actions performed by a user. Interaction describes the extent to which all the commands present in the system are used by a user. Presence describes the extent to which the systems offers tactile feedback. Each of these variables is given a value between 0 and 1 and plotted on a three-axis coordinate system. The point at 0,0,0 would be no virtual reality while that at 1,1,1 would be the ultimate in virtual reality. See **Virtual Reality (VR)**.

Air

That portion of a typed or typeset page which contains no type or illustration matter. More commonly known as **white space**.

Air Bell

An alternate term for the surface defect of a paper called a **blister** or **foam mark**. See **Blister**.

Air-Blast Nozzles

Devices on an offset press **sheet-separation unit** that direct jets of air between sheets on the **pile table** so as to separate one sheet at a time for feeding into the press. See **Sheet-Separation Unit** and **Feeder Section**.

Airbrush

A small, pencil-shaped device that sprays high-pressure watercolor-based pigment as a means of correcting **halftone**s or producing tonal variations.

The term *airbrush* also refers to a function in a digital color imaging system that serves the same purpose as a

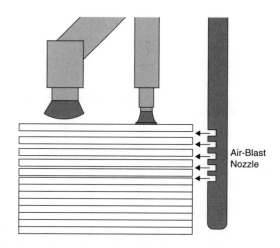

Air-blast nozzle on a sheetfed press sheet separation unit.

conventional "analog" airbrush. The airbrush function can be controlled by moving a stylus on a **digitizing tablet** or by a mouse and adjusting the speed, size, and strength of the "spray" from a menu of commands or settings.

Air Curtin

A device added to the **inking system** of some offset presses that aids in the removal of extraneous moisture by blowing jets of air against an ink roller so as to accelerate the evaporation of moisture. Although some degree of moisture is a

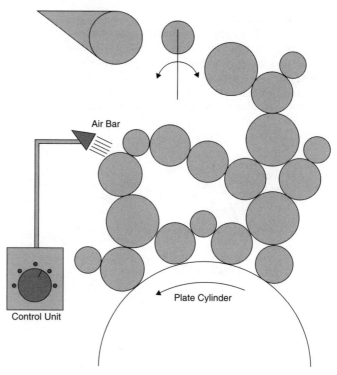

The Air Curtin™, developed by AirSystems, Inc., uses low-pressure bursts of air to remove excess moisture from an offset press inking system.

necessary component of lithographic inking systems, too much can cause poor performance and degraded print and drying qualities.

Air-Cushion Drum

Alternate term for an *air-transport drum*. See *Air-Transport Drum*.

Air-Dried Emulsion

In *screen printing*, an *emulsion* applied to the surface of the screen fabric and allowed to dry at room temperature without the use of drying equipment.

Air-Dried Pigment

A type of ink containing a pigment-resin combination that will dry at room temperature without the need for additional drying equipment or agitation of the surrounding air, commonly used in *screen printing*.

Air Drying

A method of producing high-grade *bond*, *ledger*, and writing papers by passing the wet paper *web*, with little or no tension, through an enclosure containing circulating hot air. As the drying paper is allowed to shrink unimpeded, it takes on a rough *cockle finish*.

Airing

Alternate term for *wind*. See *Wind*.

Air-Knife Coater

A device used to apply a *coating* to the surface of a paper. It operates in a manner akin to that of a *blade coater*, in that a thick layer of surplus coating is deposited on the surface of the *base stock*, but an air-knife coater uses a concentrated jet of air to level and meter the coating across the surface. (See also *Coating* and *Blade Coater*.)

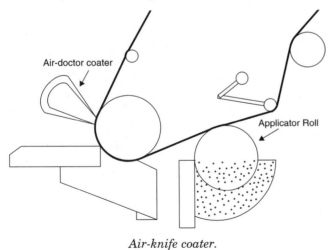

Air-knife coater.

Air Leak Tester

Term for a number of different devices that measure a paper's surface *smoothness* in terms of the rate at which a vol-

ume of air passes between a smooth surface in the machine and the surface of a paper sample. See *Bekk Smoothness Tester*, *Bendtsen Smoothness Tester*, *Gurley Smoothness Tester*, and *Sheffield Smoothness Gauge*. All of these machines are calibrated differently, so results are not interchangeable among them. (See *Smoothness*.)

Air Pull

In *screen printing*, the coating of the surface of the screen fabric with ink without forcing the ink through the screen or making an impression. Also known as *flooding*.

Air Shear Burst

A web *burst* caused by air becoming trapped in the paper roll during winding. (See also *Caliper Shear Burst*, *Cross-Machine Tension Burst*, and *Full Machine Direction Burst*.)

Air-Transport Drum

A cylinder on an offset printing press that replaces a conventional *transfer cylinder*, and is used for transporting printed sheets from the *impression cylinder* to either the *delivery pile* or to additional printing units in the press. A conventional transfer cylinder uses near-frictionless covers and coatings to ensure that the wet ink is not smudged or marked during transport. An air-transport drum (in some configurations) features a metal cylinder with a cover through which small jets of air can be pumped, providing a cushion of air on which the printed

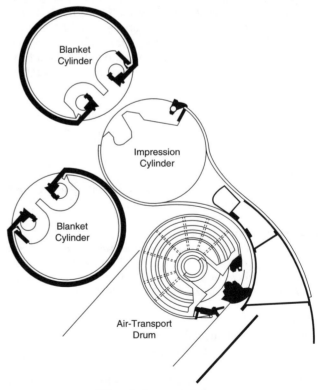

The air-transport drum.

sheet can ride, preventing it from contacting any hard surface that can mark or smudge the ink. An air-transport drum is also known as an *air-cushion drum*.

AITI

Abbreviation for *Automated Interchange of Technical Information*. See *Automated Interchange of Technical Information (AITI)*.

AIX

Abbreviation for *Advanced Interactive eXecutive*, a variety of the *UNIX* operating system manufactured by *IBM*, allowing UNIX to be run on IBM's RS/6000 *RISC* workstations, on IBM *mainframe* computers, and on the IBM PS/2 personal computer. AIX is based on AT&T's UNIX System V with Berkeley extensions.

Albumen

One of a variety of simple, sulfur-based colloidal proteins found in egg whites, blood, milk, and other animal secretions and tissues. Commercially produced albumen is used as a plate sensitizer in *offset lithography* and in some photosensitive emulsions used for *screen printing* stencils. Also spelled *albumin*.

Albumen Plate

An offset lithographic plate coated with *albumen*. It is used for book printing and capable of print-runs of up to 100,000.

Alcohol

Any of a class of organic compounds having the general formula ROH, where R is an alkyl group (which is a univalent group having the general formula C_nH_{2n+1}), and OH (oxygen and hydrogen) is a hydroxyl group. A common example of an alcohol is ethyl alcohol, C_2H_5OH. Alcohols, in addition to some obvious uses, are also commonly used as *solvent*s in printing inks and for cleaning purposes. See *Solvent*.

Alcohols are also added to the *fountain solution* of an offset press as a *wetting agent*, or as a means of reducing the surface tension of the solution. Some fountain solutions utilize *alcohol substitutes*. See *Fountain Solution*.

Alcohol Substitutes

Any of a variety of substances used as a *surfactant* or *wetting agent* in an offset lithographic press *fountain solution* instead of alcohol. See *Fountain Solution*.

Aldus Manutius

Aldus Pius Manutius (1452–1516) was the foremost editor, printer, and publisher of the Renaissance. Manutius was born in 1452 at Bassiano, south of Rome. Between 1467 and 1473 he was a student in the Faculty of Arts in the University of Rome where he developed a passion for the classics. In the late 1470s he attended the University of Ferrara, where he studied Greek under humanist educator Battista Guarino.

In 1489 Aldus abandoned teaching for publishing and moved to Venice, where he entered into a partnership with Andrea Torresano, who provided experience and resources, and Pierfrancesco Barbarigo, a member of a Venetian ducal family, who provided financial and political support. In 1490 the Aldine Press was founded, with a staff of printers and Greek scholars and compositors.

His early editions include the *Hero and Leander of Musaeus*, the *Galeomyomachia,* and the *Greek Psalter*. Between 1495 and 1509, his Greek classics included the works of Aristotle, Aristophanes, Thucydides, Sophocles, Herodotus, Xenophon, Euripides, and Demosthenes, as well as an edition of Greek orators and some of the works of Plutarch.

The Aldine Press introduced many printing innovations. The *octavo*-sized volume was an innovation popularized by Aldus. Aldus's octavo editions of the classics have often been called the precursors of the modern pocket book. This portable book was a benefit for traveling since it fit in a saddle bag.

The Aldine Press.

Aldus experimented with a number of Greek and Latin types, many of his own design. The first two fonts used by Aldus were modeled on the writing of the Greek scribe Immanuel Rhusotas, the third, from Aldus's editorial collaborator, Cretan Marcus Musurus. The last was a simplified version that represented Aldus's own handwriting. Aldus did not revolutionize roman type as much as he refined it. Aldus was the first to adopt *italic* as a printing font. The models for the Aldus's italic fonts were probably the handwriting of scribes Pomponio Leto (1428-1497) and Bartolomeo Sanvito (b. 1435). Aldus's fonts had great influence on the development of typography over the centuries.

In 1500, Aldus founded the New Academy, a school dedicated to Greek studies. He had begun his career as a teacher and saw a need for the publication of Greek and Latin classical authors, whose works ranked high on the

Renaissance humanist agenda. Many of the works of Latin and Greek authors had been published by the end of the 15th century but a large number were not in print. His development of Greek and italic fonts and the octavo format indicate a planned program for the dissemination and popularization of ancient classics. Because of Aldus, works of numerous Greek and Latin authors were published for the first time, and works by others appeared in better editions than had previously been available.

Aldus Printer Description (APD)

An Aldus software file that contains specific information about an output device, such as its *resolution*, the type of paper utilized, the feed mechanism, etc. APDs have been largely replaced by PostScript Printer Definitions (*PPD*s). Aldus itself no longer exists, having been acquired by Adobe Systems, Inc.

Alerting

In computing, the act—on the part of a computer—of making an audible or visible signal when an error has been made on the part of the user, when there is a message from the computer (such as an error message), or when electronic mail is waiting on a mail server. A specific visible alert may include the flashing of the menu bar, while an audible signal is known as an *alert noise* or *audible cue*.

Alert Noise

In computing, a sound generated by a computer (usually a beep, quack, eep, or a user-customized noise) used to warn the user of an improper keystroke or mouse-click, to let him/her know that an error message has been generated, or that a lengthy process has been completed. Also known as an *audible cue*.

Algebra

A type of mathematics in which letters (called "variables") stand in for numerical values and can be manipulated according to the laws of arithmetic. Algebra is used in mathematics (and computer programming) to describe general relational statements of values to each other. A very basic algebraic expression is:

$$x + 1 = 5$$

where x would, in this case, equal 4, or perhaps refer to another algebraic expression. One particular branch of algebra relevant to computing is known as *Boolean algebra*, which deals with logical rather than numerical relations between sets of values.

    Algebra itself was developed around the 9th century by Persian mathematician Al-Khwarizmi, but did not make its way into Europe until several hundred years later, when the Arab city of Toledo (in Spain) was sacked. Arabic knowledge (much of it mathematical) then spread throughout Europe. The word *algebra* derives from the Arabic *al-Jabr*, which some sources claim was a mathematician. The word *jabara*, however, means, in Arabic, "to set or consolidate."

Algebraic Language

In computing, a programming style in which algorithmic statements are structured to resemble expressions found in the branch of mathematics known as *algebra*. Examples of algebraic computer languages are *ALGOL* and *Fortran*.

ALGOL

A computer language that uses algorithms to concisely express arithmetic and logical programming operations and processes. (ALGOL itself is an abbreviation for "ALGorithmic-Oriented Language.") ALGOL was developed in the late 1950s by computer scientists from North America and Europe. Although it never caught on commercially, it was an important influence on later programming languages such as *Pascal* and *C*.

Algorithm

In mathematics and computing, any sequential set of ordered instructions for solving a problem or performing a function. The basis of any computer programming.

Alias

In computing, any shorthand or abbreviated name for a file. Specifically, it is used as a shortcut for opening a file that may be buried in several layers of directories (in *UNIX*) or folders (on a *Macintosh*). An alias is essentially a way of opening a file without typing long paths of directories or clicking through many hierarchical folders. The original file name and/or icon can be copied and placed in a convenient location, such as in a one-layer-deep director or folder, on the Mac desktop, or in the Mac's Apple Menu.

Aliasing

In computer graphics, an undesirable effect—also known as *jaggies*—in which the edge of an image is characterized by a stair-step appearance. Aliasing occurs when the edge of the image is offset to the closest available *pixel*, and an

The effects of aliasing (left) and antialiasing (right).

edge consisting of many small alternating horizontal and vertical lines results. Thus, straight lines (or more commonly diagonal or curved lines) on a computer monitor or low-*resolution* output device are only approximately straight. Aliasing can be rectified by *antialiasing*, or the partial lighting of intermediate pixels. (See *Antialiasing*.) Aliasing is also known as *stair-stepping*.

Align

To line up letters, characters, and words. See *Alignment*.

Align Left

Alternate term for *left justification*. See *Left Justification*.

Alignment

A term used to refer to the proper positioning of all *typefaces* and size variations along an imaginary reference line. Alignment is a necessary consideration that ensures that all styles and sizes can be mixed in the same line.

Base alignment (or *horizontal alignment*) involves aligning the bottom of each character along a horizontal *baseline*. *Vertical alignment* involves alignment of characters beneath each other along an imaginary vertical line to the left of the characters.

Optical alignment involves the use of some visual reference point. For instance, in the setting of vertical lines, characters would not be *flush left* but centered. In some cases, optical alignment may require that curved or angular characters (such as "O"s) be slightly off the baseline to achieve visual alignment. Although they may be geometrically correct, they simply will not "look right" to the eye.

Base alignment.

Alignment Mark

On a continuous form, a preprinted mark used to assist in accurately positioning entries.

Align Right

Alternate term for *right justification*. See *Right Justification*.

Aliphatic Hydrocarbon

A class of *hydrocarbon* (organic molecules containing only carbon and hydrogen atoms) in which the carbon structures can be straight-chain, branched chain, or cyclic, distinguished from the *aromatic solvents*.

Aliphatic hydrocarbons are one of several types of *solvents*, derived from petroleum oil, used in printing inks, especially those used in *flexography*. Examples of aliphatic hydrocarbons are VMP naphtha, gasoline, kerosene, etc. Although they are used often in conjunction with *Buna N* synthetic rubber plates and press rollers, they tend to cause swelling of natural and other synthetic rubbers.

Alkali

A substance that yields hydroxyl (OH⁻) ions when added to a solution. Alkalis typically have a caustic effect on many substances. The *alkalinity* of a solution is described in terms of *pH*, a scale running from 1–14, where 7 is defined as neutral and alkalinity increases with increasing pH. Alkalis turn litmus paper blue and neutralize *acid*s, substances occupying the opposite end of the pH scale. An alkali is also known as a *base*. A substance capable of functioning both as an acid and an alkali is referred to as *amphoteric*. See *pH*.

Alkali Blues

A series of *organic color pigments* used in printing inks. Alkali Blues and *Reflex Blues* (*CI Pigment Blue 56 No. 42800, CI Pigment Blue 18 No. 42770,* and *CI Pigment Blue 61 No. 42765:1*) are the strongest blue pigments available. They comprise a wide range of shades of blue (from reddish to greenish), and possess varying degrees of *lightfastness* and chemical resistance. PB 56 has the greatest color strength and the most *alkali resistance*, while PB 18 and 61 have poor alkali resistance. These blues have poor lightfastness, moderate resistance to heat, and good resistance to acids. New formulations of these types of blues have found particular use in *flexographic* inks; as *flushed colors* they are also used in *lithographic* and *gravure* inks. Alkali Blues are most commonly added to *black pigment*s to reduce their brownish tone and, interestingly, are primarily responsible for the "blackness" of some black pigments. (See *Organic Color Pigments*.)

Alkaline Paper

A type of paper having a *pH* higher than 7. Most paper is *acid paper*, since it is produced using bleaching agents, *sizing* materials, and *coatings* that impart to the paper a degree of acidity. The primary disadvantage of acid paper is its low *permanence*; acid paper tends to deteriorate very rapidly, perhaps in as short a time as 50 years or less. There has been much interest in recent years (especially from librarians and archivists) in alkaline paper (also called *acid-free paper*), the advantage of which is its much longer permanence (as long as 200 years). Alkaline paper also has enhanced brightness, whiteness, and opacity compared to acid paper. The lack of acids in papers is also believed to be more environmentally sound. One disadvantage of alkaline paper is its incompatibility with acid-based offset press *dampening system*s (when acids and bases intermingle, they react, sometimes quite strongly), especially when *calcium carbonate* is used as a *filler* or a coating. Alkaline sizing materials (such as alkyl ketene dimer or alkyl succinic anhydride) are beginning to be used in place of acid-rosin sizing, which is the chemical that, although useful for imparting water resistance to paper, is also responsible for rapid aging, yellowing, and deterioration. New developments are removing the stumbling blocks to the greater use of alkaline paper, and some experts have predicted that in the near future acid paper will no longer be available.

Acidity and alkalinity occupy opposite ends of the pH scale. A solution with a pH of 7 is defined as neutral, one with a pH of less than 7 is defined as an acid, and a solution with a pH of greater than 7 is defined as a base (or an alkaline solution). (See *pH*. See also *Acid Paper*.)

Alkali Resistance

A property of paper describing its ability to resist fading, discoloring, or deteriorating when exposed to alkaline (low-*pH*) substances such as soaps and adhesives. Alkali resistance is an important property when a paper is intended to be used in the packaging of such materials.

The term *alkali resistance* also refers to a similar ability of a printing ink to resist **bleeding**, discoloring, fading, or chemically reacting with alkaline materials. Inks intended for use in the packaging of soaps or other alkaline materials need to possess high alkali resistance. (See **Pigment**.) (See also **Soap Resistance**.)

Alkyd

Any of a variety of synthetic **resin**s used in the manufacture of printing inks, produced by reacting one of several dicarboxylic **acid**s (such as phthalic or maleic acid) with a **polyhydric alcohol** such as glycol or glycerol. See **Resin**.

Aller Undulating Ductor Roller

A segmented **ductor roller** used in the **inking system** of some printing presses used in **web offset lithography**. Each segment of the undulating roller is set off-center with respect to the other sections. Thus, some segments are picking up ink from the **fountain roller**, while others are transferring ink to the rest of the **roller train**. The Aller undulating roller accurately controls the distribution of ink laterally across the press. See **Inking System: Offset Lithography**.

Alley

Alternate term for **gutter**. See **Gutter**.

Alligator

A printing defect of **screen printing** in which an ink film contracts during drying, producing small, discrete pools of color, creating an effect that resembles the texture of alligator skin.

All Points Addressability (APA)

In computer graphics, any array of **pixel**s (or a **bitmap**) in which each specific pixel (be it on a computer screen or on an output device) can be individually manipulated. In other words, each pixel has a unique **address**. Also referred to as **page mode**.

All Rights

In publishing, the purchase of all subsidiary rights to a publication, illustration, photograph, etc., including North American and international rights, serial rights, etc.

Almanac(k)

Multiple or individual pages containing a calendar of the days, weeks, and months of the year with a record of various astronomical activity, weather predictions, and seasonal suggestions for farmers, plus miscellaneous other information, including data on the rising and setting times of the Sun and Moon, the phases of the Moon, the positions of the planets, timings of high and low tides, a register of ecclesiastical festivals and feast days, astronomical phenomena, and meteorologic and agricultural forecasts.

Although almanacs date from ancient times, the term is derived from the Spanish-Arabic almanakh (manakh, "calendar"; manah, "sundial"). In modern Arabic, *al-man-akh* is the word for the weather. The term almanac was used in Roger Bacon's *Opus majus* (c.1267) with astronomical tables showing the movements of the stars and planets. The first printed almanac appeared in Europe in 1457, but almanacs existed in some form since the beginnings of astronomy. Ancient calendars showed festival dates and days thought to be lucky or unlucky; Roman *fasti* named

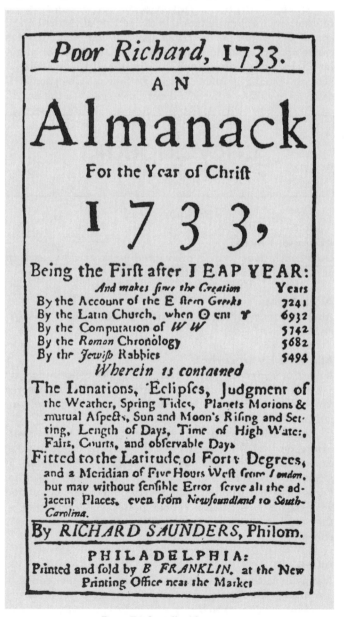

Poor Richard's Almanac.

days on which business could be conducted. Medieval psalters and missals had calendars listing holy days, and 12th-century manuscripts contained tables on the movements of the heavenly bodies. Almanacs became more popular after the development of printing. Printed almanacs in England were published by the Stationer's Company, especially *Vox Stellarum* by Francis Moore, in 1700.

The popular almanac evolved into folk literature with weather predictions, moral precepts and proverbs, medical advice and remedies, as well as jokes. Farmers were able to estimate the time to begin seasonal farm work. The first almanac printed in colonial North America was *An Almanac for New England for the Year 1639*, compiled by William Pierce and printed at Harvard College. Benjamin Franklin's brother James printed *The Rhode Island Almanac* in 1728, and Benjamin Franklin (as Richard Saunders) began his Poor Richard's almanacs in Philadelphia in 1732, which were enlivened by Franklin's humor.

The traditional almanac survives in the *Old Farmer's Almanac*, which has been continuously published in the United States since 1792. Other almanacs are handy collections of statistical, historical, and other information. English-language examples include *The World Almanac*, first published in 1868, and the *Information Please Almanac* (from 1947).

Alpha

The earliest pre-release test copy of computer software or hardware, or another product. See ***Alpha Test***.

Alpha AXP

In computing, a ***64-bit***, ***RISC***-based ***microprocessor*** manufactured by the Digital Equipment Corporation (DEC). The Alpha AXP uses ***PAL***-code, which allows it to execute ***machine code*** written for other processors to run applications created on other computer ***platform***s.

Alphabet

The letters—upper- and lowercase—used in the written form of a language.

An alphabet is a writing system that represents the sounds of a language by a set of understandable symbols for those sounds—symbols representing individual graphemes, or written forms of sounds. From "animal pictures" to "thing pictures" to ideograms to hieroglyphics ("sacred writings"), humankind has sought communication both orally or through some writing system. The alphabet evolved out of commercial necessity as Phoenician merchants sought a way to communicate with themselves and others. Every Phoenician character can be traced to a corresponding hieratic (a fast way of writing hieroglyphics) sign. But it was the alphabet known as the North Semitic, originating around the eastern shores of the Mediterranean in the period around 1600 BC, that was the first. The commercial importance of Israel, Phoenicia, and Aram, the kingdom of Sheba in southwest Arabia, and the growth of the Greek nation provided four branchings: Canaanite, Aramaic, South

Semitic, and Greek. From the Canaanite and the Aramaic evolved modern Hebrew and Arabic; Western alphabets evolved through the Greek, by way of the Phoenician.

The spread of the alphabet is still unclear. Opinions are that conquering armies carried their alphabets with them and imposed them on subjects; or the widespread trade originating around the Fertile Crescent in the Middle East caused a commingling of alphabets as a result of attempts by traders and merchants to communicate with a minimum of confusion; or that religious groups sent missionaries who spread alphabets in the form of scriptures, etc.

PHOENICIAN ALPHABET

The Phoenician alphabet, a writing system spread over the Mediterranean area by Phoenician traders, was the ancestor of the Greek alphabet and all Western alphabets. The earliest Phoenician inscription is the Ahiram epitaph at Byblos in Phoenicia dating from the 11th century BC and written in the North Semitic alphabet. The Phoenician alphabet gradually developed and was in use until about the 1st century BC. Phoenician scripts are classified as Cypro-Phoenician (10th–2nd century BC) and Sardinian (9th century BC). A third Phoenician script evolved into the Punic and neo-Punic alphabets of Carthage, which continued until the 3rd century AD. The Phoenician alphabet remained essentially a Semitic alphabet of 22 letters, written from right to left, with only consonants represented and phonetic values unchanged from the North Semitic script.

The Arabic alphabet is a descendant of the Aramaic, developed into the Kufic and the Naskhi. The Kufic does not exist but was used for stone or metal carvings, coin inscriptions, and scribing the Qur`an (Koran). The Naskhi, from which modern Arabic descends, was a more calligraphic form for handwriting. Like the Hebrew alphabet, the Arabic is almost vowelless. Only 3 of its 28 letters are used for long vowels, with 14 diacritical marks supplying not only other vowels but distinguishing between consonants and serving as noun and verb modifiers.

The Hebrew alphabet as written today came from the Square Hebrew alphabet based on an Aramaic alphabet evolved during the period of the Babylonian Captivity (586–538 BC). Square Hebrew script was standardized around the start of the Christian Era and remains virtually unchanged to this day. All Indian alphabets have their origins in a script called Brahmi, a descendant of Aramaic. From the Brahmi was developed the Gupta, which further developed into Siddhamatrka script which evolved the script used for the writing of Sanskrit, and Devanagari—the latter has remained unchanged since the 9th century AD.

GREEK ALPHABET

The Greek alphabet derived from the North Semitic script via the Phoenicians in the 8th century BC and is the ancestor of all modern European alphabets. The Greek alphabet was modified to make it more efficient and accurate for writing a non-Semitic language by the addition of several new letters and the modification or dropping of several others.

Ancient Egyptian		Phoenician	Ancient Greeks	Latin	Mœso Gothic		Cherokee			
Monumental	Cursive				Form	Sound				

A comparison of the alphabets:

Mœso Gothic

Form	Sound
λ	A
Ƃ	B
Γ	G
ᴆ	D
Ɇ	E
F	F
G	G or J
h	H
ï or I	I
К	K
λ	L
M	M
N	N
ℓ	O
Π	P
☉	HW
К	R
S	S
T	T
Ψ	TH
n	U
u	CW
V	W
X	CH
Z	Z

Latin

A B C D E F Z H — I K L M N — O P — Q R S T

Cherokee

D	a	Ꮻ	o
Ꮝ	ga Ꮒ ka	A	go
Ꮗ	ha	Ꮦ	ho
W	la	Ꮆ	lo
Ꮎ	ma	Ꭽ	mo
Ꮎ	na Ꮵ hna Gnah	Z	no
Ꮖ	qua	Ꮼ	quo
Ꮪ	s Ꮜ sa	Ꮷ	so
Ꮮ	da Ꮃ ta	V	to
Ꮬ	dla Ꮭ tla	Ꮬ	tlo
Ꮏ	tsa	K	tso
Ꮆ	wa	Ꮼ	wo
Ꮿ	ya	Ꮀ	yo
Ꭱ	e	Ꮴ	v
Ꭶ	ge	J	gu
Ꭾ	he	Γ	hu
Ꮣ	le	M	lu
Ꮉ	me	Ꭳ	mu
Ꮑ	ne	Ꮕ	nu
Ꮻ	que	Ꮜ	quu
Ꮢ	se	Ꮗ	su
Ꮪ	de Ꮦ te	S	du
Ꮣ	tle	Ꮯ	tlu
Ꮴ	tse	Ꮫ	tsu
Ꮼ	we	Ꮩ	wu
Ꮽ	ye	Ꮿ	yu
Ꭲ	i	Ꭵ	v
Ꭹ	gi	Ꭱ	gv
Ꭿ	hi	Ꮀ	hv
Ꮅ	li	Ꮑ	lv
H	mi		
Ꮒ	ni	Ꮵ	nv
Ꮹ	qui	Ꮛ	quv
Ꮖ	si	Ꭱ	sv
Ꮧ	di Ꮦ ti	Ꮂ	dv
Ꮳ	tli	Ꮅ	tlv
Ꮵ	tsi	Ꮤ	tsv
Ꮻ	wi	Ꮾ	wv
Ꭹ	yi	B	yv

A comparison of early alphabets.

The direction of writing in the oldest Greek inscriptions—as in the Semitic scripts—is from right to left, a style that was superseded by boustrophedonic (in Greek, "as the ox plows") writing in which lines run alternately from right to left and left to right. This occurred in the 6th century BC. After 500 BC Greek writing went from left to right.

Right to left

Boustro-
phedonic

Left to right

The Greek alphabet developed around 1000–900 BC and branched into eastern and western subdivisions: Ionic (eastern) and Chalcidian (western) with minor differences. The most significant offshoots of Greek were the Cyrillic and Etruscan alphabets. The Cyrillic became the script of the Russian, Ukrainian, Bulgarian, Serbian, and Belorussian peoples. The Chalcidian alphabet became the Etruscan alphabet of Italy in the 8th century BC and other Italic alphabets, including the Latin alphabet, used for most European languages. In 403 BC, Athens adopted the Ionic alphabet and almost all local Greek alphabets, including the Chalcidian, were replaced by the Ionic script, which became the classical Greek alphabet, which had 24 letters and consisted of capital letters that were suited for monuments and inscriptions. Scripts suited to handwriting were uncial, essentially the classical capitals adapted to writing with pen on paper and similar to hand printing, and cursive and minuscule, which were calligraphic scripts similar to modern handwriting forms, with joined letters. Uncial went out of use in the 9th century AD, and minuscule, which replaced it, developed into today's Greek handwriting form.

Inscriptions throughout the Hellenistic world include decrees, codes of law, lists of citizens, temple accounts, offerings, coins, lettering on vases, etc. Greek manuscripts serve as sources for the studies of ancient history, philology, philosophy, and other branches of learning. Both inscriptions and manuscripts show us the evolution of the Greek alphabet.

Offshoots from the Greek alphabet were the Gothic, Cyrillic, and Glagolitic alphabets. The Gothic should not to be confused with Gothic script, a variety of the Latin alphabet. The script consisted of 27 letters, of which most were taken over from the Greek uncial script. In Italy, two alphabets derived directly from the Greek: the Etruscan and the Messapian (Messapic). The Messapii were an ancient tribe who inhabited southern Italy in pre-Roman times. The Romans borrowed 21 of the 26 Etruscan letters. The *y* and the *z* were absorbed following Rome's conquest of Greece in the 1st century BC—imagine conquering a country for two letters. The *j* and the *v*, which had previously been written interchangeably with *i* and *u* came into being

during the Middle Ages. With the addition of the *w* from a Norman source, the Latin alphabet came to its complement of 26.

There have been attempts at an alphabet that would ideally use only one symbol for each sound of a language. One such effort resulted in the International Phonetic Alphabet, invented at the close of the 19th century. Although English has numerous cases of duplication—the same sound represented by two or more graphemes (e.g., the sound of the *j* in *jewel* and the *g* in *gentle)*, or a grapheme having no counterpart in oral form (the *g* in *paradigm,* or the *c* in *scissors)*—are due to users of a language failing to make the changes in spelling as changes have occurred in spoken usage. A similar evolution took place with the Latin alphabet. It was modified and standardized by Charlemagne who directed the development of the uncial for faster writing. Uncial letters were somewhat rounded and separate versions of capital letters or cursive forms. Minuscule letters developed from cursive writing and have simplified, small forms—our present lowercase.

Alphabetic
Descriptive of data consisting solely of letters. See **Alphanumeric** and **Numeric**.

Alphabetic Code
A computer code comprising alphabetic, rather than numeric, characters.

Alphabetic String
Any **character string** comprising letters of the same alphabet. See **Character String**.

Alphabet Length
In typography, a measurement of the length of the 26-letter Latin alphabet. The alphabet used is the lowercase *a* through *z* for any particular **typeface**. By comparing the length of these letters when set normally with standard

abcdefghijklmnopqrstuvwxyz
Tekton

abcdefghijklmnopqrstuvwxyz
Avant Garde Book

abcdefghijklmnopqrstuvwxyz
Garamond Book Condensed

abcdefghijklmnopqrstuvwxyz
Futura Book

abcdefghijklmnopqrstuvwxyz
Frutiger Roman

Alphabet lengths of several different typefaces.

letterspacing (not *condensed* or *expanded*) in the same size for different typefaces, one can evaluate comparative "mass." A typeface with a low alphabet length would set more characters in the same space than a typeface with a high alphabet length. This same relationship is also expressed as *characters per pica (CPP)*, the number of characters that fit in one pica.

Alpha Channel

In digital image-processing programs (such as Adobe Photoshop), one of two basic types of "channel" which comprise an image. A channel is essentially one portion of a digital image. There are color channels, and there are alpha channels. A color channel is one of three separate channels (one for red, one for green, and one for blue), each of which contains a grayscale image corresponding to one of the three primary colors making up the image. (For example, the red channel contains only the red portions of the image, the green contains only the green portions of an image, and the blue contains only the blue portions of an image). An alpha channel, on the other hand, is a kind of "wild card" channel, and can store other user-selected portions of an image, or even other images that can be intermingled with the other channels to provide various effects to the image as a whole. Most image-processing programs allow for many different channels to be added.

Alpha Channel (3D)

In three-dimensional graphics, an additional *channel* that is used to store transparency information pertaining to the illustration.

Alpha Pulp

High-grade, highly-refined paper *pulp* that produces the best-quality paper. See *Pulping*.

Alpha Test

The first stage in the testing of a new product—in particular, computer hardware and software—in which in-house personnel use the product in a working environment as a means of gauging the efficacy of the product's concept and design, and to identify any flaws or "bugs" in the product, allowing time for rectification. An alpha test is followed by a *beta test* involving actual users. (See also *Beta Test*.)

Alphameric

Alternate term for *alphanumeric*. See *Alphanumeric*.

Alphanumeric

Descriptive of a *character set*, used especially in computer code, comprising letters, numbers, and sometimes other special control characters or punctuation symbols. Also known as *alphameric*.

Alt

Abbreviation for the *alternate key* found on a computer keyboard. See *Alternate Key*.

Alteration

In publishing, any change made to typeset copy, indicated either by the author (*author's alteration*s), editor (*editorial change*s), or proofreader (*typographical error*s or *printer's error*s).

Alternate Characters

In typography, the term for the variations in the design of a particular letter within the same *typeface*. Some typefaces have several versions of the same letter in the *font* to allow a greater variety of typographic expression. Specimen showings normally list all character variants with numbers for identification purposes. Multiple versions of the same character allow more creativity in *display* setting. The key to their use, however, is restraint—it is best to use as few as possible. Most alternate characters are *swash* versions: they over- or underhang adjacent characters with curve-like flourishes. Although effective, the use of swash characters should be kept to a minimum.

Alternate characters in Caslon.

Some alternate characters consist of combinations of capital letters, used to reduce excess space between some letter combinations in some fonts. When these characters are used, the space between other letters in the same word often need to be reduced, to give the type a unified appearance.

Alternate Key

A key on computer keyboards used to modify another key. The Alternate Key is added to expand the number of functions that a particular key can have. See also *Command Key*, *Control Key* and *Option Key*. The Alternate Key is usually designated *Alt*, as in the common keyboard combination *Ctrl-Alt-Del*. On the *Macintosh* computer, the *Option key* is used in lieu of the Alternate key.

Alternate Mode Processing

Alternate term for *multitasking*. See *Multitasking*.

Alternate Route

In telecommunications and networking, a secondary transmission path that can be used to route a transmission when the primary path is not available.

Alternative Route

See *Alternate Route*.

ALU

Abbreviation for *arithmetic logic unit*. See *Arithmetic Logic Unit (ALU)*.

Alum

Shorthand term for aluminum sulfate—chemical formula $Al_2(SO_4)_3$—a material that is commonly added to the papermaking *furnish* during *refining* in a process called *internal sizing*. *Rosin* is added to paper *pulp* to increase resistance to water and other liquids, and alum is added to help the rosin adhere to the paper fibers. The use of rosin and alum for internal sizing imparts a degree of *acidity* to paper, causing the rapid yellowing and crumbling with age typical of *acid paper*. Synthetic sizing agents, such as alkyl ketene dimer or alkyl succinic anhydride, are used instead of rosin and alum in the production of *alkaline paper*. See *Sizing* and *Internal Sizing*.

Alumina Hydrate

A white, inorganic compound used as a *white pigment* in printing inks. Alumina hydrate (chemical composition $Al_2O_3.O \cdot 3SO_3.3H_2O$) is mined from bauxite, is highly transparent, and is used as an *extender* pigment in lithographic and screen printing inks. It is chemically resistant to most substances, with the exception of dilute hydrochloric acid. It also improves the flow of *lithographic* inks and the *gloss* of a variety of other types of inks. (See also *White Pigments*.)

Also known as *Light Alumina Hydrate*, *Lake White*, and *Transparent White* (*CI Pigment White 24 No. 77002*).

Aluminum Bronze

Powdered aluminum used as a *metallic ink* in *screen printing*.

Aluminum Ink

Powdered aluminum used as a *metallic ink* in *screen printing* to impart a metallic silver color to the printed ink.

Aluminum Plate

The most common type of image carrier used in *offset lithography*. Aluminum oxides impart a higher degree of water receptivity to nonimage areas than do other materials. See *Plate: Offset Lithography*.

Aluminum Stearate

An inorganic compound, chemical formula $Al(OH)_2C_{18}H_{35}O_2$, used as a thickening agent in *screen printing* inks.

Alychne

A mathematical construct representing the area surrounding the *CIE color space*, or the "space beyond color."

AM

Abbreviation for *amplitude modulation*. See *Amplitude Modulation (AM)*.

In networking, *AM* is an abbreviation for *access method*. See *Access Method (AM)*.

Amberlith

A two-layer *acetate* film with a transparent base and a red or amber emulsion. In the past, it was most often attached to pasteup boards in place of *halftone* images. When the *mechanical* was photographed as a *negative*, the amberlith would leave a blank space into which the halftone negative could be stripped. It was also used in the making of *color separation*s. See also *Rubylith*.

Ambient

Descriptive of any phenomenon—such as light, sound, humidity—that exists in a particular location. See *Ambient Light*, *Ambient Sound*, and *Ambient Humidity*.

Ambient Humidity

The amount of moisture in the air in a particular environment. See *Relative Humidity* and *Humidity*.

Ambient Light

The amount of light that is present in a particular room or environment.

Ambient Sound

The level and type of sound that is present in a particular room or environment.

AMD

Abbreviation for *American Micro Devices*, a manufacturer of *microprocessor*s, especially a series of clones of Intel's 80386 and 80486 chips.

American Federation of Information Processing Societies (AFIPS)

A large organization comprising many different computer-related associations and societies, such as the Institute for Electrical and Electronic Engineers Computer Group, the Association for Computer Machinery, and many others.

American National Standards Institute

See *ANSI*.

American Standard Code for Information Interchange

See *ASCII*.

Ammonium Bichromate

A chemical compound—chemical formula $(NH_4)_2Cr_2O_7$—that renders *colloid*s or *emulsion*s photosensitive. It is used in the manufacture of *photostencil*s for *screen printing*. Ammonium bichromate is also known as *ammonium dichromate*.

Ampersand

In typography, a symbol (&) used as an abbreviation of the word "and." The ampersand was originally a *ligature* (a single character formed from the combination of two separate ones, in this case *et*, the Latin word for "and") and expressed as *et per se* ("et by itself, and"), which became corrupted to *and per se and* and, finally, *ampersand*. In some ampersand designs, the *e* and *t* are distinguishable. A small-cap ampersand often works better than the standard cap version, especially when used with lowercase letters. The ampersand is commonly used in company names and titles, but in running text looks sloppy and is inappropriate.

Ampex Digital Optics (ADO)

A high-end device used to create ***digital video effects***. See ***Digital Video Effects***.

Amphoteric

A substance capable of acting as either an ***acid*** or an ***alkali***.

Amplifier

Any electronic device used to increase the power of a signal. Some examples are the amplifiers used to increase the volume of musical instruments at a concert, or an amplifier used in a home stereo system, which boosts the signals coming from the attached components and sends the increased signals to the speakers.

Amplitude

In any periodically varying quantity—in other words, a wave—such as light or sound, the height of the crest or the intensity. See also ***Frequency***.

Amplitude Modulation (AM)

In communications, a type of ***modulation*** of a signal in which the amplitude of the carrier is varied with changes in the value of the signal it is carrying. In broadcasting (such as radio broadcasting), a particular sound emanating from a radio station is converted into electrical energy, which is referred to as its signal. This signal wave is overlaid on top of a radio wave, called a carrier wave. In AM broadcasting, the amplitude (or height) of the carrier wave conforms to the changes in amplitude of the signal (or sound) being transmitted. AM broadcasting, as we are all aware, is subject to static, which occurs at the top and bottom of a wave cycle. (In contrast, ***frequency modulation*** keeps the amplitude of the carrier wave constant, thus the tops and bottoms of the signal wave can be eliminated, which is why FM radio generally remains static free.)

In data communications, a similar process of modulation is used to overlay a signal representing computer information onto a carrier wave (which is transmitted over a telephone line, rather than through the air). Amplitude modulation is a similar means of varying the amplitude of the carrier signal in accordance with changes in the data signal.

See ***Modulation***. See also ***Frequency Modulation (FM)***.

In ***halftone*** photography, the term *amplitude modulation* is used to refer to a halftoning technique (the conventional form of halftone ***screening***) in which the sizes of the ***halftone dot***s are varied according to whether they correspond to ***shadow***s (large dots), ***middle tone***s (medium-sized dots), or ***highlight***s (small dots). An alternate means of halftone screening is known as ***stochastic screening***, or ***FM screening***. See ***Halftone*** and ***Stochastic Screening***.

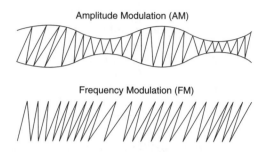

Amplitude Modulation (AM)

Frequency Modulation (FM)

Amplitude modulation (AM) vs. frequency modulation (FM).

Ampule

In packaging, a sealed glass container that is used in the distribution of pharmaceutical products. An ampule contains a single dose of a medication, commonly one used for hypodermic injection. It is formed out of a single piece of glass, and is hermetically sealed by flame at the open end. It is opened by snapping off the top along a scored portion of the stem. The important consideration in the manufacture of glass ampules is that the glass be completely inert chemically and not react in any way with the drug contained within it. Also spelled *ampul* and *ampoule*. See also ***Vial***.

Amyl Acetate

A liquid ***ester***—chemical formula $C_7H_{14}O_2$—comprising a mixture of isomers derived from amyl alcohol. Used as a ***lacquer*** in some printing ink or varnish formulations (in particular, those used in ***screen printing***) because of its low ***volatility***. Amyl acetate is also called *banana oil* since it smells like bananas. It is also used as an artificial fruit flavor in some foods and candies.

Analog

Descriptive of a continuous wave or signal, such as that produced by varying electrical voltage, as opposed to ***digital***, which refers to discrete numerical values. Analog signals—such as music, for example—can be converted to digital form (as in the production of a ***compact disc***). Digital signals—such as computer output—often must be converted to analog signals (as in the transmission of data over telephone lines or in the conversion of electro-optical signals to digital information in ***scanning***).

The term *analog* is also used to describe a computer using continuous signals of varying intensity, rather than the "on" or "off" dichotomy utilized by digital computers.

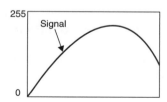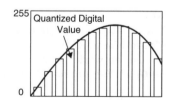

An original analog waveform (left) and a digital sample of that waveform.

Analog Computer

A computer that measures continuously changing variables—such as temperature, pressure, etc.—and translates them into discrete quantities.

Analog Data

Data that exist as non-discrete, continuous variations in voltage, amperage, density, etc., rather than as discrete numerical values (*digital data*). See *Analog*.

Analog Display

A computer monitor in which continuous signals are used to generate the image. Such monitors are separated from the main computer by a *video adapter* containing a *digital-to-analog converter* that switches the *digital* data in the *frame buffer* to varying electrical signals.

Analog Film Recorder

A *film recorder* that outputs a digital image directly from a computer screen onto film. The output image is at the same *resolution* as the screen image, which is typically much lower than the optimum resolution required for high-quality reproduction. See *Digital Film Recorder*, *Film Recorder*.

Analog Loopback

In networking and telecommunications, a means of testing a *modem* or other telecommunications equipment. Essentially, a test signal is transmitted and echoed back to the sending device. The reflected signal is then compared to the original to determine if any errors have been introduced. See *Loopback*. See also *Digital Loopback*.

Analog Monitor

See *Analog Display*.

Analogous Colors

On a *color circle*, colors in close proximity to each other that share similar *hue* and *saturation*. Analogous colors are most often used to achieve proper color harmony. Also known as *adjacent colors*. (See COLOR PLATE 6.)

Analog Scanner

An imaging device that utilizes data that exist as continuous variations in voltage in the reproduction and correction of color and tone, as opposed to a *digital scanner* which utilizes discrete numerical (or *digital*) data.

Analog Sound

Any sound wave propagating through a medium, in contrast to digital audio, which describes sound as a series of 1s and 0s. Digital audio played back on a computer in digital sound editing programs must be converted to analog sound before it can be heard.

Analog-to-Digital Converter

A device used to convert continuous (or *analog*) electrical signals into discrete *digital* signals. Such devices are often found in *trackball*s and *joy stick*s (or other computer input device) that indicate movement by electrical signals that must be converted into digital form to be understood and processed by the computer. The continuous electric signal is sampled many times per second, with each sample translated into a discrete number representing the *amplitude* and *frequency* of the continuous waveform. Analog-to-digital converters are also found in *scanner*s, where electro-optical signals generated by *CCD*s or *photomultiplier tube*s need to be translated into digital form before they can be input to a computer. Also known as an *ADC* and an *A/D Converter*. See also *Digital-to-Analog Converter*.

An analog-to-digital converter.

Analog Transmission

In telecommunications, any data signal that is transmitted as a continuously varying signal, such as a *voice-grade* telephone line, rather than as discrete bits.

Analog Video

A variable electric signal carrying images (and often sound), such as television. See also *Digital Video*.

Analysis Graphics

General description of graphics gleaned from spreadsheet or database data or models, used to analyze such things as finances, performance monitoring, and strategic planning.

Anamorphic

In graphics, enlarging or reducing the size of an image only along one axis to create a stretched or otherwise out-of-proportion image.

Anchor

In *desktop publishing*, a function enabling an illustration or other graphic object to be linked to a specific point in a text block. The illustration remains in the proper position even after text has been added and/or deleted.

Anchorage

The attachment of an *adhesive* material to a label stock or to an *anchor coat*.

Anchor Coat

A preliminary *coating* applied to the surface of paper or another *substrate* to facilitate the *adhesion* of additional layers of coating or *adhesive*. Also known as a *primer* or a *tie coat*.

Anchoring

In *flexography*, the process by which an ink adheres to the surface of the *substrate*.

Anchor Point

In computer graphics, the beginning and end points of a *Bézier curve*. When lines or curves are created in a *drawing program*, it is often possible to move either anchor point, with the program automatically changing the size, location, or shape of the object in relation to the relocated anchor point(s).

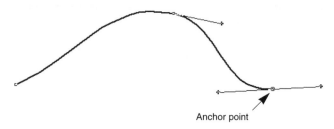

Anchor point

Anchor point for a Bézier curve.

Angle

In geometry, the distance between two lines originating at a common point, measured on a scale of degrees from 0° to 360°.

In graphics, *angle* refers to the degree to which a graphic element has been rotated from the horizontal or vertical.

In photography, the image captured by the camera, which is a function of the *focal length* of the lens. See *Wide Angle*, for example.

Angle Bar

A metal bar placed horizontally at a 45° angle to the feed direction of a printing press. An angle bar is used to turn the web when feeding from the side, or to bypass the *former folder*. Angle bars are also used on *ribbon folders*. It is often filled with air and perforated to reduce web friction.

Angle-Bar Folder

Alternate term for a *ribbon folder*. See *Ribbon Folder*.

Angle Mark

Alternate term for *register mark*. See *Register Mark*.

Angle of Attack

In *screen printing*, the angle formed under pressure between the blade of the moving *squeegee* and the plane of the screen. The flexible rubber squeegee blade will, during printing, lay at a different angle than that of the squeegee itself (known as the *squeegee angle*).

Ångstrom

Abbreviated Å, an Ångstrom is a small unit of measurement equal to 0.0000000001 meter (or 0.1 *nanometer*) used in the measurement of light wavelengths. It is named for the Swedish astronomer and physicist Anders Ångstrom. (See also *Nanometer*.)

Anhydrous

Describing a substance, compound, or solution that does not contain water.

ANI

Abbreviation for *automatic number identification*. See *Automatic Number Identification (ANI)*.

Aniline Dyes

A variety of synthetic *colorant*s manufactured from coal tar (or from derivatives of benzene found therein) and used in the dyeing of textiles and clothing and in *flexographic* and *screen printing* inks. (*Flexography* itself was at one time called "Aniline Printing.") Aniline is a colorless, oily, slightly water-soluble organic compound (chemical formula $C_6H_5NH_2$) derived from nitrobenzene and is also used in the manufacture of pharmaceuticals.

Aniline was one of the first synthetic dyes ever produced, and was the first commercially successful synthetic dye. Until the mid-19th century, most dyes and colorants were derived from minerals (such as lapis lazuli) or from a variety of plants, insects, and, of course, mollusks (octopus and squid inks) and other shellfish. These dyes were expensive, and for the most part lacked *permanence*.

In 1856, an eighteen-year-old British chemist named William Perkin had been trying to solve the problem of malaria—a disease caused by the transmission of a microorganism by *Anopheles* mosquitoes—in British colonies in the Far East. It was found that the chemical quinine was an effective remedy for malaria, and British colonists had been importing it—at great expense—from the Dutch. (Interestingly, the British colonists found that quinine—which tasted terrible—was more palatable when mixed with tonic water. It still tasted terrible, but was rendered thoroughly drinkable when a bit of gin was added. Hence, the resulting gin and tonic is probably the only alcoholic beverage that could legitimately claim to have been developed for "medicinal purposes.") However, quinine was only obtained naturally from the bark of the cinchona plant, which at that time only grew in Peru and in Indonesian colonies owned by the Dutch, who charged a hefty price for it. Attempts to grow cinchona back in England failed, so William Perkin was charged with the responsibility of developing a means of creating quinine synthetically. He turned to coal tar, a waste product of the manufacture of gas, which was found to possess substances very close in chemical structure to quinine. One of Perkin's compounds, though not quinine, did end up staining a rag deep purple. He applied some of his dye to a fabric, and the purple color resisted sunlight and laundering. This was the first aniline dye. Giving up on the search for quinine, Perkin invested his father's life savings into dye production and became quite wealthy, although he unfortunately failed to patent his discovery. First the French, and later the German, chemical industry got into synthetic dyes, and suddenly synthetic colors were everywhere. (The word *mauve*, for instance, was originally the trade name of the French version of purple aniline dye.)

Although aniline is rarely used as a dye today, it stimulated a great deal of research and investment into synthetic colorants, which eventually led to the wide variety of pigments and colorants now available.

Aniline Point

A measure of the strength of a hydrocarbon **solvent** intended for use in a printing ink, described as the lowest temperature at which the solvent can be completely dissolved in an equal amount of aniline (a synthetically produced derivative of nitrobenzene).

Aniline Printing

A former name for **flexography**, no longer in use. See **Flexography**.

Anilox Roller

An engraved metal or ceramic roller used in **flexographic** printing presses to transfer ink from the **fountain roller** (or directly from the fountain) to the printing plate. A flexographic inking system is sometimes known as an **anilox system**.

The purpose of the anilox roller is to pick up ink from the fountain roller (or, in some configurations, directly from the **ink fountain**) and deliver a predetermined, metered, uniform amount of ink to the rubber printing plate. It accomplishes this because its surface (commonly of steel that has been treated to make it suitable for engraving) is pitted with etched cells, typically only visible under magnification. (The number of cells can vary from 80–1,000 cells per inch, depending on the application.)

After the cells are engraved—most often with a steel milling machine, a diamond **electromechanical engraving** stylus (such as that used in the engraving of **gravure cylinder**s) or, more and more commonly, lasers—the surface is covered with a protective layer of chrome or ceramic to guard against wear. (In some configurations, the cells are engraved directly in a layer of ceramic.) The structure of the cells themselves also varies. The most common configuration of anilox roller cell is an inverted pyramid, each

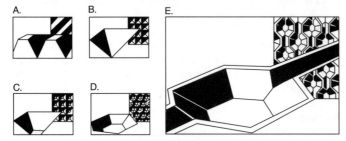

Anilox roller cell structures: (A) inverted pyramid, (B) quadrangular, (C) trihelical, (D) hexagonal, and (E) quad channel screen.

of which is exactly the same size. The volume of one specific cell can be calculated using the formula:

$$Volume = D/3[(A_1 + A_2) + \sqrt{A_1 A_2}]$$

where *D* is the depth of the cell, A_1 is the area of the opening of the cell on the surface of the roller, and A_2 is the area of the cell at its lowest point. The volume obtained, then, can be multiplied by the total number of cells on the roller to obtain the total volume of ink the roller can hold. Or, typically, the volume of a cell is obtained, converted to cubic microns, and multiplied by the number of cells in a square inch. Other cell shapes include trihelical, which is basically a long, unbroken valley etched at a 45° angle (useful for printing highly viscous inks); quadrangular, essentially a pyramid with the point cut off (which tends to release ink better, and also varies in volume less from top to bottom, mitigating against roller wear), and hexagonal (which releases ink better and is more easily chrome- or ceramic-plated). Another type of anilox cell structure is called a quad channel screen in which each cell is connected by a thin engraved channel. This type of cell structure has been found to have the most effective ink-transfer capabilities.

Cell wear is an important consideration, especially as a cell's region of greatest volume is at the surface of the roller. On an anilox roller using inverted pyramid-shaped cells, a 20% decrease in cell depth due to wear can cause more than a 40% decrease in volume. The fewer the total number of cells on the cylinder as a whole, the greater the percentage of the volume decrease. Wear is commonly gauged by the manufacturer, using a microscope. In practical application in the pressroom, a shinier roller surface or a decrease in print density of a known ink formulation are determinants of anilox roller wear.

A problem that was common in the days before rotating fountain rollers (and still occurs on occasion) is **mechanical pinholing**, in which ink starvation of the fountain roller results in ink transfer to the plate that takes on the texture of the anilox roller.

The anilox roller is also known as a **metering roller**, a **knurled roller**, and an **engraved roller**. Some web offset presses—especially those using thin, liquid inks—use an anilox roller in their inking systems as well. See **Web Offset Lithography: Inking System**.

Anilox System

Alternate term for an **inking system** used in **flexography** that transfers ink to the printing plate with a rubber-covered **fountain roller** and an engraved metal **anilox roller**. See **Inking System: Flexography** and **Anilox Roller**.

Animated Screen Capture

In computing, an application which accurately records everything that occurs on a computer screen, including mouse and cursor movement, often incorporated into instructional presentations.

Animatic

In *animation*, a rough, rudimentary animated scene comprising primarily *key frame*s and few *in between*s to give a sense of how the finished sequence will look. Depending upon the desired effect, animatics may also be used as a finished sequence.

Animating on Fields

Smoothing computer-animated motion. An animation is created as a series of still frames that, when projected in sequence at a certain rate (commonly 25 frames per second), provide the illusion of motion. In *field animation*, a particular frame comprises two *field*s that are stored separately. Thus, during the animated sequence, the viewer sees 50 half-frames per second rather than 25 whole frames per second. As a result, animated motion appears smoother.

Animation

A sequence of still images (called *frame*s) varying slightly from image to image that, when projected at high speed, produce the illusion of movement. Animation can display at any speed, but is usually somewhere between 22–30 frames per second. Most familiar types of animation are *two-dimensional (2-D) animation*, or flat images overlaid and moving against a flat background. The most common type of 2-D animation is *cel animation*, in which the animated images are drawn or painted on transparent overlays. Computer graphics programs are increasing the quality of *three-dimensional (3-D) animation*, or images that appear to have depth.

Animation Stand

In photography and videography, a motion-picture camera (or video camera) mounted vertically above a table on which artwork can be mounted for frame-by-fame photography. The camera can shoot a single frame, the artwork changed, a second frame shot, etc. The cameras may also be able to move up and down (allowing *zoom*s in and out), to *pan*, etc.

Animator

A graphic artist or illustrator responsible for designing an animated sequence. See *Animation*.

Annex

Alternate term for an *extension*. See *Extension*.

Annotate

In text or word processing, to embed comments into text that will not print, but can be viewed on screen by other readers of the document.

Annotation

In typography, an explanatory note added to an illustration. *Annotation* is also used to refer to any explanatory *footnote* or *reference* in a book, journal, magazine, etc.

Announcements

Sheets or cards of high-quality paper (such as *wedding paper*, *imitation parchment*, or high-quality *bond paper*) used, commonly with matching envelopes, for personal stationery, wedding and/or party invitations, greeting cards, and other personal, yet dignified, occasions.

Annulus

On a *scanner*, a small aperture through which the image data passes, surrounded by the *unsharp mask* aperture or mirror. See *Scanner*.

Anode

A source of positively charged ions, used in a variety of applications and devices, from *electroplating* gravure cylinders to *photomultiplier tube*s found in *drum scanner*s. A source of negatively charged particles is called a *cathode*.

Anonymous FTP

In networking, especially over the *Internet*, a means of locating and downloading a file (by means of *File Transfer Protocol*) on a remote *server* even if the user has no *account* on the server's system. Instead of a special user name and *password*, the user simply types "anonymous" as a user name and his/her Email address as a password. Anonymous FTP only works on those systems configured to allow it. See also *File Transfer Protocol (FTP)*.

ANSI

The *American National Standards Institute*, a U.S. member of the *International Standards Organization (ISO)*, that develops voluntary standards for business and industry. Graphic arts viewing standards are one example of an ANSI standard.

ANSI Character Set

In computing, an extended set of codes used in Microsoft Windows and OS/2 environments, which includes the *ASCII standard character set* among many others.

ANSI IT8

A set of standards developed by the American National Standards Institute (*ANSI*) committee governing color communication and control specifications. IT8 standards cover *RGB*, *CMYK*, scanning targets, and multivendor calibration.

ANSI Y14.5

A set of standards developed by *ANSI* (the American National Standards Institute) used in the *CAD* (computer-aided design) industry. For example, Claris CAD supports this standard. See *ANSI*.

Answer Back

In networking, a signal generated by a *terminal* or *workstation* (either automatically or manually) in response to a signal originating elsewhere. An answer back verifies that the original signal has reached the terminal, and that it is operational. The terminal *address* may also be included in the answer back, to verify that the original signal has in fact reached the terminal it wanted.

Answer Mode

In telecommunications, a *modem* function that answers incoming calls and synchronizes itself with the *protocol* being used by the calling system.

Anthraquinone Scarlet

An *organic color pigment* used in printing inks. Anthraquinone Scarlet is a transparent yellow red possessing high *lightfastness*, and good chemical resistance to most substances, save alkalis. It is often used in security inks. (See also *Organic Color Pigments*.)

Also known as *Perylene Red Y* (*CI Pigment Red 224 No. 71127*).

Anthraquinonoid Blue

See *Indanthrene Blue*.

Antialiasing

In computer graphics, reducing the undesirable stair-step pattern (*aliasing*) along the edges of images on a computer monitor or on low-resolution output. Typically, antialiasing on monitors (in programs such as Adobe Photoshop) involves reducing the intensity of intermediate *pixel*s to give the appearance of a smooth line or edge. See *Aliasing*.

Antifoaming Agent

Any of a variety of fluids added to an offset press's *fountain solution* to reduce foam or bubbles that can interfere with the proper distribution of dampening solution. Antifoaming agents are commonly silicone-based fluids or emulsions (in particular, polydimethyl siloxanes) that either dissolve a *surfactant* more thoroughly in the fountain solution, or reduce the surface tension of the fluid to prevent bubbles and foam from forming. (See *Fountain Solution*.) Also referred to as a *defoaming agent*.

Antifoaming agents are also added to any printing ink likely to form bubbles during printing.

Antihalation

In *screen printing*, a coating added to a film or to the screen fabric to eliminate blurring caused by light reflected from the base of the film or the fibers in the screen. Screen fabrics dyed yellow, orange, or red will cause *halation*.

In photography, *antihalation* refers to the elimination of a blurring effect caused by the reflection of light rays back through an exposed photographic emulsion. Antihalation of photographic films is usually effected by means of *antihalation dye*.

Antihalation Backing

In photography, a coating applied to the back of photographic film to prevent *halation*. See *Halation* and *Antihalation*.

Antihalation Dye

A substance applied to the base material of a photographic film to prevent *halation*, or a blurring of photographic images caused by light reflecting from a film's base material back through the already-exposed *emulsion*. The antihalation dye absorbs these light rays before they can be reflected. On some flexible films, the dye also serves as an anti-curl agent. Antihalation dye is dissolved out of the film during development.

Antioffset Spray

See *Antisetoff Spray*.

Antioxidant

An *inhibitor* added to a *lithographic* or *screen printing* ink to retard *oxidation* of the ink *vehicle* and thereby prevent excessive or overly rapid ink drying. Antioxidant compounds most often used are oximes (such as methyl ethyl ketoxime), phenolic antioxidants (such as butylated hydroxy toluene), and quinones (such as hydroquinone), which are slightly, moderately, and highly effective, respectively. A class of antioxidants is called *antiskinning agent*s. A chemical that slows the drying time by reducing the *evaporation* rate of the solvent is called a *retarder*.

Antipenetrant

Term for any substance—such as a paper *coating*—that impedes the penetration of ink into the surface of a *substrate*, or causes an increase in *ink holdout*.

Antipinhole Agent

A *wetting agent* added to a liquid printing ink to reduce the surface tension of the ink as well as the printing defect called *pinholing* in *gravure* printing and *chemical pinholing* in *flexography*. (See *Pinholing*.)

Antireflection Surface Panel

A special coating applied to the surface of a computer monitor or other screen to reduce *glare*.

Antique Finish

A paper *finish*, typically found in *book paper* and *cover paper*, characterized by a rough surface intended to simulate old, handmade paper.

Antisetoff Compound

A substance added to an ink to prevent *ink setoff*, the undesirable transfer of ink from a printed sheet to the back of the sheet lying on top of it in the delivery pile. Antisetoff compounds—commonly starch or silica powders—typically reduce this problem either by forming a protective layer on the surface of the ink film (their particle size is greater than the thickness of the ink film, allowing them to protrude through the surface of the film, keeping the adjacent sheet physically separated from the wet ink), or by expediting the drying time of the ink. Antisetoff compounds are favored over *antisetoff spray*s. See also *Antisetoff Spray*.

Antisetoff Spray

A powder, commonly consisting of fine starch particles that range in size from 15–65 microns, sprayed on the surface of printed sheets either to prevent *ink setoff*—the transfer of wet ink from a printed sheet to the back of the sheet lying on top of it—or to prevent a printed ink film from contacting the wet printed ink film on the back of the sheet above it. Antisetoff spray is also referred to as *spray powder*. The use of antisetoff sprays is undesirable on the part of many printers, and ink manufacturers have taken to incorporating *antisetoff compound*s directly into the ink itself. (See also *AntiSetoff Compound*.)

Antiskid Varnish

A *resin* added as a *coating* to the surface of *substrate*s used for packaging to prevent slipping during shipping, stacking, and handling.

Antiskinning Agent

A chemical substance added to ink to prevent the formation of an ink skin by impeding *oxidation* of the ink *vehicle*.

Antistatic Coating

A coating applied to the surface of a computer monitor to prevent static-electricity buildup on the display. The reduction of static charge also reduces the amount of dust that will adhere to a surface.

Antistatic Solution

A compound applied, commonly as a coating, on a printing *substrate* as a means of preventing the buildup of static electricity charges.

Antivirus Program

In computing, a software utility that scans a system or network for the presence of computer *virus*es. Essentially, an antivirus program works by searching for suspicious activity, such as unusual disk access or important system files changing in some way. The program also compares information gleaned from system activity with a database of known viruses and their effects. There are two types of antivirus programs: *terminate and stay resident (TSR)* programs are loaded into the computer's memory at startup and detect virus-like activity on the fly; others need to be loaded and launched by the user periodically, as a type of housekeeping duty. See also *Virus*.

AOS

Abbreviation for *automated office system*. See *Automated Office System (AOS)*.

APA

Abbreviation for *all points addressability*. See *All Points Addressability (APA)*.

APD

See *Aldus Printer Description*.

Aperture

In any optical system, an opening allowing the passage of light, electrons, or other forms of radiation. In photography, the *aperture* is the hole through which light passes into a camera, the size of which is controlled by the *diaphragm*. (See *Photography*.) An aperture, in this sense, is also known as an *iris*.

In a *cathode-ray tube*, the size of the aperture determines the size and shape of the electron beam.

In *screen printing*, the term *aperture* refers to one specific opening in the mesh screen through which ink passes, also known as a *mesh aperture*. (See *Screen Printing*.)

Aperture Percentage

In *screen printing*, the percentage of the total area of a screen fabric occupied by *mesh aperture*s (the spaces between the threads) or, in other words, the total amount of area capable of having ink transferred through it. Also called *mesh opening area*.

Apex

In typography, the part of a letter or other character where two stems meet at the top of the character, as in the point of a capital letter "A." See *Letter Elements*.

API

Abbreviation for *application programming interface*. See *Application Programming Interface (API)*.

Apochromatic

See *Achromat*.

Apostrophe

In typography, a *punctuation* mark (') used to denote possessive words and to stand in for omitted letters in contractions (as in *don't*).

The term *apostrophe* is also used in literature to refer to a rhetorical address to someone or something not actually present, found often in poetry, such as John Donne's "O Death, where is thy sting?" or John Milton's "Apostrophe to Light" (also called "On His Blindness").

App

Abbreviation for *application*. See *Application* (fourth definition).

Apparent Density

The density—or weight per unit volume—of a sheet of paper. It can be calculated either by dividing the *basis weight* by the *caliper* (or thickness) of a single sheet, or by dividing the *grammage* by the single-sheet thickness. Since basis weight varies according to the *basic size* of the *ream* of paper used, comparisons of apparent densities should be converted to a common basic size. In the metric system, apparent density is measured in grams per cubic centimeter.

A paper's apparent density is the result of all the myriad aspects of the papermaking process, from the consistency of the papermaking *furnish* to the degree of *calendering*, and affects nearly all the properties of paper. (See *Paper and Papermaking: Paper Properties*.)

Append
To add material to the end of a document, page, or file.

Appendix
One or more additions to the *back matter* of a book providing material that is supplementary to the main text, but not essential to it. See *Book Typography*.

Apple Desktop Bus (ADB)
On the Apple *Macintosh* personal computer, a *serial port* used to connect low-speed input devices, such as keyboards, mice, etc. Typically, up to sixteen ADB devices can be daisy-chained through the ADB port.

AppleShare
Apple Computer's networking software used to connect Macintosh computers to a central *server*. AppleShare makes use of the *AppleTalk Filing Protocol*.

Applet
In computing, any small application program used for a single specific purpose. Most operating systems include applets such as a calculator, note pad, calendar, etc. Applets are also small programs developed using Sun Microsystems' *Java* computer language, such applets being distributed on the *World Wide Web*.

AppleTalk
Apple Computer's proprietary telecommunications architecture and network *protocol* for the *Macintosh* computer. Based on the *OSI* communications model, AppleTalk is primarily used for connecting printers to the system, and as a network AppleTalk is slow (230.4 *kilobits per second*). Phase 2 of AppleTalk (released in 1989) supports *Ethernet* and *Token Ring*. Apple's *Open Transport* is replacing AppleTalk as a protocol for connecting to the Internet via *TCP/IP*, especially on newer PowerMacs.

AppleTalk Filing Protocol (AFP)
A *protocol* used in computer networks such as *AppleShare* and network protocols such as *AppleTalk* that allow workstations to store and retrieve files and applications from a centralized *server* as if they were on a local disk.

Application
Any particular end-use for a printed product.

An *application* is also used to refer to any *adhesive* decal, label, etc., attached to a surface or *substrate*.

In *screen printing*, *application* refers to any ink or color printed on a substrate. See also *Application Printing*.

In computer terminology, *application* refers to any software program—such as Adobe Photoshop, Microsoft Excel, or QuarkXPress—that applies programmed routines to handle certain tasks. Application, in this sense, is often abbreviated *app*.

Application Developer
In computing, an individual who creates (either alone or as a member of a team) a computer program. The term "developer" is used primarily to refer to the programming—rather than design or content—aspect of application development.

Application Framework
In computing, a type of "library" whose contents provide the basis for the development of a number of applications within a specific class. This library ensures that certain elements remain consistent from program to program, such as the location of common commands. An application framework, in addition to providing shortcuts for the developer, also ensures that a user who has operated other programs has at least a basic understanding of how to navigate a new program.

Application Generator
A high-level computer language that creates a program from data provided by the user. An application generator, also known as a *program generator*, allows the user to specify what data are to be processed, rather than simply how the data should be processed.

Application Layer
In networking, the seventh, and highest, *layer* in the *OSI* reference model, defining the path by which programs exchange information. See *Open Systems Interconnection (OSI)*.

Application Menu
In computing, especially using the *Macintosh operating system*, a list of open and running applications, which

Application menu from a Macintosh computer.

facilitates switching between or among them, especially when their windows are hidden by other open applications. The application menu is found at the far right of the menu bar. By clicking on the rightmost icon (which is either a computer when all applications or hidden, or the icon corresponding to the active application), a list of open programs will be displayed. In **Windows**, the application menu is called a **task list**.

Application Metering
In networking, the act of counting the number of copies of an application in use on a network at any specific time, as a means of ensuring that the number of executable copies does not exceed the limits imposed by the licensing agreement of the software. Usually, if the limit has been reached, any additional users who attempt to open the program will receive error messages.

Application-Oriented Language
A computer language whose commands or statements are designed to resemble the language of the specific user of that program.

Application Package
Any commercially available computer program, along with assorted "extras," such as **plug-in**s, system **extension**s, tutorial files, and related documentation. See **Application Program**.

Application Paper
Alternate term for **application tape**. See **Application Tape**.

Application Printing
Screen printing an ink directly on a fabric **substrate**, as opposed to using a **dye-transfer** medium.

Application Program
Any software program that allows a computer to be used for a specific task. Application programs include those for word processing (such as WordPerfect), creating spreadsheets (Excel), laying out pages for publication (QuarkXPress), manipulating digital photographs (Adobe Photoshop), or drawing illustrations (Macromedia FreeHand), among many others. An application program often comes with a wide variety of "extras," such as **plug-in**s, system **extension**s, tutorials, and other elements that add functionality to the basic program. This collection of extras (including the documentation needed to learn how to operate the program) is known as an **application package**.

Application Programming Interface (API)
In computing, a set of functions, commands, and values by which a program communicates with another program or an operating system.

API is also a specific programming interface permitting developers to write programs for IBM's **OS/2** operating

system, safe in the knowledge that their application will be compatible with future revisions of the operating system.

API also defines a means by which an application program can access the procedures of a telecommunications program, removing the need for the operator to worry unduly about dealing with connection issues directly. (See also **Messaging API**.)

Application Server
See **Server**.

Application Specific Integrated Circuit (ASIC)
In computing, a **microprocessor** chip designed and built for a particular application, rather than for a wide variety of applications.

Application System
Alternate term for an **application package**. See **Application Package**.

Application Tape
A paper—or other material—used to support the application of **pressure-sensitive adhesive** materials. Also called **application paper**.

Applicator
A machine used to automatically apply labels to a surface.

Applied Color Decorating
In **screen printing**, alternate term for **application printing**. See **Application Printing**.

APPN
Abbreviation for **Advanced Peer-to-Peer Networking**. See **Advanced Peer-to-Peer Networking (APPN)**.

APR
See **Automatic Picture Replacement**.

Apron
In **binding and finishing**, a blank portion at the edge of a **foldout** allowing for damage-free **folding** and **tipping-in**.

The term *apron* is also used to refer to a leader sheet on a set of continuous forms.

Aqueous Dispersion
A variety of **pigment** used in inks designed for the **screen printing** of fabrics. The pigments are dispersed in a water-soluble **binder** that is converted to a water-*in*soluble binder and deposited on the **substrate** when the printed fabric is cured with heat or steam.

Arabic Numerals
The numbers Americans and Europeans use most commonly, having the form 1, 2, 3, 4, 5, 6, 7, 8, 9, 0.

Although referred to as "Arabic," they originated among the Hindus in India and were transmitted to Arabia via a translation of the Indian *Siddhanta*, which was brought to Baghdad in AD 772.

In the Arabic world, numbers were originally written out in words and, eventually, certain Arabic letters began to be used as numbers (much as the Greeks had done). Once the *Siddhanta* had been translated into Arabic, the Hindu numeral system found therein was adopted by Arabic merchants, while the original letter-based system was retained by Arabic astronomers.

After a split in the Arabic empire, the Hindu number system eventually mutated into two different ones; one remained in the eastern portion of the empire, and closely resembled numerals still in use in the Middle East today. The other system eventually found its way to Toledo, in Spain, populated by dispossessed Arabs. When Toledo was toppled in 1085 by Christian mercenaries, a tremendous amount of Arab knowledge was revealed to the West, although some European scholars, who had studied in Spain, were already using and teaching the new numerals.

The first Arabic numeral proponent in Europe was a man named Gerbert (who later became Pope Sylvester II). John of Seville, in the 12th century, translated the works of the Arabic mathematician Al-Khwarizmi, and as a result the Arabic numerals became well-known, and were originally described by the word *algorism*, a corruption of Al-Khwarizmi's name which eventually mutated into the modern word *algorithm*. (The word *algebra*, by the way, also has a similar origin, coming from the name of another Arabic mathematician, Al-Jabr.) In addition to the numerals, the concept of the zero (0), unknown in *Roman numerals*, was introduced to Europe.

For the rules regarding the typography of numerals, see *Figures*. See also *Roman Numerals*.

Arbitration

In networking, the rules designed to manage competing requests for network resources.

Arc

In typography, any curved stroke or part of a letter or other character that is not a *bowl*. See *Letter Elements*.

Archie

On the Internet, a system designed to locate files available by means of *anonymous FTP*. Programs are used to regularly access all anonymous FTP sites and create and update a database of publicly available files. Most *Internet service provider*s include Archie which, when called up, accesses this centralized database, providing the location and availability of a requested file. Anonymous FTP can then be used to retrieve the file. Archie itself was named for the comic book character of that name; other related programs include *Veronica* and *Jughead*.

Architecture

The internal configuration of computer *hardware*, including its *microprocessor*, its *bus*, and the amount of data that can be addressed at any one time, among other things. A specific *operating system* is often designed specifically for a single (or a small variety of) architecture(s).

Archivable

A paper with a high *permanence*, or the ability to resist yellowing, fading, discoloring or deteriorating. This makes it suitable for printed materials that will be stored indefinitely in a library or other archive. Materials printed on *alkaline paper*s tend to be more suited for archiving than *acid paper*s. (See *Alkaline Paper*.)

The term *archivable* also describes a printed ink that retains its color strength, *opacity*, and *gloss* for a prolonged length of time.

Archival Paper

A variety of *acid-free paper* (or *alkaline paper*) designed to resist fading, yellowing, and the general deterioration characteristic of *acid paper*. Archival paper is used for permanent documents and records and other materials intended to be stored indefinitely. See *Alkaline Paper*.

Archival Storage

A medium used to store any type of computer data. Materials are maintained in archival storage until erased or altered.

Archive

When used as a noun, a particular computer data file stored on a permanent medium, such as a magnetic disk or *optical disc*, and intended to be kept for a long period of time for subsequent retrieval.

When used as a verb, to create such a file.

Archive Bit

In computing, a *bit* included in the *directory* entry for a file created in or modified by an application running on the *DOS* operating system. The archive bit can be utilized by a backup program to copy the created or modified file. It may be either cleared or retained after backup, depending upon the backup technique. See also *Differential Backup* and *Incremental Backup*.

Arc Lamp

A high-intensity electric lamp in which light is produced by the jumping or "arcing" of electricity either between two carbon rods in air or between metal electrodes in a xenon gas-filled quartz bulb. Pulsed-xenon arc lamps are still used in photography and in conventional platemaking.

ARCnet

Abbreviation for *Attached Resource Computer network*, one of the first and most popular *local area network (LAN)* architectures, developed in 1968 by Datapoint Corporation, but supplanted in recent years by *Ethernet*. ARCnet uses the *Token Ring* network *protocol*, and can be cabled with *fiber optics*, *unshielded twisted pair*, or *coaxial* *cable*s. Initially transmitting with speeds of 2.5 megabits per second, a 20-Mb/sec. version was released in 1990.

Area Array

In a *digital camera*, a set of *CCD*s arranged in a rectangular block to capture an entire image at once (as opposed to line by line, as with a *linear array*). An area array often requires three separate exposures to capture all three primary color channels. Also known as a *matrix array*. See *Digital Photography*.

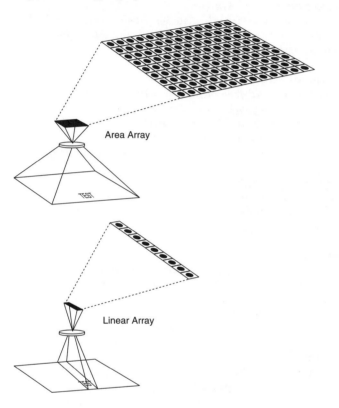

Area CCD array vs. linear CCD array.

Area Composition

In typography, setting type in such a way that as little pasteup as possible is required. The advent of *desktop publishing* rendered this obsolete.

Area Mask

In computer graphics, any outline that isolates a particular region of an image, either by predetermined shape, color, color range, or tonal value.

Argon Laser

In imaging, a strong, directional bluish *laser* light used to generate images on *orthochromatic* or blue-sensitive film, paper, or plates. An argon laser is commonly used in lieu of a *helium-neon laser*, as blue-sensitive paper—unlike the red-sensitive paper used with helium-neon lasers—can be handled safely in red or yellow light.

Argument

In computer programming, an independent variable or expression that defines the specific conditions of an instruction. An argument can either be a numerical value or a logical expression.

Arithmetic Capability

A computer system feature that performs user-defined mathematical calculations.

Arithmetic Logic Unit (ALU)

In a computer, the portion of the *central processing unit (CPU)* in which all mathematical and logical calculations and functions are executed. Also known as *arithmetic unit*.

Arithmetic Unit

Alternate term for *arithmetic logic unit*. See *Arithmetic Logic Unit (ALU)*.

ARLL

Abbreviation for *advanced run-length limited encoding*. See *Advanced Run-Length Limited Encoding*.

Arm

In typography, the horizontal or diagonal stroke extending off the *stem*, as in the capital "E." An arm connected on both sides is called a *bar*. See *Letter Elements*.

Aromatic Solvent

A variety of *hydrocarbon* compounds containing one or more benzene (or equivalent heterocyclic ring) structures, also usually characterized by an agreeable smell. Aromatic compounds such as toluene and xylene make excellent *solvent*s for use in printing inks. However, air pollution laws have drastically restricted their use.

ARP

Abbreviation for *Address Resolution Protocol*. See *Address Resolution Protocol (ARP)*.

ARPANET

Acronym for *Advanced Research Projects Agency Network*, a research network created by the Defense Advanced Research Projects Agency (DARPA). ARPANET was the precursor of the modern *Internet*.

ARQ

Abbreviation for *automatic request for retransmission*. See *Automatic Request for Retransmission (ARQ)*.

Array

Generally speaking, any set of related items.

In graphics, an *array* is any graphical representation of items, such as a chart, table, or graph. A computer display can be described as a *pixel* array. In *scanning* and *digital photography*, image capture is typically effected by a *CCD array*.

Array Processor

In imaging, a computer processor capable of calculating a new value for each **byte** stored in a data array. It allows many calculations to be made at high speed, necessary in **raster image processor**s. See **Raster Image Processor (RIP)**.

Arrow Key

One of four keys marked with arrows on a computer keyboard. An arrow key moves the **cursor** up, down, left, and right when the operator enters text, or maneuvers through menus and graphics. Used in lieu of positioning with the mouse. Also known as **cursor-movement key**s.

Arrows

In typography, a set of characters (available in **pi font**s) that are, basically, arrows, either highly decorative or strictly utilitarian and pointing in most directions. They can be used to connect a caption to a photo, to indicate the continuation of a story to another page, or for other purposes.

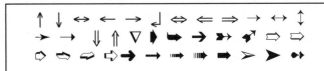

Arrows.

Art

In prepress and graphic arts, any material intended for reproduction. In page layout, the term *art* is often used to refer to any material that is not text (which is called **copy**).

Art Director

The person responsible for the visual look of a publication, as well as the acquisition of the talent needed to generate it. The art director coordinates all designers, artists, etc., and purchases outside visual material.

Article

In publishing, a non-fiction piece published in a magazine or newspaper.

In grammar (and typography), an *article* is, in English, one of three adjectives—*a, an,* and *the*—used to merely identify a noun as a noun, rather than attribute some trait to it (as is the case with conventional adjectives), as in "*a* trout" or "*the* sponge." (Other languages also have similar words.) The word *article* itself was originally used to refer to any clause, point, or statement in a contract or formal agreement (such as with God), and originally derives from the Latin word *artus*, meaning "joint," its sense eventually coming to mean "distinct parts," as in the word "articulate," which can mean to either pronounce each part of a statement distinctly or to possess distinct parts (or joints), as a limb.

Artifact

In **digital video**, distortions produced by a **compression** program and present in the playback of digital video.

In computing, the term *artifact* also refers to any extraneous characters that appear in **email** messages, word processing documents, or elsewhere.

Artificial Language

Essentially, a language whose rules regarding syntax, grammar, etc., are carefully developed prior to general usage. An example is Esperanto, whose rules were laid out deliberately before anyone learned it. Another example would be any computer language. The "opposite" of an artificial language is a **natural language**, which in most cases existed long before its rules were ever codified. The primary difference between the two is that the latter grew out of regular usage, its rules changing over the course of centuries. A natural language is learned by exposure to it (such as the primary way we tend to learn English, French, German, or whatever our primary language is) rather than by conscious study.

Artificial Intelligence (AI)

Broadly speaking, a group of related technologies that attempt to understand human thought processes and other aspects of human behavior, the goal being to create machines and computer systems that mimic human reasoning and decision-making. Pioneered by Marvin Minsky, among others, artificial intelligence is premised on the belief that the human mind is a complicated machine comprising many structures that evolved to solve certain problems. Although AI researchers are, for the most part, aware that the human brain and thought processes cannot be reduced to simple mathematic formulas, an understanding of how these structures sift through data and make decisions can result in "thinking machines" that can sort through stored knowledge and make decisions that require judgment and reasoning in the face of ambiguity. IBM's "Big Blue," a computer that recently defeated world chess champion Garry Kasparov, is one recent example of artificial intelligence at work. AI has also been successfully implemented in many fields of endeavor, such as medicine, chemistry, geology, and other systems of thought where machines have been required to engage in human-like thinking and decision-making. There are six general branches of AI research: natural-language manipulation, pattern recognition and analysis, perception, knowledge engineering, inference processing, and robotics.

Artist's Illustration Board

A **bristol paper**, produced with a **close formation** and designed for writing with pencil, pen, or watercolor paints or markers.

Art Knife

A small, sharp tool used for the delicate cutting of stencil films used in **screen printing**.

Art knife.

Art Paper

A high-quality drawing paper produced with a *close formation*, specially manufactured for pencil, pen, ink, or other drawing materials.

The term *art paper* also refers to a *clay-coated paper*, ideal for printing high-quality *halftone*s.

Artwork

Any illustration matter, or material that is not text. Most often used to refer to hand- or computer-drawn graphics, artwork can also refer to hand lettering or photographs. *Artwork* is also used as a synonym for *art*.

Arylide Yellows

See *Hansa Yellows*.

ASA

Abbreviation for *American Standards Association*, now known as the *American National Standards Institute*, and more familiarly known as *ANSI*.

In photography, *ASA* is used to refer to a measure of *film speed*, so named because the American Standards Association first applied the standardized numerical scale to film speed. See *Film Speed* and *Photography: Basic Photographic Principles*.

Ascender

In typography, the portion of some *lowercase* letters that extends above the character's *x-height*. The ascending characters are *b*, *d*, *f*, *h*, *k*, *l*, and *t*. They may not always align at the top of the ascender, although most do. One must be careful that line spacing, or *leading*, is sufficient so that the ascenders of one line do not touch the *descender*s of the previous line. In Old Roman typefaces, the ascenders were taller than capital letters. See also *Descender* and *x-Height*.

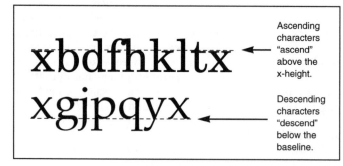

Ascenders and descenders.

Ascender Line

In typography, an imaginary horizontal line that marks the uppermost point of an *ascender*. See *Ascender*.

Ascent

In typography, the maximum distance that a *font* rises above the *baseline*. See also *Descent*.

ASCII

Abbreviation for *American Standard Code for Information Interchange*, pronounced "ASS-key," a file encoded in the industry-standard representation for text. ASCII is a set of standard codes used by most computers to symbolize letters, numbers, punctuation, and sets of commands (such as returns, etc.), but not style attributes, such as bold, italic, or other formatting commands. The *ASCII standard character set* of a microcomputer usually includes 256 characters or control codes. For example, the letter "A" is stored as ASCII 41, etc. Some ASCII "characters" do not display on the screen but instead control the display in other ways.

ASCII 8 is the backspace, 10 is the line feed, 13 is the carriage return, and 27 is escape. Other ASCII characters, consisting of letters from non-English alphabets and graphic symbols and called the *ASCII extended character set*, fall in the range from ASCII 128 to 255. These "upper ASCII" characters will not always display or print in consistent ways. The most consistent ASCII characters are those that can be seen on the keyboard; they fall in the range from ASCII 32 to 127 and are called "plain ASCII."

A "plain ASCII" file can be read by just about any program. Files created in a word processing, page makeup, or other type of program are often translated to and saved as an ASCII file (often called simply a *text file*) for transmission via modem. Text saved as ASCII can be opened in virtually any word processing program or *page makeup software*.

ASCII Extended Character Set

An additional group of characters used in *ASCII* coding schemes. See *ASCII*.

ASCII File

A data or text file consisting of only characters used in the standard *ASCII* character set. See *ASCII*.

ASCII Standard Character Set

The group of characters used in *ASCII* coding schemes. See *ASCII*.

Aseptic Packaging

In packaging, a means of ensuring that food remains sterile and free from bacteria or other harmful microorganisms. (The word *septic* refers to infection by a pathogenic organism; *aseptic* means free from such pathogens, while the more familiar term *antiseptic* refers to a substance that kills septic pathogens.)

Aseptic packaging is the final step in aseptic food processing, in which food products are continuously sterilized, ensuring that no microorganisms—which cause either food decay and/or food poisoning—are present. Aseptic packaging ensures that the containers for the food are also sterilized continuously and that the food is inserted into the container in a completely sterile environment.

Although Louis Pasteur is often the first name that comes to mind when we think about food sterilization, the process dates back to the Napoleonic Wars and, in fact, to the Napoleonic army's difficulty in obtaining food from local merchants, as the money the French Army was using (a type of currency invented by the Revolutionary government) was pretty much worthless elsewhere in Europe. In response to a prize started by Napoleon for the promotion of industry, a champagne bottler named Nicholas Appert looked into the problem of food preservation. He found that if you put food in a champagne bottle, seal it tightly, and boil it for long enough, the food within keeps for a very long time. He patented the process, and wrote a book on the subject. Preserved food eventually came out of bottles and into tin cans when the process migrated to England (curiously, the English patent for the process of preserving foods saved from financial ruin a man named John Gamble, who had lost a great deal of money when the Fourdrinier brothers' automated papermaking machine failed commercially; see ***Fourdrinier***), as tin was more plentiful in England than in France. Although the first versions of tin cans required the use of a hammer and chisel to open (no one had yet invented the can opener!), the process eventually caught on, especially once Louis Pasteur discovered exactly *why* it was that heating canned foods preserved them.

Aseptic packaging and processing can be accomplished—in modern times—in a variety of ways. The processing and packaging equipment itself is often heated to a temperature of 300–320°F for a preset amount of time. The food itself then must immediately be run through the equipment while it is sterile. The packaging itself can be sterilized by steam, heat, radiation, or hydrogen peroxide. The can was the first aseptic packaging container, but recent developments have broadened the range of containers and packages that can be filled aseptically. In the 1970s, the Irvine, California-based Scholle Corporation invented the first aseptic ***bag-in-box*** packaging, which uses flexible materials, sterilized by gamma radiation, and filled immediately after sterilization. Food products packaged in such a way include ketchup, tomato products, ice cream toppings, and sliced fruits. FDA regulations, however, restrict the bag-in-box process to acidic foods only. In the early 1980s, the use of hydrogen peroxide as a sterilizing agent was allowed by the FDA, and the aseptic packaging industry took off. Most ***form/fill/seal*** packaging machines sterilize the packaging (usually a multi-ply thermoplastic material bonded to foil, ***duplex paper***, or other type of laminate) with hydrogen peroxide and heat. Next, the device forms the material into the appropriately shaped package, fills it, and seals it. Form/fill/seal machines are widely used in industry now—not only for traditional can packaging, but also for plastic soft drink containers, milk cartons, and other plastic or plastic-laminate packaging. (See ***Form/Fill/Seal*** and ***Food Packaging***.)

A Series

In the metric system, a series of standard paper sizes based on portions of a square meter. (A square meter is the area used to determine paper ***grammage***, the metric equivalent

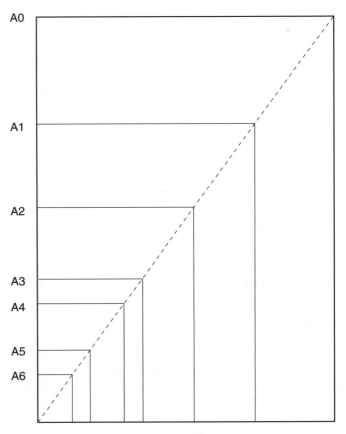

A series of paper sizes.

of ***basis weight***. Grammage is expressed as grams per square meter [g/m^2].) In the A series, the length-to-width ratio is maintained from size to size, and the area varies from size to successive size by a factor of 2 or ½. The standard size that corresponds most closely to the United States standard letter size of 8½×11 in. is ***A4***-size paper. There is also a ***B series*** of paper sizes that are intermediate A series sizes. The sizes and area of A series paper (from sizes A0 to A8) are as follows:

A#	Size (in.)	Size (mm)	Area (m^2)
A0	33.11×46.81	841×1189	1.0
A1	23.39×33.11	594×841	0.5
A2	16.54×23.39	420×594	0.25
A3	11.69×16.54	297×420	0.125
A4	8.27×11.69	210×297	0.063
A5	5.83×8.27	148×210	0.031
A6	4.13×5.83	105×148	0.016
A7	2.91×4.13	74×105	0.008
A8	2.05×2.91	52×74	0.004

See also ***Grammage***, ***B Series***, and ***ISO Paper Sizes***.

AS/400

A series of ***minicomputer***s introduced by IBM in 1988, used in networks either as a ***host*** or as an intermediate ***node***.

Ash Content

The amount of filler in a paper. Paper consists of organic **cellulose** fibers combined with inorganic **fillers** such as **clay**, **titanium dioxide**, or **calcium carbonate**, added during papermaking to increase such paper properties as **brightness**, **whiteness**, or **opacity**. For many printing processes, a filler or ash content of 15–20% may be desirable. To determine the ash content of a paper, a sample is weighed, then subjected to complete combustion (usually at 925°C ± 25°C). This removes all the organic constituents of the sample, leaving behind a residue of inorganic materials, or fillers. This is weighed, and the percentage of the original sample that remains is its ash content. Further analytical procedures can determine the chemical makeup of the ash as a means of identifying the specific fillers used.

ASIC

Abbreviation for **application specific integrated circuit**. See **Application Specific Integrated Circuit (ASIC)**.

Aspect Ratio

A comparison of the height and width of any rectangular area, be it a television screen, a movie screen, a window, or a photographic image. For example, the aspect ratio of a standard television screen is 4:3. In graphics and imaging, this ratio is important in the reproduction of images.

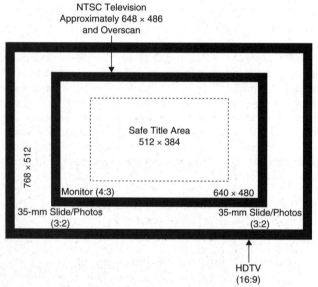

Aspect ratios of VGA monitor, NTSC television picture, 35-mm slide, and high-definition television.

Asphaltum

In **offset lithography**, a natural **resin** used to enhance and prolong the **ink receptivity** of a printing plate.

ASR

Abbreviation for **automatic send and receive**. See **Automatic Send and Receive (ASR)**.

Assemble

Alternate term for **compile**. See **Compile**.

Assemble Draw

In **binding and finishing**, the act of combining two or more sets of gathered **signature**s to form a **book block**.

Assemble Edit

A means of editing a videotape in which separate clips are placed in sequence with no **transition**s or smoothing effects other than straight cuts. **Assemble editing** is often a quick and easy way of creating a rough cut of a video presentation for preview purposes. Also referred to as **punch-and-crunch editing**, or **assemble-style editing**.

Assemble Edit also refers to any video material added to the end of a tape.

Assemble Editing

See **Assemble Edit**.

Assembler

Alternate term for a **compiler**. See **Compiler**.

Assembler Language

Alternate term for **assembly language**. See **Assembly Language**.

Assemble-Style Edit

See **Assemble Edit**.

Assembling

In **prepress**, an alternate term for **image assembly** or **stripping**. See **Stripping**.

In **binding and finishing**, *assembling* refers collectively to **collating**, **gathering**, or **inserting**—or, in other words, collecting pages or **signature**s into complete sets as a prelude to binding. See **Binding and Finishing**.

In typography, the term *assembling* referred to collecting and pasting up set type onto a **mechanical**. In hand-set and hot-metal typography, *assembling* referred to combining metal type slugs on a galley.

Assembly

In traditional **prepress**, the process of putting all the pieces of film for a particular page together in position on a carrier sheet of goldenrod paper, plastic, or film, prior to platemaking. This work is done electronically now, all these disparate elements being assembled into pages on the desktop computer. Also known as **film assembly**, **flat assembly**, **image assembly**, and **stripping**.

In publishing, *assembly* also refers to the collating together of all the various sections of a book, magazine, newspaper, etc.

Assembly Language

In computer programming, a **low-level language** that uses mnemonic or symbolic codes to represent function codes. Assembly languages are very similar to the actual *machine language* that the computer can read and, consequently, can be very difficult for humans to use.

Assembly Program

A computer program with which *assembly language* is written. See *Assembly Language*.

Assembly Sheet

In printing, an instruction sheet containing all the specifications for a job, such as the correct pagination and page sequence (including unnumbered and blank pages), the layout specifications, etc.

Asset

Any of the components—such as audio or video clips, photographs, scans, line drawings, text blocks, etc.—used as the "raw material" for a multimedia presentation or production.

Assign

In computer programming, to change the value of a *variable* during the execution of the program.

Assignment

In *three-dimensional modeling* and *rendering*, providing values for the color, opacity, and refractive index of each element of a model.

Association of Banyan Users International (ABUI)

A group, comprising about 1700 members worldwide, of users of the *Banyan VINES* networking system, as well as other related Banyan systems. See *Banyan VINES*.

Associative Dimensioning

In *computer-assisted drawing (CAD)*, the ability for a CAD program to automatically update a particular dimension when an object is stretched, moved, or resized.

Associative Storage

A computer storage device in which file locations are identified by content rather than name or position.

Asterisk

A *pi character* (*) used in *footnotes* and *references*. The asterisk is also used as a *wildcard* character in many computerized search engines. The term *asterisk* derives from the Greek word *asteriskos* (meaning "small star").

Asymmetrical Compression

A *lossy* data *compression* system often used with *digital video*. A compression algorithm is considered asymmetric when the decompressed file does not completely match the original file. When compressing video, there is so much information contained in the original file that it is not always possible to obtain a significantly compressed file. As a result, lossy compression schemes lose some data between compression and decompression. See *Data Compression*.

Asymmetrical Multiprocessing

In computing, a means of *multiprocessing* in which a specific task is handled by a specific processor. See also *Symmetrical Multiprocessing*.

Asymmetry

In typography and page design, an unpredictable pattern, specifically one in which the design is not reflected around a central axis. Asymmetric designs tend to be more dynamic. The opposite property is known as *symmetry*.

Asynchronous

Descriptive of two or more events which occur independently of each other in time, usually used to refer to *asynchronous transmission* in data communications, in which the timing of a transmission does not need to be precisely coordinated by both the sender and the receiver. See *Asynchronous Transmission*. See also *Synchronous*.

Asynchronous Communication

Alternate term for *asynchronous transmission*. See *Asynchronous Transmission*.

Asynchronous Communications Server

In networking, a *LAN* server that allows a user to dial outside the network and access the public telephone system. Also known as a *dial-in/dial-out server* and a *modem server*.

Asynchronous Computer

A computer in which an operation begins only after a previous operation has been completed. Once an operation is complete, a signal is generated, which tells the computer that the next operation can begin. In contrast, a *synchronous computer* executes operations according to a master clock.

Asynchronous Transfer Mode (ATM)

In telecommunications, a high-speed, *broadband* communications scheme used for transmitting *analog* data. The advantage of ATM is its use of *cell switching*, a combination of *circuit switching* and *packet switching*, in which transmitted data is broken into small fixed-size (53 *bytes*) cells, each containing the data and an *address*. The fixed size of the cell allows it to be handled quickly, while its small size allows many cells to be processed. As a result, ATM is well-suited to transmitting audio and video. The *CCITT* has selected ATM as the designated transmission mode for broadband *ISDN*. ATM is also known as *cell relay*. See also *ISDN*.

Asynchronous Transmission

In telecommunications, a form of *serial transmission* in which a transmitted message contains only one character, each preceded by a *start bit* (0) and followed by a *stop bit* (1). (The characters themselves comprise 7 or 8 *data bit*s.) In this way, the receiving system determines where a character begins and ends. No precise timing is required on the sending or receiving system. Also known as **asynchronous communication**. See also **Synchronous Transmission**.

AT Bus
See **Industry Standard Architecture (ISA)**.

AT Command Set
In networking and telecommunications, a set of commands and instructions used to control a variety of **modem** features. The term *AT* itself is an abbreviation for *ATtention*. For example, the command set ATDP (which stands for *ATtention Dial Pulse*) instructs the modem to use pulse dialing, while ATDT (which stands for *ATtention Dial Tone*) instructs the modem to use touch-tone dialing. The AT command set was originally developed by Hayes Microcomputer Products for its brand of modems, but is now utilized by nearly all modem manufacturers.

AT-Compatible
Abbreviation for **Advanced Technology-compatible**, descriptive of a computer that could run applications and open files created for and on an IBM AT computer, a now-obsolete system that featured an Intel 80286 **processor**.

IBM AT computer.

ATM
Abbreviation for **Adobe Type Manager**. See **Adobe Type Manager**™.

    ATM is also an abbreviation for **asynchronous transfer mode**. See **Asynchronous Transfer Mode**.

ATOS
Abbreviation for **Automated Technical Order System**. See **Automated Technical Order System (ATOS)**.

ATR
Abbreviation for an *audio tape recorder*, a device used to record sounds, speech, or music and store them magnetically on tape.

At Symbol (@)
An archaic symbol used in pricing (i.e., 2 doughnuts @ $1 ea.) now rendered ubiquitous in this age of **email**. Essentially, the "at" symbol separates the user name from the domain of the mail server in an email address. For example, "wiggly@aol.com". Also referred to as the *at sign*. Also referred to, descriptively, as a **cinnamon bun**.

Attach
In networking, to connect a **workstation** to a **file server** so as to be able to access additional servers once a network connection has been established.

    In **email** terminology, *attach* means to append a file to an email message.

Attached Resource Computer Network
See **ARCnet**.

Attachment Unit Interface (AUI)
In networking, a 15-pin connector used to link a computer to an **Ethernet** network. See **Ethernet**. Also known as an **autonomous unit interface**.

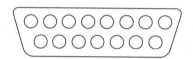

Attachment unit interface (AUI).

Attenuation
The reduction in the intensity of a light beam or electrical signal most often occurring when waves travel great distances.

Attribute
In computer graphics, any characteristic of the appearance of a **primitive**, such as color, style, width, etc.

    In typography, an *attribute* is any particular **typographic specification**, such as **typeface**, **point size**, **leading**, style, etc.

    In database terminology, an *attribute* is a **field** within a **record**, especially in a **relational database**.

Audible Cue
Alternate term for an **alert noise**. See **Alert Noise**.

Audio
Any sound, especially in electronic or digital form, or as part of a presentation. See **Analog Audio** and **Digital Audio**.

Audio Capture Board
A **digitizer board** used specifically to convert **analog audio** signals to **digital form**. See **Digital Audio**.

Audio CD
Popular term for **Compact Disc–Digital Audio**. See **Compact Disc–Digital Audio (CD-DA)**.

Audio Dubbing

In film and video production and editing, the addition of sound (such as narration, music, or pre-recorded dialogue) to a movie or presentation after the video has been shot.

Audio Engineering Society (AES)

An international organization dedicated to organizing seminars and assisting in the creation of standards for the storage and transmission of audio.

Audio Engineering Society/European Broadcast Union

See *AES/EBU*.

Audio Frequencies

Vibrations of a medium (such as air) that can be detected by a receiving party (such as human ears) and perceived as sound. Vibrations from about 15 to 20,000 *Hertz* are perceived as sound by human ears.

Audio Interchange File Format (AIFF)

In multimedia, a standard *file format* created by Apple Computer for exchanging sound files among applications. Its three-digit file extension is often *AIF*.

Audio Mixer

In sound production, an electronic board connected to several (or many) audio sources, such as microphones, individual instruments, audio playback devices, etc. In the process of *audio mixing*, the volume of each sound source can be adjusted to the desired level before the track is ultimately recorded onto tape or other medium.

Audio Mixing

In sound recording and multimedia, the creation of a custom audio track from several different audio sources using an *audio mixer* or other such device.

Audio Output

In *digital audio*, the playback of an audio file from a computer, accomplished with a *digital-to-analog converter*, which allows the sound to be heard.

Audio Processing

Customizing an analog or digital audio track, to add such special effects as echoes, feedback, reverb, etc.

Audio Response Unit

In telecommunications, a device that converts data (stored in a computer) to vocalized sounds understandable to humans. Audio response units are often used in telephone networks, and they "respond" to touch-tone keypad input. An audio response unit is also known as a *voice output unit* or a *voice synthesizer*.

Audio Segment

Any portion of a soundtrack.

Audiospace

In radio, television, motion picture, or video production, general term for the use of sound cues to create a particular impression on an audience.

Audio Stream

See *Streaming Audio* and *Streaming Video*.

Audio Synthesis

In sound production, converting a digitally stored sound to *analog* form. Audio synthesis also refers to the simulation of an analog sound (be it a non-music sound, a musical instrument, or a human voice) by digital means, often colloquially referred to as *sampling*.

Audio Track

The portion of a presentation, film, or videotape containing the audio signal.

Audio Video Interleaved (AVI)

A *file format* developed by Microsoft to store and transport *digital video* among *IBM-compatible computer*s. Intended to compete with Apple's *QuickTime*, the process of *interleaving* ensures that the audio and video portions of a video clip are synchronized. Uncompressed, the AVI format can handle only a *resolution* of 160×120 *pixel*s at a rate of 15 *frames per second*, and then only on computers having at least an 80486 *processor* and a clock speed of at least 33 *MHz*. With hardware compression, however, higher frame rates and resolutions are possible.

Audit Trail

A file that records a particular user's activities on a *network*, including a listing of files created, modified, or deleted.

Auditing

In networking, a means of closely analyzing system events and transactions, especially those that may compromise network security, such as the creation, deletion, and editing of files and/or directories. A record of such events is stored in a special log file that can only be opened by individuals with special clearance.

AUI

Abbreviation for *attachment unit interface*. See *Attachment Unit Interface (AUI)*.

Authentication

In networking, the process of validating the log-in information provided by a user desiring access to the network. The authentication process typically involves the entering of a user name (which must be one which the system identifies) and a *password*. If both pieces of information are recognized by the system, network access (the extent decided by the *access rights* assigned to the particular user) is granted. Typically, password information is encrypted before it is sent over the network. However, since this encryption is not seen by the user, it is known as ***background authentication***.

Authoring

In general computing, the process of producing new information, rather than simply manipulating or repurposing previously created data.

In multimedia, *authoring* refers to the process of creating a multimedia presentation or title, often using ***authorware***.

Authoring Language

A script-based programming language for developing multimedia productions and presentations. Authoring languages can vary in the complexity of the programming required to get the presentation to function properly. A high-level language, such as Lingo used in Macromedia Director, lets the author specify within the ***authoring system*** what should occur at a given point, but it is up to the program to determine how it gets done. In a low-level language, such as C, the author would need to directly program the specific code telling the application how to accomplish things.

Authoring System

In general, any computer application used to create multimedia presentations and productions. Authoring programs vary widely in the level of their complexity; some allow iconic or graphical insertion of sound clips, graphics, video, and text into flow charts, while others require increasing degrees of script-based programming using an ***authoring language***. In general, a presentation written in a specific programming language such as C tends to run faster and perform better than one created graphically. Authoring software is often also known as ***authorware*** (also the brand name of a program used for authoring).

Authorization

In networking and telecommunications, a tool defining a user's access rights to a computer network or system. Authorization is often confirmed by the network or system by means of double-checking user names and passwords. Once on a network or system, users may be restricted in the files or devices they may access.

Author Profile

In multimedia, a file containing information on the creator of a particular multimedia title or presentation, including the computer system and software used to create the work.

Author's Alteration

Changes made by an author to a book or other material after the initial layout has been determined. Author's alterations are typically distinguished from ***typographical errors***, ***printer's errors***, or other such minor changes. Due to the expense involved in making excessive changes at this stage, book contracts typically stipulate that the author pay for alterations beyond a certain agreed-upon minimum limit. Often abbreviated ***AA***. (See also ***Editorial Change***.)

Authorware

Any computer program used for the ***authoring*** of multimedia titles and presentations. See ***Authoring System***.

Auto-Answer

In telecommunications, a feature of a ***modem*** that enables it to automatically answer an incoming call.

Auto Assemble

In video production, the automated editing of a videotape according to an electronic ***edit decision list***. The device used for auto assembly can read the electronic information and automatically create a ***master tape***, human intervention only being required in the case of technical problems. Master tapes assembled in this manner typically use an ***insert edit*** rather than an ***assemble edit***.

AutoCAD

Brand name of the leading ***CAD*** software, originally available only for DOS-based systems, now available for most ***operating system***s.

Auto-Dial

In telecommunications, a feature of a ***modem*** that enables it to automatically open a telephone line and dial a pre-set number.

Auto-Dimensioning

In computer graphics, a feature of a program that automatically scales one dimension of an image in the correct proportion to a user-initiated change in the other dimension.

Auto Execute

In computing, an ***operating system*** utility that allows a user-determined program to launch at system start-up.

AUTOEXEC.BAT

In computing, the ***batch file*** created by the ***DOS*** computer operating system that contains the commands and instructions to be executed at system start-up. A user can enter specific commands into this file. "AUTOEXEC" is an abbreviated term for "auto execute" while "BAT" is a ***file extension*** for a "batch" file. See ***Batch File*** and ***Batch Processing***.

Auto-Join

In graphics, a feature of a ***drawing program*** that automatically connects endpoints of a line or shape that are within a certain distance to each other.

Automated Interchange of Technical Information (AITI)

In computing, a standard that defines the tape format for the exchange or transfer of technical documents.

Automated Office System (AOS)

Hardware and software, as well as personnel and procedures, designed to automate traditional office operations. Elements of an automated office system can include a computer system, word processing capabilities, *email*, automatic scheduling, networking, etc.

Automated Technical Order System (ATOS)

An *SGML* application used for producing military technical manuals.

Automatic

Descriptive of any process or device that is self-activating and/or self-regulating or, in other words, requires minimal—if any—user intervention to execute.

Automatic Answer

See *Auto-Answer*.

Automatic Backup of Files

A feature of some word processing (or other) programs which automatically generates a duplicate copy of a file each time a file is created.

Automatic Call

See *Auto-Dial*.

Automatic Calling Unit (ACU)

In telecommunications, a device that generates pulses or tones recognizable by telephone networks. An ACU allows computers or business machines to dial remote systems or devices.

Automatic Carriage Return

In word processing, a command that inserts a *carriage return* (or a *soft return*) when the last word that will fit on a line has been entered. See *Carriage Return*.

Automatic Centering

In word processing, or computerized typesetting or page layout, a feature that allows only a few keystrokes or menu selections to automatically center text on a line or between designated points.

Automatic Coding

In computer programming, the creation of *machine language* routines with the assistance of a computer.

Automatic Conveyorized Drying

In *screen printing*, a commonly-used drying mechanism that carries the printed *substrate* on a conveyor belt through a drying oven. This device is also known as a *conveyor dryer*.

Automatic Data Processing (ADP)

Alternate term (used primarily by Federal agencies) for *data processing*. See *Data Processing (DP)*.

Automatic Decimal Tab

In computerized typesetting or word processing systems, a feature that automatically aligns numbers in a column on the decimal point, allowing the typist to enter numbers without regard to alignment.

Automatic Dial

See *Auto-Dial*.

Automatic Dialing Unit

Alternate term for *automatic calling unit*. See *Automatic Calling Unit (ACU)*.

Automatic Display Power Down

In computing, one particular feature of a system having an *auto power down* function in which the monitor is shut down or dimmed if the computer is left idle for a set period of time. Automatic display power down is used as a means of reducing power consumption.

Automatic Document Feeder

An auxiliary device for as scanner, photocopier, etc., which automatically feeds a set of sheets or other flat originals—one by one—onto the imaging platen. Automatic document feeder is often abbreviated *ADF*.

Automatic File Select

In a database system, the ability of the system to find and display data files or records based on specific characters that appear in a *field*. For example, if a particular demographic database had a field that indicated how many times an individual had seen *The Sound of Music*, the system could be used to locate all those records corresponding to people who had seen it more than two times.

Automatic File Sort

In a database system, a feature of the system that allows for the automatic arranging of files or data in alphabetical, numerical, chronological, or other user-defined order.

Automatic Footers

In word processing or page layout programs, a feature that allows *footer*s to be placed at the bottom of each page of a multi-page document without the user having to manually insert them. See also *Automatic Headers*.

Automatic Footnote Tie-In

In word processing (or other) programs, a feature that automatically places a *footnote* at the bottom of the page on which it is called, moving it to a new page when the corresponding text is reflowed.

Automatic Headers

In word processing or page layout programs, a feature that allows *header*s to be placed at the top of each page of a multi-page document without the user having to manually insert them. See also *Automatic Footers*.

Automatic Hyphenation

In typography, the making of word-break decisions by computer software, not by the human operator. See *Hyphenation*.

Automatic Job Recovery

In computing, a feature that allows a computer system to continue functioning when one or more components has failed.

Automatic Line Spacing

In word processing (and other) programs, a feature that enables the user to alter the *line spacing* throughout a document without having to change the corresponding setting on the printer.

Automatic Margin Adjust

In word processing (and other) programs, a feature that allows one or both margins to be changed with a single command, automatically changing line endings and repagination without user intervention.

Automatic Message-Switching Center

In networking and telecommunications, the site at which incoming messages are automatically routed to their proper destinations.

Automatic Number Identification (ANI)

In telecommunications and networking, a means of transmitting a telephone caller's phone number over a network or telephone line, allowing the recipient to identify the caller, often a characteristic of *ISDN*. Also known as *caller ID*. The ANI can be hidden if an incoming message contains a *privacy bit*.

Automatic Page Numbering

Alternate term for *automatic pagination*. See *Automatic Pagination*.

Automatic Pagination

In typesetting, the ability of a typesetting device to automatically subdivide a multi-page document into individual pages, within certain defined specifications (such as line length, lines per page, etc.). This ability is often enjoined with the ability to automatically number the pages. Automatic pagination performed without operator interaction is known as *batch pagination*, in contrast to *interactive pagination*.

Automatic Peel

A mechanism on an automatic press used in *screen printing* that lifts the screen behind the moving *squeegee*.

Automatic Picture Replacement (APR)

A term used by Scitex to refer to a feature of its desktop-to-prepress system in which *low-resolution* image files are replaced by *high-resolution* scanned images. See also *Open Prepress Interface (OPI)*.

Automatic Programming

In computer programming, the use of a computer to do at least some of the work of writing a program.

Automatic Receive

See *Automatic Send and Receive*.

Automatic Repagination

In word processing and *desktop publishing* programs, a function that will automatically reposition the page breaks or page lengths as material is added or deleted.

Automatic Request for Retransmission (ARQ)

In networking and data communications, a means of *error detection* in which the sending device requests that the receiving device send either an *acknowledgement (ACK)* signal (indicating that all data was received intact) or a *negative acknowledgement (NAK)* (indicating that all data was not received intact).

Automatic Right-Justifying Tab

In computerized typesetting, word processing, or page layout, a function that automatically aligns column text along a preset right margin, so that the operator or keyboarder will not have to constantly justify each line.

Automatic Rollback

In *database* computing, a safety feature that restores a database to its last-saved version in the event of a system crash. As a result of this feature, all incomplete later versions (which may have been damaged by the crash) are rendered invalid.

Automatic Send

See *Automatic Send and Receive*.

Automatic Send and Receive (ASR)

In telecommunications, descriptive of a device capable of generating messages prior to connection to a transmission medium. The device stores these messages and will automatically transmit them at a later date. By the same token, these devices can also receive messages when connected to another system, and store them locally for later retrieval and/or printing. Also known as *buffered automatic send/receive*, or *BASR*.

Automatic Widow Adjust

In computerized typesetting systems or in *page layout programs*, a function of the computer software that automatically prevents the last line of a paragraph from falling on the first line of a page, or the first line of a paragraph from falling on the last line of a page. See *Widow*.

Automation

The use of machines and/or computer software to accomplish any task, especially one that used to be performed manually.

Autonomous Unit Interface

In networking, a 15-pin connector used to link a computer to an *Ethernet* network. (See *Ethernet*.) Also known as an *attachment unit interface*.

Auto-Panning

In computing, a feature of many computer programs that allows the contents of a screen *window* to be moved with the mouse *pointer* when the pointer is positioned outside the window.

Autopositive

The term used to describe photographic materials that will produce an exact black-and-white duplicate of the original.

Auto Power Down

In computing, an energy-saving feature of many computer systems. If a system is left idle for a predetermined (and often user-definable) period of time, power-consuming components shut down or enter a "standby" mode. When the user hits a key or clicks the mouse, the system "wakes" and is ready to use. The *automatic display power down* feature dims or turns off a monitor when it is left idle.

Autotrace

In computer graphics, a feature of many *drawing programs* in which a *bitmapped* graphic is converted to a *vector* graphic. A bitmap is imported into the illustration program as a template, and a path is traced around the detectable edges of the image. It is then translated into *Bézier curves* characteristic of vectors. Depending on the complexity of the bitmap, autotrace features have varying degrees of utility. See *Bitmap* and *Vector*. Also spelled as two words, *auto trace*.

AUX

In audio equipment, an abbreviation for *AUXiliary*. See *AUXiliary*.

In *DOS*-based computing, *AUX* is the name assigned to an auxiliary device, typically one connected through the default *serial port*, commonly designated COM1.

A/UX

In computing, Apple Computer's software allowing *UNIX*-based applications to run on a *Macintosh* computer.

AUXiliary

In audio equipment, an additional plug or input *jack* used to connect another sound source. Abbreviated *AUX*.

Auxiliary Equipment

Any device(s) attached to a computer not under the direct control or supervision of a *central processing unit (CPU)*.

Auxiliary Memory

Additional computer storage space supplementing its internal storage capacity, such as magnetic tape and cartridges, floppy disks, optical discs, etc. Also known as *auxiliary storage*.

Auxiliary Operation

In computing, any activity performed offline by a device not under the direct control of a *central processing unit (CPU)*.

Auxiliary Roll Stand

In *web printing*, a *roll stand* that can be mounted on top of another roll stand, used to reduce press downtime by enabling the operator to reload while the attached stand is still unwinding. Unlike a *two-roll stand*, an auxiliary roll stand cannot be used to feed two rolls into the press simultaneously. See *Roll Stand* and *Web Offset Lithography: Infeed and Web Control*.

Auxiliary Storage

Alternate term for *auxiliary memory*. See *Auxiliary Memory*.

Availability

In computing, the extent to which a system or system resource is ready to process data or execute an operation.

Available Time

Alternate term for *uptime*. See *Uptime*.

Average Access Time

In computing, a means of evaluating the time it takes to write and read data to and from a storage medium. See *Access Time*.

AVI

Abbreviation for the *audio video interleaved* file format. See *Audio Video Interleaved (AVI)*. *AVI* is also a common *file extension* used to denote files saved in the AVI format.

AWG

Abbreviation for *American Wire Gauge*, a measure of the thickness of copper wire (such as that used as a cabling medium in networks) in which the AWG number decreases with increasing wire thickness. *Thin Ethernet*, for example, uses 20 AWG wire as a cabling medium while *Thick Ethernet* uses 12 AWG wire.

Axis

On a graph or other *coordinate system*, a line along which distances are measured and positions referenced. *Two-dimensional* coordinate systems use two axes—an *x axis* and a *y axis*—while *three-dimensional* coordinate systems add a *z axis*.

Azeotrope

A mixture of two liquids with a constant boiling point (typically higher or lower than that of either component). It can be distilled in a fixed ratio and without decomposition of either component, such as the mixture of isopropyl alcohol and water, or other combinations of liquids used in printing inks.

AZERTY

A French equivalent of the **QWERTY** keyboard layout, so named because the first six alphabetic keys at the top left of the keyboard are, in fact, A, Z, E, R, T, and Y.

Azo Dye

A dye made from organic compounds comprising an azo group (an organic molecule consisting of bivalent –N=N– joined to *two* hydrocarbon groups, such as azobenzene,

$C_{12}H_{10}N_2$) used in the **screen printing** of cotton **substrate**s.

Azo Magenta G

An **organic color pigment** used in printing inks. Azo Magenta G is a bluish red and possesses high **lightfastness** and good chemical resistance to most substances. It is most commonly used in **liquid ink**s for the printing of packaging. (See also **Organic Color Pigments**.)
(*CI Pigment Red 222.*)

Azo Yellows

See **Hansa Yellows**.

B

B, b
The second letter of the Latin and English alphabets, derived from the Greek *beta*. The form of the uppercase *B* derives from the North Semitic *beth*, later adopted by the Greeks and the Romans. The lowercase *b* derives from the Greek *beta*, formed by eliminating the top loop.

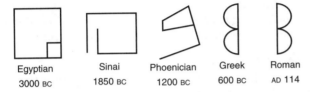

Egyptian	Sinai	Phoenician	Greek	Roman
3000 BC	1850 BC	1200 BC	600 BC	AD 114

The evolution of the letter B.

Babbling Tributary
In networking, a *workstation* in a *local area network (LAN)* that sends meaningless messages.

Backbone
Alternate term for the *spine* of a publication. See *Spine* (first definition).

In networking, a shorthand term for a *backbone network*. See *Backbone Network*.

Backbone Network
A portion of a computer network that carries the majority of the data traffic, or the part that connects different *LAN*s.

Backbone Space
In *binding and finishing*, the portion of the inside of a book cover in which the *spine* of the book fits.

Back Cylinder
Alternate term for the *impression cylinder* on a printing press. See *Impression Cylinder*.

Back Cylinder Print
An *offset* printing problem in which a printed image is transferred to the surface of the *impression cylinder* before a press sheet is in position between it and the blanket. The printed image is then transferred to the back of the press sheet. Interestingly, observation of this type of problem provided the basis for the development of offset lithography. See *Offset Lithography*.

Back-Edge Curl
A printing and paper defect characterized by the *waffling*, or *embossing*, of the rear edge of a sheet of paper. Back-edge curl has the same cause as waffling, namely, the pulling and consequent distortion of the paper when pulled by thick, tacky ink films. Back-edge curl results when heavily printed areas appear too near the rear edge of the sheet. Back-edge curl can be avoided by designing the layout of the printed material so that no solid printed areas appear at the bottom of the page. Back-edge curl is also called *tail-end hook*. (See also *Waffling*.)

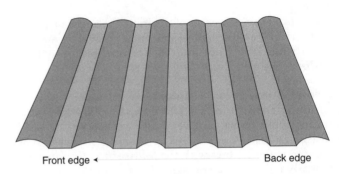

Front edge ◄ ——————————————— Back edge

An example of waffling.

Back-End Processor
In computing, a secondary *microprocessor* designed for a specific task. See *Coprocessor*.

Back-End System
In networking, the *server* portion of a *client/server* network that provides services to the *front-end application*s. Essentially, the front-end *workstation* sends a query (via an application) to the back-end system, which processes the request and returns the results to the *front end*.

Back Gluing
Alternate term for *gluing-off*. See *Gluing-Off* and *Case Binding*.

Back Gray Cloth
On a *screen printing* press, a cotton fabric placed over the *printing table*'s felt padding to protect from ink seepage.

Background
In graphic design or layout, the color, pattern, etc., on top of which other elements are placed.

On a computer display, the color on which the characters or other images are displayed.

In computer processing, *background* refers to any area outside the view of the user. See *Background Processing*.

Background Authentication
In networking and telecommunications, an *authentication* process in which some or all of the processing is not seen by the user. See *Authentication*.

Background Noise

In telecommunications, any *noise* present in a system caused by internal or external interference, typically beyond that produced by the signal itself. See *Noise*.

Background Processing

Computer operations or calculations that take place "off-screen," or behind the primary operations being performed by the computer operator, allowing unimpeded work in the *foreground*. See *Foreground Processing*.

Backing

In *case binding*, a process of widening the *spine* of a *book block* prior to *casing in* as a means of providing a shoulder on which the front and back covers rest. See *Case Binding*. See also *Rounding*.

Backing Away From Fountain

A printing defect of *offset lithography* characterized by printing that grows progressively weaker or streaked, caused by a high-*viscosity* ink (or an ink resistant to flow) failing to make contact with the *fountain roller* and consequently failing to be transferred to the *ductor roller*.

Backing Out

In networking, an alternate term for *automatic rollback*. See *Automatic Rollback*.

Backing Sheet

Any sheet of paper, plastic, or other material that serves as a support for *screen printing* stencil film, photographic film, or *adhesive* labels.

Backing Up

The process of printing on the second side of a sheet of paper or other *substrate*, commonly by making additional passes through the press, as opposed to *perfecting*, which refers to two-sided printing performed in a single pass.

Backlap

In *screen printing*, a crude, thick layer of ink on one side of the *substrate*, caused by ink pulling through the screen behind the *squeegee* at the beginning of the printing stroke.

Backlash Gear

A thin, supplemental gear attached to a *spur gear* to reduce the occurrence of *play*, an undesired, unimpeded lateral movement of meshing gears. Older offset press cylinders (such as the *plate cylinder* or *blanket cylinder*) utilize spur gears and backlash gears. Newer presses tend to use cylinders equipped with *helical gear*s, which by design reduce play themselves. (See *Plate Cylinder*.)

Back Light

In photography, the illumination of a subject from behind.

In computer display equipment, the background light used is an *LCD*. See *LCD*.

Backlining

In *case binding*, a piece of paper, muslin, or other material applied to the *spine* of a book as a means of stiffening and strengthening it. See *Case Binding*. Also spelled as two words, *back lining*, or simply referred to as *lining*.

Back Margin

An alternate term for *gutter margin*. See *Gutter Margin*.

In printing, a *back margin* on a press sheet is the total distance from the type on one page to that of the facing page, or twice the back margin of a single page.

Back Matter

In *book typography* and production, the pages of a book that follow the main text. See *Book Typography*.

Backoff Algorithm

In networking, the formula by which a *contention network* determines when to try to resend a message following a *collision*.

Backplane

Alternate term for a computer's *motherboard*. See *Motherboard*.

Back Pressure

The pressure, or *squeeze*, found in the *impression nip*, or the pressure between the *blanket cylinder* and *impression cylinder* on a printing press used in *offset lithography*. The degree of back pressure exerted during printing directly affects not only print quality but also blanket wear and damage. See *Offset Lithography: Printing Unit*, *Blanket Cylinder*, and *Packing*.

Back Printing

Printing on the reverse side or underside of a sheet or transparent film to create a text continuation or, in the case of transparent films, to provide a background for the text or other design printed on the front side. Back printing is completed with *head-to-head imposition* (the top of the copy on the back side is the same as that on the front side, as the pages of a book), *head-to-foot imposition* (the top of the copy on the back side begins at what is the foot of the copy on the front side), or *head-to-side* (the copy on the reverse side is at a right angle to the copy on the front side). It is also known as *reverse printing*. See also *Face Printing*.

Backs

Collective term for any *negative*, *flat*, or printing *plate* containing the second side of a printed sheet.

Back Slant

In typography, a left tilt or change in posture of the type characters of a *typeface*. The opposite is *italic* or *oblique*. Back slanting is not considered typographically desirable.

This is backslanted type.

Backslash

A slanted line (\), or an opposite slash (\), used in many computer operating systems to indicate a data path.

Back Spinner

On a *perfect binding* machine, a roller used to control the thickness of the *adhesive* placed on the *spine*. See *Perfect Binding*.

Back Trap Mottle (BTM)

A printing defect similar to *mottle* that occurs on multiple-unit offset presses, caused by nonuniform ink setting when the paper is still moving through the press, and aggravated by the use of *quickset ink*s and *coated paper*s that promote the quick setting of ink. When the *blanket* on the last printing unit contacts the paper, it disturbs the print, but not uniformly, which produces the mottled appearance. BTM can be reduced by using an ink that does not set as quickly, or by using paper with a different coating formulation.

Back Up

To print the second side of a previously printed sheet of paper or other *substrate*. Back up is commonly used to refer to such printing accomplished by multiple passes through the press, as opposed to *perfecting*, which is performed in one pass.

Backup

One or more copies of a computer file kept on one or more types of external (or internal) media as a safeguard against accidental deletion or damage of the original file. One can never have too many backups. Also known as a *backup copy* or *backup file*.

   Backup also refers to any duplicate apparatus to be used in case of accident to the primary unit(s). Sometimes spelled as two words, *back up*, or is hyphenated, *back-up*. See also *Differential Backup* or *Incremental Backup*.

Backup Blade

A small blade used on some *gravure* presses to strengthen and impart rigidity to the *doctor blade*. The backup blade does not contact the ink or the surface of the *gravure cylinder*. See *Doctor Blade*.

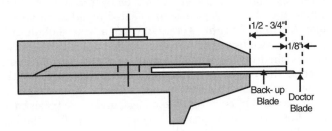

The back-up blade mounted in the same holder as the doctor blade.

Backup Program

In computing, a program used to create a *backup* of a file or disk. Although most operating systems allow the user to copy files to backup media, often specific applications for backing up files are a more effective means of archiving files. See *Differential Backup*, *Disk Duplexing*, *Disk Mirroring*, *Full Backup*, and *Incremental Backup*.

Backup Roll

Alternate term for a printing press *impression cylinder* or *impression roller*. See *Impression Cylinder*.

Backward Broadside Page

In typography, a page in which the printed text runs sideways in relation to that on the rest of the pages of the book or document.

Backward Chaining

In logic, a method of reasoning that begins with the desired goal (i.e., a hypothesis) and proceeds backward to the known facts that support it. Backward chaining is also used in computer programming; the program creates a hypothesis and works backward to compute the "rules" that support it. Specifically, the program works from the "...then" portion of a command and seeks to match it from the "if..." portion. See also *Forward Chaining*.

Backward Compatible

Alternate term for *downward compatible*. See *Downward Compatible*.

Bad Break

In typography, a term for an incorrect end-of-line *hyphenation*, or the beginning of a page or column with a *widow* or *orphan*.

Bad Copy

A *manuscript*, *typescript*, or other copy that is illegible, poorly edited, or in some other way unsuitable for typesetting or imaging.

Bad Sector

In computing, a *sector* on a *magnetic disk* or an *optical disc* which cannot be read from or written to, due to accidental damage or a manufacturing defect. Most operating systems are able to keep track of bad sectors, preventing the loss of data. When a *hard disk* contains a bad sector, the operating system keeps track of them in a *bad track table*, and thus prevents data from being placed there. Almost all disks and discs have bad sectors as a result of the manufacturing process.

Bad Track Table

In computing, a list of the defective *sector*s and/or *track*s on a *hard disk*, provided by the manufacturer. Nearly all hard disks have some bad sections as a result of the manufacturing process, and the operating system can read this bad track table and automatically cordon off those areas.

Bag

In packaging, any of a wide variety of flexible containers, made from plastic, paper, foil, or other materials.

Paper Bags

Most people are familiar with a variety of paper bags, such as *kraft* grocery bags, small paper lunch bags, and many types of small, often printed bags used to package goods at retail outlets. In packaging applications (as distinguished from consumer bags), literally billions of paper bags are manufactured each year. In the packaging industry, there are three primary classifications of paper bags: *single-ply bag*s, *duplex bag*s (or two-ply bags), and *multiwall bag*s (three-ply or greater). (Duplex bags are also often called multiwall bags.) Multiwall bags, the most commonly used in industrial and consumer packaging, often include one or more layers of plastic, foil, or other nonpaper material, depending upon the degree of vapor-barrier performance required. Such bags often require some level of moisture or air protection, especially those that are designed to contains foods or other materials which can be damaged by prevailing environmental conditions.

Materials. Paper bags, as their name indicates, are primarily manufactured from kraft paper, a strong, durable paper made from bleached or unbleached wood pulp, specifically sulfate pulp (see *Sulfate Process*). Kraft paper for paper bag manufacture is manufactured at basis weights of 25–60 lb., at a basic size of 24×36 in. Kraft paper used for industrial or commercial paper bags is often referred to as shipping-sack kraft, which is stronger than so-called "grocery kraft" paper. Paper used for bags can come in a variety of finishes, in particular, machine finish, or a type of moderately glossy finish produced by a calender. Plastics are also used in multiwall paper bags—specifically polypropylene, polyvinyl chloride (PVC), and other polymers—either as separate plys or as paper coatings. Most multiwall paper bags consist of just kraft paper, but about one fourth of all the multiwall bags produced contain a plastic ply or plastic component.

Bag Styles. There are five basic paper bag configurations recognized by the packaging industry. *Sewn open-mouth (SOM)* bags are sewn at the bottom, the top remaining open to facilitate filling. After filling, the top may be sewn, taped, stapled, or glued shut. SOM bags are often used for granular materials. *Sewn valve (SV)* are similar to SOM bags, except that both the top and bottom are sewn shut prior to filling, filling being accomplished by means of a small valve commonly located at a corner of the bag. Smaller granular materials are often put in SV bags. *Pasted open-mouth (POM)* bags are analogous to SOM bags, except that pasting rather than sewing is the primary

sealing means. *Pasted-valve stopped-end (PVSE)* bags are analogous to SV bags, both ends being pasted shut prior to filling, with filling accomplished by means of a small valve. Filled PVSE bags are characterized by a distinctively square shape which facilitates further printing, shipping, stacking, and storing. Finally, *pinch-bottom open-mouth (PBOM)* bags are manufactured by pinching shut and gluing the bottom, filling the bag, and using a *hot-melt adhesive* to glue the top shut. The PBOM bags are increasing in popularity, as the tightness of the seal produced by the pinching and the use of hot-melt adhesive result in a more secure closure than is possible by traditional sewing, reducing leakage and contamination significantly.

Filling and Closure. The bags are filled either by impellers which force material though the valve, by a belt and pulley arrangement, by a horizontal screw-like auger, by air flow means, or by simple force of gravity. Bags are closed either by sewing (the traditional method), which may then be covered over with tape, or by using heating elements to melt the plastic plys of a bag, effectively sealing it.

Printing. The printing of distinctive graphics on commercial, industrial, or consumer bags is more often than not performed using *flexographic* presses, which have increasingly been able to print at a high quality on a wide variety of substrates and with a wide variety of inks. In some cases, *gravure* presses—the original presses used for packaging—are also used.

Paper bags—of any of the above varieties or configurations of equipment—are used in five primary markets: agriculture and food (such as feed for livestock and pets, as well as flour, sugar, coffee, rice, etc.), construction material (such as cement mix, insulation, etc.), chemicals (such as fertilizer, salt, etc.), minerals (such as clay and lime), and a broad category of absorbent materials (such as kitty litter).

Plastic Bags

Plastic bags have replaced paper in many areas, but paper bags are still preferred in many heavy-duty applications.

Manufacture. Plastic bags are categorized in one of two ways: by application (see below) or by the method with which the sheets of plastic are sealed together to form a bag. A *sideweld seal* is created when a heated blade cuts and seals two layers of film. The knife passes through two sandwiched layers of plastic and, as it cuts through both sheets, the combination of heat and pressure fuses the sheets together. This type of bag is used in bread bags, ice bags, sandwich bags, vegetable bags, and some trash bags. In a *bottom seal*, a special seal bar is used to fuse the layers of plastic together at the seam, but a separate cutting action removes the bag from the rest of the bag stock. This latter method has advantages over the sideweld method in that the dwell time is easier to control. Additionally, the combination cutting/fusing action of the sideweld device can change the physical structure of the plastic at the point of the seal. The bottom weld is used on vegetable bags (especially vegetable bags that come perforated on a roll, as in a grocery store produce department), dry cleaning bags, freezer bags, and trash bags. A ***twin seal*** uses the same principle as the bottom seal, only it includes—as its name indicates—two seal bars, separated by the cutting knife. The interesting wrinkle with the twin seal method means that two separate seals on two separate bags can be made at the same time. This configuration also allows it to be used to seal bags on both sides (rather than the bottom) simultaneously. The twin seal is used on grocery bags primarily.

Application.

Bags are primarily classified in terms of their ultimate end uses, such as "bread bag," "trash bag," etc. The two primary divisions, however, are commercial and consumer. Commercial bags are those used to package another product, such as bread. Consumer bags are those sold and purchased as bags, such as sandwich bags, trash bags, etc.

There is also an extremely large specialty bag market which advanced bag-making technology has made possible, such as "handle-tie" bags, drawstring bags, deli bags, etc.

Heavy-Duty Plastic Bags.

Less than 10% of all the heavy-duty bags used in the United States are plastic; paper is still the material of choice for most heavy-duty usage. Plastic is used for materials—such as fertilizer, rock salt, ice melters, etc.—that require strong barriers to moisture. Some materials—such as industrial sulfur, pet foods, etc.—need to "breathe" in the bag, which reduces the occurrence of a variety of deleterious effects, such as growing mold or spontaneously bursting into flame. Heavy-duty plastic bags are most often formed from a single ply of a thermoplastic film, such as polyethylene, either in high-density or low-density varieties. Two-ply bags are also manufactured. These bags can either be open-mouth or valve bags, which have the same basic configuration as open-mouth and valve paper bags. Valve plastic bags tend to square at the bottom when they are filled, and are thus also known as "square-bottom bags." Various form/fill/seal technologies have been applied to heavy-duty plastic bags. As with most other types of bags, flexography is the printing method of choice.

Although heavy-duty plastic bags are more expensive to produce than paper ones, plastic can be more cost-effective in the long-run due to its increased resistance to moisture and chemicals. In the garden products industry, for example, it can be more cost- and space-effective to store overstock outside, which plastic makes possible.

Bag-In-Box (BIB)

In packaging, a type of container used for both dry and liquid products. The contents are placed in a flexible bag, which is then placed inside a (typically) cardboard carton.

Dry Products.

Dry products packaged using bag-in-box techniques include crackers, cookies, cereals, and other such foods. The concept was invented in the early years of the twentieth century when the National Biscuit Company (now Nabisco) introduced the Uneeda Biscuit. This soda cracker marked the first use of the folding carton as a package. Eventually, the carton was lined with wax paper, which prolonged freshness. Thus was born the lined carton, in which the cardboard box itself could be automatically assembled and glued, the top flaps remaining open. A second device inserts an open wax paper bag into the box, which can then be filled with the contents, and the top of the wax paper bag folded and sealed shut, followed by the closure of the box itself. A slightly later development inserted the lining prior to assembling the carton.

In the 1950s, the introduction of vertical ***form/fill/seal*** packaging machinery allowed the bag to be formed, filled, and sealed, and inserted complete into the carton, which cut the number of steps and motions involved in the packaging process. One problem that has plagued this process was occasional (or even frequent) bag-jamming, as misshapen or overloaded bags could not be easily dropped into the cartons. One means of solving this problem was the invention of devices which produced a sharp rectangular shape to the bags, which facilitated their dropping into the carton.

Liquid Products.

Liquids (or semi-liquids) packaged in bag-in-box containers include inexpensive wines and industrial chemicals, among many other substances. The components of liquid BIB packages include a flexible and collapsible inner bag commonly made from a synthetic film, a spout attached to the inner bag to easily pour desired quantities of the liquid, and an outer protective cardboard carton. The first uses of the liquid BIB container were for industrial bulk milk dispensers and for sulfuric acid used as an activator for dry-cell batteries. The inner bag (also called a barrier film) is commonly manufactured from metallized thermoplastic materials (such as ***polyethylene*** and/or ***polyvinylidene chloride***), and the most commonly used barrier film today is a three-ply film of two layers of ethylene-vinyl acetate and one layer of metallized ***polyester***. The exact composition of the barrier film, however, is dependent upon the mechanical and chemical requirements of the product to be placed within it.

The liquid BIB manufacturing process is a bit more involved than the dry BIB process. Essentially, the bag is created by sealing two layers of the desired film together and adding the spout, which, as one can imagine, must be perfectly leakproof, and must be able to withstand the filling operation. The liquid is poured into the bag, and the bag is placed into the box. The desired valve or other dispensing spout is applied to the bag, and the box may have a perforated hole allowing easy access to the spout.

The advancements in BIB packaging technology are resulting in more and more liquid or semi-liquid products being distributed in BIB containers. In fast-food restaurants, for example, condiments and soda fountain syrups are pumped on menu items and into soda machines from BIB containers, which reduces the need for recycling of metal containers.

Bagasse
The material remaining after sugarcane has been ground, used as a fibrous source for papermaking.

Baggy Paper
A paper roll defect in which the *web* does not unwind uniformly and whose width fails to support web tension, caused by inconsistent paper thickness, excessive stretching of the thicker areas during winding, or by winding the roll too tightly. Bagginess at the edges of a roll is called *slack edge* and bagginess at the center is called *slack center*. Slack edges can also be caused by the absorption of moisture at the edges of the paper roll.

Bailment
In graphics, photography, and other such fields, a legal obligation on the part of an individual to take reasonable care of original art. An example of this is when a portfolio of a freelance artist's work is left with an art director for review, or when a photograph or illustration is supplied to a magazine or newspaper for publication.

Balance
In page layout and typography, a term descriptive of the overall visual "weight" of page elements and their page position. See *Dynamic Balance* and *Formal Balance*.

Balanced Screening
A system developed by the Agfa Corporation for calculating high-quality *PostScript* halftone *screen angles*. Predetermined screen descriptions are sent to a *raster image processor (RIP)* rather than screen-calculation algorithms. See *Screen Angles*.

Ball Mill
A device used in the manufacture of ink to disperse the solid *pigment* particles in the fluid ink *vehicle*, utilizing steel or ceramic balls to chop up the pigment particles and disperse them thoroughly. The ball mill consists of a closed horizontal metal cylinder, containing the balls at the bottom. The ink *slurry* is put into the machine to partially fill the cylinder. The cylinder is rotated, and the tumbling of the balls generates frictional forces which break up and disperse the pigment particles. The nature of the sealed cylinder makes ball milling well-suited for processing of inks containing highly volatile *solvent*s, which would be likely to evaporate and escape from the mixture in an open system. Inks used in *flexography* and *gravure* printing, which have thin, volatile, solvent-based vehicles, are commonly produced in ball mills. The longer the slurry remains in the mill, the more finely the particles are broken up. Often, geometrical shapes other than spheres can be uti-

lized. (See also *Three-Roll Mill*, *Sand/Shot Mill*, and *Colloid Mill*.)

Ball Printer
A type of *impact printer* or *typewriter* in which the *character set* is carried on a small metal ball. Typefaces can be changed by simply swapping balls.

Ballistic Effect
In computing, a function of *mouse*-controlling software that varies the speed of the *pointer* with the speed of the movement of the mouse itself. For example, if the rolling speed of the mouse is decreased, the pointer decelerates, while if the rolling speed of the mouse is increased, the pointer accelerates. Often, the speed of the ballistic effect can be adjusted by the user, as different applications may require different pointer speeds. General operations are best accomplished with an accelerated pointer speed, while intricate computer drawing or *pixel* manipulation is best handled with a decelerated pointer speed.

Ballot Box
In typography, a *box*, usually possessing a drop shadow (❏), used in bulleted lists or checklists. A ballot box may also be a circle.

Balsam of Copaiba
A natural *resin*, obtained from the copaiba tree (one of several species in the genus *Copaifera*, commonly *C. officinalis*, native to South America) used as a *vehicle* for colorants in glass printing and decorating. The copaiba resin is also used medicinally as a diuretic and a laxative.

Balun
In networking, a device used to connect two different networking media (such as *twisted-pair wiring*, which is balanced, to *coaxial cable*, which is unbalanced) such that the impedances of the two media are matched. Balun is itself a contraction of "balanced" and "unbalanced."

Bamboo
General name for a variety of species of woody grasses, primarily of the genus *Bambusa*, native to tropical and subtropical regions of Asia, Africa, and North America. (The most widely used bamboo species is *Bambusa vulgaris*.) In some countries, bamboos are used as a fibrous source for papermaking.

Band
In *binding and finishing*, a strip of paper—which may or may not be printed—that is wrapped around loose sheets in lieu of proper binding.

A *band* is also a continuous ribbon of mylar or metal imprinted with characters or dots, used in certain types of impact printers. See *Band Printer*.

In video, the term *band* is used to refer to a group of 32 consecutive scan lines.

Band Buffer

In video, an area of computer storage or memory used to transfer one *band* (or 32 consecutive scan lines) of video data to a scanner.

Band Printer

A type of *impact printer* containing a metal *band* with character shapes imprinted on it. During output, the band rotates horizontally past the paper, and a hammer strikes the band opposite the appropriate character, pressing it through an inked ribbon and onto the paper. Band printers can print from 300 to 2000 lines per minute. Also known as a *belt printer*.

Banding

A press and printing problem of a *continuous-flow dampening system* used in *offset lithography* characterized by fine dark and light bands or streaks on the chrome-plated *transfer roller*, which transfer to the plate and, ultimately, to the print. Banding (also called *ridging*) commonly occurs when a *fountain solution* containing an alcohol substitute is used with a metering roller possessing a hardness, or *durometer*, of 25–30 (which is the normal durometer of rollers used with alcohol solutions). Banding is caused by the harder rollers being less water-receptive than softer ones, non-alcohol solutions having a harder time adhering to their surfaces. The solution is to use softer rollers, such those possessing a durometer of 18–22. Some roller manufacturers also produce textured, or grained, rollers which increase the amount of water that can adhere to their surfaces. (See *Fountain Solution* and *Dampening System*.)

In imaging, *banding* refers to a perceptible streakiness of *halftone dot*s, characterized by smooth gradations of dots separated by bands of dots of lighter or darker than desired density, caused by problems in *imagesetter* film feeding problems, commonly oriented perpendicular to the direction of film travel. (See also *Contouring*.)

In computer graphics, *banding* refers to the perceptible "steps" in a computer-generated gradation of *color* or *gray scale*.

A smooth gray scale vs. one with obvious banding.

Bandwidth

Generally speaking, the quantity of information capable of passing through any system. In imaging, the *bandwidth* may refer to the range of wavelengths of light that can pass through a filter. In computers, the *bandwidth* may refer to the speed—in cycles per second (hertz)—at which the *central processing unit* operates. In telecommunications, *bandwidth* refers to the information capacity—or the maximum frequency range—of a transmitted signal or communications link. In this latter sense, the size of the available bandwidth determines the type of communication link that is possible, be it voice, data, audio, video, etc.

Bandwidth on Demand

In networking, a feature of *wide area network*s that enables the user to call up additional bandwidth as desired, depending on the requirements of a specific application.

Bang

An alternate term for an *exclamation mark* (!). See *Exclamation Mark* and *Punctuation*.

In networking, telecommunications, and the Internet, *bang* is a term for an exclamation mark used in older *Email* addresses. See, for example, *Bang Path*.

Bang Path

In networking, a *UNIX*-esque *Email* address that uses exclamation marks (or *bang*s) to separate the sequence of user names and domains to arrive at the addressee.

Bank Note Paper

A high-quality, high-*cotton content* paper used for bank notes, stock and bond certificates, and other such financial uses. Such papers, it is hoped, have high degrees of *permanence*.

Banner

In typography, any large *headline*, especially one that spans the width of a page.

In networking, the term *banner* refers to a page printed at the beginning of a print job output from a network printer, containing job and user information.

Banyan VINES

In networking, a network operating system developed by Banyan Systems, based on a version of the *UNIX* System V operating system. VINES systems can support workstations running *DOS*, *Microsoft Windows*, *UNIX*, or the *Macintosh Operating System*. VINES itself is an acronym for *VIrtual NEtworking Software*.

Bar

In typography, an *arm* of a letter or other character connected to a stroke on both sides, as in the capital letter "H." See *Letter Elements*.

In packaging, the term *bar* also refers to one of the black solid lines comprising a *bar code*. See *Bar Code*.

Bar Chart

A type of *chart* or graph that represents variations of one set of values by means of rectangular bars whose respective heights are in proportion to the values they represent. Also known as a *bar graph*. See *Chart*.

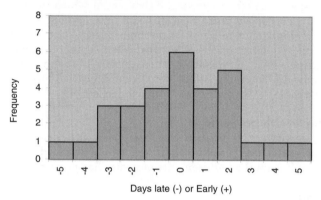

A typical bar chart.

Bar Code

In packaging and *optical character recognition (OCR)*, a series of black and white bars used to encode product and price information in a form that can quickly and accurately be read by a scanning device (called a *bar-code scanner*). Bar codes of various types are used in many different applications, from grocery and other retail pricing, to stock and inventory, to tracking shipments, to Department of Defense stock tracking.

The basic principle of the bar code is that the alternating white and black bars stand for certain binary digits which, when read by a computer, correspond to whatever the bar code symbol has been encoded to represent, such as product, inventory, and price information. Depending upon the system used to encode information, bar codes may either be discrete (in which each individual set of black bars in a larger code stand for individual characters) or continuous (in which the entire bar code encodes one set of data). There is also usually enough redundant information encoded in a bar code to ensure that data is interpreted correctly by the computer. Many bar code systems also allow the code to be scanned in any direction or orientation, thus expediting check-out procedures, for example. Despite the ubiquity and seeming homogeneity of the bar code, there are actually many different, mutually incompatible bar code systems in use.

Standard bar code.

Types of Bar Codes

UPC. Perhaps the most familiar bar code is the *Universal Product Code (UPC)*, adopted in 1973 by the grocery industry. Although originally devised as a means of expediting grocery store checkouts and stock management, the UPC symbol eventually made its way to many other forms of consumer goods, from pharmaceuticals to books to records (or CDs) to computer equipment and liquor. UPC symbols are designed to be printed on packages at a specific size. If the symbol, however, is too large for the package meant to contain it, the top may be cut off. Although in most cases a "shaved off" bar code can be scanned, it eliminates the number of orientations in which the scanner can read the symbol.

Code 39. Code 39 is the standard bar code for the United States Government, having been initially designed and adopted in 1975 by the Department of Defense to track parts and inventory supplied by contractors. Other industries—such as the automotive and health-care industries—have adopted Code 39. (The "39", by the way, refers to the fact that three of every nine bars will be wide ones.)

Two of Five. The Two of Five bar code was developed in 1968 and is used in warehouses for the tracking of inventory, in the airline industry for ticketing, baggage handling and cargo tracking, in photographic development for the tracking of jobs, and in other such in-house data processing. A revised and expanded version of the Two of Five bar code is used in shipping industries.

Codabar. Developed by a division of Pitney Bowes for retail price coding, it was supplanted by the UPC system. Codabar is now used primarily in libraries to keep track of which books have been checked out and in hospitals to code blood bags by blood type (and other information). Especially in this latter use, it is fortuitous that the Codabar system contains much redundant information to facilitate self-checking.

Plessey Code. Developed in the United Kingdom, the Plessey Code has limited use and is primarily used in the labeling of grocery store shelves.

Scanning Systems. There are a variety of scanning systems available for reading bar codes ranging from small, pen-like hand-held units, to the large, moving beam scanners built into grocery store checkout counters. (See *Bar-Code Scanner*.)

Bar-Code Printing

One crucial yet often overlooked aspect of printing on packaging is the accurate reproduction of the bar code. Inaccurately sized or printed bar codes will not scan properly (or at all), which can lead to a great deal of frustration, especially in crowded supermarkets, a situation which no doubt goes without saying. Since most packaging is printed by means of *flexography*, certain conditions in the prepress process need to be addressed. Since flexography prints from rubber or other types of elastomeric plates, there is some degree of image elongation which occurs when the plate is mounted to the plate cylinder. (Also, in the preparation of rubber flexo plates, there is also some degree of image reduction when the plate cools and hardens.) As a result, these dimensional changes need to be accounted for in the imaging of flexo plates. (See *Prepress: Printing Processes: Flexography*.)

Regardless of the printing process used (some materials containing bar codes may be printed by *gravure*, *offset lithography*, or *screen printing*), it is important that the film master from which the plates will be prepared be exposed within very strict tolerances. Special photocomposing devices are used to prepare master films of bar codes. Since every printing process has some degree of dimensional change from film master to press print, the film master must take into account these variations in size. Often, bar codes are printed separately at special bar-code printing sites onto labels, and these labels are then attached to the product they are meant to identify.

An alternative to including a bar code on a package is on-site bar-code printing. Often, the data to be encoded in a symbol cannot be predicted or "programmed" in advance, or needs to be changed or generated "on the fly." (For example, some stores use bar codes to identify lot number, weight, and other site-specific information.) As a result, bar codes can be printed on-site, using any configuration of computer printer, such as *laser printer*s, *dot-matrix printer*s, *inkjet printer*s, etc.

Bar Graph

Alternate term for *bar chart*. See *Bar Chart*.

Bar-Code Reader

See *Bar-Code Scanner*.

Bar-Code Scanner

A device used to read data encoded on a *bar code* and correlate it with the proper information stored in a computer. Bar codes and bar-code scanners are used in a variety of industrial, commercial, and consumer applications, but the most familiar bar code is the *Universal Product Code (UPC)* symbol found on just about every retail item someone is likely to purchase. (See *Bar Code: Universal Product Code*.)

Despite the wide variety of standardized bar codes in existence, all bar-code scanners essentially work according to the same principle: light—generated either by a laser, an LED, a lamp, or other source of illumination—is directed at the printed bar code, and reflected light is transferred back into the scanner optics, and the intensity of the reflected light is converted to an electrical signal. Since a bar code consists of alternating light and dark bars of varying thickness, the intensity of the light fluctuates as the light source moves across the bar code. Consequently, the electrical signal oscillates. These oscillations can be converted to digital information, as a microprocessor measures the duration of each electrical signal oscillation. The pattern of oscillations can then be correlated to the information stored in the computer. Although this principle underlies all types of bar-code scanners, they each differ in the means by which they scan the bar code.

Hand-Held Scanners. Hand-held bar-code scanners contain the light source and optics in a small, pen-like housing, which can be moved over the bar code at a constant speed. (These are often found in some retail stores, or are carried by shippers such as Federal Express.) The advantages to these devices are their portability and low cost. A disadvantage is that, unlike with larger scanners, there is a limited number of orientations which are readable to the device.

Fixed-Beam Scanners. These devices are larger than the held-held models (although there are smaller "pistol" configurations which are used in some stores) and use a non-moving beam of light to illuminate a large area in which the bar code to be read is placed. The code is focused into the device's optics, and the bars decoded. As a result of the optical configuration and the fixed beam, the distance between the device and the bar code needs to be very small, and there is little variation in orientation of the bar code allowable.

Moving-Beam Scanners. These are the devices most often found in supermarkets and other large retail outlets. The device moves the light beam back and forth in either a straight line, or in an X-shaped or star-shaped pattern. The advantage to the moving beam is that the bar code can be read regardless of the orientation it is in; backwards, forwards, upside-down, at an angle, etc. So long as the code faces the scanner, it can be read. In fact, in some newer holographic systems the bar code can be read even if it does not directly face the scanner; a three-dimensional scanning pattern is used to read a bar code on the side of a package. These latter devices are quite expensive, however.

Video-Image Scanners. A less costly alternative to moving-beam scanners is a video-image scanner, which uses a device analogous to a video camera (or, in other words, a linear photodiode array) to capture a video signal of the bar code to be read, which can then be decoded. Bar-code scanners are also known as bar-code readers.

Bare Cylinder Diameter

The diameter of a *flexographic* press *plate cylinder* before the plate is mounted.

Bareback Dampener

A *ductor roller* or *form roller* in a *conventional dampening system* on an offset press used without fabric or paper covers, allowing the *fountain solution* to transfer directly to its rubber-compound surface. Rollers that are run bareback respond more quickly to changes made to the amount of fountain solution sent to the plate. A *wetting agent* such as alcohol is needed to reduce the surface tension of the solution, allowing the fluid to form a continuous film more easily in the absence of an absorbent cover. (See *Dampening System*.)

Barium Sulfate
See *Blanc Fixe*.

Baronial Envelope
A type of square-shaped envelope, typically used for announcements, formal correspondence, and greeting cards.

Barrel
In packaging, a large container (usually made of wood) used to store and/or ship liquids. The wooden barrel, despite the antiquity of its design, is still the strongest known shipping vessel, thanks primarily to its use of the arch, which is in physics, engineering, and architecture, the strongest structure known. Its double-arch design, down its length and across its girth, imparts to the barrel its great strength.

Barrel Distortion
A distortion found on computer display monitors characterized by bowing vertical and/or horizontal lines.

Barrier Coat
In labelmaking, a *coating* applied to the surface of the *face material* to prevent the *migration* of the *adhesive* into the face material (and vice versa) and to enhance the *anchoring* of the adhesive. Also known as *primer*, *sealer coat*, and *tie coat*.

In *binding and finishing*, a *barrier coat* (or *barrier coating*) is used on food packaging to increase resistance to air, moisture, or other environmental conditions.

Barrier Polymer
Any of a variety of thermoplastic materials used in the packaging of foods, beverages, and other materials that require some degree of protection from environmental forces, such as water, oxygen, etc. Of particular importance is the ability to impede the penetration of oxygen. A polymer is described as a "barrier" when its oxygen permeability is less than [10 cm^3 • mil/100 in.^{2} • d • atm at 23°C.] Such a barrier will also impede the penetration of other gases (such as carbon dioxide) into the package, as well as other substances (such as odors) *out* of the package. Another consideration in the use of barrier polymers is the extent to which the packaging material will leech the flavor or odor of the material being packaged, as well as the extent to which the packaged material will absorb the flavor and odor of the packaging. Some commonly used barrier polymers are polyvinyl alcohol, polyacrylonitrile, ethylene–vinyl alcohol, PVCD homopolymer, *cellophane*, as well as various *polyvinyl chloride* and *polyethylene* formulations. Where once glass and metal were used as barriers in packaging, advances in polymeric formulations have replaced these materials in many applications. Even more recent advances in polymer chemistry

have resulted in packages which can be specifically formulated for certain materials.

Barrier Tape
A *pressure-sensitive label* on which diagonal red transparent stripes have been printed, for use on the rear of vehicles and street barriers as a safety or warning signal.

Barytes
An inorganic white compound used as a *pigment* in printing ink, typically as an *extender*, due to its transparent properties. Barytes, also called barite or barium sulfate (chemical formula $BaSO_4$), is a naturally occurring ore of barium. See also *Blanc Fixe*.

Base
In *screen printing*, a flat, solid surface on which the *substrate* is placed for printing.

Also in screen printing, the term *base* refers to an *extender pigment* or *transparent pigment*.

In printing ink manufacturing, *base* refers to an ink *vehicle* containing a dispersion of only one *pigment* in a high pigment-to-*binder* ratio, which is the mixture of vehicle, pigment, and binder that produces a printing ink with the desired end-use characteristics and properties.

The term *base* also refers to an alkaline substance, a material having a *pH* greater than 7. See *Alkali* and *pH*.

In mathematics, the term *base* refers to a reference value on which a numerical system is based. We are most familiar with a decimal—or "base 10"—system; most calculations in daily life are based on ten digits. In computing, the *binary* system is referred to as "base 2," as a computer can only recognize two separate digits, 0 and 1.

Base 2
Alternate term for *binary*. See *Binary*.

Base 8
Alternate term for *octal*. See *Octal*.

Base 10
Alternate term for *decimal*. See *Decimal*.

Base 16
Alternate term for *hexadecimal*. See *Hexadecimal*.

Base Address
In computing, a specific *address* which, when combined with a *relative address*, yields the *absolute address*. See *Address* and *Absolute Address*.

Base Alignment
In typography, the setting of a line of type so that all the characters appear to "sit" on the same *baseline*. Base alignment also refers to the ability of a typesetting device to mix *typeface*s and type sizes on the same line and still have the characters aligned on the baseline. Also known as *horizontal alignment*. See *Alignment*.

Baseband

In telecommunications and networking, a type of data communications comprising only one channel. With only one channel, no processing or modulation of the signal is required, allowing transmission and reception equipment to be simple and relatively inexpensive. Since all the devices in a baseband network are connected to the same channel, a network *protocol* is required to ensure that messages are sent and received correctly, also working to sort out the condition of several users sending messages simultaneously. Networks such as *Ethernet* and the older *ARCnet* are baseband networks, requiring network topologies such as *CSMA/CD* and *Token Ring*.

The alternative to a baseband network is a *broadband* network, which allows several signals to be sent along the network simultaneously, as more channels are utilized. A baseband network can simulate a broadband network by means of *multiplexing*. See also *Broadband*.

Baseband LAN

A *local area network (LAN)* utilizing *baseband* signaling. See *Local Area Network (LAN)* and *Baseband*.

Baseband Signaling

See *Baseband*.

Base Color

In *process color* printing, the first—or background—color printed, on top of which the other colors are printed.

Base Cylinder

Term for a *gravure cylinder* prior to electroplating copper to its surface. Also called a *cylinder base*. See *Gravure Cylinder*.

Base Flash

In *halftone* photography, a flash that produces the correct *shadow* dot sizes without *bump exposure*.

Base Image

Any image to which other images are added.

Baseline

An invisible horizontal line on which the feet of all characters on a line of type are set, used for proper *alignment* of type. Also known as a *z-line*. See *Alignment*.

In networking, a means of gauging the *throughput* and performance of a data communications network under what is considered to be its normal load.

Baseline Rule (BLR)

A short rule line, commonly only one *em* or *en* long, located on or just below the *baseline* of a line of type.

Baseline-to-Baseline (B/B)

In typography, the distance from the *baseline* of one line to the baseline of the next line, usually measured in points.

Base Material

Alternate term for *face material*. See *Face Material*.

Base Stock

Term for any paper to which a *coating* will be applied. Depending on the various properties desired for particular end uses, the base stock will vary in all those properties. It is necessary that the coating be compatible with these properties. It is also vital that the base stock have uniformity of *formation* and other surface properties to minimize deficiencies in the coating process. (See *Coating*.) The base stock is also called the *raw stock*, and *body stock*. The term *base stock* can also refer to the paper that will undergo any post-forming process, such as laminating, embossing, etc.

BASIC

Acronym for *Beginner's All-purpose Symbolic Instruction Code*, a popular algebraic computer programming language utilizing a small set of commands and simple statements. BASIC is widely used in personal computers.

Basic

Alternate term for *alkaline*, descriptive of a solution or material having a high *pH*. See *Alkali* and *pH*.

Basic Dye

A dye or colorant which is not dispersed in an ink *vehicle* or other type of fluid medium.

Basic Input/Output System (BIOS)

In computing, the part of an *operating system* responsible for linking computer hardware devices to software.

Basic Rate Interface (BRI)

One of two types of *ISDN* connections comprising two *B-channel*s and one *D-channel*. See also *Primary Rate Interface (PRI)*. See *ISDN*.

The baseline, an invisible set of lines, is shown here in a page-layout program.

Basic Sheet Size

Alternate term for *basic size*. See *Basic Size*.

Basic Size

Also called *basic sheet size*, the size of a sheet of a particular grade of paper at which its *basis weight* is determined. The basic size varies according to paper grade: for *book paper* it is 25×38 in., for *bond paper* it is 17×22 in., for *cover paper* it is 20×26 in., for *bristol paper* it is 22½×28½ in., for *index paper* it is 25½×30½ in., and for *tag paper* it is 24×36 in. In the metric system, used primarily outside the United States, the term *grammage* is used instead of basis weight. Grammage is simply the weight of the paper in grams per square meters of area. Grammage is independent of basic size, but there are also basic sizes in the metric system. (See *A Series*, *B Series*, and *Basis Weight*.)

Basic Telecommunications Access Method (BTAM)

In telecommunications, a means of accessing a network that allows remote devices to read and/or write data to and from each other.

Basis Weight

The weight (in pounds) of a *ream* (500 sheets) of paper cut to the *basic size* for a particular *grade* of paper. The basic size of *book paper* is 25×38 in. If 500 sheets weighs 70 pounds, then the basis weight is 70 pounds. Paper is commonly identified using basis weight: 20-lb. *bond paper*, 80-pound *coated paper*, and so on. Size-and-weight tables, however, frequently give basis weight per thousand sheets. For example, a 25×38-in. 70-lb. book paper could be listed as "25×38—140M." The "M" signifies one thousand sheets, so to use the more conventional basis weight notation, the 140 should be halved, and it is then found that the basis weight (per 500 sheets) is 70 lb. The basic size is not the same for all paper grades. Paperboards are commonly signified as pounds per 1,000 square feet.

Basis weight is occasionally called *substance*, or *substance number*. A 20-pound bond paper would then be "substance 20." The *nominal weight* is the basis weight specified when ordering paper, but can differ—usually within certain built-in and acceptable tolerances—from the basis weight of the paper actually delivered due to a host of papermaking variations, including *moisture content*. The *actual basis weight*, or the weight measured under prevailing environmental conditions, may differ from the specified basis weight due to variations in the papermaking process and the effect of moisture content on paper weight.

In the metric system, used primarily outside the United States, basis weight is referred to as *grammage* and is given in grams per square meter. Grammage exists independently of basic size. The metric system does utilize a basic size, which is called the *A series*. There is also a *B series* of intermediate sizes.

The basis weight of a paper is determined by weighing a sample cut to the basic size on a "basis weight scale" that is designed to determine the weight of 500 sheets of the paper being measured. Basis weight strongly influences the strength properties of a paper, as well as such other properties as thickness, opacity, and runnability. (See *Basic Size*, *Grammage*, *A Series* and *B Series*.) (See also *Paper and Papermaking: Paper Properties*.)

Baskerville, John

John Baskerville (1706–1775) was an English writing master who became a type designer and printer. He was born in Worcestershire, England, and began engraving tombstones and working as a calligrapher at the age of 17. In 1740 he entered the japanning trade in Birmingham, and built up a considerable fortune in less than a decade. His beautiful round roman typeface, modeled on his earlier penmanship, had an important influence on type design.

Baskerville took up printing and typefounding as a hobby, seeking to improve upon the typefaces of William Caslon. His first work, "Virgil," was published in 1757, in royal quarto (12½×10 in.) Later books include Horace, and a series of classical editions in quarto including the works of Lucretius, Terence, and Catullus. His typeface designs were delicate, with contrast in stroke widths, requiring advances in printing technology which he also pioneered. In particular, he is credited with the technique of "sock"—pressing the wet printed sheets between copper plates, smoothing the paper and drying the ink. His work was known for its rather plain, unornamented style. His typefaces are considered a transition between the old style type (Caslon) and the modern type style exemplified by Bodoni.

Baskerville's contributions include the use of woven paper, invention of rich inks that were truly black, generous space between lines, and wide letterspacing in display lines. He also introduced glossy paper instead of the rough, antique laid paper of the time. He was printer to Cambridge University from 1758 to 1768. His folio Bible of 1763 ranks as the finest example of printing in the 18th century.

BASR

Abbreviation for *buffered automatic send/receive*. See *Automatic Send and Receive (ASR)*.

Bastard Copy

In typesetting, any copy for which the *type specifications* vary from those that are typically used, such as type to be set in an unusual width or *point size*.

Bastard Progs

A set of *progressive proof*s sequentially showing every possible *four-color process* color combination.

Bastard Size

Paper that is not of a *standard size*.

Bastard Title

In *book typography* and production, a *half-title* page that is the first page of the book, preceding the *title page*. Also known as a *false title*. See *Book Typography*.

Batch

Descriptive of any processing or manufacturing operation that handles a group (or "batch") of elements at one time.

Batch Composition

A type of electronic page layout that does not allow the user to immediately view the results of changes made to the content or layout of a page (or pages), such viewing only being possible upon output. Batch composition exists in contrast to *interactive composition*.

Batch Delivery

A delivery unit used in a *collating* device that cuts web-assembled sets into the proper units.

Batch File

In computing, a file containing several (or a "batch" of) commands to be executed by the *operating system*. In *batch processing* (or the reading of a batch file by an operating system), all the instructions in the file are executed from beginning to end with no input from the user unless problems arise, in contrast to *interactive processing* in which the user is prompted for a new command after the execution of each instruction. Startup files—such as the *AUTOEXEC.BAT* file used by *DOS*—are often batch files.

Batch Mode

Term for a type of computing in which applications are run on a computer one at a time, as opposed to *multitasking*.

Batch Pagination

In typesetting, a variety of *automatic pagination*—or the assigning of page numbers to pages—performed by the typesetting device in the "background" without operator interaction, in contrast to *interactive pagination*. See *Pagination*.

Batch Process

In any manufacturing operation, the production of a single, discrete quantity of a material at one time, in contrast to a *continuous process*.

Batch Processing

In computing, one of two basic means by which a computer reads and executes instructions. A list of different commands stored in a *batch file* are executed nonstop without user interaction until an *end-of-file* command is reached. See *Batch File*. In contrast is *interactive processing*, in which commands are executed one at a time by means of prompts or dialog boxes.

In manufacturing operations, *batch processing* refers to the production of discrete quantities of a material (such as an ink) in contrast to a *continuous process*.

Batch Sample

In manufacturing, a random sampling of purportedly identical units. This sample is tested to ensure that all batches of the material produced are similar in their properties. Batch sampling is a means of ensuring batch consistency.

Battered

In typography, any type—on a *mechanical*, on a *proof*, or on a final press print—that appears damaged or worn.

Battery Indicator

An icon usually found on the screen of a portable computer which indicates how much charge remains in the battery. Usually, if the battery indicator falls beyond a certain level without any battery recharging, the user is prompted with error messages. Failure to heed both the battery indicator and the error messages can result in lost data and/or computer damage.

Baud

In telecommunications, a measure of the rate of data transmission between computers or over telephone lines. Essentially, a baud is equal to the number of "signal events" per second. In telegraphy (from whence the term originated), one baud equals one half-dot cycle per second. In modern telecommunications via modem, baud is used interchangeably with *bits per second (bps)*, which isn't entirely accurate. At low modem speeds (300 baud or less), one baud does indeed equal one bit per second. At higher speeds, however, one baud is equal to two or more bits per second. A common baud rate as of this writing is 19,200, but that will likely be deemed too slow in a very short period of time. (See also *Bits Per Second (bps)*.)

The term, *baud* itself comes from Emile Baudot, a French telegraph engineer who devised a code for rapid data transmission. (See *Baudot Code*.)

Baudot Code

In telecommunications, a code designed for the transmission of data in which one character is represented by five *bit*s. Baudot code is named for Emile Baudot, a French telegraphic engineer. See also *Baud*.

Bayonet

Alternate term for *saddle bar*. See *Saddle Bar*.

In networking and telecommunications, a type of connector used to link devices to a network or to connect video equipment. See *BNC*.

Bayonet-Neil-Concelman

See *BNC*.

BBS

Abbreviation of *bulletin board service*. See *bulletin board*.

BCC

Abbreviation for *block check character*. See *Block Check Character*.

bcc

Abbreviation for **blind carbon copy**, a somewhat anachronistic term used in **Email** to refer to recipients of a message which are not to be listed anywhere on the message (usually so as to not let the primary recipient of a message know to whom it has also been sent). The term derives from paper-based letter-writing. See also **cc**.

BCD

Abbreviation for **binary coded decimal**. See **Binary Coded Decimal**.

B-Channel

In telecommunications, a 64-**kilobit per second** ISDN channel used for all data transmissions once an **ISDN** connection has been established between two users. See **ISDN**.

BCN 1

In video production, a European standard videotape size in which the tape is one inch wide.

BCP

Abbreviation for **Bézier control point**. See **Bézier Control Point (BCP)**.

Beaconing

In networking, especially by means of a **Token Ring** network, the process of informing connected nodes that **token passing** has been halted due to an error condition.

Beak

In typography, the outer part of an **arm** or **serif** as in the capital letters "E" and "F." See **Letter Elements**.

Beam Position

On a **cathode-ray tube**, the location at any given moment of the position of an electron beam.

Beam Splitter

An optical device used to split a beam of light into two or more separate beams and redirect them. For example, a beam splitter in a color **scanner** divides the input into **red**, **green**, **and blue** beams and points each at a **photomultiplier tube**. An output beam splitter can divide a light beam as many as ten times, one to each **modulator**.

Beam Spot Size

On a **cathode-ray tube**, the diameter of the spot of illumination on the screen produced by the electron beam.

Bearer

A metal ring attached to both ends of a **plate cylinder**, **blanket cylinder** and **impression cylinder** in the printing unit of an offset printing press. On the plate and blanket cylinders, the diameter of the bearers is the true diameter of the cylinder, the main body of the cylinder being **undercut**, or possessing a shorter diameter than the

bearers, so as to allow varying degrees of cylinder **packing**. In some presses (called **bearer-contact press**es), the bearers of the plate and blanket cylinders are in direct contact with each other, the advantages being easy alignment of the cylinders and reduced gear damage. In other presses (called **non-bearer-contact press**es), the bearers are not in contact, but the manufacturer's recommended gap between plate and blanket cylinder bearers can be used to determine proper cylinder settings. (See **Plate Cylinder** and **Blanket Cylinder**.) On the impression cylinder, the bearers are undercut; the body of the cylinder is the essential measure of the cylinder diameter. (See **Impression Cylinder**.) The diameter of cylinder bearers is also equal to the diameter of the gears running the cylinder.

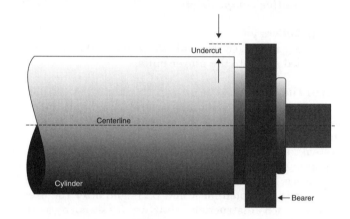

Press cylinder bearer and undercut.

Bearer-Contact Press

A type of printing press used in **offset lithography** in which the blanket and plate cylinder **bearer**s (metal rings located at each end of each cylinder body, with diameters greater than the diameter of the cylinder body) are in tight contact with each other while the press is in operation. Such presses reduce gear wear, as the pressure of the cylinders falls on the bearers rather than the gears. Proper cylinder setting and **packing** considerations vary between bearer-contact presses and **non-bearer-contact press**es. See **Bearer**, **Plate Cylinder**, **Blanket Cylinder**, and **Packing**.

Beater

Also called a refiner, a beater is an older, mechanical refining device for paper **pulp**. It is an oval-shaped tank containing metal bars mounted on a rotating beater roll in the center of the tank and stationary metal bars mounted on a bedplate attached to the wall of the tank. The fibers, suspended in a water **slurry**, are circulated through the tank and drawn between the two sets of bars. The resulting abrasion alters the fibrous structure make them suitable for forming into a paper **web**. This process, known as **beating** or **refining**, is the most crucial stage of the papermaking process.

Various *fillers*, *coatings*, or *sizing* can also be added to the pulp fibers at this point, as can dyes used to color the paper. (Paper which has had sizing added during refining is known as *beater-sized*, while paper that has had colorant added during refining is known as *beater-dyed*.) The fibers are pumped from the beater to a *conical refiner*—also called a *jordan*—for further beating.

Newer pulp refining methods employ continuous *disk refiners* in the place of the beater system. (See *Refining* and *Paper and Papermaking: Papermaking*.)

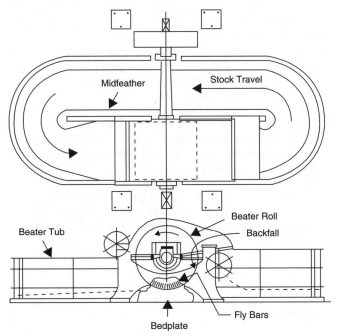

Papermaking machine's beater.

Beater-Dyed

A type of colored or tinted paper in which the dye or colorant was added to the papermaking *furnish* in the *beater* during the *refining* stage. See *Beater*.

Beater-Sized

Term for paper or pulp to which *sizing* has been added to the papermaking *furnish* during *refining*. See *Beater*.

Beating

An alternate term for the *refining* of paper *pulp*, particularly when performed in a *beater*. (See *Refining*.)

Bed

In *binding and finishing*, the flat metal surface on a *guillotine cutter* on which the paper (or other material) to be cut is placed. See *Guillotine Cutter*.

Bed Knife

On a *sheeter*, a stationary knife held firmly into position on the frame of the sheeter.

Beginner's All-Purpose Symbolic Instruction Code

See *BASIC*.

Bekk Smoothness Tester

A type of *air leak tester*, an instrument used to determine the *smoothness* of a paper surface. Air at a specified pressure is leaked between a smooth glass surface and a paper sample; the time (in seconds) for a fixed volume of air to seep between these surfaces is the "Bekk smoothness." See also *Smoothness*.

Bell Communications Standards

In telecommunications, a set of data communications standards developed in the 1980s by AT&T for *modem* manufacturing. Generally, however, these standards have been supplanted by *CCITT* standards.

Belt Press

A type of printing press used in the *letterpress* printing of books that performs two-sided printing as well as cutting, folding, and binding in one continuous pass. See *Letterpress: Belt Press*.

Belt Printer

Alternate term for a *band printer*. See *Band Printer*.

Benchmark

A set of quantifiable and measurable standards used in testing computer hardware or software used to ensure that the material being tested performs according to specifications. A specific task used to gauge the performance of a piece of hardware or software in relation to another piece of hardware or software is called a *benchmark problem*. A program used for such a purpose is known as a *benchmark program*.

Benday

A pattern of dots or lines used to mechanically effect shades and tones in line art and line plates. See *Benday Process*. Also known as as *Ben Day*.

Benday Process

A means of effecting flat tones or shades on a line drawing or line plate by means of dot or line patterns or a screen. Originally, *benday process* referred to the process used by its inventor, Benjamin Day. The term is now used to refer to any such process; however, it is an obsolete process, having been replaced by photographic *screen tint*s.

Bender

Paperboard of sufficient strength that it can be creased, folded, and/or scored without breaking or tearing.

Bendtsen Smoothness Tester

A variety of *air leak tester*, an instrument used to determine the *smoothness* of a paper surface. Air at a specified pressure is pumped between the device's gauge head and the surface of the paper sample; the rate at which the air flows between the two surfaces being a measure of the paper's smoothness. See also **Smoothness**.

Benton, Linn Boyd

While typesetting and printing speeds increased phenomenally, so did the speed of punchcutting. In 1885, Linn Boyd Benton (then of Benton, Waldo & Company, Milwaukee) invented a pantographic device that automated the previously painstaking process of creating punches.

Linn Boyd Benton (1844–1932) invented the enabling technology for mechanized typesetting. His 1882 patent was a multiple mold for casting leads and slugs. He began to work on a typesetting machine with automatic justification. He devised a system, based on his self-spacing type," that shortened the time required for justification by reducing the number of character widths in a font of type. Printing type after that was cast to pre-determined widths. By 1884 the foundry was using the first version of a pantograph machine he invented for engraving steel punches. A patent for the third version came in 1885.

As his son Morris was entering Cornell in 1892, 23 American type foundries, including the Benton firm, formed the American Type Founders Company. Boyd moved to New York where the new company had its offices. Morris Fuller Benton helped his father to further develop the punch and matrix-engraving machines, and become ATF's chief type designer in 1900. When Boyd was 86 years old, he received a patent for an improvement in the larger printing types used for newspaper headings. His inventions revolutionized the typefounding art and craft, and placed the ATF in a position of leadership. Morris Benton remained at ATF for another five years after his father's death, but it was a difficult period for the company. Profits had begun to decline, and the 1930s brought a brush with bankruptcy. In 1937, Morris Benton retired from ATF.

A step in type production was to make the characters an appropriate size for printing. Each drawing for a typeface was placed in a special delineating machine invented by Linn Benton—a refined pantograph with a microscope attachment that enabled the operator to enlarge or reduce a single character accurately. Benton's patent application for the machine was at first rejected by the Patent Office on the grounds that it described a mechanical impossibility. The crosshairs of a microscope were focused on the outline of the character being traced. Then the operator followed the outline of the design by moving the pencil holder and, in so doing, traced an enlarged outline of the character.

The next step was to create a pattern plate for each character. These were made either in wax and then electrotyped, or directly in metal, depending on whether a punch or a matrix was required. Another Linn Benton pantograph machine was used to make the pattern plates for matrix engraving. Matrices of all the regular type sizes could be cut from these pattern plates.

In Milwaukee, Benton had invented a pantographic machine for his type foundry. The matrix engraver was an adaptation of the punchcutting machine and was developed in the early 1900s when ATF decided that engraving directly into a matrix blank was more practical than cutting a punch. Matrices could be cut for different point sizes of a type design simply by adjusting the reproduction ratio between the pattern and the cutting tool. Allowable tolerance in the construction of this head was within 0.0002 in. The Benton matrix engraver could accurately reproduce the image on the pattern plate in any type size and was also capable of altering that image, deviating from exactly proportional reproductions as the operator adjusted the machine capable of infinitesimal gradations in all directions. It could be adjusted to compensate for the optical variables that occur when letter sizes change.

D. B. Updike wrote:

[A] design for a type alphabet that may be entirely successful for the size for which it is drawn, cannot be successfully applied to all other sizes of the same series. Each size is a law unto itself, and is often bettered by modifications in the original design . . . and the first types produced by punchcutting machines did seem to show a certain rigidity from the point of view of design. That there has been an improvement of late in type cut by machine is undeniable, and yet there has been practically no change in its mechanism. This improvement, I learn, has come to pass through a more sympathetic and subtle manipulation of the machine itself, and by modifications of rules by the eye of the workman who operates it.

Morris Benton used cutting slips to make certain that engraving machine operators consistently adjusted the machine for every point size. Linn Benton said "The adjustments are such that the operator is enabled to engrave the letter proportionately more extended or condensed, and lighter or heavier in face, than the pattern. Only one size of a series is cut in absolutely exact proportion to the patterns."

His machine could scale a drawing to the required size, as well as compress or expand the characters, and vary the weight slightly to compensate for the larger or smaller size—this last being a crude form of the "optical scaling" done by skilled typographers making versions of the same font for different sizes. In optical scaling, the thickest strokes retain the same relative thickness at any size; the thinnest strokes are not simply scaled up or down with the rest of the type, but made thicker at small sizes and thinner at large display sizes, so as to provide the best compromise between art and readability. Only the 36-point size of a typeface was cut exactly proportional to the pattern plate. All other sizes were derived from this "master" size. Going down in size, the face was actually extended in width but not in height and above 36-point, the letters were condensed relative to the standard. Each size of ATF's American Caslon, in sizes from 6 to 48 point, was proportional to the pattern plate. The Stempel foundry used a Benton matrix engraver with three sets of patterns for each typeface. Adjustments on the machine were only used to widen characters in the very smallest point sizes. The unfinished matrix went to a fitter, who made final adjustments on Benton's matrix fitting machine. The matrix as delivered from the Benton engraving machine required very precise trimming in order to be absolutely straight and on the proper baseline. ATF's type was then cast from a mixture of tin, antimony, lead, and a small amount of copper.

Benzidine Yellow

An organic dyestuff, derived from nitrobenzene, used as a strong yellow *toner* in *screen printing* and other inks.

Benzimidazolone Brown HFR

An *organic color pigment* used in printing inks. Benzimidazolone brown is a transparent brown possessing high *lightfastness* and chemical resistance. They are used effectively on foil and film *substrate*s. (See also *Organic Color Pigments*.) Also known as *Fast Brown HFR* (*CI Pigment Brown 25 No. 12510.*)

Benzimidazolone Carmines and Reds

A variety of *organic color pigments* used in inks. *Benzimidazolone Carmine HF 3C* is a bright, transparent bluish red possessing high *lightfastness* and resistance to acids, alkalis, soap, and heat. It is widely used in packaging, metal decoration, and other applications where its high expense is warranted. (See also *Organic Color Pigments*.)

(*CI Pigment Red 176 No. 12515.*)

Benzimidazolone Carmine HF4C is a high quality, expensive red pigment, clean in color and highly resistant to chemicals and heat, although it is not particularly lightfast. It is occasionally used as magenta in *process color* printing, but only when the expense is warranted.

(*CI Pigment Red 185 No. 12516.*)

Benzimidazolone Red HF2B is a bright, transparent medium red with moderate heat and light resistance. It also possesses the chemical resistance properties of other Benzimidazolones. It is used in liquid inks for package printing and for metal decorating.

(*CI Pigment Red 208 No. 12514.*)

Benzimidazalone Bordeaux HF 3R is a bright violet transparent red possessing high resistance to most chemical substances, save for some organic solvents. It is highly heat resistant, but not particularly lightfast. It is used primarily for liquid packaging inks and metal decorating.

(*CI Pigment Violet 32 No. 12517.*)

Benzimidazolone Orange HL

An *organic color pigment* used in printing inks. Benzimidazolone Orange HL is a dull, reddish orange possessing high *lightfastness* and heat resistance. It can also withstand exposure to many solvents used in printing inks, but

is soluble in some organic solvents. It is an expensive pigment, and is only used when the application warrants the additional expense. (See also *Organic Color Pigments*.)

(*CI Pigment Orange 36 No. 11780.*)

Benzol

A benzene *solvent*, not widely used due to its toxicity.

BER

Abbreviation for *bit error rate*. See *Bit Error Rate*.

Berkeley Software Distribution UNIX

In computing, a derivative of the *UNIX* operating system developed at the University of California, Berkeley, which is distinguished from other, earlier versions of UNIX by support for *virtual memory*, networking ability, support for additional peripheral devices, and enhanced file system and security enhancements. Often referred to as *Berkeley UNIX* and *BSD UNIX*.

Bernoulli

In computing, a brand of removable magnetic data storage cartridge manufactured by Iomega. It was so-named due to its "basis" on the Bernoulli equation, formulated by Swiss mathematician physicist Daniel Bernoulli, a fundamental equation in fluid dynamics (and applied to aerodynamics). In Bernoulli's equation, the velocity of a fluid (such as air) at a given point on a body's surface is related to the pressure exerted on that body. If the speed of the airflow is greater over the upper than over the lower surface of a body (as with a wing-shaped body), the pressure on the bottom surface will be greater than that on the top surface, and the body will rise. This is known as "lift." In the Bernoulli cartridge drive, the speed at which the disk rotates produces a similar pressure differential, allowing the top surface to rise toward the *read/write head*. The movement of air also prevented the disk surface from actually touching the read/write head (storage and retrieval of data not requiring actual physical contact between disk surface and read/write head), thus preventing damage to the disk surface. Storage capacities of Bernoulli cartridges ranged from several to several hundred *megabyte*s.

Iomega has largely discontinued the Bernoulli cartridge in favor of the less expensive and more popular Zip and Jaz cartridges.

BERT

Abbreviation for *block error rate test*. See *Block Error Rate Test*.

Beta

Abbreviation of *Betamax*, an obsolete home videotape format. See *Betamax.*

The term *beta* also refers to the condition that software or hardware is in during a *beta test*; i.e., probably containing *bug*s or other *glitch*es. See *Beta Test*.

Beta Release
See *Beta Test*.

Beta Site
A test site for an as-yet-unreleased software program or system. See *Beta Test*.

Beta Test
The first non-in-house trial of computer software or hardware, conducted among general computer users under normal working conditions as a means of detecting any *bug*s or other problems with the product, enabling their correction prior to general release. A beta test is in contrast to an *alpha test*. See also *Alpha Test*. The version of a program used in a beta test is known as a *beta release*.

Betacam
In video production, the brand name of Sony's broadcast-quality video recording and playback system, utilizing half-inch wide tape. Betacam is used widely in electronic news gathering, as the camera and recorder are housed in one lightweight unit. A higher-quality improvement on Betacam is *Betacam SP*.

Betacam SP
In video production, a high-quality brand of video recording and playback system developed by Sony. Using the same size videotape (½-in. wide) as *Betacam*, Betacam SP captures higher-quality video. This system can also capture digital PCM-sound, and the system also includes digital input and output ports. Still working with *component analog video*, it is likely to be able to record *digital component video* in the near future.

Betamax
In video, the first home videotape format. Invented by Sony, Beta tapes were ½ inch wide and incompatible with the 1-inch VHS tapes which, although of inferior quality, became the more popular. *Betamax*, when referred to at all, is commonly abbreviated *Beta*.

Between-Set Perforations
In a set of continuous forms, a series of *perforation*s, or small cuts, across a page, allowing individual forms to be separated from each other.

Bevel
An incline of any surface at an angle ≤ 90°.

Bevel Join
In computer graphics, a point of intersection between two strokes in which the join has been flattened out, as on the apexes of some typefaces, such as the capital letter "A" in Helvetica:

See also *Miter Join*.

Bézier Control Point (BCP)
In computer graphics, one of two points on a *vector*-based graphic which guide a *Bézier curve*. See *Bézier Curve*.

Bézier Curve
In computer graphics, a smooth, mathematically defined curve or line defined by two endpoints (called *anchor point*s) and two control points (called *Bézier control point*s) in a region adjacent to the curve. Since the Bézier curves are defined mathematically, rather than as *bitmap*s, it is possible to print illustrations composed of them at as high a resolution as the output device is capable of. They are also processed by the computer much more rapidly. Bézier curves are used to create graphics in *CAD* programs, as well as *vector*-based illustration programs such as Adobe Illustrator. The concept of the Bézier curve was invented by Paul Bézier to aid in the design of Renault automobiles. "Bézier" is pronounced "BEH-zee-ay." (See also *Encapsulated PostScript* [*EPS*].)

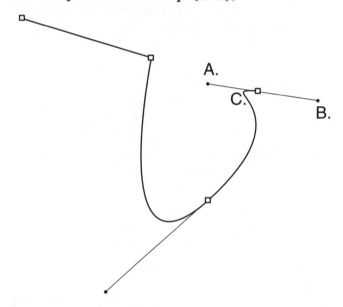

Bézier curve and control points. To change the shape of the curve at point C, the control points (A and B) can be moved.

BFMA
Abbreviation for the *Business Forms Management Association*. See *Business Forms Management Association*.

BGP
Abbreviation for *Border Gateway Protocol*. See *Border Gateway Protocol (BGP)*.

Bi-Cutter
A small, two-bladed knife used for cutting parallel lines in the preparation of *screen printing* stencils.

BIB
Abbreviation for *bag-in-box*, a type of packaging. See *Bag-In-Box (BIB)*.

Bible

The sacred scriptures of the religions of Judaism and Christianity. The Jewish Bible includes only the books of the Old Testament. The Christian Bible consists of the Old Testament and the New Testament, with the Roman Catholic version of the Old Testament slightly larger because of acceptance of certain books and parts of books not accepted by Protestants. Arrangement of the Jewish and Christian canons differ considerably but the Protestant and Roman Catholic arrangements are closely matched.

Jewish scholars have divided scriptures into: Torah ("Law"), or Pentateuch; Nevi`im ("Prophets"); and Ketuvim ("Writings"), or Hagiographa. The Pentateuch and the book of Joshua account how Israel became a nation and possessed the Promised Land. "Prophets" continues the story, describing the establishment of the monarchy and presenting the messages of the prophets. "Writings" speculate on good and evil, include poetical and historical works.

The New Testament is a collection of books, including early Christian literature. The four Gospels deal with the life and the teachings of Jesus as he was remembered. The book of Acts carries the story of Christianity from the Resurrection to the end of the career of Paul. The Letters, or Epistles, are correspondence by leaders of the early Christian church, primarily Paul, the apostle. The book of Revelation (Apocalypse) is typical of such literature in the early Christian movement.

Early translations

The Jewish Bible, or Old Testament, was written in Hebrew, with some elements in Aramaic. The New Testament books were probably written in Greek, though some may have been first written in Aramaic. When the Persian Empire controlled the Mediterranean basin, Aramaic became the esperanto of the region, and it became necessary for the Jewish community to have the Torah, or Pentateuch, translated into a common language. The resulting Targums (Aramaic for "translator") survived after original Hebrew scrolls had been lost. In the mid-3rd century BC, Greek was the ruling language, and Jewish scholars translated the Hebrew canon again, a version called the Septuagint. The spread of Christianity required translations into Coptic, Ethiopian, Gothic, and Latin. St. Jerome in about 400 AD translated a Latin version based on the Septuagint, and this version, the Vulgate, despite the errors of copyists, became the standard of Christianity for a thousand years.

Writings in the Old Testament are mostly anonymous, and it is not known whether they were compiled by individuals or groups. References to God are the primary means of distinguishing chronology of the text: the Yahwist, or J, because it used the name of the Lord in Hebrew transliterated into English as YHWH (J from the German: JHVH) and spoken as Yahweh; the Elohist, or E, by its reference to the Lord as Elohim; the Deuteronomist, or D, with its distinctive vocabulary; and the Priestly, or P, which contains ritual instructions. Most of the Old Testament authors are anonymous but New Testament sources are known from manuscripts in Greek dating from the 2nd–15th centuries AD, referred to as "witnesses."

The King James Version

Queen Elizabeth imposed a high degree of uniformity upon the church and it was requested that the English Bible be revised because existing translations were corrupt and did not match the "original." By 1604, King James I had approved a list of 54 revisers, organized into six companies, two each working at Westminster, Oxford, and Cambridge. The Bible was published in 1611, said to be more faithful to original languages, imitating the rhythm and style of the Hebrew of the Old Testament. Two editions were printed,

A reproduction of part of the Bible of Thirty-six Lines.

the "He" and "She" Bibles, because of the variant "he" and "she" in the final part of chapter 3, verse 15 of Ruth: "and he went into the city." Both printings contained errors. The Wicked Bible of 1631 comes from the omission of "not" in chapter 20 verse 14 of Exodus, "Thou shalt commit adultery," for which the printers were fined, not executed; the "Vinegar Bible" of 1717 stems from a misprinting of "vineyard" in the heading of Luke, chapter 20.

The King James Version contained weaknesses independent of typographical errors. The translators' understanding of the Hebrew tense system was often limited so that their version contains inaccurate renderings. The Greek text of the New Testament used as their base was a poor one and early Greek codices were not available. The Convocation of Canterbury in 1870 approved the revision of the King James Version. Scholars from the major Christian denominations, except the Roman Catholics (who declined to participate) were included. Parallel companies worked in the United States and England. The New Testament was published in 1881 and over 30,000 changes were made, of which 5,000 represented differences in the Greek text used as the basis of the King James Version.

The American Standard Version

In 1900 the American edition of the New Testament was produced. The American Standard Version was sensitive to the American public, produced in reaction to individual and unofficial translations into modern speech from 1885 on. The Greek of the New Testament used the common nonliterary language spoken throughout the Roman Empire when Christianity was in its formative stage. Classical, Hebraic, and theological scholarship in the United States led to a desire to produce a native American version of the English Bible. In 1928 the copyright of the American Standard Version was acquired by the International Council of Religious Education—ownership by churches representing 40 major denominations in the United States and Canada. A committee recommended a thorough revision, and in 1937 it was authorized and in 1946 the revision of the New Testament was printed. Six years later the complete Revised Standard Version (RSV) was published, the first to make use of the Dead Sea Scroll of Isaiah.

Other Bibles

Though English-speaking Jews generally utilized the King James Version and the Revised Version, the English versions contained departures from the traditional Hebrew text with Christological interpretations and renderings in the legal portions of the Pentateuch, which frequently diverged from traditional Jewish scholarship. Until 1917 Jewish translations were individual efforts. In 1892, the Jewish Publication Society of America made the first translation representing Jewish learning by English-speaking Jews and it retained Elizabethan diction. A committee of translators was established composed of professional bibli-

cal and Semitic scholars and rabbis in 1955 and the Pentateuch was issued in 1962.

The Rheims-Douay English translation of the Latin Vulgate Bible produced by Roman Catholic scholars in exile from England at the English College in Douai (now part of France). The New Testament translation was published in 1582 at Rheims. The Old Testament was not published until 1609–10, in Douai. Former Oxford men who provided the Old Testament annotations was instrumental in its production. Roman Catholic practice had restricted personal use of the Bible in the Latin Vulgate to the clergy.

Representatives of the major Protestant churches of the British Isles, with Roman Catholics as observers, published their version in 1961 and a second edition in 1970. This New English Bible was a commercial success and differed from the English Bible in that it was not a revision but a completely fresh version from the original languages. It abandoned biblical English and, except for "thou" and "thy" in addressing God rendered the original into a contemporary English idiom.

A modern Catholic translation was initiated by the Confraternity of Christian Doctrine in 1936. A New Testament version of the Latin Clementine Vulgate (1941) was a translation into simple English. Both Testaments were retranslated into modern English from the Hebrew and Greek originals. The resultant Confraternity Version (1952–61) was later issued as the New American Bible (1970). Another modern version, more colloquial, was the Jerusalem Bible (1966), translated from the French Catholic Bible de Jérusalem in 1961.

Bible Paper
Alternate term for *lightweight paper*, primarily due to its use in bibles. See *Lightweight Paper*.

Bibliographic
Descriptive of a *bibliography*. See *Bibliography*.

Bibliographic Database
A *database* consisting of references to published works such as newspapers, magazines and other periodicals, as well as books, patent documents, contracts, video and audio transcripts, or other such material.

Bibliographic Record
In a *bibliographic database*, a set of data *field*s considered as a single logical entity.

Bibliographic Reference
Data required for the complete and/or unique identification of a source of information.

Bibliography
A portion of the *back matter* of a book providing a list of books (including author, title, publisher, and year of publication) or other publications that the author has consulted while writing a book, or which will provide supplementary

material to readers interested in the subject at hand. See ***Book Typography***.

Bichromate

Shorthand term for ***ammonium bichromate*** or ***potassium bichromate*** salts used to render ***screen printing*** stencils photosensitive.

Bichromate Direct Emulsion

One of several types of ***emulsion*** used on ***screen printing*** stencils produced by the ***direct process***. The surface of these emulsions has been rendered photosensitive by application of one of the two primary ***bichromate*** salts. See ***Photostencil: Direct Process***.

Bid

In printing, a quote for a print job submitted by a printer to a client. The client typically solicits bids from several printers and chooses from among the lowest. However, there are usually other criteria involved in accepting a printer's bid, and selecting the cheapest may not always be the best idea. Other factors involved include the turnaround time, as well as the quality of the printing.

In networking, the term *bid* refers to the means by which terminals gain access to and messages get transmitted across a ***contention network***.

Bidirectional Interface

A connection between two pieces of equipment (such as a computer and a peripheral device) in which data can be transmitted in both directions. In imaging, a bidirectional interface is used to connect a scanner to a ***color electronic prepress system (CEPS)*** to allow the scanner to both transmit data into the system and to output film.

Bidirectional Printing

A type of computer printer that prints one line from left to right, then the following line from right to left. Such printing is faster than printing in one direction only, as there is no need to wait for the carriage or other imaging mechanism to return to the left margin before starting a line. Also known as ***boustrophedon printing***, a term with an interesting etymology. See ***Boustrophedon Printing***.

Bidirectional Reader

In computing, a ***magnetic tape*** reader capable of reading information in either forward or reverse direction.

Bidirectional Symbol

A type of ***bar code*** format allowing for the bar code to be read either from left to right or from right to left. See ***Bar Code***.

Biform

In typography, the intermingling of modified ***small cap*** and ***lowercase*** characters in the formation of a lowercase alphabet, giving such type a unique appearance. Biforms are derived from ***uncial*** versions of handwritten styles, the most popular of which is Peignot. Biforms are most often used in heads, subheads, or ***display*** type, but rarely in running text unless you're an eleventh-century scribe.

Big Blue

Affectionate nickname for ***IBM***, in reference to its blue corporate color as well as the fact that it is a perennial blue chip stock.

Bilevel

A means of ***scanning*** done at a ***color depth*** of ***one-bit (1-bit) color***, or in which the scanner only registers black or white. Bilevel scanning is often used for scanning ***line art***, and when levels of gray are being scanned, the tolerance— or the gray level at which all shades below are registered as white and all shades above are registered as black—can be set. Such a scanner is known as a ***two-tone scanner***, and bilevel scanning is also known as ***binary scanning***.

Bill of Materials

A feature of some ***computer-assisted design (CAD)*** systems that can examine a finished technical drawing, itemize all the parts, and produce a list of the cost of materials involved in fabricating it.

Billboard Binding

In ***binding and finishing***, a form of ***mechanical binding*** comprising a three-ring binder with clear vinyl pockets on the front, back, and/or spine, allowing for insertion of cover sheets.

Billing ID

In telecommunications, an ***ISDN*** user identification used by the telephone company for billing purposes. Companies with their own internal ***PBX***s may require one billing ID but different ***caller ID***s for individual users.

Bimetal Plate

A strong, durable printing ***plate*** used in ***offset lithography***. Bimetal plates, as their name indicates, utilize a metal base (either stainless steel or aluminum) plated with copper. Some bimetal plates also utilize a third metal. In the most common configuration, copper (highly ***oleophilic***) is plated to aluminum or stainless steel (highly ***hydrophilic***). The copper is then covered with a light-sensitive coating. The plate is brought into contact with a photographic ***negative*** of the material to be printed, and the light exposes only the image areas of the negative, hardening the coating. The nonimage areas, unexposed and unhardened, are dissolved by chemical treatment. The copper in the nonimage areas is removed with an etching solution, baring the water-receptive bottom layer of metal.

Bimetal plates, although the most durable and the most practical for the longest print runs, are also the most expensive. Bimetal plates have many other advantages. In the event of ***plate blinding*** or ***scumming***, a simple acid treatment will solve both problems at once, unlike other plates where solving one problem can increase the occurrence of the other. Bimetal plates also allow reproduction of *halftone*s with minimum *dot gain*. (See *Plate: Offset Lithography*.)

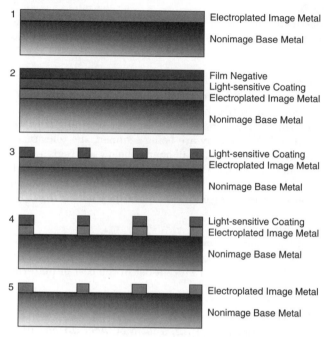

Bimetal platemaking.

Bimodal

Descriptive of a computer *device driver* that can operate in both *real mode* and *protected mode*. See *Protected Mode* and *Real Mode*.

Bimonthly

A publication (or descriptive of such a publication) that is issued every two months.

Bin

A portion of a *laser printer* which holds blank paper for input into the device, or which holds printed sheets following output.

Binary

A mathematical system based on only two numbers, 0 and 1. Computers are based on such a system, all computations, functions, etc., being represented as some pattern of these two digits. Each 0 and 1 corresponds to "off" or "on," respectively. The "on" and "off" states correspond to the states of transistors located on the microprocessor. A pattern of ons and offs—or "a completed electrical circuit" and "an incompleted electrical circuit"—is essentially what makes computers work. The more transistors that can be placed on a particular processor, the more circuits can be turned on and off; thus the more data and the faster that data can be processed. One of these digits is called a *binary digit*, more commonly known as a *bit*; eight bits equal one *byte*.

A binary system is often referred to as a base 2 system, as it is based on two digits. Other systems include *octal* (base 8), *decimal* (base 10), and *hexadecimal* (base 16).

Binary Card

Alternate term for a *punch card*. See *Punch Card*.

Binary Coded Decimal (BCD)

A computer coding system in which a single *decimal* digit is represented by four *binary* digitals (0s or 1s). For example, the decimal number 93 would be represented in BCD by 1001 0011. Also referred to as *binary decimal*.

Binary Color

Alternate term for *secondary color*. See *Secondary Color*.

Binary Decimal

Alternate term for *binary coded decimal*. See *Binary Coded Decimal (BCD)*.

Binary Digit

See *Bit*.

Binary File

A computer file or part of a software program that has been written in *binary* form (also known as *machine language*), and is thus capable of being accessed and read directly by the computer. Binary files are usually referred to in contrast to *ASCII file*s, which are text files. Material in a binary file is said to be in *binary format*.

Binary Format

See *Binary File*.

Binary Scanning

Alternate term for *bilevel* scanning. See *Bilevel*.

Binary Synchronous Communication (BSC)

In telecommunications, IBM's designation of a specific communications procedure utilizing *synchronous transmission*. See *Synchronous Transmission*.

Binary Synchronous Transmission (BST)

Alternate term for *synchronous transmission*. See *Synchronous Transmission*.

Bind

To attach pages of a book or other publication to each other with staples, adhesives, thread, wire, or other means, commonly between two covers. See *Binding and Finishing*.

Bind is also an alternate term for *link*. See *Link*.

Binder

In *binding and finishing*, a book-like device used to hold a quantity of sheets, commonly *loose-leaf* paper. Binders can either be temporary or permanent, the former allowing the easy removal and insertion of sheets, the latter not.

Binders come in all shapes and sides, but there are a few standard sizes available. Binding mechanisms can include three-ring and post binding. See **Mechanical Binding**.

In printing ink manufacture, any substance in an ink that allows the ink **pigment** to adhere to the **substrate**, or printed surface, or to keep the pigment uniformly dispersed in the fluid ink **vehicle**. Some printing processes require specially formulated binders to enable the ink to adhere to the substrate properly. Various types of **resin**s are used as binders. (See **Resin** and **Ink: Printing Requirements**.)

The term *binder* is also used in papermaking to refer to an organic or inorganic material added to the **pigment** in the manufacture of **coated paper**, which assists the pigment particles in adhering to the paper fibers. Organic binders include starch, **casein**, and soya protein. Starch is the most widely used, and is obtained from a variety of agricultural sources such as corn, wheat, potatoes, etc. Higher-quality papers use synthetic binders, typically **styrene-butadiene** and **vinyl acrylic latices**, which allow for greater **gloss**, **ink holdout**, and flexibility in post-printing operations such as folding and binding. (See **Coating**.) Binders are also known as **adhesives**.

Binder Holes

In **mechanical binding**, a set of holes or slits punched or drilled into a stack of sheets that allows them to be inserted into a **binder**. See **Mechanical Binding**.

Binder's Board

In **case binding**, a type of paperboard used for producing book covers, commonly covered with cloth or paper binding material. Binder's board is usually 70 **point**s (0.070 in.) thick.

Binder's Brass

In **binding and finishing**, a piece of brass commonly ¼ inch thick comprising a **relief** image of text or an image, used for the **die-stamping** of book covers. Also known as a **binder's die**. See **Die**.

Binder's Creep

Alternate term for **creep** in **binding and finishing**. See **Creep** (third definition).

Binder's Die

Alternate term for a **binder's brass**, especially when made of less expensive materials such as zinc or magnesium. See **Binder's Brass**.

Binder's Marks

In early bookbinding, decorative designs, initials, or names added to the covers of early bound books which contained information about the bookbinder.

Binder's Waste

In **binding and finishing**, the amount of spoilage that can occur and still permit the delivery of the specified quantity of bound articles.

Binders for Dyes

In **screen printing** or dyeing of textiles, an ink **vehicle** that serves to firmly bind the **pigment** particles in the dye to the fabric fibers.

Bindery

A facility where **binding and finishing** operations are performed following printing.

Bindery Operations

Any **binding and finishing** operations, or any operation performed on printed material following printing. See **Binding and Finishing**.

Bindery Punching

The **three-hole drilling** or punching of paper (or other **substrate**) when performed as a bindery operation, rather than prior to printing or on a sheet-by-sheet basis by the customer.

Bindery Truck

In **binding and finishing** facilities, a wheeled cart on which printed **signature**s or other book parts are stored until they are required.

Binding and Finishing

Binding and finishing are the activities performed on printed material after printing. Binding involves fastening individual sheets together, while finishing involves additional decorative actions such as die-stamping, embossing, etc.

The Evolution of Binding

The earliest "books" were essentially **papyrus** scrolls, or long sheets of papyrus (a paper-like material) rolled on a stick. After political feuds brought about the use of **parchment** and **vellum**, individual sheets were gathered into **quire**s, folded and stitched together. A leather strip was added to the **spine** to protect the pages and the stitches. The addition of leather-covered wooden boards—called **half binding**s—as the front and back formed the **codex**, a type of binding used in the late Roman Empire. This simple type of binding continued into the Middle Ages, and books produced by monks or scribes in monastery scriptoria were bound using pieces of leather sewn onto the pages.

During the Middle Ages, techniques of manuscript **illumination**—or decorating the pages of a hand-written book with illustrations, **gold leaf**, or other decorative matter—began to be applied to book bindings. Leather, silk, velvet, and other such materials began to be used for book covers, and ivory, gems, gold, and other ornamentations were used on these early book covers. These bindings were of such value that even those who could not read (which included most of Europe at that time) began to collect books. After the invention of the printing press in the mid-1400s, a common form of decorative binding was known as **gold tooling**, which involved using a heated instrument to melt gold leaf onto the book cover. Engraved dies were used to stamp patterns into the leather cover, and *fillet*s—or serrated wheels—were used to create continuous lines. One particular type of decorative cover technique was called *blind tooling*—or *blinding in*—and involved drawing a design on a sheet of paper, placing it on top of the book cover, and using heated tools to "trace" the design onto the cover. For gold tooling, the blinded-in image is first treated with *glaire*, a solution of egg white and vinegar, and a volatile oil, to ensure that the gold leaf remained flat once applied.

It was shortly after the invention of the printing press that the techniques of *imposition* were developed. The concept of imposition involves printing multiple pages on a large press sheet—called signatures—then folding and cutting the printed sheet to form the individual pages. The *folio* was the first signature size, followed by the *quarto* and, in the 1700s, the *octavo*. Currently, signatures as large as *thirty-twomo* (or a signature which contains thirty-two leaves, or sixty-four pages) are commonly printed. It was also immediately after Gutenberg's invention that the bindery trade began to be recognized as an art, and *binder's marks*—or complex illustrations, initials, or other identifying features—began to appear on books, particularly in France and the Netherlands. By the 1800s, however, cloth binding—called *case binding*, or *edition binding*—began to appear, which could be performed mechanically. As one might expect, binders began to rebel at this affront to the art and craft of hand binding books.

Bindery Operations

Although binding is a post-press function, binding considerations need to be dealt with in the prepress phase of any print job. There are many different ways to bind press sheets (see below), and certain bind margin allowances need to be made, which vary by binding type. The correct imposition needs to be determined at this time, as well. Imposition issues are usually the purview of the *stripper*, or the person responsible for the assembly of all the page elements. (See *Imposition* and *Stripping*.) A variety of layouts or dummies assist in the proper determination of correct imposition. A *mechanical* layout, provided by the designer, shows how all the disparate page elements need to be arranged.

The stripper prepares an *imposition layout* which illustrates how the page elements and whole pages need to be assembled in order to meet the printing, folding, and binding requirements. The imposition layout thus indicates page sequence, margins, trim marks, fold lines, press *gripper margin*s, *register marks*, etc. A *folding dummy* is an actual-size press sheet which has been folded into pages of the desired size and marked with page numbers to indicate the proper page imposition. The folding dummy also indicates where the gripper margin is, an allowance for which needs to be made. A *binding dummy* is essentially a folding dummy that has been trimmed and bound in the

desired fashion, to indicate how much margin is lost during binding. Some jobs—especially those that are to be saddle-stitched—may need *shingling* during stripping to compensate for *creep*, the decreasing size of the binding margin caused by increasing page count.

When thinking about binding considerations prior to printing, the various characteristics of the paper need to be accounted for. For example, the *basis weight* and *folding endurance* of a paper will affect how many times a sheet can be folded. Very lightweight paper (such as *Bible paper*) may need special equipment in order to fold and bind the sheets without damaging them. The paper's *grain direction* also affects the ease with which finishing operations can be performed.

Cutting and Trimming. Cutting of paper stock may be performed at any point in the printing and/or binding processes. Blank stock may need to be trimmed prior to printing in order to produce square, uniformly sized press sheets (more properly called *trimming*), or printed sheets may need to be cut after printing, especially when signature pages need to be separated or multiple copies of the same image were printed on the same sheet. Often, printed sheets also need to be cut in order to fit into folders or other bindery devices.

Most cutting and trimming is performed on a *guillotine cutter*, a manual or electronic device with a long, curved, heavy *knife*. A stack of sheets is placed on the bed of the cutter, and the blade cuts through it at the desired position. Some guillotine cutters, especially those used for trimming books, use a *split gauge*, a back gauge divided into three sections allowing for the trimming of three sides of a stack of pages without the need to change the trim setting. In book trimming—usually performed after binding—a *three-knife cutter* is most often used, which comprises three blades, enabling all the unbound sides to be trimmed simultaneously.

The most common knife material is stainless steel, although some cutters—especially those used for special jobs such as labels—utilize carbide inserts. The angle at which the knife contacts the sheet depends on the thickness of the material to be cut. Lightweight papers require a smaller angle, while heavier stock requires a larger angle. Some cutters also utilize high-tech accessories, such as *low-pressure air table*s, optical *cut-line indicator*s, *gripper-loading system*s, and *tilting-transfer table*s, as well as various video monitors and computers, all of which work to increase the efficiency, cost-effectiveness, and quality of the cutting operations. (See *Cutting and Trimming*.) After cutting, sheets are often placed in a *jogger*, which is a vibrating table, the action of which squares stacks of sheets.

Folding. A *folder* is an automated device which uses a variety of means to fold sheets of paper inserted into it. Most printing, as was mentioned above, is performed by printing multiple pages on large press sheets, which are then folded into signatures. There are two basic types of folder, and the choice of folder also depends on the type of fold desired. A *right-angle fold* involves making a fold in a sheet, rotating the sheet 90° and making a second fold. One fold makes four pages, two right-angle folds make eight pages, etc. A *parallel fold* involves making two or more folds in a sheet which are oriented in the same direction. Such folds are often made in leaflets, brochures, etc. Some common types of folds include the *accordion fold* (also known as a *fanfold*), which includes two or more parallel folds with additional folds in opposite directions; and a *gatefold*, or two parallel folds made such that the sheet opens from the center. Other specialty folds include the *over-and-over fold*, the *French fold*, and the *letter fold*.

A common type of folder is known as a *knife folder*, also known as a *right-angle folder*. On a knife folder—which can have any number of folding stations depending on the ultimate number of folds that need to be made to a sheet—a sheet is carried by the feeder mechanism on a flat plane. It hits a gauge, is positioned by a side guide, and a moving metal blade (or knife) pushes down on the sheet at a right angle to its surface, pushing it down between two counter-revolving metal or rubber (or combination of both) rollers. The action of the knife and rollers creates and "cements" the fold. At this point, the device carries the sheet to additional folding stations, if desired. A *jobber* is a knife folder has four folding stations and one or two parallel sections, allowing for up to four right-angle folds, two right-angle folds with a third parallel fold, or three right-angle folds and a fourth parallel fold. A *double-sixteen* knife folder is used in book production and can be used to make two separate 16-page units or one 32-page unit. A *quadruple*, or "quad," knife folder can be used to make two separate 32-page units or four 16-page units. A quad folder is often used in case binding for book production.

A second type of folder is called a *buckle folder*. A buckle folder uses diagonal rollers to position a sheet against side guides. Feed rollers push the sheet between two metal plates—collectively known as a *fold plate*—a preset stop in which causes the sheet to buckle. At this point, an additional set of rollers grasps the sheet and forms the first fold. Additional sets of rollers and fold plates make additional folds. A *combination folder* (colloquially known as a *combi*) is also used in many folding applications. Generally speaking, knife folders are used for heavier stocks, while buckle folders are used for lighter stocks.

As with cutters, new technologies can be added to folders to increase efficiency, especially by eliminating paper jams and damaged sheets. (See *Folding*.)

Collating and Gathering. Before binding, cut, trimmed, and/or folded sheets need to be placed in the correct sequence. In the process of *collating*, individual sheets are organized into sets. Collating is not often a printing or bindery operation, and is more often performed in offices for loose-leaf or mechanically bound materials. Automatic devices—such as photocopier accessories—are often used

for collating. In the process of *gathering*—which *is* a printing and binding operation—signatures are organized into sets, often using gathering machines comprising up to thirty individual pockets. Signatures are fed manually or automatically into these pockets, after which they are gathered together for binding. A variation on the gathering process—*inserting*—involves inserting one signature inside another signature. Signatures that have been gathered and are ready for binding are known collectively as a *book block*.

There are four basic means of binding sheets: *perfect binding*, *saddle-stitching* (and the related *side-wire stitching*), *case binding*, and *mechanical binding*.

Perfect Binding. Perfect binding, also called *adhesive binding*, is a means of affixing pages to a cover or spine by means of glue. An adhesive material is applied to the edges of the book block, and a cover stock is attached on top of it. Common examples of perfect bound publications include *paperback* books, magazines, telephone books, etc. After gathering, a gluing device applies a film of adhesive (usually a *hot-melt adhesive*) to the edge of the pages, usually with two applicator wheels. After application of the adhesive, a single-piece cover is applied, where nipping stations tightly press the cover over the book block. After binding, trimmers are used to cut the individual pages of the signatures apart at the top and/or bottom and remove excess paper. In perfect binding, trimming is done following the addition of the cover, as they are often designed to have *flush cover*s, or covers which have edges that are trimmed flush with the interior pages. (See *Perfect Binding*.)

Saddle-Stitching. Saddle-stitching (known with side-stitching collectively as *wire stitching*) essentially involves the use of wire staples to bind pages together. Saddle-stitching drives the staples through the center of the spine of folded sheets, and is commonly used for magazines, newsletters, and other such publications. A cursory glance at *Newsweek*, *Time*, *Business Week*, or other such magazines will provide an example of saddle-stitching. A less common variety of wire stitching is side stitching, in which staples are driven through the pages from the top of the cover down, usually oriented parallel to the bind margin. Side-stitching is most commonly used for reports, and had once been used for magazines such as *National Geographic* which are now bound by means of perfect binding.

Signatures to be side-stitched can be gathered and/or collated much like signatures destined for perfect binding, but saddle-stitched signatures must be inserted, or outer signatures laid open on top of inner signatures, which in turn are placed face down on the *saddle bar* of the saddle-stitching device.

Saddle-stitchers are best used for publications that are up to ¼ in. thick. Individual signatures for a single publication are each placed in a pocket, which feeds the signatures to the saddle bar. There, a spool of wire (the gauge or thickness of which is determined by the binding needs of the publication) is cut into individual staples by a bending mechanism, which can cut staples to the desired size. After forming the staple, it is driven through the spine of the signatures, and a clinching device bends the legs of the staples to secure each staple in place (and avoid injury to the reader). Slitters and trimmers then separate the pages and remove any excess. (See **Saddle-Stitching**.)

Thread Sewing and Case Binding. In contrast to wire stitching, **thread sewing** involves stitching a book block together by means of thread or cord, often in conjunction with an adhesive. Thread sewing is used for hardcover books, encyclopedias, Bibles, etc. It should be pointed out that thread sewing is the means by which the pages are bound together, while case binding is the attaching of the book cover to the book block. The most common means of thread sewing is called **Smyth sewing**, in which a thread is passed through the backfolds of the signatures comprising the book block. This secures the signatures to each other while still permitting the finished book to lie flat.

There are essentially two means of thread sewing, somewhat analogous to saddle-stitching and side-stitching: **saddle-sewing** and **side-sewing**. In the former, the more popular of the two, thread is driven through the centerfold of each signature, and each signature is joined to the others. In the latter, the thread is driven through the top sheet down through the signatures and along the edge of the book parallel to the bind margin. In shorter books, a continuous lockstitch or standard sewing pattern is used. In both of these, the stitches are placed in the same position on each signature. The drawback to these stitches is that if there are many signatures, **thread build-up** can cause swelling of the book. Longer books use staggered or continuous staggered stitches, which move the position of the stitches from signature to signature, reducing thread build-up.

Between thread sewing and case binding, the stitched book block passes through a series of **forwarding** operations. The first of these are **rounding** and **backing**, or a shaping of the book's spine to more securely fit a book cover. Rounding uses steel rollers to give the book's spine a concave shape, while backing flares the back of the spine outward, increasing the width of the spine which facilitates the attaching and the security of the case, and also creates the **hinge**s which allow the opening of the book. The process of **back gluing** coats the edge of the spine with an adhesive material, allowing it to maintain its concave shape. It is also at this point that the tops of the pages receive any **edge treatment**, such as **edge staining** (the coloring of the pages of a book) or **gilding** (the application of gold leaf to the edges of a book.) **Headbands**—or decorative cotton or silk reinforcements attached to the top and bottom of the spine of a book—may also be added at this time. Both these latter operations are optional, and are often only performed only when a publisher feels a book's importance warrants the additional expense.

The final stage is the process of case binding, or attaching a cloth or leather case to the pages. The prelude to casing is **smashing** (in which pressure is applied to the entire front and back surfaces of the book block) or **nipping** (in which pressure is only applied to the front and back of the spine), both of which work to compress the book block, forcing out air and eliminating the effects of thread build-up. (Hard papers undergo nipping, while soft papers undergo smashing.) The case itself is created by cutting stiff paperboard to the desired book size and covering it with cloth, the excess cloth then being folded under the boards and glued into place. Cases undergo **die-stamping** on the spine and/or cover at this time. The process of **casing in** involves the application of an adhesive to the **endleaf** papers in such a way that the front and back cover project evenly over the front and back of the book block. The process of **building in** uses pressure plates and heating elements to dry and set the adhesive.

Many book printers who handle high volumes of book work utilize fully automated printing and binding equipment. Many **hardcover**—or **casebound**—books also have a preprinted paper book **jacket** added at the end of the process. (See **Case Binding**.)

Mechanical Binding. Mechanical binding is the most basic form of binding, and includes such binding types as **comb binding**s, in which the teeth of a plastic "comb" are inserted into a series of slits drilled or punched into a stack of sheets, often used for reports and presentations; **spiral binding**, in which a continuous wire or plastic coil is threaded through holes drilled or punched into a stack of sheets, often used for notebooks; and **loose-leaf binding**, in which a set of holes (commonly three, but sometimes more or less) is drilled in a stack of sheets, allowing for insertion into standard or customized **ring binder**s or **post binder**s. The advantage of the latter is the easy removal and insertion of sheets. Loose-leaf binding is often used not only for notebooks but also for many types of prospecti, presentations, financial reports, instruction books, and other such uses that may require frequent updating.

Finishing Operations

Although the term *finishing* refers to any post-printing operation, including all the above operations of cutting, trimming, folding, and binding, it also refers to specialized decorative processes.

Embossing. **Embossing** is a process by which **die**s are used to stamp a **relief** image in a book cover or printed material. Often, an ink or other substance is used to color or accent the relief image. **Blind embossing**, however, uses no decorative inks, keeping the stamped image "as is." A similar process, **debossing**, uses a die to stamp a sunken image on the substrate. In either embossing or debossing, the substrate passes beneath an embossing plate which carries the engraved die bearing the image. Directly beneath the substrate is a "counter" die, or a die which bears a relief image of the image engraved on the emboss-

BINDING AND FINISHING OPERATIONS

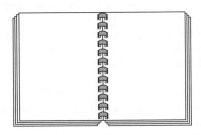

Comb binding.

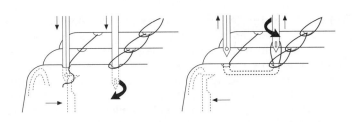

Smyth sewing.

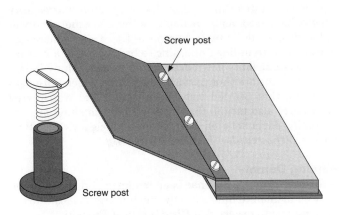

Mechanical binding.

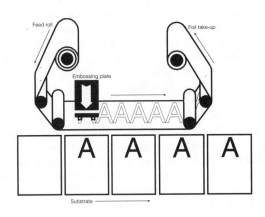

Foil stamping.

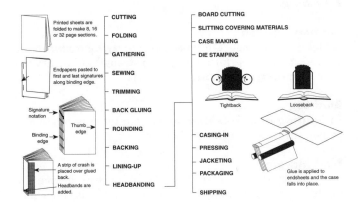

Casebinding.

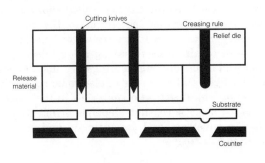

Diecutting.

ing die. When the substrate passes between these two dies and pressure is applied (forcing the two dies together), a relief image is produced on the substrate. (Debossing can occur by simply switching the positions of the two dies, or turning the substrate over.) Often, the dies are heated.

Foil Stamping. A process similar to embossing (and may also be performed at the same time as embossing) is *foil stamping*, in which a heated die presses against a roll of foil, contacting the substrate. This transfers the foil—in a pattern corresponding to the design on the die—to the substrate. In *foil embossing*, the embossing and foil stamping processes are performed simultaneously. Foil stamping replaced the earlier process of *bronzing*, in which a metallic powder was applied to the surface of a substrate. A type of foil stamping—*die-stamping* or *blanking*—is used to press an image into a hard substrate for which embossing is inappropriate, such as a book cover used in case binding.

Diecutting. The process of *diecutting* uses a different type of die, one which contains knives or creasing rules to cut a pattern into a substrate, or to cut the substrate into a particular pattern. The dies themselves are prepared and engraved for specific jobs out of a variety of materials and in a variety of ways. See *Die*.

Coating. A variety of coatings can be applied to printed products, either for extra protection or for decorative purposes. (The two uses are not mutually exclusive, of course.) There are several classifications of coatings used in finishing operations: a *primer* is used to prepare a surface for ink reception or for the application of another type of coating. A *lacquer* is a combination protective/decorative coating applied to a printed piece. A *barrier coating* is a protective coating applied to printed packaging, designed to impart resistance to oxygen, water, or other chemicals. *Overprint varnish* is a high-gloss coating which is added for decorative and protective purposes. Overprint varnish may be applied to the entire surface of a printed material, or to only select portions (in this case called *spot varnish*).

Coatings are classified according to the means by which they dry. Aqueous coatings are water-based and dry upon exposure to air, thus requiring a long drying time. Ultraviolet and electron-beam coatings dry upon exposure to ultraviolet light and to beams of electrons, respectively, which cause *polymerization* of materials in the coating.

The use of specific coatings depends primarily on the nature of the substrate and the ultimate end-use of the material. (See *Coating*.)

Laminating. *Laminating* differs from coating in that lamination involves the adhesive bonding of two separate materials or layers of material together. Often, laminating in the finishing sense refers to the sealing of a substrate between two layers of a plastic material.

There are a variety of other types of finishing operations which vary according to the specific requirements of a

job. These can include *indexing* (the addition of plastic *index tab*s or *index thumb cut*s to the edges of printed sheets as an aid to locating specific information), *padding* (the binding of a stack of sheets with a flexible adhesive from which sheets can be easily removed, used in making note pads), and other such functions as sorting, numbering, addressing, gluing (i.e., the application of a moistenable adhesive, as in envelopes or labels), or any *converting* operation. (See *Converting*.)

In-Line vs. Off-Line Finishing. Often many finishing operations are described as *in-line* processes. This means that these functions are performed by additional units attached to the end of the printing press (especially a *web press*). Finishing operations can be performed in a continuous process or as an extension of the printing process, eliminating the need to gather up the printed sheets and transport them to another location for finishing. A disadvantage of in-line finishing is that very often *makeready* time is increased, as is spoilage, as there are more individual operations to set up and prepare. There also is increased downtime with in-line units, since a breakdown at any point in the system shuts down every other system. Many finishing operations are thus performed *off-line*, which (although requiring that printed webs be rewound and transported elsewhere) also means that printing and finishing are not mutually dependent on each other's efficiency. (See *Web Offset Lithography: In-Line Finishing*.)

Binding Dummy
A *folding dummy* that has been trimmed and bound in the desired fashion to indicate how much margin is lost during binding due to *creep*. See *Binding and Finishing*.

Binding Edge
The edge of a printed sheet or paper web on which binding is to occur. Also known as the *stub edge*. See *Binding and Finishing*.

Binding Varnish
A highly viscous substance used as a *bodying agent* in the manufacturing of printing ink, or to strengthen the dry ink film. (See *Bodying Agent*.)

Bind Leg
In *binding and finishing*, one of the types of binding to be performed in a *split bind* order.

Bind Margin
The *gutter* or inner margin of a book measured from the binding to the beginning of the printed area. Also known as the *binding margin*.

Biocide
A substance added to water-based film *emulsion*s as a means to killing potentially damaging bacteria or other microorganisms.

BIOS

Abbreviation for ***basic input/output system***. See ***Basic Input/Output System (BIOS)***.

BIOS Extension

In computing, additions to the primary ***BIOS*** that allows the computer to handle add-on devices, such as ***VGA*** adapters and other such devices. BIOS extensions are added as additional ***ROM*** chips to the ***motherboard*** or as ***expansion card***s.

Bipacking

In photography, a type of ***matting*** process performed in the camera. See ***Matting***.

Bipolar

Descriptive of a semiconductor technology in which an electrical signal is propagated by means of layers of silicon having different electrical characteristics (i.e., positive and negative). In a bipolar transistor, the most common type of transistor used in integrated circuits, current is split and directed toward two different poles, a base and a collector.

Bird's-Eye View

In ***three-dimensional (3-D) graphics***, a view of a rendered scene from above—as a bird would see it—with the horizon in sight. Also called a ***helicopter view***.

Bis

In telecommunications, a term referring to a ***CCITT*** specification that is secondary—or is an alternative or extension—to a primary specification. For example, CCITT V.42 lists the recommendations for error correction, while CCITT V.42 bis lists the recommendation for data compression. The term *bis* itself means "twice" and is an interjection used to request a repetition of a musical performance, much like "encore."

B-ISDN

Abbreviation for ***broadband*** ISDN. See ***ISDN***.

Bisynchronous Communication

A network ***protocol*** used in mainframe networks that requires both the sending and receiving devices to be syn-

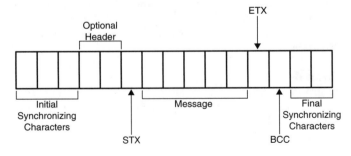

Data packet structure used in bisynchronous communications.

chronized in order for data transmission to take place. Essentially, bisynchronous transmissions transmit data in packets known as ***frame***s. The data included in each frame is enrobed by initial and final synchronization characters which allow each computer to synchronize its clock with the others. Control characters are also included for ***error detection and correction*** purposes. This type of protocol is the basis of ***SDLC***, a protocol used in IBM's ***Systems Network Architecture (SNA)***.

Bit

A contraction of the term "bi*nary* dig*it*," the smallest piece of information used by a computer, consisting of either the number 1 or 0. A computer processor is essentially a large collection of transistors; information is only understood by the computer in terms of turning these transistors on or off (in other words, whether there is an electrical connection or not). In binary, then, "1" represents "on," while "0" represents "off." Combinations of bits form larger units which convey greater amounts of information. Eight bits is known as one ***byte***, which is commonly the amount used to represent a single character or letter. One thousand bytes (or, more correctly, 2^{10}, or 1,024, bytes) is one ***kilobyte***, while one million bytes (or, more correctly, 2^{20}, or 1,048,576 bytes) is one ***megabyte***. Increasingly common computer data storage sizes are ***gigabyte***s and ***terabyte***s.

The term ***digital*** is used to refer to any information conveyed using digits, in this case 1 and 0.

Bit Block Transfer

In computer graphics, a memory management function (used by graphics adapters) in which ***pixel***s are moved about in large chunks, rather than ***bit*** by bit or ***byte*** by byte. Such adapters tend to perform better and more rapidly. A chip in a graphics ***coprocessor*** that effects bit block transfers is called a ***blitter***, while the act of executing a bit block transfer is called ***blitting***.

Bit Depth

Alternate term for ***color depth***. See ***Color Depth***.

Bit Duration

In telecommunications and networking, a measure of the time it takes for one ***bit*** of encoded data to pass a specific point on the transmission medium.

Bite

The penetration into the surface of a ***substrate*** by an ink ***solvent*** or an ***adhesive***.

Bit Error Rate

In telecommunications and networking, a measure of the quality of a data transmission consisting of the ratio between the total number of ***bit***s in a transmitted message and the number that were received in error. Commonly abbreviated ***BER***. Also known simply as the ***error rate***.

Bitmap

In computer graphics, the collection of individual dots—or *pixel*s—that make up a screen image. *Bitmapped*, or *raster*, images are defined as a series of dots. At the lowest *color depth*, *one-bit color*, each dot is either black or white, "on" or "off." At higher color depths, increasing numbers of *bit*s describe each pixel; this allows for the display of a greater number of different colors.

The computer display memory keeps a "map" of which pixels are on and off, and subsequent manipulation of screen images (such as erasures of picture elements in Adobe PhotoShop, for example) involves registering changes on this bitmap. Various *paint program*s deal with all images as bitmaps. But although manipulation of bitmapped images is simple (most paint and graphics programs let you alter images pixel by pixel), their output *resolution* is limited by the size of the pixel matrix. On a standard computer monitor that resolution is 72 pixels per inch, far below sufficient for high-quality output.

The edges of bitmapped graphics tend to exhibit the stair-step pattern known as *aliasing*. Although *antialiasing* functions can reduce this problem on the computer display, it's almost impossible to eliminate on even laser-printer output. Images, however, can be input to a computer (via a scanner, Photo CD, or other means) at resolutions sufficient for high-quality output. Although displayed on the screen at the maximum resolution of the monitor, they will output at the higher resolution.

An alternative to bitmapped images are known as *vector* graphics; although displayed as bitmaps on the display (for there is no way to display anything on a conventional

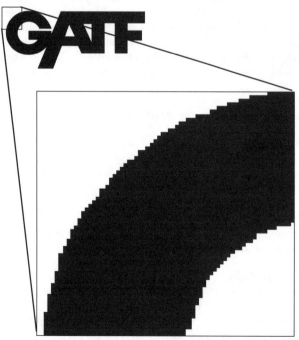

Detail of a bitmapped letter. Note that it comprises a series of dots or pixels. Note also presence of aliasing along the edges.

computer monitor except as a bitmap), they are actually defined by the computer as a series of mathematical formulas that describe circles, curves, lines, and other graphical objects which. When output as a *PostScript* (or *encapsulated PostScript [EPS]*) file, these images print smoothly and at as high a resolution as the output device is capable of. Sophisticated graphics programs can convert bitmapped images to vector images, and vice versa. Photographs and *halftone*s, however, will always need to be output as bitmaps; line art, however, should always be vector-based to ensure the fidelity of lines and curves. Vector images are also processed faster than bitmapped images, and take up less disk space and *RAM*.

Bitmap is occasionally written as two words (*bit map*); its adjective (*bitmapped*) is written as one word, but can be two words (*bit mapped*), or hyphenated (*bit-mapped*).

Bitmap Font

In digital type, a set of typographic characters that exist as *bitmap*s—or a collection of dots—rather than as outlines or mathematical descriptions of lines and curves (*outline font*s). Bitmap fonts are used as *screen font*s, which are the fonts as they are displayed on the computer screen and cannot be anything *but* bitmaps. *Printer font*s, or the fonts that are used by the output device, should never be bitmaps, as they tend to exhibit *aliasing* and can only be output at the resolution of the pixel matrix. *Scaling* bitmapped fonts rarely turns out well, so if the use of them is unavoidable, it is best to stick with the sizes included in the font. (See also *Outline Font*.)

Bitmap Format

A particular type of graphics *file format* used for saving *bitmap* graphics. Some common bitmap file formats are *TIFF*, *BMP*, *PCX*, *PIC*, *GIF*, and *TGA*.

Bitmapped

Existing as a *bitmap*, such as a graphic image or *font*, rather than as a *vector*.

Bit-Oriented Protocol

In networking, a data communications *protocol* in which data is transmitted as a series of *bit*s, rather than larger *byte*s. Sequences of bits are used as control codes. Two common examples of bit-oriented protocols are *High-Level Data Link Control (HDLC)* and IBM's *Synchronous Data Link Control (SDLC)*. See also *Byte-Oriented Protocol*.

Bitonal

In graphics and imaging, a computer graphic or image comprising only two tonal values, which can be represented by a 1 or a 0, often simply black and white. Also referred to as *One-Bit (1-Bit) Color*.

Bit Pad

A computer input device, specifically a *digitizing tablet* used with a *puck*. See *Digitizing Tablet* and *Puck*.

Bit Plane

The hardware wherein a *bitmap* is stored. See *Bitmap*.

Bit Rate

In telecommunications, the number of *bit*s of data that can be transferred per unit time, usually expressed in *bits per second (bps)* or *kilobits per second (kbps)*. Also known as the *bit transfer rate* and *data-transfer rate*.

Bit Serial

Alternate term for *serial transmission*. See *Serial Transmission*.

Bit Synchronous

In telecommunications, a type of *synchronous transmission* in which single *bit*s of data are sent in a continuous stream. See *Synchronous Transmission*.

Bit Transfer Rate

Alternate term for *bit rate*. See *Bit Rate*.

Bits Per Inch (bpi)

The number of *bit*s that can be stored in one linear inch, used as a measure of the density of magnetic storage media. See also *Characters Per Inch (CPI)*.

Bits Per Pixel (bpp)

Alternate term for *color depth*. See *Color Depth*.

Bits Per Second (bps)

In telecommunications, a measure of data or modem speed. In *synchronous* communications, one character is described by 8 *bit*s, thus a speed of one character per second would be equivalent to 8 bps. In *asynchronous* communications, one character per second is equivalent to 10 bps. The evolution of modems has resulted in ever-increasing transmission speeds. Several years ago, 2400 bps was the norm; as of this writing, 28,800 bps (or 28.8 *kbps* or *kilobit*s per second) is the norm. Bits per second is often confused with *baud*, with which it may or may not be equivalent. (See also *Baud*.)

Biweekly

A publication (or descriptive of such a publication) that is issued every two weeks.

Black

In *color*, the absence of all (or nearly all) reflected light from a surface, as in the printing of an ink with no perceptible *hue*. Technically, however, there is no such thing as a "perfect black"; even the darkest materials that have been found to exist (such as lampblack, soot, pitch, or black velvet) reflect as much as 3% of the light striking it.

Totally nonreflective blacks have been conceptualized, most notably the theoretical *blackbody* of physics, and the perhaps as equally theoretical "black hole" of astronomy. The latter of these is only totally black because its intense gravitation prevents any light from escaping. (This would not make a good basis for printing inks, however.) Both those "black" objects—so far as we know—do not really exist.

Black can be produced by mixing the three *subtractive color primaries—cyan*, *magenta*, and *yellow*—in equal proportion.

Black is also used to refer to one of four inks in *process color*—or four-color—printing, where it is denoted as the "K" (for *key*) in *CMYK*.

Black-and-White

Any original or reproduced image—generated either photographically, digitally, manually, or by other means—comprising only a single color (*black*) on a white background, as distinguished from a color image, which contains one or more colors in addition to black. Also known as *monochromatic*. In common parlance, *black-and-white* is also used to refer to an image which also contains grays or, in other words, no *chromatic colors*.

Black Box

A colloquial term for any mechanical or electronic device that alters input data for output but whose exact inner workings are a mystery to the operator.

Black Iron Oxides

A variety of *black pigment* used in printing inks. Black iron oxides are commonly natural or synthetic ferrous-ferric oxide (chemical formula $FeO\text{-}Fe_2O_3$), commonly mined as magnetite, a magnetic iron oxide.

Most iron oxides used as black pigments are produced synthetically. Black iron oxides are dense, *matte* blacks which possess high *lightfastness* and resistance to heat and chemicals (with the exception of acids, which dissolve the pigments). At temperatures above 300°F, however, these pigments turn red. Black iron oxides have been typically used in copperplate and die-stamping inks, and magnetic iron oxides are used in inks printed to be read by magnetic ink character recognition (*MICR*) equipment. Synthetically produced black iron oxides are bluer in shade than naturally occurring iron oxides. (See also *Black Pigments*.) Also known as *Mineral Blacks* (*CI Pigment Black 11 No. 77499*).

Black Letter

In typography, one of a wide variety of *typeface*s based on medieval script, commonly from thirteenth-century German writing. This style of type is also known as *Spire-Gothic* and *Old English*, and is characterized by dark, angular characters comprising thick and thin lines. This style of type is often used to set the nameplates of newspapers, such as the *New York Times*. A German-derived name for these designs is *Fraktur* (or "broken" in Latin), so-called because when medieval scribes switched from simple handwriting to the black letter style, the pen needed to be lifted off the page to make each stroke. Since these letters could not be created with one stroke, the writing flow was fractured, or broken.

Type set in black letter typefaces should never be all *caps*; as the capital letters are richly embellished, they become nearly indecipherable when formed into words.

These typefaces are also known as *Textura*, as they appear to produce a woven texture on the page.

Black Light

A somewhat inaccurate term for a form of illumination containing short-wavelength *ultraviolet* light (radiation just beyond the blue end of the visible spectrum). Although "black light" is technically invisible, it tends to cause some substances to fluoresce upon exposure. Photographic *emulsion*s (especially those that use *photopolymer*s), are susceptible to black light. Sun lamps, plant "grow" lights, lights used in discotheques, etc., are all forms of black light. Black light is also used to read "invisible" inks, such as nightclub hand stamps.

Black Patch

See *Red Patch*.

Black Pigment

Substances added to printing inks to impart a black color, generally derived from the refining of oil or natural gas. The black pigments primarily in use today are called *Carbon blacks*, which can be either *Furnace black* or *channel black*, depending on the method by which they are produced. Furnace black is derived from the "cracking" of natural gas or oil. Channel black, due to tightened air pollution laws, is no longer manufactured in the United States, although it is quite desirable, and may be imported from other countries if the added expense is warranted.

Black iron oxides can either be obtained from natural sources (primarily magnetite) or synthetic sources.

Vegetable black is the oldest black pigment, but has been replaced almost entirely by Furnace Black.

The black pigments listed above are classified and identified in the *Society of Dyers and Colorists' Color Index*. Each classification consists of two parts, corresponding to the two parts of the Index: The first part identifies each pigment with a CI number, which accompanies a description, usage, and technical information. The second part lists each pigment by chemical composition, and assigns each one a single number. Thus, carbon black above is listed in Part 1 as *CI Pigment Black 7* and in Part 2 as *No. 77266*. These two sets of identifications accompany the individual entries on each separate pigment.

Black Printer

Alternate term for *key*, a black printing plate in *process color* printing, used to increase contrast and emphasize neutral tones and detail in the *shadow*s. See also *key*, *full-scale black*, and *skeleton black*.

Black Screen of Death

Overly descriptive term used to refer to a blank computer screen that indicates a system *crash*. See *Crash*.

Blackboard Coating

A *matte* coating applied to the surface of a *substrate*, either by spray or utilizing *screen printing* apparatus so as to impart to the surface a texture suitable for writing with chalk. Also called a *chalkboard coating*.

Blackbody

A theoretical "perfect *black*" object, or one which allows absolutely no light to be reflected from its surface. Even the blackest blacks on Earth—such as lampblack, soot, etc.—reflect as much as 3% of the light that hits it. Blackbodies have historically contributed to science and physics—it was physicist Max Planck's study of blackbody radiation that led to his nascent version of quantum theory in 1900. Blackbodies are also used in the determination of *color temperature*. See *Color Temperature*.

Another perfect blackbody is the so-called "black hole" of astrophysics, a collapsed star of such high density and gravitation that no light can escape it.

Blackening

See *Calender-Blackened Spots/Streaks*.

Blackout

A period of complete loss of electrical power, caused by increased electrical demand or other problems at an electrical utility company. A less severe form of reduced electrical power is known as a *brownout*. When sudden blackouts occur in the middle of a computing session, some data loss is inevitable. Blackouts can be circumvented by means of an *uninterruptible power supply (UPS)*.

Blade

Any thin, long strip—either sharpened or not—made of metal, plastic, rubber, or other material used for cutting, slitting, scraping, folding, coating, etc. A blade used for cutting is commonly known as a knife. A blade for scraping is commonly known as a *doctor blade*.

A *blade* is also the flexible printing edge of a *squeegee* used in *screen printing*. See *Squeegee*.

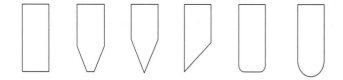

Several common squeegee blade shapes, used in screen printing.

Blade Coater

A device used to apply a *coating* to the surface of a paper. The blade coater applies a thick layer of surplus coating to a paper *web* (often utilizing an applicator roll), then uses a flexible blade to scrape away the excess coating, leaving a desired level amount of coating on the paper. A blade coater produces an extremely level coating surface.

There are a number of different types of blade coaters (see, for example, *short-dwell coater*) and blade coating is the most popular method of coating papers. (See *Coating*.) Particles caught behind the blade, however, can cause paper defects such as a *blade scratch*, a *blade cut*, or *blade streak*.

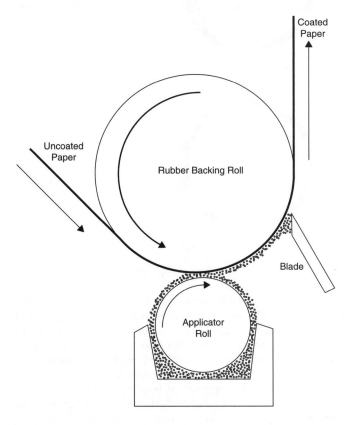

Blade coater. Note that the applicator roll applies a thick layer of coating, which is then scraped and metered by the blade.

Blade Cut

A paper defect characterized by a hairline cut through the thickness of a coated paper, running in the *grain direction*, caused by a particle becoming attached to the back of the blade on a *blade coater*, which then carves a narrow furrow in the paper as the web travels past it. A smaller particle will only carve a narrow, hairline scratch in the surface of the coating, producing a *blade scratch*, and a larger particle will cut a wider furrow than a scratch, called a *blade streak*.

Blade Extension

On a *gravure* press, the length of *doctor blade* or *back-up blade* that protrudes beyond the edge of the blade press-mounting assembly. Blade extensions should generally be in the range of ⅜–½ inch. See *Doctor Blade*.

Blade Mark

Alternate term for a *blade streak*. See *Blade Streak*.

Blade Scratch

A paper defect characterized by a hairline indentation in the surface of a paper's coating running in the *grain direction*, caused by a particle becoming attached to the back of the blade on a *blade coater*, which then carves a narrow furrow in the applied coating as the web travels past it. If the particle is large enough, it can cut right through the web, producing a *blade cut*, or carve a wider furrow than a scratch, called a *blade streak*.

Blade Streak

A paper defect characterized by a wide indentation in the surface of a paper's coating, running in the *grain direction*. A blade streak is caused by a large particle becoming attached to the back of the blade on a *blade coater*, which then carves a wide furrow in the applied coating as the web travels past it. A particle can also cut right through the web, producing a *blade cut*, or it can carve a narrow, hairline streak, called a *blade scratch*. A blade streak is also known as a *blade mark*.

Bladeless Ink Fountain

An *ink fountain* used on offset presses that replaces the *fountain blade* with a disposable sheet of polyester foil in contact with the *fountain roller*, supported by means of small cylinders. See *Inking System: Offset Lithography*.

Blanc Fixe

An inorganic material used as a *white pigment* in printing inks, typically as an *extender*. Blanc fixe is precipitated *barium sulfate* (chemical formula $BaSO_4$) with trace amounts of silicon oxide. It possesses high *lightfastness*, heat resistance, and chemical resistance. It also helps maintain the original qualities of the color with which it is mixed. (See also *White Pigments*.)

(CI Pigment White 21 No. 77120.)

Blank

Any unprinted *substrate*, be it paper, plastic film, metal, or a fabric.

A *blank* is also a term for an order form that has yet to be filled in.

To *blank* means to omit printing on a certain portion of the substrate.

In *binding and finishing*, to *blank* means to *blind emboss* a substrate, or *die-stamp* it without adding coloration. See *Embossing* and *Die-Stamping*.

Blanket

A synthetic rubber mat used in *offset lithography* to transfer—or "offset"—an image from a metal plate to the paper or other *substrate*. It is the use of a blanket that gives offset lithography its name (see also *Direct Lithography*.)

The earliest blankets were made from pure rubber that, although producing a much superior image than could be obtained with the lithographic plates in use at the time, imparted a number of problems to the process. The invention of synthetic rubbers in the 1930s eliminated most of the problems inherent in rubber-blanket offset printing. Blankets today are primarily made from synthetic rubbers such as **Buna N** or **neoprene**. A variety of substances are added to this basic rubber, such as softeners to increase resilience and other materials to toughen the surface. The rubber compound is applied to a fabric backing, which is pre-stretched to simulate the tension it will experience when it is ultimately mounted on the press. The strength of the fabric is typically greater lengthwise than across its width, as it needs to be stronger in its around-the-cylinder direction. A blanket with greater strength across its width will stretch irretrievably when mounted, and the resulting bagginess will cause poor image transfer. The direction of greater strength is called the blanket's **warp**, while that of its lesser strength is called its **weft**. Colored threads woven into the back of the blanket indicate its warp direction. Two, three, and even four plys of fabric are cemented together, and as many as 80 individual coats of rubber compound are added to its surface. Temperature, humidity, and other environmental factors need to be carefully controlled to keep the blanket thickness within the acceptable tolerances (about ±0.0005 in.) The finished blanket is then vulcanized to improve its dimensional stability and strength.

Of primary consideration in evaluating a blanket is its **release**, or how easily the blanket will let go of the press sheet as it leaves the **impression nip**. In addition to other non-blanket factors such as ink **tack**, the **squeeze** exerted in the impression nip, and the surface characteristics of the paper, the smoothness and hardness of the blanket surface also contribute to release. A hard blanket with a somewhat rough surface has anecdotally been found to give the best release, although empirical experimentation fails to confirm this. Perhaps the difficulty of accurately quantifying blanket hardness is one reason. As for smoothness, there is some debate on the desired level of smoothness that provides the best printed impressions.

Most blankets are slightly grained or textured, which doesn't affect the impression, but, it is claimed, helps drain water from the plate. Others say the graininess should be eliminated as much as possible. Regardless of the proper level of graininess, it should never be pronounced enough to print the texture of the blanket in solids. Blankets containing holes, depressions, pits, or other surface irregularities should be replaced. Blankets should also have desirable levels of **resilience**, in particular **smash resistance**—the extent to which a blanket will retain its original dimensions following an instance of printing pressure. Similarly, blanket **durability** describes the extent to which the blanket will retain its dimensional characteristics over time.

Another important characteristic is a blanket's ability to simultaneously be ink-receptive, yet not absorb the ink **vehicle** or the blanket-cleaning **solvent**s used on it. Such absorption causes blanket swelling, which distorts and degrades the printed impression. A final consideration of blanket performance is its inability to stretch. New blankets do have an inherent tendency to stretch somewhat over the course of the first few thousand impressions (and conse-

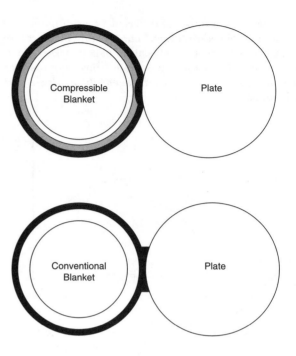

A conventional vs. compressible blanket.

quently will need to be repacked) but any stretching after that point should be minimal, primarily to keep the printing pressure consistent throughout a print run or between different pressruns. A blanket that needs to be repacked regularly may need to have the printing pressure lessened, its lockup tension increased, or its tension decreased.

One recent development in blanket manufacture that has become more and more widespread is a **compressible blanket**. A compressible blanket is manufactured in a manner similar to the conventional blanket described above, but its backing also includes one layer (or perhaps more) of a soft, resilient material such as foam rubber, cork, or loose fabric fibers. The advantage of a compressible blanket is the ability to increase the **packing** height without generating a corresponding increase in printing pressure, which can lead to a variety of press and print problems such as plate and blanket wear and/or damage, gear wear and **gear streaks**, **mottle**, **dot slurring**, and increased **picking**. Compressible blankets also contribute to the attainment of **true rolling**, or a condition of no slippage at the nip between the plate and the blanket cylinders. When a conventional blanket contacts the plate, the rubber deforms somewhat, and as a result the surface speed of the blanket is different than that of the plate, producing a slippage that can cause **slurring**. A compressible blanket, on the other hand, displaces less rubber at the nip, and as a result, the difference in surface speeds between the blanket and the plate is reduced. An added advantage is that reduced slippage leads to less plate wear, increasing the lifespan of the plate. Compressible blankets also improve **smash** recovery. ("Smash" is a undesirable, localized compression of a portion of the blanket caused by a foreign object or multiple sheets of paper passing through the impression nip.) Since, by design, these blankets compress under increased pressure, they have the ability to return to their original dimensions. (Smash recovery may be within 2–10 sheets, if the compression is not overly severe.) There is also a reduced tendency for *compression set*, a permanent, unrecoverable decrease in blanket thickness. Another advantage of compressible blankets is their ability to even out any irregularities in blanket thickness.

Regardless of the variety of blanket, it is necessary to ensure that the thickness of the blanket is accurately known. Manufacturer specifications may only report an average thickness for any particular shipment of blankets. Measurements need to confirm or refute those numbers in order to properly determine the required amount of packing to add. Uniformity of thickness throughout a single blanket may also be a problem. Micrometer measurements should be made at a variety of different locations to determine an average thickness for the blanket, and any gross irregularities may necessitate blanket replacement.

Blankets may be shipped from the manufacturer with press mounting bars already attached, or they may need to be added after receipt. When mounting a blanket, both squareness of the blanket and even tension on the cylinder need to be paid attention to. An unsquarely mounted blanket (either due to improper mounting or a manufacturing defect) will produce uneven tension. Blankets should be purchased so that their thickness necessitates the minimum use of packing. Whether one should use two-, three-, or four-ply blankets (mentioned above) depends on the size of the *undercut* of the blanket cylinder. Too much packing causes *packing creep*. When packing the blanket, only prescribed packing paper should be used; mylar packing is fine for use beneath plates, but causes many problems when used under a blanket. (See *Packing*.)

When a blanket smash occurs, and a visible depression is left in the surface of the blanket, it is typically not the rubber that is damaged, but the less compressible fabric beneath it. If the rubber surface is not cut, the blanket may be recoverable, and the fabric fibers can be returned to their original dimensions by soaking the blanket for a day or so either in water, or in water with a small amount of *wetting agent* added. The blanket is then hung up to dry by the mounting bar. When it is dry, the fabric fibers are likely to have returned to their original size. If the rubber surface or the fabric fibers are torn, however, there is no way to save the blanket. Damaged blankets, although not useful for general printing, are good to use in conjunction with perforating dies attached to the impression cylinder. Perforating dies will damage a new blanket, so it may be wise to use an already damaged, expendable blanket.

Blankets not on press should be stored in a cool, dark, dry place. Prolonged exposure to sunlight, fluorescent lighting, or heat can cause the rubber to crack. Storing blankets with the rubber surface in contact with the fabric backing of an adjacent blanket can cause the rubber to pick up the texture of the fabric, which may be permanent, and will not print well. When cleaning a blanket, a solvent that is compatible with the synthetic rubber should be used. Improper solvents can be absorbed by the blanket, causing it to swell, or can dissolve the rubber surface. Solvent should not come into contact with the edges of the blanket; the sides of a blanket are frequently not sealed, and solvent can destroy the adhesive holding the plys of fabric backing together.

Blanket Compression Set
See *Compression Set*.

Blanket Creep
An undesirable movement of the surface of an offset press *blanket*, affecting the part of the surface that is either in contact with the plate or the paper. See *Creep*.

Blanket Cylinder
The part of an offset lithographic printing press containing a rubber blanket, to which the inked image is transferred from the plate, and which then transfers the inked image to the paper or other *substrate*.

The surface of the blanket cylinder of a sheetfed offset press is commonly not an unbroken one; there is a gap (called a *cylinder gap*) which occupies about 20% of its circumference. Somewhat like the *plate cylinder*, in whose cylinder gap lie the *plate clamp*s, the blanket cylinder has reels or bars to which the blanket is attached and pulled tightly over the metal surface of the cylinder. Each end of the cylinder has a metal ring called a *bearer*, the diameter of which is the actual diameter of the cylinder, and of the gear that drives the cylinder. (Older presses utilize a *spur gear*—in which the teeth are cut straight across—while newer presses utilize a *helical gear*—in which the teeth are cut at an angle.) The gear on the blanket cylinder is in contact with and drives a similar gear on the plate cylinder. The bearers of each cylinder may or may not be in contact, but those that run out-of-contact need helical gears to minimize *play* (undesired free movement of cylinder gears). The diameter (and thus the radius) of the main body of the cylinder where the blanket is attached is slightly less than that of the bearers. The difference in radius between the bearers and the main cylinder body is called the *undercut*, and exists to provide space for blanket height adjustment, typically by means of *packing* (paper, plastic, or other material placed underneath the blanket to raise the printing surface).

The blanket cylinder is moveable, in that it can be brought in and out of contact with the plate cylinder and *impression cylinder*. However, since the gears of each of these cylinders need to remain in contact, the blanket cylinder cannot be moved very far. This backing away of the blanket is necessary to allow the mounting and washing of plates without dirtying the blanket, or to allow the mounting and washing of the blanket without dirtying the plate or plate cylinder. The distance between the blanket and the impression cylinder is adjustable to allow printing on a

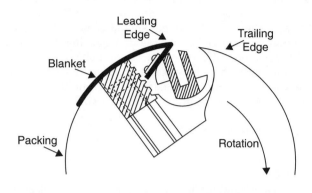

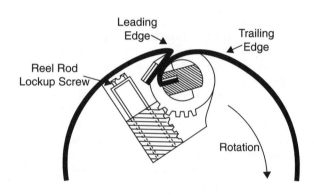

Securing the blanket to the blanket cylinder.

wide variety of substrate thicknesses. The blanket and impression cylinder can be brought out of contact with each other using an impression lever that shifts the impression cylinder's eccentric bushings. On some presses, however, the blanket cylinder is equipped with two sets of eccentric bushings, one set controlling the bearer pressure between the plate and blanket cylinders, the other set controlling the position of the blanket cylinder in relation to the impression cylinder. On presses with a single printing unit, the gear of the blanket cylinder is connected directly to the main motor of the press, and the blanket cylinder gear drives all the other cylinders.

As with inking and dampening rollers, the proper pressure that exists between cylinders is an important adjustment, and the adjustments vary slightly depending upon whether the plate and blanket cylinder bearers are in contact with each other or not. On a ***bearer-contact press***, the bearers act as not only a means of ensuring the alignment of the two cylinders, they also act to reduce gear wear, as the perfect alignment of the bearers ensures proper gear meshing. Effective use of the bearers is only possible when pressure that the bearers exert on each other is beyond that produced simply by the weight of the upper cylinder. In the process of ***preloading***, or setting the increased pressure

between the bearers, proper pressure can be set as follows. With the plate and blanket set to the proper printing height, the blanket is slightly overpacked by about 0.003 in., and thumbprints of ink are placed around both blanket cylinder bearers. With the press started up and the impression pressure engaged, the cylinders are allowed to turn through several revolutions, and the press is stopped. If the inked thumbprints are transferred evenly and thickly, the cylinder setting is fine. If not, the pressures need to be adjusted.

On a ***non-bearer-contact press***, it is necessary to determine the manufacturer's recommendation of the proper gap between the bearers. Then, a small piece of metal with a thickness equal to the required width of the gap is obtained. The blanket is slightly overpacked, and the plate is packed to its correct printing height. The press is started, and the plate, blanket, and ***impression cylinder***s are rolled into position. (The blanket cylinder should be set to exert only a 0.004-in. ***squeeze*** on the impression cylinder.) With the press stopped, the strips of metal are inserted between the plate and blanket cylinder bearers. They should fit tightly, and be moveable with only a strong pull. If they are overly loose or require a great deal of force to move them, the cylinder settings need to be adjusted.

Maintenance of the blanket cylinder simply requires ensuring that the gears and bearers are free of paper debris, dried ink, gum from the dampening solution, and other detritus that can impede gear movement and/or cause gear damage. Lubrication on many presses is accomplished automatically. (See also ***Offset Lithography: Printing Unit***, ***Plate Cylinder***, and ***Impression Cylinder***.)

Blanket-to-Blanket Press

A type of ***perfecting press*** used most commonly in ***web offset lithography***. The ***impression cylinder*** in the printing unit is replaced with a second ***blanket cylinder***, so that as a press sheet or paper web passes between the two blankets it is printed on both sides simultaneously. Successive printing units can print additional colors. See ***Perfecting Press*** and ***Web Offset Lithography***.

Blanking

Alternate term for ***blind-stamping***. See ***Blind-Stamping***.

Blanking Interval

On a ***videodisc*** player, the length of time the device displays a blank screen while searching for the next video segment or frame. See also ***blanking level***, ***Horizontal Blanking Interval*** and ***Vertical Blanking Interval***.

Blanking Level

The level or intensity of a signal sent from a ***videodisc*** player to a monitor during the ***blanking interval***, usually zero, resulting in a blank screen. *Blanking level* also refers to the intensity of the signal during the ***horizontal blanking interval*** and ***vertical blanking interval***, which needs to always be zero, or no signal, to prevent distortion of the screen by the electron gun.

Bleach

Also called *bleach determination*, bleach is a measure of the ***tinctorial strength*** of a printing ink. An ink sample is mixed with a much larger quantity of a white base, and the strength of the resulting color is compared to a predetermined standard.

Bleached Board

Any type of paperboard composed entirely of bleached ***pulp***, as opposed to unbleached ***kraft*** pulp.

Bleaching

One of the final stages in the paper ***pulping*** process, especially those employing chemical means to separate fibers of ***cellulose*** from nonfibrous materials present in wood. The presence of impurities (such as ***lignin***) in pulped wood chips gives unbleached pulp a dark brown color (for example, paper grocery bags use this unbleached pulp.) To increase the ***whiteness*** of pulp and to dissolve residual lignin and other impurities, pulps undergo treatment with bleaching chemicals in several stages, typically five (called "multistage bleaching"). Pulps produced in the ***sulfite process*** and early ***soda process*** use ***calcium hypochlorite***, a chemical similar to household bleach, as a bleaching agent in a one-stage bleaching process. This method, however, is unable to bleach pulps produced using the now-prevalent ***kraft***, or ***sulfate process***.

Multistage bleaching of kraft pulps has two primary phases: lignin-removal and enhancing whiteness. In the first stage of the bleaching process, the pulp is exposed to chlorine gas, which allows the lignin and its related impu-

rities to dissolve easily in a caustic water solution. Several passes through the system ensure that as much lignin as possible is removed. The second stage involves alkaline extraction to remove the byproducts of the previous chlorination phase. Following the lignin-removal phase is the bleaching phase. In the third stage of the process the pulp is treated with calcium (or sodium) hypochlorite to remove coloration from additional impurities in the pulp, and bring out the white color of the cellulose fibers themselves. The fourth stage uses a second alkaline extraction process to remove detritus. The fifth and final stage exposes the pulp to ***chlorine dioxide***, which removes the last of the lignin.

Mechanical pulps are bleached somewhat, but not to great extent. A side-effect of the bleaching process (related to lignin and ***hemicellulose*** removal) is a decrease in pulp yield. The main advantage of mechanical pulping is high pulp yield; excess bleaching would counteract this advantage.

The whiteness of pulp is measured using brightness test methods provided by the ***Technical Association of the Pulp and Paper Industry (TAPPI)*** and the ***International Standards Organization (ISO)***.

Bleed

A printed image that extends beyond one or more of the finished page ***margin***s and is later trimmed so that the image "bleeds" off the edge of the sheet. See also ***Full Bleed***. Also referred to as a bleed off.

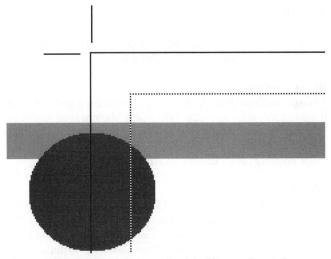

An example of a bleed created with illustration software.

Bleeder Strip

A strip of polyester, acetate, or foil used in the production of ***sheet photopolymer*** plates in ***flexographic*** platemaking, used to cover those portions of the photosensitive plate material that extend beyond the edges of the photographic negative. See ***Plate: Flexography***.

Bleeding

The running of a printing ink or ink component into an undesirable area, either while wet or due to the action of a chemical or other substance on a dry ink film. Bleeding of

The printing unit of a blanket-to-blanket press.

dry ink films is commonly a symptom of an ink with a poor amount of *chemical resistance* or resistance to moisture.

Blend

In graphics, a tool or technique used to create a transition—possessing varying degrees of smoothness—from one color or shape to another.

Blind Embossing

In *binding and finishing*, the stamping or pressing of a relief image or pattern into a *substrate* without any additional color or decoration of the image. See *Embossing*.

Blind Folio

In *book typography*, a page number, or *folio*, that is counted in the page numbering but which is not printed.

Blinding

See *Plate Blinding*.

Blinding In

Alternate term for *blind tooling*. See *Blind Tooling*.

Blind-Stamping

In *binding and finishing*, *die-stamping* performed without using ink or other colorant or decoration. See *Die-Stamping*. Also known as *blanking*.

Blind Text Capability

In a word processing (or other) program, a feature that allows some quantity of text to print on one specific hard copy but not on another, as defined by the user.

Blind Tooling

In early bookbinding, a means of decorating a book cover by drawing a design on a sheet of paper, placing it on top of the book cover, and using heated tools to "trace" the design onto the cover. Blind tooling was often performed as a prelude to *gold tooling*. Also known as *Blinding In*.

Blister

A paper defect that occurs during the *heatset drying* of coated papers, characterized by an oval-shaped bubble that protrudes from both sides of the paper. Blistering is caused by moisture trapped in paper evaporating rapidly under the increased temperature of the heatset dryer. This rapid evaporation causes the water vapor to expand. Coated paper can lack sufficient porosity to allow the water vapor to diffuse gently through the paper surface, and in some cases the water vapor will burst the paper's internal structure apart. Blistering can occur in either printed or non-printed areas, but never occurs in uncoated papers. The problem of blistering used to be a fairly common one, but recent improvements in papermaking have reduced its incidence significantly. To prevent blistering, the *moisture content* of the paper used in heatset drying must be lower than that normally used for sheetfed offset printing, and the *coatings* themselves must be porous enough to enable

the water vapor buildup to diffuse through the surface of the paper. Blistering also occurs less in papers with lower *basis weights*, as lighter paper has less moisture than heavier paper. Blistering is also rarely a problem on *coated-one-side* papers. A paper's ability to keep from blistering is called *blister resistance*. A blister is also known as an *air bell* and a *foam mark*. (See also *Blister Resistance* and *Fiber Puffing*.)

In *binding and finishing*, the term *blister* refers to a small spot on a cloth book cover where the glue has failed to adhere the cloth covering to the underlying board.

Blister Cut

A paper defect characterized by a cut in a paper *web*, usually running diagonally to the *machine direction*. It is caused by a blister-like accumulation of excess paper at the opening of a nip between rollers on the papermaking machine. As the web passes through the nip, the blister cuts the web. (See also *Calender Cut*, *Calender Spot*, *Calender-Blackened Spots/Streaks*, *Fiber Cut*, and *Hair Cut*.)

Blister Package

See *Carded Package*.

Blister Resistance

The ability of a coated paper to resist formation of *blister*s during the *heatset drying* of *heatset ink*. A blister is an oval-shaped bubble protruding from both sides of the paper *web*. Blistering is caused by moisture trapped in paper evaporating rapidly under the increased temperature of heatset drying. As the vapor expands, it may not be able to escape through the surface of the paper if the paper *coating* is of low porosity, in which case it bursts the paper's internal structure apart. In order for a coated paper to possess high blister resistance, it must have a lower *moisture content* than usual, and it must have adequate porosity and *internal bond strength*. As a paper's *basis weight* increases, so does its tendency to blister, as heavier paper will hold more moisture. *Coated-one-side* paper does not tend to blister. (See also *Blister*.)

Tests to measure a paper's blister resistance involve conditioning a coated paper to a particular *relative humidity*, then immersing the paper in a hot oil bath. The temperature of the bath can be altered to determine the temperature at which blistering will occur. Another test involves covering a coated paper with a thick lacquer (to simulate the heavy ink coverage that is one of the causes of blistering). The paper is run through an oven for a set period of time, and the paper is examined for blistering. Varying the time spent in the oven and the oven temperature help to gauge the specific blister resistance of the paper. (See also *Fiber Puffing*.)

Blitter

In computer graphics, a processing chip used in graphics adapters (especially a *graphics coprocessor*) that effects *bit block transfer*s, or *blitting*. Since a blitter is designed expressly for this activity, it is faster than a general *CPU*. See *Bit Block Transfer*.

Blitting

In computer graphics, the act of effecting a *bit block transfer*, especially by means of a *blitter*. See *Bit Block Transfer* and *Blitter*.

Block

In word processing software, any defined quantity of text which can be cut, copied, moved, and pasted by the user.

In networking and telecommunications, *block* is an alternate term for a *packet*. See *Packet*.

Block book

Block books were printed from wooden blocks into which the text and illustration for each page had to be tediously cut by hand. Such books or ephemera (smaller printed products) pre-dated printed books. After the invention of movable type, words were made up of individual metal letters, each of which could be reused, and only illustrations

This example of a book block is taken from the Bible of the Poor, printed in 1470 by Walther & Hurning in Germany.

and special images, such as initial letters, had to be carved individually in wooden blocks which were then set in forms with metal letters to print. The earliest engraved printing units were wood engravings in which the nonimage areas of an illustration were removed by carving them from the surface of a flat wood block. The oldest known illustration printed from a wooden block is a Buddhist scroll from about 750 AD. The Chinese Diamond Sutra of 868 AD incorporates a woodcut title page and text with woodcut images. Block book printing is also called xylography.

Block book printing is of Chinese origin, probably from the 6th century AD. The first examples were produced by hand-rubbing impressions from the block to rice paper. The method spread to Europe by the 15th century, and simple presses were used to impress the image from blocks. Each letter was carved each time it appeared on a page which made the method applicable for short, simple works—mostly religious. European block books were not produced after the 16th century. The earliest extant example of a European print from a wood engraving is a print entitled "St. Christopher," dated 1423. Another example of block book printing is the "Apocalypse of St. John," printed in 1450.

The printing press was initially a simple adaptation of the binding press, with a fixed lower surface (bed) and a movable upper surface (platen), moved vertically by means of a worm screw. The composed page, after being locked or screwed tight into a metal frame (form), was inked, covered with a sheet of paper to be printed, and then pressed in the vise formed by the two surfaces. This process was better than the hand brushing method used in block printing in Europe and China because it produced a sharp impression and could print both sides of a sheet.

Block Check Character

In networking and telecommunications, a character or character sequence used to determine if a larger set of characters was received correctly. Abbreviated *BCC*.

Block Color

Any color printed with the same *density* and *opacity* over the entire surface of the *substrate* without tints, gradations, or shading.

Block Diagram

Alternate term for a *flowchart*. See *Flowchart*.

Block Error Rate Test

In telecommunications and networking, a measure of the quality of a transmission, consisting of the ratio of the total number of blocks transmitted in a message to the number of blocks received in an error. Abbreviated *BERT*.

Blocking

The sticking together of printed sheets or a printed *web*, caused by *ink setoff*, the transfer of ink from a printed sheet to the sheet lying on top of it due to incomplete ink drying. See *Ink Setoff*.

In telecommunications, *blocking* refers to the state of a *PBX* system in which all lines are in use.

Blocking Factor

In computing, the number of individual (or logical) records contained in a single physical block or record on a *magnetic tape* or *magnetic disk*.

Blocking Out

In *screen printing*, the treatment of the screen fabric with a sealant (called *blockout solution*) between the edges of the stencil and the frame, to prevent ink transfer in non-image areas.

Blocking Test

See *Block Test*.

Block Length

In computing, a measure of the size of a set of data, be it *bit*s, *byte*s, characters, words, records, etc.

Block Letter

In typography, a *gothic* or *sans serif* typeface. Also called *block type*.

Helvetica, an example of block letters.

Block Move/Copy

In word processing programs, the ability to define a *block* of text, copy (or cut) it, and paste it elsewhere in the same document or in a different document.

Blockout Compound

Alternate term for *blockout solution*. See *Blockout Solution*.

Blockout Filler

Alternate term for *blockout solution*. See *Blockout Solution*.

Blockout Printing Screen

In screen printing, a screen prepared without a stencil by manually applying blockout solution in desired nonimage areas, leaving the screen open and capable of transferring ink in those regions comprising the image area.

Blockout Solution

In *screen printing*, a water-based glue or other fluid applied to the surface of the screen fabric between the edges of the stencil and the frame which, when dry, will prevent ink transfer in nonimage areas. In short print runs, a paper mask prepared from *kraft* paper is often used in lieu of blockout solution. Blockout solution is also known as *blockout compound* and *blockout filler*.

Block Protect

In desktop publishing, the ability to mark a block of text (or, usually, tabular or chart data) to ensure that it does not get separated by a page break.

Block Test

Term for any of a variety of tests used to determine the likelihood that a particular ink and *substrate* combination will result in *blocking* when printed. The factors that contribute to blocking—pressure, drying time, temperature, humidity—are varied and inflicted upon a press proof containing the ink and substrate to be printed. Block tests vary from simple "finger twist" tests, in which a press proof is twisted tightly and examined for *setoff* and ink film breakage, to elaborate tests utilizing ovens that vary the pressure, temperature and humidity to which the sample is exposed. Also known as *Blocking Test*s.

Block Text

In typography, paragraphs set without indents.

Block Type

Alternate term for *block letter*. See *Block Letter*.

Bloom

A printing ink defect in which substances from the interior of an ink film rise to the surface, producing a distortion or discoloration of the ink film, commonly caused by too-rapid evaporation of ink *solvent*. Bloom caused by solid materials is commonly referred to as *exudation*. (See also *Blushing*.)

The term *bloom* is also used to refer to the desirable rising of waxes within an ink to the surface, as a means of imparting scuff resistance to the dried ink film.

Blooming

On a computer display monitor, a type of distortion characterized by the enlargement of screen images as the brightness level is increased.

Blotch

Any irregularly shaped area of discoloration, either on a *substrate*, a plate, blanket, etc.

Blotting

A term for any form of spotting or staining.

In *screen printing*, *blotting* is the process of removing excess moisture from a developed and mounted *photostencil* by applying unprinted newsprint (or other absorbent material) to the top of the screen and rolling a *brayer* over it.

Blow-Down

A series of air holes, nozzles, or fans used in the *delivery section* of a sheetfed printing press (especially that used in *offset lithography*)—alone or in tandem with *suction* *roller*s—to slow down a press sheet as it leaves the *delivery chain* and enters the *delivery pile*. The force of the air blowing down on the sheet keeps the sheet steady as it is about to fall onto the stack. (See *Delivery Section*.)

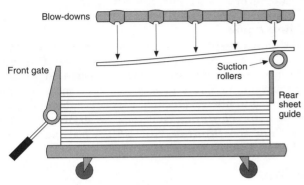

Blow-down.

Blow-In Card

In *binding and finishing*, a type of *insert*—such as a *return card* found in magazines or an errata sheet added to books—which is printed separately (usually on a somewhat heavy card stock) and inserted into a publication using compressed air to "blow" the card between the pages.

Blow Molding

In packaging, a means of forming hollow plastic packaging (such as bottles) in which air or nitrogen is "blown" into preformed plastic, causing the plastic to expand against the mold corresponding to the desired shape of the bottle. Blow molding can be performed either by injection molding (in which melted plastic is injected into a cavity around a core rod and air used to expand the plastic to the desired shape) or extrusion molding (in which the melted plastic is extruded as a tube, the mold being placed around it to form the desired shape).

Blowup

In imaging, when used as a verb, to enlarge an image or type. When used as a noun, it means the *enlargement* itself. Also spelled as two words, *blow up*. Blowing up that is performed electronically is commonly called *scaling*.

Blue

The *color* characteristic of light possessing a wavelength between 450 and 500 *nanometer*s, located on the spectrum between *green* and *violet*. Blue is one of the three *primary colors* of light. (See *Additive Color Primaries*.)

In *process color* printing, *blue* is also a secondary color produced by overprinting *cyan* and *magenta* inks. Blue is often—though somewhat incorrectly—used synonymously with cyan. (See *Subtractive Color Primaries*.)

Blue-Sensitive

A type of photographic film which is only sensitive to light in the *blue* portion of the *visible spectrum* (or, in other words, light having a wavelength between 450 and 500 *nanometer*s) and in the *ultraviolet* portion of the spectrum. Also known as *color blind* film, blue-sensitive film—unlike *orthochromatic* and *panchromatic* films—can be used somewhat safely outside a darkroom, and is often used for photoimaging utilizing ultraviolet light.

Blueline

A single-color photographic proof exposed from *negative*s prior to platemaking, used to evaluate *pagination* and location of page elements, such as text, photos, and other illustrations. Since bluelines (they can also be brown—in which case they are called *brownline*s) are produced in only one color, the color breaks are not directly exhibited, but variations in exposure can indicate somewhat crudely where divisions in color will occur.

Bluelines are also called *blues*, and have variously been known as *brown print*, *Dylux*, *silverprint*, *VanDyke*, and *Velox*, names derived from the brands of photosensitive paper used to create them.

Blues

Alternate term for *blueline*.

Blur

In imaging, to reduce the sharpness of an image. In computer graphics and image manipulation programs, a blur tool is used to soften images to achieve a variety of special effects, such as creating a soft effect.

Blurb

In book publishing, a brief summary of a book or, more commonly, a quote from a book review or established author (or other expert) placed on a book cover or jacket for promotional purposes.

Blurring

Any condition which causes printed matter to appear blurry. See also *Slurring*.

Blushing

A printing defect, commonly of *gravure* printing, characterized by a transparent printed ink film having a foggy appearance. Blushing is caused by *precipitation* or incompatibility of the substances comprising the ink, typically exacerbated by increased moisture condensation and humidity. (See also *Bloom*.)

BMP

A *file format* and *file extension* for a *bitmap* graphic. BMP files were first used in the *Windows* environment to display, for example, the desktop background ("wallpaper"). BMP files are also used in the *OS/2* operating system.

BNC

Abbreviation for *Bayonet-Neil-Concelman*, a type of bayonet connector used to connect devices to an *Ethernet* network by means of **coaxial cable**, or to connect different pieces of video equipment together.

Board

A heavy-weight, thick paper with a **caliper** exceeding 6 mil. (0.006 in.) In computing, a *board* is a circuit card on which integrated circuits are mounted.

Bodied Oil

An oil—either a **drying oil** or a **non-drying oil**—used as a printing ink **vehicle** which has been heated to increase its **viscosity**.

Bodoni, Giambattista

Giambattista Bodoni (1740–1813) was born into a printing family in Saluzzo, Italy. At the age of 18 he was hired by the Vatican printing house in Rome. By 1768, he became the director of the press of Ferdinand, Duke of Parma, which he retained for the rest of his life. Bodoni was the most successful early proponent of the "modern" typeface, distinguished by a strong contrast between the thin and thick strokes, and vertical, rather than oblique, shading. His books were produced for the wealthy and the aristocracy, and were more advanced in elegance and refinement than anything else being printed in Europe. Intended more for show, his publications were often inaccurate and difficult to read. His Greek typefaces, as seen in his masterful edition of Homer, are more successful. His enormous collection of typefaces was published posthumously in the two-volume *Manuale Tipografico* (Parma, 1818).

Body

A general term describing the thickness, consistency, **viscosity**, and stiffness of a printing ink. Inks run the gamut from very soft and fluid (such as inks used for the printing **newsprint**) to very thick and stiff (such as inks used in collotype). Some inks can possess a "false body," called **thixotropy** or **dilatancy**, or a consistency that changes, sometimes drastically, when under stress. The term *body*, when applied to inks, can also refer to the increased viscosity of an ink following the **polymerization** of the ink **vehicle** with the application of heat.

In typography, the term *body* is a shortened version of the term **body text**. See **Body Text**. Also in typography, the term *body* is a shortened version of the term **body height**, an alternate term for **x-height**. See **x-Height**.

In **binding and finishing**, the term refers to the main text of a book, exclusive of **end paper**s or covers.

Body Gum

A type of **bodying agent**, or a substance added to printing ink to increase its **viscosity**. Body gum (also called **Num-**

ber 8 Varnish) consists of thick, gummy, heat-polymerized **linseed oil**. (See **Bodying Agent**.)

Body Height

Alternate term for **x-height**. See **x-Height**.

Bodying Agent

A substance added to a printing ink to increase its **viscosity**. Bodying agents (such as **body gum** or **binding varnish**) increase an ink's **tack**, and the increased viscosity allows the ink to print images and type more sharply. When added to lithographic ink, they prevent **emulsification** and **ink chalking**, and improve drying. (See also **Body Gum** and **Binding Varnish**.) A bodying agent is also known as a **thickener**.

Body Size

Alternate term for **x-height**. See **x-Height**.

Body Stock

Alternate term for **base stock** in the **finishing** operations in papermaking. See **Base Stock**. Also called **raw stock**.

Body stock is also another term for **face material**. See **Face Material**.

Body Text

The main portion of a book or other document, excluding **front matter** and **back matter**.

Body Type

Alternate term for **text type**. See **Text Type**.

BOF

Abbreviation for **bottom of form**. See **Bottom of Form**.

Boiled Oil

An oil (typically **linseed oil**) used in a printing ink **vehicle** which has had its **viscosity** and drying rate increased by heating it to a high temperature for a short duration.

Boilerplate

Any stored text, paragraph, or document used to create a new document, often with variable text. Boilerplate is often used in connection with contracts, where various clauses and terms remain the same from contract to contract.

Bold

Shortened version of the term **boldface**.

Boldface

A type style characterized by heavier **weight** than the "plain" versions of the characters. Boldface, more commonly known as **bold**, is used primarily for emphasis or **heading**s.

This is plain type.
This is boldface type.

Bolts

In **binding and finishing**, the untrimmed, usually folded edges of a **signature** prior to trimming, not including the **binding edge**. The fold at the top of a signature is known as the **head bolt**. Uncut signature folds are called **closed bolts**. Roughly trimmed edges are called **open bolts**. Both open and closed bolts require complete trimming at the end of the binding process.

Bomb

In computers, a system failure or the abrupt termination of a program. Also used as a verb, as in "The system will bomb quite easily." Also known as a **crash**.

Bon à Tirer

The first approved **press proof**, from the French phrase meaning "good to print."

BON Arylamide Red

An **organic color pigment** used in printing inks. BON Arylamide Red is a medium, slightly bluish red possessing high **lightfastness**, and resistance to acids, alkalis, soap, water, and heat. It tends to bleed in most solvents, however. It is somewhat more expensive than similar pigments, and is used when its increased chemical resistance properties warrant it. It is also used for printing flesh tones.

Also known as **Naphthol Red FGR** (*CI Pigment Red 112 No. 12370*). (See also **Organic Color Pigments**.)

Bond Paper

A common **grade** of paper commonly used for letterhead, business forms, writing, typing, and copying. Bond papers are characterized by high **permanence** and **durability**, high surface strength to withstand writing and erasing, and high **stiffness**. Un**watermark**ed bond papers, made from **chemical pulp**, are used for invoices and other business forms. An air-dried, watermarked, **cockle finish** bond is used for high-quality letterhead. The highest quality bond papers are **cotton-content** bond papers, which are produced from a higher amount of rag-based pulp (from 25–100% cotton-fiber). High cotton-content bond papers are used for distinctive letterheads and writing papers, as well as matching envelopes.

The **basic size** for bond papers is 17×22 in., and standard **basis weight**s are 13-, 16-, 20-, 24-, 28-, 32-, 36-, and 40-pound. Most bond papers are cut to a **standard size** of 8½×11 in. Other standard sizes for bond papers are 8½×13 in., 8½×14 in., 11×17 in., 17×22 in., 17×28 in., 19×24 in., 22×34 in., 24×38 in., 28×34 in., 34×44 in..

Bonding Agent

A substance added to a printing ink (such as that used in **screen printing**) to facilitate adhesion to a **nylon** surface.

BON Maroon

An **organic color pigment** used in printing inks. BON Maroon comprises several shades, depending on the metallic salt it contains, the most common being a deep blue red possessing moderate **lightfastness**, high resistance to acids, and moderate resistance to alkalis and solvents.

(*CI Pigment Red 63 No. 15880*; *CI Pigment Red 63* [sodium]; *CI Pigment Red 63:1* [calcium]; *CI Pigment Red 63:2* [manganese].)

(See also **Organic Color Pigments**.)

BON Red

An **organic color pigment** used in printing inks. BON Red comes in a variety of shades, depending on the metallic salt it contains. Shades vary from a yellow red (sodium) to scarlet (manganese). BON Red is similar in structure to **Lake Red C**, but possesses higher degrees of **lightfastness**, heat resistance, and solvent resistance. The medium red shade, containing calcium salt, is the most commonly used BON Red. BON Red is used often in the United States, primarily for its color characteristics, but its popularity in Europe is very low.

Also known as **Lake Red C BON** (*CI Pigment Red 52 No. 15860*; *CI Pigment Red 52* [sodium]; *CI Pigment Red 52:1* [calcium]; *CI Pigment Red 52:2* [manganese]).

(See also **Organic Color Pigments**.)

Bonus Color

In multicolor **screen printing**, the production of a desired extra color by overprinting other desired colors (typically transparent inks), eliminating the need for a third stencil and press pass.

Book Block

In **binding and finishing**, all the pages and/or **signature**s of a book which have been folded and gathered, and which await binding.

Book Cloth

In **binding and finishing**, a type of plastic-coated or starch-filled cotton fabric used for **casebound** book covers.

Book Ink

A variety of **rotary ink** used in **letterpress** printing of books, produced with various formulations depending on the **hardness** and surface texture of the **book paper** printed. Book inks generally have a fluid **body**, and can be fast-drying (if used on hard papers) or somewhat slower-drying (if used on soft papers). (See **Rotary Ink**.)

Book Mark

In **binding and finishing**, a thin ribbon or cord fastened at the top of a book's **spine** under the **backlining**, designed as a decorative ornament on specialty books or **deluxe edition**s. The term *book mark* also refers to any material inserted into a book—usually by a reader—to mark one's place, including the **dogear**.

In multimedia and World Wide Web applications, a *book mark* (usually spelled as one word, *bookmark*) is an electronic marker added to an application program. On a

CD-ROM, for example, a marker can be added at certain points, given a name, and selected again at a later time from a menu, allowing the user to go directly to that point in the presentation. Bookmarks are also used in Web browsers, where they are essentially a type of *alias*, or a stored *URL*, allowing the user to go directly to a web site without having to enter often-unwieldy addresses.

Book Paper

A *grade* of paper used in the printing of text and trade books, as well as a variety of other types of printed materials. They are similar to *text paper*, but are usually less expensive, and come in a wider variety of *basis weight*s and *bulk*s. This aids in choosing the right thickness of paper depending on the desired ultimate book thickness (see *Bulk*). Finishes range from *antique* to *smooth*. There are also *coated book paper*s and *groundwood book papers*, depending on the finish and cost desired.

The *basic size* of book paper is 25×38 in., coming in *basis weight*s of 30, 40, 45, 50, 60, 70, 80, 90, 100, and 120-lb. *Standard sizes* are 17½×22½ in., 19×25 in., 23×29 in., 23×35 in., 24×36 in., 25×38 in., 28×44 in., 32×44 in., 35×45 in., 38×50 in., and 42×58 in.

Bookplate

A label with a printed design intended to indicate ownership pasted inside the front cover of a book. Bookplates originated in Germany, where the earliest bookplate dated about 1480 is found. German bookplates were art, designed

An ornately-carved bookplate, this one belonging to George Washington.

by the foremost artists of the time, including Albrecht Durer, Lucas Cranach, and Hans Holbein. French bookplates came into use about 1530, but until 1630 book owners preferred having their arms or other devices stamped on leather covers. The earliest known American bookplate, is from colonial New England, in the form of a plain printed label with the owner's name, "John Cotton, his book," 1674. Pictorial bookplates included portraits, stacks of books, views of bookcases, and landscapes. Allegorical bookplates were in favor in France during the reign of Louis XV and in England by mid-18th century. Also introduced into the design were symbols of the interests and occupations of the book's owner.

Book Typography

The setting and arrangement of the various parts of a book. In the typesetting and assembly of books, the following terms are used commonly:

Verso: the left-hand page of a two-page spread.

Recto: the right-hand page of a two-page spread.

Folio: the page number.

Running head or *running foot*: the book title, author, chapter name, or other identifying line of text appearing at the top or bottom, respectively, of each page.

Line short/long: an allowance for setting certain pages shorter or longer, respectively, than the standard page depth to eliminate *widow*s, excessively short pages, or to provide room for illustration matter.

Widow: the last line of a paragraph when it is less than one-third the width of the line, commonly used to refer to the carry-over of a hyphenated word.

Orphan: a widow carried to the top of the next page.

In printing book pages, a sheet of paper printed as one page is known as a *broadside*. Folding it once to produce four pages makes it a folio. Folding it again to produce eight pages makes it a *quarto*. Folding it again to produce sixteen pages makes it an *octavo*. Folding it yet again to produce thirty-two pages makes it a *sixteenmo*. Folding it yet again to produce sixty-four pages makes it a *thirty-twomo*.

Book production has a long history, and many of the customs and traditions are highly standardized. The order of the portions of a book are generally as follows, although not all parts need to be present in a single book.

Front Matter. Front matter is all the material that precedes the main text of the book, including (in order):

Half-title (the book title alone on a page); *fact title* or *ad card* (the list of books by the same author, commonly facing the title page); *title page* (always a *recto* page, listing title, author, and publisher); *copyright page* (commonly on the reverse of the title page, listing copyright and CIP data); *dedication* (may be on the copyright page or, more commonly, on a new recto page); *preface*, *prologue*, or *foreword* (always begins a new recto page); *acknowledgements* (commonly on a new recto or can be included with the back matter); *table of contents* (always begins a new recto); lists of illustrations, figures, maps, charts, tables, etc. (commonly begins new recto); and *introduction* (always begins new recto). Front matter is commonly paginated using lowercase **Roman numerals**.

Following the front matter is the main text of the book, which always begins on a new recto, and with Arabic pagination beginning at page one.

Back Matter. Back matter is all the material that follows the main text of the book, including:

An *afterword*, *epilogue*, *appendix* (or appendices); notes, quotations, *bibliography*, *glossary*, *index*, and the author's biographical information. Some books also include a *colophon*, providing production details about the book, the typeface used, etc.

See also *Book Publishing: Production*.

Book-Wrap Mailer

Alternate term for a *wraparound mailer*. See *Wraparound Mailer*.

Booklet

Any small, low-page count *pamphlet* commonly saddle-stitched or thread sewn. Booklets often utilize a *self-cover*, but may also use slightly heavier stock for a cover. Booklets are used for instruction manuals, promotional literature, etc., and are not often designed to be long-lived.

Boolean Algebra

In mathematics, a type of *algebra* concerned with logical objects or relations in which there are only two stable states: yes/no, true/false, on/off, etc. Boolean algebra was devised by English mathematician George Boole in 1847, but was largely ignored until the middle of the twentieth century, when it could be applied to the fields of relay switching and, consequently, electronic computers. In Boolean algebra, variables do not represent numbers, but rather statements and logical operations. By using *Boolean operator*s such as "or," "and," and "nor," computers can be instructed to do certain things. For example, a program may read something like, "If A or B = C, then do D." The computer will then wait for the conditions to be such as that A or B = C, and then it will execute whatever D corresponds to.

In database systems, *search engine*s, and on the World Wide Web, searches for information typically use Boolean algebra. See *Boolean Search*. Boolean algebra is also known as *Boolean logic*.

Boolean Operator

In computing, words such as "and," "or," and "not" used to specify logical processes in computer programming, or search for specific keywords in databases or on the *World Wide Web*. See *Boolean Algebra* and *Boolean Search*.

Boolean Search

In database systems, a *search query* in which more than one word can be searched for at one time. Each term is connected by *Boolean operator*s such as "and," "or," and "not." In a Boolean search (which is based in principles of *Boolean algebra*), two or more search criteria may be used at one time in three logical relationships. For example, to find "giant squid" you could choose "giant" *and* "squid." In this case, a text string will qualify as a "hit" if it contains both those words. Searching for "giant" *or* "squid" would yield all text strings containing "giant," and all text strings containing "squid." All text strings containing both terms will also qualify as "hits." A third alternative would be "squid" *not* "giant," and "hits" will pick up all text strings containing "squid" but not "giant."

Boot

In popular parlance, to start up a computer, also referred to by the phrase *boot up*. Technically, *boot* means to read information in a device's *ROM*, which tells the computer how to access files and read input data or, in other words, how to load the operating system. All a computer really knows how to do upon start-up is read whatever information is in ROM or on the boot sector of the hard disk (or other startup disk). "Boot" is derived from the earlier term *bootstrapping*. See also *Cold Boot* and *Warm Boot*.

Bootable Disk

In computing, any disk from which the computer can be started. Once, *floppy disk*s were used to *boot* computers, but in recent years operating systems have grown too large to be stored on low-capacity floppies.

Boot ROM

In computing and networking, a type of *read-only memory (ROM)* that instructs a *workstation* on how to access a network *file server* and read a *boot* program. This procedure is used for workstations lacking a disk drive.

Bootstrap

In computing, a program residing in *ROM*, on a startup disk, or elsewhere, containing the information the computer needs in order to know how to load the operating system. See *Boot*. Early computers needed the insertion of punch cards or strips of paper tape, a process called *bootstrapping*. The term *bootstrap* itself derives from the popular expression "pull oneself up by one's bootstraps," which is fairly descriptive of the process. A bootstrap is also known as a *bootstrap loader*.

Bootstrapping

Full term for *booting* a computer, used colloquially when computers needed to be booted by means of a punch card or strip of paper tape containing instructions on how to load the operating system and read from actual program cards or tape. See *Bootstrap* and *Boot*.

Bordeaux FRR

An *organic color pigment* used in printing inks. Bordeaux FRR is a dull but extreme blue red possessing high *tinctorial strength*, good *lightfastness* and high chemical resistance properties, especially high resistance to soaps.

Also known as *Bordeaux F4R* (*CI Pigment Red 12 No. 12385*).

(See also *Organic Color Pigments*.)

Border

In typography, a frame, decorative lines, or design used to surround typographic, pictorial, or other material. A border should be chosen so that it complements and harmonizes with the material it surrounds. It is also aesthetically important that the corners meet properly, without gaps or overhangs.

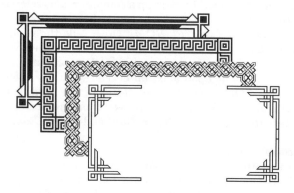

Decorative borders.

Border Gateway Protocol (BGP)

In networking, a *routing protocol* used to connect networks. BGP evaluates all the possible routes by which to transmit a message and selects the most expedient one. BGP supplanted the earlier *External Gateway Protocol (EGP)*.

Bottle Cap Printer

An offset press used to print a design onto a metallic *substrate*, which is then die-cut and formed, used—as its name indicates—as bottle caps.

Bottle Press

A configuration of *screen printing* press designed to print on cylinders (or other shapes) used—as its name indicates—for making bottles.

Bottleneck

In a computer system, the operation having the slowest speed or the least capacity. In systems with no alternative routing, the bottleneck can slow down the rate at which other operations are performed. Also called a *limiting operation*.

Bottom Seal

In packaging, a means of manufacturing plastic *bag*s. See *Bag: Plastic Bags*.

Bounce

An erratic rotation of a printing press cylinder—such as a *plate cylinder*, *blanket cylinder*, or *impression cylinder*—that results in defective impressions, caused by inconsistent reactions to plate or blanket compression under impression pressures. Also known as *whip*.

In typography, the term *bounce* refers to a typeset line containing alternating characters in an up and down position.

In data communications, the term *bounce* refers to the return of an *email* message. Such a return can be due to an error with the recipient's mail server, a discontinued email account, or a typo on the part of the sender.

Boundary Fill

See *Fill*.

Bounding Box

In *PostScript*—or any other *page description language*—the rectangular area in which a particular image is contained. See *PostScript*.

Boustrophedon Printing

An alternate term for *bidirectional printing*, or a computer printer that prints one line from left to right, and the succeeding line from right to left. The term derives from one used to refer to an ancient Greek style of writing in which each line read alternately from left to right and right to left. The word itself comes from the combination of the Greek words *bous* (meaning "ox") and *strophe* (meaning "turning"), or, in other words, a style of writing reminiscent of the way an ox plows a field, plowing first one one way, then back the other way.

Boutique

Any computer output or printing that has high quality requirements.

Bowl

In typography, the curved stroke of a letter or other character which creates an enclosed space (called a *counter*) in the character, as in the stroke that forms the center of the letter "e". A *complete bowl* is formed only by curved strokes (as in the "o") while a *modified bowl* has the *stem* forming one of the sides, as in the lowercase "a." See *Letter Elements*.

Box

In typography, a common type of *pi character* (❑), available in a variety of sizes, used for decorative or organizational purposes. Boxes should be as close as possible to the *x-height* of the text they accompany. The *point size* of the box may need to be increased so that it optically approximates the size of the text; it is generally inadvisable to make a box larger than the x-height of the accompanying text. Boxes are often used to delineate and emphasize points or examples or to signify the end of a magazine or newspaper article. They are available either closed (∎) or open (❑). A similar pi character, and as widely used, is a *bullet*.

In typography and page layout, the term *box* also refers to a delimited rectangular portion of a page, containing text and/or graphics, usually set off from other page elements by *rules*. In *page makeup software*, such as QuarkXPress, boxes containing type are called "text boxes"; those containing graphics are known as "picture boxes." In magazine and newspaper typography, a large box of related text supplementing a main article or story is known as a *sidebar*.

In packaging, a *box* is any cube-shaped structure, manufactured from paperboard, wood, or plastic.

Corrugated Boxes. *Corrugated box*es account for over 90% of all the materials shipped in the United States. Corrugated boxes are produced from two or more sheets of unbleached or bleached *kraft* linerboard separated by a corrugated material, or a fluted paperboard, used to impart strength and cushioning. There are four standard sizes of corrugated board: A-flute (33 flutes per foot, with a flute thickness of ³⁄₁₆ in.), B-flute (47 flutes per foot, with a flute thickness of ³⁄₃₂ in.), C-flute (39 flutes per foot, with a flute thickness of ⁹⁄₆₄ in.), and E-flute (90 flutes per foot, with a flute thickness of ³⁄₆₄ in.) C-flute is the most common size.

The corrugated material is adhered to the linerboard in one of four ways. *Single-faced corrugated* has the corrugating material lined on only one side with linerboard. *Single-wall corrugated* has the corrugating material lined on both sides with linerboard. *Double-wall corrugated* has two sheets of corrugating material sandwiched between three sheets of linerboard. *Triple-wall corrugated* has three layers of corrugating material sandwiched between four sheets of linerboard. Corrugated board commonly needs to have a prescribed *bursting strength*, an amount (measured by a *Mullen test*) usually required by rail and truck freight regulations (200 pounds per square inch is a common bursting test requirement.)

Corrugated boxes are often printed—when they need to be printed—by means of *flexography*. The flexo printing of boxes also includes a variety of *in-line* finishing operations such as *folding*, *scoring*, *gluing*, and *die-cutting*. The greatest usage of corrugated boxes is the food industry, while the shipment of paper products, glass, and ceramics is the next highest classification of corrugated use.

Rigid-Paperboard Boxes. Rigid-paperboard boxes are usually much smaller and possess less strength than corrugated boxes. They are also most commonly provided to the end user in finished form, where as with corrugated boxes some degree of unfolding and securing is often required. The rigid-paperboard box has its origins in Elizabethan England, when sixteenth century nobles used paperboard boxes to carry around various clothing accessories. In modern times, such boxes are manufactured out of a single sheet of paperboard, scored, cut, folded, and glued to form the finished box. A *kraft*-paper based "stay" is glued to the outside of the box, and acts to hold the box

together. These boxes are rarely printed directly; a printed paper wrapper is glued around the finished box. Various specialty procedures can add transparent cellophane windows, padded covers, hinged covers, box-in-box, pre-formed plastic inlaid trays, etc. These boxes are often used for food packaging, textiles, cosmetics and soaps, office supplies, and many other uses.

Rigid-Plastic Boxes. Rigid-plastic boxes are very similar in design and shape to the rigid-paperboard boxes mentioned above, the differences being in the materials (plastic vs. paperboard) and manufacture. Rigid-plastic boxes are manufactured either by injection molding, plastic extrusion, or thermoforming. Injection-molded boxes are the most widely used, and can be either hinged, unhinged, or telescoping. The advantage to extruding is the wide variety of shapes that can be produced, not subject to the limitations of the process, as is the case with injection molding. Thermoformed boxes are often used for one-piece hinged boxes, or plastic insert trays in paperboard boxes.

Plastic boxes are printed by a variety of printing processes, most commonly *screen printing*, with some *offset lithographic* and flexographic printing being used. Many plastic boxes are are decorated by means of *hot stamping*, or a type of *die stamping* that uses heated dies to impress a design into the plastic. One advantage of rigid-plastic boxes is their reusability.

Solid-Fiber Boxes. Solid-fiber boxes, unlike corrugated boxes, are manufactured from a single, solid layer formed from several plies of paperboard. Separate plies are glued together under pressure to form a strong, solid sheet; die-cutting or other *converting* processes are used to cut and form the sheets into the desired size and configuration of box. Solid-fiber boxes are designed and produced almost exclusively for applications requiring reuse, commonly due to their expense. A typical solid-fiber box is estimated to be able to be used 10–15 times before it has outlived its usefulness. Breweries are one of the biggest purchasers of these boxes.

Wirebound Boxes and Wooden Crates. Wirebound boxes are often also known as crates, and reinforce a wooden construction with steel binding wires fastened to the wood by staples. Any of a variety of deciduous trees can supply the wood used for such crates. (The technical difference between a box and a crate is that the former is a completely enclosed structure in which contents are placed, whereas the latter is a container of framed construction.) The advantage of wooden boxes and crates is their sturdy construction and the increased protection they afford their contents.

Boxboard

Heavy paperboard of sufficient thickness to be used for the manufacture of *box*es, including grades such as news, filled news, chip, straw, jute, patent coated, or clay-coated.

bpi

Abbreviation of *bits per inch*. See *Bits Per Inch (bpi)*.

bps

Abbreviation of *bits per second*. See *Bits Per Second (bps)*.

Braces

In typography, the characters { }, used for parenthetical expressions. Although not widely used in general text material, braces are used in mathematics (particularly in equations) and computer programming to group certain elements together. Braces—also known as *curly braces*—are usually used third in the parenthetical progression, the first being *parentheses*, the second being *brackets*, as in $a(b[c\{d + e\}])$.

Bracketed

In typography, descriptive of the curvature linking the main vertical stem of a letter (or other character) to the horizontal *serif*. A serif character with no curvature (or where the join between the stem and the serif is a right angle) is known as *square serif*. A variety of these square serif faces is collectively called *Egyptian* (named after the extensive use of these typefaces on signboards during Napoleon's Egyptian campaign). A slight curvature between the stem and the serif is known as fine bracketing, while a highly pronounced curvature is known as full bracketing. Such bracketing is also known as a *cove serif*.

Unbracketed (left) and bracketed typefaces.

Brackets

In typography, the characters [ ], used for parenthetical expressions. Brackets are often used in general text material—especially quotes and excerpts from other sources—to indicate alterations made to the original quote by an editor, such as "Now is the [summer] of our discontent [...]". Brackets are also used in mathematics (particularly in equations) and computer programming to group elements together. Also known as *square brackets*, they are usually used sec-

ond in the parenthetical progression, the first being *parentheses*, the third being *braces*, as in $a(b[c\{d + e\}])$.

Braille

A universal system of writing used by blind persons, consisting of a code of 63 characters, each made up of one to six raised dots arranged in a six-position matrix or cell. These symbols are embossed into paper and read by passing fingers lightly over them. Louis Braille, who was blinded at the age of three, invented the system in 1824 while a student at the Institution Nationale des Jeunes Aveugles (National Institute for Blind Children), Paris.

Frenchman Valentin Haüy was the first to emboss paper as a means of reading. His printing of normal letters in relief led others to devise simplified versions. Louis Braille entered the school for the blind in Paris in 1819 and learned of writing using dots as invented by Captain Charles Barbier, a French army officer. Called night writing, it was intended for night-time battlefield communications. When he was 15 years old, Braille developed a six-dot "cell" system. He used Barbier's system as a starting point and cut its 12-dot configuration in half. The system was first published in 1829.

To aid in decoding 63 different dot patterns, Braille numbered the positions 1-2-3 downward on the left and 4-5-6 downward on the right. The first 10 letters of the alphabet are formed with dots 1, 2, 4, and 5. When preceded by the numeric indicator in line 6, the signs have numeric values. The remaining letters of the alphabet and five very common words are formed by adding dots 3 and 6 to the positions in line 1. Punctuation marks and two additional common letter combinations are made by placing the signs in line 1 in dot positions 2, 3, 5, and 6. Three final letter combinations, the numeric indicator, and two more punctuation marks are formed with dots 3, 4, 5, and 6. The last seven dot patterns are formed by dots 4, 5, and 6 and have no equivalents in written language but serve as modifiers when placed before any of the other signs.

Braille's system was not adopted by the school in Paris until 1854, two years after he died. Universal Braille code for the English-speaking world was not adopted until 1932, when agencies for the blind in Great Britain and the United States approved Standard English Braille, which was fur-

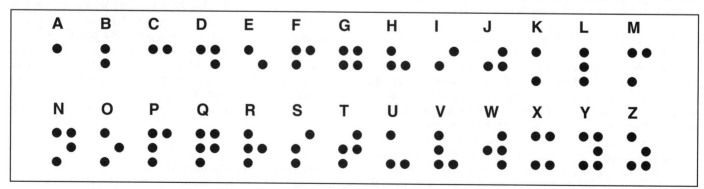

The Braille alphabet.

ther improved in 1957. The Nemeth Code of Braille Mathematics and Scientific Notation (1965) provides representation of special symbols used in mathematical and technical material. There are also Braille codes or modifications for musical notation, shorthand, and, of course, the more common languages of the world. Writing Braille by hand requires a device called a slate that consists of two metal plates hinged to allow insertion of a sheet of paper between them. The upper of the two metal plates, the guide plate, has cell-sized windows; under each of these, in the lower plate, are six slight pits in the Braille dot pattern. A stylus presses the paper against the pits to form the raised dots. The author writes from right to left and the sheet is later turned over so the dots face upward and read from left to right. Braille is also produced by special machines, with keys for each dot in the Braille cell. The first of these, the Hall Braille writer, was invented in 1892 by Frank H. Hall, superintendent of the Illinois School for the Blind. A modified form of this device is still in use today.

A recent innovation for producing Braille is an electric embossing machine similar to electric typewriters, and of course, attachments to computers.

Branch

In multimedia, one particular path a user of an interactive presentation can take. See *Branching*.

In computer programming, the term *branch* refers to one of several alternate operations or routines that may be called, depending upon the criteria and the conditions of the system.

In networking, the term *branch* refers to any direct connection between two network *node*s.

Branching

In multimedia, the creation of different paths that a user can take while navigating a particular presentation or production; the user is not relegated to following a strictly linear, predetermined path. The point at which two paths diverge is called a *branching point*.

Branching Point

In multimedia presentations or productions, the point at which two (or more) alternative paths for the user to take diverge. See *Branching*.

Brass Mounted Plate

A *flexographic* printing plate which has been premounted on a thin layer of brass and is attached to the *plate cylinder* by plate clamps or other means.

Brayer

A small, hand-held roller used for distributing and smoothing ink or other fluid, or to help in *blotting*.

Break

In *screen printing*, the release of the screen fabric from the *substrate* at the end of a printing stroke.

Also in *screen printing*, *break* refers to a tear in the screen fabric or the *stencil* due to mechanical stress.

Break also refers to a tear or complete severing of a *web* of *substrate*. See *Web Break*.

In printing ink, *break* refers to the separation of a *resin* from the rest of the *varnish*.

In networking, the term *break* refers to any interruption of data transmission.

Breakdown

Alternate term for a *cue sheet*. See *Cue Sheet*.

Break-Out

A piece of metal (such as a *burr*) that detaches itself from a *gravure* press's *doctor blade* during printing, causing a streak or other printing defect.

Breakout Box

A device used to test signals transmitted over a medium, such as a network cable. A set of LEDs in the breakout box indicates when a signal is being sent, and a set of *DIP switch*es can be used to reroute the signal. A breakout box mounted in a larger device is known as a *breakout panel*.

Breakout Panel

See *Breakout Box*.

Breaks

Printing defect characterized by broken halftone dots, the result of incomplete image transfer from the printing plate or blanket to the paper surface.

Breaks (in *gravure* printing called *snow*, *speckle*, or *skips*) are usually caused by surface or structural characteristics of paper (such as *wild formation* and low *compressibility* and *conformability*) preventing the alteration of the paper's surface contour to the extent required for the plate, *blanket* or *gravure cylinder* to completely contact the inked surface.

Breakup

Any visible interruption of a video or audio signal due to tape damage or any number of other causes.

Breathing

In animation, any undesirable change in size of an animated object from *key frame* to key frame.

Breve

In typography, an *accent* (˘) placed over a character, primarily a vowel, usually to indicate that it should be pronounced with a short vowel sound. See *Accent*.

Bridge

In networking, a hardware or software connection between two networks, such as two *LAN*s. Each connected segment must use the same *protocol*. A device that functions both as a bridge and a *router* is known as a *brouter*.

Bridge Roller

A roller used in a ***continuous-flow dampening system*** on an offset press. The bridge roller contacts both the dampening ***form roller*** and the first inking form roller, as a means of transferring moderate amounts of ***fountain solution*** into the ***inking system***. See ***Dampening System***.

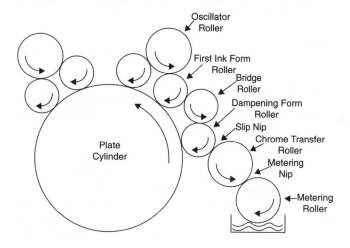

Bridge roller placement in an offset press's continuous-flow dampening system.

Bridging

In ***screen printing***, the ability of a ***photostencil*** to support itself over the gaps between screen fibers and to withstand exposure and washing.

Bright Enamel

A ***coated-one-side*** paper which has undergone ***calendering*** to impart a high surface gloss.

Brightness

Basically, the amount of light reflecting from a surface.

In printing, ***brightness*** is the amount of darkness or lightness of a printed image, described apart from the ***hue*** or ***saturation*** of the image. Brightness is typically a function of the reflectance characteristics of the paper being utilized. It is an optical property of paper that describes its reflectance of blue light, typically at a wavelength of 457 ***nanometers*** (the wavelength at which the yellowing of paper is most easily gauged).

Brilliant Yellow 8GF

See ***Fluorescent Yellow***.

Bring to Front

In desktop publishing, a command used to place one object on top of all other objects, usually as a means of either working with the object unimpeded or as a means of hiding objects beneath it. See also ***Send to Back***.

Bristol Paper

A paper ***grade*** consisting of a related variety of lightweight cardboard stocks, used for printing, filing, indexing, and mailing. Bristols possess high strength, and are often used for covers of reports, pamphlets, catalogs, etc. The surface is treated to accept ink readily with a minimum of ***ink setoff***, and the surface also has high ***abrasion resistance*** which allows it to stand up well under erasing. Printing bristol papers are manufactured using ***chemical pulp*** and ***finish***es are usually ***smooth*** or ***vellum***. Printing bristols are also usually uncoated. ***Vellum-finish bristol*** is commonly used in offset printing and has many desirable surface characteristics. ***Postal bristol*** paper is manufactured for use in postcards and has a smooth surface suited to writing with pen-and-ink. Coated bristol papers are either ***coated one side*** or ***coated two sides*** and are used for covers or for picture postcards.

The ***basic size*** for bristol paper is 22½×28½ in. and is available in ***basis weight***s of 67-, 80-, 100-, 120-, 140-, and 160-pound. ***Standard size***s are 22½×28½ in., 23×35 in., and 26×40 in. A separate paper grade, ***index paper*** is occasionally called ***index bristol***. See ***Index Paper***.

Brittleness

The property of any material—such as a ***substrate*** or an ink film—that causes it to break when stretched, creased, folded, or exposed to any other type of mechanical stress.

Broadband

In color and optics, an alternate term for ***wideband***. See ***Wideband***.

In telecommunications and networking, a type of data communications allowing the transmission of several channels simultaneously through the same cable, usually by means of ***multiplexing***. In this way, each transmission has its own unique frequency. Two-way transmission is also possible with broadband communications, accom-

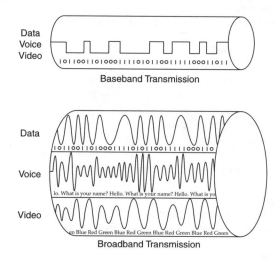

Baseband vs. broadband transmission.

plished by dividing a single channel into a forward and reverse channel. The frequency of broadband networks is measured in *megahertz (MHz)*. Analog data channels can also be combined with digital data channels. Cable television uses a broadband network; although it only allows one-way communication at the moment, many experiments and tests are being conducted to allow interactive or two-way cable television, which industry experts insist is desirable.

Broadcast

In telecommunications, to transmit a program to all those units capable of receiving it, as in radio or television.

In networking, to transmit a message to all users currently logged onto the network.

Broadcast Quality

In video production and multimedia, descriptive of any video signal which produces a picture quality in compliance with network television broadcast standards. In particular, such video equipment must produce a screen frequency and number of screen lines as specified by either of the three broadcast standards: *National Television Standards Committee (NTSC)*, *Phase Alternating Line (PAL)*, and *Séquentiel Couleur à Mémoire (SECAM)*. In general, however, broadcast quality also is a subjective measurement which is often left to the discretion of a particular broadcast station or network. For example, a poorly recorded videotape may conform to the proper number of screen lines, but be unwatchably bad.

Broadcast Storm

In networking, a situation of congestion when many *workstations* respond to a message that has been *broadcast* to the entire network.

Broadcast Video U-Matic (BVU)

A semi-professional-quality of videotape recording and playback system having a tape width of ¾ in. Often referred to simply as *Three-Quarter-Inch Tape*.

Broadside

In *book typography*, a sheet of paper printed as one page. A broadside folded once to produce four pages is called a *folio*. In commercial printing, a *broadside* is any work printed on a oversize sheet. A sheet containing text running sideways in relation to the rest of the pages in the book or document is called a *backward broadside page*.

Broken Back

In *binding and finishing*, a distorted or damaged *spine* of a book, caused by opening the book at one place and folding it back, breaking the adhesive binding.

Broken Underscoring

In typography, the underlining of multiple words separately, such as this. See also *Solid Underscoring*. See *Underscoring*.

Bromide

A type of photosensitive paper—possessing an emulsion made from silver bromide—used in phototypesetting. Also known as *phototypesetting paper*.

Bronze

A property of printed inks characterized by a metallic appearance that changes in color or shade depending on the angle at which it is viewed.

Bronze Blue

A green shade of *iron blue*, an *inorganic color pigment* used in printing inks. See *iron blue*.

Bronze Dusting

Alternate term for *bronzing*. See *Bronzing*.

Bronze Paper

A type of paperboard that has been coated with a *bronze powder* and a *binder* (commonly *pyroxylin*) to impart a metallic bronze appearance to the paper surface.

Bronze Powder

A *metallic powder*—commonly copper—used as a *pigment* in printing inks designed to have a metallic luster when printed. (See *Metallic Powders*.)

Bronze Screen

In *screen printing*, a screen fabric made of finely woven phosphor bronze threads, used primarily in the printing of wallpaper.

Bronzing

A printing and *finishing* procedure in which a *size*, or sticky-drying ink, is printed, then dusted with a metallic powder to produce the appearance of metallic printing. Also called *Bronze Dusting*. (See also *Metallic Powders*.) Bronzing, once a popular form of decorating, has largely been replaced by *foil stamping*.

Bronzing Adhesive

A clear ink or coating used in the dry application of *bronze powder* to a surface, as opposed to the use of a liquid medium for the application of such powders.

Brouter

A device used in networking that combines the functions of a *bridge* and a *router*. See *Bridge* and *Router*.

Brown

A *secondary color* produced by the mixing of *red*, *black*, and *yellow* colorants.

Brown Iron Oxides

Several types of *inorganic color pigments* used in printing inks. Brown iron oxide pigments (in nearly all cases, chemical formula Fe_2O_3) are derived from natural or synthetic sources, and are classified as either brown pigments (*CI Pigment Brown 6 and 7 No. 77491 [77492] [77499]* [synthetic or natural brown iron oxide, burnt sienna]) or red pigments (*CI Pigment Red 101 and 102 No. 77491* [synthetic or natural red iron oxides, red hematite]). They possess very high *lightfastness* and are resistant to all substances. The natural iron oxides are more difficult to process than the synthetic iron oxides, and are used less frequently. (See also *Inorganic Color Pigments*.)

Brownline

Alternate term for *blueline*, a single-color photographic printing proof used to evaluate placement of page elements. *Brownline* (or *brown print*) describes a blueline in which the images are reproduced as brown. See *Blueline*.

Brownout

Not quite a *blackout*, a *brownout* is a period of low-voltage electrical power, caused by increased electrical demand or other problems at an electrical utility company. Also spelled with a hyphen, *brown-out*.

Brown Print

Alternate term for *blueline*, a single-color photographic printing proof used to evaluate placement of page elements. *Brown print* (or *brownline*) describes a blueline in which the images are reproduced as brown. See *Blueline*.

Browser

In *Internet*, and *World Wide Web* terminology, an application program used to explore—or "browse"—Internet resources, specifically Web pages.

With a browser, the user can stroll from node to node (or page to page) without much concern for the technical details of such wandering. Some common browsers are Mosaic, Netscape, and Microsoft's Internet Explorer. See *World Wide Web*. Also referred to as a *Web browser*.

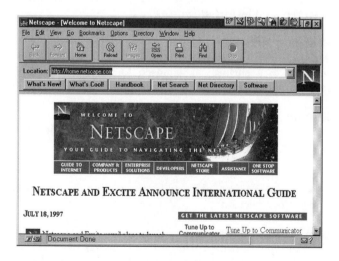

Netscape, a common browser.

Before the advent of the Web, the term *browser* referred simply to a small utility program used to scan a database or a list of files.

Browsing

In database systems, locating data by serendipity, or simply navigating through each record one by one, in contrast to deliberate *searching*.

Bruning

A high-quality page proof or *galley*, named after the brand of photocopier used to produce them.

Brunner

See *System Brunner*.

Brush Style

Any *typeface* that gives the appearance of having been drawn by hand with a brush or broad-tipped pen, used to impart a casual or informal feeling to the text set in it. Brush style typefaces are often used in greeting cards and some types of promotions, where the desired effect is one of a handwritten message. It is inadvisable to use these types of typefaces in all *caps*.

Brush Script, an example of a brush style typeface.

BS

A term used by some manufacturers of computer printers to refer to the true "business speed" of the printer, measured as the amount of time it takes from the hitting of the Print command to the output of the page.

BSC

Abbreviation for *binary synchronous communication*. See *Binary Synchronous Communication (BSC)*.

BSD UNIX

Abbreviation for *Berkeley Software Distribution UNIX*. See *Berkeley Software Distribution UNIX*.

B Series

In the metric system, series of standard paper sizes based on portions of a square meter. The basic paper sizes are known as the *A series;* the B series comprises intermediate paper sizes to the *A series*. The length-to-width ratio is maintained from size to size. The metric standard size that corresponds most closely to the United States standard letter size of 8½×11-in. is A4-size paper. The sizes and area of B-series paper (from sizes B0 to B10) are as follows:

B#	Size (in.)	Size (mm)	Area (m²)
B0	39.37×55.67	1000×1414	1.414
B1	27.83×39.37	707×1000	0.707
B2	19.68×27.83	500×707	0.354
B3	13.90×19.68	353×500	0.177
B4	9.84×13.90	250×353	0.088
B5	6.93×9.84	176×250	0.044
B6	4.92×6.93	125×176	0.022
B7	3.46×4.92	88×125	0.011
B8	2.44×3.36	62×88	0.005
B9	1.73×2.44	44×62	0.003
B10	1.22×1.73	31×44	0.001

(See also *Grammage*, *A Series*, and *ISO Paper Sizes*.)

BST

Abbreviation for *binary synchronous transmission*. See *Binary Synchronous Transmission (BST)*.

BTAM

Abbreviation for *Basic Telecommunications Access Method*. See *Basic Telecommunications Access Method (BTAM)*.

BTS

Abbreviation for *burster-trimmer-stacker*. See *Burster-Trimmer-Stacker*.

Bubble Memory

In computing, a *non-volatile* storage method by which data are stored as magnetized "bubbles" on a thin film of semiconductor material. Magnetic fields are pulsed to create these regions of magnetization.

Buckle

In *binding and finishing*, an alternate term for *gusset*. See *Gusset*.

Buckle Folder

A device used in the *folding* phase of *binding and finishing*, which uses a set of plates (collectively called a *fold plate*) to force a sheet to buckle slightly, allowing it to be pulled through a set of folding rollers. See *Folding*.

Buffer

In computers, a storage area—typically a reserved portion of *RAM*—in which data is held to await processing. A buffer is utilized by programs or by the computer's operating system itself, as a means of compensating for the speed differential between the *CPU* and any external media to or from which data is written. (See also *Frame Buffer* and *RAM*.)

In chemistry, a *buffer* is any substance or combination of substances added to a solution which has the effect of preventing a change in the overall *pH* of a solution. In printing, *buffer* refers to a compound (such as magnesium nitrate) added to an offset press *fountain solution* as a means of neutralizing acids and/or bases so as to maintain a desired level of acidity or alkalinity (*pH*). See *Fountain Solution*.

Buffer Capacity

The ability of any solution to resist a change in its *pH* when an *acid* or an *alkali* is added.

Buffer Configuration

In computing, the way that a system *buffer* is used for a specific purpose. For example, it may be split, allowing text and database information to be combined (as in a *mail merge*).

Buffered Automatic Send/Receive

Alternate term for *automatic send and receive*. Abbreviated *BASR*. See *Automatic Send and Receive (ASR)*.

Buffered Repeater

In networking, a *repeater* which is capable of controlling the flow of information to avoid collisions. See *Repeater*.

Bug

Any fault or defect—often recurring and permanent—in computer hardware or software. The goal of *alpha test*s and *beta test*s is *debugging*, or finding and fixing these errors before the hardware or software is released.

The origin of the term "bug" (in this sense) is said to come from several versions of a story dating from the 1940s. The most confirmable of these, occurring in 1945, involves a moth that was caught in a relay, crashing a Mark II electromechanical calculator the Navy had installed at Harvard. (The offending insect was apparently taped into the logbook for the session.)

The term "bug" thus came to refer to any computer error, but actually it dates from much earlier than that. In 1878, Thomas Edison used the term "bugs" to refer to "faults and difficulties" in a mechanical system. Surprisingly, even *he* didn't invent the term; it dates at least from the early days of telegraphy (Edison had worked for Western Union in his youth), and it was a common slang term even then, perhaps deriving from the ubiquitous "wildlife" in less-than-immaculate telegraph offices. (It is said that telegraphers used to compose poetry about the gymnastic feats of cavorting cockroaches.)

Bug Fix

In computing, a version of a software application released to correct *bug*s present in earlier versions of the software. Bug fixes are usually indicated by an increase in the number to the right of the decimal point in the version number. For example, version 3.1 is likely to be a bug fix to version 3.0 while version 4.0 is a major overhaul of the application.

Build

The thickness of a dried ink film.

Building-In

In *case binding*, the operation of subjecting *cased-in* books to heat and pressure as a means of keeping the case and its contents secure while the adhesive material dries. See *Case Binding*.

Build-Up

In presentation graphics and multimedia, the display of topics by revealing one line (or topic) at a time.

Build-Up Layer

In **screen printing**, a layer (or layers) of glass, plastic, board, etc., placed beneath the printing frame, used to support the stencil film to ensure a uniform, pressurized application of the stencil to the screen fabric.

Built-Up Fraction

In typography, a **fraction** created by setting the numerator over the denominator, the result being larger than the line size and requiring additional **leading**. See **Fractions**.

Bulk

The thickness of a sheet of paper, commonly called **caliper**. In book production, bulk is a factor in determining book size. (See **Bulking Number** and **Bulking Index**.)

Bulk is determined by many different variables in the papermaking process, including the amount of **refining**, the rate at which wet **pulp** is deposited on the **forming wire**, the degree of **wet pressing**, the extent of **calendering** and **supercalendering**, and the fibrous and non-fibrous content of the pulp itself. Different types of paper require different degrees of bulk, but the most important consideration is consistency of bulk along a particular paper web. Consistent thickness is required in **web offset lithography**, where varying bulk within a single roll can cause the roll to unwind with uneven tension; that uneven tension is responsible for various printing defects as well as **web break**s. Consistent thickness is also required for business forms, envelopes, and other products where a set quantity must fit into the container or packaging designed to hold it. (See **Caliper**, **High Bulk**, and **Low Bulk**.)

Bulked Up

In **binding and finishing**, descriptive of books that have been allowed to become as thick as possible.

Bulking Index

A term used in book manufacturing which designates a paper's thickness (called **bulk** or **caliper**) in inches per pound of **basis weight**. It is obtained by dividing the thickness of a single sheet by the paper's basis weight. Bulking index is used to compare the bulk of papers having the same **basic size** and varying basis weights. (See **Bulk** and **Basis Weight**.)

Bulking Number

A term used specifically in book manufacturing that refers to the number of sheets that will occupy one inch of thickness when compressed at 36 pounds per square inch (psi) for thirty seconds.

The test to determine bulking number is performed to give an indication of what paper thickness (also called **caliper** or **bulk**) is required in order for the bound book to fit in its binding. The bulking test is designed to simulate the pressure imparted to the paper by the bookbinding process (called **smashing** or **casing-in**). Measuring the caliper of a single sheet is impractical for book manufacturing, as its **smashed bulk**, or the bulk that will result when pages are subjected to the high pressure of binding, will be less than the number obtained by simply multiplying the thickness of one sheet by the total number of sheets in the book, due to a "nesting" or packing effect caused by the pressure of a binding. The bulking number is multiplied by two to provide **pages per inch (ppi)** (since each sheet contains two pages, a **verso** and a **recto**). (See also **Bulk**, **Caliper**, and **Bulking Index**.)

Bullet

In typography, a common type of **pi character** (●), used for decorative or organizational purposes. Bullets should be as close to the **x-height** of the text they accompany as possible. The **point size** of the bullet may need to be increased so that it optically approximates the size of the text; it is generally inadvisable to make a bullet larger than the x-height of the accompanying text. Bullets are often used to delineate and emphasize points or examples. They are available either closed (●) or open (○). A similar, and as widely used, pi character is a **box**.

Bulletin Board

In telecommunications, a service which can be dialed into by a remote computer system. A computer bulletin board service (abbreviated **BBS**) commonly makes software, technical support, electronic mail, and other types of files available to computer users given access.

Some BBS systems (such as those operated by companies specifically for the use of their customers) require a subscription or other means of gaining access, while others are free to all who dial in to it.

Bump Exposure

In **halftone** photography, a very brief exposure of a **continuous tone** image without the use of a **halftone screen** (usually used in conjunction with the **main exposure** using the screen).

Bump exposure is performed to increase the size of the **highlight** and **middle tone** dots while not affecting the **shadow** dots, thus compressing the screen range of the image. The length of a bump exposure is often 5–10% of that of the main exposure.

Bump Mapping

In computer graphics, the act of selectively shading the surface of a three-dimensional object to impart the appearance of a bumpy surface. Essentially, bumps are highlighted and depressions are shaded, producing an orange peel effect when the surface is viewed at certain angles. This type of surface texturing is designed to be used for regular overall texturing, not for selective texturing such as the creation of mountains in a landscape.

Bump Plate

A means of adding *extra-trinary colors* to *process color* printing. A bump plate consists of an additional plate of *cyan*, *magenta*, or *yellow* to supplement the original CMY plates and increase the density range. See *Extra-Trinary Color*. (See also *Color Substitution* and *Touch Plate*.)

Bumping Up

In video production and editing, the dubbing of a recording made on a lower-quality videotape to a higher-quality tape, such as from *VHS* to *Betacam-SP*.

Buna N

A widely used synthetic rubber produced by the *polymerization* of butadiene with acrylonitrile, invented in the mid-1930s in Germany and available in the United States just prior to the outbreak of World War II. Different grades of Buna N contain differing amounts of acrylonitrile (the amount can vary from 15–40%), greater amounts of acrylonitrile imparting greater resistance to oils. Buna N rubber is resistant to *aliphatic hydrocarbon*s, alcohols, water, and other substances, but not to *aromatic hydrocarbon*s or *ester*s.

Buna N (and other synthetic rubbers such as *neoprene*) have more stable properties than natural rubbers. It is widely used in printing press rollers (inking, dampening, and impression), as well as *blanket*s used in *offset lithography* and plates used in *flexography*. Buna N is also known as Perbunan and NBR. *Buna S*, a synthetic rubber developed at the same time as Buna N, is produced by polymerizing butadiene with styrene and is widely used for tires and other such uses.

Bundled

In computers, software (or peripheral hardware) that is included with the purchase (and is part of the purchase price) of a computer. Alternately, *unbundled* software and hardware needs to be purchased (and paid for) separately.

Bundling

In *binding and finishing*, tying up book *signature*s for any pre-*gathering* operations.

Buried Printing

A printed image applied to the underside of a transparent *substrate* and ultimately covered with an *adhesive*.

Buried printing also refers to any kind of lamination where a printed surface is covered by a transparent film, typically for protection.

Burn

To expose a photosensitive material to *actinic rays*, or the term for the exposure itself. In computers, the term *burn* is used to refer to the act of pressing a CD-ROM or other optical disc in which a laser etches tiny pits into the surface of the disc.

Burnt-In Time Code

In video production, a *time code* recorded at the same time as the video material and is thus always visible during playback. See *Time Code*.

Burr

A thin sliver of metal found on a *gravure* press's *doctor blade*, caused by excessive blade wear. Burrs can break off (at that point called a *break-out*) and cause damage to the *gravure cylinder* or generate printing defects.

Burst

In telecommunications, any quantity and sequence of data signals counted as a single unit.

Burst Binding

In *web offset lithography*, an *in-line* means of perforating or punching slits in the spine edge of a paper web to facilitate the penetration of adhesive during subsequent *perfect binding*. See *Perfect Binding*. See also *Notch Binding*.

Burst Mode

In telecommunications, a means of effecting higher transmission speeds and capacities in which the sender is able to obtain, for a short period of time, exclusive access to the transmission medium, preventing any other signal from interrupting the transmission. Once a data *burst* is sent, exclusive access is relinquished and waiting transmissions can be sent. Such a transmission is known as a *burst transmission*.

Burst Noise

In telecommunications, a sound level in excess of the desired level. See also *Noise*.

Burst Transmission

In telecommunications, a transmission of data interrupted at regular intervals, allowing devices with different transmission speeds to connect to each other. See *Burst Mode*.

Burster-Trimmer-Stacker

Finishing device attached to IBM printers. Abbreviated *BTS*.

Bursting Strength

A property of paper or paperboard used in packaging that measures its resistance to rupturing, defined as the hydrostatic pressure needed to burst a paperboard sample when it is applied uniformly across its side. Bursting strength is a function of various processes performed in the papermaking process. The increased use of *fillers* decreases bursting strength, while the increased use of longer fibers and *surface sizing* increases a paper's bursting strength.

Bursting strength is measured utilizing a rubber diaphragm that is expanded hydraulically against the paper sample. A bursting test is also known as a *Mullen test* or *pop test*, and a minimum bursting strength is required for cartons used for shipping. Bursting strength has little application to printing papers.

Bursting Test

Alternate term for a *Mullen test* of *bursting strength*. See *Mullen Test*.

Bursts

Irregular ruptures of a paper *web*, having several different characteristics and causes. See *Air Shear Burst*, *Caliper Shear Burst*, *Cross-Machine Tension Burst*, and *Full Machine-Direction Burst*.

Bus

Generally speaking, a *bus* is any means of conveying something (most familiarly people) from one place to another. It is a shortened form of the Latin word *omnibus*, the dative plural of the noun *omnis* meaning "everything."

In computing, the *bus* is the path or circuit over which all data or electrical signals are transmitted from a *CPU* to *RAM* and to peripheral devices connected to the computer. A bus contains an *address bus*, used by the system to identify specific locations, and a *data bus*, over which the actual data is sent. On any bus, all devices or components of the system receive all the data signals; it is the job of the address to ensure that only the targeted (or "addressed") device processes the signal. The number of wires in the bus determines how much memory can be addressed at any one time, and also how much data can be sent in parallel at one time. The greater the number of wires, and the greater the number of *bit*s that can be sent in parallel, the faster the system. Any unit—be it an additional device or *expansion card*—adds more addresses to the bus.

In telecommunications and networking, a *bus* is any network architecture in which stations are oriented along a linear medium, or length of cable. See *Bus Network*.

Bus Arbitration

In computing, a means of allocating *bus* resources by giving each peripheral device's signals a unique value. In the case of conflicting requests from different devices, the system dynamically determines the order in which requests are processed. An example of bus arbitration is the *Small Computer System Interface (SCSI)* in which each device is assigned (often by the user) a unique *address*.

Bus Master

In computing, any peripheral device (or other component or process) which is designed to usurp control of the system bus from the *CPU* and control the computer system, usually for its own needs.

Bus Mouse

In computing, a *mouse* connected to a special *expansion card* attached directly to the system *bus*, in contrast to a *serial mouse* which connects through a *serial port*. The only criterion in choosing a bus mouse over a serial mouse is whether a system has a free expansion slot or serial port.

Bus Network

A computer network in which all workstations and devices are connected to a common cable, each device having a unique *address*. Although all workstations and devices along a bus network receive all signals, only those with an address that matches that of a message are able to process the message. Additionally, any difficulty with one particular device in the network does not affect the other connected devices.

A bus network is easy to connect additional devices to, the only consideration being the physical extension of the common cable. Apple's *Ethernet* network is an example of a bus network.

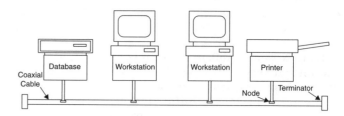

Example of a bus network.

Business Application

Any computer program that is targeted at—or is used by—an individual or organization for business purposes, such as an accounting (or spreadsheet) program, an invoicing program, a word processor, etc.

Business Data Processing

See *Data Processing*.

Business Forms Bond

A *bond paper* designed specifically for use in the production of continuous business forms.

Business Graphics

General term for graphs, charts, and other illustration material used primarily to depict and emphasize data for business purposes.

Busy Hour

In telecommunications, the 60-minute period during which communications traffic is at its highest. For many *Internet service provider*, the busy hour may be longer than 60 minutes, and usually occurs in the early evening.

Butt

The printing of two or more colors adjacent to each other with no overlapping. Also called *butt register*.

Butted

In typography and page layout, descriptive of two or more *rule line*s, images, or other page elements placed end-to-end.

Butt Label

Alternate term for *split-top label*. See *Split-Top Label*.

Button

Any physical object which makes an electrical connection when depressed, allowing the performing of some function, such as turning on a device or ringing a doorbell. Such a device is also found on a computer *mouse*.

In computing, a *button* is an analogous feature on a computer display, comprising a graphical object or *icon* found often in dialog boxes or as parts of menus in multimedia presentations. When clicked using the mouse or other means (such as a touchscreen or often by hitting the Return key), the button activates some feature or function. Such a button is often known as a *light button*.

Buttonbar

Alternate term for a *toolbar*. See *Toolbar*.

Butt Register

Alternate term for *butt*. See also *Register*.

Butyl Acetate

A colorless, fragrant, liquid *ester*—chemical formula $C_6H_{12}O_2$—used as a *solvent* in some *screen printing* ink lacquers due to its low rate of evaporation.

Butyl Alcohol

One of several types of isomeric organic *solvent*s—chemical formula C_4H_9OH—used in the manufacture of *nitrocellulose* lacquers and synthetic *resin*-based inks. Also called *butanol*.

Butyl Cellosolve

A brand of ethylene glycol mono butyl ether, a *solvent* used in many lacquer inks and coatings produced from vinyl or *nitrocellulose*, due to its high boiling point and low rate of evaporation. See also *Cellosolve*.

Buy

Term for videotaped material which will be included in the final edit or *master tape*. Also known as a *keeper*.

BVU

Abbreviation for *Broadcast Video U-Matic*.

Byline

In magazine and newspaper publishing, a line added to an article identifying the author (and other contributors, such as researchers) of the article. The byline can appear directly under the title of the article, at the end of the article, or in a special position on the page (especially if it is a regularly featured column).

Byte

A common, basic unit of computer storage or memory, commonly comprising eight *bit*s of data. (Thus, a byte is also known as an *octet*.)

One bit is one particular *binary digit*, a 1 or a 0, one byte being some eight-digit combination of them, such as "10010011." Eight of these digits is commonly the minimum amount necessary to describe a specific character, such as the letter "A," the number "5," or any other character. One byte is typically the smallest unit of main memory. 1,024 bytes (usually rounded to 1,000) is known as 1 *kilobyte*, while 1,048,576 bytes (usually rounded to one million) is known as 1 *megabyte*.

Although in general computing a byte is equal to 8 bits (the word "byte" itself is a contraction of the phrase "by eight"), other types of electronic devices have different-sized bytes. A pocket calculator, for example, uses bytes which comprise 4 bits, while some mainframe computers use 9-bit bytes.

Byte-Oriented Protocol

In networking, a data communications *protocol* in which data is transmitted as a series of *byte*s or characters, rather than smaller *bit*s. Special characters—called control characters—are used to distinguish control information for the proper data.

Most *asynchronous transmission* protocols for *modem*s utilize byte-oriented protocols. See also *Bit-Oriented Protocol*.

Byte Synchronous

In telecommunications, a means of *synchronous transmission* in which groups of *bit*s (usually a group of eight bits, or a *byte*) are transmitted as a single unit.

C

C, c

The third letter of the Latin and English alphabets. The form of the uppercase *C* derives from the North Semitic letter *ghimel*, as well as the Greek *gamma*. The letter came to the Romans through the Etruscans, in whose language there was no true distinction between the "g" sound and the hard "c" (or "k") sound. In Latin, the *C* was used exclusively as a "k" sound. The forms of the uppercase *C* and lowercase *c* were both originally more angular, resembling the uppercase Greek *gamma*, and eventually obtained their curved shape in Rome.

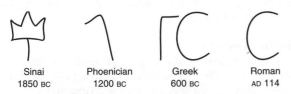

| Sinai 1850 BC | Phoenician 1200 BC | Greek 600 BC | Roman AD 114 |

The evolution of the letter C.

C

A common computer programming language, developed in 1970 by Bell Labs. It is used to create graphics software, multimedia applications, and a host of other applications. C's successor, *C++*, also facilitates *object-oriented* programming.

CA

In networking, an abbreviation for *collision avoidance*. See *Carrier Sense Multiple Access/Collision Avoidance (CSMA/CA)*.

Cable

Any group of conductive media such as wires, optical fibers, etc., that are encased in an insulating sheath and that are used as a single line to connect devices or communications systems.

The term *cable* is also short for *cable television network*. See *Cable Television Network*.

Cablecasting

In broadcasting, the transmission of television programming, computer data, or other information by means of a *cable television network*. See *Cable Television Network*.

Cable Modem

A cable that is used to connect two computers so as to allow them to communicate with each other without the need for proper *modem*s. See *Null Modem*.

Cable Television Network

Any network, usually a commercial one, that transmits television signals via cable. In its most familiar configuration, it carries many channels of programming into private homes, apartment complexes, hotels, and other such locations. Initially created as a means of providing rural areas with access to broadcast channels not easily received by conventional television aerials, cable television has in many areas replaced over-the-air television reception, thanks to its increased channel capacity and (usually) clear reception. The transmission capacity of a cable television network is about 450 *megahertz (MHz)*, although cable television networks do not currently use the entire *bandwidth* capacity, which may be used for interactive television, pay-TV transmissions, video conferencing, etc.

The term *cable television network* is also used to refer to one particular cable channel—such as The Discovery Channel, C-SPAN, or CNN—carried over a cable television network. Cable television is often abbreviated *CATV*, which actually stands for *Community Antenna TeleVision*.

Cache

See *Cache Memory*.

Cache Controller

In computing, a special processor used to manage a computer's *cache memory*. Older *PC*s use a processor such as an Intel 82385 as a cache controller. Newer *Pentium* PCs, however, integrate a cache controller in the *microprocessor* itself. See *Cache Memory*.

Cache Memory

A portion of a computer's *RAM* (or *random-access memory*) in which frequently used data (such as printer font outlines, for example) is stored for rapid access. Cache memory, also known simply as a *cache* (and is also called a *disk cache*, *memory cache*, and *RAM cache*) speeds computer operations, as the computer does not have to continually read and/or write data to a disk, which is a slower process than accessing data stored in RAM. Cache memory can be internal (or located directly in the *microprocessor*) or external (or located in special chips mounted on the *motherboard*).

There are several different types of cache memory:

In a *direct-mapped cache*, a specific location in the cache corresponds to several different locations in RAM. In this way, when a particular set of data is called by the processor it can be found quickly.

In a *fully associative cache*, data stored in RAM is kept in any free sections of the cache. In this way, the most recently used data is typically present in the cache.

In a *set-associative cache*, data stored in RAM is stored in the cache in sets, each set possibly being stored in multiple locations in the cache. Although any particular block of data may exist in more than one location, it will only be stored in one location per set.

The cache memory is typically controlled by a *cache controller*, a special processor having no other purpose but to manage data transferred to and from the cache memory.

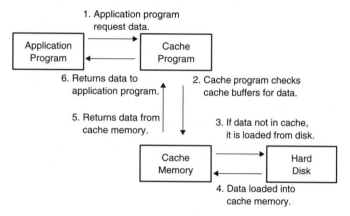

Data flow to and from cache memory.

Cache RAM

Any chip used in a computer's *cache memory*. Known as *Static Random-Access Memory (SRAM)* chips, they have an access time of 15–20 *nanoseconds*. See *Cache Memory.*

Caching

In computing, a technique used in the display of type in which a particular character is created and then stored as a *bitmap* in *RAM* or on the *hard disk*, requiring only that the bitmap be called up and re-displayed the next time the character is called for. Caching thus minimizes the time a computer spends redrawing bitmapped fonts.

CAD

Abbreviation for *computer-aided design*. See *Computer-Aided Design (CAD).*

CADAM

Acronym for *computer-augmented design and manufacturing*. See *Computer-Augmented Design and Manufacturing (CADAM).*

CAD/CAM

Acronym for *computer-aided design / computer-aided manufacturing*. CAD/CAM is a general term used to refer to the integration of computers in both the design and manufacturing processes, where technical drawings and models are made on a computer, and the computer is then used to operate some or all of the manufacturing processes, accomplished by translating a specific designed part to a numerical control language. See *Computer-Aided Design (CAD).*

CADD

Acronym for *computer-aided drafting and design*. See *Computer-Aided Drafting and Design (CADD).*

Caddy

In computing, a plastic tray in which a *CD-ROM* needs to be placed before it can be loaded into a CD-ROM drive, required on older machines. Newer computers and CD-ROM drives, however, have a servo-controlled tray built in (much like those used on *audio CD* players), obviating the need for a caddy.

Cadmium-Mercury Red

A type of *inorganic color pigment* used in printing inks and derived from various cadmium compounds, such as cadmium selenide (chemical formula CdSe), as well as mercury. Cadmium-Mercury Red also includes several shades ranging from bright red to deep red. Other cadmium-based pigments include the *Cadmium Reds* and *Cadmium Yellows*, as well as *Cadmium Oranges*. The cadmium pigments are rarely used any longer, having been replaced by less potentially toxic organic pigments, except in cases where extreme chemical resistance is necessary. (See *Inorganic Color Pigments*.)

Cadmium Orange

A type of *inorganic color pigment* used in printing inks comprising a shade of *Cadmium Yellow*. See *Cadmium Yellows*. (See also *Inorganic Color Pigments*.)

Cadmium Red

An *inorganic color pigment* used in printing inks. Cadmium Reds range in shade from orange to maroon, and they possess high *lightfastness* and high chemical resistance. However, if used with lead pigments, they can react with the lead, forming a blackish lead sulfide. Their toxicity precludes them from being used for foods, food packaging, toys, and many other applications. They can withstand excessively high temperatures, and their high alkali resistance makes them useful in certain applications. Cadmium pigments are rarely used any longer, having been replaced by less potentially toxic organic pigments. (See *Inorganic Color Pigments*.)

(CI Pigment Red 108 Nos. 77196, 77202.)

Cadmium Yellows

A type of *inorganic color pigment* used in printing inks and derived from various cadmium compounds, such as cadmium selenide or cadmium sulfide. Cadmium Yellows include shades ranging from greenish to golden yellow. Cadmium pigments are highly fast-to-light, extremely opaque, and highly resistant to heat, alkalis, and soaps, which makes them useful for printing soap packaging, but they are not acid-resistant and tend to blacken when used in conjunction with lead-based pigments. Cadmium Yellows lack *tinctorial strength* and print poorly. They are also highly toxic, and FDA regulations have prohibited their use in many applications. Other cadmium-based pigments include the *Cadmium Reds* and *Cadmium Oranges*, as well as *Cadmium-Mercury Reds*. The cadmium pigments are rarely used any longer, having been replaced by less toxic organic pigments, except in cases where extreme chemical resistance is necessary. (See also *Inorganic Color Pigments*.)

(*CI Pigment Yellow 37 No. 77199.*)

CAE

An abbreviation for *computer-aided engineering*.

CAEDS

Term for IBM's **CAD** software. See **Computer-Aided Design (CAD)**.

CAI

Abbreviation for **computer-assisted instruction**. See **Computer-Assisted Instruction (CAI)**.

Caking

Alternate term for **piling**, when describing the undesirable accumulation of dry ink **pigment** particles on a **lithographic** or **flexographic** printing plate or offset press **blanket**, or on the **impression roller** or other rollers in **gravure** printing. See **Piling**.

Calcium Bisulfite

The primary compound—chemical formula $Ca(HSO_3)_2$—in the **sulfite process**, the older and less used of the two primary **chemical pulping** processes. Calcium bisulfite is produced by combining **sulfurous acid** with limestone. Cooking wood chips in the combination of sulfurous acid and calcium bisulfite dissolves the **lignin** in the wood and liberates the **cellulose** fibers. The sulfite process is not well-suited to pulping highly resinous wood, such as pine trees. Its original calcium-based chemicals are unrecoverable, and pollution laws have resulted in newer substances being utilized, such as sodium, magnesium, and ammonia bases, the active chemical in the sulfite process being the bisulfite ion $(HSO_3{}^{2-})$. These bases are easier to recover. The sulfite process is an acidic pulping process and exists in contrast to the alkaline **soda process**. (See also **Chemical Pulping**.)

Calcium Carbonate

A bright white mineral (chemical formula $CaCO_3$) added to paper **pulp** as a **filler** in **alkaline papers** or applied as a **coating** pigment. Like **clay** and **titanium dioxide**, it is added to the papermaking **furnish** to increase **brightness** and **opacity**. Calcium carbonate is a better **optical brightener** than clay, but it is not as good as titanium dioxide. It is, however, as inexpensive as clay. Calcium carbonate cannot be used in the manufacture of **acid paper**, as it is an alkaline material that reacts strongly with acidic papermaking conditions. It is used in alkaline papermaking, which is receiving increased interest due to the longer longevity of alkaline papers. The presence of calcium carbonate in papers creates difficulty in **offset lithography**, as the alkalinity of the paper filler or coating tends to react with the acidic **dampening solution** used on the press to

keep nonimage plate regions receptive to water. Neutralization of the **dampening system** impedes its effectiveness. (See **pH**.) Calcium has also been known to react with materials in the ink and the plate, causing serious printing defects as well as damage to the plate and/or the blanket.

Calcium carbonate, the most abundant mineral on earth that is not silicon-based, is also called limestone or marble. It is found in chalk, coral, the shells of mollusks and other marine creatures, and eggshells.

Calcium carbonate is also used as a **white pigment** in many printing inks. It is a dull white but can be coated to impart greater gloss to the ink surface. Calcium carbonate is low in cost and is commonly used as an **extender** in place of the more expensive titanium dioxide. It is also highly reactive when exposed to acids and is not recommended for use in lithographic inks. Calcium carbonate may also contain trace amounts of magnesium carbonate, silicon dioxide, aluminum oxide, iron oxide, and water. (See also **White Pigments**.)

(*CI Pigment White 18 No. 77220.*)

Calendar Stock

An **offset paper** grade—produced with a **basis weight** of 50–70 lb.—that is characterized by high degrees of printability and resistance to curling, used in the printing of calendars.

Calender

A series of highly polished steel rollers at the end of a papermaking machine used to produce a desired finish on paper. (See **Calendering**.) Further calendering is performed on a separate machine called a **supercalender**. The word "calender" itself is a derivation of the word *cylindrus*, the Latin word for "cylinder."

Calender is also used to describe a similar configuration of heated rollers used to compress screen fabrics utilized in **screen printing**.

Calender-Blackened Spots/Streaks

A paper defect characterized by dark spots or streaks on a paper surface, generated during **calendering** of a paper **web**. Such marks are caused by a wet spot or streak on the web being enlarged and intensified as a result of the high compression generated by the **calender**. Also known as **blackening**. (See also **Calender Cut**, **Calender Spot**, **Blister Cut**, **Fiber Cut**, and **Hair Cut**.)

Calender Cut

A paper defect caused during **calendering** of a paper **web** and characterized by lines or fractures that tear easily under tension.

Wrinkles present on a paper's surface will impress deeply into the surface of the sheet when subjected to the pressure of the **calender** rollers and cut part way (or even completely) through the paper. (See also **Calender Spot**, **Calender-Blackened Spots/Streaks**, **Blister Cut**, **Fiber Cut**, and **Hair Cut**.)

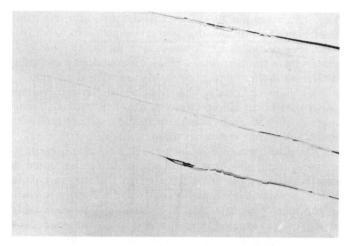

A calender cut.

Calendered Fabric

A screen fabric used in **screen printing** that has been compressed or flattened by running one or both sides through a **calender**.

Calender Finish

A glossy paper **finish** produced by running the formed paper **web** through a **calender**.

Calendering

The final operation on a papermaking machine, performed to impart to paper a desired **finish** and to increase the surface smoothness of a paper **web**. The **calender** usually consists of a stack of highly polished steel rollers. As the paper web snakes through them, the paper is compressed and surface inconsistencies are smoothed out. The degree of calendering depends on the desired level of surface **smoothness** and **gloss**. The degree of calendering improves some paper qualities at the expense of others, however. Although increased calendering increases the **apparent density**, gloss, **ink holdout**, and smoothness of the paper, it has a deleterious effect on the **brightness**, **compressibility**, **ink absorbency**, **opacity**, **porosity**, **stiffness**, and thickness of the paper. The end-use requirements of the paper are of prime consideration when deciding the degree of calendering. Additional gloss and smoothness are often achieved using off-machine **supercalendering** equipment.

Certain paper defects are generated by calendering. See **Calender Cut**, **Calender Spot**, and **Calender-Blackened Spots/Streaks**.

Calendering is also used in the forming of thermoplastic films used as printing **substrate**s. In this process, the plastic **resin** is heated to a gelatinous mass and run through heated rollers which, like paper that has been calendered, imparts to the plastic film a glossy, smooth surface.

Calender Spot

A paper defect characterized by shiny, transparent spots, generated during the **calendering** of a paper **web**. Calen-

der spots are caused by a fragment of paper stuck to the roller of a **calender** and pressed deeply into the paper web on each revolution of the roller. (See also **Calender Cut**, **Calender-Blackened Spots/Streaks**, **Blister Cut**, **Fiber Cut**, and **Hair Cut**.)

Calender Stack

Term for the stack of rollers that make up the **calender** section of a papermaking machine. See **Calender**.

Calender Wrinkle

A wrinkle or similar paper defect produced by the **calender** rollers.

Calibrated RGB Color Space

On a color computer monitor, a set of specifications that define the **red, green, and blue** (the three colors that comprise every other color that can be displayed) phosphors, a **white point** (the lightest white an output device is capable of reproducing), and other opto-electronic functions.

Calibration

In any system, the act of setting device parameters in accordance with certain prescribed or "ideal" values, especially to compensate for variables in a working environment. For example, see **Color Calibration**, which is the optimization of a scanner's settings. Computer monitors can also be calibrated to compensate for changes in **ambient light**.

California Job Case

In typography, a one-tiered type case used for transporting **handset type**.

ffi	fl	5 EM	4 EM	ˇ	k		1	2	3	4	5	6	7	8	$	£		Æ	Œ	æ	œ
j	b	c	d	e		i		s		f	g	ff 9 / fi 0		A	B	C	D	E	F	G	
?																					
!	l	m	n	h		o	y	p	w	∧	EN QUAD	EM QUAD	H	I	K	L	M	N	O		
z																					
x	v	u	t	3 EM SPACE	a	r		;	:	QUAD	P	Q	R	S	T	V	W				
q									.	-		X	Y	Z	J	U	&	ffl			

Location of handset type in the California Job Case.

Caliper

The thickness of a single sheet of paper, measured in thousandths of an inch or in **point**s, where one point equals one thousandth of an inch. In the metric system, caliper is measured in millimeters or micrometers. Caliper is measured using a **micrometer**, a device that measures minute thicknesses such as paper by applying a static load for a set period of time. As paper is compressible, careful measurements are required, frequently at different points on the paper.

Consistency of caliper throughout the paper *web* is an important consideration. An abrupt increase or decrease in caliper can affect the extent to which the printing plate or blanket contacts the paper and transfers a complete printed image, as well as other *printability* and *runnability* issues. Variations in caliper within a single paper roll cause problems in feeding web offset presses and can cause *web break*s.

The thickness of a paper itself varies according to the *basis weight* desired and other end-use considerations. Caliper can be reduced at a variety of stages in the papermaking process, such as by reducing the amount of *furnish* deposited on the *forming wire*, and by increasing the degree of *wet pressing*, *calendering*, and *supercalendering*. Caliper is related to other paper properties, and an increase or decrease in thickness affects other properties, sometimes to their detriment. (See *Paper and Papermaking: Paper Properties*.)

In *binding and finishing*, a *caliper* is a device used to measure thicknesses. A caliper is often attached to a *folding* device and detects when more than one sheet is being fed through the machine.

Caliper Shear Burst

A web *burst* or rupture in web offset lithography, caused by the paper unrolling into the press's rollers at uneven speeds due to inconsistencies in a paper's thickness throughout the roll. (See *Caliper*. See also *Air Shear Burst*, *Cross-Machine Tension Burst*, and *Full Machine-Direction Burst*.)

Call

In telecommunications, to initiate communication over a telephone or other network. When used as a noun, *call* means the communication itself.

In computer programming, *call* means to invoke a particular subroutine (or new sequence of instructions) within a program.

Call Accounting

In networking, especially in a network utilizing a *packet-switching protocol*, a means of gathering data on individual messages transmitted by a *workstation* over the network, including start and end times, as well as the amount of data and number of data *packet*s transmitted in each message.

Callback Modem

In telecommunications, a *modem* that does not answer incoming calls but instead requires the user to enter a specific code that will then allow the modem to call back the calling number. The code typically needs to match an authorized callback number; otherwise the modem will not return the call. Such modems are useful when a system

needs to be protected from unauthorized users (such as *hackers*) but accessible to authorized users. Also known as a *dialback modem*.

Called/Calling Channel

In networking, a communication channel utilized by a *local area network* that can both make and receive calls. See also *Called Channel* and *Calling Channel*.

Called Channel

In networking, a communication channel utilized by a *local area network* that can receive but not originate calls. See also *Calling Channel* and *Called/Calling Channel*.

Caller ID

Alternate term for *automatic number identification*. See *Automatic Number Identification (ANI)*.

Calligraphy

The art of beautiful writing, or a style of lettering—typically by hand—based on flat-tipped pen or brush strokes. Calligraphy is a form of lettering—the drawing of letters by hand—while typography is lettering adapted and made more orderly for special purposes, such as reproduction.

The Chancery script of the 15th century became the model for modern *italic*, and the writing masters of that period—such as Palatino—developed techniques for formal handwriting. Arthur Baker, the American calligrapher, has used Renaissance scripts for many of his models.

Hermann Zapf, the renowned German typeface designer, developed a calligraphy *font* that has been issued for typesetting by the International Typeface Corporation (ITC) under the name Zapf Chancery.

Despite the beauty of calligraphy, it does exhibit reduced legibility and should only be used sparingly. Needless to say, calligraphy—either done by hand or using calligraphic fonts—should never be all *caps*.

Zapf Chancery, a calligraphy font by Hermann Zapf.

Calling Channel

In networking, a communication channel utilized by a *local area network* that can make but not receive calls. See also *Called Channel* and *Called/Calling Channel*.

Callout

In typography, any of several different typographic elements that are, in essence, "called out" of the main *body text*, such as text pasted onto an illustration to identify specific portions of it (as on a map); a *superior* character used to indicate a *footnote*; or a *pull-quote*.

Call Packet

In telecommunications and networking, a set of data that carries *address* information as well as any other data needed to create an *X.25* circuit.

Call Request Packet

In networking, especially in which data communication is effected by means of *packet switching*, the data *packet* that is transmitted by the sender, which includes the *network user identification*, the *call user data*, and other information.

Call User Data

In networking, especially in which data communications is effected by means of *packet switching*, user information transmitted in a *call request packet*.

CALS

Abbreviation for *computer-aided acquisition and logistics support*. See *Computer-Aided Acquisition and Logistics Support (CALS)*.

CAM

Acronym for *computer-aided manufacturing*. See *Computer-Aided Design/Computer-Aided Manufacturing (CAD/CAM)*.

Camcorder

Popular term for any unit that is a combination *video camera* and *video cassette recorder*. With such a device, a scene can be videotaped and immediately played back, either through the viewfinder and/or through a connected monitor.

Camera

Generally speaking, any device used to capture still or moving images, either on photographic film, magnetic videotape, or—increasingly—in digital form. *Still cameras* (some of which are popularly known as 35-mm cameras) are commonly small, hand-held cameras used by professional or amateur photographers to take portraits of people, objects, or landscapes, news events, and other such subjects. Newer forms of still cameras fall under the heading of *digital cameras* and *electronic cameras*, as they register images directly as digital information that can be output to a computer. (See *Digital Camera* and *Digital Photography*.)

Process cameras are large devices used for graphic arts photography and the preparation of *color separations*, *line art* and *halftones* for platemaking or other prepress functions. Some process cameras are also known as *copy cameras* (or *stat cameras*) especially when used to make enlargements or reductions of original art.

Several types of cameras are used for the filming or taping of moving images. A *motion picture camera* is used to register moving images on film for television broadcast or cinematic exhibition. *Video cameras*, like motion

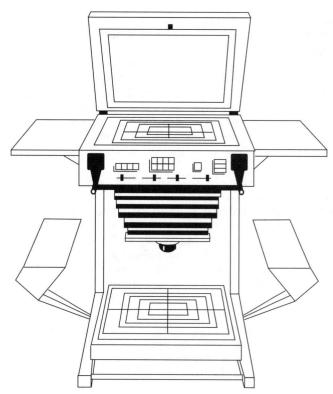

A vertical camera used in graphic arts.

picture cameras, are used to capture moving images, but the images are captured directly on videotape, eliminating the need for development. Video cameras image either on ½-in. *VHS*, ¾-in., *Super-8*, or *Hi-8* videotape, each of which has different levels of performance and image quality. Video cameras, especially those known as *camcorders*, which feature the camera and playback device in the same lightweight unit, are popular for both professional and amateur image-gathering, given their ease of use, their portability, their lack of expense, and their ability to view captured images immediately after taping.

(See *Photography*.)

Camera-Ready

Descriptive of to-be-printed copy or art that is ready to be shot as a *negative* without need for additional typesetting, redrawing, etc. See *Camera-Ready Copy* and *Camera-Ready Art*.

Camera-Ready Art

Alternate term for *camera-ready copy*, especially when involving illustration matter. See *Camera-Ready Copy*.

Camera-Ready Copy

To-be-printed copy and/or artwork that requires no additional layout, positioning, redrawing, or typesetting or, in other words, is prepared to be photographed for a *negative* or printing plate. Commonly abbreviated *CRC*. Also known as *Camera-Ready Art*.

Camera Setting

In graphic arts photography, the percent enlargement or reduction at which the original art or copy is to be photographed. On most *process cameras*, enlargement and reduction is effected by moving the *copyboard* and the *lens* certain predetermined distances from each other, depending upon the amount of size change desired. Changing the size of the reproduction also necessitates the resetting of the lens's *f-number*, as well as the *exposure time*. These changes can be handled with differing degrees of automation, depending on the camera. See *Photography: Graphic Arts Photography*.

Cameron Book Production System

A printing press used in book manufacturing consisting of thin rubber or plastic plates mounted on two moving belts and that uses *letterpress* plates, inks, and ink delivery system printing on a paper *web* to produce complete book *signature*s. Also known as a *belt press*.

Campus Network

A larger computer network used to link several *local area network*s, used in places such as college campuses, where each department may have its own *LAN*, which is then incorporated into a larger campus network. They differ from *wide area network*s in that they typically do not offer all the services common to *WAN*s.

Candela

Alternate term—especially outside the United Sates—for a *candle*. See *Candle*.

Candle

A unit of measurement for illumination, based on a standard source. At one time, the standard source was actually a candle of a specified composition and possessing specified dimensions.

Currently, the standard source is defined as a 0.16-sq.-in. theoretical *blackbody* glowing at a temperature of 1,496 K (or 1,769°C). The *candle* is thus defined as one-sixtieth of that intensity. A *candle* is also known (primarily in Europe and elsewhere outside of the United States) as a *candela*. One candle equals 12.6 *lumen*s. See also *Foot Candle* and *Lumen*.

Canned Program

In computing, a software application designed to be used "off the shelf" with little or no modification. Canned programs, unlike *custom program*s, are general enough to be used by a wide variety of businesses or individuals.

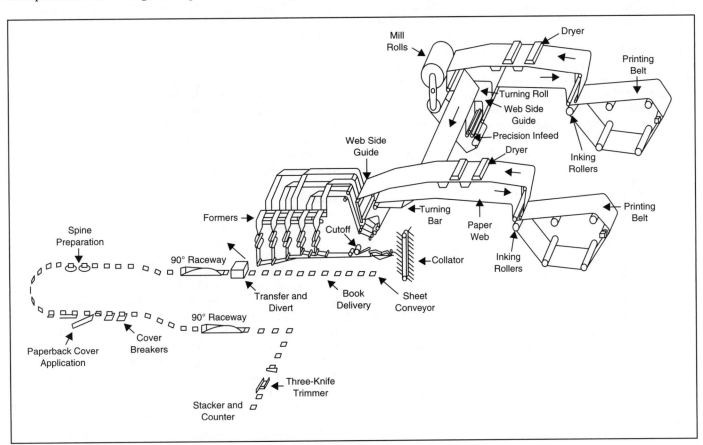

The Cameron Book Production System.

Cap

An abbreviation for a *capital*, or *uppercase*, letter. See *Uppercase*.

Capacitive Monitor

A type of *touch screen* monitor. See *Touch Screen*.

Capacity

In computing, a term used to describe the maximum amount of data that can be stored on a magnetic or optical (or magnetic optical) storage medium, measured in *characters per inch*, *bits per inch*, or—popularly—*megabyte*. The capacity of a storage medium is determined by the number of bits per inch the device can record, as well as the number of *track*s on the medium.

Cap Height

In typography, the height of a *capital* letter measured from the *baseline* to the top of the letter.

Capillary Action

A physical manifestation of the surface tension of a liquid. The molecules of some liquids—such as water, for example—have a greater attraction for solid surfaces, such as glass, than for each other, and as a result these liquids can "creep" up or down a thin tube. A thin glass tube placed in a pan of water will result in a water level higher in the tube than that of the water in the pan, the difference in height being equivalent to the difference in intermolecular forces. In the tube (and even in the pan itself) the water surface will have a pronounced concave (U-shaped) meniscus (or curvature of the surface of the liquid) as the water molecules in contact with the glass sides of the tube have a greater affinity for the glass than for other water molecules. (In contrast, a liquid such as mercury, whose molecules have a greater affinity for each other than for other

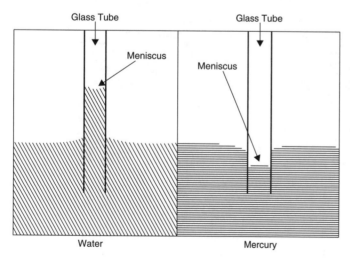

Due to capillary action, water (left) rises up a glass tube, forming a concave meniscus. Mercury (right), on the other hand, forms a convex meniscus.

surfaces, will, when subjected to the same glass-tube experiment as the water, have a convex meniscus and a level *less* than that of the mercury in the surrounding pan.) Capillary action—also known as *capillarity*—is the primary means by which plants survive and is the force that allows water to rise to the top of tall trees.

In printing processes, the degree of an ink's ability to demonstrate capillary action is one determinant of the amount of ink penetration into the surface of a *substrate* (especially a porous one—such as paper, which has many tiny capillaries throughout its surface and structure). Excessive capillary action by an ink causes such printing defects as *strike-through*, and excessive capillarity by an ink *vehicle* causes drying problems. On the plus side, capillary action is also one of the means by which ink transfer is effected in *gravure* printing (as capillarity moves the liquid ink from the engraved gravure cells to the substrate) and *flexography* (capillarity causing ink to flow from the pits of the inking *anilox roller* to the surface of the plate).

Some types of stencils used in *screen printing* are applied to the screen fabric by means of capillary action. (See *Capillary Film*.)

Capillary Film

A presensitized film used for *screen printing* stencils that is applied while wet to the screen fabric prior to exposure and development and adheres to the fabric by means of *capillary action*.

Capital

One of the letters *A* through *Z*, or *uppercase*, letters of the alphabet (as opposed to the *lowercase* letters *a* through *z*).

All-capitalized (or "all-cap" for short) words or acronyms should be set in *small caps* so that they do not appear disproportionately large. In heads, caps are usually set with minimum word spacing and, optionally, letter-spaced slightly to equalize the space between the letters. The space between words should not be greater than the space between lines. Mechanical lineup of caps on the left usually results in uneven *alignment*. *Optical alignment* requires some *kerning* to achieve better-looking alignment.

Type set in all caps has proven to be harder to read than type set in lowercase, due to the fact that the perception of words is often accomplished by means of their outline or silhouette, rather than merely the sequence of letters. Most words in lowercase have a unique outline, while those in all caps do not. Words composed in all caps, therefore, need to be deciphered letter by letter, rather than "sight-read" by outline, which makes reading all caps take longer. Proofreading type set in all caps is also more difficult, and informal studies have turned up more *typo*s in all-cap type than in upper- and lowercase type.

Capital letters are also known as *uppercase* due to their location in early typecases. Historically, capitals were known as *majuscule*s and were the dominant form of lettering until the advent of the *miniscule*—or lowercase—letters during the reign of Charlemagne.

Cap Line

In typography, an imaginary line that defines the height of capital letters of a particular *typeface*. The distance from the cap line to the *baseline* is the cap size. The cap size can be higher or lower than the *ascender*s of lowercase letters.

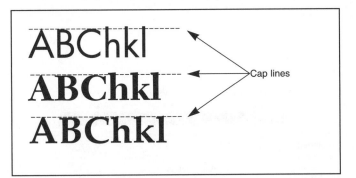

The cap line for Futura Book (top), New Caledonia Bold (middle) and Palatino Bold (bottom).

Capped Plate

A type of printing *plate* used in *flexography* produced by utilizing two separate layers of differently formulated *liquid photopolymer*s, which vary the surface and structural characteristics of the plate through its depth. See *Liquid Photopolymer*.

Capping

See *Capping and Sectioning*.

Capping and Sectioning

In *three-dimensional modeling*, features that allow a 3D model to be "cut" in any orientation to expose the interior of the object. After sectioning, the model can be capped, allowing users to view the sectioned object from a variety of perspectives.

Caps

Informal term for *capitals*, the capital letters of a *font*. See *Capital*.

Caps and Lowercase (C&LC)

In typography, the specification that each word—other than articles and prepositions—of a particular length of copy begin with a capital letter, commonly used in heads and titles. Also abbreviated *CLC*.

Caps and Small Caps (C&SC)

In typography, the specification that *lowercase* letters be replaced with *small caps* and the characters that would normally take *capitals* being set in full-size capital letters. Also abbreviated *CSC*.

Capstan

In any magnetic tape recording or playing device, or in some configurations of *imagesetter*, a spindle used to keep tape or film moving past the play, record, or imaging mechanism at a constant velocity.

Capstan Imagesetter

See *Flatbed Imagesetter*.

Caption

In typography and page layout, any strictly descriptive text accompanying an illustration, located beneath it, alongside it, or above it. Text accompanying an illustration of a more explanatory nature is called a *legend*.

Capture Board

Alternate term for a *digitizer board*. See *Digitizer Board*.

CAR

An abbreviation for *computer-assisted retrieval*. See *Computer-Assisted Retrieval (CAR)*.

Carbon Black

General term for the *black pigment* used in most printing inks. Carbon black is an amorphous (i.e., lacking a crystalline structure) form of carbon produced by partially burning *hydrocarbon*s (such as crude oil or natural gas), wood, or animal bones and tissue, and condensing the sooty flame on a cool surface. Carbon Black pigments are 90–99% carbon, with only 1–10% volatile substances.

Carbon Black pigments vary in color from a grayish blue to jet black, are not chemically reactive, are extremely fast-to-light, and have a high resistance to heat, alkalis, acids, solvents, waxes, water, soaps, and other chemicals. Carbon Blacks are classified as *Furnace Black* or *Channel Black*, which primarily describes the difference in the means of producing the pigment. (See also *Black Pigment*.)

(CI Pigment Black 7 No. 77266.)

Carbon Dummy

In the production of carbon-separated business forms, a set of sheets of paper and carbon paper hand-assembled into a set as a means of evaluating the quality of the impression.

Carbonize

In the production of *carbon release* paper, the coating of one or both sides of a sheet of paper with a carbon formula. See *Carbon Release*.

Carbonized Thread

In *screen printing*, a type of thread used in screen fabrics that has been treated to prevent the buildup of static electric charges.

Carbonless Paper

A type of paper impregnated with carbon derivatives (and other chemicals) that, when under pressure from a pen, stylus, or typewriter, transfers an impression to the sheet beneath it. Carbonless paper has largely replaced multi-ply forms separated by *carbon release* paper.

Carbon Pattern

On carbon paper, the description of the layout of the carbon on the back of the form, usually used when specifying carbon paper that does not have carbon uniformly and completely distributed.

Carbon Release

A type of image transfer between separate plys of a business form by means of interleaved sheets of carbon paper, or a paper coated with black carbon. When the top sheets are written on (either by a hard-tipped pen, or a typewriter), the pressure transfers the carbon backing of the interleaved sheets to successive forms. Carbon release paper was used in the days before photocopiers, carbonless forms, and computers were commonplace.

Carbon Shield

A sheet of metal or cloth used in conjunction with carbon paper to allow write-through of the carbon only in selected areas.

Carbon Stop

In business forms using *carbon release* paper, a narrow or short sheet of carbon paper.

Carbon Tetrachloride

A nonflammable yet highly toxic *solvent*—chemical formula CCl_4—used in the degreasing of metallic screen fabrics in *screen printing*.

Carbon Tissue

A gelatin-based emulsion used in the chemical etching of *gravure cylinder*s. The gelatinous emulsion is applied to a paper backing and is rendered sensitive to light when immersed in a 3–4% solution of potassium bichromate. After drying, it is ready for use. The carbon tissue is first exposed to a *film positive*. In those areas where the carbon tissue has received the most light (i.e., nonimage areas and highlights) the emulsion becomes thick and hard, and the thickness and hardness decreases with decreasing exposure to the light source, the emulsion being thinnest and softest in image areas corresponding to shadows and solids. After the carbon tissue is developed, it is adhered to the surface of the copper-plated cylinder. A solution of ferric chloride etchant is applied to the surface of the cylinder, where it eats away the copper through the carbon tissue. In the highly exposed areas, where the carbon tissue *resist* is the thickest and hardest, the etchant takes a long period of time to eat through the hard emulsion, while in the least exposed, thinnest regions, the etchant eats through the resist into the copper very quickly. Thus, in a given period of etching, the cells etched into the copper will be deepest (and thus will print the darkest) in those regions where the etchant has eaten through the quickest, while the cells etched into the copper will be the shallowest (and thus print the lightest) in those regions where the etchant has eaten through the slowest.

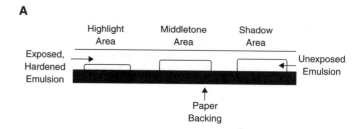

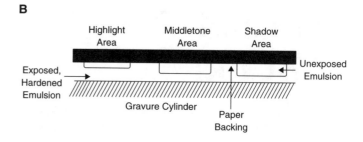

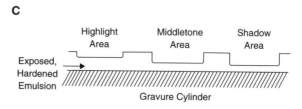

The principle of the carbon tissue resist. After exposure to a continuous-tone positive (A) highlight areas are more highly exposed and thus produce a thicker and harder emulsion than do shadow areas. After the exposed resist is attached to a gravure cylinder (B), an etchant is applied, which eats through varying thicknesses of emulsion (C).

Carbon tissue resists, the first chemical etching media, have been replaced by *photopolymer*s, and chemical etching as a whole is being increasingly replaced by *electromechanical engraving* and computer-to-cylinder *laser-cutting process*es. (See *Gravure Engraving*.)

Carbon tissue resists have also been used extensively for the manufacture of *photostencil*s in *screen printing*.

Carbon Tongue

In business forms utilizing *carbon release* paper, the portion of the carbon paper that extends beyond the edge of the plys, used as an aid in the manual removal of the carbon paper.

Carbon Wedge

In imaging and photography, a small transparent *gray scale* imprinted on a strip of film with gradually increasing densities, from completely transparent to opaque, which are either in increments or are continuous. A carbon wedge is produced using a finely grained carbon dispersion coating and does not scatter light rays greatly. As a result, a carbon wedge is often used in scanner *calibration*.

Carborundum

A solution of silicon carbide used to abrade the threads of *monofilament* mesh screen fabrics in *screen printing*.

Carbro

A *full-color* photograph used in *process color* printing.

Card

In computing, a shorthand term for an *expansion card* or *expansion board*. See *Expansion Board*.

In papermaking, *card* is occasionally used to refer to *index paper*, *tag paper*, or other thick paper.

Card Cage

In computing, a frame found within a computer that holds microprocessor circuit boards. Also known as a *card chassis*.

Card Chassis

See *Card Cage*.

Carding

In typography, the insertion of additional amounts of space (or *leading*) between lines of type, often to facilitate vertical *justification*. The term derives from hot-metal typesetting when cardboard was used for the purpose.

Cardiod Microphone

In audio/video, a sound input device having a sensitivity to sound that forms a heart-like pattern around the front of the microphone. Such a device picks up sound readily from straight ahead, somewhat less from the sides, and not at all from the rear.

Card Punch

In early computing, a device used to encode *punch card*s, often automatically.

Card Services

In computing, general term for the software (or *device driver*) required to run a *PCMCIA* card. Such card services include memory management, power management, access of the correct communications port on the computer, etc.

Caret

A symbol (^) used in proofreading to indicate where additional material is to be inserted.

Carload Lot

In papermaking, a quantity of paper rolls or skids—commonly 36,000–100,000 lb.—which will constitute a full freight carload.

Carmine F.B.

An *organic color pigment* used in printing inks. Carmine F.B. is a bluish red possessing high *lightfastness*, and resistance to acids, alkalis, solvents, soap, water, and heat.

At high concentrations, it tends to have poor flow characteristics. The high cost of Carmine F.B. has relegated its use only to those applications where its resistance properties warrant the expense. (See also *Organic Color Pigments*.)

(*CI Pigment Red 5 No. 12490*.)

Caron

In typography, an *accent* (˘) placed over a character, used often in Slavic languages. (See *Accent*.) Also called a *hacek* or a *wedge*.

Carousel

A type of multicolor *screen printing* press that contains multiple platens revolving around a central core. See *Screen Printing: Press Configurations*.

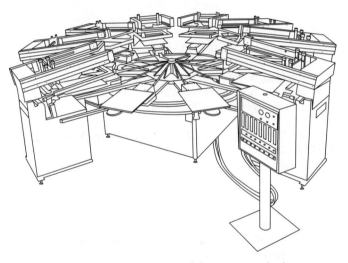

An automatic carousel press used for screen printing.

Carriage

The mechanism in a typewriter or computer printer that moves the print head along a line and to the next line.

Carriage Return

In typewriting or word processing, a manual operation or a code that signifies the end of a line, resulting in new text being added at the beginning of the following line. On a typewriter this was an actual movement of the carriage. In word processing, a carriage return can either be a *hard return* or a *soft return*. In *ASCII*, a carriage return is a *control character* (specifically, ASCII 13) that instructs the cursor or print head to move to the next line. A carriage return is sometimes referred to as a *carrier return*.

Carriage Width

Alternate term for *line width*. Also known as *carriage paper width*. See *Line Width*.

Carrier

Any electric signal maintaining a constant frequency. The modulation of such an electric signal with a second information-carrying signal essentially codes the data that is transmitted along it, allowing radio and television broadcasting, as well as *modem* and *network* communications.

Carrier Detect

In networking and telecommunications, a signal (specifically, an *RS-232* signal) sent from a *modem* to the attached computer that indicates that the modem is connected to another modem. Abbreviated *CD*.

Carrier Return

Alternate term for *carriage return*. See *Carriage Return*.

Carrier Sense Multiple Access (CSMA)

In networking and telecommunications, a protocol for a *baseband* network (such as a *LAN*) that allows all connected devices to transmit on a single channel while ensuring that only one message is transmitted at a time. CSMA protocols essentially deal with the issue of transmission collisions in two ways. See *Carrier Sense Multiple Access/ Collision Avoidance (CSMA/CA)* and *Carrier Sense Multiple Access/Collision Detection (CSMA/CD)*.

Carrier Sense Multiple Access/Collision Avoidance (CSMA/CA)

In networking and telecommunications, a *protocol* for a *baseband* network in which collisions of simultaneously transmitted messages are actively avoided. (The "feeling out" of the network before transmitting is known as *carrier sensing*.) Prior to the sending of a message by a device connected to the network, an interference signal is sent out. After a time interval, during which all the connected devices have received the signal, the message itself is transmitted. If the sending device receives an interference signal during transmission of a message, the transmission is cancelled and is resent after a random interval. Carrier Sense Multiple Access/Collision Avoidance (CSMA/CA) protocols are thus differentiated from *CSMA/CD* protocols by their reliance on "request-to-send" and "clear-to-send" signals to ensure that the network is quiet before initiating transmission. See also *Carrier Sense Multiple Access/ Collision Detection (CSMA/CD)*.

Carrier Sense Multiple Access/Collision Detection (CSMA/CD)

In networking and telecommunications, a *protocol* for a *baseband* network in which a sending device waits until a network is "quiet" before sending a message. (The "feeling out" of the network before transmitting is known as *carrier sensing*.) Prior to the sending of a message by a device connected to the network, the sending device examines the network to see if a transmission is in progress. If not, it sends its own message. If so, the message is not sent, and the transmission is attempted after a random interval. If, during transmission, another transmission is started, both are cancelled and retransmissions are initiated at later

times. See also *Carrier Sense Multiple Access/Collision Avoidance (CSMA/CA)*.

Carrier Sensing

In networking and telecommunications, a means of avoiding collisions by competing transmissions along a network by having each device determine the status of the network before transmitting. If a transmission is in progress, the sending device waits until it is finished before sending. Carrier sensing is the basis of *CSMA* network *protocol*s. See *Carrier Sense Multiple Access (CSMA)*.

Carrier Sheet

Any sheet of paper, plastic, or other material used as a backing for another material, such as labels or, in *stripping*, photographic *negative*s. Also known as a *piggyback form*.

Cartesian Coordinate

A coordinates in a *coordinate system*, typically one containing an x value and a y value, the coordinate being plotted on a two-dimensional plane or grid according to its position in relation to an x-axis (the horizontal) and a y-axis (the vertical). Named for the French mathematician, scientist, and philosopher René Descartes, who first proposed it.

Cartographic Database (CDB)

A database containing x-y coordinates defining a geographical area. When combined with other data (such as any of a wide variety of variables, such as income distribution, age, etc.), a cartographic database can be used to map the distribution of that variable within a geographical region.

Cartridge

Any magnetic tape-based medium housed in a stiff plastic shell, used for the storage and backup of computer files or other information. Cartridge media include things such as SyQuest cartridges, Zip disks, magnetic audio tape, etc. Floppy disks are not, however, considered cartridges. Such materials are also known as *data cartridge*s. Some cartridges are also known as *cassette*s.

Other materials, such as photocopier or *laser printer* toner, is also stored in cartridges.

Cascade

In computing, to link a device containing multiple *port*s to another multiple-port device, thus increasing the total number of ports available.

Cascaded Star

In networking, a network *topology* in which several *hub*s are connected to each other in a series of levels, allowing more connections than a single-level *star* topology. (See illustration on facing page.)

Cascaded Windows

In computing, especially by means of a *graphical user interface (GUI)*, multiple *window*s displayed on the

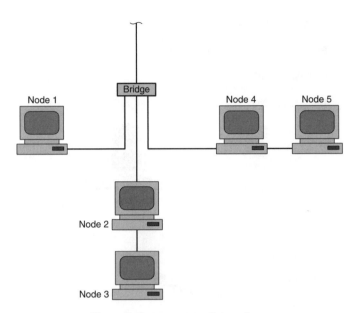

Cascaded star network topology.

screen in such a way as to have the title bar of each visible, even through the contents of each window may not be. Any window can be brought to the front simply by clicking on any visible portion of it. See also **Tiled Windows**.

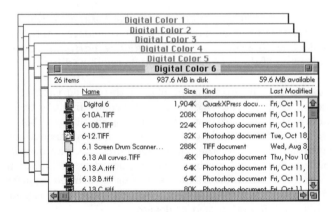

Cascaded windows.

CASE

Abbreviation for **computer-assisted software engineering**. See **Computer-Assisted Software Engineering (CASE)**.

Case

In typography, the condition of letters of the alphabet, i.e., whether they are **uppercase** or **lowercase**, capitals or non-capitals. The term "case" derives from the respective locations of the uppercase and lowercase letters in early type cases.

In **binding and finishing**, the term *case* refers to the hard covers used to bind some types of books. See **Case Binding**.

Case Binding

In **binding and finishing**, a means of binding pages together involving the sewing of printed **signature**s together with thread followed by encasing the signatures between cloth-covered cardboard covers. Case binding is used for **hardcover**—or **casebound**—books and comes in three different types: **edition binding** is the use of fully automated equipment to bind relatively large print runs; **job binding** is the binding of small quantities of books that require special bindings, often including some degree of handwork, such as leather-bound Bibles; and **library binding**, like job binding, is used for small quantities and usually involves some degree of handwork. Library binding is used to create specially reinforced bindings for library usage, and library binding services also repair and rebind damaged books.

There are three basic stages to the case binding process: thread sewing, forwarding, and casing-in.

Thread Sewing. The first step in the case binding process is **thread sewing**, in which printed signatures are stitched together by means of a needle and thread. There are two types of thread sewing: side sewing and saddle sewing. **Side sewing** passes the thread from signature to signature through the side of the book, the stitches running parallel to the **binding edge**. In side sewing, the binding is strong, but books do not lie flat when opened. Side sewing is most often used for library binding and repair work. It can be performed by hand or by special sewing machines (much like home sewing machines) that run the thread through drilled holes. **Saddle sewing**, also called **Smyth sewing**, passes the thread through the signature fold at the spine of the book. Since books that are saddle sewn tend to lie flat when opened, it is the more popular form of thread sewing.

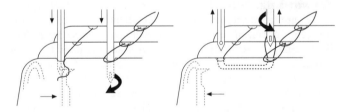

Smyth sewing.

After **gathering** of printed signatures, each signature is fed to an infeed saddle and conveyed to a sewing saddle. A complete **book block** is then automatically stitched. The type of stitch used depends upon the thickness of the book. In both the standard sewing pattern and continuous lockstitch, the stitch is placed in the same position on each signature. This results in **thread build-up**, or an increase in book thickness caused by the alignment of the thread stitches. On thin books, thread buildup can be compensated for by compressing the book block after sewing, or, on thicker books, by using a staggered sewing pattern in which the position of the stitch is offset slightly from signature to signature. A fourth variety of sewing pattern is a

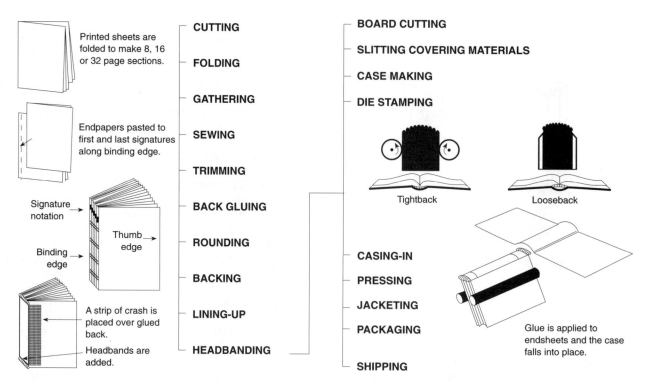

The various steps involved in case-binding a book.

continuous staggered pattern, which maintains an even spine thickness but uses more thread. The continuous staggered pattern produces the most secure bindings.

After thread sewing, book blocks are conveyed to a *three-knife trimmer* for reduction of the pages to the desired *trim size*.

Forwarding. After trimming, there are several operations, some necessary and some strictly decorative and therefore optional, known collectively as *forwarding*. The first steps—*rounding* and *backing*—are needed to shape the spine of the book so as to more effectively fit the cover. In rounding, the book block is clamped into position between two counter-rotating rollers that impart a convex shape to the spine. In backing, the book block is clamped between steel plates and the binding edges of the sewn signatures are bent outward over the clamped edges. This results in a spine that is wider than the rest of the book, and provides shoulders for the front and back covers to rest on. It also creates *hinge* creases allowing the book to be opened.

A variety of structural or decorative enhancements may also be made at this point, depending upon the nature of and the production budget allotted for the book. *Gluing-off* involves the application of an *adhesive* to the spine as a means of reinforcing the thread sewing and to maintain a convex shape. *Edge treatment*s involve such things as *edge staining*, the application of a dye or other colorant to the top, bottom, and/or side edge of the book block, or *gilding*, a similar application of gold leaf. The addition of *headband*s—decorative strips of cotton or silk attached to the

top and bottom of the spine—and/or *book mark*s—ribbons or cords that function as decorative placeholders—may also be done at this time. Special and *deluxe edition*s tend to have more of these amenities than do regular editions.

Casing-In. The attachment of a cloth-covered cardboard case is known as *casing-in*. Book cases are manufactured for a particular book just prior to casing in. Strips of board are cut and trimmed to size and fed into a casemaking machine, which fits the cloth backlining over the boards, folding the excess cloth under the boards and gluing it securely in place. Covers may either be preprinted or, after casemaking, may be *emboss*ed with the title, author, publisher, and any other text or design.

Prior to casing-in, the process of *nipping*—or an application of pressure to the spine of a book block—is performed to compress the threads (reducing the effect of thread build-up) and force out excess air. Alternately, *smashing* applies pressure to the entire front and back of the book block, rather than just the spine.

During casing in, the *endpaper*s of the bound book block are coated with adhesive, and the cloth case fitted over the pages in such as a way as to ensure that the front and back covers project evenly over the edges of the pages. After casing in, the process of *building-in* uses pressure and heat to dry the adhesive and to cause the cloth to conform to the rounded and backed spine. In trade book production, after building-in, the books can undergo *jacketing*, or the addition of a printed paper *dust jacket*.

(See *Binding and Finishing*.)

Casebound

Alternate term for a ***hardcover*** book, or a book that has been bound using ***case binding*** equipment. See ***Case Binding***.

Cased-In

See ***Casing-In***.

Case Fraction

Alternate term for ***en fraction***. See ***En Fraction***.

Casein

A protein obtained by the ***precipitation*** of milk, used in the manufacture of paper ***sizing***, adhesives, and ***coating***s, as well as printing ink ***binder***s. Casein is also the basis of cheese.

Casemaker

In ***binding and finishing***, a device used to make hardcovers for ***casebound*** books. See ***Case Binding***.

Casing-In

In ***case binding***, the operation of gluing the ***endpaper***s of a book to the case and inserting the sewn and trimmed text pages into the cover. Also spelled without a hyphen, *casing in*. See ***Case Binding***.

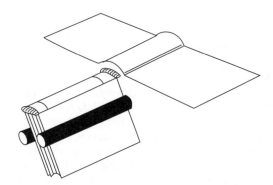

Casing-in, the attachment of the cover to the book block.

Caslon, William

William Caslon (1692–1766) was an engraver of locks and barrels for guns, who became England's first punchcutter and typefounder, developing the first major business in this field. He was born in the village of Cradley, in Worcestershire,

England. He was an apprentice engraver in London at the age of 13; by age 24 he had become a successful independent engraver. In 1720, Caslon began his career in type design by accepting a commission to create a typeface for the New Testament in Arabic. His subsequent roman typeface set an example for beauty and readability for all later type. His first spec-

imen sheet in 1734 displayed 38 of his type fonts and led to the virtual cessation of importing Dutch types, on which English printers had formerly relied. His typefaces, noted for their legibility, are among the best "utility" faces ever produced. Caslon expanded his business into Britain's first major type foundry, moving, in 1737, into the Chiswell Street Foundry, where his family would continue in the trade for over 120 years. Caslon type fell into disuse at the start of the 19th century. But in 1844, Charles Whittingham initiated a Caslon revival by using the typeface for the Chiswick Press publication of *The Diary of Lady Willoughby*. This revival was taken up in America by L.J. Johnson, who copied the Caslon face in 1858, under the name "Old Style." The Caslon typeface remains one of the most popular of all time.

Cassette

A small ***cartridge*** containing magnetic tape used as a storage medium for audio (common audiotapes), video (videotapes), or computer information.

Cast

See ***Color Cast***.

Cast Animation

In multimedia, a type of animation in which only certain components within an image are animated, rather than the image as a whole (as in ***frame animation***). Such an animated component is known as a ***cell***.

Cast Coat

To apply a paper ***coating*** utilizing a ***cast coater***. See ***Cast Coater***.

Cast-Coated Paper

Paper that has been given a high-gloss surface utilizing a ***cast coater***. See ***Cast Coater***.

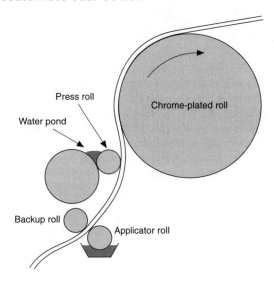

A cast coater, a device that applies coating to the surface of paper.

Cast Coater

A device used to apply a *coating* to the surface of a paper. A cast coater deposits a fluid coating on the surface of the *base stock*, then presses the paper *web* against the surface of a heated, highly polished metal drum. As the paper and coating dry, it takes on the shiny, reflective surface of the drum. Paper coated in this manner possesses high *gloss*, *ink absorbency*, and *bulk*. (See also *Coating*.)

Casting Off

In *copyfitting*, the process of calculating how many type-set or printed pages a particular length of manuscript (or other copy) will occupy. See *Castoff* and *Copyfitting*.

Casting Speed

The measure of the number of lines a *linecaster* can set per unit time. See *Lines per Minute (lpm)*.

Castoff

An estimate that is made to determine the number of typeset or printed pages a particular length of manuscript (or other copy) will occupy. A castoff is typically expressed as the total number of characters that will be typeset. See *Copyfitting*, *Character Count*, and *Characters per Pica*.

Catalog

Any directory—either in printed or digital form—of information. Common examples of catalogs are books or booklets published by stores or suppliers containing descriptions and price information on materials sold by the company.

In computers, a *catalog* is a *directory* or *folder* of disk files for a specific application. See *Directory*.

Also spelled *catalogue*.

Catalogue

See *Catalog*.

Catalyst

Any chemical or other substance that increases the rate at which a chemical reaction takes place without itself becoming permanently altered by the reaction. Platinum is one of the most effective catalysts. In printing inks, *driers* are added as catalysts, as they facilitate the chemical reactions (such as *oxidation* and/or *polymerization*) that cause an ink to dry. A substance that increases the rate of reaction but which is itself consumed or altered by the reaction is an *intermediate*. The opposite of a catalyst is an *inhibitor*.

Catching Up

The generation of the press condition of *catch-up*. See *Catch-up*.

Catchlight

Alternate term for *specular highlight*. See *Specular Highlight*.

Catch-Up

Printing problem in *offset lithography* characterized by the printing plate accepting ink in nonimage areas and printing as scum, typically occurring at the beginning of a pressrun before the flow of *dampening solution* has been adjusted properly. Catch-up is also called *dry-up*.

Catchword

In typography, especially that of dictionaries or encyclopedias, a word located at the top of a dictionary page in place of a *running head* as a means of quickly locating terms contained in the text. The term *catchword* also refers to the first word of a dictionary entry.

Category 3

In networking, a standard for *unshielded twisted pair* cabling found in 10-Mb/sec. 10Base-T *Ethernet* networks and 4-Mb/sec. *Token Ring* networks.

Category 4

In networking, a standard for *unshielded twisted pair* cabling found in 16-Mb/sec. *Token Ring* networks.

Cathode

A source of negatively charged ions, used in the *electroplating* of *gravure* cylinders, as opposed to an *anode*. (See *Electroplating*.) Cathodes are also used in *photomultiplier tubes* and many other electric and electronic devices, such as *cathode-ray tubes* used in computer monitors. See *Cathode Ray* and *Cathode-Ray Tube (CRT)*.

Cathode Ray

A beam of electrons that, when striking a phosphor-coated surface (such as the back of a television or computer screen), creates light-emitting dots or *pixels*. The motion of the ray across and down the screen is controlled by a *deflection* unit. In a *monochrome* monitor, there is a single cathode ray. In an *RGB monitor*, there are three (a red, a green, and a blue). A cathode ray is emitted by a device known as an *electron gun*.

Cathode-Ray Tube (CRT)

A type of vacuum tube and its related electronics that converts variations of voltage into patterns of images on a surface coated with phosphorous, generating light. The CRT is the basis of most television sets, computer monitors, and some *scanners* (see *CRT Flying Spot Scanner*).

A monochrome monitor (or black-and-white TV set) has a single electron gun that fires a continuous stream of electrons at the back of the display screen. Focusing lenses and deflection plates constantly control the position of the electron beam, ensuring image quality. A color CRT uses three electron guns to produce red, green, and blue dot patterns.

When used to describe computer video terminals, *CRT* has on occasion been used to refer to the entire device, including a keyboard, rather than simply the mechanism that generates the images.

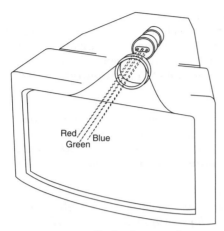

Cathode-ray tube.

CATIA

A brand of **CAD** software that is manufactured by IBM. See **Computer-Aided Design (CAD)**.

CATV

Abbreviation for **Community Antenna TeleVision**, used synonymously with cable television. See **Cable Television Network**.

CAU

Abbreviation for **Controlled Access Unit**. See **Controlled Access Unit (CAU)**.

Caution

Any procedure in any industry or manufacturing process which, if not heeded, can result in damage to equipment or software, or in bodily injury.

CAV

Abbreviation for **component analog video**. See **Component Video**.

  CAV is also an abbreviation for **constant angular velocity**. See **Constant Angular Velocity**.

Caxton, William

In 1476, William Caxton set up England's first printing press. Caxton had been a prolific translator and found the printing press a marvelous way to advance his mission of promoting popular literature. Caxton printed and distributed a variety of widely popular narrative titles including the first edition of Chaucer's *Canterbury Tales*. Caxton was an enthusiastic editor, and he determined the diction, spelling, and usage for all the books he printed. English suffered from so much regional variation that Caxton's contributions as an editor and printer have given him credit for standardizing the English language.

  William Caxton (c. 1422–91) was born in the Weald of Kent. In 1438, he became apprenticed to Robert Large, a textile merchant who became the mayor of London in 1439. After Large's death in 1441, Caxton moved to Bruges, the

center for trade between the English and Flemish, and built up a thriving textile business. He attained prominence as a merchant and by 1463 was acting governor of the Merchant Adventurers in the Low Countries. In 1464, he attempted unsuccessfully to renew a wool treaty with Phillip, Duke of Burgundy. Four years later, Caxton successfully completed the trade negotiations with Charles the Bold, Phillip's successor. Caxton was hired as an advisor to Charles' new duchess, the former Princess Margaret of York, sister of Edward IV.

  About 1471, Caxton visited Cologne, where he learned the art of printing from one of Gutenberg's workmen and later founded a press in Bruges, Belgium, before returning to England. In 1477, Caxton's press at Westminster at the sign of the Red Pale produced *Dictes or Sayenges of the Phylosophers*, the first dated book printed in England. Caxton published more than 90 editions, including works by Gower, Chaucer, and Malory, as well as his own translations of French and Latin works. It was at the request of the duchess Margaret that he resumed translation of a popular French romance, *The Recuyell of the Historyes of Troye* from the French of Raoul le Fèvre. *The Recuyell* is the first printed book in the English language (1474). His next publication, *The Game and Play of Chess Moralised* (1476), was a translation of the first major European work on chess and was the first printed book in English to make extensive use of woodcuts.

  The typefaces used by Caxton were all variations of blackletter or gothic type. His earlier works were set in an early form of French lettre bâtarde. By 1490, he had acquired a more round and open typeface, a textura originated by Parisian printer Antoine Verard and later favored by Caxton's successor, Wynkyn de Worde.

CB

Abbreviation for *coated back*.

C Band

In telecommunications, portion of the **electromagnetic spectrum**—comprising the frequencies 4–6 **GHz**—used for satellite and microwave transmission.

CBEMA

Abbreviation for **Computer and Business Equipment Manufacturers Association**. See **Computer and Business Equipment Manufacturers Association (CBEMA)**.

CBK

A **file extension** used for files created using Harvard Graphics' Chartbook program.

CBL

Abbreviation for *computer-based learning*.

CBT/CBI

Abbreviation for *computer-based training/computer-based instruction*.

cc

Abbreviation for *carbon copy*, a somewhat anachronistic term used to indicate those individuals who are to receive copies of an *Email* message. See also *bcc*.

CCD

Abbreviation for *charge-coupled device*. *See Charge-Coupled Device (CCD)*.

CCD Array

In imaging, a row of *charge-coupled device*s (*CCD*s) that pick up light reflecting off a surface from many different directions. In a *scanner*, a CCD array may only be an inch long, and can scan and measure the light impinging on it from as many as 2,048 points. Some scanners use two rows of CCDs, capable of much greater scanning capacity. See *Charge-Coupled Device (CCD)*, *CCD Scanner*, and *Digital Photography*.

CCD Scanner

In imaging, a *scanner* containing a *CCD array* rather than *photomultiplier tube*s. A CCD scanner can either be color, grayscale, or black-and-white. CCD scanners use two CCD arrays, each possessing 2,048 photosites. Consequently, a total of 4,096 photosites can capture 4,096 pixels across each scan line. See *Charge-Coupled Device (CCD)* and *CCD Array*.

CCIR

Abbreviation for *Comité Consultatif International des Radiocommunications*, or the standards for *digital component video* created by that organization. See *Comité Consultatif International des Radiocommunications (CCIR)*, *CCIR 601*, and *CCIR 656*.

CCIR 601

An international standard for digital *component video* that was devised by the *Comité Consultatif International des Radiocommunications (CCIR)*. The recommendations in the standard include signal recording on the *four-two-two (4:2:2)* format, *YCrCb* or *RGB* color coding, and an electromechanical interface described by the *CCIR 656* standard.

CCIR 656

An international standard for interfaces for digital *component video* devised by the *Comité Consultatif International des Radiocommunications (CCIR)*. The recommendations define *blanking level*, *sync signal*, and *parallel* and *serial* interfaces including the electrical characteristics of the connectors.

CCITT

Abbreviation for *Comité Consultatif International Téléphonique et Télégraphique*. See *Comité Consultatif International Téléphonique et Télégraphique (CCITT)*.

CCITT Groups 1–4

A set of standards developed by the *Comité Consultatif International Téléphonique et Télégraphique (CCITT)* for *facsimile* transmission. See *Comité Consultatif International Téléphonique et Télégraphique (CCITT)*.

CCITT V Series

A set of standards developed by the *Comité Consultatif International Téléphonique et Télégraphique (CCITT)* for data transmission. See *Comité Consultatif International Téléphonique et Télégraphique (CCITT)*.

CCITT X Series

A set of standards developed by the *Comité Consultatif International Téléphonique et Télégraphique (CCITT)* for computer networks. See *Comité Consultatif International Téléphonique et Télégraphique (CCITT)*.

CCL

Abbreviation for *common command language*. See *Common Command Language*.

CCTV

Abbreviation for *closed-circuit television*. See *Closed Circuit*.

CCU

Abbreviation for *camera control unit*. See *Camera Control Unit*.

CD

In papermaking, abbreviation for *cross-machine direction*. See *Cross-Machine Direction*.

    CD is also an abbreviation for *compact disc*, used to refer to both *compact disc–digital audio (CD-DA)* (or *audio CD*) or *compact disc–read-only memory (CD-ROM)*. See *Compact Disc (CD)*.

    In networking, *CD* is also an abbreviation for *collision detection*. See *Carrier Sense Multiple Access/Collision Detection (CSMA/CD)*.

    In telecommunications, *CD* is also an abbreviation for *carrier detect*. See *Carrier Detect*.

CD-A

Abbreviation for *compact disc–digital audio*; Also abbreviated *CD-DA*. See *Compact Disc–Digital Audio (CD-DA)*.

CDB

Abbreviation for *cartographic database*. See *Cartographic Database (CDB)*.

CD-DA

Abbreviation for *compact disc–digital audio*. See *Compact Disc–Digital Audio (CD-DA)*.

CDDI

Abbreviation for *Copper Distributed Data Interface*. See *Copper Distributed Data Interface (CDDI)*.

CD-E

Abbreviation for *compact disc–erasable*. See *Compact Disc–Erasable (CD-E)*.

Cdev

In computers, abbreviation for *control device*, an *INIT* or system *extension* that allows the main computer to control peripheral devices such as *scanner*s or *CD-ROM* drives. See *Extension*.

CD-Graphics

See *Compact Disc–Graphics*.

CD-i

Abbreviation for *compact disc–interactive*. See *Compact Disc–Interactive (CD-i)*.

CD-IV

Abbreviation for *compact disc–interactive video*, a proposed format based on the *CD-i* platform. See *Compact Disc–Interactive (CD-i)*.

CDPD

Abbreviation for *cellular digital packet data*. See *Cellular Digital Packet Data (CDPD)*.

CD-Plus

Abbreviation for *compact disc–plus*. See *Compact Disc–Plus (CD+)*.

CD+

Abbreviation for *compact disc–plus*. See *Compact Disc–Plus (CD+)*.

CD+MM

Abbreviation for *compact disc–plus multimedia*. See *Compact Disc–Plus (CD+)*.

CDR

Extension for files saved in *CorelDraw*'s native file format.

CD-R

Abbreviation for *compact disc–recordable*. See *Compact Disc–Recordable (CD-R)*.

CD-Ready

Abbreviation for *compact disc–ready*. See *Compact Disc–Ready*.

CD-ROM

Abbreviation for *compact disc–read-only memory*. See *Compact Disc–Read-Only Memory (CD-ROM)*.

CD-ROM-XA

Abbreviation for *compact disc–read-only memory–extended architecture*. See *Compact Disc–Read-Only Memory–Extended Architecture (CD-ROM-XA)*.

CD-RTOS

Abbreviation for *compact disc–real time operating system*. See *Compact Disc–Real Time Operating System (CD-RTOS)*.

CD-R-WORM

Abbreviation for *compact disc–recordable–write once, read many*. See *Compact Disc (CD)*.

CD-S

Abbreviation for *compact disc–single*. See *Compact Disc–Single (CD-S)*.

CDTV

Abbreviation for *Commodore Dynamic Total Vision*. See *Commodore Dynamic Total Vision (CDTV)*.

CD-V

Abbreviation for *compact disc–video*. See *Compact Disc–Video (CD-V)*.

Cedilla

In typography, an *accent* (‚) placed under a character, usually the letter "c", to indicate that it should be pronounced with a soft "s"-like sound. The cedilla (ç) is most commonly used in French. See *Accent*.

Cel

A shorthand term for *celluloid*, used to refer to a sheet of transparent celluloid used for each frame of an *animation*. See *Cel Animation*. Also spelled *cell*.

Cel Animation

A means of *two-dimensional (2-D) animation* in which images to be animated are drawn or painted on transparent overlays (often sheets of *acetate*) and photographed individually to create the illusion of motion. See *Animation*. Also spelled *cell animation*.

Cell

In digital prepress, shorthand term for *halftone cell*. See *Halftone Cell*.

In *gravure* printing, the term *cell* refers to one of the many small depressions etched into the image carrier used in *gravure* printing. A gravure image is composed of thousands or millions of tiny cells, the distribution and depth of which determine the density of the printed image. Cells can be etched into the *gravure cylinder* in a variety of ways. See *Gravure*, *Gravure Cylinder* and *Gravure Engraving*.

A *cell* is also one of the indentations engraved into the surface of an *anilox roller* used in *flexographic* press inking systems. See *Anilox Roller* and *Inking System: Flexography*.

In graphics and animation, the term *cell* refers to a sheet of *acetate* or other transparent sheet on which a figure to be animated is drawn. Since each figure is on a transparent sheet, they can be animated separately from other figures, such as backgrounds. Animation in such a manner is known as ***cast animation***. In this sense, *cell*—short for *celluloid*—is often spelled ***cel***.

In ***scanning***, the term *cell* is used to refer to any collection of ***pixel***s treated by the device as a single unit. Common cell sizes are 4×4 or 6×6. Larger cell sizes can include more gray levels. Analogous to a ***halftone cell***.

In spreadsheet programs, a *cell* is a particular field in which information is placed. Cells can be identified by horizontal and vertical coordinates.

In telecommunications and networking, the term *cell* refers to a particular ***packet*** of data used in ***cell switching*** protocols. See ***Cell Switching***.

The term *cell* is also a shorthand term for ***cellular***, a technology used in mobile telephony. See ***Cellular***.

Cellophane

A transparent, nonpermeable paperlike material produced from regenerated and plasticized ***cellulose*** used for packaging, food wrappers, and tape, commonly employed as a ***substrate*** in ***flexography***, ***gravure***, and other printing processes.

Cellosolve

A brand of ethylene glycol mono ethyl ether, a ***solvent*** used as a ***retarder*** in ***flexographic*** inks. A variety of Cellosolve is known as ***butyl Cellosolve***.

Cellosolve is a registered trademark of Union Carbide Corporation.

Cell Relay

Alternate term for ***asynchronous transfer mode***. See ***Asynchronous Transfer Mode (ATM)***.

Cell Switching

In telecommunications and networking, a means of data transmission—used in ***asynchronous transfer mode*** networking—that divides all network traffic into discrete packets of 53 ***byte***s. Each cell contains an ***address*** and the data itself. Since each cell has a fixed length and is small, cell switching is a fast mode of transmission.

Cellular

A technology used for mobile telephony (i.e., the increasingly ubiquitous cellular phones). Essentially, a geographic area is divided into a series of hexagonal zones (called "cells") that fit together to form a kind of honeycomb pattern. Each of these cells contains a radio transceiver and a controller. A central switch transfers calls from one cell to another, the calls originating and/or ending at a cellular phone.

Cellular Digital Packet Data (CDPD)

In telecommunications, a means of transmitting data efficiently by cellular communications and wireless modems in which any available cellular channel can be accessed. CDPD makes use of voice channels but can switch to another channel if a voice transmission begins.

Cellulose

A long-chain polymer that can be considered nature's building block, as it is the basic structural material of all trees and plants. The chemical structure of cellulose (whose basic chemical formula is $C_6H_{10}O_5$) comprises a long, repeating chain of carbon-hydrogen-oxygen units. Cellulose fiber is the most basic and important constituent of paper, and the size and quality of cellulose fibers are important considerations in the papermaking process. The greater the cellulose content of a paper ***pulp***, the higher the quality of the paper. Cotton is nearly pure cellulose, and consequently produces the best paper; woods tend to range from 50–90% cellulose, which also makes them ideally suited to papermaking, although the cellulose content of trees varies from tree to tree, or even within the same tree. The size and shape of the cellulose fibers also differ from tree to tree. The two botanical classifications of trees—***coniferous*** and ***deciduous***—each have different cellulose fiber characteristics, which can dramatically affect the quality of paper that is ultimately produced.

In its natural state, cellulose fibers are bound together with another substance called ***lignin***, the removal of which by chemical or mechanical means greatly improves paper quality. Wood and plant material also contains other carbohydrate compounds (called ***hemicellulose***s, since for many years chemists had difficulty distinguishing them from true cellulose) that also must be removed by the paper ***pulping*** process.

Cellulose, which is indigestible by all living organisms (with the exception of bacteria), is also used to make some types of plastic—such as ***cellulose acetate***, ***cellulose acetate butyrate***, ***cellophane***, and ***ethyl cellulose***—used as ***resin***s, ***film former***s, and ***substrate***s in ***gravure***, ***flexography***, and other printing processes.

Cellulose Acetate

An acetic ***ester*** produced from ***cellulose*** and acetic acid, formed as a transparent, ***thermoplastic*** film used as a ***substrate*** in a variety of printing processes, as overlays for mechanicals or other artwork, for overhead transparencies, and as a packaging material.

Cellulose Acetate Butyrate

A transparent plastic material produced from ***cellulose***, acetic acid, and butyric acid used as a ***substrate*** in several printing processes and as a packaging, coating, or laminating material.

Cellulose Fiber

The raw material for papermaking, produced from wood, cotton, or other source. See ***Cellulose*** and ***Paper and Papermaking***.

Cell Wall

The "membrane" or ridge separating one gravure ***cell*** from the next. Gravure, unlike most other printing processes, prints from ink-filled cells engraved into the surface of a copper-plated cylinder. A particular gravure image is composed of a series of cells, the thickness of the cell wall being one way of varying print density. Light areas or highlights of an image are either shallow or small cells separated from its neighbors by a thick cell wall. Shadows or other dark regions are composed of many deep, wide cells with very thin cell walls. The cell walls are needed in order to provide a surface for the **doctor blade** to scrape against (the doctor blade is the metal blade on a gravure press that scrapes off the excess ink from the nonprinting surface of the cylinder); without cell walls, the doctor blade would remove ink from the cells, or wear away the image area of the cylinder. The cell walls, along with the other nonprinting areas, are collectively known as the gravure cylinder's **land area**. See **Gravure Engraving**.

Cell wall is also used to define the ridges between the engraved cells of a **flexographic** press's **anilox roller**. See **Anilox Roller** and **Inking System: Flexography**.

Cement Exposing Method

In **screen printing**, a means of exposing a **photostencil** in which the **film positive** or **negative** is attached to the photostencil material with rubber cement.

Center Dot

Alternate term for a **bullet**. See **Bullet**.

Centered Accent

See **Accent**.

Centered Type

In typography, a line (or lines) of type centered on the **line length**. Also referred to as **quad center**.

> In typography, a line (or lines) of type centered on the line length. Also referred to as quad center.

A paragraph consisting of centered type.

Center Feed

In computing by means of paper tape, descriptive of a tape whose feed hole is positioned in the center of the tape, rather than along one side. Also known as **in-line feed**.

Center Indent

In typography, a form of **indention** in which the beginning and end of a line are indented an equal distance from the left and right margins, respectively.

Centering

In typography, the act of aligning text midway between two points, or on a line with equal amounts of space between the left and right margins.

Centerline

In prepress, a short, thin line added to original copy, a **negative**, or a **flat** to indicate the center of the trim margin of a page. A centerline is also used for **registration** purposes. Also known as a **center mark**.

Center Mark

Alternate term for a **centerline**. See **Centerline**.

Center Point

In typography, a period set centered on the **x-height** to indicate multiplication, such as 2 · 2. Also known as a **space dot**.

Center Spread

In page layout and printing, the two adjacent pages in the center of a **signature**. Also known as a **natural spread**.

Center Truck

In magazine and newspaper typography, the **two-page spread** located in the center of a magazine or newspaper.

Central Computer

A computer that controls the functions of a computer system or network.

Central Impression Press

A type of printing press used in multicolor **flexography** in which a single large-diameter **common impression cylinder** supports the **substrate** as it contacts a series of adjacent **plate cylinder**s, which lay down successive colors. Central impression presses can have anywhere from two to eight printing units, with six being the most common. See **Flexography: Press Configurations**.

Centralized Data Processing

In networking, data processing performed in a single location, to which additional **workstation**s (in this case, **dumb terminal**s) are connected.

Centralized Network

A type of **network topology** in which each **node** is connected to a central **hub** that controls network functions. See **Network Topology**.

Central Processing Unit (CPU)

The "brain" of a computer that controls the processing of all information. The CPU also possesses the arithmetic and logic capabilities of the device, and houses the **RAM** and **ROM** memory and processing chips. In **microcomputer**s, the CPU is usually a single chip.

Centrex

In telecommunications, a service in which each subscriber can be directly dialed from outside the network. Centrex switching equipment is located at the telephone company's office and is thus easy to expand. Centrex itself is an abbreviation of *CENTRal EXchange*.

Centroid

In computer graphics, the mean center point of a polygon, derived by calculating the means of the x and y coordinate points of the polygon.

Centronics

In computing, an 8-*bit*, 36-pin parallel interface for connecting printers, used by the Centronics Corporation. It has become the standard for *microcomputer*s, and is now often used synonymously for *parallel port*. See *Parallel Port*.

CEPS

Abbreviation for *color electronic prepress system.* See *Color Electronic Prepress System (CEPS)*.

Cermet

A term combining the words "ceramic" and "metallic," descriptive of a *screen printing* ink or coating formulated with conductive or insulating substances for use in printing on ceramic *substrate*s.

CF

Abbreviation for *coated front*.

CFB

Abbreviation for *coated front and back*.

CFS

Abbreviation for *contextual file search*.

CG

Abbreviation for *computer graphics*. See *Computer Graphics*.

    CG is also an abbreviation for *character generator*. See *Character Generator (CG)*.

CGA

Abbreviation for *Color Graphics Adapter*. See *Color Graphics Adapter*.

CGA Monitor

A computer monitor that will only run in concert with a *CGA* expansion card. See *Color Graphics Adapter (CGA)*.

CGATS

Abbreviation for *Committee for Graphic Arts Technology Standards*. See *Committee for Graphic Arts Technology Standards (CGATS)*.

CGI

Abbreviation for *computer graphics interface*. See *Computer Graphics Interface (CGI)*.

CGM

Abbreviation for *computer graphics metafile*, a standard *file format* used on high-end computer systems to exchange graphics files. CGM can store two-dimensional graphics in either *bitmapped* or *vector* form.

Chad

In *binding and finishing*, small bits of paper produced during three-hole punching or other paper punching or drilling operations. Also known as *confetti*.

Chain

In computer programming, a set of operations that are to be executed sequentially.

    In database systems, *chain* also means to link *record*s together in such a way that all records of a specific type are connected to each other.

Chain Dimensioning

In computer graphics, placing dimension lines end-to-end to show the dimensions of individual portions of the entire illustration.

Chaining

In database systems, the linking together of randomly located *record*s in a logical way, typically by pointers or other information (such as a *linking field*) included in the record that includes the location of the preceding and/or succeeding records in the chain. All linked records can be retrieved with a *chaining search*.

    In computer programming, the term *chaining* also refers to the ability of one program to *call* another after its own execution.

Chaining Search

In database systems, a means of retrieving all *record*s of a similar type by searching for data added to a *linking field*. See *Chaining*.

Chain Marks

A paper web defect also called *rope marks*. See *Rope Marks*.

    Chain marks also refers to the larger parallel lines about one inch apart found on *laid finish* paper.

Chain Printer

An *impact printer* in which the *character set* is mounted on an endless chain. The chain moves horizontally past each print position; when a hammer strikes the chain, a particular character is pressed against an inked ribbon and, consequently, the paper.

Chain Transfer

A method of transferring sheets from one printing unit to another on a sheetfed press (especially that used in *offset lithography*) in which sets of grippers mounted on moving chains or belts carry the printed sheet from one *impression cylinder* to the next. Because chain systems allow the sheet to contact fewer surfaces, there is less opportunity for ink marking or smudging. (See also *Single-Drum Transfer*, *Three-Drum Transfer*, and *Transfer Cylinder*.)

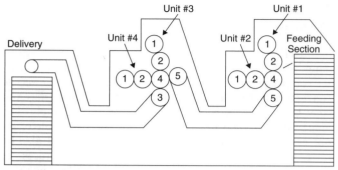

1. Plate Cylinder
2. Blanket Cylinder
3. Delivery System
4. Impression Cylinder
5. Transfer Cylinder

Chain transfer system between common impression cylinders.

Chalkboard Coating

Alternate term for **blackboard coating**. See **Blackboard Coating**.

Chalking

See **Ink Chalking**.

Chamfer

In graphics, a means of joining two lines (such as two perpendicular lines) using a third line to connect them, producing a kind of **bevel**ed corner.

Change Font

In typography, a specification added to manuscript or typescript copy indicating to the typesetter that the **font** used to set the specified material should be different from that used in the rest of the text. Typically, fonts are changed to indicate emphasis, titles, etc., or to set apart other parts of a page, such as heads. On a typewriter, change font is indicated by underlining, indicating that the italic version of the font should be used. On a typesetting device or in **page makeup software**, font changes are indicated to the device either using codes (as in old phototypesetting machines) or by highlighting the material to be changed and clicking on the appropriate font in the font menu.

Channel

In telecommunications and networking, any path for transmission between two or more points. Some networks utilize only one channel (in which it is called a **baseband** network) while other networks, through **multiplexing**, use more than one channel (in which case it is called a **broadband** network).

In graphics and image-processing software, a *channel* is one of several portions of image, usually containing all the information pertaining to a single color. Most images have a red channel, a green channel, and a blue channel, as well as some number of additional **alpha channel**s used for masking and other purposes.

Channel Black

A type of **Carbon Black**, or **black pigment**, used in printing ink. Carbon black itself is produced by the partial combustion of **hydrocarbon** compounds (such as oil, natural gas, wood, or animal bones and tissue) and the condensation of the sooty flame on a cool surface. Channel Black is produced by the contact of a natural gas flame against a metal surface. Because of stringent air pollution laws, the process used to produce Channel Black is no longer feasible in the United States, and has been primarily replaced by **Furnace Black**s. Channel Black, however, has a highly desirable bluish tint and excellent flow characteristics, and is occasionally imported from other countries when the expense of doing so is warranted.

(*CI Pigment Black 7 No. 77266.*)

Channel Capacity

In networking and telecommunications, an expression of the maximum quantity of data traffic that a **channel** can handle.

Channel Rubber

On a heated **screen printing** press, a small rubber insulating channel used to protect the metal wire screen fabric from the heated metal frame.

Channel Service Unit (CSU)

In telecommunications, a device that functions as a safe electrical circuit, used to connect a user's equipment to a larger, public telecommunications network. The CSU ensures that all signals sent over the public network are properly timed and formed, preventing improper signals from damaging public circuits. CSUs need to be approved and certified by the **Federal Communications Commission (FCC)**.

Chapbook

English and German chapbooks evolved from popular French works at the end of the 15th century. The Volksbücher or "people's books" were successful in Germany in the mid-16th century, and colonial Americans imported chapbooks from England; later they were printed locally. In the United States, magazines essentially replaced chapbooks in the 19th century. Chapbooks were small, inexpensive, self-cover, stitched, publications initially sold by itinerant dealers, or chapmen. Publications were 4.25×5.5 in. with a minimum of four pages, or multiple signatures of four pages, illustrated with woodcuts, or later, engravings. They were the supermarket tabloids of their day, containing heroic tales, legends, folklore, ballads, nursery stories, and more. Texts were usually anonymous. In the 1920s various printing and typographic associations produced small publications that continued the chapbook tradition.

Chapter

In book typography, a major subdivision of a book, usually smaller than a part, but larger than a section.

The term *chapter* is also used to refer to an addressable segment of data stored on a *videodisc*. Although specific chapters can be accessed randomly, the data within a chapter can only be accessed sequentially. The code marking the end of a chapter is called a *chapter stop*.

Chapter Head

In book typography, the opening page of a chapter, including the chapter number and/or name.

Chapter Stop

On a *videodisc*, a code used to indicate the end of a *chapter*. See *Chapter* (second definition).

Character

Any letter, number, punctuation mark, or other symbol that is typeset.

The term *character* is also used in computer terminology to refer to one particular *bit* pattern in a data code.

Character-Based Interface

An alternate term for a *command-line interface*. See *Command-Line Interface*.

Character Boundary

A *character box* is defined as the largest rectangle in which a character can be placed so that it can be read by *optical character recognition (OCR)* equipment.

Character Box

In the computerized display of text (or other) characters, the maximum amount of space or largest rectangle in which a particular character can sit. Also known as a *character boundary,* especially in *optical character recognition (OCR)*.

Character Box Element

Alternate term for a *character*. See *Character*.

Character Cell

In the computer generation of text characters (either on a screen or on a printer), the size of the matrix of dots (expressed as the number of horizontal by vertical dots) that makes up a character. A 9×9 matrix will thus allow a total of 81 dots to be used to make up a character. Also known as a *character matrix*.

Character Code

Any code—such as *ASCII*—that assigns numerical values to letters, numbers, and symbols.

Character Compensation

In typography, a means of reducing the white space on a page by reducing the width value for each character.

Character Complement

In typography, the set of characters—letters, numbers, symbols, and punctuation—available in any one *font*.

Character Count

In *copyfitting*, an estimate of the total number of characters—letters, numbers, symbols, and word spaces—in a manuscript or other copy to be set in type as a means of gauging the final length of the typeset material. A character count can be accomplished by actually counting all the characters individually, which is fine for small pieces of copy but not for a Stephen King novel, for example. For longer copy, an estimate can be made, so long as the original manuscript is typewritten. This estimate will also be fairly accurate for copy printed out from a word processor. To begin, determine an average line length and draw a vertical line down the page. Count all the characters in one full line from the left margin to this line, then multiply the result by the number of lines on the page. This will provide—roughly—the number of characters per page. On typewritten copy, it may be a bit simpler. Most older typewriters commonly have only two sizes of character: *pica* (which prints 10 characters per inch) and *elite* (which prints 12 characters per inch). Measure the distance from the left margin to the vertical line to get the length of the average line. Multiply either by 10 or 12 (depending on the typewriter used) to get the total number of characters per line. Then multiply that by the number of lines to get the characters per page.

After the characters per page has been obtained, multiply this number by the total number of pages in the copy to be typeset, making allowances if there are any blanks, full-page illustrations, etc. This will then yield a number somewhere near the total number of characters that are in the copy.

Depending on the nature of the material, it may need to be more or less accurate. If it needs to be very accurate, the characters extending beyond the vertical line may also need to counted.

Many modern word processing programs can do automatic character counts, eliminating the need for having to do it manually.

In the process of copyfitting, the *alphabet length*, or *characters per pica* count of a particular typeface can be used to determine just how many typeset lines the copy will occupy. (See *Copyfitting*.) A character count is also known as a *castoff*.

Character Dispatcher

Any computer program that creates *character*s for printing.

Character Font

A particular *font* in which a character is displayed. See *Font*.

Character Generation

The electronic creation of letters, numbers, and other typographic symbols on a computer display or through a computer printer or other output device. Character generation involves the combining of small dots (such as *pixel*s) or strokes to form a larger character.

Character Generator (CG)

In computing, a device and/or a software program designed and used to convert digital text information to patterns of dots (i.e., *pixel*s) that can be displayed on a computer monitor or output from a computer printer. Depending upon the sophistication of the character generator, special symbols in addition to the usual *character set* may be allowed, as may shapes for some types of rudimentary drawing or sketching.

Character generators are also used in video production to generate titles or other on-screen text. In this case, they are also known as *titler*s.

Characteristic Curve

In photography, a diagram created by plotting the logarithm of the *exposure time* of a photosensitive material on the *x*-axis and the *density* of the exposed materials on the *y*-axis, prepared for a particular *developer*. The characteristic curve shows the effect of every length of exposure on the image density. Also known as a a *D log E curve*.

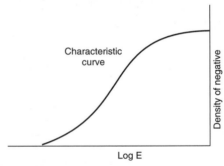

A characteristic curve, which is a plot of density versus the log of exposure.

Character Master

In typography, any master image used to create a typeset character, be it a glass *font disk*, a digital *outline font*, or other such device.

Character Matrix

Alternate term for a *character cell*. See *Character Cell*.

Character Memory

In computing, a *buffer* used to store character *bitmap*s while previously created characters are being processed. See *Caching*.

Character Mode

In computing, a mode found on a *video adapter* in which the monitor will only display text characters found in a built-in *character set*. Graphic elements, mouse pointers, etc., are not displayed. Also known as *text mode*.

Character-Oriented

In networking and telecommunications, a communications *protocol* or transmission method in which control information is encoded in fields comprising one or more *byte*s.

Character Printer

A computer printer—such as a *daisy-wheel printer* or a *dot-matrix printer*—that prints one character at a time.

Character Recognition

Generic term for the automatic input of printed characters. See *Magnetic Ink Character Recognition (MICR)* and *Optical Character Recognition (OCR)*.

Character Set

Alternate term for *font*. See *Font*.

The term *character set* also refers to a standard group of *alphanumeric* characters, punctuation marks, mathematical symbols, and control characters used by a computer. See *ASCII*, *EBCDIC*, and *Unicode*.

Character Size Control

In computing and computerized typesetting, a term used to refer to the ability of a display to alter the size of the characters on the screen, preferably in some proportion to their *point size*. Character size control is usually a function of *WYSIWYG* computer systems and monitors.

Character Spacing

Alternate term for *letterspacing*. See *Letterspacing*.

Character Spacing Display

In computing and computerized typesetting, a term used to refer to the ability of a display to alter the spacing of the characters on the screen. Character spacing display is usually a function of *WYSIWYG* computer systems and monitors.

Character Spacing Reference Line

In *optical character recognition (OCR)*, a vertical line used by the hardware and software to determine the horizontal spacing of characters.

Characters per Inch (CPI)

A measurement of type, used in *copyfitting*, that is based on the *alphabet length* of a particular *typeface*. When type needs to fit in a certain allotted portion of space, it is often necessary to determine how many characters fit in a unit of linear distance. See *Copyfitting*, *Alphabet Length*, and *Character Count*. See also *Characters per Pica (CPP)*.

CPI is also used as a measurement of the density of information that can be stored on a magnetic tape, disk, or other type of external storage medium. (See also *Bits per Inch*.)

Characters per Pica (CPP)

In typography and *copyfitting*, a means of estimating the length of typeset copy by measuring the average number of characters of a particular *typeface* that will occupy one *pica* of length. See *Copyfitting*, *Alphabet Length*, and *Character Count*. See also *Characters per Inch (CPI)*.

Characters per Second (CPS)

A measure of the number of characters that an output device can transfer to a *substrate* each second, used as a means of evaluating typesetting equipment, computer printers, and other output devices. *Kilocharacters per second* is often used to measure speeds in increments of one thousand characters per second.

Character String

In computer code, any set of characters—be they alphabetic, numeric, etc.—considered as a single unit. Also known simply as a *string*.

Character Support

Any finite *character set* that is considered complete for some purpose.

Character Triplet

In typography, any three-letter combination that has been *kern*ed. See *Kerning* and *Ligature*.

Charge-Coupled Device (CCD)

A small light-sensitive photocell or semiconductor chip. Essentially, a CCD is responsive to the amount of light being reflected from a particular image, and this light it then converts into voltages (electric charges) that can, in turn, be converted into *digital data*. CCDs are commonly used in optical devices, from video cameras to photocopiers to *scanner*s to *digital camera*s. Their small size (several thousandths of an inch wide) makes them particularly useful in desktop scanners, hand-held camcorders, and other portable or desktop devices. Although they are much smaller than *photomultiplier tube*s, which they are replacing, they are not as sensitive to small color and tone differences, especially those in *shadow*s. Consequently, photomultiplier tubes are still highly desirable for high-quality scanners. (See *Scanning*.)

Charged

Term used to refer to a material that is electrically active, either positive (and thus having an affinity for negatively charged materials) or negative (and thus having an affinity for positively charged materials). The processes of *electroplating* and *electrophotography* operate on this electrical affinity for opposite charges.

Chart

Any graphical display of information. There are four basic types of charts. A *bar chart*, in which information is represented as bars (either vertical or horizontal) on an *x-y* *coordinate system*, the respective heights of which are in proportion to the values they represent. A *pie chart* represents fractional divisions of a whole as pieces of a circle, the size of each "slice" being in proportion to its percentage of the whole. A *scatter plot* simply plots a number of points on an *x-y* coordinate system and is used occasionally to illustrate trends or groupings. A *line graph* is a type of

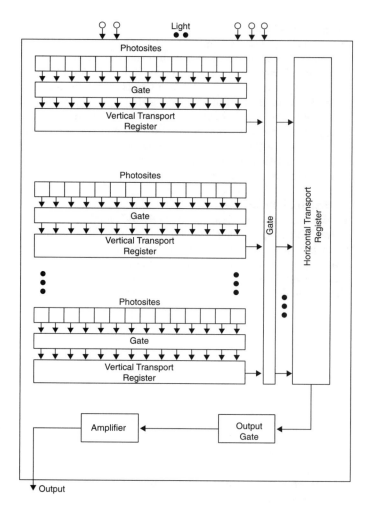

Basic CCD structure.

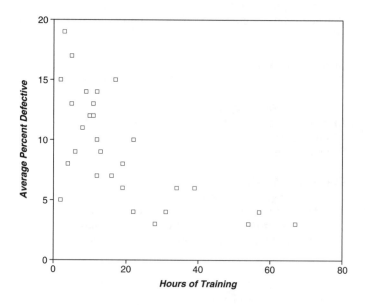

A scatter plot, one type of chart.

scatter plot in which points are connected by lines to emphasize the progression of a particular trend. The usefulness of a line graph depends upon the linearity of the plotted data.

The above charts may also be referred to as **graph**s, especially when data is plotted in a coordinate system. Many spreadsheet, desktop publishing, or other programs automatically generate charts from raw data entered into them.

A type of chart unrelated to the above is called a **flowchart**. (See **Flowchart**.) Strictly tabular data is sometimes also referred to as a chart. (See **Tabular Composition**.)

Chart Element

Any essential component of a **chart** or graph. See **Chart**.

Chart Paper

A smooth, **size**d type of **bond paper** used in the printing of charts or maps.

Chase

In **screen printing**, a screen frame possessing a means of attaching the screen fabric and adjusting its tension. See also **Floating Bar Printing Frame** and **Screen Printing: Press Configurations**.

A *chase* is also used to refer to a rectangular metal frame in which hot metal type and/or plates are positioned and locked up for **letterpress** printing.

Chatter

A jagged edge produced on a **squeegee** blade used in **screen printing** due to improper grinding or sharpening of the rubber.

Cheapernet Wire

Alternate—and not entirely unsarcastic—term for **thin Ethernet**. See **Thin Ethernet**.

Cheater

A **typeface** that is essentially an imitation of a popular copyrighted typeface. A cheater typically possesses at least three differences in design from the typeface it is imitating.

Check

In typography, a specialized character (✓) or **dingbat** used in checklists, presentations, etc. Also called a **checkmark**.

In **screen printing**, the term *check* refers to a printing defect characterized by a crack or series of cracks in the surface of a printed ink film, due to a wide variety of causes.

In computing, the term *check* refers generically to a programmed algorithm for evaluating the accuracy of transmitted, stored, or manipulated data. See **Checksum**, for example.

Check Bit

In computing, a form of **error correction**, or a means of evaluating and ensuring the integrity of the data, such as

before and after transmission over a telephone line. A check bit comprises a single **bit** added to the datastream before transmission begins.

Check Box

In computing, a means of turning on and off a setting or feature in a **dialog box**. A check box is usually a square that either contains an X (in which case the feature is activated) or is blank (in which case the feature is not activated). By clicking in the box with the pointer, the feature can be toggled on or off. An alternate to a check box is a **radio button**. At times, a check box is called a **ballot box**.

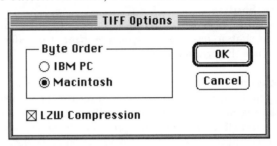

The TIFF Options dialog box in Photoshop. Notice the check box for selecting LZW compression and the radio buttons for selecting either IBM PC or Macintosh byte order.

Check Copy

A sample copy or proof of a publication, sent to the customer for approval prior to printing or **finishing**, to ensure that the printing and finishing operations are as the customer specified. The check copy is also used as the master guide for the printer and binder. Also known as an **F & G**. See **F & G**.

Check Digit

Alternate term for **check bit**. See **Check Bit**.

Check Disc

A **videodisc** produced in small quantities to test and proof the content before the actual production is initiated.

Checker

In **binding and finishing**, a person responsible for inspecting folded **signature**s and comparing the assembly of the signatures to the assembly sheet prior to binding.

Checking

A pattern of short, shallow cracks that form on a rubber or synthetic rubber surface (such as an offset press **blanket**; ink, dampening, or impression rollers; or a **flexographic** plate) due to damage from temperature, exposure to ultraviolet light, or other environmental conditions.

Checking also describes a defect of a printed ink film also known as **crazing**. See **Crazing**.

Checkmark

See **Check** (first definition).

Checkout Position

In platemaking, a term applied to all *negatives* that are properly positioned (right reading, emulsion-side down, and all pages correctly imposed on a *flat*) for platemaking.

Check Paper

Alternate term for *safety paper*. See *Safety Paper*.

Checkpoint

In computer programming, the place in a routine where the program can be interrupted, usually for debugging purposes.

Check Shot

In *graphic arts photography*, a test exposure made to ensure that a particular *exposure time* will effectively reproduce the original copy.

Checksum

In computing, a form of *error correction*, or a means of evaluating and ensuring the integrity of the data, such as before and after transmission over a telephone line. A checksum is computed by performing a mathematical operation on a data set, which is then added to the data before transmission begins. After transmission, the receiving device performs a similar checksum on what was received, and compares it to the appended, original checksum. If the two checksums are equal, then the data is correct. Also known as, and is a shorthand term for, a *summation check*.

Cheesey

Descriptive of a *plastisol*-based ink film that has been undercured.

Cheesey (or cheesy) is also descriptive of something cheap and chintzy, as a poorly printed product or a bad science-fiction movie.

Chemical Ghosting

A printing defect characterized by the faint appearance of an undesired image on the reverse side of a printed sheet, originating from the sheet beneath it. Chemical ghosting, though rare, typically occurs with oil-drying inks and are believed to be caused by gaseous emissions of a drying ink reacting with the proper drying of the ink on the adjacent sheet, producing a "phantom" image, often of less gloss than the original image. (Chemical ghosting should not be confused with *ink setoff*.) (See also *Mechanical Ghosting*.) Chemical ghosting is also called *fuming ghosting* and *gloss ghosting*.

Chemical Pinholing

A printing defect, commonly found in the *flexographic* printing of waterproof *cellophane* and other non-absorbent substrates, characterized by an incomplete ink film comprising small holes, caused by the failure of an ink to wet the entire surface of the *substrate*. The use of additives, called *antipinhole agents*, can frequently overcome the problem of pinholing, typically by reducing the surface tension of the liquid ink. (See also *Mechanical Pinholing*.)

Chemical Pulping

A method of converting wood chips into paper *pulp* for use in papermaking, accomplished by chemical cooking of the chips, as opposed to *mechanical pulping*. The purpose of *pulping* is to reduce wood (or other fibrous raw material) to individual *cellulose* fibers. A nonfibrous constituent of wood, *lignin*, binds cellulose fibers together, and is primarily responsible for reducing paper quality and *permanence*.

Chemical pulping methods produce high-quality papers as the chemical cooking dissolves most of the lignin and *hemicelluloses* present in the wood, resulting in better separation of the cellulose fibers. There are two primary means of chemical pulping. The *sulfite process* cooks wood chips in *sulfurous acid* combined with limestone to produce *calcium bisulfite*. The combination of sulfurous acid and calcium bisulfite dissolves the lignin in the wood and liberates the cellulose fibers. Sulfite pulp is soft and flexible, is moderately strong, and is used to supplement mechanical pulps (most typically in *newsprint*). Problems with the process (including limitations on the types of trees for which it is suitable, strict pollution laws, and the inability to recover some of the chemicals ejected by the system) have resulted in new chemicals being used in the process, and the wholesale adoption of new processes.

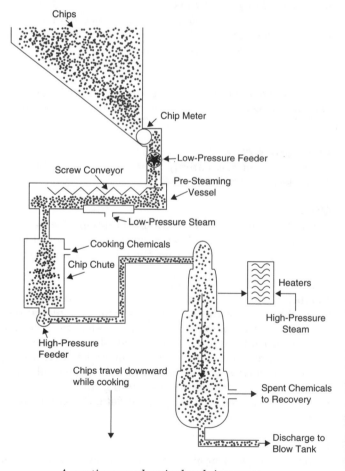

A continuous chemical pulping system.

The ***sulfate process*** is now the most widely used chemical pulping system. It evolved from the ***soda process***es developed in the 19th century, which used strong bases (alkaline solutions) such as lye to digest wood. Pulpers began adding ***sodium sulfate*** to the soda process, and a significantly stronger pulp was produced. Incorrectly termed the "sulfate" process (it was much later that chemists discovered that the active ingredient was actually ***sodium sulfide***), it is perhaps more accurately known as the ***kraft*** process ("kraft" is the German and Swedish word for "strength").

The advantages of kraft pulping include not only increased pulp strength, but also a better heat- and chemical-recovery system that reduces processing costs, its effectiveness in digesting nearly every known species of tree, and the insertion in the process of ***bleaching*** processes that increase pulp brightness. The pulp, as the name "kraft" indicates, is also much stronger than pulp produced via other methods, and the paper generated from the process runs well on high-speed presses.

To increase pulp ***whiteness*** and ***brightness*** (unbleached kraft pulp is usually a dark brown color), and to remove residual lignin, chemical pulps are bleached. It is at this point that additional nonfibrous materials called ***fillers*** are added to the pulp—a process called ***loading***—and the resulting ***furnish***—the mixture of pulp and fillers—is ready to begin the ***refining*** process.

Chemical Resistance

A property of printing inks that describes the extent to which a dried ink film will resist reacting with chemicals with which it comes in contact. Chemical resistance (in particular, the extent to which an ink formulation will resist reacting with acids and alkalis, called ***alkali resistance***) is an important property, especially in packaging. Inks that react with alkalis (such as soaps) will fade, discolor, bleed, etc., when in contact with them, producing undesirable effects when used in the printing of soap packaging. Other chemicals and materials to be packaged must also be compatible with inks used on their wrappers.

Chemical resistance is most commonly a property of the ink ***pigment***, and the choice of pigment compound directly affects the ink's resistance to various chemicals. (See ***Pigment***.) Related to chemical resistance is an ink's ***wettability***, which describes the extent to which an ink will resist ***bleeding***, fading, discoloring, etc., upon contact with moisture.

Chemical Vapor Drying

A method of ink drying in which the printed ink film is hardened by chemical reactions produced by exposure to chemical vapors.

Chemi-Thermomechanical Pulping (CTMP)

A method of ***mechanical pulping***. CTMP operates on the same basic principle as ***thermomechanical pulping (TMP)***, in which wood chips are sandwiched between the two rotating disks of a ***disk refiner*** at high temperature and pressure, but in CTMP the wood chips are chemically pretreated before refining, which increases pulp brightness and decreases the presence of ***shives***. (See ***Mechanical Pulping***.)

Cherry Picking

In telecommunications, randomly selecting data or programming being transmitted from a satellite.

Cheshire Label

A type of ***label*** designed to be applied by Cheshire® addressing equipment. Such labels are also categorized as ***four-up east-west label***s.

Chevrons

Alternate term for ***French quotes***. See ***French Quotes***.

Chiclet Keyboard

A type of keyboard designed for older microcomputers comprising small, square, widely spaced keys. This keyboard configuration (named for the small squares of chewing gum) made touch-typing difficult, and passed away into obsolescence.

Chief Information Officer (CIO)

The senior executive in charge of all ***Management Information Systems (MIS)*** functions in a company or other organization. Among the CIO's responsibilities are the selection, purchase, installation, and management of computer systems, software, and networks. The CIO also oversees the training of users within the company.

Child Window

In a computer's ***graphical user interface***, a ***window*** located within—and incapable of being dragged out of—a larger "parent" window.

Chill Roll

An internally cooled metal roller or cylinder located just beyond a web press ***dryer*** used to lower the temperature of the printed web before rewinding. Chill rolls are used to remove the heat generated either by friction on the moving web or by the heat used to dry the ink.

Chill rolls are also necessary for the second stage of the drying of ***heatset ink***s, which first need to be heated by a heatset dryer then cooled. (See ***Web Offset Lithography: Dryers and Chill Rolls***.)

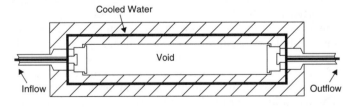

Modern chill roll design.

Chill Tower

In *web offset lithography*, the portion of the press containing the *chill roll*s. See *Chill Roll*.

China Clay

An inorganic material used as a *white pigment* in printing inks. China Clay (chemical composition $Al_2O_3 \cdot 2SiO_2 \cdot 2H_2O$) comprises several shades from white to gray and is chemically inert. It is used primarily in *letterpress* and *gravure* inks, but it is useful in a wide variety of applications, due to its low cost. (See *White Pigments*.)

Also known as *bentonite* and *kaolin clay* (*CI Pigment White 19 No. 77004*).

Chinawood Oil

Alternate term for *tung oil*. See *Tung Oil*.

Chinese Blue

A green shade of *Iron Blue*, an *inorganic color pigment* used in printing inks. See *Iron Blue*.

Chip

Any single semiconductor material, often made of silicon, onto which is etched an integrated circuit containing millions of tiny transistors. A chip—often also known as a *microprocessor* or a *CPU chip*—is the heart (or, more correctly, the brain) of a microcomputer. See *Central Processing Unit (CPU)*.

Chip Board

A thick, single-ply, low-quality grade of cardboard commonly used as a backboard in the gluing together of a pad of paper (or *padding*). Chip board is gray or brown in color and is highly moisture-absorbent. It is commonly produced from wastepaper and is used in applications where increased strength and quality are not required. Chipboard is also used in lieu of *binder's board* for the covers of inexpensive books. Also spelled as one word, *chipboard*.

Chip Family

A set of computer *microprocessor*s that are related to each other, the next in the line having evolved from the one previous to it. For example, Intel's 80X86 chip family comprises the 80286, 80386, and 80486 chips.

Chipper

A machine that cuts wooden logs to chips as a prelude to the *pulping* process in papermaking. Following *debarking*, logs must first be converted into uniformly sized chips (or other suitable form) as an aid to chemical digestion of the wood. A multiple-knife disk-type chipper consists of knives that rotate rapidly on a steel disk. Logs are fed end-first into the knives, which cut them into chips. A screening of the chips ensures that they are all of a uniform size, and foreign, nonwood material and contaminants are removed. The chips are then ready to be sent to the *digester*. (See also *Pulping*.)

Chip Set

A group of computer *chip*s needed to increase a computer's memory to a desired amount.

Chlorinated Solvent

A type of *solvent* used in printing inks, composed of carbon, chlorine and, occasionally, hydrogen. Chlorinated solvents have a high solvent strength and are capable of dissolving fats, oils, and other materials not easily dissolved by *ketone*, *ester*, or *alcohol* solvents.

Chlorine Dioxide

Very reactive gas (chemical formula ClO_2) used in the *bleaching* of chemical paper *pulp*. See *Chemical Pulping* and *Bleaching*.

Chloropleth

A type of map that uses symbols, degrees of shading, or hatching on geographical subdivisions to represent some aspect of that subdivision. For example, a state map may be subdivided into regions of varying population density, some graphic element being used to represent a particular value (or range of values) within each subdivision.

Choke

See *Spreads and Chokes*.

Chooser

On the *Macintosh operating system*, a software utility used to select and configure peripheral devices, specifically printers and fax machines.

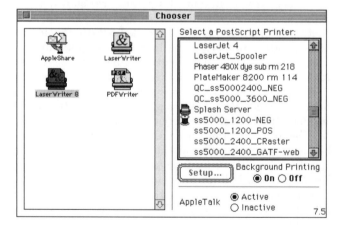

The Chooser, a software utility for the Macintosh. In this example, the computer user is in the process of selecting a PostScript printer.

Chopper Fold

A *right-angle fold* that is made on a *chopper folder*, an *in-line* folding device on a *web press*. A chopper fold is commonly the last fold made. Also known as a *quarter fold* or *cross fold*. See *Right-Angle Fold* and *Chopper Folder*.

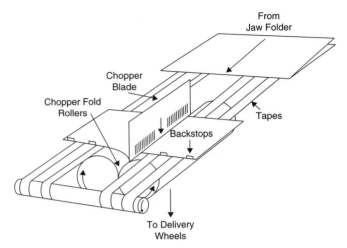

Chopper folder and chopper fold creation.

Chopper Folder

An *in-line* folding device on a *web press*, analogous to a *knife folder*, used to make *right-angle fold*s.

Chroma

The quality of a *color* that describes its amount of *saturation*, or strength, particularly according to the *Munsell color space* model. Chroma is similar to saturation, though in the Munsell color space it relates more to the amount of colorant present. It is in this definition of chroma that Munsell's color model differs substantially from all previous proposals. While the circle of hues includes all conceivable hues, and while the value axis is all-inclusive, Munsell realized that new colorants were constantly devised and chroma is therefore open-ended. See also *Saturation*.

Chroma also refers to one of the three color properties of a printing ink, and it is descriptive of its degree of *color strength* or grayness. See also *Hue*, *Value*, and *Color Mixing, Ink*.

In video production, the term *chroma* is an abbreviated term for *chrominance*. See *Chrominance*.

ChromaCom

A brand of *color electronic prepress system* (*CEPS*) manufactured by Linotype-Hell. See *Color Electronic Prepress System* (*CEPS*).

Chroma-Keying

In video production, a means of combining video images by replacing a predetermined solid color (such as a particular shade of blue or green) with another video image. A common example of chroma-keying is a television weather report. In the studio, the weather reporter is merely pointing at a blue screen. In the control room, the blue is replaced with an image of the map, satellite images, or Doppler radar. Chroma-keying is not foolproof, and often if the weather announcer is wearing clothing possessing the same blue shade, the weather map appears on his body. Also spelled as two words, *chroma keying*.

Chromatic Aberration

See *Aberration* and *Achromat*.

Chromatic Colors

Any color in which one particular wavelength or *hue* predominates. For example, *blue* and *green* are chromatic colors, while white, gray, and *black* are *achromatic colors*, as they have no dominant hue (all wavelengths are present in equal amounts within those colors). White light is considered achromatic, as it possesses no dominant hue. It is only when one particular wavelength (for example, *red*) is filtered out that the light becomes chromatic, possessing the color that is the opposite of the light that was filtered. Thus, if red light is filtered out, the opposite of red—*cyan*—will dominate. Objects and surfaces have the same effect on light, and in fact it is because they act essentially like filters that things have any color at all. An object—such as an apple—appears red because the atoms and molecules that comprise it absorb blue-green light, reflecting back the opposite color—red. (See also *Achromatic*.)

Chromaticity

The color quality of a visual impulse (i.e., light) described only in terms of its dominant *hue* (or wavelength) and its *saturation*, without needing to take into account the *value*—or *brightness*—of the color. When describing light, chromaticity refers to the proportions of two of the three *primary colors* that constitute a particular color. See *CIE Color Space* and COLOR PLATE 4.

Chromaticity Diagram

See *CIE Chromaticity Diagram*.

Chrome

A slang (and inappropriate) term for *Cromalin*. *Chrome* is also a popular colloquialism term for a *color transparency* used as original copy. See *Cromalin* and *Transparency* (second definition)

In chemistry and metallurgy, *chrome* is used to describe any compound containing chromium.

Chrome Green

A type of *inorganic color pigment* that is used in printing inks derived primarily by mixing *Chrome Yellow* (derived from lead chromate) with *Iron Blue* (a complex iron compound). Chrome-based pigments are fast-to-light (although some do darken on exposure to light, or on contact with sulfur gases), opaque, and heavy. They hold up well when mixed with solvent- and oil-based *vehicle*s, and they are generally acid and alkali resistant. (See *Inorganic Color Pigments*.)

Chrome Orange

See *Molybdate Orange*.

Chrome Scarlet

See *Molybdate Orange*.

Chrome Yellows

A type of *inorganic color pigment* used in printing inks derived primarily from lead chromate (chemical formula $PbCrO_4$). Chrome Yellows comprise several shades, ranging from primrose to orange. Chrome Yellows have a higher *specific gravity* than do other pigments, resulting in lower pigment volume than can be obtained with other materials. *Extender*s are often added to Chrome Yellows, especially to the bulkier green shades. Chrome-based pigments possess moderate *lightfastness* (although some darken on exposure to light, or on contact with sulfur gases) and are highly opaque. They hold up well when mixed with solvent- and oil-based *vehicle*s, and they are resistant to acids, soaps, and waxes but are susceptible to decomposition in the presence of a strongly alkaline substance. When exposed to heat, Chrome Yellows turn reddish in color but return to their original shade when the heat is removed. Chrome Yellows had been used as the first-down color in process color printing and are suitable for use in all types of inks, but the increased undesirability of lead-based inks has diminished their popularity and use.

Chrome Yellows can be mixed with *Iron Blues* to produce *Chrome Green*. Other chromes, derived from various shades of Chrome Yellows, include *Chrome Orange* and *Molybdate Orange*. (See also *Inorganic Color Pigments*.)

(*CI Pigment Yellow 34 Nos. 77600 and 77603.*)

Chromic Acid Treatment

One means of rendering a thermoplastic *substrate* (such as *polypropylene* or *polyethylene*) suitable for printing, involving immersion in an acid bath to reorient the material's surface electrons and make the surface conducive to ink adhesion.

Chrominance

In video production, the color portion—red, green, or blue—of a video signal as recorded by a video camera on videotape. In video terminology, chrominance (often abbreviated simply *chroma*) exists apart from *luminance*, or the brightness of a video signal. A video image that is described as high chroma is overly intense and tends to bleed, while a low chroma image looks pale and washed out. In television broadcasting, both chrominance and luminance information is broadcast. On black-and-white televisions, the chrominance information is ignored, the luminance information being the only important component needed to reproduce the image.

Chromium Antimony Titanium Buff Rutile

An *inorganic color pigment* used in printing inks. Chromium Antimony Titanium Buff Rutile is a buff-colored brown pigment possessing high *lightfastness*, heat resistance, and chemical resistance. It also possesses low *tinctorial strength*, a coarse texture, and slightly dirtier shades. It is composed of oxides of chromium (1–6%), antimony (8–12%), and titanium (80–90%) (chemical formulas

Cr_2O_3, Sb_2O_3, and TiO_2, respectively). It is used in a variety of printing processes and applications in which the low tinctorial strength and abrasive texture are not undesirable. (See also *Inorganic Color Pigments*.)

(*CI Pigment Brown 24 No. 77310.*)

Chromium Tanning

The exposure of *screen printing* photostencils (those that contain *bichromate* emulsions) to *actinic rays* that renders exposed areas hard and insoluble. See *Photostencil*.

CHT

A *file extension* appended to Chart files created by Harvard Graphics.

Chuck

On a *screen printing* press, a device or jig used to hold three-dimensional objects—such as ceramic ware—in position for printing.

Cibachrome

A brand of photographic film and paper used to make color transparencies and prints. Cibachrome is manufactured by Ilford Photo Corporation.

CIC

Abbreviation for *common impression cylinder*. See *Common Impression Cylinder (CIC)*.

Cicero

In typography, a unit of horizontal measurement used in continental Europe to measure type. One cicero equals 0.178 in. (4.51 mm) or 6 *Didot point*s. See *Didot Point* and *Point System*. A cicero is also called a *Didot pica*.

CICS

Abbreviation for *Customer Information Control System*. See *Customer Information Control System (CICS)*.

CIE

Abbreviation for *Commission International de l'Eclairage* or, in English, the *International Commission on Illumination*, an international organization that establishes specifications for the description of color, used as the basis of all color measurements. See *CIE Chromaticity Diagram*, *CIE Color Space*, and *CIE X,Y,Z*.

CIE Chromaticity Diagram

A two-dimensional representation (*COLOR PLATE 4*) of the three-dimensional *CIE color space*. See *CIE Color Space*.

CIE Color Space

In *color* measurement, a color mapping system that uses three *tristimulus values* and plots them on x, y, and z axes to create a three-dimensional representation of a color. The *CIELAB*, *CIE L*a*b**, *and* CIELUV systems utilize as these three values a lightness or darkness value

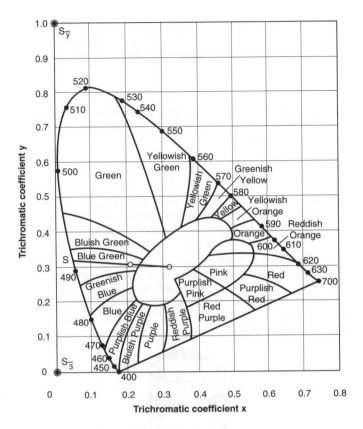

The CIE chromaticity diagram.

(denoted L or L*), a red–green value (denoted ± A, a*, or U), and a yellow–blue value (denoted ± B, b*, or V). A *colorimeter* is used to measure each of these tristimulus values and the resulting plot of a particular color can be determined.

In 1931, the Commission Internationale de l'Eclairage assembled in Cambridge, England, to establish a world standard for the measurement of color. By that time, modern instrumentation had made it possible to measure with fair accuracy the wavelength of any particular colored light. The commission took as its model the principles established sixty years earlier by Scottish physicist James Maxwell; it selected three standard colors, a particular *red, green, and blue*, with which to generate a version of the *Maxwell triangle*. The result was what is known as the *CIE chromaticity diagram*, which became a standard in the lighting industry for measuring the color of light. In 1976, the CIE chart was revised to create a more even distribution of colors. The revised chart, now indicating colors in "uniform color space," is the current standard for measuring the color of light. (See COLOR PLATE 4.)

The diagram never defines white. Somewhere in the center of the diagram is the *"white spot,"* that point where light from the three sources blends to form white light. Sunlight is one spot on the diagram and incandescent light another. This point is not fixed, as it is in the Munsell model, and is useful in describing the color of light from

various light sources without implying a deviation from some established norm. The absolute white in the Munsell model is also theoretical.

The CIE chromaticity diagram, as a two-dimensional plot of hue and saturation characteristics, is a logical point for beginning computer color mixture. Values can be added to the chart by gradually reducing the intensity (brightness) of the light source until all light is removed and absolute black is achieved. The chromaticity chart becomes a three-dimensional color model: the CIE uniform color space.

The CIE system starts with the premise that the stimulus for color is provided by the proper combination of a light source, an object, and an observer. In 1931, the CIE introduced the element of standardization of source and observer, and the methodology to derive numbers that provide a measure of a color seen under a standard source of illumination by a *standard observer*. In 1931, CIE recommended the use of standard sources *a*, *b*, and *c*, which were soon defined at standard illuminants when their spectral power distributions were measured. These sources and illuminants served the purposes of color technology well until the increased use of fluorescent whitening agents made it necessary to specify illuminants in the ultraviolet region more nearly representative of that in natural daylight.

The data representing the CIE standard observer is one of the most difficult concepts in the CIE system to understand. In an old experiment, light from a test lamp shines on a white screen and is viewed by an observer. A nearby part of the screen is illuminated by light from one or more of three lamps, equipped to give light of three widely different colors, such as red, green, and blue. These primary lights are arbitrarily selected but closely controlled. By adjusting the intensities of these lights, the observer can make their combined color on the screen match that of the test lamp. The amounts of the three primaries are three numbers describing the test color, called the tristimulus values of that color. Thus R, G, and B are the tristimulus values of the spectrum colors for this particular set of red, green, and blue primaries. In its 1931 recommendation, the CIE adopted the average R, G, and B data for a small number of observers as the experimental definition of the CIE 1931 standard observer. It was considered important to eliminate negative numbers among the tristimulus values. Therefore a mathematical transformation of the standard observer data was made, representing a change from the original red, green, and blue primaries to a new set, which cannot be produced by any real lamps, called the X, Y, and Z primaries. The tristimulus values of the equal-power spectrum colors in the CIE X, Y, Z system provide the definition of the 1931 CIE standard observer in its most used form.

In 1976, a linear adaptation of the color space was performed to try to scale color numerical differences to correspond more closely in the visual color differences. The result was the CIE Uniform Color Space, a chart which plots the available color gamut of what you can actually see and what machines can actually produce.

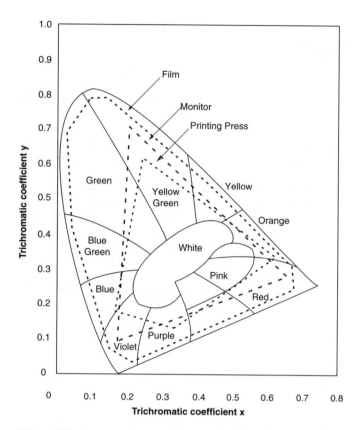

The CIE chromaticity diagram showing the approximate color gamut for film, an RGB monitor, and a four-color printing press.

The CIE Uniform Color Space is associated with CIELUV color metrics. CIELUV is based on the theory that the eye and brain code colors into mutually exclusive opponent signals: light-dark, red-green, and yellow-blue. Red-green is plotted along the horizontal U axis, with the positive values denoting red and negative values denoting green. Yellow-blue values are plotted along the vertical V axis. Light-dark values are plotted along the L axis, which is located perpendicularly to the U, V plane.

While CIE uniform color spaces still present visual nonuniformities—a color that has the same coordinates may still not look like the same color—they are considered to be the best compromises available. They have been adopted by vendors as the basis for desktop color systems and for approaches to device-independent calibration.

(See also ***Color: Color Measurement***.)

CIE Diagram
See ***CIE Color Space***.

CIELab L*a*b* Scales
See ***CIE Color Space***.

CIELUV
See ***CIE Color Space***.

CIE x,y,Y
A ***CIE color space*** utilizing the x and y coordinates from the ***CIE chromaticity diagram***, plus the ***luminance*** value, Y.

CIE X,Y,Z
The tristimulus values from which the three-dimensional systems, such as CIELAB and CIELUV, are calculated. See ***CIE Color Space***.

CIM
Abbreviation for ***computer-integrated manufacturing***. See ***Computer-Integrated Manufacturing (CIM)***.

Abbreviation for ***computer input microfilm***. See ***Computer Input Microfilm (CIM)***.

Cine-Oriented Image
An image printed on microfilm in a way that is analogous to the way a movie is printed on film, an image (or frame) being oriented at a 45° angle to the direction of film travel, each successive frame essentially "beneath" the preceding frame. See also ***Comic-Strip-Oriented Image***.

Cine-oriented image.

Cinepak
A ***codec*** used in the ***compression*** of digital video. Although able to reduce the file size of a video file considerably, its primary drawback is that it is ***lossy***.

Cinex
In photography, a test used to determine the optimum exposure for an image, especially with regard to brightness and color quality.

Cinnamon Bun
Colloquial and descriptive term for the ***at symbol***. See ***At Symbol (@)***.

CIO

Abbreviation for *chief information officer*. See *Chief Information Officer (CIO)*.

Circle Cutter

A type of compass fitted with a blade used for cutting perfect circles in hand-cut *screen printing* stencils.

Circuit

Any closed path through which an electrical current can flow.

In telecommunications, the term *circuit* refers to any communications *channel* or path through which a signal can be transmitted.

Circuit Board

In any electronic device (such as a computer), a flat, still card containing connections to which integrated circuits can be attached. Also called a *circuit card*.

Circuit Card

Alternate term for an *expansion card*. See *Expansion Card*. The term *circuit card* is also an alternate term for a *circuit board*. See *Circuit Board*.

Circuit Grade

In telecommunications, the quality or capability of a communications *circuit*. Circuit grades are defined by *telegraph grade*, *voice grade*, *subvoice grade*, and *broadband*.

Circuit Switching

In telecommunications and networking, a means of data communication in which an exclusive *channel* is established between sending and receiving stations only on a per-demand basis, which is then terminated once the connection is broken. The advantage of channel switching is that messages are unimpeded by other traffic throughout the duration of the transmission. The disadvantages, however, include the limitation of the number of connections (which can only be equal to the number of channels in the cable) and the underutilization of resources when no connection exists. See also *Cell Switching* and *Packet Switching*.

Circular Screen

A circular *halftone screen* used in the production of color *halftones*. The circular shape allows the operator to rotate the screen to obtain the proper *screen angle*s.

Circulating Matrix

In typography, a reusable mold found in linecasting machines used to cast type.

Circumferential Register

See *Running Register*.

Circumflex

In typography, an *accent* (^) placed over a character, used in French and other European languages. See *Accent*.

CISC

Abbreviation for *complex instruction-set computing*. See *Complex Instruction-Set Computing (CISC)*.

Cissing

A printing defect of *screen printing* in which a printed ink film or *varnish* recedes from portions of the *substrate* due to incomplete wetting of the surface.

CIU

Abbreviation for *computer interface unit*. See *Computer Interface Unit*.

Cladding

In *fiber optics*, glass or plastic surrounding the core of an optical fiber to keep light from passing out of the optical fiber.

Clamp Marks

In printing, undesirable marks produced on a sheet of paper by the *cutter clamp*, the device used to hold a stack of sheets in position during cutting.

Clamshell Press

A type of flatbed *screen printing* press in which the screen frame is hinged on one end, and can be raised or lowered to the printing table in a manner much like the opening and closing of a clam's shell.

Clarifier

A substance added to a printing ink that increases its transparency.

Claris CAD

A user-friendly program developed by Claris Corporation for *computer-aided design*. See *Computer-Aided Design (CAD)*.

Clarity

A property of a transparent material (such as a thermoplastic film) that describes the extent to which clear, distinct images or type can be seen through it.

Clasp Envelope

A type of envelope whose flap—which may be glued or unglued—is closed by means of a metal clasp.

Class

In computer programming, especially *object-oriented programming*, a set of objects that share common features and characteristics. Objects in the same class have similar data content, are manipulated by similar code, and share similar interfaces to that code.

Class A Certification

A *Federal Communications Commission (FCC)* certification for computer equipment. The Class A certification includes specifications for industrial and commercial computer equipment, such as mainframes and microcomputers. See also **Class B Certification**.

Class B Certification

A **Federal Communications Commission (FCC)** certification for computer equipment. The Class B certification includes specifications for residential and personal computer equipment. Specifically, the Class B certification requires that the level of **radio frequency interference (RFI)** be low enough that it will not affect television or radio reception when more than one wall and 30 ft. separate the computer equipment from the radio or television receiver. The **Class A certification**, for industrial and commercial use, does not include this 30-ft. requirement. See also **Class A Certification**.

Classified Ad

In magazine and newspaper publishing, a small, text-based ad (set in a small **point size**, commonly one known as **agate**) placed in a lengthy advertising section. Classified ads are often placed by individuals or companies looking for employees, wanting to sell items, rent and/or sell houses and apartments, etc. See also **Display Ad**.

Clay

An inorganic, fine-grained material commonly used in paper **fillers** or **coatings**. The addition of clay or other fillers to paper pulp is called **loading**.

The clay used in papermaking is usually refined from white kaolin clay, which in turn is mined from kaolinite. Kaolinite is a product of the decomposition of feldspar, which occurs when feldspar comes in contact with the atmosphere.

The addition of clay to paper pulp is done to increase one or more of a paper's properties, in particular such optical and structural properties as **opacity**, **brightness**, **smoothness**, and ink receptivity. The brightness imparted to paper as a result of the addition of clay is not as high as that imparted by other fillers such as **titanium dioxide** and **calcium carbonate**. Clay is, however, the most abundant and least expensive of the three.

The addition of fillers such as clay, however, can negatively affect other paper properties, such as strength, bulk, and stress resistance. (See also **Fillers**.)

Clay-Coated

In papermaking, descriptive of a paper or paperboard that has had one or both sides coated with **clay** so as to increase the smoothness of the surface.

CLC

See **Caps and Lowercase**.

Clean Edit

In video production, an edit made in a videotape containing no **noise**, **distortion**, or other disruption.

Clean Hole

A hole or similar paper defect caused by poor drainage of moisture out of the forming paper **web** while on the **forming wire**.

Cleaning Off

In **binding and finishing**, the removal of excess **gold leaf** from book covers following **foil stamping**.

Clean Proof

A **proof**, or **galley**, of text material that has been typeset exactly to the **type specifications** indicated on the original copy and is free from **proof marks** or other marks generated by the author, editor, or proofreader, in contrast to a **dirty proof**.

Clean Room

A enclosed area—similar to an air lock—that is pressurized so as to keep dust and other airborne foreign particles out of a room, such as one containing a **color electronic prepress system**. See **Color Electronic Prepress System (CEPS)**.

Clear

To set an entry to zero or some other default setting.

The term *clear* is also a synonym for **transparent**.

Clear Area

In **optical character recognition (OCR)**, an area of a scanned page that needs to be free of any printing or other marking not specifically related to scanning.

Clear Coat

A transparent **resin** or **varnish** applied as a protective coating to a screen printed image—such as a **decal**—to ensure maximum durability.

Clear Ink Coat

A transparent, colorless **varnish** used to screen print a clear version of the printed image as a protective coating over the proper, colored image.

Clear to Send (CTS)

In networking, a signal defined by the **RS-232-C** standard indicating that a transmission can be sent. See also **Data Set Ready (DSR)**.

Cleat-Laced Binding

In **binding and finishing**, a means of repairing a **casebound** book in which the original case and **spine** are removed. A diamond pattern of grooves is made in the new exposed spine, and thread is laced into these grooves. After sewing, the original (or new) case is attached.

Clephane, James

James Ogilvie Clephane was born in Washington, D.C., in 1842 of Scottish descent. He was a highly competent shorthand writer in that day. He was private secretary to

Secretary of State Seward during the Civil War and then was admitted to the bar of the Supreme Court. But his legal activities were concentrated on court reporting—transcribing court testimony. Clephane sought a way to transcribe his notes quickly and in multiple forms that cases in the highest tribunal demanded. The answer was not quick to come.

The typewriter was patented in 1867. It had been invented in Milwaukee by Christopher Sholes and two associates and built commercially in 1874. Clephane is reputed to have worn out the first two typewriters himself. The typewriter had solved part of Clephane's problems. He could transcribe his shorthand rapidly, but it still took as long for the printer to deliver copies. Clephane thought it would save time if somehow a machine could link with lithographic printing or make stereotypes to cast metal type. He sought the aid of Charles Moore to build such a machine. Moore went to a machine shop in Baltimore owned by August Hahl. Ottmar Mergenthaler, Hahl's cousin, felt he could improve the machine. Ottmar delivered the machine to Moore and Clephane, and it produced sharp characters, properly spaced on an endless narrow strip ready for transfer to a lithographer's stone. Sometimes a line of type would slip in the printing process. After much experimentation, it was decided that the solution lie in making a stereotype plate for final production. In trying to solve Clephane's and Moore's problems, Mergenthaler had some ideas of his own.

CLI
See *Command-Line Interface (CLI)*.

Cliche
A photoengraved steel or plastic printing plate used in *pad transfer printing* as an image carrier. See *Pad Transfer Printing*.

Click Art
In graphics, term for *clip art* distributed in digital form, either on a *floppy disk*, *CD-ROM*, or other such medium. The term derives from the need to "click" on the art with a mouse in order to use it, rather than "clip" it with scissors, as one does with traditional clip art. See *Clip Art*.

Clicking
The pressing of the button on a computer mouse to select a command or initiate a function. Often, *double-clicking* is required for some functions.

Client
In networking and telecommunications, a program or device that uses the services of another, known as the *server*. See also *Client/Server*.

Client Application
In *object linking and embedding (OLE)*, an *application* that instructs a *server application* to perform a function based in the linked and embedded data.

In *dynamic data exchange (DDE)*, a *client application* is the application that receives data from another connected application. See *Dynamic Data Exchange (DDE)*.

Client/Server
In networking and telecommunications, a network architecture that is based on a division of "labor," involving a *server* or device or program that provides a particular service, and a *client* that requests and utilizes those services.

Climatizing
Alternate term for *curling*. See *Curling*.

Clip
In video production, a piece of video or audio, also known as as *video clip*.

When used as a verb, the term *clip* means to trim a graphic image to enable it to fit into a particular space.

Clip Art
Any non-copyrighted or royalty-free graphic images—such as line drawings, cartoons, photographs, designs, borders, arrows, etc.—supplied either in printed form, on floppy disk, or on CD-ROM for use in mechanicals or digital page layouts when the cost of an illustrator or photographer would be prohibitive. Clip art is typically sold in books or disks by subject matter. When distributed in digital form, clip art is often referred to as *click art*.

Clipboard
A feature standard on both the *Macintosh* and *Windows*-based machines in which data (be it text, graphics, etc.) can be cut from one part of a document and pasted either elsewhere in the same document, in another document produced using the same application, or in another application's document.

Clip Boundary
On a computer display, the boundary of the *display area*, beyond which there is no image.

Clipper Chip
In telecommunications, an *encryption* device proposed by the United States Government that would allow business to encode sensitive information transmitted electronically, yet allow the Government to intercept and decode the message if criminal activity was suspected. Not surprisingly, this latter point has its share of opposition on the civil rights front. See *Data Encryption Standard*.

Clipping
The removing of portions of a graphic image so as to allow it to fit within a particular space.

Clipping Path
In computer graphics and imaging, a curve or polygon that defines the boundary of an image. Only the portion of the

image that is enclosed within the clipping path will be visible when the item is printed or displayed.

CLNP

Abbreviation for *Connectionless Network Protocol*. See *Connectionless Network Protocol (CLNP)*.

Clock

The portion of a computer that generates a repetitive, high-frequency electrical signal so as to precisely synchronize computer events and operations. The rate at which the clock generates signals—known as the *clock rate*—is usually measured in *megahertz (MHz)*, or millions of cycles per second. The term "speed" when used to describe a processor is synonymous with "clock" or "clock rate." As of this writing, PowerPC and Intel Pentium processors are capable of clock rates of up to 200 MHz. This is impressive when you consider that that clock rate of the original Intel 8088 chip used in the first IBM *PC* had a clock rate of 4.77 MHz. Also called a *clock generator*.

Clock-Doubling

See *Clock-Multiplying*.

Clock Generator

See *Clock*.

Clocking

In networking and telecommunications, the synchronizing of the sending and receiving devices in *synchronous transmission*. See *Synchronous Transmission*.

Clock-Multiplying

In computing, a technique used by some *microprocessor*s (such as those manufactured by Intel) that allows different parts of the computer system to run at a speed different from the internal speed of the CPU. For example, one particular Intel processor has an internal speed of 50 *megahertz (MHz)* but can communicate with other components at a reduced speed (such as 25 MHz). Specific differences in *clock speed* are known as *clock-doubling* (the above example) and *clock tripling* (utilized by such processors as the PowerPC 601).

Clock Rate

The speed at which a computer's *clock* generates electrical signals, often measured in *megahertz (MHz)*. See *Clock*. Also known as *clock speed*.

Clock Speed

Alternate term for *clock rate*. See *Clock Rate*.

Clock-Tripling

See *Clock-Multiplying*.

Clogging

In *screen printing*, the premature drying of ink within the fibers of the screen fabric, which prevents ink from flowing

through the *stencil* onto the *substrate*, producing printing defects such as voids. Also known as *drying-in*.

Clone

To create a duplicate of anything, from a photographic image (as in a *clone tool*) to a computer system. (See also *PC Clone*.) *Clone* also refers to the duplicate itself.

Clone Tool

In digital imaging, a feature of many *paint program*s that allows *pixel*s in one portion of an image (or even in another image) to be duplicated in another portion of the image.

Cloning

In imaging, a function of many *paint* or *drawing* programs that allow *pixel*s from one image area to be copied and placed elsewhere in the image.

Close Box

On a *Macintosh* computer, a small square located in the upper left-hand corner of a window which, when clicked on with the mouse, closes an open file or an open window.

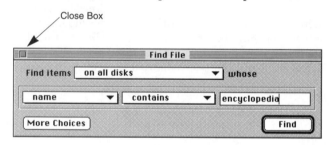

The close box for a dialog box.

In the Microsoft *Windows* environment, a *close box* is a small square, containing a minus sign, located in the top left-hand corner of every window. When clicked on, the system menu is opened. When it is double-clicked, the window or open file is closed.

Closed Architecture

Computer design that is proprietary and does not encourage nor facilitate third-party add-on devices or modifications. See also *Open Architecture*.

Closed Bolts

In *binding and finishing*, the untrimmed, folded edges of a *signature* prior to trimming, not including the *binding edge*. Roughly trimmed edges are called *open bolts*. Both open and closed *bolts* require complete trimming at the end of the binding process.

Closed Circuit

In video terminology, a private network of video cameras and monitors that, as its name implies, receives no signals from outside the network. It is most often used for surveillance and security.

Closed Head

In **binding and finishing**, an uncut top of a **signature** produced by folding. During binding, the fold is slit open. Often, however, it is desirable to leave signatures uncut until binding is nearly complete; in **thread sewing** and **saddle-stitching**, signatures that are uncut open more easily and quickly. Also known as a **closed section** or a **closed signature**.

Closed Loop

Description of any system in which system output is fed back into the system to modify further output and therefore regulate the system.

Closed/Open

In typography, a closed character or symbol is one that has been filled in, or is solid, such as a closed **bullet** (●). An open character or symbol is one that exists essentially as an outline, such as an open bullet (○).

The *open/closed* dichotomy is also used to refer to the typesetting of **dashes**. In this case, *closed* refers to a dash set without a word space at either end (such as "word—word") while *open* refers to a dash set *with* a word space at either end (such as "word — word"). On older typesetting systems, open dashes were preferred, as they allowed the typesetter more places to break lines (typesetting systems tend to look for word spaces as places to break lines), but more sophisticated devices know enough to break lines at either end of an em or en dash.

Closed Path

In computer graphics, a freely drawn line, the end of which is connected to the beginning, usually created to describe a particular shape, the interior of which can be filled with a color or pattern.

Closed Section

Alternate term for a **closed head**. See **Closed Head**.

Closed Signature

Alternate term for a **closed head**. See **Closed Head**.

Closed System

In computing, a computer system that is incompatible with other computer systems. At one time, computer manufacturers would only create computer systems that ran specific custom software. Now, it is much more common for there to be a prescribed standard defining widely used and developed-for **platform**s and file formats. See also **Open System**.

Close Formation

Term that is used to describe a paper's structure in which the **cellulose** fibers have bound together in a uniform manner throughout the sheet or **web**. (See **Formation**.) Conversely, a nonuniform distribution of paper fibers is called a **wild formation**.

Close Register

In multicolor printing, the need to lay down successive **color**s (or images) with a high degree of accuracy. Also called **tight register**. See **Register**.

Close Tolerance Printing

In **screen printing**, an alternate term for **tight register**, or the necessity of ensuring that the various printed elements (colors, designs, etc.) are as close to their position on the original as possible. Close tolerance printing is commonly an issue in the screen printing of electronic circuit boards.

Close Up

In typography, to reduce space on a page or between words or characters.

In photography and videography, a shot or scene in which the face of the subject (typically a human figure) fills the screen. In shooting scripts, close up is indicated by **CU**.

Cloudy Formation

Term (also referred to as "cloud effect") used to describe a paper's structure in which the **cellulose** fibers have bound together in an uneven manner throughout the sheet or **web**, also called a **wild formation**. (See **Formation**.) A uniform distribution of paper fibers is called a **close formation**.

Cloverleaf

In computing, particularly using an Apple **Macintosh**, term for the Command key (also called a "propeller").

CLTP

Abbreviation for **Connectionless Transport Protocol**. See **Connectionless Transport Protocol (CLTP)**.

Cluster

In computing, a unit of storage on a **floppy disk** or a **hard disk**. On a hard disk, for example, a cluster is some unit comprising multiple **sector**s (often four). On a floppy disk, a cluster may be equivalent to the size of the sector itself.

In networking, a *cluster* is a small group of workstations (which are each called a **cluster workstation**). See **Cluster Workstation**.

Cluster Controller

In networking, a workstation that controls the input and output of a small group (or **cluster**) of **cluster workstation**s. Also known as a **master workstation**.

Clustered Bar Chart

A type of **bar chart** that compares sets of data by grouping bars together. See **Bar Chart**.

Clustering

In **object-oriented programming**, storing objects in close proximity to each other on a disk or other medium for ease and expedience of access.

Cluster Workstation

In networking, a *workstation* containing its own memory but which is under the control of a *cluster controller*.

CLUT

Abbreviation for *color lookup table*. See *Color Lookup Table (CLUT)*.

CLV

Abbreviation for *constant linear velocity*. See *Constant Linear Velocity*.

C-MAC

A *component video* transmission standard for *multiplexed analog component (MAC)* video and audio signals, used in Great Britain and Norway. See *Multiplexed Analog Components (MAC)*.

CMD.EXE

In computing, especially that using the *OS/2* operating system, a program that interprets and processes commands, analogous to DOS's COMMAND.COM program.

CMIP

Abbreviation for *Common Management Information Protocol*. See *Common Management Information Protocol (CMIP)*.

CMIS

Abbreviation for *Common Management Information Services*. See *Common Management Information Services (CMIS)*.

CMOS

Abbreviation for *complementary metal-oxide semiconductor*. See *Complementary Metal-oxide Semiconductor (CMOS)*.

C-Mount

In video and motion picture photography, a system used to mount lenses on video cameras and 16-mm movie cameras.

CMS

Abbreviation for *color management system*. See *Color Management System*.

CMS is also an abbreviation for *conversational monitor system*.

CMY

Abbreviation for *cyan*, *magenta*, and *yellow*, three *process color*s or inks. See also *CMYK* and *Process Color*.

CMYK

Abbreviation for *cyan*, *magenta*, *yellow*, and *key* (black), the four *process color*s or inks. The letters are occasionally rearranged to indicate a specific *printing sequence*.

Coagulation

The congealing of a colloidal material—such as a coating—into a solid due to precipitation.

COAM Equipment

Abbreviation for "customer owned and maintained," or telecommunications equipment that is owned by the user and is connected to a *common carrier* network.

Coarse Data File

In imaging, a low-resolution image (also called a *low-resolution file* or a *viewfile*)—scanned at the resolution of the monitor itself—used to evaluate the scanner setup, the quality of the original image, or other aspects of the image. Since even a *high-resolution file* will be displayed at the resolution of the monitor, evaluations can be accomplished much more quickly by scanning at the lowest viewable resolution. Since such a low-resolution file possesses less image data than a high-resolution file, it is inadequate for high-quality output.

A coarse data file or low-resolution file is also created along with a high-resolution file and used to view an image imported into a page layout program, as a means of allowing the program to run more efficiently than it would if the entire high-resolution file were displayed. Since high-resolution files occupy a large amount of disk space and also require a great deal of *RAM* and processing power to display—all the while looking no better than a low-resolution file on screen—low-resolution files are used as *FPO* images while working on a page.

Coarse Grain

In photography, descriptive of a photosensitive film that possesses large particles (or *grain*), as opposed to *fine grain*. See *Grain* (second definition).

Coarse Mesh

A screen fabric used in *screen printing* containing threads that are not closely woven together, there being larger gaps between the threads than in a *fine mesh* screen.

Coated Board

A *coated one side* or *coated two sides* paperboard. See *Coated Paper*.

Coated Book Paper

A *coated two sides* paper available in a variety of dull to glossy *finish*es, used in a variety of printing processes. See *Book Paper*.

Coated Free Sheet

A type of *coated paper* manufactured from *pulp* containing 25% or less *groundwood* pulp.

Coated Groundwood

A type of *coated paper* manufactured from 25% or more *groundwood pulp*. See *Coated Paper*.

Coated Offset

Type of *coated paper* manufactured with high *pick resistance* specifically for use in *offset lithography*. See *Coated Paper* and *Offset Paper*.

Coated One Side (C1S)

A cover, text, or other *coated paper* that has only received its coating on one side of the sheet, commonly used for book covers, dust jackets, and postcards. See *Coating*, *Coated-One-Side Label*, and *Coated Two Sides (C2S)*.

Coated-One-Side Label

A type of *coated one side (C1S)* paper manufactured for the specific requirements of label making, including such *finishing* operations as varnishing, lacquering, *embossing*, diecutting, and, of course, the application of the label adhesive.

Coated Paper

A wide variety of papers that have undergone *coating* to impart increased degrees of *gloss*, *ink holdout*, *brightness*, and *smoothness*. *Enamel paper*s are high-gloss papers with high *bulk* and *opacity* and are ideal for offset printing. Enamel papers are also available in a variety of colors. Enamel papers are frequently produced by *supercalendering* or *cast coating*. The *basic size* of enamel papers is 25×38 in., and they come in *basis weight*s of 60, 70, 80, and 100 lb. *Dull finish* enamel papers are less glossy than regular enamel papers, yet still possess the desired qualities of high ink holdout.

*Matte-coated paper*s are low-gloss, glare-free papers that also offer many of the printing advantages of enamel papers, and their lack of supercalendering gives them greater bulk and opacity. Their basic size is also 25×38 in., and they come in basis weights of 50, 60, 70, 80, and 100 lb.

Lightweight coated papers (typically *groundwood coated paper*) are used primarily for magazines, catalogs, newspaper inserts, and coupons. Their basic size is 25×38 in., and they come in basis weights of 30 and 40 lb.

Coated papers are also formulated for the specific demands of web offset printing, in particular, for use in *heatset drying*.

Coated Screen

A screen fabric used in *screen printing* to which a photosensitive *stencil* emulsion has been applied prior to exposure. (See *Photostencil: Direct Process*.)

Coated Two Sides (C2S)

A cover, text, or other *coated paper* that has received a coating on both sides of the sheet, in contrast to *coated one side* paper. See *Coating*, *Coated One Side (C1S)* and *Coated-One-Side Label*.

Coater

In *screen printing*, a rounded, sometimes slotted, tool used to uniformly apply a photosensitive *stencil* emulsion to the surface of a screen fabric. See *Photostencil: Direct Process*. Also known as an *emulsion applicator*, *emulsion coater*, *spreader*, and *scoop coater*.

Coating

In *binding and finishing*, a finishing operation in which a printed *substrate* is covered with a clear film, such as a *primer* (usually added as a prelude to printing or other coating operations), a *lacquer*, a *barrier coat*, or an *overprint varnish*. Alternately, only a portion of a printed material may be coated, called *spot coating* or *spot varnish*ing. Coatings applied after printing may either be aqueous (water-based) that dry by evaporation, or electron-beam or ultraviolet coatings that dry by *polymerization* when exposed to electron beams and ultraviolet light, respectively. (See *Binding and Finishing*.)

In papermaking, the term *coating* refers to a paper *finishing* operation in which the surface of a paper is covered with a substance to impart a desired finish or texture to the paper and improve its *printability*. Coatings provide a smooth paper surface, and the amount and composition of a particular coating affects such properties as *ink absorbency* and *ink holdout*. Coatings also enhance the *whiteness*, *opacity*, and *gloss* of paper.

Coatings are typically made up of *pigment*s and *binder*s (also called *adhesive*s). Pigments are usually made of refined *clay* (which enhances gloss and ink holdout), *titanium dioxide* (which enhances *brightness* and opacity), or *calcium carbonate* (which enhances *ink absorbency* and brightness). Binders are added to increase the adhesion of the particles of pigment to each other and to the paper fibers. Binders are usually made from common natural sources such as starch, or synthetic sources, such as *styrene-butadiene* and *vinyl acrylic latices*. Natural binders are not water-resistant, so synthetic binders are often used in addition to or in place of them. Synthetic binders also are more resistant to cracking when the paper is folded than are natural ones.

The *coat weight* required, or how much coating is added to a *base stock* of paper, is a function of the final basis weight of the paper and other end-use considerations. Coatings can either be added on the papermaking machine (called *on-machine coating*) or on a separate machine (called *off-machine coating*). There are a variety of methods used for applying coatings, such as the use of *blade coaters*, *air knife coaters*, and *cast coaters*. Coating can be applied to one side of a paper—called *coated one side (C1S)*—such as is done with paper for labels and book jackets, or coated on both sides—called *coated two sides (C2S)*. Coated papers are best for printing *halftone*s, especially in *letterpress* printing. The removal of bits of a coating during printing and the effect of those coating particles on the printing system (for example, *coating pile*, or the collection of particles of coating on the blanket) is a consideration when determining a paper's *runnability*.

In *screen printing*, the term *coating* is also used to refer to any screen-printed material applied to a *substrate* as a continuous film.

Coating Mottle

A type of *mottle* characteristic of a *coated paper* that has undergone *calendering* consisting of small variations in the paper's *gloss* over its surface.

Coating Pile

The removal of particles of a paper's *coating* during offset printing and their collection on the press *blanket*. Various factors affect the tendency of coatings to pile on the blanket, including the interaction of the press's *fountain solution* on the coating. See *Piling*.

Coating Screen

In *screen printing*, a screen fabric designed—without a *stencil*—to print a continuous, solid background color over a large area of the *substrate*.

Coat Weight

A measure of the amount of *coating* added to a *base stock* of paper in the manufacturing of *coated paper*s. The coat weight of a particular paper is determined by such factors as the desired *basis weight* and paper *grade*. As the basis weight is decreased, the coat weight must be decreased to provide uniformity and the desired degree of *caliper*, strength, *opacity*, and other desired properties. There are a variety of different methods utilized to apply coatings to paper. (See *Coating*.) Coat weight is usually measured as pounds of coating on the surface of a 25×38-in. ream of paper.

Coax

Shorthand term for *coaxial cable*. See *Coaxial Cable*. Pronounced "KO-ax."

Coaxial Cable

A type of electrical cable consisting of a single, central copper wire surrounded by a separate, insulated woven metal shield. Both the central wire and the metal shield function

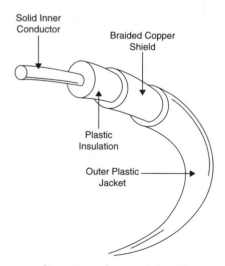

Structure of a coaxial cable.

as signal carriers, creating a signal loop. Coaxial cables are used for cable television, as well as for computer *Ethernet* or *broadband* networks. Coaxial cable is often abbreviated *coax* (pronounced "KO-ax").

Cobalt Drier

A compound of cobalt added to printing ink to hasten drying, which it accomplishes by accelerating the rate at which *oxidation* and *polymerization* of the ink *vehicle*s take place. See *Drier*.

Cobb Size Test

A test that is used to determine a paper or paperboard's water absorption, or adequacy of *sizing*, in which a paper sample is weighed, and placed in a watertight rubber-backed metal ring. The ring is filled with water, exposing the top side of the sample to water. After a set time, the water is drained, and residual water blotted off the surface of the paper, at which point the sample is weighed again. The amount of weight the sample has gained is its water absorbency.

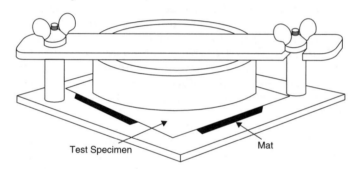

Cobb size test apparatus.

COBOL

In computing, a *high-level language* developed for creating business and data processing programs. An acronym for COmmon Business Oriented Language, it uses English-like statements. Developed in 1960, it evolved from an earlier language called FLOWMATIC, which had been developed by Grace Hopper in the 1950s.

Cobwebbing

A printing defect of *gravure* printing processes in which dried bits of ink collect in a web-like formation on the back of the *doctor blade*, on the edges of the *impression roller*, or in the engraved gravure cells.

　　Cobwebbing also describes a problem of *screen printing* in which thin strands of ink are formed between the screen fabric and the substrate, which break off the screen and leave thin, cobweb-like strands of ink on the printed *substrate*. Properly formulating the *solvent* and adjusting the printing conditions can prevent cobwebbing.

Cocking Roller

Alternate term for a *guide roller*. See *Guide Roller*.

Cockle Finish

A paper *finish* produced by *air drying*, characterized by a hard, rough surface and used most often in the production of *bond paper*s and *onionskin paper*s. See *Air Drying*.

Cockles

A paper defect comprising small ripples or spots caused by uneven moisture absorption. See *Cockling*.

In *screen printing*, *cockles* refers to lumps that have formed in screen fabric threads.

Cockling

A rippling effect imparted to the surface of a sheet of paper, caused by improper drying of the sheet or by a change in the its *moisture content* due to exposure to the atmosphere. The ripples themselves are called *cockles*. See also *Wavy Edges*.

CODASYL

Acronym for Conference On DAta SYstems and Language, an industry committee founded in 1959 to develop standards for business applications. It eventually led to the creation of the *COBOL* computer language.

Code

Any set of rules defining how data are to be represented, or how data can be translated from one representation to another. An example is computer code. Such codes are used to translate data from a representation that a human (the operator or programmer) can understand to a language that the computer can understand, and vice versa. In computer terminology, then, a *code* is any set of computer instructions.

Code Block

In computer programming, a set of statements, commands, etc., enclosed within braces—{ }—that the computer executes as a single unit.

Code Book Encoding

A means to *compress* and *decompress* digital video signals by means of a *lookup table* of values to compress and then reconstruct the signal.

Codec

Abbreviation for *coder/decoder*. See *Coder/Decoder*.

Code Conversion

In computer programming, the means by which one representation of data (or *code*) is translated into another representation of data.

Code Density

In computer programming, the number of computer *code*s that can be represented in a particular unit of space.

Coded Image

In graphics and imaging, an image containing a digital code that facilitates the storage and editing of the image.

Coded Set

Any small group of characters that represents a longer text string. A simple example is airport abbreviations; "LAX" is a three-letter coded set that represents "Los Angeles International Airport."

Code Point

In computing, an eight-*bit* (or one *byte*) number that represents one of 256 characters.

Coder

An individual who writes the specific instructions that comprise a computer program.

Coder/Decoder

In digital video production, a hardware or software application or algorithm used to code or compress and decode or decompress digital video signals. One example is a microprocessor on a digitizing board that converts analog audio or video to digital form, and back again for playback. A software example is an algorithm such as *Cinepak or* Indeo, which are used to compress video files. Abbreviated *Codec*.

Code Set

In computer programming, any specific set of characters and the rules by which those characters can be assembled to represent data. Some common code sets include *ASCII* and *EBCDIC*.

Codex

An early form of bookbinding that gradually replaced the scroll. The first codex was essentially two wooden sticks holding each end of a roll of *papyrus* or *parchment*, and it evolved into a means of binding individual leaves together—utilizing either glue or thread—with wooden boards (called *half binding*s) forming the front and back covers.

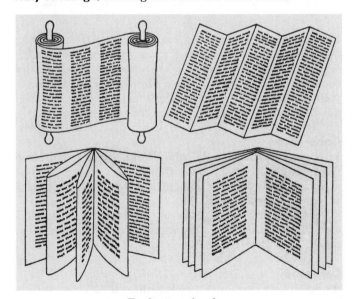

Evolution of codex.

Coding

In computer programming, writing the specific instructions and commands that tell a computer what to do.

Coefficient of Friction

The mathematical relationship of the frictional forces present between two objects in sliding contact, or how easily one object will slide against another. The coefficient of friction can be expressed as the maximum frictional force that acts just as relative motion is initiated divided by the force with which the two bodies in contact are pressed together in a direction perpendicular to their contacting surfaces. The higher the coefficient of friction, the greater the frictional forces that exist. In practical printing application where *friction* itself is important (such as in the minimization of abrasion and wear between moving surfaces), the coefficient of friction is not likely to need to be known specifically, although the lowering of the coefficient of friction is desirable. The use of lubricants (which can be liquids such as oils, greases, and waxes, or solids such as the surface roughness of a *gravure cylinder*, for example) acts to lower the coefficient of friction. (See *Friction*.)

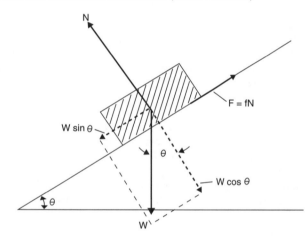

The determination of the coefficient of friction (f) is based on the equation $f = F/N$, where F is the frictional force acting as motion is initiated and N is the force with which the two bodies are pressed together in a direction perpendicular to their contacting surfaces. The angle θ is that angle at which the block just begins to slide down the inclined plane.

Coherence

In optics, the principle by which light waves remain in a fixed and predictable relationship to each other over time and/or distance. For example, a *laser* comprises light waves that possess coherence.

In a *raster display*, *coherence* refers to assigning a value to a *pixel* that is the same as that of an adjacent pixel.

Cohesion

A property of a substance that describes the ability of its component particles to stick to each other. (See also *Adhesion*.)

Cold Boot

The *boot* of a computer from an off state. See *Boot*.

Cold Colors

Alternate term for *cool colors*. See *Cool Colors*.

Cold Curing

The *curing* or hardening of an ink film that takes place at room temperature, not requiring additional heating or drying equipment.

Cold-Flow

The change in the dimensions of a plastic (such as a film or other *substrate* used in *flexography*) or other substance under stress at room temperature, caused by mechanical stretching and deformation, commonly by printing or manufacturing pressure. Cold-flow can affect proper *register* of successively printed images or colors. Cold-flow is also known as *creep* and *creeping* and, when describing the cold-flow of adhesive materials during production, *adhesive bleed*.

Cold Peel

In *screen printing* via *plastisol*-based heat-transfer materials, the condition when the removal of the release paper is not possible until the heat has been removed and the paper cooled, in contrast to *hot peel*. See also *Heat Transfer Printing*.

Cold Reboot

A drastic means of restarting a computer by depressing the reset button, turning it off and on again, or unplugging it and plugging it back in again. Such means of restarting are often required when applications or systems "freeze," but they can cause hardware and/or software damage and are only recommended as a last resort. Also known as a *hard reset*. See also *Warm Reboot*. Not to be confused with a *Cold Boot*.

Coldset Ink

A type of printing ink comprising a *resin-wax vehicle* that is a solid at room temperature and must be melted in order to be printed. Heated ink rollers, form rollers, and plates keep the ink melted long enough to print, where the ink hardens upon contact with the cool paper. Coldset inks are not used very often, save for novelty applications. (See *Vehicle*.) Coldset inks are occasionally used in *screen printing* by means of an electrically heated screen and are known as *hot-melt ink*s.

Cold Start

Alternate term for a *cold boot*. See *Cold Boot*.

Cold-Temperature Adhesive

An *adhesive* substance that can be used to bond either itself or another material or substance to a cold surface. See also *Hot-Temperature Adhesive*.

Cold Type

In typography, type produced by any means other than that used to make **hot metal type**. There is some debate about whether photographic typesetting should be included under the name "cold type"; there are those who would prefer that it refer solely to strike-on, manual, or transfer lettering. The point may now be moot, however, as type is increasingly being set digitally.

Collaborative Screen Sharing

In **video conferencing**, an interactive sharing of files and programs by conference participants. Attendants can view and edit available information publicly. Often, a **shared whiteboard** can be employed.

Collage

In graphics, any single image that has been created by combining several separate images.

The term *collage* also refers to any presentation or production in which live action (such as on video) is combined with graphics, text, or other effects.

Collate

See **Collating**.

Collating

In **binding and finishing**, the act of arranging printed pages into sets that can be bound into a book. Collating (as opposed to the similar act of **gathering**) is usually not a true bindery function and is more of an office task, frequently performed utilizing special collating assemblies attached to photocopiers.

Collating Marks

In printing, a set of numbered symbols that are printed on the folded edge of press **signature**s as a means of indicating the proper **collating** or **gathering** sequence.

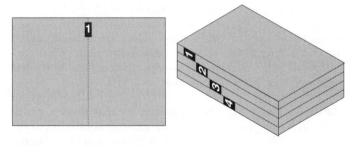

Collating marks, which are placed on the folded edge of a press signature to indicate the proper collating sequence.

Collect/Noncollect Folder

In **in-line** finishing, a **folding** device that, in conjunction with the **jaw folder** and **chopper folder**, cuts off once per half-revolution of the **plate cylinder**. This device can function as a collector—i.e., it can collect lengths of the web to form a folded and collated **signature**—or not.

Collinear

In computer graphics, a **Bézier curve** whose directional points are aligned, resulting in a straight line.

Collision

In networking, the result of the simultaneous transmission of multiple signals over the same **channel**, often causing distortion. **Carrier sensing** protocols (such as **CSMA**) work to prevent collisions. See **Carrier Sense Multiple Access (CSMA)**.

Collision Avoidance (CA)

In networking, the ability of a transmitting device to wait for an open carrier before commencing transmission. See **Carrier Sense Multiple Access/Collision Avoidance (CSMA/CA)**.

Collision Detection (CD)

In networking, the ability of a transmitting device to detect simultaneous transmissions on a shared carrier. See **Carrier Sense Multiple Access/Collision Detection (CSMA/CD)**.

Colloid

A water-soluble, noncrystalline substance comprising solid particles of a very small size (typically 0.00005–0.0000001 cm) dispersed in a solid, liquid, or gaseous medium. The particles themselves can be large protein molecules or aggregates of other substances. Common examples include **gelatin**, glue, and **albumen**. Colloids are used as vehicles in **emulsion**s used for stencils in **screen printing**, and the application of **bichromate** renders them photosensitive.

Colloid Mill

A device used in the manufacture of printing ink to further disperse the solid **pigment** particles in the fluid ink **vehicle** that utilizes a rotor-stator arrangement to chop up the pigment particles and disperse them thoroughly. The ink **slurry** is pumped into a metal chamber where it passes between a rotating blade (the rotor) and a stationary blade (the stator). The distance between these two blades determines how finely ground the particles of pigment will be. The colloid mill can be adapted to either batch or continuous processes. (See also **Three-Roll Mill**, **Ball Mill**, and **Sand/Shot Mill**.)

Colophon

A page commonly added to the **back matter** of a book providing information concerning the book's production, the **typeface** used, and perhaps the printer's imprint. The term *colophon* was originally used to refer to the emblem or insignia of a printer or publisher.

Color

Generally speaking, the quality of any substance, surface, or object with respect to the spectral component(s) of the light reflecting from it. The term *color* also refers to the quality of light possessing certain dominant wavelength(s).

Color is a vast, complex subject that encompasses nearly every aspect of human endeavor. Consequently, the following article will concentrate primarily on the application of color to the graphic arts, in particular color printing, following a short overview of color theory.

The colors of the visible spectrum include (in order of decreasing wavelength) ***red***, ***orange***, ***yellow***, ***green***, ***blue***, and ***violet***. Light or objects that appear ***blue***, for example, reflect light in that portion of the ***visible spectrum***. ***White light*** appears to have no color because all the wavelengths are present in equal amounts, effectively "cancelling" each other out. Sometimes, light beyond the range of the visible spectrum (in particular, ***ultraviolet***) is also included under the term "color." Some species of insects, for example, can see into the ultraviolet, and many types of flowers that use these insects as pollinators also include an ultraviolet component among the colors they display. (See *COLOR PLATE 3*.)

The perception or sensation of color, despite attempts to objectively quantify it, is a highly subjective phenomenon. We speak of, for example, a "red apple," but the redness of the apple is more dependent on our own peculiar visual systems than any inherent "redness" in the apple. (To organisms with different types of photoreceptors, it could appear to possess a much different color.) Even among different humans, the redness perceived is not absolute, varying according to minute physiological differences in visual acuity or according to the illumination used.

Interestingly, according to Hope and Walch in *The Color Compendium*, polls have consistently found that in Western Europe and North America over half of the adults surveyed name "blue" as their favorite color, while children under eight consistently name "red" as their favorite. (In Japan, however, over half of the people surveyed named either white or black as their favorite color.) Color preferences tend to vary by culture, not unexpectedly. This may seem like a trivial matter, but it is an important consideration in planning multinational advertising campaigns, designing products such as clothing for other markets, and other such endeavors. It also manifests itself in appropriate dress when visiting other cultures; white is not universally accepted as the bride's dress color at a wedding, for example, nor is black universally appropriate for funerals or other mourning rites. In other words, color is a cultural-specific concept; various colors are symbolic of different things, and these symbols are not universally consistent.

COLOR THEORY

Color begins with ***light***. Light is a small portion of the much larger ***electromagnetic spectrum***, a broad range of different types of generated energy, ranging from radio waves and electrical oscillations, through microwaves, infrared, the visible spectrum, ultraviolet radiation, gamma rays, and high-energy cosmic rays. All of these sources of electromagnetic radiation exist as waves, and it is the variations in wavelength and frequency that determine the precise nature of the energy. These wavelengths range in size from many meters (such as radio waves) to many bil-

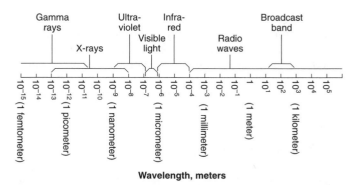

The electromagnetic spectrum.

lionths of a meter (gamma and cosmic rays). Visible light is technically defined as electromagnetic radiation having a wavelength between approximately 400 and 780 ***nanometer***s (one nanometer is equal to one billionth of a meter).

An object or surface appears to possess a certain color because of the chemical makeup of that substance. In an atom, negatively charged electrons "orbit" around a positively charged nucleus. These electrons are in certain "energy levels," each having a certain "default" energy level. When these electrons are subjected to an energy source (in this case, visible light), they absorb the energy, but only at certain wavelengths (or colors). When these wavelengths are absorbed by the electrons, the remaining wavelengths of light are—essentially—reflected back to the observer. These reflected wavelengths are the opposites of those that were absorbed. Thus, we can say that an apple appears red because the atoms within the apple absorb light corresponding to the blue portion of the spectrum, reflecting back the opposite—or red—wavelengths. (The process is actually quite a bit more complicated than this.)

All of the colors we can perceive are produced by the mixing of certain basic colors. There are three categories of colors: ***primary colors***, ***secondary colors***, and ***tertiary colors***. Primary colors are those that are not formed by the mixing of any other colors and can be said to be "pure" colors. Secondary colors are those formed by the mixing of two or more primary colors. Tertiary colors are those produced by the mixing of two or more secondary colors. What constitutes a primary color differs depending on whether one is talking about light or pigments.

Additive Color Mixing. In ***additive color theory***, which describes the interaction of different colors of light, three primary colors are recognized: red, green, and blue. Mixing these three primaries in various proportions is what creates the wide range of the visible spectrum. Mixing green light with blue light of equal strength will produce cyan, a secondary color (but see *subtractive color mixing* below); red light plus blue light yields magenta light; red light plus green light yields yellow light, while an equal mixture of all three additive primaries yields white light. Varying the intensities of these lights produces many other colors as well. Television screens and computer monitors display

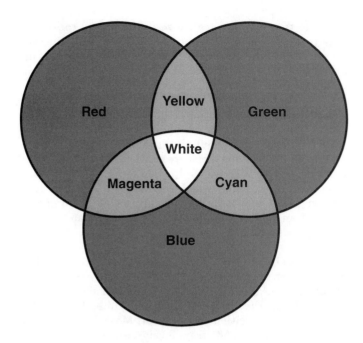

Additive color mixing.

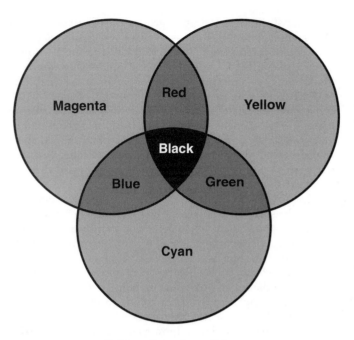

Subtractive color mixing.

colors using additive color mixing; three different projectors (a red, a green, and a blue) vary the intensity of their respective colors to produce the range of displayed colors. (See *Color Plate 2*.)

Subtractive Color Mixing. Colorants (such as inks, pigments, dyes, etc.) produce the sensation of a particular color in a different manner than does light. Since there is an extra step involved in the generation of a colorant (namely, the absorption of certain wavelengths of light, and the reflection of the opposite wavelengths), the *subtractive color primaries* are those colored substances that absorb the three additive color primaries. The subtractive color primaries are *cyan* (which absorbs red light), *magenta* (which absorbs green light), and *yellow* (which absorbs blue light). Mixing these colorants produces different color effects. Thus, if cyan ink is placed on a substrate, it will absorb the red light striking it. If a yellow colorant is overprinted on the cyan, then all the blue will also be absorbed, and the only remaining color of light that will be reflected back is green. Consequently, cyan plus yellow yields green. (Thus, subtractive color mixing operates by "subtracting" out one or more colors of light.) Varying the proportions of these colorants creates a wide variety of different colors. Cyan, magenta, and yellow are, in printing terminology, known as *process colors* since it is these pigments that are used in *process color* printing—also known as *full-color* or, when *black* ink is added, *four-color printing*. Full-color printing is accomplished by overprinting dots of these colors in varying amounts. (See *Color Separation* below.) It is for this reason that *transparent pigment*s are required for process color inks, while *opaque pigment*s are more often required for *spot color* printing. These three sub-

tractive primaries are often referred to as "blue, red, and yellow," which is not entirely appropriate. In theory, the combination of the three subtractive primaries in equal amounts should yield black, but in practice that is not always the case. (See *Color Plate 1*.)

In addition to additive and subtractive primaries, there are also *memory colors*, which are the colors we often find in daily life—the green of grass, the blue of the sky, the color of human skin, etc., which printers and color separators need to ensure are reproduced accurately.

Color Measurement

The "birth" of color as a science came in 1872, when the Scottish physicist James Maxwell attempted to apply mathematics to the description of color. He created an equilateral triangle (called *Maxwell's triangle*) that identified red, green, and blue as the three primary colors of light, each located at one of the corners of the triangle. White was located in the exact center of the triangle, the point where all spectral components exist in equal amounts. All the other colors and combinations moved inward toward white, as well as around the perimeter of the triangle. (See *Maxwell's Triangle*.)

In 1905, Alfred Munsell developed the *Munsell Color Space*, a means of expressing the relationships between colors. (See *Munsell Color Space*.)

In 1931, the Commission Internationale de l'Eclairage (CIE) developed the first *CIE color space*. The CIE system, which has been revised many times (both by the CIE itself and by other organizations), is essentially based on *tristimulus values*, derived from *standard observer* data. Essentially, these tristimulus values (plotted on a three-axis coordinate system) are derived from the relative amounts of the three additive primary colors that a particular sample comprises. These values are gathered either using *colorimeter* data (gleaned by evaluating a sample using three filters—red, green, and blue—that simulate the human eye's perception of color) or from spectral data derived from a quantitative measurement of each of the three wavelengths of light. From the three-axis coordinate system, a two-dimensional *chromaticity diagram* can be mathematically derived, which is a horseshoe-shaped chart whose curved outer rim ranges from red to blue, with the *saturation* of a particular hue decreasing toward the center of the diagram. (See *COLOR PLATE 4*.)

Later CIE (and other) color measurement systems recognize three color attributes, which are based on these tristimulus values: *hue* (which is the dominant wavelength or most easily discernible color) of a sample; *saturation* (or how "pure" the hue is, to what extent it is contaminated with other colors, or the degree of grayness); and *brightness* (the amount of light that is being reflected, or how bright the sample is). In other color spaces, saturation is known as *chroma*, while brightness is variously known as *value* or *lightness*. Three-term color spaces include *HSL* (hue, saturation, and lightness), *HSB* (hue, saturation, and brightness), *HSV* (hue, saturation, and value), and *LCH* (luminance, chroma, and hue). In all of them, the same fundamental color properties are recognized. An important distinction between HSL and HSB is that the latter is based on the RGB intensities of a computer monitor.

Different color measurement systems measure the color depending on the medium. Two variations of the CIE color space are *CIEL*a*b** (L*a*b* referring to hue, saturation, and brightness, respectively), which is designed for measuring reflective color samples, and *CIELUV* designed for color displays, such as television sets and computer monitors. The *Hunter L,a,b* values are also widely used. (See *CIE Color Space*.)

Related to color models are *color matching system*s, which are collections of printed or computer-generated color samples, used by designers and printers to match and specify colors. An advantage to these systems—used for both *spot color* and *process color*—is that they often include the proportions of colored inks required to produce the desired color. (See *Color Matching System*.)

TONE REPRODUCTION AND IMAGING

Whether prepress is performed in the traditional method or on digital systems, the evaluation of a reproduction, proof, and/or original comprises the same basic issues. One of the inherent difficulties, however, involves the dichotomy between *analog* and *digital* data. Analog data essentially refers to any continuous wave, such as sound, light, or an electrical signal. Digital refers to any information that exists as discrete bits. Digital is most often used to describe computers, as a computer can only understand two commands—on or off. A computer's *central processing unit* consists of thousands of tiny transistors, which either complete or interrupt an electrical signal. Thus, the binary language of the computer (called *machine code*) consists of only 1s and 0s (on or off, respectively). Everything the computer does is some pattern of 1s and 0s (these two digits are called *bit*s, a term that is short for *bi*nary digi*t*). Eight bits equal one *byte* (for example, 01001001). Consequently, any digital signal is composed of very small "steps" that aim to describe as closely as possible the contours of the original analog wave. In order for an analog signal to be effectively turned into a digital signal, the *sampling rate* (or the frequency with which the steps are captured by the computer) must be greater than human perception can detect, otherwise the discrete steps would be perceived. In digital color imaging, this translates into ensuring that the range of tones of an original (analog) image are accurately translated into digital form.

Gray Levels. In order for a digital image to reproduce well, it must render transitions between gray scale values imperceptibly. The greater the number of discrete steps that can be inserted between black and white, the smoother the grayscale transitions will appear. Most digital systems can accommodate 256 gray levels, which is somewhat beyond the number that research suggests that most humans can detect. The inadequacy of the number of gray levels in a digital image manifests itself in tints and gradients as the phenomenon of *banding*, or the visibility of the discrete gray levels.

Density. In imaging, *density* is a quantitative measure of the amount of light a particular surface absorbs. In a printed reproduction, density becomes a measure of how well the tone depth of an image has been reproduced. Density measurements can be made independent of hue, by using a densitometer and filters that can evaluate each color in a reproduction as a shade of gray. (See *Density* and *Density Range*.)

Contrast. The term *contrast* refers to the distribution of tones in an image. For example, an image with a great deal of *shadow* and *highlight*—but little *middle tone*—detail is considered to be high-contrast, while an image with a great deal of detail in the middle tone region would be said to be low-contrast. (See *Contrast* and *Gamma*.)

Tonal Gradation. An important issue in color reproduction is ensuring that the tonal range of the image is optimized for the printing process to be utilized. Depending on the printing process, *halftone dot*s below a certain minimum size (which will correspond to highlight areas of the image) may be lost. Consequently, prior to scanning the original image, it is necessary to map the lightest highlights to the smallest halftone dot the printing process can reproduce. For example, the smallest dot that can be printed on an offset press is about 8 microns, while the smallest dot that can be printed on a *flexographic* press is 40 microns. Similarly, dots in the darkest shadow areas should not be larger than the largest dot that can be

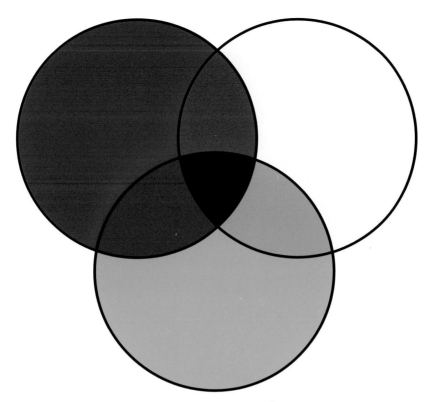

COLOR PLATE 1. *Subtractive color mixing.*

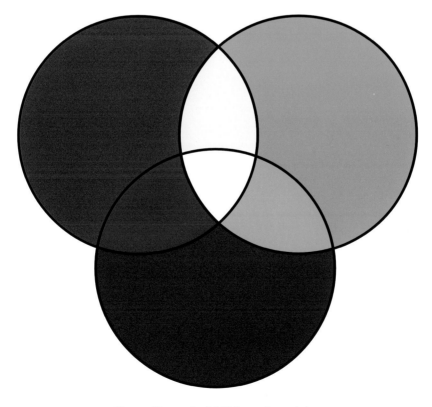

COLOR PLATE 2. *Additive color mixing.*

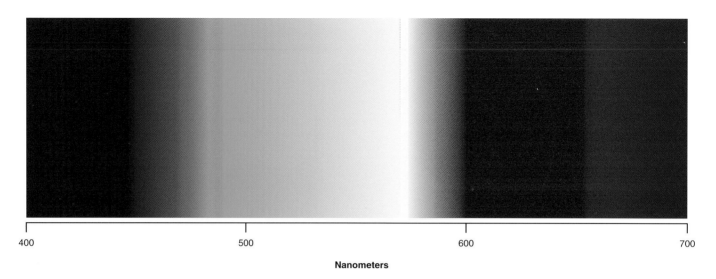

Nanometers

COLOR PLATE 3. *The visible spectrum.*

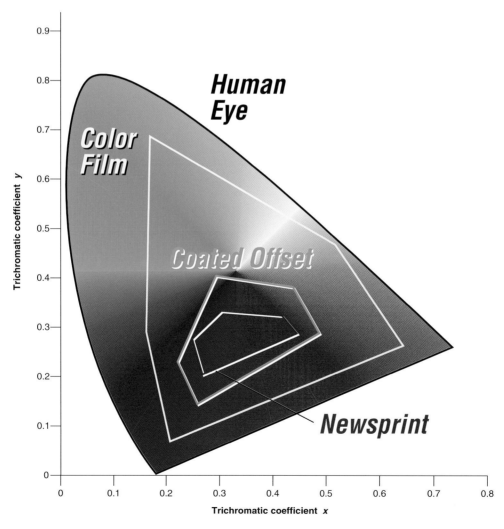

COLOR PLATE 4. *CIE chromaticity diagram showing the color gamut of the human eye, color film, newsprint, and coated offset paper.*

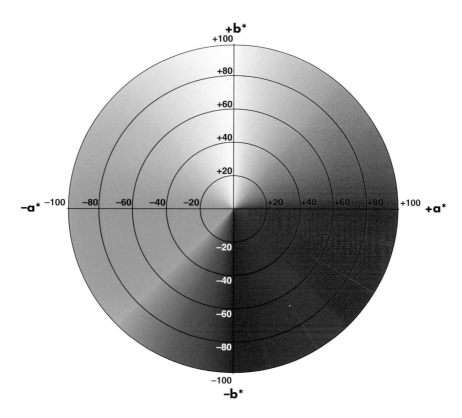

COLOR PLATE 5. *CIE L*a*b* transformation of the CIE color space.*

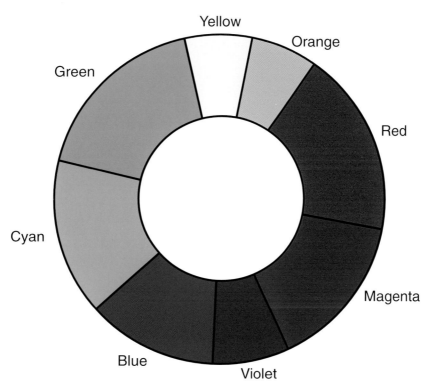

COLOR PLATE 6. *The hue component of color on an abridged color circle. The divisions on the color circle are approximate. Colors on opposite sides of the circle are complementary colors.*

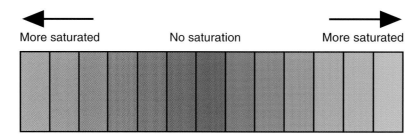

More saturated   No saturation   More saturated

COLOR PLATE 7. The saturation component of color for the magenta-green hue axis.

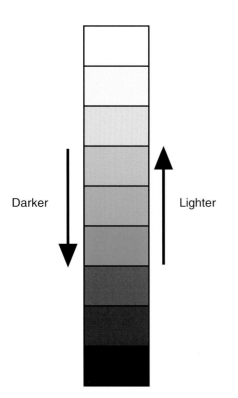

Darker   Lighter

COLOR PLATE 8. The lightness component for the color green.

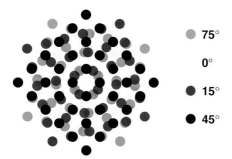

75°

0°

15°

45°

COLOR PLATE 9. The rosette that is formed when the cyan, magenta, yellow, and black halftone dots are at the proper screen angles.

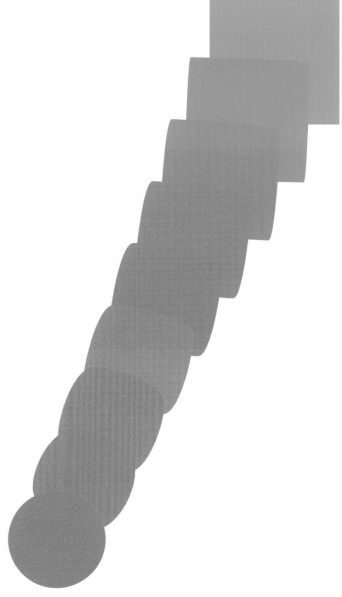

COLOR PLATE 10. An example of one object being morphed into another. A light green square has been morphed into a magenta circle with seven intermediate steps.

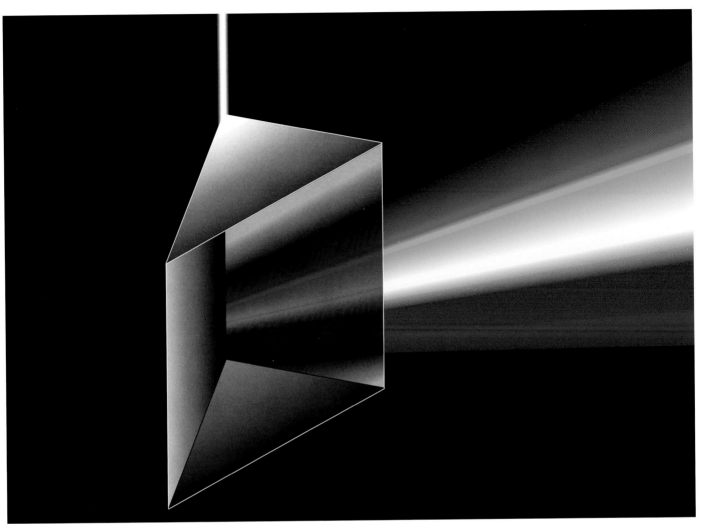

COLOR PLATE 11. An example of refraction. White light enters a prism and is refracted.

COLOR PLATE 12. Three gradients. The radial gradient at the left has red at its center, progressing to a light green at its extremities. The linear gradient at the top right progresess from blue to yellow, and the gradient at the bottom right progresses from light red to dark red.

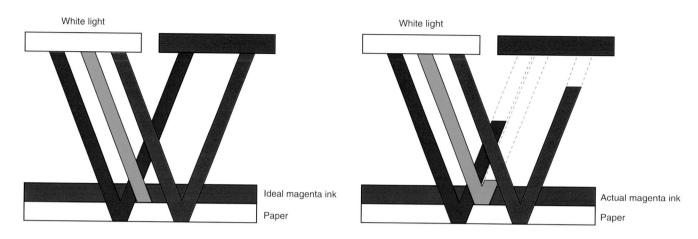

COLOR PLATE 13. The portion of the visible spectrum absorbed and transmitted by an ideal magenta ink (left) and an actual magenta ink (right).

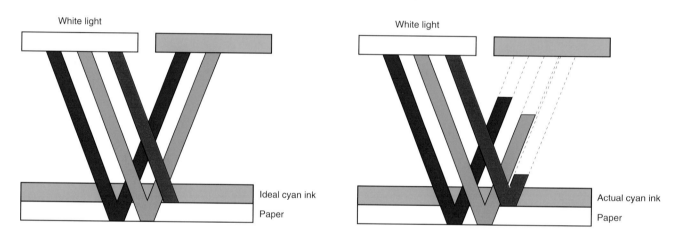

COLOR PLATE 14. The portion of the visible spectrum absorbed and transmitted by an ideal cyan ink (left) and an actual cyan ink (right).

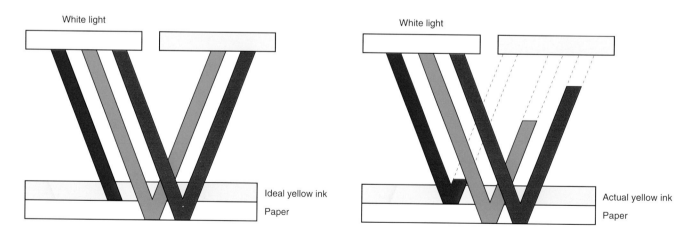

COLOR PLATE 15. The portion of the visible spectrum absorbed and transmitted by an ideal yellow ink (left) and an actual yellow ink (right).

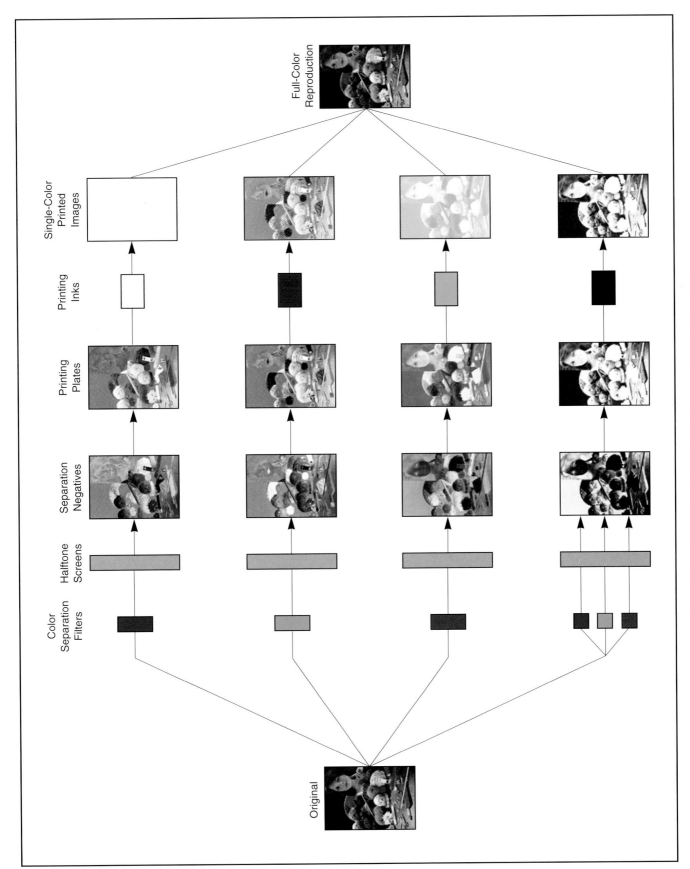

COLOR PLATE 16. The principles of color reproduction in printing.

COLOR PLATE 17. *The interference pattern, or moiré, that results due to incorrect screen angles. In this example, the cyan tint is at the proper angle, 75°, but the magenta tint is at 20°, instead of 15°.*

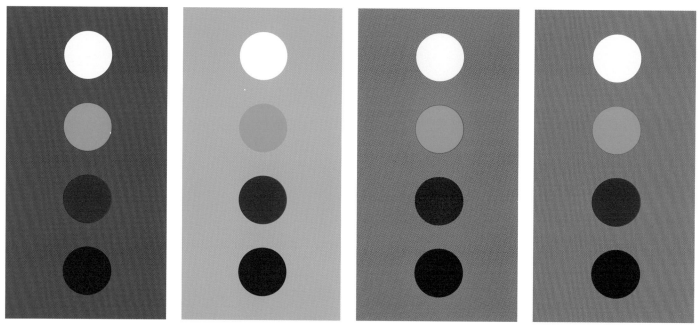

COLOR PLATE 18. *The adjacency effect of surrounding colors on color perception. In each of the four examples above, the yellow, red, green, and blue circles are identical, but the background color varies.*

COLOR PLATE 19. *A reproduction with proper gray balance (left) and an image with poor gray balance (right), which causes a color cast throughout the image.*

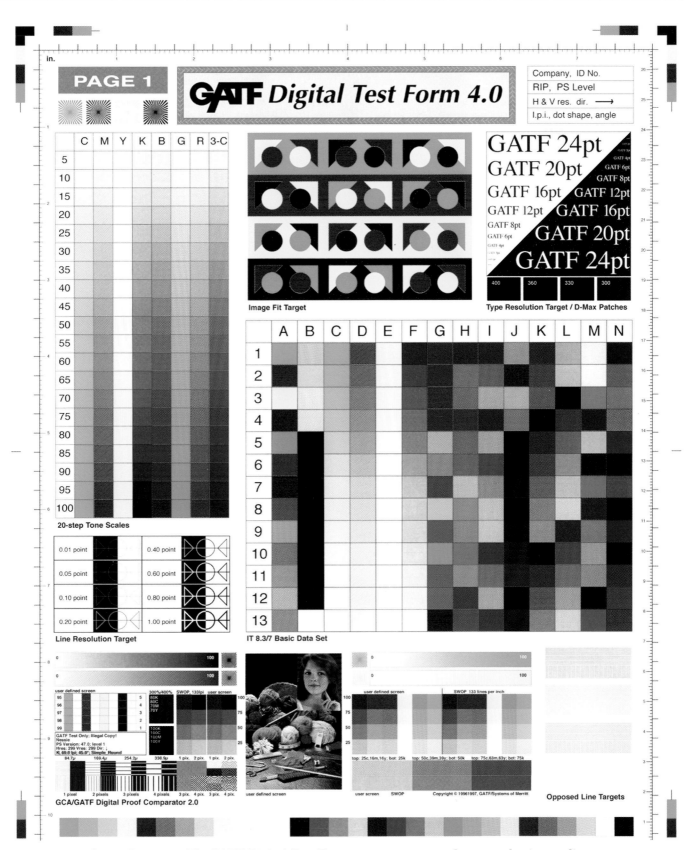

COLOR PLATE 20. The GATF Digital Test Form, a test pattern used to control print quality.

COLOR PLATE 21. A page from Gutenberg's 42-line Bible.

COLOR PLATE 22. *Examples of the same image reproduced using conventional screening techniques (top) and stochastic, or frequency modulated, screening (bottom).*

COLOR PLATE 23. Examples of the same image reproduced using cyan, magenta, yellow, and black — the four process-color inks (top) and reproduced using extra-trinary colors to expand the color gamut of the reproduction (bottom).

COLOR PLATE 24. *The use of unsharp masking to improve the appearance of a color reproduction. The original image is at the left and the sharpened image is at the right.*

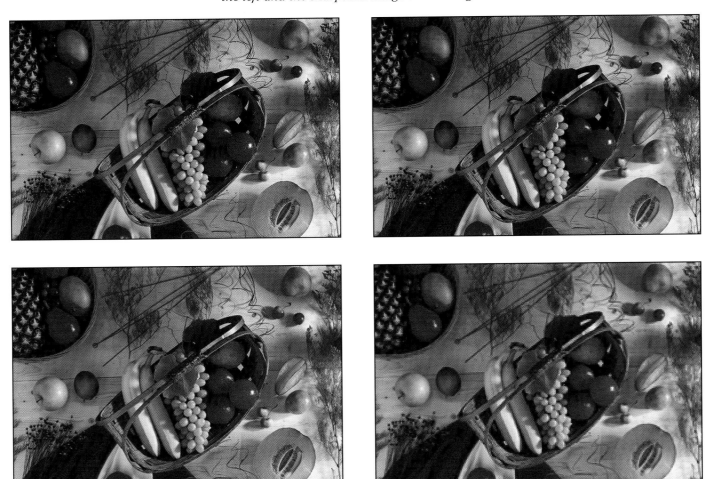

COLOR PLATE 25. *The effect that scanning at various resolutions has on color reproduction quality. The rule of thumb is to scan an image at twice the final screen ruling. All four images have been output at 150 lines/inch, but they were scanned at different resolutions: 300 ppi (top left), 225 ppi (top right), 150 ppi (lower left), and 72 ppi (lower right).*

Crystallize

Noise

Ripple

Extrude

Pointillize

Posterize

COLOR PLATE 26. Image-editing programs, such as Photoshop, can be used to apply special-effects filters to color images.

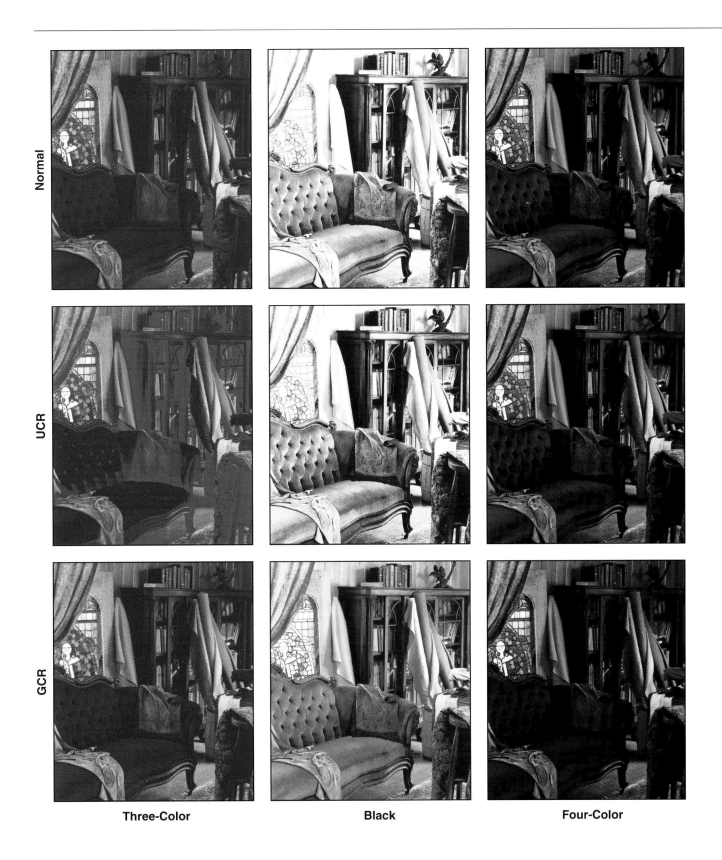

COLOR PLATE 27. *The three-color, black, and four-color prints for normal, undercolor removal (UCR), and gray component replacement (GCR).*

COLOR PLATE 28. *Effects of file compression on a color reproduction. The image at the right was compressed using the JPEG algorithm set to medium quality. Notice the slight loss of detail in the compressed image compared to the original image (left).*

COLOR PLATE 29. *A high-key image (left) and a low-key image (right).*

COLOR PLATE 30. *Two examples of a duotone made from the same original. The duotone at the left was printed using cyan and magenta inks, while the duotone at the right was printed with black and cyan inks.*

printed, otherwise the space between the dots will fill in while on press. Many image-processing programs (such as Photoshop) will let you adjust the middle tones as desired.

Resolution. When a digital image is on a computer screen, it is displayed at whatever maximum *resolution* the monitor is capable of. On the *Macintosh*, for example, that number is 72 *dots per inch (dpi)*. The screen resolution is determined by the number of *pixel*s per unit of linear space. The monitor screen resolution is usually very far below the minimum resolution needed for high-quality output. The image itself, however, will be at whatever resolution it was scanned at, which may be anywhere from 300 to 3,000 dpi. The only issue involved with resolution is the capability of the output device. Like the computer monitor, the output device describes images—be they text, *line art*, or photographs—as a grid of tiny dots. The higher the number of dots per inch, the higher the resolution and the smoother and sharper the image. A *laser printer*, for example, is capable of only as high a resolution as 600 dpi, which is fine for most type and line work, but inadequate for halftone screens. An *imagesetter*—a high-end device that exposes type and images directly on film—is capable of resolutions as high as 3,000 dpi or greater. The resolution of an original image can be changed either by downsampling (reducing the resolution by discarding image data) or upsampling (increasing the resolution by interpolating data between pixels). This latter technique rarely works effectively, and it is best to scan at the desired (or higher) resolution. However, scanning at too high a resolution though not deleterious to image quality requires more computer power, disk space and memory, and slows down quite significantly the rate at which the image can be processed and output.

When a digital file is sent to an imagesetter for output, it first needs to pass through a *raster image processor (RIP)* that maps the type and images to the grid of spots on the film recording section of the output device, effectively controlling which spots on the device's recording grid need to be exposed and which should remain unexposed. For type and line art, this is a straightforward process, but for digital halftones, there are some unique wrinkles.

Halftone Screening. All continuous-tone images—be they color or black-and-white—need to be converted to *halftone*s before they can be reproduced. Because few printing processes can lay down varying densities of ink, images must first be broken down into very small, discrete dots of varying size, density, and distribution in a process called *halftone screening*. This was originally accomplished by photographing the original image through a fine grid, or screen, of a set number of lines per inch. When the film is exposed, the image will consist of thousands of tiny dots: dark, tightly packed dots in the shadow areas, a moderate amount of dots in the middle tones, and few, light dots in the highlights. Each color separation negative is processed as a halftone. However, when successively col-

An enlarged view of a halftone image (top) and a simulated continuous-tone gray scale (bottom).

ored dots are overprinted, if the angle of the lines of dots is the same for all four colors, the lines will interfere with each other and produce an undesirable *moiré* pattern. Consequently, each screen needs to be placed at a different angle, experience generating certain specified *screen angles* that are the most effective for reducing moiré. (See *Color Plates 9* and *17*.)

On digital systems, halftoning is performed electronically. Computer output devices need to create images as a series of tiny dots (called *spot*s to distinguish them from halftone dots). These spots are much smaller than the halftone dots, and in fact each halftone dot is composed of many of these printer spots. (Thus in digital output, halftone dots are referred to as *halftone cell*s.) The problem with halftone screening is that two of the conventional screen angles are known as *irrational screen angles*. This means that the tangents of these angles (the tangent being, in trigonometry, the ratio of one side of an angle to the opposite side) are irrational numbers (in other words, a number that is not a whole integer, but an endlessly repeating number such as 3.333333.... or π—3.14159....). The upshot of this is that the computer cannot calculate irrational screen angles, and the rows of cells will not align with the grid perfectly. Rounding to the nearest rational angle helps the computer, but more often than not causes distortion and moiré. A combination of proprietary *screen algorithms* and the development of *supercell* screening has finally solved the problem of irrational screen angles. (See *Screen Angles*.)

Other aspects of the halftoning process also need to be considered, such as *dot size*, *dot shape*, *screen count*, and the screening method employed. Newer types of screening procedures are enhancing the quality of color halftone reproduction. (See *Stochastic Screening* and *Color Plate 22*.) One inevitable aspect of any printing process is *dot gain*, or an undesired increase in the size of halftone dots. Dot gain can be caused by any or all of the steps from prepress to press: imagesetter output, platemaking, and the nature of the *substrate* used in printing are all contributors to dot gain. (There is also, in addition to this *physical dot gain*, an *optical dot gain*, which is an optical illusion caused by the scattering of light at the edges of halftone dots.) Therefore, some degree of *dot gain compensation* is performed prior to final output of an image. (See *Dot Gain*.)

Color Imaging. Images are usually obtained from a variety of sources. The most common means of capturing images is by scanning them. A scanner is an optical device that converts reflected or transmitted light (depending on whether the image is a print or a transparency, respectively) to digital data for each primary color (RGB). A scanner scans each pixel of each line of an original image for each primary color and stores all the variations as a series of gray values. It can either output the color separations directly on film or, more often, store the image as an RGB file for later manipulation. Scanners come in two basic varieties: *drum scanner*s and *flatbed scanner*s. The former mounts the original image inside or on the surface of a drum, which rotates the image past the optics. The latter type of scanner places the image on a flat platen and moves the optics beneath the image. Drum scanners are high-end devices and tend to produce higher-quality scans. They also tend to cost upwards of $10,000. However, flatbed scanners are commonly available for near or under $1,000, and their quality is quickly catching up to what can be achieved on drum scanners. When scanning, transparencies tend to reproduce better than prints. (See *Scanner*.)

A scanner captures what are known as *bitmap* images, in which an image exists solely as a grid of variously colored pixels. The alternative type of graphics are *vector graphics*, in which images are stored as mathematical descriptions of lines, curves, and other shapes. Vector graphics have the advantage of taking up less disk space, can be scaled in size easily, and will print at the highest resolution the output device is capable of. The disadvantage, however, is that they cannot be as easily edited (i.e., pixel by pixel) as bitmapped images can. Vector graphics are only possible for line art; photographs cannot be saved as vectors. Bitmaps are also known as *raster* images. (See *Bitmap* and *Vector Graphics*.)

Color image files can be saved in one of many *file format*s. The choice of a file format is crucial if the image needs to be transferred to other computers or systems that use different software. A file format is essentially a scheme for organizing the digital image data. Some standard file formats can be read by a wide variety of devices and programs. For bitmapped images, *TIFF* is the most widely used file format, while *encapsulated PostScript (EPS)* is widely used for vector graphics. (See *File Format*, *TIFF*, and *Encapsulated Post Script*.)

An increasingly popular source of photographic images is the Kodak *Photo CD*, or a compact disc with prescanned images at a variety of resolutions that can then be manipulated, color corrected (if necessary) and otherwise processed for output. (See *Photo CD*.)

*Digital camera*s are also becoming popular sources for image capture. (See *Digital Camera*.)

DESKTOP COLOR AND COLOR SYSTEMS

Most color prepress these days is performed digitally, utilizing either a high-end *color electronic publishing system (CEPS)* running proprietary software, or a desktop *microcomputer* running on a *standard platform* with off-the-shelf software. Regardless of which type of system is utilized, certain basic features and considerations need to be taken into account.

Computer System. The heart or brain of any computer is the *central processing unit (CPU)*, housing the *microprocessor*(s) that execute all system functions, often measured in *MIPS*, or millions of instructions per second. (Desktop computers are still often measured in some fraction of MIPS, but that is likely to change in the near future.) The microprocessor—on IBM-compatible computers, the Intel 386, 486, or Pentium chips, and on the Apple Macintosh, the Motorola 680X0 or PowerPC chip—can operate at a variety of speeds, measured in *megahertz* (MHz). Obviously, the faster the processor, the less time that will be spent waiting for the computer to finish performing a function. Especially when dealing with large graphics files, fast processor speed is highly desirable.

The software that controls all aspects of the computer and that forms the interface between user and device is the *operating system*, or *platform*. For many years, Microsoft's text-based *DOS* (a *command-line interface*) was the dominant operating system, but it was the *Macintosh operating system*, the first commercially successful *graphical user interface* (GUI), that made the desktop publishing revolution a reality. Later, Microsoft *Windows* provided a GUI for PC clones, and although PCs are gaining momentum in desktop publishing and graphics work, the Macintosh is still the computer of choice. Workstations—such as those by Sun—commonly run on one of the many flavors of *UNIX*. High-end systems usually utilize their own proprietary and/or custom-made operating system. Although as of this writing, most operating systems are incompatible with each other, the use of standard file formats (such as TIFF or EPS or the increasingly popular Adobe *portable document format*) can allow files to be transferred from system to system. (See *Platform* and *File Format*.)

Another important consideration in computer graphics is the system's *random-access memory* (or *RAM*). Although it is only one of several types of computer memory, it is what is most often meant by "memory." RAM—these days measured in *megabyte*s—is the memory allotted by the computer for the storage of open applications, system software, and other data the computer needs to deal with at any given time. Whatever important data cannot fit in RAM is stored on the computer's hard disk, and read from it, which is a much slower process than reading from RAM. The more RAM the better; one can never have enough. Most graphics applications—especially those that deal with full-color images—are very RAM-intensive; although it is increasingly difficult to get by with 8 *MB* of RAM, it can be done, but not easily. Computer systems are increasingly being shipped with at least 16 MB of RAM, but even that is not enough for large image files. Computer systems that regularly work with very large image files should not have less than 120 MB of RAM. (See *RAM*.)

Most computers also come with at least one hard disk, frequently located internally (although external hard disks are available). The hard disk is the site of the system software and important applications. A hard disk is read and written much faster than most other types of storage devices. Hard disks are available in a large number of storage capacities. Once measured in *kilobyte*s, hard disks are more often measured in megabytes and *gigabyte*s. (One *byte* equals eight *bit*s. One kilobyte equals 1,024 bytes, one megabyte equals 1,024 kilobytes, and one gigabyte equals 1,024 megabytes. See *Bit*, *Byte*, *Kilobyte*, *Megabyte*, and *Gigabyte*.) For graphics files, a minimum hard-disk storage capacity of 200 MB is recommended, although 1 *GB* is a common size, and hard disks are getting larger all the time. Much larger disks capable of storing data measured in *terabyte*s (1,024 gigabytes, or over one *trillion* bytes) are now beginning to appear.

Peripherals. Computer peripherals are those devices that are connected to the computer, as opposed to being built in to them. The monitor or video display is not technically a peripheral but is an important "add-on" to any system. Most monitors utilize *cathode-ray tube*s (CRTs), which comprise three electron guns, one for the red, one for the green, and one for the blue signal comprising an image. The guns repeatedly scan across the screen in discrete bursts, which are known as *pixel*s (which is an abbreviation for "picture element"). The size of a particular pixel is referred to as its *dot pitch*, which is a function of the smallest point the electron beam can describe. The color of a particular pixel is controlled by a *digital-to-analog converter*, which translates the computer's internal digital "picture" of the monitor to the variations in voltage to regulate the intensity of the electron beam(s) being fired at the screen. The number of colors that can be displayed by any given pixel is determined by the *color depth* of the monitor, or a measure of how many bits describe each pixel. This can range from *one-bit color*, in which each pixel is described by one bit of information (in other words, either "on" or "off," black or white) to—as of this writing—*thirty-two-bit color*. For most graphics work, *twenty-four-bit color* is required, which means that twenty-four bits of information are used to describe each pixel, or eight bits for each of the three colors. This allows for the use of 2^{24}, or 16,777,216 possible colors for each pixel. (See *Twenty-Four-Bit Color*; see also *Eight-Bit Color* and *Sixteen-Bit Color*.) Other monitor considerations include the *refresh rate* (or how fast the electron beam scans the screen anew) and the *addressable resolution*, or the number of pixels that can be displayed on the screen. Some computers and monitors require *expansion board*s to expand the number of colors or the resolution the monitor can display.

The most commonly installed peripheral devices are storage media, which can be any of a number of devices. These roughly fall into two categories: magnetic and optical. A magnetic medium is any disk that stores information by orienting magnetic particles in a particular way. Exam-

ples include a *floppy disk* or any of a variety of removable cartridges (the most oft-used of which, as of this writing, are SyQuest cartridges and Iomega's Zip or Jaz disks). Other non-computer examples include audio- and video-cassettes. Optical media include a variety of *optical disc*s such as CDs and CD-ROMs, or magnetic-optical discs. (By the way, the word "disk" when spelled with a "k" refers to magnetic media; when spelled "disc" it refers to optical media.) External storage media are most often used to transfer files from system to system, or to create *backup file*s. One can never have too many backup files. Such media are also used for archiving, or the long-term storage of files not needed at the moment, but may eventually be needed in the future.

Many larger companies have their computers linked in a network (often called a *local area network (LAN)*, which allows for the transfer of files from computer to computer, or to and from a central data storage device. Input and output devices are also attached to the network. An *open prepress interface (OPI)*, developed by Aldus, minimizes network traffic problems by centrally storing *high-resolution file*s and only sending out *low-resolution file*s to various workstations for positioning and layout purposes. When the document or page is ultimately output, stored commands provide the system with information about how to position the high-resolution file, which is inserted by the system just prior to output. The use of low-resolution files reduces the processor and memory demands, which expedites the import and positioning of imaging in page makeup programs. Since the computer monitor is incapable of high-resolution display anyway, the use of a high-resolution file is not necessary in the layout stage. (See *OPI*.)

The Internet and other forms of telecommunications are also being used widely to send and receive image files to and from outside sources. (See *Telecommunications*.)

Data Compression. When files are stored or transmitted, it is often desirable that they take up as little disk space as possible. Several means of reducing image file size have been developed, which are collectively known as *data compression* algorithms. There are many different types of algorithms, but they all function on the same principle: most images contain a great deal of redundant data, or pixels that are similar to other pixels. (A photograph of a clear blue sky is an extreme example of this; most of the pixels are the exact same color.) Data compression works by saving the file not as a collection of tens of thousands of individual pixels, but as instructions for producing those pixels. In many algorithms, particular blocks of pixels are analyzed and, if a simple formula can be devised for describing those pixels (such as 4 blue pixels, 3 white pixels, 7 green pixels, etc.), it saves the formula as a binary code. This takes up far less room than the individual pixels. Thus, when the image is re-opened, the formula is used to "rebuild" the image. Some algorithms can reduce file sizes to a mere fraction of their original size (20:1 or 30:1 are not uncommon). However, as can be expected, the greater the compression, the more shorthand instructions are created. As a result, the image may not be reconstructed with absolutely perfect fidelity, and some data may be lost, the extent of which ranges from undetectable to egregious. Data compression algorithms that cause no discernible data loss are called, not surprisingly, *lossless*, while those that do are known as *lossy*. Some of the common compression schemes in use are *JPEG*, *Huffman encoding*, and *LZW*, to name but a few. (See *Data Compression*.)

Those are the basics of the desktop tools used to acquire and process color images. A number of software programs are used to manipulate the images themselves, such as Adobe Photoshop, Aldus PhotoStyler, and many others. Page layout programs such as *QuarkXPress* and *PageMaker* (to name two) are used to incorporate color images in pages. High-end CEPS use their own proprietary and often customized prepress software to assemble pages for output.

Let us now turn our attention to the output of color images, beginning with color separation.

COLOR SEPARATION

Color printing, in its most basic expression, involves the overprinting of colored dots at various densities to produce a wide range of secondary colors. Since each individual process color needs to be printed separately, each color needs its own plate. To make a plate, therefore, each color needs its own *negative*. The conversion of a full-color *continuous-tone* photograph (or other image) to a series of (typically four) individual color negatives or *positives* is called *color separation*.

Traditional Color Separation. Until the early 20th century, "full-color printing" typically involved printing an image in black and white and hand-coloring it. Color print-

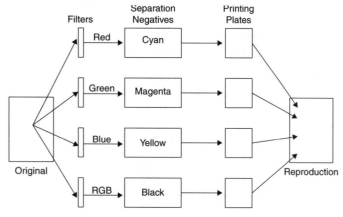

The four-color printing process requires that an original color image be separated (by means of colored filters) into the four plates needed for printing.

In digital color separation, RGB values are converted to CMY values by taking the negative values of the red, green, and blue signals.

ing as such was limited for the most part to what we now refer to as "spot color," or single localized portions of solid color that can be laid down exactly as black ink is. Advancements in photography—such as the various "processes" (the Dufay process and Warner-Powrie process, to name two)—eventually led to the relatively easy and inexpensive "process color" printing. Traditional color separations were performed either manually or, more often, photographically. Essentially, a full-color image (either *reflection copy*—such as a print—or *transmission copy*—such as a *transparency*) was photographed three times, through a red filter (which produced the cyan film), a blue filter (which produced the yellow film), and a green filter (which produced the magenta film). An additional film—black—was also needed to add shading and contrast. These four films—called *printer*s—could then be used to make plates. Often additional manual *color correction* (such as *dot etching*) was required to adjust any *hue error*s generated by the color separation process. (The shorthand term for these four process colors—*CMYK*—is the acronym of the three subtractive color primaries plus "K" for black. The "K" stands for *key*, as it was the *black printer* that was printed first and used as a guide for the subsequent *registration* of the other colors.) See *COLOR PLATE 16*.

Digital Color Separation. In the late 1970s and early 1980s, Scitex and other vendors began introducing *color electronic prepress system*s (CEPS), which quickly rendered photographic color separation processes virtually obsolete. In addition, the prevalence of the *PostScript* device-independent *page description language* has made digital color separations of higher quality and greater ease. Desktop systems—personal computers, either *IBM-compatible computer*s or Apple Macintoshes—using off-the-shelf *page makeup software* such as QuarkXPress or PageMaker are now able to generate high-quality color film or paper output. Where once high-quality color prepress was strictly the purview of high-end color electronic publishing systems, relatively inexpensive desktop systems can easily rival that quality.

Digital color separation typically functions by means of converting from one *color space* (such as CIE, RGB, or *YCC*) to the CMYK color space. (Actually, the initial conversion is to just the CMY color space; black is added later.) It is not easy to construct an algorithm that will easily convert to CMY, however; the fact that the CMY color space is a subtractive system while all the others are additive systems creates difficulties, as does the fact that printing inks and other printing variables do not act or function with the mathematical precision of a computer algorithm. In theory (and in *PostScript Level 1*), it should be possible to convert from RGB to CMY simply by subtracting the red, the green, and the blue values to get the corresponding "negative" colors (the CMY colors), but that does not work in actual practice. More complex mathematical formulas with several variables have been proposed, but the computing power needed to perform these calculations for *each pixel* of an image makes such an approach far too unwieldy. Instead, the computer (or, usually, a high-end scanner) makes use of *color lookup table*s (or *CLUT*s), which are basically lists of a number of CMY values that have been experientially determined to be the equivalent colors to the RGB (or other) colors. Since a CLUT that included every single match would still be far too unwieldy, some representative samples are included, and any RGB colors that do not have an exact match in CMY are determined computationally by interpolation. Naturally, this leaves the process open to error; the more entries in the CLUT, the more accurate the conversion. *PostScript Level 2* uses the CLUT approach to remapping the colors. Even the use of a CLUT takes a great deal of time, however, so the computations are only done very seldomly; typically, the colors are recalculated only when the scanner is recalibrated, and the same color conversions are used for most images, with some post-scan color correction performed to rectify any egregious errors.

Desktop computers that utilize CLUTs typically have much fewer entries (as they commonly lack the processing power of a scanner), but sophisticated interpolation algorithms can make it very accurate indeed. Different programs handle the CMYK conversion differently. Adobe Photoshop, for example, uses the CIE x,y,Y values prescribed by *SWOP* standards. The default values may need to be changed, depending upon the ink and substrate to be utilized. Or, some *plug-in*s and *extension*s (such as *Efi-Color*, *Kodak CMS*, and *Agfa FotoFlow*, and Pantone Open Color Environment, among other *color management system*s) can also reduce user input as much as possible. Also, since the use of CLUTs is a CPU-intensive process, accelerator boards are available for a number of different computer *platform*s that can help make color separation take less time to accomplish.

An additional process required in color separation is the generation of the black printer. Although most of the colors produced in process color printing are produced by combinations of CMY, black is added to increase the density range of the reproduction and to reduce the amount of the more expensive process inks that need to be used.

Essentially, the theory behind the various processes of *undercolor removal (UCR)* and *gray component replacement (GCR)* is as follows: one or two of the three process colors is a dominant hue in any given color. The remaining primary (or primaries) serves to make that color darker, as it (or they) is a complementary color and as such serves to add gray to the dominant hue. (In subtractive color theory, a color plus its complementary color equals neutral gray.) Since that is the only function the complementary color has, it is less expensive to simply replace that complementary color with black. So, for example, UCR replaces the primary colors in dark shadow areas, to save on process ink and to avoid exceeding the *maximum overprint*, an upper limit to the amount of ink per dot imposed on web offset printers, so as to reduce the incidence of ink smearing, to which web offset lithography is especially prone. Although UCR reduces some of the contrast and detail in shadow regions,

it tends to improve ink *trapping* and makes the *color balance* more stable, as it eliminates the *color drift* or hue shift that can occur with process inks. (By the way, there is also an *undercolor addition [UCA]*, which can be used to *add* process color dots to dark shadow areas of an image.)

A more thorough version of UCR is GCR, which replaces the gray component of complementary primaries throughout the entire tonal range of an image. The best results are usually obtained with 50% GCR; a greater percentage can lead to undesired color shifts. A problem with GCR, however, is an increased difficulty in evaluating color separations before printing. Black plates used in images that have undergone GCR also need to be moved farther back in the *printing sequence*, and the black printer needs to be more carefully controlled on press than usual; even the slightest deviation in ink density or dot gain can cause color problems. See *Color Plate 27*.

Another important aspect of proper color separation is *gray balance*. By ensuring—prior to conversion to CMYK—that the gray balance is correct, any *color cast* (or unwanted dominant hue) can be avoided. See *Color Plate 19*.

Extra-Trinary Colors. One of the problems with the subtractive primaries is their limited color *gamut*, especially in orange-red, green, and blue-violet regions. For this reason, additional plates are added to multicolor printing presses. Particularly in packaging applications, additional process color plates are added to expand the color gamut available. (Many presses used in *flexography*, for example, have up to six *printing unit*s, which can thus add three colors beyond the basic CMY colors.)

There are several means of expanding the process color printing range: *color substitution* retains the use of four colors, but the standard CMY colors are replaced with alternate colors that more closely match important colors in the original image; *bump plate*s add additional plates of cyan, magenta, and yellow to the basic three or four, which often print as solids in overprint areas, increasing the density range possible; and *touch plate*s add special colors beyond CMYK to emphasize unique colors in the original (such as a corporate logo or color scheme, for example). See *Color Plate 23*.

A number of vendors provide software plug-ins that can effect the production of bump or touch plates, and companies such as Scitex, Linotype-Hell, and PANTONE have created extra-trinary colorants that can be used to supplement the basic three. However, different CLUTs need to be used when extra-trinary colors are added; not only must the new separations be made, but existing dot values need to be altered as well, lest the original color values become distorted. Additionally, special halftone screening techniques need to be employed, to generate the most efficacious screen angles for the new colors so as to avoid moiré patterns. Stochastic screening (also called *FM screening*) eliminates the occurrence of moiré entirely and is often used when printing extra-trinary colors.

COLOR OUTPUT

Most digital output devices these days use the PostScript page description language to control the output of documents, both color and black-and-white. PostScript is essentially a programming language that creates precise mathematical descriptions of graphical objects, ensuring that all page elements are transferred exactly as specified to an output device. PostScript also implements algorithms for halftone screening. In terms of color, PostScript converts RGB or images in other color spaces to CMYK by means of CLUTs or the CIE color space. The advantage of PostScript is its device-independence; any output device that possesses a PostScript interpreter can output it. The page descriptions remain essentially immutable and in "user space"; the PostScript code is merely translated by the device ***driver***, which executes the code. Another advantage to PostScript is that it can render graphical objects and type on the same page; since the type and images are both converted to ***vector graphics***, the same means of describing them can be used. The advantage to this is, in typography, smooth characters. When adding scanned images to a page, PostScript creates a vector-based ***bounding box*** around the image, and the image itself is mapped to the page, retaining the original information such as its position, its ***resolution***, the color values for each pixel, and definitions of how to translate those color values into a particular color space.

PostScript printer drivers are provided by the computer platform or the application program, not by the output device. Therefore, PostScript files are independent of a particular output device. However, a particular file must be compatible with the output device's maximum paper size, image size, and resolution. There are several ways of outputting color separation films on an imagesetter or film recorder: (1) an RGB image can be converted to a CMYK composite image by the desktop software, and the RIP itself can remove the separate color components and generate the four films; (2) an RGB image can be converted to CMYK using the desktop software, and saved as ***five-file EPS*** using the ***Desktop Color Separation (DCS)*** format, and the RIP can process and output each color film separately; or (3) an RGB image can be sent directly to the output device, where the RIP performs the color separations using the PostScript color rendering dictionary. The process used will depend on several variables. For example, images destined for conventional platemaking and printing processes require separate color films, so a composite image will need to be color-separated either by the software (i.e., DCS) or by the imagesetter, but not all imagesetters can separate composite images. Composite images may either be in TIFF or EPS format, but separated colors must be in the DCS/EPS format, as TIFF does not at the moment support separated images. Images destined for digital printing devices, however, do not require separate plates, as they extract their own color information when printing. Therefore, a CMYK composite image is fine. Extra-trinary colors create their own brands of problems, as each additional color will require its own plate and, therefore, its own separation film. The additional color must also not be converted to process color, and the image bearing the additional color needs to be saved in a separate EPS file.

As was mentioned earlier, in the section on halftoning, before imaging actually occurs, the material to be imaged needs to be converted to ***raster*** format, or a ***bitmap***. It may at first seem somewhat illogical to spend so much time worrying about vector graphics and converting bitmaps to vectors when everything is only going to become a bitmap again anyway, but the bitmap grid used by imagesetters and film recorders is so much finer (i.e., the printer spots are so much smaller) than monitor or laser printer bitmaps, that it is not illogical at all. Essentially, the RIP analyzes the PostScript file and uses the page descriptions embedded therein to determine which spots on the raster grid will need to be exposed, and which will remain unexposed. Once that is determined, the laser in the recording section can expose the film or paper according to that raster pattern. When you consider how many individual printer spots there are in even a small image or page, it becomes obvious that a lot of processing power is required, and that RIPing is quite a time-consuming process. Both of these assumptions are true. Nowhere it is more evident than in the imaging of tints and gradations. A gradation is essentially a series of lines of successively changing tonal values. (A continuous ***gray scale*** is an example of a gradation.) Each line then becomes a separate graphical object, and the RIP or PostScript interpreter needs to process each one of them. The larger the gradation, the longer it takes to process, and the more likely a system crash is, as the processor becomes overloaded. Another problem, once RIPing and outputting is completed, is ***banding***, or the visibility of the discrete steps in the gradation, commonly caused by too-few available gray levels for smooth transitions.

When preparing color separation films for output, an important consideration is that of ***trapping***, or insuring against potential ***misregister*** of adjacent colors or images when on press. Misregister is often caused by paper and press problems (such as paper possessing low ***dimensional stability***), and an experienced anticipation of likely degrees of misregister can save a lot of time and trouble. Trapping, which also refers to a slight modification of abutting images to ensure that there is a slight degree of overlap when they print, was historically effected photographically by means of ***spreads and chokes***, or enlarging of images that would be overprinted *within* another image, and a reduction of the "hole" that image is designed to print in. Spreads and chokes are far more effective and less time-consuming when performed on the desktop, and special effects such as blends can be used to create traps. Some high-end CEPS use trapping utilities during output, which can take the form of ***vector trapping*** in which whole graphical objects are added where needed; ***raster trapping*** in which additional pixels or printer spots are added by the RIP after rasterization; or ***hybrid trapping***, which involves adding new graphical objects pixel by pixel after rasterizing. Automatic trapping tends to be more effective than desktop trapping, but the cost of these utilities is prohibitive for many uses. It is best, actually, to leave trapping up to a service bureau, as they will be more likely to know the dynamics of the press and paper the job will be printed on, and can make better judgments about the type and extent of the trapping required.

COLOR PROOFING

Since the goal of *proofing* is to spot any errors—egregious or otherwise—it is of course necessary for a *color proof* to resemble as closely as possible the final printed product and, in fact, replicating the printing process to be used and the *substrate* it is to be printed on is the best means of proofing there is. Not knowing how the colors and halftone dots will behave on press with a particular ink and paper combination can set one up for some unpleasant surprises, which may be a waste of time and money.

Proofing commonly takes place at several different stages in the production process. The earliest proofs are primarily design proofs; the designer of the piece checks the design and layout of the pages and page elements with the client, to ensure that the client's specifications have been met. Later stages in the proofing process, commonly following typesetting, check for *typographical error*s and additional aspects of the final design. Color proofs themselves typically begin immediately after color separation. In the earliest color proofs, the separations are often ganged on one substrate along with other illustrations to show how they have been made and how they will reproduce at the size desired. (These are sometimes called *random proof*s or *scatter proof*s). Various proofs are generated once the illustrations have been incorporated with the text and other page elements. *Comprehensive*s and *mechanical*s are also often used as proofs of one kind or another. In addition to these *hard proof*s is also a *soft proof*, which is really little more than a color image as it is displayed on a computer monitor. Soft proofs are useful in that changes can be instantaneously made and the time and expense of generating hard proofs are eliminated.

Digital proofing confers its share of advantages and disadvantages to the proofing process. The advantages include the ability to quickly create relatively high-quality proofs at early stages in the design and prepress processes, allowing for the correction of problems and errors before sending the digital files to a service bureau or making expensive films. There are three means by which digital proofs are made:

• *Electrostatic*. Electrostatic systems basically involve color laser printers, which are fast and economical. A drawback is that the resolution of laser printers is still fairly low.

• *Ink Jet*. High-end ink-jet printers can be used to reasonably replicate the appearance of halftones, although one major drawback to ink-jet printers of all types is that the liquid ink, if not printed on specially formulated paper, spreads and bleeds rather badly.

• *Dye Sublimation*. Dye-sublimation printers use colored waxes that are heated by small resistors and melted onto a substrate in image areas. Although, like most other proofing systems, they have a hard time simulating halftone screens, they do reproduce images very well as continuous tones with color densities that are very accurate. Their drawback is their need for special coated papers, which tend to be more expensive than the papers required for other proofing methods.

Digital proofing is particularly useful in the early stages of production when frequent alteration is still likely. During the prepress stage, however, *prepress proof*s are more commonly prepared photomechanically using the color separation negatives. There are two basic types of color proofs made from the color separation negatives: *overlay color proof*s include film positives of each color on sheets of transparent *acetate* and are "overlayed" on top of each other, to show how the full-color image looks with the separations. An alternative is a *single-sheet color proof*, which uses photographic paper and dye-transfer printing to make positives of each color separation negative, which are laminated together to form a single colored sheet. (They are commonly called *Cromalin* proofs, after the brand of photographic paper used to make them.) These proofs are also used to ensure that there are no extraneous specks or other blemishes on the films. Photomechanical proofs are quick to make and very closely approximate the finished product. However, some photomechanical proofs provide a misleading degree of gloss, which tends to make the finished product somewhat of a disappointment. Matte-finished proofing papers can reduce this, however.

Once plates have been prepared, a *press proof* is occasionally made, most effectively using the intended press, inks, and substrates. These commonly constitute a *contract proof* (also known as a *color OK* proof or an *OK sheet*), which is what the client signs off on and what he or she will expect when the job is completed. These latter proofs are used as guides throughout the printing and finishing processes. Press proofs are now more often than not prepared on special *proof press*es, which are small, sheetfed presses that can quite rapidly be set up for printing. The actual plates are mounted, the actual ink(s) may be used, and the actual substrate is used. The disadvantages to proof presses, however, are that they tend to print with less dot gain (the *squeeze* is lighter on proof presses than on production presses) and with heavier ink weights. This often can result in a misleadingly good-looking press proof that may actually be impossible to replicate on the production press. (See also *Color Proofing*.)

PRINTING

Full-color printing is possible utilizing all of the basic printing processes—*letterpress*, *offset lithography*, *gravure*, *flexography*, and *screen printing*—and each has its strengths and weaknesses with regard to color printing. (See the individual entries for each process.)

Various types of digital color printing have emerged in recent years, most designed primarily for short-run jobs. Although there has been a great deal of interest in "on-demand printing," digital printing devices are not as fast or economical as the conventional printing processes, nor do they (yet) produce as high a quality. These new processes are likely to find a niche in the in-house markets, the just-in-time markets, prototyping, and other limited-run applications. Their main advantage is their ability to accept digital data directly from the computer, which allows them to function essentially as peripheral devices. (See *Ink Jet*, *Dye Sublimation*, and *Laser Printer*.)

Some high-volume digital printers utilize dry or wet *electrophotography* (the same principle at work in a laser printer). The Xeikon DCP-1 uses up to eight printing units, and can image up to 2,100 pages an hour. Front ends by Agfa add OPI capabilities, color management, and raster image processing. The Indigo E-Print, a liquid-toner-based electrophotographic imaging system, can print at high resolutions with good highlight detail and no dot gain.

An interesting wrinkle on conventional offset lithography is the Heidelberg GTO-DI, which is essentially a small offset press that utilizes direct-imaged waterless plates, etched by a laser driven by digital information. The image resolution is comparable to that which can be obtained on an imagesetter. (See *Direct-to-Plate*.)

Color, Paper

A paper (or other material) will absorb light of only certain wavelengths, depending on its chemical composition, and reflect the remaining wavelengths back toward the observer. These reflected wavelengths are a paper's color. Dyes or other fillers added to white paper are the chief determinants of a paper's color. The human eye alone is insufficient for the proper determination of a color value of a particular paper, and a color value will also vary based on the type of illumination used, so carefully cut paper samples are put in color-matching booths, where *TAPPI*-prescribed levels of illumination (i.e., simulated daylight) are shined on a paper at right angles to its surface. It is important in color matching that the paper samples themselves be chosen with care; the paper samples should all have the same *grain direction*, and the same side (either *felt side* or *wire side*) should be illuminated. A *spectrophotometer* is an instrument that analyzes the reflected light from a paper surface wavelength by wavelength, and generates a *spectral reflectance curve*, or a graph of the degree of light reflectivity from a paper's surface against each individual wavelength along the visible spectrum.

In the human eye and brain, color is a subjective quality. An objective measurement, in addition to spectrophotometry and specular reflectance curves, involves the use of color-matching scales, which plot the degree of reflectance of the three primary colors—red, green, and blue—on a three-axis graph. These "tristimulus values" are used to define a color. (See *CIE L*a*b** scales.) Other scales use degree of blackness or whiteness, a degree of

redness or greenness, and a degree of yellowness or blueness (in other words, color oppositions). (See also *Hunter L,a,b values*.)

Colorant

The portion of a printing ink that imparts to the ink its color or *hue*, comprising *pigment* and/or *dye*. See *Pigment*.

Color Balance

In *process color* printing, ensuring a consistent ratio of the process colors of *cyan*, *magenta*, and *yellow* so as to keep all *hue*s uniform and prevent *color cast* or other types of discoloration. (See COLOR PLATE 19.)

Color Bars

A set of colored bars forming a video picture, used to calibrate a video camera or playback device. Color bars are used to set the *chrominance*, *luminance*, and *color balance*.

Color Blind

In photography, an alternate term for *blue-sensitive* film. See *Blue Sensitive*.

Color Break

The division of a single-color page proof (such as a *blueline*) to ensure that the appropriate colors will ultimately print in the correct places.

Color Burn-Out

A printing defect characterized by an undesirable discoloration of a printing ink, either in a standing quantity of the ink itself or on the printed piece, caused either by the chemical incompatibility and reaction of disparate ink components or by heat produced in a stack of printed pieces that interferes with the *oxidation* of the wet ink.

Color Calibration

A means of setting a computer monitor, scanner, or color printer to a standard set of color values so as to ensure that all the colors remain consistent throughout each step of the imaging process. This can often be aided by using a *color management system (CMS)*.

Color Cast

A *color* imbalance resulting in an overall discoloration of a reproduction (or the original), caused by a preponderance of one color (light or pigment) over the others. Color cast commonly manifests itself as a bluish red, pinkish blue, etc. A color cast affecting an original image may need to be color-corrected after scanning. A color cast may also be observable in a video picture. (See COLOR PLATE 19.)

Color Chart

A set of *color swatch*es, or samples of printed color that are used to accurately mix, match, choose, and communicate a particular color. These color swatches vary from each other in varying amounts of *cyan*, *magenta*, *yellow* and **black** inks, and each sample can commonly be closely replicated according to predetermined formulas for its mixing. The swatches can also refer to premixed colors or **spot color**s.

Color Circle

A circular chart illustrating all the colors of the **visible spectrum** in sequential order by wavelength. Complementary—or opposite—colors are opposite each other. Also known as a **color wheel**. See COLOR PLATE 6. See also **GATF Color Chart**.

Color Coding

Any means of identifying parts of a set using colored marks, paper, ink, etc.

Color Comp Print

A photographic print made from a **transparency**, used for layout and proofing purposes.

Color Compression

The reduction of the **color gamut** of an original image so as to enable it to be reproduced using the ink, paper, and printing equipment on hand.

In digital imaging, *color compression* refers to the practice of reducing of the amount of data comprising an image by removing data that is redundant or extraneous, as a means of speeding up the processing of the image or the amount of disk space occupied by the file. (See **Data Compression**.)

Color Computer

Any part of a computer program, **scanner**, or other imaging device that calculates the amount of each colorant—be it **CMYK** or **RGB**—required to replicate a particular color image. Such calculations can involve the use of **masking equations**, **Neugebauer equations**, or **color lookup tables**.

Color Control Bar

A test strip comprising a series of **grayscale** and **color** patches printed onto a **substrate** as a means of ensuring proper and uniform **color balance** during printing. One commonly used color control bar is the **GATF Standard Offset Color Bar**.

Color Correction

Any means of altering one or more **color**s in a scanned or photographed image so as to fix any undesirable tonal variations that may have accrued during imaging, to keep within the range of ink colors available, or for other reasons (such as customer request, etc.). Color correction can be accomplished photographically, manually, or digitally (in **paint program**s such as Adobe Photoshop, for example). Color correction is related to **retouching**, and can be either **global correction** (performed on the entire image) or **local correction** (performed only on specific portions of the image).

Color Corrector

In video production, a device used, often in conjunction with a **vectorscope**, to adjust the colors of a video image, as a means of preventing a **color cast** or ensuring proper **color balance**.

Color Coupler

In photography, any of a variety of organic compounds that form **color** images in color photographic films and papers. These compounds are colorless before developing; when a silver halide image is developed following exposure, these compounds mix with by-products of the chemical reactions of the developer and form **cyan**, **magenta**, and **yellow** dyes in proportion to the density of the silver halide developed on the emulsion. Other varieties of color coupling compounds are used in color photographic **negative**s as masking dyes, a **color correction** technique. It is these compounds that result in the pinkish or brownish appearance of color negatives.

Color Cycling Animation

A type of animation technique that creates the effect of movement by altering the **color lookup table**. The animator sequentially assigns colors to portions of the image. The colors in the color lookup table in the video card are rotated, achieving the desired effect. Some programs used to create animations have a menu option facilitating the execution of this function.

Color Depth

On a computer monitor, a term that refers to the **resolution** of the display. Specifically, it refers to how many **color**s can be displayed, which is a function of the number of

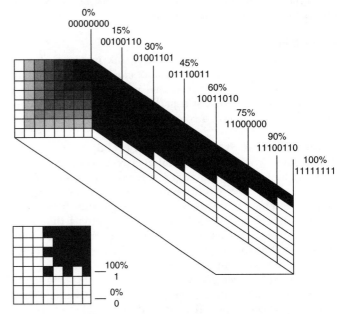

A grayscale image containing a total of 256 shades of gray thus requires eight bits (or one byte) of data per pixel.

*bit*s used to describe each screen *pixel*. (The unit for color depth measurement is thus ***bits per pixel***.) For example, a monitor with a color depth of one bit per pixel can only describe two colors (black or white), while one with a color depth of 24 bits per pixel can describe over sixteen million colors. In ***eight-bit color***, eight bits are used to describe each pixel. Thus, a white pixel (or one with no color) would be represented by the binary code 00000000, while black would be represented by 11111111. All the intermediate colors in the palette (which can often be individually selected or removed, depending on the program in use) would include the various combinations of 1s and 0s among those eight digits, represented mathematically by the figure 2^8, or 256. (White in ***twenty-four-bit color*** is represented as 000000000000000000000000, different colors being represented by different combinations of 1s and 0s among those 24 digits, or 2^{24} colors.) As you can tell, the greater the color depth, the more processing power is required. See ***One-Bit Color***, ***Four-Bit Color***, ***Eight-Bit Color***, ***Sixteen-Bit Color***, ***Twenty-Four-Bit Color***, and ***Thirty-Two-Bit Color***. Color depth is also known as ***pixel depth***. Color depth is also an important issue in *scanning*. See ***Scanning: Principles of Scanning***. Color depth is also called ***pixel depth*** and ***bit depth***.

Color Difference

In video broadcasting, a means of reducing the amount of information that needs to be transmitted by combining the three color components of a video image—red, green, and blue—into two signals. The ***Phase Alternating Line (PAL)*** video system used in Europe utilizes this technique.

Color Display

Any type of computer monitor that can display more than one *color*. See also ***Monochrome***.

Color Drift

The changing of shade of a printing ink *pigment* due to aging or when used to tint another color. Checking the ink by applying a sample of it to the intended *substrate* can determine whether or not a particular ink has undergone, or is likely to undergo, a color drift.

Color Electronic Prepress System (CEPS)

A computer system used to color-correct scanned images and assemble them into pages, a means of accomplishing digitally what has traditionally been done by hand by means of color transparencies and *stripping*. There are many different configurations of CEPS systems that vary by manufacturer. CEPS is distinguished from a desktop system in that the former tends to be high-end, high-quality, and high-cost, and runs on proprietary operating systems and customized software, whereas the latter tends to be less expensive and utilizes off-the-shelf software. As far as quality is concerned, it is now often possible to obtain a quality on a desktop system that is very nearly as high as that possible on a CEPS.

Color Enhancement

Alternate term for ***image enhancement***. See ***Image Enhancement***.

Colorfastness

The ability of a printing ink to resist discoloration and fading upon exposure to light or over time. See ***Lightfastness***. Also called ***color retention***.

Color Film Recorder

See ***Film Recorder***.

Color Filter

See ***Filter***.

Color Fixative

Any of a variety of substances applied to a colored surface to prevent color fading, running, or other deterioration.

Color Gamut

The total range of ***color***s that can be reproduced with a given set of inks (or other colorants), on a given paper stock, and on a given printing press (or other color output) configuration. Also known simply as ***gamut***. Many digital color systems or software programs utilize an ***out-of-gamut alarm*** to alert users that a particular displayed color cannot be output. (See also *Color Plate 4*.)

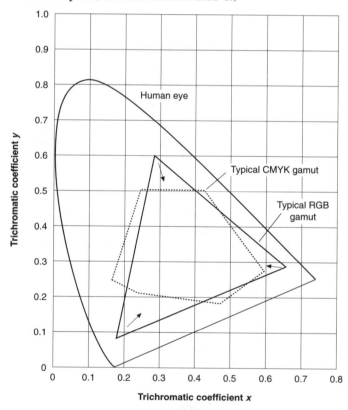

Different color devices are capable of recognizing or reproducing widely different color gamuts.

Color Graphics Adapter (CGA)

An expansion board for *IBM-compatible computer*s that provided 320×200-*pixel* resolution for color monitors (and 640×200-pixel *resolution* for *monochrome* monitors). The CGA provided four-color display, but with an 8×8-pixel cell for text, was incapable of displaying readable text or high-resolution graphics. The CGA was the first color video expansion card for IBM compatibles, but was supplanted by the Hercules Adapter. IBM also superseded CGA with the *Enhanced Graphics Adapter (EGA)*.

Color Guide

Alternate term for *color chart*. See *Color Chart*.

Color Hexagon

In color printing, a hexagon-shaped graph on which is plotted three filter densitometer readings of a color. A color hexagon is often used when comparing different sets of inks, and in the comparison of printed materials to color proofs.

Colorimeter

A device used to accurately measure the *tristimulus values* of a particular *color*. Essentially, a colorimeter consists of a vision field—either located through an eyepiece or directly with the eye—that displays, on one side, the reference—or comparison—color, produced using *red, green, and blue* light beams, the proportions of each one constituting a particular color are indicated on the device. On the second half of the vision field is the color to be tested, and either a human observer or a photoelectric detector is used to evaluate each color for matching purposes.

Colorimetry

The science of objectively quantifying *color*s and measuring the results against colors as they are perceived.

Colorization

The converting of a black-and-white image to a color image, either by hand, photographically, or digitally. *Colorization* also refers to any general changing of colors in an image.

Color-Key

A brand of *acetate*, manufactured by 3M, used for producing *overlay color proof*s. See *Overlay Color Proof*.

Color Lookup Table (CLUT)

A set of computer data containing definitions of the *red, green, and blue* components of displayed colors, used to translate from one *color space* to another, commonly by means of evaluating the correspondence between numeric codes assigned to each color and display codes utilized by the output device. Also known as a *color map*.

Color Management System (CMS)

A set of computer programs or utilities that are used to ensure *color calibration* by accurately translating from one *color space* to another. Color management systems

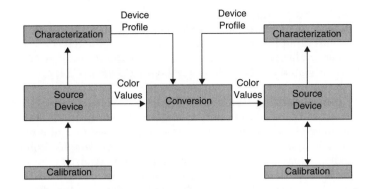

Basic color management scheme. Device profiles for input and output devices instruct the conversion algorithm how to convert one set of color values to another.

ensure consistent *color* throughout the prepress processes by calibrating the color relationships among the *scanner*s, monitors, printers, *imagesetter*s, and other devices in the chain from input to output, usually by creating a *device profile* for each device. There are three primary aspects of a color management system:

- *Device Profiles*. Device profiles utilize *CIE color space* values to represent the *gamut* of colors that can be scanned, displayed, and printed by any of the devices in the system.
- *Converters*. CMS conversion methods convert each device's *device-dependent* color space (which can be either *RGB*, *CMY*, or *CMYK*) to the *device-independent* CIE color space values.
- *Previews*. Software utilities allow for the on-screen previewing of how colors will appear when output from a particular device.

As of this writing, there are currently available four color management systems: *Kodak CMS*, *EfiColor*, *Agfa Foto-Flow*, and the *Pantone Open Color Environment*. The drawback to all of these systems (save Pantone's) is that they need to operate from within a specific application, rather than the *operating system*. Although the number of applications that support a CMS is increasing, the lack of direct operating system integration limits the efficacy of a CMS. A partial solution to this is Apple's *ColorSync*, a system extension that aims to extend the range of one of the above-mentioned systems at the operating system level. Many vendors are now creating their CMS utilities to plug in to ColorSync. Version 2.0 of ColorSync was a major breakthrough in CMS technology, especially in its use of a standard format for device profiles. Essentially, it allows color image files (either *TIFF* or *EPS* format files) to be "tagged" with a description of the color space the file uses and the source of that color data. A number of different vendors—such as Adobe, Agfa, EFI, Kodak, and Pantone—have announced support for the ColorSync 2.0 device profile format.

Color Map

Alternate term for *color lookup table* (commonly abbreviated *CLUT*). See *Color Lookup Table (CLUT)*.

Color Mapping

A form of computer-based *color correction* in which *color* values input into the system are converted to predetermined color values, such as those stored in a *color lookup table* (abbreviated *CLUT*). See *Color Lookup Table* (*CLUT*).

Color Matching System

A set of *color chart*s and/or *swatch*es—either in printed form or as computer-generated samples—used to compare, match, and specify different colors. The color samples typically include the proportions of colored inks required to produce the desired color. Color matching systems are available for both *spot color* and *process color*. (See *PANTONE*, *TRUMATCH*, and *Focoltone*.) Also known as a *color swatching system*.

Color Mixing, Ink

The mixing of inks to match a particular *color* for printing can either be done entirely by the ink manufacturer, primarily done by the manufacturer, with a modest amount of in-house adjustment, or completely performed in-house. When mixing colors in-house, base colors are matched according to *color chart*s and systems provided by ink manufacturers and other color experts. The important factor in color mixing is identifying in which particular color direction a base ink has to go to match the desired color. (For example, yellow ink can range from a greenish yellow to an orangish green; blue can range from purple to green; brown, commonly a dark orange, can either be reddish or yellowish; purple can range from red to blue; and green can range from blue to yellow.) It is also important for the ink mixer to keep on hand a sample of the mixed ink (in case more is needed), a detailed record of how the final color was arrived at, and a *press proof*, an example of how the color prints on the intended *substrate*. There are three basic stages to color mixing: matching, mixing, and testing.

Matching. In matching a color, a color chart (such as a Munsell or Ostwald chart) will indicate the key color, or the color which will form the primary component of the ink mix. A small test sample should be mixed, and a dab of the final ink placed on the intended substrate, to ensure that the ink will retain its color after printing and drying. Careful measurements should be made throughout the test sample mixing, to ensure that when the time comes to make the final batch, the proportions of the mixed colors will produce the same result.

Mixing. The primary ingredients for color mixing are the strong base colors, white inks (*transparent ink*s and *opaque ink*s), black ink, and a neutral gray. By utilizing color charts, the three color measurements—*hue* (the specific wavelength or *shade* of the color), *value* (its degree of darkness or lightness), and *chroma* (its strength)—can be determined and each of these three color aspects can be adjusted by the color mixer. The hue can be adjusted by adding the color that will bring it back in the direction it needs to go. If a blue is too purple, yellow or green may need

to be added. If the value is incorrect, the ink will need to be darkened or lightened, using either black (which has the tendency to dirty an ink, however) or a suitable dark color, or white or suitable light color. If the chroma is incorrect, adding neutral gray can help bring the color purity where it needs to go. Should too much gray be added, the original base color can be added to reverse the graying trend. Another important consideration in color mixing is to ensure that all the ingredients added are compatible chemically and mechanically: inks that dry by *evaporation* should not be mixed with inks that dry by *oxidation*, *heat-set ink*s should not be mixed with *moisture-set ink*s, inks designed for letterpress printing should not be mixed with inks designed for offset lithography, and so forth. Some mixtures can also possess a lesser degree of *permanence* than the constituent inks, a problem not typically noticed until well after the material is printed. For example, some types of yellow pigment will react with *iron blue*, causing the desired shade of green to become increasingly yellow over time. Incompatible inks may also become altered in other ways, such as in *body* and *chemical resistance*.

Testing. Testing of the ink should check three aspects: accurate color, correct drying, and runnability congruent with the printing method to be used, the press speed at which it is to run, the substrate on which it is to be printed, and the desired end-use characteristics of the printed material. Testing can be accomplished by depositing a sample of the mixed ink on a sample of the actual stock to be used (inks will behave differently on different types of paper or other surfaces), either by dabbing a small bit of the ink on the substrate in a thickness approximating the intended thickness of the printed ink film (called *drawdown*, *pat-out*, or *roll-out*), or on a proof-press of the intended printing process. Proper ink drying is commonly evaluated after an appropriate length of time (such as overnight), and the dried ink is examined for proper ink penetration (or *holdout*), *gloss*, *opacity*, and color.

The testing procedures for mixed inks are not foolproof, and the only true way to accurately gauge an ink's performance is to actually duplicate the final print run in as exact a manner as possible.

Color Model

In a graphics system, a means of describing each *color* within the *color gamut* in a particular *color space*. Examples of color models include *PHIGS* (Programmer's Hierarchical Interactive Graphics System) in which the color model is a three-dimensional coordinate system in which every displayable color is represented by a single point plotted on those three axes; *HLS* (hue, lightness, and saturation); *RGB* (red, green, and blue); and *CIELAB* (lightness, redness, and blueness).

Color Negative

A photographic *negative* made using color film from an original image, used to make *color separation*s or produce color prints.

Color Noise

A distortion in the color component of a video signal characterized by bands of color in a picture, caused by low color *bandwidth* or by *color subsampling*.

Color OK

Alternate term for *OK sheet*. See *OK Sheet*.

Color Palette

The range of *primary colors* available to an artist or other graphic designer, which can be mixed in varying amounts to produce additional, *secondary colors*. In a computer color system, the color palette is the full range of colors available in a particular software program or operating system.

Color Portability

In computer graphics, the ease with which *color* images can be transferred from one system or device to another without producing egregious tonal variations.

Color Print

Any photographic print that contains *color*, such as Anscochrome, *Cibachrome*, *dye transfer*, Kodacolor, etc.

Color Process Work

See *Process Color*.

Color Proof

In *process color* printing, a sample of the actual *substrate* to be printed using the inks that will be printed, pulled from the press prior to the actual printing of the job as a means of checking the *color balance*, *registration*, and other aspects of the job that may need to be corrected prior to printing.

Color Reference

In *process color* printing, a means of ensuring proper *color balance* in which standard *process inks* are printed at standard densities on a standard *substrate*.

Color Resolution

A measure of the sharpness of the color in a video image.

Color Retention

Alternate term for *colorfastness*. See *Colorfastness*.

Color Retouching Station

In digital imaging and graphics, a computer workstation at which *color correction* is performed after scanning (or other means of obtaining an image, such as from a *color electronic prepress system*). The digital file is retouched in whatever way is desired or necessary, and the file is output back to the *CEPS* or to another output device. A color retouching station typically does not assemble pages, obtain the images directly (i.e., *scanning*), or output directly.

Color Rotation

Alternate term for *color sequence* or *printing sequence*. See *Printing Sequence*.

Color Scanner

A *scanner* that can digitize color images. See *Scanner*.

Color Scanning System

A device, essentially a high-end *drum scanner*, used to produce *color separation*s comprising a fixed scanning head that picks up light impulses emanating from within a rotating drum (or elsewhere), on the surface of which is mounted the image to be color-separated. The light signals emanating from the original are "read" by the scanning head, separated into primary colors—*cyan*, *magenta*, *yellow*, and *black*—and then written to photographic *negative*s. Color printing requires a separate negative for each of these colors. The scanning software also has the capability of adjusting the contrast, saturation, brightness, and gray balance, increasing the sharpness of the image, or performing automatic *color correction*. Depending on the device, the separations can be output to a page makeup system, as *halftone* positives, halftone negatives, etc. (See *Scanning*.)

ColorSense

A color management program used in combination with Apple Computer's *ColorSync* to ensure that colors are kept consistent among the various components of the system—scanners, monitors, and printers. Not as powerful as some other *color management system*s available, ColorSense achieves its best results with simple applications.

Color Separation

A means of dividing a full-*color* photograph into four separate components, corresponding to the four *primary colors* used in *process color* printing—*cyan*, *magenta*, *yellow*, and *black*. Process color printing involves overprinting *halftone dot*s of each of these four colors in varying densities, the various combinations producing the wide range of reproducible colors. Consequently, a different printing plate needs to be made of each color, and this, in turn, requires separate *negative*s or *positive*s. (The term *color separation* refers to both the process and the products of that process.) The process of color separation can be accomplished photographically, electronically, or on the desktop.

Photographic Color Separation. Before the advent of electronic and digital prepress systems, all color separations were made photographically by exposing a full-color *continuous-tone* image through a series of *red*, *green*, and *blue* filters to sheets of unexposed film. Each filter would expose only that primary color in the image as a film negative, and the resulting film positive would contain the complementary—or opposite—color. The red filter images the red areas of the image on the negative, and the positive will thus contain the complementary—or opposite—color, cyan.

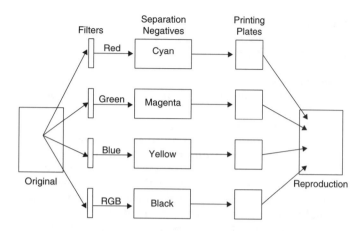

The four-color printing process requires that an original color image be separated (by means of colored filters) into the four plates needed for printing.

In digital color separation, RGB values are converted to CMY values by taking the negative values of the red, green, and blue signals.

The green filter images the green areas of the image on the negative, and the resulting positive will contain its opposite, magenta. And the blue filter images only the blue components of the image and the resulting positive will contain its opposite, yellow. In order to increase **contrast**, a fourth separation, black, is made to darken **shadow** areas and grays. When black is used, the other three colors are reduced proportionally, so as to effect proper ink transfer on press. Plates can be images from the negatives, the positives being used for proofing purposes. Often, however, **color correction** is required, and the process of **dot etching** is performed to improve specific regions of the image. Often, when using photographic separations, different regions of an image required different color densities, so it was not unusual for many different pieces of color-separated film to be spliced together, each of which had been photographed in a slightly different manner from different regions of the image.

For this reason, electronic color separation caught on quickly, and little photographic separation is performed any longer.

Electronic Color Separation. In the late 1970s and early 1980s, high-end **color electronic prepress system**s heralded the age of electronic color separation. In essence, an original (preferably a **transparency**) is mounted to the drum of a **drum scanner**, and a light source analyzes the image **pixel** by pixel. (In some early scanners, the light source could only detect one of the three RGB elements at any one time, so three passes were required; later scanners were able to split a single light beam into individual RGB signals.) All of the red components of an image are stored in the device as a range of gray values, which is essentially the range of reds. Similarly, all the green and all of the blue elements are also stored as series of grays.

At this point, one of several things can happen. Since in electronic scanning the RGB images become digital data and are no longer subject to the action of real light, converting them to **CMY** is tricky. (Adding the black becomes another issue, as well.) In older scanners, software in the scanner itself converted the RGB data to CMYK data, using algorithms that were proprietary and varied from scanner vendor to scanner vendor. These early scanners also output the color separation film immediately after scanning, utilizing a second drum inside the device. (This "double-action scanner" is rarely used today, except in cases where the film will actually be stripped into **flat**s, a technique that is quickly being replaced by electronic page layout programs.) Alternately, the RGB data can be stored in the prepress system's central computer and later output as CMYK data to a separate **film recorder**. Or, the RGB data can be sent to the central computer, and then to a graphics workstation for retouching, manipulation, and incorporation with text and other page elements into a finished page. Then, the color separation can be effected by the page makeup program and output with the rest of the page.

In the late 1980s, as desktop computers became more powerful and software made it easier to lay out pages and manipulate scanned images, desktop color separation began to increase in frequency.

Desktop Color Separation. The power and speed of **microcomputer**s, coupled with the strength of off-the-shelf **page layout software** such as **PageMaker** and **QuarkXPress**, and **PostScript**-based **imagesetter**s, enabled high-quality color output at a fraction of the cost of high-end proprietary color prepress systems. Although, at the beginning, color separation algorithms used by these desktop systems could not approach the quality of those possible on high-end systems, that is no longer the case. Desktop color separation functions almost identically to the high-end electronic separation, the primary difference being that scanners used on desktop systems cannot perform separations "on-the-fly"; they must be performed after scanning, adding a step to the process. After scanning, the image is imported into an image processing program, such as Photoshop, and any color corrections or further manipulation is performed. The grayscale data for each RGB channel is merged, so a full-color RGB image is displayed, although each channel can often be edited separately. (And using only three channels—rather than four for CMYK images—reduces the file size and processing requirements during editing, which expedites matters considerably.) The image can then be imported into a page makeup program. (Often, a **low-resolution file** is displayed at this stage. Since the monitor can only display at very low resolutions, there is no real need to use the actual **high-resolution file**, which would only slow down the system. Later, during output, the high-resolution file will be substituted.) After pages are made up, the application can effect the conversion to CMYK. The use of a **color management system** can help ensure that the colors are remapped from RGB to CMYK effectively; since a computer monitor can only display in RGB mode, what you see may be far removed from what you ultimately get. Various *digital color proof*s can be generated before actual output, which can approximate fairly closely the actual colors that will be output.

Actual separation films are output on an imagesetter (also itself known as a film recorder), where it can then be sent for platemaking, stripping, or other prepress activity.

Color Separation Negative

In *color* prepress, a black-and-white *negative* that contains an image corresponding only to the amount of a single color required to reproduce a full-color original. Full-color images are printed using four separate colors—*cyan*, *magenta*, *yellow*, and *black*—that are combined in varying amounts to produce all the interstitial colors. Consequently, a full-color original needs to undergo *color separation*, a photographic or digital means of reducing a color image to its four component colors and producing negatives for each of them. Four color separation negatives are required for *process color* work. A color separation negative is also called a *printer*. (See *Color Separation*.)

Color Sequence

An alternate term for *printing sequence*. See *Printing Sequence*.

Color Solid

A three-dimensional (or two-dimensional representation of a three-dimensional) system for plotting the three *tristimulus value*s of a *color*, which uses x, y, and z axes to plot *hue*, *saturation*, and *value*.

Color Space

A three-dimensional coordinate system that plots three different *color* qualities (generally *hue*, *value*, and *chroma*, but the names vary according to the specific color system) on x, y, and z axes. Thus, any given color sample can be quantitatively measured, plotted, and consequently described by a single point located somewhere on the coordinate system. Specific color spaces utilized include the *CIE color space* and *Munsell color space*.

Color Standard

A means of evaluating the *color* of an ink for color-matching purposes, consisting of a sample of the wet ink or a printed proof to which another sample is compared.

Color Station

On a multicolor press, an individual set of rollers and cylinders used for printing each specific *color*, comprising inking rollers, dampening rollers (in *offset lithography*), a *plate cylinder* (in offset lithography and *flexography*), a *gravure cylinder* (in *gravure* printing), and a *blanket cylinder* (in offset lithography). A two-color press has two color stations, a four-color press has four color stations, and so on. Depending upon the press configuration, each color station may have its own *impression cylinder* or the

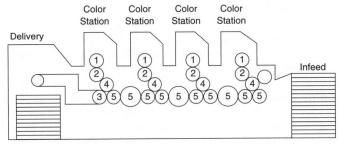

1. Plate Cylinder
2. Blanket Cylinder
3. Delivery Cylinder
4. Impression Cylinder
5. Transfer Cylinder

Multicolor offset press with four color stations.

press as a whole may have a single large-diameter *common impression cylinder* that brings the substrate in contact with each color station successively.

Color Strength

A measure of the concentration of *pigment* or other *colorant* in a printing ink to the total weight or volume of the ink. (See also *Tinctorial Strength*.)

Color Subsampling

A means of reducing the *bandwidth* of a color video image by reducing the *color resolution* of the *chrominance* of the image to a value lower than that of the *luminance* prior to transmission. The original color resolution is restored upon reception and display of the image. An undesired consequence of color subsampling is *color noise*.

Color Substitution

A means of adding *extra-trinary color*s to *process color* printing. Color substitution replaces one or more of the traditional *cyan*, *magenta*, or *yellow* primary colors with colors more closely matching special colors found in the original image. Color substitution is widely used in packaging. See *Extra-Trinary Color*. (See also *Touch Plate* and *Bump Plate*.)

Color Swatch

A sample of a specific *color*—either printed or stored digitally—used to describe a particular printing ink or combination of printing ink colors.

Color Swatching System

Alternate term for *color matching system*. See *Color Matching System*.

ColorSync

A system *extension* developed by Apple Computer for the *Macintosh* that is designed to facilitate color management for all attached devices and their respective color spaces. See *Color Management System*.

Color Synthesis

The formation of a wide range of *secondary colors* from a small number of *primary colors*, by either additive or subtractive means. See *Additive Color Theory* and *Subtractive Color Theory*.

Color Temperature

A means of *color* evaluation utilizing the temperature (in degrees *Kelvin*) to which a black object would need to be heated in order to produce light of a certain wavelength (or color). Substances, when heated, will tend to incandesce—or, in other words, as their constituent atoms or molecules absorb increasing amounts of energy, they will emit light and the wavelength of that light will vary by temperature and by substance. Iron, for example, when heated, emits light that is pale red; heated further, it emits white, then blue light. The black object described in terms of the evaluation of color temperature is essentially a theoretical "perfect *blackbody*," a substance so black that it absorbs all the light that strikes it. In theory, as it increases in temperature, it will emit colors in a predictable manner. For example, at 2000 Kelvin (or 2000 K), it will emit red light;

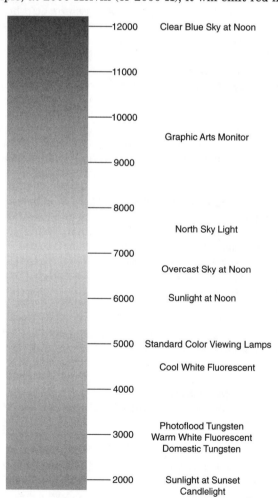

Range of color temperatures, in degrees Kelvin.

12000	Clear Blue Sky at Noon
11000	
10000	Graphic Arts Monitor
9000	
8000	
7000	North Sky Light
6000	Overcast Sky at Noon
5000	Sunlight at Noon
	Standard Color Viewing Lamps
	Cool White Fluorescent
4000	
3000	Photoflood Tungsten
	Warm White Fluorescent
	Domestic Tungsten
2000	Sunlight at Sunset
	Candlelight

at 5000 K, it will emit white light; and at 10,000 K, it will emit blue light.

Light bulbs are often described in terms of their color temperature, as it is the heating of specific substances within them that actually produces the light. A generic 100-watt incandescent bulb (which essentially produces light by heating its tungsten filament until it glows brightly) has a color temperature of 2860 K. Direct sunlight—which produces white light, or light possessing an even distribution of wavelengths (or colors)—has a color temperature of about *5000 K*, and is considered an important characteristic of the *standard viewing conditions* for the evaluation of color.

Color Transparency

In photography, a *color* original reproduced on color photographic film, characterized by the need for light to pass *through* the image in order for it to be viewed, also known as *transmission copy*. A common example of a color transparency is the Ektachrome slide, which is also—albeit inappropriately—called a *chrome*. See *Transparency*.

Color Value

See *Value*.

Color Wheel

Alternate term for *color circle*. See *Color Circle*.

Column

A vertical area of running text on a page. In *page layout software*, text that spans the entire width of a page is considered as a column, although a column is conventionally thought of as some fractional division of a page. The width of a column should be based on type size and legibility and is a function of *line length*. See *Line Length*.

Column is also used to describe any vertical row of data.

Column Balance

A feature of some *page layout program*s that has the ability to automatically spread text among columns on a page in such a way that all columns are of equal length.

Column Chart

A chart in which information and data are presented as vertical bars.

Column Gutter

Alternate term for *gutter*. See *Gutter* (second definition).

Column Head

A heading used to identify the entries to be placed in a *column*.

Column Inch

In newspaper and magazine publishing, a measurement unit of area equal to the width of a text column by one inch high. Total column inches—calculated as a means of determining advertising costs—is arrived at by multiplying the total depth of inches by the number of columns.

Column Justify

In typesetting, setting columnar data to fit a predetermined depth and to align with other other columns on the page.

Column Move

In typesetting or *page layout program*s, the ability to move an entire column of text horizontally and/or vertically.

Column Move/Delete

In a typesetting system or *page layout program*, the ability to manipulate and/or delete characters vertically within a column with a minimal number of separate commands.

Column Rule

In typography, a thin vertical line occasionally used to separate columns of type.

Column Snaking

In a typesetting system or *page layout program*, the ability to create multiple columns of text while allowing the text to wrap from column to column.

Column Space

Alternate term for the *gutter* between columns of text on a single page. See *Gutter*.

Column Wrap

In a typesetting system or *page layout program*, the ability to make a change, addition, or deletion to one column of text and have all successive columns adjust themselves accordingly.

COM

In *DOS*, a *coded set* that indicates a *serial port*, often followed by a number when the computer has more than one serial port. When configuring applications—such as communications programs—it is necessary to specify which serial port a *modem* is connected to. The specification *COM1*, for example, indicates that it is connected to the first serial port.

In computing, *COM* is also an abbreviation for *Computer Output Microfilm*. See *Computer Output Microfilm (COM)*.

Comb

A horizontal *rule* with a user-specifiable number of smaller vertical rules.

Comb Binding

A means of *mechanical binding* in which pages are bound together by means of a plastic comb. This comb consists of a plastic strip off of which extend a series of curved plastic prongs, which are inserted into drilled or punched

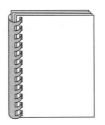
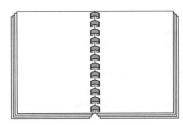

Comb binding.

holes along the *binding edge* of the pages. See *Mechanical Binding*. Also known as *plastic comb binding*.

Comber

A device—usually a set of wheels—used on a printing press, folder, or other sheetfed machine to fan out blank or printed sheets so they will feed one sheet at a time, preventing jams. Also known as *comber wheels*.

Comber Marks

A defect of printed products that have been run through a folder, characterized by smudged ink caused by the *comber wheels* passing over printed areas of a sheet.

Comber Wheels

See *Comber*.

Combi

In *binding and finishing*, a colloquial term for a *combination folder*. See *Combination Folder* and *Folding*.

Combination Folder

In *binding and finishing*, a folding device that consists of folding units of both the *knife folder* and *buckle folder* design. Also known as a *combi*. See *Folding*.

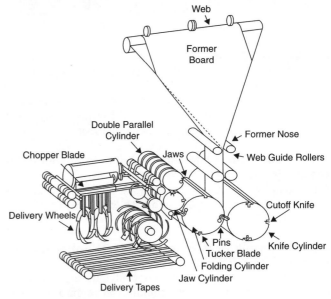

In-line combination folder.

In *web offset lithography*, a *combination folder* is an *in-line* folding device that combines the *former folder*, *jaw folder*, and *chopper folder* configurations.

Combination Plate

A printing plate used in *letterpress* or *flexography* that includes both *halftone*s and *line art*.

Combination Run

The running of two or more printing jobs simultaneously. Also known as a *gang run*.

Combination Stencil

See *Direct/Indirect Photoscreen Stencil*.

Combined Endsheet

In *case binding*, a special *endsheet* comprising two standard endsheets separated by a strip of tape.

Comic Ink

Alternate term for *newsink*, a variety of ink designed to print on newsprint, such as that used in newspapers or comic books. See *Newsink*.

Comic-Strip-Oriented Image

An image printed on microfilm in a way that is analogous to the individual panels of a comic strip, an image (or frame) being oriented parallel to the direction of film travel, each successive frame essentially "next to" the preceding frame. See also *Cine-Oriented Image*.

Comic-strip-oriented image.

Coming-and-Going Imposition

A type of *imposition* in which all the *recto* (or right-hand) pages are in numerical sequence from the front of the book to the back; when the book is flipped over, all the *verso* (or left-hand) pages are then in numerical sequence from the back of the book to the front. (See *Imposition*.)

Comité Consultatif International des Radiocommunications (CCIR)

An international organization that develops standards for audio and video equipment and broadcast. See *CCIR 601* and *CCIR 656*.

Comité Consultatif International de Téléphonique et Télégraphique (CCITT)

A international organization—one of four organizations that comprise the International Telecommunications Union (ICU)—that develops standards for data communi-

cations. The standards created by the CCITT fall into three categories:

• *CCITT Groups 1–4.* This set of standards defines the recommendations for *facsimile* transmissions. Groups 1 and 2, no longer in use, defined analog facsimile transmissions. Group 3 defined fax transmissions at a rate of 9600 *bits per second* at a *resolution* of 203×98 *dots per inch* (in standard mode) or 203×198 dpi (in fine mode). Group 4 defines standards for high-speed fax transmissions of high-resolution images (up to 400 dpi) over *ISDN* (or other digital) networks.

• *CCITT V Series.* This set of standards defines recommendations for data transmission, including transmission speed. Always in flux and changing, revised or alternative standards are indicated by the notation *bis* (the second version of a standard) or *ter* (the third version of a standard).

• *CCITT X Series.* These standards defines recommendations for *protocol*s and hardware used in computer networks, including transmission speeds, interfaces, and operation.

Comma-Delimited File

In a database, a data file in which data elements or *field*s are separated by commas. See also *Tab-Delimited File*.

Command

In computing, any instruction given to a computer—either by a programmer in the form of codes written in a computer language or by a user in the form of menu selections or typed keywords that initiate events.

COMMAND.COM

In *DOS*, a component of the operating system that executes commands. In DOS, there are two means of executing commands: externally and internally. External commands are executed by loading a file (usually one with the .EXE or .COM *file extension*, such as "WP.EXE," a file that executes the commands required to run WordPerfect) into memory and executing the commands contained therein. (Other external commands are those entered by the user, such as COPY, FORMAT, etc.) Internal commands are those commands that the user enters and that COMMAND.COM interprets and executes.

Command-Driven

Descriptive of a computer program or operating system in which operations are initiated by entering special commands, often utilizing a special language requiring an adherence to a specific syntax. See also *Menu-Driven*.

Command Interpreter

Alternate term for a *command processor*. See *Command Processor*.

Command Key

A key included on computer keyboards (especially those used by the Apple *Macintosh* computer) used to modify another key. The Command Key is added to expand the number of functions that a particular key can have and is widely used for **keyboard shortcut**s. See also **Alternate Key** and **Option Key**. The Command key is usually designated **Cmd** and is referred to as a **cloverleaf**.

Command Language

In computing, the set of rules written into a program that tells the computer how to interact with the user. For example, a command language will define the data the program will accept as input, how that data will be processed, and how the results will be reflected back to the user.

Command Line

In computing, a text line on which the user enters commands to be executed by the computer. See **Command-Line Interface (CLI)**.

Command-Line Argument

Alternate term for a **command-line switch**. See **Command-Line Switch**.

Command-Line Interface (CLI)

Any computer interface (such as BASIC or **DOS**) that mediates between the user and the computer's processor by means of text. Unlike a **graphical user interface (GUI)**, which uses **icon**s and pull-down menus that can be clicked on with a mouse to represent computer elements and files and to enter commands, a CLI utilizes user-enterable commands that must be typed at a particular prompt. Also known as a **character-based interface**.

Command-Line Switch

In computing via a **command-line interface**, a character that changes a default aspect of a command. For example, in **DOS**, the command-line switch is a slash (/) followed by a number or letter combination. In **UNIX**, the command-line switch is a character preceded by a hyphen. Also known as a **command-line argument**.

Command Port

In networking, the console or system used to monitor network activity.

Command Processor

In computing, the part of an operating system (especially one making use of a **command-line interface**) responsible for displaying **prompt**s on the screen, as well as interpreting and executing commands entered by the user. Also known as a **command interpreter**.

Command Prompt

See **Prompt**.

Command Tree

In computing, a diagram of command hierarchies that illustrates all of the possible selections from a main command menu and all the related submenus.

Comment

In computer programming, "remarks" added to a line of code that explains that line or provides other information relevant to another programmer rather than to the computer itself. Comments are usually set off from the lines of code by characters such as double hyphens (--) that the computer knows to ignore.

Commercial Match

In commercial printing, a type of paper ordered specially for a customer that is based on a sample provided to the manufacturer.

Commercial Perforation

A set of small slits (or **perforation**s) created in a printed sheet by a folder parallel to the fold at the **binding edge**. Commercial perforation is often produced so as to allow sheets to be easily separated.

Commercial Publishing

Printing and publishing in which documents and other printed materials are produced on a for-profit basis for clients or for commercial sale. Commercial publishing includes advertising, magazine and newspaper publishing, book publishing, etc.

Commercial Register

In **process color** printing, the ability to lay down successive **color**s in which the accuracy of the impression can be off by either one row or one-half of a row of **halftone dot**s. See **Register**.

Commission International de l'Eclairage (CIE)

See **CIE**.

Committee for Graphics Arts Technology Standards (CGATS)

An **ANSI**-approved, United States standards organization whose primary function is to develop standards for the graphic arts industry. Currently, they provide standards in areas not covered by other standards organizations. CGATS is also defining color measurement practices, densitometry standards, and plate dimension standards.

Commodity Paper

In papermaking, a low-quality **bond paper** or **offset paper**.

Commodore Dynamic Total Vision (CDTV)

A consumer multimedia computer system developed by Commodore Business Machines. The CDTV, perhaps the first home multimedia system, it included a **CD-ROM**/CD audio player and the Motorola 68000 microprocessor. It was based on Commodore's Amiga 500 **microcomputer**.

Commodore 64/128

The Commodore 64 was a home computer introduced by Commodore Business Machines in 1982 that ran simple programs for word processing and games, among others. Ten million Commodore 64s were sold worldwide. The Commodore 128 was an upgrade to the 64, introduced in 1986.

Common Action

In the *Windows* computing environment, a feature or function for user interaction that every program developed for Windows should provide, as defined in the *Common User Access* standard. Some examples are "OK" (not, say, "Sure") for executing an activity; "Cancel" (not, say, "Skip It") for stopping an activity; and "Help" (not, say, "Aidez-Moi") for providing information on what specifically the activity will do.

Common Carrier

Any communications company that provides voice and/or data telecommunications services to companies, organizations, or individuals. AT&T, MCI, and Sprint are examples of common carriers, as are local telephone companies.

Common Command Language

A command language used for accessing European on-line databases, especially those maintained by the *European Community Host Organization (ECHO)*. Common command language is often abbreviated *CCL*.

Common Impression Cylinder (CIC)

A large-diameter *impression cylinder* used in multicolor sheetfed and web offset printing presses that contacts the *blanket cylinder* of more than one *satellite press* (or printing unit), passing a printed sheet beneath successive *blanket*s that lay down successive colors.

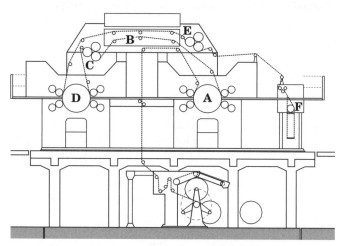

A printing press with two common impression cylinders (A, D), each having four printing couples. The web feeds into the first unit (A), which prints four colors on one side. It passes through a dryer (B) and over chill rolls (C), is turned over and enters the second unit (D), which prints four colors on the other side of the web. The web then re-enters the dryer (B), is chilled (E), and finally is folded (F) and delivered.

A common impression cylinder is also used on a *central impression press* for multicolor *flexographic* printing. On such a press, the substrate is carried around a large-diameter cylinder where it contacts four to eight different *plate cylinder*s, each printing a separate color.

See *Impression Cylinder*.

Common Language

In computing, any *machine language* or other system of coding that can be understood by another, related set of computers.

Common Management Information Protocol (CMIP)

In networking, an *Open Systems Interconnection (OSI)* protocol for network monitoring, adopted by the *International Standards Organization (ISO)* as ISO 9596. CMIP includes the management of security and accounting, configuration, and other network management functions. CMIP, however, is not in wide use. See also *Common Management Information Services (CMIS)* and *Simple Network Management Protocol (SNMP)*.

Common Management Information Services (CMIS)

In networking, a standard *OSI* set of functions for network monitoring and control. See also *Common Management Information Protocol (CMIP)* and *Simple Network Management Protocol (SNMP)*.

Common Pages

In typography and page layout, copy or type used for more than one publication, often without excessive (or even any) changes.

The term *common pages* also refers, when discussing *offprint*s, to printed leaves (each of which consists of two pages) needed for more than one article.

Common Service Area (CSA)

In computing, a storage area in a computer's memory in which data designed to be shared among concurrently executing programs is stored.

Common Tab Stop

In typewriting and word processing, a tab setting that is used to align copy or columnar items. With a common tab stop, individual spaces can be substituted with hits of the tab key to accurately position the carriage. In typesetting and word processing, tab stops are preferable to using *word space*s (via the space bar), as during *justification* small bits of space are added or deleted from word spaces to fill out or shorten a line.

Common User Access (CUA)

A standard developed by IBM to standardize certain aspects of *Windows*, the *graphical user interface* used on most *IBM-compatible computer*s. The common user access was designed to provide guidelines for developers so as to create consistency from application to application.

Such guidelines include having an application and/or open file reside in an on-screen window, the top of the window possessing a menu bar containing several pull-down menus having common commands. The guidelines also specify that the user be able to resize the window in a standard manner. The CUA standards also provide standard program behaviors for functions, including clickable buttons controlling **common action**s.

Communication
Essentially, the transmission of some form of content from one party to another.

Communication Control Character
In networking, a **control character** used to facilitate data communications.

Communication Network
See **Network**.

Communications Channel
See **Channel**.

Communications Controller
A small, dedicated computer whose sole function is to regulate and direct the flow of data to and from mainframe computers and remote terminals. Also known as a *communications control unit*.

Communications Line
Any medium—be it copper wire, fiber optic cable, etc.—over which voice, data, or other signals can be transmitted and, hopefully, received.

Communications Parameters
In telecommunications, a set of settings required for two or more computers to communicate with each other successfully. For example, when setting the communications parameters for a **modem**, such things as the **baud** rate, **data bit**s, **stop bit**s, and **parity** bits need to be set.

Communications Protocol
In telecommunications, a sequence of standard control characters used to establish **synchronous communication**s between a remote computer and a mainframe (or between any two computers).

Communications Satellite
In telecommunications, a **geostationary satellite** in earth's orbit that relays microwave transmissions from one **earth station** to another. When a satellite receives a transmission from the ground, it amplifies the received signal and retransmits it on a different frequency to another ground station.

Communications Satellite Corporation (COMSAT)
A privately owned American communications carrier and the U.S. representative in the international **INTELSAT**,

providing technical and operations services for the global organization.

Communications Server
See **Server**.

Communications Session
Any connection between two computers during which they can transmit data back and forth.

Community Antenna TeleVision (CATV)
See **Cable Television Network**.

Comp
Shorthand term for **comprehensive**. See **Comprehensive**.

Compact Disc (CD)
A popular form of digital data storage media, available in a variety of reading and writing formats. The two most common are **compact disc–digital audio (CD-DA)**, or **audio CD**, which supplanted vinyl records as the primary means of distributing music, and **compact disc–read-only memory (CD-ROM)**, a common means of disseminating computer files and multimedia titles.

The compact disc in its most familiar form is a flat platter 4.72 in. (120 mm) in diameter. It has a reflective, silvery layer into which pits are engraved (or "burned"), often by a laser. The pattern of pits and non-pits is how data is encoded, which is decoded by a laser in the reading device and transferred into analog audio data (in the case of CD-DAs) or transmitted to a computer (in the case of CD-ROMs). The CD-DA was the first CD format available and was received enthusiastically by the recording industry due to its noiseless audio reproduction ability and its high storage capacity (in excess of 72 minutes, compared to just over 50 minutes for conventional vinyl records). (A perhaps apocryphal story has it that the audio CD's playing time of 72 minutes was arrived at by a high-ranking official at Sony who wanted the medium to be just long enough to hold his favorite version of Beethoven's Ninth Symphony, which as it happened, was about 70 minutes.) The CD was quickly applied to the archiving and transport of computer information, also due to the medium's ability to retain the integrity of stored data for long periods of time and its high storage capacity (650 **megabyte**s). Both an audio CD and a CD-ROM have a total of 99 tracks; few music publishers and recording artists, however, use the full complement of tracks. (One audio CD in particular, the album *Kerosene Hat* by the rock band Cracker, uses all 99 tracks, most of which are blank, a few songs being sprinkled throughout. Perhaps they just wanted to have a song at track 99.)

There are several types of CDs loosely contained under the rubric of "CD-ROM"—the **compact disc–erasable (CD-E)**, **compact disc–interactive (CD-i)**, **compact disc–read-only memory–extended architecture (CD-ROM-XA)**, and **compact disc–recordable (CD-R)**, this latter term used to refer to the system for recording—often

A recordable CD-ROM.

at one's desktop—a CD-ROM. A ***compact disc–single (CD-S)*** is a small-format audio CD that aims to replace the 45-rpm record, while the ***compact disc–plus (CD+)*** combines the audio CD with an extra track of digital information, allowing a particular title to feature both audio tracks playable on a standard compact disc player with multimedia presentations playable on a computer.

Compact Disc Formats. All of the above mentioned variants of CD technology conform to one or more formats.

The original audio CD was defined by specifications set forth by the first CD technology developers (Sony and Philips) and was known as the ***Red Book*** standards (so-called because the binding on the publication containing the standards was in fact red). The Red Book essentially specifies the size and data format for the discs (it also includes specifications for ***compact disc graphics [CD-Graphics]***).

Sony and Philips then immediately saw how the CD format could be applied to computer data. Thus the first CD-ROM specifications were defined by the ***Yellow Book*** standards (yes, the book had a yellow binding). Although it primarily defined the specifications for CD-ROMs in terms of those for audio CDs, it also included considerations for error correction, such as ***interleaving*** data. It also defined new types of tracks; conventional audio tracks (consisting of uncompressed digital audio, the same as in Red Book), Mode 1 tracks (for computer data), and Mode 2 tracks (for compressed graphics, audio, and video). It is not unusual to find CDs that contain all three types of tracks. One draw-

back, however, is that each track can only be accessed one at a time, which is a consideration in multimedia title production. Thus, audio tracks and computer data cannot be accessed simultaneously. (A way around this is to load one track or the other into the computer's ***RAM***, which is possible only if the computer in question has a great deal of memory.)

In 1987, Philips devised a new set of CD-ROM standards to take into account new uses that were being developed for the CD-ROM format, and thus came up with the ***Green Book*** standards (you guessed it: green cover), also known as compact disc–interactive (CD-i). The primary difference with CD-i is that it was not designed to be played on a ***standard platform*** computer. Rather, like Nintendo or the older Atari systems, it required its own player (often connected to a television set) that was a small computer with its own operating system. The CD-i format is primarily used for delivering interactive games and other types of multimedia titles.

To increase the multimedia capabilities of CD-ROMs, Philips, Sony, and Microsoft developed the CD-ROM-XA standards. (They did not have their own colored book, but were rather an extension of Yellow Book Mode 2.) Essentially, the CD-ROM-XA system included ***adaptive differential pulse code modulation (ADPCM)*** and data interleaving, which allowed not only audio compression (allowing a total of 9.5 hours of stereo and 19 hours of monaural sound to be contained on the disc) but also the ability to simultaneously combine video, audio, and graphics on a single track, each one relegated to its own sector. Thus, on-screen synchronization of sound, video, and text was made possible. These tracks were known as XA tracks, each sector being either a Form 1 sector (which can contain computer data) and Form 2 sectors (which can contain compressed audio, video, or graphics). CD-ROM-XA discs require

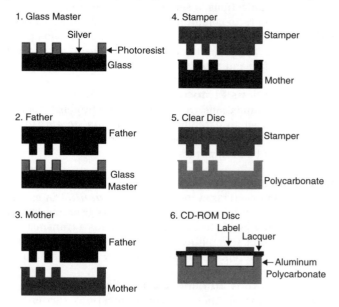

The stages of the CD-manufacturing process.

special software and hardware to record and to read, although they are playable on CD-i players. Many new CD-R devices support the XA format.

One aspect of CD-ROM pressing that has always vexed users has been the need to record everything in one session. In other words, you could not simply record some files, stop, then record more at a later time. (This was because the original CD production techniques were created while still thinking of the music-industry model; a single master is used to mass-replicate CDs.) With the development of CD-Rs and Kodak's *Photo CD* (see below), it soon became apparent that multisession CD-ROM production was desirable. Thus, the *Orange Book* standard was developed to define ways of creating multisession CD-Rs. Consequently, data can be added to a disc piecemeal until the disc is full. A catch is that both the reader and the disc must be Orange Book-compatible, and a drawback is a reduction in the amount of actual data that can be stored, since each session requires some degree of overhead.

Another type of CD-ROM was developed by Eastman Kodak for a purpose that bombed but which found a successful niche elsewhere. Kodak originally developed the Photo CD as a means of replacing photographic prints; essentially, the reasoning went, rather than have holiday snaps developed into prints, the returning vacation-goer would have his/her film transferred to CD-ROM, the images then being viewable on a special Photo CD reader hooked up to the television. That use did not quite work out, but the Photo CD found a place in digital prepress as an alternative to scanning. Photo CDs use a proprietary format but are readable on special readers manufactured by Kodak, on CD-i players, or on a computer utilizing a drive that supports the CD-ROM-XA standard. (See *Photo CD*.)

File Formats. The CD-ROM formats covered above detail how the files are recorded onto CD but do not specify how the files themselves are organized.

In 1986, representatives of the new CD-ROM industry met at Lake Tahoe high in the Sierra Nevada mountains (remember that location, it'll become important in a moment) to attempt to remedy an inherent problem with the new [multi]medium: *cross-platform* incompatibility. For example, CD-ROMs developed for a Macintosh could not be read on a PC, and vice versa. They thus came up with the *High Sierra* (get it?) standard file format. Thus, a CD-ROM with files created according to that standard would be compatible with any computer operating system, often one with the High Sierra *extension* appended to it. The High Sierra standard, rarely used any longer, was adopted and modified by the *International Standards Organization (ISO)* and became the *ISO 9660* standard file format. CD-ROMs that are desired to be read with an ISO 9660-compatible system must be premastered, or have its file directory structure organized in accordance with that specified in the standard. An alternative to the ISO 9660 format is the *HFS* format. HFS, or *Hierarchical File System*, is the file and directory structure used by the

Macintosh operating system. Thus, a CD-ROM created with this file format will look exactly like any other peripheral attached to a Macintosh. In essence, then, ISO 9660 resembles the PC file format structure while HFS resembles the Mac file format structure. (There is also a *UNIX* file format in which CD-ROMs can be created.) Thus, we still have platform incompatibilities. Recently, commercial CD-ROMs are cross-platform discs, as they contain two sets of data—ISO 9660 files for PCs and HFS files for Macs—and are thus able to be used on both platforms.

CD-ROM Readers and Recorders. Although CD-ROM drives (or readers) are sold separately, they are included in nearly every basic computer system sold today. Aside from specialized reading devices, such as the CD-i, most external drives can be hooked up to a personal computer. Of particular issue with drives is the speed of the drive. Initially, CD-ROM drives only had one speed, which was very slow (350–500 *millisecond*s). Soon, a drive was introduced that ran twice as fast and was known as a *double speed*, or 2X, drive (the original thus, in retrospect, becoming known as a 1X drive). Soon, drives were appearing that were four times (*quad speed*, or 4X) as fast as the original drive. As of this writing, 4X and 6X drives are the most common, although 8X and 10X drives are now appearing with remarkable rapidity.

Most CD-ROM drives are treated just like any peripheral device; on the Macintosh, they are linked to the *SCSI* chain. On the Windows side of things, early drives needed special adapter cards and system configurations, but now the tendency toward *plug-and-play* is making the process of installing a CD-ROM drive a painless process. And the early need to insert a CD-ROM into a special plastic caddy or cartridge before inserting it into the drive has almost entirely been done away with in favor of drives with servo-controlled pop-out trays, much like conventional audio CD players.

As of this writing, CD-ROM recording equipment has dipped below the $1,000 mark, although the software required to effect the CD-burning process may push the price back over that mark. Most CD-R devices can be easily hooked up to a computer (or are available as internal models, as well) just like any peripheral storage drive. When purchasing software, it is necessary to determine what file format you need to record in (i.e., ISO 9660, HFS, etc.) and at what speed. The situation is constantly changing, so it is best to consult with a recent round-up of CD-R devices and software packages in a major magazine, such as *New Media* or one of the plethora of CD-ROM magazines available. For issues specific to your own platform, try *Macworld* and *MacUser* or *PC World*.

CD-ROM Publishing. Because of its high storage capacity, the increasing market penetration of drives, and the ease of portability, CD-ROM publishing is expanding into markets traditionally handled only by print and is also inventing new markets. Education and reference is one market well-served by CD-ROMs; interactive interfaces, graphics, video, and audio in addition to text make the medium well-suited for encyclopedias and other teaching aids and reference books. Entertainment is also a wide-open market for CD-ROM, as video games, interactive novels, and CD+ music titles expand the range of what can be communicated in any one of the conventional media.

CD-ROM is also useful for the dissemination of any other type of data or information. Company reports, advertising, sales presentations, etc., can be easily and reasonably inexpensively produced and distributed on CD-ROM. Much computer software—which has been traditionally distributed on many floppy disks—is now distributed on CD-ROM.

There has been a proposed second generation of compact discs, designed independently by Philips/Sony and Toshiba/Time Warner. Two varieties of high-density CD allow for much higher storage capacities than conventional, first generation CDs. The Philips/Sony disc, called the *multimedia CD (MMCD)*, can hold up to 3.7 *gigabyte*s. The Toshiba/Time Warner disc, called the *super density (SD)* format, is double-sided and can hold up to 4.2 GB per side. Higher storage density is achieved by using a red laser, which possesses a shorter wavelength. However, rather than appear separately, both versions of the *HDCD* were incorporated into a new standard format adopted by the computer industry called the *digital versatile disc (DVD)* (originally called a *digital video disc*), which includes a double-sided double-layer technology developed by 3M that allows for a capacity of 4.7 GB per side per layer, for a total capacity of 17 GB. (See *Digital Versatile Disc (DVD)*.)

Compact Disc–Digital Audio (CD-DA)

The original *compact disc*, used to store in excess of 72 minutes of digital audio. The CD-DA (known simply as a *CD*, *CD-A*, or an *audio CD*) has replaced the vinyl record as the primary medium for the distribution of recorded music. See *Compact Disc (CD)*.

Compact Disc–Erasable (CD-E)

Alternate term for a *magneto-optical disc*. See *Magneto-Optical (MO) Disc*.

Compact Disc–Graphics

A type of *compact disc* containing audio, video, and graphics that plays a musical audio track accompanied by a video clip of the song and an on-screen lyric sheet. The music has had its vocal track stripped off, allowing the user to sing along. The CD-Graphics format is often used for *Karaoke*. See also *Compact Disc (CD)*.

Compact Disc–Interactive (CD-i)

A *compact disc* format that allows user interaction with video, audio, graphics, and text. Developed by Philips, the CD-i disc requires a special TV-top device to be read. The device is a small computer (using its own *operating sys-*

tem called *Compact Disc–Real Time Operating System (CD-RTOS)*, a dedicated computer and operating system designed only to run CD-i discs. It is widely used for video games, reference, and training *courseware*. See *Compact Disc (CD)*.

Compact Disc–Interactive Video (CD-IV)

See *Compact Disc-Interactive (CD-i)*.

Compact Disc + Multimedia

See *Compact Disc-Plus (CD+)*.

Compact Disc–Read-Only Memory (CD-ROM)

Any optical disc based on the *compact disc* containing digital information, in contrast to the *compact disc-digital audio*. See *Compact Disc (CD)*.

Compact Disc–Read-Only Memory–Extended Architecture (CD-ROM-XA)

A type of *CD-ROM* based on the *compact disc–interactive (CD-i)* standard that can simultaneously read interleaved audio and video, and that has a high storage capacity. See *Compact Disc (CD)*.

Compact Disc–Ready

Term for a *compact disc-interactive (CD-i)* disc that is playable in a conventional *audio CD* drive.

Compact Disc–Real Time Operating System (CD-RTOS)

The *operating system* used by TV-set-top computers used to play discs recorded in the *CD-i* format, derived from *OS-9*. See *Compact Disc–Interactive (CD-i)* and *Compact Disc (CD)*.

Compact Disc–Recordable (CD-R)

Any combination of hardware (such as a *compact disc* recording device and blank discs) and software used to press one's own compact discs, specifically *CD-ROM*s and *audio CDs*. Discs and recording systems may require all recording to be done in one session, but many systems currently available support multisession CD recording, allowing data to be added to a disc over the course of several sessions. CD-R is similar to the older *Write Once, Read Many (WORM)* discs, although WORMs are not readable by today's popular CD readers. The specifications for CD-R technology is defined in the *Orange Book* standards. See *Compact Disc (CD)*.

Compact Disc–Plus (CD+)

A *compact disc* format that is playable both as a *CD-ROM* in a computer's CD-ROM drive and a *CD-DA* playable in a conventional *audio CD* drive. Essentially, the CD+ format has tracks produced using the *Red Book* specifications for CD-DA, plus an additional track of computer information comprising digital video, graphics, and audio. The CD+ (also occasionally called *CD+MM*, or *compact disc + multimedia*) is often used for music (usually that of pop and rock artists), to feature both original songs and supplementary multimedia features highlighting the artist. One of the first discs to be recorded in this format was Sarah McLachlan's *The Freedom Sessions*. Other musicians and groups have also released titles in this format including The Cranberries (*Windows and Doors*) and The Great Kat (*Digital Beethoven on Cyberspeed*). See **Compact Disc (CD)**.

Compact Disc–Single (CD-S)

A **compact disc** format used for **compact disc–digital audio (CD-DA)**. This disc is smaller in diameter than conventional compact discs—3.13 in. (80 mm) as opposed to 4.72 in. (120 mm)—capable of holding a smaller amount of information (20 minutes of uncompressed audio, or 150 **megabyte**s of data). The CD-S is occasionally used by the music recording industry to distribute singles and extended-play song compilations, intended as a replacement to the 45-rpm vinyl record. Many older **audio CD** players required a special adapter to support the smaller format. (See **Compact Disc (CD)**.)

Compact Disc–Video (CD-V)

A type of **videodisc** developed by Philips for the distribution of analog video as well as digital or analog audio. The brand name of the CD-V is the Laser Disc. There are three configurations of CD-V: the CD Video Single that is 4.7 in. (120 mm) in diameter (the size of a general **compact disc**) with a single-sided storage capacity of 6 minutes of video and audio, or 20 minutes of just audio; the CD Video EP that is 7.9 in. (200 mm) in diameter with a capacity of 20 minutes of video and audio per side, each side being record- and playable; and the CD Video LP that is 11.8 in. (300 mm) in diameter with a capacity of 60 minutes of audio and video per side, each side being recordable and playable.

Compaction

In computing, the reduction of the storage space required to store data files.

Companding

A means of enhancing the quality of a **digital video** image.

Compandor

In telecommunications, a device used to increase the capacity of a telephone line by compressing the signal prior to transmission and decompressing after reception. Compandor is short for compressor/expander.

Compatibility

Generally speaking, the quality of a piece of hardware or software that allows it to perform in concert with an accepted standard, or in a manner akin to another piece of hardware or software.

In terms of hardware, compatibility refers to the ability of a piece of equipment to conform to an accepted model. For example, an **IBM-compatible computer** by definition will behave virtually identically to an IBM **PC**, regardless of the manufacturer. Similarly, a **Hayes-compatible modem** will behave virtually identically to a **modem** manufactured by Hayes. Also in terms of hardware, compatibility also refers to the ability to add a piece of equipment (such as a keyboard, printer, etc.) to a system and have it function properly.

In terms of software, compatibility refers to the ability to read a file created by one program (or version of a program) using another program (or another version of the same program).

Compatibility Box

In computing, especially on the **OS/2** platform, a portion of a computer's memory that is allocated for running **MS-DOS** applications from within the OS/2 system.

Compensators

In **web offset lithography**, a set of adjustable rollers found in the folding section and used to control and maintain web tension.

Compilation Time

In computer programming, the time required to translate **source code** into **object code** (or **machine language**), or, in other words, the time required to **compile**. See **Compiler**.

Compile

To translate a program written in a specific language—such as **C**—to **machine language**, or sets of instructions a **microprocessor** can understand.

Compiler

In computing, a systems program needed to translate instructions written in **source code** in a specific programming language such as **C** into **object code** (or **machine language**), instructions that the **microprocessor** can understand. Some programs are "interpreted," which means that the computer itself must first translate the source code into object code itself. Programs that are compiled beforehand tend to run much faster, since the computer can read object code directly. Also known as an **assembler**.

Compiler Language

A computer language that more closely resembles a language understandable to humans, rather than **machine language** that a computer can understand. After writing a program using a compiler language, the resulting **source code** is translated by the **compiler** into **object code**, or the machine language.

Complementary Colors

Among the **additive color primaries**, complementary colors are those that, when combined, produce white light. Among the **subtractive color primaries**, complementary colors are those that, when combined, yield a neutral gray or black. See **Additive Color Theory** and **Subtractive Color Theory**.

Complementary Flat

In the ***image assembly*** phase of ***prepress***, one of two separate ***flat***s that will be imaged on the same printing ***plate***. Complementary flats are one means of handling disparate page elements that need to be imaged on the same plate but that yield better results when imaged separately on the same plate (such as two images that need to butt each other, or need to overlap slightly). For example, in the case of abutting images, the space between the adjacent images may be too narrow to make an effective splice on the same flat.

The process of using complementary flats in platemaking is called ***double printing***. If images on each complementary flat are to overlap, it is known as ***surprinting***.

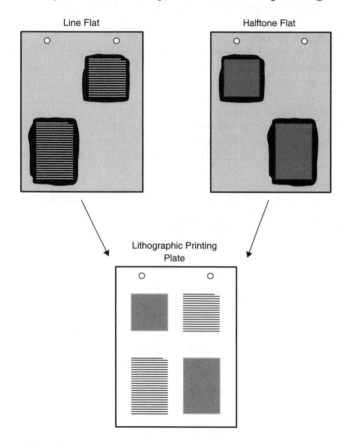

Complementary flats combined into one printing plate.

In some cases, separate images can be prepared on complementary flats and combined photographically onto a single film prior to platemaking, a process called ***photocombining***. Such a negative (or positive) is called a ***composite negative*** (or ***composite positive***). (See ***Prepress: Graphic Arts Photography and Flat Assembly***.)

Complementary Metal-Oxide Semiconductor (CMOS)

A type of ***integrated circuit*** used for computer processors and memory chips. CMOS are characterized by high speeds, low power consumption, and low heat generation. In ***PC***s,

batteries are used to constantly supply a CMOS chip with power to keep some operating parameters in memory while the computer is turned off. See also ***MOS***.

Complex Instruction-Set Computing (CISC)

Descriptive of a computer ***microprocessor*** that is able to process high-level, complex instructions. Complex instructions require fewer individual instructions in order to accomplish a single task, which makes programming less time-consuming. However, additional processing time is required for the processor to decode and execute the instructions. CISC-based processors require complex arrays of large numbers of transistors, which makes design difficult. A common alternative is a ***RISC***-based processor. See also ***Reduced Instruction-Set Computing (RISC)***.

Complexity

General term for any negative effect caused by attempting to print too many characters, graphics, rules, etc.

Compliance Color

Any non-toxic printing ink or other colorant that conforms to governmental regulations.

Component

Any small, individual part of a larger system.

Component Analog Video (CAV)

See ***Component Video***.

Component Video

In video production, a means of recording a video signal such that the ***chrominance*** (the color information) and the ***luminance*** (the brightness information) are recorded separately. Component video allows higher picture quality than ***composite video***, as in the latter the signals can interfere with each other and cause distortion. Also known as ***component analog video (CAV)***.

COM Port

On a ***PC***, especially one running ***DOS***, the designation of one of four ***serial port***s into which ***modem***s can be connected. Early PCs only supported two COM ports—designed COM1 and COM2—but later versions of DOS allowed up to four—COM1, COM2, COM3, and COM4—to be utilized.

Composed Page

In prepress and desktop publishing, a page laid out electronically that contains both text and graphics and that can only be printed on an ***all-points addressable*** output device.

Composed Text

In typesetting, text data containing specific formatting, placement, and appearance commands.

Composing Stick

In typography, a handheld tool in which metal type was assembled character by character, justified, and transferred to a *galley* for proofing, lockup, and printing. See *Type and Typography: History of Type*.

Composite

In graphics, any image comprising two or more smaller images, be they *line art*, *continuous-tone*, or some combination of them.

In video, a means of video transmission in which separate red, green, and blue signals are combined to form a picture. See *Composite Video*.

Composite Color

In video, the red, green, and blue color information contained in a single video signal. See *Composite Video*.

Composite Color File

In *DCS* (*Desktop Color Separation*), a *low-resolution file* containing the entire color image, used as a quickly viewable complement to the four *color separation* files the program generates.

Composite Negative

In *prepress*, a single *negative* that has been produced by the *photocombining* of separate *complementary flat*s.

Composite Positive

In *prepress*, a single *positive* that has been produced by the *photocombining* of separate *complementary flat*s.

Composite Sync

A television or video system containing horizontal and vertical scan controls to keep both aspects synchronized. See *Synchronization*.

Composite Video

In video production, a means of recording a video signal such that the *chrominance* (the color information) and the *luminance* (the brightness information) are combined into a single signal. Composite video produces lower picture quality than *component video*, as in the former the signals can interfere with each other and cause distortion. Television signals tend to be composite video, each of the three major broadcast standards—*NTSC*, *PAL*, and *SECAM*—providing different means of combining, encoding, and decoding the signals.

Compositing

Generally, adding two or more elements together to create a *composite*. In computer graphics, programs such as *Photoshop* and *Painter* (among many others) allow for several images to be combined with each other. In so doing, the program much calculate (or the user must set) transparency information for each separate image (or a *clipping path* for an image).

The images can often be stored on separate "layers" within the program, so that they can be edited individually. All layers can then be merged when editing is complete, yielding a composite image.

Composition

The setting of type.

Composition and Markup

The setting, formatting, and positioning of type on a page. *Composition* specifically refers to the setting of type; *markup* specifically refers to the generation of *type specification*s; a commonly used additional term, *makeup*, specifically refers to the assembly of set type and other page elements on the page.

Composition Formatting

In typesetting, the insertion of a set of formatting and positioning commands into input text.

Composition Software

Any computer program designed and used to set type. Composition software usually has advanced algorithms for the handling of typographic operations like *kerning*, *hyphenation*, and *justification*, whereas basic word processing software most likely does not.

Composition System

Any typesetting system that facilitates the positioning of type on a page, eliminating the need for additional manual or electronic pasteup.

Compositor

A person who sets type.

Compositor's Error

An error made during typesetting, also known as a *printer's error* and a *typographical error*, in contrast to an *author's alteration*.

Compound Document

In word processing or *page layout software*, a document comprising elements of various data types and formats—e.g., text, *EPS* graphics, *TIFF* images, and sounds (in the case of multimedia documents)—each file type being linked to the application that created it. Compound documents are created using a program called a *compound document editor*.

Compound Document Editor

A software application used for creating a *compound document*, or a document, file, or presentation comprising elements of various data types—such as text, graphics, sounds, video, etc. Such applications allow the importing of files created by other types of applications. Compound document editors are often known as multimedia *authoring* programs.

Comprehensive

A stage in the page layout and design process consisting of a detailed dummy or layout of the page to be reproduced, showing the exact placement of page elements (text, illustrations, etc.) in a form comparable to that of the final print. Many desktop publishing systems can easily generate comprehensives, commonly with *low-resolution* black-and-white versions of images. A comprehensive is commonly referred to as a *comp*.

Compress

To reduce the size of a file, usually by means of *data compression* algorithms. See *Data Compression*. See also *Decompress*.

Compressed Audio

Any audio data that has undergone *data compression* (usually *lossy* compression) prior to being stored onto a *videodisc*.

Compressibility

The degree to which a paper will reduce in thickness when exposed to a compressing force, as during printing. A high degree of compressibility aids in producing a good printed image, as the squeezing down of surface contours enables the printing plate or blanket to contact the paper more completely. Compressibility is a function of the paper's *apparent density*, the degree of *refining* that the fibers have received during papermaking, and the degree of *calendering* and *supercalendering*. A paper's compressibility is also increased by increased *moisture content*. The degree of compressibility required varies according to the printing process to be used, and other paper properties involved (in particular *resiliency* and *hardness* or *softness* which, with compressibility, define the paper's *printing cushion*). Generally, easily compressible paper is preferred for printing, although it is less of an issue in offset printing, and stronger paper may be required in the case of end uses involving folding or handling. A TMI Monitor/Printing Surf System can be used to quantitatively measure the compressibility of a paper. (See also *Resiliency*, *Hardness*, and *Softness*.)

The term *compressibility* also refers to the extent to which an offset press *blanket* will reduce in thickness under the pressures generated during printing. See *Blanket*.

Compressible Blanket

A rubber *blanket* used in *offset lithography* that differs from a *conventional blanket* by including one layer (or more) of foam rubber, cork, or nonwoven fabric fibers between plys of fabric backing. Compressible blankets, as their name indicates, can be compressed without causing deformations or structural damage to either the rubber surface or the fabric backing.

Advantages of compressible blankets include the ability to utilize greater amounts of *packing* without producing a corresponding increase in printing pressure

The separate plys of a compressible blanket.

(which can contribute to plate wear, blanket wear, *slurring*, and a variety of other press and printing problems), reduced slippage between the plate and blanket, and a greater ability to recover from a blanket *smash*. (See *Blanket*.)

Compression

See *Data Compression*.

Compression Ratio

The amount of *data compression* a digital file has undergone, expressed as the ratio of the original file size to the compressed file size. For example, a compression ratio of 10:1 might mean that the original file was 10 *megabytes* and has been compressed to 1 megabyte. The higher the compression ratio, the more *lossy* the compression tends to be. See *Data Compression*.

Compression Set

A nonreversible, permanent depression in or compression of any portion of an offset press blanket, caused either by a *smash* or by a lack of *resilience*, in which the blanket is unable to retain its original thickness following the exposure to the extreme pressures generated during printing. (See *Blanket* and *Smash*.)

Compression set is also used to refer to a permanent reduction in thickness of a rubber *flexographic* printing plate, the distortion being represented as a percentage of the original thickness of the rubber surface.

Computation Bound

In computing, a limitation imposed on the execution of a program or route by the speed of the processor. See also *Input/Output Bound*.

Computed Tomography

In imaging—specifically, medical imaging—a diagnostic system whereby X-rays are passed through an object (such as a human body) at a variety of angles to produce a set of cross-sectional views of that object which can in turn be used to generate a three-dimensional representation of it. Such views are then used to search for biological anomalies. Abbreviated *CT*.

Computer

Electronic device for performing stored sequences of arithmetic and logical instructions on a group of data in text, graphic and image form.

A computer is a machine that is capable of performing repetitive logical and arithmetic operations on data and storing the results of those operations. A computer consists of hardware, software, and firmware components.

Computers are generally mainframes, minicomputers, or microprocessors. These names differentiate them according to speed, capabilities, and costs.

There are several ways of indicating the power of a computer, but these are relative. Cycle time (the amount of time required to perform a series of simple operations) and word size (the amount of information stored per location in memory) are indicators of the power of the computer's central processing unit (CPU). The size of memory, expressed in thousand of words (K), is a measure of the computer's capacity.

What is called a computer, is actually a collection of machines or devices. Each of these performs some function (like a disk that stores data) and is able to communicate to other devices as well.

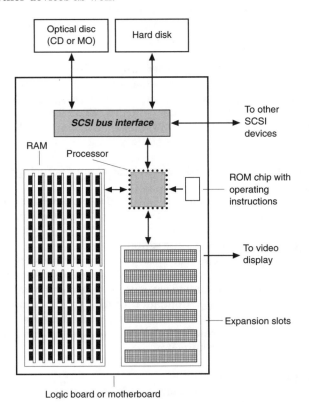

Basic elements of a desktop computer.

Devices that are not part of the CPU are called peripheral devices. Peripheral devices are on-line or off-line. An on-line peripheral is under the control of the CPU and is physically attached to it in some electronically meaningful way. An off-line peripheral does not communicate directly with the CPU.

The CPU requires data in order to perform its operations and produces new data as its result. This means that there must be a device, like a filing cabinet, in which information can be stored, and from where it can be retrieved. In addition, a control unit is needed to decide where to get data and where to put data. The CPU's "filing cabinet" is called a random-access memory (RAM). Both the RAM and CPU are subordinate to the control unit, which decides what device performs its function and when.

Data Structures. To store numbers large enough to be meaningful, bits need to be grouped into arrays. The smallest array size used in a computer is called a byte. A byte is a group of bits (binary digits) linked together, which is long enough to store a meaningful amount of information. A byte is also part of a larger organizational structure since it is either one-fourth or one-half of a computer word.

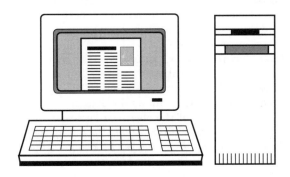

A typical personal computer.

A word is the smallest unit of computer memory that can be directly addressed or accessed for storage and retrieval of data. In the typesetting, business processors can be commonly found that utilize 16-bit words, each of which is made up of two 8-bit bytes.

When a computer is said to be 16-bit, it means that each part of the computer that deals with data from the disks and memory, to the registers in the CPU, or organized into words of that size. Storage, retrieval, and transmission of information is always done in word-size chunks.

Computer-Aided Acquisition and Logistics Support (CALS)
A computer program developed and used by the U.S. Department of Defense for the standardized management of technical data pertaining to weapons systems.

Computer-Aided Design (CAD)
An acronym for ***computer-aided design*** (sometimes also called *computer-assisted design*). In graphics, CAD systems and software are special workstations and programs that aid in architectural, engineering, and scientific design by enabling a real-time link between the computer and designer-initiated input via a graphics tablet, a light pen, or a mouse. Depending on the specific CAD program, rendered objects can appear as ***wire-frame*** models, as shaded models, or as solid objects.

CAD is frequently used in conjunction with **computer-aided manufacturing** (collectively known as **CAD/CAM**), a general category that involves the use of computers in design and manufacturing. Other related acronyms include **CADAM** (computer-augmented design and manufacturing) and **CADD** (computer-aided design and drafting).

Some of the specific functions of most CAD programs include:

Wireframe modeling, in which the object is represented as simply connected points in space. Often, wireframe representations are the most expedient model forms, as they require less processing power to change and manipulate.

Layering is a means of dividing the drawing into color-coded layers, which can be turned off to reveal additional layers of the drawing.

Solids modeling involves the "filling in" of a wireframe and enables the designer to evaluate the physical characteristics of the object being designed, such as center of gravity, mass, etc.

User-defined views enable the designer to "rotate" the object (either figuratively or literally) so as to see it from a variety of different directions.

Auto-dimensioning allows the designer to change one particular dimension of the object while the computer will then alter all the other dimensions affected by the change.

Coordinate tracking keeps the designer apprised of where he or she is on the x, y, and z axes.

CAD data can be exchanged among different designers by means of the **Initial Graphics Exchange Specification (IGES)**, a vendor-independent standard **file format** for CAD and CAD/CAM graphics.

Computer-Aided Drafting and Design (CADD)

A variety of **CAD** software used specifically in industrial design and technical drawing. See **Computer-Aided Design (CAD)**. CADD is also sometimes known as *computer-assisted drafting and design*.

Computer-Aided Instruction

See **Computer-Assisted Instruction**.

Computer-Aided Manufacturing (CAM)

See **CAD/CAM**.

Computer-Aided Publishing

The application of a computer—either a **microcomputer** or a dedicated prepress system—to the majority of page layout, design, and other prepress processes. See **Desktop Publishing**.

Computer and Business Equipment Manufacturers Association (CBEMA)

A professional trade organization founded in 1916 comprising computer vendors and business equipment manufacturers. CBEMA is concerned with the development of standards for business equipment and data processing. CBEMA also developed the **PHIGS** programming language.

Computer-Animated Graphics

Alternate term for **computer animation**. See **Computer Animation**.

Computer Animation

Graphics—ranging from simple moving bar charts to complex feature-length animated movies such as Disney's *Toy Story*—which have been drawn and animated using a computer, rather than pen or paint on paper or acetate. See **Animation**. Also known as **computer-animated graphics**.

Computer-Assisted Graphics

The creation and/or manipulation of graphical material using a computer. See **Computer Graphics**.

Computer-Assisted Instruction (CAI)

The use of computer applications—such as multimedia training programs or tutorials—to teach a particular subject.

Computer-Assisted Retrieval (CAR)

A means of accessing and retrieving micrographic images utilizing a computerized index and search engine.

Computer-Assisted Software Engineering (CASE)

In computer programming, a set of technologies that aim to facilitate designing, writing, and programming computer applications. CASE tools often include **distributed processing**, **graphical user interface**s, debugging routines, etc. CASE tools often run on **UNIX** workstations.

Computer-Augmented Design and Manufacturing (CADAM)

An alternate term for **computer-aided design/computer-aided manufacturing**. See **Computer-Aided Design**.

Computer-Controlled Animation

In video and motion picture photography, **animation** technique whereby a computer is used to automatically move the camera or an animation sequence a set amount of space each second (or less). Computer control of the process allows for a greater degree of accuracy and sophistication, not to mention a substantial reduction of labor on the part of the cameraman or animator.

Computer Family

In computing, a line of computers built around the same **central processing unit**, or which otherwise share similar characteristics. For example, Apple's Quadra family of Macintosh computers incorporates the same 680X0 processor.

Computer Game

Any type of computer software designed and used for primarily recreational purposes. Computer games began as very simple text-only narratives that allowed players to type in a limited number of words to perform actions or explore realms. Early computer graphics were also very simple, consisting essentially of large blocks that represented balls, ping-pong paddles, or game players. Nowadays, graphics have become far more sophisticated, and photorealistic computer games are *de rigueur*. They can range in subject matter from the somewhat cerebral (such as *Myst*) to the strictly visceral, shoot-em-up type (such as *Doom* and its sequels). Popular card or board games have also made the leap to cyberspace, and computer chess, Scrabble, poker, solitaire, and many others are very popular. **CD-ROM**s and the **World Wide Web** have replaced **floppy disk**s as the primary means of computer game distribution.

Computer-Generated Animation

Alternate term for **computer animation**. See **Computer Animation**.

Computer Graphics

As its name implies, graphic images created or edited on a computer. Computer graphics fall into two forms: **bitmap**s and **vector graphics**, which are somewhat analogous to the **continuous tone** and **line art**—respectively—dichotomy in conventional graphics. However, the comparison is only a generalized one; often line art can be reproduced as vectors and sometimes as bitmaps.

Computer graphics can be created either from scratch (using a **drawing program** such as **Illustrator** or **FreeHand**) or can be captured from an external nondigital; source, such as a **scanner** or **digital; camera**. After being digitized, the image can be edited, corrected, etc. Computer graphics can then be output to a laser printer or an ink-jet printer, to an imagesetter as a negative or positive for printing, to an electrostatic or ink-jet plotter for **large-format output**, or to a digital press for direct digital output. More often than not, computer graphics are incorporated into page layouts as illustrations. See **Bitmap** and **Vector Graphics**. Computer graphics also encompasses **computer-aided design (CAD)** as well as **three-dimensional** graphics.

Computer Graphics Interface (CGI)

In computer graphics programs, a two-way communication protocol between the program and any **device driver**s in the system. CGI communicates directly with these device drivers to control the output of computer graphics. CGI is usually found in **device-independent** graphics programs.

Computer Graphics Metafile

See **CGM**.

Computer-Independent Graphics

Any computer graphics software that can run on more than one computer **platform**.

Computer-Independent Language

A **high-level** computer language or set of computer commands that can be used on any computer platform or system possessing the proper **compiler**.

Computer Input Microfilm (CIM)

A system in which images recorded onto microfilm are digitized, or converted into digital form and input into a computer. See also **computer output microfilm (COM)**.

Computer Instruction

In computer programming, any set of codes that tells a computer to perform an action.

Computer-Integrated Manufacturing (CIM)

CIM integrates the office and accounting functions with the automated factory systems in a manufacturing organization. Systems for point of sale, billing, and machine tool scheduling, as well as ordering supplies are all part of a CIM system.

Computer Interface Unit

Any device used to connect another device or **peripheral** to a computer system. Abbreviated **CIU**.

Computerized Axial Tomography (CAT)

In imaging—specifically, medical imaging—a diagnostic system in which X-rays are passed through an object (such as a human body or head) to a certain depth and at a variety of directions. A computer is used to record the X-rays as they pass through the body, yielding an image of the body's internal structure. CAT—or a "CAT scan"—is used to diagnose biological anomalies, such as tumors and other growths.

Computerized Composition

Any typesetting system that has been programmed to automate typographic decisions, such as **kerning**, **hyphenation**, **justification**, etc.

Computer Language

In computing, a system of characters, symbols, words, and/or syntax used to give instructions to a computer. Computer languages are usually written in English-language form (or other foreign-language form). The instructions are then converted by a **compiler** into **machine language**, which only the computer can understand. Common computer languages include **C**, **FORTRAN**, **COBOL**, **BASIC**, and others.

Computer Literacy

The basic ability to understand and use a computer.

Computer Network

A network that connects computers together. See **Network**.

Computer Output Microfilm (COM)

In computing, **microfilm** or **microfiche** that is generated by digital data from a computer. See also **Computer Input Microfilm (CIM)**.

Computer–PABX Interface (CPI)

In a **local area network**, a **PABX** standard for both voice and data that utilizes **T1** transmission with 54-kilobit per second channels.

Computer Program

Essentially, a set of instructions that tell a computer what to do. A computer program, written in (or later converted to) *machine language*, instructs the computer what operations to perform either of its own accord or when certain user input is received. Computer programs are written to achieve specific end results. Known more broadly as an *application*.

Computer Programmer

An individual who writes the specific code that comprises a *computer program*.

Computer Resource Unit (CRU)

In computing, a measure of the *clock speed*, *memory* capacity, and other basic computer attributes, often used as a guide when pricing a computer or computer usage.

Computer Science

A branch of engineering that deals with all aspects of designing and building a computer system, including hardware manufacture and installation, as well as software programming and use.

Computer Simulation

See *Simulation*.

Computer-to-Plate (CTP)

In prepress and printing, a system in which electronic page information is used to guide lasers in the direct imaging of a printing plate, eliminating the need for a *negative* to be produced. CTP (also known as *direct-to-plate*) systems are increasingly being incorporated into all-digital prepress and printing workflows.

In a CTP system, digital information from a page file is sent in *PostScript* form to an off-press device known as a *platesetter*, which reads the file information and exposes the data onto polyester plates that are ready for press. Although imagesetters have long been able to image onto polyester plate material, the material itself was not capable of holding very high resolution images or very high line screens. New developments, however, now enable polyester plates to hold up to 133 lpi screens, and new imagesetters and platesetters can image them with increasing degrees of quality. Even newer systems can image plates while they are mounted on the *plate cylinder* of a printing press. In addition, new systems can also output color-separated files and image each of the four *process color* plates in sequence, often while on press, which ensures that successive colors remain in *register*.

CTP systems have taken off in recent years, despite the high costs of early systems. As all-digital workflows become more prevalent, CTP (and perhaps even *direct digital printing*) will play a large role in the future of printing.

Computer Typography

Use of a computer to set, format, and position type. Alternate term for *desktop publishing*. See *Desktop Publishing*.

Computer Virus

See *Virus*.

Compute Time

In networking and telecommunications, the portion of a user's *connect time* that he or she is actually utilizing the *server*'s resources. See *Connect Time*.

COM Recorder

A device used to generate *Computer Output Microfilm*. See *Computer Output Microfilm (COM)*.

COMSAT

Abbreviation for *Communications Satellite Corporation*. See *Communications Satellite Corporation (COMSAT)*.

Concatenation

In computer programming, linking together several character strings to form a single character string.

On a computer display, *concatenation* means the joining of one line on the display to the succeeding or preceding line.

Concatenator

Alternate term for a *hub*. See *Hub*.

Concentrator

In networking, a device (such as a *repeater* or *hub*) that links *channel*s from several network *node*s, coordinating the competition for and sharing of transmission channels. Concentrators also perform *bridge* and *routing* functions.

Concentricity

The state at which a circle within a larger circle within a larger circle (etc.) all have a common center. Implicit in the concept of concentricity is the perfect roundness of each circle, an important consideration in the proper running of a printing press cylinder, in which the *journal*, bearing steps, bore, and outside diameter of the cylinder all need to be as close to perfectly circular as possible and have the centers of their respective diameters all meet at the same point. (See also *out-of-roundness* and *total indicated runout*.)

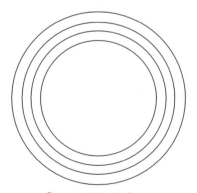

Concentric circles.

Concertina Fold

Alternate term—especially in England—for **accordion fold**. See **Accordion Fold**.

Concurrence

In video production or broadcasting, the simultaneous transmission of both audio and video.

Concurrency

In **object-oriented programming**, the property that defines an active from an inactive object. See **Object-Oriented Programming**.

Concurrent License

In computing, a software licensing agreement that allows an application to be provided on a network **file server** for the use of more than one individual in an organization. Depending upon the specific language of the agreement, only one person may be able to use the application at a time, or only a specified number of copies may be open at any one time. See also **Application Metering**.

Concurrent Processing

Alternate term for **multitasking**. See **Multitasking**.

Condensation Resin

Alternate term for an **alkyd** resin or a phenol-aldehyde resin. See **Resin** and **Alkyd**.

Condensed

In typography, descriptive of the relative narrowness of all the characters in one typeface. Condensed type is used when large amounts of copy must fit into a small space, such as in **tabular composition**.

There are four basic gradations of condensation beyond the "normal" typeface: semicondensed, condensed, extracondensed, and ultracondensed. *Narrow* and *compressed* are often used synonymously with one or more of these degrees of condensation.

Garamond Condensed
Avant Garde Condensed

Two examples of condensed typefaces.

Hot metal typography and early phototypesetting could typically only condense type by removing space from between letters, without actually altering the widths of the letters themselves. Digitized typesetters and other digital composition devices and programs have the capability of actually altering the widths of the letters themselves, by removing raster lines and defining new set widths. This 12-pt. type can be specified as 11½ set. A problem of this lat-

ter technique of condensing type optically or digitally—compared to type that has been condensed by the type designer—is that the legibility of the type will gradually diminish with increasing condensation.

A condensed typeface has an **em space** that is no longer a square formed by the value of the **point size**. Thus fixed widths will appear narrower than normal. If a typeface is condensed by changing the set width, then all the values—including the fixed spaces—will change. This would have to occur so that the fixed spaces for the figure width matches the actual width of the figures. This is important because, for condensed typefaces, the word space values must also be reduced (i.e., condensed) or the texture of the lines will seem unnaturally segmented by wider than appropriate word spaces.

See also **Expanded**.

Condition

Alternate term for **stabilize**. See **Stabilize**.

Conditional Branch

Alternate term for **conditional transfer**. See **Conditional Transfer**.

Conditioning

In telecommunications, the improvement of the quality of data transmission over a **voice-grade** channel.

Conductive Ink

A type of ink used in **screen printing** formulated with a metallic substance (such as silver, graphite, or nickel) to facilitate the conduction of electricity. These inks are commonly used in the screen printing of electronic circuit boards.

C1S

Abbreviation for **coated one side** paper. See **Coated One Side**.

Confetti

In printing, binding, and/or finishing, small bits of paper debris produced during hole punching, perforating, cutting, or trimming. Also known as **chad**.

In video production, small points of color or speckles in a video display caused by video errors or defects in the videotape.

CONFIG.SYS

A data **configuration file** used in **DOS** to instruct the computer at start-up and to load the system parameters into the computer's memory. In other words, the files that are loaded when the system is **boot**ed. The CONFIG.SYS file is easily edited by the user, as it is an **ASCII text** file.

Configuration

In computing, the setting of a user's own preferences for a computer system, expansion board, application, etc., which may differ significantly from the default settings. The user's specific preferences are stored in a *configuration file*, such as DOS's *CONFIG.SYS*.

Configuration File

In computing, a file containing the system parameters (or the *operating system* configuration) that is typically read and loaded when the system is *boot*ed.

Configuration Item

In networking, any piece of hardware or software that comprises the system under *configuration management*. See *Configuration Management*.

Configuration Management

In networking, a general term for a variety of network administration and "housekeeping" tasks, such as keeping track of *bridge*s, *router*s, and other hardware elements, so as to quickly effect changes in a network configuration should problems arise; adding new *nodes* if needed; adding new *server*s, as needed; etc.

Confirmation Prompt

On a computer utilizing *command-line interface*, a message displayed to the user asking if he or she *really* wants to initiate a command the user may or may not have entered deliberately.

Confirmation Proof

A page *proof* generated prior to a pressrun and shown to a customer as an example of how the page will print. Approval is not necessary when a customer is shown a confirmation proof, unlike an *OK Sheet*.

Confluence of Ink

In *screen printing*, the property that allows the tiny, individual bits of ink deposited through the screen fabric to flow together and give the appearance of a continuous, unbroken printed image.

Conformability

A paper quality that describes how a paper's surface will alter its surface shape to completely contact a printing surface. Conformability is an important determinant of *print quality*, in that a printing plate or *gravure cylinder* making incomplete contact with the paper will not completely transfer the printed image, which may result in *breaks* (or broken halftone dots) or, in gravure printing, *skips*, *snow*, and *speckle*. A *wild formation* or low *compressibility* can adversely affect a paper's ability to thoroughly contact an inked surface.

Congestion

In networking and telecommunications, a state in which there is too much network traffic to effectively and expediently transmit messages from node to node. Other network performance problems may also occur.

Conical Refiner

A device used for *refining* paper *pulp* fibers, also called a *jordan*. See *Jordan*.

Conic Generator

A feature of a *computer graphics* system that draws general conic shapes—circles, parabolas, arcs, ellipses, etc.

Coniferous

A cone-bearing tree, also classified as *softwood*, used in most pulping processes for the manufacturing of paper. Familiar types of coniferous trees include pines, spruces, firs, hemlocks, larches, cypresses, and cedars. They are distinguished from deciduous trees by their usually long, needle-shaped leaves. Popularly known as "evergreens" for their ability to remain green year round, some conifers—such as the larch—do shed their leaves in winter. The wood of conifers lends itself well to the papermaking process, as the fibers are of such a size and structure that produce the best-quality paper. *Coniferous* is one of two primary classifications of trees; see also *Deciduous*.

Connected Dot

*Halftone dot*s of greater than 50% dot density joined together on a photographic *negative* or plate.

Connectionless Network Protocol (CLNP)

A network *protocol* used in *Open Systems Interconnection (OSI)* for data transmission, utilizing *datagram*s containing address data to efficiently route messages from, node to node. CLNP is used in *local area network*s, and is the OSI version of *Internet Protocol (IP)*. See also *Connection-Oriented Network Service (CONS)*.

Connectionless Protocol

In telecommunications, a data communications *protocol* that does not require the sender and receiver to be connected to each other before a transmission can commence. In such a networking system, the devices and components monitor the network data stream for data *packet*s bearing their *address*. An example of a connectionless protocol is *TCP/IP*. See also *Connection-Oriented Protocol*.

Connectionless Transport Protocol (CLTP)

In networking, a *protocol* used in *Open Systems Interconnection (OSI)* for transport data addressing and error correction. CLTP, however, does not guarantee delivery of a message, nor does it effect *flow control*. CLTP is the OSI version of *User Datagram Protocol (UDP)*.

Connection Number

In networking, a number assigned to any device—such as a *workstation*—connected to a network *server*.

Connection-Oriented Network Service (CONS)

In networking, a *protocol* that is used in *Open Systems Interconnection (OSI)* for data delivery. CONS is used in *wide area networks*. See also *Connectionless Network Protocol (CLNP)*.

Connection-Oriented Protocol

In telecommunications, a data communications *protocol* that requires the sender and receiver to be connected to each other before a transmission can commence. See also *Connectionless Protocol*.

Connectivity

Generally, the ability of a computer to be linked to one or more other computers.

Connectivity is used in networking and electronic publishing to refer to the ability of all workstations, peripherals, storage devices, and output devices to be linked together in a network, allowing the easy assembly of entire pages from disparate sources.

Connect Time

In networking and telecommunications, the period of time during which a user is physically connected to a network, regardless of whether or not the user is utilizing the server's resources. See also *Compute Time*.

CONS

Abbreviation for *Connection-Oriented Network Service*. See *Connection-Oriented Network Service (CONS)*.

Consecutive Numbering

A *finishing* operation utilizing an *ink jet* or other printing device to apply different numbers to printed forms.

Consistency

A property of a printing ink (or other fluid or substance) that describes both its *body* and its *viscosity*, usually in terms such as thick, thin, buttery, watery, etc. See *Body* and *Viscosity*.

Consistent with the Physical Resolution

Property of a computer display in which the display information is within one *pixel* of its "true" position, or the position on a page as measured by the program generating it, or the position the object will be in when output from a higher-resolution device.

Console

In networking, a computer used by the network administrator (or other similar individual) to monitor the performance of the network, computer system, etc.

Constant Angular Velocity

Abbreviated *CAV*, a means of writing data on an *optical disc* in which the rotational speed of the disc remains constant regardless of where a particular track is written to or read from. Or, in other words, the same amount of data is contained on a track near the center of the disc than one near the outside edge, that amount being of necessity

defined by the size of the inner track. Consequently, data is more densely packed near the center of the disc. Although CAV allows data to be accessed quickly (each track is divided into fixed lengths called *sectors*, each of which starts at a fixed location), only half the capacity of the entire disc is used, since the outer tracks could conceivably hold more data than the inner tracks. See also *Constant Linear Velocity*.

Constant Data

Any information on a form that does not change from form to form, and which is often preprinted.

Constant Gloss Test

A test designed to evaluate the *gloss* of a paper (specifically *matte* and uncoated papers), in particular whether light reflected from the surface of the sheet will impede the readability of the material printed on it.

Constant-Illustration Presentation

In presentation graphics, a slide presentation in which the screen is never dark, as is often the case during slide shows. In a constant-illustration presentation, successive slides are transitioned to and from by means of dissolves, cuts, wipes, etc.

Constant Linear Velocity

Abbreviated *CLV*, a means of writing data on an *optical disc* in which the rotational speed of the disc changes depending on where a particular track is written to or read from. Or, in other words, more data is contained on a track near the outside edge of the disc than one near the center.

Although CLV allows as much of the total capacity to be utilized as possible, data may not be accessed quickly (although each track is divided into fixed lengths called *sectors*, each of which starts at a different location); such a disc does not contain tracks that are concentric as with *constant angular velocity* systems; rather, it contains a single track that is a continuous spiral.

As a result, the speed of rotation increases when moving from the outside of the disc toward the center. See also *Constant Angular Velocity*.

Constrain

In a *drawing program*, a tool used to draw geometrically precise lines or shapes. When drawing a circle, for example, it is not uncommon for it to come out looking like an ellipse; the constrain tool will either restore the original and desired shape after it is drawn or, more often, holding down the Option (or some other) key while drawing will allow the object to keep its shape.

Construction Line

In illustration, a faint line that is drawn on paper as a reference point and not intended to be a part of the final illustration.

Consultative Committee International for Telephone and Telegraph Communication

English translation of the organization known as the ***Comité Consultatif International de Téléphonique et Télégraphique***. See ***Comité Consultatif International de Téléphonique et Télégraphique (CCITT)***.

Consumable Textbook

In book publishing, a ***textbook***—often known as a ***workbook***—that is designed to be written in (often including perforated exercises that are occasionally passed in as homework) and discarded.

Contact Angle

On a ***gravure*** press, the angle at which the ***doctor blade*** contacts the surface of the ***gravure cylinder***. See ***Doctor Blade***.

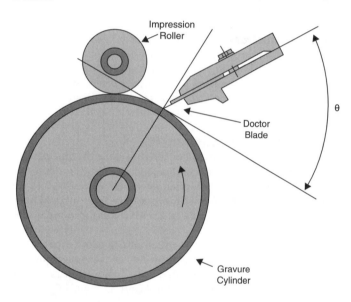

Gravure press doctor blade contact angle θ. This angle should generally be between 55 and 65°.

Contact Angle Method

A test to determine a paper's resistance to water on its surface, or the adequacy of its ***sizing***, in which a drop of water is placed on the paper's surface and after a set period of time the angle between the paper's surface and a line drawn tangent to the surface of the drop at the point where it contacts the paper's surface is observed. If the angle is close to 0°, the drop will have been almost totally absorbed into the paper. The greater the angle, the less wetting that will have occurred. If the angle is beyond 90°, the drop will have simply remained beaded on the paper's surface.

Contact Print

In photography, a print made by placing a piece of photosensitive paper in contact with a film negative or positive and exposing it to light.

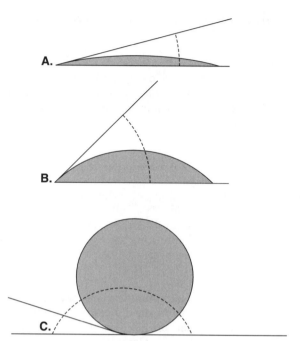

The contact angle method of measuring a paper's water resistance is based on the angle at which a drop of water remains on its surface, whether it is a small angle (A and B) or a large angle (C).

Contact Printing

In ***screen printing***, the process of printing with the screen fabric in contact with the ***substrate*** all across its surface, in contrast to ***off-contact printing***. Also referred to as ***on-contact printing***.

Contact Printing Frame

In platemaking, a vacuum-powered device used to hold ***flat***s, plates, or other reproduction materials firmly in position and in contact with each other during photographic exposure. Also called a ***vacuum frame***.

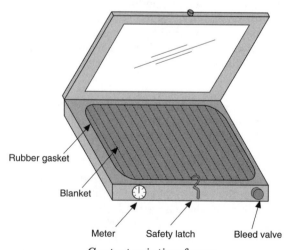

Contact printing frame.

Contact Screen

A screen used in the production of **halftone**s that is placed between and in direct contact with the original **continuous-tone** positive and the unexposed film. When light passes through the original and the screen, and strikes the film, a halftone **negative** will result.

Contended Access

In a **local area network**, an access method for the network in which connected devices gain entry to the communications medium on a first-come, first-served basis. See also **Explicit Access**.

Content

The actual information contained by a document, presentation, Web page, multimedia production, etc., independent of the structure, layout, and design.

Contention

In networking, competition or conflict between two or more **node**s for access to the transmission medium, channel, or other system resources. In order to effectively handle the occurrence of **collision**s between messages transmitted simultaneously, some form of arbitration is required. See **Carrier Sense Multiple Access/Collision Detection (CSMA/CD)**.

Content Search

In database systems, a type of **search** in which the system can read through all the text to match a user-defined character string.

Context-Sensitive Help

In computing, a feature of an application that allows the user to access instructions of **help file**s specific to the mode or status he or she is in. A context-sensitive help can also help resolve a particular error condition.

Context Switching

In computing, the ability to switch from program to program without having to quit one and launch another. Unlike true **multitasking**, however, all additional programs loaded in memory must halt when a new program is switched to. See **Multitasking**.

In **CAD** graphics, *context switching* refers to the ability to control the visibility of layers on the display by switching between or among groups that share similar attributes.

Continuity

In video, television, film, or multimedia production, the maintaining of consistency from scene to scene, shot to shot, or screen to screen. A common example in cinematic films is the water level of a glass that changes from one shot to another within the same scene. This is known as poor continuity. In multimedia, a button that is active in one screen must be active in the next.

Continuous Code

A type of **bar code** that lacks gaps between the characters comprising the code.

Continuous Envelopes

A set of envelopes produced as a long sheet, each of which is separated by perforations, so they can be pin-fed through a computer printer or other device.

Continuous-Flow Dampening System

A type of **dampening system** used in offset lithographic presses that utilizes a **metering roller** in constant contact with both the **water fountain** and a **transfer roller**, which in turn is in constant contact with the **form roller**s that contact the plate. The advantage that continuous-flow systems have over the conventional **intermittent-flow dampening system** is that periodic surges of **fountain solution** are eliminated, and the whole system itself is more instantaneously responsive to adjustments in the amount of fountain solution flowing from the fountain. There are several varieties of continuous-flow systems: **inker-feed system**s, **plate-feed system**s, and combinations of both. (See **Dampening System**.)

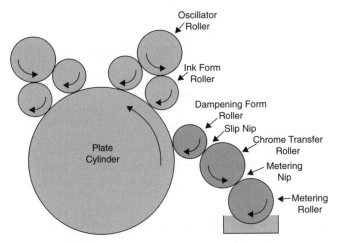

One configuration of continuous-flow dampening system.

Continuous Forms

Any blank or printed forms produced as a long sheet, separated by perforations, as opposed to forms cut into separate sheets.

Continuous Forms Stacker

An output or delivery unit that refolds and stacks a set of **continuous forms** after printing.

Continuous Leading

In typesetting, the continuous feeding of photographic material in a phototypesetter.

Continuous Process

In any manufacturing process, the ongoing production of a steady stream of material, in contrast to a **batch process**.

Continuous Self-Mailer

In business forms printing, a type of continuous form that includes glued margins, cross gluing, and coatings so as to allow an inside and outside to be printed simultaneously, as well as allow a single sheet to serve as its own envelope.

Continuous Tone

Essentially, a photographic image that is not composed of *halftone dot*s or, in other words, an image that consists of tone values ranging from some minimum density (such as white) to a maximum density (such as *black*). An example of a continuous-tone image is a photograph or a *color transparency*.

The term *continuous tone* also refers to a digital image (such as one that has been scanned or generated on the computer) prior to its being screened into halftone dots. Continuous tone also refers to the *bitmap* file of a scanned image.

Continuous tone is often abbreviated **CT** or referred to as *contone*.

Continuous-Tone Developer

Any noninfectious photographic *developer*.

Continuous-Tone Format

General term for any computer image displayed in *eight-bit color* or more.

Continuous-Tone Processing

In photography, developing film using *continuous-tone developer*.

Continuous Wedge

A type of *carbon wedge* containing a range of gray densities from *transparent* to *opaque* lacking discrete steps.

Contone

Abbreviation for *continuous tone*. See *Continuous Tone*.

Contour

In typography, the setting of type in a shape in order to create the appearance of an object. On typesetting devices, it is accomplished by means of multiple line indents. A special sheet with *pica* and *point* gradations is used to calculate the value of the indents. The sheet, usually transparent, is placed over the art or shape so that all indents can be established. Desktop publishing programs such as QuarkXPress simplify considerably the process of setting contour type. Contour type is also referred to as *runaround*.

A similar way of setting type around the shape of an illustration (or a "negative" contour) is called *wraparound*.

Although contoured type is effective in some applications, it frequently exhibits decreased legibility, especially when the contour eliminates the straight, vertical left margin, a common reference point for the eye when reading. When the left margin is staggered, it makes the eye work harder and reading more difficult.

Miscellaneous forms (also called contours) are special shapes into which type is set to achieve a desired visual effect. Type may be set in irregular forms, such as this one. As with justified copy, irregular space and hyphenation may be required to maintain the borders of the format. A comp or rough sketch should be provided to the typesetter with the manuscript. Include individual line lengths to insure a precise fit. Miscellaneous forms (also called contours) are special shapes into which type is set to achieve a desired visual effect. Type may be set in irregular forms, such as this one. As with justified copy, irregular space and hyphenation may be required to maintain the borders of the format. A comp or rough sketch should be provided to the typesetter with the manuscript. Include individual line lengths to insure a precise fit. Miscellaneous forms (also called contours) are special shapes into which type is set to achieve a desired visual effect. Type may be set in irregular forms, such as this one. As with justified copy, irregular space and hyphenation may be required to maintain the borders of the format. A comp or rough sketch should be provided to the typesetter with the manuscript. Include individual line lengths to insure a precise fit.

Type set as a contour.

Contour Character

A letter or other character having a continuous line drawn around—but not touching—the character.

Contouring

A digital imaging problem, characterized by *pixel*s possessing similar values that, when output, tend to group together, producing the appearance of spots of varying color *density*. (See also *Banding*.)

Contract Proof

In printing, a *color proof* pulled from the press that represents the agreed-upon appearance of the finished printed product by the printer and the client. It is commonly the last proof made before printing begins in earnest. Hence, it is also called a *final proof*.

Contrast

Any difference between visual items.

In typography and the graphic design thereof, contrast can include *point size* (10 pt. vs. 24 pt.), character *weight* (plain vs. bold), character width (condensed vs. expanded), character form (uppercase vs. lowercase), character placement (next to each other vs. at oblique angles to each other), character structure (*serif* vs. *sans serif*), character posture (normal vs. oblique), and various combinations of these properties. The use of contrasting type in design is useful and effective, but as a general rule the contrast needs to be strong to be effective. Varying fonts can be effective (not within a single text paragraph, of course), but there should be a large degree of difference between the fonts. Contrasting Helvetica with Times Roman is effective; contrasting Bookman with Palatino looks like an error.

In printing (or other forms of reproduction), *contrast* refers to the degree of perceptible difference between a duplicate and the original from which it was made.

Contrast is also used to refer to a specific mathematical relationship between the tonal qualities of the original and a reproduction. A *gray scale* can be used to compare and contrast each density of the original—from the *shadow*s through the *middletones* to the *highlight*s—with the corresponding densities of the reproduction. These densities can be graphed with the densities of the original on the x axis and those of the reproduction on the y axis, to generate a *gamma* curve. The slope of the resulting line is an indication of the fidelity of the reproduction. A gamma—or slope—of 1.0 describes a line at a 45° angle from both the horizontal and the vertical, corresponding to a perfect reproduction (or, in other words, each density on the original is matched identically with those on the reproduction). Portions of the curve with less than a 45° angle indicate low contrast. Commonly, color reproductions have low contrast in the shadows, but normal contrast in middletones and highlights.

The gamma can be calculated mathematically according to the following formula:

$$\gamma = \frac{DR_O}{DR_R}$$

where γ represents gamma, DR_O represents the density range of the original, and DR_R represents the density range of the reproduction.

Contrast Enhancement

In image editing and manipulation, the adjustment of an image *histogram* to redistribute the *pixel*s between the lightest and darkest portions of the image. Essentially, contrast enhancement stretches or contracts the range of intensities in an image, depending upon the desired effect.

Contrast Ratio

In graphics and imaging, the difference between the minimum and maximum brightness values in an image, or between the *shadow* and *highlight* areas, respectively.

Contrast Ratio Method

A means of measuring a paper's *opacity* by backing a paper sample with a black sheet of paper, measuring how much light is reflected back through the sample, then backing the sample with a white reflecting surface, and measuring how much light is reflected off the top of the white backing and back through the sample. The ratio of these two figures is the paper sample's contrast opacity. It is believed, however, that the *diffuse opacity method* is

more effective than the contrast ratio method in estimating potential *show-through*. (See *Opacity* and *Diffuse Opacity Method*.)

Contrast Stretching

In computer graphics, *contrast enhancement* performed on a display.

Control Ball

Alternate term for a *track ball*. See *Track Ball*.

Control Block

In computing, a data storage area in which information needed to control certain functions of a computer's *operating system* is kept and relayed to other parts of the system.

Control Bus

In computing, the path over which data is transferred from the *central processing unit* to the computer's *memory* and back again.

Control Card

Alternate term for *job control*. See *Job Control*.

Control Character

A character in a *character set* (such as in *ASCII*) that represents a command or function (such as *carriage return*, *line feed*, etc.) or formatting attribute, rather than a printing character such as a letter or number. In the ASCII character set, the first thirty-two characters are control characters. In networking and telecommunications, a *communication control character* facilitates data communication over networks.

Control Character Printout

In computing, the ability to print out typically nonprinting *control character*s. See *Control Character*.

Control Code

In computing, a sequence of characters used to control hardware devices, such as printers, modems, displays, etc. A control code typically begins with a character that instructs the printer (or other device) to interpret a set of successive characters as commands rather than text for printing. The characters used as a control code are known as *setup string*s and *escape sequence*s.

Control Code Display

In computing, the ability of a computer system to display nonprinting (or control) characters on the screen.

Control Device

See *Cdev*.

Control Field

In a database system, a *field* in which is kept the information needed to classify the *record*.

Control Function

In computing, any routine called by a *control character* that affects the processing, writing, transmission, or interpretation of data.

Control Key

A key included on computer keyboards used to modify another key. The Control Key is added to expand the number of functions that a particular key can have. See also *Alternate Key*, *Command Key*, and *Option Key*. The Control key is usually designated *Ctrl*, as in the common keyboard combinations *Ctrl-C* and *Ctrl-Alt-Del*.

Controlled Access Unit (CAU)

In networking, a *multistation access unit (MAU)* or other type of *hub* used in *Token Ring* networks that allows specific ports to be turned on or off. See *Multistation Access Unit (MAU)*.

Controller

In computing, a *processor* responsible for directing the operation of a disk drive, printer, or other device.

Control Point

See *Bézier Control Point (BCP)*.

Control Procedure

In networking and telecommunications, the transmission of data in an orderly fashion. Also known as *link discipline*. See *Protocol*.

Control Program

In computing, the instructions needed for an *operating system* to oversee the basic operations of the computer. The control program is often stored in the computer's *read-only memory (ROM)*.

Control Program for Microcomputers

See *CP/M*.

Control Punching

In printing and/or binding and finishing, the punching or drilling of holes in the marginal areas of a printed web, usually to facilitate a manufacturing or finishing operation. Often trimmed prior to delivery to the customer.

Control Read-Only Memory (CROM)

The portion of most *central processing unit*s that contains the micro code that the computer assembles into the larger, macro codes or commands that the user can select.

Control-S

A remote control device used to operate a Sony video monitor, especially one that is interlinked with others. It is analogous to commonly used television or VCR remote controls except insofar as it uses wires to transmit a control signal to the controlled device, rather than infrared rays.

Control Section

In computing, the portion of a *central processing unit* responsible for interpreting instructions within a program and overseeing their execution by other parts of the system.

Control Signal

In computing, a unique set of computer-generated codes used to control devices attached to the computer system.

Control Station

In networking, a point on a network responsible for control procedures, such as polling, among others, as well as keeping order on the network in the event of *contention* or other problems.

Control Strip

In photography, a pre-exposed piece of film used to gauge the activity or strength of a *developer*.

Control Track

The portion of a videotape containing information regarding synchronization, *time code*, or tape speed. Sometimes spelled with a hyphen, *control-track*.

Control Unit

In computing, the portion of a *central processing unit* responsible for directing the execution of operations by every other part of the computer system.

Conventional Blanket

Term for an offset *blanket* that is not a *compressible blanket*. See *Blanket*.

Conventional Color Angles

Alternate term for *traditional color angles*. See *Traditional Color Angles*.

Conventional Dampening System

An alternate term for an *intermittent-flow dampening system*, a *dampening system* that is used in offset lithographic presses. See *Dampening System: Intermittent-Flow System*.

Conventional Gravure

A means of *gravure engraving* in which the gravure cells comprising the image areas are of the same size and all maintain uniform *cell wall* thicknesses, variations in print density being controlled by cell depth. See *Gravure Engraving*.

Conventional Gravure Engraving

Alternate term for *diffusion-etch process*. See *Gravure Engraving: Diffusion-Etch Process*.

Conventional Memory

In computing by means of *DOS*, the basic 640 *kilobyte*s of *random-access memory (RAM)* used by the *operating system* to run programs. Any additional memory (called *upper* *memory*) was reserved by the system for internal use. The 640-KB figure was essentially derived arbitrarily by IBM (the original figure was 512 KB). The concept of conventional memory has been rendered passé by *Windows* and *OS/2*, whose applications use whatever memory is available. In fact, most modern applications would never be able to run with a mere 640 KB of memory. See also *Expanded Memory*.

Convergence

In a *cathode-ray tube (CRT)*, the proper alignment of the horizontal and vertical lines, ensuring that they remain perfectly perpendicular to each other. Also in a CRT, *convergence* refers to the crossing over of the three separate electron beams (the red, green, and blue) at the plane of the aperture mask.

　　In networking, the term *convergence* refers to the process of synchronizing of a network after a *routing* change has taken place. *Convergence time* is the time required for all *routers* to be updated with new routing information.

Convergence Time

In networking, the time required for all *routers* to be updated with new *routing* information. See *Convergence*.

Conversational

Descriptive of a computer program that carries on a "dialog" with the user either through command lines or *dialog box*es. The program will prompt the user for some type of input and will respond to that input in some fashion.

Conversational Language

A computer language comprising English-like grammar and syntax so as to facilitate a "dialog" between the user and the computer. *BASIC* is an example of a conversational language.

Conversational Mode

A mode of computer operation in which a program or system carries on a "dialog" with the user, using English-like words, grammar, and syntax to prompt the user for input, and respond to that input.

Conversational Timesharing

See *Timesharing*.

Conversion

The translation of one type of data file, unit of measurement, color space, etc., to another, either by manual or computer-assisted calculation.

Conversion Unit

A type of *black box* used to convert electronic data from one format or system to another.

Convertible Perfector

A type of offset *perfecting press*, used to print on both sides of a sheet of paper in one pass through the press. A

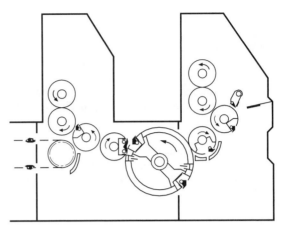

A convertible perfector.

convertible perfector comprises separate printing units, connected by special *transfer cylinder*s that flip the paper over after it leaves the first *impression cylinder*, allowing the second side to be printed by the second impression cylinder. One advantage of this type of press is that by adjusting the transfer cylinders so that they do not flip the sheet over, it can be used as a single-side, multicolor press. A variety of color and side combinations is possible with convertible perfectors. See *Perfecting Press*.

Converting

Any *finishing* operation that forms a printed product into another physical form other than simple ink-on-substrate. Bagmaking, boxmaking, bookbinding, waxing, coating, laminating, folding, gluing, diecutting, etc., are all considered converting operations. See *Binding and Finishing*.

Convert Utility

In computing, a *utility program* that allows a file to be converted from one *file format* to another, typically to facilitate output to different devices.

Conveyor Dryer

See *Automatic Conveyorized Drying*.

Cool Colors

A range of *colors*—green, blue, and violet—that produce a psychological impression of coolness, as opposed to *warm colors* (yellow, orange, and red). Any printed product or other color reproduction will instill feelings of coolness if the *color balance* as a whole imparts a bluish tone. See *Color Plate 6*. See also *Warm Colors*.

Cooling Roller

Alternate term for a *chill roll*. See *Chill Roll*.

Cooling Zone

The portion of a printing press drying system in which the heated *substrate* is cooled before handling, stacking, or rewinding.

Cooperative Multitasking

In computing, a type of *multitasking* in which all open applications must work in tandem to share system resources. In *Windows*, for example, a particular application that has been given control of system resources effectively prevents other applications from running until an operation is completed and control is given back to Windows. See also *Preemptive Multitasking* and *Time-Slice Multitasking*.

Cooperative Processing

In networking and computing, the sharing of a workload among two or more computers, such as a *personal computer* and a *mainframe*.

Coordinate

Any numerically defined position (either vertical or horizontal) relative to some point of origin. A graph—or other *coordinate system*—plots a point using a horizontal coordinate and a vertical coordinate defined with respect to an origin (0,0). Thus, a point having the coordinates (4,5) would be four units from the origin along the horizontal axis, and five units above the point of origin on the vertical axis. Three-dimensional coordinate systems add a third coordinate representing depth.

Coordinate System

Any system used to mathematically indicate location. Most coordinate systems utilize two axes (a horizontal, called an *x-axis*, and a vertical, called a *y-axis*), coordinates being plotted with respect to variables indicated along both axes. Such a system is known as two-dimensional, as only two variables are mapped; an additional *z-axis* is often added to add a third dimension. A graph is a basic coordinate system, often using only two axes. Graphics and page layout programs allow objects to be drawn or positioned by means of coordinates.

In three-dimensional modeling, different sets of coordinates are used: *world coordinates* are absolute, fixed coordinates, while *modeling coordinates* and *eye coordinates* are coordinates defined in terms of a particular viewing angle.

Coordinate Tracking

In computer graphics programs, a function that uses *x* and *y* (and sometimes *z)* coordinates to indicate to the user where the cursor or pointer is located on the screen.

Copolymer

A large molecule created by the *polymerization* of two or more smaller molecules (called *monomer*s).

Copper Distributed Data Interface (CDDI)

A network utilizing a *token-passing protocol* in which devices are connected with copper *unshielded twisted pair* wiring. CDDI, a variant of *FDDI*, supports transmission speeds of up to 100 megabits per second and uses *Ten-Base-T (10Base-T)* copper wiring.

Copper Ferrocyanide Pink

An *organic color pigment* used in printing inks. Copper Ferrocyanide Pink is used as a substitute for the *Rhodamine 6G* double and triple salts, as its color is very similar and is less expensive. It possesses less *lightfastness*, however, and less resistance to solvents and heat. It has low resistance to acids, alkalis, and soaps, but it is stronger tinctorially. It has good flow and workability characteristics and is often used for inexpensive bright shades. (See also *Organic Color Pigments*.)

(*CI Pigment Red 169 No. 45160:2.*)

Copperplate

In typography, a style of type dating from the days of *copperplate engraving* characterized by fine *serif*s at the end of each stroke. Copperplate type was originally produced by etching a copper plate with a steel scribe, creating depressions in the surface that held ink (a form of printing known as *intaglio* and is the basis of modern *gravure* printing). In order to obtain sharp corners on the strokes, a final scribe was made perpendicular to the main stroke and was allowed to extend just a bit beyond, creating the copperplate serifs. After printing—or in small *point sizes*—copperplate serifs often became indistinguishable. Copperplate typefaces often do not have a lowercase; smaller point-size caps are used in their stead. Copperplate faces therefore are rarely used for text, as all-cap type is difficult to read. In the days of metal typesetting, copperplate typefaces were widely used for business cards, stationery, and other such uses. With the advent of modern typesetting equipment and the widespread availability of many different typefaces, the use of copperplate faces has declined.

Coprocessor

An additional *microprocessor* installed in a computer so as to supplement the *central processing unit (CPU)* and expedite and facilitate certain mathematical functions (often by being designed to perform exponential arithmetic, expediting the calculation of large numbers). When the CPU encounters an instruction intended for a coprocessor, it sends it to the coprocessor and awaits a signal indicating that the calculation is completed. (If there is no coprocessor installed, an error message may be the result.) Since these coprocessors are designed specifically for certain types of calculations, they require significantly fewer instructions than a general CPU would. Many newer CPUs are now created to perform these functions. Spreadsheets, *CAD*, and some graphics programs perform significantly better when coprocessors are installed, although a program must be written specifically to take advantage of a coprocessor.

These coprocessors are sometimes called *floating-point coprocessor*s, or *floating-point unit*s.

Copy

Any material that is to be typeset, be it a *manuscript*, *typescript*, or a typewritten document with hand-written changes and edits. *Copy* is also used to refer generally to any other page elements—including illustrations, photographs, etc.—that will need to be prepared and assembled, although the term commonly is used to refer strictly to text.

The term *copy* also means to reproduce any original, be it via simple photocopying or by printing. *Copy* is also used to refer to the duplicate itself. Digital files and disks can also be copied.

Copy Area

On a *screen printing* press, the portion of the screen through which the image is to be printed.

Copyboard

The portion of a graphic arts camera comprising an adjustable frame—usually with a glass cover—on which original copy is mounted while it is photographed. Depending on the type of camera (i.e., whether it is a *vertical camera* or a *horizontal camera*), the copyboard may be oriented horizontally or vertically, respectively. When oriented vertically, the copyboard can usually be tilted to a horizontal position to facilitate the positioning of the original. The variable distance between the *lens* and the copyboard determines the reproduction size of the original. See *Photography: Graphic Arts Photography*.

Copy Camera

Alternate term for a *process camera* used in graphic arts photography. See *Process Camera* and *Photography: Graphic Arts Photography*.

Copy Dot

In *halftone* photography, to photograph dot for dot a previously screened image.

Copyedit

To perform *copyediting* on a manuscript. See *Copyediting*. Also spelled as two words, *copy edit*.

Copyediting

A stage of the publishing process during which an editor—either in-house or freelance—reviews a *manuscript* and marks grammatical, typographical, and content-related errors. The copyediting process also involves correct markup of text for typesetting and formatting. Copyediting is always performed before actual typesetting. Also spelled as two words, *copy editing*.

Copyfitting

In typography, the process of estimating the *point size* and *leading* in which a particular piece of copy will need to be set to fit in a (usually) predetermined area. Copyfitting is based on a calculation called *characters per pica (CPP)*, which varies by *typeface*, and is also a function of that typeface's *alphabet length*, or how many characters in a *font* will occupy one pica of linear distance. The process of copyfitting is generally as follows:

1. Obtain a *character count* for the manuscript to be typeset. (In other words, either count or calculate the total number of characters in the manuscript; see *Character Count*.)
2. Check the typeface, size, and line length (LL) that will be used. Look up the CPP and multiply it by the line length. For example, if the CPP is 2.81 and the line length is 25 picas, then 70.25 (2.81 × 25 = 70.25) indicates how many characters will fit in one line.
3. Divide the number of characters per line into the total number of characters (derived from the character count) to obtain the total number of lines that the job will set.
4. Multiply the number of lines by the leading value to arrive at the copy depth (in points). If the job is mostly straight text, the number of lines per page can be divided into the total number of lines to obtain the total number of pages the job will set. However, any heads, subheads, illustrations, and other non-text matter will need to be accounted for, if present.

If the type needs to fit a predetermined area (such as in magazine and newspaper articles), the type size, leading, or even the typeface may need to be altered (if cutting of the material is not possible). In automated typesetting, *white space reduction (WSR)* is also an alternative. The simplest way to find out how much space will be saved by white space reduction is to set a sample line or paragraph with the desired WSR increment and compare it to the type set in expanded letterspacing. Then determine the gain in space in rounded-off percentage points and simply deduct that percentage from the number of lines estimated for the standard letterspacing.

The general application of copyfitting is for *justified* type. There is usually no difference in the number of type lines between *justified* and *unjustified* type, but on occasion—in order to avoid poor *hyphenation*—a minimal line increase may occur in unjustified type.

Copying

The act of making any reproductions of original material.

Copy Paper

A type of paper designed for use with photocopiers.

Copy Preparation

In typography, a term originally used to refer to the proper preparation of manuscript copy for typesetting. To a large extent, "copy preparation" still refers to typewritten sheets, 8½×11 in., typed double-spaced and neatly marked with typographic instructions. In recent years, however, copy is no longer rekeyboarded by the typesetting operator (keyboarder). Copy is increasingly prepared on personal computers with word processing capabilities, and then the information is input to the typesetting process electronically. The originator thus has the benefit of sophisticated editing and correction prior to releasing the material for typesetting. An important attribute will be consistency of preparation, since the conversion of the electronic data to typesetting input will require a match-up of specific occurrences of indents, word spaces, returns, and other code and character combinations in order to change typewriter-oriented copy into typography.

Some basic rules of copy preparation, regardless of the means, are as follows:

1. Use the same number of blank spaces or a tab key for paragraph indents, but use each consistently.
2. If an extra word space is inserted at the end of a sentence, make certain that only that one additional space is inserted at each point.
3. Check with the typesetting operator about recommended use of the quote marks. The open and close quotes are the same character on a typewriter, but they are different in typesetting. In desktop publishing programs like QuarkXPress, a distinction needs to be made between proper "smart quotes" ("" ' ') and the inch marks (" ').
4. Use the special function for automatic underlining so that a change to italic can be generated. Word processing and page makeup programs can now set italic type, eliminating the need for underlining as a substitute in manuscript preparation.

Copyright

In *book typography* and production, a page—typically printed as the reverse of the *title page*—listing the copyright information of the book, and the Library of Congress Cataloguing-in-Publication (CIP) data, and on some occasions the *dedication* and any permissions information for quoted material used in the text. See *Book Typography*. Also see *Intellectual Property*.

Copy Separation

Any mechanical means of keeping consecutive copies of a printed or otherwise duplicated product distinguishable from each other.

Copy Stand

A device used for supporting and adjusting the position of a photographic or video camera so as to videotape flat art or still objects. Often, the copy stand has lamps mounted to it so as to provide appropriate illumination to the objects being filmed or taped.

CORA

In digital typography, a *page description language* used by the Linotype 202 and other related machines.

Cordless Mouse

A computer *mouse* that transmits signals to the main computer by means of radio impulses rather than electrical signals sent along a wire. Such a device affords the user greater freedom of handling.

Core

See *Core Memory*.

In *fiber optics*, the central portion of the optical cable—usually 8–12 microns (for single-mode fiber)—through which light is transmitted.

CorelDraw

A popular computer program developed by Corel used to draw *vector-based graphics*. Originally developed for *IBM-compatible computer*s, a version for the *Macintosh* has been introduced.

Core Memory

A type of computer memory—found on older machines—in which data is stored on a magnetic, doughnut-shaped core.

Core Remainder

In *web printing*, the amount of paper left on an expiring paper roll prior to splicing.

Corona

In an imaging system—such as a photocopier, laser printer, etc.—a component used to clear the photoconductive drum of the previously printed image. Damage to or dirt on the corona impedes its ability to remove the entire prior image, causing degraded quality of successive images.

Corotron

Alternate term for *corona*. See *Corona*.

Corporate Publishing

The production of documents, pamphlets, books, etc., for the support or marketing of specific products and services. In contrast to *commercial publishing*, corporate publishing is not conducted for profit-making per se, but rather to increase the profitability of the primary functions of the company.

Corrosion Inhibitor

A compound (such as magnesium nitrate) added to an offset press *fountain solution* as a means of preventing *oxidation* or other chemical reaction of the aluminum printing plate. See *Fountain Solution*.

Corrugation

A paper web defect also called *rope marks*. See *Rope Marks*.

Co-Solvent

Two *solvent*s that are both required to dissolve a particular substance.

Coster, Laurens Janszoon

Coster, also spelled Koster (c. 1370–1440), is said to be a Dutch rival of Johannes Gutenberg as the inventor of printing. In the 19th century some Dutch scholars believed that Laurens Janszoon Coster was the real inventor of book printing and that Johannes Gutenberg had stolen the idea from him. Coster's home town, Haarlem, still has his statue standing in the central square.

Coster is said to have printed with movable type as early as 1430, but proof is lacking. No surviving specimen attributed to him bears his name—documentation also missing in the case of Gutenberg. Coster's printing achievement was not recorded until a century after his death and his method of typecasting was said to be casting in sand from wooden molds.

His last name means "sacristan," a title for an official of the Great Church of Haarlem and is mentioned several times in records between 1417 and 1434 as alderman, tax assessor, and treasurer. He is presumed to have died in a plague that struck Haarlem in 1440.

Cotton-Content

Paper manufactured using *pulp* obtained from cotton, linen, or other fabrics, rather than wood. Papers can range from 25–100% cotton fibers. Cotton-content papers are typically higher in quality than wood-pulp papers. Cotton-content is also called *rag content*.

Cotton Drill

In *binding and finishing*, a heavy cotton fabric used for cloth bindings.

Cotton Linters

Short hairs remaining on cotton seeds following cotton ginning, used as a fibrous source for papermaking.

Couch Marks

A paper defect characterized by thick and thin marks in the surface of the web matching the size and shape of the holes on the *couch roll*, caused by a too-rapid removal of the forming web from the wire by the couch rolls.

Couch Roll

A rotating, perforated metal cylinder at the end of a *fourdrinier* papermaking machine's *forming section* that uses a vacuum to remove water from the wet paper *web* before the web is sent to the *press section*. After passing through the couch roll, the paper web is still about 80–85% water. (See *Fourdrinier*.)

It is called a "couch roll" because the moving felt belts of the press section were at one time called "couches." The roll that transferred the web to the couch was then called the "couch roll."

Coumarone-Indene Resin

A *thermosetting* resin derived from coal tar used in printing ink *varnish*es. Also called *cumar*. See *Resin*.

Count

In printing and *binding and finishing*, the actual quantity of finished press sheets, *signature*s, or bound publications delivered on an order.

Counter

In typography, the space in a letter or other character enclosed—either fully or partially—by the strokes of the character, as in the center of the letter "o." The lines enclosing the counter are known as the *bowl*. See *Letter Elements*.

Counterbalanced Squeegee

A *squeegee* used in *screen printing* to which a weight (equal to the weight of the squeegee) has been attached—on the opposite side of a pivot—as a means of absorbing the weight of the squeegee. A counterbalanced squeegee is used primarily to eliminate operator fatigue.

Counter-Stacker

In *binding and finishing*, a mechanical device that automatically counts and stacks bound publications as they are delivered from the binding section.

Coupling

The process of connecting two or more devices—such as computers—together in order to share resources or work loads.

Courier

A *typeface* used originally on typewriters but that is also found very often on computer systems. Courier was designed by Bud Ketler of IBM in the early 1950s. It is usually used as a default font on output devices and is a standard *fixed-width* font.

```
A typeface used originally on type-
writers but that is also found very
often on computer systems. Courier
was designed by Bud Kelter of IBM.
```

Courier, a typeface that was used originally on typewriters.

Courseware

Any set of media—books, software, videodiscs, CD-ROMs, etc.—used or recommended to supplement educational or instructional programs.

Covering

In *binding and finishing*, any process of attaching a book cover or case to a bound *book block*. See *Binding and Finishing*.

Covering Power

Alternate term for a printing ink's *opacity*. See *Opacity*.

Cover Ink

A printing ink characterized by high *gloss*, *lightfastness*, and scuff resistance, used to print report, book, magazine and other covers.

Cover Paper

Also called *cover stock*, cover paper is a thick, durable paper *grade* used for covers of pamphlets, catalogs, reports, etc. The paper quality of prime importance for cover papers is its strength, which must allow it to adequately protect the pages that are bound beneath or between it.

Cover papers come in a variety of *finishes*, *coatings*, textures, etc., as one of the prime functions of cover paper is to aesthetically represent the contents of the pages it is covering. Depending on the wishes of the graphic designer, cover paper may also need to undergo *embossing*, die-cutting, drilling, scoring, stapling, varnishing, lacquering, laminating, folding, etc., and cover paper may also be printed using a wide variety of specialty inks. Cover paper *finish*es run the gamut from *smooth* to *embossed*. Typically, cover stock that has the same *basis weight* as the text paper should have twice the thickness. *Double-thick cover stock* consists of two sheets of 65-lb. cover stock laminated together.

The *basic size* of cover papers is 20×26 in., and comes in basis weights of 50, 60, 65, 80, 90, 100, and 130 lb. *Standard sizes* for cover papers are 20×26 in., 23×35 in., 26×40 in., and 35×46 in.

Cover Stock

Alternate term for *cover paper*. See *Cover Paper*.

Cover White

Alternate term for *titanium dioxide* when used as an *opaque pigment* in printing inks. See *Titanium Dioxide* and *Opaque Pigments*.

Cove Serif

See *Bracketed*.

CPE

Abbreviation for *customer-premises equipment*. See *Customer-Premises Equipment (CPE)*.

CPI

Abbreviation for *characters per inch*. See *Characters Per Inch*.

CPI is also an abbreviation for *computer-PABX interface*. See *Computer-PABX Interface (CPI)*.

CPM

Abbreviation for *characters per minute*. See *Characters Per Minute*.

CPM is also an abbreviation for *critical path management*. See *Critical Path Management*.

CP/M

Abbreviation for *Control Program for Microcomputers*, a computer *operating system* developed in the early 1980s by Digital Research, Inc. It was eventually superseded by Microsoft's *Disk Operating System (DOS)*.

CPP

Abbreviation for *characters per pica*. See *Characters Per Pica (CPP)*.

C Print

A color photographic print produced by exposing photosensitive paper to a color *negative*. Also spelled with a hyphen, *C-print*.

CPS

Abbreviation for *characters per second*. See *Characters Per Second (CPS)*.

CPU

Abbreviation for *central processing unit*. See *Central Processing Unit (CPU)*.

CPU Busy Time

Alternate term for *CPU time*. See *CPU Time*.

CPU Chip

The heart of a computer or computer-controlled device. The CPU chip (*CPU* stands for *central processing unit*) is the determinant of what is known as the operating speed of the computer (measured—as of this writing—in *megahertz*). A CPU chip consists essentially of many tiny transistors, that repeatedly turn on and off, hence the *binary digit*s that comprise the code that a computer understands include only 1 and 0 ("open" or "closed", "on" or "off"). Computer operating speeds—as of this writing—have hit the 132+ MHz range, with under 75 MHz becoming rarer and rarer.

Chip speeds are increasing at a dramatic pace. The chips utilized in some of the IBM PCs and compatibles on the market now (which commonly run the Windows or DOS operating system) include Intel's 80386, 80486, and Pentium chips, the Pentiums being the most rapid. The Apple Macintosh computers utilize Motorola's 68020, 68030, and 68040 (commonly described generally as 680X0) or, more and more commonly, the PowerPC chip, with ever-increasing speeds.

CPU Time

A measure of the time it takes a computer's *central processing unit* to execute an instruction. Also known as *CPU busy time*. See *CPU*.

Cracked Edge

Also called an *edge tear*, a paper *web* defect characterized by a tear at the edge of the roll. Although edge tears only extend inward a very short distance, *web break*s in web offset lithography can be started by edge tears. (See also *End Damage*.)

Cracking

The breakdown of a printed ink film, characterized by thin cracks appearing in the surface of the film.

Craftsman Table

A table used in graphic arts comprising straight horizontal and vertical edges, calibrated to draw rule lines on paper, plastic, mylar, or other material.

Crane

In photography and videography, a platform mounted to a moving arm to which a camera is fixed. The arm can be moved up and down and back and forth. A crane is often used to capture overhead shots or shots from a high viewpoint.

Crash

An abrupt failure—characterized by a "freezing" or "bombing"—of a computer system or attached device, caused by a wide variety of software or hardware malfunctions. One particular type of hard disk crash is called a *head crash*. See *Head Crash*.

In *flexography*, the term *crash* refers to a condition in which excessive pressure exists between either the *plate cylinder* and the *impression cylinder* or the *anilox roller* and the *plate cylinder*, resulting in printing defects such as *halos* or double impressions.

In *binding and finishing*, *crash* is a term for a strong, coarse, open-mesh fabric used as a *backlining* in some *casebound* books, added to afford the binding extra support.

Crash Bar

Alternate term for a *safety bar*. See *Safety Bar*.

Crash Edit

In video editing, a crude *assemble edit* made by manually pressing the "record" button on a *VCR*. Crash edits often leave glitches or distortions at the edit point.

Crash Finish

A paper *finish* characterized by a coarse surface intended to simulate rough linen.

Crash Numbering

In the production of continuous forms, a consecutive numbering of printed or photocopied sheets performed on a collating device using carbon-based or carbonless materials to transfer numbers to successive plys of a collated set. A type of *crash printing*.

Crash Perforation

In the production of continuous forms (specifically multiply carbonless forms), a perforation cut through all the plys of a collated set.

Crash Printing

The impression of an image using relief pressure and carbon or carbonless forms.

Cratering

A defect of *gravure* printing characterized by small rings of color (typically visible under magnification), caused by

solvent trapped beneath a dry ink film. As the solvent is vaporized, it bursts through the surface of the ink, forming "craters" (also called *volcanoes*). Using a slower-drying ink or reducing the heat of a drying oven (if the ink is a *heat-set ink*) are ways of alleviating the problem.

Cratering also refers to a defect of *screen printing* in which depressions form in a printed ink film that may be deep enough to expose the *substrate*.

Crawl

In film, television, video, or multimedia production, any text that moves either horizontally or vertically over the screen, either to display credits or other text. In computer lingo, also known as *scrolling*.

In video production, the term *crawl* is also used to refer to a video error characterized by a glare surrounding bright portion of an image, often seen in low-quality recordings.

Crawling

A printing defect characterized by a printed ink film beading up on a *substrate* that it does not wet completely. Crawling is also a symptom of poor *trapping*, the printing of one ink on top of a previously printed ink, in which the first ink film repels the second, causing the ink to form drops. (See also *Crystallization*.)

Crawl Space

The space at the bottom of a video screen reserved for text display. See *Crawl*.

Crazing

A printing ink defect characterized by wrinkling or cracking of a printed ink film believed to be caused by a contraction of a drying ink film, occurring when *solvent* is removed too quickly from the drying ink film. Crazing occurs most often on plastic *substrate*s, typically plastics that are sensitive to solvents. Incorrect *resin* formulation can also be a cause.

Crazing is also known as *checking* and *gas crazing* (when the ink vehicle is formulated from *tung oil*).

CRC

Abbreviation for *camera-ready copy*. See *Camera-Ready Copy*.

CRC is also an abbreviation for *cyclic redundancy check*. See *Cyclic Redundancy Check (CRC)*.

Creative Director

An employee of an advertising agency responsible for the overall supervision of all aspects of the quality and nature of the agency's work for a specific client.

Credit Line

A line of type accompanying an illustration, photograph, or other graphic element indicating the photographer, artist, or basic ownership of the image, usually used in the reproduction of copyrighted materials. Credit lines may also be printed on the copyright page of a publication.

Creep

An undesirable movement of an offset press **blanket** or blanket **packing** material during printing, caused either by blanket stretching, improper tension, or an excessive number of different sheets of packing material. Creep caused by the latter condition is known as **packing creep**. See **Blanket** and **Packing**.

The term *creep* can also be used to refer to the steady deformation of a plastic (such as a **substrate** used in **flexography**) under stress, a condition also known as **cold-flow**.

In **binding and finishing**, the term *creep* refers to the gradual extension of the inner **signatures** of a **book block** beyond the edges of the signatures that surround them, resulting in inner signatures having a progressively smaller trim size. **Shingling** is one means of compensating for creep. Creep is also known as **binder's creep**, **pushout**, and **thrust**, and is commonly an issue only in publications that are bound by **saddle-stitching**.

Creeping

A printing defect characterized by a lateral movement or oozing of a wet printed ink film beyond the boundaries of the position on the **substrate** for which it was intended.

Creeping is also an alternate term for **cold-flow**. See **Cold-Flow**.

Cresol

Any of three isomeric organic compounds—chemical formula C_7H_8O—derived from coal tar and wood tar, used primarily as a disinfectant. It is also occasionally used in **screen printing** to improve the adhesion of a **stencil** by causing the screen fibers to become sticky and swollen. Cresol is not used often, due to its tendency to weaken the screen fabric and its toxicity. Cresol is also known as *methyl phenol*.

Crinkle

To severely wrinkle or crush a printed film—such as packaging or wrapping material—then examine the ink film for signs of breakage, as a means of gauging the degree of ink flexibility.

Critical Error

In computing, an error condition in which a program stops until the user rectifies the condition. An example is when the user selects "print" and there is no paper in the printer.

Critical Path

In project management, the shortest and most direct route a project can take through a workflow. **Critical path management** involves seeking the most efficient route for a project to take.

Critical Path Management

In project management, the analysis of all the steps needed to complete a project and a determination of the quickest and most efficient route through those steps. Critical path management is abbreviated **CPM**.

Critical Path Scheduling

In project planning, a means of ensuring continued progress of a project by setting deadlines for milestones, or other events or activities. See **Critical Path Management**.

Crock

A measure of the **abrasion resistance** of an ink film printed on a fabric.

Crocking

General term for the rubbing off or smudging of ink, due to any number of factors. (See **Ink: Printing Ink Defects and Problems**.)

CROM

Abbreviation for **control read-only memory**. See **Control Read-Only Memory (CROM)**.

Cromalin

A proprietary term that is used for a type of **single-sheet color proof** used to check the **registration** of the **colors**, the existence of any egregious blemishes or other undesirable marks, and to confirm size and position of page elements. The Cromalin process utilizes several sheets—commonly four, one for each **process color**—of clear photosensitive plastic. Each sheet is exposed to one of the **color separation negative**s, and, when the sheets are treated with process color toners, dots will adhere to the surface of the plastic in the image areas. The four exposed sheets of plastic—each containing a different process color—are aligned with each other in proper register and laminated together.

Cromalin is a trademark of du Pont.

Crop

To remove by cutting portions of a printed piece, a photograph, plate, or digital image. **Cropping** is done to either cut a printed product down to its desired size, or to omit extraneous detail from an illustration or photograph, allowing attention to focus on a particular region of the image. Cropping can be done in the **prepress** stage, either manually or digitally, and before or after **scanning**. The guidelines for the desired amount of cropping is indicated by **cropmarks**.

Cropmarks

Lines drawn or printed on a photograph, overlay, or printed product to indicate the proper **cropping** of the image or print in question. Also spelled as two words, *crop marks*, and also known as **trim marks**.

Cropping

Cutting off a undesired portion of a printed piece, photograph, or other image. See **Crop**.

Cropmarks that show how the photograph should be cropped.

Croque

A rough sketch of a design or illustration made by an artist, specifically a fashion illustrator.

Cross Assembler

In computer programming, an *assembler* that runs on a computer other than the one on which its output will actually be run. Also known as a *cross compiler* or *cross assembler program*.

Cross Assembler Program

See *Cross Assembler*.

Crossbar

In typography, a horizontal stroke that passes through the *stem*, as in the lowercase "t." See *Letter Elements*.

Cross Compiler

Alternate term for a *cross assembler*. See *Cross Assembler*.

Cross Direction

Alternate term for *cross-grain direction*. See *Cross-Grain Direction*.

Cross-Fade

Alternate term for a *dissolve*. See *Dissolve*.

Crossfeed

In *scanning*, a movement of the input or output optics of a scanner in a direction parallel to the axis of the scanning cylinder.

Cross Fold

Alternate term for a *chopper fold*. See *Chopper Fold*.

Cross-Grain Direction

The direction perpendicular to the *grain direction* of a paper (the direction in which all or most of the paper fibers are oriented in a sheet or *web*). Since the grain is produced on the *forming wire* of a papermaking machine in the direction of the web's travel through the machine, the grain direction is also called the *machine direction*, and the cross-grain direction is called the *cross-machine direction*. Grain direction is an important factor of such paper properties as strength and dimensional stability. See *Grain*. Also known as the *cross direction*.

Cross Hairs

On a computer, a cursor or pointer design consisting of two intersecting perpendicular lines used to accurately locate screen coordinates. Sometimes spelled as one word, *crosshairs*.

Cross Head

In page layout, a *heading* that extends beyond a single column of text.

Cross-Interleaved Reed-Solomon Code

An error detection and correction technique added to *CD-ROM*s so as to prevent slight manufacturing faults and surface scratches from rendering a disc unreadable or introducing errors into a file.

Crossline Screen

In *halftone* photography, a grid (usually made of glass) comprising opaque lines that form transparent squares, used to convert a *continuous-tone* image to a halftone. See *Halftone*. Also known as a *glass screen*.

Cross-Machine Direction (CD)

On a papermaking machine, the direction perpendicular to the direction in which the paper *web* travels as it is forming. Cross-machine direction tests are frequently made during paper production to ensure that the papermaking *furnish* is being delivered across the *forming wire* with uniform thickness, consistency, moisture content, etc. Variations in CD profiles affect the quality, *printability* and *runnability* of the paper that will ultimately form. The cross-machine direction is also called the *cross-grain direction*.

Cross-Machine Tension Burst

A *burst* or rupture in a paper *web* caused by abrupt inconsistencies in a paper's thickness across the roll's width, or by winding the roll too tightly. (See also *Air Shear Burst*, *Caliper Shear Burst*, and *Full Machine-Direction Burst*.)

Crossmarks

A type of *register marks* comprising two perpendicular lines. See *Register Marks*.

Crossover

Descriptive of a printed illustration that occupies portions of both sides of a two-page spread, essentially "crossing over" the binding edge, commonly found in newspaper, magazine, and—to a lesser extent—book publishing. When positioning and printing both parts of the illustration, it is of course crucial that the two halves line up when the final publication is assembled and that the colors match. (See also *Spread*.)

Cross-Platform

Descriptive of computer files and applications that can run on more than one computer *platform*, especially a *standard platform*. Adobe *Acrobat* files are good examples of cross-platform files, as they can be read on *DOS*, *Windows*, *Macintosh*, and *UNIX* systems.

Cross Stroke

Alternate term for the letter element known as a *crossbar*. See *Crossbar*.

Crosstalk

In telecommunications, any interference of a signal by a signal on an adjacent *channel*.

Crotch

In typography, the part of a letter or other character that forms the inside of an *apex* or a *vortex*, as in the inside of the points of a capital letter "W." See *Letter Elements*.

Crowbar

An alternate term for a *surge protector*. See *Surge Protector*.

Crowd

To apply too heavy an ink film to a plate, as a means of darkening the printed image.

Crown

In printing, the difference in the diameter of a printing press roller that exists among certain reference points along its circumference, used as a measure of *out-of-roundness*.

In *binding and finishing*, *crown* refers to the length of the staple that is visible on the *spine* of a publication that has been bound via *saddle-stitching*. See *Saddle-Stitching*.

CRT

Abbreviation for *cathode-ray tube*. See *Cathode-Ray Tube*.

CRT Flying Spot Scanner

In *scanning*, a *scanner* using as its optical mechanism a *cathode-ray tube (CRT)* that *rasterize*s an image (typically *reflection copy*). The beam generated by the CRT is reflected through the device's lens and through a *photomultiplier tube*, where it is converted to an electrical signal and, ultimately, a digital signal capable of being input into a computer. CRT flying spot scanners are capable of very high *resolution*s.

Crunching

Alternate term for *data compression*. See *Data Compression*.

Crushed Core

A paper *web* defect in which the paper roll's core is no longer round. A crushed core is a contributor to *out-of-roundness* paper rolls. See *Out-of-Roundness*.

Crushing

In *case binding*, a smashing of the *spine* of a book that occurs during *rounding*, occasionally causing an undesirable creasing of the paper (especially of low-bulk paper) along the *bind edge*.

Cryoelectronic Storage

A computer storage device made up of materials that become highly electrically conductive at extremely low temperatures.

Cryosar

A switching device used in semiconductors that becomes highly electrically conductive at very low temperatures.

Crystal Base

A colorless, transparent substance added to a *screen printing* ink as a means of adjusting the ink's viscosity, commonly utilized in *halftone* screen printing.

Crystallization

A printing defect symptomatic of poor *trapping*, the ability to print one ink on top of another previously printed dry ink, in which the dry ink film—which has been allowed to dry too hard—repels the wet ink, causing *crawling*, *mottle*, or *rub-off*. Crystallization occurs with inks that dry by *oxidation* and when the second ink is printed at a much later time than the first ink. Crystallization can commonly be avoided by reducing the amount of *drier* in the ink. (See *Trapping*.) As used in printing terminology, *crystallization* has nothing to do with the chemical term *crystallization*, which describes an entirely different phenomenon.

Crystal Violet (CFA)

An *organic color pigment* used in printing inks. Crystal Violet is a bright violet with good color qualities, but poor resistance to alkalis and soaps. Its low cost makes it acceptable for use in water-based flexographic and gravure packaging inks for applications that do not require high degrees of chemical resistance. Commonly used as an economical substitute for *PMTA Violet* pigments. (See *Organic Color Pigments*.)

(*CI Pigment Violet 27 No. 42535:3*.)

CSA

Abbreviation for *common service area*. See *Common Service Area (CSA)*.

CSC

See *Caps and Small Caps*.

C-Set

Abbreviation for *control set*. See *Control Set*.

CSMA

Abbreviation for *carrier sense multiple access*. See *Carrier Sense Multiple Access*.

CSMA/CA

Abbreviation for *carrier sense multiple access/collision avoidance*. See *Carrier Sense Multiple Access/Collision Avoidance (CSMA/CA)*.

CSMA/CD

Abbreviation for *carrier sense multiple access/collision detection*. See *Carrier Sense Multiple Access/Collision Detection (CSMA/CD)*.

CSU

Abbreviation for *Channel Service Unit*. See *Channel Service Unit (CSU)*.

CT

Abbreviation for *continuous tone*. See *Continuous Tone*.

The term *CT* is also a *file extension* appended to files saved in the Scitex CT format.

The term *CT* is also an abbreviation for *computed tomography*. See *Computed Tomography*.

Ctrl

In computing, abbreviation for the *control key*. See *Control Key*.

Ctrl-Alt-Del

A shorthand means of specifying "Control-Alternate-Delete," a three-key combination used to *reboot* (or *warm boot*) a computer, particularly one using *DOS* or *Windows* as an *operating system*. On the *Macintosh*, commonly the menu option Restart, or a reset button, effects a warm boot.

Ctrl-Break

Alternate term for the keyboard designation *Ctrl-C*. See *Ctrl-C*.

Ctrl-C

A shorthand designation for the keyboard combination "Control-C," a command in computing (especially by means of *DOS* or *Windows*) that instructs a program to stop performing a particular function, such as printing, searching etc. On the *Macintosh*, the equivalent is "command-period."

CTS

Abbreviation for *clear to send*. See *Clear to Send (CTS)*.

C2

In computing, a level of operating system security specified by the *National Computer Security Center (NCSC)*, requiring a user *password* to gain access.

C2S

Abbreviation for *coated two sides* paper. See *Coated Two Sides*.

CU

Abbreviation for *close up*. See *Close Up*.

CUA

Abbreviation for *Common User Access*. See *Common User Access (CUA)*.

Cubic Mapping

In *three-dimensional (3D) animation*, a means of simulating the reflection of light from a 3D object in which six photographs of the object are taken and projected on the six inside faces of a cube. The object itself is then placed inside a cube, and the reflections of light on the object are generated by *bitmapped* images representing the outside world. See *Mapping*.

Cue Control

In video editing, a device for rapidly fast-forwarding or rewinding a videotape so as to quickly locate a particular section.

Cue Sheet

In video production, a list of the points at which audio and video need to be synchronized. Also known as a *breakdown*.

Cumar

An alternate term for *coumarone-indene resin*. See *Coumarone-Indene Resin*.

Cure

To undergo *curing*. See *Curing*.

Curing

The conversion of a wet printing ink film to a dry one, typically by chemical means or by exposure to various types of radiation, such as ultraviolet light.

Curing also refers to the hardening and solidification of any wet or gelatinous material, such as rubber, the exposed portion of an acid *resist*, or other such substance. Curing that takes place at room temperature is referred to as *cold curing*.

Curl

A distortion of paper characterized by a lack of flatness. Curl can have a number of different causes: differences in structure between a paper's *wire side* and *felt side* cause each side to expand and contract in different ways when moisture is gained and lost, producing a curl; paper that is wrapped very near the core of a paper roll and then sheeted will have a curl (called *roll-set curl*), if it has not been decurled properly; dimensional changes caused by the addition of moisture to a paper's surface during offset printing causes a curl. Curl is usually more apparent in lower-basis-weight papers. Curl can possibly be counteracted by running the paper through a press with a blank plate and merely applying moisture to the side of the sheet opposite the curl. Failing that, two-sided offset print jobs typically print better if the first side is printed curl down. Adding moisture to this side during printing may help neutralize the curl.

Curling

The act of preparing paper for use on computer printers, consisting of such actions as removing moisture, flattening the sheets, etc. Curling is often done to prevent paper jams or other feeding problems. Also known as *climatizing*.

Curl Test Method

A test to determine a paper's water resistance or adequacy of its *sizing* in which a paper sample is floated on a water surface. It will curl toward its dry side until the water has penetrated halfway through the paper, at which point the curl will reverse its direction. The length of time from contact with the water to the point of the maximum angle of curl is the measurement of water resistance.

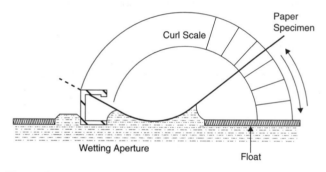

The curl test method for measuring a paper's water resistance.

Curly Braces

See *Braces*.

Curly Quotes

Alternate term for *smart quotes*. See *Smart Quotes*.

Current Directory

In computing, a *directory* or *folder* (depending upon the *operating system*) that will be searched first, or in which a file will be stored first, unless the system is directed otherwise. See also *Default Drive* and *Parent Directory*.

Current Drive

In computing, the disk drive being used at a particular moment for the reading and writing of files. See also *Default Drive*.

Current Loop

In computing, a type of *serial* communication in which either the presence or absence of an electrical signal indicates whether a 1 or a 0, respectively, is being transmitted.

Cursive

In typography, descriptive of handwriting or a *typeface* designed to resemble handwriting. Cursive is also often used as a synonym for *italic*.

Cursor

On a computer or computerized device, a moveable spot on the computer screen that indicates where the next entered character will go, or where the next action will occur. Text-entry cursors are often blinking. Cursors controlled by a mouse are often known as *pointer*s.

Cursor-Movement Key

In computing, any key on a keyboard that will move the *cursor* around the screen, in lieu of a *mouse*. These are most commonly one of four *arrow key*s, but may also involve other keys such as Home, PgUp, PgDn, End, etc.

Curtain Coater

Any device used to apply a coating—be it an *adhesive*, a paper *coating*, etc.—by spreading uniform amounts of a low-viscosity (i.e., highly fluid) coating material across a surface.

Curved Plate

A metal relief plate used on presses for *letterpress* printing that is precurved to fit the *plate cylinder* of a *rotary press*. See *Letterpress*.

Curved Screen

In *screen printing*, a specially constructed screen fabric that is mounted on a curved frame, for use in printing round or spherical *substrates*.

Customer Information Control System (CICS)

In telecommunications and networking, a communications control program that was developed by IBM to manage transaction processing in its *VM* and *Multiple Virtual Storage (MVS)* operating systems. Used on many *mainframe* systems, CICS provides activity logs, *authentication* routines, and database maintenance and searching functions.

Customization Software

Alternate term for *variable-data software*. See *Variable-Data Software*.

Customized Software

Any computer application or suite of programs that has been designed and programmed for a specific use for a specific client, as opposed to *off-the-shelf* software, which is designed and programmed for a broad range of applications.

Customer-Premises Equipment (CPE)

In telecommunications and networking, any communications equipment—be it owned or leased—located at a customer's site, rather than at a central telecommunications company office.

Cut

In printing ink, to dilute or thin an ink, *varnish*, or *lacquer* with a *solvent* as a means of reducing its *viscosity* and altering its flow characteristics.

In film and video production, an abrupt transition from one scene to another lacking any transition effect, such as a *dissolve* or a *wipe*.

Cut and Paste

In a computer application, a function of the program (or operating system) that allows portions of a document to be removed from one place and pasted in another place, even within another document or within another application. See also *Clipboard*.

Cut-Flush Binding

Alternate term for a *flush cover*. See *Flush Cover*.

Cut-In Head

In typography and layout, a heading inserted within a box of white space positioned on the side of a typeset page.

Cut-Line Indicator

An optical device used on a *guillotine cutter* that shines a thin line of light onto the stack of material to be cut, indicating where the cut will be made. See *Guillotine Cutter*.

Cutoff

A printing and/or binding defect characterized by either partially or completely missing text or artwork from a printed or trimmed sheet or publication, due to any number of causes.

Cutoff Knife

A knife or blade found in the *in-line* folding section of a *web press*, commonly located just prior to the *jaw folder*, that is used to cut a continuous printed web into individual sheets or *signature*s.

Cutoff Register Control

On a *web press*, an auxiliary electronic device that automatically controls the *register* of printed images with respect to the web *cutoff* point, or the point at which the web is cut into signatures.

Without a cutoff register control device, the colors or images may be in register with respect to each other, but the entire image may vary from page to page or signature to signature. Such devices usually use photoelectric detectors that, in combination with a signal directed by the printing unit, measure and keep consistent the interval between impressions.

Cutoff Rule

In newspaper or magazine typography, a *rule line* used to separate advertisements from text or to separate different news items.

Cutout

Alternate term for *knockout*. See *Knockout*.

Cutscore

In *binding and finishing*, a sharp-edged knife used in *diecutting* that is set lower (usually by several thousandths of an inch) than the cutting dies so as to only partially cut into the substrate. A cutscore is used primarily for *scoring* purposes to facilitate folding.

Cut-Sheet Paper

Any type of paper cut into individual sheets for use in high-speed computer laser printers, in contrast to fan-fold paper or a continuous roll.

Cut-Size Paper

A paper trimmed to a small *standard size* (commonly 8½×11 in., and up to and including 11×17 in.) for printing, copying, or other purposes.

Cutter

Alternate term for *guillotine cutter*. See *Guillotine Cutter*.

Cutter Clamp

On a *guillotine cutter*, a metal bar or plate that is used to hold a stack of sheets in position during cutting. See *Guillotine Cutter*.

Cutter Dust

Particles of paper fiber, *filler*, or *coating* that adhere to the paper (typically at the edges) produced by *sheeting* or other paper *trimming* operations. Cutter dust can interfere with a paper's *printability* and *runnability*. (See *Paper and Papermaking: Printing Problems and Defects*.)

Cut-Through

In networking, a means of speeding up *packet* forwarding on some *Ethernet* networks in which only the first few *byte*s of a packet are examined for errors. Although this does speed up transmission, some damaged data packets can slip through.

Cutting

See *Cutting and Trimming*.

Cutting and Trimming

In printing and finishing operations, the acts required to reduce sheets of paper (either blank or printed) to a desired size. *Web*s of blank stock are often cut into sheets prior to shipping to a printer. (See *Sheeting*.) Paper sheets need to be trimmed prior to printing to ensure that edges are perfectly square and straight, so as to avoid press jams and other mechanical press problems.

In **binding and finishing** operations, cutting and trimming are performed to reduce large-size press sheets to the desired **trim size**, to separate pages that have been ganged up on a single sheet, and to remove extraneous edges containing **registration marks**, etc. Cutting is often differentiated from trimming in that cutting refers to the separation of pages that have been printed together, while trimming refers to the process of removing paper from around the edges of a sheet.

Most cutting and trimming is performed on a **guillotine cutter**, a large device consisting of a flat **bed** on which the paper is stacked, and a wide, sharp steel or steel-carbide **knife**, which is lowered through the paper either manually or, increasingly, mechanically. Guillotine cutters also make use of a **cutting stick**, a piece of wood or other material imbedded within the bed of the cutter directly beneath the knife. The cutting stick provides a firm yet somewhat resilient surface for the knife to press against, enabling not only a clean cut but also preventing blade wear and damage. Side and back gauges on the cutter bed also help position the paper accurately and squarely, allowing for the ability to trim to a very accurate size. A cutter clamp holds the paper securely beneath the knife, and also expels air from the stack of sheets, eliminating distortion of sheets, which can result in improper cutting. Older cutters required manual movement of gauges back and forth whenever a change in trim size or position was needed. Now, new dimensions can easily be programmed onto the device via a keyboard, which positions the gauges automatically. Cutting and trimming are also performed by the use of **crop-marks**, lines in the trim area of the sheets that indicate the proper size of the finished stack.

The cutting of different weights of paper has different considerations. When cutting lighter-weight papers, it often happens that the knife as it cuts through the stack pulls sheets from beneath the clamp, resulting in upper sheets that are cut shorter than lower layers, a situation known as **overcut**. In contrast, harder stocks, such as cardboard, result in an **undercut**, or a small cut in an undesirable area, caused by insufficient clamp pressure.

Guillotine cutters also have a wide variety of accessory devices and are increasingly under computer control. (See **Guillotine Cutter**.) In bookbinding, trimming is often performed using a **three-knife trimmer**, which allows for the trimming of all three unbound sides of a book or **book block** simultaneously.

Cutting Stick

On a **guillotine cutter**, a wooden bar imbedded in the **bed** of a cutter directly beneath the **knife** as a means of protecting the blade from damage. See **Guillotine Cutter**.

Cyan

One of the **subtractive primary colors**—appearing blue-green—characterized by its absorption of **red** light. It is used in various proportions with the other subtractive primaries—**magenta** and **yellow**—to form many other colors. Cyan is often incorrectly used as a synonym for **blue**.

Cyan is also a term for one of the four **process color** inks used in process color printing. Also incorrectly referred to as "blue," perhaps because the word *cyaneous* refers to a deep, cerulean blue, while its etymological root, the Greek word *kyanos*, means "deep blue." Cyan is the blue component used in many types of color mixing and is also a **secondary color** in **additive color theory** produced by the mixing of red and blue.

Cybercop

A person who investigates illegal activities on the **Internet** or other computer networks, such as hacking, software piracy, computer virus dissemination, credit card fraud, etc.

Cybernaut

An explorer of **cyberspace**.

Cybernetics

Any scientific inquiry into the comparison of organic brains (i.e., those of humans and other animals) with mechanical and electronic brains (i..e, computers and other devices), the goal being to apply such knowledge to the development of robots. The results of such inquiries have already been used in the development of machines and programs that simulate human experience, such as flight simulators.

Cyberpunk

Alternate term for a **hacker**. See **Hacker**.

Cyberspace

Generally speaking, the "space" inside a computer, used commonly to refer to the sum total of all that exists on the **Internet** and the **World Wide Web**. Those who often navigate—or "surf"—the Internet are known as **cybernaut**s. The term *cyberspace* itself, although deriving from the word **cybernetics**, was coined by science fiction author William Gibson in his novel *Neuromancer*. In that novel, people accessed computer networks by hooking their brains directly to them. It has not come to that . . . yet.

Cycle Stealing

In computing, a technique in which a peripheral device briefly usurps control of the **CPU**'s regularly scheduled activities to access the computer's internal memory.

Cyclic Redundancy Check (CRC)

In networking and telecommunications, a means of error detection in which a series of two 8-**bit** block check characters representing the entire **packet** of data are created and appended to the file or packet to be transmitted. When the packet is received, the receiver checks the data and the CRC. If they do not match, the received packet is either discarded or is delivered with the indication that a CRC error has been discovered. Also referred to as a *cyclical redundancy check*.

Cylinder

A generic term for any cylindrical part of a printing press, in particular those used in the printing unit, such as a *plate cylinder*, *blanket cylinder*, *impression cylinder*, *transfer cylinder*, or *gravure cylinder*. A cylinder is also known as a *drum*.

In computing, a set of stacked tracks on a *hard disk* that can be accessed simultaneously without moving a *read/write head*. See *Hard Disk*.

Cylinder Base

Term for a *gravure cylinder* prior to the electroplating of copper to its surface. Also called a *base cylinder*. See *Gravure Cylinder*.

Cylinder Board

A form of paperboard produced in a papermaking process utilizing a *cylinder machine*. See *Cylinder Machine*.

Cylinder Gap

A break in the circumference of an offset press *plate cylinder*, *blanket cylinder*, *impression cylinder*, or *transfer cylinder* in which is typically housed the various clamps or reels that hold the plate or blanket to the cylinder or, in the case of an impression and transfer cylinder, the *grippers* that carry the paper (or other *substrate*) through the press. The cylinder gap on many offset presses is about 20% of the circumference of the cylinder. The cylinder gap on the plate cylinder also allows the *inking system* to renew itself between printed sheets. On some plate cylinders, the cylinder gap provides an inclined "ramp" back up to the surface of the cylinder, allowing the *form roller*s to smoothly return to the plate without producing streaks or bumps. (See *Offset Lithography: Printing Unit* and *Inking System: Offset Lithography*.)

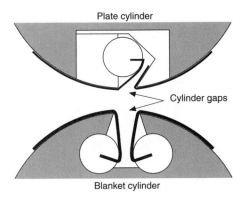

The gaps on a plate cylinder (top) and a blanket cylinder (bottom) of a web press.

Cylinder Guide Mark

A mark made on the nonimage area of a printing plate used in *offset lithography* that matches up with a similar mark on the *plate cylinder*, made to ensure that all the plates used for a particular job will be positioned accurately.

Cylinder Machine

A papermaking machine using a rotating wire-belt-covered cylinder. As the cylinder rotates, it passes through a tank containing papermaking *furnish*. As water drains though the wire toward the inside of the cylinder, the fibers form the paper *web* on the wire belt. The fibers are then transferred to the underside of a moving felt belt. As the fiber mat travels along this belt, additional cylinders add further layers of fibrous mats. Papermaking systems employing cylinder machine are somewhat slow compared to traditional *fourdrinier* machines and newer *twin-wire formers*, but they are useful in making thick, inexpensive paperboard. The ease of adjusting the composition and number of plys has high cost advantages. Printing and writing papers, however, are rarely produced on a cylinder machine, and many cylinder machines are being replaced by twin-wire formers.

The first automated papermaking machine in the United States was a cylinder machine, built by Delaware papermaker Thomas Gilpin and first put into use in 1817. The first fourdrinier papermaking machine did not appear in the United States until 1827, although it had been in operation in England since around 1803. (See *Fourdrinier*.)

Cylinder Press

Alternate term for a *flatbed press* used in *letterpress* printing. See *Flatbed Press*.

Cylinder Printer

A type of impact printer comprising a *character set* embossed on metal rings positioned around a cylinder. The cylinder moves up and down as a character is selected and the action of a hammer striking the cylinder against a ribbon "types" the character. Also known as a *drum printer*.

Cylinder Undercut

See *Undercut*.

CYMK

Abbreviation for *cyan*, *yellow*, *magenta*, and *key* (black), the four *process color*s or inks. Also known as *CMYK*.

Cyrillic

In typography, the alphabet used in Russian and other Slavic languages, brought to Eastern Europe by St. Cyril (c. 827–869), although it is unknown whether or not he actually invented it. Cyril was a Greek-born missionary whose attempts to Christianize Slavic peoples in central Europe resulted in a translation of the Bible into Slavic utilizing a modified Greek alphabet known as Cyrillic. Cyrillic is available in a wide variety of typefaces.

абвгдежзийклмнопрстуфхцчшщъы ьэюя АБВГДЕЖЗИЙКЛМНОПРСТУ ФХЦЧШЩЪЬЬЭЮЯ 1234567890

The Cyrillic alphabet.

D

D, d

The fourth letter of the Latin and English alphabets, derived from the Greek *delta*. The form of the uppercase *D* derives from the North Semitic letter *daleth*, later adopted by the Greeks and ultimately by the Romans. The lowercase *d* also derives from the Greek *delta* and from the Latin cursive letter *d*.

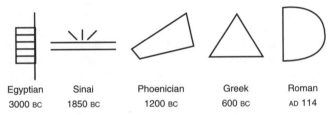

Egyptian	Sinai	Phoenician	Greek	Roman
3000 BC	1850 BC	1200 BC	600 BC	AD 114

The evolution of the letter D.

D1

A *CCIR 601* standard for digital video, utilizing a tape 19 mm wide and having a total recording time of 94 minutes. The D1 standard allows high *bandwidth* for *chrominance* and making multiple generations of copies with little quality deterioration. See also *D2*.

D2

A standard for digital *composite video* recording in *PAL* and *NTSC* formats, utilizing a tape 19 mm wide and having a total recording time of up to 208 minutes. The D2 standard differs from the *D1* standard. See also *D1*, *PAL*, and *NTSC*.

D2-MAC

A new television broadcasting system perhaps destined to replace current *NTSC*, *PAL*, and *SECAM* standards. D2-MAC boasts higher-quality video and *CD-quality* sound, as well as the ability to simultaneously broadcast speech in several languages. The picture size conforms to the current 4:3 proportion, as well as the wide-screen-TV 16:9 proportion. Currently in use in several European countries, it is considered the precursor to *high definition television*.

D3

A standard for digital *composite video* recording in *PAL* and *NTSC* formats, utilizing a tape 1 inch wide and having a total recording time of up to 245 minutes. See also *D1*, *PAL*, and *NTSC*.

DA

Abbreviation for *display adapter*. See *Display Adapter*.

    DA is also an abbreviation for *data administration*. See *Data Administration (DA)*.

DAA

Abbreviation for *data access arrangement*. See *Data Access Arrangement*.

DAC

See *Digital-To-Analog Converter*.

D/A Converter

A device (or software) utilized to convert *digital* data to *analog* form. The opposite device (or software) is known as an *A/D Converter*. See *Digital-to-Analog Converter* and *Analog-to-Digital Converter*.

Dacron

A brand of polyester fiber used for textiles. Dacron also refers to *polyester* fibers used in *screen printing* screens.

Daemon

In computing, especially in that utilizing the *UNIX* operating system, a process that performs a utility function in the background and without user intervention, such as *spooling* a document to a printer or collecting error information (such as a mail daemon that returns undeliverable *email*). Pronounced as "demon."

Dagger

A *pi character* (†) used in *footnote*s and *reference*s. The dagger is usually the second reference mark after the *asterisk*.

Daguerreotypy

A nascent method of photography (largely based on the work of French chemist Joseph Nicéphore Niepce [1765–1833], with whom Daguerre was a partner), invented in part by French painter Louis Jacques Mandé Daguerre (1789–1851). Daguerre was originally a theatrical scenery painter, who had created a diorama in the 1820s. Seeking a means of quickly and efficiently reproducing the various images in his dioramas, he hooked up with Niepce, who had been working on photographic reproduction since 1814. Niepce and Daguerre worked on developing a means of capturing photographic images by means of sunlight, but when Niepce died in 1833, Daguerre abandoned Niepce's process and devised one of his own. In the resulting daguerreotypy, announced in 1839, a polished silver plate was exposed to iodine vapors, which resulted in a light-sensitive layer of silver iodide on the plate. This plate was then exposed to light using a camera, and the *latent image* was developed using mercury vapor. The remaining unexposed silver iodide was removed using a solution of common salt (sodium chloride), which acted as a *fixing* solution. Eventually, it was discovered that sodium thiosulfate was a better fixer than was salt. Daguerre's photographs were (and still are) known as *daguerreotypes*, which are among some of the oldest photographic images still in existence.

Daisy Chain

In computing, a means of propagating an electrical or electronic signal along a *bus* such that the signal passes from one unit to the next in a serial manner until it reaches its destination. The *small computer system interface (SCSI)* is such a bus.

Daisy Wheel

A type of print head used in computer printers and electronic typewriters (called *daisy-wheel printer*s) that contains relief characters located at the tips of spokes arranged around the perimeter of the wheel. The advantage of daisy wheels is their reliability and the formation of whole, solid characters (rather than the characters made of dots typical of *dot-matrix printer*s). The spoke pattern is reminiscent of the petals of a daisy, hence the name. Also called a *print-wheel*, and also spelled as one word, *daisywheel*.

Daisy-Wheel Printer

An impact printer utilizing a plastic wheel with relief characters located on spokes along the perimeter of the wheel. When a character is selected, the wheel rotates to align that character with a hammer which forces the spoke against a ribbon, imaging the page. Daisy wheels are used in computer printers and electronic typewriters. Fonts can be changed by swapping wheels. See *Daisy Wheel*. Also spelled *daisywheel printer*.

Daisychaining

See *Daisy Chain*.

Damar

A hard and lustrous *resin* obtained from one of several types of trees from Southeast Asia, especially Sumatra and Malaya, used in *screen printing varnish*es. Also spelled *dammar*.

Damp Streaks

A paper defect caused by nonuniform pressing or drying during papermaking.

Dampeners

Collective term for the rollers on an offset lithographic press that transfer the *fountain solution* from the *water fountain* to the plate. See *Dampening System*.

Dampening Solution

Alternate term for an offset lithographic press's *fountain solution*. See *Fountain Solution*.

Dampening System

In offset lithographic printing, the system that transfers a water-based *fountain solution* to the printing plate as a means of making nonimage areas ink repellent. *Offset lith-*

ography is based on the principle that oil and water do not mix readily, thus the water-based fountain solution ensures that the oil-based ink does not collect in undesirable regions of the printing plate. (See *Offset Lithography*.)

In addition to water, the fountain solution contains a variety of other additives to enhance the performance of the fountain solution, and to prevent press problems and plate damage. The concentrated fountain solution (called *fountain concentrate*) comprises a variety of different substances depending on the composition of the ink used, but most solutions include, in addition to water, an acid—such as phosphoric acid, citric acid, or lactic acid—or a base, to control the *pH* of the solution; a *gum* (either a natural gum such as *gum arabic* or a synthetic gum) to *desensitize* the nonimage regions of the plate; a *corrosion inhibitor* which prevents *oxidation* or other chemical reaction between the dampening solution and the metallic plate and also contributes to pH adjustment; an alcohol-based *wetting agent* which allows the solution to flow more easily by reducing the surface tension of the fountain solution; a fungicide which prevents the growth of fungi, mildew, or bacteria in the fountain; and an *antifoaming agent* to prevent the generation of foam in the solution, which can have deleterious effects on fountain solution distribution through the press.

The fountain solution may also contain a *drying stimulator*, which acts to enhance the performance of the ink *drier*, typically used when ink isn't drying fast enough. Most suppliers provide premixed fountain concentrates, the printer only needing to add water and, perhaps, suggested quantities of alcohol and/or gum. Adjusting several properties of the dampening solution, particularly pH and electrical conductivity, may also be necessary. Refrigeration of fountain solution also helps prevent various press problems, such as *scumming* and *tinting*. (See *Fountain Solution*.)

There are two fundamental varieties of offset press dampening system: an *intermittent-flow dampening system*, and a *continuous-flow dampening system*.

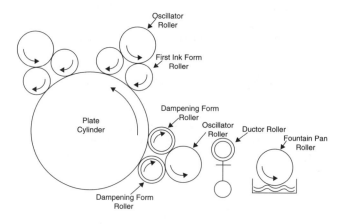

A conventional offset press dampening system.

INTERMITTENT-FLOW SYSTEM

Also known as a conventional dampening system, an intermittent-flow system closely resembles the press's inking system. However, since the fountain solution does not need to be worked to the extent that the ink does, much fewer rollers are involved. At the head of the dampening system is a water pan (also known as a fountain pan), the reservoir containing the solution. Turning in the water pan is a chrome- or aluminum-plated fountain pan roller, which picks up a film of solution as it turns. The rotation of the fountain pan roller is controlled by its own motor or, if connected to the main drive of the press, at a speed greatly slower than that of the press (produced via gear reduction) to prevent spraying of fountain solution all over the pressroom. On some presses, the fountain pan roller is covered with an absorbent material to increase the amount of fountain solution transferred to the rest of the system. A fabric-covered ductor roller alternately contacts the fountain pan roller and an oscillator, transferring the dampening solution at set intervals. Adjusting the length of time the ductor roller contacts the fountain pan roller (and, therefore, the amount of fountain solution it picks up) controls the amount of solution ultimately transferred to the plate. The chrome- or aluminum-plated oscillator, as its name indicates, not only transfers fountain solution from the ductor roller to the form rollers, but also oscillates back and forth parallel to the ductor roller to even out fountain solution distribution across the dampening system, and to ensure the transfer of solution uniformly across the surface of the plate. The rotational speed of the oscillator is commonly the same as that of the plate cylinder. The final set of dampening rollers are the form rollers, of which most presses contain two. These rollers contact the plate before the inking form rollers, and desensitize the nonimage areas of the plate before the application of ink.

Web presses utilize other configurations of dampening rollers. One common system uses a flap roller, or flapper, as a fountain roller. The flapper, as its name implies, is covered with canvas flaps that transfer fountain solution to the adjacent oscillator. Adjusting the speed of rotation of the flaps controls the amount of solution sent toward the plate. A prime advantage to this system is its elimination of the ductor roller and the consequent ductor shock. Another system uses a roller covered with stiff bristles, which flex when under pressure with the fountain roller. The bristles pick up fountain solution and, as the roller rotates, the bristles "flick" the solution at the adjacent oscillator (with which it is not in contact). A similar configuration uses adjustable flicker blades to flex and release the bristles. In this case, the bristle-covered brush roller replaces the fountain roller.

As with ink rollers, the proper setting of dampening rollers is important; the pressure of the various rollers against their neighbors can be adjusted, and correct pressure ensures the proper transfer of fountain solution. If the pressure between rollers is not strong enough, not enough solution will be transferred, and the form rollers (driven solely by pressure from the neighboring oscillator) will not turn at their proper speed. If the pressure is too strong, however, the dampening solution will be squeezed out the sides of the rollers, again preventing sufficient solution transfer. Also of consideration is the pressure between the form rollers and the plate, which should be less than that between the form roller and the adjacent oscillator. The oscillator should be perfectly parallel to the form roller, the fountain pan roller, and the plate cylinder. Various tests that gauge drag (i.e., the three-strip method) can ensure that the roller setting is correct and consistent across the length of the rollers. It is also important that the form roller not bump when passing over the plate cylinder gap.

As for regulating the amount of dampening solution transferred to the plate, there are three primary means of adjustment. The first involves changing the rate of rotation of the fountain pan roller; the faster it turns, the more solution it picks up and the more surface area it brings into contact with the ductor roller. The second involves controlling the length of time the ductor roller contacts the fountain pan roller, which also regulates the amount of dampening solution transferred to the surface of the ductor. A third means of regulating the fountain solution is with attachments called water stops, which are metal or plastic tabs, squeegees, or rollers that press against the fountain pan roller with varying pressures. These act to squeeze or "scrape" water from the surface of the fountain pan roller before it contacts the ductor, removing a preset, desired amount of solution. An advantage of water stops is the ability to loosen or tighten selected stops across the length of the fountain roller, depending on which portions of the plate require more or less fountain solution. Running dampening rollers bareback, or without fabric covers, also makes the rollers more sensitive to adjustments elsewhere in the dampening system. Rollers that run bareback commonly need wetting agents added to the solution, so as to decrease surface tension and allow the comparatively nonabsorbent roller to pick up more fluid.

This conventional dampening system is called an intermittent-flow system because the movement of the ductor roller prevents the continuous flow of solution from the fountain to the plate. This set-up causes problems when fountain solution surges through the system, and these surges are difficult to control. (A similar problem can exist in inking systems that also utilize an alternating ductor roller, but the increased number of rollers mitigates against surge problems.)

CONTINUOUS-FLOW SYSTEM

Of primary advantage with continuous-flow systems is their quick response to dampening system adjustments; there is no need to wait for the ductor roller to cycle to the fountain, then back to the oscillator before seeing changes take place. There are two varieties of continuous-flow system, which can exist separately or in some combination.

Inker-Feed. An inker-feed dampening system does away with the ductor roller and uses the first inking form roller as a dampening form roller. Fountain solution is transferred from the water pan to a resilient, rubber-covered ***metering roller***, which contacts a hard, chrome-plated ***transfer roller***, the nip between these two rollers—called the ***metering nip***—regulating the thickness of the film that is transferred. The transfer roller then contacts the first inking form roller, the nip between these latter two rollers—called the ***slip nip***—also metering the solution film ultimately transferred to the plate. The speed of the metering and transfer rollers, as well as the size of the metering nip, controls the amount of dampening solution transferred to the plate. An obvious consideration in this arrangement is ensuring that a uniform film of dampening solution will sit on top of the already-inked form roller. Using a fountain solution that is 5–10% alcohol helps. The form roller used as both an inking and dampening roller must be set harder to the plate than would a traditional dampening form roller.

Plate-Feed. A plate-feed system is set up almost identically to an inker-feed system—a hard transfer roller contacts a soft metering roller at a metering nip, which regulates the thickness of the fountain solution film—but a plate-feed system has its own dampening form roller which contacts the plate. Unlike other systems, the metering and transfer rollers can be skewed at various angles to adjust the thickness of the solution film across the rollers.

Combination Systems. Combinations of inker-feed and plate-feed dampening systems exist in a variety of configurations, all of which typically feature an oscillating or vibrating ***bridge roller*** contacting both the dampening form roller and the first inking form roller. In one system, the difference in rotational speeds between the form roller, the bridge roller, and the plate cylinder results in a kind of ***hickey***-removal system. Other configurations of combination continuous-flow systems use either skewed rollers or water stops in combination with the bridge roller to ensure an accurate and effective ink-water balance.

Some configurations of continuous-flow systems have a metering roller and a transfer roller that rotate in the same direction, producing a ***reverse slip nip*** where they meet. This means that the rollers are travelling in opposite directions at the point of contact, keeping liquid from flowing through the nip. The point is to reduce or eliminate the excess dampening solution returning from the plate, to keep it from interacting with the "fresh" metered solution from the fountain. This helps to more closely control the flow rate of the fountain solution to the plate, as the incoming solution doesn't interfere with the outgoing solution.

An interesting variation on the continuous-flow system used on some web presses is a ***spray-bar dampening system***, which sprays jets of fountain solution onto the rollers of the inking system using a row of nozzles. An advantage is that each nozzle in the row can be adjusted, allowing for flexibility in the lateral distribution of fountain solution. And since this system does not recirculate the fountain solution as other systems do, there is no need to worry about contamination or subtle changes in chemistry and/or pH. However, substances in the fountain solution itself (especially gum) can clog and/or contaminate the nozzles.

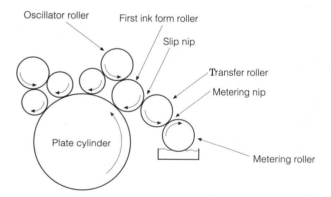

Configuration of an inker-feed dampening system.

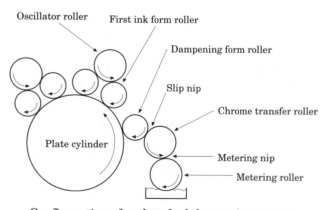

Configuration of a plate-feed dampening system.

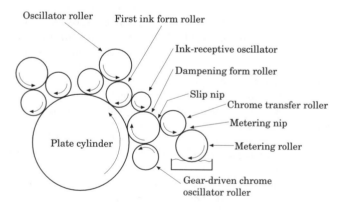

Configuration of a combination continuous-flow

ROLLER MAINTENANCE

Dampening roller maintenance has some of the same considerations as ink roller maintenance (for example, rollers should never be used if they become out-of-round, or rotate with a detectable bump). However, one of the primary dampening roller considerations is the roller cover, which over time can pick up ink, and become greasy or worn, all of which reduce their ability to properly pick up dampening solution. A covered roller that is removed must be replaced so that it rotates in the same direction as it did before, otherwise damage to the cover will result, causing bagginess, linting, and creeping. Metal uncovered rollers should be periodically treated with *gum etch* to properly desensitize them and restore their water receptivity, as they can become greasy over time. A broken or beaded-up film of dampening solution on a metal roller's surface is an indication that the roller needs to be degreased. The growth of fungi or other organisms can be prevented by using fungicidal additives, or by frequent cleaning of the dampening system. A 1:9 bleach-water solution can be flushed through the system to kill anything that may be growing, but the bleach should be thoroughly flushed out before replacing the fountain solution.

Common printing problems, such as *catch-up* (the appearance of ink in nonimage areas of the plate), and undesirable color strengthening and halftone thickening, are caused by uneven or inadequate dampening of the plate, commonly the result of improper setting of the form rollers to both the plate and oscillator, or the ductor roller to the oscillator. Dampening system effectiveness can also be affected by changes in atmospheric conditions, in particular relative humidity, and by changes in the desensitizing film on the plate caused by prolonged print runs. Problems can also be caused by too *much* dampening solution, which excessively emulsifies the ink, causing poor ink transfer. (Increasing the flow of ink only aggravates the problem.) Too much fountain solution on the plate eventually transfers it back into the inking system, where it can desensitize the ink *roller train*, causing problems such as *roller stripping*, or inability of the ink rollers to accept ink. Another type of appearance of ink in nonimage plate regions—*tinting*—can be caused by an excessive amount of dampening-solution emulsification by the ink.

Too much fountain solution also impedes the drying characteristics of the ink, causing smearing and *ink setoff*. Increased absorption of the fountain solution by the paper itself can cause varieties of drying and appearance problems, in particular expansion of the paper in the *cross-grain direction* as it absorbs water, which can cause *misregister* on multi-color jobs, or other jobs involving more than one pass through the press. Another problem is *bleeding*, or a fundamental incompatibility between the ink and the fountain solution, which causes ink *pigment* particles to be transferred to and dissolved in the dampening solution, which then results in an undesirable colored tone being printed.

A clean, well-kept dampening system with properly adjusted rollers should help minimize any problems likely to be caused by the fountain solution.

Dancer Roller

A type of roller, also known as a *floating roller*, used in the infeed section of a *web press* to regulate the speed at which the web of substrate unwinds into the press and to maintain web tension. The dancer roller is free to move up or down, forward or backward, as the press runs. The movement of the dancer, in combination with an attached brake on the *roll stand*, acts to keep the web unwinding at a constant speed. Additional dancer rollers may be added for additional web control. (See also *Web Offset Lithography: Infeed and Web Control*.)

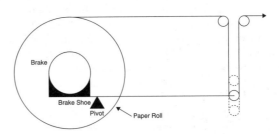

Dancer roller connected to a brake shoe in the web press infeed section.

Dandy Roll

A wire-covered cylinder located toward the end of the *forming section* of a papermaking machine that is used to squeeze excess water out of the wet paper *furnish* and even out the *formation* of the paper *web*. Raised designs woven into the dandy roll wire are used to add a *wove finish* or *laid finish* texture to the paper, as well as a *watermark*.

The dandy roll was invented in 1826 by John Marshall, a English maker of molds for watermarking handmade paper. After the invention of the papermaking machine (see *Fourdrinier*), he developed the dandy roll technique as a means of watermarking machine-made paper. (See also *Watermark*, *Laid Finish*, and *Wove Finish*.)

Dark Reaction

A premature *polymerization* of an *ultraviolet curing ink* (or other UV curing coating or substance) in the absence of exposure to *actinic light*. A dark reaction results in the conversion of the ink or emulsion into a gel-like material.

Darkroom

In photography, a special room constructed to be completely absent of white (or even any) light, used for handling and developing film. Darkrooms are often equipped with (usually) red safelights, depending upon the light-sensitivity of the film being used.

Dark Spot

An undesirable concentration of an ink *pigment* in one particular spot, commonly caused by a pit or depression in the surface of the *substrate*.

DAS

Abbreviation for *dual-attached station*. See *Dual-Attached Station (DAS)*.

DASD

Abbreviation for *direct access storage device*; pronounced "DAZ-dee." See *Direct Access Storage Device (DASD)*.

Dashes

In typography, three basic characters used either for *hyphenation*, to set off parenthetical text, or to express a numerical range. The smallest dash is the *hyphen* (-), used for breaking words or syllables at the ends of lines, or for compound or connected words (such as "mother-in-law"). The *en dash* (–) is used to replace the words *to* or *through* (as in "pages 1–9"). It is also used to connect two nouns of equal weight (as in "East–West alliance") or to replace a colon.

If an en dash is unavailable, two hyphens may be *kern*ed together. En dashes are always set *closed*. An *em dash* (—) is the largest dash available, and is used to indicate missing material (as in "Dr.— was the murderer"), for parenthetical remarks requiring special emphasis or indicative of a break in thought (as in "Good God—he shrieked in horror—what is that thing?"), or to replace a colon (as in "Here's the diagnosis—"). Em dashes may be set *closed* or open, open-set dashes providing more opportunities for end-of-line breaks, although modern typesetting equipment will break an em dash if it occurs at the end of a line.

Generally, dashes should not be carried over to the beginning of the following line, if it can be avoided. In some cases, an intermediate dash between an en and em (called a ¾ em dash) is available, and is used in narrow typefaces or *condensed* type in lieu of an em dash, as a means of reflecting the narrow feeling of the type design.

Dash Leaders

In typography, *leaders* composed of dashes or hyphens (- - - - - -) rather than dots or periods (.......), which are known as *dot leaders*. See *Leaders*.

DAT

Abbreviation for *digital audio tape*. See *Digital Audio Tape*. *DAT* is also the abbreviation for *dynamic address translation*. See *Dynamic Address Translation*.

Data

A general term for any information, facts, numbers, letters, symbols, etc. Data is commonly used in computers to refer to discrete bits of information which are processed, transmitted, etc. *Data* is the plural of the word *datum*.

Data Access Arrangement

In telecommunications, equipment for data communications provided by a *common carrier* that allows privately owned data equipment to be added to it.

Data Acquisition

In computing, the gathering of information from disparate sources for centralized processing.

Data Administration (DA)

In database management, the hardware, software, and personnel required to maintain the security, availability, and quality of data and data resources.

Data Aggregate

In a database file, any group of elements within a *record* and referred to as a whole.

Data Bank

Any collection or library of information pertaining to a specific subject.

Database

In computing, any organized, searchable collection of data, often in the form of *record*s containing individual *field*s. A database, controlled by a *database management system (DBMS)*, can store just about any information, from magazine or newspaper subscribers to 10,000 graphic arts terms.

Database Administration

An infrastructure of personnel, hardware, and software designed to organize, support, and maintain a *database*.

Database Administrator

An individual charged with the responsibility of organizing, supporting, and maintaining a *database* and its accompanying *database management system*.

Database Management System (DBMS)

A computer system designed for the storage and retrieval of information stored in a *database*. The software comprising the DBMS facilitates the formatting, storage, organization, and retrieval of the data (in *field*, *record*s, and files), as well as the integrity and security of data. A DBMS may allow remote access, and may support the printout of data. A DBMS also facilitates the searching of the database for specific *character string*s or other criteria.

Database Model

A method used by a *database management system* to organize a *database*, the most common of which is a *relational database*. See *Database Management System (DBMS)* and *Relational Database*.

Database Producer

A company which collects, organizes, formats, and sells information *database*s.

Database Server
See *Server*.

Data Bit
In data communications, the basic unit of *asynchronous transmission*s. Seven or eight data bits comprise one character. See *Asynchronous Transmission*.

Data Bus
The path between a peripheral device (or set of peripherals) to the host computer over which data is transferred.

Data Capture
Generally speaking, the digitization of any nondigital information, be it text (by means of *optical character recognition [OCR]*), graphics (by means of a *scanner*), audio and video (by means of a *capture board*), etc.

The term *data capture* also refers to the ability of a multimedia application to obtain user input (such as name, address, etc.) and export it into a database.

Data Carrier Detect (DCD)
In networking and telecommunications, a signal (specifically, an *RS-232* signal) sent from a *modem* to the attached computer that indicates that the modem is online and ready to transmit data.

Data Cartridge
Alternate term for a *disk cartridge*. See *Disk Cartridge*.

Data Circuit Terminating Equipment
In telecommunications, equipment needed to create, maintain, and ultimately terminate a connection over a *common carrier*'s line.

Data Class
In a database file, any category of related information, such as name, address, etc.

Data Collection
See *Data Acquisition*.

Data Collection Equipment
In telecommunications, the equipment required for communication between data terminal equipment and the data circuit itself.

Data Communication
Transfer of data from computer to computer by means of an electronic or electrical medium, such as a cable. Data communication is considered apart from voice communication.

Data Communications Equipment (DCE)
In networking and telecommunications, any device or configuration of devices that connects a computer to a communications network. Often used synonymously with *modem*, which is one type of DCE.

Data Compression
The process of removing redundant bits of information from a digital file (especially a graphics, audio, or video file) as a means of reducing file size and/or expediting processing and transmission over networks. Essentially, data compression works utilizing one of a variety of algorithms to remove large chunks of information, but include codes for its later restoration. When the file is reopened or recreated from the data file, the system decodes the compression algorithm, replacing the "removed" data. (Video compression algorithms are thus also known as *codec*s, standing for "compress/decompress.") However, the greater the compression, the less detail can be encoded, and the more detail is lost when the file is recovered.

As algorithms become more sophisticated, the compression ratios will increase while resulting in decreasing amounts of data loss. Currently, 10:1 is a compression ratio (in other words, the compressed file is ten times smaller than the original) that is performed without significant loss of information. Compression ratios of 30:1 are also common, but they tend to result in some degree of detail loss.

Compression algorithms that result in no data loss when the files are subsequently *decompress*ed are called *lossless*, while those that do result in some degree of data loss are called *lossy*.

Some common data compression algorithms in use include *JPEG* and *MPEG*, to name two. See also *File Compression*.

Data Connector
In networking, a *connector* used with a *Type 1* cable in *Token Ring* networks.

Data Conversion
The translating of one particular data *file format* or code structure to another, or transferring a file from one computer *platform* (such as *Windows*) to another (such as *Macintosh*).

Data Density
In electronic page layout, the ratio of text, graphics, and other page elements to white space, calculated (or estimated) as a means of determining the amount of optical storage space required for the document.

Data Dictionary/Directory
In a database management system, information about the data in the system.

Data-Encoding Scheme
In computing, a means by which a *hard disk* controller stores information on a hard or *floppy disk* (or other type of external storage medium). See *Run-Length Limited (RLL)* and *Advanced Run-Length Limited (ARLL)*.

Data Entry
The input of source information into a database system.

Data Exchange Format
See *DXF*.

Data File
Alternate term for a computer *file*. See *File*.

Data Glove
In *virtual reality*, an electronic hand covering—or glove—containing directional sensors, used to transmit electrical signals to a computer. These signals are then converted to digital form and the resulting data control objects in the virtual environment being displayed. See also *Data Suit*.

Datagram
Alternate term for a data *packet*. See *Packet*.

Datagram Delivery Protocol (DDP)
In networking, a *routing* protocol developed by Apple Computer for its *AppleTalk* network.

Data Independence
In a database system, the ability of the physical structure of the database to be altered without having to alter the application that creates and manages it.

Data Integrity
In a database system, the state of data that is well-maintained and kept free from accidental erasure, corruption, or alteration.

Data Interchange Format (DIF)
In computing, a *file format* developed for VisiCalc, the very first *spreadsheet* program. DIF is still used to transfer files from spreadsheet to spreadsheet.

Data Interface
In computing, the physical link between software and hardware, or two pieces of hardware.

Data Item
In a database, the smallest unit of data contained in a *record*. Often a *field*.

Data Link
In telecommunications, all the required hardware and software—such as a *modem*, communication channel, and communications controller—required to transmit information from one point to another.

Data-Link Layer
Alternate term for *link layer*. See *Link Layer*.

Data Management
In computing, the function of an *operating system* involving the organization, storing, and retrieving of data as well as the control of input and output devices.

Data Manipulation Language
In database systems, the *interface* between an application program and a database management system.

Data Network
Any telecommunications network designed and built specifically for data, rather than voice, communication.

Data PBX
A *private branch exchange (PBX)* that supports digital data communications rather than strictly analog—or voice—communication.

Dataphone
Initially, Bell Telephone's trade name for their brand of *modem*, now used to refer generically to any modem.

Data Processing (DP)
General term for any computing (typically performed by *mainframes* or *minicomputers*) in a business environment or data center. DP commonly involves bookkeeping, accounting, etc.

Data Processing System
The computer or network of computers required for *data processing*. See *Data Processing (DP)*.

Data Production
All the steps required to compile data from a database and prepare it for distribution, either on *CD-ROM*, over the *Internet*, etc.

Data Protection
Any safeguarding of computer information and files from any unwanted damage, loss, or disclosure. See, for example, *File Protection*.

Data Rate
Alternate term for *bit rate*. See *Bit Rate*.

Data Reduction
In a database system, the distilling of raw data into that which is the most pertinent and useful. See also *Data Refinement*.

Data Redundancy
In *data compression*, the state of data that is extraneous to a particular file, and which can be discarded to reduce the size of the file. Such data is known as *redundant data*. See *Data Compression*.

Data Refinement
Converting a set of raw data into a usable form, which can include not only deleting data that is extraneous to the desired end-use of the data, but also organizing, cataloging, tagging, and indexing it.

Data Register

A portion of a computer's ***central processing unit*** in which small amounts of information are held for processing in the near future. Data held in a data register is accessed and processed faster than that held in ***memory***. Also known simply as a ***register***.

Data Security

See ***Security***.

Data Service Unit (DSU)

In telecommunications, a device used to connect ***data terminal equipment*** to a digital communication line and to format the data for transmission on public networks.

Data Set

In a database system, any logical group of data organized in some fashion.

In telecommunications, a device that converts data into a form that can be transmitted over a communications line, or which converts transmitted data into a form that can be processed by the receiving system.

Data Set Ready (DSR)

In networking, a signal defined by the ***RS-232-C*** standard indicating that a hardware device is ready to operate.

Data Sharing

In networking, the ability for multiple users to access data stored at a single location simultaneously.

Data Shuttle

See ***Removable Hard Disk Drive***.

Dataspeed

The actual speed two ***modem***s transmit data between each other; it may or may not correspond to the advertised transmission speed. True dataspeed is a function not only of the modems but also the quality of the telephone connection.

Data Storage

In computing, the storing or archiving of data files on a ***hard disk*** or any of a variety of external storage media.

Data Stream

Any continuous flow of computer information from one point to another, such as the transmission of files over a network.

Data Structure

In a database system, the specific organization of a data set.

Data Suit

In ***virtual reality***, an electronic body covering—or suit—containing directional sensors, used to transmit electrical signals corresponding to the wearer's movements to a computer. These signals are then converted to digital form and

the resulting data control objects in the virtual environment being displayed. See also ***Data Glove***.

Data Tablet

Alternate term for a ***digitizing tablet***. See ***Digitizing Tablet***.

Data Terminal Equipment (DTE)

In networking, any device—such as a terminal, a computer, a controller, etc.—connected to a communications circuit.

Data Terminal Ready (DTR)

In networking, a signal defined by the ***RS-232-C*** standard sent from a computer to a modem indicating that the computer is ready to receive a transmission.

Data Transmission

In computing, the sending of computer information—such as a file—over a network or other form of telecommunications link.

Data-Transfer Rate

Alternate term for ***bit rate***. See ***Bit Rate***.

Dating Routine

In computing, the set of instructions the computer uses to keep track of or compute the current date.

Daughterboard

In computing, a board that is mounted on the ***motherboard***, often used for memory upgrades.

Day-Glo

A trade name for a variety of fluorescent inks and papers.

dB

Abbreviation for ***decibel***. See ***Decibel (dB)***.

DB Connector

In computing, any of a variety of ***parallel*** or ***serial*** connectors, used to connect peripheral devices to computers. "DB" (which stands for "data bus") is followed by a number indicating the number of pins the connector will typically have. Thus, a DB-25 connector can have 25 pins. (See illustration on the following page.)

DBF

A ***file extension*** used to denote files created by Ashton-Tate's dBaseII and dBaseIII programs.

D Bit

Abbreviation for ***delivery confirmation bit***. See ***Delivery Confirmation Bit (D Bit)***.

DBMS

Alternate term for ***database management system***. See ***Database Management System***.

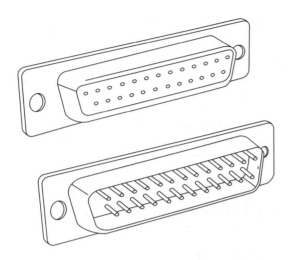

Male (top) and female (bottom) DB connectors.

dBrn

Abbreviation for **decibel above reference noise**. See **Decibel Above Reference Noise**.

DC-2000

A type of **magnetic tape** (having a tape width of ¼ inch) used for backup of computer information. With the proper level of **data compression**, up to 250 **megabyte**s can be stored.

DCA

A **file format** created by IBM for **word processing** files.

DCB

Abbreviation for **disk coprocessor board**. See **Disk Coprocessor Board**.

DCD

Abbreviation for **Data Carrier Detect**. See **Data Carrier Detect (DCD)**.

DCE

Abbreviation for **data communications equipment**. See **Data Communications Equipment (DCE)**.

D-Channel

In telecommunications, a 16-**kilobit per second** ISDN channel, used for establishing **ISDN** connections without tying up a higher-capacity **B-channel**. In **Primary Rate Interface** connections, a D-channel has a capacity of 64 Kbps. See **ISDN**.

DCS

Abbreviation for **Desktop Color Separation**. See **Desktop Color Separation**.

DCT

Abbreviation for **discrete cosine transform**. See **Discrete Cosine Transform (DCT)**.

DD

Abbreviation for **double density**. See **Double Density**.

DD1/ID1

A prescribed standard for computer data recording equipment utilizing **D1** videotape. See **D1**.

DD2

A prescribed standard for computer data recording equipment utilizing **D2** videotape. See **D2**.

DDAP

Abbreviation for **digital distribution of advertising for publications**, a standard **file format** designed for the electronic transmission of ad files sent to publishers and printers.

DDCMP

Abbreviation for **Digital Data Communications Message Protocol**. See **Digital Data Communications Message Protocol (DDCMP)**.

DDCP

Abbreviation for **direct digital color proof**, a **color proof** printed directly on the desired **substrate** from a digital file, using a **color electronic prepress system** or other type of computer system. The DDCP is output from the system utilizing one of a variety of printers—dot matrix, ink-jet, electrophotographic thermal transfer, or photographic exposure—and an advantage of the system is that it enables a color proof to be generated without the need for **halftone** film. DDCP is also known as a **digital hard proof**, as opposed to a **digital soft proof**.

DDD

Abbreviation for **direct distance dialing**. See **Direct Distance Dialing**.

DDE

Abbreviation for **dynamic data exchange**. See **Dynamic Data Exchange (DDE)**.

DDES

Abbreviation for **Digital Data Exchange Standards**, an **ANSI**- and **ISO**-approved series of protocols and formats devised to allow computer equipment manufactured by one vendor to communicate with that of another vendor.

DDL

Abbreviation for **Dynamic Linking Library**. See **Dynamic Linking Library (DDL)**.

DDP

Abbreviation for **Datagram Delivery Protocol**. See **Datagram Delivery Protocol (DDP)**.

In general computing terminology, *DDP* is an abbreviation for **distributed data processing**. See **Distributed Data Processing**.

Dead Finish

A paper *finish* characterized by a smooth, nonglare surface.

Dead Matter

Any typographic material—be it original copy, a manuscript, typescript, type, or typeset copy—that is no longer needed, as opposed to *live matter*.

Deadlock

In networking, a blockage which comes about when two or more users attempt to access the same device or facility.

Deadly Embrace

Alternate and overly descriptive term for *file lock-out*. See *File Lock-Out*.

Dead White

Any white ink *pigment* exhibiting no trace of a tint.

Debarking

The removal of bark prior to *pulping* wooden logs or sticks for use in papermaking. Wood is pulped in order to liberate *cellulose* fibers from nonfibrous materials. Bark contributes no fibrous material and adds dirt and other contaminants to the *pulp*, so must be removed. (But see also *Whole Tree Utilization*.) Pulpwood logs are debarked either mechanically in a drum-type barker, in which logs are sent through a rotating barking drum and the impact and abrasion experienced by the logs as they roll over each other knocks the bark off; or hydraulically, where logs are rotated beneath high-pressure water jets (at 1,300 pounds per square inch) that strip the bark away. Bark is then used as a fuel source or for garden mulch. The debarked logs are sent to a *chipper*, in which they are cut into small chips ready for pulping. (See also *Pulping*.)

Deblocking

In a database system, the separation of a block of data into individual *record*s.

Debossing

In *binding and finishing*, the reverse of *embossing*, or the use of heated dies to stamp or press a depressed (*intaglio*) image into a *substrate*. See *Embossing*.

Debug

In computer application and system development, to search for and—purportedly—correct *bug*s. See *Bug*.

Decal

A design printed (often by *screen printing*) on a plastic or other *substrate* intended for ultimate transfer to another surface, either by water-slide transfer, heat-transfer, or any other means. "Decal" is short for *decalcomania*, the name for the process of using a decal as a means of transferring an image.

Decal Adhesive

A colorless, transparent, water-soluble material, capable of accepting *screen printing* ink, applied to the face surface of a *decal* to facilitate the adhesion of the decal face down on another transparent surface, so to be read through the other side of the *substrate*.

Decal Varnish

A *varnish* used to apply a *decal*, in particular one designed for outdoor use and exposure to the elements.

Decalcomania

The process of transferring an image to a *substrate* (such as glassware, plastic ware, etc.) by first printing the image on a special paper, plastic, or other substrate, and then applying the printed image to the ultimate desired substrate, either by a water-slide method, heat transfer, or other means. See *Decal*.

Decentralized Network

Alternate term for a *distributed network*. See *Distributed Network*.

Decibel Above Reference Noise

A measure of the number of *decibel*s by which a sound exceeds the intensity of a reference value. See *Decibel*. Abbreviated *dBrn*.

Decibel (dB)

A measurement of sound intensity utilizing a relative scale based in the ratio of one sound intensity to another, one usually being a standard intensity.

The scale of decibel level is a logarithmic one; the decibel is defined as 20 times the common logarithm of the ratio of the pressure produced by the sound in question to that of a standard reference pressure (usually considered to be 0.0002 microbar, one microbar being equal to one millionth of an atmosphere). Thus a sound 20 dB higher than another is 100 times greater in intensity. A sound 30 dB higher than another is 1,000 times greater in intensity. A decibel is also defined as one-tenth of a Bel unit (a unit named for acoustics pioneer and telephone-inventor Alexander Graham Bell).

A *decibel* is also used to measure voltage levels.

Deciduous

A category of tree, also classified as *hardwood*, used in *pulping* processes for manufacturing paper.

Familiar types of deciduous trees include aspen, beech, birch, cottonwood, elm, maple, and oak. They are distinguished to a large extent by their yearly loss of leaves, in contrast to *conifers*, most of which retain their leaves year-round. Hardwood fibers are much shorter than *softwood* fibers (obtained from conifers), and don't lend themselves well to production of many types of paper. See also *Coniferous*.

Decimal

A number system based on 10, usually referred as "base 10." Each digit in a number essentially has 10 possibilities, comprising the numerals 0–9.

Decimal Fraction

In typography, a means of avoiding the problem of how to typeset *fractions* by simply converting a fraction to a decimal, as in ¼ = 0.25. See *Fractions*.

Decimal Tab

In typesetting systems, a tab character that aligns columns of numbers by decimal point rather than by the first character. Decimal tabs can be aligned manually, or automatically (as with an *automatic decimal tab*).

Decision Table

In computer programming, a matrix created to map out the conditions and responses to those conditions to be programmed into a software application. Often used in lieu of a *flowchart*.

Deck

In typography, one particular line of a multi-line headline.

The term *deck* is also an alternate term for a *drop-head*. See *Drop-Head*.

Deckle

A type of paper with an irregular, untrimmed edge which decreases in thickness towards the edge of the paper. Deckle-edge paper is commonly used for high-quality books, booklets, announcements, or fine art prints. The edge itself can be created either by letting the pulp dry by itself, or by spraying a jet of water or air against the edge. *Double-deckle paper*—has two parallel deckle edges.

DECnet

A line of communications and networking hardware and software developed and marketed by Digital Equipment Corp. (DEC) for use with *microcomputer*s and *workstation*s. DECnet is compatible with *Ethernet* and *wide area network*s, and is built into DEC's *VMS* operating system.

Decoating

In *screen printing* the removal of ink residue and stencil film from the screen fabric at the conclusion of a print run.

Decoded Audio Signal

An *analog audio* signal produced by a *digital-to-analog converter* in a device used to playback digital audio (such as a conventional *audio CD* player).

Decoder

A device or algorithm used to unscramble encoded data.

Decoder/Encoder

In video production, a device which separates *composite video* into separate red, green, and blue signals (a decoder),

or one which combines the separate red, green, and blue signals into a composite signal (an encoder).

de Colines, Simon

Simon de Colines (1480–1546) was a French printer who pioneered the use of italic types. He worked as a partner of Henri Estienne. Colines married his widow, and was in charge of the press until Estienne's son Robert I entered the business in 1526, by which time Colines had set up his own shop. In 1528 de Colines began to use italic type and publish many Greek and Latin classics. He is credited with the design of italic and Greek fonts and of a roman face for St. Augustine's Sylvius (1531), from which the Garamond types were derived. In 1525 he published the notable Grandes Heures de Simon de Colines, with decorations by Geoffroy Tory.

Decollate

To break up collated sets of copies. *Decollate* also means to remove carbon paper from multi-ply forms.

Decompress

To restore a data file to its proper size and *file format* following *data compression*. See *Data Compression*. See also *Compress*.

Decompression

The opposite process from *data compression*, or to restore a compressed data file to its original form. See *Data Compression*.

Decorative Paper

Any of a wide variety of stylized papers which includes different colors, *coating*s, *basis weight*s, and *finish*es.

Decorative Type

Any of a wide variety of ornamental *typeface*s, such as *script*s or those with *swash* characters, whose aesthetic attributes take precedence over those of legibility.

Decryption

The process of decoding encrypted data. See *Encryption*.

Decurler

See *Sheet Decurler*.

Dedicated

General term for any device committed to one particular purpose, such as a *dedicated line*, *dedicated server*, *dedicated system*, etc.

Dedicated Circuit

Alternate term for a *dedicated line*. See *Dedicated Line*.

Dedicated Keyboard

A keyboard which generates unique code sequences and is thus compatible with only one type of computer or typesetting machine.

Dedicated Landing Zone

On a computer storage disk (in particular, a **hard disk**), a section of the disk surface where no data is stored and where the **read/write head** sits when it is inactive. The dedicated landing zone ensures that the magnetized surface of the disk is not damaged during transport or other disk handling. Also known as the **take-off zone** and, simply, the **landing zone**. See also **Flying Height**.

Dedicated Line

In networking and telecommunications, a communications line permanently used for a single purpose (such as a modem, fax machine, etc.) and not shared by other devices or users.

Similarly, the term *dedicated line* can also refer to an electrical outlet assigned to only one device, and isolated from other electrical outlets and electrical interference.

In both senses of the term, a *dedicated line* is also called a **dedicated circuit**.

Dedicated Server

In networking, a **server** used solely for a network purpose, such as to regulate data flow, traffic, and other aspects of the network. On a dedicated server, network versions of software applications used by connected users are stored, as are data files. See **Server**. See also **Nondedicated Server**.

Dedicated System

In electronic publishing, a computer system designed and programmed used exclusively for publishing.

Dedication

In **book typography** and publishing, a page—typically appearing as a new **recto** page immediately following the **copyright** page—on which the author lists those for whom the book has ostensibly been written, such as loved ones, pets, or agents. The dedication may also appear on the copyright page. See **Book Typography**.

Deep-Etched Plate

A type of **plate** used in **offset lithography** in which the action of light during exposure to a **film positive** produces a hard coating on nonimage areas. During development, the image areas are slightly etched. Deep-etched plates are used for long runs and/or high-quality offset printing.

De Facto Standard

Any computer language, program, routine, device, etc., that through a combination of wide use and little competition has become the model upon which other languages, programs, routines, devices, etc., are based. De facto standards differ from standards consciously developed by organizations in that they tend to be accidental, unintentional, and serendipitous.

Default

Any preset value that a computer system or program will use in the processing of data when no user-specified value has been indicated. A default setting is one that the computer will "fall back on" for want of other instructions. For example, some word processing programs will by default use 12-point Geneva type on 12 points of leading, unless the user deliberately changes it. In some cases—such as imaging applications—the default settings are those believed by the software developer to be the most desirable settings. However, this is not always the case.

Default Directory

In computing, the **directory** or **folder** (depending upon the **operating system**) in which an application will store a file, unless another directory is specified by the user. See also **Current Directory**.

Default Drive

In computing, the disk drive on which an application will store a file, unless another drive is specified by the user. See also **Current Drive**.

Definition

The degree of sharpness or **resolution** of any image, either produced photographically or digitally.

Deflection

A tendency for a metal rod, tube, cylinder, or roller to bend or deform between its bearings when pressure is exerted, such as when rollers and cylinders exert increased pressures on each other.

Deflection, when occurring on inking rollers, can result in inconsistent ink transfer to the plate, blanket, and/or substrate across the press. Deflection also refers to a cylinder or roller's pressure-induced **out-of-roundness**. Deflection is also known as **flex**.

In a **cathode-ray tube**, a technique added (by means of a device called a deflection unit) that increases the angle at which the electrons beams are spread on the back of the screen. Increased angle of deflection increases the flatness of the monitor.

Deflocculant

Any chemical used for the purpose of **deflocculation**. See **Deflocculation**.

Deflocculation

The breaking up and dispersion of undesirable clusters of **pigment** particles in a printing ink. See **Flocculation**.

Defoaming Agent

See **Antifoaming Agent**.

Defragment

In computing, to restructure a **hard disk** or any other data storage medium. When a computer stores files that have been edited or altered, it doesn't necessarily store a complete new file, but rather inserts codes into the previously saved version of the file which function as pointers to the location of the changes made to the file. The changes may be located near the original file, but not always. Thus, files are said to be *fragmented*. A software utility (such as Norton's SpeedDisk) is used to combine all the file fragments into a single location or block, which increases the speed with which files can be accessed and opened.

Degauss

Generally speaking, to demagnetize any device, object, or material, commonly by means of electric coils. Degaussing was at one time (and may still be) performed on the hulls of naval vessels, as a means of removing any magnetic influence a metal hull might have on a magnetic mine (such as causing the mine to explode). Many electric and electronic devices build up magnetic charges. Often, degaussing needs to be performed on an audio tape player, as built-up magnetism affects the playback of recordings. On a computer monitor, magnetic buildup distorts the appearance of displayed colors, and degaussing can usually correct such display problems. The term *degaussing* also refers to the erasure of data stored on magnetic media, such as audio and video tapes, magnetic computer cartridges, and so forth.

The term *degauss* derives from the name of the German mathematician and scientist Karl Friedrich Gauss (1777–1855) who in the 1830s carried out some of the earliest and most influential research on magnetism.

Deglazing

Removal of *glaze* from an offset press ink roller. See *Glaze*.

Degradation

In telecommunications and networking, a deterioration in the quality or speed of a transmission, usually caused by an increased number of users accessing the network.

Degradation Factor

In a data processing system, a measure of the performance loss resulting from alteration or reconfiguring of the system.

Degradé

A tint applied to a color *halftone* that changes in both *color* strength and *hue* from one edge to the other. The color qualities may vary in both directions, depending upon the distribution of the particular *process color* used for the tint. Degradés are also known as *graded tint*s and, incorrectly, as *gradient*s. See also *Vignette*.

Deinking

A procedure performed to make *recovered fiber* usable for the manufacturing of *recycled paper* that is to be used for printing and writing papers. Deinking is the first phase of the "repulping" process for recycled papers. Mesh screens filter out large particles, and centrifugal cleaners remove other nonfibrous particles. Particles that float to the surface of the cleaning tank are skimmed off. In *wash deinking*, chemical *dispersent*s and physical collision remove ink particles from the wastepaper, allowing them to be washed away. Further chemical treatment keeps the separated ink from returning to the fibers. The fibers are

strained out of the solution, and the ink particles remain behind. This process also removes *fines* and particles of filler from the previous papermaking process, which helps produce a stronger, brighter pulp. Wash deinking, however, tends not to be a very cost-effective procedure, requiring large amounts of water.

Flotation deinking treats wastepaper with chemicals such as calcium soaps that render the ink particles *hydrophobic*, or tending to avoid water. The suspended ink particles are collected by air bubbles injected into the flotation tank, and they are carried to the surface where they can be skimmed off. Flotation deinking uses less water than wash deinking, but often both procedures must be used to make the recovered fibers suitable for writing and printing papers.

Delamination

Term that can mean either a general separation of the plys of any paper due to inadequate *surface strength*, or, in web offset lithography, a specific paper defect occurring in blanket-to-blanket perfecting presses characterized by elongated blister-like formations along the *web*, also caused by inadequate surface strength that causes the internal structure of the paper to rupture when the web wraps around both blankets, causing an alternating flexing force that pulls the paper apart.

Delay

Any pause in an activity.

In networking and telecommunications, a *delay* refers to any period of inactivity, as when system resources are unavailable for transmitting or relaying a message.

Delay Distortion

In telecommunications, a distortion of a signal due to differing speeds among various components of the signal (typically the high-frequency component) as it travels through a transmission medium. Also known as *envelope delay*.

Delayed Indent

In typography, an indent occurring only after a certain number of lines have been typeset.

Delete

Any instruction—either indicated on a marked-up manuscript or film or initiated by a computer command—to remove indicated material.

Delete Capability

In word processing and other such types of programs, term describing the smallest grammatical unit—be it pages, paragraphs, sentences, word, or individual characters—that can be deleted from a storage location.

Delete Key

On a computer keyboard, a *key* used to delete text one character at a time. On many keyboards, the delete key is in the position occupied by the backspace key on typewriters, and this key deletes characters as the **cursor** backs over a line. Some extended keyboards have a separate delete key which deletes text appearing in front of the cursor.

Delimiter

In computing, any special character used to separate individual items within a set or file. For example, some database programs use commas to separate different **field**s within a record. (Such records are then said to be "comma-delimited.") Also known as a **separator**.

In networking, a *delimiter* is a specific set of **bit**s used in **Token Ring** networks to define the limits of a **token**.

Deliquescence

A property of certain solids—such as calcium chloride or various salts—that describes their ability to absorb water from the atmosphere and become dissolved in it. See also **Efflorescence**.

Delivery

A portion of any printing press, folding or binding machine, or other device where output materials are stacked.

Delivery Chain

A belt or chain used in the **delivery section** of a sheetfed printing press (especially that used in **offset lithography**) that transfers the printed sheet from the final **impression cylinder** to the **delivery pile**. See **Delivery Section**, **Delivery Cylinder**, and **Delivery Pile**.

Delivery Confirmation Bit (D Bit)

In networking, especially **X.25** packet-switched networks, a **bit** appended to a data transmission instructing the receiving device to notify the sender that the message was received.

Delivery Cylinder

The final cylinder in an offset printing press, responsible for transferring the printed sheet to the delivery pile. A delivery cylinder is a type of **transfer cylinder**, others of which may exist in the press between printing units. The delivery cylinder is charged with the responsibility of carrying the printed sheet from the final **impression cylinder** to the grippers attached to the delivery chains. A delivery cylinder, in most configurations, is covered with **skeleton wheels**, a set of disks (which can frequently be adjusted to ensure that they only support the sheet in non-image areas) that hold the sheet as it travels to the delivery chains. (Such a delivery cylinder is also known as a **skeleton cylinder**.)

In other configurations, the delivery cylinder—like a typical transfer cylinder—is coated with a near-frictionless substance, then covered with a near-frictionless cloth that is allowed to slide freely over the surface of the cylinder, further ensuring that the wet ink won't be smudged or marked. A marked alternative to the traditional delivery cylinder is known as a BacVac, a system devised by Printing Research, Inc., in which the unprinted side of the sheet

is pulled away from the skeleton wheels by a vacuum and rollers, preventing contact between the wheels and the wet ink. This system, however, cannot be used on presses which print both sides of a sheet simultaneously. (See **Offset Lithography: Printing Unit**.)

Delivery Pile

The tray in which is stacked the pile of printed sheets following printing, also called a **delivery table**. The delivery pile also contains a series of moveable guides called **joggers** that work to keep the stack of sheets neatly piled. (See **Delivery Section** and **Jogger**.)

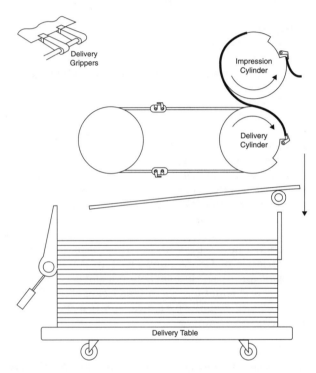

Sheetfed offset press delivery section.

Delivery System

The hardware and software requirements needed to store and/or display a multimedia production or presentation.

Delivery Table

Alternate term for **delivery pile**. See **Delivery Pile**.

Delta E (ΔE)

In **color**, a specified degree of a change in color. Delta, the Greek letter Δ, simply means—in scientific and mathematical terminology—"change in." In colorimetry, changes in **hue** and strength are measured on a computerized scale, which can automatically compute the change in a color.

Delta-YUV

In **digital video** and graphics, a means of compressing and storing digitized photographic images by reducing the amount of color information saved, while retaining all the *luminance* information. The principle behind it is that human eyes more easily detect changes in luminance than changes in color. Despite its advantages, however, it can result in a loss of contrast between *pixel*s and diminished *definition*. It is a video compression format supported by *CD-i*. Abbreviated *DYUV*. See also *YUV*.

Deluxe Edition

In *binding and finishing*, any book or quantity of a print run of a book bound in a more expensive and/or superior manner than other editions of the same title. A leather-bound edition with edge *gilding* and a ribbon *book mark* is an example of a deluxe edition.

Demand Paging

In computing, a type of *virtual memory* in which a *page* of information is loaded into memory from the disk only when needed by a particular program. See *Virtual Memory*.

Demand Priority

In networking, an alternative access method to *CSMA/CA* and *CSMA/CD* in which all workstations are connected (via a *star* topology) to a central *hub*. When a particular station wants to transmit a message along the network, it asks the hub's "permission," and the hub will maintain a connection for the duration of the transmission. (A technique known as *guaranteed bandwidth*.) The demand priority access method is an effective means of ensuring *collision avoidance*, a consideration when a common channel is used (as in a *baseband* network). With other methods—in particular the varieties of CSMA—any given transmission may have to wait for a free channel before being sent, which is particularly problematic in the transmission of multimedia (such as video or audio) where delays in transmission can disrupt picture continuity.

Demand Processing

Alternate term for *real-time processing*. See *Real-Time Processing*.

Demand Publishing

See *On-Demand Printing*.

Demibold

In typography, a *typeface* weight between normal and *bold*. See *Weight*.

Demo Disk

In multimedia or computing, any disk produced to demonstrate or test a program or presentation, usually not as slickly or efficiently produced as the full-fledged production.

Demodulation

In telecommunications, the conversion of a modulated analog signal transmitted along a *carrier* (such as data being transmitted along a telephone line) to a digital signal, or one that can be read by a computer (or a signal which can

be read by any receiving device, such as a radio receiver). The reverse process, necessary before transmission, is called *modulation*. A *modem*—a device used to perform both modulation and demodulation—is short for "modulator/demodulator."

Demountable

One type of *plate cylinder* used in *flexography*. See *Plate Cylinder: Flexography*.

Demultiplexing

In telecommunications, the reverse of *multiplexing* consisting of the separation of a compound signal back into individual signals. See *Multiplexing*.

Dennison Wax Test

A test performed to measure a paper's *pick resistance*, or *surface strength*, in which calibrated, progressively adhesive wax sticks are melted onto the surface of a paper sample and, after cooling, pulled quickly from the surface. The "wax strength number" is the highest-number wax stick that can be melted on and pulled from the paper without marring its surface. The wax test should be performed on both the *wire side* and *felt side* of the paper.

Densitometer

An instrument having a light-sensitive photoelectric eye to measures the density of images and colorants. The measurements of color densities are used in *color calibration*.

Scanning densitometer.

Density

In imaging and *color*, the perceived darkness of a substance, material, or image caused by the absorption or reflection of light impinging on the material. Differences in density as related to color are also known as *gray levels*. As the density of a material increases, the amount of light that is absorbed by the material increases, while the amount of light reflected from or transmitted by the material decreases. The absorption of light is inversely proportional to the transmission or reflectance of light, according to the formula:

$$\text{Density} = \log_{10}\frac{1}{\text{Transmittance}} = \log_{10}\frac{1}{\text{Reflectance}}$$

The term *density* also refers to the degree of blackness or darkness possessed by a type character, or to the number of characters per unit of *line length*.

Density is also used to refer to the storage capacity of a magnetic storage medium, such as a floppy disk, referring to the amount of data that can be stored in a given surface area or per linear *track* of the magnetic material. It also refers to the number of tracks the particular disk contains.

Density Range

In printing, any nonuniformity in the density of a printed image, resulting from fading, discoloration, incomplete ink coverage, or other causes.

In imaging, *density range* refers to the *gamut* of tones in an original (or reproduction), expressed as the difference between the area of maximum density (the darkest portions of an image) and the minimum density (the lightest tones). Also known as *tonal range*.

For example, the density of a *shadow* area can be calculated as 2.5. The density of a *highlight* area can be calculated as 0.10. Thus, the density range for the image as a whole would be 2.4. (For the formula regarding the calculation of density, see *Density*.) Also known as *tonal range* and *dynamic range*.

Densometer

A device used to measure the *porosity* of paper by measuring the length of time it takes for a quantity of air to pass through a paper sample. (See *Gurley Densometer* and *Porosimeter*.)

Departmental LAN

A small *local area network (LAN)* used by a limited number of people with shared system resources.

Depth

When referring to two-dimensional planes (such as pages), a measurement of the vertical dimension, synonymous with height. When referring to three-dimensional planes, a measurement of the dimension perpendicular to the plane of the viewing surface.

Depth Cueing

In the *rendering* of three-dimensional graphics, a means of creating the impression of a third dimension (or depth) by the use of perspective or by rendering "distant" points darker and blurrier than "closer" points.

Depth of Field

In photography, the range of distances from a *lens* in which objects are in focus, the object upon which the lens is focused being located within this range, and not being situated at either boundary of this zone. Altering the diameter of the *iris* changes the depth of field; reducing the iris diameter increases the depth of field while enlarging the iris diameter decreases the depth of field. Also known as *depth of focus*.

Depth of Focus

Alternate term for *depth of field*. See *Depth of Field*.

Derivative Work

Any creative endeavor overtly produced in part or in toto from an already-existing work. The term can be merely descriptive (such as a *CD-ROM* version of a book) or derogatory (such as a work touted as original but which is an attempt to duplicate another, usually successful, piece of work). In this latter sense, it differs from plagiarism or copyright infringement in that there is just enough original material to sufficiently distinguish it.

DES

Abbreviation for *Data Encryption Standard*. See *Data Encryption Standard (DES)*.

Descender

In typography, the portion of lowercase letters that extends below the character's *x-height*. The descending characters are *g*, *j*, *p*, *q*, and *y*. They may not always align at the bottom of the descender, although most do. One must be careful that line spacing, or *leading*, is sufficient so that the descenders of one line do not touch the *ascender*s of the next line. *Typeface*s are designed to meet the designer's creative feeling; thus, some descenders may be shorter (or longer) than others. See also *Ascender* and *x-Height*.

Descender Line

In typography, an imaginary horizontal line that marks the bottommost point of a *descender*. See *Descender*.

Descent

In typography, the maximum distance of a *font* below the *baseline*. See also *Ascent*.

Descreening

The removing of a *halftone* screen pattern from an image to be able to add a new screen. Descreening can be accomplished either optically or electronically.

Descriptor

Alternate term for a *keyword*. See *Keyword*.

Desensitization

The chemical treatment of a lithographic plate to impart to nonimage areas water-receptivity and ink-repellency, commonly achieved utilizing a solution of *gum arabic* or other *gum* compound. It is the offset press *fountain solution* that keeps the plate properly desensitized over the course of a print run. See *Plate: Offset Lithography*. (See also *Fountain Solution*.) Also called *gumming*.

Desensitize

To chemically treat a lithographic plate to impart to nonimage areas water-receptivity and ink-repellency, commonly utilizing a solution of *gum arabic* or other *gum* compound. It is the offset press *fountain solution* that keeps the plate properly desensitized over the course of a print run. See *Plate: Offset Lithography*. (See also *Fountain Solution*.)

In photography, a substance used to decrease the sensitivity to color of a photographic emulsion, to facilitate *development* under relatively bright light.

Design Plans

A layout or other sketch used as a guide for carrying out a proposed design.

Design Roll

An alternative to a rubber or photopolymer plate, used as an image carrier in *flexography*.

A design roll consists of any of the various configurations of *plate cylinder* to which a thin (commonly at least ⅛ inch, perhaps thicker) layer of rubber has been applied. After the rubber has undergone vulcanization and cooling, the roll can be ground and polished to ensure that the surface is smooth and as close to perfectly round as possible (or having a *total indicated runout* of no more than 0.001 inch). The image to be printed is then engraved onto the surface of the cylinder using a high-energy laser, which atomizes rubber in the nonimage areas of the plate, leaving the image areas in relief. The height of the image above the floor of the cylinder can be varied in the engraving process, depending on the level of relief desired.

Laser-engraved design rolls are used for long pressruns, typically in decorative printing applications. The most important benefit of the design roll is its seamlessness; it can be used to print continuous images or solid-color backgrounds, such as those found on packaging, wrapping, and other such applications. The elimination of image distortion and elongation (a concern on flat, flexible plates mounted on a standard plate cylinder) is also an added advantage of the design roll. Design rolls can also be used in tandem with mounted plates for multicolor or multidesign applications.

See also *Plate: Flexography*.

Design Station

Any computer workstation at which the user (a designer) can create an image or page layout. The design station may be connected to a network page or other design elements can be obtained from other workstations or produced anew.

Desk Accessory

A small program or utility in the *Macintosh operating system* folder that can be used while another application is running. Some common Mac desk accessories include the alarm clock, calculator, notepad, etc.

De-Skewing

In image manipulation, an adjustment made to an image to compensate for physical or dimensional distortions caused by errors in scanning.

Desktop

In computer terminology, *desktop* refers to any computer or peripheral small enough to fit on the top of a desk, as opposed to a *mainframe* computer. Desktop is commonly used as an adjective modifying another term, such as "publishing," "computer," or other devices or activities that at one time could not be performed on the desktop.

The term *desktop* is also used to refer to the *Macintosh* (and now *Windows*) user interface, where screen elements are cast as *icon*s or other representations that are meant to be analogous to a literal desktop. Some common elements of the "virtual desktop" approach to the *GUI* are the representation of computer files as manila folders, file delete functions as trash cans (or recycling bins), etc. Small, utility programs such as a clock or a calculator are known as *desktop accessories*.

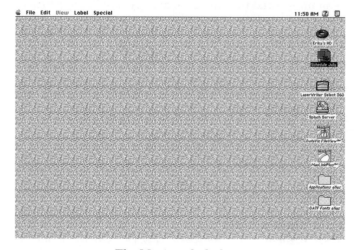

The Macintosh desktop.

Desktop Accessories

In computing, small, utility programs—such as a clock, a calculator, scrap book, notepad, etc.—added to the *desktop* of a *graphical user interface*. See *Desktop* and *Graphical User Interface (GUI)*.

Desktop Color

General term for the reproduction of *color* images (either as a part of digital prepress or for other means) on a *desktop* computer (such as a *Macintosh*, *PC*, Sun workstation, or other type of computer), utilizing a color scanner or other means of obtaining digital images such as a Photodiscs, Internet file transfers, etc. Images are imported into a program (such as Adobe Photoshop), color corrected, resized, and otherwise processed, exported into a page makeup program (i.e., *PageMaker* or *QuarkXPress*), and then output to a color printer, direct digital color proofer, or to film.

Desktop Color Separation (DCS)

A standard data file created as a means of producing *color separation*s in desktop publishing systems. DCS essentially creates five separate files: one is a *low-resolution* composite file in which the full color image is viewable (as a **PICT** file), and the other four consist only of separate color data (in **EPS** format) for each of the **process colors**—**cyan**, **magenta**, **yellow**, and **black**. Hence, any particular DCS image is often called a **five-file EPS** file. An RGB **TIFF** image can be converted to CMYK using any DCS-compatible program, such as Photoshop. This can be done before importing the image into the page makeup program, the low-res viewfile being used on the screen display. Disadvantages of DCS, however, include the increased disk space occupied by the five files, and the fact that if DCS separations are made early in the production process, any changes that will effect the halftone **screen ruling** (such as changing the paper on which page will be printed) will require new separations to be made.

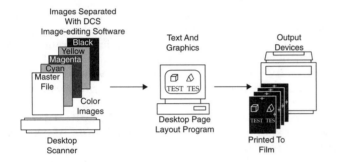

Desktop color separation (DCS) used for including original color images in a page layout program and for generating color-separated output.

Desktop Computer

Any small **microcomputer** that can literally fit on a desk, as opposed to a **mainframe**, which typically requires its own room. A desktop computer is essentially a compact unit consisting of a case containing the computer itself, including the **CPU** and other chips controlling all the peripherals that can be attached to the computer, as well as a hard disk drive, one or more floppy disk drives, and, increasingly, internal CD-ROM drives and modems. A monitor, a keyboard, and a mouse are also attached to the system.

Desktop Management Interface (DMI)

In networking, a standard **application programming interface (API)** used to automatically identify **workstation** hardware and software, usually by at least manufacturer, name, version, installation date and time, and more or less information. DMI is used to help network administrators solve configuration problems and easily spot sites for possible upgrade. Most vendors support DMI.

Desktop Publishing

A general, term referring to the process of assembling pages on a **desktop computer**, commonly accomplished using commercially available software, an input device such as a scanner, and an output device, such as a laser printer or other devices of increasing image quality and **resolution**.

Desktop publishing is enhanced (and, in fact, even made possible) by the use of **page description language**s, most notably Adobe Systems's **PostScript**. Increasing output quality has resulted in many publications—from newspapers to magazines to newsletters to corporate documents—being assembled on desktop computers rather than on traditional typesetters.

The term "desktop publishing" itself was coined in the mid-1980s by Paul Brainerd, the founder of Aldus Corporation (now owned by Adobe Systems), the company whose **PageMaker** program essentially invented the idea of publishing from one's desktop.

Although initially desktop publishing was used for little more than short-run newsletters, flyers, and brochures, the same systems are now often used to create books, slick magazines, newspapers, etc. In fact, there is now very little difference between desktop publishing and digital **prepress**.

Desktop Publishing System

Any collection of hardware (in particular a **desktop computer**) and software (in particular, **page-makeup software**) used to create and assemble finished pages for output as **camera-ready copy**, film for platemaking, or as a finished plate ready for press. See also **electronic publishing system**.

Desktop Video (DTV)

The production of video presentations using **desktop computer**s and off-the-shelf video editing software. Although images are recorded using a video camera and are initially prepared on videotape, they are often digitized (using an **expansion board** designed for the purpose) and input into a video editing program (such as Adobe Premiere or one of a host of others).

Additional software and hardware can be used to generate a variety of effects. The finished production may be distributed solely in digital form (such as on a **CD-ROM** or as part of a larger multimedia production), or output back onto videotape.

Desktop-to-Prepress

Descriptive of any ability to create and assemble pages on a **desktop publishing system** and transfer them to a more advanced, higher-quality **color electronic prepress system (CEPS)**. See **CEPS**.

Destination Address

In networking, the **address** of the recipient of a transmitted message or data **packet**. See also **Source Address**.

Destination Field

In networking, a header appended to a message that contains the address of the message's destination.

Destructive Read

In computing, erasing data from a location by reading it.

Detackifier

A substance added to a *screen printing* ink to reduce stickiness, or *tack*, and improve the ink's flow characteristics.

Detail Enhancement

In *scanning*, the process of exaggerating the edges of an image (commonly utilizing an *unsharp mask* or *peaking* feature) to facilitate the viewing of all the original image detail in the reproduction.

Detail File

Alternate term for *transaction file*. See *Transaction File*.

Detail Paper

A thin, good-quality translucent paper commonly used for layouts or tissue overlays. Also known as *layout paper*.

Developer

In photography or any photographic process, a chemical or combination of chemicals used to render a *latent image* produced in a gelatino-silver film emulsion, visible usually by converting areas that have been exposed to light (non-image areas, at least in photographic *negative*s) from a silver halide to black metallic silver.

Different types of film require different types of developer and development times. Developing is often halted by immersing the film in a *stop bath* followed by a *fixing solution*. See *Photography*.

Developer's Toolkit

In computer programming, subroutines used by programmers as an aid to writing computer applications. A developer's toolkit can include a library of routines and strings of code written in a particular programming language, as well as conventions used in the operating system for which the application is being written.

Developing Ink

A greasy, nondrying, fluid ink applied to the surface of a lithographic plate to maintain or renew the ink-receptivity of the image area during or after plate developing, etching, and gumming.

Development

In photography or any photographic process, the act of using a chemical treatment to render a *latent image* in an exposed film visible. See *Photography*.

In computer programming and multimedia, creating a computer application or multimedia presentation.

Development Time

The amount of time it takes to write and debug a new computer program.

Device

A general term referring to any piece of hardware added to a computer system or other piece of equipment.

Device Dependence

A term used to refer to any computer application or software package that generates output that can only be generated on a particular type of output device, as opposed to software that possesses *device independence*. Device-dependent files require for their proper output special codes, *driver*s, or units of measurement unique to devices having certain characteristics or manufacturers. Also known as *hardware dependence*.

Device-Dependent

Descriptive of a computer file or program that possesses *device dependence*. See *Device Dependence*. Also known as *machine-dependent*.

Device Independence

A term used to refer to any computer application or software package that can generate output that is perceptibly identical regardless of the characteristics or brand of the output device. A common example are files saved in the *PostScript* page description language, which can be output identically regardless of the computer *platform* or output device.

Color that can be reproduced identically from device to device is known as *device-independent color*. Also known as *hardware independence*.

Device-Independent

Descriptive of a computer file or program that possesses *device independence*. See *Device Independence*. Also known as *machine-independent*.

Device-Independent Color

A term descriptive of color images that retain the same color and tonal qualities regardless of what device is displaying them, be they monitors or various color output devices. See *Device Independence*.

Device Intelligence

In computing, the ability of a software application to take full advantage of an input or output device, used especially to refer to graphic programs having such an ability.

Device Name

In computing, a name used by an *operating system* to identify an attached peripheral device.

Device Number

In computing, a number assigned to a peripheral device so that it can be connected to the network.

Devices are usually identified by three numbers: a *physical address*, determined by the the connectors on the board to which the device is attached; a device code, based on the physical address; and a *logical address*, determined by the physical address in conjunction with the order in which the *device driver* has been loaded into the system's memory.

Device Profile

In a *color management system*, a *device-independent* definition of colors. Each of the devices in a particular system—from the scanner to the monitor to the printer—may not reproduce a particular color in exactly the same manner. Thus, a color management system defines the colors which can be reproduced by each device and determines and corrects colors that deviate from device to device. See *Color Management System (CMS)*.

DFX

A *file format* for *CAD* files.

DHCP

Abbreviation for *Dynamic Host Configuration Protocol*. See *Dynamic Host Configuration Protocol (DHCP)*.

Di-Litho

A printing process in which flat *offset lithographic* plates are used on *letterpress* presses to print directly onto the *substrate* without the use of a blanket.

DIA

Abbreviation for *Document Interchange Architecture*. See *Document Interchange Architecture*

Diacritical Mark

Any mark added to a character to indicate a change in pronunciation. Synonymous with *accent*. See *Accent*.

Diagnostic

Descriptive of the search, detection, isolation, and repair of hardware or software malfunction and errors. See *Diagnostic Program*.

Diagnostic Code

In computing, a numerical or alphabetic string that indicates a system condition (usually an error). The diagnostic code may be self-explanatory (i.e., "The printer is out of paper") or not ("Error of type -1072").

Diagnostic Program

Any computer application that checks the computer and/or attached peripheral devices for errors or malfunctions, such as disk errors, among many other things. It is generally a good idea to run a diagnostic program every once in a while. Most computers perform a set of diagnostic routines at start-up (called *power-on self test*s). When an error is detected, the user is presented with an error message.

Dialback Modem

Alternate term for a *callback modem*. See *Callback Modem*.

Dial Exchange

In a *PABX* system, a switch in which calls can originate.

Dial-In/Dial-Out Server

Alternate term for an *asynchronous communications server*. See *Asynchronous Communications Server*.

Dial Network

In networking, term for a network in which users can dial special numbers to establish communications links with other nodes.

Dialog

Any portion of a program—such as a command line or, more and more commonly, a *dialog box*—where human–computer interaction takes place.

Dialog Box

In computer programs, a box which asks for the user to input certain variable types of information that tell the program how to proceed with a specific command or function. The communication between user and computer is known as a *dialog*.

Dial-Up

In telecommunications and networking, descriptive of terminals, workstations, etc., which are not directly connected to a *server*, requiring instead that the terminal dial a special phone number for access.

Dial-Up Line

In telecommunications, a communications circuit established by dialing the number of the destination, and which is broken when the call is completed. See also *Dedicated Line* and *Leased Line*.

Dianisidine Orange

See *Diarylide Orange*.

Diaphragm

The part of a camera that regulates the amount of light allowed to pass through the *aperture*. See *Camera* and *Photography*.

Diarylide Orange

An *organic color pigment* used in printing inks. Diarylide orange is a bright reddish orange possessing high *tinctorial strength*. It is not very fast-to-light, but has a high degree of transparency. It is, however, the most commonly used orange pigment in printing inks, and is frequently used to replace *DNA orange* in printing on kraft paper. (See also *Diarylide Yellows* and *Organic Color Pigments*.)

Also known as *Dianisidine Orange* (*CI Pigment Orange 16 No. 21160*).

Diarylide Yellow

A type of *organic color pigment* used in printing inks derived from dichlorobenzidine. Diarylide yellows are strong pigments (stronger than the **hansa yellows** which they have replaced in many applications), and range from lemon to golden yellow and from opaque to transparent (see color index reference chart below).

Diarylide yellows range from moderately to extremely lightfast, and they have high alkali resistance and can withstand heat very admirably. Their particle size is small and they easily absorb oil, which makes obtaining desired flow characteristics somewhat difficult, but recent developments have made them more easily dispersible. They are the most commonly used yellow pigments in printing inks, especially for three- and four-color process printing. (See also **Organic Color Pigments**.)

(*CI Pigment Yellow 12, 13, 14, 17, 55, 83.*)

Diarylide Yellow Color Index Reference

Name	Shade	Transparency	Lightfastness
Diarylide AAA	Reddish	Transparent	Fair
Diarylide AAMX	Greenish	Transparent	Good to very good
Diarylide AAOT	Greenish	Opaque	Good
Diarylide AAOA	Greenish lemon	Very transparent	Very good
Diarylide AAPT	Warm reddish	Opaque	Very good
Diarylide AADMC	Warm red	Transparent	Excellent

Diazo

In organic chemistry, the term for any compound or other material containing a diazo group, which basically consists of either bivalent –N=N– or bivalent =N=N (where N is the chemical element nitrogen, – denotes a single bond, and = denotes a double bond) bonded to one hydrocarbon group and one other element or group, such as $C_6H_5N=NOH$ (benzenediazo hydroxide) and $CH_2=N=N$ (diazomethane).

The term *diazo* in platemaking and photography typically refers to a compound containing salts of diazonium, denoted by the general formula $[Ar]N_2X$, where *Ar* represents an aryl group (any organic group created by the removal of a hydrogen atom from a hydrocarbon, such as phenyl, C_6H_5-, produced by the removal of a hydrogen atom from benzene, C_6H_6) and X represents a negatively charged ion. One common diazonium salt is benzenediazonium chloride, $C_6H_5N_2Cl$, which includes a diazo group, an aryl group (phenyl), and chlorine. The mixture of a diazonium salt with an azo dye, a dye made from organic compounds comprising an azo group (an organic molecule consisting of bivalent –N=N– joined to *two* hydrocarbon groups, such as azobenzene, $C_{12}H_{10}N_2$) is sensitive to ultraviolet, violet, and blue light, and can be used effectively in light-sensitive coatings for **photolithographic** printing plates. An advantage of diazo coatings is that they are not affected by changes in temperature or humidity, which allows them to have a shelf-life in excess of that possessed by other types of plates. (See **Diazo Plate** and **Plate: Offset Lithography**.)

Diazo emulsions are also used in the production of photosensitive stencils for **screen printing**, as an alternative to **bichromate** emulsions.

Diazo Brown

An **organic color pigment** used in printing inks. Diazo brown possesses good **lightfastness**, heat resistance, and acid and alkali resistance properties, and high grease, oil, and wax resistance. Some shades do not withstand exposure to soaps and organic solvents. They are more expensive than **brown iron oxides**, and are occasionally used in lieu of the latter in cases where the enhanced resistance and lightfastness properties are required. (See also **Organic Color Pigments**.)

(*CI Pigment Brown 23.*)

Diazo Plate

A type of printing plate used in **offset lithography**. Diazo plates are characterized by an aluminum (or other metal) base to which a **diazo** coating (a light-sensitive organic compound) has been added. When making diazo plates, a film **negative** or **positive** is placed against the surface of the unexposed plate, and an intense light is shined through the negative. When using a film negative (such a plate being called a **negative-working plate**), the plate is exposed in the image area of the plate only, which causes the diazo coating to harden and become insoluble, while the coating in unexposed (nonimage) areas remains soluble. After exposure, a chemical treatment of the plate with an acid solution of lacquer and **gum etch** dissolves the coating in nonimage areas, and deposits a layer of gum in those portions of the plate that need to be water-receptive and a layer of lacquer in those portions that need to be ink-receptive. Plates that require the image areas to be treated with a special reinforcing material are known as **additive plates**, while those that are manufactured with a layer of lacquer and do not need an additive during development are known as **subtractive plates**. Additive plates are capable of print runs of up to 150,000 impressions, while subtractive plates are capable of up to 250,000 impressions. (See **Plate: Offset Lithography**.)

Dibit

In computers, a group of two **bit**s treated as a single unit. Since one bit can either be a 0 or a 1, there only four possible dibits: 00, 11, 01, and 10.

DIBK

See **Disobutyl Ketone**.

Dichroic Filter

A color filter, often used for making **color separation**s and generating **laser** light, that will only allow light of certain specified wavelengths through, causing all other wavelengths to be reflected. In contrast, a conventional filter *absorbs* all the light it doesn't transmit. A dichroic filter accomplishes this by means of several thin layers of coating that, for certain wavelengths, create **interference** reflections. The coatings can be so formulated to allow only light of a very narrow range of wavelengths to pass through, and as a result are widely used in scientific analysis. See **Filter**.

Dichroism

A phenomenon of some colored fluids or transparent objects which causes them to change in **color** with increasing thickness. For example, a thin film of blood looks yellow, but deep puddles appear deep red.

Dichromatic

Possessing two colors. Also referred to as *dichromic*.

Dictionary

In computing, a file (usually a **plug-in**) which contains a list of the correct spelling of English (or other) words. Such a file can be accessed by an application and consulted by that program's **spell checker**. This sort of dictionary may contain the words themselves, or may contain common roots, prefixes, and suffixes, as well as algorithms that instruct the program as to how to verify that words are spelled correctly.

In typesetting, a *dictionary*—in this case, known as a **hyphenation dictionary**—is a list of words and their correct hyphenation, to be consulted when end-of-line decisions need to be made. Exceptions to this dictionary (or the program's general hyphenation algorithm) are known as an **exception dictionary**.

Regardless of the type of dictionary being utilized, a **user-definable dictionary** is one in which the user him/herself may add words, such as proper names, places, or terms, that the computer doesn't already have.

Didone

In typography, alternate term for **typeface**s classified as **modern**. See **Modern**.

Didot Pica

Alternate term for a **cicero**. See **Cicero**.

Didot Point

In typography, a unit used predominantly in continental Europe to measure type. One Didot point equals 0.0148 in.; 6 Didot points equal 1 **cicero**. The Didot point is slightly larger than the point used in the English system, which equals 0.0138 in. See **Didot System** and **Point System**.

Didot System

In typography, a type measurement used in continental Europe which uses the **cicero** (1 cicero = 0.178 in.) and the **Didot point** (1 Didot point = 0.0148 in.; 6 Didot points = 1 cicero) as the basic units of measurement. The Didot system also uses units called **corps**; 1 cicero = 12 corps. See **Point System**.

Die

In **binding and finishing**, any metal plate or block etched with a design, lettering, or other pattern—either **relief** or **intaglio**—used to stamp or press these designs into a **substrate** in finishing operations such as **embossing**, **die-stamping**, or **foil stamping**.

Dies for embossing and stamping are made of brass, magnesium, or copper. Brass is especially useful for long runs. A brass die used to stamp book covers is called a **binder's brass** or, when made from other metals, a **binder's die**. The image itself can be chemically etched, machine-cut, or hand-tooled. Increasingly, dies are manufactured using lasers guided by **CAD/CAM** computer software. There are five basic configurations of dies. A single-level die is most often machine-cut, and is cut to a single uniform depth. A multilevel die has several distinct depths, and is most often machine-cut brass, used to impress images with greater levels of detail than those created with a single-level die. A bevel-edge die has a single uniform depth, but the edges of the image are usually hand-tooled at an angle, commonly 30–50°. A sculptured die has many varying depths across the image. A stamping die contains a single-level relief image and is used for foil stamping. The nonimage area is usually recessed at a depth of 0.060 in.

The term *die* is also used to refer to a pattern of sharp blades or other cutting tools used to cut a particular pattern into a substrate in the finishing process of **diecutting**. The most common type of die used in diecutting is a **steel-rule die**. See **Diecutting**.

Dieboard

In **diecutting**, a plywood board onto which cutting rules or **die**s are mounted. See **Diecutting**.

Die-Cut Label

Alternate term for **laid on label**. See **Laid On Label**.

Diecutting

In **binding and finishing**, a finishing operation involving the use of sharp steel rules or knives to cut a specific pattern into a **substrate** or to cut the substrate itself into a specific pattern. Diecutting is used to create pop-up books and games, and to cut flat printed sheets into packages or boxes for later assembly. Some diecutting devices also crease and **score** the substrate as part of the same process, a system used especially in the creation of folding boxes and cartons.

A **steel-rule die** includes a plywood base, onto which is drawn the layout pattern. A jigsaw is used to cut the layout into the wood, and the cutting or scoring rules or blades are inserted into these tracks. A release material (such as rubber) is placed between the blades and the substrate. The whole cutting die assembly is then pressed down on the substrate, where the blades cut or crease the substrate in the proper position. Diecutting presses can either use platens or cylinders, the platen presses being the more popular. On a **reciprocating platen diecutter**, one moving platen (containing the rules) contacts a stationary one. On a **jaw platen diecutter**, two moving platens contact each other. Diecutting is also spelled as two words, *die cutting*, or is hyphenated, *die-cutting*.

(See also **Binding and Finishing**.)

233

Dielectric Ink

An ink formulated for use in the **screen printing** of electronic circuit boards made from materials that will not conduct electricity.

Dielectric Paper

Paper made specifically to prevent the conduction of electricity, commonly used as an insulating material.

Dielectric Process

A type of nonimpact printing in which treated paper containing a conductive base and a nonconductive coating is given an electric charge by a set of electric styli, which produces the images.

Dieresis

In typography, an **accent** (¨) placed over a character, commonly used in European languages either to indicate that two adjacent vowels should be pronounced as separate syllables (as in *Noël*). See **Accent**. Also called an **umlaut** when used in German and Russian.

Die-Stamping

In **binding and finishing**, a finishing operation similar to **embossing** in which hard metal **die**s are used to stamp or press images or patterns into a surface, such as a cloth book cover. Die-stamping is frequently a synonym for **foil-stamping**, although ink rather than foil may be stamped onto a surface. When die-stamping is performed with no coloration, it is known as **blind-stamping**. (See **Die** and **Binding and Finishing**.)

DIF

Abbreviation for **Data Interchange Format**. See **Data Interchange Format (DIF)**.

DIF is also an abbreviation for **Drawing Interchange Format**. See **Drawing Interchange Format**.

Differential Backup

In computing, the file **backup** that is new or has changed since the last time a backup was made or, in other words, a file in which the **archive bit** is activated. After backup, the archive bit is left active. See also **Incremental Backup**.

Diffraction

In optics, a spreading out or deflection of a light wave as it passes through an opening or hits an object. A consequence of this is that, if white light is projected through a thin aperture no longer than a few wavelengths wide, the light will spread out on the far side of the aperture, the shorter wavelengths spreading farther than the longer ones. As a result, small grids possessing very small apertures (such as a **diffraction grating**) cause white light to break down into the constituent spectral colors. (See **Diffraction Grating**.) This process has the same effect as that which underlies the principle of the prism, but is a different process. (See also **Dispersion**.)

Diffraction Grating

An array of very narrow parallel slits or apertures which, when white light is projected through the openings, breaks it down into the **color**s of the spectrum, due to the **diffraction** of light waves as they pass through the openings. A diffraction grating produces a spectral effect of such a large magnitude due to the reinforcement of the light waves from adjacent slits. A spectrum produced using a diffraction grating contains all the colors in an order that is the reverse of that obtained using a prism. And, unlike a prism, a diffraction grating doesn't distort the red end of the spectrum. A prism also isn't based on the process of diffraction; see **Dispersion**.

Diffuse Highlight

A type of **highlight** in an original or in a reproduction that comprises the lightest neutral white area(s) of an image, including some detail, and which will print with the smallest **halftone dot**. See also **Highlight** and **Specular Highlight**.

Diffuse Opacity Method

A means of measuring a paper's **opacity** by backing a paper sample with a black sheet of paper, measuring how much light is reflected back through the sample, then backing the sample with a thick pile of the paper to be tested and measuring how much light is reflected off the top of the backing pile and back through the sample. The ratio of these two figures is the paper sample's diffuse opacity. It is believed that the diffuse opacity method is more effective than the **contrast ratio method** in estimating potential **show through**. (See **Opacity** and **Contrast Ratio Method**.) Diffuse opacity was once called **printing opacity**.

Diffuser

In photography, a gelatin-based **filter** used to diffuse the light striking a light-sensitive emulsion to "soften" the exposed image. In computer image manipulation, a *diffuser* is a software feature that reduces the contrast of **pixel**s that is used for the same purpose. Also known as a **diffusion filter**.

Diffusion

In optics, the scattering of light rays from a relatively straight path into a variety of paths, either as the light passes through a medium or as it is reflected off of a medium. An example of diffusion is a frosted window; the **translucent** glass prevents light from passing through it in a straight line, resulting in the blurry and unidentifiable appearance of figures seen through it.

Diffusion is also the result of **matte** surfaces (such as paper or film), which, unlike **glossy** surfaces, reflect the light waves back toward the viewer in a wide variety of directions, the result being that the surface looks flat and dull. Colors printed on a matte surface will appear softer and lighter, due to diffusion, than colors printed on a glossy surface.

Diffusion Filter

Alternate term for a *diffuser*. See *Diffuser*.

Diffusion Transfer

An imaging system based on the use of chemicals to "diffuse" an image from one material to another. Essentially, an original image is first exposed by light to a negative in the usual manner, where the image areas on the original become transparent on the negative or, in other words, have not been converted to black metallic silver, as have the nonimage areas. During development, the substrate to which the image will be diffused is placed against the emulsion side of the exposed negative. This transfer sheet contains a gelatin emulsion of silver sulfide or colloidal silver. As the negative develops, the unexposed and intact silver halide emulsion in the image areas of the negative diffuses into the emulsion of the copy paper where it converts those portions of the emulsion into black metallic silver. Where the negative has already had its silver halide emulsion converted to metallic silver (the nonimage areas), there is no diffusion of chemicals to the copy paper emulsion. Thus, a negative image on the negative becomes a positive image on the copy paper.

Diffusion transfer, also known as *photomechanical transfer (PMT)*, is also used in lithographic platemaking. Diffusion transfer is also the basis behind Polaroid film.

Diffusion-Etch Process

A means of *gravure engraving*, or transferring an image to the surface of the image-carrying *gravure cylinder*. See *Gravure Engraving: Diffusion-Etch Process*.

Digester

A vessel used in *chemical pulping* processes in which wood chips are cooked with chemicals to produce wood *pulp* for papermaking. The purpose of *pulping* is to separate fibers of *cellulose* from other nonfibrous material. The chemicals added to wood chips in the digester (utilizing either the *sulfite process* or the *sulfate*—or *kraft*—process) dissolve most nonfibrous components of wood, such as *lignin* and *hemicellulose*, leaving only cellulose and a residual amount of lignin and other substances. *Bleaching* removes further amounts of these materials. (See *Chemical Pulping*.)

Digiography

Term for the art and technology of digitizing character images. This includes digitized typesetting, as well as the electrophotographic creation of typeset characters from computer information.

Digit

Any numeral.

Digital

State of information which exists as discrete units of (typically) numeric code, such as that which is the only type of information a computer can process. In computers, digital data is a *binary* system, or some combination of 1s and 0s, the only two digits a computer can identify. The "opposite" of digital data is *analog data*, in which information exists as a continuous signal. See *Digital* and *Analog*. Analog data can be converted to digital data, and vice versa, by means of an *analog-to-digital converter* and a *digital-to-analog converter*, respectively. A somewhat common example of digital data is DNA itself, or the genetic material comprising all life on Earth. In that case, the digital data is a quaternary system, or made up of four "digits," A, C, T, G—or adenine, cytosine, thymine, and guanine—which are the four bases comprising the basis of the DNA molecule. Combinations of these four digits are what make up all life, at least on Earth.

Digital Audio

A means of converting an *analog* sound wave or signal to *digital* form, improving the fidelity and sound quality of the recorded sound. A common example of digital audio is a conventional *audio CD*, in which music exists as numerical data converted (in a CD player) to analog signals for playback.

Digital audio is used in a variety of multimedia applications, and is captured by the process of *sampling*; in other words, a digitizing device or audio *capture board* records small bits of an analog signal at a certain rate, producing a digital approximation of the continuous sound wave. The sampling rate (or the number of times per second a sample is taken) and the *resolution* (or bit depth) affects the quality of the sound recorded. Both these factors also affect the file size. Sound can also be recorded in stereo or mono.

The preceding chart indicates some common—as of this writing—sampling rates. As you can tell, to record a standard 3.5 minute song at the highest sampling rate and resolution (44.1 *KHz*, 16-bit stereo, also known as *CD-quality* and is the rate at which commercial CDs are recorded) would require 36.75 megabytes. Lower sampling rates and bit depths are used for various purposes in multimedia that do not require such high quality audio, such as brief sound effects. Most narration is recorded at least at 22.05 KHz. See also *Compact Disc–Digital Audio (CD-DA)*. See also *MIDI*.

Sampling Rate	Bit Depth	Stereo or Mono	Bytes required for one minute
5.5 KHz	8-bit	Mono	325 K
5.5 KHz	8-bit	Stereo	650 K
11 KHz	8-bit	Mono	650 K
11 KHz	8-bit	Stereo	1.3 M
22.05 KHz	8-bit	Mono	1.3 M
22.05 KHz	8-bit	Stereo	2.6 M
22.05 KHz	16-bit	Mono	2.5 M
22.05 KHz	16-bit	Stereo	5.25 M
44.1 KHz	8-bit	Mono	2.6 M
44.1 KHz	8-bit	Stereo	5.25 M
44.1 KHz	16-bit	Mono	5.25 M
44.1 KHz	16-bit	Stereo	10.5 M

Digital Audio Tape (DAT)

A type of magnetic tape used for the storage of computer data and for sound recording and distribution. Data is stored on a DAT in *digital* form (unlike a conventional magnetic tape that records in analog form), allowing the high-fidelity reproduction of music and other audio. DAT recorders and players are available for home use. Many people in the recording industry insisted that the availability of DAT technology would give "home-taping" the impetus it needed to "kill" music. It didn't.

Digital Blinders

A colloquial term for a individual's obliviousness to everything else in the universe when working with a computer or other gadget.

Digital Camera

A device that can capture photographic images and store them in either digital or analog form on an integrated circuit card, a hard disk, or a type of *RAM*.

The use of digital cameras is a desirable alternative to scanning, especially as cost, image resolution, and storage capacity of the cameras all improve. See *Digital Photography*.

Digital Computer

Any computer that reads, writes, and processes data existing as discrete 1s and 0s, rather than as continuous signals.

Digital Data

Data that exist as discrete numerical values, rather than as continuous variations in voltage, amperage, density, etc., (*analog data*). See *Digital*.

Digital Data Communications Message Protocol (DDCMP)

In networking, a *network protocol* developed by Digital Equipment Corporation (DEC) for *synchronous* communications.

Digital Data Exchange Standards

See *DDES*.

Digital Film Recorder

A type of *film recorder* that reads a digital image file and converts the *digital data* to an *analog* signal and records the image on film. Consequently, the *resolution* of the image output to the film is much higher than the resolution of the image on the computer screen. (See also *Analog Film Recorder*.) See *Film Recorder*.

Digital Font

A typographic *font* which exists as either a *bit map* or as *Beziér curves*.

Digital Hard Proof

Alternate term for *DDCP*. See *DDCP*.

Digital Highway

Another term for *information superhighway*. See *Information Superhighway*.

Digital Image

Any image that exists as *digital data* on a computer. A digital image has as its most fundamental unit a *pixel*, each of which possesses its own color. Depending upon the *color depth* of the display, a pixel may be one of two colors or one of over several million colors. When viewed on a monitor or output onto paper or film, a digital image resembles a photograph. Many software applications allow for the editing, correction, manipulation, and enhancing of digital images. Such images may be obtained via scanning, from photo CDs, or from *digital camera*s.

Digital-Image Processing

The use of any of a wide variety of hardware and software to obtain, edit, manipulate, and output *digital image*s.

Digital Loopback

In networking and telecommunications, a means of testing a *modem* or other telecommunications equipment. Essentially, a test message is transmitted, decoded and re-encoded by the receiving device, then echoed back to the sending device. The echoed message is then decoded and compared to the original to determine if any errors have been introduced. See *Loopback*. See also *Analog Loopback*.

Digital Network Architecture (DNA)

A *network architecture* developed by Digital Equipment Corporation (DEC).

Digital Photography

The process of digitizing—or converting to *digital* form—a photographic image at the same time as it is taken, typically by means of a *digital camera*. An advantage of digital photography is the elimination of the need for the intermediate step of scanning; digitally photographed images can be imported directly into a processing or page makeup program. Also, the photographs taken can be "instant," or in other words viewed almost immediately after they were taken, saving time if reshooting is necessary. Images taken with a digital camera are often displayed on a small *LCD* monitor attached to the camera, or by means of a *PCMCIA* (or *flash memory*) card added to a laptop computer. Images obtained digitally can be stored on any computer medium (such as *magnetic disk*s, *optical disc*s, *magneto-optical disc*s, *CD-ROM*s, etc.). Kodak's *Photo CD* format also allows for the archiving of digital images.

CCD vs. Film

There are several aspects to consider when deciding to use a digital camera instead of a conventional film-based camera. A digital camera, like a *scanner*, captures images by means of a *charge-coupled device (CCD)*, or a "light sen-

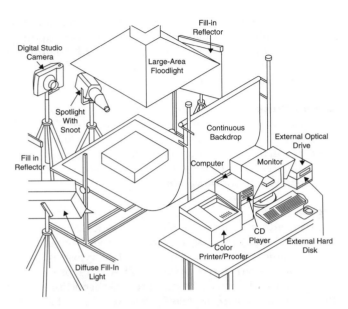

Basic digital studio setup.

sor," many of which are assembled into an array, which can either be a *linear array* (all the CCDs located in a single row) or an *area array* (the CCDs arranged in a rectangular block). With a linear array, an image is captured one row of *pixel*s at a time, whereas an area array captures an entire scene. However, the latter may require up to three separate exposures to capture all color information. There is also a *trilinear array*, which contains three linear arrays mounted side by side, each array coated with a colored dye to act as a color filter, enabling red, green, and blue color information to be captured simultaneously. However, since each color array is offset slightly from the others, the software driving the camera must accurately adjust the separate color images so that all color channels align perfectly upon output. However, since these types of arrays take some time to image all color information, no movement within a scene is possible.

Certain variations of the area array have been devised. Some use filter wheels, which require three separate exposures. Some, however, use mirrors or prisms to split incoming light into three separate beams, each going to a separate CCD, which can capture all three color channels simultaneously. However, with this technique, the low light intensity resulting from splitting the incoming light can result in poor imaging of scenes that are lit less than optimally. Other configurations split a single beam of light among a single CCD, which although it allows for rapid capture of separate color channels, can result in less-than-optimal color depth.

RESOLUTION

The number of "image details" captured per linear inch is referred to technically as the *sampling rate*, but is often popularly referred to as the device's *resolution*. Each indi-

vidual portion of an image is known as a pixel, and the greater the number of pixels per inch (and the smaller the pixels), the sharper the image. In many cases, as with scanners, software *interpolation* can "artificially" increase the number of pixels in an image. It does this by analyzing the pixels that have been captured optically and inserting additional "pre-fab" pixels between them, essentially guessing at what their color should be. Interpolation has widely variable results, as one could imagine.

COLOR DEPTH

The *color depth* (or *bit depth*) of an image refers to the number of *bit*s the computer uses to describe the image. For realistic (to human eyes) color reproduction, 256 levels for each of the three primary colors (red, green, and blue) is required. An imaging device with a bit depth of 8 bits per pixel per color (or *twenty-four-bit color*) is usually satisfactory for capturing realistic color images. Anything below that and *posterization* usually results, producing an image with visible pixels and an inadequate number of colors. (See *Color Depth*.)

LENS

The camera itself, like conventional film cameras, uses a *lens* to focus light rays onto the CCD array. An *iris* is also used to control the size of the *aperture*, which affects how much light enters the camera. The aperture size is specified by an *f-stop* number. All of these factors work to adjust the *focal length*, which focuses objects at various distances onto the plane of the CCD array. (See *Photography*.) Some cameras used for digital photography are in fact modified 35-mm film cameras, the traditional film back of the camera being replaced by a CCD array. These cameras generate the highest quality images, whereas less expensive models are limited in terms of image quality, and are thus often used for on-screen presentations, multimedia applications, or other such purposes where the limits of presentation medium (as opposed to high-quality printed reproduction) preclude high-quality imaging.

FOCAL LENGTH MAGNIFICATION

In conventional photography, the focal length of a camera is related to the size of the film. A so-called "normal" lens has a focal length that is equal to the diagonal size of the film. However, in a digital camera, a CCD array is much smaller than a piece of film. As a result, a lens mounted on a digital camera will behave differently than a lens of the same size mounted on a conventional camera. Specifically, a digital camera will behave as though a longer lens has been mounted. This effect is known as *focal length magnification* and it doesn't adversely affect image quality per se, except insofar as the knowledge of the effect is necessary to ensure consistent photographic results. In order to achieve a desired effect, a new lens may need to be obtained.

LIGHTING

As with any type of photography, lighting is a crucial element. Common types of lighting used for conventional and digital photography include tungsten lamps, which operate very much like conventional household light bulbs. Although less expensive than other types of lighting, tungsten bulbs have their limitations, such as their low *color temperature* (about 3200 K), their production of a red and yellow *color cast*, and their tendency to give off a great deal of heat, which can cause not only physical discomfort to human subjects but also damage to computer equipment.

Metal-vapor lighting is used primarily in motion-picture photography, especially since its high color temperature (5200 K) allows natural daylight to be simulated accurately. Metal-vapor lighting does tend to run hotter than tungsten lighting, however, and this high temperature also makes the bulbs very fragile.

Fluorescent lighting is bright, efficient, and doesn't run as hot as other types of lighting, but constant flickering (which is not easily perceptible by the human eye, but can be easily detected by CCD arrays and film) limits their use. The flickering occurs at a rate equal to twice the frequency of the power line. A converter can be used to increase the power-line frequency, but these can be expensive.

Strobe lights operate by sending out intermittent flashes of light. Although they are perhaps most commonly encountered in nightclubs, flash bulbs and flash lighting are forms of strobe lights. They run cool, and are very bright.

DYNAMIC RANGE

The *dynamic range* of a digital camera is analogous to the dynamic range of a scanner. In essence, it refers to the difference between the highest and lowest densities the CCD can capture. There is a relationship between dynamic range, f-number, and color depth:

f-stops	Density	Gray Levels
5	1.5	32
6	1.8	64
7	2.1	128
8	2.4	256
9	2.7	512
10	3.0	1,024
11	3.3	1,048
12	3.6	4,096
13	3.9	8,192
14	4.2	16,384
15	4.5	32,768
16	4.8	65,536

All of the aspects in the above table are variable. It is unlikely that you will ever need over 65,000 gray levels (bear in mind though that for "full-color" images, 256 gray levels per each of the three primary colors is required, not 768 total gray levels). Depending upon the density range and/or total f-stops you need, you may need to capture an image at a higher bit depth. If you only need to capture a 2.4 density range, 256 gray levels (or *eight-bit color* per channel) would be fine. If you need to capture a higher density range, you'll need to up the bit depth accordingly.

Digital Press

A configuration of printing press used in *offset lithography* in which the printing plates are imaged directly from *digital data*, either on-press or off-press. The advantage of the process is in the elimination of the need for extensive makeready. See *Computer-to-Plate*.

Digital Proof

A proof, either a *color* or black-and-white reproduction, produced directly from *digital data*, without any intermediate production of film. There are two types of digital proofs: a *digital hard proof* or *DDCP* (a proof made directly on a *substrate* by an output device connected to the computer) or a *digital soft proof* (a display of the page or image on a computer monitor).

Digital Recording
See *Digital Audio*.

Digital Scanner

A device used to optically read a color or black-and-white image (such as a photograph) and convert it to *digital form*. Typically, a digital scanner determines a particular gray density or color quality for each *pixel* that an image comprises. With the aid of software, digital scanners can automatically determine the proper color gradation and correction, with only moderate post-scan tweaking by the operator. At one time only capable of black-and-white scans, *24-bit color* scanners are now relatively inexpensive and widespread. *Analog scanners* also exist, but are becoming increasingly rare. (See *Scanner*.)

Digital Screening

The process of generating *halftone screen*s comprising halftone dots made up of *spot*s produced by a digital output device such as a *laser printer* or *imagesetter*.

Digital Signal Processor (DSP)

A computer chip designed to process *analog* data after converting them to *digital* form, used often in data communications and the processing of *digital audio* and *digital video*. A DSP, a type of *coprocessor*, is optimized to perform extensive mathematical calculations, and are programmed using their own specialized *operating system*. Consequently, the addition of new functions requires only a software upgrade, not a hardware one. See also *Native Signal Processing (NSP)*.

Digital Soft Proof

A type of *digital proof*—or early prepress rendering of a to-be-reproduced item—consisting of a reproduction of the image on a color computer monitor. Also known simply as a *soft proof*. See also *DDCP*.

Digital-to-Analog Converter

A device that converts discrete *digital* signals into continuous (or *analog*) electrical signals. Some common devices that utilize digital-to-analog converters are computer monitors, where each *pixel* is described digitally by the computer, this information needing to be converted to electrical signals controlling the intensity of the light forming each screen dot. A conventional audio CD player also uses such a converter to translate the stored digital information into the music that emanates from the speakers. Also known as a *DAC* and a *D/A Converter*.

Digital Type

In typography, type generated by a computer, as opposed to metal or photographic type. Digital type gets its name from digital computers, which are based on the binary principle of on/off. A digital image is created with dots, and the individual dot is either there or not there—on or off. The individual dot is also called a *pel* or *pixel* (both terms are shorthand for picture element), and a group of overlapping dots forming a straight or curved line is called a *raster*.

Typesetters that use line segments—or *vectors*—to outline a character still use dots as the basic building blocks. All digital typesetters use the basic principle of turning some light source on or off to create an image. That light source can be a cathode ray tube (CRT) or a laser, or it may not be a light source at all, as newer technologies apply electro-erosion, magnetography, and light-emitting diodes.

The placement of the dots for an individual character is stored in memory. Rather than turn the imaging source on and off for each dot, many devices employ a principle called run-length of coding, which allows the beam to sweep continuously over a series of "on" dots, rather than turning on and off for each one.

Because every character is made up of dots, diagonals and curves may not be as smooth and sharp in their edge resolution as straight lines. At 1,000 dots per inch (dpi), acceptable quality is produced. At 5,000 lines per inch (lpi), there is no visible difference between digital type and other photographic type.

The best place to check the quality level is the dot on a lowercase *i*—the location of the greatest curvature—or the entire typeface Optima, as it has almost no straight lines.

Digital Typesetter

A typesetter that produces *digital type*. See *Digital Type*.

Digital Typesetting

The act of using a *digital typesetter*.

Digital Video

General term for video in *digital* form—or is described in a computer as a series of discrete numerical codes (*bit*s and *byte*s)—as opposed to *analog video*. Digital video has an advantage over analog video in that it can be edited *pixel* by pixel, and it facilitates *nonlinear video* production. Digital video will also not decline in quality as subsequent copies and copies from copies are made. Among the disadvantages of digital video are the extensive processing and memory capacities required to effectively capture and process video.

Digital Video Effects

In video production, a hardware device used to edit video in digital form, used to add special effects such as transitions between scenes (such as *dissolve*s and *wipe*s). The device includes a *frame grabber* to capture and digitize *analog video* as well as a *genlock* to convert it back to analog form after editing. Abbreviated *DVE*.

Digital Video Interactive (DVI)

In video and multimedia, a standard *data compression* technique (or *codec*) developed by Intel and IBM for the compression and playback of *digital audio* and *digital video*. The DVI system includes special *microprocessor* and software to effect compression and playback. Although it has *compression ratio*s of up to 100:1 (facilitating the playback of full-motion video from *CD-ROM* of other storage medium), it is also a type of *lossy* compression scheme.

Digitization

The act of converting any *analog* signal into a *digital* form. Digitization is the basis of *scanning*, *digital audio*, and *digital video*. Even a *mouse*, keyboard, or other computer input device is based on a type of digitization: electrical signals indicating mouse movement or a keystroke are converted to digital information.

Digitize

To convert an *analog* signal to *digital* information. See *Digitization*.

Digitized Type

Any *typeface* that is designed and stored as *digital data* rather than as a photographic or metal matrix. Also known as a *digitized font*.

Digitizer

Any device used for the conversion of an *analog* signal to *digital* form. A *scanner* or an audio or video capture board is a type of digitizer, as is a *mouse*, *digitizing tablet*, *trackball*, or keyboard. See *Digitization*.

Digitizer Board

In computing, an add-on device (or *expansion board*) containing special *microprocessor*s used for the *digitization* of audio or video. Also known as a *capture board*.

Digitizing Tablet

A device attached to a computer consisting of a flat, rectangular pad on which a stylus can be moved. The software

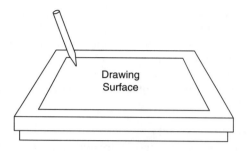

Digitizing tablet.

driving the tablet records the movements of the stylus across the pad and stores them in a digital file. Digitizing tablets are used to generate original **line art** or to trace printed line art, thereby digitizing it without the need for scanning it. Also called a **data tablet**.

Dilatancy

A property of a fluid—such as printing ink—that describes a "false body," or consistency, thickness, and **viscosity** that increases with the application of stress or other force. Some inks are somewhat fluid while in their containers, but upon the application of stress or shear forces become thicker and more viscous. Dilatancy is also called **shear thickening**. Some inks also exhibit the opposite property, **thixotropy**, in which the viscosity *decreases* when stresses are applied.

Dilatent

Possessing the property of **dilatancy**. See **Dilatancy**.

Diluent

A **solvent** or other fluid added to printing ink to reduce the ink's **viscosity**. A diluent does not necessarily have to be a true solvent (i.e., capable of dissolving the **binder** in the ink **vehicle**), but should maintain a high degree of effectiveness when used in combination with true solvents.

Dimension Sign

In typography, a "typeface-independent" cross or "3" used to indicate dimensions or the multiplication function. The character itself is centered on the **cap height** of the font in question. The dimension sign is typographically preferable to using the letter "x," although many typefaces do not include it. Also known as the **multiplication cross**.

Dimensional Stability

A measure of the extent to which a paper will resist a change in size as the result of a change in moisture content or the application of a compressing force, as during printing. The **cellulose** fibers comprising a sheet or **web** of paper have an affinity for water, which means that they readily absorb water from the atmosphere (or lose water to the atmosphere, depending on the **relative humidity** and the **equilibrium moisture content** of the paper).

When paper fibers absorb water, they expand primarily in width, but only slightly in length. (Similarly, when a paper *loses* moisture to the atmosphere, the fibers will shrink primarily in width, but only slightly in length.) Therefore, when a paper undergoes a dimensional change, it will primarily be in the **cross-grain direction**. (See **Grain** and **Moisture Content**.) The percent change in size, either by expansion or reduction, is called the paper's **hygroexpansivity**.

The addition of **fillers** to the papermaking **furnish** helps increase a paper's dimensional stability, as fillers do not absorb or lose moisture. The extent to which a paper's fibers have been refined (i.e., how short and how closely bonded the fibers are in the paper) also affects its dimensional stability; the less refined the fibers are the greater the dimensional stability. (But less refining also compromises other paper qualities.) Paper has the highest degree of dimensional stability in relative humidities of 35–50%.

Paper and printing defects such as **waffling** result from paper's being stretched past its ability to retain its original dimensions. (A paper's ability to return to its original dimensions after a stretching force is removed is called its **visoelasticity**; stretching beyond a certain point, however, destroys the paper's ability to "snap back" to its original size.) Paper is generally stronger in its grain direction, and stretching that occurs in **long-grain** paper in the cross-grain direction usually can be compensated for by other press procedures.

Some papers, depending on their end use, don't require a high degree of dimensional stability. Those that do include papers to be used for multicolor offset work, where proper registration is important, and forms that are going to be collated into a bound or padded set. Dimensional stability of a paper can be measured with an **expansimeter**.

Dimmed Command

In computing, especially by means of a **graphical user interface (GUI)**, a menu option that is not available at a particular time and consequently appears in gray rather than black type, as do available commands.

Dimple

A small pit or depression in a coating or printed image.

DIN

Abbreviation for *Deutsche Industrie Norm*, an organization responsible for setting standards in Germany. Claris CAD supports DIN standards for drafting, while **DIN connector**s and **DIN keyboard**s were designed in accordance with DIN specifications.

DIN Connector

A type of connector for computer equipment created according to **DIN** (Deutsche Industrie Norm) specifications. DIN connectors are often used for the connection of keyboards (for example, a 5-pin DIN connector connects a keyboard to a **PC**) or other **serial** devices (for example, an 8-pin DIN connector is used to connect peripherals to a **Macintosh** computer's **serial port**).

DIN Keyboard

A type of computer keyboard standard developed by **DIN** (Deutsche Industrie Norm) which includes several design parameters intended to improve **ergonomics**.

Ding

An indentation (i.e., a nick or a dent) that can be felt.

Dingbat

In typography, a decorative character which can be typeset, or an alternate term for an **ornament**. (See **Ornament**.) Although the etymology of the term *dingbat* is unknown (it also means an empty-headed, foolish person, as well as a brick or other object used as a missile), it likely originated with the term *dingus* (a somewhat informal term for any device or gadget whose exact purpose is unknown), which in turn originated with the word "thing" or non-English words meaning "thing" (such as *ding*).

Characters from the Zapf Dingbats typeface.

Dinitroaniline Red

See **DNA Orange**.

Dioxazine Violet B

An **organic color pigment** used in printing inks. Dioxazine violet B is a bright red violet, resistant to light, heat, alkalis, acids, soaps, oils, waxes, solvents, and water. It is used in a wide variety of inks. (See **Organic Color Pigments**.)

(*CI Pigment Violet 37 No. 51319.*)

Dioxazine Violet (RL) Carbazole Violet

An **organic color pigment** used in printing inks. Dioxazine violet is a strong, red, transparent purple possessing high **lightfastness**, heat resistance, and chemical resistance to most substances. It is widely used in all printing inks and processes despite its expense, by virtue of its vastly superior resistance properties. (See also **Organic Color Pigments**.)

(*CI Pigment Violet 23 No. 51319.*)

DIP

Abbreviation for **dual in-line package**. See **DIP Switch**.

DIP Switch

In computing, a small switch on a computer, printer, or other device used to adjust optional settings. **DIP** is an abbreviation for **dual-in-line package**.

Dipentene

A hydrocarbon **solvent** used—commonly in lieu of turpentine—as an **antiskinning agent** in printing inks.

Diphthong

The combination of two vowels pronounced as a single sound and typeset as a single character, such as æ, œ, Œ, or Æ.

Dipropylene Glycol

An ether alcohol used as a **solvent** in printing inks.

Direct Access File

In computing, a file in which the user can directly read or write data without the need to go through intermediate data values.

Direct Access Storage Device (DASD)

In computers, a general term for any magnetic (as opposed to optical) disk drive.

Direct Digital Color Proof

See **DDCP**.

Direct Distance Dial Network

Alternate term for a **public network**. See **public network**.

Direct Distance Dialing (DDD)

Term for the ability to place a long distance telephone call without the need for operator intervention. At one time, operator assistance was required for long distance calls (and even local calls), but now DDD is pretty much de rigeur.

Direct Distance Dialing Network

Term for the general voice telephone system.

Direct Drive

A configuration of **screen printing** press in which the movement of the **substrate** is synchronized with the movement of the **squeegee**.

Direct Emulsion

A type of liquid **polymer** emulsion used in the **direct process** of preparing **screen printing** photostencils. See **Photostencil: Direct Process**.

Direct Engraving

A type of **gravure engraving** utilizing a light-sensitive **resist** coating applied directly to the surface of the **gravure cylinder**. See **Gravure Engraving**.

Direct-Impingement Dryer

Alternate term for an **open-flame dryer**. See **Open-Flame Dryer**.

Direct/Indirect Photoscreen Stencil

A type of photostencil used in **screen printing** prepared by the **direct/indirect process**. See **Photostencil: Direct/Indirect Process**.

Direct/Indirect Printing Screen

A type of screen used in *screen printing* that is prepared by the *direct/indirect process*. See *Photostencil: Direct/ Indirect Process*.

Direct/Indirect Process

In *screen printing*, the preparation of a *photostencil* by applying a transparent backing sheet to the bottom of the screen fabric and coating the top of the screen with a photosensitive emulsion, which is exposed to a film positive of the image to be printed once the emulsion is dry. See *Photostencil: Direct/Indirect Process*.

Direct Input Typesetter

Alternate term for a *direct entry typesetter*. See *Direct Entry Typesetter*.

Direct Lithography

See *Di-Litho*.

Direct Manipulation

In computing, especially by means of a *graphical user interface (GUI)*, the ability to perform actions on screen objects by means of a mouse or other *graphic input device*, rather than through menu selections. Examples of direct manipulation include *drag-and-drop* applications, using the mouse to resize a *window*, etc.

Direct-Mapped Cache

One particular type of *cache memory* used in computers. See *Cache Memory*.

Direct Memory Access (DMA)

In computing, a means of transferring data from a peripheral device directly to the computer's *RAM* (or memory) without *CPU* intervention, resulting in faster data transfer. DMA is controlled by a specific application program, but not all computers support it.

Direct Mode

A feature of a *modem* that allows direct data transfer without *compression* or *error correction*.

Director

The individual in charge of the filming, videotaping, and editing of a motion picture or video production.

Directory

On a computer, a list of the files contained on a specific storage medium. Directories (called *folder*s in the *Macintosh Operating System*) can be created (or deleted) and files grouped into certain specific directories, for ease of access.

Directory Replication

In networking, the duplication of a master *directory* (or set of directories) from an *export server* to other designated

servers or *workstations* as a means of ensuring that all connected terminals are working with completely up-to-date directories. A directory is replicated when a new file is added or an existing file is updated.

Directory Services

In networking, a list of all network resources (such as files, applications, etc.) and users, provided as a means of helping clients locate users and files.

Directory Structure Duplication

In computing, the copying of a *directory* entry table and *file allocation table* to a separate portion of a hard disk as a means of ensuring that a copy remains if the original is damaged in some way. Duplicated directories are kept updated by means of *directory verification*.

Directory Tree

In computing, especially by means of a *graphical user interface (GUI)*, a means of pictorially representing the hierarchical structure of a directory, including its subdirectories and files.

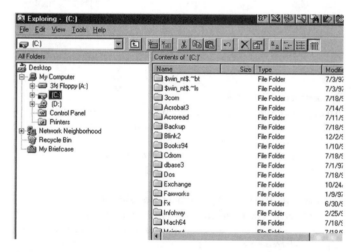

A Windows directory, showing the files on a computer's hard drive.

Directory Verification

In computing, a function of *directory structure duplication* that checks the consistency of duplicated *file allocation table*s and *directory* entry tables. On networks, directory verification is typically performed each time a *server* is started.

Direct Photoscreen Stencil

A type of photostencil used in *screen printing* produced by the *direct process*. See *Photostencil: Direct Process*.

Direct Printing Screen

A type of screen used in *screen printing* prepared by the *direct process*. See *Photostencil: Direct Process*. Also known as a *Direct Stencil*.

Direct Process

In *screen printing*, the preparation of a *photostencil* by coating the screen fabric with a photosensitive liquid emulsion and exposing it to a film positive of the image to be printed while the emulsion is still wet. See *Photostencil: Direct Process*.

Direct Screen Halftone

A *halftone* negative made by directly exposing the original *continuous tone* image through a screen to the unexposed film. Also known as a *direct halftone*.

Direct Stencil

Alternate term for *direct printing screen*. See *Direct Printing Screen*.

Direct-to-Plate (DTP)

Alternate term for *computer-to-plate*.

Direct-Transfer Process

A means of *gravure engraving*, or transferring an image to the surface of the image-carrying *gravure cylinder*. See *Gravure Engraving: Direct-Transfer Process*.

Dirt

Although "dirt" is a vague, general term in everyday use (or even in printing terminology), in papermaking it refers specifically to any foreign matter that embeds itself in the surface of the paper and which differs in color from the rest of the paper (it is usually black). Dirt may or may not be able to be lifted from the surface of the paper by a press blanket. Dirt can have deleterious results when occurring in *OCR paper*, designed for *Optical Character Recognition (OCR)* machines.

To gauge how "dirty" a paper is, a "dirt count" can be calculated, providing a measure of the total black (or "dirty") area in square millimeters per square meter.

Dirtball

A term referring to general computer printer output.

Dirty Proof

A *proof*, or *galley*, of text material that has been typeset exactly to the *type specifications* indicated on the original copy but contains uncorrected errors, as well as *proof marks* or other marks generated by the author, editor, or proofreader, in contrast to a *clean proof*.

Disable

To remove or turn off a hardware or software function. See also *Enable*.

Disaster Recovery

A means by which network services and resources are restored following some form of interruption, from a disk *crash* to an earthquake. Disaster recovery is at its most effective when it is planned before something bad happens.

Disc

A term often used interchangeably with the word *disk*. When spelled *disc*, it typically refers to *optical disc*s or *compact disc*s, rather than magnetic disks, such as *floppy disk*s. See *Compact Disc (CD)* and *Optical Disc*. See also *Disk*.

Disc Image

In computing, an exact representation of the *bit*s of data that will be burned onto a *CD-ROM*.

Disc Warp

Any distortion or bend in the surface of an *optical disc*.

Discharge Printing

In *screen printing*, a means of printing on darkly colored textiles in which a chemical (commonly sulfoxylate reducing agents) is applied to the image area(s) of the *substrate*, to lighten the color of the fabric, allowing lighter-colored inks or dyes to print. Also called *garment discharging*.

Discrete Access

In networking, especially a *local area network* having a *star* topology, in which each node has its own separate connection to the network. See also *Shared Access*.

Discrete Cosine Transform (DCT)

In *data compression*, a mathematical computation or process used by a compression algorithm (in the compression of *digital video*) that uses a specific code scheme to change picture data. Although *codec*s utilizing DCT make possible high *compression ratio*s, the result is usually a slight loss of image data. (See *Data Compression* and *Lossy*.)

Discrete Value

Any value that varies from other values only by whole, countable units, such as the determination of the number of light sources generated in a *scanner* rather than the intensity of the light. See also *Nondiscrete Value*.

Discretionary Hyphen

In typography and typesetting, an instruction given to the computer or typesetting device (or "embedded" in a text file) to indicate a point where the program may hyphenate a word if the program needs to. A discretionary hyphen will take precedence over any other type of hyphenation, such a logic program or dictionary. (See *Hyphenation*.)

Dished Roll

A paper roll defect called a *telescoped roll* in which the edge misalignment was generated during paper roll winding. See *Telescoped Roll*.

Disk

Any of a variety of flat, circular, information storage media, ranging from old vinyl records to the common 3.5-in. floppy disks.

In computer parlance, *disk* typically refers to a flat, round surface covered with a magnetic material (such as a magnetic oxide) which can store digital (or other) information. This magnetic coating can be manipulated by the writing device (or *write head*) to carry magnetic fields, the varying orientations of which can be interpreted digitally by the reading device (or *read head*) and translated into machine- or human-readable code. This is how a vast majority of computer data is stored.

Although often used interchangeably with the term *disc*, this latter term is reserved for media that store data optically, such as *compact disc*s.

Disk Array

In computing, the collection of *hard disk*s used in a redundant array of inexpensive disks.

Disk Cache

See *Cache Memory*.

Disk Cartridge

A rigid computer-storage medium which can be removed from the disk drive and replaced with another one.

Disk Controller

In computing, any device which functions as an *interface* between the *CPU* and a peripheral disk drive, controlling the manner in which the data is written to and read from disks inserted in the device. Such a device acting as the interface between the CPU and the computer's *hard disk* is known as a *hard disk controller* or a *disk coprocessor board*.

Disk Coprocessor Board

Alternate term for a *hard disk controller*. See *Disk Controller*. Abbreviated *DCB*.

Disk Crash

Any failure of a computer's disk drive to read or write data properly, due to any of a variety of causes, such as a software problem, a computer virus, a power outage or surge, excessive heat, or foreign-substance contamination. A specific type of disk crash—a *head crash*—involves a collision between the read/write head and the surface of the disk.

Disk Drive

One of several types of peripheral devices attached to a computer (or mounted within the computer) to enable data to be written to or read from magnetic, optical, or magneto-optical media. See *Hard Disk*, *Floppy Disk*, *Optical Disc*, and *Magneto-Optical Disc*.

Disk Duplexing

In networking, a process that simultaneously writes data onto two different *hard disk*s, each of which uses a different *hard disk controller*. Disk duplexing is utilized to provide redundancy of important data in the event of the

failure of one hard disk or disk controller. However, it does not stave off loss of information due to multiple disk crashes. Hence, a complete set of backups is often needed in addition to disk mirroring. See also *Disk Mirroring*.

Disk Head

Alternate term for *read/write head*. See *Read/Write Head*.

Disk Mirroring

In networking, a process that simultaneously writes data onto two different *hard disk*s (or two different *partition*s on the same hard disk), using a single *hard disk controller*. Disk mirroring is utilized to provide redundancy of important data in the event of the failure of one hard disk or partition. However, it doesn't stave off loss of information due to multiple disk crashes or failure of the controller. Hence, a complete set of backups is often needed in addition to disk duplexing. See also *Disk Duplexing*.

Disk Operating System

See *DOS*.

Disk Optimizer

In computing, a program that improves the performance of a disk by *defragment*ing the files contained thereon. See *Storage Fragmementation* and *Defragment*.

Disk Recorder

In multimedia, a *hard disk* used as a storage medium for *digital video*.

Disk Refiner

A system for *refining* paper *pulp* to impart the desired structural and binding characteristics to the *cellulose* fibers that will form the paper *web*.

A disk refiner consists of two vertical disks with serrated or otherwise contoured surfaces. One disk rotates clockwise, while the other either remains stationary or rotates counterclockwise. The fiber *slurry* is pumped between the disks through an inlet in the center of one disk. As centrifugal force pushes the fibers out toward the perimeter of the disks, the abrasion experienced by the fibers cuts, softens, rubs, and disperses them to the degree desired. The space between the disks can be widened or shortened, depending on the extent of refining appropriate to the end-use of the paper to be produced.

The disk refining system has replaced the *beater* in many larger papermills. The advantages it has over the older system include the fact that it is a continuous system, rather than a batch system, meaning that pulp qualities and degree of refining can be altered at will, depending on the grade and type of paper to be produced. (See *Refining*.)

Disk refiners are also utilized in some newer types of *mechanical pulping*. See *Mechanical Pulping*.

Disk Sector

See *Sector*.

Disk Storage

The storing of computer data on magnetic disks.

Disk Striping

In computing, a means of consolidating a series of *partition*s on separate *hard disk*s into a single volume that the *operating system* sees as a single drive, allowing fast, concurrent access to different disks. *Disk striping with parity* is a variation of the above, allowing data to be recreated from other partitions should one partition in the stripe fail.

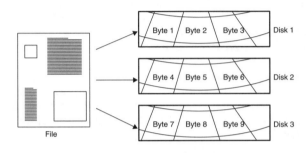

Disk striping.

Disk Striping With Parity

In computing, the inclusion of *parity* information when performing *disk striping* so to be able to recreate data from a disk when one particular *partition* fails. See *Disk Striping*.

Diskette

Alternate term for a *floppy disk*. See *Floppy Disk*.

Diskless Workstation

In networking, a *workstation* having no disk storage itself, all files and applications being read from and written to a *server*. Diskless workstations are useful when sensitive information is being accessed, as there is no danger of data being copied to a local disk since there isn't one.

Disobutyl Ketone (DIBK)

A *solvent* in the *ketone* family used as a *retarder* in vinyl printing inks, lacquers, and coatings.

Disperse Dye

A water-insoluble colorant used to color or print on textiles.

Dispersing Agent

A substance added—typically in small quantities—to a printing ink as a means of increasing the *dispersion* of the solid particles of *pigment* in the fluid ink *vehicle*. A dispersing agent is essentially a type of *wetting agent*.

Dispersion

The uniform distribution of particles of *pigment* in a printing ink *vehicle*, performed in the *mixing* and *milling* stages of printing ink manufacturing. Incomplete dispersion or *flocculation* of pigment particles is a common cause of many printing ink problems. (See *Ink: Ink Manufacturing*, as well as *Ink: Printing Ink Problems and Defects*.)

In *color*, *dispersion* refers to the separation of a beam of white light into its spectral components, caused by *refraction* rather than *diffraction*. Dispersion occurs when a beam of light passes through a *transparent* material (such as glass or water) at an angle; each separate wavelength that constitutes the light beam is bent at a different angle. Though not pronounced enough to be detectable in everyday surfaces (such as windows, glasses of water, or ponds), special transparent materials such as prisms can be produced which will magnify the dispersion effect rendering the full *visible spectrum*. Dispersion is also the cause of such phenomena in photography as *chromatic aberration*.

Display

General term for *display type*, set in larger-than-text size for headlines and other applications. See *Display Type*.

In computers, *display* is also used to refer to a computer monitor (also called a *video display*), *CRT*, or other such device. *Display* also refers to the material that is viewed on a computer display.

Display Ad

General term for a large-size print advertisement, especially one that includes artwork rather than just text, in contrast to a *classified ad*.

Display Area

The portion of a computer's monitor—or *display*—in which the image is actually displayed, exclusive of border areas.

Display Attributes

In typography, the *type specifications* for *display type*.

Display Buffer Memory

Alternate term for *frame buffer*. See *Frame Buffer*.

Display Cycle

The movements of a *cathode ray* required to image a character on a display screen or *cathode-ray tube*.

Display Equation

In typography, a mathematical equation—such as

$$E = mc^2$$

that is typeset apart from the running text on its own line.

Display Face

A *typeface*, usually a larger and bolder version of a text face, used to typeset *display type*. See *Display Type*.

Display Frame

Alternate term for *active page*. See *Active Page*.

Display Image

In computing, any group of elements that are represented together on a display or monitor.

Display Matter

Alternate term for *display type*. See *Display Type*.

Display Menu

A computer menu, especially one appearing on a computer monitor. See *Menu*.

Display Monitor

A *CRT* (or *cathode ray tube*) used as a computer *display*, or the monitor on which computer images are viewed.

Display PostScript

A version of the *PostScript* page description language that translates PostScript code to graphics and text that can be displayed on a computer monitor, facilitating the editing of PostScript files.

On most computers, a file is not converted to PostScript until output, in which case errors in the PostScript code will necessitate editing the original file and re-translating it to PostScript. Display PostScript allows direct correction of the PostScript code. However, due to the high processing power required to use Display PostScript, it is only possible on high-end prepress systems. See *PostScript*.

Display Size

A measure of the actual *display area* of a computer monitor; as with television sets, it is measured diagonally. As of this writing, display sizes range from about 13–21 in.

Display Type

In typography, type set in a larger *point size* than the text (commonly greater than 14 point), such as headlines.

Display Typesetting

In typography, a general term referring to the setting of *display type*, such as advertisements, or in fact any material other than straight text.

Dissolve

In motion picture, video, and multimedia editing, a *transition* between two scenes or shots in which the first scene is gradually faded into the second, in contrast to a *cut* or a *wipe*. Since the two images overlap for a time, the effect is also known as a *lap dissolve*.

Distance Vector Algorithm (DVA)

In networking, one of a related set of algorithms used for *routing*, determining the most expedient route by which to transmit data between adjacent *nodes*.

Distortion

Any undesirable change of shape of a roller, cylinder, bar, or other mechanical part.

Distortion also refers to any undesirable modification of an electric, audio, or video signal.

Distributed Architecture

A *network topology* in which all nodes share a single communications medium. See *Shared Access*.

Distributed Computing

In networking, the imbuing of individual *workstation*s with a greater share of the processing and computer power, as opposed to containing all of the processing ability in a central controller. See also *Distributed Processing*.

Distributed Data Processing

See *Distributed Processing*.

Distributed Database

A *database* whose constituent records are physically stored in more than one geographic location, but which are managed as a single, large database. Often redundant data is stored in more than one location as a means of preventing irretrievable data loss if something happens to one location. Such systems usually have means of facilitating the update of all redundant information.

Distributed Network

A *network topology* in which all *node*s are connected to each other either directly or through intermediate nodes. See *Network Topology*. Also known as a *decentralized network*.

Distributed Processing

In networking, an arrangement in which different nodes (or *CPU*s) perform different functions or tasks on the same file or application. Also known as *distributed data processing*.

Distributing Roller

Alternate term for a *distributor* roller on an offset press. See *Distributor*.

Distribution Medium

Any medium used to disseminate or distribute a publication, application, etc., including traditional print, *CD*, *CD-ROM*, *floppy disk* or other magnetic medium, videotape, or the *Internet*.

Distributor

One of two types of *intermediate rollers* found in the *inking system* on a printing press used in *offset lithography*. Distributors are located between two other rollers (such as between two *oscillator*s) and have a resilient nap-covered surface that serves to work the ink into a printable *viscosity* and mixes the ink with amounts of water to form an emulsion. Distributors are turned by the force of the rotation of adjacent chain-and-gear-driven rollers. Another type of intermediate roller is a *rider*. (See *Inking System: Offset Lithography* and *Offset Lithography*.)

Dither

In digital imaging, to use the values (*color*s) of two *pixel*s to determine the color of a pixel lying between them. This new pixel thus has a value that is the average of the two pixels on either side of it. *Dithering* is often used to eliminate unwanted *jaggies* (i.e., to give an image a smoother edge), or to determine the value of certain pixels when reducing the color depth of an image, as when converting from *twenty-four-bit color* to *eight-bit color*. The term *dither* also means to change a range of grayscale values to patterns of black-and-white by placing white and black dots in such a pattern as to simulate or suggest a range of grays.

Dividers

Plastic or other tabs used in *indexing*. See *Indexing*.

Divinity Calf

In *binding and finishing*, a type of dark brown calfskin used for the binding of bibles.

DLL

Abbreviation for *dynamic link library*. See *Dynamic Link Library (DLL)*.

DMA

Abbreviation for *direct memory access*. See *Direct Memory Access (DMA)*.

D-MAC

In video production and broadcasting, a transmission standard utilizing *MAC* video and *NICAM* audio.

D$_{max}$

Abbreviation for *maximum density*. See *Maximum Density*.

DMI

Abbreviation for *desktop management interface*. See *Desktop Management Interface (DMI)*.

D$_{min}$

Abbreviation for *minimum density*. See *Minimuim Density*.

DNA Orange

An *organic color pigment* used in printing inks. DNA orange is a reddish-orange pigment that possesses high *lightfastness*, heat resistance, and acid and alkali resistance, and can withstand exposure to waxes and water. It is also highly opaque. However, it does not hold up well when exposed to solvents. Its toxicity remains in doubt. DNA orange has poor flow characteristics, and is used primarily in inexpensive printing on kraft paper or polyethylene films. (See also *Organic Color Pigments*.)

Also known as *Orange 2G*, *Dinitroaniline Red (BS 3599/4)*, and *Permanent Red 2G* (*CI Pigment Orange 5 No. 12075*).

DNS

Abbreviation for *Domain Naming System*. See *Domain Naming System (DNS)*. The term *DNS* is also an abbreviation used in proofreading that stands for "do not set."

Docking Station

In computing, a hardware configuration into which a *portable computer* or *laptop computer* can be plugged to allow the portable to be used as a full-fledged desktop computer. A docking station, however, is essentially part of the portable, making it difficult to mix and match docking stations and portables from different manufacturers.

Doctor Blade

Generic term for any steel, rubber, plastic, or other type of blade used to apply or remove a liquid substance from another surface, such as those blades used in coating paper. The term "doctor blade" is believed to be derived from the name of a blade used in conjunction with ductor rolls on letterpress presses. The term "ductor blade" eventually mutated into the term "doctor blade."

In *gravure* printing, the *doctor blade* is a steel strip used to remove ink from the outside surface of the *gravure cylinder*. Although steel is preferred in most gravure applications, plastics are occasionally used, usually in conjunction with a worn cylinder as a means of prolonging its life. Steel doctor blades vary in thickness from 0.004 to 0.015 in., and are manufactured with strict tolerances.

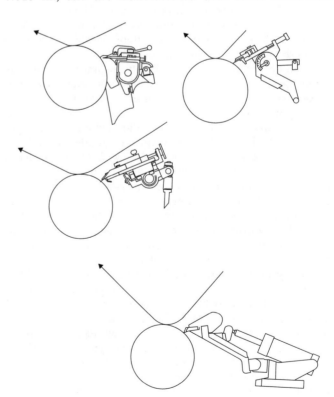

A panoply of doctor blade holder configurations.

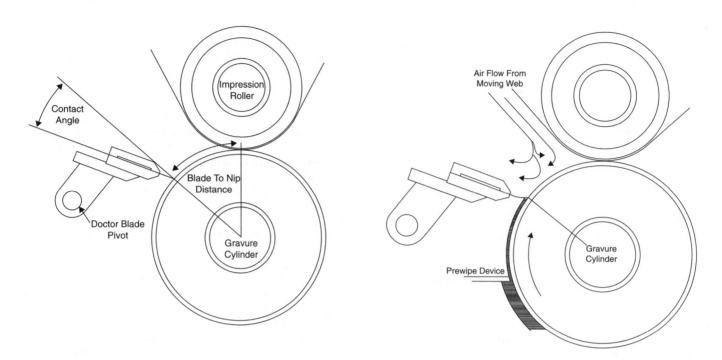

The position and common configuration of gravure press doctor blade (left). During press operation, the doctor blade bends, or deflects (right). Note also the use of a prewiping device.

(Plastic blades can be as thick as 0.060 in.) The most important consideration in the manufacture of a doctor blade is straightness, so to ensure consistent scraping pressure across the width of the gravure cylinder.

The doctor blade is fixed firmly in place by a doctor blade assembly, the amount of blade protruding from the holder being known as the **blade extension**—generally recommended to be ⅜–½ in. It is set at certain optimum angles to ensure minimal blade and/or cylinder wear. The angle at which the blade contacts the cylinder (called the **contact angle**) is generally 55–65°, with 60° being most manufacturers' specified contact angle. The angle can be varied to correct various cylinder defects and/or inking problems. The contact angle also affects the distance between the blade and the nip between the gravure cylinder and the **impression roller**. This distance needs to be small enough to prevent **drying-in**, the undesirable drying of ink in the gravure cylinder cells.

Many doctor blades oscillate across the width of the cylinder as a means of preventing cylinder wear and to remove solid bits of debris that can collect on the surface of the cylinder of the rear of the blade itself. The force or pressure with which the blade contacts the cylinder should be as minimal as possible, or should wipe the cylinder effectively but not contribute to blade and/or cylinder wear. (The process of setting the contact angle and blade contact pressure is known as **running in** or **toning in**.) A related consideration is the unavoidable **deflection** of the blade during the print run, or, in other words, a slight curvature of the

blade caused by the rotating cylinder. The contact angle and blade pressure should take into account deflection. The edge of the blade itself comes in a variety of configurations, either pre-honed by the manufacturer or honed in-house by the printer. Regardless of the configuration, the important considerations are effective wiping and the minimization of wear. Surface **roughness** of the cylinder is important for doctor blade lubrication (which refers to the ease or reduced-friction movement of one solid surface over another). Gravure cylinders that are too smooth will increase doctor blade wear and cylinder damage. On some packaging presses, **scavenger marks** are deliberately etched into non-image areas corresponding to nonprinting regions of the substrate (and which can be removed during finishing operations, such as trimming) to facilitate the removal of particles of ink or other debris from beneath the doctor blade.

Blade wear can have three different causes: abrasion (commonly produced by foreign particles or the use of abrasive ink pigments), fatigue (caused by stress), and corrosion (the result of chemical reaction, such as oxidation—or rusting—or overly acidic or alkaline ink vehicles). Most inks manufactured for gravure printing are produced with proper resin and solvent concentrations so as to minimize abrasion and facilitate lubrication.

Some gravure presses include a pre-wiping blade located between the ink fountain and the doctor blade, set close to the cylinder, but which does not contact it. Its purpose is to slough off excess ink before the doctor blade removes the remaining thin ink film.

Damaged doctor blades can produce a variety of printing defects, such as *railroading* and *railroad tracks*, or continuous streaks, marks, or lines appearing on the substrate, caused by incomplete wiping of the cylinder. Such problems are commonly caused either by nicks in the doctor blade, or by dried particles of ink or other materials stuck to the rear or back of the doctor blade. (See also *Inking System: Gravure* and *Gravure*.)

A *doctor blade* is also used in several *flexographic* inking systems. Similar in construction and function to doctor blades used in gravure, doctor blades used in flexographic presses scrape excess ink from the surface of the *anilox roller* that applies ink to the printing plate. Doctor blades tend to be more effective for ink metering than more traditional *fountain roller* arrangements. See *Inking System: Flexography* and *Anilox Roller*.

A doctor blade used in *screen printing* is called a *flood bar*. See *Flood Bar*.

Doctor Roller

Alternate term for a *flexographic* printing press's *fountain roller*. See *Fountain Roller*.

Documation

The automated distribution of a document, such as making it available on database or network that can be logged onto from a computer.

Document Exchange Format

See *DXF*.

Document Management

In networking, the storage, cataloging, and maintenance of a networked file, including such information as the creator of the file, the date and time created, and the application used to create it.

Document Processing

In computing and *database* management, the creation and processing of text documents, including indexing methods for later retrieval.

Document Structure

Alternate term for *layout structure*. See *Layout Structure*.

Document Type Definition (DTD)

A code or character set added to the beginning of a *SGML* document which describes the elements of the document and the structure of those elements. DTD allows for the rapid and uniform retrieval of documents from databases. See *Standard Generalized Markup Language (SGML)*.

Documentation

Any written and/or pictorial information (in print or electronic form, but usually the former) comprising instructions, tutorials, technical support, specifications, and other material needed to explain how to operate a device or application. Often referred to as an "instruction manual."

DOD

Abbreviation for *drop on demand*. See *Drop on Demand* and *Ink Jet*.

Dog-Ear

Part of a sheet of paper—commonly a corner—which has been folded over. Dog-ears can be caused by a number of mechanical problems, either on press or in a *folding* machine. Some of the less civilized among us also use dog-ears as bookmarks. Also spelled as one word, *dogear*.

Dolby Surround Sound

A system developed by Dolby Labs that splits a two-channel audio signal into four separate signals. With the appropriate placement of four speakers connected to an audio system with the surround sound capability, a "you-are-in-the-middle-of-everything" effect can be achieved. Originally used in movie theaters, it is now available on many types of home audio and video systems. The four-way sound is achieved using special codes, which are ignored when the surround sound hardware is not available, allowing productions recorded using surround sound to be played on non-surround-sound hardware.

Dolly

In film and video photography, a wheeled cart to which a camera can be mounted, allowing for the tracking of moving objects or for other effects. The dolly is often pulled by hand along tracks, often by a crewmember known as a "dolly grip."

In three-dimensional modeling, *dolly* is a term used to refer to similar type of movement.

Domain

In networking, a single computer, an entire department, or an entire site, used for administrative and naming purposes. Depending upon the system and the network architecture, a domain can refer to different things. On the *Internet*, the domain falls under the purview of the *Domain Naming System, (DNS)*. See *Domain Name*.

Domain Directory Services

In networking, the *directory services* within a single *domain*. Each separate *server* (or domain) within a network requires its own administration and, consequently, its own directory services. See *Directory Services*.

Domain Name

In networking, the name of a particular site's *Internet* host, usually an easy to remember name (such as aol, panix, mindspring, etc.). See also *Bang Path*, *Domain Naming System (DNS)*, and *IP Address*.

Domain Naming System (DNS)

In networking, especially on the *Internet*, an addressing system used to combine the *domain* name with the *IP* address. Some frequently encountered domains on the Internet include *.com* (a commercial organization), *.edu* (an educational institution), *.gov* (a government agency), *.int* (an international organization), *.mil* (a military institution), *.net* (a network), and *.org* (a nonprofit organization).

Dongle

A piece of computer hardware that needs to be attached to a computer system (such as through the *parallel port* or between the keyboard and the ADB port) for some software applications to function. Designed as a way of thwarting unauthorized software duplication, the software scans for a serial number embedded on the device and will not operate if it does not detect it. Also called a *hardware key*.

Don't Save

In computer programs, a command that closes an open file without saving any changes made to it since the last time it was saved.

Door Swing

In video production, a *video effect* in which an image is rotated along an axis, often used for *transition*s.

Dope

A colloquialism for the *fountain solution* used in *offset lithography*. Dope is also a colloquialism for other various varnishes, *reducer*s, and other compounds used in offset lithography.

In *screen printing*, a colloquialism for a lacquer made of *cellulose acetate*.

DOS

Abbreviation for *Disk Operating System*, one of the first operating systems used in personal computers. Developed by Microsoft in the early 1980s for use in the first IBM PCs, it for many years dominated the operating system market until being supplanted by Microsoft's own *Windows* and Apple's *Macintosh operating system*.

Essentially, the function of DOS (or any operating system, for that matter) is to control all the operations of the computer, and direct and process the flow of information to and from the hard disk drive, the floppy disk drive, and any other peripherals attached to the system, such as a monitor, scanner, modem, etc. See *Operating System*.

The version of DOS that was licensed by IBM and sold with their PCs was called *PC-DOS*. The version of DOS that was licensed by Microsoft to other computer manufacturers or sold by itself was known as *MS-DOS*. They both functioned essentially the same as each other. Applications designed to run on PC-DOS can also be run on MS-DOS.

DOS, a *command-line interface*, has for the most part given way to graphical user interfaces (*GUIs*), although Windows (and even Windows 95) is still a GUI built on top of an underlying DOS infrastructure.

DOS Prompt

A *prompt* of the type utilized by *DOS*, most familiarly, "C:>". See *Prompt*.

Dot

Strictly speaking, the smallest fundamental unit of a *halftone* image, a small point of *color*, black, or some shade of gray which, when combined with many other dots of varying color and shade, form an image.

Although more technically referred to as *spot*s, in order to distinguish them from halftone dots, computer screen *pixel*s, the smallest portions of light that a scanner can detect, the smallest bits of toner that a *laser printer* can print, and the smallest areas that an *imagesetter* or a *plotter* can expose are also often referred to as *dot*s.

Dot Area

An alternate term for *dot area density*. See *Dot Area Density*.

Dot Area Density

The size of a *halftone dot*, expressed as a percentage of the total surface area, which can range from 0% (no dot) in *highlight*s to 100% (solid ink density) in *shadow*s. By carefully measuring the dot area in various regions of an image at various stages in the reproduction of an image, dot densities can remain consistent.

In digital halftoning, dots (in this case called *cell*s) comprise much smaller printer *spot*s that, depending on the resolution of the output device, can be used to create dots of various sizes and densities. Varying the number of spots that make up a halftone cell can work to fine-tune the dot densities by increasing the number of shades of gray available as the number of spots in a cell is increased. Dot area density is also known as *dot area* or *dot density*.

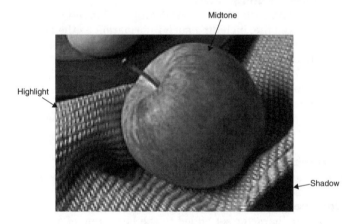

Enlarged view of a halftone image shows variations in dot area density and how they relate to the appearance of shadows, midtones, and highlights.

Dot Chart

Alternate term for a *scatter plot*. See *Scatter Plot*.

Dot Density

Alternate term for *dot area density*. See *Dot Area Density*.

Dot Etching

A means of manually altering the size of a **halftone dot** after the halftone film has already been produced. Dot etching can be performed chemically by immersing the film in an acid bath, photographically by overexposing the halftone film on other films, or digitally by altering the dot size on a computer. Dot etching is performed as a means of altering the colors in a particular image area when halftones and **color separation**s are produced photographically. Such processes, however, are increasingly being performed digitally. (See also **Dry Dot Etching**.)

Dot Font

A computer file consisting of **halftone dot**s at a range of sizes, so as to be able to produce the required dot size on the output medium.

Dot Gain

A printing defect characterized by **halftone dot**s that print larger than desired, imparting to the printed image a darker tone or color, caused, in **offset lithography**, by increased pressure between the **blanket cylinder** and **impression cylinder** of an offset press, or in other processes by ink **feathering** or **spreading** as it penetrates the surface of the **substrate**. Dot gain can have many causes, one of which being the use of paper that has too great a **porosity** or an ink that has too low a **viscosity**. Some types of offset printing plates, in particular **bimetal plate**s and **positive-working plate**s, are better at compensating for dot gain than others.

Dot gain typically increases the diameters of dots by the same amount, regardless of the size of the dots. However, the larger the circumference of the dot, the larger the area around the dot that will increase, the result being that **middle tone**s tend to be the dots most dramatically affected. In multi-color printing, dot gain can affect proper **registration**, so many prepress operations commonly reduce the dot sizes in the middle tone areas so as to compensate for gain (called **dot gain compensation**). Some often-encountered dot gain percentages include:

Coated sheetfed lithography at 150 lpi	15%
Uncoated sheetfed offset lithography at 133 lpi	20%
Coated web offset lithography at 133 lpi	22%
Newsprint web offset lithography at 100 lpi	30%

A 40% Dot On Film   The Same 40% Dot Becomes A 57% Dot When Printed

Effect of dot gain.

The variety of dot gain mentioned above is called **physical dot gain**, as the size of the dots physically increases. Another optically perceived phenomenon is known as **optical dot gain**. (See **Optical Dot Gain**.) Dot gain is also called **dot spreading** and **press gain**. (See also **Slurring** and **Doubling**.) The opposite effect is called **sharpen**.

Dot Gain Compensation

A means of allowing for the effect of **dot gain** by reducing the size of the **halftone dot**s on halftone **color separation** films. Dot gain is often the most pronounced in the **middle tone** regions of an image, and it is typically these areas that undergo dot size reduction. The percentage of the dot size gain varies according to the printing process (i.e, sheetfed or web **offset lithography**) and the paper characteristics. See **Dot Gain**.

Dot Leaders

In typography, **leaders** composed of dots or periods (.......) rather than dashes or hyphens (- - - - - -), which are known as **dash leaders**. See **Leaders**.

Dot Matrix

In computing, any grid pattern of dots that makes up an image. A dot matrix can refer to nearly any digital output or display device; a computer monitor (which constructs an image as a set of **pixel**s), a **laser printer**, **imagesetter**, or **plotter**, etc. (which constructs an image from a small set of printer **spot**s). The term *dot matrix*, however, is commonly used to refer to a type of computer printer popular before the advent of inexpensive laser and ink jet printers. See **Dot-Matrix Printer**.

Dot Pitch

On a computer monitor, a measure of the size of a screen **pixel**, or dot, measured in millimeters. For example, a monitor with a dot pitch of 0.28 contains dots that are 0.28 mm across. Dot pitch, though not specifically a measure of **resolution** per se, is what determines the resolution of a particular screen. The dot pitch is governed by the size of the **raster** scan line and the spacing of the shadow mask. The smaller the dot pitch, the more dots can fit per inch, and the greater the resolution.

The term *dot pitch*, when used to describe a computer printer or other output device, is synonymous with the **dots per inch**, or resolution. See **Resolution**.

Dot Range

The difference between the minimum and maximum **halftone dot** sizes that can be generated on a particular output device or film.

Dot Shape

The geometric appearance of a **halftone dot**, which may vary from elliptical to perfectly round to square. Depending on the application, the shape of halftone dots can be varied to eliminate such problems as **moiré** and **dot gain**. Dot gain is commonly a problem where dots join each other; elliptical dots are particularly effective in reducing that problem, as the existence of long and short directions connects dots to each other in varying ways—in the long direction, they may not connect until the **dot area** has reached 60%; in the short direction, they may not join until the dot area has reached 40%. When using perfectly round dots, areas of high **dot density**—or areas where the dots are tightly packed together—generate little star-shaped white spaces between dots which can fill in with ink, causing shadow areas to print darker than they should. As for square dots, a problem arises when the corners of the dots start to connect, which creates a similar darkening effect in shadow areas (an optical illusion called **optical jump**). (See also **Elliptical Dot**.)

In digital halftoning, the **PostScript** page description language allows for the creation of different dot shapes; as a halftone **cell** (or a halftone dot when created digitally) is composed of much smaller printer **spot**s, these spots can be oriented in a variety of ways to produce different dot shapes. One particular PostScript function uses round dots for **highlight**s and **shadow**, but switches to square dots in the **middle tone**s. This solves both the problems of optical jump in square-dot shadows and **plugging** up of the shadows. PostScript can even allow for the use of customized dot shapes for special effects, such as halftone cells in the shape of bowties or other whimsical shapes.

Dot Slurring

A printing defect of **offset lithography** characterized by smeared **halftone dot**s, especially in their trailing edges, caused by mechanical slippage of the paper against the **blanket**. See **Slurring**.

Dot Spread

Alternate term for **dot gain**. See **Dot Gain**.

Dot-Matrix Printer

A type of computer output device—or printer—that uses patterns of small dots to construct an image. Although just about any computer printer could be considered a dot-matrix printer (including a **laser printer**), the term is most commonly used to refer to a type of **impact printer** popular before the advent of inexpensive laser printers, characterized by printing on **fanfold** paper with light printing made of very large, visible dots.

Dots Per Inch (dpi)

A measure of the **resolution** of a computer monitor, **scanner**, or output device such as a **laser printer** or **imagesetter**. Each of these devices generates or displays images composed of many tiny dots (called **pixel**s or **spot**s). The resolution is determined by measuring how many of these "dots" can fit in a unit of linear distance, such as an inch. See **Resolution**. A more proper term—to distinguish screen and printer dots from **halftone dot**s—is **pixels per inch (ppi)**.

Dots Per Line (dpl)

A measure of the **resolution** of a computer monitor indicating the number of **pixel**s that are placed on a horizontal line. For example, a monitor said to have a 640×480 resolution has a resolution of 640 pixels on each of its 480 horizontal lines. See **Resolution**.

Dotted Decimal

Alternate term for **Internet address**. See **Internet Address**.

Double-Black Duotone

Alternate term for **double-black halftone printing**. See **Double-Black Halftone Printing**.

Double-Black Halftone Printing

In printing, a means of increasing the **tonal range** of printed **halftone**s by printing with two specially prepared black halftone plates. Not to be confused with a **double halftone**. Also called a **double-black duotone**.

Double Buffering

In computer animation, a means of making animation smoother. In double buffering, two separate **frame buffer**s are utilized. An image is composed in one frame buffer, and while it is being displayed, the next image is composed in the inactive buffer, which then becomes active. The two buffers alternate in this manner until the animation is complete.

Double-Clicking

In computing, the pressing of the button on a **mouse** twice in rapid succession (the rate of which can often be set in the operating system's control panel). Double-clicking, in contrast to single-**clicking**, is often required for some features and functions, such as opening an application or file.

Double-Coated Stock

A type of **coated paper** that has had two layers of coating applied.

Double-Column

Descriptive of typeset pages comprising two vertical columns of text, as opposed to **single-column**.

Double-Deckle Paper

A type of paper having two **deckle** edges, usually parallel with each other. See **Deckle**.

Double Density

A type of **floppy disk** that contains twice as many **track**s as the first variety of floppy disk, allowing twice as much data to be stored. So-called "single density" disks vanished shortly thereafter. Double-density disks were eventually supplanted by **high density** disks. Abbreviated **DD**.

Double-Dot Halftone

Alternate term for **double halftone**. See **double halftone**.

Double Draw

In **binding and finishing**, the assembly of the sections of a book in more than one stage. See **Draw** (second definition).

Double-Ending

A variety of **half-web printing** in which two half webs are printed simultaneously. See **Half-Web Printing**.

Double-Former Folder

An **in-line** folding device used on publication and commercial **web press**es that creates only one **former fold**, which serves as the **backbone** for a printed product. It is called a double-former folder because it has two **former board**s that can deliver twice as many **signature**s as a regular **former folder**. A double-former folder usually operates on the same principle as a **ribbon folder**: a blade slits the web into two halves, each of which is sent through a former folder to create two sets of printed and folded signatures. A double-former folder is also known as a **form-and-cutoff**.

Double Halftone

In prepress, a lithographic printing plate imaged from two separate **halftone** negatives, one providing the **shadow** and **highlight** regions (or, in other words, the two extremes of the **tonal range** of the image) the other providing the **middle tone** regions. A double halftone—not to be confused with a **duotone** or **double-black halftone printing**—reproduces with much greater tonal range than a conventional halftone. Also called a **double-dot halftone**.

Double-Page Spread

In page layout and printing, two facing pages of a book, magazine, newspaper, or other publication on which the text, artwork, or other page elements span the **bind margin**, one portion of the image falling on the **verso**, the other portion falling on the **recto**. The **imposition** and printing of double-page spreads require that the two portions of the image be perfectly aligned when the publication is assembled, and that the colors be identical. See also **Spread**. Also called a **two-page spread**.

Double Paper

Alternate term for **duplex paper**. See **Duplex Paper**.

Double-Period Directory

In computing, especially by means of a system utilizing a **hierarchical file system**, the use of a double period (..) to designate a **parent directory**. The **current directory is thus designated with a single period (.) and is consequently known as a** period directory. This shorthand means of referring to directories is often used in **DOS**, **OS/2**, and **UNIX** operating systems.

Double Printing

In **prepress**, refers to the imaging of two separate **flat**s on the same **plate**. See **Complementary Flat** and **Prepress: Graphic Arts Photography and Flat Assembly**.

Double-Roll Stand

In **web printing**, a **roll stand** which holds two rolls of paper (or other **substrate**) at a time and can feed both into the press simultaneously. Also called a **dual-roll stand**. See **Roll Stand**. See also **Single-Roll Stand**.

Double Rotary Cutter

A device used in the **sheeting** of paper rolls consisting of two rotating knives that cut the paper **web** moving between them. The speed of the rotating knives is adjusted relative to the speed of the paper web. Sheeting is also performed on a **single rotary cutter**. (See **Sheeting**.)

Doubles

In **binding and finishing**, the result of a malfunction of **gathering** equipment consisting of two like **signature**s being gathered and assembled where only one should be.

Double-Sheet Detector

A device attached near the interface between a sheetfed press's **feedboard** and **sheet-separation unit** that detects when more than one sheet is being fed through at one time.

A double-sheet detector can either be mechanical or electric, and is attached to a caliper roller placed between the **forwarding roller**s. When paper beyond a certain preset thickness passes beneath the roller, the detector shuts off the feeding unit and/or the printing unit. Electric detectors have a set of electrical contacts that, when paper beyond a certain thickness passes beneath the caliper roller, are brought into contact, tripping the shutoff of the feeder. Needless to say, the sheet detector needs to be set precisely to the thickness of the paper being printed. On a **stream feeder**, in which the sheets overlap while feeding,

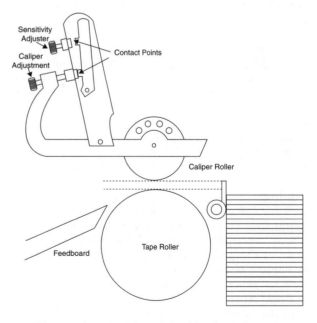

Electrical contact-based double-sheet detector.

it is necessary to set the double-sheet detector to trip when *three* sheets pass beneath it. When printing larger-size paper with a stream feeder, however, is it not uncommon for there to be points when three sheets overlap. Consequently, the double-sheet detector needs to be set to trip when *four* sheets pass beneath it. (On presses equipped with stream feeders, double-sheet detectors are commonly referred to as ***extra-sheet detector***s.)

A *double-sheet detector* is also used on some ***folding*** machines as a means of detecting when more than one sheet is being fed into the mechanism.

Double-Sided Diskette
See ***Dual-Sided Diskette***.

Double-Sixteen
In ***binding and finishing***, a type of ***knife folder***. See ***Folding: Knife Folder***.

Double-Speed (2X)
Descriptive of a ***CD-ROM*** drive capable of reading and transferring data at a speed twice as fast as a single-speed drive. A ***single-speed*** CD-ROM drive, in retrospect designated 1X, could process data at a speed of 150 ***kilobyte***s per second. A ***double-speed (2X)*** CD-ROM can thus process data at a speed of 300 kilobytes per second. Later triple-speed drives process data at a speed of 450 kilobytes per second. Newer drives have even faster access times: 600 kilobytes per second (***quad speed***, or 4X, drives), 900 kilobytes per second (6X drives), 1200 kilobytes per second (8X drives), 1500 kilobytes per second (10X drives), and 1800 kilobytes per second (12X drives).

Double-Thick Cover Stock
A ***cover paper*** produced by laminating together two sheets of 65-pound cover stock. See ***Cover Paper***.

Doubletone Ink
A type of printing ink containing a soluble ***toner*** that, upon printing, bleeds to generate a secondary color in the image, producing a two-color printing effect in one impression.

Double Varnish
The application of two coats of ***overprint varnish*** as a means of affording a printed piece additional protection from handling, or contact with fluids or other substances.

Doubling
A printing defect of ***offset lithography*** characterized by a faint duplicate of a printed impression out of register with the solid image, caused by ***prekissing***, or the premature contact of the paper and the printing blanket before the true impression is made. Prekissing can be caused by such things as paper deformations and static electricity. (See also ***Prekissing*** and ***Slurring***.)

In ***die-stamping*** or ***foil stamping***, a defect characterized by a doubled impression, caused by successive

stamping operations that do not accurately register the second impression over the first.

Doughnut Hickey
A printing defect characterized by a solid printed area ringed by a blank unprinted area, typically caused by an ink-receptive particle adhering to the surface of the printing plate, offset ***blanket***, ***gravure cylinder***, or other image-carrying surface. Sources of doughnut hickey-generating particles are bits of ink skin (called ***ink hickey***s), dirt from the press, chips of flaking ceiling paint, or other various dust and debris that pick up ink, but as raised surfaces, do not allow the surrounding area to print. Doughnut hickeys are typically not caused by paper ***lint***, which tends to produce ***void hickey***s. Some lint can begin as a doughnut hickey and turn into a void hickey. (See ***Hickey***.)

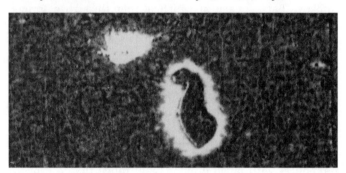

Doughnut hickey.

Dowel
In prepress and printing, a short metal or plastic pin to which a ***flat*** and/or ***plate*** can be attached so as to accurately register subsequent film or plates for ***step-and-repeat*** exposures or multi-color printing.

Downlink
An orbiting satellite that can transmit data to an ***earth station*** on the ground. See also ***Uplink***.

Download
To receive a data file on one's computer from another computer (which can be a file server, a ***bulletin board service***, an Internet USENET group, or another individual's computer), typically via modem. The opposite, ***upload***, means to *send* a data file from one's computer to another computer. Similarly, ***laser printer***s and other output devices frequently *download* data (such as the file to be printed, and the ***font***s with which to print it) from the computer. (See ***Downloadable Font***.)

Downloadable Font
In computers and ***desktop publishing*** systems, a ***digital font*** that can be sent to an output device (commonly a ***laser printer***) from the computer's hard disk and loaded into the printer's memory, as opposed to a font that needs to be stored on a plug-in cartridge. Also known as a ***soft font***.

Downsizing

In computing, the redevelopment of applications originally designed for use on **mainframe** computers so that they will run on smaller and less powerful **PC**s, often within a **local area network**. Although some advanced features of such applications need to be discarded to ensure performance on smaller computers, that may not always need to be the case, as a networked series of PCs can be collectively more powerful than a single mainframe.

The term *downsizing* is also an unhappy term used to refer to the process by which a large company eliminates a percentage of its workforce, usually to save money.

Downstream

In a **cable television network**, the direction of a transmitted signal from the **head end**. The direction *to* the head end is referred to as **upstream**.

Down Time

In any mechanical, electronic, digital, or telecommunications system, an unscheduled stoppage of equipment due to malfunction, system maintenance, or a variety of other reasons. Also spelled as one word, *downtime*.

Downward Compatible

In computing, descriptive of software that will run on earlier versions of the hardware for which it was developed. An exmple would be a program developed for a **Pentium** computer that can run on a 80486 machine. Also referred to as **backward compatible**. See also **Upward Compatible**.

DP

Abbreviation for **data processing**. See **Data Processing**.

dpl

Abbreviation for **dots per line**. See **Dots Per Line (dpl)**.

DPSS

Abbreviation for **direct printer services subsystem**. See **Direct Printer Services Subsystem**.

DR-DOS

In computing, a **DOS**-compatible **operating system** developed by Digital Research and later acquired by Novell, Inc.

Draft-Quality Printer

A high-speed computer printer (or mode on a variable-speed printer) which prints documents rapidly, but at less than typewriter quality. Used for the quick printing of drafts or internal documents for which high quality is not essential.

Drag

In computer graphics or page layout programs, to move selected images, objects, columns, text blocks, or other items from place to place on the screen, commonly using a mouse. See **Drag-and-Drop** and **Direct Manipulation**.

In printing, *drag* is an alternate term for **slur**. See **Slur**.

Drag-and-Drop

An application, especially in a **graphical user interface (GUI)**, activated or launched when another object (such as a file) is dragged (using the mouse) and placed on top of it. An example of drag-and-drop is Aladdin's StuffIt Expander, which, when a StuffIt archive is dropped on top of it, will decompress the compressed file without having to launch the StuffIt application.

Dragging

In computer graphics, moving a selected image, object, column, text block, or other item across the screen. See **Drag**.

Dragout

A printing defect of **gravure** characterized by excessive thicknesses of ink surrounding shadow areas of a printed image, commonly caused by either cells that have been etched too deeply, or by poor ink drying on a coated paper.

Dragout also refers to the accumulation of printing ink pigment on the gravure **doctor blade** which can become detached from the blade and print on the substrate.

Drain

To output all the pages of a document without interruption.

DRAM

Abbreviation for **dynamic RAM**. See **Dynamic RAM**.

Draw

To generate an illustration or illustration vector either manually (using pen and ink on a substrate) or digitally (using a **drawing program**).

In **binding and finishing**, the term *draw* refers to the gathered sections (or **signature**s) of a book. Depending upon the number of signatures vs. the number of stations on the **gathering** machine, book sections may need to be assembled in more than one stage. A **double draw** is two batches of sections that are assembled, while a **triple draw** is three batches to assemble.

In **cutting and trimming**, the term *draw* also refers to any dragging motion of a cutting knife.

Drawdown

A means of evaluating the color mixing of a printing ink by depositing a layer of the mixed ink on the surface of a **substrate** using a smooth-edged knife. Drawdown is one of three basic tests used to determine the accuracy of color matching and mixing processes, the compatibility of the various inks combined, the performance of the ink on the substrate, and the drying characteristics of the ink. Drawdown is also called **pulldown**. (See **Color Mixing, Ink**. See also **Pat-Out**.)

Drawing

Any illustration or other form of nontext material or artwork that was created by hand, as opposed to a photograph. Commonly also referred to as a **line drawing** or **line art**.

The term *drawing* also refers to a computer application used for creating line drawings and illustrations, commonly using a mouse or stylus and *digitizing tablet* to replace a pen, pencil, or other mechanical tool. Drawing programs commonly utilize *vector* graphics, in contrast to *paint* programs that use *bitmap* graphics.

Drawing File

A graphics file containing all the *vector* information needed to generate the contents of the illustration. Usually used when discussing drawings created in drafting programs.

Drawing Interchange Format

In computer graphics, a *file format* used to transfer *CAD* files from system to system, supported by AutoCAD, among other applications. Abbreviated *DIF*.

Drawing Paper

Any paper designed and manufactured specifically for pen and/or pencil drawing. There are a wide assortment of papers available for this purpose, their fiber content ranging from 100% *cotton content* to 100% *groundwood*.

Drier

A substance, or *catalyst*, added to a printing ink to increase the speed at which the ink dries, typically by speeding up the rate at which the vehicle undergoes *oxidation* and *polymerization*. There are two basic types of driers: liquid driers and paste driers.

Liquid driers are produced by the conversion of certain types of organic acids to heavy metal salts and soaps (commonly called *metallic soaps*), which are soluble in oils or other *solvent*s and can then be mixed into the ink. The amount of metal used in a drier varies; typical metal composition of liquid driers is from 3–18%, although lead and zirconium-based driers can be 24–36% metal. Liquid driers typically make up about 0.5–4% of an ink. Other factors such as paper *pH*, surface characteristics and porosity of the paper, temperature, and humidity all affect drying time of an ink. Typically, inks dry faster at higher temperatures, but slower at high relative humidities.

The most popular drier is cobalt, which is also the most powerful drier. Cobalt-based driers are violet in color, but turn brown following oxidation. As a result, a drawback of cobalt driers is their tendency to discolor white images and tints. Cobalt driers are also soluble in organic acids, and can be removed easily from the ink by the *fountain solution* and contaminate the water fountain. Cobalt acetate, however, can be added to the fountain solution as a *drying stimulator*.

Other metals used as driers in printing inks include manganese, which has less of a catalytic effect than does cobalt, but is less likely to tint or leach into the fountain solution than is cobalt. However, manganese driers typically work only in the presence of increased heat. Lead is used only sparingly, as it is slow-acting, and the use of lead is becoming increasingly restricted. Lead is commonly used in combination with manganese soaps, but has primarily been replaced by lithium, zirconium, and cerium soaps. Calcium and zinc, which are relatively ineffective as drying catalysts, are used infrequently, and then only in some white inks. Calcium is used to modify the catalytic action of other metallic soaps. Iron-based driers are used in *tung oil* varnishes.

Paste driers commonly comprise *linseed oil* varnishes in which are dispersed ground organic lead and manganese salts, the most common being lead acetate and manganese borate (typical composition being about 40% lead acetate and 8% manganese borate). Cobalt is rarely, if ever, used in paste driers. Paste driers are slower drying than liquid driers, and improve *trapping* in multicolor printing, as they allow overprinting of successive colors to a much greater degree than does cobalt. Inorganic peroxides are occasionally used as driers, particularly in lithographic inks.

A drier can either be a *through drier* or a *top drier*, which will either dry the ink throughout the interior of the ink film, or on the surface of the ink film, respectively.

The addition of an excessive amount of drier produces ink skin and causes it to dry while it is still on the press. In some cases, the addition of too much drier can actually impede ink drying, and cause problems like *ink setoff*. *Greasing* and *scumming* are symptoms of excessive drier in lithographic inks, and the addition of water to counteract it can result in excessive water absorption by the paper and hampered drying of the ink off-press.

The enhanced absorption of the drier by the *substrate*, or a drier's chemical reaction with a *pigment* can deprive a particular chemical of its drying power, a problem called *drier dissipation*. On occasion, *antioxidants* and *antiskinning agents* are added to the ink to prevent excessive drying.

An ink drier (or other means of expediting the drying time of an ink) is also known as an *accelerator*.

Drier Dissipation

A loss in the effectiveness of a *drier*, a substance added to printing ink to speed up the rate at which *oxidation* and/or *polymerization* dry an ink. Drier dissipation is commonly caused by enhanced absorption of the drier into the *substrate* or by chemical reaction between the drying compound and a *pigment*. (See also *Drier*.)

Drift

The change in hardness, or *durometer*, of a rubber *screen printing* squeegee blade, due either to chemical deterioration or abrasive wear.

Drilling

In *binding and finishing*, the act of punching holes in press sheets, *signature*s, books, etc., to facilitate *mechanical binding*, commonly in *ring binder*s or *post binder*s. The specific punching of three holes for three-ring binders is known as *three-hole drilling*. Drilling is also known as *punching*. Drilling is often performed on special drilling devices or, when done on small quantities, on a common three-hole punch. When performed as a bindery operation, it is known as *bindery punching*.

Driography
An ill-fated early form of *waterless lithography* developed by 3M in the late 1960s. See *Waterless Lithography*.

Drip Through
A premature transfer of ink through a *screen printing* stencil either prior to a stroke or during press downtime.

Drive
Any computer component or peripheral in which a *hard disk* or other type of removable medium can be inserted or removed. Examples are *floppy disk* drives, *CD-ROM* drives, *optical disc* drives, and others.

Drive Letter
On a *personal computer*, a letter used to specify a disk drive. For example, the *hard disk* is usually designated "C" while the *floppy disk* drive is usually designated "A".

Driver
A computer software utility or program that operates a specific attached peripheral device or interface. The peripheral device, such as a printer, requires certain commands and signals in order for it to function; the driver (also called a *device driver*), typically supplied on a floppy disk or other media with the device, serves as an interface between the main computer or application (such as a word processing program) and the device itself, interpreting and processing the data from the application to the appropriate form for the proper operation of the device. Some computer operating systems include drivers for commonly used peripheral devices, such as laser printers.

Driving Side
The side of a *flexographic* printing press on which the gears are located, as opposed to the *operating side*. Also called the *gear side*.

Drop
In networking, one particular connection point or *node* on a communications medium.

Drop Cable
In a *local area network*, a cable connecting the *data terminal equipment* to the main network cable.

Drop Cap
Alternate term for a *sunken initial*. See *Sunken Initial*.

Drop Folio
In *book typography*, page number, or *folio*, that is printed at the bottom of a page. Also known as a *foot folio*. See *Folio*.

Drop-Frame Time Code
In video production, a *SMPTE* time code used in *NTSC* which drops frame numbers :00 and :01 every minute (except for every tenth minute). This is due to the fact that the effective speed of NTSC is 29.7 frames per second, while most counters measure video frame speed as 30 frames per second.

Drop-Head
In typography, a smaller, secondary headline set directly beneath a larger, primary headline. Also known as a *deck*.

Drop Initial
Alternate term for a *sunken initial*. See *Sunken Initial*.

Drop-Out
In telecommunications, any momentary interruption of a transmission, due to *noise* or any other disturbance of a signal.

The term *drop-out* also refers to any momentary loss of an audio or video signal, most often due to a physical defect of the tape (or other medium).

In computing, the term *drop-out* refers to any error in the reading of data from a magnetic storage medium.

The term *drop-out* is also spelled as one word, *dropout*.

Drop-Out Halftone
A *halftone* containing *specular highlight*, or *highlight*s which print with no dot. The term *drop-out halftone* also refers to any halftone photographed as *line art*; i.e., solely as black and white with no shades of gray.

Drop-Out Highlight
Alternate term for *specular highlight*. See *Specular Highlight*.

Drop-Out Type
Alternate term for *reverse type*. See *Reverse Type*.

Drum
A generic term for any printing press cylinder, such as a *plate cylinder*, *blanket cylinder*, *impression cylinder*, or *gravure cylinder*.

In *offset lithography*, an alternate term for an *oscillator* roller found in the *inking system* of an offset press. See *Oscillator*.

Drum Imagesetter
A type of *imagesetter*, a device used for *high-resolution* laser output of digitally created pages or *color separation*s. On a drum imagesetter, the digital file is converted to film format, and the film to be exposed is, in an *external drum imagesetter*, mounted on the surface of a drum or, in an *internal drum imagesetter*, mounted inside the drum. Digital information is used to guide the laser in the line-by-line exposure of the film. An alternate type of imagesetter is a *flatbed imagesetter*, in which the film is

An internal (top) and external (bottom) drum platesetters.

exposed by moving it with rollers past the imaging source. Of the two, drum imagesetters are widely believed to generate the better quality output. (See also ***Imagesetter***.)

Drum Machine

An electronic musical instrument that uses digital sampling technology to imitate the sound of a drum.

Drum Printer

Alternate term for ***cylinder printer***. See ***Cylinder Printer***.

Drum Scanner

A high-end optical ***scanning*** device used to convert an image to digital form for later manipulation and output as part of a page, as a color-separated image, or by itself.

In a drum scanner, the original image (usually a ***color transparency***) is attached to a transparent revolving drum—or cylinder—while a small point of light illuminates the image from within the drum, where this light is split, passed through ***red, green, and blue*** filters, and picked up by a ***photomultiplier tube***, which analyzes each row, ***pixel*** by pixel, storing the particular color or grayscale information for each pixel in a digital file. When one revolution is complete, the light source moves one pixel to the side, and images the next row, continuing this process until the entire picture is imaged. In the photomultiplier tube, the amounts of ***cyan***, ***magenta***, and ***yellow*** contained by the image are derived from the amounts of red, green, and blue light hitting it. The device stores the cyan, the magenta, and the yellow values for each pixel as one of 256 shades of gray. Alternatively, and more commonly, the device records the RGB signals for later conversion to CMYK. (The device also analyzes how much black makes up the image, based on the "heaviness" of the other three colors; if all three colors are heavy, then there is a significant amount of black present. If only two of the three colors are heavy, then it is likely that the colors are saturated, and there is thus little black involved.)

After scanning, the grayscale levels corresponding to each constituent color are "reassembled" either as one large digital file (if the image needs further manipulation) or as individual color-separated films.

Other types of scanners—such as desktop ***flatbed scanners***—utilize a ***charge-coupled device (CCD)*** rather than a photomultiplier tube. Although these devices are less expensive than high-end drum scanners, they tend to produce lower-quality scans.

Most high-end drum scanners are both digital and analog scanners; the original scan gleans analog data, which is later converted to digital information to be read by the computer. Strictly digital scanners obtain information in digital form at the outset. (See ***Scanner*** and ***Scanning***.)

Dryback

A decrease in the ***gloss*** of an ink during drying. The ultimate gloss of a printing ink is a function of the thickness of the ink, the ***ink absorbency*** of the paper, and the gloss of the paper. Dryback increases with increased penetration of the ink ***vehicle*** into the paper, which makes the ink dry faster than it should. Dryback can be avoided by ensuring that the paper's absorbency allows the proper amount of time for ink drying.

Dry Color

A printing ink ***pigment*** in powder form, or in the absence of water or other fluids.

Dry Dot Etching

A means of ***dot etching***, or altering the sizes of the ***halftone dots*** in a particular image or specific area of that image, commonly done to adjust the ***color*** gradations. Although dot etching can be performed in a variety of ways, dry dot etching specifically refers to the photographic over-exposure of positive or negative contact films made from the halftone separation films, a procedure which enlarges or reduces the dots as desired. (See also *Dot Etching*.)

Dry Dusting

A technique for determining the amount of surface debris a paper contains. Dry dusting consists of running a number of sheets of the paper to be tested (200, for instance) through a press containing a clean black *blanket*. A strip of cellophane tape is attached to the blanket and then pulled off (to remove the debris from that portion of the blanket covered by the tape). A *densitometer* is used to examine the dirty and clean areas of the blanket, and the difference in reflection density indicates the amount of debris generated by the paper.

Dry dusting examines superficial surface debris (see also *Pickout*), which consists of *lint*, *fines*, fiber, or coating particles generated during cutting and trimming, or general overhead dust. This material can result in various printing defects such as *hickeys* and *specks*.

Dryer

In *web offset lithography* (or other type of web printing), an oven through which the printed web passes. The dryer—operating at a temperature of up to 600°F, heats the web itself to a temperature of about 330°F. Most *blanket-to-blanket press*es require *floating dryer*s, as the web has ink on both sides. A dryer is needed when printing with *heatset ink*s which dry and set only with the application of heat. Most dryers are either *open-flame dryer*s or *high-velocity hot-air dryer*s. There are also combination open-flame, medium-velocity hot-air dryers. After drying, the web needs to pass through the cooled *chill rolls*.

Dry Finish

A type of paper *finish* produced by not steaming or dampening the formed paper before running it through the *calender* rollers.

Dry Imager

Alternate term for *toner*. See *Toner*.

Dry Indicator Method

A test used to measure the water resistance of paper, or the adequacy of its *sizing*, in particular, the time it takes for a liquid to completely penetrate the paper. A powder containing a water-sensitive dye is sprinkled on one side of a paper sample, and the reverse side of the sample is floated on water. The amount of time between the paper's initial contact with the water and the appearance of the pronounced color of the indicator dye is the time it takes water to penetrate the paper.

Drying-In

A problem of *gravure* printing characterized by the drying of ink within the cells of the *gravure cylinder*, causing a loss of color in light-tone areas of the printed image. The use of a slower-drying *solvent* or *vehicle* system can alleviate the problem.

In *screen printing*, the term *drying-in* is an alternate term for *clogging*. See *Clogging*.

Drying Oil

One of a variety of substances used in printing inks that harden by *oxidation* and *polymerization*, used in *drying oil vehicle*s. See *Drying Oil Vehicle*.

Drying Oil Vehicle

A type of ink *vehicle*—the fluid carrier of the ink *pigment*—that dries by *oxidation* (the absorption of and chemical reaction with oxygen) of the vehicle, rather than by *evaporation* or absorption into the *substrate*. Once an ink vehicle has absorbed oxygen, it hardens by a process called *polymerization*, or the combining of simple molecules to form a long, chain molecule called a *polymer*. *Linseed oil* is the drying oil most commonly used in inks, which must be boiled to impart the desired *viscosity* to the vehicle.

Other oils used for drying oil vehicles include castor oil, *tung oil*, cottonseed oil, fish oil, petroleum drying oils, rosin oil, soybean oil, and various types of synthetic oils. Synthetic *resin*s and other substances may be added to the vehicle to prevent absorption of the vehicle by the substrate, as *high-gloss ink*s require a high degree of *ink holdout* in order to dry with the desired level of gloss. Paper that has a low degree of *ink absorbency* is required for these types of inks. Drying oil vehicles are commonly used in *letterpress* and *offset lithographic* inks. (See *Vehicle*.)

Drying Section

A part of a papermaking machine, following the *press section*, in which steam-heated cast iron cylinders evaporate as much residual moisture from the paper *web* as possible. The paper web snakes through a series of cylinders (as many as thirty in some systems) which alternately expose the web's *wire side* and *felt side* to the heated cylinders, to ensure consistent drying on both sides of the paper. It is necessary to keep the paper web under tension to prevent distortion and shrinkage.

A paper's water content is about 60–70% before entering the drying section, and ranges from 2–8% at the end of the drying section, depending on its end-use requirements. In general, about two pounds of water are evaporated for every pound of paper produced.

Different desired paper characteristics can also vary the drying method used. (See *Yankee Dryer* and *Air Drying*.) *Surface sizing* is also performed in the drying section. (See *Size Press*.)

After drying, the paper web is sent to the next and final section of a traditional papermaking machine, the *calender*, which controls various surface characteristics of the paper.

Drying Stimulator

A substance, such as cobalt chloride or cobalt acetate, that is added to the *fountain solution* of an offset press to accelerate or enhance the drying capabilities of the ink. Drying stimulators commonly supplement *drier*s that have been added to the ink. (See *Drier*, *Fountain Solution*, and *Dampening System*.)

Drying Time

The length of time it takes for a printed ink film to solidify from a liquid state and become free from smudging or smearing, either by *evaporation*, *oxidation*, *precipitation*, or other drying methods. See also *Natural Drying Time*.

Dry Method

A means of producing a *carbon tissue* stencil for use in *screen printing* by drying the tissue after photosensitizing it, the exposure performed while the carbon tissue is dry. See also *Wet Method*.

Dry Mount

To attach a photograph (or other type of print) to a stiff background by means of a special adhesive and a heated press.

Dry Offset

Alternate term for *letterset* printing. See *Letterset*.

Dry Pick Resistance

The extent to which a paper will resist *picking* in the absence of moisture (as opposed to *wet pick resistance*, in which a paper's *pick resistance* is diminished by exposure to water). (See *Pick Resistance* and *Picking*.)

Dry Picking

Picking, or the rupturing of a paper's surface during printing, not caused by exposure to water (in contrast to *wet picking*). (See *Picking* and *Pick Resistance*.)

Drypoint Positive

A film positive used in making *photostencil*s for *screen printing* produced by scratching lines in the surface of a sheet of plastic and filling them in with ink.

Dry Trapping

In *process color* printing, the ability to successfully lay down a wet ink film on top of a previously printed, dry ink film. See *Trapping* (second definition).

Dry-Up

Alternate term for the press condition *catch-up*.

DS

In telecommunications, a *common carrier* digital transmission service, comprising several levels and speed of service: DS-0 (also known as fractional T1) features 64 *kilobit* per second service. DS-1, designated *T1*, features speeds of 1.544 *megabit*s per second. DS-1C *multiplex*es two DS-1

channels into one 3.152 megabit-per-second channel. DS-2 multiplexes two DS-1C channels into one 5.312 megabit-per-second channel (designated *T2*). DS-3 utilizes seven DS-2 channels multiplexed into one 44.726 megabit-per-second channel (designated *T3*). DS-4 features six DS-3 channels multiplexed into one 274.176 megabit-per-second channel (designated *T4*).

DSK

Abbreviation for *Dvorak Simplified Keyboard*. See *Dvorak Simplified Keyboard*.

DSP

Abbreviation for *document storage processor*. See *Document Storage Processor*.

    DSP is also an abbreviation for *digital signal processor*. See *Digital Signal Processor (DSP)*.

DSR

Abbreviation for *Data Set Ready*. See *data set ready*.

DSU

Abbreviation for *Data Service Unit*. See *data service unit*.

DTD

Abbreviation for *document type definition*. See *Document Type Definition (DTD)*.

DTE

Abbreviation for *data terminal equipment*. See *Data Terminal Equipment (DTE)*.

DTP

Abbreviation for *direct-to-plate*. See *Computer-to-Plate*.

    DTP is also an abbreviation for *desktop publishing*, a generic term referring to the layout and production of *camera-ready* (or plate-ready, as the case may be) page layouts on a *desktop computer*. See *Desktop Publishing*.

DTR

Abbreviation for *data terminal ready*. See *Data Terminal Ready (DTR)*.

DTV

Abbreviation for *desktop video*. See *Desktop Video*.

Dual-Attached Station (DAS)

In networking, a device used in a *fiber distributed data interface (FDDI)*. A DAS connects to both of the dual, counter-rotating rings in the interface, and provides fault tolerance for *concentrator*s, *bridge*s, and *router*s. See also *Single-Attached Station (SAS)*.

Dual Column

The ability of a typesetting system, word processing program, or *page layout program* to convert a single column of text to two side-by-side text columns.

Dual Homing

In an *FDDI* network, a means of cabling *concentrator*s in a tree-like topology so as to provide an alternate route for data transmission should the primary route fail.

Dual In-Line Package

See *DIP Switch*.

Dual-Roll Stand

Alternate term for a *double-roll stand*. See *Double-Roll Stand*.

Dual-Sided Diskette

A computer storage medium using both sides of a magnetic disk to store data. Also called a *double-sided diskette*.

Dub

To copy an audio- or videotape. An exact copy of the video and audio tracks of a videotape (i.e., with no editing) is known as a *window dub*.

The term *dub* also means to add an audio track to a video track. See *Audio Dubbing*.

Ductor Roller

A roller found in the *inking system* or *dampening system* of a press used in *offset lithography*.

In a press inking system, the ductor roller is the first roller in the *roller train*, and is the roller that alternately is in direct contact with the *fountain roller* and with the first *oscillator*. The ductor roller's rate of movement between the fountain roller and the oscillator can usually be adjusted, and is commonly timed to the revolution of the plate cylinder, either contacting the oscillator once for every revolution of the plate cylinder, or once every three or four revolutions.

Regardless of the rate at which the ductor roller moves, an effectively timed ductor roller only contacts the oscillator while the *form roller*s—the ink rollers that directly contact the printing plate—are over the *cylinder gap*, especially during the initial contact of the ductor and the oscillator, which sends a vibration through the press known as *ductor shock*. The length of time that the ductor roller is in contact with the fountain roller—known as *dwell*—can also be adjusted, and controls the quantity of ink that flows through the rest of the system. Dwell is also related to the rate at which the fountain roller turns; the faster it turns (or the greater the arc it turns through—or sweep—) the more surface area of the ductor roller that is covered with ink and, consequently, the more ink that flows ultimately to the plate. The ductor roller may also have the tendency to skid when making contact with the oscillator, which results in uneven ink flow through the system, and can be corrected by using a lighter-weight roller or a special braking device appended to the inking system. (Some *web press*es use a variation on the ductor roller called an *Aller undulating ductor roller*. See *Aller Undulating Ductor Roller*.)

The proper setting of the ductor roller is crucial. Ductor rollers can be set (or, in other words, the pressure between the ductor and the oscillator adjusted) using the *strip method* (which can be either the *three-strip method* or the *folded-strip method*), in which specially cut strips of paper, plastic, or *packing* material are inserted between the rollers, and pulled out, the extent of the drag experienced being a determination of not only the general pressure existing between the rollers, but also a gauge of the uniformity of the pressure between the rollers across their width. (See also *Inking System: Offset Lithography*, and *Offset Lithography*.)

In the dampening system of an offset lithographic press, the ductor roller has a similar function; it alternately contacts the *fountain pan roller* (located in the *water pan*) and an oscillator (in contact with the dampening form rollers). The amount of *fountain solution* that is ultimately transferred to the plate can be controlled by adjusting the amount of time the dampening ductor roller is in contact with the fountain pan roller.

The dampening ductor roller is made of a rubber compound and covered with a molleton fabric, which increases the amount of fountain solution it can hold. The proper setting of the dampening ductor roller is also very important to ensure uniform and adequate distribution of fountain solution. The setting of the ductor roller to the oscillator can be evaluated using the same strip methods indicated above. Dampening systems utilizing ductor rollers are called *intermittent-flow dampening system*s, in contrast to *continuous-flow dampening system*s, which do away with the alternating ductor roller. (See *Dampening System*.)

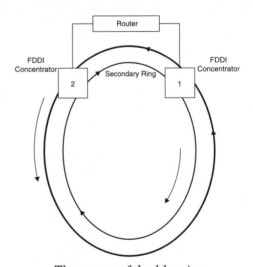

The process of dual homing.

Ductor Shock

A vibration or ripple sent through the *inking system* of an offset press when the *ductor roller*, alternately contacting the first *oscillator* (an ink roller) in the *roller train* and the ink *fountain roller*, first makes contact with the oscillator. Ductor shock does not have serious consequences for print quality as long as the *form roller*s are over the plate *cylinder gap* when the shock occurs. (See *Inking System: Offset Lithography* and *Offset Lithography*.)

Dull-Coated Finish

A paper *finish* characterized by a smooth surface and low *gloss*.

Dull Ink

A printing ink that dries with a low-*gloss*, or *matte*, finish, in contrast to *high-gloss ink*.

Dumb Terminal

In a network, a computer *terminal* that can only function when connected to a host computer, not by itself.

Dummy

A detailed sample page layout indicating the approximate position and style of the various page elements—text, line art, photos, etc.—used as a guide for the actual page makeup. A dummy can describe such a sample page at any level of completeness; it can refer to a simple *thumbnail* sketch drawn with a pencil, to a full-sized *rough* which indicates more detail, to a *comprehensive* which is highly detailed.

The term *dummy* also refers to a printed *signature* folded to check the page *imposition*. (See also *Imposition Layout*, *Folding Dummy*, and *Binding Dummy*.)

Dummy Folio

In *prepress*, a "fake folio"—or page number—added for position only or for effect, to be changed before the page is printed. Dummy folios often appear on table of contents pages prepared as samples or which appear in early proofs before the final pagination has been set.

Dump

In *hot-metal* composition, a table on which lead type may be assembled and corrected.

Duochrome

Alternate term for *duotone*, especially one created using two colored, non-black inks. See *Duotone*.

Duotone

A two-color *halftone* produced by overprinting two halftone screens made from the same photograph (usually a black-and-white photograph), as a means of generating a *monochromatic* image with a full range of tonal gradations.

In the creation of a duotone, two halftone plates are made, one for black, which picks up the *highlight* and *shadow* regions, and one for *middle tones*, either other shades of black, or another color.

When two non-black colors are used in the production of a duotone, it is often called a *duochrome*. Duotones are often made to increase detail in the black regions of an image, or as a special effect. Often, only one halftone is

printed, the second plate being a solid color, thus creating what is known as a *fake duotone*. See also *Tritone* and *Quadratone*.

Dupe

Any duplicate made of an original (when used as a noun), or to make such a duplicate (when used as a verb).

A duplicate *transparency* or slide made from an original as a means of altering size or making additional copies. Also known as a *second generation original*.

Duplex

In printing, the placement of images on both sides of a *substrate*.

The term *duplex* also refers to any substrate which possesses a different color or surface characteristic on each side, also referred to as *duplex paper*.

Duplex also refers to a *laser* (such as that used in a *laser printer*) that can image both sides of a sheet of paper at the same time.

In telecommunications, *duplex* refers to a system allowing an operator to simultaneously send and receive data, also referred to as *full duplex*, in contrast to *half duplex*, which describes a system whereby the user may send or receive data, but not at the same time. See also *Simplex* (second definition).

Duplex Bag

In packaging, a paper *bag* formed from two *ply*s or layers of paper. See *Bag: Paper Bags*.

Duplex Decal Paper

Alternate term for *duplex paper* when used for *decal*s. See *Duplex Paper*.

Duplex Fonts

In typesetting, two *font*s possessed by a typesetting device, each of which has identical *escapement* values for corresponding characters.

Duplex Paper

Any type of paper *stock* produced—typically via lamination—with a different color on each side.

In *screen printing*, *duplex paper* is a type of paper used for the printing of *decal*s in which a thin, water-absorbent tissue is laminated to a heavier stock. The decal design is commonly printed face down on the tissue side, and the decal is commonly affixed to its ultimate substrate by means of water or a varnish. Also known as *duplex decal paper* and *double paper*.

Duplicate Directory

In computers, a backup *directory* of the files stored on a particular disk.

Duplicate Transparency

A copy of a photographic *transparency*.

Duplicating Film

In graphic arts photography, a special film used to make duplicate copies of color transparencies.

Duplicator

A small printing press (typically capable of printing sheets no larger than 11×17-in.) used in **offset lithography** for quick, single-color, short-run print jobs. Duplicators are typically simpler, stripped-down versions of more advanced and automated offset presses. (See **Offset Lithography**.)

Duplicator Paper

A hard, smooth **bond paper** with controlled absorbency designed for use in **spirit duplicator**s. See **Bond Paper**.

Durability

A paper property that measures the extent to which a paper will retain its chemical, structural, and optical properties over time with continued handling (in contrast to **permanence**, which merely describes a paper's ability to retain its properties over time itself, neglecting the usage aspect). Papers do not necessarily have to be both permanent and durable. (See **Paper and Papermaking: Paper Properties**.)

The term *durability* also refers to the extent to which an offset press **blanket** will retain its thickness, dimensions, and structural integrity over the course of its lifetime, during which it is repeatedly subjected to the increased tension of press mounting and the high pressures of printing. (See **Blanket**.)

Durometer

A device (also called a **type-A durometer**) used to measure the hardness of the surface of an offset printing ink roller, offset **blanket**, or gravure **impression roller**, and the term for the roller or blanket's hardness itself. Durometer is measured on a scale of 0–100, where 0 is an extremely flexible surface, and 100 is an extremely inflexible surface, such as cast iron. A roller's surface (i.e., the compound—such as rubber—that comprises its surface) must maintain a certain degree of flexibility and resilience in order to effect proper ink transfer. However, the required hardness or softness depends on the specific type of ink roller (i.e., a **form roller**, **oscillator**, etc.); a form roller should have a more resilient surface (thus a lower durometer) than a **distributor**, for example. A roller's durometer increases with age, as exposure to such things as light, heat, solvents, and so on, cause chemical reactions in the surface compound, causing a progressive hardening and shrinking. *Glazing* is also a common cause of roller hardening. An increase of 10–15 durometer points is common over the course of a roller's lifetime, but increases beyond that cause a degradation of ink transfer and print quality. (See also **Type-A Durometer**, and **Impression Roller**.)

The flexibility of a **squeegee** blade used in **screen printing** is also measured in terms of durometer.

An example of a durometer.

Dust Cover

Alternate term for **jacket**. See **Jacket**.

Dusting

Alternate term for **powdering** (**piling**.) See **Powdering**.

Duty Cycle

In computing, term used to refer to the durability of a computer printer, measured as the number of pages per month the manufacturer recommends printing.

DVA

Abbreviation for **distance vector algorithm**. See **Distance Vector Algorithm (DVA)**.

DVE

Abbreviation for **digital video effects**. See **digital video effects**.

DVI

Abbreviation for **Digital Video Interactive**. See **Digital Video Interactive (DVI)**.

Dvi File

Abbreviated term for a **device-independent** file. See **Device-Independent**.

Dwell

The length of time the **ductor roller** is in contact with the ink **fountain roller**. On a printing press used in **offset lithography**, the fountain roller is that roller in direct contact with the **ink fountain**, or the trough containing the ink. The ductor roller alternates between contacting the fountain roller (and picking up a quantity of ink from it) and contacting an **oscillator** roller that is in direct contact with the rest of the inking system, terminating at the plate itself. Adjusting dwell is one of several ways of controlling how much ink ultimately flows to the plate. (See *Inking System: Offset Lithography* and *Offset Lithography*.)

Dwell also refers to any time interval in which two surfaces, substances, or objects are in contact with each other.

DX4

In computing, a 32-bit *microprocessor* developed by Intel and based on its 80486 chip. The DX4 is available in clock speeds of 75, 83, and 100 *megahertz*.

DXF

Abbreviation and *file extension* for *Data Exchange Format*, a *file format* developed by AutoCAD for the import and export of 2D and 3D *CAD* images. Also referred to as *Document Exchange Format*.

Dycril Plate

A relief plate used in *letterset* printing. See *Letterset*.

Dye

A coloring material used in printing inks, distinguished from a *pigment* by its vehicle-solubility, which *pigment*s lack. Dyes, though more commonly used in the coloring of textiles, are frequently used in inks to impart a set of desired optical properties—such as transparency, purity, and color strength—not achievable with pigments. Dyes are most commonly used in liquid inks (such as those used in *gravure* and *flexography*), but special formulations allow some dyestuffs to be added to paste inks used in *lithography* and *screen process* printing. However, the classification of a dye often overlaps with some pigments. Dyes are frequently used as *toner*s. Some common dyes include *Eosine*, *Methyl Violet*, *Victoria Blue*, *Rhodamine B*, and many others. (See also *Pigment*.)

Historically, most dyes were obtained from natural sources, notably the woad plant (*Isatis tinctoria*), a source of blue dye; the indigo plant (*Indigofera tinctoria*), a source of indigo dye; and some species of madderwort (several species of the genus *Rubia*, most notably *R. tinctorum*), a source of a deep red dye (also called madder). Many dyes were also obtained from animals, such as mollusks and insects. However, it took 20,000 mollusks to dye one square yard of fabric, so dyed materials were rare and expensive.

The first synthetic colorants were developed in the eighteenth and nineteenth centuries, most notably *Prussian Blue*, the first important synthetic pigment, invented in 1704. The first important synthetic dye, *aniline dye*, was created by accident in 1856 by William Perkin, who was actually trying synthesize quinine. (See *Aniline Dye*.)

Dye Emulsion

A type of *screen printing* emulsion ink used for printing on textiles. The colorant is a *dye* rather than a *pigment*.

Dye Ink

A type of *screen printing* ink used in printing textiles, consisting of *dye*s (rather than *pigment*s) dispersed in a vehicle of inert thickening agents. Also known as a *dye paste*.

Dye Migration

In the *screen printing* of textiles, the transfer of a *dye* from the cloth to another ink that has been printed on top if it, commonly caused by the addition of heat.

Dye Paste

Alternate term for a *dye ink*. See *Dye Ink*.

Dye Sublimation Printer

A device used to produce digital *color proof*s that utilizes a *sublimable dye* imprinted on a carrier sheet to transfer images to a receiving sheet by placing them in direct contact with each other. See also *Heat-Transfer Printing*.

Dye Transfer Print

A full-color photographic print made by color separating the image into three *colors—cyan*, *magenta*, and *yellow*—and using those separations to make gelatin-based matrices (one color per matrix), which are then used to transfer dye solution to gelatin-coated recieving paper.

Dylux

Alternate term for *blueline*, specifically when using Dylux paper. See *Blueline*.

Dynamic

In computing, any operation performed "on the fly," or while the program that called the operation is running.

Dynamic Balance

Quality of a page layout that is not truly *symmetric*, but appears to be visually balanced. See also *Formal Balance*.

Dynamic Data Exchange (DDE)

A communication *protocol* used in Microsoft *Windows* and IBM *OS/2* operating system environments to transfer data and commands back and forth between applications. In Windows, DDE is supplemented by *object linking and embedding (OLE)*, while in OS/2 it is supplemented by *OpenDoc*.

Dynamic Focusing

A technique used in computer monitors to ensure that the *pixel*s at the edge of the display are round, preventing image distortion.

Dynamic Host Configuration Protocol (DHCP)

In networking, a protocol used to configure network setups, including such things as *IP* addresses. See *TCP/IP*.

Dynamic Link Library (DLL)

In computing, a module containing a set of routines and code that can be utilized as a common resource by other applications. A DLL is linked to an application when the application is launched, and is unloaded when no longer required.

DLL files are often used in **Windows** and **OS/2** applications. An advantage is that using a single DLL file to house often-called routines helps preserve disk space and keep down the size of .EXE files, as a particular routine need not be repeated in each .EXE file.

Dynamic RAM (DRAM)

In computing, a type of **random-access memory (RAM)** which is constantly refreshed (by means of electrical regeneration), even when no data is being read from or written to it. DRAM is often used when memory access is expected to be frequent. See also **Static RAM (SRAM)**.

Dynamic Range

Alternate term for **density range**. See **Density Range**.

The term *dynamic range* is also used to refer to the measure of the sensitivity of any optical device. See **Scanning**.

Dynamic Routing

In networking, especially when data communications is effected by means of **packet switching**, a system feature that allows the network to find a clear route between sender and receiver, and to seek an **alternate route** when a primary route is disabled or busy.

Dynamic Tension

In **screen printing**, the measure of the tension of the screen fabric increased by the force of the **squeegee**.

DYUV

Abbreviation for **Delta-YUV**. See **Delta-YUV**.

E

E, e
The fifth letter of the Latin and English alphabets, derived from the North Semitic *he*, a consonant somewhat reminiscent of the modern letter *h*. The form of the uppercase *E* derives from the Greek letter *eta*, which became a vowel, although the North Semitic *he* (resembling the modern *h)* was used in some places to represent the long *e* sound. It was eventually adopted by the Romans. The lowercase *e* derives from the *uncial* version of uppercase *E*.

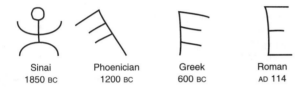

Sinai	Phoenician	Greek	Roman
1850 BC	1200 BC	600 BC	AD 114

The evolution of the letter E.

E
Abbreviation for the prefix *exa-*. See *Exa-*.

Ear
In typography, a short stroke extending off the *stem*, *bowl*, or other portion of a letter or other character, such as the small protuberance from the bowl of a lowercase *g*. See *Letter Elements*.

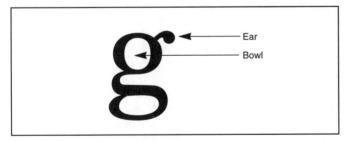

An ear, a short stroke extending off the bowl of the letter "g."

Earth Colors
A rarely used class of *inorganic color pigment*s including sienna, umber, and ochre, which are dull in color and are occasionally used in special applications.

Earth Station
An earth-based parabolic antenna or satellite dish, and the associated electronic equipment used for sending and receiving transmissions to and from orbiting satellites.

EBCDIC
Abbreviation for *Extended Binary Coded Decimal Interchange Code*, pronounced "eb-se-dik." EBCDIC is an eight-bit *character set* used primarily in IBM *mainframe*s. Like *ASCII*, a set of numeric codes are used to present letters, numerals, and *control character*s. Unlike ASCII, however, EBCDIC has a discontinuous placement of letters. There is also no direct character-to-character correspondence when converting from EBCDIC to ASCII (and vice versa).

EB-Curing Ink
See *Electron-Beam-Curing (EB-Curing) Ink*.

EBU
Abbreviation for *European Broadcast Union*. See *European Broadcast Union (EBU)*.

ECC
Alternate term for *error correcting code*. See *Error Correcting Code*.

Echo
In telecommunications, a signal that is reflected back to the sender with an intensity strong enough to be distinguished from the original signal. Echo is often heard as a type of interference when making long-distance telephone calls.

In networking, the term *echo* is a mechanism used to test network *node*s. Essentially, a message sent from a host or server is echoed back from each receiving station. Also known as an *echo check*.

In telecommunications, the term *echo* also refers to a function of a communications program that repeats characters typed by the sender to the sender's terminal, allowing the sender to see what he or she is typing.

ECHO
Abbreviation for *European Community Host Organization*. See *European Community Host Organization*.

Echo Cancellation
In telecommunications, a means of removing unwanted interference (or *echo*) on long-distance transmissions by which a *modem* (a device known as an *echo suppressor*) "listens" for a delayed replication of an original signal, then adds a reversed version of the transmission to the channel containing it. In this way, the crests of the duplicated waveform correspond to troughs on the reversed signal (and vice versa), effectively cancelling out the echoed signal.

Echo Check
In networking, a means of testing network *node*s in which a message transmitted from a *host* or *server* is repeated back from each receiving station to ensure that the message was received properly. See *Echo* (second definition).

Echoplex

In telecommunications, an *echo* of a user's keystrokes when connected to another system, especially that using *full-duplex* transmission to ensure that typed data was received by the remote system correctly.

Echo Suppressor

A mechanism used for *echo cancellation*. See *Echo Cancellation*.

ECU

Abbreviation for *extreme close-up*. See *Extreme Close-Up*.

EDC

Alternate term for *error detecting code*. See *Error Detecting Code*.

EDG

Abbreviation for *electronic dot generation*. See *Electronic Dot Generation*.

Edge Acutance

A measure of the sharpness of a screen-printed image, dependent upon the quality of the *stencil*, the tension of the screen fabric, the consistency and formulation of the ink, and other such factors.

Edge Bleed

An unwanted coloration of the edge of a sheet caused by a cutting machine.

Edge Detection

In computer image-manipulation programs, a means of locating the boundary of an image and defining a region of the screen (or image) by this perimeter.

Edge Enhancement

In *scanning*, a means of increasing the sharpness of the edge of a reproduced or scanned image by increasing the *contrast* between the light and dark sides of the point where two colors meet. One common means of edge enhancement is known as *unsharp masking*. See *Unsharp Masking*.

Edge Gilding

In *binding and finishing*, a type of *edge treatment* that involves coating the trimmed edges of book pages with *gold leaf*. Also known simply as *gilding*. Gilding all three unbound edges is known as *full gilding*.

Edge Staining

In *binding and finishing*, a type of *edge treatment* involving application of a dye or other colorant to the trimmed edges of a book. Edge staining may be performed on all three unbound edges, only on the side edge, or only on the top edge. In the latter case, the process is known as *top staining*. Edge stains added in an irregular or spatter pattern are known as *sprinkled edges*.

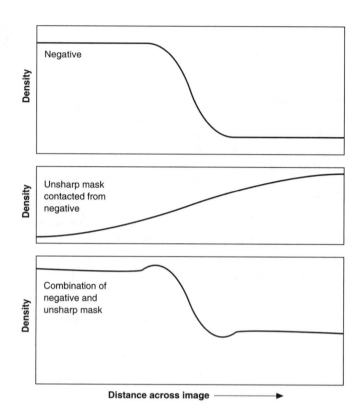

Edge enhancement.

Edge Tear

A paper *web* defect, also called a *cracked edge*. See *Cracked Edge*.

Edge Tearing Resistance

A paper property that measures a paper's ability to withstand being torn when the tear is started at the edge of the paper. See *Tearing Resistance*.

Edge Treatment

In *binding and finishing*, any of a variety of decorations applied to the trimmed edges of a book. Common edge treatments include *edge staining* (the application of a colorant) and *gilding* (the application of gold leaf).

EDI

Abbreviation for *electronic data interchange*. See *Electronic Data Interchange (EDI)*.

Editability

A term used to refer to the ability to open or reopen any computer data file and alter its content, using ordinary software. A *PostScript* output file is not considered to be editable, as there are not many programs or applications capable of manipulating the PostScript code.

Edit Decision List (EDL)

In video production, a handwritten or electronic log of the edits to be made in a videotape, usually including *time code*s corresponding to start and end points. The EDL can be used as a guide in manual tape editing or can be used to auto-assemble a master tape by an electronic *edit controller*.

Editing

Modification of any data, either in print or electronically. In book, magazine, and newspaper publishing, editing involves correction—for content, spelling, grammar, etc.—and *copyfitting* of a manuscript or article. In graphics and imaging, editing refers to changing specific aspects of an image, such as cropping, color correction, etc. In audio, film, and video production, editing involves assembling raw footage or clips into a tight, cohesive production. In this latter sense, editing also involves adding *video effects* and *transition*s between scenes and shots.

Editing Terminal

In computerized typesetting, a video display and attached keyboard through which a user interacts with the computer, most commonly to make changes to already entered data.

Edit In/Out Points

In video editing, the frames chosen to begin and conclude an edit, respectively.

Edition

The version of a publication, which might include the number of copies published at one time, the time or day that it is published, a special issue for a specific day or purpose, such as a Sunday or an international edition, or one of the issues of a newspaper in a single day, such as a city, late, or a bulldog edition. Other editions are:
• *Trade or mass-market edition,* a book planned for general distribution
• *Text or el-hi or academic edition,* a book prepared for use in schools and colleges
• *Paper or pocket edition,* a paperback and/or smaller version
• *Limited edition,* a collectible book advertised to be limited to a small number of copies
• *First edition,* copies of a work first printed

Edition Binding

In *binding and finishing*, any commercial *casebound* book manufactured as part of a large-scale, automated production line, as opposed to a *job binding* or *library binding*, each of which may involve some degree of handwork.

Editor

An individual responsible for *editing*, either in the publishing or video sense. See *Editing*.

An *editor* is also a term for any software utility or feature within another application that allows rudimentary text entry and editing, but without the extensive formatting capability of a full-fledged word processor. A program used for telecommunications, for example, will have an editor in which the user can type messages for transmission. In this sense, an editor is also known as a *text editor*.

Editorial Change

The graphics and color printing equivalent of *author's alterations*, or changes requested by a customer to certain aspects of an image during *color separation*. See also *Author's Alteration*.

Editorial System

In *electronic publishing*, a dedicated system designed and used specifically for copy creation, *editing*, and manuscript preparation.

Edits More Than One File On-Screen

In some word processing programs, the ability to open additional *window*s while a document is open. Material can be cut-and-pasted from another file in a different window.

Edit Source

In video editing, any video source generating a signal to be recorded in an editing session.

EDL

Abbreviation for *edit decision list*. See *Edit Decision List (EDL)*.

EDP

Abbreviation for *electronic data processing*. See *Electronic Data Processing (EDP)*.

EDTV

Abbreviation for *enhanced-definition television*. See *Enhanced-Definition Television (EDTV)*.

Edutainment

Alternate term for *infotainment*, used especially in the classification of *CD-ROM*s and other multimedia productions. See *Infotainment*.

EEMS

Abbreviation for *Enhanced Expanded Memory Specification*. See *Enhanced Expanded Memory Specification (EEMS)*.

EEPROM

A type of *erasable read-only memory*, especially one that is erased by means of an electrical current. See *Erasable Read-Only Memory (EROM)*.

Effective Address

Alternate term for *absolute address*. See *Absolute Address*.

Efflorescence

A property of certain solids in an aqueous solution that describes their ability to dehydrate when exposed to the atmosphere, and remain behind as a powder or other form of crystalline solid, as opposed to other solids in solution that evaporate along with the water. See also *Deliquescence*.

Efflux Cup

One of several configurations of cup designed to measure the *viscosity* of a fluid, in particular, a printing ink. Essentially, an efflux cup is a container with a hole at the bottom. The cup is lowered into the ink to be measured, then lifted out. When the hole is above the surface of the ink reservoir, a stopwatch is started, and the time it takes a fixed quantity to flow out of the hole can be measured. Efflux cups come in a variety of shapes and sizes, such as a Ford Cup, a Zahn Cup, a Shell Cup, and a GRI Hiccup. Each configuration of cup comes with a set of different hole sizes, suitable for inks with a range of viscosities. For example, a thicker, more viscous ink requires a larger hole than a thinner, less viscous ink. Several different readings should be taken for the same ink and averaged, as long as each reading is within ±0.5 second of each other. The measurement of an ink's viscosity is an important factor in many printing processes, in particular *gravure* and *flexographic* printing. (See also *Viscosity*.)

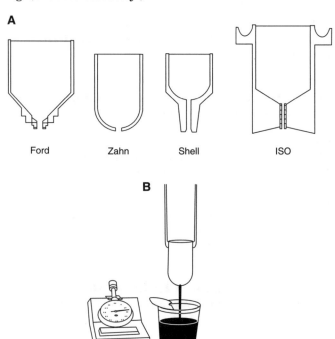

A

Ford   Zahn   Shell   ISO

B

Several types of efflux cups used to measure ink viscosity, as viewed in cross-section (A), and an efflux cup in action (B).

EfiColor

A *color management system*—a set of computer programs or utilities that ensures consistent color throughout the prepress processes by calibrating the color relationships among the scanners, monitors, printers, imagesetters, and other devices in the chain from input to output—developed by Electronics For Imaging (EFI). The EfiColor system uses device profiles to convert from *color space* to color space, allowing users to manually or automatically remap or adjust colors that cannot be accurately matched. Although originally available only as part of spe-

cific applications (such as *QuarkXPress* and Photoshop), an all-purpose CMS called EfiColor Works can be used to ensure complete input-to-output color management. An integral part of EfiColor Works is a System Profile, which allows device-by-device customization of any element in the system according to such aspects as *gamma*, *screen angles*, *dot area density*, *dot shape*, *screen ruling*, *gray component replacement*, or a variety of other image attributes. (See *Color Management System [CMS]*.)

EFP

Abbreviation for *electronic field production*. See *Electronic Field Production (EFP)*.

EGA

Abbreviation for *Extended Graphics Adapter*. See *Extended Graphics Adapter*.

EGA/CGA Monitor

A computer display capable of alternating between two modes of display, *CGA* and the later *EGA*. See *Color Graphics Adapter (CGA)* and *Enhanced Graphics Adapter (EGA)*.

Eggshell Antique

A type of paper characterized by a rough *finish* not unlike the texture of an eggshell.

EGP

Abbreviation for *External Gateway Protocol*. See *External Gateway Protocol (EGP)*.

Egyptian

A *typeface* characterized by heavy, square *serif*s. Also called *slab serif* and *square serif*.

Lubalin Graph
Glypha

Two examples of typefaces that are classified as Egyptian.

EIA

Abbreviation for *Electronic Industries Association*. See *Electronic Industries Association (EIA)*.

EIA SYNC

A standard signal designed for the *synchronization* of image scanning, developed by the *Electronic Industries Association (EIA)*.

EIA/TIA 586

A standard for telecommunications wiring developed jointly by the *Electronic Industries Association (EIA) and the* Telecommunications Industries Association(TIA). The 586 standard defines the wiring system for commercial buildings, as well as media types, connections, terminations, and a basis for the compatibility of competing products and services. The 586 standard applies to all *unshielded twisted pair* cabling systems, such as *Ethernet*, *Token Ring*, *ISDN*, etc.

Eight-Bit (8-Bit) Color
On a computer monitor, a color display in which each *pixel* (or smallest point of *color*) is described by 8 bits of information. (One *bit* is either a 1 or a 0; 8-bit color can be thought of as one of these two numbers taken to the eighth power; thus $2^8 = 256$ possible colors.) The color of a pixel on a computer display is commonly expressed as some amount of *red, green, and blue*. Greater numbers of combinations of these amounts require more processing power on the part of the computer. At 8 bits per pixel, a total of 256 colors can be described and displayed. (Some programs allow you to specify which colors can be included in that palette.) The 8-bit, 256-color monitor is also known as *VGA* (*Video Graphics Array*), and is a default setup for many monitors. Although this color depth is the standard and/or required setting for many CD-ROMs and multimedia programs, it is insufficient for high-quality graphic arts reproduction. See also *Sixteen-Bit Color*, *Twenty-Four-Bit Color*, and *Thirty-Two-Bit Color*. Computer monitors can also display *one-bit color* (black and white, or any two colors) and *four-bit color* (16 colors).

Eight Millimeter (8 mm)
In videography, a popular videotape size for amateur recording (usually by means of a *camcorder*). Tapes are 8 mm wide, and cassettes are about the same size as an audiocassette.

EIP
Abbreviation for *electronic integrated processes* for print, a term coined by Dunn Technology to describe the interconnection of all electronic prepress units—from page layout to film output to platemaking—as a means of eliminating the need to re-input images or other data.

EISA
Abbreviation for *Enhanced Industry Standard Architecture*. See *Enhanced Industry Standard Architecture (EISA)*.

Elastic Elongation
The maximum length a material—such as a paper or other *substrate*—can be stretched without breaking, expressed as a percentage of the material's original length. See also *Tensile Strength*.

Elasticity
The extent to which a material—such as a paper or other *substrate*—will return to its original dimensions after being stretched.

Elasticity Reserve
An extraneous amount of resilience in a taut screen fabric used in *screen printing* to compensate for any curvature of the *substrate*.

Elastomer
Any elastic substance, produced either naturally (such as natural rubber) or synthetically (such as *Buna N* synthetic rubber). Elastomers are often used for offset press *blanket*s and a variety of printing press *inking system* and *dampening system* rollers.

Elastomeric
Having the properties of an *elastomer*—flexible, elastic and resilient.

Electrodeposition
Alternate term for *electroplating*. See *Electroplating*.

Electroformed Printing Screen
A screen used in *screen printing* produced by electroplating a developed, photosensitive metal sheet and attaching it to the screen fabric.

Electroluminescent Display
A type of enhanced *liquid crystal display (LCD)* monitor that generates its own source of illumination. See *Liquid Crystal Display(LCD)*.

Electrolysis
An electrochemical process that consists of passing an electric current through an ionized, charged solution (called an *electrolyte*), causing negative ions in the solution to collect at an *anode* and positive ions to gather at a *cathode*. The process of electrolysis is used in the copper- and chrome-plating of cylinders that are used in *gravure* printing, and for *anilox rollers* that are used in *flexography*. (See *Electroplating*.)

Electrolyte
A solution containing electrically charged particles (or ions) used as a medium in the processes of *electrolysis* and *electroplating* copper and chrome to a *gravure* cylinder or flexographic *anilox roller*. See *Electroplating*.

Electromagnetic Interference
In electronics, any electromagnetic radiation that is emitted by an electrical or electronic device that interferes with the proper operation or performance of another electrical or electronic device. Electromagnetic interference, often abbreviated *EMI*, is produced by any number of electronic devices that are found in offices, ranging from computers and photocopiers to fluorescent lighting. The *Federal Communications Commission (FCC)* has regulations and certifications that limits the extent of EMI a device (designed for commercial use) can emit. Also known as *radio-frequency interference*.

Electromagnetic Spectrum

A continuum comprising all of the various sources of electromagnetic radiation. Essentially, radio waves, microwaves, heat, visible light, ultraviolet light, X-rays, gamma rays, cosmic rays, etc., are all versions of the same phenomenon: energy radiated through space. (This is why sound waves are not typically considered part of the electromagnetic spectrum, since sound requires a medium—such as air or water—through which to propagate, whereas electromagnetic waves have little difficulty in radiating through the vacuum of space.)

This radiated energy is in the form of waves (light, however, creates some difficulty, since in some cases it tends to behave like discrete particles—or quanta—rather than waves, but color theory and many other sciences dealing with light require that it be considered a wave). All the various forms of this radiated energy differ in terms of wavelength and frequency, both of which are mathematically related to each other.

The variations in wavelength are what produce the different perceived effects of various types of radiation. The longest (and believed by some to be the most benign) wavelengths belong to radio waves, while the shortest and most damaging wavelengths belong to the gamma rays and cosmic rays. Electromagnetic waves, regardless of their wavelength or frequency, all generally have the same source: accelerating electric charges, which can either consist of tiny yet powerful electron jumps between energy states within atoms (which generate visible light, ultraviolet light, X-rays, and gamma rays), or by "extra-atomic" electron conduction, as in an electric circuit (which produce radio waves).

The wavelengths that are covered by the electromagnetic spectrum range from 0.00003 *Ångstrom*s (Å) (or 0.000000000000003 m) for cosmic rays, to 300 m for radio waves. (See also *Visible Spectrum* and COLOR PLATE 3.)

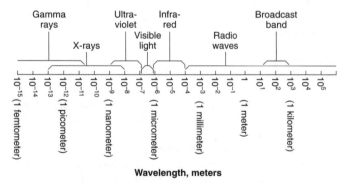

The common subdivisions of the electromagnetic spectrum and their respective wavelengths.

Electromechanical Engraving

A means of *gravure engraving*, or transferring an image to the surface of the image-carrying *gravure cylinder*. See *Gravure Engraving: Electromechanical Engraving*.

Electromechanical engraving techniques (comprising a diamond engraving stylus that etches a predetermined pat-

tern in a metal-plated cylinder or roller) are also used in the etching of cells in the surface of a *flexographic* press's *anilox roller*. See *Anilox Roller*.

Electron Beam

A concentrated beam of electrons, used in *cathode-ray tube*s and as a drying mechanism for *electron beam curing ink*.

Electron-Beam-Curing (EB-Curing) Ink

A type of *photoreactive vehicle* ink that dries, or sets, with the application of a beam of electrons, in a manner similar to that of *ultraviolet-curing ink*. The EB-curing ink *vehicle* is composed of fluid *oligomer*s and *monomer*s that, when exposed to a beam of high-energy electrons, release *free radical*s that cause the *polymerization* of the vehicle, which hardens to a dry ink film containing the *pigment*. EB- and UV-curing inks are designed to replace *heatset ink*s whose *solvent*s emit potentially toxic and environmentally unsound gaseous emissions.

The expense of UV-curing inks is obviated by EB-curing inks, as the reactive materials used in UV inks are very expensive; EB-curing inks can utilize less-expensive and less-reactive materials, and do not require costly initiators. The real expense involved in EB-curing inks is the cost of equipping a press to utilize them. There is also a danger of EB-curing equipment producing X-rays.

The equipment for electron-beam curing is either a scanned beam generator (electrons are produced from a cathode and shot at a positively charged screen, which uses a magnetic lens to focus them to a thin beam), or a linear cathode beam generator (producing electrons from a cathode but not focusing them into a beam, merely allowing them to bombard the wet ink in a shower. The latter type is the more popular, as it is smaller and more effectively shielded against X-ray leakage. (See *Photoreactive Vehicle*.)

Electron Gun

In a *cathode-ray tube*, an electrostatic device used to shoot and focus a beam of electrons (or a *cathode ray*) on the back of a phosphor-coated screen. The action of the

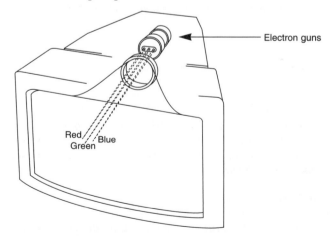

The three electron guns of an RGB monitor.

electron beam causes the phosphors to glow, producing an image. In an *RGB monitor* or color television, there are three electron guns, one for the red, one for the green, and one for the blue components of an image.

Electronic Camera

A type of camera that captures images electronically on magnetic media rather than on film. Although an electronic camera captures images using *analog data*, this type of camera is capable of storing the images as either analog or *digital data*, information that can later be displayed on a computer monitor. (See also *Digital Camera* and *Digital Photography*.)

Electronic Composition

General term for the setting of type using a computer. See *Desktop Publishing*.

Electronic Data Interchange (EDI)

In telecommunications, a standard for transmission of business forms and other documents. Used commonly for electronic transmission of invoices, order confirmations, etc., the electronic documents are translated into a predetermined format prior to transmission.

Electronic Data Processing (EDP)

See *Data Processing (DP)*.

Electronic Dot Generation (EDG)

The digital production of *halftone dot*s on paper or film in *raster* format, rather than through the use of a screen. Electronic dot generation is performed by multiple exposure of the paper or film to a *laser* (or other light source) through fiber optic media.

Electronic Editing

Any means of *editing* a videotape without physically altering (by cutting or splicing) the tape.

Electronic Field Production (EFP)

General term for taping video productions on location (rather than in a studio), using portable equipment (such as a *camcorder*) and often including multi-camera setups. See also *Electronic News Gathering (ENG)*.

Electronic Gray Scale

A strip of paper or film that contains a range of gray densities or *halftone dot*s originally produced from a *scanner*'s calibration software and that is used to calibrate a scanner's output.

Electronic Industries Association (EIA)

A U.S.-based organization similar to Europe's *CCITT* that defines standards for data communications. The standards developed by the two organizations are virtually identical. See *Comité Consultatif International Téléphonique et Télégraphique (CCITT)*.

Electronic Keyboard

A keyboard attached to a computer or other electronic device that generates characters through electronic means (i.e., on a computer screen) rather than directly on a *substrate* as a typewriter does.

Electronic Mail

See *Email*.

Electronic Pasteup

General term for the design, layout, and composition of pages on a computer (or other electronic system), rather than by manual *pasteup*. See *Desktop Publishing* and *Page Makeup Software*.

Electronic Printer

Alternate term for a printer that images paper by means of *electrophotography*. See *Electrophotography*.

Electronic Publishing

A broad term that describes any means of designing, laying out, composing, assembling, and outputting pages using electronic means, such as computers and electronic printing systems. *Desktop publishing* is one particular category of electronic publishing system, referring to the assembly of pages on a personal desktop computer operating on a standard platform using off-the-shelf software. Electronic publishing also refers to high-end electronic publishing systems and mid-range systems. (See illustration on next page.)

Electronic Publishing System

Any collection of hardware devices and software applications that assist in the digital design, typography, and production of pages. See *Electronic Publishing*.

Electronic Still Photography

The capture of images utilizing either an *electronic camera* or a *digital camera*, or photography where the image is at some point in electronic form. See also *Digital Photography*, *Electronic Camera* and *Digital Camera*.

Electronic Typewriter

A device that attempts to bridge the gap between the typewriter and the word processor. An electronic typewriter is microprocessor-based and allows electronic display of typed material (usually up to a line) prior to actual printout. Additional memory storage and enhanced demi–word processing features are also included on many models.

Electronic Viewfinder

A small, usually black-and-white *cathode-ray tube* or *liquid crystal display* built into a video camera, used to see what the camera is seeing prior to taping a scene.

Electrophotographic Plate

A type of printing plate used in *offset lithography* that is produced utilizing the process of *electrophotography*, or

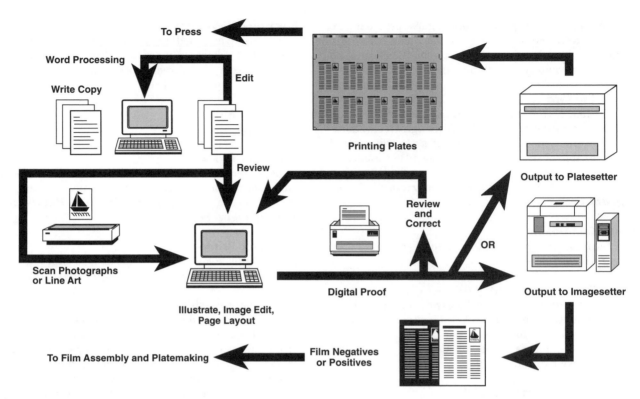

An example of the workflow in electronic publishing.

electrostatic printing commonly found in photocopiers and laser printers.

There are two means of exposing electrophotographic plates. The first utilizes an inorganic photoconductor, typically selenium or cadmium sulfide, applied to the surface of a drum. A corona sensitizes the drum to light using an electrostatic charge. Light reflected by nonimage areas of the original dissipates the charge from the nonimage portions of the drum, the charge remaining in the image portions. A dry or liquid **toner**, oppositely charged, is attracted to the charged (image) portions of the drum and adheres to it, transferring then to the paper (or other **substrate**) passing beneath the drum. Plates produced in this fashion require special treatment and are used typically for only very short runs or in **reprography**.

A second variety of electrophotographic plate utilizes the same principle outlined above, except that the photoconductor (organic in this case) is applied directly to the surface of the desired substrate rather than a drum. The toner is either fused directly to the surface of the photoconductor, or is transferred to another substrate. Plates produced in this fashion for high-speed laser imaging have a base of anodized aluminum, and the photoconductive coating must be removed from nonimage areas prior to printing. Nonprinting areas need to be sensitized using **gum arabic** and **fountain etch** to impart the desired level of water-receptivity. This chemical treatment, however, tends to damage halftone dots, making these plates not ideally suited for fine screen work. (See **Plate: Offset Lithography**.)

Electrophotography

A type of imaging system, commonly used in photocopiers, laser printers, etc., that utilizes an inorganic photoconductor—such as zinc oxide in electrofax, or selenium in xerography—applied to the surface of a drum. A corona sensitizes the drum to light using an electrostatic charge. Light reflected by nonimage areas of the original image dissipates the charge from the nonimage portions of the drum, the charge remaining in the image portions. A dry or liquid

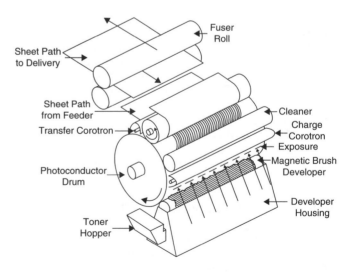

The principle of electrophotography.

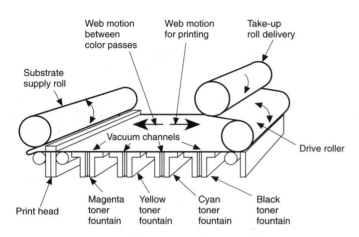

A multicolor, webfed electrophotographic process.

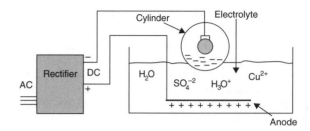

The principle of electroplating. The gravure cylinder base is given a negative charge and thus acts as a cathode. A copper anode is given a positive charge. Copper ions are thus forced into the solution, where—being positively charged—they bond with the negatively charged cylinder.

toner, which is oppositely charged, is attracted to the charged (image) portions of the drum and adheres to it, transferring to paper (or other **substrate**) passing beneath the drum.

Electroplating

A means by which an ionized metal is transported through an **electrolyte** and non-ionized metal is fused to another substance. The process of passing an electric current through an electrolyte (or a solution containing negatively and/or positively charged ions) is called **electrolysis**. An electric current is passed through an electrolyte, resulting in negatively charged ions migrating to the positive electrode (or the **anode**) and positively charged ions migrating to the negative electrode (or **cathode**). Electroplating typically involves utilizing the metal to be plated as the anode, and the surface to which it is to be plated as the cathode.

In **gravure** printing, electroplating is the means by which a **gravure cylinder** is first coated with a layer of copper (which will be engraved with the cells transferring the image; see **Gravure Engraving**) and then by a thin protective layer of chrome. In a basic plating tank, the steel gravure cylinder acts as the cathode, and is attached to a rectifier that generates DC current and allows the cylinder to supply electrons. At the bottom of the tank is a thin, positively charged anode, also attached to the rectifier, which imparts to it a positive charge by removing electrons. Charges can only be imparted to substances by adding or removing electrons, the negatively charged particles. Although protons are positively charged particles, they can only be added or removed in the processes of nuclear fusion and fission, respectively, techniques that are impractical for cost-effective electroplating.

The anode is commonly composed of the metal to be plated. The cathode and anode sit in an electrolytic bath, typically (in gravure cylinder plating) an acid copper electrolyte, comprising copper sulfate ions (Cu^{2+} and SO_4^{2-}) and sulfuric acid ions ($2H_3O^+$ and SO_4^{2-}). The copper of the anode is ionized by the application of the charge, and the positively charged copper atoms are then attracted to the

negatively charged cathode. (When an atom is ionized, it has electrons either added or removed, depending upon the electron shell configuration of the atom. "Shells" can be thought of as concentric rings around the nucleus of an atom. Each shell can hold a certain number of electrons, and when the outermost shell is close to containing its full complement of electrons, it will accept electrons from other sources readily. When its outermost electron shell is nearly empty, it will readily give up electrons. This is the basis of most chemical reactions. When the outermost shell is full to capacity, it will not readily accept or give up electrons, and is said to be inert, such as the so-called noble gases.) The negatively charged cathode provides the electrons needed by the copper ions to fill their outermost shells, and the copper "adheres" to the surface of the cylinder.

The amount of amperage needed to deposit a quantity of metal equal to its equivalent weight (in other words, the weight of the atom divided by its valence, or the amount of its charge) is the same for all elements, and has been determined to be 26.8 Ampere hours (Ah). To determine how much metal can be deposited at that amperage, the equivalent weight is divided by 26.8 Ah. Thus, for copper in an acid bath, the atomic weight is 63.6 and its valence is 2+, thus the equivalent weight (in grams) is 63.6 ÷ 2, or 31.8 grams. Dividing that by 26.8 Ah yields an electrochemical equivalent of 1.186 g/Ah, or how much material will be deposited per Ampere hour.

After the layer of copper is deposited and engraved, a very thin layer of chrome is deposited on top of the copper, as a means of affording the engraved surface a degree of protection from the abrasive effect of the **doctor blade** during printing. The process of chrome plating is similar in principle to copperplating, although the chrome material is not supplied through the anode, but is instead added to the solution in the form of chrome salts added to the tank at various intervals. The chrome-plating process is much less efficient than the copperplating process.

A number of variables affect gravure cylinder plating, such as the composition of the electrolyte, polarization of the electrolyte (where charges cluster in specific regions in the plating tank, rather than distribute evenly throughout), the efficiency of the electrolyte (or how much of the electrical energy being applied to the system is being applied to the process of electroplating itself), the immersion factor of the cathodic cylinder (or how much of its surface area is immersed in the tank), the distance between the cathode and the anode, the temperature of the electrolyte, and the throwing power of the electrolyte (the ability to cover the cathode with copper evenly). An important factor in electroplating that has the potential to affect print quality is called *epitaxy*, which is the tendency for the layer of the anodic substance to follow the surface contours of the cathode exactly. Metal deposited in a thick layer, however, has a levelling effect. This effect is negated when the deposited layer is not of sufficient thickness to compensate for any surface irregularities in the copper layer.

After plating, the cylinder undergoes polishing, cutting, and other processes to impart the desired degree of surface *roughness* and *waviness*, as well as the intended cylinder diameter and circumference.

Similar electroplating techniques are used to plate a thin layer of chrome to the surface of an engraved *anilox roller*, used in most *flexographic* inking systems. See *Anilox Roller*.

Electroscopic Ink

A *screen printing* ink that contains finely ground pigment particles which are capable of becoming statically charged, for use in *electrostatic decorating*. See *Electrostatic Decorating*.

Electrostatic Assist (ESA)

A device used on *gravure* printing presses to overcome some of the limitations inherent in gravure printing. Since gravure prints from depressed, ink-filled cells engraved in the surface of a metal cylinder, a recurring problem is the incomplete transfer of ink from the cells to the substrate passing above it. Although a resilient *impression roller*

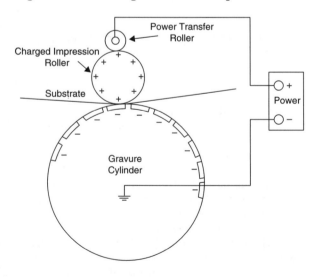

The principle of the electrostatic assist (ESA).

works to force the substrate down into the cells, where capillary action completes the ink transfer, there are limitations to the efficacy of this process, and printing defects such as *snowflaking*, *skips*, and other voids and missing halftone dots tend to recur.

Since it is impractical to further force the substrate into the cells, the Gravure Research Institute (now the *Gravure Association of America [GAA]*) developed the concept of the Electrostatic Assist unit that attempts to bring the ink to the substrate. The principle of ESA is to generate an electric field in the region of the nip between the impression roller and the *gravure cylinder* (where ink transfer takes place). Electrostatic repulsion generated between the ink and the gravure cylinder is alleviated by electrostatic attraction between the ink and the impression roller (which lies just beyond the substrate). The ink is then pulled electrostatically onto the substrate. Although the process works most effectively with polarized inks (inks and ink solvents containing molecules and atoms that ionize readily), nonpolar inks have also been used successfully.

ESA works by imparting a charge to the impression roller, either using a backup roller connected to an electrical source that runs in contact with the impression roller and transfers the charge to it, electrodes that transfer a charge to the impression roller by brushes or fingers, or by charging the core of the impression roller itself. Common ESA systems in use today include the Hurletron ESA (which uses a separate power source that transfers the charge by either an applicator or a core-charging mechanism), the Crosfield Heliostat ESA (which uses a charged backup roller configuration), and the Eltex ESA (which also uses an external electrode conveying the charge via an applicator).

The benefits of ESA have included spectacular improvements in print quality, especially on less-expensive stock, less waste, reduced need for high impression pressures, faster press speeds, decreased impression roller heat buildup, and a resultant increase in roller life.

Electrostatic Decorating

A variety of *screen printing* that utilizes the principle of electrostatic attraction to transfer an ink (whose particles carry a positive static-electric charge) to a negatively charged *substrate*.

Electrostatic Printer

Alternate term for a printer that works by means of *electrophotography*. See *Electrophotography*. Also known as a *xerographic printer*.

Electrostatic Process

Alternate term for *electrophotography*. See *Electrophotography*.

ELF

Abbreviation for *extremely low-frequency*. See *Extremely Low-Frequency (ELF)*.

Elite

In typography, a 12-pitch (12 characters per horizontal inch) typewriter *font*. See also *Pica*.

```
The elite type version
of the typeface Courier.
```

Elite type, which has 12 characters per horizontal inch.

Ellipsis

In typography, the three periods (. . .) used to indicate that something is missing (as in the shortening of a quotation) or that a conversation has stopped. An ellipsis is commonly set open (i.e., a word space before and after it, as in "The end is near, or . . . it seemed to be"). If the ellipsis occurs at the end of a sentence, and the sentence is complete, the period is set close, followed by the three points (as in "The end is near, or at least it seemed to be. . . ."). The dots of the ellipsis should be set with spaces between them, but they should be fixed spaces, as some *justification* programs may vary the spacing between them depending upon the justification requirements of the line in question.

Ellipsoid

A solid, three-dimensional geometric shape in which each plane describes an ellipse, or oval, like a squashed sphere or a football.

Elliptical Dot

A *halftone dot* that is shaped like an ellipse (or oval), rather than a perfect circle or square. Elliptical dots are often used in the *middle tone* regions of images as a means of reducing the occurrence of *dot gain*, a frequent problem of middle tone areas where the increased *dot size* and joining of dots makes them more susceptible to gain. (See also *Dot Shape*.)

Elmendorf Test

A test performed to gauge the *tearing resistance* of paper.

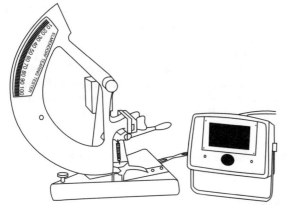

Elmendorf tester for measuring the internal tearing resistance of a paper.

ELS

Abbreviation for *extreme long shot*. See *Extreme Long Shot*.

Em

In typography, a *fixed space* having a height and a width equal to that of the *point size*. For example, in a 12-pt. *font*, an *em space* is 12 pt. wide and 12 pt. high. An *em dash* is a *dash* equal to the size of an em in a particular typeface at a particular size. An *en* is defined as a fixed space half the size of the em. Thus, in 12-pt. type, an *en space* would be 6 pt. wide. (See *Fixed Space* and *Dash*.) The em was originally defined as a square the size of a capital letter "M," which extends to the *descender* line. This definition is no longer accurate. Also called a "mutt."

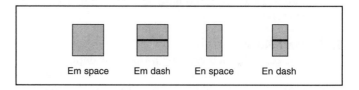

The em space, em dash, en space, and en dash for 24-pt. type.

Email

Shorthand and popular term for *electronic mail*, or the sending of messages over the *Internet* (or other network), in contrast to so-called *Snail Mail* (term used by Internet avatars to refer to conventional post-office-based mail). Email is a basic feature of any network or *Internet service provider (ISP)*. In this latter manner, a message is composed in an *editor* and sent to a mail server (or a *pop*) where it is sent to the indicated address. An email address comprises at least three basic elements: a name, usually a single word in all caps or all lowercase letters (i.e., jsmith); a *domain*, preceded by the "at" sign (@) and indicating the server that distributes mail to the individual (i.e., aol for America Online); and a three-letter extension indicating the nature of the domain such as *.com* for a general communications domain, *.net* for a local network, *.edu* for an educational domain like a university, *.org* for an organization such as PBS, or *.gov* for a government organization. Email is increasingly being supplied as a basic part of a computer's *operating* system. Most email systems allow for attaching files.

Email Address

In telecommunications and networking, address information that must be included in an *email* message in order for

Email address.

it to be delivered. An email address usually involves a user name, followed by a *domain name*. See *Email*. Also known as an *Internet address*.

Embedded Commands

In computer typesetting, word processing, etc., any formatting or other commands and codes included within a document. Such commands include font, size, and style changes, as well as returns, word spaces, etc.

Embedment

A *screen printing* process in which an image, design, or other matter is printed onto rice paper and encased in a translucent or transparent polyester/fiberglass *resin*, to provide increased permanence and durability. Embedment is commonly used for large outdoor signs that need to be weather resistant.

Embossed Finish

A paper *finish* characterized by a raised or depressed surface intended to simulate wood, leather, cloth, or other texture or pattern, produced by *embossing*. (See *Embossing*.)

Emboss Filter

In digital image manipulation programs (such as Adobe Photoshop), a tool that adds shading to a selected image or portion of an image imparting to it a three-dimensional effect, or the resemblance to a design produced by conventional *embossing*. An emboss filter is often used in the creation of on-screen *button*s for multimedia presentations.

Embossing

In *binding and finishing*, a process in which images, patterns, or text are stamped or pressed into a *substrate*. In the embossing process, a relief *die* or embossing form is mounted to a platen beneath the substrate to be stamped. A counter embossing form—or a sunken die into which the relief die fits exactly—is mounted to a platen directly above the substrate. During embossing, the two dies are pressed together through the substrate, which creates a raised image. Often, the dies are heated. Embossing that simply stamps an image with no additional coloration or decoration of the pattern is known as *blind embossing*. Embossing that is combined with *foil stamping* to transfer a foil image to the embossed pattern is known as *foil embossing*.

In the process of *debossing*—which is the reverse of embossing, or the created of a sunken image—the positions of the relief die and the counter die are reversed. A similar process in which a sunken image is pressed into a hard book cover or other such substrate is known as *die-stamping*.

Embossing dies are made of brass, magnesium, or copper. Brass is especially useful for long runs. A brass die used in stamping book covers is called a *binder's brass* or, when made from other metals, a *binder's die*. The image itself can be chemically etched, machine-cut, or hand-tooled. Increasingly, dies are manufactured using lasers guided by *CAD/CAM* computer software. Embossing can be

Dieboard with counter embossing form

Substrate

Relief embossing form

Typical embossing configuration.

done before or after printing. See *Die* and *Binding and Finishing*.

In papermaking, *embossing* is a paper *finishing* operation in which paper is impressed with a raised design. A machine used for embossing is similar to a *supercalender*, in which a hard steel roll containing the raised design to be stamped on the paper is in contact with a soft compressible roll. As the paper *web* passes through the nip of these rolls, the design is stamped on it. The process is used for *embossed finish* papers, and papers with other heavily textured surfaces.

In printing, *embossing* is also an alternate term for the printing and paper defect known as *waffling*. (See *Waffling*.)

Em Dash

In typography, a dash one *em* long (—), used to set off parenthetical text, replace missing text matter, or function in lieu of a colon. It is used in contrast to a *hyphen* or an *en dash*. See *Dashes*.

EME

Abbreviation for *electromechanical engraving*, a means of transferring an image to the image-carrying surface of a *gravure cylinder*. See *Gravure Engraving: Electromechanical Engraving*. Electromechanical engraving is also used to etch the cells into the surface of a *flexographic* press's *anilox roller*. See *Anilox Roller*.

Em Fraction

In typography, a *fraction* set as a single character having a width of one *em*, consisting of a numerator and denominator separated by a slash, such as "¼." Em fractions are in contrast to *en fraction*s and *piece fraction*s. See *Fractions*.

EMI

Abbreviation for *electromagnetic interference*. See *Electromagnetic Interference*.

Em Leader

In typography, two dots, such as periods, spaced evenly within the width of one *em*. See *Leaders*.

EMM

Abbreviation for ***Expanded Memory Manager***. See ***Expanded Memory Manager (EMM)***.

Emphasis

In typography, the use of variations in style to emphasize information. Although italic type is the most common means of emphasis, bold type is also effective (although should be used sparingly). Although underlining—the only means available on a typewriter—is redundant in typography, it is occasionally used for aesthetic or stylistic reasons. All caps can also be used. Variations on and combinations of the above are also possible, such as:

ALL CAPITALS

SMALL CAPITALS

CAPS & SMALL CAPS

Underlined

Italic

ITALIC CAPS

ITALIC SMALL CAPS

ITALIC CAPS & SMALL CAPS

Bold

BOLD CAPS

BOLD CAPS & SMALL CAPS

BOLD SMALL CAPS

Bold Italic

ITALIC BOLD CAPS

ITALIC BOLD CAPS & SMALL CAPS

ITALIC BOLD SMALL CAPS

Some writers tend to use all of these forms of emphasis, sometimes in the same paragraph.

Empty-Slot Ring

In networking, especially by means of a ***ring*** topology utilizing a ***token-passing protocol***, a network in which a free data ***packet***, or ***token***, constantly cycles through each node, a ***bit*** in the packet indicating wether or not the token contains a message for a particular node. See ***Ring*** and ***Token***.

EMS

Abbreviation for ***expanded memory specification***. See ***Expanded Memory Specification (EMS)***.

Em Space

In typography, a ***fixed space*** one ***em*** in length. See ***Em*** and ***Fixed Space***. In the past, an em space has been colloquially referred to as a ***mutt*** or ***mutton***.

Em Square

In typography, the square one ***em*** wide and one em high. See ***Em***. The em square received its name from the capital "M" that filled the piece of type body in early printing days.

Emulate

In computing, to mimic the behavior of a different hardware or software system, facilitating data communications (see ***Terminal Emulation***) or software compatibility. In this latter sense, by means of ***emulation*** a program written for one hardware/software configuration can be run on another hardware/software configuration. Strictly in hardware terms, an ***EGA*** monitor was often used to emulate the behavior of a ***CGA*** monitor. In terms of computer printers, many brands are designed to emulate more popular "standard" brands. Any software utility designed for purposes of emulation is called an ***emulator***.

Emulator

Any software and/or hardware configuration that allows one computer system to mimic the behavior of another, for purposes of software and/or hardware compatibility. See ***Emulate***.

Emulsification

The formation of a colloidal suspension, or the dispersion of particles of a solid, liquid, or gas in another substance. In lithographic printing processes, ***fountain solution*** is emulsified into the ink. Improper emulsification of water and ink is the cause of a variety of printing problems. (See ***Ink: Printing Ink Defects and Problems***.)

Emulsifying Agent

Any substance that promotes the ***emulsification*** of two other substances. See ***Emulsification***.

Emulsion

In general chemical terms, an emulsion is the colloidal suspension of one liquid in another. In photography, an emulsion is any light-sensitive coating—made from a variety of materials, most commonly a silver halide suspended in ***gelatin***—used in photographic processes. An emulsion will react to ***actinic light*** when exposed, forming a reproduction of that image, either negatively or positively. This is the basis of photography.

Emulsion Applicator

In ***screen printing***, alternate term for a ***coater***. See ***Coater***.

Emulsion Coater

In ***screen printing***, alternate term for a ***coater***. See ***Coater***.

Emulsion Side

The surface of a photographic film to which the light-sensitive ***emulsion*** has been applied, and which is the side of the film that can be exposed. It commonly has a less shiny appearance than the non-emulsion side.

En

In typography, a unit of measurement exactly one-half as wide as, and as high as, the ***point size*** being set. In 12-pt. type, the en is 6 pt. wide and 12 pt. high. An en or ***en space*** is also defined as a **fixed space** having a width half as wide as an **em**. See **Fixed Space**. An **en dash** is a **dash** as wide as the en for that particular typeface and type size. See **Dashes**.

Enable

To restore or turn on a hardware or software function. See also **Disable**.

Enamel Paper

A type of high-gloss **coated paper**. See **Coated Paper**. See also **Bright Enamel**.

Encapsulated Ink

A type of printing ink containing **pigment** particles encased in a coating that provides a dry, free-flowing system. With the application of heat and/or pressure—as in "scratch-and-sniff" applications—materials within the ink coating (such as aromas) are activated.

Encapsulated PostScript (EPS)

A graphics file format developed by Adobe Systems, Inc.; a device-independent **PostScript** representation of a graphic or other object (or page). It stores files not only as a series of **Bézier curve**s (or **vector**s), but also includes a low-resolution **bitmap** representation of the file for quick on-screen viewing. **Drawing** programs such as Adobe Illustrator (and even some paint programs like Adobe Photoshop) can save graphics (most commonly line art) as EPS files, which means that they will print with smooth lines and curves (i.e., not exhibiting the stair-step pattern of bitmapped graphics) at whatever resolution the output device can achieve. The **Macintosh** viewfile is in the **PICT** file format, while on the **PC** it is in the **TIFF** or Microsoft **Windows** metafile format. *EPS* is also sometimes referred to as **EPSF** (Encapsulated PostScript Format).

Encapsulation

In computer programming (specifically, **object-oriented programming**), the grouping of both data and the computer code that manipulates it into a single object.

In networking, *encapsulation* refers to the means by which a **frame** header and information from a high-level **protocol** is inserted into the frame of a lower-level protocol.

Enclosed Inking System

An **inking system** used on some **flexographic** printing presses, comprising an **anilox roller** located between two **doctor blade**s and accepting ink directly from the **fountain**. Also known as a **manifold inking system**. See **Inking System: Flexography**.

Encryption

The conversion of computer data into unique codes that can only be decoded by a receiving party possessing the proper decryption algorithm. Encryption is used for security purposes, especially for the transmission of sensitive or private

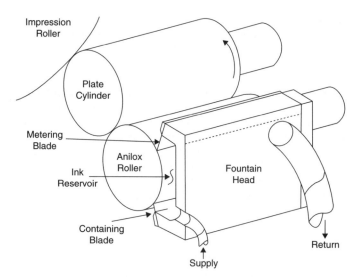

Enclosed inking system, used on some flexographic presses.

material (such as credit card numbers) over the Internet. Encryption can be either "asymmetric" (the **encryption key** needs to be known by both sender and receiver) or symmetric (half of a bit sequence is used to encrypt data but the other half is needed to decrypt the data). So far it is unknown just how effective encryption is. The decoding of encrypted data is known as **decryption**. See also **Data Encryption Standard (DES)**.

Encryption also refers to encoding special **hint**s into the digital descriptions of Adobe **PostScript** fonts (only **Type 1 PostScript font**s, however). These encrypted hints are used to improve the quality of the type when it is output, and is especially useful when small **point size**s are output.

Encryption Key

In telecommunications, a unique number used for data **encryption** when transmitting sensitive data over unsecure networks, so as to keep such data from falling into unauthorized hands. See **Encryption** and **Data Encryption Standard (DES)**.

Encyclopedia

A work that contains information on branches of knowledge or comprehensively covers a particular branch of knowledge in articles arranged alphabetically, as with this publication.

Encyclopædia Britannica (one of the few that uses the æ diphthong in its name) is the oldest and largest English-language encyclopedia and has been published since 1768, when it first appeared in Edinburgh, Scotland. It was conceived by two printers, Andrew Bell and Colin Macfarquhar, and edited by printer William Smellie. Initial pieces of the work began to appear in 1768, and the whole work was completed in 1771 in three volumes of 2,391 pages, with 160 copperplates engraved by Bell. The work consolidated subjects into comprehensive treatises plus shorter, dictionary-level articles on technical terms and other subjects. This encyclopedia follows that model.

The second edition was ten volumes totaling 8,595 pages and appearing in parts from 1777 to 1784. The scope of the second edition was enlarged by the inclusion of biographical articles and the expansion of geographic articles to include history. The editor was James Tytler.

The tenth edition (1902–03) was published under the sponsorship of The Times of London. It added eleven supplementary volumes to those of the ninth edition, updating much of the material. The eleventh edition was issued in twenty-nine volumes by the Cambridge University Press in 1910–11. This edition marked a departure from previous editions in its splitting up of the traditional lengthy, comprehensive treatises into somewhat more particularized articles. The eleventh edition had 40,000 articles, double the ninth edition's 17,000.

In 1920 Britannica was bought by the Chicago mail-order firm Sears, Roebuck and Company. In 1941 William Benton, a former advertising executive and a vice president of the University of Chicago, obtained the rights to the *Britannica* as a gift to the university. When the trustees decided not to undertake the financial risks, Benton supplied the working capital and became chairman of the board of directors and majority stockholder.

In 1952, with Britannica's publication of its *Great Books of the Western World* began the association of philosopher Mortimer J. Adler. A vast editorial effort resulted in the publication of *Britannica 3,* or the fifteenth edition, in 1974. It consisted of three parts serving different functions: the Micropædia (Ready Reference), Macropædia (Knowledge in Depth), and Propædia (Outline of Knowledge). There were over 4,000 contributing authors from over 100 countries.

Annual revisions of the set continued, supplemented by a major revision of the fifteenth edition in 1985. The set consisted of thirty-two volumes. In the early 1990s, *Britannica* was made available for electronic delivery on a number of CD-ROM-based products, including the *Britannica Electronic Index* and the *Britannica CD* (providing text, illustrations, and a dictionary, along with proprietary retrieval software, on a single disc). During this period, the company developed Britannica Online, an electronic reference service for delivery over the Internet. In 1994 it debuted on the World Wide Web at *http://www.eb.com*.

In the United States, the first edition of *The New International Encyclopaedia* was issued in 1902–04 and was subsequently supplemented by yearbooks. The *Encyclopedia Americana,* which traces its ancestry back to an English-language adaptation (1829–33), has enjoyed growing success through its policy of following the continuous revision system, and yearbooks have supplemented it from 1923 onward. In 1950–51 *Collier's Encyclopedia* appeared in twenty volumes, and subsequent editions have been supplemented by yearbooks since 1960.

France has produced three encyclopedias of note in the 20th century. The *Encyclopédie Française* (1935–66) is a collection of monographs by scholars and specialists, arranged in classified form and available in loose-leaf binders, supplemented by a continuously revised index. The articles are notable for their almost total concentration on contemporary issues in the fields considered.

Other important encyclopedias and handbooks issued in recent years include *The Encyclopedia of Photography* (1949); the *McGraw-Hill Encyclopedia of Science and Technology* (1960; seventh edition, 1992); and the *Encyclopedia of Library and Information Science* (1968–83 and supplements).

In 1985 Grolier, Inc., issued its *Academic American Encyclopedia* on CD-ROM. The text version added illustrations in 1990, and audio and video in 1992, becoming the *New Grolier Multimedia Encyclopedia.* Multimedia versions were issued in 1989 by Compton's MultiMedia Encyclopedia, then owned by Encyclopædia Britannica. In 1993 Microsoft Corporation released *Microsoft Encarta Multimedia Encyclopedia,* which enhanced the text of *Funk & Wagnall's New Encyclopedia* with extensive graphics, audio, and video. World Book and Encyclopædia Britannica issued the texts of their print sets on CD-ROM between 1989 and 1993. In 1994, illustrations were added to World Book's *Information Finder,* and in 1995 the *Britannica* CD was released with all 44 million words of the print edition supplemented by illustrations and *Merriam-Webster's Collegiate Dictionary.*

END

Abbreviation for **equivalent neutral densities**. See **Equivalent Neutral Densities (END)**.

End Damage

Any damage or defect at the edge of a paper **web**, such as **cracked edge**s, nicks, bruises, gouges, or other such problems typically caused by indelicate handling. Any type of end damage can cause a **web break** in web offset lithography. (See also **Stuck Edge**.)

En Dash

In typography, a dash one **en** long (–), used to represent the words *to* or *through*, or function in lieu of a colon. It is used in contrast to a **hyphen** or an **em dash**. See **Dashes**.

Endleaf

In **case binding**, a strong paper designed to secure the body of a book into its case. Endleaf papers, also called **endpaper**s and **endsheet**s, may be blank white sheets, colored papers, or they may be printed, containing maps, diagrams, or other designs and illustrations pertinent to the subject matter of the book. See **Case Binding**. Also spelled as two words, *end leaf*.

Endmatter

Alternate term for the **back matter** of a book. See **Book Typography** and **Back Matter**.

End Node

In networking, a **node** that can send and receive data solely for its own use and cannot transmit messages to other nodes.

End Note

A *footnote* or *reference* that appears at the end of a book or other publication. See *Footnote*.

End-of-Data

In computing, a code added to the end of a magnetic tape indicating the point at which the data ends. Abbreviated *EOD*.

End-of-File

In computing, a code added to a file stored on a magnetic tape indicating the point at which the data comprising the file ends. Abbreviated *EOF*.

End-of-Input-File

Alternate term for *end-of-file* See *End-of-File*.

End-of-Line

In computing, a code added to a document indicating at what point a line ends, used to instruct the computer or output device to move to the next line. Abbreviated *EOL*.

End-of-Page Stop

A code or command set used by some computer printers (i.e., those that only print one page at a time) instructing the system to stop printing until the operator has inserted a new sheet of paper.

End-of-Tape

On a magnetic tape (such as that used for computer storage or audiovisual recording), a physical or digital marker—ranging from a reflective strip, transparent tape, or a *bit* code—indicating the end of a recordable section of the tape. Usually abbreviated *EOT*.

End-of-Text

In computing and telecommunications, a code added to a file indicating the point at which the data comprising the file ends. Abbreviated *ETX*.

End-of-Transmission

In telecommunications, a *bit* pattern or other code indicating the end of a data transmission. Abbreviated *EOT*.

End Page

In *binding and finishing*, an alternate term for an *endsheet*. See *Endsheet*.

In computers, end page refers to the page at the end of a tree-structured database.

Endpaper

Alternate term for *endleaf* paper. See *Endleaf*. Also spelled as two words, *end paper*.

Endplay

A lateral movement of an offset press ink roller's shaft within its bracket, caused by excessive wear and/or poor fit.

The lateral movement, if more than 0.02 in., can cause printing defects such as *slurring* and streaking. Endplay can be stopped with the use of shims, but only if there is no possibility for increased wear to damage the shaft or bracket (or other parts of the roller) irretrievably. (See also *Play*.)

End Point Densities

In *halftone* photography, the densities that yield the optimal *highlight* and *shadow* dot sizes.

Endsheet

Alternate term for an *endleaf* paper. See *Endleaf*. Also spelled as two words, *end sheet*.

End User

In any manufacturing or production system, the individual or organization that will ultimately be the recipient of the item being produced.

En Fraction

In typography, a *fraction* set as a single character having a width of one *en*, consisting of a numerator positioned directly over the denominator, separated by a horizontal line. En fractions are in contrast to *em fraction*s and *piece fraction*s, and are also known as *case fraction*s and *stack fraction*s. See *Fractions*.

English Finish

A paper *finish* characterized by a smooth, calendered, low-*gloss* surface, commonly used for book or magazine papers. English finish paper is the smoothest finish that can be obtained on a paper machine and has a very *close formation* and a high *filler* content.

Engrave

To etch or cut a pattern or other image into a surface such as an *intaglio* printing plate, *gravure cylinder*, *anilox roller*, or acid *resist* surface.

Engraved

In typography, alternate term for *in-line*. See *In-line*.

Engraved Roller

Alternate term for a flexographic *anilox roller*. See *Anilox Roller*.

Engraving

The act of etching an image into a plate or other image carrier in relief form (as in *letterpress* printing) or in *intaglio* form (as in *gravure* printing). When used as a noun, *engraving* refers to the etched image itself. Engraving is also known as *etching*. (See illustration on facing page.)

Enhanced-Definition Television (EDTV)

A television system boasting advanced encoding and transmission techniques, but not as sophisticated as *high-definition television*.

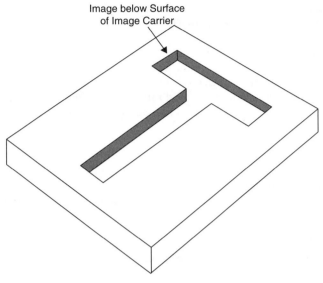

An intaglio engraving.

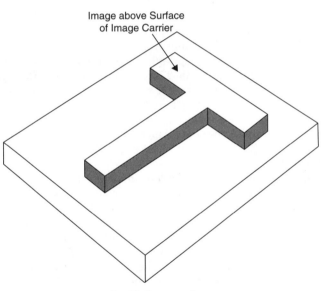

A relief engraving.

Enhanced Graphics Adapter (EGA)

An IBM expansion card added to a computer system, enabling a color monitor to display 16 colors at a screen *resolution* of up to 640×350 pixels at 21.8 kilohertz (KHz). It was an improvement over *CGA*, but still was only capable of displaying text with an 8×14-dot character cell. It was superseded by *VGA*.

Enhanced Industry Standard Architecture (EISA)

In computing, a term for a 32-bit *bus* used in a *microcomputer*. EISA, designed to supersede the previous *ISA* bus, boasted higher transmission capacity and data speed, but required expensive additional hardware and as a result never truly caught on. Also referred to as *Extended Industry Standard Architecture*.

Enhanced Small Device Interface (ESDI)

In computing, a standard *interface* for computer peripheral devices such as *hard disk* drives, *floppy disk* drives, *magnetic tape* drives, etc. ESDI, capable of data transfer rates of 10–20 *megabit*s per second, is most commonly used for large-capacity hard disks.

Enlargement

Any reproduction that is larger than the original. Also known as a *blowup*. See also *Reduction*.

En Leader

In typography, two dots, such as periods, spaced evenly within the width of one *en*. See *Leaders*.

ENS

Abbreviation for *Enterprise Network Services*. See *Enterprise Network Services (ENS)*.

En Space

In typography, a *fixed space* half as wide as the *em space*, or as wide as an *en* in that typeface and type size. See *En* and *Fixed Space*. An en space has been known colloquially as a *nut*.

Enter Key

In computing, a keyboard key used to insert a *carriage return* in a document, or to initiate a function or execute a command. Often used interchangeably with the *return key*.

Enterprise Network

A computer network comprising every computer in a particular business, organization, or corporation, even including those in disparate geographic locations and those that may run disparate operating systems. An enterprise network may also be composed of even smaller *departmental network*s. The enterprise network also runs the company's *mission-critical application*s.

Enterprise Network Services (ENS)

In networking, a software application that is based on Banyan's *StreetTalk* and that provides *directory services* for networks.

Envelope

A folded and pasted sheet of paper in which other pieces of paper or materials can be placed, often for mailing or other transportation.

In computer graphics, an *envelope* is the outline of an object used by *drawing program*s. The editing of the shape of an object's envelope allows the object's shape to be changed. Such editing also produces a number of other special effects.

Envelope Delay

Alternate term for *delay distortion*. See *Delay Distortion*.

Envelope Feeder

A tray, cartridge, or other device attached to a photocopier or computer printer that feeds envelopes—rather than flat sheets—into the device for imaging.

Envelope Pattern Gluer

An *in-line* finishing device found on a *web press* that is used to apply an adhesive.

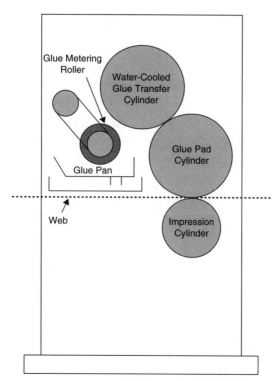

Basic pattern gluer.

Environment

Generally speaking, *environment* refers to the conditions in which an individual and/or computer operates. These may be simply whatever conditions happen to prevail in a particular location or may involve special conditions necessary for the proper operation of the equipment. For example, some systems need to be in an air-conditioned environment.

In computing, the term *environment* refers to the particular hardware and software configuration available to a computer user. Most commonly, the term *environment* refers to a particular *operating system*, such as a *Windows environment*.

In computing by means of *DOS*, the term *environment* refers to an area of computer memory in which system information is stored, such as *command prompt* data. In DOS, "environmental" settings are created by means of the SET command.

Environmental Immersion

A term for the highest level of *virtual reality*. See *Virtual Reality*.

EOF

Abbreviation for *end-of-file*. See *End-of-File*.

Eosine

A red, organic, crystalline, water-insoluble solid used as a brilliant red *dye* or *pigment* in printing inks. Eosine is also called eosin, bromeosin, and tetrabromofluorescein (chemical formula $C_{20}H_8Br_4O_5$). A lead *lake* of eosine is called *phloxine*.

EOT

Abbreviation for *end-of-transmission*. See *End-of-Transmission*.

EOT is also an abbreviation for *end-of-tape*. See *End-of-Tape*.

EP

Abbreviation for *electronic publishing*. See *Electronic Publishing*.

Epitaph

An inscription on a tombstone. The earliest surviving epitaphs are those of the ancient Egyptians on sarcophagi or on the walls of burial chambers.

The oldest existing epitaphs in Britain are those of the Roman occupiers, in Latin. The earliest epitaphs in English churches are usually a simple statement of name and title, with the phrase *hic jacet* ("here lies"). By Elizabethan times epitaphs on stone monuments, in English, became common, and this practice spread to America.

Epitaxy

A physical principle in *electroplating*, especially that of *gravure cylinder*s, in which a layer of metal will closely conform to the shape and structure of the cathode. Even though electroplated metals of a certain thickness will also contribute a leveling effect, the thinness of the chrome layer deposited precludes the correction of any surface defects or irregularities in the copper surface. Consequently, all nonuniformities in the copper surface need to be ironed out before the layer of chrome is deposited. (See *Electroplating*.)

Epoxy

Any of a variety of thermoplastic *resin*s derived from the *polymerization* of any of the epoxides (a class of organic compounds containing an oxygen atom bound to two other atoms, specifically carbon).

Epoxies are strong adhesive materials that are used to produce printing inks that dry with a thick, tough film that is resistant to chemicals, water, and other environmental conditions.

EPROM

An abbreviation for the term *erasable programmable read-only memory*. See *Erasable Read-Only Memory (EROM)*.

EPS

See *Encapsulated PostScript (EPS)*.

EPS is also an abbreviation for *electronic publishing system*. See *Electronic Publishing System*.

EPS is also an abbreviation for *external page storage*. See *External Page Storage*.

EPSF

Abbreviation for *encapsulated PostScript format* (or *encapsulated PostScript file*). See *Encapsulated PostScript (EPS)*.

EPS5

Alternate term for a file in the *DCS* graphics *file format*. See *Desktop Color Separation (DCS)*.

Equalization

In telecommunications, a means of compensating for signal *attenuation* and/or *delay distortion* by balancing a circuit by reducing the frequency and phase distortion such that it transmits all frequencies equally. In general, the higher the transmission rate, the greater the need for equalization.

In graphics and imaging, the term *equalization* refers to the process of expanding the number of shades of gray in an image so as to improve its appearance.

Equalize Filter

In digital image manipulation programs, a tool that is used to decrease the difference in brightness between the lightest and darkest areas of an image, such as a scanned photograph.

Equilibrium Moisture Content

The amount of moisture contained by a paper when its own *relative humidity* is equal to that of the surrounding atmosphere, and the point at which paper will neither gain nor lose moisture to the atmosphere. The primary constituents of paper, fibers of *cellulose*, have a strong affinity for water and will gain (or lose) it readily, depending on the amount of moisture in the air. This *hygroscopic* characteristic of paper makes it dimensionally unstable, as the length and/or width of a paper can change depending on how much water the paper has gained or lost.

The equilibrium moisture content of a paper depends on its percentage of *fillers*—inorganic materials added to paper during papermaking—that neither gain nor lose moisture. *Coatings* also affect the moisture content of paper. Fillers and coatings increase a paper's *dimensional stability*, which improves *printability* in many printing processes.

The equilibrium moisture content of paper is also dependent on past exposure to moisture. (See *Moisture Content* and *Relative Humidity*.) The equilibrium moisture content will remain unchanged unless the relative humidity is changed; lowering the relative humidity of the environment will result in the paper losing moisture until a new equilibrium moisture content is reached. Similarly, increasing the relative humidity of the environment will result in the paper gaining moisture until a new equilibrium moisture content is reached. Generally speaking, if the relative humidity is 20–65%, a 10% increase or decrease in humidity will effect a 1% change in a paper's equilibrium moisture content. A related measurement is *equilibrium relative humidity*.

Equilibrium Relative Humidity

The *relative humidity* of the atmosphere at a particular temperature at which paper will neither gain nor lose moisture. At equilibrium relative humidity, paper can be exposed to air without the environment effecting a change in its length and/or width. The primary constituents of paper, fibers of *cellulose*, have a strong affinity for water and will gain (or lose) it readily, depending on the amount of moisture in the air. This *hygroscopic* characteristic of paper makes it dimensionally unstable, as the length and/or width of a paper can change depending on how much water the paper has gained or lost. (See *Moisture Content* and *Dimensional Stability*.)

The equilibrium relative humidity of a paper depends on its percentage of *fillers*—inorganic materials added to paper during papermaking—that neither gain nor lose moisture. *Coatings* also affect the moisture content of paper. Fillers and coatings increase *dimensional stability*, which improves *printability* in many printing processes. A related measurement is *equilibrium moisture content*.

Equivalent Neutral Density (END)

In color printing, the respective densities of the three *process color*s—*cyan*, *magenta*, and *yellow*—required to produce neutral gray.

Equivalent Weight

A term used to describe the respective *basis weight*s of the same paper at two different sheet sizes.

Erasable CD

Alternate term for a *magneto-optical disc*. See *Magneto-Optical (MO) Disc*.

Erasable Optical Disc

A variety of *optical disc*, or type of external storage media, that allows the deletion and rewriting of information, unlike a *CD* or *CD-ROM*, which are read-only optical discs. An erasable optical disc allows high-capacity storage (600 MB or more) and their durability has made them useful for archival storage. See *Magneto-Optical Disc*.

Erasable Read-Only Memory (EROM)

A type of *read-only memory* chip that can be erased and programmed with new data. EROM chips are used for *flash memory*. See *Flash Memory*. EROM is also called *EPROM* (for *erasable programmable read-only memory*). EROM memory can be erased using ultraviolet light. EROM that is erased using an electrical current is known as *EEPROM*.

Erase

To remove information from a computer screen, page, computer storage, or other area.

Erase Head

On an audio or video recorder, a separate head that contacts the tape surface before the record head and erases the previously recorded signal before rerecording. Many low-end recorders simply use the record head as an erase head, while high-end systems use *flying erase head*s, which yield the best results and allow the highest-quality edits to be made.

Ergonomics

The study of the human body and the effects of machines on it, especially for the purposes of designing productive and healthy work environments. Ergonomics studies the effect of keyboard arrangements (especially as it affects the occurrence of carpal-tunnel syndrome and other repetitive-stress disorders), monitor placement, chair comfort, illumination levels, etc. A device described as "ergonomic" has purportedly been designed in accordance with principles of health, comfort, and productivity.

EROM

Abbreviation for *erasable read-only memory*. See *Erasable Read-Only Memory (EROM)*.

Errata

Errors discovered in a book after printing, which may consist of either simple typographical errors or more serious content-related errors. Errors are often corrected either directly in the text in subsequent printings or by adding a loose page (called an *errata sheet*) to the book during binding.

Errata Sheet

A sheet inserted or pasted into a book during binding containing corrections of errors discovered in the text after printing. The most interesting use of the errata sheet is described by physicist Murray Gell-Mann in his book *The Quark and the Jaguar*, where he reports having once seen a book-length collection of random numbers—which contained an errata sheet.

Error

A mistake of any kind.

In computing, a discrepancy between a predetermined correct value or behavior and the actual observed value or behavior. Errors in computing can be fairly trivial (such as an attempt to write data to a disk drive that contains no disk) and will provoke a gentle (if occasionally cryptic) rebuke from the computer (an *error message*). A particular action may also result in a *fatal error*, which can render the system inoperative and/or cause it to *crash*.

Error Burst

In telecommunications, any series of defective *bit*s in a transmitted data stream, often requiring retransmission.

An error burst can be the result of *noise* or other problem with the transmission medium.

Error Condition

The state a computer is in during the generation of an *error message*. See *Error Message*.

Error Control

Alternate term for *error correction and detection*. See *Error Correction*.

Error Correcting Code

Any calculation or encoding scheme added to transmitted data so as to detect and correct errors. See *Error Correction*. Often abbreviated *ECC*.

Error Correction

In computing, any technique, calculation, or other means of evaluating and correcting errors in data or data transmission. A computer's main memory contains hardware that checks for errors in *parity*. Data to be transmitted along a network or other medium has various calculations added to it to determine if any errors have been introduced into the stream during transmission. Such calculations—or *error correcting code*—include *checksum*, *cyclic redundancy check*, and *cross-interleaved Reed-Solomon code*. The term *error correction* is also used in concert with *error detection*.

Error Detection

In computing, any technique, calculation, or other means of locating errors in data or a data transmission. See *Error Correction*.

Error Detection Code

In computing, a code written such that each expression is constructed according to certain predetermined rules, allowing violations of those rules (which can result in errors or problems) to be detected. Also referred to as *self-checking code*. Abbreviated *EDC*.

Error Diffusion

A means of eliminating the graininess of a digital image by changing the values of adjacent *pixel*s to average pixel values.

Error Handling

In computing, the means by which a program or system deals with the occurrence of errors as the program is running. Some programs—those that are well-written—handle errors or unexpected problems well, and simply inform the user (by means of an *error message*) that something untoward has happened and may instruct the user as to how to rectify it. Other programs—those that are poorly written—freeze the system upon encountering even the slightest error. It could perhaps be argued that a program's error handling technique is reflective of that of the individual who created it.

Error Message

In computing, a command line or dialog box that tells a user when an *error* has been generated. Often, the error message will tell the user what the specific problem is (such as one that reads "printer is out of paper"), the solution being explicitly or implicitly provided. Sometimes, error messages are more cryptic (such as one that reads "error of Type 1") and references specific programming problems that the user may or may not be able to interpret.

Error Rate

See *Bit Error Rate*.

ESA

See *Electrostatic Assist (ESA)*.

ESC

Abbreviation for a computer keyboard's *escape key*. See *Escape Key*.

E-Scale

A transparent plastic scale containing the letter "E" in a variety of *point size*s. The E-scale is used to gauge the size of set type.

Escape Key

In computing, a keyboard key and/or *control character* whose function varies from program to program. Generally, however, the escape key is a shortcut for quitting out of a program, returning a program to a prior state, or transferring control to another portion of the program.

Escapement

In typography, the width of a typeset character, gauged in relative units, and set so that adjacent characters do not overlap each other. On typewriters, all characters have the same escapement value. On most typesetters, each character has its own escapement value; for example, the letter "m" has a different value than the letter "i." Some characters on some systems—such as accents—have a zero escapement value, and are used in concert with other characters:

$$´ + e = é$$

The accent has a zero escapement, allowing placement of the "e" directly beneath it.

The term *escapement* also refers to the mechanism in mechanical *phototypesetter*s that proportionally spaces the characters. Some devices print a character, then escape the width of that character, while other systems print a character, then escape the width of the *next* character before printing it. Laser typesetters, however, do not utilize the concept of escapement.

Escape Sequence

Alternate term for a *setup string*. See *Setup String*.

ESDI

Abbreviation for *Enhanced Small Device Interface*. See *Enhanced Small Device Interface (ESDI)*.

Esparto

A species of grass (*Stipa tenacissima*) native to southern Spain and northern Africa used as a fibrous source for papermaking in Europe and Africa.

ESPRIT

See *European Strategic Programme for Research and Development in Information Technology (ESPRIT)*.

Essential Facilities

In networking, the standard facilities of a network utilizing *packet switching*.

Establishing Shot

In motion picture, television, or video production, a short scene (usually an exterior of a building or other location) intended to indicate where the action of a subsequent interior scene is taking place.

Ester

A class of organic compounds formed by the reaction of an organic acid with an alcohol in which a molecule of water is released. Esters such as *ethyl acetate* and *ester gum* are used extensively as *solvent*s in the manufacture of printing inks. So-called "fruit esters"—such as the ethyl and isoamyl esters of formic, acetic, butyric, and valeric acids—are produced in plants, and provide the characteristic taste and odors of raspberry, cherry, grape, rum, and other flavors, which can also be synthesized artificially.

Ester Gum

Any of several types of *resin* produced by the esterification (or the reaction between an acid and an alcohol, with the elimination of a water molecule) of *rosin*.

Estienne, Henri

Henri Estienne II (also spelled Etienne, in Latin: Stephanus) (1528–1598), scholar-printer, grandson of Henri Estienne, founder of the family printing firm in Paris, and son of Robert I Estienne, who left Paris to establish a printing firm in Geneva. Educated in classical literature, Estienne traveled in Italy, England, and Flanders, studying ancient manuscripts and visiting scholars. He joined his father in Geneva and began publishing the results of his own researches in the first printed editions of ancient Greek texts.

In 1566 Estienne published a Latin edition of *Herodotus,* accompanied by a French version. As Estienne's most famous work, it caused Estienne trouble in Geneva. Designed to show how the strange stories in *Herodotus* are paralleled by equally strange ones in modern times, it was bitterly satirical of his own age. Estienne was arrested and tried and forced to cancel the offending pages. Even so, the book went through 12 editions in 16 years. His Greek dictionary, *Thesaurus graecae linguae*, 5 vol. (1572), a masterpiece and a monument of lexicography, appeared in new editions as late as the 19th century. After 1583 he spent much time away from his home, wandering from city to city in search of a patron. The later publications of his press thus suffered to some extent from neglect. He died on a visit to France.

Etch

Alternate term for *fountain concentrate*, the undiluted chemicals used in an offset press *fountain solution*. See *Fountain Concentrate* and *Fountain Solution*.

In *gravure* printing, *etch* refers to the act of engraving—either chemically or electromechanically—cells onto the surface of the image-carrying *gravure cylinder*. See *Gravure Engraving*.

Etchant

Any chemical used to etch an image area in an *intaglio* plate, a *gravure cylinder*, or a *flexographic* press's *anilox roller*. The most common etchant in use is ferric chloride. See *Gravure Engraving* and *Anilox Roller*. An etchant is also used in flexographic platemaking. See *Plate: Flexography* and *Gravure Engraving*.

Etch Out

Alternate term for *polish out*. See *Polish Out*.

Etch Resist

See *Resist*.

Etch Stick

Alternate term for *snake slip*. See *Snake Slip*.

Ethernet

In networking, a popularly used local area network (*LAN*) standard developed in the early 1970s by Xerox, Intel, and DEC, in which computers are linked together by means of *coaxial cable*s, *twisted-pair cable*s, or *fiber optic* cabling. Ethernet networks are characterized by the transmission of data in *packet*s, and the use of *CSMA* protocols for data delivery. As many as 1,024 workstations can be hooked up to a particular Ethernet network, and communication as fast as 10 million *bits per second (bps)* is possible. Some applications (such as graphics and multimedia) require higher-capacity networks, hence the development of *Fast Ethernet*.

Ethernet Address

Alternate term for a *hardware address*. See *Hardware Address*.

Ethernet Packet

In networking, a data *packet* used on an *Ethernet* network, typically comprising a *synchronization* header (called a *preamble*), a *destination address*, a *source address*, a type code field, a data field (which contains the message itself, and can hold from 46 to 1500 *byte*s), and a *cyclic redundancy check*.

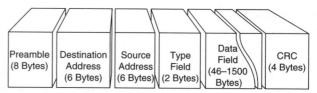

Structure of an Ethernet data packet.

EtherTalk

In networking, an *AppleTalk* protocol used by Apple computers to communicate on *Ethernet*. EtherTalk utilizes *coaxial cable* and can transmit data at the Ethernet rate of 10 *megabit*s per second.

Ethyl Acetate

A volatile *ester* (chemical formula $C_4H_8O_2$) formed from the reaction of ethyl alcohol and acetic acid (in the presence of a catalyst), used as a *solvent* in inks designed for *flexographic* and *rotogravure* printing processes. It is also widely used in the manufacture of *nitrocellulose* lacquers.

Ethyl Alcohol

The most common type of alcohol—chemical formula C_2H_5OH—obtained from the yeast fermentation of some carbohydrates (such as grains, molasses, starch, or sugar, for example), or produced synthetically. It has a wide variety of uses, from *solvent*s in printing inks to beverages. Also called *ethanol*.

Ethyl Cellulose

An ethyl ether of *cellulose* formed by treatment of pulped wood with an alkali, used as a *film former* in *gravure* printing inks. Ethyl cellulose is also available as a transparent film and is used as a *substrate* in *gravure* and *flexographic* package printing.

Ethyl Lake Red C

An *organic color pigment* used as an orange pigment in printing inks. Ethyl Lake Red C is a yellow shade of *Lake Red C* and possesses high brightness and *tinctorial strength*. However, it possesses low *lightfastness* and *alkali resistance* and has a tendency to bleed in many solvents. It is often used for printing on unbleached kraft stock. (See also *Organic Color Pigments*.)

(*CI Pigment Orange 46 No. 15602.*)

ETX

Abbreviation for *end-of-text*. See *End-of-Text*.

Euro Connector

Alternate term for a *scart*. See *Scart*.

European Broadcast Union (EBU)

A group of European broadcasting organizations set up to advise the *CCIR* about the development of broadcast standards. See *Comité Consultatif International des Radiocommunications (CCIR)*.

European Community Host Organization (ECHO)

An organization—based in Luxembourg—established in 1980 to create a common market for information services in the European Community. ECHO not only maintains and provides access to information services but also serves to guide and train users not previously exposed to advanced information services.

European Print Stroke

In *screen printing*, a printing stroke (i.e., the movement of the *squeegee* across the screen fabric) in which the squeegee is pulled toward the front of the press when making an impression, commonly used on many European screen printing presses.

European Strategic Programme for Research and Development in Information Technology (ESPRIT)

An organization that was created to develop European technologies and to give European companies a competitive advantage over those from the United States and Japan, as well as foster cooperation among European companies and develop international standards for information technologies.

Evaporation

The changing of a liquid into a gas, which occurs at a liquid's boiling point. In printing ink terminology, evaporation refers to a method of drying in which an ink *vehicle* containing a low-boiling-point *solvent* evaporates out of the ink film (either at room temperature or in the presence of heat), leaving the dried *pigment* on the *substrate*.

Evenly Weighted

In typography, descriptive of a *typeface* in which all of a character's strokes are drawn with the same thickness.

Even Parity

In computing, a *parity check* used to detect and correct errors in data transmission by adding an extra *bit* (either a 1 or a 0) to a character code so as to ensure that the total number of 1s in the code is an even number. See *Parity*. See also *Odd Parity*.

Event-Driven

A type of computer programming in which a program executes commands only as a reaction to messages that are sent to it.

Event Queue

In computing, a sequential list of commands awaiting execution. Often, priority can be given to certain commands—either by the user or by the computer—sending them to the front of the queue.

Eventstore

In electronic video editing, a form of memory in which editing actions are stored.

Evocative Typography

The use of *typeface*s to create a mood or feeling by their appearance alone. For instance, the typeface Manhattan evokes a feeling of the 1920s; the typeface Caslon Antique is used to create a feeling of colonial America.

Evocative typography is most often used in display or headline type. Display has been defined since hot-metal days as any size over 14-point, and faces were specifically designed for display use. Today, electronic sizing makes it possible for any typeface to be used as display.

Optical spacing becomes more critical in larger sizes, and one must review the typeset word or line for consistency of spacing. Because of this, *ligature*s are not usually set in display, although *swash* and *alternate characters* are.

Novelty typefaces are also used for display or evocative purposes. Typefaces formed with flowers, bullet holes, rope, people, or other elements are rarely used. With literally thousands of display faces, fewer than 100 are used very frequently.

Exa-

A *metric prefix* denoting 1,000,000,000,000,000,000 (one quintillion, or 10^{18}) units. In computing, *exa-* refers to 2^{60}, and one *exabyte* (EB) of storage (should such a thing exist some day) is approximately equal to one quintillion *byte*s of data (actually 1,152,921,504,606,846,976 bytes). See *Metric Prefix*. See also *Kilo-*, *Mega-*, *Giga-*, *Tera-*, and *Peta-*. *Exa-* is usually abbreviated *E*.

Exabyte

An uncommon unit of computer storage, comprising 1,024 *petabyte*s or 1,152,921,504,606,846,976 *byte*s. *Exa-* is the prefix meaning "quintillion," so it is common to consider 1 exabyte as equal to 1 quintillion bytes, although that is not entirely accurate. Exabyte is abbreviated EB.

Exception Dictionary

In typography, a *dictionary* containing only those words that will not be hyphenated properly by a typesetting device's *hyphenation* program. See *Dictionary*.

Excess Pressure

Extraneous amounts of *squeeze* generated by any two contacting parts of an *offset lithographic* press—such as between a plate and *blanket cylinder*—that cause distortion, tension, or other such phenomena. See *Squeeze*.

Exclamation Mark

In typography, a form of *punctuation* that is used to indicate emphasis (!) or enthusiasm. Many people tend to use exclamation marks with unbridled enthusiasm!!! Also called an *exclamation point*, *screamer*, or *bang*. See *Punctuation*.

Exclamation Point

Alternate term for an *exclamation mark*. See *Exclamation Mark*.

EXE

In computing, a *file extension* for applications or other functions that need to be executed by the computer.

Execute

In computing, to carry out some function (on the part of the computer), usually as the result of a user directive.

Execution Time

In computing, the length of time the computer requires to *execute* a command or function.

Executive Size

A paper size of 7¼×10½ in., often used for stationery.

Exit

In computing, to close and quit a program or routine within a program. When used as a noun, *exit* refers to the point at which a program can be quit.

Expandability

In computing, the ability to expand a computer system or, in other words, add devices or enhanced features to it. In terms of hardware, *expandability* may refer to the ability to add more memory, storage, or input/output devices. In terms of software, *expandability* may refer to the ability to add network users and/or other *node*s.

Expanded

In typography, descriptive of the relative wideness of all the characters in one *typeface*. Expanded type is used in heads, subheads, and small blocks of ad copy.

There are four basic gradations of expansion beyond the "normal" typeface: semiexpanded, expanded, extra-expanded, and ultraexpanded. *Extended* and *wide* are often used synonymously with one or more of these degrees of expansion. Some typefaces, such as Century Expanded, expand the characters in the *x-height* direction, rather than in width. When Century Expanded was designed at the turn of the century, it had a very large x-height and was described as having as "expanded x-height," so it was called Century Expanded for its height, not its width. This made the typeface applicable for newspapers and books since x-height is related to readability.

Digitized typesetters can modify character set widths electronically to create wider characters. Expansion can also be accomplished optically.

If a digitized typesetter is used to reduce set size, then all values are changed, including the fixed spaces. This would have to be the case, since the figure space width (which is often the *en space*) would have to increase the width of the figures. When using expanded type, it is important to ensure that the word space standards are also expanded, otherwise words will tend to run together. Expanded type should also not be used with narrow line lengths, as it looks awkward. Expanded type also has reduced legibility, so its use should be sparing. (See also *Condensed*.)

abcdefghijklmnopqrstuvwxyz
Century Expanded

abcdefghijklmnopqrstuvwxyz
Eurostile Extended

abcdefghijklmnopqrstuvwxyz
Univers Extended

An example of three expanded typefaces. Century Expanded is not "expanded" in its width like the other two typefaces, but rather it has an expanded x-height.

Expanded Characters

Very wide type characters. See *Expanded*.

Expanded Memory

See *Expanded Memory Specification (EMS)*.

Expanded Memory Manager (EMM)

In computers, especially those running on the *MS-DOS* operating system, a *device driver* that enabled 80386 computers to make use of additional memory. In DOS, the program was called EMM386.EXE. See *Expanded Memory Specification (EMS)*.

Expanded Memory Specification (EMS)

In computers, especially those utilizing the *MS-DOS* operating system, an add-on piece of hardware that allowed applications to access more memory than their allotment (640 *kilobyte*s) of the 1 *megabyte* upper limit of early DOS computers, although this additional memory could only be used for storage, not running the program. EMS required that additional memory be divided into 64-*kilobyte* blocks, only one of which was accessible at any one time, although the hardware enabled the blocks to be switched between very rapidly. Using a special *driver* called an *expansion memory manager*, EMS essentially "tricked" the computer into thinking that a particular 64-KB block was within the 1-MB range, when in actuality it was on the EMS *expansion board*. Since modern computers no longer have a 1-MB limit to memory, EMS is no longer used and has been supplanted by the *extended memory specification (XMS)*.

Expander

Alternate term for a *synthesizer*, especially one lacking a keyboard. See *Synthesizer*.

Expansimeter

A device that measures a paper's *dimensional stability*, or change in length and/or width as a result of the gain or loss of moisture from the air, as a function of *relative humidity*. See *Dimensional Stability* and *Relative Humidity*.

Expansion Board

A circuit board that is added to a basic computer setup (often to an *expansion bus*) so as to enable the system to handle additional features or functions beyond those the basic system can handle, such as recording or playing audio and video, adding memory, operating certain displays, etc. Also known as an *expansion card*.

Expansion Bus
The part of a computer containing electronic plugs and connectors that allows addition of *expansion board*s to the system. See *Expansion Board*.

Expansion Card
Alternate term for *expansion board*. Also known simply as a *card*. See *Expansion Board*.

Expansion Slot
One of several spaces provided on a computer's *expansion bus* that allow installation of *expansion board*s, or circuit boards that enhance the computer's basic capabilities. On a *portable computer*, a *PCMCIA* connection provides an expansion slot for a *PC card*. (See *Expansion Board*.) The term *expansion slot* also refers to the ability of the *CPU* to effectively handle the addition of expansion boards.

Expansivity
See *Hygroexpansivity*.

Expert
A person who is regarded as being knowledgeable or all-knowing about a particular subject.

Expert Set
In typography, a *font* containing a set of *accent*s (with their respective vowels), *small caps*, *fractions*, and other specialized characters, in addition to the basic character set.

Explicit Access
In a *local area network*, an access method for the network in which connected devices are allowed entry to the communications medium for a specific period of time. Although every *node* gets a chance to transmit, it must wait for its turn. See also *Contended Access*.

Export
To output data from a computer file created in one software application in a format that can be read by a different application. See also *Import*. Also referred to as *text out*.

Export Server
In networking, a *server* on which *directory* information is stored, allowing it to be replicated for distribution to connected *workstation*s. See *Server* and *Directory Replication*.

Exposure
A measure of the amount of light hitting a photosensitive surface—be it paper, film, plate, or *CCD*—and the length of time the surface was hit by the light.

Exposure Latitude
Alternate term for *exposure tolerance*. See *Exposure Tolerance*.

Exposure Level
A measure of the amount of light that impinges on a photosensitive surface, be it film, paper, *CCD*, etc.

Exposure Time
In *photography*, the length of time that a camera's shutter remains open, exposing the film. See *Photography*.

Expressed Folio
In *book typography*, a page number that is printed, in contrast to a *blind folio*. See *Folio*.

Extended
Alternate term for *expanded*. See *Expanded*.

Extended Architecture
In computing, general term used to refer to operating systems or other system components that are capable of transferring more data faster than previous versions. Often used to refer to 32-bit buses. Abbreviated *XA*.

Extended Binary Coded Decimal Interchange Code
See *EBCDIC*.

Extended-Definition Television
Alternate term for *enhanced-definition television*. See *Enhanced-Definition Television (EDTV)*.

Extended Font
A collection of type characters to support languages that require more than 256 (the maximum number of characters that can be contained in a computer font) characters.

Extended Graphic Character Set
A set of characters in a type font that require two *byte*s (rather than the usual one byte) of computer data to represent a character. An example is the *Kanji* character set.

Extended Industry Standard Architecture
Alternate term for *Enhanced Industry Standard Architecture*. See *Enhanced Industry Standard Architecture*.

Extended Memory
See *Extended Memory Specification (XMS)*.

Extended Memory Manager
A *device driver* used to support the *Extended Memory Specification* on *IBM-compatible computer*s. See *Extended Memory Specification (XMS)*.

Extended Memory Specification (XMS)
In computers, especially those running the *MS-DOS* operating system, a successor to the *expanded memory spec-*

ification (EMS) that allowed 80X86 computers to access additional memory, both for storage and for running applications. XMS required a 16-*bit* processor, but with the advent of 32-bit processors all extended and expanded memory features are available directly within the *microprocessor*.

Extender

A class of *white pigments*, also known as *transparent pigments*, used to "extend" the quantity of other, perhaps more-expensive color pigments, or to reduce a particular pigment's *opacity*, *color strength*, or other properties. Extenders are also used to increase the volume of an ink without altering its overall viscosity. See *Transparent Pigments*. In *screen printing*, an extender is known as an *extender base*.

In computing, an *extender* is a device that increases the distance over which data can be sent from a computer to a printer.

Extender Base

Alternate term for *transparent pigment*, especially in *screen printing*. See *Transparent Pigment*.

Extensible

A property of a material, such as a plastic film used as a *substrate*, that describes its ability to be stretched, or undergo elongation, during printing and/or finishing.

Extensible Paper

A paper that will withstand a sudden shock without rupturing or tearing.

Extension

A general term for any software program or utility that expands the functionality of a larger program or computer system, acting as if they were part of that program or system. On the *Macintosh*, system extensions (in this case, also called *INIT*s) work as part of the Mac operating system, adding such features as the ability to play back video or audio, or read certain types of files. In a program such as Photoshop, extensions (in this case, also called *plug-in*s) supply an additional set of filters and ways of manipulating images, or allow for scanner software to work from within the program. Extensions are also called *addition*s or *annex*es.

The term *extension* is also an abbreviated term for a *file extension*. See *File Extension*.

Exterior Durability

A measure of the extent to which a screen-printed product can survive exposure to sunlight, rain, weather, or other outdoor conditions.

External Command

In computing, any *DOS* command existing as a separate program in the main DOS directory, such as FORMAT, BACKUP, etc. See also *Internal Command*.

External Drum Imagesetter

A type of *drum imagesetter*, a device that is used for *high-resolution* laser output of digitally created pages or *color separation*s, in which the film to be exposed is mounted on the surface of a drum, as opposed to within the drum (see *Internal Drum Imagesetter*). See *Drum Imagesetter*.

External Gateway Protocol (EGP)

In networking, a *routing protocol* used to connect networks. Although EGP can determine whether or not a particular network is reachable, it does not select the most expedient route by which to transmit a message. The external gateway protocol was supplanted by the later *Border Gateway Protocol (BGP)*.

External Mail Gateway

In networking, a *gateway* that allows members of a *local area network* to exchange *email* with users outside the network. See *Gateway*.

External Memory

In computing, any "memory" (or storage space) that is located on a peripheral device, such as a *floppy disk*, a *magnetic disk*, an *optical disc*, etc., in contrast to *internal memory*.

External Modem

In computing, a *modem* that exists as a *standalone* device and connects to the computer via a cable connected to the

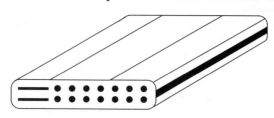

An external modem.

serial port, in contrast to an *internal modem*. An external modem, possessing a set of *LED*s that indicate modem status, can be connected to different computers easily.

External Page Storage

In computing, a portion of a *hard disk* used to store *page*s of information while other pages are loaded in memory. See *Virtual Memory*.

External Sizing

Alternate term for *surface sizing*, *sizing* added to paper after its has formed. See *Surface Sizing*.

Extra Leading

In typography, a set amount of *line spacing* set between two blocks or lines of type to set off one portion of the copy from another.

Extra-Sheet Detector

Alternate term for a ***double-sheet detector***, especially on a press equipped with a ***stream feeder***. See ***Double-Sheet Detector***.

Extra-Trinary Color

Any additional ***color*** beyond the basic ***cyan-magenta-yellow*** triumvirate added to a printed reproduction. Most ***process color*** printing is accomplished using cyan, magenta, yellow, and ***black*** (CMYK). Additional colors (which may be process colors or special colors) may be needed to increase the ***density range*** of a reproduction or to reproduce unique colors that more closely approximate those used in the original image. Extra-trinary colors require additional ***color separation*** films and additional plates. Extra-trinary colors can be applied by means of ***color substitution***, a ***bump plate***, or a ***touch plate***. Also known as *HiFi Color*. (See COLOR PLATE 23.)

Extreme Close-Up

In ***photography*** (still, motion picture, or video) a ***close-up*** in which the subject extends beyond the frame of the shot. Abbreviated and specified (i.e., in shooting scripts) as ***ECU***.

Extreme Long Shot

In ***photography*** (be it still, motion picture, or video) a ***long shot*** in which the subject is a long distance away, as in a shot of a mountain climber appearing as merely a dot on a mountain.

Extremely Low-Frequency (ELF)

A type of electromagnetic radiation having a frequency of 5–2,000 ***Hertz***, generated by computer monitors and other electrical and electronic devices. ELFs are referred to in the context of ***electromagnetic interference***.

Extruding

In computer graphics, a means of creating a three-dimensional object from a series of two-dimensional objects depicting each of several views. Essentially, a top view, a front view, a side view, and a bottom view are combined to create the object. Extruding is a type of ***lofting***. See ***Lofting***.

Extrusion

Processing a hot thermoplastic material through an opening or orifice to produce a thin, continuous sheet of film, such as those used as ***substrate***s in ***gravure*** and ***flexography***.

In computer graphics, *extrusion* refers to ***rendering*** of a three-dimensional (3D) object from a two-dimensional (2D) one by essentially grabbing a line and stretching it out along a new third axis, accomplished in the same manner as a square is turned into a cube.

Extrusion Coating

A type of laminating or paper ***coating*** in which a thermoplastic material is applied to the surface of a paper by the process of ***extrusion***.

Exudation

A printing ink defect in which solid substances from the interior of an ink film rise to the surface, producing a distortion or discoloration of the ink film. (See also ***Bloom*** and ***Blushing***.)

Eye Coordinates

In computer graphics, a ***coordinate system*** produced relative to the viewer's position, used to give three-dimensional objects the illusion of depth. Eye coordinates are produced from ***world coordinates***.

Eyedropper

In computer graphics programs, a tool used to sample a color from an image and have it become the active color, allowing a particular shade to be matched accurately elsewhere in the image.

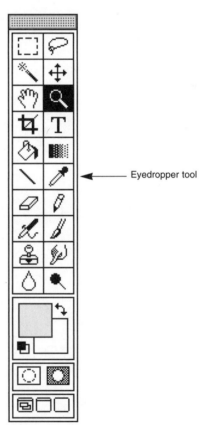 ◄— Eyedropper tool

The eyedropper tool in Photoshop.

Eyemarker

A small image (such as a rectangle) printed toward the edge of the web of ***substrate*** on a ***flexographic*** press as a means of activating an electronic position regulator to ensure proper ***register*** of successive images or colors. Also known as an ***eyespot***.

Eyespot

See ***Eyemarker***.

F

F, f

The sixth letter of the Latin and English alphabets, derived from the North Semitic letter *waw*, a letter usually denoted by a symbol resembling a modern *Y*. A variant of this North Semitic letter was eventually adopted by the Greeks, who called it *digamma*, and used a symbol resembling a modern *F* to represent it. However, it has a *w*-like sound, and eventually fell out of use as a letter (although it remained as a numeral). In early Latin, the *f* sound was usually denoted by the *wh* letter combination, the *h* eventually being discontinued, and the *F* eventually coming into greater use. The lowercase *f* derives from the scribal cursive letter *f* which came from the capital.

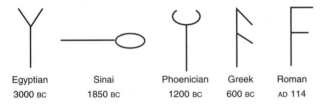

Egyptian	Sinai	Phoenician	Greek	Roman
3000 BC	1850 BC	1200 BC	600 BC	AD 114

The evolution of the letter F.

F & G

In **binding and finishing**, abbreviation for *folded and gathered*, referring to book pages which have been folded into **signature**s and gathered together into complete books, but which have not yet been bound. F & Gs are often used to proof the signatures and **book block** prior to actual binding. An F & G is also known as a **check copy**.

Fabric Stretcher

In **screen printing** a device used to mechanically stretch the screen fabric accurately over the frame.

Fabritecture

Obsolete term for **screen printing**. See **Screen Printing**.

Face

The printing surface of a piece of metal type.

The term *face* is also a shortened form of the term **typeface**. See **Typeface**.

Face is also used in computer graphics to refer to one particular plane in a **wireframe** model. See **Wireframe**.

Face Cut Label

A type of **label** that has been cut from a larger sheet of **substrate**, the substrate material left attached after diecutting the labels. See also **Laid On Label**.

Face Margin

Alternate term for **thumb edge**. See **thumb edge**.

Face Material

Any paper, plastic, or other surface used to carry **pressure-sensitive labels**, **decal**s, or other **adhesive** material, which will eventually be applied to another surface. Also known as **body stock**, **face stock**, and **base material**.

Face Printing

Printing on the "front side" or top side of a sheet or transparent film, in contrast to **back printing**, which is printing on the reverse of a sheet or film. See also **Back Printing**.

Face Stock

Alternate term for **face material**. See **Face Material**.

Facility

In networking and telecommunications, an alternate term for a **channel**. See **Channel**.

Facsimile

An identical reproduction of an image.

The term *facsimile* is also used to refer to the transmission of images or text over phone lines, known more popularly as **fax**. See **Fax**.

Facsimile Modem

A device, commonly a **modem**, that allows a computer to send and receive **fax**es. A facsimile modem (also known as a **fax modem**) can either be internal (i.e., inserted as an **expansion card** into the computer), in which case it is known as a **fax board**, or external (i.e., is an additional capability of an **external modem**).

Fact Title

In **book typography** and production, a list of alternate titles by the same author, commonly included as a **verso** page preceding the **title page**. Also known as an **ad card**. See **Book Typography**.

Fade

In motion picture and video production, and in audio recording, any gradual increase or decrease in the intensity of an image or signal, such as from black or silence (**fade-in**), to black or silence (**fade-out**), or to another image or audio signal (**cross fade** or **dissolve**). The term *fade* is also used as a verb meaning to effect any of these fades.

In printing, *fade* means to reduce in intensity, such as of a printing ink, over time or upon exposure to light or other conditions.

Fade-Down

In motion picture and video production, to decrease the intensity of a picture or signal, usually to a slightly lower value. In audio recording, *fade-down* refers to a decrease in the intensity of an audio signal. See also **Fade-Up**.

Fade-In

In motion picture and video production, to increase the intensity of a picture or signal, usually from zero, such as fading in a picture from black at the beginning of a production. In audio recording, *fade-in* refers to an increase in the intensity of an audio signal, usually from silence. See also **Fade-Out**.

Fading

A progressive decreasing of the **color strength** or **brightness** of a printing ink, paper, or other material upon exposure to light, heat, or with age. (See **Permanence** and **Lightfastness**.)

In telecommunications, *fading* refers to any decrease in intensity—or **attenuation**—of a signal. See **Attenuation**.

Fade-Off Tone

A problem of **gravure** printing characterized by the production of a **halftone dot** so small that it is not visible when printed.

Fade-Ometer

A device used to measure a paper's **lightfastness**, or its ability to resist yellowing and fading upon exposure to light, by exposing the paper to light radiation produced from a carbon arc or xenon tube. A Fade-Ometer is also used to measure the fading resistance of inks and other pigments. (See **Lightfastness**.) A variation of the Fade-Ometer is a **Weather-Ometer**, basically a Fade-Ometer equipped with a water jet to simulate the effects of weather. (See **Weather-Ometer**.) Also spelled *Fadeometer*.

Fade-Out

In motion picture and video production, to decrease the intensity of a picture or signal, usually to zero, such as fading out a picture to black at the end of a production. In audio recording, *fade-out* refers to a decrease in the intensity of an audio signal, usually to silence. See also **Fade-In**.

Fade-Up

In motion picture and video production, to increase the intensity of a picture or signal, usually from only a slightly lower value. In audio recording, *fade-up* refers to an increase in the intensity of an audio signal. See also **Fade-Down**.

Fail-Safe

Descriptive of a computer system that is designed to continue operating and not lose data when some part of the system fails or malfunctions. See also **Fail-Soft**.

Fail-Soft

Descriptive of a computer system that is designed to continue operating at a reduced capacity and with a slight amount of data loss when some part of the system fails or malfunctions. See also **Fail-Safe**.

Fake Color Printing

A form of multi-color printing in which a **color** ink (commonly a **transparent pigment**) is printed over a previously printed color, to create a third, darker shade.

Fake Duotone

A type of two-color printing using one solid **color** and one halftone **screen tint** to simulate the appearance of a true **duotone** (which is produced using two halftones). See **Duotone**.

Fake Fraction

Alternate term for a **shilling fraction**. See **Shilling Fraction** and **Fractions**.

Fake Root

In computing, a sub-**directory** that functions as the **root directory**. See **Root Directory**.

False Body

A liquid—such as a printing ink—whose **body** and **viscosity** change when stresses are applied. A false body can either be **thixotropic** (the substance thins when forces are applied) or **dilatent** (the substance thickens when forces are applied). See **Thixotropy** and **Dilatancy**.

False Color

In digital image processing, any color added to a black-and-white image used solely to differentiate portions of an image during processing.

False Title

Alternate term for **bastard title**. See **Bastard Title**.

Family of Type

See **Type Family**.

Fan Book

In one of the many **color matching system**s in existence, a collection of small color charts or swatches that are clasped at one corner, and can be separated for easy comparison of a color sample to a matching color patch.

Fan Delivery

In printing, one or more rotary units used to transfer folded **signature**s from the **in-line** folding sections to the **delivery** section.

Fanfold

Alternate term for **accordion fold**. See **Accordion Fold**.

Fanfold Paper

A continuous sheet of paper whose individual sheets are separated by *accordion folds* and perforations, used in computer printers. Often, fanfold paper contains tractor feed holes along the right and left sides.

Fanning

In *binding and finishing*, an operation following *edge gilding* in which the leaves of a book are separated.

Fan-Out

The undesirable expansion of a sheet of paper on the press, caused either by moisture absorption or by mechanical stretching of the paper. Fan-out produced mechanically commonly occurs on the *impression cylinder*, as the pressure exerted in the nip of the impression and *blanket cylinder*s irons the sheet out, causing it to expand at its tail end just prior to being printed. After leaving the impression nip, the sheet returns to nearly its original dimensions, but the image is narrowed at its tail end. When the sheet is then passed through successive printing units, the sheet will fan out again, but the successive images will print with narrower tails than the preceding ones, resulting in poor registration of images.

One means of reducing the effects of fan-out is by bowing the *gripper*s (or adjusting the grippers so that the center gripper is slightly out of alignment with the others) on the impression cylinder or on other mechanisms in the *infeed section* of the press. Another corrective method uses a *gripper-bowing device*, which exaggerates the effect of fan-out produced by the first impression cylinder, resulting in a much narrower tail-end of the printed image. Consequently, successive images will align properly on the first. (See *Infeed Section* and *Gripper-Bowing Device*.)

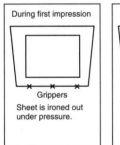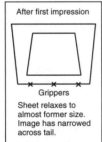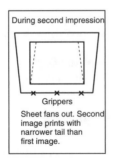

An example of fan-out.

FAQ

In *Internet* lingo, an abbreviation for "frequently asked questions," pronounced "fak." A FAQ is generally a file or document posted to a *USENET* group containing, as its name indicates, the questions that new subscribers (or *newbie*s) ask. FAQs are designed to provide answers to questions that longer subscribers have grown weary of answering. Asking a question that is in the FAQ is a good way of getting *flame*d.

Fast Brown HFR

See *Benzimidazolone Brown HFR*.

Fast-Drying Ink

A variety of *glycol vehicle* ink that dries primarily by *precipitation*. See *Glycol Vehicle*.

Fast Ethernet

In networking, a variety of the *Ethernet* network characterized by a transmission speed of 100 megabits per second and *unshielded twisted pair* cabling. As its name indicates, it is faster than traditional Ethernet. See *Ethernet*.

Fast Orange F2G

An *organic color pigment* used in printing inks. Fast orange F2G is a bright reddish orange possessing high transparency, *lightfastness*, and alkali, acid, and heat resistance. It is most effectively used in oil-based inks, where high gloss can be achieved. (See also *Organic Color Pigments*.) (CI Pigment Orange 34 No. 21115.)

Fast Select

In networking by means of *packet switching*, a calling method that transmits a small amount of data (such as 128 *kilobyte*s) along with the call-request packet, rather than in the data packets that follow. This expedites the transfer of information.

Fast Solvent

A *solvent* used in printing inks that imparts rapid drying, due to its low boiling point and high *volatility*.

Fast-to-Light

Describing a paper that is able to resist yellowing and fading upon exposure to light. See *Lightfastness*.

The term *fast-to-light* also describes a printing ink that is able to resist fading or changing color upon exposure to light. See *Lightfastness*.

Fast-to-Light Dye

A substance added to paper which increases the paper's ability to resist yellowing upon exposure to light, primarily added to papers intended for outdoor use, such as posters and signs, or for use under fluorescent lighting, such as business records and packaging. (See *Lightfastness*.)

Fat

Term descriptive of an oil-based printing ink that flows smoothly. See also *Lean*.

FAT

Abbreviation for *file allocation table*.

Fat Bit

In computer image manipulation, an enlarged *pixel* capable of being altered by means of *fat bit editing*. See *Fat Bit Editing*. Also spelled as one word, *fatbit*.

Fat Bit Editing

In computer image manipulation programs, the ability to enlarge a computerized image and edit it *pixel* by pixel, the enlarging process increasing the size of the pixels comprising the image to a size which can be easily manipulated.

Fatal Error

Any computer *error*—caused either by the user or by a *bug*—that renders an *operating system* useless.

Fatties and Skinnies

Alternate term for *spreads and chokes*, respectively, procedures performed to facilitate *trapping* in *process color* printing. See *Spreads and Chokes* and *Trapping*.

Fatty

A printing defect characterized by an excess of ink in a particular portion of a printed image.

Fault

Any physical condition that causes a mechanical or electronic system to fail, such as a broken wire, a frayed cable, a short circuit, etc.

Fault Management

In networking, a type of network management concerned with the detection and correction of faults on the network, as defined by the *ISO* and *CCITT*.

Fault Tolerance

In computing, a type of computer system design that provides redundancies among its component parts, so as to safeguard against failure. For example, multiple CPU chips and circuits, and the ability to bypass the failing component are parts of a fault-tolerant design. Similarly, additional disk drives are often included, as is an *uninterruptible power source*, to provide the system with power in the event of a *blackout*. Sometimes, an entire computer system is duplicated in a remote location.

Fax

Short for *facsimile*, a term referring to the transmission of text, illustrations, or other material over telephone lines, either by means of a "fax machine" or a *facsimile modem*. In its most basic form, the fax machine at the transmission site scans the image to be sent and transmits it to another fax machine as a series of impulses. The receiving device reads these impulses as a series of dots, and prints the reconstructed image onto either special thermal paper or on plain paper utilizing an ink cartridge.

With a facsimile modem, either the sender or receiver—or both—may be a computer which, with the use of special software and peripheral devices, can perform the same functions as a standalone fax machine.

Fax Board

A type of *facsimile modem* (or *fax modem*) mounted as an *expansion card* within a computer. See *Facsimile Modem*.

Fax Modem

Shortened term for *facsimile modem*. See *Facsimile Modem*.

Fax Server

See *Server*.

FBA

Abbreviation for *fixed block architecture*. See *Fixed Block Architecture (FBA)*.

FCB

Abbreviation for *forms control buffer*. See *Forms Control Buffer (FCB)*.

FCC

Abbreviation for *Federal Communications Commission*. See *Federal Communications Commission (FCC)*.

FCC Certification

Written approval by the *Federal Communications Commission* that a computer meets the FCC standards for *radio frequency interference* or other *electromagnetic interference* emissions. There are two classes of FCC certification. See *Class A Certification* and *Class B Certification*.

FDDI

Abbreviation for *fiber distributed data interface*. See *Fiber Distributed Data Interface (FDDI)*.

FDM

Abbreviation for *frequency division multiplexing*. See *Frequency Division Multiplexing (FDM)*.

FDX

Abbreviation for *full duplex*. See *Full Duplex*.

Feather Edge

A thin, rough edge found on carbon or carbonless papers that extends beyond the edges of other sheets in multi-ply forms.

Feathering

A printing defect characterized by ink spreading at the edges of a printed area, typically caused by irregularities in ink distribution on the surface of the paper. Also known as *wicking*.

Feathering also refers to a paper *sizing* test. See *Feathering Test*.

In typography, the term *feathering* refers to the act of adding small amounts of *leading* to aid in vertical *justification* of a column.

Feathering Test

A test performed to measure a paper surface's degree of water resistance, or how effectively the paper has been sized. (See *Sizing*.) In the feathering test, lines are drawn on a paper sample with a pen and a water-based ink. The extent of *feathering*, or spreading of the lines as ink is absorbed into paper, indicates the efficacy of the paper's sizing for pen-and-ink uses.

Feature

Any useful aspect of an application, program, or device.

In motion picture or video production, a *feature* is any production with a running time greater than 60 minutes, as a "feature film." Any production with a shorter running time is known as a ***short***.

Federal Communications Commission (FCC)

A United States Governmental agency created for the regulation of radio, television, telecommunications services, and equipment.

The FCC assigns bandwidths to radio and television stations, and attempts to ensure that they operate "in the public interest," as specified in the Communications Act of 1936 (the act that also created the FCC). The FCC also must certify all computer equipment before it can be sold in the United States, as such equipment needs to meet certain criteria with regard to radio and conductive interference, lest such devices interfere with commercial broadcasts. See ***FCC Certification***.

Feed

To carry a ***substrate*** through any imaging or printing mechanism.

Feed Cable

Any cable that connects a video source—such as a camera or VCR—to a monitor.

Feed Roller

On a sheetfed printing press, one of a set of rubber wheels that transports a sheet of paper from the ***pile table*** to the ***grippers***.

Feedboard

A conveyor belt-like platform separating the ***pile table*** and ***sheet-separation unit*** from the ***infeed section*** and printing unit on a sheetfed press (especially one used in ***offset lithography***). After a sheet has been lifted from the pile, it passes through a set of ***forwarding rollers*** at the rear of the feedboard. Located between these rollers may be one or more ***double-sheet detectors***, which shut the feeder off if more than one sheet is being fed at a time.

Once through the forwarding rollers, the sheet travels down the feedboard, which uses a set of rollers, balls, and/or brushes to press the sheet against moving feed tapes that carry the sheet to the front guides at the head of the feedboard, where it pauses at a set of stops. Side guides ensure that any lateral movement of the sheet has been compensated for, assuring proper positioning of the sheet for printing. The paper commonly travels along feed tapes, the number of which is determined by the width of the press and the size of the paper. Feedboards can possess as

few as four or as many as eight, and the tapes are spaced approximately 4–6 inches apart and kept under proper tension for accurate paper transport.

It is important that the various devices located on the feedboard be kept clean; ink buildup can cause the sheets to stick or become crooked as they travel. Sheet bridges are also placed across the feedboard where the feed tape is wound around its driving cylinder or roller, to ensure that the sheet isn't carried into the bowels of the press by the feed tape. Some feedboards also contain suction devices to keep the sheet flat once it hits the front guides, special detectors (such as a ***safety bar***) that can identify foreign objects (such as crumpled paper) and prevent them from getting into the printing unit, and ***sheet detector***s that identify sheets arriving early or late to the front guides, which can cause further feeding and/or printing problems.

The front guides themselves ensure proper squaring of the sheet and timing of its entry into the printing unit, ensuring consistent positioning of the printed image. Proper spacing (and number) of the front guides depends on the size of the sheet, but they must be positioned accurately to ensure that the sheet pressing against them isn't supported wholly by one of them, which can cause crooked feeding into the printing unit. Folding the paper into equal sections (four sections for shorter paper, eight or more for longer paper) and lining the guides up with the creases is a good rule of thumb for setting front guides. Setting the position of the front guides along the lead edge of the feedboard also affects ***gripper bite***, or how much of the sheet is grabbed by the grippers that pull the sheet into the

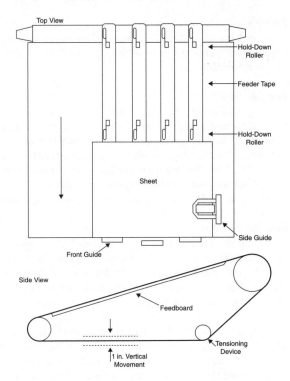

Offset press feedboard.

impression cylinder. The height of the front guides depends, naturally, on the thickness of the stock, and a useful means of setting this height is to place two sheets of the stock to be printed beneath the front guides, which are adjusted until they just barely clear the sheets. A third strip is inserted on top of the other two, and the guide height adjusted until it takes a slight amount of additional force to remove the third sheet.

As the sheet is held against the front guides, a moveable side guide slides automatically and pushes or pulls the sheet against a ***register block***, a metal block or plate precisely adjusted to keep the lateral register of the sheet consistent and accurate. The register block must be absolutely parallel to the sheet, and a smoother attached to the top of the register plate (which may or may not be attached, but when it is it keeps the sheet from moving up at right angles to the surface of the feedboard) must be adjusted to the thickness of the stock. (The same clearance as that created by the front guides is typical and effective.) The side guides, which square the sheet against the register block, can use a roller or a foot that pivots down onto the sheet and pulls it toward the register block. Side guides can also use a ***suction plate*** that sucks the paper downwards, then slides it over to the register block. Regardless of the type of side guide utilized, it is imperative that the tension of the device be compatible with the thickness of the stock, in order to avoid buckling.

Once the sheet is in register with the front guides and the register block, it is ready for transfer to the ***infeed section*** of the press. (See ***Infeed Section*** and ***Feeder Section***.)

Feeder

The portion of a printing press that separates sheets of paper and properly orients them prior to printing. See ***Feeder Section***.

Feeder Foot

An adjustable device attached to the rear of a sheetfed press's ***feeder section*** used to set the correct height of the paper pile to ensure proper feeding into the press. It also contains a nozzle that blows a jet of air beneath the topmost sheet lifted by the ***pickup suckers***. (See ***Feeder Section: Sheetfed Offset Lithography*** and ***Sheet Separation Unit***.) The feeder foot is also called a ***pressure foot***.

Feeder Section

The portion of a printing press in which the paper (or other ***substrate***) is stored and fed into the press for printing.

On an offset press, the feeder section separates individual sheets of paper from the ***pile table*** by means of a ***sheet-separation unit*** and transfers them to a ***feedboard***, on which they are jogged into the correct position and then transferred to the ***infeed section*** of the press. There are two basic configurations of feeder section: a ***stream feeder*** sends sheets through the press, at speeds slower than that of the press, in such a way that more than one sheet is on the feedboard at any one time; and a ***single-***

sheet feeder sends sheets though the press, at speeds equal to that of the press, so that only one sheet is on the feedboard at any one time. Both types of feeders utilize essentially the same methods for transferring sheets. For the specific differences between the two systems, see ***Stream Feeder*** and ***Single-Sheet Feeder***.

The pile table can be raised or lowered to permit adding paper stock. Stock must be added, and the pile table itself positioned, so that the paper is exactly centered when it enters the press, or it will not be registered properly and either the resulting print will be off center or the paper will jam in the press. The paper should also be preconditioned to the ***relative humidity*** of the pressroom, as ***wavy edges*** and ***curl*** can cause feeding problems. The paper should also be neatly stacked in the press, and all ream markers and damaged sheets (such as those with bent corners or tears) should be removed. Manufacturer specifications indicate the correct margins required to compensate for grippers and pile guides. Some pile tables are continuous-feeding, allowing for additional stock to be added without necessitating press stoppage. (See ***Pile Table***.) Other configurations allow rolls of paper to be fed into the machine and cut into sheets by the feeding section just prior to printing. (See ***Roll Sheeter***.)

A ***sheet-separation unit*** is responsible for accurately plucking one sheet from the top of the pile and sending it to the feedboard. Typically, nozzles direct bursts of air under the topmost half dozen or so sheets, and vacuum-powered ***pickup suckers*** at the rear of the pile lift the top sheet. A ***feeder foot*** drops and holds down the rest of the pile, while nozzles blow a cushion of air beneath the top sheet. A set of pickup suckers toward the front of the pile (called ***forwarding suckers***) then pull the sheet to the ***forwarding rollers***. (On a ***stream feeder***, the rear pickup suckers are already picking up the next sheet in the pile before the first sheet has completely cleared the pile.) The pressure of the air and the force of the vacuum, as well as the pressure of the feeder foot and other elements of the sheet-separation unit (such as

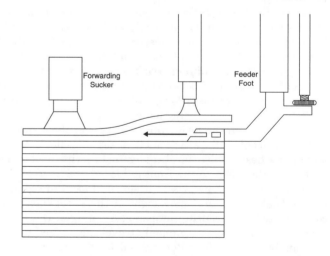

Feeder foot.

*separator brush*es and *separator finger*s), can be adjusted and need to be set to ensure that more than one sheet is not fed through at a time. (See *Sheet-Separation Unit*.)

The forwarding rollers mark the boundary between the sheet-separation unit and pile table and the feedboard. Between the forwarding rollers is a *double-sheet detector*, a device that shuts off the feeder if more than one sheet is passing by at once. Once on the feedboard, a series of rollers, balls, brushes, and feed tapes keep the paper moving toward the front of the feedboard, where it hits a series of *front guides* and pauses. *Side guides* close in and ensure that the paper's lateral movement down the feedboard has been compensated for, and that the paper is in proper position for printing. Once the paper is positioned, the *infeed section* is responsible for transferring the sheet to the printing unit.

The sheet control devices on the feedboard can vary from press to press and need to be adjusted depending on the characteristics of the paper being used (see *Feedboard*), and the position of the forwarding rollers adjusted (see *Forwarding Roller*). The double-sheet detector also needs to be calibrated depending on the job (see *Double-Sheet Detector*). At the front of the feedboard, many presses also have additional *sheet detector*s that gauge whether a sheet is early or late.

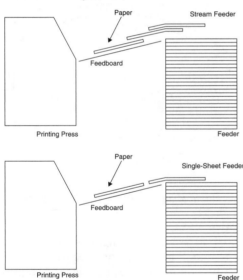

Stream feeder vs. single-sheet feeder.

Felt Finish

A paper *finish* characterized by a wool- or felt-like texture, produced at the *wet end* of the papermaking machine by pressing woven wool or patterned synthetic felts into the forming paper *web* during *wet pressing* to impart the texture to the paper. Felt finish paper is also called *felt mark*, *genuine felt finish*, and *felt marked finish*.

Felt Mark

Alternate term for a *felt finish* paper. See *Felt Finish*.

Felt-Marked Finish

Alternate term for a *felt finish* paper. See *Felt Finish*.

Felt Side

The top side of a sheet or *web* of paper, or the side that has not formed in contact with the papermaking machine's *forming wire*, as opposed to the *wire side*. As water drains down through the wire mesh belt from the papermaking *furnish*, small fibers (called *fines*), *fillers*, and *sizing* are lost through the mesh. Consequently, the felt side contains more fines, fillers, and sizing than the wire side. The paper's *grain* is also less pronounced on the felt side, and the felt side also has a less "wild" *formation*. Since the felt side contains more filler, it is somewhat weaker than the wire side, and is often not the preferred side for printing. Paper that is to be folded also has a greater tendency to crack when the felt side is on the outside of a fold. Since it also has more fines, many of which remain as loose particles, printing on the felt side results in greater *piling* of paper debris on the blanket. However, the felt side of paper is preferred for other printing applications, especially for writing with a pen and ink, as *feathering* is minimal on the felt side. Letterheads are typically printed felt side up, and envelopes folded felt side out. A watermark will read forward from the felt side.

A paper's *two-sidedness* is primarily caused by using a traditional single-wire *fourdrinier* paper machine. The disparity between the two sides can be minimized by using a *twin-wire former* which sandwiches the papermaking furnish between two wires, imparting to the paper two wire sides. (See also *Wire Side*.)

Female Connector

Any type of electrical cable connector possessing holes or slots designed to receive a set of pins on a corresponding *male connector*.

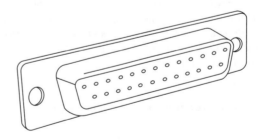

Female connector.

FEP

Abbreviation for *front-end processor*. See *Front-End Processor (FEP)*.

Festoon

On a *web press*—especially one utilizing a *zero-speed splicer* to splice together rolls of substrate—a set of pneumatically controlled, collapsible rollers through which an unwinding web of paper snakes. With enough paper stored in the festoon, the press can draw from that supply while the unwinding roll is stopped and spliced to a fresh roll. See **Zero-Speed Splicer**.

A festoon is also required to give the web of paper a long lead time into the press, to provide a tightly wound paper roll enough time to retain its original dimensions. See **Festooning**.

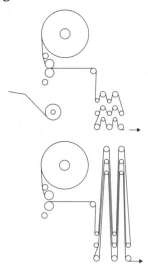

The principle of the festoon. The top diagram shows the collapsed festoon after a splice has been made. The bottom shows the festoon rewound, ready for the next splice to be made.

Festooning

In **screen printing**, the act of suspending printed material over rods or other such structures so as to facilitate drying without having the printed **substrate**s contact each other.

In **web offset lithography**, *festooning* refers to the act of giving an unwinding paper roll a long lead time before it enters the printing section of the press. This is often needed to give tightly wound paper rolls a chance to "relax" and retain their original dimensions, lest **registration** problems occur. The set of collapsible rollers used to accomplish this is known as a **festoon**.

FF

Abbreviation for **form feed**. See **Form Feed**.

Fiber

The basic unit of a paper's structure. See **Cellulose** and **Paper and Papermaking**.

The term *fiber* is also used in telecommunications to refer to a **fiber optic** cable used for data communication. See **Fiber Optics**.

Fiberboard

Fiber sheets produced with a thickness that makes them suitable for use as containers, corrugated board, or other high-stiffness packaging **substrate**s. Thicknesses of fiberboard range from 0.06–0.14 in.

Fiber Channel

In telecommunications and networking, a network **protocol** currently under development (as of this writing) that allows for use of both copper wire and **fiber optics** cabling. Currently allowing transmission speeds of up to 1062 megabits per second, it is conceivable that transmission speeds of gigabits per second can be achieved.

Fiber Cut

A paper **web** defect characterized by a short, smooth, straight cut in the paper web, caused by a **shive** slitting the paper surface as it passes through the **calender**. A fiber cut can cause a **web break** in web offset lithography, in particular if it runs in the **cross-machine direction** and/or is located at the edge of the web. (See also **Blister Cut** and **Hair Cut**.)

Fiber Distributed Data Interface (FDDI)

A network utilizing a **token-passing protocol** in which devices are connected with **optical fiber** wiring. FDDI supports transmission speeds of up to 100 megabits per second. FDDI equipment is expensive, however, and is only used when the traffic volume warrants it. See also **Copper Distributed Data Interface (CDDI)**.

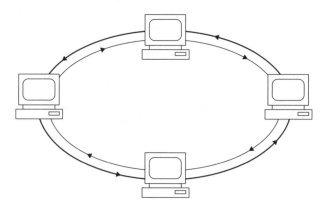

Basic structure of an FDDI network.

Fiber Optics

The science and technology of light as a means of transmitting information. Fiber optics involves strands of thin (thinner than a human hair) glass, plastic, or fiberglass (called **optical fiber**s) which are bundled together to form a cable that transmits light, the light representing digital data. Because of the internal reflectivity of the cables, light is only transmitted through the glass and does not dissipate to the exterior, except at the end of the cable, where it exits into whatever the ultimate reception point is. The fibers can also be made to bend around corners, transmit at a much higher data capacity than traditional copper wires, and are not susceptible to interference from nearby electrical sources. Fiber-optic cables occupy less space than traditional forms of wiring, and are rapidly becoming used for a variety of applications, from computer data transmission to voice communication.

Fiber Orientation

The direction in which a paper's *fiber*s are aligned. Synonymous with *grain* and *formation*.

Fiber Puffing

A paper defect of coated *groundwood*-pulp papers generated during *heatset drying*. Groundwood pulps (unlike most chemical pulps) frequently contain bundles of fiber resulting from incomplete grinding of the logs during *pulping*. During heatset drying, the heat from the dryer explodes these fiber bundles, producing a rough, abrasive surface on the paper. Fiber puffing can be reduced by reducing the temperature of the dryer. (See also *Blister*.)

Field

In a database, one particular data element in a record, such as a street address in one record of a mailing-list database, for example. A *fixed field* only allows a certain number of characters to be used in the field, regardless of how much data a particular record contains, while a *variable field* is designated with start and end codes and thus can vary from record to record depending upon the amount of actual data in the field.

In television and video, a *field* is essentially one-half of a video picture. When a video signal is scanned onto a screen, first all the even-numbered horizontal lines are scanned from the top of the screen to the bottom, then all the odd-numbered lines are scanned. Each of these "halves" is known as a field. Two fields make up one *frame*.

Field Accuracy

In video production, the ability to edit a videotape at the level of the *field*. See *Field* and *Frame Accuracy*.

Field Dominance

In television and video, the property possessed by the *field* that is scanned first. See *Field*.

Field Frequency

In television and video, the number of *field*s that an imaging system scans per second, approximately twice the

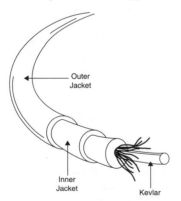

Structure of a fiber optic cable.

frame rate, as there are two fields per frame. In *NTSC* (which scans at 29.7 frames per second) the field frequency is 59.94 *Hertz*, while in *PAL* and *SECAM* (which scan at 25 frames per second) the field frequency is 50 Hertz.

Field Size

The size at which a photographic reproduction will be imaged on a film.

FIFO

Abbreviation for *first-in, first-out*. See *First In, First Out*.

Figure Space

In typography, a fixed amount of white space (typically equal to an *en space*) used in typeset material to align columns of *figures*.

Figures

In typography, a term used to refer to numerals. The numbers 1 through 0 come in two versions: *oldstyle figures* (also known as *old face*) which are nonaligning or *hanging figures*, which means that some numerals have *ascender*s or *descender*s and may not line up perfectly with each other. The other variety is modern, or *lining figures*, in which all the numerals are the same size, without ascenders or descenders and will all line up on a line.

The set of figures in common use throughout the world is called *Arabic numerals*, since ancient Arabic merchants and scholars first used them (although they originated in India). Another common system of enumeration, still in use today, are *Roman numerals*.

In text, numbers under 100 are usually spelled out, unless they relate to references. Numbers should always be spelled out at the beginning of a sentence.

In tabular copy, all figures must be the same width to allow for their lineup; this does not apply to dates, however. The numeral 1, because of its narrowness, looks ill-spaced with other figures. Some fonts have a *fitted 1*. See also *Arabic Numerals* and *Roman Numerals*.

The term *figure* is also used to refer to any line illustration or photograph used in publications, such as a graph, chart, exploded view, rendering, halftone, or any other illustration.

File

In computers, a collection of data, often named, which consists of a single document, image, illustration, or page, considered by the computer—or the user—as a single unit. Computers allow files to be saved, copied, moved about, opened, and edited.

File Allocation Table

In computing, a type of "map" or directory used by *DOS* to store, locate, and retrieve files on a particular disk. The file allocation table, abbreviated *FAT*, also indicates used and available disk space.

File Compression

In computing, a means of reducing the size of a file so that it occupies less space on a disk. File compression is useful not only to save space on disks, but also to reduce the amount of time it takes to transfer a file electronically (such as on a network or over the Internet). Depending on the file, *compression ratio*s can be as high as 50%. Many operating systems (both for PC and networks) can provide a *file-compression program* or scheme. There are many commercially available programs available, however, such as Aladdin's StuffIt. A compressed file needs to be decompressed (or expanded) before it can be opened. Often, a compressed file can be saved as a *self-extracting archive*, which allows the compressed file to be decompressed by itself, without the need for a special program. However, such self-extracting files may not be as small as regular compressed files.

File-Compression Program

A computer application that compresses files, allowing them to take up less space on a disk. Some file-compression programs are built into operating systems, while others are proprietary standalone programs. Some programs can compress more than one file at a time (into an archive), while others can compress every file on a disk or within a particular disk *partition*.

Although compressed files need to be expanded before they can be opened, some programs allow files to be compressed into *self-extracting archive*s, which allows them to be decompressed without the need for a special program. Some common file-compression programs include PKZIP, LHArc, and StuffIt. Some are available for purchase, while others are available as *shareware* or *freeware* on the Internet. See *File Compression*.

File-Conversion Program

A computer application that converts a file saved in one type of *file format* to another. Such a program may also be used to convert a file created on one computer *platform* to another platform. Such programs are most often used to convert a file from *Windows* to *Macintosh*, or vice versa. See also *File-Transfer Program*.

File Extension

A (typically) three-character addition to a computer *file name*. With some computer *platform*s (in particular, *DOS*), the name of a file is limited to eight characters, followed by a period and a three-character extension (such as "FILENAME.EXT"). The extension is often used to indicate the *file format* in which the file was saved. Some common extensions used for graphics files include ".eps" (*encapsulated PostScript*), ".pct" (*PICT*), ".tif" (*TIFF*), etc. File extensions are useful means of indicating and determining file type. Also known as a *file-name extension*.

Many common file extensions used in DOS, Windows, and OS/2 include:

AI	Adobe Illustrator
AIF	Audio Interchange File Format
BAK	Backup copy of an edited file
BMP	Bitmap graphic
CDR	Corel Draw vector graphics
CMD	OS/2 command file
COM	DOS command file
DOC	ASCII text document
DLL	Dynamic link library
EPS	Encapsulated PostScript file
EXE	Executable file, or machine language file
GIF	Graphics Interchange Format file
HLP	Help file
ICO	Icon
INI	Initialization file
JPG	JPEG file
MID	MIDI file
PCT	PICT file
PCX	Zsoft bitmap file
PDF	Portable Document Format file
PIF	Program Information File
PS	PostScript file
SEA	StuffIt self-expanding archive
SIT	StuffIt (compressed) archive
SYS	Operating system component
TEX	TEX or LATEX document
TGA	TARGA graphics file
TIF	TIFF graphics file
TMP	Temporary file
TXT	ASCII text file
WAV	Sound wave file
WKQ	Quattro spreadsheet file
WMF	Windows MetaFile
WKS	Lotus 1-2-3 worksheet file
XLS	Microsoft Excel worksheet file
ZIP	PKZIP-compressed file

File Format

A specification for the structure with which a computer data file is saved and stored, often requiring certain programs or computers to reopen and/or edit the information within. Many formats are proprietary, meaning that only certain software can be used to open the file. Other file formats are defined by various software-independent file standards, such as *ASCII*, *PICT*, *TIFF*, *EPS*, etc., requiring only that a particular program support that format.

File Fragmentation

Alternate term for *storage fragmentation*. See *Storage Fragmentation*.

File Gap

In computing, a short length of blank magnetic tape separating files, usually between a *file mark* (denoting the end of the previous file) and the start of the next file.

File Lock-Out

In computing (especially in a *multitasking* environment), a condition which occurs when two active programs request the same two files. Typically, one program will be allowed access to one file, while the other program will be allowed access to the second file. If both programs need both files to proceed with a function, neither program can proceed. Also called, rather descriptively, *deadly embrace*.

File Locking

In computing, especially on networks or other multi-user environments, a means of preventing a single file from being updated or altered by two different users simultaneously. File locking, usually imposed by a *database management system*, thus allows only one user to access a file at any one time, effectively locking out all others. After a file is closed, the next user to attempt to open it can, again locking out all others. In a large database file, however, locking out all users except one can seriously slow down progress. Consequently, some systems use *record locking* instead. See also *Record Locking*.

File Maintenance

Keeping a particular computer file current.

File Manager

In computing, any application program used to keep track of computer files, and effect such user-designated commands as copying, deleting, viewing, etc. A file manager may also allow for editing the *directory* structure of a disk, on which a set of files resides.

File Name

In computing, the name of a file on a disk. No two files in the same *directory* can have the same name. In *DOS* and early versions of *Windows*, file names could only have up to eight characters, plus a three-digit *extension* often added by a program to indicate file type. Windows 95 has done away with this, allowing many more characters to be used in a file name. On the *Macintosh*, file names can possess up to 31 characters.

File-Name Extension

See *File Extension*.

File Protection

The use of software or "hardware" (i.e., the plastic tabs on a *floppy disk*) to prevent accidental erasure of a computer file or disk.

File Purging

Erasing data files from a storage medium to make room for new data.

File Recovery

In computing, the ability to rescue data from a damaged or deleted file or disk. Typically, a file remains on a disk when it is deleted; the only true deletion is that file's *directory* entry. The data itself remains intact until it is overwritten with other data. Some programs can facilitate the "undeleting" of files inadvertently deleted. File recovery is also important when some portion of the file's control information is damaged and the file cannot be opened in a normal fashion.

File Select

Abbreviated term for *automatic file select*. See *Automatic File Select*.

File Server

See *Server*.

File-Server Protocol

In networking, a protocol that allows applications to share files over the network.

File Sharing

In networking, the ability for two or more users or *workstation*s to access a file. File access is often controlled by *file locking* or *record locking* to prevent more than one user from accessing the file at any one time.

File Sort

Abbreviated term for *automatic file sort*. See *Automatic File Sort*.

Filespec

In computing, a specification used to denote a file's complete *path*, including drive letter, directory name, file name, or any other path information. The term *filespec* itself is a contraction of the term *file specification*.

File System

In computing, the means by which an *operating system* organizes, stores, and names files. Typically, an operating system has some form of file system installed (such as *Hierarchical File System*, *file allocation table*, *High Performance File System*, and the *NT File System*), or additional file systems can be installed.

A file system is also used as part of a *database management system* as a means of managing individual records and files and creating a system for relating them to each other.

File Transfer, Access, and Management

See *FTAM*.

File-Transfer Program

In computing, a program used to convert a file created on one computer *platform* to one that can be read by a program running on a different platform. (An example is a program such as MacLink Plus, which allows files created on a *Macintosh* to be run on an *IBM-compatible computer*, and vice versa.)

File Transfer Protocol (FTP)

In networking and telecommunications, a specific (and eponymously named) *file-transfer protocol* used for logging into remote computer networks, browsing and searching directories, and *downloading* or *uploading* files without data loss. FTP, typically used on *TCP/IP* in *UNIX*-based networks, supports a wide variety of file formats and file types, such as *ASCII*, *EBCDIC*, etc.

File-Transfer Protocol

In networking and telecommunications, any means by which data is transferred from one system to another, usually by means of a *modem* and a telephone line or network cable. Such a protocol typically breaks the data into smaller units (such as *bit*s or *byte*s) which can then be processed and transmitted in sequence. Common file-transfer protocols are *Xmodem*, *Ymodem*, *Zmodem*, *Kermit*, *Gopher*, and the eponymously named *File Transfer Protocol (FTP)*.

Filet

See *Fillet* (last definition).

Fill

In graphics, any solid coloring, shade, or pattern added within the boundaries of a geometric shape. Also known as a *boundary fill*. Specific types of fills include *fountain fill*s, *linear fill*s, and *radial fill*.

In sound and music recording, a *fill* is a small piece of music (usually percussion) used to fill the transition between two music clips.

Fill Area

In graphics, a shape in which a *fill* is applied. See *Fill*.

Fill Font

Alternate term for an *outline font*. See *Outline Font*.

Fill Pattern

In graphics, the specific solid coloring or pattern used to effect a *fill*. See *Fill*.

Fill-In

A printing defect similar to *dot gain* characterized by printing ink between *halftone dots*, or in small, nonimage areas in type or *line art*. Fill-in is commonly caused by the presence of debris such as *lint*, paper fibers, coating particles, or other random detritus trapped in the ink. Ink that has not been well-ground and contains larger and a greater number of *pigment* particles than usual, that possesses low *viscosity* and high *tack*, or even various press conditions can contribute to fill-in. Fill-in is also called *specking*. (See also *Doubling* and *Slurring*.)

Fill-In Light

In motion picture and video production, a light used to eliminate shadows not filled in by the *key-light*. The fill-in light is less intense but more diffuse than the key-light.

Filler

Inorganic, nonfibrous material added to paper *pulp* prior to papermaking. Adding fillers is called *loading*. The combination of pulp and filler is the papermaking *furnish*.

The basic constituent of paper is *cellulose* fiber, but fillers are added to alter one or more of a paper's properties, depending on the desired end-use characteristics. Loading modifies such paper properties as texture, *opacity*, *brightness*, *basis weight*, *dimensional stability*, *ink absorbency*, and overall *printability*. It is important for fillers to scatter light well to increase opacity, impart high brightness, be nonabrasive, and not be chemically reactive with either the printing system to be used or with any proximate end-use materials.

The most commonly used fillers are *clay* and *titanium dioxide*, the latter of which is ideal for increasing opacity. *Calcium carbonate* is used in producing *alkaline paper*s. Other fillers that are used on occasion are talc, calcium sulfate, barium sulfate, hydrated alumina, silicas or silicate pigments, and zinc pigments. Fillers added for *internal sizing* include acid or alkaline *rosin* and *alum*. Gums, starches, and synthetic polymers are added to aid in sheet formation. Dyes and pigments are added to alter the color of a paper. In writing and printing papers, filler content can range from 5–30% of a paper's weight.

Although fillers primarily improve the optical properties of paper, it is not without compromising other properties. Increasing the amount of fillers in general increases brightness, dimensional stability, ink absorbency, opacity, and smoothness, but it can decrease a paper's strength and stress endurance. Fillers reduce paper *bulk* and *stiffness*, which may or may not be desirable.

Adding fillers is a function of the intended printing method and end-use requirements of the paper. (See also *Paper and Papermaking: Paper Properties*.)

In typography, the term *filler* refers to any extraneous material added to a page to fill out a short column.

Fillet

In *binding and finishing*, any narrow rule, line, or other ornamentation, especially when added to the *spine* of a book. The term *fillet* also refers to any tool (such as a hand-held wheel) used to produce such a design.

In graphics, a *fillet* is any rounded corner.

In typography, the term *fillet* refers to any arc used to connect two perpendicular lines of a border, providing a rounded edge, or a round corner connecting *serif*s to main strokes on letters. In this case, it is occasionally spelled *filet*.

Filling-In

Creating a printing defect called a *fill-in*. See *Fill-In*.

Film

General term for any thin (less than 0.010 in.), flexible, unsupported material used as a printing *substrate*. A substrate with a thickness of more than 0.010 in. is called a *sheet* or *sheeting*.

In photography and other types of imaging, a material—commonly comprising a photosensitive **emulsion** on an **acetate** base—which receives images either photographically by exposure to **actinic light** or by lasers driven by digital data. Film often needs to be chemically processed to develop the **latent image**s. In phototypesetting, photosensitive paper is also called *film*.

Film Assembly
Alternate term for **stripping**. See **Stripping**.

Film Chain
In a television studio or other such facility, an arrangement of film projectors, slide projectors, or other such devices used to transfer a filmed image to a videotape, or directly to a television camera for broadcast. In both cases, the image from the film is projected into the lens of a camera, where it is either then recorded or broadcast.

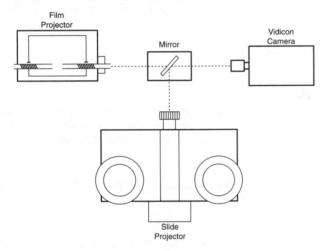

Basic film chain.

Film Coating
A lightweight paper **coating** applied to the surface of uncoated **book paper**s to increase **smoothness**. Film coating is typically applied on the papermaking machine at the **size press**. Also called **wash coating**.

Film Feed
A mechanism used in typesetting machines to move the photosensitive paper through the device.

The term *film feed* also means to add an extra length of unimaged photo paper at the beginning of a typeset galley.

Film Former
Any of several types of natural or synthetic **resin**s used in printing ink **vehicle**s to form a strong, continuous ink film. Commonly used film formers include **nitrocellulose**, **polyamide**s, **polystyrene**, and **polyvinylidene chloride**. Film formers are commonly used in **gravure**, **flexographic**, and **screen printing** inks.

Film Mechanical
A **mechanical** (or layout of all page elements) in the form of **film positive**s stripped into position on a carrier sheet. Also called a **photomechanical**.

Film Negative
A **negative**, when exposed on photosenstive film, as opposed to a **paper negative**. See **Negative**.

Film Plotter
In a color system, a type of **plotter** or device that uses a **laser** or a **light-emitting diode (LED)** to expose type or other line or **halftone** images on photographic film. Unlike an **imagesetter**, a film plotter has no **raster image processor (RIP)** directly connected to it.

Film Positive
Alternate term for **positive**. See **Positive**.

Film Processor
A device used to develop, fix, and wash the exposed film output from an **imagesetter**.

Film Recorder
A computer output device used to generate color-separated film directly from a computer image file. Technically the same type of device as an **imagesetter**, although the term *film recorder* is used to refer to high-quality imagesetters. Also known as a **color film recorder**.

A *film recorder* is also a device which generates a computerized image as a 35-mm or 4×5-inch color transparency, also, in this case, known as an **image recorder**.

Film Separation
In **screen printing**, a failure of the **stencil** to properly adhere to the screen fabric.

Film Solvent
In **screen printing**, a **solvent** used to remove the **stencil** from the screen fabric at the completion of a print run.

Film Speed
A quality of photographic film related to the shutter speed of the camera; in other words, how quickly an image will register on the film. It is commonly measured according to the **ASA** exposure time index, a set of whole numbers referring to a particular fraction of a second. For example, a film speed of 800 can be said to refer to a shutter speed of 1/800th of a second. Film speed is an important consideration when dealing with either fast motion (as in sports photography) or when levels of illumination are low. The less light there is, the faster a film should register an image. However, there is a tradeoff with fast film. The higher the film speed, the larger the grains of silver in the film, and thus the grainier the resulting photograph will be. Very fast speed (speeds over ASA 500 or so) tend to produce the

grainiest images and will consequently not enlarge or reproduce well. Slower speeds have much finer grains which are less perceptible upon development. See *Photography*.

Film Strip

A long piece of film with successive frames of still images (each usually 18×24 mm), used in educational environments. When projected through a film strip projector, each frame is displayed one after the other, usually turned by hand according to cues on an accompanying audio presentation.

In phototypesetting, a *film strip* is a chemically treated photosensitive strip of film or paper on which character images are exposed. Also spelled as one word, *filmstrip*.

Filter

In *photography*, a plate of glass or gelatin of a particular *color* placed between an original and the lens of a camera. The filter separates out certain colors, thus allowing only certain other colors to register on the film. Filters—also called *color filters*—are used to make *color separation*s, or four negatives that will be used to print the four *process colors* of *cyan*, *magenta*, *yellow*, and *black*. The original is thus photographed four times using different color filters. The choice of colors for the filters is based on *additive color theory*; a blue filter is used to produce the yellow *printer*; a green filter is used to produce the magenta printer; a red filter is used to produce the cyan printer; and a combination of all three filters is used to generate the *black printer*. See also *dichroic filter*.

In digital imaging, a *filter* is a software function (available as a native part of the image-processing application or as a *plug-in*) that alters an image in a particular way, changing either the *color balance*, or adding special effects such as a "ripple" effect, a motion blur, etc.

Filter Factor

The additional exposure required when a color *filter* is used during photography.

Filtering

In imaging, the application of a *filter* to an image, either photographically or digitally. See *Filter*.

In networking and telecommunications, *filtering* refers to the ability of a *bridge* or *router* to prevent certain data *packet*s (such as some source and destination addresses) from passing into other portions of a network.

Filtration

The final stage of the printing ink manufacturing process in which the dispersed mixture of *pigment* and *vehicle* is passed through bag or cartridge filters to remove dirt, undispersed pigment particles, and other debris and detritus. Careful attention must be paid to the *viscosity* of the ink; too great a flow, or a clog in the filter, will build up excessive pressures in the filtration chamber and rip bits of fibers out of the filter into the ink, defeating the purpose of filtration.

One of the "contaminants" of ink that filtration cannot remove is trapped air, bubbles of which have the capacity to promote the premature production of an ink skin, typically in inks that dry by *oxidation*. In lithographic ink that dries by a mechanism other than oxidation, the air bubbles are less of a problem, as the press dampening system will negate any detrimental effects likely to be caused by the bubbles.

Final Copy

A finished, perfectly typed document or manuscript.

Final Negative

A photographic *negative* created in the *prepress* phase of printing from which plates can be made. In order to properly expose photosensitive plate material, the negatives must be right-reading, emulsion-down.

Final negatives are produced from *intermediate negative*s, which are oriented right-reading, emulsion-up. See *Negative*.

Final Proof

Alternate term for a *contract proof*. See *Contract Proof*.

Finder

The "virtual desktop" which is the basic user interface on the *Macintosh operating system*. The portion of the Finder that facilitates *multitasking* is the *Multi-Finder*.

Fine Data File

Alternate term for a *high-resolution file*. See *High Resolution File*.

Fine Etching

In platemaking, *dot etching* performed on metal plates or *gravure cylinder*s to correct tone values.

Fine Grain

In photography, descriptive of a photosensitive film which possesses small particles (or *grain*), as opposed to *coarse grain*. See *Grain* (second definition).

Fine Mesh

A screen fabric used in *screen printing* containing threads that are closely woven together, with much smaller gaps between the threads than in a *coarse mesh* screen.

Fineness-of-Grind

A measure of the uniformity of *pigment* particle dispersion in a printing ink *vehicle*. Inadequate dispersion, or excessively large pigment particles, can generate various ink and printing defects and problems. (See *Ink: Printing Ink Defects and Problems*.) The fineness-of-grind can be quantitatively measured using a *grindometer*.

Fine Paper

Any high-quality paper used for writing or printing.

Fines

Small paper fibers that either drain through the papermaking machine's *forming wire*, or bond only loosely to the surface of the *felt side* of the paper and which can collect as lint.

Finger

In telecommunications and the *Internet*, a *UNIX* utility used to find and display information about a user, such as name, log in time, and physical location, as well as *email address*. Some configurations also display profiles.

Fingerprinting

The testing of a printing press prior to beginning the actual print run as a means of determining the exact degree of *dot gain*, ink density, *trapping*, and other printing characteristics. Each print job has its own particular "fingerprint," or set of subtle (or not so subtle) variations in the above-mentioned qualities. This fingerprint needs to be determined to properly customize the *color separation*s and ensure proper *register* of successive color images.

Finial

In typography, a particularly decorative form of *terminal*, or free-ending letter stroke. See *Letter Elements*.

Finish

The surface smoothness of paper, which differs greatly according to variations in one or more aspects of the papermaking process, including use of and the design attached to a *dandy roll* in the *forming section*, the degree of wet pressing in the *press section*, and the use of felts, *calenders* and *supercalenders*, *embossing* rolls, or *coatings* applied to a paper surface. Common paper finishes include *Antique*, *Calender*, *Cockle*, *Crash*, *Dead*, *Dry*, *Dull-Coated*, *Eggshell*, *Embossed*, *English*, *Felt*, *Granite*, *Handmade*, *High*, *Kid*, *Kromecote*, *Laid*, *Linen*, *Low*, *Mottled*, *Natural*, *Pebble*, *Plate*, *Ripple*, *Satin*, *Smooth*, *Suede*, *Vellum*, *Water*, and *Wove*. Papers with varying smoothness have varying degrees of printability, ink receptivity, and absorbency.

Finished Art

Alternate term for *camera-ready art*.

Finishing

Any of a variety of processes performed to a document or publication after printing. Finishing can include *cutting*, *trimming*, *folding*, and *binding*, as well as such decorative operations as *embossing*, *foil stamping*, and *laminating*. See *Binding and Finishing*.

In papermaking, a general term for the final processes that prepare paper for delivery after the papermaking process has been completed. This can include adjusting the paper's *finish* via such operations as *supercalendering*, *embossing*, or *coating*, or such final preparations as *rewinding*, *sheeting*, *trimming*, and packaging.

FIPP

A set of European standards and guidelines for color proofing when printing on *coated paper* by *offset lithography* devised by the International Federation of Publishers Press. See also *SWOP* and *SNAP*, two United States printing and proofing specification systems.

Fire Reds

A type of *organic color pigment* or *toner* used in printing inks that are fast-to-light and somewhat transparent, but are dirty in tone. They are widely used in poster and label inks. (See *Organic Color Pigments*.)

Firewall

In networking, an impermeable barrier created by a *router* that allows transmissions to leave a *local area network* but will not allow transmissions to enter, often as a means of preventing unwanted intruders into the network.

Firmware

Any software—stored in a computer's *read-only memory (ROM)*—used to control hardware components. Firmware—which is "firmly" programmed into the computer—cannot be erased or reprogrammed by the user.

First Color Down

In *process color* printing, the first color printed on the *substrate* as it passes through the press. The first color down is usually—but not always—*black*.

First-Generation Typesetter

The first configuration of phototypesetter, incorporating the photo technology with older *linecasting* technology. Essentially, a *film negative* was inserted in a linecasting matrix and each character image on the negative was successively placed between a light source and photosensitive paper.

First In, First Out

In computing, a means of manipulating data such that the first data entered into the system is the first data processed. Abbreviated *FIFO*. See also *Last In, First Out*.

First Line Form Advance

In word processing and computing, a feeding device attached to a word processor (used for continuous forms) that feeds the paper to the top of the next form when one form is finished printing.

First Parallel Fold

On *in-line* folding equipment, a *parallel fold* made in the *jaw folder* immediately after the *former fold*, and often after the web has been slit in half in the direction of web travel. A fold made in this manner produces eight-page multiples of the number of webs produced. The size of the *signature* created is one-half the *cutoff* length by one-half the width of the web. Also called a *tabloid fold*.

First Proof

The first typeset pages of a document that are checked against the original copy and corrected before being sent to the author or customer for further *proofing*.

First Rate Read

A measure of the accuracy of a *bar code scanner*, expressed as a percentage of the correct readings that will be obtained in one pass of a scanner over a *bar code*.

First Side Bearing

In typography, a measure of the white space between the left side of a character and the left edge of its *em square*. See also *Second Side Bearing*.

Fish Eye

A defect of *screen printing* characterized by a circular bubbling of a printed ink film and a dispersion of the ink *pigment* therein, resulting in a nonuniformity of color resembling, as its name implies, the eye of a fish.

In graphics, *fish eye* refers to an effect imparted to a flat image that makes it look as if it were mounted to the surface of a sphere.

Five-and-one-quarter (5¼-Inch)

In computing, descriptive of a common size of *floppy disk*. See *Floppy Disk*. Also in computing, the term *5¼-inch* is also descriptive of a standard size of internal devices and the housings used to contain them.

Five-File EPS

Any image or file in *DCS* format. See *Desktop Color Separation (DCS)*.

Five-Point Curve Control

In color, the process of changing the contrast or gradation of a color *scanner* by manipulating five points on the tone scale: *highlight*s, *quartertone*s, *middle tone*s, *three-quartertone*s, and *shadow*s. See also *Three-Point Curve Control*.

Five Thousand (5000) K

In *color*, the intensity of the light source in standard viewing conditions used in the evaluation of transparencies and *reflection copy*. "K" is the abbreviation for *Kelvin*, a unit of temperature—including *color temperature*.

Fixative

See *Color Fixative*.

Fixed Accent

Alternate term for a *pre-positioned accent*. See *Accent*.

Fixed-Beam Scanner

A type of *bar-code scanner* in which a stationary beam of light reads the *bar code* printed on products that are moved past it. See *Bar Code* and *Bar-Code Scanner*.

Fixed Disk

Alternate term for a *hard disk*. See *Hard Disk*.

Fixed Field

In a database, a *field* which contains the same number of characters in all the records of a set, regardless of how much data the field in a particular record actually contains. See also *Variable Field*.

Fixed Focus

In photography, a camera with a nonadjustable *lens* and *depth of field*.

Fixed Font

In typography, a *font* containing characters with fixed widths, such as Courier, as opposed to fonts with *proportional width* characters. (See also *Proportional Font*.)

Fixed-Length Record

In a database, one record of a set containing fixed fields. Fixed-Partition Memory Management
In computing, the subdivision of a computer's memory into some number of equal sections.

Fixed Pitch

In typography, a typeface in which every character has the same width, in contrast to *proportional width*.

Fixed Point

The typesetting or representation of numbers with no digits to the right of the decimal point.

Fixed Space

In typography, a blank space of a fixed increment, used where a constant-width blank space is required, since typographic word spaces vary in width according to the *justification* needs of a line.

The most common widths are the *em space* (a square formed by the value of the *point size*; a 9-point em space will be 9 points wide no matter what the face), the *en space* (a size half that of the em), and the *thin space* (either ¼ or ⅓ of an em). The *figure space* would have the same width as the numerals 1–0 and the dollar sign, although the en may be used for this in some systems. Some people occasionally confuse em and en spaces with caps M and N, which is no longer appropriate. If the fixed space requirement is a certain number of points, it may help to recall that the em is as wide as the point size. If two picas of horizontal space are required, two ems in 12-point (1 pica = 12 points) can be used.

In most type families, the em space is designed as a square of the point size. For example, in 12-point type, the em space would be 12 points wide by 12 points high. The en space would therefore be proportionately half as large and the thin space proportionately ¼ or ⅓ as wide. *Condensed* or *expanded* type varies the widths of these spaces, however.

Fixer

A combination of chemicals used in the *fixing* phase of *development* of a photographic film. See *Fixing*.

Fixing

In photography, the immersion of a developed film in a chemical solution designed to remove the unexposed silver halide from the emulsion, leaving the exposed metallic silver intact. *Fixing solution*, often made of sodium or ammonia thiosulfate, renders the silver halide water-soluble, allowing it to be washed out of the film in a water bath, often the last stop of a film. Fixing—also known as *stabilization*, especially when combined with the washing phase—is necessary to render a photographic image permanent.

FL

Abbreviation for *focal length*. See *Focal Length (FL)*.

Flagging

In web printing, the act of indicating the position of a *splice* on the roll as a means of facilitating removal of the *signature* bearing the splice from the delivery.

Flaking

A defect of *screen printing* characterized by detachment of ink bits from the printed film, caused by a lack of adhesion between the ink and the *substrate*.

Flame

In *Internet* colloquial terminology, an intentionally insulting *email* message or post to a *USENET* group, often directed at a particular individual. A newsgroup post that deliberately provokes a flame is referred to as *flame bait*.

Flame Bait

In *Internet* colloquial terminology, a post to a *USENET* newsgroup deliberately provoking other members of the group to *flame* the originator of the message. A prolonged posting of flames and flame bait is called a *flame war*.

Flame Resistance

Property imparted by treatment of paper with chemicals that prevent the paper from promoting the spread of a flame, should the paper catch fire. Papers used for drapes and curtains, paper-based garments, hats, tablecloths, streamers, or other party favors are required by government ordinances to be flame-resistant. Flame resistant papers are not fireproof, however; flame resistance merely allows a flame to be contained, not avoided completely.

Flame resistance is quantitatively gauged by the length of time an ignited paper continues glowing, and the size of the remaining portion of paper once the flame has ceased.

Flame War

In *Internet* colloquial terminology, a prolonged series of *flame*s between two or more subscribers to a *USENET* group. See *Flame* and *Flame Bait*.

Flap

In *binding and finishing*, the portion of a book's *jacket* which folds under the cloth cover holding the jacket on the book. Book flaps often contain promotional copy and author information.

In copy preparation, a *flap* is an overlay containing type (or other page element), used in conjunction with the type (or other page element) on the *mechanical* beneath the flap. Flaps are used when two pages have common elements; the mechanical (with the flap up) is photographed for one page, and photographed again (with the flap down) for the second page.

Flap Roller

In *offset lithography*, a roller used in an offset press *dampening system* comprising canvas flaps which transfer *fountain solution* from the *fountain* to an adjacent *oscillator*. Also known as a *flapper*. See *Dampening System*.

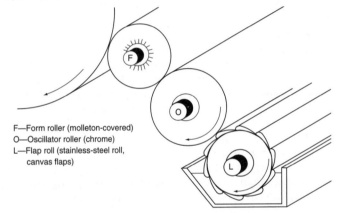

F—Form roller (molleton-covered)
O—Oscillator roller (chrome)
L—Flap roll (stainless-steel roll, canvas flaps)

Levey flap roller.

Flapper

Alternate term for *flap roller*. See *Flap Roller*.

Flare

In photography, an undesirable quantity of stray light that strikes the film plane of a *camera*, caused by internal reflection, lighting conditions, diffraction of light due to dust, etc.

Flash

In phototypesetting, to shine a light source through a character image, exposing the character onto photosensitive paper. The *flash* is also the device that controls this character exposure.

In typography, the term *flash* also refers to emphasized text, such as that printed as a *reverse*, in a different color, or with a frame of some sort.

In computing, *flash* also refers to *flash memory*.

Flash Exposure

In *halftone photography*, additional exposure to enhance the dots in the *shadow* regions of halftone negatives.

Flash Memory

In computing, a type of computer memory comprising *erasable read-only memory (EROM)* chips, which is a kind of middle-ground between *RAM* and *ROM*. A computer's *random-access memory (RAM)* can be constantly erased and reprogrammed, and is also known as *volatile memory*, as data stored there is erased once the power supply is cut off. In contrast, a computer's *read-only memory (ROM)* cannot be erased or reprogrammed, and is known as *nonvolatile memory*, as it remains intact even if the power is turned off. Flash memory, however, allows data to be stored, removed, deleted, reprogrammed, etc., and it is also nonvolatile. The *access time* required to retrieve data stored in flash memory is very fast (it's measured in *nanosecond*s), but the time required to reprogram it is very slow. Also known as *flash ROM*.

Flash ROM

See *Flash Memory*.

Flat

In *prepress*, a group of properly positioned photographic *negative*s or *positive*s from which a printing plate will be made by exposing the photosensitive plate to the flat. A flat can consist of the negatives or positives attached to the back of a sheet of goldenrod (called a *goldenrod flat*), with holes cut only over those areas of negative/positive that correspond to regions denstined for exposure. The flat contains all the page elements in the proper position for exposing a plate. (See *Stripping*.)

In printing, the term *flat* is also used to refer to a set of pages that are in the proper position for folding a *signature*.

In *photography*, the term *flat* refers to a photographic image that lacks *contrast*.

In *gravure* printing, the term *flat* refers to the size of the nip between the *gravure cylinder* and the *impression roller*. See *Impression Roller*.

Flat Assembly

Alternate term for *stripping*. See *Stripping*.

Flat Back

Any type of *binding* on which the *spine* is not rounded, as opposed to a *round back*. Also known as *square back*.

Flatbed

Any flat (as opposed to cylindrical) surface used to mount a printing plate or typeform in *letterpress* printing. See *Letterpress: Flatbed Press* and *Letterpress: Platen Press*.

In imaging, the term *flatbed* is descriptive of any optical input or output device—such as a *scanner* or *imagesetter*—that images the original from a flat surface (rather than a cylinder) or exposes film or paper on a flat surface. See *Flatbed Imagesetter*, *Flatbed Plotter*, and *Flatbed Scanner*.

Flatbed Cutter

Alternate term for *guillotine cutter*. See *Guillotine Cutter*.

Flatbed Imagesetter

A type of *imagesetter*, a device used for *high-resolution* laser output of digitally created pages or *color separation*s. On a flatbed imagesetter, the digital file is converted to film format, and the film to be exposed is fed from a roll through rollers (called a capstan) past a light source. Digital information is used to guide the laser in line-by-line exposure of the film.

An alternate type of imagesetter is a *drum imagesetter*, in which the film is exposed by moving it around a cylinder. Of the two, drum imagesetters are widely believed to generate the better quality output. (See also *Imagesetter*.) A flatbed imagesetter is also known as a *roll-fed imagesetter* or a *capstan imagesetter*.

Flatbed Press

A configuration of press used in *letterpress* printing, in which an *impression cylinder* carries the paper or other *substrate* into contact with an inked typeform or flat printing plate mounted to a *flatbed*. See *Letterpress: Flatbed Press*. A flatbed press is also used for generating *color proof*s before the job is transferred to a large production press. See *Flatbed Proof*.

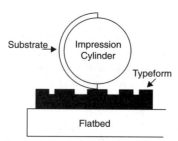

A flatbed press used in letterpress printing.

Flatbed Proof

A *color proof* produced by applying ink to the *substrate* using a special *flatbed press* to simulate the printed image before the job is transferred to a production press. The flatbed press used for generating proofs is generally fed by hand, sheet-by-sheet.

Flatbed Scanner

An optical scanning device used to convert an image—such as a photograph—to digital form, in order to allow later manipulation and output as part of a page, as a color-separated image, or by itself.

In a flatbed scanner, the original image (either a print or transparency) is placed face-down on a glass platen. A light source illuminates the image line by line from beneath the platen and moves across or down the image. The light is picked up by an array of *charge-coupled devices*

(CCDs), which analyzes the image **pixel** by pixel and stores the particular **color** or **grayscale** information for each pixel in a digital file, commonly by use of colored filters that pass over the CCD array. (Some newer CCD scanners have multiple arrays of CCDs, each of which is responsible for a particular color.) When one line is complete, the light source moves and images the next one, continuing this process until the entire picture is imaged. Scanners that have multiple CCD arrays are faster than those that have only one array, as the scanner needs to only make one pass (rather than three) to glean all the color information it needs.

After scanning, the image is processed as one large digital file (if the image needs further manipulation) or as separate color-separated films.

Other types of scanners—such as high-end **drum scanners**—utilize **photomultiplier tube**s rather than CCD arrays. Although these devices produce much higher-quality scans than flatbed scanners, they are far more expensive. Flatbed scanners—due to the fixed, flat copyboard—also allow scanning images from books and other sources that would be hard to image on a drum scanner. See **Scanner** and **Scanning**. See also **CCD Scanner**.

Flatbed scanner.

Flat Bond

A type of **bond paper** produced solely from wood fibers; a bond paper with no **cotton conent**.

Flat Color

A form of **color** printing in which color dots are not printed on top of each other; each colored ink is printed as is, as opposed to **process color** in which dots of one color are **overprinted** on dots of one or more other colors to produce blends.

Flat Screen

In computing, a thin video display, in contrast to larger, more perceptibly bowed **cathode-ray tube**s.

Flat Shading

In computer graphics, coloring a three-dimensional object in a flat, unrealistic way, used primarily to make a quick examination of the effect of a particular lighting.

Flat Text

In telecommunications, uncoded text (i.e., text containing no formatting commands, such as typeface, point size, italic, bold, etc.) sent electronically from one computer to another. Also known as **raw text**.

Flat Tint

A printed image containing "halftone" dots that are all of uniform size, as opposed to a **halftone** or **vignette**, which use variable-size dots to simulate a range of tones or shades. Often called simply **Tint**.

Flatting Agent

Any of a variety of substances added to a printing ink to reduce the **gloss** of the printed film.

Flax Tow

Linen fibers obtained from flax plants (several species of the genus *Linum*, in particular the common flax, *L. usitatissimum*) used as a fibrous source in papermaking.

Fleuron

In typography, any ornament used to mark the beginning of a paragraph, or for some other strictly decorative purpose.

Flex

Alternate term for **deflection**. See **Deflection**.

Flex also refers to the ability of any material or substance—such as a printing **substrate**—to be bent.

Flexible Disk

Alternate term for a **floppy disk**. See **Floppy Disk**.

Flexo

An abbreviation of **flexographic**, used as an adjective for **flexography**. See **Flexography**.

Flexo Gravure

A type of **offset gravure** printing performed on a **flexographic** press. See **Gravure: Offset Gravure** and **Flexography: Hybrid Flexographic Presses: Flexo Gravure**.

Flexographic

Pertaining to or descriptive of the printing process of **flexography**. See **Flexography**. The adjective *flexographic* is also commonly abbreviated as **flexo**.

Flexographic Technical Association (FTA)

An international organization devoted to the promotion and development of **flexographic** printing, with a focus on testing and evaluating new developments and providing educational material on **flexography**.

Flexography

A form of printing that uses flexible rubber relief plates and highly **volatile**, fast-drying inks to print on a variety of **substrates**, commonly used in package printing.

Flexography has its origins in the development of natural and synthetic rubbers. Natural rubber is obtained by the treatment of latex, a milky exudation of various trees and plants primarily native to the tropics. It was used by many pre-Columbian civilizations in Central and South America (such as the Mayas). Samples of rubber were sent back to Europe by missionaries and explorers in the sixteenth century, and in the late eighteenth century British chemist Joseph Priestley (famous primarily as the discoverer of oxygen) found that latex rubber, when heated, would erase pencil marks. From this "rubbing" ability, he coined the term "rubber."

In 1839, Charles Goodyear accidentally discovered a means of strengthening natural rubber, a process he called "vulcanization." In the mid- to late-1800s, various rubber products and patents began appearing.

In the late 1800s, letterpress (printing from raised type, typically bits of metal) was the dominant form of printing, with the alternate processes of *lithography* and *gravure* still in their formative years. It was found that *letterpress* type could be set into plaster and that unvulcanized liquid rubber could be poured into the mold and, after heating and cooling, could make a workable rubber stamp. Soon, it was found that the rubber stamp concept could be applied to the manufacture of printing plates, which could be useful for printing on surfaces that did not yield good results with conventional letterpress processes, in particular corrugated paperboard.

The invention in the 1930s of synthetic rubbers made the properties of the rubber stamps and plates much more reliable than they were with unreliable natural rubber. Advances in rubber platemaking were pioneered by the Mosstype Corporation, which developed effective processes for both *aniline printing* (as flexography was known until the 1950s) and for letterpress printing. In the 1940s, Mosstype developed effective off-press plate-mounting systems, which minimized downtime and made aniline printing more efficient. In 1938, two men at the International Printing Ink Corporation devised a way of accurately and effectively metering the film of ink transferred to the rubber plate. Their system was inspired by the etching of gravure cylinders, which transfers ink from cells to the substrate. They developed an ink roller, engraved with a controlled size and number of cells, and plated with copper and chrome that effectively metered the ink film transferred to the aniline

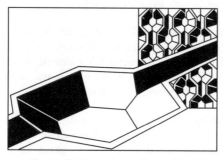
One cell from an anilox roller.

printing plate. They called their roller an *anilox roller*, and it is still the basis of modern flexographic presses.

In the first decades of the twentieth century, as was mentioned, flexography was known as "aniline printing," taking its name from the type of dyestuff used in the inks. In the 1930s, the *aniline dye*s were declared toxic by the FDA. Although aniline printers were by then using different types of inks, the name remained. In the late '40s, it grew apparent to industry leaders that the name "aniline printing" had to go, as the name had bad connotations, since the process was widely used for printing food packaging. In 1951, the Mosstype Corporation, in its company newsletter, held a contest to rename the process. Alternate names were solicited, and a final choice would be voted on. Two hundred suggestions came in from printers around the country, and a special committee formed by the Packaging Institute pared the list down to three: permatone process, rotopake process, and flexographic process. On October 21, 1952, it was announced that the overwhelming choice was "flexographic process," or "flexography."

Like other printing processes, there are a wide variety of press configurations. In its most basic form, however, the flexographic press comprises the following parts.

INK FOUNTAIN

Flexo ink, typically a thin, volatile liquid ink, is stored in an *ink pan*, where a rubber-covered *fountain roller* rotates. The fountain roller picks up a thick film of ink and transfers it to a *metering roller*, typically known in flexography as an *anilox roller*. The anilox roller is a chrome- or ceramic-covered roller whose surface contains small, engraved pits or *cell*s (typically from 80–1,000 cells per in.)

The pressure between the fountain roller and the anilox roller is set so that the excess ink pools up at the top of the nip between them. The difference in revolution speed of the two rollers (the fountain roller typically turns at a slower rate than the anilox roller) causes a wiping effect on the anilox roller. The goal is to ensure that only the ink stored in the engraved cells on the anilox roller's covering is transferred to the plate. The difference in speed also eliminates a problem in flexography called *mechanical pinholing* (sometimes also called *ghosting*, and related to *mechanical ghosting* found in *offset lithography*), in which ink is not replenished uniformly to the surface of the anilox roller, causing the texture of the roller to be transferred to the substrate.

Some alternate configurations include a chambered or enclosed system, in which the anilox roller sits in the ink fountain itself (removing the need for a fountain roller), the ink metering performed by a *doctor blade* (a strong strip of steel, plastic, or other material) that is placed between the fountain and the nip between the anilox roller and the plate cylinder. The angle and pressure of the doctor blade ensure a controlled and uniform ink metering. Another fountain roller-less configuration pumps ink from an ink tank to the surface of the anilox roller (which sits above an ink pan, the latter acting as a catch basin). A doctor blade is also used in this configuration to meter the ink film. Another more elaborate system, called an ***enclosed inking system***, features two doctor blades—one at the bottom of the anilox roller, the other at the top, the ink reservoir located between them. Ink is pumped onto the surface of

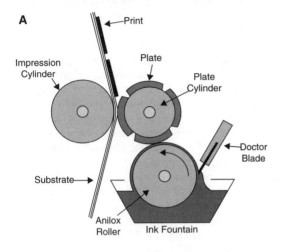

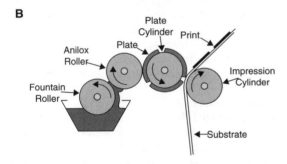

Two configurations of flexographic inking systems: two-roller (A) and three-roller (B).

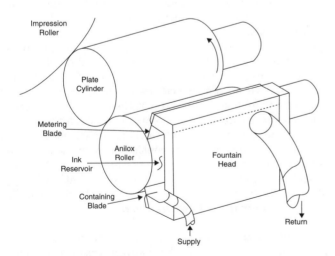

Enclosed inking system.

the anilox roller, where the top doctor blade is responsible for metering. This system is typically used on high-speed presses, and is popular due to the fact that, since the inking system is not exposed to the air, ink ***viscosity*** can be tightly controlled.

PRINTING UNIT

The inked anilox roller is adjacent to the ***plate cylinder***, a steel drum on which the rubber flexographic plate is mounted (usually by means of an adhesive backing, rather than the plate clamps used in offset lithography). The raised impression on the flexo plate picks up the ink and transfers it to the substrate passing between the plate cylinder and the smooth, steel ***impression cylinder***. The plate cylinder can either be ***integral*** (the cylinder body, end-caps, and shafts are all one piece), ***demountable*** (the shafts are removeable), ***sleeve*** (the cylinder face is slid onto a bored cylinder using high-pressure air), and ***magnetic*** (the cylinder is magnetized, allowing metal-backed plates to be mounted magnetically, rather than by means of adhesive). (See ***Plate Cylinder: Flexography***.)

In some applications (typically those in which ink ***strike-through*** is a problem, and is likely to cause ink buildup on the impression cylinder), the impression cylinder is replaced with an ***impression bar***, a ¼- to ½-inch-diameter steel rod clamped into the proper position behind the web. The bar does not rotate, and as a result the moving web wipes off any ink likely to accumulate on it.

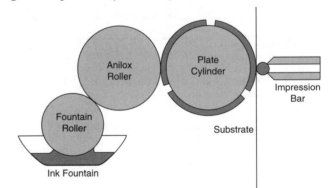

Flexographic press using an impression bar instead of a roller.

PLATES

There are three types of image carriers in flexography, two of which can be categorized as plates:

Rubber Plates. A negative of the image to be printed is placed on top of a metal alloy coated with a light-sensitive acid ***resist***. When exposed to light, the resist hardens in the exposed image areas, and remains soft and soluble in the unexposed, nonimage areas. The unhardened resist is washed away after exposure, and an ***etchant*** is applied to the surface, which engraves those areas not protected by the hardened resist. The result is a metallic relief plate. A mold—or matrix—is then made of the relief plate. After cooling the mold, a rubber sheet is pressed into the matrix which, after cooling, will be a rubber relief plate. Various finishing operations optimize the plate for flexographic printing.

Photopolymer Plates. Manufactured either from *sheet photopolymer* or *liquid photopolymer* materials, a photographic negative is placed on top of the photopolymeric material and exposed to ultraviolet light, which hardens the photopolymer in those areas through which it passes (the image areas), leaving the unexposed regions unhardened. After exposure, washout procedures remove the unhardened photopolymer from the nonimage areas, leaving the image areas in relief.

Plates are mounted on the plate cylinder either by an adhesive backing or by other means, such as plate clamps. See *Plate: Flexography*.

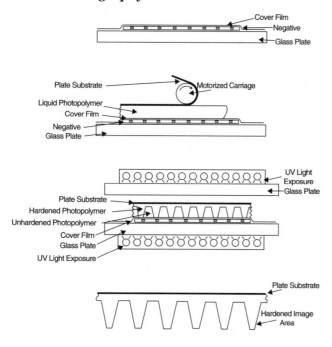

Liquid photopolymer plate makeup.

Design Rolls. A third type of image carrier is called a *design roll*, which consists of a layer of vulcanized rubber applied as an unbroken "jacket" on the surface of the plate cylinder itself. The imaging of the plate is commonly performed using high-energy lasers, which atomize the nonimage portions of the rubber surface, leaving the image areas in relief.

Design rolls, due to their seamlessness, are useful for printing continuous background patterns such as those found in packaging, wrapping, and other forms of decorative printing applications. They are also capable of higher print runs than conventional plates, with which they are occasionally used in tandem. (See *Design Roll*.)

SUBSTRATE CONTROL

There are two main portions of the substrate control system on a flexographic press (as on many other webfed presses).

Infeed Section. The feeding systems used to control the movement of the web to the press vary. Flexography is used to print a wide variety of substrates, primarily those used for packaging, so each feeding and tension-control system needs to be tailored to the specific requirements of the substrate in question. Typically, the web is placed on a *reel stand*, which can either be a single-position unwind (one roll is mounted at a time, the primary advantage of which is its ability to accomodate a wide variety of roll widths and diameters) or a flying-splice unwind (a second roll is mounted above the first one, which is then spliced—with varying amounts of automation, depending on the device— onto the end of the expiring roll).

Single-position unwinds are useful when roll changes do not need to be made very often. Flying-splice unwinds, however, do not allow the wide variety of roll sizes that single-position units do. Flying-splice stands used for packaging can accomodate up to 24-in. diameter rolls, while stands for paper or other heavy substrates can accomodate up to 72-in. diameter rolls. One basic problem that needs to be accounted for is the out-of-roundness of the core, which always exists to some degree. If kept within certain tolerances, it is acceptable, but the unwind stand must be sufficiently sturdy to guard against any vibration caused by the nonconcentric core disrupting the printing units of the press.

The unwinding stand is one of the several "tension zones" on a web-fed press. Unwinding tension is important for proper register, and to prevent web breaks. Enough tension needs to be created to properly feed the substrate into the printing unit, yet too much can cause slippage elsewhere in the press. There are a wide variety of mechanisms that control web tension such as braking systems or a *dancing roll*, a roller connected to an air cylinder that can be adjusted to apply the appropriate amount of force to the web. A dancing roll is especially useful in that it can compensate for the decreasing diameter of the roll as it unwinds into the press, the diameter change altering the tension on the web.

The final portion of the press just prior to the printing unit is known as the *infeed unit*, which consists of two steel rollers and one rubber roller, the point being to brake the web and create a "tension barrier" between the unwind section and the printing section. This barrier ensures that the web tension beyond it is consistent, regardless of what is happening to the web prior to reaching it. This tendency to isolate regions of web tension ensures that any anomalies are dealt with before the printing unit. (See also *Web Offset Lithography: Feeding Section*.)

Outfeed Section. After the printing unit comes the *outfeed unit*, also known as the *cooling drum unit*, which acts to pull the web through the printing unit, create another tension zone separate from the printing unit, and guide the web to the rewind unit. This section commonly uses *chill roll*s, which are rollers cooled with water, brine, or some other substance that removes heat (generated by friction and/or from the drying portion of the printing unit) from the web prior to rewinding. The printed web is rewound on one of two types of rewinders, a *surface rewinder* (using a moving roller to wind the roll by frictional contact with the outside surface) or a *center rewinder* (winding the roll by means of a shaft inserted through the core.) See *Web Offset Lithography: Rewind Equipment*.

INKS AND SUBSTRATES

Flexographic presses typically use liquid inks that possess low viscosity and dry primarily by evaporation of the vehicle. Flexographic presses use either water inks (occasionally on nonabsorbent substrates such as polyolefins and laminated surfaces and, in the past, on various types of paperboard) or solvent inks (for use on surfaces such as cellophane). Water-based flexographic inks, however, have a longer drying time on less absorbent substrates and dry with a low degree of gloss.

Water-based inks are undergoing further research and development due to the desire to decrease the dependence on solvent-based flexographic inks, which contribute to air pollution. Currently, however, water-based inks do not perform very well when printed on nonabsorbent substrates. Ultraviolet curing inks are also extensively used in flexographic printing. (See also *Ink: Printing Requirements: Flexography*.)

Paper and Paperboard. Flexographic printing is done on *kraft* board, in particular corrugated board. White, bleached, and clay-coated linerboard are also often printed, the latter providing the best degrees of *ink holdout* and *ink receptivity*. Other types of paper- and paperboard-based flexo products include envelopes, folding cartons, milk cartons, coated paper-based gift wrapping, *groundwood*-based mass market paperback books, multi-layer bags used to package pet foods, fertilizer, and gardening supplies, wax paper- and *glassine* paper-based food packaging, and *vegetable parchment* used to line meat packaging. As with most other printing processes, the paper's *moisture content* can affect printability and runnability, in particular the drying characteristics of the ink. A moisture content greater than 5–7% can cause difficulties with flexo ink drying.

Non-Paper Substrates. *Polyethylene* is the most commonly printed film substrate used, encompassing end uses from adhesive tape to "boil-in-bag" TV dinners. The typical film manufacturer will produce over 1,000 different products. Some films need to be "treated," which involves re-orienting the surface electrons, a process that improves ink adhesion and *trapping*. However, overtreating can cause *ink setoff* and *blocking*.

Polyester films tend to be stronger and have more desirable characteristics for flexographic printing and are increasing in popularity. Originally used in photography, microfilm, audio- and videotape, and leisure suits, polyesters are finding more and more applications in flexo-printed packaging. Its high degree of chemical stability, which makes it desirable as a packaging material, also makes it difficult to print on, however. Chemical treatment of the surface of polyester films can help alleviate this problem. One particular problem with polyester films (and indeed many types of plastics) is their reduction in tensile strength at high temperatures, such as those generated by friction during printing. This can make these materials more susceptible to expansion and/or shrinkage, causing registration and aesthetic problems.

In an average year, 350 million pounds of *polypropylene* film is used for flexible packaging, 22% of which is for snack food wrappers alone. (This variety of polypropylene is called "oriented polypropylene".) Although it is widely used, its bare surface characteristics do not facilitate wetting by inks; frequently, it needs to be "activated" either by a corona, high-voltage discharge, or by exposure to a flame. (The latter treatment is not performed often.) Polypropylene films also lose much of their resistance to stretching beyond 140°F, temperatures commonly encountered in printing and converting equipment.

A variety of *vinyl film* used as a common flexo substrate is *polyvinyl chloride (PVC)*, about 240 million pounds of it being used for packaging each year. Other types of vinyl film are specifically produced for particular applications. Vinyl films are widely used for their chemical and water resistance. Unlike many other types of plastic films, treatment of the surface to improve ink adhesion is rarely necessary.

Other films used as flexographic substrates include *polystyrene*, *cellophane*, metal-coated films, synthetic papers, latex papers, and a variety of other surfaces. As in any printing process, the compatibility of substrate with ink constituents is crucial; some substrates, such as polystyrene, can be easily damaged by some solvents used in flexo inks.

PRESS CONFIGURATIONS

There are three basic press configurations used in flexography (with many different variations, depending on the manufacturer). A *stack press* is used for multi-color printing, and each *color station* is, as its name indicates, stacked vertically. Some configurations use two parallel stacks of printing units, sending the moving web in a U-shaped path. Stack presses include two to eight separate color stations (the most common stack presses possessing six stations), each with its own inking rollers, plate cylinder, and impression cylinder. The advantage of a stack press is the ease of reversing the web, allowing both sides of the substrate to be printed in essentially one pass. The accessibility and independence of each color station also make such a press easily

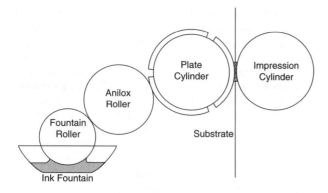

Basic flexographic printing unit.

adjustable to each specific application. The increased web tension produced on a stack press, however, sometimes precludes its use for very thin or highly extensible substrates, as stretching can cause misregister.

A second type of flexo press is a ***central impression press***, which uses a large-diameter ***common impression cylinder*** to carry the web around to each color station. The advantage of such a press is the ease of maintaining proper registration. The use of larger impression cylinders (up to 83 in. in diameter) has, in the past, led to an increase in press speed, but as drying methods have improved there is no longer a strict correlation between larger impression cylinders and increased speed. Central impression presses are not overly useful for facilitating reverse printing, however.

An ***in-line press*** is a third type of multicolor press; separate color stations are mounted in a horizontal line from front to back. They can handle a wider variety of web widths than can stack presses, but as with stack presses it can be difficult to maintain accurate register on some substrates. The in-line press can also make use of ***turning bars*** to "flip" the web over, allowing easy reverse printing.

SHEETFED FLEXOGRAPHY

Flexographic presses are rarely sheetfed, although most, if not all, corrugated board is printed in sheets rather than as continuous webs. The rigidity of the substrate enables it to be kept horizontal throughout its trip through the press. The sheets are essentially pushed into a set of feeder rollers, which send them through the impression nip(s) and finally to the outfeed stack. Printing can be accomplished either by printing on the top of the sheet or on the bottom.

HYBRID FLEXOGRAPHIC PRESSES

There are several varieties of "hybrid" printing processes that combine aspects of flexography with other methods.

Flexo Gravure. *Flexo Gravure* is a form of ***offset gravure***. Offset gravure printing essentially replaces the flat offset plate with a longer-lasting ***gravure cylinder***, transferring the image to a rubber blanket that, in turn,

transfers the image to the substrate. In flexo gravure, offset gravure is performed on a flexographic press, with the gravure cylinder replacing the anilox roller. A rubber blanket (such as that used in offset lithography) is mounted on the flexo plate cylinder. The ink is transferred to the engraved cells of the gravure cylinder (which, unlike conventional gravure, need to be engraved so that the image is right-reading); the image is then offset onto the rubber blanket (where the image becomes wrong-reading), and is finally transferred onto the substrate. Flexo and offset gravure are utilized when the desire for the high-quality gravure image carrier and long life of the gravure cylinder are needed for substrates that are not easily printed by traditional gravure. The flexible rubber blanket ensures high-fidelity image transfer on a wide variety of surfaces.

Offset Flexo *Offset flexo* is a hybrid of flexography and offset lithography in which the anilox roller transfers the ink to a flexo plate (its image in positive-reading form), which then offsets the image to an offset blanket cylinder mounted between the plate and the impression cylinder. Cylindrical plastic containers need to be printed in this manner. In some presses, all the color stations are positioned around a single blanket cylinder, and a multi-colored image is registered on the blanket, a single multi-color image being transferred to the substrate in essentially one pass.

The main advantage of flexographic printing, as was mentioned earlier, is its ability to print on many different types of substrates. There are far too many flexo substrates used to provide a comprehensive list here; flexo presses print everything from breath-mint wrappers to plastic packages that hold king-size mattresses. In the past, different types of polymers (i.e., plastics) mixed together tended to yield poor substrates with low print characteristics, but new advances in chemistry and manufacturing are producing new blends of plastics—known as "plastic alloys"—that can impart different qualities to the final product, such as increased strength, chemical resistance, resistance to the penetration of oxygen or other gases, etc. As the substrates change, so must the ink; cooperative efforts between ink manufacturers and the manufacturers of substrates ensure that for each new substrate a compatible ink will enable printers to utilize it effectively, efficiently, and economically.

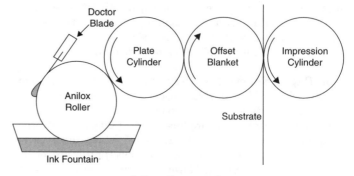

Offset flexography.

Flexural Stiffness

A paper property that describes its resistance to an externally applied bending force. See *Stiffness*.

Flicker

A perceptible fluctuation in the intensity of a computer monitor's display, produced during *refresh* cycles when the *refresh rate* exceeds the persistance of the phosphors coating the back of the screen. Flicker is also observed in a television or video picture when the two *fields* of a particular *frame* are not properly synchronized. A particular type of flicker—called *interlace flicker*—is a condition that affects monitors whose image is formed by means of *interlacing*. See *Interlacing* and *Interlace Flicker*.

Flicker Blade

In *offset lithography*, a set of blades or fingers used in the *dampening system* to flex and release a bristle-covered *fountain roller*. The action of the flicker blades transfers *fountain solution* to an adjacent oscillator roller. See *Dampening System*.

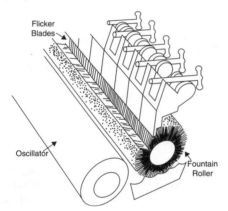

Brush dampening roller with flicker blades.

Flier

See *Flyer*.

Flint Glazing

A means of producing a high-gloss *finish* on a paper by polishing the web with a smooth stone or burnishing device as it moves through the papermaking machine. Paper produced in this manner is known as *flint paper*.

Flint Paper

A type of *coated-one-side* paper characterized by bright color and high gloss, produced by *flint glazing*.

Floating Accent

Alternate term for a *centered accent*. See *Accent*.

Floating Bar Printing Frame

In *screen printing*, a screen frame possessing extra moveable bars within the solid frame, which can be attached via wing nuts or other means. The screen fabric can be attached to the moveable bars and the tension of the screen adjusted by moving the bars. Such a frame also allows for adjustment of *register*.

Floating Dryer

A type of *dryer* that is used on *blanket-to-blanket press*es in *web offset lithography*. A floating dryer allows the web to simply pass through a heated region of air, rather than contact a surface, as on blanket-to-blanket presses the web contains wet printing on both sides. Floating dryers can either be *open flame dryer*s or *high-velocity hot-air dryer*s.

Floating Load

A shipment of paper loaded into a freight car in such a way that it can shift to some degree during shipping without becoming damaged.

Floating Palette

In a computer graphics (or other) program, a *window* containing a set of icons representing various tools at the user's disposal. The windows are described as floating when they are visible even when other windows are active. Very often, these windows can be closed when the tools are not required, and re-opened when they are needed.

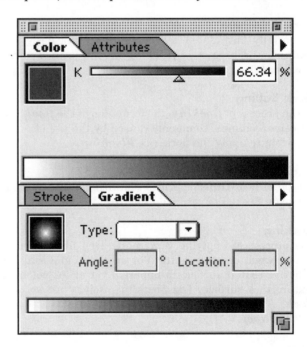

Floating palette, in this example the color and gradient palettes from Adobe Illustrator.

Floating-Point

In computing, descriptive of a mathematical feature which produces more accurate calculations of large numbers. See *Floating-Point Coprocessor*.

Floating-Point Coprocessor

In computing, a **microprocessor** (often installed as a **coprocessor**) capable of rapid calculation of large numbers, as it is relies on exponential arithmetic. Also known as a *floating-point processor*, a **floating-point unit**, and simply **FPU**. See **Coprocessor**.

Floating-Point Unit

Alternate term for a **floating-point coprocessor**. See **Floating-Point Coprocessor**.

Floating Roller

Alternate term for a **dancer roller**. See **Dancer Roller**.

Flocculation

Ink problem characterized by particles of **pigment** becoming "undispersed" and "flocking" together in clumps, commonly caused by addition of a substance that "shocks" the particles out of suspension.

Ink that has undergone flocculation tends to print with decreased **color strength**, and occasionally with decreased **gloss**. Adding **solvent** to the ink may alleviate the problem, although adding an excessive amount of solvent will result in an excessive decrease in **viscosity**. (See also **Sedimentation**.) The dispersion of clustered pigment particles is called **deflocculation**.

Flock Adhesive

A specially formulated **screen printing** ink designed to facilitate the process of **flocking** on the printed surface. See **Flocking**.

Flock Balling

In the process of **flocking**, the formation of the **flock** fibers into small clumps, commonly caused by the use of a rotating drum to apply the flock. See **Flocking**.

Flock Transfer

A type of heat-transfer printing utilizing a screen-printed image on flocked paper. See **Flocking**.

Flocking

The process of applying very short, dyed fibers of rayon, cotton, wool, or other natural or synthetic material to an adhesive-coated surface to impart a velvet- or velour-like texture to a surface. The fibers themselves are known as **flock**. A paper that has been flocked is also known as **velvet paper**.

Flocs

Premature clots of paper fibers that form before the water-suspended **pulp** mixture is delivered to the **forming wire** on a papermaking machine. The presence of flocs results in poor paper formation. Constant agitation of the fiber solution in the paper machine's **headbox** prevents clots from forming.

Flood Bar

On a **screen printing** press, a type of metal or plastic **doctor blade** which aids in **flooding** the screen fabric. The flood bar commonly precedes the actual printing stroke and moves the ink in the opposite direction from the **squeegee**. A flood bar is also called a **return blade**.

Flood Coat

In **screen printing**, a thin layer of ink applied uniformly to the top of the screen fabric without making an impression, performed prior to the actual printing stroke. The flood coat can either be applied by the **squeegee** or, on automated presses, by a **flood bar**.

Flood Coating

In **screen printing**, an alternate term for **flooding**. See **Flooding** (screen-printing definition).

Flooding

A printing problem of **offset lithography** characterized by an excessive amount of ink on the printing plate, caused by too much ink flow from the ink fountain, too little water flow from the water fountain, or an inadequate amount of etching material in the **fountain solution**.

The term *flooding* also refers to a printing ink defect characterized by separation (on the surface of the ink) of one type of **pigment** from others.

Flooding also refers to a printing problem in **flexography**, in which more ink is transferred to the plate in the center than the sides, commonly caused by **deflection** of the **fountain roller**.

In **screen printing**, *flooding* is an alternate term for **air pull**, or coating the top of the screen fabric with ink without making an impression. Also called **flood coating**.

Flood Stroke

In **screen printing**, the movement of either the **squeegee** or a **flood bar** that applies the **flood coat** to the screen fabric. See **Flood Coat**.

Flop

To create a mirror-image of a photograph or other image by "flipping" it around a central axis (either lengthwise or widthwise), commonly by exposing it from the "wrong" side of the negative, or by rotating it in any of the image processing programs available. Also known as **flopping**.

Flopping

See **Flop**.

Floppy Disk

A flexible (or "floppy") magnetic storage disk secured in a protective case, either soft or hard plastic shell (in which case it is often called a **diskette**). The floppy disk was one of the original computer storage media, predating even *hard disk*s. Before the invention of the hard disk, floppies were used to store programs and files; after the advent of the hard disk, they became a popular back-up medium and the primary means of distributing and transferring software. As programs become larger and exceed even the capacity of several floppy disks, and other, higher-capacity media become more prevalent, the floppy is decreasing in popularity. Many programs are now distributed on *CD-ROM* (or over the Internet) and most back-up and file transfers are done using other types of magnetic cartridges.

There are two sizes of floppy disk—5½-in. and 3½-in.—the latter of which is the most common. Both sizes are available in one of two densities: *double density (DD)* 5½-in. disks have a total capacity of 360 *kilobyte*s (KB), and **high density (HD) 5½-inch disks have a total capacity of 1.3** megabytes (MB). Double density 3½-in. disks have a total capacity of 720 KB, while the high density 3½-in. disks have a total capacity of 1.44 MB. An extended density 3½-in. disk has a capacity of 2.88 MB.

Floptical Disc

A type of magnetic storage medium comprising a 3½-in. *floppy disk* in concert with the laser tracking of *optical disc*s to increase the storage capacity of a conventional floppy to as high as 20 *megabyte*s. The floptical required a specialized drive, which could also read and write conventional 3½-in. floppies. The floptical—perhaps living up to its name—never caught on commercially, although the technology lives on in *magnetic optical* discs.

Flotation Deinking

A method of removing ink and making *recovered fiber*s suitable for production of *recycled paper*. See *Deinking*.

Flow

A property of printing ink (and other fluids) that describes its ability to spread across a surface, into a thin film, or to and from the rollers of a printing press. The measure of a fluid's flow is *viscosity*. See *Viscosity*.

Flowchart

A diagram used to graphically represent the workings of a process. Essentially, a flowchart consists of a series of variously shaped boxes which indicate individal actions or decision choices. Each box is connected to others by a series of lines or arcs, which indicate what action will result from another action or decision.

Flow Control

In computing, a means of regulating the transfer of data between two devices, specifically working to prevent the loss of information once a particular device's *buffer* is full.

In networking, the term *flow control* refers to the means by which the network operating system keeps traffic from becoming congested, typically by re-routing data transmissions around troublesome portions of the network.

Flowing-In

A printing defect of *screen printing* characterized by a post-impression flowing of a printed ink film, ruining any fine detail that was printed.

Flow-Mark

A defect of *screen printing* characterized by a waviness of the surface of a printed ink film.

Flow Out

The ability of a *screen printing* ink to manifest a small degree of flow following printing, to "erase" the texture of the screen fabric from the surface of the ink film.

Fluff

Alternate term for *lint*, also called *fuzz*. See *Lint*.

Fluorescence

A physical process of converting high-frequency radiation (most commonly *ultraviolet* light) into visible light. Fluorescent materials—such as *fluorescent pigment colors*—absorb ultraviolet light and discharge it as bright visible light. A common example of other fluorescent materials are the phosphors coating the inside of a *cathode-ray tube*, which fluoresce to produce the components of a computer or television display. Ultraviolet light is used to detect certain naturally fluorescent materials—for example, fungi and other organisms responsible for food spoilage will fluoresce, and ultraviolet light can be used to detect them. Fluorescent dyes are also used in medicine, where they can be used to identify tumors and other medical problems. Fluorescent materials are also used in laundry detergents, and it is the fluorescence of these materials which produces the brightening effect of whites and colors.

Fluorescent Pigment Colors

A type of *pigment* used in printing inks characterized by high brilliance when viewed under an *ultraviolet* light source. They are commonly used in screen printing, where they produce the best results. Although fluorescent pigments are used in other printing processes, their performance is less than optimal since they typically require thick ink films or multiple passes to produce an effective printed image. Fluorescent pigments are only available in a few colors, and they don't intermix well to produce intermediate colors as well as nonfluorescent pigments.

Fluorescent Yellow

Also known as *Brilliant Yellow 8GF*, fluorescent yellow is a greenish fluorescent yellow *organic color pigment* used in printing inks. Although fluorescent yellow is resistant to soaps, it possesses low *lightfastness* and low resistance to heat and solvents. It is used for specialty applications such as display packaging, cartons, and greeting cards, often in conjunction with other fluorescent inks. It has also been used as a first-down color in process printing to increase lightness, and as a gold pigment in foil applications. It is used in *letterpress*, *lithographic*, *gravure*, and *screen printing* processes. Recent innovations have improved its lightfastness and its suitability for a wider variety of applications. (See also *Organic Color Pigments*.)

(*CI Pigment Yellow 101 No. 48052*.)

Flush

In typography, any type which lines up vertically along some invisible reference line. See *Justification*. The term *flush* itself in this sense is believed to derive from hydraulic *quadding* units used to position type on a line.

Flush Cover

Any book cover that is trimmed to the same size as the body pages, as on a paperback book. Also called a *cut-flush binding*. Such books are known as *trimmed flush*.

Flushed Colors

A type of ink *pigment* produced by dispersing the pigment particles in oil rather than water. See *Flushing*.

Flushing

A process used to produce a printing ink *pigment* that involves dispersing the pigment particles in oil, rather than water. Typically, pigments begin life as a water suspension of pigment particles, which are then filtered out of the suspension and dried into a press cake. In flushing, the particles are not dried after filtering, but are left with a water content of 30–80%; the resulting press cake is mixed with oil, which then disperses the water. The remaining bits of moisture are removed via suction and/or heat. Flushing is performed on pigment particles that, in the traditional method of drying, form hard-to-grind clumps. The paste generated by flushing produces finer-dispersed particles. In some cases, the manufacture of pigment is faster, easier, and less expensive when pigment is produced using the flushing process. Pigments can be flushed in a variety of different liquids, depending on the end-use characteristics of the ink. *Newsink* is flushed using mineral oils, and other types of inks use anything from litho oils to gloss ink varnishes. Pigments produced by flushing are called *flushed colors*.

Flush Left

Alternate term for *left justification* or *quad left*. See *Left Justification* and *Quadding*.

Flush Paragraph

A paragraph typeset without indenting the first line of text.

Flush Right

Alternate term for *right justification* and *quad right*. See *Right Justification* and *Quadding*.

Flutter

A defect of an audio recording comprising a high-pitched noise heard during playback, caused by either a defect in the original recording or as a result of the motor of the playback device running at an irregular speed. Usually used in concert with the term *wow*. See *Wow*.

Fly-By

In computer graphics and three-dimensional modeling, a moving *bird's-eye view* of a three-dimensional object or environment.

Fly Fold

Alternate term for a *four-panel fold*. See *four-panel fold*.

Flyer

A small publication consisting essentially of a single sheet of paper, either folded or unfolded, often used to promote retail stores, sales, promotions, etc. Also spelled *flier*.

Fly Knife

On a *sheeter*, a rotating knife that cuts paper.

Fly-In

In video production, a *transition* in which one picture is reduced in size and made to appear as if it is disappearing into another picture. The outgoing picture may also be rotated to add perspective.

Flying

Alternate term for *ink misting*. See *Ink Misting*.

Flying Erase Head

In video editing, an erase head on a VCR that is oriented at the same angle as the recording and playback heads, resulting in smooth transitions and pinpoint accuracy in editing. In a conventional VCR, the erase head is oriented vertically, resulting in *noise* and choppy transitions.

Flying Height

On a computer's *hard disk*, the distance between the *read/write head* and the surface of the disk. Also known as the *head gap*.

Flying Paster

Alternate term for a *flying splicer*. See *Flying Splicer*.

Flying Splicer

A device found in the infeed section of printing presses used in *web offset lithography* which splices a fresh roll of paper to an expiring roll.

A flying splicer, in contrast to a *zero-speed splicer*, operates while the web is unwinding at the speed of the press. Sensing devices keep track of the roll diameter and, when it shrinks to below ½ inch, the splicing function is initiated. The position of the leading edge of the new roll, which has been accelerated to press speed, is monitored. An adhesive is applied to this *nose end* and, when it is in the proper position relative to the expiring roll, a pressure roller drops and the two edges are pressed together, ensuring that the splice is perfectly straight and that there are no air bubbles or wrinkles. The remainder of the expiring roll is cut away, and the old roll replaced with a new one to await the next splice. On a flying splicer, the whole operation, from initiating the splicing equipment to the actual splice, takes only several minutes, while the splice itself is effected in a mere fraction of a second.

Flying splicers can either be **two-arm splicer**s (two rolls can be mounted) or **three-arm splicer**s (three rolls can be mounted.) A flying splicer is also known as a **flying paster**. (See also **zero-speed splicer** and **Web Offset Lithography: Infeed and Web Control**.)

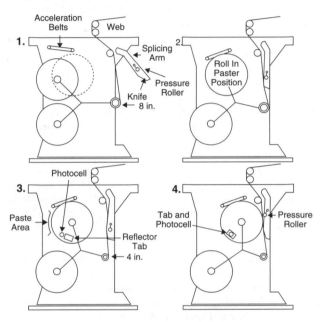

Use of a flying splicer.

Flying Spot Scanner

Any **scanning** device which utilizes a moving beam of light to scan an image. See **Scanner** and **Scanning**. See also **CRT Flying Spot Scanner**.

Flyleaf

In **case binding**, a set of unprinted sheets of heavy paper which follow or precede the **endleaf** papers. Also spelled as two words, *fly leaf*.

Fly-Out Menu

In computing, especially by means of a **graphical user interface**, a secondary menu that appears to the side of a **pop-up menu** or **pull-down menu**, providing a list of options or commands within one option on the larger menu.

Fly-Through

In computer graphics and three-dimensional modeling, a video of **three-dimensional animation** in which the camera passes over an object or through a location in a single continuous motion.

FM

Abbreviation for **frequency modulation**. See **Frequency Modulation (FM)**.

FM Screening

Abbreviation for **frequency modulation** screening, an alternate term for **stochastic screening**. See **Stochastic Screening**.

F-Number

See **F-Stop System**.

Foam Mark

An alternate term for the surface defect of a paper called a **blister** or **air bell**. See **Blister**.

Foaming

A problem of **gravure** ink, commonly observed in the summer, that manifests as **volcanoes** in the printed image. Foaming is caused by entrapped air in low-**viscosity** inks. The use of additives and ensuring that the ink fountain is full are ways of alleviating the problem.

Focal Length (FL)

In optics, the focal length of a **lens** is the distance between the lens-air interface and the focal point of the lens, or the point at which all the light rays entering the lens converge to form a sharp image of the object from which the light rays have been reflected. In photography, the focal length is defined as the distance from the center of the lens to the

Multiple levels of fly-out menus, here showing the font menu in QuarkXPress, with options for a particular font.

sharp image of an object (i.e., focal point), when the lens is focused at infinity. (See **Photography**.)

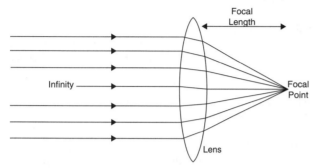

The focal length of a lens.

Focal Plane

In optics and photography, a planar surface containing the **focal point** of a lens. See **Focal Point** and **Photography**.

Focal Point

In optics and photography, the point at which all the light rays passing through a lens converge along a principal axis to form a sharp image of the object from which the light is reflecting. See **Lens** and **Photography**.

FOCOLTONE®

A **color matching system** used to specify and match **process color**s. The FOCOLTONE Color System consists of samples of 763 four-color combinations of the **process colors**, in single tints of all four inks from 5% to 85%. On the FOCOLTONE charts, each line contains a four-color process color and the 14 combinations that can be produced from it—four single colors, six combinations of two colors, and four combinations of three colors.

The FOCOLTONE system is supported by most of the commonly used **page layout program**s, such as **Page-Maker** and **QuarkXPress**. (See also **PANTONE** and **TRUMATCH**.)

Focus

In photography or an optical system, the point at which an adjustable lens hones incoming light (or electron beams) to the smallest spot, usually producing the sharpest image. It also refers to the act of adjusting a lens to sharpen an image.

Focus Servo

On an **optical disc** player, a mechanism that keeps the **read/write head** on a particular track, added to compensate for any minor distortions or defects in the disc surface, or any vibrations caused by the drive's motor.

Fogging

A defect of **gravure** printing, characterized by accumulating ink on the nonprinting areas of the **gravure cylinder** (which then is transferred to the substrate). Fogging is caused by the attraction certain inks have for the

chromium surface of the cylinder, or by poorly ground pigment particles adhering to the cylinder and failing to be wiped off by the doctor blade. Fogging may also be caused by surface irregularities in a new chrome cylinder, which cause ink to collect there. One way of remedying this problem is by using a fast-drying **solvent** ink, which will dry on the surface of the cylinder before contacting the **substrate**. Fogging is also called **scumming**.

Foil

A very thin (under 0.006-in.) printing **substrate**, composed either entirely of metal (such as aluminum) or a tissue-like material coated on one or both sides with metal or a metal coloring. A metallic substrate over 0.006 in. is called a **sheet**.

Foil Embossing

In **binding and finishing**, a finishing operation combining **embossing** (the stamping or pressing of images or patterns into a **substrate**) with **foil stamping** (the application of a layer of foil in a particular design or pattern to a substrate). See **Embossing** and **Foil Stamping**.

Foil Stamping

In **binding and finishing**, a finishing operation in which a design or other image is pressed onto a **substrate**. In foil stamping, a heated **die** containing a **relief** (raised) image presses down on a roll of foil passing above the **substrate** to be decorated. As the die hits the foil, it is transferred to the substrate. Many paperback books, hardcover book **jacket**s, and various types of packaging are foil stamped. Foil is available in many different colors, patterns, finishes, textures, etc. Foil stamping replaced an earlier process known as **bronzing**. Foil stamping that occurs in tandem with **embossing** is known as **foil embossing**.

See also **Die** and **Binding and Finishing**.

Foils

Suction cup-shaped plastic objects, placed beneath a papermaking machine's **forming wire** to support the wire and

aid in water removal from the paper **web** passing overhead on the wire. Foils are one of several means of water removal, and can be used instead of **table rolls**, or in concert with oscillation of the forming wire (called **shake**).

Folded-Strip Method

One of the varieties of **strip method** (or **sandwich method**) for testing the **roller setting** of offset printing ink or dampening rollers. See **Three-Strip Method**.

Folder

A printed sheet containing one or more folds.

A *folder* is also a device used in the **folding** phase of **binding and finishing**. See **Folding**.

A *folder* is also a large sheet of heavy paper or paperboard that has been folded to form a pocket, in which sheets can be filed and stored.

The term *folder* is also used to refer to the file organization system on a ***Macintosh*** or other ***window***-based operating system. Computer files on any computer are stored in sets of hierarchical directories that, on ***GUI***-based systems, use ***icon***s representing file folders as directories. The folder is intended to perpetuate the "desktop" metaphor common to the Macintosh and other similar systems.

Folding

In ***binding and finishing***, an operation performed—commonly after printing and ***cutting***—to fold a press sheet into a ***signature***. Folding is performed using special devices—either ***in-line*** or ***off-line***—called ***folder***s.

In addition to folding press sheets into signatures (which will eventually be bound and slit), folding is also performed to create brochures, magazine and newspaper inserts, maps, newspapers, etc.

Folds. Signatures for books are said to be ***folded-to-print***, which means that the folds are made in such a way to ensure that ***header***s, ***footer***s, ***folio***s, and other page elements, as well as ***backup printing***, are kept aligned from page to page throughout the signature. Other types of printed materials (in particular sheets with printing on only one side) are said to be ***folded-to-paper***, which means that such attention to alignment is not necessary. Folding-to-paper is acceptable in cases where all sheets exist independently of each other, as opposed to book signatures that do not.

There are two basic types of folds that can be made to a sheet: a ***right-angle fold*** is made at a 90° angle to a previous fold, while a ***parallel fold*** is oriented in the same direction as the previous fold. It is the combination of right-angle and parallel folds in various locations on a sheet that provide the wide array of folding configurations, including the ***accordion fold***, the ***gatefold***, the ***over-and-over***

fold, the ***French fold***, and the ***letter fold***, for example. The number of folds made to a press sheet determines the number of leaves (and pages) in that signature. See ***Folio***, ***Quarto***, ***Octavo***, ***Sixteenmo*** and ***Thirty-Twomo***.

FOLDERS

Machines used for folding are high-speed, high-tech devices that use combinations of knives and rollers to rapidly and accurately fold sheets. There are two basic types of folder:

Knife Folders. A ***knife folder*** has a folding unit comprising moving tapes or belts that feed a sheet along a flat plane until it contacts and is stopped by a gauge. The sheet is positioned squarely against a side guide. Beneath the sheet is a pair of counter-rotating folding rollers. The gauge and side guides position the sheet so that the desired location of the fold is above the nip of the two rollers. A metal knife presses down at a right angle to the sheet and forces it down between the rollers, which creates the fold. Additional folding units (of a similar configuration) are located at right angles to the previous folding unit and create additional folds in the sheet. Most knife folders also contain perforating units, which pierce the folds enough to allow air to escape, preventing wrinkles and other defects, as well as paper jams.

Three different configurations of knife folder include the ***jobber***, which contains four folding units and one (or two) parallel folding sections. The jobber allows up to four right-angle folds, two right-angle folds and one fold parallel to the second, or three right-angle folds and one fold parallel to the third; the ***double-sixteen*** is designed for producing 16-page or 32-page signatures; and a ***quadruple*** is designed to produce four 16-page or two 32-page signatures.

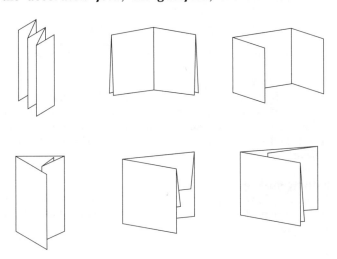

Some common folds, including (from top left) accordion, 8-page signature, gate, over-and-over, French (heads in), and letter.

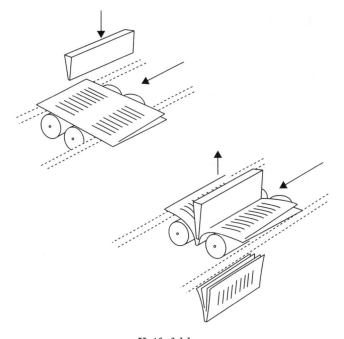

Knife folder.

Buckle Folders. A ***buckle folder*** has a folding unit which uses moving tapes or belts to carry a sheet up a slight incline between two metal plates (collectively called a ***fold-plate***). When the sheet hits a pre-positioned stop gauge at the top of the fold plate assembly it buckles slightly at the base of the fold plate. This buckle is grabbed by a set of rotating rollers and pulled downward, creating the fold. The sheet is then passed to additional fold plates and folding units to create the desired number and orientation of folds.

Each type of folder is used for different types of jobs. Right angle folds are primarily the purview of knife folders, while parallel folds are often made using buckle folders. Lighter-weight papers perform better on a buckle folder, while heavier-weight papers are often folded with a knife folder. Large-signature sheets produced in book printing are more often folded with a knife folder.

There are also ***combination folder***s that comprise folding units of both knife and buckle configurations. These tend to be more flexible than either/or devices.

Some common problems experienced with folders are worn or improperly positioned sheet deflectors, which can cause ***dog-ear***s, or a bend in the corner of a sheet. ***Double-sheet detector***s are also used on folders as a means of preventing more than one sheet from feeding into the machine at a time, which can cause paper jams and spoilage.

There are many accessories available for folders, which act to make the folding operations as trouble-free as possible. Air nozzles are used to provide as complete sheet separation as possible. Newer fold-plate designs can account for different stock weights. Stackers improve efficiency. Automated counters accurately measure the number of units passing into and out of the machine, allowing precise logs of a particular job. (See also ***Binding and Finishing***.)

Folding Dummy

In ***prepress***, an actual-size press sheet that has been folded into pages of the desired size and marked with page numbers to indicate the proper page imposition. The folding dummy also indicates where the ***gripper margin*** is, an allowance for which needs to be made.

Folding Endurance

A paper property that refers to the ability of a paper to be folded repeatedly without tearing. The number of folds it can withstand before it breaks is its folding endurance. Folding endurance varies according to ***grain direction***, and is greater ***against the grain***. In the Schopper method, a metal blade repeatedly folds a strip of paper back and forth between several rollers until it breaks. In the MIT method, an oscillating folding head repeatedly folds a paper sample back and forth until it breaks. The MIT method allows greater variability in the paper samples, and tension can be adjusted based on the thickness of the sample.

Folding endurance is enhanced by increased paper fiber ***refining***, being a function of the interlacing bonds between the paper fibers. nonfibrous additives such as ***fillers***, ***sizing***, and ***coating***s to the papermaking ***furnish*** or finished paper surface reduce folding endurance. Mois-

ture loss also considerably decreases folding endurance. The degree of folding endurance desired depends on the end-use requirements of the paper. The procedures that increase folding endurance also work to the detriment of other, perhaps more-desirable paper properties. (See ***Paper and Papermaking: Paper Properties***.)

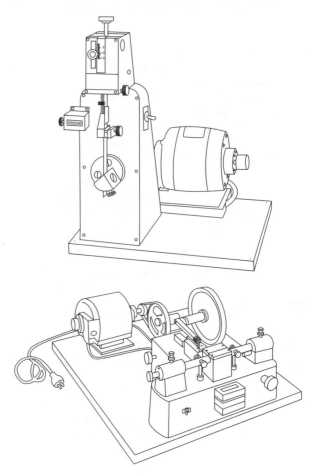

Two configurations of folding endurance testers.

Folding Plate

On a ***folding*** device (specifically a ***buckle folder***), a combination of two metal plates between which a sheet of paper is fed. A stop gauge in the fold plate determines the position of the fold on the sheet of paper. See ***Folding: Buckle Folder***.

Folding-to-Paper

A means of ***folding*** in which creases and folds are made without regard to the alignment of ***header***s, ***footer***s, or other image areas. Folding-to-paper is often performed on sheets that will eventually stand alone, in contrast to ***folding-to-print***. See ***Folding***.

Folding-to-Print

A means of ***folding*** in which creases and folds are made so that all ***header***s, ***footer***s, and other image areas are kept

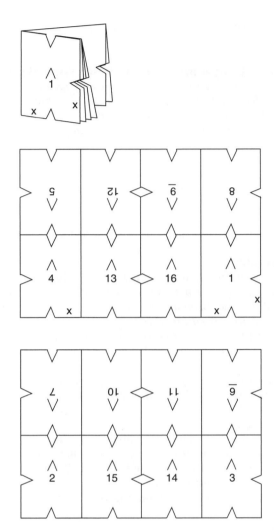

Folding dummy for this open sixteen-page layout.

aligned throughout the sheets created by the fold. Folding-to-print is often performed on sheets that form *signature*s, in contrast to *folding-to-paper*. See *Folding*.

Fold Marks

A set of marks added to a *negative* or *flat*—in the margins of a page—added as a guide for post-press *folding*.

Foldout

A printed insert which is designed to be bound into a book or other publication, but printed separately.

The width of a foldout is wider than the page of the publication in which it is to be bound. Consequently, one or more folds are needed to ensure that it doesn't protrude beyond the edge of the book. Foldouts are usually bound by the process known as *tip-in*.

Folio

In typography, a page number, commonly placed outside the *running head* at the top of the page. Folios are also commonly set *flush left* on *verso* pages and *flush right* on *recto* pages. They can also be centered at the top of the page. A folio that appears at the bottom of a page is called a *drop folio*. A folio counted in page numbering but which is not actually printed is called a *blind folio*. A folio that is printed is also called an *expressed folio*.

In printing, a *folio* refers to any printed sheet that is folded once to produce four pages. See also *quarto*, *octavo*, *sixteenmo*, and *thirty-twomo*.

Folio Lap

Alternate term for *lip*. See *Lip*.

FONT

In computing, an archaic resource name for a *Macintosh* bitmap font size.

Font

In typography, a set of all characters in a *typeface*.

A type font contains all of the alphanumerics (letters and numbers), punctuation marks, special characters, ligatures, etc., contained in a typeface. The term *wrong font (wf)* refers to a character that does not belong to the font. Examples of fonts are Palatino, Times, and Souvenir. The word *font* itself derives from *funditus*, a verbal corruption of the Latin word *fundere* ("to pour"). *Funditus*, in popular parlance, meant "a pouring, molding, or casting," referring to casting hot metal type.

In older typesetting terminology, *font* was used to refer to only those characters of a particular size, weight, and style (italic, bold, etc.). Thus, one typeface could have many fonts. In desktop publishing terminology *font* is used interchangeably with *typeface*.

The term *font* has also been used to refer to the specific physical device used to store the characters in a font, such as a film strip, disc, grid, or case (in metal type). (Whence the British term for font, *fount*.)

Although many fonts have the same name, different sources may subtly vary some elements within a typeface. Helvetica, for example, may be somewhat different when purchased from two different places.

Font Cartridge

A cartridge containing laser printer *font*s that needs to be plugged into the printer in order for it to be able to print the indicated fonts, as opposed to systems that allow fonts to be downloaded to the printer directly from the computer's hard disk. (See also *Downloadable Font*.)

Font/DA Mover

An application included with older versions of the *Macintosh operating system* that handled the loading of *font*s and desk accessories into the system.

Font Data

In computing, encoded *bitmap*s used to print characters of specific *font*s.

Font Database

In computing, the portion of a software program that stores *font* information.

Font Disk

In phototypesetting, a type of *font master*. A glass disk contains character shapes for a particular *font* which, when placed between a light source and a photosensitive paper, image the character on the paper. A focusing lens is also used to enlarge or reduce a character to a specified *point size*.

Font Downloader

In computers, a software program or utility used to effect the transfer of digital *font* information from the computer's hard disk to the output device, so as to allow the printer to print the specified font. Some printers require special plug-in *font cartridge*s.

Font Family

See *Type Family*.

Font File

A computer file containing *font* information.

Font Master

In phototypesetting, the medium on which character shapes of a particular *font* are stored, including a glass *font disk*, a film strip mounted on a revolving drum, a grid matrix, etc. The "original" version of a computer font from which all size variations are made is known as the *master font*.

Font Number

In computerized typesetting, a shortcut used during composing in which each available *font* is assigned a number, which the keyboard operator could enter when that font was desired.

Font Size

See *Point Size*.

Fonts On-Line

In phototypesetting, the total number of *font*s that are available on a particular system.

Font Stress

See *Stress*.

Font Substitution

In desktop publishing and digital prepress, the automatic replacement of an indicated but unavailable *font* in a document with an available font that most closely resembles it. A program that practices automatic font substitution analyzes the characteristics of the desired font—weight, syle, size, etc.—and attempts the best match it can. This may or may not generate good results, and a poor substitution can dramatically alter a page layout.

Font Weight

See *Weight*.

Food and Drug Administration (FDA) Regulations

A set of regulations governing the use of paper or paperboard in food and pharmaceutical packaging that concerns issues like contaminants, offensive odors, and other safety rules for packaging substrates and printing inks.

Foolscap

A standard British paper size—8×13 in.—now being replaced by the *A4* paper size. See *A Series*.

Foot

The bottom of a book, page, or column. See also *Head*.

Foot Candle

A measure of illumination, defined as the illumination of a one *candle* object at a distance of one foot. One foot candle is equal to one *lumen* per square foot. In the *ANSI*-prescribed *standard viewing conditions* (such as a color booth used for color analysis), the illumination is 200 foot candles. (Also commonly spelled as one word, *footcandle*.)

Foot Folio

Alternate term for a *drop folio*. See *Drop Folio*.

Foot Margin

In typography, the amount of blank space allowed between the bottom of the last line of text (or other bottommost page element) and the bottom edge of the sheet. Depending upon the user or typesetter, the foot margin may or may not include any *foot folio*s or *running feet*.

Footage

The total amount of all film or tape that has been shot for a specific production. See also *Shooting Ratio*.

Footer

In typography, any text that appears at the bottom of a page but is not part of the body text, such as a title, author, chapter title, etc. A footer appearing on every page is called a *running foot*.

Footlambert

A measure of *luminance*, one *lumen* per square foot.

Footnote

In typography, a reference relating to the main body of text, positioned at the bottom of the page. Footnotes are referenced by certain symbols (*, †, ‡, etc.), letters, or numbers, most often in *superior* or superscript form.

A footnote begins on the same page as its reference call, but it may be carried over to the bottom of successive pages. A short rule or additional space should separate the footnote from the text. The first line of each footnote is normally slightly indented.

Point sizes for footnotes are usually 7- or 8-point. By law, footnotes in financial forms, annual reports, prospectuses, and other SEC documents must be no smaller than the text size, which is 10-point.

The most common sequence of footnote reference marks is:

1. asterisk (*)
2. dagger (†)
3. double dagger (‡)
4. paragraph symbol (¶)
5. section mark (§)
6. parallel rules (‖)
7. number sign (#)

If more are required, they can be doubled up: double asterisks (**), double single daggers (††), double double daggers (‡‡), etc. However, when many footnotes are used, it is more practical to use numbers to identify each footnote.

Footnote Capability

The ability of a word processing, page layout, or other program to automatically number *footnote*s and ensure that they are located on the same page as their reference in the text, and remain that way even when text is reflowed.

For Position Only (FPO)

On a *mechanical*, a written designation applied to a *low-resolution* or inferior-quality image (such as a xerox of a photograph or *line art*) to indicate that the image (as seen) has only been added to the mechanical to indicate its position on the layout and thus is not indicative of the appearance of the final printed image. The actual *transparency* or artwork will be stripped in or otherwise added later.

Foreground

The portion of computer space where processing can be observed and interacted with by the user. In *multitasking* environments, the foreground is usually given higher priority than the *background*.

Foreground Job

See *Foreground Processing*.

Foreground Processing

In a computer system that does not support *multitasking*, any activity that the computer will execute to the exclusion of all others until it is finished, such as printing. In a system that *does* support multitasking, foreground processing refers to the computer paying attention to whatever activity the user happens to be working on, all other tasks occurring at the same time being referred to as *background processing*. If a particular *foreground job* happens to require extensive computer involvement, it is given priority of system resources over background processes.

Foreword

A type of *introduction* to a book, especially when written by someone other than the author. Nothing upsets a book editor more than confusing the word *foreword* with *forward*. See *Book Typography*.

Form Feed

In computing, a *control character* used to instruct a printer to advance *fanfold paper* from the last line on one page over the perforation to the top of the next page. Abbreviated *FF*.

Form Roller

One of several rollers found in the *inking system* and *dampening system* of a printing press used in *offset lithography*, which are in direct contact with, and transfer ink or dampening solution to, the printing plate. There are usually three to four form rollers in the *roller train*, commonly of different diameters to help prevent the printing problem known as *mechanical ghosting*. The form rollers can be lifted off the plate manually if desired, or automatically, as when the press is not printing. When the form rollers are raised from the plate, the *ductor roller* is removed from contact with the *fountain roller* and ink flow through the system ceases.

Proper setting of the form rollers is crucial. Form rollers that are set with too much pressure against the plate cylinder can cause streaking (caused by a bouncing generated as the form rollers pass over the *cylinder gap*), as well as *slurring* and *dot gain*, not to mention accelerated plate and roller wear and damage. Drastically unequal pressure between the form rollers and the *oscillator* at one end, and between the form rollers and the plate cylinder at the other end can also cause skidding and streaking. Increased pressure between the form rollers and the oscillator adjacent to them can cause warping and out-of-roundness of the form rollers, which produces a bounce when rolling against the plate, generating streaks and other blemishes. Form rollers can be set using the *strip method* (either the *three-strip method* or the *folded-strip method*), in which specially cut strips of paper, plastic, or *packing* material are inserted between the rollers and pulled out. The extent of the drag experienced during the pulling is a determination of not only the general pressure existing between the rollers, but also a gauge of the uniformity of the pressure between the rollers across their width.

Setting of form rollers can also be accomplished using a less subjective *roller-setting gauge*. The form rollers should always be set to the oscillator before setting them to the plate cylinder. Setting the form rollers to the plate can be accomplished in the same manner as setting them to the oscillator, although form rollers should be set slightly lighter to the plate so that the form rollers are driven by the oscillator and not the plate cylinder. Form roller setting can be evaluated using the *picture method* (also called the *ink stripe method*).

Some presses are also equipped with an *oscillating form roller* that moves laterally as it turns. This not only smooths out the ink film before it contacts the plate, but also helps to reduce mechanical ghosting. (See also *Inking*

System: Offset Lithography, and *Offset Lithography*.) In some presses, the first inking form roller also doubles as a dampening form roller. (See *Inker-Feed System*.)

In the dampening system of an offset press, the form rollers (of which there are typically two) also contact the plate directly, just prior to the inking form rollers. *Fountain solution* is transferred to the first dampening form roller by the dampening oscillator. Dampening form rollers that are driven by pressure from the oscillator are made of rubber, and are either covered with cloth or paper, or are run *bareback*. The proper setting of dampening form rollers to the plate and to the oscillator are also important, to ensure consistent and adequate transfer of fountain solution to the plate. The strip methods indicated above can also be used to evaluate the setting of the dampening form rollers. In some *continuous-flow dampening system*s, the dampening form rollers do not exist, the first inking form roller doubling as a dampening form roller. (See *Dampening System*.)

The term *form roller* is also used to refer to one of a series of rollers (commonly three) that perform a similar function on presses used for *letterpress* printing. In this case, the form rollers transfer the ink to the flat typeform or the plate cylinder, depending upon the press configuration. See *Letterpress*.

In *flexography*, the term *form roller* is used occasionally to refer to the *anilox roller*, or other type of roller that transfers ink to the surface of the plate. See *Anilox Roller* and *Inking System: Flexography*.

Formal Balance

In page layout, a page designed so that it is geometrically symmetric. See also *Dynamic Balance*.

Form-and-Cutoff

Alternate term for a *double-former folder*.

Format

In typography, any combination of *point size*, line spacing (*leading*), *line length*, *typeface*, placement, and style that contributes to producing a specific typographic appearance. This may relate to a character, word, line, paragraph, section, page, group of pages, or an entire publication.

In computerized typesetting, a *format* can be stored as a series of codes (which can be used repetitively). When those previously stored codes are to be used, the format is "called" or invoked by its given name or number.

In computers, the term *format* refers to the exact arrangement and orientation with which file data or computer command codes are stored.

The term *format*, when used as a verb, also means to create a specific typographic appearance for typeset copy by specifying the typeface, point size, spacing, etc.

When used as a verb, *format* also means to set up a floppy disk (or other type of computer storage media) to receive data in the form used for a particular system or device. For example, a floppy disk used to store *Macintosh* files needs to be formatted for a Macintosh computer.

Format Codes

In word processing, desktop publishing, or other programs, visible or invisible commands inserted in a document (either manually or automatically) used to control the format of text elements, such as *font*, *point size*, etc.

Formation

Paper characteristic describing the uniformity of its structure, especially to the extent that it relates to paper *smoothness*. When *cellulose* fibers form the paper *web* on the papermaking machine, nonuniform distribution generates "peaks" and "valleys" in the surface of the paper (visible as dark and light regions when the paper is held to the light). An excessive degree of nonuniformity is referred to as a *wild formation*, while a high degree of uniformity is referred to as a *close formation*. The degree of *wet pressing*, and such post-forming operations as *calendering* and *supercalendering* help even out these variations. A close or wild formation affects such other paper properties as *opacity* (a wild formation results in variable degrees of opacity across a paper's surface) and surface levelness. It can also have deleterious effects on *ink absorbency* and can result in ink *show-through* and incomplete ink transfer, especially in *letterpress* and *gravure* printing. (Wild formation doesn't typically cause problems in offset printing, due to the flexibility of the rubber blanket which can counteract the problems of inconsistent formation.) Prolonged fiber *refining* also helps improve formation uniformity. Close formation, however, can also compromise other desired paper properties. (See *Paper and Papermaking: Paper Properties*.)

Formatted Capacity

In computing, the *capacity* of a storage medium after it has been formatted. Formatted capacity may be somewhat less than the total capacity of the medium due to the space required for directory, timing, and other information required by the *disk drive* and computer system to accurately locate and organize files.

Formatter

In computing, term for software that allows word processing programs to *format* text in available *font*s, styles, etc,.

Formatting

In typesetting and page layout, application of predetermined *type specification*s to text. See *Type Specification*.

In computing, the term *formatting* refers to the act of configuring a storage medium (such as a magnetic disk) such that it will accept data transferred to it from the *CPU*. See *Format*.

Former Board

A triangular, downward-pointing piece of metal located at the beginning of the folding section on a *web press*. The former board is used to create a *former fold*, which is made as the moving web passes through the nip of two rollers located at the bottom of the former board. Also called a *plow*.

Former Fold

On a *web press*, a fold created by an in-line folder (called a *former folder*). A former fold is essentially a single fold made parallel to the direction of web travel, created as the web is pulled over a triangular metal *former board*. The former fold is usually the first fold made, and, depending on the application, a former fold may be the only fold required. A former fold is also called a *newspaper fold* or a *plow fold*. See also *Jaw Fold* and *Chopper Fold*.

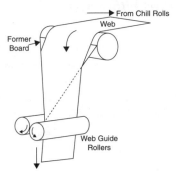

Making a former fold.

Forming Section

Part of a papermaking machine where a water suspension of paper *pulp* fibers is formed into a *web* of paper. The fiber solution flows from the *headbox* at the *wet end* of the machine, where the mixture is agitated to prevent premature fiber clotting, and delivered onto the continuous wire mesh belt of the forming section through the *slice*. Suction cup-shaped *foils*, rotating *table rolls*, or oscillation of the *forming wire* (called *shake*) drains water from the fibers. In a traditional *fourdrinier* machine, the forming section utilizes a single wire belt. The side of the paper that forms against the wire—called the *wire side*—has a different structure and texture than the top side of the paper—called the *felt side*. This *two-sidedness* of paper has deleterious consequences in many printing processes. Recent innovations such as *twin-wire formers* sandwich the fibrous solution between two wire belts, producing paper that has two virtually identical wire sides.

The forming section of the paper machine also contains a *dandy roll*, a wire-covered cylinder that may be used to stamp a *watermark* or the markings of *laid finish* paper in the forming paper web. The forming section ends with a *couch roll*, a perforated cylinder employing a vacuum to suck additional water from the paper web before it is sent to the *press section* of the papermaking machine. At the end of the forming section, the paper web is about 80–85% water.

Forming Wire

The continuously moving mesh wire belt on a papermaking machine on which *cellulose* fibers are bonded together into a paper mat. A solution of fibrous paper *pulp* is sent from the *headbox* (at the *wet end* of the papermaking machine) to the forming wire at a uniform speed, thickness, and consistency, to ensure that the paper that forms has uniform structural properties. As the fibrous solution travels along the forming wire, additional layers, or plys, are deposited on top of previous ones, and suction cup-shaped *foils*, rotating *table rolls*, or oscillations of the wire (called *shake*) supplement the force of gravity in draining water from the fibers. Traditional *fourdrinier*-type papermaking machines utilize a single forming wire; the side of the paper *web* that forms in contact with the wire (called the *wire side*) will have different structural and surface properties than the top side of the paper. Recent innovations such as *twin-wire formers* help reduce this *two-sidedness* of paper. (See *Fourdrinier*.)

Forms Feed

In computing, a means of advancing *fanfold paper* through a computer printer, usually by means of a tractor feed mechanism.

Forward Acting Code

Term for an *error correcting code*. See *Error Correction*.

Forward Channel

In telecommunications, *channel* carrying the voice or data from the calling to the called party.

Forward Error Correction

In networking and data communications, a means of controlling errors in transmissions by adding redundant *bit*s of data to a message prior to sending, then examining the redundant data upon reception. See *Error Correction*.

Forwarding

In *case binding*, any of a variety of operations performed on a *book block* between *thread sewing* and *casing-in*. Forwarding procedures can include *rounding*, *backing*, *back gluing*, *edge treatment*, and/or *headbanding*. See *Case Binding*.

In networking, *forwarding* refers to the act of transferring a data *packet* from one *local area network* to another by means of a *bridge*.

Forwarding Roller

A device on a sheetfed printing press that transfers paper from the *sheet-separation unit* to the *feedboard*. The number of rollers (typically an even number) varies according to the width of the press and/or the size of the paper, but they should be evenly spaced across the width of the paper. Folding the sheet into even sections and placing the rollers on the outermost creases is a good rule of thumb for setting their position. The tension of the rollers should be compatible with the thickness of the paper; inserting a 0.004-inch thick strip of paper between the roller and the feed tape and lowering the roller until the strip can be pulled out with only a slight amount of drag is typical. Regardless of the tension, it is imperative that all rollers be set with identical amounts of tension, or the paper is likely to be fed through them at an angle. (See ***Feeding Section: Sheetfed Offset Lithography*** and ***Feedboard***.)

Forwarding Sucker

A vacuum-powered suction cup used in a sheetfed offset press ***sheet-separation unit*** to pick up the topmost sheet of the pile and transfer it to the ***feedboard***. On a ***stream feeder***, the forwarding suckers are located toward the middle or front of the pile; they lift the topmost sheet and transfer it to the feedboard.

At the rear of the pile, the ***pickup sucker***s initially pick the sheet from the top of the pile. A jet of air ensures that the top sheet is clear, and the pickup suckers release the sheet as the forwarding suckers take it. On a ***single-sheet feeder***, one set of pickup suckers is located at the gripper (or front) edge of the pile and performs both lifting and fowarding jobs. See ***Sheet-Separation Unit*** and ***Feeder Section***.

Forward Prediction

A type of ***data compression*** used for ***digital video*** in which only the differences between adjacent frames are recorded.

Foul Proof

Any re-typeset or output pages that have had one or more sets of corrections made.

Foundry Type

Type cast in hard metal, used in handset typography. No longer in use.

Fountain

The portion of a printing press (typically a metal trough) in which either ink or, in ***offset lithography***, ***fountain solution*** is stored for controlled distribution to the printing plate, ***gravure cylinder***, or ***screen printing*** frame. See ***Inking System*** and ***Dampening System***.

Fountain Blade

A metal plate, either continuous or segmented, or plastic strip found in the ***ink fountain*** of an offset printing press. The fountain blade acts as a barrier between the trough or pan containing the ink, and the ***fountain roller*** which transfers ink to the rest of the ***inking system***. The thin gap between the ink fountain and the fountain roller regulates the amount of ink that flows through the press. The width of this gap can be adjusted using the ***fountain keys***, or screws that move either all or portions of the fountain blade toward or away from the fountain roller.

Perhaps the simplest part of an offset press, the fountain blade should not be neglected; dried ink can collect on the bottom of it, preventing the fountain keys from turning properly, and the blade itself (either with age, extreme use,

or improper fountain key tightening) can become warped or distorted, preventing effective and accurate control of ink flow. Blade wear can also result in worn corners, causing ink seepage out of the fountain. (See ***Inking System: Offset Lithography*** and ***Offset Lithography***.)

Fountain Cheek

A metal bar or block, two of which form the sides of an ***ink fountain*** on an offset press. The fountain cheeks lie at right angles to the ***fountain blade*** and ***fountain roller***, and abut the fountain roller tightly to prevent ink leakage out of the fountain. (See ***Inking System: Offset Lithography*** and ***Offset Lithography***.)

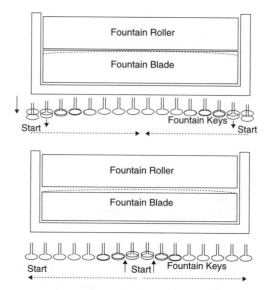

Offset press fountain blade, with adjustable fountain keys.

Fountain Concentrate

Term for the undiluted substances comprising an offset press's ***fountain solution***. Fountain concentrate commonly consists of alcohol or an alcohol substitute, a ***wetting agent***, a ***gum***, a fungicide, and perhaps a ***drying stimulator*** and/or an ***antifoaming agent***, with variations on the actual composition in order to be compatible with the chemistry of the ink and/or ***substrate*** used. Fountain concentrate is often premixed by the supplier. Adding a recommended quantity of water produces the fountain solution itself. (See ***Fountain Solution*** and ***Dampening System***.) Fountain concentrate is also called ***fountain etch*** and ***etch***.

Fountain Etch

Alternate term for ***fountain concentrate***, the undiluted chemicals used in an offset press ***fountain solution***. See ***Fountain Concentrate*** and ***Fountain Solution***.

Fountain Fill

In graphics, a type of ***fill*** comprising two different colors, one at each end of the ***fill area***, a smooth ***blend*** in between. A fill in which the blend forms a straight line from one end to the other is known as a *linear fill*. A fill in which the blend radiates out from the center is known as a *radial fill*.

Fountain Height Monitor

Alternate term for *ink leveler*. See *Ink Leveler*.

Fountain Keys

A series of screws found in the *ink fountain* on a printing press used in *offset lithography*. The fountain keys, which can either be hand-turned or motor-driven, adjust the gap that exists between the *fountain blade* and the *fountain roller*. The width of this gap determines how much ink is allowed to pass from the fountain to the rest of the inking system. The fountain keys are lined up in a series across the width of the ink fountain, and can be adjusted one by one, depending on which portions of the plate require more or less ink. A plate that needs additional ink in its center requires that the fountain keys in the center of the fountain be loosened, for example. Resetting fountain keys should be done carefully, and typically moving from the center to the edges, to avoid mechanical warping or other distortion of the fountain blade. (See *Inking System: Offset Lithography* and *Offset Lithography*.)

Fountain Pan Roller

A metal, chrome-, or aluminum-plated roller found in the *dampening system* of a printing press used in *offset lithography*. In an *intermittent-flow dampening system*, the fountain pan roller rotates at a set rate in the *water pan* where it picks up a film of *fountain solution* on its surface. An alternating *ductor roller* contacts the fountain pan roller, picks up a quantity of fountain solution, then separates from the fountain pan roller to contact an *oscillator* roller. The amount of dampening solution sent to the ductor roller can be adjusted by controlling the rate at which the fountain pan roller turns (the faster it turns, the more of its surface is coated with the fountain solution), the length of time the ductor roller spends in contact with the fountain pan roller (the longer the two are in contact, the more of the surface of the ductor roller that is covered with solution), or by adding *water stops*. In *continuous-flow dampening system*s, the fountain pan roller is replaced with a *metering roller*, which is in constant contact with a *transfer roller*. (See *Dampening System*.)

Fountain Roller

A metal roller found in the *ink fountain* on a printing press used in *offset lithography*. The fountain roller is in direct contact with the ink from the fountain, the amount of ink transferred to it being regulated by the gap between the roller and the *fountain blade*. The *fountain keys* adjust the width of this gap, allowing more or less ink to transfer to the fountain roller. Contacting the fountain roller at set intervals is the *ductor roller*, which transfers ink from the fountain roller to the rest of the ink *roller train* and, ulti-

mately, to the plate. The fountain roller can rotate at varying rates, depending upon how much ink is ultimately required by the plate. A fountain roller that turns through a longer distance will transfer more ink to the surface of the ductor roller, and a longer amount of contact between the ductor and fountain rollers (called *dwell*) also affects how much ink is sent through the system. The best results can generally be obtained by allowing the fountain roller to have a long sweep—or turn through a longer distance—but a thin ink film. This allows a greater sensitivity of the rest of the system to ink flow adjustments made with the fountain keys. (See *Inking System: Offset Lithography* and *Offset Lithography*.)

A *fountain roller* is also found on a press used in *letterpress* printing, and is also used to transfer the ink from the ink *fountain* to the rest of the roller train.

A *fountain roller* is also used in some *gravure* inking systems. A gravure fountain roller is an absorbent roller that absorbs ink from the bottom of a shallow *ink fountain* and squeezes it into the engraved cells of the *gravure cylinder* rotating above it. (See *Inking System: Gravure*.)

A *fountain roller* is also used in many *flexographic* ink fountains, typically having a natural or synthetic rubber surface that transfers ink to the surface of an *anilox roller*. A fountain roller used in flexography is also known as a *doctor roller*. See *Inking System: Flexography*.

In *screen printing*, a fountain roller rotates in the fountain and agitates the ink, helping it retain its flow characteristics. See *Inking System: Screen Printing*.

Fountain Solution

A mixture of water and other chemicals distributed by the *dampening system* on a printing press used in *offset lithography*. Lithographic printing operates on the principle that oil and water do not mix to any great extent; offset presses first treat metal printing plates with a fountain solution, which works to *desensitize* the nonimage areas, rendering them ink-repellent. The fountain solution is applied to the plate through a series of rollers in a variety of configurations. (See *Dampening System*.)

The fountain solution itself can consist solely of water, but such solutions lose their effectiveness on any but the shortest press runs. Other chemicals added to the solution keep the plate desensitized much longer than water alone. In addition to water, fountain solutions typically consist of:

- An acid or base (depending upon the desired *pH* of the fountain solution)
- A *gum* (such as *gum arabic*) to desensitize the nonimage areas of the plate
- A *corrosion inhibitor* (such as magnesium nitrate) to prevent *oxidation* or other chemical reactions which may damage the plate
- A *wetting agent* (commonly an alcohol such as isopropanol, or an alcohol substitute) to reduce the surface tension of the solution and enable it to flow more easily

- A fungicide to help kill any organic growth in the fountain or elsewhere in the dampening system
- An *antifoaming agent* to, as its name indicates, reduce the tendency of the solution to foam or bubble, which can cause distribution problems on the printing press.

The fountain solution may also contain a *drying stimulator* (commonly cobalt chloride) that works to enhance the effectiveness of the *drier* in the ink. A drying stimulator is typically added when ink is not drying fast enough to prevent such problems as smudging, *ink setoff*, and/or *blocking*. The concentrated fountain solution is known as *fountain concentrate*, *fountain etch*, or *etch*, and can comprise a variety of different substances, depending upon the ink and *substrate* used. For example, a *metallic ink* or the use of *alkaline paper* may require a high-pH fountain solution, in contrast to the typical fountain solution, with a moderately acidic pH of 4.0–5.5. (See *pH*.) The following are the primary constituents of fountain solution.

Water. The largest component of fountain solution is water, and it is important that the water used be as free from impurities as possible. Water with a high concentration of magnesium and calcium ions is known as "hard" water; water free of such substances is known as "soft" water. Water straight from the tap can be fairly unpredictable, especially in a large metropolitan area. Water hardness is measured in terms of the water's electrical conductivity, as a higher ion concentration in the water increases its conductivity. The total dissolved solids (TDS) in parts per million (ppm) is multiplied by 1.5 to yield the conductivity in micromhos per centimeter (μmhos/cm). Local authorities, such as the water department, can provide the water hardness figure for the area. Water with a hardness above 220 ppm (thus a conductivity of greater than 330 μmhos/cm) may need to be purified for better performance on press, as the higher the water hardness, the more it can raise the solution's pH. But more important than actual water hardness is the consistency of water hardness, which many printers ensure by mixing "raw" water with purified water of a predetermined and consistent hardness.

Wetting Agents. An important property of a fountain solution is its ability to quickly form a thin film on the rollers and the plate or, in other words, to rapidly "wet" these surfaces. The wettability of a solution is a function of the surface tension of the liquid, measured in dynes per centimeter. (A dyne is a unit of force, 1 dyne being equal to the force that will produce a one-centimeter-per-second acceleration per second on a mass of one gram.) Pure water has a surface tension of 72 dynes per centimeter, and a 10–25% concentration of wetting agents (commonly isopropyl alcohol or non-alcohol *surfactant*s) reduce this to about 35–45 dynes per centimeter, suitable for forming a quick, thin film.

Alcohol. The use of alcohol in press fountain solutions has many advantages in addition to reducing surface tension. It is efficient (alcohol concentrations as low as 5% can be used effectively on many presses) and it increases the *viscosity* of the solution allowing a thicker film to be applied to the rollers and/or the plate. The high *volatility* of alcohol means that it will evaporate more quickly before being transferred to the blanket; its tendency to emulsify the ink to a lesser extent than other liquids reduces *snowflaking* (small, white, unprinted specks in printed solids and type), and alcohol tends to allow greater print quality right at startup—a cost-effective benefit. However, Environmental Protection Agency (EPA) and Occupational Safety and Health Administration (OSHA) regulations (such as those calling for the reduction of volatile organic compounds) are limiting, if not eliminating, the use of alcohol in dampening solutions.

Several of the disadvantages of alcohol—such as its expense, toxicity, flammability, and need for adequate ventilation in areas of use—are causing alcohol substitutes to be more frequently utilized. These substitutes include derivatives of glycol and glycol ethers, frequently in combination with ethylene glycol. These substitutes can either completely replace isopropanol or they can be added as a supplement to it, reducing the total isopropanol concentration. The advantages of these substitutes include a lower volatility, which cuts down on toxic emissions; their effectiveness at lower concentrations than alcohol (5% or less); increased print quality, including less ink and water necessary for good color printing, sharper halftone dots and reduced *dot gain*; and their lack of odor improves workplace conditions. However, their disadvantages include increased *piling* of paper debris on the blanket; increased amounts of dampening solution transferred to the blanket; inability to mix directly with concentrated amounts of gum; increase of ink drying time; press problems such as *roller stripping*; and incompatibility with nonpaper substrates such as plastic, film, or other nonabsorbent surfaces. They also increase the tendency for the *metering roller* (in continuous-flow dampening systems) to become ink-receptive. The use of 1:32 *gum etch* can help eliminate the problem.

Another metering-roller problem, namely, *banding* (the formation of light and dark bands on the roller that cause streaks on the plate and print), happens when using alcohol substitutes on a hard roller (i.e., one with a *durometer* of 25–30). The use of a lower-durometer roller (18–22) will alleviate the problem, as will using a metering roller with a slightly grained surface, which allows more water to be carried by the roller. The low volatility of alcohol substitutes (which can be lower than that of water) can also result in an increase in substitute concentration over the course of a print run as the water evaporates. As there is no easy way to gauge the concentration of alcohol substitutes on the fly, the only preventive measure that can be taken is to replace the fountain solution at least once a week. Some alcohol substitutes also increase the tendency for *foaming*. Antifoaming agents will help alleviate this problem. Some substitutes also require greater amounts of wetting agents to be added, indicated by **plugging** of halftone dots or small type. Another roller problem is caused by the deposit of salts (a white solid material) on the metering roller, typically a problem when the press is idle for an extended period of time (such as overnight). The metering roller should be cleaned and desensitized before letting it stand overnight. Alcohol substitutes also have no effect on fountain solution viscosity, which requires higher roller speeds in **continuous-flow dampening system**s. Refrigerating the solution, however, can help increase the viscosity.

Refrigeration of dampening solution has other benefits as well. **Hot-weather scumming**, more commonly called **tinting**, is characterized by the accumulation of ink in non-image areas of the plate, and is caused by the particles of ink **pigment** bleeding into the dampening solution, a tendency that increases with temperature. Keeping the temperature of the fountain solution low can reduce this problem. Keeping the temperature of the fountain solution low can reduce this problem. Refrigeration also helps ensure that the fountain solution stays at a constant temperature. As viscosity decreases with increasing temperature, keeping the solution at a constant temperature keeps the viscosity constant, eliminating the need for frequent adjustments of the **metering nip** in continuous-flow dampening systems. Refrigeration also reduces the evaporation of alcohol in alcohol-based fountain solutions, which helps prolong the fountain solution and cuts down on the concentration of the health-hazards of evaporated alcohol in the pressroom air. However, refrigeration is not without its problems. One such difficulty could arise when the warm press and fountain pan cause condensation of water drops on the bottom of the pan containing cool or cold fountain solution. These drops can drip onto the paper, damaging it. Cold fountain solutions can also increase the ink's **tack**, or its stickiness, increasing such problems as **picking**, **splitting**, and **tearing** of the paper.

pH. A solution's pH is a measure of how acidic or alkaline (basic) the solution is, measured as the concentration of hydrogen (H^+) or hydroxyl (OH^-) ions. A solution with a pH of 7 is described as neutral, with the solution becoming more acidic as the pH decreases, and becoming more alkaline as the pH increases. (See **pH**.) Not only is the fountain solution's initial pH important, but so is consistency of pH over the course of the pressrun. Most fountain solutions are slightly to moderately acidic, as the gum arabic used to desensitize the plate loses its effectiveness if the pH rises above 5 (i.e., becomes less acidic). In this case, it loses its ability to adhere to the plate, and ink begins to adhere to the plate in the nonimage areas, a problem known as **scumming**. However, excessive acidity can also cause scumming (as the acid eats away the protective plate coating), as well as **plate blinding**, in which the acid eats away the image areas of the plate, causing a lack of ink receptivity.

Increased acidity can also cause roller stripping, or the lack of ink receptivity of the ink rollers. Another problem involving pH is the use of alkaline paper, or paper contain-

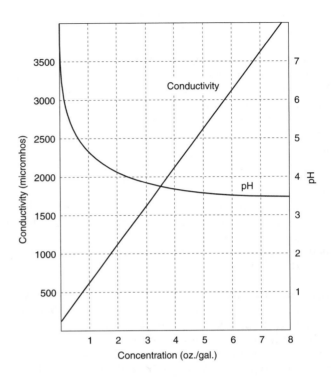

Graph of concentration vs. pH and conductivity for a hypothetical combination of dampening solution concentrate and water.

ing calcium carbonate either as a filler or a coating. Calcium carbonate is an alkaline material, and when particles of it come into contact with an acidic dampening solution, deleterious effects can occur. (When acids and bases come into contact with each other, they react with each other, sometimes quite strongly.) The growing trend away from the use of acid paper in favor of longer-lasting alkaline paper has resulted in the need for alkaline fountain solutions. These solutions do not use gum as a desensitizing agent, and contain sodium carbonate or sodium silicate, which increase the solution's pH. Such solutions require the addition of a sequestering agent to prevent the precipitation of various compounds (such as those containing magnesium and calcium) out of the solution. Additional wetting agents are also required. A solution's pH can be measured using dyes (changing color depending on the acidity or alkalinity of the solution), litmus paper (turning red or blue depending on pH), and electronic pH meters, which can determine pH to within 0.01–0.05 pH.

Electrical Conductivity. As was mentioned above, electrical conductivity is used as a measure of water purity, or hardness. Pure water has an electrical conductivity of close to 0 micromhos (μmhos). (A *mho*, as its name may imply, is a unit of measurement equal to the reciprocal of an *ohm*, a measure of electrical resistance. A micromho is equal to one-millionth—or 0.000001—of a mho.) As the amount of dissolved solids in water increases, so does its electrical conductivity, in direct proportion to the concentration of total dissolved solids (with slight variations depending on the actual minerals dissolved). So-called "soft water" has a conductivity of 0–225 µmhos, "hard water" having a conductivity greater than 450 µmhos. Average water straight from one's faucet may have a conductivity of 200 µmhos or greater. In order for a dampening solution to be effective and trouble-free, its conductivity must fluctuate by no more than ±50 µmhos. Conductivity fluctuations of at least 200 µmhos are a sign that water purification is necessary. A relationship exists among concentration of the solution, the pH, and the electrical conductivity, all of which need to be in balance when mixing an effective fountain solution.

As was indicated in the graph on the preceding page, the conductivity and pH need to be rechecked periodically throughout the pressrun, as various substances from ink, paper, and elsewhere can contaminate the fountain and alter the pH while on press.

Fountain Splitter

A vertical metal bar or block (similar to a *fountain cheek*) added to an offset printing *ink fountain* that essentially divides the fountain pan into two separate pans, allowing the use of two different colors at once, for use in *spot-color printing*. Typically, two fountain splitters are used in two-color work, creating a four-inch "buffer zone" that prevents the two colors from mixing either in the fountain or farther along on the *roller train*.

When doing two-color spot-color work, the lateral movement of the *oscillator*s should be kept to a minimum (ideally, less than the width of the fountain splitter). This kind of spot-color work requires that the different-colored images be far enough apart on the plate so as to avoid the possibility of color intermingling.

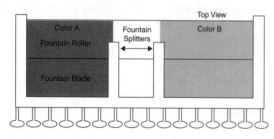

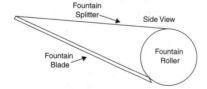

The fountain splitter.

Fountain Stops

Alternate term for *water stops*. See *Water Stops*.

Four-Bit (4-Bit) Color

On a computer monitor, a color display in which each *pixel* (or smallest point of *color*) is described by 4 bits of information. (One *bit* is either a 1 or a 0; 4-bit color can be thought of as one of these two numbers taken to the fourth power; thus $2^4 = 16$ possible colors.) The color of a pixel on a computer display is commonly expressed as some amount of *red, green, and blue*. Greater numbers of combinations of these amounts require more processing power on the part of the computer. At 4 bits per pixel, a total of 16 colors can be described and displayed. (Some programs allow you to specify which colors can be included in that palette.) See also *One-Bit Color*, *Eight-Bit Color*, *Sixteen-Bit Color*, *Twenty-Four-Bit Color*, and *Thirty-Two-Bit Color*. Computer monitors can also display *one-bit color* (black and white, or any two colors).

Four-Color Printing
See *Four-Color Process*.

Four-Color Process

In multi-color printing, the printing of *process color* by means of *color separation*s corresponding to the four process colors: *cyan*, *magenta*, *yellow*, and *black*. Combinations or overprinted dots of these four colors are what create the wide range of colors discernible to the human eye that can be reproduced. *Flat color* is used to refer to multi-color printing using these four process colors but without overprinting them, so that each color only is reproduced as itself. See *Process Color*.

Fourdrinier

The oldest and still the most prevalent machine for making paper, utilizing a continuously moving wire mesh belt to produce long rolls or *web*s of paper.

Following *stock preparation* and *refining*, the papermaking *furnish*—a water suspension of paper *pulp* fibers and any nonfibrous additives or *fillers*—is diluted to a concentration of about one part fibers to 200 parts water and delivered to the fourdrinier machine's *wet end*. Here, the pulp solution is kept in the machine's *headbox*, which keeps the fibers from bonding together prematurely. From the headbox, the furnish is sent through the *slice*—an adjustable rectangular slit—to the continuously moving *forming wire*. The headbox and slice ensure that the furnish is deposited on the wire with a uniform speed, thickness and consistency.

The *forming section* consists of the moving forming wire made of bronze or plastic. As the furnish is deposited on the wire, water drains through the mesh. Suction cup-shaped *foils* or *table rolls* beneath the wire increase water removal by suction. Some paper machines also oscillate the wire back and forth, producing a *shake* that also contributes to water drainage. As the water is removed, the fibers bond together forming the paper web. Additional lay ers of fibers are then deposited on top of previous ones. As the web forms, the side that forms in contact with the wire—called the *wire side*—will have a somewhat different texture than the top side—called the *felt side*. This *two-sidedness* of paper has consequences in certain types of printing, and new techniques and devices—in particular, a *twin-wire former*, an alternative to the traditional fourdrinier machine—have been developed to reduce differences in the wire and felt sides of paper. After the foils, table rolls, shake, and gravity itself have removed as much water as possible, the web passes over vacuum boxes that suck out more water. At this point, the web may pass beneath a *dandy roll*, a wire-covered cylinder that compresses the web fibers. In some papers, a *watermark* is produced utilizing a raised design on the dandy roll. (Watermark-like designs on the dandy roll also impart *laid*-like marks to some paper.) At the end of the forming section of the fourdrinier machine is a *couch roll*, a perforated cylinder that uses a vacuum to suck out more water before the web is sent to the *press section*.

The paper is 80–85% water when it reaches the press section. As its name implies, the purpose of the press section is to compress the fiber web to improve fiber bonding and regulate the ultimate thickness, bulk, and finish of the paper. The degree of pressing at this stage can be adjusted, depending on the desired bulk and finish of the paper. When the web leaves the press section, it is 60–70% water, and is ready to be sent to the *drying* section, where a series of heated cylinders evaporate residual moisture. The method of drying also depends on the desired characteristics of the paper. (See also *Yankee Dryer* and *Air Drying*.) The drying section also includes a *size press*, which adds a *sizing* solution to many types of papers. Following drying, paper may be subjected to various degrees of *calendering* to impart the desired finish, thickness, or other characteristics.

The difficulties created by the two-sidedness of paper have resulted in the search for modifications or replacements to the conventional fourdrinier machine. (See also *Twin-wire Former* and *Cylinder Machine*, as well as *Paper and Papermaking: Papermaking*.)

The fourdrinier machine has a fairly complex history that begins around the period of the French Revolution in a papermill run by St. Leger Didot. During the Napoleonic Wars, most of his skilled papermakers were conscripted

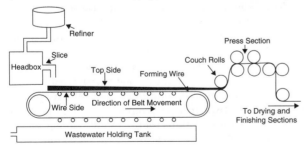

Basic schematic diagram of a fourdrinier papermaking machine.

into the army. Didot hired a new personnel director, Nicholas Robert, who had a talent for engineering and told Didot his idea for an automated papermaking machine. Didot agreed to financially support Robert in this endeavor. Robert produced a working model, and applied for a French patent. Soon, Didot and Robert fought over who actually held the rights to the machine, the result being that Didot agreed to buy the rights from Robert. A short time later, Robert sued to regain the rights and won, but Didot bought them back again. Robert, never actually getting paid by Didot, tried for the rest of his life to sell his invention but failed, and died broke.

Didot, having come to believe that there was no market for a papermaking machine, gave the idea to his brother-in-law, John Gamble, in London. There, Gamble took the idea to two stationer brothers, Henry and Sealy Fourdrinier, who agreed to help build the machine. In 1801, Gamble received a patent for the machine in Britain and the Fourdriniers started getting the machines manufactured. The man employed in their mill who was put in charge of the project also ran a foundry elsewhere, and passed all the paper-machine work to one of his foundry employees—Bryan Donkin—who was coerced into building the machine based on Robert's original design. Donkin improved on the machine, and set it up in a papermill at Frogmore in Hertsfordshire in 1803, primarily to manufacture wallpaper. The new papermaking machines, however, did not sell well, and other manufacturers infringed on the patent. Eventually, the court costs of the patent infringement suits drove the Fourdrinier brothers into bankruptcy.

Four-Panel Fold

A fold created in a sheet of paper by folding the sheet in half, forming four panels or pages. Also called a *fly fold*.

Four-Sided Trim

In *binding and finishing*, a *trimming* operation performed on all four sides of a bound book or pile of sheets. Also called *trim four*.

Four-Stop Photography

An obsolete term for *measured photography*. See *Measured Photography*.

Four-Up East-West Label

A type of *label*, designed to be applied by Cheshire® addressing equipment, that comes on sheets of four rows across, sequenced (for example, in ZIP code order) from left to right (east to west). See also *North-South Label*.

Four-Wire Channel

Alternate term for *four-wire circuit*. See *Four-Wire Circuit*.

Four-Wire Circuit

In networking and telecommunications, a channel or circuit in which two *half-duplex* circuits (comprising two wires each) are combined to create a *full-duplex* circuit, allowing simultaneous two-way communication. Also known as a *four-wire channel*. See also *Two-Wire Circuit*.

Foxed

Descriptive of a brown discoloration of a paper, especially old papers or books. The discoloration may appear over the entire surface of the paper or as spots.

FPO

See *For Position Only (FPO)*.

fps

Abbreviation for *frames per second*, a measure of *frame frequency*. See *Frame Frequency*.

FPU

Abbreviation for *floating-point unit*, or *floating-point processing unit*. See *Floating-Point Coprocessor*.

Fractal

A recently developed type of geometry that describes a large pattern or shape as a collection of infinite and progressively smaller copies of the image. A fractal image is derived from a mathematical computation repeated as often as is desired. Fractal geometry and software for describing it are used in the graphic arts primarily for the creation of beautiful images and designs, as well as for *fractal compression*.

Fractal Compression

A type of *data compression* system devised for the compression of *digital video*. Essentially, fractal compression is based on the concept of *fractal* geometry. A particular image is compressed and defined by a set of mathematical formulas, or the same formulas used to describe fractals (infinitely and increasingly small repeating patterns of shapes), the playback being effected by the "playing" of these formulas. Fractal compression boasts high *compression ratios* and no perceptible degradation of image quality. However, although reconstruction of the image from the formulas during playback is accomplished quickly, it can take quite a long time to compress the image.

Fraction Bar

Alternate term for a *slash*. See *Slash*.

Fractional T1

In telecommunications, some fraction of a *T1* circuit that can be leased by customers in 64 *Kbps* increments without needing to lease the entire 1.544 Kbps T1 circuit. See *T1*.

Fractions

In typography not affected by the metric system and the decimalization of numbers, a numeric symbol indicating a portion of a whole number. A fraction is made up of a numerator, a denominator, and a dividing line. There are several ways of typesetting fractions:

*Em fraction*s are the most common form, each fraction on the *em* width, with a diagonal stroke. Most devices have the ¼, ½, and ¾ as standard. In some desktop publishing programs, this can be a bit more difficult.

*En fraction*s are set on the *en* width, with a horizontal stroke. They are used when a vast number of odd fractions—16ths, 32nds, etc.—are required. En fractions are also called *case fraction*s or *stack fraction*s.

*Piece fraction*s are en or em fractions with only the denominators. The numerators are "created" using special numerals, such as the *superior*s, which are positioned with the denominator to form the full fraction.

*Fake fraction*s are formed from the normal numerals separated by a slash, such as "1/4." When using fractions with whole numbers, a hyphen needs to be added to make "1 1/4" look like "1-1/4." These are used only if there is no alternative.

*Decimal fraction*s do away with the whole problem by expressing all fractions as their decimal counterparts, for example ¼ = .25, and so on.

And, of course, there is the last resort of spelling the fraction out: ¼ = "one quarter" or "one fourth."

Type-font suppliers often substitute fractions from one typeface for others that are closely related. It is important to ensure that the fractions fit with the typeface in both weight and design.

Fragmentation

Abbreviated term for *storage fragmentation*.

Fragmented

Desciptive of computer files that have not been saved in a contiguous manner. See *Storage Fragmentation*.

Fraktur

In typography, a German term for *black letter* typefaces. See *Black Letter*.

Frame

In layout, a rectangle (or other shape) placed on a page and filled with text or graphics. In *page makeup program*s, such as *QuarkXPress*, frames are also used to create specific regions for the placement of text or graphics. Frames can either have borders or be borderless.

The term *frame* also refers to any screenful of information on a computer monitor.

In television and video, a *frame* is used to describe one particular complete video picture, comprising two interlaced *field*s. In *NTSC*, one frame equals 525 horizontal lines written in approximately one-thirtieth of a second.

In motion pictures, animations, or film strips, a *frame* is a single picture in a sequential group of pictures, the rapid movement of which creates the illusion of movement.

In networking, the term *frame* refers to one particular unit of data sent over a network, also known as a *packet*. See *Packet*. The subdivision of data into individual frames is called *framing*.

Frame Accuracy

In video production, the ability to edit a videotape at the *frame* level, rather than merely "in the ballpark." Frame accuracy was virtually impossible until the advent of the *time code*. Computer-based video editing systems are now able to edit at the *field* level, a quality of editing known as *field accuracy*.

Frame Animation

A means of animation in which each *frame* of the sequence is a completely new drawing that, at a typical rate of 30 frames per second, can be extremely time-consuming to produce, although they are of the highest quality. An alternative to frame animation is known as *cast animation*, where only selected elements of a frame are redrawn from frame to frame. See *Cast Animation*.

Frame Buffer

A portion of a computer's main memory or an add-on card that stores the contents of a displayed image *pixel*-by-pixel and that is used to *refresh* the screen display. The color depth of the frame buffer—be it *eight-bit color*, *sixteen-bit color*, etc.—determines the number of bits per pixel—or, in other words, the total number of different colors—that can be displayed. Also known as a *screen buffer*, and *display buffer*.

Frame Clamp

Alternate term for *screen holder*. See *Screen Holder*.

Frame Differencing

In *data compression* of *digital video*, a type of compression scheme that only records differences between adjacent *frame*s, used often in *production-level video*.

Frame Frequency

In television and video, the number of times per second that a *frame* is scanned. In *NTSC*, the frame frequency is 29.7 (usually rounded to 30) frames per second, while in *PAL* and *SECAM*, the frame frequency is 25 frames per second.

Frame Grabber

In *digital video*, a type of *digitizing board* added to a computer that, when a VCR, video camera, *videodisc* player, or other such device is attached, allows for video and audio signals to be captured and digitized, enabling digital editing to be performed. Frame grabbers can capture a single frame of a video, usually at very high resolution and with a color depth of 24 bits per pixel. A frame grabber can also capture the entire video, at a resolution, size, and frame rate dependent upon the power of the processor and the amount of *RAM* possessed by the system. In this latter sense, it is more often referred to as a *video capture board*.

Frame Relay

In telecommunications, a type of *packet switching* network *protocol* used in *wide-area network*s, particularly useful for the transmission of multimedia presentations and graphics. Frame relay is not especially fast, however.

Frames Per Second (fps)

A measure of *frame frequency*. See *Frame Frequency*.

Framing

In photography and videography, the process of setting up a shot, especially with regard to the correct and desired placement of objects.

In networking and telecommunications, *framing* refers to the division of to-be-transmitted data into small *frame*s or *packet*s, provided with a header, a *checksum*, and the *bit*s that comprise the data. In *asynchronous transmission*, the inclusion of *start bit*s and *stop bit*s is part of the framing process.

Franklin, Benjamin

Benjamin Franklin was born in Boston on January 17, 1706, into a Puritan family. His father, Josiah, was a candlemaker and mechanic who raised 13 children—survivors of his 17 children by two wives. In Ben Franklin's simultaneous careers as printer, publisher, moralist, essayist, civic leader, scientist, inventor, politician, statesman, diplomat, businessman, and philosopher, he became a symbol for the American character. With less than two years of formal schooling, Franklin was pressed into his father's trade. He devoured books at home, and, after being apprenticed to his brother James, printer of *The New England Courant*, he read virtually every book that came to the shop. He absorbed the values and philosophy of the English Enlightenment. Like his favorite author, Joseph Addison, whose essays in the Spectator he memorized, Franklin added good sense, tolerance, and urbanity to his Puritan ethic.

At age 16, Franklin secretly wrote articles for the Courant signed "Silence Dogood," in which he satirized the Boston authorities and society. In one essay he argued that "hypocritical Pretenders to Religion" more injured the commonwealth than those "openly Profane." At one point James Franklin was imprisoned for similar statements, and Benjamin carried on the paper himself. Ben refused to suffer his brother's domineering attitude and in 1723 ran away to Philadelphia. Though penniless and unknown, Franklin soon found a job as a printer. After a year he went to England, where he became a master printer and lived among the aspiring writers and thinkers of London. Returning to Philadelphia in 1726, he soon owned his own newspaper, the *Pennsylvania Gazette*, and began to print

James Franklin's newspaper, on which Benjamin Franklin served his apprenticeship. Close examination will show that this issue includes an article by "Silence DoGood."

Franklin began another career when in 1740 he invented a fireplace called the Franklin stove, which soon heated buildings in Europe and North America. He read about electricity and the experiments he proposed showed that lightning was in fact a form of electricity. His famous kite experiment, in which he flew a kite with the wire attached to a key during a thunderstorm, further established that laboratory-produced static electricity was akin to a previously mysterious and terrifying natural phenomenon. The Royal Society in London published these discoveries, and the lightning rods he invented appeared on buildings all over America and Europe and Franklin became world famous. He was elected to the Royal Society in 1756 and to the French Academy of Sciences in 1772. His achievements included a theory of heat absorption, a stove, charting the Gulf Stream, tracking storm paths, and inventing bifocal lenses.

The first issue of the Pennsylvania Gazette after its purchase by Benjamin Franklin.

Poor Richard's Almanack (1732). His business expanded further when he contracted to do the public printing of the province, and established partnerships with printers in other colonies. He also operated a book shop and became clerk of the Pennsylvania Assembly and postmaster of Philadelphia. In 1748, Franklin, at age 42, retired to live off the income from his businesses, managed mostly by others.

The sayings of "Poor Richard" are well known: "Early to bed and early to rise make a man healthy, wealthy, and wise" and his philosophy for moral virtue was presented in his *Autobiography*, Franklin summarized his view of how the poor man may improve himself by hard work, thrift, and honesty. *Poor Richard's Almanack* sold widely in America, and a version known as *The Way to Wealth* was translated into many languages.

In 1751, Franklin was elected to the Pennsylvania Assembly and began over 40 years as a public official. He had intended to enlist political support for his various civic enterprises, but politics soon engulfed him. He opposed the Proprietary party that sought to preserve the power of the Penn family in Pennsylvania affairs, and as the legislative strategist and recorder for the so-called Quaker party, he defended the powers of elected representatives.

From April 1775 to October 1776, Franklin served on the Pennsylvania Committee of Safety and in the Continental Congress, submitted articles of confederation for the united colonies, proposed a new constitution for Pennsylvania, and helped draft the Declaration of Independence. He signed the Declaration, thus becoming a revolutionary at the age of 70. Franklin and his two grandsons sailed for France in 1776, where he gained critical French aid for the Revolutionary War. Parisian literary and scientific circles hailed him as a living embodiment of Enlightenment virtues. Wigless and dressed in plain brown clothes, he was called le Bonhomme Richard.

France wanted to injure Britain but could not afford to help the American rebels unless eventual success seemed assured. Franklin worked behind the scenes to send war supplies across the Atlantic, thwart British diplomacy, and make friends with influential French officials. He overcame his own doubts about the possibly dishonest dealings of his fellow commissioner (Silas Deane) in channeling war materials to American armies, but the third commissioner, Arthur Lee bitterly condemned both Deane and Franklin. Despite these quarrels, in 1778, following news of the American victory at Saratoga, the three commissioners were able to sign the vital French alliance.

Franklin became the first American minister to France and for seven years acted as diplomat, purchasing agent, recruiting officer, loan negotiator, admiralty court, and intelligence chief—he was generally the main representative of the new United States in Europe and oversaw the dispatch of French armies and navies to North America, supplied American armies with French munitions, outfitted John Paul Jones—whose ship Bonhomme Richard was named in Franklin's honor—and secured loans from the nearly bankrupt French treasury.

The loss at Yorktown (1781) persuaded British leaders that they could not win the war and Franklin made secret contact with peace negotiators sent from London. In these negotiations he proposed treaty articles close to those finally agreed to, such as complete American independence, access to the Newfoundland fishing grounds, evacuation of British forces from all occupied areas, and a western boundary on the Mississippi River. With John Jay, Franklin represented the United States in signing the Treaty of Paris (1783), by which the world's foremost power (Great Britain) recognized the independence of the world's newest nation. Franklin came home in 1785.

In his 80th year he accepted election for three years as president of Pennsylvania and resumed active roles in the Pennsylvania Society for Promoting the Abolition of Slavery, the American Philosophical Society, and the University of Pennsylvania.

At the Constitutional Convention of 1787, although he was too weak to stand, Franklin's good humor and gift for compromise helped to prevent bitter disputes. Franklin's final public pronouncements urged ratification of the Constitution and approved the inauguration of the new federal government under his admired friend George Washington. He wrote friends in France that "we are making Experiments in Politicks," but that American "affairs mend daily and are getting into good order very fast." Still cheerful and optimistic,

Benjamin Franklin died in Philadelphia on April 17, 1790. In his will he left 800 pounds, to gain interest for 100 years, to the cities of Boston and Philadelphia to aid in the education of yound people. At the turn of the century both cities erected Franklin Institutes and put some of the money back in the bank for another 100 years. In the 1990s the funds were used to enhance the Institutes.

He was the quintessential American and defined the spirit of a nation. His epitaph, which he penned when he was in his 40s asked that he be remembered for one thing—that he was a printer.

Free Memory

In computing, term for any *random-access memory (RAM)* that is available to an application after an *operating system* and all related *device driver*s, *system extension*s, etc., have been loaded.

Free Page

A page of a document or publication that has been designed in a different format than surrounding pages.

Free Radical

An extremely reactive atom or molecule bearing an unpaired electron that destabilizes other atoms or molecules. Free radicals are typically produced as the products of other chemical reactions (such as combustion). Their presence in several types of printing ink *vehicle*s (in particular those of *radiation-curing ink*s) starts rapid chain reactions that cause the *polymerization* of the vehicle, that hardens to a dry ink film containing the *pigment* (called *free radical polymerization*).

Free Radical Polymerization

A chemical reaction in which the presence of transient, highly reactive atoms or molecules (called *free radical*s) produces complex, high-molecular-weight molecules (*polymer*s) from several simple, low-molecular-weight molecules. Free radical polymerization is responsible for drying certain types of printing inks. See *Free Radical* and *Polymerization*.

Free Sheet

Any paper manufactured without **mechanical pulp**.

Free-Standing Insert (FSI)

In **binding and finishing**, a separately printed, self-contained **signature** bound into a newspaper.

French Fold

Type of fold in which a sheet printed on one side is folded first vertically, then horizontally, to produce a four-page **folder**.

French Quotes

In typography, an early type of **quotes** that originated in France (« ») and were placed in the center of the type body so that the same character could be used for either the open or closed position. English printers refused to use the French form and used an inverted comma (') for the open position and the apostrophe (') for the closed. See **Quotes**. Also called **chevrons** and **guillemets**.

French Spacing

In typography, the practice of adding an extra word space following punctuation marks and between sentences.

Frequency

Generally speaking, the number of occurrences of an event in a specific time interval.

The term *frequency* is commonly used to refer to the number of cycles per second a musical pitch, electrical signal, or other **analog data** repeats, commonly measured in **hertz** (corresponding to one cycle per second). Since analog signals—such as sounds or electrical signals—are essentially waves, the frequency is a measure of how many crests (or troughs) at a given amplitude pass a given point per unit time. In terms of sound, for example, low frequencies correspond to bass sounds; high frequencies correspond to treble.

In computers, the term frequency, expressed in megahertz (MHz), or millions of cycles per second, is a measure of a **CPU**'s **clock rate**.

Frequency Division Multiplexing (FDM)

In telecommunications, a means of transmission in which the available **bandwidth** is divided into smaller parallel paths, each separated by "guard bands" of varying frequency. In this manner, multiple signals can be transmitted simultaneously. FDM is utuilized most commonly in **analog** transmissions, such as over a telephone line or **baseband** network.

Frequency Histogram

A graphical analysis of data obtained from a given sample indicating how many times a specific occurrence took place. In scanning, a color **scanner** may often generate an electronic frequency histogram to indicate how many occurrences of each color there were in a given scan, so as to accurately determine and adjust the **middletone** placement for an original image.

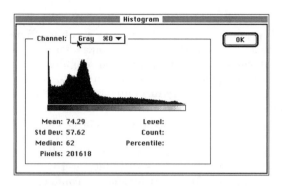

Adobe Photoshop's frequency histogrram.

Frequency Modulation (FM)

In communications, a type of **modulation** of a signal in which the frequency of the carrier is varied with changes in the value of the signal it is carrying. In broadcasting (such as radio broadcasting), a particular sound emanating from a radio station is converted into electrical energy, which is referred to as its signal. This signal wave is overlayed on top of a radio wave, called a carrier wave. In FM broadcasting, the frequency of the carrier wave conforms to the changes in the frequency of the signal (or sound) being transmitted. **AM** broadcasting, as we are all aware, is subject to static, which occurs at the top and bottom of a wave cycle. In contrast, frequency modulation keeps the amplitude of the carrier wave constant, thus the tops and bottoms of the signal wave can be eliminated, which is why FM radio generally remains static free.

In data communications, a similar process of modulation is used to overlay a signal representing computer information onto a carrier wave (which is transmitted over a telephone line, rather than through the air). Frequency modulation is a similar means of varying the frequency of the carrier signal in accordance with changes in the data signal. See **modulation**. See also **amplitude modulation (AM)**.

In **halftone** photography, the term *frequency modulation* is used to refer to a halftoning technique (also known as **stochastic screening**) in which the sizes of the **halftone dot**s remain constant but their distribution within an image is varied according to whether they correspond to **shadow**s (lots of dots), **middle tone**s (a moderate amount of dots), or **highlight**s (few dots). See **Halftone** and **Stochastic Screening**.

Frequently Asked Questions

See **FAQ**.

Friction

The resistance to relative motion that exists between two different substances in contact, be they two solids, a solid and a liquid, a solid and a gas, a liquid and a gas, etc. The difficulty in sliding a heavy box along a flat surface is one example of friction, while the force of a **doctor blade** against a **gravure cylinder** would be another. Friction is the force responsible for **abrasion** and the damage caused thereby.

Static friction is defined as the resistance of an object to the initiation of sliding, while *kinetic friction* is the force that resists an object's continued sliding once it has been initiated. The *coefficient of friction* is one means of mathematically determining the frictional forces that exist between two sliding objects.

Frictional Resistance

A property of paper that refers to its ability to keep from slipping or sliding. (Friction is the force that resists one object's sliding over another.) There are two basic types of friction that need to be taken into account: *static friction*, the force that resists an object's beginning to slide from a stationary position, and *kinetic friction*, the force that resists a moving object's continued sliding. A paper's frictional resistance is primarily an issue in paper and paperboard manufactured for use in cartons and other packaging, in which excessive slippage during shipping and handling can result in damage to the contents of the packaging, or to the contents of other cartons or packages. Paperboard surfaces are often treated with antiskid treatments to help increase frictional resistance. Frictional resistance is rarely a concern in most printing applications. A greater degree of frictional resistance can prevent sheets from sliding over each other easily, which can either cause feeding problems in the press or generate a buildup of static electric charges.

Friction Feed

In computing, a feeding system that uses rollers to move a sheet of paper through a computer printer.

Fringe

In *screen printing*, an alternate term for *halo*. See *Halo*.

Frisket

Any material—paper, plastic, or other substance—used to mask a portion of artwork during *retouching*, *airbrushing*, or printing.

In *letterpress* printing, a *frisket* is a strong, protective paper used to cover any portion of a printing plate not intended to print.

Frisket Knife

In *screen printing*, a small knife used to cut stencils.

Front

In *binding and finishing*, the edge of a book opposite the *binding edge*. Also known as the *thumb edge*.

Front End

In computing, term for a computer system responsible for whatever control and conversion of data is required before the data can be output. The front end (also known as a *front-end processor* or *front-end system*) in typesetting, for example, is that system in which the user enters text to be typeset. The front end then converts this data to a form

that is readable by the remainder of the system, which can then output it in typeset form. In telecommunications, the front-end processor manages all the aspects of communications with other systems or networks, freeing the central processor for all other data processing. Also known as a *front-end computer* and, in telecommunications, *host front end*, *front-end communications processor*, or *network front end*.

Front-End Application

In networking and telecommunications, the computer program that functions as an *interface* between the *front-end system* and the *back-end system*, performing such tasks as *email* composition, *database* management, etc.

Front End Communications Processor

See *Front End*.

Front-End Computer

See *Front End*.

Front-End Processor (FEP)

See *Front End*.

Front-End System

See *Front End*.

Front Guides

A set of metal tabs or plates attached to the front end of a sheetfed printing press's *feedboard*, which aid in properly positioning a sheet of paper before it is transferred into the printing unit. See *Feedboard*.

Front Matter

In *book typography* and production, the pages of a book that precede the main text. See *Book Typography*.

Front Projection

Alternate term for *front-screen projection*. See *Front-Screen Projection*.

Fronting

Printing the front of a sheet, as opposed to *backing up*.

Frontispiece

In book typography, an illustration facing the *title page* of a book, usually on the *verso* page. Often, a frontispiece is printed separately on higher-quality *enamel paper* and *tipped-in* during binding. Also known as a *frontis*.

FSI

Abbreviation for *free-standing insert*. See *Free-Standing Insert (FSI)*.

F-Stop System

In photography, a set of values used for setting camera lens *aperture*s. Essentially, a specific f-stop (also called an *f-number*) is the ratio of the *focal length* of the lens to the diameter of the aperture. Thus, a camera (such as a *process camera*) with an 8-in. focal length and a 1-in. aperture diameter would have an f-number of f/8 (8 ÷ 1 = 8). Reducing the aperture to ½ in. would yield an f-number of f/16 (8 ÷ ½ = 16).

Although in theory any f-number can be produced, lens manufacturers and photographers recognize a given set of f-stops: f/1.4, f/2, f/2.8, f/4, f/5.6, f/8, f/11, f/16, f/22, f/32, and f/64. The greater the f-number, the smaller the diameter of the aperture. Each f-stop also differs by a factor of 2 in the amount of light that is allowed to pass into the camera. Using f-stops, it is possible to gauge the *exposure time* required; adjusting the lens aperture and f-stop can yield shorter (or longer) equivalent exposure times. (See *Photography: Basic Photographic Principles*.)

FTA
See *Flexographic Technical Association*.

FTAM
Abbreviation for *File Transfer, Access, and Management*, an *OSI* standard *file-transfer protocol* for the remote transfer of files between computer systems manufactured by different vendors.

FTP
Abbreviation for *File Transfer Protocol*. See *File Transfer Protocol (FTP)*.

Fugitive Colors or Inks
A variety of inks produced from *pigment*s or *dye*s that lack *permanence*, and fade or discolor rapidly upon exposure to light, heat, moisture, or other substances and conditions.

Full Backup
The complete backup of a file from a *hard disk* to an additional storage medium, regardless of whether changes have been made to it or not.

Full Binding
In *binding and finishing*, a book cover or case consisting of a single piece of material. See also *Half Binding* and *Quarter Binding*.

Full Bleed
A printed image that extends to the edge of the page on all four sides. See *Bleed*.

Full-Color Printing
See *Four-Color Process*.

Full Contact Printing
In *screen printing*, an impression made with the screen fabric touching the substrate at all points during a stroke.

Full Duplex
In telecommunications, a system in which bi-directional channels are opened, affording the communicating parties the ability to both send and receive data simultaneously. A full duplex environment also allows the terminal to *echo* the characters typed by the sending party, or have them sent back to the sender and displayed on the screen. In a *half duplex* environment, only one-way transmission is possible. See *Half Duplex*. Abbreviated *FDX*.

Full-Duplex Ethernet (FDE)
In networking, a type of *Ethernet* in which data can be transferred in two directions simultaneously, greatly increasing data transfer rates.

Full Flush
Alternate term for *justification*. See *Justification*.

Full Gilding
In *binding and finishing*, an *edge gilding* applied to all three unbound edges of a book. See *Edge Gilding*.

Full Immersion
A level of *virtual reality*. See *Virtual Reality*.

Full Machine-Direction Burst
A *burst* or rupture of a paper *web* characterized by a complete rupture of the web running parallel to the roll's *machine direction*, caused by a winding of the roll that exceeds the paper's *tensile strength*. (See also *Air Shear Burst*, *Caliper Shear Burst*, and *Cross-Machine Tension Burst*.)

Full Measure
In typography, descriptive of a line set to the entire *line length*.

Full-Motion Video
In *digital video*, term for video that is shown on a computer at a *frame frequency* that approximates that of video seen on television or an *analog video* tape. Or, in other words, digital video that plays back at a rate of 30 frames per second (in *NTSC*) or 25 frames per second (in *PAL* or *SECAM*).

Full-motion video is rarely possible on typical *microcomputer*s, due to the enormous processing power, *RAM*, and specialized hardware required to achive it. Although advances in technology are moving closer to full-motion video (and its partner, *full-screen video*) as of this writing compromises in either decreased frame rate and/or decreased image size are often made.

Full-Page Display
Any computer monitor large enough to display an entire page of text without the need for constant scrolling.

Full-Range Black

See *Full-Scale Black*.

Full Resolution Video Display

In digital imaging, the display on a computer monitor of every *pixel* in a particular data file or portion of a data file. Because of the large amount of data that exists in a graphics file, only a small portion of the image can be displayed on the screen at any one time. A full *resolution* video display is used for retouching and other types of intricate image manipulation, and is in contrast to a *coarse data file*, a low-resolution version of the image used mainly for viewing and crude manipulation purposes. See also *High-Resolution File*.

Full-Scale Black

A *black printer*—or *key*—*color separation* containing the full range of tonal gradations, from white *highlight*s to dark *shadow*s. Consequently, dots are printed in every part of the image, as opposed to the *half-scale black*. See *Half-Scale Black*. Full-scale black is also known as *full-range black*.

Full-Screen Video

In *digital video*, term for video that is shown on a computer that fills the entire screen. Full-screen video is rarely possible on typical *microcomputer*s, due to the enormous processing power, *RAM*, and specialized hardware required to achieve it. Although advances in technology are moving closer to full-screen video (and its partner, *full-motion video*) as of this writing compromises in either decreased frame rate and/or decreased image size are often made.

Fully Associative Cache

One particular type of *cache memory* used in computers. See *Cache Memory*.

Fully Connected Network

Alternate term for a *mesh network*. See *Mesh Network*.

Fully Formed Character

Printed characters (as from a computer printer) that are formed all at once, usually from relief typeforms, rather than as a series of dots. See *Letter-Quality*.

Fumaric Resin

A synthetic resin used in printing inks derived from the chemical reaction of fumaric acid and *rosin*. See *Resin*.

Fuming Ghosting

Alternate term for *chemical ghosting*. See *Chemical Ghosting*.

Function

Generally speaking, any task or process that a mechanical device (or individual) is capable of performing.

In computing (via algebra), the term *function* refers to any algebraic expression that describes a relation between two or more variables.

Function Generator

Hardware device designed and installed to perform a specific *function*, such as moving the cursor about the monitor.

Function Key

In computing, one of (usually) ten or twelve programmable keys (labelled F1–F10 or F1–F12) used to perform special control tasks. The precise tasks activated by function keys usually vary from application to application, although there is some degree of consistency (F1 usually calls up *help files*.) Often, using the function keys in conjunction with shift, control, option, and command keys expands the range of functions available, and some programs come with transparent overlays that provide easy reference. Some applications allow the user to program some or all of the function keys him/herself.

Function Keypad

The portion of a computer keyboard containing the *function key*s. See *Function Key*.

Function Menu

In computing, a list of words or icons that, when selected, perform specific functions, such as "delete," "copy," "save," etc.

Furnace Black

A variety of *Carbon Black*, or *black pigment*, used in printing ink, produced by the "cracking" of petroleum oil. Crude oil is essentially a complex mixture of *hydrocarbon* compounds. Cracking, or the exposure of these hydrocarbons to high temperatures and pressures, weakens and decomposes the carbon-to-carbon bonds in the molecules, and as various substances are boiled off, other residual substances are left behind. The partial burning of these hydrocarbons and the condensation of the flame on a cool surface produces carbon black. (Carbon black obtained from the cracking of natural gas is typically referred to as *thermal black*.)

Furnace Black pigments vary in shade from a grayish blue to jet black, and possess high *lightfastness* and resistance to heat, alkalis, acids, solvents, soaps, water, and other substances. (See also *Black Pigments*.)

(*CI Pigment Black 7 No. 77266.*)

Furnish

Term for the water-suspended mixture of paper *pulp* and nonfibrous additives such as *fillers*, dyes, or *sizing*, from which paper or paperboard is made. After all the disparate materials are added to the papermaking furnish, it undergoes *refining* to dissolve the pulp into a *slurry* before it is sent to the *beater* and, ultimately, the *forming section* of the paper machine. (See also *Pulping* and *Paper and Papermaking: Papermaking*.)

Fuser

In photocopiers and *laser printer*s, the part of the printing system that uses heat, chemicals, and/or pressure to "fuse" the particles of *toner* to the paper.

345

Fusing

One of several procedures used to "fuse" particles of *toner* to a sheet of paper during photocopying or laser printing, which can involve heat (usually around 400°F), pressure, and/or chemicals.

Fust, Johann

Johann Fust (c.1400–1466), a German money-broker, was the financial backer of Johannes Gutenberg. The money advanced by Fust in 1450 and an additional loan in 1452 enabled Gutenberg to develop his printing process and to buy the necessary materials and equipment. A prominent goldsmith and money-lender, Fust lent Gutenberg 800 guilders in 1450 to perfect his movable-type printing process. An additional 800 guilders was invested about two years later. Gutenberg's 42-line Bible and his 1457 Psalter were almost finished, but Fust sued in 1455 for 2,020 guilders to recover his money with interest. The court found in Fust's favor, and Gutenberg lost his equipment. Gutenberg could not repay the first loan; Fust foreclosed and took possession of Gutenberg's press and materials. With Peter Schöeffer, who had been Gutenberg's assistant and foreman, Fust finished the 42-line Gutenberg Bible around 1455 and the Psalter in 1457, the first example of color printing. Both volumes had been designed and initiated by Gutenberg and are generally credited to him. Fust's firm later produced the Benedictine Psalter (1459), the 48-line Bible (1462), and an edition of Cicero's *De Officiis*. Fust later died on a trip to Paris to sell his bibles, and Schöeffer inherited the business. The spread of printing was accelerated by Adolf of Nassau's 1462 invasion of Mainz. The printers, fleeing the city, spread the art throughout Europe.

Fuzz

Alternate term for *lint*, also called *fluff*. See *Lint*.

Fuzzy Fonts

In computerized typesetting, gray *pixel*s inserted in the blank spaces between solid black (or other color) pixels to eliminate the stair-step pattern on *bitmap font*s known as *jaggies*. Fuzzy fonts are a form of *antialiasing*.

G

G, g
The seventh letter of the Latin and English alphabets, derived from the North Semitic letter *ghimel* and the Greek *gamma*, also the sources for the letter *C* (see *C, c*). In the Etruscan language, there was no distinction made between a *g* sound and a *k* sound, consequently the hard *c* and the *g* were used interchangeably. In Latin, when this distinction needed to be made, the small stroke was added to the lower portion of the *C*. The lowercase *g* was a scribal variation of the capital, coming down in its present form from the Carolingian script.

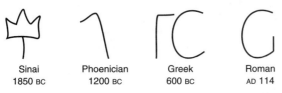

Sinai 1850 BC   Phoenician 1200 BC   Greek 600 BC   Roman AD 114

The evolution of the letter G.

G
Abbreviation for the prefix *giga-*. See *Giga-*.

GAA
Abbreviation for *Gravure Association of America*. See *Gravure Association of America*.

Gaffer
In movie, television, and video production, an individual who builds and dismantles sets. See also *Grip*.

Gain
See *Dot Gain*.
   In telecommunications, an increase in voltage, power, or signal, expressed in *decibels*.

Galley
In typography, a length of typeset material output for *proofing*. The term derives from the days of hot metal, where a *galley* was a metal tray with raised edges that held about 20 in. of metal type, which was then proofed and handled. *Galley* thus came to refer both to the amount of material and its state. Since a galley proof was made right after type was set, it was a first, or reading, proof. Subsequently, the material would be corrected and organized into pages, creating final page or repro proofs, made up with elements in position. Thus, a galley is a rough proof or copy of a length of typeset material.
   Today, galleys are not usually of equal lengths, although systems can be programmed to make them so. In book publishing, there are several types of galleys, com-

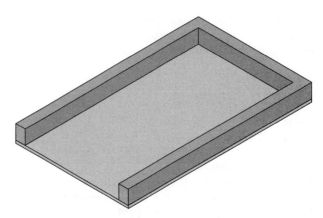

A galley for holding metal type.

monly considered as "first-pass pages," which are the first typeset pages of a book, and "second-pass pages," which are revised and corrected proofs and are commonly close to the final pagination of the book. "Bound galleys" are first-pass proofs cut into pages, bound with a cover, and sent out to early reviewers or used for promotional material. In electronic publishing systems, sheets of type, not yet assembled into final pages, output to a laser printer are often referred to as *galleys*.

Galley Proof
See *Galley*.

Gallium Arsenide
A crystalline and highly toxic semiconductor compound, chemical symbol GaAs, used in *laser*s, *LED*s, and other electronic devices. GaAs is also used to make computer chips, which results in *microprocessor*s that are faster and require less power than traditional silicon.

Galvanized
Alternate term for the mottled appearance of a printed image. See *Mottle*.

Galvano Screen
A special screen used in rotary *screen printing* capable of long print runs.

Gamma
A measure of the *contrast* of a photographic image. See *Contrast*.

Gamma Correction
A modification of the *contrast* of a photographic image by means of adjusting the *tone curve*s for the image. Essentially, gamma correction involves increasing or decreasing the *middletone* value, depending upon the desired correc-

tion. For example, a reproduction of a red fire hydrant may reproduce too dark. By reducing the middletone, the dark color—**cyan**—will be reduced, allowing the lighter color—**magenta**—to peek through to a greater extent and make the image brighter. Gamma correction—also called **tone correction**—is often incorrectly confused with **color correction**. (See also **Contrast**.)

Gamma Curve
See **Contrast**.

Gamut
See **Color Gamut**.

Gamut Compression
The process of squeezing the **color space** represented in an image to one that can be reproduced in a second image generation, such as ink on paper or a digital color proof.

Gamut Mapping
In **color**, a means of matching the **color space** of one particular device with that of another device, commonly accomplished by means of **color lookup table**s.

Ganged Images
A collection of discrete images that are digitized, scanned, or otherwise captured all at one time, as a time-saving measure. Ganged images can often be separated into individual image files and further edited, color corrected, and output after capture.

Ganged Separations
The grouping of several color transparencies on a single carrier sheet to make several **color separation**s at one time.

Ganging
Grouping images, photographs, or other original art together for shooting **negative** or **color separation**s, rather than making each exposure separately.

Gang Run
Alternate term for a **combination run**. See **Combination Run**.

Garamond, Claude
Claude Garamond (also spelled Garamont) (1490–1561) was a French type designer and publisher. About 1510, he apprenticed to Antoine Augerau, and by 1520, he was working with the typefounder Geoffroy Tory. His first romans and grecs du roi were cut for the firm of Robert Estienne. As a French punchcutter, he designed many typefaces in renaissance roman styles, as well as two italics. Many of his punches survive today at the Plantin-Moretus Museum in Antwerp and at the Imprimerie National in Paris. Though most of today's typefaces called Garamonds are actually based on the work of Jean Jannon, there are a few bearing Garamond's name that are based directly on his work, and

---

abcdefghijklmnopqrstuvwxyz
Garamond Condensed Book

abcdefghijklmnopqrstuvwxyz
Garamond Book

abcdefghijklmnopqrstuvwxyz
Garamond 3

Examples of Garamond type.

countless others including Jan Tschichold's Sabon owe large elements of their design to Garamond.

In 1545 he began to publish books; apparently he was not successful in business, for he died in poverty. Garamond, who was one of the first punchcutters to work independently of printers, influenced European punchcutters for 150 years. His Greek type set the pattern for Greek printing until the early 19th century. Modern typefaces bearing his name were patterned after other faces mistakenly attributed to Garamond, mostly those of Jean Jannon.

Garbage
Any unwanted or meaningless information stored in a computer file.

Garbage In, Garbage Out
Incorrect or inaccurate output caused by incorrect or inaccurate input, due to the fact that a computer is only capable of processing the data that is input to it and incapable of anything beyond that. Abbreviated **GIGO**.

Garment Discharging
Alternate term for **discharge printing**. See **Discharge Printing**.

Gas Crazing
See **Crazing**.

Gas Plasma Display (GPD)
Alternate term for **plasma panel**. See **Plasma Panel (PP)**.

Gatefold
In **folding**, a four-page insert or configuration of **foldout**. A large page is folded with two **parallel fold**s to produce a center spread revealed by opening two folded flaps.

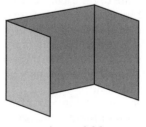

A gatefold.

Gateway

In networking and telecommunications, a link or **node** connecting two networks that utilize different **protocol**s. The gateway is an intelligent hardware device that allows conversion from one protocol type to another. **AppleTalk** and **TCP/IP** are two types of gateways used on personal computers, especially when connecting to the Internet.

Gateway Server

In networking, a communications **server** that allows access between different networks using different access **protocol**s.

GATF

Abbreviation for **Graphic Arts Technical Foundation**. See **Graphic Arts Technical Foundation**.

GATF Color Circle

A means of analyzing and evaluating colored inks utilizing a circular graph containing plotted **hue**s and grays of **color**s.

GATF/RHEM Light Indicator

In color analysis and **color proofing**, a device used to verify that a particular viewing environment conforms to standard lighting conditions.

GATF Standard Offset Color Bar

In **process color** printing, one of a large variety of **color control bar**s available from GATF. Like other color control bars, it is printed beyond the image area of a press sheet and consists of a series of color solids, tints, and sharpness guides, used to maintain uniform color and tonal reproduction during proofing and throughout a pressrun.

Gathering

In **binding and finishing**, the process of assembling printed **signature**s and placing them in the correct sequence for binding. Gathering is often performed by automated gathering machines that operate much like collating machines: each signature placed in a different pocket, and after all the pockets have been filled, the machine assembles them in the desired sequence. A type of gathering in which signatures are wrapped around other signatures (such as the prelude to **saddle-stitching**) is called **inserting**, while the gathering of individual sheets (rather than of signatures) is called **collating**. See **Binding and Finishing**.

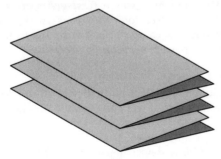

The process of gathering signatures.

Gauge

Generally speaking, any device used to measure and/or evaluate a quantity.

The term *gauge* is also a means of measuring the thickness of a wire or cable. See **AWG**.

Gauze

A designation of a class of screen fabrics used in **screen printing** manufactured from a blend of natural and synthetic fibers. Typically a European designation.

GB

Abbreviation for **gigabyte**. See **Gigabyte**.

GCA

Abbreviation for **Graphic Communications Association**. See **Graphic Communications Association (GCA)**.

GCA/GATF Proof Comparator

In **color proofing**, a set of **process color** (or **four-color**) test targets to which a press proof is compared.

GCA T-Ref

See **T-Ref**.

GCR

Abbreviation for **gray component replacement**. See **Gray Component Replacement**.

GCR Guide

An informative poster supplied by the **GCA** detailing many aspects of **gray component replacement (GCR)**.

GD

Abbreviation for **graceful degradation**. See **Graceful Degradation**.

Gear Side

Alternate term for the **driving side** of a **flexographic** press. See **Driving Side**.

Gear Streaks

A printing defect of **offset lithography** characterized by light and dark bands in solids and halftones parallel to the **gripper edge** of a press sheet, the distance between which being equal to the distance between the teeth of the cylinder gear. Gear streaks are a consequences of excessive **packing**, or the production of too much pressure, or **squeeze**, between the plate and blanket cylinders, which causes the cylinders to slip. Streaks then begin to appear on the blanket, which are then transferred to the paper.

Gel

A jelly-like, semirigid colloidal suspension of a solid with a liquid. In printing ink terminology, *gel* is an undesirable transformation of the **body** of an ink into a jelly-like consistency. (See also **Livering**.)

Gelatin

A proteinous *colloid*, typically derived from animal bones, used as a coating for *carbon tissue* resists and other types of photographic *emulsion*s. Gelatin is soluble in water, but insoluble in alcohol and other solvents.

Gelatin Stencil

A type of *screen printing* stencil containing a *gelatin*-based *emulsion* or coating.

GEM

Abbreviation for *graphical environment manager*. See *Graphical Environment Manager (GEM)*.

GEM is also a *file extension* for files produced by GEM Paint or GEM Graph.

GEM/IMG

See *IMG*.

Gender

In cabling terminology, term used to describe whether a connector has pins and is thus designed to be plugged into another device (a *male connector*) or has slots or holes into which a plug is inserted (a *female connector*). Special intermediate connectors called *gender changer*s are often required to make one cable or connector attach to another properly.

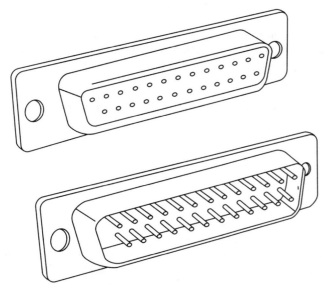

A female connector (top) and a male connector (bottom).

Gender Changer

A device or connector used to change a *male connector* into a *female connector* (or vice versa) to facilitate the attaching of different electrical or electronic components.

Generalized Sort/Merge Program

In *database* management, a computer program designed to organize *record*s and prevent inadvertent duplicates.

General MIDI

In multimedia and audio recording, a standardization of channel numbers used for *MIDI*, allowing MIDI files to be transferred from system to system while still having each synthesized instrument remain the same. For example, a violin on one system will remain a violin on another system. See *Musical Instrument Digital Interface (MIDI)*.

General Protection Fault (GPF)

In computing, particularly by means of an operating system that operates in *protected mode*, an error condition caused when an application attempts to access a portion of computer memory reserved for another purpose. See *Protected Mode*.

General-Purpose Bond

A type of paper (used for making forms) that is *translucent* when viewed under *ultraviolet* light but *opaque* enough for printing to be legible.

General-Purpose Computer

Any computer designed to perform a wide variety of tasks, rather than being manufactured and programmed for one specific purpose.

General-Purpose Interface Board

See *General-Purpose Interface Bus (GPIB)*.

General-Purpose Interface Bus (GPIB)

A standard IEEE-488 eight-bit parallel interface that fits inside a desktop computer and is used to connect peripheral devices—in particular, *scanner*s—to desktop computer systems. Also known as a *general-purpose interface board*.

General-Purpose Operating System

Any *operating system* designed for a wide variety of applications, rather than being designed and programmed for one specific purpose. See *Operating System*.

Generation

In imaging and photography, each successive stage of reproduction. A copy of an original is first generation; a copy of the copy is second generation, etc.

The term *generation* is also used to refer to a particular stage or level of technology. For example, the very first phototypesetting machine was a *first-generation phototypesetter*; the next "version" was the second generation, and so on. In terms of computer software, the term *generation* is synonymous with *version* or *revision*.

Generation Loss

In video production, the loss of quality of an *analog video* picture when it is copied from one tape to another.

Genlock

In *digital video*, a device used to synchronize *analog video* signals with digital video signals. The analog signals are imported from an external source (such as a VCR) and merged with a digital image. A genlock allows the overlay of computer-generated graphics or other video signals on a video signal, used in video editing, multimedia, teleconferencing, and other such applications. *Genlock* is an abbreviation for **synchronization generator lock**.

Genuine Felt Finish

Alternate term for a **felt finish** paper. See **Felt Finish**.

Geographic Information System (GIS)

In computing and databases, a system for storing maps and demographic data digitally, allowing for ease of access as well as ease of updating the data.

Geometric Model

In graphics, any quantitative representation of a two-dimensional or three-dimensional object utilizing **Cartesian coordinates**.

Geometric Printing

A general term for **screen printing** three-dimensional objects, such as glassware, ceramics, plastic objects, and other such nonflat **substrate**s.

Geostationary

Descriptive of an orbit around a planet (as a satellite in orbit around the Earth) in which the orbiting object travels at a velocity equal to that of the rotation of the Earth, so that the object is stationary with respect to a particular point on the Earth's surface. Also referred to as **geosynchronous**.

Geostationary Satellite

A type of **communications satellite** placed in Earth's orbit at 22,300 miles up and set to orbit the Earth at such a speed as to allow it to make one revolution every 24 hours, thus causing the satellite to appear to be in the same position above the Earth at all times. Also called **geosynchronous**.

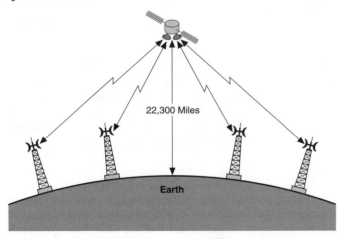

A geostationary satellite.

Geosynchronous

Alternate term for **geostationary**. See **Geostationary**.

Ghost Halftone

A very light **halftone** often overprinted with text.

Ghost Image

In **screen printing**, an ink stain (commonly in the image areas) on the screen fabric, resulting from improper cleaning. More caustic and vigorous cleaning methods are thus necessary.

Ghosting

An offset printing defect characterized by the appearance of faint replicas of printed images in undesirable places, produced in one of two ways. **Mechanical ghosting** is characterized by the appearance of a "phantom" image on the printed side of the sheet; it appears during printing and is easily detectable in the delivery tray. It can be caused by such things as ink starvation, as heavily inked areas on the plate are not always adequately reinked by the form roller, or by incorrect-diameter form rollers. **Chemical ghosting**, also called **gloss ghosting** or **fuming ghosting**, is characterized by a "phantom" image on the reverse side of a sheet originating from the sheet below it (not caused by **ink setoff**), and typically results from an ink reacting with and altering the drying of the ink on the sheet on top of it. (See **Mechanical Ghosting** and **Chemical Ghosting**.) Ghosting can also refer to a faint reproduction of an image without actual ink transfer.

Ghosting is also an alternate term for a **flexographic** printing problem more commonly known as **mechanical pinholing**. See **Mechanical Pinholing**.

The term *ghosting* also describes a defect of **screen printing**, characterized by a faint reproduction of the printed image beyond the edges of the **stencil**, caused by

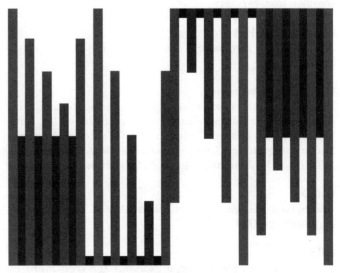

A mechanical ghosting form, showing the effects of ink starvation due to the design of the form.

an improperly tensioned screen fabric which, following a *squeegee* stroke, creeps in the direction of the stroke. *Ghosting* in screen printing also refers to the reproduction of a printed image on the reverse of the substrate lying on top if it, caused by ink setoff.

GHz

Abbreviation for *gigahertz*, a measure of *frequency*. See *Gigahertz*.

GIF

Abbreviation for *Graphics Interchange Format*. See *Graphics Interchange Format (GIF)*.

Giga-

A *metric prefix* denoting 1,000,000,000 (one billion, or 10^9) units. In computing, *giga-* refers to 2^{30}, and one *gigabyte* (GB) of storage is approximately equal to one billion *bytes* of data (actually 1,073,741,824 bytes). See *Metric Prefix*. See also *Kilo-*, *Mega-*, *Tera-*, *Peta-*, and *Exa-*. *Giga-* is usually abbreviated *G*.

Gigabit

A unit equal to approximately 1,000,000,000 (actually 1,073,741,824) *bit*s. See *Bit*.

Gigabyte

An increasingly common unit of computer storage, comprising 1,024 *megabyte*s or 1,073,741,824 *byte*s. *Giga-* is the prefix meaning "billion," so it is common to consider 1 gigabyte as equal to 1 billion bytes, although that is not entirely accurate.

It is not uncommon to find hard disks and magnetic cartridge media with storage capacities in excess of 1 gigabyte. Gigabyte is abbreviated GB, or, colloquially, "gig." 1,024 gigabytes equal 1 *terabyte*, which may yet become a common disk capacity.

Gigahertz (GHz)

A measure of *frequency*, equal to one billion cycles per second.

Gigascale Integration

In computer *microprocessor* manufacturing, term for the design and production of *integrated circuit*s with a component density of over 1 billion transistor gates. See *Large-Scale Integration (LSI)*, *Very-Large-Scale Integration (VLSI)*, and *Ultralarge-Scale Integration*.

GIGO

Abbreviation for *garbage in, garbage out*. See *Garbage In, Garbage Out*.

Gilding

In *binding and finishing*, a form of *edge treatment* in which gold or other metallic leaf is applied to the edges of a book. Also called *edge gilding*.

Gill, Eric

Eric Gill (1882–1940), stone carver, wood engraver, essayist and typographer, was born in Brighton, England. His father was a curate and his mother a singer. Early in life, he displayed a talent for drawing and an eye for proportion, inspiring his family to enroll him in an art school in Chichester. In 1900, his father apprenticed him to the architect of the Ecclesiastical Commissioners. He began to study lettering in evening classes with Edward Johnston. After three years, he abandoned architecture to start his own business in letter cutting and stone carving. In 1907, he joined an artists' community in Ditchling, Sussex, where he had his first experiences with printing and typography. In 1925, Stanley Morison approached Gill with the idea of creating a new typeface for the Monotype Corporation, consequently he designed Perpetua, and a sans-serif, Gill Sans, that has become the leading British sans serif, sometimes described as the "national typeface of England." Although he never considered himself primarily a typographer, he designed eleven typefaces of beauty and subtlety, and wrote an influential *Essay on Typography*.

abcdefghijklmnopqrstuvwxyz
Gill Sans

abcdefghijklmnopqrstuvwxyz
Gill Sans Condensed

Two examples of Gill Sans.

Gilsonite

A black, bituminous, extremely pure asphalt mined in Utah and Colorado used to manufacture black printing inks. Gilsonite is also called *uintaite*.

GIS

Abbreviation for *geographic information system*. See *Geographic Information System (GIS)*.

GKS

Abbreviation for *Graphical Kernel System*. See *Graphical Kernel System (GKS)*.

Glaire

In early bookbinding, a solution of egg white and vinegar applied to book covers as a prelude to *gold tooling*, or a means of melting *gold leaf* onto a book cover. Glaire facilitated the adhesion of the gold leaf to the cover material. See *Binding and Finishing* and *Gold Tooling*.

Glare

The reflection of light from a surface, usually undesirable. Glare is often a problem when trying to read a computer display, as the reflection of the *ambient light* impedes clear viewing. A monitor made with an *antireflection surface panel* can help reduce or eliminate glare.

Glass

A hard, brittle, noncrystalline (and usually transparent) material produced from the melting and fusion of silica and other silicates. Glass is essentially a very viscous liquid and is thus seemingly solid. Glass is used in a wide variety of materials, from camera lenses to light bulbs, to windows to protective covers on camera *copyboard*s, etc.

The term *glass* is also an abbreviated term for a magnifying glass.

Glassine

A high-gloss, *transparent* or *translucent* paper made from highly refined *chemical pulp*, possessing high air, moisture, and grease resistance, widely used for dust jackets and food packaging.

Glass Master

In multimedia and *CD* production, a glass disc on which the data from a *master tape* are stored. It is used to stamp an impression in the *stamper*, creating a pattern that is the reverse of a *compact disc* (i.e., *pit*s on a CD exist as *land*s and vice versa on the stamper), which is then used to stamp multiple copies of a CD.

Glass Screen

Alternate term for *crossline screen*. See *Crossline Screen*.

Glaze

A buildup of ink *pigment* particles, dried ink *vehicle*, dampening solution gum, particles of paper fiber and *coating*, and other material on ink rollers, a problem occurring on offset presses. The accumulation of glaze (typically on resilient rollers, such as *form rollers*) is caused by a combination of press chemistry and improper cleaning and maintenance. Ink rollers effect the transfer of ink by virtue of the presence of tiny protrusions on the surface of the rubber coating, and the flexibility of these protrusions allow

Photomicrographs of the surface of a new roller (left) and a glazed roller (right).

consistent and effective ink coverage. The materials that cause glaze fill up the space between these protrusions and reduce their flexibility, resulting in the decreased efficacy of ink transfer. Glazed rollers can cause streaking, inconsistent ink coverage, and other such problems. The process of *deglazing* rollers can be effected using basic washup techniques and properly formulated cleaning *solvent*s. (Improper solvents are also a cause of glaze.)

Glazed Paper

A type of *coated paper* that has been polished and burnished to produce a very high-gloss *finish*. See also *Unglazed Paper*.

Glazed Rollers

Offset press ink rollers suffering from an accumulation of *glaze*. See *Glaze*.

Glazing

The accumulation of *glaze* on offset press ink rollers. See *Glaze*.

Glitch

Any abrupt, temporary error or malfunction in a mechanical, electrical, or electronic system. In a video signal, a glitch is usually a brief deformation of the picture.

Glitter

A decorative, high-gloss material added to a printing ink to produce a sparkling effect on the printed ink film.

Global

Any phenomenon, alteration, or variable that occurs throughout a system, file, or program rather than simply in one location.

Global Correction

A type of *color correction* performed on an entire image (such as altering the shade of red throughout an image), as opposed to *local correction*, which refers to a color correction performed on only a portion of an image.

Global Directory Services

In networking, any *directory services* that treat the entire network as a single unit, allowing all resources, users, servers, etc., to be defined in one place and at one time. See *Directory Services*.

Global Log-in

In networking, the ability for a remote user to access all parts of the network at once, rather than requiring that he or she constantly log into different *server*s.

Global Network

A *really* *wide area network* that includes all departments, branches, and offices of a multinational corporation, which may be located throughout the world.

Gloss

The quality of a paper that causes it to appear shiny. When light hits a paper's surface, the orientation of the reflected light rays (or **specular reflectance**) determines a paper's gloss. A paper that has undergone extensive **calendering**, **supercalendering**, or **coating**, or has had its surface highly polished will reflect the light primarily as parallel rays, or all in the same direction. This is what causes a paper surface to be shiny, or "glossy." The opposite of a glossy surface, a **matte** surface, is much less polished, so the light rays that strike it are reflected in different directions (or more diffusely) due to small surface contours. Gloss is related to paper smoothness, but there is no clear correlation between the two qualities. Glossy papers are used in some printing jobs to increase the gloss or color brilliance of the printing ink (glossy paper reflects light back through the ink), and less glossy papers are used in other printing jobs to reduce eyestrain (the high degree of reflected light makes text printed on glossy paper hard to read).

Paper gloss is measured using a **glossmeter**, which compares the amount of light reflected from a paper surface to the amount of light hitting it. Paper gloss may differ with **grain** direction, so separate glossmeter readings may be taken **with the grain** and **against the grain** and then averaged. Since papers also exhibit **two-sidedness** (i.e., **wire side** vs. **felt side**), an average gloss level may be provided for each side of the paper. "Perfect gloss," as determined by referencing a gloss standard (i.e., polished black glass), is near 100 gloss units. Matte papers register generally less than 20 gloss units, while **dull-finish** papers range up to 40 gloss units.

The term *gloss* also refers to the degree of shine of a printed ink. Certain inks, such as **high-gloss ink**s, dry to a high degree of gloss. The key to glossy inks is the maximization of **ink holdout**, as it is premature absorption of the ink **vehicle** into the paper before it can dry by **oxidation** that decreases gloss.

Glossary

A portion of the **back matter** of a book providing definitions of the technical or subject-specific terms bandied about in the main text. See **Book Typography**.

Gloss Ghosting

Alternate term for **chemical ghosting**. See **Chemical Ghosting**.

Gloss Ink

A printing ink formulated with an additional amount of **varnish** to impart a glossy appearance to the dry ink film. See **High-Gloss Ink**.

Glossmeter

A device used to measure the amount of **gloss** possessed by a paper, expressed as the ratio of the amount of the paper sample's reflected light to the light falling on it as compared to a gloss standard (polished black glass) of 100

"gloss units." Gloss is measured at a determined angle from the paper's surface; for coated papers, it tends to be 15° from the paper's surface (for extremely glossy papers, best results can be obtained at 20° from the paper's surface). The glossmeter shines a light of known intensity on the paper and calculates the amount reflected back at the chosen angle of reflectance. Gloss can differ with **grain direction**, so readings in both the grain and **cross-grain direction** are typically taken. (See **Gloss**.)

Gloss White

An inorganic **white pigment** used as an **extender pigment** in printing inks, derived from the co-**precipitation** of **alumina hydrate** and **blanc fixe**.

Glossy

A term describing any surface or substance—such as paper or ink—that appears shiny. (See **Gloss**.)

Glossy Print

A photographic print produced on a high-gloss photosensitive paper.

Glow

Any halo of light surrounding, blending into, or otherwise disfiguring a photographic or videographic image.

Glow Lamp

A type of discharge lamp containing a vacuum tube filled with a gas that, when ionized by electrons, gives off an intense glow. The intensity of the light could be varied according to the voltage applied to it. Glow lamps were used in early **drum scanner**s.

Glueability

A property of paper or paperboard that determines the speed and strength of a bond generated by the application of an adhesive to the paper surface. Glueability is important in the manufacture of paper and paperboards to be used as cartons or other packaging. The adhesive used to glue the sides of the box together must maintain a strong bond both when the carton is empty and when it is full. Glueability is also an issue in the binding of books and other publications.

Glued-On Cover

In **binding and finishing**, any cover that has been attached to the book body by glue, as opposed to staples or sewing. See **Perfect Binding**.

Glue-Off Machine

In **case binding**, a device used to apply an **adhesive** to the sewn pages or **signature**s of a book, prior to **casing in**.

Glue Pot

In **binding and finishing**, the portion of the gluing section of a **perfect binding** system in which the adhesive material for binding is stored. See **Perfect Binding**.

Gluer

Any device used in **binding and finishing** (either **in-line** or **off-line**) to apply glue or **adhesive** material to a substrate. See **Perfect Binding** and **Adhesive**. On in-line finishing equipment used in **web offset lithography**, types of commonly used gluers include **paster wheels**, **remoistenable pattern gluer**s, **backbone gluer**s, and **envelope pattern gluer**s. See **Web Offset Lithography: In-Line Finishing: Gluers**.

Gluing Off

In **case binding**, the process of applying an **adhesive** to the sewn pages or **signature**s of a book prior to **casing-in**. See **Case Binding**. Also known as **back gluing**.

Glycol Vehicle

A type of ink **vehicle**—the fluid carrier of the ink **pigment**—that dries by **precipitation** of the pigment out of the vehicle, rather than by absorption of the vehicle into the **substrate** or by **oxidation** of the vehicle. Also called **moisture-set ink**s, glycol vehicle inks are made from water-insoluble **resin**s that are dissolved in glycol (an alcohol also used in antifreeze). Glycol itself is water-soluble, and when moisture comes in contact with this type of vehicle, the glycol is dissolved, and the resin precipitates out, dragging the pigment with it. A variation on the glycol vehicle inks are fast-drying inks, which neutralize an acidic resin with an amine and dissolve the resulting resin salt in glycol. When printed, the amine is absorbed into the paper, de-neutralizing the resin, which is abruptly rendered insoluble in glycol and precipitates out and hardens on the surface of the substrate. The hardening of the resin happens very quickly and without the use of moisture. Glycol vehicles are commonly used in **letterpress** printing. (See **Vehicle**.)

Glyph

Any **pictogram** used to convey information (such as a hieroglyph). A glyph is also a coding system used in computing that utilizes printed symbols. After scanning, these symbols are converted into data by the computer. A **bar code** is a type of glyph.

GMF

A **file extension** used to denote metafiles created by Lotus Freelance Plus.

Gobo

In still and motion picture photography, a black screen used to deflect studio lighting from directly entering a camera lens. A gobo is also used to create shadow effects.

Golden Mean

In mathematics and fine arts, the ratio between two portions of a line or two dimensions of a plane figure (such as a rectangle) in which the lesser of the two dimensions is to the greater of the two dimensions as the greater dimension is to the sum of the greater and the lesser dimensions. This "golden mean" works out to about 0.618:1 (usually also denoted as a 3:5, which works out somewhat closely). For example, in the case of a rectangle, the shorter dimension would need to be 3 in., while the longer dimension would need to be 5 in. This ratio of two dimensions is often used in architecture and graphic design due to its purportedly pleasing appearance.

In mathematics, the *golden mean* is known as the *golden section*, and the statement of it dates from the days of the Greek mathematician Pythagoras (about the 6th century BC). The original statement of the problem involves the cutting of a line segment into the extreme and mean ratio. So, for line segment AB, point P would divide AB internally in the ratio AB : AP = AP : PB. Euclid dealt with the problem, as well, and eventually used it to construct a regular decagon and a regular pentagon. He went on to show that if AB is denoted by a and PB is denoted by b in the above proportion, then $a + b : a = a : b$, whence $a : b = b : a - b$, which then shows that if b is cut off from a, then a and $a - b$ are also two parts of a golden section. This process can be repeated infinitely. The concept of the golden section influenced ancient Greek ethics (the "Golden Mean" has also been used to describe the Aristotelian concept of moderation) and medieval theology, as well as art itself.

Golden Plast

In **stripping**, a carrier sheet used in lieu of **goldenrod paper** in the making of **flat**s. Also known as **orange plast**.

Goldenrod Flat

A **flat**, especially one made using photographic **negative**s attached to goldenrod paper. See **Stripping**.

Goldenrod Paper

In **prepress**, a coated, stiff, yellow or orange carrier paper used for **flat**s in **stripping**. (See **Stripping**.) A flat made using goldenrod paper is called a **goldenrod flat**.

Gold Ink

A series of related shades of metallic ink produced by mixing flakes of bronze, copper, and/or other metals, with a **varnish**, used in inks designed to impart a metallic luster to the printed image. See **Metallic Powders**.

Gold Leaf

In **binding and finishing**, a very thin sheet of 18- or 22-carat gold used for cover decorating and **foil stamping**. See also **Imitation Gold Leaf**.

Gold Tooling

In early bookbinding, a means of decorating a book by using a heated instrument to melt gold leaf onto the cover.

Good-Enough Color

Somewhat colloquial term for **process color** printing derived from low-end to mid-range **desktop publishing** systems that, although suitable for a particular customer, is below the level of quality attainable on high-end systems.

Gopher

In *Internet* terminology, a popular *client/server* application used to facilitate information searches on the Internet. Essentially, Gopher—typically provided by an *Internet service provider*—presents all Internet resources as a series of menus, and despite the fact that many different *IP* addresses and *access method*s are represented, the user is oblivious to this. The menus that Gopher presents can contain viewable documents or downloadable files. Alternately, the user may be able to jump directly to a selected Gopher *server* and view that server's directory of files. All the resources available via Gopher are collectively known as *Gopherspace*. The term itself derives from the common colloquialism *gopher*, referring to an individual who "goes for" things. *Hypertext* linking on the *World Wide Web* is supplanting Gopher to a large degree.

GOSIP

Abbreviation for *Government Open Systems Interconnection Profile*. See *Government Open Systems Interconnection Profile (GOSIP)*.

Gothic

Alternate term for *black letter*. See *Black Letter*.

The term *gothic* is sometimes inappropriately used in the United States to refer to *sans serif* typefaces. Gothic typefaces are also often referred to as *grotesk* (also spelled *grotesque*).

Goudy, Frederic W.

An American printer and typographer (1865–1947) who designed more than 120 typefaces, Goudy taught himself printing and typography while working as a bookkeeper. In 1895, in partnership with an English teacher, C. Lauren Hooper, he set up the Camelot Press in Chicago, which printed the Chap-book for Stone & Kimball publishers, widely praised for its fine design. He sold the first typeface he designed, called Camelot, to a Boston printer for $10. In 1903, with his wife, Bertha, and Will Ransom, he started the Village Press in Park Ridge, Illinois. Goudy and the Village Press landed in Marlborough, New York, in 1923. The workshop and type foundry burned in 1939. From 1920 to 1940 he was art director of the Lanston Monotype Company. He produced such faces as Goudy Old Style, Kennerly, Garamond, and Forum for the American Type Founders and Lanston companies. He was the author of *The Alphabet* (1918), *Elements of Lettering* (1922), *Typologia* (1940), and the autobiographical *A Half-Century of Type Design and Typography, 1895–1945* (1946).

In 1908, he created his first significant typeface for the Lanston Monotype Machine Company: E-38, known as Goudy Light. However, in that same year the Village Press burned to the ground, destroying all of his equipment and designs. In 1911, Goudy produced his first "hit," Kennerly Old Style, for an H.G. Wells anthology published by Mitchell Kennerly. His most widely used type, Goudy Old Style, was released by the American Type Founders Com-

abcdefghijklmnopqrstuvwxyz
Goudy Regular

abcdefghijklmnopqrstuvwxyz
Goudy Extra Bold

abcdefghijklmnopqrstuvwxyz
Goudy Heavy Face

Examples of Goudy type.

pany in 1915, becoming an instant classic. The graceful letterforms of Goudy Old Style made it visually appealing, while its shortened descenders allowed printers to squeeze more type on a page.

In the early years of his career, Goudy designed mostly display faces for advertising. As he progressed as a designer, his interests moved toward the perfecting of the traditional roman typeface. He drew his letters by hand and eschewed the mechanical way that companies such as Monotype produced matrices for his typefaces. In 1923 he set up a foundry in his home in Marlborough, New York, in order to produce type in a more creative way. By 1927, he was engraving the matrices himself. But in 1939 Goudy's work was destroyed by fire. The rest of his life was mainly devoted to teaching and lecturing.

Goudy is credited with personally designing over 120 typefaces. He is, however, best remembered for a series of types known variously as Goudy Old Style, Berkeley, University of California Old Style, and others. Goudy's type is reminiscent of Jenson's famous model from 1470. Goudy set the standard for contemporary type designers with new, distinctive types while remaining faithful to the old models, particularly those of the Venetian Renaissance.

Gouraud Shading

In computer graphics, a technique used for coloring three-dimensionally-rendered objects in which the area to be colored is divided into triangles, the solid colors being placed at the corners of a triangle, the remainder of the area of a triangle being filled with a gradient extending from corner to corner. Although this system avoids complicated calculations, it does not always produce smooth gradients.

Government Open Systems Interconnection Profile (GOSIP)

A set of standards based on the *Open Systems Interconnection (OSI)* reference model and used by the United States Government. A degree of GOSIP support is required for any government networking setup.

Government Size

Cut paper sheets commonly used by the United States government. Government letter size is 8×10½ in., and government legal size is 8×8 in.

GPD

Abbreviation for *gas panel display*, an alternate term for a *plasma panel*. See *Plasma Panel (PP)*.

GPF

Abbreviation for *general protection fault*. See *General Protection Fault (GPF)*.

GPIB

Abbreviation for *General-Purpose Interface Bus*. See *General-Purpose Interface Bus (GPIB)*.

Grab Utility

In computing, a small software utility residing in the computer's *RAM* that allows the user to make a *screen capture* in any program and import it into any other program for imaging and output.

Graceful Degradation

A gradual and often imperceptible deterioration in the quality or speed of data transmission caused by an increase in the number of users accessing a computer or computer network.

Grace Log-in

In networking, the ability for a user to log into a network using an expired *password*. Typically, a user is allowed a finite number of grace log-ins.

Gradation

Alternate term for *contrast*. See *Contrast*.

Grade

A method of categorizing different types of paper by size, weight, *pulp* composition, manufacturing procedure, thickness, and end use. There are hundreds of different paper grades and subgrades. See *Bond Paper*, *Bristol Paper*, *Coated Paper*, *Cover Paper*, *Duplicator Paper*, *Imitation Parchment*, *Index Paper*, *Ledger Paper*, *Manifold Paper*, *Mimeograph Paper*, *Newsprint*, *Offset Paper*, *Onionskin*, *Safety Paper*, *Tag Paper*, *Text Paper*, and *Wedding Paper*.

Graded Tint

Alternate term for *degradé*. See *Degradé*.

Gradient

In graphics, any smooth progression from one color or gray value to another, usually comprising a series of steps that,

A gradient, progressing from light gray to dark gray.

ideally, should be imperceptible. In digital output, one particular defect of gradients is *banding*, or the visibility of the discrete steps of a gradient, usually produced when the system or output device cannot generate enough gray or color levels to render a smooth gradient. (See COLOR PLATE 12.)

Grain

The direction of fibers in a sheet or *web* of paper, generated during paper formation. As paper moves forward along the *forming wire* on a papermaking machine, the fibers align themselves in a direction parallel to the direction of wire travel through the machine (also called *machine direction*). When paper is cut into sheets, it will be either *long-grain* (or *grain-long*) if the fibers are aligned parallel to the sheet's longer dimension, or *short-grain* (or *grain-short*), if the fibers are aligned parallel to the sheet's shorter dimension. Paper will tear and fold more easily *with the grain* and with greater difficulty *against the grain*.

Grain direction is an important consideration in printing processes such as sheetfed offset lithography (in particular multicolor work), especially in connection with dimensional stability, or how well a particular sheet of paper will retain its original length and width upon exposure to moisture. When paper fibers absorb water, they will expand in width, but not in length. Therefore, the direction of greater dimensional change will be in the *cross-grain direction*. Long-grain paper is generally preferred to short-grain paper for offset lithography, as the total dimensional change due to moisture will be less if the expansion is in the shorter dimension. This is an important consideration when separate colors in multicolor jobs need to align properly. In some cases, however (primarily in black-and-white and single-color jobs), short-grain paper is preferred, as register is not a concern. In addition, since paper is stronger against the grain, paper that is fed into the press against its grain will be less likely to suffer from structural deformities such as curling, stretching, or *waffling* as a result of tensile forces. When pages are to be bound, as in books and catalogs, the grain should be parallel to the binding edge. Pages bound with the grain perpendicular to the binding edge do not lie flat or turn easily.

There are a variety of ways of determining the grain direction in a particular sheet of paper. One test is to moisten one side of a paper square. It will curl toward its dry side, and the two opposite edges that curl up will be parallel to the grain direction. Another test is to cut two long, thin strips at right angles to each other from the same sheet. Put one strip on top of the other, align them, and hold them together between the thumb and forefinger from the short edges, letting them dangle. Then, turn them over. When on the bottom, the short-grain strip will bend toward the ground more than the long-grain strip. (See also *Bursting Test* and *Tensile Test*.)

In *binding and finishing*, the term *grain* refers to an artificial or exaggerated grain pattern imparted to binding materials, commonly by *embossing*. See *Graining*.

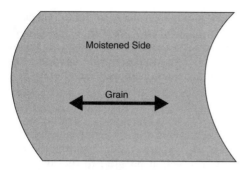

Curl test for determining grain direction.

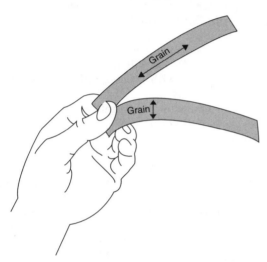

Flex test for determining grain direction.

In photography, *grain* is used to refer to the size of the particles—or, in other words, the visual texture—forming the exposed image. The size of the grain (be it *fine grain* or *coarse grain*) determines not only how visible or "grainy" the image ultimately is, but also the smallest size of the image that can be recorded on it.

In platemaking, the term *grain* refers to the irregular surface texture of a lithographic *plate*.

Grain Direction

The direction in which all or most of the paper fibers are oriented in a sheet or *web*. Since the grain is produced on the *forming wire* of a papermaking machine in the direction of the web's travel through the machine, the grain direction is also called the *machine direction*. The direction perpendicular to the grain direction is the *cross-grain direction*. Grain direction is an important factor of such paper properties as strength and dimensional stability. See *Grain*.

Graininess

Also called *graininess of halftones* or *grainy halftone dots*, a printing defect characterized by a somewhat patterned unevenness of tone in *halftone dots*. Graininess is typically the result of nonuniform *ink absorbency* across a

paper's surface, which can be caused by fluctuations in surface characteristics such as *wild formation*, inadequate *smoothness*, or incomplete *coating* on coated papers. Similar, less patterned defects are called *breaks* or, in *gravure* printing, *skips*, *snow*, or *speckle*.

Graining

In *binding and finishing*, the production of an artificial or exaggerated *grain* pattern in a cover or other binding material, commonly by *embossing*.

Grain-Long

Alternate term for *long-grain*. See *Grain*.

Grain-Short

Alternate term for *short-grain*. See *Grain*.

Grainy Edges

In papermaking, a surface roughness along the edges of a paper web that occasionally develops during drying.

Grammage

Metric system equivalent of a paper's *basis weight*. Basis weight, expressed in pounds, is typically the weight of one ream (500 sheets) of a paper cut to its *basic size*, which can vary by paper *grade*. Grammage is defined as the weight (in grams) of a square meter of paper, and is expressed in grams per square meters (g/m^2). To convert from a known basis weight and basic size to g/m^2:

Trade size	g/m^2 to lb.	lb. to g/m^2
17×22 in.	0.266	3.760
20×26 in.	0.370	2.704
24×36 in.	0.614	1.627
25×38 in.	0.675	1.480
1000 ft.^{2}	0.205	4.831

So, to find the grammage of a 20-lb. 17×22-in. bond paper, multiply the basis weight (20 lb.) by 3.760 to get 75.2 g/m^2. Similarly, to find the basis weight of a 103.6 g/m^2 book paper, multiply the grammage by the conversion factor corresponding to the basic size of a book paper (25×38) to get $103.6 \times 0.675 = 69.93$, or approximately 70-lb. paper.

The metric system also has its own basic sizes. (See *A Series* and *B Series*.)

Granite Finish

A *paper finish* characterized by the addition of different-colored fibers to the papermaking *furnish* to impart a mottled appearance intended to resemble the texture of granite.

Graph

In graphics, alternate term for a *chart*, especially one in which data is plotted in a *coordinate system* See *Chart*.

The term *graph* is also an abbreviation for *paragraph*. See *Paragraph*.

Graph Area

The area within a ***coordinate system*** where data is plotted.

Graphic

Any visual matter—such as an illustration, photograph, symbol, etc.—included on a page or within a document.

Graphical Environment Manager (GEM)

An early ***graphical user interface (GUI)*** or windowing system, developed by Digital Research, designed to run on top of ***MS-DOS***. It was ultimately replaced by Microsoft ***Windows***.

Graphical Kernel System (GKS)

A ***device-independent***, standard ***file format*** developed by the ***International Standards Organization (ISO)*** for ***vector graphics***. GKS is used for creating two-dimensional and three-dimensional graphics, as well as ***bitmapped graphics***. As it is a standard file format, it can easily be transferred from system to system or application to application, so long as the application to which it is imported supports the GKS format.

Graphical User Interface (GUI)

A computer interface (i.e., the means by which the user and the computer communicate with each other) that uses visual, graphical ***icons***, windows, pull-down menus, and a pointing-clicking-dragging device (such as a mouse) to manipulate screen objects, rather than relying on a straight, somewhat cryptic and technical text, to convey messages and accept commands. Early personal computers used ***BASIC***, ***DOS***, ***UNIX***, or some other text-based interface, called a ***command-line interface (CLI)***, which consisted of sometimes obscure commands and proper syntax to locate, open, save, and copy files and programs, or perform any other computer function. The GUI was first developed by Xerox at the Palo Alto Research Center (PARC) in the early- to mid-1970s. The first true GUI-based personal

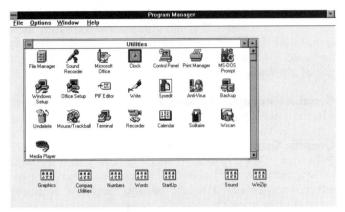

The Program Manager in Microsoft Windows 3.1, another graphical user interface.

computer was the early Apple Lisa and, shortly thereafter, the ***Macintosh***. Microsoft Windows is a GUI that is merely a layer of user-friendliness sitting on top of the DOS infrastructure.

With a GUI (pronounced "GOO-ee"), files are represented on the screen (which is designed to look like—and is called—a ***desktop***) as pieces of paper, and directories are represented as folders. A feature unique to GUIs is their reliance on a mouse, or other type of pointing device, to move objects around the screen and "click" on files to open them. It could be argued that the GUI was responsible for the proliferation of personal computers in the 1990s. A GUI, relying as it does on the use of icons, is sometimes called an ***iconic interface***.

Graphic Artist

Any visual artist working in the ***graphic arts***. See ***Graphic Arts***.

Graphic Arts

The field or technology encompassing graphic design, applied art, typesetting, imaging, printing, telecommunications, publishing, advertising, and other related artistic and creative endeavors involving information or knowledge in visual form. The ***graphic arts*** includes all technologies that involve the realization of art—the conversion of ideas into visible form. Because of the inclusion of computer-generated approaches, the term ***graphic communications*** is also applied.

Graphic Arts Technical Foundation (GATF)

The Graphic Arts Technical Foundation is a nonprofit, scientific, technical, and educational organization dedicated to the advancement of the graphic communications industries worldwide. Its mission is to serve the field as the leading resource for technical information and services through research and education.

For 73 years the Foundation has developed leading edge technologies and practices for printing. GATF has a staff of

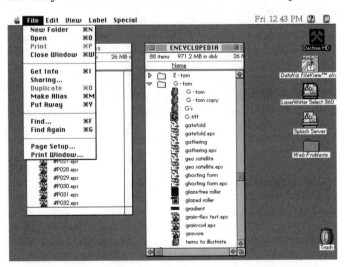

The Macintosh desktop, a popular graphical user interface.

researchers, educators, and technical specialists who help printers worldwide. Through conferences, satellite symposia, workshops, consulting, technical support, laboratory services, and publications, GATF strives to advance a global graphic communications community.

Graphic Character Repertoire
Alternate term for *character set*. See *Character Set*.

Graphic Communications Association (GCA)
A division of the Printing Industries of America (PIA) comprising printers, publishers, color separation experts, and advertisers dedicated to the advancement and improvement of color printing.

Graphic Designer
A *graphic artist* who utilizes elements of illustration, typography, and photography to design pages, publications, book covers, *Web* pages, multimedia presentations, or other graphic communications materials.

Graphic Display Device
Alternate term for a computer *monitor* or *display*. See *Monitor*.

Graphic Elements
Any material placed on a page or within a document. There are essentially three classes of graphic elements: text, geometric elements (such as lines, curves, and other *vector*-based elements), and photographic images.

Graphic Input
Any computer input digitized by means of a *graphic input device*. See *Graphic Input Device*.

Graphic Input Device
Any device attached to a computer used to digitize or create digitized graphic material. Such devices can be as complex as *scanner*s or as simple and basic as a *mouse*.

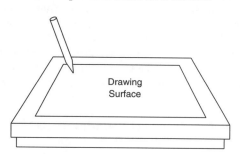

Drawing
Surface

An acoustic tablet, one of many graphic input devices.

Graphic Output Device
Any device attached to a computer used to output digitized graphic material. Such devices include a monitor (for "outputting" a *soft copy*), or any of a wide variety of printers, *imagesetter*s, *plotter*s, etc.

Graphic Primitive
Alternate term for *primitive*. See *Primitive*.

Graphics
Any visual presentation of information, generally consisting of *line art* and *halftone*s. Graphics can be produced manually (by drawing), photographically, or digitally.

Graphics Accelerator
An add-on card or integrated *microprocessor* that accelerates the *refresh rate* on computer monitors or, in other words, speeds the rate at which graphic images are displayed. Also known as an *accelerator board*.

Graphics Adapter
Alternate term for a *frame buffer*. See *Frame Buffer*.

Graphics Board
Alternate term for a *graphics card*. See *Graphics Card*.

Graphics Card
A card or board installed into a computer that can convert computer images and send them to a video device, such as a monitor, projector, or VCR. It can capture video frames and transfer them to a computer display.

Graphics Coprocessor
In computing, an additional *microprocessor*, commonly installed on a *video adapter*, used to increase the processing speed of graphic data.

Graphics Display
Alternate term for a *computer monitor*. See *Monitor*.

Graphics Formats
Any of a wide variety of *file format*s used for the storage and transfer of graphics files. See *EPS*, *PICT*, *PICS*, *JPEG*, *TIFF*, *GIF*, *PCX*, *BMP*, *MSP*, *TGA*, and *CT*.

Graphics Interchange Format (GIF)
A standard *file format* that was developed by CompuServe for the transmission of *bitmapped graphics* via modem to computer *bulletin board* systems and Internet USENET groups. GIF images are capable of displaying images in only *eight-bit color*, or with a display of up to 256 colors. This low color depth helps keep image file sizes small, thus facilitating and expediting telecommunications transfer.

Graphics Processor
See *Graphics Coprocessor*.

Graphics Resolution
The highest number of *pixel*s, or *spot*s, an output device is capable of printing per inch, measured horizontally and vertically. The higher the graphics resolution, the clearer and sharper the image. (See *Resolution*.)

Graphics Scanner
See *Scanner*.

Graphics Terminal
In computing, a monitor or *terminal* capable of displaying pictures or other images, either in *raster* form or, less commonly, *vector* form. Some common graphics terminals of the recent past have included the *CGA*, *EGA*, *VGA*, etc.

Graphic Visualization
A means of presenting data—such as in scientific and engineering research—in a graphic or visual way, such as by means of charts, graphs, etc. Often, data from *spreadsheet* or database programs can be imported into graphics programs that will facilitate its conversion to visual form.

Graphic Window
In computing, a *pixel* matrix or grid in which each pixel can be specified by the user as either black or white.

Grave Accent
In typography, a left-pointing *accent* (`` ` ``) placed over a character such as "è." The accent pointing in the opposite direction is called an *acute accent*. See *Accent*.

Gravure
A printing method that utilizes engraved cylinders or, infrequently, cylinder-mounted plates as the image carriers. The image areas are etched into the surface of the cylinder as a collection of tiny cells. The cylinder rotates in an ink fountain and ink collects in the cells, the excess ink being scraped from the nonimage areas by a *doctor blade*. The paper (or other *substrate*) is passed between the

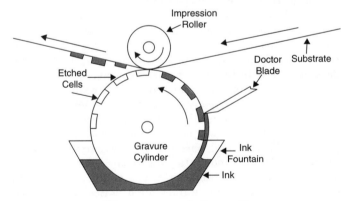

The gravure printing unit.

gravure cylinder and a rubber-coated *impression roller*, and ink is transferred by a combination of capillary action and the pressing of the substrate into the engraved cells of the cylinder, helped by the rubber surface of the impression roller. Most gravure printing performed today is web-fed *rotogravure* printing, with occasional sheetfed use. Gravure is also well-suited to the printing of packaging on a variety of nonpaper substrates.

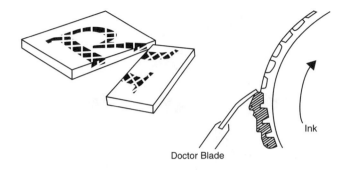

The two basics of gravure printing—the recessed image and the doctor blade.

Gravure printing is a direct descendent of older *intaglio* printing (gravure and intaglio, commonly used synonymously, are different processes; all gravure printing is intaglio, yet all intaglio printing is not gravure—for example, *copperplate printing*, which is an intaglio process without being considered a gravure process), developed around the same time as Gutenberg was developing relief-based printing (the mid-15th century). Intaglio, primarily an artist's medium, was essentially a wooden (and soon metal) block on which the image to be printed was etched. A thin ink was poured into these etched lines or dots, and the paper on which the design was to be printed was brought into contact with the inked image carrier in such a way as to force the paper into the cells where it could pick up the ink. A porous substrate allows capillary action to enhance this process. Around 1440, the first metal plates began to be used, commonly made from copper (hence the term *copperplate engraving*). Intaglio was used primarily for illustration matter and playing cards. Around the same time, Gutenberg's letterpress-based printing press was increasing in popularity, and the use of intaglio for text was not actively pursued, as the intaglio plates were incompatible with the relief method of printing. Still, intaglio represented a more artistic rather than commercial medium, perhaps best exemplified by the woodcuts and other engravings of German artist Albrecht Dürer in the late 15th and early 16th centuries, as well as engravings by other noted artists such as Rembrandt van Rijn and Peter-Paul Rubens.

In the first half of the 16th century, the invention of chemical etching of intaglio plates was a great leap forward for the process. Rather than laboriously scrape away the metal itself, artists could now simply scrape away a soft coating (known as a *resist*), which would allow the penetration of an acid only in certain areas, which would then etch the copper beneath the coating chemically. Chemical etching made the intaglio process even more favored by artists, and intaglio printing proved to provide better-quality illustrations than did letterpress, so it was not uncommon for the text of a book to be printed using letterpress, and illustrated pages to be printed using intaglio, the separate pages being collated together after printing. Denis Diderot's great and controversial *Encyclopédie*, published

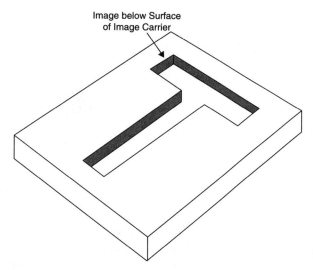

Intaglio printing, in which the image is below the surface of the image carrier.

in seventeen volumes of text from 1751 to 1755, was supplemented by several additional volumes of intaglio illustrations, which served to primarily illustrate various manufacturing processes as part of Diderot's extolling of the virtues of artisans. (This would be a contributing factor in the French Revolution of 1789.) Intaglio-based printing was also widely used for the reproduction of sheet music, as well as maps, needed more than ever once the New World was found and colonized. The invention of the ***mezzotint*** (an early means of representing shades of gray in copperplate engraving; "mezzotint" itself literally means, in Italian, "halftone") in the 1600s further refined the use of intaglio for high-quality pictorial reproduction.

Following the invention of ***lithography*** at the tail-end of the 18th century, and its further development in the 19th century, the search was on for a means of printing utilizing cylinders, rather than flat plates, stones, or locked-up bits of type. The one desperate need of any printing press is, as its name indicates, *pressure*. It is easier and less laborious to produce suitable and uniform printing pressure in the nip of two cylinders than over the surface of a flat plate, but the question was how to accomplish it; a litho stone could not be bent into a cylinder, the individual letters, or even lines, of type were impractical for rotary printing, and intaglio techniques were not able to keep the ink from spilling out of the cells. The development of ***stereotype*** platemaking eventually solved the problem for letterpress printing, and the later use of zinc and aluminum plates eventually solved it for lithography. Interestingly, the first cylinder-based printing press was a gravure press, originally developed for printing on textiles in 1680. The quality was most likely not very high, but its primary usage was in the printing of calico patterns on cheap clothing. In 1783, British textile printer Thomas Bell patented a rotary intaglio press for use in higher-quality textile printing. His patent drawings show a system very much like that still in

use in gravure printing today, but for non-textile printing, the idea of a rotary press languished.

The invention of photography in the 1820s and 1830s resulted in the search for a means of transferring a photographic image to an intaglio plate. William Henry Fox Talbot devoted himself to the search for photoengraving materials and techniques. Using gelatin-based coatings for metal plates, he was able to achieve photographic etching initially for only line art, but eventually he devised formulations that would enable the selective variation of image density, which would print at varying shades. Fox Talbot soon hit upon the halftone screen, which broke up continuous images into very small, discrete dots that could be varied in size and shade of gray. This was the breakthrough photoengravers (and printers everywhere) needed. Letterpress and lithographic platemaking were the direct beneficiaries of this process, however. The intaglio process was desired by most people for little more than fine art reproductions and illustration material.

The problem for gravure still remained: how to produce a photographic coating for a cylinder that could be used for etching. The English engraver J.W. Swan solved the problem in the early 1860s with a ***carbon tissue***, which was a gelatin resist coating on a light-sensitive material applied to the surface of paper. After exposure, the paper could be removed, and the exposed coating applied to another surface, such as a metal plate—or a cylinder.

Thus, all the disparate elements needed for modern gravure printing existed, and it remained for someone to put them all together. That someone was Karel Klic (in German spelled Karl Klietsch), from Bohemia (now the Czech Republic). Combining Bell's rotary intaglio textile press, Fox Talbot's halftone screen process, and Swan's carbon tissue coating, Klic developed the first gravure printing press. Still used exclusively in the printing of textiles, however, Klic made his way to England and teamed up with Samuel Fawcett, an engraver at Story Brothers and Company, a textile printing company. In the early 1890s, they developed new techniques for photoengraving, and began commercial printing of intaglio art prints, conducted with such secrecy that company employees were not allowed to venture into rooms other than those they were assigned to, lest they become exposed to all of the various parts of the process. A bit paranoid, perhaps, but the company—under the name of Rembrandt Intaglio Printing Company—held a monopoly on the process for over a decade. In 1903, an employee of Klic's came to the United States and revealed Klic's process. The jig was up.

Meanwhile, in 1860, a French publisher named Auguste Godchaux developed a rotogravure press that printed on rolls (or ***web***s) of paper, a design very similar to modern rotogravure press designs. In the early 1900s, gravure presses began turning up in the United States, and the *New York Times* in 1913 was the first to print rotogravure newspaper supplements. Other newspapers began to take notice of the high-quality reproduction of photographs the new system afforded. (Today, most Sunday newspaper sup-

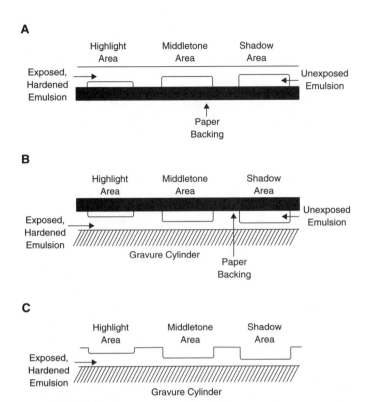

The principle of the carbon tissue resist. After exposure to a continuous-tone positive (A) highlight areas are more highly exposed and thus produce a thicker and harder emulsion than do shadow areas. After the exposed resist is attached to a gravure cylinder (B), an etchant is applied, which eats through varying thicknesses of emulsion (C).

plements—such as the *New York Times Magazine*, *Parade*, *USA Weekend*, and other color supplements across the country—are printed on rotogravure presses.) In the 1930s, gravure presses began to be used in the printing of packaging; a single-color gravure press in 1933 was set up to print Tootsie Roll wrappers. In 1938, multicolor gravure presses were used for the printing of Jell-O boxes. These so-called "Jell-O presses" were the largest and fastest yet designed; together, they were capable of printing up to 36,000 cartons an hour and were in use until 1987.

Modern advances in engraving technology have made gravure printing a high-quality printing operation. The expense of producing and imaging the gravure cylinders, however, still continues to make gravure printing an expensive process, and gravure is rarely used economically for print-runs of under 200,000 or so. An advantage of gravure printing, though, is the relative simplicity of the press, which does not require the intricate series of ink and dampening rollers that a lithographic press requires.

Gravure Presses

The gravure printing press has several basic elements: gravure cylinder, ink fountain, impression roller, and substrate control.

Gravure Cylinder. A gravure press most often prints from a gravure cylinder, which comprises a steel base, that can either be a *sleeve cylinder* or a *shaft cylinder*. A sleeve cylinder requires a shaft to be attached when it is mounted on the press, or when it is mounted in the engraving mechanism. The inaccuracies inherent in the fitting of a separate shaft have brought about the development of a shaft cylinder, which comes with shafts already mounted, and they are the dominant gravure cylinder bases currently utilized. Aluminum bases have be devised to hopefully replace steel, especially in presses used in the printing of packaging, but although they are lighter they are also harder to electroplate. Newer plastic cylinder bases are being developed that are much lighter than metal bases, and contain special surface coatings (most of which are proprietary) that facilitate *electroplating*.

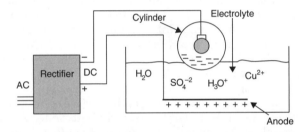

The principle of electroplating. The gravure cylinder base is given a negative charge and thus acts as a cathode. A copper anode is given a positive charge. Copper ions are thus forced into the solution, where—being positively charged—they bond with the negatively charged cylinder.

To the cylinder base is electroplated a layer of copper, which has historically been—and continues to be—the dominant surface material for gravure cylinders—and is commonly electroplated to the base utilizing a sulfuric-acid electrolyte. On top of the copper, after engraving, is plated a thin layer of chrome, which is applied to protect the etched copper surface from the abrasion of the doctor blade during printing. After print runs, the cylinder needs to be resurfaced. (See *Electroplating*.)

The copper surface of the cylinder, prior to printing, is etched or engraved. A particular image printed in gravure is essentially a collection of many tiny cells that are etched with varying depths (darker regions of a print utilize deeper cells that can hold more ink, while lighter regions utilize shallower cells that hold less ink). This is why gravure-printed type can look fuzzy when examined under magnification. But due to this printing mechanism, gravure can print halftones extremely well. Before the development of *electromechanical engraving* in the 1960s, most gravure cylinder etching was performed photochemically, using carbon tissue resist coatings and ferric chloride etchants to chemically etch the image areas. Now, the artwork to be engraved is often placed before an optical scanning device, which uses photodiodes to receive the image, and the image is transformed into digital data, which is then used to drive an engraving head (typically a diamond stylus), which can produce as many as 5,000 cells per second. New developments in direct computer-to-engraving-head imaging are removing the need for a film positive from which to obtain the information to drive the engraving head.

One particular consideration with the gravure cylinder is ensuring that it is as close to perfectly round as possible (and that the circumference of the cylinder is large enough to carry the image to be printed). *Total indicated runout (TIR)* is used to indicate the roundness of the cylinder, and gravure cylinders are manufactured—and need to be kept—within strict tolerances. (See *Gravure Cylinder* and *Gravure Engraving*.)

Ink Fountain. The *inking system* for a gravure press is far less complex than that used for *offset lithography*. The gravure cylinder is partially submerged in a large pan of thin, highly fluid ink. (Ink is pumped into the pan as needed from a sump, typically located below the fountain pan.) As the cylinder rotates in the ink, its surface becomes covered with ink, and the cells fill. A thin, flexible steel doctor blade, either alone or in tandem with other pre-wiping devices, scrapes the excess ink from the surface of the cylinder before the inked cells contact the substrate. Some gravure inking fountains utilize a *fountain roller*, a cloth-covered roller that is partially submerged in the ink fountain and that contacts the surface of the gravure cylinder. In some configurations, ink is sprayed onto the surface of the cylinder by a nozzle. (See *Inking System: Gravure*.)

action transfers the ink to the substrate. The pressure exerted on the substrate as it passes though the nip can be adjusted. The impression roller typically has a smaller diameter than the gravure cylinder and consequently rotates at a faster rate. However, in the nip between the two cylinders, the rubber is deformed slightly by the pressure of impression roller against the gravure cylinder. Faster press speeds in recent years, however, have resulted in excessive heat buildup in smaller impression rollers. Consequently, many presses now utilize larger-diameter rollers, which also have the added advantage of reducing stress on the web, as the increased size of the nip results in the same total amount of pressure being applied but over a larger surface area. Too large an impression roller, however, can cause printing defects, as the substrate remains in the nip for a longer period of time. As with the gravure cylinder itself, the TIR of an impression roller should be carefully monitored. The excessive friction caused during web gravure printing can also result in high static charge buildup. These charges can exceed 25,000 volts and can cause such printing problems as *whiskering*, or health hazards such as severe electrocution. A related phenomenon, but one that is induced deliberately and that has positive effects, is known as *electrostatic assist*, in which the impression roller is given a static charge that attracts the droplets of ink from the gravure cells to the substrate and helps to more completely transfer ink and reduce the occurrence and severity of such problems as *snowflaking*. (See *Impression Roller*.)

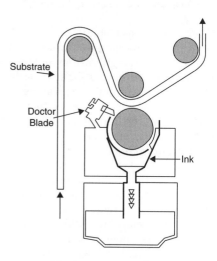

Basic gravure inking system.

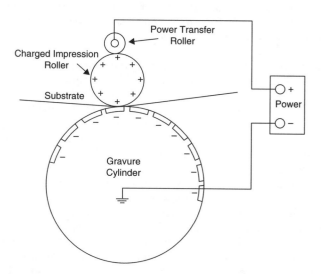

The principle of the electrostatic assist (ESA).

Impression Roller. The gravure impression cylinder, or *impression roller*, is a hard cylinder covered with a synthetic rubber lying directly above the gravure cylinder. The purpose of the impression roller is to exert pressure on the substrate passing through the nip between the impression roller and gravure cylinder. This forces the substrate partially into the cells on the gravure cylinder, where capillary

Substrate Control. The feeding systems used to control the movement of the web of paper (or other material) through the press vary by press. Since gravure is used for a wide variety of different types of substrates, all of which contribute various feeding problems, web handling equipment comes in a number of different configurations. Plastics, films, and other nonpaper substances are often heat-sensitive, nonabsorbent, and easily stretched beyond their ability to return to their original dimensions. Paper, on the other hand, is more resistant to stretching, is less heat-sensitive, and is more absorbent. But it is also bulkier and, more often than not, needs to be printed on both sides simultaneously. Consequently, web handling units for packaging films requires a more tension-controlled path, less heat for drying and, consequently, a faster-drying ink. Immediately after the printing unit, it is not uncommon for the web's drying path to be a vertical one; the web travels vertically up to a fixed distance, allowing it time to dry—expedited by hot-air dryers—and either out to the finishing section of the press, or back down again, depending upon how much drying time is specifically required. It has become more common for drying paths to be varied according to the job by add-on modules that provide more or less drying space. This has become increasingly necessary on higher-speed presses; modern packaging presses print at speeds of up to 1,000 ft./min., while publication presses can print at speeds exceeding 3,000 ft./min.

The web roll is placed on a ***reel stand***, which has developed over the years from simply holding one roll at a time (which required press stoppage when the roll ran out and needed to be replaced) to a two-roll stand (which required a good deal of operator skill to switch to the new roll when the first one ran out) to fully automated, two-roll unwinding systems. Most webs—either paper or packaging—tend to have 3- or 6-in.-diameter cores, made primarily out of cardboard, with plastic and metal cores becoming more popular, as they tend to retain their roundness more easily. (Cores that are out-of-round will result in the roll unwinding with a bump, which will cause feeding problems and perhaps web breaks.) The most common type of reel stand consists of two metal arms, one fixed, the other moveable. Attached to each is a cone that fits into the core of the roll. The roll is mounted first on the fixed arm, then the second is moved in to engage the other side and hold it firmly. The centering of the roll for travel into the press can be performed by moving the arms in or out, as may be necessary. Some reel stands also make use of an earlier configuration involving a metal bar that runs through the center of the roll. Many configurations involve two unwind stands at the end of a long central arm, the whole assembly looking rather like a see-saw. One basic problem that needs to be accounted for is, as was mentioned, the out-of-roundness of the core, which always exists to some degree. If kept within certain tolerances, it is acceptable, but the reel stand must be sufficiently sturdy to guard against any vibration caused by the nonconcentric core disrupting the printing units of the press. When one roll runs out, the new one must immediately and carefully be spliced to it, the point being to avoid having to stop the press. Often, this system is automated, but it still requires careful preparation on the part of the press operator. The appropriate amount of web tension is carefully regulated by running the web around a ***dancing roll***, a roller connected to an air cylinder that can be adjusted to apply the appropriate amount of force to the web. Newer systems carefully measure the diameter of the roll repeatedly as it is unwinding (to account of any eccentricities or out-of-roundness), either by ultrasound sensors or other means, and automatically adjust the speed of the motor driving the unwinding reel.

The final portion of the press just prior to the printing unit is known as the ***infeed tension unit***, which is little more than two rollers, the nip of which the web passes through to reach the printing unit. This nip, regulated by a mechanism similar to a dancing roll, ensures that the web tension beyond it is consistent, regardless of what is happening to the web prior to reaching the nip. This tendency to isolate regions of web tension ensure that any anomalies are dealt with before the printing unit. (See also ***Web Offset Lithography: Feeding Section***.)

SHEETFED GRAVURE

Most of the gravure presses in operation are web-fed presses, but occasional sheetfed gravure work is done, such as for printing proofs, fine art posters and prints, cartons, and other high-quality work for which sheetfed offset lithography is inappropriate (such as the printing of metallic inks that are incompatible with offset press chemistry). Sheetfed gravure presses consist of a ***pile table*** on which the sheets are stacked and are fed into the press, through the printing unit (a standard gravure cylinder-impression roller-doctor blade arrangement, with the cylinder typically inked by a fountain roller), transported by a series of ***transfer cylinder***s, over several drying nozzles, and finally to the ***delivery pile***. Some configurations of sheetfed gravure presses also replace the gravure cylinder with a flat gravure plate.

A variety of intaglio plates are used for high-quality, specialty printing such as bank notes, postage stamps, money, securities, and other such documents. These can either be sheetfed or web-fed, and are more commonly known as copperplate printing. See ***Copperplate Printing***.

OFFSET GRAVURE

Some substrates (such as those with irregular surfaces) are printed by a process called ***offset gravure***, or ***indirect gravure***, which comprises the standard gravure printing unit, except that the image is first transferred from the gravure cylinder to a rubber-covered ***transfer roller*** which first receives the image from the gravure cylinder, then transfers it to the substrate passing between the transfer roller and the impression roller. (This is based on essentially the same principle as ***offset lithography***.) Products printed by this method include decorated metals and woods, and other types of irregular surfaces. The resilience of the rubber image-carrying blanket makes printing on hard surfaces such as these much easier. A variety of offset gravure takes place on a flexographic press, where the ***Anilox roller*** of the flexo press is replaced by a gravure cylinder. The gravure cylinder transfers the image to a rubber blanket, which has been mounted to the flexo plate cylinder. The blanket then transfers the image to the substrate. This is known as *flexo gravure* and is used to print high-quality packaging, advertising, and other materials commonly printed by traditional flexographic means, but with the increased quality of gravure printing. Gravure units are also occasionally added to regular flexographic presses, for the overprinting of various elements, such as prices, store addresses, and other design elements that need to be changed several times over the course of a print run, on products whose other elements are printed by traditional flexography.

Gravure, like other printing processes, has specific ink requirements that produce the best results, specifically, highly fluid liquid inks with volatile solvents. (See *Ink: Printing Requirements: Gravure*.) Gravure presses also require paper substrates with certain characteristics to produce the best results. (See *Paper and Papermaking: Printing Requirements: Gravure*.) Gravure is also well-suited for printing on a host of other types of substrates, such as foils, plastics, etc. When used on plastic packaging, most gravure presses require the use of fast-drying solvents.

Gravure Association of America (GAA)

An organization dedicated to the advancement and dissemination of information about the *gravure* printing industry and related industries. GAA is also involved in the production of educational materials, textbooks, and other materials related to gravure printing. They also perform valuable research and publish recommended guidelines and technical specifications for printers and manufacturers.

Gravure Cylinder

The engraved image carrier used in *gravure* printing. Unlike *letterpress* or *lithographic* printing processes (which use raised and flat printing surfaces, respectively) gravure prints from cells or depressions etched in a metal cylinder that are filled with ink and transferred to the *substrate*.

A gravure cylinder comprises a (typically) steel *cylinder base*, or an underlying metal structure that supports the engraved image-carrying layer. The two primary types of cylinder bases are *sleeve cylinder*s and *shaft cylinder*s. A sleeve cylinder differs from a shaft cylinder in that it needs to have shafts attached prior to installing it on the press, whereas a shaft cylinder, as its name indicates, comes with shafts attached. The disadvantages of a sleeve cylinder include the fact that different shafts (with their own peculiar inaccuracies) are used during different stages of production—engraving, preparing, and printing—which create inaccuracies in the engraved image and, ultimately, in the printed image. Shaft cylinders, utilizing the same shafts at each stage of production, are remarkably accurate and, not surprisingly, are the most widely used cylinder bases. Although steel is the most-often used material for cylinder bases, aluminum bases are utilized occasionally, primarily for their light weight (making shipping less costly and handling easier), but aluminum is more difficult to electroplate the image-carrying copper to and is less resis-

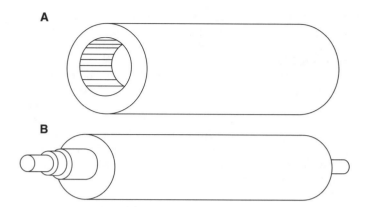

Two varieties of gravure cylinder: sleeve (A) and shaft (B).

tant to wear than steel. New plastic materials are also starting to be utilized in gravure cylinder manufacture, which can be modified to facilitate electroplating, and are also much lighter and less expensive than conventional steel. As the cylinder is for the most part hollow, *deflection* needs to be taken into consideration. Deflection is defined as the deformation of the circumference of the cylinder (also referred to as *out-of-roundness*) due to the pressure exerted by the *impression roller* during printing. Wider cylinders are more prone to deflection than shorter ones, and frequently the walls of the cylinder are reinforced to increase structural rigidity. Cylinders that become out-of-round produce a variety of printing defects. Defects are also caused by cylinders that are not perfectly balanced, or in which the center of gravity does not lie along its rotational axis. The result of an imbalanced cylinder is the generation of vibrations as it rotates. Holes and metal plugs are added to various portions of the cylinder as a means of redistributing the mass and bringing it back into balance.

Onto the gravure cylinder base is electroplated a layer of copper, into which the image will be etched. Copper has been used as the image-carrying layer since the earliest days of intaglio printing, and it provides the highest degree of predictable, structural, and functional results. It is easy enough to electroplate and to engrave, and it also withstands increased printing pressure without causing breakdowns in the walls of the cells comprising the image. (See *Electroplating*.) After the copper is plated to the cylinder base, the copperplated surface is ground down to a reduced size, if necessary. Polishing and finishing operations ensure that inaccuracies inherent in the copperplating procedure are compensated for.

After copperplating and polishing, the gravure cylinder is engraved in one of the several different engraving methods in use today. Gravure engraving etches the image into the copper surface, the image comprising many tiny cells, the distribution and depth of which determine the lightness/darkness of a particular image area. The unengraved portions of a gravure cylinder are known collectively as the *land area*. (See *Gravure Engraving*.)

To impart an added degree of protection and lower the coefficient of friction (thus increasing the run length of the cylinder) a thin (about 0.00023 in.) layer of chrome is electroplated on top of the engraved cylinder. Chrome polishing is the final stage of gravure cylinder production. A crucial measurement prior to printing is the ***total indicated runout (TIR)*** of the cylinder, which means that a cross-section of the cylinder must be as close to a perfect circle as possible, to avoid generating any "bumps" or printing distortions. The ***roughness*** of the surface—or, in other words, minute surface irregularities—is important to prevent doctor blade wear; too smooth a surface does not provide enough doctor blade lubrication, and causes chrome wear. A related but different property of the cylinder surface is ***waviness***, which describes much more pronounced surface irregularities. Too much waviness can result in an inability of the doctor blade to effectively remove excess ink, causing printing in undesirable areas. Prior to engraving, the hardness of the copper surface needs to be determined, to ensure that the copper layer is ductile enough to allow effective image etching. After chrome-plating, similar measurements are made, and it should be cautioned that due to the thinness of the chrome layer, any undesirable aspects of the copper layer cannot be compensated for during chroming. Proper doctor blade lubrication is the result of extremely thin cracks in the chrome layer, a cracks-per-inch count of around 150 being the most effective.

After engraving and chrome-plating, a test proof is printed, and any corrections are carefully made, which involves either re-etching or replating problematic areas.

After printing, the cylinder can be re-used, but not before the chrome and copper layers are removed and replated. (See also ***Gravure***.)

Gravure Engraving

Collective term for the various means of engraving or etching the image onto the ***gravure cylinder***. Gravure, unlike most other printing processes, prints from depressed, ink-filled cells produced on the surface of a copper-plated cylinder. The ink in the cells is then transferred to the desired ***substrate***.

The four basic means of engraving the image into a gravure cylinder are the diffusion-etch process, the direct-transfer process, electromechanical engraving, and the laser-cutting process.

Diffusion-Etch Process. Also called ***conventional gravure engraving***, diffusion-etch is the oldest method of gravure cylinder engraving. It uses two film positives, one of which is a film positive of the image (solid areas, text, or continuous-tone, variable-density image) the other being a special gravure screen, containing between 100–200 lines per inch. The screen is used to "convert" the solid image into many tiny cells (similar to making a halftone from a continuous-tone photograph, for example), which are small squares oriented at a 45° angle to the direction of web travel through the press (diamonds, basically). The positive

A. Diffusion-Etch

Shadow   Highlight

B. Two-Positive

Shadow   Highlight

C. Direct-Transfer

Shadow   Highlight

D. Electromechanical

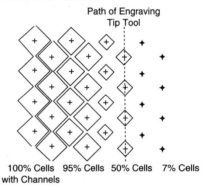

100% Cells   95% Cells   50% Cells   7% Cells
with Channels

Cell structure as produced by chemical etching techniques: diffusion-etch (A), two-positive (B), and direct-transfer (C), as well as variable cell structure produced by electromechanical engraving (D).

image and the screen are placed on top of a ***carbon tissue***, a water-soluble paper covered with a light-sensitive gelatin ***resist***, and consecutively exposed to ultraviolet light. After exposure, the least exposed image areas are soft and soluble, while the most highly exposed nonimage areas are hard and insoluble, and those midtone regions are slightly exposed and produce a slightly hard and insoluble emulsion. The carbon tissue is then adhered to the surface of the gravure cylinder and developed. The cylinder with the developed resist is placed in an acid bath (commonly a ferric chloride etchant), where the etchant eats through the resist and into the copper at varying rates, depending on the hardness of the emulsion. In the highlight areas—those that have received the most exposure—the etchant eats through very slowly, so that in a given period of etching time the cells engraved into the copper are very shallow (and thus print the lightest), while in the shadows and solids—areas that have received the least exposure—the etchant eats through the resist and into the copper very quickly, so that the engraved cells are deeper (and thus print the darkest). The midtone regions—which have had varying degrees of exposure, spending on the density of the image—allow a moderate amount of etchant through, producing cells that are not as deep as shadows and not as shallow as highlights. Nonimage areas possess the thickest portions of the emulsion and thus allow the copper surface to remain unetched. The time required for the completion of the etching process is about half an hour.

In the diffusion-etch process, all cells are the same size, and the thickness of the membrane between cells—called the ***cell wall***—remains constant. The amount of light the resist received determines the depth of the cells; highlights and light areas produce shallow cells (which do not hold much ink) while the shadows and darker areas produce deeper cells (which hold more ink). A variation of this etching system is called a ***two-positive system***, which operates the same basic way, but the gravure screen is replaced by a halftone screen made from continuous-tone illustration matter, while a standard gravure screen is used for solids and text matter. The advantage of this system is that the halftone screen allows the cells to vary in area, not just depth. This allows greater degrees of sharpness and detail. Another variation is known as ***Hard Dot Engraving*** in which the depth of each cell is the same, but the area of each cell varies, depending upon whether it is a highlight or a solid.

Direct-Transfer Process. Also called the ***Single-Positive System***, the direct transfer process is, like the diffusion-etch process, a chemical etching process. The primary difference is in the composition of the resist, which replaces the carbon tissue with high-contrast, high-resolution ***photopolymer*** emulsions. The emulsion is applied (by a spray, ring coater, or other means) directly to the copper-plated surface of the gravure cylinder itself. A single screened positive is brought into contact with the emulsion on the cylinder and exposed to ultraviolet light. As in the diffusion-etch process, the exposed (nonimage) areas become hard, while the unexposed (image) areas remain soft. A solvent is used to wash away the unexposed resist, and the photopolymeric resist produces cells that print with smoother edges than cells etched by electromechanical engraving. Etchant is applied, as before, and engraves cells at a rate that varies according to the thickness of the resist. The film positive is carried by clear mylar belts between the emulsion of the gravure cylinder and a mercury-vapor lamp, which enables the engraver to expose the resist in a circumferential fashion. The direct-transfer process is also quicker than the diffusion-etch process, taking only about 4–10 minutes to etch a cylinder.

Despite the quickness and ease of the previous forms of chemical engraving, they have been replaced for the most part by newer techniques, primarily by the ***electromechanical process***, while newer digital computer-to-laser systems are making inroads into the gravure engraving process.

Electromechanical Engraving. Electromechanical engraving uses an electronically controlled diamond-stylus to cut the the cells into the surface of the gravure cylinder. The original copy is scanned into a computer and digitized. Each scanned and digitized image is converted to halftone-like dots, each having an electronic signal, ranging in intensity from 0–100%, depending upon the darkness or lightness of the image. (For this reason, early-generation electromechanical engraving devices could not scan in pre-screened images—such as halftones—or it would create its own dots on top of the already-existing dots, producing moiré patterns.) The image is then converted back into an analog signal that then drives the engraving head, telling it how deep to carve the cell on the cylinder. (Cell depth and cell area are varied simultaneously by using a tapered engraving head.) The computer then controls the engraving head, which moves across and around the cylinder, engraving cells of varying depths. The thickness of the cell walls can also be varied; at 100% depth, the diamond-shaped cells interlock with those of the rows on either side of it, with just a tiny cell wall. At 10%, however, the cells are much reduced in size, and a good deal of space is between them. With computerized engraving, the angle of the cells themselves can be altered as well, by producing elongated or compressed diamond-shaped cells as necessary. Electromechanical engraving devices take much longer than chemical processes; for example, a 40-in.-wide cylinder with a 30-in. circumference has over 25 million cells. At an average speed of 3,200 cells per second, it takes nearly 2½ hours to engrave a single cylinder.

Electromechanical engraving is also referred to as ***EME***.

Laser-Cutting Process. The most recent development in gravure engraving is the use of computer-directed lasers, which, like the electromechanical method, cut cells of varying depths and sizes. The original is scanned into a computer, the various image densities are determined, and lasers etch the cylinder. Due to the high light reflectance of copper, however, it is not particularly useful for laser etching. Consequently, other materials such as special alloys or plastics can be used to coat the cylinder. The real advantage of the laser processes is the speed; at 30,000 cells per second, the 40-in.-wide, 30-in.-circumference cylinder mentioned above would only take about 13 minutes.

Regardless of the system used (chemical engraving still has its adherents, but the increasing tendency toward computer-generated originals is making direct computer-to-cylinder processes more and more popular), after engraving the cylinder is electroplated with a layer of chrome to offer protection against the abrasive action of the ***doctor blade***.

Gravure Etching
See ***Gravure Engraving***.

Gravurescope
A microscope used to examine engraved ***gravure cylinder*** or ***anilox roller*** cells as a means of evaluating cell depth, the cell opening, and ***cell wall*** thickness.

Gray
A color lacking a ***hue*** (also called an ***achromatic color***), or possessing all the wavelengths of light in equal amounts so

that none predominates. Grays are produced by the mixture of white and black pigments, or by mixing **complementary colors**.

Gray Balance

In color printing, combinations of **cyan**, **magenta**, and **yellow** inks that produce neutral shades of gray. Improper proportions of any of these colorants will result in one particular dominant **hue**, which may or may not be desirable. Regardless, it is necessary to ensure a consistency of the gray balance throughout the proofing and printing processes.

Gray Component Replacement (GCR)

A means of producing more consistent color and increased **shadow** detail in a printed reproduction by reducing the sizes of the **cyan**, **magenta**, and **yellow** halftone dots that contribute to the darkening effect—or gray component—of an image. This has the effect of lightening an image without changing the actual colors reproduced, as the size of the black dots is increased to compensate for the gray removal. (See COLOR PLATE 27.)

Grayed Command

Alternate term for a **dimmed command**. See **Dimmed Command**.

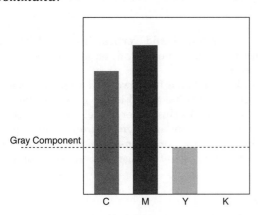

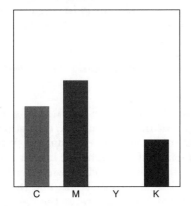

Removing equal amounts of each of the three process colors and replacing them with black keeps the gray component of an image yet reduces the amount of process ink that is required.

Gray Level

In describing color image input (scanning) and processing, a discrete shade of gray as viewed through a **color separation** filter. During scanning, the device's optics read each of the three **primary colors** (**red, green, and blue**) during successive passes of the light source, an appropriate color filter being used to read only the color the device is scanning during any one pass. All the various shades and gradations of one of these colors are stored in the device as a series of gray levels, which are then translated back into the appropriate shades during output or subsequent digital manipulation. The more gray levels the device can detect and store, the greater the color range (and the greater the smoothness of the color transitions) of the ultimate reproduction. Early scanners were only capable of storing 64 discrete shades of gray; 256 is the common number now, which is usually sufficient for most color work. Some high-end scanners are now able to detect and store up to 1,024 gray levels.

In terms of output, the term *gray levels* refers to the total number of discrete tonal variations that can be recorded on film or paper. In this case, the number of gray levels depends on the **resolution** of the output device and the type of **halftone screen** used. An insufficient number of gray levels can cause the problem known as **banding**.

Grayness

A measure of the amount of gray content a particular color possesses, commonly obtained by examining a color using a densitometer and three RGB filters.

Gray Scale

A thin strip of paper or film containing 15–20 shades of gray, increasing in density (typically in a logarithmic, not linear, fashion) from white to black, used to analyze and optimize the **contrast** of color and black-and-white images.

A 15-step gray scale.

Gray scales come in a variety of different forms, for different types of reproduction. A gray scale can be supplied on film, as either **continuous tone**s or **halftone dot**s. If it is on film and comprises discrete stages of gray, it is called a **step tablet**. If it is on film and comprises a single continuous strip of progressively dense gray, it is called a **continuous wedge**. If it is on film and comprises halftone dots in discrete levels of gray, it is called a **halftone scale**. Gray scales are often printed beyond the trim boundaries of printed pages as a means of ensuring the consistency of the print characteristics.

On a computer monitor, gray scales are produced by varying the intensity of the **pixel**s, on a scale of white to black. Images saved in the **TIFF** file format convert gray scale information into printer commands, which instruct the printer to construct a **bitmap** plotting all the levels of gray for each **spot** in the output. The more levels of gray that a computer and printer can discern, the smoother and more realistic the image.

Gray Stabilization

The maintaining of a consistent, neutral **gray balance** throughout the production of a color reproduction. See **Gray Balance**. Gray stabilization can be effected by **gray component replacement (GCR)**.

Gray Value

In computer displays, a number used to specify the intensity or level of gray in a particular **pixel**, on a scale from white (0% gray) to black (100% gray).

Grease-Proof Ink

An ink formulated with a **varnish** that will prevent the ink from **bleeding** or discoloring upon exposure to greases, fats, and oils. Grease-proof inks are useful for the printing of various food packaging.

Grease-Proof Paper

A type of paper produced from **chemical pulp** that has had **sizing** or **coating** materials added to make the paper impermeable to greases and oils.

Greasing

An alternate term for offset lithographic **tinting**, or the presence of ink in nonimage areas of the printing plate. See **Tinting**.

Greek Characters

In typography, the letters of the Greek alphabet, used mainly in mathematics, but also in theological, philosophical, literary, or other books. As in English, Greek letters also come in upper- and lowercase.

ΑΒΧΔΕΦΓΗΙϑΚΛΜΝΟΠΘΡΣΤΥςΩΞΨΖ
αβχδεφγηιφκλμνοπθρστυϖωξψζ

The Greek alphabet.

Greeking

In computing, a means of speeding up the display **redraw rate** of a computer monitor by representing text characters below a certain size as gray lines, boxes, or illegible dummy type.

Green

The **color** characteristic of light possessing a wavelength between 500 and 570 **nanometer**s, located on the spectrum between **yellow** and **blue**. Green is one of the three primary colors of light. (See **Additive Color Primaries** and COLOR PLATE 3.)

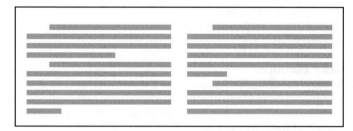

Greeking type by using gray lines to represent text below a certain point size.

In **process color** printing, *green* is also a secondary color produced by the overprinting of **cyan** and **yellow** inks. (See **Subtractive Color Primaries**.)

Green Book

In multimedia, a set of standards developed by Philips for the **compact disc** format known as **compact disc–interactive (CD-i)**. The Green Book standard (so-named because the publication containing the specifications had a green cover) describes the structure of the disc, the steps required to produce a CD-i application, the recording equipment, and the playback equipment. See **Compact Disc–Interactive (CD-i)** and **Compact Disc (CD)**.

Grid

Any pattern of horizontal and vertical lines and coordinates. A **bitmap** is one type of grid, as is a conventional **halftone screen**.

A grid is also used as a framework in page layout and design, page elements being added to the grid at geometrically precise locations. In this latter sense, each horizontal or vertical line is known as a **guideline**. Often, these guidelines are "magnetic", or **snap-to** guides, which automatically "grabs" the edge of a page element and aligns it along the line.

Grid Image

In computer output devices, any pattern overlaid on the device coordinate system (or **grid**) used to define the **resolution** of the device.

Grind Gauge

Alternate term for **grindometer**. See **Grindometer**.

Grindometer

A device used to measure the **fineness-of-grind** of the particles of **pigment** in a printing ink, consisting of two metal troughs with numerical marks ranging from zero to the maximum depth of the trough. The ink samples to be tested are placed in the troughs and drawn toward the zero mark by a highly polished scraper blade, and the point at which pigment particles begin to scratch the metal surface of the scraper blade (or ink flow is interrupted) is the measure of the fineness-of-grind. (See **Fineness-of-Grind**.) A grindometer is also called a **grind gauge**.

Grindometer, which is used to measure the fineness-of-grind of pigment particles.

Grin Through

In *screen printing*, a decrease in color strength of printed textiles caused by a stretching of the *substrate*, resulting in the unprinted fibers showing though the printed image.

Grip

In motion picture and video production, an individual responsible for mounting or placing the camera in the locations indicated by the director, cameraman, or director of photography. Some types of grips are responsible for pulling a *dolly*-mounted camera along the tracks laid down for it (the "dolly grip"). See also *Gaffer*.

Gripper

A row of metal tabs or clips located on an *impression cylinder*, *transfer cylinder*, or other device in an *infeed system* that grab a sheet of paper and feed it through a printing press. See *Infeed Section*.

Gripper Bite

The amount of paper, or the margin, that is held by the *gripper*s that feed the sheet through a printing press. The amount of margin grabbed by the grippers is an important consideration when designing the material to be printed (i.e., image areas that fall in the gripper margin will not print). Another important consideration is the pressure exerted on the paper by the grippers, which, if excessive, can damage the sheet or, if uneven across the press, can cause wrinkling of the sheet and misregister of printed images. (See *Infeed Section*.)

Gripper-Bowing Device

A device attached to the *infeed system* of a printing press (especially one used in sheetfed *offset lithography*) that compensates for the effect of *fan-out*, an undesirable expansion of a sheet of paper caused by pressure between the *impression cylinder* and the *blanket cylinder*. This increased pressure causes the sheet to expand its tail end

just prior to printing. When the sheet leaves the printing unit, it relaxes nearly to its original dimensions, but the image that is printed will consequently have a narrower tail end. When the sheet passes into a second printing unit, the sheet fans out again, but this second image will have a narrower tail than the first and will thus be out of alignment. A gripper-bowing device reduces this problem by altering the alignment of the *gripper*s (typically on the rotating drum feeding the sheet from the *feedboard* to the impression cylinder). The gripper bar (the bar containing the set of grippers) is bowed, setting the center gripper forward by as much as 0.008 in., so that the sheet encounters a convex surface and distorts slightly. This exaggerates the fanning out of the sheet and causes the first image to print with a narrower tail end than would be printed with a normal gripper bar. As a result, the narrow images printed by successive printing units (whose grippers are not bowed) will fit the first printed image. The key to this system is ensuring that the exaggerated fanning out of the sheet in the first printing unit produces a narrowed image equal to that produced by normal degrees of fanning out in successive printing units.

A gripper-bowing device can also be used to bow the grippers *in*, which has the effect of widening an image at its tail end, which may be desirable in some printing conditions.

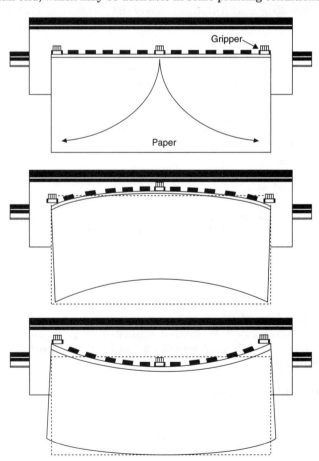

The principle of the gripper-bowing device.

Gripper Edge

The edge of a sheet of paper passing through a sheetfed press containing the *gripper margin*, or, in other words, that edge of the sheet which is grasped by the *gripper*s of the press.

The term *gripper edge* also refers to the edge of a wraparound printing plate that is secured by the plate clamp.

Gripper-Loading System

A device used on a *guillotine cutter* that automatically transfers stock from a *jogger* to the *bed* of the cutter. See *Guillotine Cutter*.

Gripper Margin

A space at the leading edge of a sheet of paper—usually ⅜–½ in. wide—in which, on a sheetfed press, printing cannot take place. This margin is reserved for use by the *grippers*, or the mechanisms that carry the sheet through the press. The edge of the sheet containing the gripper margin is known as the *gripper edge*. During the layout phase of prepress, allowance must be made for the gripper in the design of any page.

Groove

In *binding and finishing*, one of the two channels or valleys on a *casebound* book running parallel to the *spine*.

Grooving the Cylinder

Damage sustained to a *gravure cylinder* due to the presence of an abrasive foreign substance.

Grotesk

In typography, synonymous with *gothic* or *sans serif*. Sometimes spelled *grotesque*.

Grotesque

See *Grotesk*.

Ground Glass

In graphic arts photography, a plate of translucent glass attached to the back (i.e., darkroom side) of a *process camera* that is used to check the focus and placement of copy to be photographed prior to making the actual photographic exposure.

Groundwood

Wood that has been ground against a rotating abrasive stone to be used in *groundwood pulp*. See *Mechanical Pulping*.

Groundwood Book Papers

A variety of *book paper* manufactured using *groundwood*, or *mechanical pulp*. They are typically high in *bulk*, *smoothness*, and *printability*. Although groundwood pulps present problems (see *Pulp*), these difficulties may be obviated by the low cost of groundwood book papers. (See *Book Paper*.)

Groundwood Pulp

An alternate term for a type of paper *pulp* produced by mechanically grinding logs of wood against a rotating stone (also called mechanical pulp; see *mechanical pulping*). Groundwood pulp, having a high level of impurities such as *lignin* (in contrast to pulp produced using chemical methods), is used for low-quality paper such as that used in newspapers, telephone directories and other nonpermanent printing jobs. (See also *Pulping*.)

Group

In a *drawing program* or *page layout program*, the act of combining two or more drawing or page elements so as to allow for their simultaneous positioning or manipulation. The grouped elements can also be separated, or *un-group*ed, whenever it is necessary to manipulate them individually.

In networking, the term *group* refers to a collection of network users assigned to a specific group such that they all have access to the same directories. Each group thus has its own *security* level.

Groupware

A software program, a single copy of which can be used over a network by several different users. One such application, Lotus Notes, effectively drove the concept of groupware.

G.Series

In broadcasting and sound recording, a series of standards for audio equipment and the transmission of audio signals.

G704

In networking, a signal standard for connecting devices to a digital network.

Guaranteed Bandwidth

In networking and telecommunications, the ensured transmission capacity of a specific connection. See *Bandwidth*.

Guard

In *binding and finishing*, a thin strip of muslin, paper, or other material to which *insert*s (or other *tipped-in* materials) are attached for binding into a book or other publication. A guard is often wrapped around a *signature* prior to sewing. A guard wrapped around the first and last signatures of a book is called a *reinforced endsheet* or a *guarded signature*. The process of adding a guard to a signature is called *guarding*.

Guarded Signature

Alternate term for *reinforced endsheets*. See *Reinforced Endsheets*.

Guarding

In *binding and finishing*, the attaching of a *guard* to one or more *signature*s. See *Guard* and *Reinforced Endsheets*.

GUI

Abbreviation for *Graphical User Interface*. See *Graphical User Interface*.

Guide Edge

In printing, the edge of a sheet of paper at right angles to the *gripper edge*, or an edge that contacts the *side guide* of the printing press.

Guideline

One of the horizontal or vertical lines on a *grid* used in *page layout program*s for the accurate positioning of page elements.

Guide Marks

Alternate term for *register marks*. See *Register Marks*.

Guide Roller

On a *web press*, a roller located on a *roll stand* between the roll and the first *dancer roller*, used during paper infeed to compensate for variations in paper roll conditions. Also called a *cocking roller*.

Guide Word

Alternate term for *telltale*. See *Telltale*.

Guillemets

Alternate term for *French quotes*. See *French Quotes*.

Guillotine Cutter

An automatic or manual device used to cut and trim paper and other *substrate*s. Guillotine cutters are available in a variety of configurations and with varying degrees of automation and computer control, but all essentially comprise the following: a flat *bed* made of metal on which the material to be cut is placed; a long, heavy steel or steel-carbide *knife* that is mounted to a bar located near the front of the machine and that is either mechanically or electronically brought down through the material to be cut; a *cutting stick* imbedded in the bed directly beneath the knife, so as to prevent blade damage; a *cutter clamp*, a metal bar or plate that is lowered onto the stack of material to be cut, compressing the air out of it and holding it firmly in place while the knife cuts it; and stationary side guides and a moveable back gauge, which hold the stack of sheets squarely in place in the desired position on the bed to cut the sheets to the desired size. On some cutters, a *split gauge* is used, which is divided into two or more segments allowing for more than one edge of a stack to be cut without changing the back gauge setting between cuts.

Of particular concern with the use of guillotine cutters is the angle at which the knife contacts the sheets. Average weight papers—such as writing paper or common printing papers—are accurately cut with a knife angle of 22°, but thinner or heavier papers may require smaller or larger angles, respectively. The clamp pressure also may be too high or too low, depending upon stock thickness. Experi-

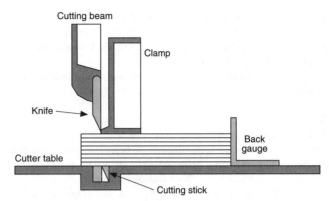

Principal parts of a guillotine paper cutter.

ence and experimentation are the best indicators for these materials.

Although the earliest guillotine cutters were operated simply by pulling a large metal handle to bring the knife down through the stock, a variety of high-tech improvements have made the cutter a remarkably efficient and computerized device. On many models, desired sizes can be programmed into a computer, and the back guide automatically moved to the correct position between cuts. This has the desired effect of eliminating the need for the operator to put his hands under the knife to move the stock into position.

The numerous electronic and mechanical accessories to cutters have not only improved safety but have also increased production capacity. These include *low-pressure air table*s, which have improved the feeding and flow of materials to the cutter; *cut-line indicator*s, which use a thin line of light to indicate on the stock where a cut will be made, eliminating the need to tentatively lower the knife to the stock to ensure that an image area will not be cut; *gripper-loading system*s, which automatically remove stock from *jogger*s and feed it directly to the rear of the cutter bed, and *tilting transfer table*s, which have enhanced the ability to automatically feed large-size sheets. Cutting information for several jobs can be programmed into a computer off-line and sent to the cutter via modem or by inserting a diskette, eliminating downtime between jobs. *Lifting table*s utilize sensors to detect pile height and

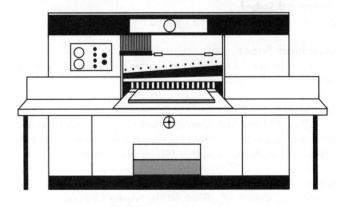

Guillotine paper cutter.

accurately load it into position on the cutter, and post-cutting **vertical storage system**s automatically stack cut piles, often utilizing a jogger to ensure that stacks are kept square and straight.

(See also **Cutting and Trimming** and **Binding and Finishing**.)

Gum

Any of a variety of water-soluble, resinous plant or tree exudations used in the formulation of printing inks and **var-nish**es, in particular **gum arabic** or **gum tragacanth**. Gums are also used in **offset lithography**, both in the production of printing plates and in press **fountain solution**s as a means of desensitizing the nonimage areas of the plates and keeping them ink-repellent. (See **Fountain Solution**.)

Gum Arabic

A gummy, water-soluble substance exuded by several species of tree of the genus *Acacia* (in particular *A. senegal*) used in the manufacture of many different products, from inks to candy, from ceramics to pharmaceuticals. In ink manufacture, it is used as a **vehicle** in certain types of printing inks (see **Water-Soluble Gum Vehicle**). Gum arabic is also called *gum acacia*.

Gum arabic is also applied to the surface of offset printing plates to prevent ink accumulation in nonprinting areas. Gum arabic is also a component of offset press **fountain solution**s, used to **desensitize** the nonimage areas of the plate and enable them to retain their ink-repellency. (See **Fountain Solution**.)

Gum Etch

Also called 1:32 gum etch, a substance, produced by mixing one part 85% phosphoric acid with thirty-two parts of 14° Bé gum arabic, used to **desensitize** offset printing plates and/or chrome-plated **dampening system** rollers as a means of restoring their ink-repellency and water-receptivity. Metal **dampener**s can lose their water-receptivity over time or with use, as grease collects on their surfaces, and become increasing receptive to ink, which can produce a variety of press and printing problems. (See **Dampening System**.)

Gummed Label

A label with an **adhesive** applied to one side.

Gummed Paper

A type of paper, in a variety of grades, coated with an adhesive material on one side.

Gumming

In **offset lithography**, an alternate term for plate **desensitization**, performed by applying a solution of **gum arabic** to the plate surface. See **Desensitization**.

Gum Streaks

A printing defect of **offset lithography** characterized by streaks in the printed image, particularly in printed *halftone*s, caused by nonuniform desensitization of the plate by the gum, resulting in a partial desensitization of the image area.

Gum Tragacanth

A gummy, water-soluble substance exuded by several species of Asian shrub of the genus *Astragalus* (in particular *A. gummifer*) used as a stiffening agent in pills, throat lozenges, and other such applications. It is also used as a **binder** in water-vehicle solutions, such as those used to make **screen printing** stencil emulsions.

Gurley Densometer

A device used to measure the **porosity** of a paper by measuring the length of time it takes for a specified volume of air (usually 100 cm^3) to pass through a particular area (usually 1 in.^{2}) of a paper sample under a constant temperature and pressure. A slowly descending piston forces the quantity of air through the paper at the bottom of the shaft, while a timing device times how long it takes for all the air to diffuse through the paper. (See also **Porosimeter**.)

Gurley Smoothness Tester

A variety of **air leak tester**, an instrument used to determine the **smoothness** of a paper surface, in which air at a specified pressure is leaked between a smooth glass surface and a paper sample, and the time (in seconds) for a fixed volume of air to seep between these surfaces is the smoothness of the paper. See also **Smoothness**.

Gusset

In printing, an undesirable wave, wrinkle, or crease produced at the top of the inner page of a **closed-head** press **signature**. The production of gussets is called **gusseting**. Gussets are also known as **buckle**s.

Gusseting

The production of **gusset**s. See **Gusset**.

Gutenberg, Johannes

Johannes Gensfleisch zur Laden zum Gutenberg (c.1400–68) was born into a patrician family of the city of Mainz, Germany. His early training was in goldsmithing. His father was Friele zum Gensfleisch, a goldsmith. Gutenberg took his mother's last name for his own, following the custom that one son should carry on the mother's family name.

Gutenberg conceived the idea for movable type and brought together the technologies of paper, oil-based ink, and the screw-press to print books. The printing press was not a single invention. It was the aggregation of technologies known for years before Gutenberg, who gets credit for an invention that is thought to have been developed simultaneously in Holland and in Prague. The inventions brought together by Gutenberg in his pursuit of printing were:

1. The adaptation for printing of the wine or olive oil, screw-type press that had been in use for many years, throughout Europe and Asia.

2. The development of oil-based inks. These had been around since the 10th century, impressed on vellum with woodblocks. Handwritten religious manuscripts used an egg-based tempura that was unsuitable for printing with metal type.

3. The development of a punch and mold system that allowed the mass production of the movable type used to reproduce a page of text. These letters would be put together in a type tray, which was then used to print a page or pages of text. If a letter broke down, it could be replaced. When the printing of the copies of one page was finished, the type could be reused for the next page or the next book.

4. The adaptation of wood block-print technology—xylography—known in Europe since the return of Marco Polo from Asia at the end of the 13th century.

5. The development of mass production papermaking techniques. Paper was brought from China to Italy but was originally thought too flimsy for books.

There are very few direct pieces of information about the person who invented the most important communication system of all time. Most of the information about his life comes from documents of financial or legal transactions. Exiled from Mainz in the course of a struggle between the guilds of that city and the patricians, Gutenberg moved to Strassburg (now Strasbourg, France) between 1428 and 1430 and records put his presence there from 1434 to 1444. He engaged in crafts such as gem cutting, "stone polishing," and metalworking, and he taught those skills to a number of business associates.

As a goldsmith and maker of mirrors, he experimented with metal casting. He had been working on a mass-

A bas-relief on a monument to Gutenberg in Mainz, Germany.

production technique for "spiegeln" or mirrors. As a maker of these artifacts, he had borrowed a significant amount of money from business partners to invest in the manufacture and selling of mirrors at a pilgrim convention in Aachen. Unfortunately, in 1438, they discovered that they got the year of the festival wrong, and it was actually two years away. His partners asked him to teach them something else that he had been secretly working on. In 1438, a five-year contract was drawn up between him and Hans Riffe, Andreas Dritzehn, and Andreas Heilmann. A clause stated in case of the death of one of the partners, his heirs were not to enter the partnership but were to be compensated financially. When Andreas Dritzehn died in 1438, his heirs sued Gutenberg, demanding to be made partners. They lost the suit, but the trial revealed that Gutenberg was working on an invention that had something to do with metal casting, a press with a screw mechanism, and paper. Witnesses testified that a carpenter named Conrad Saspach built a wooden press, and Hans Dünne, a goldsmith, declared that he had sold to Gutenberg, in 1436, 100 guilders' worth of casting materials. This very tantalizing fragment offers only a glimpse into history.

After March 1444, Gutenberg's activities are unknown for a number of years. In October 1448, Gutenberg was back in Mainz to borrow more money from a relative. In 1450, Gutenberg went into partnership with a wealthy Mainz money-broker, Johann Fust. Fust invested 800 guilders to become a partner.

In this shop he set type for a Turkenkalender (Turkish Calendar), which was printed in 1454, and two indulgences. His printing experiments had apparently reached a considerable degree of refinement, in order to persuade Fust to lend him 800 guilders—a substantial capital investment, for which the tools and equipment for printing were to act as security. Two years later Fust made an investment of an additional 800 guilders in installment payments for a partnership in the "work of the book" with the work itself as collateral. Fust and Gutenberg became estranged as Fust, apparently, wanting a quick return on his investment, while Gutenberg aimed at perfection rather than promptness. Fust foreclosed.

Fust won the suit against him, the record of which is preserved, in part, in what is called the Helmasperger Notariatsinstrument (the Helmasperger notarial instrument), dated November 6, 1455, now in the library of the University of Göttingen. Gutenberg was ordered to pay Fust the total sum of the two loans and compound interest (probably totaling 2,020 guilders). It has been said that this settlement ruined Gutenberg, but recent scholarship suggests that it favored him, allowing him to operate a printing shop through the 1450s and 1460s.

The printing of certain books mentioned in the record of the trial refers to the 42-line Bible that was Gutenberg's masterpiece. It is called the 42-line Bible because most of its pages are 42 lines long; it was completed in 1455 at the latest. The sale of the 42-line Bible alone would have produced many times over the sum owed Fust by Gutenberg, and there exists no explanation as to why these assets were not counted among Gutenberg's property at the trial. Fust gained control of the Bible and of the type for Gutenberg's second masterpiece, the Psalter, and some of Gutenberg's printing equipment. Fust continued to print, using Gutenberg's materials, with the assistance of Peter Schöffer, his son-in-law, who had been Gutenberg's skilled assistant and a witness against him at the 1455 trial.

Gutter

On a ***screen printing*** press, the taped interior edge of the screen fabric running parallel to the direction of the ***squeegee***.

In typography, the term *gutter* refers to the space between columns of type, usually determined by the number and width of columns and the overall width of the area to be filled. Sometimes a rule is used instead of blank space. When laying out pages, gutters should not be so narrow that columns run together. In these cases, the rule line is often used. With standard text type sizes, one pica is the standard gutter space (also called ***column space***). For large type sizes, more gutter space should be used. For type set ***ragged right***, a slightly smaller gutter space works better. Since almost all lines in ragged type are not in full line measure, a small amount of gutter space is "built in." The gutter is also referred to as the ***column gutter***.

In a ***two-page spread***, the gutter is the space between the two pages where the pages are attached to the spine or other binding. This gutter is also known as a ***gutter margin***, ***back margin***, or ***blind margin***.

Gutter Jumper

In page layout, a headline, picture, or other page element that extends across the ***gutter*** of a ***double-page spread*** from one page to the next.

Gutter Margin

See ***Gutter*** (third definition).

H

H, h

The eighth letter of the Latin and English alphabets. The form of the capital *H* has its origins in the North Semitic alphabets, as well as the Greek capital letter *eta*, which although denoting an *E* sound was written as the modern *H*. Although earlier alphabets utilized the form of the letter *H,* it was not until the advent of English that it took on an aspirate pronunciation.

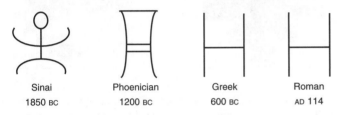

The evolution of the letter H.

H.261

In *digital video*, a *CCITT* standard for video *data compression*.

H.320

In telecommunications, a standard format for *videoconferencing*, defining the specifications for connected conferencing devices.

H & J

See *Hyphenation and Justification (H&J)*.

Hacek

Alternate term for a *caron*. See *Caron*.

Hacker

In computing, an individual unparalleled in computer expertise who delights in creating mischief, usually over networks such as the Internet. Hackers can be mischievous (by playing practical jokes via computer), dangerous (by creating computer viruses or breaking into government or corporation computer systems), or felonious (stealing credit card numbers over the Internet). Hackers are also known as *cyberpunk*s. Although the term *hacker* now has negative connotations, that was not always the case. Originally, the term simply referred to anyone skilled in computer programming, or who, in other words, was capable of (and interested in) "hacking through" all the complexities needed to create a working computer program. Computer programmers—the original "hackers"—use the term "cracker" to refer to a malicious hacker.

Hair Cut

A paper *web* defect characterized by a short, smooth, straight cut in the paper web, caused by a stray hair slitting the paper surface as it passes through the *calender*. A hair cut can cause a web break in web offset lithography, in particular if it runs in the *cross-machine direction* and/or is located at the edge of the web. (See also *Fiber Cut*.)

Hair Space

In typography, the thinnest space that can be made. In hot metal typography, it was 0.167 pica. In phototypesetting, it is 0.5 point.

Hairline

In typography, the thinnest line that can be reproduced. See *Hairline Rule*.

In *binding and finishing*, the term *hairline* refers to very thin lines die-stamped on book covers. Often spelled as two words, *hair line*.

Hairline Register

In *process color* printing, abutting successive colors with no color overlap. See *Register*.

Hairline Rule

In typography, a very thin *rule line* typically less than 0.5 pt. wide. On some output devices, the hairline rule is as thin as the smallest *printer spot* the device can image. On 600 ppi laser printers, the hairline rule is effective; however, on high-resolution (2400+ ppi) *imagesetter*s, it can be essentially invisible. See *Rule Line*.

Halation

In photography, a halo-like blurring effect of highlights or other bright areas of a photographic image. Halation is caused by light rays, after passing through the light-sensitive *emulsion* and the base material, reflecting from the bottom of the base material and passing back up through the emulsion, essentially re-exposing the film. Halation is eliminated on modern films by the use of *antihalation dye*, which absorbs the light rays before they can be reflected back up through the emulsion.

Half Binding

In *binding and finishing*, a type of bookbinding in which the material used for the *spine* and corners is different than that used for the front and back. See also *Quarter Binding* and *Full Binding*.

Half Duplex

In telecommunications, a system in which a channel is only opened in one direction, allowing communicating parties to only send or receive data, but not both simultaneously. A

377

half duplex environment also prevents the terminal from "echoing" the characters typed by the sending party—or having them sent back to the sender and displayed on the screen—thus requiring that the terminal itself be responsible for displaying the characters as they are typed. In a *full duplex* environment, two-way transmission is possible. See *Full Duplex*. Abbreviated **HDX**.

Half-Inch Video

In video, a popular videotape size and format. There are essentially two formats of ½-in. tape, **VHS** (which is the most commercially popular tape format) and *Betamax* (a failed, although technically superior, format). Half-inch tapes are rarely used for broadcast, as their quality is inferior to other tape eizes and formats. *Betacam*, Sony's follow-up to Betamax, is a commonly used, broadcast-quality, ½-in. tape.

Half-Scale Black

A *black printer*—or *key—color separation* containing only a partial range of tonal gradations, in particular those in the darkest regions of the print—the *quartertone*s and the *shadow*s. Consequently, dots are only printed in the dark portions of the image, as opposed to the *full-scale black*. See *Full-Scale Black*. Half-scale black is also known as *skeleton black*.

Half-Title

In *book typography* and production, a *recto* page on which is printed the title of the book, and which falls between the *front matter* and the first page of the main text of the book. A half-title page also falls as the very first page of the book, preceding the *title page*, and in this case is also known as a *bastard title* or *false title*.

Halftone

Any image—such as a photograph—that exists as a series of small dots of varying size and color density, which serve to simulate the appearance of continuous gradations of tone. Halftones are necessary in the reproduction of photographic images; most printing presses cannot print *continuous tone*s, so photographic images must first be converted to a series of dots in order to be effectively printed.

Lightness and darkness of portions of an image are effected by varying the size and density of the dots; small dots spaced far apart produce light areas (*highlight*s), while large dots clustered more closely together produce dark areas (*shadow*s).

Halftones are produced either as film *positive*s or *negative*s by photographing a continuous tone original through a *halftone screen* or fine grid. The screen pattern and frequency of the dots produced determine the ultimate quality of the reproduction. A 150-line screen, for example, will produce 150 rows and 150 columns of dots, or 22,500 dots per square inch. Halftones can also be produced electronically, using digital data. (See *Electronic Dot Generation*.)

Halftone Cell

In digital *halftone* production, a *halftone dot* generated on an *imagesetter* or *laser printer*, comprising a collection of smaller printer *spot*s. Since digital output devices generate images as a series of very small spots, each halftone dot must be composed of smaller printer spots. These printer spots are arranged in discrete "cells" or grids, which correspond to the halftone dots. The number of printer spots in a particular cell can be varied; the more printer spots that are grouped in a halftone cell, the darker the larger the cell appears.

Two halftone cells, comprising 25 printer spots (left) and 100 printer spots (right). The larger the matrix, the greater the number of printer spots, and the greater the number of gray levels.

Halftone Device

Any *graphic output device* that can produce any number of *gray value*s beyond basic black-and-white.

Halftone Dot

The basic indivisible unit of some printed images—commonly photographs—produced by photographically exposing or digitally imaging a *continuous tone* image to a screen, which breaks the image up into discrete dots. Since most printing processes are incapable of printing continuous tone images, such images need to be broken down into individual dots of varying shades of color or gray, each tiny solid dot printing discretely and which together give the illusion of a continuous tone image. See also *Halftone* and *Dot*.

Halftone Gravure

Term for a *gravure cylinder* produced in one step from a single pre-screened film *positive*, as opposed to other gravure engraving procedures using multiple steps to first expose the light-sensitive *resist* to the image and then to a gravure screen. See *Gravure Engraving*.

Halftone Ink

A printing ink possessing high *color strength* and finely dispersed *pigment* particles, formulated especially for high-quality reproduction of *halftone dot*s on *coated paper*s.

Halftone Negative

A photographic *negative* film produced by exposing a *continuous-tone* image through a *halftone* screen. A halftone negative is also called a ***screened negative***. See ***Halftone***.

Halftone Plate

A somewhat incorrect term occasionally used in ***screen printing*** to refer to a screen fabric suitable for printing ***halftone*** images.

Halftone Positive

A photographic ***positive*** film produced by exposing a ***continuous tone*** image through a ***halftone*** screen. Also called a ***screened positive***. See ***Halftone***.

Halftone Scale

A type of ***gray scale*** that exists on film and comprises ***halftone dot***s in discrete levels of gray. See ***Gray Scale***.

Halftone Screen

See ***Screen*** (second definition) and ***Halftone***.

Halftone Screen Algorithm

Alternate term for ***screen algorithm***. See ***screen algorithm***.

Halftone Tint

Alternate term for ***screen tint***. See ***Screen Tint***.

Halftoning

The conversion of a ***continuous tone*** image to a ***halftone***, by photographic or digital means. See ***Halftone***.

Half Web Press

A printing press used in ***web offset lithography*** that measures 17³⁄₄×26 in. See ***Web Press; Web Offset Lithography***.

Half-Web Printing

In ***web offset lithography***, a means of ***perfecting*** in which a paper web of half the diameter of the ***plate*** and ***plate cylinder*** is run through the press. The "half web" is aligned with one edge of the plate and run through the press. It is dried, flipped over, and aligned with the other edge of the plate, where the second side is laid down. In some configurations—a process referred to as ***double-ending***—two half webs are run through simultaneously. See ***Web Offset Lithography: Press Configurations***.

Halo

See ***Halo Effect***.

The term *halo* also refers to a defect of ***screen printing*** characterized by a faint doubling of the printed image, caused by movement of the ***stencil*** under the pressure of the ***squeegee***, typically due to an improperly tensioned screen fabric. A *halo* is also used in screen printing to refer to an enlarged halftone dot, stemming from one of many causes. (Also known as ***fringe***.)

In ***halftone*** photography, a *halo* is a characteristic of a ***soft dot***. See ***Soft Dot***.

Halo Effect

A letterpress and ***flexographic*** printing defect characterized by the accumulation of excess ink at the edges of printed letters and dots, and/or by a colored region surrounding the ink "piles" caused by excess spreading of the ink ***vehicle***. It may also be caused by excessive pressure between the plate and impression cylinders.

Halt

In computing, any stoppage of a fucntion or operation due to user intervention or some form of error.

Hamming Code

A type of ***error detection*** and ***error corection*** technique that is capable of detecting and correcting single-***bit*** errors during data transmission.

Essentially, using Hamming code, the sending device appends three verification bits to every four bits of data, while the receiving device does the same, to ensure that the four data bits were received correctly. Hamming code is a type of ***forward error correction***.

Hand

In ***binding and finishing***, a somewhat vague term designating a quantity of ***signature***s or books equal to that which can be held in one's hand.

Hand-Cut Stencil

A ***stencil*** used in ***screen printing*** not prepared by photographic means. See ***Stencil***. Also called ***knife-cut stencil***.

Hand-Held

Descriptive of any gadget (usually an electronic one) that is truly portable, typically being able to fit in the palm of one's hand. Such a device is occasionally known as a ***palmtop***. See also ***Portable Computer***.

Hand Letterer

A ***graphic artist*** who creates ***logotype***s or other forms of custom lettering by hand.

Handling Stiffness

A paper property that describes the ability to support its own weight in various handling applications. See ***Stiffness***.

Hand Machine

Alternate term for ***hand unit***. See ***Hand Unit***.

Handmade Finish

A paper ***finish*** characterized by a rough surface intended to simulate the texture of ancient handmade paper.

Handmade Paper

Paper that has been manufactured, sheet by sheet, by hand, rather than by a papermaking machine. Such paper commonly has a ***deckle*** edge. Also known as ***mouldmade***.

Hand Processing

An obsolete term for manual *screen printing*.

Handset

Descriptive of type that has been set by hand in hot-metal composition.

Handshake

In telecommunications, an exchange of signals between two modems and communications programs as a means of verifying that they are properly connected, compatible with each other, and ready to proceed with the communications session.

Handshaking

In telecommunications, an exchange of *handshake*s between two connected computers, performed to synchronize the devices and ensure that communication has been established.

Hand Table

Alternate term for *hand unit*. See *Hand Unit*.

Hand Unit

A configuration of *screen printing* press operated entirely by hand and without automation, from feeding to stacking. Also known as *hand table*, *hand machine*, and *manual unit*.

Handwork

Any activity that can only be performed manually.

Handwriting Recognition

Property possessed by any computer system or other similar device that can receive handwritten input (such as by means of a stylus on a *digitizing tablet*) and convert it to machine-readable text. The Apple Newton is one particular system capable of handwriting recognition.

Hanging Figures

In typography, a style of numerals—also called *oldstyle figures*—in which certain numerals have *ascender*s and *descender*s, in contrast to *lining figures*, in which all digits align on the *baseline*. See *Figures*.

Hanging Indent

In typography, a form of *indention* in which the first line or first few lines of a paragraph are set *flush* with the left margin, while rest of the lines of that paragraph are indented a specified distance. A hanging indent may also refer to an indent from the right margin. See *Indention*.

Hanging Punctuation

In typography, punctuation marks (commonly hyphens) that extend beyond the left and/or right margin of *justified* type. Purportedly a modern invention—it is commonly performed for purposes of optical justification—it was actually employed by Gutenberg in his Bible. Also called *hung punctuation*.

Hanging-In

In *perfect binding*, an inclusive term for *gluing off* the spine of a *book block*, affixing the book cover, and applying pressure to facilitate setting.

Hangout

In *perfect binding*, the amount of binding edge of a *book block* that protrudes from the clamps holding it. See *Perfect Binding*.

Hansa Yellows

A type of *organic color pigment* used in printing inks, also called *azo yellows* or *arylide yellows*. Hansa yellows are strong, opaque pigments (about three to five times stronger than *chrome yellow*s), are fast-to-light, and possess a high degree of resistance to chemicals. They vary from a greenish yellow to a bright, warm yellow (see color index reference chart below), and are often used to enhance the color of chrome yellows. They are used in both paste and liquid inks, and work well in *letterpress* and *lithographic* processes, and are especially used on soap packages. Their color strength is less than that of *diarylide yellows*, and have been replaced by diarylides in many cases.

The term *Hansa* is a trade name, and these dyes are more properly known as aceto-acetarylamides. (See also *Organic Color Pigments*.)

(CI Pigment Yellow 1, 3, 4, 65, 73, 74, 97, 98.)

Name	Shade
Arylide G	Warm Yellow
Arylide 10G	Greenest Yellow
Arylide 13G	Slightly Green
Arylide RN	Reddish Yellow
Arylide GX	Bright Yellow
Arylide 5GX	Strong Lemon Yellow
Arylide FGL	Bright Yellow

Arylide Yellow color index reference.

Hard

In computing, descriptive of a physical rather than strictly digital representation of something, usually copy (as in *hard copy*, or printed output, vs. *soft copy*, or a screen or disk copy). See also *Soft*. Also in computing, *hard* refers to a magnetic disk that is rigid (as a *hard disk*) rather than "floppy" (as a *floppy disk*).

Hardbound

Alternate term for *casebound*. See *Casebound*.

Hard Card

In computing, an *expansion card* containing a *hard disk*.

Hard-Coded

Descriptive of a computer program that has been written in such a way that it is incapable of great degrees of flexibility or expandability, such as having program variables written indelibly in the code rather than as promptable user-input.

Hard Copy

Any page, document, publication, or other data that exists as some kind of output, be it on paper, film, etc., rather than as an item on a computer display, or *soft copy*.

Hardcover

A type of nonflexible, cloth-covered paperboard used for binding and covering *casebound* books. See *Case Binding*.

The term *hardcover* also refers to a book bound in such a manner.

Hard Disk

Generally speaking, a rigid computer storage medium; a term once used to distinguish it from a *floppy disk*. In current use, the term *hard disk* commonly refers to any high-capacity rigid magnetic storage medium, distinguished by rapid speed and low access time, as well as large data capacity, measured in either *megabyte*s or, increasingly, *gigabyte*s. Essentially, a hard disk contains a series of magnetized aluminum platters, each of which contains its own read/write head. Hard disks are usually internally mounted within the computer, and most desktop systems these days have at least one internal hard disk. Hard disks can also be attached externally as peripherals. The hard disk as we know it today was developed by IBM and originally called a Winchester disk, a name by which it still occasionally goes.

Hard Disk Controller

See *Disk Controller*.

Hard Dot

A *halftone dot* that has been imaged on film using a laser or contact with another film, characterized by a sharp, well-defined edge that will resist a variation in dot size during platemaking. See also *Soft Dot*.

Hard Dot Engraving

A variation of the *diffusion-etch process*. See *Gravure Engraving: Diffusion-Etch Process*.

Hard-Disk Interface

In computing, the means by which a computer accesses the data on (and writes data to) a *hard disk*. There are several different hard-disk interface standards: *ST506 Interface*, *Enhanced Small Device Interface (ESDI)*, *Integrated Drive Electronics (IDE)*, and *Small Computer System Interface (SCSI)*, to name a few.

Hard-Disk Type

In computing, a number used to identify specific *hard disk* characteristics, such as number of *read/write head*s,

cylinders, etc. This number is usually stored in a PC's *CMOS* memory, and is not accessible to the user. Some systems, however, allow the hard-disk type to be accessed via special configuration programs or through the *BIOS* setup program.

Hard Edge

In *halftone* printing, a defect of a halftone image (usually a *vignette*) characterized by an outer edge that prints as a dark line rather than fading into the color of the substrate.

Hardener

A substance—such as *hydrogen peroxide*—applied to a water-soluble *screen printing* stencil to make it waterproof.

Hardening

In the *screen printing* of textiles, a process in which the mounted *stencil* is treated with a lacquer to make it resistant to the acid or alkali dyes used in printing fabrics, and to enable the stencil to withstand long press runs. After lacquering, compressed air is used to force open the image areas of the stencil.

Hard Hyphen

In typography, a hyphen that is always typeset, regardless of where on the line it falls. Such a hyphen would be one of those in the word "mother-in-law."

Hardness

The degree to which a paper will resist a reduction in thickness when exposed to a compressing force, as during printing, writing, or typing. (The degree to which a paper will allow a reduction in thickness is called its *softness*.) A low degree of hardness aids in producing a good printed image, as the squeezing down of surface contours enables the printing plate or blanket to contact the paper more completely.

The degree of hardness required varies according to the printing process to be used, and other paper properties involved (in particular *resiliency* and *compressibility* which, with hardness and softness, define the paper's *printing cushion*). Generally, easily compressible paper is preferred for printing, although it is less of an issue in offset printing, and stronger paper may be required in the case of end uses involving folding or handling. (See also *Resiliency*, *Compressibility*, and *Softness*.)

The term *hardness* is also used to describe the surface properties of printing press rollers and cylinders (either the ink or dampening rollers, and *blanket* used in *offset lithography*, or the *impression roller* used in *gravure*). Each type of roller, printing process, and substrate require differing degrees of roller or cylinder hardness.

Hardness of rollers and cylinders is measured in, and is also referred to as, *durometer*. (See *Inking System: Offset Lithography*, *Dampening System*, *Blanket*, *Impression Roller*, and *Durometer*.)

Hard Proof

A *color proof* produced on a *substrate* (commonly one similar to the ultimate printing substrate) either using *color separation* films, or directly from digital data. In the latter case, it is often also known as a *direct digital color proof (DDCP)*. A color proof that exists solely on a computer monitor is known as a *soft proof*.

Hard Reset

Alternate term for a *cold reboot*. See *Cold Reboot*.

Hard Return

In word processing, a *carriage return* inserted by the user when a line is desired to break at a certain point, such as the end of a paragraph. See also *Soft Return*. See *Carriage Return*.

Hard-Sectored

In computing, descriptive of a magnetic storage disk which cannot vary the size of the *sector* on it. A file stored on such a disk must either fit within a sector, or else be subdivided among more than one sector.

Hard-Sized

Paper that has had a large amount of *internal sizing* added to impart a high degree of water resistance. (See *Sizing* and *Internal Sizing*.)

Hard Spot

A paper *web* defect, also called a *ridge*. See *Ridge*.

Hard-Wired

In computing, descriptive of a computer system component that is irremovably attached to the computer system, rendering that part of the system incapable of future expansion. The term *hard-wired*, in networking, also refers to any device attached directly to the network, such as a printer.

Hardware

The physical, mechanical and electrical components of a computer system. Hardware includes such elements as the *CPU*, *hard disk*, *motherboard*, input devices (such as a keyboard, mouse, etc.), output devices (printers), *scanner*s, *modem*s, and all related wiring and cabling, as opposed to *software*.

Hardware Address

In networking, the *address* assigned to a device's *network interface card* by either the original manufacturer or by the network administrator. The hardware address locates a device on the network, and allows messages sent to it to find it. Also known as a *physical address*, *media-access-control address*, and *Ethernet address*.

Hardware Dependence

Alternate term for *device dependence*. See *Device Dependence*.

Hardware Independence

Alternate term for *device independence*. See *Device Independence*.

Hardware Interface

In computing, the means by which the hardware components of a computer system communicate with each other. See *Interface*.

Hardware Interrupt

In computing, any signal generated by an attached device and sent to the *CPU*, its intention being to interrupt the CPU from what it is doing and process the new signal. Since many signals may all be clamoring for attention at any given moment, each hardware interrupt signal is assigned a specific priority. The CPU uses the assigned priority to determine the order in which to process incoming signals. See *Interrupt*.

Hardware Key

A perhaps more dignified term for a *dongle*. See *Dongle*.

Hardwood

Wood that is obtained from *deciduous* trees, especially when used in papermaking. *Softwood*, also used in papermaking, comes from *coniferous* trees. See *Coniferous* and *Deciduous*.

Harmonic Drive

In *web printing*, a system of rollers used to control web tension.

Hashing

In computing, a means of locating and retrieving data from a disk. Essentially, a key used to identify the data references a numbered *address* or disk location of the data. Hashing allows swift access of data.

HASP

Abbreviation for *Houston Automatic Spooling Program*. See *Houston Automatic Spooling Program (HASP)*.

Hayes-Compatible Modem

In telecommunications and computing, any *modem* that supports and recognizes the *AT command set*, a means of software control of modems originally defined by Hayes Microcomputer Products and now an industry standard. Nearly all modems manufactured are Hayes-compatible, or can be easily configured as such.

Haze

A printing defect of *gravure* characterized by printing in nonimage areas, caused by incomplete ink removal from the surface of the *gravure cylinder* by the *doctor blade*.

The term *haze* also refers to any milky discoloration of a transparent film or liquid solution, such as a printing ink, in any printing process.

HBA

Abbreviation for *host bus adapter*. See *Host Bus Adapter (HBA)*.

HDCD

Abbreviation for *high-density compact disc*. See *High-Density Compact Disc (HDCD)*.

HDLC

Abbreviation for *High-Level Data Link Control*. See *High-Level Data Link Control (HDLC)*.

HDTV

Abbreviation for *high-definition television*. See *High-Definition Television (HDTV)*.

HDX

Abbreviation for *half duplex*. See *Half Duplex*.

Head

The top of a book, page, or column. See also *Foot*.

In typography, the term *head* is also an abbreviation for the term *heading*. See *Heading* and *Display Type*.

In electronic recording and/or playback equipment, *head* refers to any part of the device that writes to or reads from a magnetic storage medium. On a disk drive, a *read/write head* is used to write data to and read data from the disk. See *Read/Write Head*.

Head-and-Tail Tester

A device used to measure the force required to pull out a page of a bound book—at both the head end and the tail end—as a means of gauging the strength of the binding of an adhesive-bound book.

Headband

In *case binding*, a thin strip of cotton or silk added to the top and bottom of a book, between the bound pages and the cloth cover, used for reinforcement and decoration.

Headbanding

In *case binding*, the addition of *headband*s to a *casebound* book. See *Headband* and *Case Binding*.

Head Bolt

In *binding and finishing*, an uncut *signature* fold located at the top of the signature. See *Bolts*.

Headbox

The initial portion of the *forming section* (or *wet end*) of a papermaking machine that deposits the water-suspended solution of *pulp* fibers, or the papermaking *furnish*, to the *forming wire*.

The functions of the headbox are to swirl and agitate the pulp mixture to keep premature clots (or *flocs*) from forming, and to regulate the speed, thickness, and consistency at which the furnish is delivered onto the wire. The furnish exits the headbox through an adjustable *slice*, with which variations in paper weight can be made.

Head Clamp

One of two *plate clamp*s found on the *plate cylinder* of an offset printing press. The head clamp is the device to which the top, or leading edge, of the plate is attached, as opposed to the *tail clamp*. See *Plate Clamp* and *Plate Cylinder*.

Head Crash

A *crash*, or hardware malfunction, occasionally occurring on a computer's *hard disk* in which the read/write head—which is normally supposed to "float" above the surface of the disk—collides with the surface of the disk.

The results of this can range from simple data loss to more severe hard disk damage. Head crashes are commonly caused by some kind of contamination such as fingerprints, dust particles, etc. A head crash is one particular variety of a more general *disk crash*.

Head End

Catchall term for the hardware at the start of any transmission system, usually a two-way *broadband* network (such as a *cable television network*).

The head end is responsible for routing transmission signals from the network to the various nodes connected to the network, as well as to distribute the available *bandwidth*s.

Header

In typography, any text that appears at the top of a page but is not part of the body text, such as a title, author, chapter title, etc. A header appearing on every page is called a *running head*.

In computing, *header* is a shorthand term for *header information*. See *Header Information*.

In digital imaging, a *header* is also a term for information located at the beginning of a *sector* on a *CD-ROM*, used to quickly access data for playback.

Header Information

In computing, information located at the beginning of a data file (usually not visible to the user) that provides necessary information to an application or computer as to the file's *file format*, file name, application program, etc.

Head Frame

In video production, the first *frame* of either the audio or video portion of an image.

Head Gap

Alternate term for *flying height*. See *Flying Height*.

Heading

In typography, *display type* used to emphasize copy, act as a book, chapter, or section title, or otherwise introduce or separate text. More commonly referred to as simply a *head*.

Heading Band

In presentation graphics, any graphic element—such as a trademark, logo, line, or color—that sets the title of a chart apart from the subtitle.

Headline

In typography, a prominent piece of text, usually short and attention-grabbing, to announce, summarize, or draw attention to the contents of accompanying text, as in newspapers.

Headliner

A device designed specifically to set type in large *point sizes*, usually one character at a time, most often for *headlines* and other *display* material.

Head Margin

In typography, the amount of blank space allowed between the top of the first line of text (or other topmost page element) and the top edge of the sheet. Depending upon the user or typesetter, the head margin may or may not include any *folios* or *running heads*.

Head-Mounted Display

In *virtual reality*, a helmet containing two built-in screens, used to simulate a three-dimensional environment. By projecting each of the two images at slightly different angles, the illusion of 3D or stereoscopic vision can be produced. Sensors built into the helmet sense the movements of the user's head, and adjust the perspective of the images accordingly (known as *head tracking*). Often abbreviated *HMD* and also known as a *visette*.

Head Section

In *binding and finishing* or *folding*, especially of a two-up form, the section containing *closed heads*. The head section usually has lower page numbers than the *tail section*.

Head-to-Foot

In *foil stamping*, descriptive of the movement of the foil in a direction parallel to the height of the book, or from the top to the bottom. See also *Across-the-Cover*.

Head-to-Foot Imposition

A form of *back printing* such that the top of the copy (or other printed image) on the back side of the sheet is "next"

to the bottom of the copy on the front side of the sheet, read by turning the page over from top to bottom. See also *Head-to-Head Imposition* and *Head-to-Side Imposition*. Also known as *Head-to-Toe Imposition*.

Head-to-Head Imposition

A form of *back printing* such that the top of the copy (or other printed image) on the back side of the sheet is the same as the top of the copy on the front side of the sheet, read simply by turning the page over, as the pages of a book. See also *Head-to-Foot Imposition* and *Head-to-Side Imposition*.

Head-to-Side Imposition

A form of *back printing* such that the top of the copy (or other printed image) on the back side of the sheet is at a right angle to the top of the copy on the front side of the sheet. See also *Head-to-Foot Imposition* and *Head-to-Head Imposition*.

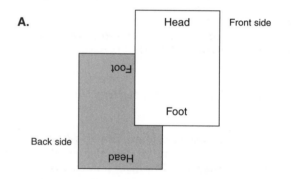

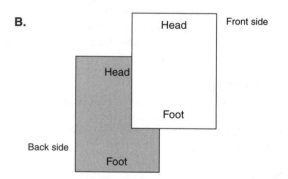

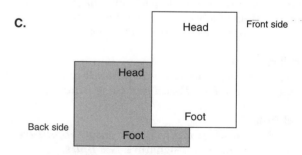

Different impositions, including (A) head-to-foot, (B) head-to-head, and (C) head-to-side.

Head Tracking

In **virtual reality**, the use of sensors built into a **head-mounted display** to register changes in the position of the wearer's head and adjust the perspective of the displayed image accordingly.

Head Trim

In **binding and finishing**, the amount of paper that is trimmed off the top of a book or page.

Heartbeat

In networking, a somewhat anthropomorphic term for an **Ethernet** test signal, used to determine whether or not a particular component is functioning and capable of **collision detection**. Also known as a **signal quality error**.

Heat Activation

The process of converting an **adhesive** material from a dry state to a "wet," sticky state by applying heat.

Heat Curing

The process of drying and/or hardening a material—such as an ink film—by the application of heat.

Heat-Release Decal

A decal that has been printed face down (commonly by **screen printing**) on a release paper; it is transferred to the desired **substrate** by means of heat and pressure.

Heat Seal Paper

A label paper on which the **adhesive** is activated by heat as opposed to moisture, a process known as **Heat Activation**.

Heat-Sensitive Plate

A type of printing plate used in **offset lithography** comprising a metal (or other material) base coated with a layer of thermally sensitive **polymer**s, allowing the plate to be imaged with heat rather than light. Infrared lasers expose the image areas of the plate, which then need to be processed chemically. The primary advantage of these types of plate is the lack of need for special lighting conditions (required for handling other light-sensitive plate coatings.) Thermal curing after processing also imparts a high degree of durability to the image areas, allowing them to be used for print runs of over 1,000,000. (See **Plate: Offset Lithography**.)

Heatset

Any chemical that is hardened or dried at elevated temperatures, such as a **heatset ink**. See **Heatset Ink**. Any process of drying or curing with the application of heat is known as **heat curing**.

Heatset Drying

A method of drying certain types of printing ink (called **heatset ink**) that require drying by **evaporation**, chemical reaction promoted by heat, and cooling. This is accomplished by passing the printed paper **web** through a dryer at a temperature of 250–500°F and then cooling it to 75–90°F. (See **Heatset Ink**.) **Coated paper**s can cause problems in heatset drying, especially when their **moisture content** is high and the **porosity** is low. (See **Blister** and **Fiber Puffing**.)

Heatset Ink

A quick-drying type of ink that dries by **evaporation** of its **solvent** in a high-temperature drying oven followed by cooling to set the ink. Heatset inks comprise the **pigment**, a solvent (a heatset oil), a litho **varnish**, and a wax compound modifier. In **heatset drying**, the printed **web** is passed through a high-temperature dryer (typically at 250–500°F) that evaporates the solvent. A chilling procedure (utilizing **chill rolls**) then cools the ink down to about 75–90°F. Chemical reactions and absorption also set the ink. (See also **Heatset Drying**.)

Heatset inks are used in **letterpress** and **offset lithography**, typically in web presses, and have the advantage of quick drying, which reduces the risk of excessive ink spread and absorption. The process, however, can cause problems in **coated paper** that, if of insufficient **porosity**, can **blister** during heatset drying. (See **Blistering** and **Fiber Puffing**.)

Heat Transfer Printing

A means of transferring a design to a **substrate** using an intermediate step. In heat transfer printing, a design is printed in reverse (typically by **screen printing**) on a special release paper using a **plastisol**-based ink (or other type of **sublimable dye**). The printed image is then placed against the desired substrate (commonly a fabric, such as a T-shirt) and subjected to high temperature (commonly 375°F) and pressure (60 pounds) for a short period of time (12–15 seconds is common). After the substrate has cooled, the release paper is peeled away and the image will have been transferred to the substrate. This process is commonly used for "iron-on" decals. Also known as **screen flex heat transfer**.

Variations on the above include **lithographic flex heat transfer**, a process for the heat transfer of photographs. The primary difference is that the image is commonly printed on release paper by means of **offset lithography**. **Nylon heat transfer** uses a specially formulated screen printing ink designed to adhere to nylon. **Screen glitter heat transfer** involves the use of **glitter** inks to provide a glittery, disco look to the final printed image.

Heat Tunnel

In shrink-wrap packaging, the enclosed "oven" through which a package travels. The intense heat within causes the plastic wrapping to contract such that it tightly conforms to the material it encloses.

Heavy-Bodied Ink

An ink possessing a high **viscosity** and a stiff consistency. See **Body** and **Viscosity**.

Hebrew

A Semitic language closely related to Phoenician. Spoken in ancient times in Palestine and supplanted by the western dialect of Aramaic in the 3rd century BC. It was revived as a spoken language in the 19th and 20th centuries and is now the official language of Israel. The history of the Hebrew language has four major periods: Biblical/Classical, until the 3rd century BC, in which most of the Old Testament is written; Mishnaic/Rabbinic, the language of the Mishna about AD 200 ; Medieval, from the 6th to the 13th century AD, when words were borrowed from Greek, Arabic, and other languages; and Modern, the language of Israel today.

The language is written from right to left in a script of 22 letters. Early Hebrew was the alphabet used by the Jewish nation in the period before the Babylonian Exile (6th century BC). The Early Hebrew alphabet had only consonants, and was more closely related in letterform to the Phoenician than to the modern Hebrew. Between the 6th and 2nd century BC, Classical, or Square, Hebrew displaced the Aramaic alphabet, which had replaced Early Hebrew in Palestine. Square Hebrew became established in the 2nd and 1st centuries BC and developed into the modern Hebrew alphabet over the next thousand years. Classical Hebrew showed three distinct forms by the 10th century AD: Square Hebrew, a formal or book hand; Rabbinical or "Rashi-writing," employed by medieval Jewish scholars; and various cursive scripts, of which the Polish-German type became a modern cursive form.

Hectograph

A process or device used for duplication of small documents utilizing a gelatin-based surface to which an original has been transferred. Rather like a mimeograph, a hectograph process is used for very small runs of memos, letters, etc.

Hectographic Paper

A type of duplicator paper used on a **hectograph**.

Helical Gear

A gear used to drive printing press rollers or cylinders, in which the teeth are cut at an angle to the surface of the cylinder. Helical gears, found on newer presses, by design reduce **play**, the unimpeded (and undesirable) movement between gears. The older **spur gear**, on which the teeth are cut parallel to the surface of the cylinder, generally requires a **backlash gear** to reduce play. Cylinders in which the **bearer**s (metal rings attached to the ends of the cylinder) of the **plate cylinder** run in contact with those of the **blanket cylinder** commonly use spur gears, while those that run out of contact use helical gears to reduce play and provide a smoother drive. (See **Plate Cylinder**, **Blanket Cylinder** and **Spur Gear**.)

Helical Scan

The means by which a **head** on a videocassette recorder scans the magnetic tape. The playback head on a VCR is not aligned perfectly with the tape transport mechanism,

but is rather skewed at a 30° angle. It is thus able to contact and process more of the tape surface. The video head also rotates as the tape moves past it, making one rotation per **frame**. The addition of a second play head allows each **field** to be read separately.

Helicopter View

Alternate term for a **bird's-eye view**. See **Bird's-Eye View**.

Heliogravure

A term, no longer in use, used to refer to **gravure** printing whose image was derived from a photoengraving.

Helium-Neon Laser

In imaging, a strong, directional red light—with an output of up to 632.8 **nanometer**s—used to generate images on red-sensitive film, paper, printing plates or press cylinders. A helium-neon laser is occasionally used in lieu of an **argon laser**, as helium-neon lasers are deemed more stable and less expensive than argon lasers, although the latter do have their advantages in that the blue-sensitive paper used with argon lasers—unlike the red-sensitive paper used in conjunction with helium-neon lasers—can be handled safely in red or yellow light. A helium-neon laser is abbreviated **HeNe**, from the chemical symbols for helium and neon, respectively.

Hell Angles

Term for **screen algorithms**, algorithms used to create digital halftones, that solve the problem of the **irrational screen angles**, developed and patented by Linotype-Hell. They are proprietary, licensed by other **CEPS** manufacturers. See **Screen Angles** and **Irrational Screen Angles**.

Help

In computing, any message or file that provides information on how to use a particular application. Many applications now feature extensive **help file**s, which provide an indexed and serachable list of topics.

Help File

A computer file, accessible from within a software program, that contains instructions and tips—commonly easily searchable—for use of the software, geared to supplement the instruction manuals for a particular program.

Helvetica

Proper name of the most common **sans serif** typeface, used in a wide variety of text and display applications. Helvetica (the Latin word for Switzerland) was designed by Max Mei-

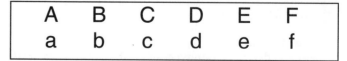

The Helvetica typeface.

dinger for the Haas Foundry. It was released for the Linotype in the early sixties and for phototypesetting in the seventies. It is the most popular sans serif typeface.

Hemicellulose

General term for a collection of polysaccharides found in wood, having a chemical structure similar to that of *cellulose* (hence the name "*hemi*cellulose"). In papermaking, the only necessary ingredient from the wood or plant source is cellulose, and hemicelluloses and *lignin*—a material that binds the cellulose fibers together—are contaminants that reduce paper quality and *permanence*; they must be removed from paper pulp before papermaking begins. (See *Pulping*.)

HeNe

Abbreviation for *helium* and *neon*, in particular, for *helium-neon laser*. See *Helium-Neon Laser*.

Heraldry

The devising, blazoning, and granting of armorial insignia and of tracing and recording genealogies. From the second quarter of the 12th century in western Europe, heraldic designs are found representing nobles and royals. A similar system was found in Japan, dating from the 12th century. The complex heraldic practice was best known in western Europe.

From 1150 to 1500, the use of heraldry was utilitarian: on armor in warfare, and on seals in peace. From the beginning, the use of arms had been associated with higher feudal castes and heraldry provided an identification with the concept of gentility that persists to this day. To bear arms was the mark of a gentleman, and those arms were inscribed with the gentleman's insignia. Thus, to possess gentility, one needed armorial bearings for social distinction.

Seals flourished in Mesopotamia to authenticate documents (baked clay on papyrus or vellum) on which they were stamped. Literate and illiterate alike were able to recognize the symbol of a ruler or a noble. Flags can be heraldic—that of the United Kingdom is formed by the amalgamation of the crosses of St. George, St. Andrew, and St. Patrick. These symbols are borne only by the reigning king or queen or the head of the high-ranking family. In Scottish heraldry this is rigidly enforced, but it has fallen into decay, except in the case of the British royal family. An extension of medieval heraldry was connected with guilds or associations of trades whose object was to uphold standards of craftsmanship. Military heraldry has continued to the present. Corporate heraldry is actually growing as banks, insurance companies, and other commercial concerns use arms, as do professional, educational, and trade associations.

Hercules Adapter

In computing, a *video card* developed by Hercules Computer Technology in 1982 to increase the *resolution* (to 720×348 *pixel*s) of IBM's original *CGA* monitor. The Her-

cules Adapter became the standard for *monochrome* monitors, but its lack of color support rendered it obsolete when IBM introduced the *EGA* monitor.

Herringbone Perforator

A type of *perforator* used to cut herringbone-shaped (or cross-hatched) slits in a paper, usually at the top of 5½×8½-in. *signature*s to reduce *gusseting*.

Hertz

A unit of frequency equal to one cycle per second, used in the measurement of electrical signals and electromagnetic waves, including sound and light. Essentially, *hertz* is a measure of the number of times an electrical event repeats in one second, and is used to describe the "clock rate" of a computer's *central processing unit* (usually described—as of this writing—in *megahertz*, or "millions of hertz"). Hertz is abbreviated *Hz*, and was named for German physicist Heinrich Hertz, who first described electromagnetic waves.

Heterogeneous Network

A network comprising *host* computers made by different manufacturers or differing in some other way from each other. See also *Homogeneous Network*.

Hewlett-Packard Graphics Language (HPGL)

A *file format* for *CAD* files, developed by Hewlett Packard originally to drive *pen plotter*s, but now used primarily for the storage and exchange of graphics files.

Hex

Abbreviation for *hexadecimal*. See *Hexadecimal*.

Hexadecimal

A number system based on 16, usually referred to as "base 16." Each digit in a number essentially has 16 possibilities, comprising the numerals 0–15. In the hexadecimal system, as applied to computers, the digits 0–9 are utilized as is, the digits 10–15 representing the letters A–F. The hexadecimal system is widely used in computer applications, as it can be easily reduced to *binary* figures, and all 16 hexadecimal digits can be represented in four *bit*s, two hexadecimal digits (each representing a set of four bits) can be stored in one *byte* of data. Many *email* systems convert attached files to hexadecimal form for compact and rapid transmission over the Internet or other networks. Hexadecimal is usually abbreviated *hex*.

HFS

Abbreviation for *Hierarchical File System*. See *Hierarchical File System (HFS)*.

Hi-8

A brand of consumer and semiprofessional-level videotape developed by Sony that records video on 8-mm tape. Hi-8 tape is used in compact *camcorders*.

Hickey

Any printing defect caused by a particle either of paper or other source of debris attaching itself to the printing plate, **blanket**, **gravure cylinder**, or other image-carrying surface. Debris produces either a blank, unprinted spot in a printed area (a **void hickey**) or a solid printed area ringed by a blank unprinted area (a **doughnut hickey**). The type of hickey produced depends on the ink receptivity of the particle; ink-repellent particles such as loose paper fibers rid themselves of ink on the plate or blanket and print as void hickeys; ink-absorbent particles pick up the ink and print as spots, but being raised particles, they do not allow the surrounding area to print and manifest themselves as doughnut hickeys. Doughnut hickeys produced by particles of ink skin collecting on the blanket or plate are called **ink hickey**s. (See **Doughnut Hickey** and **Void Hickey**.) Offset presses can also add a special roller, called a **hickey-picking roller**, which can either remove or lessen the effects of hickeys.

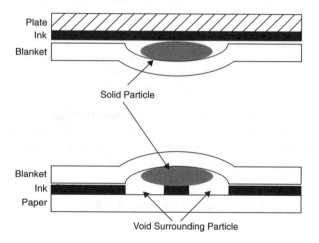

Plate
Ink
Blanket

Solid Particle

Blanket
Ink
Paper

Void Surrounding Particle

The birth of a hickey.

Hickey-Picking Roller

In **offset lithography**, a press roller, typically installed as the first **form roller**, that has a special fibrous surface to either pick a **hickey**-causing particle from the plate, or surround the particle with ink to eliminate the characteristic white ring. Careful and frequent cleaning of this roller is important in order for it to maintain its usefulness. The position of the roller in the **roller train** also has effects on its efficiency, and its ability to cause other problems. Installing it as the last form roller contacting the plate can cause **mottle** or **graininess**, and if the first form roller is a combination ink/dampening roller, the hickey-picking roller should be placed second. The closer the roller is to the plate, however, the less coarse its surface fibers should be to avoid transferring the texture of the roller to the plate.

Hidden File

In computing, a file with a set of **control character**s indicating that information about the file should not appear in a **directory**, for security or other reasons. Other limitations may also be imposed on the file, such as the inability to move, copy, delete, or display its contents.

Hidden Weight

A term used to refer to the weight of additional items you will need to schlep around with you in order to make a portable computer actually work, an amount not usually indicated in ads for portable computers. Such items include AC adapters and power cords, battery rechargers, extra batteries, and a heavy, padded bag to carry it all in.

Hidden-Line Removal

In computer graphics, a means of **rendering** three-dimensional (3D) objects in which the software determines (and deletes) the lines of a **wireframe** at a certain angle that would not be visible if the object were solid and opaque. **Hidden-Surface Removal** works on the same principle.

Hidden-Surface Removal

In computer graphics, a means of **rendering** three-dimensional (3D) objects in which the software program determines (and removes) the surfaces of a **wireframe** at a certain angle of viewing that would not be visible if the object were solid and opaque. **Hidden-Line Removal** works on the same principle.

Hide

In **binding and finishing**, any animal skin, especially one used as a binding or book cover material, such as leather for **deluxe edition**s.

Hierarchical File System (HFS)

A **file system** (used by the Apple **Macintosh**, as well as some other types of computers) that stores data in a top-to-bottom (or hierarchical) organizational structure. Data access thus starts from the top of the hierarchy and proceeds downward. HFS, on the Macintosh, replaced the older **Macintosh File System (MFS)**.

Hierarchical Link

In animation, a linking of two objects in a parent-child relationship, which means essentially that changes visited upon the parent are inherited by the child, but not the reverse. For example, if animating the head of a rabbit, moving the head (parent) would change the position of the ears (child), but moving the ears would not change the position of the head. This sort of link is the basis of the animation technique of **inverse kinematics**.

Hierarchical Storage Management (HSM)

In networking, a model used to define specifications for the storage and management of network data. Essentially, data is stored on a medium based on the frequency of its use; often-used files are stored on **hard disk**s, while less frequently used data is kept on other storage media, such as **optical disc**s, etc.

Hieroglyphic

Hieroglyphic writing is a system that employs pictures as a form of communication. These signs, called hieroglyphs, may be read either as pictures, as symbols for pictures, or as symbols for sounds. The word hieroglyphic is the Greek word for "sacred carving" or "sacred sign" and refers to Egyptian writing. Greeks labeled as hieroglyphic the symbols that they found on temple walls and public monuments. The Greeks distinguished this writing from two other forms of Egyptian writing that were written on papyrus or on other smooth surfaces. These were known as the hieratic, which was employed during the time of the ancient Greeks for religious texts, and the demotic, the cursive script used for ordinary documents.

From 2800 BC to AD 300 hieroglyphic writing was used for inscribing stone monuments and appears in Egyptian high relief and bas-relief, in painted form, on metal, in cast form and sometimes incised, and on wood. Hieroglyphics have been found on the walls of temples, tombs, memorials, gravestones, statues, coffins, and vessels and tools. Hieroglyphic writing was used for secular texts—inscriptions, music, legal and scientific documents—and also for religious subject matter. These inscriptions were decorative monumental writing, and not suitable for everyday writing purposes. For popular use, hieratic script was developed, an abbreviated form of the picture symbols for writing with brush and ink on surfaces like papyrus and wood.

Hieroglyphic, in its strict meaning, designates only the writing on Egyptian monuments. The word has been applied to the writing of other peoples who have used picture signs as writing characters, such as the scripts of the Indus civilization, the Hittites, the Mayan, the Incan, and Easter Islanders. Colloquially, the word means any illegible or poorly legible writing.

Hieroglyphs were difficult to write and were supplemented by more convenient scripts. Changes occurred in the characters of hieratic simply because they could be written rapidly on papyrus.

Hieratic was written in one direction only, from right to left. In earlier times the lines had run vertically and later, about 2000 BC, horizontally. Later the papyrus scrolls were written in columns of changing widths. There were ligatures in hieratic so that two, but no more than two, signs could be written in one stroke. The spelling of the hieratic script was more rigid than that of hieroglyphic writing. Hieratic used diacritical marks to distinguish between two signs that had grown similar to one another because of cursive writing.

Commonplace documents were written in hieratic script, as were literary and religious texts. In the life of the Egyptians, hieratic script played a larger role than hieroglyphic writing and was also taught in the schools. Hieratic was replaced by demotic in the 7th century BC.

ROSETTA STONE

An ancient Egyptian stone bearing inscriptions in multiple languages. The decipherment of this stone led to the understanding of hieroglyphic writing. An irregularly shaped stone of black basalt 45 in. long and 28 in. wide, with a corner broken. It was found near the town of Rosetta, northeast of Alexandria in 1799. After the French surrender of Egypt in 1801, it passed to the British and is now in the British Museum.

The inscriptions, written by the priests of Memphis, summarize benefactions conferred by Ptolemy V (205–180 BC) and were written in the ninth year of his reign. Inscribed in Egyptian and Greek, and three writing systems, hieroglyphics, demotic script (a cursive form of Egyptian hieroglyphics), and the Greek alphabet, it provided a key to the translation of Egyptian hieroglyphics. The decipherment was the combined work of Thomas Young of England and Jean-François Champollion of France. The hieroglyphic text on the Rosetta Stone contains six identical cartouches (oval figures enclosing hieroglyphs). Young deciphered the cartouche as the name of Ptolemy. By examining the direction in which the bird and animal characters faced, Young also discovered the way in which hieroglyphic signs were to be read. In 1821–22 Champollion, starting where Young left off, and eventually established an entire list of signs with their Greek equivalents. He was the first Egyptologist to realize that some of the signs were alphabetic, some syllabic, and some determinative, standing for the idea or object expressed.

High Bulk

A type of paper having a thickness (called *bulk* or *caliper*) greater than that of other papers of the same *basis weight*. High-bulk paper is specially manufactured, and is usually used for book paper to increase the thickness of low-page-count books, such as fiction and children's books. (See also *Low Bulk*.)

High Contrast

Descriptive of a photographic reproduction of an image in which the difference in *density* between adjacent regions of the image is greater than that of the original.

High-Definition Television (HDTV)

A new standard for television broadcasting, still under development as of this writing. The advantages of HDTV include sharper resolution, increasing the number of scan lines on a screen from 525 (in *NTSC*) or 625 (In *PAL* and *SECAM*) to 1250, and an *aspect ratio* increase from the current 3:4 to 9:16. In addition to sharper picture quality and a wider screen, HDTV will also produce new standards in hardware, graphics processors, and compression schemes.

High-Density Compact Disc (HDCD)

The proposed second generation of *compact disc*s, developed independently by Philips/Sony and Toshiba/Time Warner. Two varieties of HDCD allow for much higher storage capacities than conventional first-generation CDs. The Philips/Sony disc, called the *multimedia CD (MMCD)*, can hold up to 3.7 *gigabyte*s. The Toshiba/Time Warner disc, called the *super density (SD)* format, is double-sided and can hold up to 4.2 gigabytes per side. Higher storage density is achived by using a red laser, which possesses a shorter wavelength.

However, both versions of the HDCD were incorporated into a new standard format adopted by the computer industry called the *digital versatile disc (DVD)*, which includes a double-sided, double-layer technology developed by 3M that allows for a capacity of 4.7 gigabytes per side per layer, for a total capacity of 17 gigabytes. See *Digital Versatile Disc (DVD)*.

High DOS Memory

In computers running on the *DOS* platform, term for the memory capacity of early PCs between 640 *kilobyte*s and 1 *megabyte*. See *Expanded Memory Specification*.

High-End

Descriptive of any system or device that is both highly expensive and of superior quality, compared to other similar yet lower-priced systems and devices. For example, in scanning, a high-end *drum scanner* is likely to cost tens of thousands of dollars, but produces the best image quality, as compared to a *low-end* flatbed scanner, which costs around $1,000, fits on a desktop, and generates relatively inferior (but still workable) image quality.

High-Energy Dye

A type of *sublimable dye* that requires a very high temperature (over 400°F) in order to be transferred to the *substrate*. Since these dyes undergo *sublimation* at very high temperatures, they are less susceptible to washing out of the fabric on which they are printed. However, some high-energy dyes are only transferred at temperatures which would cause damage to fabric, and are used in other types of applications. See also *Low-Energy Dye*.

High Finish

A paper *finish* characterized by a smooth, hard surface achieved through extensive *calendering* or other *finishing* procedures.

High-Gloss Ink

A variety of printing ink produced with an additional quantity of *varnish* that allows the ink to dry with a highly glossy finish, typically by *oxidation* and *polymerization*. High-gloss inks achieve their best results when used on paper (typically *coated paper*) that allows a high degree of *ink holdout*, or does not allow rapid penetration of the ink *vehicle* into the paper surface.

Rapid drainage of the fluid vehicle hampers oxidation and reduces printed gloss. The application of heat to expedite ink drying also works to reduce printed gloss. High-gloss inks are manufactured for use in both *letterpress* and *offset lithographic* printing processes.

High-Key Transparency

A type of photographic *transparency* that is very light and may have been overexposed. A high-key transparency contains most of its important image detail in *highlight* areas, with very few *shadow* regions. See also *Low-Key Transparency*.

High-Level Data Link Control (HDLC)

In telecommunications, a *bit-oriented* protocol for *synchronous transmission*, used in *X.25* packet-switching networks. HDLC transmits data as subdivided, variable-length units known as *frame*s or *packet*s, with *error correction* at the *data-link layer*. HDLC is an *ISO* standard protocol, although many manufacturers supply their own proprietary version of it, one common example being IBM's *Synchronous Data Link Control (SDLC)*.

High-Level Language

A computer language in which statements written with English-like syntax correspond to many instructions in *assembly language*. The advantage of a high-level language is that programs can be written using words, symbols, and commands, rather than arcane codes that, essentially, only a machine can understand. Examples of high-level languages are BASIC and FORTRAN. See also *Low-Level Language*.

Highlight

The brightest area(s) of an image, printed with the smallest amount of ink transfer and/or the smallest *halftone dot*, in contrast to *shadow*s and *middletone*s. A highlight that comprises the whitest neutral area and prints with the smallest dot is known as a *diffuse highlight*, in contrast to a *specular highlight*, which is a reflection of a light source within an image and contains no detail nor any halftone dots at all.

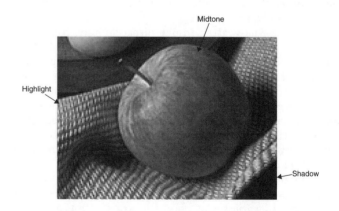

The highlight, midtone, and shadow areas of a halftone.

Highlight Halftone

Alternate term for a *dropout halftone*. See *Dropout Halftone*.

Highlighting

A feature of a computer display that allows user-selected text to be reversed, recolored, made to blink, etc., to indicate selected text intended to be deleted, copied, or moved.

High Memory Area

In computers running on the **DOS** platform, term for the first 64 **kilobyte**s of memory above the first **megabyte**, a portion of memory that could only be addressed by 16-bit processors. Often abbreviated **HMA**.

High-Performance File System (HPFS)

A file management system used by the **OS/2** operating system, affording high-speed access to files via **cache memory** and supporting file names up to 254 characters.

High Quality Screening (HQS)

A system developed by Linotype-Hell for calculating high-quality **PostScript** halftone **screen angles** using **supercell** screen-calculation algorithms. See **Screen Angles**.

High-Res

See **High-Resolution**.

High-Res File

See **High-Resolution File**.

High-Resolution

Descriptive of an image—either on a computer display or in printed form—that has a high number of dots per square inch. On computer screens and digital output devices, images are essentially composed of very small dots (technically called **spot**s) that, when put together in certain shapes, form the text or image that is output. The more spots per square inch, the sharper the image, and the greater the **resolution**. A high resolution image on a computer monitor is defined roughly as 1,000×1,000 **pixel**s per 12-inch diagonal display, a resolution that tends to generate the most realistic-looking images and most effective color transitions. On output devices, high resolution may be 600 spots per inch or greater, depending on the image. Also called **high-res**. (See **Resolution**.)

High-Resolution File

A digital image containing all the information needed to generate high-quality output, existing on the computer disk with its sampling rate—at least four **pixels** per dot of output—intact. On many **color electronic publishing systems**, high-resolution files are created separately from **viewfile**s. They are versions of the image generated at the resolution of the computer monitor (far less than what an output device, such as an **imagesetter**, is capable of), which speeds image processing and manipulation. Any changes made to the low-resolution viewfile are automatically made to the high-resolution file, which then becomes the file that is ultimately output. Also called a **high-res file**.

High Sierra

The first standard format for **CD-ROMs**, named after the region surrounding Lake Tahoe high in the Sierra Nevada mountains where industry representatives gathered to propose specifications for the new format. The High Sierra format eventually mutated into the **ISO 9660** format. See **Compact Disc (CD)**.

High-Speed Precision Printing

A variety of automated **screen printing** at a very high impressions-per-hour rate, while maintaining very tight **register**.

High-Velocity Hot-Air Dryer

A type of **dryer** found on presses used in **web offset lithography** that, unlike **open-flame dryer**s, blows jets of hot air at the printed web. Such dryers also include exhaust vents to remove solvent-laden air to keep it from recondensing back onto the dry web. The nozzles of these dryers can also be oriented to impart a controlled rippling effect to the web, which may help avoid web tension problems further down the line, specifically in the **chill rolls**. See **Dryer** and **Web Offset Lithography: Dryers and Chill Rolls**.

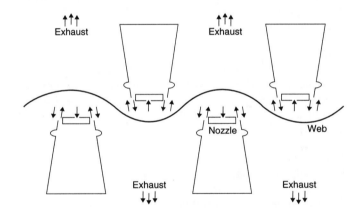

Using a high-velocity hot-air dryer to add a ripple to the web.

Higonnet, René

Louis Marius Moyroud (1914–) and Rene Alphonse Higonnet (1902–1983) developed the first practical phototypesetting machine. Born in Moirans, Isere, France, Moyroud attended engineering school from 1929 to 1936 and graduated as an engineer from Ecole Nationale Superieure des Arts et Metiers of Cluny, France. He served in the military as a second lieutenant from 1936 to 1938 and as a first lieutenant in 1939 and 1940. He joined the LMT Laboratories, a subsidiary in Paris of ITT, in 1941 and left in 1946 to spend all of his time on photocomposition. Moyroud and Higonnet first demonstrated their first phototypesetting machine, the Lumitype—later known as the Photon—in

September 1946 and introduced it to America in 1948. The Photon was further refined under the direction of the Graphic Arts Research Foundations.

The first book to be composed by the Photon was printed in 1953, titled *The Wonderful World of Insects*. Composed without the use of metal type, it might someday rank in the historical importance of printing with the first book printed from moveable type, the Gutenberg Bible.

Higonnet was born in Valence, Drome, France. The son of a teacher, he was educated at the Lycee de Tournon and the Electrical Engineering School of Grenoble University. He was granted a scholarship by the International Institute of Education in New York in 1922, went to Carleton College in Minnesota for one year, and subsequently spent one term at the Harvard Engineering School. He was an engineer with the Materiel Telephonique, a French subsidiary of ITT, from 1924 to 1948. He then became a transmission engineer and worked on long distance cables in Paris-Strasbourg, London-Brussels, and Vienna-Budapest. He was also associated with the Patent and Information Department of ITT.

Hinge
In *case binding*, a flexible joint on the front and back of a *casebound* book where the covers intersect with the *spine*. The hinge allows the book to open without breaking the spine. Also known as a *joint*.

Hints
A variety of computer algorithms—such as those encrypted in *Type 1 PostScript font*s—that improves the appearance of characters, especially those at small sizes, by rendering screen fonts more uniformly shaped across the set of characters.

Histogram
Generally speaking, a graph—usually a bar graph—of frequency distributions, in which the x-axis (horizontal) represents a series of definable quantities (such as, for example, a range of weights of members of a population), while the y-axis (vertical) represents how often those quan-

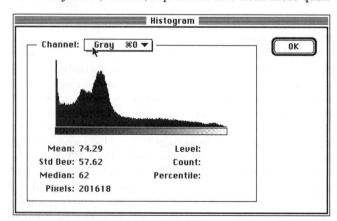

Frequency histogram from Adobe's Photoshop.

tities occur in the sampled population. The actual data accumulated is represented as a series of rectangles, with bases equal to the division of definable quantities and heights that represent the frequency with which those quantities occur.

In *color* analysis, a histogram (also called a *frequency histogram*) is used to determine the distribution of colors in a scanned image. See *Frequency Histogram*.

Hit
In *binding and finishing* and *die-stamping*, an impression made using a stamping *die*.

The term *hit* also refers to an occurrence of a user arriving at a particular Web page.

A *text unit* identified as matching the search request. A hit may be a *false positive* or a true positive. Text units that should have been hits but were missed are *false negatives*.

Hit Point
In motion picture and video productions, a dramatic moment that requires the introduction of new music.

HLS
A *color system* utilizing the three basic values of *hue*, *lightness*, and *saturation*, using the values for each of those qualities to compute accurate color models. Sometimes referred to as *HSV* (hue, saturation, and *value*). Also referred to as *HSL* or *HSB*. See Color Plate XX.

HMA
Abbreviation for *high memory area*. See *High Memory Area*.

HMD
Abbreviation for *head-mounted display*. See *Head-Mounted Display*.

HMI Light
In photography, a hydrargyrum medium-arc-length iodide light source used to illuminate a scene.

HMSF
Abbreviation for *hours:minutes:seconds:frames*, the structure of a *time code*. See *Time Code*.

Hoe, Robert
British-born American printing-press manufacturer (1784–1833) who, as head (1823–33) of R. Hoe and Company, acquired and improved Samuel Rust's patent for a wrought-iron framed printing press manufactured as the "Washington" press. Hoe emigrated to the United States in 1803 and became a partner with two brothers, Matthew and Peter Smith, in a newly founded enterprise, Smith, Hoe and Company, New York City, manufacturers of printers' equipment. Among several innovations was the introduction of the cast-iron frame to replace the wooden frame

in presses. In 1829 he began improving upon the Napier cylinder press imported from England and supplanted British-made presses in the United States. Hoe acquired rights to a steam-powered press patented by Isaac Adams and manufactured it.

Holdout

See *Ink Holdout*.

Hologram

A laser-generated image that, when viewed under ambient light, appears three-dimensional. A hologram is also known as a *holograph*.

Holostore

A means of storing three-dimensional (3D) images using light-sensitive crystals capable of distinguishing patterns of light.

Home Computer

Any *microcomputer* designed to be used in one's home, either for personal business such as accounting or writing a novel, or for playing games.

Home Page

On the *World Wide Web* (the graphics-based part of the *Internet*), the starting point for a company or individual's set of linked pages or other Internet resources. Typically, a company or individual provides potential users with a web address (or *Universal Resource Locator (URL)*) that corresponds to a home page. Once the user has reached that page, s/he can view an overview of the company or individual, as well as a list of other *hypertext* links.

Homogeneous Network

A network of computers which have all been made by the same manufacturer. See also *Heterogeneous Network*.

Homographs

In typography, words that are spelled the same, but pronounced and hyphenated differently (e.g., in-val-id, in-va-lid; pre-sent, pres-ent). (Homonyms are those words that are only pronounced the same, e.g., "to" and "too.") The process of *hyphenation* in America is based upon pronunciation (in England, it's based on the word's derivation). Computer programs that hyphenate automatically cannot effectively handle homographs, because the computer would have to discern the meanings of the words. In any case, the hyphenation of these words depends upon the mind of the person who wrote them.

Hooked Vector

In computing, an *interrupt* vector that calls a new *interrupt service routine*, rather than the original one. A hooked vector is created by altering the computer's *interrupt vector table*. Hooked vectors are often used by *terminate-and-stay-resident* programs.

Hop Count

In networking, the number of links during *routing* that a message needs to cross when traveling from a source to a destination. Hop count is often used by networking systems to calculate the most expedient route by which to transmit a message.

Hopper

Any storage bin.

In *binding and finishing*, a pocket located on a *collating*, *gathering*, or *inserting* device in which printed and folded *signature*s are stored prior to binding.

Horizontal Alignment

Alternate term for *base alignment*. See *Base Alignment*.

Horizontal Blanking Interval

In a *cathode-ray tube*, the amount of time required for an *electron gun* to move from the end of one horizontal line to the beginning of the next one. See also *Vertical Blanking Interval*.

Horizontal Camera

A type of graphic arts *process camera* in which the *copyboard*, *lens*, and *filmboard* are aligned in a horizontal plane, as opposed to a *vertical camera*. See *Photography: Graphic Arts Photography*.

Horizontal Page

Alternate term for a *landscape* page orientation. See *Landscape*.

Horizontal Resolution

The number of *pixel*s that a *scanner* can distinguish in a horizontal line. See *Resolution*.

Horizontal Scaling

The distortion of a graphic by expanding or reducing its size in only the horizontal direction, altering the original proportions of the image.

Horizontal Scan Rate

On a computer monitor, the speed at which the electron beam producing the screen image moves from left to right across the display. The horizontal scan rate is measured in *kilohertz*. See also *Vertical Scan Rate* and *Refresh Rate*.

Horizontal Scrolling

On a computer display, the ability to scroll left or right to display text or parts of an image or page that do not fit onto the screen. See also *Vertical Scrolling*.

Hornbook

A form of children's educational primer used in England and America from 1600 to 1800. A sheet with the letters of the alphabet and numerals was mounted on a wooden frame and covered with transparent plates of horn. The frame was shaped like a ping pong paddle, with a handle, and was usually hung by the child's belt. They contained a large cross, from which the hornbook was called the Christ's Cross row, or crisscross row.

Host

In networking, any computer that controls or provides the computing power for workstations and peripheral devices connected to the network. Also known as a *host computer*.

Host Bus Adapter (HBA)

Alternate term for a *hard disk controller*. See *Hard Disk Controller*.

Host Front End

See *Front End*.

Host Interface

In networking, the link between a network and/or communications processor and the *host* computer.

Host Site

In networking, the physical location or address of the *host* computer. See *Host*.

Hot Colors

Alternate term for *warm colors*. See *Warm Colors*.

Hot Key

Any computer keystroke or combination of keystrokes that initiates a function within a program or operating system.

Hot Metal

See *Hot-Metal Type*.

Hot Peel

In *screen printing* via *plastisol*-based heat-transfer materials, the condition when the removal of the release paper is possible immediately after application without having to wait for paper cooling, in contrast to *cold peel*. Hot peel allows transfer of much thinner ink films, since the release paper is in contact with the substrate for a shorter period of time. See also *Heat Transfer Printing*.

Hot Press

In *binding and finishing*, to perform *embossing* or *die-stamping* with heated *die*s.

Hot Spot

In a video image, an extreme highlight, caused by the reflection of light.

Hot Stamping

In *binding and finishing*, *die-stamping* performed using heated *die*s. Hot stamping is often performed on plastic materials, such as *rigid-plastic box*es.

Hot Text

In multimedia, a precursor to *hypertext* in which a bold, colored, or otherwise distinctive word can be clicked on with the pointer, initiating an activity.

Hot Type

Metal type produced by mechanical typesetting machines.

Hot Zone

Alternate term for *hyphenation zone*. See *Hyphenation Zone*.

Hot-Melt Adhesive

Any adhesive material that is a solid at room temperature and must be heated in order to be applied. Hot-melt adhesives dry by cooling back into a solid. See *Adhesive*.

Hot-Melt Ink

A type of ink used in *screen printing* that is melted to the proper printing consistency by means of an electrically heated screen, rather than a *thinner* or other *solvent*. See *Cold-Set Ink*.

Hot-Metal Composition

The setting of type either by hand or by using a linecasting device, such as a *Linotype*.

Hot-Metal Type

Type cast by pouring molten metal in a brass letterform matrix. An incorrect term for *foundry type*.

Hot-Temperature Adhesive

An *adhesive* substance that can be used to bond either itself or another material or substance to a hot surface. See also *Cold Temperature Adhesive*.

Hot-Wax Screen

A type of screen used in *screen printing* that can be heated electrically for use with *hot melt ink*s.

Hot-Weather Scumming

Alternate term for the press and printing condition known as *tinting*, especially when it tends to increase in occurrence as the temperature of the *fountain solution* increases. See *Tinting*.

HotJava

In *World Wide Web* terminology, a web *browser* developed by Sun Microsystems to play interactive applications written in *Java*. See *Java*.

Hourglass

In computing, especially by means of the *Windows* operating system, an icon that replaces the *pointer* when the computer is performing a function and cannot receive new input.

On the *Macintosh*, a similar icon is the *watch*.

House Style

Any page design, *type specification*s, etc., used repeatedly.

Houston Automatic Spooling Program (HASP)

In computing, IBM software that controls a variety of computer functions and operations, such as *spooling* as well as conducting communications between processors and *Remote Job Entry* stations.

HP-UX

In computing, the version of the *UNIX* operating system developed by Hewlett-Packard. See *UNIX*.

HPFS

Abbreviation for *High-Performance File System*. See *High-Performance File System (HPFS)*.

HPG

In computing, a *file extension* used to denote a file saved in *HPGL*.

HPGL

Abbreviation for *Hewlett-Packard Graphics Language*. See *Hewlett-Packard Graphics Language (HPGL)*.

HPIB

Abbreviation for *Hewlett-Packard Interface Bus*. See *GPIB*.

HQS

Abbreviation for *High Quality Screening*. See *High Quality Screening (HQS)*.

HSB

Abbreviation for *hue*, *saturation*, and *brightness*. See *HLS*.

HSL

See *HLS*.

HSM

Abbreviation for *hierarchical storage management*. See *Hierarchical Storage Management (HSM)*.

HSV

Abbreviation for *hue*, *saturation*, and *value*. It is essentially an alternate term for *HLS*. See *HLS*.

HTML

Abbreviation for *Hypertext Markup Language*. See *Hypertext Markup Language (HTML)*.

HTTP

Abbreviation for *Hypertext Transport Protocol*. See *Hypertext Transport Protocol (HTTP)*.

Hub

In networking, any system or other equipment that acts as the point of distribution of a network, all terminals, output devices, etc., connected to each other through the hub. A network utilizing a hub from which workstations radiate is known as a *star* configuration.

An *active hub* boosts signals transmitted from point to point on the network, while a *passive hub* merely relays transmissions to and from the *server*. Also known as a *concatenator*.

Hub Polling

In networking, a means of *polling* in which one network *node* sends an inquiry to the next node in the sequence to determine if it has data to transmit. The asked node then asks the *next* node in sequence, and so on. See *Polling*.

Hue

The primary and most basic attribute of a *color* that makes it distinct from another color, determined by its dominant wavelength of light on the *visible spectrum*. In ink manufacturing and color matching, hue is more commonly known as *shade*. Two other aspects of color, in addition to hue, are *value* and *chroma*. (See *Color Mixing, Ink*.)

Hue Angle

On the *CIE color space*, the angle of the dominant wavelength of a hue.

Hue Circle

Alternate term for a *color circle*. See *Color Circle*.

Hue Error

A measure of the degree of contamination of one *process color* ink by another. For example, often a purportedly *magenta* ink will appear more distinctly red than a pure magenta (which is more of a purple-red) would, because of contamination by yellow pigments. Software (or other means) used to generate *color separation*s needs to take hue error into account, commonly accomplished by reducing the *dot size*s of the unwanted shades. The hue error for a particular ink can be calculated by making three *densitometer* measurements—one with a red filter, one with a green filter, and one with a blue filter—and recording the high, middle, and low densities.

Hue error can be calculated by using the formula:

$$\text{Hue error (\%)} = \frac{M - L}{H - L} \times 100$$

where H equals the highest density, M equals the middle density, and L equals the lowest density.

Huffman Encoding

A popular *lossless* algorithm used for *data compression*. Essentially, Huffman encoding replaces frequently occurring code strings with shorter ones, often by means of a *look-up table* explaining what the shorter codes mean. See *Data Compression*.

Humectant

A substance (such as glycerin) added to a printing ink to prevent the loss of moisture.

Humidity

General term for the presence of water vapor in the air, commonly expressed as the amount of moisture in the air. Control of humidity is important in the printing process, and is a vital concern in the papermaking process. Because of paper's *hygroscopic* properties, it adds or loses moisture readily, depending on both its *moisture content* and the moisture content of the surrounding air. (See *Dimensional Stability*, *Moisture Content*.)

Humidity can be measured in terms of specific humidity (the ratio of the mass of the moisture vapor in the air to the total mass of air and water vapor), *absolute humidity* (the mass of the water vapor present in the atmosphere), or *relative humidity* (the amount of water vapor in the air expressed as a percentage of the total amount of water vapor the air could hold at that particular temperature). A related term is *dew point*, the temperature at which the air needs to be cooled for it to become saturated and for dew to form. Relative humidity is the most important measurement of the humidity as it relates to paper and its properties. (See *Relative Humidity*.)

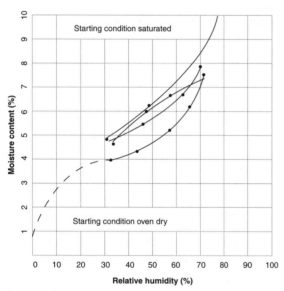

Effects of changes in relative humidty on the moisture content of paper.

Hung Punctuation

Alternate term for *hanging punctuation*. See *Hanging Punctuation*.

Hung-In

In *binding and finishing*, descriptive of a book which has been glued only along the spine.

Hunter L,a,b Color Solid

A three-dimensional *color* model, similar to the *CIE Color Space*, that utilizes three values to plot a particular color sample on a three-dimensional coordinate system. See *Hunter L,a,b Values*.

Hunter L,a,b Values

Scales for the accurate measurement of *color* developed by Dr. Richard Hunter, providing an alternative to the *CIE Lab L*a*b* scale*. The Hunter L,a,b scales, like the CIE scales, utilize three values to create a three-axis graph on which the values can be plotted and color determined. The three values utilized by Hunter are *L*, or luminosity (the degree of lightness from black to white), ± *a*, the degree of redness or greenness on a scale from red to green, and ± *b*, the degree of yellowness to blueness on a scale from yellow to blue. These scales are based on the perception of color as a series of three oppositions: black vs. white, red vs. green, and yellow vs. blue. These scales are utilized to provide an accurate and consistent description of color.

Hybrid Computer

A computer incorporating both *analog* as well as *digital* components, allowing for the processing of both types of data signals. A hybrid computer includes *digital-to-analog converter*s and *analog-to-digital converter*s to effectively handle both types of data.

Hybrid Network

A *local area network* that comprises a variety of different topologies and access methods. See *Topology*.

Hybrid Plate

A type of printing plate used in *offset lithography* comprising a metal base coated with two layers of a photosensitive coating. The bottom coating is essentially the same as that used on a *photopolymer plate*, a substance that when exposed to light forms hard, durable, heavy molecules (polymers). The top coating is similar to that used to coat a *silver halide plate*, an emulsion that is exposed and developed much like a photographic negative, either optically using light or by lasers directed by computer information. During the burning of hybrid plates, the top layer is exposed either via light shined through a photographic negative or with lasers, and the bottom layer is exposed to ultraviolet light in the image areas of the original. After burning, the top layer is completely removed, and the bottom layer is processed to create the image area/nonimage area dichotomy necessary for lithographic printing. (See *Plate: Offset Lithography*.)

Hybrid Trapping

In digital prepress, a means of ensuring the *registration* of multi-color images performed on digital systems in which *vector*-based graphics are *rasterized* (or converted to *bit maps*), analyzed for potential *trapping* problems, and new objects are added to the original file where needed. Hybrid trapping is a combination of ***vector trapping*** and ***raster trapping***. See ***Trapping***.

Hydration

In papermaking, subjecting paper ***pulp*** to an increased degree of ***refining*** to increase the ***moisture content*** of the paper.

Hydrocarbon

Any of a class of organic compounds containing only carbon and hydrogen atoms, the simplest hydrocarbon being methane (chemical formula CH_4). The different varieties of hydrocarbon—be they alkanes (or paraffins), alkynes (or acetylenes), alkenes (or olefins), or aromatics (such as benzene)—describe different numbers and arrangements of the carbon and hydrogen atoms. Many hydrocarbons are used as ***solvent***s in printing inks, and form the starting point for many other organic compounds, such as alcohols, ethers, esters, amines, ketones, aldehydes, etc.

Hydrogen Peroxide

A compound—chemical formula H_2O_2—used as a ***hardener*** for ***screen printing*** stencils.

Hydrophilic

A quality of certain papers, components of paper, or non-image areas of lithographic plates that causes them to absorb and/or be receptive to water.

In ***offset lithography***, a hydrophilic substance is likely to be receptive to water and ***fountain solution***s and repellent to oils and oil-based inks. Hydrophilic substances are also ***lipophobic***. (See also ***Hydrophobic***.)

Hydrophobic

A quality of certain papers, components of paper, or the image areas of lithographic plates that causes them to repel water. Hydrophobic substances are likely to be receptive to oils and oil-based inks. Hydrophobic substances are also called ***oleophilic*** or ***lipophilic***. (See also ***Hydrophilic***.)

Hygroexpansivity

A measure of a paper's expansion or reduction in size due to variations in its ***moisture content***, expressed as a percentage of the paper's original size. (See ***Dimensional Stability*** and ***Moisture Content***.)

Hygroscopic

Readily absorbing moisture from the air; used to describe paper. A paper's primary constituents, ***cellulose*** fibers have a strong affinity for water (which is how plants and trees—composed primarily of cellulose—survive). Changes in the ***relative humidity*** of a paper's environment can result in a gain or loss of moisture on the part of the paper, which affects its ***dimensional stability***, or its ability to retain its original width and/or length. Such changes in size have deleterious effects on many printing processes. As paper gains moisture, the cellulose fibers increase primar-

ily in width (but not as much in length), so paper tends to expand in the ***cross-grain direction*** (see ***Grain***). (See also ***Dimensional Stability***.)

Hypermedia

Essentially, the combination of ***hypertext*** and ***multimedia***, or an application that allows hypertext links to retrieve and view not only text and graphics, but also animation, video, and audio.

Hypertext

A type of text that can be used interactively, often used on the ***World Wide Web*** and in multimedia presentations. Essentially, predetermined "links" (indicated by colored, bold, or underlined words) are used to access different data files. The link is effected by means of clicking on the highlighted word or link. Based on the principle of ***hot text***, hypertext is the foundation of ***HTML*** (or ***hypertext markup language***), a type of programming language used to link data files.

Hypertext Link

A connection of one data or text file to another, accessed interactively by means of ***hypertext***. See ***Hypertext***.

Hypertext Markup Language (HTML)

On the ***World Wide Web*** (the graphics-based portion of the ***Internet***), a standard ***hypertext*** language used to create Web pages and other hypertext-based documents. Essentially, an HTML document creates text, as well as codes corresponding to linked files, which can be graphics, video, audio, or other pages. Thus, when you access a particular Web page, the pictures you view actually exist in separate files, which the HTML code imports from those linked files. The most notable feature of an HTML document is highlighted text (usually blue, but that depends on one's particular Web ***browser***), which, when clicked on, opens another document. That document can be on the same computer system, or on a computer system thousands of miles away. Essentially, the HTML code includes the ***Universal Resource Locator (URL)*** for the linked document and the ***Hypertext Transport Protocol (HTTP)*** controls the manner in which linked documents are accessed and opened. Since HTML is a markup language and not a program per se, any program capable of producing text can be used to create a Web page, although there are a panoply of programs on the market to facilitate the construction of Web pages. Many desktop publishing programs also now feature the ability to add HTML coding to documents, allowing pages to be prepared both for print and electronic distribution essentially simultaneously.

Hypertext Transport Protocol (HTTP)

On the ***World Wide Web*** (the graphics-based portion of the ***Internet***), the ***protocol*** used to manage the means by which one ***hypertext*** document is linked to another. The term *HTTP* is perhaps most familiar as the first four characters of any Web address (called a ***Universal Resource Locator***), which is the means by which a Web ***browser*** is instructed to use HTTP to access a ***hypertext link***.

Hyphen

In typography, a very small dash (-) used to break words or syllables at the ends of lines, or to connect parts of compound or connected words. It is used in contrast to an ***em dash*** or an ***en dash***. See ***Dashes***.

Hyphenation

In typography, the breaking of a word into syllables and inserting hyphens, manually or automatically, so that word spaces remain consistent—within prescribed limits—for proper justification.

There are several basic rules for hyphenation:

1. There must be at least two characters on both sides of the hyphen.
2. Numerals should not be hyphenated except, in an emergency, at a comma point.
3. It is not good practice to hyphenate in a headline.
4. A one-syllable word should never be hyphenated, though some systems will certainly try.
5. A word should be divided on a double consonant, unless the word root ends with a double consonant (e.g., miss-ing, not mis-sing).
6. More than three hyphens should not be used in a row. Too many hyphens in a row (or too many hyphens in a text block) is referred to as ***pig bristles***.

An incorrect word division is called a ***bad break***. For maximum legibility, hyphenation should be used as little as possible.

A ***discretionary hyphen (DH)*** is inserted in a word during input to give the system a specific point to hyphenate, and that point will take precedence over any logic-generated point. Often, a DH at the beginning of a word tells the system not to hyphenate the word at all.

Logic hyphenation refers to a system where the computer is programmed with certain logical rules for hyphenating words at the ends of lines. However, no program is infallible. Hence, the need for an "exception dictionary," a collection of the program's incorrectly hyphenated words held in the computer's memory. With luck, the system will search the exception dictionary before consulting the logic program.

Hyphenation is often considered together with ***justification***, forming a joint concept called ***hyphenation and justification (H & J)***.

Hyphenation and Justification (H & J)

In typography, the practice of setting copy so that the lines are ***justified***, or align evenly on both the left and the right,

accomplished by expanding or contracting the word spaces and by hyphenating words at the end of a line as needed. (Both are separate processes; see ***Hyphenation*** and ***Justification***.) In most typesetting systems, both terms are used together, as one enhances the efficacy of the other.

Hyphenation Dictionary

In typography, a ***dictionary*** containing a list of words and their correct ***hyphenation***. See ***Dictionary***.

Hyphenation Zone

In typography, a "zone" established by a typesetting device or software toward the end of a line, within which the system can hyphenate words. A hyphenation zone is commonly used in ***ragged right*** copy (***justified*** copy has its own set of problems). The setting of a hyphenation zone is a way of controlling the number of hyphens that will appear in the set copy. Also known as a ***hot zone***.

Hyphenless

In typography, ***justification*** performed only by adjusting the word and ***letterspacing***, without hyphenating words at the ends of lines.

Hypo

A term for sodium thiosulfate, a chemical used as a ***fixer*** in photography. The term *hypo* is short for *hyposulfite*, as the chemical is also known as sodium hyposulfite. See ***Fixer***.

Hysteresis

The difference in paper's ***moisture content*** at a particular ***relative humidity*** due to changes in the paper's conditioning. The primary constituents of paper, fibers of ***cellulose***, have a strong affinity for water and will gain (or lose) it readily, depending on the amount of moisture in the air. For a particular paper, its moisture content at increasing relative humidities can be plotted on a graph, and a moisture content curve drawn. However, a paper's moisture curve will vary, depending on whether the paper has started at a high relative humidity and then been conditioned to lower relative humidities or whether it has started at a low relative humidity and then been conditioned to higher ones. Thus, two papers of the same type will possess different moisture contents at the same relative humidity depending on its previous "moisture history." This difference, hysteresis, is important when determining a paper's ***equilibrium moisture content***. (See also ***Moisture Content***.)

Hz

Abbreviation for ***hertz***, a measurement of ***frequency***. See ***Hertz***.

I

I, i

The ninth letter of the Latin and English alphabets. The form of the capital "I" has its origins in the North Semitic *yodh* (a consonant, equivalent to the English "Y"), which mutated into the Greek vowel *iota*. The form of the lowercase "i" was first written with a dot in Medieval Latin, to distinguish it from the lowercase "m" and "n" (which at the time utilized three and two—respectively—vertical strokes without the connecting curves).

| Egyptian 3000 BC | Sinai 1850 BC | Phoenician 1200 BC | Greek 600 BC | Roman AD 114 |

The evolution of the letter I.

IAB

Abbreviation for **Internet Architecture Board**. See **Internet Architecture Board (IAB)**.

IBM

Abbreviation for *International Business Machines* Corporation, the Armonk, New York-based computer manufacturer. Long a maker of high-end **mainframe** computers, in the early 1980s the company introduced the IBM **PC**, or **personal computer**, a low-cost desktop system that stimulated the explosion of the PC market. It used as its operating system a version of **DOS** (called **PC-DOS**) developed by Microsoft, and other computer manufacturers—in particular, Compaq, Packard Bell, and many others—also arranged to license a version of DOS (called **MS-DOS**) and reverse engineer the PC architecture, resulting in a vast **clone** market. (See **IBM-Compatible Computer**.) Although the clone machines, being lower-priced than IBM's devices, captured a greater share of the PC market than IBM, the first PC—and later systems—set the standard for personal computers.

IBM Cabling System

Alternate term for **type 1–9 cable**. See **Type 1–9 Cable**.

IBM-Compatible Computer

Any computer manufactured by a company other than **IBM** that functions virtually the same as an IBM **PC** and that can share software with IBM PCs. IBM-compatible computers are now referred to generically as "PCs," usually to distinguish them from the Apple **Macintosh** when describing a particular computer **platform**. PCs commonly use either **MS-DOS** or **Microsoft Windows** (or both) as an operating system, although IBM has developed its own operating system, called OS/2. IBM-compatibles are the

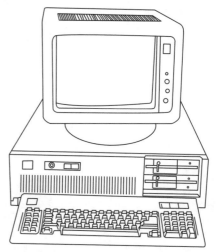

An IBM-compatible computer.

most commonly used computers, primarily because of their low cost and the wide availability of software, although ease of use is easily surpassed by the Macintosh.

IC

Abbreviation for **integrated circuit**. See **Integrated Circuit**.

Ice Cap

A cooling unit installed in computers running with an Intel 80486 **microprocessor**, used to prevent overheating. Fast processors have the potential to generate heat that can raise the temperature above 85°C, which can promote system malfunctions or even a breakdown. The ice cap keeps the processor at a constant temperature of 20–25°C.

Icicles

In **gravure** printing, a term referring to dried ink hanging stalactite-like from any of the parts of the **gravure cylinder** assembly.

ICMP

Abbreviation for **Internet Control Message Protocol**. See **Internet Control Message Protocol (ICMP)**.

Icon

Generally speaking, a simple pictorial representation of an object or concept, usually comprising an image that readily conveys what it represents.

In Russia, icons are portraits of religious figures, such as Christ, while here in the West in the 20th century, icons are used to convey such things as traffic laws (the octagonal shape and red color of a stop sign), conveniences (the symbols found on rest room doors), etc.

In computers, icons are the basic elements that constitute a ***graphical user interface (GUI)***, which is also sometimes called an ***iconic interface***. Files, programs, utilities, disks, etc., are represented as pictorial symbols—a document looks like a small piece of paper, a directory or subdirectory looks like a manila folder, a disk looks like a disk, a delete function looks like a trash can, etc.—which can be moved about the screen, copied to other media, deleted, or clicked on (using a mouse). Various applications use icons to represent menu items; a symbol of a printer may represent a print function, for example.

The goal of a good icon is to convey what it means directly and simply. As we know from experience, however, this is not always the case.

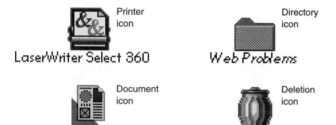

Printer icon
LaserWriter Select 360

Directory icon
Web Problems

Document icon
Letter I

Deletion icon
Trash

Icons used with a graphical user interface.

Iconic Interface
Alternate term for a ***graphical user interface (GUI)***, especially one that represents screen elements, files, and menu items as ***icon***s. See ***Graphical User Interface (GUI)*** and ***Icon***.

I.D.
Abbreviation for the *inside diameter* of a cylindrical object, such as the core of a roll of paper (or other ***substrate***) or a press cylinder or roller. See also ***O.D.***

IDE
Abbreviation for ***Integrated Drive Electronics***. See ***Integrated Drive Electronics (IDE)***.

Ideogram
A picture or symbol that represents an idea, concept, or noun. Chinese and Japanese, for example, are languages made up entirely of ideographs. Common ideographs in modern life are a skull and crossbones (representing poison) or the symbols found on rest room doors. Also known as an *ideograph*. See ***Pictograph***.

Idiot Mode
In typesetting, any mode in which the user does not have to make the line-ending decisions.

Idler Roller
On a ***web press***, any free, rotating roller used to support and guide the paper web. Also known as a ***web lead roller***.

An example of an ideogram indicating that the motorist is approaching a school crosswalk.

Idle Time
The period of time that a computer system (or any electronic or mechanical device) is available but not in use.

IEC
Abbreviation for ***International Electrotechnical Commission***. See ***International Electrotechnical Commission (IEC)***.

IEEE
Abbreviation for ***Institute of Electrical and Electronic Engineers***. See ***Institute of Electrical and Electronic Engineers (IEEE)***.

IEEE 802.3
In networking, a standard for ***Ethernet*** devised by the ***IEEE*** that defines a ***CSMA/CD*** access method on a ***local area network*** with a ***bus*** topology.

IEEE 802.4
In networking, a standard devised by the ***IEEE*** that defines a ***token passing*** access method on a ***local area network*** with a ***bus*** topology.

IEEE 802.5
In networking, a standard devised by the ***IEEE*** that defines a ***token passing*** access method on a ***local area network*** with a ***ring*** topology.

IEEE 802.12
In networking, the standard for 100Base-VG networking.

IEEE Project 802
A group set up by the ***IEEE*** to develop the IEEE 802 set of ***local area network*** standards.

IETF
Abbreviation for ***Internet Engineering Task Force***. See ***Internet Engineering Task Force (IETF)***.

IFEN

Abbreviation for *intercompany file exchange network*. See *Intercompany File Exchange Network (IFEN)*.

IFS

Abbreviation for *installable file system*. See *Installable File System (IFS)*.

IGES

Abbreviation for *initial graphics exchange specification*. See *Initial Graphics Exchange Specification (IGES)*.

Illumination

An exposure of light to an object.

In layout and design, *illumination* refers to the use of any non-text material (such as a drawing, photograph, or other decorative element) to enhance or clarify written material. Historically, *illumination* referred to the decorative illustration of handwritten manuscripts prepared by medieval scribes and monks.

An example of the use of illumination to enhance or clarify written material.

Illumination Model

Alternate term for a *reflectance model*. See *Reflectance Model*.

Illustrator

Generally speaking, any graphic artist who has the ability to generate visual images using pen, paint, computer graphics programs, collages, etc., to communicate a pictorial message or visually complement accompanying text material. An illustrator is distinguished from a photographer in that the former typically relies on the generation of images by hand (using a variety of mechanical and/or electronic tools), rather than photographing something.

The term *Illustrator* (capitalized) also refers to a popular software program developed by Adobe Systems, Inc., that allows those who have mastered the program's intricacies to create *vector*-based line art and illustrations, which can then be saved as *EPS* files and imported into page makeup (or other) programs. The earliest versions of Illustrator pioneered the use of vector-based drawings and although many similar programs are currently on the market, Adobe Illustrator is still the most versatile and complex. Versions of Illustrator are available for most major computer *platform*s.

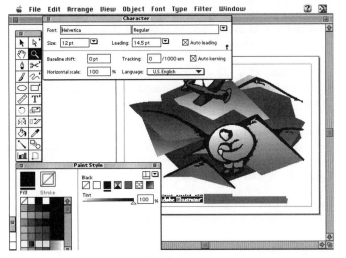

Adobe Illustrator.

IMA

Abbreviation for the *International MIDI Association*. See *International MIDI Association (IMA)*.

Image

Any pictorial representation of an object, be it a type character, a photograph, a drawing, etc., that exists either in printed form, on a *glass disc* (as a font image used in phototypesetting), or digital form. The generation and/or reproduction of images is known as *imaging*.

In data processing, an *image* is any array of data that has been copied from one storage location to another. For example, a *disc image* is a copy of the *bit* pattern of a *CD-ROM*.

Image Area

Any portion of a photographic negative or positive, printing plate, **gravure cylinder**, offset **blanket**, **stencil**, or other image-carrying surface that contains the image(s) to be printed.

Image Area Piling

A form of **piling** characterized by an accumulation of paper debris (such as **lint**, particles of **filler**, or dislodged bits of **coating**) that collects on the image areas of the blanket or plate and collects ink, and the mixture of debris and ink makes the ink tackier and attracts more debris. If the image area piling becomes severe enough, it can affect **print quality**, especially if it occurs in halftones. A chief cause of image area piling is using a paper with low **pick resistance**, some of the piling being bits of paper or coatings picked from the paper surface by the ink. Excessively tacky inks also contribute to image area piling. (See also **Piling**.)

Image Assembly

Alternate term for **stripping**. See **Stripping**.

Image Bitmap

A digital representation of an image, or an image existing as a pattern of **bit**s, each of which is mapped to a specific **pixel**. See **Bitmap**.

Image Board

In computing, an accelerator board that expedites the compression, decompression, and processing of images.

Image Compression

Any **data compression** algorithm designed and used specifically for the compression of images, such as **JPEG** or **LZW**. See **Data Compression**.

Image Data

Alternate term for **raster data**. See **Raster Data**.

Image Digitizer

In a video camera, a **CCD array** that uses electron beams to convert light into a set of electronic signals.

Image Graphics

A computer display of a **bitmapped** image. See **Bitmap**.

Image Management

All of the processes involved in keeping track of the location of a particular image on a **CEPS** or other such system, as a means of ensuring that the image can be located when needed.

Image Memory

In digital imaging, the portion of a computer's memory that contains the data pertaining to a particular image's **bitmap**. See **Bitmap**.

Image Packet

In networking and telecommunications, a **packet** of compressed data ready for transmission.

Image Pacs

The specifications of the five **resolution**s of images supplied on a **Photo CD**. These resolutions are (in **pixel**s): 128×192, 256×384, 512×768, 1024×1536, and 2048×3072. See **Photo CD**.

Image Processing

The editing and manipulation of **digital image**s as a means of altering their characteristics, depending upon the output requirements, aesthetic considerations, or operator whim. Image processing can involve such things as improving image **contrast**, making **color correction**s, applying any special effects, if desired, or changing any of hundreds of different aspects of an image, depending upon operator judgment.

Imager

Alternate term for a **digital camera**. See **Digital Camera**.

Image Recorder

A type of **film recorder** used to record a digital image as a 35-mm slide or a 4×5-in. **transparency**. See **Film Recorder**.

Image Scanner

A type of **scanner** that only recognizes the dot pattern of an original image and saves it as a **bitmap**, as opposed to a **text scanner**, which recognizes scanned text and can save it as an **ASCII** text file. See **Scanner**.

Imagesetter

A **high-resolution** output device that takes **bitmapped** data generated by a **raster image processor**—such as a digital text or image file—and writes it to film or paper, commonly by means of a **laser** that exposes the film or paper line by line. An imagesetter is commonly distinguished from a typesetter in that the former can also

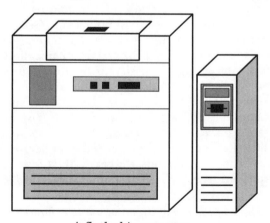

A flatbed imagesetter.

output high-resolution *halftone*s and other graphics, as well as type. Imagesetters are also used to output *color separation*s. Imagesetters are considered *high-end* devices and come in essentially two varieties: *drum image-setter*s and *flatbed imagesetter*s. Of the two, the former is deemed to produce the higher quality output.

Image Setting

The setting of type, and the output of graphics and *halftone*s using digital means, as opposed to setting type and exposing halftones photographically.

Imaging

The capture and/or generation of images by a wide variety of means, be it photographic or digital. See *Photography*, *Digital Photography*, and *Scanning*.

Imaging Area

Alternate term for the *live area* of a page. See *Live Area*.

IMG

A *file format* used for *bitmapped* images created in programs running on the *graphical environment manager (GEM)* windowing system. See *GEM*.

Imitation Gold Ink

A type of ink designed to impart a metallic gold luster to a printed image, utilizing aluminum powder to provide the sheen and a yellow *colorant* to provide the gold hue. "Non-imitation" *gold ink*s use bronze or copper flakes. (See *Metallic Powders*.)

Imitation Gold Leaf

In *binding and finishing*, a thin sheet of brass used in place of *gold leaf* (for reasons of economy) for cover decorating and *foil stamping*. See also *Gold Leaf*.

Imitation Parchment

A type of paper manufactured to resemble the mottled surface properties and texture of ancient *parchment* (which was actually the split and rubbed skin of sheep), or the appearance of modern *vegetable parchment*, by producing paper with a *wild formation*, or an uneven distribution of fibers. It is used for wine lists, menus in expensive restaurants, certificates, diplomas, coupons, or any other end use requiring a dignified paper.

IMPACT

Abbreviation for *Information Marketing Policy Actions*. See *Information Marketing Policy Actions (IMPACT)*.

Impact Printer

A general term describing a computer printer that images paper by striking an inked ribbon with a relief typeform, as opposed to a *nonimpact printer*. Two common examples of impact printers are *daisy-wheel printer*s and *band printer*s.

Impedance

A property of any electrical or electronic cable or wire that describes the cabling medium's apparent resistance to the flow of a current (in particular, alternating current) at a specific frequency. Impedance combines the properties of capacitance, inductance, and resistance, and it is measured in ohms.

Implementation

In computer software development, the final stage in which software is installed in hardware for ultimate distribution to users. The term *implementation* also refers to the act of adding new hardware, software, or features to a pre-existing system or application.

Import

To input data from a computer file created in one software application to another software application. The imported data thus needs to be in a format that can be read by different software applications. Many page makeup applications—such as *QuarkXPress* or Adobe *PageMaker*—allow importing of various types of files, as a means of assembling both text and graphics in a single file. See also *Export*.

Import/Export Capabilities

Features available in many different software applications that describe a program's ability to *import* data saved in different *file format*s or to *export* data in a particular file format for importation into a different program.

Imposition

The positioning of pages on a press sheet in such a manner that when the sheet is folded into a *signature* and cut, the pages will be in the correct sequence. Imposition involves not just the correct positioning of pages on the same side of the sheet, but also the *back printing*, or the pages printed on the back of the sheet. Back-printed pages can be oriented in a variety of ways; *head-to-head imposition* involves aligning the back printing so that the top of the page on the front is opposite the top of the page on the reverse; *head-to-foot imposition* involves aligning the back printing such that the top of the page on the front is opposite the bottom of the page on the reverse; *head-to-side imposition* involves back printing that is at a right angle to the printing on the front. *Coming-and-going imposition* is a type of page sequencing in which the *recto* (or right-hand) pages are in numerical sequence from the front of the book to the back, but the *verso* (or left-hand) pages are sequenced such that when the book is flipped over, they are then in sequence from the back of the book to the front.

Based on the size of the press and the press sheets to be used for a particular print job, film *negative*s or *positive*s of pages are stripped into the proper imposition during the film assembly stage of *prepress*. Newer digital prepress processes also allow the output of properly imposed pages as

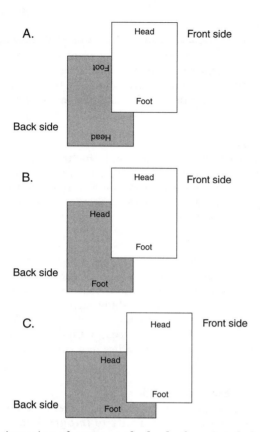

The orientation of pages on the back of a printed sheet: (A) head-to-back imposition, (B) head-to-head imposition, and (C) head-to-side imposition.

film negatives directly from an *imagesetter*. (See also *Stripping*, *Prepress: Graphic Arts Photography and Flat Assembly*, and *Prepress: Digital Prepress*.)

Imposition Layout

In *prepress*, a layout prepared by the *stripper* that illustrates how the page elements and whole pages need to be assembled in order to meet the printing, folding, and binding requirements. The imposition layout thus indicates page sequence, margins, trim marks, fold lines, press *gripper margin*s, *register marks*, etc.

Impression

The pressure necessary to transfer a printed image from a printing plate, *blanket*, or other image carrier to the paper or other *substrate*. The term *impression* is also used to refer to a printed image.

Impression Bar

A small-diameter (typically ¼–½ in.) steel rod used on some *flexographic* presses in place of a conventional *impression cylinder*. In some cases, the *substrate* to be printed is porous enough to allow significant *strike-through* of ink, which then can collect on the impression cylinder. Ink buildup can result in a variety of printing defects or in dam-

age to the plate. The use of a stationary steel bar eliminates the problem of ink buildup since, as it does not rotate, the substrate is constantly wiping the bar clean. A flexo impression bar is also known as a *tympan bar*. (See *Impression Cylinder* and *Flexography: Printing Unit*.)

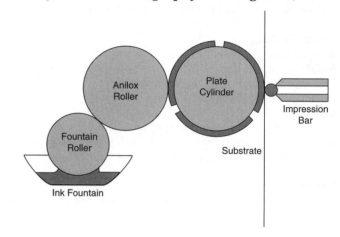

An impression bar, occasionally used in lieu of an impression cylinder on a flexo press.

Impression Cylinder

The part of an offset lithographic printing press that carries the paper or other *substrate* through the printing unit and beneath the inked press blanket. The impression cylinder also provides a hard backing that allows the blanket to press a strong, solid impression on the paper. (Hence an impression cylinder is also known as a *back cylinder* or *backup roll*.) Like the *plate cylinder* and *blanket cylinder*, the impression cylinder has a *cylinder gap* interrupting its circumference, in which is located the *gripper*, a shaft containing fingers that grasp and hold the incoming sheet of paper and hold it in register under the blanket, before releasing the printed sheet to be sent to the next printing unit or *delivery pile*.

Unlike the plate and blanket cylinders, the surface of the impression cylinder possesses no *undercut*, and the true diameter of the cylinder is equal to the diameter of the *bearer*s of the other two cylinders. On the impression cylinder, it is the *bearers* that are undercut.

The position of the impression cylinder with respect to the blanket cylinder can be controlled in one of two ways. On some presses, the impression cylinder is mounted on eccentric bushings, an impression lever being used to shift the impression cylinder away from or toward the blanket. On other presses, it is the blanket cylinder that has the eccentric bushings, one set controlling the bearer pressure between the plate and blanket cylinders, and a second set controlling the distance between the blanket cylinder and the impression cylinder.

Controlling the distance between the impression and blanket cylinder bearers is set in much the same way as that between the plate and blanket cylinders in a *non-bearer-contact press*. The manufacturer's recommended gap between the bearers of the two cylinders is determined by feeler gauges that are inserted between the bearers on a properly packed press.

In some press configurations, a **common impression cylinder** is used. A common impression cylinder is an impression cylinder that contacts more than one blanket, passing a single sheet beneath successive blankets, commonly used in multicolor printing. (See **Blanket Cylinder**, **Plate Cylinder**, and **Offset Lithography: Printing Unit**.)

The term *impression cylinder* is also used to refer to the *impression roller* of a *gravure* printing press. See **Impression Roller**.

On a **flexographic press**, an *impression cylinder* is used much the same way, as a hard backing for the substrate, which is also in contact with the **plate cylinder**. The flexo impression cylinder is smooth and highly polished, and its speed of rotation must be the same as that of the plate cylinder and the **anilox roller**, otherwise smearing and other printing defects can occur. As with other cylinders and rollers, the roundness of the impression cylinder is crucial. The **total indicated runout (TIR)** (a measure of a cylinder's **out-of-roundness**) must not exceed 0.0005 in., otherwise the cylinder will rotate with a slight or pronounced "bump" (depending on the degree of out-of-roundness), causing a variety of printing defects. Another aspect of the impression cylinder that must be checked is the extent to which it is parallel with the plate cylinder. Since the impression cylinder is commonly the only cylinder that cannot be moved within its support frames, all other cylinders and rollers must be set parallel to it, to ensure uniform printing pressure in the nip between the impression and plate cylinders.

Some flexographic printing presses replace the impression cylinder with an **impression bar** (also called a **tympan bar**). In some cases, porous substrates are printed, through which the ink seeps and collects on the impression cylinder. Ink buildup then can affect print quality, or damage the plate. Flexographic presses on which ink **strikethrough** is likely to be significant use a small-diameter (typically ¼–½ in.) steel rod as a firm backing for the substrate. Since the impression bar does not rotate, it is constantly wiped clean by the moving substrate. In some impression-bar configurations, a hollow bar is cooled with water or other means to prevent heat buildup and the consequent expansion of the metal.

Many flexographic presses (in particular, multicolor ones) use a **common impression cylinder**, a large-diameter impression cylinder surrounded by two to six plate cylinders. The substrate is carried around the impression cylinder where it contacts each printing unit in sequence, which lay down successive colors in essentially one pass. Such a press is known as a **central impression press**. (See also **Plate Cylinder: Flexography** and **Flexography: Press Configurations**.)

An impression cylinder is also used for similar purposes in **rotary press**es and **flatbed press**es used in **letterpress** printing. See **Letterpress**.

Impression Nip

The nip between the **blanket cylinder** and the **impression cylinder** on an offset press or, in other words, the space in which a press sheet is passed to be printed. (See **Offset Lithography: Printing Unit**.)

On a **gravure** press, the impression nip is the line of contact between the image-carrying **gravure cylinder** and the resilient **impression roller**, through which the substrate passes. (See **Gravure** and **Impression Roller**.)

On a **flexographic** press, the impression nip is the line between the **plate cylinder** and the **impression cylinder**, through which the substrate passes. See **Flexography**.

Impression Roller

A resilient cylinder or roller found on a **gravure** press forming a nip with the **gravure cylinder** through which the **substrate** passes. (This nip is referred to as the **impression zone**.) The impression roller (typically located above the gravure, or image-carrying, cylinder) forms a hard yet resilient backing for the substrate. Its rubbery surface facilitates squeezing the substrate into the individual inked cells of the gravure cylinder where ink is transferred by capillary action.

The impression roller is a steel tube covered by an elastic polymer, such as natural rubber, or synthetic rubbers such as **neoprene**, **Buna N**, and polyurethanes (the coating having a thickness varying from ½ to ¾ in.). It is driven by frictional forces generated by contact with the motor-driven gravure cylinder. The impression roller is usually smaller than the gravure cylinder, and consequently runs at a higher RPM than the gravure cylinder. The pressure at the nip also causes a deformation of the resilient surface of the impression roller, which slows down its rotation at the nip. Consequently, rotation of the impression roller is not uniform, and the velocity differential also puts additional strain on the web. The pressure of the impression roller against the gravure cylinder can be adjusted, and printers commonly adjust it to the least amount of pressure needed to generate the desired print quality, as increased pressure causes structural damage to the press bearings, the gravure cylinder, and the roller covering. The increased frictional forces also produce more heat, which can adversely affect print quality. Another impression roller setting factor is **wrap**, or how much contact the **web** of substrate has with the impression roller, described in terms of the angle formed by the web before and after the impression zone. A wrap of 120° is typical, but varies according to the substrate and the diameter of the roller; a 4- to 6-in.-diameter roller will typically have a wrap of greater than 90°; a larger-diameter roller and less wrap is desirable for heavier stock.

One type of gravure impression roller uses a system called **electrostatic assist (ESA)**. ESA imparts opposite charges to the impression roller covering and the ink, the ink being attracted toward the substrate (behind which is the oppositely charged impression roller). (See **Electrostatic Assist [ESA]**.)

An important consideration in the use of the impression roller is heat buildup in the rubber covering, which can cause expansion, softening, and deterioration of the covering, all of which adversely affect print quality and web runnability. Expansion of the rubber due to heat can also increase the pressure in the nip enough to cause distortions in the gravure cylinder itself, or affect the cells and the ink therein, causing premature drying, *drying-in*, or a loss of detail in the highlights of the image. Some impression rollers utilize a method of cooling such as running cold air or water through the core, from a separate roller (which produces condensation problems, however), or utilizing a separate heat-exchange unit.

A major problem with impression rollers (especially wide ones) is their tendency to deflect. *Deflection* is a tendency for a cylinder or roller—especially one with a large width—to bow when pressurized or under pressure itself. Deflection commonly manifests itself in nonuniform ink transfer to the substrate. Some methods used to compensate for deflection include a three-roll system, in which a small-diameter impression roller is sandwiched between the gravure cylinder and a hard, larger-diameter backup roller that applies pressure from the other side of the impression roller. This system is commonly used with small-diameter impression rollers. A drawback of it is the excess heat generation caused by an additional nip. Heat generation on a three-roll system can be at least twice as much as is generated by the impression nip itself. A centrally supported, two-roll system reinforces the center of the core of the impression roller, transferring the site of the pressure from the edges of the impression roller to the center. A third means of deflection prevention is a cambered two-roll system, which uses a curved rubber surface on the impression roller to compensate for deflection of the gravure cylinder. However, this system needs to be tailored for each specific size of gravure cylinder, which may or may not be easy. Other systems being developed and utilized include a NIPCO-roll system and an Albert Frankenthal K-type roller—both of which use a hydrostatic, internally pressurized impression roller—and a Cerutti flexible impression roll and Motter CDR impression roll.

As with rollers and cylinders in other printing press configurations, gravure impression rollers require various specifications for best results. Roller *hardness* is measured in *durometer*, and the covering should typically have a hardness between 60 and 95 durometer (for most commercial substrates). Consistency of hardness across the width and around the circumference of the roller is also important. The *Gravure Association of America (GAA)* recommends a soft impression roller with a durometer of 60 for light, smooth substrates (such as foil, cellophane, and some coated papers), or perhaps as high as 80 for the smoothest substrates. GAA recommends a moderately hard roller possessing a durometer of 80–90 for calendered, laminated paper or coated paperboard. For rough paper (such as kraft or most paperboard), GAA recommends an impression roller with a durometer of greater than 90.

The *total indicated runout (TIR)* (or *out-of-roundness*) of an impression roller should not exceed 0.003 in. Surface roughness should also be kept to a minimum. The rubber covering should also not be adversely affected by fumes generated by solvent-based inks.

The setting of the impression roller pressure, as was mentioned earlier, is an important consideration. A typical means of determining the impression pressure is to measure the width of the nip area (called the *flat*). This checks several important aspects: ensuring that the impression roller and the gravure cylinder are exactly parallel, determining if there has been any expansion and/or softening of the rubber coating on the impression roller, and checking (somewhat crudely, but fairly effectively) the impression pressure. One means of accomplishing this is to apply grease and *carbon black* to the impression roller, insert bits of paper between the impression roller and gravure cylinder, and engage the impression. The size of the nip can then be determined by measuring the size of the black grease stain on the papers. A more convenient and less messy means of measuring the flat is to apply a strip of transparent adhesive tape to the carbon side of a sheet of carbon paper. Several of these tape/carbon combinations are placed strategically along the impression nip (while the web is still in the machine) and the impression is engaged, then released. A dark stripe of carbon will be apparent through the tape where the increased pressure was applied. The different sandwiches can be measured and compared.

The impression roller and incorrect settings thereof are responsible for several common gravure printing problems and defects. One potentially dangerous problem is the buildup of static electricity, caused by the rapidly moving web. This buildup (which can exceed 25,000 volts) can cause fires or dangerous electric shocks. Static is also the cause of *whiskering*, which manifests itself as hairlike tendrils extending off a printed image into nonimage regions of the substrate. The static buildup pulls the ink from cells in undesirable directions as the substrate leaves the impression nip. Moistening the web is one way of eliminating static electric buildup.

(See *Gravure*.)

Impression Time

In *screen printing*, the period of time necessary for the *squeegee* to make one printing stroke.

Impression Zone

Term for the nip between a gravure press's *gravure cylinder* and *impression roller* where image transfer takes place. See *Gravure*, *Gravure Cylinder*, and *Impression Roller*.

Imprimatur

Latin for "let it be printed," signifying the permission of the Roman Catholic church, under canon law and granted by a bishop, for the publication of a work on scripture or any writing with significance to religion or morality. The imprimatur is a concession preceded by the judgment of a censor and has come to imply ecclesiastical approval of the publication. It is not an endorsement of content but does state that nothing offensive to faith or morals is in the work.

Imprint

To impress, to fix indelibly or permanently (as on paper or memory). Something imprinted or printed, as a mark or depression made by pressure. An identifying name (as of a publisher) placed conspicuously on a product, the name under which a publisher issues books.

In-Betweening

In animation, the act of creating a series of frames "in between" two *key frame*s. In conventional (i.e., manual) animation, the professional animator draws the key frames, while assistants usually draw the frames in between them, the in-between frames comprising the movements of an animated object required to have it move from the point in the first key frame to the point in the second key frame. For example, the first key frame of a sequence may involve a whole egg on a table, while the second key frame may have a broken egg on the floor beneath the table. The in-between frames would then involve all the individual frames needed to have the egg roll off the table and break. Many computer-animation programs will automatically create in-between frames. Also referred to as *tweening*.

Inches-to-Metric Conversion

A conversion factor used to convert units of length expressed in the English system (i.e., inches) to a metric measurement (i.e., centimeters), as 1 in. equals 2.54 cm. Thus, to convert to centimeters, the number of inches is multiplied by 2.54 (i.e., a length that is 5 in. long would be converted as 5 × 2.54 = 12.7 cm). To convert to millimeters, the number of inches is multiplied by 25.4 (as there are 10 mm in a centimeter, and 25.4 mm in an inch). Thus, a 5-in. length would be converted as 5 × 25.4 = 127 mm.

To convert from metric to inches, the number of inches in one centimeter can be used as a conversion factor. (See *Metric-to-Inches Conversion*.)

Inching

Intermittently operating a printing press for small increments to facilitate cleaning of the press, or mounting and positioning of a plate or blanket. Also known as *jog*.

Incident Light

The light that is illuminating an object or surface, coming from all directions. The *color* of the incident light is one factor in the perception of the color of the object. An object's color is a function of the wavelengths that a particular material absorbs and reflects (i.e., whatever wavelengths an object does not absorb will be reflected). White light, containing all the wavelengths of visible light, falling on an apple will have the blue and green wavelengths absorbed by the apple, reflecting back the red wavelengths.

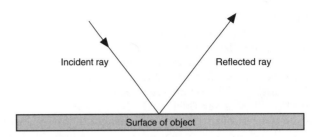

Incident light and reflected light.

Incline Press

A configuration of *screen printing* press in which the screen and frame print in a position parallel to the printing bed, but which is lifted diagonally during the feeding of the *substrate*.

Incremental Backup

In computing, the *backup* of a file that is new or which has changed since the last time a backup was made, or, in other words, a file in which the *archive bit* is activated. After backup, the archive bit is deactivated. See also *Differential Backup*.

Incunabula

The Latin word for "cradles," describing books and other matter printed during the earliest period of typographic printing from metal, from the invention of the art in Europe in the mid-1400s to 1500. The word was first used of early printing in 1653. The first attempt to catalog incunabula was made by Georg Wolfgang Panzer in the five volumes of *Annales Typographici ab Artis Inventae Origine ad Annum MD* (1793–97) that listed books chronologically under printing centers, which were alphabetically arranged. Others followed in other languages as interest in book collecting grew. The total number of editions produced by 15th-century European presses is between 35,000 and 50,000 based on how you count ephemeral literature (single sheets, devotional materials, etc.).

Indanthrene Blue

An *organic color pigment* used in printing inks. Indanthrene Blue is a reddish transparent blue pigment possessing high *lightfastness* and resistance to heat, acids, alkalis, solvents, and soaps. Indanthrene Blue is well-suited for use in all types of inks, but its expense limits its use to applications whose chemical resistance requirements make the expense warranted, such as in the gravure printing of soap wrappers and packaging. (See also *Organic Color Pigments*.)

Also known as *Anthraquinonoid Blue* (*CI Pigment Blue 60 No. 69800*, while a chlorinated version is a redder shade and is categorized as *CI Pigment Blue 64*).

Indelible Ink

A variety of ink used in the printing of fabrics designed to resist fading or bleeding during laundering.

Indent

In typography, the positioning of the text of one or more lines a fixed distance from one or both margins of a page. The most common indent is the *paragraph indent*, or an indention of the first line of a paragraph from the left (or right) margin. The reverse is a *hanging indent*, in which the first line is set flush with the left (or right) margin, while the rest of the lines of the paragraph are indented. A *nested indent* is an indent relative to the previous indent, rather than from the margin. A *runaround indent* is the indention of a certain number of lines to make room for an illustration or other page element the text is intended to flow around. A *skewed indent* is a varied indenting of subsequent lines, giving the margin a slanted appearance. A *delayed indent* is an indent that does not manifest itself until after a specified number of lines have been set. (See also *Indention*.)

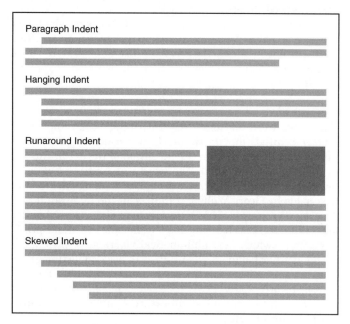

Four common types of indents.

Indention

In typography, a form of placement for text and display type showing the relation of items to one another. The simplest indent is the *paragraph indent*, which denotes the beginning of a text block. This indent should be proportional to the line length; if the line is under 24 picas, the paragraph indent should be 1 *em space*. If the line length is between 25 and 36 picas, the indent should be 1½ em spaces. If the line length is 37 picas or greater, the indent should be 2 em spaces. However, since the size of an em space is based on the *point size*, indenting a larger head the same amount of space as smaller text beneath it will result in misalignment; the same point size needs to be selected for both indents.

A *hanging indent* is the reverse of a paragraph indent, with the first line set to the full measure and sub-

sequent lines in the paragraph indented. Both of these indents apply primarily to blocks of copy and may be indented from the left, right, or both margins.

The term *indention* should not be confused with the term *indentation*.

Indeo

In *digital video*, a *codec* developed by Intel used for *data compression* of video files. The Indeo codec is available either as hardware or software.

Index

On an automated *screen printing* press, to move the *substrate* into position beneath the screen prior to making an impression.

In *book typography*, a portion of the *back matter* of a book providing a comprehensive alphabetized list of terms, names, subjects, or other material used in the book and on what page(s) they can be found, for easy location of specific material in the text.

A symbol or number used to identify a particular value in a series of similar values.

Index Hole

A physical opening in the plastic shell of a *floppy disk* marking the start of the first *sector*.

Indexing

In *binding and finishing*, a finishing operation in which *index tab*s are attached to the edges of sheets as a means of affording easy location of material contained within. Indexing may also involve the production of *index thumb cut*s. See *Binding and Finishing*.

In computing, the term *indexing* refers to a means of storing and retrieving data using an index key, or a list of the contents (i.e., records) of a database as well as their location, allowing the rapid access of data.

Index Paper

Also called *index bristol*, a lightweight cardboard, or paper *grade* characterized by high *stiffness* and thickness, as well as possessing a high degree of receptivity to writing inks. Index stock is typically used for index cards, but has a wide variety of usage whenever a low-cost, but stiff and attractive paper is required. It is available in *smooth finish* or *vellum finish*, and it is manufactured entirely from *chemical pulp*.

The *basic size* of index stock is 25½×30½ in. Index stock has *basis weight*s of 90, 110, 140, and 170 lb. *Standard size*s are 20½×24¾ in., 22½×28½ in., 22½×35 in., and 25½×30½ in.

Index Sequential

A method of organizing computer disk files for random access, whereby overflow material from one addressable location contains the address of the next portion of the computer data.

Index Tab

In *binding and finishing*, a plastic marker attached to a sheet in a larger publication as a means of allowing easy reference. See *Indexing*.

Index Thumb Cut

In *binding and finishing*, a semi-circular hole cut in the *front* edge of a book or other publication, allowing the book to be opened at a particular location. An index thumb cut is often used in dictionaries.

India Paper

A type of strong, *opaque*, lightweight paper used for thick publications such as bibles, dictionaries, and other reference works. Sometimes also known as *bible paper*.

Indicia

In typography and *prepress*, an identifying mark that is used as a guideline for the placement of copy or other page elements.

In *binding and finishing*, an indicia is a mailing permit preprinted on an envelope.

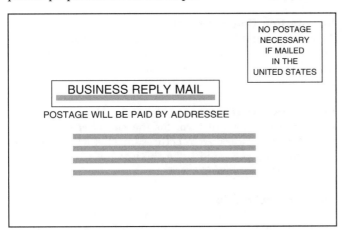

A business-reply envelope with an indicia in the upper right-hand corner.

Indirect Gravure

Alternate term for *offset gravure*. See *Gravure: Offset Gravure*.

Indirect Printing Screen

In *screen printing*, a screen prepared by the *indirect process*. See *Photostencil: Indirect Process*. A screen containing a *knife-cut stencil* is also referred to as an indirect printing screen.

Indirect Process

In *screen printing*, the preparation of a *photostencil* by means of a photosensitive emulsion applied to a plastic backing sheet, which is exposed to a film positive of the image to be printed and mounted on the screen. See *Photostencil: Indirect Process*.

Indirect Stencil

In *screen printing*, a *photostencil* prepared by the *indirect process*. See *Photostencil: Indirect Process*.

Individual Negative Letterspacing

Alternate term for *kerning*. See *Kerning*.

Industry Standard Architecture (ISA)

In computing, an 8-bit *bus* standard for *expansion card*s developed by IBM for the original *PC* (also known as the *PC/XT bus*). When IBM came out with the later AT line of computers, a 16-bit ISA bus (called the *AT bus*) was introduced. This latter bus supported both 8-bit and 16-bit expansion cards.

Infeed

The unit or section of a printing press responsible for transporting sheets or webs of *substrate* into the press and, in the case of *web printing*, maintaining proper *web tension*. See *Infeed Section* and *Web Offset Lithography: Infeed and Web Control*. Also spelled with a hyphen, *in-feed*.

Infeed Section

The portion of a sheetfed printing press (especially that used in *offset lithography*) that transfers a properly registered sheet from the *feedboard* to the *impression cylinder* in the printing unit.

The three basic configurations of infeed section are swing-arm system, rotary-drum system, and overfeed system.

Swing-Arm System. When the paper stops at the *front guides* at the head of the feedboard, it is jogged into position. The front guides move out of the way, and grippers attached to the front of an arm mechanism swing down, clamp onto the front of the sheet, and bring it into contact with the grippers on the impression cylinder.

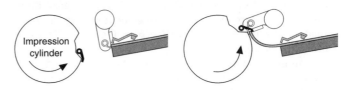

Swing-arm infeed system.

Rotary-Drum System. A rotary-drum infeed system is configured nearly identically to the swing-arm system, except that instead of a swinging arm, the grippers used to transfer the sheet from the feedboard to the impression cylinder are mounted on a rotating drum, transferring one sheet per revolution.

Overfeed System. After the front guides at the head of the feedboard move out of the way, feed rollers or a vacuum belt force the sheet against a stop on the impression cylinder, causing the paper to buckle slightly. The grippers on the impression cylinder then clamp onto the sheet. The

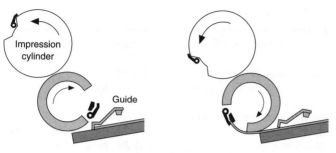

Rotary-drum infeed system.

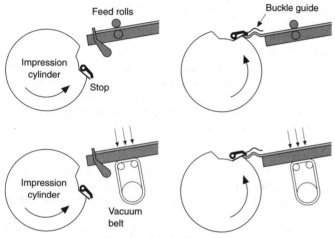

Overfeed infeed system.

extent of paper buckling can be carefully controlled to retain proper register.

On some infeed systems, the grippers on the impression cylinder, or on the infeed drum, are bowed (i.e., the center gripper is slightly—up to 0.008 in.—out of alignment with the others) to compensate for sheet *fan-out*, or the expansion of the tail end of the sheet, which causes poor alignment of printed images. Often, a *gripper-bowing device* is added to the infeed system. (See *Fan-Out* and *Gripper-Bowing Device*.)

The grippers themselves need to be properly adjusted for paper thickness and to ensure that the *gripper bite* is consistent across the press. Uneven gripper bite can cause sheet wrinkling and poor registration of the printed image. Grippers that are set too tightly can distort, damage, and/or tear the sheet, and cause transfer and delivery problems.

The infeed on a *web press* involves unwinding a roll of paper (or other substrate) into the press, ensuring that *web tension* remains consistent throughout the pressrun. See *Web Offset Lithography: Infeed and Web Control*.

Inferior

In typography, characters set in a smaller point size and positioned below the *baseline*, also called a *subscript*. Inferior characters are used for chemical equations (such as "H_2O"), etc. They are most often numerals, but letters can be used as well. Inferiors can be "manufactured" by chang-

ing to a smaller size and reversing the line spacing (if this capability is available) for positioning. See also *Superior*.

Infinite Loop

A *bug* in a computer program that results in an endless repetition of a single instruction or set of instructions.

Infinitely Variable Stroke

A *screen printing* system in which the speed of the printing stroke (the movement of the *squeegee* across the top of the screen fabric) can be varied at will.

Info Highway

An even more colloquial term for the already colloquial term *information superhighway*.

Infomercial

A long television commercial designed and produced to resemble a documentary, talk show, or other type of actual program. Infomercials are usually shown late at night or early in the morning and superficially resemble an informative program.

Information Conversion Unit

A device used to transfer files—be they text or image files—from one system to a different one by converting the data format, syntax, and protocol of the file to one that is compatible with the new system.

Information Highway

Generic and colloquial term for the *Internet* and related *broadband* network architectures (most of which have not been invented yet), said to be the wave of the future. See *Information Superhighway*.

Information Junkie

An individual who can not get enough information, characterized by a tendency to read anything and everything, cruise the *Internet* for hours, watch CNN religiously, or by other obsessive-compulsive behaviors.

Information Marketing Policy Actions (IMPACT)

A European program designed to foster cooperation among businesses for the purposes of creating a market for and supplying information services.

Information Path

In computing, the route within a computer or from the computer to connected devices that data takes when it is transferred. Often, the user needs to specify a particular path for data to take. For example, in *DOS*, saving a file requires the typing of the full *pathname* of the storage location, such as "C:\MOIST\EELS.TXT." This specifies that an open file will be saved on the "C" disk in a directory named MOIST with the file name EELS.TXT. The backslash (\) is used in DOS to indicate a path. Even on the *Macintosh*, specifying linked files (in multimedia applications, for example) also requires the user to type paths, especially when different drives and sub-sub-sub-folders are involved.

Information Processing

In computing and *database* management, all of the functions required to gather, store, provide, search, and retrieve information.

Information Retrieval

The accessing of any data file (be it text or images) using a computer, either on-site or from a remote location by modem. Information retrieval also involves the ability to easily search for specific files or data.

Information Retrieval System

A complete computer system designed for the purposes of *information retrieval*. See *Information Retrieval*.

Information Superhighway

A euphemism for the *Internet* and the underlying digital communications infrastructure. There are two major components in a digital information highway: a switching system to direct traffic on the network, and a transport medium for delivering the information.

The vision of data transmission is a single network that merges support for audio, video, graphics, and computer data. Fiber optics is a favored medium because it has hundreds of megabits per second of transmitting capacity, and it reliably delivers excellent picture quality. Fiber uses less than 1% of its theoretical bandwidth, and a single strand of fiber could carry the nation's radio and television traffic and still have significant capability left. Fiber optics has greater potential bandwidth because it transmits signals as pulses of light at a far higher frequency than electric signals in wire or microwave radiation to satellites. Combined with other wire communication, satellite and microwave transmission, the telecommunications infrastructure is thus formed. With the Internet and all of its protocols and methods, the base currently exists to move virtually any amount of information and data to anyone in digital form.

Infotainment

Colloquial term for any television program, book, or multimedia production that imparts information or educational materials in an entertaining way. Infotainment is also known as *edutainment*.

Infrared

The region of the *electromagnetic spectrum* located just below the visible portion (i.e., just beneath the red end) of the spectrum, which consists of wavelengths from 780 *nanometer*s (or 0.000001 mm) to 1 mm. Infrared radiation is also used as a source of heat, particularly in the drying of certain types of inks (such as *super quickset infrared inks*). (See *Electromagnetic Spectrum*.)

Infrared Data Association (IrDA)

A trade association comprising many hardware and software companies created for the purpose of fostering research in and the specification of standards for *wireless communications*.

Infrared Monitor

A type of *touch screen* monitor. See *Touch Screen*.

Infrared Transmission

In electronics, a means of wireless transmission of signals that utilizes a portion of the *infrared* spectrum. The frequency used by such devices (which include, most commonly, remote controls for televisions, VCRs, etc.) is just below that of visible light.

Infrared Web Temperature Control

In *web offset lithography*, a system that uses *infrared* sensors to monitor the temperature of the web as it leaves the *dryer* and automatically adjusts the temperature of the dryer to compensate for any variations.

Inhibitor

Any chemical or other substance that decreases or stops the rate at which a chemical reaction takes place. Substances such as *antioxidants* inhibit the chemical reactions (such as *oxidation* and/or *polymerization*) that cause an ink to dry. An inhibitor is also called a *poison*. The opposite of an inhibitor is a *catalyst*.

In-House

Descriptive of any graphics, prepress, or printing system operating within a company to service the company's own needs. Also spelled solid, *inhouse*, and also called *in-plant*.

In-House Publishing

A publishing operation located within a larger company designed to perform all aspects of the graphics, prepress, and printing processes for the company of which it is a part. In-house publishers tend not to solicit work from outside clients and usually do not depend on outside firms to handle parts of the publishing process. Also called *in-plant publishing*.

INIT

Short for *initial*, a small utility program or system *extension* for the *Macintosh* computer that loads into the system at start-up and adds some degree of additional functionality to the system. See *Extension*. (See also *cdev*.)

Initial

In typography, a large letter—typically the first letter of the first word of the line—placed at the beginning of a chapter, page or paragraph. The oldest style is the *sunken initial*, or *drop cap*, position, in which the initial letter is set down within the copy, not rising above the top line of the text. The second style is the *raised initial*, or *stickup initial*, in which the initial letter rests on the baseline of the first or subsequent line of text and rises above the top line of the text. The use of initial letters (or *initial caps*) dates back to the artistic application of them in handwritten books. Early printed books, such as Gutenberg's 42-line Bible, had colorful initial caps drawn by hand. Today, initials are used primarily to break up the gray monotony of long text blocks or simply as decorative elements.

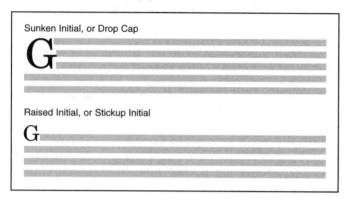

Two styles of initial capitals.

The most important aspect in the use of initial letters is their fit, or how they align with the rest of the text on the page. The space around the initial letter should be optically the same on the side as it is on the bottom. A raised initial letter must also rest on the *baseline*, with *kerning* applied where necessary. Raised letters may also be indented. If quotes are to be set (for example, if the initial letter is the beginning of a quote), they should be in a size between the text size and the initial letter size. They may even be eliminated (which is advisable). Traditionally, the first word following the initial is set in small caps or caps. Often, the lines of text adjacent to the cap are contoured to flow around the curves or strokes of the letter.

Initial Cap

Alternate term for an *initial* letter. See *Initial*.

Initial Caps

In typography, capital letters used at the beginnings of principal words in a title.

Initial Graphics Exchange Specification (IGES)

In computing, a vendor- and *device-independent*, ANSI standard *file format* for the transfer of *CAD* graphics files. IGES has become a widespread and popular CAD file format and is used to transfer CAD files from one system to another. Any program that supports the IGES format (and most now do) can open and edit such files.

Initialization

In computing, the act of setting up a computer system application, or other component of a system. Initialization also refers to the placing of magnetic *address* markers on a magnetic or optical storage medium as a prelude to its use. Initialization also refers to setting up memory and *register* locations performed by a computer application when it is first launched.

Initialize

To set up a computer system or to format an external storage medium for use. See *Initialization*.

Ink

The earliest forms of written communication had been carved cuneiform tablets, used in Sumerian and Babylonian civilizations around 3000 BC. The earliest use of writing on a paper-like substance (*papyrus*) with ink took place in ancient Egypt. Around 2500 BC, black ink was produced by mixing soot and vegetable gums in water; a pen consisted of a reed with a small brush mounted on the end of it. Five thousand years later, the manufacture of printing ink is far more complicated than that of the earliest inks.

The remainder of this article will deal exclusively with inks used in printing.

ELEMENTS OF INK

Modern printing inks come in two basic types: *liquid inks* (which are fluid and watery) and *paste inks* (which are thick and tacky). They typically comprise three fundamental types of substances: a *vehicle*, a *pigment*, and a variety of additives, such as *driers*.

Vehicle. The ink vehicle is the fluid part of the ink that, as its name implies, transports the pigment onto the *substrate*. The type of vehicle to be used in a particular ink is dependent upon the type of drying system utilized. Inks that dry by absorption utilize *non-drying oil vehicles* that do not dry by other means before they can be absorbed into the paper. Inks that dry via *oxidation* and/or *polymerization* require *drying oil vehicles* and paper qualities that do not allow the vehicle to be drained away before oxidation can take place. Inks that dry via evaporation utilize low-boiling-point *solvent-resin vehicles*. Inks that dry by *precipitation* require a water-soluble *glycol vehicle* in which are dissolved water-insoluble resins. When water is added to the vehicle, the glycol is dissolved, but the resin (containing the pigment) is not and precipitates out onto the surface of the paper. (Such inks are called *moisture-set inks*.)

Inks that use a combination of drying mechanisms, such as *quickset inks*, have a portion of the vehicle—a *solvent*—absorbed first into the paper, and a resin-oil mixture left behind that dries by oxidation and polymerization. Quickset inks use a *resin-oil vehicle*. Inks called *coldset inks* use a *resin-wax vehicle*, which is solid at room temperature, is melted by special heated rollers on a press, applied to the paper, then dried by turning back into a solid. Other, lesser-used vehicles include *water-soluble gum vehicles*, such as in watercolor inks, and *photoreactive vehicles*, which "set" upon exposure to various types of radiation. (See *Vehicle*.)

Pigment. The pigment is the part of the ink that imparts gloss, color, texture, and other characteristics to the printed image. Pigments can be ***black pigments*** (consisting primarily of various types of ***carbon black***), ***white pigments*** (which are either ***opaque pigment***s or ***transparent pigment***s), and color pigments that can be produced from either mineral sources (the ***inorganic color pigments***) or from organic derivatives of coal tar (the ***organic color pigments***). Other materials such as ***metallic powders*** can be used for various specialty inks. (See ***Pigment***.)

Printing ink additives include driers, which speed up the drying of inks; ***bodying agent***s, which increase the ***viscosity*** of an ink; and waxes such as microcrystalline, polyethylene, paraffin, beeswax, carnauba wax, and ozokerite, which are used to prevent such printing defects as ***ink setoff*** and ***blocking***, and to increase the ink's ***scuff resistance***. Other materials such as teflon can also be added to help "shorten" an ink. Other compounds can be used to reduce an ink's ***tack***. Lubricants and greases are added to not only reduce tack but also to help the ink distribute on the plate, blanket, or substrate more consistently and uniformly. Reducing oils and solvents such as thinner can be added to increase the ink's setting capacity. ***Antioxidant***s and ***antiskinning agent***s can be added to keep ink from oxidizing and setting while it is still on the press. Corn starch is added for body and to reduce ink setoff, while surface active agents are used to enhance the dispersion of pigments in the vehicle.

PRINTING INK MANUFACTURE

The primary function of the manufacture of printing ink is the dispersion of the pigment (the solid portion) in the vehicle (the liquid portion). The vehicle is prepared first and contains all of the important performance, setting, and consistency properties. Once the vehicle is prepared, it goes through three basic stages of production: ***mixing***, ***milling***, and ***filtration***. Although in many cases mixing is the only stage necessary, the desired end properties of the ink and the nature of the vehicle and of the pigment determine whether the ink will need to undergo milling or filtration.

Mixing. At this stage, the pigment, or coloring material—which can be in flushed (i.e., produced by ***flushing***), chip, or pulp form—is added to the vehicle in batch mixers or vats, which can hold anywhere from 5 to 1,000 gal. (Only a few types of inks, in particular newsinks, are produced in continuous mixing processes.) The type of ink ultimately produced and the nature of the pigment to be dispersed determine the speed at which the mixture is stirred—anywhere from a few to hundreds or thousands of revolutions per minute. The number of blades and the blade configuration of the mixer also affect the speed at which the mixture is stirred. When pigment materials have been predispersed, ink can be mixed to its desired end-use specifications in a one- or two-step mixing process. Inks that need further milling or grinding need to proceed to the next stage.

Milling. The principle of milling an ink ***slurry*** (the combination of pigment material and the vehicle) involves exposing the mixture to a greater shearing and mixing force than can be produced in the mixing stage. A variety of different machines are available for milling the ink slurry, such as a ***three-roll mill***, a ***ball mill***, a ***sand/shot mill***, and a ***colloid mill***. All of these devices expose the ink slurry to a shearing force, either by forcing the slurry through the nips of steel rollers, by spinning the slurry in a cylinder containing steel balls, by forcing the slurry through a layer of special sand or metallic pellets, or by pumping the slurry through a rotor-stator arrangement. A variety of other devices are used for milling ink, generally based on pumping the slurry through a turbine or high-speed rotor. The nature of the desired ink and the printing process in which the ink will be used determines the nature of the milling and the equipment required. (See ***Printing Requirements*** below.)

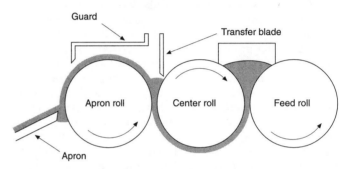

Three-roll mill.

Filtration. Liquid inks frequently undergo filtration to remove dirt, fibers, grit from the mill, and other impurities. The type of filter used can affect the final end properties of the ink, especially its viscosity. For paste inks, filters can also be used. However, changing filters between batches of different colors (so as to prevent color contamination) is time-consuming, so the volume of ink to be filtered must justify the effort. The limitations on filtration, however, include its inability to remove small air bubbles that may have been inadvertently injected into the ink during mixing or milling. In offset lithography, the grittiness of the ink due to trapped air bubbles will not affect print quality due to the dampening system, but other printing methods may have difficulties. Inks that dry by oxidation are more difficult to manufacture using filtration processes, as air bubbles can increase the formation of ink skins. In filtration methods, one problem that can arise is the clogging of the filter, which builds up pressure in the ink and can pull bits of fiber from the filter into the ink, defeating the purpose of filtration.

INK PROPERTIES

The three basic groups of ink properties are optical properties, structural properties, and drying characteristics.

An ink's color is a function of the pigment used, and an ink's other optical properties are primarily determined by the pigment characteristics. An important consideration is color matching, or the ability to precisely duplicate another color. Color matching tests can be done visually under specific lighting conditions, or utilizing a **spectrophotometer** and computer programs that can match a color wavelength by wavelength. Color matching charts and ink mixing formulas and procedures are provided by various companies. (See **Color Mixing, Ink**.)

An ink's **opacity** describes how opaque or transparent an ink is, or to what degree the ink allows or prohibits the transmission of light through it and how well the background on which the ink has been printed can be seen. Some inks are required to be opaque; some are required to be transparent. Another important property is the **permanence** of an ink pigment, or the extent to which an ink will retain its color strength and brightness with time or upon the exposure to light. A pigment's resistance to chemicals, in particular, how well it will retain its permanence or resist bleeding in the presence of acids, alkalis, or other substances is another important consideration—properties that determine on what types of materials an ink can be used. A similar property is the ink's **wettability**, or the ability of an ink to refrain from bleeding when exposed to water.

An ink's **body** refers to its consistency, or hardness or softness. An ink's body can be very soft and fluid, such as newsprint and gravure inks, or hard and stiff, like collotype inks. An ink's flow characteristics can be measured in terms of its viscosity, or the degree of its resistance to flow. (See **Viscosity**.) Some inks also demonstrate a deceptive body, properties called **thixotropy** and **dilatancy**. A thixotropic ink is thick and viscous while in its container, but when stress or shear forces are applied, it loses its viscosity and flows quite freely. (It is due to thixotropy that offset presses require so many ink rollers.) The opposite condition is called **dilatancy**. (See **Thixotropy** and **Dilatancy**.)

Another important structural property of ink is its **length**, which is related to its consistency and describes the ability of an ink to form long stringy filaments. Inks that are **long** have increased flow characteristics and form long threads of ink when pulled. Inks that are **short** flow very poorly and have a kind of buttery consistency. Excessively long and excessively short inks are undesirable. (See

Comparing two inks for length.

Length.) An ink's **tack** is a measure of how sticky the ink is, or the force required to split the ink film between the plate or blanket and the substrate. Although highly tacky ink is required for many printing applications, an ink's tack should not exceed the paper's **surface strength**, or tearing can result. (See **Tack**.)

Another major consideration in terms of ink is its drying method, or the means by which the vehicle is removed from the pigment, allowing the pigment to harden and solidify on the surface of the substrate. As we saw earlier, inks dry by oxidation, absorption, polymerization, evaporation, precipitation, or any combination thereof. The suitability of an ink's drying mechanism with a particular substrate and printing process is important in preventing problems such as **ink strike-through**, **ink setoff**, and **ink chalking**. (See **Vehicle**.)

TYPES OF PRINTING INKS

The various classifications of inks are based primarily on their drying methods, which, in turn, are based on the vehicle each ink uses.

Quickset Inks. These types of inks utilize a resin-oil vehicle, consisting of a resin-oil-solvent mixture. The solvent drains very quickly into the substrate leaving the remainder behind to oxidize and polymerize on the surface. Quickset inks are among the most commonly used in offset lithography and yield extremely good results when printed on **enamel paper** and **cast-coated paper**.

Heatset inks. These inks utilize a solvent-resin vehicle that dries primarily by evaporating the solvent from the vehicle, then recooling the remaining ink components. Heatset inks accomplish this by utilizing a solvent with a high boiling point, and the ink must then be dried in a special drying oven. Although commonly used, especially in web offset lithography, their drawbacks involve the additional equipment required, such as a drying unit and chill rolls to cool the heated ink.

Moisture-Set Inks. These inks utilize a glycol vehicle that dries primarily by precipitation. The pigment and a water-insoluble resin are dissolved in a water-soluble glycol. Upon contact with moisture, the glycol is dissolved, but the resin and pigment are not and precipitate out of solution onto the surface of the paper.

Radiation-Curing Inks. These inks utilize complex vehicles that harden and polymerize upon exposure to radiation, either ultraviolet light (as in **UV-curing ink**), beams of electrons (as in **EB-curing ink**), or infrared light (as in **super-quickset infrared ink**).

High-Gloss Inks. These inks essentially are produced with an additional quantity of **varnish**, which allows them to dry with a highly glossy appearance. High-gloss inks are dependent upon the properties of the substrate to be truly effective; a high degree of ink holdout is necessary to keep the vehicle from draining into the paper before it can dry by oxidation.

Metallic Inks. These inks are used for specialty applications and to produce a printed image with a metallic luster. The pigments used in these inks comprise flakes of metallic powders.

Magnetic Inks. These inks were developed for use in banks and are used primarily for printing on ***MICR (Magnetic Ink Character Recognition) Check Paper*** and read with MICR equipment. The pigments used in these inks have the ability to be magnetized after printing (or are composed of magnetite, a black, magnetic oxide of iron), and MICR ink and printing must be performed to precise specifications, depending upon the sensitivity of the equipment.

Fluorescent Inks. These inks lack permanence but make use of ultraviolet light to reflect back light in brilliant colors. Limited for many years solely to screen printing, recent innovations and formulations have produced fluorescent inks that can be printed in a variety of ways. Their semi-transparency makes them useful for overprinting on other inks, and fluorescent pink is occasionally printed as a fifth color in four-color printing to enhance skin tones and magentas. When used alone, fluorescent colors need to be printed on white paper, and they achieve their best effect when contrasted with darker colors.

Scuff-Resistant Inks. Inks that are able to withstand the wear and tear of shipping and handling are available in a variety of grades and formulations.

PRINTING REQUIREMENTS

Each printing process requires ink specially formulated for the mechanics and chemistry of the process.

Letterpress. Letterpress uses paste inks whose tack varies according to the speed of the press (though ink of moderate tack is generally preferred), and which typically dry by absorption, oxidation, or evaporation (or a combination of drying methods). The letterpress process, however, is falling into disuse in favor of other printing methods, such as offset lithography and flexography (letterpress now accounts for less than 5% of all printed packaging, for example). The varieties of ink used in letterpress printing are ***rotary ink***, ***heatset ink***, ***moisture-set ink***, ***water-washable ink***, ***newsink***, and ***job ink***. Rotary inks are commonly used in letterpress printing of books, magazines, and newspapers. ***Book ink*** is a somewhat fluid ink, and book inks are formulated to be compatible with the surface of the ***book paper*** on which it is to be printed. For example, a paper with a high degree of surface ***hardness*** requires a fast-drying ink. Rotary inks also include heatset inks. (See ***Rotary Ink***.) Moisture-set inks, as was mentioned earlier, utilize glycol vehicles that set fairly fast and

are odor-free, which is why they are frequently used in printing food wrappers and packaging. (See ***Moisture-Set Ink***.) Water-washable inks set very fast, are water-resistant when dry, and are used to print on ***kraft*** paper and paperboard. (See ***Water-Washable Ink***.) Newsink, used for printing on ***newsprint***, dries primarily by absorption of the vehicle into the substrate, and consequently needs to have a fluid consistency. Like newsprint—which is made from inexpensive and somewhat low-quality ***groundwood pulp***—newsinks also are made from inexpensive and perhaps less-than-optimal raw materials. The faster the press, the thinner the ink must be. An ink that is too thick will smudge when the paper is folded or generate ink setoff. An ink that is too thin can soak all the way through the paper, producing a printing defect known as ***strike-through***. Most newspapers, however, although originally printed by letterpress, are now printed using web offset lithography. Job inks have a medium body and a drying process that can be used on as wide a variety of paper as possible. Job inks tend to be a standard default ink in many letterpress print shops and need to be compatible with many paper types and many types of presses. Letterpress printing processes also use various other types of inks on occasion, such as ***non-scratch ink*** that is needed for labels, covers, and other end uses that require a scratch-resistant ink, quick-set inks, and high-gloss inks.

Offset Lithography. The suitability of the offset lithographic process for printing on a wide variety of surfaces has resulted in a large number of inks available for the process. Typically, lithographic inks (which are paste inks) are more viscous than other types of inks, and since the ink film is thinner with offset printing, the pigment content must be higher. (Offset presses deposit ink films that are about half the thickness of films deposited by letterpress presses.) And since offset lithography is premised on the fact that oil and water do not mix, inks designed for the process must contain significant amounts of water-repellent materials.

Sheetfed offset presses primarily use quickset inks, which dry rapidly without the need for additional equipment, such as drying ovens necessary for heatset inks. Some sheetfed offset presses, however, do use various radiation-curing devices, as is needed for super-quickset infrared ink, ultraviolet-curing ink, and electron-beam-curing ink.

Lithographic inks primarily set by a combination of absorption of oil-based vehicle components into the substrate, followed by oxidation and polymerization of the remaining components of the vehicle. Web offset lithographic presses utilize higher press speeds and consequently need to lay down an ink film more rapidly. The ink must be absorbed into the substrate more quickly to avoid smudging and setoff during folding processes at the end of the press. Hence, web offset inks tend to be more fluid and have less tack than sheetfed lithographic inks. Newsinks have seen improvements recently, especially from ***soy ink***, which is made from the latest development in vegetable oil vehicles, soybean oil. Web presses also utilize heatset inks, which dry as the printed paper *web* is passed through a high-temperature drying oven. Web presses also utilize radiation-curing methods.

The most important criterion for offset inks, however, is their insolubility, as they must resist bleeding in the presence of the water-based press dampening systems. Problems with the drying of offset inks that dry by oxidation include *emulsification* of the fountain solution into the ink. An excessive amount of dampening solution (or one with a high *pH*) can impede proper ink drying, and the use of papers with a low pH also has a deleterious effect on ink-drying properties. (See *Acid Paper* and *Alkaline Paper*.) Lithographic processes are also well-suited to printing on surfaces other than paper. Lithographic inks used for printing on metals (such as the printing of cans and other metallic packaging) contain synthetic resin varnishes that dry in high-temperature ovens. *Letterset ink*s and *waterless ink*s are also available for recent developments in waterless offset printing processes.

Flexography. Flexographic presses typically use liquid inks that possess low viscosity and dry primarily by evaporation of the vehicle. Flexographic presses use either water inks (typically on nonabsorbent substrates such as polyolefins and laminated surfaces and, in the past, on various types of paperboard) or solvent inks (for use on surfaces such as cellophane). Water-based ink vehicles are composed of ammonia, protein (solubilized by amine), casein, shellac, esterified fumarated rosins, acrylic copolymers, or mixtures thereof. They have a high degree of *printability*, perform well on the press, and clean up easily. Water-based inks are used extensively in flexographic newspaper printing as they are almost totally smudgeproof. Water-based flexographic inks, however, have a longer drying time on less-absorbent substrates and a low degree of gloss. Water-based inks are undergoing further research and development due to the desire to decrease the dependence on solvent-based flexographic inks, which contribute to air pollution. The vehicle for solvent-based inks is a solvent-resin mixture, formulated to suit the surface to be printed, as well as the press plate and other parts of the press it will be in contact with. Incompatible solvents can distort and damage the rubber flexographic plates. The solvent is made up of an alcohol—ethyl, propyl, or isopropyl. To produce optimal resin solubility, glycol ethers, aliphatic hydrocarbons, acetates or esters may be added. These additives also contribute to the desired viscosity and drying speed. The resins themselves must be chosen with care, as they affect the end properties of the ink. Typical resins used in flexographic inks include acrylics, cellulose esters, *nitrocellulose*, polyamides, modified rosins, and ketone resins.

Gravure. Unlike most inks produced for other printing processes, gravure inks comprise a pigment, a *binder* to keep the pigment uniformly dispersed and to bind the pigment to the surface of the substrate, and a solvent to dissolve the binder and eventually evaporate away in the drying phase. Depending on the solvent used and what it is capable of dissolving, a wide variety of materials may be used as binders. They are chosen according to the end properties desired, such as gloss, resistance to water or other substances, flexibility, etc. Some binders, such as film formers, dissociate themselves from their solvents rapidly after printing, which enables the ink to dry quickly. Finishing operations such as rolling, diecutting, etc., can be performed immediately as is the case with types of wrapping and packaging. In rotogravure printing, the most important considerations in terms of solvents are their dissolving of the film-forming resins, the rate at which they dry, whether or not they have deleterious effects on previously printed ink (as in multicolor jobs), their toxicity, and whether they release harmful vapors. Pigment particles must also be more finely ground than in other printing processes, lest damage be incurred by the gravure cylinder. As part of the effort to reduce the usage of solvent-based inks, water-based gravure inks are being developed but have not yet met with resounding success.

Screen Printing. Screen process printing requires paste inks that are thick and able to print sharply through the screen. They must also perform well under the action of a squeegee. The binder added to screen process ink must be compatible with the surface on which it will be printed. The solvents used should also not be overly volatile, as excessively early evaporation would cause the remaining ink components to clog the screen. Screen inks typically utilize a drying oil vehicle.

Ink-Jet Printing. The inks used in ink jet printers—typically used for computer printouts, labels, etc.—consist of dyes mixed with a highly fluid vehicle or carrier that form very small drops, can pick up an electrical charge, and can be deflected properly to fall in the right place for the formation of a printed character or image.

Copperplate and Die Stamping. Copperplate printing is commonly used to print stamps, bank notes, securities, and other high-quality decorative applications. These processes utilize a somewhat viscous, heavy ink that allows the designs etched in the printing plate to be completely filled in, much like in gravure printing. The vehicles for these inks utilize light litho oils and fluid resins mixed with low-volatility solvents that evaporate very slowly.

Electrostatic Printing. Also called *xerography*, electrostatic printing is commonly found in photocopying machines and computer laser printers. The "ink" used in these processes—commonly referred to as *toner*—consists of a fine, dry powder coated with the desired color imparted by a colored resin binder. The important consideration is not only particle size but also electrical properties, as electrostatic printing works by attracting particles electrostatically to a charged drum, the point of attraction on the drum being the printing areas.

END USES AND SUBSTRATES

As printing processes increase in speed and in the ability to print on a wider variety of substrates, new ink formulations must keep pace with new innovations to ensure high print quality. The considerations involved in proper ink formulation include the speed of the printing process, the nature of the printing process, the surface properties of the intended substrate, and the ultimate end-use characteristics of the finished printed piece. As we saw above, each printing process requires inks with specific characteristics to ensure compatibility with press chemistry and mechanics. Ink characteristics such as permanence depend on the end use; newspapers do not necessarily need to be permanent, but inks used in books do. Chemical resistance is necessary in various types of packaging, a longer degree of permanence is necessary to maintain an attractive appearance for products whose packaging is intended to entice consumers into purchasing them.

In terms of substrates, two basic divisions must be taken into account: paper and nonpaper.

Paper. An uncoated, *unsized*, highly absorbent paper such as newsprint used on high-speed web offset presses requires thin, less-viscous inks that dry primarily by absorption; yet, as we have seen, too fluid a vehicle will produce strike-through. Similarly, newsprint (or *roto news paper*) formulated for high-speed rotogravure printing of newspaper supplements and Sunday magazine sections also requires fluid inks that dry by absorption. Uncoated papers (such as *bond paper*, *antique finish* paper, and *vellum finish* paper, for example) have low surface gloss and high absorbency (depending on the amount of water-resistant *sizing* added). Inks for printing on uncoated papers are typically moderately viscous paste inks that dry by oxidation or absorption. A wide variety of surface features and absorbencies are available in uncoated papers, and inks are typically formulated with drying properties and viscosities dictated by what will work best on the paper.

Coated and *smooth finish* papers and papers that have undergone some degree of *calendering* or *supercalendering* are typically glossy and water-repellent, with high degrees of ink holdout. Inks formulated for use on these papers tend to dry by oxidation, although heatset inks are becoming more and more prevalent. To reduce smudging, setoff, and blocking, inks that dry quickly are highly desired for printing on these kinds of papers. The increased quality of these papers also allows the effective use of high-gloss inks to provide a higher-quality printed image. The use of high-speed web presses with these papers also demands that the inks be quick setting.

Multicolor printing processes also impose their own demands on the inks used. (See *Printing Ink Defects and Problems* below.) Printing hard paperboard and corrugated packaging requires abrasion-resistant and scuff-resistant inks, as well as inks that dry quickly. All the printing processes are employed in the printing of various

types of packaging as well, which also places additional demands on the ink formulation. Letterpress and offset lithographic inks utilized in paperboard printing are commonly oxidation-drying inks, and flexographic and gravure inks are commonly absorption-drying and evaporation-drying inks. Glassine papers (such as wax papers used to wrap food products) are highly repellent surfaces, commonly printed using gravure and flexography. Various types of imitation parchment are used to produce high-quality documents, such as diplomas, and are printed using copperplate or letterpress processes.

Various types of parchment are also used for wrapping food products, and inks formulated need to be greaseproof and resistant to other types of materials in the foods. They must also be odorless and resist bleeding. Decorative papers such as wrapping paper are primarily printed by gravure, flexography, and screen printing, which requires taking into account the ink requirements of the particular process as well as the aesthetic requirements of the end use. Kraft papers used for grocery bags and other such uses are typically printed with flexographic processes, utilizing rapidly drying inks so as to complete cutting, folding, and bundling in rapid succession without smudging or setoff.

Nonpaper. Nonpaper substrates include the following: plastics and metal.

Plastic substrates are frequently used in printing wrappers and other packaging. An important consideration is minimal (or no) absorbency of the ink by the stock. Quickly evaporating solvent- or water-based inks (printed using flexography) are commonly used. Gravure presses are also commonly used for film packaging. Compatibility of the binder to plasticizing materials in the substrate is also an important consideration, as intermingling of plasticizing materials and ink binding substances can soften the binder, causing smudging, setoff, and blocking. The type of plastic film used—be it cellophane, polyethylene, polypropylene, or other petrochemical substances—is also important. Solvents used in inks also help the ink adhere to the surface of some plastics better than to others, in particular, to cellophane. Often, plastic-coated paper, paperboard, or foils are utilized, and the ink must adhere to both surfaces. In many cases, these "dual-substrates" are used in food wrappers, where solvent-retention by the dry ink film must be avoided, so as to prevent both delamination of the surfaces and leeching of the solvent into the food.

Aluminum sheets or foils are commonly used in various types of packaging and are printed most commonly with flexography or gravure presses. Often, the foil is covered with a layer of shellac, nitrocellulose, or other material to improve the adhesion of the ink, and frequently thin sheets of foil are laminated on other substrates, such as paper, to reduce the quantity of metal required. Aluminum or steel sheets are used in the printing of beverage and food cans, which undergo stamping, rolling, folding, or soldering immediately after printing. Rapid drying (usually by steam or baking processes) is therefore a necessity. The dry ink film must also stand up to the finishing processes (as well as filling, shipping, and handling processes) without chipping, smearing, flaking, or abrading. Offset lithography is often used for the printing of aluminum or steel sheets, primarily for the great ability of the rubber blanket to conform to the surface of the metal, as metal sheets themselves are fairly incompressible, at least under the pressures generated in printing operations. *Overprint varnish* is often used on printed metal surfaces. Screen printing is also utilized for some metal printing applications, such as toys.

Other Factors. When determining the proper ink to be used for a particular job, other general factors are also important to bear in mind, in particular, the amount of coverage a particular ink is likely to provide on a given stock. An important measurement in this respect is *specific gravity*, which is a measure of an ink's density (or weight per unit volume) compared to the weight of an equal volume of water. The higher the specific gravity of an ink, the smaller the volume, and the less coverage that can be expected. Another factor is the *tinctorial strength* (or color strength) of the ink; the weaker the color, the thicker the ink film that may be required to provide the desired hue. The surface properties of the paper, as we have seen above, also affect ink quantity; absorbent and/or rough paper surfaces require thicker ink films than smooth papers to provide the desired print density and/or gloss. Another consideration affecting ink coverage is the content of the material to be printed; type requires less ink than solids.

PRINTING INK DEFECTS AND PROBLEMS

As we have seen above, it is important that all the disparate elements in the printing process be compatible with each other. Inks must be chosen that will run on the desired printing press; papers or other substrates must be chosen that also are suitable for use in a particular process and will allow the ink to dry by its designed drying method. Problems caused by printing on substrates that impede an ink's proper drying method can result in problems such as ink setoff and blocking—the sticking of printed sheets in the delivery pile. The separation of blocked sheets can result in torn paper.

One particular problem in printing is incorrect color, which can be a function of incompatibilities between the ink and the substrate, too much or too little ink transfer, contamination from improperly cleaned press rollers or blankets, inconsistencies in the stock itself, and *color drift*, a tendency on the part of some pigments to alter their shade upon aging.

Another printing problem is *mottle*, a nonuniform appearance to a printed image, which can be caused by hard, nonabsorbent or nonuniformly absorbent papers, poor ink distribution on the plate or blanket, incorrect ink viscosity, or the presence of too much dampening solution. Ink whose tack exceeds the *picking resistance* of the substrate can result in *picking*, or the pulling off of paper and/or paper coating particles, which collect on the blanket

or plate and create printing defects called *hickey*s. Too much drier can cause premature oxidation of the ink while it is still on the rollers, resulting in an increase in ink tack that can also cause picking. Other contaminants such as dust and other stray debris from the pressroom and/or the press can also produce hickeys. Debris can also contribute to *fill-in*, or the printing of stray ink between halftone dots or in nonprinting regions of small type (an example would be an "O" that had a filled-in center), which produces an undesirable, speckled appearance to printed halftones. Other press and ink conditions, such as using excessively heavy inks, inks that are poorly ground or milled, solvents that evaporate too quickly for the press speed, or heavy press roller settings can also produce fill-in. Related to fill-in is *feathering*, or the printing of ragged edges of type or images. It can have the same cause as fill-in (especially in flexographic printing), or it can result from incompatibilities between the ink and the paper.

A problem commonly attributed to poor drying is *rub-off*. The symptom of this problem is ink that is dry but is easily rubbed off. The cause of rub-off is the use of a binder (or the inadequate use of a binder) that does not properly hold the pigment to the surface of the substrate. Excessive and/or premature vehicle absorption can also contribute to rub-off.

In addition to the *piling* of paper debris on the plate or blanket (producing various printing defects and hickeys), ink can also contribute to piling and *caking*. Accumulation of dry bits of ink on the rollers, plate, or blanket are typically caused by an inadequate amount of, or low viscosity, ink vehicle being unable to hold the pigment particles in suspension. Excessively absorbent substrates can also drain the vehicle away too quickly while the ink is still on press, leaving pigment particles behind on the blanket or plate.

The adhesion of ink to nonimage areas of the plate, called *tinting*, occurs only with offset lithographic inks and is caused by emulsification, or the formation of an oil/water emulsion, of the ink by the fountain solution, which then begins to adhere to the water-receptive areas of the plate. A similar problem, called *scumming* or *greasing*, is characterized by the nonimage areas of the plate gradually becoming sensitized to the presence of ink, resulting in the accumulation of ink in undesirable areas. Tinting and scumming can be caused by inadequately water-resistant inks, improperly cleaned or set rollers, a high- or low-pH dampening solution, or excessive pressure between the plate and blanket. A somewhat opposite problem is called *stripping*, or the loss of adhesion between ink and metal press rollers, commonly caused by a transfer of dampening solution to the ink rollers by the ink. Stripping tends to occur when too much fountain solution is in the press. In gravure printing, scumming (also called *fogging*) is characterized by the accumulation of ink on the cylinder outside the etched cells, which some inks cause due to an affinity for the cylinder's chrome surface. In other cases, it is caused by surface roughness of a chrome cylinder to which ink adheres.

Problems involving the visibility of a printed image on the reverse side of the paper can either be caused by low paper *opacity* (called *show-through*) or by excessive ink vehicle penetration (called *strike-through*). Strike-through commonly results from the use of a thin ink, and can be reduced by utilizing a thick ink or less-absorbent paper stock.

Mechanical ghosting, a problem occasionally encountered on small presses with a small number of form rollers, results from a plate image removing ink from the form rollers, which is then not replaced on the roller, the result being a faint image of the previous form on a later printed impression. Utilizing more form rollers, varying the diameters of form rollers, or installing oscillating rollers can remedy the problem of mechanical ghosting. *Chemical ghosting* is caused by the reaction of the vapors of a drying ink with other drying inks, and typically produces a faint impression on the opposite side of the sheet. The use of a faster-evaporating ink solvent will help remedy the problem.

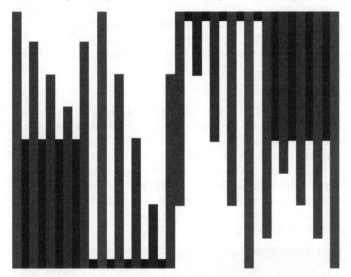

A mechanical ghosting form, showing the effects of ink starvation due to the design of the form.

Ink *flying* or *misting* is observed on high-speed presses and results from the use of excessively long inks. Misting is characterized by a spray or fog hovering over the press and coating the outside of the press, the floor, and the walls. Not a printing defect per se, it can certainly be a mess. The use of shorter inks will remedy the problem.

In wet multicolor printing, a second ink that is tackier than the previously printed ink can impede *trapping*, or the adherence of the second color on top of the first. If the first color has dried too quickly, *crystallization* of subsequent inks can occur, which will cause them to *crawl*, mottle, or be rubbed off easily. These problems can be avoided by utilizing less drier in inks slated to be printed first.

The printing of progressively fainter images is referred to as an ink "printing too sharp," which can be caused by either too tacky an ink being used or an excessively acidic fountain solution *etching* the image areas of the plate, making them more ink-repellent.

A problem encountered in the flexographic printing of nonporous substrates—particularly waterproof cellophane—is *chemical pinholing*, or printing a discontinuous ink film containing small voids or holes. It is caused typically by the failure of the ink to completely wet the surface of the substrate. Another form of *pinholing*, called *mechanical pinholing*, is characterized by the reproduction of the texture of the engraved form roller (or *anilox roller*). It is commonly caused by a variety of ink problems, such as inadequate viscosity, accelerated drying, or an insufficient ink quantity. Pinholing is also a problem found in gravure printing and has a similar cause to that of flexographic chemical pinholing. In gravure, however, pinholing can also be caused by air bubbles in the ink picked up by the gravure cells and printed as voids.

Another flexographic problem, typically associated with *nitrocellulose ink*s, is *souring*, characterized by a precipitation of the nitrocellulose out of the vehicle due to absorption of atmospheric moisture by water-receptive solvents in the ink. *Precipitation* is also a general flexographic problem characterized by resins that come out of solution at inopportune moments, as the resins used in flexographic inks require a great deal of auxiliary solvents to remain dissolved. Flexographic printing also has its own form of *picking*, in which the plates carrying successive colors remove bits of the previously printed colors. Ensuring that the first-down color dries faster than the successive ones can alleviate this problem. (Note that this is the opposite of the remedy for crystallization in wet multicolor offset printing.)

Problems unique to gravure printing include *skips* (also called *snow* or *speckle*), which are characterized by specks on unprinted areas. They are caused by dirt and debris, by trapped air bubbles behind the doctor blade, or by an insufficient ink supply. *Snowflaking* is characterized by randomly distributed voids and is commonly caused by using stock with an irregular surface or that lacks sufficient *compressibility* to allow the gravure cells to transfer complete images. Using harder impression rollers or lower viscosity inks can alleviate the problem. *Screening*, characterized by a screen-like pattern in the printed image area (commonly observed in multicolor gravure printing), is also caused by incomplete ink flow from the cells to the substrate. Adjusting (i.e., thinning) the ink viscosity helps, but if the problem is due to trapping difficulties generated by the printing of successive colors, adjusting the drying rate of each ink may help.

The presence and printing of ink beyond the edge of the engraved cells of the gravure cylinder is known as *spilling*, *drag-out*, and *squeeze-out*, and it can either be caused by the use of low-viscosity ink or by cylinder over-etching that results in the deterioration of the cell walls. The formation of *volcanoes* (also known as *cratering*) is characterized by rings of color (typically visible under magnification) and is caused by an evaporating ink solvent trapped beneath an already dried ink surface, bursting through and collapsing the ink film. Some inks contain phosphoric acid (such as inks used for printing on foil), and others contain a rubber chlorinate that can produce hydrochloric acid. Both of these acids can dissolve the chrome surface of the gravure cylinder, etching new faux cells that can print in undesired areas.

Inks that dry quickly can cause **drying-in**, which is a premature drying of the ink inside the cells of the gravure cylinder, typically manifesting itself as a loss of color in light areas of the print. Gravure ink can also be susceptible to **sedimentation**, or the precipitation of dispersed pigment particles out of the vehicle, if the ink is stored unused for an extended period of time. Sedimentation tends to occur with ink containing particles of larger size. A similar problem is **flocculation**, in which the addition of another material causes the pigment particles to fall out of suspension in the vehicle. Both sedimentation and flocculation can be characterized by a decrease in color strength and gloss. A problem that generates defects similar to cratering is called **foaming**, which involves entrapped air in the ink.

As the printing processes change and evolve, so does the ink needed to run on those processes. What the ink of tomorrow will be like is based on several factors. The first is the speed and nature of the printing processes themselves. As web presses continue to increase in speed and prevalence, the ink must change to effectively print at accelerated speeds. Flexographic processes are becoming more and more popular, and water-based flexographic inks for high-speed flexo newspaper printing are currently undergoing major developments. Such processes—web offset and flexographic printing—are replacing letterpress systems, so the development of letterpress inks is declining. Government regulations, in particular Environmental Protection Agency (EPA) and Occupational Safety and Health Administration (OSHA) policies (to reduce air pollution and workplace toxicity, respectively), are spurring the development of water-based inks to decrease the need for environmentally and biologically harmful solvent-based inks, especially in flexographic printing. The Food and Drug Administration (FDA) and the Department of Agriculture have stiff regulations regarding the types of inks that can be used in the printing of food packaging, and they are also watching the development of new types of inks (especially those that contain materials believed to be carcinogenic). The desire to decrease reliance on petroleum products (begun during the oil shortage of the 1970s) is also spurring the search for alternate materials. Radiation-curing inks are receiving much attention, as are other types of "next generation" inks that employ new advances in chemistry, in the development of inks that will satisfy the industry's conditions of printability, print quality, and cost-effectiveness, and other interests in environmental protection and pressroom safety.

Ink Absorbency

A paper characteristic that determines the quantity of ink that will penetrate its surface, or the rate at which ink will penetrate a paper's surface. The desired amount of ink absorbency (or its converse, **ink holdout**) is dictated by the type of ink used and the nature of the printing job itself. In some high-quality sheetfed offset presswork, the paper must be absorbent enough to prevent **ink setoff**, yet not so

absorbent that ink that primarily dries by exposure to air is absorbed before it has a chance to dry. Ink holdout is primarily responsible for printed gloss. Lack of printed gloss and even **ink chalking** can result if the ink vehicle is drained from the ink film by absorption. On the other hand, in high-speed web printing, fast ink vehicle absorption is necessary to prevent smudging. In newspaper printing, rapid absorption of the ink vehicle traps the pigment on the surface of the paper, which is why newspaper ink never dries enough to keep from blackening the reader's hands.

A variety of interrelated paper properties affect ink absorbency and ink holdout. Primary among them is **porosity**, or the size and quantity of tiny interfiber air spaces in paper. It is by capillary action that inks and other fluids are absorbed into paper. Various procedures, such as the **refining** of paper fibers, the addition of **fillers**, the degree of **calendering** or **supercalendering**, and the application of various types of **coatings** affect ink absorbency. (See **Porosity** and **Paper and Papermaking: Paper Properties**.)

Various tests can determine the ink absorbency of a paper. (See **Vanceometer Test** and **K and N Ink Absorbency Test**.)

Ink Agitator

A device added to many offset press **inking system**s consisting of a motorized revolving metal cone that runs along the **ink fountain** continuously stirring the ink. Ink agitators are commonly used with excessively **thixotropic** inks that increase in **viscosity**, or decrease in desired flow characteristics, while sitting. Ink agitators not only keep ink at a workable consistency, they also help reduce the formation of dried ink skins, which contribute to printing defects known as **hickey**s.

Ink agitator.

Ink Chalking

A defect in printing characterized by improperly dried ink being easily rubbed off the paper, although **ink setoff** rarely occurs. Chalking is caused by an incompatibility between the ink and a coated paper that results in the inactivation of the drier in the ink. Ink that is chalking right off the press will eventually dry completely, although

GATF has found that it can sometimes be days or even weeks before ink that has not been properly formulated for a particular paper *coating* will dry.

Ink Cuff

An accumulation of dried ink on the ends of an offset press's ink roller, commonly caused by improper or infrequent cleaning. The primary hazard of ink cuffs is their tendency to break off during printing and contribute to the production of printing defects known as *hickey*s.

Ink cuff.

Ink Dot Scum

A printing problem found on aluminum plates used in *offset lithography* characterized by thousands of tiny, inked dots in nonimage portions of the plate. Ink dot scum is caused by corrosion of the aluminum, which forms thousands of tiny pits that, when the film of *fountain solution* wears off, fill with ink. The corrosion is commonly caused by adding a layer of water to the surface of the plate and allowing it to evaporate slowly, providing enough time for *oxidation* of the metal surface to occur. It is also found frequently in a band corresponding to the position of a wet dampening roller. If the scumming is caught in time, and its effects are still localized within a small region of the plate, a solution of phosphoric acid and *gum arabic* can be used to eliminate it. If it has progressed far, the plate may be unusable.

Ink Drum

See *Drum*.

Inker-Feed System

A type of *continuous-flow dampening system* used on an offset lithographic press, consisting of a *metering roller* transferring *fountain solution* from the *water pan* to a *transfer roller* and, ultimately, to the first inking *form roller*, which doubles as a dampening form roller. The width of the *metering nip* between the metering and transfer rollers controls the amount of fountain solution ultimately sent to the plate. Inker-feed systems differ from other dampening systems in that other systems have specially designated dampening form rollers. The obvious consideration with inker-feed systems is ensuring that the inking form roller will accept a film of dampening solution. The use of alcohol-based *wetting agent*s in the fountain solution help alleviate this difficulty. See *Dampening System*.

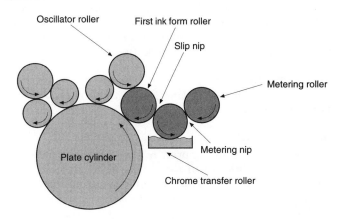

An inker-feed dampening system.

Ink Flotation Method

A test to determine the water resistance of paper, or the adequacy of its *sizing*, in which a paper is floated on the surface of a pool of dark-colored ink. The amount of time between the paper's contact with the ink and its appearance on the reverse side is a gauge of the efficacy of the sizing.

Ink Fountain

A reservoir on a printing press that holds ink and allows it to be transferred, by rollers or other means, to the printing plate or cylinder for ultimate transfer to the paper or other *substrate*. Each printing process has a different ink fountain setup. See *Inking System*.

Ink Hickey

A *doughnut hickey* produced by particles of ink skin collecting on the image area of a plate, press blanket, *gravure cylinder*, or other image-carrying surface. See *Hickey* and *Doughnut Hickey*.

Ink Holdout

The ability of paper to prevent ink from penetrating into its surface (in contrast to *ink absorbency*). Inks that produce the best result by drying via *oxidation* (as opposed to drying via absorption into the paper) require paper that has sufficiently low *porosity*. Too much ink holdout, however, can cause *ink setoff*. Inks achieve greater levels of gloss and better image quality when they dry on the surface of paper, rather than when they are absorbed. However, in some printing processes (such as high-speed web printing for newspapers), it is desirable to obtain rapid ink penetration and drying, a case where increased ink holdout is undesirable.

The degree of ink holdout is a function of porosity, as well as *moisture content* and a variety of other paper characteristics. (See *Ink Absorbency* and *Paper and Papermaking: Paper Properties*.)

Inking Control Console

On newer offset presses, a computerized mechanism that allows the press operator to automatically and electronically regulate the amount of ink fed through the press, as well as a variety of other press operations, from a single remote location, such as the inspection table.

Inking Mechanism

Alternate term for a printing press's *inking system*. See *Inking System*.

Inking System

The portion of a printing press responsible for transferring ink from the *ink fountain* to the printing plate. The nomenclature of the inking system depends on the type of printing process and press utilized.

OFFSET LITHOGRAPHY

In offset lithographic presses, the inking system (also called the *inker*) consists of a train of at least ten (often more) rollers of various types, all leading back to an ink fountain, a pan or trough containing the ink. A *fountain blade* (which can be adjusted using manual or motorized *fountain keys*) forms a barrier between the pan of ink and the *fountain roller*, and two *fountain cheeks* form the sides of the ink pan, contacting the edge of the fountain roller and the fountain blade to keep undesired amounts of ink from flowing through the remaining system.

A *ductor roller*, the first roller in the *roller train*, alternately contacts the fountain roller and an *oscillator* roller, transferring a set amount of ink. The timing of the action of the ductor roller can be set in relation to the rotation of the plate cylinder, the timing of the oscillator, or at some other rate. It is important to ensure that the ductor roller only contacts the oscillator when the *form rollers* (the ink rollers that directly contact the plate) are over the plate *cylinder gap*, especially during the vibration that results when the ductor first contacts the oscillator (called *ductor shock*). The ductor roller is a crucial linking roller from the fountain to the rest of the roller train, making its proper setting and maintenance of vital importance to print quality. (See *Ductor Roller*.) Some web presses use continuous rollers in place of ductors, which are covered with bristles or raised designs to help transfer predetermined amounts of ink. Some web presses also use an *Aller undulating ductor roller*, which is a segmented roller, each segment mounted off-center in relation to the others. Some segments thus are in contact with the fountain roller while others are in contact with the adjacent drum roller. After a set period of time, the segments switch positions. This helps with the lateral distribution of ink across the lithographic printing press.

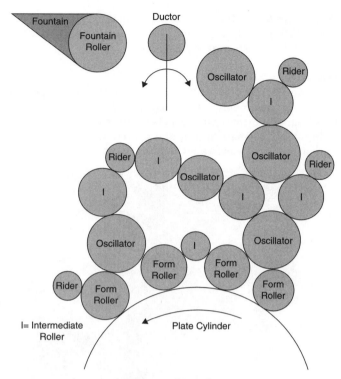

A typical lithographic inking system.

An offset inking system contains several oscillator rollers (also called *drum*s or *vibrator*s) that move laterally, or at right angles to the rest of the roller train. Their purpose is to not only work the viscous ink and make it thinner and workable (see *Thixotropy*), but also to ensure that faint images from the plate are not propagated through the inking system (see *Mechanical Ghosting*). Their lateral movement is typically set to the rate of plate cylinder revolution, but can be adjusted based on the *body* of the ink. Too frequent oscillation can result in ink starvation on the plate (in some cases), while too seldom oscillation can cause overinking. Oscillators in contact with the *form roller*s should oscillate at the maximum rate possible. The oscillators are moved by gears and chains, and they move adjacent rollers in the train by movement against their surfaces.

A variety of *intermediate rollers* occupy various positions within the roller train. These intermediate rollers are called *distributor*s or *rider*s. Distributors typically sit between two other rollers, such as oscillators, and move by surface contact with the adjacent chain-and-gear-driven rollers. Distributor rollers are responsible for mixing the ink with small amounts of water to form a uniform emulsion. Riders are typically connected to only one other roller, such as an oscillator, and function solely to condition ink by sending it off on a kind of detour. Lithographic ink commonly attains a workable *viscosity* only after extensive working. Riders also collect various types of paper and ink debris. Having the smallest diameter of all inking rollers, riders therefore have the greatest number of rotations per minute, and they move due to surface contact with adjacent oscillators.

A printing press can have up to four form rollers, which transfer ink from the roller train directly to the printing plate. The form rollers can be lifted from the plate either automatically (as when the press is idle) or manually, should the press operator desire it. When the form rollers are not contacting the plate, the ductor roller is lifted from the fountain roller, cutting off ink flow through the system. One specific problem with form rollers involves the brief period of time when the form rollers pass over the plate cylinder gap. As they are still in contact with the rest of the roller train and make one complete revolution, they can become overloaded with ink, and their first revolution over the returning plate deposits a greater-than-desirable thickness of ink, commonly ending with a streak. Varying the diameters of the form rollers can help alleviate the problem. Another problem involves mechanical ghosting. Mechanical ghosting can be avoided by properly timed oscillators, or by use of an **oscillating form roller**. The setting of the form rollers to the plate has important consequences for the resulting print. Too much pressure on the plate can cause **slurring**, streaking (especially if the form rollers bounce at the end of the cylinder gap), and roller/plate wear and damage. The setting of the form rollers to the oscillators is also important (See **Form Roller**.)

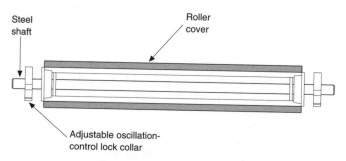

An oscillating form roller.

Adjusting the amount of ink sent through the system can be done in two ways. The first is using the fountain keys to control the space between the fountain blade and the fountain roller, which controls the lateral distribution of ink through the system. These keys are usually adjusted based on the ink requirements of the particular plate. The second is by adjusting the **dwell**, or the amount of time the ductor roller contacts the fountain roller. The rate at which the fountain roller turns is also significant and is referred to as its sweep, or the distance it moves before being contacted by the ductor roller. In general, it is a good idea to let it rotate through a longer distance and adjust the fountain keys so that a thinner film of ink is on the fountain roller. This allows the ability to make quick adjustments if necessary. Especially when printing colors, the fountain roller's sweep should be as constant as possible. All these basic settings should be made during **makeready**, with only intermittent fine-tuning needed during the pressrun.

Some **web press**es utilize variations on this basic theme, such as a cam or eccentric roller controlled by a lever that controls the amount of ink transferred to the fountain roller. Other web presses—such as those used for printing newspapers—borrow from **flexography** the engraved **anilox roller** to transfer a finely metered film of ink to the remainder of the roller train.

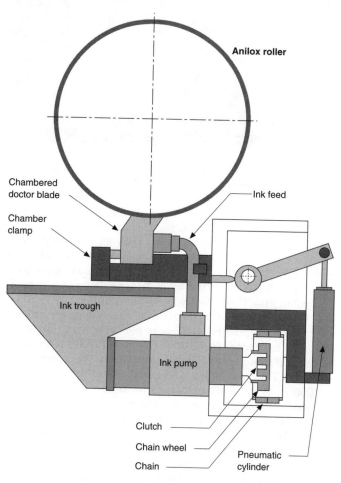

A lithographic inking system that uses an anilox roller.

Various inking system and print quality problems can be caused by ink rollers that are out-of-round, due to either dropping them during cleaning (or other similarly originating damage), or by excessive pressure from other rollers in the roller train. Out-of-round rollers tend to bump when contacting the plate and cause streaking. Metal oscillating rollers made from steel can become susceptible to **roller stripping**, or a loss of ink affinity. Another serious problem with ink rollers is **glazing** (also called **glazed rollers**). Glazing is an accumulation of dried ink **pigment** and **vehicle**, gum from the dampening system, and particles of paper **coating** or fiber caused by the ramifications of press chemistry and inadequate cleaning. The result of glazing is that ink rollers become increasingly unable to effectively transfer ink to and from each other. Glazing also reduces

Photomicrographs of the surface of a new roller (left) and a glazed roller (right).

roller friction, which manifests itself in skidding and streaking. Ink rollers are susceptible to various types of ink buildup (in addition to glazing), such as *ink cuffs*. The fountain blade can also become damaged, and bits of dried ink can collect under it, preventing the fountain keys from moving it properly. If the blade becomes worn or warped, controlling ink flow effectively becomes difficult.

The various characteristics of the rollers are important. A roller must be as close to perfectly round as possible. A roller's *total indicated runout (TIR)* is a measure of the difference in a roller's radius from its center to its surface. The maximum tolerance allowable for TIR is 0.0005 in. A roller's hardness is measured using a *type-A durometer*, which measures the resilience of a surface from 0 (a very soft surface) to 100 (a very hard surface, such as cast iron). Rollers can increase in undesirable hardness with age, due to glazing. A roller whose hardness (also called its *durometer*) exceeds certain preset tolerances causes problems such as mechanical ghosting, streaking, and other problems. (See *Durometer*.)

Some offset lithographic inking systems also employ add-on devices, such as an *ink agitator* to automatically stir a viscous ink that gets thicker upon standing; a *fountain splitter* to enable the press to perform two-color *spot-color printing* in one pass; a *hickey-picking roller* to remove dust and debris that can generate printing defects; an *ink leveler* to automatically keep the ink fountain replenished, and an *Air Curtin*™ to remove excess moisture from the inking system.

(See also the specific entry on *Offset Lithography*.)

LETTERPRESS

Letterpress printing uses thick paste ink that is similar to lithographic ink, and consequently the thixotropic nature of much letterpress ink also requires the use of a long series of ink rollers to apply the proper force. A letterpress inking system consists of a *fountain*, or pan, into which the ink is put. A *fountain roller* transfers a set amount of ink to a series of inking rollers (commonly three or four), which then transfers the ink to the *form rollers* (of which there are commonly three). The form rollers then transfer the ink to the flat typeform or curved printing plate, depending upon the press configuration. (See *Letterpress*.)

GRAVURE

The inking system for gravure printing is perhaps the simplest, consisting of little more than an ink-filled trough that runs the width of the press, called the *ink fountain*. The image carrier, the *gravure cylinder*, is partially submerged in the pool of ink. As the cylinder rotates, ink fills the *cell*s engraved on the surface of the cylinder. Excess ink is wiped from the surface of the cylinder by a *doctor blade* and the inked cells contact the substrate passing above them. A compressible *impression roller* forces the substrate down into the cells, where the ink is transferred by means of capillary action. The ink used in gravure printing is highly fluid liquid ink (in contrast to the thick, tacky paste ink used in offset lithography), and it is the high fluidity and low viscosity of the ink that makes the process work effectively. However, at high press speeds, heat generated by the friction of the impression roller pressing against the gravure cylinder can warm the ink, causing it to decrease in viscosity (i.e., become thinner) and can cause the ink to dry prematurely, producing *drying-in*. This results in a loss of print density, particularly in the highlights. Often, ink in the fountain is kept cool, commonly using a chiller tube, a heat-exchange device, or chilled water. Gravure ink performs well at temperatures as high as 70–80°F, but temperatures higher than that can result in decreased viscosity and too-rapid solvent evaporation. On the other hand, if the ink is chilled too much, viscosity can increase, requiring a greater concentration of solvent to thin it, resulting in weaker printing. Viscosity of gravure ink is important to measure and monitor (every 30 minutes is a good rule of thumb; some presses have automatic

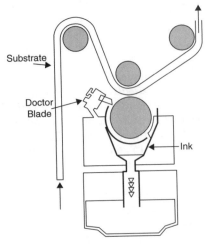

A typical gravure inking system.

424

viscosity controls, which make life simpler). A quick and easy means of doing so is the use of an ***efflux cup***, which is a way of timing the rate at which a given quantity of ink flows through an opening of a given diameter. (See ***Efflux Cup*** and ***Viscosity***.)

There are a couple of variations on the gravure ink fountain. One configuration uses an absorbent rotating ink ***fountain roller*** located beneath and slightly off to one side of the gravure cylinder to absorb ink from a shallow fountain and squeeze it into the cylinder cells, ensuring that ink coverage is complete. Another configuration, commonly found on presses used to print packaging, uses a completely enclosed fountain that pumps ink from the reservoir through a wide nozzle onto the surface of the cylinder, which also ensures complete ink coverage. Some presses supplement the doctor blade with a pre-wiping blade that sloughs off a thick film of ink before the proper doctor blade wipes of the remaining thin film.

(See also the specific entry on ***Gravure***.)

FLEXOGRAPHY

There are many different flexographic press configurations, but there is a "standard" system that is used in many general applications. Essentially, a flexo inking system comprises an ***ink fountain*** or pan, in which the ink is stored. In many configurations, called "two-roll systems," a ***fountain roller*** rotates in the ink fountain, picking up a film of ink on its rubber-covered surface. The speed of rotation of the fountain roller—which is independent of the speed of the other rollers and cylinders in the press—is varied according to the application. The point of the fountain roll is to effectively deliver ink to the surface of the adjacent ***anilox roller***. No set rule exists about the ratio of the rates of rotation between the fountain and anilox rollers. All that needs to be maintained is a supply—or pool—of ink over the nip between the two rollers. This will also depend on the direction the ***web*** of substrate is moving: when the web is traveling through the press in the downward direction, the rollers are turning in such a way that the ink pool is on the nip at the top of the rollers; when the web is traveling in the up direction through the press, the roller are turning such that the pool is on the nip at the bottom of the rollers. Thus, in the latter configuration, gravity will keep the ink from collecting in as a high a volume as it will in the former configuration. As a result, on presses possessing a "bottom nip" the fountain roller needs to turn at a faster rate than it does on a "top nip" press. As long as the pool is thick enough, the fountain roller is turning at a sufficient rate.

Another factor in effective ink metering is the pressure between the fountain and anilox rollers. Some methods of fountain roller setting are performed mechanically, while more prevalent systems use pneumatically or hydraulically set rollers. In mechanically set rollers, the hardness—or ***durometer***—of the rubber becomes an issue, as softer rubber will carry more ink. Mechanically set systems also have a tendency to vary in ink metering over the course of the run, as heat buildup causes rubber expansion. The impor-

tant consideration, regardless of the type of roller setting, is consistency of the setting across the press throughout the run. Variations in ink metering will result in color changes on the printed substrate.

Fountain rollers are also susceptible to ***deflection***, or a bowing due to increased pressure. This will result in more ink being transferred in the center than at the sides (a condition known as ***flooding***). One means of compensating for deflection and flooding is to attach the fountain roller at a skewed angle, so that more metering is done in the middle than at the ends. A number of different variables affect the proper skewing angle, such as the respective roller diameters, ink viscosity, etc.

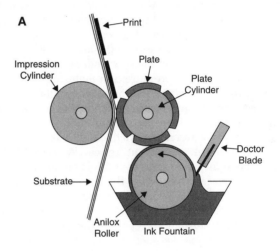

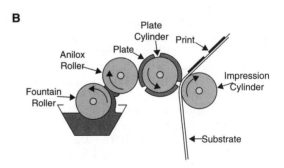

Two configurations of flexographic inking systems: two-roller (A) and three-roller (B).

The anilox roller is a chrome-plated or ceramic-covered roller containing many pyramid-shaped cells embedded in its surface (other shapes can be used, as well). The function of the anilox roller is to deliver a predetermined amount of ink (ideally, just the ink contained in the cells) to the adjacent printing plate. Since all the cells are the same size, the ink capacity of the roller itself can be calculated. The total number of cells varies from roller to roller, depending on the application. The cells are engraved in a specially treated copper or ceramic surface. Copper anilox rolls are commonly plated after engraving with a layer of chrome, to protect the cells against wear. When wear does occur, the cells lose their regions of greatest volume (i.e., the bases of pyramids) and the ink-carrying ability of the roller goes into sharp decline. (See ***Anilox Roller***.)

A number of alternative inking configurations are commonly used on flexo presses. One of the most prevalent uses a reverse-angle ***doctor blade*** that scrapes the ink from the surface of the anilox roller. The doctor blade is most effective when contacting the roller at an angle of 30° from a line tangent to the point at which the blade contacts the surface. (The interior of the angle should also face *toward* the plate cylinder.) This is similar to the doctor blade system used in gravure inking systems. When using doctor blade systems, it is important that the anilox roller be manufactured specifically for use with a doctor blade, lest increased wear and roller damage occur. The ***total indicated runout*** of the roller should also not exceed 0.0005 in. (although the tolerances are higher for shorter rollers and lower for longer rollers), or blade pressure and metering will not be consistent around the circumference of the roller.

A third, newer configuration is known as an ***enclosed inking system*** and utilizes an anilox roller in an enclosed cartridge, usually with one or two doctor blades. The anilox roller contacts an ink fountain at its rear. A doctor blade at the top of the fountain ensures that ink is metered correctly to the roller surface, while one at the bottom keeps a pool of ink in contact with the roller. Such enclosed systems are preferable when ink viscosity is overly crucial; reduced exposure to the atmosphere keeps viscosity more consistent than in open systems, as open systems tend to result in excessive evaporation of volatile ink solvents.

Flexo inks need to be fast-drying and, as a result, premature drying during press downtime is an issue. When the press has stopped, it is often necessary to keep the anilox and fountain rollers moving, to prevent drying. Thus, many presses allow the anilox roller to be separated from the plate cylinder. By the same token, the plate cylinder can also be separated from the impression cylinder and the web of substrate. In many cases, ink needs to be cleaned from the plate when the press is stopped, and if it remains in contact with the web, the drying ink can cause the plate to stick to the web, causing a web break when the press is restarted.

A flexographic inking system is sometimes known as an ***anilox system***.

(See also the specific entry on ***Flexography***.)

SCREEN PRINTING

In its most basic form, the inking system for ***screen printing*** consists of little more than an informal reservoir of ink applied to any nonprinting portion of the top of the printing screen. Prior to printing, the ink is distributed across the screen (especially over the stencil) either by the ***squeegee*** or by automatic ***flood bar***s. In some automated and semi-automated press configurations, ink is placed in a special ***fountain*** and fed to the printing screen automatically. (See ***Screen Printing***.)

Ink Jet

A type of nonimpact printing process, used most frequently in computer output devices, that utilizes tiny droplets of highly fluid ink that are given an electric charge. During printing, these droplets are sprayed in a continuous fashion toward the ***substrate***, their positions being governed by oppositely charged deflection plates, the position of the plates themselves being driven by the printer ***driver*** and the application from which the printing is being coordinated. This is known as ***continuous-flow*** ink-jet printing.

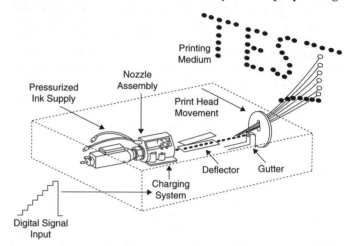

Continuous-flow ink-jet printing.

Another variety of ink-jet printing is known as ***drop-on-demand***, an intermittent system in which discrete bursts of ink are directed at the proper position on the page by a moving ink-jet printing head.

Ink-jet printers have increased dramatically in ***resolution***; early devices were capable of only about 50–80 ***dpi***; newer high-end devices have reached 720 dpi. Although that is better than most ***laser printer***s, a variety of problems severely limit ink-jet output quality. In particular, the highly liquid ink soaks into most paper easily, causing blurring, distortion, and paper wrinkling. Special coated papers designed for use with ink-jet printers have helped overcome such problems. One of the primary advantages of ink-jet

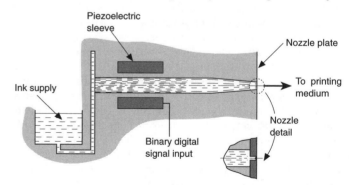

Drop-on-demand ink jet.

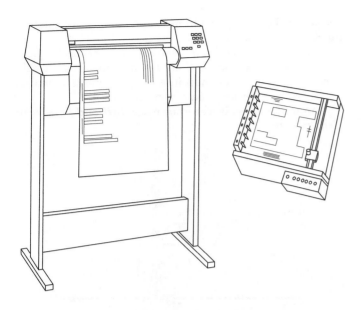

A large-format ink jet printer.

printers, however, is the ease of color printing; multicolor ink-jet printers allow for printing either **spot color** or **process color** in one pass through the printer. The low cost of these printers have made them ideal for home or small-office use, and they are used to create a wide variety of personal and professional materials. They are also used to generate **color proof**s.

In **binding and finishing**, ink-jet printers are also used for addressing magazines and other publications, as well as for the printing of personalized messages on printed matter.

Ink-Jet Printer

A printer that utilizes **ink jet** technology. See **Ink Jet**.

Ink Leveler

A device added to the **ink fountain** of some offset presses that uses an ultrasonic sensor to monitor the level of the ink in the fountain. When the ink level reaches a certain depth, the device automatically triggers a pneumatic pump to add more, removing the need for manual inspection and refilling. An ink leveler (also called a **fountain height monitor**) is most commonly used on presses for printing cartons.

Ink Misting

A condition generated on high-speed presses by rapidly moving ink rollers that spray out filaments and threads of ink. Ink misting more commonly occurs when excessively **long ink** is used. Ink misting is also called **flying**, **spitting**, **spraying**, and **throwing**.

Inkometer

A device used to measure the **tack**, or stickiness, of a printing ink by means of determining the torque produced by a series of rotating inked rollers. Inkometers are frequently used to compare and contrast the tack of various inks to be used in wet multicolor printing processes, where the tack of the first ink printed must exceed that of the ink printed on top of it. An Inkometer is also called a **Tackoscope**.

Ink Pan

Alternate term for an **ink fountain**, the part of a printing press—be it one used in **letterpress**, **lithography**, **gravure**, or **flexography**—containing the ink. See **Ink Fountain** and **Inking System**.

Ink Receptive

A property of paper, other **substrate**, or printing plate that describes the extent to which it (or portions of it) will accept the transfer of ink to its surface. A paper or other substrate that is ink-receptive will also absorb some or all of the **vehicle**, as opposed to a substrate that is **ink repellent**. Ink-receptive surfaces tend to be water-repellent.

Ink Receptivity

The extent to which a paper, other **substrate**, or printing plate will accept the transfer of ink to all or part of its surface. See **Ink Receptive**.

Ink Repellent

A property of paper, other **substrate**, or printing plate that describes the extent to which it will not accept the transfer of ink to all or part of its surface in favor of water, as opposed to a surface that is **ink-receptive**.

Ink Resistance

Alternate term for **ink holdout**, the extent to which a paper or other **substrate** will refrain from absorbing some or all of the fluid ink **vehicle**. See **Ink Holdout**.

Ink Setoff

Printing defect characterized by the transfer of wet ink to the reverse side of the sheet lying on top of it in the press delivery tray. Ink setoff can be prevented by ensuring that the combination of ink and paper are compatible enough to promote rapid ink vehicle penetration. When sheetfed offset lithographic inks dry, their **vehicle** is absorbed into the paper in seconds, which leaves the pigment compact and immobile on the paper surface and free to completely dry at its leisure. Basis weight is also a factor in preventing ink setoff.

When paper is sent to the delivery tray, it sits on a cushion of air on top of the previous sheet, not directly against its surface. Eventually, the air leaks out from between the sheets, and the paper pile is compacted. The time it takes for the air cushion to leak away is usually sufficient for a substantial amount of ink drying. Using heavier weight paper, however, diminishes that air cushion faster. Setoff is also increased by static electricity, which causes paper to cling together in the delivery tray. Additives such as an **antisetoff compound** or a post-printing **antisetoff spray** can also be employed to reduce setoff.

The sticking together of paper sheets due to ink setoff is called **blocking**. Separation of blocked sheets can result in severe damage to one or both of them.

Ink Stability

Alternate term for **screen stability**. See **Screen Stability**.

Ink Stripe Method

Alternate term for **picture method**, a test designed to evaluate the setting of an offset press's **form roller**s. See **Picture Method**.

Ink Trap

See **Trap** (second definition).

Inkwell

The blocked-out portion of a **screen printing** screen used as an ink **fountain** or reservoir. Also known simply as a **well**.

Inlay

In **binding and finishing**, a decoration added to a book cover by first cutting or **blanking** apertures into the cover. See also **Onlay**.

In-Line

In typography, a style of type that has a chiseled effect, as if chipped out of stone. Although classic in appearance, their use in small doses is most effective, and they are often used in display type and are especially well-suited to dropping out from a dark background. At small sizes, however, the letters tend to fill in. Also referred to as **engraved**.

In-line is also descriptive of any series of processes connected in a logical sequence, requiring little user intervention. For example, **in-line press**es have a variety of finishing devices—folders, diecutters, binders, etc.—attached in the proper sequence after the printing unit, so that a printed piece passes directly through all the printing and finishing stages without being taken off press and placed in another set of devices. (See **Web Offset Lithography: In-Line Finishing**.) Some **imagesetter**s also have in-line processors that develop the exposed film as it comes out of the device, eliminating the need to physically remove the film and re-insert it in a processor.

In-Line Covering

In **perfect binding**, any binding system on which covers are attached on gathered and glued **signature**s in a single process.

In-Line Feed

In computing by means of paper tape, alternate term for **center feed**. See **Center Feed**.

In-Line Press

A printing press connected directly to any of several finishing operations, such as stamping, diecutting, sheeting, creasing, folding, etc., so that the printed **substrate** does not need to be demounted from the press and remounted on the finishing equipment.

The term **in-line press** also refers to a multicolor press in which all the **color station**s are mounted in a straight horizontal line, rather than in a circle around a **common impression cylinder** or in a vertical stack.

An in-line press is also known as a **tail-end printer** or a **tailprinter**.

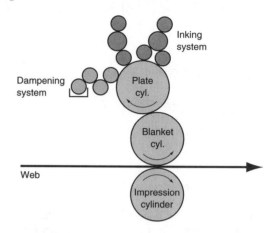

One color station of a multicolor in-line printing press.

In-Line Problem

A problem of **process color** printing characterized by one page on a printing press requiring different amounts of ink than a page printing below it.

Inorganic Color Pigments

Pigments used in ink manufacture derived from inorganic mineral sources (in contrast to **organic color pigments**). There are several different varieties of inorganic pigments, classified primarily by their source.

The inorganic pigments listed below are classified and identified in the Society of Dyers and Colorists' Color Index. Each classification consists of two parts, corresponding to the two parts of the index: the first part identifies each pigment with a CI number, which accompanies a description, usage, and technical information. The second part lists each pigment by chemical composition and assigns each one a single number. Thus, Cadmium Yellow below is listed in Part 1 as *CI Pigment Yellow 37* and in Part 2 as *No. 77199*. These two sets of identifications accompany the individual entries on each separate pigment.

Chromes. Chromes are generally derived from various lead compounds, are fast-to-light (although some do darken on exposure to light, or on contact with sulfur gases), opaque, and heavy. They hold up well when mixed with solvent- and oil-based **vehicle**s, and they are generally acid and alkali resistant. **Chrome Yellows** and **Chrome Reds** (comprising several shades ranging from greenish to orange) are produced from lead chromate mixed with other lead compounds, such as lead sulfate. **Chrome Green** is a mixture of Chrome Yellow and Iron Blue. Other chromes include *Orange Chrome*, *Chrome Scarlet* and *Molybdate Orange*, which are shades of Chrome Reds.

Cadmiums. Cadmiums are derived from various cadmium compounds, such as cadmium selenide or cadmium sulfide, are fast-to-light, and are highly resistant to alkalis and soaps, which makes them useful for printing soap packaging or for long outdoor use. Cadmium-based pigments include *Cadmium Red*, *Cadmium Yellow*, and *Cadmium Oranges*, as well as *Cadmium-Mercury Red*s. The chrome and cadmium pigments are rarely used any longer, having been replaced by less potentially toxic organic pigments, except in cases where extreme chemical resistance is necessary.

Irons. Irons are derived from various iron oxides and include *Iron Oxide Yellows* and *Iron Blues*. *Brown Iron Oxides* can either be classified as red pigments or brown pigments.

Earth Color. A lesser-used class of inorganic pigments include the *earth colors,* which are mined from sienna, umber, and ochre. Earth colors are dull in color and and are occasionally used in special applications. *Ultramarine Blue* and *Ultramarine Violet* possess high color purity and high resistance and lightfast qualities. *Chromium Antimony Titanium Buff Rutile* is used often as a brown pigment.

(See also *Organic Color Pigments*, and individual entries on the separate inorganic pigments.)

In-Plant

Alternate term for *in-house*. See *In-house*. Also spelled solid, *inplant*.

In-Plant Printing

Alternate term for *in-house publishing*, especially with regard to the printing unit of an in-house publishing operation. See *In-house Publishing*.

In-Point

In video editing, the *frame* at which an edit begins. See also *Out-Point*.

Input Bound

See *Input/Output Bound*.

Input Device

Any hardware device that is attached to a computer and converts electronic signals to digital signals, allowing the input of data to the computer system. Examples of input devices are keyboards, mice, *track ball*s, *digitizing tablet*s, *scanner*s, etc. See also *Output Device*.

Input Image

Any image that is digitized and stored as a file on a computer.

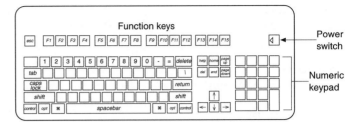

A keyboard, one example of an input device.

Input/Output Bound

In computing, descriptive of a computer capable of functioning only as rapidly as its input and output ports. The process of inputting data and/or outputting data is much more time-consuming than the actual processing of that data by the *central processing unit (CPU)*. See also *Computation Bound*.

Input/Output (I/O)

General term for devices that are connected to a computer system and can either send information to the computer or receive information from it, or both. Input/output devices are usually connected to one of several of the computer ports; examples of input/output devices are keyboards, drives, and printers.

Input Scanner

A type of scanner used to convert an image into *digital data* and display it as a collection of *pixel*s on a computer monitor, as opposed to a scanner designed to merely generate *color separation*s. See *Scanner*.

Insert

In typesetting or editing, when used as verb, *insert* means to add material to a body of text. When used as a noun, it means the material that has been added.

In *binding and finishing*, an *insert* is one printed *signature* that has had another signature wrapped around it. See *Inserting*.

The term *insert* also refers to any preprinted page or set of pages that are placed into a separately printed publication. Examples of inserts are advertising supplements, maps, or *foldout*s. A *free-standing insert* is a single signature added to a newspaper.

Insert Edit

In video production, the insertion of new video material or the overwriting of old information on a videotape, performed without altering the *control track*.

Inserting

In *binding and finishing*, a means of assembling printed *signature*s for binding in which one signature is wrapped around another signature. Publications to be bound by *saddle-stitching* are often assembled in this manner. See *Binding and Finishing*.

Insert Position

In a text-editing program, the location of the *cursor* on the screen where new text is entered.

Inspection

See *Acceptance Sampling*.

Inspector Gadget

An obsessive-compulsive individual who needs to possess every new electronic or mechanical device that comes along. Named for the cartoon character.

Install

In computing, the process of adding new software or hardware (and its related software *driver*) to a computer system. Often, an application has an automated *installation program* that copies all the appropriate files from the original *CD-ROM* (or *floppy disk*) to the proper directories or folders on the computer's *hard disk*. These installation utilities may also assist the user in configuring the software for his/her use.

Installable File System (IFS)

In computing, a *file system* that is loaded by the *operating system* when needed. In some computer systems, different file systems are used for different purposes, each one capable of being loaded dynamically as required.

Installation Program

In computing, a special application used to install a program on a computer. A new program, as it exists on its original *CD-ROM* or *floppy disk*(s) is a complex set of many files and folders, often *compressed*. These files need to be decompressed and copied to the correct directories (or folders) on the user's *hard disk* before the program can be used. An installation program simplifies this process, performing all file decompression, copying, and directory selection itself, requiring the user merely to indicate on which drive the application should be installed (or to perhaps also insert a large number of floppies). Depending on the application to be installed and the installation program itself, some degree of configuration of the new application may also be included in the installation process, including registration.

Instant Jump

On a *LaserVision* videodisc recorder, a feature that provides the ability to "jump" either forward or backward a distance of up to 50 *frame*s without generating a *blanking interval*.

Institute of Electrical and Electronic Engineers (IEEE)

An international society of professional engineers that issues networking standards for the computer and communications fields.

Instruction Register

Alternate term for *program register*. See *Program Register*.

Instruction Set

In computing, a complete set of directions (written in *machine language*) that a computer's processor can recognize and execute. In *complex instruction set computing (CISC)*, there may be hundreds of directions in the instruction set, while in *reduced instruction set computing (RISC)*, there may be only be a few.

Intaglio

Term for any printing or imaging process in which image areas are etched into a surface, filled with ink, and transferred to a *substrate*. Although derived from older engraving methods, modern versions of intaglio printing include *gravure* and *copperplate printing*.

The word *intaglio* is an Italian term (and is more properly pronounced "in-TAL-yo" although the pronunciation "in-TAG-lee-oh" has become prevalent and accepted) meaning "engraved." The earliest uses of intaglio date back perhaps to the ancient Sumerians in the fourth millennium BCE who produced engraved seals. Intaglio was used in China to print books, the text being cut into wood blocks, inked, and transferred to paper. In the West, the practice survived through the Roman era, and declined after the fall of Rome. It was revived again in the 15th century and was the primary means of reproducing illustration matter, even after Gutenberg's *letterpress*-based printing press was invented. Playing cards, religious prints, and other illustrations were produced using intaglio techniques, including newly developed means of engraving images on metal plates. Until the development of gravure printing in the 19th century, intaglio remained almost entirely an artist's medium, perhaps best demonstrated in the engravings of the German Renaissance artist Albrecht Dürer. (See *Printing* and *Gravure*.)

The term *intaglio* is also used to refer to the engraved image or design itself. It is also used to refer to the pattern of cells engraved on a *flexographic* press's *anilox roller*.

In *finishing*, *die*s used for *embossing* or *foil stamping* may be *intaglio* dies, or have a depressed image area.

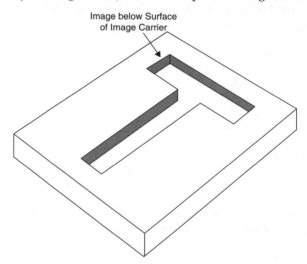

Image below Surface of Image Carrier

An intaglio engraving.

Integral

One type of *plate cylinder* used in *flexography*. See *Plate Cylinder: Flexography*.

Integrated Circuit (IC)

A plastic or ceramic object or "substrate" about 2 in. long, ¾ in. wide, and ⅛ in. thick. Within this body is the *microprocessor*, or "chip," that is the brain of a computer, a set of many electrical "gates" or circuits, the "on" or "off" state of each corresponding to the 1 or 0 of *binary* code. Although the term *integrated circuit* is used interchangeably with the word "chip," it is not entirely correct.

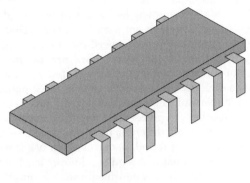

An integrated circuit.

Integrated Drive Electronics (IDE)

In computing, a standard *interface* for *hard disk* drives, capable of high data transfer rates and is thus widely used for hard disks having storage capacities of 40 *megabyte*s to 1–2 *gigabyte*s. With IDE, all the control circuitry is located on the drive itself, a separate *hard-disk controller* card not being required.

Integrated On-Line Database Service

A company or organization that produces and allows remote access to *database*s.

Integrated Services Digital Network (ISDN)

A worldwide digital telecommunications network that, as of this writing, is becoming prevalent not only in high-speed network access but also for high-speed *Internet* access. Many *Internet service provider*s are now offering ISDN connections to their customers.

The advantage of ISDN—in contrast to telecommunications using voice-grade telephone lines, or even other connections used in networks—is much faster speed and its ability handle greater volumes of data. At the moment, two types of ISDN connections are possible: *Basic Rate Interface (BRI)*, comprising two *B channel*s each with a capacity of 64 kilobits per second, and one *D-channel*, with a capacity of 16 kilobits per second (the two B channels can be used simultaneously); and *Primary Rate Interface (PRI)*, which comprises 23 B channels and one D channel, each channel having the same capacity as those used for the BRI. In Europe, however, PRI comprises 30 B channels

and one D channel. A "broadband ISDN" (or *B-ISDN*), an ISDN standard slated to support transmission speeds of up to 135 megabits per second, is currently in development. It will allow the transmission of multimedia applications, as well as facilitate video conferencing, high-resolution television, and other such high-capacity data.

Integrated Software

In computing, any application software that combines several different program types—such as database, spreadsheet, word processing, communications, and/or business graphics—into a single package comprising several modules, usually with a single, simple *interface* from module to module. The advantage to integrated software—also known as an *integrated software package*—is that data can be easily transferred from module to module. A disadvantage, however, is that each module lacks the advanced features that a *standalone* version of the application possesses. Microsoft Works and Claris Works are two popular integrated software packages. See also *software suite*.

Intellectual Property

Intellectual property is the term for all creative expressions of human thought, research, science, and entertainment. It includes the legal right of an individual or company to publish, print, perform, record, film, or tape a literary, artistic, musical, software program, or other work of creativity. It is codified by the laws of each country and international agreements.

We are surrounded by text and sound and graphics. The World Wide Web Browsers let you download all manner of material. The ability to store, transmit and access text, data, sound, images, and other types of information in digital form has led to the explosion of the new media market. With this rise in the use of multimedia, the integration of computer, communications, entertainment, music, and publishing industries has become more apparent with more challenges to intellectual property.

DEFINING MEDIA

A media product could be print, or it could include text, sound, and images that are assembled and then accessed interactively by the user via his or her computer. The user is prompted to use the mouse or keyboard to "click" from screen to screen. Digital media is a combination of software and multiple forms of content, in digital form, stored and delivered using computer technology, and used in an interactive and nonlinear manner.

Digital media contains different combinations of sound (usually spoken words, music, or sound effects), images (such as photographs, graphics, motion picture clips, or animation), and some sort of software to run the program. This software is used to make the program actually operate. The result is a seamless production of content and form.

Since digital media products are digital in nature, they are usually produced in machine-readable form. This can be anything from a magnetic disk to a compact disk with read-only memory (CD-ROM) or a stored file on a Web server. Delivery of new media products can take many forms. The most common form is on CD-ROM or floppy disk. With the use of a modem, users can also download software and multimedia packages from an online service and be billed for the transaction through a credit card or an account. Digital media must be delivered to be used. Since most new media products are interactive, that is, they use some sort of action or reaction from the user to prompt them to continue, by making objects available on the screen to "click" or select. Multimedia products provide what is called "nonlinear" access—the user can move around from place to place in the program by clicking on objects that link them to other parts of that program. This is unlike traditional ways were the user is typically expected to read or listen to the work from start to finish—passively.

There is no single governmental body overseeing the new media industry. Instead, it is comprised of existing laws that are applicable to the development, protection, and distribution of the product. These include copyright law (probably the biggest source of protection and concern), trademark and unfair competition law, laws protecting one's right of publicity and privacy, defamation law, trade secret laws, and patent laws. These are all of great concern to information developers and designers.

All media products, including all of the content generated, are automatically protected by federal copyright from the instant of their creation. This law creates a valuable form of protection for all media works that you personally produce. This law also acts as a double-edged sword in that it provides an obstacle for content that is created by others in the event that your creation is similar to another or uses parts of another. Originality is the key. Some information produced by others is public domain, free to use without permission from the creator. However, this part of the copyright law is interpreted by the federal law in different ways, and the law itself can create problems because some of it does not seem to make sense.

RIGHT OF PUBLICITY AND PRIVACY

When you produce the digital media disk or Web site of the Mickey Mouse Club, the creator of that good old rodent may not wish him to be a part of the production. This is their right under the Publicity Law—to negate the use of Mickey in your production. If in the production of your new media package you use the names of people, living or dead, those people have the right to refuse you the use of their name under the Privacy Law. Even deceased people have rights, believe it or not.

If your program or project says something really nasty about Barney the Dinosaur, that he likes to eat Boy Scouts for lunch, you could get sued under Defamation Law. It could be seen as injuring the reputation of a large stuffed object and making false statements about purple dinosaurs. If you used an outside company to produce the graphics used in a digital media production and this company used union talent, the union contract may have the

right to collect certain payments. This may include payment to many different unions.

All software used to create a new media product, unless you created your own programs, including authoring and editing tools, is copyrightable. Any controlling software that is needed to run the program falls under the same copyright laws. Most programs have a "player" or "viewer" that are specifically given away so that productions can be played or viewed.

TRADE SECRET AND PATENT LAW

In the creation of your multimedia product, you may have needed to use valuable information from another company that wishes this information be kept a secret. Under the Trade Secret Law, you must not pass on any facts that would harm the company that you borrowed the information from. Like copyright laws, trade secret laws are automatically obtained. But you must not let the secret out or you lost them.

Because of a law passed in November 1993, patent law became an important consideration for digital media creators. If you developed a process of navigating through a program and it is uniquely different from everyone else's, then you can get a patent on it and no one else can use it without your permission. It must be unique and never used before.

Virtually all content of a new media work is qualified for copyright protection. This includes text and databases, musical works, sound recordings, pictorial and graphic works, and motion pictures and other audio, visual, or textual works. Text by itself is protected by copyright. This includes items such as books, plays, poems, articles, editorials, as well as other works expressed in text form. Both fiction and nonfiction books are obviously copyrightable as well.

Databases as a whole are copyrightable. This copyright holds true if the database is comprised of text or numbers or images. This database could hold images for certain clients of a company, and without their permission, the images would not be usable by outside groups. An example of a database that may not be copyrightable is one comprised of names and addresses, but a compilation copyright might be granted for the order or structure of the database.

Fictitious characters that exist in visual form such as Batman and Daffy Duck usually carry a copyright on them for their use in works. These characters are copyrightable in image or pictorial form, and not so as much as in text form. Assume all cartoon characters are copyrighted.

MUSICAL WORKS

Any kind of musical work—verbal, written lyrics, or the music itself—is copyrightable. Lyrics by themselves do not sufficiently qualify for a copyright, but with the combination of sound and tone they do qualify. To use music, you may require rights from several different parties depending on whether or not you record the music from its source or use the performance of a third party. Rights in music are quite complicated.

Mechanical rights include the basic right to use a musical composition and do not include the right to publicly perform the music. A mechanical license often does not permit the use of the music with still or moving images—such use requires a "synchronization" license. Copyright law provides a compulsory license for mechanical rights, but most licensees prefer to obtain these rights commercially through the Harry Fox Agency or other agencies. This preference is based on the payment and accounting requirements imposed by the "compulsory" license in the Copyright Act.

If the music is to be synchronized with still or moving images on a screen, the licensee must obtain a "synchronization" license. Although these rights may also be handled by the Harry Fox Agency, in some cases you may need to contact the music publisher directly.

You will also need a license for public performance if shown to an audience. Most music publishers permit either ASCAP or BMI to license their public performance rights. These rights do not apply to a particular performance by a particular individual or group to use the particular recording of a performance of the musical composition. Obtaining a mechanical license to "Feelings" would not permit you to use a particular artist's performance of the song.

If you have rights to a particular performance or recording and you desire the musical composition to be performed by a particular group or individual, you must also obtain the right of the copyright holder for that particular performance. Unless you have new artists record the music, you must negotiate with the holder of the rights. These rights are generally held by record companies. Sound recordings that incorporate music, the spoken word, and other sounds, such as sound effects, are copyrightable. You could have a case where two sounds sound alike but were both recorded as original sounds.

PHOTOGRAPHS AND STILL IMAGES

Whether drawn graphics or photos of art, they all are copyrightable. This can include two- and three-dimensional works of art, photographs, and prints of art reproductions. Illustrations such as architectural and technical drawings are also copyrightable. A picture of a statue is protectable.

Copyrights for photographs are owned by the photographer, although they may either be assigned to another party or transferred to the photographer's employer under the work-for-hire contract. The determination of who owns the appropriate rights in the photograph can be very difficult and time-consuming because of fragmentation in this industry. For example, the fact that a photograph appeared in Forbes does not necessarily mean that Forbes owns the copyright in the photograph. Forbes may only have a license to use it once in its magazine. The licensing of photographs includes the use of color, the medium (newspapers, magazines, etc.), and attribution as well as others.

AUDIO AND VISUAL WORKS

It is clearly stated in the Copyright Act of 1976 that all motion pictures and other related audio and visual works are copyrightable. Video is a related audio and visual work.

You must distinguish between video that you have created and video for which you need to obtain rights. The "authors" of a videotape may include the actors, directors, scriptwriters, music composers, and the camera people. To avoid the problems of joint ownership of copyright, you should obtain the appropriate agreements from all individuals involved.

The use of the short video clips from a particular event may require multiple clearances, including clearing the music used in the clip, obtaining a license from the copyright owner, paying reuse fees to any entertainment unions, and clearing the rights of publicity of the participants. If you use the "scripted" performances, you will have to pay reuse fees.

Stock footage is available from stock houses in many cities and ranges from historical footage of various locations or events to local commercials. Other institutions, such as television stations, may also license their newscasts. These institutions generally base their royalty on the type of use of the film or video. Different royalties are established for use on national television or local broadcasts.

The creation of a new media production is very complicated. Whether it be for navigating or searching your disk the software as well as the content is copyrightable. Copyright protects both content and software that go into the work, plus there is a copyright on the entire package itself. One digital media work could have copyrights that belong to different parties. Since parts of a multimedia production use someone else's art or design, the copyrights can become quite numerous since these items are used solely with permission.

WHAT RIGHTS DO COPYRIGHT OWNERS HAVE?

Article I, Section 8 of the Constitution authorizes Congress to create a copyright system to promote the "Progress of Science and useful Arts, by securing for limited Times to Authors the exclusive Right to their Writings." The last major revision of its copyright law in 1978 specifies that copyright subsists in original works of authorship fixed in any tangible medium. Under this legislation, copyright extends to computer programs. The Act accords to copyright owner the exclusive right to reproduce and distribute their work, or derivative works with the general term of copyright protection as the life of the author plus 50 years. Copyrights prior to 1978 last 28 years from the date originally secured with the second term of an existing copyright renewable for an additional 47 years.

The Copyright Act of 1978 grants the owner of the copyright of a work a limited monopoly of the use of the work. To accomplish this, the copyright owner is given the right to do the following:

1. Make copies of the work yourself for whatever purpose (reproduction right).
2. Prepare derivative works (adaptation right).
3. Distribute copies of the work publicly by sale, rental, lease, or lending (distribution right).
4. Perform or display the work publicly in front of an audience (display and public performance right).

When someone other than the copyright holder performs any of the above, they are in direct infringement of the copyright law unless given the permission of the copyright owner.

OWNERS' REPRODUCTION RIGHT

The Copyright Act gives you, the copyright owner, an exclusive right to reproduce and to authorize the work to be reproduced or used by others. Because the owner of the copyright is the only person granted the right to authorize reproduction of a copyrighted work, the process of digitally scanning or capturing a copyrighted photograph from a magazine and then storing it onto a disk constitutes making a copy, and also constitutes copyright infringement. Copying a sound recording to a disk without authorization by the copyright owner also constitutes copyright infringement.

With respect to the creation of media work:
1. You can create your own text and graphics.
2. In certain cases, you can use existing content without permission (fair use of content).
3. You can obtain permission to use preexisting content from the owners of the rights of that content that you want to use.

WHAT WORKS ARE PROTECTED BY COPYRIGHT?

In reference to the Copyright Act of 1978, virtually everything that goes into any digital media production is copyrightable. To fully understand the extent of copyright on digital or multimedia productions, we need to understand three areas: copyright protection for content (for example, text and music); copyright protection for the technology (software for writing programs); and the completed digital media product itself. They synthesize into one protectable unit.

Copyright protection is available for all "works of authorship." This includes the following types of works that are of interest to the multimedia developer:
• *Literary (text-based) works*—novels, nonfiction prose, poetry, newspaper articles, magazine articles, journal articles, computer software, software manuals, training manuals, technical manuals, catalogs, brochures, ads (text), and compilations such as business lists and directories.
• *Musical (music-based) works*—songs, operas, musicals, ad jingles, and instrumentals.
• *Dramatic works*—plays, operas, and skits.
• *Pictorial and sculptural works*—photographs, posters, maps, paintings, drawings, graphic art, display ads, cartoon strips, cartoon characters, stuffed toys, statues, paintings, and fine art.
• *Motion pictures and other visual works*—movies, documentaries, travelogues, training videos, television shows, television ads, and interactive multimedia works.
• *Sound (sound-based) recordings*—recordings of music, sounds, or words.

COPYRIGHT PROTECTION

Copyright protection is automatic when an "original" work of authorship is "fixed" in a tangible medium of expression.

Registration with the Copyright Office is optional (but you have to register before you file an infringement suit.) Registering early may make you eligible to receive attorney's fees and statutory damages in a future lawsuit.

A work is original as far as copyright is concerned if it is original to the author and was not copied from some preexisting work or works.

A work is "fixed" when it is made "sufficiently permanent or stable to permit it to be perceived, reproduced, or otherwise communicated for a period of more than transitory duration." Even copying a computer program into RAM has been found to be of sufficient duration for it to be "fixed" (although some legal scholars disagree with this conclusion).

Neither the "originality" requirement nor the "fixation" requirement is stringent. An author can "fix" words, for example, by writing them down, typing them on a typewriter, dictating them into a tape recorder, or entering them into a computer. A work can be original without being novel or unique—or even correct.

Minimal creativity is required to meet the originality requirement. No artistic merit or beauty is required. A work can incorporate preexisting material and still be original. When preexisting material is incorporated into a new work, the copyright on the new work covers only the original material contributed by the author. A digital media work might incorporate a number of photographs that were made by a photographer (who gave the developer permission to use the photographs in the work). The copyright on the digital media work does not cover the photographs, only the material created by the developer.

SCOPE OF PROTECTION

Copyright protects against copying the expression in a work as opposed to the idea of the work. The difference between idea and expression is one of the most difficult concepts in copyright law. The most important point to understand is that the protection of the expression is not limited to exact copying—either of the literal words of a novel or the shape of a stuffed bear. Copyright infringement extends to new works that are substantially similar. A copyright owner has five exclusive rights in the copyrighted work:
• *Reproduction right.* The reproduction right is the right to reproduce, duplicate, transcribe, or imitate the work in fixed form.
• *Modification right.* The modification right (also known as the derivative works right) is the right to modify the work to create a new work. A new work that is based on a preexisting work is known as a "derivative work."
• *Distribution right.* The distribution right is the right to distribute copies of the work to the public.
• *Public performance right.* The public performance right is the right to show the work at a public place or to transmit it to the public. In the case of a motion picture or other audio or visual work, showing the work's images in sequence is "performance." Some types of works, such as sound recordings, do not have a public performance right.

• *Public display right.* The public display right is the right to show a copy of the work directly or by means of a film, slide, or television image at a public place or to transmit it to the public. In the case of a motion picture or other audiovisual work, showing the work's images out of sequence is considered "display."

In addition, certain types of works of "visual art" also have "moral rights" that limit the modification of the work and the use of the author's name without permission from the original author. Anyone who violates any of the exclusive rights of a copyright owner is an infringer.

An artist scanned a photographer's copyrighted photograph, altered the image by using digital editing software, and included the altered version of the photograph in a multimedia work that the artist sold to consumers. If the artist used the photograph without permission, the artist infringed the copyright by violating the reproduction right (scanning the photograph), the modification right (altering the photograph), and the distribution right (selling the altered photograph in his or her work). Three counts and you're out!

A copyright owner can recover actual or, in some cases, statutory damages (which can be as high as $100,000 in some cases) from an infringer. In addition, courts have the power to issue injunctions (legal orders) to prevent or restrain copyright infringement and to order the impoundment and destruction of infringing copies.

The extent (term) of copyright protection depends on three major factors:

1. Who created the work.
2. When it was created.
3. When it was first distributed commercially.

For copyrightable works created on and after January 1, 1978, the copyright term for those created by individuals is the life of the author plus 50 years. The copyright term for work made for hire is 75 years from the date of first publication (distribution of copies to the public) or 100 years from the date of creation, whichever expires first.

The copyright is owned by the person (or persons) who create the work. If the work is created by an employee within the scope of his or her employment, the employer owns the copyright because it is a *work for hire.* The copyright law also includes another form of *work for hire* that applies only to certain types of works that are specially commissioned works. These include audio and visual works, which will include most interactive media projects. In order to qualify the work as a *specially commissioned* work for hire, the creator must sign a written agreement stating that it is a *work for hire* prior to commencing the project.

Most foreign jurisdictions do not recognize the *specially commissioned* work for hire, and you need an assignment to transfer rights in some countries. Do not assume foreign law is the same as U.S. law.

The Universal Copyright Convention (1952) in Geneva, under the auspices of UNESCO, adopted the following:

• A copyright notice must appear in all copies of a work and consist of the copyright symbol, name of the copyright owner, and the year of first publication.
• No nation should accord domestic authors more favorable copyright treatment than the authors of other nations.
• The term of copyright is the life of the author plus 25 years.
• All signatory nations must grant an exclusive right of translation for seven years.

The Universal Copyright Convention and the Berne Convention were revised in 1971 to consider developing countries in regards to teaching, scholarship, and research. In 1988 the United States reversed its long opposition to the Berne Convention and joined the Berne Union. U.S. Copyright Law is slightly different in its treatment of "moral rights," which includes the right of an author to preserve his or her work from alteration. The Berne Convention recognizes a "right of integrity," while U.S. copyright law does not.

AVOIDING INFRINGEMENT

Current technology makes it too easy to combine material created by others—audio and video segments, music, graphics, photographs, text—into a digital media product. The technical ease of copying does not give one the legal right to do so. The use of copyrighted material owned by others without permission can incur legal liability for thousands or even millions of dollars in damages.

Most of the third-party material you will want to use in a multimedia product is protected by copyright. Using copyrighted material without getting permission—either by obtaining an "assignment" or a "license"—can have disastrous legal consequences. The owner of the copyright can prevent the distribution of your product (an injunction) and obtain damages for infringement, even if you did not intentionally include their material. An assignment is generally understood to transfer all of the intellectual property rights in a particular work, although an assignment can be more limited in scope. A license provides the right to use a work and is generally quite limited in its scope.

Most published works must present a copyright notice. However, for works published on or after March 1, 1989, the use of copyright notice is optional. Even if a work does not have a copyright notice does not mean that the work is not protected.

It is correct that *de minimis* copying (copying a small amount) is not copyright infringement. Unfortunately, it is rarely possible to tell where *de minimis* copying ends and copyright infringement begins. Copying even a small amount of a copyrighted work is infringement if that which is copied is a qualitatively substantial portion of the copied work. As example, a magazine article that used 300 words from a 300,000-word autobiography was found to infringe the copyright on the autobiography. Even though the copied material was only a small part of the autobiography, the copied portions were among the most important passages in the autobiography.

Copying any part of a copyrighted work is fraught with danger. If what you copy is truly a tiny and nonmemorable part of the work, you may get away with it (the work's owner may not be able to tell that your work incorporates an excerpt from his or her work). However, there is the risk of having to defend your use in expensive litigation.

If you give credit to the author, you are not a plagiarist because you are not pretending that you authored the copied work. However, attribution is not a defense in cases of copyright infringement. You cannot escape liability for copyright infringement by altering or modifying the work you copy. If you copy and modify elements of a copyrighted work, you will be infringing the copyright owner's modification right as well as the copying right. Ideas and facts are not protectable, but the expression of those ideas or facts is. You do not need a license to use a copyrighted work if:

- Your use is fair use.
- The work you use is in the public domain.
- The material you use is factual or an idea.

It is often difficult to tell whether a particular use is fair or unfair. Determinations are made on a case-by-case basis:

1. Courts are likely to find fair use where use is noncommercial, such as book reviews or school projects.
2. Courts are likely to find fair use where the copied work is factual rather than creative.
3. Courts are likely to find fair use where a small, but unsubstantial, amount of the protected work is used.
4. Courts are likely to find fair use where new work is not a substitute for the copyrighted work.
5. Courts are likely to find fair use if the new work does not compete, either in whole or in part.

If your new media work serves traditional fair use purposes—criticism, comment, news reporting, teaching, scholarship, research—you are within the bounds of fair use more than if your work is sold for commercial gain.

PUBLIC DOMAIN

Public domain works—works not protected by copyright—can be used by anyone. Because these works are not protected by copyright, no one can then claim the exclusive rights of copyright for such works. The plays of Shakespeare are in the public domain; there was no copyright then. Works enter the public domain because the term of the copyright expired, the copyright owner failed to "renew" their copyright under the Copyright Act of 1909, or the copyright owner failed to properly use a copyright notice—for works created before March 1, 1989. After that, copyright notice became optional.

You do not need a license to use facts or ideas from a protected work. Copyright protection is limited to original works of authorship. Nor do you need a copyright license for material that you create yourself. The rules regarding ownership of copyright are complex. You should not assume that you own the copyright if you pay an independent contractor to create the work (or part of it). The copyright for a work is owned by the individual who creates it, except for full-time employees working within the scope of their employment and copyrights that are assigned in writing.

THE PERTINENCE OF PATENT LAW

This law protects inventions and processes ("utility" patents) and ornamental designs ("design" patents). Inventions and processes protected by utility patents can be electrical, mechanical, or chemical in nature. Works protected by design patents include a design for a lamp, a design for silverware, or a design for a machine, as examples. Typefaces are not patentable unless linked to special hardware, such as machine-readable fonts. There have been notable lawsuits, even one suing the Patent Office, but typeface designs are not protectable. Their names can be trademarked, and the software programs that created them can also be protected.

A utility patent covers an invention that must be new, useful, and "nonobvious." To meet the "new" requirement, the invention must not have been known or used by others in the United States before the applicant invented it or been patented or described in a publication in the U.S. or a foreign country before they invented it. The policy behind the novelty requirement is that a patent is issued in exchange for the inventor's disclosure to the public of the details of the invention. If the work is not novel, the inventor is not adding to the public knowledge, so the inventor should not be granted a patent.

To meet the nonobvious requirement, the invention must be sufficiently different from existing technology and knowledge so that, at the time the invention was made, it as a whole would not have been obvious to a person having ordinary skill in that field. The policy behind this requirement is that patents should only be granted for real advances, not for mere technical tinkering or modifications of existing inventions. Utility patents are granted for a period of 17 years. Design patents are granted for a period of 14 years. Once the patent on an invention or design has expired, anyone is free to make, use, or sell the invention or design.

TRADEMARK LAW

Trademarks and service marks are words, names, symbols, or devices used by manufacturers and marketers and service providers to identify their goods and services, and to distinguish their goods and services from goods manufactured and marketed by others. For trademarks used in commerce, federal trademark protection is available under the federal trademark statute, the Lanham Act. Many states have trademark registration statutes that resemble the Lanham Act, and all states protect unregistered trademarks under the common law (nonstatutory law) of trademarks.

Trademark protection is available for words, names, symbols, or logos capable of identifying or distinguishing the owner's goods or services from the other goods or services. A trademark that merely describes a class of goods rather than distinguishing the trademark owner's goods is not protectable. "Corn flakes" is not protectable as a trademark because it describes a type of cereal that is sold by a number of companies rather than distinguishing one brand from another. It is said to be "generic." A trademark that is so close to a trademark already in use in the U.S. as to be likely to cause confusion is not protectable. Trademarks that are "descriptive" of functions, quality, or character of goods or services have special requirements before they will be protected, and these are quite complex.

The most effective trademark protection is obtained by filing a trademark registration application in the Patent and Trademark Office. Federal law also protects unregistered trademarks but is limited to the geographic area in which the mark is used. State trademark protection under common law is obtained by adopting a trademark and using it in connection with goods or services but is limited to the geographic area in which the trademark is actually used. State statutory protection is obtained via application with the state trademark office.

Several other areas of law deal with the right of individuals to control their image and reputation. Libel and slander laws protect an individual against the dissemination of falsehoods. To be actionable, the falsehood must injure the individual's reputation or subject them to hatred, contempt or ridicule. The individual can obtain monetary losses as well as damages for mental anguish.

IntelliDot

A digital *halftone* screening process developed by Optronics, capable of generating high-quality halftones.

Intelligent Device

Any device, such as one of a variety of consumer electronics devices, possessing its own computer.

Intelligent Terminal

In a network, a computer *terminal* that can function by itself and does not need to be connected to a host computer to be able to execute instructions.

Intensity

The degree of brightness, strength, or luminescence of a surface, such as a *CRT* screen, a printed ink film, etc.

Interactive

In general computing, descriptive of any computer program that solicits user participation, allowing the user to make decisions about what the program actually does. See *Interactive Processing*.

In multimedia, the term *interactive* refers to any presentation or production that allows the user to directly affect the course of a narrative. In conventional media such as movies, television, and video, the narrative unfolds in a linear manner, from start to finish. In interactive multimedia, there are *branching points*, at which the user is prompted for a direction to take. In this manner, information can be accessed in any order and—theoretically—the

presentation will be coherent regardless of what route the user takes.

The term *interactive* is also used to refer to a developing technology known as *interactive television*, a two-way *cable television network* that allows the viewer to influence the presentation of the programming. See *Interactive Television*.

Interactive Composition

A type of electronic page layout that allows the user to immediately view the results of changes made to the content or layout of a page (or pages). Interactive composition exists in contrast to *batch composition*.

Interactive Device

Any computer hardware that supports the input and output of graphics controlled by the user, usually by means of a dialog.

Interactive Graphics

Any computer graphics display system that supports user modification of graphics by means of input devices.

Interactive Processing

In computing, one of two basic means by which a computer reads and executes instructions. At the conclusion of each command, the computer stops and prompts the user for the next command, usually by means of a command line or *dialog box*. In contrast is *batch processing*, in which commands (usually contained in a *batch file*) are executed nonstop by the computer.

Interactive Session

In computer graphics, the set of activities, processes, and computations with which the *CPU*, the display, the keyboard, and the *mouse*—as well as the user—are currently occupied with.

Interactive Teletext

A two-way transmission of *teletext* using a *cable television network* to transmit information *to* the viewer, and a simultaneous telephone-line connection to transmit information *from* the user. Essentially, the viewer sees text and graphics on the television screen, and the keypad on a telephone is used to control the display of that text and graphics, as well as respond to its content (such as in the ordering of products and services). See also *Teletext*. Interactive teletext is often abbreviated *i.txt*, and is also known as *interactive videotext*.

Interactive Television

In telecommunications, a two-way transmission of information to and from television viewers, usually over a *cable television network* or other type of *broadband* network. The advantages of interactive television, which is still under development as of this writing, is that remote viewers can influence the course of the programming, from such things as selecting movies on demand (called *video-on-demand*) to other more elaborate decisions, such as choosing a desired camera angle during sporting events. Tests in various communities have been conducted for at least two decades, and viewer response has been less than encouraging. However, the increasing marriage of the *World Wide Web* with television (as opposed to one's computer, as is now the case) may open new doors for the concept of interactive television.

Interactive Video

Essentially, the marriage of computers and video, allowing the user to interact with the video material, which can involve such things as selecting what program will be shown, as well as making decisions that affect the linear progression of the narrative. Interactive video is currently distributed on *videodisc*s and *CD-ROM*s.

Interactive Videotext

See *Interactive Teletext*.

Interblock Gap

Alternate term for *block gap*. See *Block Gap*.

Intercharacter Spacing

A form of positive *letterspacing* performed specifically to ensure that a line is *justified*.

Intercompany File Exchange Network (IFEN)

In computing, a means by which peripheral devices can be linked together to workstations in a network, allowing for multiple-user access to files stored on external media.

Interface

In physical and chemical terms, an interface is the line or point of contact between two separate media, such as between water and air. In computing, the term *interface* has several meanings.

The most common definition of *interface* refers to the way a computer interacts with the user (and vice versa), usually used to describe either a *command-line interface*, in which text-based and somewhat cryptic commands are entered via a keyboard, or a *graphical user interface*, in which icons, windows, and dialog boxes are clicked on using a mouse or other similar device. The latter is often described as more *user-friendly*. See *Command-Line Interface (CLI)* and *Graphical User Interface (GUI)*. This type of interface is commonly known as a *user interface* or *software interface*.

The term *interface* also refers to the means by which two hardware components of a computer system interact with each other, usually involving some means of software control. For example, different computer systems have different interfaces between the *CPU* and *peripheral* devices connected to it. On the Apple *Macintosh* and increasingly *Windows*-based PCs, the *Small Computer System Interface (SCSI)* is the means by which attached disk drives,

CD-ROM drives, scanners, etc., communicate with the CPU. Peripheral devices—including printers and modems—also need *device driver*s, which are the primary software component of the interface. This type of interface is commonly known as a *hardware interface*.

The term *interface* also refers to the means by which a computer is connected to a network, facilitating the transfer of data from node to node.

Interface Standard

In computing, any standard means of connecting one device to another device, the specifications usually involving cabling and the transfer of data through those cables. Some common interface standards include *Small Computer System Interface (SCSI)*, *Integrated Drive Electronics (IDE)*, *Enhanced Small Device Interface (ESDI)*, among others.

Interference

In optics, the interaction of light waves with each other. When beams of light are split or deflected—such as when they pass through a *diffraction grating*—the resulting waves will interact with each other. As waves, they will each possess crests and troughs; when interacting waves are "in phase" with each other, the crests of one wave will line up with the crests of another, magnifying the intensity of the light wave (known as "constructive interference"). On the other hand, if the two waves are "out of phase" with each other, the crests of one wave will line up with the troughs of another, and they will essentially cancel each other out (known as "destructive interference"). It is the effect of constructive interference that makes a diffraction grating so effective at breaking white light into individual spectral components.

Interframe Coding

Alternate term for *interframe compression*. See *Interframe Compression*.

Interframe Compression

A means of *data compression* used for the compression of *digital video*, *animation*, or other moving images. Interframe compression is based on the encoding of—or creating a shorthand notation for—portions of a frame that possess the same color. Such coding is the basis behind *MPEG* encoding. See *Data Compression*.

Interlaced

Descriptive of a *cathode-ray tube* whose image is generated by means of *interlacing*. See *Interlacing*.

Interlaced Fields

A monitor that is scanned by means of *interlacing* the two separate *field*s comprising a *frame*. See *Interlacing*.

Interlaced Scanning

Alternate term for *interlacing*. See *Interlacing*.

Interlace Flicker

On a **cathode-ray tube**, a perceptible **flicker** of the image caused by a difference in brightness between odd and even scan lines on an **interlaced** monitor. See **Interlacing**.

Interlacing

A scanning technique used in **cathode-ray tube**s in which the **electron gun** scans a line with each vertical passage as well as with each horizontal passage. Or, essentially, the gun constructs an image with two separate **fields**. Usually, the gun draws first the even-numbered lines, then draws the odd-numbered lines, each set of lines being considered a field. Interlacing is used on television sets, but rarely on computer monitors with a **resolution** less than 1024×768 **pixel**s. Screens that are **interlaced** tend to produce a flicker (called **interlace flicker**) whereas a **non-interlaced** screens tend to have a more settled image. Also known as **interlaced scanning**.

Interleave

To insert sheets of a non-adhering material (called **slip sheet**s) between printed materials as they come off press to prevent **ink setoff** and **blocking**.

In computing and multimedia, the term *interleave* means to integrate different types of data or files. For example, in many multimedia applications (especially those created using the **CD-i** system), text, graphics, audio, and video are intermingled to produce presentations that play synchronized sound and video. See **Audio Video Interleaved (AVI)**, for example.

Interleaved Memory

In computing, a means of increasing the speed of computer system operation that involves dividing **dynamic RAM** (also known as **DRAM**) into separate "banks." One system limitation inherent in computing is the need to update the system's DRAM every thousandth of a second, and while this updating is taking place the **processor** cannot read the contents of DRAM. By dividing DRAM into separate banks, it can be updated by cycling through each memory bank. In this way, there is always at least one bank that can be read by the processor at any one time.

Interleaving

In printing, the insertion of **slip sheet**s between prints as they come off press. See **Interleave** (first definition).

In computing, the term *interleaving* refers to the division of a computer's **dynamic random-access memory** (known as **DRAM**) into separate memory "banks" as a means of enhancing system performance. See **Interleaved Memory**.

In computing and multimedia, *interleaving* also refers to the act of combining various data types and files into a seamless whole. See Interleave (second definition).

Interletter Spacing

Alternate term for **letterspacing**. See **Letterspacing**.

Interline Spacing

Alternate term for **leading** or **line spacing**. See **Line Spacing**.

Intermediate

Any chemical or other substance that increases the rate at which a chemical reaction takes place, but which itself is consumed and/or altered by the reaction. In printing inks, **drier**s are added as **catalyst**s, as they facilitate the chemical reactions (such as **oxidation** and/or **polymerization**) that cause an ink to dry. A substance that increases the rate of reaction but that is *not* affected by the reaction is called a catalyst. A substance that acts to retard the rate of a chemical reaction is called an **inhibitor**.

Intermediate Material

Term used to describe the **asset**s used to construct a **videodisc**, such as original video, prints, slides, etc.

Intermediate Negative

A **negative** prepared in the **prepress** phase of printing that is oriented right-reading, emulsion-up. Intermediate negatives cannot be used to make plates; they must be further exposed emulsion-to-emulsion to produce **final negative**s. See **Negative**.

Intermediate Rollers

Term for one of two types of rollers found in the **inking system** of a printing press used in **offset lithography**. Intermediates are resilient-surface rollers found adjacent to gear-and-chain-driven, hard-surface rollers (such as **oscillator**s) and are turned by the force generated on their surfaces by contact with the adjacent rollers. Intermediates (known as **distributor**s when falling between two other rollers or as **rider**s when they contact only one other roller) serve the function of working the ink into the necessary **viscosity** needed for proper printing, and of mixing the ink with amounts of water to form a proper emulsion. (See **Inking System: Offset Lithography** and **Offset Lithography**.)

Intermittent-Flow Dampening System

A **dampening system** used in many offset lithographic presses that utilizes a **ductor roller** to alternately contact the **fountain pan roller** attached to the **water fountain** and an **oscillator**, a roller in contact with the **form roller**s.

Intermittent-flow systems, as their name implies, do not provide a continuous flow of fountain solution to the plate, which can cause problems in dampening system performance, as well as the lack of an instantaneous effect of changes to the quantity of **fountain solution** sent forth from the water fountain. Since intermittent-flow systems have been traditionally the most common dampening systems used in offset presses, they are also known as **conventional dampening system**s. (See also **Continuous-Flow Dampening System**.) See **Dampening System**.

See illustration on the next page.

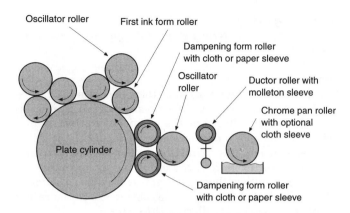

An intermittent-flow dampening system.

Internal Bond Strength

A measure of the strength of a paper to resist rupturing in the direction perpendicular to the plane of the paper surface. Paper strength is measured in three dimensions: the **grain direction** (or "X-direction"), the **cross-grain direction** (or "Y-direction"), and the direction at right angles to the paper (or "Z-direction"). When paper fibers are deposited on the **forming wire** during papermaking, successive layers of fibers are placed on top of each other. The internal bond strength refers to the strength of the bonding of these separate fibrous layers, and the **plybond strength** refers to the force needed to "delaminate," or separate, these layers. The internal bond strength is an important consideration in offset printing, to ensure that the paper sheet will not delaminate when subjected to the Z-direc-

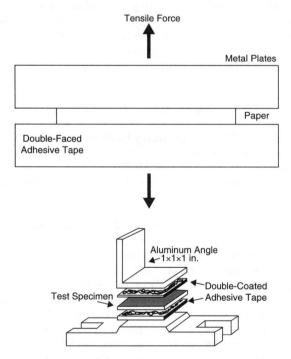

Two means of testing a paper's internal bond strength.

tional force caused by the peeling of the sheet from a press blanket containing tacky ink. Low internal bond strength of coated paper is also a factor in **blistering** during **heatset drying**.

Internal bond strength of paper is tested in a variety of ways, all of which gauge the amount of force needed to delaminate a paper sample. In one test, the sample is sandwiched between and adhered to two metal plates. A force is applied at right angles to the sample, and the force required to pull the sample apart is recorded, usually in pounds per square inch (psi) or kilopascals. Another test (utilizing an internal-bond impact tester) adheres a paper sample to the underside of an L-shaped metal anvil. A swinging pendulum contacts the side of the anvil, which applies a force at right angles to the paper sample. The force needed to delaminate the sample is recorded as its internal bond strength. Internal bond strength is also known as its **Z-directional tensile strength**.

Internal Command

In computing, any **DOS** command that does not exist as a separate program in the main DOS directory and is thus always available to the user. Examples of internal commands are COPY and DIR. See also **External Command**.

Internal Drum Film Recorder

Alternate term for **internal drum imagesetter**. See **Internal Drum Imagesetter**.

Internal Drum Imagesetter

A type of **drum imagesetter**, a device used for **high-resolution** laser output of digitally created pages or **color separations** in which the film to be exposed is mounted inside a cylinder, and the light source moves around the inside of the drum, as opposed to an **external drum imagesetter**. See **Drum Imagesetter**. Also called an **internal drum film recorder** and an **internal drum plotter**.

Internal Drum Plotter

Alternate term for an **internal drum imagesetter**. See **Internal Drum Imagesetter**.

Internal Font

In computing, **font** data that is housed within the device utilizing the font(s) in question. Internal fonts do not need to be loaded into the device memory before use.

Internal Modem

In computing, a **modem** that does not exist as a **standalone** device, requiring installation on an **expansion bus**, in contrast to an **external modem**.

Internal Sizing

Materials added to the papermaking **furnish** at the beginning of the paper machine's **forming section** to improve the paper's resistance to water or other liquids. Substances used for internal sizing include **rosin** and printer's **alum**, which is short for aluminum sulfate (which helps the rosin adhere to the paper fibers). Rosin used for sizing is slightly acidic, so **alkaline paper** is sized using synthetic alkaline sizing agents. Although internal sizing is added to prevent water penetration, it does not make the paper waterproof. Internal sizing is also called **beater sizing**, as it is often added in the **beater**, a device used for paper pulp **refining**. Papers that have a minimal amount of internal sizing are called **slack-sized**, while papers that have a large amount of internal sizing are called **hard-sized**. Papers destined for sheetfed offset printing need to be hard-sized in order to withstand repeated exposure to the press's water-based dampening system. Unsized papers used for paper towels, blotter papers, or other uses that require high levels of water absorbency are called **waterleaf**.

A number of tests are used to determine the degree of a paper's internal sizing. (See **Feathering Test**, **Contact Angle Method**, **Dry Indicator Method**, **Ink Flotation Method**, **Curl Test Method**, **Cobb Size Test**, and **Water Immersion Method**.) Internal sizing differs from **external sizing**, also called **surface sizing**. See **Sizing**.

Internal Storage

Any computer storage space mounted within the computer, such as an **internal hard disk**, as opposed to an external disk drive.

Internal Tearing Resistance

A paper property that measures its ability to withstand being torn when the tear has already been started. See **Tearing Resistance**.

International Electrotechnical Commission (IEC)

An international organization, comprising several different committees from around the world, that meets to develop standards and specifications for electrotechnical hardware and software. They are very closely related to the **International Standards Organization (ISO)**.

International MIDI Association (IMA)

A worldwide organization that meets to develop standards and specifications for **MIDI** applications. See **Musical Instrument Digital Interface (MIDI)**.

International Prepress Association (IPA)

A trade organization devoted to the improvement of the processes of **color separation** and other prepress issues.

International Publishers Association (IPA)

A professional association of book and periodical publishers. The organization supports and promotes the publishing industry.

International Standard Book Number (ISBN)

A ten-digit number assigned to a book or edition, which identifies the work's national, language, or other group, and its publisher, title, edition, and volume number. The

ISBN is part of the International Standard Bibliographic Description (ISBD), which was prescribed by the International Organization for Standardization, adopted in 1969. The ISBN is a standard for the arrangement of bibliographic information in single- and multivolume publications; its numbers are assigned by publishers and administered by designated national standard book numbering agencies, such as R.R. Bowker in the United States, Standard Book Numbering Agency Ltd. in the United Kingdom, National Library in Brazil, and the Staatsbibliothek Preussischer Kulturbesitz (Prussian State Library) in Germany.

International Standard Serial Number (ISSN)

An eight-digit number that provides an identification code for serial publications. Unlike the **International Standard Book Number (ISBN)**, this number is a unique identification of a particular publication and does not record subject, language, or publisher. The ISSN is used by librarians, publishers, and subscription services for administration, copyright, ordering, and inventory control. The ISSN was developed by the International Organization for Standardization and registrations are made through the U.S. Library of Congress.

International Standards Organization (ISO)

An international organization operating with a view towards improving quality, expanding trade, increasing productivity, lowering costs, and transferring technology around the globe. One of the primary duties of the ISO is to set international standards on products, services, and testing in nearly all industries.

In the paper and pulp industry, the ISO sets standards on the procedures used to evaluate various paper properties. These ISO standards complement tests and standards set by the **Technical Association of the Pulp and Paper Industry (TAPPI)** and in many cases vary little from TAPPI standards. They also set standards on international paper sizes. (See **ISO Paper Sizes**, **A Series**, and **B Series**.)

High Level Data Link Control (HDLC) is an ISO protocol. ISO developed the Open Systems Interconnection (OSI), a seven-layered model for communications processing.

The International Standards Organization set standards for most of Europe, including drafting standards. Claris CAD supports this standard.

International Telecommunications Union (ITU)

An international organization that develops standards and specifications for telecommunications hardware and software. Responsible to the United Nations, the ITU is the parent organization of the **CCITT**.

Internegative

A photographic **negative** made of a print, **transparency**, or slide from which further prints or transparencies (or enlargements thereof) will be made.

Internet

Essentially, a world-wide computer network in which smaller networks and individual computers are connected to each other by means of a complex system of *router*s and *gateway*s. Originally created by the United States Department of Defense, it is now a popular consumer-oriented network, especially thanks to the *World Wide Web*, a graphics-based portion of the Internet. Access to the Internet can either be direct (which is how educational institutions, government departments, organizations, etc. connect) or through a third party known as an *Internet service provider (ISP)*, such as America Online, CompuServe, or MindSpring, to name but three. In this latter case, a consumer (usually through a personal computer equipped with a *modem*) dials into a central *server* that then allows access to other Internet resources.

The Internet has several distinct features, including email, USENET, Internet relay chat, and the World Wide Web.

Email. Perhaps the most widely used of all Internet resources, *electronic mail* (or *email*) allows for the (usually) instantaneous transmission and reception of messages from one user to another. The sender and receiver can be in adjacent offices, or separated by thousands of miles. Email is transmitted based on an *Internet address* (or *email address*), which typically includes the user's name, followed by the *at-sign* (@) and the user's *domain*, or the *local area network* in which the user (or the user's *mail server*) is located.

USENET. A *USENET* group, also known as a *newsgroup*, is a kind of electronic bulletin board, in which subscribers can post and download messages to and from each other, usually pertaining to a single topic, be it taoism, socialism, conspiracy theories, television programs, music groups, artists, computers, and (not surprisingly) sex. There are literally thousands of newsgroups on every conceivable topic.

Internet Relay Chat. *IRC* allows for a number of different users to "meet" in a single location and converse with each in real time. IRC (known colloquially as *chat room*s) is kind of a real-time USENET group, where users can discuss a wide variety of topics.

The World Wide Web. The World Wide Web is the fastest-growing portion of the Internet, being as it is graphics-based. Essentially, the Web is an interlinked collection of "pages," which correspond to files on widely separated computers. These pages can be instantaneously accessed by means of *hypertext link*s. The Web can be used (by means of a *browser*, or a software utility that can read *HTML* code) to view graphics, as well as hear sounds, see video and animation, or download files. Various *search engine*s make it easy to locate specific topics on the Web, and many companies and individuals now routinely provide their Web address (called a *Universal Resource Locator*) in ads, on business cards, etc.

Other Internet Resources. Before the advent of the World Wide Web (and in many cases afterward), files were located and obtained by means of searching utilities such as *Gopher*, *WAIS*, *Archie*, *Veronica*, *Jughead*, etc. The resources and utilities available to search the Internet are changing daily.

Internet Activities Board

Former name of the *Internet Architecture Board*. See *Internet Architecture Board (IAB)*.

Internet Address

See *Email Address*.

Internet Architecture Board (IAB)

A committee formed to coordinate and manage the generally unwieldy *Internet*. The two subcommittees that comprise the IAB are the *Internet Engineering Task Force (IETF)*, which recommends standard protocols for Internet transmission of data, and the *Internet Research Task Force (IRTF)*, which explores new technologies and the manner in which they can be applied to the Internet. The IRTF refers their findings to the IETF. See *Internet*. Formerly called the *Internet Activities Board*.

Internet Control Message Protocol (ICMP)

In networking and telecommunications, a portion of *TCP/IP* that facilitates *network-layer* management.

Internet Engineering Task Force (IETF)

A subcommittee of the *Internet Architecture Board*. See *Internet Architecture Board (IAB)*.

Internet Package eXchange (IPX)

In networking, a communications *protocol* developed by Novell for use in NetWare that creates, terminates, and sustains connections between devices (such as *workstation*s, *server*s, etc.) connected to the network.

Internet Protocol (IP)

See *Transmission Control Protocol/Internet Protocol (TCP/IP)*.

Internet Research Task Force (IRTF)

A subcommittee of the *Internet Architecture Board*. See *Internet Architecture Board (IAB)*.

Internet Service Provider (ISP)

In computing, a company or organization that provides users and subscribers with remote *Internet* access and usually a host of other services. An ISP is, essentially, a centralized *server* to which users can connect from a personal computer, the server then allowing further connections to other Internet sites. An ISP usually also allows the sending and receiving of *email*, *USENET* group subscriptions, *file transfer protocol (FTP)* connections, *Gopher* Internet searching, and *World Wide Web* browsing. Many ISPs also have their own sites and groups, and many companies and organizations have their own sites on specific ISPs (such as America Online, CompuServe, etc.). Internet Service Providers are usually local services, although many are national and international. Even national ISPs allow connections through local dial-up numbers, although in some metropolitan areas there may not be enough dial-up numbers for all the subscribers that make use of them. Although most ISPs once charged subscribers hourly, most now offer flat monthly rates. See also *On-Line Service*.

Internetwork Router

In a *local area network*, a device used to transmit messages between subnetworks.

Internetworking

In networking and telecommunications, the communication between different networks, commonly achieved by means of *bridge*s and *gateway*s.

Interoperability

In networking, the ability to run applications from different vendors over computer networks, typically a function of programs conforming to national and international standards.

Interpolated Resolution

In *scanning*, a measure of the maximum *resolution* at which a *scanner* can capture an image using its optics in combination with *interpolation* software, which can be used to "artificially" increase resolution. See *Scanning*. See also *Optical Resolution* and *Interpolation*.

Interpolation

In imaging and *scanning*, a means of "artificially" increasing the *resolution* of a scanned image. The new *interpolated resolution* supplements the *scanner*'s *optical resolution*. Essentially, interpolation works by taking the scanned *pixel* values and averaging sets of them, inserting new pixels between the originals. Interpolation generates varying degrees of image quality. Although it does not add detail to a scan, it can smooth transitions between gray or color gradations, eliminating such undesirable effects as *banding*. (See *Scanning* and *Resolution*.)

This is the process of re-sizing an image by computing new pixel values as weighted averages of existing pixel values. It is slightly more complex than a simple average. This system uses interpolation, including reducing the size of files to be sent to the host. The host specifies the reduction size with a whole number called an integer interpolation factor. Thus, if the host requests an image with an integer interpolation factor of 2, the system will send the image only after it has reduced it by a factor of 2 from 4 megabytes to 2 megabytes, for example.

Computers usually store images as numbers that represent the intensity of the image at discrete points. It is frequently necessary to determine the intensity of the image between those discrete points. Interpolation is a mathematical technique that generates those in-between values by looking at the surrounding intensities.

Interpress

A *page description language* developed by Xerox. See *Page Description Language (PDL)*.

Interpreter

In computer programming, a type of *compiler* that allows hardware to read and execute *source code* without needing to output intermediate *object code* (or *machine language*). Programmers often use an interpreter to quickly view a program for debugging purposes. See also *Compiler*.

Interprocess Communication

In computing, the ability for different applications to share information, either in a *multitasking* environment or over a computer network. At the most fundamental level, interprocess communication (abbreviated *IPC*) consists of the ability to cut data from one application and paste it into another. Beyond that is *Dynamic Data Exchange (DDE)*, the ability for pasted data in one document to be automatically updated when the corresponding data in another document is updated. The highest level of IPC is *Object Linking and Embedding (OLE)* in which one program can "borrow" the capabilities of another. See *Dynamic Data Exchange (DDE)* and *Object Linking and Embedding (OLE)*.

Inter-Repeater Link (IRL)

In networking, a portion of an *Ethernet* network connecting two *repeater*s but lacking any network *node*s.

Interrobang

In typography, a new form of punctuation proposed (not surprisingly) in the 1960s comprising a combination *exclamation mark* and *question mark*. It was designed to replace the "!?" combination, which is occasionally used. The interrobang, however, has not quite caught on.

Interrupt

In computing, a break in the processing of a command or a routine such that the processing can be continued at a later time. Any activity requiring the processor's attention is considered an interrupt. When an interrupt signal (called an *interrupt request*) is received, the processor branches to an *interrupt service routine*.

In networking, *interrupt* is a feature of some access methods in *ring* and *bus* networks that allows a particular *node* to instruct the *server* to put whatever it is doing on hold and process a request. After the node's request is completed, the server resumes the interrupted process.

Interrupt Controller

In computing, a *processor* used to deal with *hardware interrupt*s, prioritize them, and pass the information on to the main processor.

Interrupt Handler

In computing, a software routine called when an ***interrupt*** signal is received by the processor. Each type of interrupt signal—be it from a keyboard, mouse, etc.—possesses its own interrupt handler, which are stored by the computer in an ***interrupt vector table***.

Interruptible Display

In computing, a feature of many application programs that discontinues a ***screen redraw*** as the user initiates a new process. Since the user then does not have to wait until the screen is finished redrawing to begin a new process, a considerable amount of time can be saved.

Interrupt Request (IRQ)

In computing, a signal generated by a hardware device that indicates that an event has occurred that the processor needs to deal with.

Interrupt requests are usually given a unique numerical address (controlled by an ***interrupt controller***); for example, a keyboard may be assigned interrupt request 1, while the hard disk may be assigned interrupt request 5. Some computers (such as those using an ***ISA*** bus) have a limited number of interrupt requests, and it is often the case that system additions may inadvertently be configured to utilize the same interrupt request code. In this case, the conflicting device needs to be located and its interrupt request address altered. Interrupt request is abbreviated ***IRQ***.

Interrupt Service Routine

In computing, a routine that is called when a processor receives an ***interrupt*** signal. The processor suspends whatever it is working on when an interrupt service routine is called. After the interrupt service routine is completed, the system returns to the activity that was suspended. Interrupt service routine is abbreviated ***ISR***.

Interrupt Vector Table

In computing, a list of addresses corresponding to specific ***interrupt handler***s. See ***Interrupt*** and ***Interrupt Handler***.

Intertype

An automated linecasting device, manufactured by the International Typesetting Machine Company, that operated in a manner similar in principle to that of the ***Linotype***. See ***Type and Typography: History of Type*** and ***Linotype***.

Interword Spacing

In typography, the addition or subtraction of word spaces as a means of text ***justification***. See ***Justification***.

In-Text Equation

In typography, a mathematical equation or expression run in with text, such as $E = mc^2$, as opposed to a ***display equation***.

Intraframe Coding

Alternate term for ***intraframe compression***. See ***Intraframe Compression***.

Intraframe Compression

In ***digital video***, a means of ***data compression*** in which a still image is compressed as part of a video compression. Intraframe compression uses ***discrete cosine transform*** to look for redundancy of data in consecutive images. See ***Data Compression***. Also known as ***intraframe coding***.

Introduction

A portion of a book appearing immediately prior to the main text and serving to provide an overview of the text before it actually begins. An introduction is commonly distinguished from a ***foreword*** (which is commonly written by someone other than the author) and a ***preface*** (which tends to be a shorter statement about the text rather than an introduction to it). See ***Book Typography***.

Intruder

In networking and telecommunications, an unauthorized user on a network or computer system, often one with malicious intent. See also ***Hacker***.

Intumescent

Descriptive of an ink or coating material that swells or produces foam when exposed to heat.

Inverse Color Highlighting

Alternate term for ***reverse video***. See ***Reverse Video***.

Inverse Kinematics

A means of ***three-dimensional (3D) animation*** that makes use of ***hierarchical link***s and a feedback mechanism to animate objects. In inverse kinematics, a "child" object (say, a rabbit's ears) will be animated and, due to the feedback mechanism, the "parent" object of that child (say, the rabbit's head) will also move from a certain point. In turn, the parent of the parent (say, the rabbit's body) will also move.

Inverse Landscape

Alternate term for ***tumble landscape***. See ***Tumble Landscape***.

Inverse Portrait

Alternate term for ***tumble portrait***. See ***Tumble Portrait***.

Inverse Video

Alternate term for ***reverse video***. See ***Reverse Video***.

Inverted Backbone

A type of network architecture in which the ***hub*** and ***router***s are placed at the center of the network, all network ***node***s and segments attaching to this central hub. See ***Backbone Network***.

Inverted Index

A file structure that contains each value that can be used as a search parameter, together with pointers to identify the record within the data file from which each search value was extracted.

A file created from the full-text file or other database to facilitate searching. Sometimes called an "inverted file," an index consists of all terms that are not stopwords and are found in a given *field* (if fields exist in the file). In the initial step of creating an index, the terms are listed in the order of their occurrence in the full-text file. Then they are alphabetized ("inverted") and stored with the addresses of the text locations where they occurred. When the user enters a search request, the term(s) can be found quickly in the alphabetized listing. the associated addresses may be used for a further test such as proximity and are then translated into the set of text units that are the *hit*s of the search.

Inverted Page

A page that is upside-down.

I/O

Abbreviation for *input/output*. See *Input/Output (I/O)*.

I/O Bound

See *Input/Output Bound*.

Iodine Number

A measure of the speed at which a *vegetable oil*-based ink *vehicle* will dry. The higher the iodine number, the faster the ink will dry.

The iodine value also can be used to determine whether an oil is a drying oil, a semi-drying oil, or a non-drying oil, an important consideration in the formulation of an ink vehicle. (See *Vehicle*.)

IP

Abbreviation for *Internet Protocol*. See *Transmission Control Protocol/Internet Protocol (TCP/IP)*.

IPA

Abbreviation for *International Prepress Association*. See *International Prepress Association (IPA)*.

Abbreviation for *International Publishers Association*. See *International Publishers Association (IPA)*.

Abbreviation for *isopropyl alcohol*. See *Isopropyl Alcohol (IPA)*.

IPA Standard Color Reference

A set of *color swatch*es or samples of *SWOP* inks published by the *International Prepress Association (IPA)*, used as color standards for publication proofing and printing. One set of color samples, the Hi-Lo Reference, indicates the maximum and minimum density of each ink, while the Single-Level Color Reference indicates the optimum density of a particular ink, based on SWOP standards.

IPX

Abbreviation for *Internet Package eXchange*. See *Internet Package eXchange (IPX)*.

IrDA

Abbreviation for the *Infrared Data Association*. See *Infrared Data Association (IrDA)*.

Iris

In photography, an alternate term for *aperture*. See *Aperture*.

In video production, the term *iris* also refers to a video *transition* effect in which an image disappears into a subsequent image in spirals.

IRIX

In computing, an *operating system* developed by Silicon Graphics based on version 4 of the *UNIX* operating system. IRIX is used for Mips' *RISC*-based processors.

IRL

Abbreviation for *inter-repeater link*. See *Inter-Repeater Link (IRL)*.

Iron Blue

A variety of *inorganic color pigments* used in printing inks, derived from a complex iron compound, generally potassium ferric ferrocyanide—with the chemical formula $KFe(Fe[CN]_6) \cdot H_2O$—although the potassium may be replaced by sodium, ammonium, or some combination of both. Iron Blues range from highly transparent (some of the lighter shades) to highly opaque (the darker shades). Iron Blues possess high *lightfastness* and resistance to acids, oils, waxes, and heat, but react strongly to alkalis. They are also prone to spontaneous combustion if the undispersed pigment particles are left unmilled. They are highly popular pigments, however, primarily due to their low cost and high strength. Tinted Iron Blues can degrade upon storage, turning green and dirty. Various shades of Iron Blue include *Chinese Blue*, *Milori Blue* (or *Bronze Blue*), *Prussian Blue*, and *Toning Blue*. (See *Inorganic Color Pigments*.)

(*CI Pigment Blue 27 No. 77510.*)

Iron Oxide

Any of a variety of iron-oxygen compounds used as *pigment*s in the manufacture of printing inks. Iron oxides vary in color from yellow to brown, from brown to red, and from red to black. Iron oxides can occur naturally (such as the mineral hematite and rust) and can be specially manufactured. Some iron oxides are useful in *magnetic ink* (such as magnetite), and iron oxide is also used as a coating for recording tape. Iron oxide is also called ferric oxide. Iron oxide pigments are used frequently in *screen printing* inks.

Iron Oxide Yellows

A variety of *inorganic color pigment* that are used in printing inks. Iron Oxide Yellows are derived from hydrated ferrous oxide, possess excellent chemical resistance and **lightfastness**, and can withstand exposure to weather. Iron Oxide Yellows are used in printing applications involving exposure to high degrees of light and heat. Their advantages over other inorganic yellow pigments also include low toxicity and low cost. (See also **Inorganic Color Pigments**.)

(*CI Pigment Yellow 42 No. 77492*.)

IRQ
Abbreviation for **interrupt request**. See **Interrupt Request (IRQ)**.

Irrational Screen Angle
A **screen angle** that is used in the production of **halftone**s, distinguished by having a tangent that is an irrational number. (See also **Rational Screen Angle**.) See **Screen Angles**.

IRTF
Abbreviation for **Internet Research Task Force**. See **Internet Research Task Force (IRTF)**.

ISA
Abbreviation for **Industry Standard Architecture**. See **Industry Standard Architecture (ISA)**.

ISBD
Abbreviation for *International Standard Book Description*. See **International Standard Book Number (ISBN)** and **International Standard Serial Number (ISBN)**.

ISBN
Abbreviation for **International Standard Book Number**. See **International Standard Book Number (ISBN)**.

ISDN
Abbreviation for **integrated services digital network**. See **Integrated Services Digital Network (ISDN)**.

ISO
Abbreviation for **International Standards Organization**. See **International Standards Organization (ISO)**.

Isobutyl Acetate
An organic **solvent** used as a **thinner** in lacquer compounds.

Isochronous Service
In telecommunications, a means of data transmission in which preallocated **bandwidth** is used to deliver time-synchronized transmissions. Isochronous service is required for such transmissions as voice, video, audio, and other types of data for which delays in **packet** delivery would be unacceptable.

Isolated Text
In typography, one or two concluding lines of a paragraph carried over to the top of a new page or column, or a partial word occurring as the final line of a paragraph. (See also **Widow** and **Orphan**.)

Isolation
In videography, a means of simultaneously videotaping the same scene with several different cameras, each connected to its own recorder. During **editing**, the separate shots are viewed and evaluated and edited together.

Isomorphic
In graphics, **scaling** performed simultaneously in the horizontal and vertical directions.

ISO 9660
In computing, one of the first standards developed for the production of **compact disc**s, based on the earlier **High Sierra** standard. See **High Sierra** and **Compact Disc (CD)**.

ISO/OSI Model
See **Open System Interconnection (OSI)**.

ISO Paper Sizes
Standard sizes of international paper set by the **International Standards Organization (ISO)**. ISO paper sizes all maintain a constant width-to-length ratio of 1:1.414. When a sheet is cut in half, both new sheets will still retain that size ratio. (See **A Series** and **B Series**.)

Isophorone
A compound in the **ketone** family—chemical formula $C_9H_{16}O$—produced by the condensation of **acetone** and used as a **solvent** in printing inks (such as those used in **screen printing**) containing **vinyl resin**s, cellulose esters, and other such substances, due to its high solvent power and high boiling point. It is also mixed with other, less powerful solvents for use as a **retarder** in some lacquer formulations.

Isopropyl Alcohol (IPA)
A **monohydric alcohol**—chemical formula C_3H_8O—widely used in **shellac** and other lacquers, as well as in rubbing alcohol and antifreeze, or as a **solvent**.

ISO/TC 130 (Graphic Technology)
A committee within the **International Standards Organization (ISO)** that sets standards for the graphic arts.

ISP
Abbreviation for **Internet service provider**. See **Internet Service Provider (ISP)**.

ISR
Abbreviation for **interrupt service routine**. See **Interrupt Service Routine**.

ISSN
Abbreviation for **International Standard Serial Number**. See **International Standard Serial Number (ISSN)**.

Italic

In typography, a variation in the posture of the characters in a particular *typeface*, specifically, a slant to the right (*such as this, for example*). Today, italic type is used for emphasis, or in the setting of the titles of books, movies, etc.

Italic as a typeface was created in 1500 and was first utilized in books printed by Venetian printer Aldus Manutius. Its use then, however, was strictly one of economy; since italic type is narrower than *roman* type, more characters could be fit on a page, and fewer pages would be required, an important consideration in the days of escalating paper costs. Aldus Manutius's books were the first "pocket editions," designed to fit in a horseman's saddlebag. Eventually, roman faces were designed more narrowly, and replaced italic, primarily because italic was too difficult to read at great length.

There are three kinds of italics. *Unrelated italic*s are "pure" styles, based on 15th-century hands. *Related italic*s are designed to blend with a specific roman face but are still more or less pure italic. *Matching italic*s are essentially the same design as a particular roman typeface. Digitized typesetting devices that can modify characters electronically create matching italics, although purists call them *oblique*. Only electronically created italics are fully matching, since designed italics differ somewhat from romans.

The slant of a particular italic will vary, but a good standard is about 78°, or 12° from vertical. Certain characters change form when they make the transition from roman to italic. It's better to use generic (specially drawn) italics instead of electronically created italics due to the latter's proportional distortion of letters.

Tilting characters to the left (*back slant*) or right (oblique) so as to change their posture is called *slant*. This is

abcdefghijklmnopqrstuvwxyz
Avant Garde Book Oblique

abcdefghijklmnopqrstuvwxyz
Century Expanded Italic

abcdefghijklmnopqrstuvwxyz
Eurostile Oblique

abcdefghijklmnopqrstuvwxyz
New Baskerville Italic

Examples of italic and oblique typefaces.

optical or electronic distortion, and it is different from a true italic. Italics of *sans serif* designs usually look poor, and electronically italicized sans serifs almost always look bad, since italics were based on handwriting, and sans serifs are far-removed from any handwriting style.

Back-slanted type is nonfunctional, as the direction of letters goes against reading flow, and although modern digitized typesetters allow back slanting, there is no real reason to ever use it.

Typographically speaking, the terms *italic, cursive,* and *oblique* are all synonymous. In English-speaking countries, "italic" is the preferred term, although other countries commonly use "cursive," which means "flowing" or "running." The term "oblique" was most commonly associated with the Futura, or sans serif, family of typefaces. In this case, oblique is used rather than italic or cursive because the designer, Paul Renner, felt that the Futura italic was not a true italic and that it should have a name that more accurately described it. So he called it "oblique," which simply means "slanted."

Modern digitized typesetters can electronically slant characters to create oblique fonts. Oblique often refers to a somewhat mechanical slanting of characters; italic faces, however, are designed along more calligraphic lines.

In markup, italic is indicated by an underline. Copy that is traditionally put in italic type includes titles of publications, names of ships, trains, and aircraft, foreign words and phrases, scientific names, mathematical unknowns, protagonists in legal citations, words quoted by name, quotations, names of shows or plays (but quotation marks are used for TV shows), and works of art.

Alternatives to italic for highlighting or emphasizing are underline or bold face. All-capital italic lines should be avoided, since the uniform outline shape of all-cap words reduces legibility.

IT8

See *ANSI IT8*.

ITU

Abbreviation for the *International Telecommunications Union*. See *International Telecommunications Union (ITU)*.

i.txt

Abbreviation for *interactive teletext*. See *Interactive Teletext*.

J

J, j

The tenth letter of the English alphabet. The letter *J* did not exist as a letter until Medieval Latin, when it was used interchangeably with the letter *I*. It was also pronounced as the letter *I*, its only distinction being that it tended to be used as an initial letter and as a consonant (similar to the *Y* sound). In recent times, under the influence of French, it began to be used as the *dg* sound we use often today.

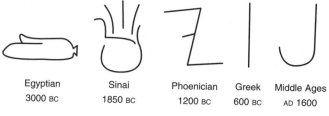

Egyptian	Sinai	Phoenician	Greek	Middle Ages
3000 BC	1850 BC	1200 BC	600 BC	AD 1600

The evolution of the letter J.

Jabber

In networking, any constant spewing of *garbage* (or meaningless transmissions) by a *workstation* that is connected to a *local area network (LAN)*, tying up the network. Jabber is usually caused by a circuit or logic problem at the workstation.

Jack

A connection port on a electronic device to which a *plug* can be connected. The term *jack* may also refer to the plug itself. See also *Modular Jack*.

Jacket

In *binding and finishing*, a printed, decorative paper wrapper placed around a *casebound* book, as a means of affording the underlying cloth cover protection, as well as for advertising and promotional reasons. Also known as a *dust cover* or *dust jacket*. See *Case Binding*.

Jacketing

In *binding and finishing*, the addition of a paper dust *jacket* to a *casebound* book.

Jaggies

Alternate term for the results of *aliasing*. See *Aliasing*. Also known as *stairsteps*.

Jam

A mechanical problem of any sheetfed device (printer, printing press, folder, etc.) during which sheets of paper do not feed properly and become wedged in the device.

Jannon, Jean

The French punchcutter and printer Jean Jannon was born in 1580. He designed a series of Baroque romans and italics. Much of Jannon's original material survives at the Imprimerie Nationale in Paris, where his typefaces are known as the Caracteres de l'Universite. They wound up there when Cardinal Richlieu attacked the Protestant stonghold of Sedan and confiscated Jannon's print shop and types. The types eventually ended up in the French National archives and were used in 1890 for the Centennial of the French Revolution, since they were thought to be Garamond's. Beatrice Warde discovered the error in the 1920s, but by then many Jannon types were issued as Garamond types.

Japan

A type of *varnish* that dries to a hard, glossy film.

Japan Art Paper

A type of paper with a mottled finish, manufactured in *basis weight*s from 50 to 150 lb.

Java

A programming language developed by Sun Microsystems for creating small, executable, rapidly downloaded applications for distribution on the *World Wide Web*. These programs can be used by the user to display animations or other multimedia presentations, and to perform other tasks.

Jaw Fold

On a *web press*, a fold made by a *jaw folder*. A jaw fold is created as the paper web travels around a cylinder, where it is tucked into a set of jaws on a second cylinder by a *tucker blade*. A jaw fold is usually at right angles to the former fold. If a second jaw fold is made, two *parallel fold*s are the result. A jaw fold is also known as a *tucker fold*. (See illustration on the following page.)

Jaw Folder

An *in-line* folding device on a *web press*. The jaw folder essentially consists of a set of cylinders. As a paper web is carried around one cylinder, it is cut into individual sheets or signatures, each of which is forced by a *tucker blade* (which creates a slight protrusion on paper) into a set of jaws on an adjacent cylinder. As the web is forced through these jaws, a fold is created. The jaw folder is essentially used to cut and fold a web into individual cylinders. (See illustration on the following page.)

Jaw Platen Diecutter

A type of *diecutting* press comprising two moving platens, one of which contains the cutting *die*, as opposed to a *reciprocating platen diecutter*. See *Diecutting*.

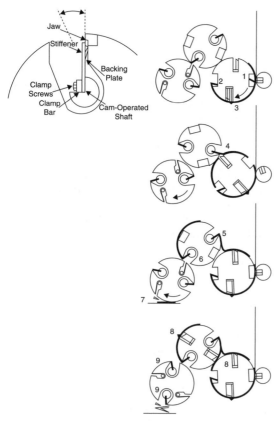

The making of a jaw fold.

Jelling

Alternate term for *livering*. See *Livering*.

Jenson, Nicolas

Nicolas Jenson (c. 1420–1480) was a publisher and printer best known as the person who developed the roman typeface. Apprenticed as a painter and then a cutter of dies for coinage, Jenson later became master of the French Royal Mint at Tours. In 1458 he went to Mainz and probably learned printing in Gutenberg's shop in Eltville. In 1470 he opened a printing office in Venice, and, in the first work he produced, the printed roman lowercase letter took on the proportions, shapes, and form that marked its transition from an imitation of handwriting to the typographic style that has remained in use throughout the centuries. Jenson also designed Greek-style type and blackletter type. He composed his types meticuously but did not always print them that way as he published more than 150 titles. The Jensonian roman would be the model for all roman typefaces that would ever follow it. The Roman family of types used by Aldus for printing Latin books—six fonts—were probably modeled on those of Nicolas Jenson, from whom Torresano had learned the trade and whose plant Aldus subsequently purchased. Jenson is credited with the invention of roman type, but roman style type-

faces had preceded him by five years or more. Jenson's type is remarkably similar to that of John de Spira. It probably was not de Spira's types that inspired Jenson's, they each may have used a similar manuscript hand as a model. Jenson's rounder, slighter, roman letter results in a gray, not a black page. The roman style is a typical Renaissance product, just as the blackletter is a gothic style. It may be said that Jenson was more famous for his type than the printing he produced.

Jet

A qualitative term descriptive of the blackness of black or near-black inks. Jet derives from the name of a black coal used to make beads and other types of jewelry.

Jewel Box

A plastic container in which *compact disc*s are distributed, usually comprising a transparent (or tinted) hinged cover, a set of prongs on the inside of the cover that holds a booklet or other sheet containing information on the disc, a round set of clasps that holds the disc in the box, and a transparent bottom where other decorative and/or informative artwork can be displayed. Also known as a *jewel case*.

Jewel Case

Alternate term for *jewel box*. See *Jewel Box*.

Jitter

Any instability in a video, electronic, or electric signal, due to a variety of causes. In video, jitters may be caused by synchronization and tracking problems, or problems encountered holding the camera still during taping.

In networking and telecommunications, *jitter* is any similar instability and/or distortion of a communications line that results in data-transmission errors.

Jittervision

A somewhat sarcastic term for a video or motion picture image that was apparently photographed or taped by a camera operator with a shaky hand.

Jobber

In *binding and finishing*, a type of *knife folder*. See *Folding: Knife Folder*.

Job Binding

In *binding and finishing*, any *casebound* book manufactured in small quantities, with some degree of handwork, such as special leather bible bindings, as opposed to *edition binding*, which is a fully automated, high-quantity production system.

Job Envelope

A large envelope used to store all the particular elements, films, mechanicals, original images, etc. for a particular print job.

Job Ink

A generic type of ***letterpress*** ink designed to be printed and dried on a wide variety of paper surfaces. Job ink is commonly used as a kind of "default" ink in many letterpress shops, and does not require special surface characteristics to dry properly (as is the case with many other types of inks that require the right degree of paper ***porosity*** to absorb the ***vehicle*** at the proper rate). They are also useful for printing a wide variety of images, from text to halftones.

Job Lot

Any shipment of paper that turns out to be unsuitable for a particular job. It may be ultimately resold at a discount.

Job Separation

A mechanism used in ***binding and finishing*** equipment that has the ability to keep separate jobs distinguished from each other.

Job Tracking

In printing and prepress, the careful recording of the location and status of each of the elements required for a particular job, as well as the time taken to produce each aspect of the job.

Jog

To align or even sheets of paper to a common edge to produce a neat stack.

Alternate term for the process of ***Inching***. See ***Inching***.

Jogger

A device comprising a vibrating table, the action of which squares and neatly stacks a pile of sheets of paper.

In sheetfed ***offset lithography***, a *jogger* is one of three moveable devices typically found on the ***delivery pile*** of a sheetfed printing press (especially that used in ***offset lithography***) to ensure that the printed sheets remain neatly stacked. Joggers are usually oriented on three sides of the delivery pile, a fixed front gate forming the fourth side.

Jogger-Stacker

In ***binding and finishing***, an accessory device on a ***folder*** that *jog*s and stacks folded ***signature***s as they come out of the folder.

Joint

Alternate term for ***hinge***. See ***Hinge***.

Joint Editing

In telecommunications and networking, an ***ISDN*** feature that allows a voice connection to be made simultaneously with a data connection, allowing two connected parties to both speak with each other and view or edit a computer file. Also known as ***screen sharing***.

Joint Photographic Experts Group

See ***JPEG***.

Joint Work

Any production authored by several individuals, each of whose individual contributions cannot be distinguished.

Jones Diagram

A plot used to measure the tonal values of a reproduction compared to the original. See ***Tone Reproduction***.

Jordan

Also called a ***conical refiner***, a jordan is a chamber used for ***beating*** and ***refining*** paper ***pulp*** in preparation for papermaking. The jordan contains metal bars mounted on the inside of a cone-shaped rotor, which contact stationary metal bars mounted on the shell of the device. The fiber ***slurry***, following ***refining*** in a ***beater***, is pumped into an inlet in the smaller end of the jordan and squeezed between the two sets of bars, the resulting abrasion working to brush and cut the fibers. The fibers are then pumped out through a discharge tube in the larger end of the jordan. (See ***refining***.)

The jordan is named after the American inventor, Joseph Jordan, who developed it.

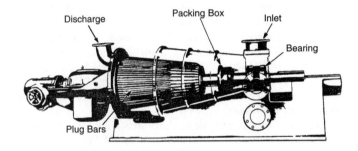

Conical refiner (jordan) used in papermaking.

Journal

An end shaft on which a cylinder or roller rotates.

Joyscroll

In video editing, to review a videotape using an editing station with a ***joystick*** controller.

Joystick

A computer input device that utilizes a 360° rotatable lever to move screen images, commonly used in video games.

A *joystick* is also a similar device used in video editing. It can be moved up or down (which accesses different connected VCRs) and left or right to rewind or fast forward the videotape.

JPEG

Abbreviation for ***Joint Photographic Experts Group***, an ***ISO*** committee that has defined standards for the digital compression of graphical images.

JPEG is a ***data compression*** scheme (and a ***file format***, based on similar algorithms) for still photographs.

JPEG algorithms can be used to compress still images (i.e., make them smaller) by removing as much extraneous material from the file as possible and replacing it with a kind of coded "shorthand" notation of how to reconstruct what was taken out. When the file is opened again, the program reads the code and tries its best to put back what was removed. Specifically, each image to be compressed is divided into 8×8-*pixel* blocks, or a square containing 64 pixels. Each pixel is then mathematically described relative to the pixel in the upper left hand corner of each block. Since the *binary* notation of this mathematical relationship takes up far less space than 64 individual pixels, the data can be stored in a smaller file.

Depending on how drastic the compression is, it may be *lossless* (meaning no, or no significant amount of, data was lost) or *lossy* (meaning some information was lost and the image quality is not what it used to be). Usually, the greater the compression, the greater the loss of data. Typically, visible degradation begins to occur after a compression ratio of about 20:1. JPEG algorithms can reduce a 580K file down to as much as 20K, although a great deal of data is lost. The egregiousness of the lost data depends on the resolution of the image, and the image itself. High *contrast* areas, for example, are likely to be poorly reconstructed when the image is compressed.

JPEG is also a standard *file format* for saving digital images, which can be read by several programs, such as Photoshop and *QuarkXPress*. Pictures posted to Internet USENET groups also frequently utilize the JPEG file format. The file format also employs some level of JPEG compression to the image.

JPEG compression algorithms are also used to compress full motion digital video. (See also *MPEG*.)

JPEG++

A proprietary extension to the *JPEG* data compression algorithm, developed by Storm Technology. With JPEG++, a portion of an image can be designated as either foreground or background, and the compression level of each designation can be set separately. For example, when compressing an image file containing a portrait of a person, the foreground can be compressed only slightly while the background can be compressed to a much greater extent. As a result, the lossiness of the image is reduced. See also *JPEG*.

Jukebox

A device used to store multiple optical discs that, when connected to an online server, can rapidly access files contained on them.

Jumbo Roll

A roll of paper over 24-in. diameter and weighing more than 500 lb.

Jumbo roll also refers to a roll of any type of *substrate* that possesses an inside diameter larger than the standard size for that substrate.

Jump

In page layout, the continuation of an article on another page. The *jump line* (usually) indicates the page number on which the article is continued.

In computing, *jump* refers to a computer instruction telling the program to go to a new set of instructions.

In film and video editing, an abrupt cut or change in scene. (See *Jump Cut*.)

Jump Cut

In motion picture and video editing, a visually and deliberately jarring *cut* used between scenes, especially when a new scene has shifted to a new location and time.

Jumper

In any electrical system or network, a small cable or wire used to create a temporary circuit, usually for diagnostic purposes.

Jump Line

In page layout, a typeset line at the bottom of a column or page indicating the page on which an article is continued. A jump line also appears at the top of a column or page, indicating from what page the article has continued.

Jump Out

In motion picture and video production, any perceptible discontinuity caused by poor editing or poor continuity.

Junior Carton

A shipment or package of paper containing 8–10 *ream*s.

Justification

In typography, setting lines of text so that they line up on the left and right, as opposed to *ragged right*, in which the lines do not line up on the right.

The earliest books, handwritten by scribes, began as unjustified, but were later justified by the medieval scribes to speed writing, to fit as many characters on a line as possible, and for aesthetic reasons. Gutenberg (and other early printers) desired their printed books to look as much like handwritten manuscripts as possible, so lines were set with numerous contractions and *ligature*s to achieve justification. Later, metal type required even copy blocks to allow lockup into page form.

Justification is accomplished by filling a line until the last possible word or syllable fits and then dividing the remaining space by the number of word spaces. The result is placed at each word space. This is why word spaces vary in width from line to line, expanding or contracting as needed to space the line out to its justification width. Margins are the imaginary vertical demarcations for text or tabular columns. Overall or primary margins are established by the line length function or the cumulative total of secondary margins (tab or text columns). Ragged right (or *unjustified*) is recommended for continuing text, since the eye needs an imaginary reference line on the left. The advantages of ragged right include fewer (or no) hyphenations, even word spacing, white space at line ends to allow type to "breathe," a more relaxed look, and no *river*s.

Justification is often described in conjunction with *hyphenation*; see *Hyphenation and Justification*.

This is justified type. This is justified type. This is justified type. This is justified type. This is justified type. This is justified type. This is justified type. This is justified type. This is justified type. This is justified type. This is justified type. This is justified type. This is justified type. This is justified type. This is justified type. This is justified type. This is justified type. This is justified type.

This is ragged-right type. This is ragged-right type. This is ragged-right type. This is ragged-right type. This is ragged-right type. This is ragged-right type. This is ragged-right type. This is ragged-right type. This is ragged-right type. This is ragged-right type. This is ragged-right type. This is ragged-right type. This is ragged-right type.

Justification Range

In typography, a zone a specific distance from the right margin inwards, within which the computer will evaluate acceptable line breaks before actually justifying the line.

Justification Space

In typography, a word space (produced by striking the spacebar on the keyboard) that the computer can expand or contract to fill out or compress a line of type so to produce a *justified* line. See *Justification*.

Justified

Type that aligns on both the left and the right. See *Justification*.

Justified Composition

Alternate term for *justified* text. See *Justified*.

Justified Text

Alternate term for *justified* text. See *Justified*.

Justified Type

Alternate term for *justified* text. See *Justified*.

Justify

To set text so that both the left and right margins are aligned. See *Justification*.

Jute

A fiber obtained from the plants *Corchorus capsularis* and *C. olitorious*, which are native primarily to India, Pakistan, and Brazil. Long used for bags and wrapping materials, jute fiber is also used as a fibrous source for papermaking.

Jute Board

A strong form of paperboard that can be easily folded. Despite its name, it is not produced from *jute* fibers.

K

K, k
The eleventh letter of the English alphabet, deriving from the North Semitic *kaph* and the Greek *kappa*. Although the Romans borrowed the form of the *K* from the Etruscans, Latin had three letters corresponding to the *K* sound (*C, K,* and *Q*) and consequently the *K* fell into disuse. It did not reappear until after the Norman conquest of England in 1066, when it began to be used in place of the hard *C,* especially to identify native words. (It replaced, among many other things, the *C* in "knife"—which was originally "cnif"—and was pronounced with the hard *C.*)

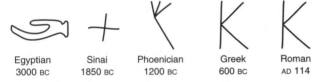

| Egyptian 3000 BC | Sinai 1850 BC | Phoenician 1200 BC | Greek 600 BC | Roman AD 114 |

The evolution of the letter K.

K
Abbreviation for the prefix *kilo-*. See *Kilo-*.

The letter *K* is also used as a colloquial abbreviation for the term *kilobyte*.

K is also the abbreviation for *Kelvin,* a temperature scale.

K and N Ink Absorbency Test
A test used to quickly determine the degrees of *ink absorbency* for various papers, in which a nondrying ink containing a soluble dye is thickly applied to several overlapped paper samples and allowed to sit for two minutes. The ink is then wiped off the samples, and the different degrees of color depth of the ink stains on the various samples are compared, the greater density of color indicating

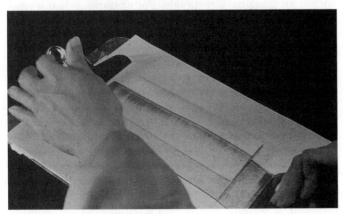

K and N ink absorbency test.

the highest ink absorbency. The K and N test provides best results on coated papers and can also be used to test the uniformity of ink absorption across the surface of a single sheet. (See also *Ink Absorbency* and *Vanceometer Test*.)

Kanji
A special *font* or character set consisting of about 5,000 symbols used in Japanese ideogrammatic writing. Kanji characters are derived directly from earlier Chinese characters. In the computerized setting of Kanji, each character is described by two *byte*s of data. Kanji is also known as *honji*.

Kaolin Clay
See *China Clay*.

Karaoke
A form of entertainment in which the vocal track from a song is stripped off, allowing individuals to sing along. The music can be on an optical disc or magnetic tape, and in more advanced systems, the lyrics and other graphics can be viewed on a screen. Karaoke is popular in nightclubs, and is also a fairly popular type of multimedia presentation.

Kauri-Butanol Value
A quantitative measure of the *solvent* power of a *hydrocarbon* compound, or how well a solvent will dissolve a material, which utilizes a reagent comprising kauri gum and butanol. The low end of the scale (indicating poor solvents) is 20, while the high end of the scale (excellent solvents) is 105. The kauri-butanol value is abbreviated *KB value*.

KB
Abbreviation for *kilobyte*. See *Kilobyte*.

Kbps
Abbreviation for *kilobit*s per second. See *Bits per Second*.

Kbs
An alternate abbreviation for *kilobit*s per second. See *Bits per Second*.

KB Value
See *Kauri-Butanol Value*.

Kbyte
Abbreviation for *kilobyte*. See *Kilobyte*.

Kchar/s
Abbreviation of *kilocharacters per second*, or a speed of 1,000 characters per second. See *Characters per Second (CPS)*.

Keeper
Alternate term for a *buy*. See *Buy*.

Keep Standing
An instruction to a printer to store set type as printed, in preparation for a reprinting order.

Kelvin
An absolute temperature scale used primarily in scientific specifications, devised by British physicist William Thomson, Lord Kelvin. On the Kelvin scale, absolute zero (the point at which all molecular motion has effectively ceased, −273.16°C and −459.69°F) is 0 K. The temperature intervals are exactly the same as those of the Celsius temperature scale, only 273.16 degrees greater. Thus, on the Kelvin scale, the freezing point of water (0°C and 32°F) is 273.16 K, while the boiling point of water (100°C and 212°F) is 373.16 K.

The Kelvin scale is also used to measure the *color* of a light source, by means of determining the temperature to which a black object would need to be heated in order to

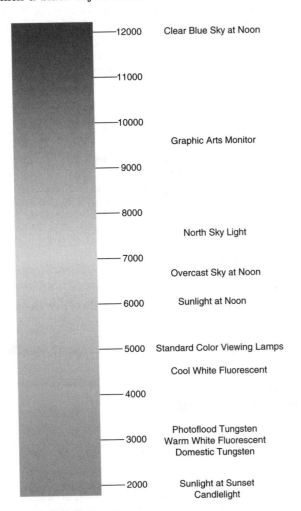

Range of color temperatures, in degrees Kelvin.

produce light of a certain wavelength or color. (See *Color Temperature*.) Kelvin is abbreviated **K** and does not take the degree sign (°).

Kenaf
A plant of the mallow family, also called Deccan hemp (*Hibiscus cannabinus*), native to India and other tropical regions, used primarily for rope and coarse fabrics, and whose bark is a fibrous source for papermaking.

Kermit
In telecommunications, a *file-transfer protocol* created at Columbia University (but placed in the public domain). Kermit is used to transfer files between remote *PC*s and *mainframe*s. Data transmission comprises variable-length blocks up to 96 characters in length, each block being checked by Kermit for errors. When an error is detected, Kermit initiates repeat transmissions. "Kermit" was in fact named after the frog.

Kern
In typography, to remove space from between two characters so as to cause them to appear closer together. See *Kerning*. The term *kern* also refers to the part of a letter (or other character) that hangs over the body of the letter itself, as the top curl on a lowercase "f."

Kernel
In computing, the most fundamental part of an *operating system* that is always resident in memory, is invisible to the user, and is responsible for basic functions such as *memory management*, the *file system*, disk operations, etc. Most computer operating systems have but a single, large kernel that always remains resident in memory. But see also *Microkernel*.

Kerning
In typography, the reduction of letterspacing between certain character combinations in order to reduce the space between them, performed for aesthetic reasons. Typeset characters have specific width values and are positioned within an imaginary rectangle. For example, when a capital "W" is set next to a lowercase "a," the right side wall of "W" will touch the left side wall of the "a," but because of the shape of these two letters, a space will result.

In the process of kerning, no matter what imaging technology is used, the space is reduced by "fooling" the typesetting machine. A certain number of units is subtracted from the width of the "W," the typesetter positioning system then moves fewer units than would normally be required, and the subsequent letter overlaps to visually reduce the intercharacter space. Most computer typesetting systems can kern over 200 character pairs automatically. This becomes an issue because after the 20 or so primary pairs have been kerned, further pairs are then limited to a hundred or so. And, if those hundred are kerned, another hundred should be kerned, due to the imbalance caused by

1. Yo	6. Wo	11. P.	16. T.
2. We	7. Tu	12. Ty	17. Y.
3. To	8. Tw	13. Wa	18. TA
4. Tr	9. Ya	14. yo	19. PA
5. Ta	10. Te	15. we	20. WA

The top 20 kern pairs.

some pairs kerned and some not kerned—thus creating a situation of inconsistency. If kerning cannot be performed infinitely, then it is perhaps more desirable to remain with the top 20.

Kerning is essentially an optical function, whereby the space between certain letter combinations is reduced until it looks right. Kerning can be described as ***individual negative letterspacing***; removing space from all characters is referred to as ***universal negative letterspacing***. A new concept known as ***topographic kerning*** defines characters not in terms of a rectangle, but in terms of the shape of each letter, resulting in the ability to kern on an almost infinite basis.

Kern Pair

In typography, a particular combination of letters that has undergone ***kerning***. See ***Kerning***.

Ketone

A class of organic compounds composed of a carbonyl group (a double-bonded carbon and oxygen group) attached to two alkyl groups (a variety of hydrocarbons having the general formula C_nH_{2n+1}), such as acetone, whose chemical formula is CH_3COCH_3. Ketones are highly volatile liquids commonly used as ***solvent***s in inks produced for ***gravure*** and ***flexographic*** printing.

Key

An alternate term for ***black*** ink used in multicolor printing. When ***letterpress*** was the dominant printing process, black was always the first ink down, the ***registration*** of all the subsequent colors being keyed to the black. In ***process color*** terminology, the "K" in CMYK stands for "key," or black. A ***black printer*** is a key plate made that includes only a range of black tonal gradations, used to enhance the ***contrast*** of the image as a whole and improve the detail in the ***shadow***s. Black printers can either be ***full-scale black*** or ***half-scale black***.

The term *key* also means, in prepress, to precisely identify page elements prepared separately but destined to be printed on the same page. See ***Keying*** (first definition).

In video production, the term *key* also means to insert one video image onto another. See ***Keying*** (second definition).

Keyboard

A computer input device that allows the entry of letters, numerals, and symbols. It is based on the original typewriter keyboard arrangement.

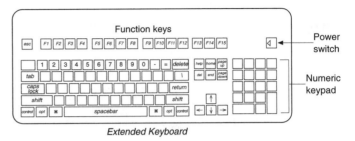

Extended Keyboard

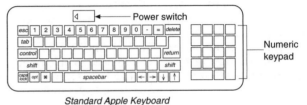

Standard Apple Keyboard

Two types of keyboards.

Keyboard Buffer

In computing, a small area of a computer's memory in which recently typed characters are stored. Some ***utility program***s allow typed keystrokes and/or commands to be saved and edited at a later time. Also known as the ***type-ahead buffer***.

Keyboarding

Typing text on a typewriter, or entering text into a word processor or typesetter using a ***keyboard***.

Keyboard Shortcut

In computing, a keystroke or series of keystrokes (such as Control-Option-D) that activates a command or feature, without first having to access a menu.

Keyboard Template

In computing, a plastic plate that fits over a set of keys on a keyboard (usually ***function key***s) as a quick reference for commands, functions, and shortcuts available. Keyboard templates are application-specific.

Keyboard Terminal

A workstation or ***terminal*** with a keyboard. See ***Terminal***.

Key Combination

In computing, a set of keystrokes (either held down all at once or in sequence) used to initiate a function or command, commonly as a ***keyboard shortcut***.

Keyer

In video production, a device—usually part of a ***genlock***—used to superimpose graphics over a video image, as in the creation of titles, credits, etc. See ***Keying***.

Key Frame

In *animation*, a frame that marks the beginning or the end of a particular animated sequence. The drawing of frames to connect start and end key frames is known as *in-betweening*.

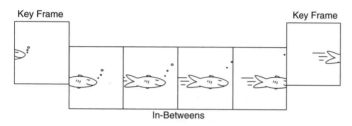

Key frames and in-betweens.

Keying

The process of identifying and labeling all the separate pieces of art, copy, or film that will need to be stripped into a single *flat* or that will be printed on the same page. Keying typically involves ensuring that both a *continuous-tone* image or *halftone* are supplied separately and the "holes" on the *mechanical* or *negative* are clearly marked, so that the stripper and/or printer inserts the correct image into the correct position.

In video production, the term *keying* refers to the process of overlapping or superimposing one video image on another. See *Chroma-Keying* and *Genlock*.

Key Light

In still and motion picture photography, as well as videography, the primary source of illumination for a scene or subject, usually a *quartz-iodine light*.

Keyline

A box or frame drawn—either by hand or on a computerized page layout—on a *mechanical* that indicates a region in which a solid color or some form of artwork or image will be placed.

The term *keyline* is also occasionally used as an alternate term for *mechanical*.

Keylining

The act of producing a *keyline*. See *Keyline*. Keylining is also used by some (especially in the Midwest) as a synonym for *pasting up*.

Key Plate

One of a set of printing plates for a color printing job that contains the most detail and is used as a guide for proper *registration* of the other plates.

Key Redefinition

In computing, the ability for the user to assign different functions to various keyboard keys (such as the *function keys*). Some application programs allow the user to redefine the keys.

Key Signal

In television and video, an electronic signal that indicates the beginning of each separate video image, as well as the end of each scan line.

Keystoning

A deformation of a projected image—as from a slide or movie projector—that results when the *lens* of the projector and screen onto which the image is projected are not at right angles to each other. If the lens is directed upwards, for example, the projected image will be greater in width at the top than at the bottom. Also known as the *keystone effect*, the term deriving from the trapezoidal shape of keystones used in architecture.

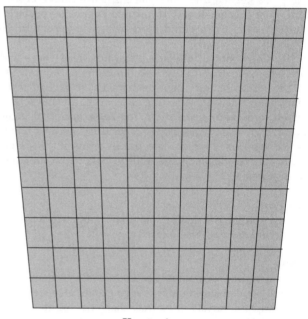

Keystoning.

Keystroke

The depression of a single *keyboard* key. Often, a keystroke (or some quantity of them per unit time) is a measure of worker productivity.

Keystroke Storage

Alternate term for a *keyboard buffer*. See *Keyboard Buffer*.

Keyword

In databases or other searching mechanisms, any significant and representative word used to locate a particular file, document, Web page, etc.

In computer programming, any word used in a particular programming language.

Kid Finish

A paper *finish* characterized by a surface texture intended to simulate soft kid skin.

Kill

In typesetting, printing, etc., a directive to either delete copy or type, or to stop a particular function or operation.

Killer App

See *Killer Application*.

Killer Application

Any computer *application program* that is so useful that it alone justifies the purchase of the computer system, for which it was designed, as well as any peripheral or collateral software or hardware. For example, for the original Apple II personal computer, the "killer application" was Visi-Calc, the first spreadsheet program. In the case of the original IBM PC, the "killer application" was a word processing program. For the Apple Macintosh, the "killer application" was graphics and desktop publishing. In all these cases (and many more), a single application was the impetus for sales of a system. Also colloquially referred to as a *killer app*.

Kilo-

A *metric prefix* denoting 1,000 (one thousand, or 10^3) units. In computing, *kilo-* refers to 2^{10}, and one *kilobyte* (KB) of storage is approximately equal to one thousand *byte*s of data (actually 1,024 bytes). See *Metric Prefix*. See also *Mega-*, *Giga-*, *Tera-*, *Peta-*, and *Exa-*. *Kilo-* is usually abbreviated *k* or *K* (when referring to computer-related quantities).

Kilobaud

A unit equal to 1,000 *baud*. See *Baud*.

Kilobit

A unit equal to approximately 1,000 (actually 1,024) *bit*s. See *Bit*.

Kilobyte

A common unit of computer storage, comprising 1,024 *byte*s. *Kilo-* is the prefix meaning "thousand," so it is common to consider one kilobyte as equal to one thousand bytes, although that is not entirely accurate.

It was once common to find hard disks, magnetic storage media, and *RAM* capacities measured in terms of kilobytes, but the larger *megabyte* (and increasingly the even larger *gigabyte*) has now become a more prominent capacity. Fortunately, however, most text files are still measured in only tens or hundreds of kilobytes.

Kilobyte is abbreviated KB, or, colloquially, "K." 1,024 kilobytes equals one megabyte.

Kilocharacters per Second

See *Kchar/s*.

Kilohertz (kHz)

A measure of *frequency*, equal to one thousand cycles per second.

Kinetic Friction

One of two basic types of *friction*, referring to the force that resists a moving object's continued sliding. See *Friction* and *Static Friction*.

Kiss Impression

Alternate term for *kiss pressure*. See *Kiss Pressure*.

Kiss Pressure

The minimum pressure required to produce the proper ink transfer from the blanket to the paper or other *substrate* (in *offset lithography*) or from the plate to the substrate (in *flexography*). It can also refer to the minimum pressure required to transfer ink from the *form roller* or *anilox roller* to the plate. Kiss pressure is also called *kiss impression*.

Knife

On a *guillotine cutter*, a long, heavy steel blade that is used—either manually or electronically—to cut large stacks of paper or other *substrate*. See *Guillotine Cutter*.

On a *folding* machine—specifically a *knife folder*, a *knife* is a metal blade used to force sheets of paper through a set of folding rollers. See *Folding* and *Knife Folder*.

The term *knife* is also used to refer to any of a large number of handheld implements used in graphic arts for cutting *frisket*s (a *frisket knife*), screen printing *stencil*s (an *art knife*), or other such work. One popular form of handheld cutting implement is called an *X-Acto Knife*.

An art knife, often referred to as an "X-Acto knife."

Knife Coating

A paper *coating* applied by means of a *doctor blade* or knife.

Knife-Cut Film

A film applied to a transparent sheet, into which a design can be cut, used for making mechanical *stencil*s for *screen printing*. Knife-cut film can also be used for cutting a mask for making photostencils for screen printing.

Knife-Cut Label

Alternate term for *split-top label*. See *Split-Top Label*.

Knife Folder

A device used in the *folding* phase of *binding and finishing*, which uses a metal blade to force a sheet through a set of folding rollers. Also known as a *right-angle folder*. See *Folding*. (See illustration on next page.)

Knife Roller

A type of hard, small-diameter roller used in an offset press *inking system* to remove ink skin particles, *lint*, and other

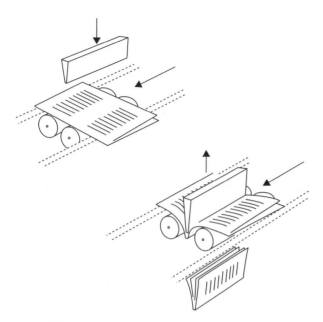

The operating principle of a knife folder.

debris from the ink, keeping the inking system clean and reducing the production of *hickey*s and other printing defects.

Knockout

A space—or *keyline*—left in a document for the later insertion of some form of graphic image. Also known as a *cutout*.

The term *knockout* is also used to refer to "white type" or, in other words, type that prints as a reverse, or, in fact, does not really *print* at all, allowing the color of the page to show through a background in the shape of type. Sometimes spelled as two words, *knock out*, or with a hyphen, *knock-out*.

An ink agitator

A knockout: type that prints in reverse.

Knockout Mask

A mask created in graphics software, used to ensure that a layered image prints directly on the paper and not on top of the image beneath it.

Knurled Roller

Alternate term for a flexographic *anilox roller*. See *Anilox Roller*.

Kodak CMS

A *color management system*—a set of computer programs or utilities that ensure consistent color throughout the prepress processes by calibrating the color relationships among the scanners, monitors, printers, imagesetters, and other devices in the chain from input to output—developed by Kodak. Of primary advantage with the Kodak Precision CMS is the vast library of device profiles, or files that indicate the color space utilized by the various devices in the system. Additionally, the Kodak CMS allows users to create new profiles for devices that may not be in the default library. Based on the *CIELUV* color space, the Kodak CMS uses advanced and proprietary *transformation algorithms* to accurately match colors from one space to another. It also includes *gamut* mapping and *gamut compression* to compensate for the differences in gamut from one device to another. (See *Color Management System [CMS].*)

kp-Height

In typography, the distance between the top of the *ascender* of the lowercase "k" and the bottom of the *descender* of the lowercase "p." See also *x-Height* and *Baseline*.

The kp-height of 48-pt. Palatino type.

Kraft

The most prevalent method of *chemical pulping* used in papermaking (or a term for the pulp itself).

The kraft process derived from the *soda process*, developed in the mid-19th century that dissolved wood chips using a strong base (alkaline solution) such as lye. In 1879, *sodium sulfate* was added to the process, and a stronger pulp was produced. As a result, the process became known as the *sulfate process*, and kraft pulping is still known by that name, even though the active ingredient has since been found to be *sodium sulfide*. "Kraft" is a more accurate term since it is the German and Swedish word for "strength." The kraft process soon supplanted other chemical processes (such as the *sulfite process*) by virtue of its ability to effectively digest the wood of nearly every species of tree, its efficient heat- and chemical-recovery system that helps keep down processing costs, and the strong, high-quality pulp it produces. The addition of *bleaching* systems to increase the brightness and decrease the lignin content of the pulp also helped make the kraft process the most popular pulping process.

The term "kraft" is also used to refer to paper or paperboard made using unbleached pulp produced by the kraft process. Unbleached kraft pulp is generally dark brown in color and strong. Papers produced from unbleached kraft pulp include brown wrapping paper, paper bags, envelopes, etc.

Kromecote

An extremely glossy, highly polished, mirror-like paper *finish*.

Ku Band

In telecommunications, a data transmission network conducted via satellite with a transmission capacity of 12 *gigahertz*.

L

L, l

The twelfth letter of the English alphabet, deriving from the North Semitic *lamed* and the Greek *lambda*. The current form of the uppercase *L* came about in ancient Latin, the lowercase being a cursive variation of the capital.

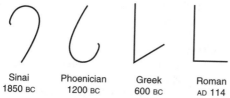

Sinai	Phoenician	Greek	Roman
1850 BC	1200 BC	600 BC	AD 114

The evolution of the letter L.

L*a*b Color Space

Alternate term for *CIE color space*. See *CIE Color Space*.

Label

A strip of paper or other *substrate* that can be attached—typically with some form of *adhesive*—to another surface for purposes of identification. A label can be a *face-cut label*, *laid-in label*, *pressure-sensitive label*, *gummed label*, *punched-out label*, *roll label*, *sheet label*, *split-top label*, *tamper proof label*, *tarnish proof label*, *Cheshire label*, *coated one-side label*, *north-south label*, or *transparent label*.

One or more characters, within or attached to a set of data, that contains information about the set, including its identification. A set of symbols or a name used to identify or describe an item, record, message, file, or storage address. An identification written electronically at the beginning of a magnetic tape to describe its content or name.

Label Paper

Any type of *coated-one-side* paper that can be used for wrapping or labelling, with the other side being either uncoated or coated with an *adhesive*, respectively.

Lacquer

A clear or colored *resin*-based solution, either added to a printing ink or applied as a *coating* to the surface of a printed piece, that forms a thin film upon *evaporation* of the *solvent* in which it is dissolved. Lacquer is used to afford a printed piece protection, or to impart a high level of *gloss* to the ink or to the printed sheet as a whole.

Lacquer Stencil

A type of knife-cut *stencil* used in *screen printing*, produced from a *lacquer* rather than a water-soluble *gelatin* or other substance.

Ladder

In typography, a term for three, four, or more hyphenated lines in a row, considered typographically undesirable. Ladders are usually a consequence of *justified* lines, especially those set using unsophisticated *hyphenation and justification* features.

Lag

In *screen printing*, the period of time during which the screen fabric is in contact with the *substrate* immediately following the printing stroke.

Laid Finish

A type of *bond paper* or *book paper* finish imprinted with evenly spaced parallel lines that are visible when the sheet is held up to the light.

This "laid finish" is produced in the same manner as a *watermark*; the lines are woven from wire and attached to the surface of the *dandy roll* in the *forming section* of the papermaking machine. As the wet paper *pulp* passes beneath it, the laid design is imprinted into the pulp, decreasing the paper opacity in the image areas. Laid paper is commonly used for company letterhead. (See *Dandy Roll* and *Watermark*.)

Laid-In Label

A type of *label* that has been cut from a larger sheet of *substrate*, the substrate material being discarded after removing the labels. See also *Face-Cut Label*. Also called *diecut label*.

Lake

An organic *pigment* used in printing inks produced by combining (either chemically or by other means) a water-soluble dye with a metallic base to make the dye insoluble in water. (See *Organic Color Pigments*.)

The term *lake* is also used to refer to any depression in the surface of a rubber *flexographic* plate.

Lake Red C

An *organic color pigment* used in printing inks. Lake Red C is used to refer to one of three types of related pigments (versions of *CI Pigment Red 53*), most commonly the pigment containing barium salt. It is a yellowish red with a blue undertone possessing good chemical resistance properties, but only moderate *lightfastness*. As it contains barium, it is also toxic. It is the most commonly used red organic pigment, as its brightness and color strength work in conjunction with its low cost. (See also *Organic Color Pigments*.)

(*CI Pigment Red 53* [sodium]; *CI Pigment Red 53:1* [barium]; *CI Pigment Red 53:2* [calcium].)

Lake Red C BON
See *BON Red*.

Lake White
See *Alumina Hydrate*.

Laminated
Descriptive of a printed sheet that has been coated with a layer of clear plastic, for preservation, protection, or other purposes. See *Lamination*.

Lamination
A layer of clear plastic applied to a sheet of paper (or other material) for preservation, protection, or other purposes. *Lamination* also refers to the process of applying such a clear plastic layer.

Lampblack
A form of *carbon black*, composed of nearly pure carbon, collected as soot from the combustion of vegetable oils, petroleum, asphalt, or gas, used as an intense, dull black *pigment* in printing inks.

LAN
See *Local Area Network (LAN)*.

LAN-Aware
In networking, term for an application having *file locking* and *record locking* mechanisms. See *File Locking* and *Record Locking*. The term is also used to refer to any application capable of running over a network.

Land Area
The unengraved portions of a *gravure cylinder* that contact the *doctor blade* during printing. The thin *cell wall*s also count as part of a cylinder's land area.

Landing Zone
See *Dedicated Landing Zone*.

Land Line
Any copper wire or *fiber optic* cable used to transmit data, either voice- or computer-generated.

Lands
On a *compact disc*, the portions of the reflective surface of the disc between the engraved (or "burned") *pits*. See *Compact Disc (CD)*.

Landscape
A page format in which the correct reading or viewing orientation is horizontal; the width of the page is greater than its height. See also *Portrait*.

Language
Any organized system for conveying information, either orally or by means of written representation. A language not only refers to a means of communication between humans, but also between humans and computers. A computer (or any similar electronic device) at its most basic level cannot understand any human language, except the strictly mathematical *binary* system of 1s and 0s. Software *interpreter*s and *compiler*s are needed to translate a language a human can understand (and program in) into *machine language*, or the language the computer can understand.

LANLORD
Pun-based term for the administrator of a *local area network*. See *Local Area Network (LAN)*.

Lanston, Tolbert
Inventor of the Monotype. The Monotype Corporation began in 1897 in England after securing an investment to aid in the final development of Tolbert Lanston's typecasting machine. Lanston (1844–1913), an American civil war veteran, inventor, law school graduate and government pension clerk, patented his typecaster in 1887. The Type-Caster featured a separate keyboard, encoded paper tape system, and caster for single pieces of type, one at a time (hence Mono-type). Production of typecaster began in Salfords England in 1902.

Like its better-known cousin, Linotype, a keyboard operator sets the type, but unlike Linotype the product is a galley of individual letters cast in lead type. The chief advantage of monotype is that the individual characters can be changed or corrected (in the case of a minor error) without having to re-keyboard the entire line, as is required with Linotype. Monotype is a two-step process, in that the keyboard operator punches a paper tape, which is then used to drive the casting machine. The matrix case houses the matrices from which the type is cast. Each letter has its own matrix, and it takes anywhere from 225 to 272 mats to make up a diecase.

The Monotype keyboard is a miracle of mechanical ingenuity, combining the functions of typewriter and calculator. The operator could not see what they are typing, because the only "output" is a paper tape about four inches wide punched with holes that tell the casting machine which character to cast and how wide to make the word spacing. The paper tape gives a location code to the casting machine so that the die-case can be properly positioned over the mold. Compressed air is forced through the holes in the paper tape, which raises tiny pistons which limit the movement of the die-case on an x-y axis.

The Linotype machine is a kind of cross between a casting machine, a typewriter, and a vending machine. The Monotype machine was a complete typefoundry as much as it is a composing machine. By the early decades of the twentieth century, companies like Monotype and Linotype held a virtual monopoly on commercial printing, and kept it right up to the digital era. Where type had once been cut and cast by individual printers, it was later "issued" by the Monotype Corporation and others.

It is said that Lanston got the idea for separating the input and the output mechanisms because of a device invented by a fellow worker at the Census Bureau—Herman Hollerith had deveopled the punch card and tabulating machine.

Lap

Alternate term for *lip*. See *Lip*.

LAP

Abbreviation for *Link Access Procedure*. See *Link Access Procedure (LAP)*.

LAP-B

Abbreviation for *Link Access Procedure-Balanced*. See *Link Access Procedure-Balanced (LAP-B)*.

Lap Dissolve

See *Dissolve*.

Lap Mark

In *screen printing* (especially that of glass surfaces), a ridge produced where two separate colors overlap.

Lapping Color

Alternate term for *lap register*. See *Lap Register*.

Lap Register

In multi-color printing, the process of *trapping*, or overlapping of a thin strip of a second (or later) color at the edges of a previously printed color. See *Register* and *Trapping*. Also known as *lapping color*.

Laptop Computer

A *personal computer* that has the processing power and speed of a desktop computer, but is compact and lightweight enough to—in theory—fit on a person's lap. A larger version of the laptop was the *luggable* computer, which was not as lightweight as today's laptops. Most laptops (as of this writing) weigh up to 14 pounds (but see also *Hidden Weight*). In terms of memory, storage, and other aspects of the system, most laptops are comparable to desktop computers, the exception being that the monitor of necessity must be smaller than desktop system displays, and the mouse is usually replaced by a *trackball* or *touchpad*. See also *Portable Computer*.

Large-Scale Integration (LSI)

In computer *microprocessor* manufacturing, term for the design and production of *integrated circuit*s with a component density of 200–20,000 transistor gates, or computer chips that are very fast and powerful, and are capable of more diverse functions. LSI has been supplanted by *very-large-scale intregration (VLSI)* which ups the component density to 10 million transistors. Looming on the horizon are *ultralarge-scale integration* and *gigascale integration*.

Laser

An acronym for *Light Amplification by Stimulated Emission of Radiation*. A laser is essentially a thin, intense beam of coherent light. It differs from light emitted by conventional light bulbs in that traditional light is *in*coherent; light waves are radiated in all directions independently of each other, and the crests and troughs of the wave do not coincide with each other and therefore possess little energy. In a laser, all the light waves are emitted in the same direction and with their crests and troughs aligned with each other. The beam thus has a great deal of energy. The light rays, as they travel along the beam, are kept as close to being parallel with each other as possible and, as a result, the waves diverge very slightly. As an example, in 1962 a one-foot-wide laser beam was pointed at the moon and, when it reached the moon, illuminated a two-mile-wide area. An ordinary light beam making the same journey would cover a 25,000-mile-wide area.

Essentially, a laser is created by stimulating certain substances to emit light, which involves adding energy until the low-energy-level atoms have absorbed enough energy to trigger an emission of energy in the form of electromagnetic radiation—i.e., light. The first lasers utilized ruby crystal rods. Today's lasers utilize gases or liquids as the laser material.

Lasers have a wide range of uses in a variety of industries. In imaging and printing, fine beams of laser light are used to image light-sensitive printing plates and *imagesetter* films, and lasers are used in computer *laser printer*s to expose a charged metal plate in regions corresponding to image areas, allowing toner to adhere to it and transfer to the paper passing beneath it. Lasers are also used in optical discs, such as audio CDs and CD-ROMs, to either write or read the tiny pits in the surface of the disc which can then be translated into digital or analog data. Lasers are also used for a variety of surgical procedures.

The laser was a successor to an earlier device called a *maser*, which stood for *Microwave Amplification by Stimulated Emission of Radiation*. Once, lasers were merely the stuff of science fiction; now most homes in the United States have at least one.

DEVELOPMENT OF THE LASER

Albert Einstein, in 1917, hypothesized that light can be produced by atomic processes. An atom consists of a nucleus and one or more electrons in motion around it. The electrons and the nucleus are related in terms of energy levels and the electrons normally occupy the lowest energy level, a ground state. Electrons can occupy higher energy levels, leaving some of the lower energy states vacant. Electrons can change from one energy state to another by the absorption or emission of light energy, via radiative transition. Electrons can absorb energy from the transfer of the energy of a photon directly to an orbital electron. The increase in the energy of the electron causes it to jump to a higher energy level; the atom is then said to be in an "excited" state. Electrons can accept only the precise amount of energy needed to move from one energy level to another. Only photons of the exact energy acceptable to the electron can be absorbed. Photons of similar energy will not be absorbed. Another means used to excite electrons is where energy is supplied by collisions with electrons accelerated by an electric field. The result of excitation is that the absorption of energy places an electron in a higher energy level. The atom is said to be excited.

SPONTANEOUS EMISSION

Atomic structures tend to exist at the lowest energy state. An excited electron in a higher energy level will "de-excite" itself and some of its energy may be converted to heat. Another means of de-excitation is the spontaneous emission of a photon. As it is released by an atom and is de-excited it will have a total energy equal to the difference in energy between the excited and lower energy levels—called spontaneous emission. An example is a neon sign. Atoms of neon are excited by an electrical discharge through the tube and they de-excite themselves by emitting photons of visible light.

Einstein stated that a photon released from an excited atom, upon interacting with a second excited atom, could trigger the second atom into de-exciting itself with the release of another photon. The photon released by the second atom would be identical in frequency, energy, direction, and phase with the triggering photon, and the triggering photon would continue, unchanged. If a medium contains a large amount of excited atoms and de-excitation occurs by spontaneous emission, the light output will be equal in all directions. Stimulated emission can cause a photon cascade—an amplification of the number of photons traveling in a particular direction. A direction is established by placing mirrors at the ends of an optical cavity and the number of photons traveling along the axis of the two mirrors increases and Light Amplification by the Stimulated Emission of Radiation occurs and with enough amplification, a laser beam results. Stimulated emission will not produce a noticeable amplification of light unless "population inversion" occurs. The higher the percentage of atoms in an excited state, the higher the probability of stimulated emission. When there are more atoms excited than not excited, they are said to be inverted.

LASER ARCHITECTURE

A laser consists of a lasing medium, a "pumping" system, and an optical cavity. The laser material must have a metastable state in which the atoms or molecules can be trapped after receiving energy from the pumping system. The pumping system imparts energy to the atoms, enabling them to be raised to an excited "metastable state" creating a population inversion. Optical pumping uses photons provided by a source such as a gas flash lamp or another laser to transfer energy to the lasing material. The optical source must provide photons that correspond to the allowed transition levels of the lasing material. Collision pumping relies on the transfer of energy to the lasing material by collision with the atoms of the lasing material. Energies which cor-

respond to the transitions must be provided, often by electrical discharge in a pure gas, or gas mixture. Chemical pumping systems use the binding energy released in chemical reactions to raise the lasing material to the metastable state. An optical cavity provides the amplification in the laser and selects the photons traveling in the desired direction. As the first atom or molecule in the metastable state of the inverted population decays, it triggers the decay of another atom or molecule in the same state via stimulated emission. If the photons are traveling in a direction that leads to the walls of the lasing material, a rod or tube, they are lost and amplification terminates. If one of the decaying atoms releases a photon parallel to the axis of the lasing material, it can trigger the emission of another photon and both will be reflected by a mirror on the end of the lasing rod or tube. The reflected photons pass back through the material triggering further emissions along the same path, which are reflected by mirrors at the ends of the lasing material. As amplification or gain exceeds the losses in the cavity, laser oscillation occurs, and a concentrated beam of coherent light is formed. Lasers are commonly designated by the lasing material employed:

- Gas
- Dye
- Solid state
- Semiconductor

Solid-state lasers employ a lasing material distributed in a solid matrix. An example is the Neodymium-YAG laser. The term YAG is an abbreviation for the crystal Yttrium Aluminum Garnet, which serves as the host for Neodymium ions. This laser emits an infrared beam at the wavelength of 1.064 micrometers or 1,064 nanometers (1 nm = 10^{-9} m). Internal or external devices convert the output to visible or ultraviolet wavelength.

Gas lasers use a gas or a mixture of gases within a tube. The most common gas laser uses a mixture of helium and neon (HeNe) with a primary output of 632.8 nm, which is a visible red color. It was first developed in 1961 and has proved to be the forerunner of a whole family of gas lasers. Gas lasers are similar in construction and behavior. For example, the CO_2 gas laser radiates at 10.6 micrometers in the far-infrared spectrum. Argon and krypton gas lasers operate with multiple-frequency emissions principally in the visible spectra. The wavelengths of argon lasers are 488 nm and 514 nm.

Dye lasers use a laser medium that is a complex organic dye in liquid solution or suspension. The major feature of these lasers is their "tunability." Choice of the dye and its concentration allows the production of laser light over a broad range of wavelength in or near the visible spectrum. Dye lasers commonly employ optical pumping, although some types use chemical reaction pumping. A common dye is Rhodamine 6G, which provides tunability over a 200-nm bandwidth in the red portion (620 nm) of the spectrum. Semiconductor lasers (also referred to as diode lasers) should not be confused with solid state lasers. Semiconductor devices consist of two layers of semiconductor material sandwiched together. These lasers are small and of modest power but may be built into larger arrays. A common diode laser is the Gallium Arsenide diode laser with an emission of 840 nm.

Continuous-wave lasers operate with a stable average beam power. In higher-power systems, the power can be adjusted, but in low-power gas lasers, such as HeNe, the power level is fixed by design, and performance degrades with use. Single-pulsed (normal mode) lasers have pulse durations of a few hundred microseconds to a few milliseconds, referred to as long pulse or normal mode. These lasers result from an intracavity delay that allows the laser media to store a maximum of potential energy. Under optimum gain conditions, emission occurs in single pulses of 10^{-8} second time units.

Repetitively pulsed or scanning lasers involve pulsed lasers operating at a fixed (or variable) pulse rate from a few pulses to 20,000 pulses per second. The direction of a continuous wave laser can be scanned with optical systems to produce the equivalent of a repetitively pulsed output. Mode-locked lasers operate as a result of the resonant modes of the optical cavity, which affect the characteristics of the output beam. When the phases of different frequency modes are synchronized, or "locked together," the different modes will interfere with one another to generate a heat effect. The result is laser output as regularly spaced pulsations.

LASER TYPES

Helium Neon. The first continuous-wave laser system was the helium neon (HeNe) gas mixture. Best known operating at the red 633 nm, some HeNe lasers can emit at other wavelengths (594 nm, 612 nm, 543 nm). Earlier HeNe lasers were excited by radio frequency (RF) discharge but all HeNe lasers are driven by a small DC discharge between electrodes in the laser tube. The HeNe laser operates by an excitation of the helium atoms from the ground state. This energy excess is coupled to an unexcited neon atom by a collisional process with the net result of an inversion in the neon atom population, thus allowing laser action to begin. Power levels available from the HeNe laser ranges from a fraction of a milliwatt to about 75 milliwatts in the largest available systems. The HeNe laser is known for its high-frequency stability and single mode operation, and is one of the most widely used lasers.

Ion. The family of ion lasers utilizes argon, krypton, xenon, and neon gases to provide over 35 laser frequencies, ranging from the near ultraviolet (neon at 322 nm) to the near-infrared (krypton at 799 nm). It is possible to mix the gases to produce either single frequency or simultaneous emission at ten different wavelengths, ranging from the violet through the red spectrum. The design of an ion gas laser is similar to the HeNe with the major difference that the electrical current flowing in the laser tube will be 10–20 amperes, sufficient to ionize the gas. Population inversion is obtained only in the ionized state of the gas. A feature of

COMMON LASER WAVELENGTHS

Laser Type	Spectrum	Wavelength (Nanometers)
Gas Lasers		
Argon Fluoride	Excimer—UV	193 nm
Krypton Chloride	Excimer—UV	222 nm
Krypton Fluoride	Excimer—UV	248 nm
Xenon Chloride	Excimer—UV	308 nm
Xenon Fluoride	Excimer—UV	351 nm
Nitrogen	Excimer—UV	337 nm
Helium Cadmium	UV	325 nm
Helium Cadmium	Violet-UV	441 nm
Argon	Blue	488 nm
Argon	Green	514 nm
Krypton	Blue	476 nm
Krypton	Green	528 nm
Krypton	Yellow	568 nm
Krypton	Red	647 nm
Xenon	White	multiple
Helium Neon	Green	543 nm
Helium Neon	Yellow	594 nm
Helium Neon	Orange	612 nm
Helium Neon	Red	633 nm
Hydrogen Fluoride	MIR	2,700 nm
Carbon Dioxide	FIR	10,600 nm
Metal Vapor Lasers		
Copper Vapor	Green	510 nm
Copper Vapor	Yellow	570 nm
Gold Vapor	Red	627 nm
Solid State Lasers		
Doubled Nd:YAG	Green	532 nm
Gallium Arsenide	Diode-NIR	840 nm
Neodymium:YAG	NIR	1,064 nm
Erbium:Glass	MIR	1,540 nm
Erbium:YAG	MIR	2,940 nm
Holmium:YLF	MIR	2,060 nm
Holmium:YAG	MIR	2,100 nm
Chromium Sapphire	Ruby—Red	694 nm
Titanium Sapphire	NIR	840–1,100 nm
Alexandrite	NIR	700–815 nm
Dye Lasers		
Rhodamine 6G	VIS	570–650 nm
Coumarin C30	Green	504 nm
Semiconductor Lasers		
Galium Arsenide (GaAs)	NIR	840 nm
Galium Aluminum Arsenide	VIS/NIR	670–830 nm
Ultraviolet		200–400 nm
Visible	VIS	400–700 nm
Near Infrared	IR-A (NIR)	700–1,400 nm
Middle Infrared	IR-B (MIR)	1,400–3,000 nm
Far Infrared	IR-C (FIR)	3,000 nm–1 mm

these lasers is the very stable high output power of up to 20 watts/CW. Commercial models have a wavelength selector (a prism) within the cavity to allow operation at any one of the wavelengths available.

Argon-ion lasers produce the highest visible power levels and have up to 10 lasing wavelengths in the blue-green spectrum. These lasers are rated by the power level (usually 1–10 watts) produced by all of the six major visible wavelengths from 458 to 514 nm. The most prominent argon wavelengths are 514 and 488 nm. Wavelengths in the ultraviolet spectrum at 351 and 364 nm available by changing resonator mirrors. To dissipate the large amount of generated heat, larger argon ion laser tubes are water cooled and some lasers have separate heat exchangers. Simple pulsed versions of argon ion lasers also are available. Since the duty cycle ("on" time divided by the time between pulses) is low, the heat generated is small, and usually only convective cooling is needed. The average power output may be as high as several watts, thought the peak powers can be as high as several kilowatts. Pulse widths are approximately 5–50 microseconds, with repetition rates as high as 60 Hz.

Carbon Dioxide. The carbon dioxide laser is the most efficient and powerful of all CW laser devices with powers reported above 30 kilowatts in the infrared wavelength. An electrical discharge is initiated in a plasma tube containing carbon dioxide gas. CO_2 molecules are excited by electron collisions to higher levels, from which they decay to the metastable level; which has a lifetime of 2×10^{-3} seconds at low pressure. Establishing a population inversion leads to lasing transitions at 10.6 micrometers, while a population inversion between other levels can result in lasing transitions at 9.6 micrometers. Lasing can be obtained in a plasma tube containing CO_2 gas alone, but various gases are added, including N_2, He, Xe, CO_2 and H_2O to increase the operating efficiency. Carbon dioxide lasers can produce tremendous amounts of output power, because of the high efficiency of about 30%, compared to less than 0.1% for HeNe lasers. The difference between the CO_2 and other gas lasers is that the optics must be coated to be reflective or transmissive at the far infrared wavelengths.

There are laser cavity configurations of the CO_2 laser. The first is the gas discharge tube. Second is the axial gas flow, where the gas mixture is pumped into one end of the tube and taken out the other. The gas flow allows for the replacement of the CO_2 molecules depleted by the electrical discharge. Nitrogen or helium are added to increase the efficiency of the pumping process. The last method is the transverse gas flow that can produce CO_2 laser emissions at power levels approaching 25 kW.

Nd:YAG Lasers. A popular laser source for moderate to high power uses a neodymium doped crystal Yttrium Aluminum Garnet (YAG), commonly designated Nd:YAG and belonging to the class of solid-state lasers. The Nd:YAG laser is optically pumped by tungsten or krypton pump

amps and is capable of continuous wave outputs at 1,000 W at the 1.06 micrometers wavelength. The crystal ends, usually in the form of a rod, are lapped, polished, and may be coated to provide the cavity mirrors. Solid-state lasers are unique. The first operational laser medium was a crystal of pink ruby (a sapphire crystal doped with chromium) and the term "solid-state laser" is used to describe a laser whose active medium is a crystal doped with an impurity ion. Solid-state lasers are heavy duty and capable of generating high power. Crystals of refractive index variations distort the laser's wavefront and mode structure. High-power operation causes thermal expansion of the crystal, which alters the effective cavity dimensions and thus changes the modes. The laser crystals are cooled by air or liquids for high repetition rates. Solid-state laser output is not continuous, but consists of a high number of separated power bursts. As the repetition rate increases, the exit energy per pulse decreases. Some systems produce up to ten joules per pulse at a repetition rate of 10 Hz.

Excimer Lasers. High-power ultraviolet (UV) lasers could produce a focused beam of submicrometer size. In 1975 the first of a family of new UV laser devices was discovered by Searles and Hart. This type laser was to be referred to as an excimer laser, an abbreviation for the term "*Excited Dimer*." Excimer lasers operate using reactive gases such as chlorine and fluorine mixed with inert gases such as argon, krypton, or xenon. The various gas combinations, when electrically excited, produce a pseudo molecule (called a "dimer") with an energy level that causes the generation of a specific laser wavelength emission that falls in the UV spectrum.

Laser Media	Wavelength (nanometers)
Argon Fluoride	193
Krypton Chloride	222
Krypton Fluoride	248
Xenon Chloride	308
Xenon Fluoride	351

An excimer operates in a repetitively pulsed mode of 30–40 ns pulses at pulse rates up to 50 Hz with pulse energies of 1–2 joules/pulse. Some use x-rays to pre-ionize the excimer gas mixture to enhance lasing efficiency and increase output power. Excimer lasers were used as a UV source or to serve as a "pumping" or exciting source to generate visible laser emissions. The excimer's UV output is directed into a tunable dye laser module and converted into a moderate power visible emission.

Semiconductor Diode Lasers. The semiconductor or diode injection laser is a solid-state laser. Energy levels are produced by charge carriers in the semiconductor and may be pumped optically, by electron beam bombardment, or by an externally applied current. They operate in the near-infrared spectral region, but visible laser diodes are being made and many are tunable by varying the current, changing temperature, or applying an external magnetic field. Laser diodes are used for communications, in disc players, retail scanners, and printers. Semiconductor lasers are used in distance detectors and remote sensing systems, and for voice and data communications. Many of the diode lasers are operated on a continuous wave basis.

Other Lasers. Dye lasers were the first tunable lasers. Using different organic dyes, they are capable of emission from the ultraviolet to near infrared, in the visible with tunable emissions at almost any wavelength. The organic dye lasers are optically pumped and the most common dye is Rhodamine-6G in solution. They may be flashlamp pumped, or pumped with another laser such as an Argon or Nitrogen laser. Using dye solutions, an argon-ion laser as a pump, and a prism, the dye laser is tunable across most of the visible spectrum. Tunable dye lasers are used in atomic spectroscopy.

Lasers in Platemaking. There are five lasers that are used in platemaking systems:
- Argon ion (blue—488 nm)
- Double frequency Nd:YAG (green—532 nm)
- Nd:YAG (IR 1064 nm)
- Low power visible laser diodes (670 nm)
- High power IR laser diodes (780-908 nm)

Lasers are used in all aspects of the graphic arts, but most commonly in laser printers, laser imagesetters and computer-to-plate systems.

Laser Diode
A small *laser* light-emitting device in some *imagesetter*s.

Laser Disc
Generally speaking, any optical storage medium written and read by a *laser*. See *Compact Disc (CD)* and *Videodisc*. The term *LaserDisc* (one word, capitalized), however, is a trade name of a type of videodisc created by Philips, also known as *Compact Disc–Video*. See *Compact Disc–Video (CD-V)*.

Laser Platemaking
The use of lasers in the imaging of plates. See *Computer-to-Plate*.

Laser Printer
A computer-driven, plain-paper output device used to generate proofs, masters, or general on-demand output. Most laser printers can output text, photographs, *halftone*s, or other images. Laser printers are increasingly the standard output device attached to home and office computers, having replaced in most cases the old dot-matrix printer, especially as laser printers have come down in price and increased in quality.

A laser printer works generally on the same principle as a photocopier, imaging on paper by means of *elec-*

trophotography. A laser printer contains an electrically charged, light-sensitive metal drum or cylinder. Controlled by information received from the printer *driver* installed in the computer, the laser exposes the charged drum in those regions corresponding to image areas, forming an image out of many tiny, virtually microscopic dots (more correctly called *spot*s, especially to distinguish them from *halftone dot*s). The areas of drum exposed by the laser become oppositely charged from the rest of the drum, and will accept oppositely charged particles of *toner*, a fine black or colored powder. The toner adheres to the drum in those regions exposed by the laser, and is transferred to the *substrate* passing beneath it. Heat and pressure are then used to fuse or "fix" the toner to the substrate, preventing it from being easily rubbed off.

One of the drawbacks of most laser printers (as of this writing) is that their maximum resolution is 600 *dpi*, which is adequate for most text and line-art output, but inadequate for *halftone* output, which usually need—depending upon the screen count—around 1200–1500 dpi. Color laser printers are also increasing in popularity and coming down in price. Laser printers are primarily used to generate galleys, proofs, and general output, while high-end *imagesetter*s are typically used to generate high-quality, camera-ready output or film.

As laser printer resolution has evolved from 300 to 600 and now to 1,200 dpi we have seen plain-paper output used for camera-ready copy by small and quick printers with camera-platemaking systems. Many books are output at 600 dpi or better and photographed to imposed film or plate using step-and-repeat systems. Plain-paper laser printers are also used to output special offset plate material.

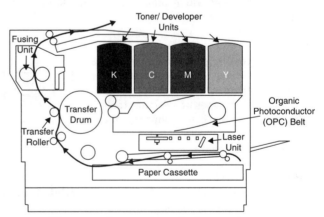

The general operation of a laser printer.

Laser Printing
General term for printing or other imaging performed by means of *laser*s. See *Laser Printer* and *Imagesetter*.

Laser Servo
A device used to increase storage capacities on magnetic media that writes a control track on the disk with a much finer tolerance than standard magnetic *read/write head*s.

Laser Videodisc

See *Videodisc*.

Laser-Cutting Process

A means of *gravure engraving*, or transferring an image to the surface of the image-carrying *gravure cylinder*. See *Gravure Engraving: Laser-Cutting Process*.

LaserVision (LV)

The trade name of an analog *videodisc* system manufactured by Philips, used to distribute color video with two channels of audio (up to 35 minutes per side) and color stills (up to 54,000 per side). The LaserVision disc was 30 centimeters in diameter, and resembles a cross between an old vinyl record and a *compact disc (CD)*. It was written and read by a laser employing the *constant angular velocity (CAV)* principle. Although the LV was primarily an analog storage medium, some digital data was used to guide the operation of the disc. An all-digital version of the LV is known as the *LV–ROM*, while the LaserVision disc itself was changed to the *LaserDisc* (also known as *Compact Disc Video*) in the early 1990s. See *Compact Disc–Video (CD–V)*.

LaserVision–Read-Only Memory (LV-ROM)

An interactive video distribution medium, a hybrid of the *compact disc–read-only memory (CD–ROM)* and the *videodisc*. Essentially, the LV–ROM is a 12-in. wide digital video disc capable of storing two digital sound channels, 54,000 analog images, and up to 324 *megabyte*s of computer data. The computer data can be loaded into the memory of the LV–ROM player (essentially a videodisc player) and can accompany video information. Also known as an *LD–ROM*.

Lasso Tool

In many types of graphics programs, a selection tool used to define an irregular area of an image with which to work, in contrast to other types of selection tools— such as rectangular or elliptical *marquee*s—that are able to select only very basic geometric shapes.

Last Color Down

In *process color* printing, the last color printed on the *substrate* as it passes through the press.

Last In, First Out

In computing, a means of manipulating data such that the last data entered into the system is the first data processed. Abbreviated *LIFO*. See also *First In, First Out*.

Latent Image

In photography, term for an image exposed on a light-sensitive material (such as film) that remains invisible until developing.

In *electrophotography*, a *latent image* is the "pattern" of static electric charges imparted to the photoconductive drum prior to the application of toner. See *Electrophotography*.

Latex

A milky exudation of certain types of plants used in the making of natural and synthetic rubber, as well as paints, paper *coating*s, and other such materials.

Lathe

In computer graphics, a means of *rendering* three-dimensional objects by rotating a two-dimensional object around the horizontal or vertical axis. For example, a sphere can be created by rotating a circle.

Lattisnet

In networking, the first implementation of *Ethernet*, developed by Synoptics. Lattisnet utilized a *star* topology, connected by *twisted-pair wiring*, and ran at 10 megabits per second.

Launch

To start a computer program by double-clicking on its icon (in a *graphical user interface*) or entering the name of the program's *EXE* file (in a *command-line interface*).

Lavaliere

In television and video, a small microphone designed to clip onto the wearer's lapel or be worn around the neck. The term derives from the French word *lavaliere*, used to refer to a jeweled pendant worn around the neck that, in turn, was named after the Duchesse de La Vallière, one of the mistresses of King Louis XIV.

Lay

The position of a printed image on a press sheet. The desired lay of an image is typically squarely in the center of the sheet. The lay of an image is usually gauged at the start of a job by running through one or more *lay sheet*s. Improper lay may necessitate a repositioning of the plate on the *plate cylinder*.

Layback

The portion of a printing plate used in *offset lithography* that does not print, typically considered the region between the plate edge and the *gripper margin*, plus the gripper margin.

Laydown Sequence

Alternate term for *printing sequence*. See *Printing Sequence*.

Layer

In image-processing software applications (such as Adobe Photoshop, for example), a digital "overlay" used to keep image elements separate for ease of editing and manipulation. For example, a background may exist on one layer, while on top of it could be a figure intended to be superimposed on that background. By keeping the superimposed figure on a separate layer, it can be altered or deleted without disrupting the *pixel*s forming the background.

In networking, *layer* refers to one of seven networking functions or aspects described in the *OSI* reference model. See *Open Systems Interconnection (OSI)*.

Layering

In a computer *drawing* program, a means of dividing an illustration into several transparent "overlays" which can be turned on or off, allowing attention to be focused on specific portions of the image.

In audio recording, *layering* refers to the combination of several sound sources so as to produce a fuller, richer sound.

Layflat Adhesive

An *adhesive* substance that will resist warping.

Layout

In typography, a drawing, sketch, or other plan indicating how a printed piece will look, including the placement of text, illustration matter, and other page elements, and perhaps *type specifications*.

In prepress and design, the manual or electronic *pasteup* of pages.

In platemaking, a marked sheet used for *step-and-repeat* exposures.

Layout Object

One particular element of a page *layout*.

Layout Paper

Alternate term for *detail paper*. See *Detail Paper*.

Layout Proof

Any working copy of laid-out pages.

Layout Sheet

Alternate term for *imposition layout*.

Lays

A set of two fixed guides on the printing bed of a *screen printing* press used to *register* the *substrate* prior to printing. The edges of the substrate that contact the lays are known as *laysides*.

Lay Sheet

A preliminary sheet run through a printing press at the beginning of a job to evaluate the positioning of the image on the sheet (called the *lay*). Improper *register* or line-up may require repositioning the plate on the *plate cylinder*.

Laysides

In *screen printing*, the two edges of a *substrate* that contact the *lays*, or guides used to *register* the substrate.

LC

Abbreviation for *lowercase*. See *Lowercase*.

LCD

Abbreviation for *liquid crystal display*. See *Liquid Crystal Display (LCD)*.

LCD Monitor

A computer monitor comprising a *liquid crystal display*. See *Liquid Crystal Display (LCD)*. LCD Monitors are used on most *laptop computer*s.

LCD Panel

A device that can be connected to a personal computer and placed on an overhead (or other) projector, allowing computer data to be projected on a large screen, used in computer-based presentations and lectures. See *Liquid Crystal Display (LCD)*.

LCH

Abbreviation for *luminance*, *chroma*, and *hue*. See *HLS*.

LD–ROM

Abbreviation for *LaserDisc–read-only memory*, an alternate term for *LaserVision-read only memory*. See *Laser Vision–Read-Only Memory (LV-ROM)*.

Lead

Pronounced "ledd." In metal type, a strip of metal used to space successive lines of type. In phototypesetting and electronic page make-up, the distance, measured in *point*s, from the *baseline* of one typeset line to the baseline of an adjacent line. See *Leading*.

Leader Characters

In typography, any characters (primarily dots or hyphens) used as *leaders*, to fill up the space between tabs, such as in tables of contents. See *Leaders*.

Leadering

In typography, the setting of *leaders*. See *Leaders*.

Leaders

In typography, dots (called dot leaders) or dashes (called dash leaders) that lead the eye from one side of a line to the other. Hairline rules or dashes under type can sometimes replace leaders. In hot metal, leaders were unique characters, with one leader dot centered on an en width or two leader dots set on an em width. Dots come in varying weights, ranging from fine, light dots to heavy, bold ones. The linecaster provided various styles of leaders to meet different publishing and printing requirements. They varied primarily in weight of dot or stroke, in dots or strokes to the em, and—in hot metal—in depth of punching:

Regular leaders, in dot or hyphen style, in two, four, or six dots (or strokes) to the em. *Universal leaders* had a uniform weight of dot or stroke. *Thin leaders* were used with either the regular or universal style (four dots or strokes to the em) for close *justification*. *Newspaper leaders* were the regular dot or hyphen leader, supplied in two dots or strokes to the em. *Radial leaders* were designed for newspaper use with a uniform weight of dot for all point sizes. They were made with a rounded or radial printing surface to prevent perforating paper and damaging press blankets. *Dash leaders* are en- or em-width hairline dashes (0.004 weight) punched to cast type high and present a continuous, unbroken line. *Leader-aligning dashes* cast a continuous, unbroken line.

Today, however, the period is used most often as the leader dot. However, it often does not work to the best advantage. Better-looking leaders are often found in lower point sizes, rather than setting the leader dots in the same point size as the text. Leaders need to be aligned vertically as well as horizontally, which is typically accomplished automatically by the typesetting device.

A common problem with the use of leaders is related to the mathematics of dividing their width into the line length. For example, a 9-point leader would divide into a 20-pica line 26.66 times ($20 \times 12 = 240$ points; $240 \div 9 = 26.66$). The resulting blank space needs to be placed somewhere, and the device may not place it in the most opportune location.

The best way of setting leaders is to select the narrowest possible width that will achieve the desired look, the en being the most popular. Then, key a word space at the beginning or end of the line as a place for the excess space to go. Finally, reduce to a smaller point size. This process allows more leader dots or strokes to fit on a line providing for the extraneous space.

For tables of contents, it is occasionally best not to use leaders at all, but to instead simply place the page number (after an en or em space) immediately after the story or chapter title.

The term *leader* also refers to the length of a *magnetic tape*, on which no data is recorded, used to wind the tape around the reel.

The term *leader*, in motion picture photography and videography, also refers to the opening images of a film or video, usually including the opening titles.

Lead-In

In typography, the first two or three words of a block of text set in a different, contrasting *typeface* or style (such as small caps or boldface).

Leading

In typography, an alternate and more popularly used term for *line spacing*, pronounced "ledding," See *Line Spacing*. The word leading derives its name from the strips of flat metal, usually lead, used to space lines of metal type.

Leading Edge

In *screen printing*, the edge of the *squeegee* blade that contacts the screen fabric during a printing stroke.

Leading Scale

In typography, a strip of clear *acetate*, calibrated in *point*s, used as a scale to measure the *leading* of typeset copy. See *Line Spacing*.

Lead Screw

A type of screw found inside a *scanner* that controls the movement of the scanner's optics as it moves across the image. Also known as a *spindle*.

Leaf

Term for a sheet of paper in a book or other publication. One leaf contains two pages—a *verso* and a *recto*.

The term *leaf* also refers to a colored material, usually a foil of some kind, used in *foil stamping*. One example is *gold leaf*. See *Foil Stamping*.

Leafing

In printing ink terminology, the formation of a flat layer of metallic *pigment*s parallel to the surface of a printed piece imparting a high metallic sheen.

Leakage

Term for the sound that seeps out of the headphones worn by an individual listening to a portable *compact disc* player or stereo.

Lean

Term descriptive of an oil-based printing ink that does not flow smoothly. See also *Fat*.

Learning Curve

A type of "graph" (referred to more figuratively than literally) in which the time it takes to master a particular skill (such as dexterity with a certain computer program) is plotted against the time spent working on that skill. For example, a complicated new program with many unfamiliar features may take some time to master. Such a program is thus said to have a "steep learning curve."

Leased Line

In telecommunications, a communication line or channel rented or leased by a company or individual for its exclusive use for data transmission.

Leatherette-Finish Paper

A paper *finish*, typically found in *cover paper*s, that has been *embossed* to simulate the look and texture of leather.

Leatheroid

In *binding and finishing*, a paper-like material used as a substitute for leather.

LED

Abbreviation for *light-emitting diode*, a type of digital display that generates pulses of visible or infrared light. Essentially, an LED works by removing and injecting digitally controlled pulses of electrons. As electrons are removed from the diode, they create gaps in the atoms they vacated which, when filled by newly arriving electrons, stimulate the emission of light in either visible (as in an indicator light on an automobile dashboard, or the display on a calculator) or infrared (as in hand-held remote control devices for garage doors, VCRs, televisions, etc.). *Binary* information controlling the flow of electrons into and out of the diode is what generates the desired pattern of illumination. LEDs are also used to expose photosensitive film and paper in some imaging devices.

Ledger Paper

A *grade* of paper similar to *bond paper*, but is typically manufactured in higher *basis weight*s for reasons of *durabilty*. Ledger paper is commonly used in business applications for keeping records, or in legal applications such as wills, deeds, etc., and consequently requires a high degree of *permanence*. Paper qualities typical of ledger papers are high strength, *stiffness*, and a surface suitable for pen and ink, erasing, and computer printing devices. The paper *finish* may be smooth, or slightly roughened (called a *posting finish*), for machine posting of data. Ledger papers are made from all *chemical pulp*, typically with a high (or total) *cotton-content* pulp.

The *basic size* of ledger papers is 17×22 in., and typical *basis weight*s are 24-, 28-, 32-, and 36-lb. *Standard size*s are 17×22, 17×28, 19×24, 22×34, 24×38, and 28×34.

Left Justified

In typography, copy that is set so that all the lines align on the left margin. Also known as *flush left*. See also *Right Justified*.

Left-Handed Coordinate System

A means of specifying the *coordinate system* in three-dimensional mathematical modeling: the left hand is extended palm out, fingers up in front of the viewer. The positive values on the *x-axis* (or horizontal axis) are indicated by the thumb, which points to the right; the *y-axis* (or vertical axis) is indicated by the index finger, which points up; and the negative values of the *z-axis* (or axis providing depth) are said to emerge from the palm, pointing away from the viewer. See also *Right-Handed Coordinate System*.

Leg

A *letter element* synonymous with *tail*. See *Tail*.

Legacy System

A computer system that has been in use for a very long period of time, such as a corporation's *mainframe* or an older *personal computer*. The trouble with so-called legacy systems is that, since they typically have a much slower *microprocessor* and less *random-access memory (RAM)*, they may not be able to run new applications or upgraded versions of older applications. (See also *Legacy Wiring*.)

Legacy Wiring

In networking, wiring or cabling that has been in use for a great deal of time, or was preinstalled at some point in the perhaps not-so-recent past. Such wiring may or may not be suitable for modern computer networks. See also *Legacy System*.

Legal Size

A size of paper originally designed to correspond to the standard size for legal briefs, which is 8½×14 in. "Legal size" paper has now become the dominant large-size paper for use in many other businesses.

Legend

Any explanatory text attached to (or placed near) an illustration or chart, as distinct from a strictly descriptive *caption*.

Legibility

In typography, the ease with which typeset copy is read. Related to legibility is *readbility*, which describes how clearly what is typeset has been written and can be understood. Copy can be readable but not legible, legible but not readable, both legible and readable (the ideal situation), or neither legible nor readable (the worst situation).

Legibility is related to the way we read. The human eye fixates on something each quarter of a second and takes in a group of words. It then jumps to the next fixation, etc. Each of these fixations is called a saccad, and saccadic jumps move the eye from one saccad point to another. Speed-reading approaches usually try to train the reader's eyes to make larger jumps and take in more words at one time.

Legibility has been reflected in the design of letterforms. Large *x-height* serif faces with a bolder print to them tend to score highly in legibility research. Additionally, it has been found that word spacing should be the width of a lowercase "i" and the leading should be slightly larger than the word spacing. Legibility research also has found that narrower line lengths, consistent word spacing, upper- and lowercase lettering (as opposed to all caps), and well-designed typefaces aid in efficient reading.

Lempel-Ziv-Welch

See *LZW*.

Length

A property of printing ink that describes its ability to flow, and to form threads when stretched. *Long ink*s flow well, and form long filaments when stretched. Although long inks have desirable flow characteristics, excessively long inks have a tendency to produce problems such as *ink misting* or *flying* when used on high-speed presses. *Short ink*s form short filaments, have a butter-like consistency, and poor flow characteristics. Excessively short inks can cause *piling* or *caking* on the blanket, plate, or rollers. The best inks, therefore, are those that are not excessively long or short. The extent to which an ink will form threads is also called ***stringiness***.

Lenox-Cut

A continuous means of paper ***cutting and trimming*** designed to eliminate out-of-square corners and dished reams.

Lens

An optical device, usually made of glass or quartz, used, basically, to focus light. The first lens is believed to have been a magnifying glass, evidence suggesting that the ancient Chaldeans in Babylonia knew of rudimentary optics. Essentially, a lens is based on the principle of light ***refraction***. The curved surface of a convex lens will contain light passing into it at a variuety of angles in relation to a principal axis (i.e., described by a ray of light hitting the exact center of curvature). All the rays passing through this curved surface will converge at a single point along the principal axis, called the ***focal point***. The distance between the point on the principal axis where it meets the exterior of the curved surface and the focal point is known as the ***focal length***. Convex lenses with different degrees of curvature will have different refraction effects (and concave lenses also have different effects). The most common examples of lenses are those found in our own eyes; called a crystalline lens (and not made of glass, to be sure), it works to focus light passing through the pupil onto the retina. In many of us, the focal lengths of our eyes have changed over time, the result being that the focal point of our lenses now falls either behind or in front of the retina. As a result, blurry vision occurs. Artificial lenses (i.e., eyeglasses or contact lenses) are used to reposition the focal point of light entering the eye so that it falls directly on the retina, allowing clear vision.

The lens of a ***camera*** operates in much the same way, working to focus light rays at a specific point corresponding to the film plane. The ability to adjust the lens allows for

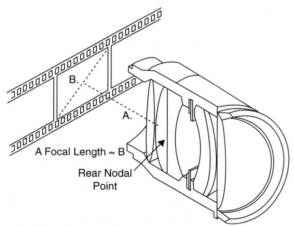

Standard focal length lens. Typically, a lens is chosen such that the focal length is approximately equal to the diagonal size of the image.

the focusing of images at a variety of distances from the camera. (See ***Photography***.)

The principle of the lens is also used for simple magnification in some types of cameras, in magnifying glasses, telescopes, microscopes, and a variety of other devices.

Lens Hood

A cylindrical lens cap attached to the end of a camera ***lens*** used to keep ***ambient light*** from inside the camera.

Letter Elements

In typography, the various portions of a type character, which include:

The ***apex*** is the top junction of two stems, such as the point of the capital "A" or the center of the capital "W." The opposite of an apex (or the bottom junction of two stems) is the ***vortex***. The capital "W" has one apex and two vortex points. The inside of an apex or a vortex is known as a ***crotch***.

The ***counter*** is the fully or partially enclosed part of a letter, as in the lowercase "e," which has a full counter above and a partial counter below. The term *counter* refers to the space itself, while the term ***bowl*** refers to the lines enclosing the counter. The proportion of the counter to the character is important to legibility. A complete bowl is formed by curved strokes only, and a modified bowl has the stem forming one of the sides. A ***loop*** is a bowl that serves as a flourish, as in the descending part of some lowercase "g" characters.

The ***stem*** is the main vertical stroke or principal stroke in an oblique character or face and is the dominant element in most characters. Elements that are perpendicular to the stem or connected to it or to other main parts of the letter include the ***arm*** (a horizontal or diagonal stroke starting from the stem, as in the capital "E" or "F"), the ***bar*** (an arm connected on both sides, as in the capital "H"), the ***crossbar*** (a horizontal stroke that crosses through the stem, as in the lowercase "t"; the capital "T" stroke is more accurately two arms), the ***ear*** (a short stroke extending from the bowl of a lowercase "g" or from the stem of a lowercase "r"), the ***tail*** (a downward-sloping short stroke, ending free), the ***beak*** (the outer portion of arms and serifs of the letters "E," "F," "G," "T," and "Z"), the ***arc*** (any curved stroke that is not a bowl), and the ***spine*** (the main curved arc section of the letter "S").

A ***terminal*** is a free-ending stroke of a letter, commonly with some kind of special treatment, which can be *acute* (having the angle of an acute ***accent***), *concave* (rounded out), *convex* (rounded in), *flared* (extended), *grave* (having the angle of a grave accent), *hook* (looped), *pointed* (coming to a point), *sheared* (sliced off), *straight* (even with the stroke itself), or *tapered* (graduated). A type of terminal is the ***finial***, a more decorative, alternative ending to a stroke, such as a *ball* (having a rounded shape), *barb* (the end of an arc), *beak* (commonly a half-serif), or a *swash* (a flourish).

The variations of these letter elements are what distinguish one typeface from another.

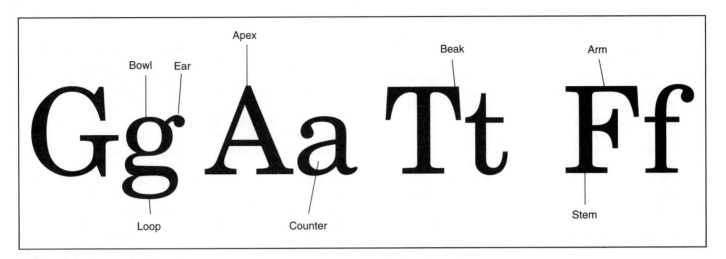

The elements of a typographic letter.

Letter Fold

In **binding and finishing**, a type of fold consisting of two or more **parallel fold**s, all oriented in the same direction, with the creases wrapping around an inner leaf. See **Folding**.

Letter Quality

Descriptive of computer printer output produced as whole characters (rather than collections of dots), as from a **daisy-wheel printer**, which resembles typewriter type and is suitable for personal correspondence (i.e., letters).

Letter Size

A **standard size** of paper, 8½×11, and the most common size of paper available commercially. Commonly used for letters, but also for scores of other uses.

Letter-Quality Printer

Any computer output device that generates text of **letter quality**. See **Letter Quality**.

Letterfit

In typography, the degree of the legibility or aesthetic palatability of the **letterspacing**. See **Letterspacing**.

Letterforms

General term referring to all typographic characters and symbols.

Letterpress

The oldest of the major printing processes distinguished by its use of raised metal type. The type can be either individual characters or plates made with raised type. Although the first printing presses ever created were letterpress devices, the use of letterpress printing has been declining due to advances in other forms of printing, especially **offset lithography** and **gravure**. The legacy of letterpress lives on in **flexography**, a type of relief printing utilizing flexible rubber plates. The decline of letterpress is due primar-

ily to the extensive and expensive makeready procedures required. Letterpress plates exert varying amounts of pressure on the **substrate** during printing. For example, for a given amount of impression pressure, more pressure will be exerted on small **highlight** dots than on larger blocks of solids or **shadow**s. Consequently, it takes a great deal of effort to ensure that that small highlight areas do not pierce the substrate and that the solids print with uniform density (in flexography, the resilience of the rubber plate eliminates this problem). The use of **photopolymer** plates is reviving letterpress to an extent, however. There are several parts to a letterpress press:

IMAGE CARRIER

Johann Gutenberg's important contribution to printing was not really the *idea* of the printing press, but an effective image carrier. He solved the problem by casting type, or forming a matrix with a punch that made a mold of a particular letter. He then poured molten lead into the mold and let it cool. These could all be fit into a frame, inked, and printed. Eventually, others developed means of casting type a line at a time or, even more efficiently, making a mold of an entire page of locked-up type and making a solid plate out of it, which could then be wrapped around a cylinder. Two versions of these early letterpress plates are **stereotype**s and **electrotype**s, two different ways of creating a solid, curved metal plate from a locked-up typeform. (See **Type**.) Molded rubber **photopolymer plate**s have for the most part replaced the older metal stereotypes and electrotypes, and are prepared in a manner not unlike plates produced for flexography. There are essentially four types of letterpress presses:

Platen Press. A **platen press** utilizes a flat plate or typeform mounted on the bottom—or **flatbed**—of the press. A **platen** closes over the inked typeform and substrate, exerting pressure and transferring the ink from the type to the paper. Small platen presses are used to print short-run jobs, such as invitations, announcements, stationery, etc.

Flatbed Press. On a *flatbed press*, the typeform is again placed on a flatbed, but the substrate is carried on a rotating *impression cylinder*. In some configurations, the flatbed moves beneath the rotating cylinder, effecting ink transfer. In some configurations, the typeform is in a vertical position and both the flatbed and the cylinder move.

Rotary Press. A *rotary press* utilizes a rotating *plate cylinder* to which a curved metal relief plate is mounted. The curved plate is brought in contact with a rotating impression cylinder, the paper passing through the nip between the two cylinders. Rotary sheetfed presses are a casualty of the declining market for letterpress printing, but some web-fed rotary presses are still utilized. Narrow web rotary presses utilizing photopolymer plates and *ultraviolet curing ink* are capable of high-speed multicolor letterpress printing, and can handle web widths of up to 24 in. These presses are also often used inline with other types of presses, such as flexo and lithographic, or with finishing equipment such as embossers and diecutters.

Belt Press. A *belt press* is used for high-speed production of books. The press consists of two belts, one containing a set of plates for the *recto* pages, the other belt containing a set of plates for the *verso* pages. A paper web is fed through the press at speeds of up to 1,200 feet per minute, where it contacts all the plates on one belt, is allowed to dry, then is sent through to contact all the plates on the other belt, thus printing both sides of all the sheets. The printing unit of this press is inline with finishing equipment that cuts and folds the pages into *signature*s, collates them together into books, and binds them into the covers.

INKING SYSTEM

Letterpress uses thick, *paste ink*s that, due to *thixotropy*, need to be heavily worked by means of a long series of ink rollers in order to achieve the desired flow properties for ink transfer. The ink is stored in a *fountain*, essentially a pan or trough. A *fountain roller* rotates in the fountain,

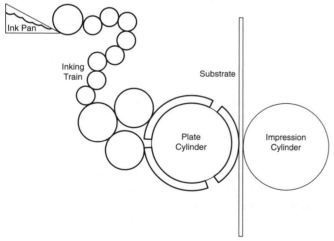

Basic letterpress printing unit.

transferring a specified amount of ink to the ink rollers (commonly four), which then transfer it to the *form roller*s (commonly three). The form rollers then transfer the ink to the typeform on the flatbed or to the plate on the plate cylinder, depending on the press configuration. The image carrier is commonly inked following each impression.

Dry Offset. A variety of letterpress printing has some specialty applications. In the process of *dry offset*, a relief plate is mounted on an offset press, where it is inked, and brought into contact with a rubber *blanket*, similar to that used in offset lithography. The image is transferred to the blanket which, in turn, transfers the image to the substrate. It is called "dry offset" because the use of a raised plate precludes the need for a *dampening system*. Although this process has difficulty printing fine detail or *halftone*s and does not have wide commercial use, it is useful for printing on rough or irregular surfaces, such as aluminum cans.

Letterset

A hybrid of *letterpress* printing and *offset lithography* that uses a metal relief plate mounted to a *plate cylinder* to transfer the ink to a rubber blanket, similar to that used in offset lithography. The blanket then transfers the ink to the *substrate*. The use of a raised image carrier eliminates the need for a *fountain solution*. Dry offset is not widely used commercially, as it has difficulty reproducing fine line detail or *halftone*s, but is useful for printing on rough or irregular surfaces, such as aluminum cans. Also known as *dry offset* and *offset letterpress*.

Letterset Ink

A variety of ink used in *letterset* printing (also called *dry offset*), in which ink is transferred from a relief (*letterpress*) printing plate to an offset blanket and then to the *substrate*. The use of the letterpress plate allows the printing process to operate in the absence of water. The lack of water allows an unlimited variety of *pigment*s to be utilized in the ink formulation, as excessive *emulsification* by the fountain solution is no longer an issue. Letterset inks possess greater strength than do conventional letterpress inks, but possess less strength than conventional offset inks, as letterset inks are not diluted by a fountain solution. (See also *Waterless Ink*.)

Letterspacing

In typography, the space between typeset letters or other characters. There are two varieties of letterspacing: positive and negative.

Positive Letterspacing. Adding space between letters in uniform increments for one or more of the following reasons:
1. Automatic letterspacing, activated so that word spaces are not too wide during *justification*. Called into action when word spaces reach a preset maximum amount. This approach interrupts the even texture of text typography and impairs legibility.

2. Selective letterspacing for certain character combinations. In serif type, the serifs provide natural boundaries against negative letterspacing (serifs should not overlap). More caution is necessary with sans serif type, although when too tight, certain letter combinations (such as "rn" or "ol") may flow together (to look like "m" or "d").
3. Word letterspacing for aesthetic reasons, such as all-capital titles or headings.

All in all, positive letterspacing is not recommended, because of poor legibility, although aesthetic considerations may prevail.

Negative Letterspacing. Also known as *minus letterspacing*, subtracting space equally from between all letters in small units of space for one or more of the following reasons:
1. Tight spacing (*white space reduction*) is desirable for artistic reasons.
2. Selective subtraction (*kerning*) is required for certain character combinations.

When tight type is reduced photographically, letters also will flow together, perhaps necessitating an alteration of letterspacing.

The concept of *tracking* is simply presetting of *universal negative letterspacing* into degrees of spacing to allow type specifiers to select the desired "look" or "color" for the typeface and size in use. The variations, in order of increasing space, are touching, very tight, tight, normal, open, or open (foundry, a greater degree of letterspacing than open).

Levant

In *binding and finishing*, a type of irregularly grained leather cover material made from goatskin. Also called *Levant morocco*, morocco being a type of goat-based leather.

Level 2 Cache

In computing, a secondary memory *cache* typically located between the primary RAM cache and the rest of the computer system. The level 2 cache is often larger—but slower—than the primary cache. See *Cache Memory*.

Leveling

In *perfect binding*, the process of cutting a small amount of paper from the *spine* of a book to impart to the book a perfectly square spine. See *Perfect Binding*.

Levelness

Alternate term for a paper's *smoothness*. See *Smoothness*.

Level One Videodisc

A *videodisc* possessing a few—but not very many—interactive features. Unlike a *level zero videodisc*, which can only play and stop playing a disc, a level one disc allows the access of certain positions on the disc by entering a *frame* number on the player's remote control keypad. A level one

disc has its data stored in fixed segments (called *chapter*s), and as a result can only be stopped and started at certain points. A *level two videodisc* and a *level three videodisc* both allow increasingly greater degrees of interactivity. See *Videodisc*.

Level Three Videodisc

A *videodisc* possessing a high number of interactive features and possibilities. Unlike a *level zero videodisc*, which can only play and stop playing a disc, a *level one videodisc*, which only allows certain frame numbers to be accessed, or a *level two videodisc*, which allows a considerable but limited degree of interactivity, a level three disc makes use of an external computer that can be connected to the disc player, thus allowing a high degree of interactivity. See *Videodisc*.

Level Two Videodisc

A *videodisc* possessing a significant number of interactive features. Unlike a *level zero videodisc*, which can only play and stop playing a disc, or a *level one videodisc*, which only allows certain frame numbers to be accessed, a level two disc contains an operating program that can utilize the disc player's internal microprocessor and up to 10 *kilobyte*s of memory, thus allowing a considerable degree of interactivity and specialized programming. A *level three videodisc* allows a greater degree of interactivity. See *Videodisc*.

Level Zero Videodisc

A *videodisc* possessing no interactive features. Essentially, a level zero disc can only be played from beginning to end, unlike a *level one videodisc*, a *level two videodisc* and a *level three videodisc* that allow increasingly greater degrees of interactivity. See *Videodisc*.

Lexical

Descriptive of text or tabular material, or content that would be found in a lexicon.

LF

Abbreviation for *line feed*. See *Line Feed*.

Library

Any organized and easily accessed collection of information, be it physical (a building full of books) or virtual (an on-line database of documents).

In computer programming, a *library* is a collection of standard functions and operations used by programming languages to execute certain tasks. The purpose of a library and the advantage of a well-stocked one is that it can significantly cut down the time required to develop a new computer application, as standard routines can simply be obtained from the library and combined with new codes, routines, etc., that the programmer creates. These new routines can also be added to the library, should they be required again.

Desktop publishing programs have a Library function for reuseable type and art elements, and many programs have libraries of metal type.

Library Binding

In *binding and finishing*, a *casebound* book bound in accordance with the standards of the American Library Association. Library bindings having strong *endleaf* papers, *reinforced endsheets*, four-cord thread, canton-flannel backlining, and covers of Caxton buckram cloth, with round corners.

Library binding also refers to any *case binding* process involving low-quantity production, some degree of hand-work, and some amount of binding repairs.

Library Buckram

In *binding and finishing*, a trade name for a strong cloth used for book covers that have been manufactured in accordance with United States Bureau of Standards binding specifications.

Licensed Font

A special, high-quality *font*—digital or otherwise—that is purchased from a type manufacturer (or foundry) and requires licensing agreements in order to be used.

LIFO

Abbreviation for *last in, first out*. See *Last In, First Out*.

Lift

In *binding and finishing*, an informal measure of a quantity of printed sheets or books consisting of the amount contained in a convenient handful. See also *Hand*.

Lifting

A defect of *screen printing* characterized by wrinkling a printed ink film, caused by the penetration of a second printed ink film into the first.

Ligated

In typography, descriptive of character pairs that are connected, as *ligature*s. See *Ligature*.

Ligature

In typography, two or more characters designed as a distinct unit and commonly available as a single character. There are five f-ligatures (fi, fl, etc.) plus the diphthongs (Æ, Œ, etc.). Gutenberg's font had many ligatures in order to simulate handwriting and to achieve even word spacing in his *justified* text columns.

The traditional ligatures are easily and automatically generated on command. Although book production most often finds them mandatory, advertising typography rarely finds them useful—and, in fact, they cannot be used in copy set tighter than normal spacing, since the space within ligatures cannot be manipulated. Computer automation will usually allow any ligature to be selected without operator intervention—an incentive for the expansion of ligature design and use until we someday develop a modern version of the Gutenberg font, which, research suggests, may increase legibility.

The diphthongs are also considered ligatures. Historically, ligatures were developed for metal type so that certain letter combinations that contained space buried between them could be used more closely together. Different languages had additional ligatures for often-used letter combinations. In German, for example, "ch" and "ck" were ligatures. The word ligature itself comes from the Latin word *ligatus*, the past participle of the word *ligare*, meaning "to tie or bind." Ligature also refers to any medical procedure in which arteries or tubes are "ligated" or tied, as in tubal ligation.

Light

The visible portion of the *electromagnetic spectrum*, perceived either as *white light* (light containing each wavelength of color in equal amounts and thus lacking any particular *hue*) or as light of a particular color, depending on which wavelengths are dominant. The portions of the electromagnetic spectrum that surround the *visible spectrum*—namely, the *infrared* and *ultraviolet*—are also occasionally referred to as "light," although they cannot be detected visibly. Ultraviolet light is occasionally—and not entirely correctly—referred to as *black light*.

Depending upon the experiment, light can either be a wave, as was first proposed by Dutch physicist Christian Huygens, or as a series of discrete particles, as was first proposed by Sir Isaac Newton. The particulate nature of light was the predominant theory of the nature of light until the early 1800s, when Thomas Young and Augustin-Jean Fresnel demonstrated in experiments the *diffraction* and *interference* of light, which could only occur if light was a wave. In 1864, James Clerk Maxwell demonstrated that light was a form of electromagnetic radiation, which boosted support for the wave theory of light. However, in 1905, Albert Einstein reconceived the notion of light as discrete particles (or photons, or quanta) in order to explain the photoelectric effect, or the emission of electrons produced when light strikes an object. Eventually, it was decided that light could be both a wave and a series of particles.

The intensity (or *luminosity*) of a light source is measured in *candle*s. The intensity of light reflected from a surface (or *luminance*) is measured in candles per square meter, or *foot candle*s, or *footlambert*s. (See *Color*.)

Light Alumina Hydrate

See *Alumina Hydrate*.

Light Button

Alternate term for a *button*, appearing as a graphical object on a computer display. See *button* (second definition).

Light-Emitting Diode

See *LED*.

Lightface

A *typeface* possessing a *weight* that is lighter than the standard weight for that typeface.

Aa Bb Cc Dd Ee Ff
Aa Bb Cc Dd Ee Ff

Futura typeface (top) and Futura Light (bottom).

Lightfastness

A paper property that measures the extent to which a paper will retain its original color, *brightness*, and *whiteness* with exposure to light. Various chemical constituents in paper *pulp* reduce its lightfastness, in particular the presence of *lignin*, a naturally occurring chemical found in wood that binds fibers of *cellulose* together, and is responsible for paper darkening and yellowing upon exposure to light. It is the goal of many *pulping* systems to remove as much lignin as possible from the wood pulp before paper-making. Various *chemical pulping* procedures, and the use of *bleaching* agents remove nearly all lignin from wood pulp, but *groundwood* pulp still contains a high amount of lignin, so paper composed of some quantity of it yellows very quickly (such as newsprint). Bleaching and the use of *fast-to-light dyes* help increase a paper's lightfastness, but no paper can be completely lightfast.

Tests to gauge lightfastness involve exposing a paper sample to a carefully controlled light source for a set period of time using a *Fade-Ometer*.

Lightfastness also refers to a printing ink's ability to retain its color strength and resist fading upon exposure to light. Tests to gauge an ink's lightfastness are performed in a manner similar to measures of a paper's lightfastness. Lightfastness is also referred to as *colorfastness*.

Light Integrator

An electronic device on a *process camera* that controls the *exposure time* of the camera as a function of the intensity of the light to produce a constant exposure on film or plates.

Lightness

One of the three basic qualities of a color on most *color models*, describing the degree of darkness or brightness of a particular color, plotted on most three-dimensional color coordinate systems independently of *hue* and *saturation*. See *CIE Color Space*, for example.

Lightness also refers to the general brightness or darkness of a black-and-white or color image in general. (See *Color Plate 8*.)

Light Pen

In computing, a graphic input device comprising a stylus containing a photoelectric cell. When the point of the stylus is brought into contact with the computer display, the coordinates of the point the stylus touched can be recorded by the computer, and a specific action or function can be initiated.

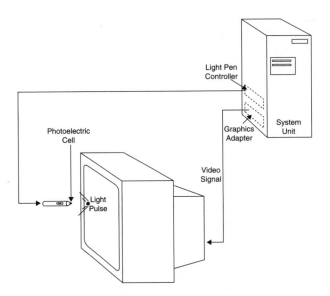

The basic principle of the light pen.

Light Table

A glass-topped table or other surface illuminated from below, used to facilitate tracing and *stripping*.

Lightwave Communications

Alternate term for *fiber optics*. See *Fiber Optics*.

Lightweight Paper

Formerly called *bible paper*, lightweight papers include a variety of different types of low-thickness, high-*opacity* papers used in bibles, handbooks, dictionaries, encyclopedias, and other uses that require low bulk or low weight (for example, in material that will be mailed). The *basic size* of lightweight papers is 25×38 in., and comes in *basis weight*s of 17–40 lb.

Lignin

A complex, organic material in wood that binds fibers of *cellulose* together. One of the purposes of the *pulping* process is to separate the cellulose fibers from the lignin and other nonfibrous materials such as *hemicelluloses*. It is the presence of lignin in paper *pulp* that reduces paper permanence and contributes to the yellowing of paper over time. Wood consists of approximately 45–60% cellulose, 15–35% lignin, and 15–25% hemicelluloses, depending on the tree.

Chemical pulping, which dissolves these extraneous materials, is the only pulping method that can almost completely remove lignin and hemicelluloses.

Mechanical pulping methods make no real attempt at lignin removal, being a method that generates a high pulp yield, due in part to a high lignin content. (See also *Pulping*.)

Likesidedness

The condition of a paper having the same color, texture, and *finish* on both sides.

Limiter

A user-defined minimum amount of **highlight** or **shadow** that a **scanner** or other imaging system will record when making **color separation**s. Operators will define limiters when the printing process to be utilized has certain basic limitations on the amount of highlight or shadow it can accurately reproduce.

Limiting Operation

Alternate term for a **bottleneck**. See **Bottleneck**.

Limp Binding

In **binding and finishing**, a type of leather, imitation leather, etc., book binding that is soft and easily flexed. Often used on bibles.

Line

In typography, a single row of characters. In graphics, an object formed by directly connecting two points, also called a **rule**. In telecommunications, a circuit or channel connecting two devices, be they modems or telephones.

Line Adapter

In telecommunications, a device such as a **modem** used to convert a **digital** signal (as from a computer) to a form suitable for transmission over a communications line.

Line Analyzer

In telecommunications, a device used to monitor and troubleshoot a communications channel.

Lineale

Alternate term for a **sans serif** typeface. See **Sans Serif**.

Linear Array

In a **digital camera**, a **CCD** array that captures an image one line of **pixel**s at a time. See **Digital Photography**.

Linear Editing

In video production, the editing of video clips by physically placing them in the correct order on a storage medium, unlike **nonlinear editing**.

Linear Fill

In graphics, a type of **fountain fill** in which one color is blended into another in a straight line, the angle of which can typically be altered at will. See also **Radial Fill**. (See Color Plate 12.)

Linear Play

In media, the sequential playing of a tape, **CD**, or vinyl record from beginning to end with no interaction.

The term *linear play* also refers to a **videodisc** which is written to and read from according to the **constant linear velocity (CLV)** principle. See **Constant Linear Velocity (CLV)**.

Linearization

The process of optimizing an imaging system as a means of controlling all the optical and physical variables involved in the generation of an image, be it it electronic (via **scanning**) or photographic. Linearization involves the proper setting of such disparate elements as film type and speed, exposure time, the type and intensity of the light source, the focus, and the electrical factors involved, such as amperage and voltage. The goal of linearization is to generate an image—on film or in digital form—with predictable and consistent results.

Line Art

Any illustration material that contains no **halftone**, **continuous tone**, or **tinted** images.

In digital and/or electronic imaging, *line art* is defined as illustration matter that can be displayed by **pixel**s described by only one **bit** of information—i.e., black or white, on or off (or blue and white, white and gray, etc., depending upon the color **palette** being utilized). Digital line art is frequently created and output using **vector**-based graphics rather than **bitmap**s. A drawing which exists as line art (rather than a painting, water color, etc.) is known as a **line drawing**.

Line Art Scan

A digital image that has been captured and is displayed using only one **bit** of information per **pixel**—i.e., either black or white. During scanning, the device examines the original pixel-by-pixel and determines if each dot is dark enough to represent as black, or light enough to represent as white. Line art scanning does not include any gray values; everything is either black or white.

Linecaster

Any early typesetting device that assembled a row of character molds one line at a time and injected molten metal into them to create a slug of an entire line. An example of a linecaster is the **Linotype**. See **Type and Typography: History of Type**. (See illustration on next page.)

Line Chart

A type of **chart** in which values are plotted on an x-y **coordinate system**, a line then being drawn to connect each point, often used to illustrate the progression of a particular trend. See **Chart**.

Line Conditioner

A device attached to the AC cord that protects electronic devices against sudden surges or drops in electric current. Also called a **surge protector**.

Line Copy

Text or artwork containing no tonal values, or shades of gray, and which can be imaged and printed without the need for **halftone** screens. See **Line Art**.

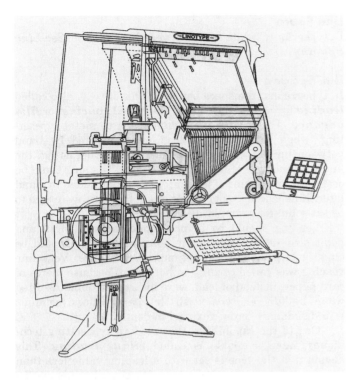

The linecaster assembled lines of character matrices to create a line of metal type for letterpress printing.

Line Device

Any of a variety of computer printers or electronic typewriters that accepts and prints data one line at a time. Also known as a *line printer*.

Line Driver

In telecommunications, a device (either a transmitter or a receiver) used to boost the transmission distance between computers that are connected to each other via *leased line*s. A line driver is required at both ends of such a connection.

Line Editing

A means of video editing in which an *edit decision list* is prepared to later *auto assemble* a videotape.

Line Feed

In computing, a control character that instructs the printer to begin printing on the next line. Abbreviated *LF*.

Line-for-Line

In typography, an instruction used to specify that copy should be typeset with the exact same number of characters per line.

Line Gauge

A ruler used in typography and graphics that measures *point*s and *pica*s. See *Type Gauge*.

Line Graph

Alternate term for a *line chart*. See *Line Chart*.

Line Justification Display

The ability of a typesetting device, composition system, or word processor to display justified text on the monitor. See *WYSIWYG*.

Line Length

In typography, the overall width of a typeset line, usually the area between two margins. Also called *measure, column width,* or *line measure*. There are several long-held rules for establishing line length (essentially a function of *point size*) that ensure maximum *legibility*. The following chart indicates the recommended line lengths (in points) for a variety of common text point sizes:

Type Size	Minimum Length	Optimum Length	Maximum Length
6	8	10	12
7	8	11	14
8	9	13	16
9	10	14	18
10	13	16	20
11	13	18	22
12	14	21	24
14	18	24	28
16	21	27	32
18	24	30	36

Sometimes the formula *point size × 2* is used to determine the optimum line length. *Lowercase alphabet × 1.5* is also used. For maximum legibility, a line should comprise 55–60 characters, or 9–10 words.

Wider typefaces look best with wider line lengths; condensed faces look best with narrow line lengths. Instead of wide line lengths, double or multiple columns of smaller line lengths should be used.

Line Measure

Alternate term for *line length*. See *Line Length*.

Linen Finish

A paper *finish* characterized by a surface texture intended to simulate linen cloth, used primarily on *bond paper*. Linen-finish paper was originally produced by pressing the paper against linen cloth, but the linen finish is now imparted to the paper by *embossing*.

Line Negative

A photographic *negative* containing only text or *line art*, no *halftone*s, *continuous tone*s, or other matter containing shades of gray.

Linen Tester

Alternate term for a *mesh counter*. See *Mesh Counter*.

Line-of-Business Application

Alternate term for *mission-critical application*. See *Mission-Critical Application*.

Line-of-Sight

In broadcasting and telecommunications, descriptive of a signal's transmission path that is direct and unobstructed from sender to receiver. A line-of-sight path is required for laser, microwave, infrared, and other forms of **wireless communication**.

Line Pairing

A **video error** characterized by the overlapping of adjacent scan lines. A single television or video **frame** is created by the scanning of two separate **field**s: one field consists of all the even-numbered scan lines, and the second field consists of all the odd-numbered scan lines. Ideally, the lines should not overlap.

Line Plate

A printing plate consisting solely of **line art**, with no **halftone**s.

Line Printer

Alternate term for **line device**. See **Line Device**. See also **Page Printer**.

Line Screen

Alternate term for a halftone **screen**. See **Screen**.

Line Screen Frequency

Alternate term for **screen ruling**. See **Screen Ruling**.

Line Segment

Any small portion of a larger line.

Line Sharing

In telecommunications, the ability for two separate devices—such as a fax machine and a telephone—to share a single communications line. Switching from device to device can either be effected manually by the user, or automatically by means of a **line-sharing device**. See **Line-Sharing Device**.

Line-Sharing Device

A device used to allow two separate devices (such as a fax machine and a conventional telephone, or a fax machine and an answering machine) to share a single communications line.

A line-sharing device answers an incoming call and listens for the telltale high-pitched tone that indicates that a fax machine is calling. If it is present, the signal is routed to the fax machine. If it is not present, the signal is routed to the answering machine or telephone.

Line Short/Long

In **book typography**, setting a page one line longer or shorter than the specified page depth as a means of eliminating **widow**s, **orphan**s, and short pages, or to make allowances for illustration matter.

Line Space

In typography, white space between lines of type. See **Line Spacing**.

Line Spacing

In typography, the space between lines of type, also called **leading** (pronounced "ledding"), **vertical spacing**, or **film advance**. The term *leading* dates back to metal typesetting, when thin strips of lead were inserted by hand between lines (i.e., lines were leaded). In linecasting, the line was one unit of metal called a *slug*. The slug could be cast with an amount of leading "built-in" or added by hand later. If no leading was present at all, the lines were said to be set solid (for example, 10/10).

Leading should be in proportion to line length and point size—about 20% of the point size—or it should be slightly larger than the optimum word space. Very fine spacing was called *carding* in hot metal, because pieces of card paper, instead of lead, were inserted; trouble resulted when liquid (i.e., type wash) hit paper slices: columns would suddenly "grow" (expand in depth).

One of the capabilities that modern typesetting techniques make available is called **minus leading**. This means that the type is set with a leading value less than the point size, for example, 9 on 8½. Usually, this can be done only with faces that are small on body (small **x-height**), have short **ascender**s and/or **descender**s, or for all caps.

Small x-height faces and some sans serifs should have minimal or minus leading. Large x-heights and bold type need more leading. To calculate the minimum amount of leading required between two lines when changing point sizes, take one-third of the present point size and add it to two-thirds of the point size to be used on the next line. If the leading is not properly set, the lines could overlap.

The most important point to remember is that all leading is measured from **baseline** to baseline. In hot metal, it was merely the incremental space between slugs. Today, it is the total space between lines, defined by the baseline.

Line Speed

In telecommunications, the maximum rate at which a signal can be transmitted over a particular communications channel, measured in **baud** or **bits per second**. Line speed is typically a function of the capacity of the transmitting equipment.

Lines Per Inch (lpi)

A measure of **resolution**, or the number of "dots"—be they screen **pixel**s or printer **spot**s—that comprise an image. Lines per inch, in this sense, is somewhat synonymous with **pixels per inch (ppi)** or **dots per inch (dpi)**; since lines are composed of pixels and dots, the number of lines in an inch will equal the number of dots per inch. The greater the number of lines—or dots—per inch, the greater the resolution and the sharper the image.

In *halftone* generation, halftone screens are measured in lines per inch, which is equivalent to the number of halftone dots per linear inch. Thus, a screen described as 150-line would contain 150 rows and 150 columns of dots, or 22,500 dots per inch.

Lines Per Minute (lpm)

A measure of the speed of a typesetting device, especially an older *linecaster*. Lpm is measured in the number of 30-character, 11-pica lines of 9-point type a device can set in one minute. Also known as *casting speed*.

Line Up

To center or properly position copy or an image in front of a camera lens, on a printing press sheet, etc.

Line Width

A measure of the widest paper a computer printer can accommodate. Also known as *carriage width*.

Line Work (LW)

Generally speaking, any image or image carrier—be it an original, a scan, a *negative* or *positive*, or printing plate—that contains to *halftone* or *continuous tone* images, or shades of gray. In other words, images consisting solely of *line art*. See *Line Art*.

In some *color electronic publishing systems (CEPS)*, *line work* describes files saved in a linework *file format*.

Lining

See *Backlining*.

Lining Figures

In typography, a style of numerals in which all the numerals align with each other at the top and bottom, and are commonly the same height as the capital letters of a given typeface, in contrast to *hanging figures*, in which all digits do not align. See *Figures*.

Lining-Up

In *case binding*, the addition of *backlining* and *headband*s to a *book block* before *casing-in*. See *Case Binding*.

Link Access Procedure (LAP)

In telecommunications, a *CCITT*-recommended protocol for communications between *data communications equipment (DCE)* and *data terminal equipment (DTE)*. See also *Link Access Procedure-Balanced (LAP-B)*.

Link Access Procedure-Balanced (LAP-B)

In telecommunications, a *CCITT*-recommended protocol for communications between *workstation*s and *personal computer*s and networks (specifically, those that transfer data by means of *packet switching*).

LAP-B is a *bit-oriented*, *data-link layer* protocol and is analogous to *HDLC*. See also *Link Access Procedure (LAP)*.

Link Discipline

Alternate term for *control procedure*. See *Control Procedure*.

Linking Field

A *field* added to a database *record* that includes information pertaining to the location of the preceding and/or succeeding records in a chain of interconnected records. See *Chaining*.

Link Layer

In networking, the second of seven *layer*s in the *OSI* reference model, defining the means by which adjacent *node*s transmit data to each other. See *Open Systems Interconnection (OSI)*. Also known as the *data-link layer*.

Link Level

In telecommunicatons, a *CCITT* standard that defines the link access protocol for data communications. See *Link Access Procedure (LAP)* and *Link Access Procedure-Balanced (LAP-B)*.

Link-State Routing Algorithm

In networking, one of a related set of algorithms used for *routing* that broadcasts the state of each link to each *node*, reducing the number of routing loops.

Link-Support Layer (LSL)

In Novell's *Open Data-Link Interface (ODI)*, the portion of the interface that links the server's *local area network* and other communications protocols such as *IPX* or *TCP/IP*.

Linoleate

Any of a variety of salts or soaps of fatty acids derived from *linseed oil*. Linoleates of cobalt and manganese are commonly used as *drier*s in the manufacture of printing inks.

Linotron Unit

A measurement used in typography that is equal to one-eighteenth of a *point*.

Linotronic™ Output

Although referring specifically to *PostScript* output generated on a Linotype-Hell Linotronic *imagesetter*, the term has come to mean any generic imagesetter output.

Linotype

An early typecasting machine, invented in the late 1800s by Ottmar Mergenthaler. The Linotype was the first device that enabled an operator to set type by typing on a keyboard, which automatically cast hot-metal type one line at a time. See *Type and Typography: History of Type*.

Linseed Oil

A natural oil obtained from the seeds of the flax plant (any of several plants of the genus *Linum*, especially *L. usitatissimum*), used as the basis of **drying oil vehicle**s and **varnish**es in the production of printing inks. Linseed oil that has been refined by exposure to high temperatures is called **stand oil**, a term also used in the United Kingdom to refer to linseed oil in general. Soaps or fatty acids of linseed oil are called **linoleates** and are frequently used in the manufacture of printing ink **drier**s.

Lint

Loosely bonded surface fibers on a paper that build up on a blanket in printed image areas, absorb water and repel ink, causing **void hickey**s. Lint can also become attached to the printing plate or blanket (which causes blanket **piling**), which affects print quality. Lint is also called **fuzz** and **fluff**.

Lip

An allowance made for publications to be bound by **saddle-stitching** or **saddle-sewing** comprising a short overhang (usually about ⅜ in.) of one side of a signature over the other. A lip is needed to allow the gripper mechanism of the binding device to be able to pick up and open the signature during **inserting**. (See **Saddle-Stitching**.) Also known as a **lap** and a **pickup**.

Lip Synchronization

In video editing, the **synchronization** of sound and video evaluated by ensuring that speech matches the lips of the speaker. Often abbreviated *lip sync*.

Lipophilic

A quality of certain papers, components of paper, or the image areas of lithographic printing plates that causes them to have an affinity for oils and oil-based inks. Lipophilic substances are likely to repel water. Lipophilic substances are more commonly called **oleophilic** and are considered **hydrophobic**. (See also **Lipophobic**.)

Lipophobic

A quality of certain papers, components of paper, or the nonimage areas of lithographic printing plates that causes them to be repellent to oil-based inks and have an affinity for water. Lipophobic substances are more commonly called **oleophobic** and are considered **hydrophilic**. (See also **Lipophilic**.)

Liquid Crystal Display (LCD)

A type of display used for computer monitors (especially those found in **laptop**s), as well as many other electronic devices such as fax machines, photocopiers, cellular phones, digital watches, video games, etc. Essentially, an LCD forms a picture by the selective absorption and reflection of light. Two light polarization filters enclose a group of liquid crystals. When light passes through the first polar-

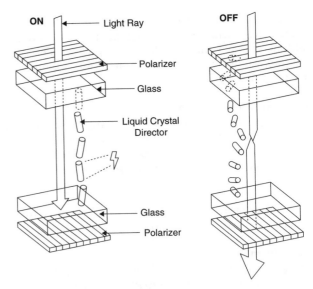

The mechanics of a liquid crystal display.

ization filter, it is polarized, or in other words the light rays are oriented in one particular direction. Each **pixel** of the display is controlled by the liquid crystals. When an electric field (produced by a transistor) is imparted to the crystals controlling the display of a pixel, it causes the liquid crystals to align, which then causes the light ray to pass unimpeded through the crystal layer. When it hits the second polarization filter, it is absorbed and does not pass out of it. If there is no electric field imposed on the crystals, they cause the light ray to orient itself in the direction that will allow it to pass through the second polarization filter.

There are two varieties of **LCD**s. A **passive-matrix** display has one transistor that controls a whole line of pixels by itself. In contrast, an **active matrix** has one transistor per pixel, and consequently has faster screen updates and allows the display to be clearly viewed at wider angles. Active-matrix LCDs, however, are substantially more expensive and consume more power.

Liquid Frisket

A latex solution used in some **resist** stencils for **screen printing** that are water-soluble when wet but become insoluble when dry. Also called **maskoid**.

Liquid Ink

One of two primary classifications of printing inks, characterized by low **viscosity** and a fairly watery body. Liquid inks are commonly used in **gravure** and **flexographic** printing processes. See also **Paste Ink**. (See **Ink**.)

Liquid Laminate

A plastic **coating** material used in papermaking.

Liquid Photopolymer

One of two types of **photopolymer** plates used in **flexography**, in contrast to a **sheet photopolymer**.

A liquid photopolymer plate is made by placing the negative of the image to be engraved emulsion-side-up on the exposure unit, covered by a transparent sheet. A motorized roller evenly and uniformly spreads a liquid photopolymeric resin on top of the transparent cover sheet. It also adds a substrate sheet—or plate base—on top of the polymer, which has been treated to adhere to the liquid photopolymer. The liquid photopolymer is enhanced by exposing the base side of the plate to ultraviolet light, hardening the photopolymer on the reverse side of the plate. Increasing or decreasing the exposure time varies the depth of penetration into the photopolymer of the radiation which varies the ultimate relief height of the plate. (For example, the longer the exposure, the deeper the penetration, and the shallower the floor of the plate.)

A second exposure to UV light from below (i.e., through the negative) hardens the photopolymer in the image areas of the plate, with the hardness of the photopolymer decreasing with decreasing exposure to radiation. The non-image areas are left unexposed, soft and soluble. The exposed plate is removed from the exposure unit, and the cover film peeled from the exposed plate surface. The exposed plate is then sent to a washout unit which removes the unhardened photopolymer from the plate surface, leaving the exposed image areas in relief. In some cases, the plates can be pre-washed by hand (using a squeegee or an automated device) to remove the unexposed photopolymer and allow it to be reused. (This process is called resin reclaim.) A mild detergent is applied to the plate in a

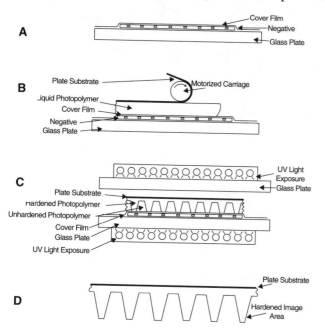

Producing a liquid photopolymer plate: (A) a negative is mounted on a glass plate, where it is coated with the liquid photopolymer (B). The plate is then exposed (C), producing a hardened image area (D) after development and post-exposure.

washout unit to remove any residual unhardened resin. A final exposure to UV light further hardens the plate surface. Although liquid photopolymer plates are amber-colored (which is more effective for UV light transmission), it is sometimes desirable to dye the plates prior to mounting, which may aid in proofing, inspection, and mounting. Any water-soluble fabric or industrial dye can be used on flexographic plates.

Some liquid photopolymer plates, called **capped plate**s, are processed using two layers of differently formulated photopolymers, which vary several plate characteristics, such as hardness, resilience, and image geometry, from the raised image areas to the plate floor. The advantages of capped plates include deeper reverse etch depth, less distortion, and wider impression latitude.

The composition of the liquid photopolymer can either be oil and water resistant or solvent resistant. The latter are the more compatible with highly volatile alcohol- or acetate-based solvent inks.

See also **Sheet Photopolymer**, **Plate: Flexography**, **Photopolymer**, and **Flexography**.

Listserv

Abbreviation for **listserver**. See **Listserver**.

Listserver

On the **Internet**, a computer program used to send out mass **e-mail**ings. Typically, one sends an e-mail message to a group of people by entering one address in the "to" line, and cc-ing everyone else. With very large mailing lists (such as newsletters, for example), this is impractical, so the message is sent to a single e-mail address, which then automatically distributes the message to all those on the mailing list. Listserver is abbreviated **listserv**. Some common listservers that are encountered are "majordomo," "mailserv," and "almanac."

Litho Pencil

A grease-based pencil used for marking instructions and specifications on **camera-ready copy**. Historically, a litho pencil was used for drawing on lithographic stones.

Lithographic Flex Heat Transfer

See **Heat Transfer Printing**.

Lithographic Image

The term for the ink-receptive image on a printing plate used in lithographic printing, distinguished by its existing on the same plane (in other words, not raised or depressed) as the nonimage areas of the plate. (See **Lithography**.)

Lithography

A term describing a printing process in which the image area and the nonimage area co-exist on the same plane, in contrast to **letterpress** (printing from raised type) or **gravure** (printing from etched or engraved cells). Lithographic printing is based on the principle that oil and water do not mix readily (although a minute amount of mixing *is* necessary for lithography to work); the image area of a lithographic printing plate will attract a greasy, oil-based ink, while the nonimage areas will attract water, mutual chemical repulsion keeping the two regions separate. The term *lithography* (which comes from the Greek words *lithos* meaning "stone" and *graphia* meaning "writing") originally referred to the use of special stones (a variety of calcium carbonate) on which lithographic printing was first performed (see below).

In modern parlance, lithography refers to the use of aluminum plates that have replaced lithographic stones (also called, more accurately but less popularly, *planography*). *Offset lithography* refers to lithographic printing in which the inked plate first transfers the image to a rubber blanket, and the blanket then transfers the image to the paper or other surface. Lithography encompasses such processes as sheetfed offset lithography, *web offset* printing, *direct lithography* (also called *Di-Litho*), and *waterless printing*.

The inventor of lithography, Alois Senefelder (1771–1834) was the son of a German actor, and had attended the University of Ingolstadt in Bavaria, hoping to pursue a career in law. In 1792, his father died, and he could no longer afford to pursue his studies. He turned to writing plays, and, trying to find a way to inexpensively print them, spent a good deal of time researching various types of printing. He began with copperplate engraving, and since a certain type of Bavarian limestone was less expensive than copper, he tried using the principle of copperplate engraving on the stone. It is said that by accident he stumbled acoss the idea of *lithography*, but actually he had been carefully researching the idea for some time.

Using a slab of limestone (in particular, that from Kelheim in Bavaria), Senefelder was able to transfer a grease-based design or text to the surface of the stone, which was porous enough to accept a greasy ink. The nonimage areas of the stone would, with the application of water, repel ink. Thus, lithography does not use a raised printing surface with which to make the impression. Senefelder was given by the Prince-Elector of Bavaria, Max Joseph, an exclusive 15-year license to develop the process of lithographic printing. In 1809, the King of Bavaria appointed him the Royal Inspector of Lithography, and he spent the rest of his life—profiting quite nicely from the invention—further developing and refining the process. In 1817, he created a working model of a lithographic printing press, and at the same time developed paper printing plates, with which he wanted to replace the bulky and unwieldy lithographic stones. He travelled throughout Europe extolling the virtues of the process and, in 1834, died. Unlike many of the inventors in the history of printing and the graphic arts, Senefelder was monetarily successful, won many prizes and medals for his invention, published books on the process, and was roundly praised and appreciated by his contemporaries.

Initially, lithography was used primarily for artistic expression and illustration, but advances in photography,

press design, and platemaking made it a viable and popular commercial printing medium. The advantages of the lithographic printing process included the ability to print on rougher substrates than was possible with traditional letterpress methods. At the beginning of the twentieth century, however, lithography was falling behind letterpress, as new photomechanically produced image carriers were better suited to letterpress process than stone printing. The stones themselves were taken out of the process and replaced with zinc and aluminum plates, a substitution that Senefelder himself had suggested some time before they actually went into widespread use.

Between 1881 and 1906, the process known as *offset lithography* was developed by accident, which added to the lithographic system the press blanket. Thus, in offset lithog-

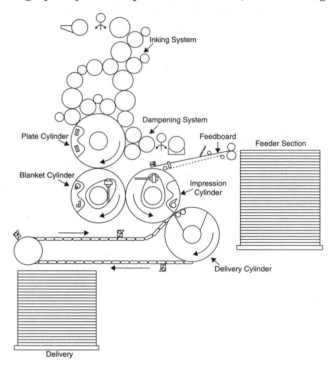

Sheetfed offset lithography.

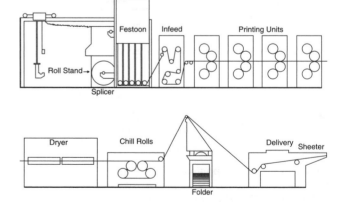

Web offset lithography.

raphy, the plate does not come in contact with the substrate; the inked plate transfers the image to the rubber blanket, which then transfers it to the paper. The advantages of this process include the ability to print with a softness and richness of tone hitherto unknown; the conformability and flexibility of the blanket also created the ability to print on a wider variety of surfaces than was previously possible. Although offset lithography had inauspicious beginnings, during and after World War II lithographic platemaking and ink formulating vastly improved the quality and efficiency of the process.

Offset lithography is the most common printing process today, and has spawned several varieties, including sheetfed offset (which, as its name implies, prints onto individual sheets of paper or other material), **web offset lithography** (which prints onto a continuous paper **web** or roll), **direct lithography** (or the printing of lithographic plates directly onto the substrate without an intermediate, offsetting blanket), and **letterset** (in which specially formulated silicon-based plates are designed to be used without the need for water). (See **Offset Lithography**.)

Lithol®* Red

An **organic color pigment** used in printing inks. Lithol reds comprise a variety of shades, depending upon the metallic salt contained in them. The Lithols come in vivid yellow red (sodium), bright bluish red (barium), and deep blue red (calcium). They possess low **lightfastness** and low resistance to acids, alkalis, and heat. They are somewhat resistant to oil.

Despite many poor resistance properties, they are occasionally used in quick, inexpensive applications, and the strong color qualities make them well-suited for inexpensive liquid inks. Lithol reds are the standard reds for publication gravure printing in the United States. (See also **Organic Color Pigments**.)

(CI Pigment Red 49 No. 15630; CI Pigment Red 49 [sodium]; CI Pigment Red 49:1 [barium]; CI Pigment Red 49:2 [calcium].) *Lithol® is a registered trademark of the BASF Corporation.

Lithol®* Rubine 4B

An **organic color pigment** used in printing inks. Lithol rubine 4B refers to a variety of different red shades, depending upon the metallic salt contained. The shade containing calcium is the most commonly used, and is a brilliant bluish red possessing moderate **lightfastness** and good resistance to solvents, oils, and waxes. It has moderate resistance to heat and is moderately weatherpoof (though it has a poor resistance to water). It has poor resistance to acids and alkalis. It has excellent working properties, however, and recent improvements are enhancing its resistance to water. Lithol rubine 4B is used as magenta in many inks used in process color printing. (See also **Organic Color Pigments**.)

(CI Pigment Red 57 No. 15850; CI Pigment Red 57 [sodium]; CI Pigment Red 57:1 [barium]; CI Pigment Red 57:2 [calcium]; CI Pigment Red 57:3 [strontium].) *Lithol® is a registered trademark of the BASF Corporation.

Lithopone

An inorganic material used as a **white pigment** in printing inks. Lithopone is composed of barium sulfate (60–72%) and zinc sulfide (28–40%) (chemical formulae $BaSO_4$ and ZnS, respectively). It is an opaque pigment used as an **extender** in many inks. It is chemically inert, but is susceptible to decomposition when in contact with acids. (See **White Pigments**.)

(CI Pigment White 5 No. 77115.)

Live Area

In typography and page layout, the portion of a page within the prescribed margins where type, graphics, and other page elements can be added. Also sometimes called the *live matter area*.

Live Matter

Any typographic material—be it original copy, a manuscript, typescript, type, or typeset copy—that is still needed for a particular job, as opposed to **dead matter**.

Livering

A problem of printing inks characterized by an irremediable increase in **body**, **viscosity**, and thickness, or the transformation of the ink into a **gel** or jelly-like susbtance, caused by a chemical change in the ink during long-term storage. Also known as **jelling**.

Liveware

A colloquial term for the human being who uses a computer.

LLC

Abbreviation for **logical link control**. See **Logical Link Control (LLC)**.

Load

To enter data into a computer.

Load Balancing

In networking, a means of increasing network and **bandwidth** efficiency by distributing network traffic along parallel paths, or moving a user's job from a heavily congested resource to a less-congested one.

Load Point

In computing, a predetermined point at which a **magnetic tape** is positioned under the drive's **read/write head**.

Load Sharing

In networking, the distribution of a set of tasks among a number of different **workstation**s or **node**s.

Also in networking, the term *load sharing* refers to the construction of parallel **bridge**s, allowing a different bridge to be used if one should fail.

Loading

The addition of *fillers* to paper *pulp* in papermaking. Fillers are typically fine particles of inorganic materials such as *clay*, *titanium dioxide*, or other such substances. The basic constituent of paper is *cellulose* fiber, but fillers are added to alter one or more of a paper's properties, depending on the desired end-use characteristics. Loading modifies such paper properties as texture, *opacity*, *brightness*, *basis weight*, *dimensional stability*, *ink absorbency*, and overall *printability*. Other types of fillers include starches, gums, and synthetic polymers, as well as dyes and pigments. The combination of paper pulp and fillers is called the papermaking *furnish*. (See also *Fillers* and *Sizing*.)

In computing, the term *loading* refers to the act of transferring data into a computer, either manually or automatically, as when a program is "loaded" into the computer's memory.

Local

Generally speaking, term for any two or more components of a system in close geographical proximity to each other. A *local area network*, for example, comprises a set of computers in a single building, or at the very least, a set of buildngs clustered fairly close together. A *local disk* is a *hard disk* connected directly to a *workstation*, rather than to a central *server*.

The term *local* is also used to refer to any correction, change, etc., performed only in an isolated area, as opposed to one that is *global*. See, for example, *Local Correction*.

Local Application Numerical Control (LANC)

A *video control* system incorporated in many video devices that consists of a two-way communication link between the controller and the device, allowing the transfer of information such as *time code* data, etc. See *Video Control*.

Local Area Network (LAN)

A network of linked computers occupying a small geographic area, such as an office, in contrast to a *wide area network*, which encompasses a larger area. Essentially, a cable connects the various workstations, as well as peripheral devices such as CD-ROM drives, printers, etc. LANs typically do not use such international or national networks such as *ISDN*, or even the telephone network.

Local Area Transport (LAT)

In networking, a *protocol* developed by Digital Equipment Corporation to effect virtual terminal access over an *Ethernet* network.

Local Bus

In computing, a data *bus* possessing a very short path between the main processor and the input/output processor. A local bus is often used for such functions as high-resolution displays that require very fast inout/output speeds.

Local Correction

A type of *color correction* performed only on selected portions of an image (such as altering the shade of red of an apple appearing in a small section of the image), as opposed to *global correction*, which refers to a color correction performed on the entire image.

Local Disk

In networking, a *hard disk* (or other form of storage medium) that is directly connected to a *workstation* rather than to a central file *server*. A local disk is often housed in a *local drive*.

Local Drive

In networking, a *disk drive* that is directly connected to a *workstation* rather than to a central file *server*. A local drive often houses a *local disk*. See also *Network Drive*.

Local Intelligence

In networking, a property of an *intelligent terminal*, or one which possesses its own processor and memory. See *Intelligent Terminal*.

Local Loop

In telecommunications and networking, the portion of a communications line that connects a customer's equipment to the local telephone company exchange.

Local Printer

A computer printer that is directly connected to a *workstation* rather than to a central file or print *server*.

LocalTalk

In networking, the hardware that is required to set up and transfer data over an *AppleTalk* network or, in other words, a network of Apple Macintoshes. LocalTalk is essentially an inexpensive, 230.4 kilobit-per-second cabling system for Apple computers.

Locator Device

Alternate term for an *input device*, especially one used in computer graphics to determine object coordinate data. See *Input Device*.

Lock Up

In *letterpress* printing, to secure the metal type (either as individual characters, lines, or plates) in a frame (called a *chase*) to hold them in position during printing.

Locked File

In computing, a file that can be opened and read, but cannot be changed, written to, or deleted.

Lofting

In computer graphics, a means of *rendering* a single three-dimensional (object from multiple two-dimensional objects. There are two elements to this type of rendering: a "backbone," or a path along which the 3D object is to be created, and the 2D objects that form the outline of the rendered object. The 2D outlines are plotted along the path, the spaces betweeen them filled in with solid objects based on the 2D objects.

Log

Any record of events, operations, or actions.

In telecommunications, the term *log* refers to connecting to or disconnecting from another computer system. See *Login* and *Logoff*.

In *binding and finishing*, a *log* is any tightly compressed stack of book *signature*s.

Logical Drive

In computing, a subdivision of a *hard disk* that is recognized by the system as a separate storage entity. Frequently, large hard disks are subdivided into smaller logical drives for the sake of convenience and efficient file management.

Logical Link Control

In networking and telecommunications, the upper sublayer of the *link layer* of the *Open System Interconnection (OSI)* reference model that provides a protocol for data "repackaging" when data is transferred between different network types.

Logical Object

A specific division of a long document's *local structure*, such as a part, chapter, section, or paragraph.

Logical Structure

The division of a long document—such as a book—into progressively smaller portions, such as parts, chapters, sections, and paragraphs. Each of these specific aspects of the logical structure is called a *logical object*.

Logical Unit (LU)

In networking, especially utilizing IBM's *Systems Network Architecture (SNA)*, a set of protocols used to control communications functions, comprising transmission- and flow-control layers (LU0), control host sessions (LU1, LU2, LU3), *peer-to-peer* and *client/host* communications (LU4), and *APPC* protocol (*LU6.2*).

Logic Hyphenation

In typography, a set of rules for proper *hyphenation* programmed into a computer. See *Hyphenation*.

Login

In networking, to gain access to a computer network, or a command (such as a username and/or a password) used to gain access to a computer network. The disconnection of a user from a network is known as *logout*. Also spelled with a hyphen, *log-in*, or as two words, *log in*. Also referred to as *logon*.

Login Script

In computing, networking, and telecommunications, a *script* (such as a small file or *macro*) that a user calls to execute an often-used series of instructions when logged onto a network. Such instructions may map disk drives, launch programs, retrieve *email*, etc.

Logo

Shortened form of *logotype*. See *Logotype*.

Logoff

Alternate term for *logout*. See *Logout*. Also spelled with a hyphen, *log-off*, or as two separate words, *log off*.

Logon

Alternate term for *login*. See *Login*. Also spelled with a hyphen, *log-on*, or as two words, *log on*.

Logotype

In typography, a symbol representing a company or product. Originally, in metal typesetting, logotypes were letter combinations or words cast together as one body (for letters or words used frequently) to speed up the typesetting process. (*Logos* is the Greek word for "word.") Today, a logotype (referred to popularly as a "logo") is usually a specifically designed company name (often with a symbol). A logo is a design that emphasizes typography, in contrast to a *symbol*, which is usually an abstract, nontypographic image. Logotypes and symbols are usually included in special *pi font*s.

Logout

A command used to disconnect from a computer network. See also *Login*. Also spelled with a hyphen, *log-out*, or as two words, *log out*, and also often known as *logoff*.

Long

Descriptive of *long ink*. See *Long Ink*.

Long-Grain

Also called *grain-long*, term for a sheet of paper having its *grain* direction parallel to the longer sheet dimension. (Paper with its grain direction parallel to the shorter

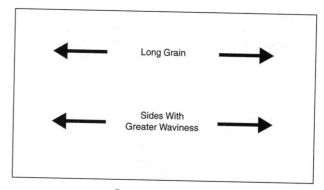

Long-grain paper.

dimension of the sheet is called **short-grain**.) Whether a paper is long-grain or short-grain is an important consideration in many printing processes, as the grain direction affects **printability** and **runnability**, especially in connection with sheet strength and **dimensional stability**. See **Grain**. See illustration on following page.

Long-Haul Modem

In telecommunications, a **modem** capable of transmitting information over long distances (usually beyond 25 miles). See also **Short-Haul Modem**.

Long Ink

A printing ink characterized by its ability to flow and to form long threads when stretched, in contrast to **short ink**. Ink that is long has desirable flow characteristics, performs well on the ink rollers, has desirable water-resistant qualities, and transfers to the plate, blanket, and **substrate** well. Ink that is excessively long, however, has a tendency to produce problems such as **ink misting** when used on high-speed presses. (See **Length**.)

Longitudinal Magnetic Recording

The means by which data is recorded on a **magnetic tape**. See **Magnetic Tape**.

Longitudinal Register

See **Running Register**.

Longitudinal Time Code (LTC)

In video production, a **time code** recorded as an audio signal on a linear track of a videotape. Such a code is not visible on the screen. See **Time Code**.

Long Play

Descriptive of a **videodisc** which is written to and read from by means of the **constant linear velocity (CLV)** principle. See **Videodisc** and **Constant Linear Velocity (CLV)**.

Long Shot

In photography—still, motion picture, or video—a shot in which the subject is far from the camera, as, for example, an individual sitting on a park bench photographed from across the street. A long shot is distinct from a **medium shot** and **close up**, and usually serves to provide a means of determining a subject's geographic location, especially when used as an **establishing shot**. See also **Extreme Long Shot**. In shooting scripts, a long shot is indicated by **LS**.

Lookup Table (LUT)

In computers, any table of values that can convert one set of computer codes to another set. Thus, any set of values that are input into the system can be converted to the proper values for accurate output. In digital imaging, for example, the color and brightness values for a particular image can be converted from the display to the output device. See also **CLUT**.

Loop

In typography, the part of a letter or other character consisting of a **bowl** that serves as a flourish, as in the bottom portion of the lowercase "g." See **Letter Elements**.

In computing, any command or series of commands that endlessly repeats until the system is instructed to stop.

In networking, a *loop* is used to refer to a network configuration in which each node is linked, in series, in a circular manner, data being set from device to device until it reaches the node it is addressed to. In such topologies, there is no central controller.

Loop Stitching

In **binding and finishing**, a form of **saddle-stitching** in which the staples used for binding are formed into semicircular loops, allowing the publication to be inserted into a three-ring binder. Loop stitching eliminates the need for three-hole drilling. See **Saddle-Stitching**.

Loopback

In networking and telecommunications, a means of testing communications equipment by sending a signal from one station to another, then back again. When the signal has made its round trip, it is analyzed for intensity and data content, measurements which are then compared to the corresponding aspects of the original signal. The two components of such a diagnostic test are known as **analog loopback** (testing the signal) and **digital loopback** (testing the encoded/decoded data).

Loose

Type set with a judicious amount of white space between characters, words, or lines, as opposed to **tight**.

Loose Back

A type of **binding** in which the **spine** is not glued to the **binding edge** of the sheets. See also **Tight Back**.

Loose-Leaf Binding

A means of **mechanical binding** in which pages are bound together by means of inserting the metal rings or poles of a three-hole **binder** into drilled or punched holes along the **binding edge** of the pages. See **Mechanical Binding**.

Loose Line

In typography, a line with excessive **word spacing**.

Loose Register

In multi-color printing, the ability to print successive colors with a somewhat decreased degree of accuracy, or where the absolute position of each successive color (or image) is not especially critical. See **Register**.

Lossless

Any **data compression** algorithm that will reduce the size of a particular file with no—or no appreciable—loss of data. (See also **Lossy**.) See **Data Compression**.

Lossy

Any *data compression* algorithm that will reduce the size of a particular file with varying degrees of data loss. (See also *Lossless*.) See *Data Compression*.

Loupe

A small magnifying lens mounted in an eyepiece used to closely examine *halftone dot*s or other areas of output.

Low Bulk

A type of paper having a thickness (called *bulk* or *caliper*) less than that of other papers of the same *basis weight*. Low-bulk paper is specially manufactured, is characterized by a smooth surface, and is frequently used for book paper to reduce the thickness of high-page-count books, such as encyclopedias or bibles. (See also *High Bulk*.)

Low-End

Descriptive of any system or device that is both inexpensive and of inferior quality, compared to other higher-priced systems and devices. For example, in scanning, a high-end *drum scanner* is likely to cost in the tens of thousands of dollars, but produces the best image quality, as compared to a *low-end* flatbed scanner, which costs around $1,000, fits on a desktop, and generates relatively inferior (but still workable) image quality.

Low-Energy Dye

A type of *sublimable dye* that does not require a very high temperature (commonly under 375°F) in order to be transferred to the *substrate*. See also *High-Energy Dye*.

Low Finish

A paper *finish* characterized by a dull, low-*gloss* surface.

Low-Frequency Suppression

In audio or video production, the elimination of any sound having a *frequency* of less than 20 *Hertz*, a sound that is inaudible to human ears but which can cause mechanical vibrations and increase power consumption.

Low-Key Transparency

A type of photographic *transparency* that is very dark and may have been underexposed. A low-key transparency contains most of its important image detail in *shadow* areas, with very few *highlight* regions. See also *High-Key Transparency*. (See COLOR PLATE 29.)

Low-Level Language

In computing, a programming language in which instructions have close to a one-to-one correspondence with the *machine language*. *Assembly language* is considered a low-level language. See also *High-Level Language*.

Low-Pressure Air Table

A device used on a *guillotine cutter* to transport materials to be cut to the cutter *bed*. See *Guillotine Cutter*.

Low-Res

See *Low-Resolution*.

Low-Res File

See *Low-Resolution File*.

Low-Resolution

Descriptive of an image—either on a computer display or in printed form—that has a low number of dots—or *pixels*—per square inch. On computer screens and digital output devices, images are essentially composed of very small pixels that, when put together in certain shapes, form the text or image that is output. The more pixels per square inch, the sharper the image, and the greater the *resolution*. A low-resolution image on a computer monitor is defined roughly as less than $1,000 \times 1,000$ pixels per 12-inch diagonal display, resolutions which tend not to generate realistic-looking images or effective color transitions. On output devices, low resolution may be less than 600 pixels per inch or greater, depending on the image. Also called *low-res*. See *Resolution*.

Low-Resolution File

Alternate term for *coarse data file*. See *Coarse Data File*.

Lower Rail

A device on a *hot metal* typesetting device containing the primary *typeface* for a particular job. Such devices could also shift to an *upper rail* containing an alternate typeface. See *Rail*.

Lowercase

Small letters, as opposed to *uppercase*—or capital—letters. The term originally referred to the layout of the printer's typecase, which had the capital letters in the upper part (the "upper case") and the small letters in the lower part (or the "lower case"). Eventually, the *California job case* combined both the upper and lower cases into a single case (purportedly to enable traveling printers to better carry them on horseback during the California Gold Rush). Though no longer strictly appropriate, especially after the advent of the *Linotype* and *phototypesetting*, the terms upper- and lowercase have nevertheless stuck.

Much of the history of written communication involved only capital letters. Lowercase letters evolved in the Middle Ages as scribes tried to write faster and faster. Two handwriting styles—the formal hand of the church and the informal hand of the scholars—developed over the centuries. The Caroline *miniscule* (named after Charlemagne) is the direct ancestor of modern lowercase letters.

The evolution of alphabetic characters was spurred by three separate forces: Phoenician, Greek, and Roman. Until the invention of printing, there was little in the way of standardized forms of writing. In the Middle Ages, as scribes tried to write faster to keep up with the increasing demand for written material, short cuts were made so as to make serifs and terminal strokes with more fluid motions of the pen. Hence, the development of *cursive* writing. It primarily produced speed, but a welcome by-product was the beauty, symmetry, and simplicity of cursive writing. At this point, the *uncial* (from the Latin word *uncus* meaning "crooked") was still a capital letter—or a *majuscule*—that rounded the straight lines. Hurriedly written Roman capital letters were called *Rustica*. The uncial eventually mutated into the *half-uncial*, which was the dominant manuscript style by the eighth century. Charlemagne commissioned the Caroline alphabet—a true small-letter alphabet—from a monk named Alcuin. The Caroline miniscule eventually evolved into the *gothic*—or *black letter*—hand, the style of writing that Gutenberg sought to emulate with the first metal type, and which became a prevalent type style during the nascent days of printing.

As might be expected, there were many regional and national differences in lettering styles, but it was Charlemagne who decreed that the Caroline miniscule was to be the dominant form of lettering used throughout his kingdom. The variations in metal type design that became widespread after the advent of printing were resurrections of characteristics of national handwriting styles.

As for the number of letters themselves, it was only in 1585 that the *v* and *j* began to be used as consonants and that *u* and *i* began to be used as vowels, thanks to Louis Elzevir. Even then, this did not become universally accepted until 1822. Typecases therefore did not have allotted spaces for the *j* and the *u*.

Lp

Symbol for *sound pressure level*. See *Sound Pressure Level (Lp)*.

lpi

Abbreviation for *lines per inch*. See *Lines Per Inch (lpi)*.

lpm

Abbreviation for *lines per minute*. See *Lines Per Minute*.

LPTx Port

On a *PC*, especially one running *DOS*, the designation of one of the computer's *parallel port*s into which printers can be connected. The first parallel port, LPT1, is most commonly the port in which the printer is connected. DOS supports up to three parallel ports, while *OS/2* supports up to 9.

LQ

Abbreviation for *letter quality*. See *Letter Quality*.

LS

Abbreviation for *long shot*. See *Long Shot*.

LSI

Abbreviation for *large-scale integration*. See *Large-Scale Integration (LSI)*.

LTC

Abbreviation for *longitudinal time code*. See *Longitudinal Time Code (LTC)*.

LU

Abbreviation for *logical unit*. See *Logical Unit (LU)*.

LU6.2

The specific protocols that define *advanced program-to-program communications*. See *Advanced Program-to-Program Communications (APPC)*.

Lucey

An optical projection device used in art studios to enlarge or reduce original images to facilitate tracing.

Ludlow

A *hot-metal* type casting device used to produce slugs of *display type* utilizing brass matrices assembled by hand.

Luggable

Term for a *portable computer* between 14–20 lb., only carried around with great difficulty. The true *portable computer*s reduced this weight to the point where they are easily carried. *Laptop computer*s weigh even less.

Lumen

A unit of measurement of a light source, 12.6 of which equal one *candle*. See *Candle*.

Luminance

In color models (such as the *CIE color space*), an alternate term for *lightness*. See *Lightness*.

Luminance is also defined as the luminous intensity of a surface or object, or the amount of light that is radiated or reflected by that surface or object. Luminance is measured in terms of the photometric brightness of a surface as viewed from a given direction per unit of area of the surface in that direction, such as *candle*s per square meter or *lumen*s per square foot (also called *footlambert*s).

In video and television production, *luminance* refers to the brightness of a video signal. It can be controlled independently of *chrominance* (color information.)

Luminosity

A rather obsolete synonym for *brightness*. See *Brightness*.

LUT

Abbreviation for *lookup table*. See *Lookup Table (LUT)*.

LUV

Shortened term for *CIELUV*. See *CIE Color Space*.

Lux

An *ISO* unit of illumination equal to 1 *lumen* per square meter, or 0.1076 *footcandle*s.

LV

Abbreviation for *LaserVision*. See *LaserVision (LV)*.

LV-ROM

Abbreviation for *LaserVision-read only memory*. See *LaserVision–Read-Only Memory (LV-ROM)*.

LW

Abbreviation for *line work*. See *Line Work*.

Lw

Symbol for *sound power level*. See *Sound Power Level*.

LZW

Abbreviation for *Lempel-Ziv-Welch*, a type of *lossless* algorithm used for *data compression*. This algorithm compacts image files (such as those saved in the *TIFF* and *GIF* file formats) by looking for repeating patterns of colored *pixel*s (such as "yellow-red, yellow-red . . .") and reducing them to a kind of binary shorthand, which it can later use to reconstruct the file. (See also *Huffman Encoding*.) See *Data Compression*.

M

M, m

The thirteenth letter of the English alphabet, deriving from the North Semitic *mem*, obtaining its current form—in both upper- and lowercase—with the Greek *mu*.

Egyptian	Sinai	Phoenician	Greek	Roman
3000 BC	1850 BC	1200 BC	600 BC	AD 114

The evolution of the letter M.

M

Abbreviation for the prefix *mega-*. See *Mega-*. The letter *M* is also used alone to signify the number 1,000, deriving from the *roman numeral M*.

Mac

Abbreviation for *Macintosh*, any of a number of personal computers manufactured by the Apple Computer. See *Macintosh*.

MAC

Abbreviation for *Magazine Advertising Canadian Specifications*, a set of specifications for *color separation* and *color proofing* similar to those outlined by *SWOP*.

In networking, the acronym *MAC* is also an abbreviation for *media access control*. See *Media Access Control (MAC)*.

In telecommunications, abbreviation for *multiplexed analog components*. See *Multiplexed Analog Components (MAC)*.

Macadam Unit

In *color* analysis and evaluation, an elliptical region on a *chromaticity diagram* that indicates a barely detectable variation in all three of the diagrammed color attributes.

MacBinary

In telecommunications and computing, a protocol used by the Apple *Macintosh* to transfer files from system to system via a *modem*. Although most Macintosh communications programs support MacBinary, programs running on other platforms rarely do.

Mach

In computing, an *operating system* developed at Carnegie Mellon University. Originally based on *UNIX* and designed to support *multitasking* and *multiprocessing*, it differs from UNIX in that it operates by means of a *microkernel*, which provides only basic, essential operating system functions, such as *virtual memory*, *interrupt* handling, etc., while add-on modules are used to handle other more-or-less optional functions such as file management, networking, etc.

Machine Clothing

In papermaking, a generic term for the *felt*s and wires of a papermaking machine.

Machine Coated

See *On-Machine Coating*.

Machine Code

Alternate term for *machine language*. See *Machine Language*.

Machine-Dependent

Alternate term for *device-dependent*. See *Device-Dependent*.

Machine Direction (MD)

The direction that is parallel to the direction of the movement of the *forming wire* on a papermaking machine. It is the forward movement of the forming paper *web* on the forming wire that induces the paper's *grain*. The machine direction is also called the *grain direction*. The direction perpendicular to the machine direction is known as the *cross-machine direction (CD)*, or the *cross-grain direction*.

Machine-Finish

In papermaking, a variety of paper that has had its *finish* applied while still on the papermaking machine. See *Finish*.

Machine-Glazed

A high-gloss paper *finish* produced by allowing the wet paper *web* to dry against a highly polished metal cylinder, also called a *yankee dryer*. See *Yankee Dryer*. Paper that has been machine-glazed is occasionally called *MG paper*.

Machine-Independent

Alternate term for *device-independent*. See *Device-Independent*.

Machine Language

In computing, the *binary* code that is read directly by the computer. Although binary code is the only code that can be read by a computer, it differs from computer type to computer type. A *low-level language*, machine language—also known as *machine code*—is rarely written directly by human programmers, as machine language is extremely difficult for humans to understand. Essentially, programmers create applications using a ***high-level language*** that comprises (depending upon the language) more or less understandable symbols, words, and statements that often have an English-like syntax. (These comprise what is known as ***source code***.) After the application is written in this high-level language, a ***compiler***, ***assembler***, or ***interpreter*** is used to translate the application to machine language. Machine language is also known as ***object code***.

Machine-Readable

Essentially, any form of data that is in ***digital*** format and can be read by a computer. In the early days of computing, *machine-readable* referred to information encoded on punch cards and paper tape, but the term now refers to any—usually magnetically or optically stored—data. The term can also refer to text that has been typed in such a manner that it can be scanned by ***optical character recognition (OCR)*** equipment.

Machine-to-Machine Communication

A general term referring to any transmission of data between computers (as in a network or telecommunications link) or between a ***CPU*** and any other connected device, especially an output device.

Machine-Trimmed Paper

A seemingly contradictory alternate term for ***untrimmed paper***. See ***Untrimmed Paper***.

Machine Unit

In typewriting, a measure of the smallest distance the escapement mechanism of the typewriter can move.

Macintosh®

A type of personal computer manufactured by Apple Computer, Inc., distinguished primarily by its use of the ***Macintosh operating system***, the first popular ***GUI***. The Macintosh computer was introduced in 1984, being a direct descendent of an earlier Apple device called the Lisa, which had in turn derived from a primitive GUI devised by Xerox at its Palo Alto Research Center in the 1970s. The Macintosh is also distinguished by its ease of use. The Mac's GUI approach to computing as well as the Mac's support for the ***PostScript*** page description language were primarily responsible for the creation of ***desktop publishing*** in the mid- to late-1980s. Although the Macintosh does not have the market share enjoyed by ***IBM-compatible computer***s, it has long been the computer of choice for designers and computer artists.

The PowerMac, or PowerPC, is the latest line of Macintosh computers, distinguished by the increasingly fast performance (up to 240 MHz, as of this writing), as well as the ability to also run ***Microsoft Windows*** and files created therein.

In 1997, Apple acquired Next, Inc., also founded by Steve Jobs, in order to develop the next generation of graphical user interface.

Macintosh Client

In networking, any ***Macintosh*** computer connected to a network.

Macintosh File System (MFS)

In computing, a "flat" (or nonhierarchical) file system used by older ***Macintosh*** computers. It has been replaced in recent versions of the ***Macintosh Operating System*** by the ***Hierarchical File System (HFS)***.

Macintosh Operating System

The ***operating system*** used by Apple ***Macintosh*** computers to control all computer functions, from finding files, opening applications, formatting external media, etc. The Macintosh OS was the first popular ***GUI*** (graphical user interface) and its ease of use and ***WYSIWYG*** display helped create ***desktop publishing***. There are many versions and updates to the operating system, but System 8.0 is the most recent as of this writing. Apple has recently begun licensing the Macintosh OS to other computer manufacturers, such as PowerComputing and Radius, with the hopes of spawning a wide ***clone*** market, as was the case with the ***IBM-compatible computer***.

MacPaint

A ***paint program*** dating from the earliest days of the ***Macintosh*** computer, used to create ***bitmapped*** graphics. The term *MacPaint* also refers to the ***file format*** in which MacPaint files were saved.

Macro

In computers, any sequence of instructions, keystrokes, or commands that can be stored en masse and invoked with a single command, as a means of automating certain often-used functions.

Macron

In typography, an ***accent*** (¯) placed over a character, primarily a vowel, usually to indicate that it should be pronounced with a long vowel sound. See ***Accent***.

Madder Lakes

A type of red ***organic color pigment*** used in printing inks. Although dirtier in color than other red pigments, Madder Lakes are highly lightfast and have a high resistance to bleeding. (See ***Organic Color Pigments***.)

Mag

Abbreviated term for ***magnetic***, used to refer to any type of magnetic storage medium.

Magazine

In publishing, any periodical, or regularly published publication, containing a mix of staff-written or freelanced articles and features, usually pertaining to one particular subject. Magazines may be slick and colorful, or they can be black-and-white and less elaborate. They also usually contain some quantity of photographic content. Most magazines also obtain the bulk of their revenue from the selling of advertising space. The point at which a *newsletter* becomes a magazine is blurry, but the latter tends to be less slickly and expensively produced, and relies less on advertising than subscription fees for revenue.

The word "magazine" itself dates from the Arabic word *makhazin* and the Italian word *magazzino*, both of which meant "storehouse." In English, the word "magazine" also had (and retains in many cases) this meaning. In 17th-century English, the word "magazine" was first used to refer to a publication that was a "storehouse of information."

The word *magazine* also refers to any container or device used to store objects or materials, as in an artillery magazine that holds ammunition. In *hot-metal* typesetting, the term also had this meaning, referring to a container in which the type matrices were sorted and stored. *Typefaces* could be changed by removing one magazine and inserting another.

Magenta

One of the *subtractive primary colors*—appearing purple red—characterized by its absorption of *green* light. It is used in various proportions with the other subtractive primaries—*cyan* and *yellow*—to form many other colors. Magenta is often incorrectly used as a synonym for *red*. (See COLOR PLATE 1.)

Magenta is also a term for one of the four *process color* inks used in multicolor printing. Also incorrectly referred to as "red" (or *process red*), it is the red component used in many types of color mixing.

The word *magenta* derives from the name of one of the first synthetic dyes developed by French chemists, named in 1859 after the victory of the French army in the Italian town of Magenta.

Magnetic

One type of *plate cylinder* used in *flexography*. See *Plate Cylinder: Flexography*.

Magnetic Card

A small, plastic card containing a thin strip of a magnetic material on which data can be recorded in a manner akin to recording on *magnetic tape*. Such cards are used for credit cards, bank cards, parking cards, and other specific applications.

Magnetic Disk

In computing, a general term describing a wide variety of data storage media in which information is stored by selectively magnetizing the surface of a flat, circular, metallic plate. Contrast *Optical Disc*.

Magnetic Ink

A type of ink produced using *pigment*s that can be magnetized after printing so as to enable the printed material to be read using *Magnetic Ink Character Recognition*

(MICR) equipment, originally developed for use in the electronic processing of bank checks. Magnetic inks must be produced along strict guidelines and must print clearly, so as to facilitate the reading of the material by machine. Magnetic inks can also contain *black pigments* produced from magnetite, a naturally occurring magnetic oxide of iron.

Magnetic Ink Character Recognition (MICR)

A predecessor of *optical character recognition (OCR)*, in which character images were printed utilizing *magnetic ink* and read by a machine, commonly used for encoding numbers on checks. Sometimes called *E13B* characters, they were designed to be deciphered by machines. The metallic ink content allowed the machine to "read" the magnetic pattern and match it to its memory. The characters were designed to eliminate confusion pairs, so that each pattern was unique. (See also *MICR Check Paper*.) See *Optical Character Recognition (OCR)*, which has largely replaced MICR.

Magnetic Media

Any magnetically coated substance or surface used for the storage of computer data, as opposed to *optical media*. See *Magnetic Disk* and *Magnetic Tape*.

Magnetic Optical

See *Magneto-Optical Disc*.

Magnetic Tape

A mass storage medium for *analog* and *digital* data. Its most common configuration is its use in audiocassettes, used for distributing music, speech, or for other uses, such as in answering machines. Essentially, magnetic tape is a metallic or plastic strip coated with a magnetic substance such as an *iron oxide* (usually ferric oxide—Fe_2O_3—obtained from hematite or magnetite). The electromagnetic record heads alter the magnetic polarity of different portions of the tape, and the play head converts the pattern of magnetized spots to an electronic signal that can be converted to sound waves or computer data. Magnetic tape is used as a storage medium for computer information, but the ability to only access the tape serially (i.e., from beginning to end, not at random, as with other *magnetic media*) makes it impractical for general use. Magnetic tape is also used for the strips on *magnetic card*s such as credit cards. Magnetic tape stored in a hard plastic cartridge is known as a *tape cartridge*.

Magneto-Optical Disc

A type of computer storage medium that combines the principles of the *magnetic disk* and the *optical disc*. Essentially, an *MO* disc consists of four layers of material: a very thin (i.e., only a few atoms thick) crystalline metal layer and a thin aluminum layer, which are sandwiched between two layers of transparent plastic. The thin crystalline layer can have the polarity of its crystals altered by exposure to a magnetic field. Thus, some crystals have their polarities adjusted to a configuration that signifies a "1," while unaltered crystal polarities signify "0s." (Computer data can only be some combination of 1s and 0s; see *Digital*.) Data written to the disc is erased by heating it with a high-energy laser to a certain critical level (i.e., the temperature at which the crystal polarity is "reset" to all 0s). To record new data, the magnetic head again switches the polarity of certain crystals to 1s. When the disc is read, a low-energy, polarized laser beam is reflected from the aluminum layer beneath the crystalline layer. As the light is reflected back up, the polarization of the light is altered with respect to the polarization of the magnetic crystals. Thus, unaltered crystal polarity (0s) and altered crystal polarity (1s) can be distinguished by the laser, and the proper *bit* pattern transferred to the computer.

Magneto-optical discs, unlike optical discs such as *CD-ROM*s or *WORM*s, can be erased and rewritten repeatedly. MO discs are increasing in speed and storage capacity and decreasing in expense. However, many imaging and prepress service bureaus are discontinuing support for them.

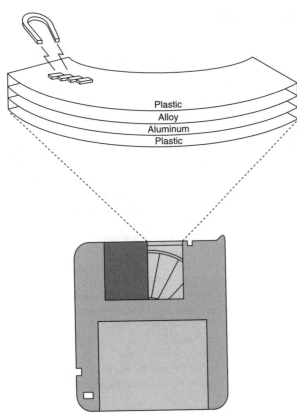

Schematic of a magneto-optical (MO) disc.

Magnification

A measure of the relationship of the size of a reproduced image to the size of the original image, commonly by means of the following formula:

$$M = \frac{I}{O}$$

where *M* is the magnification factor, *I* is the size of the reproduced image, and *O* is the size of the original. Thus, an original image with a width of 4 in. that was reproduced with a width of 8 in. would have a magnification factor of 2.

Mail-Aware Application

In computing, any computer program capable of sending and receiving *email* and, perhaps, other services such as enhanced handling and organization of email, workflow automation, etc. See *Email*. Also known as a *message-enabled application* or a *mail-enabled application*.

Mailbox

In telecommunications and networking, an alternate term for a *mail folder*. See *Mail Folder*.

Mail-Enabled Application

Alternate term for a *mail-aware application*. See *Mail-Aware Application*.

Mail Folder

In networking, or in an *email* program or *server*, a disk-based "folder" in which the user's sent and received email is stored until the user deletes it. Also known as a *mailbox*.

Mail Merging

A function of many word processing programs that allows database records to be combined with a word processor-based text file, used most commonly for individually addressing a single form letter to multiple recipients. Many mail merging features also allow for the insertion of database record-specific text into the body of the letter, making it seem as if the letter was personally written to the recipient.

Main Exposure

In *halftone* photography, a camera exposure that is made of a *continuous-tone* image through a halftone screen made to reproduce all the areas of a photograph except the deepest *shadow* areas.

Maintenance Release

In computing, a minor software upgrade that corrects small *bug*s or adds a limited number of minor features. Such a release is usually indicated by a change in the decimal portion of the application's version number, while the whole number portion indicates a major upgrade. For example, an application numbered 3.2 contains only minor changes and bug fixes from version 3.1. Version 4.0, however, could be a drastically revamped version of the program from version 3.0.

Majuscule

An alternate term for a capital letter. See *Capitals*.

Makegood

A reprinting and rerunning of a printed advertisement, performed gratis, as a result of an *ad complaint* on the part of the publisher or advertiser.

Makeover

Any print or other job that needs to be remade in order to incorporate corrections or to correct defects in the original run.

Makeready

Collective term for all of the operations necessary to set up a printing press for printing, including inking and ink adjustment, dampening solution adjustment, ink and dampening roller adjustment, plate and blanket cylinder adjustment, and other procedures performed to preclude the need for wasted time and paper once the job itself has started. Makeready also involves the printing of *color proof*s, and ends with the client or customer signing an *OK sheet*.

Makeup

In prepress and graphics, the assembly of text, graphics, and other page elements onto a *mechanical*. Synonymous with *pasteup* and *layout*. Used as a noun and a verb. Also spelled as two words, *make up*, or with a hyphen, *make-up*.

Making Order

A quantity of paper, not of a standard size or type, manufactured by a papermill to customer specifications. Most mills impose a minimum quantity of such papers.

Malachite Green

A green, rarely used *lake* that serves as a *pigment* in printing inks.

Male Connector

Any type of electrical cable connector possessing a set of pins designed to be inserted in a set of holes or slots on a corresponding *female connector*. One does not need to think too hard to derive the etymology of this.

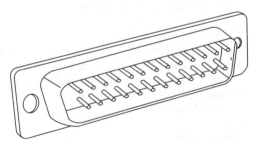

Male connector.

Maleic Resin

A synthetic *resin* produced from the reaction of maleic acid with *rosin*, used in printing inks to impart high degrees of hardness to the printed ink film. See *Resin*.

MAN

Abbreviation for *municipal area network*. See *Municipal Area Network (MAN)*.

Also the abbreviation for *metropolitan area network*. See *Metropolitan Area Network (MAN)*.

Management Information Base (MIB)

In networking, a network configuration database used by *Common Management Information Protocol (CMIP)* and *Simple Network Management Protocol (SNMP)* to manage, monitor, and change network settings and resources.

Management Information System (MIS)

A computer system used to facilitate *job tracking* and *image management*—or, in other words, to record and analyze data pertaining to production, such as cost of materials, time spent on a particular job, the locations of files, etc. Nearly all industries and corporations have some sort of MIS system to provide detailed information about the business.

Manchester Encoding

In telecommunications, a means of encoding both data and timing signals in the same *bit* stream in which the state of the signal (i.e., 0 or 1) during the first half of a bit period indicates the value of the data while a transition to the opposite state mid-way through the bit period acts as the timing signal.

Mandatory Entry Field

In computing, any blank space in a user *interface* (such as in a command line or dialog box) in which the user must enter requested input before the system can continue. An example of a mandatory entry field is a username and/or password that must be entered before a user can gain access to a network.

Mandrel

A shaft on which printing press cylinders or rollers are mounted.

Mandrel is also an alternate term for a *sleeve cylinder*, a type of *gravure cylinder*. See *Sleeve Cylinder*.

Manganese Drier

A compound of manganese added to printing inks to accelerate ink drying by speeding up the rate at which the ink *vehicle* undergoes *oxidation* and *polymerization*. See *Drier*.

Manifold Inking System

Alternate term for an *enclosed inking system* used on some *flexographic* presses. See *Inking System: Flexography*.

Manifold Paper

A lightweight *bond paper* either unglazed or *machine-glazed* (on one side or on both sides) closely related to *onionskin* used for making carbon copies or for reports, airmail stationery, or envelope enclosures. See *Bond Paper*.

Manila

A type of moderately heavy paper characterized by high tear strength and durability, used for envelopes, folders, wrapping paper, and other such uses. Manila paper is often made from *Manila hemp*.

Manila Hemp

Popular name for abacá (*Musa textilis*), a tree-like herb of the banana family native to the Philippines. Primarily used for making rope, manila hemp is also used as a fibrous source for papermaking, especially for **Manila paper**.

Manual Unit

Alternate term for **hand unit**. See **Hand Unit**.

Manufacturing Automation Protocol (MAP)

A communications protocol developed in 1982 by General Motors to provide a set of common standards for the interconnection of computers and programmable manufacturing tools. An accompanying protocol, called **Technical and Office Protocol (TOP)**, was developed by Boeing Computer Services to standardize the front-office networking of manufacturing systems.

Manuscript

Any original handwritten or typed copy from which type will be set. Although the term *manuscript* (deriving from the Latin terms *manus*—"hand"—and *scriptus*—"written") technically only refers to copy written by hand, it is commonly used to refer to what could more properly be called a **typescript**. *Manuscript* is commonly abbreviated **ms.**, and the plural is abbreviated **mss.**

Manuscript Cover

A type of **cover paper**, commonly light blue in color, used as a cover sheet for legal documents and **manuscript**s.

Map

In graphics and imaging, to assign colors or levels of gray to one or a set of **pixel**s, as per data contained in the original image. See **Color Mapping**.

In general computing, the term *map* also means to assign a drive letter to a particular **information path** or **directory** such that when a drive letter is entered, the assigned path or directory is accessed.

MAP

Abbreviation for **Manufacturing Automation Protocol**. See **Manufacturing Automation Protocol (MAP)**.

MAPI

Abbreviation for **messaging application programming interface**. See **Messaging API**.

Map Paper

A sturdy, moisture-resistant, yet easily folded (though not easily re-folded) paper, usually made from pulp of high **cotton content** or produced via **chemical pulping** methods, used in the printing of maps.

Mapping

In graphics and imaging, an abbreviated term for **color mapping**. See **Color Mapping**.

Also in graphics and imaging, *mapping* also refers to the act of transforming an image or graphic from one coordinate system to another.

Mapping also refers to the act of assigning characters to specific keys on a keyboard.

In three-dimensional object **rendering**, the term *mapping* refers to the means by which a texture is added to the surface of an object. In mapping, the texture must be added correctly with respect to the shape of the object, as well as the orientation of the "lighting" and the position of the viewer. Also, if the object is to move, the mapped texture must move with the object, as well.

Mapping Function

See **Mapping** (second definition).

Marching Ants

Overly descriptive, alternate term for a **marquee**. See **Marquee**.

Margin

Any deliberately unprinted space on a page, especially surrounding a block of text. Margins are used not only to aid in the aesthetics and the readability of a page, but also to provide allowances for trimming, binding, and other postpress operations. (See **Bind Margin**.) Although *margin* most commonly is used to refer to the blank space to the left and right of a text passage (but not usually the space between columns of text on a single page; see **Gutter**), there is also a **head margin** and a **foot margin**, which refer to the blank space at the top and bottom of a page, respectively. The margin at the fold is usually slightly narrower so visual space is not overwhelming.

Marginal Copy

Any text or copy printed in the **margin**s of a page.

Marginal Notes

Any written or typeset material appearing in the **margin**s of a page. Often, marginal notes are handwritten on a manuscript or within a book as notes to the author or to other readers concerning the type specifications and/or content of the text. Also called **side notes**.

Marginal Side Heads

Any **head** appearing in the **margin** of a page, beyond the text area of the page. Marginal side heads are often used in reference works and textbooks, as a means of facilitating the location of specific topics.

Mark

Any special symbol, character, or image that is added to the nonprinting or marginal regions of a **mechanical**, film, plate, or print, used for such purposes as ensuring proper **registration** of images or colors, or to indicate the **trim size** of a final print. See also **Register Marks** and **Crop Marks**.

A *mark* is also any symbol or value added to a computer code or other data set to facilitate the locating of a particular item.

Marking Engine

The part of a computer printer, of any of a variety of types, that creates the image to be printed on the *substrate*.

MARKOLOR™

A proprietary means of *color separation* in which all full-color graphic information is processed through special filters or scans to two separate films or files. These files can then be printed on a wide variety of *substrate*s utilizing two colors, such as red and green, green and black, or red and blue.

Mark Parity

In computing, a *parity check* used to detect and correct errors in data transmission by adding an extra *bit* (a 1) to a character code. See *Parity*. See also *Space Parity*.

Marks Flat

See *Master Flat*.

Markup

In typesetting, the specification of the desired characteristics of the type to be set, including *point size*, *typeface*, style, alignment, *leading*, *line length*, etc. See *Composition and Markup*. Also spelled as two words, *mark up*, or with a hyphen, *mark-up*.

The term *markup* also refers to a *markup language*. See *Markup Language*.

Set head as
14/18 Helvetica Bold
on 18 picas

Set text as
10/12 Times on 18
picas, ragged right

`History of Web Offset Printing`

`Prior to World War II, almost all lithographic`

`presses were sheetfed; the trend was toward`

`larger multicolor presses.`

`   A few web offset presses were in opera-`

`tion; however, these were used mostly for`

`single-color and simple two-color work. These`

`web offset presses had no heated dryers`

`through which to pass the freshly printed web.`

A typewritten manuscript that has been marked up for the typesetter.

Markup Language

A set of codes and formatting commands used to consistently identify elements of a document, such as chapter, heading, subheading, etc. Most software developers, however, tend to use their own markup system, which makes consistency and compatibility from application to application difficult. Various attempts have been made to standardize formatting commands. See, for example, *Standardized Generalized Markup Language (SGML)*.

Marquee

In many computer programs, a *selection tool* that identifies the selection object (or portion of an object) by means of an animated dashed line bounding the selection. The term *marquee* is derived from the animated effect, which looks like a theater marquee. A perhaps more descriptive colloquial term for the marquee tool is *marching ants*.

Mar Resistance

Alternate term for *abrasion resistance*. See *Abrasion Resistance*.

Martini Binder

An *in-line* device used on *web press*es to produce paper-bound books. The martini binder assembles *signature*s, adhesive-binds them, and adds the covers.

Mask

Any material or substance used to block off portions of an area for a variety of purposes. In *screen printing*, some form of solid or liquid masking material is used to block portions of the screen from allowing ink to pass through. In photography, masks are used to block off portions of an image or film that should not be exposed to light. In digital imaging, masks can be created electronically to also block off portions of an image. (See also *Area Mask*, *Outline Mask*, and *Unsharp Mask*.)

A mask, used to isolate background or foreground objects.

Masking Equations

In multicolor printing, mathematical equations that describe the relationship between the amount of ink printed and the densities or reflectances of the resulting red, green, and blue ink films, computed as a means of correcting *hue error*s. (See COLOR PLATE 15.)

Masking Paper

In prepress, term for the carrier sheet—usually *goldenrod paper* or other similar material—to which negative films are stripped for platemaking. See *Stripping*.

Maskoid

Alternate term for *liquid frisket*. See *Liquid Frisket*.

Mass Storage

In computing, term for any medium used to store large quantities of computer data. See *Magnetic Disk*, *Magneto-Optical Disc*, *Optical Disc*, and *Compact Disc (CD)*, for example.

Masstone

The *hue* reflected from a quantity of ink, used to evaluate its color characteristics.

Master

In printing and duplicating, any original image-bearing copy used for making reproductions.

Similarly, in media and multimedia, an original copy of an audio or video recording or an interactive presentation from which copies will be made.

Master Flat

In color *prepress*, a separate flat prepared alongside the flats bearing the *color separation*s with all the *registration mark*s, *crop mark*s, etc., for the print run. Also called a *marks flat*. See *Prepress: Graphic Arts Photography and Flat Assembly*.

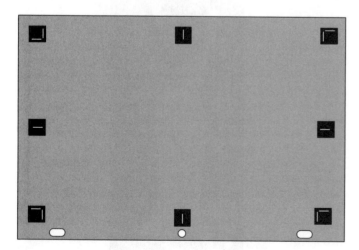

A master marks flat punched for pin register.

Master Font

In computerized typesetting, the "original" *font* outline from which all size variations are scaled.

Master Image

In typography, any *character master* from which type is set by photography or other means.

The term *master image* also refers to any image—be it a print, transparency, mechanical, scan, etc.—from which subsequent copies will be made.

Mastering

In mass *CD* production, an optical recording process that transfers digital information (stored on a *premastering* tape) to a *glass master*, or a glass disc containing an image of the *pit* and *land* pattern desired on the ultimate CD. The glass master is used to create a metal *stamper* that can then be used to stamp multiple copies of a disc. A glass master can also be generated from an *analog* master tape.

Master Page

In graphics, a template or page layout to which all or most pages in a publication or document will conform. Many *page layout program*s allow the creation and application of master pages.

Master Proof

A *galley proof* containing flagged items and questions for the editor or author. Also known as a *printer's proof* and a *reader's proof*.

Master Tape

In audio and video production, an edited tape from which copies will be mass-produced for distribution.

Master Workstation

Alternate term for a *cluster controller*. See *Cluster Controller*.

Masthead

In newspaper and magazine publishing, the listing of the publication's staff, management, address, etc., commonly printed toward the beginning of the publication.

That term *masthead* is often confused with the flag or logo, which is a newspaper or other publication's nameplate.

Matching Italic

In typography, a type of *italic* type created with the same design as a corresponding *roman* type, as opposed to "pure" or *unrelated italic* that is designed to stand alone. Digitized typesetters create matching italic by electronically modifying the roman version of the typeface and imparting a slant to it. See *Italic*.

Matchprint™

A *single-sheet color proof* produced off-press using materials—similar to *Cromalin*—manufactured by 3M.

Mathematics

Special characters available in some fonts used for the typesetting of mathematical material. Here are some of the more popular math symbols:

$$+ - \times \div = \pm \mp \,^{\circ} \,' \,'' \,''' \, \sqrt{} \, \infty + (\,) [\,]$$
$$\{\,\} \langle \rangle \int \Sigma \pm \mp \equiv < \leqslant \geqslant > | / \nless \ngtr$$

Mathematical symbols.

Math Functions

In a word processing program, a feature that allows the program to be used as a calculator without having to leave the program and open a utility program to do calculations.

Matrix

Any type of mold used for casting metal type.

In *flexographic* platemaking, a *matrix* is a mold made from an engraving or a metal relief master into which softened rubber is pressed. See *Plate: Flexography: Rubber Plates*.

In graphics, the term *matrix* is used to refer to any *coordinate system* or *grid*. See *Grid*.

In typesetting, a *matrix* is a metal mold or photographic image of a type character used to generate copies of that character during the setting of type.

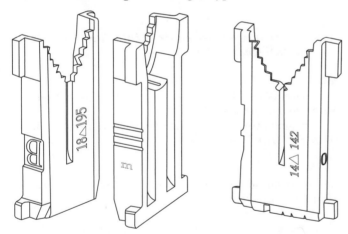

In hot-metal typesetting, the matrix was a mold for each letter.

Matrix Array

Alternate term for an *area array*. See *Area Array*.

Matrix Printer

See *Dot-Matrix Printer*.

Matte

Any surface characterized by a rough, dull, and/or unshiny appearance, produced by the surface reflecting less light back toward the eye. Colors printed on matte surfaces appear less dense.

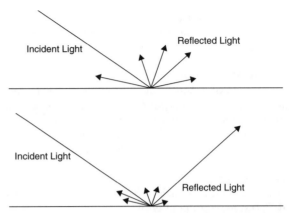

Reflection of light rays from a matte surface (top) is more diffuse than that from a glossy surface (bottom).

In papermaking, *matte* refers to a paper surface that has a low level of *gloss* and that does not appear shiny. Paper that has a high degree of gloss reflects the light rays that hit its surface back nearly all in the same direction, while paper that has a low degree of gloss reflects the light back more diffusely, or in different directions, which imparts a dull surface to the paper. Whether a paper's surface is glossy or matte is related to the paper's smoothness. Increasing *calendering*, *supercalendering*, or *coating* tends to increase a paper's gloss.

A paper's level of gloss is measured using a *glossmeter*, and the value obtained is compared to a "perfect" gloss of 100 gloss units. Matte papers tend to register less than 20 gloss units. (See also *Gloss*.)

In video and motion picture production, a *matte* is a means of producing composite pictures by *keying* one video source over a second source. See *Matting* and *Chroma-Key*.

Matte-Coated Paper

A type of low-gloss *coated paper*. See *Coated Paper*.

MAU

Abbreviation for *multistation access unit*. See *Multistation Access Unit (MAU)*.

The acronym *MAU* is also an abbreviation for a *medium attachment unit*. See *Medium Attachment Unit*.

Maximum Density

In imaging, the greatest image *density* achievable with a particular configuration of devices or *substrate*s. On one particular press using *coated paper*, for example, the maximum density may be 3.0, while on the same press printing on *newsprint* it may be 1.5. Also known as D_{max}. See also *Minimum Density*.

Maximum Interword Space

In typography, the maximum amount of space allowed between words, used in the setting of tolerances for *justification*. See also *Minimum Interword Space* and *Justification*.

Maximum Partition Size

In computing, the largest amount of memory that is available for a program to ensconce itself in. See **Partition**.

Maximum Resolution

Generally speaking, the greatest number of **pixel**s, or dots, a computer display or output device is capable of producing per inch, measured in **pixels per inch (ppi)**. The higher the maximum resolution, the sharper and clearer the image can be displayed or printed. (See **Resolution**.)

Maxwell's Triangle

The first attempt to scientifically and mathematically quantify the perception of **color**.

In 1872, James Maxwell, a Scottish physicist, developed a chart in the form of an equilateral triangle and suggested that all known colors could be located within this triangle. The Maxwell triangle identifies **red, green, and blue** as the three primary components of light, the **primary colors** at the corners of the triangle. These are the same colors that are the basis of television and computer color monitors. They are the primary colors of light, rather than of pigment. In the center of the chart is white—the color produced by the combination of all components of the spectrum. All colors can be arranged within the triangle. As one moves along its edges, the transitions are experienced: red changes to **orange**, then to **yellow**, and finally to green; green changes to blue; blue changes to **violet**, to **purple**, and back to red. Moving from the edge to the center of the triangle, the brilliance of each primary color is lost in a transition from full saturation at the edge to white at the center. Maxwell superimposed grid lines, drawn parallel to each edge of the triangle, in order to establish a system of color notation. Any point within the triangle identifies a specific color sample and was assumed by Maxwell to be definable by the quantities of the primary color it contains. This quantity can be measured by the distance from each primary color. In Maxwell's triangle any point—any color—is defined by only two dimensions, the distance from point 1 and point 2.

Maxwell's triangle paved the way for the **Munsell color space** and the **CIE color space**. See **Color: Color Measurement**.

MB

Abbreviation for **megabyte**. See **Megabyte**.

Mbit/s

Abbreviation for **megabits per second**. See also **Bits per Second**.

MBONE

Shorthand term for **Multicast Backbone**. See **Multicast Backbone (MBONE)**.

Mbyte

Abbreviation for **megabyte**. See **Megabyte**.

MCA

Abbreviation for **microchannel architecture**. See **Microchannel Architecture (MCA)**.

MCGA

Abbreviation for **multicolor graphics adapter**. See **Multicolor Graphics Adapter (MCGA)**.

MCI

Abbreviation for **media control interface**. See **Media Control Interface (MCI)**.

MD

In papermaking, abbreviation for **machine direction**. See **Machine Direction (MD)**.

In computing, MD is also an abbreviation for **MiniDisc**. See **MiniDisc (MD)**.

MDA

Abbreviation for **Monochrome Display Adapter**. See **Monochrome Display Adapter (MDA)**.

Mealiness

A term for a defect of **gravure** printing used to refer to **snowflaking** that occurs in middletone regions of the print. See **Snowflaking**.

Mean Line

Alternate term for **x-height**. See **x-Height**.

Mean Time between Failures (MTBF)

In computing, the average length of time—derived statistically—that a computer system or system component will operate before it fails, expressed (perhaps optimistically) in tens of thousands of hours. Also referred to as *mean time before failure*. See also **Mean Time to Repair (MTTR)**.

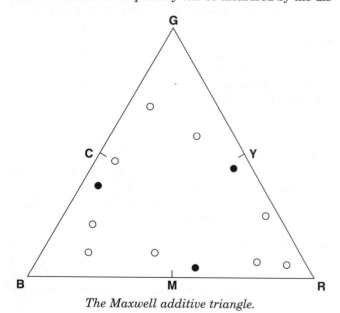

The Maxwell additive triangle.

Mean Time to Repair (MTTR)

In computing, the average length of time—derived statistically—that it takes to repair a computer system or system component. See also **Mean Time Between Failures (MTBF)**.

Measure

The quantitative determination of any value, be it length, width, height, storage capacity, speed, etc. Or, when used as a verb, to make such a determination.

In typography, *measure* is synonymous with **line length**. See **Line Length**.

Measured Photography

A means of ensuring the proper illumination of a to-be-photographed scene, accomplished by carefully measuring the level of illumination in all of the regions of the scene that will be captured by the camera. Measured photography is performed so as to ensure that no areas of the resulting image will be too dark or too light to reproduce properly. Once called **four-stop photography**.

Mechanical

Camera-ready art consisting of typeset text, heads, **line art** or other illustration matter, and other page elements pasted up into the proper position and ready for the making of **negative**s or plates. *Mechanical* also refers to the rigid paper or paperboard on which these materials are pasted up. Mechanicals are increasingly being generated digitally, however.

The term *mechanical* is also used to refer to any process or function performed by a machine, in contrast to "manual," "chemical," or "electronic." (In some cases, though, mechanical *does* refer to a process performed manually.)

Mechanical Adhesion

The force that attaches one surface or material to another by physical interlocking of component particles, rather than by chemical means.

Mechanical Binding

A means of fastening sheets of paper together using metal or plastic attachments inserted through punched or drilled holes in the paper. Ironically, of the four major methods of binding, "mechanical" binding is the least mechanized. The three primary types of mechanical binding are loose-leaf binding, spiral binding, and comb binding.

Loose-Leaf Binding. **Loose-leaf binding** is the simplest and most common form of mechanical binding. In one variety, pages are placed in a book, or **binder**, and held together by means of a metal clamp. In others, plastic strips also serve as clamps to hold pages together. Slightly more elaborate types of loose-leaf bindings are the popular **ring binder**s (most often found in a three-ring variety). Metal rings mounted inside the binder can be fitted through holes punched or drilled in the sheets. Ring

binders (and similar **post binder**s) have the advantage of allowing sheets to be inserted or removed easily, which makes them well-suited for publications, presentations, and other such documents that will be updated with some degree of frequency. The holes can be punched prior to printing (some letter-size paper is sold pre-drilled) or afterward, either by a professional bindery or using a hand-held hole punch widely available at office supply stores.

Spiral Binding. In **spiral binding**, a long series of small holes is punched or drilled along the length of the **binding edge**, and a continuous wire or plastic coil is threaded through the holes. The ends of the coil are then crimped, and the pages within are secure and can be opened flat. Spiral binding is often used for notebooks, cook books, instruction manuals, or other types of publications that need to remain flat when opened. **Wire-O binding** is one variety of spiral binding.

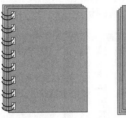

Spiral binding.

Comb Binding. **Comb binding**s consist of a strip of solid plastic with curved teeth or prongs extending off it. These prongs can be inserted into slits drilled or punched into the binding edge of the sheets. Comb bindings have the same advantages as spiral bindings, an added advantage being that there are no crimped wires to come uncrimped and slowly unravel, an occasional problem with some heavily used spiral-bound notebooks.

In spiral and comb binding, covers can be added to the top and bottom. In loose-leaf binding, the binder itself acts as a cover, and some loose-leaf binders allow for cover sheets to be inserted into clear plastic pockets on the front of the binder.

Mechanical binding is inexpensive, but it is used primarily on very short-run jobs and/or internal documents and publications.

See **Binding and Finishing**.

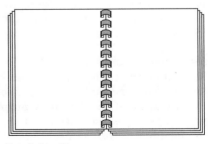

Comb binding.

Mechanical Color Separation

Any process for generating **color separation**s performed by hand, rather than by photographic or electronic means. In mechanical color separation, the art for each separate color is prepared manually on separate boards or transparent overlays.

Mechanical Ghosting

A printing defect characterized by the appearance of an undesirable image on a printed sheet. Mechanical ghosting (in contrast to **chemical ghosting**) is exclusively found on the printed side of a sheet and is typically the result of ink starvation, as the form rollers are sometimes not adequately reinked, especially on heavily inked areas of the plate. Incorrect-diameter form rollers and a blanket that has a swollen or compressed spot are the usual causes of mechanical ghosting. (See also **Chemical Ghosting**.)

Mechanical ghosting also refers to a **flexographic** printing problem more typically referred to as **mechanical pinholing**. See **Mechanical Pinholing**.

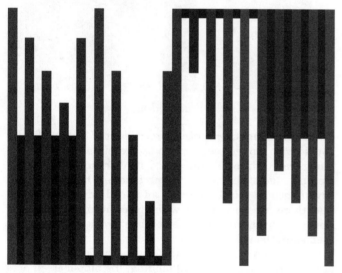

A mechanical ghosting form, showing the effects of ink starvation due to the design of the form.

Mechanical Pinholing

A printing defect of **flexographic** printing, characterized by an incomplete ink film that has reproduced the pattern of the press's **anilox roller** on the **substrate**. Mechanical pinholing can be caused by overly rapid ink drying, insufficient ink quantity, or an inadequate degree of **viscosity**. (See also **Chemical Pinholing**.)

Mechanical Pulping

Method of converting logs or wood chips into paper **pulp** for use in papermaking accomplished by mechanical grinding, as opposed to **chemical pulping**. The purpose of **pulping** is to reduce wood (or other fibrous raw material) to individual **cellulose** fibers. A nonfibrous constituent of wood, **lignin**, binds the cellulose fibers together and is primarily responsible for reducing paper quality and its permanence.

Traditional mechanical pulping involves forcing logs against a revolving stone, which grinds the logs into pulp by abrasive action. The stone is sprayed with water to remove fibers from the pulp stone and to prevent fiber damage due to friction-generated heat.

The production of mechanical pulp (also called **groundwood**) results in little removal of lignin content and consequently produces paper that is not of as high a quality as other pulping methods that remove significant amounts of lignin. The advantages of mechanical pulping are its high pulp yield (100 lb. of wood can generate as much as 95 lb. of pulp), its low cost, and the paper that it produces has several desirable printing qualities, such as high ink absorbency, compressibility, opacity, and bulk. Disadvantages, however, include low strength, low permanence, and a tendency to yellow with time (primarily caused by high levels of lignin). Paper made with mechanical pulps also contain **shives**, or incompletely ground fiber bundles.

Mechanical pulps are primarily used in newsprint, as well as papers used in telephone directories, catalogs, "pulp" magazines, and paper towels and tissues.

Many pulps are bleached following pulping to increase brightness and whiteness and to dissolve additional amounts of lignin. Mechanical pulps are bleached, but not to any great degree. Although some lignin is removed from groundwood pulps by **bleaching** (and some lignin is softened and lost by the heat generated by the grinding process), extensive bleaching can result in a decrease of pulp yield, defeating the primary advantage of the process. About 23% of the pulp used in the world is mechanical pulp. In most usages, however, groundwood pulp is combined with pulps produced chemically, to counteract the disadvantages of paper made with mechanical pulps.

The above method of producing groundwood pulp is the oldest pulping process. New mechanical pulping methods are reducing the disadvantages without compromising the advantages of mechanical pulping. **Refiner mechanical pulping (RMP)** sandwiches wood chips between two revolving disks. Heat due to friction softens the lignin and allows greater separation of the cellulose fibers, while contributing less fiber damage. RMP has greater strength than traditional groundwood, which reduces the need to supplement it with chemical pulps. RMP pulpmills, however, have been supplanted by even newer pulping techniques. **Thermomechanical pulping (TMP)** operates similar to RMP but under higher temperature and pressure. (In many cases, the wood chips are preheated.) The higher temperatures and pressures soften the lignin even more than can be accomplished using frictional heat, and fiber separation is easier. Additional passes through the system increases defiberization. Thermomechanical pulp is stronger than refiner mechanical pulp, and still retains the high-yield and cost-effectiveness of mechanical pulps. **Chemi-thermomechanical pulps (CTMP)** use mild chemicals, which

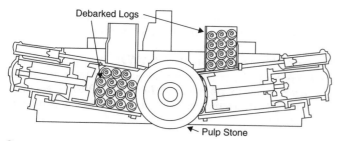

One configuration of mechanical pulping device. Logs are pressed against a revolving pulp stone.

increases pulp brightness and reduces shive content. **Pressurized groundwood (PGW)** is similar to traditional groundwood pulping, but operates under high pressure, which helps overcome some of the disadvantages of the process.

Media

Generally speaking, the plural of the word *medium*, used to refer to any means of transferring or propagating something. In pop culture terms, the term *medium* refers to any means of transmitting programming or information, such as television or radio. In computing, a *medium* is any form of **mass storage** device, such as a **magnetic disk**, a **magneto-optical disc**, etc.

Media Access Control (MAC)

In networking, a component of the **link layer** of the **Open System Interconnection (OSI)** reference model that governs access to the transmission medium. Media access control is used primarily in **Token Ring** and **CSMA/CD** local area networks.

Media Access Control Address

Alternate term for a **hardware address**. See **Hardware Address**.

Media Access Control Protocol

Alternate term for **access protocol**. See **Access Protocol**.

Media Control Interface (MCI)

In multimedia, a standardized control system for multimedia applications, allowing for the operation of different files and devices. Each device possesses its own **device driver** that utilizes a standard set of controls, such as stop, play, rewind, fast forward, etc.

Media Filter

In networking, a device that is used in **Token Ring** networks to convert an output signal from the adapter board to a form (or transmission speed) capable of being transmitted along the specific type of wiring used as the transmission medium.

Medium

Singular form of the word **media**. See **Media**.

Medium Attachment Unit

In networking, a transceiver connected to an **Ethernet** adapter's **attachment unit interface** port, used to allow further attachment to a specific transmission medium, be it **fiber optic** cable, **unshielded twisted pair** wiring, etc. Abbreviated **MAU**.

Medium-Format Camera

In photography, a camera with a picture size larger than 35 mm, but smaller than a **view camera**, including such film sizes as 60×60 mm, 60×70 mm, and 60×90 mm.

Medium Shot

In photography—be it still, motion picture, or video—a shot of a subject at some distance between a **close-up** and a **long shot**. In shooting scripts, medium shot is indicated by **MS**.

Meg

In computing, a common, informal abbreviation for **megabyte**. See **Megabyte**.

Mega-

A **metric prefix** denoting 1,000,000 (one million, or 10^6) units. In computing, *mega-* refers to 2^{20}, and one **megabyte** (MB) of storage is approximately equal to one million **byte**s of data (actually 1,048,576 bytes). See **Metric Prefix**. See also **Kilo-**, **Giga-**, **Tera-**, **Peta-**, and **Exa-**. *Mega-* is usually abbreviated **M**.

Megabit (Mb)

A unit equal to approximately 1,000,000 (actually 1,048,576) **bit**s. See **Bit**.

Megabyte (MB)

A common unit of computer storage, comprising 1,024 **kilobyte**s or 1,048,576 **byte**s. *Mega-* is the prefix meaning "million," so it is common to consider one megabyte as to be equal to one million bytes, although that is not entirely accurate. It is now common to find hard disks, magnetic cartridge media, and computer memory measured in megabytes. Megabyte is abbreviated MB, or, colloquially, **meg**. 1,024 MB equals one **gigabyte**, which is also becoming a common disk capacity.

Megahertz (MHz)

A measure of **frequency**, equal to one million cycles per second.

Megapixel

In computing and digital imaging, term for a **bitmapped** image containing more than one million **pixel**s. For example, a 1,024×1,024-pixel image contains 1,048,576 pixels and would thus be called a *megapixel*.

MEK

See **Methyl Ethyl Ketone**.

Memory

The internal storage capacity of a computer, usually temporary. When computer memory is spoken of, it is usually *random-access memory (RAM)* that is meant, rather than disk size, which is technically known as *storage*, not memory. Memory may be volatile (erased when power is disconnected) or nonvolatile (remaining in memory without external power).See *RAM*.

Memory Address

In computing, the precise location in a computer's *RAM* that a particular item of data is stored.

Memory Bank

In computing, the smallest logical unit of memory, such as the slot in which a memory chip can be installed.

Memory Board

In computing, a circuit board that houses either *memory chip*s or sockets for the addition of additional memory chips.

Memory Cache

See *Cache Memory*.

Memory Card

A type of *magnetic card* containing *flash memory* chips used as a substitute for a disk drive.

Memory Chip

In computing, a *chip* used to store data or instructions, either temporarily (as in the case of *random-access memory*; see *RAM*) or permanently (as in the case of *read-only memory*; see *ROM*).

Memory Colors

*Color*s of familiar objects, such as a blue sky, a red apple, green grass, etc. Such colors are borne in mind by *color separator*s when performing *color correction*s, to ensure that familiar colored objects are reproduced properly and have a natural appearance.

Memory Management

In computing, the way in which the computer and *operating system* divide and utilize the available *RAM* (or *random-access memory*). In earlier days, the *DOS*-based personal computer divided available RAM into conventional memory, which was any memory below 640 *kilobyte*s (KB) and *upper memory*, which was 384 KB of memory beyond the conventional memory and was reserved strictly for system hardware. There were also extended memory and *expanded memory*, which increased the amount of memory that was available beyond the original one-*megabyte* limit. Modern computers no longer have this upper limit, and any memory beyond what the system software itself requires is fair game for applications. Memory management now also tends to refer to how the user allots memory to various

applications, especially when *multitasking* is involved. (See also *Memory Management Unit (MMU)*.

Memory Management Unit (MMU)

In computing, the portion of a *processor* that maps *memory address*es to *physical address*es. Once a separate chip, the MMU is now an integral part of most modern *CPU chip*s.

Memory Map

In computing, a chart or list of the amount of memory used by an *operating system*, as well as that used by each open application.

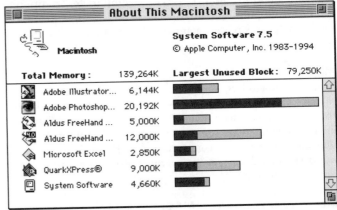

Memory map used by the Macintosh operating system, showing the amount of total memory, available memory, and memory used by the system as well as each open application.

Memory-Resident Program

Any computer program or utility described as *terminate-and-stay-resident*. See *Terminate-and-Stay-Resident*.

Menu

Any detailed list of choices—from restaurant dishes to computer functions. In computers, a menu is a list of available options, functions, etc., from which the user can

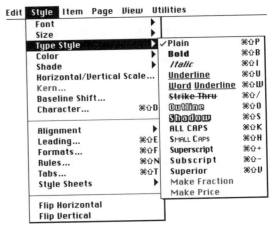

The style menu in QuarkXPress.

choose, depending upon what the user would like the computer to execute. Computer menus can either be text-based (the user types in the menu item itself or a letter or number corresponding to the menu item), pull-down, or pop-up (the user points and clicks with the mouse on a particular region of the screen and a list of items drops down or pops up, through which the user can scroll, clicking on the desired option), or a combination of both (options that exist on pull-down/pop-up menus are often executable using keyboard shortcuts).

Menu-Driven

Descriptive of any computer program or operating system that functions via *menu* options the user can select, commonly by pointing and clicking with a mouse, rather than by typing commands. Software that runs on *GUI*-based computer systems is typically menu-driven. In many cases, however, clickable menu options are also available by using keyboard shortcuts, or combinations of keys that perform the specified function, such as *Command-D* and *Command-Z* (a common combination!). See also *Command-Driven*.

Menu Traversing

In *menu-driven* computer programs or operating systems, the movement among items within a menu, or movement between different menus.

Menu Tree

In *menu-driven* computer programs and operating systems, the hierarchical organization of menus or menu items.

Merged

In *desktop publishing*, a term descriptive of a page that has some combination of disparate page elements (such as fonts, line art, halftones, etc.) on the same page that will be output at one time.

Mergenthaler, Ottmar

Ottmar Mergenthaler (1854–1899) was a German-American whose invention of the Linotype machine made a significant contribution to the printing industry. Apprenticed to a watchmaker in his native Germany at the age of 14, he emigrated to the United States in 1872 and became a citizen in 1878. While employed in the Baltimore machine shop of August Hahl (his cousin), he worked on building a "writing machine" that later helped him solve the problems involved in mechanizing the tedious work of typesetting. His machine used a keyboard to assemble lines of matrices prior to casting a one-piece slug in molten metal. From this prototype, Mergenthaler received financial backing from groups of newspaper publishers. A group of publishers headed by Whitelaw Reid bought controlling interest in the National Typographic Company, which later was renamed the Mergenthaler Linotype Company. The company exists today as a part of the Heidelberg press company and produces imaging equipment. The first machine was installed in the *New York Tribune* in 1886.

Mergenthaler could not solve the problem of automatic justification since the answer was a patent owned by J. W. Shuckers for the variable wedge, later called the spaceband. Eventually the Linotype company acquired the company that had the patent, and the Linotype machine enjoyed almost two decades without a serious contender, until a group of engineers from Linotype started the Intertype Company in 1911 when some of the original patents expired. For the next 70 years, these two companies controlled typesetting machinery around the world, with minor competition from Monotype and Ludlow.

The company he founded, the Mergenthaler Linotype Company, was renamed Allied Linotype in 1980, the Linotype Company in 1984, Linotype-Hell in 1991, and today is a division of the Heidelberg company.

Mesh Aperture

A space between two threads of a *screen printing* fabric, through which the ink passes.

Mesh Count

Alternate term for *mesh number*. See *Mesh Number*.

Mesh Counter

A magnifying lens used to count the number of threads per inch in a *screen printing* fabric. Also known as a *Linen Tester*.

Mesh Marks

A defect of *screen printing* in which the cross-hatched pattern of the screen fabric is exhibited by the dried ink film, caused either by inadequate *flow out* of the ink or improper tensioning of the screen fabric. Also called *screen marks*.

Mesh Network

A *network topology* in which each *node* is connected directly to every other node on the network. Multiple links to and from each device are also valuable for providing network link redundancy.

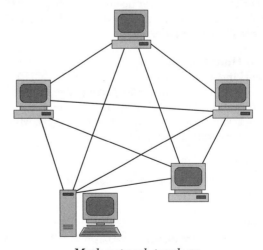

Mesh network topology.

Mesh Number

A count of the number of *mesh aperture*s—or spaces between the threads of a *screen printing* fabric—per inch. A finer mesh will have a higher mesh number than a coarser one. Also known as *mesh count*.

Mesh Opening

In *screen printing*, a measure—in microns—of the distance across a *mesh aperture*.

Mesh Opening Area

Alternate term for *aperture percentage*. See *Aperture Percentage*.

Mesh Volume

In *screen printing*, the area (width × length) of a *mesh aperture* multiplied by the thickness of the fabric.

Message

In networking and telecommunications, a name give to any data transmission.

In general computing, any statement from the computer to the user, reporting on the status of a function or process, providing instructions or caveats about a certain command, or cryptically indicating that some form of error has occurred.

Message Channel

In computing, a means of *interprocess communication* used in some *multitasking* environments that allows two open applications to share data with each other. See *Interprocess Communication* and *multitasking*.

Message-Enabled Application

Alternate term for a *mail-aware application*. See *Mail-Aware Application*.

Message Handling Service (MHS)

In networking, a popular *protocol* for the storage, management, and exchange of *email*, originally developed by Action Technologies and later licensed to Novell. MHS handles email efficiently by means of *store-and-forward* technology. See *Store-and-Forward*.

Message Handling System

In networking and telecommunications, a CCITT *X.400* standard protocol for *store-and-forward* email transmission. The system defines, among other things, the type of data a message may contain, to the means by which one data type is converted to another.

Message Switching

An alternate term for *packet switching*. See *Packet switching*.

Messaging API

An *interface* for applications written for *Windows* that adds messaging capabilities, or, in other words, the ability to send and receive *email* messages from within any application. Messaging API stands for *messaging application program interface* and is further abbreviated as *MAPI*.

Messaging Application Programming Interface

See *Messaging API*.

Metafile

A type of *device-independent* file format for computer illustrations, which was originally developed by the *National Bureau of Standards* as a means of exchanging illustrations to be used in government publications. The advantage of a metafile is that both a *bitmap* version and a *vector* version of an illustration can co-exist in the same file.

Metallic Inks

A variety of printing ink made with *metallic powders* so as to impart a metallic luster to the printed image. See *Metallic Powders*.

Metallic Paper

A paper that has been coated with a layer or layers of metallic materials.

Metallic Powders

Fine metal flakes that are mixed with a varnish and used as a *pigment* in some types of printing inks to impart silver, gold, or other types of metallic luster to the printed image. Metallic powders used in inks are produced in different grades and with varying degrees of fineness, depending on the desired end-use characteristics. Despite such names as *silver* or *gold*, less precious metals are typically used. "Silver" is actually made from aluminum, and "gold" is made from brass, copper or other metals, depending on the shade desired (from pale gold to rich gold). Specially made *vehicle*s are needed to carry these pigments to ensure proper binding to the *substrate* and to impart the desired level of brightness. Metallic powder-based inks, especially bronze powders used in "gold" inks, need to be mixed just prior to using, as they tarnish rapidly. The vehicle is designed to dry rapidly, so as to prevent a minimum of post-impression tarnishing. (See *Pigment*.) Often, metallic powders are added to the substrate following the printing of a highly tacky, nondrying ink, a process called *bronze dusting*.

Metallic Soaps

Metallic compounds, typically derived from manganese, cobalt, iron, copper, zinc, or zirconium, used as *drier*s in the manufacture of printing inks. Metallic soaps, and other materials added as driers, work as *catalyst*s to expedite the *oxidation* of chemicals in the fluid ink *vehicle*, allowing the ink to set more rapidly, preventing smudging and problems such as *ink setoff* caused by the handling of still-wet printing. (See *Drier*.)

Metal Screen Fabric

A screen fabric used in **screen printing** comprising threads of stainless steel, copper, bronze, or nickel, used either when **absolute register** is crucial or when printing abrasive inks on ceramics or glass—inks and substrates that are likely to quickly damage silk or synthetic fiber screens.

Metamer

A **color** that displays the same perceived **hue** as another color, although it may have a different spectral energy distribution than the apparently similar color. The apparent similarity in color may disappear under a different source of illumination. (See **Metamerism**.)

Metameric Color

A **color** that possesses the property of **metamerism**, or changes its perceived **hue** under varying sources of illumination. See **Metamerism**.

Metamerism

A phenomenon in which two **color**s match each other under one light source (for example, under tungsten light) but fail to match each other under a different one (for example, sunlight), or in which one color varies in its perceived shade under varying light sources. Procedures for the color evaluation of papers and inks, therefore, require standard, consistent sources of illumination. A color that changes its perceived hue under varying sources of light is called a **metameric color**.

Metaphor

In computing, especially utilizing a **graphical user interface**, a term describing an **icon** or other aspect of the **interface** that is designed to represent something else. The **Macintosh operating system**, for example, uses as its central metaphor the **desktop**, complete with **folders**, a trash can, etc. See **Graphical User Interface (GUI)** and **Icon**.

The word *metaphor*, as applied to computer terminology, of course derives from the literary use of the word *metaphor*, in which some object stands in for something else, or some object is used to convey a particular meaning. In Greek, the word *metaphora* lent itself to the literary terminology, but in contemporary Greece it also has a much more prosaic meaning. Paleontologist and author Stephen Jay Gould, in an essay in his book *Dinosaur in a Haystack*, reports seeing vans and luggage carts labeled *metaphora*, adding that "Metaphors can carry luggage as well as ideas."

Metering Nip

The line of contact between a soft, rubber-covered **metering roller** and a hard, chrome-covered **transfer roller** found in an offset press's **continuous-flow dampening system**. The width of the metering nip controls how much **fountain solution** is delivered from the fountain to the plate, and this nip can be varied. The angle at which the two rollers contact each other can also be varied, providing more or less metering of the film of fountain solution at the edges or the center, depending on the fountain solution requirements of the plate. (See **Dampening System**.)

Metering Roller

A resilient, rubber-covered roller used in an offset press's **continuous-flow dampening system**, in conjunction with a hard, chrome-covered **transfer roller**. The line of contact between the two rollers, called the **metering nip**, can be varied in width, depending on the desired thickness of the film of **fountain solution**. The metering roller (and/or the transfer roller) may be used as the fountain roller, or as the roller adjacent to the fountain roller. Adjusting the angle of the metering roller's contact with the transfer roller varies the thickness of the fountain solution film across the length of the rollers, depending on whether the edges or the center of the plate require greater quantities of fountain solution. (See **Dampening System**.)

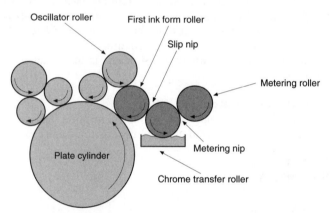

An inker-feed dampening system, showing the location of the metering nip and the metering roller.

In **flexography**, a *metering roller* is an alternate term for an **anilox roller**, a pitted metal roller used to transfer a metered film of ink from the **ink fountain** to the surface of the flexographic printing plate. See **Anilox Roller**.

Methanol

Alternate term for **methyl alcohol**. See **Methyl Alcohol**.

Methyl Alcohol

A **monohydric alcohol**—chemical formula CH_4O—obtained from the distillation of wood, the incomplete oxidation of natural gas, or by the synthetic combination of carbon monoxide and hydrogen. Highly toxic, methyl alcohol is used as a fuel, in antifreeze, or the manufacture of formaldehyde. It is also a powerful **solvent** and is used in printing inks and lacquers when high volatility is important. It is also used as a solvent or a thinner in some **screen printing** blockout solutions or to remove stencils from screen fabrics after a print run. Methyl alcohol is also known as **methanol**.

Methyl Carbitol

A trade name (and perhaps a more easily memorable name) for diethylene glycol mono methyl ether, a high-boiling-point **solvent** used widely in printing inks.

Methyl Cellosolve®

A brand of ethylene glycol mono methyl ether, a **solvent** used in many lacquer formulations, having high solvent power for **cellulose acetate**. See also **Cellosolve**.

Cellosolve is a registered trademark of Union Carbide Corporation.

Methyl Chloride

A colorless, poisonous gas—chemical formula CH_3Cl—used in combination with **ethyl alcohol** in some types of **solvent**s for **blockout solution**s in **screen printing**.

Methyl Ethyl Ketone (MEK)

A fast-drying but flammable organic **solvent**—chemical formula C_4H_8O—in the **ketone** family used in **flexographic** printing inks. It will readily dissolve **nitrocellulose** and vinyl lacquers, but it will cause swelling of **Buna N** synthetic rubber and, in large amounts, natural rubber. Methyl ethyl ketone, abbreviated **MEK**, is also known as *butanone*.

Methyl Isobutyl Ketone (MIBK)

A flammable organic **solvent**—chemical formula $C_6H_{12}O$—in the **ketone** family used in lacquer compounds and **resin**s.

Methyl Violet

See **PMTA Violet**.

Metric

A system of measurements used widely in most advanced countries, with the exception of the United States. The metric system uses the meter (equal to 3.3 ft., or 39.6 in.) as its basic unit of length, the liter (equal to 1.06 qt.) as its basic unit of volume, the gram (equal to 0.035 oz.) as its basic unit of mass (weight), and the Celsius degree as its basic unit of temperature. Most software programs allow measurements to be made in either English or metric units. Most **high-end** scanners and other devices use metric measurements, as well. (See also **Metric-to-Inches Conversion** and **Inches-to-Metric Conversion**.) Multiple quantities of **byte**s are also measured using **metric prefix**es. See **Metric Prefix**.

Metric Prefix

A prefix appended to a unit to indicate some multiple of that unit, usually multiples of 1,000. For example:

Kilo- (K)	10^3	Thousand
Mega- (M)	10^6	Million
Giga- (G)	10^9	Billion
Tera- (T)	10^{12}	Trillion
Peta- (P)	10^{15}	Quadrillion
Exa- (E)	10^{18}	Quintillion

In computing, metric prefixes are used to indicate multiple quantities of **bit**s and **byte**s. For example, one **kilobit** is equal to approximately 1,000 bits. (Actually, since computing is based on a **binary** system, not a decimal one, "kilo-" is used to refer to 2^{10}, which equals 1,024, the closest number to 1,000). See **Kilo-**, **Mega-**, **Giga-**, **Tera-**, **Peta-**, and **Exa-**.

Metrics

In computer typography, complete set of **font** information, such as size, leading, width, **kerning**, etc.

Metric-to-Inches Conversion

A conversion factor used to convert units of length expressed in the metric system (i.e., centimeters) to an English measurement (i.e., inches), as 1 cm equals 0.394 in. Thus, to convert to inches, the number of centimeters is multiplied by 0.394 (i.e., a length that is 12.7 cm long would be converted as 12.7 × 0.394 = 5 in.). To convert to millimeters, the number of inches is multiplied by 0.0394 (as there are 10 mm in a centimeter, and 0.0394 in. in a millimeter). Thus, a 127-mm length would be converted as 127 × 0.0394 = 5 in.

To convert from inches to metric, the number of centimeters in one inch can be used. (See **Inches-to-Metric Conversion**.)

Metropolitan Area Network (MAN)

In telecommunications and networking, a high-speed, public network capable of transmitting both voice and data (at a speed of up to 100 **megabit**s per second) over a distance of up to 50 miles. A MAN is larger than a **local area network (LAN)** yet smaller than a **wide area network (WAN)**. Also referred to as a **municipal area network**.

Meyer Bar

A wire-covered metal bar used to apply a controlled and consistent thickness of printing ink to the surface of a **substrate** as a means of testing a mixed ink's color, performance, appearance, and drying properties. A Meyer bar is also called a "Meyer rod."

Mezzotint

An early technique in copperplate engraving, invented in the 17th century by Ludwig von Siegen, that involves etching a copper or steel printing plate with a pattern of crosshatched lines or dots to provide the illusion of **continuous tone** images and gray values. The denser the pattern of lines or dots, the darker the tone. The mezzotint process eventually gave birth to **halftone** photography. In fact, the word *mezzotint* itself means, in Italian, "halftone." Mezzotinting is still used in design and illustration primarily as a special effect. (See illustration on next page.)

MFS

Abbreviation for **Macintosh File System**. See **Macintosh File System (MFS)**.

A mezzotint, in which dots represent continuous tones.

MG Paper

Abbreviation for paper that has been *machine-glazed*. See *Machine-Glazed*.

MHS

Abbreviation for *Message Handling Service*. See *Message Handling Service (MHS)*.

MHz

Abbreviation for *megahertz*, a measure of *frequency*. See *Megahertz*.

MIB

Abbreviation for *Management Information Base*. See *Management Information Base (MIB)*.

MIBK

See *Methyl Isobutyl Ketone (MIBK)*.

Mic

Abbreviated term for *microphone*. See *Microphone*. Also spelled *mike*.

Mice Type

In typography, a slang term for an extremely small *type size* or credit line.

MICR

See *Magnetic Ink Character Recognition (MICR)*.

MICR Check Paper

A type of *safety paper* designed specifically for checks printed with magnetic ink for use in *Magnetic Ink Character Recognition (MICR)* equipment.

Microchannel Architecture (MCA)

In computing, a 32-bit *expansion bus* developed by IBM in 1987 for its line of *personal computer*s. MCA was developed to facilitate *multiprocessing*, allowing various *expansion board*s to have a unique address and thus be more easily identified by the system, eliminating conflicts among various boards.

Microcode

A computer instruction that specifies what a *microprocessor* is supposed to do when it executes a particular *machine language* instruction.

Microcom Networking Protocol (MNP)

In networking and telecommunications, a set of communications protocols originally developed by Microcom but that has now become standard for *data compression* and *error detection*. The MNP standard comprises definitions for hardware error control (MNP 1–4), a means of data compression capable of a 2:1 *compression ratio* (MNP 5), a communications *protocol* starting with *V.22 bis* modulation, but switching to *V.29* if possible (MNP 6), another means of data compression that is capable of compression ratios as high as 3:1 (MNP 7), a means of allowing *half-duplex* devices to function as *full-duplex* devices (MNP 8), a means of providing high performance over a wide variety of data-link types (MNP 9), and a powerful error detection and correction program (MNP 10).

Microcomputer

An alternate term for a *personal computer*, or other type of small, inexpensive, low-capacity computer (as compared to larger *minicomputer*s and *mainframe*s) consisting of a simple *microprocessor*, input and output devices, memory, and peripherals.

Microfiche

A strip of film (such as microfilm) used to store photographic images of printed materials (such as back issues of a newspaper or magazine). A microfiche reader is required to enlarge the image to a size that is readable. Many readers are also capable of providing a hard copy of the displayed image.

Microkernel

In computing, a stripped-down *kernel* design developed by Carnegie Mellon University for use in its *Mach* operating system. Whereas most *operating system*s have but one large *kernel* that is always resident in the computer's memory and is responsible for such disparate system functions as *memory management*, the *file system*, networking, etc., the microkernel is a small kernel designed to only handle the most basic of system functions, such as loading and running applications, task-scheduling, etc., other more or less "optional" functions—such as networking, *virtual memory*, etc.—being available as add-on modules that run on top of the microkernel.

Micrometer

When pronounced with the accent on the second syllable, a device used to measure minute thicknesses utilizing a fixed deadweight pressure. A micrometer is used in measuring the thickness of paper *caliper*, or the packing of the plate and blanket on a printing press.

When pronounced with the accent on the first syllable, a unit equal to 0.000001 meter (one-millionth of a meter), also called a micron.

Microphone

A device for converting acoustic energy into electric signals that have similar wave characteristics. Sound-pressure variations in the air are converted into corresponding variations in electric current. The sound wave impinges on a slightly flexible surface (diaphragm), causing it to move in a manner corresponding to the movement of the air particles. The diaphragm by its motion causes a corresponding change in an electric circuit. Telephone transmitters comprise the largest class of microphones, but the term is applied mostly to other varieties, such as hearing aids, sound-recording systems (magnetic and digital tape recorders), dictating machines, and public-address systems. Microphones are extensively used in communications systems, radio or wire.

Microprocessor

A single chip containing all the integrated circuits that make up a computer's *central processing unit*. The microprocessor, in desktop computers, is essentially synonymous with the central processing unit, as it is the device responsible for performing all calculations and functions required by other areas of the computer. IBM *PC*s and *IBM-compatible computer*s use microprocessors manufactured by Intel (including the 286, 386, 486, and Pentium series of chips) while the Apple Macintosh utilizes microprocessors manufactured by Motorola (including the 680X0 and PowerPC series of chips).

Microprocessors are also the main components of other types of computerized devices, such as calculators.

Microsecond

A measure of time or rate of speed equal to one millionth (0.000001, or 10^{-6}) of a second. The speeds of some computers are measured in microseconds. See also *Millisecond* and *Nanosecond*.

Microsoft Mouse

In computing, a standard *mouse* developed by Microsoft that makes use of two buttons. Some standard mice use one button or three buttons.

Microsoft Windows™

See *Windows™*.

Micro-to-Mainframe

Any communications link between a *microcomputer* and a *mainframe*. Typically, the microcomputer (or *PC*) desir-

ing the connection needs to utilize software (called *terminal emulation* software) that allows it to access the data stored on the mainframe system.

Microwave

A form of electromagnetic radiation (or section of the *electromagnetic spectrum*) possessing a wavelength between 1 millimeter and 30 centimeters, and a very high *frequency* (between 1 and 30 gigahertz). Microwaves are used not only for cooking purposes (in microwave ovens) but also for *broadband* communications. Since microwave transmission requires *line-of-sight* communication, long-distance transmissions require repeater stations every 20 miles or so, to compensate for the Earth's curvature. Typically, microwaves are used to transmit information from an *Earth station* to a communications satellite and back to another Earth station.

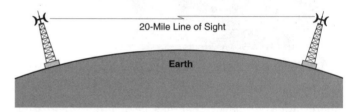

Microwave transmission.

Middletone

The tones or shades of a printed image or original lying between the *highlight*s and the *shadow*s. Also spelled as two words, *middle tone*, or abbreviated *midtone*.

Middletone Placement

In *halftone* reproduction, a means of determining the sizes of the *middletone* dots, accomplished during *scanner* setup by indicating the points on the input setup *grayscale* where *shadow*s, *diffuse highlight*s, and *middletone*s are to lie, to ensure proper *contrast* in the final reproduced image. This controls the ultimate sizes of the middletone dots that, if not done properly, results in poor color reproduction. Other factors that must be taken into account during middletone placement are the anticipated *dot gain* from the printing process and the type of paper to be utilized. Also of importance is the *screen ruling* that will be used to generate the halftone itself.

MIDI

Abbreviation for *Musical Instrument Digital Interface*. See *Musical Instrument Digital Interface (MIDI)*.

Midrange

Descriptive of any system or device—in particular, a page makeup system—that is more expensive and of higher quality than *low-end* desktop systems, but less expensive and of lesser quality than *high-end* color electronic publishing systems. Midrange refers more to cost than output quality, however. Midrange systems usually are cannibalizations of both the desktop and high-end systems; they may use desktop computers but with high-end *film recorder*s, *image-setter*s, or scanners. They may use off-the-shelf software, or special applications, and may or may not use *PostScript* output. A midrange system is generally considered to be in the $250,000 range for a computer, scanner, proofing device, and film recorder.

Midsplit

In telecommunications and networking, a *broadband* cabling system used to divide available frequencies into two sets, one for transmission and one for reception.

Midtone

Abbreviation for *middletone*. See *Middletone*.

MIF

Abbreviation for *minimum internetworking functionality*. See *Minimum Internetworking Functionality (MIF)*.

Mil

A unit of length equal to 0.001 in. (one one-thousandth of an inch) used for measuring wire diameters or paper thicknesses. The word *mil* is derived from the Latin word *millesimus*, meaning "thousandth."

Mileage

Term for the total amount of surface area a given quantity of ink (or paper *coating*) will cover, an important factor in the informed ordering of ink quantities.

Milking

A form of *piling*, characterized by the accumulation of paper debris on the nonimage areas of the printing *blanket*. Milking differs from *powdering* in that milking tends to comprise particles of non-moisture-resistant *coating*s that are loosened by the wet areas of the blanket and are transferred to the blanket. Milking becomes severe typically only when being run through multicolor presses, as the loose coating particles are continually pulled off by successive impressions. Milking is accelerated by water on the blanket. Powdering, on the other hand, is accelerated by the lack of water on the blanket. If milking and powdering become severe enough, they can interfere with ink transfer at the edges of image areas, and accelerate plate or blanket wear. See *Piling*.

Mill Boards

Thick, high-*basis weight* cardboard used for bookbinding and box-making.

Milling

A secondary step in the manufacturing of printing ink, following *mixing*, in which particles of *pigment*, or coloring matter, are further ground and dispersed in the fluid ink *vehicle*. In the mixing stage, the solid pigment is mixed with the fluid vehicle, and in the production of many types of ink only one or more mixing stages is necessary. In some types of ink, however, the particles of pigment are large and/or hard enough to warrant further refining and dispersion in one of several types of milling devices, which vary in method and configuration, but all are based on the principle of applying shearing and/or frictional forces to the ink *slurry* (the mixture of vehicle and pigment) to break up and disperse the particles.

Depending on the nature of the ink produced, one of several types of mills may be utilized. *Flexographic* and *gravure* inks, due to their thin, highly volatile *solvent*-based vehicles, need to be milled in closed systems, such as a *ball mill* or a closed *sand/shot mill*. Heavy *letterpress* inks may be milled in ball mills, but their heaviness may necessitate the use of more powerful mixing and milling systems, such as high-speed dispersers.

(See *Three-Roll Mill*, *Ball Mill*, *Sand/Shot Mill*, and *Colloid Mill*.)

Milling Head

In *perfect binding*, a device used to remove the folded *spine*s of book *signature*s prior to the application of the adhesive. See *Perfect Binding*.

Millisecond

A measure of time or rate of speed equal to one thousandth (0.001, or 10^{-3}) of a second. The speeds of some computers are measured in milliseconds. Abbreviated *ms*. See also *Microsecond* and *Nanosecond*.

Milori Blue

A green shade of *Iron Blue*, an *inorganic color pigment* used in printing inks. See *Iron Blue*.

MIME

An abbreviation for *Multipurpose Internet Mail Extensions*. See *Multipurpose Internet Mail Extensions (MIME)*.

Mimeograph

A type of imaging and duplication process in which an image is transferred to absorbent paper *substrate*s by means of a chemical dye.

Mimeograph Paper

A variety of *bond paper* with a rough, absorbent surface designed specifically for use in *mimeograph* machines. See *Bond Paper*.

Mineral Blacks

See *Black Iron Oxides*.

Mineral Oil

Any of a variety of high-molecular-weight *hydrocarbon* compounds derived from petroleum sources and used in printing ink *vehicle*s.

Mineral Spirits

A *volatile* naphtha distillate of petroleum (commonly an intermediate product between gasoline and benzene) widely used as a *solvent* and a *thinner* in printing inks, especially paint-type inks used in *screen printing*.

Minicomputer

A computer system that is smaller and less powerful than a *mainframe*, yet larger and more powerful than a *micro-computer* (i.e., a desktop personal computer or workstation). Minicomputers have an advantage over both mainframes and microcomputers in that they tend to be more modular than mainframes, allowing them to be modified to fit into specialized computer systems, and they have a greater capacity and power than microcomputers, which allows them to be used in smallish multi-user (i.e., up to 10) systems.

MiniDisc (MD)

A type of *magneto-optical disc* developed by Sony, which is written to and read from in accordance with *Orange Book* specifications.

Mini-Hard Disk

A *hard disk* housed on a *PCMCIA* card. See *PCMCIA*.

Minimize

In computing, especially by means of a *graphical user interface*, to replace an open *window* with an icon. When an open application is hidden from view, its open windows are replaced with a small icon representing that application. When the program is desired to be active again, the icon can be clicked on and the open windows can be restored to the display.

Minimum Density

In imaging, the lowest image *density* achievable with a particular configuration of devices or *substrate*s. Also known as D_{min}. See also *Maximum Density*.

Minimum Internetworking Functionality (MIF)

In networking, a guiding principle behind *ISO* standards for *local area network* workstation complexity when connecting to systems, computers, or networks external to the *LAN*.

Minimum Interword Space

In typography, the minimum amount of space allowed between words, used in setting tolerances for *justification*. See also *Maximum Interword Space* and *Justification*.

Miniscule

Alternate term for a *lowercase* letter. See *Lowercase*.

Minus Leading

In typography, the typesetting of copy utilizing less than the minimum recommended amount of *leading*, i.e., 12 on 11½. See *Line Spacing*.

9-pt. New Caledonia, Set Solid
In typography, the typesetting of copy utilizing less than the minimum recommended amount of leading, i.e., 12 on 11½. See Line Spacing.

9-pt. New Caledonia, Leading of 8.5 Points
In typography, the typesetting of copy utilizing less than the minimum recommended amount of leading, i.e., 12 on 11½. See Line Spacing.

Minus leading.

Minus Letterspacing

In typography, the subtraction of space between letters or other characters. See *Letterspacing*.

9-pt. New Caledonia, Normal Letterspacing
In typography, the typesetting of copy utilizing less than the minimum recommended amount of leading, i.e., 12 on 11½. See Line Spacing.

9-pt. New Caledonia, –2 Units of Letterspacing
In typography, the typesetting of copy utilizing less than the minimum recommended amount of leading, i.e., 12 on 11½. See Line Spacing.

9-pt. New Caledonia, –4 Units of Letterspacing
In typography, the typesetting of copy utilizing less than the minimum recommended amount of leading, i.e., 12 on 11½. See Line Spacing.

Minus letterspacing.

Minutes, Seconds, Frames

A form of *time code* used for multimedia productions and *audio CD*s. Abbreviated *MSF*. See *Time Code*.

MIPS

Abbreviation for *millions of instructions per second*, a measure of the average rate at which a computer can process and execute machine-language instructions. A *mainframe* is capable of on the order of 2.0 MIPS (or 2,000,000 instructions per second), while a personal computer may only be capable of about 0.5 MIPS (or 500,000 instructions per second).

Mirror

In graphics and imaging, the reversal of an image about a central axis.

Mirror Resist

A type of ink used in *screen printing* for printing on glass that will be made into a mirror. A mirror resist ink is composed of materials that will withstand the silvering acids used in the "mirrorizing" of glass.

MIS

Abbreviation for *management information system*. See *Management Information System (MIS)*.

Misread

In computing and telecommunications, descriptive of a transmission to the **host** computer that has been decoded incorrectly.

Misregister

A printing defect in which successive passes of a printed sheet through a press do not print an image in the spot they were intended to, typically a problem in multicolor printing. Misregister typically occurs due to changes in a paper's dimensions, either from moisture gain or loss, or from mechanical stretching. An overabundance of **fountain solution** can contribute to the dimensional changes of paper that contribute to misregister. (See **Dimensional Stability** and **Moisture Content**.) Misregister is commonly caused on web presses by poor side-to-side alignment of the web with the printing unit or variations in web tension. See **Register**.

Mission-Critical Application

Any computer program that is vital to the interests and functioning of a corporation using it. Also known as a **line-of-business application**.

Mistake

Any human error made when dealing with machines (or, some would say, even dealing with machines in the first place). Mistakes are distinguished from **crash**es, **bug**s, or **glitch**es that are strictly machine errors, although mistakes can be responsible for crashes, bugs, and glitches.

Misting

See **Ink Misting**.

Miter Join

In computer graphics, a point of intersection between two strokes in which the join comes to a point, but one that the angle is limited, as on the apexes of some typefaces, such as the capital letter "A" in Palatino:

See also **Bevel Join** and **Miter Limit**.

Miter Limit

In computer graphics, the number of degrees that the angle formed by the intersection of two strokes is limited, so as to prevent excessively pointed joints. See **Bevel Join** and **Miter Join**.

Mitography

An alternate term for **screen printing**, coined by Albert Kosloff and derived from the Greek words *mitos* ("thread of fibers") and *graphein* ("to write"). See **Screen Printing**.

Mix

In audio and video production, to combine two or more audio or video sources into a single tape. See also **Audio Mixing**.

Mixing

The primary stage in ink manufacturing, in which the solid particles of **pigment**, or coloring matter, are introduced and dispersed into the fluid ink **vehicle**. The pigment particles can be in flake, chip, flushed, or predispersed form. Depending upon the desired end-use characteristics of the ink and the size and hardness of the particles themselves, the ink **slurry** (the combination of pigment and vehicle) may require one or more passes through the mixer, or may require further **milling** to further grind and disperse the particles. Many inks today, such as inks used in web offset lithography, utilize **flushed color** pigments that are then dispersed into the vehicle by high-speed and high-shear mixers or high-speed dispersers, and are then sent right to the **filtration** stage without the need for further milling.

In typography, the term *mixing* refers to the setting of a word, line, or block of type containing more than one **typeface** or **point size**.

Mixing White

Any type of **white pigment**, either transparent or opaque, added to printing inks to produce tints of other colors.

MJ

Abbreviation for **modular jack**. See **Modular Jack**.

MMC

Abbreviation for the **Multimedia Marketing Council**. See **Multimedia Marketing Council (MMC)**.

MMCD

Abbreviation for **multimedia CD**. See **Multimedia CD**.

MMJ

Abbreviation for **modified modular jack**. See **Modified Modular Jack**.

MMU

Abbreviation for **memory management unit**. See **Memory Management Unit (MMU)**.

Mnemonics

Term for names, abbreviations, etc., used to help an individual remember longer pieces of information. An example would be "HOMES," a simple word used by grade-school children to recall the five Great Lakes (*H*uron, *O*ntario, *M*ichigan, *E*rie, *S*uperior). Similarly, a more complicated mnemonic—"Martha Visits Every Morning, Just Stays Until Noon, Period"—comprises a purportedly easy-to-recall sentence used to remember the names of the planets of the solar system in order of distance from the Sun (usually; at this writing, Pluto's eccentric orbit has actually brought it temporarily closer to the Sun than Neptune).

In computing, mnemonics are used to improve the efficiency of computer memories by using abbreviations of **address** terms. Also, in computer programming, mnemonics are used by various **assembly language**s as an aid to the programmer, reducing complex sets of functions, routines, and formats to short, easy-to-remember symbols or terms.

The word *mnemonic* itself is pronounced "nemonic," and it derives from the Greek word *mnemonikos*, meaning "of, or pertaining to, memory."

MNP

Abbreviation for *Microcom Networking Protocol*. See *Microcom Networking Protocol (MNP)*.

Mobile Computing

The ability to work on a computer without needing to be tied to a central location, such as an office. Mobile computing usually involves the use of a *laptop computer*, a *portable computer*, or even a *luggable* (if increased upper-body strength is desired). Such computing can be accomplished from home, from a train or plane, from a beach in the Bahamas, or some other remote (and perhaps undisclosed) location. The use of modems can put one's remote computer in direct contact with an office, while cellular phones, pagers, and call-forwarding can all be used to give a *road warrior* all the benefits of working back at the office without needing to actually be there.

Mock-up

Alternate term for a *dummy*. See *Dummy*.

Modeling

In 3D image creation or *CAD* graphics, one of several steps in creating an illustration—either as a still image or as part of an animation—that has the illusion of three dimensions, surface texture, and detail. Geometric modeling programs typically use mathematical equations to describe lines, curves, and other aspects of the illustration. The program must also be able to describe various shapes in the proper spatial relationship with other shapes. The three basic types of modeling are wireframe, surface, and solid.

Wireframe. A *wireframe model* is the least processor-intensive type of model, consisting solely of connected lines and curves that resemble wires. They are used to provide a rough general shape and detail. Also called a *skeleton*.

Surface. A *surface model* is used by some graphics programs to provide a 3D image with the illusion of solidity, commonly by "filling in" a wireframe with the specified surface detail, and removing any hidden lines that one would not be able to see if it had been an actual physical object. Unlike *solid model*s below, surface models are not solid all the way through; the surface texture is merely a kind of "skin" stretched over the wireframe.

Solid. A *solid model* is the most complex and advanced type of 3D modeling in which the object is treated by the program as being completely solid, or having both surface and internal structure. A solid sphere could have a tunnel cut into it, which would resemble a tunnel cut through an actual solid sphere. Solid modeling is the most processor-intensive form of modeling.

It is primarily the technique of shading—or applying different shades of the primary *hue*—that provide the illusion of three dimensions in both surface and solid modeling. The texture of an orange peel, for example, is rendered by means of applying the least predominant color to selected portions of the image. Too much of such a color, however, will result in an overall darkening of the image.

Modeling Coordinates

A *coordinate system* used for three-dimensional *modeling* in which each object possesses its own set of coordinates that can then be converted to a set of *world coordinates*.

Modem

An abbreviated term for "modulator/demodulator," or a peripheral device that converts (or modulates) digital computer data into *analog* audio signals for transmission along telephone lines. A modem also receives transmitted analog signals from over the phone line and converts it to digital data. The modem also performs *error detection and correction*, *data compression*, and controls the speed at which data is transmitted.

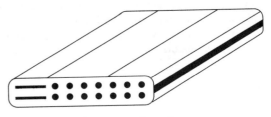

An external modem.

Modem Eliminator

In telecommunications and networking, any device that allows two *personal computer*s to be connected to each without the need for a proper *modem*. In *synchronous* systems, such a device needs to provide timing and synchronization functions. In an *asynchronous* system, however, such a device need only be a *null modem* cable.

Modem Server

Alternate term for an *asynchronous communications server*. See *Asynchronous Communications Server*.

Modern

Descriptive of a *typeface* designed in the early 19th century characterized by high contrast between thick and thin strokes and thin, straight *serif*s. Based on a modified version of Old Style, they were originally developed by Firmin Didot and Giambattista Bodoni. Also called *didone*.

Modern typefaces are identifiable with straight, flat serifs, no bracketing, and thicker vertical strokes. The Bodoni typeface was popular with newspapers for over 100 years.

Modified Modular Jack

A variety of *modular jack* developed by Digital Equipment Corporation, comprising a six-pin connector used to connect *serial* cables to computer hardware devices. A modified modular jack (abbreviated *MMJ*) is distinguished from a conventional *RJ-11* modular jack (used to connect telephone lines to wall outlets) by having a side-locking rather than a center-locking tab.

Modular

Descriptive of any system or objects (such as furniture or computer system components) available in small, discrete units that can be combined in a wide variety of ways so as to suit a range of conditions.

Modular Jack

Any of a variety of different types of *plug*s or *jack*s used to connect telephones and telephone equipment to wall outlets. See, in particular, *RJ-11*. See also *Modified Modular Jack*. Modular jack is often abbreviated *MJ*.

Modulation

In communications and broadcasting, a process by which one characteristic of a signal or waveform is varied in accordance with another characteristic. Modulation is performed so as to transform an originating signal (such as from a computer) into one that is compatible with the transmission medium and communications equipment. Upon reception, the modulated signal needs to undergo *demodulation*. (Hence the term *modem*, which is a device that performs both modulation and demodulation functions, is a contraction of "*mod*ulator/*dem*odulator.")

In broadcasting, *modulation* refers to a similar process of overlaying an electrical signal (derived from the sound wave produced by, say, a radio station) onto a carrier wave. See *Amplitude Modulation (AM)* and *Frequency Modulation (FM)*.

See also *Pulse Code Modulation (PCM)*.

Modulator

A device used in imaging equipment that varies the output of each beam of light exposing photosensitive film, paper, printing plates, or press cylinders. Modulators can be optical, acoustical, or crystal.

Module

Any interchangeable component of a system. See *Modular*.

In *bar code* scanning, the term *module* refers to the narrowest bar or space in a bar code.

In computer programming, a *module* is any small, self-contained portion of a larger program, written and tested separately from the rest of the program. Typically, a module is designed to perform only one specific task or function.

Moiré

An undesirable optical effect found in *halftone* reproductions resulting from *interference* patterns caused by incorrect *screen angles*. Moiré patterns (in optics, called the *moiré effect*, and named after a type of woven fabric also called "moiré," etymologically deriving from the word "mohair") are characterized by the appearance of lines or dots at points where different sets of halftone lines or dots conflict, the points of conflict serving to reinforce the undesirable optical pattern. Also spelled "moire," without the accent over the "e," but always pronounced "mwah-RAY." See *Screen Angles*. (See Color Plate 17.)

An undesirable *moiré* pattern is also found in television and video images, also caused when two patterns interfere. This is most often seen when a person in a televised image wears a finely striped jacket or shirt. The odd vibrating effect seen between the stripes is an example of moiré.

Moiré effects.

Moisture Content

The amount of water contained in paper expressed as a percentage of the paper's total weight. The primary constituents of paper, fibers of *cellulose*, have a strong affinity for water and will gain (or lose) it readily, depending on the amount of moisture in the air, or the *relative humidity* of the surrounding environment. This *hygroscopic* characteristic of paper makes it dimensionally unstable, as the length and/or width of a paper can change depending on how much water the paper has gained or lost. The moisture content of paper also affects its various mechanical, surface, and electrical properties, and contributes to the qualities of *printability* and *runnability* in the various printing processes.

When cellulose fibers absorb water, they expand primarily in width, and only slightly in length, which means that paper has less dimensional stability *against the grain* than *with the grain*. This consideration affects whether *long-grain* or *short-grain* paper is required for a particular printing process (see *Grain*). For example, a 5% moisture gain will result in a 0.05% expansion with the grain, but a 0.23% expansion against the grain. (The percentage of a paper's expansion or reduction as a result of water gain or loss is called its *hygroexpansivity*.) Dimensional changes, however, vary according to the degree of fiber *refining* that has been done, and the amount of inorganic *fillers* that have been added. Fillers, being inorganic materials like *clay* are resistant to the loss or gain of moisture and contribute to a paper's dimensional stability. Moisture loss or gain can also occur in varying degrees across the surface of a paper, depending upon which portions of the paper are exposed to the atmosphere. Paper sheets exhibiting *wavy edges* or paper rolls with baggy edges have gained moisture from the atmosphere, while paper sheets or paper rolls with tight edges have lost moisture to the atmosphere. Since paper is generally two-sided (i.e., having a *wire side* and a *felt side*), and the grain is more pronounced on the wire side, absorption of moisture will occur unevenly, and the paper will curl. (Generally, increased moisture content will cause a curl toward the felt side of the paper.) The moisture content of paper will also vary according to how it has been conditioned. (See *Hysteresis*.)

Dimensional changes usually cause the most problems in multicolor printing work, as dimensional changes that occur between passes through the press can result in misalignment of successive colors. For sheetfed offset paper, determining a paper's *equilibrium moisture content* (its moisture content when equal with the relative humidity of the pressroom) or the *equilibrium relative humidity* of the room (the relative humidity that is equal to the moisture content of the paper) is important. Generally speaking, paper should be printed when it is in equilibrium with the environment, but for multicolor work, the best results are obtained when the paper's moisture content is slightly higher than its equilibrium moisture content. The length of the paper's contact with the press *dampening system* (i.e., slower sheetfed offset presses versus high-speed web offset presses) also affects its moisture content. The moisture content is less of a consideration with web paper than with

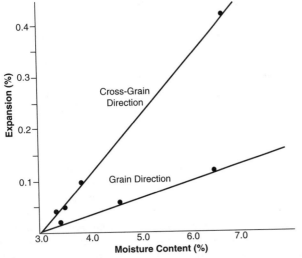

Effect of moisture content on paper size. Note that paper size expands with increasing moisture content, the effect being more pronounced in the cross-grain direction.

sheet paper. But paper also tends to print better when its moisture content is on the high side. Low moisture content tends to produce hard, brittle papers that generate web breaks, do not provide a good printing cushion, and tend to crack when folded. However, coated papers with high moisture content tend to cause *blistering* during *heatset drying*. (See *Blister*.)

A paper's moisture content is determined in a variety of ways. One method is the "oven-drying method," in which a sample is weighed, placed in an oven at 221°F for an hour, and weighed again. The difference in weight divided by the original weight times one hundred is the percent moisture of the paper. Quick determinations of moisture content made during papermaking are accomplished with infrared or microwave sensors. Results from these sensors can be used to alter the moisture content of the paper if necessary. A moisture meter, containing sensors that use measures of electrical resistance or electrical holding power, can also be used to gauge moisture content of paper.

Moisture-Set Ink

An ink that dries, or "sets" by *precipitation* of the pigment out of the *vehicle*. Moisture-set inks typically utilize glycol-based vehicles. Water-insoluble *resin*s are dissolved in a water-soluble solvent, usually glycol (an alcohol also used in antifreeze). When moisture comes in contact with this type of vehicle, the glycol is dissolved, and the resin precipitates out, dragging the pigment with it. Glycol vehicles are commonly used in *letterpress* printing, and their lack of odor makes them useful for printing food packaging. Moisture-set ink in which the moisture is provided in the form of water vapor or steam is called *steamset ink*. (See *Glycol Vehicle*.)

Moisture Welt

A paper web defect characterized by either a raised welt, band, or wrinkle located near the outer portion of the roll and run in the *machine direction*, caused by *cross-grain* expansion of the outer layers of paper due to absorption of moisture. Moisture welts result when a roll is exposed to higher *relative humidity* or to warm air. Moisture welts typically only affect the outer layers of the paper roll and can usually be cut off. Running a roll containing moisture welts through the press will cause *misregister*.

Molding Press

A platen press used for making molded rubber *flexographic* plates or the molds from which the plates are made. See *Plate: Flexography: Rubber Plates*.

Molleton

A thick fabric made from cotton used as a covering for offset press *dampening roller*s. See *Dampening System*.

Molybdate Orange

A chrome-based *inorganic color pigment* used in printing inks. Molybdate Orange is one of several shades of orange red pigment, with good *lightfastness*, but a tendency to become dark when exposed to air. They are highly opaque and are resistant to heat, but susceptible to reaction with acids and alkalis. As with many of the inorganic pigments, its use is waning due to its toxicity. (See also *Inorganic Color Pigments*.)

Other related shades are *Chrome Scarlet* and *Orange Chrome* (*CI Pigment Red 104 No. 77605*).

Monitor Routine

Alternate term for *executive routine*. See *Executive Routine*.

Monochlorbenzene

A high-power *solvent* used with *vinyl resin* inks and lacquers, as well as inks and other substances containing *ethyl cellulose*.

Monochromatic

Possessing a single color. Synonymous with *monochrome*.

Monochrome

Literally, "one color," used to refer to any image that comprises a single color, although the term is most often used to refer to a black-and-white image.

Monochrome Display Adapter (MDA)

A type of computer monitor introduced in 1981 by IBM with the original *PC*. The MDA featured a 720×348-*pixel* display, a nonvariable 9×14-pixel character matrix, 80 columns per screen, and 18 *kilohertz* operation. It was also a *monochromatic* monitor (the single color being green). The MDA monitor was designed solely for word processing and was soon superseded by the *CGA* monitor. See *CGA*.

Monofilament

Any strand (such as that which comprises a *screen printing* fabric) made of a single thread, as opposed to a *multifilament*.

Monofilament Polyester

A *screen printing* fabric woven from single threads of *polyester*. Such screens are called *monofilament polyester screens*.

Monofilament Polyester Screen

A *screen printing* screen made from single strands of *polyester*.

Monohydric Alcohols

A family of organic compounds containing one hydroxyl group (–OH), used as *solvent*s in *gravure* and *flexographic* printing inks, characterized by their high *volatility* (or ability to evaporate quickly at low temperatures), that expedites ink *vehicle* drying and ink setting. Examples of monohydric alcohols are methyl alcohol, ethyl alcohol, propyl alcohol, and isopropyl alcohol. (See also *Polyhydric Alcohol*.)

Monomer

A low-molecular-weight compound that can be reacted and united with other low-molecular-weight compounds to form a long, higher-molecular-weight chain-like *polymer*. The formation of polymers—a chemical process called *polymerization*—is the basis of the drying of many types of printing inks, commonly preceded by the chemical process of *oxidation*, and many printing ink *resin*s are produced by the process of polymerization. A monomer is considered the basic structural unit of a polymer, and various smaller combinations of monomers are described as dimers, trimers, or *oligomers*.

Monospaced

In typography, descriptive of characters of a typeface all having the same width. The lowercase "i" and "m"—which would have different widths in *proportional width* typefaces—are identical in monospaced typefaces. Consequently, it is necessary to extend the "i" and condense the "m" to keep their spacing consistent relative to other characters. Typewriters and line printers are the primary users of monospaced typefaces. These are usually 10-pitch, or 10 characters to the inch (also called *pica*), or 12-pitch, 12 characters to the inch (called *elite*). Newer approaches offer finer *escapement*, thus allowing these faces to have quasi-proportional spacing. However, a monospaced character is a monospaced character, no matter how you space it.

ABCDEFGHIJKLMNOP
abcdefghijklmnop

Courier, a monospaced typeface in which all characters have the same width.

Monotone

Any artwork reproduced in only one color. Usually descriptive of black-and-white reproductions.

Monotype

A mechanized typecasting device that enabled a keyboard operator to set type by punching holes in a paper ribbon, which then triggered the casting of individual letters. See *Type and Typography: History of Type*.

Montage

In imaging, a series or combination of pictures, portions of pictures, or other images placed in a certain order so as to convey a story.

Morgue

In desktop publishing, term for a collection of reference materials, such as an encyclopedia, dictionary, thesaurus, and materials from a *swipe file*, such as *clip art*.

Morison, Stanley

Stanley Morison (1889–1967), English typographer, scholar, and historian of printing, born in Wanstead, Essex, is best remembered for his design of Times New Roman, which first appeared in print in 1932 in London's *Times,* later called the most successful new typeface of the first half of the 20th century. He was typographic adviser to Monotype Corp. (1923) and Cambridge University Press (1923–59); editor of *The Fleuron,* a typographic journal (1926–30); and author of *Four Centuries of Fine Printing* (1924) and *First Principles of Typography* (1936). In the second decade of the 20th century, the Monotype Corporation had begun to develop a version of the Caslon (1734) type for their machines.

Morison joined Monotype in 1922 for their revival of a Garamond type (actually a revival of a revival cut by Jean Jannon in the 1620s). Over the next nine years and under Morison's direction, Monotype released revivals of roughly a dozen historic roman faces, including Centaur, a revival of Jenson's type designed by the American Bruce Rogers; Bembo and Poliphilus, adapted from Francesco Griffo's roman types; and eventually in 1931 Morison's own Times New Roman, based on 17th century styles and which would become one of the century's most used typefaces. Morison was not so much a designer as a champion of designs. One of his greatest achievements is the rediscovery of Francesco Griffo's work, especially the type in Pietro Bembo's *De Aetna* of 1495. Before Morison, few typographic scholars had much to say about the Aldine types, generally preferring Jenson's specimens. Blaming the poor reputation of Griffo's type on the poor specimens that had come down to contemporary scholars, Morison encouraged the development of Monotype's Bembo, released in 1929, and demonstrated that it was this type that had been the model for the popular French "old-faces" of Claude Garamond in the mid-16th century. Bembo was one of the most popular revivals ever released by Monotype. In Morison's words, "In the pages of *De Aetna,* the type, then new, looks almost as fresh as if it had come off a present-day typecaster."

Morphing

In computer graphics and imaging, a means by which one image is gradually (or quickly) changed into another by means of animation. Essentially, morphing operates on the same principle as typical *animation*: the two images (the "before" and the "after") are considered as *key frame*s, and the computer performs the *in-betweening* in very small increments, so the shape and color of the first image seamlessly turns into those of the second image. The first popular example of this was in Michael Jackson's video for the song "Black and White," but by now it has become very com-

Morphing a square into a circle, with five intermediate steps.

monplace, especially in science fiction and horror movies. (See *COLOR PLATE 10.*)

Morris, William

In the late 1880s William Morris, a businessman, socialist, and key figure in the Arts & Crafts movement in England, began work on new typefaces that would be the basis of the Kelmscott Press. Morris saw a need to revitalize printing. Morris felt that the art of book printing had reached its peak in 15th-century Venice and that it had been going downhill ever since. His aim was to produce books that lived up to the standards of the early Venetian printers. Morris cut three typefaces for the Kelmscott Press: two blackletter and a roman that was based on his interpretation of Jenson's roman of 1470—which Morris saw as the epitome of roman letters. The Kelmscott Press was a revival of handpress practices and almost medieval workmanship. Morris engaged in monumental efforts in woodblock engraving and decoration, and held true to the earliest standards of fine printing: that the page be as "black" as possible, by way of a combination of heavy type, rich illustration, tight leading, and close word spacing. The fifty books produced by the Kelmscott Press are works of art and transcended the so-called "private press" movement because of their impact on British printing as a whole. William Morris fought against the degeneration in typography. He printed books with handpresses and handmade paper. He revived gothic blackletter types to combine with heavy woodcut borders, creating richly decorated but difficult-to-read art objects.

Mortise

In video production, to reduce the size of a video image and surround it with a (usually) black or white border.

Mortise Copy

In page layout, text that is typeset over an illustration by removing portions of the picture area so as to allow the text to be legible.

Mosaic

The first *World Wide Web* and *Internet* browsing software, developed by the National Center for Supercomputer Applications. Although it was Mosaic that stimulated the widespread interest in the Internet and the Web, it has largely given way to the more popular Netscape program. See *Web Browser*.

Mosaic Filter

A special effect that can be applied to digital images that breaks an image up into small shaded squares that causes the image to look as if it were made up of small mosaic tiles.

Motherboard

In computing, the main circuit board containing the *central processing unit (CPU)* chip, the *random-access memory (RAM)* chips, the *read-only memory (ROM)* chip, and on occasion any installed *coprocessor*s.

Motif

In computing, a ***graphical user interface*** developed for the ***UNIX*** operating system by Open Software Foundation.

Motion Blur

In ***animation***, a means of more effectively simulating the illusion of motion by drawing or painting in the wake of an object a vague blur in the shape of the object. This helps the eye of the viewer more easily fix on the path of the object.

Motion-Control Photography

In motion picture photography and videography, the use of computers to accurately control the movements of one or more cameras.

Motion Graphics

Alternate term for ***animation***. See ***Animation***.

Motion Picture Experts Group

See ***MPEG***.

Motion Video

Any video recording or production containing moving images. Although this is what is usually meant by the term *video*, see also ***Still Video***.

Mottle

A printing defect characterized by a spotty, nonuniform appearance in solid printed areas. Different print characteristics have different types of mottle; there is a density mottle, a gloss mottle, or a color mottle, depending on what aspect is being affected. All forms of mottle are typically the result of nonuniform ink absorbency across the surface of the paper. A mottled appearance is also called ***galvanized***. A complex type of mottle is called ***back-trap mottle (BTM)***. (See ***Back-Trap Mottle [BTM]***.)

A type of mottle characteristic of calendered papers is known as ***coating mottle***.

In ***binding and finishing***, the term *mottle* is used to describe a type of ***edge staining***, a decorative treatment of the trimmed edges of a book. See ***Edge Staining*** and ***Sprinkled Edges***.

Mottled Finish

A paper ***finish*** characterized by an intentional nonuniform distribution of blotches of high and low ***gloss***.

Mouldmade Paper

A ***deckle*** edge paper produced on a ***cylinder machine***. *Mouldmade* is also an alternate term for ***handmade paper***. See ***Handmade Paper***.

Mount

To attach a piece of art, copy, etc., to a surface, such as a ***process camera*** copyboard, a ***scanner*** drum, etc., for processing, photography, scanning, etc. *Mount* also means to attach a plate (or other image carrier) to a printing press.

In computing, the term *mount* means to load a disk or other volume into a system so that it can be read from and/or written to.

In networking, the term *mount* refers to a means by which a network ***node*** accesses network resources.

Mounting Board

A stiff paperboard, produced by laminating a high-quality paper onto a heavier board, used to mount photographs and prints.

Mouse

In computing, an input device used to move a pointer or cursor about the screen, for positioning text-insertion points or for drawing, painting, or other graphics functions. Essentially, a mouse contains a rotating ball. As it moves on a flat surface, electrical signals within it describe its coordinates relative to the screen, and these signals are converted to the digital information needed to show its current position on the computer display. Most mice have one, two, or three buttons used for selecting (or ***clicking*** and ***double-clicking*** on) screen objects. (See ***Mouse Button***.) The mouse was so-named because the three-button variety, with a wire protruding from the back, vaguely resembled the rodent, replete with eyes, nose and tail. As if to firmly cement the metaphor, it has been found, albeit informally, that cats do in fact like to play with them.

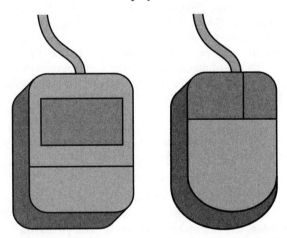

A one-button mouse (left) and a two-button mouse (right).

Mouse Button

One or more buttons on a computer ***mouse***. Different computer systems and different manufacturers make mice with varying number of buttons, each configuration altering the way objects can be selected and features activated. The simplest configuration is the ***Macintosh*** mouse, which has but one button with which all ***clicking*** and ***double-clicking*** is performed. The ***Microsoft Mouse*** has two buttons, while the ***Mouse Systems Mouse*** has three. Some mice have more than three buttons. Usually, the extra buttons can be programmed by the user to control specific functions.

Mouse Systems Mouse
In computing, a standard *mouse* developed by Mouse Systems that makes use of three buttons. Some standard mice use one button, two buttons, or even more than three buttons.

Moving-Beam Scanner
A type of *bar-code scanner* in which a moving beam of light reads the *bar code* printed on products that are moved past it. See *Bar Code* and *Bar-Code Scanner*.

Moving Pictures Experts Group
See *MPEG*.

Moyroud, Louis
Louis Marius Moyroud (1914–), together with Rene Alphonse Higonnet (1902–1983), developed the first practical phototypesetting machine. Born in Moirans, Isere, France, Moyroud attended engineering school from 1929 to 1936 and graduated as an engineer from Ecole Nationale Superieure des Arts et Metiers of Cluny, France. He served in the military as a second lieutenant from 1936 to 1938 and as a first lieutenant in 1939 and 1940. He joined the LMT Laboratories, a subsidiary in Paris of ITT, in 1941 and left in 1946 to spend all of his time on photocomposition.

Moyroud and Higonnet first demonstrated their first phototypesetting machine, the Lumitype—later known as the Photon—in September 1946 and introduced it to America in 1948. The Photon was further refined under the direction of the Graphic Arts Research Foundation.

The Wonderful World of Insects, printed in 1953, was the first book to be composed by the Photon. Composed without the use of metal type, it might someday rank in the historical importance of printing with the first book printed from moveable type, the *Gutenberg Bible*.

MPC
Abbreviation for *multimedia personal computer*. See *Multimedia Personal Computer (MPC)*.

MPEG
Abbreviation for *Motion Picture Experts Group*, a committee working by arrangement with the *ISO* and *CCITT* to standardize algorithms for *data compression*. The term *MPEG* is also the name given to a set of algorithms used to compress a wide variety of file types. Such as:

• *MPEG 1*. A compression scheme for *full-motion video* and *digital audio*, used in the production of *compact discs*. Although very high *compression ratio*s are possible (*intraframe compression* ratios of 100:1 and 200:1 are possible), the *resolution* of the decompressed image is usually about half that of the *NTSC* and *PAL* television standards. New compression algorithms and *expansion board*s are greatly improving image quality.
• *MPEG 2*. A compression scheme for transmitting *digital video* over the *cable television network*, as well as for the upcoming *DVD* (or *digital versatile disc*). The image resolution is congruent with current television standards.

• *MPEG 4*. A compression scheme for developing technologies, such as video telephony, video conferencing, etc., that does not boast very high image quality.

ms
Abbreviation for *manuscript*. See *Manuscript*. The plural is *mss*.

The term *ms* is an abbreviation for *millisecond*. See *Millisecond*.

MS
Abbreviation for *medium shot*. See *Medium Shot*.

MSAU
One of two abbreviations used for *multistation access unit*. See *Multistation Access Unit (MAU)*.

MS-DOS
Abbreviation for *Microsoft Disk Operating System*. A version of *DOS* sold by Microsoft to non-IBM computer manufacturers, as opposed to *PC-DOS*. See *DOS*.

MS-DOS Extension
In computing, especially that using the *DOS* operating system, software originally needed to allow the original versions of DOS to access computer files that were greater than 32 *megabyte*s, which was the original DOS limit. Such a software extension is no longer necessary.

MSF
Abbreviation for *minutes, seconds, frames*. See *Minutes, Seconds, Frames*.

MSP
A *file extension* used to denote files saved using the Microsoft Paint program.

MSS
Abbreviation for *mass storage system*. See *Mass Storage*.

mss
Abbreviation for more than one *manuscript*. See *Manuscript*. The singular form is *ms*.

MTBF
Abbreviation for *mean time between failures*. See *Mean Time between Failures*.

MTTR
Abbreviation for *mean time to repair*. See *Mean Time to Repair*.

Muddy Media
Somewhat derogatory term for a multimedia presentation or production that is of poor quality, poor quality being defined as low degrees of interactivity, little meaning to content, garish and/or tasteless use of color, lack of typo-

graphical knowledge, etc. Such "muddy media" are particularly heinous when they fail to take full advantage of the possibilities of multimedia.

Mullen Test

A test performed to measure the **bursting strength** of paper or paperboard. In a Mullen test (also called a **pop test**), the paper sample is placed between two ring-like clamps in a device called a **Mullen tester**, and hydraulic pressure is used to inflate a rubber diaphragm, which expands against the sample stretching it. The measure of the total hydraulic pressure expanding the diaphragm at the time the sample ruptures (usually expressed in either pounds per square inch or kilopascals) is its bursting strength. Mullen tests are performed for each side of a paper or paperboard, and the bursting strength can be expressed as the average of both sides. Bursting strength expressed as a percentage is called the **percent Mullen**. Mullen tests are typically performed on papers and boards designed for use in packaging, bags, and envelopes. It is rarely performed on printing or writing papers. See **Bursting Strength**.

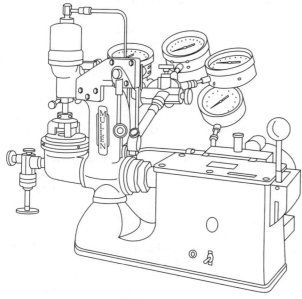

Mullen tester.

Mullen Tester

A device used to test a paper's bursting strength. See **Mullen Test** and **Bursting Strength**.

Muller

A glass (or other material) surface used for testing printing ink **pigment**s by grinding them in a **varnish**. Automatic mullers use two rotating glass grinding surfaces.

Multicast

In telecommunications, a type of broadcast transmitted to more than one receiving station, but not to all possible receiving stations.

Multicast Backbone (MBONE)

In computing, an experimental means of transmitting **real-time** digital video over the **Internet**. Although various types of digital video files can be **download**ed from Internet and **World Wide Web** sites, MBONE is an attempt to allow real-time viewing of video on the Internet. One basic problem that needed to be overcome is that the basic protocols used for transmitting data on the Internet—namely, **TCP/IP**—are designed to get files from one system to another reliably, but always with some delay. These delays, although fine for text, graphics, and other files, is unsuitable for real-time audio or video. Compounding that problem is the fact that existing Internet hardware cannot support real-time transmissions. Consequently, a new **backbone network** needed to be created that will also be able to accommodate new hardware capable of real-time audiovisual transmission.

Multicolor Graphics Adapter (MCGA)

A video standard created specifically for the PS/2 Models 25 and 30. MCGA does not work with **EGA** software.

Multicolor Printing

Printing in two or more colors. The most common variety of multicolor printing is four-color, or process-color printing, which uses cyan, magenta, yellow, and black inks.

Multicolor Press

Two or more connected printing units.

Multidrop Line

In networking, a communications circuit containing more than one **node** on a single link. Such nodes—considered secondary stations—are controlled by a primary station. A multidrop line—also known as a **multipoint line**—is used frequently in IBM's **Systems Network Architecture (SNA)**.

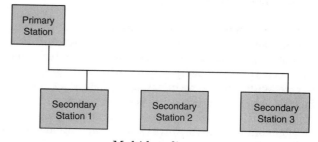

Multidrop line.

Multifilament

A type of thread used in **screen printing** fabrics composed of multiple strands of thread woven together, as opposed to a **monofilament**.

MultiFinder

In computing, the portion of the **Macintosh operating system** that facilitates **multitasking**, or the simultaneous loading of more than one program into the computer's memory at a time.

Multi-Image

A slide show or other similar presentation that utilizes two or more synchronized projectors.

Multilink

In computing, a circuit board comprising several layers of circuitry laminated together to which different components can be connected.

Multilith

A small printing press or *duplicator* used in *offset lithography*. A multilith is often used for small-run jobs such as letterhead. See *Offset Lithography*.

Multilith Master

Alternate term for a *paper master*. See *Paper Master*.

Multimedia

A technology for creating interactive presentations that incorporate sound, graphics, video, and text, usually playable on a computer (albeit one with a certain set of minimum hardware requirements; see below), and distributed on a variety of computer storage media, most notably *compact discs* (such as *CD-ROM*s), *videodisc*s, and, increasingly, the *Internet* and *World Wide Web*.

In the past, the term *multimedia* referred to presentations involving one or more forms of audiovisual presentation media, such as multiple slide projectors, film projectors, videocassette recorders, audio devices, or some combination of them. Today, it usually means an interactive presentation or production distributed digitally.

MULTIMEDIA DESIGN AND PRODUCTION

There are a myriad of personnel, hardware, and software requirements for the design, production, and development of multimedia applications.

Personnel. In many cases, such as short business presentations, one person can somewhat easily design and develop the entire production. In the case of a computer game or interactive encyclopedia, many different people with diverse skills need to be involved to produce a quality production. Although the specific personnel may vary according to the budget and scope of the project, multimedia development typically involves some combination of the following individuals:

• *Project Manager.* In some ways, the project manager is much like the producer of a television program of motion picture. The project manager is responsible for overseeing all the aspects of the production, coordinating designers, developers, writers, etc., as well as planning the budget and schedule, motivating team members, and all other day-to-day operations.

• *Content Provider.* The content provider is essentially the "screenwriter" for the project. The content provider is responsible for not only all the aspects of the production that a traditional scriptwriter handles (such as character,

linear action, point of view, dialogue, or whatever specific scripting requirements there are) but also generating the interactivity of the production. The content provider may generate completely original material or repurpose material from other media (such as books, movies, etc.). Often, several different writers will be responsible for different aspects of the scripting; content will be created by one person or group, and the results of that labor will be synthesized by another writer into text that actually appears on the screen.

• *Designer.* The two types of designers who work on multimedia projects are graphic designers and interface designers. A graphic designer is responsible for the look and feel of what is on the screen. How text is displayed (i.e., typeface, point size, etc.), the layout of text and graphics, the color scheme, button design, consistency of the design from screen to screen, etc., are all the purview of the graphic designer. The interface designer, on the other hand, needs his/her work to be completely invisible to the end-user. The interface is essentially how the user interacts with the production. The interface designer thus creates the "map" of the production, including navigation pathways, where a particular button sends the user, what screen comes after what, etc. The less obtrusive an interface is, the more successful it will be. These designers are often supplemented by an instructional designer, who ensures that the subject matter being presented (in the case of reference and educational productions) is clear and correct.

• *Video Specialist.* In productions that involve digital video, a person (or a team) is responsible for the taping, the editing, the digitizing, and the compression of the video material. In some cases, where video is not an especially important part of a production, the video specialist can be one person with a video camera. In other cases, such as interactive movies and games, it may be an entire production crew, not unlike that which would be involved in the taping and editing of a television program.

• *Audio Specialist.* Again, an audio specialist can be an individual or a team, but the responsibilities include the recording and editing of music, sound effects, dialogue, alert noises, etc. Or, in other words, the entire sonic feel of the presentation. An audio specialist may also be a musical composer and/or musician, providing original music for the project, or may contract original music from outside sources. The audio specialist may also repurpose and digitize music from other sources, as well.

• *Programmer.* Also known as a developer, the programmer is responsible for writing the actual computer code that makes all the above aspects of the production work. This may involve either authoring using an authoring program (such as Macromedia Director) or writing actual code in a specific programming language such as C++. Without a skilled and talented programmer, all of the above elements are produced in vain.

There is a great deal of variation in multimedia production, and depending upon the requirements of the project, one person may fulfill some combination of the above.

The project manager may also be the content provider; the video specialist may also do audio; the designer may do video, etc. It is rare for one person to handle all functions except in the simplest of productions, however. It should be pointed out as well that group dynamics can make or break a project, and it is up to the project manager to ensure that all team members are working together.

Hardware. Like the individuals who comprise a production, all the hardware elements used in production and development must work with, not against, each other. Hardware changes almost weekly, with new machines coming out regularly, each new version more powerful than the next.

• *Computer.* Although for some time the Apple *Macintosh* was the only computer up to the task of multimedia production, that situation is changing rapidly. The Mac is still the machine of choice, but the *IBM-compatible computer* (running on the *Windows* platform) is making strong inroads in multimedia production. Although the Macintosh inherently supports high-resolution graphics, audio, and (via the *QuickTime* system extension) digital video, the Windows-based computer, supplemented with a *Super VGA* monitor, a *sound card*, and its own video extension, can be used just as readily. Increasingly, the trend is toward cross-platform development, and more and more programs (most notably the Macromedia Director authoring program) are making it a simple process to convert from the Mac to Windows. As far as specific system requirements go, there is a great deal of flexibility. The two most important system considerations are the *central processing unit (CPU)* of the computer, and the total amount of *random-access memory (RAM)*. Multimedia applications and the elements (graphics, sound, video) needed to produce them require a large amount of computing power and memory, as these files take up a great deal of memory. On the Macintosh side, a lot of multimedia was produced on pre-PowerMac machines, with 68040 *microprocessor*s running at speeds of only 33 *megahertz (MHz)*. Now, with machines containing *PowerPC* chips boasting speeds of up to 200 MHz, it is becoming simpler and faster to produce even complicated productions. On the Windows side, a *Multimedia Personal Computer (MPC)* with an Intel 80486 processor is fine for multimedia, but the *Pentium* series of processors works even better. As far as memory is concerned, it is difficult to get by with less than 24 *megabyte*s of RAM. Remember, you can never be too rich, too thin, or have too much RAM.

• *Monitor.* The size of the monitor needed for multimedia is for the most part dependent upon how much scrolling the user likes to do. The de facto standard monitor size is 640×480 *pixel*s, which is the resolution most commercially available multimedia CD-ROMs shoot for. As for actual screen size, a 13-in. monitor will work fine, but larger monitors may require a video card to speed up screen redraws. Most RGB monitors will display up to *twenty-four-bit (24-bit) color* (or over 16 million colors), but few authoring programs can effectively handle graphics with a *color depth* greater than *eight-bit (8-bit) color*. What is typically done is to prepare graphics at 24-bit then reduce them to 8-bit using a customized color palette. It is becoming somewhat common, however, to keep the final color depth at 16-bit, as more powerful processors can handle it and most monitors currently in use support it.

• *Storage.* Multimedia files can be very large indeed, and there needs to be someplace to store it all. (Backing up files should be done often.) In addition to the computer's internal *hard disk*, there is a wide variety of storage media available, both for temporary and permanent storage. The earliest mass storage devices were the *SyQuest* and *Bernoulli* cartridge drives. Although the Bernoulli cartridges are no longer available, SyQuest cartridges are, with storage capacities in excess of 270 MB per cartridge. Iomega's *Zip* and *Jaz* disks are also inexpensive and popular, and provide a great deal of storage capacity. In addition, *magneto-optical (MO)* discs are also reliable and provide large amounts of storage space. For permanent storage, *CD-R* devices allow for the archiving of files on CD-ROM.

• *Other Devices.* Depending upon the specific needs of a project, other devices may be required, primarily audio and video digitizing devices. Some computers—such as the AV series of Macintoshes—have built-in digitizers for both sound and video, but more often than not a high-quality digitizing board may be required. These devices allow an external audio or video player (such as a CD player, a tape deck, a VCR, or videodisc player) to be connected to the system. Audio and/or video can be captured directly from source material and edited in an audio or video editing program. (See *Digital Audio* and *Digital Video*.)

A *scanner* may also be a requirement, if there are a lot of still images that need to be digitized. (See *Scanner* and *Scanning*.) Alternatives to the scanner are the Kodak *Photo CD* and a *digital camera*, which contain still images already in digital form. (See *Photo CD* and *Digital Photography*.)

Other devices that may or may not be required are speakers for higher audio output quality than can be provided by the built-in speaker, projectors and *LCD panel*s for the presentation of projects, a *modem* for the electronic transfer of files either over a *local area network (LAN)* or over the Internet, and a CD-ROM drive and/or recorder for *premastering*, *mastering*, or archiving.

Software. The software requirements for multimedia depend on the nature of the production, but the following list includes some of the most basic requirements. The specific software mentioned in the following section should not be construed as an endorsement, but rather as the most prevalent in the industry.

• *Paint Programs.* These are *bitmap*-based image manipulation programs that allow for the editing of digitized images as well as the creation of original bitmapped images. A whole host of paint programs are on the market, but the most popular by far is Adobe Photoshop, the most recent version being 4.0, as of this writing.

• *Drawing Programs*. These are ***vector-based graphics*** programs that allow for the creation of original ***line art***. There are several popular programs, such as Adobe Illustrator, Macromedia FreeHand, and CorelDraw, to name but three.

• *3D and CAD Drawing*. Three-dimensional modeling and drawing, as well as ***computer-aided drawing (CAD)***, are widely used in multimedia, usually to create simulated environments, objects, and "virtual" worlds. Some popular 3D modeling programs include Strata Studio, Infini-D, and others, while two popular CAD programs are Claris CAD and AutoCAD.

• *Sound and Video Editing*. Digital audio can be captured by even as simple a program as SimpleText (on the Macintosh), but more advanced digital audio editing programs include Macromedia's SoundEdit 16, which supports CD-quality sound. Many audio programs also support ***Musical Instrument Digital Interface (MIDI)***, a standard for the digital simulation of musical instruments. As for video, there are a wide variety of video capture and editing programs, which also support a host of ***transition***s, ***chromakeying***, and other video effects. A popular one is Adobe Premiere.

Other utilities and programs are available for a variety of specialized purposes, such as ***data compression***, as well as text editing and World Wide Web authoring and design.

• *Authoring Software*. Authoring software falls into two basic categories: simple presentation tools and full-fledged authorware. Presentation tools, as the term implies, allows for the simple combination of text, graphics, sound and video into slide shows. Screen-, card-, or page-based programs create a series of slides that can be flipped to in any order the creator desires, while icon-based programs lay out a presentation as a type of flowchart or map of navigational links. Full-fledged authoring programs are often time-based, which means that events are organized along a time line, or as a series of movie-like frames that can be played back at a rate set by the developer. The most flexible programs are those that require some degree of programming or scripting. Macromedia Director, to work to its full advantage, requires knowledge of its own scripting language called Lingo. The more that is programmed with Lingo, the more control the developer has over how things work. Writing the entire production in a programming language (such as ***C*** or ***C++***) allows the greatest degree of control.

ELEMENTS OF MULTIMEDIA

As was mentioned earlier, multimedia is the combination of text, sound, images, and video into a single presentation. Let's look briefly at each of these elements of a multimedia presentation:

Text. The principles of typography and design do not change much when moving from the printed page to the computer screen. There are, however, some important differences.

One of the most significant aspects of typography in multimedia is legibility. Since the resolution of a computer monitor (72 ***pixels per inch***) is much less than that of a printed page (300–2400 ppi), fonts do not display as cleanly on screen as they do in print. Some fonts, though, do look better on screen than others, so the designer needs to evaluate each font on screen and ensure that it looks not only legible, but also is appropriate to the content. Italic type can be very hard to read on screen and should be used sparingly. Too much text packed onto a single screen can be very hard to read, as can type that is too small. On screen type should rarely be less than 18–24 points, especially if the presentation is one that is going to be projected on a screen and be read from a distance. On the other hand, too little text on a screen may be easy to read but may necessitate scrolling or the turning of "pages" by the user, which can get irritating. Various effects can be used to make text more readable, such as ***anti-aliasing*** or drop shadows. When large blocks of text are used (as in an encyclopedia entry, for example), the font should be selected for legibility above aesthetics. Text is always harder to read on screen than on paper, so it should be made as easy as possible.

Text must also be used for navigation purposes. Although ***icon***s may be used to communicate some things (an arrow can be used to illustrate "go back" or "go forward"), sometimes there is no easy way to communicate something graphically. Short text lines (a word or two, or in other words a word or phrase about the length of a menu item) can be surrounded with a button-like background or frame, indicating that it is something to be clicked on.

Screen text can be enhanced by the use of a ***utility program*** such as ***Adobe Type Manager***, which is used to improve the display of ***PostScript*** fonts.

Audio. There are two ways of adding audio to a presentation. The first is by sampling a sound. A sound digitizer essentially receives an analog input (the sound wave as an electrical signal) and uses numbers (***bit***s) to represent what the analog wave is doing at any given period of time (usually some fraction of a second). These discrete digits approximate very closely the original sound wave. The drawback, however, is that sampled digital audio takes up a great deal of file space. (See ***Digital Audio***.)

Another way of creating sound in multimedia is by ***MIDI***, a standard way of using commands to describe various musical instruments and the notes they are supposed to play in digital form. So, for example, when the MIDI representation of a particular musical score is fed to a MIDI output device, the commands are used to recreate the sound of, say, a pipe organ playing "Louie, Louie." MIDI is not sound but is merely the recipe for making a particular sound or series of sounds. Using MIDI can result in file sizes that are 200–1000 times smaller than corresponding digital audio files. However, since the sound that is produced is a function of the MIDI playback device, a single file may sound different when transferred from one machine to another. MIDI also cannot be used to recreate human voices. (See ***Musical Instrument Digital Interface [MIDI]***.)

When audio needs to be imported into a multimedia authoring program, it is important to pay attention to the ***file format*** that the program needs a sound to be in. On the Macintosh, most authoring programs support ***AIFF*** sound files. Not all programs support MIDI, however.

Video. Digital video is perhaps the most complex element of a multimedia application, especially as the means of capturing, editing, compressing, storing, and playing it are still being refined. The problem with digital video is the immense amount of memory it requires. For example, consider that a still, full-screen (i.e., 640×480 ppi) color image can require as much as 1 megabyte of memory to display. At the normal video display rate of 30 frames per second, that means the computer needs to display 30 still images per second, requiring 30 megabytes of memory every second, which does not even take into account the audio portion of a video signal. Even without audio, one minute of full-screen, full-motion video would require up to 1.8 ***gigabyte***s of memory. Since this is beyond the capacity of most computers, digital video is often compressed and is rarely displayed at full-screen and with full-motion. (Often, however, full-screen, full-motion video can be generated by means of a video compression board—such as an ***MPEG*** board—which can quickly compress and decompress video with a facility beyond what is capable with software alone.) After capture and editing, video is often compressed by means of a ***codec*** (a shorthand term for ***compressor/decompressor***), which looks for redundant information from frame to frame and saves it as a series of codes that function as a kind of shorthand. Upon playback, the computer needs to decode the shorthand and replace the missing information, usually "on-the-fly" during playback. Most digital video codecs are ***lossy***, meaning some information is lost during compression. Some high-end compression systems are nearing ***lossless*** compression. (See ***Data Compression***.) To achieve a balance between what the computer can handle and what is aesthetically pleasing, sacrifices must be made. For example, often full-screen video is not possible, so a reduced image size is used. Or a full 30 frame per second rate is not possible, so the frame rate is reduced. See ***Digital Video***.

Animation. Like video, animation is a series of still images that, when viewed in rapid succession, produce the illusion of movement. Animation, however, can be produced somewhat simply in a good authoring program and does not always require the high memory capacities of digital video. Animation has been traditionally produced by hand: a series of still images were drawn or painted on sheets of celluloid and photographed in succession (known as ***frame animation***). Alternately, there is also what is known as ***cast animation***, in which only certain elements are redrawn from frame to frame, while static portions of the image—such as a background—remain unchanged. Anima-

tion is often prepared by the primary animator as a series of ***key frame***s, or frames that mark the beginning and end of a specific sequence. The process of ***in-betweening*** involves simply creating—either by computer or by the use of animation assistants—the intermediate frames that link the beginning and end of the sequence.

A variety of animation is known as ***morphing***, in which one image segues into another. This technique is often used in horror movies, and initially achieved widespread popularity in the Michael Jackson video "Black and White." (See ***Animation***.)

DELIVERING MULTIMEDIA

Multimedia can be delivered in a variety of ways, depending upon the application and the desired end user. One means of delivery, for basic presentations and slide shows, is directly from a computer hard drive, the computer being hooked up to an LCD panel and projected onto a screen to a roomful of people. This is a common means of providing interactive audiovisual material as a supplement to a corporate presentation. Another means of delivery is an interactive ***point of information*** or ***point of sale***, usually comprising a kiosk in a public location, such as a shopping mall, museum, etc., which allows users to view interactive presentations that provide information on exhibits and events, or information on items for purchase.

Although any computer storage medium can be used to deliver multimedia (even the ***floppy disk***, containing less than 2 megabytes, has been used as a delivery system for multimedia), the most common is the compact disc. The most common model for multimedia production involves a series of tests before actual mass production begins. After the initial development and production, a production is given an ***alpha test***, in which in-house personnel (and perhaps some outside individuals) are given copies. These individuals use the application as an end-user would, the goal being to find trouble spots that can range from content-based problems such as an unclear interface or navigation scheme to flaws (or ***bug***s) in the programming, causing unusual things to occur, which can include the benign (such as jumping to the wrong screen when a button is pressed) to the less benign (crashing the system). After all the problems discovered during the alpha test have purportedly been fixed, it is then prepared for ***beta test***ing, in which outside individuals are given copies and asked to report any problems. There may be several beta versions, depending upon the number and severity of problems. The production is then mass-produced and distributed. (See ***Compact Disc [CD]***.)

The Internet, especially the World Wide Web, is increasingly being used as a distribution medium for multimedia, and some major authoring programs now have plug-ins that facilitate the playback of interactive productions over the Internet. Although still in the early stages of development, the Internet (and, if ***Web TV*** catches on, the home television) may become the primary means of multimedia distribution.

529

Multimedia CD (MMCD)

Alternate term for a type of **high-density compact disc** designed by Philips/Sony. See **High-Density Compact Disc (HDCD)**.

Multimedia Extension

In computing, any **system extension** that allows a computer system and/or application to control time-based data, such as music, **audio**, **video**, **animation**, or other **multimedia** element. Such extensions may also function as **device drivers** and synchronization controllers for attached hardware devices.

Multimedia Marketing Council (MMC)

A group of computer hardware and software manufacturers organized to create the specifications for **multimedia personal computer**, specifically, the minimum hardware configuration a **DOS** machine should possess in order to run multimedia applications. See **Multimedia Personal Computer (MPC)**.

Multimedia Personal Computer (MPC)

A **personal computer** with a hardware configuration in accordance with the **Multimedia Marketing Council**'s specifications. The following chart illustrates the specifications for MPC Level 1 (published in 1990) and Level 2 (published in 1993).

MPC Level 1	MPC Level 2
CPU: 386SX or equivalent	CPU: 486SX at 25MHz or
RAM: 2 MB	equivalent
Storage: 30 MB	RAM: 4–8 MB
Video: VGA (16 colors)	Storage: 160 MB
Optical Disk: 1X	Video: VGA+ (64K colors)
Audio: 8-bit	Optical Disk: 4X
	Audio: 16-bit

Specifications for MPC Level 1 and Level 2.

Multimedia System

In computing, all the hardware and software required to incorporate photographic images, line art, **animation**, **still video**, **motion video**, sound, text, and computer data into an interactive presentation. The term *multimedia system* also refers to the minimum system requirements needed to view such a presentation on one's computer.

Multimode Fiber

In networking and telecommunications, a **fiber optic** cable with a wide core, allowing light waves to travel by alternate routes. However, light waves cannot travel as far as those using a **single-mode fiber**.

Multipart Forms

A type of paper stock grouped into sets, each set separated by **carbon release** paper (or each sheet of a set containing special **carbonless** materials). Such forms can only be printed by **impact printer**s.

Multiple Master

In digital typography, a means—developed by Adobe Systems—of describing **outline font**s in terms of **weight**, **width**, and **style**, each aspect of which comprises a sliding scale between extremes. The user can thus adjust any or all of these type characteristics.

Multiple Media

In publishing, the combination of more than one form of medium in a single package, such as a book and a **CD-ROM**, a video and an audiotape. The term *multiple media* should thus not be confused with **multimedia**. See **Multimedia**.

Multiple Passes

The exposure of more than one image on a single piece of film.

Multiple-Roll Sheeting

A variation of **sheeting**, or the cutting of manufactured paper rolls into individual sheets, in which two or more rolls are sheeted simultaneously. See **Sheeting**.

Multiple-Up

The printing of more than one page or image on a sheet of paper. See **One-Up, Two-Up** . . . .

Multiple Virtual Storage (MVS)

In computing, a standard **operating system** developed by IBM for its large **mainframe** computer systems.

Multiple Virtual Storage/Enterprise System Architecture (MVS/ESA)

In computing, a version of IBM's **Multiple Virtual Storage** operating system that uses expanded storage to enhance system efficiency. MVS/ESA is designed to handle applications that require the processing of large amounts of data, such as artificial intelligence, etc.

Multiple Virtual Storage/Extended Architecture (MVS/XA)

In computing, a version of IBM's **Multiple Virtual Storage** operating system based on a 32-bit addressing architecture.

Multiplex

In telecommunications, to simultaneously transmit two or more signals over the same **channel**. See **Multiplexer**.

Multiplexed Analog Components (MAC)

In telecommunications, a proposed standard for the transmission of television signals in which the **chrominance** (color) and **luminance** (brightness) components of the signal are transmitted one after the other and are combined (or **multiplexed**) upon receipt. In this way, color interference—which can occur in both the **NTSC** and **PAL** systems—can be eliminated.

Multiplexer

In telecommunications, a device used to simultaneously transmit more than one message on a single channel. This can be accomplished in several different ways: different messages can be sent at different frequencies along the same channel, or different *packet*s of data can be sent at staggered intervals. Multiplexer is sometimes abbreviated *mux*.

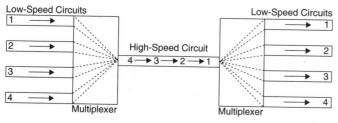

Multiplexer.

Multiplication Cross

Alternate term for the *dimension sign*. See *Dimension Sign*.

Multiplication Dot

In typography, a small dot, larger than a period and centered on the *cap height* of a *font* (·) used to indicate multiplication (i.e., 2 · 2 = 4). The multiplication dot is also used in Europe as a decimal point.

Multipoint Line

Alternate term for a *multidrop line*. See *Multidrop Line*.

Multiprocessing

In computing, the ability for a computer to use more than one *central processing unit (CPU)*, each one charged with different tasks and functions. The tasks given to a particular processor may be predetermined (*asymmetrical multiprocessing*) or determined at start-up, based on system resources (*symmetrical multiprocessing*). See *Asymmetrical Multiprocessing* and *Symmetrical Multiprocessing*.

Multiprogramming

Alternate term for *multitasking*. See *Multitasking*.

Multipurpose Internet Mail Extensions (MIME)

In *Internet* terminology, a specification for Internet data transmission that allows users to transmit and receive multipart *email* messages, the content of which may comprise data types other than generic *ASCII text*, such as *PostScript* files, binary files, images, audio, video, etc. See also *uuencode* and *uudecode*.

Multiserver Network

A computer network utilizing more than one *file server*.

Multisession

In *CD-ROM* recording, descriptive of the ability to write data to a disc in more than one session. The first *compact*

disk–recordable (CD-R) devices required all data to be written onto the disc at one time and were thus known as *single-session*. See *Compact Disc (CD)*.

Multistation Access Unit (MAU)

In networking, a device or wiring *hub* that allows terminals, printers, and other peripherals to be connected to a *star* or *Token Ring* network. Sometimes also abbreviated *MSAU*. See also *Controlled Access Unit (CAU)*.

Multitasking

In computing, a feature of some *operating system*s that allows more than one program or other function to be in operation at one time, usually dependent upon the amount of memory available in the system. Also spelled with a hyphen, *multi-tasking*. See also *Multithreaded* and *Context Switching*.

Multithreaded

In computing, descriptive of an *operating system* that allows a single program to perform more than one task simultaneously. The concurrent performance of these interrelated tasks—called "threads"—requires much less processing power than would be required by conventional *multitasking*. See also *Multitasking*.

Multiuser

Descriptive of a computer system that allows more than one individual to access files, applications, and other facilities simultaneously. Each user has his/her own terminal and keyboard connected to a single *CPU*.

Multiwall Bag

In packaging, a paper or plastic *bag* formed from two *ply*s or layers of paper and/or plastic. See *Bag: Paper Bags*.

Municipal Area Network (MAN)

In networking, any network (larger than a *local area network* but smaller than a *wide-area network*) that serves a city or other municipality, a college campus, a business complex, or other single "site" possessing widely separated buildings. Also referred to as a *metropolitan area network*.

Munsell Color Space

A type of color model, or means of quantitatively and objectively classifying a perceived color, based on the tristimulus attributes of *hue*, *value*, and *chroma*.

The Munsell color system was developed in 1905 by Alfred Munsell as a means of expressing relationships between colors. Munsell was looking for a way to move from one color to another through a path of orderly, progressive steps. The Munsell chart was developed through experiments in which subjects were asked to arrange color chip samples under conditions of constant illumination and surroundings. It consists of a color "tree" of these chips separated into "leaves" according to hue. Within each hue leaf, chips are arranged in a grid, with discernible progressions of chroma (**saturation**) along the horizontal *x* axis and discernible progressions of value (**lightness**) along the vertical *y* axis. Unlike the mathematically symmetrical grids of the typical lookup table, the resulting color space more closely captures the geometric irregularities of human visual perception. Each leaf is different because within different hues, the number of discernible colors varies with degrees of value and chroma. The Munsell system provides a straight-line progression of steps in equal increments along both chroma and value dimensions. This characteristic provides a natural foundation for color navigation.

Hue was defined by Munsell as a circle of hues. He chose to designate red, yellow, green, and purple as **primary colors**. These colors, together with their complements—yellow-red, green-yellow, blue-green, purple-blue, and red-purple—provide a ten-part division that reminds one of a decimal system. The hues are spaced equally around the hue circuit. By colorimetric measurement they represent consistent steps of hue change in equal gradations.

Munsell called the second color dimension *value*, and it is similar to lightness, though related to pigment, not light. Black and white form the vertical axis of the color model. This axis extends from white, absolutely pure white (the presence of all color) on the top, to ideal black (the absence of all color) on the bottom. Although neither of these ideal poles is attainable in pigment, the steps between them are highly definable as grays. They are numbered from 1 to 10.

Chroma, Munsell's term for the third dimension of color is similar to saturation, though to Munsell it relates more to the amount of colorant present. It is in this definition of chroma that Munsell's color model differs substantially from all previous proposals. While the circle of hues includes all conceivable hues, and while the value axis is all-inclusive, Munsell realized that new colorants were con-

stantly devised and chroma is therefore open-ended. (See also **Maxwell's Triangle**, **CIE Color Space**, and **Color: Color Measurement**.)

Musical Instrument Digital Interface (MIDI)

An industry-standard digital protocol for controlling digital musical instruments and other MIDI-compatible devices such as lights or sound effects. This communication protocol is used for synchronization and control of MIDI musical instruments and other devices.

Must

The date by which some manufacturing or other production process absolutely has to be completed.

Mute

In audio, video, television, and multimedia, to turn off or down the sound level of a speaker.

Mutt

In typography, slang term for an **em space**. See **Em Space**. Short for **mutton**.

Mutton

In typography, slang term for an **em space**. Often abbreviated to **mutt**.

Mux

Abbreviation for **multiplexer**. See **Multiplexer**.

MVS

Abbreviation for **Multiple Virtual Storage**. See **Multiple Virtual Storage (MVS)**.

MVS/ESA

Abbreviation for **Multiple Virtual Storage/Enterprise System Architecture**. See **Multiple Virtual Storage/ Enterprise System Architecture (MVS/ESA)**.

MVS/XA

Abbreviation for **Multiple Virtual Storage/Extended Architecture**. See **Multiple Virtual Storage/Extended Architecture (MVS/XA)**.

M Weight

A means of describing the **basis weight** of paper in pounds of 1,000 sheets cut to a specific size. See **Basis Weight**.

Mylar

A clear, strong, thin polyester film used in the manufacture of photographic film, recording tapes, insulation, etc. Mylar® films are used as printing **substrate**s, as well as travelling belts in some press systems.

Mylar is also used as a type of film designed for **plotter**s, distinguished by its high **dimensional stability**, an important consideration in the output of architectural and engineering graphics drawn to scale.

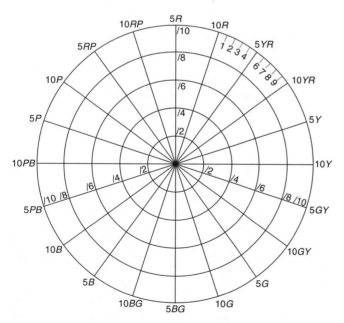

Munsell hue spacing and chroma.

N

N, n
The fourteenth letter of the English alphabet, deriving from the North Semitic *nun*, obtaining its current form in the Greek *nu*.

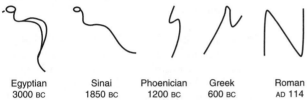

| Egyptian 3000 BC | Sinai 1850 BC | Phoenician 1200 BC | Greek 600 BC | Roman AD 114 |

The evolution of the letter N.

NAB
Abbreviation for the **National Association of Broadcasters**. See **National Association of Broadcasters (NAB)**.

Nailhead
In **binding and finishing**, term for a paperbound book that is widest at its **spine** resembling, in profile, a nail.

NAK
Abbreviation for **negative acknowledgment**. See **Negative Acknowledgment (NAK)**.

Named Pipe
In networking, a communications **Application Program Interface (API)** that provides a connection between an application located on a **server** and the **client** attempting to use the application. The named pipes allow the use of routines for the opening, reading, and writing of files that are similar to those used by a program in non-networking environments. See also **Pipe**.

Nameplate
In **newspaper typography**, the name of the newspaper printed at the beginning (commonly toward the top of the front page), most often in a highly stylized, decorative design.

Nanometer
Abbreviated nm, a nanometer is a small unit of measurement equal to 10^{-9} (0.000000001 or one-billionth) of a meter, used to measure a wavelength of light. To make numbers less unwieldy, frequently the **Ångstrom** (1 Å = 0.0000000001 meter, or 0.1 nanometer) is used.

Nanosecond
A measure of time or rate of speed equal to one billionth (0.000000001, or 10^{-9}) of a second. The speeds of some computers are measured in nanoseconds. Abbreviated **ns**. See also **Millisecond** and **Microsecond**.

Naphtha
Any of a variety of **aliphatic solvent**s, or a class of **hydrocarbon** compounds that are derived from petroleum distillation, used as a solvent in printing ink **vehicle**s. See **Solvent**.

Naphthenate Drier
A compound formed by the reaction of cobalt, manganese, or other metal with naphthenic acid, added as a **drier** in printing inks, that acts as a **catalyst** in the **oxidation** of chemicals in the printing ink **vehicle**, expediting the drying time of the ink.

Naphthol Red FGR
See **BON Arylamide Red**.

Naphthol Reds and Rubines
An **organic color pigment** used in printing inks. *Naphthol Red* possesses moderate **lightfastness** and good resistance to soap and heat. It is primarily used in the printing of packaging, but its unremarkable lightfastness and high cost limit its use.

(*CI Pigment Red 17 No. 12390.*)

Naphthol Red Light differs from naphthol red in its chemical structure (it lacks a methyl group [$-CH_3$]) and in its shade (yellow red.) It also possesses moderate lightfastness and similar chemical resistance properties. Like naphthol red, its expense and unspectacular lightfastness limit its use.

(*CI Pigment Red 22 No. 12315.*)

Naphthol Red Dark differs somewhat more significantly from naphthol red in chemical structure, and is a dark blue red, but shares similar lightfastness and chemical resistance properties.

(*CI Pigment Red 23 No. 12355.*)

Naphthol Red F4R is a bluish red possessing moderate lightfastness, and good resistance to soap and heat. Its use is limited by its expense and its poor lightfastness, but is used in multicolor process color printing of soap packaging.

(*CI Pigment Red 8 No. 12335.*)

Naphthol Carmine FBB is a bluish red pigment, and possesses high lightfastness and chemical resistance properties. It is used in liquid and paste inks, as well as for metal decorating inks. It is also a highly expensive pigment, and is used whenever its desirable properties make the added expense warranted.

Also known as *Permanent Carmine FBB* (*CI Pigment Red 146 No. 12485*).

Naphthol Red F5RK is a brilliant, strong bluish red that possesses high lightfastness and chemical resistance properties. It is suitable for use in inks of all printing processes and applications, but its high cost limits its use.

(CI Pigment Red 170 No. 12475.)

Naphthol Rubine F6B is similar to caphthol carmine FBB in shade, but stronger. It has the high chemical resistance properties of naphthol carmine FBB, but has low lightfastness. It is used for liquid inks in the printing of packaging, and for inks utilized in metal decorating.

(CI Pigment Red 184.)

Naphthol Red F6RK is stronger and bluer than naphthol red F5RK, and possesses high resistance to acids, alkalis, soap, wax, and heat, but poor lightfastness. It is used primarily in liquid inks for the printing of packaging.

(CI Pigment Red 210.)

Naphthol Red LF is a bright, transparent red possessing high lightfastness and resistance to alkalis and heat. It tends not to withstand exposure to strong solvents, however.

(CI Pigment Red 9 No. 12460.)

(See also *Organic Color Pigments*.)

NAPIM

Acronym for *National Association of Printing Ink Manufacturers*. See *National Association of Printing Ink Manufacturers*.

NAPS

Abbreviation for *negative-acting proofing system*, a type of *overlay color proof*, similar to 3M's *Color-Key*, prepared using materials manufactured by Hoescht.

Narrowband

Descriptive of an optical system or color *filter* characterized by a small *bandwidth*, or one that does not allow the passage of a great deal of information, such as light of only certain wavelengths or colors. See also *Wideband* (first definition).

In telecommunications, *narrowband* is used to refer to any communications facility that can handle up to 200 *bits per second*. See also *Wideband* (second definition).

National Association of Broadcasters (NAB)

A U.S. organization of radio and television station owners and other companies involved with American broadcast networks.

National Association of Printing Ink Manufacturers (NAPIM)

A nonprofit organization composed of professionals from the printing ink industry devoted to the development and improvement of ink manufacturing. NAPIM also acts as an interface between the industry and the government, the public, and related industries. NAPIM also has international affiliates.

National Computer Security Center (NCSC)

A branch of the United States National Security Agency that defines standards and classifications for computer and network security, ranging from "A1" (the highest level of computer security) to "D" (the lowest level of security or, essentially, no computer security whatsoever). The "C" security classification can be used in commercial environments, but at the "B" level, the access-control mechanisms become too unwieldy for commercial use. Security levels are defined in Department of Defense Standard 5200.28.

National Information Infrastructure (NII)

A proposed public, high-speed information service network accessible from homes, business, and schools.

National Television Standards Committee (NTSC)

The American committee that establishes standards for color television broadcasting and video recording. The NTSC standard for television—used in North America and Japan—specifies 29.97 *frames per second*, a screen frequency of 59.94 *hertz*, and a screen consisting of 525 video lines. In Europe, two other standards—*Phase Alternating Line (PAL)* and *Séquentiel Couleur à Mémoire (SECAM)* are used. It is sometimes said in jest that NTSC stands for Never The Same Color. This standard will change with the development of High Definition television.

Native Signal Processing (NSP)

The processing of *analog* data in real time by a computer's native *microprocessor*, rather than by means of a *digital signal processor*, used often in data communications and the processing of *digital audio* and *digital video*. Very few *microprocessor*s are capable of the calculations required for NSP. See also *Digital Signal Processor (DSP)*.

Natural

In papermaking, descriptive of a paper color such as cream, white, or ivory.

Natural Drying Time

The amount of time that elapses from the point at which a printed web exits the final printing unit to the time it encounters the high temperature of the drying unit.

Natural Finish

A paper *finish* characterized by a soft, slightly fuzzy texture.

Natural Spread

Alternate term for a *center spread*. See *Center Spread*.

NBS

Abbreviation for *National Bureau of Standards*, now known as the *National Institute of Science and Technology*. See *National Institute of Science and Technology (NIST)*.

NCB

Abbreviation for *network control block*. See *Network Control Block (NCB)*.

NCP

Abbreviation for **network control program**. See **Network Control Program (NCP)**.

NCSC

Acronym for the **National Computer Security Center**. See **National Computer Security Center (NCSC)**.

NDIS

Abbreviation for **Network Driver Interface Specification**. See **Network Driver Interface Specification (NDIS)**.

Near-End Crosstalk (NEXT)

In networking and telecommunications, a type of **crosstalk** that occurs near a connector at one or both ends of a cable.

Near-Instantaneously Companded Audio Multiplex (NICAM)

In telecommunications, a system by which **CD-quality** audio can be transmitted along with a television signal, **data compression** being required to keep the transmission within its proper **bandwidth**. So far, NICAM is used only in Europe.

Near-Letter Quality

Descriptive of the print quality of some types of computer printer that, although they do not generate **letter quality** output (since they are still **dot-matrix printer**s, and do not produce images from relief typeforms), overtype the final characters in such a way as to produce elegant and moderately high-quality type.

Near-Typeset Quality

Descriptive of a computer printer (such as a **laser printer**) capable of an output **resolution** greater than 300 **pixels per inch (ppi)** on plain paper. Typeset quality is defined as film or photographic paper output at resolutions of 1200 ppi or greater (such as an **imagesetter**).

Nebraska Scale

In multimedia, a scale developed by the Nebraska Videodisc Design/Production Group to classify the level of **interactivity** of a multimedia production, **videodisc**, or other system. The scale runs as follows:

Level 0. A system in which productions possess a strictly linear narrative and no interactivity, such as a feature movie.

Level 1. A system allowing a small, limited amount of interactivity like basic fast forward and rewind capabilities or some individual frame selection, such as a **level 1 videodisc**.

Level 2. A system utilizing a **microprocessor** that allows increased interactivity by reading the program from a **hard disk** or other such storage medium.

Level 3. A system utilizing a complete **microcomputer**, with the storage medium and the drive playing the production as separate entities (such as a CD-ROM drive connected to a personal computer). This allows unlimited interactivity.

Level 4. A system in which the drive, **operating system**, and microprocessor are complete in one unit, the entire system being dedicated solely to interactive productions (such as Philips' **CD-i**).

Neckline

In typography, the spacing beneath a **head**.

Negative

Generally speaking, a reversed photographic image produced on acetate-based film (a **film negative**) or photosensitive, resin-coated paper (a **paper negative**). On a black-and-white negative, white images become black and black images become white; on color negatives, each tone value is reversed. In most prepress operations, film negatives need to be prepared from **mechanical**s (either pasted-up artwork or digitally generated pages), and it is from film negatives (in particular, from **final negative**s) that plates are exposed. The process camera that makes the negatives from mechanicals is the "camera" in **camera-ready art**. On most negatives, black areas commonly correspond to nonprinting areas. During prepress, prior to platemaking, film negatives need to be stripped into **flat**s. (See **Stripping** and **Prepress: Graphic Arts Photography and Flat Assembly**.)

Negative Acknowledgment (NAK)

In telecommunications and networking, a **control character** used by some network **protocol**s to indicate that a message has not been received intact and should thus be retransmitted. See also **Acknowledge (ACK)**.

Negative-Working

Descriptive of any prepress or printing procedure (such as platemaking) in which additional imaging or reproduction is performed using film **negative**s rather than **positive**s. See **Negative** and **Negative-Working Plate**.

Negative-Working Plate

One of two types of **photolithographic** printing plates produced by bringing an unexposed plate into contact with a photographic **negative** of the image to be printed, and exposing it to a high-intensity light. The plate's coated metal surface is exposed in the image areas (where light passes through the negative) and unexposed in the nonimage areas (where light does not pass through). The exposure to light renders the image areas hard and insoluble. After platemaking the plate is chemically treated to dissolve the unhardened nonimage areas, rendering that portion of the plate water-receptive, the exposed image areas remaining hard, durable, and ink-receptive. The nonimage areas are then treated with a solution of **gum arabic** (or other gum, either natural or synthetic), which **desensitize**s the nonimage areas, adding a higher degree of water-receptivity.

Although negative-working plates are the most prevalent, a disadvantage of them is that they tend to reproduce **halftone** images with a higher degree of **dot gain** than plates made from **positive**s. (See also **Positive-Working Plate**.) (See **Plate: Offset Lithography** and **Platemaking**.)

Neon

In graphics, a special effect achieved through the use of glows and highlighting to impart a look to a graphic or piece of text that is reminiscent of neon light.

Neoprene

A synthetic rubber, developed in 1931 by the du Pont Chemical Company (based on research conducted by J.A. Nieuwland at the University of Notre Dame). Neoprene is produced by polymerizing acetylene to vinyl acetylene, then adding hydrochloric acid to produce chloroprene, which is then polymerized to neoprene. Neoprene is oil, chemical, and heat resistant, and has a wide variety of uses in hoses, gloves, and gaskets. It is also used in the manufacture of **flexographic** press rollers, **offset lithographic** press blankets, and **squeegee** blades used in **screen printing**, due to its excellent resistance to alcohols, **Cellosolve®**, water, **aliphatic hydrocarbons**, and **ester**s. It is not, however, resistant to **aromatic hydrocarbons**. Synthetic rubbers such as neoprene and **Buna N** have more stable physical and mechanical properties than natural rubbers.

Nested Indent

In typography, a form of **indention** in which each subsequent indent is set relative to the previous indent, rather than from the left (or right) margin.

NetBIOS

Abbreviation for **Network Basic Input/Output System**. See **Network Basic Input/Output System (NetBIOS)**.

NetBIOS Extended User Interface (NetBEUI)

In networking, a network **protocol** developed by Microsoft that conforms to the **NetBIOS** programming interface, used in PC-based **local area network** operating systems.

Netiquette

In **Internet** terminology, colloquial term for "network etiquette," or a set of informal, unwritten rules governing polite and courteous discourse through **email**, **USENET**, and other aspects of the Internet. Think of netiquette as "Miss Manners in Cyberspace."

Netscape

A popular (perhaps the most popular) **browser** for accessing information and sites on the **World Wide Web**, capable of a wide range of features, including not only storing **bookmark**s (or shortcuts to a user's favorite Web sites), but also sending, receiving, and managing **email**, subscribing to **USENET** groups, searching the **Internet**, and a wide range of other things.

The browser evolved in 1994 through work done at the University of Illinois at Champaign-Urbana where students developed Mosaic, a graphical user interface for presenting hypertexted information. Netscape is developed and marketed by Netscape Communications Corporation and, although Microsoft's Internet Explorer has been making some headway in the browser market, Netscape is still the browser for which most pages are written. See **World Wide Web (WWW)**.

NetView

In networking, a brand of mainframe network-management software developed by IBM for its **Systems Network Architecture (SNA)**.

Netware

A proprietary networking system of protocols and features developed by Novell, Inc.

Network

Essentially, any interconnection of separate components, be they computers, television or radio stations, etc., each **node** or station of which is capable of transmitting some form of information to another node or station.

In terms of computer networks, they can either be small and localized—a **local area network (LAN)**—or progressively larger—such as a **metropolitan area network (MAN)** or **wide area network (WAN)**. The largest network of all—which spans the globe—is the **Internet**. See **Networking**.

Network Adapter

In computing and networking, a card added to a **microcomputer** to allow the computer to be connected to a network. Different network **protocol**s (such as **ARCnet**, **Token Ring**, **Ethernet**, etc.) require different cards.

Network Administrator

An individual who is charged with the responsibility of organizing, supporting, and maintaining a computer network. The duties of a network administrator may involve monitoring network performance, changing passwords and other security issues, adding and removing new users and/or **node**s, backing up and archiving files, troubleshooting network problems, installing upgrades of hardware and software both of applications used on the network and for the network itself, etc. See also **Configuration Management**.

Network Analyzer

In networking, a device used to monitor and troubleshoot data transmitted over a network. A network analyzer may be a hardware device, or it may be a software program, or some combination of both.

A network analyzer usually operates by encoding, transmitting, receiving, and decoding data **packet**s, and searching for transmission errors.

Network Architecture

Essentially, the structure and organization of a computer network, or the means by which different *node*s are connected to each other and data is transferred between or among them, either locally as LANs or over high-speed, wideband, long-distance interconnections linked over telecommunications facilities. This includes hardware, software, *protocol*, *topology*, etc. There have been several well-received and popular standards for network architecture, in particular the *International Standards Organization*'s *Open System Interconnection (OSI)* model, as well as IBM's *Systems Network Architecture (SNA)*. Each of these models structures network functions into several layers comprising hardware and software. See *Open System Interconnection (OSI)* and *Systems Network Architecture (SNA)*.

Network Basic Input/Output System (NetBIOS)

In networking, a *network protocol* developed by IBM and Sytek to control the exchange of data, as well as network access. Essentially, NetBIOS provides an *API* with a standard set of commands that allows an application to transfer data from *node* to node without needing to go through the basic network operating system.

Network Board

Alternate term for a *network interface card*. See *Network Interface Card*.

Network Control Block (NCB)

In networking, term for the structure of a data *packet* used in the *NetBIOS* protocol. See *NetBIOS*.

Network Control Program (NCP)

In networking, a program transmitted to a *communications controller* in a network (especially one using an *SNA* environment) that controls the operation of the communications controller, and manages such network functions as *routing*, *error detection*, *error correction*, etc.

Network Device Driver

In networking, a *device driver* used to control the *network interface card*. See *Device Driver* and *Network Interface Card*.

Network Directory

In networking, a *directory* of computer files located on a *server*, or a computer other than the one on which a particular user is working.

Network Drive

In networking, a *disk drive* located on a central *server*, or a computer other than the one on which a particular user is working, in contrast to a *local drive*.

Network Driver Interface Specification (NDIS)

In networking, a specification—developed by Microsoft and 3Com in 1990—for a *network device driver* that is inde-pendent of the *network protocol* and network interface card being used in a particular networking environment. NDIS also allows for the "multiplexing" of protocols, allowing more than one protocol to be used on the same computer.

Network File System (NFS)

In networking, a file-sharing system developed by Sun Microsystems that allows a computer to access the files and peripheral devices of another networked computer, as if they were local. NFS runs on any computer *platform*, and has been licensed by many different vendors.

Network Interface Card (NIC)

In networking, an *expansion card* installed in a personal computer, *server*, or other device that interfaces with the *network operating system* to allow the device to become part of the network. The NIC is attached directly to the network transmission medium (cabling of some kind, be it *fiber optic*, *unshielded twisted pair*, etc.).

Network Layer

In networking, the third of seven *layer*s in the *OSI* reference model, defining the protocols with which computers transfer data between and among each other. See *Open Systems Interconnection (OSI)*.

Network Management Protocol (NMP)

In networking, a set of standard specifications for controlling *modem*s, *T1* multiplexers, and other network devices, developed by AT&T.

Network Operating System (NOS)

In networking, the system software used to coordinate all the disparate functions of a computer network, such as user accounts and passwords, access methods, resource access and sharing, power monitoring, file and message transfers, error detection and correction, etc.

In most *local area network*s (especially those that use a *client/server* architecture), a large portion of the network operating system runs on the *file server*, while a small component of the NOS runs on each *node* or *workstation* connected to the network. Examples of these types of network operating systems include Novell's NetWare, Banyan VINES, and Microsoft LAN Manager.

In *peer-to-peer* networking, each node or workstation has its own component of the NOS, which then runs on top of each computer's own operating system. Examples of these types of network include LANtastic, Windows for Workgroups, Personal NetWare, etc.

Network Printer

Alternate term for a *print server*. See *Print Server*.

Network Topology

In networking, the physical structure and organization of a network. Topologies can be *centralized* (in which all the individual *node*s, or workstations, are connected to a central *hub*) or *distributed* (each node is connected to every other node, with no central controller). Some common network topologies are *star*, *bus*, *ring*, and *tree*.

Neugebauer Equations

A set of three equations that are used in *color proofing* to predict the *red, green, and blue* reflectances that are likely to result from printed *halftone dot*s. The Neugebauer equations are based on the specific dot sizes used to make a particular reproduction, and are extraordinarily complicated to solve, and even then require more trial and error than anything. However, new computer models and software packages are replacing such trial-and-error methods.

Neutral Color

Alternate term for *achromatic* color. See *Achromatic*.

Neutral Density

A term used to describe a photographic image that contains no dominant *hue*, or possesses a gray optical density.

Neutral Gray

Any shade of gray—running the gamut from white to black—that possesses no discernible color or *hue* or that resembles a gray shade found on a *gray scale*.

Neutral pH

A *pH* of 7.0, descriptive of a solution or substance possessing no *acidity* or *alkalinity*. See *pH*.

Newbie

In colloquial *Internet* terminology, term (perhaps derogatory) for an individual who is either new to a particular *USENET* group or to the on-line environment in general.

Newsink

A type of printing ink used for printing on *newsprint*. Like newsprint, which is an inexpensive, low-quality paper made from *groundwood pulp*, newsink in turn is an inexpensive ink produced from low-cost raw materials, primarily mineral oils and *Carbon Black*. Newsprint has a high degree of *ink absorbency*, and the high speed of web offset presses makes rapid *vehicle* absorption necessary to prevent smudging and *ink setoff*. Newsink, then, has a highly fluid *body* and low *viscosity* that allows for quick absorption. The addition of *resin*s to the ink also helps reduce the capacity for smudging. Ink that is too fluid or oily, however, can soak through the paper producing ink *strike-through*. Newsink is also specially formulated for *letterpress* printing, although very little newspaper printing is done on letterpress machines any longer.

Newsletter

Any smallish publication produced for a select readership. The content of a newsletter is usually much more sharply focused than that of a *magazine* or newspaper. The line between a newsletter and a magazine may be a thin one,

although a magazine is usually larger, more expensively produced, and has a broader (though not always) readership and more of a dependence on advertising to cover operating costs.

Newspaper Fold

Alternate term for a *former fold*. See *Former Fold*.

Newspaper Line

In typography, an archaic copy measurement consisting of a line of type 11 picas long comprising 30 characters per line. The newspaper line was also at one time used as a gauge for the performance of a typesetter (used as the "line" in "lines per minute").

Newspaper Typography

Generally speaking, type that is used in the composition of newspapers.

A great deal of research and development has been done since the 1930s to create special *typeface*s for newspaper use. The problems of high-speed web printing, paper shrinkage, and image legibility combined to present a challenge to the type designer. One reason for the somewhat "heavier" weight of the normal typeface cut was that the paper is slightly gray (not white), ink is dark gray (not black); hence, type needs to stand out more.

*Nameplate*s at the beginning of newspapers—the name of the paper—were originally set by hand in the largest type available; now they are being specially designed. The *masthead* is the area, usually on the editorial page, that lists the newspaper's editors and management.

Newsprint

An inexpensive, uncoated paper *grade* manufactured primarily from *groundwood* or other mechanical *pulp* used for newspapers, and has high *opacity*, a good *printing cushion*, and is able to rapidly absorb ink, which makes it useful for high-speed web offset printing. Newsprint has a *basic size* of 24×36 in., and comes in *basis weight*s from 28–35 lb., with 30-lb. newsprint being the most widely used.

Newton's Rings

An undesirable optical effect found on photographic films— such as transparencies mounted on a scanner drum or film in a glass contact frame—characterized by irregularly shaped rings of color surrounding a transparent center. This phenomenon was first described by Sir Isaac Newton (hence its name) when he attempted to reproduce the colors of the spectrum by laying a thin convex glass lens on a pane of glass and shining a white light on it.

The point of direct contact by the beam of light was uncolored, but surrounding the "blank" spot were rings of colors, such as a ring of blue, followed by a ring of white, followed by orange, red, violet, blue, and green. Although Newton did not know it at the time (he did not agree with Dutch physicist Christian Huygens that light could be described in terms of waves), these rings were caused by *interference* effects, caused by the light as it is refracted from the various surfaces of the lens. It is essentially the same principle as that underlying a prism. This phenomenon occurs in photographic film when the *transparency* or other type of film is not pressed tightly against a transparent screen.

NEXT

Abbreviation for *near-end crosstalk*. See *Near-End Crosstalk (NEXT)*.

NeXTstep

In computing, an *operating system*, based on *UNIX*, distinguished by the fact that it is the first *object-oriented* operating system. Initially, the NeXTstep operating system was only compatible with specific NeXT hardware, it can now be run on any system using an Intel *microprocessor* more powerful than the 80486.

NFS

Abbreviation for *Network File System*. See *Network File System (NFS)*.

Nib

Any foreign material that juts out from the surface of a printed ink film.

NIC

Abbreviation for *network interface card*. See *Network Interface Card (NIC)*.

NICAM

Abbreviation for *near-instantaneously companded audio multiplex*. See *Near-Instantaneously Companded Audio Multiplex (NICAM)*.

Nick

Any scratch, hole, or other such imperfection in a blade or other surface.

In *binding and finishing*, *nick* refers to a small tear at the top of the pages of a book that has been bound by *saddle-stitching*. This defect is caused by the blade during *trimming*.

Nigrosine

Any of a variety of deep blue or black *dyes* derived from the oxidation of *aniline*, used as a *colorant* in printing inks. Also called *nigrosin*.

NII

Abbreviation for *National Information Infrastructure*. See *National Information Infrastructure (NII)*.

Nine-Chip Module

In computing, a type of *single in-line memory module (SIMM)* containing nine 1-megabit chips. A 9-chip module, like a *three-chip module*, is used to add *random-access memory (RAM)* to a computer.

Nine-Track Tape

A type of ½-in. *magnetic tape* used for the backup of computer information and files, comprising nine parallel *track*s, eight of which are used for data, the ninth being used for *parity* information. Often used on some *minicomputer* systems, although *digital audio tape*s tend to be more popular for networks.

Nip

The line of contact between any two cylindrical objects, such as rollers, cylinders, drums, etc.

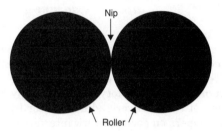

Schematic of a nip.

Nipper

One of two clamps used in the *building-in* stage of *case binding*, used to apply pressure to the bound book and expedite the drying and setting of the binding adhesive. See *Case Binding*.

Nipping

In *case binding*, the compressing of the spine of a book prior to *casing in*. Nipping forces out air from the pages of a *book block* and also compensates for *thread build-up*. In contrast, *smashing* is the application of pressure to the entire surface of the book block. See also *Smashing* and *Case Binding*.

NIST

Abbreviation for the *National Institute of Science and Technology*. See *National Institute of Science and Technology (NIST)*.

Nitrocellulose

A resinous component of *flexographic*, *gravure*, and *screen printing* inks and lacquers widely used as a *film former*. Its presence in inks can cause a printing defect known as *souring*. Nitrocellulose is also known as cellulose nitrate and is any of a variety of nitric *esters* of *cellulose*, in particular those types containing less than 12.4% nitrogen. Nitrocellulose is also known as *pyroxylin*.

NLQ

Abbreviation for *near-letter quality*. See *Near-Letter Quality*.

NMP

Abbreviation for *Network Management Protocol*. See *Network Management Protocol (NMP)*.

No-Read
A failed attempt by a *bar-code scanner*.

No-Screen Exposure
Alternate term for *bump exposure*. See *Bump Exposure*.

Node
In networking, any device (such as a *workstation*, printer, etc.) connected to the network that can be independently addressed, or independently send and/or receive messages.

In graphics, the term *node* also refers to a linking point on a *Bézier curve*.

Node Number
In networking, a unique number assigned to the *network interface card* of each device—or *node*—connected to a network, used for addressing and identification purposes. The node number may be factory-set (as in many *Ethernet* networks) or set by a network administrator by means of switches or jumpers on each network interface card.

Nodule
A small, rounded or irregularly shaped protuberance on the surface of a *flexographic* press's *anilox roller*, either due to a defect in chrome *electroplating* or from some other source, which requires increased polishing to remove.

Noise
Any unwanted signal—be it an audio, video, or electronic signal—that "contaminates" an audio or videotape, an electrical system, or a voice or data transmission. In audio and voice-grade telecommunications, noise is characterized by static; in video, it is characterized by bursts of snow; in data transmissions, it can be characterized in retrospect as garbled data or errors.

Noise Immunity
In telecommunications, the quality of a device that enables it to distinguish between valid signals and *noise*, accepting the former and rejecting the latter.

Noise Power Emission
In audio recording, *noise* produced by the audio source.

Nominal Velocity of Propagation
The speed at which a signal travels through a transmitting medium, such as a cable, expressed as a fraction or percentage of the speed of light. The nominal velocity of propagation is often measured as a means of determining cable lengths.

Nominal Weight
The *basis weight* specified when ordering paper, and the basis weight the papermaker tries for, within certain acceptable manufacturing tolerances, but that may vary from the basis weight of the actual paper, due to variations in the papermaking process. See *Basis Weight*.

Non-Alignment
In typography, a condition—either desired or undesired—in which all the characters or words on a line do not align along the *baseline*. The effect of non-alignment is called *bounce*. Non-alignment can often be caused by device error.

Non-Bearer-Contact Press
A type of printing press used in *offset lithography* in which the blanket and plate cylinder *bearers* (metal rings located at each end of each cylinder body, with diameters greater than the diameter of the cylinder body itself) do not contact each other while the press is in operation. Whether a press is a non-bearer-contact press or a *bearer-contact press* affects proper cylinder setting and *packing* considerations. See *Bearer*, *Plate Cylinder*, *Blanket Cylinder*, and *Packing*.

Noncollate
In *binding and finishing*, to not arrange printed or otherwise duplicated sheets in order or in sets.

Nondedicated Server
In networking, a *server* on which software applications used by connected users are stored. See *Server*. See also *Dedicated Server*.

Nondiscrete Value
Any value that can be quantitatively distinguished from another value only by the degree of precision allowed by the measurement system or device used or, in other words, cannot be differentiated from another value by whole, countable units. For example, the intensity of the light generated in a scanner would be a nondiscrete value, as compared to the number of light sources in the scanner. See also *Discrete Value*.

Non-Drying Oil
An oil used in printing ink *vehicle*s that does not dry upon exposure to the atmosphere. See *Non-Drying Oil Vehicle*.

Non-Drying Oil Vehicle
A type of ink *vehicle*—the fluid carrier of the ink *pigment*—that dries by absorption of the vehicle into the surface of the *substrate*, rather than by *evaporation* or *oxidation*. Non-drying oils are composed primarily of petroleum and rosin oils that do not dry upon exposure to the atmosphere, but penetrate the surface of the paper, leaving the hardened pigment on the surface. To the vehicle are added various *resin*s to provide the necessary *viscosity* or *tack*. Non-drying oil vehicles are used in inks that are printed on highly absorbent paper, such as *newsprint*. (See *Vehicle*.)

Nonfogging Film
A transparent thermoplastic film used as a *substrate* that does not become cloudy when exposed to changes in atmospheric temperature or humidity.

Nonimage Area

Any portion of a photographic negative or positive, printing plate, *gravure cylinder*, offset *blanket*, *stencil*, or other image-carrying surface that does not contain the image(s) to be printed.

Nonimpact Printer

Any of a wide variety of computer output devices that produce images on a substrate without striking the sheet, in contrast to an *impact printer*. Some common examples of nonimpact printers are *laser printer*s, *ink-jet printer*s, and *thermal printer*s.

Non-Interlaced

Descriptive of a *cathode-ray tube* whose image is not generated by means of *interlacing* or, in other words, is drawn as a single frame rather than as a frame comprising two separate *field*s. See *Interlacing*.

Nonlinear

Descriptive of a computer storage medium with which data can be accessed in random order, rather than serially. Such non-linear devices include *hard disk*s, *floppy disk*s, and *optical disc*s, as opposed to *magnetic tape*.

Nonlinear Editing

In video production, a means of editing video clips by storing video images on a *nonlinear* storage medium, such as a *hard disk*, *videodisc*, etc., and editing them together simply by indicating new *edit in/out point*s and clip orders. In contrast, *linear editing* requires all clips to be physically placed in the correct order.

Nonpareil

In metal typography, a term for a slug of type six *point*s thick, used to refer to six-point type prior to the advent of the *point system*.

Nonpreemptive Multitasking

In computing, a variety of *multitasking* in which an operating system cannot halt a task that is executing and begin a new task. See *Preemptive Multitasking; Multitasking*.

Nonprinting

In computing, any characters displayed on the screen that will not ultimately print out. Nonprinting characters include formatting and other commands. Nonprinting characters can be removed from the display, as well.

Nonrepro Blue

In prepress, a shade of blue that is invisible to photographic film and is thus used to mark guidelines, instructions, etc., on *camera-ready copy*.

Nonreproducible Color

Any color found in nature that is beyond the *gamut* of colors that can be reproduced using combinations of *process*

*ink*s. For example, the deep red color characteristic of burgundy wine cannot be reproduced using process inks.

Nonreproducing

In prepress and graphics, descriptive of any marks made on a *mechanical* or other *camera-ready copy* that will not be captured by a photographic reproduction process. Such marks are often made using "non-reproducible blue" pen, a shade of blue that does not register on graphic arts film.

Non-Scratch Ink

A printing ink that (when dry) has a hard, abrasion-resistant surface, used to print labels, cartons, covers, and other *substrates* that receive increased wear-and-tear from handling. (See also *Scuff-Resistant Ink*.)

Nonswitched Line

Any telecommunications link in which dialing is not necessary to make a connection.

Nonvolatile Memory

In computing, any computer memory that is not erased when the power is shut off. Computer storage—such as *hard disk*s or other magnetic and optical media—is defined as non-volatile memory, as are certain read-only Memory (ROM) chips, which hold data that cannot be modified, erased, or deleted when power is removed. See also *Volatile Memory*.

Nonwoven

In *binding and finishing*, a material used for "cloth bound" books made from a material other than cloth.

Normal

In graphics (and geometry), a line oriented at a right angle to a surface, indicating the curve of the surface.

Normal Viewing Orientation

The way a sheet of paper of a particular size is traditionally oriented, i.e., in the *portrait* orientation, in the case of an 8½×11-in. sheet.

North Pulse

An operator-defined point at the top of a to-be-scanned image, used as a reference point by a *drum scanner*.

North-South Label

A type of mailing *label* that comes on accordion-folded sheets one label wide.

NOS

Abbreviation for *network operating system*. See *Network Operating System (NOS)*.

Notch Binding

In *binding and finishing*, the gouging of grooves (commonly ¼ in. wide) in the spine of a *book block* to facilitate the penetration of adhesive during subsequent *perfect binding*. See *Perfect Binding*. See also *Burst Binding*.

Notebook

A type of portable computer smaller than a *laptop* but larger than a *hand-held* device. A notebook computer typically weighs less than eight pounds (but see also *Hidden Weight*).

ns

Abbreviation for *nanosecond*. See *Nanosecond*.

NSFNET

A computer network set up by the National Science Foundation (NSF) that, though not the *Internet* itself, makes up a portion of it.

NSP

Abbreviation for *native signal processing*. See *Native Signal Processing (NSP)*.

NT File System (NTFS)

In networking, the file system used by Microsoft's Windows NT operating system, which allows file sharing, and utilizes the *file allocation table* and *High Performance File System* used by *OS/2*.

NTFS

Abbreviation for *NT File System*. See *NT File System (NTFS)*.

NTSC

Abbreviation for *National Television Standards Committee*. See *National Television Standards Committee (NTSC)*.

NuBus

In computing, a fast, 32-*bit* bus used on older Apple *Macintosh* computers. NuBus is increasingly being replaced by the newer *PCI* bus. See *Bus*.

Nucleus

In computing, the section of a computer's main memory in which the *operating system* is located. Also known as the *supervisor*.

Nudge

In page layout programs, to move a selected object up, down, left, or right in very small increments, typically by using special arrow keys rather than the mouse.

Null

In computing, a code that represents the absence of information, usually zero.

Null Modem

In computing, an *RS-232-C* cable used in lieu of a *modem* to connect two computers together. The null modem cable connects to each computer's *serial port*, with several wires being crossed over such that the wires used by one computer for transmitting data can be used by the other computer for receiving data, and vice versa. See also *Modem Eliminator*.

Number

Either a *figure* (or digit) or a collection of figures (or digits) used to represent an arithmetical value. So, although 1, 6, 9, and 4 are each figures and digits, the quantity 1,694 is a number. Figures can also be numbers when a single figure represents such a value. See *Figures*.

Number 8 Varnish

Alternate term for *body gum*, a *bodying agent* added to printing inks. See *Body Gum*.

Numeric

Descriptive of data consisting solely of numbers. See also *Alphabetic* and *Alphanumeric*.

Numeric Character

One of the *Arabic numerals*. See *Arabic Numerals* and *Figures*.

Numeric Database

A *database* comprising primarily numeric information, such as statistics.

Numeric Processing Unit

Alternate term for a *coprocessor*. See *Coprocessor*.

Nut

In typography, a slang term for an *en space*.

Nut Segment

In a *scanner*, a nut that rides on the *lead screw* to regulate the movement of the scanner's optics.

Nylon®*

Any of a variety of *polyamide* compounds, formed by the interaction of dicarboxylic acid with a diamine compound (a molecule containing two $-NH_2$ groups) used as a synthetic *resin* in printing inks and as a screen fabric in *screen printing*.

*Nylon® is a registered trademark of the du Pont Chemical Company.

Nylon Heat Transfer

See *Heat Transfer Printing*.

O, o

The fifteenth letter of the English alphabet, deriving from the North Semitic consonant *ayin* and ultimately the Greek *omicron*. The form of the *O*, in both upper- and lowercase has changed little since then.

Egyptian	Sinai	Phoenician	Greek	Roman
3000 BC	1850 BC	1200 BC	600 BC	AD 114

The evolution of the letter O.

Object

In graphics, any graphical entity—such as a circle—perceived as such by an application program or computer system. An object is treated as a single unit by the system, whereas in a *paint program*, for example, every image is treated merely as a set of *pixel*s.

In computer programming, the term *object* refers to a single programming entity that can contain both code and data. See *Object-Oriented Programming (OOP)*.

In computing, the term *object* refers to a single data entity used in *Object Linking and Embedding*. See *Object Linking and Embedding (OLE)*.

Object Code

In computing, the *machine language* output from a *compiler*, which is used to convert *source code* to the object code that the computer can understand. Object code can be directly executed by the computer, or it can be further processed to produce a code suitable for execution by the computer.

Object Editor

Any software that is used to *render* and/or edit *three-dimensional (3D) graphics*.

Object Linking and Embedding (OLE)

In computing, especially on the *Windows* platform, a means of linking Windows-based files and sharing the data contained within them. Essentially, as the name indicates, a particular data object can be embedded within a program's data file. In this case, there are two copies of any particular data object or set of objects: the original data as created by the user in the original file or document, and a duplicate set embedded in a linked file or application. Alternately, data can merely be linked; rather than embedding multiple copies of a data set in several applications or files, pointers to the original data can be embedded in a linked file or application, so the system knows where to find the original data. The advantage of this latter method is that one set of data need only be altered once to have the changes reflected in all linked documents. On the *Macintosh* platform, a competitive method is called *OpenDoc*.

Object-Oriented

Descriptive of computer graphics that are based on *vector*s rather than *bitmap*s. See *Vector Graphics*. The term *object-oriented* also refers to *object-oriented programming*. See *Object-Oriented Programming (OOP)*.

Object-Oriented Graphic

Alternate term for a *vector graphic*. See *Vector Graphics*.

Object-Oriented Programming (OOP)

In computing, a means of programming in which a program comprises not individual, separate lines of code, but rather groups of programming lines that represent specific objects that have specific functions. Each of these objects is self-contained, and can be used in different programs for similar functions. Object-oriented programming allows programs to be written much faster.

Object Program

A computer program that exists as executable *object code*. See *Object Code* and *Machine Language*.

Object Rotation

A feature of a *three-dimensional (3D) graphics* program that allows the rendered object to be rotated on the screen.

Oblique

In typography, an alternate term for *italic*, or a term descriptive of a right-leaning change in the posture of the characters in a particular *typeface*. Although oblique can refer to any italic version of a typeface, it is often used to

abcdefghijklmnopqrstuvwxyz
Avant Garde Book Oblique

abcdefghijklmnopqrstuvwxyz
Century Expanded Italic

abcdefghijklmnopqrstuvwxyz
Eurostile Oblique

abcdefghijklmnopqrstuvwxyz
New Baskerville Italic

Examples of italic and oblique typefaces.

describe a **matching italic** face, or an italic created by merely slanting the roman characters electronically (or by other means). See **Italic**.

Oblong Binding

In **binding and finishing**, a book that has been bound along its short dimension. See also **Upright Binding**.

OCR

Abbreviation for **Optical Character Recognition (OCR)**. See also **Optical Character Reader**.

OCR Paper

A type of business form paper with a high level of **whiteness** to be used with **Optical Character Recognition (OCR)** equipment. The various optical properties need to be within certain specifications dictated by the OCR devices themselves.

Octal

A numerical system based on eight digits. An octal system is occasionally used by computer systems as it is based on a **binary** system. See **Binary** and **Digital**.

Octavo

In **book typography** and production, any printed sheet that has been folded three times to yield eight leaves or sixteen pages. Abbreviated *8vo* and *8°*. *Octavo* is also used to refer to the book size produced by folding pages in this manner (commonly 6×9 in.). See also **Folio** and **Quarto**.

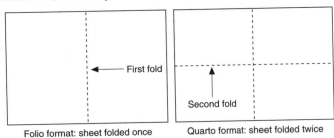

Folio format: sheet folded once   Quarto format: sheet folded twice

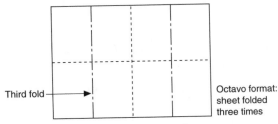

Folio, quarto, and octavo formats.

Octet

Alternate term for a **byte**. See **Byte**.

Octothorpe

The actual name for the cross-hatch symbol (#) used as an abbreviation for the word "number," or as a special function key on telephone keypads. It is more commonly known as the **pound sign**.

O.D.

Abbreviation for the *outside diameter* of a cylindrical object, such as the core of a roll of paper (or other **substrate**) or a press cylinder or roller. See also **I.D.**

ODBC

Alternate term for **Open Database Connectivity**. See **Open Database Connectivity (ODBC)**.

Odd Parity

In computing, a **parity check** used to detect and correct errors in data transmission by adding an extra **bit** (either a 1 or a 0) to a character code so as to ensure that the total number of 1s in the code is an odd number. See **Parity**. See also **Even Parity**.

Odd Size

Any paper size that is not a **standard size**. Also called a **bastard size**.

ODI

Abbreviation for **open data-link interface**. See **Open Data-Link Interface (ODI)**.

ODI/NDIS Support

See **Open Data-Link Interface/Network Driver Interface Specification Support (ODINSUP)**.

ODINSUP

Abbreviation for **Open Data-Link Interface/Network Driver Interface Specification Support**. See **Open Data-Link Interface/Network Driver Interface Specification Support (ODINSUP)**.

OEM

Abbreviation for **original equipment manufacturer**. See **Original Equipment Manufacturer**.

Off Color

Descriptive of any paper and/or ink that do not match their corresponding samples.

Off-Contact Printing

In **screen printing**, making a printed impression with the printing screen adjusted so that it does not contact the

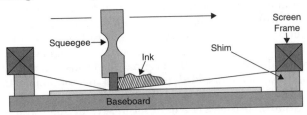

Off-contact screen printing.

substrate except along the line directly beneath the *squeegee*. The distance (when the screen is not under the load of the squeegee) between the stencil and the substrate can range from ¹⁄₁₆–⅛ in., the distance occasionally being as great as ⅜–½ in.

Off-Line

Descriptive of **binding and finishing** operations that are performed separately from the printing process or from each other, as opposed to **in-line** processes.

In computing, the term *off-line* refers to the state of a computer, network **node**, printer, etc., that does not have an active connection to the network, controller, or other system. See also **On-Line**. Also spelled as a single, hyphenless word, *offline*.

Off-Line Editing

In video editing, a kind of "pre-editing" during which videotape is reviewed on a conventional VCR or other inexpensive system (i.e., not an editing system) and an **edit decision list** is compiled, along with a list of **edit in/out** points, as well as desired effects. It is on this initial off-line editing session that an **on-line editing** session is based.

Off-Line Reader

In **Internet** terminology, a program that allows a **USENET** newsgroup subscriber to automatically **download** postings to the newsgroup and read them at leisure without needing to remain connected to the Internet. An off-line reader also lets the user compose replies or posts of his/her own, which will then be **upload**ed the next time the user connects to the Internet. An off-line reader is not only valuable when connecting through **Internet service providers** that charge by the hour, but also for basic **netiquette** in that a single user is not tying up a connection for an inordinate period of time.

Off-Machine Coating

The **coating** of the surface of a paper performed after it has come off the papermaking machine, as a separate operation, often by a mill that specializes in coating. The advantages of off-machine coating are the speed and efficiency of utilizing special equipment designed just for coating, and the **base stock** produced by more than one papermaking machine or process can be coated using one machine. Disadvantages include the necessity of winding, packing, and shipping paper rolls. See also **Coating** and **On-Machine Coating**.

Off-Press Proof

A **color proof**, typically prepared photographically or digitally—by exposing a negative or positive to light-sensitive materials, or generating color output from a computer, respectively—designed to simulate the appearance of a printed piece. Off-press proofs can either be **overlay proof**s (such as **NAPS** or **Color-Key**) or **single-sheet proof**s (such as **Cromalin** or **Matchprint**). An off-press proof differs from a **press proof** in that the latter is prepared on a printing press. Also known as a **prepress proof**.

Offprint

In printing, any printed sheet beyond the quantity originally ordered.

Offset

To transfer ink from a printed **substrate** to the reverse of the sheet lying on top of it after printing, an undesirable condition. See **Ink Setoff**.

The term *offset* is also an alternate term for **offset printing** in general and **offset lithography** in particular.

Offset Alignment

The calibration or adjustment of a color **scanner**'s internal analog color computer.

Offset Flexo

A hybrid form of **flexography** that utilizes a rubber **blanket**—similar to that used in **offset lithography**—to transfer the image from the flexo plate to the substrate. See **Flexography: Hybrid Flexographic Presses: Offset Flexo**.

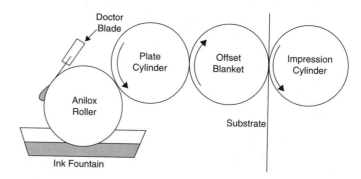

An offset flexo printing unit.

Offset Gravure

A variety of **gravure** printing in which the image is transferred from a **gravure cylinder** to a rubber-covered **transfer roller** and, ultimately, to the substrate. See **Gravure:**

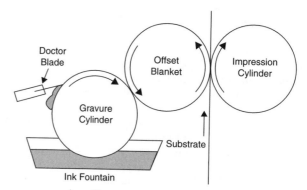

An offset gravure printing unit.

Offset Gravure. Offset gravure is also known as ***indirect gravure***, and offset gravure that is performed on a flexographic press is known as ***flexo gravure***.

Offset Lithography

A term describing the most common form of ***lithography*** (a printing process in which the image area and the non-image area co-exist on the same plane, rather than from raised or etched type, as in ***letterpress*** and ***gravure*** printing, respectively; see ***Lithography***) in which a printed image is transferred first to a rubber blanket, and the blanket then transfers (or "offsets") the image to the paper or other surface. Other forms of lithography include ***direct lithography (or*** di-litho) and ***waterless lithography***. The two basic varieties of offset lithography are sheetfed and ***web offset lithography***. The remainder of this article will deal primarily with sheetfed offset printing. See also ***Web Offset Lithography***.

EVOLUTION OF OFFSET LITHOGRAPHY

The offset press as we know it today was invented around 1905 by Ira Rubel, a papermill owner in Nutley, New Jersey, who also used the contemporary lithographic stone presses to print bank deposit slips. At that time, stone-based lithographic presses used a natural rubber blanket wrapped around the ***impression cylinder*** (the cylinder providing a hard backing to the paper, allowing a clear, firm impression by the plate), and the stone plate transferred the image directly to the paper. Occasionally, the feeder (which in those days was a person manually inserting paper into the press) would miss a sheet, and the plate would accidentally transfer the image to the blanket. When this happened, the next sheet through the press would print on both sides, a right-reading image on the top of the sheet transferred by the plate, and a wrong-reading image on the bottom of the sheet, transferred by the still-wet image on the blanket. Rubel noticed, as many others had, that the image transferred by the blanket was clearer and sharper than that transferred by the stone plate, and decided to build a printing press using the rubber blanket as the means of transferring the image to the paper.

Rubel joined forces with a Chicago-based printer, A.B. Sherwood, and together they created the Sherbel Syndicate. Hoping to monopolize the new printing process, they set strict rules concerning how many offset presses could be built; they decided on only one per region of the country. Twelve offset presses were built initially, but internal strife within the Sherbel Syndicate, the desire on the part of printers for more machines than the syndicate was willing to allow, and Rubel's death in 1908 ruined any chance of a monopoly succeeding. It did, however, quickly produce a competitor, who would be more successful than Sherbel: the Harris Automatic Press Company.

In 1906, a Harris salesman tried to sell a lithographic stone press to the Goes Lithograph Company, a Chicago print shop. Charles Goes, head of the company, was not interested but had recently been irked by Sherwood and the

Sherbel Syndicate's rules, and told the Harris salesman that if they could build a press like the one Sherbel was manufacturing, he would buy one. This was reported to Charles Harris, an engineer at the Harris Company, and an offset press was designed and built. By the end of 1906, Harris shipped four offset presses; six more were shipped in 1907. Much later, in 1927, Harris bought the company that had been manufacturing Rubel's presses.

Offset lithography was heralded as a triumph by many, though there were some pockets of resistance. By 1912, there were 560 offset presses in operation in the United States, and by the 1930s it was the dominant form of lithography—stone lithography had ceased to exist. Further refinements in the component parts of the press—from plates, which began to be composed of metal, to the rollers, to the blanket itself, which was made less troublesome after the invention of synthetic rubber in the 1930s—eventually made it the rapid, efficient, and overwhelmingly popular printing process that it is today.

The basic parts or systems of an offset printing press are the inking system, dampening system, printing unit, and infeed and sheet control.

INKING SYSTEM

As one would expect, the ***inking system*** primarily functions to transfer ink from the ***ink fountain*** to the printing plate, to add enough force to break the thick, viscous ink down into a thinner, more workable ink film (see ***Thixotropy***), and to prevent the existence of faint reproductions of the printing image on the ink rollers (see

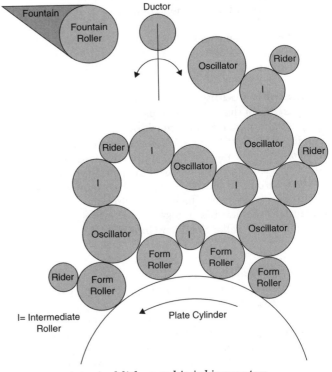

A typical lithographic inking system.

Mechanical Ghosting). Offset inking systems can comprise as many as ten (or perhaps more) different rollers, which include *ductor roller*s, *oscillator*s, *distributor*s or *vibrator*s (collectively called *intermediate rollers*), and *form roller*s. The entire series of rollers is called the *roller train*. The amount of ink that is sent to the rest of the press can be controlled either by adjusting the ink fountain's *fountain keys*, which vary the amount of ink transferred to the *fountain roller*—the roller that contacts the first roller in the train—or by adjusting the *dwell*—the amount of time that the first ductor roller contacts the fountain roller. (See *Ductor Roller*.) Controlling the ink film thickness, or the amount of ink that is ultimately deposited on the plate, is a function of the form rollers, which actually contact the plate itself. (See *Form Roller*.)

A printing ink thickness of 0.2–0.4 mils (0.0002–0.0004 in.) generally produces the best results, depending on other aspects such as ink color. Too great an ink thickness transferred to the plate results in such problems as *ink setoff*, *graininess*, and *dot gain*, as well as ink drying problems, increased *emulsification* of the ink, and inaccurate color reproduction. Too thin an ink film can result in such problems as *picking*, *hickeys*, decreased *color strength*, decreased ink *gloss*, and poor ink coverage of the paper. Desired inking levels can be determined utilizing the concept of *print contrast*, a formula based on the printing density of solids and tints. (See *Print Contrast*.)

Some printing presses have auxiliary inking system devices attached. An *ink agitator* helps prevent ink from *backing away from the fountain*, a problem experienced with certain inks that tend to thicken up readily and need to be stirred frequently to properly transfer to the fountain roller. The agitator is a motorized cone-shaped device that

Ink agitator.

moves back and forth across the ink fountain, automatically keeping the ink stirred. A *fountain splitter* is used occasionally in *spot-color printing* to separate two different colors of ink in the same fountain, enabling the two different colors to be printed at the same time, provided that the colors appear far enough apart on the substrate. Printing problems called hickeys (caused by particles of debris

from dried ink skins, paper *lint* and dust, or other particulate matter adhering to the printing plate or blanket) can be reduced with a *hickey-picking roller*, a roller covered with synthetic fibers that contacts the plate and either picks off the offending particle, or surrounds it with ink, eliminating the white halo characterizing a *doughnut hickey*. Some presses also benefit from the installation of an *ink leveler*, a device that uses ultrasonic vibrations to determine the level of the ink in the fountain, and automatically triggers a pneumatic pump to add ink to the fountain when the level gets low enough. An *Air Curtin*™ is used on some presses to remove excess moisture from the inking system by directing concentrated streams of air at a particular roller, which evaporates the water being transferred through the system. (See *Inking System: Offset Lithography*.)

DAMPENING SYSTEM

Lithographic printing is based on the principle that oil and water do not mix readily (although a very slight amount of mixing is what makes the system work). Therefore, the dampening system of an offset press keeps nonimage areas of the plate moistened so that they will repel ink. The nonimage areas of a plate have been desensitized during platemaking to facilitate water receptivity. An offset press *dampening solution*, commonly referred to as a *fountain solution*, can consist entirely of water. As this is generally ineffective for long print runs, synthetic desensitizers are added to the fountain solution to maximize the ink repellency of the nonimage areas of the plate. The substances added to the fountain solution depend on the type of ink being used, but typically a fountain solution consists of water, an acid or base (depending on the desired *pH* of the solution), a gum (such as *gum arabic* to desensitize the nonimage plate regions), a *corrosion inhibitor* to prevent the solution from reacting with the metallic plate, an alcohol-based *wetting agent* to reduce the fountain solution's surface tension, a *drying stimulator* to increase the effectiveness of the ink *drier*, a fungicide to prevent the growth of mildew, fungi, and bacteria, and an *antifoaming agent* to prevent the production of foam in the dampening system. Fountain solution is usually premixed by the supplier, requiring only the addition of water and alcohol by the printer. (See *Fountain Solution*.)

A typical dampening system closely resembles an inking system, but since water does not need to be worked the way ink does, fewer rollers are used. One of the rollers in the dampening system is the *water pan*, which holds the fountain solution. A *fountain pan roller* rotates in the water pan and transfers the solution to the rest of the dampening system. A *ductor roller* alternately contacts the fountain pan roller and an *oscillator roller*. The oscillator roller, like that used in the inking system, moves laterally across the press to even out the distribution of solution, then transfers the solution to the *form roller*s, which then transfer the solution directly to the plate. The dampening form rollers (of which there are typically two)

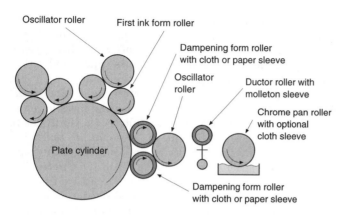

A conventional, or intermittent-flow, dampening system.

contact the plate before the ink form rollers, desensitizing the nonimage areas of the plate before the application of the ink. As with ink, the amount of water flowing to the plate must be carefully metered, which can be accomplished either by adjusting the rate at which the fountain pan roller turns, the length of time the ductor roller contacts the fountain pan roller, or by using *water stops*, a set of squeegees, tabs, or rollers that press against the fountain pan roller and squeeze excess water off it. The pressure of the water stops can be controlled, the highest pressure squeezing the greatest amount of water off the fountain pan roller and transferring the least amount of fountain solution through the press.

The dampening system described above is known as a *conventional dampening system* or an *intermittent-flow dampening system*, as the movement of the ductor roller does not allow the continuous flow of fountain solution through the press. *Continuous-flow dampening systems*, which can transfer the fountain solution either through the inking system (called an *inker-feed system*), directly to the plate (called a *plate-feed system*), or both through the inking system and directly to the plate, do away with the ductor roller and provide, as their name indicates, a continuous flow of fountain solution. Continuous-flow systems help eliminate some of the common dampening

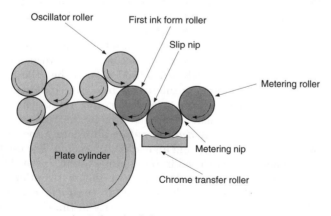

An inker-feed dampening system.

system problems and allow instantaneous response to adjustments in the system. (See *Dampening System*.)

PRINTING UNIT

The basic printing unit of an offset press contains three (or sometimes more) cylinders: a *plate cylinder*, to which the plate is attached, a *blanket cylinder*, to which the offset blanket is attached, and an *impression cylinder*, which carries the paper through the printing unit and provides a hard backing against which the blanket can impress an image on the paper. Many presses also contain some number of *transfer cylinder*s, which carry the paper either to additional printing units (in multicolor presses) or to the delivery tray. The last transfer cylinder that sends the printed sheets to the delivery tray is called the *delivery cylinder*. Some presses, in lieu of a transfer or delivery cylinder, utilize an *air-transport drum* that reduces the potential for ink smearing by carrying the paper on a cushion of air.

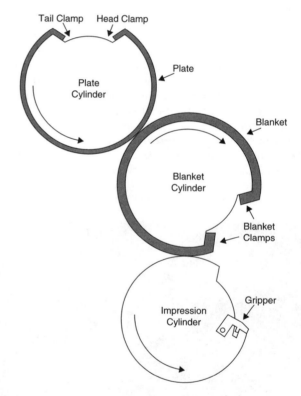

The three cylinders that comprise a sheetfed printing unit.

The arrangement of the cylinders can vary depending on the press, so long as the proper cylinders are adjacent to each other. The plate cylinder is typically the topmost cylinder and is in contact with the inking and dampening form rollers. The plate contains a right-reading image that is inked by the inking system. As the plate cylinder rotates, it is brought into contact with the blanket cylinder beneath it. (The blanket cylinder can be backed away from the plate cylinder, to facilitate removal and adjustment of the plate.)

The inked image areas of the plate transfer to the rubber blanket, the image now being wrong-reading. The paper (or other substrate) is carried by the feeder system to the impression cylinder and is sent through the nip between the blanket and impression cylinders. There, the blanket transfers the image to the substrate. The substrate then is transferred to the delivery cylinder (if the press is a single-color press) or to a series of transfer cylinders that send it to other printing units (if it is a multicolor press).

As with the various rollers of the inking and dampening systems, proper cylinder setting and maintenance are important to ensure the proper fidelity of the printed image. Various adjustments can also be made to the cylinders, depending on the print job. An important aspect of offset printing is proper *packing*, or height adjustment, of the plate and blanket cylinders, which has important consequences in terms of print quality. (See *Packing*.) (See also *Plate Cylinder*, *Blanket Cylinder*, *Impression Cylinder*, and *Transfer Cylinder*.)

INFEED AND SHEET CONTROL

The sheet control and feeding mechanisms on an offset press are concerned with proper transfer of paper into the press, between printing units (if a multicolor press), and, finally, out of the press into a delivery tray. Consequently, the sheet control system as a whole comprises four basic subparts.

Feeder Section. At an offset press's *feeder section*, sheets are removed from the top of a paper pile. The feeder section consists of an adjustable *pile table* on which the stack of paper is placed, a *sheet-separation unit* (jets of air and/or a vacuum to ensure that only one sheet is sent through the press at any one time), and a *feedboard* (a platform or ramp on which the paper is sent to the devices that properly position the paper for printing). The most widely used type of sheet feeder is a *stream feeder*, in which more than one paper sheet, traveling slower than the speed of the press, is on the feedboard at any one time, in contrast to a *single-sheet feeder* in which only one sheet, traveling at the speed of the press, is on the feedboard at one time. (Both stream and single-sheet feeders share the various elements of the feeder section.) The paper stock is stacked on the pile table, precisely centered to the feeder. Even slight variations in stock position can cause feeding problems, necessitating press stoppage. Some pile tables can be continuous-feeding, meaning that the press does not need to be stopped to reload. Configurations vary. (See *Pile Table*.)

A variation of the continuous-feed system is called a *roll sheeter*, in which a roll of paper is cut into sheets just prior to being sent into the press. (See *Roll Sheeter*.) The sheet-separation unit uses blasts of air to separate a batch of the topmost sheets, while suction feet lift the top sheet and forward it to the feedboard. The strength of the air blasts and the vacuum can be adjusted to the thickness of the stock. Brushes and fingers can also be added to the

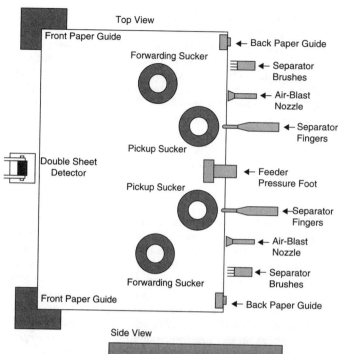

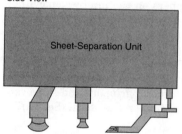

Sheet-separation unit.

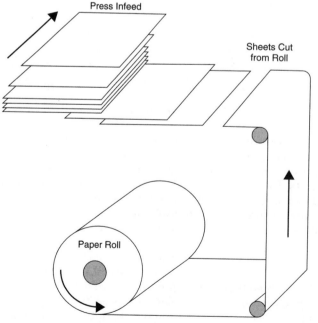

Principle of roll sheeting.

sheet-separation unit, which enhances paper control. (See *Sheet-Separation Unit*.) Before transfer to the feedboard, a series of *forwarding roller*s and *sheet detector*s ensure that only the proper number of sheets are sent through at any one time. The configuration and sensitivity of the feeder rollers and the sheet detectors can be adjusted. The feedboard consists of a series of rollers, brushes, balls, and feed tapes that carry the sheet to a set of stops, ensuring that any lateral movement of the paper is compensated for. Various feedboard configurations can also ensure that foreign objects are not sent into the press, and they can detect early or late sheets, preventing paper jams or *misregister*.

Infeed Section. Once a sheet is aligned properly at the head of the feedboard, it needs to be transferred by the *infeed section* to grippers on the impression cylinder. Three basic configurations accomplish this end: a *swing-arm system* in which a swinging gripper arm grabs the sheet of paper from the feedboard and carries it to the grippers on the impression cylinder, a *rotary-drum system* in which a rotating drum armed with grippers picks up the sheet from the feedboard with each rotation and transfers it to grippers on the impression cylinder, and an *overfeed system* in which the paper is forced by vacuum belts, or rollers, against a stop located on the impression cylinder itself. The paper buckles against this stop until impression cylinder grippers grab it. It is the careful calibration of this buckling effect that ensures proper paper alignment. The configuration of grippers and stops can be adjusted or varied, depending on the stock. (See *Infeed System*.)

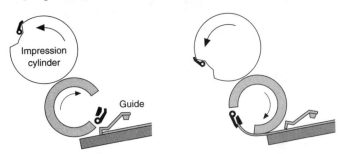

Rotary-drum infeed system.

Transfer Section. As we saw above, sheets are moved between printing units by a transfer cylinder. (In some presses, however, the paper is transferred between printing units by transfer cylinder-powered chains. See *Chain Transfer*.) The exact configuration of the transfer system varies by press and can involve one or three transfer cylinders of varying diameters. Each cylinder is equipped with grippers that pick up the paper from the previous cylinder (either transfer or impression) and transfer it to the next (either transfer or impression). (See *Single-Drum Transfer*, *Three-Drum Transfer*, and *Transfer Cylinder*.) On a *perfecting press*, specially adjusted transfer cylinders flip the sheet over so that additional printing units can print on the reverse side of the paper. (See *Perfecting Press*.)

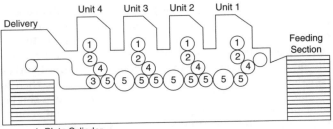

1. Plate Cylinder
2. Blanket Cylinder
3. Delivery Cylinder
4. Impression Cylinder
5. Transfer Cylinder

A printing press with a three-drum transfer system.

Delivery Section. Once the printed sheet leaves the final impression cylinder, grippers on the delivery cylinder pick up the sheet and deposit it either on a moveable delivery chain, which carries the sheet to the *delivery pile*, or directly onto the delivery pile itself. On the delivery pile, moveable guides jog the sheets into a neat pile. (See *Delivery Section* and *Delivery Cylinder*.)

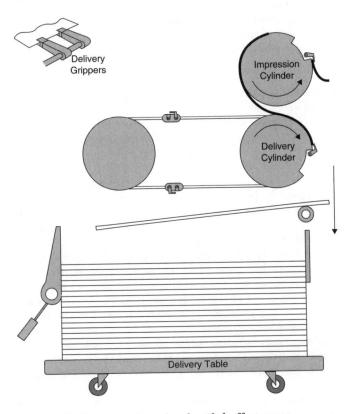

Delivery section of a sheetfed offset press.

As was mentioned above, unlike most other printing processes, offset lithography uses not only a metal plate but also a rubber blanket to transfer the image to the substrate. Both of these elements of the press have certain considerations.

PLATES

The process of lithographic platemaking ensures that the image areas of a plate are **lipophilic** (or **oleophilic**) and **hydrophobic** (in other words, receptive to oil—namely, ink—and repellent to water) while the nonimage areas are **lipophobic** (or **oleophobic**) and **hydrophilic** (in other words, repellent to oil and receptive to water). These chemical principles ensure that the ink will only adhere to the image areas of the plate. On the press, the water-receptive coating on the nonimage areas must be increased, a process called **desensitization**. A gum, such as gum arabic, is typically used to accomplish this. Gum additives in the press fountain solution ensure that the plate remains desensitized over the course of the pressrun. (See **Plate: Offset Lithography**.) Before mounting, plates are inspected for scratches and other defects, and occasionally minor corrections can be made to the plate. Unwanted specks or other small, undesirable image areas can be erased, then treated with etch and gum; voids in solid image areas can be filled in by scratching the plate, then applying ink to the area. Such plate doctoring should only be performed on the most minor of defects. At this point, the degree of **packing** should be determined. (See **Packing**.) Mounting is performed according to the press manufacturer's recommendations, and the image **lay**, or position of the printed image on the paper, determined. At this point, the plate may need to be repositioned, to keep the image centered, or in register with previously printed images on the paper. Properly formulated and applied fountain solution will more often than not obviate the need for continual plate maintenance while on press. Extended press shutdowns, however, such as overnight, should not occur while the plate is still inked. Gum that dries on the image areas causes **plate blinding**.

Plates can be subject to two primary defects: **scumming** and blinding, which are ink receptivity in nonimage areas and ink-repellency in image areas, respectively. (See **Scumming** and **Plate Blinding**.) Most plate problems are caused by improper formulation or application of fountain solution.

BLANKETS

An offset blanket is commonly made of a synthetic rubber, and the most important feature of the blanket is its **release** capability, or the ease with which it will let go of the sheet passing through the **impression nip**. Release is primarily a function of the smoothness of the surface of the blanket, though things like ink **tack**, impression nip **squeeze**, and the surface characteristics of the paper also play a part. Printers often have found hard blankets to provide the best release, although empirical research has not borne this out. (Problems relating to the accurate measurement of blanket hardness no doubt contribute to this lack of evidence.) A blanket's **smash resistance** (its ability to return to its normal thickness after being subjected to printing pressure) and its **durability** (its ability to withstand the force of printing pressures over time) are also of importance. Whether a

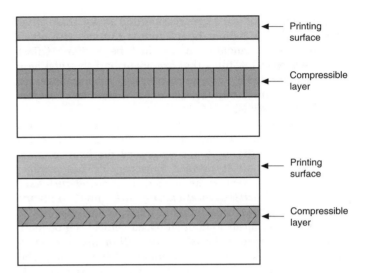

A compressible blanket.

blanket is a conventional or **compressible blanket** is also important. Prior to mounting, the packing requirements of the blanket should be determined. (See **Packing**.) One problem that blankets can be subject to is **blanket smash**, or a small, depression in the blanket surface, typically caused by a foreign object passing through the impression nip. Blanket smashes can cause various printing defects, so it is typical to replace the blanket with a spare, or repair the blanket before continuing with it. Any blanket that has more grievous problems, such as rips or tears, should be replaced immediately. Blankets may also experience **piling**, the accumulation of paper fibers or coating particles, which can produce printing defects such as **hickey**s. (See **Blanket**.)

Each printing process also has certain ink and paper requirements that, although the exact nature is typically governed by the print job itself, achieve the best results with a minimum of printability and runnability problems.

PAPER AND INK

Offset lithography uses tackier inks than other methods, so the paper used must have high surface and internal-bonding strength. It must also have high water resistance to maintain its surface strength in the presence of water from the dampening system. The paper surface must be free of dust, lint, or other debris to keep foreign material from piling on the blanket or upsetting the press's chemical balance. If successive printings on each sheet are required, the paper must have high dimensional stability, and its equilibrium moisture content must approximate the relative humidity of the pressroom, to prevent register misalignment. Long-grain paper is also required for multicolor jobs. Various types of nonpaper surfaces, such as metals, foils, plastics, etc., can also be utilized.

The suitability of the offset lithographic process for printing on a wide variety of surfaces has resulted in a large number of inks available for the process. Typically, lithographic inks are more viscous and tacky than other types of inks, and since the ink film is thinner with offset printing, the pigment content must be higher. (Offset presses deposit ink films that are about half the thickness of films deposited by letterpress presses.) Inks designed for the process must contain significant amounts of water-repellent materials.

Sheetfed offset presses primarily use quickset inks, which dry rapidly without the need for additional equipment, such as drying ovens necessary for heatset inks. Some sheetfed offset presses, however, do use various radiation-curing devices, as is needed for *super-quickset infrared ink*, *ultraviolet-curing ink*, and *electron-beam-curing ink*. Lithographic inks primarily set by a combination of absorption of oil-based vehicle components into the substrate, followed by *oxidation* and *polymerization* of the remaining components of the vehicle. The most important criterion for offset inks, however, is their insolubility, as they must resist bleeding in the presence of the water-based press dampening systems. Problems with the drying of offset inks that dry by oxidation include *emulsification* of the fountain solution into the ink. An excessive amount of dampening solution (or one with a high pH) can impede proper ink drying, and the use of papers that have a low pH also has a deleterious effect on ink-drying properties. (See *Acid Paper* and *Alkaline Paper*.) Lithographic inks used for printing on metals (such as cans and other metallic packaging) contain synthetic resin *varnish*es that dry in high-temperature ovens.

PRESS CONFIGURATIONS

The many different types of sheetfed offset presses tend to fall into one of three categories.

A single-color press has one set of printing unit cylinders to print one color at a time on only one side of the sheet. Additional colors, or the second side, can be printed following reinking and the mounting of separate plates. One particular consideration of multicolor printing on a single-color press is *dry trapping*, or the ability of the wet ink film to lay on top of the dried ink from previous passes.

A multicolor press contains more than one printing unit lined up in series, through which the press sheet passes before being sent to the delivery pile. A consideration of multicolor presses is *wet trapping*, or the ability of the wet ink film to lay on top of still-wet ink films deposited by previous printing units. Press sheets are transferred between printing units by the transfer cylinders mentioned above, their numbers varying according to press configuration but that needs to comprise an odd number of transfer cylinders between units to keep the printed side of the sheet from facing the impression cylinder.

A *perfecting press* is a press that prints at least one color on both sides of the sheet simultaneously. A *convertible perfector* has more than one printing unit and uses special reversing cylinders to turn the sheet over before it contacts the second printing unit. By adjusting the transfer cylinders, this type of perfecting press functions either as a

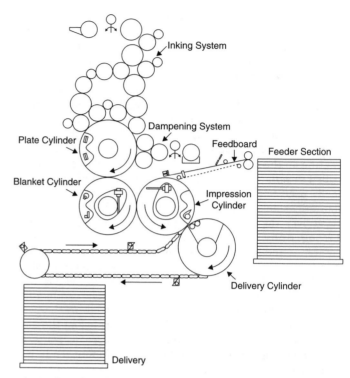

A single-color sheetfed offset lithographic printing press.

single-side multicolor press or as a two-sided perfector. A variety of perfecting press is a *blanket-to-blanket press*, in which the blanket cylinder of a second set of printing cylinders replaces the impression cylinder, allowing the press to print both sides of the paper simultaneously. Blanket-to-blanket presses are found most commonly in web offset printing.

A fourth type of press that is gradually falling into disuse is a *proof press*, a small, stripped-down offset press used to produce a proof from a particular plate, negative, or

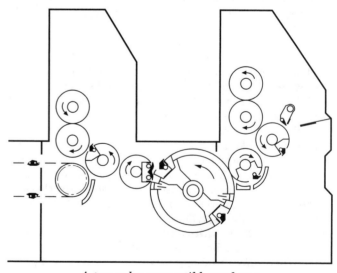

A two-color convertible perfector.

positive. A proof press varies from a typical production press in that it lacks automated feeding, inking, and dampening systems, and most configurations feature the plate and paper mounted on flat beds, a rolling blanket cylinder being used to first pick up the inked image from the plate and then transfer it to a single sheet at a time. Proofing is now done in a variety of other ways, such as on a production press (or, often, the press that will actually be used for the job), or using special photosensitive papers, colored films, etc. Such means are known as *off-press proofing* and can involve single sheets or colored overlays taped together in register. A fast-growing form of proofing is *direct digital color proofing (DDCP)*, using computer information to digitally image proof paper or film. (See *Color Proofing*.)

A fifth type of offset press is known as a *duplicator*, which is a small press (typically one that prints paper sizes less than 11×17 in.) without cylinder bearers and used for small, quick jobs. Their simplicity and low cost had made them ideal for small copy centers. Newer machines retain the simplicity of the duplicator but add some of the advanced automated features of full-size offset presses.

A new breed of *intelligent copier/printer (IC/P)* bridges the gap between the standard offset press and the photocopier, providing the advantages of photocopying—quick turnaround time and practically no makeready—as well as acceptable quality for many applications. Many printers are supplementing their larger offset presses with IC/Ps, which enable them to use the latter for quick, single-color jobs while reserving the former for larger, multicolor jobs. Newer generations of IC/P have higher print resolutions and can print directly from computer data. Add-on finishing and binding devices enhance the speed and efficiency of the process. New technologies are also enhancing color printing, especially technologies that allow direct computer imaging (often via PostScript files) of printing plates. Digital printing, in a variety of forms, is becoming more and more common as technology allows higher quality and faster speeds than could be previously obtained. (See *Digital Prepress*.)

Offset Paper

General term for a variety of paper *grades*, similar to *book paper*, manufactured especially for *offset lithography*. Increased amounts of *sizing* enhance its ability to repel moisture when in contact with offset press dampening systems. Specific types of offset papers include *coated offset paper* and *uncoated groundwood-free offset paper*.

Off-the-Shelf

Descriptive of any product—usually computer software, however—that can be purchased at a retail outlet, rather than custom-made for a particular task or company. The opposite is generally considered a *proprietary system*.

Oil Absorption

A measurement used in the manufacture of printing inks that describes the amount of oil required to completely wet a given weight of *pigment*.

Oil Mounting

The process of attaching a *color transparency* to the drum of a *drum scanner* by means of a layer of oil (such as paraffin oil or mineral oil) in order to avoid scratching the transparency or producing *Newton's rings*.

Oiticica Oil

An oil derived from the seeds of the oiticica tree (*Licania rigida*), a member of the rose family native to Brazil. Oiticica oil, by virtue of its high drying qualities and its *chemical resistance*, is used in the manufacture of printing ink *vehicles*.

OK Sheet

A *color proof* or early press sheet that is evaluated by the printer and the customer as to the quality of the color reproduction. Once "okayed" by the customer, it is then used as a color guide for the length of the pressrun. Also known as a *color OK* or a *pass sheet*.

Old Style

In typography, a *typeface* design dating from the early days of printing, specifically those utilized by Venetian printers in the late 15th century, or typefaces derived from those early styles. Such faces are characterized by variations in stroke and width, bracketed *serif*s, and diagonal strokes. Some common examples include Bembo, Caslon, and Garamond.

ABCDEFGHIJKLMNOPQ
abcdefghijklmnopqrstuvwxyz
Caslon

ABCDEFGHIJKLMNOPQRST
abcdefghijklmnopqrstuvwxy
Garamond Book

Two examples of old style typefaces.

Old Style Figures

Alternate term for *hanging figures*. See *Hanging Figures*.

OLE

Abbreviation for *object linking and embedding*. See *Object Linking and Embedding (OLE)*.

Oleophilic

A quality of certain papers, components of paper, or the image areas of lithographic printing plates that causes them to have an affinity for oils and oil-based inks. Oleophilic substances are likely to repel water. Oleophilic substances are also called *lipophilic* and are considered *hydrophobic*. (See also *Oleophobic*.)

Oleophobic

A quality of certain papers, components of paper, or the nonimage areas of lithographic printing plates that causes them to repel oil-based inks and have an affinity for water. Oleophobic substances are also called *lipophobic* and are considered *hydrophilic*. (See also *Oleophilic*.)

Oligomer

A type of small *polymer*, a high-molecular-weight compound formed by the reacting and uniting—or *polymerization*—of a small number of *monomer*s. An oligomer with only two monomers is called a dimer, one with three monomers is a trimer, etc. The polymerization of monomers and oligomers into much longer chain polymers is a means of drying and solidifying some printed inks, as well as producing many different synthetic *resin*s used in the manufacture of printing ink.

Omnidirectional Microphone

A microphone that picks up sound equally from all directions.

Omnifont

Descriptive of the ability of any *optical character recognition* (or *magnetic ink character recognition*) device to recognize characters printed in a variety of different type styles.

On

In typesetting, a term used to specify the *leading* to be used in combination with a certain *point size*. For example, "10 on 12" means that 10-point type should be set with two extra points of leading between each line.

On-Contact Printing

An alternate term for *contact printing*. See *Contact Printing*.

On-Demand

Descriptive of printed output that is generated only as needed, rather than printed in bulk and allowed to sit around on shelves or in warehouses. See *On-Demand Printing*.

On-Demand Printing

On-demand is basically one of short notice and quick turnaround. If you want a movie or fax on-demand you push a button or make a phone call—you give short notice and get quick turnaround. In the printing industry, the term is also associated with shorter printing runs and printing in multiple locations so as to be closer to the customer. When we put all this together, the definition of *on-demand printing* becomes "short notice, quick turnaround of short, economical print runs distributed beyond a single printing facility." When all criteria are met, it results in lower inventory costs, lower risk of obsolescence, lower production costs, and reduced distribution costs. In general most traditional printing does not fulfill this criteria and does not result in

these advantages. The disadvantage of traditional long-run printing is that the reproduced information can become out-of-date, which requires the disposal of material and re-manufacture of new material. In the United States, it is estimated that 31% of all traditional printing is discarded because it becomes obsolete.

Publications	11%
Promotional	41%
Specialty (forms, etc.)	13%
Other	35%

Printing discarded because of obsolescence.

Approximately one-third of all magazines displayed on a newsstand today are discarded. Many books are never sold and are discarded by the bookseller, who may return the torn-off cover for credit. Tractor trailers filled with forms or data/specifications sheets go to the land fill or dump because of product changes.

No particular technology is associated with the concept of on-demand. If you are clever or efficient or high tech, you could produce on-demand printing with a traditional press. It does not matter what technology you use. The customer probably does not care. In addition, most customers today use the terms *printing* and *copying* interchangeably, without any thought as to what they signify. An on-demand system is any device that can print short runs, on short notice, relatively quickly, in a cost-efficient manner. This could be done with a traditional printing press, a high-speed copier, a direct-imaging press (plate imaged on press), a high-quality digital printer, or a color copier. The terms "on-demand printing" and "demand printing" are used interchangeably.

DIGITAL PRINTING

The definition of digital printing is a little harder. A simple definition is that *digital printing is any printing done from digital files.* Two points must be noted: we avoid discussing specific technologies, and, when talking about digital printing, we eliminate the short-run aspect. A digital press may be capable of printing short runs economically, but digital printing on printing presses is well suited for longer runs. For example, a Heidelberg GTO-DI is definitely a digital press, but it may or may not be an on-demand press. Therefore on-demand printing is economical, fast, and oriented to short runs, while digital printing is printing from digital files but is not restricted to short runs. Demand printing could be done with digital files or conventional film or plates, while digital printing is only done with digital files. The point is that on-demand printing is possible with virtually any technology.

VARIABLE PRINTING

Traditional printing does not allow you to print variable information easily. Traditional printing uses a fixed image plate; however, ink jet may be added to the back end of the systems. With traditional printing, you perform the pre-press work, make the plates, and run them on the press. As a result, you end up with thousands of pages that look exactly the same. We could say that the information is static (not variable) and that the pages are static (not variable).

Most of the digital presses (presses that print from digital data) can print variable information, which results in variable printing. On different pages you could have different names and addresses. The ability to print variable information, and result in variable printing, is the critical component of customized printing. Although traditionally accomplished with high-speed ink jet devices, many of the digital presses offer this ability. Digital presses can take information from a database and create different information on different pages. An added advantage is that these devices are not limited to six or twelve lines of copy, as many of the ink jet devices are, but some can customize the entire page.

These abilities allow you to vary the contents of any single document or group of documents during a run. For instance, a cataloger could print 5,000 catalogs in lots of 500, each with a different cover. This could be used to test-market different covers. This would have been almost impossible or cost-prohibitive with traditional techniques. The building blocks of customized printing is the combination of variable information with output devices without any intermediate films or plates. They are true digital printing systems in that all or part of the image area can be changed from impression to impression.

Only digital presses allow the use of 100% variable information. If you look at the amount of mailings you receive where your name is built into the message, you will get some idea of the tremendous market for personalization and customization of text and images. The object of any direct mail piece is to encourage you to read it. Personalization accomplishes this because you are more apt to read something that grabs your interest.

In the definition of on-demand printing, what is a *short run*? The problem is that different companies that use different printing technologies define short runs differently. What might be a short run for gravure, might be a long run for sheetfed. Run lengths from 1 to 2,000 are the ideal for the digital color presses.

The most popular definition of a short run is one that is less than 5,000 impressions. The next question is, "How much work is done at this run length?" Many people are surprised at the answers. Almost 62% of commercial, book, and office printing including duplicating and copying is in the category. Only 3% of all this printing is done in four or more colors (1996). By the year 2000, the amount of process printing in this run-length market will more than quadruple to 15%. Color will increase as a percentage of total reproduced pages as it becomes easier to accomplish on new and traditional equipment.

Traditional printing presses generally operate in the long-run category and above. Also, technology advances that can be applied to traditional presses, such as quick-change

1	Ultimate Short Run (USR)
2–100	Very Very Short Run (VVSR)
101–250	Very Short Run (VSR)
251–500	
501–1,000	
1,001–1,500	Short Run (SR)
1,501–2,000	
2,001–3,000	
3,001–4,000	Moderate-Short Run (MSR)
4,001–5,000	
5,001–6,500	
6,501–8,000	Moderate Run (MR)
8,001–10,000	
10,001–25,000	
25,001–40,000	Average Run (AR)
40,001–50,000	
50,001–70,000	
70,001–100,000	Moderate-Long Run (MLR)
100,001–250,000	
250,001–400,000	
400,001–600,000	Long Run (LR)
600,001–750,000	
750,001–1,000,000	
>1,000,000	Very-Long Run (VLR)

Run length ranges.

(1996) Run Lengths	% of Total Market	% of Run in 4-Color	% of Total Market in 4-color or More	
			1994 est.	2000 est.
<100-500	16.6	1.0	0.2	3.5
500-2,000	33.5	3.0	1.0	5.5
2,000-5,000	22.3	10.0	1.8	6.0
5,000-10,000	13.8	16.0	2.2	5.0
10,000-100,000	5.6	25.0	1.4	1.5
>100,000	8.2	41.0	3.4	5.5
Average %	100.0		10.0	27.0

Color printing as a percentage of total reproduced pages.

plate capability and on-press densitometry and calibrated adjustments, as well as waterless offset, could move some presses into the short-run category. It is possible for clever printers to accomplish on-demand printing with traditional presses. Based on market projections, short run will take place in the 1 to 2,000 copy range. Above that, newer printing presses will compete, and below 2,000, newer plain-paper color printers/presses will evolve.

With short-run work, it will be necessary to automate the job submission approach so that all information about the job accompanies the actual data file. This is only one aspect of on-demand that escapes potential users. Short runs imply more jobs passing through a facility, with average runs of under 1,000. This will change workflow and billing procedures. Currently there are three specific on-demand strategies: on-demand printing, distributed demand printing, and demand publishing.

Except for rare occasions when traditionally prepared and printed short runs are fast and economical, most of the time the expression "on-demand" means that the data is stored and printed in electronic form. Any reproduction process can be on-demand or short run.

Distributed demand printing workflow requires that the files are electronic because the files are transmitted to other locations and printed locally. These distributed locations can store and print the products as needed and ship them locally. This is an implementation of the "distribute and print" philosophy as opposed to the traditional "print and distribute" philosophy. The traditional long-run printing strategy is to print large volumes in a central location and then ship them both long (nationally) and short distances (regionally). Decentralization reduces shipping costs but does not eliminate storage and distribution costs. You need to combine on-demand printing with decentralization to get the best results.

The third general strategy is demand publishing in which the data is stored in paginated form and transmitted for immediate printout. Large-volume magazines do this—which allows them to provide regional inserts. Portable document formats, such as Adobe Acrobat or No Hands Common Ground, are being used to distribute the paginated and print-ready page and document files.

Digital printing is any form of printing that uses a rasterization process to produce image carriers or to replicate directly to substrate from digital document files. Ultimately, on-demand printing requires both an imaging engine and a means of combining in consecutive, uninterrupted operations the printed pages into finished products—college textbooks, out-of-print books, insurance policies, research reports, business proposals, or any other reproduced products. Printing with in-line finishing puts very stringent demands on the condition and reliability of the equipment used. The definition of demand publishing will not be limited to paper output. In the future, powerful computers, with flexible file formats and cross-platform equipment will allow us to output documents to a wide variety of devices, including file servers, networked storage devices, or CD- and DVD-ROM drives.

One-Bit Color

On a computer monitor, a color display in which each *pixel* (or smallest point of *color*) is described by 1 bit of information. (One *bit* is either a 1 or a 0; 1-bit color can be thought of as one of these two numbers taken to the first power; thus $2^1 = 2$ possible colors.) The color of a pixel on a com-

puter display is commonly expressed as some amount of *red, green, and blue*. Greater numbers of combinations of these amounts require more processing power on the part of the computer. At 1 bit per pixel, a total of only two colors (typically black and white, or any other two colors) can be described and displayed. See also *Four-Bit Color, Eight-Bit Color, Sixteen-Bit Color, Twenty-Four-Bit Color*, and *Thirty-Two-Bit Color*. Scanning done at a color depth of one-bit is known as *bilevel* scanning.

100Base-T

In networking, a network *protocol*, derived from *100VG-AnyLAN* and using the *CSMA/CD* protocol, capable of transmission speeds of up to 100 megabits per second. Also known as *fast Ethernet*.

100VG-AnyLAN

In networking, a network *protocol* co-developed by Hewlett-Packard, IBM, and AT&T as an alternative to *100Base-T*. Capable of transmission speeds of up to 100 megabits per second, it uses *demand priority* as its access method. As a protocol, its ability to guarantee *bandwidth* makes it especially useful for the transmission of multimedia applications.

One-Inch

In video production, a videotape format utilizing a tape 1 in. wide. Type B and Type C are two different formats of 1-in. tape.

One-Man Squeegee

In *screen printing*, a large squeegee counterbalanced so as to enable it to be operated by only one person.

1.44

Abbreviation for a specific capacity of *floppy disk*, having a diameter of 3.5 in. See *Floppy Disk*.

1.22

Abbreviation for a specific capacity of *floppy disk*, having a diameter of 5.25 in. See *Floppy Disk*.

One-Up, Two-Up . . .

Descriptive of any activity in which some number of things are done at the exact same time. Printing done one-up, for example, prints one page on one sheet of paper using one plate. *Two-up* printing would involve printing two pages on the same sheet with the same plate, etc.

Onionskin

A lightweight *bond paper* typically used for airmail stationery, carbon copies of documents, legal documents, etc. Onionskin is made from chemical wood *pulp*, or 25% to 100% cotton-content. Onionskin commonly undergoes *air drying* for a *cockle finish* or *calendering* for a smooth finish.

The *standard size* of onionskin is 17×22 in. and comes in *basis weight*s of 8 or 9 lb.

Onlay

In *binding and finishing*, a decorative color illustration or other image printed separately and applied to a book cover by means of adhesive. An onlay, unlike an *inlay*, is added without first *blanking* the cover to create a space for it.

On-Line

In computing, descriptive of the state of a computer, network *node*, printer, etc., that has an active connection to the network, controller, or other system, and can thus transmit, receive, or process data. See also *Off-Line*. Also spelled as one word, *online*.

On-Line Editing

In video editing, the assembly of a videotape production using a fully equipped editing console (usually an *A/B roll* as well as other equipment). On-line editing is often accomplished by means of an *auto assemble* device operating in accordance with an *edit decision list*. On-line editing, more meticulous and expensive than *off-line editing*, results in a *master tape*.

On-Line Processing

Computer processing performed *on-the-fly*, or immediately as the commands are received from the user.

On-Line Service

In computing, a company or other organization that provides remote access to a network, the *Internet*, or other networked resources, usually for a fee or subscription charge.

    An on-line service may provide only specialized resources—such as a *bulletin board service* or other specialized database service—or a wide range of services, usually including the Internet and the *World Wide Web*. In this latter case, the on-line service is more commonly known as an *Internet service provider (ISP)*. See *Internet Service Provider (ISP)*.

On-Machine Coating

The *coating* of the surface of a paper performed while it is still on the papermaking machine. The advantages of on-machine coating involve elimination of the necessity of winding, packing, and shipping paper rolls of *base stock* to a separate coating plant. Disadvantages include the necessity of having to shut down the entire papermaking process if difficulties in the coating section arise (as well as the necessity of shutting down the coating of paper if difficulties in the other portions of the papermaking system arise), and the fact that on-machine coating processes are not suitable for all paper *grade*s. See also *Coating* and *Off-Machine Coating*.

On-Screen Slide

In presentation graphics, an image displayed and viewed on the computer monitor.

On-the-Fly

Descriptive of computer operation, function, processing, or calculation performed in real time, or as it is needed with no perceptible delay in its execution.

On-the-Fly Compression/Decompression

In computing, a means of compressing and decompressing a file in which compression/decompression takes place during the writing to/reading from (respectively) a storage medium. The advantage of this is that the user does not need to actively compress or decompress the file. Also known as *real-time compression/decompression*.

OOP

Abbreviation for *object-oriented programming*. See *Object-Oriented Programming (OOP)*.

Ooze

Alternate term for *adhesive bleed*. See *Adhesive Bleed*.

Opacimeter

A device used to measure the *opacity* of a paper by gauging how much light is being reflected back through paper, using either the *diffuse opacity method* or the *contrast ratio method*. See *Opacity*.

Opacity

In optics, the extent to which an object or surface will impede the transmission of light through it. A completely *opaque* object is one that allows no light to pass through it. See also *Translucency* and *Transparency*.

    In papermaking, *opacity* is a property of paper that describes the amount of light transmitted through it. Paper that has a high degree of opacity does not let much light pass through it, while paper that has a low degree of opacity is more translucent, or allows much light to pass through it. A paper's opacity determines the extent to which printing on a particular side of paper will be visible from the reverse side (called *show-through*).

    Cellulose fibers, the primary constituents of paper, are transparent, but the piling up of them in a paper *web* diffuses the light passing through the sheet, imparting a paper's opacity. *Fillers* such as *clay*, *titanium dioxide*, and *calcium carbonate* are added to increase the diffusion of light through a paper, thereby increasing its opacity. The best opacifiers, however, tend to be the most expensive, so the majority of papers are at best translucent. Tinting and dyeing of papers also increase their opacity, as does increasing a paper's *basis weight*, *bulk*, or *coating*. Increasing a paper's *whiteness* tends to decrease its opacity, as does increasing its degree of *calendering*, *supercalendering*, or fiber *refining*.

    The measurement of a paper's opacity is accomplished utilizing an *opacimeter* employing either the *contrast ratio method* or the *diffuse opacity method*. The contrast ratio method compares the amount of light reflected back through a paper when it is backed by a black sheet of paper to the amount reflected back though a paper when it is backed by a white surface. The diffuse opacity method differs from the contrast ratio method in that the white surface is replaced by a stack of the paper being tested.

The degree to which printing will show through to the reverse side of a sheet of paper may be the result not of diminished opacity but of an increase in ink absorption and penetration through the paper, being not an optical problem but a structural one.

The term *opacity* also refers to the extent to which a printed ink will permit or prevent the transmission of light through it, either blotting out or allowing to be seen what is beneath it. *Opaque pigments* do not allow light to pass through them, instead reflect it back, and are used to print solid colors. *Transparent pigments* allow varying amounts of light to pass through them, revealing the background printing or substrate. Transparent pigments are used to reduce color strength of more opaque inks, aid dispersion of color pigments, and "extend" a quantity of more expensive pigments. (See *Pigment*.) Ink opacity is also referred to as its *covering power*.

Opaque

When used as an adjective, *opaque* is descriptive of any substance or material that does not allow the transmission of light through it, or possesses a high degree of *opacity*. The opposite of opaque is *transparent*. A middle-ground is a *translucent* substance or material, which allows some light to pass through it, albeit diffusely.

The term *opaque*, when used as a verb, means to apply a thick fluid to portions of a photographic *negative* prior to platemaking, as a means of eliminating unwanted images or specks, known as *opaquing* or *spotting out*.

Opaque, when used as a noun, refers to the thick, typically red or black fluid used for blocking out the aforementioned undesirable specks or images on photographic negatives. Also known as *opaquing fluid*. A special red felt-tip marker used for the same purpose is also called *opaque*.

Opaque Pigment

White pigments used in printing inks that do not let light pass through them, and are used for printing white, or for mixing with other colors to increase *opacity* or lighten the color. The most opaque white pigment, *titanium dioxide*, is also called *cover white*. Other opaque white pigments include *zinc sulfide*, *lithopones*, and zinc oxide. Frequently two or more of these pigments are mixed together to obtain the desired results. (See also *Transparent Pigment*.)

Opaquing

The process of applying a thick, light-blocking fluid to small pinholes in a photographic *negative* prior to platemaking, as a means of ensuring that unwanted blemishes on the negative do not print. See *Opaque*.

Opaquing Fluid

See *Opaque* (third definition).

Open Architecture

The design of a computer system such that specifications are made public as a means of encouraging third-party developers to market add-on hardware and software. A computer running on a *standard platform* typically has an open architecture. Such a system is known as an *open system*.

Open Bolts

In *binding and finishing*, the roughly trimmed edges of a *signature* prior to final trimming, not including the *binding edge*. Uncut signature folds are called *closed bolts*. Both open and closed *bolts* require complete trimming at the end of the binding process.

Open Database Connectivity (ODBC)

In computing, an *Application Program Interface (API)* developed by Microsoft that facilitates the accessing of several different file and database types by a single application.

Open Data-Link Interface (ODI)

In telecommunications and networking, a standard developed by Novell that allows a single system to use different network *protocol*s over the same cable and *network adapter*.

Open Data-Link Interface/Network Driver Interface Specification Support (ODINSUP)

In networking, an interface developed by Novell that allows two separate network driver interfaces—Novell's own *Open Data-Link Interface (ODI)* and Microsoft/3Com's *Network Drive Interface Specification (NDIS)*—to run on the same system or network. ODINSUP allows a particular *workstation* to connect to networks using different protocols through a single *network interface card*.

OpenDoc

In computing, an *object-oriented* linking scheme by which elements of files created in different programs can be compiled and combined. An added advantage is that changes made to a linked file are reflected in the file in which the link is called. OpenDoc, developed jointly by Apple Computer, IBM, and WordPerfect, is a competitor to Microsoft's *Object Linking and Embedding (OLE)*.

Open-End Envelope

An envelope with its opening on the shorter dimension. See also *Open-Side Envelope*.

Open-Face Vacuum Frame

On a *graphic arts camera*, a board or frame to which the film to be exposed is mounted, the film held in place by suction from below. An open face vacuum frame does not possess a glass or plastic covering.

Open-Flame Dryer

A type of *dryer* (or *floating dryer*) used on a *web press* in which a heat source heats the air within an enclosed space through which the web passes to a very high temperature (often as high as 600°F). The open-flame dryer (also called a ***direct-impingement dryer***) is the oldest form of drying equipment. A commonly used alternative is the ***high-velocity hot-air dryer***. See ***Dryer*** and ***Web Offset Lithography: Dryers and Chill Rolls***.

Open Look

In computing, a ***graphical user interface (GUI)*** designed by AT&T and Sun and based on the ***X Windows*** system.

Open Negative

In graphic arts photography, a film ***negative*** that has been slightly underexposed or underdeveloped to produce an image slightly larger than the original. An open negative will result in more darkly printed images.

Open Prepress Interface (OPI)

A workflow protocol developed by Aldus Corporation used in electronic prepress to link desktop publishing systems and high-end ***CEPS***. Essentially, ***high-resolution*** color

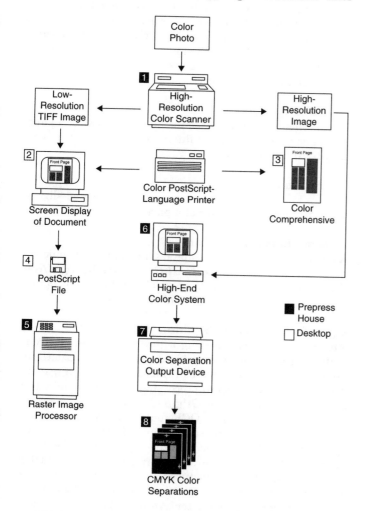

OPI facilitates both page layout and color separation.

images are stored on a central network server, to which all the workstations are connected. ***Low-resolution*** files are sent by the server to individual computers working on page layout. The low-res images are imported into the page (in a kind of ***FPO*** way), positioned, and comments sent back to the OPI server provide specific cropping, scaling, positioning, and color information about the image. The server's ***PostScript*** driver inserts the proper instructions into the PostScript code. When the page is ultimately output to an ***imagesetter*** connected to the network, the high-resolution image is swapped for the low-res one, and the indicated instructions as to cropping, etc., are executed.

OPI is useful for minimizing high-resolution-file travel on networks; their large file size can make traffic screech to a halt. And by utilizing only low-resolution viewfiles on workstations, processing speed is increased. The efficacy of OPI is contingent upon the use on the workstations of OPI-compatible software; many page layout programs are increasingly including support for OPI, although some OPI specifications for color separation have not been effectively nailed down yet. Although OPI is often compared to ***DCS***, the latter is strictly a color separation protocol, while the former is more of a workflow protocol.

Open Press

Descriptive of any lithographic printing press having a ***blanket***-to-steel ***impression cylinder*** printing unit.

Open Shortest Path First (OSPF)

In networking and telecommunications, a protocol used by ***TCP/IP*** for ***routing*** that maintains a current "map" of a network and the status of each link and is thus able to transmit messages by the shortest available route from node to node.

Open-Side Envelope

An envelope with its opening on the longer dimension. See also ***Open-End Envelope***.

Open System

In computing, a computer system that has had part of its ***source code*** released so as to facilitate and encourage the development of programs by third-party developers. See also ***Closed System***.

Open System Interconnection (OSI)

In telecommunications, an ***ISO*** standard for data communications that acts as a model for setting up networks, connecting nodes, transferring data, etc. The OSI model comprises seven "layers" that describe the specific aspects of the system:
• *Layer 1 (Physical Layer)*. The physical configuration of the network, including the hardware required.
• *Layer 2 (Data-Link Layer)*. The ***protocol***s that will be required to link parties and make connections.
• *Layer 3 (Network Layer)*. The ***network topology*** required.

• *Layer 4 (Transport Layer)*. The protocols required for data transfer.
• *Layer 5 (Session Layer)*. The means of communication once a connection has been established.
• *Layer 6 (Presentation Layer)*. The adaptation and conversion of a connection.
• *Layer 7 (Application Layer)*. The application of the above-mentioned items. Often referred to, palindromatically, as the **ISO/OSI Model**.

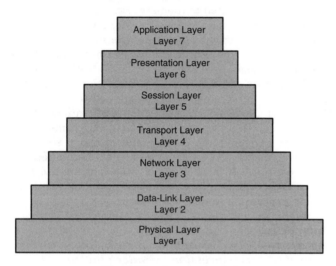

The OSI reference model.

Open Systems Foundation (OSF)
A nonprofit organization founded by Mitch Kapor (who also founded Lotus) dedicated to keeping the Internet free and open, without censorship or limitation.

Open Up Shadows
In scanning, a command programmed into the scanner allowing for the reduction of three-quartertone areas, commonly performed to increase detail in shadow areas.

OpenView
A popular network management application package developed by Hewlett-Packard.

Operating Side
The side of a **flexographic** printing press on which the printing adjustment controls are located, as opposed to the **driving side**. See also **Driving Side**.

Operating System
In computing, a set of computer programs, files, and applications used to tell the hardware how to operate or, in other words, how data gets read, written, and stored, how applications get loaded into memory and unloaded again, how commands get interpreted, etc. The operating system that a computer possesses is often what defines the computer's **platform**. Although many high-end and mid-range system (especially those designed for one particular purpose) have

their own proprietary operating systems, most **microcomputers** have one of the widespread and standard operating systems: **DOS** (which stands for **Disk Operating System**, developed by Microsoft for the original IBM **PC**; the **Microsoft Windows** interface is not truly an operating system, but is rather a **graphical user interface** that sits on top of DOS); the **Macintosh Operating System**; **UNIX**; and **OS/2**. The operating system a computer uses is determined by the hardware configuration. For example, you cannot run DOS/Windows on the hardware designed to run the Macintosh OS (although it is becoming increasingly possible).

Operating System/2
See **OS/2**.

Optical Alignment
In typography, the use of visual reference points to align a row or column of type. See **Alignment**.

Optical Brightener
A material (typically a fluorescent dye) added to paper to increase its **brightness**. As an optical brightener absorbs **ultraviolet** radiation impinging on the paper, it reflects it back as visible light, which can increase a paper's brightness to as high as 90 or more. (See **Brightness**.) Also known as an **optical whitener**.

Optical Brightness
In papermaking, an increase in the **brightness** of a paper by means of the addition of fluorescent dyes or other types of **optical brightener**s.

Optical Center
In page layout and graphic design, a point located slightly above the geometric center of a page.

Optical Character Reader
A device used to convert graphic symbols to electronic signals, such as is used in **Optical Character Recognition**. See **Optical Character Recognition (OCR)**. The optical character reader itself is also abbreviated *OCR*.

Optical Character Recognition (OCR)
An imaging process utilizing a device that can electronically read typewritten or printed pages and translate the characters into codes that can then be saved as a text file and imported into a word processing program, eliminating the need for keyboarding. Originally, OCR devices required special machine-oriented OCR fonts, but as scanners and scanning software increased in sophistication, many other types of fonts (almost any printed typeface) can be recognized. OCR scanning is often performed using special **OCR Paper**, specially manufactured to be as free from dark spots or blemishes as possible, as any non-text markings would register as a character. An early form of OCR was called **magnetic ink character recognition (MICR)**.

Optical Density

In imaging (especially *scanning* and *photography*), the logarithm of the *opacity* of a material or portion of an image. See *Density*.

Optical Disc

In computing, a type of *mass storage* medium, used to describe one of several types of discs that are read and/or written using a laser to detect a pattern of engraved *pit*s. See *Compact Disc (CD)* and *Videodisc*. The magnetic/optical hybrid—known as a *magneto-optical disc*—is also often known as an optical disc.

Optical Dot Gain

An optically perceived increase in the size of a *halftone dot* when printed, caused by light that should reflect off the surface of the paper becoming trapped under the edge of the dot(s), increasing the *density* in those areas. Finer halftone screens or more roughly textured papers can help reduce the effect of optical dot gain. (See also *Dot Gain* and *Physical Dot Gain*.)

Optical Drive

In computing, a disc drive used to read from and write to an *optical disc* and *magneto-optical disc*. See *Optical Disc* and *Magneto-Optical Disc*.

Optical Fiber

See *Fiber Optics*.

Optical Jump

A problem of *halftone*s, commonly those comprising square-shaped *halftone dot*s, in which the corners of the dots in areas of high *dot density* begin to connect with each other, creating a visual darkening of those areas. Altering the shape of halftone dots can alleviate that problem. (See *Dot Shape*.)

Optical Media

Any of a variety of computer storage devices characterized by being written to and read from by a laser, as opposed to *magnetic media*. See *Optical Disc*, *Compact Disc (CD)*, *Magneto-Optical Disc*, and *Videodisc*.

Optical Memory Disc Recorder

A device that writes information to a non-erasable *optical disc*, typically a *compact disc*. See *Compact Disc (CD)*.

Optical Resolution

In *scanning*, a measure of the maximum *resolution* at which a *scanner* can capture an image using its optics alone, exclusive of any *interpolation* software, which can be used to "artificially" increase resolution. See *Scanning*. See also *Interpolated Resolution*.

Optical Scanner

A *scanner* that optically analyzes and digitizes an image. See *Scanner*.

Optical Spacing

In typography, the "look" of the typeset letters in relation to each other, which may or may not be geometrically accurate due to optical illusions caused by the proximity of various letter shapes. In good *typeface* design, spacing between lowercase letters is "built in."

Letters come on three basic shapes, oval (such as an "O"), inclined (such as a "V"), or vertical (such as an "I"). The combined appearance of the spacing between letters is called *optical volume*, which can vary depending upon the shape of the letters. For example, the space between two squares may look different than that between two circles, even though they may be quantitatively the same. On modern typesetting and page makeup devices and software, automatic and manual *kerning* options can solve the problem of optical volume.

Optical Storage

Storage of computer data by means of *optical disc*s. See *Optical Disc*.

Optical Tape

Any tape used for data storage coated with an optical rather than magnetic recording material.

Optical Volume

In typography, the combined appearance of the spacing between letters that cannot always be gauged quantitatively. Different letter-shape combinations generate the illusion of more or less space between them, resulting in the need for *kerning*. See *Optical Spacing*.

Optical Whitener

Alternate term for *optical brightener*. See *Optical Brightener*.

Option Key

A key included on computer keyboards used to modify another key. The Option Key is added to expand the number of functions that a particular key can have. See also *Alternate Key*, *Command Key*, and *Control Key*.

Option Module

Alternate term for an *expansion board*. See *Expansion Board*.

Orange

The *color* characteristic of light possessing a wavelength between 590 and 610 *nanometer*s, located on the spectrum between *red* and *yellow*. Orange is a *secondary color* produced—in *additive color theory*—by mixing red and yellow light. Orange is also a secondary color produced in multicolor printing by overprinting dots of *magenta* and yellow. (See COLOR PLATE 3.)

Orange Book

In multimedia, a set of standards developed for the *compact disc–recordable (CD-R)* format. The Orange Book standard (so-named because the publication containing the specifications had an orange cover) describes the structure of the disc and the instructions for creating not only CD-Rs, but also *magneto-optical discs* (in Orange Book 1) and *CD-R-WORM*s (Orange Book 2). See *Compact Disc–Recordable (CD-R)* and *Compact Disc (CD)*.

The term *Orange Book* is also used to refer to the Department of Defense standard for computer security. See *National Computer Security Center (NCSC)*.

Orange Peel

A *mottle*-like printing defect of *flexography*, *gravure*, and *screen printing* characterized by a granular image reminiscent of the texture of an orange peel, caused by a failure of the ink to flow out to a smooth, uniformly thick film.

Orange Plast

Alternate term for *golden plast*. See *Golden Plast*.

Orange 2G

See *DNA Orange*.

Ordinate

One of two coordinates in a two-dimensional *coordinate system*, often the vertical one (denoted y).

Organic Color Pigments

Pigments used in the manufacture of printing inks derived from derivatives of coal tar (organic pigments are frequently referred to as "coal tar colors"), in contrast to *inorganic color pigments*, which are derived from mineral sources. The inorganic pigments are classified according to chemical makeup (chromes, cadmiums, etc.), while the organic pigments are classified by color. The organic pigments listed below are classified and identified in the Society of Dyers and Colorists' Color Index. Each classification consists of two parts, corresponding to the two parts of the index. The first part identifies each pigment with a CI number, which accompanies a description, usage, and technical information. The second part lists each pigment by chemical composition, and assigns each one a number. Thus, Para Red below is listed in Part 1 as *CI Pigment Red 1* and in Part 2 as *No. 12070*. These two sets of identifications accompany the individual entries on each separate pigment.

There are literally thousands of organic pigments, many of which are no longer in use or which are used very seldomly. The pigments listed below are among the most commonly used in the industry, as of this writing.

Yellows. Yellows comprise the *Yellow Lakes*, which are transparent pigments used as a yellow to cover other inks but not hide them, *Tartrazine Yellow Lake* (also called FD&C Yellow No. 5 and used as a dyestuff in foods), *Hansa Yellows*, and *Diarylide Yellows*, which are the most common yellow pigments used in printing inks. *Fluorescent Yellow* is also used in some specialty applications. Organic Yellows are commonly used to replace *Chrome Yellows*.

Oranges. The most common orange pigment is *Diarylide Orange*, a transparent yet not very fast-to-light pigment. Other assorted orange materials tend to be used where orange pigments are necessary, and include *DNA Orange*, *Pyrazolone Orange*, *Fast Orange F2G*, *Benzimidazolone Orange HL*, and *Ethyl Lake Red C*.

Reds. Reds include *Para Reds*, *Toluidine Red*, *Permanent Red "R"*, *Carmine F.B.*, *Naphthol Reds and Rubines*, *Permanent Red FRC*, *Bordeaux FRR*, *Rubine Reds*, *Lithol® Reds*, *BON Red*, *Lithol® Rubine 4B*, *BON Maroon*, *Rhodamine 6G*, *Lake Red C*, *BON Arylamide Red*, *Quinacrinone Magentas*, *Copper Ferrocyanide Pink*, *Benzimidazolone Carmines and Reds*, *Azo Magenta G*, *Anthraquinone Scarlet*, and *Madder Lakes*.

Blues. Blues include *Phthalocyanine Blues* (the most commonly used group of organic blue pigments), *PMTA Victoria Blue*, *Victoria Blue CFA*, *Ultramarine Blue*, *Indanthrene Blue*, *Alkali Blues*, and *Peacock Blue*.

Violets. Violets overlap slightly with some of the bluer reds (such as *Benzimidazolone Bordeaux HF 3R* (see *Benzimidazolone Carmines and Reds*) and also include such pigments as *PMTA Rhodamine*, *PMTA Violet* (also known as *Methyl Violet*), *Dioxazine Violet (RL) Carbazole Violet*, *Crystal Violet*, *Dioxazine Violet B*, and *Thioindigoid Red*.

Greens. A common series of greens are the *Phthalocyanine Greens* as well as the *PMTA Greens*.

Browns. Brown pigments include *Diazo Brown* and *Benzimidazolone Brown HFR*.

Also available in the organic class of color pigments are the *fluorescent pigment colors*, which are used primarily in screen printing. They lack the lightfastness, variety, and mixability of the regular pigments, and they are more expensive and require application of thick films or multiple passes to achieve the desired effectiveness. (See *Fluorescent Pigment Colors*.)

See individual entries on separate pigments.

Organic color pigments, unlike the (usually) straightforward inorganic color pigments, are chemically described by complex ring structures that, for the sake of clarity, have been omitted from the individual entries. Detailed molecular structures for each of these pigments can be found in *The Printing Ink Manual* or in the *Color Index* published by the Society of Dyers and Colorists.

Organosol

An organic *solvent* that contains a suspension of particles (commonly particles of *polyvinyl chloride* resin in a *plasticizer*). An organosol containing less than 5% of volatile solvents by weight is known as a *plastisol*. See also *Plastisol*.

Org Chart

Alternate term for a *flowchart*. See *Flowchart*.

Orientation

The relation of printed material to the longer and shorter dimension of the sheet of substrate on which it is printed. Two categories of orientation are *landscape* (lines of text are parallel to the longer dimension) or *portrait* (the lines of text are parallel to the shorter dimension). In specifying document or page size, the width is expressed first; thus, a portrait orientation would be specified 8½×11 in., while a landscape orientation would be specified 11×8½ in.

Original

Any copy—be it a *mechanical*, artwork, or other material—from which reproductions are to be made. The term *original* commonly refers to photographs used for *halftone*s or to original *line art*.

Original Equipment Manufacturer (OEM)

In the manufacture of computer systems, a supplier or manufacturer of specific portions of a system that are incorporated into a system, often at the point of purchase. So, for example, if you purchased a Compaq computer, the *hard disk* within it may not have been manufactured by Compaq, but rather by an OEM.

Ornament

In typography, a symbol or other decorative element, commonly available in supplementary fonts (called *pi fonts*). Ornaments can be created as additions to fonts (i.e., a company *logotype*). *Borders* can be created by repeating an ornament or any other symbol. An ornament is also called a *dingbat*.

Orphan

In typography, the last line of a paragraph when it is less than one-third the width of the line—especially when it is

> Today, office workers are using the computer more and more for word processing, databases, spreadsheets, and desktop publishing. As a result, printed documents are being produced more often and in much greater
>
> quantity. ◀— Orphan
>
> Typeset materials are easier to read and the most professional looking. Typesetting creates an air of quality that typewriters and computer printers cannot match. ◀—— Widow

In the text above, the word "quantity" at the top of the second column is an orphan, and the word "match" at the bottom of the second column is a widow.

the carry-over of a hyphenated word—carried to the top of a new page or column. An orphan is essentially a *widow* found at the top of a page or column.

Orthochromatic

Descriptive of the sensitivity of photographic films or other photosensitive materials to *blue*, *green*, *yellow*, *orange*, and *ultraviolet* light, but not to *red* light. An advantage to orthochromatic film is that it can be handled safely in a red darkroom light, unlike *panchromatic* film, which is sensitive to light of all wavelengths.

OS

In computing, abbreviation for *operating system*. See *Operating System*.

In motion picture photography and videography, *OS* is an abbreviation for *over-the-shoulder*. See *Over-the-Shoulder*.

OS-9

In computing, a real-time *operating system* on which Philips' *CD-RTOS* is based. The CD-RTOS is used to run systems that play *Compact Disc–Interactive* discs. See *Compact Disc–Interactive (CD-i)*.

OS/2

Abbreviation for *Operating System/2*, a 32-bit *operating system* started by Microsoft and finished by IBM, designed for use on *IBM-compatible computer*s. OS/2, a *graphical user interface*, allows *multitasking* and *virtual memory* and can run *DOS*, *Windows*, and its own native applications. OS/2 has not caught on as well as Windows, however. Version 3.0 of the OS/2 operating system is called *OS/2 Warp*.

OS/2 Client

In networking, any *workstation* running on the *OS/2* platform.

OS/2 Warp

In computing, the name for version 3.0 of IBM's *OS/2* operating system, its name a reference to "warp speed," a term used in science fiction (most familiarly *Star Trek*) to refer to faster-than-light speed. OS/2 Warp, thus, runs faster than previous versions, but in other respects is very similar. See *OS/2*.

Oscillating Form Roller

A variety of *form roller*—the roller that directly contacts and transfers ink to the printing plate—found in the *inking system* of an offset press that, unlike conventional form rollers, moves laterally as it rotates. The oscillation of the form roller should be at a rate different from that of the nearest *oscillator*, a standard ink roller that itself oscillates back and forth. Oscillating form rollers are added not only to further smooth the ink before it is transferred to the plate but also to help eliminate the press problem known as

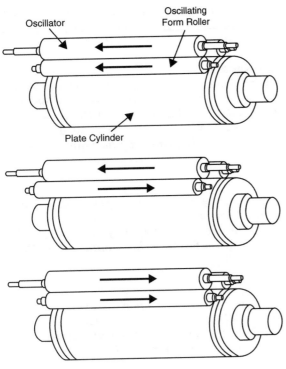

Oscillator

Oscillating
Form Roller

Plate Cylinder

The action of an oscillating form roller.

mechanical ghosting, commonly caused by allowing the image area of the plate to continuously remove ink from the same portion of the roller. (See also *Form Roller*.)

Oscillator

One of several rollers found in the *inking system* or *dampening system* on a press used in *offset lithography*. An offset lithographic printing press can have as many as five (or more) oscillator rollers. In addition to occupying several other positions within the ink *roller train*, oscillators are also the rollers that are in direct contact with the *ductor roller* and the *form roller*s. Oscillators (also called *vibrator*s or *drum*s) are typically made of steel, covered with a *lipophilic* (oil-receptive) material such as copper or nylon to prevent a printing problem known as *roller stripping*. Oscillators, as their name implies, move laterally as they rotate, which has the effect of not only smoothing and working the ink but also preventing the transfer of images from the plate to the rest of the inking system (see *Mechanical Ghosting*). The rate of oscillation can be adjusted, although it is generally preferable to set the rollers to the highest amount of oscillation; a lesser amount of oscillation can result in overinking, but in many cases a greater amount of oscillation can cause ink starvation. Oscillators rotate by means of chains and gears, and move adjacent *intermediate rollers* by friction. (See *Inking System: Offset Lithography* and *Offset Lithography*.)

In the offset press dampening system, only one oscillator is used. A dampening oscillator is in intermittent contact with a dampening ductor roller (which operates in a manner

similar to an inking ductor roller) and in constant contact with the first dampening form roller, which contacts the plate. Dampening oscillators are not covered, and have a chrome- or aluminum-plated surface. They are motor-driven and move the adjacent form rollers by surface pressure.

OSF

Abbreviation for *Open Systems Foundation*.

OSI

Abbreviation for *Open System Interconnection*. See *Open System Interconnection (OSI)*.

OSPF

Abbreviation for *Open Shortest Path First*. See *Open Shortest Path First (OSPF)*.

OSS

Abbreviation for *Operating System Software*.

Outdent

In typography, term for the first line of a paragraph that extends into the left margin, the rest of the lines of the paragraph being set flush left.

Outline

Any set of closed lines, curves, etc., used to define a particular region or shape.

In typography, a typeface with no insides. Outline faces are used in display work and lend themselves to colored or tinted layouts, allowing the type to drop out of the background. The insides of letters (normally white) can be used for special effect in color or dropout of color. Since these are "busy" typefaces, they should be used sparingly and only in display sizes. Also known as *outline characters*.

Outline Characters

See *Outline*.

Outline Font

In computerized typography, a *font* comprising characters described as a series of mathematical descriptions corresponding to curves and lines, as opposed to collections of dots

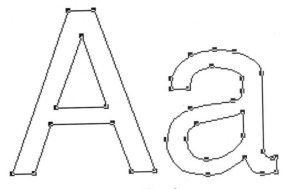

An outline font.

(or *bitmap*s). Outline fonts are easily scaled and can be output at whatever resolution the output device is capable of. (See also *Bitmap Font*.) Also called a *fill font*.

Outline Format
Alternate term for a *vector* format. See *Vector*.

Outline Halftone
Alternate term for *silhouette halftone*. See *Silhouette Halftone*.

Outline Mask
On *CEPS* or desktop publishing systems, a silhouette created in digital image manipulation programs that isolates one particular region or element of a picture from the rest.

Out-of-Gamut Alarm
In digital imaging software programs, a feature that alerts the user that a particular *color* displayed on the video monitor is not one that the electronic color system can output, or is beyond the system's color *gamut*.

Out of Register
In multicolor printing, a condition in which successively printed *color*s (or images) are not positioned correctly with respect to each other, caused by a variety of different factors, from a change in the dimensions of the *substrate* to inaccuracies in platemaking, or any of a host of other causes. See *Register*.

Out of register is also used to describe a condition of two-sided printing in which a sheet's *back printing* does not accurately line up with the *face printing*.

Out of Roundness
A paper *web* defect characterized by a paper roll that is not perfectly round, caused by storing a roll on its side, excessive clamp pressure, dropping the roll on its side, or any other similar indignity. Running an out-of-round roll through a web press will cause it to unroll in a jerky manner, and it will unwind into the press with uneven tension,

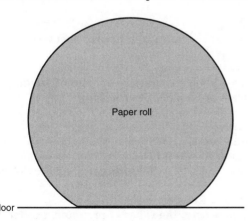

An out-of-round roll of paper, caused by storing the paper on its side.

causing *misregister*, distortion of printed images, and other problems with *printability* and *runnability*. (See also *Crushed Core*.)

Out of roundness is also a consideration of any ideally round object, such as printing press rollers and cylinders. The measurement of the out-of-roundness of press rollers and cylinders is called its *total indicated runout (TIR)*.

Out-Point
In video editing, the *frame* at which an edit ends. See also *In-Point*.

Output
In computing, any information that is transferred out of the computer. Generally, the term *output* refers to *hard copy* of data or a document as generated from a printer or other *output device*, but it may also refer to a file written to a disk or even information viewed on the computer display (called *soft copy*).

The term *output* in computing also refers to the results of the processing of data that has been input, such as a mathematical function, graph, computer model, etc.

Output Bound
See *Input/Output Bound*.

Output Hopper
The part of a computer printer in which printed sheets are collected.

Output Optics
On an output device, such as an *imagesetter*, all the related devices—lenses, focusing devices, light sources, beam splitters, modulators, etc.—which make up the part of the machine that exposes the output film.

Output Tube
Alternate term for a computer *display* or *monitor*. See *Monitor*.

Outside Margin
Alternate term for the *thumb edge* of a book. See *Thumb Edge*.

Outsourcing
The process of hiring an outside individual organization to provide a service of some kind, such as data processing, producing graphics or other multimedia, etc., rather than maintaining an in-house staff and equipment.

Over-and-Back Fold
Alternate term—especially in England—for *accordion fold*. See *Accordion Fold*.

Over-and-Over Fold
A type of fold consisting of two or more *parallel fold*s, creating a kind of "spiralling" effect. See *Folding*.

Overcorrection

An extreme form of *color correction* occurring when, as a means of eliminating *hue error*, too much of a particular *hue* is removed, resulting in a loss of detail and too light printing of that particular hue. See also *Undercorrection*.

Overcut

A problem of *cutting and trimming* in which the sheets at the top of a stack are cut shorter than the bottom sheets of a stack, caused commonly by improper *cutter clamp* pressure. See *Cutting and Trimming*.

Over-Dub

In audio and/or video production, the recording and addition of a new soundtrack (or portion of a soundtrack). Overdubbing is often used to add music and sound effects, as well as to add re-recorded dialogue that did not record clearly when the video was shot. It is also performed to replace dialogue in a foreign language with a translation. Also spelled as one word, *overdub*.

Overfeed System

One configuration of the *infeed section* of a printing press, especially one used in *offset lithography*. See *Infeed Section*.

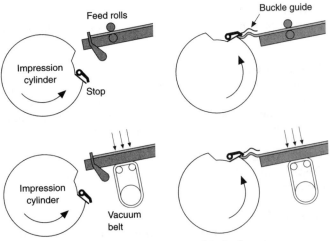

The principle of the overfeed infeed system.

Overhang

In *binding and finishing*, the extension of the edges of a book cover over the trimmed pages it surrounds. A cover possessing an overhang is called an *overhang cover*.

Overhang Cover

In *binding and finishing*, a book cover whose edges extend beyond the edges of the pages it surrounds, in contrast to a *flush cover*.

Overhead Scanner

A type of *scanner* designed to *digitize* material on an *overhead transparency*.

Overhead Transparency

A type of audiovisual projection medium consisting of an image (or text) printed on transparent *acetate* and projected on a screen. Often used in classroom settings, seminars, lectures, and other such forums.

Overinked

Descriptive of a printing press or printing plate that is receiving too much ink, resulting in heavy print that tends to smudge.

Overlap

In computing, to perform two processing operations simultaneously, such as printing one document while working on another document.

Overlay

To place one or more images on top of another image, each image being essentially a separate layer. Images can be superimposed either on a *mechanical* board by means of sheets of tissue paper or acetate, or on a computer monitor.

Overlay Color Proof

One of two primary types of *color proof*, comprising a set of thin, transparent sheets of plastic or film, each of which contains one of the four *process color*s—*cyan*, *magenta*, *yellow*, and *black*—superimposed on top of each other to simulate the appearance of the final, full-color reproduction. Two common trade names that are used as synonyms for overlay color proofs are *Color-Key* and *NAPS*. See also *Single-Sheet Color Proof*.

Overlay Module

A part of a computer program that is not loaded into the computer's memory until the functions it contains are specifically called for. After the functions contained in the overlay module have been completed, it can be overwritten by other parts of the program. In this way, computer memory—which is invariably in short supply—can be most effectively managed.

Overleaf

The opposite side of any given page or sheet of paper.

Overpacking

In printing, adding an excessive amount of *packing* material to a plate or blanket. See *Packing*.

Overpressure

On a printing press, a condition in which the impression pressure is greater than is strictly necessary, resulting in a variety of printing defects, such as *plugging* and/or *dot gain*.

Overpressure Range

In *screen printing*, the range of pressures exerted by the *squeegee* beyond that capable of producing a high-quality print.

Overprint

To print one printed impression on top of another, or to apply a layer of *varnish* on top of another.

The term *overprint* also refers to the printing of dots of one *process color* over the dots of a different color, to produce a *secondary color* that is the combination of the *primary color*s. Such colors are called *overprint colors*.

Overprint Colors

Colors produced by the printing of dots of one *primary color* on top of the dots of a second primary color to produce a third color that is the combination of the two primaries. Overprint colors are also called *Secondary Colors*. (See also *Overprint*.)

Overprinting

Printing that is done on top of a previously printed area. See *Overprint*.

Overprint Varnish

A *varnish* that is applied to a printed piece as a *coating* after printing, in contrast to the application of varnish to the formulation of the ink *vehicle* itself before printing. Overprint varnishing is typically performed—either on-press or as part of the *finishing* processes—for aesthetic purposes or to protect the printing from moisture, from abrasion, or from other potential sources of damage. (See also *Spot Varnish*.)

Overrun

Any quantity of printed materials that is greater than what was specified in the original order. See also *Underrun*.

Overscan

Any computer image that extends beyond the edges of the visible display, typically to prevent a black border from forming around the image. Accessing the nonvisible portions of the image is accomplished by means of *scrolling*. See also *Underscan*.

Overset

In typography and typesetting, a line of type that exceeds the specified *line length*.

Oversetting may be done deliberately to avoid other typographically undesirable effects, such as *widow*s or *orphan*s. See also *Underset*.

Oversewing

In *binding and finishing*, a means of repairing *case-bound* books by removing the case and *spine* of the book, *side sewing* small groups of pages, tying the lot together, *gluing off* the spine, and reattaching the case. Books that are oversewn do not lie flat due to the side stitching.

Oversize

In page layout, any image or block of text positioned such that it extends beyond a standard page boundary, but not designed to be a *bleed*.

Overstrike Characters

Any set of characters that are printed on top of another set of characters.

Over-the-Shoulder

In motion picture photography and videography, a camera shot wherein the camera is shooting over the shoulder of an individual in a particular scene, usually at another individual. Over-the-shoulder shots are often used in scenes involving conversations between individuals. In shooting scripts, over-the-shoulder is denoted by *OS*.

Oxidation

A chemical reaction involving the combination of oxygen with any other substance. One of the most common, yet least desired, results of the process of oxidation is the rusting of iron, which consists essentially of the combination of oxygen with iron (typically in the presence of moisture). Oxidation is caused by the fact that, due to the chemical structure of oxygen, it will bond with nearly anything (basically, the oxygen atom is two electrons short of having a full outer "shell," and it will hunt mercilessly for them). Although this process is the basis for respiration, it also has deleterious effects on many substances, and is the cause of such unpleasantnesses as the souring of milk, the tarnishing of silver, the spoiling of wine, and the spoilage of food, not to mention rusting. In fact, it is the reaction of oxygen with human cells that is the basis of the aging process. (Interestingly, at one point early in the history of life on Earth, there was very little atmospheric oxygen. Nearly all of the vegetation inhabiting the planet breathed nitrogen or sulfur. When green plants evolved and began emitting oxygen as a waste product, it built up to heavy concentrations in the atmosphere and killed off many of the earlier anaerobic life forms, to which oxygen was a potent poison. Oxygen, then, was the original air pollutant.) The word "oxygen" itself was named after the Greek word *oxys*, meaning "acid" and *gen*, meaning "to be born," as it was believed that oxygen was present in all acids (we now know this to be false).

In printing, oxidation is the process by which many inks dry. As the oxygen from the air is absorbed by and reacts with the substances in the ink *vehicle*, the fluid vehicle is hardened into a solid ink film. (See *Drying Oil Vehicle*.) Another chemical process called *polymerization* also contributes to hardening of ink films. Drying by oxidation should not be confused with drying by *evaporation*, which occurs when a *solvent* with a low boiling point simply turns into a gas and diffuses out of the ink, leaving the *pigment* behind. (See also *Vehicle*.)

P

P, p

The sixteenth letter of the English alphabet, deriving from the North Semitic *pe* and, phonetically, the Greek *pi*. The form of the uppercase *P*, bears little resemblance to its Greek and Etruscan progenitors, and even in early Latin resembled a candy-cane, eventually closing the top loop in later Latin. The lowercase *p* is derived from the uppercase version simply by extending the descender.

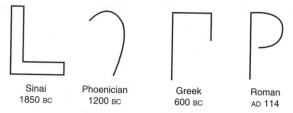

| Sinai 1850 BC | Phoenician 1200 BC | Greek 600 BC | Roman AD 114 |

The evolution of the letter P.

P6

In computing, a 32-bit *microprocessor* in Intel's 80X86 line of chips, capable of running at 133 *megahertz*.

PABX

Abbreviation for *private automatic branch exchange*. See *Private Automatic Branch Exchange (PABX)*.

Pack-Up

In *screen printing*, material placed behind the screen to raise the surface of the printing bed; facilitates *stencil* adhesion.

Package

In computing, a set of software programs (and at times related hardware) developed for a specific application and sold as a bundle.

Packet

A unit of data sent over a network, consisting of information concerning the sender, the receiver, and *error correction*, as well as the actul data that was sent. The size of the packet and the specific contents thereof depend upon the network *protocol* used. Also known as a *data packet*.

Packet Assembler/Disassembler (PAD)

A device attached to a *packet-switched network* that bundles a stream of serial data (as that from a *bridge* or *router*) into individual *packet*s suitable for transmission. A PAD also disassembles data packets back into a stream of serial data after transmission. PADs are used to attach various nodes or terminals to packet-switched networks. See *Packet Switching*.

Packet Filter

In networking and telecommunications, a means of controlling network traffic by identifying various characteristics of a data *packet*—such as *protocol*, *domain*, etc.—and relegating it to one portion of a network.

A packet filter is applied to a *bridge*, which monitors incoming traffic and sorts each packet according to a set of predetermined specifications.

Packet Switching

In networking and telecommunications, a type of data transmission method in which data to be sent is divided into small, fixed-length units (or *packet*s). Each packet has a network *address*, which includes the address of the recipient and the sender. When the message hits the network, the network controller creates a *checksum* (a means of *error correction and detection*) for each packet, which is then sent through one by one.

Depending on the network traffic, different packets may take different routes from sender to recipient. (This re-routing of data packets to avoid traffic is known as *switching*.) Upon reception, the network controller then attempts to replicate the checksum to ensure that all data has been transmitted accurately, and, if so, an *ACK* signal is sent to the sender of the message. If not, a request to resend the data is transmitted to the sender.

The advantage of packet switching is that since the data are broken down into small units, each of which can be sent by a variety of routes, there is no need to set up a direct connection between sender and recipient, which may not always be possible on busy networks. As a result, data transmission is very rapid.

A disadvantage, however, is that the data packets do not always arrive at the receiver in the same order that they were sent; it is up to the receiving terminal to examine the order information in each packet and reassemble the original message. Consequently, some types of data—such as sound or video—are not effectively transmitted using packet switching. Some common network *protocol*s that use packet switching techniques are *X.25* and *frame relay*. (See also *Circuit Switching* and *Cell Switching*.)

Packet-Level Procedure (PAP)

A *protocol* that is used in *X.25* networks for the *full-duplex* transfer of *packet*s between a computer and a *modem*.

Packet-Switched Network

A computer network that transfers data from *node* to node by means of *packet switching*. See *Packet Switching*. The term *packet-switched network* is commonly used to refer to a network using the *X.25* standard.

Packing

Paper, plastic, or other material inserted underneath an offset press plate or *blanket* on the press to raise the printing surface or increase the circumference of either the *plate cylinder* or *blanket cylinder*. (The process of inserting these materials is also referred to as "packing.") Each of these cylinders is *undercut*, or possesses a difference between the radius of the cylinder body and the cylinder *bearer*s, to allow varying degrees of packing. Packing is frequently necessary when the printing pressure is too light to produce a good image, either on the blanket or on the *substrate*, or when the printing length needs to be adjusted.

There are three reasons for packing: it allows use of many different plate and blanket thicknesses, enables the printing pressure to be varied (depending upon the desired print density), and allows for compensation of paper stretching or expansion during multicolor printing (by varying the ratio of plate to blanket diameter, a print that has expanded can be accurately matched). The packing materials themselves need to be manufactured with accurate and consistent thicknesses, must be able to retain their thickness under printing pressure, and retain dimensional stability. *Kraft* paper has traditionally been used for packing in the past, but the use of plastic—especially polyester—is becoming more frequent, due to its increased toughness. Paper designed primarily for printing should not be used as packing; the thickness can vary considerably from sheet to sheet, and its compressibility, although important for printing, makes it unsuitable for packing. Packing can be as wide as the plate or blanket, but due to seepage from the *dampening solution* (which causes the packing to swell,) many press operators leave a small amount of space (anywhere from ⅟₁₆ to ½ in.) between the edge of the blanket and the packing.

There is no specific or practical measure of the pressure existing between the plate and blanket cylinders, so the term *squeeze* (measured in inches) is commonly used. If each cylinder is packed so that their diameters are the same size and exactly equal to the size the undercut (so that each surface is just touching), there is no squeeze. If a 0.002-in. sheet of paper is added to the packing of one cylinder, the squeeze then becomes 0.002 in. Each thickness of packing material subsequently added increases the squeeze by the thickness of the sheet added.

In addition to squeeze, the pressure exerted by squeeze is also important. An equal amount of squeeze will exert differing amounts of pressure, depending on the resiliency of the two surfaces being squeezed. For example, the squeeze between the plate and the blanket (a hard surface meeting a resilient surface) will exert more pressure than an equal squeeze between blanket and paper (where two resilient surfaces are meeting). Consequently, it is generally recommended that blankets generate a squeeze of 0.002–0.004 in., although this can vary. A rule of thumb is generally to overpack the blanket by 0.001 in., as blanket compression tends to occur during printing. The type of blanket used—whether a *conventional blanket* or a *compressible blanket*—also affects the degree of packing. (See *Blanket*.)

Another hurdle involved in the packing question is compression of the metal bearers on the cylinder. Especially on older presses, the steel bearers can deform under pressure, changing the size of the undercut by as much as 0.002 in. The actual packing height can be measured using a *packing gauge*, which will account for any bearer compression (or other pressure-generated packing anomalies), but quantitative measurements are no comparison for experiential observation of print quality and packing height. A good qualitative test involves packing the press to a working height, and a plate containing solids and halftones is printed so that a good, solid image is printed. Then, packing is removed until the solids will no longer print. At that point, packing material is replaced 0.001 in. at a time until the solids once again print well. This, then, is the minimum pressure the press requires. The packing gauge can be used to quantitatively measure what has just been achieved, the aim being to reproduce it consistently for other print jobs.

The thickness of packing material, plates, and blankets tends to vary, although plates and blankets obtained from the same manufacturer will probably not vary by much, if at all. Still it is always a good idea to carefully measure the thicknesses of all these elements—using a *micrometer*—just to be on the safe side. Blankets especially can vary, and it is best to take up to nine separate readings in various locations on the blanket surface, an average thickness being computed for the entire surface. When measuring the thickness of paper packing, it is best to allow the material to reach equilibrium with the relative humidity of the pressroom, as paper thickness changes with increased or decreased moisture content.

Determining the amount of packing to use is a case of simple arithmetic. If the plate needs to be 0.005 in. above the bearers, and it is known that the undercut is 0.020 in., then the plate-plus-packing height needs to be the sum of those two numbers, or 0.025 in. If it is then known that the plate is 0.015 in. thick, subtracting that from the plate-plus-packing height yields 0.010 in., which is the total thickness of the packing required. Similar calculations can be done to determine the packing required for the blanket.

Determining the squeeze generated between the plate and blanket on a particular *bearer-contact press* is also a case of simple math, and is simply the height of the plate above the bearers added to the height of the blanket above the bearers. (If the blanket is packed below the height of the bearers, its height is subtracted from the height of the plate above the bearers.) In determining the squeeze on a *non-bearer-contact press*, the math proceeds in two stages. First, the height of the plate above the bearers is added to the height of the blanket above the bearers, and from this total is then subtracted the distance between the bearers, yielding the squeeze.

Improper packing and inadequate or excessive amounts of squeeze can have many deleterious effects on both print quality, and the integrity of the plate and/or blanket. Squeeze in excess of 0.004 in. while using a conventional blanket (or in excess of 0.008 in. if using a compressible blanket) causes *dot gain*, and streaking, as well as plate wear, *scumming*, and *plate blinding*, as the excessive friction of the blanket on the plate abrades the surface of the plate, removing the desensitizing film of dampening solution from nonimage areas and rubbing off the image(s). Too much squeeze between the impression cylinder and the blanket contributes to paper deformations and increased *picking*. (Too much squeeze can also be caused by damaged press cylinders, such as cylinders that have had low spots impressed into them, perhaps by a wad of towel or other lumpy foreign substance passing through the nip of press cylinders.) As might be expected, squeeze generally less than 0.002–0.003 in. results in light, faded images. A cause of this is not taking into account compression of the blanket, bearers, etc., when determining packing. A common but incorrect solution is to increase ink flow, which generates a variety of printing defects, such as *snowflaking*, *dot slurring*, excessively thick printing, and a variety of other defects. In nearly all of these cases, problems of inadequate or excessive squeeze can be avoided by carefully measuring all the various elements that contribute to plate and blanket height and squeeze, and understanding the degree to which various elements can be compressed during the increased pressures generated during printing.

Another advantage of packing is the ability to adjust the length of the print by varying the diameters of the plate and blanket cylinders. When paper is stretched, or comes into contact with moisture (such as offset press dampening systems), it changes its dimensions. (Since paper changes direction primarily in the *cross-grain direction*, image-size adjustment is typically effective only on paper whose grain runs perpendicular to the direction of transport through the press; if, for example, 8½×11-in. paper is run through the press with its longer direction parallel to the direction of travel, the grain should be parallel to the shorter dimension. Such paper is called *grain-short*. Conversely, if the paper is run through the press with its *shorter* direction parallel to the direction of travel, the grain should be parallel to the *longer* dimension. Such paper is called *grain-long*.)

When paper changes its dimensions, the image changes size, and additional colors or images will print out of register. One way to rectify this is using variations in packing height to enlarge or reduce a printed image. Adding more packing to the blanket cylinder, thus increasing its circumference, lengthens an image, while adding more packing to the plate cylinder shortens an image. The procedure varies slightly depending on whether the press is a bearer-contact press or a non-bearer-contact press.

IMAGE ENLARGEMENT

Bearer-Contact Press. Remove packing from the plate cylinder, decreasing its height, and add it to the blanket cylinder, increasing *its* height by the same amount. Decrease the squeeze between the impression and blanket cylinders by an amount equal to the change in packing. Increase inking and dampening settings, if necessary.

Non-Bearer-Contact Press. Remove packing from the plate cylinder, reducing its height. Increase the squeeze between the plate and blanket cylinders and between the blanket and impression cylinders by an amount equal to the packing removed. Increase the inking and dampening settings, if necessary.

IMAGE REDUCTION

Bearer-Contact Press. Remove packing from the blanket cylinder, reducing its height, and add it to the plate cylinder. Increase the squeeze between the impression and blanket cylinders by an amount equal to the change in packing. Decrease inking and dampening settings, if necessary.

Non-Bearer-Contact Press. Add packing to the plate cylinder, raising its height. Decrease the squeeze between the plate and blanket cylinders by an amount equal to the change in packing. Increase the squeeze between the blanket and impression cylinders by an amount equal to the packing change. Decrease the inking and dampening settings, if necessary.

It may have been observed that on non-bearer-contact presses only one cylinder—the plate—needs to have the packing adjusted. The extent of image enlargement possible depends on the packing conditions at the start of the job. If there is slippage between the plate and blanket initially, any adjustment of packing beyond 0.004 in. could cause further slippage and print distortions such as *slurring*. With no slippage initially, packing changes beyond 0.004 in. may cause no problems. If the paper is expected to stretch, it may be best to print a slightly shorter image the first time, then restore the packing to normal for successive colors.

There is no substitute for experience in determining possible print length increases due to paper dimensional instability, but there is a quick way to approximately predict any dimensional changes: on a flat plate, etch four lines on the plate, one in either corner, ensuring that they fall within the print area of a press sheet. Measure the distance between the lines. Put the plate on the press and print a few sheets. Measure the distance between the lines on the print, and subtract from it the distance between the lines on the plate. Then, divide the difference in total print size by the distance between the lines on the plate. The result will be the average size of the length gain per inch.

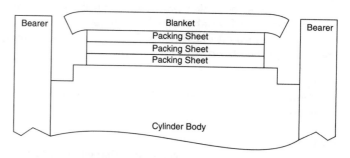

Packing the blanket cylinder.

In computer graphics, *packing* also refers to the instructions used to effect ***data compression***, or the reduction in size of a computer file. See ***Data Compression***.

Packing Creep

An undesirable movement of offset press blanket *packing* material during printing, commonly caused by an excessive number of different sheets of packing material. See ***Blanket*** and ***Packing***.

Packing Cut-Off

A defect of ***offset lithography***, characterized by printing that is too light or is cut off at the top or bottom of a sheet, caused by insufficient *packing* or by *packing creep*.

Packing Gauge

A device used by offset printers to determine the ***packing*** height of a plate or blanket. The main body of a packing gauge is placed on the plate or blanket, with an additional feeler contacting the ***bearer***, the metal ring attached to either end of a press cylinder. The dial on the device indicates the difference in height between the plate/blanket and the cylinder bearer. Packing height needs to be measured extremely accurately. See ***Packing***.

Pad

In ***cutting and trimming***, an alternate term for a ***cutting stick*** on a ***guillotine trimmer***. See ***Cutting Stick***.

In ***binding and finishing***, when used as a verb, *pad* means to apply a flexible adhesive to a stack of paper allowing sheets to be pulled off one at a time. See ***Padding***. The term *pad*, when used as a noun, refers to such a bound stack of sheets.

PAD

Abbreviation for ***packet assembler/disassembler***. See ***Packet Assembler/Disassembler (PAD)***.

Padded Cover

A book cover used in ***case binding*** containing a layer of felt or other flexible material between the cloth and the underlying board, used to impart a spongy effect to the cover.

Padding

In ***binding and finishing***, a finishing operation in which a flexible adhesive—called ***padding glue***—is applied to one edge of a stack of sheets. When the adhesive is dry, sheets can be torn off individually. Padding is used to create notepads. See ***Binding and Finishing***.

Padding Glue

In ***binding and finishing***, a flexible ***adhesive*** used in *padding*. See ***Padding***.

Pad Transfer Printing

A type of printing, used on irregularly shaped ***substrate***s, in which the image is transferred from a metal or plastic photoengraved (or ***intaglio***) plate (called a ***cliche***) to an intermediate silicone rubber pad and, ultimately, to the substrate. Ink is supplied to the engraved portions of the cliche after each impression.

Page

One side of a sheet of paper. Two pages make up a ***leaf***. Page is abbreviated *p* or *pg*. The plural, pages, is abbreviated *pp*.

In computing, the term *page* refers to a segment of a program or application. A computer system (especially one utilizing ***virtual memory***) will subdivide a program into several pages of a certain length, and load as many as will fit into memory. The rest it will save on a dedicated portion of the hard disk. See ***Virtual Memory***.

Page Composition

Alternate term for ***layout*** See ***Layout***.

Page Description Language (PDL)

A computer language or software—such as ***PostScript***, the most popular page description language—that describes an entire page—including text, graphics, lines, and ***halftone***s—as a series of codes, allowing for viewing or output on any device capable of decoding the language.

Paged Memory Management Unit

In computing, a special ***processor*** or chip used to manage a computer's ***virtual memory***. Abbreviated ***PMMU***. Most ***microprocessor***s being manufactured these days have PMMU functions built in.

Page End

In computing, a command indicating where a page ends.

Page Flex

In ***binding and finishing***, the number of times a book page can be flexed before it comes loose from the binding.

Page Geometry

The position, shape, and orientation of each element appearing on a composed page.

Page Layout Program

Alternate term for ***page makeup software***. See ***Page Makeup Software***.

Page Layout Software

Alternate term for ***page makeup software***. See ***Page Makeup Software***.

PageMaker®

One of the very first ***page makeup software*** programs, created by Aldus Corporation (and since bought by Adobe Systems, Inc.), that allows assembly of disparate page elements—text, ***line art***, ***halftone***s, etc.—in a single document. Designed originally to run on the Apple ***Macintosh*** computer, PageMaker is now available for a variety of *plat-forms*, in particular, *IBM-compatible computers* running Microsoft *Windows*. The development of PageMaker in the mid-1980s, coupled with the creation of the Apple Macintosh and the *PostScript* page description language, were instrumental in the invention of desktop publishing.

Page Makeup

The art and process of assembling all page elements—text, graphics, *line art*, *halftone*s, and other material—into *camera-ready copy*. At one time accomplished using hot metal, it was until recently performed primarily by pasting up output text and other page elements onto a pasteup board. Pages are now increasingly composed electronically and digitally, using *page makeup software*.

Page Makeup Software

A computer program used to assemble pages electronically and/or digitally, with all page elements capable of being viewed on a computer monitor in positions approximating their location on the final output page. Page elements can also be "cut" and "pasted" on the screen, a digital equivalent of earlier manual pasteup processes. Page makeup software—ranging from off-the-shelf programs such as *PageMaker* and *QuarkXPress* to customized *CEPS* applications—allows importation and generation of many types of images in a variety of *file format*s. They commonly allow the assembly of text, line art, photographs, and *halftone*s in a single file, with the capability of generating high-end output, such as that produced by an *imagesetter*. Page makeup software invented desktop publishing.

Page Map

Alternate term for *page definition*. See *Page Definition*.

Page Memory

In computing, the portion of *video memory* in which information pertaining to a complete video page is stored. Depending upon the capacity of the *video adapter*, more than one image may be able to be loaded into page memory simultaneously, expediting the display of subsequent images.

Page Mode

Alternate term for *all points addressability*. See *All Points Addressability (APA)*.

Page-Mode RAM

In computing, a means of memory management designed to speed up *dynamic RAM (DRAM)* performance. Essentially, page-mode RAM uses specialized DRAM chips that divide memory into smaller units called *pages*. The use of consecutive *memory address*es in the same page of RAM speeds up the rate at which data can be accessed.

Page Printer

Any computer output device that only produces one page at a time.

Page Proofs

Samples of a page or document produced prior to a press-run as a means of checking for errors.

Page Scrolling

In word processing and page makeup programs, a feature allowing the user to quickly flip through all the pages of a multipage document, usually in both forward and reverse order.

Page Segment

In page layout programs, any object that can be placed on a page; it can include text and/or graphics.

Pagination

In typography, the assembly of type into pages. Typesetting is the process of setting type; pagination is the process of putting pages together with that type and other graphic elements. There are a variety of ways that pages can be assembled:

1. Affixing reproduction-quality typeset printout to a carrier sheet to form a *camera-ready* mechanical. Also called *pasteup* or *keylining*. This process is being replaced almost entirely by digital techniques (see #3 below).
2. Assembling *film positive* printout on clear acetate carrier sheets to form a master for contact exposure to form a *negative* film. Also known as *stripping*.
3. Electronically reviewing and/or assembling type on a page makeup screen or, more and more commonly, in a *page makeup program* such as *PageMaker* or *QuarkXPress*, to create finished pages that will be sent to an output device—or, increasingly, direct-to-plate—in position. (See *Desktop Publishing*.)

The basic building blocks of a page are text blocks, display lines such as heads, boxes and rules, line illustrations, photographs, captions, footnotes, tabular blocks, and page numbers (called *folios*).

A page is usually designed as an image area defined by the margins and/or borders. A grid is created to position blocks consistently within the image area. Columns must align at the top and bottom of the image area. The image area is also known as the *live matter area*. A rough assembly of pages to see how they will look prior to final assembly is called a *dummy*.

The term *pagination* also refers to the process of numbering the pages, commonly done by *automatic pagination* features of a typesetting device or page makeup software.

Paint

Abbreviated term for a *paint program*.

Paint Brush

In computer graphics, a tool of many paint and drawing programs that functions much like a paintbrush, allowing a variety of strokes, line widths, and textures to be added to an image or drawing.

Paint Program

A computer program used to produce original graphics, or manipulate existing **bitmapped** images. The difference between a paint program and a **drawing** program is that the latter is used to produce **vector**-based graphics, useful for the smooth, clean output of **line art**. Paint programs, being bitmapped graphics, are both displayed on the computer monitor and output as **bitmap**s, the **resolution** on-screen being dependent on that of the monitor. The advantage of paint programs is that images can be manipulated **pixel**-by-pixel, the color depth of each pixel varying only by what the monitor is capable of displaying. Paint programs are occasionally useful for generating original artwork; they are more commonly used for manipulating scanned or otherwise imported graphic images. (See **Bitmap**.)

PAL

Abbreviation for **Phase Alternating Line**. See **Phase Alternating Line (PAL)**.

Palette

An alternate term for a **color palette**. See **Color Palatte**.

In many types of computer graphics programs, the term *palette* is also used to refer to any window full of icons representing various tools at the user's disposal. Many of these are known as **floating palette**s.

Palette Shift

In computer imaging, an undesirable color change in a displayed image caused by the use of more colors than the monitor can effectively process. For example, an image created in RGB mode with a palette of millions of colors will not display accurately on a monitor capable of (or set to) only 256 colors.

Pallet

A wooden platform on which cartons and other materials can be placed, secured, and shipped. Pallets usually have openings in the side to allow movement by means of a forklift. Also known as a **skid**.

Palmtop

Alternate term for **hand-held**. See **Hand-Held**. Also spelled with a hyphen, *palm-top*.

Pamphlet

Any publication commonly possessing fewer than 80 pages, saddle-stitched or thread sewn, and utilizing a **self-cover**, or a slightly heavier stock for a cover. Small pamphlets are known as **booklet**s.

Pan

In motion picture photography and videography, to move a camera horizontally, either while following a moving subject, or to view all of a large stationary subject, as a landscape.

The process of translating all elements of a picture with a workstation transformation to give the appearance of movement to a point or object of interest.

In computer graphics, to move an object from side to side or up and down. On the Macintosh we call this scrolling. On non-Macintosh CAD systems it is called panning. It simply means moving around to different parts of the drawing.

Panchromatic

Descriptive of the sensitivity of photographic films or other photosensitive materials to all wavelengths of light. Panchromatic film is commonly used to make photographic **color separation**s. A disadvantage of panchromatic film is that it cannot be handled safely in a red darkroom light, unlike **orthochromatic** film, which is sensitive to all colors except **red**.

Panel

In **finishing**, a solid color of ink or foil applied to all or part of the cover of a **casebound** book to provide a background for additional **foil stamping** or **die-stamping**.

Panel Pictures

In **halftone** photography, two or more individual **continuous-tone** images (such as photographs) pasted up adjacent to each other and photographed as a single halftone.

PANTONE

The brand-name for a popular **color matching system**, or series of printed **color swatch**es used to match, specify, identify, and display specific colors or colored ink combinations. PANTONE systems are available for both **spot color** and **process color**.

Spot Color. The PANTONE Matching System (**PMS**) is PANTONE's spot color matching system, which comprises a series of books of color swatches containing 1,012 PMS colors, mixed from 12 different base inks. PMS colors are specified for uncoated and coated papers, since the type of paper used can significantly vary the quality of the color that is produced. Each swatch is numbered, and instructions for the ink mixing are also included. Thus, designers, when for example deciding which color to use for a company's logo on a letterhead, can specify "PMS 620" and the printer will be able to match that color with a great degree of accuracy. On desktop color systems, however, color output (from **laser printer**s or other digital printing devices) can only approximate PMS spot colors, as they utilize four **CMYK** colorants rather than premixed inks.

Process Color. Called the *PANTONE Process Color System* (to distinguish it from the spot-color PMS) specifies over 3,000 different colors, expressed as percentages of CMYK. This system is available for various software applications, and also includes a version designed to comply with **SWOP** specifications.

Matching spot color to a corresponding process color is not always possible. A third PANTONE swatching system, the PANTONE Process Color Imaging Guide, includes over 1,000 spot color swatches along with a sample of the process color that most closely matches it. This system is a boon to designers as it allows them to determine at the outset which colors can be reproduced with process inks and which require strictly spot inks.

PANTONE systems are the most widely used color matching systems, at least in North America, and are supported by most of the popular *page makeup program*s. (See also *TRUMATCH* and *FOCOLTONE*.)

PANTONE Open Color Environment

A *color management system*—a set of computer programs or utilities that ensure consistent color throughout the prepress processes by calibrating the color relationships among the scanners, monitors, printers, imagesetters, and other devices in the chain from input to output—developed by *PANTONE*. Most other color management systems are based on the *CIE color space*, but the PANTONE Open Color Environment (abbreviated POCE) utilizes an original color model called Appearance Equivalency (AeQ). POCE allows color matching from device to device for both *spot color* and *process color*, as well as for *continuous-tone* color images. Like other color management systems, it utilizes device profiles, which can be user-modified, but unlike other systems it operates at the *operating system* level, and even supports cross-platform color matching among *Macintosh*, *Windows*, and *UNIX* platforms. (See *Color Management System [CMS]*.)

PAP

Abbreviation for *Packet-Level Procedure*. See *Packet-Level Procedure (PAP)*.

The acronym *PAP* is also an abbreviation for *Printer Access Protocol*. See *Printer Access Protocol (PAP)*.

Paper

The earliest writing materials are believed to have been stone and brick. Many examples of the ancient Sumerian cuneiform writing—characters engraved on clay tablets—have been found, and the practice was adopted by other early civilizations such as the Babylonians, the Chaldeans, the Persians, and the Egyptians. Preserving important documents as engravings on metals such as bronze was customary in ancient Rome. Writing on leaves (usually palm, but those of other trees as well) was also popular in Ancient Rome, and the term "leaf" still denotes the page of a book today. The Romans also wrote on the bark of trees. (The word *liber* was the Latin word for "inner bark," and soon came to denote a book itself. It is the etymological root of English words such as "library.") Ancient civilizations also made use of *parchment*, which was made from the split skin of sheep, and *vellum*, made from calfskin, goatskin, or lambskin (the word "vellum" itself derives from the same etymological root as "veal," denoting a calf). The use of

parchment and vellum continued well into the era of the printing press, and still continues for important documents today. It is said that the skins of three hundred sheep were needed to produce one Gutenberg Bible. *Papyrus*, although bearing similar characteristics, is not paper in the true sense of the term, although it is made by splitting the stalks of the papyrus plant (*Cyperus papyrus*), laying them side by side, and hammering them together to provide a smooth writing surface. Papyrus was popular in ancient Egypt, where the papyrus plant grew, and later spread elsewhere. Although the species is now nearly extinct in Egypt, it still grows along the upper Nile and in Ethiopia. The first true paper is believed to have been produced in China, by Ts'ai Lun in AD 105. The Chinese closely guarded the manufacture of paper, and it took 500 years for the craft to make it even to Korea. By the mid-twelfth century, however, papermaking had reached Europe, most likely by way of Arabia.

Until the late eighteenth century, the bulk of the paper produced in Europe was made from linen and cotton, whose high *cellulose* content (higher than that of wood *pulp*) still makes them the best materials for papermaking. (In fact, in the economic boom that followed the ebbing of the Black Death in Europe in the fourteenth century, the rage for new clothes—in particular, underwear—resulted in a lot of discarded old clothes. The all-too-familiar "bone man," who collected the remains of plague victims, became the "rag and bone man" who also collected old clothing, which went to the papermakers. It was this surplus of paper that provided the impetus for the invention of printing. Without an inexpensive material to print on, it would hardly have become as popular as it did.) Eventually, however, the surplus of cotton and linen turned into a shortage. A substitute—wood pulp—was suggested by the French physicist and naturalist René Antoine Ferchault de Réaumer, who got the idea by observing wasps build paper-like nests by chewing wood into pulp. Scientists seized on the idea of using materials other than cotton rags to make paper, and much of the eighteenth century consisted of various suggestions of plants that could be used. These included seaweed, swamp moss, vines, hemp, corn husks, potatoes, reeds, and the bark, leaves, and wood of various trees and shrubs. (A book was even published which was printed on paper made of asbestos.) In the nineteenth century, the technology to produce wood-pulp paper was in place, but a public slow to favor it over cotton- and linen-based paper made it less than economical. It wasn't until the 1880s that wood-pulp paper was accepted, and now, one hundred years later, the only rag-based paper the average person is likely to encounter is United States currency.

Other sources of pulp are also being sought, and include *bagasse* (a fibrous material left after the processing of sugarcane), *esparto* (a wild grass native to northern Africa and southern Spain, which has been used in England for a long time as a source of paper pulp), *bamboos* (any of several types of tall, woody grasses that grow in tropical regions), *manila hemp* and *sisal hemp* (obtained from used rope), *jute* (scraps of burlap), *cotton linters* (fibers from cotton seeds, left after cotton ginning), *flax tow* (another source of linen fiber), and *kenaf* (a plant native to India). Economy and renewability are of prime consideration in the choice of a fibrous source for mass papermaking.

PAPERMAKING

There are two basic stages in the papermaking process. The first is *"pulping"*—extracting fibrous material from the wood or other raw material—and interleaving these fibers together to create paper. Before wood can be pulped, it must undergo *debarking*. Bark contains little or no fibrous material, and contributes dirt and other contaminants to the pulp, and is removed either mechanically or hydraulically. Debarked logs are then sent to a *chipper* where they are chopped into small pieces ready for *digesting*. The purpose of pulping is to separate the cellulose fibers from the other nonfibrous material in the wood, in particular *lignin*, an organic material that binds fibers of cellulose together. It is the presence of lignin that is primarily responsible for a paper's low durability and yellowing with age. Pulping can be done either by mechanical, chemical, or semichemical (a combination of mechanical and chemical) means. (See *Pulping*, as well as individual entries on *Mechanical Pulping*, *Semichemical Pulping*, and *Chemical Pulping*.)

Mechanical (or *groundwood*) pulping is typically used for low-quality papers used for newspapers, directories, catalogs, and "pulp" magazines. Most printing and writing papers are made from chemical pulp, in particular that utilizing the *kraft* process. The advantages of kraft pulping include its ability to handle nearly every known type of wood, its efficient chemical and heat recovery system (which lowers processing costs), and its ability to produce a strong, high-brightness pulp. The replacement of batch pulping systems with continuous pulping systems and the use of monitoring operations via computer has also improved speed, economy, and quality of pulp. Modified chemical processes are used to pulp nonwoody plants. Although extracting cellulose is easier, their fibrous content tends to be less than that of wood. Cotton and other textile remnants generate higher fiber content; they are used for high-quality and permanent writing papers and are also pulped using a modified alkaline chemical process. *Recycled paper* is also being used increasingly as a source of pulp.

Wood pulp is brown in color (due primarily to the presence of residual lignin), and can often be used as is for brown wrapping paper or paper bags. More often, however, pulp must be bleached in order to produce printing and writing papers. Prolonged chemical pulping results in severe fiber degradation, so *bleaching* is typically done to remove or alter the lignin without harming the cellulose fibers. Bleaching of mechanical pulps also helps remove some of its lignin content, but is done on a limited basis to prevent fiber loss and decreased pulp yield. Bleaching increases the whiteness of mechanical pulps, but not to the extent that it does for

chemical pulps. Bleached mechanical pulp also lacks the brightness, stability, and permanence of chemical pulps.

At the end of the pulping process is when *loading* occurs. Loading is the addition of various *fillers*, or nonfibrous raw materials that alter the properties of the paper, depending on what qualities the paper is desired to have. Loading is done to modify such paper characteristics as opacity, brightness, printability, texture, weight, color, etc. The most common fillers are *clay* (refined from naturally occurring kaolin), *titanium dioxide*, and *calcium carbonate*. Fillers account for 5–30% of a paper's total weight, depending on the end-use requirements of the paper. (See *Fillers*.) *Sizing*, such as *rosin* and *alum*, are often added at this point, as well, which make the paper resistant to water. (See *Sizing*.) Pulp and nonfibrous additives are known collectively as the papermaking *furnish*.

Prior to papermaking, the furnish undergoes *stock preparation*, which includes *refining* and mixing of fibrous and nonfibrous materials. Fibers are dissolved in water in a pulper, which is a heavy tank containing high-speed blades which help dissolve the pulp into a *slurry*. The slurry is sent to undergo *beating* (or refining), either in a *beater* and a *conical refiner* (also called a *jordan*), which is an older, batch refining system still in use in many small paper mills, or a *disk refiner*, which is a newer, continuous process. In both systems, the beating process brushes, cuts, frays, and shortens the fibers. It also swells the fibers, increasing their surface area as an aid to bonding. Nonfibrous additives may be added at this point. In the disk refining system, which allows for greater flexibility, the furnish can be altered at will, depending on the final ultimate paper grade or other desired end-use factors.

There are three basic types of paper machines: a *fourdrinier* machine, a *twin-wire former*, and a *cylinder machine*. Each differs primarily in the *forming section* or *wet end*. At the beginning of the process, the furnish is diluted with water to a fiber-water ratio of 1:200. Centrifugal force removes foreign particles such as bits of metal, dirt, plastic, and other extraneous material. It is also necessary to keep the fibers from clumping together until it is on the *forming wire*. Premature clots of fibers (or *flocs*) result in poor paper formation. The paper machine's *headbox* keeps the fibers from clotting and regulates the rate at which the fiber suspension is sent to the forming section. The *slice* is an adjustable rectangular slit that regulates the width, thickness, and consistency of the furnish, ensuring that the paper that ultimately forms has properties that are uniform. As the furnish travels through the slice, the individual fibers begin to align in the direction of their flow, forming the *grain* of the paper.

In a traditional fourdrinier machine, the water-fiber mixture flows through the slice onto a moving wire mesh belt. As the mixture moves forward, water drains through the mesh and the fibers begin to interlace, forming a mat. More fibers are deposited on top of the previous layer. The belt is supported by suction-cup-shaped *foils* or turning *table rolls* that also aid in drainage, usually by suction.

Some paper machines increase drainage by oscillating the wire, producing a *shake* in the direction perpendicular to the direction the wire is moving. The side of the fiber mat that forms on top of the belt is called the *wire side* of the paper while the reverse is called the *felt side* of the paper. Since some amount of fine fibers and fillers drain through the wire with the water, the felt side of the paper will have a somewhat different composition and texture than the wire side. Recent innovations have reduced the *two-sidedness* of paper. As the wire continues with the newly formed paper *web*, it passes over vacuum boxes, which suck out water that is beyond the reach of the foils, shake, table rolls, or gravity itself. In many machines, the web now passes under a *dandy roll*, a hollow, wire-covered roller that improves paper formation. Designs on the dandy roll also add a *watermark* or the markings typical of *laid finish* paper. At the end of the forming section of the paper machine, the web passes the *couch roll*, a perforated cylinder that uses a vacuum to remove even more water. At this point, the web is about 80–85% water, and is ready to be sent to the *press section*, which uses pressure and suction to remove and evenly distribute as much moisture as possible, and to increase fiber bonding and consequently sheet strength. The press section also affects the paper's final *bulk* and *finish*. When it leaves the press section, the web is about 60–70% water by weight. It is further dried in the *drying section*, where heated cylinders evaporate residual moisture. It is necessary to keep the web under tension to prevent distortions and shrinkage. When the web is dried, its water content will be 2–8%, depending on its end-use requirements. The method of drying also depends on the paper's specific end-use requirements. (See also *Yankee Dryer* and *Air Drying*.) *External sizing*, materials added to improve the paper's resistance to fluids and to seal the surface fibers to increase sheet strength, is also added at the *size press*, which is located within the drying section. (See also *Surface Sizing*).

The final step for the paper web on the machine is *calendering*. The machine's *calender* comprises several steel rollers which impart a dense, smooth surface with consistent thickness. The degree of calendering depends on the desired finish of the paper. Paper is wound into a full-width machine roll, and rewinders reduce the roll to the desired width and diameter. The creation of the paper roll is a more complex operation than one would expect. The requirements of any paper roll are *printability* and *runnability*, and as press speeds increase, new demands are placed on the roll-building technology. Tests are made that generate *cross-machine direction* profiles of the paper as it comes out of the slice and monitor variations in *moisture content* and *caliper* or, in other words, variations in the thickness of the forming web. Any variation beyond certain acceptable tolerances will prevent the web from winding correctly. It is necessary for printers to utilize rolls that unwind with even tension across the roll. If it is wound too tightly, the paper will be stretched beyond its ability to return to its original dimensions. Winding that is slack near the core but tight on the outer portion of the roll will result in a *telescoped* or *starred roll*, specific distortions and defects in the paper. New innovations, such as electronic drives and computer controls have contributed greatly to the creation of optimally wound rolls.

Finishing refers to the final preparations of paper, depending on the specific end-use requirements. It can include *rewinding*, *sheeting*, *trimming*, or altering the finish by *embossing*, *supercalendering*, or *coating*.

PAPER PROPERTIES

The many properties a particular paper possesses affect its *printability*, *print quality*, and *runnability*. Once produced, paper is tested by methods produced by the *Technical Association of the Pulp and Paper Industry (TAPPI)*. Each paper property has a specific test and guideline prescribed in the *TAPPI Official Test Method*. Tests that do not have an official method, but have practical applications, are known as *TAPPI Useful Test Methods*. Since paper responds to environmental conditions such as temperature and humidity, tests must be conducted in a tightly controlled environment.

Surface Properties. Cleanliness of a paper's surface is an important consideration. Various surface contaminants are an unwanted byproduct of the papermaking process, however. Loosely bonded surface fibers, particles of fibers, fillers, or coatings detached by cutting and trimming operations performed with inadequately sharpened blades, *lint*, dust from the air, or fabric fibers from machine felts all contribute to generating surface debris that causes blanket *piling* and various printing defects. *Dirt* is a term that in papermaking specifically refers to specks or particles embedded in the paper, contrasting with the color of the paper itself. *Ink absorbency* and its opposite property, *ink holdout*, are functions of a paper's *porosity*, as well as other surface and structural properties. A lack of uniform ink absorbency results in a *mottled* or *galvanized* appearance, or visible inconsistency in ink density, color, gloss, or other aspect. Variable color density and gloss result from variations in the paper's gloss and point-to-point variations in the capacity for ink holdout. (See *Ink Holdout* and *Ink Absorbency*.) Printing *smoothness* refers to how complete the contact between the paper and the printing surface is. The smoothness of paper affects the appearance of the printed image, involving as it does the variations in surface contour. Smoothness is primarily a *formation* issue, and the type and length of fibers used, the extent of wet pressing, the amount of filler, the extent of calendering, and the use of coatings all affect the ultimate levelness of the paper's printing surface. (See *Smoothness*.)

A paper's *conformability* is the degree of contouring that will take place when a printing surface applies pressure to the paper to bring it in more complete contact with the ink on the printing plate. Poor formation of the paper or low *compressibility* will result in incomplete image transfer to the paper. The **surface strength**, also called **pick resistance**, is the ability of paper to resist rupturing under forces that act at right angles to its surface, as when the film of ink splits between the paper surface and the plate or blanket during printing. **Picking** refers to any ink-transfer damage, such as the pulling off of coating fragments, the separation of paper plys below the printed surface, or any blistering or rupturing. (See **Picking**.)

Also affecting the smoothness and printability of paper is the two-sidedness of paper. Coatings applied to papers usually reduce the differences in the two sides. Paper manufactured on newer twin-wire formers also ensure that both sides of the paper are roughly similar in texture and smoothness. (See also individual entries for **Wire Side** and **Felt Side**.)

The **compressibility** of a paper is a function of its hardness, density, moisture content, and the relative humidity, and refers to its change in thickness under pressure. **Resiliency** is the paper's ability to return to its original thickness and surface contour when pressure is removed. **Hardness** and **softness** are, respectively, the extent to which a paper will resist or allow indentations made by a pen, printing plate, or other surface. All of these structural characteristics are collectively described as its **printing cushion**. Although high softness is preferred, different end-use requirements necessitate differing degrees of hardness and resiliency.

Structural Properties. **Formation** is a paper quality that describes the uniformity of its minute surface contours. "Hills" and "valleys," seen as light and dark regions when paper is held up to a light source, affect the smoothness and levelness of the paper's surface. Calendering, or compressing the "hills," is only a partial solution, as the "valleys" still remain, and printing on such paper will have a blotchy or mottled appearance. **Grain** direction is the result of the fibers aligning themselves with direction of their travel through the paper machine (called **machine direction [MD]**).

A paper's grain direction is called **long-grain** when the grain direction is parallel to its longer dimension. **Short-grain** paper has its grain direction parallel to its shorter dimension. Grain direction is important, particularly for sheetfed printing, as long-grain paper will be more dimensionally stable than short-grain paper. (See **Grain**.) A paper's strength is described not only in terms of its grain and **cross-grain direction**s, but also in a direction perpendicular to the plane of the paper's surface. The **internal bond strength**—also called the **plybond strength**—refers to the force needed to separate the two plys of a single sheet of paper. Internal bond strength is a consideration when forces in printing act on a paper's surface, such as tacky inks and blanket-to-blanket web presses. (See **Internal Bond Strength**.) A paper's **porosity** is described as the amount of interfiber space that exists in the paper. A paper's porosity affects its ability to absorb ink. High-porosity paper is needed for rapid ink vehicle penetration and setting, and to decrease ink holdout and to resist

smudging during folding processes. Other printing methods require low-porosity paper to increase ink holdout, decrease ink penetration and reduce strike-through. (See **Porosity**.)

Also important is a paper's **dimensional stability**, which is a paper's ability to retain its original dimensions under printing stresses and changing environmental conditions. All papers will expand or shrink in size with changing moisture content, but a lesser degree of refining (producing paper with a loose fibrous structure) and the use of fillers can increase dimensional stability. A paper's tendency to absorb or release moisture to the atmosphere is an important consideration when doing multiple-color press work where the paper must run through the press two or more times. (See **Dimensional Stability**.) Low dimensional stability can result in bad register of successive colors. A paper's **viscoelasticity** refers to its ability to return to its original dimensions after being stretched. Beyond a certain tensile strength, however, some permanent distortion is inevitable. (See **Waffling**.)

An important consideration in web printing is a coated paper's **blister resistance**. During **heatset drying**, water vapor generated will increase a paper's tendency to **blister**, especially if a paper's porosity does not adequately allow the release of vapor pressure that is built up within the paper as it is exposed to heat. Related to blistering is **fiber puffing**, in which fibers in coated groundwood paper explode during drying, which mars the surface of the paper.

All of these surface and structural properties determine a paper's **printability**, or how well a printed image is transferred to the paper, and a paper's **runnability**, or its ability to run through a press or other printing means without affecting the printing process itself, such as contaminating a press's fountain solution, transferring paper debris to the plate or blanket, generating the need to frequently adjust the press, or any other defect in the paper that reduces press speeds. On a web press, runnability is described in terms of web breaks per 100 rolls. Runnability is a fairly quantifiable property, but so far various attempts at quantifying the printability of paper has been elusive, but devices such as the Prüfbau, IGT, and Huck gravure **printability testers** are occasionally used toward this end, as are printing presses themselves, but the problems of evaluating printability stem from the more subjective aspects of the term, which defy objective quantification.

Chemical Properties. A paper's chemical composition determines not only the texture of the paper but its performance on the press. If a paper is to be used on a sheetfed offset press, it will need to be water-resistant, while paper running on a web offset press runs more quickly, so does not need to be. Coatings must also be compatible with ink-drying systems, and must not transfer any of the coating materials to the printing system, which would contaminate the chemical balance of that system. The type of fibers used in the paper (cotton vs. wood, for instance) affects a paper's attributes, as does the pulping method used. Groundwood pulp provides high opacity and ink absorbency, but low strength, brightness, and permanency. The type and quantity of fillers also affect paper characteristics. Fillers, as their name implies, fill up pores and capillaries between paper fibers, dividing large capillaries into many smaller ones. Ink (and other fluid) absorbency works by capillary action. Increasing the number of capillaries increases the absorbency of the paper, although the capacity of the paper to hold moisture is decreased. (Many smaller pores will absorb more but hold less than fewer large pores.) Fillers also make paper less susceptible to changes in moisture content, improving dimensional stability. (The determination of the amount of filler is called its *ash content*. See *Ash Content*.)

Paper is able to absorb moisture from the air. As cellulose fibers take on water, they expand primarily in width (but not greatly in length), and when they lose water, they shrink primarily in width (but not greatly in length), which affects the dimensional stability of paper, causing distortion problems in printing. Moisture loss results in paper curling by disrupting the stresses between the felt side and the wire side of the paper, as the wire side has greater fiber alignment in the grain direction than the felt side. The *moisture content* of paper itself must be varied depending on the end-use requirements. Paper that is too dry is hard and brittle, reducing the quality of the printed impression. Paper that is too moist can blister during heatset drying. Book papers that have varying moisture contents and varying abilities to accept or lose moisture can change dimensions after binding and trimming, forming uneven edges among different *signature*s. The *equilibrium moisture content* of paper is the moisture content of paper when it neither loses nor gains moisture from the surrounding air, and depends on the *relative humidity* and the fiber and filler content of the paper. (A variation is the *equilibrium relative humidity*, or the level of humidity in the atmosphere at which paper will neither lose nor gain moisture.) Interestingly, the equilibrium moisture content of a paper will be lower if the paper starts at a low relative humidity and progressively is conditioned to higher ones than if the paper starts at a high relative humidity and is conditioned to lower ones. This difference is called *hysteresis*, and describes a paper's equilibrium moisture content in the context of its entire moisture history. Another problem involving a paper's moisture content involves the buildup of electrical charges, which occurs if the relative humidity of the paper falls below 35%. If the paper cannot dissipate its electrical charges, static cling occurs. (See *Moisture Content*.)

Another important chemical property is a paper's *pH*, which refers to its acidity or alkalinity. The term "pH" itself means "potential of the hydrogen ion (H^+)". A solution that contains an excess of hydrogen ions is said to be an "acid," while a solution that contains an excess of hydroxyl (OH^-) ions is said to be a "base," or an "alkaline" solution. A paper's pH is regulated by the *internal sizing* used, and any changes in pH arecontributed by a paper coating. Most paper is currently *acid paper*, but *alkaline paper* is receiving great interest, as alkaline papers retain their

brightness and strength over time, unlike acid papers which tend to deteriorate, sometimes quite rapidly. The life expectancy for alkaline papers is about 200 years, compared to 50 years for acid papers. (See *pH*.)

A paper's resistance to water is also important, and therefore the desired amount of *sizing*, or treatment to prevent water penetration (and whether it will be *internal sizing* or *external sizing*), depends on the end-use requirements of the paper. *Waterleaf* is *unsized* paper that absorbs water readily, and is used for towels, blotting paper, and other papers designed expressly for the absorption of fluids. *Slack-sized* paper has a minimal amount of *internal sizing*, and *hard-sized* paper has a large amount of internal sizing. Internal sizing hinders the penetration of fluids into the paper, but it does not make the paper waterproof or hamper its ink absorbency. Internal sizing is typically used to protect the paper from press dampening systems, and usually consists of a *rosin* added to the papermaking furnish during the stock preparation phase. Acid-rosin sizing is increasingly being replaced by alkaline-rosin sizing, as the interest in alkaline papers increases. *External sizing* (also called *surface sizing*) usually consists of a starch that is added to the web before it is completely dry. External sizing contributes little water resistance; its purpose is primarily to seal the surface fibers, increasing surface strength. (See *Sizing*.)

Optical Properties. A paper's *whiteness* refers to the extent to which all wavelengths of light are reflected from a paper's surface, and *brightness* refers to the degree that blue light is reflected from a paper's surface. (See *Whiteness* and *Brightness*.) *Color* refers to the extent to which paper selectively absorbs light of certain wavelengths, the remaining wavelengths being reflected back to the observer, imparting to the paper surface its color. (See *Color, Paper*.) *Gloss* refers to a paper's *specular reflectance*, or the condition of a paper surface that causes it to be shiny or *glossy*. The opposite of a glossy surface, a *matte* surface, reflects light diffusely, imparting a dull finish to the surface. (See *Gloss*.) *Opacity* refers to the extent to which light passes through a paper, which is an important consideration in printing. Low opacity results in a greater degree of *show-through*, or the visibility of the printing on the reverse of a sheet of paper. (See *Opacity*.)

End-Use Properties. One important criterion is a paper's ability to accept adhesives, either an adhesive backing for labels and tapes, or the various adhesives used in binding processes. The composition of a coated paper's coating must allow the application of adhesives if it is to be used for such purposes. (The binding strength of an adhesive-bound book is determined using a *head and tail tester*.) A related property important in the production of cartons and packaging is a paperboard's *glueability*, or the speed and strength with which an adhesive bond is formed when two sections of a paperboard are glued together. Papers and paperboards used in packaging must be produced in line with ***FDA regulations*** if they are going to be used to package foods and pharmaceuticals. A paper used in the packaging of edible products cannot emanate strong odors, while papers used for packaging silver- or iron-based metals should not contain chemicals that will corrode or chemically react with the materials being packaged. Papers used to package soaps, detergents, or other alkaline materials should be able to resist discoloration. Other types of packaging should also be able to withstand penetration by various types of liquids such as oil, grease, blood, etc. Paper used in electrical work (such as for wrapping cables) must be chemically neutral. Some papers need to possess ***flame resistance***. (See ***Flame Resistance***.) Paper produced with a high lignin content, such as groundwood-based paper, is, as we saw earlier, susceptible to yellowing upon exposure to sunlight or fluorescent lighting. Papers that are likely to be exposed to such lighting will need to maintain a high level of ***lightfastness***, or be able to resist yellowing and fading. (See ***Lightfastness***.)

A paper's ***permanence*** refers to its ability to resist structural, chemical, or other changes in its properties over time. ***Durability*** is similar to permanence, but refers to a paper's ability to resist deterioration with repeated usage and handling. Papers can be durable but not permanent (paper bags and boxes), permanent but not durable (paper towels or toilet tissue), or both permanent and durable (high-quality bond paper). (See ***Permanence*** and ***Durability***.)

A paper's level of water absorbence also has end-use considerations. Paper towels need to have a high degree of water absorbency, while packaging needs to have a low degree of water absorbency. To protect packaged items from damage due to contact with moisture in the form of water vapor, a paper or paperboard's ***water vapor transmission rate*** must be determined. Barriers to water vapor are created by coating a paper with wax, plastic, aluminum foil, or other protective materials. Paper or paperboard to be used in packaging needs to possess a high ***bursting strength***, or the force needed to rupture a paper. Bursting strength is primarily a measure used for packaging, bags, cartons, etc., and has little application in printing papers. (See ***Bursting Strength***.)

A paper may also need to have a high degree of ***folding endurance***. (See ***Folding Endurance***.) Folding endurance tests are also useful for determining permanence and durability of paper. ***Stiffness*** is a measure of a paper's resistance to bending. ***Flexural stiffness*** is the ability of paper to resist a bending force. ***Handling stiffness*** is a paper's ability to support its own weight. All paper has a higher degree of stiffness when bent against its grain. (See ***Stiffness***.) ***Tearing resistance*** refers to a paper's ability to resist being torn. ***Internal tearing resistance*** is defined as the force required to tear a paper a specific distance once a tear has been started. ***Edge tearing resistance*** is the force required to tear a paper when that tear has started at its edge. In web printing, an important consideration is ***tensile strength***, or a paper's resistance to the stretching forces generated in web presses. ***Tensile***

breaking strength is the tensile stress that a paper will endure before breaking. ***Wet-tensile breaking strength*** is the ratio of the breaking strength when the paper is wet to the breaking strength of the same paper when it is dry. ***Tensile energy absorption (TEA)*** is the amount of energy the paper can absorb, or the extent to which it can withstand a tensile shock. Tensile strength absorption is useful for measuring paper toughness, or, for example, whether a paper bag will burst if it is dropped, or if a paper web will break if the press suddenly speeds up. ***Tensile-at-the-fold*** is a measure of to what extent a coated paper can endure the application of heat and folding without splitting along the fold. ***Wet strength***, as its name implies, is a paper's tensile strength after it has been saturated with water. (See ***Tensile Breaking Strength***.)

A paper's ***abrasion resistance*** is important in writing and typing papers (for example, how well will it stand up to an eraser) and packaging (for example, how well it will resist scuffing and other types of abrasion encountered in shipping, handling, etc.) ***Frictional resistance*** describes how well one sheet of paper slides over another. (***Static friction*** is the force that will resist an object's sliding when in a stationary position, while ***kinetic friction*** is the force that resists the continuation of sliding once it has begun.) Frictional resistance is important not only in determining the slippage and sliding likely to be experienced by cartons and other forms of packaging (less slippage is desirable), but also in paper runnability on a printing press (more slippage is desirable). The resistance of one sheet to sliding over another not only causes feeding problems, it also can cause static electric buildup.

Weight and Size. A paper's ***basis weight*** is the weight (in pounds) of a ***ream*** of paper cut to its basic size. (A ream is almost exclusively 500 sheets.) ***Basic size*** is the sheet size (in inches) at which the basis weight is calculated. Paper also comes in a variety of ***standard size***s, which are pre-cut sheet sizes and are consequently less expensive and quicker to obtain than custom sizes. A paper's ***apparent density*** is its weight per unit volume. The term ***substance number*** is sometimes used instead of basis weight to describe the weight of writing papers. ***Nominal weight*** is the basis weight actually specified when ordering paper and which is the target weight in manufacturing. The actual basis weight varies somewhat from the nominal weight due to variations in moisture content and other variables in the papermaking process. ***Grammage*** is the weight of a single sheet of paper (in grams) having an area on one side of 1 square meter. Grammage is a metric system value and is sometimes used in place of basis weight. A paper's basis weight affects many paper properties such as opacity, thickness, strength, printability, and runnability, as well as end-use properties. (See ***Basis Weight***, ***Basic Size***, ***Apparent Density***, and ***Grammage***.) Paper thickness is popularly known as ***caliper***, which is the thickness of a single sheet. In book manufacturing, the ***bulking number*** (the number of pages that will bulk 1 in. under a specified pressure), ***pages per inch (ppi)*** (the bulking number times two, since each sheet usually contains two pages), and ***smashed bulk*** (the thickness of a book's pages when bound, which can be smaller than the bulking number due to the added compression of a binding) are important figures when specifying the page thickness for a book. (See ***Bulk*** and ***Bulking Number***.)

PROPERTY INTERACTION

None of the above-mentioned properties exists independently of the others. Changing one property in the paper-making process changes one or more of the other properties; improving one property can compromise others.

Increasing the length of the fibers in papermaking increases the bursting strength, folding endurance, tearing resistance, and tensile strength, but decreases the levelness and smoothness of the surface, and generates a "wilder" formation.

Bleaching increases whiteness and brightness, but decreases opacity.

Increasing the amount of mechanical refining of fibers will increase folding endurance, bursting strength, tensile strength, apparent density, hardness, ink holdout, internal bond strength, and smoothness and makes the formation less "wild," but decreases caliper, compressibility, dimensional stability, and porosity. However, refining is only beneficial to the above-mentioned properties up to a point; over-refining will have a deleterious effect on the properties for which moderate refining has a beneficial effect.

The adding of fillers will increase brightness, dimensional stability, uniform ink absorbency, opacity, and smoothness, but decrease bursting strength, caliper, folding endurance, internal bond strength, picking resistance, stiffness, tearing endurance, and tensile strength.

Increasing the amount of surface sizing, a treating of uncoated papers for enhanced performance and surface strength in offset printing, will increase the bursting strength, ink holdout, stiffness, surface strength, and tensile strength, but decrease the brightness, opacity, porosity, and folding endurance.

Increasing the degree of calendering, which primarily is done to create a desired paper finish, increases the apparent density, gloss, ink holdout, and smoothness, but decreases the brightness, compressibility, ink absorption, opacity, porosity, stiffness, and thickness.

Increasing the amount of coating applied will increase smoothness, ink holdout, print quality, gloss, and opacity, but decrease its folding endurance and blister resistance. Also, if the coating weight is increased, in order to keep the basis weight consistent, the weight of the base stock must be reduced, which will decrease caliper, stiffness, strength, and provide a decrease in opacity that will offset any increase in opacity from the coating.

There is also a complex interdependent relationship among basis weight, caliper, and paper finish of uncoated papers. At a constant basis weight, increasing the caliper will roughen the finish, and increase the porosity and ink absorbency. At a constant caliper, increasing the basis weight will smoothen the finish, and decrease the porosity and the ink absorbency. At a constant finish, increasing the basis weight will increase the caliper, but not affect the porosity and the ink absorbency much.

So, when choosing a paper all these interdependencies must be taken into account, and the end-use requirements of the paper evaluated in order to determine which are the most important properties to enhance, and which are the least important.

PRINTING REQUIREMENTS

Although end-use requirements are important in determining the paper to be used, the various printing processes also have their own inherent paper requirements.

Sheetfed Offset Lithography. This printing method uses tackier inks than other methods, so the paper must have high surface and internal bonding strength. It must also have high water resistance to maintain its surface strength in the presence of water from the dampening system. The paper surface must be free of dust, lint or other debris, to keep foreign material from piling on the blanket or upsetting the press's chemical balance. If successive printings on each sheet are required, the paper must have high dimensional stability, and its equilibrium moisture content must approximate the relative humidity of the pressroom, to prevent register misalignment. Long-grain paper is also required for multicolor jobs.

Web Offset Lithography. Many of the same considerations for sheetfed offset printing are required for paper destined for web printing. Web printing inks are generally not as tacky as those used in sheetfed offset, there is less moisture involved in web printing, and the paper moves faster through the system than in sheetfed printing, the result being that web presses can handle lower basis weight papers, and papers that are weaker have less pick resistance. The moisture content of web rolls tends to be lower than paper used for sheetfed offset printing, to reduce moisture loss and web shrinkage. High-speed web presses also reduce many of the problems inherent in sheetfed offset printing. But web printing requires paper rolls that unwind with even tension and flatness, and have a minimum of defects to prevent web breaks. It is generally damage to rolls that causes the most problems in web offset printing.

Gravure. Because of the nature of gravure printing (ink is transferred to the paper from ink-filled cells engraved in the press cylinder), smoothness of the paper surface is the most important criterion. Compressibility and softness are also crucial. Minute pits or depressions in the paper's surface can cause incomplete ink transfer, as can low compressibility. Gravure presses, however, print well on low-quality, lightweight papers.

Flexography. Flexographic printing can handle many different types of papers. Flexographic inks are not very tacky, so pick resistance is not a major concern. (Paper rolls used in rollfed flexographic presses must be free of the same defects as those used in web offset printing.) Flexography is used for many types of packaging, wrappers, cartons, corrugated boards, and books.

Screen Printing. Screen printing can handle many different types of surfaces. Smoothness is not a critical issue, but may affect ink drying. Crucial considerations for screen printers are sheet flatness and freedom from curling or wavy edges. The ability to withstand and maintain dimensional stability during heat-based ink drying is necessary. Thickness is also a consideration when using heavy inks, so to prevent warping.

Letterpress. Like paper needed for gravure printing, paper destined for letterpress printing must have an extremely smooth surface to allow complete ink transfer. Inks used in letterpress tend to be heavy, so the paper surface must be able to prevent spreading of halftone dots. The paper must also be able to withstand the pressures imposed on it during printing. (The ability to accept letterpress images is called a paper's *impression tolerance*.) Since inks are heavy, the paper must have high pick resistance, and high surface cleanliness. Supercalendered coated papers or coated papers with high finish are often used for fine halftone printing.

Electrostatic Printing. Electrostatic printing, including photocopiers, laser printers, and other forms of nonimpact printing based on electrostatic attraction of toner, requires little more than paper that will not curl or cause other feeding problems at high or low speeds—runnability issues similar to those for other printing processes. A specific requirement for electrostatic printing paper is high electrical resistivity. Paper is made specifically for use in electrostatic printing machines (sometimes called xerographic paper).

Ink-Jet Printing. A requirement of ink-jet printer paper (used primarily in addressing, coding, and computer printouts) is that it absorb ink quickly and minimize spreading and feathering, so to produce sharp images. Specially coated papers are manufactured specifically for use in high-resolution ink jet printers.

END-USE REQUIREMENTS

There is a vast number of end-uses for paper, and even within types of paper products there are a variety of factors that determine what type of paper should be used. Here are a few of the larger paper markets and some general guidelines for the paper(s) used for each.

Advertising. The paper used must be aesthetic and functional. If multicolor printing is to be used, paper suitable for multiple passes is required, and must also possess the desired texture and color. Offset lithography and gravure processes are most frequently used, so the paper must also work functionally and economically with the appropriate process, and conform to the customer's issues of print quality and cost. Advertising that includes return mail cards must meet postal thickness requirements.

Books. In addition to printing and binding requirements, aesthetic factors must also be taken into account. The subject matter should dictate the paper texture, finish, and shade. Illustration matter must be on such paper that allows for acceptable reproduction. Bulk is a consideration, as the signatures must fit into the predesigned case. High-bulk paper is generally required for low-page-count fiction and children's books, while low-bulk papers are required for high-page-count encyclopedias and Bibles. Opacity, consistency of shade, and strength along binding edges are also important. Groundwood papers are used for low-quality short-life books, while books destined for long-term archival and storage are typically printed on alkaline papers. (See also *Cameron Book Production System*.) *Endleaf* papers that secure the pages to the binding must be strong and tear-resistant. Book covers and dust-jackets must have high durability and tear resistance. *Coated-one-side (C1S) label* paper is used for printed book jackets. A type of *coated one side* paper, also known as *bristol paper*, is used for paperback covers.

Business Forms. Special paper, called *business forms bond* is used primarily for business forms. Quick ink absorption is a special consideration. Multiple colors are used for separate copies, and issues of tear resistance and ease of perforation are important. Clear transfer of carbon images or, increasingly, carbonless images is also necessary. Forms used in *optical character recognition (OCR)* systems must provide compatibility with OCR scanning equipment.

Cartons and Containers. Printed paperboard and rigid containers provide packaging for cigarettes, cereals, candies, milk, cosmetics, and pharmaceuticals. Print quality and aesthetic considerations are of prime importance, as are FDA regulations. They must also be able to withstand procedures such as diecutting, folding, scoring, gluing, laminating, and processing on high-speed packaging equipment. They must also be highly rigid and strong, resist fading and abrasion, repel moisture, be chemically inert, nontoxic, and sanitary, as well as be compatible with flexography, gravure, letterpress, and sheetfed and web offset lithography.

Catalogs. Low-basis-weight papers are used for mail-order catalogs, for postal cost considerations, and catalogs distributed through other means use a variety of other basis weights. *Newsprint*-type paper is used extensively, and catalogs are mostly printed by web offset and rotogravure printing processes.

Checks. The surface of check paper must be uniformly smooth, and allow for writing, printing, typing, and the printing of *magnetic ink character recognition (MICR)* ink. It must also be strong enough to withstand repeated handling and check sorting. Regular considerations of its prominant printing methods—letterpress and offset lithography—are also required.

Company Reports. Annual reports and other corporate print jobs must utilize paper that will cleanly reproduce financial material and illustration matter (such as graphs or halftones). Ease of reading numbers (either in tabular or pictorial form) is the prime consideration, and different types of paper can be used in the same report, depending on the availability of paper that will meet all the required needs. Glossy papers, because of their glare, are typically not used. Offset lithography is primarily the reproduction process, which adds additional considerations to the choice of paper stock.

Envelopes. Standard envelope paper is often used, as are coated and uncoated *book paper*s, and papers that match accompanying letterhead and stationery. Preprinted envelopes for direct-mail and other uses are printed with their accompanying material and as self-mailers on business forms paper, and are often done all at once on a web press. The paper requirements also include other aesthetic and functional requirements, as well as the ability to withstand repeated handling and postal sorting equipment. Envelopes are printed by offset lithography, flexography, letterpress, thermography, and steel-die engraving, adding further considerations.

Greeting Cards. In addition to aesthetic considerations, paper used for greeting cards must have high folding endurance and must be adequately stiff and rigid. Textured surfaces, like vellum, are also required, as are operations such as embossing, bronzing, flocking, diecutting, and thermography. A *papeterie* type of paper is used for greeting cards, and offset lithography is almost exclusively used for printing, with the occasional use of letterpress and screen printing.

Labels and Packaging. Label papers must be able to withstand printing, varnishing, lacquering, diecutting, embossing, andautomated labelling equipment, and they must adhere well to their intended surfaces, as well as be compatible with their primary printing processes—gravure, letterpress, sheetfed offset, flexography, and, to a minor extent, screen printing. Packaging uses include wrapping paper (decorative and otherwise), book dust covers, food wrappers, etc. All must have adequate strength and high ink holdout. Box wraps must endure lamination, and food wrappers must comply with FDA regulations. All must be compatible with flexography and rotogravure, the primary packaging printing processes.

Legal Forms and Financial Reports. Low-basis-weight, high-opacity papers are typically used for business prospectuses, financial and stockholder reports, and other corporate jobs. Permanent and durable high-grade *bond* and *ledger paper*s are used for legal documents such as contracts, leases, wills, mortgages, etc. All must be compatible with letterpress and offset lithography, the primary printing methods for such documents.

Maps. The requirements for map paper are dimensional stability (to keep the scale of miles or other required measurement scales accurate), high tear resistance, tensile strength, and folding resistance (so the map will survive extensive handling, unfolding, and refolding), and high wet-strength (a must for maps intended for outdoor use, such as camping or hiking). Maps are almost always printed using offset lithography.

Menus. The two most important requirements for menu paper are aesthetics (a variety of specialty papers, such as *imitation parchment*, are used) and *stiffness* (for ease of reading in an upright position). Menu paper should also possess a high degree of tear resistance, tensile strength, and folding endurance (to keep menus intact with repeated handling). It's also probably a good idea for menu papers to have a high degree of wet strength. Menus must also endure embossing, stamping, and printing using letterpress or offset lithography.

Newspapers. Most newspapers are printed on high-speed web presses, using primarily inexpensive groundwood pulp-based *newsprint*.

High opacity, good printing cushion, and rapid absorption of ink are necessary considerations. The source of most web-printing problems comes from inadequate winding of the paper rolls themelves. Paper having inconsistent bulk throughout the roll will unwind with uneven tension and cause deformations in the printed image while on-press, and even cause web breaks.

Newspaper Supplements. Newspaper supplements are printed on "roto news" paper designed for high-speed rotogravure presses. Roto news paper is produced with a higher filler content and is calendered to a high finish, such as that required for rotogravure printing. Sunday supplements and magazine sections of newspapers, such as *Parade* magazine, use supercalendered uncoated rotogravure papers.

Periodicals. High-circulation magazines are printed on high-speed rotogravure presses, and *lightweight paper*s are often used to keep down mailing costs. Often, *coated groundwood paper* is used. Covers and advertising inserts are typically printed on higher-quality *coated paper*s and reply cards on *postal bristol* or other heavier-weight card stock.

Phone Books. High opacity and low thickness are requirements, and lightweight, uncoated, mechanical-pulp-based papers are used for phone books. The ability to reproduce small type legibly, as well as clear advertisements in yellow-page sections, is important. Most phone books are printed on web offset presses.

Postcards. Heavy bristol papers (such as postal bristol) are used for postcards, which must not only accept pen-and-ink readily, but also be stiff and rigid enough to withstand postal sorting equipment. Coated-one-side bristols are used for picture postcards, and offset lithography is typically the printing process used.

Sheet Music. Of prime importance is high whiteness, brightness, and opacity. The paper must be free of dirt, which could be construed as notes or other types of musical notation. Pages must remain flat when bound. Sheet music is primarily printed using offset lithography.

Stationery and Letterhead. Aesthetic and functional requirements are necessary considerations for business and personal stationery. Business letterhead is commonly printed on watermarked chemical pulp bond, or watermarked *cotton-content* bond. Envelopes and other paper products are designed to match the letterhead. Acceptance of pen, typing, and, increasingly, laser printing are requirements for this type of paper.

Personal stationery is typically printed on white or pastel *papeterie*, a filled uncoated paper with a smooth, vellum, or embossed finish.

Tags and Tickets. Depending on the specific end-use requirements, most tags, tickets, punch cards, etc., use *tag papers*, which have the highest strength and durability. Depending on the desired print quality, coated tag stock may be used, and wet strength may be required. Tickets and laundry tags need to be stiff and durable, yet also tear properly at perforations. Letterpress and offset lithography are the primary tag and ticket printing processes.

PAPER GRADES

Paper is categorized by its end use characteristics and its basis weight into a variety of different *grade*s. There are hundreds of different grades and subgrades, but there are a few common, basic paper subdivisions. Each grade has a separate set of available basis weights, and one particular basic size at which the basis weights are calculated. For specific information about some common individual paper grades, see also *Bond Paper*, *Bristol Paper*, *Coated Paper*, *Cover Paper*, *Duplicator Paper*, *Imitation Parchment*, *Index Paper*, *Ledger Paper*, *Manifold Paper*, *Mimeograph Paper*, *Newsprint*, *Offset Paper*, *Onionskin*, *Safety Paper*, *Tag Paper*, *Text Paper*, *Vegetable Parchment*, and *Wedding Paper*.

PAPER AND PRINTING PROBLEMS AND DEFECTS

All the paper properties listed earlier work in concert to increase or decrease a paper's printability and runnability. Both of these factors contribute to various printing defects affecting both print quality and trouble-free running of paper through a press.

Here are some of the most common printing problems caused by paper imperfections.

Defects due to blanket contamination, or particles of paper debris, *lint*, *pickouts* (the pulling of particles of paper or coatings from the paper surface), or debris from elsewhere in the pressroom contribute to *hickey*s. (See *Hickey*.) The accumulation of particles on the blanket, called blanket *piling* when it is present in such quantity as to cause a degradation of print quality, is called either *whitening*, when it occurs in the nonimage area of the blanket, and *image area piling* when, as its name indicates, it occurs in the image area of a blanket. (See *Piling*.)

The appearance on a printed sheet of undesirable images is called *ghosting*. (See *Ghosting*.) Printing problems resulting from premature contact between the paper and the blanket—called *prekissing*—results in halftone blemishes such as *doubling*, or the printing of a phantom halftone dot slightly offset from the proper halftone dot, which distorts the printed halftone image. *Slurring* is a smearing of the edges of text or line art, while *dot slurring* is the smearing of halftone dots, both types of slurring typically occurring at the trailing edges of the images in question. (See *Doubling* and *Slurring*.)

Paper with inadequate pick resistance or low basis weight results in a printing defects called *waffling*, or *embossing*, and *back-edge curl* (or *tail-end hook*), in which the pull of a tacky ink as the paper is peeled from the blanket pulls the image area of the paper with it and creates distortions in the paper. (See *Waffling*.) Other similar problems include *picking*, in which bits of paper are ripped out and stick to the blanket. (See *Picking*.)

In web presses, ink tack also contributes to *delamination*. (See *Delamination*.) Paper that has a wild formation can cause *graininess* of halftones, in which halftones dots are not printed uniformly. (See *Graininess*.)

Ink chalking is a problem of coated papers that occurs when ink drying is hampered by an incompatibility between the ink and the paper coating. (See *Ink Chalking*.) Other ink-related distortions include *ink setoff* and *blocking*, *mottle*, *show-through*, *tinting*, and *misregister*. (See individual entries.) Problems with ink drying include *dryback* and *blistering*.

Problems that affect runnability of paper include *curl*, *wavy edges*, and other problems related to dimensional instability. In web offset printing, a primary cause of runnability problems is roll defects. (See *Baggy Paper*, *Cracked Edge*, *Telescoped Roll*, *End Damage*, *Fiber Cut*, *Slime Spot*, *Moisture Welt*, *Out of Roundness*, *Ridge*, *Rope Marks*, and *Bursts*.)

All of these various aspects mentioned above work together in the manufacture and printing of paper. There is a lot of technology in a piece of paper.

Paperback

In *binding and finishing*, a book that has been bound with a heavy paper cover rather than cloth-covered cardboard. Most paperback books are bound using *perfect binding*. A paperback book is also known as *softcover* or *paperbound*.

Paperboard

Strong, thick paper or cardboard used for boxes and other types of packaging. Paperboard can either be bleached or unbleached, coated or uncoated, and produced in a variety of thicknesses, depending on the end use requirements.

Paperbound

Alternate term for a *paperback* book. See *Paperback*.

Paper Grade

A means of categorizing paper. See *Grade*.

Paperless Office

A perhaps over-optimistic term for an office in which all data is stored in electronic form.

Paper Master

In *offset lithography*, a paper plate containing a hand-drawn or typewritten image; the image carrier on a *duplicator*.

Paper Memory

A paper property describing the ability of a sheet to become permanently curled if it has been rolled up tightly enough.

Paper Negative

A photographic *negative* exposed on a photosensitive, resin-coated paper, as opposed to a *film negative*, which is exposed on acetate-based film. Paper negatives are generally inferior in image quality to film negatives. See *Negative*.

Paper Path

The route a sheet or web of paper takes through a computer printer or printing press.

Paper Sensing Switch

In a computer printer, a switch or detector that tells the printer where the paper is located.

Paper Source

General term for any of a variety of paper trays, cartridges, or feeders attached to a computer printer.

Paper Stencil

In *screen printing*, a *stencil* made out of thin paper adhered to the bottom of the screen fabric either by the ink itself or by coating the stencil with *shellac* and applied by means of a hot iron.

Paper Surface Efficiency

A measure of a paper's *printability*. See *Printability*.

Paper Tape

In computing, the successor to the punch card and the precursor to the *floppy disk* as a medium for computer storage. Essentially, paper tape was a length of paper between ⅛–1 in. wide, perforated with holes which represented data in 6-, 7-, and 8-bit units. The coding system was called TTS for TeleTypeSetter.

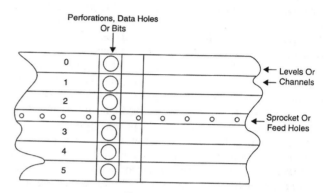

Paper tape.

Papeterie

A high-filler-content, uncoated paper used for manufacturing greeting cards or personal stationery. Papeterie can have a smooth, vellum, or embossed *finish*.

Papyrus

An early paperlike material used in Egypt and Europe before the development of paper. Although papyrus is a paperlike surface, it is not true paper. (Paper is primarily described as being manufactured from the dissolved and processed fibers of plants. Papyrus could be used to make paper, however, but rarely is.) To form papyrus into a suitable writing surface, stalks of the papyrus plant (*Cyperus papyrus*) are split lengthwise, wetted, laid side-by-side until the desired width was reached, other strips were placed crosswise on top of these, then hammered together. The surface of the "page" was then polished and smoothed with shells, ivory, or other hard surface until surface aberations were evened out.

The word "paper" derives from the Greek word *papyros*. The Greek word for written sheets or rolls of papyrus was *biblia*, from *biblos*, denoting the inner fibers of the papyrus plant. (*Biblia* is the etymological root of many book-related terms today, such as "bibliography," "bibliophile," and foreign terms such as *bibliotheque*, the French term for "library." The word "Bible" has as part of its etymology the Greek phrase *ta biblia*, or "the rolls.") The use of papyrus as a writing medium developed in Egypt, where the papyrus plant grew in abundance. It is a testament to the efficacy of the process of papyrus-making that many ancient documents written on papyrus still survive to this day. The use of papyrus continued through the ages of Greece and Rome, until, as a result of a papyrus embargo on the part of Ptolemy VI of Egypt around 193 BC, the use of *parchment* became widespread. The development of papermaking from cotton and linen rags (and, later, wood pulp) supplanted papyrus as the basis of the written medium.

Paradigm

Any model, template, example, or illustration of process.

Paragraph

In typography, any block of text ending with a hard (carriage) return. The first line may or may not be indented. The paragraph is the basic unit of English composition. Research has found that frequent breaks—in contrast to long unbroken blocks—are important for good *legibility*. Paragraphs should also contain only one particular thought or subject; each new thought should be a new paragraph.

An alternative means of distinguishing text blocks uses additional line spacing between paragraphs. In this case, the use of an indent at the beginning of subsequent paragraphs is redundant. Another means of visually separating text blocks is to run all the paragraphs together, separating them from each other only with a special character, such as the *pilcrow* (¶), also referred to as a "paragraph symbol."

A short line at the end of a paragraph, if less than one-third the line length, is called a *widow*. Alternately, *widow* may also refer to carry-over letters of a hyphenated word to the next line if there are no other characters on that line. A widow carried to the top of a column or page is called an *orphan*, and should be avoided. Similarly, a new paragraph should never begin as the last line of a column or page.

Paragraph Indent

In typography, an indent found at the beginning of the first line of a paragraph. See *Indention*.

Parallel

Descriptive of data transfer by a computer that is not performed sequentially—or in *series*—or, in other words, not *bit* by bit. In a parallel connection (such as through a computer's *parallel port*), one *byte* (or eight bits) of data is sent through eight of the connections at once, the other connections being used to transmit check signals back and forth from the computer to the attached peripheral device. See *Parallel Port*. See also *Serial* and *Serial Port*.

Parallel Communication

Alternate term for *parallel transmission*. See *Parallel Transmission*.

Parallel Fold

Any fold made in a sheet of paper (or other *substrate*) that is oriented in a direction parallel to a previous fold. (See also *Right-Angle Fold*.) See *Folding*.

Parallel Input/Output

See *Parallel* and *Parallel Port*.

Parallel Interface

In computing, data transmission by a *parallel port*.

Parallel Port

One of two types of ports on a personal computer to which peripheral devices can be connected. In contrast to a *serial port*, a parallel port transmits one *byte* (or eight *bit*s) of data at one time, rather than one bit at a time. Printers, for example, are commonly connected to *PC*s by means of a DA-25 connector on the computer and a *Centronics*-36 connector on the printer. Larger computers have larger parallel connectors and can transmit larger increments of data in parallel at one time. See also *Serial Port*.

Parallel Printer

A computer printer that connects to a computer's *parallel port*. See *Parallel Port*.

Parallel Processing

In computing, the processing of more than one task or event at one time, often by means of the *microprocessor* in conjunction with a *coprocessor*.

Parallel-Receding Press

A *screen printing* press configuration in which the screen frame remains parallel to the printing bed at all times, the frame being moved away from the printing bed by an assembly that moves up and back (or up and sideways).

Parallel Run

The operation of a newly acquired or developed computer system in tandem with an older system until the reliability of the new system is confirmed.

Parallel Transmission

A means of transmitting data in *parallel* (or in greater amounts than one *bit* at a time) rather than in *series*. See *Parallel* and *Parallel Port*. Also referred to as *parallel communication*.

Para Reds

A type of *organic color pigment* used in printing inks. Para reds vary in shade from yellow to blue, and possess moderate to good *tinctorial strength*, but with a dull tone. They also possess high *lightfastness*, but when diluted become less fast to light. They are also resistant to acids and alkalis, but not to soaps, oils, and solvents. They had once been widely used in poster and label inks, but their tendency to bleed has caused their growing disuse. (See *Organic Color Pigments*.)

(CI Pigment Red 1 No. 12070.)

Parchment

A material, made from the split skin of sheep, used as a writing surface before the invention of paper. To prepare parchment, the skin is split, washed, rubbed with lime (which imparts a paperlike feel to the surface), and scraped with a knife to eliminate pits and bumps in the surface. The skin is stretched on a wooden frame, and the scraping continues until the entire skin acquires a uniform thickness. The flesh side of the skin provides a better writing surface than the hair side, and the difference in texture between the two sides can be felt on some old books. Later developments, such as the use of chalk and pumice, eliminated much of this "two-sidedness" of parchment.

The word "parchment" itself derives from the name Pergamum, a city and library in Asia Minor. Although parchment was originally developed in the East perhaps as early as 1500 BC, its widespread use began in the city of Pergamum during the reign of Eumenes II (197–159 BC). Pergamum's rulers, especially Eumenes II, were devotees of the Greek world, and looked with envy upon the cultural and intellectual achievements of the Ptolemaic kings in Egypt (in particular, the library at Alexandria), and founded the Pergamene Library in 196 BC, quickly attracting the finest Greek scholars. In a short time, the library at Pergamum was said to have rivaled that at Alexandria.

Hoping to cease the growth of Pergamum, King Ptolemy VI of Egypt forbade the export of *papyrus* (a paper-like material made by hammering together the stalks of the papyrus plant) from Egypt, which was at that time the most widespread writing material. In response to this, Eumenes II supported the use of the treated skins of sheep as a writing material and soon this material (eventually called "parchment") supplanted papyrus as the chief medium of communication and literature. Its use flourished in Rome, and continued to some extent after papermaking had been developed, but its use in the printing of books did not continue to any large degree beyond AD 1500. (British and American patent documents were printed on parchment until the nineteenth century.) As for the Pergamene Library, in 46 BC (distrustful of his sons, King Attalus III had bequeathed the city to Rome in 133 BC) Mark Antony gave it as a gift to Cleopatra to replace the portion of the Alexandrian library which had been burned during an uprising against Julius Caesar in 48 BC. By then, it was said the collection included 200,000 volumes. It is thanks to this collection that much ancient Greek prose has survived. (See also *vellum* and *imitation parchment*.)

Parchment Paper

A type of high-quality, durable, hard-surfaced cotton-fiber paper designed to resemble *parchment* (which was actually the split skin of sheep). It is used for wills, deeds, diplomas, and other dignified and elegant documents.

Parent Directory

In computing, a *directory* in a *hierarchical file system* that is "above" (or which contains) another directory, such as the *current directory*.

Parity

In computing and telecommunications, a means of *error detection and correction* in *asynchronous* serial con-

nections in which an extra *bit* of data (called the *parity bit*) is added to each transmitted character. One bit is either a 0 or a 1, and thus the parity bit can either be a 0 or a 1. Some systems use one of four types of *parity check*: *odd parity*, which means that all character codes must have an odd number of 1s in it. If it already does, then the parity bit is set at 0 to maintain the odd number. If it does not, then the parity bit is set at 1 to make the number of 1s odd. *Even parity* works the same way; each character code needs to have an even number of 1s, the parity bit being added to ensure that. *Mark parity* always sets the eighth bit to 1, while *space parity* always sets the eighth bit to 0. In this way, the extra bits can be examined after transmission to see if any errors have been introduced. New, faster error detection and correction techniques are gradually replacing these parity checks. (A computer's main memory still uses parity to check for errors, however.)

Parity Bit

In data transmission, a *bit* (either a 1 or a 0) added to a character code to ensure that the total number of 1s in the code is either an even or an odd number, used as a means of *error detection* in *asynchronous* serial connections.

Parity Check

A type of *error detection* used in data communications.

Parity Error

In data communications, a mismatch in *parity bit*s that signifies that a transmission error has occurred. See *Parity*.

Parser

An algorithm or routine used in computing to break down user input to basic logical units that can be easily converted into *machine code*.

Parsing

In computer programming, the breaking down of a sentence or language statement into smaller units that can be easily converted into *machine code*, usually by means of a routine or algorithm known as a *parser*.

Part-Title

In *book typography*, a (usually) *recto* page indicating the number and/or name of a part (or section) or a book. A part-title is usually backed by a blank page.

Partial Immersion

A level of *virtual reality*. See *Virtual Reality*.

Partial Page

Any page not containing all the elements it was designed to.

Particle Animation

The *animation* of small, equal-size particles that move according to basic laws of physics, turbulence, gravity, etc., such as rain, snow, explosions, swarms of bees, etc.

Partition

In computing, a subdivided region of a computer's **RAM**. Certain programs require a certain size partition in which to be loaded. The largest partition available to a program is known as the **maximum partition size**.

The term *partition* also refers to a subdivided portion of a computer's **hard disk**, which can be named and addressed separately. Each partition may also have its own size.

Passive Hub

In networking, a point of distribution of a network (or **hub**) which relays transmissions to and from the **server**. See **Hub**. See also **Active Hub**.

Passive-Matrix

A type of **liquid crystal display (LCD)** in which one transistor controls a whole line of **pixels** by itself. As a result, passive-matrix displays do not produce as bright or sharp an image as do **active-matrix** displays. See also **Active-Matrix**. See **Liquid Crystal Display (LCD)**.

Pass Sheet

Alternate term for **OK sheet**. See **OK Sheet**.

Password

In telecommunications and networking (or other aspect of computing), any unique character set that a system needs to identify before a user is allowed access to a network or database. It can be a random string of numbers and letters (such as "8hgtd") or a number with some meaning to the user (such as a birth date) or a word the user is likely to recognize (such as "swordfish").

Password Protection

In networking, the utilization of more than one **password** to gain access to a computer system or network.

Paste

See **Cut and Paste**.

Paste Drier

A type of **drier** used in printing inks, typically comprising a mixture of lead and manganese compounds.

Paste Ink

One of two primary classifications of printing inks, characterized by high **tack** and high **viscosity**. Paste inks are commonly used in **letterpress**, **lithographic** and **screen printing** processes. See also **Liquid Ink**. (See **Ink**.)

Pasteup

The composition of a page by assembling the disparate page elements, either manually or electronically, into a **mechanical** or other form of **camera-ready copy**. For many years, pasteup was performed manually, by means of sheets of output text and graphics that were literally pasted into position on a pasteup board, then photographed by a process camera to make **negatives** for platemaking. Increasingly, however, pasteup is performed digitally, either on a **desktop publishing system** or a **CEPS**. Pasteup is also known as **page makeup**, which is becoming the dominant term, as digital systems are rendering the term pasteup obsolete.

Pasted Open-Mouth (POM)

In packaging, a type of paper **bag** in which the bottom is glued shut prior to filling, leaving the top unglued. After filling, the top is sealed by gluing or by other sealing means. See **Bag: Paper Bags**.

Pasted-Valve Stepped End (PVSE)

In packaging, a type of **bag** in which the bottom and top are glued shut prior to filling. Filling is effected by means of a small valve in the corner of the bag. See **Bag: Paper Bags**.

Paster

Any device used to apply an adhesive material.

In **web offset lithography**, *paster* is an alternate term for a **splicer**. See **Splicer**.

Paster Wheels

A set of driven wheels found on **in-line** gluers on **web press**es that apply a film of adhesive to printed materials, usually to bind **signature**s together.

Pasting

The process of using an adhesive to bind any two materials together.

In desktop publishing and word processing, *pasting* refers to the digital insertion of a block of text into another document or block of text.

Patch

In electronics and wiring, a temporary electrical connection.

In audio-video equipment, the term *patch* means to connect an audio or video device to another by means of cables or through a central panel.

In computer programming, the term *patch* refers to a series of codes added to a program to modify or fix it in some way without performing a major rewrite. When used as a verb, *patch* means to add such a set of codes.

Patch Panel

In networking, a central panel containing rows of **modular jack**s to which network devices are connected. A patch panel is used to allow a **network administrator** to easily add or remove devices to or from the network.

Patent Base

In **letterpress** printing, a perforated metal base on which the **electrotype** is secured during printing.

Path

In **vector-based graphics**, a single unit of linked segments, curves, or points that define a specific object.

In general computing, the term *path* also refers to an *information path*. See *Information Path*.

Pathnames

In computing, the specification of the *information path* of a file. See *Information Path*.

Pat-Out

A means of testing color-mixed ink for proper *hue*, *substrate* compatibility, and drying performance by dabbing a spot on the intended substrate with the finger, and distributing it to approximate the actual thickness with which it will be printed. (See also *Drawdown*.) Also called *tap-out*.

Pattern Storage

Alternate term for *raster-pattern storage*. See *Raster-Pattern Storage*.

Pay TV

In television, any programming service to which one subscribes (and pays a subscription fee) to view it. Pay TV is usually provided by a *cable television network*. Although a cable system itself could be considered pay TV, the term usually refers to channels requiring an additional subscription beyond regular cable subscriptions. A variety of pay-TV programming is known as "pay-per-view," which is usually a one-time-only showing of an event (such as a boxing match or a concert event) and requires additional payment to see.

PB

Abbreviation for *petabyte*. See *Petabyte*.

PBOM

In packaging, an abbreviation for *pinched-bottom open-mouth*, a type of paper *bag*.

PBX

Abbreviation for *private branch exchange*. See *Private Branch Exchange (PBX)*.

PC

Abbreviation for *personal computer* in general, but commonly used as a synonym for *IBM-compatible computer*, or those based on the *IBM* Personal Computer and running either *DOS* and/or Microsoft *Windows*. PC is commonly distinguished from *Mac*, the Apple *Macintosh*.

In printing, the term *PC* is an abbreviation for *print contrast*. See *Print Contrast*.

PC Card

See *PCMCIA*.

PC Clone

Alternate term for *IBM-compatible computer*. See *IBM-Compatible Computer*.

PC-Based Router

In networking, a *router* which can be installed on a standard *personal computer*. See *Router*.

PC-Card Slot

In computing, a slot in a *portable computer* in which a *PC card* can be installed. See *PCMCIA*.

PC-DOS

Abbreviation for *Personal Computer Disk Operating System*. A version of *DOS* developed by Microsoft and licensed to IBM for use in its first line of personal computers, as opposed to *MS-DOS*. See *DOS*.

PC/XT Bus

See *Industry Standard Architecture (ISA)*.

PCC

A *file extension* used to denote files created by the PC Paintbrush program.

PCI

Abbreviation for *Perpipheral Component Interconnect*. See *Peripheral Component Interconnect (PCI) Bus*.

PCL

Abbreviation for *Printer Command Language*.

PCM

Abbreviation for *pulse code modulation*. See *Pulse Code Modulation (PCM)*.

PCMCIA

Abbreviation for *Personal Computer Memory Card International Association* and used to refer to a specific *memory card*—about the size of a credit card—which can be inserted into a personal or portable computer. These cards add *flash memory* to the system, and are also used to accommodate *modem*s, network connections, and other peripheral devices and services. Also known as *PC card*s.

PCQ

A *file extension* used to denote files created by the RIX EGA Paint 2005 program.

PCS

Abbreviation for *personal communications services*. See *Personal Communications Services*.

PCT

A *file extension* for files saved in the Macintosh's *PICT* format. See *PICT*.

PCU

Abbreviation for *Printer Control Unit*.

PCX

A computer **file extension**—short for *PC* Paintbrush EXtension—attached to files created with PC Paintbrush, a **bitmapped** graphics program and **file format** originating with ZSoft's PC Paintbrush program. PCX is now a widely used graphics file format on **PC clone**s.

PDA

Abbreviation for **personal digital assistant**. See **Personal Digital Assistant (PDA)**.

PDE

Abbreviation for *Page Description Entry*.

PDF

Abbreviation for **Portable Document Format**. See **Portable Document Format (PDF)**. *PDF* is also the abbreviation for *Program Development Facility*.

PDL

Abbreviation for **page description language**. See **Page Description Language**.

 PDL is also a **file extension** used to denote files created by Lotus Manuscript.

PDN

Abbreviation for **public data network**. See **Public Data Network**.

PDX

Abbreviation for *Printer Description Extension*, a **file extension** specification devised by Adobe Systems, Inc., used with **PPD**s (PostScript Printer Description) to define specific output requirements of **PostScript** files.

PE

Abbreviation for **printer's error**. See **Printer's Error**.

Peacock Blue

A type of **organic color pigment** used in printing inks. There are two types of peacock blue: fugitive (several greenish shades of blue that are not very lightfast and tend to bleed in water, but are inexpensive) and permanent (much more lightfast, stronger, and more expensive than the fugitive variety, although they are not as clean and brilliant). (See **Organic Color Pigments**.)

Peaking

In **scanning**, a function of **unsharp masking** that increases **edge enhancement** of a particular image.

 The term *peaking* also refers to edge enhancement performed on **color separation negative**s by increasing the difference in density at image edges.

Pearlescent

A blend or mixture of inorganic materials used in printing inks to impart a luster characteristic of mother-of-pearl.

Pearlescents—commonly co-precipitates of **titanium dioxide** and mica or other minerals—produce nonmetallic shades from silver and gold. They are transparent pigments, with a high refractive index. They are also heat resistant up to 1470°F.

 The multiple reflection of light is responsible for pearlescent pigments' luster, and they are used in screen, lithographic, gravure, and flexographic inks in applications to impart a metal-like sheen when the use of **metallic powders** is precluded. (See also **Pigment**.)

 (CI Pigment White 6 and 20.)

Pebble Finish

A paper **finish** characterized by a finely embossed, or rippled texture intended to simulate a "pebbling" effect.

Pedestal Up/Down

In motion picture photography and videography, the raising/lowering of the camera.

Peel Adhesion

A measure of the extent to which a pressure-sensitive label is attached to a surface, consisting of the force required to pull a test strip of the material in question from a test surface at a specific angle and speed. In some cases, the peel adhesion of a particular label can increase over time due to **adhesion buildup**.

Peeling

A printing defect in which the printed ink film as a whole (or a portion of it) detaches itself from the **substrate** due to inadequate adhesion to the substrate.

 In **screen printing**, *peeling* also refers to the premature detachment of the **stencil** from the screen fabric.

Peer-Quality Graphics

Graphics produced and reproduced with a quality that, although probably not acceptable for commercial use, is good enough for use within an in-house presentation or report.

Peer-to-Peer

Descriptive of a networking architecture in which any **node** can function both as a **client** and as a **server**. See **Peer-to-Peer Network**.

Peer-to-Peer Communications

See **Peer-to-Peer**.

Peer-to-Peer Network

A type of network configuration in which all connected computers can function either as **server**s or **workstation**s. Also known as **peer-to-peer communications**.

Pel

An abbreviation for **picture element**, more commonly known as a **pixel**. See **Pixel**.

Pen

A mechanical imaging device held in one's hand. A pen images a sheet of paper (or other surface) by means of ink.

In computing, a *pen* is any graphical input device that transmits coordinate information to the computer and display by either light (see *Light Pen*) or by moving it on a *digitizing tablet*. See also *Pen-Based PC*.

Pen Computer

Alternate term for a *pen-based PC*. See *Pen-Based PC*.

Pen-Based PC

A type of *palm-top* computer which receives input by means of a stylus. The user "writes" on an *LCD* with the stylus, and his/her scribbling (within reason) is recognized as text characters and converted to digital information. Also often known as a *personal digital assistant*.

Penetration

The extent to which a printing ink *vehicle*, *solvent*, or *varnish* (or any other liquid, such as water) is absorbed into the surface of a *substrate*. Inks that dry by absorption of the vehicle require a paper (or other surface) that will allow a high degree of penetration (but not enough to allow the fluid to soak through to the opposite side of the sheet), while inks that dry by other means, such as *evaporation* or *oxidation*, require a low degree of penetration.

Pentium

A *microprocessor* manufactured by Intel as a successor to its 80486 chips. The Pentium uses a combined *RISC/CISC* architecture with a 64-*bit* bus. The Pentium chip is used in *IBM-compatible computer*s running *Windows 95* and *Windows NT*, and the Pentium's ability to emulate the Intel 80486DX chip allows it to be used for running *DOS* and earlier versions of *Windows*. The Pentium chip can also be used to run varieties of *UNIX*, as well. (Although the Pentium chips could conceivably be called 80586 chips, due to a court decision prohibiting Intel from maintaining control over the X86 chip designation, they opted to give the new series of chips a proper, copyrightable name.)

Percent

In typography, the symbol representing percentage (%), commonly available in most standard *fonts*. In the event the symbol is not available, the alternative is to spell out "percent." When the symbol is imported from another *typeface*, it is important that the symbol blend with the text it will be appearing alongside.

Percent Elmendorf

The tearing strength of a paper, expressed as a percentage.

Percent Mullen

The expression of a paper or paperboard's *bursting strength*, determined using a *Mullen test*, as a percentage. (See *Mullen Test* and *Bursting Strength*.)

Percent Tensile

The *tensile strength* of a paper, expressed as a percentage. See *Tensile Strength*.

Perfect Binding

In *binding and finishing*, a means of binding utilizing an adhesive to hold pages together. Perfect binding, also known as *adhesive binding*, applies an adhesive to the *spine* of gathered pages that, when dry, keeps them securely bound. Commonly, a soft paper or paperboard cover (or *paperback*) is attached over the binding adhesive. Perfect bound publications have rectangular backbones. Publications bound by perfect binding include paperback books, telephone books, catalogs, and magazines. (About 40% of national magazines are perfect bound.) There are six basic units in a perfect binding line:

Gatherer. After printing and *folding*, book *signature*s are gathered together in the correct sequence, commonly using *gathering* machines comprising several pockets to hold individual signatures. At the gathering phase, any separately printed *insert*s (such as advertising supplements, subscriber reply cards, etc.) or *foldout*s also need to be assembled and included. Gathering devices can be rotary or swinging-arm devices. Once signatures have been gathered together, the book-length pile of them is called a *book block*.

Backbone Cutter. In perfect binding—unlike other types of binding such as *saddle-stitching* or *case binding*—the signature folds at the spine need to be removed and the pages aligned squarely with each other at the binding edge, which facilitates the effect of the adhesive. After gathering, the book blocks, spine down, are carried by clamps to the binding section. The spine protrudes from the bottom of the clamps, where knives, saws, or shredders cut off or grind away the signature folds. After cutting away the folds, the spine must be roughened to improve the application of the adhesive. In *notch binding*, large ¼-in. grooves are cut into the spine. The depth and spacing of the notches depend on the paper type and the composition of the adhesive. In *burst binding*, perforations are made in the crease of a fold either on press or on the *folder*. This eliminates the need to actually cut away the signature folds, as the punched holes allow for the penetration of glue. A variety of burst binding is *punch perforation*, in which slots are cut into the binding edge prior to the last fold.

After spine cutting, the book block is ready for the application of the adhesive.

Gluer. While still clamped together, the book block is carried to the gluing station, where applicator wheels force the adhesive onto the spine, a *back spinner* metering the thickness of the adhesive (usually about 0.020 in.). Often, multiple *glue pot*s are used to apply separate layers of different adhesives. Paperback books, for example, have one layer of a low-viscosity *hot-melt adhesive* applied to bind the pages together, while a layer of a high-viscosity hot-melt adhesive is used to adhere the book block to the cover. Thicker publications, such as metropolitan telephone books or heavy catalogs, use three different types of adhesives.

Most of the adhesives used in perfect binding are hot-melt adhesives, a mixture of **resin**s and **polymer**s which become fluid at high temperatures and dry by cooling back to a solid state. Most hot-melts achieve their best combination of flow characteristics and bonding strength when applied at a temperature between 350–400°F. In addition to hot-melts, **polyvinyl acetate**-based adhesives are often used. These do not need to be heated in order to be applied, but require special ovens to dry. They do, however, provide a more flexible spine than do traditional hot-melt adhesives. A third type of adhesive increasing in popularity is a polyurethane reactivate (PUR) adhesive. PUR-bound materials tend to lie flatter than material bound using other adhesives, PUR bindings tend to dry faster, and tend to be more durable. PUR, however, is more expensive and emits toxic vapors when heated.

Cover Feeder. After applying the adhesive, the cover is applied to the book block. A feeding mechanism scores the cover where it is to be folded around the book block, and the cover is pressed onto the backbone. **Nipper**s pinch the cover around the spine, while clamps press the front, back, and sides securely around the block. The bound book is then dropped onto a conveyor belt where it is sent for trimming.

Trimmer. Once the adhesive is cool, the tops of the folded signatures of the book block need to be split, and trimming around the other sides may also be necessary. Often, **three-knife trimmer**s—located in-line or off-line—can trim all three unbound sides at once. In some cases, binding is done **two-up**, where two books are bound together as one unit. In this case, the two individual books must be split apart prior to trimming. Some books can be trimmed **two-on**, or one book on top of another. This is more effective when used with thinner books.

Counter-stacker. The final step in the perfect binding process is the **counter-stacker**, a device which counts the number of individual units coming off the finishing line and stacks them for shipping.

Perfect binding equipment can bind up to 18,000 units an hour, with trimming stages slowing the process down somewhat; three-knife trimmers operate only up to about 6,000 units per hour. Any overflow can be diverted directly to stackers and trimmed off-line.

Despite the name of the process, perfect binding is not truly "perfect." Inflexible adhesives can result in books not lying flat, and the spines of paperback books can often be distorted almost beyond recognition, primarily by sloppy readers. The Swedish textbook manufacturer Otava has invented the "Otabind process" of perfect binding which uses two applications of a quick-drying adhesive along the spine. The binding is reinforced with additional layers of hot-melt adhesive along both sides of the book block, which are topped with crepe paper or cloth, followed by another layer of adhesive to secure the cover. The cover, in turn, has been scored several times, which in effect creates "hinges" which make the spine very flexible.

Perfect bind is also used occasionally in conjunction with case binding, where an adhesive is applied to the spine of a book block after sewing. Many book publishers use the same book blocks for hardcovers and their corresponding trade paperbacks. If there is a significant number of hard-cover books left in the warehouse, the trade paperback is produced by stripping off the cloth case and perfect binding a paperback cover onto the book blocks, rather than printing a whole new edition. This is an economical way of producing paperback versions of hardcovers which have not sold as well as had been anticipated, the only drawback being is that corrections or updates to the text cannot be made.

(See **Binding and Finishing**.)

Perfect Casebinding

In **binding and finishing**, a combination of two separate types of binding—**perfect binding** and **case binding**—in which **signature**s are bound together with adhesive prior to attaching the case. Perfect casebinding is performed to eliminate the **thread sewing** characteristic of traditional case binding.

Perfecting

The printing of the reverse side of an already-printed sheet, especially when it is performed on a **perfecting press**, utilizing either special **transfer cylinder**s or printing units to print on two sides during one pass through the press. See **Perfecting Press**. Printing on the reverse side of a printed sheet by means of successive passes through a press is commonly referred to as **backing up**.

Perfecting Press

A printing press, especially one used in **offset lithography**, that allows printing on both sides of a sheet of paper in one pass through the press. There are two basic configurations of offset perfecting presses. In a **convertible perfector**, special **transfer cylinder**s between successive printing units flip the paper over after it leaves the first **impression cylinder**, allowing the second unit to print on the reverse side of the sheet. Such presses have the advantage of being able to be used for single-side multicolor printing, simply by adjusting the transfer cylinders to keep them from flipping the sheet over. A second type of perfecting press, used primarily in **web offset lithography**, is called a **blanket-to-blanket press**, and utilizes one printing unit in which the impression cylinder is replaced by a second **blanket cylinder** directly below the first. As the sheet or paper web passes between the two blankets, images are printed on both sides at the same time. (See also **Offset Lithography**.)

Perfector

Alternate term for a ***perfecting press***, an offset press capable of printing on both sides of a sheet of paper in one pass through the press. See ***Perfecting Press***.

Perfect Press

See ***Perfecting Press***.

Perforating

In ***binding and finishing***, any operation that punches tiny slits or holes in a sheet of paper or other ***substrate***. Perforating is performed either on press or off press using perforating dies. Materials are perforated either to allow a portion to be easily removed (such as an order form or coupon), or to allow air to escape from folded signatures, which helps prevent wrinkling. The amount of paper between the perforations—called a ***tie***—can be adjusted. Perforating may also be effected directly on an offset press by means of a ***perforating rule***.

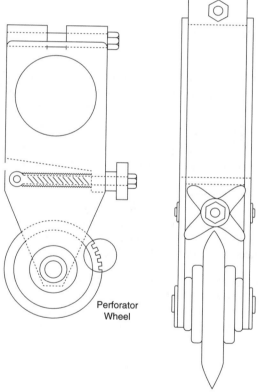

Perforating wheel.

Perforator
Wheel

Perforating Rule

A device used for on-press ***perforating***, consisting of a spiked strip attached to the blanket or impression cylinder of an offset press.

Perforation

A series of slits or cuts made in paper or other substrate, used for portions of a page intended to be removeable.

Perforation Tear Strength

A measure of the ease with which a ***perforation*** is torn.

Perfumed Ink

A printing ink to which has been added a small quantity of perfume (or other scent) as a means of making the printed sheet aromatic.

Perilla Oil

An oil obtained from the seeds of mints of several plants in the genus *Perilla* (most commonly *P. frutescens*) used as a drying oil in some printing ink ***vehicle***s.

Period Directory

In computing, especially by means of a system utilizing a ***hierarchical file system***, the use of a single period (.) to designate the ***current directory***. The current directory's ***parent directory*** is thus designated with two periods (..) and is consequently known as a ***double-period directory***. This shorthand means of referring to directories is often used in ***DOS***, ***OS/2***, and ***UNIX*** operating systems.

Peripheral

Any hardware device connected to a computer and which is under the control of the ***CPU***. Peripheral devices include printers, modems, and any of a variety of magnetic or optical storage media.

Peripheral Component Interconnect (PCI) Bus

In computing, a ***local bus*** specification for ***personal computer***s, introduced in 1992 by Intel. PCI supports up to 10 ***expansion card***s in a single computer, so long as at least one of them is a PCI controller card. Other expansion cards including ***video card***s, ***network interface card***s, and ***SCSI*** interfaces can be added. The PCI bus operates with a bus speed of 32 MHz, with a maximum ***throughput*** of 132 ***megabyte***s per second (with a 32-bit data path) or 264 megabytes per second (with a 64-bit data path).

Permanence

A paper property that measures a paper's resistance to changes in its chemical, structural, or optical properties over time. Permanence includes such things as resistance to yellowing and fading upon exposure to light (***lightfastness***) over time, and the paper's ability to retain its strength over time. Paper permanence is measured using ***accelerated aging*** conditions, and describes its brightness loss and yellowing. A paper's retention of ***folding endurance*** over time is also a useful test for determining how well a paper will retain its strength. Some of the factors that affect a paper's deterioration over time are the deterioration of the ***cellulose*** fibers themselves (which moisture accelerates), and the use of acid-rosin ***sizing***. ***Acid paper*** tends to be less permanent than ***alkaline paper***. Permanence is related to ***durability***. (See ***Durability***.)

The term *permanence* also refers to the ability of a printing ink to resist fading or changing color upon exposure to light or weather. The permanence of an ink is generally governed by the **lightfastness** of the **pigment** used. (See **Pigment**.) A substance's permanence is also known as **age resistance**.

Permanent Adhesive
An **adhesive** with a high degree of **ultimate adhesion**, or retaining its adhesive bond for a long period of time.

Permanent Font
In desktop publishing, a **font** which, after being downloaded to a printer, remains in memory until the power is turned off. This may not sound especially permanent, but it refers to the fact that a particular font does not need to be downloaded more than once in a particular job or session. See also **Transient Font**.

Permanent Internal Font
On a personal computer, one of several system **font**s that are always resident in the computer's memory.

Permanent Red 2G
See **DNA Orange**.

Permanent Red FRL
An **organic color pigment** used in printing inks. Permanent Red FRL is a bluish-orange red possessing good **lightfastness** and resistance to chemicals and heat. It is used in many printing applications for its resistance properties. (See also **Organic Color Pigments**.)
(CI Pigment Red 10 No. 12440.)

Permanent Red FRR
An **organic color pigment** used in printing inks. Permanent Red FRR is a strong, bright yellowish red possessing moderate **lightfastness** and high resistance to acids, alkalis, and soaps. Permanent Red FRR is used in **letterpress** and **lithographic** inks primarily for cartons (especially soap packaging). (See also **Organic Color Pigments**.) Also known as *Naphthol Red*.
(CI Pigment Red 2 No. 12310).

Permanent Red "R"
An **organic color pigment** that is used in printing inks. Permanent Red "R" is a bright orange red that possesses high **lightfastness** and acid and alkali resistance, but low heat resistance. Permanent Red "R" is inexpensive and used in many different applications, but printability problems make it difficult to produce effective formulations. (See also **Organic Color Pigments**.)
Also produced as *Chlorinated Para Red* (CI Pigment Red 4 No. 12085).

Permanent Swap File
In computing, a **swap file** created for **virtual memory** management that, once created, is reused over and over again. See **Swap File**. See also **Temporary Swap File**.

Permanent Violet
A **dye** used in printing inks that comprises either **Methyl Violet** reacted with tungsten or molybdenum compounds, or **Dioxazine Violet (RL) Carbazole Violet**, which possesses a high degree of **lightfastness**.

Permanent Virtual Circuit (PVC)
In telecommunications, a communications channel that is open and maintained even when no data is being transmitted through it. See **Virtual Circuit**. See also **Switched Virtual Circuit (SVC)**.

Permission
In networking, the ability for a user to access certain network resources and files, based on the **rights** assigned to that user by the **network administrator**.

Persian Orange
A transparent, brilliant orange **organic ink pigment**, characterized as a **lake**, that is used as a **colorant** in printing inks.

Persistence of Vision
A strange fluke of the human visual system that allows television and motion pictures to work. Essentially, a motion picture, like an animation, is a series of still images which, when projected at a certain minimum speed (about 30 frames per second) appears as continuous motion.

Personal Communications Services
In computing, a set of applications and utilities pertaining to **wireless communications** for **portable computer**s.

Personal Computer
Alternate term for a **microcomputer**, especially one designed for use by a single individual. *Personal Computer* is also the name of a specific brand of microcomputer manufactured and marketed by IBM. Abbreviated **PC**.

Personal Computer Memory Card International Association (PCMCIA)
A trade organization that sets standards for devices—specifically memory cards—that are added to personal computers. The term **PCMCIA** is commonly used to refer to a specific **memory card** that adds **flash memory** to a personal computer. See **PCMCIA**.

Personal Digital Assistant (PDA)
A small, **palm-top** computer device which accepts handwriting as input. Such a device has **fax** and **email** capabilities, as well as various personal organization software. The term *Personal Digital Assistant* was first coined by Apple Computer (whose Newton is the most common example of the device), although the term has entered the popular lexicon. Many companies now market similar devices. The personal digital assistant is also known more generically as a **pen-based PC**.

Personal Information Manager (PIM)

In computing, a set of small application modules—such as a database, word processor, etc.—used for personal organization, such as storing names and addresses, notes, memos, etc. PIMs are often used in *personal digital assistant*s.

Persplex

A transparent, thermoplastic polymer—similar to Plexiglas—used in the production of scanner drums. Also known—primarily in England—as *perspex*.

Perylene Red Y

See *Anthraquinone Scarlet*.

Peta-

A *metric prefix* denoting 1,000,000,000,000,000 (one quadrillion, or 10^{15}) units. In computing, *peta-* refers to 2^{50}, and one *petabyte* (PB) of storage (should such a thing exist some day) is approximately equal to one quadrillion *byte*s of data (actually 1,125,899,906,842,624 bytes). See also *Kilo-*, *Mega-*, *Giga-*, *Tera-*, and *Exa-*. *Peta-* is usually abbreviated *P*.

Petabyte

An uncommon unit of computer storage, comprising 1,024 *terabyte*s or 1,125,899,906,842,624 *byte*s. *Peta-* is the prefix meaning "quadrillion," so it is common to consider 1 petabyte as equal to 1 quadrillion bytes, although that isn't entirely accurate. Petabyte is abbreviated PB. 1,024 petabytes equal 1 *exabyte*.

PGA

Abbreviation for *Professional Graphics Adapter*. See *Professional Graphics Adapter (PGA)*.

PGF

Abbreviation for *Presentation Graphics Facility*.

pH

Abbreviation for "potential of the hydrogen ion (H^+)," a measure of how acidic or alkaline paper (or any other substance) is. An excess of H^+ ions makes a substance acidic, while an excess of hydroxyl ions (OH^-) makes a substance alkaline (an alkaline solution is also called a base). Equal concentrations of both ions produce a neutral substance. pH is represented as the logarithm of the reciprocal of the concentration of H^+ ions in gram atoms per liter. The pH scale runs from 0 to 14, and each change in pH number indicates an exponential change in ion concentrations. A pH of 7 indicates a neutral solution, while decreasing numbers indicate exponentially greater acidity (a solution with a pH of 6 being weakly acidic, and a solution with a pH of 0 being one million times more acidic than a solution with a pH of 6) and increasing numbers indicate exponentially greater alkalinity (a solution with a pH of 8 being weakly alkaline, and a solution with a pH of 14 being one million times more alkaline than one with a pH of 8). A substance capable of functioning both as an acid and an alkali is referred to as *amphoteric*.

The pH of an offset press's *fountain solution*—typically around 4.0–5.5, or slightly to moderately acidic—needs to be carefully set, checked, and kept consistent. *Gum arabic*, added to a fountain solution to desensitize the nonimage areas of a printing plate, loses its effectiveness when the pH of the fountain solution exceeds about 5.0. Other problems such as *tinting*, *plate blinding*, and *roller stripping* can be traced to incorrect or inconsistent pH. Various dampening solutions can also be produced with alkaline formulations. (See *Fountain Solution: pH*.)

A paper's pH can have a number of important effects on various printing properties, one of the most important being a paper's permanence. *Acid paper* has been found to last for a significantly shorter period of time than *alkaline paper* (acid paper has an estimated life span of about 50 years or less, compared to a life span of 200 years for alkaline paper). The switch to using alkaline paper has been ongoing in Europe, and has been strongly supported by librarians and archivists worried about the deterioration of books and documents printed on acid paper. (Actually, the pH of "alkaline paper" is only slightly higher than 7.0.) Aside from permanence, paper pH affects the printing process itself, primarily in offset printing. Low pH (either in the paper or in the press dampening system) can interfere with the proper drying of quickset and drying-oil inks, while high-pH paper can interfere with the acidic dampening system of the press (when acids and bases come into contact with each other, they react, sometimes quite strongly, depending on the respective pH concentrations). A paper's *sizing* is one of the chief determinants of a paper's pH; *rosin* sizing is generally acidic, while synthetic materials are now used to impart alkalinity to paper. The materials used in a paper's *coating* also affect its pH. For example, the use of *calcium carbonate*, which produces alkalinity, as a coating material has been known to have deleterious effects when particles of coating contaminate a press's dampening system.

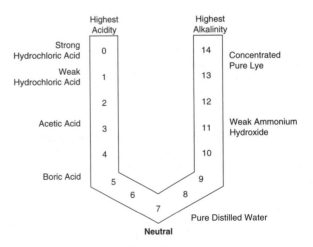

The pH scale.

A paper's pH can be determined using a water extraction of a paper sample and a glass-electrode pH meter. The pH of the paper's coating can also be obtained by slicing a sample of the coating off the paper, producing a water extraction of it, and using a pH meter.

Phenolic Resin

Any of several types of *thermosetting* resins produced from the condensation of phenol (a poisonous organic compound, a hydroxyl derivative of benzene), or a phenol derivative, with formaldehyde (or other type of aldehyde) used in printing inks to impart high degrees of *gloss*, hardness, and rapid drying properties. See *Resin*.

PHIGS+

An *extension* to the *PHIGS* graphics standard. See *Programmers Hierarchical Interactive Graphics System*.

PHIGS

Abbreviation for *Programmers Hierarchical Interactive Graphics System*. See *Programmers Hierarchical Interactive Graphics System (PHIGS)*.

Phloxine

A bluish red *pigment* used in printing inks. Phloxine, used for magenta in process color, is a lead *lake* of *eosine*. Due to government restrictions on lead-based ink pigments, phloxine is rarely used.

Phonetics

An alternative alphabet used in pronunciation guides.

Phong Shading

In three-dimensional graphics, a technique used to apply color to the surface of rendered objects with which the color of each *pixel* of the object's surface is calculated. Phong shading yields the highest-quality results of all the various coloring and shading methods.

Phosphor

A substance applied to the back of a *cathode-ray tube* that, when struck by an *electron beam*, emits light, a property known as *phosphorescence*. It is the action of phosphors under the action of a moving electron beam (or, in color monitors, three electron beams) that produce an image on a computer screen or television set.

Phosphorescence

A property of a substance—such as an ink film or coating or the back of a *cathode-ray tube*—produced from *phosphor*s that have the ability to become luminous at certain wavelengths when exposed to heat, light, or ultraviolet rays.

Photocombining

In the *image assembly* phase of *prepress*, the use of *complementary flat*s (or separate flats containing different images that will ultimately be imaged on the same plate) in which the separate flats will be combined photographically onto a single negative (or positive) prior to platemaking. Such negatives (or positives) are known as *composite negative*s (or *composite positive*s).

Photocompositing

Other term for *phototypesetting*. See *Phototypesetting*.

Photocomposition

Other term for *phototypesetting*. See *Phototypesetting*.

Photo Conversion

In graphics, a photomechanical process for converting a photograph into a simulation of a *line drawing*.

Photo Detector

Any device found in a *scanner*, *digital camera*, or *optical disc* drive used to detect light.

Photodiode

A photocell mounted on a computer chip used to measure the amount of light striking it. Photodiodes (or *photodiode array*s) are used in many types of *scanner*s to sense the tonal value of each *pixel*.

Photodiode Array

A set of *photodiode*s used in many types of *scanner*s that are arranged in rows to detect the tonal values of regions of an original image corresponding to *pixel*s. See *Photodiode*.

Photoengraving

In *letterpress* printing, a process by which an acid *resist* containing a photosensitive emulsion is adhered to a sheet of metal, exposed to a film negative, developed, and then the surface is treated with a chemical etchant, which eats through the resist quickly and dissolves the metal in the unexposed, nonimage areas, and eats through the resist more slowly in the most highly exposed image areas, failing to etch the metal in the portions of the image corresponding to solids and shadows. The process of photoengraving is reminiscent of a stencil process; the depth of engraving is not variable as it is in some *resist* etching systems. This process results in a metal relief plate.

A very similar process is used to make molded rubber *flexographic* plates, the metal relief plate then being impressed into a mold consisting of cellulose fibers and phenolic resins, the rubber then added to the hardened mold to form a raised rubber plate. (See *Plate: Flexography: Rubber Plates*.)

Photographic Element

In graphics, an array of *pixel*s or printer *spot*s used to create a photographic image.

Photographic Justification

In typography, making a line *justified* by uniformly expanding all the characdters and *word space*s on a line.

Photographic Proof

Any type of *proof* produced from photographic *negative*s or *positive*s.

Photographic Screen Printing

General term for *screen printing* performed using screens prepared by the *direct process*, or from *stencil*s exposed while the photosensitive emulsion is already applied to the screen. Such a screen is called a *photoscreen*. See *Photostencil: Direct Process*.

Photographic Screen Printing Plate

Alternate term for *photoscreen*, the result of the *direct process* of preparing a *photostencil*. See *Photostencil: Direct Process*.

Photography

Etymologically, *photography* derives from two Greek words that essentially mean "writing with light," which is an accurate description of the process. In its most basic expression, photography is the exposure of a light-sensitive material to light, typically through a lens or other means of focusing light into a sharp point. After chemical development of the light-sensitive material, the image of the objects off which the light striking the film has reflected will appear.

Photography has many uses, most of which are beyond the scope of this article. Photography is used for portraits of people, holiday snapshots, art, journalism, and the preparation of materials for printed reproduction. The following article will briefly discuss the history of photography, and then discuss the various elements needed for modern photography. The article will then turn to graphic arts photography, or the shooting of line art and *halftone*s for printed reproduction. The article will conclude with an overview of the newly emerging digital photographic techniques, from Photo CDs to digital cameras.

HISTORY OF PHOTOGRAPHY

Odd as it may seem, the camera preceded what we think of as photography by over 700 years. In 1039, the Arab scholar Alhazen described a device in use at the time (later called the camera obscura) which essentially consisted of a dark, box-like room with a small hole cut in one wall. Light passed into the room through the hole and cast the image of scenes taking place outside the box on the opposite wall. People could sit in the box and watch a "picture show" of activities transpiring outside. In the mid-sixteenth century, several Italian scientists fitted the camera obscura hole with a lens and diaphragm apparatus to provide a sharper image. The camera obscura was used for a type of "photography," but there was no way of capturing the images except by manually drawing what was cast on the wall, which is how many painters actually worked. (The Dutch painter Jan Vermeer [1632–75], for example, is believed to have used a camera obscura for his highly detailed domestic scenes.)

Meanwhile, in 1727, the German physicist Johannes Heinrich Schulze discovered the sensitivity of certain silver salts to light. However, Schulze's interest in the chemistry of the process blinded him to the commercial exploitation of it. Several advances were made in the use of the silver salts for the capture of images, and several years later the English chemists Thomas Wedgwood and Humphry Davy were able to coat a paper with silver salts and photographically create silhouettes of leaves and other objects. However, unexposed salts could not as yet be dissolved away, the result being that the captured images were not permanent. In the 1820s, French chemist Joseph Nicéphore Niepce duplicated the work of Wedgwood and Davy, but found that bitumen (a material similar to asphalt) became insoluble when exposed to light. He coated bitumen on metal plates, exposed them to an image, and dissolved the unexposed bitumen (corresponding to nonimage areas). Applying acid to the plate, the acid did not dissolve the exposed bitumen, and Niepce therefore had a relief plate which could be used on a *letterpress* printing press. Image quality, however, was not very high. Niepce also applied the camera obscura to this technique and the first attempts to combine a camera and a photosensitive material were made. Although Niepce called the process heliography (literally "sun writing"), the world's first true photograph, of the view outside Niepce's window, was made in 1826.

Niepce (and, after Niepce's death in 1833, his son Isidore) formed a partnership with the French painter Louis Jacques Mandé Daguerre to develop the photographic techniques. Daguerre abandoned bitumen as the photosensitive material and returned to silver compounds. In 1839, Daguerre announced the process of *daguerreotypy*, in which a polished silver plate was exposed to iodine vapor. The resulting layer of silver iodide was light-sensitive, and after exposure mercury vapor was used to develop the plate. Common salt could then be used to remove the unexposed silver iodide. The process caught on, and soon better materials (first sodium thiosulfate and then a mixture of silver iodide and silver bromide) were found to yield better results and reduce the required exposure time enough to make portrait-taking practical.

At about the same time that Daguerre was preparing his paper on the daguerreotype process, an English archaeologist and philologist named William Henry Fox Talbot had invented a similar process, which he called calotypy (also known as the talbotype process). Talbot exposed silver iodide-treated paper with a camera and developed it in gallic acid. This process produced a paper *negative*, which could then be transferred to a second sensitized paper to produce a *positive* print. Talbot's images, however, ended up much grainier and blurrier than Daguerre's (due to the coarseness of the paper Talbot used), but the process of making a single negative from which multiple positives could be made became the basis of modern photography.

Until it was realized that silver salts were only light-sensitive when in the presence of certain organic media (such as that found in paper), the use of other base materials for photographic plates (glass in particular) was impossible. However, in the mid-1840s, Niepce de Saint-Victor discovered this, and by coating glass plates with a layer of **albumen** (an organic colloid found in egg whites), potassium iodide, and sodium chloride, the added silver nitrate was rendered light-sensitive. Saint-Victor was able to produce negatives on glass plates, which produced much sharper images than Talbot's original paper negatives. In 1851, Frederick Scott Archer invented the wet-plate process, which replaced the albumen with a substance called collodion (essentially a solution of guncotton in ether and alcohol). These glass plates needed to be exposed and developed before they were allowed to dry (they lost their sensitivity to light when dry), but the process was very popular among some photographers, who built portable darkrooms so as to be able to photograph events "on location." In particular, famed Civil War photographer Matthew Brady used the wet-plate process. The wet-plate process was very popular for studio work, however, especially early graphic arts photography, but for portable photographic work a solution wasn't found until 1871, when English physician Richard Maddox developed an emulsion made from **gelatin** rather than collodion, and further refinements made the resulting dry plates practical.

Meanwhile, the camera itself was undergoing changes. The first daguerreotype cameras essentially comprised two wooden boxes, one being slid in or out of the other one for focusing. In 1861, the first single-lens reflex camera (a camera in which light was reflected through the lens—which could be focused without moving the rest of the camera—both to the film and to the viewfinder) was invented, and in 1880 the twin-lens reflex camera (which had two lenses, one which led to the viewfinder and one which led to the film) was invented. In 1888, George Eastman introduced the first roll-film camera. The first model of the Kodak camera (named, legend has it, after the sound the camera makes when the shutter button is pressed, although some believe this to be apocryphal) used photographic paper coated with a gelatin emulsion, which could be peeled off and transferred to glass for developing. Subsequent models replaced the paper backing with celluloid-based film (invented several years earlier by John Corbutt). The small size of the Kodak cameras made amateur photography extraordinarily popular. In 1885, a pocket camera was introduced which, designed by Frank Brownell, was known familiarly as the "Brownie." The earliest Kodak cameras came pre-loaded with film which, after shooting all the pictures, was sent—camera and all—back to the company for developing. These were replaced by reloadable cameras, but in the 1990s the so-called "disposable camera" made a comeback. *Plus ça change, plus c'est la même chose.*

The problem with celluloid film—which, by the way, also made possible the motion picture industry, as its transparency meant that light could be projected *through* it after development—was that it was highly flammable. (Celluloid, made from guncotton mixed with alcohol and camphor, was invented by John Hyatt, an Albany, New York,

printer for a completely different purpose than film: he wanted to win a prize offered by a billiard-ball manufacturer who had been having difficulties obtaining ivory, the original material for the balls. Although Hyatt's billiard balls caught on, the celluloid was rather unstable, and during a game of billiards they had a tendency to explode, or at the very least emit a sound much like a gunshot. When used in Western saloons filled with trigger-happy cowboys, one can imagine a variety of unfortunate events arising.) At any rate, nonflammable celluloid acetate "safety film" was introduced in the 1920s, and had completely replaced the flammable celluloid film completely by the 1950s.

Further refinements over the years have made high-quality cameras smaller and more portable, color photographs possible and of greater tonal quality, film faster, and exposure times much quicker.

Basics of Photography

Although new digital cameras and other technologies may someday make film obsolete, it still remains one of the essential parts of the photographic process. And who knows? Someday, maybe even the camera itself will become obsolete!

Camera. Any camera, regardless if it is a small hand-held model or a room-sized graphic arts **process camera**, is essentially the same device: a light-proof box with a **lens** at one end that can focus incoming light onto securely mounted film for a set period of time. A lens is a curved piece of glass that refracts incoming light and focuses it at a specific point, producing a sharp image of whatever it is that the light is reflecting off of. A camera's **focal length** is a measure of the distance between the center—or node—of the lens and the point at which distant objects are in focus, or the **focal point**. Portable cameras have focal lengths measured in millimeters, but in graphic arts cameras they may be measured in inches. In most cameras (except movie cameras), the focal length is equal to the diagonal size of the negative.

Light passes through the lens into the camera through an **aperture**, a small hole which is opened for set periods of time (the length of time the aperture remains open, allowing light to strike the film, is also called the *aperture*). Light entering the camera is controlled by the **shutter**, the "door" that when closed prevents light from entering and when open allows light to enter. The amount of time the shutter remains open is called the **shutter speed**. In addition to shutter speed and aperture, the aperture diameter (adjusted by means of a **diaphragm**) is also an important measurement in photography. The diameter of the aperture and the focal length are related mathematically to each other by means of the **f-stop system**. A camera's **f-number** is essentially the ratio of the focal length to the aperture diameter. For example, if a camera has a focal length of 8 in. and the aperture diameter is set at 1 in., then the f-stop value would be f/8 (f-number = focal length ÷

aperture diameter, or 8 ÷ 1 = 8). If the aperture diameter were reduced to ½ in., then the f-stop value would be f/16 (1 ÷ ½ = 16). Although in theory any f-number can be created, there is a set of default f/stops prescribed by lens manufacturers, which are f/1.4, f/2, f/2.8, f/4, f/5.6, f/8, f/11, f/16, f/22, f/32, and f/64. This set of f-numbers is based on a factor of 2; moving from one f-number to the next doubles the amount of light entering the camera. (For a constant focal length, the higher the f-number, the smaller the aperture. Thus changing from f/32 to f/22 doubles the aperture, while changing from f/16 to f/22 halves it.) As a result of this relationship, an equivalent exposure time can be determined, as a means of minimizing the length of exposure while at the same time ensuring that the same amount of light strikes the film. Thus, at f/16 with an exposure time of 60 seconds, an equivalent exposure could be determined to be 30 seconds at f/11. Since f-stop values are mathematical ratios of focal length to aperture diameter, they are not specific to any single camera. On both a 35-mm portable camera and a large graphic arts process camera, an f-stop of f/16 will allow the same quantity of light to enter the camera.

Another factor involved in photography is the field, both the size and depth of field. In most cameras, the field (or the size of the area the lens can capture) for any given lens is related to the focal length. A lens with a focal length of 50 mm would be able to cover about a 53° field. The **depth of field** is that range of distances at which all objects will be in acceptable focus when the lens is focused on a particular point. So, for example, a lens focused on an object 16 f.t away would have all objects within the range of 13–25 ft. in acceptable focus. Depth of field varies with lens size (i.e., focal length). (See **Lens**.)

Another important consideration in photography is shutter speed, or the length of time the shutter remains open. This can range from fractions of a second to several minutes, depending on the illumination level, the type of film used, the type of lens used, and other such factors.

Film. The basis of film (or any photosensitive material) is the chemical change in an emulsion that occurs when light of a specific wavelength strikes it. Most photographic film is formulated to be sensitive to light in the **visible spectrum**. Other materials (such as printing plate materials, for example) are sensitive to light in the **ultraviolet** portion of the **electromagnetic spectrum**. Basically, photographic film consists of an **emulsion** containing silver halides (a class of chemicals including bromides, iodides, and chlorides) suspended in a gelatin, which is then applied to a plastic or paper base. After exposure to an image (or, rather, light reflecting off an image), immersion of the film in a **developing solution** converts the silver halide to metallic silver in direct proportion to the amount of exposure received; the greater the exposure, the less metallic silver is produced. The light areas of the original are represented (on a photographic negative) by heavy deposits of silver, while the dark areas of the original are very light or transparent, containing very light silver deposits. (On a

film or paper positive, the reverse is the case.) Different types of film require different types of developing chemicals and developing temperatures to be effective. During developing, when the desired image density is reached, the action of the developing chemical must be stopped, often using an acid- or water-based **stop bath**. Immersion in a **fixing solution** (often sodium or ammonia thiosulfate) dissolves the residual silver halide and effectively "fixes" the image on the film. Automated film processing machines are widely used to save time and produce consistent results.

A photographic negative is used to prepare either film positives or prints. A recurring problem with photographic films and papers (especially now that glass is no longer used as the backing material) is the dimensional stability of the plastic or paper. Such materials tend to increase or decrease in size with changes in temperature. In cases where high degrees of **registration** are vital, a variety of base materials are available that keep their shape (and thus prevent image distortion) readily.

Some films exhibited the problem of **halation**, or a blurring effect of photographic images caused by light passing through the emulsion and base material, striking the back of the base material, and passing back out through the emulsion, essentially exposing the film twice. Films now use an **antihalation dye**, which is applied to the back of the base material and effectively absorbs the light striking it, preventing the light from bouncing back up through the emulsion.

Different types of films demonstrate different types of color sensitivity, or in other words, each type of film is sensitive to light in certain portions of the spectrum. **Blue-sensitive** film, as the name indicates, is only sensitive to light in the **blue** and **ultraviolet** portion of the spectrum, and is also often known as **color blind** film. **Orthochromatic** film is sensitive to all the wavelengths of the spectrum except for **red**. Orthochromatic (often called simply "ortho") film is the most commonly used, since its lack of sensitivity to red light means that it can be developed in a darkroom under a red safelight. In contrast, **panchromatic** film is sensitive to all wavelengths of visible light and as a result must be developed in total darkness. The color sensitivity of a film is usually indicated by a **wedge spectrogram**, which is a graph or **histogram** that shows the relative sensitivity of a film across a range of wavelengths.

A film's **contrast** refers to the degree to which the tones of the original (either a graphic arts mechanical or a "real-life" scene) have been compressed or expanded. Film manufacturers often provide a characteristic curve, or a graph illustrating the film density as a function of exposure time, for various films.

Another important issue in photographic film is **film speed**, which essentially refers to the length of time the film needs to be exposed in order to register an image, or in other words how much light is required. "Fast" film requires less light, while "slow" film requires more light. Film speed is measured using the **ASA** system; the higher the ASA rating, the faster the film. Although conventional film is given a general ASA number, detailed exposure indexes give different ASA values for different light sources.

Effective photography—be it conventional or graphic arts—is a balancing act between all the above-mentioned variables: f-number, shutter speed, exposure time, film speed, and a variety of lighting conditions.

GRAPHIC ARTS PHOTOGRAPHY

There are basically two varieties of photography: creative and graphic arts. Creative photography—the variety with which most everyone is at least slightly familiar, includes professional portrait photography, amateur holiday photography, and photojournalism, among many other things. Graphic arts photography, on the other hand, comprises those **prepress** processes used to prepare copy and art for printed reproduction. Although digital prepress processes are working to replace graphic arts photography, some of the basic principles involved in optimizing copy and art apply to both photographic and digital processes.

Graphic arts cameras (also called *process cameras*) are very large devices. They commonly have a camera area under regular room light, while the camera back and controls are built into the wall of a darkroom (and are thus called **darkroom camera**s), which allows the operator to load and remove film without having to leave the darkroom. Other models, called **galley camera**s, operate under ambient light and the film needs to be loaded into special light-tight containers and brought out of the darkroom and loaded into the camera. Some process cameras have components—such as suspension units—attached to either the floor or ceiling. Most graphic arts cameras possess a horizontal image plane (in which case they are also known as **horizontal camera**s); some cameras—called **vertical camera**s—have the copyboard, lens, and camera back aligned vertically. Vertical cameras have an advantage over horizontal models in that they save space.

Graphic arts cameras use symmetric coated lenses, ground within very strict tolerances to reduce and/or eliminate distortion as much as possible. Most are of the **achromat** type (also called **apochromatic**) which fully corrects the lens for any color deviations throughout the visible spectrum. Process camera lenses have f-numbers ranging from f/8 to f/11, which—due to the large focal lengths (ranging from 8 to 48 in., depending on the size of the camera) correspond to small aperture diameters. Due to the large size of some mechanicals, process cameras need to be able to capture images up to 40-in. square.

Process cameras use high-resolution, high-contrast films, which are characterized by slow film speeds. As a result, high-intensity pulsed xenon lamps (for color reproduction) or quartz iodine lamps (for monochrome reproduction) are used. Lamps are often built onto the unit itself, one lamp on the right and one on the left, and are oriented such that the incident light rays strike the copyboard at a 45° angle. Many advanced cameras utilize computer-controlled light integrators which use photoelectric cells to monitor the intensity of the light and automatically adjust the exposure time to compensate for any deviations. The lamps are often controlled by the camera shutter; when the shutter opens (controlled by a user-set timer) the lights usually click on. When the shutter closes, the lights turn off.

The original art is mounted on a **copyboard**, a glass-covered frame facing the lens. On horizontal cameras, the copyboard is oriented vertically, but can usually be rotated to a horizontal position to facilitate the mounting of copy. The copyboard can also be moved toward or away from the lens, depending upon whether enlargement or reduction, respectively, is desired. When moving the copyboard—often by means of rotating wheels on the control panel of the camera—the lens also usually needs to be adjusted and refocused. Accurate enlargement and reduction percentages can be effected using line-up tapes, guide numbers, or via computer-controlled mechanisms. During enlargement or reduction, the distance of the copyboard from the light source also changes, which can be accounted for either by varying the f-number or by using the above-mentioined light integrators.

Enlargements and reductions are denoted as percentages of the original copy. A reproduction that is 100% of the original is the same size as (or is at a 1:1 ratio to) the original. Percentages lower than 100% are reductions (such as 50%, which is half the size of, or at a ratio of 1:2 to, the original), while those greater than 100% are enlargements (such as 200%, which is twice the size of, or at a ratio of 2:1 to, the original).

At the other end of the camera is the **filmboard**, a flat plane to which the film is mounted, commonly using a vacuum system to hold it in place. The filmboard, like the copyboard, can be in a horizontal position for easy mounting of film, and is swung into a vertical position behind the lens for exposure.

During exposure, a **step tablet** or **grayscale** is placed on the copyboard next to the copy to be photographed (but not in a position that obscures detail of the original copy!) A step tablet consists of a series of discrete steps of gray progressing from white to black. When the film is developed, the individual steps darken with increasing development, which serve as important cues in the proper development of the image. When a predetermined gray step has filled in, it is time to stop the developing process. Afterward, the grayscale can be evaluated to gauge the usability of the film.

Graphic arts photography is used to make photostats of line art and other elements, which can then be pasted onto a mechanical, or it can be used to generate the negatives (or positives) for **stripping** and platemaking, or it can be used to make **color separation**s. (See **Prepress: Graphic Arts Photography and Flat Assembly** and **Color Separation**.) Regardless, however, there are two basic varieties of graphic arts photography that must be recognized: line photography and halftone photography.

Line Photography. Like **line art**, line photography involves the photographing of simple lines, shapes, text matter, solids, etc. (as opposed to continuous-tone images).

Line photography is essentially high-contrast photography: either black or white, ink or no ink. Line photography is relatively simple to accomplish, and is often performed using orthochromatic film. Line photography is used in the preparation of negatives of text and line art for stripping. Although most such photography consists of the making of negatives from original copy, **contact print**s are often made as well. Contact printing essentially involves the exposure of a previously exposed positive or negative to a piece of film, producing a negative or positive, respectively. Special duplicating film is used to make negatives from other negatives and positives from other positives.

Halftone Photography. The conventional printing processes are essentially "binary" media; they are incapable of printing continuous tones. As a result, any continuous-tone image (such as a photograph) that is to be printed needs to be converted to a series of very small, discrete dots. Such an image that consists of dots is called a halftone. Each dot is some shade of gray (or color) and it is the packing of these dots in specific densities that provides the illusion of a continuous-tone image. In order to optimize a continuous-tone image for printing, then, it needs to be converted to a dot pattern. This is accomplished using either a **halftone screen** or, more and more commonly, **electronic dot generation**. (The remainder of this section on halftones will primarily concern itself with the photographic techniques for halftone production; see also **Halftone** for a discussion of electronic dot generation.)

Originally, halftones were produced by shooting a continuous-tone image through a glass screen, which was essentially two glass "sheets" cemented together, each of which contained a grid of inked lines which, when placed together at right angles to each other, formed a fine screen that separated the contone image into small discrete square dots. The glass screen is now obsolete, but the principle survives in the use of the **contact screen**. Contact screens are a descendent of glass screens (and are usually prepared from them), but are on film (i.e., acetate) bases and utilize **vignette**d dots, with gradient density from the center of each dot (the greatest density) outward to the perimeter. There are a variety of different types of screens, such as gray screens on which the dots are in silver, and magenta screens in which the dots are formed using a magenta dye. Other screen patterns include elliptical and square dots, as well as other shapes, which produce different effects to enhance different portions of an image, such as **shadow**s, **midtone**s, or **highlight**s. Contact screen photography includes placing the screen against the unexposed film, and exposing it to the original continuous-tone image. The density variation of the dots on the screen leaves variations in the density of the original as smaller or larger dots, depending upon whether a region is a highlight or a shadow, respectively, or, in other words, based on how much light is being reflected or transmitted by the original. Various additional processes can enhance certain aspects of the image: **flashing**—or exposing the film as a whole to a yellow light—reduces contrast in shadow regions, while **no-screen exposure** (also called **bump exposure**)—or removing the screen for a short period of the exposure—increases contrast in the highlights. The specially dyed screens also help increase or reduce contrast in desired portions of an image.

The screen process most commonly yields a halftone negative which is stripped into a **flat** prior to platemaking, but in some cases, a screen print can be made from a negative which can then be added to a mechanical and shot with line art prior to stripping. Called **copy-dot reproduction**, it is most often used in newspapers, catalogs, in-house newsletters and reports, etc. These prints are most often made by a **diffusion transfer** method.

(See **Halftone**.)

Color Separation. When printing **process color**—or "full-color" photographs or other images—all the reproducible colors that exist are produced by overprinting halftone dots of the four process colors (**cyan**, **magenta**, **yellow**, and **black**) at various densities to create **secondary colors**. As a result, each of those four colors needs its own plate, and therefore its own negative. These negatives are produced from color separations in which a full-color, continuous-tone image is photographed four times through a series of color filters, to produce negatives or transparencies of just one color at a time. Although color separations were once produced exclusively photographically, they are more often than not performed digitally these days. (See **Color Separation**.)

There is an increasing trend in recent years toward **digital photography**, and the dissemination of digital images on a **Photo CD**. See **Digital Photography** and **Photo CD**.

Photogravure
Printing from a **gravure cylinder** or **intaglio** plate that has been imaged photographically. See **Gravure**.

Photoinitiator
A chemical or other substance used in printing ink **vehicle**s that, when exposed to light, forms **free radical**s, which promote **free radical polymerization**, a means of drying and hardening some ink films.

Photolettering
In typography, type produced utilizing one of a variety of devices that compose type—typically display and headline type—by photographic means. Photolettering is typically distinguished from **phototypesetting** in that the latter is frequently performed with computer assistance, while the former is not.

Photolithographic
Term describing an offset printing plate whose image has been imparted to the surface of the plate by means of photographic exposure, typically utilizing an intense light shined through a photographic negative or positive onto a light-

sensitive coating on the surface of the plate, which then needs to be developed chemically following exposure. See *Plate: Offset Lithography*.

Photomechanical

Descriptive of any photographic reproduction or imaging process.

Photomechanical Transfer (PMT)

Alternate term for *diffusion transfer*. See *Diffusion Transfer*.

Photomultiplier Tube (PMT)

A type of phototube, an electronic device that emits electrons when exposed to light. The phototube and the principle of photoemission are based on quantum mechanics, specifically the science of dealing with the light as discrete "quanta," or "particles" of energy (in contrast to the sciences of *color* and photography, which treat light in terms of waves). In a phototube, a "photon" of light strikes a metallic surface, which contains electrons. As the photon hits an electron, it disappears, imparting all of its energy to the electron. This additional energy causes the electron to flow from the metallic surface. And it is the flow of electrons that produces an electric current. The electrons are collected by an anode which then allows the electric current produced to accomplish whatever it was designed to accomplish. In a photomultiplier tube, the electrons released by a phototube hit an additional electrode called a "dynode," which generates a set of secondary electrons. This secondary set of electrons is much greater in number than the original number of electrons hitting it. These secondary electrons hit a second dynode, generating even more electrons, and so on for several stages, until finally being collected by an anode. Essentially, then, the photomultiplier tube converts a small amount of light into a strong electric current.

In digital imaging devices, in particular *drum scanners*, photomultiplier tubes are used to sense very low levels of light and amplify them into strong electronic signals, which can then be converted to digital information describing color values. It is the high sensitivity of the photomultiplier tube that allows drum scanners to excel at producing a *color separation*, as even small amounts of tonal variation can be detected.

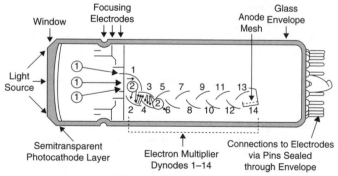

Photomultiplier tube.

Photopolymer

A soluble, light-sensitive, organic substance that undergoes *polymerization* when exposed to light. A photopolymer coating is applied to several types of printing plates used in *offset lithography*. Commonly used photopolymers are esters of cinnamic acid (produced by reacting cinnamic acid—denoted $C_9H_8O_2$ and derived from cinnamon—with an alcohol, resulting in the release of a molecule of water). When light comes into contact with these molecules, they form large chain molecules. (See *Polymerization*.) The advantages of photopolymer plates are their high abrasion resistence and durability, as well as their ability to resist temperature and humidity changes. Thermal curing of photopolymers after plate processing enhances their durability, and results in the ability to use such plates for print runs in excess of 1,000,000 impressions. (See *Photopolymer Plate* and *Plate: Offset Lithography*.)

Photopolymer emulsions are also used as *resist* coatings for use in chemical etching of an image-carrying *gravure cylinder*. See *Gravure Etching: Direct-Transfer Process*. Photopolymers are also widely used in exposing printing plates for *flexography*. See *Plates: Flexography*. Photopolymers are also used as emulsions in photostencils used in *screen printing*. See *Photostencil*.

Photopolymer Plate

A type of printing plate used in *offset lithography* based on the same principle as *diazo plate*s. A light-sensitive coating is applied to the surface of an aluminum plate; it is then exposed to light via a photographic negative or positive, which causes the coating to harden in image areas and remain soluble in nonimage areas (when exposed via a photographic negative; see also *Positive-Working Plate*). A chemical treatment after exposure removes the coating in the nonimage areas, making those portions of the plate water-receptive, while the hard, durable image areas remain ink-receptive. Photopolymer plates utilize coatings that provide more durable and abrasion-resistant image areas than do diazo coatings, and consequently photopolymer plates can be used for longer print runs (up to 250,000 impressions). Upon exposure to light, the molecules in the coating undergo *polymerization*, or the joining together of smaller molecules to form long chains of higher-molecular-weight molecules, which are responsible for the high degree of durability. (See *Photopolymer*.) Special thermal curing processes after exposure and developing make the image areas even more durable, and have been known to be able to last for print runs in excess of 1,000,000 impressions. New developments in photopolymer plates include dye-sensitized photopolymers that can be etched by lasers, making them well-suited for use in computer-to-plate platemaking. (See *Plate: Offset Lithography*.)

A *photopolymer plate* also refers to one of two types of plates used in *flexography*. The photopolymers used in flexo plates can be either *sheet photopolymer*s or *liquid photopolymer*s. See *Plate: Flexography*, *Sheet Photopolymer*, and *Liquid Photopolymer*.

Photoposterization

In graphics, a *posterization* effect achieved photographically. See *posterization*.

Photo-Reactive Vehicle

A type of ink *vehicle*—the fluid carrier of the ink *pigment*—that dries upon contact with various types of radiation, designed to obviate the need for spray powders in sheetfed printing and to eliminate air pollution generated by the *solvents* in traditional *heatset inks*. Photo-reactive vehicles contain *resins*, along with *monomers* and special chemicals called "initiators" that, upon exposure to high amounts of ultraviolet radiation, release *free radicals* that polymerize and harden the vehicle, leaving behind the hard, solid resin.

These inks do not require heat (but they do require UV radiation) and due to their complex chemistry tend to be much more expensive than traditional inks. However, they emit no harmful or *volatile* substances. There are currently two varieties of photo-reactive vehicles. See *Ultraviolet (UV) Curing Ink* and *Electron Beam (EB) Curing Ink*. (See also *Vehicle*.)

Photorealism

A goal of three-dimensional (3D) modeling that aims to render objects as they would look if encountered in the real world, i.e., accurate light reflection, accurate shading, perspective, etc.

Photoreceptor

Any electronic light-sensing device, especially one used in a *scanner*. See *Scanner*.

Photorepro

A type of *reproduction proof* of phototypeset copy generated directly by a phototypesetter, or by contact printing of negatives of phototypeset material.

Photoresist

Shorthand term for a *photosensitive resist*. See *Resist*.

Photoscreen

A term used in *screen printing* to refer to either a *photostencil* in general, or a screen fabric that has had a photosensitive *emulsion* applied prior to exposure in the *direct process*. See *Photostencil: Direct Process*.

Photoscreen Stencil

Alternate term for *photostencil*. See *Photostencil*.

Photosensitive Resist

See *Resist*.

Photosensitizer

Any chemical or other material that can be applied to an *emulsion* to render it sensitive to light, or which undergoes chemical reactions when exposed to *actinic rays*.

Photostat

A photographic print made of *line art*.

Photostencil

Any type of stencil used in *screen printing* that is coated with a photosensitive *emulsion* and exposed to the original artwork to be printed, in contrast to a *hand-cut stencil*. There are three processes used to prepare photostencils:

Indirect Process. The *indirect process* employs a dry photosensitive emulsion which has been coated onto a clear plastic backing sheet. A film positive is placed in contact with the transparent backing sheet and exposed to ultraviolet light. The ultraviolet light shines through the positive and the base in the nonimage areas hitting the emulsion beneath, and post-exposure development (utilizing either hydrogen peroxide or water, depending upon the exact nature of the emulsion) hardens those portions of the photostencil emulsion. The ultraviolet light does not penetrate the image areas of the positive, and consequently the corresponding portions of the emulsion remain soft and insoluble and can consequently be washed away with water (or other fluid) after exposure and developing, forming the open regions of the stencil. This washout procedure also varies according to the stencil material, and can utilize either hot water (95–105°F) or cooler water (about 70°F).

The stencil is washed until a clear, sharp stencil image appears, and the development process can usually be stopped (or, in other words, the image "fixed") with cold water. The stencil is then applied to the bottom of the screen, typically using only the water from the washout process, and, when dry, the plastic backing sheet is removed. *Blockout solution* is then applied to the open portions of the screen fabric beyond the edges of the stencil, and the solution is also used to touch up any pinholes that turned up in the stencil during exposure. Once the blockout solution is dry, the stencil is ready to print.

Direct Process. In the *direct process*, a liquid emulsion—often composed of *polyvinyl chloride*, a *gelatin*-based substance, or some combination thereof plus a *bichromate*-based photosensitizer—is applied directly to the surface of the screen fabric (commonly by means of a *scoop coater*). Similar to the indirect process, a film positive of the image to be printed is placed in contact with the wet emulsion and exposed to ultraviolet light, which, as above, hardens the nonimage areas and leaves the image areas soft and soluble. The image areas are then washed away after exposure, producing the openings in the stencil. When the emulsion is dry, the screen is ready for printing. A printing screen prepared in this manner is known as a *photoscreen*.

Direct/Indirect Process. As its name implies, the *direct/indirect process* is a combination of the previous two processes. An unsensitized film backing is placed on the stencil side of the screen fabric. On the top side of the

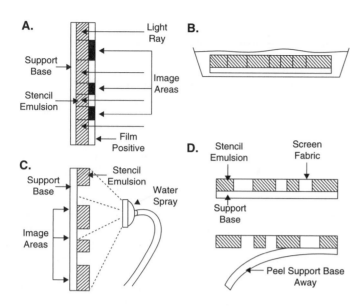

The process of exposing an indirect stencil: (A) a film positive allows light to strike only the nonimage areas, which then harden during development (B). After exposure, the unhardened image areas are washed away (C), leaving those areas of the stencil open. Finally, the stencil is adhered to the screen fabric (D).

screen, a liquid emulsion and a photosensitizing agent are applied, and seep through the screen to coat the backing film. When the emulsion/sensitizer mixture are dry, the film backing is removed, leaving the emulsion on the screen. At this point, a similar exposure as outlined above is performed. The primary advantage of this process is the ability to produce a uniform emulsion thickness throughout the stencil.

There is no simple formula for determining proper exposure times for photostencil emulsions. Each manufacturer has specific recommendations, but these can vary according to the application. The use of a **step wedge** is often used to calibrate photostencil emulsion times. (See **Step Wedge**.)

Phototypesetter

In typography, a device used to set type photographically, generally with some degree of computer assistance. The machine exposes and outputs photosensitive paper or film according to the signals that it receives.

The term *phototypesetter* also refers to the person who sets type using phototypesetting equipment.

Phototypesetting

In typography, the setting of type or the preparation of copy for printing in which light is shined through a photomatrix (or outline of the character to be imaged) onto a photosensitive film or paper which, after development, bears the set type with the specifications indicated during input. Also called **photocompositing** and **photocomposition**.

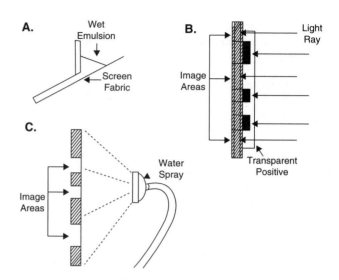

The process of exposing a direct stencil: (A) a wet emulsion is applied directly to the screen fabric, and exposed to actinic light through a film positive (B), where nonimage areas harden. After exposure, washing (C) removes the unhardened image areas, leaving holes in the stencil.

Phototypography

Any photographic typesetting process.

Photounit

The housing for the optics, energy source, and photographic materials on which a typographic image is produced in **phototypesetting**.

PhotoYCC

A **color space** used in the Kodak **Photo CD**. See **Photo CD**.

Phthalocyanine Blues

A series of **organic color pigments** used in printing inks. Most of the Phthalocyanine Blues mentioned below are categorized as *CI Pigment Blue 15*, each one differing from the others in one respect or another, and are modifications of PB 15.

Phthalocyanine Blue (Alpha Form) is a strong red shade of blue, and possesses high **lightfastness** and resistance to acids, alkalis, heat, waxes, oils, solvents, and soaps. It is the least used of the PB 15 pigments, but is occasionally used in newsinks. This variety is a solvent-unstable form of PB 15. (*CI Pigment Blue 15 No. 74160.*)

Phthalocyanine Blue (Alpha, Solvent-Stable) is a bright red shade of blue, and possesses high lightfastness and resistance to acids, alkalis, heat, waxes, oils, solvents, and soaps. It is the most commonly used of the PB 15 pigments, accounting for 25% of the PB 15 use. It is more resistant to heat and more solvent-stable than the alpha form above.

Also known as *Phthalo Blue NC Alpha (CI Pigment Blue 15:1 No. 74160 or 74250 .)*

Phthalocyanine Blue NCNF (Alpha Form, Solvent-Stable, Nonflocculating) is a bright red shade of blue, and possesses many of the same properties as PB 15:1, differing in that the pigment particles have been treated to prevent *flocculation*, or undesirable clumping together of the particles. It is more expensive than PB 15 or 15:1, but accounts for about 5% of PB 15 use.

(*CI Pigment Blue 15:2 No. 74160 or 74250.*)

Phthalocyanine Blue NC (Beta Form, Solvent-Stable) is a bright green shade of blue, and possesses high lightfastness and high resistance to acids, alkalis, heat, waxes, oils, solvents, and soaps. It is transparent, solvent-stable, has strong tinting strength, but is weaker than alpha forms of Phthalocyanine Blue. It is the most commonly used cyan in process color printing, as it is usable in every type of ink and printing process.

(*CI Pigment Blue 15:3 No. 74160.*)

Phthalocyanine Blue B NCNF is a bright green shade of blue possessing all the high resistance properties of the other PB 15 pigments. This version, like PB 15:2, has been treated to prevent flocculation of the pigment particles. It is used primarily in liquid inks, and is also useful as a process color cyan.

(*CI Pigment Blue 15:4 No. 74160.*)

Phthalocyanine Blue (Epsilon Form) is a strong red shade of blue, and possesses all the high resistance properties of the Phthalo Blue series. It is the only solvent-stable reddish shade in the series, and finds most of its use in liquid-ink applications.

(*CI Pigment Blue 15:6 No. 74160.*)

Phthalocyanine Blue (Copper Free) is the greenest shade of Phthalo Blue, and possesses the high resistance properties of other Phthalo Blue pigments, although it tends to be less heat resistant than other versions. (Its primary difference, as its name indicates, is the lack of copper in its molecular structure.) It is more expensive than other Phthalo Blues, and is limited to use in applications requiring a metal-free ink.

(*CI Pigment Blue 16 No. 74100.*)

(See also *Organic Color Pigments*.)

Phthalocyanine Greens

An *organic color pigment* used in printing inks. *CI Pigment Green 7 No. 74260* is a blue-green pigment with high *lightfastness* and chemical resistance to most substances. It is also transparent and possesses high tinting strength. It is the green standard in most printing inks.

CI Pigment Green 36 No. 74265 is used to expand the range of shades not covered by Pigment Green 7 above, ranging from blue to yellow. (Adding more bromine atoms to the molecule increases the yellowness of the pigment.) It retains the lightfastness and the remarkable resistance properties of Green 7, though it is more expensive. (See *Organic Color Pigments*.)

Physical Address

In computing, the *address* of an attached peripheral device determined by settings on the board or adapter to which it is attached.

Physical Dot Area

Alternate term for *dot area*. See *Dot Area*.

Physical Dot Gain

A physical increase in the size of a *halftone dot* when printed, as opposed to *optical dot gain*, an optical phenomenon that gives the illusion of dots increasing in size. See *Dot Gain*.

Physical Drive

An actual, tangible disk drive that can be attached to a computer, as opposed to a *logical drive*. A single physical drive may be subdivided into several logical drives.

Physical Layer

In networking, the first of seven *layer*s in the *OSI* reference model, defining the electrical and mechanical means by which different devices are connected to each other. See *Open Systems Interconnection (OSI)*.

Physical Page

A page that one can physically hold in one's hand, such as a sheet of paper, in contrast to an electronic page.

Physical Unit (PU)

In networking, especially by means of IBM's *Systems Network Architecture (SNA)*, any physical device connected to the network and its attendant resources. See also *Logical Unit (LU)*.

Pi Characters

In typography and typesetting, a collection of special characters, such as *mathematics*, *fractions*, monetary symbols, or decorative symbols, such as $\sum$, $\sqrt{}$, $\int$, ½, ¼, ⅛, \$, ¥, £, *, •, %, etc. *Accents* are also available as pi characters. (The characters themselves—whether they are available in a standard typeface or not—are called *pi characters*; when available only in special fonts—such as Zapf Dingbats—they are referred to as *pi font*s.)

A type manufacturer can create customized pi fonts for special needs, and new software programs allow for the easy creation of special digital fonts. Special fonts were developed for television listings, for example. Other types of pi characters include ®, ‰, °, ¢, §, ¶, π, #, @, etc.

In handset metal type, *pi* also referred to the type of one style mistakenly put in the storage drawer of another style. When setting handset type, one of these mismatched letters would be thrown into a box of "pi type," also known as the *hell box*, to be sorted out later or returned to the type foundry for a credit. *Pi* also referred to handset type that had spilled or collapsed, a feared occurrence blamed on the *printer's devil*—the apprentice.

It is unknown if the etymology of "pi character" has anything to do with the Greek letter (and mathematical symbol) *pi* (π). It may even come from the common word "pie" (indicative of something "jumbled together"), and *pi type* is also known as *pied type*.

Pi Font

In typography, a special *font* containing *pi characters*. See *Pi Characters*.

Pi Type

In typography, metal type characters of one *font* that have been mixed up—purportedly accidentally—with characters of another font. *Pi type* also refers to unexpected or garbled phototypesetter output, and to *pi characters*. See *Pi Characters*. The aggravation of mixing similar letters in the same tray resulted in the dictum to printers' apprentices to "mind your p's and q's."

PIC

A *file extension* denoting a variety of *bitmap* files, such bas those created by PC Paint, among others. This *file format*, however, is limited to 256 colors.

Pica

A basic unit of measurement in typography. One pica equals 12 *point*s, and 6 picas equal approximately 1 in. (Actually, 6 picas equal 0.996 in.) See *Point System*.

The term *pica* also refers to a 10-pitch (10 characters per horizontal inch) typewriter *font*. See also *Elite*.

Pica Point

In typography, the basic unit of type measurement used in North America and Great Britain, equal to approximately ¹⁄₇₂ in., or ¹⁄₁₂ *pica*, in contrast to the *Didot point* widely used in Europe. See *Point System*.

Pick

When used as a noun, the degree to which a substance (such as paper) will allow bits of its surface to be removed by a tacky printing ink. See *Picking*. When used as a verb, the act of removing these surface materials.

Pick also refers to an event triggered by an electronic pointing device that reports identifying data for the detected display item and the segment containing it.

Pick Resistance

Also called *surface strength*, the extent to which a paper can withstand a force applied at right angles to its surface (such as that generated by a sticky ink film during printing) without rupturing, or *picking*. Picking can include either a delamination of the plys of a paper and/or a partial or total removal of a paper *coating*. Pick resistance is enhanced by increased *internal bond strength*, as well as increased fiber *refining* prior to papermaking, a decreased use of *fillers*, increased *surface sizing*, or a more liberal use of *binders* in *coatings*. However, pick resistance is increased to the detriment of other properties (see *Paper and Papermaking: Paper Properties*.) Pick resistance is more of a concern in *letterpress* and *offset* printing than in other printing processes. The term *wet pick resistance* refers to a paper's ability to resist picking after it has been exposed to moisture (in contrast to its *dry pick resis-*

tance). Moisture can decrease a paper's surface bond strength, making it more susceptible to picking (called *wet picking*, in contrast to *dry picking*).

Various tests can determine the pick resistance of a paper. (See *Dennison Wax Test* and *Printability Tester*.) The pick resistance for offset papers is best determined, however, in conditions that best simulate printing processes using progressively tackier inks and a *pick tester*.

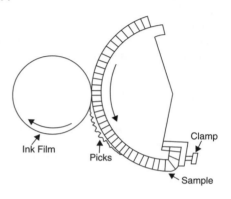

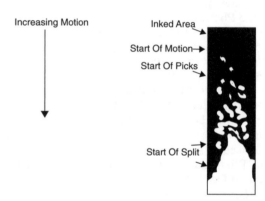

Pick test using an IGT printability tester.

Pick Tester

A device used to determine a paper's *pick resistance* by means of a series of inks with progressively greater degrees of tack. (See *Picking* and *Pick Resistance*.)

Picking

Rupturing or other deformation of a paper's surface caused during ink transfer by the force of a sticky ink either separating the layers of a paper, forming a blister-like protrusion in the paper, or removing portions of the paper's *coating*. Picking occurs when the force of an ink film exceeds the paper's *pick resistance*, or *surface strength*. (See *Pick Resistance*.) There are two forms of picking: *dry picking* happens when water is not present; *wet picking* is the result of decreased pick resistance stemming from exposure to moisture prior to printing. *Tearing* is an extreme form of picking that rips off the paper surface, leaving a delaminated portion on the press sheet, and *splitting* is the tearing off of large areas of the paper surface, which then stick to the blanket. Small particles that are picked out of the paper surface are called *pickouts*. Picking is also called *plucking*.

Picking also describes a similar problem of *gravure* printing in which bits of the substrate are transferred to the *impression roller* or other roller.

The term *picking* also refers to a printing problem occurring in multicolor flexographic printing in which the plates of successive colors remove bits of the first printed color, commonly caused by printing on still-wet ink. Flexographic picking can be alleviated by ensuring that the first-down color has the most rapid drying time.

Pickout

Term for any foreign particle embedded in a paper surface that is pulled out of the paper by the press's blanket during printing. The most common cause of pickouts are random bits of particles of *filler*, *sizing*, *coatings*, etc., that collect on papermaking machine rollers, felts, or drying cylinders and get pressed into the moving paper *web*. Common sources of pickouts are scale, rust, and *slime spots*. (See also *Calender Spots*.)

Pickup

Alternate term for *lip*. See *Lip*.

Pickup Sucker

A vacuum-powered suction cup used in a sheetfed offset press *sheet-separation unit* to pick up the topmost sheet of the pile and lift it for transfer to the *feedboard*. On a *stream feeder*, the pickup suckers are located toward the rear of the pile and work to lift the topmost sheet, while a second set of *forwarding sucker*s grabs the sheet and moves it to the feedboard. On a *single-sheet feeder*, one set of pickup suckers is located at the gripper (or front) edge of the pile and performs both lifting and fowarding jobs. See *Sheet-Separation Unit* and *Feeder Section: Sheetfed Offset Lithography*.

Picon

In computer graphics, an *icon* representing a graphics file, comprising a small version of the illustration, used for preview and quick identification purposes.

PICT

A *file format* for *Macintosh*-based *vector* and *bitmapped* images. It is primarily used for clipboard images and *screen capture*s, among other things. There are two varities of the PICT format: PICT (known in retrospect as PICT1) can store only eight colors (white, black, cyan, magenta, yellow, red, green, and blue), and *PICT2*, an expanded version of the format capable of either *eight-bit (8-bit) color* (or 256 different colors) or *twenty-four-bit (24-bit) color* (or 16.7 million different colors). Although the PICT formats are widely used for multimedia images, they are limited in usefulness for other applications.

PICT2

See *PICT*.

Pictograph

In graphic communication, a symbol representing an object, such as an ox or a house. Pictographs were an early stage in the development of the alphabet; hieroglyphics were a form of pictograph. The term *pictograph* derives from the Greek words *pictus* (meaning "painted") and *graphein* (meaning "writing"). It was a forerunner of true writing used either for descriptive-representational purposes (such as a series of pictographs "describing" a hunting expedition, which may consist of representations of buffalo or oxen, followed by pictures of men holding spears, etc.) or for identifying-mnemonic purposes (such as pictures which indicate the order of specific rites to be performed at a ceremony, or the verses to be sung in a song). Pictographs are often described in connection with *ideogram*s (from the Greek words *idea*—meaning "idea"—and *gramma*—meaning "something drawn or written"), which were pictorial representations of ideas (such as "love" or "home"), regardless of whether they were concrete, recognizable pictures. (The terms "picto*gram*" and "ideo*graph*" are also used interchangeably with "pictograph" and "ideogram.")

Pictographs and ideograms were used by early peoples to express a message directly, or to represent aspects of the spoken language. In the latter case, they became the earliest versions of what we would now call "true writing," in which a picture stood for a word or a part of a word. Such systems as Chinese, Egyptian hieroglyphics, Hittite, and Sumerian cuneiform were early examples of true writing based on pictorial representations of words and word-parts. As the writing evolved, gradually, more and more symbols became non-pictographic, as it became more economical in terms of both time and a writing surface to use simpler symbols than elaborate pictures. Sometimes, however, both pictographs and less elaborate symbols were used, depending upon the context. Early Egyptians, for example, had three systems of writing: hieroglyphic, hieratic, and demotic, in decreasing order of pictorial detail. Hieroglyphic writing was used on temples, tombs, and other ceremonial objects, where they were engraved into stone and then painted. Hieratic and demotic, which used simpler symbols, were used for official records and letters, where they were written on *papyrus*. It was from these early post-pictographic symbols that modern letterforms derived. One of the earliest true alphabets was Greek, from which the Roman alphabet later derived.

Picture Element

Full term for *pel* or *pixel*. See *Pixel*.

Picture-in-Picture (PIP)

In television and video, a means of showing one video image within another, one image apperaring in a small box in a corner of the larger image. PIP is often found in television sets and in video equipment.

Picture Method

A test performed to evaluate the ***roller setting*** of offset printing press ***form roller***s, consisting of essentially an inked representation of the roller setting. To determine the setting of the form rollers to the plate, the rollers are inked, the plate is packed to printing height and positioned underneath the form rollers, the form rollers are lowered to the plate to allow ink transfer, then are lifted up again. When the plate cylinder is rotated back around, there will be a set of printed stripes, the size and uniformity of which indicate the efficacy of the setting (and the condition of the rollers). In general, an ink stripe should be $\frac{1}{16}$ in. wide for every inch of roller diameter (for example, a 4-in.-diameter form roller should produce a stripe about ¼ in. wide). The stripes should be uniform in thickness across the plate. If a stripe is heavier at one end than at the other, the setting of the rollers is uneven and should be adjusted. If the stripe is wider in the center than it is at either end, or if the stripe is wider at *both* ends than it is in the center, roller damage is indicated, and they should be replaced or repaired. To test the setting of the form roller to the oscillator, the press is run for several seconds without contact between the form rollers and the plate, the press is then stopped, allowed to sit for about half a minute, then the cylinders are moved about 2–3 in. The stripe that appears on the oscillator (produced by the form roller at rest) should be examined for the same nonuniformities as the stripes on the plate. However, the stripe on the oscillator should be thicker than that on the plate, as the form roller should be set tighter to the oscillator than to the plate. The picture method is also called the ***ink stripe method***.

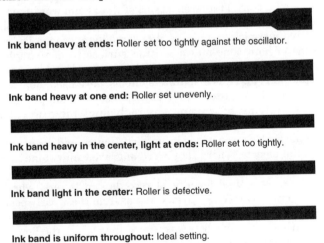

Ink band heavy at ends: Roller set too tightly against the oscillator.

Ink band heavy at one end: Roller set unevenly.

Ink band heavy in the center, light at ends: Roller set too tightly.

Ink band light in the center: Roller is defective.

Ink band is uniform throughout: Ideal setting.

Proper and improper roller stripes produced using the picture method of checking roller settings.

Picture Stop

On a ***videodisc***, a command that allows a moving video image to be stopped at the beginning of a predetermined ***chapter***. See ***Videodisc***.

Piece Accent

Alternate term for a ***centered accent***. See ***Accent***.

Piece Fraction

In typography, a type of ***fraction*** typeset using special characters consisting of the denominator and the slash, which are set in concert with other characters, such as superiors, for the numerator. These are available as ***em fraction***s or ***en fraction***s. The en variety is also known as a ***split fraction***. See ***Fractions***.

Pie Chart

A type of ***chart*** in which fractional divisions of a whole are represented as wedge-shaped "slices" of a circle. The size of each slice is typically in proportion to its fraction of the whole. See ***Chart***.

Pied Type

Alternate term for ***pi type***. See ***Pi Type***.

Piezo Electric Force Transducer

A type of computer monitor containing crystals which produce an electric signal when under pressure, often used for ***touch screen*** monitors.

PIF

Abbreviation for ***program information file***. See ***Program Information File (PIF)***.

PIG

A ***file extension*** denoting files created by Ricoh's IS30 Pixel Image Generation program.

Pig Bristles

In typography, term for text that contains too many hyphenated words. See ***Hyphenation***.

Piggyback Form

Alternate term for ***Carrier sheet***. See ***Carrier Sheet***.

Pigment

In papermaking, pigments are fine, inorganic particles added to fill, color, or coat paper. Pigments such as ***clay***, ***titanium dioxide***, and ***calcium carbonate*** are used as ***fillers*** and ***coatings*** in papermaking. When used as a paper coating, the pigment is applied in the presence of a ***binder***, which assists the pigment particles in adhering to the paper fibers. (See ***Coating***.)

In ink manufacturing, pigments are fine, insoluble, organic or inorganic particles of ***colorant*** that are suspended in the ***vehicle*** (which carries the pigment in the ink-transfer process and helps the pigment adhere to the ***substrate***) and provide not only the color of ink, but also such specific properties as transparency, ***opacity***, ***specific gravity***, and resistance to heat, chemicals, water, or oils.

Pigments, therefore, help determine the suitability of the ink to a particular printing process or end use.

Pigments can be primarily divided into black, white, and colored pigments, and there are a variety of different types of each. **Black pigments** include the **Carbon Blacks** (including **Furnace Black**—the most common type of black pigment—and **Channel Black**), **Vegetable Black**, and **Black Iron Oxides**.

White pigments come in two varieties, **opaque pigment**s and **transparent pigment**s. Opaque pigments, as their name implies, reflect light from their surface, and are used to hide the background on which they are printed. Transparent pigments allow light to pass through them, and are commonly added to other, more expensive inks to "pad them out" and reduce the use of expensive pigments. (Transparent pigments are also called **extender**s.) They are also used to reduce the color strength of other inks and to produce tints.

Inorganic color pigments include pigments of varying colors derived from mineral, or inorganic, sources. Inorganic color pigments include "Chromes," "Cadmiums," and "Irons." (See **Inorganic Color Pigments**.) A type of mixture containing co-precipitates of titanium and mica (or other minerals) is used to make a **pearlescent**, which are transparent and highly light-refractive, imparting to the ink film the luster characteristic of mother-of-pearl. (See **Pearlescent**.)

Organic Color Pigments are the most widely used pigments and are derived primarily from derivatives of coal tar. Organic color pigments tend to be brighter and stronger than their inorganic counterparts, and the presence of lead in inorganic pigments results in the desire for less toxic substitutes. (See **Organic Color Pigments**.)

Metallic powders are, as their name implies, produced from flakes of metal, in varying degrees of fineness and grade. Despite some of their names (such as "Rich Gold" and "Silver"), however, few metallic powder pigments come from precious metals. (See **Metallic Powders**.)

Flushed colors are colored pigments produced in a manner (called **flushing**) different from typical pigment manufacture. Typically, pigments begin life as a water suspension of pigment particles, which are then filtered out of the suspension and dried into a presscake. In flushing, the particles are not dried after filtering, but are left with a water content of as much as 80%, and the resulting presscake is mixed with oil, which then disperses the water. Flushing is performed on pigment particles that, in the traditional method of drying, form hard to grind clumps. The paste generated by flushing produces finer-dispersed particles.

Pigment Emulsion

An **emulsion**-type **screen printing** ink containing pigment particles to impart the desired color to the printed **substrate**.

Pigment Paper

A type of tissue paper possessing a **gelatin**-based pigmentized emulsion used as a **resist**. See **Resist**.

PIL

See **Publishing Interchange Language**.

Pilcrow

Actual name for the "backwards P" symbol (¶) used to signify the beginning of a new **paragraph** or as a **footnote** symbol. Derivation unhknown.

Pile Feeder

A mechanism attached to a sheetfed printing press which separates sheets of paper and feeds them into the press. See **Feeder Section** and **Pile Table**.

Pile Table

A platform that can be raised or lowered, on which the paper (or other **substrate**) to be used for printing is stored on a printing press. The stack of paper to be printed needs to be fanned, and stacked neatly on the platform, about ¼ in. off center (away from the moveable side guide on the table). Any observably defective sheets of paper (as well as other extraneous objects like ream markers) need to be removed. Paper with bent corners, tears, **wavy edges**, or **curl** need to be removed as well, as paper jams or poor prints will result. Once paper is loaded, the pile table is raised to the feeding height specified for the press and feeding mechanism. It is then the responsibility of the **sheet-separation unit** to feed the paper into the press. (See **Sheet-Separation Unit** and **Feeder Section: Sheetfed Offset Lithography**.)

With traditional pile tables, the press needs to be stopped when paper needs to be reloaded. However, some feeding systems allow for continuous feeding. The configuration of continuous systems varies from press to press, but

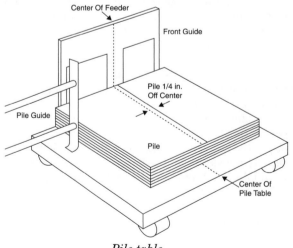

Pile table.

most involve either a secondary pile table that can be moved into position just as the stock on the first table is about to run out, or a pile supported by flat metal strips, which allows the pile table itself to be lowered and refilled without disturbing the feeding of the remaining sheets. The most obvious consideration with continuous systems is ensuring that the height of the pile being fed is not altered during reloading. Other feeders utilize a *roll sheeter*, in which a continuous roll of paper is inserted, and the feeding mechanism cuts the roll into individual sheets just prior to being fed into the press. (See *Roll Sheeter*.)

Pile Wedge

A wood or plastic *wedge* used in the *delivery pile* of a sheetfed printing press (especially that used in *offset lithography*) at the beginning of a pressrun. Two or more wedges are placed on the bottom of the delivery pile to support the back edge of the sheets and counteract the effects of *tail-end hook*, a deleterious curl at the back end of a press sheet. (See *Delivery Section*.)

Piling

A printing problem characterized by the accumulation of paper fibers (called *lint*), bits of detached *coating* particles, or other debris (such as *pickout*s) on the printing plate or blanket, in either image or nonimage areas, that affect *print quality*. Piling can result from a variety of causes in addition to basic surface debris, such as the use of tackier inks that overcome the paper's *pick resistance*, changes in the blanket's surface stickiness or increased blanket slippage, the chemical composition of the press's dampening system reacting with that of the paper, and various stresses imposed on a paper during feeding. Piling can be classified in a variety of ways, depending on the characteristics of the material. (See *Whitening*, *Powdering*, *Milking*, and *Image Area Piling*.) Piling not only affects print quality but can increase the rate of plate or blanket wear.

The term *piling* also refers to the accumulation on the plate or blanket of dry particles of ink. Ink piling commonly is caused by the inadequate *viscosity* of the ink *vehicle*, or an inadequate amount of vehicle, preventing the pigment from being transferred to the *substrate* with the vehicle and remaining behind on the plate or blanket. In some cases, an overly absorbent substrate will drain the vehicle away from the pigment while on the press, leaving the pigment to pile on the plate or blanket. In cases where the paper is to blame, the only solution is to use different paper. If the ink vehicle is inadequate, the addition of *body gum* may alleviate the problem, if there is no time for ink reformulation. Ink piling is also called *caking*.

Piling also refers to dried particles of ink that can collect on the *impression roller* or other rollers used in *gravure* printing.

PIM

Abbreviation for *Personal Information Manager*. See *Personal Information Manager (PIM)*.

Pin Feed

In a computer printer, a means of feeding paper through the imaging mechanism by means of a series of pins or pegs mounted on a rotating wheel that fit into holes punched into the sides of the paper. Also called *tractor feed* and *sprocket feed*.

Pin Register

A set of accurately positioned holes punched on films, *mechanical*s, *flat*s, etc., and a set of corresponding metal pins used during the various phases of *prepress* to ensure that multiple films, mechanicals, or flats to be imaged on a single page are kept in *register*.

Pin-Compatible

In computing, descriptive of a chip (be it a microprocessor, memory module, etc.) that has the same number and configuration of pins as another similar device. Pin compatibility facilitates upgrading and expansion of system components, as a newer chip can easily replace an older one. See also *Plug-Compatible*.

Pinch-Bottom Open-Mouth (PBOM)

In packaging, a type of paper *bag* in which the bottom is pinched and sealed shut, the top being left unsealed prior to filling. After filling, the top is sealed shut using a *hot-melt adhesive*. See *Bag: Paper Bags*.

Ping

In networking, to transmit a diagnostic data *packet* to a *node* on the network to verify that the node in question is connected properly to the network. Typically, the test packet is an *echo* request, thus forcing the receiving node to send a packet back to the original sender. "Ping" may or may not be an acronym for "Packet Internet Groper" (especially when used with *TCP/IP* systems).

Pinhole

In *gravure*, *flexography*, and *screen printing*, the result of *pinholing*. See *Pinholing*.

In photography, pinholes are small, transparent dots that appear in nonimage areas of a negative (or small black dots that appear in the nonimage areas of a positive) produced by dust on the lens, copy, copyboard, or film. Pinholes also appear in nonimage areas of *photostencil*s.

In papermaking, pinholes are small imperfections in the surface of a paper, produced by foreign particle contamination during forming.

Pinholing

A printing defect, commonly found in *flexographic* and *gravure* printing processes (and occasionally in *screen printing*), characterized by an incomplete ink film comprising small holes, caused by the failure of an ink to wet the entire surface of the *substrate*. The use of additives can frequently overcome the problem of pinholing. In gravure printing, pinholing can also be caused by the presence of air bubbles in the ink, which transfer to the cells and print as voids. In flexography, there are two varieties of pinholing: ***chemical pinholing*** and ***mechanical pinholing***.

Pinouts

In an electric or electronic ***connector***, term for the function and configuration of each pin.

PIP

Abbreviation for ***picture-in-picture***. See ***Picture-in-Picture (PIP)***.

Pipe

Term for the short vertical symbol (|) found as the shift of the ***backslash*** key on computer keyboards. Not often typeset, it is primarily used in computer documentation.

In computing, the term *pipe* refers to a portion of a computer's memory that is used by a specific command to transfer data to a second command for processing. A specific type of pipe used in ***interprocess communication*** is called a ***named pipe***. In some operating systems, a pipe is symbolized by the pipe symbol (|).

Pipe Roller

A type of hard, small-diameter roller used in an offset press ***inking system*** to remove ink skin particles, ***lint*** and other debris from the ink, keeping the inking system clean and reducing the production of ***hickey***s and other printing defects.

Pipelining

In computing, a means of queueing up successive instructions for the processor to ensure that there is never any idle time. As soon as one instruction is processed, the next instruction is ready.

Pitch

In typography, a term for the number of characters a ***fixed pitch*** typewriter or printer will print per inch. Ten-pitch, or ***pica***, is used to refer to a pitch of 10 characters per inch. Twelve-pitch, or ***elite***, is used to refer to a pitch of 12 characters per inch.

In printing ink terminology, *pitch* is used to refer to a black, bituminous, asphaltic material added as either a solid or semi-solid to printing inks as a means of increasing ink ***length*** or decreasing ink ***viscosity***.

Pits

Laser-engraved depressions in the surface of a ***compact disc***, the pattern of which is how information is encoded. The pattern is controlled by the size of the interstitial ***lands***. See ***Compact Disc (CD)***.

Pixel

Shorthand term for *picture element*, or the smallest point or dot on a computer monitor. Any computer display is divided into rows and columns of tiny dots, which are individual

points at which the scanning electron beam has hit the phosphor-coated screen. The pixel is the smallest indivisible point of display on a monitor. The ***dot pitch*** is the measure of the diameter of an individual pixel; a monitor with a dot pitch of 0.28, for example, is composed of pixels 0.28 millimeter in diameter. The number of pixels per inch or lines of pixels per inch is a measure of screen ***resolution***. It is commonly expressed as the horizontal and vertical dimensions of the ***pixel array***; for example, a monitor described as 640×480 possesses 640 pixels across by 480 pixels down. The greater the number of pixels per inch, the better the resolution. The measure of the number of ***bit***s used to describe a pixel is known as ***color depth***. (See ***Color Depth***.) A pixel is also known as a ***pel***, which is also short for *picture element*.

The term *pixel* is also used to refer to the smallest point that a ***scanner*** can detect, or is synonymous with the ***sampling rate*** of the scanner. A scanner that takes 500 samples per inch (or, in other words, 500 discrete points of imaging each inch) can be said to have a resolution of 500 pixels per inch (also known as ***dots per inch (dpi)***). The resolution at which a scanner will capture an image can be varied.

The term *pixel* is also used to refer to the individual printer ***spot***s that make up an image produced on a ***laser printer*** or ***imagesetter*** or other digital output device. These pixels are more commonly down as "dots" or, more correctly, "spots."

Pixel Array

On either a computer monitor or digital output, the two-dimensional grid of ***pixel***s that define the form and color of a digital image.

Pixel Density

Alternate term for ***resolution***, especially of a computer monitor. See ***Resolution***.

Pixel Depth

Alternate term for ***color depth***. See ***Color Depth***.

Pixelization

A special effect available in image-processing programs that converts ***continuous-tone*** images into large rectangular blocks, used to deliberately impart a "digitized" look to an image. *Pixelization* is also an undesirable condition of digital images in which the individual pixels are large enough to be egregiously visible. Also called ***pixellation***.

Pixellation

See ***pixelization***.

Pixel Manipulation

Altering the color or position of individual ***pixel***s in a digital image.

Pixel-Oriented

Alternate term for ***bitmapped***. See ***Bitmapped***.

Pixel Replication

A type of *upsampling* of a digital image, effected by increasing the number of *pixel*s in an image, but without adding any data or detail. The new colored pixels are often interpolated using the original pixels. Image quality is not often very high when images are enlarged in this manner.

Pixel Swopping

An image-manipulation procedure in which pixels from one area of a digital image are copied and pasted into another section of the image, used either to slightly retouch images (such as removing a facial blemish from a portrait) or significantly alter the image's content (such as replacing the nose of a person in a portrait with a third eye).

Pixels Per Inch (ppi)

A measure of the *resolution* of a computer monitor, *scanner*, or output device such as a *laser printer* or *imagesetter*. Each of these devices generates or displays images that are composed of many tiny dots (called *pixel*s or *spot*s). The resolution is determined by measuring how many of these pixels can fit in a unit of linear distance, such as an inch. See *Resolution*. Also referred to as *dots per inch (dpi)*.

Plain Edges

In *binding and finishing*, trimmed edges of a book which have had no *edge treatment*.

Plain Paper

Descriptive of a computer printer or fax machine which can print on regular cut-sheet paper, rather than specially cut or coated papers.

Planographic

Referring to a printing process, in particular *lithography*, in which the image area of the plate carrying the image to be printed is the same height (or on the same plane) as the nonimage areas. Planographic printing processes use the principle of chemical repulsion between oil-based inks and water to keep image areas and nonimage areas separate. (See *Lithography*.)

Planography

A printing process, in particular *lithography*, in which the image area of the plate carrying the image to be printed is the same height (or on the same plane) as the nonimage areas, as opposed to relief or *letterpress* printing (where the image areas are raised above the nonimage areas) or *gravure* (where the image areas are engraved *below* the nonimage areas). Planographic printing processes use the principle of chemical repulsion between oil-based inks and water to keep image areas and nonimage areas separate. The process of *lithography* (which literally means "stone writing") is less commonly, but more appropriately, called *planography*. See *Lithography*.

Plasma Panel (PP)

A type of computer display comprising a grid of electrodes enclosed in a gas-filled space. When a difference in electrical potential is generated by adjacent electrodes, the gas in that area is ionized (the term "plasma" refers not only to a component of blood, but also to ionized gas) and emits light. Also known as a *gas plasma display (GPD)*.

Plastic Comb Binding

See *Comb Binding*.

Plastic Laminated Paper

A *cover paper* coated with a layer of plastic to impart protection or enhanced *gloss* to the paper.

Plastic Plate

A reproduction of a printing plate used in *letterpress* printing that, due to its decreased weight, can be easily and inexpensively shipped.

Plasticizer

Any of a wide variety of substances added—in either solid or liquid form—to a *substrate* or to a printing ink as a means of increasing flexibility, *viscosity*, or softness.

Plastisol

An organic fluid containing a suspension of particles (commonly *polyvinyl chloride* resins) in a *plasticizer*, similar to an *organosol* but containing no *solvent*s.

Plate

The basic image-carrying surface in a printing process, which can be made of a variety of substances, such as various metals (as those used in *letterpress* and *lithography*), rubber, or plastic (such as those used in *flexography*). The image areas of a printing plate may either be raised above the nonimage areas (such as in letterpress or flexography) or on the same plane as the nonimage areas (as in lithography). The exact nature, composition, and method of *platemaking* depend on the printing process to be utilized.

Plates used in the various printing processes are detailed below. *Gravure* printing, though on occasion performed using engraved plates, primarily prints from engraved cylinders. See *Gravure Cylinder*. In *screen printing*, a screen with a mounted stencil is also known as a plate. See *Screen Printing*.

OFFSET LITHOGRAPHY

Plates used for lithography are commonly *photolithographic*, and can be produced in a variety of ways and from a variety of substances (commonly aluminum in combination with another metal, such as copper). All lithographic plates share a common feature: the image areas are rendered *oleophilic*, or receptive to oils—such as ink—and *hydrophobic*, or repellent to water, while the nonimage areas are rendered *oleophobic*, or repellent to oils, and *hydrophilic*, or receptive to water. Consequently, since oil and water do not mix with each other readily, the image areas are transferred to the *substrate* (commonly by means of an intermediate *blanket*) while the nonimage areas do not. It is up to the offset press *dampening system* to keep the nonimage areas properly ink-free. There are several types of lithographic plates in use today.

Diazo Plates. These utilize a *diazo* (an organic compound) coating, are *presensitized*, and can be made either from photographic negatives or positives (but are most commonly made from negatives). After exposure to high-intensity light, an emulsion developer (comprising an acid solution containing a lacquer and a gum-etch) is added to the surface. The unexposed portion of the coating (which, when made from photographic negatives, comprises the nonimage areas of the plate) is dissolved by the solution, and a treatment of gum makes these areas water-receptive. When diazo plates are made from photographic positives (in which case it is the image areas that are unexposed) special solvents are required to protect the image areas. Diazo plates can be used for print runs as large as 150,000. Special pre-lacquered diazo plates can be used for runs as large as 250,000. (See *Diazo Plate*.)

Photopolymer Plates. These are produced in a manner very similar to diazo plates, but the coatings used are more inert and abrasion resistant, and can consequently be used for longer print runs than is possible with diazo plates. Special thermal curing processes can give photopolymers an increased strength, allowing them to be used for print runs as high as 1,000,000. (See *Photopolymer Plate*.)

Silver Halide Plates. These utilize light-sensitive coatings similar to, although slower than, those used on photographic films. Silver halide plates can be exposed either photographically or by lasers guided by computer data. They are commonly used to print single-color documents from digital artwork. Silver halide emulsions can be used to coat anodized aluminum, and these are often used for color printing produced from digital artwork. (See *Silver Halide Plate*.)

Electrophotographic Plates. These, like the principles of electrostatic printing found in many photocopiers, use a photoconductor (either mounted on a drum or on the substrate) that is sensitized to light utilizing a corona discharge that impart a charge to the photoconductor. Upon exposure to light in the nonimage areas, the charge is dissipated, it remaining in the image areas, which then attracts an oppositely charged toner. A drum-type photoconductor uses a selenium or cadmium sulfide cylinder to receive the image, which is then transferred to paper or other substrate, which can then be used as a printing plate. In another type, the photoconductor is a coating on the substrate itself, the toned image being formed directly on the substrate. Such plates then need to be desensitized in a manner akin to other *photolithographic* plates. (See *Electrophotographic Plate*.)

Bimetal Plates. These are plates that are useful for long print runs. Copper, which is highly oleophilic, is electroplated on a hydrophilic metal, such as aluminum or stainless steel. Negative-working platemaking exposes the image areas to light, hardening the coating on top of the copper. The unexposed coating is then dissolved away, baring the copper, which is in turn removed chemically, baring the second metal beneath it. Some plates use a tertiary metal, which serves to merely support the other two and plays little role in the actual printing surface of the plate. Of primary advantage to these plates is their virtual indestructibility. (See *Bimetal Plate*.)

Ablation Plates. These are primarily used in computer-to-plate systems, and consist of digital information controlling laser diodes, which burn small holes in a coating applied to the surface of a polyester or metallic plate. Of primary advantage is the lack of chemical processing, which allows them to be mounted and imaged directly on the press. (See *Ablation Plate*.)

Heat-Sensitive Plates. These plates utilize heat (in the form of infrared radiation) rather than light as the means of exposing the image vs. nonimage areas. Their coatings typically consist of heat-sensitive polymers, etched by infrared laser diodes. With post-exposure curing processes, these plates can be made capable of print runs in excess of 1,000,000. (See *Heat-Sensitive Plate*.)

Hybrid Plates. These utilize two separate coatings, a conventional photopolymer as the bottom layer, a silver halide coating providing the top layer. As the top layer is exposed—either with lasers or conventional, high-intensity light—the bottom layer is exposed by ultraviolet light. Removal of the upper layer and chemical processing of the bottom layer produces the image and nonimage areas of the plate, printing being done from the bottom layer.

Of increasing importance and use today is the computer-to-plate system. (See *Platemaking*.)

Most lithographic plates are *surface plate*s, whose surfaces contain an oleophilic, light-sensitive coating. There are two basic categories of lithographic plates determined by the means used to expose them (in systems that do not utilize digital platemaking techniques): *negative-working* and *positive-working*. To produce negative-working plates, a negative of the piece to be printed is placed against the plate. Light shines through the negative in the image areas only, rendering only those regions of the plate hard and insoluble. Consequently, after exposure, the unexposed coating in the nonimage areas of the plate are dissolved away, or subtracted (this type of platemaking is thus called *subtractive*, especially when the coating has been pretreated with an image-reinforcing compound). A solution of *gum arabic* (or other gum, either natural or

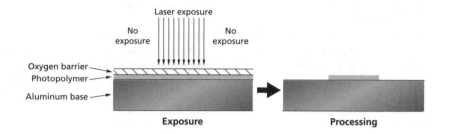

Photopolymer plates.

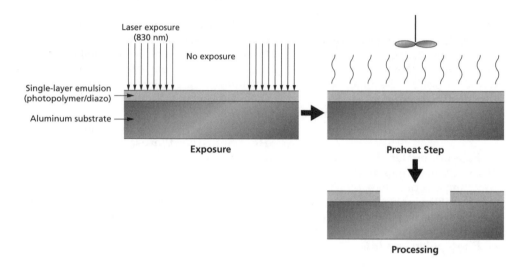

Thermal plates

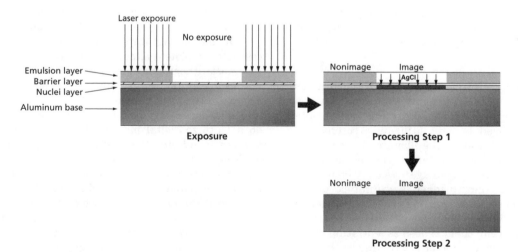

Silver halide plates on metal bases.

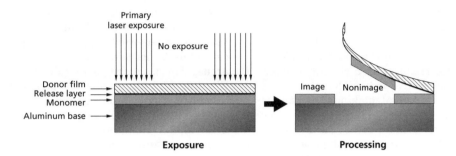

Laser ablation transfer.

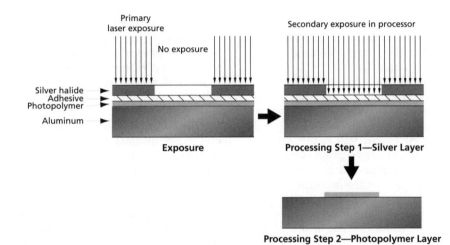

Hybrid plates.

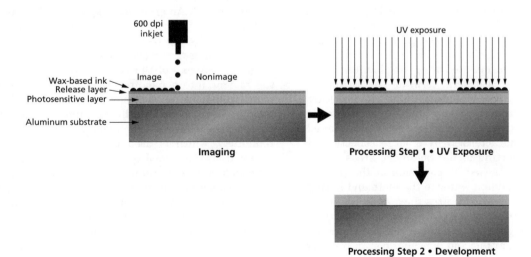

Ink jet plates.

synthetic) is used to further ***desensitize*** the nonimage areas of the plate, rendering them even more water-receptive. Some negative-working plates require the addition of a substance to reinforce the strength and durability of the plate coating in the image areas, and are thus called ***additive***. Positive-working plates are produced in a similar manner, except that a photographic positive is brought into contact with the unexposed plate during platemaking. The plate is exposed through the nonimage areas and un-exposed in the image areas. The coating is formulated so that the areas that are exposed to high-intensity light (i.e., the nonimage areas) are rendered soluble, and after exposure to light, chemical treatment removes the exposed portions of the plate. (See ***Platemaking***.) Both negative- and positive-working plates behave virtually identically on press.

After platemaking, the plate is mounted on the press's ***plate cylinder***. According to the press manufacturer's recommendation, the appropriate amount of ***packing*** (paper or plastic material) is inserted underneath the plate to raise the height of the plate surface. (See ***Packing***.) Once the plate is mounted, it is inked up to determine the ***lay***, or the position of the printed image on the paper (or other substrate). It may be necessary to adjust the position of the plate in order to center the image squarely on the paper. Once the pressrun is started, a properly formulated and adjusted inking and dampening system will keep the plate properly inked and dampened. Prolonged press stoppages, such as overnight, should be accompanied by a thorough cleaning of the plate; hardened gum on the image areas will render them ink-repellent. A finisher, such as an asphaltum-gum etch, can be applied to the surface of a plate, which will preserve the appropriate degrees of ink repellency and receptivity in nonimage and images areas, respectively.

As was mentioned earlier, a properly formulated ***fountain solution*** is important to prevent the accumulation of ink in nonimage areas of the plate, especially in those that lie between halftone dots. The film of hydrophilic gum added during initial plate desensitization wears off during the course of a print run, and it is the gum in the fountain solution that maintains this film. Improper retention of this film due to poorly formulated or applied fountain solution causes ***scumming***, a general term for the accumulation of ink in nonimage areas. Modern aluminum plates are easy to desensitize and keep desensitized, but scumming is still occasionally a problem. A variety of scumming, called ***ink dot scum***, is characterized by a large collection of small dots of ink collecting in the nonimage areas of the plate and is typically caused by corrosion of the plate—frequently a result of adding water to the plate and letting it evaporate so slowly that it oxidizes the aluminum, forming tiny pits in the surface of the plate that can collect ink. If ink dot scum is caught soon enough, it can be eliminated with a solution of gum arabic and phosphoric acid. If it has progressed too far, the plate is unusable.

A problem that can be considered as the reverse of scumming is ***plate blinding***, or a lack of ink receptivity in image areas, commonly caused by an abrasive force—such as ***form roller***s set too hard to the plate, too much pressure between the plate and ***blanket cylinder***, or excessively abrasive paper—rubbing off the image. Blinding can also be caused by a poor adhesion of the plate coating to the image areas, which can begin to rub off during the print run. Blinding is also caused by the gum in the dampening solution beginning to desensitize the image areas, which can be the result of too much gum in the dampening solution, too little ink flow from the ink fountain, a waterlogged ink, or a fountain solution that is too acidic, all of which gives the desensitizing gum a better foothold on undesirable regions of the plate. (See also ***Offset Lithography: Printing Unit***, ***Offset Lithography: Plates***, and ***Fountain Solution***.)

FLEXOGRAPHY

The first plates developed for flexographic printing were made of natural or, more commonly, synthetic rubber, and were manufactured much like letterpress plates. Although ***photopolymer plate***s are now widely used in flexographic platemaking, rubber still has its adherents, primarily because of its economy, its simplicity, and its compatibility with ink solvents that cannot be used with photopolymer plates.

Rubber Plates. Molded rubber plates are produced from etched metal masters, which are used to make molds, or matrices. A photographic negative of the image is placed on top of a metal sheet—typically magnesium, although photosensitive nylon photopolymers are becoming common for making masters—whose surface is coated with an acid ***resist***. The photosensitive resist is exposed to ultraviolet light through the image areas, causing those portions of the resist to harden and become insoluble. This leaves the nonimage areas unhardened, with varying degrees of hardness in between, depending on the amount of exposure received by the resist. After exposure, the metal sheet is washed, which dissolves the unexposed resist, leaving the exposed portions intact. An ***etchant*** is applied to the surface of the metal, where it engraves the plate only in those areas unprotected by the hardened resist (i.e., in the nonimage areas), leaving the image areas in relief. After etching, a mold—or matrix—of the relief plate is made by pressing the master into a molding sheet composed of a phenolic resin (commonly a thermosetting resin, which hardens upon exposure to heat), cellulose, and mineral fibers. Some matrix sheets also use a phenolic molding powder called Bakelite®, which is used to achieve extra depth of the image areas (i.e., when the image height on the final plate is needed to be more than 0.125 in.), which is necessary for some applications, such as the printing of corrugated board. Generally speaking, rubber plate relief height obtainable with sheet matrices ranges from 0.020–0.125 in. The matrix is produced in a molding press by pressing the metal relief master face down into the matrix material at high temperatures (300–310°F) for approximately 8–10 minutes. After curing, the master is removed from the matrix and the mold is allowed to cool. Brushing removes any foreign matter. When the matrix is ready to be used for molding the rubber plate, the correct thickness of the rubber sheet needed is determined by measuring the diameter of the plate cylinder on which it is to be mounted and ensuring that the thickness of the rubber will be enough to ensure proper contact with the inking *anilox roller* and the *impression cylinder*. The rubber sheet is pressed into the matrix at high pressure (600–1,000 psi) and temperature (300–310°F) for about 10 minutes. After removing the finished plate from the matrix, it is examined for undesirable variations in thickness and other defects. In many cases, excessive thickness can be corrected by grinding.

Photopolymer Plates. As was mentioned in the above discussion of photopolymer plates used in offset lithography, photopolymers are materials that, when exposed to light, undergo polymerization, or the chemical conversion of many small molecules into long-chain molecules. The result is that they will be harder and more insoluble in exposed areas and softer in unexposed areas. There are two basic types of photopolymer plates used in flexographic platemaking.

Sheet Photopolymers. As its name indicates, these plates are supplied as sheets, typically precut to the desired size. They are first exposed to ultraviolet light on one side to cure—or harden—the plate base. After exposure, the plate is flipped over, and a negative of the image to be exposed placed on top of it. The plate is again exposed to ultraviolet light, which exposes the image areas through the negative. After exposure, the plate is processed with chemicals that remove the unexposed nonimage areas, lowering those portions of the plate surface and leaving the image areas in relief. Post-exposure drying and a final dose of ultraviolet light cures and hardens the whole plate, making it printable.

Liquid Photopolymers. To manufacture liquid photopolymer plates, the film negative of the image to be exposed is placed on a glass plate and protected by a plastic transparent cover film. A layer of a liquid photopolymeric substance is applied to the surface of the cover film, typically accomplished by a motorized device that controls the thickness of the photopolymer and ensures that the application is uniform. It also applies on top of the liquid photopolymer a coated sheet that will bond with the photopolymer and serve as the plate base. Exposure on the base side of the plate facilitates the bonding of the photopolymer to the base. Then, a second ultraviolet light source below the negative exposes the photopolymer in the image areas of the negative, which causes those regions to solidify. The nonimage areas remain liquid, and are washed off after exposure, leaving the hardened image areas in relief. A final dose of ultraviolet light cures the whole plate.

Liquid photopolymer plates tend to have several advantages over solid sheet photopolymer plates, including shorter drying times, since the washout procedure only involves soap and water, whereas sheet photopolymers use solvents that impregnate the plate surface and need longer periods of time to be leached out. The thickness of the liquid photopolymer can also be varied at will, as opposed to having to rely on a standard set of sheet thicknesses.

One of the problems inherent in the use of flexible plates that are exposed flat, and then wrapped around a cylinder, is that of image elongation. Often, the film negative must be shrunk to compensate for image enlargement once the plate has been mounted on the press. A common formula for calculating the percentage that the negative needs to be reduced to compensate for image elongation is

$$\% \text{ reduction} = \frac{K}{R} \times 100\%$$

where K is a constant (provided by plate manufacturers) and R is the printing circumference of the plate cylinder (expressed as the repeat length of the cylinder). The K factor is dependent upon the plate thickness.

Because rubber plates have had the longer history of the two types of plates, there are more variations in rubber platemaking. The most widely used is known as a *plain-backed plate* and, as its name implies, it is simply the molded rubber plate with no special backing. A *shrink-controlled plate* sandwiches a sheet of fabric between layers of rubber, to ensure that no shrinkage of the plate occurs during molding, used primarily when print size and proper register of successive colors or images is important. A somewhat similar type of plate is a *metal-backed plate*, which molds and vulcanizes the rubber to a metal backing. Such plates, like some of those used on offset presses, have prepunched holes for accurate mounting on plate cylinder registration pins. Such plates tend to be easier to mount and more accurate than traditional adhesive-backed plates. Several types of *remounted plates* are produced on a removable metal cylinder or sleeve that can be slid onto the plate cylinder. Some varieties also produce the plate on a mountable carrier sheet. *Magnetic plates* have the rubber surface applied to a magnetic backing material, allowing the plate to be mounted on the plate cylinder magnetically, which allows for easy mounting and removal, as well as register adjustment.

One particular alternative to flexographic plates is a *design roll*, which is a printing cylinder containing a layer of rubber. The image areas are engraved directly on the rubber-covered cylinder, commonly using lasers. They are used primarily when seamless printing is required, such as for gift-wrapping, linerboard, security paper, etc. (See *Design Roll*.) (See also *Platemaking: Flexography* and *Flexography*.)

Plate Blinding

A printing problem of *offset lithography* characterized by a printing plate's loss of ink receptivity, commonly caused by an excessively acidic *fountain solution* eating away at the image areas of the plate. A solution is to raise the *pH* (i.e., make it less acidic) of the fountain solution. (See *Fountain Solution: pH*.)

Plate Clamp

Either of two devices located in the *cylinder gap* of an off-set press's *plate cylinder*, consisting of metal fingers that grasp both the leading and trailing edges (called the *head clamp* and *tail clamp*, respectively) of the offset plate and fasten it tightly and securely to the cylinder. There are a variety of configurations of plate clamps, some utilize a single quick-release cam, others involve a series of independently released metal fingers. Some can also be operated electronically from a press console to tilt the plate, if necessary. All clamps, regardless of configuration, allow the plate to be moved up or down or laterally, so as to position the image on the press sheet. On many newer configurations, plate clamps comprise a series of register pins that correspond to holes punched in the plates, allowing for proper positioning with a minimum of, if any, further adjustment. (See *Plate Cylinder*.)

Plate Cylinder

The part of a printing press to which a *plate* is attached and which transfers the inked image to either a rubber *blanket* (as in *offset lithography*) or directly to the substrate itself (as in *letterpress* and *flexography*.)

Offset Lithography. The part of an offset press to which the metal plate is attached, and which transfers the inked image areas to the rubber blanket. The surface of the plate cylinder commonly contains a *cylinder gap* which occupies about 20% of its circumference. The purpose of the gap is two-fold: it houses the *plate clamp*s, to which the plate is attached and secured, and it allows the inking system to renew a full quantity of ink between sheets. Each end of the cylinder has a metal ring called a *bearer*, the diameter of which is the actual diameter of the cylinder, and of the gear that drives the cylinder. (Older presses utilize a *spur gear*—in which the teeth are cut straight across—while newer presses utilize a *helical gear*—in which the teeth are cut at an angle.) The gear on the plate cylinder is in contact with and driven by a similar gear on the *blanket cylinder*. The bearers of each cylinder may or may not be in contact, but those that run out of contact need helical gears to minimize *play* (undesired free movement of cylinder ends). The diameter of the main body of the cylinder where the plate is attached is slightly less than that of the bearers. The difference in radius between the bearers and the main cylinder body is called the *undercut*, and exists to provide space for plate height adjustment, typically by means of *packing* (paper, plastic, or other material placed underneath the plate to raise the printing surface).

The plate is attached by means of the plate clamps, commonly including a *head clamp* and a *tail clamp* which grip the top and bottom of the plate, respectively. Clamps come in a variety of configurations, but all hold the plate securely in place while printing, and allow the move-

ment of the plate either up or down or laterally to adjust the position of the printed image, if necessary. Some clamps utilize pins that align with holes punched in the plate, which provide proper positioning of the plate and the image, with minimal (if any) necessary adjustments.

Some plate cylinders are marked with a *start-of-print line*, engraved about an inch below the cylinder gap, which indicates the topmost boundary of the plate that will print. Needless to say, all image areas on the plate should fall below the start-of-print line. Above the line, the cylinder gradually tapers down into the gap, which allows the inking rollers to smoothly return from the cylinder gap to the plate surface proper.

As with inking and dampening rollers, the proper pressure that exists between cylinders is an important adjustment, and the adjustments vary slightly depending upon whether the plate and blanket cylinder bearers are in contact with each other or not. On a *bearer-contact press*, the bearers act as not only a means of ensuring the alignment of the two cylinders, they also act to reduce gear wear, as the perfect alignment of the bearers ensures proper gear meshing. Effective use of the bearers is only possible when the pressure that the bearers exert on each other is beyond that produced simply by the weight of the upper cylinder. In the process of *preloading*, or the setting of the increased pressure between the bearers, proper pressure can be set as follows.

With the plate and blanket set to the proper printing height, the blanket is slightly overpacked by about 0.003 in., and thumbprints of ink are placed around both blanket cylinder bearers. With the press started up, and the impression pressure engaged, the cylinders are allowed to turn through several revolutions, and then the press is stopped. If the inked thumbprints are transferred evenly and thickly, the cylinder setting is fine. If not, the pressures need to be adjusted. On a *non-bearer-contact press*, it is necessary to know the manufacturer's specification for the proper gap between the bearers. Then, a thickness gauge with a thickness equal to the required width of the gap is obtained. The blanket is slightly overpacked, and the plate is packed to its correct printing height. The press is started, and the plate, blanket, and *impression cylinder*s are put on impression. (The blanket cylinder should be set to exert only a 0.004-in. *squeeze* on the impression cylinder.) With the press stopped, the thickness gauges are inserted between the plate and blanket cylinder bearers, and they should fit tightly and be moveable with only a strong pull. If they are overly loose, or require a great deal of force to move them, the cylinder settings need to be adjusted.

Maintenance of the plate cylinder is a straightforward case of ensuring that the gears and bearers are free of paper debris, dried ink, gum from the dampening solution, and other detritus that can impede gear movement and/or cause gear damage. Lubrication on many presses is accomplished automatically. (See also *Offset Lithography: Printing Unit*, *Blanket Cylinder*, and *Impression Cylinder*.)

Flexography. On a flexographic press, the plate cylinder is the part of the press to which the rubber or photopolymer plate is attached. The flexo plate cylinder can be removed and swapped with cylinders of varying diameters, depending upon the application. The plate is inked by the adjacent *anilox roller*, and transfers the raised images directly to the web of substrate passing between the plate cylinder and the *impression cylinder*. As can be expected, one important aspect of the plate cylinder is to ensure that it is exactly parallel with the impression cylinder. One way of checking this is by inserting strips of cellophane between the anilox roller and the image areas of the plate at various spots along the nip, lowering the plate cylinder to the impression cylinder, and pulling each one out. Each strip should be able to be pulled out with the same amount of force. As with the offset lithographic cylinders, the concentricity of the flexo plate cylinder is important. The *total indicated runout (TIR)* of the cylinder should not exceed 0.0005 in. (a TIR of 0.001 in. is acceptable if the press is not printing process color work). As always, gears must be clean and free of grease, dirt, and other foreign materials, and *play* must be kept to a minimum. There are four basic configurations of flexo plate cylinder:

• *Integral.* The entire cylinder, including the body, end-caps, and shafts, are all a single unit.
• *Demountable.* The cylinder body is manufactured without pre-attached shafts, and can be made to any diameter and later mounted onto an existing shaft.
• *Sleeve.* The plate is mounted on a removable cylinder sleeve which is slid onto the main cylinder. High-pressure jets of air expand the sleeve slightly allowing easy mounting and removing.
• *Magnetic.* A variety of integral cylinder that produces a magnetic field, allowing the mounting of metal-backed plates (commonly iron), which eliminates the need for adhesive-backed plates.

As in any inking and printing unit, the surface speeds of the cylinders and rollers in contact are an important consideration in flexography. The anilox roller, the plate cylinder, and the impression cylinder are all geared together to ensure that they all turn at the same speed. Any difference in surface speed of these three components can cause smearing.

A *plate cylinder* is also used in some types of presses used in *letterpress* printing. See *Letterpress*.

Plate-Feed System

One of two basic types of *continuous-flow dampening systems* utilized on offset lithographic printing presses. Unlike an *inker-feed system*, which uses the first inking *form roller* as a dampening roller, a plate-feed system uses its own designated dampening form roller. Similar to inker-feed systems, however, a plate-feed system uses a rubber-covered *metering roller* as a fountain roller, which transfers *fountain solution* to a hard chrome *transfer roller* at a *metering nip*, which then delivers the solution to the form roller and, ultimately, the plate. As with other continuous-flow dampening systems, the advantages include an unbroken stream of fountain solution to the plate, as well the ability to supply a carefully metered film of fluid by varying the width of the metering nip. The metering or water pan roller can be attached at an angle or skewed, which provides more or less metering at the ends or in the center of the rollers, depending on the dampening solution requirements of the plate. There are also several types of combination inker-feed and plate-feed dampening systems in use on offset presses. (See *Dampening System*.)

Plate Finish

A paper *finish* characterized by a very smooth, high finish produced by *supercalendering*.

Plate Flaking

A printing problem of *offset lithography*, characterized by portions of the image areas of the plate flaking off. Plate flaking is primarily a problem of plates utilizing copper-based coatings that harden in the image areas, forming the ink-receptive portion of the plate. Poor *adhesion* of the copper layer results in a chipping off of the copper, which can result in the chips adhering to the *blanket*, elsewhere on the plate, or in the ink *roller train*, which can produce *hickey*s or other printing defects.

Platemaking

The process of imaging a *plate* (or other image carrier) for use in printing. See *Plate*.

Platen

A flat portion of a *letterpress* printing press that carries the *substrate* to be printed and lowers it onto the inked typeform, or printing plate, under enough pressure to effectively transfer the ink. See *Letterpress: Platen Press*.

Platen Press

A configuration of *letterpress* printing press that presses a sheet of paper (or other *substrate*) onto a flat inked typeform or plate. See *Letterpress: Platen Press*.

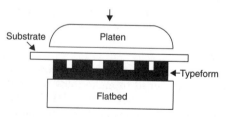

General configuration of a platen press used in letterpress printing.

Plate Scanner

A device used in *offset lithography* to measure the various densities of the printing plate's image areas prior to mounting the plate on the press. The evaluation of image densities allows for an accurate presetting of ink *fountain keys*, which varies the thickness of the ink film sent to the plate across the width of the plate, so that image areas that require greater amounts of ink receive it, while areas that require lesser amounts are not adversely affected, and vice versa.

Platform

In computers, the basic computer architecture utilized by a particular model or series of models, which defines a certain standard to which application developers must adhere when writing software intended for it. The term *platform* more commonly refers to the specific **operating system** utilized by a particular computer (such as the **standard platform**s of **Macintosh**, **DOS**, **Windows**, **UNIX**, and **OS/2**) or specialized system software, such as network management software, etc. Software that can run on more than one standard platform is known as **cross-platform**.

Platform-Specific Router

In networking, a **router** that is only compatible with a certain hardware architecture.

Play

The free, unimpeded lateral movement of a roller shaft within the roller bracket, or between gears (such as those found on the **plate cylinder** and **blanket cylinder** of an offset press) due to wear or poor fit. For ink rollers, a small degree of play is acceptable and will not have deleterious effects on inking or print quality. On press cylinders or other gears, play needs to be reduced as much as possible. **Spur gear**s, which are most susceptible to play, need to be supplemented with **backlash gear**s, while **helical gear**s, by design, reduce play. (See also **Roller Setting**, **Endplay**, **Spur Gear**, **Helical Gear**, and **Plate Cylinder**.)

Plenum Cable

A cable used in networking that is covered with a special **Teflon** coating, designed for use within walls, between floors, or within suspended ceilings. The Teflon coating provides flame and smoke reduction in the event of a fire.

Plow Fold

Alternate term for a **former fold**, especially one made using a **plow folder**. See **Plow Folder**.

Plow Folder

An **in-line** folding device used on **web press**es, often in lieu of a **former folder**, used to make folds in the direction of web travel. The moveability of the plow heads allows for greater flexibility than a former folder in the number and width of folds that can be made in a web.

PLT

A **file extension** denoting files created by the AutoCAD program.

Plucking

Alternate term for **picking**. See **Picking**.

Plug

Any connector used to make an electrical or electronic connection. Plugs usually connect to **jack**s.

Plug-and-Play

In computing, a rather optimistic term for computer equipment, peripherals, or software that can be installed (or "plugged in") simply and quickly, without a great deal of extensive formatting, initialization, and instruction. Although the term is in general usage, Plug-and-Play is actually a standard developed by Microsoft, Compaq, Intel, and Phoenix. Plug-and-Play adapters contain configuration information stored in **nonvolatile memory**, each adapter thus capable of being isolated and identified by the computer's operating system. Plug-and-Play is often abbreviated **PnP**. See also the more sarcastic term **Plug-and-Pray**.

Plug-and-Pray

In computing, a rather sarcastic, colloquial term for a **Plug-and-Play** system that does not live up to its expectations. See **Plug-and-Play**.

Plug-Compatible

In computing, descriptive of any hardware device or peripheral that will connect to a system and work essentially like any other similar device. For example, any external **serial** device (such as a printer or a modem) is said to be plug-compatible, as they will all plug into a computer's **serial port** without elaborate recabling. See also **Pin-Compatible**.

Plug-In

Alternate term for **extension**, especially when describing any small software program or utility that can be "plugged into" a larger program. See **Extension**.

Plugged

In printing, descriptive of characters or images that have experienced **plugging**. See **Plugging**.

Plugging

A press and printing problem in **offset lithography** characterized by filled-in **halftone** shadows and small reverse type, commonly occurring when using a **fountain solution** comprising an alcohol substitute, caused by incomplete wetting of the plate due to a lack of reduced surface tension of the solution. Adding a **wetting agent** to increase the solution's ability to form a thin, continuous film can help alleviate the problem. (See **Fountain Solution**.)

PLV

Abbreviation for **production-level video**. See **Production-Level Video (PLV)**.

Ply

Any single layer of a paper or plastic. Multiple plys of paper or plastic laminated together are referred to as *two-ply* or *duplex*. More than two plys, in packaging terminology, is referred to as *multiwall*.

Plybond Strength

The measure of the force acting at right angles to a paper's surface required to separate the plys comprising the paper. See *Internal Bond Strength*.

PMA

An abbreviation for phosphomolybdic acid, used to describe a printing ink *pigment* produced by combining the original dyestuff with a "double salt" of this acid. See also *PTMA* and *PTA*.

PMMU

Abbreviation for a *paged memory management unit*. See *Paged Memory Management Unit*.

PMS

An abbreviation for the *PANTONE* Matching System. See *PANTONE*.

PMT

An abbreviation for *photomultiplier tube*. See *Photomultiplier Tube*.

An abbreviation for *photomechanical transfer*. See *Photomechanical Transfer*.

PMTA

An abbreviation used in the classification of printing inks, stands for "phosphoric, molybdic, tungstic acid." PMTA color pigments are produced by combining the original dyestuff with "triple salts" of these three acids. Many pigments are also produced from "double salts" containing phosphoric acid and molybdic acid salts (PMA), phosphoric acid and tungstic acid salts (PTA), or a silicomolybdic acid salt (SM) alone. (See *PMTA Pink*, *PMTA Greens*, *PMTA Victoria Blue*, and *PMTA Rhodamine*.)

PMTA Greens

A series of *organic color pigments* used in printing inks. *PMTA Deep Green* is a bright bluish green possessing moderate *lightfastness*, but with a tendency to darken when exposed to the sun. It is not effectively resistant to alkalis, soaps, or strong solvents. It is used in all types of printing inks and applications requiring an intense shade. *PMTA* refers to the presence of phosphotungstomolybdic acid, the "triple salt" of which is contained by the pigment.

(*CI Pigment Green 1 No. 42040:1*.)

PMTA Vivid Green is a mixture of PMTA Deep Green and a yellow PMTA pigment (*CI Pigment Yellow 18 No. 49005:1*), which produces a brilliant emerald green, possessing poor lightfastness and low heat and alkali resistance. It is used when the shade is desired, but its low resistance characteristics limit its use. (See also *Organic Color Pigments*.)

(*CI Pigment Green 2*.)

PMTA Pink

See *Rhodamine 6G*.

PMTA Rhodamine

An *organic color pigment* used in printing inks. PMTA Rhodamine, classed as a violet pigment, is a strong magenta commonly used as a bluish red. Although possessing high *tinctorial strength*, it tends to darken upon exposure to light, however, and has poor resistance to water, solvents, oils, and soaps. Although it is usable in water-based inks, it is unusable in lithographic printing, and its use is declining. Like other *PMTA* pigments, it is a "triple salt" of phosphotungstomolybdic acid. It is also produced from double salts, as well. (See also *Organic Color Pigments*.)

(*CI Pigment Violet 1 No. 45170:2*.)

PMTA Victoria Blue

An *organic color pigment* used in printing inks. PMTA Victoria Blue is a bright reddish blue of high *tinctorial strength*; it possesses good *lightfastness* when used at full strength, but succumbs to darkening when reduced. It also possesses poor resistance properties. It is used in most types of inks, despite the expense of the pigment, primarily because the hue cannot be replicated with other pigments. Like other *PMTA* pigments, it is produced using a "triple salt" of phosphoric, molybdic, and tungstic acids. "Double salt" varieties using phosphoric acid and one of the two other acids can also be produced, though these tend to be stronger in color, but not as lightfast. (See also *Organic Color Pigments*.)

Also known as *PMTA Brilliant Blue* (*CI Pigment Blue 1 No. 42595:2*).

PMTA Violet

An *organic color pigment* used in printing inks. PMTA Violet is a bright blue violet possessing good *lightfastness* and heat resistance. It has good water resistance and resistance to some solvents, but does not withstand exposure to most solvents or soaps. Like other *PMTA* pigments, it is produced using a "triple salt" of phosphoric, molybdic, and tungstic acids. "Double salt" varieties using phosphoric acid and one of the two other acids can also be produced, though these tend to be stronger in color, but not as lightfast. (See also *Organic Color Pigments*.)

Also known as *Methyl Violet* (*CI Pigment Violet 3 No. 42535:2*).

Pneumatic Screen Printing Machine

A variety of semi-automatic or fully automatic *screen printing* press powered by compressed air rather than an electric motor or other means.

Pneumatic Stretcher

A device used in *screen printing* that uses compressed air to stretch a screen fabric in order to properly tension it before it is mounted on the frame.

PnP

Abbreviation for ***Plug-and-Play***. See ***Plug-and-Play***.

PNT

A ***file extension*** denoting files created by the MacPaint program.

Pocket

In ***binding and finishing***, one of many stations on a ***gathering*** device in which a ***signature*** is placed prior to ***assembling***.

The term *pocket* also refers to any pouch produced from cloth, vinyl, or paper and attached to the inside of a book or binder.

Pocket Fold

In ***folding***, a sheet of paper folded such that it will fit into an envelope or ***pocket***.

Pocking

The production of dimples or other small pits on the surface of a printed ***substrate***, produced by a variety of causes.

POH

Abbreviation for ***power-on hours***. See ***Power-On Hours***.

POI

Abbreviation for ***point of information***. See ***Point of Information (POI)***.

Point

See ***Point System*** and ***Point Size***.

In papermaking and in ***binding and finishing***, one *point* equals one thousandth of an inch. Thus, ***binder's board*** having a thickness of 80 points is 0.080 in. thick.

Point of Information (POI)

A computer system and ***interactive*** program, usually presented on a kiosk, in a public space that provides information to the general public. POIs are often located in public parks, museums, recreation areas, post offices, exhibitions, etc. POIs usually provide historical information, or information on the services offered at a particular location. A variety of POI, called a ***point of sale (POS)***, is often found in retail areas, such as shopping malls and individual stores, and provides information on products for purchase.

Point of Presence (POP)

In telecommunications, any connection to a telephone company or long-distance carrier.

Point of Sale (POS)

See ***Point of Information (POI)***.

Point of View

In motion picture photography and videography (as well as three-dimensional modeling), a camera angle or position intended to represent the view of an individual in the production. The viewer of the film or video thus sees what the character sees. In shooting scripts, point of view is denoted by ***POV***. In three-dimensional modeling, the point of view is the object's position and orientation in relation to the viewer.

Point Size

In typography, a measure of the height of the characters of a font, measured in points.

The ***point*** is the basic unit of measurement used in typography, and all other measurements derive from it. Historically, each individual size was referred to using a name not a number (such as Diamond, Brevier, Pica, Great Primer, etc.; only one of these names—*agate*—is still used; see ***Agate***), but this became inadequate for quantitatively specifying type sizes above and below it. In the late nineteenth century, the ***point system***—devised a century earlier by Pierre Fournier—was adopted by the printing industry.

The point is used to describe the difference in size among ***typeface***s, ***leading***, and other aspects of composition. It is not without its confusion, however. In the United States and Great Britain, the point is approximately 1/72 in. (0.351 mm), or 1/12 ***pica*** and is called a ***pica point***. In Europe, the point is a little bigger (0.376 mm) and is called a ***Didot point***. (There is also a third ***point system***, used primarily in Belgium, called the Mediaan system, but is has largely fallen out of use; see ***Point System***.) In both the American-British and the Didot systems, points have always been used to describe the length of one metal chunk of type. A 72-point "H," in metal type, is a character cast onto the top of a metal block, which carries the character through all the subsequent printing operations. The block's surface itself is exactly 72 points (or 1 in.) in height. However, the actual size of the letter that is printed will be slightly smaller than the overall size of the metal block that carries it. Thus, the point size refers to a specific dimension of the metal, not the letter, an important distinction due to the occasional appearance of ***ascender***s and ***descender***s. If the type is to line up evenly and securely, the characters must be cast onto oversize metal blocks that are large enough to allow for these extremes of projection above and below the ***baseline***. Therefore, all the metal blocks end up being equal in height, this height being the determinant of the point size of the typeface.

Consequently, point size is merely an expression of the distance from ascender to descender, with a small amount of space allowed above and below to compensate for the metal block, and as such cannot describe the proportional relationship of a typeface's ***x-height*** to its ascenders and descenders.

When specifying very small type, it is better to deal in round numbers than in fractions of inches or millimeters. In the United States, only pica points were used until about 1960, with the exception of some typefaces—such as Bauer, Bodoni, and the original Helveticas—which had been available in Didot points for quite some time. When typefaces from Europe began to be used in **Linotype** and **Monotype** systems, these faces were cut in Didot points.

So, a font of 24-point characters may have been adapted from **hot type** 24-pica-points high, hot type 24-Didot-points high, or from **photolettering** that had some tenuous point designation. It may even have been designed originally for phototype, in which case the capital letters might have been 24 points high (pica *or* Didot).

In modern typesetting, the traditional point measurements associated with hot type are a hindrance. Type is no longer composed using metal slugs, but appears directly on a sheet of film or paper, commonly produced digitally. A system could easily be employed using actual letter-image heights, which would be much simpler and more logical.

The term **photolettering** originally referred to headline and display work. The master size on the photomatrix was usually 1 in. (72 points), and all enlargements and reductions modified this basic size. Thus, the concept of standard type sizes was lost, since one could specify any size necessary to fit a layout and the past increments—6, 7, 8, etc.—were rendered meaningless. **Phototypesetting** utilized three approaches for type sizing:

1. Each photomatrix had a different master size and characters were photographed at a 1:1 ratio.

2. The photomatrix had one master size (8-point, for example) and lenses enlarged or reduced the character image as necessary.

3. There were ranges of master sizes so that a photomatrix with the 8-point master would only be used for enlargement up to 12-point, and another photomatrix would have a master size of 12-point for enlargement up to 18-point, for example.

Some type suppliers made their master sizes all the same size and worked from constant-sized artwork. Thus, all typefaces would be 7 in. and reduced to the 8-point master size. In many cases, this effectively limited x-height variability; all sizes were then the same.

In more recent digitized typesetting, the image is not a photographic master. It is made up of thousands of dots, overlapping to create lines (called **raster**s). Thus, the number of type sizes is increasing as technology changes the typesetting process.

Point System

A measurement system used in typography. The system dates from early handset metal type, where the sizes of type cast by type founders were graduated on a uniform "point" scale. Each size is described by its number of points (called its **point size**; see **Point Size**), which referred to the height of the body on which it is cast. Calculations are simplified by assuming each point is $\frac{1}{72}$ in. At one time, there were three point systems in use worldwide:

American-British System. This is the point system used throughout North America and Great Britain. The standard of measurement is the 0.166-in. **pica** and the 0.01383-

in. point. One point is equal to $\frac{1}{12}$ pica. Thus, 1,000 lines of pica (or 12-point) matter measure 166 in., and 1,000 lines of 6-point matter measure 83 in. Point is abbreviated **pt**.

Didot System. Used primarily in Europe, the Didot system uses the **cicero** as its basic unit, which is equal to 12 **corps**, or 0.178 in. The Didot corps (or **Didot point**) measures 0.0148 in.

Mediaan System. Once used principally in Belgium, the Mediaan system has a corps (or point) equal to 0.01374 in. The Mediaan em, or cicero, measures 0.165 in. The Mediaan system, however, has largely been replaced by the Didot system.

For general, practical measurement purposes, three decimal places (thousandths of an inch) are deemed sufficient significant digits.

In the American-British system, it is convenient to remember 6 picas equal one inch, 12 points equal one pica, and 72 points equal one inch—but it's not exactly true. Picas and points do not have an exact relationship to inches. Thus, 30 picas—or approximately 5 in.—actually equal 4.98 in.

It should be noted, however, that much of Europe is moving to purely metric measurements.

Point-to-Point

In telecommunications, descriptive of an exclusive link between two stations.

Point-to-Point Network

In networking, a network in which only two nodes or devices share the same transmission line at the same time. See **Point-to-Point**.

Point-to-Point Protocol (PPP)

In networking, telecommunications, and **Internet** terminology, a protocol used in **TCP/IP** to transmit **IP** data **packet**s over telephone lines. PPP allows a personal computer to directly access the Internet by **modem** through a **host** computer (such as one maintained by a user's **Internet service provider**). PPP thus allows such a personal computer to appear to the host as if it were a node on the host's own network. Point-to-Point Protocol is gradually replacing the older **Serial Line Internet Protocol (SLIP)**.

Pointer

In computing, especially by means of a **graphical user interface**, a (usually) arrow-shaped **cursor** that is moved around the screen by the **mouse**, used to select menu items, among other things. See **Cursor**.

A variable that contains a memory address. A key element in the efficiency of C, pointers allow a programmer to indirectly address the contents of a variable at a memory address.

An address stored in memory that provides a link to a related field, file, record, or control block.

Pointillism

In digital image manipulation, a special effect that transforms a **continuous-tone** image into small dots. Essentially, dots of pure colors are placed adjacent to each other, the viewer perceiving that various intermediate shades are present. (This is somewhat different than **halftone** production.) The term derives from (and is meant to simulate) a style of painting popularized by several Impressionists of the late nineteenth century (most notably Georges Seurat), also called *pointillism*.

Poison

An alternate term for an **inhibitor**, or a chemical substance that decreases or eliminates the efficacy of a chemical **catalyst**. See **Inhibitor**. The term *poison* also refers to any substance hazardous to one's health, especially if ingested.

Polar Solvent

A **solvent** containing oxygen, such as water, **ester**s, **ketone**s, alcohols, and other organic compounds, as opposed to nonpolar solvents which comprise compounds made from **hydrocarbon**s. A characteristic of polar solvents is their electrical conductivity which enables them to prevent the buildup of static charges, a degree of difficulty commonly found in nonpolar solvents.

Polishing

A printing defect characterized by an intended **matte**-finish ink increasing in **gloss** when dried ink film is rubbed.

Poll

In computing, to continuously and sequentially monitor (by the **central processing unit**) each device connected to a computer to determine if the device requires processing.

Polling

In networking, a means of determining whether a connected **node** on a **shared circuit** or **multidrop line** has any data to transmit. An inquiry is made, and if a node *does* have data to send, it sends an acknowledgment, and transmission commences. Polling is performed in one of three ways. In **roll-call polling**, a central node runs down a list of connected nodes, "asking" each one if it has data to transmit. In **hub polling**, one node asks the next node if it has data to transmit, which then asks the node after that if it has data to transmit, and so on. In **token-passing polling**, a **token** passes from node to node which can either pick up a message or simply pass to the next node in sequence.

Polyamide

A polymeric compound containing amide groups (ammonia derivatives, chemical formula $-NH_3$) used in fluid inks intended for **flexographic** and **gravure** printing processes, in particular for printing on **film**- and **foil**-based **substrate**s. A common polyamide compound is **nylon**, used for **screen printing** fabrics or as substrates.

Polyethylene

A plastic **polymer**, chemical formula $(C_2H_4)_n$, derived from the **polymerization** of ethylene gas under pressure, used as a **resin** in printing inks. Polyethylene films are also used as **substrate**s in **flexography**, **gravure**, and **screen printing**. In Great Britain, polyethylene is known as *polythene*.

Polyhydric Alcohol

A family of organic compounds containing two or more hydroxyl groups (–OH) used as **solvent**s in printing inks, characterized by their much lower **volatility** (ability to evaporate quickly at low temperatures) than **monohydric alcohol**s. An example of a polyhydric alcohol is glycerol.

Polymer

A large, high-molecular-weight molecule formed by the combination of many smaller **monomer**s in a process known as **polymerization**. It is the formation of polymers from the constituent parts of substances in printing ink **vehicle**s that is responsible for the drying and hardening of many types of ink films. (See **Vehicle**.)

The chemical formulae of polymers are typically of the form $(X_a Y_b ...)_n$, where X and Y indicate the component elements having the atomic quantities indicated by the numerals a and b. The formula enclosed in parentheses is the **monomer** or **oligomer**, and the n indicates that an unspecified and variable number of the monomers comprise the chain. For example, polyethylene is a polymer of ethylene, and has the chemical formula $(C_2H_4)_n$, where each monomer (an ethylene molecule) contains two atoms of carbon bonded to four atoms of hydrogen, the n indicating that many of these molecules are strung together.

Polymerization

A complex chemical reaction that takes place in drying printing inks. Several relatively simple, low-molecular-weight compounds (called monomers) combine to form a long, high-molecular-weight chainlike molecule (called a polymer). Polymerization commonly takes place in the presence of a **catalyst**, which can be another compound, heat, or light. Polymerization is responsible for the hardening and drying of printed ink films and commonly occurs following **oxidation** of components of the ink **vehicle**.

Polymerization is also the basis of the creation of several types of plates used in **offset lithography** and **flexography**, in which **photopolymer**s (molecules that are polymerized by light) are applied to the surface of a plate, and exposure of these coatings, via light shined through a photographic negative or positive or by lasers, causes the image areas of the original to form hard, durable polymers in the appropriate regions of the plate. Chemical treatment after exposure removes the unexposed coating from nonimage areas of the plate. (See **Plate: Offset Lithography** and **Plate: Flexography**.) Polymerization is also involved in the preparation of **photostencil**s used in **screen printing**. See **Photostencil**. Polymerization—brought about by exposure to either ultraviolet light or electron beams—is also the basis of the drying of many types of *coating*s used in *finishing* operations. See *Binding and Finishing: Finishing: Coating*.

Polyolefin
Any of a wide variety of thermoplastic compounds produced by the *polymerization* of olefins, such as styrene or ethylene. Hence, polyolefins include such plastics as *polystyrene* and *polyethylene*.

Polypropylene
A plastic *polymer*, chemical formula $(C_3H_5)_n$, derived from the *polymerization* of propylene gas, used as a *resin* in printing inks. Polypropylene films are also used as *substrate*s in *flexographic* printing. Polypropylene can be formed into bottles, and is often used for *screen printing*.

Polystyrene
A *thermoplastic* polymer, chemical formula $(C_8H_8)_n$, derived from the *polymerization* of styrene, used as a *film former* in printing inks. Polystyrene films are also used as *substrate*s in *flexography*, *gravure*, and *screen printing*.

Polyvinyl Acetate (PVA)
A plastic *polymer*, chemical formula $(C_6H_4O_2)_n$, derived from the *polymerization* of vinyl acetate, used as a *resin* in printing inks, coatings, and adhesives. Polyvinyl acetate is also one of the primary adhesives used in *perfect binding*.

Polyvinyl Alcohol
A *thermoplastic*, water-soluble *polymer* derived from the hydrolysis (the splitting of a compound into separate compounds through chemical reaction with water) of *polyvinyl acetate*, used as a *resin* in printing inks. An emulsion of polyvinyl alcohol is also widely used—in combination with either of the *bichromate*s—in the preparation of *screen printing* stencils and screens.

Polyvinyl Chloride Acetate
A plastic *polymer* derived from the co-*polymerization* of a mixture of vinyl chloride and a small quantity of vinyl acetate, used as a *resin* in printing inks.

Polyvinyl Chloride (PVC)
A *thermoplastic*, water-insoluble *polymer*, chemical formula $(C_2H_3Cl)_n$, derived from the *polymerization* of vinyl chloride, used as a *resin* in printing inks and coatings. Polyvinyl chloride films are also used as *substrate*s in *flexographic* printing.

Polyvinyl Fluoride (PVF)
A *thermoplastic*, water-insoluble *polymer* derived from the *polymerization* of vinyl fluoride, used as a *resin* in printing inks and coatings. Although it is a tougher resin than *polyvinyl chloride*, it is not as widely used.

Polyvinylidene Chloride (PVDC)
A *polymer*, chemical formula $(C_2H_2Cl)_n$, derived from the *polymerization* of vinylidene chloride, popularly known as *saran* (as in Saran Wrap), used as a *film former* in printing inks (and as a food wrapping) by virtue of its increased ability to prevent the transmission of moisture.

POM
In packaging, an abbreviation for *pasted open-mouth*, a type of paper *bag*. See *Pasted Open-Mouth (POM)*.

POND
Abbreviation for *print on demand*. See *on-demand printing*.

Poor Trapping
In *process color* printing, the inability to print an ink on top of a previously printed ink. See *Trapping* (second definition).

POP
Abbreviation for *point of presence*. See *Point of Presence (POP)*.

Pop Test
An alternate, somewhat onomatopoeic, term for a *Mullen test* of a paper's *bursting strength*. See *Mullen Test* and *Bursting Strength*.

Pop-Up Menu
In computing, especially that utilizing a *graphical user interface (GUI)*, a menu of commands and functions that "pops up" from another menu item when that particular menu item is clicked on. See also *Pull-Down Menu*.

Porosimeter
A device used to measure the *porosity* of a paper by measuring the rate of the flow of air through a paper sample. See *Sheffield Porosimeter*.

Porosity
A measure of the extent to which a paper surface will allow the penetration of a gas or liquid, such as air or ink, through its surface. The nature of paper is such that the bonding of the paper fibers produces many tiny air passages throughout the paper, which can either be completely submerged in the paper, extend from the surface down into the interior of the paper, or penetrate completely through the sheet. The porosity of a paper is a function of the various stages of the papermaking process. An increased level of fiber *refining* causes the fibers to bond together more strongly and tightly, making the paper denser, and reducing the network of air passages and thus the porosity. *Surface sizing*, *coating*, *calendering* and *super-calendering* all work to seal or compress surface fibers, reducing the paper's porosity.

Different printing methods require paper of differing porosities, as porosity affects how thoroughly and how quickly inks are absorbed into a paper, which occurs primarily by capillary action. Paper with high porosity increases **ink absorbency**, and in some printing processes can increase the risk of **show-through** and/or **strike-through**. Paper with low porosity increases **ink holdout**, and increases the risk of smudging during post-printing processes such as folding. The low porosity of coated papers is one of the causes of **blistering** during **heatset drying**, as water quickly converted to water vapor inside the paper can't escape through the surface easily and ruptures the internal structure of the paper. High-speed web offset printing, such as the printing of newspapers, requires highly porous paper for rapid ink absorption, while sheetfed offset printing often requires nonporous papers to promote proper ink drying and to increase ink gloss. Low-porosity papers are also more likely to curl and have greater problems with **dimensional stability** as a result of changing **moisture content**.

Porosity of paper is measured quantitatively as either the length of time it takes for a quantity of air to pass through a paper sample, or the rate of the passage of air through a sample, using either a **Gurley densometer** (in the first case) or a **Sheffield porosimeter** (in the second case).

A paper's porosity is also related to other important paper properties, and changes in porosity effect changes in other characteristics, sometimes to their detriment. (See **Paper and Papermaking: Paper Properties**.)

Port

In computing, to transfer an application, file, or operating system from one **platform** to another. In this sense, the term *port* is an abbreviation for **portability**.

Also in computing, the term *port* refers to any physical point (usually a **jack** or **plug**) at which a device is connected to a computer.

Port Multiplier

In networking, a **concentrator** used to provide more than one connection to a network.

Portability

In computing, general term for the ability of one program, file, etc., to run on more than one **platform**. The term *portability* also refers to a computer that can be easily moved from place to place. See **Portable Computer**.

Portable

In computing, descriptive of software, files, or hardware that possesses **portability**. See **Portability**.

Portable Color

See **Color Portability**.

Portable Computer

A **personal computer** that is is small and lightweight enough to be easily carried from place to place. The earliest "portable computers" were more appropriately known as

luggable computers, as they required a good deal of upper body strength to carry around. Modern portable computers fall into roughly three categories: **laptop computer**s are roughly briefcase-size and are easily carried, and can conveniently be used while sitting in airplane seats, for example. They are powerful enough to run most common **operating system**s and most applications. Most also possess an internal battery. **Notebook computer**s are about the size of a college textbook and can easily fit inside a briefcase. They are also powerful enough to run most operating systems and applications. **Hand-held computer**s are capable of fitting in the palm of one's hand (and are also known as **palmtop**s) and are used for small, personal organization tasks and memos. Although portable computers are getting smaller and more powerful, see also **Hidden Weight**.

Portable Operating System Interface for UNIX (POSIX)

In computing, an **IEEE** standard language interface between applications and the **UNIX** operating system, designed to facilitate the **portability** of programs when transferred from one UNIX system to another. Varieties of POSIX are also available for other operating systems.

Porting

The conversion of a software application or file from one computer **platform** to another. See **Port** (first definition).

Portrait

A page format in which the correct reading or viewing orientation is vertical; the height of the page is greater than its width. See also **Landscape**.

POS

Abbreviation for **point of sale**, a variety of information kiosk. See **Point of Information (POI)**.

Position Proof

A **color proof** used to check the position, location, and proper **register** of various page elements (text, graphics, etc.) The colors appearing on a position proof may not be the proper **hue**s or strengths; as a position proof is only meant to verify position, other color proofs are used to verify correct color.

Positive

Any image, especially a photographic film or paper print, possessing the same tonal orientation as the original—i.e., black text on a white background—as opposed to a **negative**, which is tonally reversed. Although negatives are used most often for platemaking, positives may also be used, depending upon the photosensitive plate material. (See **Positive-Working Plate** and **Negative-Working Plate**.)

Positive Printing

In **offset lithography**, printing performed using **positive-working plate**s. **Halftone** positive-working plates when made tend to decrease the ***middletone*** dot size by about 5%, but when used on web presses, the ***dot gain*** inherent in web printing compensates.

Positive-Working

Descriptive of any prepress or printing procedure (such as platemaking) in which additional imaging or reproduction is performed using film ***positive***s rather than ***negative***s. See ***Positive*** and ***Positive-Working Plate***.

Positive-Working Plate

One of two basic types of ***photolithographic*** printing plates produced by bringing an unexposed plate into contact with a photographic ***positive*** of the image to be printed, and exposing it to a high-intensity light. The plate's coated metal surface is exposed in the nonimage areas—where light passes through the positive—and unexposed in the image areas—where light does not pass through. The exposure to light renders the nonimage areas soluble, and after platemaking the plate is chemically treated to dissolve the nonimage areas, rendering that portion of the plate water-receptive, the unexposed image areas remaining hard, durable, and ink-receptive. Some positive-working plates can be thermally cured, which further hardens the image areas, making them suitable for longer than usual pressruns. The nonimage areas are then treated with a solution of ***gum arabic*** (or other gum, either natural or synthetic), which ***desensitize***s the nonimage areas, adding a higher degree of water-receptivity. The advantage of positive-working plates is that they tend to reproduce halftone images with less ***dot gain*** than plates made from negatives. (See also ***Negative-Working Plate***.) (See ***Plate: Offset Lithography*** and ***Platemaking***.)

POSIX

Abbreviation for ***Portable Operating System Interface for UNIX***.

Post

Abbreviated term for ***post-production***. See ***post-production***.

POST

Abbreviation for ***power-on self test***.

Postal Bristol

A type of ***bristol***, a light paperboard, used primarily for postcards. Its surface is smooth, and its ***finish*** is uniform, allowing both pen-and-ink writing and processing with postal sorting equipment. (See ***Bristol***.)

Postal Telephone and Telegraph

In telecommunications, an official government committee or organization that oversees the telecommunications systems in many European countries.

Post Binder

A ***binder*** used in ***loose-leaf binding*** that uses metal (or plastic) posts inserted through punched or drilled holes in the pages to hold sheets together, in contrast to a ***ring binder*** that uses metal rings to bind pages together. An advantage of post binders is the ability of the post to be lengthened as the size of the binder contents increases. (See also ***Ring Binder***.) See ***Loose-Leaf Binder***.

Posterization

The conversion or reproduction of a ***continuous-tone*** image to one with only a few distinct tones, or having a flat, poster-like quality. When images are posterized photographically, high-contrast film is used to separate the continuous tones into a few distinct shades. Multiple exposures and colored gels are used to create a color-composite image. Posterization can also be performed digitally, in a photo manipulation program, commonly by specifying a set number of gradient steps.

Posterize

To impart to an image the effect of ***posterization***. See ***Posterization***.

Post Hardening

An additional exposure of a ***screen printing*** photostencil to ultraviolet light after initial exposure and washout, as a means of rendering the developed image harder and more resistant to wear.

Posting Finish

A ***finish*** imparted to ***ledger paper*** designed for use in data-entry equipment. See ***Ledger Paper***.

Post-Production

In motion picture and video production, any process that takes place after filming or taping, such as editing, additional sound recording and over-dubbing, the ***keying*** of graphics (such as credits and titles), the addition of special effects and transitions, etc.

PostScript®

A ***page description language*** invented by Adobe Systems, Inc., that consists of software commands which, when translated through a ***RIP (raster image processor)*** forms the desired image on an output device, such as a ***laser printer*** or an ***imagesetter***. PostScript is commonly used for both text and ***line art***. In the latter case, it is often referred to as ***encapsulated PostScript (EPS)***.

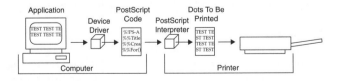

PostScript's advantage is that the code is rasterized in an interpreter in the output device, not the computer.

Essentially, PostScript allows for **device independence**, or the ability to generate virtually identical output on devices made by different manufacturers, so long as they can interpret PostScript commands. The original version of PostScript (sometimes known as **PostScript Level 1**) was one of the most important elements in the invention of **desktop publishing**. A secondary, revised version of PostScript (called **PostScript Level 2**) included support for **process color** output.

PostScript Clone

Any **RIP** (**raster image processor**) that can read and interpret **PostScript** files, but which has been manufactured without the authorization or license from Adobe Systems, the creator of and license-holder for PostScript. PostScript clones typically generate images that are virtually identical to those generated by a true PostScript output device. PostScript clones are also described using the term **PostScript-compatible**.

PostScript-Compatible

Decriptive of a **PostScript Clone**. See **PostScript Clone**.

PostScript Level 1

The original version of the **PostScript** page description language, created by Adobe Systems, Inc. However, PostScript Level 1 was not actually called that until the release of **PostScript Level 2** in 1991. See **PostScript**.

PostScript Level 2

A revision and re-release of Adobe Systems' popular **page description language**, which among other things provided support for **process color** output, in particular defined **color space**s and algorithms for the **data compression** of color images. See **PostScript**.

Post-Treatment

In **offset lithography**, any additional treatment of the non-image areas of a plate to effect maximum desensitization.

Posture

In typography, the vertical inclination of type characters, such as **oblique**, **italic**, etc.

Potassium Bichromate

A chemical compound—chemical formula $K_2Cr_2O_7$—used to render colloids or emulsions photosensitive, used in the manufacture of **photostencil**s for use in **screen printing**. Potassium bichromate is also known as *potassium dichromate*.

Pound Sign

Common name for the cross-hatch symbol (#) used as an abbreviation for the word "number," or as a special function key on telephone keypads. The actual name for this symbol is an **octothorpe**.

POV

Abbreviation for **point of view**. See **Point of View**.

Powder Gravure

A type of **gravure** printing that replaced liquid ink with a fine powder similar to **toner**, imaging being effected by electrostatic means.

Powdering

A form of **piling**, the accumulation of visible particles of **lint** or paper-cutter dust on the nonimage areas of a printing plate or **blanket**, which can have deleterious effects on **print quality**, and even accelerate blanket or plate wear. Powdering is typically found in those areas of the blanket or plate that contact the outer edges of the paper sheet or **web**, especially powdering caused by dust from paper trimmers. (See **Piling**.) Powdering is also called **dusting**.

Power Conditioning

In computing, the use of any of a variety of devices to ensure that electrical power of a constant voltage is fed into a computer or system. In particular, power conditioning guards against **surge**s, **spike**s, and other irregularities of incoming voltage, which can damage computer components. The devices involved include a **power stabilizer**, **surge protector**, or **uninterruptible power supply**.

Power Consumption

In computing, the amount of electrical power used by a peripheral device or by the computer itself. If a peripheral device **uses PC power supply**, the device's power consumption should not exceed the amount available.

PowerLAN

A popular **network operating system** developed by Performance Technology that provides **peer-to-peer** networking fo **Windows**-based computers.

Power Mac

The most recent line of Apple **Macintosh** computers, based on the **PowerPC** microprocessor. Although using a different chip and architecture than earlier Macintosh computers, the Power Mac behaves nearly identically and is capable of running the same software, although with varying degrees of performance. Power Macs are also capable of running **DOS** and **Windows** software by means of the Soft-Windows emulation program.

Power-On Hours (POH)

Alternate term for **mean time between failures**. See **Mean Time Between Failures (MTBF)**.

Power-On Self Test

In computing, a **diagnostic** routine performed by a PC at start-up. See **Diagnostic Program**. Abbreviated **POST**.

PowerOpen

In computing, a variety of the *UNIX* operating system designed for the *PowerPC* microprocessor, developed by IBM and Apple and based on IBM's *AIX* and Apple's *A/UX*.

PowerPC

In computing, a powerful *microprocessor* developed jointly by Apple, IBM, and Motorola. The *RISC*-based PowerPC chips, used in most new *Macintosh* computers, are the successors to Motorola's 680X0 chips, used in older Macintoshes. The PowerPC chip, however, is also used in IBM's PCs.

PowerPC Reference Platform (PReP)

In computing, a standard developed by IBM for computers using a *PowerPC* microprocessor, detailing technical specifications for system software, as well as input and output devices, add-on cards, etc.

Power Stabilizer

In computing, a transformer to which a computer or system's AC power cord is connected to ensure that a constant voltage is fed to the system. See also *Surge Protector*.

Power Supply

In computers (or any other electronic device), a transistor that converts high-voltage alternating current (AC) coming from a wall outlet to low-voltage (usually 5–12 volt) direct current (DC) that the internal workings of the computer require. If the power supply is not functioning, nothing else in the computer will function.

Power Surge

A brief, sudden increase in electrical voltage that can damage the internal components of a computer or other electronic device. Power surges can have many causes, ranging from nearby electric appliances (such as photocopiers) to lightning strikes. Power surges are often combatted by means of a variety of *power conditioning devices*, in particular *surge protector*s.

Power User

Term for an individual who not only spends a great deal of time working at a computer, but is also highly proficient and can learn new applications quickly and readily. A power user may also be capable of installing new hardware devices or upgrading old ones.

PP

Abbreviation for *plasma panel*. See *Plasma Panel (PP)*.

PPCC

Abbreviation for *Page Printer Communication Component*.

PPD

Abbreviation for *PostScript Printer Description*, a *PostScript* file specification, set by Adobe Systems, Inc., used in many *page makeup software* applications. PPDs contain various specifications on specific output devices, and are referred to as a means of ensuring that any particular PostScript file is within the limits of the intended output device.

PPFA

Abbreviation for *Page Printer Formatting Aide*.

PPM

Abbreviation for *pages per minute*. See *Pages Per Minute (PPM)*.

PPP

Abbreviation for *Point-to-Point Protocol*. See *Point-to-Point Protocol (PPP)*.

Precipitation

A chemical process in which a substance dissolved in a *solvent* becomes insoluble (either by chemical reaction or by saturation) and separates from (or "precipitates out of") the solution. In ink terminology, precipitation is a form of drying utilized by *moisture-set ink*, or ink containing a *glycol vehicle*, in which a water-insoluble *resin* (containing the *pigment*) is dissolved in glycol, which *is* water soluble. When water comes into contact with the glycol, the glycol is dissolved in the water, but the resin is not, and the resin and pigment "precipitate out" onto the *substrate*. Variations of this process can also occur in the absence of water. (See *Glycol Vehicle*.)

The term *precipitation* also describes a problem encountered in flexographic inks that utilize hard-to-dissolve resins that require many additional solvents to keep them in solution. Frequently, a resin will precipitate out of the solution. The use of a more powerful solvent will help alleviate the problem. (See also *Souring*.)

Precision

A measure of the degree of exactness with which a measured quantity is stated. In scientific measurements, precision refers to the degree to which a quantity in a set of specific measurements agrees with the mean value for that set. In this sense, precision should not be confused with *accuracy*.

Precision Sheeting

A method of *sheeting*, or converting paper rolls to individual sheets, that aims to accurately control the sheet dimensions to make further *trimming* unnecessary. Although precision sheeting devices tend not to make every sheet in a single pile of exactly uniform dimensions (a *guillotine cutter* does), precision sheeting does result in more accurate sheet dimensions throughout an entire load. (See *Sheeting* and *Trimming*.)

Preemptive Multitasking

In computing, a variety of *multitasking* in which an operating system executes a task for a set period of time (determined by the task's assigned priority status), at the end of which it is preempted and a new task is executed for its pre-determined period of time. See also ***Nonpreemptive Multitasking*** and ***Multitasking***.

Pre-Etching

In platemaking for ***offset lithography***, the act of applying a thin film of ***gum arabic*** to the surface of the plate prior to coating it completely.

Preface

A portion of a book preceding the main text that comprises a formal statement by the author concerning the content of the book. It is commonly distinguished from an ***introduction*** (often part of the main text), and a ***foreword*** (frequently written by someone other than the author). It is similar to a ***prologue***. In actual fact, however, authors often include prefaces, forewords, and introductions with little regard to the formal distinction among them. See ***Book Typography***.

Preferences

In computing, a file created by a program containing user-defined settings. Preference files are read by the program each time it is launched, eliminating the need for the user to re-enter the settings. Changes to settings are overwritten into the preferences file.

Prekissing

A premature contact between the paper and the offset press ***blanket***. Prekissing produces a printing defect known as ***doubling***, a distortion of a printed image in which a faint "pre-impression" of halftone dots is made out of register with the proper dots of the actual printing impression. Prekissing is caused by paper distortions such as ***wavy edges*** or by static electricity. (See also ***Doubling***.)

Preloading

On a ***bearer-contact press*** used in ***offset lithography***, preloading is the process of increasing and setting the pressure that the plate and blanket cylinder ***bearer***s exert on each other, the pressure exerted by the weight of the upper cylinder on the lower one not being sufficient for proper and effective operation. Proper bearer setting and pressure enables not only an accurate determination of plate and blanket ***packing***, but also reduces wear on the gears driving the cylinders and provides a smoother driving of the cylinders. Although considered a factory operation, press operators may occasionally need to gauge and adjust the bearer pressure. See ***Plate Cylinder*** and ***Blanket Cylinder***.

Premastering

In ***videodisc*** and ***compact disc*** production, the creation of a ***master tape*** containing all the video, audio, graphics, and other files that will ultimately go onto the final disc. The resulting tape can then be tested to ensure that everything works correctly and is present before the ***mastering*** phase.

Pre-Positioned Accent

See ***Accent***.

PReP

Abbreviation for the ***PowerPC Reference Platform***. See ***PowerPC Reference Platform (PReP)***.

Prepress

Generally speaking, the term *prepress* includes all the steps required to transform an original into a state that is ready for reproduction by printing. Prepress includes the following steps: art and copy preparation (including typesetting), graphic arts photography (i.e., shooting ***negative***s), image assembly and ***imposition*** (***stripping***), and platemaking. Depending on the nature of the original, other included aspects of prepress may also include ***halftone*** photography, ***color separation***, or other procedures. Prepress should not be confused with ***makeready***, which is the preparation of the printing press. This article will begin with the traditional prepress methods, and will then cover newer digital prepress processes, which are replacing in large part the conventional ones. The article will conclude with the specific prepress considerations that vary according to the printing process to be utilized.

ART AND COPY PREPARATION

Strictly speaking, the term *copy* refers to text material only, while *art* refers to text as well as other page elements such as illustration matter (***line art*** and photographs), decorative borders, etc.

Manuscript. Copy is supplied by the author (or other content provider) in ***manuscript*** form. (Although the term *manuscript* is used to refer to any original text matter, it technically refers only to handwritten copy, a no-no in modern copy preparation. The more correct term for a typed manuscript is ***typescript***.) Since the setting of type needs to be done as quickly and as accurately as possible, there are certain manuscript conventions that should be followed, although the exact requirements can vary according to the temperament of the publisher and/or typesetter. Manuscript copy should always be typed (or output from a word processing program) and should be double-spaced. The pages should be consecutively numbered from the first page to the last page, never by chapter. Typing should only be on one side of the sheet, never on the reverse. Pages should always be 8½×11 (in the United States), although A4-size paper is acceptable in many cases. (See ***A Series***.) Copy produced on a typewriter should have uniformly sized characters, to ensure an accurate ***character count***. Copy prepared using a word processing program may not need to be; most such programs can automatically generate character and/or word counts. Line- and copy-editing alterations should be clearly indicated, preferably using standard ***proof marks***. If the number of corrections on a certain page is excessive, the page should be retyped. As many corrections as possible should be made in the manuscript phase; after typesetting, it becomes increasingly expensive to make all but the most minor of changes. (Large-scale changes to typeset copy made beyond the simple correction of *typographical errors* are known as *author alterations*, and most publishers charge an author when the changes exceed a certain amount.)

Type Specifications and Copyfitting. It is often the job of a copy editor, designer, or other such person to indicate on the manuscript copy the *typeface*, *point size*, *line length*, *leading*, etc., in which the copy is to be set. This includes both the text type and the *display type*, if any. A prime determinant of the type specifications, aside from aesthetics and the nature of the copy itself, is the amount of space in which the type needs to fit. In book typography, the amount of space available is dependent upon the desired final page count of the book, which is determined by the length of the manuscript and by the desired cost of the book. Since books are printed in *signature*s of varying size, it is often desirable to allow the page count to come as close as possible to the end of a signature, to reduce the amount of blank pages at the end of the book. In magazine, newspaper, and other such typography, there are strict space requirements for a particular article, with little leeway. Additionally, most magazines also have predetermined type specifications as part of the magazine's overall design, so cutting and/or adding of copy is often performed by an editor to fit the copy to the prescribed length. Other forms of typography, such as brochures, ads, etc., also have certain space requirements, but adhering to a certain design is not often a consideration in such "one-shot" jobs.

In all the cases mentioned above, the process of *copyfitting* is performed to fit the type in the alotted space as economically as possible. A *character count* is often performed to gauge the total number of characters in a particular manuscript. This number is often compared to the *alphabet length*s of various typefaces, to determine how much space will be occupied by the type when set in a particular *font*. Depending upon the nature of the piece to be printed, this may be performed with more or less accuracy. (See *Type and Typography*, *Copyfitting* and *Character Count*.)

Art Preparation and Layout. In the simplest of cases, such as a novel, text can be set as straight type. In many cases, however, art needs to be included. Art preparation begins with a layout, or a blueprint that aims to show how all the disparate elements of a page will be organized. The specific layout of a particular piece is dependent upon the nature of that piece, and what the piece is supposed to actually do and for whom it is intended. The layout for a beer ad aimed at purportedly "hip" young adults would probably be very different than that for an academic book jacket aimed at Civil War historians. Regardless of the nature of the layout, the steps involved in the production of it are the same. At the outset, a sketch of the intended design is prepared, with varying degrees of completeness. The roughest sketch

of a layout is a *thumbnail*, or a very crude pen or pencil diagram showing where text and images will be placed on a page. Thumbnails do not have to be the exact size as the ultimate page, can use wavy lines to indicate text, and can be prepared on any type of paper. They have even been prepared on cocktail napkins. A *rough* sketch is slightly more formalized than a thumbnail, and is closer to the actual size of the page. Thumbnails and roughs are often used during the brainstorming phase of design, and are used primarily to garner approval for a particular design idea. Once a rough has been approved, a *comprehensive* is produced, which is the most formalized of the early layout phases. It may be crudely drawn, but must be accurate with regard to page size, image size, and type size, as it is the primary guide that will be used to generate the *camera-ready art*.

Once a layout has been approved, a *mechanical* is prepared. The mechanical is where all the actual elements are assembled for reproduction. The set and corrected type is pasted to the mechanical in the proper position, and line art and other nonphotographic elements are also pasted to the mechanical board. (Hence, a mechanical is also known as a *pasteup*.) In the case of photographs, which need to be converted to halftones, commonly rough copies (such as xeroxes) or strips of *rubylith* are pasted into the proper position, simply to indicate where they will be inserted (and are often marked *FPO*, or "for position only"). The actual halftone negatives will be inserted into the page during stripping.

Line Art vs. Continuous-Tone. There are two basic types of original art: line art and photographs. Line art consists of art that, as the name imples, are simply lines, shapes, or other similarly rendered illustration. Type itself could be considered line art. Photographs are known as continuous-tone images, as they include gradations of color or gray, and are not simply black (or some other single color) or white. Most printing processes are incapable of reproducing continuous-tone images, so such images must be converted to a collection of tiny dots (called halftones). Each tiny dot is some level of gray (or color) and the packing together of these variably sized dots provides the illusion of continuous tones. Since negatives for halftone reproduction need to be photographed separately from line art and type, they cannot be added to the same mechanical. An FPO copy or strip of rubylith is used to create a hole or window in the negative, into which the halftone can be inserted. (See *Halftone*.) Other types of continuous-tone illustrations—such as paintings—also need to be converted to halftones.

Image Acquisition. Images can be generated or acquired in a variety of ways. Line art can be produced by hand, using pen and ink on paper, the only requirements being that the lines are clearly and solidly drawn, and that the paper be a background (such as white) that won't interfere with the image when it is photographed for a negative. Line art can also be produced in a computer *drawing program* (such as Adobe Illustrator, Corel Draw, etc.) and output from a *laser printer*, or higher *resolution* device. Continuous-tone images can either be ***reflection copy*** (such as prints) or ***transmission copy***, such as slides or transparencies. The terms *reflection* and *transmission* refer to the manner in which they are photographed (for negatives) or scanned (in digital prepress): for reflection copy, light is bounced off the surface of the copy where it is captured by the camera lens or scanner optics, while for transmission copy, light is passed through the image. Line art can also be reflection or transmission copy, as well.

Color Prepress. The are two basic types of color reproduction: ***spot color*** and ***process color***. Spot color is essentially an additional single color used to print specific page elements as a means of highlighting them. An example would be a black-and-white page of type that had a head printed in blue, or a company logo printed in red. Spot colors are physically separated from each other on the page, and are rarely overprinted. Each spot color will ultimately require its own plate, so it can be prepared on a separate mechanical or, more commonly, on a transparent overlay attached to the mechanical. The mechanical itself should only contain the ***key*** color, or the color that comprises the bulk of the page (this is commonly black). Spot color overlays are taped into position over the key and can be exposed separately.

Process color is more complex, and is used to print "full color" or ***four-color*** illustrations. There are four basic process colors: ***cyan***, ***magenta***, ***yellow***, and ***black***. The inks used to print the process colors are somewhat transparent (unlike the opaque spot color inks), and it is the overprinting of halftone dots of these four colors in varying densities that produces the full range of reproducible colors. Depending on how tight the ***register*** of the colors needs to be, the different colors can be indicated on transparent overlays, with the color and screen percentage marked on each sheet, or combined on one layer of the mechanical board, the color breaks indicated on a tissue overlay. The actual ***color separation negatives***, however, are always prepared separately and stripped in during flat assembly.

Process color images need to be color-separated during the prepress phase in order to produce a set of four different negatives so that four separate plates can be prepared. Although color separation has historically been performed photographically by exposing a full-color image to different color filters, most color separation is now performed digitally. (See ***Color Separation***.)

Image Sizing. When assembling graphic images on a mechanical, it is rare that the size of the original image will correspond exactly to the apportioned size on the layout. Two means of resizing photographs can be used, either independently or in conjunction with one another. ***Scaling*** is the resizing of an image that changes the dimensions of the image without altering the ratio of the width to the height, which can be performed photographically or digitally. ***Cropping*** is the cutting of certain sections of an image, either to allow it to fit in a prescribed areas, or to eliminate unwanted and/or unnecessary portions of the image.

The Final Mechanical. The final mechanical that is sent for graphic arts reproduction contains the pasted-up type and usually any line art. Black-and-white halftones and color images are represented by black or red shapes that correspond eactly to the size and shape of the image(s) to be inserted. It is important that all images not supplied on the mechanical be clearly identified and correlated with a marking on the mechanical (called ***keying***) to ensure that the correct image is placed in the correct position. It is at this point that the mechanical is sent out to be converted to negatives.

It should be pointed out at this point that much of the foregoing began—in the mid-1980s—to be replaced by digital means, all type and art being assembled in ***page makeup program***s such as ***QuarkXPress*** and ***Page-Maker***. Mechanicals, negatives, and color separations can be output directly from the computer. Increasingly, too, the printing plates themselves are imaged directly from digital data. (See ***Digital Prepress*** below.)

GRAPHIC ARTS PHOTOGRAPHY AND FILM ASSEMBLY

Although this article has talked primarily about producing negatives for graphic reproduction, this is only true in the case of some of the major printing processes. Some require film ***positive***s in order to properly prepare the final image carrier, while others require negatives. Some processes can utilize either negatives or positives. Plate for the most common printing process, ***offset lithography***, are imaged from negatives and are referred to as ***negative-working plates***. Lithographic plates can also be imaged from positives; these plates are called ***positive-working plates***. Each type of plate has somewhat different performance characteristics, but the preparation of the flat for platemaking is essentially the same. Thus, the term "negative" will be used throughout this article, but bear in mind that the term "positive" may also be appropriate. Where the processes of preparing the two types of film differ, distinctions will be made.

Graphic Arts Cameras and Films. Unlike portable (or even not-so-portable) cameras used for creative photography, photojournalism, or holiday snapshots, graphic arts cameras are very large devices, which, once installed, are rarely moved and are commonly attached to the darkroom in which the films are developed. There are several different configurations of graphic arts cameras, but they all share certain common features. The copyboard is where the mechanical is attached for exposure, and many cameras also include ***transparency*** holders, allowing for the imaging of both reflection and transmission copy. (In color separation and halftone photography, higher image quality is achieved with transmission copy.) Lenses used in graphic arts cameras differ from other types of camera lenses. Graphic arts camera lenses commonly have ***f-number***s between f/8 and f/11 (the higher the f-number, the smaller the lens ***aperture*** and the longer the exposure time required) and ***focal length***s that can range from 8–48 in., depending on the size of the camera. (In contrast, a typical 35-mm camera has a 2-in. focal length.) Lenses for graphic arts cameras are also prepared to generate as few aberrations and distortions as possible, and are also prepared to reproduce the colors of the visible spectrum as accurately as possible. The exposure times for graphic arts films are comparatively long, thus the lighting needs to be of much higher intensity than that required for other types of photography. Many graphic arts cameras also include suspension systems to minimize vibrations of the camera during exposure, and some have computer-controlled exposure systems which measure the intensity of the light source and vary the exposure time accordingly. Some varieties of cameras are vertical models, on which the copyboard, lens, and lensboard are aligned in a vertical plane, rather than the more typical horizontal system. The chief advantage of vertical cameras is their economical use of space.

Films used in graphic arts photography are similar to those used in other types of photography: an **emulsion** consisting of silver halides suspended in a gelatin is applied to a plastic or paper base. After exposure to an image, the light areas of the original are represented (on a photographic negative) by heavy deposits of silver, while the dark areas of the original are very light or transparent. (On a film or paper positive, the reverse is the case.) A photographic negative is used to prepare either film positives or prints. Different types of films are required for different types of originals, be they halftones, color separations, or line art.

Photographic films after exposure contain latent images, which only become visible after immersion in a developing solution. The solution transforms the silver halide to metallic silver in proportion to the amount of light to which the emulsion was exposed. Thus, in less exposed areas of a photographic negative (the image areas), less silver halide is converted to silver, while in the more highly exposed areas, more silver halide is converted to metallic silver. Fixing solutions after developing convert the unexposed silver halide in image areas to a soluble form, which can then be washed away. (Film positives operate in an opposite manner.) The chemical composition of the developing solution, the temperature at which the film needs to be developed, and even the color of the darkroom's safelight all vary according to the type of film used. (See **Photography: Graphic Arts Photography**. See also **Photography: Halftone Photography** and **Color Separation**.)

Image Assembly. The process of image assembly is known by a variety of terms, including imposition and stripping, although *stripping* is a term considered by some to be technically exclusive to offset lithography. All the terms, however, refer essentially to the assembly of negatives (or positives) into pages and signatures for platemaking and printing.

The guidelines for assembling page negatives are governed by the number of pages that will comprise a signature; that is, in turn determined by the size of the printing press and the paper to be used. In printing, it is desirable (both in terms of time and cost) to minimize the number of individual pressruns. Thus, a number of pages is printed on one side of a large press sheet, backed up, then the completed sheet is folded and cut into individual pages. As an example, say you want to print an eight-page newsletter, each page being 8½×11 in. You could of course run four sheets of 8½×11-in. paper through the press twice, but that amounts to eight separate pressruns, and eight separate plates, which is scarcely time- or cost-effective. A more efficient solution is to make only two pressruns. Using paper that is 22×17 in., four pages can be printed at a time. The imposition would look like this for one pressrun:

5 (inverted)	4 (inverted)
8	**1**

while the printing on the reverse would look like this:

3 (inverted)	6 (inverted)
2	**7**

Folding and cutting yields the proper number of pages. (And on a **perfecting press**, which prints both sides of the sheet simultaneously, only one pressrun is required.) This one 22×17-in. sheet is known as a signature. (More specifically, it is known as a **quarto**, or a single printed sheet of paper that is folded twice to yield eight pages.) Book printers can create signatures of up to 64 pages. (See **Book Typography**.) Consequently, the size of the signature that can be produced needs to be known prior to beginning image assembly.

The process of image assembly involves the attaching of a photographic negative of a page to a carrier sheet. For single-color printing, this carrier is most often a sheet of opaque goldenrod paper. The negative is attached to the back of the sheet, and holes are cut in the front over the image areas. (The entire assembly of negatives attached to a carrier sheet is called a **flat**.) This will allow light from the platemaking apparatus to pass through the transparent image areas, exposing the plate only in those areas. After the holes have been cut, the process of **opaquing** involves placing the negative on a light table and using a thick fluid or opaque marking pen to cover up any extraneous pinholes or other undesirable transparent regions of the negative, thus ensuring that unwanted spots, speckles, or marks will not be imaged on the plate. During opaquing and stripping, the stripper may also add crop marks, register marks, or other guides for the printer. Additionally, *pin register* systems—used throughout the prepress processes—use devices to punch holes or slots in nonimage areas of film and copy, while pins are fitted into the holes to ensure that successive pieces of film and/or copy are positioned correctly with respect to each other. Pin register systems are most often used when making multiple images on plates or films, especially in multicolor production.

The size of the flat is at least equal to the size of the press sheet to be utilized. The negative for each page to be printed on that sheet is stripped into the proper position on the flat, with certain allowances for trimming and binding considerations. (In particular, *shingling*, or the progressive increase of the size of the gutter margin of folded sheets to make allowances for the increase in thickness of a document that is bound by saddle-stitching, is set at this point.) It is also at this point that individual negatives that have been prepared separately (such as halftones) are inserted, making use of the transparent window that strips of rubylith have provided.

PLATEMAKING

The final process in prepress is platemaking. Platemaking is a general term that refers to the act of exposing the image carrier for the printing process to be utilized, and not all printing processes use plates specifically; *gravure* prints from an engraved *gravure cylinder* while *screen printing* utilizes a handcut or photographically prepared *stencil*. Each specific printing process—or application within that process—requires different plates or platemaking considerations. See *Plate: Offset Lithography*, *Plate: Flexography*, *Gravure Cylinder* and *Stencil*. See also the prepress considerations for each of the major printing processes mentioned below.

DIGITAL PREPRESS

The prepress processes outlined above are increasingly being replaced by digital methods. The history of digital prepress is one of evolution and revolution.

Before the 1950s, when *letterpress* was still the dominant form of printing, type was set using linecasters by trade typesetters, and color separations were made by engravers or other specialized trade shops. The advent of offset lithography and the photographic means of preparing plates were applied to the photographing of a letterpress-printed sheet. In the 1960s, phototypesetting eliminated this step in the process. Color separations were eventually made using electronic color scanners that could output the separations directly to film. In the late 1970s, the invention

of the *raster image processor (RIP)* and the raster-based *imagesetter* allowed the output of high-quality and high-*resolution* images and type directly on film, eliminating much of the need for graphic arts camera work. In the mid-1980s, the introduction of the Apple *Macintosh* personal computer, *page makeup software* (such as Aldus Page-Maker [now Adobe PageMaker]), and the Adobe *PostScript* page description language allowed the output of digital pages either as proofs on low-resolution *laser printer*s or as film on high-resolution imagesetters. Additionally, these systems (and later versions of these systems) also devised means of making color separations on the desktop, as well.

Essentially, advances in digital prepress have served to bring the front end (i.e., the acquisition of text and images) closer to the back end (i.e., the printed page). Some of the newest systems can image plates directly on press, while some can generate high-quality output directly on paper. Prepress systems range from low-end desktop systems that use a personal computer, off-the-shelf page makeup software, desktop scanners, and perhaps an imagesetter to generate digital pages for output to film or plate to high-end *color electronic prepress system*s (*CEPS*) that use high-quality *drum scanner*s, large computer systems often including many workstations connected together in a network, proprietary page makeup software and color separation programs, and high-end imagesetters. The difference between the systems—aside from price—is the quality of the output, especially halftone images and color separations. However, it should be pointed out that the gulf in output quality is rapidly closing, as low-end desktop systems increasingly generate quality on a par with much more expensive proprietary systems. Regardless of whether prepress is digital or "analog," the same basic processes need to be performed.

Copy and Art Preparation. In digital prepress, text material can be obtained in a variety of ways. It can either be typed directly into a program such as QuarkXPress or PageMaker while the page is being prepared, or it can be imported from a word processing, spreadsheet, database, or other program. The ability of these page makeup programs to allow the importing of text from other programs means that authors or other content providers do not necessarily need to have the same program as the typographer. Imported text can be edited and formatted with ease directly on the page (or "mechanical"), prior to film or paper output, unlike conventional typesetting that involved a good deal of literal cutting and pasting. Text can also be sent over the Internet (or transmitted from system to system by modem or by means of networking and/or telecommunications), where it is transferred as *ASCII text* and can be imported into the page makeup program. The drawback to ASCII text, however, is that it is incapable of representing formatting commands, such as italics, bold, etc.

Line art can be obtained in a variety of ways. Often, drawing programs are used by illustrators and artists to create digital line drawings, using either a conventional computer mouse to move a digital "pen" around the screen or other types of input devices such as *digitizing tablet*s. These drawings can be saved in a PostScript file format (*encapsulated PostScript [EPS]*) and input directly into a page makeup program in the proper position, and can be resized and cropped if necessary. They can also be output with the rest of the page or separately, if need be. Line art can also be drawn by hand on paper, digitized using a scanner, and converted to EPS format. There are many commercially available drawings programs, the most popular of which include Adobe *Illustrator*, Corel Draw, and Macromedia FreeHand.

The acquisition of photographic images is undergoing some turbulent changes. The earliest (and still common) means of obtaining photographic images is to use a scanner to digitize a transparency or print, edit, fix, color correct, or otherwise manipulate it using image-processing software (such as Adobe Photoshop), insert a low-resolution version of it in the page (comparable to the low-quality FPO image in mechanical pasteup), and generate a separate halftone negative or color separation negatives using the digital data. Newer means involve the use of *electronic camera*s and *digital camera*s to take photographs directly as digital information. These cameras can be plugged into a computer system and the images are already in digital form, eliminating the need for film developing and scanning. These cameras are still in their infancy, however, but an intermediate technology devised by Kodak (called the *PhotoCD*) is increasing in popularity. The PhotoCD is a technology allowing photographic images shot with conventional film cameras to be digitized by the developer from the original film and supplied to the customer on a CD-ROM, eliminating the need for scanning. Regardless of the means of digitizing an image, attention needs to be paid to the *file format* in which an image has been saved. For importing and exporting to and from page makeup programs, certain file formats produce the best quality or have the fewest compatibility issues. The most common formats for photographic images are *TIFF* and EPS. Images sent via the Internet or World Wide Web are often in the *GIF*, *JPEG*, or other format, and have often had some means of *data compression* performed on them, to reduce the size of the file that is transferred.

Bitmaps vs. Vectors. All of the types of copy and art mentioned above (and this includes text type) fall into one of two forms: *bitmap*s or *vector*s. A bitmap is essentially a computer display or output in which a screen object is described by a series of dots called *pixel*s. If you look closely at your computer monitor, you'll notice that each character comprises a series of dots. (Computer output—such as from a laser printer or even an imagesetter is also made of pixels, but these latter dots, technically called *spot*s to distinguish them from halftone dots—are so much smaller than screen pixels that they are barely perceptible.) When a computer system or program describes a bitmap, it essentially saves in its memory a grid corresponding to the display area of the screen, and the status of each pixel is

noted. Most paint programs and image-processing software make use of bitmapped images, which is the only practical means of handling photographic or other continuous-tone images. Type and line art, however, when described as bitmaps, tend to exhibit the stair-step pattern known as *aliasing* (or *jaggies*). This is because straight lines, for example, are made up of discrete dots which become visible at certain angles. Bitmapped type and line art tend to result in output that is not smooth. A solution to this problem is the use of *vector graphics*, in which type characters and line illustrations can be represented by mathematical formulas or descriptions of lines, angles, and curves. This results in much smoother output, and also requires less processing power than bitmaps. Vector graphics, however, cannot be manipulated on a pixel-by-pixel basis. (See *Bitmap* and *Vector Graphics*.)

PostScript. In the early days of personal computing, all output was bitmapped, which was fine when dot matrix printers were the most common output device. In order for personal computers to make any headway into the world of prepress, however, some means of generating high-quality, high-resolution output needed to be devised. Enter PostScript, a *page description language (PDL)* introduced in 1985. The important advantage to PostScript was its ability to describe typographic characters as vectors or outlines, rather than as bitmaps (although computers do need bitmaps to display the font properly on the screen). Essentially, the PostScript language is a text-based description of a page, another advantage of which is its device independence, the ability to print a page virtually identically on any output device (regardless of manufacturer) that can interpret the language. These devices can include laser printers and imagesetters, among other devices. Occasionally, errors occur in a PostScript file, and although a PostScript file is theoretically editable, sometimes that's easier said than done. Later versions of the PostScript language included algorithms for color separations and, in particular, halftone *screen angles*. (See *PostScript*.)

Output. As was mentioned earlier, the traditional mechanical has moved from the pasteup board to the computer screen. Where once the mechanical was photographed by a graphic arts camera to produce ready-for-stripping negatives, most electronic pages are output (either directly or by sending the computer file to a service bureau or prepress house) as film negatives from an imagesetter. An imagesetter is an output device separated from the actual computer by a raster image processor (RIP). The PostScript file describing a page is sent to the RIP, where it is converted to a bitmap, each possible point on the output film being addressed. (Despite what was said earlier about the desirability of vectors over bitmaps, the resolution—or number of pixels that can fit into a particular unit of length—of most imagesetters is so high that jaggies are rarely a problem.) After *ripping*, the laser in the output device moves across the film, exposing each individual dot according to the instructions provided by the RIP. At this point, the output negatives may include any halftones already in position, or text and halftones may be output separately and manually stripped into flats. Some devices can output large negatives including all the pages properly imposed, or, once again, individual pages can be imposed manually on traditional goldenrod flats. Additionally, some systems allow for the direct laser imaging of plates, in some cases directly on the press. This is particularly useful when a particular print job will contain multiple plates for a single page (such as multicolor printing), which must remain in register.

Additionally, some newer systems skip intermediate film output and platemaking entirely and generate the actual printed output directly from digital data. (See *On-Demand Printing*.) See also *Color*, *Color Separation*, *Halftone*, *Screen Angles*, *Imaging*, *Graphics*, and *Scanning*.

PRINTING PROCESSES

Each of the major printing processes uses different image carriers, press configurations, inks, and press chemistries to transfer an image to a substrate. As a result, some of the prepress steps vary from process to process. What follows is an overview of the specific considerations to take into account when preparing copy and art for printing.

Offset Lithography. The image carriers for offset lithographic presses can be either positive-working plates or negative-working plates, the major difference (in terms of prepress) is that the former are produced from film positives while the latter are prepared from film negatives.

Film Assembly. Negatives for single-color jobs are commonly attached to goldenrod paper as was mentioned above. For multicolor jobs, however, a different flat material may be required, such as orange vinyl, masking film, or clear polyester to which an orange vinyl mask may be attached. On this negative carrier sheet (also known as a layout sheet), which is often slightly larger than the size of the plate on which the film will be imaged, the press gripper and plate bend allowances are marked, and lines are drawn to indicate the proper positioning of the films. Trim marks and other reference points are etched into the negative, beyond the image area, so to aid in registration of successive colors or to indicate trim margins for the finisher. The carrier sheet is positioned wrong-reading on a light-table, and the negatives are positioned emulsion-side-up, and taped into position. The carrier sheet is flipped over, and holes that are large enough to reveal the entire image area(s) are cut. At this point, the film assembler inspects the revealed image areas for any defects and performs any necessary opaquing.

In many cases, it is desirable to use film positives. (Generally, positive-working plates produce less *dot gain* in the printing of halftones than negative-working plates, and are frequently used in web offset lithography.) Stripping of film positives is performed essentially in the same manner as that of negatives, with the exception that they are stripped emulsion-side-up on a clear plastic carrier. As a result, there is no masking material to cut away.

At this stage, any inserts (or additional negatives or positives) may be inserted, so long as they are going to be part of the same flat. Such inserts include halftone negatives, which can be attached to the flat in the transparent window created by the use of black or red material on the mechanical. Sometimes, however, such inserts are prepared on separate flats (called *complementary flats*). Both the line and halftone flats are exposed to the same plate. In some cases, a particular plate needs to include a *screen tint*. When a screen tint is to serve as a background for type, it may be prepared by reversing the type into a dark tint or *surprinting* type over a light tint. Multiples of the same image that will appear in different locations on the final print can be prepared by making multiple negatives, or by a *step-and-repeat* platemaking process that uses a single film to repeatedly expose the plate in several locations.

In process-color printing, a single flat needs to be made for each of the colors to be printed. (However, if each color prints in a distinctly different location, a single flat can include all four colors, and separate plates prepared by masking all but the color to be imaged at any one time.) More often, however, one *key* flat is prepared using one of the four color separation negatives. This is most commonly the *black printer* (and the designation of black as "K" in *CMYK* stands for "key"), and all other flats are prepared in register with the black.

In process-color image assembly, registration, trim, and fold marks are included on a separate flat, called a *master flat* or a *marks flat*. Negatives are made just of the various marks needed, which are stripped into position on a carrier sheet.

Trapping. Multicolor printing requires different degrees of registration and, depending upon the application, the degree of fit between one color or image and an adjacent one has more or less latitude. Hairline register refers to the need to maintain very strict tolerances between one image or color and the next. In contrast, loose register means that the separate images or colors are fairly independent of one another, and some degree of leeway is possible when preparing flats and making plates. In many cases, lap register, or trap, is required, which refers to a small degree of overlap between adjacent colors. An example is yellow type on a blue background; the blue prints around the type, leaving a white hole. When the yellow prints, it fills the hole. An incorrect fit will result in either a line of white between the blue and the yellow or an overprinting of the two colors beyond the hole created for the yellow. In lap register, a small amount of overlap (commonly equivalent to one row of halftone dots) is acceptable and preferable to white space. In some cases, elaborate photographic techniques are performed to improve the trapping of successive images or colors. (See, for example, *Spreads and Chokes*.) Trapping, by the way, not only refers to the manipulation of successive images, but also to the ability of one ink film to adhere to a previously printed ink film. (See *Trap* and *Trapping*.)

Digital Prepress. Digital processes have replaced some of the above-mentioned procedures, but film assembly may still need to be performed manually as a prelude to platemaking. Some digital programs allow for the output of line and halftone images on the same negative, and the output of the individual color separation negatives. The output of entire properly imposed flats may eliminate the need for extensive stripping. And, of course, direct-to-plate systems avoid the issue of negatives entirely. (See also *Plate: Offset Lithography*.)

Gravure. The advantages of the gravure printing process include a greater tonal range, producing a print quality that is essentially unmatched by any other printing process. The very simple inking system also means that ink/water balance need not be a concern, and consequently the color drifts that occur in offset printing tend not to occur with gravure. *Dot gain* is also not an issue in gravure printing. (The disadvantage, of course, is the expense of the process. Although it is used for high-quality art prints and other illustration matter and packaging, it is not cost-effective for short-run jobs.)

In terms of the prepress considerations, however, there are several limitations to the gravure process that need to be kept in mind. The first is that since the gravure image carrier—the engraved *gravure cylinder*—uses depressed cells to transfer ink to the substrate, this means that essentially all artwork—be it type, line art, or continuous-tone images—is screened, much like a halftone, the result being that some *typeface*s and *point size*s reproduce less well than others. Another consideration in gravure prepress is the increased need to proof all materials carefully before the preparation of the gravure cylinder. In offset lithography (and other processes), it is not significantly expensive or time-consuming to correct or even remake plates (although it can be). In gravure, however, the removal of the copper plating and the re-engraving of a cylinder is extremely expensive and time-consuming, although some extremely minor corrections can be made by hand on the cylinder.

Copy and Art Preparation. Designers and typesetters preparing originals for gravure reproduction need to be aware that the gravure screen can interfere with the legibility of some typefaces, especially those that have fine *serif*s, extreme thick and thin strokes, or extremely light weights. Point sizes below six points are not advised generally, but especially not in gravure printing. In some cases, typefaces do not reproduce well even at six points.

In terms of other types of original artwork, gravure is able to reproduce line art and photographs, as well as many other types of illustration matter. The process for producing a mechanical is the same as it is for offset lithography.

Color Separation and Halftones. In the 1980s, a set of standards was devised that created what is known as **halftone gravure**, or the ability to image the gravure cylinder using films designed for offset lithography. This came about because advertisers would often submit film to more than one publication, some of which were printed using lithography, and some of which were printed using gravure. The need for a common set of standards resulted in language in the **SWOP** standards covering the use of offset films for gravure printing. The important consideration is that gravure cannot reproduce halftone dots below 5% density, so art directors keep in mind that halftone dots smaller than that will not reproduce on gravure presses.

The process of color separation is the same for gravure as it is for offset lithography. Photographic separation has been replaced in large part by digital separations prepared on color electronic publishing systems or, more and more commonly, desktop systems. Unlike offset lithography, however, some gravure systems allow halftone screens in four-color images to all be at the same angle, eliminating the headaches that the **screen angle** issue can cause. (See **Screen Angles**.)

Cylinder Etching. Historically, gravure cylinders were engraved using photographic negatives or positives exposed through a special gravure screen (similar to a halftone screen) onto a photosensitive resist coating on the copper-plated gravure cylinder which, when developed and exposed to a strong acid, etched the image areas into the copper. The most common means at the moment of gravure cylinder engraving is known as **electromechanical engraving**, and involves the use of a diamond-tipped stylus physically etching the cells into the surface of the cylinder. The engraving head is driven by information gleaned from a scanned image—the mechanical—or an image obtained from some other source. The screen pattern, screen angle, dot count, dot shape, etc., are all preprogrammed into the system beforehand. This method of engraving reduces the need for negatives in many cases. It is also possible to drive the engraving head from negatives (as in the case of halftone gravure). In the case of prescreened original halftones, the optics of the scanner can be adjusted to ignore any dot patterns, thus ensuring that the original screen pattern is not added to the screen pattern generated by the engraving mechanism. It is also possible to drive the engraving head directly from digital data. Newer systems are also beginning to etch the gravure cylinder using lasers driven by digital information. (See **Gravure Engraving**.)

Flexography. Since flexographic printing is done on a wide variety of substrates on a wide variety of press configurations and with a wide variety of inks, the exact materials to be used in a particular job will determine the limitations imposed on type and art to be utilized. When preparing copy and art, industry standards commonly recommend no smaller than six-point type for wide-web presses (and no smaller than eight-point type for any reverse copy), while no smaller than four-point type (or six-point for reverse copy) is recommended for narrow-web jobs. Flexography can also print any copy or art that can be printed with other methods, including line art and halftones. When preparing halftones, however, the substrate will determine the best screen count to use; on corrugated board, 45- to 65-line screens will suffice, while plastic film-based web printing requires screen counts between 65 and 150, depending on the press. In multicolor flexographic printing, tight register is typically to be avoided, as the overprinting of adjacent colors can yield undesirable third colors. The tolerances—or amounts of space that should be left between successively printed colors—vary by press, from ¼ in. for **stack press**es printing on corrugated board to ¹⁄₆₄ in. for narrow-web presses.

The Flexographic Plate. Flexography's use of natural or synthetic rubber plates presents a series of difficulties to the prepress process. Specifically, when rubber plates are prepared, there is some degree of shrinkage of the original image during platemaking, followed by a stretching of the image as the plate is attached to the plate cylinder. As a result, these deformations need to be accounted for in the preparation of copy and art, as these plate expansions and shrinkages can result in distorted type and images which affect not just the aesthetics of a job, but also the functionality. For example, **Universal Product Code** symbols on packaging are often printed flexographically, and distorted prints can render them unreadable to the bar-code scanning devices. Plate deformations can also affect proper register. Additionally, different portions of the plate may deform in varying amounts.

Given the variety of plate materials, press configurations, substrates, etc., it is impossible to provide a detailed list of tolerances and degrees of compensation. Each production manager should check with the printer to know what is likely to occur during the prepress and printing processes. Generally speaking, however, it is safe to say that molded natural or synthetic rubber flexographic plates shrink about 1½–2% in length, width, and plate thickness when the molded rubber cools (assuming no shrink-control materials have been added). As a result, if these plates are to be used for a particular print job, the artwork on the mechanical needs to be reduced by this amount. As for **photopolymer plate**s, shrinkage doesn't occur during the platemaking process, but any image carrier—and this applies to metal plates, as well—will distort when it is stretched around a cylinder. Although mathematical formulas can be used to calculate the amount of stretch per inch, all the various aspects of the press, substrate, plate thickness, etc., can affect the numbers obtained. As a result, it is often preferable to make test plates to obtain an accurate, custom-calculated degree of plate stretch. It should be born in mind, however, that not all jobs are affected dramatically—or even significantly—by plate elongation. Jobs with small image areas, or images printed in large open spaces, will not be affected unduly. Increasing the complexity of a job, however, results in an increased need to pay attention to elongation. Jobs needing close register of successive colors need careful attention paid to stretch.

Copy and Art Preparation. Like the other printing processes that have already been discussed, flexographic plates are also prepared from negatives or positives, which in turn are prepared by photographing (or digitally outputting) a mechanical. Mechanicals for flexography are prepared in exactly the same way as those for other printing processes. In some cases, intricate designs and artwork may be attached to the mechanical in an enlarged size, but will need to be reduced to the proper size during the preparation of negatives. Single-color jobs require but one mechanical, one negative, and one plate, and are produced very straightforwardly. Color separations, halftones, spot color, etc., are all prepared and laid out in a manner similar to that which has already been discussed. It is at the mechanical stage that plate elongation compensation may be performed. When preparing halftones, dot gain is commonly about 10–20%. The engraved cells of the flexographic **anilox roller** (the primary inking roller on the press) can also interfere with halftone dots, creating undesirable **moiré** patterns. Since the cells of an anilox roller usually run at a 45° angle to the direction of web travel, screen angles need to be significantly offset to avoid undesirable patterns.

As one can imagine, digital prepress equipment and processes have made strong inroads in the flexographic prepress process. The process is virtually the same for flexography as for other printing processes, with attention paid to the flexo-specific issues and considerations mentioned above.

Film Assembly. Assembly (stripping) of film negatives for flexo platemaking is exactly the same as that for offset lithography, or even gravure, with the exception that photographic techniques to compensate for image elongation or distortion during platemaking may be performed prior to stripping.

After image assembly, flexographic plates are ready to be made. (See **Plate: Flexography**.)

Screen Printing. The prepress processes involved in **screen printing** differ from those used in the other major printing processes. Screen printing uses as its image carrier a **stencil** mounted to a finely-woven cloth screen. The stencil contains holes that correspond to image areas, and ink is forced through these image areas using a **squeegee**.

There are two basic ways of preparing a stencil, and there are consequently two sets of prepress procedures.

Handcut Stencils. The simpler of the two means of stencil preparation is the hand- or knifecut method. In this case, the mechanical is placed beneath a transparent or translucent stencil material, and the image areas are literally cut out of the stencil using an X-ACTO knife or other similar implement. Additionally, smaller mechanicals can be placed in a photo enlarger, and the size of the original mechanical adjusted up or down. The stencil material is placed on top of the surface bearing the enlarged or reduced image, and the cuts made. As one can imagine, this means of preparing a stencil has severe limitations on the type of original art which can be imaged. Handcut stencils are used for very simple line illustrations and geometric shapes, not commonly type or photographic images. The complexity of the image, however, depends upon the skill of the person performing the cutting.

A similar variety of manually-prepared stencil is known as the *tusche-and-glue* method, which involves "drawing" the stencil directly on the screen using *tusche*, a special type of glue. This method is typically used only by screen artists, rarely in industrial screen printing.

Photostencils. The basic principle behind the *photostencil*, or a screen printing stencil that is imaged photographically, is the exposure of a film positive of the mechanical to the stencil material which, after developing, creates holes in the stencil material in image areas, but remains solid and impermeable to ink in the nonimage areas, rather like a photographic negative. The process of preparing photostencils can handle mechanicals including type, line art, and halftones. Multicolor screen printing can also be performed by creating different stencils for each of the colors to be printed.

Halftone Screen Printing. The preparation of photostencils for halftone reproduction creates some problems in screen printing that require additional steps in the prepress process to overcome. Although screen-printed halftones can be larger, printed in shorter runs economically, and use more brilliant inks than those printed using other processes, the dot sizes must be more carefully controlled. For example, highlight dots in screen printing below 10–15% or shadow dots above 85–90% will not likely reproduce. The halftone *screen count* for screen printing needs to remain coarse; in many facilities, an 85-line screen is the best bet, although some more advanced facilities can achieve good results with up to a 110-line screen.

In many cases, a finer screen (such as the common 133-line screen) can be used in concert with a film enlarger to produce a film positive that artificially creates the equivalent of a 65-line screen, which is well-suited for screen printing halftone images. Another problem inherent in the screen printing of halftones is a moiré pattern produced when the halftone screen pattern interferes with the pattern of the printing screen, commonly experienced when too coarse a *mesh count* is used. This can be alleviated by placing the film positive bearing the halftone image on the screen and rotating it to an angle at which the moiré disappears. This angle can be noted and the stencil can be adhered at this angle.

(See also *Photostencil.*)

Letterpress. Although letterpress—the printing from raised type—is a rarely used process these days, a direct descendent lives on in flexography. Letterpress is distinguished from flexography in that the former uses curved metal plates (although flexible photopolymer plates similar to those used in flexography are also used) and viscous, lithographic-like inks. Plates are prepared from negatives, which are prepared in a manner similiar to those produced in other printing processes. Letterpress plates are prepared in a manner similiar to that used to produce flexographic plates. (See *Plate: Letterpress.*)

Other Printing Processes. Although the above-mentioned printing processes are the five most common in the printing industry, new technologies are creating new types of presses. In some types of printing—such as laser printing and *ink jet* printing—prepress is not much of an issue; these types of printing are commonly used to output computer information, either to make proofs of jobs that will be printed by the conventional methods or as general office printouts. In the latter case, "prepress" simply refers to the input and formatting of the copy and/or art on the computer screen. Printing *device driver*s then output the file to the printer. In the former case, "prepress" will commonly be whatever processes are used to produce the art for the printing process to be utilized.

The trend in new printing technologies has been to bring the back end closer and closer to the front end, so that new "on-demand printing" devices function essentially as large laser printers or imagesetters, being able to (relatively) quickly output large numbers of copies of black-and-white or color pages.

Prepress has gone through some remarkable transformations since the early days of this century. It is interesting in that the latest round of developments—digital prepress—has essentially sought to eliminate it as much as possible. Economically, this makes sense. The elimination of the need to output type, paste it into mechanicals, shoot negatives, and then shoot plates reduces many steps in the process, saving time, money, and materials. The CEPS and imagesetter combination did away with the need to create physical mechanicals; negatives could be output directly from the screen. Now, direct-to-plate systems are eliminating the need to output negatives. Eventually, it could be argued, direct-to-substrate printing may become viable, although one doubts that the quality produced by such systems will ever surpass that produced by the conventional printing processes. The term *prepress* itself is sometimes hyphenated, *pre-press*.

Prepress Proof
Alternate term for an *off-press proof*. See *Off-Press Proof*.

Preprinted Form
Any sheet of paper reproduced in some quantity with some amount of constant data, to which variable data can be added. Invoices, with constant company name, address, etc., and variable charges, are examples of preprinted forms.

Pre-Production

In motion picture and video production, any process that takes place before filming or taping commences, such as scriptwriting, storyboarding, hiring production crews and talent, arranging shooting schedules, etc.

Pre-Roll

In video editing, to rewind a video tape a short distance before an *in-point* to ensure that the tape is up to speed when the edit is made, preventing *distortion* or other video errors. The ability to pre-roll tapes is standard on nearly all professional and semi-professional editing equipment.

Prescan Analysis

A preliminary examination of a *color transparency* prior to *scanning* to evaluate its tonal characteristics as a means of properly setting up and calibrating the *scanner*. A prescan analysis can be performed either by direct measurement or by the use of reference transparencies.

Prescreen

In prepress, a low-contrast *halftone* on glossy photographic paper that is pasted up with *line art* and text, to avoid having to strip in a halftone negative when assembling a *flat*.

Presensitized Plate

A printing plate used in *offset lithography* that has been pretreated with a light-sensitive coating. See *Plate: Offset Lithography*.

Presentation Graphics

Application programs (or the results thereof) designed to create high-quality audiovisual aids for business presentations, including graphs, charts, decorative line art, logos, photographs, or even sound and video. Usually, these programs generate "slide shows," which consist of screens accenting points made by the presenter. There is usually some degree of *interactivity* in these presentations, such as single-screen "builds" of points or figures.

Presentation Layer

In networking, the sixth of seven *layer*s in the *OSI* reference model, defining the means by which data is formatted, presented, and encoded. See *Open Systems Interconnection (OSI)*.

Pre-Separated Art

Any art prepared for reproduction in which each color—be it *spot* or *process color*—exists on a separate overlay.

Presscake

The term for the mixture of water and pigment particles following filtration and prior to either drying or *flushing*. The moisture content of the presscake can range from 30–80%. (See *Ink: Ink Manufacturing*.)

Press Gain

Alternate term for *dot gain*. See *Dot Gain*.

Press Proof

A *color proof* produced using the actual ink(s) and *substrate* that will be used in the pressrun proper, as a means of evaluating how a particular set of inks performs on a particular substrate, and to ensure that the desired colors can be achieved. The printing press used may or may not be that which will be used for the actual pressrun, and may be a *proof press*.

Pressrun

The actual printing of the desired number of copies of a print job, immediately following *makeready*. The length of a particular pressrun may need to be taken into account to gauge production costs.

Press Section

A part of a papermaking machine, consisting of a series of two-roll presses, through which the wet paper *web* passes after leaving the *forming section*. When the web reaches the press section, it is about 80–85% water. In each two-roll section, the web travels through the nip of the rolls, which squeezes out moisture, evens out the paper's *formation*, and presses the fibers together, improving their bonding and, ultimately, sheet strength. The press section and the degree of *wet pressing* affect the ultimate *finish* and *bulk* of the paper. Those papers that require high bulk and low finish need less wet pressing than those that require low bulk and high finish. After the press section, the paper—still about 60–70% water—is sent to the *drying section*. (See *Fourdrinier* papermaking machine.)

Press Sheet

In printing, a full-size sheet of the actual paper that will be used for a particular job on the printing press. The term can refer to blank stock or to the printed sheets.

Pressure Foot

Alternate term for a *feeder foot*, a device located in a sheetfed press's *feeder section*. See *Feeder Foot*.

Pressure-Sensitive Adhesive

A form of *adhesive* that, in dry form, will remain sticky at room temperature and will bond to another surface under minimal pressure and without moistening.

Pressure-Sensitive Label

A paper to which a *pressure-sensitive adhesive* has been applied. (See *Pressure-Sensitive Adhesive*.) Also known as a *pressure-sensitive paper*.

Pressure-Sensitive Paper

A paper to which a *pressure-sensitive adhesive* has been applied. See *Pressure-Sensitive Adhesive*. Also known as a *pressure-sensitive label*.

Pressurized Groundwood (PGW)

A method of *mechanical pulping* in which wood is ground against an abrasive rotating stone, as with *groundwood*, but under high pressure and at temperatures in excess of 100°C. PGW also generates a better quality pulp than traditional groundwood. (See *Mechanical Pulping*.)

Pressurized Screen Printing

A configuration of *screen printing* press that uses air pressure to force ink through the screen fabric, eliminating the need for a *squeegee*.

PRI

Abbreviation for *Primary Rate Interface*. See *Primary Rate Interface (PRI)*.

Primary Colors

Any set of colors within a particular color system that are the most basic colors for that system. All other colors can be produced from the primaries, but the primaries cannot be produced by combinations of other colors. In two particular systems, there are three primary colors. The *additive color primaries*, or the primary colors of light, are *red, green, and blue*. The *subtractive color primaries*, or the primary colors of pigments or colorants, are *cyan, magenta*, and *yellow*. All other colors—called *secondary colors*—are derived from combinations of these primaries.

Primary Font

In typography, the *font* in which the bulk of the text or other print matter has been typeset.

Primary Indent

In typography, an *indent* placed at the beginning of a line (usually at the beginning of a *paragraph*), often preceded by an *end-of-paragraph code*. See also *Secondary Indent*.

Primary Leading

In typography, the *leading* (or *line spacing*) utilized in the main body of text, or in a particular set of lines, as opposed to *secondary leading*. See *Line Spacing*.

Primary Rate Interface (PRI)

One of two types of *ISDN* connections comprising 23 *B-channel*s (in the United States and Japan) and one *D-channel*. In Europe, PRI utilizes 30 B-channels. PRI is primarily used by businesses rather than individual users. See also *Basic Rate Interface (BRI)*. See *ISDN*.

Primary Side Head

In *book typography*, the title given to the largest subdivision (such as a part or section) of a chapter, printed in the margins of the text. See also *Secondary Side Head*.

Primer

Alternate term for *anchor coat*. See *Anchor Coat*.

Alternate term for *barrier coat*. See *Barrier Coat*.

Primitive

Any fundamental constituent of a graphic image, be it a point, dot, line, geometric shape, or alphanumeric character. The extrapolation or combination of primitives creates more complex objects or entities and, ultimately, the desired graphic image.

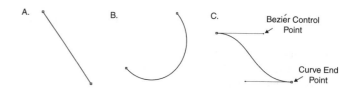

The three basic graphical primitives used by PostScript— the line, the arc, and the curve.

Printability

A term describing the interrelationships of paper properties that result in accurate, high-quality printed images. Factors affecting printability include surface properties (smoothness, levelness, ink absorbency, cleanliness, gloss, finish, etc.) and structural properties (bulk or thickness, weight, pick resistance, dimensional stability, etc.). Although various attempts at quantifying printability have been proposed (see *Printability Tester*), it still remains primarily a subjective quality. Printability is often described in concert with *runnability*, or how well a paper will perform on press without interfering with the operation of the printing process.

Printability Tester

A device used to quantitatively measure the *printability* of a paper. The concept of printability is a highly subjective one, and over the years many attempts have been made to make it more objective, including the use of printing presses in laboratory conditions, as well as specific printability testing devices (such as the Prüfbau, IGT or Huck printability testers) to measure a host of paper properties, such as print density, paper smoothness, *pick resistance, ink setoff, ink transfer*, and many other interrelated properties that affect *print quality*. So far, however, a widely accepted numerical value gauging printability has yet to be devised. (See *Paper and Papermaking: Paper Properties*.)

Printable Area

That portion of a sheet of paper where a computer printer can place an image.

Print Block

Any area of a page occupied by printed material. Also called a *print box*.

Print Contrast (PC)

A method of evaluating and optimizing the *density* of the ink deposited on the *substrate* during printing. The ink strength—or print contrast—is determined to take into account the solid ink density, the density of the ink in *shadow* areas of the image, and the **dot gain**. Print contrast is calculated by measuring the ink density of a solid area and the ink density in a 75% tint. The print contrast is calculated according to the formula:

$$\text{Print Contrast} = \frac{D_s - D_{75}}{D_s} \times 100$$

where D_s is solid area density, and D_{75} is the 75%-tint density.

Printer Access Protocol (PAP)

In networking, a **protocol** used in **AppleTalk** networks to manage network printing.

Printer Description Language

Alternate term for **page description language**. See **Page Description Language**.

Printer Driver

A **driver** used to control a printer. See **Driver**.

Printer Emulation

In computing, the ability of a printer to **emulate** a printer manufactured by another vendor.

Printer Font

A computer file—either in **PostScript** format or other **page description language** format—containing mathematical descriptions or image outlines of a particular **typeface**. Printer fonts can be downloaded to the printer (or other output device) and called up when a document utilizing a particular font is sent to the printer. Most fonts available for computers contain printer fonts, which, being **vector**-based, rather than **bitmapped**, ensure that the output is at as high a resolution as the output device is capable of. Such fonts also contain **screen font**s, which are **low-resolution**, bitmapped versions of the fonts used to display the font on the computer monitor. Computer fonts possessing only screen fonts rather than printer fonts tend to output at low resolution and with inferior typographic quality, especially at large point sizes. (See also **Screen Font**.)

Printer Paper

Any paper designed specifically for any type of computer printer. Printer paper may be distinguished by having holes to accomodate feeding mechanisms, or special coatings to improve image quality.

Printer's Error (PE)

An error in typesetting made by a keyboard operator during input, which needs to be corrected at the proof stage, also known as a **typographic error**, in contrast to an **author's alteration**.

The term *printer's error* also refers to any mistake made in any prepress (negative-making, platemaking, etc.) or printing operation.

Printing

The production of multiple copies of a document, book, etc., by the use of plates or other surface to transfer an impression to a **substrate** For much of the history of printing, **letterpress** (or "relief") was employed, but advancements since the nineteenth century have produced a wide variety of printing processes.

HISTORY OF PRINTING

The history of printing begins in a parallel course with that of movable type. Although Johann Gutenberg, a goldsmith from Mainz, Germany (c. 1400–c. 1468), is regarded as having invented both movable type and the printing press, the former dates back to eleventh-century China, and the latter to eighth-century Japan and ninth-century China. Between 1058 and 1061, Pi Sheng used clay, and later tin, to create type. The nature of the Chinese language (the lack of a true alphabet and the presence of more than 40,000 characters) made the invention and practical use of movable type a near impossibility. Pi Sheng's type was not widely used, and didn't catch on in the East until a couple hundred years later. Metal type was invented in 1403 in Korea, primarily due to the dearth of hardwood necessary to create workable blocks of type, and was quickly endorsed and adopted by the Korean emperor T'ai Tsung as an aid to government and the preservation of civilization.

The idea of using raised blocks of wood to create an impression on a substrate (initially clay) derived from seals (used in impressing signatures). (The Chinese word for "print" is the same as that for "seal.") In the second century, classical texts were stamped into stone; around the fifth century, ink was applied to the blocks. The earliest known printed book is the "Diamond Sutra," printed by Wang Chieh in 868. Many other books, most in roll form but one in the cut-sheet form we are familiar with today, were found that date from around the same time. Shortly thereafter, the idea of printing was adopted by religious adherents to promote their doctrines and prayers, hymns, and other ecclesiastical materials were widely duplicated and disseminated. The other primary use of printing, dating from around 969 or earlier, was the production of playing cards. In the tenth century, the emperor agreed to (and financed) the printing of the Chinese classics, which led to a widespread revival of learning and education during the time of the Sung Dynasty (known as the Sung Renaissance). Also in the tenth century, printing was enthusiastically applied to the production of paper currency, which had the effect of introducing to China the concept of inflation.

The invention of block printing had a dramatic effect on Chinese culture and the democratization of knowledge; by 972, five thousand volumes of the Buddhist canon had been printed, and hundreds of volumes of Dynastic histories appeared soon thereafter, followed by encyclopedias, dictionaries, as well as compilations and anthologies of literature. There was, in a word, a riot of scholarship. The downside, however, is that due to a prohibition on the use of printing for commercial (i.e., money-making) purposes, all printed texts were given away by the government. This helped stifle the further development of printing technology; movable metal type, created in Korea, had a brief popularity, then died away. The prevalence of movable type could have been effected by the adoption of a simplified, twenty-four character alphabet devised by King Sajong of Korea, but interest in things Chinese (rather than Korean) prevented this. Typesetting (as we now know it) only became popular in China after Gutenberg's invention and the principles and techniques of Eastern typography were introduced by missionaries, after having first been carried from Korea to Europe, probably by Arab traders. What goes around comes around.

In Europe, there is evidence (albeit inconclusive) that printing utilizing movable type was first practiced in the 1430s in Haarlem, Holland, by Laurens Coster. If that was the case, it didn't catch on, as the next recorded Dutch use of the technology was in 1470, when German printers set up a press in Utrecht.

The birth of the printing press in Europe can be traced back to the demand for religious indulgences. Following the ebbing of the Black Death in the late fourteenth century, there was a great economic boom, and general sense of revelry in Europe. As a result of all the "moralistic infractions" going on at the time, there was a great need for indulgences (basically, religious documents absolving sinners of their sins). Indulgences (from which there was big money for those providing and writing them) could be obtained at any of a variety of religious shrines and popular pilgrimage spots throughout Europe. Also to be obtained at these pilgrim "conventions" were any number of religious artifacts—trinkets, special mirrors with which one was supposed to catch the image of oneself standing before the shrine, and other sorts of "souvenirs." Makers and sellers of these items pursued their craft with a vigor and determination similar to that employed by carnival or fair hawkers of today. One particular maker of these artifacts had borrowed a significant amount of money from his business partners to invest in the manufacture and selling of these items at a big pilgrim convention in Aachen in the mid-1400s. Unfortunately, in 1439, he discovered to his horror that he got the year of the festival wrong and missed it. Heavily in debt to his partners, he assured them that he had been secretly working on something else that was likely to be a goldmine (literally). He was a goldsmith from Mainz, Germany, born Johann Gensfleisch (the German word for "gooseflesh"); understandably, he preferred to use his mother's maiden name, Gutenberg. Although he wasn't the first person in Europe to print from movable type, he was the first to make it practical, and devised the metal punch, metal matrix to receive the punched—or engraved—metal letters, numbers, and punctuation marks, and a mold to hold the appropriate metal characters in a line for printing. (The printing press itself was essentially a modified press used in papermaking.) In 1450, Gutenberg mortgaged his printing press to a goldsmith named Johann Fust. The first things that were printed—dating from 1454, or per-

haps even as early as 1451—were indulgences. In 1455, Gutenberg, who had not yet repaid his mortgage to Fust, was sued. Unable to pay, Gutenberg's press was confiscated by Fust, and the printing work was carried on by Peter Schöffer, Gutenberg's typesetter. (Actually, it is believed by many that the important developments of movable type were devised by Schöffer.) In 1456, Gutenberg borrowed more money and set up another printing press, on which he produced the first printed book—the "Gutenberg Bible." The spread of printing was accelerated by Adolf of Nassau's 1462 invasion of Mainz. The printers, fleeing the city, spread the art throughout Europe. As for Gutenberg, he ended up in Eltville, set up another press, and, after several years of unending financial crises, died in 1468.

It is probably small consolation to Gutenberg that the printing press had an infinitely profound effect on European culture, and was in fact the goldmine he had promised it would be (for everyone but him, alas). At the time, however, there was enough demand for such a process in Europe that someone was likely to have invented it. (The Plague had killed off many of the scribes, and those who were left were expensive.) The speed at which the printing press spread throughout Europe was lightning-fast; within fifty years there were over 200 presses operating in Europe, and eight million books printed. The effect of the printing press was profound; William Caxton's introduction of the press into England in the 1460s resulted in not only the professional career of Geoffrey Chaucer, but also the standardization of the English language (in other countries, other vernaculars became standardized as well; printers must have realized that the bulk of the book-buying public didn't know Latin). The Protestant Reformation was accelerated by the use of printing; Martin Luther had used printing to disseminate his problems with the Catholic church. The printing and consequent rediscovery of ancient Greek and Roman texts resulted in the Renaissance. The literacy rate of the European population soared, as more people had access to books, which were far more inexpensive than books produced by scribes. (Interestingly, great advances in the manufacture and availability of eyeglasses appeared shortly before the printing press.) Whereas before printing, knowledge and learning were the privilege of a rare few (such as monks and university scribes), many people now had access to it. Writers who had previously been unable to get their work disseminated (scribes, in particular monks, would frequently fail to copy manuscripts they felt were heretical, and many manuscripts that came their way were erased and the paper "recycled") could flourish.

The earliest printers were only interested in reproducing texts cheaply and quickly, and had also wanted to preserve the look of the older handwritten manuscripts. Soon, however, printers such as Johann and Wendelin da Spira, Nicolas Jenson, and many others began to design distinctive "typefaces" specifically for book printing, called "roman" typefaces. The great Venetian printer Aldus Manutius not only printed the first "pocket editions" but also pioneered the use of italic type (as a means of fitting more characters per page and thus making the books cheaper to produce; eventually, italics came to be used merely for emphasis or titles; see *Type*).

The next 400 years consisted of improvements on and mechanization of the typesetting and printing processes. Type was inserted character-by-character into a composing stick, which comprised a line of type. The characters from the composing stick were then transferred en masse to a metal or wooden tray called a galley. After the galley was proofed, it was broken down into pages, and running heads, folios, etc., were added. Each page of type was then locked up, to be sent for platemaking or to the pressroom if the material was going to be printed directly from type. Presses at that time were flatbed or platen, presses in which the type was locked onto a flat platen and the substrate was pressed over it, either sheet by sheet, or, later, by a rotating cylinder. In 1725, Scottish printer William Ged invented a process for making plates from locked-up type. It was refined and officially named *stereotyping* shortly afterward by Firmin Didot. In stereotyping, locked-up type is covered with a wet paper or mat, and pressure applied to stamp the impression of the type in the mat. The paper or mat is allowed to dry. The mat is then removed, and placed in a casting machine, where molten metal is added to cast an entire page of type as a single plate.

In 1811, the German printer Friedrich König adapted the printing press to steam power, allowing the duplication of greater volumes of printed material. In 1846, the American printer Richard Hoe created a cylinder-type press (in contrast to the flatbed type previously employed), in which the type could be locked into place on a rotating cylinder. In 1869 English printers began using curved stereotype plates on cylinder-based presses, which replaced the assembled type forms. These developments were the most significant advances in printing technology towards the attainment of greater volume and speed. In the late 1800s, machine composition of type was developed by Ottmar Mergenthaler (who invented the *Linotype*, or a machine for producing type line by line, rather than character by character), and Tolbert Lanston (who invented the *Monotype*, or a device that uses a typewriter-like keyboard to punch holes in a paper tape, which is then fed back through a casting machine to automatically determine what characters get cast). Later developments such as the *Varityper* also improved and expedited the setting of type. (See *Type*.)

MAJOR PRINTING PROCESSES

Letterpress. The printing process utilized for most of the history of printing is what we could today term "letterpress"; a raised image or text area (the movable type of Gutenberg's day, stereotype plates of the 1800s, or modern letterpress plates) is inked and the image transferred to a surface, primarily paper. Letterpress printing, although still used today, has been largely replaced by *offset lithography*, or a descendent of letterpress printing known as *flexography* (see below). (See *Letterpress*.)

Lithography. Lithography, or printing utilizing a flat surface on which an oil-based ink-receptive image area and a water-receptive nonimage area are the same height and kept separate by the chemical repulsion between oil and water, was invented in 1796 by Alois Senefelder, a Bavarian playwright searching for a way to cheaply produce his plays. He discovered that a certain type of Bavarian limestone was ideally suited to the process. (The word "lithography" itself is derived from Greek words meaning "stone writing.") He devised the first lithographic press, and eventually zinc and aluminum plates replaced the stones, and around 1905 Ira Rubel was the first to realize that a rubber blanket produced a higher-quality image than did the stone plates. Many had noticed this (a rubber blanket initially covered the impression cylinder on lithographic stone presses, and feeding problems often resulted in accidentally printing on the blanket, which then erroneously transferred to the paper) but Rubel was the first to construct a press that used a rubber blanket as an image carrier. And so was born the offset press. New technological refinements have made offset lithography the dominant form of printing in the world. (See *Lithography* and *Offset Lithography*.)

Gravure. The early precursors to true gravure printing go back to 9th century China, but became prevalent in the West around the middle of the 15th century. Early gravure—or *intaglio*—methods of printing commonly comprised engraved wood or metal blocks into which ink was poured and then transferred to a substrate. In 1879, Viennese printer Karel Klic adapted such disparate elements as line-engraving, etching, mezzotinting, etc., to a printing process, called gravure printing. The gravure printing process uses a metal cylinder engraved with the text or design matter to be printed. (The engraved portions of the gravure cylinder are called *cell*s.) The cylinder rotates in an ink fountain, where ink collects in the depressed cells and is wiped off the outside of the cylinder. As the paper (or other surface) is brought into contact with the cylinder, the ink is transferred out of the cells onto the substrate by *capillary action* (or a transfer of a liquid from one place to another by virtue of the surface tension of the liquid) generated by pressure of the substrate on the surface of the cylinder. The gravure process can also be used to print at high speeds on fast-moving paper webs, a process called *rotogravure*. (See *Gravure*.) A variety of intaglio printing (considered as a separate process from gravure) is *copperplate printing*, such as that commonly used for currency. (See *Copperplate Printing*.)

Flexography. The youngest of the major printing methods, *flexography* is a variety of rotary letterpress printing utilizing flexible rubber or plastic plates to transfer a highly liquid ink to a wide variety of substrates, primarily plastic films, corrugated board, and other types of packaging material. Flexography has its origins in the early twentieth century and developments in the vulcanization of rubber and the consequent invention of rubber stamps. The process of making a metal relief plate (as in letterpress), making a depressed mold from it, and making a relief rubber plate was used initially to print on surfaces—such as corrugated board—that did not yield good results with conventional letterpress processes. Early flexo printing—then called *aniline printing*—used *aniline dye*s. The invention of synthetic rubbers and the *anilox roller* (used to effectively meter and transfer ink to the plate) was a boon to the process, and it began to have more and more applications. The proliferation of plastic packaging materials proved to be ideal substrates for aniline printing. However, aniline dyes were banned by the FDA after it was found that the dyes were toxic. Although aniline printers had by then been using different types of less toxic colorants, the name still remained, and in 1952 the name of the process was, after a contest held by the Packaging Institute, officially renamed "flexography." Flexography today is primarily used for various types of plastic packaging, but also has applications in printing on paper, as well. (See *Flexography*.)

Screen Process. Screen process printing is also known as *screen printing*, *silk screening*, and *serigraph*, and derives from older practices of stencil printing. The screen process was devised in Germany and Scotland in the late 1800s. In 1907, Englishman Samuel Simon created a process of screen printing utilizing a cut stencil of the intended design mounted on a finely-woven silk screen, a brush being used to force the ink through the screen in the cut-out areas of the stencil. (This was a direct descendent of an older *pochoir* method of stencilling.) In 1914, American John Pilsworth devised a system for the silk screening of banners, and until the late 1930s silk screening was used primarily for commercial purposes, eventually becoming favored among artists.

Silk screening today still retains the simplicity of earlier forms of it; a hand-cut or photographically produced stencil is mounted on the bottom of a fine mesh screen, which has been stretched taut on a wooden frame. A fairly viscous ink (formerly paint) is placed on the screen, and a squeegee pulls the ink down over the stencil, where it prints the design onto the intended substrate (commonly textiles, such as T-shirts and other decorative materials

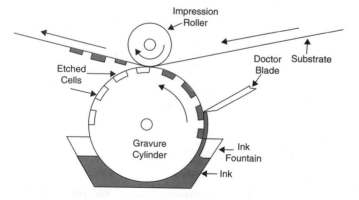

Basic rotogravure image transfer.

such as posters). Screen process printing is not used for other traditional types of printing, such as books, newspapers, etc. (See *Screen Process*.)

Other varieties of printing are being constantly developed, in particular *electrostatic printing* and *xerography*, printing methods involving the attraction of electrostatically charged pigment particles (called *toner*) to an oppositely charged metal drum. Such printing methods are utilized in photocopying machines and computer laser printers. (See *Electrostatic Printing*.) Another variety of printing common in computer markets is *ink jet* printing, in which tiny electrically charged droplets of ink are aimed at the substrate, and as they travel they are deflected to the proper position on the paper by means of a charged deflector plate. (See *Ink Jet Printing*.)

Each printing process has different ink and paper requirements to generate the best possible printed image which is, after all, the goal of any printing process. (See *Paper and Papermaking: Printing Requirements* and *Ink: Printing Requirements*.)

Printing Area

In *screen printing*, the total area of the region under the screen frame on the *printing bed* on which the *substrate* is placed, as opposed to the *image area*, which is only that area containing the image itself.

Printing Base

Alternate term for *printing bed*. See *Printing Bed*.

Printing Bed

The portion of a *screen printing* press beneath the screen frame on which the *substrate* is placed and which provides a hard backing for printing. Some configurations have *lays*, a vacuum system or other means of registering the substrate. Also known as the *printing base* and *printing table*.

Printing Couple

In *offset lithography*, overall term for all the parts of a printing press required to print one color on one side of a sheet of paper: *inking system*, *dampening system*, *plate cylinder*, *blanket cylinder*, and *impression cylinder*. The bare minimum requirements for offset printing.

Printing Cushion

The combination of the paper qualities of *compressibility*, *resiliency*, and *hardness* or *softness*, which determines the extent to which a paper's surface will deform under a compressing force to allow complete ink transfer from a printing plate or blanket, and be able to return to its original dimensions when the compressing force is removed. They are all determined by such factors in the papermaking process as the degree of *refining* of the paper fibers, and the degree of *calendering* or *supercalendering*. Generally, a soft, easily compressible paper is desirable, but different degrees of each of these characteristics may be required, depending on the printing process to be used, and the end-use characteristics of the paper. *Letterpress* and *gravure* require more compressible and resilient papers than *offset lithography* or *flexography*, while offset lithography needs harder papers to withstand the stress of being peeled off an inked blanket. The degree of strength required—such as *folding endurance*, or the ability to withstand other types of handling—may also be the determining factor in the combination of printing cushion qualities.

The softness or compressibility of a paper can be quantified with an air-leak method, in which a paper sample is inserted into a device which presses a metal plate on top of it and measures the rate of air leakage between the surface of the paper and the metal plate. As the metal plate will press more deeply into softer paper, the rate of air leakage will be greater for harder paper.

Printing Head

The portion of a *screen printing* press consisting of the printing frame, the *squeegee*, the *flood bar*s (if included on the press in question), and the press operator controls.

Printing Nip

The nip between the *blanket cylinder* and the *plate cylinder* on an offset press. (See *Offset Lithography: Printing Unit*.)

Printing Opacity

See *Diffuse Opacity Method*.

Printing Plate

Any surface that carries an image that will eventually be used to transfer printed impressions to a *substrate*. Each printing process requires plates of particular formulations and orientations. See *Plate*.

Printing Press

Any device—typically mechanical, but not necessarily—that transfers an inked image, or—more often—many copies of an inked image to a surface. There are a wide variety of printing presses, generally categorized by the half dozen or so major printing process, but with many different variations on a basic theme. See *Letterpress*, *Offset Lithography*, *Gravure*, *Flexography*, and *Screen Printing*. Printing presses are also categorized according to whether they are webfed (print on continuous rolls of *substrate*) or sheetfed (print on single sheets, fed into the press in a variety of ways).

Printing Pressure

Any force or pressure required to transfer an inked impression from the image carrier to the *substrate*. Printing pressure is determined by the amount of pressure that exists between either the *plate cylinder* and the *impression cylinder* (in *flexography*), between the *blanket cylinder* and the impression cylinder (in *offset lithography*), or between the *gravure cylinder* and the *impression roller*

(in *gravure*, for example.) The required printing pressure varies from process to process and from specific application to specific application.

Printing Screen

In *screen printing*, general term for the screen fabric, the frame supporting the fabric, and the stencil attached to the fabric. Also sometimes referred to as a *plate*.

Printing Sequence

In *process color* printing, the order in which the colors are printed. In *offset lithography*, for example, the common printing sequence is *black*, *cyan*, *magenta*, and *yellow*. Also called *color sequence* and *laydown sequence*.

Printing Stroke

In *screen printing*, the movement of the *squeegee* along the *printing screen*, forcing ink through the screen and onto the *substrate*. A printing stroke is also known as *pull*.

Printing Table

Alternate term for *printing bed*. See *Printing Bed*.

Printing Unit

The portion of a printing press where printing actually takes place, consisting of image carrying surfaces (*plate*s, *blanket*s, *gravure cylinder*s, and, *impression cylinder*s or rollers.)

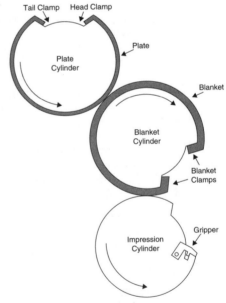

Basic printing unit of an offset press.

Printout

Any hard copy of computer data.

Print Position

Alternate term for *addressable point*. See *addressable point*.

Print Quality

Term describing the quality of a printed image compared to the quality that was originally intended, used in the context of the interrelationships of a paper's properties. (See also *Printability*.)

Print Queue

In computing, a sequential list of printing commands awaiting execution, as when a printer is connected to a network and receives print commands from different workstations. Often, priority can be given to certain print commands, sending them to the front of the queue.

Print Server

See *Server*.

Print Spooler

In networking, the portion of the *network operating system* (or an individual computer's operating system) that keeps track of print jobs sent to a shared printer. Each job is stored in a separate file in the *print queue* until the printer becomes free. See also *Spooler*.

Printwheel

Alternate term for a *daisy wheel*. See *Daisy Wheel*.

Privacy Bit

In telecommunications, a *bit* added to *ISDN* transmissions that instructs the receiving switch to hide the *caller ID*.

Private Automatic Branch Exchange (PABX)

In telecommunications, an automatic telephone system serving a particular location (such as a company office). A PABX allows connections from one extension to another within the location, as well as connections to an external telephone network. Some PABXs are capable of transmitting computer data. See also *Private Branch Exchange (PBX)*.

Private Branch Exchange (PBX)

In telecommunications, a local switching system installed in a particular location (such as a company's office) that allows telephone connections from one extension to another as well as connections to the external telephone network. See also *Private Automatic Branch Exchange (PABX)*. A *data PBX* is capable of transmitting digital data, rather than analog (or voice) data. A PBX can also be connected to a *PRI* system for *ISDN* transmission.

Private Leased Circuit

A *leased line* connected from one location to a remote site that is available 24 hours a day, 7 days a week.

Private Line

In telecommunications, a telephone line that is not connected through a central office, but rather is available for the exclusive use of a single individual.

Privilege Level

In networking, the *rights* granted to a user (or group of users) by a *network administrator* for reasons of *security*. See *Rights*.

In computing, a type of protection built into Intel *microprocessors*, comprising two basic types of protection: one assigns each task a separate *address space*, the other subdivides a task into four privilege levels which work to render portions of the operating system and processor inaccessible to applications. The four privilege levels range from level 3 (least privileged), which is available to applications, to level 0 (the most privileged). Levels 1 and 2 are reserved for use by the operating system and system extensions.

Privileged Mode

In computing, especially by means of Intel processors, a mode within the *protected mode* that allows the *operating system* and some types of *device driver* to control parts of the system, such as *port*s, memory, etc.

PRN

On a *PC*, especially one running *DOS* or *OS/2*, the device name for a printer, most commonly located in the first *parallel port*. See also *LPTx Port*.

Process

Any means by which something is accomplished.

In computing, the term *process* refers to a computer program or a portion of a computer program, especially in a *multitasking* environment. When used as a verb, the term *process* means to perform or execute a function.

Process Camera

A large *camera* used for graphic arts photography, such as shooting negatives and positives as a prelude to platemaking, making *color separation*s, or screening continuous-tone images into *halftone*s. See *Photography: Graphic Arts Photography*. A process camera is also known as a *stat camera* and a *copy camera*. (See illustration on the following page.)

Process Color

The printing of "full color" images utilizing a photographic *color separation* process in which each of three *primary colors—cyan*, *magenta*, and *yellow*, plus *black*—are separated from the original art and given their own printing plate. Successive runs through the press or multiple printing units lay down inks of each of these colors in combinations that allow for the reproduction of many colors of the spectrum. Process color is also called *four-color process* when four separations are made. See *Color: Color Separation*.

Process Colors

The four colors used in *process color* printing: *cyan*, *magenta*, *yellow*, and *black*, the combinations of which allow for the reproduction of many colors of the spectrum. See *Process Color*.

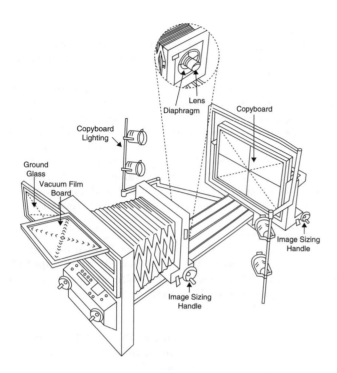

Process camera used for graphic arts photography.

Process Control

In any manufacturing system, the means by which the products of the manufacturing process are kept within certain acceptable limits of variation.

Process Inks

Inks used in *process color* printing of "full color" illustrations and halftones. The colors utilized are *cyan*, *magenta*, *yellow*, and *black*. See *Process Color*.

Process Lens

In graphic arts photography, a highly corrected lens used on a *process camera* designed to shoot flat copy, rather than subjects that require some degree of depth as in traditional photography.

Process Printing

Printing performed using two or more color *halftone* plates (or other image carriers) to print intermediate shades of the basic primary colors. See *Process Color*.

Processing

In computing, general term referring to the manipulation of data within a computer, or to the execution of programmed tasks.

Processor

The portion of a computer that reads, interprets, and executes instructions. See *Microprocessor* and *Coprocessor*.

In printing, a device that automatically develops exposed light-sensitive materials, such as plates and film.

Production

The manufacture of any product.

In motion pictures, television, video, and multimedia, *production* refers to the filming or taping of images and/or sound. Consequently, the term *pre-production* refers to all design, scripting, etc., activities that take place prior to fiming, while *post-production* refers to all editing and additional processes performed after filming. The term also refers to the final program or presentation itself.

Production Control Room

In television and video production, especially live or live-on-tape programs, a room containing monitors, speakers, switching boards, effects generators, and other equipment, used to monitor and edit a program on-the-fly, or as it is being taped.

In much television production (especially half-hour comedies, talk shows, and variety programs), an entire program is acted out live, while a multi-camera set-up is used to tape the action from a variety of angles. In the control room, the director decides which camera is going to be recording the actual image at any given moment. In such productions, there is inevitably some degree of *post-production* editing and correction.

Production Editing

General term for the *pasteup* and assembly of pages, as well as negotiations with the printer.

Production-Level Video (PLV)

A form of *data compression* used in *DVI* to compress *digital video*. PLV uses high-powered computers and yields the highest quality.

Professional Graphics Adapter (PGA)

An IBM color monitor standard which could display 256 colors at a time (from a total palette of 4096) with a screen *resolution* of 640×480 *pixel*s.

Prog

Shortened form of the term *progressive proof*. See *Progressive Proof*.

Program

When used as a noun, a *computer program*. See *Computer Program*.

When used as a verb, *program* means to create a set of computer-executable instructions. See *Programming*.

Program Control Statement

In a computer *programming language*, especially *C*, a written statement that regulates the flow of a program. Some examples are *while*, *for*, and *dowhile* (which regulate program loops); *if* and *switch* (which tell the program what to do based on conditions set up by the program); *goto*, *continue*, and *break* (which instruct the computer as to what to do once a loop has been completed); etc.

Program Information File (PIF)

In computing in the *Windows* environment, a file containing information about a specific application, such as its name, its *information path* and location, the monitor color depth it requires, etc.

Program Register

In computing, a *register* in which the current program instruction is stored. Also known as *instruction register*.

Programmer

An individual who writes *computer program*s, or who writes the computer code for an application.

Programmers Hierarchical Interactive Graphics System (PHIGS)

In computer graphics, a set of standards—developed jointly by *ANSI* and *ISO*—comprising a graphics system and language used for two-dimensional and three-dimensional images that acts as a device-independent *interface* between an application and a graphic subsystem. PHIGS, however, is a comprehensive system that requires high-end workstations and host processors. An extension, *PHIGS+*, adds data to three-dimensional models concerning lighting and shading.

Programming Language

Any of a large number of languages used to write a program that a computer can understand and execute. Commonly, a programming language uses faintly English-like vocabulary and syntax to compose a set of instructions, which are then translated (by means of a *compiler*) to the *machine language*, or the series of 1s and 0s that the computer can understand. There are close to 200 different programming languages, which range from *high-level languages* (such as C, Pascal, etc., highly reminiscent of English) to *low-level languages* (such as *assembly language*, more closely resembling machine language). Although some popular programming languages (such as C) are used for a wide variety of applications, many are used for very specific purposes, such as scientific and mathematical analysis (FORTRAN and APL), artificial intelligence (LISP and Prolog), etc.

Progression

In typography, one particular *typeface* in a particular style displayed at a range of sizes.

Progressive Proof

A set of *color proof*s produced on-press using the four *color separation negative*s exposed to separate plates and printed in *printing sequence* using the *process ink*s intended for the pressrun. A set of progressive proofs (commonly known as *prog*s) is likely to include the following: the *yellow* plate alone; the *magenta* plate alone; a combination of yellow and magenta; *cyan* alone; yellow, magenta, and cyan in combination; *black* alone; and all four colors in combination, or the full-color image. Progressive proofs are a preferred way of checking the color separation negatives,

and are also used—by referencing them to press sheets—to maintain press control during the pressrun.

Prompt

In computing, a line used on a *command-line interface* at which operator instruction needs to be entered. Prompts can appear alongside specific questions, or simply be a disk drive letter followed by a greater-than sign, i.e., "C:>" (a *DOS prompt*). Also known as a *command prompt*.

Proof

Any early copy of to-be-reproduced material produced as a means of checking for *typo*s or other similar errors, as well as positional errors, layout problems, and color aspects. See *Proofing*.

Proof Marks

In typography, uniform marks are used to identify corrections on manuscript or typeset copy. Proof marks are standardized to facilitate clear understanding among all the parties that may be involved, such as authors, clients, line editors, copy editors, and typesetters. (See illustration on the following page.)

Proof Press

A small, often hand-fed and hand-operated printing press used to make proofs of *process color* (or often *spot color* jobs, prior to running the job on a production press. Proof presses print multicolor jobs one color at a time, registration being accomplished with a scope or other device. Proof presses are used to check the color balance and the efficiacy of *ink color mixing*.

Proofing

In *prepress*, the act of making a proof or *color proof*, either on a *proof press*, the actual press on which the job will be printed, on a variety of digital output devices, or other means.

There are several reasons for making proofs, not the least of which is to show the customer or client how the job was typeset and how the job will print. Proofs of text material are looked over by the typesetter and (in book publishing) proofreaders and the author, where *typographical error*s are flagged for later correction. At this stage, *author alteration*s may also be indicated. The designer of the piece also examines the proofs to ensure that the *type specification*s have been enacted properly. All the corrections from the various copies of the proofs are then collated into one set of master proofs which is then sent back to the typesetter for correction. In book publishing, there are usually three sets of proofs: the *first-pass pages*, or the very first typeset pages; *second-pass pages*, or the pages with the corrections indicated on the first-pass pages having been made, plus final pagination. These second-pass pages are rarely sent to an author, and in-house and freelance proofreaders go over them again, looking for typographical errors. These proofs are followed by *reproduction proof*s

Symbol	Meaning	Symbol	Meaning
⊙	Period or full point		Set in Boldface Type
	Comma	Bf	Boldface Type (In Margin)
	Hyphen		Capitalize Material
;/	Semicolon	cap	Capitalization (In Margin)
	Apostrophe		Set in Italic Type
!/	Exclamation Mark	ital	Italics (In Margin)
/en/ /N/	En Dash	∧ ∨	Caret
/em/ /M/	Em Dash	#	Insert Space
(I)	Parentheses	hr#	Insert Hair Space
	Quotation Marks (Double)	□	Indent One Em Space
	Quotation Marks (Single)		Delete or Take Out
	Align Horizontally		Delete and Close Up Space
‖	Align Vertically		Close Up
	Move to the Left	[?]	Query to Author
	Move to the Right	.....	Let Indicated Material Remain as It Is
	Move Matter Up	stet	Let It Stand (In Margin)
	Move Matter Up		Transpose Material
× ⊠	Broken Letter	tr	Transpose (In Margin)
ꓘ	Set in Lowercase		
lc	Lowercase (In Margin)		

Proof marks.

(or **repro** for short), which are the camera-ready pages, gone over one last time for any egregious errors. **Bluelines** are also prepared prior to printing, as a means of checking the positioning of page elements, broken characters, and other non-content-related issues.

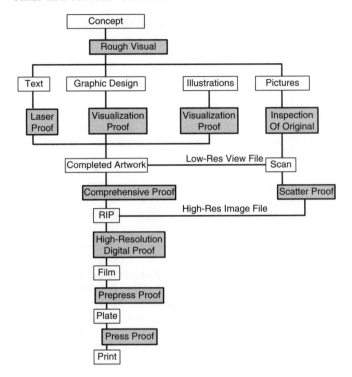

The basic proofing and approval cycle.

Color proofs are prepared photographically (see **overlay color proof**s or **single-sheet color proof**s) or digitally (see **direct digital color proof [DDCP]**) in order to show how the **color separation**s have been made and how accurate they have been. Color proofs can also be made on press, preferably using the inks and **substrate** that will be used for the actual job. One set of these proofs constitutes the **contract proof** (or **color OK**), a color proof that is okayed by the customer and which serves as a master guide for the pressrun. A set of **progressive proof**s is also used to ensure that the colors conform precisely to the contract proof. (See **Color Proofing**.)

The term *proofing* also refers to the act of **proofreading**, or checking typed or typeset text for typographical errors or other mistakes.

Proofing Stock

A special type of paper used for printing **color proof**s, with an eye towards ensuring that they look as close to the final reproduction as possible.

Proofreader

A person who reads proofs of typeset material and marks errors for correction using standardized **proof marks**.

Book publishers often hire freelance proofreaders at several points in a book's production.

Proofreader's Marks
See **Proof Marks**.

Proofreading

The reading of typeset (or other to-be-disseminated) copy as a means of locating misspellings or other errors introduced during keyboarding.

Prop

In motion picture, television, and video production, objects and materials needed either to decorate a set (such as furniture), "equip" a character (such as a cigarette case, a wallet, or keys), or serve an integral function in the production (such as a sled or a light saber).

Propagation Delay

In telecommunications, the delay between the time a signal is transmitted and the time it is received. Propagation delays are most commonly a result of large geographic distances between sender and receiver. For example, in a **local area network**, there is a minimal propagation delay, whereas in satellite communications, the delay can be quite considerable indeed.

ProPhoto CD

A variety of **Photo CD** designed for professional use, rather than consumer use. The primary difference is that the ProPhoto CD includes high-resolution images, in addition to the five standard **resolution**s (thumbnail, 6×6 cm, 6×7 cm, 6×9 cm, and 4×5 in.) See **Photo CD**.

Proportion Rule

A device used in graphic arts design and photography to determine the percentage reduction or enlargement an image requires, based on a ratio of the size of the original to the size it needs to fit. A proportional rule may, in one configuration, be two attached movable disks, the size of the original on one disk, the size of the reproduction on the other. When the original size is lined up with the reproduction size, a window in the middle of the scale indicates the reproduction percentage required. Also known as a **proportion scale**.

Proportion Scale

Alternate term for **proportion rule**. See **Proportion Rule**.

Proportional Font

In typography, a **font** containing characters with **proportional width**s, as opposed to fonts utilizing fixed width characters. (See also **Fixed Font**.)

Proportional Spacing

In typography, the spacing of characters in relation to their individual widths or **escapement** values. See **Proportional Width**.

Proportional Type
See *Proportional Width*.

Proportional Width
In typography, individual character-width relationships based on character shape and typeface design. For example, the letter "i" has a narrow width, while the letter "m" has a wide width. (The opposite is *monospaced*, which refers to characters all having the same width value; a lowercase "i" and a lowercase "m" would have the same width.)

Proportionally-Spaced Type
See *Proportional Width*.

Proprietary Alcohol
Ethyl alcohol that has been denatured (had a substance added to it to make it unfit for drinking) for use as a *solvent* in printing inks.

Proprietary Software
Any computer software that is custom-designed and manufactured for a specific application or client and not generrlly available outside the company that created or commissioned it. Typically the opposite of *off-the-shelf* software.

Proprietary System
Any computer system (such as a publishing or prepress system) that is custom-designed and manufactured for a specific application or client. Typically the opposite of an *off-the-shelf* system or software.

Propylene Glycol
A *polyhydric alcohol*—chemical formula C_3H_8O—used in the production of printing inks and coatings.

Protected Mode
In computing, especially by means of Intel *processor*s, an operating state that refers to the means by which microprocessors and applications can access computer memory.

Essentially, in protected mode, a processor exerts a certain amount of control over how programs gain access to memory locations. The processor can cordon off portions of memory, thus preventing applications from usurping the resources of other applications (or even the *operating system*). Such attempts at memory conquest result in the *general protection fault* error condition. (In contrast, applications running on a *real mode* operating system take whatever memory they can.)

The advantage to protected mode operation is that the microprocessor can be used to its full potential, and directly address all available memory. In 16-bit protected mode (supported by the 80286 and higher processors), the *CPU* can directly address up to 16 *megabyte*s of memory. In 32-bit protected mode (supported by the 80386 and higher processors), the CPU can directly address up to 4 *gigabyte*s of memory. However, some operating systems can only operate in real mode. *DOS*, for example, is a real-mode

operating system. *Windows*, though operating in protected mode, has a DOS underpinning, resulting in DOS operating needing to run in real mode. *OS/2*, however, is a completely protected-mode operating system. See also *Real Mode*.

Protection Master
Any copy of a *master tape* of a *videodisc*, *compact disc*, etc., that is hidden or secreted (often in a safe-deposit box) to prevent damage, loss, or erasure in the event that it is needed again.

Protocol
In networking and telecommunications, a predetermined set of rules and procedures for data transmission and reception, *error detection and correction*, *data compression*, etc.

Some protocols, known as low-level, set transmission speeds, data encoding schemes, interfaces, and the means by which *node*s can access the network during data transmission. Other protocols, known as high-level, control a greater number of network aspects, such as printing, file sharing, servers, etc. Some common network protocols are *Ethernet*, *ARCnet*, *Token Ring*, *LocalTalk*, *Copper Distributed Data Interface (CDDI)*, *Fiber Distributed Data Interface (FDDI)*, *Intergrated Services Digital Network (ISDN)*, and *Asynchronous Transfer Mode (ATM)*.

In telecommunications, protocols determine the means by which data is transmitted and errors are detected and corrected. Some common telecommunications protocols are *XModem*, *YModem*, *ZModem*, and *Kermit*.

Protocol Analyzer
In networking, a hardware/software package used to troubleshoot network problems by decoding network *protocol* data.

Protocol Converter
In networking and telecommunications, a hardware/software package used to convert one *protocol* to another, used when two networks utilizing different protocols are connected to each other. A protocol converter is often used in a *gateway*.

Protocol Stack
In networking, the various levels of software that comprise a network *protocol*. Also known as a *protocol suite*.

Protocol Suite
Alternate term for a *protocol stack*. See *Protocol Stack*.

Prototype
In any manufacturing process—but in terms of graphic communications, especially computer software and multimedia productions—a working but not fully implemented model of a proposed device or application, used for demonstration purposes, and to get approval and/or funding to continue further.

Proxy File

Alternate term for *low-resolution file*. See *Low-Resolution File*.

Prussian Blue

A red shade of *Iron Blue*, an *inorganic color pigment* used in printing inks. See *Iron Blue*.

PS

Abbreviation or file *extension* for *PostScript*. See *PostScript*. On some computer systems, the file extension letters are not capitalized, *ps*.

PSAF

Abbreviation for *Print Services Access Facility*.

Pseudo-Color

Alternate term for *false color*. See *False Color*.

Pt.

Abbreviation for *point*, a common type measurement. See *Point System*.

PTA

An abbreviation for phosphotungstic acid, used to describe a printing ink *pigment* produced by combining the original dyestuff with a "double salt" of this acid. (See also *PTMA* and *PMA*.)

PTOCA

Abbreviation for *Presentation Text Object Content Architecture*.

PTR

Abbreviation for *printer*. See *Printer*.

PTT

Abbreviation for *Postal Telephone and Telegraph*. See *Postal Telephone and Telegraph (PTT)*.

PU

Abbreviation for *physical unit*. See *Physical Unit (PU)*.

Public Data Network (PDN)

In networking and telecommunications, any government-controlled *packet-switched network*.

Public Domain

Any work for which the copyright has expired.

Public Key Encryption

In data communications, an *encryption* scheme that utilizes two keys: a public key to encode data and a private key to decode the data following transmission. See *Encryption*.

Public Network

Term for the general voice telephone system. Also known as the *direct distance dialing network*.

Publishing Interchange Language (PIL)

A computer file standard used to exchange *page geometry* data between different *page makeup programs*.

Puck

A movable, rectangular, hand-held computer input device, often used by graphics professionals in lieu of a mouse. A puck is used in concert with a *digitizing tablet* to move images and the cursor around a computer display.

Puddle Method

In *screen printing*, the development of a *photostencil* without completely immersing the stencil in developing fluid.

Puff Ink

A type of specialty ink commonly used in *screen printing* that, when heated, expands to create a three-dimensional ink film. Commonly used in printing on T-shirts.

Pull

In *screen printing*, an alternate term for a *printing stroke*. See *Printing Stroke*.

In photography, *pull* means to reduce the development time of a film as a means of compensating for overexposure. See also *Push*.

Pull Quote

In magazine publishing (and occasionally elsewhere), a small extract of text from a story or article and set off from the main text, often in a larger *point size* and/or different *typeface*, and may be surrounded by a border or *rule*. Often used for emphasis.

Pull Test

In *binding and finishing*, a test used to gauge the strength of a *perfect binding*, consisting of a measure of the amount of pull required to rip a page from the binding.

Pull-Down Menu

In computing, especially that utilizing a *graphical user interface (GUI)*, a menu of commands and functions that scrolls down from a menu bar (usually located at the top of a screen or window) when a particular menu name is clicked on. See also *Pop-Up Menu*.

Pulldown

Alternate term for *drawdown*. See *Drawdown*.

Pulp

The fibrous material forming the basis of *paper*, the production of which is the first stage in the papermaking process. Pulp is produced either mechanically, chemically, or semichemically from fibrous raw material, primarily wood, cotton, or linen. (See *pulping*, *mechanical pulping*, *chemical pulping*, and *semichemical pulping*.) The goal of pulping is to liberate fibers of *cellulose* from other impurities in the raw material. The higher the cellulose content of a paper, the better the quality, so the best pulps are those that contain cellulose exclusively and little else. Cotton, being nearly 100% cellulose, produces the best pulp, as do linens and other textile materials, but are more expensive than other fibrous sources. Wood, having a lower cellulose content, produces pulp that is not as good as cotton or linen pulps, but chemical treatment reduces the amount of impurities and enhances the quality of the pulp. The type of pulping method used also directly affects the quality of the paper that is produced. Mechanically produced pulp (also called *groundwood* pulp) has a high *lignin* content, which reduces the *permanence* of paper, and is chiefly responsible for the yellowing of paper over time. Mechanical pulp is used for low-quality papers used in newspapers, catalogs, directories, and "pulp" magazines. Semichemical pulps have a somewhat reduced lignin content, and are higher in quality than mechanical pulps. Pulps produced chemically (especially utilizing the *kraft* process) are used for high-quality printing and writing papers. Wood pulp is brown in color (due primarily to the presence of residual lignin), and can often be used as is for brown wrapping paper or paper bags. More often, however, pulp must be bleached in order to produce printing and writing papers. Chemical pulping can only be done for so long before severe fiber degradation occurs, so *bleaching* is typically done to remove or alter the lignin without harming the cellulose fibers. (Mechanical pulps are also bleached, but not to the extent that chemical pulps are, as bleaching decreases pulp yield, defeating the purpose of the mechanical pulping process.)

It is at the end of the pulping process that the addition of nonorganic *fillers*—a process called *loading*—occurs. The degree of *refining* of the pulp also dramatically affects the paper quality. (See *Paper and Papermaking: Paper Properties*.)

Pulping

A process that extracts fibrous material, *cellulose*, from wood or other raw material as a prelude to papermaking. The purpose of pulping is to liberate cellulose fibers from other chemicals and impurities in the wood (or other fibrous source).

Before wood can be pulped, it must undergo *debarking*. Bark contains little or no fibrous material, and is removed either mechanically or hydraulically. Debarked logs are then sent to a chipper where they are chopped into small pieces ready for pulping. Pulping can be done either by mechanical, chemical, or semimechanical (a combination of mechanical and chemical) means.

Mechanical pulping uses revolving disks to grind wood chips into pulp. Water is added to the process to reduce wood damage due to heat and friction. One of the nonfibrous elements that is not removed during mechanical pulping is *lignin*, an organic material that binds fibers of cellulose together in the wood. It is the presence of lignin that is primarily responsible for low *durability* and yellowing with age. Mechanical (or *groundwood*) pulp is in-

expensive to produce and generates the highest yield (100 pounds of wood will yield 80–95 pounds of pulp with this method). Groundwood pulp has many qualities that make it ideal for printing, but also has many disadvantages, such as low strength, low brightness, low permanency, and the tendency to yellow with time. Paper made from mechanical pulp also has a high quantity of imperfections called *shives*, or bundles of fiber that were torn from the wood during grinding. Groundwood pulp is used for low-quality papers used for newspapers, telephone directories, catalogs, and "pulp" magazines, as well as household items such as paper towels, tissues, and sanitary papers. Recent technological innovations are improving the quality of mechanical pulps while retaining their cost and yield advantages. (See also *Mechanical Pulping*, *Refiner Mechanical Pulp*, *Thermomechanical Pulp*, *Chemi-Thermomechanical Pulping*, and *Pressurized Groundwood*.)

Semimechanical pulping, as its name implies, is a two-stage process that uses a chemical mixture (most commonly *sodium sulfite* and alkaline salts) to soften lignin, followed by a disk refiner to fiberize the cooked chips. However, a substantial portion of the lignin still remains, and pulp yield (60–80% of the original wood) is less than that of mechanical pulping. Semimechanical pulping produces stiff fibers, and is generally used for corrugated board, roll cores, and containers. Semimechanical pulp is not used for paper intended for writing or printing. (See also *Semichemical Pulping*.)

Chemical pulping results in near-total removal of lignin and other nonfiber constituents of wood. Chemical pulps produce the highest-quality printing and writing papers, but fiber yield is generally 50–55%, lower than the other pulping methods. There are several different chemical pulping methods. In the *sulfite process*, wood chips are cooked with a solution of *sulfurous acid* and *calcium bisulfite* to dissolve lignin. Sulfite pulp is moderately strong, and is soft and flexible. It is used to supplement mechanical pulp. Over the years, stronger pollution laws have resulted in the use of different chemicals. The sulfite process was for a time the most important chemical pulping process, but has been largely replaced by *alkaline pulping*. In the 1850s, the *soda process* was devised, which used lye (a caustic soda) to remove lignin from wood chips. Two decades later, *sodium sulfate* was added to the soda process, resulting in a pulp with greater strength. The advantages of this process—called *kraft* pulping, after the German word for strength—resulted in its becoming the dominant chemical pulping method. Although kraft pulping is often called the *sulfate process*, the active chemical has since been discovered to be not sodium sulfate, but rather *sodium sulfide*. The advantages of kraft pulping include its ability to handle nearly every known type of wood, its efficient chemical and heat recovery system which lowers processing costs, and its ability to produce a strong, high-brightness pulp. The replacement of batch pulping systems with continuous pulping systems and the use of monitoring operations via computer has also improved, speed, economy, and quality of pulp. Wood pulp is brown in color (due primarily to the presence of residual lignin), and can often be used as is for brown wrapping paper or paper bags. More often, however, pulp must be bleached in order to produce printing and writing papers. Chemical pulping can only be done for so long before severe fiber degradation occurs, so bleaching is typically done to remove or alter the lignin without harming the cellulose fibers.

Modified chemical processes are used to pulp nonwoody plants. Although extracting cellulose is easier, their fibrous content tends to be less than that of wood. Cotton and other textile remnants generates higher fiber content, and is used for high-quality and permanent writing papers and is also pulped using a modified alkaline chemical process. *Recycled paper* is also being used increasingly as a source of pulp.

Pulpwood

Any wood used to make paper *pulp*; it can be in the form of wood chips, sawdust, scrap lumber, or whole logs. See *Pulping*.

Pulse Code Modulation (PCM)

A means of modulating a signal to create a quantized and coded form that can be ultimately interpreted as *digital* data. In the creation of *optical discs* (such as *compact discs* and *videodiscs*), the *binary* numbers representing the data on the *master tape* are encoded as a series of pulses. This series of pulses then drives a laser which etches it as a pattern of *pits* on the surface of the disc. This process is also used to digitally store audio.

In telecommunications, PCM is used to demodulate an analog signal (such as comes over a telephone line to a modem) and glean digital data from it. It does this by measuring the analog signal at a rate of 8000 times per second, encoding each measured unit with eight *bit*s. This works out to a rate of 64,000 bits per second, or 64 kilobits per second. (See also *Adaptive Differential Pulse Code Modulation (ADPCM)*.

Punch Perforation

In *binding and finishing*, a perforation of the binding edge of a *book block* prior to *perfect binding*. Punch perforation is similar to *burst binding*, save that it is performed *off-line*. See *Perfect Binding*.

Punch-Down Block

In telecommunications and networking, a connecting device used for telephone lines in which metal teeth strip away the insulation and ensure a tight connection. Also known as a *quick-connect block*.

Punched-Out Label

A type of *label* that has been cut with a die to remove it from (or "punch it out of") the *substrate*. Punched-out labels come in two varieties: those still attached to the sub-strate (*face-cut label*s) and those completely removed from the substrate (*laid-on label*s).

Punching

Alternate term for *drilling*. See *Drilling*.

Punctuation

In typography, symbols used to break up or end sentences, such as the period (.), comma (,), question mark (?), exclamation point (!), apostrophe ('), and quotation marks ("", ''). There is also the colon (:), semicolon (;), and hyphen(-).

Aldus Manutius, the great Venetian printer, was one of the first to use punctuation marks to break up text. Prior to the advent of printing, punctuation was rarely and inconsistently used, and served primarily as cues for the proper reading of text aloud in church. The period was used as a full stop at the end of a sentence, while the solidus (/) was used as a comma, to indicate a brief pause in the reading, and was introduced into English printing in 1521, although it was used in Venetian printing before 1500.

The question mark was derived from the Latin word *quæstio* (meaning "for what"), and came to England in 1521. The *exclamation mark* (also called a *screamer* or a *bang*) came from the Latin word *io* (meaning "joy") and dates from much later. The semicolon didn't appear in England until 1569, but only became widely used after 1580. The open single quote (') and the close single quote (') were used interchangeably in such abbreviations as *th'* for "the", and *'t'is* (for "tis") and were common in the Elizabethan period.

In display typography, the word space placed after a comma or an abbreviation period should be reduced slightly to compensate for the excess space created optically by the punctuation mark. A variety of word spacing called *French spacing* places an additional space between sentences, and was common in printed books through the nineteenth century. In typewriting, this is accomplished by means of an additional word space; in typesetting, a *thin space* can be used rather than a second word space to achieve French spacing, for those who desire it.

Modern computerized desktop publishing programs are creating another stylistic punctuation problem involving quotation marks. Most word processing programs and some page makeup programs use the single/double quote key to set inch marks (") and foot marks ('). These are typographically unacceptable as quotation marks, and often option or shift-option combinations are needed to set *smart quotes* (also called *curly quotes*).

Purple

A color which exists strictly as an intermediate between *red* and *blue*, or as the complementary—or opposite—of *yellow*. The color purple doesn't exist in the spectrum of light, as it has no dominant wavelength, being formed only as a mixture of red and blue. It is often incorrectly confused with *violet*.

Push

In photography, to increase the development time of a film as a means of compensating for underexposure. See also *Pull*.

Pushout

Alternate term for *creep* in *binding and finishing*. See *Creep* (third definition).

PVA

See *Polyvinyl Acetate*.

PVC

Abbreviation for *polyvinyl chloride*. See *Polyvinyl Chloride (PVC)*.

The term *PVC* is also an abbreviation for *permanent virtual circuit*. See *Permanent Virtual Circuit (PVC)*.

PVDC

See *Polyvinylidene Chloride*.

PVF

See *Polyvinyl Fluoride*.

PVSE

An abbreviation for *pasted-valve stepped end*, a type of paper *bag*. See *Pasted-Valve Stepped-End (PVSE)*.

Px64

Alternate term for *H.261*. See *H.261*.

Pyrazolone Orange

An *organic color pigment* used in printing inks. Pyrazolone Orange is a yellow shade of orange, is somewhat opaque, and is resistant to acids, alkalis, soaps, waxes, water, and heat. It also possesses high *tinctorial strength*. However, it has poor flow characteristics, and often fails to print well. Although suitable for many *lithographic*, *gravure*, *letterpress*, and *flexographic* applications, it is frequently used in liquid inks to print packaging. See also *Organic Color Pigments*.

Also known as *Permanent Orange G (CI Pigment Orange 13 No. 21110)*.

Pyroxylin

Alternate name for *nitrocellulose*. See *Nitrocellulose*.

Q

Q, q
The seventeenth letter of the English alphabet, derived from the North Semitic *qoph*, used to represent a guttural "k" sound. The *Q* as a separate letter did not exist in Greek (*kappa* was used for the "K" sound; see *K, k*), but the Etruscan *Q* was carried over into Latin to represent a labialized "k" sound. The *Q* was also used in combination with *U* and was pronounced much as it is today. In Old English, the *QU* combination was represented as *CW* or *KW*.

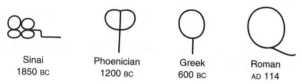

Sinai	Phoenician	Greek	Roman
1850 BC	1200 BC	600 BC	AD 114

The evolution of the letter Q.

QIC

Abbreviation for *quarter-inch cartridge*. See *Quarter-Inch Cartridge (QIC)*.

Q-60

A calibration kit for color *scanner*s developed and marketed by Eastman Kodak.

QT

Abbreviation and *file extension* for *QuickTime* movies. See *QuickTime (QT)*.

Quad

When used as a verb, *quad* means, in typography and typesetting, to space out the blank portion of a line to its full measure. See *Quadding*.

When used as a noun, *quad* means, in metal typography, a blank piece of metal—more formally called a *quadrat*—used to fill up a line of type, forcing the rest of the characters into a desired position on the line. Quads were used to set a line *flush left*, *flush right*, or centered.

In *binding and finishing*, the term *quad* is also a shorthand term for a *quadruple* folder. See *Folding: Knife Folder*.

Quad Center

In typography and typesetting, copy set so that it is centered on the line and not aligned with the right or left margin. See *Quadding*.

Quad Center Lock

In typography, the setting of type such that every line ending with a return will be centered. See *Quadding*.

Quadding

In typography, another term for *placement*. The word "quadding" comes from a short form of *quadrat*, a blank metal cube used for filling blank space in handset type. All type had to lock up, and this necessitated that lines with only one word on them, for example, be filled with nonprinting blanks. The blanks then positioned the type. For example, a line aligned at the left margin with blanks extending to the right margin was known as *quad left*. A line aligned at the right margin with blanks extending to the left margin was called *quad right*. A line centered between the two margins, with blank spaces extending both left and right was called *quad center*; the reverse, where one portion of a line aligned at the left while another aligned at the right, with blank spaces in the middle, was called *quad middle*.

Linecasters mechanized the process with semiautomatic attachments that filled the blank areas of a line with metal. These quadders were either mechanized, hydraulic, or electric. The popularity of the latter unit led to the use of the term *flush* as a verb for positioning. Today, both flush and *quad* are used interchangeably, although with the advent of desktop publishing, the term *quad* is being used less and less often.

The function of quadding always takes place on the *baseline* between preset margins. The term *quad lock* describes the function of repetitive quadding to the same position. Thus, a *quad center lock* indicates that every line ending with a return will be centered.

Quad Fold

In *folding*, a means of producing four *signature*s from one *press sheet*.

Quad Left

In typography and typesetting, copy set to align with the left margin. Also called *flush left*. See *Quadding*.

Quad Lock

In typography, the function of repetitive *quadding* to the same position. See *Quadding*.

Quad Middle

In typography and typesetting, copy set so that one portion of a line is flush with the left margin, while the second portion of the line is set flush with the right margin, blank spaces filling out the center of the line. See *Quadding*.

Quadratone

A four-color *halftone* image that is produced by overprinting four different screens of the same image, each possessing a different set of tonal values. See also *Duotone* and *Tritone*.

Quadrature Amplitude Modulation

In telecommunications, a means of encoding several *bit*s on a single *carrier*.

Quad Right

In typography and typesetting, copy set to align with the right margin. Also called *flush right*. See *Quadding*.

Quadruple

In *binding and finishing*, a type of *knife folder*. Also known as a *quad*. See *Folding: Knife Folder*.

Quads

In prepress, collective term for the four *color separation* films—*cyan*, *magenta*, *yellow*, and *black*.

Quad-Speed (4X)

Descriptive of a *CD-ROM* drive capable of reading and transferring data at a speed that is four times as fast as a single-speed drive. A *single-speed* CD-ROM drive, in retrospect designated 1X, could process data at a speed of 150 *kilobyte*s per second. A *double-speed (2X)* CD-ROM can thus process data at a speed of 300 kilobytes per second, and a quad-speed drive at a speed of 600 kilobytes per second. Newer drives have even faster access times: 900 kilobytes per second (6X drives), 1200 kilobytes per second (8X drives), and 1500 kilobytes per second (10X drives).

Quality Control

In any manufacturing or other process (such as printing), all the activities that ensure that the ultimate end-user or customer is pleased with a product or service. This includes *batch sampling* or other means of ensuring consistency of the product during production, as well as customer service, process control, and other ways of generating customer satisfaction.

Quantizer

Alternate term for a *digitizer*. See *Digitizer*.

QuarkXPress®

A popular *page makeup program* developed by Quark, Inc., widely used to assemble page elements—from text to *line art* and *halftone*s—for output to a *laser printer*, *imagesetter*, or other device (commonly a *PostScript* device). QuarkXPress also allows for the specification of *spot color* or desktop *color separation*. QuarkXPress, originally available only on the *Macintosh* platform, is now available for *Windows* with only minimal differences in functionality. One of the advantages of QuarkXPress is its support for *QuarkXTensions*, modular *plug-in* programs available from outside vendors that increase and enhance the functionality of the original program.

QuarkXTension™

General term for a wide variety of modular *plug-in* programs available from third-party vendors that increase and

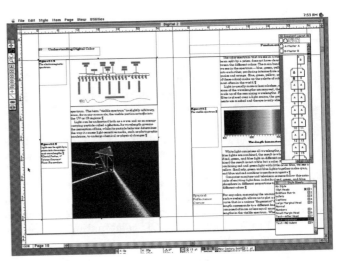

QuarkXPress, a page layout program.

enhance the functionality of *QuarkXPress*, a popular *page makeup program*.

Quarter Binding

In *binding and finishing*, a type of bookbinding in which the material forming the *spine* is different than that forming the front and back. See also *Half Binding* and *Full Binding*.

Quarter-Inch Cartridge (QIC)

A series of *magnetic tape*s used for computer data storage, which range in capacity from 60 *megabyte*s to 4 *gigabyte*s.

Quartertone

In imaging and photography, the portions of an image (such as a photograph) with tonal values between those of *highlight*s and *middletone*s, containing *halftone* dot sizes of approximately 25% *dot area*.

Quarto

In *book typography* and production, any printed sheet that has been folded two times to yield four leaves or eight pages. Abbreviated *4to* and *4°*. *Quarto* is also used to refer to the book size produced by folding pages in this manner (commonly 9½×12 in.). See also *Octavo* and *Folio*.

Quartz-Halogen Lamp

A light-source used in color *scanner*s comprising a quartz envelope filled with halogen gas that uses a tungsten filament to illuminate the original image during *scanning*. Also known as a *tungsten-halogen lamp*. Quartz-halogen lamps are also used in photographic studio lighting. Also known as a *quartz-iodine light*.

Quartz-Iodine Light

Alternate term for a *quartz-halogen lamp*. See *Quartz-Halogen Lamp*.

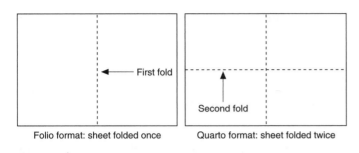

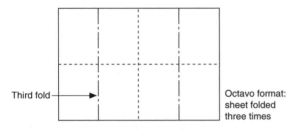

Folio, quarto, and octavo formats.

Quartz Lighting
See *Quartz-Halogen Lamp*.

Query
In database computing, a command sent by the operator to the computer designed to elicit a response from the system. Such a command typically involves a search for data stored within the database.

Query Language
In database computing, a programming language designed to allow users to request, create, or modify data. One such language is *Structured Query Language (SQL)*.

Question Mark
In typography, a *punctuation* character (?) in many languages that indicates that the foregoing text is interrogative in tone. See *Punctuation.*

   The **question mark** is also used as a *wildcard* character in many computer *operating systems* to represent a character in a file name.

Queue
In computing, a sequential list of items awaiting some type of processing. See, for example, *Print Queue* or *Event Queue*.

Quick-Connect Block
Alternate term for a *punch-down block*. See *Punch-Down Block*.

QuickDraw™
A *page description language* incorporated into the *Macintosh operating system*, which is a useful part of many Macintosh applications. QuickDraw, although rarely used for high-quality output to an *imagesetter*, is quick and

adequate for daily office tasks, and many *laser printer*s are driven by QuickDraw commands. For high-quality output, however, QuickDraw files are converted (by Quick-Draw itself) to *PostScript* format. Color QuickDraw extensions allow for the support of *32-bit color*.

   Like PostScript, QuickDraw essentially converts page elements to mathematical formulas that describe lines and curves, and it is used for two-dimensional text or images. Apple's latest version of QuickDraw—called QuickDraw 3D—allows for the rendering of three-dimensional images.

Quickset Ink
A type of printing ink comprising a balanced *solvent*-resin-oil *vehicle*. When quickset inks are printed, the solvent quickly drains out of the ink film through absorption into the *substrate*, leaving behind a film of *resin* and oil, which then quickly hardens by *oxidation* and *polymerization*. (See *Resin-Oil Vehicle*.) Quickset inks are used frequently in *letterpress* and *offset lithography* for their rapid drying and compatibility with *cast-coated* and *enamel paper*s. Quickset inks have high gloss. A recent problem with quickset inks, typically occurring on multiunit presses, is a printing defect called *back-trap mottle*. (See *Back-Trap Mottle*.) A new innovation in quickset inks is *super-quickset infrared ink* that utilizes the application of heat energy—in the form of infrared radiation—to accelerate the drying process. (See *Super-Quickset Infrared Ink*.)

Quicksetting
The rapid drying of *quickset inks*. See *Quickset Ink*.

QuickTime (QT)
An *extension* to the *Macintosh operating system* for the *compression*, *decompression*, and display of *digital video*. The first version of QuickTime only allowed a frame rate of 12 frames per second (and that at a size only one-sixteenth the size of the screen), although new versions (released regularly) are increasing the frame rate and display size. Although QuickTime began as solely a Macintosh extension, it is now available for *Windows*.

QuickTime VR
An application developed by Apple Computer for the creation of realistic, three-dimensional scenes, for use in multimedia applications. Essentially, the QuickTime VR (the "VR" stands for *virtual reality*) application employs the means of creating a 360° panoramic image as well as the means of being able to view objects from virtually all angles by either moving around them or moving and rotating them. The panorama itself is created as a series of overlapping still photographs that cover all 360°. (QT VR can also create maneuverable panoramas of completely computer-rendered scenes.) In addition to moving around the scene, the user can also zoom in or out, and by clicking in certain regions, the user can activate video clips, audio links, etc. Of additional advantage is that a single panoramic scene only occupies one *megabyte* of disk space. The first commercially

available example of QuickTime VR was a CD-ROM called *The Star Trek Interactive Technical Manual*.

Quinacridone Magentas
A series of *organic color pigments* used in printing inks.

Quinacridone Magenta Y. *Quinacridone Magenta Y* is a bright blue red possessing high *lightfastness* and resistance to acids, alkalis, soap, water, and heat. Quinacridone Magenta Y is expensive and possesses low *tinctorial strength*, resulting in its use in only a limited number of applications. (See also *Organic Color Pigments*.)

(*CI Pigment Red 122 No. 73915.*)

Quinacridone Magenta B. *Quinacridone Magenta B* is the most lightfast of the Quinacridones and is slightly redder than Quinacridone Magenta Y. It also shares its chemical resistance properties and its expense. It is usable in all printing processes and is reserved for high-quality applications.

(*CI Pigment Red 202.*)

Quinacridone Violet. *Quinacridone Violet* comprises several shades from yellowish red to bright violet and possesses high lightfastness and chemical resistance to most substances. It is an expensive pigment and is reserved for those applications where its superior properties warrant the expense.

(*CI Pigment Violet 19 No. 73900.*)

Quire
An archaic measure of paper quantity, consisting of 24 sheets of a uniform size. One *ream* was originally defined as "20 quires," or 480 sheets.

In binding, a *quire* is a somewhat obsolete term for a group of pages that have been gathered as a prelude to binding. See *Binding and Finishing*.

Quoin
In handset typography, a wooden or metal wedge used to secure type in the frame after hand tightening.

Quotes
In typography, the opening and closing *punctuation* marks—" " ' '—indicating verbal statements or defining or emphasizing certain words.

Double quotes are normally used in American books, with single quotes being used within double quotes, as in "Doubles on the outside, 'singles' on the inside," although in Britain this is reversed. The single close quote is also an apostrophe.

Quotes (or "quotation marks") were originally only commas, placed in the outer margin, and first began to be used by Morel of Paris in 1557. A century later, they resembled the so-called *French quotes* (« ») that were placed in the center of the type body so that the same character could be used for either the open or closed position. English printers refused to use the French form and used inverted commas for the open position and the apostrophe for the closed. This resulted in nonsymmetrical quotes.

In some cases, it is necessary to use a small space to separate quotes from certain letters, and between single and double quotes where they abut each other.

Usually the punctuation at the end of a quote negates the need for additional space at the close. For good display typography, sometimes it is best to use quotes one size smaller so they are not too overbearing.

R

R, r

The eighteenth letter of the English alphabet, derived from North Semitic, by way of the Greek *rho*. The form of the uppercase *R* in Latin came from a variant of *rho* in Greek script, which added the short stroke below the top loop. The lowercase *r* comes from the Roman cursive form of the capital.

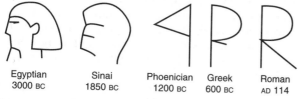

Egyptian	Sinai	Phoenician	Greek	Roman
3000 BC	1850 BC	1200 BC	600 BC	AD 114

The evolution of the letter R.

R4X00

A series of *microprocessor*s developed by MIPS Technologies, used primarily in *UNIX* systems, especially those manufactured by Silicon Graphics.

The R4000 and R4400 chips are *RISC*-based processors boasting a 64-*bit* bus. Applications designed for other processors can be used by installing the MIPS-Application Binary Interface (ABI).

RACE

Abbreviation for *Research and Development in Advanced Communications Technologies in Europe*. See *Research and Development in Advanced Communications Technologies in Europe (RACE)*.

Radial Fill

In graphics, a type of *fountain fill* in which one color is located in the center of the *fill area*, and blends into a second color out toward the perimeter of the shape. See also *Linear Fill*. (See COLOR PLATE 12.)

Radiation-Curing Ink

A variety of printing ink composed of complex *oligomer*s, *monomer*s, and other compounds that dry or "set" by *polymerization* upon exposure to various forms of radiation, such as ultraviolet light, beams of electrons, or infrared radiation, rather than traditional drying methods such as *evaporation*, absorption, precipitation, or *oxidation*. See *Ultraviolet (UV) Curing Ink*, *Electron Beam (EB) Curing Ink*, and *Super-Quickset Infrared Ink*.

Radio Button

In computing, a means of turning on and off a setting or feature in a *dialog box*. A radio button is usually a small circle that either contains a black dot within it (the feature is activated) or is empty (the feature is not activated). By clicking in the circle with the pointer, the feature can be toggled on or off. An alternate to a radio button is a *check box*.

Radio-Frequency Interference

Alternate term for *electromagnetic interference*. See *Electromagnetic Interference*. Abbreviated *RFI*.

Radius Printing

A *screen printing* press configuration designed for printing on conically shaped *substrate*s, in which the *printing screen* moves in a circular arc while the *squeegee* remains stationary.

Rag

See *Ragged*.

Rag Content

Alternate term for *cotton-content*, describing paper produced from pulp composed either entirely or partially of cotton-based *pulp*. (See *Cotton-Content*.)

Rag Left

See *Ragged Left*.

Rag Paper

A paper containing at least 25% rag or cotton pulp. (See *Cotton-Content*.)

Rag Pulp

A type of paper *pulp* derived from cotton or linen rags, as opposed to pulp derived from wood. Rag pulp produces the highest quality paper. (See *Cotton-Content*.)

Rag Right

See *Ragged Right*.

Ragged

In typography, lines of type that are not *justified*; that is, they do not align at the right margin. (Also called *ragged right*.) The *quad*, or optimum, word space values should be used. Justified and *unjustified* texts usually result in the same number of lines.

There is continuing argument about how ragged text should be and whether *hyphenation* should be allowed. There are no rules; it is up to the designer's discretion. "Soft" ragged refers to subtle differences in the length of adjacent lines, while "hard" ragged refers to severe differences. "Soft" ragged usually allows hyphenation.

Although ragged right is more common, in some applications, lines can be aligned along the right margin, but be ragged along the left (called *ragged left*).

Ragged is also informally referred to as *rag*.

Ragged Left

In typography, an alternative to *justified* type in which the lines are aligned along the right margin but not along the left. See also **Ragged Right** and **Justification**. Also informally known as *rag left*.

Ragged Right

In typography, an alternative to *justified* type in which the lines are aligned along the left margin but not along the right. See also **Ragged Left** and **Justification**. Also informally known as *rag right*.

RAID

Abbreviation for *redundant array of inexpensive disks*. See **Redundant Array of Inexpensive Disks**.

Rail

In the days of *hot metal* typesetting, a device containing an alternate *typeface* or type style (such as *italic*), which could be shifted to. The **upper rail** often contained the alternate typeface while the **lower rail** contained the original one.

Early computerized typesetting devices retained the concept of the upper and lower rail, although it increasingly became a metaphor for programming and formatting commands rather than an actual device. A line or part of a line set in a different typeface or style from the surrounding text was thus known as a *rail line*.

Rail Line

In typography, a line or part of a line set in a different *font*, *typeface*, or type *style* than the surrounding text. The term derives from the use of an **upper rail** and a **lower rail** on *hot metal* typesetting devices to switch between different fonts. See **Rail**.

Railroad Tracks

A defect of *gravure* printing characterized by a set of continuous streaks that print in nonimage areas of the *substrate*, caused by nicks in the *doctor blade*, specifically an oscillating doctor blade. The nicked area fails to wipe the ink from the portion of the *gravure cylinder* passing beneath it. Railroad tracks usually comprise a thick line produced at the end of an oscillating blade's stroke, with thinner lines produced in between them.

Railroading

A defect of *gravure* printing characterized by a continuous streaks or marks printed in nonimage areas of the *substrate*, caused by dried particles of ink or other material stuck to the back of the *doctor blade*. Such particles also commonly lead to scratching of the *gravure cylinder*.

Raised Initial

In typography, an *initial* letter that rests on the *baseline* of the first (or a subsequent) line of text and juts above the top line of the text. See **Initial**.

RAM

Abbreviation for *random-access memory*. RAM is essentially the "working" memory a computer uses to store temporary information.

RAM can be read from and written to, as its name indicates, in a random sequence, and is used to store data from open applications as well as the operating system itself. Unlike **ROM** (or *read-only memory*), which can only be read from, RAM is "cleared" or emptied when the power is turned off. Data is not often stored in RAM in a contiguous fashion; this is why very often it appears as if less RAM is available than the system indicates.

RAM is housed on memory chips or boards (such as **SIMM**s and **DIMM**s, which are known collectively as **RAM chip**s), and can be expanded by adding more chips. On **desktop computer**s, RAM was once measured in *kilobyte*s (or increments of 1,024 *byte*s) but is now almost exclusively measured in *megabyte*s (or increments of 1,024 kilobytes).

Most personal computers—as of this writing—ship with at least 8 megabytes (MB) of RAM, but as computer operating systems and applications become larger, even this amount is becoming inadequate, and many systems now come with a minimum of 16 MB.

A computer accesses RAM much faster than it can access a hard drive or any external media, which is why when playing or recording audio or video, it is best to play them directly from RAM rather than from the disk on which they are stored. This presupposes, of course, that the system has enough RAM to effect this form of playback.

In computer parlance, the term "memory" is commonly a synonym for RAM, and both terms should not be confused with "storage," or the amount of disk space available. *Cache memory* (or **RAM cache**) is a cordoned off section of RAM used to store frequently accessed data, such as font outlines, which allows for much faster processing of often-performed activities, as the computer then does not have to continually read from the hard disk.

RAM-Animation

In computer *animation*, an animated sequence that has been sufficiently *compressed* to allow it to fit entirely in a computer's **RAM**, or memory. Animations run faster when played back directly from RAM than when read from a disk or other medium.

RAM Cache

See **Cache Memory**.

RAM Chip

A semiconductor added to a computer to expand its *random-access memory (RAM)*. See **RAM**.

RAMDAC

Abbreviation for *random-access memory digital-to-analog converter*. See **Random-Access Memory Digital-to-Analog Converter**.

RAM Disk

Alternate term for a *RAM drive*. See *RAM Drive*.

RAM Drive

In computing, a portion of a computer's *random-access memory (RAM)* that can be used as a *disk drive*, albeit a temporary one. This is useful when playing back animations or digital video, as the access speed from RAM is much much faster than that from a conventional disk drive. However, since RAM is *volatile* memory, it is erased when the power is turned off. Also known as a *virtual drive* or a *RAM disk*.

Ramp

Collective alternate term for the color gradations known as *degradé* and *vignette*. See *Degradé* and *Vignette*.

Random Access

In computing, the ability for a disk drive—or other data storage device—to immediately retrieve data stored at a particular *memory address* without needing to progress sequentially through the storage medium from the beginning. See also *Sequential Access*.

Random-Access Editor

In video editing, a videotape editing system that can access any *in-point* or *out-point* instantly, make an edit, and play back the results immediately, expediting the video editing process. Most of these systems are digital.

Random-Access Memory

See *RAM*.

Random-Access Memory Digital-to-Analog Converter

The means by which data from the *central processing unit* is displayed on the screen. The *RAMDAC* chip on a *graphics card* (or *video adapter*) converts *digital* information representing *pixel*s to *analog* signals (variations in voltage) that control what points of the display are illuminated.

Random Lines

Alternate term for *ragged* (or *ragged left* and *ragged right*). See *Ragged*. Also referred to as *random setting*.

Random Proof

A type of *color proof* comprising a set of color images reproduced on the same sheet of *substrate* without regard to the correct positioning of these elements, produced as a cost-effective way of evaluating the color reproduction of completed scans prior to *stripping* and/or *color correction*. Also known as a *scatter proof*.

Random Setting

The typesetting of *ragged* lines. See *Ragged*.

Raster

Generally speaking, an alternate term for *bitmap*. *Raster* refers to images or type that has been input either by *scan-*

ning, keyboarding, or other means, processed, and/or output line-by-line. Raster images exist as discrete *byte*s, *pixel*s or lines of pixels, rather than as *vector*s, or mathematically described lines and curves. See *Bitmap*.

In television and video, the term *raster* refers to the pattern of horizontal scan lines traced by an *electron gun* on the back of the television screen. A typical raster display (in television equipment) has 525 scan lines per screen (in *NTSC*; in *PAL* and *SECAM*, there are 625 scan lines). A computer monitor works on the same principle, and is also known as a raster display. A computer monitor, however, is simpler in design and construction (as it does not need to decode a broadcast signal), but has a greater number of scan lines, which are in turn subdivided into smaller pixels. A computer monitor, as of this writing, can have over 1,000 scan lines per screen, which includes over one million *addressable point*s.

Raster Data

The information used to represent a computer image as a grid of *pixel*s, or, in other words, as a *bitmap*. See *Bitmap*. Also referred to as *image data*.

Raster Graphics

Alternate term for *bitmapped* graphics. See *Bitmap*.

Raster Image File Format

See *RIFF*.

Raster Image Processor (RIP)

In computer graphics and imaging, the hardware and software configuration used in output devices to determine what value each *pixel* or *spot* of output should possess, driven by commands from a *page description language* such as *PostScript*. All computer-generated output (such

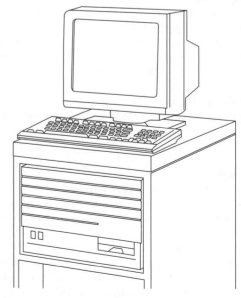

EFI Fiery raster image processor.

as that produced on an *imagesetter*) is composed of very small spots. The RIP converts a *vector*-based image, or an image—such as type or *line art*—stored by the computer as a series of mathematical formulas that describe lines and curves, into the pattern of spots needed to generate the output. (The conversion of a vector image to a *raster* image is called *ripping* or *RIPing*.) Essentially, an interpreter in the hardware converts a PostScript file into a display list, which is then converted into a *bitmap* describing the page. Most PostScript output devices have a RIP built into the hardware.

The earliest RIPs had difficulty with *halftone* screening, but PostScript screening (via *PostScript Level 2*) is now of very high quality. Another problem service bureaus have had with PostScript-driven RIPs is the occasional PostScript error and the lack of editability of the PostScript file, which often necessitated going back to the original application file and modifying it. Newer PostScript interpreters allow the editing of the display list before ripping, enabling operators to clean up problematic PostScript files.

Raster Pattern

In computer graphics and imaging, a set of *pixel*s arranged in rows and columns to form an image. See *Raster* and *Bitmap*.

Raster Scanning

In computer display imaging and *scanning*, producing or capturing (respectively) an image by means of an intensity-controlled, line-by-line sweep across the surface of the display or the image. In computer monitors, raster scanning is the means by which a *cathode-ray tube* moves across the back of the screen, illuminating phosphors according to the *bitmap* indicated in the *frame buffer*.

Raster Trapping

In digital prepress, a means of ensuring the *registration* of multicolor images performed on digital systems in which graphics are *rasterized* (or converted to *bitmap*s), analyzed for potential *trapping* problems, and new *pixel*s are added where needed. See *Trapping*.

Raster-Pattern Storage

The portion of a computer's *RAM* or another storage location in which the *bitmap*s describing fonts and images are held.

Rasterization

The process of converting a *vector*-based or other image into a *bitmap*. See *Bitmap*. Also known as *ripping*, especially when performed by a *raster image processor (RIP)*.

Rational Screen Angle

A *screen angle* used in the production of *halftone*s, distinguished by having a tangent that is a rational finite number. (See also *Irrational Screen Angle*.) See *Screen Angles*.

Raw Data

Any computer data that has not been processed or manipulated.

Raw Stock

Alternate term for *base stock* in the *finishing* operations of papermaking. See *Base Stock*. Also called *body stock*.

Raw Text

In computing, any text lacking formatting commands, such as that sent over the Internet or transferred from system to system. In word processing or page layout programs, raw text is formatted and cleaned up.

RC Paper

Abbreviation for *resin-coated paper*, a type of paper used for both photographic processing and high-quality typesetter and *imagesetter* output.

RC paper comprises a paper base and an *emulsion*, plus a resin coating that renders it waterproof during processing. RC paper is processed three times as rapidly as, and possesses a much higher degree of *permanence* than, other types of imaging paper, such as *stabilization paper*. The processing equipment used to develop RC paper is more expensive, however.

RCP

Abbreviation for *Remote Communications Processor*.

Re-Etch

To apply additional amounts of etchant to a lithographic plate as a means of modifying the image.

Reaction Shot

In motion picture photography and videography, a brief cutaway to a *close up* of a character's face to gauge his/her reaction to a particular event.

Read

In computing, to access and retrieve a stored data file, as opposed to *write*.

Readers

In prepress, non-reproduction-quality proofs of typeset copy used to check the material for typos or other errors.

ReadMac

Alternate term for a *MacPaint* file. See *MacPaint*.

README File

In computing, a text file included with distributed software that provides information about that software, such as licensing agreements, known system conflicts or incompatibilities, or installation instructions. Information in a README file may or may not be in other documentation for that software, and it often pays to read it.

Read-Only

In computing, descriptive of a diskette, disk, or other data storage medium that the system may only read; data on read-only media may not be altered or erased, and no additional data may be written to that media.

Read-Only Memory

See *ROM*.

Read-Out

In computing, the display of the contents of a data file, either on the computer monitor or as a *printout*. Also spelled as one word, *readout*.

Read/Write Head

On a computer disk drive, an electromechanical or optical device used to read data from and write data to a magnetic or optical storage medium.

Real Estate

Colloquial term for the storage space on a *magnetic disk*, *optical disc*, *videodisc*, or *magnetic tape*.

Real Hyphenation

In typography, the use of hyphens to separate compound words, in contrast to hyphens used to break a word at the end of a line. Such hyphens are necessary.

Real Image

In imaging, an image obtained from the "real world" (i.e., from a camera, be it still, motion picture, or video) as opposed to one drawn by hand or generated by computer.

Real Mode

A computer operating mode in which the processor can directly address up to 1 *megabyte* of memory. In contrast, *protected mode* allows the computer to access more memory and allows the processor to run faster. Real mode was the operating state of the original 8088/8086 *central processing unit*. Later processors in the 80X86 family run in protected mode by default, but support real mode. In this latter case, they function similarly to 8088/8086 processors, only faster. See also *Protected Mode*.

Real Time

Descriptive of a computer function that is executed at the same time the operator initiates it, or an instantaneous computer response to digital input. For example, in imaging, "real time" would describe processing and displaying changes to a manipulated *high-resolution file* as the operator is making them, rather than at a later time. Processing performed in real time is also said to be performed *on-the-fly*.

Real-Time Animation

In computer *animation*, animation that will consistently play back at the frame rate set by the animator or pro-grammer. Whether or not this can occur is a function of the speed of the computer processor on the playback system, as well as from what medium the animation is played back. For example, *RAM-animation*, or an animated sequence that fits in the computer's *RAM*, will come the closest to the ideal of real-time animation. Animation played back from certain disks or recorded media will be slower than from the computer's internal storage.

Real-Time Compression/Decompression

Alternate term for *on-the-fly compression/decompression*. See *On-the-Fly Compression/Decompression*.

Real-Time Image Generation

Alternate term for *real-time animation*. See *Real-Time Animation*.

Real-Time Operating System

A computer *operating system* that does not allow any significant delay in processing. Such systems are used in standalone applications, such as *CAM* systems.

Real-Time Video (RTV)

A means of *data compression* used in the *digital video interactive (DVI)* standard.

Ream

For most types of papers, a ream is 500 sheets of paper of a single size. In the past, a ream comprised 20 "quires," a quire containing 24 sheets of a uniform size. Therefore, a ream used to consist of only 480 sheets. In fact, a ream of certain types of papers—tissue and wrapping papers—is still 480 sheets. A ream is the quantity of paper used to determine *basis weight*. (See *Basis Weight*.)

Ream Marker

In printing, any sheet of colored paper or other material used to mark the divisions between *ream*s, either as a means of keeping an accurate count of the number of prints made, or to separate different jobs from each other.

Rear Projection

Alternate term for *rear-screen projection*. See *Rear Screen*.

Rear Screen

In film or audiovisual terminology, a translucent screen made of glass, acrylic, or other substance that enables an image projected from behind to be viewable from the front. Rear screens (and *rear-screen projection*) were often used in movie-making; a pre-filmed sequence was projected on a screen that was located behind the actors in a stationary automobile, producing the illusion that the car was moving.

Rear-Screen Projection

See *Rear Screen*.

Reboot

To **boot** a computer without turning off the power. See **Boot**.

Reciprocating Platen Diecutter

A type of **diecutting** press comprising a moving platen, which contains the cutting **die** and one stationary platen, as opposed to a **jaw platen diecutter**. See **Diecutting**.

Reclaimed Screen

In **screen printing**, a previously used screen fabric that has had the stencil and excess ink removed (and any reconditioning or repairing performed), ready to have a new stencil mounted.

Reclaiming

In **screen printing**, the act of removing a stencil and excess ink from a screen fabric after the completion of a print run for reuse in a later job.

Reclaiming Solution

In **screen printing**, a **solvent** used in the process of **reclaiming**. See **Reclaiming**.

Recommended Specifications for Web-Offset Publication

See **SWOP**.

Record Locking

In computing, especially on networks or other multiuser environments, a means of preventing a single record within a database file from being updated or altered by two different users simultaneously. Record locking, usually imposed by a **database management system**, thus allows only one user to access a specific record at any one time, effectively locking out all others. After a record is closed, the next user to attempt to open it can, again locking out all others. Some systems use **file locking** rather than record locking, which locks all users but one out of the entire database file. See also **File Locking**.

Recorder

Generally speaking, any device used to record analog, digital, or other types of information on some form of medium—such as an audio tape recorder, a videotape recorder, etc.

In imaging, the term *recorder* is also a shorthand term for **film recorder**. See **Film Recorder**.

Recovered Fiber

Fibrous paper source that has been made into paper in the past and is undergoing repulping, for use in **recycled paper** (in contrast to **virgin fiber**). See **Recycled Paper**.

Recto

The odd-numbered page on the right side of an open book, or the front or top of a printed sheet, from the Latin phrase *recto folio*, meaning "on the right-hand leaf." See also **Verso**.

Recursion

In computer programming, the ability for a particular routine or subroutine to be able to repeat itself, as when certain processing steps need to be repeated.

Recycled Paper

Paper produced using discarded paper, or **recovered fibers**, rather than **virgin fibers** as a source of **pulp**. About 80% of the recovered paper in the United States is used to produce paperboards, and the primary sources of the recovered fibers are discarded cardboard containers and packaging, old newspapers, catalogs and directories. Recovered paper used for paperboard typically does not undergo **deinking**. Since the early 1970s, recycled pulp has been increasingly used to manufacture newsprint, and deinked recycled paper is increasingly used to manufacture writing, typing, printing, and xerography papers, as well as tissues and other sanitary papers. Recovered paper can either come from post-consumer sources, such as discarded paper, or from pre-consumer sources, such as waste from the papermaking process itself. The expense of recovering paper and making it usable—especially for high-quality writing and printing papers—is still an impediment to the widescale production of recycled papers. Concern over deforestation and the mushrooming size of landfills (40% of material occupying United States landfills is paper products) has spurred the use of recycled paper. Printing and writing papers utilized by the federal government must contain 50% recovered fibers, and according to an Executive Order, beginning in 1995 government-purchased paper must contain 20% post-consumer fibers, the percentage to rise to 30% by 1999.

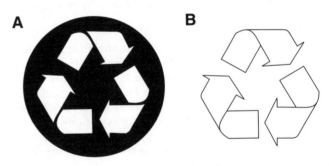

A   B

Two recycling symbols. The filled symbol (A) indicates that the paper has been recycled. The outline symbol (B) indicates that the paper can be recycled.

Red

The **color** characteristic of light possessing a wavelength between 610 and 780 **nanometer**s, located at the very end of the visible spectrum, between **infrared** and **orange**. Red is one of the three **primary colors** of light. (See **Additive Color Primaries**.)

In multicolor printing, *red* is also a **secondary color** produced by the overprinting of **yellow** and **magenta** inks. Red is often—though somewhat incorrectly—used synonymously with *magenta*. (See **Subtractive Color Primaries**.)

Red Book

In multimedia, the original set of standards developed by Sony and Philips in 1982 for the *compact disc*, technically called the *compact disc–digital audio*. The Red Book standard (so-named because the publication containing the specifications had a red cover) describes the physical structure of the disc and the instructions for creating CDs. See *Compact Disc–Digital Audio (CD-DA)* and *Compact Disc (CD)*.

Redesign

To modify a pre-existing design to create a new product, as a means of avoiding the need to create a new design from scratch. In the '90s, this is also known as *repurposing*.

Red, Green, and Blue (RGB)

The three *additive color primaries*, or the three basic components of visible light, the various combinations of which produce all the colors of the spectrum. (See *Additive Color Primaries*.)

In computer graphics, *RGB* refers to a type of color image display (called an *RGB monitor*) or *color space* in which each of those three color components is stored and transmitted to the display separately, the intensity and percentage of each varying by *pixel*, by an amount determined by the *color depth* of the monitor.

In printing, red, green, and blue are *secondary colors* produced by overprinting dots of the *subtractive color primaries*—*cyan*, *magenta*, and *yellow*. (See *Subtractive Color Primaries*.)

Redirector

In networking, a software program or module loaded on individual *workstation*s that processes file-sharing and printer-sharing requests. The redirector intercepts these requests and relays them to the *file server* for handling. A redirector is also known as a *requester*.

Redline

In proofing, to mark corrections on a *printout* or *galley* pages, so-named due to the use of a red pen or pencil.

Red Patch

In traditional prepress, a square or other shape of *rubylith*, *amberlith*, etc., pasted to a *mechanical* in the exact position of a desired *halftone* or other illustration. When the mechanical is photographed as a *negative* prior to *stripping*, it will appear as a transparent window, into which the halftone negative can be placed. Also called a *black patch*.

Reduced Instruction-Set Computing (RISC)

Descriptive of a computer *microprocessor* that is able to process small, optimal sets of instructions, rather than large, complex sets of instructions. As a result, many types of applications (such as those for graphics) can be processed more quickly. However, since the processor has fewer instructions, the applications themselves must supply a large percentage of the instructions and thus can be larger and more unwieldy (and require more memory to run). An alternative is a *CISC*-based processor. See also *Complex Instruction-Set Computing (CISC)*.

Reducer

A substance—such as a *varnish*, *solvent*, oil, grease, or wax—added to a printing ink to decrease the ink's *tack*, or improve its consistency.

Reduction

Any reproduction that is smaller than the original. See also *Enlargement*.

Reduction Rate

Alternate term for *compression ratio*. See *Compression Ratio*.

Redundancy Check

See *Cyclic Redundancy Check*.

Redundant Array of Inexpensive Disks

A computer storage system developed by IBM in 1977 comprising a set of linked *hard disk*s. The advantage of this system, abbreviated *RAID*, was the increased storage capacity.

Redundant Data

See *Data Redundancy*.

Reel Curl

Alternate term for *roll-set curl*. See *Roll-Set Curl*.

Reel Rods

In *offset lithography*, a set of metal rods located on the *plate cylinder* and the *blanket cylinder* used to fold the plate and blanket onto the cylinder.

Reference

In typography, a *footnote*, specifically one that appears at the end of a book or other publication. Also known as an *end note*. See *Footnote*.

Reference Marks

In typography, symbols such as asterisks (*), daggers (†), superscript numerals (¹), etc., used to indicate *footnote*s or *reference*s. See *Footnote*.

Refiner Mechanical Pulping (RMP)

A recent development in *mechanical pulping* in which wood chips are sandwiched between the two revolving disks of a *disk refiner* in the presence of water and at atmospheric pressure. Heat due to friction softens the lignin and allows greater separation of the cellulose fibers, while contributing less fiber damage. Refiner mechanical pulp has greater strength than traditional groundwood, which reduces the need to supplement it with chemical pulps.

RMP also is able to utilize more tree species, as well as various types of scrapwood and waste chips. Most RMP pulpmills, however, have been supplanted by even newer pulping techniques.

Refining

The mechanical treatment of paper *pulp* fibers to impart to them the appropriate characteristics for papermaking. A part of the *stock preparation* phase of papermaking, refining is the most important aspect of the process, as it is here that the characteristics of the *cellulose* fibers and the composition of the papermaking *furnish* that comprise paper are determined, affecting how the fibers bind with each other during the formation of the paper *web* and what the various optical, structural, and chemical properties of the paper will be.

There are two basic methods for pulp refining. The first, an older batch system, uses an oval tank called a *beater*. The beater is equipped with rotating metal bars that squeeze the fibers between stationary metal bars. The water-suspended fibers are repeatedly passed through the rotating bars, the end result of which is that the fibers become frayed, shortened lengthwise, swollen in diameter and softened. Their surface area is increased to facilitate the binding of fibers in subsequent stages of the papermaking process. *Loading*, or the addition of nonfibrous additives such as *fillers*, can take place at this point.

The furnish is sent to a *conical refiner* (also called a *jordan*) for further refining. The furnish enters at the smaller end of the conical refiner, is swirled between a rotating plug and stationary metal bars, and is ejected out the larger end. In larger papermills, the beater/refiner batch system has been replaced by continuous *disk refiners*, which are rotating disks having serrated or otherwise contoured surfaces. One disk rotates clockwise, while the other rotates counterclockwise, or is stationary. The furnish is pumped through the center of one of the disks and as centrifugal force throws the furnish toward the perimeter of the disks, it is sandwiched between them. The action of the rotating disks rubs, rolls, cuts, frays, and softens the fibers. The space between the disks can be adjusted, depending on the degree of refining desired. In continuous refining systems, the type of pulp, the degree of refining, and the type and quantity of fillers can be altered easily depending on the type of paper that is to be produced.

A variety of paper properties are a direct result of the refining process. If the fiber length is decreased, the strength and resistance to tearing of the paper produced will decrease, but the surface levelness and smoothness will increase, and the print quality will become better. As the degree of refining is increased, the density, hardness, ink holdout, smoothness, and internal bond strength will increase, but thickness, compressibility, dimensional stability, and porosity will decrease. Complicating matters is the fact that with initial refining, resistance to tearing will increase, due to the enhanced ability of the fibers to bind with each other and resist pulling away, but further refining will work to decrease tearing resistance, as the shortening of the fibers has a deleterious effect on paper strength. In other words, increased refining will work to shorten paper fibers, which enhances smoothness and printability, but diminishes strength and resistance to stresses. (See also *Paper and Papermaking: Paper Properties*.)

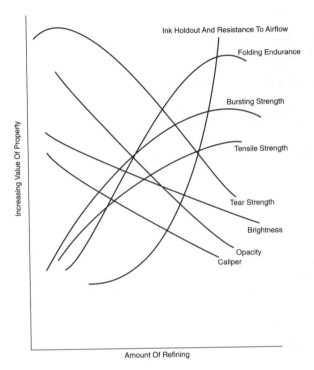

Effect of the amount of refining on various paper properties. Notice that the optimization of any specific paper property may compromise other properties.

Reflectance

In imaging, the ratio of the total amount of light striking a surface to the amount of light that is reflected from that surface. The calculation of reflectance is part of the measurement of image *density*. See *Density*.

Reflection

The bouncing of light rays off of a surface. In optics, the law of reflection holds that the angle at which a light ray is reflected will be equal to the angle of incidence. On a *matte* surface, however, light is reflected diffusely, or in a variety of different directions, the result being that the color of that surface will appear lighter.

Reflection Copy

Any original copy of a to-be-reproduced image that exists on an opaque *substrate* (such as a photographic print) which must be photographed or scanned by reflecting light from its surface, as opposed to *transmission copy*.

Reflective Beads

Tiny orbs of glass that are embedded into the surface of an ink film—in the production of *reflective ink*—or an *adhesive* coating material—in the production of *reflective sheeting*—to reflect light, imparting a sparkling effect to the dried film or sheet.

Reflective Ink

A printing ink that has had tiny glass beads—called *reflective beads*—embedded in it to produce a sparkling effect in the dried ink film.

Reflective Sheeting

A sheet of *substrate* that has had tiny glass beads—called *reflective beads*—embedded in it to produce a sparkling effect in the sheet surface.

Reflex Blue

See *Alkali Blues*.

Refraction

The bending of light rays as they pass from one medium to another, such as from air to water or glass. As light travels into a denser medium (such as into glass from air, or from the vacuum of space to the Earth's atmosphere), it will be bent toward a line perpendicular to the interface (the border of the two media). Additionally, light rays of shorter wavelengths—such as the blue end of the visible spectrum—will be bent to a greater extent than rays of longer wavelengths. It is this principle on which a prism is based.

Printing inks are also based on the principle of refraction. The size and dispersion of the particles of *pigment* in an ink *vehicle* determine the index of refraction of that ink; the greater this index of refraction, the more *opaque* the ink film will appear when printed. *Refraction* is also the principle upon which a camera lens is based; light passing through a suitably shaped piece of glass can focus the rays on a single point, allowing a clear (or less clear) image. (See *Color Plate 11*.)

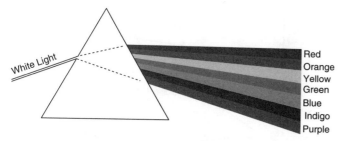

White Light

Red
Orange
Yellow
Green
Blue
Indigo
Purple

The refraction of light as it passes from one medium to another (such as into a prism and back out into air) bends different wavelengths in varying amounts.

Refresh

The process of redrawing a computer display by the electron beam scanner. Since the phosphors coating the inside of the computer screen do not retain an image for more than an instant, the raster scanner needs to repeatedly "refresh" the image. The number of times per second the beam redraws the screen display is known as the *refresh rate*.

The term *refresh* also refers to the process of reading then rewriting the data on a magnetic storage medium, which has the effect of refreshing the magnetic charge on the surface.

Refresh Cycle

See *Refresh Rate*.

Refresh Rate

The frequency with which a *raster* beam repeats the scan of a computer monitor (or other *cathode-ray tube*), or the number of times per second the screen redraws itself. The faster the refresh rate of a monitor, the less of a discernible flicker it will have. Generally speaking, a refresh rate of at least 70 hertz (Hz)—or, in other words, 70 screen redraws per second—is the minimum for flicker-free monitors. Depending on the monitor's brightness setting and the lighting of the room it is in, however, even somewhat higher refresh rates can generate a flicker. By the way, it is the difference in the scan rate of a computer monitor and a television screen that causes the visibility of the raster line when a computer display is shown on TV.

Register

The degree to which successively printed *color*s (or images) are accurately positioned with respect to each other. Accurate register ensures that a final printed piece has the effect of a "single image," with no color gaps or overlaps. Register is initially set by correct exposure, positioning, and mounting of printing plates (or other image carriers), but proper register on the printed piece can be mitigated against by many different variables, such as dimensional changes in the *substrate* due to changes in *moisture content* and/or mechanical stretching, deficiencies in the press feeding section, web tension, or changes in the image-carrying portions of the press, such as blanket compression (in *offset lithography*) or plate swelling (in *flexography*), among many other factors.

Depending on the application, accuracy of registration may be more or less necessary. See *Absolute Register*, *Close Register*, *Commercial Register*, *Hairline Register*, *Lap Register*, and *Loose Register*. Inaccuracies in registration are known as *misregister*. *Process color* printing is usually performed utilizing *register marks*, small shapes on successive plates that aid in the setting of proper register.

Register is also used to refer to a storage area in a computer. See *Data Register*.

In the computer language "C," variables may be declared as register, instructing the compiler to keep the value of these variables in the register of the central processing unit (CPU) rather than in memory, where variables are conventionally stored. Operations performed on register variables are therefore very fast.

Register Block

An adjustable metal plate attached to the side of the *feed-board* of a sheetfed printing press used in tandem with a *side guide* to properly position a sheet of paper before it is transferred to the printing unit. See *Feedboard* and *Feeder Section: Sheetfed Offset Lithography*.

Register Marks

Small designs, shapes, or other patterns (most commonly a circle or oval with a cross through it) placed in nonimage areas of negatives, positives, color separations, and plates to ensure correct *register*—or alignment—of successive colors and/or images. Register marks should not be confused with crop marks, corner marks, or other marks designed for finishing operations. See *Register*. Also known as *Angle Marks*.

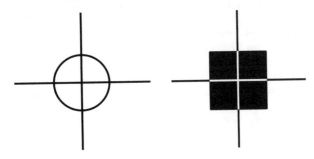

Two types of register marks.

Register Motor

In *offset lithography*, an auxiliary device used to make adjustments to the *plate cylinder* (to control *register*) from a master control panel.

Register Paper

A thin *bond paper* used for *multipart forms*.

Register Plate

Alternate term for *register block*. See *Register Block*.

Registration

The extent to which successively printed colors or images are positioned on the final print, with respect to each other or to their position on the original copy. See *Register*.

Registration Mark

See *Register Marks*.

Reinforced Endsheets

In *case binding*, a means of strengthening the binding by adding a strip of tape (usually muslin), called a *guard*, around the fold of the first and last *signature*s of the *book block*. Also known as a *guarded signatures*.

Related Italic

In typography, a more or less "pure" *italic* type designed to blend with a corresponding *roman* typeface. See *Italic*.

Relational Database

A type of *database* in which data appear as sets of rows and columns. The rows contain the individual *record*s in the database, while the columns contain the separate *field*s for each record.

Relative Humidity

A measure of the amount of water vapor present in the air expressed as a percentage of the total amount of water vapor the air could hold at the same temperature and pressure.

Relative humidity is an important consideration in printing and papermaking, as paper's *hygroscopic* tendency makes it absorb and lose water readily, affecting several paper properties, not the least of which is *dimensional stability*. (See *Moisture Content* and *Dimensional Stability*.) Most paper produced in North America is manufactured at 35–50% relative humidity. Many pressrooms have humidity control and maintain the relative humidity within that range to prevent as much water loss or gain as possible, so the paper remains flat before, during, and after printing. When printing jobs require more than one pass through the press (such as multicolor work), paper should have a relative humidity 5–8% higher than the relative humidity of the room, so that its rate of moisture loss to the atmosphere will be offset by its rate of water absorption from the press dampening system.

In some pressrooms, varying levels of *humidification* (adding moisture to the atmosphere) or *dehumidification* (removing moisture from the atmosphere) may have to be performed to ensure that paper and pressroom are of congruent moisture content. (See also *Equilibrium Relative Humidity*, and *Equilibrium Moisture Content*.)

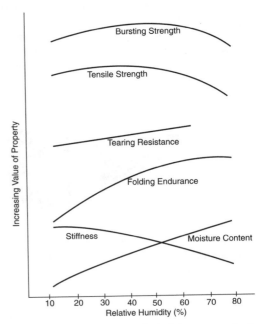

Effect of increasing relative humidity on selected paper properties.

Relative Unit

In typography, a measure of space in relation to an ***em space***. Since the size of an em space is dependent upon the ***point size***, the fractional divisions of an em are also dependent upon the point size. Common relative units are defined as relative-unit spaces per em, and include 18, 36, 54, 72, and 108. In the first case, then, the relative unit consists of 18 units per em, the exact width of which is a function of the point size. See ***Unit System***.

Release

The degree to which an offset press ***blanket*** will let go of the paper as it leaves the ***impression nip***. Although release is a function of many aspects of the offset printing process—such as ink ***tack***, the extent of the ***squeeze*** between the ***blanket cylinder*** and ***impression cylinder***, and the surface characteristics of the paper—the structural characteristics of the blanket also play an important role. It is the unanimous opinion of press operators that hard blankets release the paper better than soft ones (although empirical research has yet to confirm this, perhaps due to the inadequacy of effective quantification of blanket hardness), and somewhat rough surfaces release paper better than smooth ones. (See ***Blanket***.)

Release Paper

A sheet of paper (or other ***substrate***) that functions as a carrier and a backing for ***pressure-sensitive label***s, allowing easy removal for application to the ultimate desired substrate.

Relief

Any printing or imaging process that transfers an image to a ***substrate*** by means of a raised image-carrying surface, in contrast to ***gravure*** (or ***intaglio***), which prints from an etched surface, or ***lithography***, which prints from a flat surface. Relief printing is commonly used synonymously with ***letterpress*** printing, but can also be used to refer to ***flexography***. In ***finishing***, ***embossing*** processes involve the use of dies to create a raised—or *relief*—image to a ***substrate***.

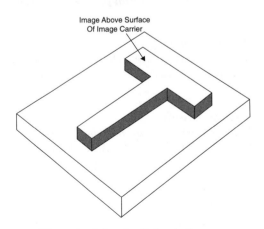

The principle of relief printing.

Remoistenable Pattern Gluer

An ***in-line*** finishing device found on a ***web press*** that is used to apply an adhesive, a fragrance, or a "scratch-and-sniff" material to a printed product, utilizing a raised plate mounted to a cylinder. A transfer roller meters the film of the material to be applied and transfers it to the plate cylinder, which in turn transfers it to the printed web passing between the plate and impression cylinders. Such devices are often used for direct mail pieces, envelopes, and insert cards (such as perfumed cards) for magazines, newspapers, and other such publications.

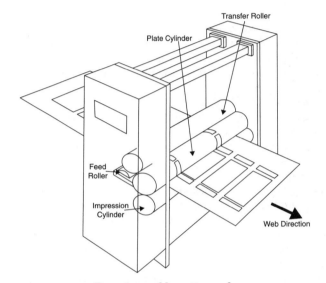

Remoistenable pattern gluer.

Remoisturizer

In ***web offset lithography***, a device comprising a set of applicators that increase the moisture of a printed and dried paper web. A remoisturizer is often used to minimize static electric buildup prior to ***sheeting***.

Remote

In networking and telecommunications, descriptive of a computer, ***workstation***, or user that is connected to a larger computer or ***server***, while not necessarily being geographically proximate. See ***Remote Access*** and ***Remote Terminal***.

Remote Boot

In networking, the ***boot***ing of a ***workstation*** from the central ***file server*** rather than from a drive attached to the workstation itself. See ***Boot***.

Remote Control

Any small electronic device (usually handheld) used to control a piece of equipment from some distance away. The most common example is the television remote control. Remote controls are also used to control VCRs, home audio equipment, as well as professional video editing systems.

Most remote controls use infrared rays to beam information from the remote to the device, while others use a physical wire connecting the remote and device.

Remote Terminal

Any individual computer or **workstation** that is connected to a larger computer, **mainframe**, or **server**. A remote terminal may or may not have its own processing capabilities.

Remote User

Any computer operator accessing a computer system from some geographical distance away. See **Remote Access**.

Removable Adhesive

An **adhesive** substance characterized by higher degrees of **cohesion** than **adhesion**, or that can be removed from the surface to which it is adhered with minimal difficulty.

Removable Hard Disk

A **magnetic disk** that has all the characteristics of a conventional **hard disk** (also known as a **fixed disk**), save that it is stored in a plastic case from which it can be removed.

Rendering

An alternate term for **rasterization**. See **Rasterization**.

In digital imaging and three-dimensional **modeling**, the application of shading and color variations to an image to provide the illusion of depth, or a third dimension. Computerized rendering utilizes mathematical formulas to determine the location of a light source in relation to the object being rendered, and calculates the manner in which the light source would affect shadows, highlights, and color variations.

Flat Rendering. A simple shading scheme that assigns all pixels in a polygon the same color.

Gouraud Rendering. A shading algorithm devised by Henri Gouraud in which each pixel on a surface is calculated as an average from the color and illumination at the corners of the wireframe polygon in which it is located.

Phong Rendering. A shading algorithm due to Phong Bui Tuong that computes each pixel of a surface based on the color and illumination at that pixel. This is more accurate than Gouraud shading, but also more compute-intensive. However, it is less demanding than ray tracing. Phong rendering provides the coloring, shading and modeling to allow an image to simulate reality.

Rep

Abbreviated term for *representative*.

Repeatability

A measure of the extent to which an **imagesetter** or **film plotter** will place a specific dot in exactly the same position on successive pieces of film.

Repeater

In networking (especially those utilizing **Ethernet**), a device that receives transmitted signals and repeats them—in an amplified and restored version—in an additional circuit (or circuits). A repeater is used to compensate for distortion or attenuation, especially when a signal is being transmitted over long distances. A repeater capable of controlling the flow of data to avoid collisions is known as a **buffered repeater**.

Repertoire

Alternate term for a **character set**, or set of available characters in a font. See **Character Set**. The term *repertoire* also refers, in computing, to any other complete group of commands and functions.

Replenisher

In photography, a chemical added to a **developer** to allow it to retain its strength for an extended period of time.

Replication

The process of mass-producing **compact disc**s and other forms of **optical disc**. The process of replication, like the earlier means of pressing vinyl records, involves the use of a relief template, in the case of optical discs, that is a **glass master**. This master has been encoded (using data from the **master tape**) with a series of pits and lands, which correspond to the **pits** and **lands** to ultimately be stamped on the disc. These pits and lands are stamped into a metal plate, called a **stamper**, which thus contains a "negative" of the pit/land pattern. The stamper then stamps one side of the disc, under high pressure and temperature. Then, the stamped side is covered with a thin layer of aluminum, to create a reflective layer. A protective coating is then applied, and a label is added to the reverse side. The final step involves punching the center hole (by which the disc is accurately held in the reader or drive). See **Compact Disc (CD)**.

Reprint Rights

In publishing, the contractual and therefore legal right to reprint or reproduce text, illustrations, photographs, etc., that have already been published elsewhere.

Repro

Abbreviation for **reproduction proofs**. See **Reproduction Proofs**.

Reproduction Paper

A high-quality, **coated one side** paper used in the making of **reproduction proofs**, or for fine **screen printing** or color printing.

Reproduction Proofs

In publishing, a set of **page proofs** typeset and output in the best-quality form, to be used as **camera-ready copy**. Reproduction proofs—also known simply as **repro**—are also read one last time for any typesetting mistakes or other errors. Any corrections are output as small two- or three-line bits of type and pasted over the original portion of text, a more economical means of making last-minute corrections without needing to re-output the entire set of proofs.

Reproduction Ratio

The amount of **enlargement** or **reduction** of an original that is required to yield a reproduced image at the desired size. The reduction ratio is often expressed as a percentage of the original image, where 100% is a 1:1 ratio.

Reprographic Paper

An uncoated paper commonly used in office photocopying or computer printing equipment.

Repurposing

The act of modifying pre-existing content or design to create something new. In this age of multimedia, one can consistently repurpose one's own material to generate books, CD-ROMs, videos, etc.

Requester

Alternate term for a **redirector**. See **Redirector**.

Rerun

To print a job again from existing negatives or plates.

Rescreen

A **halftone** negative made of a preprinted halftone, produced using a special diffusion filter to prevent the two screens from interfering with each other and producing **moiré**.

Research and Development in Advanced Communications Technologies in Europe (RACE)

A European program set up to research and develop standards for **broadband** networks, including hardware, cabling, and network **protocol**s not only for computer data transmissions, but also **HDTV** and other such applications. The RACE program, designed to set up the infrastructure for such networks, was completed in 1995 and has been followed up by the **Advanced Communications Technologies and Services (ACTS)** program that is designed to develop specific applications.

Reservoir

In **screen printing**, the term for an **ink fountain**, or the portion of the printing press in which the ink to be printed is stored and gradually fed to the **printing screen**. The reservoir can consist of simply a portion of the printing screen beyond the edges of the stencil from which the **squeegee** picks up ink at the start of each printing stroke.

Reset

To return a device or software program to an initial state, to eliminate any custom settings. See also **Hard Reset**.

In typography, *reset* means to typeset a job again, either with different **type specification**s, or due to loss or irremediable damage to the original.

Resident

In computing, descriptive of any data—be it a command, a font, or a program—that is stored in and is readily available from the computer's (or other device's) **RAM**. See **Terminate-and-Stay-Resident (TSR)**.

Resilience

A measure of an offset press blanket's ability to return to its original thickness following its exposure to the increased pressure produced during the production of a printed impression. Resilience is commonly thought of as synonymous with **smash resistance**. (See **Blanket**.)

Resiliency

The extent to which a paper is able to restore its original dimensions and surface contours after a compressing force has been removed, as in printing. The degree of a paper's resiliency, along with its **compressibility**, and **hardness** or **softness** define its **printing cushion**. Such factors in the papermaking process as degree of fiber **refining**, **calendering**, and **supercalendering** affect a paper's resiliency, as do **density** and **moisture content**. Resiliency is more of an issue in **letterpress** and **gravure** printing and less of one in **flexography** and **offset lithography**. Other considerations such as hardness and an ability to withstand handling and folding may obviate the desire for a paper with high resiliency. (See **Compressibility**, and **Hardness** and **Softness**.)

Resin

A material, either solid or semi-solid, used as a printing ink **binder** in ink **vehicle**s to assist the ink **pigment** in adhering to the **substrate**. Resins also determine the ink qualities of gloss, hardness, and adhesion. Resins are either derived from natural sources (such as **rosin**, derived from the distillation of turpentine obtained from the sap of pine trees) and lac (secreted by the lac insect, used in **shellac**), or are synthesized by the **polymerization** of other materials. Commonly used resins include **alkyd**s, **asphaltum**, **coumarone-indene resin**, **fumaric resin**, **gum**, **maleic resin**, **Nylon®**, **phenolic resin**, **polyethylene**, **polypropylene**, **polyvinyl acetate**, **polyvinyl alcohol**, **polyvinyl chloride**, **polyvinyl chloride acetate**, and **shellac**. Resins are also used in **varnish**es, **lacquer**s, and other materials. (See **Vehicle**.)

Resin Reclaim

A post-exposure process in **flexographic** platemaking in which unexposed **liquid photopolymer** is washed from the exposed plate, collected, and reused for later plates. See **Liquid Photopolymer**.

Resin-Oil Vehicle

A type of ink **vehicle**—the fluid carrier of the ink **pigment**—that dries by rapid absorption followed by **oxidation** and **polymerization** of the vehicle. Also known as **quickset ink**s, resin-oil vehicles are produced from a combination of **solvent**s, oils, and resins. The solvent is rapidly absorbed by the **substrate**, leaving the **resin** and oil mixture to dry and harden by polymerization (the combining of smaller molecules to form a longer one, called a polymer). These inks dry quickly upon contact with paper, and are used in **letterpress** and **offset** printing. (See **Vehicle**.)

Resin-Wax Vehicle

A type of ink **vehicle**—the fluid carrier of the ink **pigment**—that dries by the cooling of a wax-based vehicle. Resin-wax vehicle inks, as their name implies, are made from a combination of resins and waxes, and are solids at room temperature. Presses designed to print these inks (called **coldset ink**s) must have heated ink rollers, form rollers, and plates to melt the ink and keep it liquefied long enough to make an impression on the **substrate**, where it then cools and hardens. Coldset inks are not widely used. (See **Vehicle**.)

Resist

A paper, emulsion, or other substance that can be rendered light-sensitive, exposed to a film positive, and developed so that when the exposed emulsion is applied to the surface of a **gravure cylinder**, the unexposed image areas are soft and soluble, while the exposed, nonimage areas become hard and insoluble. The resist, as its name indicates, resists penetration by an acidic etchant, used to engrave the cells into the image-carrying surface of the gravure cylinder, in varying degrees, according to the amount of UV exposure that portion of the resist received. The hardest portions of the resist offer the most resistance to penetration by the etchant, ensuring that engraving does not occur in the nonimage areas. Highlight sections of the image also offer resistance to the etchant, and only very shallow etching occurs there. Shadows and solids, however, have little resistance to the etchant, so cells can be engraved rather deeply. In midtone regions, moderate amounts of engraving occur. Resists, formerly **carbon tissue**, are now produced from **photopolymer**s. (See **Gravure Engraving**.) Resists are also used in the exposure of **flexographic** printing plates. (See **Plate: Flexography**.) A resist is also known as an **acid resist** and an **etch resist**.

Resistive Monitor

A type of **touch screen** monitor. See **Touch Screen**.

Resolution

A measure of the extent to which the human eye can distinguish between the smallest discrete parts of an image. In terms of human vision, though, this is more or less a subjective measurement, due to the variability among individuals in how well their eyes can resolve small images. A person's ability to perceive small images, as we are all aware, changes (and not for the better) as we get older.

In computer graphics and imaging, the term *resolution* can mean a variety of different things, depending on the image and which particular aspect of a graphics system one is talking about.

Screen Resolution. Screen resolution can refer to both the *color depth* (i.e., *eight-bit color* vs. *twenty-four-bit color*, or the total number of colors that can be displayed) and intensity of the displayed image, or to the number of *pixels* displayed per unit of length. (Though not really a measure of resolution per se, a monitor's *dot pitch* is a measure of the diameter of one screen pixel. The smaller the dot pitch, the greater the resolution.) When describing *vector* displays, *screen resolution* refers to the number of horizontal lines per inch. When describing *raster* displays, *screen resolution* refers to the number of horizontal and vertical *pixel*s that can be displayed (i.e., 640×480).

Output Resolution. Although **dots per inch (dpi)** is commonly used as a measure of output resolution, a more preferable measure is of the number of discernible line pairs per inch (or millimeter), as in many types of output the dots are deliberately made to overlap, skewing the "dots per inch" measurement.

In **desktop publishing**, "dots per inch" or, more correctly, **pixels per inch (ppi)** (to distinguish pixels from halftone dots), is the measurement of choice, and is the unit most often used in input and output device specifications. For example, a Macintosh monitor has a resolution of 72 ppi; a **laser printer** has a maximum resolution of 300–600 ppi; and an **imagesetter** has a resolution of 1270–3386 ppi. On the input side of things, a desktop scanner has a resolution of 300–600 ppi, while a high-end **drum scanner** has a resolution of up to 10,000 ppi. Resolution, therefore, is a combination of both the input resolution and the total number of dots (actually, more correctly called **spot**s, to, again, distinguish them from halftone dots, which are themselves composed of printer spots) that the output device can print per inch.

As a general rule, the higher the resolution the better, but there is a caveat. Although scanning an image at the highest resolution that the device will allow may seem like a good idea, it is in vain if the output device's resolution is lower. And since digital file size increases with increasing resolution, one may be doing oneself a disservice by scanning higher than one needs to, which will result in longer image processing time, larger file sizes, and more RAM needed to work with the image. (See **Scanning**.)

Resolution-Independent

Any text or graphics file or file description language (such as **PostScript**) that will output a file at the highest **resolution** the output device is capable of, in contrast to a **resolution-dependent** file or language (such as the original version of **QuickDraw**) that only allows certain predetermined resolutions (such as **screen resolution**) to be printed.

Resource Sharing

In networking, the hardware and software that allows certain peripheral devices—such as printers, modems, etc.—to be shared by all connected users.

Respi-Screen

In **halftone** photography, a **contact screen** with a screen ruling of 110 **lines per inch (lpi)** in **highlight** portions of an image, and 220 lpi in **middletone** and **shadow** portions. Respi-screens thus generate halftones with smoother tonal gradations in light areas of the image.

Response Time

In computing and networking, the time it takes for a host computer to react to a command initiated by a connected workstation, including the transmission to the host, the processing of the desired command, and the transmission of the results back to the workstation.

Restart

To **reset** a computer routine, or return it to a specific location, due to error. *Restart* also means to **boot** a computer again.

Restore

To open a backup copy of a file or document if an error occurs or damage is incurred by the original.

Restructured EXtended eXecutor (REXX)

In computing, a **macro** designed to automate the **OS/2** operating system and the applications that run on it.

Retarder

A low-volatility **solvent** added to a printing ink **vehicle** to slow down the rate at which the ink dries by impeding solvent **evaporation**, commonly used in **flexographic**, **gravure**, **screen printing**, and **heatset** inks. Retarders that slow an ink's drying time by preventing **oxidation** from taking place are called **antioxidants**.

Reticulation

A printing defect characterized by a large-scale withdrawal of a printed ink film from portions of the **substrate**, caused by incompatibilities between the ink formulation and the surface of the substrate.

Retouching

Any manipulation of an image—either manually, photographically, or digitally—ranging from a manual "airbrushing" out of unsightly facial blemishes on a publicity photo, to a digital insertion of Napoleon on the moon. Retouching refers to essentially any alteration in an image's appearance, and can include **color correction** or other rectification of image flaws, or complete changes in the design or content of an image.

Retrieval

See **Information Retrieval**.

Return Blade

Alternate term for a **flood bar**. See **Flood Bar**.

Return Card

A **blow-in card** or detachable form or coupon inserted in magazines and other publications for the convenience of readers wishing to respond to an offer or to subscribe.

Return Key

A computer keyboard key that is now virtually interchangeable with the **enter key**. See **Enter Key**.

Reversal Film

In photography, any film used for making contact prints that preserves the black and white values on the original. For example, a negative will be produced from a negative, and a positive will be produced from a positive, in contrast to typical contact film that produces a positive from a negative, and vice versa.

Reversal Processing

In photography, the **development** of an exposed film such that it will appear as a **positive** rather than a **negative**.

Reverse

Essentially, the **negative** of an image, or the producing of the negative of an image.

The term *reverse* also refers to type or other matter that is designed to print as white on black (or colored), rather than as the typical black on white.

The term *reverse* should not be confused with the physical reversing of the orientation of an image, which is more correctly known as **flopping**.

Reverse Folio

In **book typography**, a **folio** that is set **flush right** on **verso** pages and **flush left** on **recto** pages, the opposite of the positioning of a traditional folio.

Reverse Leading

In typesetting, the act, on the part of a phototypesetter, of reversing the imaging film resulting in the placement of a successive line higher on the page than a previous line.

Reverse Overlay

In prepress, copy—to ultimately be reproduced as a *reverse*—pasted onto an **overlay** over other page elements.

Reverse Printing

See **Back Printing**.

Reverse Slip Nip

In an offset press's **continuous-flow dampening system**, the line of contact between two rollers rotating in the same direction, typically a hard **transfer roller** and a **form roller**, either belonging to the **dampening system**, or shared by the dampening and **inking system**s. When two adjacent rollers rotate in the same direction (either clockwise or counterclockwise), at the line of contact (the nip) they are moving in *opposite* directions, preventing the **fountain solution** transferred by the rollers from flowing into the nip. A reverse slip nip is occasionally produced in presses as a means of preventing interaction between excess fountain solution returning from the plate and "fresh" fountain solution flowing out of the fountain pan. Preventing this interaction allows greater control, or metering, of the fountain solution flowing to the plate. A more or less "conventional" nip between two rollers rotating in opposite directions is called a *slip nip*. (See *Dampening System*.)

Reverse Type

In typography, a form of *special effect* in which the background is the printed image while the type itself remains the color of the *substrate*. Also called *dropout type*.

Reverse Video

On a computer monitor, a means of highlighting a character, word, etc., by reversing the background and foreground colors of the display. For example, if a monitor is displaying black text on a white background, a highlight word would comprise white text on a black background.

Revise

In typography, a *proof* generated after the first proof has been corrected. It is also the proof that bears the *proof marks*.

Rewetting

The ability of an *overprint* to cause the underlying printed ink film to resoften.

In *screen printing*, *rewetting* refers to the ability of an ink to soften dried ink particles clogging the screen fabric.

Rewinding

A *finishing* operation performed at a papermill consisting of slitting and rewinding a large, finished paper roll into smaller rolls for delivery to the customer. Rewinding procedures include such operations as slitting machine rolls to make rolls having a specified width and/or diameter, winding on specially constructed cores, removing paper containing defects and splicing rolls back together, and packaging rolls for delivery.

Rewritable Consumer Time Code

In video, a *time code* format designed by Sony for use in the *video system control architecture (VISCA)*. Like the *SMPTE time code*, it measures a video production in hours:minutes:seconds:frames (*HMSF*).

Rewritable Optical Disc

See *Erasable Optical Disc*.

REXX

Abbreviation for *Restructured EXtended eXecutor*. See *Restructured EXtended eXecutor (REXX)*.

RFTEDCA

Abbreviation for *Revised Format Editing Document Composition Architecture*.

RGB

Abbreviation for *red, green, and blue*. See *Red, Green, and Blue (RGB)*.

RGB Color Space

Collective term for the *red, green, and blue* signals produced by a color computer monitor. The RGB signals are used to calculate and store the variations and intensities of these three colors.

RGB Monitor

A color computer monitor that sends a separate color signal to the display for each of the *additive color primaries—red, green, and blue*—required for the display of high-resolution images. See *Red, Green, and Blue (RGB)*.

Rhodamine 6G

An *organic color pigment* used in printing inks. Rhodamine 6G is a bright rose pink that can be produced in several varieties: triple salts produced by combining the original dyestuff with phosphoric, molybdic, and tungstic acids (referred to as PMTA), or double salts produced by combining the dyestuff with phosphoric and molybdic acids (referred to as PMA), phosphoric and tungstic acids (referred to as PTA), or with silicomolybdic acid by itself (referred to as SM). The triple salt variety tends to possess higher *lightfastness*, and neither the triple nor double salts are alkali or soap resistant. The double salts tend to be less expensive and stronger in color. Rhodamine 6G is used as magenta in many inks used in four-color process color printing, as well as a variety of other applications. (See *Organic Color Pigments*.)

Also known as *PMTA Pink* (*CI Pigment Red 81 No. 45160:1*).

Ribbon Folder

An *in-line* cutting and folding device found on a *web press* used to cut a web into two halves (or ribbons). Each half is run through a set of angle bars where it is folded (commonly by a *jaw folder*) and ultimately bound separately. A ribbon folder is also known as an *angle-bar folder*. (See the illustration on the facing page.)

Rice

In prepress, a term for a *proof* or *galley* made on a thin, translucent paper, such as *rice paper*.

Rice Paper

A type of thin, translucent paper, found commonly in China, Japan, and elsewhere in Asia, made from the straw of rice, or from one of several trees and shrubs of the ginseng family.

Rider Roller

A hard-surfaced variety of *intermediate roller* found in the *inking system* of a printing press used in *offset lithography*. Riders, in contrast to *distributor*s, typically only contact one other roller (such as an *oscillator*) and do not transfer ink, their purpose being primarily to provide an added "detour" that adds additional forces to the ink to work it into a suitable *viscosity* and thickness for proper printing, needed due to the *thixotropic* nature of litho-

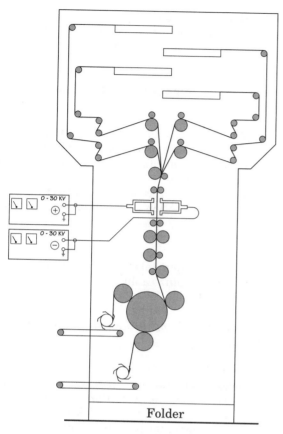

Ribbon folder.

graphic printing ink. Riders have the smallest diameters of all the rollers on an offset press, and consequently have the highest number of revolutions per minute. They turn by action of frictional forces generated on their surface by adjacent gear-and-chain-driven rollers. (See *Inking System: Offset Lithography* and *Offset Lithography*.)

Ridge

A paper web defect characterized by a ring running around the circumference of the paper roll, caused by inconsistent *cross-machine* thickness. The areas of higher thickness build a ridge around the perimeter of the roll higher than the rest of the web's width. (See also *Rope Marks*, *Chain Marks*, and *Corrugations*.) A ridge is also called a *hard spot*.

Ridging

Alternate term for the press and printing condition known as *banding*. See *Banding*.

RIFF

Abbreviation for *raster image file format*, a graphics file format developed by Letraset as a supplement to *TIFF* (or *tag image file format*). RIFF was designed to store *CMYK* or *RGB* mask data as grayscale images. RIFF is primarily used in Letraset software, but newer versions of TIFF have replaced it in general use.

Right Justified

In typography, copy that is set so that all the lines align on the right margin. Also known as *flush right*. See also *Left Justification*.

Right-Angle Fold

Any fold made in a sheet of paper (or other *substrate*) that is oriented at a 90° angle to a previous fold. (See also *Parallel Fold*.) See *Folding*.

Right-Angle Folder

Alternate term for a *knife folder*. See *Knife Folder* and *Folding: Knife Folder*.

Right-Handed Coordinate System

A means of specifying the *coordinate system* in three-dimensional mathematical modeling: the right hand is extended palm out, fingers up in front of the viewer. The negative values of the *x-axis* (or horizontal axis) are indicated by the thumb, which points to the left; the *y-axis* (or vertical axis) is indicated by the index finger, which points up; and the negative values of the *z-axis* (or axis providing depth) are said to emerge from the palm, pointing away from the viewer. See also *Left-Handed Coordinate System*.

Right-Reading

Descriptive of any film or paper image that can be read normally—i.e., from left to right and top to bottom—as opposed to *wrong-reading*.

Rigid Disk

Alternate term for a *hard disk*. See *Hard Disk*.

Rigidity

In papermaking, alternate term for *stiffness*. See *Stiffness*.

In ink terminology, *rigidity* refers to a condition of an ink that will not flow readily.

Ring Binder

A *binder* used in *loose-leaf binding* that uses metal (or plastic) rings inserted through punched or drilled holes in the pages to hold sheets together. (See also *Post Binder*.) See *Loose-Leaf Binder*.

Ring Crush

A test used to gauge the on-edge stiffness of paperboard, linerboard, and corrugated boxes, consisting of inserting a sample of the paperboard to be tested into a holder with a circular groove and determining the amount of force required to crush it.

Ring Network

A *network topology* in which each workstation is connected in series to the adjacent workstation. A transmitted message is sent from the point of origin around the ring through each workstation until it reaches its destination. Ring networks—such as Apple's *LocalTalk* or IBM's *Token Ring*—are not useful for large networks, and the number of devices and nodes that can be connected is usually limited. Additionally, the serial arrangement means that if one node fails (i.e., one workstation computer crashes), any devices or workstations beyond that point cannot be accessed.

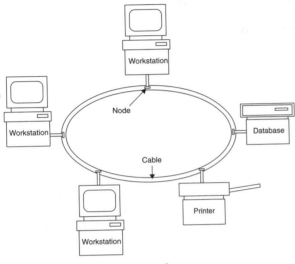

Ring topology.

RIP
Abbreviation for *raster image processor*. See *Raster Image Processor (RIP)*.

RIPing
Alternate spelling for *ripping*, or converting an image to a *bitmap* utilizing a *raster image processor*. See *Raster Image Processor (RIP)*.

Ripped
Converted to a *bitmap* via a *raster image processor*. See *Raster Image Processor (RIP)*. Also spelled *RIPed*.

Ripping
The act of using a *raster image processor (RIP)* to convert a *vector*-based image into a *bitmap*. See *Raster Image Processor (RIP)*. Also spelled *RIPing*.

Ripple
In graphics, a type of special effect added to an image to provide a dream-like effect.

Ripple Finish
A paper *finish* characterized by a dimpled surface produced by *embossing*.

RISC
Abbreviation for *reduced instruction-set computing*. See *Reduced Instruction-Set Computing (RISC)*.

RISC-Based Workstation
Workstation comprising a full-fledged *personal computer*, particularly one that utilizes a *RISC*-based processor.

Riser
Term for a bar on a *bar chart*. See *Bar Chart*.

River
In typography, a optical path of white space that sometimes occurs when word spaces in successive lines of type occur immediately below each other and continue for several lines. This is distracting to the eye and aesthetically undesirable, and may be corrected by moving words from line to line in order to reposition the word spaces. Also known as a *river of white*.

RJ-45
In networking, an 8-pin telephone connector used with *unshielded twisted pair* cabling.

RLE
Abbreviation for *Run Length Encoding*. See *Run Length Encoding (RLE)*.

Road Warrior
A colloquialism for an individual possessing the number of portable devices—such as a *laptop* computer, cellular phone, etc.—needed to be able to work unimpeded away from one's office, home, town, state, country, or planet. A road warrior is kind of an *inspector gadget* possessing creative purpose.

Rock Ridge
In multimedia, a proposed *compact disc* standard format designed to specify updatable *directory* files allowing *multisession* compact disc recording. As of this writing, the Rock Ridge format is only used for multisession *Photo CD*s.

Roll
A long, continuous length of paper or paperboard that has been wound around a cylindrical core to a specified diameter. Also commonly referred to as a *web*, a paper roll is the form in which paper comes out of the papermaking machine. It can either be subsequently cut into individual sheets or shipped as rolls.

Roll-Call Polling
In networking, a means of *polling* in which a central network *node* uses a list of attached nodes to determine if any node has data to transmit. See *Polling*.

Roll Coating
A paper *coating* applied by means of rollers.

Roller Controller
An advanced *trackball* used for video games developed on the *CD-i* platform. See *Compact Disc–Interactive (CD-i)*.

Roller Setting

The process of adjusting the pressure that one offset press ink or dampening roller generates on an adjacent roller or cylinder. The important rollers to set are the ***ductor roller*** to its adjacent ***oscillator***, a ***form roller*** to its adjacent oscillator, and a form roller to the ***plate cylinder***. The amount of pressure that one roller exerts on another has serious consequences on the ultimate press performance and print quality. (See ***Ductor Roller*** and ***Form Roller***.) The setting of rollers can be performed using a ***strip method*** and/or a ***roller-setting gauge***. (See ***Strip Method*** and ***Roller-Setting Gauge***.)

The final setting can be tested and evaluated using the ***picture method*** or ***ink stripe method***. It is also somewhat common to gauge the roller setting by noting the degree of bounce made by the form rollers as they cross over the plate ***cylinder gap***, although this bounce can be the result of a host of other factors, such as ***play***, roller wear, roller ***durometer***, and other varieties of damage to either the roller, their bearings, or their brackets. Another problem that may be noted at this time is ***endplay***, a lateral movement of the form rollers caused by an improper fit between the roller shaft and bracket. The lateral movement is commonly exacerbated by the movement of the oscillators. Endplay of less than 0.002 in. is acceptable, but beyond that can cause printing defects such as ***slurring***, streaking, and plate wear.

Another consideration with roller setting is the mechanical action that occurs at the nip of a hard, metal roller (such as an oscillator) and a rubber, resilient roller (such as a form roller). With increased pressure, the harder roller impresses itself into the softer one, making it out of round. On the press, this is beneficial, as it increases the shear forces on the ink, which makes it thinner and more workable. The degree that an ink is worked at the nips of resilient and hard rollers is known as its ***work ratio***. Although a moderate work ratio is beneficial, an excessive amount reduces the workability of the ink. (See ***Work Ratio***.)

Roller Stripping

In ***offset lithography***, the removal of ink from the metallic ink rollers due to the presence of too much ***fountain solution***, which has been transferred by the ink itself and which makes the ink rollers ink-repellent. Decreasing the strength or the flow of the fountain solution may help alleviate the problem, as will the addition of ***emulsifying agent***s such as laketine. Copper rollers are also an effective solution.

Roller stripping can also be caused by ***glazed*** rollers, or by the use of a fountain solution with too low a ***pH***. Generally speaking, roller stripping that occurs at the beginning of a press run is typically caused by a glazed roller, while stripping that occurs in the middle of a run is caused by excessive or excessively acidic fountain solution.

The term *roller stripping* also refers to the act of removing excess ink from ink rollers by running a sheet of heavy paper through them.

Roller Train

Collective term for the rollers that comprise the ***inking system*** in a printing press used in ***offset lithography***. The roller train begins with the ***ductor roller***, which transfers ink from the ***fountain roller*** to the ***oscillator***s, ***intermediate rollers*** (***distributor***s and ***rider***s), and the ***form roller***s, the end of the train that transfers the ink to the plate. (See ***Inking System: Offset Lithography*** and ***Offset Lithography***.)

Roller-Feed Scanner

Alternate term for ***sheetfed scanner***. See ***sheetfed scanner***.

Roller-Setting Gauge

A device used to measure the ***roller setting***, or the pressure that exists between two offset press ink or dampening rollers. A roller-setting gauge measures the amount of force generated when the device's metal strip is pulled through the nip of the two rollers being set. A roller-setting gauge can also be used in concert with less objective methods such as the ***three-strip method*** and the ***folded-strip method***.

Rollerball

Alternate term for a ***track ball***. See ***Track Ball***.

Roll-Fed Imagesetter

See ***Flatbed Imagesetter***.

Roll Hardness Tester

A device used to measure the degree of tightness with which a roll of paper has been wound.

Roll Label

A ***label*** that is part of a long, continuous (commonly accordion-folded) sheet or roll.

Roll Nose

In ***web offset lithography***, the leading, adhesive-coated edge of a paper roll that is to be spliced to the end of an expiring paper roll during printing. See ***Web Offset Lithography: Infeed and Web Control: Splicing***.

Roll-Out

A means of testing the efficacy of a color-mixed ink by applying a sample of the ink to a surface using a small hand roller, or ***brayer***. See ***Color Mixing, Ink***.

Roll-Set Curl

A paper deformity characterized by a tendency to curl. Paper that is wrapped very near the core of a paper roll and then sheeted will have a curl if it has not been decurled properly. Roll-set curl always occurs ***across the grain***. Roll-set curl will not usually occur in every sheet, but rather at various intervals throughout the pile. Roll-set curl is incurable, the only solution being to pull the curled sheets from the paper pile and discard them. (See ***Curl***.) Roll-set curl is also called ***wrap curl*** or ***reel curl***.

Roll Sheeter

A device attached to the *feeder section* of a sheetfed offset lithographic press that allows a continuous roll or *web* of paper to be used in lieu of cut sheets. A roll sheeter automatically cuts a roll of paper into individual sheets just prior to feeding into the press. It is typically synchronized to the speed of the press, allowing printing to occur at full speed. The advantages of a roll sheeter include the economy of purchasing paper rolls rather than cut-sheet paper, the elimination of the need to stack paper, and the prevention of downtime caused by having to reload sheets of paper into the press. It also saves on makeready, and as the size of the

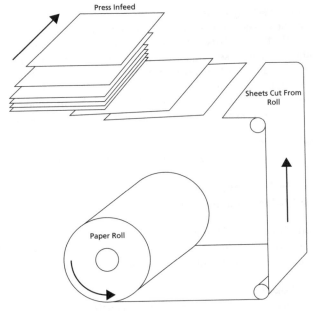

Basic roll sheeter.

sheets can be set, the most economically sized paper can be used with little waste. Some even come with a bar that automatically eliminates any curling caused by roll winding. Roll sheeters can be attached to work in tandem with a conventional feeding system in minutes. Most roll sheeters also cut the sheets accurately to within ±0.01 in. (See also *Pile Table* and *Feeder Section: Sheetfed Offset Lithography*.)

Roll Stand

A device used in *web offset lithography* (or on other types of *web press*es) to hold a paper roll and feed it with consistent and controlled tension into the printing unit of the press. Metering rollers and one or more *dancer rollers* are often part of the roll stand. Roll stands may be *single-roll stand*s (holding only one roll of paper at a time) or *double-roll stand*s (holding two rolls of paper at a time). An *auxiliary roll stand* may also be used. The roll stand is commonly located directly behind the first printing unit of the press, but some configurations use a *side roll stand*, in which the roll stand is located to the side of the press, the web being transferred into the printing unit by angle

guides. Such arrangements are useful in pressrooms lacking enough space to keep the roll stand in line with the rest of the press. (See *Web Offset Lithography: Infeed and Web Control*.)

Roll Up

In *offset lithography*, the process of applying ink to the plate just after mounting.

Roll-Up Menu

In computing, especially by means of a *graphical user interface*, a menu that remains on the screen without requiring that the user hold down the mouse button. Such a menu can be "rolled up" (by clicking a button at the top of it) so that only its title bar displays.

ROM

Abbreviation for *read-only memory*, a general term for any type of computer storage medium (such as a *CD-ROM*) which, unlike *RAM* (or *random-access memory*) allows only the reading, not writing, of data.

Information stored in ROM cannot be edited, altered, or amended in any way. A computer has ROM permanently built-in to a solid-state chip housed on the motherboard and contains often-accessed information the system needs to function. The data stored in ROM is programmed at the time of the computer's manufacture, and is also often called *firmware*, implying that it is "firmly" embedded in place. Although most computer ROM is hard-wired into the computer, some ROM dwells on external cartridges that need to be inserted into special ports.

Roman

In typography, an all-encompassing term for *typeface*s based on the *serif* variations developed by the ancient Romans and further developed by Italian humanistic lettering. In current usage, *roman* is used to indicate the primary typeface in a *type family*; in other words, the main text face that is not bold or italic. On desktop publishing programs, "roman" is replaced by the word "plain." Although Roman should not be used to refer to *sans serif* typefaces, it occasionally is.

There were five historical influences of the development of the roman typeface, the first being the roman capital, illustrated by the inscription on the Trajan column. Further developments included the *uncial* and *black letter* variations on the roman caps, the Caroline miniscules, the typefaces designed by Venetian designer Nicolas Jenson (under the name Eusebius), and the typefaces of William Caslon, John Baskerville, and Giambattista Bodoni. These Trajan letter shapes, cut into the stone panel several feet above the ground in the pedestal of the column, are considered the perfect roman-proportioned form and still guide type designers. They are not all the same size, because they were taken from different lines, graduated in height to look the same to the ground-based viewer.

Three varieties of roman typefaces are worth considering: old roman, modern, and transitional.

Old Roman. A characteristic style of roman typefaces characterized by very little differentiation between thicks and thins, diagonal stress, capitals shorter than **ascender**s, and serifs that are small and graceful. The "feelings" evoked by old Roman faces are warm, friendly, and traditional.

Modern. A characteristic style of roman typefaces characterized by vertical stress, hairline serifs, and maximum contrast between thicks and thins. Modern faces evoke formal, classic, and cold feelings.

Transitional. A characteristic style of roman typefaces between old Roman and modern, characterized by sharper thick/thin contrast, sharper and thinner endings to serifs, and vertical stress. These faces evoke the best of the old Roman and modern faces.

Roman Numerals

In typography, the style of numeral used exclusively until about the tenth century AD. The Romans—generally speaking—used letters as numbers, such as I (1), V (5), X (10), L (50), C (100), D (500), and M (1,000), but the co-opting of the alphabet to stand in for the number system did not begin that way. For example, it is believed that the symbol V for 5 was merely representative of an open hand with the fingers held together and the thumb apart, kind of like the Vulcan salute, while the X for (10) is merely a double V, or two crossed hands. The original symbol for 1,000 was a circle with a vertical line through it (similar to the Greek letter *phi*—Ø), and the D for 500 is believed to have been simply one-half of this symbol. The original symbol for 100 was a circle with a horizontal line through it (similar to the Greek letter *theta*—Θ). The use of C and M may have come from the first letters of the words *centum* (meaning "100") and *mille* ("1,000").

Numbers between these main numbers were typically additive; II was 2, III was 3, VI was six, XI was 11, CI was 101, etc. The subtractive principle came about later; VIIII was often used for 9 in ancient Rome, while today IX is. The Romans were not a mathematically inclined people, so large numbers were rarely called for.

Roman numerals are typeset just like capital letters are. The **front matter** of many books is typically paginated using lowercase Roman numerals (i, ii, iii, iv, etc.).

At the beginning of the second millennium AD, the so-called **Arabic numerals** (actually of Indian origin) were introduced into Western Europe, and within a few centuries proponents of the new numerals defeated those of Roman numerals and by the beginning of the fifteenth century were becoming widely used. (See also **Arabic Numerals**.)

ROP Colors

An abbreviation for *run of press* colors, or colors formerly accepted as standard color inks for use in newspaper printing. ROP colors have since been replaced by new standards prescribed by the Newspaper Association of America (NAA).

Rope Marks

A paper web defect characterized by bands of uniform width running around the perimeter of a paper roll in the **machine direction** within which are patterns resembling rope or tire treads caused by variations in paper thickness across the width of the web and by greater stretching of the web during **calendering** and winding. Rope marks are also called **chain marks** and **corrugations**. (See also **Ridge**.)

Rosette

In color printing, a very small circle of **halftone dot**s, formed when two or more **process color screen**s are overprinted at the correct screen angles with the proper dot sizes. Unlike a **moiré** pattern, a rosette pattern is desirable. (See COLOR PLATE 9.)

Rosin

A material, also called rosin **sizing**, that is commonly added to the papermaking **furnish** during **refining** in a process called **internal sizing**. Rosin is added to paper **pulp** to increase resistance to water and other liquids. **Alum** (short for aluminum sulfate) is added to help the rosin adhere to the paper fibers. The use of rosin and alum for internal sizing imparts a degree of acidity to paper, and they are responsible for the rapid yellowing and crumbling with age typical of **acid paper**. Synthetic sizing agents, such as alkyl ketene dimer or alkyl succinic anhydride are used instead of rosin and alum in the production of **alkaline paper**. See **Sizing** and **Internal Sizing**.

Rosin is also used as a resinous material in the manufacture of printing ink **vehicle**s, **varnish**es, and **lacquer**s. It remains when the **volatile** contents of turpentine are boiled away. The turpentine from which rosin is obtained is distilled from oleoresin, or crude turpentine, which is in turn obtained from the sap of **coniferous** trees, in particular the longleaf pine (*Pinus palustris*) native to the southeastern United States. Rosin is also called *colophony*. A widely used rosin, called **tall oil rosin**, is obtained from **tall oil**, a resinous by-product of the **sulfate process** of paper **pulp** production.

Rotary Cutter

A device used in the **sheeting** of paper rolls, consisting of a rotating knife contacting a fixed knife that cuts the paper **web** moving between them. (See **single rotary cutter** and **double rotary cutter**.) See **Sheeting**. (See illustration on the following page.)

Rotary Ink

A type of printing ink commonly used for **letterpress** printing of books, magazines, and other publications. There are essentially two varieties of rotary ink: **book ink** and **heatset ink**. Book inks are fairly fluid, and vary in **tack** and consistency depending on the surface **hardness** (and other properties) of **book paper** on which it is to be printed. Heatset inks for letterpress printing consist of synthetic resins mixed with low-volatility hydrocarbon **solvent**s,

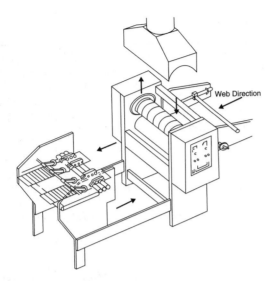

Basic rotary cutter.

which have boiling points in the range of 400–500°F and evaporate very quickly in that range of temperatures. (See **Heatset Ink**.)

Rotary Press

Any type of printing press that uses a curved image carrier mounted on (or as) a cylinder, in contrast to a flatbed press.

A *rotary press* is also used to specifically describe a type of cylinder-based press used in **letterpress** printing. See **Letterpress: Rotary Press**.

Rotary Printing

Any type of printing in which the **substrate** is passed between two cylinders, one of which is the image carrier. In most printing processes, rotary presses are more desirable than flatbed presses, as it is easier to generate the required uniform printing pressure in the nip between two cylinders than all across the surface of a flat platen.

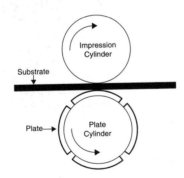

Configuration of a rotary press used in letterpress printing.

Rotary Screen Printing

A variety of **screen printing** performed on a press comprising a revolving cylindrical screen, the **squeegee** being located within the cylinder.

Rotary Union

On a **web press**, a connector used to join the **chill roll**s to the plumbing that brings cold water to the rolls.

Rotary-Drum System

One configuration of the **infeed section** of a printing press, especially used in **offset lithography**. See **Infeed Section**.

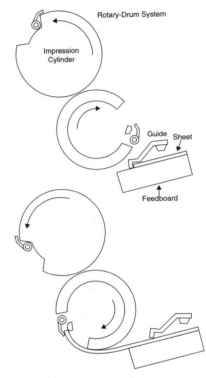

Rotary-drum infeed system.

Rotate

In graphics, to effect a **rotation**. See **Rotation**.

Rotation

In typography, an alternate term for a **font**. See **Font**.

In imaging, *rotation* refers to the act of tilting an image a certain number of degrees. On digital imaging systems, images can be rotated to fit them into predetermined designs or frames. Rotation is also often performed to fix images that were not scanned straight. Rotation, however,

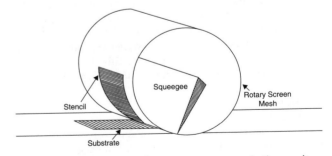

Basic configuration of a rotary screen printing unit.

is often extremely time-consuming and—when not done in increments of 90°—degrades image quality. It is often more expedient to rescan the image at the correct angle.

In computer modeling, the turning of a modeled or rendered object about an axis.

Roto News Paper

A heavily calendered and/or supercalendered, mechanical pulp-based paper used for *rotogravure* printing, primarily of newspaper supplements and magazine sections. Roto news paper is similar to *newsprint*, but is manufactured to possess the adequate levels of ink receptivity, ink holdout, compressibility, and softness required for rotogravure printing.

Rotogravure

Webfed *gravure* printing utilizing a cylinder to carry the image, used for the economical printing of long-run jobs such as newspaper supplements and Sunday magazine sections. In the early part of the 20th century, newspaper supplements were called "rotogravure sections." See *Gravure*.

Rotoscope

A device that projects an image on the bottom of a glass plate, allowing it to be traced or redrawn. It is often used in preparing *hand-cut stencil*s for *screen printing*, or many other graphic arts uses.

A rotoscope is also used in *animation*, especially when an animated sequence needs to follow the motion of an object that has been recorded on video or film. Each frame can be projected on the surface of the rotoscope, and a frame of the animation can be traced.

Rough

A sketch or enhanced *thumbnail* of a page design or layout that depicts a somewhat accurate representation of the final size and position of all page elements. Roughs are usually drawn on tracing paper by hand. A more formalized design sketch is a *comprehensive*.

Rough Cut

In *binding and finishing*, a style of edge trimming on trade books consisting of edges that are ragged, not neatly and squarely trimmed. See also *Rough Front and Foot*.

The term *rough cut* also refers to a preliminary edit of a video production or presentation, used to approximate the final *master tape*.

Rough Front and Foot

In *binding and finishing*, a style of edge trimming on trade books consisting of a *front* and *foot* edge that are ragged, not neatly and squarely trimmed. See also *Rough Cut*.

Roughening

In *screen printing* the process of abrading the screen—commonly by means of a silicon carbide powder—fabric to facilitate the adhesion of the stencil.

Roughness

A surface property of a *gravure cylinder* that describes the uniformity of the copper or chrome plating. The plating and polishing of the copper surface of the gravure cylinder yield a certain degree of minute peaks and valleys which, depending on the *substrate*, need to be minimized as much as possible.

Coated papers and other substrates with smooth surfaces are susceptible to poor print quality when surface roughness is moderately high; uncoated papers or other rough substrates are less sensitive. A high degree of peaks and valleys on the surface of the copper plating results in ink transfer in nonimage areas. However, too smooth a surface results in poor lubrication of the *doctor blade* (a metal blade that scrapes excess ink off nonimage areas of the cylinder) and results in blade and cylinder wear and damage.

Although the gravure cylinder's copper surface is covered with a layer of chrome following engraving, the combination of the thinness of the chrome layer and the physical principle of *epitaxy* (the tendency for the electroplated chrome to follow the contours of the copper to which it is plated exactly) allow for no correction or smoothing out of irregularities in the copper surface. Consequently, the roughness of the chrome layer is measured in the same way.

Copper and chrome roughness is measured by moving a diamond across the surface and measuring the peaks and valleys.

A related property is *waviness*, which is similar to roughness but on a larger scale. (See also *Waviness*.)

Round Back

Any type of *binding* on which the *spine* is curved, as opposed to a *flat back*.

Round Table

In *binding and finishing*, a circular work table used for hand *gathering* of *signature*s.

Rounding

In *case binding*, the process of imparting to the *spine* of a *book block* a rounded, convex shape to facilitate fitting the pages into the cover. See *Case Binding*.

Router

In networking, a device that connects two or more networks, much like a *bridge* or a *gateway*. Unlike these other devices, however, a router has the ability to decide the most expedient route by which to transmit a message. A device that functions both as a bridge and as a router is known as a *brouter*.

Routing

In *letterpress* printing, the removing of the nonprinting areas of a plate.

Royalty

In publishing (or other freelance or creative endeavor), monies paid to an author or other content provider based on some percentage of the revenue earned by the publisher from sale of the publication to which the author has contributed. The amount actually paid to the author is the author's share of the revenue less any *advance on royalties*.

RP 125

A *SMPTE* standard for the *parallel* connection by which *component video* signals are transmitted. The term is short for SMPTE *Recommended Practice 125*.

RPM

Abbreviation for *Remote Print Manager*.

RPMF

Abbreviation for *Remote Print Management Facility*.

RRDS

Abbreviation for *Relative Record Data Set*.

RTV

Abbreviation for *real-time video*. See *Real-Time Video*.

Rubber Plate

One of several types of printing plate used in *flexography*. See *Plate: Flexography*.

Rubberbanding

In computer graphics, the act of connecting two anchored points with a line, "grabbing" the line at some point along its length with the cursor, and stretching the line, bringing the original point to a new position. This can either be done in a *drawing* program, or on tone lines and gradient curves that control the *density* and *contrast* of images in image processing programs.

Rubine Reds

An *organic color pigment* used in printing inks. *Rubine 2B* comprises a variety of shades that owe their color to either the presence of sodium (medium red), barium (bright, yellow red), calcium (very blue red), strontium (lighter blue red), or manganese (scarlet) salts. Rubine 2Bs possess moderate degrees of *lightfastness* and resistance to acids and solvents. They have good resistance to heat and oil, and are not resistant to alkalis. They are economical, however, and are widely used in a variety of different ink formulations and applications. The colors are clean and have excellent flow and workability properties. Varieties of rubine reds containing barium have been essentially discontinued due to their toxicity, and strontium-based shades are also infrequently used. (See also *Organic Color Pigments*.)

Also known as *Permanent Red 2B* and *BON Reds*. (*CI Pigment Red 48 No. 15865*; *CI Pigment Red 48* [sodium]; *CI Pigment Red 48:1* [barium]; *CI Pigment Red 48:2* [calcium];

CI Pigment Red 48:3 [strontium]; *CI Pigment Red 48:4* [manganese].)

Rubine Red 6B is a bluish red (bluer than *Lithol®️ Rubine 4B*), with poor chemical resistance properties, but high brightness, purity, and *tinctorial strength*.

(*CI Pigment Red 200 No. 15867*.)

Rub-Off

A printing defect characterized by the printing of ink that is to all appearances dry but that rubs off easily. Rub-off is commonly caused by an inadequate *binder* formation, or an inadequate quantity of binder present in the ink, both of which impede the adhesion of the *pigment* particles to the *substrate*. It can also be caused by excessive or premature absorption of the ink *vehicle* into the substrate.

Rub-off can be compensated for by mixing a *varnish*, a heavier resin, or wax with the ink prior to printing. If rub-off is a problem after printing, an *overprint varnish* may alleviate the problem. Also known as *scuffing*.

Rubometer

A device used to quantitatively measure the ability of a printed ink film to resist scuffing and rubbing. A rubometer is also called a *rub tester*.

Rub-Proof

Descriptive of a *scuff-resistant* ink. See *Scuff-Resistant Ink*.

Rub Resistance

Alternate term for *abrasion resistance*. See *Abrasion Resistance*.

Rub Tester

Alternate term for *rubometer*. See *Rubometer*.

Rubylith

A two-layer *acetate* film comprising a transparent base and a red or amber emulsion.

Although it has many uses in graphic arts, rubylith was most often attached to pasteup boards in place of *halftone*s so that, when the *mechanical* was photographed as a *negative*, would leave a blank space into which the halftone negative could be stripped. (It is thus called a *red patch* or a *black patch*). It is also used in the making of *color separation*s. See also *Amberlith*.

Rule

In typography and graphics, abbreviated term for a *rule line*. See *Rule Line*.

Run

In printing, any single job. Also known as a *pressrun* or *print run*.

In *binding and finishing*, the quantity required of any single binding.

Runaround

In typography, copy set so that it will create a "hole" on the page to fit an illustration, photo, or other page element. Commonly produced by varying the *indention* value and/or *line length* for subsequent lines. Also known as *wraparound*.

The term *runaround* is also used to refer to *contour type*, or type that is set to form a shape. See *Contour*.

Runaround Cut

In typography, an illustration or other artwork that requires type to flow around it. See *Runaround*.

Runaround Indent

In typography, a form of *indention* in which lines are indented to make room for an illustration or other page element that the text is meant to flow around.

Rundown

In video production, an outline of the contents of a program, used in lieu of a script, especially where detailed scripting is not possible (as an interview).

Run-In

In typography, any copy—specifically a *head*—designed to be set in the same line as the text.

Run-Length Encoding (RLE)

A type of *data compression* that reduces the size of image files by counting the occurrence of identical *pixel*s in an image and saving merely that count. For example, in a black-and-white image, a series of pixels with the values "white-white-white-white-white-white-white-white-black-black-black-black" would simply be encoded in the file as "eight white pixels and four black pixels." In images with much redundant data (i.e., images that have a great deal of a single solid color), a high degree of data compression is possible, while in complex images, little compression is possible. RLE is a commonly used *lossless* compression scheme, and is utilized in the *PICT* file format, in the Adobe Photoshop-native file format, and even in fax machines. (See *Data Compression*.) RLE is also used during scanning.

Runnability

A term describing the interrelationships of a paper's properties that determine how a paper performs on press. Considerations of a paper's runnability include a variety of structural and surface properties, such as cleanliness of the surface (loose paper fibers cause problems such as *piling* on the blanket), how well particles of *fillers* and *coatings* remain bonded to the paper (loose filler and coating particles can contaminate the chemistry of an offset printing press), how well a paper maintains its dimensional stability (changes in size due to changes in moisture content can affect not only the quality of the printed image, but also cause feeding problems), and other factors such as curling, wavy edges, and chemical composition that have the potential to interfere with the efficient functioning of the printing process.

Runnability is usually described together with *printability*, or how well a paper's properties allow a high-quality printed image.

Running Foot

In *book typography*, a "heading"—such as a book title, chapter title, or author—that is located at the bottom of consecutive pages, in contrast to a *running head*. A running foot may also include a *folio*.

Running Head

In *book typography*, a heading—such as a book title, chapter title, or author—that is located at the top of consecutive pages, in contrast to a *running foot*. A running head may also include a *folio*.

Running In

The process of setting the proper pressure and *contact angle* of a *gravure* press *doctor blade*. See *Doctor Blade*. Running in is also called *toning in*.

Running Register

A *flexographic* and *lithographic* printing press control that is used to accurately position the impression produced by each *color station* in the direction of web travel through the press. Also known as *circumferential register* and *longitudinal register*.

Running Text

In typography, a text block in which lines are broken near the right margin at random, rather than by design. Running text—a characteristic of paragraphs, pages, and other continuous, narrative material—is broken utilizing a "soft return" while deliberate line breaks are achieved utilizing a "hard return."

Run Time

In computing, the amount of time needed to execute a program or other operation.

The term *run time* is also used to refer to a version of an application development program with limited functionality. Usually, run times are supplied to allow a user to view an application created with the full version of the program.

S

S, s

The nineteenth letter of the English alphabet, derived from North Semitic, by way of the Greek *sigma*. In North Semitic, the letter representing the *S* sound resembled the modern *W*, while the Greek *sigma* essentially rotated that letter 90° to the right. The curved form of the *S* in both upper- and lowercase forms was developed in Latin.

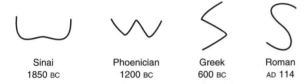

Sinai	Phoenician	Greek	Roman
1850 BC	1200 BC	600 BC	AD 114

The evolution of the letter S.

Saddle Bar

In *binding and finishing*, metal frame or bar on which *signatures* are placed for *saddle-stitching*. (See *Saddle-Stitching*.) Also known as a *bayonet* or *sword*.

Saddle Sewing

In *binding and finishing*, a type of *thread sewing* in which thread is driven through the centerfold of printed *signatures*. See *Case Binding*.

Saddle-Stitching

In *binding and finishing*, a means of binding pages together by driving staples though the centerfold of a *signature* or group of signatures. Saddle-stitching and *side-stitching* (see below) are collectively known as *wire stitching*. Side-stitching is rarely used any longer. Many magazines and newsletters—such as *Time, Newsweek, Natural History*, and many others—are bound by saddle-stitching. Although *perfect binding* has replaced much saddle-stitching, the latter is still the most effective method for binding materials that are up to ¼ in. thick.

Prepress Considerations. Two primary allowances must be made in the prepress phase of publications designed to be saddle-stitched. The first is for *creep*. Since signatures to be saddle-stitched need to be inserted within each other (as opposed to simply stacked on top of each other, as in other binding methods), the cumulative thickness of the publication will cause the edges of the inner signatures to gradually protrude beyond the edges of the outer ones. Although trimming will eventually make all the edges even anyway, the result will be progressively thinner margins on inner pages. The prepress process of *shingling*, or a slight staggering of the location of the pages on the paper, is often performed to eliminate the effects of creep. (See *Creep* and *Shingling*.)

The other allowance that needs to be made for saddle-stitched publications is an "overhang" on one side of a signature. Since the saddle-stitching device needs to open each publication from the center in order to drive the staples through the center of the spine, one side of the signature must hang over the other side, allowing the gripper mechanism to grab it and hold it open during stitching. This overhang, called a *lip* or *lap*, is commonly about ⅜ in. long.

The saddle-stitching production line comprises three basic units:

Inserter. In the process of *inserting* (analogous to *gathering* in *perfect binding* or *case binding*), printed and folded signatures are dropped into pockets on a gathering device. The device carries the signatures to a *saddle bar*, the frame on which stitching takes place. The inserter transfers the innermost signature to the saddle bar, where grippers and vacuum nozzles open it to its centerfold and place it face down over the bar. Additional pockets drop additional signatures in order over the first one. At this point, other *insert*s—such as subscription cards, ads, and other pages printed separately—are added to the pockets and dropped onto the saddle bar in the correct position. *Blow-in card*s are added at this point, as well, using compressed air to force printed cards between pages. At this point, also prior to stitching, ink-jet equipment is used to either address mailable magazines (those magazines that do not use labels) or to add personalized messages to subscribers.

Stitcher. After an entire publication has been assembled on the saddle bar, it is carried toward the stitching heads. Electronic detectors are used to find any copies that deviate from the proper thickness of the job (i.e., have more or less than the correct number of signatures), and these anomalies are ejected. The stitcher heads feed continuous rolls of wire, which are cut to the desired size and shaped into staples. When the publication is in position, the stitching

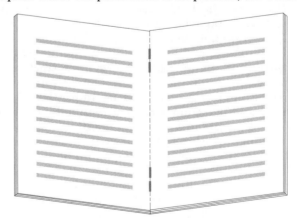

A saddle-stitched publication.

head drives the staples down through the spine fold. Devices beneath the publication bend the legs of the staples over, so as to secure the pages together. The size of the staple and of the *crown* (the length of wire visible on the spine of the publication) can be adjusted.

Accessories to saddle-stitchers include *take-off spinner*s, or large (70-lb.) spools of wire mounted to the floor, which eliminates the need to reload the stitcher frequently; *narrow stitching head*s, which are used to bind small-size publications or produce stitches that are closer together; and *oblique sheet monitor*s, which detect and eject improperly jogged or oriented signatures prior to stitching.

Trimmer. After stitching, the bound publications are closed and squeezed shut, to force out excess air and reinforce the fold. They are then transferred to a *three-knife trimmer*, which trims the unbound sides of the publication, removing signature folds from the top and any lip allowance from the right edge.

As with other binding and finishing equipment, a variety of other equipment can be added onto the saddle-stitching line. Folders can be added to the front of the line, allowing signatures to be folded and fed into the inserter in one step; stackers and counters can be used to automatically count and stack units as they come off the line; *tip-in* devices can automatically glue additional inserts into the publication or add *end paper*s to saddle-stitched books, etc.); bundling units can automatically package preset quantities as they come off the line; hole punches can three-hole-drill publications in-line, which is popular for newsletters and reports; and a variety of mailing and postal sorting equipment can make the carrying out of those functions part of the binding process.

Not all saddle-stitching equipment is on such a large-scale. Many print shops that have rudimentary binding capacities have small mechanical models, which are really little more than big staplers. A triangular metal platen functions as a saddle bar and allows the publication to be opened on top of it and stapled, one piece at a time.

One particular variety of saddle-stitching is *loop stitching*, or saddle-stitching in which the staples are formed into wire loops, allowing a saddle-stitched publication to be bound in a three-ring binder. Loop stitching eliminates the need to have to three-hole-drill a publication and, consequently, increase the *binding margin* of the text.

Side-Stitching. An alternate type of wire stitching is known as side-stitching, in which the staples are driven not through the center of the spine fold, but rather through the binding edge. The binding system is essentially the same, save there is no need to worry about inserting or shingling. The gathering device transports flat printed sheets beneath the stitching heads, where the staples are inserted. The drawbacks, however, are that pages tend not to open flat and some margin is lost along the binding edge of the pages. Advancements in *perfect binding* adhesives have reduced the desirability for side-stitching.

(See also *Binding and Finishing*.)

A side-stitched publication.

Safe Edge

In *screen printing*, a blank edge of a *photostencil* created by exposing it with an opaque strip, included as a means of allowing handling of the stencil without it incurring any damage.

Safelight

A colored lamp used in a photographic darkroom. The color of the light—usually red—is designed to be one to which a particular film is not sensitive.

Safe Title Area

On a television screen, the region that is always visible, regardless of *overscan* or loss of picture around the perimeter due to the frame, housing, etc. In television and video production, this region needs to be taken into account, especially for title and credit placement. Also known simply as the *safe area*.

Safety Bar

A device attached to the *feedboard* of a sheetfed printing press used to identify foreign objects being fed into the press, such as crumpled sheets of paper, wooden wedges used on the *pile table*, or other nonpaper objects that fall into the press. A safety bar is typically a metal strip placed over the feedboard with a clearance between the stock and itself of about ¼ in. (See *Feedboard*.) A safety bar is also called a *crash bar*.

Safety Paper

Paper especially formulated with a protective background to show erasures, or other means to expose forgery or document alterations. Safety papers are used for checks, bonds, bank slips, coupons, tickets, warranties, and legal forms. They must possess high *durability*, in particular paper used for checks, which must withstand payer and payee handling, as well as check-sorting equipment. (See also *MICR Check Paper*.) The *basic size* of safety papers is 17×22 in., and safety paper comes in a *basis weight* of 24 lb.

Sagging

A tendency of a thick, wet ink film to flow in the direction of gravity when placed on a vertical surface.

Sample

The smallest unit of any digitized image or sound, the size and frequency of which are determined by the *sampling rate* of the digitizing device. In *scanning* of images, sampling rate is measured in *pixels per inch (ppi)*, the size being determined by the size of the scanning beam and the amount of space it moves as it captures the image. In the digitizing of audio, the sampling rate is measured in *kilohertz (kHz)*, or the number of discrete "bursts" of sound occurring every second.

Sample Pages

In typography, a set of representative pages of a publication generated by the designer to indicate and seek approval for the layout of the piece before composition begins. Also known as *specimen pages*.

Sample-Playback

Alternate term for a *synthesizer*, especially one that uses digital sounds to create voices. See *Synthesizer*.

Sampler

A device—usually a plug-in board—that converts analog audio signals into digital signals (or *sample*s) for storage and manipulation in a computer.

Sampling Frequency

Alternate term for *sampling rate*. See *Sampling Rate*.

Sampling Rate

In the digitizing of images, sounds, and video, the *frequency* with which points are recorded.

In *scanning*, the sampling rate is measured as the number of samples taken per inch (or millimeter), both horizontally and vertically. Operator-controlled variations of the sampling rate include the *pixel* size to be sampled and the *resolution* at which the image is to be sampled. Also referred to as the *sampling frequency*.

Sampling-Synthesizer

Alternate term for a *synthesizer*, especially one that uses digital sounds to create voices. See *Synthesizer*.

Sand/Shot Mill

A device used in the manufacture of ink to further disperse the solid *pigment* particles in the fluid ink *vehicle*. The sand or shot mill uses sand or small metal pellets (like steel shot) to chop up the pigment particles and disperse them thoroughly. A sand or shot mill consists of a chambered metal cylinder, which contains the sand or the pellets. The ink *slurry* is piped in through the bottom of the cylinder, where rotating metal disks force the slurry upward, through the sand or shot, and finally out through a screen

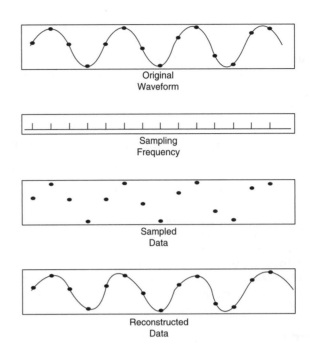

When the sampling rate of a sound, for example, is too low, the computer cannot reconstruct the waveform accurately.

at the top. Reducing the disk-rotation speed increases the amount of time the slurry remains in the machine, and the more finely ground the pigment particles are. A metal jacket can be filled with cold water and placed around the cylinder to cool it, should the heat buildup inside become high enough to compromise the consistency and *viscosity* of the ink.

The advantage of a sand or shot mill is that it can be adapted to a continuous process, rather than remaining strictly a batch process like closed *ball mill*s. Sand and shot mills are also less expensive than ball mills to install, and they provide the same high level of milling that can be obtained with a ball mill. Closed shot mills are frequently used in the production of *flexographic* and *gravure* inks, which require closed systems to prevent the *evaporation* and escape of their thin, highly volatile *solvent*-based vehicles. *Letterpress* inks are also produced in shot mills, but due to the heaviness of many types of letterpress inks, other types of more powerful milling systems may be required. (See also *Three-Roll Mill*, *Ball Mill*, and *Colloid Mill*.)

Sandwich Method

Alternate term for a *strip method*—either the *three-strip method* or the *folded-strip method*—of testing the setting of an ink or dampening roller on an offset press. See *Strip Method*.

Sans Serif

In typography, characters (or *typeface*s) without *serif*s, which are lines crossing the free end of the stroke. "Sans serif" itself means "without serif."

In the United States, the term **gothic** was sometimes used—albeit incorrectly—as a synonym for sans serif. (Sans serif type is also referred to as **grotesk**.) Serif type is easier to read in text; sans serif is generally more easily perceived in headlines.

ABCDEFGHIJKLMNOPQRSTUVWXYZ
abcdefghijklmnopqrstuvwxyz0123456789

Helvetica, an example of a sans serif typeface.

Most sans serif typefaces have a "neutral" or "cold" feeling; some sans serif typefaces, however, have touches of serifs in some of their letters—such as "a," "g," and "t"—to give them more character. The more popular sans serif typefaces today have a calligraphic feel to them. Other sans serif typefaces are geometric in design, with stark curves and lines. (See also **Serif**.)

Saran

Formerly the trademarked name (as in Saran Wrap) of a plastic packaging material, now fallen into common parlance as the popular name of **polyvinylidene chloride**, used as a **resin** in printing inks. See **Polyvinylidene Chloride**.

Satellite Press

On a printing press utilizing a **common impression cylinder**, one of several printing units that the substrate contacts during printing. See **Common Impression Cylinder**.

Satin Finish

A paper **finish** characterized by a smooth surface, intended to simulate the feel of satin.

Saturation

The point, at a given temperature and pressure, at which all the solute that can be dissolved by a **solvent** into a particular solution has been dissolved. In some cases (usually the result of changes in temperature and/or pressure) a solution can become *supersaturated*, in which case *more* solute than can typically be dissolved does go into solution. However, in the case of supersaturated solutions, the addition of a small solid particle or the jostling of the container can cause the extraneous solute to precipitate out.

In **color** terminology, *saturation* refers to a color attribute and one of the three axes on various color models (such as the **CIE Color Space**) that describes a particular color's intensity, lightness or darkness, or the degree to which a color departs from a gray of comparable lightness. In other words, the extent that a particular color comprises a selected **hue** rather than white. (See *Color Plate 7*.)

SAW

Abbreviation for *surface acoustical wave*, a type of **touch screen** display. See **Touch Screen**.

Saws

In **offset lithography**, a set of crescent-shaped wheels on a printing press used to support printed sheets as they move from the printing unit to the delivery section. They function in a manner similar to **skeleton wheel**s.

Sawtooth

In **screen printing**, an inadequate adhesion of the stencil to the screen fabric, wherein the stencil material follows the contours of the screen mesh, distorting and creating a notched effect where straight lines on the design meet the fabric mesh. **Filling in** and insufficient **bridging** and are causes of the sawtooth effect.

Scalable Font

In typography, a computer **font** that is designed to be output in a wide variety of **point size**s. Such fonts are described by the computer as a series of mathematical formulas describing lines, curves, and other shapes. When a new size is desired, it is a simple computation to recalculate the formula, creating the new size.

Such fonts are said to be **resolution-independent**, as they can be output at the highest resolution the output device is capable of. Many **bitmapped** fonts, in contrast, are created using different images for different sizes. One advantage to the **PostScript** page description language is that it uses scalable fonts.

Scalable Processor ARchitecture (SPARC)

A **RISC**-based **microprocessor** developed by Sun and Weitek used as a **central processing unit** in computers running the SunOS or various **UNIX** operating systems.

Scale

When used as a noun, any range of values between a minimum and maximum amount. For example, a **gray scale** is a series of progressively darker gray values, beginning at white and ending at black.

A 15-step gray scale.

When used as a verb, *scale* means to express a quantity in other units, with the new quantity being in some ratio to the original quantity. For example, a model that has been scaled (or a "scale model") can be measured in units (such as inches) that are more easily represented than the original units (such as feet, yards, or miles). The scale of miles found on maps is an example of this; a certain number of miles is "scaled" down to a certain number of inches, so that large land areas can be accurately represented on a convenient size of paper.

In imaging, *scale* means to resize an image—either enlarging or reducing it by some amount (called a **scale**

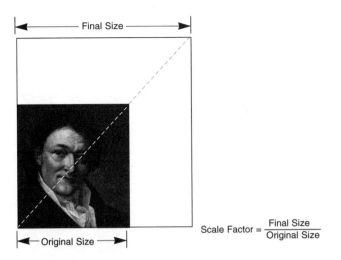

$$\text{Scale Factor} = \frac{\text{Final Size}}{\text{Original Size}}$$

The diagonal-line method of scaling a photograph.

factor)—to fit in a predetermined area, accomplished either photographically or digitally.

Computer **PostScript** fonts are also scaled; typically, the computer information includes the outline for a particular **typeface** at only one size. To achieve all other desired sizes, the computer recalculates the formula describing the structure of the characters, allowing it to be cleanly printed at the new size. Other graphic images are also scaled in a similar manner.

The term *scale* also refers to a paper defect characterized by a slightly discolored, highly glossy blotch on the paper surface, caused by dry particles of paper coating embedded into the paper during **calendering**.

Scale Compression

In **photoengraving**, a reduction of the **tonal range** of the image as a means of compensating for the lateral etching of dots to achieve the desired depth of cells.

Scale Factor

The value by which an image size has been enlarged or reduced. See **Scale**.

Scaling

The act of—or the computer function that facilitates— altering the size of an image or **font** proportionately. See **Scale**.

Scan

When used as a verb, *scan* means to look at a page or set of pages (or other information) quickly. When used in terms of computers, to *scan* means to detect which of the computer's ports or channels are open and which have devices connected to them. In imaging, to *scan* means to either produce an image (such as on a computer display or output substrate) or capture an image (as in a **scanner**), often by means of a beam of light or electrons. When used as a noun, *scan* refers to the movement of such light or electron beams

in imaging or image capture. In **scanning**, *scan* also refers to a captured, digitized image.

Scan-a-Web

In **web printing**, a piece of auxiliary equipment comprising a rotating mirror—which can be set to match the speed of the press—used to examine the printed image on the web as the press is running.

Scan Conversion

The process of converting a **vector**-based image to a **bitmap**, either for video display or for output.

Scan Converter

A device used to alter the scan rate of a video signal, allowing high-resolution computer-generated or -based graphics and images to be viewed on video screens that utilize **NTSC**, **PAL**, or **SECAM** signals.

Scan Line

Any single horizontal row of **pixel**s, especially on a computer display.

Scanned Art

Any image or artwork that has been digitized and input into a computer, commonly by means of a **scanner**.

Scanned Image

Any image that has been converted to a **bitmap** or **pixel** matrix and input to a computer, commonly by means of a **scanner**.

Scanner

A device used to analyze an original image and either generate **color separation**s and/or digitize the image and store it in a computer for later manipulation and output. Essentially, a scanner records one row of the image at a time, and converts the original into an electronic matrix of **pixel**s (or a **bitmap**). Each pixel is recorded as some level of gray for each of the **red**, **green**, and **blue** components of an image, and the scanner then collates them back into the appropriate (or closely approximating the appropriate) color for each pixel.

One basic distinction between scanners is whether it is an image scanner or a text scanner. An image scanner images all originals as a bitmap, regardless of whether it is text or a photograph. A text scanner—utilizing **optical character recognition (OCR)** software—can scan text material and convert it to **ASCII** text. Some desktop scanners can function as both, depending on which software is used, while dedicated image or text scanners can only function as one or the other.

Another important distinction in prepress is **drum scanner** versus **flatbed scanner**. A drum scanner is a high-end machine that utilizes a highly sensitive **photomultiplier tube** to capture subtle variations in tone, and it is capable of digitizing images at very high **resolution**s.

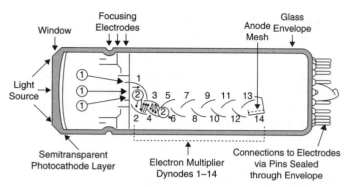

The basic principle of a photomultiplier tube (PMT).

Flatbed scanners are much less expensive, but their use of **charge-coupled devices** (CCDs) makes them less sensitive to subtle color variations. Drum scanners are beginning to come down in price, and flatbed scanners are beginning to improve in quality, so at some point the twain shall meet. Some flatbed scanners are also sheetfed scanners and have automatic stacking and/or document-feeding functions. Some flatbed and most drum scanners can scan

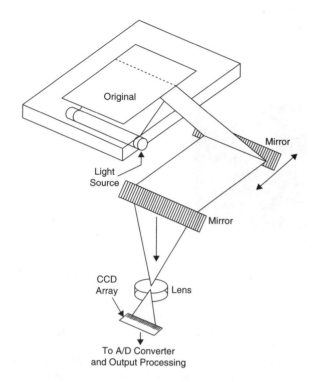

Schematic of a typical flatbed scanner.

transparencies rather than simply **reflective copy**. (See **Drum Scanner** and **Flatbed Scanner**.)

Many scanners have the ability—through software—to display previews and allow color modifications prior to scanning, enabling the operator to optimize the **contrast** and color attributes prior to image capture. Post-scanning image manipulation using programs such as Photoshop can be used to further refine and manipulate a scanned image.

Not all scanners feature **user-selectable resolution**, and thus offer only a handful of fixed resolutions (i.e., 100, 200, 300 . . . dpi), while some allow any resolution to be specified (i.e., 331 dpi). Other functions common to most scanners and scanning software include the ability to scan only a selected portion of an image and the ability to **scale** an image (either enlarging or reducing it) prior to scanning. (See **Scanning**.)

Scanner Engine
Collective term for the electro-optical mechanism used by a **scanner**.

Scanner Lamp
The light source used by a **scanner** to illuminate the original image during **scanning**. Most scanners utilize a **quartz-halogen lamp**.

Scanning
Although the term *scanning* can refer to any process—be it analog, digital, or strictly optical—it will be used in the following article (and the related cross-references) to refer to

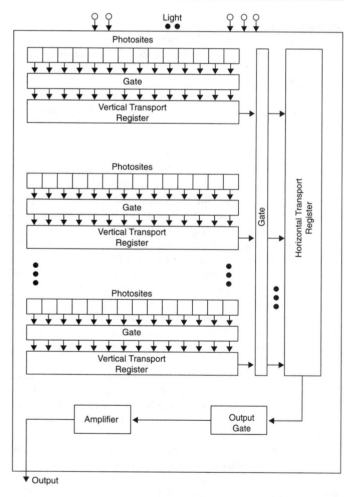

The basic principle of a charge-coupled device (CCD).

the process of capturing images electronically for conversion to digital form, primarily to obtain color and black-and-white images for *prepress* or *multimedia* purposes. Scanning is performed using a device called a *scanner*, which essentially uses transmitted or reflected light to capture an image in tiny increments (*pixel*s) of an image. The size of these increments is one of several ways that a good scan is separated from a bad scan.

Some people consider scanning to be merely a bridge or transitional technology, linking earlier photographic processes to nascent *digital camera* technologies. That may very well be the case, but for now scanning is an integral part of the prepress and imaging processes.

PRINCIPLES OF SCANNING

Each of the several different types of scanners operate somewhat differently (see below), but they all use different means to do the same thing: convert analog (i.e., optical) data into digital data.

Bit Depth. All digital information exists as *bits*, or combinations of 1 and 0. Thus, each *pixel* (or individual dot making up an image) is represented or described using combinations of these two numbers. The number of bits per pixel that a scanner can store thus determines how much color information it can recognize. For example, in a simple black-and-white scanner, the device can only handle one bit: black or white, "image" or "no image." This is fine for *line work* or even text, but is inadequate for photographs or other *continuous-tone* images. Scanners thus can store increasing numbers of bits per pixel, the more the better. Two bits per pixel can add light gray and dark gray to the basic black-and-white dichotomy, increasing somewhat the level of detail possible. (Increasing the number of bits increases exponentially the number of levels of gray or colors that can be captured, since one bit can be one of two values. For example, one bit can express pixels that are either black or white. This is represented by taking the number 2, the number of possible values per pixel, to a power equal to the number of bits the device can store (e.g., 2^1 which equals 2). Two-bit systems would be represented as 2^2, or 4, equal to black, white, light gray, or dark gray. Four-bit would be represented as 2^4, and so on. See *One-Bit Color*, *Two-Bit Color*, *Eight-Bit Color*, etc.)

Because of the number of gray levels that the human eye can detect, a scanner needs to be able to capture a high number of gray levels in order to capture photographic detail and render it with acceptable accuracy. The human eye can differentiate a little over 200 shades of gray, so using less than that results in the phenomenon of *banding*, or the visible detection of the discrete gray levels. Thus, most grayscale scanners utilize eight bits per pixel, which results in 256 levels of gray, which is more than adequate to create smooth blends in grayscale images.

Thus, when a scanner scans a photograph (popularly referred to as black-and-white but technically considered "grayscale"), the light source generated by the machine's optics move along the image pixel by pixel, measuring the level of gray and storing it as a particular value, or combination of bits. A light gray, for example, may be represented by 01110110. When the image ultimately appears on the computer screen after scanning, those pixel descriptions will be converted back to the appropriate gray level.

In color scanning, eight bits per pixel is inadequate to represent the vast range of colors available. In many multimedia applications, however, eight-bit color is the most a system can handle, but for high-quality color prepress it is of too low a quality to be useful. A color scanner generally makes use of *twenty-four-bit color*. It does this by making three passes over the original color image, each pass using a different *filter* to capture one of the three *additive color primaries*: red, green, or blue. It stores the color information for each of these passes as 256 gray levels, or eight bits per pixel per color. Since, say, red, in some color models consists of a pure *hue* with varying degrees of *lightness* or grayness, each gray level captured for red is equivalent to one of 256 shades of red. (See *COLOR PLATE 8*.) This is true for the blue and the green components as well. When the final scanned image is ultimately displayed on screen, the program being used to display and process the image creates a composite image of these three grayscale images. (In Adobe Photoshop, for example, each of these *channel*s can be viewed and adjusted separately.) This process is very similar to the principle behind *process color* printing, in which three or four different plates, each of which contains only shades of a single color, are overprinted to yield a much wider color spectrum.

Many scanners now, in the interest of efficiency, make only one pass with the scanner mechanism, which successively captures the three colors per pixel. This is called *strobing*, and it is one way of eliminating *color drift*s caused by tracking errors that can creep in during successive passes of the scanner optics. This does not always avoid color drifts, however, and some degree of *color correction* is often needed following scanning.

Resolution. One important means of measuring the performance of a scanner is by *resolution*. Resolution is defined as the number of pixels per linear unit, in this case, *pixels per inch (ppi)* (popularly but somewhat incorrectly referred to as *dots per inch [dpi]*). The greater the number of pixels per inch, the smaller and less distinguishable those pixels are, which increases the detail that is captured and hence increases image quality. In the case of scanners, resolution is a function of *sampling rate*. A pixel captured by a scanner is called a "sample," and the frequency with which a sample is taken determines the pixel size and how many of those pixels occur in a unit of linear space. A scanner with a maximum resolution of 1200 ppi can fit 1200 pixels in an inch or, in other words, takes a sample every $\frac{1}{1200}$ in.

There is a difference between a scanner's *optical resolution*—or the resolution that can be achieved by the scanner's optics alone—and its *interpolated resolution*. Scanner software uses *interpolation* to "artificially" increase the resolution captured by the device. Interpolation routines average the grayscale values of sampled pixels and places new pixels between them. This works more or less well, depending on the image. Although interpolation does not add any detail to a scan, it does tend to smooth out transitions between grays. In some cases, the resolution of an image can be doubled by interpolation. A caveat concerning resolution is that more is not always better. Capturing an image at a resolution substantially greater than the highest resolution possible by the output device will not improve image quality but will require more time to process an image and will require higher levels of processing power, **RAM**, and disk storage space. (See *COLOR PLATE 25.*)

Dynamic Range. In addition to resolution, a scanner's ***dynamic range*** is important to consider in choosing a scanner. Dynamic range is defined as the ability of any reproduction to capture both ***highlight*** and ***shadow*** detail, or in other words detail in the lightest and darkest portions of an image, respectively. Dynamic range is measured logarithmically; a highlight that is ten times as bright as a shadow is said to have a dynamic range of 1.0. One that is 100 times as bright would have a dynamic range of 2.0. The higher the dynamic range, the greater the level of detail that is captured at both ends of the image spectrum. Desktop scanners have a dynamic range of about 1.8 to 3.8, while high-end scanners can go as high as 4.0. Dynamic range is a function not only of the inherent capabilities of the scanner optics but also of the bit depth per pixel. In many images, even 8 bits per pixel per color is not enough to capture as much shade gradation and detail as the image warrants; some systems can go as high as 16 bits per pixel per color, which can eventually be distilled by the software down to 8-bit. Some scanner protocols work with a total of 48-bit-color rather than 24-bit. As of this writing, **PostScript**-based output systems can only handle 24-bit color, so a 48-bit image needs to be distilled just prior to output.

Just as there are a wide variety of imaging requirements, so too there is a wide variety of scanner configurations, which run the gamut from small, hand-held units used for scanning business cards to high-end scanners costing hundreds of thousands of dollars. Generally speaking, however, color scanners can be distinguished in four ways:

Flatbed Scanners. At the low-end of the price and performance spectrum are the ***flatbed scanner***s. These cost about $1,000, sometimes a little more, and sometimes, increasingly, a little less. Also known as ***CCD scanner***s, these use as their light detectors an array of ***charge-coupled devices (CCDs)***, which are very small photocells. Their small size is what enables the devices utilizing them to fit on a desktop. The drawback, however, is that they are less sensitive to subtle gradations of color and gray values than larger ***photomultiplier tube***s are. Flatbed scanners

A flatbed scanner.

are most often used for scanning ***reflection copy*** (or prints, rather than ***transmission copy*** such as slides and transparencies), although some models do have attachments for transmission copy. An image is placed face down on a glass platen, while the scan head (comprising a light source and a ***CCD array***) moves down the length of the original, measuring the intensity of the reflected light pixel-by-pixel. The drawback to flatbed scanners—in addition to low dynamic range and maximum optical resolutions of under 1000 ppi—is that they cannot optically enlarge an image. This presents no problems if an image is going to be reduced in size or used at 100%, but loss of detail will occur at enlarged sizes. With reflection copy, this may not be a problem, since prints can be very large to begin with. When using transparencies (the standard size of which is 4×5 in.) or the even smaller 35-mm slides, the original size is already very small and upsampling to the desired dimensions may degrade image quality unacceptably.

Slide and Transparency Scanners. A ***slide scanner*** works on the same basic principle as the flatbed scanner—a light source illuminates the image and sends it to a CCD array, which converts it to electrical signals that in turn

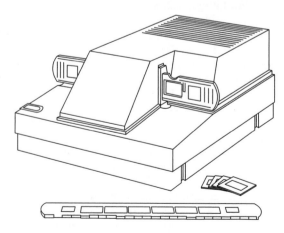

A slide scanner.

can be translated to digital information—but is specifically designed to overcome the transmission copy limitations found on conventional flatbed scanners. In this case, the light source shines *through* the image onto the CCD array. These may soon become more popular than flatbed scanners, as transmission copy in general is capable of a much greater dynamic range than is reflection copy. Compared to prints, slides and transparencies are also much easier to handle, store, and transport. Many slide scanners can capture images at up to 16 bits per pixel per color and at a resolution high enough for quality reproduction.

Desktop Drum Scanners. A *drum scanner* is a high-end device that uses photomultiplier tubes (PMTs) to record and capture color information. A transparency is mounted on a rotating (or stationary, depending on the type of scanner) transparent drum. As it rotates (or the optics rotate), a light source illuminates the image, where the PMTs detect it and send it to the computer. The use of PMTs makes these devices very sensitive to gradations in shade and color. Desktop drum scanners—descendants of much superior and more expensive high-end drum scanners—are becoming widely used for high-quality color work. They lack many of the "frills" and accessories of the high-end devices, many of which are not really needed any longer.

High-End Drum Scanners. The high-end scanners—which can be the size of a piano and cost even more—were the first scanners developed and continue to be used as part of a high-quality *color electronic prepress system (CEPS)*. Not only do these scanners have the best possible imaging systems, but many also include built-in color computers that can convert from color space to color space (such as from *RGB* to *CMYK*) on the fly, but many also output directly to film using built-in *film recorder*s. These were widely used for making *color separation*s, and still are, although more and more often captured images are output to a computer for additional manipulation and incorporation into electronic pages. (See *Scanner.*)

(The above devices are all used for color scanning of images and are thus known as *image scanner*s. There are other types of scanners, however. For example, *OCR scanner*s are used in *optical character recognition*, which uses an optical scanner—often the same type of scanner used for capturing images, only running different software—to capture a page of text. The software can then recognize the characters that have been scanned and convert it to *ASCII text* for importation into a word processing program or database. *OCR* scanners and software are used in lieu of keyboarding, saving time. *Bar-code scanner*s are used in retail shops and elsewhere to read *bar code*s. See *Optical Character Recognition* and *Bar Code*.)

SCANNING SOFTWARE AND IMAGE ENHANCEMENT

Most scanners come bundled with some type of software that is used to control the scanning process, adjust contrast, set resolution and ultimate image size, crop the image, etc.,

prior to making the actual scan. Many flatbed scanners come with either full-fledged or "limited edition" versions of popular photo manipulation programs such as Photoshop. Many scanning software programs can function as *plug-in*s to programs like Photoshop, which means that images can be scanned directly into those programs. Many programs now also are compatible with the *TWAIN* standard, which allows the use of different scanners without requiring a variety of different *device driver*s. A variety of third-party scanning software utilities allow enhanced image calibration and color correction prior to scanning.

Resolution and File Size Revisited. An important consideration, as was mentioned above, is to scan at the proper resolution. Most scanners and scanning software utilities allow the user to adjust the resolution (and image size) in advance. Some programs allow *user-selectable resolution*, which lets users enter a specific number (i.e., 221 ppi), while others have preset resolutions in increments (i.e., 200, 300, etc.). When scanning line art, it is best to scan at the resolution of the output device. For best results, between 600 and 1,000 ppi is the best resolution for text and line art. For *halftone*s, it is in general good practice to scan at a resolution that is double the *screen count* of the halftone screen that will be used. Thus, if a 150-line screen is going to be used, a 300-ppi scan would be required. This is not a hard and fast rule, though; sometimes a resolution of 1.6 to 1.8 times the screen count will produce high-quality images, as well.

However, when images are to be enlarged, the situation changes. The resolution will need to be doubled in proportion to the enlargement ratio. So if an image is to be enlarged by a factor of 2:1 (or, in other words, doubled) the resolution should be twice what it would be at 1:1. So the 300-ppi halftone image should now be scanned at 600 ppi. It is easy to see that depending on the respective sizes of the original and the desired image, the resolution may need to go very high indeed. Enlarging a 4×5-in. transparency, for example, to a 24×30-in. poster is an enlargement of 6:1. If a 150-line screen were still going to be used, the scanning resolution would need to be about 1800 ppi. Greater enlargements (such as those made from 35-mm slides) and higher screen counts require even higher scanning resolutions. Up to 3,000 ppi is not unusual.

As one would expect, file size increases as resolution (and image size) increases. File sizes are measured in units known as *byte*s. One byte equals eight bits. One thousand bytes (actually 1,024 bytes) equals one *kilobyte* (abbreviated *KB*), and one million bytes (actually 1,048,576 bytes) equals one *megabyte* (abbreviated *MB*). Let's use this example to determine file size: an 8×10-in. grayscale image scanned at 100% at 300 ppi at 8 bits per pixel. The image is thus 2400 pixels wide (300 ppi × 8 in.) by 3000 pixels deep (300 ppi × 10 in.), having a total of 7,200,000 pixels (2400 × 3000). At eight bits (one byte) per pixel, it takes a total of 7,200,000 bytes to describe this image, or 7.2 MB. If this were an RGB color image at 24 bits per pixel, it would require 21.6 MB (7.2 × 3) to describe. If it were converted to CMYK, it would require 28.8 MB. And that was only at a relatively low resolution of 300 ppi.

Consequently, it is easy to see the pitfalls of scanning at a much higher resolution than will actually be needed. Large files take a very long time to process, even on fast computers, and take up a lot of disk space, which may be in short supply. Generally, though, it is better to scan high and have to reduce than to scan low and have to increase. Increasing the resolution (in Photoshop or other such program) after scanning rarely results in very good-looking images.

Scanning Originals. The manual process of placing an original in or on a scanner for scanning has its own share of considerations. Needless to say, flatbed scanners should have their glass platens as free of dust, dirt, and other detritus as possible. Transparencies and prints should also be inspected for dust, scratches, or other visible problems that may be magnified by the scanning process. When attaching a transparency to a drum scanner, it is important that all parts of the image be flat against the drum; if any part of the image varies in distance from the scanner optics than the rest of the image, distortions in the scanned image will be evident. Sometimes, *oil mounting* is performed so as to eliminate an optical problem known as *Newton's rings*, or haloes of color caused by refraction of light passing through a transparency. Adhering the transparency to the drum by means of a clear oil can reduce this problem.

Image Correction and Enhancement. There are a variety of ways of fixing and correcting scans. Depending on the scanner and the scanning software, it may be possible to do this prior to or during scanning. Often, however, especially with flatbed scanners, such processes can only be handled after scanning, in an image manipulation program such as Photoshop.

Some of the most common activities include *sharpening*, variously known as *edge enhancement* or *unsharp masking*. (See COLOR PLATE 24.) In the latter designation, abbreviated *USM*, the scanner includes a separate photomultiplier tube that captures a slightly out-of-focus signal. This somewhat blurry (or "unsharp") signal is added to the sharp signal. The effect of this combination—used for many years in photography—is to sharpen the contrast at the edges of boundaries between separate portions of an image. (When USM is performed after scanning in a program such as Photoshop, it is effected by calculating the differences between the values of adjacent pixels and increasing the contrast between them.) Too much unsharp masking, however, can produce excessive noise and distortion in an image.

Tonal adjustments can also be made in a scanned or to-be-scanned image. This can take the form of adjusting the endpoints of an image (i.e., whitest white and blackest black, or *highlight* and *shadow*, respectively) or adjusting the midpoint of the image or the distribution of tones in the

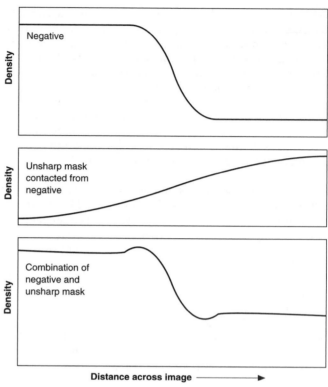

Edge enhancement.

image. Similarly, *color correction* may be needed, depending on the quality of the scanner. Sometimes, a scanner will impart a *color cast* to an image, and at other times a few of the colors in the image will be off. *Global correction* is the correction of the color throughout the entirety of the image, which can consist of darkening all the reds, for example. *Local correction* is the changing of the color of one particular portion of an image, such as only the red of a fire hydrant present in the image.

Depending upon the nature of the image and the context in which it is ultimately to appear, further types of manipulations may be required, including forming collages, removing elements from the image, inserting elements in the image, etc.

There is no hard and fast rule to these adjustments, of course; most good software and scanning programs have "preview" functions that allow the user to see what the effects of a particular adjustment will be before they are actually made. The best judge of any image or color correction operation is the human eye.

BEYOND SCANNING

It has been suggested that scanning may ultimately be replaced by other forms of imaging, especially *digital cameras*, which capture images directly in digital form. There is widespread popularity and enthusiasm for these devices, but so far quality and price issues have impeded their widespread use. But they are gaining ground. The popularity of the *Photo CD*, which many perceive to be a transitional medium, is an indicator that prepress departments and other users of digital images would like to eliminate the scanning phase as much as possible.

Scanning Mode
In *scanning*, a term referring to whether a *scanner* is set to digitize photographs, line art, color, grayscale, etc.

Scanning Spot
On a *scanner*, the point on the surface of an image where the scanning beam used for digitizing is focused.

Scanning Velocity
In computing, the speed with which a laser reads the tracks on an *optical disc*, usually expressed in meters per second.

Scan Rate
In *scanning*, the speed (measured in seconds per page) at which a *scanner* can digitize text or images.

The term *scan rate*, when used in reference to computer monitors, is an alternate term for *refresh rate*. See *Refresh Rate*.

Scart
A standard *connector* used to connect audio and video equipment to televisions, VCRs, etc. Also known as a *Euro connector*.

Scatter Diagram
Alternate term for a *scatter plot*. See *Scatter Plot*.

Scattergram
Alternate term for a *scatter plot*. See *Scatter Plot*.

Scattergraph
Alternate term for a *scatter plot*. See *Scatter Plot*.

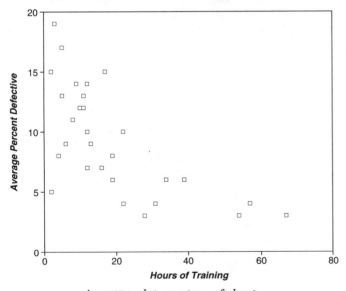

A scatter plot, one type of chart.

Scatter Plot
A means of graphing a set of data on a *coordinate system* by placing a dot, point, or other symbol at the data point. If there is a correlation between multiple data points, a line or curve is drawn that connects them. Also referred to as a *scatter diagram*, a *dot chart*, or a *scattergram*.

Scatter Proof
Alternate term for a *random proof*. See *Random Proof*.

Scavenger Marks
Deliberate etching of nonimage areas of the *gravure cylinder* to facilitate the removal of trapped particles of ink (or other material) from the back of the *doctor blade*. Scavenger marks are most commonly used on packaging presses, and need to correspond to nonprinting areas of the *substrate* that can eventually be removed in finishing operations. See *Doctor Blade*.

Scene
In motion picture, television, and video production, the smallest unit of a production, usually a period of action that occurs in one particular geographical location for a short period of time (such as a conversation in a restaurant). Usually, one scene is filmed or taped several times from a variety of angles, the various *take*s edited after filming or taping. Multiple takes are made so as to capture the best performance and/or camera angle, as well as to allow a variety of angles to be incorporated into the final presentation.

Schöffer, Peter
Peter Schöffer (c. 1425–1502) was a German printer who assisted Johannes Gutenberg and later ran the printing shop. Schöffer studied in Paris, where he supported himself as a copyist, and then became an apprentice to Gutenberg in Mainz. He entered the printing business as the partner of Gutenberg's creditor, Johann Fust, whose daughter he later  married. The best-surviving examples of his craftsmanship are the 1457 Mainz *Psalter* and the 1462 48-line *Bible*. The *Psalter* was the first printed book to give the date and place of printing and the printers' names. Schöffer cast the first metallic type in matrices and used it for the second edition of the *Vulgate Bible*. By the time of his death, he had printed more than 300 books.

School-Book Perforating
In *binding and finishing*, a *perforation* made parallel to the *spine* of a *jaw fold* in *signature*s produced for school workbooks. The perforation allows answer sections to be removed and passed in (or eaten by the student's dog, as the case may be), leaving the questions bound in the book.

Schopper Test

In papermaking, a test used to gauge the *folding endurance* of a paper. See *Folding Endurance*.

Scoop Coater

In *screen printing*, an alternate term for a *coater*. See *Coater*.

Score

See *Scoring* (first definition).

Scoring

In *binding and finishing*, the *stamping* of a crease in a sheet of paper or other *substrate* as a means of indicating the position of folds as well as facilitating the making of those folds.

In typography, *scoring* is an alternate term for *underlining* or *underscoring*. See *Underscoring*.

Screamer

Alternate term for an *exclamation mark*. See *Exclamation Mark*.

Screen

The portion of a computer monitor or a *cathode-ray tube* on which the image is displayed.

In process photography, a *screen* is a sheet of film with a particular set of dot patterns that is used to convert a *continuous-tone* image into a *halftone*, or a series of discrete dots of varying density. The term *screen* can also be used as a verb that means to produce a halftone from a continuous-tone image. (See *Halftone*.)

In digital halftone production, *screen* refers to the *screen algorithms* that convert the stored gray levels of the original image to the proper pattern of dots upon output.

Screen Algorithms

Mathematical calculations performed by computer software in the production of *digital halftones*. The algorithms essentially convert the *pixels* of each *process color* of the digital image—which are stored as gray values—into *halftone dots* (or, more accurately, *halftone cells*) of a particular shape, size, and *screen angle*. Different systems utilize different screen algorithms to effect the conversion of digital halftones, and many are proprietary. For many years, one particularly sticky problem was *irrational screen angle* calculation. See *Screen Angles*.

Screen Angles

In *process color* prepress and printing, the angle at which the rows of *halftone* dots run in relation to the horizontal. In order to eliminate undesirable *moiré* patterns when the four *color separation* halftones are overprinted in multi-color printing, each screen needs to be placed at a different angle, as the dots of one color interfere with those of another color, creating the distinct moiré patterns. Ideally, moiré is kept minimal when screens are 30° from each other. How-

ever, since there is only a total of 90° (at least for perfectly round dots) in which to rotate the screens, each screen can not be 30° from each other when printing four colors (30 × 4 = 120°). Experience, though, has resulted in a standard set of default screen angles that work very well in a wide variety of applications. The screen angle of the *yellow* separation is 0°, or perfectly horizontal. The *magenta* separation is 15° from the horizontal. The *black* separation is 45° from the horizontal, and the *cyan* separation is 75° from horizontal. Generally speaking, the further a separation is from either the horizontal or vertical axis, the less intrusive it tends to be. (Even in black-and-white halftone production, a perfectly horizontal screen angle results in more of a visual discernment of the individual dots than does a 45° angle.) Therefore, yellow, which is the lightest color, is best left along one of these axes, while black, the darkest color, is best kept as far from both as possible (or 45°, the midway point between vertical and horizontal). Depending on the application, these angles may be varied, but only by an experienced color separator. (See COLOR PLATE 9.)

In the older photographic halftone screening, generating proper screen angles was a simple question of turning the screen to the desired angle before exposing the films. Digital halftoning creates another set of screen angle problems. Since each digital halftone dot is made up of smaller printer spots (collectively called a *halftone cell*), the computer output device (in particular, the device's *raster image processor [RIP]*) needs to calculate a screen angle at which to set a particular row of dots. But the screen angles available for output are dependent upon the device *resolution*, and it may not be possible to produce a desired screen angle on a particular device. Unfortunately, moiré can appear with even the slightest deviation in screen angle (even as little as 0.01°). Hence, *rational screen angles* and *irrational screen angles* come into play. Screen angles are described in terms of their tangents, or the ratio of the opposite and adjacent sides. At some angles, such as 45° and 0°, that ratio is a rational number (a rational number being one that can be expressed evenly as the

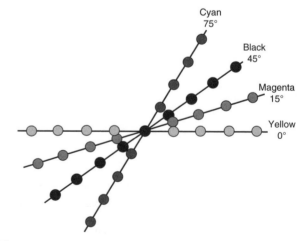

The conventional screen angles for process color printing.

ratio of two integers) while for some other angles (such as 15° and 75°), that ratio is an irrational number (an irrational number is one that can*not* be expressed evenly, consisting of decimal places that continue on perhaps forever without ever repeating—like pi [π], which equals 3.14159...). This becomes important in digital halftone output because at rational screen angles, each halftone cell can fit properly on the grid (or bitmap) of the recording device; each halftone cell will intersect the grid at the corners of a printer spot, which will allow all the halftone cells to have the same size. At irrational screen angles, however, the cells do not fit properly on the recording grid, which results in variably shaped halftone cells and cells comprising different numbers of spots. This is problematic unless each halftone cell can be described individually, rather than en masse. Needless to say, this requires a very powerful computer. However, it has been done, and several vendors have invented and licensed special screening hardware that has the power to effectively handle irrational screen angles.

As desktop computers did not have the power to deal with irrational screen angles in the same way as the high-power Linotype-Hell (now a division of Heidelberg) systems, halftones created on them possess cells that are all the same shape, but of different sizes. A consequence of this is that the cells do not always line up with the recorder grid at all screen angles, specifically the irrational ones. Adobe sought to solve this problem with **RT Screening**, a screen algorithm devised by Linotype-Hell and licensed by Adobe in **PostScript Level 1**. Halftones created with this process attempted to eliminate moiré by rounding the irrational angle to the nearest rational angle. Consequently, all halftone cell shapes are identical, and fit properly on the recorder grid. However, this didn't solve the moiré problem. A partial solution came in 1989, when Adobe introduced the Adobe *recommended RT angles*, a revised set of screen angles and screen frequencies. The two rational screen angles—black and yellow at 45° and 0° respectively—remain, but the cyan screen angle was set at 71.5° and the magenta angle at 18.5°. The new frequencies also vary the number of lines per inch of a particular screen. For example, on a 133-line screen, the cyan and magenta screens are 128.514963 lpi, while the yellow screen is 135.466667 lpi, and the black screen is 143.684102 lpi. These new angle and frequency specifications were incorporated into later revisions of PostScript, and are built into **PPD**s. They reduce moiré patterns, but not entirely.

A new and strikingly successful solution to the irrational screen angle problem came in 1992, when several different vendors introduced the concept of **supercell** screening. Adobe's **Accurate Screens**, Linotype-Hell's **HQS** screening, and Agfa's **Balanced Screening** all use large "clusters" of halftone cells (called "supercells") which, when the supercell is large enough, allows a much closer approximation of the optimal irrational angle than was available with RT Screening—74.9998° compared to 74.9°, for example, which is very close to 75°, and yet is still a rational number. Although some of the cells within the supercell still vary in shape, the supercell can begin with a printer spot exactly aligned to the recorder grid, which thus allows for the rotation of the supercell to any desired (rational) angle. The supercell just needs to be large enough. The drawback, of course, is that it requires a lot of computer memory and power to describe each cell within the supercell, and the effectiveness of supercell screening is dependent upon the amount of memory the system has available. But enhanced memory-management of **RIP**s utilizing **PostScript Level 2** and the development of **RISC**-based chips and Adobe's PixelBurst coprocessor speed this process considerably.

The three supercell screening methods mentioned above differ slightly in their approach (Balanced Screening still uses preset screen values to unburden the RIP), but they all produce superior desktop color separations that stand up favorably alongside output from high-end color systems.

Screen Buffer

Alternate term for **frame buffer**. See **Frame Buffer**.

Screen Burn-In

In computing, a problem with a **cathode-ray tube** or computer monitor in which a permanent afterimage of a displayed image remains visible. Essentially, an image remains "burned" into the phosphors of the screen and will be visible through whatever other image is on the screen. Screen burn-in is caused by leaving the same image on a monitor for an extended period of time. Although at one time screen burn-in could occur in about a day, modern computer displays would require that the same image remain on screen for at least a year for burn-in to occur. Nevertheless, the threat of screen burn-in has opened up a very lucrative market for the manufacturers of **screen savers**.

Screen Capture

Alternate term for **screen dump**. See **Screen Dump**.

Screen Carriage

The portion of a **screen printing** press that contains all the hinges, pivots, **screen holders**, or mechanical devices to which the printing screen frame is attached and that facilitates its movement toward or away from the **printing bed**.

Screen Coordinate System

The grid or **bitmap** that a computer uses to turn monitor **pixel**s on and off. See **Bitmap**.

Screen Curve

In digital imaging, a graph used to plot the relationship between a particular **pixel**'s gray level and the size of the **halftone dot** that will output from it. Screen curves are generated during the **linearization**—or calibration—of a scanner.

Screen Dump

A "photograph" of the contents of a computer screen, saved either as a graphics file or output to paper. Also called a *screen capture*.

Screened Negative

An alternate term for *halftone negative*. See *Halftone Negative*.

Screened Positive

An alternate term for *halftone positive*. See *Halftone Positive*.

Screened Print

Alternate term for a *halftone*, especially one produced as a photographic print rather than as a *negative*. See *Halftone*.

Screen Fabric

In *screen printing*, the material used to make the screen to which the stencil is attached and through which the ink is transferred. Screen fabrics include such substances as silk, *polyester* fibers, *nylon*, or metal wire.

Screen Flex Heat Transfer

See *Heat Transfer Printing*.

Screen Font

A computer file containing *bitmap* outlines of a particular *typeface* used to display that *font* on the computer monitor. As bitmaps, screen fonts occasionally look fine and legible at the *resolution* of the computer display, but are of too low a resolution for high-quality typographic output. Most computers also utilize *vector*-based *printer font*s that can be downloaded to the printer. See also *Printer Font*. Also called a *bitmap font*.

Screen Frequency

Alternate term for *screen ruling*. See *Screen Ruling*.

Screen Glitter Flex Heat Transfer

See *Heat Transfer Printing*.

Screen Holders

On a *screen printing* press, the devices or clamps on a *screen carriage* to which the screen frame is attached.

Screening

A printing defect of *gravure* printing characterized by a screen-like pattern appearing in solid portions of the printed image, caused by inconsistent ink flow from the cells of the cylinder. Decreasing the ink's *viscosity* with the addition of *solvent* will help alleviate the problem. Screening also occurs in multicolor gravure printing as successive inks can redissolve the first-down ink, which then interferes with the second-down ink, which in turn impedes the flow of ink from the cylinder. Increasing the speed at which the first ink dries is one way of alleviating the problem, as

is ensuring that all the inks in the system are compatible with each other.

The term *screening* is also used in *flexographic* printing as an alternate term for a defect called *mechanical pinholing*. See *Mechanical Pinholing*.

In prepress and photography, the term *screening* is used to refer to the act of converting a *continuous-tone* image into a *halftone*, or the act of producing any other kind of *screen tint*.

Screening Filter

In digital halftoning, a software function that allows the removal of a *halftone screen* applied to a digital file, so as to allow the application of a new *screen algorithm*.

Screening in Continuous Tones

A type of *screen printing* process in which two or more inks are placed on the *printing screen* at once, to create a color blend on the *substrate* without a clearly defined boundary between them.

Screen Marks

Alternate term for *mesh marks*. See *Mesh Marks*.

Screen Opener

A substance—commonly an aerosol—used to remove ink particles *clogging* the screen.

Screen Printing

A form of printing in which a thick *paste ink* is forced through a stencil attached to a finely woven mesh screen, transferring ink to the desired *substrate* in those areas not covered by the stencil. Screen printing, also known as *screen process* and *serigraphy*, is used to print almost any surface imaginable, from T-shirts and other textiles to posters to signs to tablecloths to shower curtains to leather goods. At one time called *silkscreening* (and, more obscurely, "fabritecture" and "mitography"), as the screen through which the ink was forced was made of silk, the term is no longer in use in the screen printing industry.

Screen printing derives from older practices of stencil printing, such as the *pochoir* method of stencilling. Essentially, a design is cut or punched into a sheet of paper, metal, or other material, and ink is applied with a brush to the surface of the stencil, where it passes through the openings onto the desired surface. Stencil printing was popular in Japan until the early 19th century, and early forms of European stencil printing date back at least to AD 1500, in particular, for printing playing cards. (Just about every printing method had its origins in the printing of playing cards, perhaps indicative of the emphasis that has always been—and probably always will be—placed on that particular form of diversion.) The screen process as we now know it was devised in Germany and Scotland in the late 1800s. In 1907, Englishman Samuel Simon created a process of screen printing utilizing a cut stencil of the intended design mounted on a finely woven silk screen, a brush being used

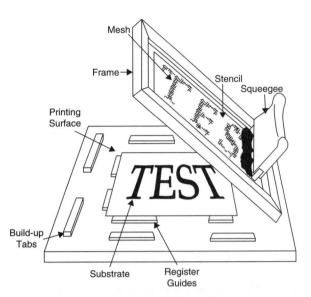

Basic screen printing unit.

to force the ink through the screen in the cut-out areas of the stencil. In 1914, American John Pilsworth devised a system for the silkscreening of banners, and until the late 1930s screen printing was used primarily for commercial purposes, eventually becoming favored among artists. Screen printing today still retains the simplicity of earlier forms of it; a hand-cut or photographically produced stencil is mounted on the bottom of a fine mesh screen, which has been stretched taut on a wooden frame. A fairly viscous ink (formerly paint) is placed on the screen, a glue is applied to the nonprinting areas beyond the edge of the stencil, and a squeegee pulls the ink down over the stencil, where it prints the design onto the intended substrate. Despite its simplicity and compatibility with a virtually unlimited variety of substrates, screen printing cannot economically compete with *offset lithography*, *gravure*, or *flexography* in the high-speed, high-volume printing of books, newspapers, etc.

The screen printing apparatus contains several basic elements: screen, stencil, and squeegee.

Screen. The *printing screen* is a fine mesh, composed of filaments of natural fibers such as silk or—more commonly—synthetic fibers such as *polyester*, *nylon*, etc. In some screen printing applications, a *metal screen fabric* is used. (See *Metal Screen Fabric*.) The fibers used for the mesh can either be *monofilament* or *multifilament*, which describes whether each fiber is composed of a single thread or several threads tightly braided together, respectively. Multifilaments provide a greater cross-sectional area and allow for a better adhesion of the *stencil*. They also retain their dimensional stability more easily, ensuring consistent ink transfer over the course of a print run. Monofilaments, although capable of facilitating ink passage through the *mesh opening* more readily, are smoother than multifilaments and consequently must often undergo *roughening* in order to properly adhere the stencil. (The

surface roughness of a monofilament screen fabric necessary to adhere a stencil material is known as its *tooth*.)

The *mesh number*, or the number of *mesh apertures* in a given unit area or length of fabric, affects the image quality of the print. For fine line art, a finely woven fabric will hold the stencil better and pass a fine film of ink. A coarser fabric will pass a thicker layer of ink but will fail to hold a stencil containing fine detail. Another consideration with respect to mesh number and the size of the mesh aperture is the type of ink to be used. Some inks contain large pigment particles, which may not be able to pass through a finely woven fabric. An ink that will not dry quickly on the screen (causing a problem called *clogging*) is also necessary.

The screen fabric is stretched across a frame, which can be any of a variety of configurations. The only considerations of the printing frame is that it be large enough to hold the fabric (and accommodate the stencil), be sturdy enough the hold the fabric without warping, and be deep enough to hold the necessary quantity of ink. The frame, as a general rule, should be about 4 in. longer and wider than the stencil it is to accommodate. The amount of tension required varies by fabric type, and each fabric manufacturer has specific recommendations. As a general rule, polyester fabrics are stretched from 1% to 4% of their original dimensions, nylon from 4% to 7%, and silk from 3% to 4%. Mechanical stretching devices can be adjusted to stretch the fabric over the frame with the proper tension, and the fabric is then stapled securely into place. After the fabric is attached to the screen, it must be cleaned and degreased, after which point it is ready to accept a stencil.

Stencils. The stencil is a paper or, more commonly, a water-based or lacquer-based emulsion attached to a plastic backing sheet that can be either hand-cut or photographically prepared so as to provide openings in the image areas for the ink to pass, while remaining hard and durable in the nonimage areas. Stencils prepared by hand are known as *hand-cut stencil*s, while those produced photographically are called *photostencil*s. Hand-cut stencils are prepared by cutting the emulsion from the backing sheet with a knife. The stencil is then adhered to the screen with water or a special adhesive material. The backing sheet is then removed. A photostencil is composed of a photosensitive emulsion applied to a plastic backing sheet (or to the screen fabric itself) and is exposed via ultraviolet light to a film positive, which hardens the emulsion in the nonimage areas, leaving the unexposed image areas unhardened, and capable of being washed away during developing, creating image-area openings in the stencil. There are a variety of means of preparing photostencils. (See *Photostencil*.)

Once the stencil is applied to the screen fabric and the plastic backing sheet removed, the portions of the screen not covered by the stencil must be masked, either with a paper mask (which is effective only on short-run jobs) or with a liquid *blockout solution*. Once dry, the screen will now only transfer ink through the openings in the stencil. (See also *Stencil*.)

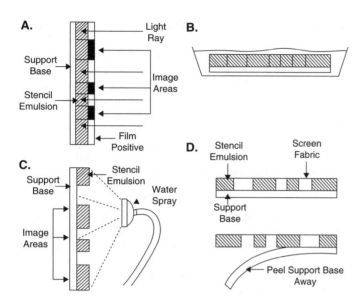

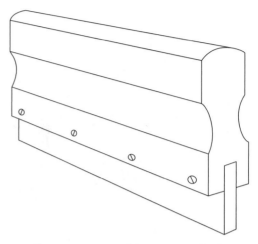

Squeegee, as used in screen printing.

The process of exposing an indirect stencil: (A) a film posi-tive allows light to strike only the nonimage areas, which then harden during development (B). After exposure, the unhardened image areas are washed away (C), leaving those areas of the stencil open. Finally, the stencil is adhered to the screen fabric (D).

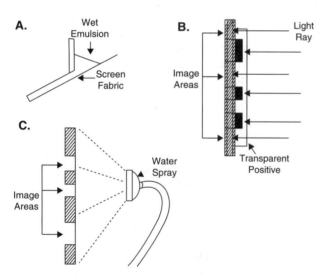

The process of exposing a direct stencil: (A) a wet emulsion is applied directly to the screen fabric, and exposed to actinic light through a film positive (B), where nonimage areas harden. After exposure, washing (C) removes the unhardened image areas, leaving holes in the stencil.

Squeegee. Printing is accomplished by means of placing a quantity of ink on top of the screen, and forcing the ink through the screen by means of a *squeegee*, essentially a flexible rubber or plastic blade attached to a handle. The shape, hardness, and chemical composition of the squeegee blade can vary by application. (See *Squeegee*.)

Printing. The two basic means of screen printing are **on-contact printing**, in which the screen, stencil, and sub-strate are in direct contact with each other throughout the pressrun, and **off-contact printing**, in which the screen and stencil are only in contact with each other during a printing stroke, directly under the line of the squeegee and the **train**. A problem with on-contact printing is that the substrate occasionally sticks to the bottom of the screen, and needs to be peeled away after each impression. On occasion, adhesive tapes or vacuum-backed printing beds can be used to prevent sticking.

Prior to a printing stroke, the ink is placed in the **inkwell** or **reservoir**, on the top of the screen away from the image area of the stencil. The process of **flooding**—or applying a **flood coat**—involves coating the printing area of the screen with a film of ink without making an impres-sion, which can either be accomplished by the squeegee (manually or automatically) or with automatic **flood bar**s. When the substrate is properly positioned, the printing stroke can be made, which essentially involves holding the squeegee at the appropriate **squeegee angle** and drawing it across the image area with a uniform pressure, speed, and angle. (Since the blade is flexible, its angle—called the **angle of attack**—will be different than the squeegee angle.) The squeegee should not be stopped until it is well out of the image area of the printing screen.

In multicolor screen printing, like other printing pro-cesses, proper **registration** is important, and any of a vari-ety of means can be employed to ensure that successive

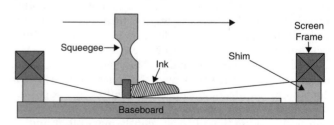

Off-contact screen printing.

colors or images print where they are supposed to, from registration marks to register guides—called **lays**. Each color requires a separate stencil. Some substrates, especially fabrics, may stretch during printing, and its return to its normal dimensions after each impression may result in some degree of difficulty in replicating the stretch to achieve the proper color fit on successive passes.

After printing, in the process of **reclaiming**, the stencil and blockout solution can be removed, either with water or with a solvent. The screen must be completely cleaned of ink, blockout solution, and cleaning solvent before it can be reused for a successive print run.

Inks and Substrates. As was mentioned several times above, screen printing is suitable for printing on an almost infinite variety of substrates. The most important consideration is ensuring that the ink used is suitable with the surface, both in terms of chemical compatibility and the facilitation of proper drying. Screen printing commonly requires paste inks that are thick and able to print sharply through the screen. They must also perform well under the action of a squeegee. The solvents used should also not be overly volatile, as excessively early evaporation would cause the remaining ink components to clog the screen. Screen inks typically utilize a drying-oil vehicle, although **ultraviolet-curing ink**s and other forms of fast-drying inks are making strong inroads in screen printing. Often, in the decoration of fabrics, glassware, and ceramics, **heat transfer printing** is utilized, which involves screen printing the design onto a **decal** (in one of a variety of ways; see **Decal**), then transferring the design (which is composed of **sublimable dye**s) to the desired end substrate by means of exposing the decal to increased heat and pressure. (See **Heat Transfer Printing**.)

Press Configurations. The most fundamental screen printing press configuration involves what could be described as a **clamshell press**, in which the printing screen frame is hinged at the back or side to the printing bed, and the screen can be lowered onto the substrate in a manner reminiscent of a clamshell opening and closing. These types of presses are hand-operated, and as a result are only capable of a few impressions per hour. Various types of automated screen presses exist. Some presses operate by means of a lever; these are still considered manual presses, but the action of the lever lowers the screen into position and moves the squeegee across it, requiring only one operation per impression. Semiautomatic presses automate the lowering of the screen and the motion of the squeegee, leaving the operator responsible only for the insertion, registration, and removal of the substrate. The automatic movement of the printing screen and squeegee may be set to make an impression at a fixed rate, or only after the operator hits a foot pedal. Some screen presses are also fully automated, from feeding to printing to delivery.

Some presses have been specially designed to print directly on three-dimensional objects (called **geometric**

printing), such as bottles, cans, balls, etc., and several press designs have arisen to handle these objects, such as **radius printing**, for example. Wallpaper and other forms of continuous images are printed by **rotary screen print-**

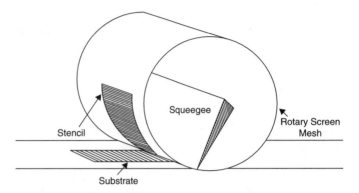

Rotary screen printing.

ing, or printing utilizing seamless screen cylinders. In these presses, the squeegee dwells inside the cylinder. For multicolor printing, a **carousel** press is commonly employed. A carousel unit has a printing bed that rotates around a central hub, carrying the substrate beneath a series of printing stations that successively lay down colors.

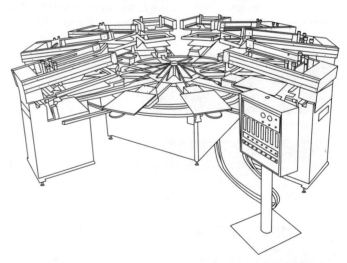

One configuration of an automatic carousel press used for screen printing.

Screen printing has a strong commercial presence, and as press speeds increase (modern cylinder-based screen presses are capable of 4,000–6,000 impressions per hour) and ink-drying systems decrease the drying time of the inks, the true potential of the process—which in principle has changed very little from the days of silkscreening—can be realized.

Screen Process
Alternate term for **screen printing**. See **Screen Printing**.

Screen Proper

In *screen printing*, the part of the *printing screen* occupied by the *stencil*.

Screen Range

In *halftone* photography, the *density range* (or the difference between the densities of the *highlight* and *shadow* areas) that a halftone screen is capable of reproducing.

Screen Refresh

See *Refresh*.

Screen Ruling

In *halftone* photography, the number of lines of *dots per inch (dpi)* on a *halftone screen*. Each line (or row) and each column contain a certain number of dots at a particular density. For example, a 150-line screen contains horizontal rows of 150 dots per inch and vertical columns of 150 lines per inch, for a total of 22,500 dots per square inch. The screen ruling is also measured in *lines per inch (lpi)*. Halftone screens are used to break a *continuous-tone* image into many tiny dots of varying color or gray, necessary for most forms of printing.

The smaller the dots (or, in other words, the higher the screen ruling), the less discernible the individual dots are and the more closely the printed image approximates a continuous-tone image. Although the more dots the better, the screen ruling that can be implemented is limited by the intended printing process and *substrate*.

150-lpi screen ruling

25-lpi screen ruling

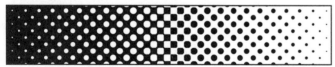
10-lpi screen ruling

The greater the screen ruling, the less obvious the constituent dots of a halftone. At 10 lines per inch (lpi), the dots are quite obvious. At 25 lpi (center), the dots become less obvious, while at 150 lpi (bottom), the dots are scarcely visible.

Black-and-white *web offset* printing on newsprint typically prints with 75-line screens, while color newspaper printing often uses 90- to 100-line screens. Although some processes allow for very high screen rulings (*waterless lithography*, for example, allows screen rulings as high as

600 lpi), 150–200 lpi is the most commonly used screen ruling for commercial printing.

In digital halftoning, the screen ruling that can be obtained is dependent upon the *resolution* of the output device. On *imagesetters* and other digital output devices, each halftone dot is created of much smaller printer *spot*s (and in this case halftone dots are known as halftone *cell*s) inserted into a matrix. This matrix thus describes the number of spots that can make up a cell, and this determines the screen ruling. For example, an imagesetter with a resolution of 2,400 dpi can produce a 16-spot by 16-spot halftone cell. Dividing 2,400 by 16 yields 150; thus this imagesetter can output films with a screen ruling of 150 lpi. On the other hand, a 300-dpi laser printer, capable of only a 5×5 cell matrix, can only output a screen ruling of 60 lpi. Related to these resolution numbers is the number of gray levels each cell matrix can produce, which is determined by the number of spots in the matrix, which affects the dot density. The 16×16 matrix can produce 256 levels of gray (16 × 16 = 256), while the 5×5 matrix can only display 25 shades of gray (plus white, for 26 total). The human eye can detect slightly more than 100 different shades of gray.

Screen ruling is also known as *screen frequency*.

Screen Saver

A computer program designed to prevent *screen burn-in*, which can occur if the same, unmoving image remains on a computer display for an extended period of time. A screen saver is a program that varies the screen image if no keyboard or mouse movement is detected within a specified period of time (usually user-definable). Although screen burn-in is not really a threat to most modern computer monitors (a static image would need to remain on the display for at least a year), screen savers are nevertheless a feature of many operating systems, and third-party screen saver programs are very popular in the consumer market. Although their efficacy is open to some debate, many screen savers are very entertaining, often more so than much more expensive video games.

Screen Seepage

A printing problem of *screen printing* characterized by an undesirable oozing of ink through open portions of the *stencil*, caused by a prolonged stoppage of printing while excessive amounts of ink are still over the stencil.

Screen Sharing

Alternate term for *joint editing*. See *Joint Editing*.

Screen Size

The dimensions of a *cathode-ray tube*, usually measured diagonally.

Screen Stability

In *screen printing*, a measure of the ability of a particular ink to print for a long period of time without *clogging* the screen. Also known as *ink stability*.

Screen Tint

A *halftone* characterized by dots that are all the same size over the entire area of the image.

Screentone

Alternate term for a *screen tint*. See *Screen Tint*.

Scribe

In prepress, to manually remove a portion of the emulsion of a *negative* to produce a straight, uniform line.

Scribe Lines

Thin horizontal and vertical lines engraved on the surface of a *flexographic* press's *plate cylinder* used for the accurate positioning and mounting of flexo plates. Scribe lines can be used in conjunction with fine engraved marks on the nonprinting portions of the plate itself to facilitate accurate plate mounting.

Scriber

A small, pencil-like steel-tipped tool, used to *scribe*, or etch, lines on *negative*s.

Scrim

In photography and videography, a circular wire mesh placed over or within a source of lighting to diffuse and dim the illumination during a shoot.

Script

In typography, a *typeface* designed with connecting characters in imitation of fine handwriting. There are various levels of script, ranging from informal (*brush style*) to Spencerian styles. All are calligraphic in nature. In script typefaces, letters are connected; in *cursive*, letters are not connected. Effective and decorative, script fonts should only be used sparingly, and never in all caps. Script typefaces are used for invitations, announcements, and other purposes evoking elegance.

The term *script* also refers to a fundamental element in film, video, television, and multimedia production. Essentially, a script contains the "instructions" for making a production, including scenes, scenery, props, characters, and the complete character dialogue and actions. Some scripts, called shooting scripts, may contain specific camera angles. In multimedia, scripts also need to indicate the structure of the presentation, the level of interactivity, the interface design, etc.

Script X

A computer language designed for multimedia scripting. Developed by Apple and IBM, Script X allows developers to create hardware- and software-independent multimedia applications.

Scroll

In computing, to move a displayed page or image left, right, up, or down, so as to access other portions of the image that do not fit within the screen dimensions.

Scroll Bar

In computing, especially that utilizing a *graphical user interface (GUI)*, a bar, usually located on the side and/or bottom of a screen or window that facilitates *scrolling* to portions of an image that exist outside the dimensions of the display. Usually, the scroll bar includes arrows for scrolling in small increments, or a *scroll box* that can be pulled along the bar to move to more distant portions of an image. See *Scrolling*.

Scroll Box

In computing, especially by means of a *graphical user interface (GUI)*, a small box located on a window's *scroll bar*, used to indicate the position of the displayed window within the document. The scroll box can be moved up or down (or left or right) to access different portions of the document. Also called a *thumb*.

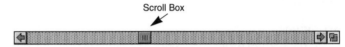

A scroll bar for scrolling in the horizontal direction.

Scrolling

Moving from one displayed portion of a page or image to one beyond the dimension of the computer screen. See *Scroll*.

Scroll-Lock Key

In computing, a key located on many keyboards that keeps the *cursor* anchored to a certain point on the screen as *scrolling* text flows under it.

SCS

Abbreviation for *Standard Character String*.

SCSI

Pronounced "SKUH-zee," an abbreviation for *small computer systems interface*, a communications standard and specification for attaching peripherals to desktop computers. Each device (which may include the internal hard drive and internal CD-ROM drive, as well as external media such as magnetic media, magnetic optical disc drives, scanners, etc.) is linked in series along a SCSI chain, or bus, and each device is given a SCSI address—on the Macintosh, typically a number from 0 to 6. No two devices may have the same SCSI address. Typically, the only devices not included on the SCSI chain are printers and modems. The SCSI standard allows for rapid transfer of data from device to device, or from device to computer. An updated version of the SCSI standard—*SCSI2*—has a greater *bus* width, allowing greater *throughput*.

SCSI2

A upgraded version of the *small computer systems interface* standard (familiarly abbreviated *SCSI*) that increases the *bus* width from 8 to 32 *bit*, allowing throughput of up to 20 *megabyte*s per second. See *SCSI*.

Scuffing

See *Rub-Off*.

Scuff-Resistant Ink

A printing ink to which a wax has been added to impart to the dry ink film a tough, hard surface able to withstand the scuffs and shocks experienced during shipping and handling. Most types of ink have scuff-resistant formulations, which are used primarily for printing on cartons and other packaging. (See also *Non-Scratch Ink*.)

Scum

The results of the process of *scumming*. See *Scumming*.

In *screen printing*, *scum* refers to a residue deposited on the surface of a photostencil during processing and developing that can collect in the stencil openings and impede proper washout of the stencil, resulting in the printing of voids.

Scumming

In *offset lithography*, scumming is a generic term for the presence of ink on nonimage areas of the printing plate, which can be caused by a variety of press conditions, in particular the use of a *fountain solution* that is too acidic, where the solution begins to eat away at the surface of the metal plate and its protective coating, or by a fountain solution that is too alkaline, as the desensitizing properties of *gum arabic* are lost at a *pH* greater than 5.0. (See *Fountain Solution: pH*.) Scumming characterized by the dispersion of ink *pigment* particles in the fountain solution, which increases as temperature increases, is known as *tinting* or *hot-weather scumming*. Scumming is also called *greasing*. See *Tinting*.

In *gravure* printing, *scumming* is an alternate term for a similar problem called *fogging*. See *Fogging*.

SD

Abbreviation for *super density*. See *Super Density (SD)*.

S/DIF

Abbreviation for *Sony/Philips Digital Interface*. See *Sony/Philips Digital Interface*.

SE

Abbreviation for *systems engineer*.

SEA

File extension used to denote a *self-extracting archive*. See *Self-Extracting Archive* and *File Compression*.

Sealer Coat

Alternate term for *barrier coat*. See *Barrier Coat*.

Search String

In computing, a sequence of characters purportedly located within a database that a user has requested the system locate.

SECAM

Abbreviation for *Séquentiel Couleur à Mémoire*. See *Séquentiel Couleur à Mémoire (SECAM)*.

Secondary Color

In *additive color theory*, a color created by the combination of (or, in *subtractive color theory*, the *overprinting* of) *primary* colors. See *Additive Color Theory* and *Subtractive Color Theory*. (See COLOR PLATES 1 and 2.) In printing, secondary colors are also called *overprint colors*. Combinations of secondary colors produce *tertiary colors*.

Secondary Font

In typography, the *font* in which the second largest portion of the text or other print matter has been typeset.

Secondary Indent

In typography, an *indent* placed at the beginning of the second and all subsequent lines of a *paragraph*), often until an *end-of-paragraph code* is encountered. See also *Primary Indent*.

Secondary Leading

In typography, the amount of *leading* (or *line spacing*) used to separate paragraphs, blocks of copy, or specific lines, different from the line spacing used for the majority of the text. (See also *Primary Leading*.) See *Line Spacing*.

Secondary Side Head

In *book typography*, the title given to the second largest subdivision (such as a chapter or section) of a book. See also *Primary Side Head*.

Second-Generation Original

Alternate term for *dupe*. See *Dupe*.

Second Parallel Fold

On *in-line* folding equipment, a *parallel fold* made in the *jaw folder* immediately after and parallel to the *first parallel fold*. A fold made in this manner produces sixteen-page multiples of the number of webs produced. The size of the *signature* created is the *cutoff* length by one-half the width of the web.

Second Side Bearing

In typography, a measure of the white space between the right side of a character and the right edge of its *em square*. See also *First Side Bearing*.

Section

In *book typography*, any major subdivision of a book, especially of handbooks and manuals. In other types of books, sections are known as parts or chapters.

Sectioning

See *Capping and Sectioning*.

Section Sign

A symbol (§) used, primarily in legal citations, to mark sections of a longer document. It may also be used as a *footnote* symbol.

Sector

In computing, the smallest portion of a *magnetic disk* in which data can be written. Several sectors equal one *track*.

Sedimentation

A problem of *gravure* inks characterized by the settling of the solid ink *pigment* out of the fluid *vehicle* as a result of long-term storage. Frequent agitation of the ink container may help alleviate the problem.

Inks possessing higher *viscosity* (even the "false viscosity" characteristic of *thixotropic* inks) will be less susceptible to sedimentation than thinner inks, and inks produced with larger and/or more poorly dispersed pigment particles will be more susceptible to sedimentation. (See also *Flocculation*.)

Seed Fill

In digital painting and drawing programs, a means of filling a solid, single-color space with a particular color.

Seek Access Time

Alternate term for *access time*. See *Access Time*.

Segment

Any smaller portion of a larger whole, such as a *line segment*, which is a portion of a line.

Segue

In film, video, or audio production, any smooth, gradual crossover from one video or audio segment to another.

Select

In computing, to activate a particular screen object or window by clicking on it with the mouse or other pointing device.

Selection Tool

In computer graphics programs, any of a wide variety of tools used to *select* objects (or parts of objects). Common examples include the *pointer*, *lasso*, *marquee*, etc.

Self-Checking Code

Alternate term for *error detecting code*. See *Error Detecting Code*.

Self-Cover

In *binding and finishing*, the cover of any book or other publication that is made of the same paper as the inside pages.

Self-Extracting Archive

In computing, a compressed file that does not need a special program to be decompressed; double-clicking on the archive expands it into the original file. Self-extracting archive is usually denoted by the file extension *SEA*. See *File Compression*.

Self-Stretching Frame

A *screen printing* frame configuration that includes a special screw for the built-in ability to adjust fabric tension.

Semichemical Pulping

Method of converting wood chips to paper *pulp* for papermaking utilizing a combination of chemical and mechanical means. The purpose of *pulping* is to separate individual fibers of *cellulose* from other nonfibrous components of wood, in particular, *lignin*, an organic material that binds cellulose fibers together and is a detriment to papermaking. Wholly *mechanical pulping* generates high pulp yields and costs comparatively little, but it removes little lignin. Wholly *chemical pulping* removes most lignin, but it is expensive and has low pulp yields.

In semichemical pulping, wood chips are first subjected to mild cooking in, most commonly, *sodium sulfite* combined with a small quantity of alkaline salts, such as *sodium carbonate*, *sodium bicarbonate*, or *sodium hydroxide*. The cooked chips are then sandwiched in a *disk refiner*—or two rotating serrated disks—that separate the individual fibers of cellulose. The pulp is then washed to remove the chemicals.

Some of the advantages of chemical pulping, including higher lignin removal, and of mechanical pulping, such as high pulp yields, are realized. Pulp yields in semichemical processes are generally from 60–80% of the original wood, and much of the residual lignin still remains. Semichemical pulping results in stiff fibers, and the process is used to make corrugated paperboard, cardboard roll cores, and containers.

See also *Mechanical Pulping* and *Chemical Pulping*.

Semiconcealed Cover

In *mechanical binding*, a single-piece cover that has been drilled or punched but that forms a closed *spine* on the bound publications.

Send to Back

In desktop publishing, a command used to place one object beneath all other objects. See also *Bring to Front*.

Senefelder, Alois

Aloys, or Alois, Senefelder (1771–1834) of Germany was the inventor of lithography. His invention of a new printing process came about by chance while he was seeking a method of reproducing plays and musical scores. Writing in reverse on a piece of limestone with greasy chalk and then dampening the stone, he found that an inked roller would deposit ink only on the chalk. He was

working on a method to improve copperplate engraving and was experimenting on Bavarian limestone in place of the more costly copper. His experiments led to the discovery that polished stone, when properly inked and treated with chemicals would transfer its image onto paper. Thus was born stone printing, or, as Senefelder called it, chemical printing, the forerunner of lithography. The practical aspects of lithography were immediately apparent, and in 1799 the prince-elector of Bavaria gave Senefelder an exclusive 15-year privilege to exploit his invention. Just one year after Senefelder submitted his model for an automated press in 1817, the first lithograph was published in the United States by Bass Otis.

Senefelder was unable to continue at the University of Ingolstadt after his father's death (his father was an actor at the Theatre Royal in Prague) and supported himself as a performer and author. He learned printing in a printing shop, purchased a small press, and sought to do his own printing. Desiring to publish plays and music that he had written but unable to afford the engraving of printing plates, because music could not be set in metal type, Senefelder tried to engrave them himself.

His work on copper plates was unsuccessful when an accident led to his discovery in 1796. Senefelder records that he jotted down a laundry list with grease pencil on a piece of Bavarian limestone. It occurred to him that if he etched away the rest of the surface, the markings would be left in relief. Two years of experimentation eventually led to the discovery of flat-surface printing (modern lithography). In 1818 he documented his discovery in *Vollständiges Lehrbuch der Steindruckerey* (*A Complete Course of Lithography*). "I had just ground a stone plate smooth in order to treat it with etching fluid and to pursue on it my practice in reverse writing, when my mother asked me to write a laundry list for her. The laundress was waiting, but we could find no paper... I wrote the list hastily on the clean stone... As I was preparing afterwards to wash the writing from the stone... I became curious to see what would happen with writing made thus of prepared ink, if the stone were now etched with aqua fortis (nitric acid). I thought that possibly the letters would be left in relief and admit of being inked and printed like book types or woodcuts." Later, plates of zinc, iron, brass and copper were ground with pumice and chalk and wrapped around a cylinder to substitute for stone. Photography later made it possible to fix an image onto a photosensitive metal plate by light exposure through a film negative. In offset lithographic printing, the first image is printed onto a rubber blanket before being transferred to the paper stock.

Sensitivity Guide

In prepress, a thin, calibrated ***continuous wedge*** (or ***gray scale***), with the tones being numbered.

Sensitization

The chemical treatment of a lithographic printing plate to impart ink-receptivity and water-repellency to image areas. See ***Plate: Offset Lithography***.

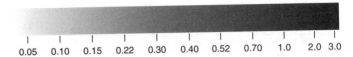

A sensitivity guide, with densities shown.

Sensitize

To chemically treat a lithographic printing plate to impart ink-receptivity and water-repellency to image areas. See ***Plate: Offset Lithography***.

Sensitizer

In photography, any of a wide variety of materials—such as silver, iron, or chromium salts, ***diazo*** compounds, etc.—used to make an ***emulsion*** (or other photographic surface) sensitive to light.

Separations

See ***Color Separation***.

Separator

Alternate term for a ***delimiter***. See ***Delimiter***.

Separator Brush

One of a set of small, brushlike attachments found in a sheetfed press's ***feeder section*** that sit on top of (or just above) the paper pile and ensure that the ***pickup sucker***s of the ***sheet-separation unit*** lift only one sheet at a time. Separator brushes may be supplemented with brushless ***separator finger***s. See illustration on facing page. (See ***Sheet-Separation Unit*** and ***Feeder Section: Sheetfed Offset Lithography***.)

Separator Finger

One of a set of small attachments found in a sheetfed press's ***feeder section*** that sit on top of (or just above) the paper pile and ensure that the ***pickup sucker***s of the ***sheet-separation unit*** lift only one sheet at a time. Separator fingers may be supplemented with ***separator brush***es. See illustration on facing page. (See ***Sheet-Separation Unit*** and ***Feeder Section: Sheetfed Offset Lithography***.)

Sequencer

In computing, the portion of a ***microprocessor*** that controls the sequence in which instructions will be executed.

In a database or database program, a *sequencer* is the portion of the system or program that sorts individual records according to the user's specifications.

In audio production, a *sequencer* is a device that controls digital musical instruments, often in accordance with the ***MIDI*** standard.

Sequential Access

In computing, the retrieval of data from a ***magnetic tape*** (or similar means of storage) by passing through all locations on the tape between the current location of the read head and the desired location. See also ***Random Access***.

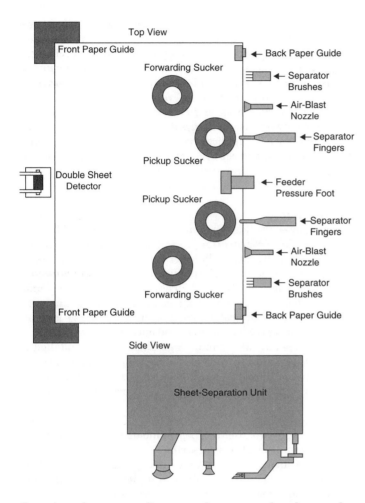

Location of separator fingers and separator brushes on the sheet-separation unit.

Sequential Storage

In computing, the storage of computer data in a linear (i.e., not random) manner on a medium such as **magnetic tape**. See **Sequential Access**.

Séquentiel Couleur à Mémoire (SECAM)

A standard for television broadcasting and video, used in France, Russia, and Eastern Europe, usually as an alternative to **PAL**. SECAM consists of 625 image lines per screen, like PAL, but its use of 819 actual "scan lines" produces a higher-quality image than PAL. The screen frequency of SECAM is 50 Hertz. See also **National Television Standards Committee (NTSC)** and **Phase Alternating Line (PAL)**.

Sequestering Agent

A substance added to an alkaline **fountain solution** to prevent calcium and magnesium compounds (added to prevent plate corrosion or for other purposes) from precipitating out of the solution, their solubility decreasing with increasing **pH**. (See **Fountain Solution**.)

Serial

Descriptive of data transfer by a computer performed sequentially or in **series** or, in other words, **bit** by bit. In a serial connection (such as through a computer's **serial port**), one bit of data is sent through the connection at one time, the rest of the bits in the transmission following behind in a single line. See **Serial Port**. See also **Parallel** and **Parallel Port**.

Serial Access

Alternate term for **sequential access**. See **Sequential Access**.

Serial Interface

In computing, data transmission by means of a **serial port**. See **Serial** and **Serial Port**.

Serial Mouse

In computing, a **mouse** connected to the computer's **serial port** rather than to a special **expansion card** attached directly to the system **bus** (which would then be called a **bus mouse**). The only criterion in choosing a bus mouse over a serial mouse is whether the system has a free expansion slot or a serial port.

Serial-Parallel

In computing, the transmission of data by a combination of **serial** and **parallel** means, such as transmitting characters one at a time (serial), but transmitting the eight bits (usually) that make up a character at one time (parallel). See **Serial** and **Parallel**.

Serial Port

One of two types of ports on a personal computer to which peripheral devices can be connected. In contrast to a **parallel port**, a serial port transmits data in a linear fashion, one **bit** at a time, rather than as a larger collection of bits. Printers, for example, are commonly connected to **Macintosh**es by means of a serial connector. Mice and other input devices are also connected to both Macs and **PC**s by means of a serial connector. See also **Parallel Port**.

Serial Printer

A computer printer that prints one character at a time, as opposed to a **line printer** or a **page printer**.

Serial Processing

In computing, the processing of one task or event at one time, in contrast to **parallel processing**.

Serial Transmission

A means of transmitting data in **series** (or one **bit** at a time) rather than in **parallel**. See **Serial** and **Serial Port**.

Series

Any sequential set of data, documents, publications, etc.

In typography, *series* is a shorthand term for **type series**. See **Type Series**.

Serif

In typography, an all-inclusive term for characters that have a line crossing the free end of a stroke. The term *serif* refers to both that finishing line and to characters and *typeface*s that have them.

It is said that the Romans invented the serif as a solution to the technical problem of getting a chisel to cut a neat, clean end to a character. Later, it became an emulation of handwriting, with flat "pens" producing thick and thin curves, based on the angle of the pen.

Serif characters tend to be easier to read, as they provide a horizontal guideline for the eye to "tie" the letters of a word together. It is generally better to use serif faces (rather than *sans serif* faces) when typesetting long stretches of copy, such as books with few illustrations, since serif faces cause less fatigue of the eyes. According to one study, there is reader preference for, and better legibility of, serif faces. Half-serifs on horizontal *arm*s are sometimes called *beak*s, and serifs at the end of *arc*s are called *barb*s. A character exhibiting a curvature of the transition from the main stroke to the serif is referred to as *bracketed*. A character in which the angle from the main stroke to the serif is a right angle is described as *square serif*. See also *Sans Serif*.

Serifs are bracketed or unbracketed. Bracketed serifs tie the serif to the main stroke with a small curved line. In the illustration below, all but Lubalin Graph are bracketed.

```
ABCDEFGHIJKLMNOPQRSTUVWXYZ
abcdefghijklmnopqrstuvwxyz1234567890
New Century Schoolbook

ABCDEFGHIJKLMNOPQRSTUVWXYZ
abcdefghijklmnopqrstuvwxyz1234567890
Caslon

ABCDEFGHIJKLMNOPQRSTUVWXYZ
abcdefghijklmnopqrstuvwxyz1234567890
Lubalin Graph

ABCDEFGHIJKLMNOPQRSTUVWXYZ
abcdefghijklmnopqrstuvwxyz1234567890
Goudy
```

Examples of typefaces with serifs.

Serigraphy

Alternate term for *screen printing*, especially that of fine art prints. The word is derived from the Greek words *ser* (meaning "silkworm") and *graphein* (meaning "writing [or printing]").

Serrated Knife

In *binding and finishing*, a circular blade having notches cut at regular intervals, used for *perforating*.

Server

In networking, a processor or computer system that provides a specific service to the other systems connected to the network (which are known as *client*s). Servers are usually identified according to the service they provide. For example, a *file server* provides file and data interchange; a *print server* keeps track of print commands and the *print queue*; a *mail server* sends, receives, and sorts *email*; a *communications server* or *access server* facilitates remote network access; a *fax server* sends and receives faxes for network users; an *application server* is designed to handle specific applications; a *database server* facilitates the search and retrieval of information stored in *database*s; etc. A computer system with no other purpose but to serve the network is called a *dedicated server*.

Service Bureau

A company—also known sometimes as a prepress house—that provides *imagesetter* output of digital files. Service bureaus typically form a link between desktop publishers—who compose a document or publication using *page makeup software* such as *QuarkXPress* or *PageMaker*—and printers, who require madeup pages on film for platemaking. Service bureaus typically take the digital files (so long as they're *PostScript*-compatible) and output them to film. Service bureaus may also handle high-end scanning and digital *color separation*. In contrast, trade shops commonly use a combination of manual page makeup processes and electronic prepress equipment to assemble film for printing.

Set

In typography, to create typographic-quality copy from an original manuscript or typescript.

Set is also used to refer to the overall appearance of copy that has been typeset, an evaluation based on the relative widths of the characters. See *Set Width*.

In database systems, a *set* is a collection of all of the records found during a search. The set can be displayed, printed, or saved to disk, and additionally analyzed, processed, etc.

In film, video, and television production, a *set* is the location where filming or taping takes place.

Set-Associative Cache

One particular type of *cache memory* used in computers. See *Cache Memory*.

Setback

In platemaking, the distance between the edge of the printing *plate* and the image area, used to indicate the amount of space available for the addition of the *plate clamp*s, as well as for the *gripper margin*.

Set-In

In *prepress*, an alternate term for *strip-in*. See *Strip-In*.

In *binding and finishing*, to position an *insert* toward the *binding edge* of a publication.

Setoff

See *Ink Setoff*.

Setoff Joint

In **binding and finishing**, a concealed cloth or muslin joint placed before the first **signature** and after the last signature, but without attaching it to the signatures. When eventually **casebound**, the setoff joints will allow the covers to be easily opened away from the signature.

Set Size

Alternate term for **set width**. See **Set Width**.

Set Solid

Descriptive of type set with **leading** equal to the **point size** (i.e., 12/12, 10/10, etc.) or, in other words, without any additional space between successive lines. One caveat about setting type solid is that the **descender**s of one line may touch—or appear to touch—the **ascender**s of the line beneath it. (See **Leading**.)

Setting

The first stage of the drying process of printing inks in which, although not fully dry, printed sheets can be picked up and handled without smudging.

Set-Top Box

A device that can be connected to a home television set to provide a variety of interactive services, such as reception of a **cable television network**, playing of a **CD-i** disc, reception of **interactive television**, or—in the not too distant future—browse the **World Wide Web**.

Setup String

In computing, a set of characters used in **control code**. See **Control Code**. Also known as an **escape sequence**.

Set Width

In typography, a concept applied to character width that is no longer universally applicable. All characters of a **typeface** can be output in a particular **point size**. The width of the characters increases as the size does; and the widths are programmed to relate to the size. Thus, a 9-pt. font has widths that are 9-set (width); 18 pt. is 18-set. Some faces are designed to be somewhat narrower; for example, 9-pt. on 8.5-set. Some typesetters allow you to change the set size by machine command. Actually, what changes is the space on either side of the character (its total width), but the actual width of the character itself does not change. Thus, 9-pt., 8-set actually tightens the character spacing. More appropriately, **negative letterspacing** commands, in either actual or relative unit values, are used to tighten up spacing (**white space reduction**).

The concept of set, however, is different as practiced by digitized typesetters and page makeup programs. Here, because characters are made up of dots, one can actually condense the width of a character electronically. A 9-pt. character can be output at various levels of condensation (or expansion). But here again, the use of the word *set* is not accurate. The characters are being condensed (or expanded)

in programmable increments (12% units or 1% units, for example).

720K

Abbreviation for a specific capacity of **floppy disk**, having a diameter of 3.5 in. See **Floppy Disk**.

Sewn Book

Any book or other publication that has been bound using thread to attach **signature**s together. See **Case Binding**.

Sewn-On Tape

Alternate term for **headband**. See **Headband**.

Sewn-Open Mouth (SOM)

In packaging, a type of paper **bag** in which the bottom is sewn shut prior to filling, leaving the top unsewn. After filling, the top is sealed by sewing or by other sealing means. See **Bag: Paper Bags**.

Sewn-Valve (SV)

In packaging, a type of paper **bag** in which the bottom and top are sewn shut prior to filling, filling itself being effected by means of a small valve located in the corner of the bag. See **Bag: Paper Bags**.

SGML

Abbreviation for **Standard Generalized Markup Language**. See **Standard Generalized Markup Language (SGML)**.

Shade

In printing ink terminology, an alternate term for **hue**, or the primary attribute of **color**, namely its dominant wavelength or place in the **visible spectrum**. Shade can also refer to the alteration of a color by adding small amounts of black ink.

Shaded

In typography, a **typeface** designed with a third dimension, such as a drop shadow or a drop outline. It lends itself to two-color display applications, since open areas inside letters may be printed in color.

Helvetica (top), Palatino (middle), and Tekton type (bottom) that have been stylized in QuarkXPress to have a drop shadow.

Shading

The process of altering the brightness and/or **color** of an image to simulate a third dimension.

Image processing technique that indicates light source in a three-dimensional display. Sensitivity changes of the electronic camera tube are used in image digitizing.

Techniques used to render an object, based on how light sources are positioned. It has also come to describe techniques used to render polygonal models, as:
• *Flat shading.* Facets of a polygonal model are rendered as a single color based on their orientation to the light and the viewer. The objects appear to have facets like a cut diamond.
• *Smooth shading.* Techniques that smooth over the facet edges, so the resulting object looks smooth.
• *Gouraud shading.* A smooth-shading technique that computes different colors at the corners of a polygon and then interpolates these colors across the surfaces.
• *Phong shading.* A smooth-shading technique that interpolates a surface normal over a polygon and then shades, generating highlights that behave more naturally than those produced by Gouraud shading.

Shadow

The darkest portion(s) of a print or an original. In *halftone*s, shadows have the largest dots. See also *Highlight* and *Middletones*.

Shaft Cylinder

One of two primary types of *gravure cylinder* in which the shafts (which are used to hold the cylinder in the press, engraving device, or elsewhere) are manufactured as part of the cylinder base. A shaft cylinder is more expensive than a *sleeve cylinder* (which requires shafts to be added),

A shaft cylinder, one of two varieties of gravure cylinder.

but the fact that the same shafts are used for every stage of the gravure engraving, preparation, and printing processes mitigates against decreased print quality caused by the compounding of shaft inaccuracies. (See also *Sleeve Cylinder*.) See *Gravure Cylinder*.

Shake

The side-to-side oscillation of a papermaking machine's forward-moving *forming wire* performed to aid in water removal from the forming paper *web* and in consistent fiber distribution. Shake is only used on slow-moving paper machines.

Shared Access

In networking, an access method in which several nodes share a single connection to the network. Two varieties of shared access are *contended access* and *explicit access*. See also *Discrete Access*.

Shared Whiteboard

In videoconferencing by means of *collaborative screen sharing*, a virtual white board or chalkboard, visible to and editable by all participants.

Sharpen

A process by which the printing size of *halftone dot*s is reduced and is often performed to reduce the effects of *dot gain*. On *color separation negative*s, sharpening is accomplished by means of *dot etching* or overexposure of the negative. On *positive working plate*s (printing plates prepared from film *positive*s), the sharpening effect tends to happen automatically, often referred to as negative dot gain.

Sharpen is also descriptive of an unwanted tendency for halftone dots to print smaller than those on the original, due to any of a wide variety of causes.

The term *sharpen* also means to increase and enhance the *contrast* around the edges of an image. (See *Sharpness*.)

Sharpness

An attribute of any image that describes the degree of clarity of the edge(s) of that image. Sharpness is applied to photographs, digital images, scans, proofs, line art, a computer video display, a printed reproduction, type characters, or any graphic image whatsoever. As the edge of an image is sharpened, detail increases, with an appearance that looks more "in focus." Too much sharpening, however, can diminish image quality. Image edge sharpness is increased—photographically or digitally—by means of *unsharp masking*. (See COLOR PLATE 24.)

Sharpness Filter

A tool in digital image manipulation programs to increase the *sharpness* of an image. See *Sharpness*.

Shave

To cut or trim a very small amount of paper from the edges of a bound book or blank stack of sheets.

Shear Adhesion

A measure of the extent to which a label or decal can be slid along a surface in a direction parallel to the surface.

Shear Thickening

Alternate term for the property of *dilatancy*, or a fluid's increase in *viscosity* with increasing shear force. See *Dilatancy*. (See also the opposite property, *Thixotropy*.)

Shear Thinning

Alternate term for the property of *thixotropy*, or a fluid's decrease in *viscosity* with increasing shear force. See *Thixotropy*. (See also the opposite property, *Dilatancy*.)

Sheet

An individual, rectangular piece of paper, as opposed to a continuous paper *web*, cut to a particular *standard size* or *odd size*.

The term *sheet* also refers to a metal **substrate** greater than 0.006 in. in thickness (a metal substrate thinner than 0.006 in. is called a **foil**), and any plastic or plasticized substrate with a thickness greater than 0.010 in. (A substrate with a thickness of less than 0.010 in. is called a **film**.)

Sheet Decurler

A device on some sheetfed printing presses (especially those used in **offset lithography**) located between the last **impression cylinder** and the **delivery pile** that works to remove the curl from press sheets. A typical sheet decurler consists of two rollers or semicircular plates over which the press sheet passes. As it passes over the nip of these two rollers (but not *through* it) a vacuum pulls down on the sheet, eliminating any curling tendencies on the part of the paper.

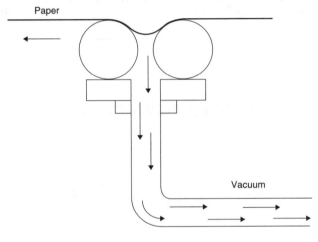

Sheet decurling.

Sheet Delamination
See **Delamination**.

Sheet Detector

A device mounted at the front end of the **feedboard** of a sheetfed printing press, used to detect paper arriving early or late, a condition that would cause improper positioning of the image on the paper. A sheet detector can be one of four types:

A mechanical sheet detector identifies late sheets, and consists of a moving pin which, when a sheet arrives at the **front guides** of the feedboard at the proper time, is prevented from entering a hole at the bottom of the feedboard. When a sheet is late, the pin enters the hole, causing the stoppage of the feeding mechanism.

An electromechanical sheet detector consists of a pair of open electrical contacts that are moved out of the way when paper arrives at the proper time. When the sheet is early, however, it hits the bottom contact, pushing it into the other contact. When the circuit is complete, the feeding action of the press stops.

A photoelectric sheet detector is timed to the front guides of the feedboard. One photoelectric cell is located

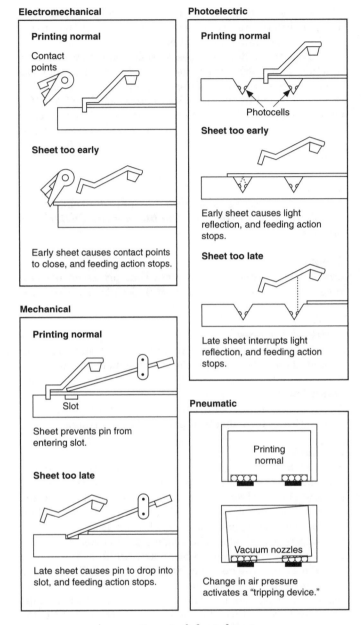

An assortment of sheet detectors.

beyond the front guides and detects early sheets. When an early sheet is not stopped by the front guides, it slides over the cell and causes an adjacent lamp to reflect into the cell, making an electrical contact and shutting off the feeder unit. A second photo cell located in front of the front guides has a lamp that turns on when the front guides are lowered. In normal printing operation, an on-time sheet reflects the light into the photocell, initiating an electrical contact. When a sheet is late, no contact is made, and the feeder unit shuts off.

A pneumatic sheet detector identifies sheets that arrive at the front guides crooked. A series of vacuum nozzles along the front guides is timed to the arrival of a sheet.

Whenever the air pressure between one set of nozzles and another differs (due to incorrect positioning of the sheet), the feeder mechanism is shut off.

All of the different types of sheet detectors can malfunction if they are not cleaned daily. In addition, they can be subject to wear due to abrasion from moving paper. They should be tested frequently. (See *Feeder Section: Sheetfed Offset Lithography* and *Feedboard*.) A different type of sheet detector, located earlier in the feeder section, detects more than one sheet being fed at once. (See *Double-Sheet Detector*.)

Sheeter

A device used to cut a paper *web* into individual sheets. See *Single Rotary Cutter* and *Double Rotary Cutter*, and *Sheeting*.

Sheetfed

Descriptive of any printing press that prints on discrete sheets of paper (or other *substrate*). See also *webfed*. Also spelled with a hyphen, *sheet-fed*.

Sheetfed Scanner

A type of *scanner* that automatically feeds originals (mounted on rolls) through the imaging mechanism.

Sheet Feeder

An auxiliary device added to a computer printer used to automatically feed sheets of paper into the printer.

Sheeting

A paper *finishing* operation that involves the cutting of manufactured paper rolls into individual sheets, typically performed on a *sheeter*. A sheeter consists of a backstand, where the paper roll is held, a *single rotary cutter* or *double rotary cutter*, and a layboy, which is used for stacking and jogging cut sheets. The single rotary cutter has a stationary bed knife contacted by another knife mounted on a rotating cylinder. The paper *web* is cut when the rotating knife contacts the stationary knife. A double rotary cutter replaces the stationary knife with a second rotating knife. The speed with which the rotating knife turns is adjusted relative to the speed of the paper web moving through the blades to produce the specified sheet size. Variations include *multiple roll sheeting*, which runs more than one roll through the sheeter at once, saving time. Sheeted paper then undergoes *trimming* so that the sheet size is exact. New processes such as *precision sheeting* utilize more accurate sheeters in order to make additional trimming unnecessary.

The term *sheeting* also refers to a *substrate* (in particular a *film*) with a thickness of more than 0.010 in. Also called a *sheet*.

Sheet Label

A *label* that comes on an individual sheet, rather than a long continuous roll.

Sheet Photopolymer

One of two types of *photopolymer* plates used in *flexography*, in contrast to a *liquid photopolymer*.

A photopolymer plate is supplied in a variety of thicknesses, depending upon the *plate cylinder* undercut. Both sides of the plate are sensitive to ultraviolet light. Before exposing the image to the plate, the "back" side is exposed to UV light, which hardens the material, allowing it to be suitable as the base of the plate. Variations in the power of the UV lamp used (which declines over time) and variations in photosensitivity among different batches of plate material require the careful determination of proper exposure time. Test strips of plate material can be exposed beforehand, as a means of gauging the correct dose of UV light needed to cure a strong backing and provide the necessary relief depth. The plate is turned over, and a negative of the image to be printed is placed on top of it. Occasionally,

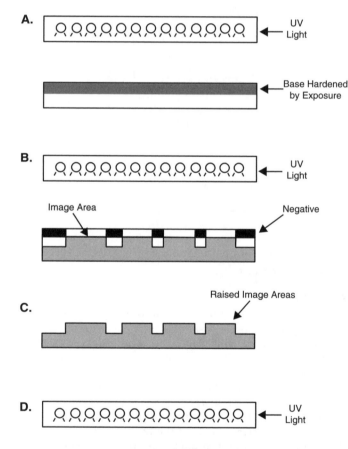

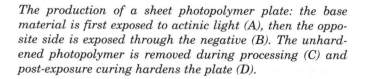

The production of a sheet photopolymer plate: the base material is first exposed to actinic light (A), then the opposite side is exposed through the negative (B). The unhardened photopolymer is removed during processing (C) and post-exposure curing hardens the plate (D).

bleeder strips (made of foil or plastic) are placed over the areas of the plate that exceed the dimensions of the negative. A second dose of UV light only exposes the photopolymer in the image areas, which renders them hard and insoluble. The amount of exposure varies according to the nature of the image to be exposed; halftone screens and fine type require more exposure to bring out detail than do solids. After exposure, the plate is washed to remove the unhardened polymeric material, leaving the exposed image areas in relief on the plate surface. As with exposure time, the required degree of washing may vary. Too little washing results in a relief image that is not well pronounced, as well as an uneven "floor" (the unraised portions of the plate) and scum produced by residual polymeric material. Too *much* washing, however, can produce damaged and missing type, a loss of detail, as well as plate swelling and uneven surface characteristics.

After washing, the plates may appear swollen, as a result of the flexible material absorbing some of the processing solvent. Drying the plates in an oven after washing removes excess solvent and provides clean, sharp images. A post-exposure of UV light ensures that the floor of the plate is effectively cured and hardened, and a variety of finishing techniques—including chemical treatment with solutions of chlorine, bromine, or iodine, additional exposure to high-energy UV lamps, or spraying or dusting with a variety of powders—can remove any additional tackiness of the plate surface.

See also *Liquid Photopolymer*, *Plate: Flexography*, *Photopolymer*, and *Flexography*.

Sheet-Separation Unit

A device located in the *feeder section* of a sheetfed offset press that is responsible for ensuring that only one sheet is fed into the press at any one time. A sheet-separation unit varies slightly in configuration, depending upon whether a press uses a *stream feeder* or a *single-sheet feeder*.

In a stream feeder, the *pile table*, which holds the pile of paper (or other *substrate* to be fed), raises the pile of sheets to the proper feeding height. *Air-blast nozzles* on the sheet-separation unit blow jets of air at the pile, raising the top half dozen or so sheets. At that point, a set of *pickup suckers* at the rear of the pile use a vacuum to lift the top sheet, after which a *feeder foot* at the rear of the pile drops onto the remaining pile. The nozzles (either on the feeder foot or attached elsewhere) then blow air underneath the raised sheet, keeping it from dropping back down on the pile. A set of vacuum-powered *forwarding suckers* toward the front of the pile then lift the sheet and send it toward the *forwarding rollers* and onto the *feedboard*. As the forwarding suckers move the top sheet away, the second sheet is lifted by the rear pickup suckers, and begins its journey toward the feedboard.

When a stream feeder is being used, successive sheets overlap each other somewhat. Sets of *separator brush*es, *separator finger*s, and guides contribute to accurate sheet separation.

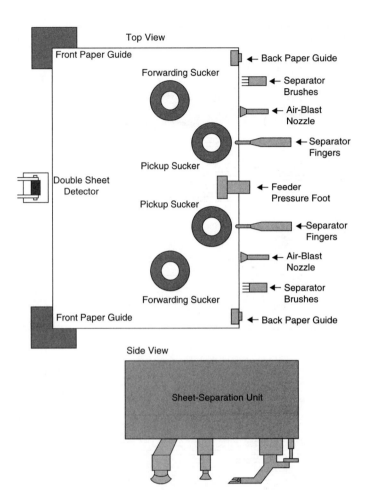

The sheet-separation unit.

Pile height is an important factor in proper sheet separation. A pile that is too high may end up feeding through two or more sheets at once, while a pile that is too low may result in no sheets being fed. Adjusting the weight of the feeder foot, moving the sheet-separation unit up or down, or tilting it, are means of adjusting the height of the paper pile. Some units lack the feeder foot.

The positioning of sheet steadiers is important. Sheet steadiers should be located on the rear of the pile, one located one-quarter of the length of the paper from the right

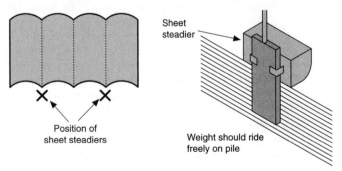

Positioning sheet steadiers.

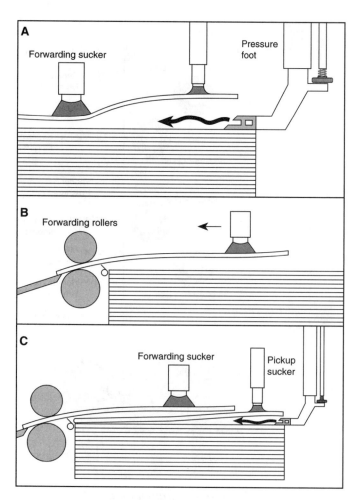

Basic principle of sheet separation on a stream feeder. After the air-blast nozzles separates the top sheets of the pile and the rear pickup suckers lift the top sheet, the pressure foot blows air beneath the top sheet so that forwarding suckers can pick it up (A), forwarding suckers transfer the sheet to forwarding rollers (B), and the rear pickup suckers, pressure foot, and forwarding suckers work together to feed a stream of sheets (C).

margin, the other one-quarter of the length of the paper from the left margin. The weight should rest freely on the top of pile and should neither exert too much or too little pressure. Separator brushes or fingers should be located at the rear of the pile, about 3/16 in. from the back of the pile and either just touching the top of the stack or at most 1/16 in. above it. However, the thickness of the paper will determine the best location of the steadiers, brushes, and fingers. The force of the vacuum used in the suckers is also determined by the thickness of the stock, and the suckers are frequently adjusted so that they tilt up slightly when grabbing a sheet, lifting the rear edge of the sheet, allowing air to blow underneath it, enhancing the separation efficiency. The row of suckers should be perfectly parallel to the pile and should not be more than 3/16 in. nor less than 1/16 in. from the top of the pile. The air nozzles should be

adjusted so that they initially lift no more than 10 and no less than 5 sheets from the pile. Once the topmost sheet has been lifted by the suckers, the air nozzle should effectively provide a cushion of air that lifts the gripper (or front) edge of the sheet.

On a single-sheet feeder, the arrangement is similar, except that one set of pickup suckers are located at the gripper (or front) edge of the pile. Air lifts the top 6–10 sheets, and the suckers pick up the top sheet, transferring it to a set of wheels or rollers at the rear of the feedboard. (See ***Feeder Section***.)

Sheetwise

Descriptive of a means of printing both sides of a sheet of paper in which one side is printed, then the printed sheets are turned over and printed with another plate, the sheets retaining the same ***gripper edge*** and side guide.

Sheet Work

A general term referring to all ***binding and finishing*** operations. See ***Binding and Finishing***.

Sheffield Porosimeter

A device used to measure the ***porosity*** of a paper by measuring the rate of the flow of air through a paper sample. The device forces air up through an adjustable orifice and through the paper, past a gauging head that measures how fast the air is moving once it comes out of the paper. The orifice can be adjusted, depending on the density of the paper to be tested. (See also ***Densometer***.)

Sheffield Smoothness Gauge

A type of ***air leak tester***, an instrument that is used to determine the ***smoothness*** of a paper surface, in which air at a specified pressure is pumped through a smooth glass column and seeps between a groove in the device's gauge head and the surface of the paper sample. An air-suspended metering float in the glass column moves up or down, the level of the float in the column indicating the rate of airflow and is thus a measure of the paper's smoothness. See also ***Smoothness***.

Shell

In ***binding and finishing***, an alternate term for a ***slip case***. See ***Slip Case***.

In computing, a *shell* is an outer "layer" of a program, or the interface between the user and the ***operating system***. The shell's purpose is to simplify user-computer communications, in particular to allow the user to switch between or among applications without having to close an open application.

Shellac

A type of ***resin*** or ***varnish*** produced by dissolving lac in an alcohol or other ***solvent***. Lac is a resinous material excreted by the lac insect (*Laccifer lacca*, a member of the order Homoptera and related to the aphid) and found encrusting the branches of various southern Asian trees (most commonly *Croton laccifera*). Shellac is widely used as a resin in the manufacture of *flexographic* inks.

Shell Back

In *binding and finishing*, a type of book binding in which a tube-like piece of *kraft* paper is inserted between the *spine* of the *book block* and the case. The result is a book that opens more freely than a conventional *casebound* book.

Shielded Twisted-Pair

A type of *twisted-pair wiring* comprising two insulated pairs of cables, each pair containing two individual wires twisted around each other. See *Twisted-Pair Wiring* and *Unshielded Twisted-Pair*. Shielded twisted-pair is usually abbreviated *STP*.

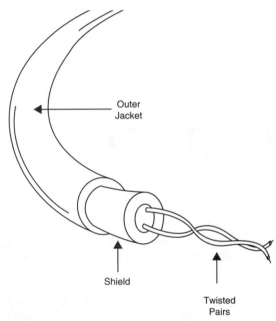

Structure of shielded twisted pair cabling.

Shielding

In computing, any metal casing installed around electronic devices or components used to isolate electromagnetic fields that may interfere with other devices or components.

Shift

In typography, a function on typewriters, typesetters, and computer keyboards used to generate an *uppercase* character. The term derives from the days of *hot-metal* typesetters when the shift key "shifted" the font-matrix sorting mechanism to a position that could access uppercase characters.

In spreadsheet or other data programs, *shift* means to move all characters in a row or column en masse to an adjacent row or column.

Shilling

Alternate term for a *slash*. See *Slash*.

Shilling Fraction

In typography, a *fraction* typeset by simply using standard numerals, separated by a shilling mark (or slash, /). Also called *fake fraction*s or *adaptable fraction*s. See *Fractions*.

Shingling

A means of positioning type in books, magazines, newsletters, or other publications designed to be bound by means of *saddle-stitching* that compensates for *creep*, an increasing book thickness through the interior of the publication, by progressively narrowing the *bind margin* from the outside pages to the center pages, and increasing the bind margin from the center pages to the back pages. Shingling is performed so that text appears to be in the same position on all pages. See *Saddle-Stitching* and *Creep* (third definition).

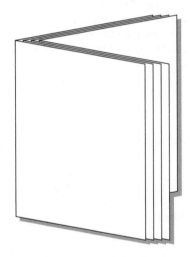

The effects of creep on saddle-stitched publications.

Shipping-Sack Kraft

In packaging, a type of strong *kraft* paper used in the manufacture of paper bags used for shipping. See *Kraft* and *Bag: Paper Bags*.

Shives

Bundles of *cellulose* fiber that were not adequately separated from each other during *mechanical pulping* or torn whole from the log during grinding. Shives are also bundles of fibers not completely digested during *chemical pulping*. (See *Pulping*.)

Shoot

In photography or videography, to capture an image on film or videotape by means of a *camera*. When used as a noun, *shoot* refers to any photography or videography session, usually one "on-location."

Shooting Ratio

In film and video production, the ratio of the total *footage* filmed or taped to that actually used in the final production.

Short

Descriptive of *short ink*. See *Short Ink*.

In printing, descriptive of any quantity of printed materials that is less than what was specified in the original order. Characteristic of an *underrun*.

In motion picture or video production, a *short* is any production with a running time of one to thirty minutes. Any production with a running time greater than 60 minutes is known as a *feature*.

Shortcut

See *Keyboard Shortcut*.

Short-Dwell Coater

A type of *blade coater*, a device used to apply a *coating* to a paper surface, utilized primarily for the high-speed coating of lightweight papers. Coating is deposited on the moving paper *web* through a slot, and a metering blade immediately smooths out the coating, filling in the "valleys" in the paper surface. (See *Coating* and *Blade Coater*.)

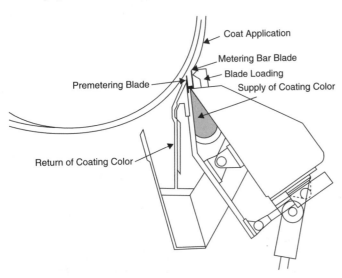

Short-dwell coater.

Short-Grain

Also called *grain-short*, term for a sheet of paper having its *grain* direction parallel to the shorter sheet dimension. (Paper with its grain direction parallel to the longer dimen-

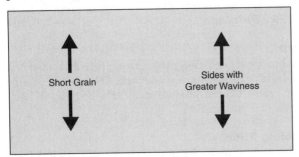

Short-grain paper.

sion of the sheet is called *long-grain*.) Whether a paper is long-grain or short-grain paper is an important consideration in many printing processes, as the grain direction affects *printability* and *runnability*, especially in connection with sheet strength and *dimensional stability*. See *Grain*.

Short Ink

A printing ink characterized by a limited ability to flow and to form short threads when stretched, in contrast to *long ink*. Ink that is short has poor flow characteristics and tends to not perform well on the press. Ink that is excessively short has a tendency to result in *piling* on the ink rollers, plate, or blanket. (See *Length*.)

Shot

In photography, any exposure made on a camera.

Shoulder

In typography, a curved stroke forming part of a letter, such as that of the letters "h," "m," or "n". See *Letter Elements*.

Shoulder.

Shower-Door Effect

A defect of video that has been compressed with a *lossy* compression algorithm, characterized by portions of the image that are in motion and portions that are not. In essence, the picture looks as if it were being viewed through multifaceted glass, such as one would find on shower doors. The shower-door effect tends to worsen as the *compression ratio* increases.

Showing

A display of samples of the *font*s and other *ornament*s available from a system or type foundry. Also called a typographic specimen, a type showing presents all or some of the characters in a font to visually demonstrate the look and color of the typeface on paper.

Show Reel

A collection of films or videos produced by an individual or a studio used as an example of a person's or studio's work.

Show-Through

The visibility of printing on the reverse side of a sheet of paper under normal lighting conditions. Show-through is typically a function of a paper's *opacity*, while show-through resulting from increased ink absorption and penetration through the paper is referred to as *strike-through*.

Shrink

Alternate term for *compress*. See *Compress*.

Shrink Band

In packaging, a plastic film—commonly printed—that is placed around a product or container and, with the application of heat, shrinks around the product. Shrink bands are used as identifying labels, tamper-evident seals, decorative ornaments (as in the plastic or plasticized foil covering the cork on wine bottles), or promotional devices. Shrink bands can be placed around only the neck of a container (as a bottle) or around the bulk of the product or container itself. Shrink bands are also used to attach other items to a product, or to join two products together as in the case of "buy one, get one free" offers.

Shrunk Negative

Alternate term for a *choke*. See *Spreads and Chokes*.

Shutter

In photography, a device located either in front of or behind a camera lens that allows or impedes the passage of light into the camera. The shutter remains closed most of the time, and the camera operator, when the time comes to take a photograph, clicks the shutter button (or other means of control) that opens the shutter for a set period of time (called the *exposure time*). The amount of time the shutter stays open (which can range from some fraction of a second in 35-mm cameras to several minutes in process cameras) is known as the *shutter speed*.

Shutter Speed

In photography, the amount of time that a camera's *shutter* remains open, exposing the film. See *Exposure Time* and *Photography*.

SHW

A *file extension* denoting a slide show file created by Harvard Graphics.

Siccative

Any substance that hastens or promotes the drying of another substance, as an ink *drier*. See *Drier*.

Sidebar

In graphics and page layout, text and/or graphics set off from the primary text to impart additional or peripheral information. Sidebars can be set off using *rule lines*, *borders*, or *screen tints*. Sidebars may also be typeset using a different *font* than the main text.

Side Bearing

In typography, a measure of the white space between the side of a character and the edge of its *em square*, or the space separating one character from the next. The *first side bearing* refers to the left side, and the *second side bearing* refers to the right side.

Side Guide

One of several devices attached to the *feedboard* of a sheetfed printing press that, in tandem with a *registration plate*, aids in laterally positioning a sheet of paper before transfer into the printing unit. A side guide can comprise either a roller, a pivoting foot, or a suction-powered plate. See *Feedboard*.

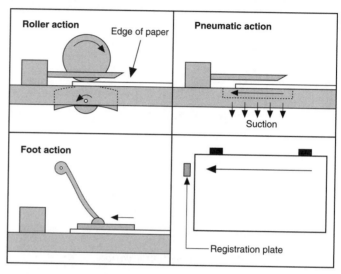

Side guiding methods: roller action (upper left), pneumatic action (upper right), and foot action (lower left). All three pull the sheet against a registration plate (lower right).

Sidehead

In typography, a *head* set on a line by itself (i.e., not *run-in* with the text) and *flush* with the margin.

Sidelay

In *web printing*, the lateral placement of a paper web as it travels through the printing unit and subsequent *in-line* folding devices.

Side Notes

Alternate term for *marginal notes*. See *Marginal Notes*.

Side Roll Stand

In *web printing*, a *roll stand* located to the side of the printing press rather than directly behind it. Side roll stands are used in cases where the pressroom is not large enough to allow an in-line roll stand. The paper web is guided into the printing unit by angle guides. See *Roll Stand* and *Web Offset Lithography: Infeed and Web Control*.

Side Sewing

In *binding and finishing*, a type of *thread sewing* in which thread is driven through the sides of printed *signatures* parallel to the binding edge, as opposed to *saddle sewing*. See *Case Binding*. Also spelled as one word, *sidesewing*, or hyphenated, *side-sewing*.

Side-Stitching

In **binding and finishing**, a means of joining pages together by driving thin metal wire (i.e., staples) through the cover of a publication along the binding edge. Side-stitching is similar to, but less often performed than, **saddle-stitching**. Publications that are side-stitched do not lay flat when opened. Also spelled as one word, *sidestitching*, or as two separate words, *side stitching*. See **Saddle-Stitching**.

A side-stitched publication.

Sideweld Seal

In packaging, a means of manufacturing plastic **bag**s. See **Bag: Plastic Bags**.

Signal Generator

A device—commonly comprising a revolving disk etched with thin lines—found inside a **scanner** or other imaging device that produces an electronic pulse that controls the rate at which a sample is taken of an original image. The fine lines on the disk allow the repeated passage of a light beam that, when striking a photocell, instructs the device to take a sample.

Signal Quality Error

Alternate term for a **heartbeat**. Abbreviated **SQE**. See **Heartbeat**.

Signal-to-Noise Ratio

In any electronic device, the ratio of a valid and desired data signal to unwanted signals, such as optical and electrical disturbances or static.

Signature

In printing and publishing, any single press sheet on which multiple pages have been imposed which, when folded and cut, forms a group of pages. Most books and other publications are printed as groups of signatures, the multiple **imposition** allowing a significant reduction in the number of independent pressruns required to print all pages. The number of pages that are imposed on a single signature varies by publication and by press size. Some common sig-

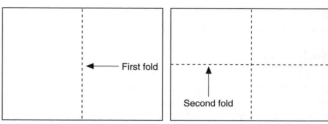

Folio format: sheet folded once   Quarto format: sheet folded twice

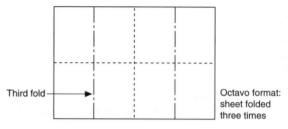

Folio, quarto, and octavo signature formats. A folio has four pages (two on each side), a quarto has eight pages (four on each side), and an octavo has sixteen pages (eight on each side).

nature sizes include **broadside**, **folio**, **quarto**, **octavo**, **sixteenmo**, and **thirty-twomo**. (See **Book Typography** and **Imposition**.)

Sign On

Alternate term for **login**. See **Login**.

Silhouette

Generally speaking, an outline or profile of a shape or object, commonly filled with a solid **color** (such as black).

A **silhouette halftone** is a portion of a **halftone** image that has been outlined and separated from the surrounding image areas by removing the dots that surround it.

In digital imaging, in particular on **color electronic publishing systems**, *silhouette* refers to a function that allows the isolation of a particular area of an image for **local correction** or other image manipulation. Silhouettes can be created on these systems when the desired area differs significantly in **density** from the surrounding image areas.

Silhouette Halftone

A means of **halftone** reproduction in which a specific portion of the image is outlined (or silhouetted) by removing the **halftone dot**s that surround it. (See illustration on facing page.) Also known as an **outline halftone**.

Silicone

Any of a variety of fluid, resinous, and/or rubbery **polymer**s composed of alternating silicon and oxygen atoms, having a wide variety of uses, such as in adhesives, lubricants, insulation, and cosmetics. Silicone is also used as an additive in printing inks to increase **flow out**.

A silhouetted halftone (left) and the original image (right).

Silicone Applicator

In **web printing**, an auxiliary device used to apply a thin layer of silicone and water to the printed web, as a means of preventing ink smearing, as well as of adding moisture as an aid to **folding**.

Silkscreening

An obsolete term for **screen printing**. See **Screen Printing**.

Silkscreen Printing

An obsolete for **screen printing**. See **Screen Printing**.

Silver Halide Plate

A type of printing plate used in **offset lithography** that utilizes a film- or metal-based plate coated with a silver halide emulsion (similar to that used in photographic film) to allow transfer of the image to be printed to the surface of the plate. Silver halide plates can be exposed using photographic negatives, which are brought into contact with the surface of the plate and then exposed to light, which only exposes the plate surface in the image areas. After exposure, the plate needs to be developed. Unlike some other types of plates that can be developed in regular, ambient light, silver halide plates are sensitive to blue light, so developing of the plates needs to be performed in a darkroom equipped with yellow-filtered light. Newer varieties of silver halide plates allow exposure to be performed by lasers, allowing direct computer-to-plate platemaking. A drawback to silver halide plates involves their processing chemicals, which contain heavy metals (in particular, silver) which, due to pollution regulations, need to be specially treated or sent to special treatment plants. Silver halide plates used for monocolored forms and other documents are film-based, while those used for color printing (either spot color or process color) are aluminum-based and are commonly exposed using digital information. (See **Plate: Offset Lithography**.)

Silver Ink

A shade of metallic ink that is produced by mixing flakes of aluminum with a **varnish**, used in inks designed to impart a metallic luster to the printed image. See also **Metallic Powders**.

Silverprint

Alternate term for **blueline**. See **Blueline**.

SIMM

Abbreviation for **single in-line memory module**, or a module that is added to a computer to increase the amount of **random-access memory (RAM)**. See **Single In-Line Memory Module (SIMM)**.

Simplex

The printing of an image on only one side of a sheet of paper. See also **Duplex** (first definition). Operators of office copiers use the terms simplexed and duplexed, where printing press operators use the terms singled-sided or perfected.

In telecommunications, *simplex* is used to refer to a circuit that can only transmit data in one direction, such as a television. See also **Duplex** (fourth definition).

Simplex Decal

A **decal** that has been printed (typically by **screen printing**) on a water-absorbent paper and coated on its face with a water-soluble adhesive. Upon immersion in water, the decal is released from the paper backing and can be slid onto the desired surface. Common examples of simplex decals are the decals that come as part of model airplane kits. Also called **slide-off decal**, **water slide-off decal**, and **water-slide transfer**.

Simplex Tipping Machine

In **binding and finishing**, a machine used for **tip-on**s.

Simulation

An **interactive** computer presentation or model designed to imitate a real object or environment. Essentially, a simulation is a mathematical description of an object or situation that uses further mathematical computations to evaluate changes to the object or situation. Examples of simulations include flight simulators that use elaborate graphics and sound to train pilots (some are so effective that they even spawn a very real phenomenon known as **simulation sickness**). **Virtual reality** is also a kind of simulation.

Simulation Sickness

Any sickness that occurs as the result of working with some types of **simulation**s, such as flight simulators, which can produce effects not unlike air sickness.

Simulator

A device or computer program designed to simulate reality, either for training or entertainment purposes (such as a flight simulator). See **Simulation**.

Simultaneous Contrast

In **color**, any changes in the appearance of a color relative to the background or to any adjacent colors. (See COLOR PLATE 18.)

Simultaneous Peripheral Operations On-Line (Spool)

See **Spool** and **Spooler**.

Single-Drum Transfer

A method of transferring sheets from one printing unit to another on a sheetfed press (especially that used in *offset lithography*) in which a large-diameter *transfer cylinder* carries the printed sheet from one *impression cylinder* to the next. The actual size of the transfer cylinder varies according to press design, and the transfer cylinder may be designed to hold one or more sheets at any one time. The transfer cylinder typically possesses one of a variety of devices or means to avoid marking or smudging wet ink, and it may contain a *gripper-bowing device*. It may also be an *air-transport drum*. (See also *Air-Transport Drum*, *Chain Transfer*, *Three-Drum Transfer*, and *Transfer Cylinder*.)

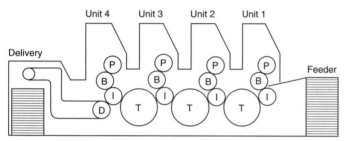

P	Plate cylinder	**Note:** For clarity, the inking and
B	Blanket cylinder	dampening systems are not shown.
D	Delivery cylinder	
I	Impression cylinder	
T	Transfer cylinder	

A printing press with a single-drum transfer system.

Single-End

A *flatbed press* containing only a single plate or typeform, thus allowing printing on only one side of a sheet.

Single-Frame Controller (SFC)

In video production, an electronic device used to control a video recorder (specifically a *single-frame recorder*). Often used for computer animations, the system processes a single image (frame) and records it onto the tape. The SFC keeps the tape accurately positioned by means of a *time code*.

Single-Frame Recorder

A video recorder that can record a single *frame* at a time, usually in conjunction with a *single-frame controller*. See *Single-Frame Controller (SFC)*.

Single In-Line Memory Module (SIMM)

A semiconductor memory module that is added to a computer to increase its amount of *random-access memory (RAM)*. A single SIMM contains several memory chips, usually rows of eight or nine individual chips, each with a capacity of 256 kilobits, 1 megabit, or 4 megabits. SIMMs are mounted to the computer's motherboard and are usually used on *Macintosh* desktop computers. Newer Macs utilize *double in-line memory modules*, also known as

*DIMM*s. A SIMM is much like a *single in-line package*, save that the SIMM plugs into the motherboard by means of a contact slot.

Single In-Line Package (SIP)

A semiconductor memory module that is added to a computer to increase its amount of *random-access memory (RAM)*. A single SIP contains several memory chips, usually rows of eight or nine individual chips, each with a capacity of 256 kilobits, 1 megabit, or 4 megabits. SIPs are mounted to the computer's motherboard by means of pin connectors, unlike SIMMs that connect by means of a contact slot.

Single-Lens Reflex Camera

A type of camera that lacks a separate veiwfinder, a mirror arrangement being used to cast the image coming through the lens *aperture* up to the eyepiece. Such cameras allow the photographer to see exactly how the image is likely to appear on the film, at least as far as focusing is concerned. Usually abbreviated *SLR*.

Single-Ply

Descriptive of any paper that comprises only a single layer. *Single-ply* is also used to refer to any plastic film consisting of only a single sheet.

Single-Ply Bag

In packaging, a paper *bag* formed from a single *ply* or layer of paper. See *Bag: Paper Bags*.

Single-Positive System

Alternate term for the *direct-transfer process* of *gravure engraving*. See *Gravure Engraving: Direct-Transfer Process*.

Single-Roll Stand

In *web printing*, a *roll stand* that holds only one roll of paper (or other *substrate*) at a time. See *Roll Stand*. See also *Double-Roll Stand*.

Single Rotary Cutter

A device used in the *sheeting* of paper rolls consisting of a rotating knife contacting a fixed knife, which cuts the paper *web* moving between them. The speed of the web and of the rotating knife determine the sheet size. Sheeting is also performed on a *double rotary cutter*. (See *Sheeting*.)

Single Screen

In presentation graphics, a type of presentation in which all images are projected (and often superimposed) on the same screen area.

Single-Session

In *CD-ROM* recording, descriptive of the inability to write data to a disc in more than one session, symptomatic of early *CD-R* devices. Newer devices are capable of *multisession* recording. See *Compact Disc (CD)*.

Single-Sheet Color Proof

One of two basic types of **color proof** used to check the **registration** of the colors, the existence of any egregious blemishes or other undesirable marks, and to confirm size and position of page elements. Single-sheet color proofs—unlike **overlay color proofs**—are generated on a single sheet of **substrate** using special toner, dye, or other type of colorant. Some common types of single-sheet color proof, named for the proprietary materials used to produce them, are **Cromalin** and **Matchprint**.

Single-Sheet Feeder

One of two basic types of systems used to feed sheets of paper into a sheetfed offset printing press (in contrast to a **stream feeder**). A single-sheet feeder feeds paper into the press at a speed equal to that of the press itself, which provides less sheet control than that obtained when using a slower stream feeder. As its name indicates, a single-sheet feeder feeds one sheet at a time, the first sheet completely clearing the **pile table** before the next sheet is pulled from the pile. (A single-sheet feeder is also known as a *successive sheet feeder*.) The configuration of a single-sheet feeder is basically the same as that described in **Feeding Section: Sheetfed Offset Lithography** and is thus very similar to a stream feeder. However, there are some differences in the configuration of the pile table and the **sheet-separation unit**. In contrast to a stream feeder, sheet separation on a

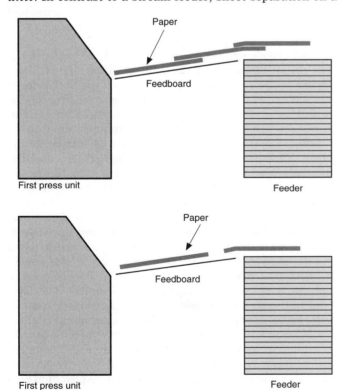

A stream feeder (top) and a single-sheet feeder (bottom). Notice the overlap of press sheets on the feedboard of the stream feeder.

single-sheet feeder typically occurs at the front (or **gripper**) edge of the sheet, rather than at the rear. Consequently, rear guides on the pile table are oriented somewhat differently. When utilizing a single-sheet feeder, the **double-sheet detector** (a device that determines and shuts off the feeder when an increased thickness of paper is passing beneath it) needs to be set differently than that used with a stream feeder. (See also **Stream Feeder**.)

Single-Speed (1X)

Descriptive of a **CD-ROM** drive capable of reading and transferring data at a speed of 150 **kilobyte**s per second. This was the original speed of the first generation of CD-ROM drives, only designated "single-speed" after successive generations. A **double-speed (2X)** CD-ROM drive can thus process data at a speed of 300 kilobytes per second. Later triple-speed drives process data at a speed of 450 kilobytes per second. Newer drives have even faster access times: 600 kilobytes per second (**quad speed**, or 4X, drives), 900 kilobytes per second (6X drives), 1200 kilobytes per second (8X drives), and 1500 kilobytes per second (10X drives).

There is no doubt that the speed of CD-ROM drives will increase, perhaps to 20X speeds. However, the advent of DVD (digital versatile disk) technology at 12X speeds will wean users away from CD-ROMs.

Sink

In typography, abbreviated term for **sinkage**. See **Sinkage**.

In computing, the receiving station of a data transmission or electrical connection.

Sinkage

A printing defect characterized by a blotchy appearance or **mottle** in a printed ink film, caused by an excessive penetration of an ink into a porous **substrate**.

In typography, *sinkage* refers to an amount of additional white space on a page above chapter, part, or section titles, which is greater than that allowed at the tops of most of the other text pages in the book. Also referred to as **sink**.

SIP

Abbreviation for **single in-line package**. See **Single In-Line Package (SIP)**.

Sisal Hemp

A plant (*Agave sisalana*) native to tropical America and Africa used primarily for rope but also as a fibrous source for papermaking.

Sixteen-Bit (16-Bit)

Descriptive of computer systems (especially **microprocessors**) and software that process data as 2-**byte** units (one byte equals 8 **bit**s). The greater the number of bytes that a system can process at any one time, the faster the system. The Intel 8086/8088 and 80286 were 16-bit processors. See also **Thirty-Two-Bit (32-Bit)** and **Sixty-Four-Bit (64-Bit)**.

Sixteen-Bit (16-Bit) Color

On a computer monitor, a color display in which each *pixel* (or smallest point of *color*) is described by 16 bits of information. (One *bit* is either a 1 or a 0; 16-bit color can be thought of as one of these two numbers taken to the sixteenth power; thus 2^{16} = 65,536 possible colors.) The color of a pixel on a computer display is commonly expressed as some amount of *red, green, and blue*. Greater numbers of combinations of these amounts require more processing power on the part of the computer. At 16 bits per pixel, a total of 65,536 colors (commonly referred to simply as "thousands of colors") can be described and displayed. This color depth is greater than the standard and/or required setting for many CD-ROMs and multimedia programs (which usually have difficulty handling greater than *eight-bit color*), but it is usually insufficient for high-quality graphic arts reproduction. See also *Eight-Bit Color*, *Twenty-Four-Bit Color*, and *Thirty-Two-Bit Color*. Computer monitors can also display *one-bit color* (black and white, or any two colors) and *four-bit color* (16 colors).

Sixteenmo

In *book typography* and production, any printed sheet that has been folded four times to yield sixteen leaves or thirty-two pages. Also called *sextodecimo*, and abbreviated *16-mo* or *16°*. *Sixteenmo* is also used to refer to the book size produced by folding pages in this manner (commonly 4×6 in.).

Sixty-Four-Bit (64-Bit)

Descriptive of computer systems (especially *microprocessors*) and software that process data as 8-*byte* units (one byte equals 8 *bit*s). The greater the number of bytes that a system can process at any one time, the faster the system. The Intel *Pentium* and DEC *Alpha AXP* chips are 64-bit processors. See also *Sixteen-Bit (16-Bit)* and *Thirty-Two-Bit (32-Bit)*.

Size

In papermaking, an alternate term for *sizing*. See *Sizing*.

In ink manufacturing, *size* is an ink that retains a considerable degree of *tack*, or stickiness, after it has dried, allowing for the application of *metallic powder* (or other types of powders) to provide an additional metallic luster to the printing (a process called *bronze dusting*).

In *binding and finishing*, *size* is a mixture (often containing *albumen*) that is used in *gilding* or *foil stamping* to facilitate the adhesion of the *gold leaf* to the book cover.

Size Press

A set of two rollers located near the end of a papermaking machine's *drying section* used to apply *surface sizing* to paper. As the partially dried paper *web* travels through the nip of these rollers, a starch solution coats the surface of the paper. Surface sizing is added as a paper fiber sealant, which improves sheet strength and resistance to a variety of stresses. Other materials may be used in addition to or instead of a starch solution to impart different surface sizing characteristics, such as increased resistance to water, ink, oils, or grease.

Sizing

The application of various materials either to wet paper *pulp* (called *internal sizing*) or to the surface of partially dried finished paper (called *surface sizing*) to provide a desired degree of resistance to water or other fluids and to increase surface strength. Papers that are unsized (called *waterleaf*) readily absorb moisture and are used for towel, tissue, and blotting papers. Internal sizing typically consists of an acid- or alkaline-based *rosin* and papermaker's *alum* (used to help the sizing adhere to the paper fibers) added to the papermaking *furnish* during the *stock preparation* phase prior to its reaching the *forming wire* of the papermaking machine. (Sizing that is added during the *refining* stage is sometimes called *beater sizing*, after the vessel—the *beater*—in which the process occurs.) Internal sizing does not make a paper waterproof, or increase its wet strength, but it does hinder the penetration of water through the paper and contributes greater *dimensional stability* to the paper. *Slack-sized* paper has a minimal amount of internal sizing, while *hard-sized* paper has a greater degree of internal sizing. Hard-sizing is used for papers that must withstand repeated exposure to offset press dampening systems without absorbing significant levels of moisture. Sizing is also added to prevent glues and other adhesives from penetrating the paper when applied to labels and packaging.

Surface sizing is added to partially dried paper on the *size press*, located near the end of the paper machine's *drying section*. Surface sizing typically consists of a starch solution added to the surface of the paper *web* by rollers. Surface sizing is typically applied as a surface fiber sealant, improving strength and stress resistances, as well as impeding the penetration of ink far into the surface of the paper. Variations in the surface-sizing process and the materials used confer different advantages on the paper, such as increased water resistance and the ability to repel grease, oil, or other substances.

The use and degree of both internal and surface sizing varies according to paper type and the desired characteristics. Papers used in *offset lithography*, as well as bond and writing papers, and *cover*, *index*, and *bristol* papers are both internally and externally sized. Papers used in high-speed *web offset lithography* are usually not surface-sized but may be internally sized, while papers used in *letterpress* printing do not need to be sized at all.

Measures of the degree of sizing are related to tests to determine water resistance. Three basic groups of tests are used to measure the degree of sizing and water resistance: those that measure surface water absorption (see *Feathering Test* and *Contact Angle Method*), those that determine how long it takes liquids to penetrate the paper (see *Dry Indicator Test*, *Ink Flotation Method*, and *Curl Test Method*), and those that determine how much liquid a quantity of paper can absorb in a set period of time (see *Cobb Size Test* and *Water Immersion Method*).

See also *Internal Sizing* and *Surface Sizing*.

In graphics, layout, and graphic arts photography, *sizing* refers to the act of determining and indicating on original copy the amount or percentage of *enlargement* or *reduction* required.

Skeleton Black

See *Half-Scale Black*.

Skeleton Cylinder

Alternate term for a *delivery cylinder*, used in an offset printing press, especially such a cylinder containing *skeleton wheels*. See *Delivery Cylinder*.

Skeleton Wheels

A set of moveable disks attached to the surface of a *delivery cylinder*, used to transfer printed press sheets from the *impression cylinder* to the delivery tray. Skeleton wheels can be moved laterally so as to ensure that the wheels only contact the paper in the nonprinted areas of the sheets. See *Delivery Cylinder*.

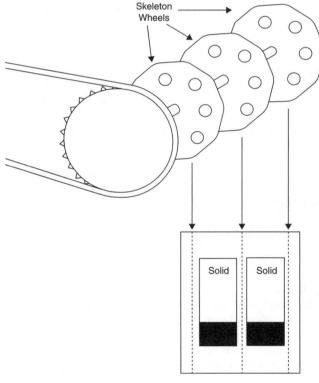

Positioning the skeleton wheels to avoid printed areas.

Skew

In *screen printing*, the movement of the *squeegee* during a printing stroke with its blade at an angle not absolutely perpendicular to the direction of travel. Also called *snowplow*.

Skewed Indent

In typography, a form of *indention* in which each line is indented a different amount than the previous line, to provide a slanted appearance to the margin.

Skid

In shipping and *packaging*, an alternate term for a *pallet*. See *Pallet*.

In papermaking, an informal measure of a quantity of paper, usually about 3,000 lb., or the amount of paper that can be packed and shipped on a skid.

In printing, *skid* means to slide about, as one object against another. As a means of preventing the skidding of printed materials, *antiskid varnish* is often used.

Skid Tag

In printing and finishing operations, a paper tag on a completed pressrun (placed on the *skid* containing the finished sheets) indicating the job number, often color-coded to indicate subsequent *binding and finishing* operations.

Skinnies

Often used in combination with *fatties* as an alternate term for *spreads and chokes*, in the process known as *trapping*. See *Spreads and Chokes*.

Skips

Printing defect characterized by broken or missing halftone dots, the result of incomplete image transfer from the cells of the *gravure cylinder* to the paper surface. Skips (also called *snow*, or *speckle* in *gravure* printing, and *breaks* in other printing methods) are usually caused by surface or structural characteristics of paper (such as *wild formation* and low *compressibility* and *conformability*) preventing the alteration of the paper's surface contour to the extent required to completely contact the inked surface.

Slab Off

A quantity of paper that is removed from the outer circumference of a paper roll. Such paper is often damaged from shipping. Several layers of the paper may have to be removed to get at the undamaged layers before the roll is mounted on press.

Slab Serif

Alternate term for *square serif*. See *Square Serif*.

Slack Center

A paper roll that is baggy at its center. See *Baggy Paper*.

Slack Edge

A paper roll that is baggy at the edges. See *Baggy Paper*.

Slack-Sized

Descriptive of a paper that has had a minimal amount of *internal sizing* and is therefore only slightly water resistant. (See *Sizing* and *Internal Sizing*.)

Slant

In typography, any tilt given to the characters of a *typeface* either to the right to create an *italic* or *oblique* version or to the left to create a *back slant*. See *Italic*.

Slash

In typography, a slanted line (/) used to create fractions, or otherwise separate one type character from another. Also called a *shilling*, a *virgule*, *fraction bar*, or *solidus*. On many computer keyboards and operating systems, a *backslash* (\) is often needed to indicate data paths.

SLD

A *file extension* denoting files created by AutoCAD.

Sleeve

One type of *plate cylinder* used in *flexography*. See *Plate Cylinder: Flexography*.

Sleeve Cylinder

One of two primary types of *gravure cylinder* in which the shafts (which are used to hold the cylinder in the press, engraving device, or elsewhere) are not manufactured as part of the cylinder base. The shafts for a sleeve cylinder

A sleeve cylinder, one of two varieties of gravure cylinder.

must be inserted into bores located on either end of the cylinder. A sleeve cylinder is less expensive than a *shaft cylinder*, but due to the fact that different shafts are used for different stages of cylinder engraving, preparation, and printing, small inaccuracies inherent in each different set of shafts may not be compatible with those in another set of shafts, producing somewhat lower quality images. A sleeve cylinder is also called a *mandrel*. (See also *Shaft Cylinder*.) See *Gravure Cylinder*.

Slice

An adjustable rectangular slit in a papermaking machine's *headbox* that regulates the rate, thickness, and consistency at which the papermaking *furnish* is deposited on the *forming wire*, necessary for consistent paper formation.

Slide

In photography, a 35mm *transparency*.

In presentation graphics, *slide* refers to any image projected onto a screen.

Slide-Off Decal

Alternate term for *simplex decal*. See *Simplex Decal*.

Slide Scanner

A *scanner* that can digitize images from slides or other forms of *transmission copy*. See *Scanner*.

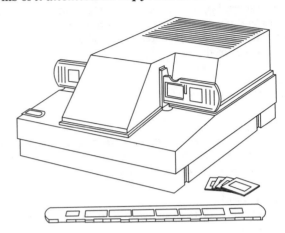

A slide scanner.

Slide-Show Feature

In graphics, a series of images that can be displayed one after the other. The term also describes the ability of a computer program to facilitate the assembly of images for such a display.

Slide-Show Option

In presentation graphics, a feature of some presentation software packages (such as Adobe Persuasion) that allows the assembly of *slide*s (containing text, images, or even sound and video) into a presentation. Slides may be displayed on the computer screen consecutively, in some other predetermined sequence, or randomly. The computer can also segue from slide to slide automatically, or in response to input—such as a mouse click or keystroke—from the presenter.

Slime Spot

A paper defect characterized by a thin spot or a hole in a paper *web* caused by the growth of bacteria during papermaking and that were formed into the paper. Slime spots and holes are a source of *web break*s.

Slip Case

In *binding and finishing*, a decorative box—usually made of cardboard—in which finished books are inserted, allowing the spine(s) to remain visible. Special editions of books, multivolume sets of books, or gift packs are often sold in slip cases. Also known as a *shell*.

Slip Compound

A printing ink additive, such as a wax, that provides the dried ink film with lubricating qualities.

Slip Nip

In an offset press's *continuous-flow dampening system*, the line of contact between two rollers rotating in opposite directions, typically a hard **transfer roller** and a **form roller**, either belonging to the **dampening system**, or shared by the dampening and inking systems. The nip between two rollers rotating in the same direction is called a **reverse slip nip**, occasionally produced on presses as a means of preventing the excess **fountain solution** returning from the plate from interacting with the "fresh" fountain solution coming from the fountain. (See **Dampening System** and **Reverse Slip Nip**.)

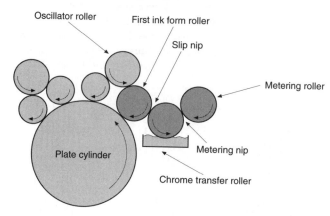

An inker-feed dampening system. Notice the slip nip between the form roller and the chrome transfer roller.

Slip Sheet

A sheet of blank—or discarded—paper inserted between two printed sheets to prevent **ink setoff** and **blocking**. The process of inserting slip sheets is called **interleaving**.

Slip-Sheeting

Alternate term for **interleaving**. See **Interleaving**.

In **binding and finishing**, *slip-sheeting* refers to the act of placing sheets of (usually colored) paper between folded **signature**s or **book block**s prior to trimming, as a means of keeping completed books separate from each other.

Slitter

A device used to slit a large press sheet or web into two or more separate sheets. See **Slitting**.

Slitter Edge

In printing and in **binding and finishing**, the edge of a sheet of paper formed during **slitting**. See **Slitting**.

Slitting

In printing or in **binding and finishing**, the cutting of a large press sheet into two or more smaller sheets. The edge of the new sheets where they had been cut is called the **slitter edge**.

Slow Motion

In television, video, or film production, the display of moving images in the final production at a speed slower than that at which the images were recorded. Slow motion is often used for dramatic effect in motion pictures, or for analytic purposes, as in sports broadcasting.

SLR

Abbreviation for **single-lens reflex**. See **Single-Lens Reflex Camera**.

Slug

In **hot-metal** typography, a strip of metal containing a line of set characters.

In magazine and newspaper typography, *slug* refers to a line or two of text used to identify the content of a story.

Slur

A blurred printed image, due typically to mechanical problems on the press. (See **Slurring**.) Also used as a verb. Also known as **drag**.

Slurring

A printing defect characterized by the smearing of the trailing edges of a printed impression, which is typically caused by slippage of the paper, resulting—in **offset lithography**, for example—from increased pressure between the plate and the **blanket** or between the blanket and the paper. It can also be caused by using a loose blanket, too soft a blanket, too soft an ink, or by the excessive use of ink. It can also be generated by using deformed paper, such as paper with **wavy edges** or other distortions. When slurring occurs in halftone images, it is called **dot slurring**. (See also **Doubling**.)

Slurry

A mixture of water and dissolved paper **pulp** produced during the **stock preparation** phase of papermaking. Pulp must be dissolved in water and constantly agitated before undergoing **refining** to keep paper fibers from prematurely clotting, which would have a deleterious effect on the paper produced. The **loading** of nonfibrous additives is also facilitated when fibers are suspended in water.

In ink manufacturing, *slurry* refers to the mixture of the liquid ink **vehicle** and solid **pigment** particles that undergo **mixing** and **milling**.

Slur Stick

A small wooden rod used to remove dried bits of ink or other foreign particles from a **gravure** press's **doctor blade**, particles that can contribute to a variety of printing defects and **gravure cylinder** damage.

Small Caps

In typography, capital letters designed to match the **x-height** of a particular **typeface** and size.

These are small caps.

Since many fonts today do not have small caps, they are created by reducing the **point size** by two sizes (or

80%), setting capital letters, and then returning to the original size. These are not true small caps, however, and may be lighter than the caps and look out of place. True-cut small caps are the same height as the x-height and are usually equal to the normal cap width: they are slightly expanded because they were on the same hot-metal matrix as the capital character and had to have the same width as the wider character. Digitized typesetting devices have the advantages of being able to reduce size in smaller increments and to electronically expand characters horizontally to form small caps.

Words in text that are specified as all caps could look better (in terms of the *typographic color* of the page) in small caps. This is also true of lining figures: they look best slightly smaller. Old Style figures look best with small caps. Also, the use of full-cap initial letters with small caps is not advised. All small caps is better. Small caps should be used for abbreviations of awards, decorations, honors, titles, etc., following a person's name.

Small Computer System Interface
See *SCSI*.

Smart Quotes
In typography, properly typeset quotation marks (" ") distinguished from the "ditto" marks found on typewriters ("). See *Quotes*. Also known as *curly quotes*.

Smash
A small depression in the surface of an offset press *blanket*, caused by the accidental running of a foreign object or multiple sheets of paper though the *impression nip*. A blanket that has been smashed but is incapable of returning the depression back to its original thickness needs to be repaired or replaced. The indentation itself is typically not a problem of the rubber surface, but is rather one of the fibers of fabric forming its backing. When the fibers are compressed beyond their ability to recover, the blanket is smashed. Soaking the blanket for a day or so in water, or in water mixed with a *wetting agent*, then hanging it up to dry may help allow the fibers to return to their original dimensions. A nonreversible compression of any portion of a blanket, either the rubber or the fabric, is known as *compression set*. (See *Blanket*.)

Smashed Blanket
An offset press *blanket* that has experienced a *smash*, or an indentation in its surface. See *Smash* and *Blanket*. A smashed blanket is also called a *weak blanket*.

Smashed Bulk
In book manufacturing, a term referring to the number of sheets of paper that will occupy a unit area of thickness under the abrupt application of pressure and compression, as during the *casing-in* operation, or binding the pages in a book cover. Due to the "nesting" or packing together of the pages during this operation, the thickness of the book will

be less than the number obtained by simply multiplying the thickness (or *bulk*) of a single sheet by the total number of sheets. (See *Bulking Number*.)

Smashing
In *case binding*, the compressing of the pages of a book prior to *casing-in*. The pressure generated during smashing causes the pages of the book to press very close together, forcing out air, and have a "nesting" or packing effect, which makes the thickness of a book less than the total thickness of all the pages separately. Smashing also compensates for *thread buildup*. (See *Bulk*.) Smashing, as opposed to *nipping*, involves the application of pressure to the entire surface of a *book block*. See also *Nipping* and *Case Binding*.

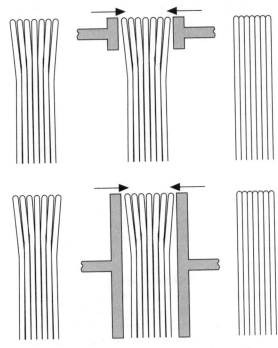

Nipping (top) and smashing (bottom).

Smash Resistance
The ability of an offset press *blanket* to return to its original thickness following its brief exposure to the increased pressure generated during the printing of an impression. Smash resistance is one of two measures of blanket *resilience*. A blanket that does not readily return to its original dimensions will print inconsistently over the course of a print run. (See *Blanket*.)

SME
Abbreviation for *subject matter expert*.

Smear
In computer graphics, a software feature that blends adjacent colors.

In multimedia, the term *smear* refers to an effect used to stretch or compress right angles in an image.

Smearing

A printing defect characterized by a blurry and unclear printed image, caused by a wide variety of press and handling conditions.

Smooth Finish

A paper *finish* characterized by a level surface free of irregularities and contours, produced by a high degree of *wet pressing* or by *calendering*.

Smoothness

Measure of the evenness or lack of contour of a paper's surface. In terms of basic printability, a surface as free as possible of irregularities is desirable, but smoothness is also a function of the interrelationship of other paper properties, and varies with assorted manufacturing processes. Smoothness tends to be characterized by a *wild formation*, which is dependent on the degree of fiber *refining*, the extent of wet pressing, the extent of *calendering* and *supercalendering*, the use of *coatings*, and the desired paper *finish*. (See *Paper and Papermaking: Paper Properties*.) Also known as *levelness*.

A measure of paper smoothness is made using an *air leak tester*, which determines the time it takes for a volume of air to seep between a smooth glass plate and the paper sample. Smoothness can also be measured using a *Bekk Smoothness Tester* or a *Gurley Smoothness Tester*. More rapid measurements can be made with a *Sheffield Smoothness Gauge* or a *Bendtsen Smoothness Tester*. All these devices utilize rates of air flow over a paper surface as an indicator of smoothness (although they all do it in different ways).

The term *smoothness* is also used to refer to the surface characteristics of an offset press printing *blanket*. See *Blanket*.

SMP

Abbreviation for *symmetrical multiprocessing*. See *Symmetrical Multiprocessing*.

SMP/E

Abbreviation for *system modification program extended*.

SMPTE

Abbreviation for *Society of Motion Picture and Television Engineers*. See *Society of Motion Picture and Television Engineers (SMPTE)*.

SMPTE Time Code

In video production, an eight-digit code used to identify video images: HH/MM/SS/FF, or "hours:minutes:seconds: frames." The SMPTE time code was developed by the *Society of Motion Picture and Television Engineers (SMPTE)* and is a universally adopted synchronization standard for audio, video, and film. The SMPTE code also has a built-in compensation for *drop-frame*s in *NTSC* broadcasting.

Smyth Sewing

Alternate term for *saddle sewing*, a form of *thread sewing* used to attach pages together for *case binding*. See *Case Binding*.

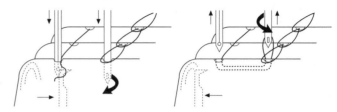

Smyth sewing.

SNA

Acronym for *Systems Network Architecture*. See *Systems Network Architecture (SNA)*.

Snake Slip

A stick or rod composed of powdered pumice and flint used in *offset lithography* to remove foreign material from the surface of the plate. Also known as an *etch stick*.

Snap-Off

In *screen printing*, the distance between the bottom of the screen and the top of the *substrate*.

Snap To

In computer graphics and page layout programs, a means of accurately positioning or drawing objects in which "magnetic" grid lines are placed on the screen (or page) and objects brought within a certain distance to these lines will "snap" to them, the edge of the object aligning along the grid line.

Sneakernet

The alternative when one's network goes down and a file needs to be transmitted: copy the file to a removable disk and walk to its intended destination, presumably while wearing sneakers. The term *sneakernet* is also used as a disparaging term for a network that transmits graphics files so slowly that it would be faster to walk the file to its destination.

Snow

Alternate term for *skips*, a printing defect in *gravure* printing. See *Skips*.

Snowflaking

A defect of *gravure* printing characterized by a nonuniform distribution of voids, or unprinted areas, commonly found in the printing of paper or paperboards with a hard, uneven surface of low *compressibility*, caused by the incomplete transfer of ink from the engraved cells of the *gravure cylinder* to the *substrate*. A harder *impression roller*, a lower-*viscosity* ink, and/or a slower-drying ink may help alleviate the problem. The use of an *electrostatic assist*

(ESA) unit will also help prevent snowflaking. Snowflaking that occurs in middletone areas of the print is also referred to as *mealiness*. *Snowflaking* is also a defect of *offset lithography* characterized by tiny white, unprinted specks in type and solids, caused when ink is excessively emulsified.

Snowplow

Alternate term for *skew*. See *Skew*.

Soap Resistance

A property of printing inks that describes the extent to which a dried ink film will resist fading, discoloring, deterioration, and bleeding when in contact with soaps, an obviously important consideration in the printing of soap packaging. Other chemicals and materials to be packaged must also be compatible with inks used on their wrappers. Soap (and other chemical) resistance is most commonly a property of the ink *pigment*, and the choice of pigment compound directly affects the ink's resistance to soaps and other alkalis. (See *Pigment*.) (See also *Chemical Resistance* and *Wettability*.)

Society of Motion Picture and Television Engineers (SMPTE)

An American organization comprising broadcasters, audiovisual equipment suppliers, television and film producers, etc., that forms committees to set standards and make recommendations for film and television broadcasting. The *SMPTE time code* is one familiar example of their work.

Socket

Generally speaking, any connection into which a *plug* can be inserted. The term *socket* has been expanded to include links between Internet browser software and telecommunications software.

In computing, a *socket* is any *expansion slot* into which an *expansion card* can be inserted.

In telecommunications, a *socket* is a standard for data communications by which a program can access the *Transmission Control Protocol/Internet Protocol (TCP/IP)*.

Soda Process

An alkaline *chemical pulping* process in which wood chips are digested in a caustic soda containing lye (NaOH), produced by adding *sodium carbonate* (Na_2CO_3) to lime (CaO). The soda process is useful for digesting *softwood* or *hardwood*. The first commercial production of soda pulp was in 1851, and it is used infrequently in the present-day due to the superiority of newer processes. In 1879, sodium sulfate (Na_2SO_4) was added to the soda process, and a much stronger pulp resulted. This process, dubbed the *sulfate process*, replaced the traditional soda process, although it was found later that the ingredient primarily responsible for the increased strength was not sodium sulfate, but rather sodium sul*fide* (Na_2S). The sulfate process is also called the *kraft* (after the German and Swedish

word for "strength") process and is the most prevalent chemical pulping system currently in use.

Pulps produced using the soda process are called *soda pulp*. (See also *Pulping* and *Chemical Pulping*.)

Soda Pulp

Paper *pulp* produced using the *soda process*. See *Soda Process*.

Sodium Bicarbonate

A substance (chemical formula $NaHCO_3$) used in *semichemical pulping* processes to pre-cook wood chips prior to grinding. See *Semichemical Pulping*.

Sodium Carbonate

A substance (chemical formula Na_2CO_3) used in *soda process*es of paper *pulping* to produce lye (NaOH), a caustic soda used to digest wood chips. See *Chemical Pulping* and *Soda Process*.

Sodium Hydroxide

A substance (chemical formula NaOH), also called lye, used in *semichemical pulping* and *chemical pulping* processes (in particular the *soda process*) to digest wood chips. See *Semichemical Pulping*, *Chemical Pulping*, and *Soda Process*.

Sodium Sulfate

A compound, whose formula is Na_2SO_4, that was for a time believed to be the substance responsible for the production of high-quality wood *pulp* in papermaking. Sodium sulfate was originally added to the older *soda process*, and a much stronger pulp resulted. (It has since been found, however, that the responsible chemical was actually *sodium sulfide*.) The pulping process has since been somewhat erroneously known as the *sulfate process*, although its alternate name, the *kraft* process (after the German and Swedish word for "strength"), is perhaps more accurate. (See also *Chemical Pulping*.)

Sodium Sulfide

A compound, chemical formula Na_2S, that is the primary ingredient in the *sulfate process* of *chemical pulping* in papermaking. The advantages of sodium sulfide pulping (yet to be named the "sulfide process," perhaps because of its phonetic similarity to the *sulfite process*) include a stronger pulp (the alternate name for the sulfate process, the *kraft* process, means "strength" in German and Swedish), the ability to effectively pulp nearly every species of tree, and its adaptability to efficient and cost-effective chemical-recovery systems. (See also *Chemical Pulping*.)

Sodium Sulfite

A compound, chemical formula Na_2SO_3, that is employed as a reducing agent in the manufacture of paper pulp. Paper pulp may be made in the sulfite process from wood chips cooked under pressure in a solution of sulfurous acid and one of its base salts, such as sodium. Sulfurous acid and limestone are next reacted to form calcium bisulfite. This process solubilizes lignin during cooking and produces what is known as sulfite pulp. It has been replaced by the alkaline pulping process.

Soft

In computing, a term that refers to a file or document that exists solely within the realm of the computer, either as a saved file or as a screen representation of it. See also **Hard**.

Softbot

Contraction of the term **software robot**, in turn an alternate term for an **agent**. See **Agent** (fourth definition).

Soft Copy

Any page, document, publication, or other data that exists on a computer display, rather than as a **printout**, or **hard copy**.

Softcover

Alternate term for a **paperback** book. See **Paperback**.

Soft Dot

In **halftone** photography, a **halftone dot** possessing a soft halo or fringe surrounding a solid core, commonly caused by the use of a **contact screen**. When a plate is made from

Soft dot (left) and a hard dot (right). Notice the fringe surrounding the solid core of the soft dot.

negatives or **positive**s containing soft dots, the fringe will allow the passage of light resulting in an improperly sized halftone dot on the plate. See also **Hard Dot**.

Soften

In imaging, to decrease the **contrast** of an image, usually by means of filters.

Softening Point

The temperature at which a plastic will begin to deform without the addition of an external force or stress.

Soft Font

Alternate term for a **downloadable font**. See **Downloadable Font**.

Soft Ink

A thick, viscous ink, such as that used in **offset lithography**.

Softness

The degree to which a paper will allow a reduction in thickness when exposed to a compressing force, as during printing, writing, or typing. (The degree to which a paper will resist a reduction in thickness is called its **hardness**.)

A high degree of softness (also known as **compressibility**) aids in producing a good printed image, as the squeezing down of surface contours enables the printing plate or blanket to contact the paper more completely. The degree of softness required varies according to the printing process to be used, and other paper properties involved (in particular **resiliency** and **compressibility** which, with hardness and softness, define the paper's **printing cushion**).

Generally, easily compressible paper is preferred for printing, although it is less of an issue in offset printing, and stronger paper may be required in the case of end uses involving folding or handling. (See also **Resiliency**, **Compressibility**, and **Hardness**.)

The term *softness* also refers to the degree to which an offset press **blanket** will reduce in thickness during printing. See **Blanket**.

Soft Proof

See **Digital Soft Proof**.

Soft Return

In word processing, a **carriage return** inserted automatically by the program when the last word that will fit on a line has been entered. See also **Hard Return**. See **Carriage Return**.

Software Interface

Alternate term for a **user interface**. See **User Interface** and **Interface**.

Software Robot

Alternate term for an **agent**. See **Agent** (fourth definition).

Softwood

Wood obtained from **coniferous** trees, especially when used in papermaking. **Hardwood**, also used in papermaking, comes from **deciduous** trees. See **Coniferous** and **Deciduous**.

Solid

In typography, a block of type to which no **leading** has been added. See **Set Solid**.

In printing, an image area containing no **halftone**s, comprising an unbroken film of ink.

One possible representation of the interior of a fill-area or polygon primitive. The interior of the image is filled with the solid color specified by the fill-area or polygon color-index attribute.

The term *solid* also refers to a characteristic of a computer program that has been completely debugged and works as it was intended.

Solids Content

The amount of non-*volatile* material in a particular compound, mixture, or solution expressed as a percentage of the total weight of the mixture.

Solid Underscoring

In typography, the underlining of multiple words utilizing a single continuous line, such as this. See also *Broken Underscoring*. See *Underscoring*.

Solidus

Alternate term for a *slash*. See *Slash*.

Solvent

Any substance capable of dissolving another to form a solution. A common, everyday solvent is water, in which substances like sugar, salt, or instant coffee can be dissolved. In many printing inks, a solvent is used to dissolve the *vehicle* and the *pigment* and aid in transport and drying of the ink. Low-boiling-point solvents evaporate quickly, leaving the pigment on the surface of the *substrate*. Other solvents are absorbed rapidly by the paper, again leaving the pigment on the surface of the substrate.

Common solvents used in inks are a variety of organic compounds, such as *hydrocarbon*s (such as *aliphatic solvents* like *naphtha*; paraffin hydrocarbons like pentane, hexane, heptane, isooctane, and *mineral oil*; and *aromatic solvents* like benzene, toluene, and xylene), alcohols (*monohydric alcohols* like methyl, ethyl, propyl, and isopropyl alcohols, and *polyhydric alcohols* like glycol and glycerol), *ketone*s (such as *acetone*, methyl ethyl ketone, methyl isobutyl ketone, and cyclohexanone), *ester*s (such as *ethyl acetate*, propyl acetate, butyl acetate, isobutyl acetate, and amyl acetate), and other organic substances such as ethers (like diethyl ether, isopropyl ether, and tetrahydrofuran).

Hydrocarbons, composed solely of hydrogen and carbon atoms, are the simplest and least expensive of the solvents, save for the aromatic hydrocarbons such as benzene and other chemicals having cyclic (or ring) molecular structures, which tend to be more expensive. Hydrocarbons are also characterized by high flammability and toxicity, as well as low solvent power for many types of materials. (The solvent power of hydrocarbons is measured using a *kauributanol value*.) The other varieties of organic solvents contain other types of atoms, in particular oxygen, and are called *polar solvents*. Although they are more expensive, polar solvents are less flammable, less toxic, and more powerful as solvents.

Another important characteristic of a solvent is its boiling point. High-*volatility* organic solvents have very low boiling points (room temperature or slightly above) and evaporate rapidly. Other solvents are much less volatile. The desired degree of volatility of a solvent is a function of the drying mechanism of the ink in which it is to be used. Inks that need to dry quickly by *evaporation* require highly volatile solvents, while those that dry by other means, such as *oxidation* or by the application of heat, may require less volatile solvents. (See *Vehicle*.)

See also *Diluent*.

Solvent Release

A property of a printing ink *binder* that describes its ability to control the rate at which the *solvent* present in the ink *vehicle* evaporates, an important consideration in the manufacture and use of inks that dry via *evaporation*.

Solvent-Resin Vehicle

A type of ink *vehicle*—the fluid carrier of the ink *pigment*—that dries by *evaporation* of the vehicle, rather than by absorption of the vehicle into the *substrate* or by *oxidation*. In solvent-resin vehicles, a low-boiling point *solvent* is rapidly evaporated out of the ink, either with or without the application of heat (as in *heatset ink*), leaving the hardened pigment on the substrate. The solvent may be composed of *hydrocarbon*s modified by the addition of gums and rosins (as in gravure inks), alcohols, water, or other *volatile* solvents (as in *flexographic* inks, although the composition of the substrate itself primarily determines the solvent), or somewhat less volatile (in other words, evaporating at a higher temperature) petroleum solvents in which are dissolved rosin esters or hydrocarbon resins (as in heatset inks for *letterpress* and *offset lithography*, which handle well on the press, and dry extremely quickly with the application of heat). (See *Vehicle*.)

SOM

In packaging, an abbreviation for *sewn open-mouth*, a type of paper *bag*. See *Sewn Open-Mouth (SOM)*.

Sony/Philips Digital Interface (S/DIF)

In video and multimedia, a consumer version of the *AES/EBU* standard for the electrical connection of digital, stereo, and audio equipment.

Sorts

In *hot-metal* typography, a set of characters used to augment the standard character set on the linecasting device.

Sound Card

In computing, an *expansion card* installed in a computer that allows it to output audio signals such as sound and music, which can then be sent to connected audio equipment.

Sound Effects

In film, television, video, and multimedia production, any sounds added to the soundtrack of a production, with the exception of voices and music.

Sound Power Level (Lw)

In audio production, the intensity of an audio signal, expressed in *decibel*s and measured as the sound intensity in watts per square meter. See also *Sound Pressure Level (Lp)*.

Sound Pressure Level (Lp)

A measure of sound intensity, or the pressure of the wave generated by an audio signal, expressed in **decibel**s and measured as the pressure of the sound wave in pascals per square meter. See also **Sound Power Level (Lw)**.

Source

In computing, the disk drive from which data is being copied. See also **Target**.

Source Address

In networking, the **address** of the sender of a transmitted message or data **packet**. See also **Destination Address**.

Source Code

In computer programming, the instruction set, written in a programming language based on usual English (or other natural language) but with a syntax unique to the programming language. Source code is used to change and extend a program and needs to be **compile**d (or translated to **machine code**) before the program can be run, not only so that the computer itself can understand it, but also so the user cannot make any changes to the source code.

Source Language

Alternate term for **source code**. See **Source Code**.

Source Program

A **computer program** written in a specific **programming language**—such as Fortran, Pascal, C, BASIC, COBOL, etc.—rather than in **machine language**.

Souring

A printing defect that occurs in **flexography** or **screen printing** with **nitrocellulose**-based inks utilizing **hygroscopic** (absorbing moisture readily) **solvent**s, in which the nitrocellulose, being water-insoluble, precipitates out of the ink when the solvent picks up water from the atmosphere. Although the addition of other substances (such as **ester**s) will help to alleviate the problem, the best defense against souring is to minimize the exposure of the ink to humid environments by using lids and fountain covers, or to use a small amount of ink in the ink fountain and refresh the ink frequently.

Soy Ink

A recent development in vegetable oil-based printing inks obtaining its oil-based **vehicle** from soybean oil. The use of vegetable oil-based vehicles has improved the printing characteristics of many inks. Soy ink has achieved excellent results when used in **newsink** and helps eliminate smudging. Other types of vegetable oils used include rapeseed and **linseed oil**s.

Space

In graphics and layout, the portion of a page containing no image areas.

In typography, *space* refers to any fixed- or variable-width regions separating one character, word, or line from another. See **Letterspacing**, **Line Spacing**, and **Word Spacing**.

Spaceband

In typography, an alternate term for a **word space**, derived from the name of a wedge-shaped object used to separate words on a **hot-metal** typesetting device. After assembly the spacebands were pushed upward to expand the word spaces equally and justify the line of type. See **Word Space**.

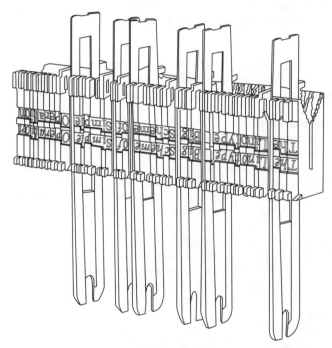

A line of matrices and spacebands ready for molten metal to form the line of type. The wedge-shaped spacebands are used to fill out a line of type in hot-metal typesetting.

Space Dot

Alternate term for **center point**. See **Center Point**.

Space Parity

In computing, a **parity check** used to detect and correct errors in data transmission by adding an extra **bit** (a 0) to a character code. See **Parity**. See also **Mark Parity**.

Spacing

In typography, the amount of space that exists between characters (called **letterspacing**), words (called **word spacing**), lines (called **line spacing**), or paragraphs. The careful adjustment of spacing increases type **legibility**.

Spam

In colloquial **Internet** terminology, term for junk **email** or repetitive mass emailings or mass posts to a **USENET** group. The term actually derives from a popular skit on the television program *Monty Python's Flying Circus* in which the word "spam" is repeated endlessly.

S Paper

Abbreviation for **stabilization paper**. See **Stabilization Paper**.

SPAR

Abbreviation for *systems problem analysis request*.

SPARC

Abbreviation for **Scalable Processor ARChitecture**. See **Scalable Processor ARChitecture (SPARC)**.

Spec'd

Shorthand term for *specified*, or copy that has had its printing and binding specifications—such as paper and ink, binding and finishing, etc.—indicated.

Special Effects

In typography, type set in a modified form for decorative or other aesthetic reasons.

Type may be reproduced in a variety of artistic forms:
• *Screened*. Tints or tones may be screened over the type or the type may drop out of the screened area. Display type may have certain parts of the characters screened.
• *Reverse*. Type may be dropped out of a black or colored background. Light or condensed typefaces are not advised for this purpose, as they tend to fill in.
• *Curves*. Type may be cut (manually or electronically) and curved around an arc for display purposes.
• *Perspective*. Type may be re-created in three-dimensional form.
• *Bleeding*. Type characters or words may be repeated as a design element and then printed as a page background by bleeding type areas off the page.

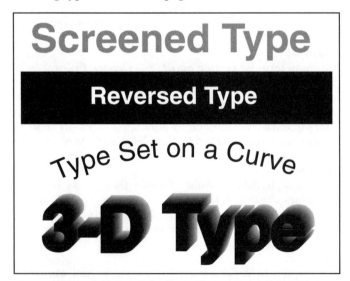

A sampling of the special effects that are possible with type.

• *Type in color*. Certain type lines may be printed in color for emphasis or for artistic reasons. Usually it is not good practice to put blocks in lighter colors.
• *Word or character pictures*. The use of light, bold, condensed, and expanded characters can visually combine to create an image (for example, a face of a person). These are created usually when there is not much work to do in the department.

Special effects are effective in many applications, but the use of special effects is most effective when done in moderation.

Specific Adhesion

A measure of the force required to remove a decal adhesive from a particular surface or **substrate**.

Specific Gravity

The ratio of the density of a substance to the density of another standard substance. For liquids, such as printing inks, specific gravity is the ratio of the weight per unit volume of the liquid to the weight of an equal volume of water.

Specific gravity is an important factor to take into account when estimating the amount of ink required for a particular print job. A printing ink with a specific gravity of 1.5 will cover twice as much **substrate** per pound than will an ink with a specific gravity of 3.0, for example (all other factors, such as temperature, being equal).

Specifier

In printing, the individual working on a particular job responsible for determining the exact type of paper to be used for the print run.

Specimen Book

A book prepared by a type foundry (or other modern **typeface** supplier) showing all the typefaces, type families, and type sizes available. Specimen books are often prepared on CD-ROM these days.

Specimen Pages

Alternate term for **sample pages**. See **Sample Pages**.

Also called a *typographic showing*, a type specimen presents all or some of the characters in a font to visually demonstrate the look and color of the typeface on paper.

Specking

Alternate term for the printing defect known as **fill-in**. See **Fill-In**.

Speckle

Alternate term for **skips**, a printing defect in **gravure** printing. See **Skips**.

Specs

An abbreviation for the terrm **type specifications**. See **Type Specifications**.

Spectral Color

Any color that corresponds to a wavelength on the *visible spectrum*. (See *COLOR PLATE 3*.)

Black, white, and gray, which are produced by the combinations of wavelengths, are not considered to be spectral colors.

Spectral Energy Distribution

A diagram that illustrates the constituent wavelengths of a color, or the energy output of a source of light.

Spectral Reflectance Curve

A curve that illustrates the reflectance of light from a surface, such as paper, wavelength-by-wavelength throughout the visible spectrum, as a means of determining the *color*

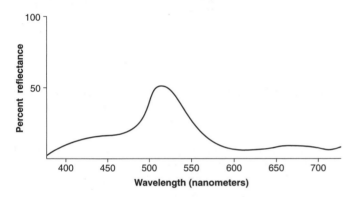

Spectral reflectance curve.

of that surface. Spectral reflectance curves are used to determine paper color, *brightness*, and *whiteness*, important optical properties that dramatically affect the quality of material printed on the paper surface. See *Color*, *Brightness*, and *Whiteness*.

Spectrophotometer

A device that measures and analyzes wavelength by wavelength the reflected light of a surface. Spectrophotometric readings are used to generate a *spectral reflectance curve* for the surface in question as a means of determining its color. See *Color* and *Color, Paper*.

Specular Highlight

In a printed or to-be-reproduced image, a type of *highlight*—the brightest area(s) of an image—produced by a reflection of a light source within an image. A specular highlight, unlike a *diffuse highlight*, contains no detail nor any *halftone dots* at all. Also known as a *drop-out highlight* and a *catchlight*. See *Highlight*.

Specular Reflectance

The extent to which light rays are reflected from a surface at an angle equal to the angle at which they hit the surface. Measures of specular reflectance at particular angles are used to determine a paper's *gloss*.

Speculation

The accepting of an assignment without any guarantee that payment will be made after the work has been completed. Producing a manuscript and submitting it to a publisher is considered speculation. Such work is usually referred to as being done "on spec."

Spelling Checker

A feature of many word processing, page layout, and other text-based programs that checks the spelling of each word of a document and compares it to that of words included in a dictionary. Words that it cannot verify the spelling of are flagged for the user.

Many programs allow the user to add specialized terms or proper names that may not be included in the default dictionary. Spelling checkers should be used with care; they are incapable of finding words that become other words when misspelled. Also referred to as *spell checkers*, and the term *spell-check* has become a verb meaning "to proofread a document using a spelling checker."

SPI

Abbreviation for *spots per inch*, an alternate term for *pixels per inch*. See *Pixels per Inch (ppi)*.

Spin-Coating

In *optical disc* manufacturing, a means of applying a thin protective coating on a disc in which a small drop of fluid is placed in the center of the disc. When the disc is spun at a high speed, the drop spreads out and coats the surface of the disc with an equal thickness throughout. When the fluid dries, it forms a transparent, protective layer.

Spindle

Alternate term for *lead screw*. See *Lead Screw*.

Spine

In book production, the bound edge of a book, where the pages are held together, commonly to the binding. The spine of a book also commonly bears the title and author of the book on the outside edge. Also known as the *backbone*.

In typography, the main curved stroke of the capital or lowercase letter "S." See *Letter Elements*.

Spine-See Binding

An alternate term for *spiral binding*, or other form of continuous-wire *mechanical binding*. See *Spiral Binding*.

Spiral Binding

A means of *mechanical binding* in which pages are bound together by means of a wire or plastic coil threaded into drilled or punched holes along the *binding edge* of the pages. See *Mechanical Binding*. Spiral binding is also known as *spine-see binding*.

Spitting

Alternate term for *ink misting*. See *Ink Misting*.

Splice

A seam resulting from the joining of two portions of a paper roll. When defects appear in paper rolls, the web is typically cut, the offending portion of paper removed, and the rest of the roll spliced back together again. It is crucial that the two spliced sections be perfectly aligned and parallel, and that the unwinding tension across the splice be perfectly even otherwise a *web break* will occur when the roll is unwound into a web offset press at high speeds. (See also *Splice Failure*.)

Splice Failure

The breaking of a *splice* joining two sections of a paper web. A splice failure can be either paper-caused (an improperly made splice) or press-caused. Any splice made in which the two sections of the web are not in perfect alignment will cause wrinkling and perhaps a *web break*. (See *Splice*.)

Splicer

In *web offset lithography*, a device attached to the *roll stand* of a web press that automatically splices a new paper roll to the end of an expiring roll. A splicer may either be a *flying splicer* or a *zero-speed splicer*. See *Web Offset Lithography: Infeed and Web Control: Splicing*. Also known as a *paster*.

Spline

In computer graphics, a curve constructed by the computer connecting user-defined points. Rather than connecting points with a series of straight lines, the computer can create a smooth curve containing all points. See also *Bézier Curve*.

Split Bind

In *binding and finishing*, a bind order in which a single book or publication will have some quantity bound in one manner (i.e., *perfect binding*) and another quantity printed in another manner (i.e., *case binding*). Each of the binding types is known as a *bind leg*. Some books are bound using conventional *case binding*, while some copies are bound in special *deluxe edition*s.

Split Fountain

A means by which two different colored inks are printed simultaneously on an offset lithographic press, used for *spot color* printing. See *Fountain Splitter*.

Split Fraction

In typography, an *en fraction* constructed in the manner of a *piece fraction*. The numerator and denominator are separate units. See *Piece Fraction*.

Split Galleys

Half-length *galley proof*s, usually prepared for reviewers.

Split Gauge

A type of back gauge on a *guillotine cutter* that is divided into two or more segments so as to allow more than one

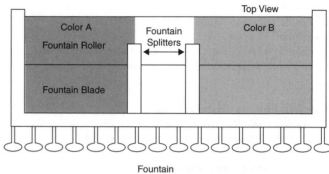

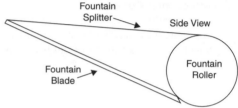

A split ink fountain.

edge of a stack of sheets to be cut without needing to change the gauge setting between cuts. See *Guillotine Cutter*.

Split Screen

In motion picture photography and videography, a type of special effect that abuts two different video sources, each on one half of the screen. Often used, for example when on-screen characters are talking to each other on the telephone. Multiple split screens allow more than two images to appear on the screen simultaneously.

Splitting

An extreme form of *picking* in which the pull of a thick, tacky ink tears off large portions of a paper's surface which then stick to the offset blanket. See *Picking*.

Split-Top Label

A label produced so that at least one edge abuts that of an adjacent label, with no extraneous *substrate* between them, so that one cut of a die can create the edges of two labels. A *split-top label* is also known as a *butt label* and a *knife-cut label*.

Spool

In computing, a set of data output from a computer awaiting a print device. *Spool* is an acronym for *simultaneous peripheral operations on-line*. See *Spooler*.

Spooler

In computing, a memory location in a computer printer (or in the computer itself) in which data to be printed is stored until the printer is ready to output it, thus allowing the computer to work on other tasks. The spooler is where the *print queue* is located. The data awaiting output itself is known as a *spool*, which is actually an acronym for *simultaneous peripheral operations on-line*.

Spray-Bar Dampening System

Spooling

In computing, the temporary storage of data in a computer printer's memory (or **spooler**) or elsewhere until the output device is ready to process the data, allowing the computer to get on with other tasks. Spooling is performed especially with slow output devices. See **Spool** and **Spooler**.

Spot

On input devices such as scanners, the smallest point that the device can detect. Also known as a **pixel**.

On an output device, such as an **imagesetter**, **film recorder**, or **plotter**, the smallest point that the laser can image. These spots are what form the image, and the number of spots in a unit of linear distance (such as an inch) is what determines the output device's **resolution**. Although resolution of output devices is often measured in **dots per inch (dpi)**, and spots are often referred to as *dots*, the use of this latter term is technically incorrect; the word *spot* is preferred as a means of distinguishing between the "dots" generated by the output device and **halftone dot**s. Many spots are used to make up a halftone dot (which, when made up of spots, is known as a **halftone cell**).

Spot Color

In multicolor printing, a **color** that is added in an individually specifiable region of a printed sheet, used to highlight individual page elements, such as logos, headlines, **line art**, etc., distinguished from **process color** in that spot color can be added simply by imaging a second **negative** and making a second plate, without requiring the complexities of **color separation**s. Spot color commonly uses different types of ink, and spot colors are not commonly overprinted to generate additional colors. (Being **opaque**, unlike **transparent** process inks, they do not overprint very well.) Spot color inks, when not consisting of primary colors, are usually mixed prior to printing, and they are specified by the use of **color matching system**s, such as the **PANTONE** Matching System (**PMS**). See also **Process Color**. Spot color is sometimes called a **tint**.

Spotlight

In film, television, and video production, a high-intensity light source used to provide a **scene** with additional depth during filming or taping, as shadows are created behind the subject being illuminated.

Spot Size

The diameter of the **spot** that a scanner can detect or an output device can image. The spot size is the determining factor in a device's **resolution**: the smaller the spot, the more that can fit in a particular unit of linear distance, and the smoother the image that will be scanned or output. See **Spot** and **Resolution**.

Spots per Inch (SPI)

Alternate term for **pixels per inch**. See **Pixels per Inch (ppi)**.

Spotting Out

Alternate term for **opaquing**. See **Opaquing**.

Spot Varnish

A **varnish** applied only to portions of a printed piece after printing, rather than to the entire sheet, typically for aesthetic purposes. Spot varnishing is commonly found on book covers, in which only portions of the cover are high in **gloss**, in contrast to the surrounding **matte** texture.

Spray-Bar Dampening System

A type of **dampening system** found on some printing presses used in **web offset lithography**, consisting of a row of nozzles that spray a fine mist of **fountain solution** onto the inking rollers. A spray-bar system is often used in lieu of a conventional roller-oriented dampening system. Its advantages include more accurate dampening control, as the spray of each nozzle across the width of the press can be individually set. There is also no recirculation—and thus no contamination—of the fountain solution with this system. One drawback of a spray-bar dampening system, however, is that some fountain solution ingredients can

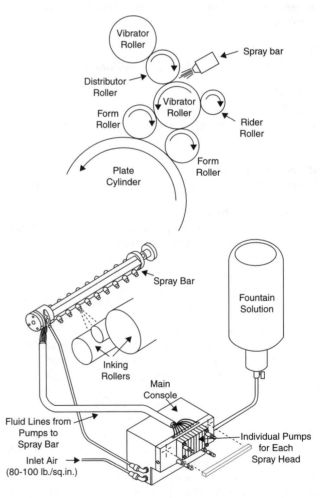

The principle of the spray-bar dampening system.

contaminate and/or clog the nozzles. Some types of spray-bar dampening systems may require their own set of rollers connected to the inking rollers. (See *Dampening System*.)

Spraying

Alternate term for *ink misting*. See *Ink Misting*.

Spray Powder

Alternate term for *antisetoff spray*. See *Antisetoff Spray*.

Spread

In page layout and printing, any two facing pages of a book, magazine, newspaper, or other publication. When designing pages, it is important to ensure that both pages of a spread are taken into account when laying out pages and evaluating things such as *typographic color*. A spread in which one portion of the image is printed on the *verso* and the other portion of the image is printed on the *recto* is called a *double-page spread*.

Spreader

In *screen printing*, an alternate term for a *coater*. See *Coater*.

Spreader Bar

Alternate term for a *yoke bar*. See *Yoke Bar*.

Spreading

An enlarging of a printed image or type due to ink *bleeding* or capillary action of the ink in porous paper. (See also *Feathering*.)

Spread Negative

Alternate term for a *spread*. See *Spreads and Chokes*.

Spreads and Chokes

In prepress and multicolor printing, a *trapping* technique, or means of effecting accurate *registration* on press by adjusting the size of an image and the opening in which it will be inserted. A choke is a photographic enlargement of the background color in which a second image will print. This has the effect of reducing the size of the hole in which a foreground object will be printed. Or, in other words, the opening is "choked." A spread is the slight photographic enlargement—or "spreading"—of the image that will print within the choked image. This combination of reducing the opening and enlarging the image creates a slight overlap when the images ultimately print, eliminating unwanted white spaces or gaps between the two images.

Spreads and chokes can be prepared in many ways, and each printer or prepress house may have a pet process. Essentially, the process of making a spread or a choke involves creating a sandwich of the original photographic negative (or positive), a diffusion sheet, and a variety of clear spacer sheets. When light is then passed through the original negative, it is scattered, and as a result, it will fall

in a slightly larger area on the unexposed film. The spacer sheets can control the extent of the scattering, adjusting the size of the spread or choke. Controlling the length of the exposure also affects the size of the spread or choked image. In some cases, the camera operator manually shakes a diffusion sheet between the light and the films, creating randomly scattered light. This is not always efficacious.

Spreads and chokes are also called *fatties and skinnies*, respectively.

Spreadsheet

In computing, a program in which a screen is divided into a grid of rows (horizontal) and columns (vertical) of *cell*s, or boxes in which text, numbers, mathematical operators, or functions can be entered. The rows are identified with numbers and the columns with letters, allowing specific cells to be addressed directly; for example, cell C5 is in the fifth row of the third column. Cells can be linked with mathematical formulas, and numerical values added, subtracted, multiplied, divided, etc. The advantage is that changing one number in a linked cell causes the program to recalculate all other links automatically. Data from spreadsheets can be exported to other programs as well, creating charts, graphs, models, etc. Spreadsheets are widely used in accounting, as well as many other fields.

The first spreadsheet program was called Visi-Calc, which was the *killer application* that sold the Apple II personal computer in the late 1970s. Popular spreadsheet programs today include Lotus 1-2-3 and Microsoft Excel, among others.

Sprinkled Edges

In *binding and finishing*, a type of *edge staining* in which the edges of a trimmed book are spattered with a dye or other colorant. A type of sprinkled edge, in which a dye is applied by sponge in an irregular pattern is known as *mottle*.

Sprocket Feed

Alternate term for *pin feed*. See *Pin Feed*.

Spur

In typography, a *letter element* corresponding to a small projection off a main stroke, as that found on many capital "G"s. See *Letter Elements*.

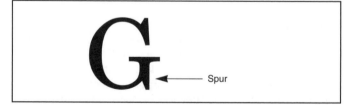

A spur, a small projection of a main stroke.

Spur Gear

A gear used to drive printing press rollers or cylinders in which the teeth are cut parallel to the surface of the cylinder. Spur gears on offset press printing unit cylinders are commonly found more often on older machines, having been replaced on newer presses by **helical gear**s. Spur gears generally require the addition of a second gear, called a **backlash gear**, so as to reduce **play**, the unimpeded (and undesirable) lateral movement between gears. Helical gears by design reduce play. Cylinders in which the **bearer**s (metal rings attached to the ends of the cylinder) of the **plate cylinder** run in contact with those of the **blanket cylinder** commonly use spur gears, while those that run out of contact use helical gears to reduce play and provide a smoother drive. (See **Plate Cylinder**, **Blanket Cylinder** and **Helical Gear**.)

A spur gear.

Spur Serif
In typography, a **serif** that comes to a point, unlike a **square serif**. See **Serif**.

SQE
Abbreviation for **signal quality error**. See **Signal Quality Error**.

SQL/DS
Abbreviation for *Structured Query Language/Data System*.

Square Back
Alternate term for **flat back**. See **Flat Back**.

Square Brackets
See **Brackets**.

Square Finish Halftone
Alternate term for a **square halftone**. See **Square Halftone**.

Square Halftone
In graphic arts photography and prepress, a **halftone** having four sides that are straight and perpendicular to each other. Also known as as **square finish halftone**.

Square-Pixel Digitizing
In video production, a means of correcting the **aspect ratio** of a television signal in a **frame grabber** to reduce distortion. In **NTSC**, distortion can be as great as 11%, while in **PAL** it can be up to 7%, which results in circular images becoming more elliptical.

Squares
In **binding and finishing**, an alternate term for **overhang**, especially when describing the amount of cover visible around the bound **endsheet**s on the inside covers of a **casebound** book.

Square Serif
In typography, a **serif** character or **typeface** characterized by serifs that are as heavy or heavier than the bodies of the letters, and that have no curvature between the main stroke and the serif. (See **Bracketed**.) See **Serif**. Also referred to as **slab serif**.

ABCDEFGHIJK
abcdefghijklm

Lubalin Graph, a typeface with square serifs.

Square Sheet
A sheet of paper containing an equal degree of strength and **tear resistance** in both its **grain direction** and its **cross-grain direction**.

Squeegee
A tool possessing a wooden or metal handle to which is attached a thin, flexible rubber or plastic blade. A squeegee is used in **screen printing** to force ink through the **printing screen** and onto the **substrate**. The configuration of the squeegee handle is a matter of printer comfort and has little direct bearing on the printing impression, but the shape of the blade is a factor that affects the thickness of the ink deposited and the sharpness of the printed image. The **squeegee profile** is a cross-sectional representation of the squeegee blade and is used to gauge blade shape. The most common shape for most general purposes is square, and it is used primarily for printing on flat substrates with standard poster inks. A flat-point, double-bevel shape (essentially a cut-off triangle) is used for printing on uneven surfaces, especially ceramics. A general double-bevel without a flat point is useful for depositing a fine ink film, such as when the **stencil** contains intricate line art. A single-bevel blade shape is used for printing on glass. A square blade with rounded corners is used for printing lighter colored inks on top of dark backgrounds. A round edge is used

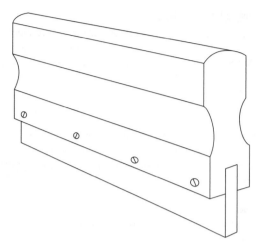

Squeegee, as used in screen printing.

for printing on textiles, such as T-shirts. When sharp blade edges are required, a squeegee blade sharpener is used to grind the blade to the proper profile.

Although the squeegee blade is generically described as "rubber" or "plastic," the specific chemical makeup of the blade needs to be compatible with the type of solvent and ink combination used. Blades designed for printing on vinyls or acetates, for example, are often water-soluble, and consequently a water-based ink cannot be used. Some blades are made of polyurethane, but *neoprene* (a synthetic rubber) is the most common all-purpose blade material.

A third important blade characteristic is its flexibility, described in terms of hardness or *durometer*. A general all-purpose blade has a durometer of 60, but a softer blade (i.e., having a durometer of 50 or less) will deposit a thicker ink film, while a harder blade (having a durometer of 70+) will produce a thinner but sharper ink film.

Screen frames and stencils can come in a variety of widths, and, consequently, the squeegee must be wide enough to completely cover the stencil image. A general rule recommends that each edge of the squeegee blade extend ½ in. beyond the edge of the stencil.

The squeegee blade should be completely cleaned after a print run. Dried ink remaining on the blade will alter the blade profile, contaminate successive inks, or cause other mechanical or chemical problems.

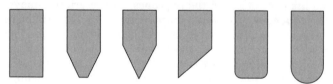

Various blade profiles for squeegees.

Squeegee Angle

In *screen printing*, the angle formed between the face of the blade of the *squeegee* (the side of the blade facing in the direction of the printing stroke) and the plane of the screen. The squeegee angle is measured with the squeegee in printing position but not under printing pressure. A similar measurement, but with a different value due to the flexibility of the rubber squeegee blade, is the *angle of attack*, or the angle formed by the face of the squeegee blade when under printing pressure.

Squeegee Carriage

An assembly on a *screen printing* press that holds the *squeegee* at the proper angle for effective ink transfer and impression pressure. Although small presses have the squeegee manually drawn across the screen, the mechanization of the printing stroke is particularly useful on larger screens.

Squeegee Holder

The part of a *screen printing* press—be it an automated or manual press—that holds the *squeegee* in position during printing.

Squeegee Pressure

In *screen printing*, the force exerted by the *squeegee* on the screen fabric that brings it into contact with the *substrate* and effects proper ink transfer through the mesh.

Squeegee Printing Edge

In *screen printing*, the edge of the *squeegee* blade that contacts the screen fabric during a printing stroke.

Squeegee Profile

In *screen printing*, the cross-sectional shape of the *squeegee* blade—be it rectangular, rounded, etc.

Squeeze

Somewhat colloquial term for the pressure exerted between two offset press cylinders (such as the *plate cylinder* and the *blanket cylinder*) or between the blanket cylinder and the paper or other *substrate*. Squeeze, which is measured in thousandths of an inch, is an important determination of proper printing pressures, governed primarily by the extent of plate or blanket cylinder *packing*. See *Packing*.

SRAM

Abbreviation for *Static Random-Access Memory*. See *Static Random-Access Memory (SRAM)*.

SSE

Abbreviation for *systems software engineer*.

SSI

Abbreviation for *subsystem interface*.

Stabilization

In photography, an alternate term for *fixing*, a stage of film *development*. See *Fixing*.

The feature on some video camera-recorders that can smooth out a wobbly picture.

Stabilization Paper

A photosensitive paper used in ***phototypesetting***. The advantage to stabilization paper is that the developer is embedded in the ***emulsion*** of the paper. As a result, processing is inexpensive and quick. A drawback, however, is that the final image is not permanent, although it can remain intact for up to several weeks. Two chemicals were used: an activator and a stabilizer. Also called ***S Paper***.

Stabilize

In printing, to ensure that the ***moisture content*** of a paper is equal to that of the surrounding atmosphere. See ***Moisture Content***.

Stacked Bar Chart

A type of ***bar chart*** in which the bars are placed on top of each other, rather than adjacent to each other. See ***Bar Chart***.

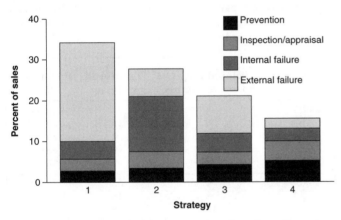

A stacked bar graph that plots the cost of quality efforts (vertical axis) for four different quality strategies (horizontal axis).

Stacker

A device used in ***binding and finishing*** (or ***in-line*** finishing operations) to collect, jog, and bundle printed and folded ***signatures***. Some configurations include ***CounterStacker***s, which keep a count of the number of signatures delivered to the unit.

Stack-Feed Capacity

In a photocopier, computer printer, etc., the number of sheets of paper that can be added to a paper tray, which thus determines the total number of printed pages that the device can print while left unattended.

Stack Fraction

Alternate term for an ***en fraction***. See ***En Fraction***.

Stack Press

A type of multicolor press used in ***flexography*** in which all the ***color station***s—from one to eight stations, with six being the most common—are oriented in a vertical stack, the ***substrate*** passing through each one, which lays down

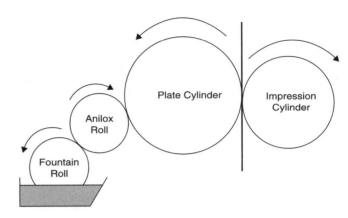

Stack-type flexographic press using two-roller system.

successive colors. Some stack presses comprise two parallel stacks, the web of substrate taking a U-shaped path through the press. Each color station possesses its own independent set of inking rollers, plate cylinder, and impression cylinder, in contrast to a ***central impression press*** that utilizes a large-diameter ***common impression cylinder*** that brings the substrate into contact with each color station. See ***Flexography: Press Configurations***.

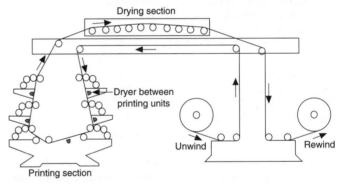

A flexographic stack press with six color stations.

Staging

In any production environment, the gathering together of all the components of a job as a prelude to the efficient completion of the job.

Stained Edge

See ***Edge Staining***.

Staining

In multicolor printing, a third, undesirable color produced by the overlapping or touching of two adjacent colors.

Stainless Steel Screen

A fabric used for ***screen printing*** screens made from thin strands of extruded stainless steel.

Stair-Stepping

Alternate term for ***aliasing***. See ***Aliasing***.

Stairsteps

In *screen printing*, an alternate term for *sawtooth*. See *Sawtooth*.

In digital imaging, an alternate term for *jaggies* or the effects of *aliasing*. (See *Aliasing*.) Stair-stepping results when resolution is too low and the individual line segments that are used to "build" a character are visible to the eye.

Stamper

In *compact disc* manufacturing, a metal plate that bears a "negative" of the *pit* and *land* pattern of the *glass master*. The stamper is pressed against a blank disc to make a "positive" of the pit and land pattern. A stamper is used in the mass production of CDs.

Stamping

Any of several *finishing* operations involving the use of hard metal *die*s to press an image into a surface or *substrate*. See *Embossing*, *Die-Stamping*, and *Foil Stamping*.

Stamping Die

A *die* used in *die-stamping*. See *Die* and *Die-Stamping*.

Stamping Press

In *finishing*, a strongly constructed press, often fitted with heating devices, used for finishing operations such as *embossing*, *die-stamping*, *foil stamping*, etc. See *Binding and Finishing: Finishing*.

Standalone

Any computer (or other type of device) that is capable of functioning perfectly without needing to be connected to another device for control and guidance, although the device may itself control another device, or need to receive media from another device. *Standalone* may also refer to a device that is housed separately from other devices to which it is connected. For example, some *raster image processor*s are standalone devices, which exist physically as separate units, although they control *imagesetter*s connected to them. Occasionally spelled with a hyphen, *stand-alone*.

Standard Generalized Markup Language (SGML)

An *International Standards Organization* standard (ISO 8879) for identifying and coding the various elements of a document, such as titles, subtitles, headings, sub-headings, paragraphs, tables, etc. SGML, supported by the American Association of Publishers, is used to mark text for a variety of purposes, including typesetting and electronic publishing. In an SGML document, data is stored in a generic text format (*ASCII text*), allowing it to run on virtually any *operating system*, and the codes are linked to the original document according to a user-defined structure, which is stored as a code or character set called a *document type definition (DTD)*. Originally designed solely for the *UNIX* platform, SGML has increased in popularity to such an extent that many word processing and page layout programs now incorporate SGML features. SGML is also used for information retrieval from databases, and designing *World Wide Web* pages as well.

Standard Platform

A type of computer *platform*—the basic computer architecture utilized by a particular model or series of models, which defines a certain standard to which application developers must adhere when writing software intended for it—utilized by commonly available computers, such as Apple *Macintosh*es, *IBM-compatible computer*s, and *UNIX* systems. The term *standard platform* is also descriptive of the particular operating system utilized by these computers, comprising the standard platforms of *Macintosh operating system*, *DOS*, *Windows*, *UNIX*, and *OS/2*. See *Platform*.

Standard Size

One of several sizes to which paper has been pre-cut, depending on the paper *grade*. Paper is typically less expensive and more readily available when ordered in a standard size than when ordered in a custom size. In addition, less

Page Size (in.)	Printed Pages in One Signature	Signatures per Sheet	Paper Size (in.)
4×9	4	12	25×38
	8	12	38×50
	12	4	25×38
	16	6	38×50
	24	2	25×38
4¼×5⅜	4	32	35×45
	8	16	35×45
	16	8	35×45
	32	4	35×45
4½×6	4	16	25×38
	8	8	25×38
	16	4	25×38
	32	2	25×38
5½×8½	4	16	35×45
	8	8	35×45
	16	4	35×45
	32	2	35×45
6×9	4	8	25×38
	8	4	25×38
	16	2	25×38
	32	2	38×50
8½×11	4	4	23×35
	8	2	23×35
	16	2	35×45
9×12	4	4	25×38
	16	2	38×50

Courtesy International Paper Pocket Pal.

Cutting chart showing smaller, popular sizes cut from larger, standard sheet sizes.

paper is wasted when standard sizes are used. Standard sizes can be cut evenly to produce all of the popular trimmed sizes currently in use. The cutting chart on the previous page indicates the smaller, popular sizes that can be obtained from the larger, standard sizes.

Standard Viewing Conditions

A set of specific, *ANSI*-prescribed conditions for the optimum viewing and evaluation of *color* transparencies and prints. Due to the tendency for different lighting conditions and other environments to alter any or all of the values of a color and a color's interaction with others, the standard viewing conditions were devised as a means of attempting to objectively evaluate color.

Standard viewing conditions are a neutral gray surround, a light source with a temperature of *5000 K*, and an illumination intensity of 200 *footcandles*. A large transparency should have a 2- to 4-in. gray border and should not have a white surround.

Stand Oil

A thick *drying oil* used in printing ink *vehicle*s produced by heating *linseed oil* to high temperatures (such as 600°F and above) and allowing impurities to settle out. The term *stand oil* is also used in the United Kingdom to refer to linseed oil in general.

Stapling

Attaching or binding printed sheets together using wire staples. Also known as *wire stitching*. The binding of publications by means of staples driven though their folded spines is known as *saddle-stitching*.

Star Network

In networking, a *network topology* in which all *node*s are connected to a central controller or *server*, which in some configurations is called a *hub*. The arrangement of nodes around the central hub resembles a star, hence the name. The advantage of the star topology is that it is a simple matter to connect additional nodes, be they workstations or peripherals such as printers. A disadvantage, however, is that if the hub crashes or fails, the network is effectively shut down.

Starred Roll

A defect in paper roll winding that results in a roll with an end forming a star-shaped pattern due to buckling of loosely wound inner paper layers under pressure of more tightly wound outer layers. Starred rolls (and other roll defects) are the result of inconsistencies in moisture content and thickness produced during the papermaking process. Thicker portions of the paper *web* will wind more tightly than thinner portions, and the differential tension will result in the variations of the roll that cause starring. Advanced *cross-machine direction (CD)* monitoring procedures in the *forming section* of the papermaking machine can ensure that the papermaking *furnish* delivered across

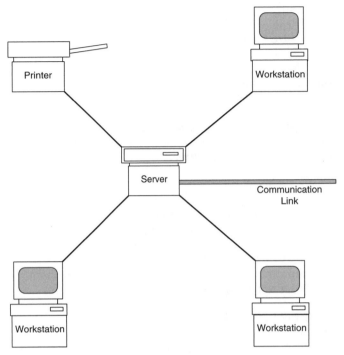

Star network topology.

the *forming wire* is consistent in thickness and moisture content, so as not to present problems when building the final paper roll. Variations in the forming of the paper web can also be rectified in subsequent stages of the papermaking process, such as *calendering*.

Defects in the paper roll have serious consequences for printers utilizing web presses. Rolls that do not unwind into the machine with uniform tension across the web stretch and deform, often beyond their ability to return to their original dimensions, causing various printing distortions. Problems with paper rolls can also cause web breaks. (See also *Telescoped Roll*.)

Start Character

In packaging, a pattern of bars and spaces identifying the beginning of a *bar code*.

Starting Point

In scanning, a specified minimum tone value at which a particular *scanner* function, such as *undercolor removal*, begins.

Start-of-Print Line

A line etched in the gutters of some offset press *plate cylinder*s, indicating the topmost boundary of the area that will print. Image areas on the plate that is mounted on such a cylinder should all lie below that line.

The start-of-print line is commonly located an inch below the *cylinder gap*, and the portion of the cylinder between the start of the gap and the line forms an inclined surface, allowing the *form roller*s to return from the gap to the surface of the plate smoothly and without bumping, which can generate streaks or other printing problems. (See *Plate Cylinder*.)

Stat

Shorthand term for a *photostat*. See *Photostat*.

Stat Camera

Alternate term for a *process camera* used in graphic arts photography. See *Process Camera* and *Photography: Graphic Arts Photography*.

Static Friction

One of two basic types of *friction*, referring to the force that resists an object's beginning to slide from a stationary position. See *Friction* and *Kinetic Friction*.

Static Random-Access Memory (SRAM)

In computing, a type of *RAM* chip used for *cache memory*. See *RAM* and *Cache Memory*.

Statistical Multiplexing

In telecommunications, a means of *multiplexing* in which the capacity of the *multiplexer* is distributed over all the channels that are transmitting at any given moment. As a result, the channels that are transmitting at any one time can receive a boost in transmission capacity.

Status Line

In some computer applications (such as word processing), a line or bar, often located at the bottom of the screen, that provides information concerning an open document, such as the page being displayed, the line the *cursor* is on, etc.

Status "T"

An *ANSI*-prescribed set of specifications defining the spectral response characteristics of a *densitometer*.

Steamset Ink

A term for *moisture-set ink* in which the moisture required for the setting of the ink *pigment* is provided in the form of water vapor or steam. See *Moisture-Set Ink*.

Steel-Rule Die

In *diecutting*, a series of metal blades or creasing rules mounted on a plywood *dieboard*, used to cut a particular pattern into a *substrate*, or to cut the substrate into a particular pattern. See *Diecutting*.

Stem

In typography, the primary, straight vertical stroke of a letter or other character, or the primary diagonal stroke in an *oblique* character. See *Letter Elements*.

Stencil

In *screen printing*, an emulsion—either cut by hand or etched photographically—attached to the bottom of the

printing screen. The stencil is open in the image areas, and hard and durable in the nonimage areas. Consequently, ink can only be forced through the stencil in the open areas, where it then contacts the *substrate*. The two basic types of stencils used in screen printing are *hand-cut stencils* and *photostencils*. A third type of stencilling is performed typically on art prints. Called *tusche-and-glue*, it involves drawing the image directly onto the screen by hand. See *Tusche-and-Glue*.

Hand-Cut Stencils. A *hand-cut stencil* is the oldest form of stencil-making, involving as it does the manual cutting away of the image areas to be printed. Originally, thin sheets of paper were cut and attached to the bottom of the screen, but then a variety of lacquers were experimented with. In the 1930s, it was discovered that if a coat of lacquer was spread on a hard surface, it would solidify and be able to be pulled off the surface as a single piece. The formation of this lacquer film, its application to a plastic support sheet, the cutting away of the image areas of the lacquer, the adhesion of the remaining lacquer to the screen, and, finally, the removal of the backing sheet, is still the basic process of hand-cut stencils. New formulations are being developed—such as water-soluble stencil emulsions—that serve the same ink-blocking purpose, but they are easier to adhere and remove from the screen. The lacquer- or water-based emulsion is applied to the surface of a plastic sheet. With a *frisket knife*, *art knife*, or other form of sharp cutting implement, the image areas are cut out of the emulsion, though it is important that the plastic support sheet itself not be marked, cut, or embossed. The original can be a photographic tracing, or an original design. It is necessary to leave at least a 2-in. margin on all four sides of the stencil, so as to ensure proper adhesion to the screen fabric.

A hand-cut stencil is applied to the screen commonly using only water. A *build-up layer* of glass, plastic, or other hard material, is used to raise the height of the *printing bed* for application of the stencil. The stencil is placed, emulsion-side up, on the top of this layer. The screen is placed, *well-side* up, on top of it. A layer of moisture is gently applied to the top of the screen with a sponge, and the stencil sticks to the bottom of the screen. The stencil is dried, and at that point the backing sheet can be peeled off. Alternatively, the stencil can be applied with the screen upside-down. Lacquer-based stencils require special adhering fluid to soften the lacquer emulsion and allow it to stick to the screen fabric.

Photostencils. A *photostencil* is based on the original principle of the *carbon tissue* resist, in which a photosensitive emulsion is exposed to a film positive (or negative), and the resist hardens in either the image or nonimage areas (depending upon the nature of the resist), the soft portions being washed away. A photostencil is made by exposing the stencil to a film positive of the image. The ultraviolet light cures—or hardens—the emulsion in the nonimage areas, leaving the unexposed image areas soft

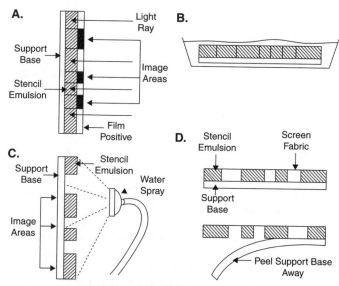

The process of exposing an indirect stencil: (A) a film positive allows light to strike only the nonimage areas, which then harden during development (B). After exposure, the unhardened image areas are washed away (C), leaving those areas of the stencil open. Finally, the stencil is adhered to the screen fabric (D).

and soluble. Developing and washout procedures remove the emulsion from the image areas, opening them. The stencil is then chemically fixed, to keep the image permanent, and applied to the screen fabric. Photostencils are ideal for intricate work, halftones, and other forms of images that would be difficult to accomplish with traditional, knife-cut stencils.

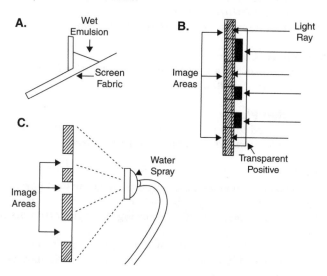

The process of exposing a direct stencil: (A) a wet emulsion is applied directly to the screen fabric, and exposed to actinic light through a film positive (B), where nonimage areas harden. After exposure, washing (C) removes the unhardened image areas, leaving holes in the stencil.

Photostencils are prepared in one of three different ways: the ***indirect process***, the ***direct process***, and the combination ***direct/indirect process***. See ***Photostencil***.

After applying the stencil to the screen fabric, it is necessary to mask the portions of the screen that the stencil does not cover. This can be accomplished with kraft masking paper, but this is only practical for short runs. A ***block-out fluid***, which is commonly employed for this purpose, is applied to both sides of the screen fabric; when dry it resists the penetration of the ink vehicle through it. It can also be used to touch up any pinholes, or other imperfections in the stencil itself. An advantage to commercially available screen printing blockout fluids is their ability to be washed out of the screen readily at the conclusion of a print run.

After printing, most water-soluble screen stencils can be removed with water alone, but often different types of stencils require specially formulated solvents or enzyme solutions to effectively remove the stencil.

Stencil Design Area

In ***screen printing***, only that portion of the stencil that contains the design to be printed.

Stencil Fabric

Any of a variety of woven materials used in ***screen printing*** on which a stencil is mounted to selectively allow ink to be transferred to the ***substrate***. Stencil—or screen—fabrics can be woven from silk (the original fabric material, hence the obsolete term ***silkscreening***), synthetic fibers (such as ***dacron***), or finely woven metal filaments, specifically stainless steel.

Stenciling

Any form of printing, drawing, or painting by means of a ***stencil***. See ***Stencil***.

Stencil Volume

In ***screen printing***, the area (width times length) of a ***mesh aperture*** multiplied by the total thickness of the fabric and stencil, in contrast to the ***mesh volume***, which does not take into account the thickness of the stencil.

Step-and-Repeat

In platemaking, a means by which multiple images from a single-image ***flat*** are exposed onto a plate in accurate ***register***. For example, when printing labels, several copies of the same label may be printed on a large size of stock, which can then be cut into individual labels during finishing. Rather than create several negatives and image the plate once, a single negative can be made of the label and repeatedly exposed to the plate in different locations. Step-and-repeat can be effected manually or by a photocomposing device.

Step Backward

On a ***videodisc*** or similar medium, the movement of the ***read/write head*** of disk drive back one increment of space, which may be a ***frame***, a ***segment***, etc. See ***Step Forward***.

Step Forward

On a **videodisc** or other such medium, the movement of the **read/write head** of disk drive forward one increment of space, which may be a **frame**, a **segment**, etc. See also **Step Backward**.

Step Frame

The playback of a **videodisc** frame by **frame**, either forward or backward.

Stepping Motor

An electric motor used in **scanner**s that, under the control of digital data, moves precisely controlled distances. A stepping motor is used to drive the **lead screw** controlling the movement of the optics in a **drum scanner**.

Step Tablet

A type of **gray scale**, particularly one that has been imaged on film (rather than paper) and consists of levels of gray in discrete—not continuous—shades of gray, ranging from white to black. Step tablets are commonly used to monitor the exposure of printing plates. See **Gray Scale**. Also known as a **Step Wedge**.

A step tablet with 15 discrete steps.

Step Wedge

A film positive or negative comprising lines of type at various sizes—some at hard-to-reproduce sizes—used to determine the exposure time for **photostencil**s used in **screen printing**. By covering various portions of the step wedge and exposing portions of it for varying amounts of time, upon development, washing, and mounting the best exposure time for a particular photostencil material can be gauged. See **Photostencil**.

Step *wedge* is an alternate term for a type of **gray scale** known as a **step tablet**. See **Step Tablet** and **Gray Scale**.

Stet

In typography and **proofing**, a proofreader's command written in the margin of marked up proofs (or corrected manuscript or typescript copy) to indicate that marked corrections should be disregarded, and the original copy should stand as it was. The word "stet" derives from the Latin word *stet*, the present subjunctive third person singular of the verb *stare*, meaning "to stand." Some people say that it means "leave it alone."

Stickup Initial

Alternate term for a **raised initial**. See **Raised Initial**.

Stickyback

A double-sided adhesive used on some presses to mount **flexographic** plates on the **plate cylinder**. Other types of presses use clamps, magnetic plate backing, and other mounting devices.

Stiff

Descriptive of a printing ink with too great a **body**. See **Body**.

Stiffness

A paper property that measures its ability to withstand a bending force. Paper has two basic varieties of stiffness: **flexural stiffness**, which is a paper's resistance to an externally applied bending force, and **handling stiffness**, which is a paper's ability to support its own weight. Thickness (or **caliper**) and **basis weight** are the chief determinants of a paper's stiffness; generally, a paper's stiffness varies as the cube of thickness (a doubling of caliper produces an eight-fold increase in stiffness). A paper's stiffness is also greater when the bending force is in the **cross-grain direction**, often by a ratio of two-to-one. The degree of stiffness required varies according to end use requirements.

Still Development

In photography, the **development** of an exposed film without agitating the tray of chemicals. Although this reduces the effects of infectious development, it produces lower **contrast** negatives.

Still Frame

A stationary video image, equal to one **frame** or one-twenty-fifth of a second.

Still Video

A video image containing no motion, generated either by freezing a **videotape** or **videodisc** at a single **frame**, or by capturing an image using a **still video camera**.

Still Video Camera

Alternate term for an **electronic camera**. See **Electronic Camera**. Abbreviated **svc**.

Still Video Player

A device used to view images photographed by means of an **electronic camera**. See **Electronic Camera**.

Sting

In television and video production, a short musical passage, such as a commercial jingle, designed to catch the viewer's attention and keep him/her humming it despite attempts to stop.

Also in television or video, a *sting* is a very brief musical note or chord used to emphasize a dramatic moment, such as in a soap opera.

Stipple

In **binding and finishing**, a background pattern of very small dots engraved in stamping **die**s to add special effects to book covers.

Stochastic Screening

A type of digital *halftone* screening that varies the pattern of dots while keeping the size of the dots constant. In contrast, conventional halftone screening varies the size of the dots while keeping their frequency per line constant. (See COLOR PLATE 22.)

Conventional screens exhibit *amplitude modulation*, which, in the case of halftone screens, means that the

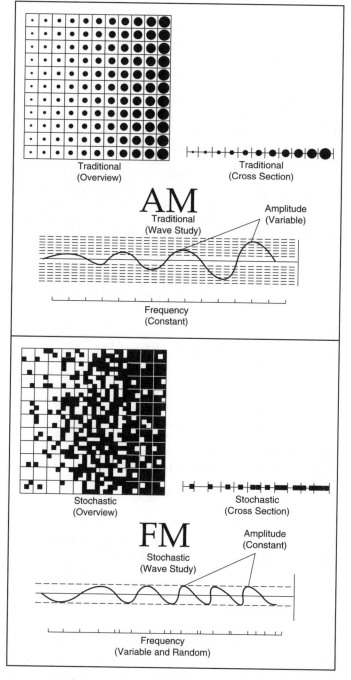

A comparison of conventional, or AM, screening (top) and stochastic, or FM, screening (bottom).

sizes of the dots are modulated or varied, while the frequency remains constant. Stochastic screening exhibits *frequency modulation*, which means that the frequency of the dots is modulated or varied, while the size remains constant. (For this reason, stochastic screening is also known as *FM screening*.) Stochastic screens use *microdot*s that are typically 15–20 microns in diameter and vary in line count by the tonal qualities of a particular section of an image. Of particular advantage is the fact that this seemingly random dot arrangement eliminates the necessity of worrying about *screen angles* when printing multiple colors; the irregular pattern of dots eliminates the interference of screen lines that causes *moiré*. Additionally, stochastic screening reduces digital file size and the time required for *ripping*. On the printing side, the random dot placement increases image *contrast* without decreasing *shadow* detail and allows for greater ink density, which enhances the reproduction of detail and color *saturation*. Stochastic screening also has the advantage of minimizing *dot gain*, as the small dots increase in size much less than conventional dots. On the down side, however, the tiny dot size creates difficulties in proofing and platemaking, but the advantages of stochastic screening are engendering the desire to quickly solve these somewhat minute problems.

Stochastic screening was originally only available on *raster image processor*s from a handful of companies, in particular Linotype-Hell (now part of Heidelberg) and Agfa. Now, there are over 20 products. It is currently used primarily for the color printing of complicated images involving complex textures (such as that of woven fabrics such as tweeds and silks), repeating backgrounds, and other geometric shapes that tend to cause interference problems when printed using conventional screens. Additionally, stochastic screening is useful in the printing of *extra-trinary colors* (additional *process color*s beyond the basic *CMY* triumvirate), which are nearly impossible to print using conventional screens (the additional screens cannot be placed at angles to eliminate moiré). (See COLOR PLATE 23.) Although still in its infancy, stochastic screening has the potential to become widely used in color prepress and printing, especially as it exhibits improved image quality and reduced file size.

Stock

Term for any surface to be printed to which ink will adhere. The stock, also called *substrate*, is typically paper, but can also be plastics, *foil*, metal, cloth, or any other surface to which printing ink will be applied.

Stocking Items

Any paper manufactured in a popular size, weight, color, finish, etc., of which an adequate stock is maintained regularly and that is thus readily obtained.

Stock Preparation

Collective term for the *loading*, *beating*, and *refining* of paper *pulp* fibers to produce the desired characteristics of the papermaking *furnish*. The degree of refining, beating, and the addition of specific types and quantities of *fillers* and *sizing* all affect the paper that ultimately emerges at the end of the papermaking process. Stock preparation is performed after the papermill receives the pulp from the pulpmill, either in wet or dry form. The *cellulose* fibers comprising the pulp must be in a water suspension both for *loading* and to control the fiber bonding as the paper *web* forms.

Stock preparation systems can either be batch or continuous. Batch systems swirl the pulp in a *beater* followed by a *conical refiner*. The purpose of beating is to swell and soften the fibers, which facilitates the later binding of the fibers to form the paper web. Continuous systems utilize *disk refiners* that facilitate abrupt changes, depending on what the ultimate end-use of the paper is destined to be.

Differences in the nature and extent of refining and of the type and quantity of fillers and additives directly affect the paper that is produced, as refining is the determining factor in how the cellulose fibers bind with each other. (See *Paper and Papermaking: Papermaking*.)

Stock Weights

Frequently used *basis weight*s of paper kept in stock by a printer or paper supplier. See *Basis Weight*.

Stoddard Solvent

A *solvent* used widely in *screen printing* for removing ink from the screen following a print run.

Stone

In *letterpress* printing, alternate term for the *flatbed* on which metal type is locked up.

Stop Bath

In photography, an acidic or water-based solution used to stop the action of the chemical *developer* during film *development*, thus preventing overdevelopment. The stop bath is also used to "rinse" the developed film and prevent developing solution from contaminating the *fixing solution*.

Stop Character

In packaging, a pattern of bars and spaces identifying the end of a *bar code*.

Stopping Out

In prepress, an alternate term for the application of *opaque* to a *negative* during *stripping*. See *Opaque* (second definition).

Stopping out is also used to refer to the application of a lacquer during the process of *dot etching*. See *Dot Etching*.

Stopping out also refers to a chemical protection of certain areas of *halftone* plates which have been deep-etched, as a means of preventing ink from collecting on the protected areas.

Storage

Any internal or external portion of a computer in which data can be held for later retrieval.

Storage Capacity

See *Capacity*.

Storage Fragmentation

In computing, especially on a *Windows*, *DOS*, or *Macintosh* computer system, the noncontiguous storage of files. When a computer stores files that have been edited or altered, it does not necessarily store a complete new file, but rather inserts codes into the previously saved version of the file that function as pointers to the location of the changes made to the file. The changes may be located near the original file, but not always. Thus, files are said to be *fragmented*.

A software utility (such as Norton's SpeedDisk) is used to *defragment* files, or combine all the file fragments into a single location or block, which increases the speed with which files can be accessed and opened. Defragmenting files periodically improves the computer's performance.

Storyboard

In film, television, video, and multimedia production, a visual or graphic outline of the narrative and/or structure of a production, illustrating—comic-strip style—key scenes, transitions, camera angles, etc. Dialogue, action, and other notes are written as captions beneath the picture to which they correspond.

Stoving

The process of drying a printed ink film by exposing it to temperatures in excess of 175°F.

STP

Abbreviation for *shielded twisted-pair* wiring. See *Shielded Twisted-Pair*.

Straight Copy

In page layout, copy that contains no charts, graphs, illustrations, or other graphic elements beyond text.

Straight Edge

A metal, plastic, or wood tool (such as a ruler) used to draw a straight line.

Straight Matter

In typography, a block or page (or more) of text that is typeset without heads or other mixing of *typeface*s or *point size*s, although the use of italic and bold versions of the text face of the same typeface is included in the designation of a length of type as "straight matter."

Streak

A printing defect characterized by elongated blotches of ink in nonimage areas, commonly caused by mechanical problems with the press, such as damaged rollers (in lithography), or by improper wiping of a *gravure cylinder* by the *doctor blade* (due to dried ink fragments attached to it, or other such problems).

Stream Feeder

One of two basic types of systems used to feed sheets of paper into a sheetfed offset printing press (in contrast to a *single-sheet feeder*). A stream feeder feeds sheets, at a speed slower than that of the press, such that the rear edge of a sheet of paper overlaps the front edge of the successive sheet. The advantages of this type of feeding system include greater sheet control. Since the sheets are moving slower

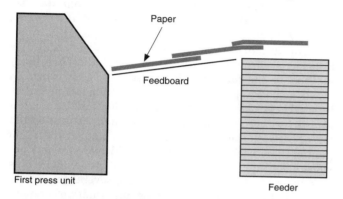

The baisc principle of a stream feeder, whereby press sheets overlap slightly on the feedboard.

than the speed of the press, they do not bounce as much on the *feedboard*, and it is easier to control their position, preventing *misregister* and paper jams. When using a stream feeder, a *double-sheet detector* (a device used to detect when more than the proper number of sheets are being fed) needs to be calibrated to take into account the overlap of sheets. The number of sheets overlapping at any one time varies by the size of the paper. If a smaller size is being used, no more than two sheets will overlap at any one time on the feedboard. If a larger size is being used, three sheets may be overlapping at any one time. (Consequently, a double-sheet detector when used with a stream feeder may more properly be known as an *extra-sheet detector*.) The basic configuration of a stream feeder is described in *Feeding Section: Sheetfed Offset Lithography*. (See also *Single-Sheet Feeder*.)

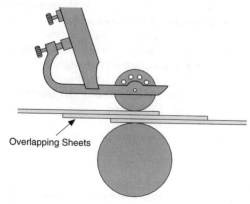

Setting the double-sheet detector according to the number of sheets that overlap on the feedboard.

Streaming Tape

Alternate term for a *tape streamer*. See *Tape Streamer*.

Strength Test

Any of a wide variety of tests used to gauge a paper's strength against tearing, bursting, folding, delamination, etc. See *Paper and Papermaking: Paper Properties*.

Stress

In typography, the gradation in curved strokes from thick to thin. The original lettering of scribes had strong diagonal stress caused by the pen. Today's refined designs usually have a vertical stress. *Sans serif* type, however, tends to have no stress at all.

Stretch

In *animation*, an effect used between two *key frame*s to simulate movement in which the subject is stretched in both directions simultaneously.

Stretch Cloth

In *binding and finishing*, a cotton-based fabric that has been Sanforized (treated to resist shrinking), used primarily on cloth-based covers for books bound via *perfect binding*.

Stretch Frame

A screen frame on a *screen printing* press that, once the fabric is attached, can allow additional adjustments of tension by means of rods, bolts, cams, or other such devices.

Stretch Ink

Any type of ink—for example, a *plastisol*-based ink—that remains elastic after curing and hardening. When printed on an elastic *substrate*, it will contract with the substrate upon the release of tension without cracking or distorting.

Striation

A printing defect (commonly of *flexography* or *screen printing*) characterized by thin, parallel streaks, commonly in the direction of web travel.

Strike

In film, television, and video production, to remove all the *prop*s from a *set*, usually at the conclusion of a shoot.

Strike-on

Descriptive of type that has been set by direct impression (or by *impact printing*) as by a typewriter.

Strike-on Type

Any characters transferred to a surface by means of a key or needle striking a carbon- or ink-coated ribbon, such as is found on a typewriter.

Strike-on Typesetter

A typesetter that produces character images by means of *strike-on type*. The first of the strike-on typesetters was the Varityper, followed by the Friden Justowriter and the IBM Composer. All were based on typewriters applying proportionally designed typefaces.

Strike-Over

In typography, type that has been set with a line through it, ~~such as this~~. In desktop publishing software, it is known as *strike-through*.

Strike-Through

The visibility of printing on the reverse side of a sheet of paper due to excessive ink penetration through the paper, in contrast to *show-through* in which printing is visible on the reverse of a sheet due to low *opacity*. See also *Show-Through*.

Strike-through is also an alternate term for *strike-over*. See *Strike-over*.

String

See *Character String*.

String-and-Button Envelope

A type of envelope having two reinforced paper buttons applied to the flap and the area just below the flap. The envelope is sealed by winding a string around the two buttons.

Stringiness

The property of a printing ink that describes the extent to which it is able to form long threads or filaments when stretched. See *Length*.

String Substitution

In computing, the substitution of one *character string* with another, different character string.

String Tie

Term for the automated binding of a bundle of papers, magazines, or other publication together with string, often as a prelude to shipping or postal handling.

Strip

In prepress, to attach a film *negative* to a carrier sheet (such as goldenrod) to create a *flat* for platemaking. *Strip* also means to insert an additional negative (such as a *halftone*) into an already assembled flat. (See *Stripping* and *Prepress: Graphic Arts Photography and Flat Assembly*.)

In *binding and finishing*, to attach reinforcements of muslin or other material to printed *signature*s, linings, or *insert*s.

Stripe

In video production, to lay a *time code* signal into the time code channel of a recorded videotape as a prelude to editing.

Strip-in

In prepress, a film *negative* (such as a *halftone*) that needs to be combined with another film negative to produce

a single negative of a page for platemaking. Also known as *set-in*. See *Stripping*.

Strip Method

A means of testing the *roller setting* of an offset press's ink or dampening *ductor roller* or *form roller*s using strips of thin paper or plastic inserted in the nips of the rollers, then pulled out. This method tests the pressure that exists between the two rollers, the size of the nip itself, the hardness (or *durometer*) of the rollers, and any *glazing* that may have occurred.

Two varieties of the strip method of roller testing (also called a *sandwich method*) are used: the *three-strip method* or the *folded-strip method*, both of which are based on inserting several "sandwiches" of paper at various intervals between either the ductor roller and its adjacent *oscillator*, between the form rollers and adjacent oscillator, or between the form rollers and the plate cylinder, and pulling them back out, the ease or difficulty of which provides a subjective but effective determination of the pressure between the rollers. By inserting several sandwiches along the length of the roller nips, uniformity of pressure can also be gauged. (See *Three-Strip Method* and *Folded-Strip Method*.)

Stripper

In prepress, a person who prepares *flat*s for offset platemaking. See *Stripping*.

Stripping

In prepress, the attaching of film *negative*s of a page—which can either be a single negative or the combination of one or more additional negatives exposed separately (such as *halftone*s or other types of *strip-in*)—on the back of a carrier sheet such as goldenrod. All the pages must be assembled on a single sheet of goldenrod in the correct *imposition*. Holes are then cut in the front of the carrier sheet over the image areas of the negative, and extraneous pinholes or other undesired images are blotted out with a thick red or black fluid or pen (a process called *opaquing*). The process of stripping produces a *flat* that is then used to expose a plate prior to printing. (See *Prepress: Graphic Arts Photography and Flat Assembly*.)

In electronic publishing systems, a type of electronic stripping places all the page elements and pages in the proper position and imposition on the digital layout.

In ink terminology, the term stripping is a shortened term for *roller stripping*. See *Roller Stripping*.

In *binding and finishing*, stripping refers to the affixing of muslin or other cloth reinforcements to *signature*s, linings, or *insert*s to impart added strength in *case binding*.

Strobing

In *scanning*, the digitizing of a color image by making only one pass across the image with the *scanner* optics. All three *primary color*s—red, green, and blue—are captured successively per *pixel*. Strobing is an alternative to making three entire passes across the image. See *Scanning*.

The term *strobing* also describes a phenomenon of the human visual system that manifests itself as a "double object," usually experienced when viewing *animation* that does not contain enough *frames per second*.

Stroke

In typography, the primary line or curve making up a letter or other character.

Stroke is also a shorthand term for *keystroke*, or a single instance of a typewriter or keyboard key being depressed.

In phototypesetting and imaging, *stroke* also refers to a character image produced as a series of lines on a photosensitive material by means of a moving point of light.

Stroking

In computer graphics, the drawing of lines around page elements or objects as a means of creating *spreads* for proper *trapping*. See *Spreads and Chokes*.

Stub Edge

Alternate term for *binding edge*. See *Binding Edge*.

Stub Roll

A paper roll on which little paper remains, or a paper roll with a small diameter. See also *Butt Roll*.

Stuck Edge

A paper *web* defect characterized by one or more layers of the roll being stuck together, caused by water, glue, or other such substance getting on the end of the roll, generally accidentally. A stuck edge can cause a *web break* in web offset lithography.

Style

Generally speaking, the unique attribute(s) of any creative individual; e.g., an artist, photographer, etc.

In typography, *style* is also a shorthand term for *typestyle*. See *Typestyle*.

Style Pages

In page design and layout, a set of pages created to convey their intended design, such as the *type specifications*, paragraph formatting, *folios*, *running heads*, etc.

Style Sheet

In electronic publishing systems and *page makeup software*, a set of type formats (such as *font*, *point size*, *leading*, color, etc.) that can be stored and applied to blocks of text, eliminating the need to recreate the type characteristics from scratch each time a format change needs to be made.

Stylus

A pencil-like object that is used to "draw" on a *digitizing tablet* as a means of inputting coordinate data to a computer. See *Digitizing Tablet*.

Styrene-Butadiene

A synthetic latex used as a *binder* in the *coating* of high-quality coated papers. Synthetic binders, which help the coating *pigment* adhere to the paper fibers, are often used in place of more popular organic binders as they provide high *gloss*, increased *ink holdout*, and increased strength and endurance for such post-printing operations as folding. (See *Binder* and *Coating*.)

Subhead

In typography, a secondary *heading*, often in a smaller *point size* and set below the primary head.

Sublimable Dye

A type of colorant that undergoes *sublimation*, or the direct transformation from a solid into a gas without passing through the liquid phase. Sublimable dyes are commonly used in *heat-transfer printing*.

Sublimation

A chemical process by which certain solid substances are converted by heat directly to a gas without first passing through a liquid stage. Upon cooling, they turn back into a solid again, also without passing through a liquid stage. Some common examples are the evaporation of snow and ice from sidewalks or streets without first melting, or the evaporation of mothballs (which are composed of naphthalene or para-dichlorobenzene). Generally speaking, it is small, compact rigid, relatively nonpolar molecules that will sublime readily, so long as their molecular weight is not high enough to preclude their *volatility*. Sublimation is used to purify some substances, such as commercial iodine; iodine molecules are readily sublimed, and they can be volatilized directly to a gas, and the vapor cooled back down to a solid on a cooled surface, separating out less easily sublimed impurities.

Some types of colorants (called *sublimable dye*s) used in heat-transfer printing take advantage of this process.

Sublime

To undergo the chemical process of *sublimation*.

Subscript

See *Inferior*.

Substance

Alternate term for the *basis weight* of *bond* and other writing papers, also known as *substance number* or *substance weight*. See *Basis Weight*.

Substance Number

(Also referred to as *substance weight*.) Alternate term for the *basis weight* of *bond* and other writing papers, also called simply *substance*. See *Basis Weight*.

Substance Weight

Alternate term for *basis weight*. The weight in pounds of a ream (500 sheets) of paper cut to a given standard size for that grade: 25×38 in. for book papers, 20×26 in. for cover papers, 22½×28½ in. or 22½×35 in. for bristols, and 25½×30½ in. for index. For example, 500 25×38-in. sheets of 80-lb. coated paper will weigh 80 lb. Because of various ream sizes specified for various grades of paper, a table of equivalent weights is sometimes necessary to correlate sheets of different grades. An alternative metric system used mostly outside the United States is grams per square meter (g/m²), which has a constant basis for all grades.

Substrate

Term for any surface to be printed to which ink will adhere. The substrate, also called *stock*, is typically paper, but can also refer to plastics, *foil*, metal, cloth, or any other surface to which printing ink will be applied.

Subtractive Color Primaries

In *color*, the colorants *cyan*, *magenta*, and *yellow*, which can be combined to produce other colors, such as green, orange, violet, etc. (See COLOR PLATE 1.) Colors produced using these primaries differ from *additive color primaries* (COLOR PLATE 2) in that it is the selective absorption of light by these colors that produces the intermediates. See *Subtractive Color Theory*.

See also *Additive Color Primaries* and *Color: Color Theory*.

Subtractive Color Theory

In *color*, the production of intermediate colors by mixing the *subtractive color primaries*, or colorants that correspond to *cyan*, *magenta*, and *yellow*. (See COLOR PLATE 1.) Colored substances differ from colored light in that it is their selective absorption of light of certain wavelengths that imparts their color. For example, a cyan pigment absorbs red light, so it appears blue-green; a magenta pigment absorbs green light, so it appears reddish; and a yellow pigment absorbs blue light, so it appears yellow. The combination of all three of these pigments tends to produce black, at least in theory. (*Additive color theory* involves the use of light—rather than colorants—which, although producing roughly the same effect, works on a very different principle; see *Additive Color Theory*. (See also COLOR PLATE 2.)

Inks, dyes, and other materials used in printing, for example, produce many of the colors discernible to the human eye by means of subtractive colors. Varying the amounts of the three primaries (and, in printing, the use of *black*) produces all the shades in between. It should be noted, however, that the color a printed or dyed material is perceived as will depend upon the color of the light used to view. Adjacent colors also influence the perception of a color. (See COLOR PLATE 18.) Under normal white light, a yellow ink will look yellow, since the red, green, and blue light (or the *additive color primaries*) are all present in equal proportion, and the blue light is being absorbed by the colorant, the light reflecting back consisting of red and green light, thus mixing to appear yellow. If the yellow ink were viewed using only a green light, it would appear

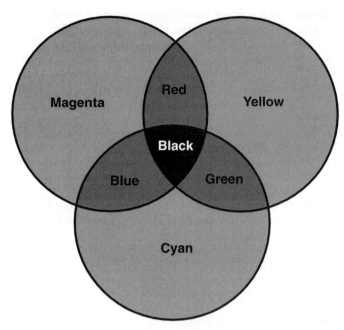

Subtractive color theory.

green, since no blue light is present, and only the green will be reflected back to the eye.

Color computer monitors display colors utilizing the additive colors, while inks to be printed utilize the subtractive colors. It is the difference between the additives and the subtractives that makes color reproduction originating on a computer screen difficult.

Subtractive Plate

A type of printing plate used in *offset lithography*, in contrast to an *additive plate*, in which light shined through a photographic negative hardens image areas on the plate, the nonimage areas remaining soluble. The coating in the nonimage areas then needs to be removed—or subtracted—from the surface of the plate following exposure. A subtractive plate does not need the addition of an image-reinforcing material. See also *Additive Plate*. See *Plate: Offset Lithography*.

Sucker

Any rubber suction cup (typically perforated to allow the use of a vacuum) used on a printing press's *sheet-separation unit* to feed paper into the press. On a *stream feeder*, suckers can either be *pickup suckers* or *forwarding suckers*. (See *Sheet-Separation Unit* and *Feeder Section*.)

Suction Box

In papermaking, a vacuum device used to remove water from the forming paper web on the *forming wire*.

Suction Feed

On a printing press or other device, an alternate term for a *sucker*. See *Sucker*.

Suction Roller

A type of vacuum-powered roller used in the *delivery section* of a sheetfed printing press (especially one used in *offset lithography*)—alone or in tandem with *blowdown*s—to slow down a press sheet as it leaves the *delivery chain* and enters the *delivery pile*. The force of the vacuum pulling down on the sheet keeps the sheet steady as it is about to fall onto the stack. (See *Delivery Section*.)

Suede Finish

A paper *finish* characterized by a texture intended to simulate the feel of velvet or suede.

Suitcase

A program developed for the *Macintosh* for font management, allowing different font packages (themselves called suitcases) to be loaded only when needed. Many computer systems, such as those used in digital prepress, utilize many different types of fonts, which can absorb a lot of computer memory. By selectively and expediently loading only those fonts that are needed, time and memory can be saved. The concept is now applied to all operating systems as a method for applying typefaces.

Sulfate Process

The most prevalent method of *chemical pulping* in papermaking. Also called *kraft*. See *Kraft*.

Sulfate Pulp

Paper *pulp* produced utilizing the *kraft* process (also called the *sulfate process*). See *Kraft*.

Sulfite Process

A *chemical pulping* method of converting wood chips into paper *pulp*. The purpose of *pulping* is to reduce wood (or other fibrous raw material) to individual *cellulose* fibers. A nonfibrous constituent of wood, *lignin*, binds cellulose fibers together and is primarily responsible for reducing paper quality and *permanence*. The *sulfite process*, the older and less used of the two primary chemical pulping processes, cooks wood chips in *sulfurous acid* combined with limestone to produce *calcium bisulfite*. The combination of sulfurous acid and calcium bisulfite dissolves the lignin in the wood and liberates the cellulose fibers. *Sulfite pulp* is soft and flexible, is moderately strong, and is used to supplement mechanical pulps (most typically in newsprint). The sulfite process was the most prevalent chemical pulping process until the mid-20th century. The sulfite process is not well-suited to pulping highly resinous wood, such as pine trees. Its original calcium-based chemicals are unrecoverable, and pollution laws have resulted in newer substances being utilized, such as sodium, magnesium, and ammonia bases (the active chemical in the sulfite process is the bisulfite ion— HSO_3^{2-}). These bases are easier to recover. The sulfite process is an acidic pulping process and exists in contrast to the alkaline *soda process*. The sulfite process has been replaced in very large part by the *sulfate* or *kraft* process.

Pulps produced using the sulfite process are called *sulfite pulp*. (See *Chemical Pulping* and *Kraft*.)

Sulfite Pulp

Paper *pulp* produced using the *sulfite process*. See *Sulfite Process*.

Sulfurous Acid

An acid (chemical formula H_2SO_3) produced in the *sulfite process* of *chemical pulping* by burning sulfur to produce sulfur dioxide, then reacting the sulfur dioxide with water. Sulfurous acid is reacted with limestone to produce *calcium bisulfite*, and the mixture of calcium bisulfite and sulfurous acid dissolves *lignin* present in wood. (See also *Chemical Pulping* and *Sulfite Process*.)

Summation Check

Alternate term for *checksum*. See *Checksum*.

Sunken Initial

In typography, an *initial* letter set such that the top of the initial is even with the top of the first line of type. See *Initial*.

Super

In *case binding*, an alternate term for *crash*. See *Crash* (third definition).

In video production, *super* is also an abbreviated term for *superimposition*. See *Superimposition*.

SuperATM

An *extension* to the *Adobe Type Manager (ATM)* utility that is distinguished by its ability to imitate fonts not available in a particular system. If, for example, a document contains text originally set in Caslon, and it is opened on a system that does not contain Caslon, SuperATM uses *multiple master* technology to create an ersatz Caslon which, though perhaps differing slightly from true Caslon, will possess the proper character widths. As a result, the layout of the document will not change.

Supercalendering

A paper *finishing* operation consisting of an additional degree of *calendering* performed on a special machine not connected to the main papermaking machine. The supercalender gives paper a high-gloss finish, the extent of supercalendering determining the extent of the gloss. A supercalender is a vertical alternating stack of hard polished steel and soft cotton (or other resilient material) rolls. The hard roll is pressed heavily against the soft roll, compressing the material. As the paper *web* passes through this nip, the force generated as the soft roll struggles to return to its original dimensions "buffs" the paper, generating the additional luster and enamel-like finish typical of supercalendered paper. Supercalendering, in enhancing some paper properties, diminishes others in the same way that regular calendering does. (See *Calendering*.) See illustration on the next page.

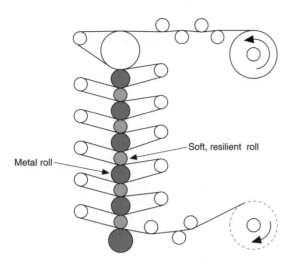

A supercalender.

Supercase

In phototypesetting, a set of special characters that were neither *lowercase* not *uppercase*, but were rather accessed by hitting a special *supershift* key (or code).

Supercell

In digital *halftone* screening, a large collection of *halftone cell*s (which are in turn composed of many printer *spot*s) which can be moved as a single unit, as a means of optimizing certain *screen angles*. See *Screen Angles*.

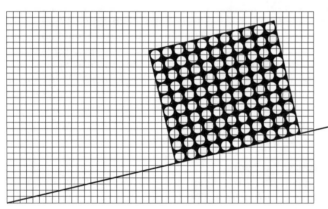

A large enough supercell can create a digital halftone of any screen frequency.

Super Density (SD)

Alternate term for a type of *high-density compact disc* designed by Toshiba/Time Warner. See *High-Density Compact Disc (HDCD)*.

Superimposition

In film, television, video, or multimedia production, the placing of one image over another and displaying them together on one screen. One video image may be placed over another, a computer-generated image may be placed over a video image (and vice versa), or graphics may be placed over a video or computer-generated image (as in the creation of titles or credits). A superimposed image is also called an *overlay*. In video editing, often superimposition is effected by means of *chroma-keying*.

Superior

In typography, characters set in a smaller point size and positioned above the *baseline*, also called a *superscript*. Superior characters are used for exponents (such as "10^{13}"), *footnote*s ("[2]See *The GATF Encyclopedia of Graphic Communications*. . ."), etc. They are most often numerals, but letters can be used as well. Superiors can be "manufactured" by changing to a smaller size and advancing the line spacing (if this capability is available) for positioning. See also *Inferior*.

Superior characters align at the cap height or the ascender height. Most systems produce and position them automatically.

Super-Quickset Infrared Ink

A type of *quickset ink* whose drying (or "setting") is facilitated by the application of heat energy in the form of *infrared* radiation. The ink *vehicle* consists of synthetic resins combined with special *solvent*s and a trace of drying oil. Super-quickset inks dry ten times faster than traditional quickset inks, even without the application of heat. (See *Quickset Ink*.)

Superscript

See *Superior*.

Supershift

An additional level of meaning assigned to a shift or precedence key on a keyboard. Typewriter keys allow two meanings for every key—shift and unshift mode. The supershift introduced additional meaning to keyboard keys if a special key is pressed first. This code or character signals the computer that the following data or character will have a different meaning than usual, or signals a change of mode. Also called a precedence code, it may be a shift or supershift character, which will change the mode of the input until another similar precedence code is used, or allowing the operator to use standard characters for command sequences. For instance, on a key sequence "precedence code" L20 might be a command for a leading of 20 points. User instruction to the computer or program, generally given through a keyboard or interactive device, can be a word, mnemonic, or character that causes a computer to perform a predefined operation. Typeset characters are what you see; typesetting commands determine how and where you will see them. Commands tell the typesetter or system how wide you want the measure, what point size, typeface and leading, the type of indention, and placement of copy. Some commands are as simple as one keystroke, but others, because they contain variable data (information that differs from job to job) must somehow be segregated from typeset characters.

Super Storyboard

A set of documents that describes all the audio, video, graphic, and control aspects of a *videodisc* program, especially one with a high degree of *interactivity*.

Super VGA

See *Super Video Graphics Array (SVGA)*.

Super-VHS

An upgrade to the *Video Home System (VHS)* videotape format that provides a sharper image quality (by recording more image lines) and a new tape composition allowing less *noise* to be recorded and more *generation*s to be made with less loss of quality. Abbreviated *S-VHS*.

Super-Video

A video signal format, used in the *Hi-8* and *Super-VHS* tape formats, that produces high-quality images by transmitting the *chrominance* and the *luminance* information separately, according to the *YC* method. Often abbreviated *S-Video*.

Super Video Graphics Array (SVGA)

A video card that can be added to *VGA* computer monitors to increase the screen *resolution* to 1024×768 *pixel*s, with a total simultaneous display of 256 colors. See *Video Graphics Array (VGA)*.

Supervisory Routine

An alternate term for *executive routine*. See *Executive Routine*.

Surface Acoustical Wave Monitor

A type of *touch screen* monitor. See *Touch Screen*.

Surface Mapping

An alternate term for *texture mapping*. See *Texture Mapping*.

Surface Plate

The most common type of printing plate used in *offset lithography*, which consists of a metal—typically aluminum—covered with a light-sensitive coating. Light shining through the image areas of a photographic negative hardens this coating, which remains on the plate when chemical treatment is added to remove the unexposed, nonimage areas of the plate. (See *Plate: Offset Lithography*.)

Surface Sizing

Materials (usually a starch solution) added to the surface of a partially dried paper *web* as a means of sealing surface fibers and increasing sheet strength and resistance to stresses. Additional substances may be used in addition to or instead of starch to impart other desired surface properties to the paper, such as increased water repellency, or resistance to penetration by other types of fluids, such as ink, oil, or grease. Surface sizing also reduces *fuzz*, loose paper fibers that cause blanket *piling* on offset presses. Surface sizing is added using a *size press*, a set of two rollers located near the end of a papermaking machine's *drying section*. As the still-damp paper web passes through the nip of these rollers, the sizing solution coats the surface of the web. Surface sizing differs in application and purpose from *internal sizing*. The addition of surface sizing depends upon the ultimate end-use requirements of the paper and the printing process for which it is destined. Paper that is to be run on high-speed web presses requires no surface sizing, as ink must be absorbed rapidly by the paper. Sheetfed offset printing may require paper that is surface-sized, to decrease blanket piling. Surface sizing that is added by running the paper web through a tub of the sizing solution is called tub sizing. Surface sizing is also called *external sizing*. (See also *Sizing* and *Size Press*.)

Surface Strength

Alternate term for *pick resistance*. See *Pick Resistance*.

Surfactant

An organic chemical added to an offset press *fountain solution* to reduce the surface tension of the solution and to better allow it to quickly form a thin film on, or "wet," the rollers and the plate.

In fountain solutions containing alcohol, the alcohol itself acts as a surfactant, or surface-active agent, but in non-alcohol fountain solutions, the fluid replacing the alcohol needs to have its wetting properties supplemented. Surfactants gather at the interface between the fountain solution and the surrounding air (or ink) and insinuate themselves between the molecules of water, which have a high tendency to cohese and impart to water a high surface tension, which is undesirable for lithographic printing. The action of a surfactant can be illustrated by the example of a drop of water on a nonabsorbent surface. The angle formed by a line drawn tangent to the point at which the drop contacts the surface and the surface (called the "contact angle") is typically greater than 90°. A surfactant added to the drop will reduce that contact angle to less than 90°, as the drop loses its sphericity and spreads out across the surface in a thinner film.

In high-speed presses, these air/ink-fountain solution interfaces are destroyed and reformed very quickly, and good surfactants must be able to diffuse to the new interfaces rapidly, in order to ensure that the fountain solution retains its ability to form a thin, continuous film. An excessive amount of surfactant in the solution, however, can cause excessive *emulsification* of the ink, which generates its own variety of press and printing problems. (See *Fountain Solution*.)

A wide variety of surfactants are available, and they can be divided into several groups. An anionic surfactant contains electrically polarized portions of molecules that carry a negative charge. These negative regions attract the positive charged regions of molecules in the substance to which the surfactant is added. All the portions of the molecules at the surface of the liquid, then, are negatively charged. The mutual repulsion of like-charged areas reduces the cohesion between molecules and reduces surface tension. (Common soap, whose cleaning ability is based on increased wetting of surfaces, is an anionic surfactant.) Cationic surfactants function essentially like anionic surfactants, except that the polar groupings in the surfactant

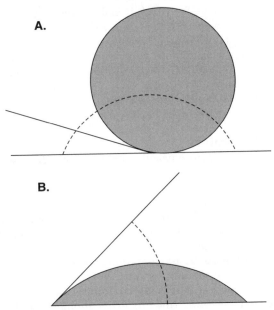

Contact angle of a typical drop on a surface (A), and the contact angle that results after the addition of a surfactant (B).

are positively charged, attracting the negatively charged portions of molecules in the substance and leaving positive charges at the surface. Amphoteric surfactants contain molecules with both positive and negative groupings and can behave anionically or cationically, depending upon the makeup of the substance to which it is added. Other, nonionic surfactants may also be used, which operate by containing molecules having portions that are attracted to a particular compound in the substance and portions that are repelled by the same substances. The mechanics are the same as those found with ionic surfactants.

Surfactants are also added to printing inks to reduce the tendency for *flocculation* of the ink *pigment*.

Surge
See *Power Surge*.

Surge Protector
A device attached to the AC cord of an electronic or electric component that absorbs *surge*s in voltage. Such electrical surges may be caused by lightning, nearby electric motors, etc. Although early personal computers could be easily damaged by electrical surges, most contemporary microcomputers have effective surge protection built in. An external surge protector never hurts, however.

Surprinting
In printing, an alternate term for *overprinting*. See *Overprinting*.

In *prepress*, *surprinting* refers to the imaging of two separate *flat*s on the same *plate*, such that there is some amount of overlap between images on the two flats. (See *Complementary Flat* and *Prepress: Graphic Arts Photography and Flat Assembly*.)

SV
In packaging, an abbreviation for *sewn valve*, a type of paper *bag*. See *Sewn Valve (SV)*.

SVC
Abbreviation for *still video camera*, itself an alternate term for an *electronic camera*. See *Electronic Camera*.

SVGA
Abbreviation for *Super Video Graphics Array*. See *Super Video Graphics Array (SVGA)*.

S-VHS
Abbreviation for *Super-VHS*. See *Super-VHS*.

S-Video
Abbreviation for *super-video*. See *Super-Video*.

Swap File
In computing, a portion of disk space used to manage *virtual memory*. The operating system creates this file in which to store data that would ordinarily be stored in *random-access memory (RAM)*. Such a file may be a *temporary swap file* (in which case it varies in location on the disk from session to session, and also varies in size) or a *permanent swap file* (in which case it is fixed in size and position). Swap files are not always listed in a disk's *directory*, depending upon the operating system. Some applications use a type of swap file (known as a *swap space*) to store their own temporary data.

Swapping
A technique used to manage *virtual memory*. See *Swap File*.

Swap Space
In computing, a *swap file* that is created by a specific application (rather than by the *operating system*) for the temporary storage of application-specific data. See *Swap File*.

Swash Letters
In typography, a set of letters—loosely based on italics—but with elaborate flourishes, tails, *ascender*s, and *descender*s.

Swatch
Shorthand term for a *color swatch*. See *Color Swatch*.

Swatch Book
A collection of **color swatch**es bound into book form and used to identify and specify colors. Each company with a **color matching system** (such as **PANTONE**) has one or more swatch books.

Swatching Out
A technique for the evaluation of **color proof**s in **gravure** printing that compares the proofs to **color swatch**es of specified **density** and **dot area** values produced on the intended printing press to be utilized, as a means of ensuring that the color appearing on the proofs and films will reproduce accurately.

Sweep Speed
In **screen printing**, the speed at which the **squeegee** is pulled across the **printing screen** during a printing stroke. When the sweep speed is increased, but the squeegee is not in the **overpressure range**, excessively thick ink deposits on the **substrate** will result. If the squeegee is in or over the overpressure range, however, thinner ink deposits will result.

Sweetening
In film, TV, and video production, any **post-production** optimization of a soundtrack, be it the elimination of **noise** for a higher-quality audio signal or adding **sound effects**, music, a laugh track, etc.

Swell
In **binding and finishing**, the precise thickness of a book at the **binding edge**.

Swing-Arm System
One configuration of the **infeed section** of a printing press, especially one used in **offset lithography**. See **Infeed Section**.

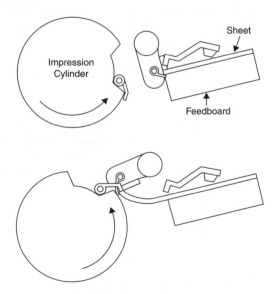

Swing-arm infeed system.

Swipe File
In graphic arts and design, a type of "scrapbook" or collection of examples of good design—such as published advertisements, page designs, etc.—from which an artist can draw for inspiration. A swipe file, despite its name, is not meant to promote or facilitate plagiarism, but rather to stimulate one's own creative juices.

Switchable
Descriptive of a computer printer that can be turned online or offline.

Switcher
In television and video production, a device usually found in a **production control room** used to instantaneously alter the source of a video signal, usually from camera to camera (in live-on-tape productions using a three-camera setup), from a pre-recorded tape, or other source. Also known as a **video switcher**.

Swivel
A rotating stand on which a computer monitor is placed or mounted, allowing it to be adjusted to a position of optimum viewing.

SWOP
Abbreviation for the recommended *Specifications for Web-Offset Publications*, a set of standards for **color proofing** developed by a joint committee of the American Association of Advertising Agencies, American Business Press, American Photoplatemakers Association, Graphic Arts Technical Foundation, Magazine Publishers Association, National Association of Printing Ink Manufacturers, and the International Prepress Association. SWOP standards were designed to ensure that colors were reproduced consistently among different publishers and publications. The SWOP standards focus on the ability of a particular printer to accurately evaluate and reproduce a color proof on-press. Consistency is further achieved by the utilization of **SWOP inks** and the generation of a **SWOP inspection report**, which is a report of the analysis of color proofs and **color separation negative**s as a means of determining if they meet the SWOP standards.

SWOP Inks
A set of inks that have been manufactured to meet the specifications outlined by **SWOP**. See **SWOP**.

SWOP Inspection Report
In multicolor web offset printing, a form that is completed following the production and evaluation of a set of **color separation negative**s as a means of determining whether the negatives meet the specifications outlined by **SWOP**. See **SWOP**.

Sword
Alternate term for **saddle bar**. See **Saddle Bar**.

Symbol Font
Alternate term for a *pi font*. See *Pi Font*.

Symmetrical Compression
A type of *data compression* algorithm in which the decompressed file is identical to the original file. In many cases, as when compressing video, so much information is contained in the original file that it is not always possible to obtain a significantly compressed file. As a result, some compression schemes lose a slight to considerable amount of data between compression and decompression, which is known as *lossy* or *asymmetrical compression*. See *Data Compression*.

Symmetrical Multiprocessing
In computing, a means of *multiprocessing* in which tasks are assigned to processors at start-up, based on available system resources. Symmetrical multiprocessing, abbreviated *SMP*, tends to be more flexible than *asymmetrical multiprocessing*. See also *Asymmetrical Multiprocessing*.

Symmetry
In typography and page design, a predictable pattern or arrangement, in particular one in which the design is reflected around a central axis. Symmetry implies order and balance, but it is also dull to some people. The opposite property is called *asymmetry*.

Sympathetic Ink
Also known as *invisible ink*, sympathetic inks are invisible until a chemical or thermal treatment renders them visible.

The use of sympathetic inks dates back to the 3rd century BC, when Philon of Byzantium first described a method of writing with the extract of nutgalls (excrescences formed on trees), which only became readable after the treatment of the paper with a copper salt containing iron. The Roman poet Ovid (author of *The Art of Love*) recommended that lovers compose their clandestine missives in milk, which can then be read by dusting the paper with soot. Muslim priests are said to have used invisible inks to inscribe the name of Mohammed on stones which then became visible under the heat of one's palm, a trick not long afterward adopted by magicians and purported mystics. In the Renaissance and afterward, the Vatican as well as various governments used sympathetic inks to convey sensitive diplomatic correspondence. The British and Americans used such inks during the American Revolution in the late 18th century, and the wartime use of sympathetic inks continued until as recently as World War II. Currently, however, invisible inks of nearly all formulations can be detected by scientific means, if one is looking for secret writing.

Scholars of invisible inks disagree about the best way of classifying them—according to substance used, according to the nature of the writer (a prisoner or a free person), according to the color of the ink when developed, or according to the methods required to develop them. In terms of the substances used, these can include body fluids (blood, saliva, perspiration, urine, and others), foods and juices, chemicals (such as acids and bases), as well as various soap solutions, glues, adhesives, and so on. Common materials that are utilized include vinegar (acetic acid), citrus-fruit juices (in particular lemon juice), baking soda, salt, sugar, rice, water, aspirin, *gum arabic*, boric acid, starch, ammonia, Epsom salts, silver nitrate, and many others. As for detecting sympathetic inks, there are basically four classifications: optical (the use of special lighting such as infrared or ultraviolet, special angles of viewing or special angles of lighting, or viewing through special materials), mechanical (dusting the encoded substrate with a fine powder such as graphite, exposing the substrate to fumes of iodine, or moistening the surface with water, an iodine solution, or a dye solution), thermal (exposing the substrate to heat or a flame), or chemical (exposure to ammonia vapor, immersing in chemical baths, or other procedures reminiscent of photographic developing).

Sync
Shorthand for *synchronization*. See *Synchronization*.

Sync Generator
A device used to generate pulses to keep the horizontal and vertical scanning mechanisms in *synchronization*. See *Synchronization*.

Synchronization
In video and film production, the playing of video and corresponding audio such that the audio perfectly matches the video. For example, the sound of an explosion that occurs at the same instant that something on-screen explodes is said to be synchronized. On the other hand, recorded dialogue that does not correspond to the flapping of a character's lips is said to be out of sync.

In television transmission, a video signal consists of horizontal and vertical pulses. If these pulses are not properly synchronized, picture problems will result, such as rolling, glitches, and other errors.

Synchronization Generator Lock
See *Genlock*.

Synchronous
Descriptive of two or more events that occur simultaneously, usually used to refer to *synchronous transmission* in data communications, in which the timing of a transmission needs to be precisely coordinated by both the sender and the receiver. See *Synchronous Transmission*. See also *Asynchronous*.

Synchronous Transmission
In telecommunications, a form of *serial transmission* in which a transmitted message comprises a single package containing all the characters of the message. In this way, the time of transmission needs to be coordinated by both sender and receiver, in contrast to *asynchronous transmission*,

no precise timing on the part of the receiving system is needed. A synchronous transmission also has control characters attached to the data, as a means of *error detection and correction*. See also *Asynchronous Transmission*.

Sync Signal

In video production, a pulse or signal that is used to synchronize two video recorders, often generated by a *time-base corrector*.

Synthesizer

An electronic musical instrument used to create artificial sounds, either imitative of actual musical instruments or musical tones that are not designed to sound like anything else. Other unconventional sounds can also be *sample*d and played back through a synthesizer. Often, a synthesizer has a built-in piano keyboard. If not, it is known as an *expander*. Some synthesizers, called *sample-playback*s or *sampling-synthesizer*s, are used for artificially producing voices.

SyQuest

A popular brand of removable *magnetic cartridge* used for the storage and transport of computer files and data. SyQuest cartridges are available in a variety of sizes and capacities: the first size was a 5.25-in. cartridge with a capacity of 44 *megabyte*s (MB), which was followed by an 88-MB version. There is also a 3.5-in. size, with capacities up to 270 MB. Although for many years SyQuest cartridges were the most popular brand of external storage and transport medium, the incompatibilities between drives and disk capacities (for example, for a while a drive designed to read and write to an 88-MB cartridge could only read 44-MB cartridges, and so forth) as well as the appearance of less expensive media (in particular Iomega's *Zip* disks) has eroded their prevalence.

System Brunner

A method of controlling and optimizing color proofing and reproduction—in particular, effectively compensating for *dot gain*—devised by Felix Brunner.

System Bus

See *Bus*.

System Menu

In computing, especially by means of *Windows* and *OS/2* operating systems and interfaces, a *pull-down menu* found in the upper lefthand corner of every window in which certain basic system commands are located.

System 8

An operating system from Apple Computer on Macintosh computers. It includes true multitasking and an improved user interface.

System 7.X

The seventh version of the *Macintosh operating system*, distinguished by its ability to easily transfer data between different applications and between different users linked to a network, and to address in excess of 128 MB of *RAM*. System 7.5 was another major revision of the system (System 8.0 is—as of this writing—the most recent re-revision of the system software) that is designed to run with the PowerPC architecture.

After System 8.X a totally new operating system, now called Rhapsody, will incorporate advanced features.

Systems Network Architecture (SNA)

In computing, the description of logical structure, formats, protocols, and operational sequences for transmitting information units through, and controlling the configuration and operation of, networks.

The layered structure of SNA allows the ultimate origins and destinations of information—the end users—to be independent of and unaffected by the specific SNA network services and facilities used for information interchange.

System Utilities

In computing, a set of *utility program*s that facilitate the organization and maintenance of files on *hard disk*s or other storage media.

T

T, t

The twentieth letter in the alphabet, derived from the North Semitic *taw*, by way of the Greek *tau*. The form of the *T* has scarcely changed since its origin.

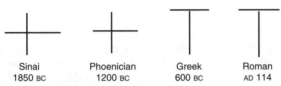

Sinai	Phoenician	Greek	Roman
1850 BC	1200 BC	600 BC	AD 114

The evolution of the letter T.

T

The abbreviation for *tera-*. See *Tera-*.

Tab

In typography, a column in which type—usually *tabular* material—is to be arranged, or the keyboard key used to jump to start points of columns.

In printing, a *tab* is a type of *skid tag* attached to stacks of printed sheets, used to indicate those sheets that are to be bound and/or folded separately from the rest.

In *binding and finishing*, *tab* is also an abbreviated term for an *index tab*. See *Index Tab*.

Tabbing

In *binding and finishing*, the application of *index tab*s on the edges of pages. See *Indexing*.

Table

Any matrix of numerical data. See *Table Chart*.

Table Chart

In typography, a form of *tabular composition* containing numbers or other elements in the form of a chart or table. See *Tabular Composition*. Also known as a *tabular chart*.

Table Entry Copy

In graphics and typography, the text which is to be set in *tabular* form.

Table Heading

In typography, a *heading* used to identify the data in a particular *tabular column*.

Table Lookup

The act of gleaning information from a *table*. See also *Lookup Table*.

Table of Contents

A portion of a book listing the chapter names and pages on which they begin, for easy reference and quick locating of desired material. See *Book Typography*. Often abbreviated *TOC*.

Table Roll

A rotating roller placed beneath the *forming wire* on a papermaking machine; the table roll supports the wire and aids in removing water from the forming paper *web* above it. Table rolls can be used in place of suction cup-shaped *foils* or in concert with oscillation of the forming wire (called *shake*).

Table Time

In prepress, the length of time required for the *stripping* of *negative*s into *flat*s.

Tabloid

In newspaper publishing, a page size of a newspaper corresponding to 11¾×15 or 17 in. long, or roughly half the size of a standard size newspaper. As tabloid size paper was often used to print so-called "scandal sheets," the term "tabloid" itself has come to refer to splashy, attention-grabbing (and, some would say, somewhat "sleazy") journalism, hence the popular term "tabloid TV."

Tabloid Fold

Alternate term for *first parallel fold*. See *First Parallel Fold*.

Tab Stop

See *Common Tab Stop*.

Tabular Chart

See *Table Chart*.

Tabular Column

In typography, any page composition utilizing multiple columns.

Tabular Composition

In typography, a vertical alignment within multiple columns. A combination of *en space*s (or *figure space*s) and *thin space*s is used to line up tabular material. Depending upon the nature of the columns that need to line up, alignment may be consistent (left) or inconsistent (right).

911	101.05
411	75
711	10.4
	.06

It is necessary to use *fixed space*s to create the electronic version of *quadding*. In word processing and computer systems, the same lineup can be achieved by means of automatic decimal alignment. The use of *rule lines* as boxes can be used to connect related tabular elements, forming charts that are easier to read and understand than simple "floating" numbers.

Tabular Format

In typography, any page or page design that contains tabular elements. See *Tabular Composition*.

Tabular Material

Any material typeset utilizing *tabular composition*. See *Tabular Composition*.

Tabular Work

Any typographical design that uses multiple columns.

Tabulating Board

An *index paper* used for manufacturing computer punch cards, used in machine processing. Tabulating board must possess a high degree of *dimensional stability*, must not curl, and must have high *tear resistance*. It must also be cut to very precise dimensions.

Tack

A property of printing inks that describes the *cohesion* that exists between particles of the ink film, the force required to split an ink film or, in other words, its stickiness. An ink with a high degree of tack (or a tacky ink) requires more force to split than does a less tacky film. Offset lithographic inks require tackier inks than do other printing processes to avoid excessive *emulsification* of the ink by the fountain solution, and to print sharp halftone images. Tacky inks, however, do not print solids very well. The tack of the ink should not exceed the *surface strength* of the paper, or *picking*, *splitting*, and *tearing* of the paper will occur. In multicolor printing, the first ink printed must have greater tack than the ink that will be printed on top of it, or the latter will not trap on the first ink. The tack of an ink can be measured with an *Inkometer* or a *Tackoscope*.

Tackoscope

A variety of *Inkometer*, used to measure the *tack* of an ink. See *Inkometer*.

Tag

In computers, a character, set of characters, or code attached to a set of data that contains information about that data, such as its identification, and any formatting information pertaining to that data set.

In desktop publishing, a code attached to a specific piece of text that provides instructions for its formatting. Tags applied to text include its *font*, *point size*, *leading*, the paragraph formatting (i.e., *ragged* or *justified*), and any other text attribute. Tags can be applied and manipulated within a specific program (such as *QuarkXPress*) as a shortcut for formatting blocks of text, or added to straight *ASCII* text composed in another application for input to a page makeup program. For example, tags used by QuarkXPress can be applied to generic text created in FileMaker and then imported into QuarkXPress, eliminating the need to format each aspect of the text file individually, which saves time when creating large Quark documents from FileMaker files, such as an encyclopedia of 10,000 graphic arts terms.

In papermaking, the term *tag* also refers to a paper *grade* characterized by high thickness, strength, density, tear resistance and water resistance, used in many heavy-duty applications such as tags, folders, and covers. The surface of tag stock allows printing, writing, stamping, and folding. It is manufactured from any of the various *pulping* methods—*sulfite*, *sulfate* or *kraft*, and *mechanical*. Tag papers also undergo *calendering* to produce a smooth, hard surface. Coated tag stock possesses enhanced *printability*, and is used for some printing applications. Tag is also manufactured in a variety of colors, primarily white and manila.

The *basic size* of tag stock is 24×36 in., and comes in *basis weight*s of 100-, 125-, 150-, 175-, 200-, and 250-lb. *Standard size*s are 24×36, 22½×28½, and 28½×45 in.

Tag Image File Format

See *TIFF*.

Tagged Image File Format

See *TIFF*.

Tagging

In computing, the process of adding additional characters to *ASCII text* to identify structural or typographic elements in the text. See *Tag* and *MarkUp*.

Tail

In typography, the downward-sloping short stroke on a letter or other character ending free, as in the *descender* of a lowercase "y" or the stroke differentiating the capital letter "Q" from an "O." See *Letter Elements*.

Tail Clamp

One of two *plate clamp*s found on the *plate cylinder* of an offset printing press. The tail clamp is the device to which the bottom, or trailing edge, of the plate is attached, as opposed to the *head clamp*. See *Plate Clamp* and *Plate Cylinder*.

Tail Margin

In typography, the margin between the last line of text and the bottom of a page.

Tail Section

In *binding and finishing* and/or *folding*, especially that of a two-up form, the section not containing *closed head*s. The tail section usually has lower page numbers than the *head section*.

Tail-End Hook

Alternate term for *back-edge curl*, a printing defect similar to *waffling*. See *Back-Edge Curl*.

Tail-End Printer

Alternate term for an *in-line press*. See *In-Line Press*.

Tail-Piece

In *book typography*, a small design (usually an uncomplicated line drawing) at the end of a chapter or other section.

Tailprinter

Alternate term for an *in-line press*. See *In-Line Press*.

Take

In typesetting, the quantity of copy that will be set and output at one particular time, such as a *galley*.

In cinematography and videography, any run-through of a *scene* by the actors while the camera is running.

Take-Off Zone

Alternate term for *dedicated landing zone*. See *Dedicated Landing Zone*.

Take-Up Reel

An empty reel on which *magnetic tape*, film, or other material is wound during recording or playback.

Talent

In motion pictures, videography, and multimedia, more or less accurate term to describe those individuals who will be filmed or taped for inclusion in a production.

Taligent

In computing, an *object-oriented* operating system under development by IBM and Apple.

Talking Head

In television and video production, somewhat colloquial term for a static shot of an individual's head and shoulders for any prolonged period of time. Used to refer to personages on talk shows and newscasts.

Tall Oil

A resinous byproduct of the *sulfate process* of paper *pulp* production, comprising fatty and rosin acids, used as an oil in the manufacture of printing ink *vehicle*s. The distillation of tall oil also produces *tall oil rosin*. The name *tall oil* itself derives from the Swedish word *tallolja*, "tall pine tree."

Tall Oil Rosin

A *rosin* derived from *tall oil* which is currently the most widely used rosin in the manufacture of printing inks.

Tally Light

In television and video production, a red light mounted on the top or front of a camera that indicates when the camera is running, used to indicate to those about to be taped in which direction to look.

Tamper-Proof Label

A *label* produced so that the label cannot be removed and reused, the removal process destroying the label. Such labels are used as price tags, for example.

Tandem Coating

Paper *coating* applied in successive layers by a series of applicator rollers, each possessing its own backup roller.

Tandem Roll Stand

In *web printing*, a *roll stand* used in conjunction with another roll stand to feed two rolls into the press simultaneously. See *Roll Stand*.

Tape

See *Magnetic Tape*.

Tape Backup

A type of file storage and/or file transfer medium, such as nine-track tape or smaller magnetic tape cartridges, used commonly to keep *backup* copies of files.

Tape Cartridge

A *magnetic tape* stored within a protective plastic shell. See *Magnetic Tape*.

Tape Drive

A device used to read and/or write data to a *magnetic tape*. See *Magnetic Tape*.

Tape Reader

A computer device or peripheral capable of reading information stored on magnetic or paper tape and inputting that data into the computer system.

Tapes

In *case binding*, term for strips of cloth or tape (such as *backlining*) glued or sewn to the *spine* of a book to increase the strength of the binding. See *Case Binding*.

Tap-Out

Alternate term for *pat-out*. See *Pat-Out*.

TAPPI Official Test Method

A procedure for evaluating a specific property of paper that is officially authorized by the *Technical Association of the Pulp and Paper Industry (TAPPI)*. There is at least one Official Test Method for each of the vast multitude of paper properties. A TAPPI Official Test Method must provide accurate and reproducible results among different paper testing laboratories over a period of time. Test methods also describe the calibration of testing equipment, the procuring of representative paper samples, and the creation of a carefully controlled environment. The addition, revision, and excision of Official Test Methods by paper professionals and laboratories around the world is constant. Procedures that are not sanctioned as official by TAPPI but which are useful in practical application are called **TAPPI Useful Test Methods**.

TAPPI Useful Test Method

A procedure for evaluating a specific property of paper that is not officially authorized by the **Technical Association of the Pulp and Paper Industry (TAPPI)**, but which TAPPI recognizes as having practical use. TAPPI Useful Test Methods are used to supplement **TAPPI Official Test Methods**.

Tare Weight

The weight of a particular unit of a packing material—such as a carton, **skid**, **pallet**, etc.

TARGA

Abbreviation for *TrueVision Advanced Raster Graphics Adapter*, a **file format** for **twenty-four-bit color** graphics files developed by TrueVision for use in image-capture boards, its advantage being that it supported **NTSC** video standards. Also used on some **MS-DOS**-based computers, the TARGA format is now almost completely obsolete. It is commonly abbreviated as **TGA**. Also called **TrueVision TARGA**.

Target

In computing, the disk drive to which data is being copied. See also **Source**.

In database terminology, the term *target* also refers to a sequence of characters (such as a word) that is being searched for.

Tarnish-Proof Label

A label formulated with substances or adhesives that will not cause discoloration or blemishing of copper, silver, or other such surfaces.

Tartrazine Yellow Lake

An **organic color pigment** used in the manufacture of printing inks, derived from aluminum salts. Tartrazine yellow lake is certified by the Food and Drug Administration for use in food packaging (and, when used in food, is known as FD&C Yellow No. 5). It is used in metal decorating inks and lacquers for food packaging. (See also **Organic Color Pigments**.)

(CI Pigment Yellow 100 No. 19140.)

Task

In computing, any function in progress at a given moment.

Task List

In computing, especially using the **Windows** operating system, a list of open and running applications, that facilitates switching between or among them, especially when their windows are hidden by other open applications. The task list is accessed by double-clicking on the desktop. On the **Macintosh**, the task list is called an **application menu**.

TB

Abbreviation for **terabyte**. See **Terabyte**.

TBC

Abbreviation for **time-base corrector**. See **Time-Base Corrector (TBC)**.

TCP/IP

Abbreviation for **Transmission Control Protocol/Internet Protocol**. See **Transmission Control Protocol/Internet Protocol (TCP/IP)**.

Tear

To rip, rupture, or remove bits of a paper. Also, when used as a noun, the rip or rupture itself.

The term *tear* is also used to refer to a paper's **tearing resistance**. See **Tearing Resistance**.

Tearing

An extreme form of **picking** in which the pull of a thick, tacky ink tears off portions of a paper's surface, leaving a delaminated area on the press sheet. See **Picking**.

Tearing Resistance

General paper property that takes into account two measures of a paper's ability to withstand being torn. **Internal tearing resistance** refers to the work required to tear a paper sample through a specified distance once the tear has been started. **Edge tearing resistance** refers to the work required to tear a paper sample by starting the tear at the edges of the sheet. Lighter papers are more susceptible to edge tears than to internal tears, so the latter measurement is frequently the more useful one. Tearing resistance is an important property in many end-use applications, from cover, wrapping, bristol, and bond papers to map and envelope papers.

As with most paper properties, tearing resistance is a function of the degree of fiber **refining**; greater interfiber bonding enhances tearing resistance, but excessive refining tends to shorten the fibers, which works to decrease the tearing resistance. The addition of **fillers** decreases tearing resistance. The procedures that increase tearing resistance sometimes diminish other desirable properties. (See **Paper and Papermaking: Paper Properties**.) Also known as **tearing strength** or simply **tear**.

Tearing Strength

See **Tearing Resistance**.

Tear Sheet

Any printed page torn from a book, magazine, newspaper, or other publication, used for promotional, **proofing**, or other purposes.

Tear Strength

Alternate term for a paper's *tearing resistance*. See *Tearing Resistance*.

Tear Test

A test used in papermaking to determine either the *grain direction* or the *tearing resistance* of a paper. See *Grain* and *Tearing Resistance*.

Teaser

In magazine and newspaper typography, a short phrase— set in a small *point size*—above a main *heading*. Also known as a *kicker*.

Tech.3235-E

In telecommunications, the standard created by the *European Broadcast Union* defining the specifications for television and video transmission. More commonly known as *Phase Alternating Line (PAL)*.

Technical and Office Protocol (TOP)

A communications protocol developed by Boeing Computer Services to standardize the interconnection of computers used for engineering, design, and manufacturing. TOP is designed for use in the front-office network, while its accompanying protocol, *Manufacturing Automation Protocol (MAP)*, is designed to connect computers running programmable machine tools in automated manufacturing systems.

Technical Association of the Pulp and Paper Industry (TAPPI)

An international organization of professionals devoted to research and technical advancement in the paper and related industries. In the United States, TAPPI has established standards and testing procedures for the manufacture of pulp and paper. TAPPI's officially recognized test standards are known as the *TAPPI Official Test Methods*, while those testing procedures not considered Official Methods but of practical use for papermakers and others are described in *TAPPI Useful Test Methods*. Internationally, TAPPI tests and standards exist alongside standards and procedures set by the *International Standards Organization (ISO)*. Many TAPPI tests are similar to ISO testing methods. There is at least one TAPPI Official Test or Useful Method for every paper property. (See *Paper and Papermaking: Paper Properties*, as well as separate entries for individual properties.)

Technical Material

In typography, any copy to be typeset that includes special symbols (such as *mathematics*), *tablular copy*, scientific and technical terms, and other material that requires greater degrees of formatting than straight text.

Teflon®*

A specific brand of polytetrafluorethylene, chemical formula $(C_2F_4)_n$, a polymeric *resin* or plastic produced from the *polymerization* of fluorinated ethylene, used as a *film former* in the manufacture of printing inks. Most popularly noted for its use on frying pans, Teflon is inert and widely used for its heat-resistant and nonstick properties.

*Teflon® is a registered trademark of the du Pont Chemical Company.

TekHVC

A type of *color space* or color data standard developed by Tektronix. TekHVC is essentially a variation of *CIELUV*.

Telecommuting

Working at home, rather than at an office, by means of a *modem* connected to the central computer of the organization for which one works. Also known as *teleworking*.

Teleconferencing

The ability for two or more people to conduct a meeting from widely separated geographical distances, by means of sound and/or video connections. See also *Videoconferencing*.

Telematics

Contraction of the terms *telecommunications* and *informatics* (computer science), a hybrid field that develops technologies for controlling remote computers.

Telemetry

The electrical and/or radio transmission of measurements from a remote sensing instrument to a perhaps very distant recording station. Telemetry is often used in space travel and observation, medicine, and for *pay TV*.

Telerecording

The remote recording of data, be it scientific measurements such as temperature or still or moving images, as in video recording. In telerecording, the measured or captured values are converted to electrical impulses that are in turn converted to *binary* data for transmission to a recording medium, be it paper or *magnetic media*.

Telescoped Roll

A defect in paper roll winding that results in a roll with progressively misaligned edges due to slippage of the paper layers. Telescoped rolls (and other roll defects) are the result of inconsistencies in moisture content and thickness produced during the papermaking process. Thicker portions of the paper *web* will wind "harder" than thinner portions, and the differential tension will result in telescoping of the roll when a force acts on the roll. Advanced *cross-machine direction (CD)* monitoring procedures in the *forming section* of the papermaking machine can ensure that the papermaking *furnish* delivered across the *forming wire* is consistent in thickness and moisture content, so to not present problems when building the final paper roll. Variations in the forming of the paper web can also be rectified in subsequent stages of the papermaking process, such as *calendering*.

Defects in the paper roll have serious consequences for printers utilizing web presses. Rolls that do not unwind into the machine with uniform tension across the web stretch and deform, often beyond their ability to return to their original dimensions, causing various printing distortions. Problems with paper rolls can also cause web breaks. A telescoped roll is called a *dished roll* when the edge misalignment is generated during roll winding. (See also *Starred Roll*.)

Teleshopping

The purchasing of consumer products and services by telephone, by *interactive television*, or over the *Internet*. The Home Shopping Network is one common example of teleshopping.

Teletext

In telecommunications, general term for the one-way transmission of digital text and graphics transmitted to a viewer's television, usually over a *cable television network*. A two-way transmission of teletext is known as *interactive teletext*. Teletext is also known as *videotext*.

Television Signal Standard

The specifications required to transmit televised images. The three common standards in use today are *National Television Standards Committee (NTSC)* (in North America), *Phase Alternating Line (PAL)* (in Europe), and *Séquentiel Couleur à Mémoire (SECAM)* (also in Europe).

Teleworking

Alternate term for *telecommuting*. See *Telecommuting*.

Telltale

In reference book publishing, the first and/or last item, word, or topic on a page, indicated on the top and/or bottom of a page as an aid to easily locating material within the book. Also called *guide word*s.

Template

In page layout, a background grid, image, or shape used to indicate where page elements are to be inserted. Templates are used to define the default page layout for a publication. In computer-based page layout, templates are created digitally, and function much like the nonreproducible blue lines drawn on *mechanical*s, indicating where column and page margins are to be, where *folio*s, *running heads*, etc., should be positioned.

Temporary Adhesive

An *adhesive* substance possessing a low degree of *ultimate adhesion*, or which will lose its adhesive strength in a short time.

10Base-2

Alternate term for *thin Ethernet*. See *Thin Ethernet*.

10Base-5

Alternate term for *thick Ethernet*. See *Thick Ethernet*.

10Base-T

In networking, an IEEE standard for *Ethernet* cabling. The 10Base-T standard prescribes the cabling (*unshielded twisted-pair* cabling), the connection (an *RJ-45 jack*), and the *network topology* (*star* topology), and the transmission speed of the connection (10 megabits per second).

Tensile-at-the-Fold

A test for coated papers to be used in *heatset drying* that aims to determine how well the paper will withstand folding and degradation due to heat without cracking along the fold. In a hot oven, a paper sample is subjected to conditions that simulate those of heatset drying. After a prescribed amount of time, the paper sample is taken out and folded and the *tensile strength* at the fold is determined.

Tensile Breaking Strength

A property of paper that indicates its ability to withstand a stretching force without breaking. The paper's maximum elongation due to tensile stress is expressed as a percentage of its original length. Paper has greater tensile strength in its *grain direction*. Although tensile breaking strength has little application to sheetfed printing processes, it is an important consideration in wrapping papers, packaging papers, business forms, web offset lithographic processes and other uses in which paper is subjected to high degrees of stretching. Tensile breaking strength is increased with increased fiber *refining* and fiber length, wet-pressing, and *basis weight*, and decreased with increasing addition of *fillers* to the papermaking *furnish*. (See also *Wet-Tensile Breaking Strength*, *Wet Strength*, and *Tensile Energy Absorption*.)

Tensile Energy Absorption (TEA)

A measure of the capacity of paper to withstand a shock when subjected to sudden high tension. The tensile force applied to a paper is graphed against the percentage elongation of the paper as a result of that force. The mathematical determination of the area beneath the resulting curve is described as its tensile energy absorption, which provides an accurate gauge of toughness, an important consideration in paper used for bags (for example, how far and with what force could a full grocery bag be dropped without splitting open) and other packaging materials, as well as paper designed for web offset printing (what is the likelihood of a web break when a press starts up suddenly). (See also *Tensile Breaking Strength*.)

Tensile Strength

Catchall term for a paper's ability to withstand a stretching force. See *Tensile Breaking Strength*, *Wet-Tensile Breaking Strength*, *Tensile-at-the-Fold*, *Tensile Energy Absorption (TEA)*, *Wet Strength*, and *Z-Directional Tensile Strength*.

Tensile strength is also a general term describing the extent to which any substance or material can be stretched without breaking.

Tensile Test

A means of testing a paper's *tensile strength* that clamps a strip of paper vertically between two jaws and stretches the paper until it breaks. Tensile strength is expressed in pounds per inch-width strip of paper, or in kilonewtons per meter. The test is performed in the paper's *grain direction* and *cross-grain direction*, and is also used when the paper is wet to measure the *wet-tensile breaking strength*. See *Tensile Breaking Strength*.

Tensioning

In computing, the backward and forward movement of a *magnetic tape* to take up excess slack prior to recording.

Tension Span

In *web printing*, the portion of a paper web's travel through the press between printing units or rollers where it is unsupported. See *Web Offset Lithography: Infeed and Web Control*.

Tera-

A *metric prefix* denoting 1,000,000,000,000 (one trillion, or 10^{12}) units. In computing, *tera-* refers to 2^{40}, and one *terabyte* (TB) of storage is approximately equal to one trillion *byte*s of data (actually 1,009,511,627,776 bytes). See *Metric Prefix*. See also *Kilo-*, *Mega-*, *Giga-*, *Peta-*, and *Exa-*. *Tera-* is usually abbreviated *T*.

Terabyte

A still-uncommon unit of computer storage, comprising 1,024 *gigabyte*s or 1,009,511,627,776 *byte*s. *Tera-* is the prefix meaning "trillion," so it is common to consider 1 terabyte as equal to 1 trillion bytes, although that isn't entirely accurate. It is uncommon to find hard disks and magnetic cartridge media with storage capacities in excess of 1 terabyte, although some high-capacity drives are measured in terabytes. Terabyte is abbreviated TB.

Terminal

In typography, the free-ending stroke of a letter or other character, commonly with a special decorative treatment. A special variety of terminal is called a *finial*. See *Letter Elements*.

In networking, a workstation comprising a keyboard and monitor. A *dumb terminal* has no processing power itself, requiring connection to a central controller for instructions to be executed. An *intelligent* terminal has its own processing power and is capable of becoming a stand-alone device.

Terminate-and-Stay-Resident (TSR)

In computing, any program that is loaded into the computer's *RAM* and stays there throughout the duration of a computer session. The program remains dormant until called by a specific key combination or menu selection. *Screen capture* programs, *anti-virus program*s, and other such utilities are examples of TSR programs. Also referred to as a *memory-resident program*.

Tertiary Color

In color printing, any color produced by *overprinting secondary colors*, or dots of all three *process color*s. Tertiary colors include orange-green, violet-orange, green-violet, etc. See also *Primary Color* and *Secondary Color*.

Test Pattern

In printing and prepress, any page containing lines and characters output by a computer printer, printing press, or other form of output and used to evaluate print quality.

In broadcast media, a special card or pattern of color bars used to calibrate and check the color balance of a camera and/or televised signal.

Text

In typography, another term for *text type*. See *Text Type*.

In computing and telecommunications, *text* refers to unformatted alphanumeric characters that can be input into any text-processing program. Often refers to *ASCII text*.

Textbook

In book publishing, any book written and designed to be sold through schools and universities and used for educational purposes.

Text Box

In desktop publishing and page layout, a box or frame in which text is entered and formatted. The size and position of the text box can be varied, and multiple text boxes can be linked together, allowing text to flow from one place to another.

In general computing, a *text box* is also any space within a *dialog box* in which user-defined data or parameters are entered.

Text Control

In any computerized typesetting or desktop publishing program, specification of the placement and appearance of text.

Text Editing

The capability of any software application—such as a word processor, page layout program, telecommunications software, etc.—to facilitate the formatting, altering, adding, and deleting of text material. The portion of the program that handles text editing is known as the *text editor*.

Text Editor

See *Editor* (second definition).

Text Face

See *Text Type*.

Text File

Any computer-generated text that has been saved as an *ASCII file*, commonly as a prelude to sending it via modem or the Internet. See *ASCII*.

Text Font

In typography, any *font* suitable for use in the typesetting of text. See *Text Type*.

Text Mode

General reference to the particular *typestyle* in which a block of text is displayed, such as *bold*, *italic*, etc.

In computing, *text mode* is an alternate term for *character mode*. See *Character Mode*.

Text Orientation

A characteristic of text or type with regard to the direction of its appearance on the page and its rotation. See also *Orientation*.

Text Out

Alternate term for *export*. See *Export*.

Text Paper

A paper *grade* that offers highly aesthetic yet functional papers with a variety of colors, textures, surfaces, and *finish*es. Text papers can be wood-pulp or *cotton-content* paper. Text papers are elegant and durable, and are used for programs, menus, annual reports, advertising circulars, announcements, etc.

The *basic size* of text paper is 25×38 in., and comes in *basis weight*s of 60, 70, 80, and 100 lb.

Text String

In computing, a *character string* comprising text characters, usually characters intended to be printed.

Text Type

In typography, copy set as paragraphs between 6-point and 12-point; in other words, blocks of copy. Over 80% of the type that is set and read is text, and thus should follow certain rules for legibility based on *point size*, *leading*, *typeface*, format, intercharacter *spacing*, and *line length*.

Point size. A determination of the most appropriate size is first necessary. Newspapers use 8- or 9-point type; books use 10- to 12-point; ads use 9- to 11-point. One particular issue involved with point size is the size of the space that needs to be filled.

Typeface. A determination of the typeface to be used is also necessary. The typeface should not only be one designed specifically for text (i.e., *serif* faces are much more legible than *sans serif* faces when set as text) but should also be compatible with the content. For example, a slickly designed, futuristic-looking face is inappropriate for, say, a history of 10th-century Italian monastaries. Also,

depending on how much copy has to fit in how much space, the *alphabet length* of various faces may need to be compared. Some faces use larger characters (regardless of point size) than others.

Leading. A determination of the amount of line spacing is needed, based on the typeface and size to be used. Large *x-height* faces need more leading; small x-height faces need less leading.

Line Length. The relationship between line length and point size needs to be recalled (see *Line Length*) and considered in relation to the typeface and point size chosen. So, for example, would two narrow columns be better than one wide one?

Format. A decision on whether the lines should be *ragged right* or *justified* needs to be made. Ragged lines have consistent word spaces and are more legible, but in wider text blocks, justified lines would work as well.

Intercharacter Spacing. The level of negative letterspacing that would work best with the face and size in use needs to be determined. The design of the typeface has a significant effect on the use of tight spacing.

Decisions on the separation of paragraphs also need to be made. Paragraphs can be defined by indents at the start of each unit, additional line spacing between paragraphs, a combination of indent and spacing, or by initial capital letters. Which would be the most appropriate?

Many typeset documents also utilize extracts, quotes, and call-outs, which are copy blocks indented on one or both sides with or without additional line spacing to set the block apart from the rest of the text. How should these be handled?

When designing pages and text blocks, it should be recalled that white space, or nontype areas, is important for producing a balanced, legible page. The use of margins, gutters, space around heads and illustrations, and leading are areas where white space may be applied.

Text Wrap

Alternate term for *word wrap*. See *Word Wrap*.

TGA

Abbreviation and *file extension* for *TARGA*, a graphics *file format*. See *TARGA*.

Thermal Black

A variety of *Carbon Black*, or *black pigment* used in printing ink produced by the "cracking" of natural gas. Natural gas is essentially a complex mixture of *hydrocarbon* compounds. Cracking, or the exposure of these hydrocarbons to high temperatures and pressures, weakens and decomposes the carbon-to-carbon bonds in the molecules, and as various substances are boiled off, other residual substances are left behind. The partial burning of these hydrocarbons and the condensation of the flame on a cool surface produces Carbon Black. (Carbon Black obtained from the cracking of petroleuim oil is typically referred to as *furnace black*.) See *Carbon Blacks*.

Thermal Print

Output produced using a *thermal printer*. See *Thermal Transfer*.

Thermal Printer

An output device used for *thermal transfer*. See *Thermal Transfer*.

Thermal Transfer

A means of printing or imaging utilizing a colored wax (similar to a crayon) that is melted and fused to special coated papers. Thermal transfer is utilized by some types of inexpensive color desktop printers manufactured by QMS, Océ, Seiko, and Tektronix, which have the ability to generate *PostScript* output.

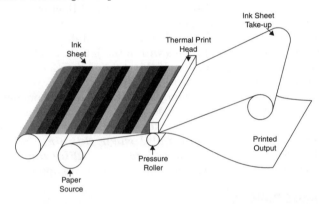

Principle of thermal printing. The ink sheet contains strips of CMY (and sometimes K) colorants which are vaporized or melted onto the substrate by the print head.

Thermal-Transfer Printer

An output device used for *thermal transfer*. See *Thermal Transfer*.

Thermography

A printing process designed to simulate raised printing by dusting the wet printed ink film with a *resin*-based powder and fusing the resin particles together with heat to produce a raised effect.

Thermomechanical Pulp

Paper *pulp* produced by *thermomechanical pulping* means. See *Thermomechanical Pulping (TMP)*.

Thermomechanical Pulping (TMP)

A method of *mechanical pulping*. Like *refiner mechanical pulping (RMP)*, TMP sandwiches wood chips between the two rotating disks of a *disk refiner*, but under higher temperature and pressure. (In many cases, the wood

chips are preheated.) The higher temperatures and pressures soften the lignin even more than can be accomplished using frictional heat, and fiber separation is easier. Additional passes through the system increases defiberization, and longer fibers and fewer *fines* are generated. Thermomechanical pulp is stronger than refiner mechanical pulp, and still retains the high yield and cost effectiveness of mechanical pulps. Newsprint made with TMP has been found to possess higher *runnability* on the press. (See *Mechanical Pulping*.)

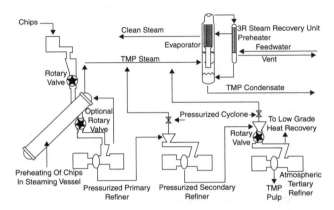

Three-stage thermomechanical pulping system.

Thermoplastic

Descriptive of a material, such as plastic, that becomes soft and flexible when exposed to heat, without a permanent alteration of its basic properties, used to describe any of a variety of polymeric substances used as *resin*s in a wide variety of printing inks or as *substrate*s in *gravure* and *flexographic* printing.

Thermoset

Descriptive of a material that hardens when heated, but does not reharden when reheated, as certain ink films.

Thermosetting

Descriptive of a printing ink that undergoes *setting* by *polymerization* upon exposure to heat. See *heatset ink*.

Thesaurus

A reference document (available in either print or electronic form) that contains a list of words and their synonyms (and perhaps also their antonyms), to aid in effective writing. Some word processing programs also have a thesaurus available as a *plug-in*. And, no, there is no synonym for *thesuarus*.

Thick Ethernet

A wide-gauge *coaxial* cable used in some *Ethernet* networks. Thick Ethernet cable is expensive, but has the advantage of being able to be laid at lengths of up to 600 meters without the need for signal amplification. See also *Thin Ethernet*.

Thickener
Alternate term for *bodying agent*. See *Bodying Agent*.

Thickness
Alternate term for *caliper*. See *Caliper*.

Thin Ethernet
A thin-gauge *coaxial* cable used in some *Ethernet* networks. Thin Ethernet cable is inexpensive, but cannot be laid at very long lengths without signal amplification. See also *Thick Ethernet*. Also known as *cheapernet wire*.

Thinner
A *solvent*, *diluent*, oil, or other substance added to a printing ink to reduce its *tack*, *body*, and *viscosity*.

Thin Space
In typography, a small *fixed space* equal in width to a comma or period (or somewhere between ¼ to ⅓ of an *em space*). Thin spaces were often used in *hot metal* typography and phototypesetting to achieve line *justification*.

Thioindigoid Red
An *organic color pigment* used in printing inks. Thioindigoid Red (classified as a red, but is actually a violet shade) is a red violet possessing high *lightfastness*, heat resistance, and chemical resistance to most substances. It is a high-quality pigment commonly used in security inks. (See *Organic Color Pigments*.)
(CI Pigment Violet 88 No. 73312.)

Thirty
In newspaper publishing, a symbol ("–30–") added to the original copy to indicate the end of a story.

Thirty-Two-Bit (32-Bit)
Descriptive of computer systems (especially *microprocessors*) and software that process data as 4-*byte* units (one byte equals 8 *bit*s). The greater the number of bytes that a system can process at any one time, the faster the system. The Intel 80386 and 80486 and Motorola 680X0 chips are 32-bit processors. See also *Sixteen-Bit (16-Bit)* and *Sixty-Four-Bit (64-Bit)*.

Thirty-Two-Bit (32-Bit) Color
On a computer monitor, a color display in which each *pixel* (or smallest point of *color*) is described by 32 bits of information, or 8 bits are used to describe each of the *red, green, and blue* values, while another 8 bits are used to describe any mask layers or other uses. The color of a pixel on a computer display is commonly expressed as some amount of red, green, and blue. Greater numbers of combinations of these amounts require more processing power on the part of the computer. This color depth is greater than the standard and/or required setting for many CD-ROMs and multimedia programs (which usually have difficulty handling greater than *eight-bit color*), and is even greater than the minimum that is sufficient for high-quality graphic arts reproduction. See also *Eight-Bit Color*, *Sixteen-Bit Color*, and *Twenty-Four-Bit Color*. Computer monitors can also display *one-bit color* (black and white, or any two colors) and *four-bit color* (16 colors).

Thirty-twomo
In *book typography* and production, any printed sheet that has been folded 5 times to yield 32 leaves or 64 pages. Abbreviated *32-mo* and *32°*. *Thirty-twomo* is also used to refer to the book size produced by folding pages in this manner (commonly 3¼×5½).

Thixotropic
Possessing the property of *thixotropy*. See *Thixotropy*.

Thixotropy
A property of a fluid—such as printing ink—that describes its "false body," or a consistency, thickness, and *viscosity* that decreases with the application of stress or other forces. Some inks, such as offset inks, are stiff and thick while in their containers, but upon being worked become thinner and more fluid, typically due to an unstable structure formed by the solid particles within the ink that is broken down when force is applied. If thixotropic ink is left undisturbed, it will thicken again. Thixotropy is one reason why offset presses require so many ink rollers, to apply enough stress to the ink to make it less viscous and more easily transferred to the plate, blanket, and ultimately the *substrate*. Thixotropy is also called *shear thinning*. Some inks also exhibit the opposite property, *dilatancy*, in which the viscosity *in*creases when stresses are applied.

Thread Build-Up
In *thread sewing* and *case binding*, an increase in the thickness of a book's *spine* caused by the thread used to bind the *signatures* together. Thread build-up can be decreased by staggering the location of a stitch from signature to signature. See *Case Binding*.

Thread Sewing
In *case binding*, the use of nylon (or other fabric) thread to hold printed *signatures* together. See *Case Binding*.

Three-Arm Paster
Alternate term for *three-arm splicer*. See *Three-Arm Splicer*.

Three-Arm Splicer
A type of *flying splicer* used on *web press*es to hold three rolls of substrate, in contrast to a *two-arm splicer*. See *Flying Splicer*. Also known as a *three-arm paster*.

Three-Chip Module
In computing, a type of *single in-line memory module (SIMM)* containing two 4-megabit and one 1-megabit chips. A three-chip module, like a *nine-chip module*, is

used to add **RAM** to a computer. A three-chip module is a memory chip providing an additional 1 **megabyte** of memory, and can only be used on newer computers.

Three-Color Black

In **process color** printing, a neutral gray comprising only **cyan**, **magenta**, and **yellow** inks. When **overprinted** at equal dot sizes, however, the term *three-color black* is somewhat of a misnomer, as impurities in the ink impart a brownish, rather than gray, color to the image.

Three-Color Process

Process color printing that eliminates the **black** plate.

Three-Dimensional (3D)

Descriptive of **two-dimensional** objects drawn or rendered in a three-axis coordinate system, or, in other words, appear to have depth, as well as width and height. *Three-dimensional* is also used to describe objects in the real world.

Three-Dimensional (3D) Animation

The **animation** of objects (usually using a 3D **modeling** program) in which a third dimension (beyond the two dimensions of height and width) is simulated, allowing the object to move in a "virtual" 3D space, or in other words, move in perspective on the screen. See also **Two-Dimensional (2D) Animation**.

Three-Dimensional (3D) Digitizer

In computer graphics, one of several devices used for the **scanning** of **three-dimensional** objects and storing the image as digital data within a computer. One type of 3D digitizer uses a surface **scanner**, which uses laser beams or a camera to image an object. Such objects are stored as **wire frame** models. Specific color, fill, and surface texture information may also be captured by the scanner, and is stored as an attached **bitmap** file. When the image is displayed, the bitmap is overlayed on the wire frame.

A 3D digitizer is also used in medical imaging.

3DO

In multimedia, a popular format and system (designed by the 3DO company) used to create and playback full-motion and full-screen interactive video and multimedia. Presentations are stored and distributed on at least a double-speed CD-ROM. A complete 3DO system includes a CD-ROM drive, development software, and specific compression and decompression algorithms. A competitor to the 3DO system in the computer gaming and entertainment markets is **CD-i**.

Three-Drum Transfer

A method of transferring sheets from one printing unit to another on a sheetfed press (especially that used in **offset lithography**) in which a set of three **transfer cylinders** carries the printed sheet from one **impression cylinder** to

the next. The actual sizes of the transfer cylinders vary according to press design, and may be designed to hold one or more sheets at any one time. The transfer cylinders typically possess one of a variety of devices or means to avoid marking or smudging wet ink, and may contain a **gripper-bowing device**. They may also be **air-transport drum**s. (See also **Air-Transport Drum**, **Chain Transfer**, **Three-Drum Transfer**, and **Transfer Cylinder**.)

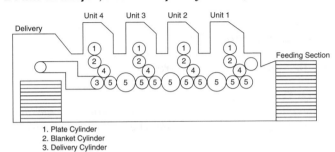

Three-drum transfer.

Three-Hole Drilling

In **binding and finishing**, the **drilling** of three holes in finished press sheets, **signature**s, etc., as a means of enabling them to be bound in a **ring binder** or **post binder**. Three-hole drilling, also known as **three-hole punching**, may also be performed on blank paper stock. See **Drilling** and **Mechanical Binding**.

Three-Hole Punching

Alternate term for **three-hole drilling**. See **Three-Hole Drilling**.

Three-Knife Trimmer

In **binding and finishing**, a type of cutting device (similar to a **guillotine cutter**) comprising three knives, two parallel knives and one right-angle knife, used to trim three sides of a bound book simultaneously. Three-knife trimmers are commonly automatic operating devices, and are located at the end of a binding line. See **Binding and Finishing**.

Three-Piece Case

In **binding and finishing**, a book cover in which the **spine** is covered with one type or color of cloth, while the front and back covers are covered with a different type or color of cloth. Also known as a *three-piece cover*. See also **Two-Piece Case**.

Three-Point Curve

In computer graphics, an object or shape described by two end points and a third point at the top of the image.

Three-Point Curve Control

In **color**, the process of changing the contrast or gradation of a color scanner by manipulating three points on the tone scale: **highlight**s, **middletones**, and **shadow**s. See also *Five-Point Curve Control*.

3.5-Inch

In computing, descriptive of a common size of *floppy disk*. See *Floppy Disk*.

Also in computing, the term *3.5-inch* is also descriptive of a standard size of internal devices and the housings used to contain them.

Three-Quarter-Inch Tape

Alternate colloquial term for *Broadcast Video U-Matic*. See *Broadcast Video U-Matic (BVU)*.

Three-Quartertone

In imaging and photography, the portions of an image (such as a photograph) with tonal values between those of **middletone**s and **shadow**s, containing **halftone** dot sizes of approximately 75% **dot area**.

Three-Roll Mill

A device used in the manufacture of ink to further disperse the solid **pigment** particles in the fluid ink **vehicle** that utilize three steel rollers revolving in opposite directions at varying speeds to chop up the pigment particles and disperse them thoroughly. The ink **slurry** is put into the machine's hopper, and as it passes through the nips of the rollers the shearing force breaks up the particles and disperses them, and the milled ink flows out of the front of the machine into a container. The hardness of the pigment particles may necessitate additional passes through the machine. The speed of the rollers, the size of the nips, and the temperature of the system can be adjusted to improve the milling efficiency. (See also *Ball Mill*, *Sand/Shot Mill*, and *Colloid Mill*.)

360K

Abbreviation for a specific capacity of *floppy disk*, having a diameter of 5.25 in. See *Floppy Disk*.

Three-Strip Method

One of the varieties of *strip method* (or *sandwich method*) testing of the *roller setting* of offset printing ink and dampening rollers. In the three-strip method, nine strips of 0.004-in.-thick packing paper are cut, three of which are 12×1 in., the other six being 12×2 in. Three "sandwiches" are made, inserting one 12×1 strip between two 12×2 strips. The sandwiches are then inserted into the nip of the two rollers to be tested, one at the left end, one in the center, and one at the right end. The size of the nip is then adjusted to the proper setting, or so that the paper sandwiches are gripped firmly but not excessively tightly. Beginning with the center sandwich, the inner strip of paper is pulled out evenly with one hand, in a straight line. With the same hand and with the same amount of force, the other two inner strips are also pulled out. They should pull out easily, without excessive drag, and each strip should

pull out with the same force. If the setting is too tight, or if the strips pull out with unequal force across the rollers, the setting needs to be adjusted, and the test tried again. This method can be used to test the setting between either the **ductor roller** and its adjacent **oscillator**, the first **form roller** and *its* adjacent oscillator, or the last form roller and the plate cylinder.

A slight variation of this procedure is the **folded-paper method**, in which instead of six 12×2-in. strips, three 24×2-in. strips are cut and folded in half lengthwise, the three 12×1-in. strips then placed in the center.

A perhaps more objective and quantitative measurement can be made utilizing a **roller-setting gauge**.

Threshold

In **scanning**, especially scanning of **line art**, a setting to determine the level of gray at which a particular **pixel** is interpreted as black or white. In **one-bit color**, pixels can only be one of those two values. Setting the threshold enhances the ability of the device to capture shades of gray.

In graphics and image manipulation programs, *threshold* refers to a setting controlling how many pixels in the image are affected by a particular operation, in particular various forms of **edge enhancement** (e.g., **unsharp masking**.)

Through Drier

A **drier** added to a printing ink as a means of increasing the rate at which the ink undergoes **oxidation** and **polymerization**. A through drier differs from a **top drier** by working to slowly solidify the ink film throughout its interior, rather than to form a hard surface. (See **Drier**.)

Throwing

Alternate term for *ink misting*. See *Ink Misting*.

Thrust

Alternate term for **creep** in **binding and finishing**. See *Creep* (third definition).

Thumb

Alternate term for a **scroll box**. See *Scroll Box*.

Thumb Edge

The outside edge of a book, opposite the **binding edge**. Also known as the **front**, **trim margin**, **face margin**, or **outside margin**.

Thumbnail

A small, crude sketch of a proposed page layout, usually generated in bunches during the brainstorming phase of design. Used primarily to seek approval as to which design warrants further development. A slightly more finalized layout sketch is known as a **rough**.

Thumbpad

In computing, a graphic input device that controls the position of the **cursor** on the screen by having the user rub the thumb over a pressure-sensitive pad. The pad registers the direction of the movement and transmits this information as electrical signals to the computer, which converts it to digital information needed to move the cursor correspondingly. An accompanying button usually allows the thumbpad to function identically to a mouse. Thumbpads are often used on *laptop* computers. Also called *touchpad*s.

Tie

The amount of paper between *perforation*s.

Tie Coat

Alternate term for *anchor coat*. See *Anchor Coat*.

Alternate term for *barrier coat*. See *Barrier Coat*.

Tie-Together

In prepress, small *flat*s taped in the proper position to each other to create a large, full-size flat.

TIFF

Abbreviation for *Tag Image File Format* (or, sometimes, *Tagged Image File Format*). In computer graphics, TIFF is the most commonly used *file format* for saving and transporting *bitmap* images. The TIFF format was developed by Aldus Corporation, and is useful for saving a wide variety of image types, from 8-bit grayscale to 24-bit color *RGB* or *CMYK* images. Essentially, TIFF saves an image with little information beyond the values of the pixels contained in the image, and a header (or tag) describing the output size and the resolution of the image. The TIFF format is often used to save scanned images, and can be imported by nearly all *page makeup software* applications, such as *QuarkXPress* and *PageMaker*.

An advantage to the TIFF format is that when saving CMYK images prior to *color separation*, no further separation may be necessary once that file is imported into the page makeup program; depending on the program, it may be able to print each channel separately. A drawback is that TIFF files tend to be very large, although some *data compression* algorithms (in particular, *LZW*) are *lossless* and can compress an image quite substantially. Another drawback, however, is that LZW-compressed TIFF images often take longer to save and reopen. The TIFF format may vary somewhat from application to application, although compatibility issues are rarely a problem any longer. The TIFF format may also vary by computer *platform*; the *Macintosh* TIFF may differ from the *PC* TIFF. (Depending on the microprocessor chip being utilized—i.e., Motorola vs. Intel—the *byte* order in which the file is saved may vary.) However, many image-processing programs can handle both Mac and PC versions of TIFF. TIFF is sometimes further abbreviated as *TIF*, especially when used as a three-character *extension*.

Tight Back

A type of *binding* in which the *spine* is glued to the *binding edge* of the sheets. See also *Loose Back*.

Tight Edges

A paper defect characterized by warpage and distortion of its edges, caused by a loss of *dimensional stability* due to decreased *moisture content* after exposure of paper edges to lower *relative humidity*, or from exposure to cooler air. The distortion is greater in the paper's *cross-grain direction*, and causes *misregister* when printing multicolor work. See also *Wavy Edges*. (See *Moisture Content* and *Dimensional Stability*.)

Tight Line

In typography, a line of type with little or no *word spacing* or *letterspacing*, often a consequence of *justification*.

The term *tight line* is also used in typography to refer to a line that will not fit in the prescribed *line length*.

In *hot-metal* typesetting, a *tight line* was a slug of type which would not fit into the vice jaws that transported the characters, causing the device to jam.

Tight Negative

In graphic arts photography, a *negative* that has been overexposed or overdeveloped to produce printed images sharper than those that would be printed otherwise.

Tightness

In typography, a quality relating to the proximity of characters and/or words to each other. See *Loose*.

Tight Register

See *Close Register*.

Tilde

In typography, an *accent* (˜) placed over a character, usually the letter "n" in Spanish, to indicate that it should be pronounced with a "ny" sound. See *Accent*. The tilde is also set centered by itself on the *cap height* (~) and is used as a character in *World Wide Web* addresses.

Tile

On a *GUI*, to position each "window" on the monitor adjacent to each other in a particular pattern, much like floor tiles, rather than overlapping them.

In page layout, to break down a large image into smaller sections, used for oversize pages or documents when an output device is incapable of imaging the entire page. After output, individual "tiles" are reassembled manually.

Tiled Windows

In computing, especially by means of a *graphical user interface (GUI)*, multiple *window*s displayed on the screen adjacent to each other, so that the contents of each window remain visible. See also *Cascaded Windows*.

Tilt

In motion picture photography and videography, a camera move comprising a swinging up and/or down in a straight vertical line, a kind of vertical *pan*.

Tilting Transfer Table

A device used on a *guillotine cutter* which automatically transfers stock from a *jogger* to the *bed* of the cutter. Tilting transfer tables are particularly effective when used for large-size sheets. See *Guillotine Cutter*.

Time Base

In television and video, the *synchronization* of the horizontal and vertical scanning pulses in a video image.

Time-Base Corrector (TBC)

In video, a device (commonly utilizing a *waveform monitor*) used to synchronize various video signals, such as two VCRs, allowing them to be used in *synchronization* with each other.

Time Code

In video production, a system whereby an electronic "marker" is encoded (or *stripe*d) into every frame of a video signal, usually on a spare channel dedicated to it. The time code typically encodes each frame with the hour, minute, second, and frame corresponding to the frame's position relative to the beginning of the tape. The inclusion of a time code, usually performed just prior to editing, allows for precise editing of material on the tape. See, in particular, *SMPTE Time Code*.

Time Code Generator

In video production, a device used to *stripe* a *time code* onto a videotape. See *Time Code*.

Time Slot

In networking, a repetitive, fixed interval during which data can be transmitted over the network. If the time slot is full to capacity, a transmission is interrupted until a new time slot opens up.

Tinctorial Strength

A property of a printing ink that describes the ability of the ink's *colorant* to impart a particular *color* to the ink.

Tint

In printing, an alternate term for *flat tint*. See *Flat Tint*.

The term *tint* is also occasionally used as an alternate term for *spot color*. See *Spot Color*.

In *subtractive color theory*, *tint* refers to a primary *hue* to which some quantity of white pigment has been added.

The term *tint* is also an alternate term for *saturation*, or how white (or light) a particular hue is. See *Saturation*.

In ink mixing, a colored printing ink to which a quantity of *extender* or *white pigment* has been added in order to reduce the *color strength* of the primary color.

In *halftone* photography, *tint* refers to a halftone produced with a dot percentage of less than 100%.

Tint Block

In printing, a small area of *color* on which an illustration or type is printed.

Tinting

A general scum that forms on nonimage areas of the printing plate and is transferred to the paper. Originally believed to be caused by contaminants from coated paper, it is now known that tinting is more a function of plate *desensitization*, various ink formulations, *fountain solution* problems, and other aspects of press chemistry, in particular the *emulsification* of the ink by the fountain solution. In particular, tinting occurs when particles of ink *pigment* bleed into the fountain solution, and are transferred to the nonimage areas of the plate, printing as a colored tint. The tendency for tinting to increase with increasing temperature has resulted in its also being known as *hot-weather scumming*. Tinting is rarely a problem anymore. Tinting is also known as *washing*, and in *waterless printing* is known as *toning*.

Tinting Strength

A property of a printing ink that describes the extent to which an ink can be diluted with a *white pigment* to produce a *tint* of a desired strength. (See also *Color Strength* and *Tinctorial Strength*.)

Tip-In

In *binding and finishing*, to bind a *foldout* or other *insert* into a book by means of an adhesive.

Tip-On

In *binding and finishing*, to attach *endleaf* papers (or other sheets) to the outside of folded *signature*s by means of adhesive.

Tipped-In

See *Tip-In*.

Tissue Overlay

An *overlay* comprised of thin, translucent paper. See *Overlay*.

Titanium Dioxide

A bright white, insoluble powder (chemical formula TiO_2) added to paper *pulp* as a *filler* or applied as a *coating* pigment, and is the most efficient means of increasing paper *brightness* and *opacity*. Of the three primary optical brighteners, it is more effective than *clay*, or *calcium carbonate*, but is also the most expensive. Titanium dioxide is an oxide of the metal titanium, and is used widely in the manufacture of other materials, such as plastics, leathers, face powders, linoleum, and paints. (See also *Fillers*.)

Titanium dioxide is also used as a *white pigment* in printing inks, and has the highest degree of opacity of any white pigment. It accounts for 80% of all the white pigments in use. It is extremely fast-to-light, and resistant to nearly all substances. There are two major grades of titanium dioxide: anatase (bluer, harder, and more opaque) and rutile (less opaque and softer). Various coatings of aluminum, silicon, or zinc oxides can also be added to obtain a variety of desired properties. Titanium dioxide is used in every type of printing ink manufactured. When used in printing ink, titanium dioxide is also called **cover white**. (See also **White Pigments**.)

(*CI Pigment White 6 No. 77891.*)

Title Bar

In computing, especially by means of a **graphical user interface (GUI)**, a label located at the top of a **window**, usually indicating the name of the document or folder it contains.

Title Generator

In television and video production, a device used to create and superimpose titles, credits, or other screen graphics over a video image.

Title Page

In **book typography** and production, a **recto** page at the beginning of the book listing the title, author, and publisher. See **Book Typography**.

Titler

An alternate term for a **character generator**, especially one used to create titles for video productions. See **Character Generator (CG)**.

TOC

Abbreviation for **table of contents**. See **Table of Contents**. Also spelled with a small "o," such as *ToC*.

Toggle

When used as a noun, *toggle* refers to a computer function or command that allows a feature to be turned on and off.

In image-processing programs, a toggle function allows a rapid alternating of "before" and "after" images, allowing the comparison of an image before and after a particular change was made to it. When used as a verb, *toggle* means to use a toggle function.

Token

In networking, especially a network that utilizes a **token passing** protocol, a special pattern or **packet** of **bit**s that continuously circulates around the network, passing each connected **node**. If a particular node wants to transmit a message, it waits for the token to come around, which then picks up the message and carries it around to the destination. Possession of the token provides exclusive access to the network for the duration of the transmission. See **Token Passing**.

Token Bus

In networking, the procedure used to access a **token passing** network. See **Token Passing**.

Token Passing

A **network protocol** used commonly in **ring** networks in which a **token**, or a special pattern or **packet** of **bit**s that continuously circulates around the network, passing each connected **node**. If a particular node wants to transmit a message, it waits for the token to come around, which then picks up the message and carries it around to the destination. Possession of the token provides exclusive access to the network for the duration of the transmission. When the recipient of a message wants to reply, that node waits for the token to come around yet again, and the new message is sent. One particular network, developed by IBM, that utilizes a token passing protocol is **Token Ring**. (See also **Network Topology** and **Network Protocol**.)

Token-Passing Polling

In networking, a means of **polling** in which a **token** makes the rounds of network **node**s to determine if any node has data to transmit. See **Polling**.

Token Ring

A **ring** network utilizing a **token passing** network protocol developed by IBM for use in its **System Network Architecture (SNA)**. The transmission speed of the Token Ring network is 16 megabits per second. The Token Ring protocol is an IEEE standard.

Token Talk

In networking, a low-level **network protocol** used to let **AppleTalk** data be transmitted by means of **Token Ring** hardware.

Toluidine Red

An **organic color pigment** used in printing inks. Toluidine Red is a dull scarlet shade of moderate **tinctorial strength** and possesses high **lightfastness** and **alkali resistance**, but does not withstand exposure to solvents and tends to discolor when exposed to heat. It is an inexpensive pigment, and is most effective undiluted and in water-based inks. (See also **Organic Color Pigments**.)

(*CI Pigment Red 3 No. 12120.*)

Toluidines

A type of **organic color pigment** used in printing inks that are fast-to-light and somewhat transparent, but are dirty in tone. They are widely used in poster and label inks. (See **Organic Color Pigments**.)

Toluol

An **aromatic solvent**—chemical formula C_7H_8—similar in odor and chemical structure to benzene, used as a solvent for synthetic **resin**s. It is a **volatile** liquid and tends to reduce the drying time of inks in which it is used. Toluol is also called *toluene*.

Tonal Range

Alternate term for *density range*, or the *gamut* of tones in an original or reproduced image. See *Density Range*.

Tone

As a noun, *tone* refers to the lightness or general quality of a *color*. When used as a verb, *tone* means to alter a color.

Tone Compression

The reduction of the *tonal range* of an original image to one that can be reproduced using the intended inks, *substrate*, and printing process.

Tone Correction

Alternate term for *gamma correction*. See *Gamma Correction*.

Tone Curve

A graph illustrating the relationship between the *density range* of an original image and that which can be indicated on a scanner's *dot area* meter. A tone curve is used during *scanner* setup to optimize the dot area range.

Tone-Line

In prepress, to photographically convert a *continuous-tone* image into *line art*.

Toner

A type of very concentrated *pigment* or *dye* used in printing inks to alter the color strength of an ink.

Toner is also a term used to refer to the fine powder used to create an image in *electrophotography*, such as in *laser printers* and photocopiers. Toner is often contained in a *toner cartridge*.

Toner Cartridge

A removable plastic cartridge containing *toner*, a fine powder used as a pigment in *electrophotography*. Toner cartridges are commonly used in *laser printers* and small photocopiers, and are installed and removed by the user. Toner cartridges—especially those used in photocopiers— may also contain the coronas used in the imaging process.

Tone Reproduction

The degree to which all the tonal elements of a reproduced image—such as the final print and the intermediate films— approximate those on the original image. Tone reproduction can be expressed graphically, using a four-quadrant Jones Diagram. *Tone reproduction* is often used interchangeably with *contrast*, *gamma*, and *gradation*.

Toning

The adhesion of ink to nonprinting areas of a printing plate, which then transfers the ink to undesirable areas of the *substrate*. In *waterless printing*, a variety of offset lithography utilizing a silicone compound rather than water as a means of repelling ink from nonimage plate areas, the plates are very temperature-sensitive, and increases in ink temperature cause the silicone compounds to lose their ink-repellent properties, resulting in accumulation of an ink film in undesired areas. Toning is also known as *scumming*.

Toning Blue

A shade of *Iron Blue*, an *inorganic color pigment* used in printing inks. See *Iron Blue*.

Toning In

Alternate term for *running in*. See *Running In*.

Toolbar

In computing, especially by means of a *graphical user interface (GUI)*, a row of small icons or buttons along the top of a screen, providing a quick means of activating commonly used commands. Also known as a *buttonbar*.

The toolbar in Microsoft Word.

Toolbox

In many computer graphics and *page makeup program*s, a set of commonly used functions (such as drawing tools, image-manipulation functions, etc.) grouped together in a palette and displayed on the screen, allowing easy access to them. The example to the right is the toolbox in Adobe Photoshop.

Tooth

Term used to describe the surface roughness of a paper that allows it to accept ink readily.

In *screen printing* *tooth* refers to the roughness of a *monofilament* screen fabric that allows it to accept the adhesion of a *stencil*.

TOP

Abbreviation for *Technical and Office Protocol*. See *Technical and Office Protocol (TOP)*.

Top Drier

A *drier* added to a printing ink as a means of increasing the rate at which the ink undergoes *oxidation* and *polymerization*. A top drier differs from a *through drier* by working to form a thick, hard surface on the top of the ink film, rather than dry it throughout its interior. (See *Drier*.)

Top Side of Paper

Alternate term for the *felt side* of a paper. See *Felt Side*.

Top-Sizing

The addition of *sizing* to a paper while it is on the *forming wire*, beyond what was added to the *furnish* in the *beater*.

Top Staining

In *binding and finishing*, the application of a dye or other colorant to the trimmed top edge of a book. Top staining is a specific form of *edge staining* or *edge treatment*. Also spelled with a hyphen, *top-staining*.

Top-Wire Former

A type of papermaking machine, an alternative to the traditional *fourdrinier* machine that has as its *forming section* a horizontal *forming wire* through which the wet pulp drains, as well as another forming wire which contacts the *web* on its top side, allowing water drainage through both sides. Top-wire formers, in addition to *twin-wire formers*, aim to reduce or eliminate the *two-sidedness* of paper, or the production of a *wire side* and a *felt side*.

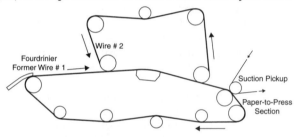

Top-wire former.

Topographic Kerning

In typography, a type of *kerning* process whereby a character is defined by the typesetting device in terms of the specific shape of the letter, rather than as the character positioned within a rectangle. This allows for an almost infinite variety of *kern pairs*. See *Kerning*.

Topology

See *Network Topology*.

Total Density

Alternate—through incorrect—term for *total printing dot*. See *Total Printing Dot*.

Total Indicated Runout (TIR)

A measure used to gauge the roundness of a printing press roller, be it an ink or dampening roller used in *offset lithography*, an *impression roller* or *gravure cylinder* used in *gravure*, or an inking roller used in *flexography*. TIR is the difference in the lengths of a roller's radius as measured from the center to the outside surface. (A perfectly round roller would have a difference of 0 between different radii, as the radii of a circle are always equal regardless of where they are measured.)

TIR is typically measured using a laser; the manufacturing tolerance of TIR is ±0.0005 in., meaning that a roller can be out-of-round by that much before being deemed defective. An older roller that develops a TIR of greater than ±0.0005 in. should be replaced or repaired. *Out-of-roundness* of ink rollers is an important consideration; rollers that are elliptical (or eccentric) rotate with a bump that can cause streaking and other ink-transfer problems. An offset press roller's out-of-roundness can also be gauged using the *stripe method* of roller setting. (See also *Impression Roller* and *Gravure Cylinder*.)

Total Printing Dot

In *halftone* photography and reproduction, the total surface area of a press sheet or *color separation negative* occupied by *halftone dot*s. Often incorrectly known as *total density* (it's not really a measure of *density*).

Touch-and-Seal Envelope

An envelope to which a special latex-based sealant has been added, allowing the flap to be sealed shut simply by pressure, rather than moistening or tying.

Touching

In typography, descriptive of type set such that each character in a word touches those adjacent to it, or has very tight *letterspacing*.

Touch Monitor

Alternate term for a *touch screen*. See *Touch Screen*.

Touchpad

Alternate term for *thumbpad*. See *Thumbpad*.

Touch Plate

A means of adding *extra-trinary color*s to *process color* printing. A touch plate consists of a plate of a special color beyond the traditional *cyan*, *magenta*, or *yellow*. Touch plates are used to reproduce a color which is out of the *gamut* of CMY mixing, used especially to reproduce a unique color in the original artwork. See *Extra-Trinary Color*. See also *Color Substitution* and *Bump Plate*.

In multicolor *screen printing*, a *touch plate* is a fifth (or otherwise additional) screen for the printing of so-called nonreproducible colors such as fluorescents or whites.

Touch Screen

A type of computer monitor by which the computer receives input by means of pressure on the surface of the screen. A touch screen, also called a *touch monitor*, can be used in lieu of a keyboard in many applications. Although all touch screens allow the user to touch a particular portion of the screen and activate a specific function, there are several means by which this is accomplished:

Capacitive. A *capacitive monitor* utilizes four oscillator circuits (located at each corner of the screen) and a capacitive surface coating (i.e., electrically charged). When an area of the screen is touched, it activates the oscillator circuits, which then determine the precise location that was touched.

Infrared. An ***infrared monitor*** utilize a "layer" of infrared beams covering the surface of screen that, when broken by the user's finger (or other object) transmits location information to the computer. Infrared monitors have the advantage that the infrared beams are sensitive up to one millimeter from the actual surface of the screen, so actual physical contact with the screen is not really necessary.

Resistive. A ***resistive monitor*** utilizes a double screen with contacts distributed in the space between the two screens that are activated when touched.

Surface Acoustical Wave (SAW). A ***surface acoustical wave monitor*** uses sonic waves to detect varying pressure over the surface of the screen.

Touch screens are used in interactive kiosks in many public locations, as well as in some special situations such as ticketing offices.

Touch Sensitive

Descriptive of a technology allowing a computer to receive input by means of a ***touch screen***. See ***Touch Screen***.

Touch-Sensitive Display

Alternate term for a ***touch screen***. See ***Touch Screen***.

Tower

A personal computer constructed so that its components fit in a tall, narrow case, often a space-saving option that allows for a smaller ***footprint*** on one's desk, or which can be placed on the floor next to the desk at which the user sits. Towers also tend to have more space for ***add-on cards*** and other devices.

TPL

A ***file extension*** denoting a template file created by Harvard Graphics.

Trace

In graphics, to create a path around the contour or outline of an object or shape. Tracing can either be done by hand (such as using translucent tracing paper to redraw an image) or by computer (such as the process of creating a ***vector*** graphic from a ***bitmap***. See also ***Autotrace***.

A computer diagnostic technique which allows an examination of a storage disk or of the result of each processing step.

Capture utility in which every byte of data involved in file transfer between two devices is captured in readable form. All data, including control codes, text, and encoded data are captured.

Track

A portion of, or a path created on, any computer or analog storage medium—such as a ***magnetic tape***, a ***magnetic disk***, an ***optical disc***, etc.—on which data can be stored. When a computer disk, for example, is initialized or for-matted, the disk drive's write head subdivides the surface of the disk into concentric circular (or spiral) tracks, which are then sub-subdivided into sectors, allowing for the organization and rapid retrieval of stored data.

On a ***CEPS***, the term *track* is used to refer to one complete circuit. Only one function can usually be performed on one track at any given time.

Track Advance

On a ***videodisc*** or ***audio CD***, to move the ***read/write head*** to the beginning of the next ***track*** (relative to its current location). See also ***Track Reverse***.

Track Ball

A computer input device comprising a mounted, moveable ball that can be rotated to generate coordinate data, which moves and positions the cursor on the screen. Although originally used primarily on video and arcade games, track balls can essentially be likened to an upside-down mouse; a mouse consists of a rotatable ball on the bottom of the device, which is moved around a surface to control the position of the cursor. A track ball mounts that same rotatable ball on top of the device. Track balls are preferred on portable computers and laptops, as they do not require as large a surface as does a mouse. Also spelled as one word, *trackball*, and also known as a ***control ball*** or a ***rollerball***.

Tracking

In typography, the adjusting of the ***letterspacing*** throughout a piece of typeset copy. See ***Letterspacing***.

In video, the term *tracking* refers to a faulty playback of a videotape, caused by an incomplete reading of the ***control track*** or by a damaged control track. On most VCRs, tracking can be compensated for by adjusting the tape speed (the "tracking" control button).

Track Reverse

On a ***videodisc*** or ***audio CD***, to move the ***read/write head*** to the beginning of the ***track*** it is currently playing. If the read/write head is already located at the beginning of a track, it is sent to the beginning of the previous track. See also ***Track Advance***.

Tractor Feed

Alternate term for ***pin feed***. See ***Pin Feed***.

Trade Book

In book publishing, any book marketed and distributed through book stores to the general public.

Traditional Color Angles

The ***screen angles*** used commonly in photographic ***color separation***, the respective angle at which the ***halftone dots*** for each ***process color*** interfere with each other less and eliminate undesirable ***moiré*** patterns. These angles are: ***yellow*** at 0° from the horizontal (or, in other words, perfectly horizontal); ***magenta*** at 15° from the horizontal;

black at 45°; and **cyan** at 75°. Digital halftone screening systems have trouble with the 15° and 75° angles, as their tangents turn out to be irrational numbers. Consequently, a variety of approaches to the problem of these **irrational screen angles** have been devised. See **Screen Angles**.

Traffic

Term for the movement of data over a telecommunications network.

Train

In **screen printing**, the moving part of the screen that adheres to the **substrate** during a printing stroke and trails behind the **squeegee**.

Tranny

Colloquial term for **transparency** used in Great Britain, New Zealand, and Australia. See **Transparency**.

Transactional

In multimedia, descriptive of a **kiosk** or other type of inter-active machine that allows a user to make some form of transaction. A common example of a transactional kiosk is a bank's automatic teller machine (ATM), which allows users to deposit and withdraw money.

Transceiver

In networking, a device needed to convert a digital signal from a computer or workstation to a signal capable of being transmitted along the networking medium (cable). A transceiver is also needed at the receiving end to convert the transmitted signal back into digital data.

Transceiver Cable

In networking, a cable used to connect a **transceiver** to the network controller, allowing **node**s to be located some distance from the network medium.

Transfer Cylinder

The part of an offset printing press that transfers the printed paper from the **impression cylinder** to the delivery tray, or to additional printing units. The last transfer cylinder in a press before the delivery tray is more commonly known as a **delivery cylinder**. In multicolor presses (i.e., those with more than one printing unit), an odd number of transfer cylinders is located between printing units. Transfer sections have three basic configurations. (See **Chain Transfer**, **Single-Drum Transfer**, and **Three-Drum Transfer**.)

An important concern with respect to transfer cylinders is ensuring that they do not smudge or mark the wet ink. Consequently, transport rollers are covered with a variety of surfaces or substances to eliminate this problem, such as a near-frictionless ink-repellent coating, which is then covered with a near-frictionless cloth, which moves unimpeded over the surface of the cylinder, preventing a rubbing action which can damage the inked image. Some

transfer cylinders also contain a thin bit of adhesive-backed foam rubber on the portions of the cylinder that correspond to nonimage areas of the printed sheets, which prevent the inked image areas from contacting the surface of the cylinder at all. Needless to say, the foam needs to be replaced and customized for each job.

Some presses replace the transfer cylinder with an **air-transport drum** which transfers the printed sheets on a cushion of air.

Transfer cylinders or drums are also used to transfer sheets through sheetfed gravure presses.

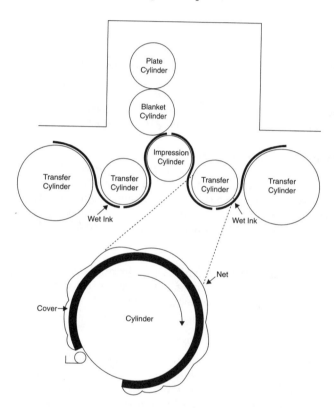

One configuration of transfer cylinder.

Transfer Film

Alternate term for a **photostencil** prepared by the **indirect process**. See **Photostencil: Indirect Process**.

Transfer Lettering

Alternate term for **transfer type** See **Transfer Type**.

Transfer Roller

A hard, chrome-covered roller used in an offset press's **continuous-flow dampening system**, in conjunction with a soft, rubber-covered **metering roller**. The line of contact between the two rollers, called the **metering nip** can be varied in width, depending on the desired thickness of the film of **fountain solution**. The transfer roller (and/or the metering roller) may be used as the fountain roller, or as the roller adjacent to the fountain roller. Adjusting the angle of the transfer roller's contact with the metering roller varies the thickness of the fountain solution film across the length of the rollers, depending on whether the edges or the center of the plate require greater quantities of fountain solution. (See **Dampening System**.)

The term *transfer roller* also refers to a rubber-covered roller or cylinder used **offset gravure** printing, which is a type of gravure printing utilizing a **blanket** similar to that used in **offset lithography**. In offset gravure, the image is transferred from a **gravure cylinder** to the rubber transfer roller and, finally, onto the substrate. (See **Gravure: Offset Gravure**.)

Transfer Stencil
Alternate term for a **photostencil** prepared by the **indirect process**. See **Photostencil: Indirect Process**.

Transfer Type Printing Screen
Alternate term for a **photostencil** prepared by the **indirect process**. See **Photostencil: Indirect Process**.

Transformation Algorithm
In computer graphics, an alternative to a **lookup table** consisting of a mathematical equation used to translate input or output data from one set of conditions to another. Transformation algorithms are often used to convert images from one **color space** to another—such as from **RGB** to **CMYK**.

Transient Font
A computer **font** that remains in a printer's memory only until a particular document is finished printing and thus needs to be reloaded for each new print job. See also **Permanent Font**.

Transition
In film, television, video, and multimedia production, any means by which one **scene** segues into the next. Common transitions, in addition to the basic **cut**, are the **dissolve** and the **wipe**. A variety of specialty transitions are also often used. See **Video Effects**.

Transitional
Any **typeface** design that incorporates elements of both **Old Style** and **Modern**. An example is Baskerville.

Translucency
In optics, the property of an object or surface that will allow the passage of light through it, but only in a very diffuse manner—such as a frosted window—such that objects cannot be clearly seen or read through it. In contrast, **opacity** is an optical property that describes the inability to pass light through an object, while **transparency** describes the ability to transmit a great deal of light.

Translucent
In optics, descriptive of a surface or object that allows for the passage of light through it, but in a highly diffuse manner, such that objects cannot be clearly seen or read through it. (See **Translucency**.) Objects which are **opaque** allow no light to pass through them, while objects which are **transparent** allow a great deal of—if not all—incident light to pass through them.

Translucent Paper
A type of paper that possesses a slight or moderate degree of **opacity**, or, in other words, allows some degree of light to pass through it, but which is not **transparent**.

Transmission Control Protocol/Internet Protocol (TCP/IP)
A **network protocol** (essentially composed of two separate protocols) that allows individual computers and networks to communicate with each other. The basic protocol, IP, is a **packet switching** protocol that facilitates the transfer of data. IP is supplemented by TCP, which basically involves **error correction and detection**, as well as establishing a fault-free connection between systems. TCP/IP was originally developed by the Department of Defense for ARPANET, but has now become a standard both for **LAN**s that connect to **UNIX** and other **minicomputer** systems, as well as for individual connection to the Internet.

Transmission Copy
Any original copy of a to-be-reproduced image that exists on a transparent **substrate** (such as a photographic **transparency**) which must be photographed or scanned by transmitting light through it, as opposed to **reflection copy**. Also known as **transparent copy**.

Transmittance
A measure of the amount of light that can be transmitted through an object or surface (such as a **transparency**) expressed as the ratio of the amount of light transmitted through the surface to the total amount of **incident light** striking it.

Transparency
In optics, the degree to which an object or surface is transparent, or allows light to pass through it. See also **Translucency** and **Opacity**.

In photography and imaging, a *transparency* is a photographic color **positive** on transparent film. Common proprietary types of transparency films are Kodachrome, Agfachrome, and Fuji Chrome. Transparencies are often used to generate **color separation**s, and are used often in scanning. Common standard sizes of transparency are 35 mm, 2¼×2½ in., 4×5 in., and 8×10 in. Due to the higher **resolution** potential of transparencies, they are preferred over prints as the original copy for scanning. A transparency is often colloquially referred to as a **chrome** or a **tranny**.

In computers, *transparency* is a property of a computer function which takes place automatically, unbeknownst to the operator. See **Transparent Function**. See also **Transparent Software**.

Data communications mode that enables equipment to send and receive bit patterns of any form, without regard to interpretation as control characters. The user is unaware that this is taking place.

Manner of transmitting electronic data in which bit patterns are not interpreted, acted upon, or transformed by transmitting or receiving devices, or by intervening devices.

Transparency Viewer

A small light box containing a filtered *5000K* light source used for viewing a *transparency* or other type of *transmission copy* under optimum lighting conditions, commonly employed when proofing color-corrected copy or prints against the original transparency.

Transparency Viewing Lamp

A light source located on a *drum scanner* used to view a *color transparency* mounted on the drum. The transparency viewing lamp is typically a *5000K* fluorescent lamp and is larger than the light source used for the actual imaging.

Transparent

In optics, descriptive of a material that allows light to pass through it relatively unimpeded, or possesses a high degree of *transparency*. The opposite is an *opaque* substance.

In computers, *transparent* is descriptive of any function or operation performed by the computer automatically while the user is performing another, perhaps unrelated function. A *transparent function* is not apparent to the operator (or even to other devices). *Transparent software* is a computer program that can be added to an original program and function seamlessly with that program without the operator having to re-learn the program.

Transparent Copy

Alternate term for *transmission copy*. See *Transmission Copy*.

Transparent Function

Any computer operation or function that takes place automatically and without being apparent to the operator, who may be performing a completely different function. See *Transparent* (second definition).

Transparent Inks

See *Transparent Pigment*.

Transparent Label

A *label* whose content is printed on a transparent *substrate* so the surface to which the label is attached can be seen through it.

Transparent Pigment

A type of *white pigment* used in printing inks that does not reflect light, but rather allows light to pass through it. The most significant use for transparent pigments is to "extend" pigments of other colors, thus reducing the cost of more expensive pigments and substances. (Hence, transparent pigments are also called *extender* pigments.) Transparent white pigments are also used to tint other color inks, to decrease the color strength of other pigments, and assist in the dispersal of particles of other pigments.

Commonly used transparent white pigments include *alumina hydrate* (sometimes called simply "hydrate"), magnesium carbonate (sometimes called simply "magnesia"), *calcium carbonate*, *blanc fixe*, *barytes*, and clays. (See also *Opaque Pigments* and *White Pigments*.) In *screen printing*, a transparent pigment is known as an *extender base*.

Transparent Programming

Alternate term for *transparent function*. See *Transparent Function*.

Transparent Software

Any computer program that can be added to an original program (such as a *plug-in* or upgrade) and function seamlessly with that program, without the need for the operator or user to re-learn the original program or the aspects of the new program. Such software is thus "invisible" to the user.

Transparent White

See *Alumina Hydrate*.

Transponder

In telecommunications, the hardware in a satellite that relays sound, video, and data signals from one *Earth station* to another.

Transpose

To exhange the position of a character, word, line, graphic element, negative, etc., with another. Often used when describing typographic errors, where two letters are inadvertently reversed, such as *htis*. Such an exchange of position is called a *transposition*.

Transposition

See *Transpose*.

Transputer

One particular computer *microprocessor* of a microprocessor array that performs one portion of any required calculation at the same time as other microprocessors are performing other portions of the calculation.

Trap

In multicolor printing, an allowance of overlap for two *colors* printed adjacent to each other, as a means of compensating for *misregister* and to avoid gaps between colors.

In typography, an indentation cut into the intersection of strokes on a letter, particularly in early photographic typesetting and especially when setting bold typefaces. The problem of *bleed* arose often, due to changes in focus, light-exposure intensity, and ink bleeding during printing. Any alteration of one or more of these factors resulted in the intersections of the letters not looking sharp on the final print. As a means of compensating for this problem, *traps* are cut into these problem spots, so that photographic and ink bleed will bring the intersection optically out where it belongs. As can be expected, this form of type needs to be redesigned a number of times before the correct amount of compensation is achieved.

One particular problem with traps is that they become visible when setting large *point size*s.

Trapping

In prepress, the compensation for *misregister* of successive colors or images. Trapping and trapping techniques ensure that there are no unsightly gaps or overlaps of successively printed colors or images. *Trapping* in this sense is referred to by many different terms, ranging from *spreads and chokes*, *fatties and skinnies*, *lap register*, and *making grips*.

In conventional (i.e., nondigital) *lithography*, trapping is accomplished using photographic techniques called *spreads* and *chokes*, also known as *fatties* and *skinnies*, respectively. A spread is a photographic overexposure of an image to make it larger than it is on the original. Thus, when it is overprinted onto another image, it will "spread" into the other image by a predetermined amount, eliminating gaps between the two. Spreads are more commonly used on foreground images or objects; backgrounds are often modified by chokes, which is a photographic enlargement of the background color or object, which "chokes" the subsequently overprinted color or image with an overlap of a set amount. (See *Spreads and Chokes*.)

In an ideal world, trapping would not be needed. Trapping is only needed because of misregister during the printing process. The various parts of the process that lead to misregister almost always involve the fact that paper is too flexible and dimensionally unstable. Misregister occurs because of paper twisting or bouncing as it moves through the press, from gripper to gripper, because it can be stretched by the feeding mechanisms, and it can change size due to its ability to absorb moisture from the environment. (In *flexography*, the stretching of rubber plates as they are mounted on the press cylinder is also a cause for misregister. Also in flexographic printing, nonpaper substrates, very fast press speeds, and many different spot colors result in the need for special trapping considerations. Traps for flexography need to be in the range of 0.006–0.01 in.) Misregister also results from improper film assembly during prepress, or from a dimensional instablity on the part of the film used to make negatives. Errors in platemaking also cause register problems on press.

The amount of trapping required in a particular print job depends not only on the desired degree of fit between successive color or images, but also on the type of press and *substrate* used. Sheetfed offset lithographic presses often require 0.003 in. of trapping, while web offset presses (especially those using highly absorptive newsprint as a sub-

strate) require more. The following chart provides general trap amounts:

Press Config.	Substrate	Screen Count (lpi)	Trap (in.)
Sheetfed offset	Glossy coated	150	0.003
Sheetfed offset	Uncoated	150	0.003
Web offset	Glossy coated	150	0.004
Web offset	Uncoated	133	0.005
Web offset	Newsprint	100	0.006
Flexography	Coated	133	0.006
Flexography	Newsprint	100	0.008
Flexography	Kraft	65	0.010
Screen Ptg. (wet)	Fabric	Any	0
Screen Ptg. (dry)	Any	100	0.006
Gravure	Glossy coated	150	0.003

Courtesy: The Complete Guide to Trapping

The above chart illustrates basic "default" trap amounts by printing process, but the trap may vary depending on prevailing press and substrate conditions. The amount of trapping can also be calculated from the line count of the halftone screen being used, and can essentially equal half the diameter of a halftone dot. A way of determining this is to find out the screen count of the halftone (for example, 133 lines per inch), divide into 1 in. to obtain the diameter (in inches) of the halftone dot (or $1 \div 133 = 0.0075$). Divide the diameter of the halftone dot by 2 to get the suggested trap amount (or $0.0075 \div 2 = 0.004$). In contrast, an 85-line halftone screen (commonly used on newsprint) would require more trapping, or $1 \div 85 = 0.012 \div 2 = 0.006$ in.

Also of concern in trapping is the question of which color should trap and which should be trapped. In general, lighter colors should be spread into darker colors, but it is not very often that the dark/light dichotomy is obvious. Often, a *color wheel* is utilized. A color wheel is essentially a circular graph or plot of all the reproducible colors. Around the circumference of the wheel are all the "pure" hues—red, magenta, blue, cyan, green, and yellow, in order proceeding clockwise. Each hue gets progressively grayer (or increases in *value*) towards the center of the wheel, where black is plotted. Any to-be-reproduced color can be plotted on this wheel by first determining its primary hue and then moving towards the center until the precise shade is found. This can then be compared to a second color, and the relative brightnesses of them can be compared by means of lighter/darker arrows indicated on the wheel. Although this is a rather simplistic means of evaluating color differences for purposes of trapping, it is useful in a variety of situations.

One means of trapping (rarely used in conventional film-based prepress) involves the creation of a screen tint of just the trap line, which avoids the unsightly creation of third colors when two other colors overlap. This is very difficult and time-consuming to accomplish photographically (essentially, a negative needs to be made of just the trap line, and a screen tint applied to the negative. Since the trap line is only several thousandths of an inch thick, this can be hard to manage. However, in digital prepress systems and programs, it is very simple to accomplish, and the high-quality results include a less obtrusive trap line. Other solutions include the elimination of trapping altogether; when colors overprint, they create a third, *secondary color* that is the mixture of the two primaries being combined. Thus, rather than printing a background color with a knockout and printing the foreground color in the box (which creates the perfect breeding ground for misregister), the foreground object is overprinted directly on the background. The inks are chosen such that when the foreground object overprints, its color will mix with the background color to produce the desired color. Another solution is to bound each separate color with thin black lines, thus letting black do the trapping. This works only so long as each separate color can be outlined with black.

Although at one time trapping was effected by the printer during prepress, the advent of digital prepress systems has resulted in less of an opportunity for printers to be able to create the trap. Printers once were responsible for shooting negatives, generating color separations, etc., and thus could trap to their heart's content. In contrast, more often than not negatives and color separations are generated via imagesetter output from digital systems, either from a publisher or from a prepress house or service bureau, with the printer involved long after the time for trapping has passed. Thus, it is up to the designer to handle any trapping (or properly communicate to a service bureau the trapping requirements). However, page make-up and image processing programs make trapping reasonably simple to effect, and each program has its own means of performing accurate trapping. There are also specialized programs just for trapping that can be purchased and utilized.

The term *trapping*, in printing, has a different meaning from the above definition, and refers to the action of printing an ink film on top of another ink film, as in process color printing. Proper trapping results in well-printed materials, while poor trapping results in successive inks that do not adhere properly and bead or rub off readily. **Wet trapping** refers to trapping performed in wet multicolor printing, where one ink is laid down on top of a previously printed, still-wet ink. If the second ink has greater **tack** than the first ink, poor trapping will occur. **Dry trapping** is a multicolor printing process in which one ink is laid down on top of a dry ink. (See also **Crystallization, Crawling, Cissing**, and **Ink: Printing Problems and Defects**.)

Tray

A cartridge or other mechanism used to store paper for feeding into a computer printer, photocopier, or other such device.

T-Ref

A standard color reference developed by the Graphic Communications Association (GCA) used for calibrating a *den-*

sitometer (specifically, a **Status "T"** densitometer). Essentially, the calibration is performed by printing **SWOP** inks on a **substrate** at specified densities and analyzing the printed samples with a **spectrophotometer**.

Trichromatic

In **color**, containing three colors. In graphics and imaging, trichromatic usually refers to the three **additive color primaries** of **red, green, and blue**.

Triethylene Glycol

A low-**volatility** ether-alcohol used in printing inks and coatings as a **plasticizer** for **resin**s.

Trilinear Array

In a **digital camera**, a set of three **CCD** arrays, used to capture all three primary color components of an image in one exposure. See **Digital Photography**.

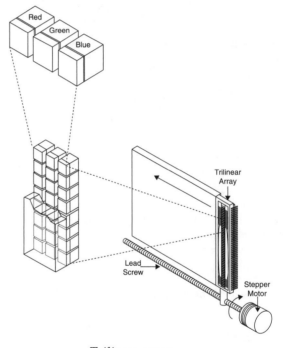

Trilinear array.

Trim

To cut away a small portion of an edge of a stack of sheets or a **book block**, either to reduce a set of sheets to a desired size or to cut away **signature** folds. See **Cutting and Trimming**. It is also used as a noun to refer to the **trim size**.

In graphics, *trim* means to cut away a portion of a line, arc, or circle.

In video production, *trim* means to select specific frames for inclusion in a master tape.

Trimetal Plate

A strong, durable printing **plate** used in **offset lithography**. Trimetal plates, as their name indicates, utilize a metal base (either stainless steel or aluminum) plated with copper. The copper layer is then plated with a thin layer of chromium. During platemaking, the chromium is etched away from the image areas, baring the copper below. The chromium remains to form the nonimage areas of the plate. Trimetal plates (as well as *bimetal plate*s) are expensive, but are particularly useful for long print runs.

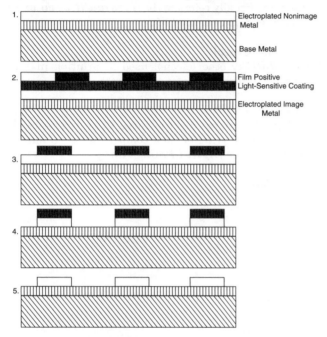

The process of trimetal platemaking. (1) Electroplate a nonimage metal over an image metal. (2) Coat with light-sensitive material and expose through a positive. (3) Dissolve and remove unhardened coating from image areas. (4) Etch through nonimage metal in image areas. (5) Remove hardened coating from nonimage areas

Trim Four

Abbreviated term for *four-sided trim*. See *Four-Sided Trim*. Also expressed as *trim 4S*.

Trim Margin

Alternate term for *thumb edge* of a book. See *Thumb Edge*.

Trim Marks

Alternate term for *cropmarks*. See *Cropmarks*.

Trimmed Flush

See *Flush Cover*.

Trimming

A paper *finishing* operation following *sheeting*, or the cutting of manufactured paper rolls into individual sheets. Trimming is necessary in sheeting systems that do not generate accurate sheet sizes. Trimming is usually performed on a *guillotine cutter*, which reduces the sheeted paper to the exact size specified by the customer. The use of *precision*

sheeting, which utilizes more accurate sheeting devices, removes the need for the secondary operation of trimming.

See also *Cutting and Trimming*.

Trim Size

The ultimate, desired size of a printed piece, which may or may not be a *standard size*, but is often arrived at by trimming the printed sheets following printing.

Triple Draw

In *binding and finishing*, the assembly of the sections of a book in more than one stage. See *Draw* (second definition).

Triple-Speed (3X)

Descriptive of a *CD-ROM* drive capable of reading and transferring data at a speed which is three times as fast as a single-speed drive. A *single-speed* CD-ROM drive, in retrospect designated 1X, could process data at a speed of 150 *kilobyte*s per second. A *double-speed (2X)* CD-ROM can thus process data at a speed of 300 kilobytes per second, and a triple-speed drive at a speed of 450 kilobytes per second. Newer drives have even faster access times: 600 kilobytes per second (*quad speed*, or 4X, drives), 900 kilobytes per second (6X drives), 1200 kilobytes per second (8X drives), 1500 kilobytes per second (10X drives), and higher.

Triplex Fonts

In typesetting, three *font*s possessed by a typesetting device, each of which has identical *escapement* values for corresponding characters.

Tristimulus Values

In a particular *color model*, the respective amounts of the three *additive color primaries (red, green, and blue)* that make up a given color. These three values are obtained by measuring a color sample through red, green, and blue filters. The tristimulus values are usually indicated using letters, such as the "LUV" in *CIELUV* or the L*a*b* in *CIEL*a*b**.

Tritone

A three-color *halftone* image produced by overprinting three halftone screens made from the same image, each possessing a different set of tonal values. See also *Duotone* and *Quadratone*.

Trogg

A typesetting language created for *UNIX* operating systems.

Truck

In motion picture photography and videography, a camera shot where the camera is mounted on a movable tripod (or *dolly*) and moved sideways, often used while following cars or other moving objects.

True Cut

Descriptive of a *typeface* or individual characters within it that are not distorted by a digitized typesetter.

True Rolling

Term that is used to describe the ideal condition of an offset plate and blanket, in which there is no slippage at the *printing nip*.

Conventional rubber blankets have a tendency to deform when they are pressed against the hard metal plate. As a result, the surface speed of the blanket is different than that of the plate, which causes a degree of slippage. This slippage can cause printing defects such as *slurring*, as well as increased plate wear. The use of a *compressible blanket* can bring the blanket and plate closer to the condition of true rolling. (See *Blanket*.)

TrueType™

A type of computer *font* format created by Apple Computer (and adopted by Microsoft) as an alternative to Adobe *PostScript font*s. TrueType fonts can be used both for *bitmapped* screen display and for *vector*-based output, the goal being to eliminate the need for two sets of fonts: *screen font*s and *printer font*s. Systems cannot utilize both TrueType fonts and fonts running with *Adobe Type Manager (ATM)*.

PostScript fonts are still the fonts of choice for high-quality output. Additionally, when dealing with a service bureau, a thing to remember is that most service bureaus have spent years compiling libraries of PostScript fonts, so very few use TrueType fonts. TrueType fonts are often used on office computers, and some prominent multimedia authoring programs (such as Macromedia Director) support TrueType over ATM.

TrueVision TARGA

See *TARGA*.

TRUMATCH™

The brand-name for a popular *color matching system*, designed specifically for digital prepress systems. Before digital halftoning, halftone screen percentages were only available in increments of 5%, which meant that each *process color* could only be specified to the nearest 5% (for example, you could specify 45% *cyan*, but not 49% cyan). This limited somewhat the number of colors that could be reproduced, since all process colors are created by overprinting each of the *CMYK* inks at various percentages. Digital prepress and desktop color systems allow colors to be specified in 1% increments, which opens up the range of colors that can be produced. The TRUMATCH Swatching System facilitates this, by including digital samples of over 2,000 process colors, each sample including the CMYK percentages required to reproduce it. In addition, the TRUMATCH system organizes each color by *hue*, or primary color component, then by *saturation*, and then by *brightness* (in other words, the *HSB* color model). The TRUMATCH system includes 50 hues, subdivided into 50 shades of each hue.

The TRUMATCH system is supported by most of the commonly used *page makeup program*s, such as *Page-Maker* and *PageMaker*, as well as a variety of popular *drawing* programs. TRUMATCH swatches are also available in book form. (See also *PANTONE* and *FOCOLTONE*.)

TSR

Abbreviation for *terminate and stay resident*. See *Terminate and Stay Resident (TSR)*.

Tub-Sizing

Alternate term for *surface sizing*, or *sizing* added to a partially dried paper *web* while it is still on the papermaking machine. (See *Surface Sizing*.)

Tuck Envelope

An envelope that is not sealed in the conventional sense, i.e., with adhesive or tying. Rather, the contents of a tuck envelope are secured in the envelope by tucking the envelope flap into the envelope.

Tucker Blade

On a *jaw folder*, a metal blade used to "tuck" the paper web into the jaws of the jaw folder. A tucker blade is also used to force the web between the rollers of a *chopper folder*.

Tucker Fold

Alternate term for a *jaw fold*. See *Jaw Fold*.

Tumble

A graphic effect in *three-dimensional* modeling and in video production that rotates an image or object about a central axis while the axis itself also rotates.

Tumble Duplex

Alternate term for *head-to-foot imposition*. See *Head-to-Foot Imposition*.

Tumble Landscape

A sheet printed with a *landscape* orientation, the *reverse printing* being inverted with respect to the *face printing*. Also known as *inverse landscape*.

Tumble Portrait

A sheet printed with a *portrait* orientation, the *reverse printing* being inverted with respect to the *face printing*. Also known as *inverse portrait*.

Tung Oil

A yellow-colored *drying oil* that is derived from the seeds of the tung tree (any of several trees of the genus *Aleurites* native to China, especially *A. fordii*) used as a printing ink *vehicle* or *varnish* due to its excellent drying and *chemical resistance*. Tung oil is also known as *chinawood oil*.

Tungsten-Halogen Lamp

Alternate term for *quartz-halogen lamp*. See *Quartz-Halogen Lamp*.

Turn-In

In **binding and finishing**, a quantity of the cloth used in **casemaking** that extends beyond the edges of the underlying boards, and is folded under the boards. A common size of turn-in is ⅝ in.

Turnaround

The length of time needed to complete a job, expressed as the length of elapsed time from the time all materials were received to the time the completed job was delivered.

The time required to reverse the direction of transmission in half-duplex devices.

Turning Bars

A set of stationary bars on a **web** printing press that guide the moving web such that it is flipped over, allowing it to then be printed on the reverse side. See also **Angle Bars**.

Turnkey System

Any computer system purchased complete and, once installed, ready to use for its intended application, without the need for additional hardware, software, or other modifications. In other words, "turn the key," and you're off. Publishing systems are sometimes sold as turnkey systems.

Turnover

In a word processing system utilizing **word wrap**, successive lines that align at the left margin with the first line.

Turpentine

Any of a variety of **volatile** oleoresins derived from several types of coniferous tree, most commonly the long-leafed pine, *Pinus palustris*, used widely as a cleaning **solvent** in **screen printing**, especially in the cleaning of screen fabrics at the conclusion of a print run.

Tusche

In **offset lithography**, a liquid emulsion ink handdrawn on a printing plate to form the image areas that will be printed.

In **screen printing**, a black, waxy material handdrawn on a screen fabric to act as a stencil. See **Tusche-and-Glue**.

Tusche-and-Glue

In **screen printing**, a **printing screen** made manually by drawing on the screen fabric with **tusche**, coating the opposite side of the fabric with a water-soluble glue, and dissolving the tusche with **mineral spirits**. The tusche is placed in the printing portion(s) of the design, which, after dissolving, are now open.

TWAIN

In **scanning**, a standard protocol used to transfer information between specific applications and peripheral devices. For example, TWAIN-compliant applications such as Adobe Photoshop can be used to drive a **scanner**.

The term TWAIN itself is so-named because it stands "twain" (as in "never the twain shall meet") the application and the device. Depending on whom you ask, it could also mean "Technology Without An Interesting Name."

Tweening

Colloquial variant of the term **inbetweening**. See **Inbetweening**.

Twenty-Four-Bit (24-Bit) Color

On a computer monitor, a color display in which each **pixel** (or smallest point of **color**) is described by 24 bits of information, or 8 bits for each of the three colors of **red, green, and blue**.

(One **bit** is either a 1 or a 0; 24-bit color can be thought of as one of these two numbers taken to the twenty-fourth power; thus $2^{24} = 16,777,216$ possible colors.)

The color of a pixel on a computer display is commonly expressed as some amount of red, green, and blue. Greater numbers of combinations of these amounts require more processing power on the part of the computer. At 24 bits per pixel, a total of 16,777,216 colors (commonly referred to simply as "millions of colors") can be described and displayed. This color depth is greater than the standard and/or required setting for many CD-ROMs and multimedia programs (which usually have difficulty handling anything greater than **eight-bit color**), but it is the color depth required for high-quality graphic arts reproduction.

See also **Eight-Bit Color**, **Sixteen-Bit Color**, and **Thirty-Two-Bit Color**. Computer monitors can also display **one-bit color** (black and white, or any two colors) and **four-bit color** (16 colors).

Twin Seal

In packaging, a means of manufacturing plastic **bag**s. See **Bag: Plastic Bags**.

Twin-Wire Former

A variation on the traditional **fourdrinier** papermaking machine utilizing two wires rather than one in its **forming section**. In conventional fourdrinier machines, the papermaking **furnish** is deposited on a single continuous wire mesh belt, which drains the water from the furnish through the bottom. The result of this process is that the side of the paper **web** that dries against the wire—called the **wire side**—has a different texture than the top side of the web—called the **felt side**. This **two-sidedness** of paper has undesirable consequences in many types of printing.

A twin-wire former sandwiches the papermaking furnish through two wire mesh belts, allowing drainage from the top and bottom of the furnish, producing paper with two wire sides. Alternate variations, such as **top-wire former**s, also employ the sandwiching of paper fibers between two wires as a means of increasing the likesidedness of paper. (See **Fourdrinier**.)

See illustration on the following page.

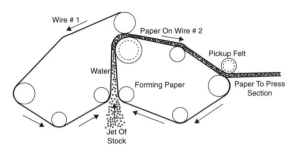

Twin-wire former.

Twisted-Pair Wiring

A type of cabling used in computer networks and other communications systems comprising several small wires grouped into pairs and twisted, usually at a rate of one twist per foot. Twisting the cable tends to offset the production of **noise**, reducing interference. Twisted-pair wiring is usually classified as **shielded twisted-pair** or **unshielded twisted-pair**.

Two-Arm Paster

Alternate term for a **two-arm splicer**. See **Two-Arm Splicer**.

Two-Arm Splicer

A type of **flying splicer** used on **web press**es that can hold two rolls of substrate, in contrast to a **three-arm splicer**. See **Flying Splicer**. Also known as a **two-arm paster**.

2B+D

Alternate term for **Basic Rate Interface**, one of the two **ISDN** services. See **Basic Rate Interface (BRI)** and **Integrated Services Digital Network (ISDN)**.

Two-Dimensional (2D)

Descriptive of a drawing or other image possessing only height and width, as opposed to **three-dimensional** which also possesses depth.

Two-Dimensional (2D) Animation

The **animation** of images in which movement is only in two dimensions, either horizontal and/or vertical. Essentially, it is the animation of flat images. Often a third dimension is simulated to create **three-dimensional (3D) animation**.

Two-On Binding

In **binding and finishing**, a **trimming** operation in which two books, one on top of the other, are trimmed at the same time.

Two-Page Spread

Alternate term for a **spread**, especially a **double-page spread**. See **Spread** and **Double-Page Spread**.

Two-Part System

Alternate term for **two-pot system**. See **Two-Pot System**.

Two-Piece Case

In **binding and finishing**, a book case made from one type of cloth, with a second type of cloth wrapped over the **spine** and a portion of both the front and back covers. See also **Three-Piece Case**.

Two-Piece Cover

In **binding and finishing**, a cover used in **mechanical binding** in which the front and back cover are two separate pieces. Not to be confused with a **two-piece case** used in **case binding**.

2.88

Abbreviation for a specific capacity of **floppy disk**, having a diameter of 3.5 in. See **Floppy Disk**.

2.5-D

In graphics, a **two-dimensional** graph with a simulated **z-axis** to produce the illusion of a third dimension.

Two-Positive System

A variation of the **diffusion-etch process** of **gravure engraving**. See **Gravure Engraving: Diffusion-Etch Process**.

Two-Pot System

A printing ink or paper **coating** comprising two reactive substances that are only combined immediately prior to printing. Also called **two-part system**.

Two-Sheet Detector

Alternate term for a **double-sheet detector**. See **Double-Sheet Detector**.

Two-Shot

In motion picture photography and videography, a camera shot of two individuals, both of whom take up an equal portion of the screen. In shooting scripts, the two-shot is abbreviated *2S*.

Two-Sidedness

A paper property that describes the difference in texture, appearance, and printability between the side of the paper formed in contact with the papermaking machine's **forming wire** (the **wire side**) and that which formed on the top, away from the forming wire (the **felt side**). (See **Wire Side**, **Felt Side**, and **Fourdrinier** paper machine.)

Two-Tone Scanner

In **scanning**, a **scanner** that only distinguishes black and white, or **one-bit (1-bit) color**. See **Bilevel** and **one-bit (1-bit) color**.

Two-Up

Descriptive of any activity in which two things are done at the exact same time. For example, printing two-up involves printing two identical pages on the same sheet using the same plate. ***Two-up binding*** involves binding two books at the same time as a single unit, subsequent trimming operations being needed to separate the individual books.

Two-Up Binding

In ***binding and finishing***, the binding of two books together as one unit, then cutting them apart into separate books. See ***Perfect Binding***.

TXT

A ***file extension*** used to indicate an ***ASCII text*** file.

Tympan Bar

Alternate term for an ***impression bar*** used on some ***flexographic*** presses. See ***Impression Bar***.

Tympan Paper

A hard paper used on ***letterpress*** printing presses as a means of ***packing***—or adjusting the height of—the image carrying surface.

Type 1 PostScript Font

A variety of ***PostScript*** font developed by Adobe Systems that includes in its font description special ***encryption*** algorithms (or ***hint***s) that make them more quickly rendered, more compact in file size, and more appealing aesthetically than ***Type 3 PostScript font***s. Type 1 fonts can also be displayed on screen by ***Adobe Type Manager***. Type 1 fonts are the more commonly used of the two font types.

Type 3 PostScript Font

A variety of ***PostScript*** font developed by Adobe Systems that does not include in its font description special ***encryption*** algorithms (or ***hint***s). Consequently, they are less quickly rendered, bulkier in file size, and less appealing aesthetically than ***Type 1 PostScript font***s. Type 3 fonts, however, can contain grayscale fills, as well as complex and stroked characters. However, Type 3 fonts cannot be displayed on screen by ***Adobe Type Manager***. Type 1 fonts are the more commonly used of the two.

Type and Typography

The term *type* is used generally to mean letters and other characters assembled into pages for printing or other means of reproduction. *Typography* refers to the rules and conventions that govern the assembling (or ***composition***) of type into aesthetically appealing and legible pages.

HISTORY OF TYPE

Although in this age of desktop publishing we tend to take type for granted, typography was at one time considered something akin to an art form.

The invention of movable type is inextricably linked to the invention of printing; it was movable type that made printing commercially viable. The first use of movable type was in China in the middle of the eleventh century. Pi Sheng used clay to make raised letters from which prints could be made. Tin eventually replaced clay, but neither of these two types gained widespread use. In 1314, Wang Chên used wood in the making of type, which was more practical at the time. The first use of metal type dates from 1403 Korea, and printed books from these types began to appear in large numbers.

The invention of printing from movable metal type in Europe is commonly attributed to Johannes Gutenberg, a German goldsmith who, in the mid-fifteenth century, produced the first printed books, notably his "Gutenberg Bibles." It is believed that the Dutch developed the process first, a man named Coster believed to have invented printing. It was only after Gutenberg, and after his process spread through Europe, that printing became a force to rival handwritten manuscripts. (See ***Printing***.) Even though Gutenberg may or may not have invented the process, it was he who first made it practical. His enhancements of the process centered around his knowledge—as a goldsmith—of the punch, the matrix, and the adjustable mold. His process was to punch a character—say, the letter "a"—into a bar of metal, fit it into a matrix, fill it with molten metal, and let it cool. When it was removed, he had a raised letter which could then be assembled into a frame with other letters of the same size, inked, and transferred to paper. Initially, printers strove to duplicate the style of lettering used in manuscripts—the ***black letter***, or ***gothic*** style found in Gutenberg's Bible is one particular example of this—but as the process caught on designers began to create new and distinctive varieties of type. In 1469, Johannes and Wendelin da Spira, the first printers to set up shop in Venice, were the first to use ***roman*** rather than gothic typefaces. French-born Nicolas Jenson, at the age of 70, moved to Venice and in 1471 printed a version of St. Augustine's *De civitate Dei* (*City of God*) in a form of black letter he had designed; he also designed a roman alphabet that has since become the model for many old style typefaces. The most successful early Venetian printer was Aldus Manutius who, in the early sixteenth century, was the first to use ***italic*** type. Although today we use italic for emphasis and other special uses, Manutius used it for the entire text, essentially as a way of fitting more characters on a page and thus reducing the amount of paper he would have to use in a book.

One of the most influential type founders was Claude Garamond who, in a new turn of events, was not a printer himself. Garamond created a number of roman faces based loosely on Jenson's roman alphabet, and also designed and cut a number of other types of alphabets, including Greek characters, used widely in the printing of Bibles and classical works, which were very popular during the Renaissance. Although, unlike Garamond, most printers designed and cut their own type, they still bought Garamond's type—or the matrices and punches used to create them—in great quantity, as they were widely recognized for their great beauty. The centerpieces of Garamond's collections were his *Caractères de l'université* and *grecs du roi* that, like his other specimens, became the property of the French government.

Other early and influential type founders included Parisian printer Robert Granjon who introduced—in about 1557—a type of gothic cursive handwriting popular at the time; Jean Claude Fournier, and his son Pierre Simon Fournier, who ran the LeBé type foundry, the most successful French foundry at the time, the younger Fournier inventing the ***point system*** for the measurement of type size still in use today; François Ambroise Didot, who not only designed type but also refined the point system devised by Fournier, which today still bears his name (see ***Didot System***); William Caslon, the best-known English type founder whose 1734 roman and italic faces are used widely today; John Baskerville, another English founder whose 1762 specimens are also still in use today; and Giambattista Bodoni, an eighteenth-century Italian printer and founder, whose modern roman faces departed dramatically from the old style roman faces.

In the twentieth century, American and European type designers developed some of the most beautiful and/or creative typefaces yet seen, especially once printed advertising became popular. One of the most prolific of the American designers was Frederic Goudy. In the 1920s, new trends in the world of art, architecture and design—such as the works of the German Bauhaus school—manifested themselves in the highly stylized faces such as as Futura, Kabel, and Erbar, which were in vogue for a number of years.

The typeface in general was for the first couple of centuries an individual type design created by printers for their own use; eventually, independent type founders—who may or may not have been printers themselves—began supplying type to large numbers of printers. By the early- to mid-twentieth century (when handset type began to be replaced by mechanized linecasters and typesetters), the average printer had hundreds of typefaces to choose from, few of which—if any—he had designed himself.

For most of the history of printing, type was composed by hand. Type was stored by typeface and size in special typecases, each slot corresponding to a particular letter or character. Each of these cases often had two trays: the lower case contained the ***miniscule*** characters—or, as they came to be known, the ***lowercase*** letters—while the upper case contained the ***majuscule*** characters—or, likewise, the ***uppercase*** letters. (In the mid-1800s, the California job case, invented purportedly for the convenience of travelling printers during the Gold Rush, combined both upper- and lowercase letters in the same tray, the ***caps*** on the right, the lowercase letters on the left.) These typecases contained letters whose quantity varied according to the frequency of letter usage; the slot to hold the "e," for example, was larger and held more characters than the slot of the "z." Their position in the typecase also varied by frequency of use, the heavily used characters near the center, the less used ones toward the outside of the case. The cases also included ***punctuation*** characters, blank slugs for word spaces, and ***quad***s which were used to fill out short lines.

The compositor—or the person who composed the type—inserted each letter one by one into a ***composing***

stick, which could be adjusted to the proper ***line length***. Once all the type was inserted into the stick, it was then transferred to a metal or plastic tray called a ***galley***. It was from the galley that the type was proofed and corrected, and the term "galley" is still used to refer to typeset copy used for proofing. The galley, once corrected, was then broken into individual pages, the appropriate ***running head***s and ***folio***s (page numbers) added, and then transferred to a lock-up table or stone, where it could then be inked and printed. Once the print job was completed, the type was replaced bit by bit back into the type case. Occasionally, the type wasn't replaced in the correct slot, or case, resulting in mixed fonts in a single case. These became known as ***pi fonts***, a term which has also come to mean specialized fonts containing characters not often used.

In the late 1800s, several machines were developed to mechanize the process of typesetting. The first was invented in Baltimore by Ottmar Mergenthaler and patented in 1884, deriving its name from the exclamation of Mergenthaler's business partner and financier Whitelaw Reid, "You've done it, Ottmar! A line of type." It was called, of course, the ***Linotype***. On the Linotype (and on a similar machine developed in 1912 by the International Typesetting Machine Corporation called the ***intertype***), composition is accomplished in essentially one mechanism. A pot melts down the metal. Meanwhile, a set of brass matrices for each letter and character in several sizes, as well as spaces, is located above the machine. Attached to the machine is a keyboard. As the operator types the line to be set, each matrix corresponding to the letter typed slides into position on a composing area. When a line is completed, enough spaces to fill out the line to the desired line length are keyed, and a flip of a lever slides the line of matrices into position over a mold chamber. The machine then pours the molten metal into the mold and matrices, sends it to a trimming mechanism, and ejects the finished slug. The completed lines could then be added to a galley, locked up, and printed. Refinements on this basic device allowed for the mixing of roman and italic type, and the changing of point size.

A third automated linecasting device was invented by Tolbert Lanston and patented in 1887. Called the ***Monotype***, it used two separate operations to set lines of type. In the first stage, the keyboard operator typed what was to be set, and the keyboarding punched holes into a paper ribbon. The device kept track of how close to the end of a line the type was coming (the ***font***—typeface and size—was specified prior to keyboarding) a bell would sound, and a lighted scale would indicate how many points were left on the line. After keyboarding, the ribbon was removed and fed into the casting mechanism, where the punched holes—similar to the principle of the player piano, Jacquard loom, or later computer punch card—trigger the appropriate matrices to slide into position one by one, where molten metal is injected into them and the mold, and each character is ejected one by one in the proper order, where the page(s) could be proofed, locked up, and printed. An advantage of the Monotype over the Linotype was that since each letter was cast separately, corrections could be made easily by hand by simply plucking out an incorrect character and replacing it with the correct one, so long as the size and typeface matched.

As printing progressed, handset type began to be disposed of earlier in the printing process, once the concept of the printing *plate* was devised. The first type of plate was the *stereotype*, invented in 1725 by William Ged of Scotland and later improved by Firmin Didot. In the stereotyping process, the locked-up typeform is placed face up on a molding table. A wet paper mat is impressed on it, allowing each character to form an impression in its surface. When dried, the mat is placed in a casting machine, where molten metal is poured into it, creating a relief plate which after cooling and trimming, can be printed from. *Electrotype* plates superseded stereotypes by the 1940s.

Although handset type was no longer being used directly as a printing surface, it was still required for platemaking. The development of *phototypesetting* marked the death of handset—or even linecast—type.

Phototypesetting involved the use of glass or plastic photomatrices bearing a typeface at a particular size. Copy was keyboarded into a terminal, appropriate commands indicating the point size, line length, leading, type style, etc., were also input where needed. These commands then controlled the photomatrix which was adjusted to expose each character to a sheet of photosensitive film or paper. Depending on the configuration of the machine, there was either a different matrix for each type size, or, more commonly, lenses photographically enlarged or reduced the characters depending on the specified point size. The film or paper was output, developed, and commonly pasted up on to pasteup boards, with all the type in the proper position for further *prepress* operations, such as making and stripping negatives and, finally, making printing plates.

Later digitized typesetters set type digitally, or as a set of tiny dots, called *raster*s, computer commands adjusting the placement of these dots which would form the character at the specified size and typeface.

In the 1980s and 1990s, an increasing amount of type began to be set on desktop computers, using page make-up—or "desktop publishing"—programs such as Page-Maker and QuarkXPress. See *Desktop Publishing*.

CHARACTERS OF TYPE

Type can be characterized a number of ways, by *letter elements*, by size, and by *type specifications*.

Letter Elements. A letter can be described in terms of the orientation of the strokes and curves that it comprises. The most basic division of typefaces is into *serif* and *sans serif*. A serif is essentially a finishing line on the ending stroke. (An example of a serif is one of the horizontal lines at the top and bottom of this capital letter "I.") Serif typefaces are most commonly used for text as they tend to be more legible than sans serif typefaces, which lack such finishing lines, as in this capital letter "I." (See *Serif* and *Sans Serif*.)

Letter height is described of in terms of its *x-height*, or the size of the main body of a letter. Some letters are also characterized by their possession of *ascender*s (strokes that extend above the x-height, such as on the lowercase b, d, f, h, k, l, t) or *descender*s (strokes that extend below the *baseline* on which the characters sit, such as on the lowercase letters g, j, p, q, y).

Other letter elements include *apex*es, *counter*s, *stem*s, and *terminal*s. See *Letter Elements*.

Typefaces, Fonts, and Families. The terms *type series*, *type family*, *typeface*, and *font* are often bandied about interchangeably. Here are the distinctions among them:

Type Family. The basic design of the type, including all the related weights and widths. For example, Helvetica.

Typeface. The type family narrowed down to a specific weight and width. For example, Helvetica Light Condensed.

Point Size. The height of the characters that will be set. For example, 10-point.

Font. The type family, narrowed down to a specific weight, width, and point size. For example, 10-point Helvetica Light Condensed.

Type Series. The range of point sizes available for a specific font of a specific typeface in a specific type family. For example, 6- to 18-point Helvetica Light Condensed.

In the new world of desktop publishing, the distinction among these terms is becoming increasingly irrelevant.

Point Size. Characters need to be specified in terms of point size, or how high each character is. There are several *point system*s in use worldwide, but in the United States and Great Britain, the point system is based on the *pica point*, or a point which is $\frac{1}{72}$ in. Point size is no longer strictly relevant as a unit of measure, and could easily be replaced by metric measurements, which is in fact the case in Europe. (See *Point System*.) At one time, prior to the adoption of the point system, type was specified using names. The last of these to still be used is known as *agate*, used to refer to 5½-point type used commonly in newspaper classified advertising. (See *Point Size*.)

Line Length. When setting type, one of the factors that will affect the type chosen is the desired *line length*, or the width of a line. Of primary consideration is how many characters per line are required in order to fill the total number of lines required. In the process of *copyfitting*, the measurement of *characters per pica (CPP)* (based on a particular typeface's *alphabet length*) is used to determine how much space copy set in a particular typeface will occupy. (See *Line Length*.)

Leading. In metal typography, lines were separated from each other by pieces of metal known as "leads," whence comes the term *leading*, which is a popular term for *line spacing*, or the amount of space that is placed between lines. Conventional rules for legibility involve formulas for the proper amount of leading required for a particular point size. (See *Line Spacing*.)

Letterspacing. Legibility also manifests itself in the correct amount of space that exists between letters, called *letterspacing*. Some character combinations, due to the shapes of the letters, require adjustment of the space between them, either positively or negatively. (See *Letterspacing*.) A particular variety of *negative letterspacing*—or moving two characters closer together—is known as *kerning*. (See *Kerning*.) Kerning is only performed between upper- and lowercase letters or between uppercase letters. As famed type designer Frederic Goudy once observed, "Anyone who would letterspace lowercase would steal sheep."

Hyphenation and Justification. Depending upon the desired attributes of a text block, lines may be set *ragged right* (the lines do not line up evenly at the right margin) or *justified* (the lines *do* line up evenly at the right margin. Of particular issue in the combined processes of *hyphenation and justification (H&J)* is the means by which justification is accomplished, typically involving variable *word space*s, i.e., the spaces between words are compressed or expanded to fill out or shorten a line. Some typesetting systems or page make-up programs handle this better than others, and some operator tweaking may need to be done to ensure that word spacing is not egregiously varied. *Hyphenation* involves the rules concerning the correct breaking of words when they do not entirely fit on a line, which may also require operator intervention. (See *Hyphenation* and *Justification*.)

Lines may also be set *ragged left*, or centered, depending upon the desired plans of the designer. The term *quadding* refers to the positioning of lines that do not fully occupy the line length. The term itself derives from the *quadrat*, a blank metal cube used to fill out short lines to allow proper lock-up of handset type. *Quad right* refers to aligning an incomplete line with the right margin (using spaces to fill out the line to the left), *quad left* refers to aligning an incomplete line with the left margin (and using spaces to fill out the line to the right), while *quad center* refers to centering a line within the line length, using spaces on either side of the text. These terms now have become more popularly known as *flush right* and *flush left*, phrases derived from hydraulic quadding mechanisms used in the mid-1900s. (See *Quadding*.)

Spacing. There are several means by which spacing is measured in typography. The *em* is essentially a blank space forming a square containing a width and height equal to the point size (i.e., an em space in 12-point type would be 12 points wide and 12 points high). An *en* is half the size of an em (i.e., an en space in 12-point type would be 6 points wide). (There are also *em dash*es and *en dash*es that are the width of one em or en, respectively.) Em and en spaces are also known as *fixed space*s. See *Fixed Spaces*.

Indention. Paragraphs are the basic text-block units, and can be separated from each other in a variety of typographically acceptable ways. The most common is to end the paragraph with a hard return and *indent* the first line of a succeeding paragraph. Alternatively, two line spaces can be used to separate one paragraph from another, and in some cases all the paragraphs can be run together, separated only by the paragraph symbol (¶). The rules governing proper *indention* also need to be taken into account. (See *Indention* and *Paragraph*.)

Non-Letter Characters. Type consists of many other types of characters than letters, each of which have their own typographic rules for maximum legibility. The most common are *figures*, or numbers, which commonly include both *Arabic numerals* and *Roman numerals*. (See *Figures*.)

Another set of characters are those used for *punctuation*, such as periods (.), commas (,), *quotes* (" "), etc. (See *Punctuation*.) Commonly used characters also include the *ampersand* (&), the *percent* (%), mathematical symbols ($\sqrt{}$, +, =), *superior* (^{2}) and *inferior* ($_2$) characters, *reference marks* (*, †, ¶), *dashes* (-, –, —), *ellipses* (. . .), *boxes* (■), *bullets* (•), *ligature*s (fi, fl), *rule line*s and *leaders*, *initial*s, *borders*, *alternate characters*, *ornaments*, *arrows*, *logo*s, or *Cyrillic* and *Greek characters*. Some of these characters are available in standard fonts, while some can only be obtained in special *pi font*s. (See *Pi Characters*.)

Many foreign languages require the use of *accents*, such as acutes (´), graves (`), circumflexes (ˆ), umlauts (¨), tildes (~) and others, which often need to be set above or below other characters (such as é, or ü). Depending on the typesetting device or software program, these may exist as a single character in the font or may exist as separate characters which can be added to each other during typesetting. (See *Accents*.)

Specific typographic applications (i.e., books, newspapers, etc.) also have their own rules and conventions. See *Book Typography* and *Newspaper Typography*.

As typography becomes more digital and situated increasingly on the desktop, it is becoming less of an art form and falling more and more in the purview of those who do not understand the proper rules for legibility. Changes in terminology also reflect that much of type's history is being forgotten, which is unfortunate. (See also *Digital Type* and *Desktop Publishing*.)

Type-A Durometer

A device used to measure the hardness (also itself called the *durometer*) of the surface of a printing ink roller, flexographic plate cylinders and rollers, and other rollers used in a variety of printing process. Durometer or hardness is a property that has significant effects on print quality and ink transfer. (See *Durometer*.) A type-A durometer measures the resistance of a surface to the pressure generated by a spring-loaded probe, the result being indicated on a dial (using units called "durometer units") graduated from 0 (extremely flexible) to 100 (extremely inflexible). The durometers used in roller measurement typically have a

1-kilogram (kg) mass mounted above the probe, which tends to provide more reproducible results. When durometer readings are measured in the pressroom, it should always be performed when the roller is still on the press. If that is not possible, it should be removed and placed in a notched rack. An ink roller should never be placed on a flat surface, lest it develop problems such as out-of-roundness.

Type-Ahead Buffer
Alternate term for *keyboard buffer*. See *keyboard buffer*.

Typeface
In typography, a specific variation within a *type family*, such as *roman*, *italic*, *bold*, etc. In other words, the basic design of the type (for example, Palatino) combined with the weight characteristics (such bold), and the width characteristics (such as condensed). Thus, we have just described the typeface Palatino Bold Condensed. See also *Font*, *Type Family*, and *Type Series*.

Garamond Light
Garamond Book
Garamond Bold
Garamond Ultra
Garamond Light Italic
Garamond Book Italic
Garamond Bold Italic
Garamond Ultra Italic
Garamond Light Condensed
Garamond Book Condensed
Garamond Bold Condensed
Garamond Ultra Condensed
Garamond Light Condensed Italic
Garamond Book Condensed Italic
Garamond Bold Condensed Italic
Garamond Ultra Condensed Italic

All the typefaces in the Garamond type family, set in 12-point type with 14 points leading.

Typeface Family
See *Type Family*.

Type Family
In typography, a group of *typeface*s created by common design characteristics. Each member may vary by weight (bold vs. regular) and width (expanded vs. condensed) and may have related italic versions.

Type Gauge
In typography, one of several different types of instruments used to measure *points* and *pica*s. Also called a *line gauge*.

Type High
In relief printing, the distance from the base of a type character to the printing surface. The value was 0.918 in.

Type Metal
A metal alloy composed of lead with smaller amounts of tin and antimony, used for making type slugs in *hot-metal* typography.

Type Page
The *live matter area* of a book page.

Type Series
In typography, the range of sizes of a particular *font* in a particular *typeface*. In metal typesetting, it meant the series of a given typeface available from the foundry, sometimes a rather limited supply. Today, practically all desired series can be generated from a master font.

Type Size
See *Point Size*.

Typescript
A more accurate term for a *manuscript* that has been typewritten, as "manuscript" literally means "written by hand."

Typesetter
A device that arranges type on a page in a printable manner, either mechanically, photographically, or digitally.

The term *typesetter* also refers to the person who sets the type or keyboards the copy into the device which sets the type.

Typesetting
The keyboarding of (or other means of assembling) copy into a printable form. Type can be set by hand, by typewriter, by phototypesetter, or by computer.

Type Specifications
In typography, a set of instructions given to a typesetter that specifies the *typeface*, *point size*, *leading*, *line length*, and *indention* required by a particular piece of copy. The point size and leading are often expressed as a fraction; for example, "10/12" means 10-point type on 12 points of leading.

Typestyle
In typography, the distinguishing characteristic of a *typeface*, which can refer to *roman*, *italic*, *bold*, *condensed*, *expanded*, etc.

Typestyle can also refer to a collection of *type families* that have a specific feature in common, such as *roman*, *sans serif* or *serif*, *gothic*, or *script*.

Type Surface
Alternate term for the *live matter area* of a page. See *Live Matter Area*.

Typo

Abbreviation of ***typographical error***. See ***Typographical Error***.

Typographer

A person who specifies and/or sets type.

Typographic Color

In typography, the overall shade of gray perceived by the eye, which may be interrupted by bad word breaks, inconsistent character spacing, or uneven ***leading***. Typographic color can only be determined by reviewing type after setting. ***River***s are patterns of white that result from the occurrence of word spaces too near each other in adjacent lines, resulting in the appearance of continuous streams of white flowing through several lines.

Other typesetting problems which affect typographic color include inconsistent word spacing (commonly a problem in ***justified*** copy), ***widow***s and ***orphans***, poor letterspacing (which can be rectified via ***kerning***), uneven right margins caused by too many hyphens in a row, and an uneven, inconsistent appearance (including the density, or blackness, of the type).

Typographical

Descriptive of the process known as ***typography***. See ***Typography***.

Typographical Error

Alternate term for a ***printer's error*** occurring during typesetting. See ***Printer's Error***. Commonly called a ***typo***.

Typographical Parameters

Alternate term for ***type specifications***. See ***Type Specifications***.

Typography

The art and process of specifying, setting, or otherwise working with print-quality type, as opposed to typewriting. Typography involves the proper placement, positioning, and specification of type to ensure not only maximum legibility but also high aesthetic appeal. See ***Type and Typography***.

U

U, u

The twenty-first letter of the English alphabet, which developed as the North Semitic *waw* and was transformed to the Greek *upsilon*. The Etruscans, however, represented the "U" sound with the letter *V*, as did the Romans. In Roman monument writing, the *V* was used interchangeably with *U*, but by the Middle Ages the two letters began to part company; *U* was used primarily in monument carving, while *V* was used in manuscripts. The two letters only took on their own unique identities after the Middle Ages.

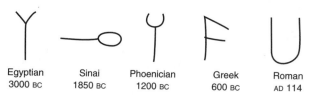

| Egyptian 3000 BC | Sinai 1850 BC | Phoenician 1200 BC | Greek 600 BC | Roman AD 114 |

The evolution of the letter U.

U&LC

See *Upper- and Lowercase*. Also written *u/lc*.

UART

An abbreviation for *universal asynchronous receiver/transmitter*. See *Universal Asynchronous Receiver/Transmitter (UART)*.

UCA

Abbreviation for *undercolor addition*. See *Undercolor Addition (UCA)*.

UCR

Abbreviation for *undercolor removal*. See *Undercolor Removal (UCR)*.

UDK

Abbreviation for *user-defined key*. See *User-Defined Key (UDK)*.

UGRA Wedge

A variety of control strip comprising a series of test images, used to accurately regulate the exposure of photographic film and printing plates.

UHF

Abbreviation for *ultra-high frequency*. See *Ultra-High Frequency (UHF)*.

U Interface

In networking, a single set of *twisted-pair* wiring used to connect an *ISDN* switch and an *NT1*.

u/lc

See *Upper- and Lowercase*.

Ultimate Adhesion

A measure of the fully formed bond between an adhesive material (such as a label or decal) and a particular *substrate*.

Ultra-High Frequency (UHF)

In telecommunications, any frequency between 300 and 3000 *megahertz*. UHF is used for television broadcasting and comprises those channels above 13. See also *Very-High Frequency (VHF)*.

Ultralarge-Scale Integration

In computer *microprocessor* manufacturing, term for the design and production of *integrated circuit*s with a component density of 10 million to 1 billion transistor gates. Ultralarge-scale integration is on the verge of supplanting *very-large-scale integration (VLSI)* that generates a component density of up to 10 million transistors. Looming on the horizon is *gigascale integration*.

Ultramarine Blue

An *inorganic color pigment* used in printing inks, derived from powdered lapis lazuli (or similar artificial pigment)—chemical formula $Na_{6-8}Al_6Si_6O_{24}S_{2-4}$. Ultramarine Blue is a clean red blue ranging from transparent to semiopaque, possessing high *lightfastness* and resistance to oils, waxes, heat, solvents, and alkalis. It fades, however, when in contact with dilute acids. Ultramarine Blue is primarily used in screen process printing, die-stamping, and water-based inks, although special grades can be prepared to make it suitable for lithographic printing. Ultramarine Blue is also suitable for use in the printing of food packaging, and the FDA allows it to be used in certain foods and cosmetics. (See *Inorganic Color Pigments*.)
   (*CI Pigment Blue 29 No. 77007*.)

Ultramarine Violet

An *inorganic color pigment* used in printing inks. Ultramarine violet (chemical formula $H_2Na_{4-6}Al_6Si_6O_{24}S_2$) is a bright reddish violet with good *lightfastness* and heat resistance. It is used in inks produced for metal decorating, primarily to tone white enamels so as to prevent yellowing. (See *Inorganic Color Pigments*.)
   (*CI Pigment Violet 15 No. 77007*.)

Ultraviolet

A form of electromagnetic radiation (or section of the *electromagnetic spectrum*) possessing a wavelength between 4 and 400 *nanometer*s, located on the spectrum just beyond *violet*. Also known erroneously as *black light*,

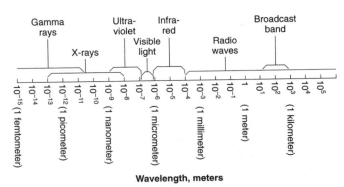

The common subdivisions of the electromagnetic spectrum and their respective wavelengths. Notice the location of ultraviolet just to the left of visible light.

ultraviolet "light" is invisible to human vision but can be detected due to its effects on substances. Ultraviolet light causes some substances—such as printing inks—to undergo *polymerization* (see *Ultraviolet-Curing Ink*), some photographic surfaces to become exposed (see *Photopolymer*), and some substances to fluoresce (see *Fluorescence*). Ultraviolet light also causes suntanning, sunburning, and the development of melanomas. Abbreviated *UV*.

Ultraviolet-Curing (UV-Curing) Ink

A type of radiation-curing ink that dries, or "sets," with the application of ultraviolet light. UV-curing ink *vehicle*s are composed of fluid oligomers (small *polymer*s), *monomer*s (lightweight molecules that bind together to form polymers), and initiators that, when exposed to ultraviolet radiation, release *free radical*s (extremely reactive atoms or molecules that can destabilize other atoms or molecules and start rapid chain reactions) that cause the *polymerization* of the vehicle, which hardens to a dry ink film containing the *pigment*. UV-curing inks are designed to replace *heatset ink*s whose *solvent*s emit potentially toxic gaseous emissions. However, UV-curing inks are as much as three times the cost of regular heatset inks, and they are used only in specialty printing, such as liquor cartons, cosmetic packaging, metal decoration, screen printing, and flexography.

The most common configuration of UV-curing equipment is a mercury vapor lamp. Within a quartz glass tube containing charged mercury, energy is added, and the mercury is vaporized and ionized. As a result of the vaporization and ionization, the high-energy free-for-all of mercury atoms, ions, and free electrons results in excited states of many of the mercury atoms and ions. As they settle back down to their ground state, radiation is emitted. By controlling the pressure that exists in the lamp, the wavelength of the radiation that is emitted can be somewhat accurately controlled, the goal being of course to ensure that much of the radiation that is emitted falls in the ultraviolet portion of the spectrum, and at wavelengths that will be effective for ink curing. UV radiation with wavelengths of 365–366 nanometers provides the proper amount of pen-

etration into the wet ink film to effect drying. (See *Photoreactive Vehicle*.) A newer variation of radiation-curing inks, *electron-beam-curing (EB-curing) ink*s, have some advantages over UV curing inks, but although the formulation of the inks is less expensive, the EB-curing equipment is more expensive. (See *Electron-Beam-Curing [EB-Curing] Inks*.)

UM

Abbreviation for *Unscheduled Maintenance*.

U-Matic

See *Broadcast Video U-Matic (BVU)*.

Umlaut

Alternate term for a *dieresis*, especially in German. See *Dieresis*.

Unbleached

Paper that has not undergone *bleaching* and thus is light or dark brown in color. An example of unbleached paper is *kraft* stock. See *Bleaching*.

Unbundled

See *Bundled*.

Uncial

In typography, a type of modified *majuscule* letterform. *Uncial* comes from the Latin word *uncus* (meaning "crooked") and was a capital letter that rounded the straight lines. Uncials were essentially *biform* characters making the transition from *caps* to *lowercase* as scribes tried to write faster and faster. The progression continued through the *half-uncial* letterform to the Caroline *minuscule*.

Uncoated Groundwood-Free Offset Paper

A variety of uncoated papers made from all-chemical or cotton-content pulp, used in a variety of printing applications, such as letters sent out as part of mass mailings, or for specific book manufacturing requirements. They also come in a variety of *finish*es. The *basic size* of uncoated groundwood-free offset papers is 25×38 in., and they come in *basis weight*s of 45–120 lb.

Uncoated Paper

Paper that has not had a *coating* applied. See *Coating*.

Uncoded Text

Alternate term for *raw text*. See *Raw Text*.

Uncut Pages

In *binding and finishing*, the pages of a *signature* that still contain *closed head*s.

Undercolor Addition (UCA)

In *process color* printing, a means of lightening dark *neutral gray* areas of a reproduction by adding dots of *cyan*, *magenta*, and *yellow* ink to the *color separation* films. (See also *Undercolor Removal [UCR]*.)

Undercolor Removal

A technique used to reduce the magenta, cyan, and yellow dot percentages in neutral areas by replacing them with increased amounts of black ink. To improve trapping and reduce ink costs in process color web printing, color separation films are reduced in color in areas where all three colors (cyan, magenta, and yellow) overprint, and the black film is increased an equivalent amount in these areas. (See *Color Plate* 27.)

Undercorrection

An insufficient amount of *color correction* occurring when, in an attempt to eliminate the *overcorrection* of *hue error*, too little of a particular *hue* is removed, resulting in a reproduced image in which one or more (or even all) hues will appear to be contaminated. The image will also print darker than it should. (See also *Overcorrection*.)

Undercut

On an offset lithographic printing press cylinder (in particular, the *plate cylinder* and the *blanket cylinder*), the difference between the radius of the cylinder's *bearer*s (metal rings at each end of the cylinder) and that of the cylinder body itself. The cylinder body—the portion of the cylinder where the plate or blanket is attached—is lower than that of the "true" diameter of the cylinder (indicated by the diameter of the bearer). The cylinder is undercut so as to provide room for plate or blanket *packing*, or adjustments in the height of the plate or blanket. (See *Plate Cylinder*, *Blanket Cylinder*, and *Packing*.) On the press *impression cylinder*, it is typically the bearers that are undercut, as the impression cylinder does not require packing.

In *cutting and trimming*, an *undercut* is a short undesirable cut caused by weak pressure of the *cutter clamp*. See *Cutting and Trimming*.

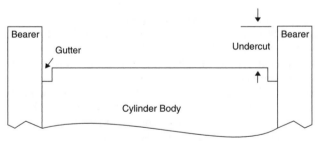

Cylinder undercut.

Underinked

Descriptive of a printing press or printing plate that is not receiving enough ink to make a dark, solid impression.

Underlay

In printing, a sheet of paper or other material used to increase the height of a printing plate. See *Packing*.

Underrun

Any quantity of printed materials that is less than what was specified in the original order. (See also *Overrun*.)

Underscan

A means of reducing a video image (usually by about 20%) so as to allow it to fit on a computer monitor. See also *Overscan*.

Underscoring

In typography, the underlining of a word or words, usually for emphasis when *italic* is not available. Underscoring multiple words with a single continuous line is called *solid underscoring*, while underlining each word separately is called *broken underscoring*.

Underset

In typography and typesetting, a line of type that is shorter than the specified *line length*. (See also *Overset*.)

Undertone

The *hue* or color of a printing ink film as viewed on a white sheet of paper (or other white *substrate*), or by light passing through the ink film.

Undertrapping

A defect of multicolor printing in which the first-down color shows through an *overprint* designed to conceal it. See *Trapping*.

Undertrimmed

In *binding and finishing*, descriptive of a book or stack of sheets that has been trimmed to a size smaller than the desired *trim size*.

Undo Command

In many computer software applications, a command that allows the user to delete the last action performed or alteration to a block of text or a graphic image made. Most programs only allow one level of undo.

Unglazed Paper

A nonglossy paper that has not undergone any *coating* or *finishing*. (See also *Glazed Paper*.)

Uninterruptible Power Source (UPS)

A device attached to a computer that supplies the system with power should the primary power supply fail. The UPS may supply the system with power continuously for an extended period of time, or for just long enough to properly shut the system down and thwart any data loss.

Unit

In printing, a shorthand term for a *printing unit*. See *Printing Unit*.

In typography, some fraction of an *em space* that, due to the variation of the size of an em according to *point size*, varies from point size to point size. (See **Relative Unit**.) The greater the number of units into which an em can be divided, the greater the latitude in the assigning of character widths. See **Unit System**.

Unitack

Any set of printing inks that possess equivalent degrees of **tack**.

Unit Count

Alternate term for **unit system**. See **Unit System**.

Unit Cut Mat

In **hot-metal** typography, a matrix device having character widths corresponding to those utilized in the **unit system**. See **Unit System**.

Unitized Font

A type of **font** using a system that is an alternative to the **unit system**. A unitized font utilizes an **escapement** value assigned to each character appropriate to a particular **typeface**, allowing greater character fit than is possible under the unit system.

Unit Perfecting Press

Alternate term for **blanket-to-blanket press**. See **Blanket-to-Blanket Press**.

Unit System

In typography, a series of relative width values assigned to characters as a means of describing the relation between their widths.

When Tolbert Lanston invented the **Monotype**, he wanted to separate the functions of input and output, and he needed a method that would let the operator know when to end a line for **justification**. Arithmetic was the best idea: he would add up character widths. To store the widths of every character in every **point size** of every **typeface** would have been prohibitive, so he created relative widths. In any typeface, all characters are proportional to one another, and from point size to point size that proportionality remains the same. Thus, if the width of every character is described as a multiple of some value, then those numerical relationships will still be valid, no matter what the size is.

For example, the relative width of an "a" in 9-pt. type might be eight-eighteenths, and the "a" in 72-pt. type would also be eight-eighteenths. The real width that these characters occupy is differentiated by multiplying those relative values by the point size:

$$9 \text{ pt.} \times 8\text{-unit "a"} = 72$$
$$72 \text{ pt.} \times 8\text{-unit "a"} = 576$$

Thus, one set of values serves for all sizes of a particular typeface. Lanston's base was 18, which served photo-typesetting for many years. In order to speed up film-font

manufacture, suppliers moved to 36-, 54-, and 72-unit systems. Also known as the **unit count system**.

(See also **Unitized Font**.)

Unit Value

The fixed unit width assigned to a character under the **unit system**. See **Unit System**.

Universal Asynchronous Receiver/Transmitter (UART)

A **microprocessor** that controls the **serial** communication of a computer, found most commonly in **microcomputer**s. The 8250 UART chip allowed a transmission speed of 9600 **bits per second (bps)** with a one-**byte** memory buffer. Its follow-up, the 16450 UART, supported higher transmission speeds but still retained the one-byte buffer. The 16550 UART provided two 16-byte buffers and even higher transmission speeds.

Universal Negative Letterspacing

In typography and typesetting, the process of removing space from between all of the characters, also known as **tracking**, as opposed to **individual negative letterspacing**, also known as **kerning**. See **Kerning**.

Universal Product Code (UPC)

A type of **bar code**, used for encoding price and inventory information on retail products. See **Bar Code**.

Universal product code (UPC).

Universal Resource Locator (URL)

On the **World Wide Web**, a "Web address," or the specific location of a Web site. A URL comprises an access method (which is almost always **hypertext transport protocol**, or **HTTP**, but could also be **FTP** or **Gopher**), followed by two slashes, the server name, and the names of the specific directories and files that correspond to the Web page. Thus, the address "http://www.splinky.com/printing" indicates that a particular site is on the server "splinky" and is a file called "printing."

UNIX

One of the three **standard platform**s (or operating systems) for computer systems—from **mainframe**s to **microcomputer**s—developed in the early 1970s by AT&T's Bell Labs. UNIX was written in the **C** language and was the first operating system to allow **multitasking**, or the simultaneous running of separate applications. UNIX is also used on computers linked to a network and a mainframe, such as university computers. It is also a useful operating system for the development of other applications. UNIX is a popular operating system, primarily for engineering and manufacturing firms, as well as academic institutions. There are also several different types of the UNIX system, which were developed in different places, and the different versions are rarely completely compatible with each other. The Internet itself was originally designed for computers running UNIX. (See *Platform*.) Varieties of UNIX include both *CLI*- and *GUI*-based interfaces.

UNIXWare

In computing, a 32-bit *UNIX*-compatible *operating system* developed by Novell that provided a *graphical user interface* as well as standard UNIX features such as *multitasking* and *multiuser* capabilities.

Unjustified

Type that does not align on both the left and the right; see *Justification* and *Ragged Right*.

Unrelated Italic

In typography, a type of "pure" *italic* type designed without the consideration of having to blend with a corresponding *roman* typeface. Unrelated italic type is based in 15th-century handwriting styles. See *Italic*.

Unsharp Mask

In *color separation* photography, a somewhat blurry, low-*contrast* photographic *negative* produced from a *transparency* and placed on top of the transparency (as a *mask*) when exposing the color separation negatives. The light passing through the mask is altered, resulting in a *color correction* that compensates for the *hue error*s of *process ink*s. An added benefit of the unsharp mask is that the edges of the images on the transparency are enhanced (or exaggerated), which produces greater detail on the color separation negatives. This process is called *unsharp masking*.

Digital image-processing programs and scanners also employ types of unsharp masks to sharpen the edges of images. See *Unsharp Masking (USM)*.

Unsharp Masking (USM)

In image processing, an *edge enhancement* process performed either photographically (when exposing *color separation negatives*), optically (by a *scanner*), or digitally (in image-processing programs such as Photoshop). The latter two methods derive from the photographic process, in which a blurry *unsharp mask* is used when exposing color separation negatives from a *transparency*. The photographic method is commonly employed for reasons of *color correction*, a side benefit being an exaggeration and enhancement of the edges of images. (See *Unsharp Mask*.)

Optical unsharp masking is performed during scanning utilizing two types of apertures: the small, primary

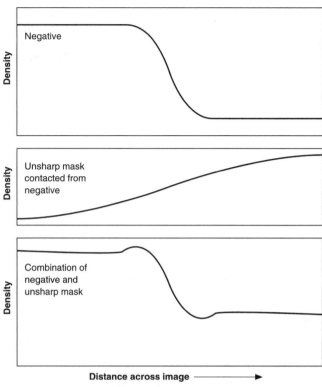

Edge enhancement.

signal aperture, which captures the individual *red, green, and blue* image signals, and a larger unsharp masking aperture, which captures a larger amount of the same signal. The two signals are combined to create a single exaggerated signal that causes an enhancement where image edges occur.

Digital unsharp masking utilizes the application software to analyze each set of adjacent *pixel*s of a digital image, locate where the edges occur, and adjust the tonal values of the pixels on either side of the edge in opposite directions, increasing the contrast along the edge. Some advanced programs allow the user to specify the number of pixels to modify, allowing greater or lesser degrees of unsharp masking.

Unlike photographic USM, neither the optical nor the digital USM techniques can be used to color correct the image, and actually neither of them technically use "unsharp masks." (See COLOR PLATE 24.)

Unshielded Twisted-Pair

A type of *twisted-pair wiring* comprising either four pairs or two pairs of cables, each pair containing two individual wires twisted around each other. Unlike *shielded twisted-pair* cables, the pairs are not insulated from each other. Unshielded twisted-pair cables (abbreviated *UTP*) are inexpensive and are often used in network connections. UTP cables are classified in one of five categories of increasing transmission capacity. Cables of category 5 are capable of transmission speeds of up to 100 megabits per second.

However, UTP cables can be laid only a relatively shorter distance (unlike *thick Ethernet* cabling) without requiring any form of signal amplification to compensate for attenuation of transmitted signals. See *Twisted-Pair Wiring* and *Shielded Twisted-Pair*.

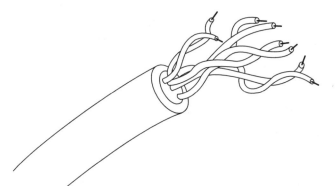

Structure of unshielded twisted-pair cabling.

Unshift Code
On typesetting devices, a code used to indicate an exit from the *shift* mode, or to return to using *lowercase* letters.

Unsized
Paper that has had no *sizing* added, either internally or externally. Unsized, or *waterleaf*, paper absorbs water readily and is commonly used for paper towels. See *Sizing*.

Untrimmed Paper
A paper that has been sheeted from a web using a *rotary cutter* and that may not be sufficiently square for use on press. Also known as *machine-trimmed paper*.

Unwanted Color
Any *process color* that ends up in a portion of a reproduced image in which it does not belong, such as *cyan* ending up in a *yellow*.

Up
Reference to the number of copies of a single image that are placed on the same plate and printed at the same time. See *One-Up, Two-Up . . .*

UPC
Abbreviation for *Universal Product Code*, a type of *bar code*. See *Bar Code*.

Update
In computing and database management, to make a file or the data within a file current. The term *update* is also a synonym for *upgrade*. See *Upgrade*.

Update Hell
An often self-imposed purgatory in which one compulsively needs to possess the newest versions of hardware and software. However, some update hells are imposed externally;

as one accrues more and more computers, it may become necessary to keep all hardware and software compatible with each other. An update (or *upgrade*) of one may require the update of them all.

Updike, Daniel Berkeley
Daniel Berkeley Updike (1860–1941), a typographer, was born in Providence, Rhode Island. He established the Merrymount Press and was a leader in the revival of classical typography in the United States. Updike was also a lecturer on printing at Harvard University from 1910 to 1917 ("Printing Types—Their History, Form and Use" and "Some Aspects of Printing").

Upgrade
In computing, to install new and/or advanced versions of hardware and software, especially those that offer greater performance, more features, or other improved aspects. The term *upgrade*, when used as a noun, also refers to an advanced version of a hardware device or software program.

Uplink
An *earth station* on the ground that can transmit data to an orbiting satellite, for retransmission to another earth station. See also *Downlink*.

Upload
To send a data file from one's computer to another computer (which can be a file server, a *bulletin board service*, an Internet USENET group, or another individual's computer), typically via modem. The opposite, *download*, means to *receive* a data file on one's computer from another computer.

Upper- and Lowercase (U&LC)
In typography, the specification that copy be typeset using upper- and lowercase letters, rather than all caps.

Uppercase
An alternate term for capital letters. See *Capitals*.

Upper Rail
A device on a *hot metal* typesetting device containing an alternate *typeface*, which could be shifted to from the *lower rail* when the alternate face was desired. See *Rail*.

Upright Binding
In *binding and finishing*, a book that has been bound along its long dimension. (See also *Oblong Binding*.)

UPS
Abbreviation for *uninterruptible power supply*. See *Uninterruptible Power Supply (UPS)*.

Upstream
In a *cable television network*, the direction of a transmitted signal to the *head end*. The direction *from* the head end is referred to as *downstream*.

Upstyle

In typography, the use of a *capital* letter as the first letter of each word of a phrase, title, etc., excluding words such as articles, prepositions, and conjunctions.

Upward Compatible

In computing, descriptive of software that will run on upgraded or later versions of the hardware for which it was developed. It is also descriptive of files created with one version of an application that can be opened and edited with upgraded or later versions of that application. An example is a file created with Photoshop 2.0 that can also be opened and edited by Photoshop 4.0. See also *Downward Compatible*.

Urethane

Any of a variety of thermoplastic material used as printing *substrate*s, or in coatings, inks, adhesives, etc.

URL

Abbreviation for *universal resource locator*. See *Universal Resource Locator (URL)*.

US ASCII

The variety of *ASCII* used in the United States. See *ASCII*.

USENET

An abbreviation for *USEr NETwork*. See *USEr NETwork (USENET)*.

User

In computing, an individual (usually a human one) operating a computer.

User-Definable Dictionary

In computing, a *dictionary* that allows the user to add his or her own terms, such as those the computer is not likely to have. See *Dictionary*.

User-Defined Key (UDK)

In computing, a key that can be programmed by the computer to record a set of keystrokes and repeat them with the touch of a single key.

User-Defined Views

In *three-dimensional* modeling, the ability for the user to instruct the program to display a rendered object in a variety of views, such as front, back, top, etc.

User-Friendly

Descriptive of any aspect of computing (although it usually pertains to software *interface*s) that can be utilized with relative ease by a person who is not especially familiar with computer programming jargon. In other words, a user interface that is fairly self-explanatory and capable of providing some degree of help. A *graphical user interface (GUI)* is considered more user-friendly than a *command-line interface (CLI)*, for example.

User Group

An organization (usually regional) of users of a particular computer platform or program who meet periodically to solve problems or compare notes on the subject of their interest. User groups can also have a great deal of influence with vendors in terms of improving their products.

User Interface

The means by which a computer interacts with the human user, and vice versa. See *Interface*.

USEr NETwork (USENET)

On the *Internet*, a linked set of *newsgroup*s. See *Newsgroup*.

User-Selectable Resolution

In *scanning*, a function of scanner-control software that allows the user to scan at precise, user-determined resolutions—i.e., 221 *ppi*—as opposed to a limited, preset series of resolutions (i.e., 200 ppi, 300 ppi, etc.). See *Scanning*.

Uses PC Power Supply

In computing, a specification that indicates that a particular device (such as a *hard disk* drive) obtains its power from the computer's own power supply, rather than from a direct AC connection.

USM

Abbreviation for *unsharp masking*. See *Unsharp Masking (USM)*.

Utility

In computing, any computer program (usually small) containing routines for various service, maintenance, or housekeeping functions, such as disk copying, disk *defragmentation*, etc.

Utility Program

See *Utility*.

Utility Routine

In computing, any specific routine performed by a *utility* program. See *Utility*.

UTP

Abbreviation for *unshielded twisted-pair* wiring. See *Unshielded Twisted-Pair*.

UV

Abbreviation for *ultraviolet*. See *Ultraviolet*.

UV-Curing Ink

See *Ultraviolet-Curing Ink*.

U,v,L

A *color space* described by Kodak in its Designmaster and Prophecy color electronic publishing systems.

V

V, v

The twenty-second letter of the English alphabet, which had no written counterpart in North Semitic or Greek. The *V* as we know it was developed by the Etruscans, who used it to represent the "U" sound, as did the Romans. (There is no "V" sound in Latin; so Caesar's famous phrase *"veni, vidi, vici"* is actually pronounced "weni, widi, wici.") The form of the *V* was used interchangeably with the *U* until the Middle Ages, when the *V* began to develop its own pronunciation. (See *U, u.*)

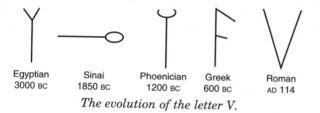

Egyptian	Sinai	Phoenician	Greek	Roman
3000 BC	1850 BC	1200 BC	600 BC	AD 114

The evolution of the letter V.

Vacuum Back
On a graphic arts *process camera*, a frame that uses suction to hold film in place during exposure. Also called a *vacuum frame*.

Vacuum Frame
See *Vacuum Back*.

Value
One of the three attributes of a color, descriptive of its degree of lightness or darkness. See also *Hue*, *Chroma*, *Color Mixing*, *Ink*, and *Color Space*.

Value-Added Network (VAN)
A privately owned and operated communications network authorized by the government to lease services from a *common carrier*, enhance those services, and resell it to the public.

Value-Added Reseller (VAR)
A company that purchases a basic system or device from an *original equipment manufacturer (OEM)*, enhances it (or adds value to it) by means of better documentation, technical support, additional features, etc., and resells it to the public.

VAN
Abbreviation for *value-added network*. See *Value-Added Network (VAN)*.

Vanceometer Test
A test performed to measure a paper's *ink absorbency*, in which an oil is spread on the surface of a paper, imparting a certain level of *gloss*, and a *glossmeter* is used to measure the decrease in gloss as the oil is absorbed into the paper. (See also *Ink Absorbency* and *K and N Ink Absorbency Test*.)

VanDyke
Alternate term for *blueline*, especially when using VanDyke paper. See *Blueline*.

Vapor Phase Inhibitor (VPI)
See *Volatile Corrosion Inhibitor*.

Vaporware
A colloquial (and not unsarcastic) term for a software program that has been announced by a company yet never shipped.

VAR
Abbreviation for *value-added reseller*. See *Value-Added Reseller (VAR)*.

Variable
In mathematics (specifically, the branch of mathematics known as *algebra*), a quantity that represents any value. Variables are used to describe general mathematical principles or functions.

In computer programming, variables are used in programs to represent data that will change. For example, a program may be instructed to print A, in which case, A will represent whatever actual value the user has defined.

Variable Area Engraving
Alternate term for *hard dot engraving*, a variation of the *diffusion-etch process* of *gravure engraving*. See *Gravure Engraving: Diffusion-Etch Process*.

Variable Data
Any specific data that is not part of a page design and that varies from form to form or page to page.

Variable-Data Software
In printing, specifically digital printing, computer applications (either standalone or incorporated into prepress or printing systems) used to customize output. In other words, such software allows different data to be printed on successive pages utilizing a common page layout. Common applications for variable-data software can include printing a different PIN code in successive telephone or bank cards, different mailing addresses on successive magazine covers or letters, or other such uses. Although variable-data software is still in its infancy (only a handful of companies are marketing it), it is receiving a lot of attention. The most commonly used variable-data packages allow for the defining of

variable text boxes in page layout programs such as **QuarkXPress** or **PageMaker**, and the variable data can be imported from a database file into these boxes during **ripping**. When sent to a digital press, each successive page contains different data within the consistent page design.

Users of these new systems have reported marginal success. However, the manufacturers—Barco, Agfa, Xeikon, Indigo, and IBM to name five—are releasing upgrades at a steady clip.

Variable Field

In a database, a **field** that contains a variable number of characters from record to record, the number dependent upon the amount of data the field actually contains. See also **Fixed Field**.

Variable-Length Record

In a database a **record** in a file in which all records differ in length. See also **Fixed-Length Record**.

Variable Text

See **Variable Data**.

Varnish

In the production of printing ink, varnish can refer to either a combination of oils, **resin**s, waxes, **solvent**s and other materials used as an ink **vehicle**. The use of varnish tends to increase the gloss of a printed ink.

The term *varnish* also refers to an overcoating applied to a printed piece following printing, performed on or off the press. Varnish is typically added to a finished printed piece either for aesthetic reasons (i.e., to increase gloss and provide a better overall look) or to protect the printing from wear and tear due to handling or contact with moisture or chemicals. Varnish that is applied to an entire printed surface after printing is called **overprint varnish**; varnish that is applied only to certain portions of a printed surface, primarily for aesthetic reasons (as on book covers) is called **spot varnish**. If the varnish is added as an overcoating after printing, it is important to ensure that the formulation of the varnish is compatible with that of the ink, or **bleeding** and other printing defects can occur.

Varnish-On Decal

A form of **decal** in which a clear lacquer is printed onto the backing paper, followed by a reverse-reading image of the design, followed by another coat of lacquer. The decal is transferred to the ultimate **substrate** by means of an adhesive varnish.

VAX

Abbreviation for *Virtual Address Extension*, a line of 32-bit **minicomputer** systems introduced by Digital Equipment Corporation (DEC) in 1977. The VAX family of computers are used primarily for data processing, and, on occasion, image archiving, but not for the processing of images. VAX systems range from small desktop systems to large **mainframe**s.

VCR

Abbreviation for **videocassette recorder**. See **Videocassette Recorder (VCR)**.

VDT

Abbreviation for **video display terminal**. See **Video Display Terminal (VDT)**.

Vector

In mathematics, an entity (such as a line segment) that possesses both magnitude and direction, represented by an arrow pointing in the direction of the quantity the length of which is equivalent to the magnitude of the quantity, commonly used to represent forces or trajectories.

Vectors are used in computer graphics to describe lines, curves, and other, more complex geometric shapes, which the system or application describes utilizing the complex mathematical formulas that describe the shape. See **Vector Graphics**.

Vector-Based Graphics

See **Vector Graphics**.

Vector Device

A computer output device—such as a **plotter**—that images film or paper by drawing lines or **vectors**, as opposed to a **raster** device, which generates output as a **bitmap**.

Vector Display

A type of video display—similar to an oscilloscope—that generates screen images as a series of lines—or **vectors**—by moving an electron beam across a cathode-ray tube between defined points, as opposed to a conventional computer display that generates a screen image as a **bitmap** comprising many tiny, individually illuminated **pixel**s.

Vector File

A computer file created utilizing **page-makeup software** that contains commands and codes describing the start and end positions, as well as the length of each line, rather than storing a page as a **bitmap**. Such files may also contain the mathematical descriptions of any **vector graphics** included. See **Vector Graphics**.

Vector Generator

In computer graphics, a computer processor or software function that translates the draw and move functions input by the user to the lines displayed on the screen.

Vector Graphics

A type of computer graphics system that describes a computer image as a series of complex mathematical formulas and coordinates that describe lines, curves, and other geometric shapes, as opposed to **bitmap graphics**, in which the image is represented as a large grid of variously colored **pixel**s. (Consequently, vector-based graphics are also referred to as ***object-oriented***, as elements within an image can be grouped together and considered by the software as individual "objects.") Vector images take up less disk space and require less processing power and ***RAM*** to create and manipulate. As they are described mathematically, they can be output at as high a ***resolution*** as the output device is capable of generating, so long as the ***file format*** in which the file is saved is one that can handle vectors. The most commonly used file format for vector graphics is ***encapsulated PostScript (EPS)***. *PostScript* printer fonts are typically vector-based descriptions of letters, numbers and other characters. A disadvantage to vector graphics is that they can be more difficult to create and manipulate than bitmaps, but vector graphics are commonly the only way of producing ***line art*** that prints out smoothly.

Despite whether a file is a vector or bitmap image, however, a conventional computer monitor can only display an image as a bitmap, so a vector graphic will never look as smooth on screen as it does when output, as it will always have to be displayed at the resolution of the monitor, which is much less than that of ***imagesetter***s or even ***laser printer***s.

Vectorscope

A device used to test and calibrate the color portion of a video signal comprising a round monitor on which a pattern is displayed. The pattern contains certain points of reference and the video signal is adjusted until the points of reference on the monitor match the optimum values.

Vector Trapping

In digital prepress, a means of ensuring the ***registration*** of multicolor images performed on digital systems in which ***vector***-based graphics are analyzed for potential ***trapping*** problems and new objects are added where needed. See ***Trapping***.

Vegetable Oil

An oil derived from agricultural sources and used in many oil-based printing ink ***vehicle***s. Commonly used vegetable oils include rapeseed and ***linseed oil***s, which need to undergo processing before becoming suitable for use in ink. The most recent development in vegetable oil-based ink vehicles is ***soy ink***, utilizing soybean oil. Soy ink, especially when used in ***newsink***, has excellent print qualities and helps eliminate the smudging of newsprint.

Vegetable Parchment

A type of paper intended to resemble ancient ***parchment*** (which had actually been made from the split skins of sheep). Vegetable parchment (in contrast to ***imitation parchment***) is produced by passing the paper through a tub of sulfuric acid, which fuses the paper fibers into an undifferentiated mass. It has high ***wet strength*** and is greaseproof. Vegetable parchment has a distinctive appearance and is used for greeting cards, reproductions of ancient documents, and greaseproof package enclosures. Vegetable parchment, having a greaseproof surface, needs to be printed using special inks.

Vehicle

The liquid component of ink that holds the ***pigment*** and binds it to the printed surface (or ***substrate***) after drying. The speed at which the vehicle is absorbed into the paper or other surface affects the ultimate quality of the ink; in inks that dry by ***polymerization*** and ***oxidation***, rapid absorption of the vehicle impedes proper ink drying and can lead to ***ink chalking***. In some printing processes (such as high-speed ***web offset lithography***), slow absorption of the vehicle can lead to smudging during finishing operations. (See ***Ink Absorbency***.)

The composition of ink vehicles varies greatly, depending on the printing process and the substrate to be used.

Nondrying oil vehicle inks dry primarily by absorption of the vehicle—petroleum or rosin oils—into the paper, and are used for ***letterpress*** news printing on highly absorbent ***newsprint*** paper.

Drying oil vehicle inks dry primarily by ***oxidation*** of the vehicle—such as ***linseed oil***, a common drying oil vehicle, as well as fish oil, cottonseed oil, castor oil, ***tung oil***, petroleum oils, synthetic oils, etc.—in which the oil absorbs oxygen and then undergoes ***polymerization***, or the hardening and solidification of the oil. Drying oil vehicle inks are the most commonly used inks in letterpress and offset printing.

Solvent-resin vehicle inks are composed of pigments dissolved in a resin-based ***solvent***, and they dry primarily by ***evaporation*** of the solvent, leaving behind a dry pigment on the substrate. Solvent-resin vehicle inks are used in gravure, flexographic, and offset printing, and are the vehicles that form the basis of ***heatset ink***s.

Glycol vehicle inks form a category of inks known as ***moisture-set ink***s, which dry by ***precipitation***. Pigments and resins are dissolved in a glycol solvent, which is solubilized in the presence of moisture. When water contacts the glycol solution, the resin and pigments precipitate out and are deposited on the substrate. The advantages of moisture-set inks include a lack of odor, and are consequently used in food-packaging printing.

Resin-oil vehicle inks dry by a combination of absorption and oxidation (called ***quicksetting***). The solvent is absorbed by the substrate quickly, and the remaining film of resin and oil finishes hardening by means of oxidation. These types of inks are known as ***quickset ink***.

Resin-wax vehicle inks dry by a process called ***cold-setting***. These inks are solid at room temperature, applied to the substrate with heated rollers, plates, and dampening systems, essentially melting the ink onto the paper, which then hardens as it cools. Since special heated presses are required for cold-set inks, they are not widely used.

Water-soluble gum vehicle inks, also called "watercolor" inks, use ***gum arabic*** or other gum that is soluble in water. These inks are not widely used.

Photoreactive vehicle inks dry upon exposure to ultraviolet radiation. (See *Ultraviolet-Curing Inks* and *Electron-Beam-Curing Inks*.)

Vellum

A material, made from the split skin of calves, goats, or lambs, used as a writing surface before the invention of *paper*. It is similar to, and prepared in much the same way as *parchment*. To prepare vellum, the skin is washed, rubbed with lime (which imparts a paperlike feel to the surface), and scraped with a knife to eliminate pits and bumps in the surface. The skin is stretched on a wooden frame, and the scraping continues until the entire skin acquires a uniform thickness. Unlike parchment, vellum uses the entire skin (it is not split into two layers the way parchment is), and this process results in a more irregular surface texture than is produced in the production of parchment. (See *Parchment*, *Vellum Finish*.)

Vellum Finish

A paper *finish* characterized by a rough, absorbent surface, intended to simulate the texture of ancient *vellum*.

Vellum-Finish Bristol

A type of *bristol* paper given a roughened finish and commonly used in offset printing for its aesthetic surface characteristics that allow quick drying of ink, high bulk, and high strength. See *Bristol Paper*.

Velox

Strictly speaking, the trade name of a type of chloride papers developed by Kodak for producing photographic prints. The term *Velox* is commonly used to refer to a *glossy* black-and-white photographic print of *halftone* images or *line art* used for proofing *negatives*.

Velvet Paper

A paper that has had *flock* added to its surface to impart a velvet-like texture. See *Flocking*.

Vendor Independence

In computing, the ability of devices manufactured by different companies to communicate with each other.

Verification

In computing, a means of ensuring that data has been written to a disk correctly; the computer reads the original data and compares it to what it has just written.

Veronica

On the *Internet*, a search engine for *Gopher* that searches Gopher menus for desired files. Search results are displayed as another Gopher menu, which can then be used to access the desired resource. Although Veronica is purported to stand for "Very Easy Rodent-Oriented Net-wide Index to Computer Archives," it joins *Archie* and *Jughead* as Archie Comics-related Internet search applications.

VersaCAD

In computer graphics, the brand name of a popular *CAD* program, available for both *PC* and *Macintosh* computer *platform*s.

Version

In computing, a means of identifying a specific hardware or software release, commonly for compatibility purposes. Most major software or hardware revisions increase the whole number, while minor revisions and bug fixes are indicated by changing the decimal number. For example, version 2.0 indicates a major revision to version 1.0, while version 1.2 would indicate merely a minor revision.

Decimal-number revisions are usually compatible with each other, while major revisions tend not to be. Some programs add a third number to indicate even more minor revisions, such as 1.2.2.

Verso

The even-numbered page on the left-hand side of an open book, or the reverse of a printed sheet, from the Latin phrase *in verso folio*, meaning "on the turned leaf." See also *Recto*.

Vertex

A letter element also known as a *vortex*. See *Vortex*.

Vertical Alignment

In typography, the aligning of a vertical column of type along an imaginary vertical line located on the left of each character. See *Alignment*.

Vertical Application

A computer program created for a very narrow market, such as a program for dental office management.

Vertical Blanking Interval

In a *cathode-ray tube*, the amount of time required for an *electron gun* to move from the end of the last horizontal line on the screen back to the beginning of the top line. In this very short period, certain data can be sent, in particular a *time code* (called a *vertical interval time code*). See also *Horizontal Blanking Interval*.

Vertical Camera

A type of graphic arts *process camera* in which the *copyboard*, *lens*, and *filmboard* are aligned in a vertical plane, as opposed to a *horizontal camera*. See *Photography: Graphic Arts Photography*. (See illustration on the facing page.)

Vertical Frequency

Alternate term for *refresh rate*. See *Refresh Rate*.

Vertical Interval Time Code (VITC)

In video, a *SMPTE time code* that has been *strip*ed in the *vertical blanking interval* of a videotape.

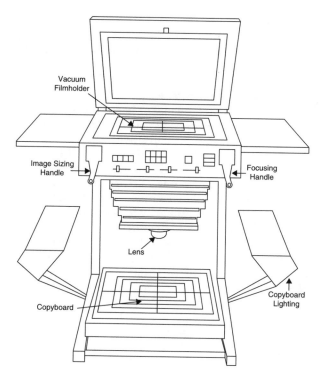

Vertical graphic arts camera.

Vertical Justification

In typography, a means of aligning the tops and bottoms of adjacent columns by adding or removing space between lines or paragraphs.

Vertical Page

Alternate term for *portrait* page orientation. See *Portrait.*

Vertical Resolution

The number of horizontal lines a computer monitor can display down the screen. (See *Resolution*.)

Vertical Retrace

In a *cathode-ray tube*, the repositioning of an electron beam at the first pixel of the top line of the screen after the conclusion of a screen redraw.

Vertical Scan Rate

On a computer monitor, the speed at which the electron beam producing the screen image moves from top to bottom down the display. The vertical scan rate is measured in *kilohertz*. See also *Horizontal Scan Rate* and *Refresh Rate.*

Vertical Scrolling

On a computer display, the ability to scroll up or down to display text or parts of an image or page that do not fit onto the screen. See also *Horizontal Scrolling.*

Vertical Setting

In typography, setting type with letters over and under one another, in a variety of orientations. One particularly undesirable form of vertical setting is vertical stacking.

Sometimes vertical setting (above) is used with regular horizontal type arrangement for attention-getting purposes. It is best to use only one (short) line, not several.

Another common site of vertical setting is a standard book edge. For book spines, the type is set in the downward direction. Thus, when the book is flat on a table with its cover up, the type on the spine can be read easily. (In Europe, book spines are commonly printed in the *up* direction.)

Vertical Spacing

In typography, the number of lines per inch on a page from top to bottom.

Vertical Tab

A *tab* oriented in the vertical direction, or a vertical skip to preselected points down the length of a page.

Very-High Frequency (VHF)

In telecommunications, any frequency between 30 and 300 *megahertz*. Television transmissions in this range occupy channels 2–13. See also *Ultra-High Frequency (UHF).*

Very-Large-Scale Integration (VLSI)

In computer *microprocessor* manufacturing, term for the design and production of *integrated circuit*s with a component density of 100,000–10,000,000 transistor gates, or computer chips that are extremely fast and extremely powerful. VLSI supplanted *large-scale integration (LSI)* and is likely to be supplanted itself by *ultra-large-scale integration* and *gigascale integration.*

VESA

See *Video Electronics Standards Association (VESA).*

VESA Local Bus

In computing, a *local bus* architecture in which up to three bus adapter slots are built into the computer's *motherboard*, which allows for such devices as hard-disk controllers, network interface cards, and video adapters to be added to the system.

VGA

Abbreviation for *Video Graphics Array.* See *Video Graphics Array (VGA).*

VGA/EGA/CGA Monitor

A computer monitor capable of switching among the three successive modes of display. See *Video Graphics Array (VGA)*, *Enhanced Graphics Adapter (EGA)*, and *Color Graphics Adapter (CGA)*.

VHF

Abbreviation for *very-high frequency*. See *Very-High Frequency (VHF)*.

VHS

Abbreviation for *video home system*. See *video home system*.

Vial

In packaging, a sealed glass container used in the distribution of pharmaceutical products. A vial contains a single dose or multiple doses of a medication, commonly one used for hypodermic injection. It is formed out of a single piece of glass, and is hermetically sealed by inserting a rubber stopper and a crimped aluminum ring at the open end. Medication is withdrawn from a vial by inserting a syringe through the rubber.

The important consideration in the manufacture of glass ampules is that the class be completely inert chemically, and not react in any way with the drug contained within it. See also *Ampule*.

Vibrator

Alternate term for *oscillator* rollers found on an offset lithographic press. See *Oscillator*.

Victoria Blue CFA

An *organic color pigment* used in printing inks. Victoria Blue CFA is a bright royal blue shade that possesses greater chemical, light, and heat resistance than *PMTA Victoria Blue* for which it is often substituted, primarily for cost reasons. Its shade, however, is not as bright as PMTA Victoria Blue. It is often used in gravure and flexographic packaging inks. (See *Organic Color Pigments*.)

Also known as *Copper Ferrocyanide Blue (CI Pigment Blue 62 No. 42595x)*.

Video Adapter

In computing, an add-on card that converts the digital data from the computer to *red, green, and blue* (or black and white) signals needed to display an image on a computer monitor.

Video Analyzer

A device used to display a *color transparency* or *color separation*s on a color monitor as a means of analyzing how the image will reproduce when printed.

Video Capture Board

A type of *digitizer board* used specifically for converting *analog video* signals to *digital form*. Also known as a *frame grabber*. See *Frame Grabber*.

Videocassette

A plastic case or shell used to house and protect magnetic *videotape*. See *Videotape*. Sometimes spelled as two words, *video cassette*.

Videocassette Recorder (VCR)

A device—either for professional or home use—that writes video signals to and reads video signals from a magnetic *videotape* (the videotape usually housed in a *videocassette*). VCRs for home use at one time included *Betamax*, but despite the superior image quality, consumers preferred the *Video Home System (VHS)*, still the most popular video format. Other home formats include *Super VHS* and *Hi-8*, the latter used primarily in *camcorder*s. Professionally, the *Betacam SP*, *Broadcast Video U-Matic*, and *BCN* systems are the most prevalent. A videocassette recorder is also known as a *videotape recorder (VTR)*. It is also sometimes spelled as three words, *video cassette recorder*.

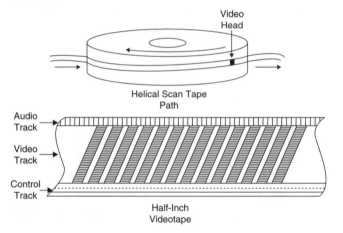

Schematic of videotape path across play head (top) and diagram of half-inch videotape structure (bottom).

Video CD

A motion video standard for *compact disc*s (described in the *White Book* standards) that can be read by any *CD-ROM-XA* device and a computer system equipped with an *MPEG* decoder.

Video Clip

See *Clip* (first definition).

Video Conferencing

In telecommunications, technology that allows participants from diverse geographical locations to attend a meeting, conference, etc., by means of video terminals, computers, and communications equipment. In many configurations, individuals at one location meet in a video conferencing room, or a room outfitted with the proper equipment such as microphones, cameras, and monitors, which is then connected to other video conferencing rooms at other locations. Often, members who are connected can view the same computer files and make individual edits to them (known as *joint-editing*). Video conferencing has the advantage of being less expensive to effect than long-distance business trips. Also spelled as one word, *videoconferencing*.

Video Control

A system for controlling—usually remotely—a *video-cassette recorder (VCR)*, involving both the connection (be it by wire or infrared) and the command structure of the operating system. See, for example, *Control-S*, *Local Application Numerical Control (LANC)*, and *Video System Control Architecture (VISCA)*.

Video Controller

In computing, the processor on a *video adapter* that converts digital data from the computer to electrical signals needed to display an image on a monitor.

Videodisc

A type of *optical disc* used for the storage and retrieval of still and motion video as well as sound. The videodisc is written and read in much the same way as a *compact disc (CD)*, although the videodisc is much larger, varying in size from 120–300 mm (4.73–11.81 in.) diameter. The 120-mm discs can be recorded on only one side, while both the 200- and 300-mm versions can be recorded on both sides. A videodisc contains high-quality analog and digital sound and video, with digital data present for the control system. A videodisc also offers differing levels of interactivity. A *level zero videodisc* (the most basic) allows simple playback of stored data, with perhaps some random access to different frames or tracks. A *level three videodisc* (the most advanced) allows far greater degrees of user interaction. See *Level Zero Videodisc*, *Level One Videodisc*, *Level Two Videodisc*, and *Level Three Videodisc*. Videodiscs are commonly used for the distribution of movies, a higher-quality alternative to the *VHS* videotape.

See also *Compact Disc (CD)*.

Videodisc Map

In *videodisc* design and production, a chart or table listing each audio and video segment, as well as the specifications for each of those segments.

Videodisc Player

A device, comprising an *optical disc* reader, used to play a *videodisc*. Usually, such devices are level-independent.

Video Display

A type of *raster*-based computer monitor. A video display uses *analog* signals to create the picture. A *digital-to-analog converter* transforms the digital data from the computer to an analog video signal.

Video Display Terminal (VDT)

A color or *monochrome* computer monitor with an attached keyboard. The term *VDT* is also used to stand for

video display tube, which essentially describes the computer monitor sans keyboard, and in this sense is synonymous with *CRT*. See *Cathode-Ray Tube (CRT)*.

Video Display Tube

Alternate term for a *video display terminal*. See *Video Display Terminal (VDT)*.

Video Display Unit

Alternate term for a *video display terminal*. See *Video Display Terminal (VDT)*.

Video Driver

In computing, the software needed to control a *video adapter*, or that functions as the *interface* between the computer (or an application) and the video adapter.

Video Effects

In television and video production, special effects added digitally or by other means. Video effects usually involve such things as *transition*s between scenes or shots, such as *dissolve*s, *wipe*s, *door-swing*s, *fly-in*s, *iris* effects, *tumble*s, *fade-in*s and *fade-out*s. See also *Digital Video Effects*.

Video 8

See *Eight Millimeter (8 mm)*.

Video Electronics Standards Association (VESA)

An organization of video monitor manufacturers that defines standards for personal computer display equipment, most importantly the *Super VGA* system. See also *VESA Local Bus*.

Video Error

Any defect in a video signal, due to a wide variety of causes. Common video errors include *breakup*, *confetti*, *noise*, *tracking*, *moiré*, etc.

Video for Windows

In *digital video*, software that allows *IBM-compatible computer*s running on *Windows* to record and play digital video. Video for Windows, developed by Microsoft, allows video that has been compressed with *Indeo* or *Cinepak* to play back at a screen size of 160 *pixel*s by 120 pixels at a frame rate of 15 frames per second. A PC with an Intel 80486 *microprocessor* running at 33 *MHz* is the basic system requirement. Larger screen sizes and frame rates are possible with additional hardware decompression.

Video Gain

In television and video, the *gain*, or intensity, of a video signal.

Video Graphics Array (VGA)

An expansion board for *IBM-compatible computer*s that provided 640×480-pixel resolution and a display of 256 colors for color monitors. VGA was the display standard for IBM's PS/2 line of personal computers and is still widely used in ***IBM-compatible computer***s. VGA superseded ***EGA*** and the earlier ***CGA***. It was itself superseded by ***XGA***. An extension to the VGA standard that increases the resolution of a VGA monitor is known as ***Super Video Graphics Array***. See ***Super Video Graphics Array (SVGA)***.

Video Home System (VHS)

The most popular ***videotape*** format, developed by JVC, comprising ½-in. magnetic tape. Despite the popularity of VHS, it provides a low-quality image and is rarely used for professional videography. In the consumer arena, VHS won out over Sony's technically superior ***Betamax*** format in the early 1980s. A higher-quality VHS tape is called Super-VHS (S-VHS).

Video Memory

Portion of a computer's memory where data regarding the screen display (or the ***bitmap***) is stored. Each ***pixel*** of the display is described by at least one ***bit*** of data, increased ***color depth*** requiring more bits per pixel. See ***Color Depth***.

Video Mode

In computing, one of several preset ***resolution***s and ***color depth***s of a computer monitor. For example, one particular video mode would be 640×480 ***pixel***s at a color depth of eight bits per pixel. Depending on the particular ***video adapter*** installed, different setups may be required when moving graphics files from computer to computer. See ***Resolution*** and ***Color Depth***.

Video Monitor

An alternate term for a computer ***video display terminal***. See ***Video Display Terminal (VDT)***.

Video-on-Demand

One of the proposed features of ***interactive television*** that will allow subscribers to view a particular program or movie whenever they like, rather than at set start times. See ***Interactive Television***.

Videophony

A service (or the hardware used thereby) by which audio and video are transmitted over telephone lines, allowing two (or more) callers to not only hear but also see each other.

Video Player

See ***Videodisc Player***.

Video Random-Access Memory (VRAM)

In computing, the ***random-access memory (RAM)*** available in a ***video adapter***, accessed by both the ***central processing unit*** and the graphics processor. This simultaneous access to VRAM results in a faster screen display and redraw.

Video Scanning

A means of electronically capturing an image by utilizing a device that records an image as ***analog data*** (essentially a video signal), which is then converted to ***digital*** form for further image processing.

Video Splitter

A device used to send a single video signal to more than one destination.

Video Switcher

See ***Switcher***.

Video System Control Architecture (VISCA)

In video production, a platform-independent ***video control*** system developed by Sony that allows up to seven video devices (such as ***VCR***s) to be connected to each other in series through the ***serial port*** of a computer. The software for controlling each device is supplied in specific applications that support the VISCA standard.

Videotape Recorder (VTR)

An alternate term for a ***videocassette recorder (VCR)***, especially one that records sound and video directly from a video camera and microphone. See ***Videocassette Recorder (VCR)***. Some times spelled as three words, *video tape recorder*.

Videotex

In telecommunications, a system used to transmit text and graphics between video terminals (usually from a centralized system) by way of conventional telephone lines. It is sort of an advanced ***teletext*** system, used for such commercial transactions as obtaining travel information, placing orders, making reservations, etc. Also known as ***viewdata***.

Video Toaster

One of the first digital video production systems, created by Newtek for the Amiga computer platform, including a character generator, a special effects generator, four video input switchers, and allowed for computer-based video production.

Viditel

A Dutch information service, similar to ***teletext***, accessed by subscribers via a computer ***modem*** over telephone lines. The Viditel system displays many pages of text data, each page containing twenty-five 40-character lines. Viditel provides information supplied by the government on the economy, legislation, etc., as well as product and service information supplied by companies and individuals.

Vidiwall

A type of video display comprising several rows of television screens stacked on top of each other, displaying a single large image, each screen displaying a portion of the larger image.

View Camera

In photography, a camera with a picture size of 4×5 in. or greater, usually used to describe a graphic arts *process camera*. See *Process Camera*.

Viewdata

Alternate term for *Videotex*. See *Videotex*.

Viewfile

Alternate term for *low-resolution file* or *coarse data file*. See *Coarse Data File*.

Viewing Direction

In *three-dimensional* graphics, the orientation of an object with respect to the window in which it is viewed.

Vignette

An illustration in which the background color gradually decreases in strength (but not *hue*) as it gets closer to the edges of the image, until it gradually segues into the color of the paper. A vignette should not be confused with a *degradé*, in which both the hue *and* the strength of the background color gradually fade out.

Vinyl

Chemically speaking, any organic compound containing a vinyl group, the univalent C_3H_3, derived from ethylene. The term *vinyl* also popularly refers to any *resin* produced by the *polymerization* of compounds containing a vinyl group.

Vinyl Acrylic Latices

Synthetic latexes used as *binders* in the *coating* of high-quality coated papers. Synthetic binders, which help the coating *pigment* adhere to the paper fibers, are often used in place of more popular organic binders as they provide high *gloss*, increased *ink holdout*, and increased strength and endurance for such post-printing operations as folding. (See *Binder* and *Coating*.)

Vinyl Plastic

A plastic, such as *polyvinyl chloride*, produced from *resin*s created from *vinyl* monomers.

Violet

The *color* characteristic of light possessing a wavelength between 400 and 450 *nanometer*s, located at the end of the *visible spectrum*, between *blue* and *ultraviolet*. Violet is the complementary—or opposite—color to *yellow*.

Violet is often confused with *purple*.

VIP

Abbreviation for *Vector Image Processor*.

Virgin Fabric

In *screen printing*, a screen fabric that has not yet been used for printing.

Virgin Fiber

Fibrous paper source used for the first time, in contrast to *recovered fiber* used in *recycled paper*.

Virgule

Alternate term for a *slash*. See *Slash*.

Virtual

Generally speaking, descriptive of computer software that is designed to imitate a piece of hardware. For example, *virtual memory* uses software to access part of the *hard disk* and use it as *random-access memory*. In terms of *virtual reality*, software (and connected hardware) is used to simulate a particular environment. Virtual has come to mean anything that is not real, but is simulating or representing somthing that is real.

Virtual Circuit

In networking and telecommunications, a temporary communications circuit that appears to be a *dedicated* circuit, but that disappears once a call or transmission is ended.

Virtual Device

In computing, an idealized nonexistent device that supports features common to a host of real devices. Graphics applications that are *device-independent* generate commands designed to drive a virtual device, these commands then being converted by a specific *device driver* to commands that drive a real device.

Virtual Drive

Alternate term for *RAM-drive*. See *RAM-Drive*.

Virtual-86 Mode

A mode found in Intel 80386 and later *microprocessors* that allows the computer to emulate several different PC environments simultaneously.

Virtual Memory

In computing, a means of extending the amount of *random-access memory (RAM)* a computer has. In essence, virtual memory uses part of the *hard drive* to supplement the RAM. What tends to happen, however, is that when a program (or more than one program) is loaded into RAM, it is divided into small segments called *page*s and the system loads as many of these pages as will fit in the actual memory. It will then save the rest to the hard disk (in a location known as *external page storage*). When a command or other data is called for that is not in RAM, the computer will swap an unused "page" in RAM with the one from the hard disk that is needed at the moment. Although virtual memory can be a useful alternative to installing more memory, it tends to be slow and is not always compatible with many applications.

Virtual Page

In page layout, the area of a page that will be printed.

Virtual Reality (VR)

A computer-simulated environment (known as a *virtual space*) that provides users with the impression of actually being in a particular place or doing a particular thing. There are several levels of virtual reality:

Desktop. At the desktop level, a two-dimensional representation of a three-dimensional scene is displayed on the computer screen. This is basically the level at which many computer games—such as *Myst*, for example—exist.

Partial Immersion. At the level of *partial immersion*, an additional degree of "you-are-there"-ness is imparted, typically by means of special 3D glasses, a mouse, or a *data glove*, allowing displayed objects to be "picked up" and moved about.

Full Immersion. In *full immersion*, the complete experience is simulated by means of a *head-mounted display*, a *data glove*, and a *data suit*. All of these items contain electronic sensors that measure the wearer's movements and relay them to the central computer, which then alters the display (contained in stereoscopic screens within the head-mounted display helmet) accordingly.

Environmental Immersion. In *environmental immersion*, the user is placed in a room whose walls bear projections of the virtual environment. By means of 3D glasses, the projected images contain depth. The room itself contains strategically placed sensors to measure the user's movements around the environment and to make changes to the display.

One particular model of virtual reality is known as the *AIP Cube*, which plots the degree of three variables (autonomy, interaction, and presence) on a three-axis coordinate system. See *AIP Cube*.

Virtual Space

In *virtual reality*, a computer-simulated environment. See *Virtual Reality*.

Virtual Storage

See *Virtual Memory*.

Virtual Telecommunications Access Method (VTAM)

In networking and telecommunications, software developed for IBM's *MVS* or *VM* operating system that controls data communications in the *Systems Network Architecture* environment.

Virus

A computer program created and disseminated with malicious intent. Essentially, a computer virus acts like its human analogue; it sneaks into an "infected" disk or *Email* transmission and is transferred surreptitiously to a hard drive. These programs usually contain code that instructs the host system to replicate them in a certain place, where they then execute other, more damaging instructions, such as erasing a disk. Viruses cannot infect a system simply by downloading a file; they need to reside in executable programs before they can do their damage. Several software developers sell antivirus programs that scan a system for virus-like activity.

VISCA

Abbreviation for *video system control architecture*. See *Video System Control Architecture (VISCA)*.

Viscometer

A device that is utilized to measure a fluid's *viscosity*. See *Viscosity*. In Great Britain, a viscometer is called a *viscosimeter*.

Viscosimeter

See *Viscometer*.

Viscosity

The property of a fluid, such as a printing ink, that describes the degree of its resistance to flow, or its ability to adhere to a surface. A fluid that is highly viscous (such as molasses) is sticky and glutinous, and does not flow easily. A fluid that is not very viscous, or "inviscid," (such as water or alcohol) flows freely. In ink terminology, viscosity refers to the extent to which ink will resist flowing. The viscosity of an ink will depend on the printing process it is designed for, and the nature of the *substrate* to which it will adhere. An ink's viscosity is a component of its *body*. The viscosity of a particular ink can vary according to the stresses to which it is subjected. (See *Thixotropy*.)

Viscosity is measured in a metric unit called a poise, which is equal to the viscosity of a fluid in which one dyne per square centimeter is required to maintain a difference in velocity of one centimeter per second between two parallel planes in the fluid that lie in the direction of flow and are one centimeter apart.

Visette

Alternate term for a *head-mounted display*. See *Head-Mounted Display*.

Visible Spectrum

That portion of the entire *electromagnetic spectrum* visible to human eyes as light of various color. The visible spectrum occupies the region of the electromagnetic spectrum from between 400 to 780 nanometers, between *infrared* and *ultraviolet*. The whole visible spectrum, when each wavelength of light is present in equal quantities, is only discernible as white light. It is only the selective absorption and emission of some of these wavelengths by other objects and substances that cause us to see colors.

Viscoelasticity

Paper quality that describes its ability to be stretched and return to its original dimensions following the release of the stretching force. Paper can only be stretched up to a certain point before it no longer will be able to return to its original size. (See *Dimensional Stability*.)

Visual Display
Any electronic display of computer data, such as a *video display terminal*.

Visualization
See *Graphic Visualization*.

VITC
Abbreviation for *vertical interval time code*. See *Vertical Interval Time Code (VITC)*.

VL Bus
See *VESA Local Bus*.

VLSI
Abbreviation for *very-large-scale integration*. *Very-Large-Scale Integration (VLSI)*.

VM
A computer *operating system* developed by IBM for use on small *mainframe* computers.

VMS
A computer *operating system* developed by Digital Equipment Corp. for its *VAX* computers.

VO
Abbreviation for *voice over*. See *Voice Over*.

Voice-Grade Channel
A communications circuit possessing a frequency range of 300–3000 *hertz*, capable of transmitting human speech as well as *analog* or *digital* data.

Voice Input Device
A computer input device that recognizes human speech (usually a limited number of well-enunciated words) and can process it as if it were keyboarded text commands.

Voice Mail
Originally, voice mail referred to software designed to transmit voice messages over computer networks. Now, voice mail refers to any means by which voice messages can be left, such as an answering machine.

Voice Output Unit
Alternate term for an *audio response unit*. See *Audio Response Unit*.

Voice Over
In film, television, video, and multimedia production, any spoken dialogue not attributed to anyone actually in a scene, such as a narrator. In shooting scripts, voice over is abbreviated *VO*.

Voice Print
A *sample* of a voice, commonly used for security purposes.

Voice Recognition
In computing, the ability for a computer to recognize and process spoken commands.

Voice Synthesizer
A *synthesizer* used to artificially produce human voices. See *Synthesizer*.

Void
Any printing defect characterized by a small or large unprinted area, due to any number of causes. See also *Void Hickey*.

Void Hickey
A printing defect characterized by a blank, unprinted spot in a printed area, commonly caused by *lint* or other ink-repellent surface contamination from the paper adhering to the printing area of the press *blanket*, *gravure cylinder*, or other image-carrying surface. See *Hickey*.

Volatile
Tending to evaporate, or turn from a liquid to a gas rapidly, readily, and at low temperatures. See *Volatility*.

Volatile Corrosion Inhibitor
A substance possessing a low boiling point, commonly added to the surface of a paper which, when volatilized, produces a gas that inhibits corrosion of plates or press parts. Also known as a *vapor phase inhibitor*.

Volatile Memory
In computing, any computer memory that is erased when the power is shut off. *Random-access memory (RAM)* is defined as volatile memory. See also *Nonvolatile Memory*.

Volatility
A property of a liquid that describes the ease with which it will evaporate, or turn into a gas. Volatile liquids, such as many organic *solvent*s, typically have low boiling points, and readily evaporate.

Liquids or solvents with a low degree of volatility have rather high boiling points and require the addition of heat and/or pressure to evaporate. The volatility of a solvent is an important consideration in the manufacture of a printing ink *vehicle*; inks that dry via *evaporation* of the vehicle require the use of a solvent that will evaporate at room temperature, or at the temperature of the drying oven in which the printed material will be placed. Solvents used in inks that dry by other methods may require less volatile solvents. (See *Vehicle*.)

Volcanoes

A printing defect of **gravure** printing caused by a process called **cratering**. See **Cratering**.

Volume

In mathematics, chemistry, and physics, the amount of space occupied by a three-dimensional object, commonly calculated as the length times the width times the height. Volume thus refers to the physical size of something.

In audio and video, the term *volume* refers to the intensity or loudness of an audio signal or a sound.

The term *volume* also refers to a unit of computer storage, usually referring to a single entire disk. In some cases, a volume can be a subdivided portion of a disk.

Lastly, volume refers to a printed and bound book, usually one of a series, but also a stand-alone entity. A set of encyclopedias. for example, is comprised of volumes.

Volume Element

See **Voxel**.

Volume Label

In computing, the name assigned to a specific disk, usually determined by the user.

Volume Pixel

See **Voxel**.

Volume Rendering

In **three-dimensional graphics**, an image-creation technique that allows the interiors of solid objects to be rendered. This may include the interiors of human bones or tissues (as in medical imaging), or the interiors of machine parts.

Volume Table of Contents (VTOC)

In computing, a **control block** on a disk that contains information as to what data the disk contains and where it is located.

Vortex

In typography, the part of a letter or other character where two stems meet at the bottom of the character, as in the points of a capital letter "W." See **Letter Elements**.

Voxel

In three-dimensional rendering, a three-dimensional **pixel**, or a pixel that has not only height and width, but also depth. The term *voxel* itself is a contraction of the term **volume element** or **volume pixel**.

VPI

Abbreviation of **vapor phase inhibitor**, an alternate term for **volatile corrosion inhibitor**. See **Volatile Corrosion Inhibitor**.

VRAM

Abbreviation for **video random-access memory**. See **Video Random-Access Memory (VRAM)**.

VT100

In computing, a type of **asynchronous** terminal manufactured by Digital Equipment Corp.

The VT100 uses specific control codes for display management, and is widely used in **mainframe**s. As a result, many **terminal emulation** programs and communications packages emulate the VT100 so as to facilitate communications between systems.

VTAM

See **Virtual Telecommunications Access Method**.

VTOC

See **Volume Table of Contents (VTOC)**.

VTR

Abbreviation for **videotape recorder**. See **Videotape Recorder (VTR)**.

 **W, w**
The twenty-third letter of the English alphabet, which was created as a separate letter in the 11th century AD to distinguish two *U*s from a *U* and a *V* (hence the name of the letter, "double-u"). The sound currently represented by the *W* was originally represented by the North Semitic letter *waw* and the Greek letters *digamma* and *upsilon*. There was no *W* in Latin.

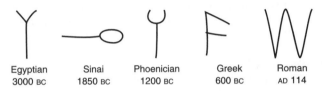

Egyptian	Sinai	Phoenician	Greek	Roman
3000 BC	1850 BC	1200 BC	600 BC	AD 114

The evolution of the letter W.

Waffling

Printing and paper defect caused by the mechanical stress of thick offset printing ink and the *blanket* pulling on a paper surface. As a paper is peeled from the blanket in offset printing, the force of the ink stretches heavily printed areas past their ability to retain their original dimensions. (See *Dimensional Stability* and *Viscoelasticity*.) Also called "embossing," waffling is characterized by embossed bands in heavily printed areas, where the pull of the ink in these regions has stretched the paper excessively, causing it to curl in these regions. Using paper that has high strength in its *cross-grain direction* or using a higher *basis weight* paper are ways of avoiding waffling.

Waffling is rarely a problem in web offset printing. Waffling that occurs toward the rear edge of the paper is called *back-edge curl* or *tail-end hook*. (See *Back-Edge Curl*.)

WAIS

Acronym for *wide area information service*. See *Wide Area Information Service (WAIS)*.

Wait State

In computing, a computer clock cycle in which no instructions are executed. Wait states occur when the processor is waiting for data to be retrieved from memory. New memory chips are resulting in *zero-wait-state computer*s that, as their name implies, run without wait states.

Walking Copy

In page makeup, text that flows from page to page, rather than remaining confined to a single page. Also known as *automatic text flow*. Almost all page assembly programs integrate this feature.

Walk-Off

In *offset lithography*, the deterioration of the image area of a plate during printing, resulting in a loss of print density in the affected area(s) of the press sheets.

WAN

Abbreviation for *wire area network*. See *Wide Area Network (WAN)*.

W & F

Abbreviation for *work-and-flop*, a means of printing more commonly known as *work-and-tumble*. See *Work-and-Tumble*.

Warm Boot

To restart a computer while it is already on, often to allow changed preferences, system extensions, installed programs, or other changes to load into the computer's memory. On the *Macintosh* a warm boot is performed using the Restart command. On a Windows device, a variety of keyboard key combinations (such as *Ctrl-Alt-Del*) will restart the computer. Typically, a warm boot, unlike a *cold boot*, bypasses self-testing and diagnostic routines performed when the system is first powered on.

Warm Colors

A range of *color*s—red, yellow, and orange—that produce a psychological impression of warmth, as opposed to *cool colors* (green, blue, and violet). Any printed product or other color reproduction will instill feelings of warmth if the *color balance* as a whole imparts a reddish tone. See also *Cool Colors*.

Warp

Lengthwise threads in a woven fabric, and typically the fabric's direction of greater strength. See also *Weft*.

Warp is also a term for the direction in which an offset press *blanket* has the greatest strength, which should ideally be in the direction of its length, or around-the-cylinder direction. An offset press blanket has been prestretched during manufacture to compensate for any stretching that may occur when it is mounted around the *blanket cylinder*. A blanket with greater strength across its width will become baggy on press, and cause *slurring* of printed images. The direction of least strength is called its *weft*. See *Blanket*.

In video production, the term *warp* refers to a *digital video effect* used as a *transition* between scenes in which the incoming image is rotated and enlarged to cover the outgoing image. Alternately, the outgoing image may be rotated and reduced to reveal the incoming image.

In computing, *Warp* refers to version 3.0 of the *OS/2* operating system. See *OS/2 Warp*.

Warping

In *binding and finishing*, a defect of *binder's board*s characterized by edges that have expanded to a greater degree than the center, resulting in wavy edges or similar structural defects. Usually caused by moisture or stress.

In graphics, *warping* refers to the transformation of an image in such a way that the size of one dimension (such as height) is altered to a different extent than the other dimension (such as width). The result is an image that is distorted.

Wash Deinking

A method of removing ink and making *recovered fiber*s suitable for the production of *recycled paper*. See *Deinking*.

Washout Ink

A type of water-washable ink used for printing on textiles and fabrics that is easily washed out.

Washup

In printing, the cleaning up of ink rollers, plates, cylinders, or other image-carrying surfaces, and perhaps the ink fountain itself, often performed at the completion of a job. Automatic washup systems are now in use.

Waste

In typography, a quantity of type that is set but that is ultimately not used.

In printing, *waste* is characterized by sheets of paper (or other substrate) used to set up the press before the print run proper begins.

Watch

In computing, especially by means of the *Macintosh operating system*, an icon that replaces the *pointer* when the computer is performing a function and cannot receive new input. In the *Windows* environment, a similar icon is the *hourglass*.

Water Ball Roller

A type of roller located in the *water pan* of an offset press's *dampening system*.

Watercolor Ink

Alternate term for *water-soluble ink*. See *Water-Soluble Ink*.

Watercolor Paper

A type of rough-textured, *hard-sized* paper designed and used for watercolor painting.

Water Drop

A defect of *offset lithography* characterized by *dampening solution* dripping onto the substrate, caused by too much dampening solution being fed to the plate. Water drops can cause blemishes on printed sheets or, in *web printing*, a *web break*.

Water Finish

A glossy paper *finish* produced by moistening the formed paper web before running it through the *calender* rollers.

Water Fountain

Alternate term for *water pan* or *fountain pan*, the metal trough on an offset lithographic press in which the *fountain solution* is kept. See *Water Pan* and *Dampening System*.

Water Immersion Test

A test to determine a paperboard's water resistance or degree of *sizing* in which a paperboard sample is weighed, then immersed in water for a set period of time, at which point it is removed, blotted dry, and weighed again. Its gain in weight is its water immersion number and is a gauge of the adequacy of its sizing.

Water in Ink

In *offset lithography*, a press condition characterized by too much *dampening solution* being fed to the plate, resulting in extensive *emulsification* of the ink, causing it to break down.

Waterleaf

A type of *unsized* paper used for paper towels, tissues, and blotting papers. The lack of *internal sizing*, a material added to most paper *pulp* to impart water resistance, gives waterleaf papers the ability to absorb water or other fluids readily and instantly. (See *Sizing*.)

Waterless Ink

A variety of ink formulated for use in *waterless lithography*, a type of offset lithography that uses silicone rubber (or other silicone compounds) in nonimage areas of the plate to repel ink, thus eliminating the need for a dampening system as in traditional offset lithography. Despite the advantages of waterless printing, a disadvantage is *toning* of the nonimage areas of the plate, typically due to heat effects; for example, a 10°F rise in ink temperature can cause toning. Waterless inks are designed to resist temperature fluctuations. Temperature-controlled ink rollers are also used on waterless presses to prevent such problems. Waterless inks are also similar in composition to *letterset ink*s. (See also *Letterset Ink*.)

Waterless Lithography

A variety of *offset lithography* that eliminates the need for a *dampening system* by utilizing water-repellent *silicone* rubber plates.

Waterless lithography is the descendant of an ill-fated printing process developed by 3M in the 1960s called *driography*, a means of printing from dry lithographic plates. Plate sensitivity and ink performance difficulties (most of which are no longer problems thanks to modern temperature-control systems) doomed the process and it never caught on. In 1977, Japan's Toray Industries introduced a presensitized waterless offset plate that, after several refinements, became commercially viable.

The waterless lithographic plate comprises an aluminum base, covered with a primer layer, a photosensitive *photopolymer* layer, a silicone rubber layer, and a final protective layer of transparent film. Waterless plates can either be *positive-working* or *negative-working*. During platemaking (utilizing a positive-working plate), a film positive is brought into contact with the plate and exposed to ultraviolet light, which fuses the silicone to the photopolymer in the nonimage areas. During developing, the plastic

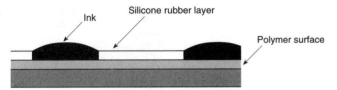

A waterless lithographic printing plate.

protective layer is removed and the silicone layer can be washed away from the plate in the image areas, revealing the photopolymer layer. In a negative-working waterless plate, the plate is exposed to a film negative. However, the plates are formulated such that the exposure to ultraviolet light weakens the bond between the silicone and photopolymer layers in the image areas. A post-exposure treatment (following removal of the protective film) strengthens the bond between the two layers in the unexposed nonimage areas, and the silicone can then be washed off the plate in the image areas. Positive-working plates can achieve screen resolutions of up to 800 lines per inch, while negative-working plates can achieve up to 300 lines per inch.

One of the problems with waterless lithography is the necessity to carefully control the temperature on press; a 10°F rise in ink temperature can result in *toning*, or the appearance of ink in nonimage areas of the plate. Temperature on waterless lithographic presses is commonly controlled in one of two ways: a special chilled ink *oscillator* roller to which cooled water is pumped from a water chilling device attached to the press, and a less effective configuration that pumps the cooled water to the *plate cylinder*. (A water heating device can be substituted in these config-

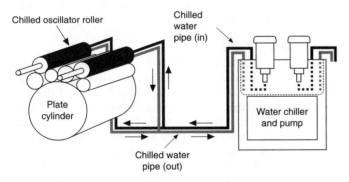

Roller cooling system for waterless lithography.

urations, depending on the direction the temperature needs to go.) The inks themselves used in the process are specially formulated to resist changes in temperature and as a result tend to be more expensive than traditional offset inks.

A variety of press configurations exist to accommodate waterless lithography; conventional offset presses can be retrofitted to include the temperature control system necessary, and specifically manufactured waterless lithographic presses can also come with a dampening system, both systems providing the printer with the option to print wet or dry.

Although waterless lithography (also known as *waterless printing* and *waterless offset*) boasts superior print quality, faster makeready, and the environmental benefits of not requiring an alcohol-based dampening solution, the expense of setting up the process, the strict temperature tolerances required, ink-viscosity problems, and toning have made many printers wary of the process. However, the process is still in its infancy and new technological developments are working to overcome its shortcomings.

Watermark

A design stamped in wet paper *pulp* as it is forming in a papermaking machine. Watermarks are created by running the wet paper *web* under a *dandy roll*, which is a wire-covered cylinder. The design to be pressed into the paper is woven in wire and attached to the wire cover of the dandy roll, decreasing the paper's opacity in the image area of the design, which becomes visible when the dried paper is held up to the light.

The idea of stamping a watermark in paper dates from about the year 1270, when an Italian papermaker created a wire mold of a cross inscribed in a circle, attached it to his papermaking mold, and dipped it into the vat of diluted pulp. The sheet of paper that formed was thinner along the wire than elsewhere, creating a transparent design. This technique of "hand-making" watermarks continued fundamentally unchanged until the 19th century. Not much outside attention was paid to watermarks until the 18th century, but papermakers appear to have indulged their whimsy over the centuries, as the variety of watermark designs that have been discovered covers every conceivable object: many types of animals, human forms and specific body parts, all sorts of flowers, ships, boats, ceramic containers, tools, instruments, and thousands of other images, many of which defy description. No one is quite sure what watermarks were supposed to mean, if anything. Since the 19th century, however, nearly all watermarks have simply been the papermaker's trademark. In the mid-1800s, William Henry Smith created light-and-shade watermarks, which used a wire screen made from a wax mold to impart to the watermark varying degrees of lightness and density in the manner of a photograph. This technique never caught on the United States, but it has found use in Europe in the printing of paper currency, primarily as a deterrent to counterfeiting. In 1826 in England, as papermaking machines began to proliferate, John Marshall, a maker of watermark molds, invented the dandy roll as a means of imprinting watermarks in machine-produced paper, a technique that is still used today. However, since dandy roll watermarks are pressed onto moist pulp from above, machine-made watermarks are not as clear and brilliant as watermarks in hand-made paper, where the furnish forms directly on top of the watermark mold.

Water Pan

A metal trough at the end of the *dampening system* on a printing press used in *offset lithography* in which the *fountain solution* is kept. In *intermittent-flow dampening systems*, a *fountain pan roller* picks up the fountain solution from the water pan and transfers it to a *ductor roller* that alternately contacts the fountain pan roller and an *oscillator*. In *continuous-flow dampening systems*, a rotating *metering roller* transfers the fountain solution from the water pan directly and continuously to a *transfer roller*. *Water stops* can be added to the water pan, which squeeze set amounts of fountain solution from the fountain pan roller, allowing greater control over the amount of dampening solution transferred to the plate. (See *Dampening System*.) The water pan is also called the *fountain pan*, the *water fountain*, or, generically, the *fountain*.

Waterproof Paper

Any of a wide varieties of paper that have been *hard-sized* and *coated* so as to impart high degrees of *water resistance*.

Water Resistance

The resistance of a paper to the penetration of water. See *Paper and Papermaking: Paper Properties*

Water Slide-Off Decal

Alternate term for *simplex decal*. See *Simplex Decal*.

Water-Slide Transfer

Alternate term for *simplex decal*. See *Simplex Decal*.

Water-Soluble Gum Vehicle

A type of ink *vehicle*—the fluid carrier of the ink *pigment*—that dries by *evaporation* and absorption of the vehicle. Also known as "watercolor" inks, these are produced by dissolving *gum arabic* in water, glycerine, or other *solvent*. When the watercolor ink is deposited on the *substrate*, absorption and evaporation remove the solvent, leaving the gum and pigment behind. Watercolor inks are not widely used, except for novelty applications. (See *Vehicle*.)

Water-Soluble Ink

A type of printing ink made from *pigments* that are readily dissolved in water, used in *screen printing*, *flexography*, and *gravure*. Also known as *watercolor inks*.

Water Stops

A set of plastic or metal tabs, squeegees, or rollers added to the *dampening system* of a printing press used in *offset*

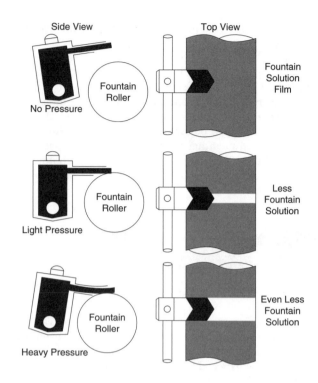

Water stops.

lithography. The water stops contact the *fountain pan roller* (the dampening roller that rides in the *water pan*, the trough containing the *fountain solution*) and squeeze or scrape a quantity of the fountain solution film from the surface of the roller. The pressure with which each stop contacts the roller can be adjusted, allowing variations in the amount of fountain solution sent through the dampening system, depending on which portions of the printing plate require more or less of the solution. (See *Dampening System*.)

Water-Washable Ink

A type of printing ink designed primarily for the *letterpress* printing of *kraft* paper and paperboard, as for packaging. The ink *vehicle* consists of a glycol solvent in which is dissolved a rosin soap. The vehicle sets quickly to become water-resistant, a useful trait for ink printed on packaging. The wet ink itself can be washed away easily with water, facilitating press cleanup.

Water Vapor Transmission Rate

A measure of paper or paperboard used for packaging that determines its efficacy as a moisture barrier. The purpose of many types of packaging materials is to prevent the penetration of moisture, ensuring that the material contained in the packaging is not damaged. The water vapor transmission rate is the weight of the water that permeates from one side of a 1-m^2 area of paperboard to the other in a one-day period. Variations in temperature and *relative humidity* can provide an accurate moisture-transmission profile for a particular paperboard. Various additional materials can be added to a packaging paper or paperboard—such as wax, aluminum foil, plastic, etc.—to increase its effectiveness as a barrier against moisture.

WATS

Abbreviation for *Wide Area Telephone Service*. See *Wide Area Telephone Service (WATS)*.

Waveform

The visual representation of a wave (such as an electrical or video signal), making visible the frequency, wavelength, and amplitude. See *Waveform Monitor*.

Waveform Monitor

A device used to evaluate the characteristics of a video signal by representing the video signal as a *waveform* on a *vector display* monitor. In this way, the intensity of the signal (the *video gain*) and the *synchronization* pulses can be checked. A *time-base corrector* is used to adjust the sync pulses while a *vectorscope* is used to evaluate the color components of the video signal.

Waviness

A surface property of a *gravure cylinder* that describes the large-scale uniformity of the copper or chrome plating. The plating and polishing of the copper surface of the gravure cylinder yield a certain degree of large peaks and valleys that need to be minimized as much as possible. A high degree of waviness on the surface of the copper plating results in ink transfer in nonimage areas, due to incomplete ink removal by the *doctor blade*. Although the gravure cylinder's copper surface is covered with a layer of chrome after engraving, the combination of the thinness of the chrome layer and the physical principle of *epitaxy* (or the tendency for the electroplated chrome to follow the contours of the copper to which it is plated exactly) allow for no correction or smoothing out of irregularities in the copper surface.

Copper and chrome waviness is measured by moving a diamond across the surface and measuring the peaks and valleys. A related property is *roughness*, which is similar to waviness but on a smaller scale. (See also *Roughness*.)

Wavy Edges

A paper defect characterized by warpage and distortion of its edges, caused by a loss of *dimensional stability* due to increased *moisture content* after exposure of paper edges to higher *relative humidity*, or from exposure to warmer

Wavy-edged paper (left) and tight-edged paper (right).

air. The distortion is greater in the paper's *cross-grain direction* and causes *misregister* when printing multicolor work. See also *Tight Edges* and *Cockling*. (See *Moisture Content* and *Dimensional Stability*.)

Wax Coater

A device used in the days of mechanical *pasteup* that applied a thin layer of adhesive wax to the back of copy and *line art* for use in pasting it to a *mechanical* board.

Waxer

An alternate term for a *wax coater*. See *Wax Coater*.

Wax Test

See *Dennison Wax Test*.

Wayzgoose

An entertainment for journeymen printers *by* journeymen printers. The word *wayz* means a "bundle of straw," and *wayzgoose* a "stubble goose," the crowning dish of the entertainment. The term dates to the early 17th century as a printer's festival held about the time of the feast of St. Bartholomew in August.

Weak Blanket

An alternate term for *smashed blanket*. See *Smashed Blanket*.

Weak Plate

Any type of printing plate on which all or part of the image area does not print clearly or distinctly.

Weather-Ometer

A device utilized to evaluate a paper or ink's ability to retain its properties when exposed to inclement weather, basically consisting of a *Fade-Ometer*'s *lightfastness*-measuring equipment supplemented with a water jet that intermittently sprays the test sample with water, to simulate the effects of weather. (See also *Fade-Ometer*.)

Web

Term for a continuous *roll* of paper that forms on a papermaking machine, or the paper roll that is used uncut in *web offset lithography*. Paper webs can either be cut into sheets at the papermill, or sent to printers in roll form.

A *web* also refers to any roll of *substrate*—be it paper, paperboard, or a plastic film—used in webfed *gravure* and *flexography*.

In *Internet* terminology, the term *Web* is a shorthand term for the *World Wide Web*. See *World Wide Web (WWW)*.

Web Break

The breaking of a paper web when it is on-press, which can occur at any point from start to finish and which is caused by many factors. A web break can either be paper-related (caused by a web that unwinds into the machine with uneven tension due to varying thickness across the width of the roll, a poorly made splice that caused the portion of the roll beyond the splice to feed into the machine differently than the portion before the splice, or by various cuts, tears, and holes in the web, such as *edge tear*s, *slime spot*s, *hair cut*s, etc.) or press-related (for example, a drying oven that is too hot can make the paper brittle, etc.). If a web break occurs at the same spot each time, it's likely that the press is the culprit, not the paper. The cause of web breaks may not even be able to be determined. For example, in a Swedish study of 250,000 newsprint rolls, it was found that web defects accounted for 9.1% of web breaks, roll defects accounted for 18.1%, transportation mishandling accounted for 4.6%, the press accounted for 31.7%, and the causes of the remaining 36.5% of web breaks could not determined.

Web Break Detector

In *web printing*, an auxiliary device that automatically detects the site of a *web break* and immediately shuts down the press.

Web Cleaner

In *web printing*, a vacuum-cleaner-like device located on the first *printing unit* and used to suck up foreign particles that might damage and/or contaminate the plate and blanket.

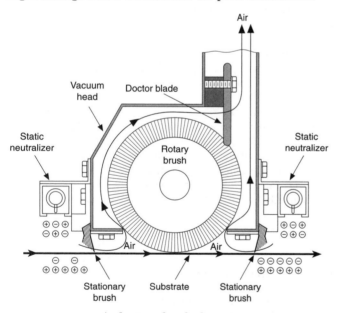

A sheet and web cleaner.

Courtesy Louis P. Batson Co.

Web Direction

The direction parallel to the direction of travel of a roll of paper. Also called *machine direction*.

Webfed

Descriptive of any printing press that prints on continuous rolls of paper, rather than individual sheets. See also *sheetfed*. Also spelled with a hyphen, *web-fed*.

Web Lead

In *web printing*, the length of paper that is in the press when the press is threaded and prepared to run.

Web Lead Rollers

In *web offset lithography*, term for an *idler roller*, especially one located between the printing units on a *blanket-to-blanket* press. Web lead rollers are used to support the paper web between printing units and to prevent *doubling* caused by web bounce.

Web Offset Lithography

Unlike sheetfed *offset lithography*, web offset lithography prints at high speeds on large rolls—or *web*s—of paper, often on both sides of the paper simultaneously, using in-line printing units and in-line finishing systems. Web presses are bulky and expensive, but they are widely used for many large-volume applications, most notably newspapers. The basic principle of web offset lithography is the same as that for the sheetfed variety. This article will concern itself primarily with the specific differences of web printing versus sheetfed printing. For a general discussion of offset lithography, see *Lithography* and *Offset Lithography*.

EVOLUTION OF WEB PRINTING

In the late 1700s, Alois Senefelder had invented the concept of lithography, and lithographic stone printing began in earnest not long afterward. Advancements such as steam-powered presses and later the rotary press enhanced the process. In the 1850s, the newspaper industry was booming. A need arose for high-speed printing, and in 1856 the first *perfecting press* was invented, which allowed for the simultaneous printing on both sides of the paper. A second distinguishing feature of this press was that it printed on a continuous roll of paper. And so was born web printing. Subsequent *finishing* devices—such as *folder*s—increased the efficiency of the process. Still lithography languished as primarily an artistic medium rather than a commercially viable means of printing. (Most presses were still *letterpress* presses.) In the early 20th century, the accidental discovery that a rubber blanket transferred images to paper more efficiently and with greater quality than lithographic stones (the "offset" in offset lithography) gave the printing process the impetus it needed for wide commercial acceptance.

Technical problems hampered the development of offset lithography until the 1940s, when lithographic platemaking (replacing litho stones with metal plates) was finally perfected. Taking advantage of *heatset ink*s and drying systems originally developed for letterpress presses, web offset lithography by the 1960s was expanding rapidly. The improvement of inks, blankets, plates, and other aspects of the process boosted growth tremendously. In the 1960s, many newspapers began switching from letterpress to lithographic presses, and more and more books began bring printed on webfed lithographic presses. The quality and popularity of web offset lithography has continued

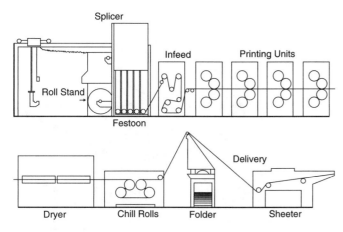

A four-unit heatset web offset printing press.

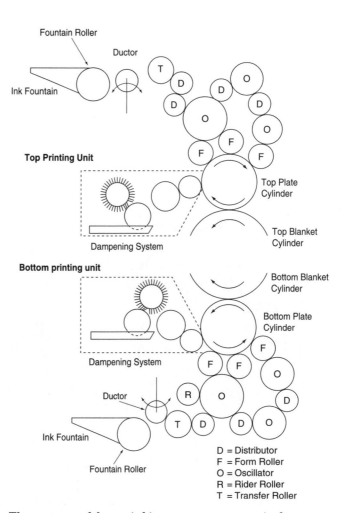

The upper and lower inking systems on a typical commercial web offset press.

unabated, and today web presses are used for everything from newspapers to periodicals to books to business forms. And offset lithography in general is the most widely used printing process in the world today.

INKING SYSTEM

The *inking system* primarily functions to transfer ink from the *ink fountain* to the printing plate, to add enough force to break the thick, viscous ink down into a thinner, more workable ink film (see *Thixotropy*), and to prevent the existence of faint reproductions of the printing image on the ink rollers (see *Mechanical Ghosting*). Offset inking systems can comprise as many as ten (or perhaps more) different rollers, which include *ductor roller*s, *oscillator*s, *distributor*s or *vibrator*s (collectively called *intermediate rollers*), and *form roller*s. The entire series of rollers is called the *roller train*. The amount of ink that is sent to the rest of the press can be controlled either by adjusting the ink fountain's *fountain keys*, which vary the amount of ink transferred to the *fountain roller*—the roller that contacts the first roller in the train—or by adjusting the *dwell*—the amount of time that the first ductor roller contacts the fountain roller. Alternately, some newspaper presses utilize an eccentric roller or cam located beneath the fountain blade. This device adjusts the opening between the fountain blade and the fountain roller, which can be opened or closed by a lever.

Another form of ink-film control device is borrowed from *flexography*: the *anilox roller*, a metal roller covered with very small pits or depressions that transfer controlled, metered amounts of ink to the remainder of the roller train. An attached *doctor blade* is used to scrape excess ink from the surface of the anilox roller. The anilox system is especially useful for newspaper printing, which requires highly fluid inks. The amount of ink being sent toward the plate can be more easily metered using the anilox setup. It also eliminates the need for fountain keys, or other such ink-flow control mechanisms.

The ductor roller alternately contacts the fountain roller and the first roller in the train. Controlling the speed

at which the ductor moves back and forth, coupled with the ratios of the sizes and rotations of the other rollers, helps unify the ink flow to the plate.

The ductor roller is an intermittent inking roller. Some press configurations utilize continuous-feed systems, employing bristle-covered rollers, metal rollers, or rollers with relief patterns on them, allowing only a predetermined surface area of a roller to transfer ink. However, these alternate systems are often inadequate for providing the lateral ink-flow control that may be desired and/or required. A solution has been devised in the concept of the *Aller undulating ductor roller*, a segmented ductor roller in which each segment is mounted slightly off-center in relation to the others. During inking, some segments are picking up ink from the fountain roller, while others are transferring ink to the adjacent oscillator.

Controlling the ink film thickness, or the amount of ink that is ultimately deposited on the plate, is a function of the form rollers, which are the ones that actually contact the plate itself. Web presses can have anywhere from one to four form rollers. (See *Form Roller*.)

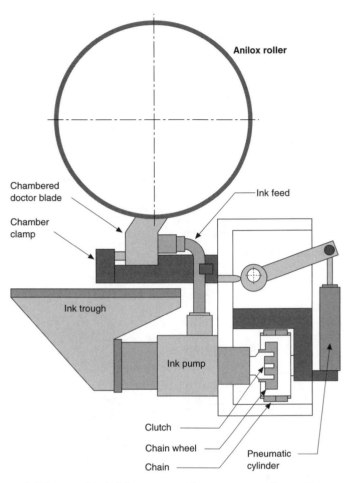

A lithographic inking system that uses an anilox roller.

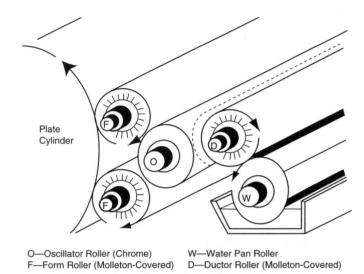

O—Oscillator Roller (Chrome)   W—Water Pan Roller
F—Form Roller (Molleton-Covered)   D—Ductor Roller (Molleton-Covered)

The conventional dampening system.

Like sheetfed offset presses, web presses also use some number of intermediate rollers between the ductor roller and the form rollers. (See *Inking System: Offset Lithography*.)

DAMPENING SYSTEM

A web offset press's *dampening solution*, commonly referred to as a *fountain solution*, can, like that for sheetfed presses, consist entirely of water, but as this is generally ineffective for long print runs, synthetic desensitizers are added to the fountain solution to maximize the ink repellency of the nonimage areas of the plate. The substances added to the fountain solution depend on the type of ink being used, but typically a fountain solution consists of water, an acid or base (depending on the desired *pH* of the solution), a gum (such as *gum arabic* to desensitize the nonimage plate regions), a *corrosion inhibitor* to prevent the solution from reacting with the metallic plate, an alcohol-based *wetting agent* to reduce the fountain solution's surface tension, a *drying stimulator* to increase the effectiveness of the ink *drier*, a fungicide to prevent the growth of mildew, fungi, and bacteria, and an *antifoaming agent* to prevent the production of foam in the dampening system. Fountain solution is usually premixed by the supplier,

requiring only the addition of water and alcohol by the printer. (See *Fountain Solution*.)

A typical dampening system closely resembles an inking system, but since water does not need to be worked the way ink does, fewer rollers are used. The dampening system includes a *water pan*, which holds the fountain solution. A *fountain pan roller* rotates in the water pan and transfers the solution to the rest of the dampening system. A *ductor roller* alternately contacts the fountain pan roller and an *oscillator roller*. The oscillator roller, like that used in the inking system, moves laterally across the press to even out the distribution of solution, then transfers the solution to the *form roller*, which then transfers the solution directly to the plate. The dampening form roller (most presses use only one, but some use two) contacts the plate before the ink form rollers, desensitizing the nonimage areas of the plate before the application of the ink. As with ink, the amount of water flowing to the plate must be carefully metered, which can be accomplished either by adjusting the rate at which the fountain pan roller turns, the length of time the ductor roller contacts the fountain pan roller, or by using *water stops*, a set of squeegees, tabs, or rollers that press against the fountain pan roller and squeeze excess water off it. The pressure of the water stops can be controlled, the highest pressure squeezing the greatest amount of water off the fountain pan roller and transferring the least amount of fountain solution through the press. As with inking rollers, the proper roller setting also needs to be made to transfer the proper amount of fountain solution to the plate.

One particular alternate dampening system device is known as a *flap roller*, or *flapper*, which is a fountain roller covered with canvas flaps that transfer the solution to the oscillator directly (eliminating the need for a ductor roller). Adjusting the rotation of the flapper regulates the amount of water flowing toward the plate. An advantage of this system is that thanks to the elimination of the ductor

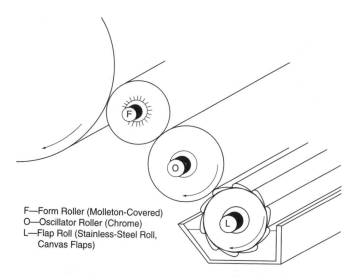

F—Form Roller (Molleton-Covered)
O—Oscillator Roller (Chrome)
L—Flap Roll (Stainless-Steel Roll,
    Canvas Flaps)

A dampening system that uses a flap ductor.

roller, ductor shock is also eliminated. A drawback, however, is that the water flow cannot be controlled laterally across the press. Another common configuration of intermittent-flow system uses a bristle-covered roller. In one such brush dampening system, a row of *flicker blades* press against a brush roller mounted in the pan; the flicker blades flexes the bristles. As the brush roller rotates, the bristles "flick" fountain solution at the adjacent oscillator (which is not in contact with the flicker roller).

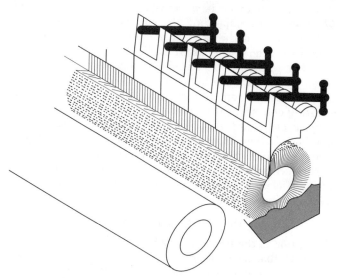

A brush dampener using flicker blades.

The dampening system described above is known as a *conventional dampening system* or an *intermittent-flow dampening system*, as the movement of the ductor roller does not allow the continuous flow of fountain solution through the press. *Continuous-flow dampening system*s, which can transfer the fountain solution either through the inking system (called an *inker-feed system*), directly to

the plate (called a *plate-feed system*), or both through the inking system and directly to the plate, do away with the ductor roller and provide, as their name indicates, a continuous flow of fountain solution. One configuration of continuous-flow system uses spray nozzles to direct jets of fountain solution onto the oscillator.

Continuous-flow systems help eliminate some of the common dampening system problems and allow instantaneous response to adjustments in the system. (See *Dampening System*.)

PRINTING UNIT

The basic printing unit of an offset press—be it sheetfed or webfed—contains three (or sometimes more) cylinders: a *plate cylinder*, to which the plate is attached, a *blanket cylinder*, to which the offset blanket is attached, and an *impression cylinder*, which carries the paper through the printing unit and provides a hard backing against which the blanket can impress an image on the paper.

The arrangement of the cylinders can vary depending on the press, so long as the proper cylinders are adjacent to each other. The plate cylinder is typically the topmost cylinder and is in contact with the inking and dampening form rollers. The plate contains a right-reading image that is inked by the inking system. As the plate cylinder rotates, it is brought into contact with the blanket cylinder beneath it. (The blanket cylinder can be backed away from the plate cylinder, to facilitate removal and adjustment of the plate.) The inked image areas of the plate transfer the image to the rubber blanket, the image now being wrong-reading. The paper (or other substrate) is carried by the feeder system to the impression cylinder, and is sent through the nip between the blanket and impression cylinders.

Unlike sheetfed presses, web presses more often than not are set up for perfecting of some kind or other. On a general perfecting press, two complete printing units (along with two complete sets of inking and dampening rollers) are placed in a line, with one unit printing one side, followed by the second unit printing the second side. Other types use a *blanket-to-blanket* printing unit, in which the blanket cylinders of two printing units run in contact, allowing for simultaneous perfecting. Another variation to the printing unit is the *common impression cylinder*, a large-diameter impression cylinder that transports the substrate from one printing unit to another, often used in multicolor printing to lay down successive colors in one press pass. (See *Press Configurations* below.)

As with the various rollers of the inking and dampening systems, proper cylinder setting and maintenance are important to ensure the proper fidelity of the printed image. Various adjustments can also be made to the cylinders, depending on the print job. An important aspect of offset printing is proper *packing*, or height adjustment, of the plate and blanket cylinders, which has important consequences in terms of print quality. (See *Packing*.) (See also *Plate Cylinder*, *Blanket Cylinder*, *Impression Cylinder*, and *Transfer Cylinder*.)

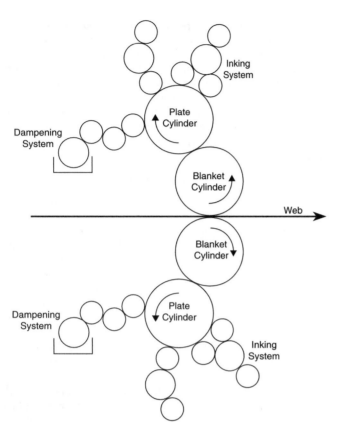

A typical blanket-to-blanket printing unit.

PLATES

The process of lithographic platemaking ensures that the image areas of a plate are *lipophilic* (or *oleophilic*) and *hydrophobic* (in other words, receptive to oil—namely, ink—and repellent to water) while the nonimage areas are *lipophobic* (or *oleophobic*) and *hydrophilic* (in other words, repellent to oil and receptive to water). These chemical principles ensure that the ink will only adhere to the image areas of the plate. On the press, the water-receptive coating on the nonimage areas must be increased, a process called *desensitization*. A gum, such as gum arabic, is typically used to accomplish this. Gum additives in the press fountain solution ensure that the plate remains desensitized over the course of the pressrun. (See *Plate: Offset Lithography*.) Before mounting, plates are inspected for scratches and other defects, and occasionally minor corrections can be made to the plate. Unwanted specks or other small, undesirable image areas can be erased, then treated with etch and gum; voids in solid image areas can be filled in by scratching the plate, then applying ink to the area. Such plate doctoring should only be performed on the most minor of defects. At this point, the degree of *packing* should be determined. (See *Packing*.) Mounting is performed according to the press manufacturer's recommendations, and the image *lay*, or position of the printed image on the paper, determined. At this point, the plate may need to be repositioned, to keep the image centered, or in register

with previously printed images on the paper. Properly formulated and applied fountain solution will more often than not obviate the need for continual plate maintenance while on press. Extended press shutdowns, however, such as overnight, should not occur while the plate is still inked. Gum that dries on the image areas causes *plate blinding*.

Plates can be subject to two primary defects: *scumming* and blinding, which are ink receptivity in nonimage areas and ink-repellency in image areas, respectively. (See *Scumming* and *Plate Blinding*.) Most plate problems are caused by improper formulation or application of fountain solution.

BLANKETS

An offset blanket is commonly made of a synthetic rubber, and the most important feature of the blanket is its *release* capability, or the ease with which it will let go of the web passing through the *impression nip*. Release is primarily a function of the smoothness of the surface of the blanket, though things like ink *tack*, impression nip *squeeze*, and the surface characteristics of the paper also play a part. Printers often have found hard blankets to provide the best release, although empirical research has not borne this out. (Problems relating to the accurate measurement of blanket hardness no doubt contribute to this lack of evidence.) A blanket's *smash resistance* (its ability to return to its normal thickness after being subjected to printing pressure) and its *durability* (its ability to withstand the force of printing pressures over time) are also of importance. Whether a blanket is a conventional or *compressible blanket* is also important. Prior to mounting, the packing requirements of the blanket should be determined. (See *Packing*.) One problem that blankets can be subject to is a *blanket smash*, or a small depression in the blanket surface, typically caused by a foreign object passing through the impression nip. Blanket smashes can cause various printing defects, so it is typical to replace the blanket with a spare, or repair the blanket before continuing with it. Any blanket that has more grievous problems, such as rips or tears, should be replaced immediately. Blankets may also experience *piling*, the accumulation of paper fibers or coating particles, which can produce printing defects such as *hickey*s. (See *Blanket*.)

INFEED AND WEB CONTROL

Just prior to the first printing unit is all the infeed equipment. Unlike sheetfed presses, web presses need to be concerned with the proper tension of the paper web throughout the press, not only to ensure image quality but also to avoid web breaks, which can bottleneck any printing operation.

Infeed Unit. The paper roll itself is mounted on the *roll stand*, commonly located in a straight line with the rest of the press. In some configurations, however, especially where space is an issue, the roll stand can be located to one side of the press and the web is turned at a right angle into the press. Some roll stands are located below the press on a separate level of the building housing the pressroom. The most basic roll stand configuration is a ***single-roll stand*** which, as its name indicates, holds only a single roll. (There are also multiple-roll stands—the ***double-roll stand*** being the most common—that hold more than one roll at a time and allow for the feeding of multiple webs through the press at any one time.) A roll is held securely onto the roll stand by means of a shaft passing through the hollow core of the roll.

The speed at which the roll unwinds into the press is regulated by a series of rollers located between the roll itself and the first printing unit. The most important of these rollers is the ***dancer roller*** (also called a ***floating roller***). A dancer roller is free to move up or down, or backward or forward, during the pressrun. Essentially, the dancer creates a downward path for the paper as it comes off the roll and then sends it upward again. If the amount of paper unwinding from the roll just before the dancer roller is the same as the amount of paper feeding into the press just after the dancer roller, then the dancer is kept in a "normal" position. If these two amounts of paper differ, the loop formed by the paper path will increase or decrease in size, and the dancer moves up or down, simultaneously releasing or applying a brake (which can be electromechanical, hydraulic, pneumatic, or magnetic) on the roll stand. This effectively keeps the web tension constant during infeed. A second dancer roller may also be added just before the first printing unit as a means of further controlling web tension.

If web tension during infeed were the only consideration, a roll stand and dancer roller would be the only infeed devices needed. However, the web must be flat and taut as it enters the printing unit. Consequently, additional "metering" rollers are located between the dancer and the printing unit. These rollers (two of which are driven by gears connected to the press motor) work to keep the web speed close to that of the press speed (tolerances often need to be within ±0.3% of press speed).

Web tension and drawing speed metering are important considerations, as variations in web tension throughout the press can cause ***registration*** problems, ***slurring***, ***doubling***, and other printing defects and problems as well as web breaks. Although the configuration of the infeed system accurately controls web speed and tension, it cannot compensate for variations in paper structure. Consequently, paper itself needs to be manufactured within very close tolerances.

Splicing. It is very rare that a print run will be completed just prior to the exhaustion of a paper roll. Changing rolls manually results in downtime and wastage that is always undesirable. Consequently, press infeed sections are equipped with continuous-roll feeding devices—splicers, also known as pasters—that automatically splice a fresh roll to an expiring one. The two types of splicers are the flying splicer and the zero-speed splicer.

A ***flying splicer*** splices an expiring roll to a fresh roll "on the fly," or while the press is running at full speed. A photoelectric cell detects when the diameter of a paper roll

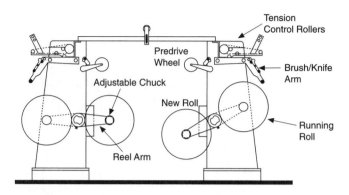

Typical two-arm flying splicer in tandem, with rolls in running position.

is as small as 8 in., and the splicing process is initiated. The pasting device is moved from a loading position to a splicing position, and the new roll is accelerated to press speed. When the amount of paper remaining on the roll reaches ¼ in., the actual splicing process begins. (Any paper left on the roll when the diameter is under ¼ in. is considered core waste and is not used.) The leading edge of the new roll (or ***roll nose***), containing an adhesive is pressed against the expiring roll under pressure, where the adhesive sets, joining the two rolls together. (Photoelectric eyes and other detectors monitor the position of the roll nose accurately). During the attaching of the roll nose to the expiring roll, it is important that pressure be applied along the entire length of the splice, otherwise a loose adhesive-coated edge may be left exposed, causing jams or other problems in the press. Beneath the pressure roller, a knife severs the expiring roll with enough of a tail to completely cover the adhesive. A ***two-arm splicer*** (which holds one roll in addition to the running roll) or a ***three-arm splicer*** (which holds two rolls in addition to the running roll) may be used. After splicing, the expired roll can be removed, and a fresh roll installed to await the next splicing sequence.

A ***zero-speed splicer*** joins two rolls while they are both stationary, but while the press is still running. As a paper roll starts expiring, a ***festoon***—or a collapsible set of rollers—expands to store a reserve of paper from the expiring roll. This allows the expiring roll to be stopped, paper being drawn only from that within the festoon. When the expiring roll is stopped, the new roll is spliced on and brought up to press speed. The paper stored in the festoon is replenished, and it is expanded to its full height. The expired roll is removed, and a fresh roll is added to await the next splicing sequence.

In some cases, a splice needs to be cut to a certain shape. The shape is dictated by the configuration of the paster, and splice patterns are not interchangeable from paster to paster. Consequently, when using a particular paster, it is important to prepare a splice template to ensure that the required shape is accurate for each splice. And, needless to say, the new roll must be spliced on perfectly straight, otherwise feeding problems and web breaks will occur.

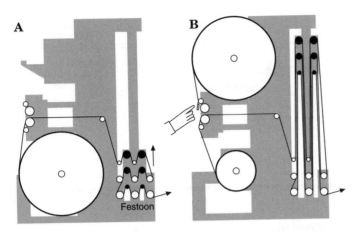

A zero-speed splicer with festoon. (A) The roll is feeding into the press and the festoon is rising. (B) The festoon has expanded to its full capacity, approximately 80 ft., a new roll is mounted, and the operator has prepared the lead edge of the new roll for the splice.

Web Tension. As was mentioned earlier, maintaining a consistent and proper web tension is important not only for reasons of image quality but also for proper mechanical operation of the press. Web jams and breaks cause undesirable downtime and paper wastage.

Throughout the press, tension is controlled by rollers at certain points, the region between these points being known as *tension span*s. It is the goal of the tension points to produce even tension throughout the spans. This is a function of several different variables.

The first is web, or surface, speed, or the speed at which the web is travelling through the press. This speed should remain constant, but the rollers used to effect this affect it in different ways. The composition of the rollers affects the amount of slippage that the web experiences (for example, rubber-covered rollers can unpredictably alter the speeds of webs passing through their nips), and the diameters of rollers and cylinders themselves (i.e., blanket packing, taping chill rolls, etc.) affect their speed of rotation and the speed they impart to the web. Surface speed is also affected by slippage in any of these rollers. The degree to which the web slips in the nips of rollers cannot always be predicted.

Another problem affecting tension is the fact that paper is not a dimensionally stable material. The elasticity of a paper causes it to stretch in one or both of its dimensions when under tension. When tension is released, the paper may return to its original dimensions, although there is often some degree of permanent stretch. What this means is that registration may be difficult if paper stretches and contracts from one printing unit to another. The *moisture content* of a paper also causes it to expand and/or contract, a particular concern in lithographic printing due to the use of a water-based fountain solution. In web printing, the use of high-temperature dryers also affects the dimensions of a paper.

When paper rolls are wound at the paper mill before shipping, a great deal of pressure is used to produce tightly wound rolls. As a result, the paper tends to "relax" when unwound into a press. This causes it to expand somewhat. When this occurs in the infeed section it may be acceptable, but if it occurs between or within printing units, it can cause registration problems. Therefore, the paper is often given a long lead-in to the printing unit during infeed (called *festooning*, an additional use of the festoon also used for splicing). This allows the paper to relax and recover as much as it needs to before entering the printing units.

Tension tends to decrease through a press, caused by, among other things, the printing units. Moisture picked up from the dampening system causes elongation and affects tension unpredictably, and blanket pull (a function of the impression pressure generated during printing) also works to increase tension. Consequently, blanket pull needs to be monitored and kept constant throughout the pressrun.

The longest tension span on a web press is between the last printing unit and the *chill roll*s, where the drying mechanism is. As a result of an unsupported span and the heat of the dryer, wrinkles can form on the web. Problems at the drying and cooling end of the press can be reduced by creating no-slip nips between the chill rolls.

DRYERS AND CHILL ROLLS

Although most newspaper printing uses *quickset ink*s and inks that dry by absorption of the *vehicle* into the substrate, modern web offset printing is still dominated by *heatset ink*s, inks that require the application of high temperatures to dry. As a result, web presses that utilize such inks need a dryer and *chill roll*s attached after the last printing section.

Dryers. Depending upon the inks used and the capacity of the dryer, the temperature to which the printed web is subjected may be as high as 500°F. And even though a single portion of the web may spend less than a second in the dryer, it will still exit with a temperature of up to 300°F. Since blanket-to-blanket presses print on both sides of the web simultaneously, such presses must utilize floating

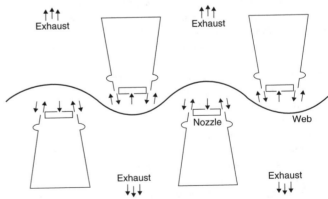

A high-velocity hot-air dryer putting a controlled ripple into the web.

dryers, or dryers through which the web can pass without being touched by a surface, so as not to smear the ink. An **open-flame dryer** (also known as a **direct-impingement dryer**) is the oldest type of dryer and simply generates a high-temperature zone through which the web passes. Alternately, a **high-velocity hot-air dryer** uses nozzles to direct hot air at the web. Such devices also include exhaust vents to pipe out the solvent fumes generated during the drying of solvent-based heatset inks. The fumes are then carried to a combustion chamber where the solvent is safely burned away. Some dryers use a combination of the open-flame and hot-air configurations, often employing medium-velocity jets of heated air. The aerodynamics of the moving web cause a thin layer of air to move along with it. In open-flame dryers, this layer of air becomes saturated with solvent from the ink, and more heat becomes necessary to remove it all, which reduces the efficiency of the drying process. Solvent-saturated air that is carried out of the dryer can condense back onto the web and/or the chill rolls. This will cause the ink to resoften, marking the chill rolls and resulting in marks being transferred to subsequent portions of the web. The high-velocity dryers, however, add turbulence to the air in the dryer, which prevents solvent from saturating the air surrounding the web. Another particular problem that can be encountered during drying, especially during the early uses of high-velocity hot-air dryers, is the production of ripples in the web which then get pressed into wrinkles by the chill rolls. A solution to this problem is the use of spaced air nozzles to produce a controlled rippling of the web. This controlled rippling has the effect of imparting to the web a greater dimensional stability than if it had been left to its own devices.

Chill Rolls. Heatset inks not only require heat to set but also require cooling. (Such inks work by evaporating the volatile solvent from the ink in the dryer and then cooling down the residual vehicle where it can set by **polymerization**.) Thus, after drying, the web is passed between the chill rolls, a set of moving steel drums through which cold water is pumped. Early designs of chill rolls filled the entire interior of the rollers with cold water, but the cooler portions of the liquid remained near the middle of the roll, causing the ends of the rollers to gradually become heated. This resulted in inconsistent cooling across the web. Newer designs use baffle plates or, more often, a thin shell around the surface of the roller and an empty center to keep the surface of the roller equally cool over its entire length. The speed of the chill rolls, as was indicated earlier, can be

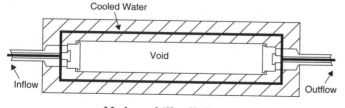

Modern chill roll design.

adjusted over a wide range, so as to control web tension through this longest tension span. One particular problem that can be encountered in the chill rolls is slippage of the web as it passes through the nip. Such slippage can cause ink from the web to mark the rolls, which can then be transferred back to the web. Attention needs to be paid to the plumbing of the chill rolls; mineral deposits from hard water or other sources can decrease the cooling efficiency of the rollers.

IN-LINE FINISHING EQUIPMENT

Although most complex and high-volume **binding and finishing** operations are best handled at a bindery, many web presses have **in-line** finishing devices, which eliminate the time and expense of rewinding a printed job and sending it out to a bindery. However, in-line equipment does have the disadvantage of shutting down the entire press when one particular stage is shut down.

Folders. Even if no other finishing operations are involved, most web presses are designed to deliver folded sheets, or **signature**s. They accomplish this by having one (or more) configurations of folding devices attached to the delivery end of the press. In-line folders make three primary types of folds: a **former fold**, which is accomplished by pulling the web over a triangular-shaped former board, which folds

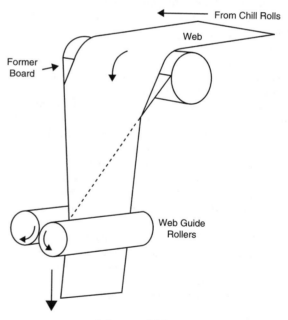

A former folder.

the web in half lengthwise in the direction of web travel; a **jaw fold**, in which the web is carried around a cylinder and is "tucked" (using a **tucker blade**) into the jaws of an additional cylinder, making a fold; and a **chopper fold**, the final folding operation in which a signature is carried along a flat conveyor, the previously made folded edge forward, where it passes underneath a metal blade that forces the

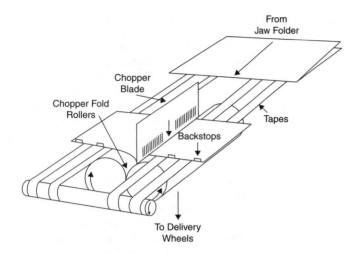

Chopper folder and chopper fold creation.

signature down at a right angle to the plane in which it was traveling and through a set of rollers. The chopper fold thus forms the **spine** of the signature. It is typically after the jaw fold is made that a **cutoff knife** is used to cut the web into individual signatures. Any, some, or all of these folds can be made in tandem. If all folds are going to be made in a single signature, a combination folder—which combines the **former folder**, the **jaw folder**, and the **chopper folder** into one device—is used. (See **Former Folder**, **Jaw Folder**, and **Chopper Folder**.)

In some publication work, a **ribbon folder** may be employed, which uses a slitter wheel to cut a web into two halves, or "ribbons," each of which will form different pages. The ribbons are carried to jaw folders, where they are folded into the form required for the publication they will form. Some publication presses also utilize **double-former folder**s. (See **Ribbon Folder** and **Double-Former Folder**.)

Several types of auxiliary folders are used to increase the variety of materials that can be produced as part of an in-line process. A **prefolder** is used to shift the web in a certain direction prior to folding (usually folding performed using a **plow folder**). A plow folder itself is most commonly used in the production of kraft paper bags (such as grocery bags). The plow folder is more variable in configuration than a traditional former folder and allows for greater flexibility in the location and number of folds possible. An **insert folder** is used to fold 8½×11-in. sheets to a size suitable for stuffing (or inserting) into an envelope or other mailing application.

Gluers. Although the **backbone** gluing for paperback books and other large publications is commonly done during post-press bindery operations, some printed materials are glued during an in-line gluing process. On some presses, paster wheels are used to apply adhesive to printed signatures, gluing them together. Hypodermic needles may also be used. A **backbone gluer** is used to adhesive-bind books directly as part of an in-line finishing operation.

A *remoistenable pattern gluer* is used in a variety of related applications, from the application of an adhesive in specific directions, to the application of fragrances (as in perfume or cologne ads) or "scratch-and-sniff" materials. One common configuration for a remoistenable pattern gluer uses two rollers to meter a predetermined film of adhesive, a transfer roller being used to transfer the adhesive to the web of substrate passing beneath it. The combination of a rubber-plate cylinder and a backing impression cylinder allows the adhesive (or other material) to be "printed" in the desired pattern. The use of segmented glue pans and transfer rollers increases the flexibility of remoistenable pattern gluers.

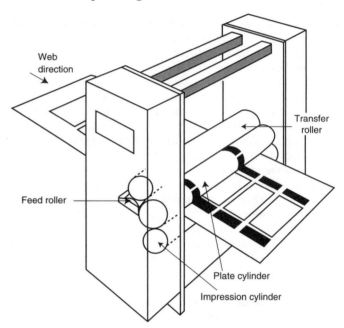

A remoistenable pattern gluer.

Sealing the edges of envelopes is the purview of an **envelope pattern gluer**, while a **spot gluer** is useful for applying glue in only certain selected "spots" across the web.

Perforating and Numbering. *Perforating* and pattern perforating are commonly used for coupons and other types of "removable" portions of a printed product. Perforators are often located immediately after the chill rolls, and utilize adhesive-backed perforating strips mounted on a plate cylinder. As the web is passed between these strips and a blanket or backup cylinder the perforation is made. Ink-jet or other types of printing heads are used in conjunction with the perforating system to successively number materials. *Scoring* can also be done at this point, which will facilitate any successive folding operations.

Sheeters. As their name indicates, sheeters cut the printed web into individual sheets. When used in conjunction with folders and other in-line finishing equipment, they can be produce a wide variety of printed products, eliminating the need for any further binding and finishing operations. Rotary cutters can also be used to produce both bleed and nonbleed products cut to final size. Many also perform final trimming operations. *Diecutting* is also a function of many types of rotary cutters.

Depending upon the space available in the pressroom, many finishing lines may be oriented in a vertical direction or at right angles to the main printing line. Depending upon the complexity and nature of the product, all binding and finishing may be done in-line, or further binding and finishing in a specific bindery setting may be required. (See also *Binding and Finishing*.)

PRESS CONFIGURATIONS

The speed and efficiency of web printing are increased by doing as much printing in as few steps as possible.

In-Line Printing Units. Multicolor and *process color* printing is often performed by including several *color stations* in a line, through which the web passes. As it passes through each of these printing units, a successive color and/or image is laid down.

Common Impression Cylinder. One popular type of multicolor press uses a *common impression cylinder (CIC)* and is thus known as a common-impression-cylinder press. Essentially, a single large-diameter impression cylinder is used to carry the web to a series of color stations (called in this case *satellite press*es) mounted in a circle around the impression cylinder. The use of two common impression cylinders in a row allows for perfecting. This can be accomplished by printing one side of the web, drying the ink, flip-

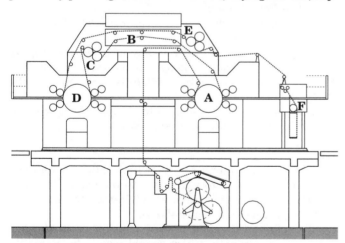

Each unit (A, D) has four printing couples. The web feeds into the first unit (A), which prints four colors on one side. It passes through a dryer (B) and over chill rolls (C), is turned over and enters the second unit (D), which prints four colors on the other side of the web. The web then re-enters the dryer (B), is chilled (E), and finally is folded (F) and delivered.

ping it over, and running it through a second CIC unit. Another often-used configuration is called *half-web printing* or *double-ending*: the web is only half the width of the plate cylinder and is aligned with one end of the plate. The web is sent through the printing unit where one side is printed. It is dried and cooled, then turned over and aligned with the second half of the plate where the second side prints. Paper can be run on both sides of the press simultaneously, which can essentially cut the time of the print run in half.

Blanket-to-Blanket Press. Another common web press configuration is a *blanket-to-blanket press*, which perfects in a single pass. Essentially, the impression cylinder in one printing unit is replaced with the blanket cylinder of another printing unit. With this system, more careful attention needs to be paid to the respective packing heights of the two blanket cylinders so as to ensure a proper impression on both sides of the web simultaneously.

INK AND PAPER

An ink consists of essentially two basic components: a fluid *vehicle* and a somewhat solid *pigment* The particles of pigment are dispersed in the vehicle and transferred to the substrate. How the vehicle is removed—either by evaporation, oxidation, polymerization, or absorption—to leave the dried pigment on the substrate is one common means of classifying printing inks. Three types of inks are commonly used in web offset lithography: newsinks, heatset inks, and nonheatset inks.

Newsinks. *Newsink* is commonly used, as its name indicates, in newspaper printing. These inks dry by absorption; that is, the liquid vehicle is absorbed into the paper, leaving the pigment on the surface. Although these inks—when printed on highly absorbent newsprint—"dry" very fast, they do not really dry at all, allowing the pigment to be easily rubbed off, as we all know from reading newspapers. A drying oil can be added to these inks to impede the rubbing off of the pigment.

Heatset Inks. *Heatset ink*s dry by evaporating a volatile vehicle at high temperatures, then setting the pigment by cooling it down. The drying of heatset inks is the function of the dryer and chill rollers.

Nonheatset Inks. Depending upon the substrate and the end-use of the printed product, other types of nonheatset inks may be used. These can include *quickset ink*s, which dry by a combination of absorption, oxidation, and polymerization. Newer types of "high-tech" inks include *ultraviolet-curing ink*s and *electron-beam-curing ink*s, which dry as a result of chemical reaction initiated by exposure to radiation. Special lamps are attached to the press to effect the drying of these inks.

One common ingredient in printing inks—save for newsinks—is a *drier*, which, as its name impliess, speeds up the drying process by acting as a catalyst in the chemical reactions that set an ink.

See also *Ink*.

Substrates. Web offset lithography is primarily used to print on paper substrates (unlike gravure or flexography that are widely used to print on plastic materials). The type of paper required depends on the end-use requirements of the print job. The type of paper chosen will to a large extent also dictate the best ink to use, as well. *Newsprint*, an uncoated, highly absorbent paper made entirely from *groundwood* pulp is widely used in the printing of newspapers. Other types of paper of varying quality include *offset paper*, *coated free sheet*, *supercalendered*, etc. Literally hundreds (or even thousands) of different paper types are available. Web printing allows for a wide variety of them to be used, the most important consideration being consistency of *formation* and *caliper* throughout the web. This is to keep the tension throughout the print run consistent and to prevent web breaks. Lighter papers are used less frequently on web presses, as their low tensile strength causes problems when exposed to the stresses and tension involved in web printing. (See also *Paper and Papermaking: Printing Requirements*.)

Web offset presses, like many other presses these days, are supplemented by a variety of computerized controls that monitor things like ink height, dampening solution, and feeding, and nearly every other aspect of the printing process, increasing the speed and efficiency of the process.

Web-Over Roller

On a *web press*, a roller used to guide a web of paper (or other substrate) over a printing unit, splicer, or other unit that the web needs to bypass. See also *web-under roller*.

Web Paper

A continuous *roll* of paper used on *web press*es. See *Web* and *Web Press*.

Web Press

A printing press that prints from large rolls of paper or other *substrate*, as opposed to a *sheetfed press*, which prints from individual cut sheets. *Gravure* and *flexographic* presses are more commonly web presses. (See *Gravure* and *Flexography*.) Presses used in *offset lithography* are either sheetfed or web. (See *Offset Lithography* and *Web Offset Lithography*.)

Web Printing

Any type of printing onto a *substrate* that is fed into the press as a continuous roll or *web*, rather than as discrete sheets. Any of the major printing processes—*offset lithography*, *gravure*, *flexography*, and *letterpress*—are used for web printing. Also known as *web process*.

Web Process

Alternate term for *web printing*. See *Web Printing*.

Web Tension

In *web offset lithography*, the pull applied to a web of paper as it travels through the press. See *Web Offset Lithography: Infeed and Web Control*.

Web-Under Roller

On a *web press*, a roller used to guide a web of paper (or other substrate) under a printing unit, splicer, or other unit that the web needs to bypass. See also *web-over roller*.

Web Weave

In *web printing*, an out-of-round paper roll that will rotate with a bounce creating variations in *web tension* that may affect printing *register* or cause *web break*s.

Wedding Paper

An elegant, highly refined, nonglare paper used for wedding announcements, invitations, personal stationery, and other such uses. Wedding papers have a very *close formation* and a surface that permits engraved characters. Wedding papers are made from chemical wood pulps, or from wood pulps with a cotton content ranging from 25–100%. The *basic size* of wedding paper is 17×22 in., and it comes in *basis weight*s of 28, 32, 36, and 40 lb. Wedding papers are also manufactured with basis weights characteristic of *bristol paper*, for business cards, RSVP cards, announcements, etc.

Wedge

A three-dimensional shape or object that is thick or wide at one end and gradually tapers to a point. A wedge is often used to split wood, stop doors, or support the back edge of blank sheets of paper in the *delivery section* of a printing press. See *Pile Wedge*.

In graphics, a *wedge* is a term for a "slice" of a *pie chart*. See *Pie Chart*.

In photography, a *wedge* is any of a variety of *gray scale*s used to monitor image densities. See *Carbon Wedge*, *Continuous Wedge*, *Step Wedge*, and *UGRA Wedge*.

The term *wedge* is also used to describe the spaceband used in linecasting. (See also *Spaceband*.)

Weft

The threads of a fabric that run horizontally across the width of the fabric, interweaving with the *warp*. The weft is commonly a fabric's direction of lesser strength. Also known as the *woof*. See also *Warp*.

Term for the direction in which an offset press *blanket* has the least strength, which should ideally be across its width, not in its around-the-cylinder direction. A press blanket has been prestretched during manufacture to compensate for any stretching that may occur when it is mounted around the *blanket cylinder*. A blanket with greater strength across its width will become baggy on press and cause *slurring* of printed images. The direction of greatest strength is called its *warp*. See *Blanket*.

Weight

In typography, the lightness or darkness in print of a particular *typeface*, based upon its design and thickness of line.

The standard gradations of weight are extralight, light, semilight, regular, medium, semibold, bold, extrabold, and ultrabold (also called heavy or black). Extremely light typefaces are often called hairline. There is no standardization

abcdefghijklmnopqrstuvwx
Univers Regular

abcdefghijklmnopqrstuvw
Univers Bold

abcdefghijklmnopqrstuv
Univers Black

abcdefghijklmnopqrst
Univers Extra Black

Various weights of the Univers Extended typeface.

of any of these weight designations, however; Helvetica Medium may be the same weight as a Univers Bold.

Due to such variables as the condition of processor chemicals, length of time since processing the *galley* (fading), and the density setting on the typesetting machine, differences in weight may be artificially created.

When trying to identify the typeface on a previously printed piece, it is necessary to consider the thickness, or density, of the ink, the amount of bleed, and the number of photographic steps that the image went through.

A bold lead-in, where the first word of a paragraph is bold, should have the same face and size as the text. If not, at least base-align the copy.

Brightness contrast is the contrast between "blackness" of letters and "whiteness" of papers. It is important in maintaining typographic color.

Weight Tolerance

An acceptable amount of variation in the *basis weight* of a paper that is shipped, as compared to what was ordered, commonly within 5% of the paper's *nominal weight*.

Weitek Coprocessor

In computing, a *coprocessor*, developed by Weitek, designed to accelerate the processing of *CAD* files on 80386 and 80486 *PC*s.

Weld

In drawing programs, a function used to join one line to another.

Well

Alternate term for *inkwell*. See *Inkwell*.

Well Side of the Screen

In *screen printing*, the top of the *printing screen*, where the ink is placed. The opposite side contacts the *substrate*.

Wet End

Alternate term for the *forming section* of a papermaking machine, or that section between the *headbox* (which contains the fibrous paper *pulp* solution) and the *drying section* where the paper *web* is formed. (See *Forming Section*.)

Wet Method

A means of producing a *carbon tissue* stencil for use in *screen printing* by exposing it while the carbon tissue is still wet or damp. See also *Dry Method*.

Wet Picking

Picking, or the rupturing of a paper's surface during printing, caused by an exposure to water diminishing a paper's surface bond strength. (See *Picking* and *Pick Resistance*.)

Wet Pick Resistance

The extent to which a paper will resist *picking* after it has been exposed to moisture. A paper's *pick resistance* is typically diminished after it has been dampened. (See *Pick Resistance* and *Picking*.)

Wet Pressing

Process performed in the *press section* of a papermaking machine, which subjects the wet paper *web* to a degree of pressure by feeding it through rollers. The pressure exerted on the paper web, to squeeze out water and compact the paper fibers, can be adjusted to provide either a slight amount of wet pressing or a great deal. The amount of wet pressing a paper receives affects many of its structural and optical properties. (See *Press Section* and *Paper and Papermaking: Paper Properties*.)

Wet Printing

In multicolor printing, the printing of subsequent colors while the previously printed colors of ink are still wet. See *Trapping*.

Wet Roll

A paper roll defect characterized by paper having been bonded together due to contact with water.

Wet Rub Test

A test that is performed to evaluate a paper's resistance to *moisture*.

Wet Strength

A property of paper that indicates the strength it retains after it has been saturated with water. It is calculated by computing the percentage of the ratio of a paper's *tensile breaking strength* to its *wet-tensile breaking strength*. Few papers retain a significant percentage of their dry strength when wet, as the interfiber bond strength in the paper is dissolved by exposure to water. Wet-strength paper is specifically made for end uses that require a significant degree of wet strength, typically by adding materials to the papermaking *furnish* to shore up the interfiber bonds and enable them to retain much strength when wet. Papers whose end uses include intentional exposure to water—such as towels or labels, or maps and charts that must withstand weathering—require a great deal of wet strength.

Wettability

A property of printing inks that describes the ability of the dry ink film to resist *bleeding*, discoloring, fading, etc., upon exposure to moisture. An ink's wettability is an important consideration in packaging and other printing applications that involve exposure to weather. Frequently, inks are formulated with *vehicle*s utilizing *varnish*es, or printed pieces are coated with a layer of *varnish* to increase the printed ink's water resistance.

The term *wettability* also refers to the ease with which an ink *pigment* can be completely wet by the *vehicle*.

Wet-Tensile Breaking Strength

A property of paper that indicates its ability to withstand a stretching force without breaking while saturated with water. The paper's maximum elongation due to tensile stress is expressed as a percentage of its original length. The wet-tensile breaking strength, combined with the (dry) *tensile breaking strength*, is used to determine a paper's *wet strength*. (See *Wet Strength* and *Tensile Breaking Strength*.)

Wetting

A procedure performed in the ink-manufacturing process in which the particles of *pigment* are coated with *varnish* so as to enable them to be ground more easily and finely and disperse more completely in the ink *vehicle*. (See *Ink: Ink Manufacturing*.)

Wetting Agent

A substance added—typically in small quantities—to a liquid in order to reduce its surface tension and allow solids to be more completely wet by the liquid. A variety of wetting agent used in the manufacture of printing inks is called a *dispersing agent*. Wetting agents are also an important ingredient of offset press *fountain solution*s so as to increase the solution's ability to rapidly form a thin, continuous film.

In many fountain solutions, alcohol or substances called *surfactant*s are added as wetting agents. (See *Fountain Solution*.)

Wetting Up

In *screen printing*, the period just before the actual print run when ink is placed onto the *printing screen* and distributed evenly across the surface (*flooding*).

Wet Trapping

In wet *process color* printing, the ability to successfully lay down a wet ink film on top of a previously printed, still-wet ink film. See *Trapping* (second definition).

Whip

Alternate term for *bounce*. See *Bounce*.

Whirler

A device used in platemaking to apply a photosensitive coating to printing plates that have not been presensitized or are not *wipe-on plate*s.

Whiskering

A defect of *gravure* printing characterized by printed areas possessing hairlike tendrils of ink sticking out into non-image areas, caused by the buildup of static charges on the moving web that attract oppositely charged drops of ink from the *gravure cylinder* cells as the substrate is leaving the *impression zone*. Such buildup can be caused by low humidity in the pressroom, fast press speed, or wet ink solvent on the substrate, and it can be reduced by moistening the paper web, by using static brushes or tinsel, or by dusting the impression roller with talcum powder.

An example of whiskering.

White Alignment

The calibration of a *color scanner* prior to scanning consisting of the balancing of the *red, green, and blue* signals, commonly accomplished utilizing a *step tablet*. White alignment is also performed to prevent a *color cast* from permeating the scanned image (in which case it is also referred to as *white out*).

White Balance

In videography, the calibration of a video camera to the frequency of light that corresponds to white, so as to enable all other colors to register correctly. Usually, a camera is white-balanced by focusing on a sheet of white paper. Setting the white balance avoids unpleasant *color cast*s in videotaped images.

White Book

In multimedia, a set of standards that describes the specifications for recording data on a *video CD*, often used for *karaoke*. The White Book standard (so-named because the publication containing the specifications had a white cover) allows up to 74 minutes of audio and video compressed by *MPEG*-1 data compression techniques.

White Light

The *visible spectrum*, in which all the individual wavelengths that correspond to specific colors are present in equal quantity, resulting in essentially "uncolored" light. The individual components of white light can be seen by refracting the light through a prism or through raindrops (as in a rainbow). See *Visible Spectrum*. (See COLOR PLATE 3.)

Whiteness

An optical property of paper that describes the degree to which a paper diffusely reflects light of all wavelengths (i.e., colors) of the visible spectrum. The ideal white standard (a powder of barium sulfate) reflects 100% of all the light falling on it. Whiteness is described in terms of the amount and uniformity of light reflectance over the visible spectrum (from 400 to 700 *nanometers*, or from the violet to the red end of the spectrum) as compared to the light reflectance of the ideal white standard. The comparative whiteness of various papers is determined by comparing their *spectral reflectance curves*.

Whiteness is an issue in paper production due to its relationship to print quality. There is more of a contrast between the paper and a colored or black ink the whiter the paper is. The greater the whiteness of the paper, the greater the contrast—and the readability—of the ink. (See also *Brightness*.)

Whitening

A form of *piling* characterized by the accumulation of a fine, white dust on the nonimage areas of a printing plate or blanket. Whitening consisting of large, visible particles is called *powdering*. See *Piling* and *Powdering*.

White Out

See *White Alignment*.

White Pigments

Several types of ink *pigments* used for either printing opaque whites (called *opaque pigment*) or for tinting, extending, or reducing the strength of other color pigments (called *transparent pigment*). Commonly used white pigments include *Zinc White*, *Titanium Dioxide*, *Zinc Sulfide*, *Lithopone*, *Alumina Hydrate*, *Calcium Carbonate*, *Blanc Fixe*, *Barytes*, talc, silica, and *China Clay*.

The white pigments listed above are classified and identified in the Society of Dyers and Colorists' Color Index. Each classification consists of two parts, corresponding to the two parts of the index: The first part identifies each pigment with a CI number, which accompanies a description, usage, and technical information. The second part lists each pigment by chemical composition and assigns each one a single number. Thus, calcium carbonate above is

listed in Part 1 as *CI Pigment White 18* and in Part 2 as *No. 77220*. These two sets of identifications accompany the individual entries for each separate pigment.

White Space

The total amount of nonimage area on a page, particularly *gutter*s and *margin*s. *White space* also refers to the space on either side of typographic characters, which can be reduced with tracking.

White Space Reduction (WSR)

In typography, the reducing of the amount of space a character is allotted, used when the *white space* between characters is optically excessive and egregious.

Whole-Tree Utilization

A concept of *pulp* making in which an entire tree is cut at ground level and its entire trunk (bark and all), branches, and foliage are all converted into wood chips for use in *pulping*. This provides a more economical use of wood, and helps reduce the pressure on future paper fiber suppliers. As new innovations make it easier to remove the contaminants and undesirable materials from whole-tree-based pulp, whole-tree utilization is becoming more and more practical as an effective source of *pulpwood*. Other materials, such as waste from sawmills and lumber yards, as well as the use of *recycled paper* are reducing the need for *virgin fiber*.

Wicking

The absorption of moisture by a paperboard through the raw edge.

Wide-Angle Lens

In photography, a *lens* with a short *focal length* that allows the capture of a wide angle.

Wide Area Information Service (WAIS)

In networking and the *Internet*, a service in which users can access text databases over the Internet. WAIS utilizes English-language queries and can search through the text of documents, unlike *Gopher* (its predecessor), which can only search the names of resources. Although WAIS has largely been superseded by the *World Wide Web*, it is good for searching through *USENET* newsgroups and newspaper archives.

Wide Area Network (WAN)

A network of linked computers or other networks that are scattered over large geographic areas. WANs are often connected by means of telephone lines and/or satellite transmissions, in contrast to a *local area network*, which occupies a much smaller area.

Wide Area Telephone Service (WATS)

In telecommunications, a service provided by a local telephone company that allows customers to make station-to-station calls on a special access line based on a flat monthly charge, rather than on a per-call basis. Calls on a WATS line are only permitted at certain periods of time.

Wideband

Descriptive of a color *filter* containing very small optical openings (measured in *nanometer*s) that allow for the transmission of light over the entire *visible spectrum*. In contrast, *narrowband* filters are used only to transmit light of selected wavelengths or colors. (See also *Narrowband*.)

In telecommunications, a *bandwidth* capable of transmitting more frequencies than a standard 3-kilohertz voice channel.

Wideband Channel

See *Wideband* (second definition).

Widow

In typography, the last line of a paragraph when it is less than one-third the width of the line, especially when it is the carry-over of a hyphenated word. *Widow* can also refer to one word or word part standing alone in a line of a heading or a caption. Widows are undesirable typographically and can be eliminated by adding or deleting words to or from the previous line to either fill out the widow line or remove it entirely. Adjusting the *set width* or *tracking* of the line can also eliminate the occurrence of widows. A widow carried to the top of a new page or column is called an *orphan*.

Today, office workers are using the computer more and more for word processing, databases, spreadsheets, and desktop publishing. As a result, printed documents are being produced more often and in much greater	quantity. ◄─ Orphan Typeset materials are easier to read and the most professional looking. Typesetting creates an air of quality that typewriters and computer printers cannot match. ◄── Widow

---

In the text above, the word "quantity" at the top of the second column is an orphan, and the word "match" at the bottom of the second column is a widow.

Width Card

In typesetting, a card, panel, or box attached to a typesetting device or keyboard that contains the *escapement* values for characters in a particular *font* in use. Also known as a *width plug*.

Width Plug

Alternate term for a *width card*. See *Width Card*.

Width Tables

In typography, information stored in an electronic typesetting system pertaining to how much horizontal space each character in a *font* should occupy. Width tables also include data concerning *kern pair*s.

Width Value

Alternate term for *escapement*. See *Escapement*.

Width Value Table

See *Width Table*.

Wildcard

In computing, a character (such as an asterisk or question mark) used in search engines that can represent any character or set of characters, used when searching for data (as in databases) whose exact descriptor is not entirely known.

Wild Formation

Term used to describe a paper's structure in which the *cellulose* fibers have bound together in an uneven manner throughout the sheet or *web*, also called a *cloudy formation*. (See *Formation*.) A uniform distribution of paper fibers is called a *close formation*.

Winchester Disk

In computing, the first *hard disk*, created by IBM and still the basis of most hard disk technologies. Essentially, the Winchester disk includes several metallic magnetic platters that rotated in an airtight unit. As a disk rotates, it creates a cushion of air that keeps the *read/write head* from actually touching the disk surface. When the disk is stopped, the air cushion disappears, and the read/write head settles to

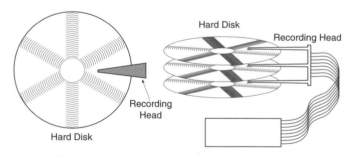

A Winchester disk.

the surface. Since the read/write head will damage data if it touches a storage location (a condition known as *head crash*), it is "parked" over a portion of the disk surface in which no data is written (called the *landing zone*) before the disk is spun down. The airtight sealing of the unit also prevents contaminants from entering the unit.

Wind

Pronounced with a short "i," to separate printed sheets so as to allow them to be ventilated by air, often needed for effective drying of some ink *vehicle*s. Also referred to as *airing*.

Window

A subdivided rectangular region of a computer display, in which different images, directories, or programs can be displayed. Operating systems and software applications that allow *windowing* typically allow more than one element to be displayed on a screen at any one time, such as different computer directories (or "folders"), different application menus, or even different files or programs. A typical window contains a *title bar* along the top, usually bearing the name of the document or directory it contains; a *menu bar* bearing the names of various *pull-down menu*s that can be accessed; a *scroll bar* (containing a *scroll box*) down the right side of the window (and perhaps another along the bottom of the window), allowing the user to quickly move to different portions of a document; and a close box, or a quick means of closing a window with a click of the mouse. Windows can be repositioned on the screen, resized, opened, closed, and can be either *tiled windows* or *cascaded windows*. The *Macintosh operating system* utilizes windows, as does the aptly named *Microsoft Windows*.

In prepress, the term *window* is used to refer to a hole cut in the front of a *flat* uncovering the image area(s) of a *negative* for platemaking. *Window* can also describe a clear, commonly rectangular "hole" in a line negative used to later strip in a *halftone*. (Also known as *window clipping*.)

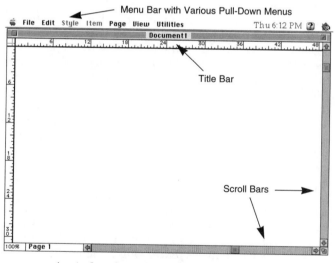

A window for a QuarkXPress document.

Window Clipping

Subdividing a computer display into individual *windows*. See *Window* (first definition).

Window clipping also refers to a transparent "hole" created in a *negative* in which a *halftone* negative is later stripped in. See *Window* (second definition).

Window Dub

An identical copy of the audio and video portions of a videotape containing the *time code* information displayed on the screen.

Windowing

Subdividing a computer display into smaller individual *windows*. See *Window*.

Window Patch

In typography and composition, a block of typeset text (commonly comprising one or more lines, or even individual words) pasted over original typeset text to effect a correction of a *typo* or other error. The size of the patch depends on the extent that the corrected text alters successive lines.

Windows

A *graphical user interface (GUI)* developed by Microsoft, used as an operating system (or, in early versions of Windows, an interface between the user and *DOS*) on *IBM-compatible computer*s.

Like the *Macintosh operating system*, Windows allows the user to interact with the computer via *icon*s and mouse-based clicking and pointing on screen, rather than the cryptic and at times complex text utilized by DOS and other *CLI*-based operating systems.

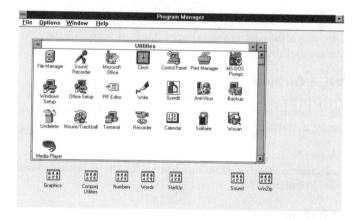

The Program Manager in Microsoft Windows 3.1, a graphical user interface (GUI).

Windows and Windows-based machines are the most widely used personal computers, and a wide variety of applications are available to run on Windows. The most important early version of Windows was version 3.1, which is still widely used and is favored by many over the newer Windows 95, a major overhaul of the Windows operating system.

Windows Accelerator

An add-on card or special *video adapter* for *personal computer*s running on the *Windows* platform that contains a fast processor and *VRAM* to increase the speed of the video display.

Windows Environment

Any computer whose display consists of *window*s, especially one utilizing the Microsoft *Windows*™ operating system. See *Window*.

Windows NT

In computing, a 32-*bit* operating system that was developed by Microsoft, that supports *multitasking* and that runs on *Pentium*-based microcomputers.

Windows Open Services Architecture (WOSA)

In computing, a set of *application programming interfaces* used to link *Windows* applications, as well as Windows and other operating systems. See *Application Programming Interface (API)*.

Wing Mailer

A device used to automatically (or semi-automatically) apply mailing labels to cartons, envelopes, publications, or books.

Wipe

In motion picture, video, and multimedia editing, a *transition* between two scenes or shots in which the second scene is rapidly "wiped" onto the first, or moved over the first image along a visible border, in contrast to a *cut* or a *dissolve*. Wipes can be from top to bottom (rather like pulling a shade over the first image), bottom to top, left to right, right to left, diagonally, out from the center, and in a variety of special customized shapes, such as stars, stripes, circles, or silhouettes of Elvis.

Wipe-On Plate

A printing plate used in *offset lithography* on which a light-sensitive coating is applied or wiped on either by hand or by a machine.

Wire

In papermaking, a shorthand term for the *forming wire*. See *Forming Wire*.

Wireframe

In *three-dimensional* graphics, a 3D image represented by a series of line segments, resembling pieces of wire, that outline the surface of the shape. Wireframe models are the least processor-intensive mode of 3D graphics. Final *rendering* adds surface, texture, and lighting effects to the wireframe.

Wireless

Descriptive of any means of electronic communication conducted without any physical connection between sender and receiver. Some common means of wireless communications involve the use of infrared and radio waves. Television remote controls, cordless phone, and *cellular* communications are common wireless applications.

Wire Mesh

Alternate term for *metallic screen fabric*. See *Metallic Screen Fabric*.

Wire-O Binding

A type of *spiral binding* comprising a double set of wire loops inserted into punched or drilled holes along the *bind-*

Wire-O binding, a type of spiral binding.

ing edge of a set of pages. See *Spiral Binding* and *Mechanical Binding*.

Wire Screen

Alternate term for *metallic screen fabric*. See *Metallic Screen Fabric*.

Wire Service

An organization—such as Associated Press (AP), United Press International (UPI), or Reuters—that collects and distributes news items via satellite to a network of subscribers, usually newspapers or radio and television news departments. Wire services also deliver advertising to member newspapers in digital form.

Wire Side

The side of a sheet or *web* of paper that has formed in contact with the papermaking machine's *forming wire*, as opposed to that formed on the top side of the paper, called the *felt side*. As water drains down through the wire from the papermaking *furnish*, small fibers (called *fines*), *fillers*, and *sizing* are lost through the mesh. Consequently, the wire side contains less fines, fillers, and sizing than the felt side. The paper's *grain* is also more pronounced on the wire side. Since the wire side contains less filler, it is somewhat stronger than the felt side, and it is often the preferred side for printing. Paper that is to be folded also resists cracking better when the wire side is on the outside of a fold. Since it also has less fines, many of which remain as loose particles on the felt side, printing on the wire side results in less piling of paper debris on the blanket. However, the felt side of paper is preferred for other applications, especially for writing with a pen and ink, as *feathering* is minimal on the felt side. Letterheads are typically printed felt side up, and envelopes folded felt side out. A watermark will also read backwards from the wire side.

A paper's *two-sidedness* is primarily caused by using a traditional single-wire *fourdrinier* paper machine. The disparity between the two sides can be minimized by using a *twin-wire former* that sandwiches the papermaking furnish between two wires, imparting to the paper two wire sides. (See also *Felt Side*.)

Wire Stitching

In *binding and finishing*, the use of a thin metal wire (i.e., staples) to bind pages together. Wire stitching includes both *saddle-stitching* and the less common *side-stitching*. See *Saddle-Stitching*.

With-the-Grain

The direction parallel to the orientation of the paper fibers (or *grain*), as opposed to *against-the-grain*. See *Grain*.

WK1

A *file extension* denoting a worksheet file created by Lotus 1-2-3, version 2.

WKS

A *file extension* denoting a worksheet file created by Lotus 1-2-3, version 1A.

WMF

A *file extension* denoting a Windows GDI metafile.

Woodcut

An illustration carved in relief on a block of wood, with lines and shapes of varying thickness, used to make prints. Woodcut printing preceded Gutenberg.

Woof

Alternate term for *weft*. See *Weft*.

Word

A popular *word processing* program developed by Microsoft.

Word Length

In computing, the number of *bit*s that comprise a word. The word length of most microcomputers is 8, 16, 32, or 64.

WordPerfect

A popular *word processing* program, originally created by the WordPerfect Corporation. It was later bought by Novell and is now owned by Corel.

Word Processing

The use of hardware and software to input, edit, and output text. Or, in other words, the processing of words. See *Word Processor*.

Word Processing Program

See *Word Processor*.

Word Processing System

See *Word Processor*.

Word Processor

A computer program that is used to input (by keyboard), edit, and output text. Although early word processing programs rarely allowed any serious formatting of text documents (underlining and bold was about it, really), most now seem to offer as many formatting options as *page layout program*s.

Word Space

In typography, a space placed between words. Unlike a typewriter, on which all word spaces have the same width, typography utilizes word spaces that are variable: they expand or contract based on the length of the line and the number of characters and word spaces on the line. In early writing, there were no word spaces; all the letters were tied together.

It is important to recognize that the *justification* process can only work with variable word spaces. Consequently, a word space cannot be used as an *indent* or in other places where a fixed (constant-width) space is required. Typists who are accustomed to keying two word spaces at the end of a sentence (known as *French spacing*) will find that this practice is not applicable (and unnecessary) in automated typography.

Word spaces are usually within certain ranges—minimum, optimum, maximum—which, in many cases, can be tailored by users to their own taste. The minimum word space is the value below which the space will not go, to eliminate the possibility that a line would be set completely tight (with no discernible word spaces). The maximum word space is the widest value that would be allowed, which is usually the threshold point where automatic letterspacing (if allowable) might be employed. The optimum word space is the value that would most often be desired for good, even spacing (this is just about the width of the lowercase "i" of the font and size). In *ragged* setting, the optimum value is usually used throughout. Too much word space creates *rivers* (white space running vertically in text columns). For short line widths, it is better to use *unjustified* (*ragged right*) lines to avoid drastically uneven word space and/or rivers. Less word space, or evenly *kern*ed word spaces, often looks better after commas, periods, apostrophes, or quotes.

Word Spacing

In typography, the amount of space placed between words, which is typically variable. See *Word Space*.

WordStar

The first *word processing* program developed for *microcomputer*s, introduced in 1978 by WordStar International. Although it is still in existence, it has been superseded by other word processing programs such as Microsoft *Word* and Corel *WordPerfect*.

Word Wrap

In word processing programs (and other text-editing programs), a feature that automatically relocates a word to the next line when it will not fit on the current line. In the early days of typesetting and word processing, the user had to insert line endings. The ability to word wrap enabled faster typing.

Word-Wrapping

See *Word Wrap*.

Work-and-Flop

Alternate term for *work-and-tumble*. See *Work-and-Tumble*. Abbreviated *W & F*.

Work-and-Roll

Alternate term for *work-and-tumble*. See *Work-and-Tumble*.

Work-and-Tumble

In *prepress* and printing, an *imposition* or layout in which one plate contains all the images (pages) to be printed on both sides of a sheet. Once one side of a job has been printed, the pile of printed sheets is turned over, the edge of the sheet that was the *gripper edge* for the first side becoming the back edge for the second side. After

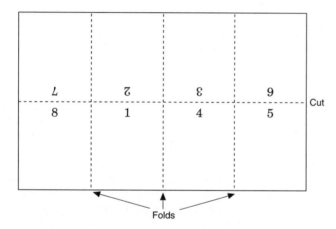

A work-and-tumble layout. After the first side is printed, the paper pile is inverted so that the back edge becomes the gripper edges for the second printing.

printing, the sheet is cut in half, yielding two identical units. Work-and-tumble layouts, with their use of different gripper edges, may have *registration* problems. See also *Work-and-Turn* and *Work-and-Twist*. Also known as *work-and-flop* and *work-and-roll*.

Work-and-Turn

In *prepress* and printing, an *imposition* or layout in which a printing plate containing both the front and the back of a sheet are mounted on the press at the same time and printed on a double-size sheet of paper. Thus, half the sheet is the top printing, while the other half of the sheet is the "back printing."

When half the required number of sheets have been printed, the printed sheets are flipped over (keeping the same *gripper edge*) and are run through the printing press again. This will result in the respective back printing on both halves of the sheet. After cutting the printed sheets in half, the job will be done, and it required half the number of impressions that would have been required with standard one-up printing. See also *Work-and-Tumble* and *Work-and-Twist*.

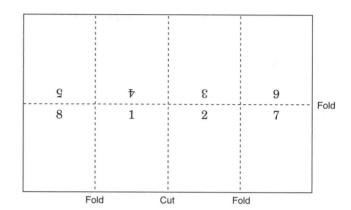

A work-and-turn layout. After the first side is printed, the paper pile is turned over so that the same gripper edge is used for the second printing.

Work-and-Twist

In *prepress* and printing, an *imposition* or layout in which one negative *flat* is used to make two images on a plate. After the negative has produced one image on the plate, the flat is rotated 180° and a second exposure made. Work-and-twist layouts are used in *two-up* printing. See also *Work-and-Tumble* and *Work-and-Turn*.

Workbook

In book publishing, any book (often paperbound and published as a companion to a *textbook*) containing exercises and quizzes to be completed by students. Pages are often perforated, to allow easy removal for passing in as homework.

Workbox

Alternate term for a *toolbox*. See *Toolbox*.

Workflow

In any production environment, all the stages through which a project or job must pass until it is completed. Workflow also refers to the physical set up of equipment and resources used to complete a project.

Work-for-Hire

In publishing, an expression used in contracts signed by freelance writers, artists, photographers, etc., that stipulates that the commissioning party (or the party hiring the freelance individual) is the owner of the copyright of the work being commissioned.

Workgroup

In networking, two or more individuals working on the same projects, or who otherwise need to share computer files, databases, programs, or other system resources. *Local area networks* are usually designed around specific workgroups.

Working Head of Ink

In *screen printing*, ink located immediately in front of the *squeegee* blade and pushed along during a printing stroke.

Workprint

In video production, a copy of the ***raw footage*** of a program or production used in ***off-line editing***.

Workstation

In networking, a ***node*** connected to the network comprising a computer ***terminal*** (more and more frequently a ***smart terminal*** such as a personal computer rather than a ***dumb terminal*** containing no processor of its own) running (typically) the ***UNIX*** operating system, and loading programs via a network controller. Some specialty workstations—such as those with specialized graphic input devices beyond the simple ***mouse***—are also widely used in networks.

Work-Up

A defect of ***letterpress*** printing characterized by ink spots in nonimage areas of the ***substrate***, caused by foreign material typically located beneath the raised image but which, under pressure during printing, is forced up to the surface of the type or plate.

World Wide Web (WWW)

The highly interconnected universe of hypertext servers (HTTP servers) that allows text, graphics, sound, and video files to be displayed. Developed by Tim Berners-Lee at CERN so that scientists could share documents.

The Internet started in 1969, as the ARPANET, the first distributed packet-switched computer network. In 1977, it became one of the Internet's backbone networks, and the protocol research done on the ARPANET was influential in the development of the TCP/IP protocols currently in use on the Internet. ARPANET's technology became obsolete and it was retired in 1990.

In 1973 the Defense Advanced Research Projects Agency (DARPA) initiated a project on internetworking to link packet-switching networks. There were 35 nodes at that time. ARPA established the Internet Configuration Control Board in 1979. By 1983, these joined networks became the Internet. In 1991 the World Wide Web, created by Tim Berners-Lee, a British citizen working at the CERN Particle Physics Laboratory in Switzerland, goes public with 1,313,000 hosts (systems or nodes, not networks). The Internet is then carrying 5.5 terabytes of data per month. In 1995, the World Wide Web alone carries 4.8 terabytes of the Internet's load. The Internet has been turned over to the private sector, since it was no longer applicable for national security purposes. In 1996, over 7 million hosts had access to the Internet, which carries over 25 terabytes of information per month.

The Internet, which is the world's largest computer network, has been doubling in size (number of hosts and networks) every year since 1988. Once the exclusive domain of research and education groups, the Internet is gaining stature with business users. The Internet is owned by approximately 30,000 organizations worldwide, from large corporations to military services and government agencies. The U.S. government was very influential in the development of the Internet but currently owns or funds only a small fraction.

Most of the Internet is privately owned and consists of local area networks inside companies. In fact, commercial connections are growing faster than educational ones. Most wide-area Internet connectivity providers are privately owned and operated and will carry any traffic that users pay for. Password protection is the common security measure on the network today. You can also set up other defenses, including prohibiting incoming network connections, limiting incoming connections to specific services, or prohibiting incoming connections for certain hosts or networks for each service. *Do not share your password.*

With the low cost of connection—often a flat monthly fee for leased line or dial-up access—business users have access to commercial and noncommercial services in the U.S. and 70 other countries. Electronic mail (email) is the most popular application on the network. While on some networks, an email message may take hours or days to reach its destination, on the Internet it usually takes seconds to minutes. Internet mail protocols handle queue congestion and flow control automatically.

Costs came down because Internet services are carried over the transmission control protocol/Internet protocol (TCP/IP), which multiplexes mail messages (and other services) across common links. This maximizes bandwidth use, minimizing cost and permitting continuous connection. Business users are not confined to one-to-one communications, however; group information exchange happens through the Internet's large base of mailing lists and newsgroups. Mailing lists enable a user to send a single mail message to a mail alias. Software then automatically sends the message to everyone on the list, saving time in retyping addresses.

The World Wide Web was made so that scientists could transfer hypertext documents (written in hypertext markup language) over the Internet and information could be shared. This was because research was being done at many sites, and using the old way of transferring text and graphics on the Internet was cumbersome. They began work on a text-mode browser and a graphical browser that would eliminate *file transfer protocol* (FTP) and Telnet and image viewers that were used. CERN had finished the first of these browsers by the end of 1990, and in 1991, it was released for use at CERN. In 1992 CERN began publicizing the World Wide Web Project, which made many people interested and caused more servers to be set up and more interfaces to be created for the Web. At the end of 1993, many software corporations were releasing browsers, which became the easiest way to access information on the Internet.

There are over 50,000 sites on the Web in many locations around the globe compared to the mere 50 sites in 1993. These sites are created with hypertext markup language (HTML). HTML not only hyperlinks information and sites, it also supports high-resolution graphics, audio, and video. It also allows Web page designers to organize and lay out titles, headings, and body text. HTML is what a Web browser translates into an easy-to-use page of information. In a Web page there may be other links pointing to similar information or recommended Web sites. They are called links because of the hyperlinking that occurs and connects the user to another server or computer. Links are highlighted images or text. Web browsers also handle email, news groups, and wide-area information services.

Transmission control protocol/Internet protocol (TCP/IP) is the language of the Internet. You can get connected through your local area network (LAN) or by the use of a modem to an Internet service provider (ISP). If you are going through an ISP you need to use a special communications protocol called *serial line internet protocol* (SLIP) or a *point-to-point protocol* (PPP). Improvements are being made to many of the browsers, and connections speeds are increasing, making it easier to access information in a shorter period of time. One of the first browsers to come out was Mosaic. It was created by computer science students at the National Center for Supercomputer Applications (NCSA) on the University of Illinois campus. It was the first program to take Web files and their links and display them in a graphically appealing manner. When Mosaic was introduced, it shifted the use of the Web from scientists and academics to commercial and consumer users. Mosaic started as a freeware program. Its older versions are still free. In late 1994, Netscape Communications introduced Netscape Navigator. It was written by some of the people that worked on NCSA Mosaic and was led by Marc Andressen, who had graduated from University of Illinois. It is said that 75% of the people that access the Web use Netscape. Netscape downloads text before graphics and also performs multiple/simultaneous downloads. When a user finds an interesting site, the user can mark that page with a bookmark, which makes it more easily accessible later. Netscape also makes it easy to navigate through USENET groups.

There are many extensions for Netscape that help it handle other file formats during downloads. Netscape is freeware, but if you pay for the commercial version you get a manual and tech support. Adobe and Netscape have integrated the portable-document format software, Acrobat, into Netscape Navigator. Adobe has a plug-in for Netscape that will allow users to link PDF documents together on the Internet. Current versions of Netscape display Acrobat PDF documents. Netscape has also worked with Macromind on a program called Shockwave to allow cross-platform playback of Macromind Director files.

Internet Explorer from Microsoft entered the market in 1996 and has secured a base of users on the Windows and other platforms.

ONLINE ADVERTISING

The World Wide Web is the answer to an advertiser's prayer. In a champagne ad from the latest issue of a magazine on the Web, readers click their mouse to play a game, hear a joke, order merchandise, or search for drink recipes. It is enough to keep a reader busy in the brand message for

perhaps half an hour. But another button lurking on that PC screen also makes such interactivity an advertiser's nightmare. Labeled "back," it causes the ad to disappear as quickly as it arrived.

As of 1993, virtually no major ad agency had a group assigned to interactive advertising. Today, all of them do. Still, they are competing with specialized agencies that have spent as much as a decade designing interactive sales demos, computerized shopping information kiosks, and promotional diskettes. To become bigger players in the interactive arena, some established agencies have made acquisitions. Clients are eager to begin interactive advertising. 60% of major U.S. corporations have plans for advertising or promotion on the World Wide Web in addition to the 19% already marketing products there. The Web's draw is its environment of full-color graphics and the ease with which users can jump from one site to the next by simply clicking on a highlighted word or image. To attract customers to their sites, companies buy "banner" or "Web pointer" ads on popular Internet locations.

Newspaper and magazine publishers have been the first to stake claims on the Internet. They are still tinkering with the advertising models for their fledgling World Wide Web sites, and many publishers ventured into cyberspace assuming that advertising alone could carry the load. Advertisers have been skittish about pumping money into a medium with an audience whose size and habits are nearly impossible to gauge. Although several publishers with Web sites, from *The New York Times* to *USA Today*, can say that they are ahead of advertising projections, none has turned a profit.

Publishers expected ad revenue to cover their Internet costs and have resisted charging users for fear of limiting their audience. But as publishers become more adept at working in cyberspace, they are setting up premium zones on their sites that charge an admission fee. Only a few prominent sites, such as *The Interactive Wall Street Journal*, have been successful in charging users for access to news or information. Publishers are hedging their bets. *The New York Times* will charge users for different services on its site, while the *Boston Globe*, a sister publication, has no plans to charge users. A hybrid of free material supported by ads and premium material with an admission fee is popular with publishers on the Web. Hundreds of newspapers across the globe publish on the World Wide Web. Many just dump the print edition on to the Net without tailoring it for electronic publishing. This is called "shovelware" and explains why most newspapers are available free on the Internet. Persuading people to pay for information on the Internet may be the real challenge.

WORM

Abbreviation for *write-once, read-many*, a type of *optical disc* used for the storage and archiving of digital information. On such a storage medium, data is "burned" into the surface of a blank disc (usually by a laser) and, once written, cannot be edited, deleted, or supplemented, although it can be read (also with a laser) as many times as one wants. WORM was the original name for a **CD-ROM** (or "compact disc–read-only memory"), but WORM is also used to refer to other permanent, indelible optical storage media.

WOSA
Abbreviation for **Windows Open Services Architecture**. See **Windows Open Services Architecture (WOSA)**.

Wove Finish
A paper **finish** that bears the characteristics and smoothness of the wire covering of the **dandy roll**. An unmarked, smooth paper finish, lacking the lines typical of **laid finish** paper, which is produced by attaching specially woven wire molds to the dandy roll.

Wow
A defect of an audio recording comprising a humming sound, usually varying in pitch, heard during playback, caused by either imperfections in the drive mechanism of the playback device or by problems with the sound medium. Usually used in concert with the term **flutter**. See also **Flutter**.

Wrap
In **binding and finishing**, to put **jacket**s on **casebound** books.

In binding, *wrap* also refers to any **signature** printed separately from the rest of a book, which is wrapped around

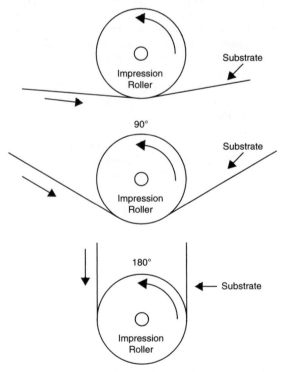

A variety of wrap angles.

other signatures prior to binding. Examples of materials prepared in this way are maps or color plates printed on special paper.

In packaging, *wrap* also refers to the encasing of materials in **kraft** paper, plastic sheets, etc., for protection during shipping.

In webfed gravure printing, *wrap* refers to the degree of the arc of contact the web has with the **impression roller**, or the angle formed by the web before it enters and after it leaves the **impression zone**. Also known as **wrap angle**. See **Impression Roller**.

Wrap Angle
See **Wrap** (fourth definition).

Wraparound
Alternate term for **runaround**. See **Runaround**.

In **prepress**, the term *wraparound* refers to a **gutter** allowance created during **shingling**. See **Shingling**.

In **binding and finishing**, the term *wraparound* refers to a sheet, **folio**, or **insert** placed around a **signature** prior to binding.

Wraparound Mailer
In packaging, a single sheet of corrugated board that is wrapped around a book and stapled or glued shut at both ends. Often used by book clubs, publishers, and distributors to afford protection to books shipped individually. Also known as a **book-wrap mailer**.

Wraparound Plate
In printing, a thin, one-piece relief plate wrapped around the **plate cylinder**, much like an offset plate.

Wrap Curl
Alternate term for **roll-set curl**. See **Roll-Set Curl**.

Wrapper Band
A paper band, either printed or unprinted, wrapped around a stack of loose sheets to keep them neatly stacked, or around collated sets.

Wratten Gelatin Filter
A thin, plastic color **filter** used in the photographic generation of **color separation**s. A Wratten filter is optically pure, and the various colored filters are identified by number, the most often-used filters being #25 (red), #58 (green), and #47B (blue).

Wrinkles
Creases that form in paper or other **substrate** during papermaking, printing, or any of a variety of finishing operations.

Wrinkles are also formed on the surface of a printed ink film that dries unevenly.

Wristwatch
See **Watch**.

Write

In computing, to transfer data from a computer's memory to a magnetic or optical storage medium, such as a **hard disk**, **floppy disk**, **optical disc**, etc. *Write* also means to record a copy of a file on another medium. See also **Read**.

Write-Once Read-Many

See **WORM**.

Write Protect

To prevent the data on a computer disk from being erased or overwritten, usually by means of a plastic tab that can be slid into a position that renders a disk "read-only." See **File Protection**.

Writing Paper

A **bond paper** characterized by a smooth, nonabsorbent surface, designed for writing with pen and ink.

WRK

A **file extension** denoting a worksheet file created by Lotus Symphony, version 1.

WR1

A **file extension** denoting a worksheet file created by Lotus Symphony, Version 1.1.

Wrong Font (WF)

In typography, an indication made on a **galley** indicating that a particular character, word, line, or other subdivision of text has been typeset in a **font**, **typeface**, style, or size other than that which was indicated on the original copy.

Wrong Overturn

In typography, term for half a line of text that appears at the top of a page or column, a carry-over from the bottom of the previous page or column. Wrong overturns, like **orphan**s and **widow**s, are undesirable typographically.

Wrong-Reading

Descriptive of any film or paper image that cannot be read normally—i.e., from left to right, top to bottom—or is, in other words, a mirror image, as opposed to **right-reading**.

WSR

Abbreviation for **white space reduction**. See **White Space Reduction (WSR)**.

WWW

Abbreviation for the **World Wide Web**. See **World Wide Web (WWW)**.

WYSIAAWYG

Abbreviation for "What You See Is Almost Always What You Get," a sarcastic play on the perceived overstatement of **WYSIWYG**, referring to the inability of computer monitors to accurately display what will eventually be output. See **WYSIWYG**.

WYSIMOLWYG

Abbreviation for "What You See Is More or Less What You Get," another sarcastic play on the perceived overstatement of **WYSIWYG**, referring to the inability of computer monitors to accurately display what will eventually be output. See **WYSIWYG**.

WYSINWYG

Abbreviation for "What You See Is Not What You Get," perhaps the most sarcastic play on the perceived overstatement **WYSIWYG**, referring to the inability of computer monitors to accurately display what will eventually be output. See **WYSIWYG**.

WYSIWYG

Abbreviation for "What You See Is What You Get," a term used in a variety of situations. Most often, it is used to describe the ability of desktop computers to display text, graphics, **color**, and other page elements on the screen exactly (or at least approximately) the way they will eventually print, showing the same **font**, line breaks, leading, etc. There are a variety of variations on *WYSIWYG*, not all of them unsarcastic. See also **WYSIAAWYG**, **WYSIMOLWYG**, and **WYSINWYG**.

The phrase "what you see is what you get" is also used in nondigital situations such as in the reassurance by a printer that the customer will receive a reproduction that looks as it does on the **color proof**.

X

X, x

The twenty-fourth letter in the alphabet, derived from the North Semitic letter *taw*, although *taw* primarily represented the "T" sound. In Greek, it became the letter *chi*, possessing the same form as the modern *X*, and represented a "kh" sound (as in the Scottish *loch*). It eventually passed into Latin, where it became used to represent the "ks" sound. Interestingly, the Greek letter *chi* (or *X*) was used in the Middle Ages to represent the name "Christ." As a result, we have the modern word "Xmas" to refer to "Christmas." Although some people find the word "Xmas" to be the height of modern, late-twentieth-century tackiness, it actually is not, and has a long historical tradition.

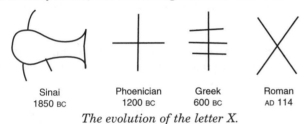

Sinai	Phoenician	Greek	Roman
1850 BC	1200 BC	600 BC	AD 114

The evolution of the letter X.

X.21

In networking, a *CCITT* standard for networks that defines the protocol for a *circuit-switching* network.

X.25

In networking, a *CCITT* standard for networks (particularly *public display network*s) that defines the interface between the network and a *packet switching* protocol, specifically detailing the creation of a *virtual circuit*, the movement of data through that circuit from one device to another, and the demolition of the circuit when transmission has been completed. X.25 is often used for personal computer *BBS* networks.

X.25 Gateway

Alternate term for the *X.75* standard. See *X.75*.

X.28

In networking, a *CCITT* standard for networks—specifically, public data networks located entirely within the borders of a single country—that defines a *data terminal equipment/data communications equipment* interface for a *packet assembler/disassembler*.

X.29

In networking, a *CCITT* standard for networks that defines the transfer of control information between *data terminal equipment* and a *packet assembler/disassembler*.

X.75

In networking, a *CCITT* standard for networks that defines the means by which two separate *packet-switching* networks are connected. Also known as an *X.25 gateway*.

X.200

In networking, the *CCITT* standard that defines the *Open Systems Interconnection* model for communication between computers. See *Open Systems Interconnection*.

X.400

An international, *CCITT* standard for *email exchange*.

X.500

In networking, a *CCITT* and *Open Systems Interconnection* standard for networks that defines an international system for locating *email* users using *X.400* systems.

XA

Abbreviation for *extended architecture*. See *Extended Architecture*.

X-Acto Knife

Tradename for a small, handheld cutting tool used in many graphic arts applications, such as the cutting of film, copy, *stencil*s, etc.

x-Axis

In geometry, the horizontal line or axis of a *coordinate system* on which the *x coordinate* is plotted. See also *y-Axis* and *z-Axis*.

XCCS

Abbreviation for *Xerox Character Code Set*. See *Xerox Character Code Set (XCCS)*.

x Coordinate

The horizontal coordinate of a *coordinate system*, plotted on the *x-axis*. See also *y Coordinate* and *z Coordinate*.

Xdm

In computing, especially on *UNIX* systems that utilize *X Windows*, the *client* program that starts the *server*, somewhat analogous to *DOS*'s *AUTOEXEC.BAT*.

XENIX

A variety of the *UNIX* operating system, developed by Microsoft for use on *microcomputer*s.

Xenon Lamp

A type of light source used in *process camera*s, *scanner*s and other optical devices comprising a tube filled with xenon gas. Xenon lamps are also capable of short-duration, high-intensity flashes, and are often used to photograph moving images without blurring.

Xerographic

Descriptive of the process of *xerography*, a type of *electrophotography*. See *Electrophotography*.

Xerographic Drum

In *xerography* or *electrophotography*, a photoreceptive, electrostatically charged metal drum used as an image carrier. See *Electrophotography*.

Xerographic Engine

In a photocopier or other imaging device that images by means of *electrophotography*, the part of the device that develops the image on the *xerographic drum*, transfers it to the substrate, and fuses it prior to output. See *Electrophotography*.

Xerographic Paper

A type of *bond paper* manufactured specifically for use in electrostatic printing process, such as photocopiers and laser printers, in which the primary consideration is a high degree of electrical resistivity.

Xerography

An electrophotographic printing and imaging process, used mostly in photocopiers and *laser printers*. See *Electrophotography*. *Xerox* is a trade name for the process.

Xerox

A corporation known for its imaging equipment. The pioneering photocopiers it developed—utilizing a proprietary system of *electrophotography* or *xerography*—led to the use of the term *xerox* to refer to any photocopy.

Xerox Character Code Set (XCCS)

In computing, a means of encoding 16-*bit* characters such that all written languages—including those that do not use the Roman alphabet—can utilize a single character set.

Xerox Integrated Composition System (XICS)

An electronic *composition* system for text that outputs to Xerox high-speed laser printers.

Xerox Network Systems (XNS)

In networking, a *protocol* developed by Xerox that was used in early *Ethernet* networks. Although some later versions and variations of XNS are still in use, it has been replaced in many cases by *TCP/IP*.

XGA

A graphics standard for *IBM-compatible computers* that provided 1024×768-*pixel* resolution and a display of 256 colors for color monitors. XGA superseded *VGA* and the earlier *EGA* and *CGA*.

x-Height

In typography, the height of the lowercase letter "x," representing the most important area of a letterform for 90% of *lowercase* characters. A character's x-height does not take into account *ascender*s or *descender*s and is thus a more realistic measurement of the size of a typeface than *point size*. Also known as *body height* and *body size*. Also occasionally known as *z-height*.

XICS

Abbreviation for *Xerox Integrated Composition System*. See *Xerox Integrated Composition System (XICS)*.

Xlib

In computing, especially on *UNIX* systems running *X Windows*, a library interface for the *C* computer language.

Xmodem

In networking and telecommunications, a popular *file-transfer protocol* for asynchronously transferring files between personal computers. Xmodem breaks a file down into small blocks, each block containing a header, a block number, 128 *byte*s of data, and a *checksum*. Xmodem has been superseded by *Ymodem*, *Zmodem*, and *Kermit*.

XMS

Abbreviation for *extended memory specification*. See *Extended Memory Specification (XMS)*.

XNS

Abbreviation for *Xerox Network Services*. See *Xerox Network Services (XNS)*.

XON/XOFF

In data communications, a *protocol* (and the control characters used therein) used for flow control, or to ensure that a transmission is sent at a speed that is no faster than the receiver can receive. The control characters instruct a sending terminal to begin transmission (XON) and end transmission (XOFF).

XPress

See *QuarkXPress*.

XTension

A computer *extension*, or *plug-in* designed for *QuarkXPress*. See *QuarkXTension*.

Xterm

In computing, especially on *UNIX* systems running *X Windows*, a standard X Windows *terminal emulator*, which emulates the DEC VT102 and Tektronix 4014.

X Windows™

A *windows environment*, or *GUI*, designed for the *UNIX* operating system, also widely used on other types of graphics workstations. The advantage of X Windows is that it is designed for use in networks, and allows graphics created on one workstation to be displayed on others in the network.

Xylol

One of three isomeric benzene-like *aromatic solvent*s— chemical formula C_8H_{10}—used as solvents for synthetic *resin*s.

Xylol is a *volatile* liquid, though it evaporates more slowly than *toluol*. Xylol is also called *xylene*.

XYZ Space

Alternate term for the *CIE X,Y,Z* three-dimensional color space, consisting of tristimulus values such as CIELAB and CIELUV. See *CIE X,Y,Z*.

Y

Y, y
The twenty-fifth letter in the alphabet, derived from the North Semitic letter *yodh* by way of the Greek letter *iota*. The form of the *Y* goes back to the North Semitic *waw*. The *Y* did not exist in Latin until the Roman conquest of Greece in the first century, where it was primarily used to transliterate the "Y" sound from Greek.

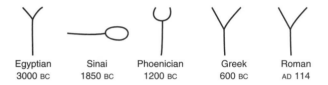

Egyptian	Sinai	Phoenician	Greek	Roman
3000 BC	1850 BC	1200 BC	600 BC	AD 114

The evolution of the letter Y.

Yankee Dryer
A variation of the multiple-cylinder *drying section* of a papermaking machine consisting a single large, highly polished, heated metal cylinder used for producing a *machine-glazed finish*. The wet paper is pressed against the smooth surface of the cylinder, and as it dries it takes on a very smooth, glazed surface. Tissue and crepe papers are produced in a similar manner, followed by a further process that imparts softness and creping.

y-Axis
In geometry, the vertical line or axis of a *coordinate system* on which the *y coordinate* is plotted. See also *x-Axis* and *z-Axis*.

YC
In video, a means of video signal coding and decoding in which the brightness information (or *luminance*, denoted "Y") and the color information (or *chrominance*, denoted "C") are carried in separate channels, resulting in a higher-quality picture. *Broadcast Video U-Matic*, *S-VHS*, and *Hi-8* video systems use YC. The letters "Y" and "C," as it happens, are also the first two initials of the inventor of the process, Yves C. Faroudj. Also spelled *y/c*.

YCC
In digital imaging, a means of *data compression* used by Kodak in its *Photo CD*s. The "Y" refers to the *luminance* information, while the two "C"s refer to two channels of color information. The YCC algorithm results in high *compression ratio*s. See *Photo CD*.

y Coordinate
The vertical coordinate of a *coordinate system*, plotted on the *y-axis*. See also *x Coordinate* and *z Coordinate*.

YCrCb
A coding system for digital *component video* in which the *luminance*, or brightness (Y) information, is digitized at a rate of 13.5 *MHz* while the *color difference* between two color signals (Cr and Cb) are digitized at 6.77 MHz. This is a means of encoding color difference information used in, for example, the *CCIR 601* standard.

Yellow
The *color* characteristic of light possessing a wavelength between 570 and 590 *nanometer*s, located on the spectrum between *orange* and *green*. Yellow is one of the three subtractive primary colors, absorbing *blue light*. It is also one of the four *process color*s in printing. See *Subtractive Color Primaries*. (See COLOR PLATE 1.)

Yellow Book
In multimedia, the set of standards developed by Sony and Philips in 1985 for the *compact disc–read-only memory (CD-ROM)*. The Yellow Book standard (so-named because the publication containing the specifications had a yellow cover) describes the physical structure of the disc, the size of the *sector*s on the disc, the rotational speed of the disc, and the specifications for reading and writing data from and to the disc. See *Compact Disc–Read-Only Memory (CD-ROM)* and *Compact Disc (CD)*.

Yellow Lakes
A type of *organic color pigment* used in printing inks, produced from derivatives of coal tar. Yellow *Lakes* are transparent, vary in levels of permanence, and are useful for printing yellow colors over darker colors without hiding them. (See *Organic Color Pigments*.)

YIQ
In video, term for the video signal used in the *NTSC* television broadcasting standard comprising the *luminance*, or brightness (Y), signal and the *color difference* signals (I and Q).

YMCK
Abbreviation for *yellow*, *magenta*, *cyan*, and *key* (black), the four *process color*s or inks. More commonly known as *CMYK*.

YModem
In networking and telecommunications, a popular *file-transfer protocol* for asynchronously transferring files between personal computers. Xmodem breaks a file down into small blocks, each block containing a header, a block number, 1 *kilobyte*s of data, and a *checksum*. Ymodem superseded *Xmodem* and was itself superseded by *Zmodem* and *Kermit*.

Yoke Bar
A metal bar or yoke used on *sheeting* equipment to span a paper roll and lift it. Also known as a *spreader bar*.

Young-Helmholtz Theory
A theory about color vision that was proposed in the early 19th century. It suggests that humans perceive color based on the message received from three receptors in the eye, one of which is particularly sensitive to red, and the other to the green and blue areas of the spectrum respectively.

YUV
In video, term for the *component video* signal comprising the *luminance*, or brightness (Y), signal and the *color difference* signals (U and V). The U and V values are coupled with the *PAL* subcarrier to yield a color signal for an image.

Z

Z, z

The twenty-sixth letter of the English alphabet, which derived from the North Semitic letter *zayin* by way of the Greek *zeta*. Although the Z character was adopted by the Etruscans, there was no Z in Latin until after the Roman conquest of Greece in the first century BC, when it was developed to transliterate Greek works.

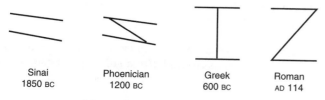

| Sinai | Phoenician | Greek | Roman |
| 1850 BC | 1200 BC | 600 BC | AD 114 |

The evolution of the letter Z.

Zapping

In television, term for rapidly "surfing" from channel to channel with the remote control, which has been known to drive many spouses insane.

z-Axis

In geometry, a line or axis of a *coordinate system* drawn at right angles to both the horizontal (*x-axis*) and vertical (*y-axis*) axes, on which the *z coordinate* is plotted. In three-dimensional graphics, it is the z-axis that provides depth. See also *x-Axis* and *y-axis*.

z Coordinate

In a *coordinate system*, a coordinate plotted on the *z-axis*. See *z-axis*. See also *x Coordinate* and *y Coordinate*.

Z-Directional Tensile Strength

A measure of the strength of paper in the direction perpendicular to the plane of its surface, also called *internal bond strength*. See *Internal Bond Strength*.

Zero

A numeral (0) representing nothing when used alone, and a decimal position for tens, hundreds, thousand, etc., when used in combination with other numerals. The numeral zero is often confused with the letter O, although in most typefaces they are designed somewhat differently. In some cases where confusion of the two characters is likely, a slash is put through the zero. (See also *Figures*.)

Zero Insertion Force Socket

In computing, a socket designed to facilitate the replacement of computer chips. A zero insertion force (ZIF) socket uses a small lever to gently raise the chip's pins from their holes. The chip can then be slid out, the new one inserted, and the lever lowered again. A ZIF socket minimizes damage to computer chips.

Zero-Slot LAN

In networking, a *local area network (LAN)* to which a computer can be connected via an existing *serial port* or *parallel port* rather than a special *network interface card*.

Zero-Speed Splicer

A device found in the infeed section of printing presses used in *web offset lithography* that splices a fresh roll of paper to an expiring roll.

A zero-speed splicer, in contrast to a *flying splicer*, operates while the expiring roll and the new roll are both stationary. The press, however, continues to print. This is accomplished by expanding a *festoon*, or a collapsible series of rollers. While splicing is taking place, the press can draw from the paper snaking its way through the fully expanded festoon. The expiring roll is stopped, the new roll is spliced to it, and the new roll is expanded to press speed.

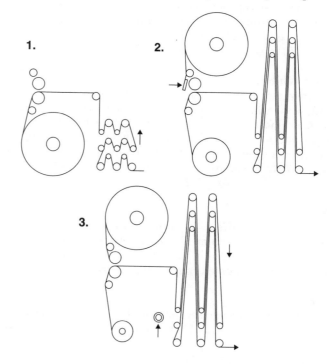

Principle of the zero-speed splicer. (1) The collapsed festoon rolls rise while paper feeds into the press. (2) The festoon is fully expanded before a splice is made. (3) The original paper roll is stopped and paper feeds from the festoon while the top web is spliced to the finished one.

This collapses the festoon, which can then be expanded the next time a splice needs to occur. (See also *Flying Splicer* and *Web Offset Lithography: Infeed and Web Control*.)

Zero-Wait-State Computer

A computer possessing a *static RAM* and *paged-mode RAM* chips that can store information without the need to be constantly refreshed by the *processor*. As a result, these computers eliminate the *wait state*, or the clock cycle during which no instructions are being executed.

z-Height

Alternate term for *x-height*. See *x-Height*.

ZIF Socket

See *Zero Insertion Force Socket*.

Zinc-Air

A type of lightweight battery capable of storing large amounts of energy, used for powering portable electronic equipment.

Zinc Sulfide

An inorganic material used as a *white pigment* in printing inks. Zinc sulfide (chemical formula ZnS) may also contain trace amounts of zinc oxide and other substances. It is an opaque white pigment that is chemically resistant to all substances except for acids. It also possesses high *abrasion resistance*. It is often used as an *extender* in many inks. (See *White Pigments*.)

(*CI Pigment White 7 No. 77975.*)

Zinc White

An inorganic material used as a *white pigment* in printing inks. Zinc white is almost entirely composed of zinc oxide (chemical formula ZnO). It is a clean white pigment of moderate *opacity* that tends to discolor when exposed to copper or when heated. It is used as an *extender* in many inks. (See *White Pigments*.) Also known as *Chinese White* (*CI Pigment White 4 No. 77947.*)

ZIP

In computing, a *file extension* denoting a file compressed using PKZIP, a popular file *compression* program for *PC* files. PKZIP can also be used to create a *self-extracting archive*, the file extension for which is *EXE*.

Zip

In computing, a magnetic disk developed by Iomega Corporation. Zip disks can hold 100 *megabyte*s of data, and are noted for their rapid read and write times, as well as low cost. They are currently extremely popular for transferring files to and from prepress service bureaus. See also *Jaz*.

z-Line

Alternate term for a *baseline*. See *Baseline*.

Zmodem

In networking and telecommunications, a popular *file-transfer protocol* for asynchronously transferring files between personal computers.

Zmodem is similar to its predecessors—*Xmodem* and *Ymodem*—but it transfers files with fewer errors and handles errors with greater efficiency. Zmodem has been superseded by *Kermit*.

Zone

In networking, especially by means of a *local area network (LAN)* such as *AppleTalk*, a subgroup of connected users within a larger group of interconnected networks.

Zoom

In motion picture photography and videography, to adjust a *lens* during filming or taping, bringing the subject nearer to or further away from the camera. See *Zoom Lens*. The term *zoom* in this sense has also been applied to computer graphics to refer to any enlargement or reduction of a screen image or icon.

Zoomable Icon

In multimedia, a small animation or video image which, when clicked on by the user, increases in size to display the animation or video at a larger size.

Zoom Box

In computing, especially by means of a *graphical user interface (GUI)*, a small, square icon located in the corner of some program windows that, when clicked on, causes the window to expand and fill the screen. If clicked on again, the window will shrink to its original size.

Zoom Command

In graphics programs, a command used to enlarge (*zoom in*) or reduce (*zoom out*) a screen image. See *Zoom*.

Zoom Lens

In motion picture photography or videography, a *lens* having a continuously variable *focal length* while the focal plane remains stationary, allowing the lens to bring the subject nearer or farther.

Time Line of Communications History

Prehistory

9000 BC Notches on animal bones in Africa and elsewhere for record keeping, a prelude to writing.

8000 BC Clay "tokens" in use as counters in the Middle East.

3300 BC In Sumeria, in Uruk, and in Iraq, crude pictographs of business transactions on clay tablets are earliest known form of writing.

3100 BC Mesopotamian cuneiform in use.

3000 BC Dust abacus is invented, probably in Babylonia.

3000 BC Egyptian hieroglyphics, sacred engraved writing, consist of pictures and symbols inscribed on temples and monuments.

2800 BC In Sumeria, pictographs evolve to cuneiform. From Latin *cuneus*—wedges—form consists of signs read from left to right.

2600 BC Egypt has a new job description—scribe.

2500 BC Travelers to the Near East take cuneiform with them, and the writing system spreads.

2500 BC Indus Valley people using seals for stamping and signing property, pictorial symbols—script—identify owner.

2400 BC In Korea, engraved ivory seals identify the writer through stamping.

2200 BC Oldest existing document written on papyrus in Egypt.

1800 BC Seals and clay tablets in Crete inscribed with sequential pictographs, first true form of writing—Linear A script.

1800 BC Babylonian mathematician develops algorithms to resolve numerical problems.

1800 BC Cretan Linear A inscriptions are in common use.

1450 BC Chinese create ideographs that are carved onto bones and bronze. Ideographs are characters that represent entire ideas.

1400 BC A cuneiform alphabet is fashioned in Ugarit trading port of Syria. This is the first complete alphabet.

1270 BC Syrian scholar compiles an encyclopedia; not much to include.

1000 BC Early Phoenician alphabet lays ground for future spell checkers.

900 BC China has an organized postal service for official use.

900 BC Greece and Mediterranean regions gain precursor of modern alphabet as Phoenicians spread the idea.

530 BC In Greece, a knowledge archive is created—a library.

510 BC Chinese scholars write on flattened bamboo with reeds dipped in black pigment.

506 BC Persia tries a form of pony express.

500 BC Greek "telegraph" consists of human relays.

500 BC Bead and wire abacus for addition and subtraction originates in Egypt.

400 BC A modern alphabet, with vowels, developed by the Greeks. It is phonetic, written from left to right.

400 BC Chinese write on silk, wood, bamboo.

220 BC Gazettes circulated to Chinese officials.

200 BC Bound pages written on parchment and vellum in Greece.

100 BC Chinese create paper but keep it a closely guarded secret.

59 BC Julius Caesar orders postings of Acta Diurna.

Advertising	Broadcasting	Computer	Information	Media
			100 Roman couriers carry official mail across the Empire's network of roads.	
		200 Saun-pan computing tray is used in China; soroban computing tray used in Japan.		
			300 Romans adopt Christianity as the official religion of the Empire. Christian scribes preserve the art of writing as they copy the Bible, gospels, and other religious teachings.	
			350 In Egypt, parchment books bound with wooden covers.	
			394 Last use of Egyptian hieroglyphics.	
			600 Chinese discover the value of nothing as the zero is applied.	
			765 Picture books are printed in Japan.	

Photo Imaging	Printing & Paper	Telecommunication	Typesetting	Word Processing
				100 Dead Sea Scrolls in Aramaic/Hebrew script.
	105 T'sai Lun may have invented paper.			
				175 Chinese classics carved in stone.
	250 Paper spreads throughout central Asia.			
	350 Parchment—refined leather—rivals papyrus use.			
	450 Ink on seals is stamped on paper in Korea and China. Chinese words for printing and seal are almost the same.			
	700 Sizing agents added to paper to improve quality.			
	751 Knowledge of papermaking spreads through Islamic cities as the Chinese secret is revealed. Paper manufactured outside of China, in Samarkand by Chinese captured in war.			

Advertising	Broadcasting	Computer	Information	Media
			770 Charlemagne revives arts and culture, employs the greatest minds to retrieve and copy books and other classical and historical information.	
			868 The *Diamond Sutra* is a block book printed in China.	
			950 Folded books in place of scrolls appear in China.	
		1000 Gerbert of Aurillac or Pope Sylvester II devises a more efficient abacus.		
			1116 Chinese make stitched books with sewing techniques.	
			1200 European monasteries communicate by rudimentary communication system.	
			1200 University of Paris has messenger service for members.	

Photo Imaging	Printing & Paper	Telecommunication	Typesetting	Word Processing
	875 Travelers to China see toilet paper; civilization begins.			
	950 Paper use spreads; moves west to Spain.			
	950 Bored women in a Chinese harem are said to invent playing cards.			
	1000 Mayas in Yucatan make paper from tree bark.			
	1035 Japanese use waste paper to make new paper; recycling begins.			
	1058–1061 Pi Sheng invents movable type with clay.			
	1140 Cloth is stripped from mummies to make paper.			
	1147 Crusader who was taken prisoner supposedly returns to Europe with paper-making art.			
	1241 In Korea, metal type is used.			
	1283 Watermarks added to paper.			

Advertising	Broadcasting	Computer	Information	Media
			1305 Private postal service in Europe.	
			1450 A few newsletters begin circulating in Europe, forerunners of newspapers.	
			1464 King of France establishes postal system.	

Photo Imaging	Printing & Paper	Telecommunication	Typesetting	Word Processing
	1298 Marco Polo records use of paper money in China.			
	1300 Wooden type discovered in central Asia.			
	1309 Paper is used in England for the first time.			
	1391 Koreans have a type foundry to produce bronze characters for imprinting.			
	1423 Europeans begin Chinese method of block printing, xylography.			
	1450 Johannes Gutenberg develops the printing press, prints a calendar in 36-line font.			
	1452 Metal plates are used in printing.			
	1455 Printing of the 42-line Bible, which Gutenberg started, is completed.			
	1458 Nicolas Jenson learns printing in Mainz.			
	1477 Production of an atlas from an intaglio engraving.			
	1477 William Caxton sets up shop in London.			
	1489 Aldus Manutius sets up shop in Venice.			
	1490 Printing of books on paper becomes commonplace in Europe.			
	1495 First paper mill is established in England.			

Advertising	Broadcasting	Computer	Information	Media
				1500 Approximately 35,000 books have been printed, about 10 million copies since the invention of printing about 1450.
		1520 Spectacles let more people read which leads to smarter people and the eventual invention of computers to aid in knowledge storage and dissemination.		
			1533 First postmaster in England.	
			1560 Regulated private postal systems develop in Europe.	
				1609 First regularly published newspaper appears in Germany.
		1617 John Napier uses bones to show division by subtraction and multiplication by addition in Scotland.		
		1622 William Oughtred develops the slide rule in England.		
		1624 Wilhelm Schickard builds four-function calculator-clock at the University of Heidelberg.		
			1627 France introduces registered mail.	
				1631 A French newspaper carries classified advertisements.

Photo Imaging	Printing & Paper	Telecommunication	Typesetting	Word Processing
	1513 First printing on paper from etched plates.			
			1545 Claude Garamond designs his typeface; forms first independent foundry.	
	1546 Printing of a book of portraits of French kings taken from engravings on copper.			
	1550 Wallpaper introduced to Europe from China by traders.			
				1565 The pencil makes its point.

Advertising	Broadcasting	Computer	Information	Media
			1639 In Boston, a person is appointed to handle foreign mail.	
		1642 Blaise Pascal builds first numerical calculating machine in Paris.		
				1650 Leipzig has a daily newspaper for the elite.
			1653 Parisians drop their postage-paid correspondence in mail boxes.	
			1659 Londoners get the penny (one pence) post.	
			1661 Postal service within the colony of Virginia. Tom Jefferson receives mail.	
		1673 Gottfried Leibniz builds mechanical calculating machine that multiplies, divides, adds, and subtracts.	**1673** Mail is regularly delivered on a route between New York and Boston.	
				1689 Newspapers are printed as unfolded broadsides. Long arms required for reading.
			1698 A public library opens in Charleston, South Carolina.	
				1702 *Daily Courant* is London's first daily newspaper.
				1704 A newspaper in Boston carries display advertising.

Photo Imaging	Printing & Paper	Telecommunication	Typesetting	Word Processing
	1639 First printing press in the American colonies; Elizabeth Glover and Stephen Daye at Harvard.			
1640 Kirchner, a German Jesuit, builds a magic lantern to project holy images.				
	1696 England has 100 paper mills.			
	1710 German engraver Jakob Christof Le Blon develops three-color printing process.			
				1714 Henry Mill receives patent in England for a typewriter-like machine.

Advertising	Broadcasting	Computer	Information	Media
			1732 In Philadelphia, Ben Franklin begins a circulating library.	
			1755 Regular mail ship sails between England and the colonies.	
			1768 *Encyclopaedia Britannica* is published.	
			1775 Continental Congress authorizes Post Office; Franklin becomes first Postmaster General.	
		1780 Benjamin Franklin flies a kite and discovers electricity.		
			1785 Stagecoaches carry mail and packages between towns in U.S.	
			1792 Mechanical semaphore signaler demonstrated in France. Predecessor of sign language.	

Photo Imaging	Printing & Paper	Telecommunication	Typesetting	Word Processing
	1719 René Réaumur proposes using wood by-products to make paper.			
	1725 Scottish printer develops stereotyping system to make duplicate printing plates.			
1727 Schulze concocts science of photo-chemistry.				
			1750 Baskerville typeface.	
				1770 The eraser is first application of "undo."
	1774 Swedish chemist invents a future paper-whitening agent.			
				1780 Steel pen points replace quill feathers to speed writing.
	1784 French book published with paper made without rags, from vegetable fiber.			
			1788 Bodoni typeface.	
		1791 French "Optical Telegraph Network" using cross-arms and pulleys for signals. Code book has 25,392 entries.		

Advertising	Broadcasting	Computer	Information	Media
			1792 Postal Act establishes mail delivery and scheduling throughout U.S.	
			1794 Letter carriers are a common sight on American city streets.	*1794* Panorama, a forerunner of future movie theaters, opens. No popcorn.
			1800 Letter takes three weeks to travel from Maine to Georgia.	
			1801 Joseph-Marie-Jacquard adapts a loom to run from holes in cards. Establishes basis for information storage and machine automation.	
			1810 An electro-chemical telegraph is demonstrated in Germany. It uses wires instead of mechanics.	
			1810 U.S. postal services consolidates private contracts and standardizes mail system.	
			1813 Congress legalizes steam boat carriage of mail.	

Photo Imaging	Printing & Paper	Telecommunication	Typesetting	Word Processing
	1798 Nicolas Louis Robert has papermaking machine operating in France.			
	1798 In Germany, lithography is invented by Alois Senefelder.			
	1800 Paper now routinely made from vegetable fibers instead of rags.			
	1805 Henry and Sealy Fourdrinier invents continuous web papermaking machine. Paper can now be supplied in rolls instead of sheets.			*1805* First use of carbon paper. By 1870s, it will become major enabler of telegraphy and typewriting.
1807 Camera lucida lets artists trace images.				
				1808 Turri of Italy builds a typewriter for a blind contessa—no need for White-Out.
	1814 A steam-powered rotary press prints *The Times* in London.			

Advertising	Broadcasting	Computer	Information	Media
			1815 America has 3,000 post offices.	
				1816 Newspapers given special postal rate: two cents.
			1818 Jöns Jakob Berzelius isolates selenium and discovers its electric conductivity in reaction to light—essential element for electro-photography.	
		1820 Arithmometer is mechanical device that is forerunner of the calculator.		
	1821 Sir Charles Wheatstone stores and reproduces sound in Great Britain.			
		1822 In England, Charles Babbage designs a Difference Engine to calculate logarithms.		
		1823 Babbage builds a subset of a calculating machine.	*1823* In England, Ronalds builds a telegraph in his garden; interest does not grow.	
				1825 Persistence of vision demonstrated with Thaumatrope.
	1827 Wheatstone constructs a microphone to work with his sound system in England.			

Photo Imaging	Printing & Paper	Telecommunication	Typesetting	Word Processing
1816 Joseph Nicephore Niépce captures an image on photo material after 8-hour exposure.				
	1819 David Napier builds an extensive rotary printing press.			
1822 Niépce makes a real photograph in under 8 hours.			**1822** William Church invents first type-composing machine in England.	
		1824 Samuel Finely Breese Morse, art instructor, learns of electromagnetism.		
1829 Louis Daguerre works with Niépce to pursue photographic quest.				**1829** William Austin Burt gets the first U.S. patent for a typewriter-like device, but does not call it that.
	1830 Gloss calendered paper is produced in England.			

Advertising	Broadcasting	Computer	Information	Media
				1832 Stroboscope in Austria and Phenakisto-scope in Belgium on the road to moving pictures.
		1833 Babbage Analytical Machine follows instructions from punch-cards—a general-purpose computer.	*1833* A telegraph line is constructed nearly two miles long in Germany.	*1833* Read all about it: a penny for a New York newspaper.
			1835 Samuel Morse exhibits the electric telegraph in the U.S.	*1835* James Gordon Bennett publishes the first of his penny press editions. Books for the masses.
			1836 Rowland Hill re-organizes British postal system. London has underground railway system only for mail.	
				1838 Wheatstone's stereoscope shows pictures in almost 3-D.
			1840 In Great Britain, postage stamps are available.	
1841 New! Improved! The advertising agency comes into being in London. Let's run it up the flagpole.				

Photo Imaging	Printing & Paper	Telecommunication	Typesetting	Word Processing
		1831 Joseph Henry demonstrates electro-magnetic telegraph. One mile run in Albany, New York.		
1837 Daguerre reduces photographic exposure time to 20 minutes.		*1837* Morse demonstrates the electric telegraph, running a distance of 1700 feet in a room at New York University.		*1837* Isaac Pitman publishes a book on shorthand in England.
		1837 Wheatstone and W.F. Cooke set up British electric telegraph. Quarrel hampers effort.		
1838 Daguerre-Niépce methods excite interest in photography.		*1838* Morse demonstrates telegraph to U.S. Congress, 10 miles of wire in a room.		
1839 William Henry Fox Talbot in England prints photographs from negatives.	*1839* In Russia, Moritz Jacobi invents electro-typing, for image reproduction.			
	1839 Electricity runs a printing press.			
			1841 A crude type-composing machine is almost used in London.	

Advertising	Broadcasting	Computer	Information	Media
		1842 Lady Ada Byron, Countess of Lovelace, daughter of poet Lord Byron, documents and writes programs for Babbage.		*1842* Illustrated *London News* filled with line art drawings.
			1845 Postal reform bill cuts postage and regulates domestic and international service.	
			1848 Forerunner of the Associated Press comes to life in New York.	
				1850 Associated Press utilizes telegraphy to transmit articles to American newspapers.

Photo Imaging	Printing & Paper	Telecommunication	Typesetting	Word Processing
	1842 The Christmas card is born.			
1843 The photographic enlarger is big deal.		*1843* U.S. Congress approves telegraph funding. Also funding for "Study of Hypnotism."		
		1844 Morse's telegraph connects Washington and Baltimore—"What hath God wroth?" is first message sent.		
		1844 First "official" telegram—Morse receives message in Supreme Court Building.		
		1845 English Channel telegraph cable is laid.		
		1845 American Morse Code becomes telegraph standard.		
		1845 Morse Magnetic Telegraph Company a success. Tariff equals 1¢ per four characters.		
		1845 Morse Magnetic Telegraph Company profits up, total revenue: $21.23.		
1846 Carl Zeiss manufactures lenses in Germany.	*1846* Double-cylinder rotary press prints 8,000 sheets an hour.			*1846* The typewriter ribbon is born, carbon paper in a roll.
	1847 A Philadelphia newspaper is printed on a rotary printing press for the first time.	*1847* Telegraph applied as business communication tool—transmits stock quotes.		
		1847 Bakewell shows a copying telegraph, which records messages.		
1849 Photographic slides are shown.				

Advertising	Broadcasting	Computer	Information	Media
			1851 U.S. newspaper mailing subsidized: postage cut in half; free distribution within country.	
			1853 Envelopes assembled by paper folding machine.	
		1854 Irishman George Boole publishes *The Mathematical Analysis of Logic* using the binary system, now known as Boolean algebra.		
		1855 George and Edvard Scheutz of Stockholm build first practical mechanical computer based on Babbage.	**1855** U.S. postage prepayment of letters made compulsory. **1855** Registered letters are new U.S. postal service.	
			1858 Mail boxes conveniently located on American street corners.	
			1860 Pony Express relays carry mail between St. Joseph, Missouri, and Sacramento, California.	
			1861 Telegraph kills Pony Express. Ponies downsized.	**1861** Oliver Wendell Holmes improves stereoscope for picture viewing.
			1862 In Italy, Caselli sends a drawing over a wire; fax is born.	

Photo Imaging

1851 Frederick Scott Archer develops wet-plate photography.

1851 Talbot takes a flash photograph at 1/100,000 of a second exposure.

1858 First aerial photograph is taken from a balloon.

1859 Cameras can now have wide-angle lenses.

1861 First chemical approaches to color photography.

Printing & Paper

1851 Paper is made from wood fiber.

1854 Early demonstration of curved stereotype plate for high-speed presses.

1856 Blotting paper replaces sand boxes and a lot of breath.

1856 Louis Adolphe Poitevan *practices* photolithography.

1856 Finishing machine folds newspapers, sheets for books.

1862 In U.S., paper currency is printed.

Telecommunication

1851 The Pennsylvania & Lake Erie Railroad depends on the telegraph for control and communication.

1854 Telegraph goes to war in Crimea.

1854 Bourseul constructs an experimental telephone.

1855 Printing telegraph developments in the U.S.

1858 First efforts at transatlantic telegraph service fail.

1861 First transcontinental telegraph link: New York to San Francisco.

Typesetting

1857 Another crude machine to set type is demonstrated in U.S.

Word Processing

1858 Eraser is integrated with the end of a pencil; a complete word processing system.

Advertising	Broadcasting	Computer	Information	Media
			1863 First international postal conference in Paris.	
			1864 Railway post office workers sort mail on trains.	
			1864 The railroad train takes on a mail car.	
			1870 Stock ticker extends the reach of Wall Street.	
1873 James Clerk Maxwell publishes a theory of radio waves.		*1873* Lord William Thomson Kelvin uses a machine to calculate the tides.	*1873* One penny postcard debut in U.S.	*1873* Illustrated daily newspaper hits the street in New York.
			1874 Universal Postal Union convened.	
			1875 In the U.S., Carey designs a selenium mosaic to transmit a picture.	

Photo Imaging	Printing & Paper	Telecommunication	Typesetting	Word Processing
		1864 Wireless electro-magnetic waves are transmitted 14 miles through Virginia countryside.		
		1865 Atlantic cable links Europe and U.S. for telegraph communication.		
		1866 Western Union dominates wire communication.		
				1867 Christopher Latham Sholes patents single-letter typewriter in Wisconsin.
				1868 Sholes calls writing machine a "Type-Writer"; so is the first typist, his daughter.
1869 Color photography via the subtractive method.	*1869* From Austria, picture postcards wish you were there.	*1869* Carbon paper commonly used by telegraphers.		
	1871 Halftone process lets newspapers print pictures.			
		1872 Simultaneous transmission from both ends of a telegraph wire in U.S.		
1873 First color photographs are seen in England.		*1873* In Ireland, May uses selenium to send a signal across the Atlantic cable.		*1873* Remington starts manufacturing Sholes & Glidden typewriter with the QWERTY keyboard.
		1874 Telephone is invented by Alexander Graham Bell; 30–40 messages on same phone wire.		
	1875 Thomas Alva Edison invents the mimeograph with assistant Albert Blake Dick.			

Advertising	Broadcasting	Computer	Information	Media
			1876 Edison's carbon transmitter sends speech over long distances.	
	1877 In America, Edison invents a phonograph.			
1878 Full-page newspaper ads.	*1878* The dynamic microphone is invented in the U.S. and Germany.			*1878* In France, praxinoscope, an optical toy, moves toward movies.
	1878 David Hughes invents the microphone.			*1878* First telephone directories are issued.
	1878 Cathode-ray tube is invented by William Crookes, English chemist.			
			1880 First parcel post is smashing success.	
			1880 Leblanc theorizes transmitting a picture in segments.	
		1880 Edison invents the electric light; now people can have ideas.		
			1882 In England, primitive wirephotos.	

Photo Imaging	Printing & Paper	Telecommunication	Typesetting	Word Processing
		1876 Bell patent for analog voice network.		*1876* James Clephane says "I want to bridge the gap between the typewriter and the printed page."
		1876 Bell Telephone founded to make telephone available to the public.		
		1876 Alexander Graham Bell invents "harmonic telegraphy."		
		1877 Bell Telephone Company grows to a 1000-phone network.		
1878 Eadweard Muybridge photographs a horse in motion.				
1878 Dry-plate photography.				
	1879 Benday process aids newspaper production of illustrations, drawings.	*1879* Telephone numbers replace names at switching offices; business rate $40/month, residential rate $20/month.		
	1880 Photos in newspapers, using halftones now routine.	*1880* 50,000 telephone lines in the U.S.		
		1881 Demise of "Optical Telegraph Networks."		
		1881 "Electric Telegraph" proposed by Francis Ronalds in Britain. Admiralty declares electric telegraph "wholly unnecessary."		
		1881 John Carty accidentally hooks two wires between phones; evolves to "unshielded twisted pair" and beginning of the telecommunications explosion.		
		1882 First manual switchboard connects telephones and people.		

Advertising	Broadcasting	Computer	Information	Media
	1883 Edison bumps into "Edison effect"— basis of broadcast tubes.			
	1884 In Germany, Nipkow scanning disc, early version of television.	*1884* Herman Hollerith applies for patents for automatic punch-card tabulating machine.	*1885* U.S. Post Office offers special delivery.	
		1884 Electric tabulator introduced for commercial use.	*1885* Trains are carrying newspapers daily for service in other cities.	
	1885 Dictating machines are used in business offices.			
	1886 Graphophone wax cylinder and sapphire stylus improve sound quality.	*1886* William Burroughs develops the first commercial mechanical adding machine. Later patents a printing version.		
1887 Montgomery Ward mails out a 540-page catalog.	*1887* Music from a flat disc stamped out by machine.	*1887* Comptometer, a multifunction adding machine is manufactured.		
	1888 Edison's phonograph is manufactured for sale to the public.			
	1888 Heinrich Hertz proves the existence of radio waves.			
		1889 Herman Hollerith takes the census with punch cards. Forms Computing & Tabulating Company, later IBM.		
	1890 Branly's coherer conducts radio waves in French experiment.			*1890* Friese-Greene builds kinematograph camera and projector in England.
				1891 Edison's assistant, Dickson, builds the Kinetograph motion picture camera; peep-show is born.
			1893 Addressograph speeds up addressing.	
				1893 Dickson builds a motion picture studio in New Jersey.

Photo Imaging	Printing & Paper	Telecommunication	Typesetting	Word Processing
		1884 Long-distance phone calls, but not that long—New York to Chicago.		
1885 George Eastman makes coated photo printing paper.				
		1886 Richard Sears sells watches via telegraph—telemarketing is born with Sears, Roebuck & Co.	*1886* Ottmar Mergenthaler demonstrates Linotype machine for setting type at *New York Tribune*.	
1887 Celluloid film; it will replace glass plate photography.				
1888 Kodak box camera makes picture taking simple.		*1888* Interstate Commerce Commission (ICC) formed to regulate telephone service.		
		1888 Coin-operated public telephone.		
		1889 Almon Strowger, a Kansas City undertaker, develops automatic telephone exchange.		
	1890 A. B. Dick markets the mimeograph machine.	*1890* Telephones number 250,000 in the U.S. as Bell's patent expires.		*1890* Typewriters are in common use in business offices.
1891 Telephoto lens is attached to a camera.	*1891* Letterpress press prints and folds 90,000 four-page newspapers an hour.			
	1892 A four-color rotary press is demonstrated.	*1892* Automatic telephone switchboard in use.		*1892* Portable typewriters take typing on the road.

Advertising	Broadcasting	Computer	Information	Media
	1894 Flat phonograph disc competes with the cylinder.			
			1896 Rural free delivery (RFD) brings mail to American farms.	*1895* France's Lumière brothers have a portable movie camera.
				1895 Paris audience sees movies projected.
		1896 Herman Hollerith constructs a sorting machine.	*1897* In England, postpeople deliver mail to every home.	
1898 New York State passes a law against misleading advertising of any kind.				
	1899 The loudspeaker blares its birth.			
	1899 Sound is recorded magnetically by Valdemar Poulsen in Denmark.			
	1899 American Marconi Company is created; predecessor to RCA.			
	1901 Sale of phonograph record made of hard resinous shellac.		*1902* Photoelectric scanning can send and receive a picture.	
	1901 Guglielmo Marconi sends a radio signal across the Atlantic; transatlantic service begins.			
	1902 U.S. Navy installs radio telephones aboard ships.			

Photo Imaging	Printing & Paper	Telecommunication	Typesetting	Word Processing
	1894 Rotogravure worked on secretly by the Rembrandt Intaglio Printing Co., Lancaster, England.	*1894* Guglielmo Marconi demonstrates wireless telegraphy.		
		1895 Dial telephones in the Milwaukee, Wisconsin, city hall bypass operator.	*1895* In England, Friese-Greene invents primitive photo-typesetting machine.	
		1895 Marconi has wireless telegraphy.		
1896 X-ray photography is born.	*1896* Electric power runs a paper mill.		*1896* The Monotype sets type by machine as single characters; separates the functions of input and output.	*1896* "What you see is what you get"—Underwood typewriter permits typists to see what they are typing; errors still occur.
1898 First photographs taken with artificial light.				
1900 Kodak Brownie camera makes photography cheaper and simpler.		*1900* AT&T formed with merger of Bell and other companies.		
		1900 Michael Pupin's loading coil reduces telephone voice distortion.		
				1901 First electric typewriter, the Blickensderfer.
1902 Germany's Zeiss invents the four-element Tessar camera lens.	*1902* Etched zinc engravings start to replace hand-cut wood blocks.	*1902* Trans-Pacific telephone cable connects Canada and Australia.		

Advertising	Broadcasting	Computer	Information	Media
	1903 Technical improvements in radio, telegraph, phonograph, movies, and printing lay groundwork for future developments.	*1903* Nikola Tesla, a Yugoslavian who worked for Edison, patents electrical logic circuits, known as gates or switches.	*1904* Korn transmits a photograph by telephone or radio in Germany.	*1903* *London Daily Mirror* illustrates only with photographs.
	1904 The double-sided phonograph disc.			*1904* *The Great Train Robbery* is first movie with a plot; creates demand for movies with a story.
	1904 John Fleming invents the diode to improve radio communications.		*1905* In New Zealand, the postage meter is introduced.	*1904* Zooks! — the comic book.
	1905 The juke box; 24 choices; no rock n' roll.			*1905* In Pittsburgh, the first nickelodeon opens.
				1905 In France, Pathé colors black-and-white films by machine.
				1905 The Yellow Pages.
	1906 A program of voice and music is broadcast in the U.S.			*1906* An animated cartoon film is shown in U.S.
	1906 Lee de Forest invents the three-element vacuum tube.			*1906* An experimental sound-on-film motion picture.
	1906 Dunwoody and Pickard build a crystal-and-cat's-whisker radio.			*1906* In Britain, new process-color books are inexpensive.
	1906 Fessenden plays violin for startled ship wireless operators.			
	1907 DeForest begins regular radio music broadcasts.			*1907* Bell and Howell develop a film projection system.
	1907 In Russia, Rosing develops theory of television.			*1907* Daily comic strips.
				1908 In U.S., Smith introduces true color motion pictures.
	1909 First editorial broadcast; the subject is women's suffrage.			
	1910 Sweden's Elkstrom invents "flying spot" camera light beam.			

Photo Imaging	Printing & Paper	Telecommunication	Typesetting	Word Processing
	1904 Offset lithography demonstrated.	*1904* A telephone answering machine is invented.		
	1905 Photography, printing, and post combine in picture postcards.			
1906 The Haloid Co., Rochester, New York, founded to manufacture and sell photographic paper.	*1906* Chester F. Carlson, inventor of xerography, born in Seattle.	*1906* Strowger advances automatic dial telephone switching.		
1907 Lumière brothers invent still color photography process.				

Advertising	Broadcasting	Computer	Information	Media
		1911 Computer-Tabulating-Recording Co. is formed through a merger of the Tabulating Company (founded by Hollerith), the Computing Scale Company, and the International Time Recording Co.		*1911* Efforts are made to bring sound to motion pictures.
	1912 U.S. passes law to control radio stations. *1912* Feedback and heterodyne systems usher in modern radio.		*1912* First mail carried by airplane.	*1912* Motorized movie cameras replace hand cranks.
	1914 Better triode vacuum tubes improve radio reception. *1914* Radio message is sent to an airplane.	*1914* Thomas J. Watson becomes president of Computing-Tabulating-Recording Company. *1914* In the U.S., Goddard aims for the sky with rocket experiments.		
	1915 The electric loudspeaker.			*1915* *Birth of a Nation* sets new movie standards.
	1916 David Sarnoff envisions radio as "a household utility." *1916* Radios get tuners. *1917* Condenser microphone aids broadcasting, recording. *1917* Frank Conrad builds a radio station, later KDKA.			
			1918 First regular airmail service — Washington, District of Columbia, to New York City.	

Photo Imaging	Printing & Paper	Telecommunication	Typesetting	Word Processing
	1911 Rotogravure aids magazine production of photos.			
			1913 Intertype line-caster competes with Linotype as original Mergenthaler patents expire.	
1914 In Germany, the 35-mm still camera from Leica.				
		1915 Wireless radio service connects U.S. and Japan.		
		1915 Radio-telephone carries speech across the Atlantic.		
		1915 First transcontinental phone call, takes 23 minutes to set up call; charge is $20.70.		
1916 Cameras get optical rangefinders.				
		1918 Multiplexing combines two or more voice channels on one wire.		

Advertising	Broadcasting	Computer	Information	Media
		1919 Flip-flop circuit invented; computers count on it.		
	1920 Sound recording is done electrically rather than mechanically.		*1920* First cross-country airmail flight in the U.S.	
	1920 The first radio broadcasting stations are started.		*1920* Post Office accepts the postage meter.	
	1920 KDKA in Pittsburgh broadcasts first scheduled programs.			
	1921 Quartz crystals keep radio signals from wandering.	*1921* Czech word robot is used to describe mechanical workers in the play R.U.R. by Karel Capek.	*1921* Western Union begins wirephoto service.	
1922 A radio commercial is broadcast; cost is $100 for ten minutes.	*1922* Recording artists desert phonograph horn mouths for acoustic studios.			*1922* Technicolor introduces two-color process for movies.
				1922 Germany's UFA produces a film with an optical sound track.
				1922 Experimental 3-D movie, requires spectacles with one red and one green lens.
				1922 *Nanook of the North* is first cinema documentary.
	1923 Ribbon microphone becomes the studio standard.		*1923* A picture, broken into dots, is sent by wire.	*1923* 16-mm nonflammable film makes its debut.
	1923 Vladimir Zworykin's electronic iconoscope camera tube and kinescope display tube debut.			
1924 The Eveready Hour is the first sponsored radio program.	*1924* At KDKA, Frank Conrad sets up a short-wave radio transmitter.		*1924* Daily coast-to-coast air mail service.	
	1924 2.5 million radio sets in the U.S.		*1924* Experimental pictures are transmitted over telephone lines.	
			1924 Notebooks get spiral bindings. Idea falls flat.	

Photo Imaging	Printing & Paper	Telecommunication	Typesetting	Word Processing
		1919 Callers can now dial telephone numbers themselves.		
		1919 Shortwave radio is invented.		
			1920 Bauhaus typography.	
		1923 People on one ship can talk to people on another ship by radio telephone.		
		1923 Bell rate structure contains 206 different local rates.		

Advertising	Broadcasting	Computer	Information	Media
	1925 All-electric phonograph is demonstrated.	*1925* Vannevar Bush builds a large scale analog calculator, the differential analyzer, at MIT.	*1925* Commercial picture facsimile radio service across the U.S.	*1925* From France, a wide-screen film.
	1925 A moving image, the blades of a model windmill, is telecast.			
	1926 Some radios get automatic volume control, a mixed blessing.	*1926* Robert Goddard launches liquid-fuel rocket.	*1926* Commercial picture facsimile radio service across the Atlantic.	*1926* In U.S., the first 16-mm movie is shot.
	1926 John Logie Baird demonstrates an electromechanical TV system.		*1926* Bell Telephone Labs transmit film by television.	*1926* The Book-of-the-Month Club.
	1926 National radio network, NBC, is formed.			
	1927 Negative feedback makes hi-fi possible.			*1927* Al Jolson's *The Jazz Singer* is the first movie "talkie."
	1927 NBC begins two radio networks, Red and Blue; CBS formed.			*1927* Movietone offers newsreels with sound.
	1927 Philo Farnsworth assembles a complete electronic TV system.			*1927* Glorious technicolor developed.
	1927 First public demonstration of television.			
	1927 Radio-telephone operational between London and New York.			
	1928 In Schenectady, New York, the first scheduled television broadcasts.	*1928* IBM adopts the 80-column punch card.		*1928* *Steamboat Willie* introduces Mickey Mouse and an empire is born.
	1928 Baird demonstrates color TV on an electromechanical system.			*1928* A motion picture is shown in color in Hollywood.
	1928 Russian immigrant, Vladimir Zworykin, patents the cathode-ray tube (CRT).			
	1928 Television sets are put in three homes, programming begins.			

Photo Imaging	Printing & Paper	Telecommunication	Typesetting	Word Processing
			1926 Walter Morey conceives the idea of driving linecasting machines from coded paper tape. The process is supported by Frank Gannett of Gannett Newspapers and the result is TTS— Tele-TypeSetting—which permitted the transmission of data for typesetting. The concept lays the foundation for the automation of the typesetting process, but will not be fully implemented until 1951, when the newspaper unions relax their objections.	
		1927 U.S. Radio Act declares public ownership of the airwaves.	*1927* Futura typeface.	
		1928 The teletype machine makes its debut.		

Advertising	Broadcasting	Computer	Information	Media
	1928 Baird invents a video disc to record television.			
	1928 In an experiment, television crosses the Atlantic.			
	1929 In Germany, magnetic sound recording on plastic tape.		*1929* Brokers watch stock prices on an automated electric board.	
	1929 The car radio.		*1929* Air mail flown from Miami to South America.	
	1929 Experiments begin on electronic color television.		*1929* Bell Lab transmits stills in color by mechanical scanning.	
	1929 Television studio is built in London.			
	1929 Zworykin demonstrates cathode-ray tube "kinescope" receiver, 60 scan lines.			
	1930 "Golden Age" of radio begins in U.S.			
	1930 Lowell Thomas begins first regular network newscast.			
	1930 TVs based on British mechanical system roll off factory line.			
	1931 Electronic TV broadcasts in Los Angeles and Moscow.	*1931* First calculator, the Z1, is built in Germany by Konrad Zuse.		
	1931 NBC experimentally doubles transmission to 120-line screen.			
				1932 Disney adopts a three-color Technicolor process for cartoons.
				1932 Stereophonic sound in a motion picture, *Napoleon*.
	1933 Edwin Howard Armstrong invents FM, but its real future is 20 years off.		*1933* Singing telegrams.	
	1933 Phonograph records go stereo.			

Photo Imaging	Printing & Paper	Telecommunication	Typesetting	Word Processing
		1929 Telegraph ticker sends 500 characters per minute.		
		1929 Ship passengers can phone relatives ashore.		
1930 Photo flashbulbs replace explosive flash powder.	*1930* Four-color offset press.	*1930* AT&T picture phone blurs TV and telephone.		
		1930 Telephone network outgrows telegraph network.		
1931 Exposure meters go on sale to photographers.		*1931* Commercial teletype service.		
1932 Kodak introduces 8-mm film for home movies.			*1932* The *Times* of London uses its new Times New Roman typeface by Stanley Morison.	
1932 Zoom lens is invented, but has a long way to go.				
1932 The light meter.				
1933 Multiple-flash sports photography.				

Advertising	Broadcasting	Computer	Information	Media
	1934 Half of the homes in America have radios.		*1934* Associated Press starts wirephoto service.	*1934* Drive-in movie theater opens in New Jersey.
	1934 Mutual Radio Network begins operations.			*1934* Three-color Technicolor used in experimental film.
	1934 In Germany, a mobile television truck roams the streets.			
	1935 In Germany, audio tape recorders go on sale.			*1935* The pocket Penguin paperback book hits the market.
	1935 A. C. Nielsen's Audimeter tracks radio audiences.			
	1935 All-electronic VHF television comes out of the lab.			
	1936 Berlin Olympics are televised closed circuit.	*1936* Alan Turing's "On Computable Numbers" describes a general-purpose computer.	*1936* Coaxial cable connects New York to Philadelphia.	
		1936 Bell Labs invents a voice recognition machine.		
	1937 A recording, the Hindenburg crash, is broadcast coast to coast.	*1937* George Stibitz builds the first binary calculator at Bell Telephone Laboratory.		*1937* *Snow White* is the first feature-length cartoon.
	1937 NBC sends mobile TV truck onto New York streets.			
	1938 Broadcasts can be taped and edited.	*1938* Hewlett-Packard Co. is founded to make electronic equipment.	*1938* Chester Carlson makes first xerographic image in Astoria, in the New York City borough of Queens.	
	1938 CBS "World News Roundup" ushers in modern broadcast newscasting.			
	1938 Radio drama, "War of the Worlds," causes national panic on Halloween.			
	1938 Bill Baird demonstrates live TV in color.			
	1938 Allen DuMont markets television receiver for the home.			

Photo Imaging	Printing & Paper	Telecommunication	Typesetting	Word Processing
		1934 Communications Act of 1934 creates Federal Communications Commission.	**1934** In Scotland, teletypesetting sets type by phone line.	
1935 German single-lens reflex roll (SLR) film camera synchronized for flash bulbs.				**1935** IBM's electric typewriter comes off the assembly line.
1935 Eastman Kodak develops Kodachrome color film.				
		1937 Pulse code modulation points the way to digital transmission.		
1938 Strobe lighting brightens photographic market.				**1938** Biro brothers invent the ballpoint pen in Argentina.

Advertising	Broadcasting	Computer	Information	Media
	1939 New York World's Fair shows TV to public.	*1939* John J. Atanasoff designs a prototype ABC (Atanasoff-Berry Computer) with the help of graduate student Clifford Berry at Iowa State College. In 1973 a judge will declare it the first automatic digital computer.	*1939* Air mail service across the Atlantic.	
	1939 Regular TV broadcasts begin.			
	1940 First color TV broadcast.		*1940* Photostat process invented.	*1940* *Fantasia* introduces stereo sound to the American public.
	1941 Stereo is installed in a Moscow movie theater.	*1941* Zuse's Z3 is the first computer controlled by software.		
	1941 FCC sets U.S. television standards.			
	1941 CBS and NBC start commercial television transmission.			
	1941 Peter Goldmark at CBS experiments with electronic color TV.			
		1942 Atanasoff, Berry build the first electronic digital computer.		
	1944 NBC presents first U.S. network newscast, a curiosity to many viewers.	*1944* Mark I (IBM ASCC) is completed, based on the work of Professor Howard H. Aiken at Harvard and IBM. It is a relay-based computer.		
	1945 A 1941 FCC ruling requires RCA to divest itself of one of its two networks; NBC Blue is sold in 1943 to Edward Noble for $8 million, and it will become ABC in 1945.	*1945* Vannevar Bush (science advisor to President Roosevelt) proposes MEMEX, a conceptual machine that stores information, with the ability to create information trails, links to related texts and illustrations, for future reference.		
	1945 Wartime ban on new TV stations lifted. Over previous four years, FCC had applications for station licenses but took no action. There were fewer than 7,000 working TV sets in the country and only nine stations; three in New York, two in Chicago and Los Angeles, and one in Philadelphia and Schenectady, New York.	*1945* John von Neumann paper describes stored-program concept for EDVAC.		

Photo Imaging	Printing & Paper	Telecommunication	Typesetting	Word Processing

1941 Microwave transmission.

1942 Kodacolor process brightens color prints.

1944 IBM offers a typewriter with proportional spacing, the Executive.

1945 It is estimated that 14,000 products are made from paper.

1945 Author Arthur C. Clarke envisions geosynchronous communication satellites. 30 years later he will transmit manuscript from home in Sri Lanka to his New York publisher.

Advertising	Broadcasting	Computer	Information	Media
	1946 Jukeboxes go into mass production.	**1946** University of Pennsylvania's ENIAC heralds the modern electronic computer.		
		1946 Binac (Binary Automatic Computer), the first computer to operate in real time, is started by Eckert and Mauchly; it will be completed in 1949.		
		1946 Eckert-Mauchly Computer Corporation is formed as the Electronic Control Co. to design a Universal Automatic Computer (UNIVAC).		
	1947 "Howdy Doody," a children's series, premieres live on NBC, remains on the air until 1960.		**1947** Haloid acquires license to Chester Carlson's basic xerographic patents from Battelle Development Corp. of Columbus, Ohio.	
	1947 NBC debuts "Meet the Press." It will go on to become the oldest series on network TV.			
	1947 The zoom lens covers baseball's World Series for TV.			
	1948 The LP record arrives on a vinyl disk.	**1948** IBM introduces the 604 electronic calculator.	**1948** Shannon and Weaver of Bell Labs propound information theory.	**1948** Hollywood switches to non-flammable film.
	1948 Advertisers accept TV: 933 sponsors buy TV time, a rise of 515% over 1947.	**1948** IBM builds the Selective Sequence Electronic Calculator (SSEC), a computer with 12,000 tubes.	**1948** Haloid and Battelle announce development of xerography.	
	1948 Early cable systems are born in remote areas of Pennsylvania and Oregon. Known as Community Antenna Television, its function was to bring TV signals into communities where off-air reception was either poor because of interfering mountains or distance.	**1948** Transistor is invented by William Bradford Shockley with John Bardeen and Walter H. Brattain. It will eliminate vacuum tubes.		
	1948 Milton Berle debuts as the master of ceremonies on "The Texaco Star Theater," which will run until 1956. The show earns the highest rating ever recorded—86.7% of all TV households.			

Photo Imaging	Printing & Paper	Telecommunication	Typesetting	Word Processing
		1946 Automobile radio telephones connect to telephone network.	*1946* French engineers build a phototypesetting machine.	
1947 Hungarian engineer in England invents holography.				
1948 Land's Polaroid camera prints pictures in a minute.				

Advertising	Broadcasting	Computer	Information	Media
	1948 Public clamor for television begins; FCC freezes new licenses.			
	1948 Airplane re-broadcasts TV signal across nine states.			
	1949 RCA offers the 45-rpm record.	**1949** Whirlwind at MIT is the first real-time computer.	**1949** Model A copier (Ox Box) is first commercial xerographic product; manual process.	
	1949 Number of TV stations grows to 98 (in 58 market areas) from 18 (in 12) the previous year.	**1949** Magnetic core computer memory is invented.		
	1949 Network television in U.S.			
	1950 A.C. Nielsen's Audimeters track viewer watching.	**1950** Remington-Rand acquires Eckert-Mauchly Computer Corp.		
	1950 Regular color television transmission.			
	1950 Vidicon camera tube improves television picture.			
	1951 CBS broadcasts first color program, but only 25 receivers accommodate mechanical color. Viewers of 12 million existing black-and-white sets see only a blank screen.	**1951** UNIVAC I is installed at the Bureau of Census using a magnetic tape unit as a buffer memory.		**1951** Cinerama will briefly dazzle with a wide, curved screen and three projectors.
		1951 Wang Laboratories, Inc. is founded by An Wang in Boston.		
	1951 The number of TV households grows to 20 million, up 33% from previous year. U.S. advertisers spend $288 million on TV time, an increase of 38.8% from 1951.	**1951** Computers are sold commercially.		
	1952 Sony offers a miniature transistor radio; you can even walk around with it.	**1952** EDVAC takes computer technology a giant leap forward.		**1952** 3-D movies finally offer thrills to audience.
	1952 Bing Crosby's company tests videotape recording.	**1952** UNIVAC I predicts an Eisenhower landslide with 7% of the votes, just one hour after the polls close.		
	1952 Zenith proposes pay-TV system using punch cards.			

Photo Imaging	Printing & Paper	Telecommunication	Typesetting	Word Processing
			1949 Intertype Fotosetter is first generation of phototypesetting.	
			1949 "Petunia" is early version of Photon second-generation phototypesetter by René Higgonnet and Louis Moyroud.	
			1950 Intertype introduces the Fotosetter, a photographic typesetter based on the linecaster. First announced in 1948, it and the Monophoto later categorized as the first generation of phototypesetting, mechanical and optical.	*1950* Changeable typewriter typefaces in use.
1951 Still cameras get built-in flash units.		*1951* Coaxial cable reaches coast to coast.		
		1952 Telephone area codes.		

Advertising	Broadcasting	Computer	Information	Media
	1953 Color broadcasting officially arrives in the U.S. when FCC approves modified version of an RCA system.	*1953* First high-speed printer is developed by Remington-Rand for use on the UNIVAC.		
	1953 NTSC color standard adopted.	*1953* IBM ships its first stored-program computer, 701, a vacuum-tube, or first-generation, computer.		
	1953 CATV system uses microwave to bring in distant signals.			
	1954 Radio sets in the world outnumber daily newspapers.	*1954* FORTRAN is created by John Backus at IBM. Harlan Herrick runs first FORTRAN program.		
	1954 Sporting events are broadcast live in color.	*1954* Gene Amdahl develops the first operating system, used on IBM 704.		
		1954 USSR launches Sputnik, the first artificial earth satellite.		
	1955 Music is recorded on tape in stereo for first time.		*1955* Debut of Xerox Copyflo, semiautomatic xerographic printer; continuous copies on plain paper.	
	1956 Videotape is introduced by Ampex Corp. at a CBS-TV affiliate's station. Most TV shows are produced by the kinescope process.	*1956* T. J. Watson, Jr. assumes presidency of IBM.	*1956* Rank Xerox Limited formed as joint venture of Haloid Co. and Rank Organization.	
	1957 During a typical week, viewers encounter 420 commercials totaling 5 hours, 8 minutes.	*1957* FORTRAN becomes the first high-level programming language.		*1957* First book to be entirely phototypeset is offset-printed, *The Wonderful World of Insects* (Beacon Press).
	1957 A surgical operation is televised.	*1957* Dot matrix printer from Centronics.		
		1957 Advanced Research Projects Agency (ARPA) formed within Department of Defense to establish lead in science and technology applicable to military.		
	1958 Commercial stereo recording systems introduced.	*1958* First virtual memory machine, Atlas, installed in England by Feranti, was developed at University of Manchester by R. M. Kilburn.	*1958* The Haloid Company becomes Haloid Xerox Inc.	
	1958 Broadcast bounced off rocket, pre-satellite communication.			

Photo Imaging	Printing & Paper	Telecommunication	Typesetting	Word Processing

Typesetting

1954 Mergenthaler Linotype Company introduces the Linofilm phototypesetter. The leading hot-metal typesetting supplier enters the new technology late.

Telecommunication

1955 Tests begin to communicate via fiber optics.

1956 Bell tests the picture phone for real.

1956 First regular transatlantic telephone calls by cable.

1957 Letraset dry transfer lettering.

1958 Data moves over regular voice-grade phone circuits.

Advertising	Broadcasting	Computer	Information	Media
	1958 Cable carries FM radio stations.	**1958** First electronic computers are built in Japan by NEC.		
	1958 There are 525 cable TV systems serving 450,000 subscribers in the U.S.	**1958** Frank Rosenblatt builds the Perceptron Mark I using a CRT as an output device.		
	1958 Ad expenditures in radio and TV cross the $2 billion mark.	**1958** LISP is developed on the IBM 704 at MIT under John McCarthy.		
		1958 Seymour Cray builds the first fully transistorized super-computer for Control Data Corp., CDC 1604.		
		1958 Laser is shown. It will change the world.		
	1959 Local announcements, weather data, and local ads go on cable.	**1959** IBM introduces the 1401 computer. Over 10,000 units will be delivered during its lifetime.	**1959** Xerox manufactures first plain-paper copier.	
	1959 French SECAM and German PAL systems introduced for television.	**1959** IBM ships its first transistorized, or second-generation, computers, the 1620 and 1790.	**1959** Xerox 914 copier.	
			1959 Xerox purchases from Battelle all worldwide patents on xerography.	
		1959 Jack S. Kilby at Texas Instruments files a patent for the first integrated circuit.		
		1959 The microchip is the building block of new electronic processors.		
		1959 Bell Labs experiments with artificial intelligence.		
	1960 The first of four "great debates" between John F. Kennedy and Richard Nixon is broadcast on September 26, breaking new ground in presidential campaigning.	**1960** Benjamin Curley develops the first mini-computer, the PDP-1, at Digital Equipment.		**1960** A movie gets Smell-O-Vision, but public turns up its nose.
	1960 Zenith tests subscription TV; no buyers.	**1960** COBOL runs on UNIVAC II and RCA 501.		
		1960 Removable disks appear.		
	1961 Boxing match test is a knockout; shows potential of pay-TV.	**1961** The time-sharing computer is developed. Time-sharing runs at MIT on IBM 709 and 7090 computers.		
	1961 FCC approves FM stereo broadcasting; spurs FM development.			

Photo Imaging	Printing & Paper	Telecommunication	Typesetting	Word Processing
			1959 Helvetica typeface introduced.	
			1959 Lithomat changes its name to Photon, Inc.	
		1960 Echo I, a U.S. balloon in orbit, reflects radio signals to Earth.		
		1960 First electronic switching central office opens in Chicago.		
				1961 IBM introduces the "golf ball" typewriter, Selectric.

Advertising	Broadcasting	Computer	Information	Media
	1961 ABC stretches the station break between programs to 40 seconds from 30. The other networks follow. **1961** FCC Chairman Newton Minow delivers speech in which he denounces U.S. TV as a "vast wasteland." **1962** Cable companies import distant signals for local broadcast. **1962** FCC requires UHF tuners on TV sets.	**1962** APL (A Programming Language) is developed by Ken Iverson, Harvard University, and IBM. **1962** IBM markets 1311 using removable disks. **1962** IBM's U.S.-based revenues from computer products at $1 billion; surpasses other revenue. **1962** H. Ross Perot founds Electronic Data Systems in Dallas, Texas. **1962** The minicomputer arrives.	**1962** Haloid Xerox, Inc., becomes Xerox Corporation. **1962** Xerox acquires University Microfilms, Inc. Fuji Xerox is joint venture of Rank Xerox and Fuji Photo Film. **1962** Telstar satellite transmits an image across the Atlantic.	
	1963 From Phillips in Holland comes the audio cassette. **1963** CBS and NBC TV newscasts expand to 30 minutes in color. **1963** On Nov. 22, President Kennedy is shot in Dallas, and TV coverage of the assassination and funeral grip the nation and the world. Jack Ruby shoots accused assassin Lee Harvey Oswald on an NBC live broadcast as he is being transported by law officials. **1963** TV surpasses newspapers as an information source; poll indicates 36% of Americans find TV more reliable source, compared with 24% who favor print.	**1963** PDP-8 becomes the first popular minicomputer. **1963** Control Data acquires Bendix Corp. computer division. **1963** Conversational graphics consoles developed by General Motors (DAC-1) and MIT Lincoln Labs (Sketchpad), resulting in computer-aided design (CAD). Sketchpad uses first light-pen, by Ivan Sutherland. **1963** Tandy acquires Radio Shack (9 stores).	**1963** Postal zip codes introduced. **1963** Xerox 813 is first desktop copier to make copies on ordinary paper; five copies per minute.	

Photo Imaging	Printing & Paper	Telecommunication	Typesetting	Word Processing
		1962 Comsat created to launch, operate global system.		
		1962 Paul Baran, Rand Corp., authors "On Distributed Communications Networks."		
1963 Polaroid camera instant photography adds color.		*1963* Communications satellite is placed in geosynchronous orbit.		

Advertising	Broadcasting	Computer	Information	Media
	1963 Instant replay adds a new dimension to televised sports when featured in a telecast of an Army-Navy football game. In 1964, it becomes a standard technique.			
	1964 FCC issues its first cable regulation. There are about 1 million homes wired for cable in the U.S. at the time.	*1964* IBM System 360, the first family of compatible computers.	*1964* LDX, Long Distance Xerography, uses scanners, networks, and printers for high-speed document facsimile transmission.	
	1964 73 million viewers tune in to the appearance of the Beatles on the "Ed Sullivan Show."	*1964* Control Data Corporation introduces the CDC 6000, which uses 60-bit words and parallel processing. CDC ships the 6600, the most powerful computer for years, designed by Seymour Cray.	*1964* 2400 copier/ duplicator is first Xerox duplicator; 40 copies per minute.	
	1964 Olympic Games in Tokyo telecast live globally by satellite.			
	1964 From Japan, the videotape recorder for home use.	*1964* BASIC (Beginners All-purpose Symbolic Instruction Language) created by Tom Kurtz and John Kemeny of Dartmouth. First time-sharing BASIC program runs.		
		1964 Graphic tablet is developed by M.R. Davis and T.D. Ellis at Rand Corporation.		
		1964 Russian scientists bounce a signal off Jupiter.		
	1965 Cartridge audio tapes go on sale.	*1965* Computer time-sharing becomes popular.		*1965* Color news film.
	1965 Satellites begin transmitting television signals; domestic TV distribution in Soviet Union.	*1965* Digital Equipment ships the first PDP-8 minicomputer.		
	1965 Color TV booms as NBC's nighttime schedule is broadcast in color, along with all major programs, sports events, and specials. About 2.7 million color sets are sold, more than twice as many as in 1964.	*1965* IBM ships System 360, its first integrated circuit-based, third-generation, computer.		
	1965 Solid-state equipment spreads through the cable industry.			

Photo Imaging	Printing & Paper	Telecommunication	Typesetting	Word Processing
		1964 Touch Tone telephones and Picturephone service. *1964* Intelsat, international satellite organization, is formed.	*1964* The Mergenthaler Linofilm Quick and Photon 713 are introduced. They bring cost of second-generation phototypesetting down to under $50,000.	
1965 Kodak offers Super 8 film for home movies.		*1965* Electronic phone exchange gives customers extra services. *1965* Communications satellite Early Bird (Intelsat I) orbits above the Atlantic. *1965* ARPA sponsors study on "cooperative network of time-sharing computers." *1965* TX-2 at MIT Lincoln Lab and Q-32 at System Development Corp. (Santa Monica, California) are directly linked without packet switches.		*1965* Ted Nelson coins the word "hypertext."

Advertising	Broadcasting	Computer	Information	Media
		1966 Honeywell acquires Computer Control Company, a mini-computer manufacturer.		
		1966 Scientific Data Systems (SDS) introduces Sigma 7.		
		1966 Texas Instruments offers the first solid-state hand-held calculator.		
	1967 Dolby eliminates audio hiss.	*1967* Computers get the light pen as input/control tool.		
	1967 Pre-recorded movies on videotape sold for home TV sets.	*1967* DEC introduces the PDP-10 computer.		
		1967 A. H. Bobeck at Bell Laboratories develops bubble memory.		
	1968 Approximately 200 million TV sets in the world, 78 million in U.S.	*1968* The RAM microchip reaches the market.	*1968* Xerox 3600 I and III copier/duplicators; 60 copies per minute.	
		1968 UNIVAC introduces the 9400 computer.		
	1968 Manufacturers churn out 11.4 million new TV sets, up from the 5.7 million receivers made in 1960.	*1968* Integrated Electronics (Intel) Corp. is founded by Gordon Moore and Robert Noyce.		
	1969 Astronauts walk on the moon; then send live photographs from the moon to earth.	*1969* Xerox acquires Scientific Data Systems.	*1969* 3M announces Color in Color copier. Does not result in a marketable product.	
	1969 Sony's U-Matic puts videotape in a cassette.	*1969* Edson deCastro leaves DEC to start Data General and introduces Nova, first 16-bit mini-computer.		

Photo Imaging	Printing & Paper	Telecommunication	Typesetting	Word Processing
1966 Telecopier is first desktop Xerox facsimile machine.		*1966* Fiber optic cable multiplies communication channels.	*1966* Hell of Germany introduces the Digiset, world's first CRT photo-typesetter. This later becomes the RCA Video-comp and still later the Information International Comp80. Third generation of phototype-setting, these units have output speeds of 1000 characters per second.	
		1967 Cordless telephones get some calls.	*1967* Mergenthaler Linotype and CBS Labs Linotron phototypesetter outputs at 1,000 characters per second.	
		1967 About 200 million telephones in the world, half in the U.S.		
		1967 ACM Symposium on Operating Principles. Plan for a packet-switching network.	*1967* Alphanumeric, Inc. introduces the APS CRT typesetter. It is later sold to IBM and introduced as the IBM 2680, then returned to Alphanumeric, which acquires Autologic to manufacture the device.	
		1967 First design paper on ARPANET published by Lawrence G. Roberts.		
		1967 Andreas van Dam and others build the Hypertext Editing System.	*1967* Linotype installs the Linotron 1010 CRT typesetter at the U.S. Government Printing Office, developed in conjunction with CBS Laboratories.	
		1968 FCC approves non-Bell equipment attached to phone system.	*1968* At Chicago's Print 68 show, Compugraphic introduces a second-generation phototype-setter for under $10,000. The 2900/4900 quickly aids in the conversion from hot metal to photo-typesetting. The price point allows the technology to reach the mass of users. By this time the infrastructure is in place to allow that use: paper-tape keyboards and systems, computer type-setting programs, and reliable paper and film consumables.	
		1968 Intelsat completes global communications satellite loop.		
		1968 PS-network presented to the Department of Defense's Advanced Research Projects Agency (ARPA), forms foundation for Internet.		
		1968 Doug Engelbart demonstrates NLS, a hypertext system.		
		1969 ARPANET commissioned by Department of Defense for research into networking.	*1969* ATF, AM Vari-typer, Star Parts, and Harris all introduce phototypesetters.	

Advertising	Broadcasting	Computer	Information	Media
	1969 Public Broadcasting Service begins, launching "Sesame Street," one of the most influential achievements in children's TV.	**1969** IBM unbundles hardware and software; introduces a minicomputer line, System/3.		
	1969 On July 20, astronaut Neil Armstrong takes mankind's first step on the moon as millions of U.S. viewers watch the historic event live on TV.	**1969** PASCAL compiler is written by Nicklaus Wirth and installed on the CDC 6400.		
		1969 Xerox Palo Alto Research Center in California established.		
		1970 The computer floppy disk shows its flexibility; from Shugart Associates.	**1970** Postal Reform Bill makes U.S. Postal Service a government corporation.	
		1970 DEC ships its first 16-bit minicomputer, the PDP-11/20.	**1970** U.S. Post Office and Western Union offer Mailgrams.	
		1970 Data General ships SuperNova.		
		1970 Honeywell acquires General Electric's computer operations.		
		1970 IBM ships its first System 370, a fourth-generation computer.		
1971 The transition from 60 seconds to 30 seconds as the standard length for commercials takes hold.		**1971** Intel builds the microprocessor, "a computer on a chip."		
		1971 IBM 370/135 and 370/195 mainframe computers.		
		1971 Floppy disks load the IBM 370 microcode.		
		1971 Intel Corporation has first microprocessor, the Intel 4004, developed by a team headed by Ted Hoff.		
		1971 Sperry-Rand takes over the RCA computer product line.		
	1972 HBO initiates limited pay-TV service for cable.	**1972** "Pong" starts the video game craze; market goes up and down.		
	1972 New FCC rules lead to community access channels.	**1972** Cray Research is founded.		

Photo Imaging	Printing & Paper	Telecommunication	Typesetting	Word Processing
		1969 Bolt, Beranek and Newman (BBN) create a network for ARPA that connects university, military, and defense contractors.		
1970 In Germany, a videodisc is demonstrated.	*1970* Xerox 4000 copier.	*1970* ARPANET hosts start using Network Control Protocol (NCP).		
		1971 Ray Tomlinson of BBN has email program to send messages across a distributed network, derived from intra-machine email program (SNDMSG) and experimental file transfer program (CPYNET).	*1971* First video editing terminal introduced by Harris. Edits paper tapes. Competing unit introduced later that year by Hendrix Electronics of Londonderry, New Hampshire. These devices let you edit text input from paper tape and then produce a new paper tape.	*1971* Wang 1200 is company's first word processor.
1972 Sony's Port-a-Pak, a portable video recorder.

1972 Polaroid camera can focus by itself. | *1972* Xerox 1000 copier is last of 914 copier technology machines; 15 copies per minute. | *1972* The BBC offers "Ceefax," a two-way cable information system.

1972 "Open Skies" means any U.S. firm can have communication satellites. | | |

Advertising	Broadcasting	Computer	Information	Media
		1972 First electronic pocket calculator is developed by Texas Instruments. *1972* Gary Kildall at Naval Postgraduate School writes PL/1, the first programming language for the Intel 4004 microprocessor. *1972* Prime Computer is founded. *1973* Winchester disk drives are first introduced by IBM, which uses the term as a code name for its Model 3340 direct-access storage device. *1974* Intel introduces the 8080, an 8-bit microprocessor that will be used in numerous personal computers.	*1973* Xerox 6500 color copier makes full-color copies on plain paper and transparencies. *1974* In England, the BBC transmits Teletext data to TV sets. *1974* Xerox 4500 copier.	

Photo Imaging	Printing & Paper	Telecommunication	Typesetting	Word Processing
		1972 Landsat I, "eye-in-the-sky" satellite, is launched.		
		1972 International Conference on Computer Communications opens with demonstration of ARPANET between 40 machines and the Terminal Interface Processor (TIP).		
		1972 InterNetworking Working Group (INWG) created to address need for establishing agreed-upon protocols with chairman Vinton Cerf.		
		1972 Telnet specification (RFC 318) is published.		
	1973 Xerox 1200 computer printing system is first nonimpact xerographic printer for computer output.	*1973* First international connections to ARPANET.	*1973* Over 11 firms have video editing terminals or systems and phototypesetter models.	*1973* IBM's Selectric typewriter is now "self-correcting."
		1973 Bob Kahn poses Internet problem, starts internetting research program at ARPA.	*1973* Photon suffers financial crisis. Bought out by Dymo, which has acquired Star Parts. Result is Dymo Graphic Systems. Dymo then bought out by Esselte, and is sold to Litton Industries which acquires Itek, which has a phototypesetter division. The market is not as big as everyone thought.	*1973* Redactron shows cassette-based word processor, first firm to challenge IBM dominance of word processing market.
		1973 Vinton Cerf draws gateway architecture on back of envelope in hotel lobby in San Francisco.		
		1973 Cerf and Kahn present basic Internet ideas at INWG at University of Sussex, U.K.		
		1973 The Defense Advanced Research Projects Agency (DARPA) initiates a project on internetworking to link packet switching networks. There are 35 nodes at this time.		
		1974 Cerf and Kahn publish "A Protocol for Packet Network Intercommunication" which specifies in detail, the design of a Transmission Control Program (TCP).	*1974* First multi-terminal video editing systems introduced by Harris, Hendrix, and Tal-Star, primarily for newspapers. These systems automate the editorial part of the process.	
		1974 BBN Telenet is first public packet data service (a commercial version of ARPANET).		

Advertising	Broadcasting	Computer	Information	Media
	1975 Time Inc. links satellite programming to cable systems with international launch of Home Box Office. The heavyweight boxing championship bout between Joe Frazier and Muhammad Ali is broadcast from Manila.	*1975* The microcomputer, in kit form, reaches the U.S. home market.	*1975* Sony's Betamax and JVC's VHS battle for public acceptance.	
		1975 Cray-1 supercomputer is introduced.		
		1975 Homebrew Computer Club is first personal computer users group.		
		1975 MITS Altair personal computer, named after a Star Trek episode. This kit cost $397 for a 256-byte computer. The I/O consists of switches and lights, designed by Ed Roberts and Bill Gates.		
		1975 Microsoft is founded after Bill Gates and Paul Allen adapt and sell BASIC to MITS for the Altair PC.		
		1975 The first computer store opens in Santa Monica, California.		
		1975 Xerox withdraws from the mainframe computer industry.		
	1976 Ted Turner delivers programming nationwide by satellite.	*1976* Apple 1 computer shown by Jobs and Wozniack.	*1976* Last Xerox 914 copier order, although field service on the machine continued.	
	1976 British TV networks begin first teletext system.	*1976* Seymour Cray engineers and delivers Cray 1 with 200,000 freon-cooled ICs and performance of 100 million floating point (MFLOP) operations per second.		
	1976 Ted Turner's WTBS, Atlanta, becomes a "superstation" via cable TV.	*1976* Kurzweil Reading Machine reads books to the blind.		

Photo Imaging	Printing & Paper	Telecommunication	Typesetting	Word Processing
			1974 AM Varityper shows first phototypesetter with video editor connected, the Comp/Set. Within two years, every competitor has a similar device.	
				1975 ZOG (now KMS), a distributed hypermedia system, debuts at Carnegie Mellon University.
1976 Still cameras are controlled by microprocessors.		*1976* UUCP (Unix-to-Unix CoPy) developed at AT&T Bell Labs and distributed with UNIX one year later.		

Advertising	Broadcasting	Computer	Information	Media
	1977 Columbus, Ohio, residents try two-way cable experiment, QUBE.	*1977* Xerox acquires Shugart Associates, first floppy disk maker.		
	1977 More than 75% of TV homes are able to receive color on one or more sets.	*1977* Apple Computer founded formally with Apple II personal computer.		
	1977 Gross TV advertising revenues rise to $7.5 billion—20% of all U.S. advertising.	*1977* DEC first 32-bit superminicomputer, the VAX-11/780.		
	1978 PBS goes to satellite for delivery, abandoning telephone lines.	*1978* Texas Instruments introduces the Speak-and-Spell educational toy featuring digital speech synthesis.		*1978* *TypeWorld* magazine founded by Frank Romano.
	1978 Viacom's Showtime cable network.	*1978* Total computers in use in the U.S. exceed 500,000 units.		
	1979 Videotext provides data by television on command.	*1979* Ethernet local area network connects workstations, printers, and other equipment.	*1979* Xerox 9500 duplicator produces halftones and line copy comparable to offset; 120 copies per minute.	
		1979 VisiCalc, first electronic spreadsheet software, shown at West Coast Computer Faire.		
		1979 Speech recognition machine has a vocabulary of 1,000 words.		
	1980 Sony Walkman tape player starts a peripatetic fad.	*1980* Total computers in use in the U.S. exceed million units.		*1980* In France, a holographic film shows a gull flying.
	1980 Addressable converters pinpoint individual homes.			
	1980 Ted Turner's Cable News Network, 24-hour news channel, is born.			

Photo Imaging	Printing & Paper	Telecommunication	Typesetting	Word Processing
	1977 Xerox 9700 electronic printing system is first xerographic laser printer; 120 pages per minute.	*1977* Tymshare launches Tymnet.		
	1977 Xerox 9400 duplicator automatically copies on both sides of paper; automatic document handler accepts virtually all kinds of originals; 120 pages per minute.	*1977* Theorynet by Larry Landweber at University of Wisconsin provides electronic mail to researchers in computer science (using a locally developed email system and Telenet).		
		1977 First demonstration of ARPANET/ Packet Radio Net/ SATNET operation of Internet protocols with BBN-supplied gateways.		
1978 From Konica, the point-and-shoot camera.			*1978* Combined video editing/phototypesetters introduced by Mergenthaler, Compugraphic, AM Varityper, and Itek.	*1978* Electronic typewriters go on sale.
			1978 Mergenthaler Linotype shows the Linotron 202, first of the under $50,000 phototypesetters. Shortly followed by Autologic, Compugraphic, Alphatype, Itek, and others.	*1978* Word processing evolves into multi-terminal systems with central data storage.
				1978 The Aspen Movie Map, first hypermedia videodisc, shown at MIT.
1979 From Holland comes the digital videodisc read by laser.		*1979* In Japan, first cellular phone network.		*1979* WordStar, word processing program for PCs, from Micropro.
		1979 ARPA establishes the Internet Configuration Control Board (ICCB).		
1980 Public international electronic fax service, Intelpost, begins.	*1980* Xerox 5700 laser printing system combines word processor printing, electronic mail, remote computer printing and copying in a single unit.	*1980* Intelsat V relays 12,000 phone calls, two-color TV channels.		
	1980 Diablo 630 computer daisywheel printer sets industry standard.			

Advertising	Broadcasting	Computer	Information	Media
		1981 450,000 transistors fit on a silicon chip one quarter-inch square.		
		1981 The IBM PC legitimizes the personal computer.		
		1981 The laptop computer is introduced by Radio Shack.		
		1981 The first mouse pointing device.		
		1981 Commodore VIC-20 home computer, which sells over one million units.		
		1981 Osborne Computer Osborne 1 is the first portable computer.		
		1982 Compaq Computer incorporates.		*1982* *USA Today* pages output in regional plants by satellite communication.
		1982 Sun Microsystems is founded.		
		1982 Microsoft licenses MS-DOS to 50 microcomputer manufacturers in first 16 months.		
		1983 Computer chip holds 288,000 bits of memory.	*1983* ZIP + 4, expanded 9-digit ZIP code is introduced.	*1983* Lasers and plastics improve newspaper production.
		1983 *Time* names the computer as "Man of the Year."	*1983* American video-text service starts, fails.	

Photo Imaging

1982 From Japan, a camera with electronic picture storage, no film.

1982 Kodak camera uses film on a disc cassette.

Printing & Paper

1981 Xerox 8700 electronic printing system produces and prints computer-generated text, business forms and other images at up to 70 pages per minute.

1981 Xerox 2700 laser printer.

1981 Canon introduces LBP-CX which will become most prolific engine for laser printing at the desktop. Within three years, it is adopted by Hewlett-Packard, Apple, and scores of other companies and millions will be shipped worldwide.

Telecommunication

1981 Minitel (Teletel) is deployed across France by France Telecom.

1981 BITNET, the "Because It's Time NETwork." Starts as a cooperative network at the City University of New York, with the first connection to Yale. Featuring electronic mail and listserv servers to distribute information, as well as file transfers.

1981 CSNET (Computer Science NETwork) is the collaboration of computer scientists and University of Delaware, Purdue University, University of Wisconsin, Rand Corp., and BBN funded by NSF to provide networking services (email) to university scientists with no access to ARPANET.

1982 AT&T agrees to give up 22 Bell companies, settling a 13-year lawsuit brought by the U.S. Justice Department.

1982 DCA and ARPA establish Transmission Control Protocol (TCP) and Internet Protocol (IP) as the protocol suite for ARPANET. Leads to first definition of an "internet" as a connected set of networks, specifically those using TCP/IP.

1982 TCP/IP suite to be standard for Department of Defense.

1982 External Gateway Protocol (RFC 827) specification between networks.

1983 Cellular phone network starts in U.S.

1983 Switch from NCP to TCP/IP.

1983 AT&T forced to break up; seven Baby Bells are born.

Typesetting

1982 Linotype shows its Linotron 101 laser typesetter.

Word Processing

1981 Ted Nelson conceptualizes "Xanadu," a central, pay-per-document hypertext database encompassing all written information.

Advertising	Broadcasting	Computer	Information	Media
		1983 Compaq ships its first computer in January and marks up $111 million in sales—the greatest first-year sales in the history of American business.		
		1983 Cray 2 computer introduced with performance of one billion FLOPs (floating point operations per second).		
		1983 Lotus 1-2-3 replaces VisiCalc as spreadsheet software of choice for microcomputers.		
		1983 Total computers in use in the U.S. exceed ten million units.		
1984 During the third quarter of the Super Bowl, Apple Computer introduces Macintosh computer with 60-second commercial called "1984," created by Chiat/Day. The spot cost $400,000 to produce and $500,000 to broadcast in its single national paid airing.	**1984** A television set can be worn on the wrist.	**1984** Portable compact disc player arrives.	**1984** Xerox introduces 6500 color copier. Just marginally successful because it uses only three toners.	
		1984 The 32-bit microprocessor.		
		1984 One megabyte memory chip.		
		1984 Apple introduces the Macintosh computer.		
		1984 IBM PC AT (Advanced Technology) merges with Rolm Corp. to form telecommunications subsidiary.		
		1984 Tandy 1000 personal computer becomes the best selling PC-compatible in first year.		
		1984 Experimental machine can translate Japanese into English.		
	1985 Sony builds a radio the size of a credit card.	**1985** CD-ROM can put 270,000 pages of text on a CD record.		
	1985 U.S. TV networks begin satellite distribution to affiliates.	**1985** IBM delivers the new 3090 Sierra systems.		
	1985 In Japan, 3D television; no spectacles needed.	**1985** Synthetic text-to-speech computer pronounces 20,000 words.		
	1985 Pay-per-view cable channels open for business.			

Photo Imaging	Printing & Paper	Telecommunication	Typesetting	Word Processing
		1983 CSNET/ARPANET gateway put into place.		
		1983 ARPANET split into ARPANET and MILNET, the latter integrated with the Defense Data Network.		
		1983 Desktop workstations, many with Berkeley UNIX, include IP networking software.		
		1983 The ARPA-joined networks become the Internet.		
1984 *National Geographic* puts a hologram on its cover.	*1984* Canon LBP-CX starts laser printer revolution; 8 pages per minute at 300 dots per inch becomes Hewlett-Packard Laserjet, Apple Laserwriter.	*1984* Internet Domain Name Server (DNS) introduced. Number of hosts breaks 1,000.		*1984* Telos introduces Filevision, a hypermedia database for the Macintosh.
1984 Japanese introduce high-quality facsimile.		*1984* JUNET (Japan Unix Network) established using UUCP.		
1984 Camera and tape deck combine in the portable camcorder.		*1984* "Neuromancer" written by William Gibson; coins term "cyberspace."		
1985 Digital image processing for editing stills bit by bit.		*1985* Cellular telephones go into cars.		*1985* Janet Walker creates the Symbolics Document Examiner.
1985 A Sony TV screen measures 40 meters × 25 meters.		*1985* The Internet consists of 100 linked networks.		*1985* Intermedia, a hypermedia system, is conceived at Brown University by Norman Meyrowitz and others.

Advertising	Broadcasting	Computer	Information	Media
	1986 HBO scrambles its signals.	*1986* Burroughs merges with Sperry to form Unisys Corporation, second only to IBM in computer revenues.	*1986* Xerox 1005 color copier reduces and enlarges; five, 3-color copies a minute.	
	1986 Cable shopping networks debut.	*1986* Compaq introduces its first Intel 80386-based PC.	*1986* Canon Color Laser photocopier is first to use four toners.	
		1986 Hewlett-Packard introduces its Spectrum line of reduced instruction set computers (RISC).		
		1986 Tandy has 7,300 retail outlets including 4,800 company-owned Radio Shack stores.		
		1986 The number of computers in the U.S. exceeds 30 million.		
		1986 Apple Computer HyperCard, first widely available hypermedia authoring tool.		
	1987 Government deregulates cable industry.	*1987* IBM introduces its PS/2 family and ships over one million units by year end.		
	1987 20th Century Fox owner Rupert Murdoch launches Fox Broadcasting Co.	*1987* Cray Research introduces the Cray 2S, which is 40% faster than the Cray 2.		
	1987 More than 50% of U.S. households are wired for cable.	*1987* Sun Microsystems introduces its first workstation based on a RISC microprocessor.		
		1987 Apple introduces the Macintosh II and SE.		
		1987 IBM introduces its Systems Applications Architecture (SAA).		
		1987 Compaq reaches a billion dollars in sales in its fifth year of operation.		
		1987 Apple spins off application software business as separate company, Claris.		

Photo Imaging	Printing & Paper	Telecommunication	Typesetting	Word Processing
	1986 Xerox 4050 laser printer. *1986* 9790 and 8790 high-volume laser printing systems, high-capacity storage and central processing power to print text and graphics, the 9790 at up to 120 pages per minute, the 8790 at up to 70 pages per minute.	*1986* NSFNET creates backbone speed of 56 Kbps. *1986* National Science Foundation (NSF) establishes five supercomputing centers to provide high-computing power for all. This allows an explosion of connections, especially from universities. *1986* First Freenet (Cleveland) on-line under the auspices of Society for Public Access Computing (SoPAC). *1986* Network News Transfer Protocol (NNTP) to enhance Usenet news performance over TCP/IP. *1987* Number of Internet hosts exceeds 10,000. *1987* Number of BITNET hosts breaks 1,000.		*1986* OWL introduces GUIDE, a hypermedia document browser. *1987* Hypertext '87 Workshop.

Advertising	Broadcasting	Computer	Information	Media
		1987 A version of the Sun workstation is available for less than $10,000 (down from $50,000). Increased interest in UNIX programs and systems because of multi-tasking functionality.		
	1988 Widespread use of videocassette recorders zap away at the TV viewing audience. At the start of the year, almost 60% of TV households have a VCR—up from 4% in 1982.	**1988** DEC introduces VAXstation 8000.	**1988** Government brochure mailed to 107 million addresses.	
		1988 Cray Research introduces the Cray Y-MP, a $20 million super-computer.	**1988** IBM and Sears joint videotex venture starts operation under the PRODIGY name.	
		1988 IBM introduces a new mainframe computer operating system called MVS/ESA.	**1988** Xerox 5090 duplicator copies at 135 copies per minute; touch-sensitive, color video screen; reduces, enlarges, makes two-sided copies, staple-stitches and thermal-binds pages, inserts covers and dividers.	
		1988 IBM mid-range computers called AS/400.		
		1988 Motorola 88000, a RISC microprocessor.		
		1988 Sun Microsystems surpasses $1 billion in sales; introduces 80386-based workstations.		
		1988 A consortium of PC companies led by Compaq introduces EISA counter-standard to IBM's PS/2 MicroChannel bus.		
		1988 Next unveils innovative workstation using erasable optical disks as the primary mass-storage device. IBM licenses Next's graphical user interface.		
		1988 Kurzweil Personal Reader is the first portable reading machine for the blind.		
	1989 Pay-per-view becomes a familiar part of cable TV service, reaching about one-fifth of all wired households.	**1989** DEC workstation using Mips Computer's RISC microprocessor.		**1989** Tiananmen Square demonstrates power of media to inform the world.
	1989 The broadcast networks reach an all-time low of 55% of the total TV audience.	**1989** Intel 80486 microprocessor and I860 RISC/coprocessor. Both chips have over one million transistors.		
		1989 Hewlett-Packard acquires Apollo for $476 million.		

Photo Imaging	Printing & Paper	Telecommunication	Typesetting	Word Processing
		1988 Nondestructive worm spreads via Internet and brings several thousand computers to their knees.		
		1988 Department of Defense adopts OSI and sees use of TCP/IP as an interim approach.		
		1988 OSI Los Nettos network created with no federal funding support by regional founders: Caltech, TIS, UCLA, USC, ISI.		
		1988 NSFNET backbone to T1 (1.544-Mbps) speeds.		
		1988 FidoNet gets connected to the Net, enabling the exchange of email and news.		
		1988 Countries connecting to NSFNET are Canada, Denmark, Finland, France, Iceland, Norway, Sweden.		
	1989 Autologic demos first computer-to-plate system.	*1989* Number of Internet hosts breaks 100,000.	*1989* Standardization of font libraries in PostScript form as almost every major foundry releases type styles in one format. Over 30,000 fonts available.	
		1989 First relays between commercial electronic mail carrier and the Internet—MCI Mail through Corporation for the National Research Initiative (CNRI), and Compuserve through Ohio State.		

Advertising	Broadcasting	Computer	Information	Media
	1989 Time Inc. & Warner Communications close $14 billion merger deal.	**1989** Sun Microsystems SPARCstation, a low-end RISC workstation at $9,000.		
		1989 IBM Officevision software uses SAA protocol, runs on PS/2, LAN, AS/400 and mainframe computers.		
		1989 Cray restructures into two companies, Cray Research, with its current business, and Cray Computer Corp., headed by Seymour Cray, which will develop a gallium arsenide-based supercomputer.		
		1989 Apple Computer introduces its first portable Macintosh.		
		1989 Worldwide number of computers in use surpasses 100 million units.		
		1989 Battery-powered notebook computer becomes a full-function computer including hard and floppy disk with the arrival of Compaq's LTE and LTE/286.		
		1989 The number of computers in the U.S. exceeds 50 million units.		
		1989 The first EISA-based personal computers arrive.		
		1989 The first 80486-based computers are introduced.		
	1990 Most 2-inch videotape machines are gone.	**1990** Motorola introduces the 68040 microprocessor.		
		1990 IBM announces its RISC Station 6000 family of high-performance workstations.		
		1990 Digital Equipment introduces a fault-tolerant VAX computer.		

Photo Imaging	Printing & Paper	Telecommunication	Typesetting	Word Processing
		1989 Corporation for Research and Education Networking (CREN) formed through merger of CSNET and BITNET.		
		1989 Internet Engineering Task Force (IETF) and Internet Research Task Force come together.		
		1989 "Cuckoo's Egg" by Clifford Stoll tells the true tale of a German hacker group that infiltrated U.S. facilities via the Internet.		
		1989 Tim Berners-Lee proposes World Wide Web project.		
		1989 The Internet consists of 500 linked networks.		
1990 Videodisc returns in a new laser form.	*1990* Xerox DocuTech Production Publisher is electronic document publishing product that bridges the gap between computer workstations and business publishing; first in a series that will use advanced technologies in scanning, filing, printing, finishing, and networking.	*1990* ARPANET dead.		*1990* IBM discontinues Selectric typewriter, a sign of the typewriter's passing.
		1990 Archie released by Deutsch, Emtage, and Heelan at McGill.		*1990* Hytelnet released by Peter Scott (University of Saskatchewan).
		1990 ISO Development Environment (ISODE) to provide an approach for OSI migration for the Department of Defense. ISODE software allows OSI application to operate over TCP/IP.		

Advertising	Broadcasting	Computer	Information	Media
		1990 Cray Research entry-level super-computer, Y-MP2E, with a starting price of $2.2 million.		
		1990 Microsoft introduces Windows 3.0.		
		1990 IBM ships the PS/1, a computer for consumers and home offices.		
		1990 Apple has low-end Macintoshes.		
		1990 Intel launches a parallel processing supercomputer using over 500 860 RISC microprocessors.		
		1990 Sun Microsystems brings out the SPARC-station 2.		
1991 CNN dominates news coverage world-wide during Gulf War.		*1991* Xerox sells Ventura Software, Inc., to Corel Corp.	*1991* Xerox 5775 Digital Color Copier is controlled by a touch-screen, color video monitor shows the progression of copies; can add color to copies made from black-and-white originals; 7.5 pages per minute.	
1991 Live TV news switching between world capitals during Gulf War looks simple.		*1991* Notebook PCs are introduced by most PC vendors.		
1991 Denver viewers can order movies at home from list of more than 1,000 titles.		*1991* Hewlett-Packard RISC-based 9000 Series 700 workstations with exceptional price-performance.		
1991 More than 4 billion video cassette tape rentals in U.S. alone.		*1991* Intel introduces the 486SX, a lower-priced 486 chip.		
1991 Three out of four U.S. homes own VCRs; fastest selling domestic appliance in history.		*1991* NCR agrees to be acquired by AT&T in a $7.4 billion deal.		
		1991 Apple releases the System 7.0 operating system for Macintosh.		
		1991 Microsoft rolls out DOS 5.0.		
		1991 Apple and IBM sign a historic deal—including two joint ventures—Kaleida will develop multimedia products, Taligent will develop object-oriented operating software and eventually disappears.		

Photo Imaging	Printing & Paper	Telecommunication	Typesetting	Word Processing
		1990 Countries connecting to NSFNET are Argentina, Austria, Belgium, Brazil, Chile, Greece, India, Ireland, South Korea, Spain, and Switzerland.		
		1990 The Internet consists of over 2,200 linked networks.		
	1991 Xerox 4135 laser printer is a cut-sheet production printer; up to 135 pages per minute.	*1991* Baby Bells get permission to offer information services.		
	1991 Heidelberg and Presstek introduce GTO-DI with first platemaking on press.	*1991* Bell companies receive permission to enter the on-line information services market.		
		1991 Wide Area Information Servers (WAIS), invented by Brewster Kahle, Thinking Machines Corporation.		
		1991 Gopher released by Paul Lindner and Mark P. McCahill from the University of Minnesota.		
		1991 World Wide Web (WWW) implemented by CERN; Tim Berners-Lee developer.		
		1991 NSFNET backbone upgraded to T3 (44.736 Mbps).		
		1991 NSFNET traffic passes 1 trillion bytes per month and 10 billion packets per month.		
		1991 The Internet consists of 4,000 linked networks.		

Advertising	Broadcasting	Computer	Information	Media
		1991 Apple PowerBook notebook and Quadra Macintosh PCs.		
		1991 IBM reorganizes itself into more autonomous business units and some divisions become subsidiaries.		
		1991 First general-purpose pen-based notebook computers.		
		1991 IBM has its first revenue decline in 45 years.		
		1991 IBM says it sold over 25,000 RISC System 6000 computers with revenue of over $1 billion in 1990.		
		1991 Hewlett-Packard color inkjet printer, the PaintWriter, for $1,395.		
		1991 Frame Technology FrameMaker 3 for Sun Workstations and Macintosh.		
		1991 Adobe upgrades to Photoshop 2.0 for the Macintosh.		
		1991 Intel debuts 50-MHz 486 microprocessor and outlines a 66-MHz, also P5 (586).		
		1991 Apple and IBM and Motorola sign pact to develop Power PC that can run Windows and Macintosh software.		
		1991 Moviegoers astonished by computer morphing in *Terminator 2*.		
1992 Cable TV revenues reach $22 billion.		**1992** Wang Laboratories files for Chapter 11 bankruptcy.		
1992 At least 50 U.S. cities have competing cable services.		**1992** Silicon Graphics buys Mips Computer in a $400 million stock swap.		
		1992 IBM releases OS/2 Version 2.0 and ships over one million units.		

Photo Imaging	Printing & Paper	Telecommunication	Typesetting	Word Processing
		1991 Countries connecting to NSFNET are Croatia, Czech Republic, Hong Kong, Hungary, Poland, Portugal, Singapore, South Africa, Taiwan, Tunisia.		
	1992 DocuTech Network Publisher accepts electronic and hard-copy originals in large printing and publishing applications. The DocuTech Network Publisher II accepts only electronic input over networks. *1992* Xerox DocuPrint Publishing Series.	*1992* Internet Society (ISOC) is chartered. *1992* Number of Internet hosts breaks one million. *1992* First multicast backbone (MBONE) audio multicast and video multicast.	*1992* Adobe Multiple Master digital fonts.	

Advertising	Broadcasting	Computer	Information	Media
		1992 Microsoft releases Windows 3.1 and ships nearly 10 million units.		
		1992 Sun Microsystems new generation of SPARC computers, SPARCstation 10 family.		
		1992 Compaq has new lines of PCs to become a price trendsetter.		
		1992 Digital Equipment next-generation computer architecture, RISC-based Alpha.		
		1992 Microsoft introduces Windows for Workgroup.		
		1992 Intel says its next microprocessor will be called Pentium instead of 586.		
		1992 Novell acquires UNIX Systems Laboratory, including Univel, from AT&T for $350 million.		
		1992 DOS Windows formally shipped. Most programs migrate to Windows.		
1993 Demand begins for "V-chip" to block out violent television programs.		*1993* IBM reports its worst year in history with a loss of $4.97 billion on revenues of $64.5 billion.	*1993* U.S. National Information Infrastructure Act.	*1993* Dinosaurs roam the earth in *Jurassic Park* because of computer animation.
1993 98% of U.S. households own at least one TV set, 64% have two or more.		*1993* IBM chairman John Akers resigns and after the most publicity ever for an executive search, Louis Gerstner becomes the new chairman and CEO.		
		1993 Next sells its hardware business to Canon to concentrate on Nextstep software.		
		1993 Microsoft unveils Windows NT.		
		1993 Pentium-based systems start shipping.		

Photo Imaging	Printing & Paper	Telecommunication	Typesetting	Word Processing
	1992 Xerox DocuTech Model 90. *1992* Hewlett-Packard LaserJet 4, a laser printer with a resolution of 600×600 dots per inch.	*1992* Veronica, a gopherspace search tool, is released by University of Nevada. *1992* Countries connecting to NSFNET are Cameroon, Cyprus, Ecuador, Estonia, Kuwait, Latvia, Luxembourg, Malaysia, Slovakia, Slovenia, Thailand, Venezuela.		
	1993 Xerox 4450—midrange production-class laser printing system—50 pages per minute. *1993* 4700 II Color Document Printer offers enhanced color printing capabilities to those featured in the 4700 (1992), including compatibility with IBM and other systems.	*1993* Mosaic takes the Internet by storm; WWW proliferates at a 342,000% annual growth of service traffic. *1993* The World Wide Web goes public with 1,313,000 hosts (systems or nodes, not networks). The Internet is carrying 5.5 terabytes per month.		*1993* International Workshop on Hypermedia and Hypertext Standards, Amsterdam.

Advertising	Broadcasting	Computer	Information	Media
		1993 Apple ships the Newton Personal Digital Assistant.		
		1993 Compaq Presario, a PC family targeted for the home market.		
		1993 IBM debuts its first workstations based on the PowerPC chip.		
		1993 IBM announces OS/2 for Windows.		
		1993 One in three Americans does some work at home instead of commuting to work.		
1994 Blockbuster Entertainment and Viacom complete a $7.6 billion merger after Viacom buys Paramount Communications for $9.5 billion.		***1994*** Aldus and Adobe merge in a transaction worth $525 million to form a $5 billion+ company.	***1994*** To reduce Western influence, a dozen nations ban or restrict satellite dishes.	
			1994 Prodigy bulletin board fields 12,000 messages in one afternoon after L.A. quake.	
	1995 Sony demonstrates flat TV set.		***1995*** CD-ROM disk can carry a full-length feature film with compression.	
			1995 Volume of copies made on printers exceeds those made on copiers.	

Photo Imaging	Printing & Paper	Telecommunication	Typesetting	Word Processing
	1994 DocuPrint 390HC is highlight color, high-speed, PostScript compatible printer; 92 pages per minute in black, black plus one color; 300 dots per inch. *1994* Xerox Production Systems created with merger of two business divisions for printing and publishing products, Document Production Systems and Printing Systems. *1995* Kodak thermal plate sets stage for future developments in processless plates.	*1994* After 25 years, U.S. government privatizes management of the Internet. *1994* U.S. Senate and House provide information servers. *1994* NSFNET traffic passes 10 trillion bytes per month. *1995* Major U.S. dailies create national on-line newspaper network. *1995* *Time* magazine declares 1995 "the year of the Internet." *1995* WWW surpasses ftp-data as service with the greatest traffic on NSFNet based on packet and byte count. *1995* Online dial-up systems (Compuserve, American Online, Prodigy) begin to provide Internet access. *1995* Technologies of the Year are WWW, search engines, mobile code (JAVA), virtual environments (VRML), collaborative tools.		

Advertising	Broadcasting	Computer	Information	Media
		1996 Apple Computer acquires Next . . . and Steve Jobs is back again.	*1996* America Online (AOL) suffers 19-hour outage, bringing into question whether internet service providers will be able to handle growing numbers of users.	
1997 Advertising agencies struggle to implement advertising on the World Wide Web, given the lack of reliable demographic data.	*1997* New regulations introduce competition into the cable industry as user rates soar.	*1997* Apple receives $150 million investment from Microsoft.	*1997* The World Wide Web continues to grow with users and sites.	*1997* Book, newspaper, and magazine publishers continue to seek profitable models in new media.

Photo Imaging	Printing & Paper	Telecommunication	Typesetting	Word Processing
		1995 The World Wide Web alone carries 4.8 terabytes of the Internet's load. The Internet is turned over to the private sector, no longer applicable for national security purposes.		
		1996 Over 7 million hosts have access to the Internet, which carries over 25 terabytes of information per month.		
1997 Digital photography growing strongly with many new cameras; everyone must learn Photoshop.	*1997* Direct imaging (computer-to-plate on press) sees new entrants at Print 97 mega-show in Chicago. Digital printing more than ready for prime time.	*1997* High-speed transmission services offered by many firms help printers and their customers send and receive files more rapidly.	*1997* The typographic industry no longer controlled by large companies, hundreds of "personal" foundries now design and promote new type designs.	*1997* Typewriters no longer made in the U.S. as word processing moves to the desktop computer and printer.

Bibliography

Adams, J. Michael, Faux, David D., and Rieber, Lloyd J. *Printing Technology.* 4d ed. Albany, NY: Delmar Publishers, 1996.

Ajayi, A'isha, and Groff, Pamela. *Understanding Electronic Communications: Printing in the Information Age.* Pittsburgh, PA: Graphic Arts Technical Foundation, 1996.

Andersson, Mattias, et al. *PDF Printing and Publishing: The Next Revolution after Gutenberg.* Torrance, CA: Micro Publishing Press, 1997.

Andrews, Christopher. *The Education of a CD-ROM Publisher.* Wilton, CT: Eight Bit Books, 1993.

Bakker, Marilyn, ed. *The Wiley Encyclopedia of Packaging Technology.* New York, NY: John Wiley & Sons, 1986.

Blatner, David, and Fraser, Bruce. *Real World Photoshop 3.* Berkeley, CA: Peachpit Press, 1996.

Bruno, Michael H. *Pocket Pal.* 16th ed. Memphis, TN: International Paper, 1995.

Bruno, Michael H. *Principles of Color Proofing.* Salem, NH: GAMA Communications, 1986.

Bunzel, Tom. *Digital Video on the PC: Video Production on Your Multimedia PC.* Torrance, CA: Micro Publishing Press, 1997.

Bureau, William H. *What the Printer Should Know about Paper.* Pittsburgh, PA: Graphic Arts Technical Foundation, 1995.

Cavuoto, James, and Beale, Stephen. *The Color Scanner Book.* Torrance, CA: Micro Publishing Press, 1995.

Cavuoto, James, and Beale, Stephen. *Guide to Desktop Publishing.* 2d ed. Pittsburgh, PA: Graphic Arts Technical Foundation, 1995.

Covington, Melody Mauldin. *Dictionary of Desktop Publishing.* Hauppauge, NY: Barron's Educational Series, 1995.

Cowan, Les. *CD-ROM: Publishing Medium—Publishing Tool.* Torrance, CA: Micro Publishing Press, 1995.

DeJidas, Lloyd P., and Destree, Thomas M. *Sheetfed Offset Press Operating.* 2d ed. Pittsburgh, PA: Graphic Arts Technical Foundation, 1995.

Dyson, Peter. *Dictionary of Networking.* Alameda, CA: Network Press, 1995.

Foundation of Flexographic Technical Association. *Flexography: Principles and Practices.* 4th ed. Ronkonkoma, NY: Foundation of Flexographic Technical Association, 1991.

GATF Staff. *Web Offset Press Operating.* 4th ed. Pittsburgh, PA: Graphic Arts Technical Foundation, 1996.

Graham, Ian S. *HTML Sourcebook.* New York, NY: John Wiley & Sons, 1995.

Gravure Association of America. *Gravure: Process and Technology.* Rochester, NY: Gravure Association of America, 1991.

Green, Phil. *Understanding Digital Color.* Pittsburgh, PA: Graphic Arts Technical Foundation, 1995.

Hope, Augustine, and Walch, Margaret. *The Color Compendium.* New York, NY: Van Nostrand Reinhold, 1990.

Kieran, Michael. *Understanding Desktop Color.* Toronto, Ontario: Desktop Publishing Associates, 1994.

Jeffrey, Noel. *Digital Printing: A Guide to the New World of Graphic Communications.* Torrance, CA: Micro Publishing Press, 1996.

Lawler, Brian P. *The Complete Guide to Trapping.* 2d ed. Indianapolis, IN: Hayden Books, 1995.

Leach, R.H., ed. *The Printing Ink Manual.* 4th ed. Wokingham, Berkshire, England: Van Nostrand Reinhold (International) Co. Ltd., 1988.

Lyman, Ralph. *Binding and Finishing.* Pittsburgh, PA: Graphic Arts Technical Foundation, 1993.

Magee, Babette. *Screen Printing Primer.* Pittsburgh, PA: Graphic Arts Technical Foundation, 1985.

Molla, R.K. *Electronic Color Separation.* Montgomery, WV: R.K. Printing and Publishing, 1988.

National Association of Printing Ink Manufacturers, Product and Technical Committees. *Printing Ink Handbook.* 5th ed. Harrison, NY: National Association of Printing Ink Manufacturers, 1988.

Romano, Frank J. *Desktop Typography with QuarkXPress, Second Edition.* Blue Ridge Summit, PA: TAB Books, 1992.

Romano, Frank J. *Digital Media: Publishing Technologies for the 21st Century*. Torrance, CA: Micro Publishing Press, 1996.

Romano, Frank J. *Machine Writing and Typesetting*. Salem, NH: GAMA, 1986.

Romano, Frank J. *The Pocket Guide to Digital Prepress*. Albany, NY: Delmar Publishers, 1996.

Romano, Frank J. *The TypEncyclopedia*. New York, NY: R.R. Bowker Company, 1984.

Screen Printing Association International. *Technical Guidebook of the Screen Printing Industry*. Screen Printing Association International, 1987.

Shapiro, Charles, ed. *The Lithographers Manual*. 5th ed. Pittsburgh, PA: Graphic Arts Technical Foundation, 1974.

Southworth, Miles, McIlroy, Thad, and Southworth, Donna. *Complete Color Glossary*. Livonia, NY: The Color Resource, 1992.

Southworth, Miles, and Southworth, Donna. *Color Separation on the Desktop*. Livonia, NY: Graphic Arts Publishing, Inc., 1993.

Southworth, Miles, and Southworth, Donna. *Pocket Guide to Color Reproduction*. Livonia, NY: Graphic Arts Publishing, Inc., 1995.

Spencer, Donald D. *Computer Dictionary*. 4th ed. Ormond Beach, FL: Camelot Publishing Company, 1993.

Stevenson, Deborah L. *Handbook of Printing Processes*. Pittsburgh, PA: Graphic Arts Technical Foundation, 1994.

Stevenson, George A., revised by Pakan, William A. *Graphic Arts Encyclopedia*. 3d ed. New York, NY: Design Press/McGraw-Hill, 1992.

Vaughan, Tay. *Multimedia: Making It Work*. 2d ed. New York, NY: McGraw-Hill, 1994.

Witkowski, Mark. *The PDF Bible: The Complete Guide to Adobe Acrobat 3.0*. Torrance, CA: Micro Publishing Press, 1998.

About the Authors

Principal Authors

Frank J. Romano is the author of sixteen books, contributor to major encyclopedias and dictionaries, and the author of numerous articles. His most recent books are *Pocket Guide to Digital Prepress* and collaborations with GATF experts Howard Fenton and Richard Adams on on-demand printing and computer-to-plate technology. His career has spanned over 30 years in printing and publishing. He has founded eight publications, serving as publisher or editor or both for *TypeWorld* (now *Electronic Publishing),* founded in 1977, *Computer Artist, Color Publishing, The Typographer, EP&P,* and both the *NCPA* and *PrintRIT Journals.* He lectures extensively and consults for major corporations, publishers, government, and other users of digital publishing. He has been quoted in the *New York Times, Wall Street Journal, Times* of London, and other publications, as well as on TV and radio.

He now serves as the Melbert B. Cary, Jr. Distinguished Professor of Graphic Arts at the Rochester Institute of Technology, College of Imaging Arts and Sciences.

Richard M. Romano is senior associate editor of *Digital Imaging* magazine and coordinator of the book publishing division of Micro Publishing Press in Torrance, California. He graduated from Syracuse University *cum laude* with a degree in communications and received a certificate from New York University in multimedia publishing.

He worked as an assistant editor for St. Martin's Press in New York City and served for four years as editorial assistant to Marilyn vos Savant, *Parade* magazine columnist. In her book *I've Forgotten Everything I Learned in School,* she says, "A special acknowledgment goes to Richard Romano, my own guy Friday, who did all the research for this book . . . kept a sharp eye out for errors, and taught me the value of a really bad joke."

Editorial Staff

Thomas M. Destree is editor-in-chief of GATF*Press.* He supervises a staff of writers and editors in preparing material to be published in textbooks, reference books, audio-visuals, and various reports and brochures.

Destree is the co-author of *Sheetfed Offset Press Operating; Graphic Arts Photography—Color;* and *Desktop Publishing Opportunities for the Printer and Service Bureaus.* He is author of *Guide to Hardware and Software for Desktop Publishing,* and editor of the ninth edition of the *Lithographers Manual.*

Erika L. Kendra is a technical editor for GATF*Press.* She serves as a copywriter, editor, and project manager on a variety of publications ranging from books and *GATFWorld* articles to promotional materials. She acts as liaison between GATF*Press* and both internal and external writers and designers to develop and secure up-to-date information and illustrations.

Kendra graduated *summa cum laude* from the University of Pittsburgh Honors College with B.Phil. degree in history and English.

Art Staff

Robert J. Romano is the technical illustrator at O'Reilly & Associates, a book publisher with production facilities in Cambridge, Massachusetts. He created over 300 of the line illustrations in this encyclopedia using Adobe Illustrator. He graduated *cum laude* from Mount Ida College in Newton, Massachusetts with a degree in graphic design. He is a member of the Phi Theta Kappa honor society and a U.S. Army veteran of Desert Storm. He is enrolled in the Continuing Education Division of Northeastern University in Boston for advanced courses in art and design.

About GATF

The Graphic Arts Technical Foundation is a nonprofit, scientific, technical, and educational organization dedicated to the advancement of the graphic communications industries worldwide. Its mission is to serve the field as the leading resource for technical information and services through research and education.

For 73 years the Foundation has developed leading edge technologies and practices for printing. GATF's staff of researchers, educators, and technical specialists partner with nearly 2,000 corporate members in over 65 countries to help them maintain their competitive edge by increasing productivity, print quality, process control, and environmental compliance, and by implementing new techniques and technologies. Through conferences, satellite symposia, workshops, consulting, technical support, laboratory services, and publications, GATF strives to advance a global graphic communications community.

The GATF*Press* publishes books on nearly every aspect of the field; learning modules (step-by-step instruction booklets); audiovisuals (CD-ROMs, videocassettes, slides, and audiocassettes); and research and technology reports. It also publishes *GATFWorld,* a bimonthly magazine of technical articles, industry news, and reviews of specific products.

For more detailed information on GATF products and services, please visit our website *http://www.gatf.org* or write to us at 200 Deer Run Road, Sewickley, PA 15143-2600 (phone: 412/741-6860).

GATF*Press:* Selected Titles

Air Pollution Engineering Guide for the Graphic Arts Industry. Jones, Gary A.

Binding and Finishing. Lyman, Ralph.

Book Design and Manufacturing. Blyden, Vincent.

Careers in Graphic Communications: A Resource Book. Flecker, Sally Ann and Pamela J. Groff.

Chemistry for the Graphic Arts. Eldred, Dr. Nelson R.

Color and Its Reproduction. Field, Gary G.

Computer-to-Plate: Automating the Printing Industry. Adams, Richard M. II, & Frank J. Romano.

Digital Photography: New Turf for Printers. Milburn, David L., with John L. Carroll.

Environmental Awareness and Solutions Manual. Witherly, Rita and Gary A. Jones.

The Essentials of Computer-to-Plate. Limburg, Michael.

Flexography Primer. Crouch, J. Page.

The GATF Encyclopedia of Graphic Communications. Romano, Frank J. and Richard M. Romano.

Glossary of Graphic Communications. Groff, Pamela J.

Graphic Arts Photography: Black and White. Cogoli, John E.

Graphic Arts Photography: Color. Wentzel, Fred, Ray Blair and Tom Destree.

Gravure Primer. Kasunich, Cheryl L.

Guide to Desktop Publishing. Cavuoto, James, & Steven Beale.

Handbook of Printing Processes. Stevenson, Deborah L.

Implementing Quality Management in the Graphic Arts. Apfelberg, Herschel L. & Michael J. Apfelberg.

The Lithographers Manual. Destree, Thomas M.

Lithography Primer. Wilson, Daniel G.

Lithographic Press Operator's Handbook. Groff, Pamela J. et al.

The Magazine: Everything You Need to Know to Make It in the Magazine Business. Mogel, Leonard.

Materials Handling for the Printer. Geis, A. John and Paul L. Addy.

Nonimpact Printing. Nothmann, Gerhard A.

On-Demand Printing: The Revolution in Digital and Customized Printing. Fenton, Howard M. & Frank J. Romano.

Printing Plant Layout and Facility Design. Geis, A. John.

Printing Production Management. Field, Gary G.

Screen Printing Primer. Ingram, Samuel T.

Sheetfed Offset Press Operating. DeJidas, Lloyd P. and Thomas M. Destree.

Solving Sheetfed Offset Press Problems. GATF Staff.

Solving Web Offset Press Problems. GATF Staff.

Total Production Maintenance: A Guide for the Printing Industry. Rizzo, Kenneth E.

Understanding Digital Color. Green, Phil.

Understanding Digital Imposition. Hinderliter, Hal.

Understanding Electronic Communications: Printing in the Information Age. Ajayi, A'isha, & Pamela J. Groff.

Web Offset Press Operating. GATF Staff.

What the Printer Should Know about Ink. Eldred, Dr. Nelson R. and Terry Scarlett.

What the Printer Should Know about Paper. Wilson, Lawrence A.